Goldmine® Jazz Album PRICE GUIDE

3rd Edition

DAVE THOMPSON

Published by

Krause Publications, a division of F+W Media, Inc.
700 East State Street • Iola, WI 54990-0001
715-445-2214 • 888-457-2873
www.krausebooks.com

To order books or other products call toll-free 1-800-258-0929
or visit us online at www.krausebooks.com

ISBN-13: 978-1-4402-4698-2
ISBN-10: 1-4402-4698-X

Cover Design by Dave Hauser
Designed by Rebecca Vogel
Edited by Paul Kennedy

Printed in the United States of America

10 9 8 7 6 5 4 3 2 1

Contents

LISTINGS A-Z

INTRODUCTION By Dave Thompson

Of all that we heard and read as this was book was being researched, one sentence in particular sticks in the mind: "A few years ago, you'd have struggled to give this record away. Now it's selling for...."

We are all familiar, because the headlines keep reminding us, with the soaring values attached to the heaviest hitters of the jazz world – Blue Note and Prestige early pressings, Miles Davis and so forth.

The heavy hitters, however, are not the only batsmen on the field today.

It was inevitable that prices would rise throughout the decade-plus since the last edition of this book was published. But many have skyrocketed. In 2004, Ayler's *Spiritual Unity* (ESP-Disk 1002) was listed with a $25 value. Today, a near-mint copy is rated close to 40 times that amount. And that is by no means a solitary example.

We are aware, of course, that auction prices should often be taken with a grain of salt, whether they are realized in traditional surroundings, online from a specialist dealer, or in the Wild West preserves of eBay. But even so, when high three-figure and midrange four-figure sums regularly change hands for so many different records, it is clear that the market for collectible jazz records is not simply in rude health. It might well be the most robust field in all of record collecting.

Just 14 LPs are cataloged at $5,000 in the latest edition of the *Goldmine Standard Catalog of American Records* – that is, our listing of every album released in this country since 1950. Of these, just three of these could be considered "regular" releases; that is, albums that were not, for whatever reason, withdrawn or even canceled before their official appearance, and two of them are in this catalog: Sonny Clark's Cool Struttin' (Blue Note BLP-1588) and Jutta Hip's With Zoot Sims (Blue Note BLP-1530). (The third is the mono pressing of Jimi Hendrix's *Axis Bold As Love*, released just as the US industry abandoned mono for stereo).

Dip down a few notches. There are 139 albums priced at $1,000 in the full catalog. No less than 58 of them – or 42 percent – appear here. Half that price and a similar ratio can again be found; of 337 LPs that list at $500, 134 are jazz records.

We should, of course, note that we are discussing records in the most uncommon of states – upwards of half-a-century old in many cases, and still looking and sounding like new; Near Mint condition is as close as you can get to un-played and unopened as it is possible to voyage, without coming upon a copy that has just left the pressing plant; and, needless to say, that is not something that a lot of original record buyers would ever have considered.

Records are made to be opened; records are made to be played; and records are made to be enjoyed. They were the soundtracks to our lives, after all – in those days before radio and television, cassettes and mp3s,

Internet streaming and laptop playlists transformed music into a commodity that sometimes feels no more precious than wallpaper, listening to records was tantamount to a sacred ritual, and one that would be indulged at every available moment.

Jazz was scarcely better served by the media of the day than any other genre outside of the easiest of easy listening – and less so, in fact, than most. For many people listening in the 1950s, memories of the day seem to revolve around broadcasts of NBC's *Monitor*, debuting in 1955 as a weekend-only mix of chat, comedy, sport and interviews, but featuring a live jazz session from clubs around New York. The rest of the time, the fan was thrown back on his record collection, or, at parties, on the collection of others.

The lack of airtime, of course contributed to the principle reason why many of these records are now so scarce. Even among the giants of the era, sales were low – so much so, in fact, that it was 1986 before any jazz album whatsoever was awarded a platinum disc (Herbie Hancock's *Future Shock*), while the Blue Note label was forced to wait until 2001 before it received its first gold award for a jazz album, John Coltrane's *Blue Train* – most of whose sales were apparently racked up following its reissue on CD (BLP 1577). It remains Blue Note's only "classic era" release to sell more than 1 million copies.

So, records got played, records got worn, records got scratched. Covers grew tatty. Inner bags were replaced. Even the most careful purchaser would eventually find age and use taking its toll. And yes, maybe if they'd had any idea of the future fortunes that were spinning on the turntable, they might at least have changed the stylus before it was dulled into a chisel.

But they didn't because who would? It is only over the last couple of decades that collectors have learned the lessons of the past, and become obsessed with keeping new purchases mint and poly-sleeved, and dealers in any of a hundred collecting disciplines can tell you what a waste of time and space (and polysleeves) that turned out to be.

Future rarities, after all, are seldom the items that everybody thinks they will be (and certainly not the ones that are marketed as such), and which they lock in the bank vault unopened. It's the ones that nobody bothers to save that turn out to be hardest to find.

But again, records are made to be opened, records are made to be played.... and the collecting market prices those "lesser" copies accordingly. Or it should – I still remember, after 20 years, discovering one particular rarity at a record fair and, never having handled a copy before, let alone seen one priced so reasonably ($60, if I remember correctly, at a time when $600 was a more realistic cost), I removed it from its sleeve to inspect the vinyl. At which point, the dealer spoke.

"It's practically un-played, VG+ at least." And he was right; it was, apart from the great crack that ran from the outer edge to the spindle hole.

I replaced the record in the rack.

The point is, if you're a buyer, not to be discouraged by the highest prices in this book – and, while that is probably not the best story with which to illustrate this point, still the records you need are out there somewhere, affordably priced and playable too. And if they're not, or while you're awaiting their appearance, there are plenty more to be looking for.

You might want to hurry, though. As prices elsewhere throughout the jazz canon evidence (not to mention the remark with which we opened this introduction), the last few years have become very much a voyage of (re)discovery for many fans and collectors. Records that were, indeed, once impossible to give away have found voracious new audiences – a symbol not only of changing tastes, but also of changing times.

Artists whom past generations regarded as mere bandwagon jumpers (or worse) are constantly being re-evaluated by new audiences... the dollar or two for which their records might sell is a small price, after all, to pay for what might prove to be a great discovery, and social media ensures that word is not slow to spread.

We offer no examples – everybody reading this has probably passed such judgment on one artist or another. But from the meekest *jazz-lite* to the most unfused jazz fusion, audiences are eschewing the received wisdom of what is "good" and "bad" jazz, and simply having fun finding the sounds that match their own interpretations of those qualities.

Which, in turn, offers another indication of just how healthy the market for the music has become. People no longer want to hear only what they're told to listen to. They want to hear everything they can, and if they can be in on the ground floor of the next hero-in-waiting, all the better.

Of course, even amidst the free-for-all that necessarily ensues from there, the most rarified strata of greats remains unchanged and largely unchallenged. That said, it is instructive to offer a few more comparisons between this edition of the price guide and the last.

In 2004, the highest price listed for a Sun Ra album, 1968's *A Black Mass*, was $300, with others marked for as low as $40. Today, $300 is itself at the low end of the scale, and inflation alone is not wholly responsible for the increase in values.

Appreciation of, and interest in Sun Ra has also skyrocketed in the 21st century, not only from a purely musical point of view, but philosophically, too. An artist who once inhabited the outermost reaches of the popular consciousness has been accepted if not into the commercial mainstream, then at least its cultural equivalent. The already pronounced scarcity of his earliest (and, indeed, later) recordings became even sharper accordingly.

Hank Mobley, *Hank Mobley*, Blue Note BST-1568, "deep groove" version with W. 63rd St. address, **$400**.

Similar tales abound throughout this volume, but one more will suffice, as we inspect the output of New York City's ESP-Disk label – home to the likes of the aforementioned Albert Ayler, Burton Greene, Karl Berger and Milton Graves. A dozen years ago, you could pick up more-or-less each artist's entire ESP-Disk catalog for less than you would today expect to pay for a single album.

No matter that few of the label's signings are in any way regarded as household names, even in the households where their records are collected. Like Blue Note, like Riverside, like Prestige and Savoy, ESP-Disk's very name has become known as a trademark of quality – an accolade that has never been a secret among its original supporters, of course. But which was certainly welcome news to anybody discovering the label in more recent years.

This upsurge of interest in artists, labels and even sub-genres who might once have been considered cultish, even "marginal," is not a phenomenon that is unique to jazz. Across the musical spectrum, the last decade or so has seen any number of once forgotten (or at least, generally overlooked) figures elevated to a degree of popular acclaim, whether by a piece of music well-placed within a television commercial or popular drama, or simply through word-of-mouth - again, the impact of social media cannot be overlooked whenever one encounters a sudden surge in some hitherto unknown artist's popularity.

Jazz just seems to have a lot of artists who fit the billing.

Also playing a significant role has been the recent rush of CD box sets gathering together both the rarest, and the best known, of a given artist's catalog – often at prices that could easily compete with a more-or-less complete collection of the same music on LP. The

curious buy the box set. The converts pick up the vinyl.

Indeed, another factor is the much-vaunted, and much-welcomed, rebirth of vinyl on the new release racks. In March 2016, industry news sources reported that, for the first time ever, vinyl revenues had not only eclipsed those raked in by the ad-supported music streaming sites, but were closing in on subscriber-funded services, too. To this can be added a massive 52.1% rise in vinyl revenues in just the past year, compared to a 32.5% *decline* in CDs, and still one is seeing only a fraction of the overall picture.

For used record sales, too, are booming, not only in terms of individual values but also across the board, from the most humble dollar box to the most exclusive rarities. And this book celebrates that fact.

Collecting has never, after all, been purely a matter of simply joining the dots in an artist's discography, and counting down the days until the collection is "complete." It has always been a voyage of discovery, a journey into musical unknowns that are as labyrinthine as your curiosity allows them to be.

It is our fervent hope, as you sit down with this, the third edition of the *Goldmine Jazz Album Price Guide*, that we will be able to help illuminate that labyrinth, not only showing you what your records are worth in monetary terms, but illustrating their value in musical and cultural terms, as well.

Happy hunting!

THE LOWDOWN

Inside this book is one of the largest and most comprehensive listings of jazz on vinyl LPs anywhere. In a broad sense, you can define "jazz" by the 40,000-plus albums listed in this book.

We also chose not to end the listings in a particular year. Though most of the "action" in jazz is with the original issues from the 1950s and 1960s, we don't stop there. The number of listings begins to taper off around 1989, the last year that vinyl was truly mass-produced in the United States. But the resurgence of vinyl from those dark days means that more modern albums can now be found.

We chose not to restrict our definition of "jazz" to any one style. Music from New Orleans-style Dixieland to avant-garde is found in this book. Male and female singers are included, as are vocal groups. Records by soloists are listed, as are records by huge bands. Every instrument on which it is possible to "swing" and/or improvise is covered, from the expected (saxophone,

trumpet, piano, guitar) to the unexpected (bagpipes, bassoon, harp, steel drums).

Also, many "borderline" jazz artists are included. Most of these are vocalists or groups who are better known in the pop or rock realm; many of the singers received their musical educations with the big bands, and even after they left, they often had accompaniment in keeping with their swing roots. In some cases, we have included their entire recorded output, because it is too difficult to look at their catalogs and decide what is and isn't "jazzy." In others, we have been more selective, because it is easier to determine what the artist's intent was.

The *Goldmine Jazz Album Price Guide* lists only LPs – microgroove 10-inch or 12-inch records that generally play at 33 1/3 rpm. Because we chose not to include other formats, that does not mean they are not collectible, it simply means we have decided to focus on the area of most interest by collectors. .

GRADING GUIDE

This book lists records in Near Mint condition. For most collectors, records of lower quality are only OK as placeholders – a stopgap until a better copy comes along – or as examples of truly rare records that are almost never found in more collectible condition and might be out of the collector's price range in a more lofty state.

Most records are graded *visually*. That is because most record dealers sell in quantity and don't have the time to play their entire stock. That said, some defects are easy to see, such as large scratches and warps. Others are subtle, such as groove wear from using a cheap or poorly aligned tone arm.

When grading albums, do so under a strong light. Look at everything carefully, and then assign a grade based on your overall observations.

Some records will be worthy of a higher grade except for small defects, such as writing, tape or minor seam

splits. *Always mention these when selling a record.* For some collectors, they will be irrelevant, but for others, they will be a deal-breaker. For all, they are important to know.

Other records will have promotional indicators such as timing strips, gold "don't sell this record or we'll take your firstborn" stamps, or other markings. Again, for some collectors, these mar the cover and make it worth less; for others, it doesn't matter, and for still others, they increase the desirability. Again, *always mention these when selling a record!*

One of the obstacles to the further growth of record collecting, jazz or otherwise, is poor grading and a lack of consensus as to what constitutes a Very Good Plus or Near Mint record or cover. Over the years, the *Goldmine* Grading Guide has tried to standardize this. But we recognize that there are many variables to grading a record. As a seller, you are better off grading

conservatively and surprising the buyer with a better record than was expected, than by grading based on wishful thinking and losing a customer.

That said, here are the standard grades for LPs, from best to worst:

MINT (M)

These are absolutely perfect in every way. Often rumored but rarely seen, Mint should never be used as a grade unless more than one person agrees that the record is truly in this condition. There is no set percentage of the listed Near Mint value these can bring; it is best negotiated between the buyer and seller.

NEAR MINT (NM or M–)

A good description of a NM record is "it looks like it just came from a retail store and was opened for the first time." In other words, it's nearly perfect. Many dealers won't use a grade higher than this, implying (perhaps correctly) that no record is ever truly perfect.

NM covers should have no creases, folds, seam splits or any signs of human handling. A Near-Mint cover also should have no cutout markings of any kind. It also will have no ring wear.

NM records are shiny, with no visible defects. Writing, stickers or other markings cannot appear on the label, nor can any "spindle marks" from someone trying to blindly put the record on the turntable. Major factory defects also must not be present; a record and label obviously pressed off center is not Near Mint. If played, it will do so with no surface noise. (NM records are not necessarily "never played"; a record played on an excellent turntable can remain NM after many plays if the record is properly cared for.)

These are high standards, and they are *not* on a sliding scale. A record from the 1950s must meet the same standards as one from the 1990s to be Near Mint! It's estimated that no more than 2 to 4 percent of all records remaining from the 1950s and 1960s are truly NM. This is why they fetch such high prices. Do not assume your records are Near Mint. They *must* meet these standards to qualify!

VERY GOOD PLUS (VG+)
or Excellent (E)

A good description of a VG+ record is "except for a couple minor things, this would be Near Mint." Most collectors and people who want to play their records will be happy with a VG+ record, especially if it is toward the high side of the grade (sometimes called VG++)

VG+ covers are close to their Near Mint counterparts. A cover might be marred by a cutout marking (cut corner, small hole punch, a cut in the spine) or promotional stamp; there might be some slight signs of handling, such as light creasing at the corners. There also can be slight signs of wear at the most vulnerable areas and even a tiny bit of ring wear. But all in all, except for a few minor imperfections, this would be a copy you could sell at retail in a store.

VG+ records may show some slight signs of wear, including light scuffs or very light scratches that do not affect the listening experience. Slight warps that do not affect the sound are OK. Minor signs of handling are OK, too, such as telltale marks around the center hole, but repeated playing has not misshaped the center hole. There may be some very light ring wear or discoloration, but it should be barely noticeable.

VERY GOOD (VG)

Many of the imperfections found on a VG+ record are more obvious on a VG record. That said, VG records – which usually go for no more than 25 percent of a Near Mint record – are among the biggest bargains in record collecting, because most of the "big money" goes for more perfect copies. For many listeners, a VG record will be worth the money.

VG covers have more signs of wear, such as minor (and we mean minor) seam splits. The most common spots for seams to split are at the bottom center, the middle of the spine, and at the upper and lower right, where the record is removed from the cover. These will not be overwhelming. Also, minor writing, tape or a sticker will detract from this cover. Other signs of handling will be more evident; ring wear, especially at the top, bottom and middle of the cover, will be visible, and it might affect the entire cover to a minor degree. Though a VG cover will still be pleasing to the eye, there is no way it could ever pass as new.

VG records have more obvious flaws. They lack most of the original gloss found on factory-fresh records. Groove wear is evident on sight, as are light scratches, deep enough to feel with a fingernail. When played, a VG record has surface noise, perhaps even an occasional audible light scratch, especially in soft passages and during a song's intro and ending. But the noise will not overpower the music otherwise. Just as with a VG cover, minor writing, tape or a sticker will detract from the label of the disc. Many collectors who have jukeboxes will use VG records in them and not think twice. They remain a fine listening experience, just not the same as if the record were in better condition.

LESSER GRADES

Good (G), Good Plus (G+) or Very Good Minus (VG–) records go for 10 to 15 percent of the Near Mint value, if you are lucky.

Good does not mean bad! The record still plays through without skipping, so it can serve as filler until something better comes along. But it has significant surface noise and groove wear, and the label is worn, with significant ring wear, heavy writing, or obvious damage caused by someone trying to remove tape or stickers and failing miserably. A Good to VG-minus cover will have more significant seam splits, perhaps to the point where they were taped closed, and highly obvious

ring wear and heavier writing, such as the huge letters a radio station might have put on a cover to deter theft.

If the item is common, it's probably better to pass it up, but if it's something you've been seeking for a long time, get it cheap and look to upgrade.

Poor (P), Fair (F) records go for 0 to 5 percent of the Near Mint value, if they go at all. More likely, they end up going in the trash. Records are cracked, impossibly warped, or skip and/or repeat when an attempt is made to play them. Covers are so badly seam spilt that they are fortunate to keep the record inside of it. Only the most outrageously rare records ever sell for more a few cents in this condition – again, if they sell at all.

SEALED ALBUMS

It is best to treat sealed albums (sometimes abbreviated "SS" for "Still Sealed") with caution, especially if you are offered one as an original edition from a bygone era at an outrageous price.

For one thing, the record might have been re-sealed, regardless of intention. For example, if you see an album with a hole or indentation indicating a cutout, and there's no hole in the shrink wrap at that spot, it was re-sealed.

With a few exceptions, the only way you can tell if a record is the specific pressing you seek is to look at the record label. Often, the covers stayed the same for years. Records with back-cover dates of 1958 can have discs inside that were pressed in the 1980s! You don't really know unless you look at the record.

And you also have no way of knowing what condition the record is in. "Sealed" is *not* equivalent to "Mint" or "Near Mint"! The record inside could have been pressed badly, or it might even be the wrong record. The author has opened sealed albums, only to find a different album inside!

Yes, legitimate sealed albums from the 1960s still exist, and sometimes they bring fancy prices. But that's only if there can be no confusion about the vintage of the record inside. Tread carefully.

COMMON COLLECTING ABBREVIATIONS

In addition to the letters used to designate a record's grade, it's not uncommon to see other abbreviations used in dealer advertisements. Knowing the more common ones helps to prevent confusion. Here are some that pertain to albums:

boot: bootleg (illegal pressing)
cc: cut corner
co: cutout
coh: cut-out hole
cov, cv, cvr: cover
dh: drill hole
dj: disc jockey (promotional) record
gf: gatefold (cover)
imp: import
ins: insert
lbl: label
m, mo: monaural (mono)
nap: (does) not affect play
noc: number on cover
nol: number on label
obi: not actually an abbreviation, "obi" is the Japanese word for "sash" and is used to describe the strip of paper usually wrapped around Japanese (and occasional US) pressings of LPs.
orig: original
pr, pro, promo: promotional record
q: quadraphonic
re: reissue

rec: record
ri: reissue
rw: ring wear
s: stereo
sl: slight
sm: saw mark
soc: sticker on cover
sol: sticker on label
ss: still sealed
s/t: self-titled
st: stereo
sw: shrink wrap
toc: tape on cover
tol: tape on label
ts: taped seam
w/: with
wlp: white label promo
wobc: writing on back cover
woc: writing on cover
wofc: writing on front cover
wol: writing on label
wr: wear
wrp: warp
xol: "x" on label

HOW YOU CAN HELP

Over 40,000 albums by performers of all jazz styles and eras are in this book. Many readers have helped point out missing performers and albums in the years since the first edition came out; much of that feedback is directly reflected in the pages of this book. We appreciate all constructive input to what we've done, and read all of it.

It's possible that we missed someone in the book, or something, that needs to be included. If so, you can send information to:

Paul Kennedy
Editorial Director
Goldmine Jazz Album Price
700 E. State St.
Iola, WI 54990-0001
Or by e-mail:
Paul.Kennedy@fwcommunity.com
If you write, please include either a daytime (Central Time) phone number or an e-mail address in your letter, so we can reach you if we have questions.

ACKNOWLEDGMENTS

First, we'd like to thank everyone who buys our books. Your support has shown that the record collecting community needs and appreciates a book on jazz albums.

This book is pulled from a database featuring hundreds of thousands of artists. Krause Publications database developer Steve Duberstein is a true rock star behind the scene. He makes all this possible. Designer Rebecca Vogel makes sense out of all the pulled data.

There are countless others who contribute their talents to this project and many others on collecting records. It is impossible to name everyone but please know that it truly takes a community to create a reference such as this. Thank you to all who make it possible.

RECORD LABEL IDENTIFIER

For the most part, the most collectible records are original pressings. Those are the ones that presumably were available at the time the album was first issued.

To tell for sure, you have to know the labels.

As opposed to 45s, which often were deleted quickly and replaced by "golden oldies" reissues, albums could stay in print in covers looking ostensibly the same for years, sometimes decades! With only some superficial differences, the same album cover can contain a copy of *Kind of Blue* that was pressed in 1959, 1969 or 1989. The same is true of an album such as *Time Out* by the Dave Brubeck Quartet; it was in print from 1958 until vinyl was phased out. In that time, Columbia went through several different label designs. It's only the originals that are most sought after.

Thus we present this rough guide to many of the most common and collectible jazz labels.

Eventually, with your help, we'd like this to be even more thorough. Instead of listing label variations by approximate year of changeover, we'd like to nail down exact numbers where a label changed from one to another. Sometimes, because of printing plant overlap, this will not be possible. But the closer we get, the better the guide gets.

This list focuses on labels that had, or have, a significant jazz presence. Some of the labels below may not have had any jazz releases, but the majority did.

By the way, this guide does not attempt to delve into the various promotional labels record companies used.

Most of the time, though, they are white versions of the labels that were in use at the time. Not every label used promo labels; others used them at some times, but not at all times.

Enough ado, let's go:

A&M

1963 (101 only?): Yellowish label, brown print, "A&M Records" logo at top, unboxed.

1963-64 (102?-at least 106): Brown label, "A&M Records" logo at top, now in familiar white box with red "A&M."

1965-73: (starting at 107?): Brown label, "A&M Records" logo at left.

1974-86: Silver gray label with fading A&M logo. A couple albums in the 1980s are known to exist on A&M's 1981-86 singles label, which was red with a black ring along the outer edge,

1986-end: Black label with five gold, black and white rounded squares across the center and A&M logo at right.

ABC; ABC-PARAMOUNT

1956-61: Black label, "ABC-Paramount" multicolor logo at top, "A Product of Am-Par Record Corp." in white at bottom.

1962-66: Black label, "ABC-Paramount" multicolor logo at top, "A Product of ABC-Paramount Records Inc." in white at bottom.

1966-67: Possible transition label with "abc" in a white

circle at top of label, but not in a multicolored box.

1967-72: "abc" in a white circle at top of label surrounded by a multicolored box.

1973: "ABC" in a white triangle spelled out in children's blocks. Very short-lived label. Quickly replaced by 1967-72 label again until another new label was created.

1974-77: Multicolored (yellow, orange, purple) "target" label with "abc Records" at top of label between two lines.

1977-79: Multicolored (yellow, orange, purple) "target" label with "abc" in an eighth note at top of label. In 1979, the label was bought by MCA, which gradually replaced ABC albums with MCA pressings.

ABC DUNHILL – See DUNHILL.

ABC IMPULSE! – See IMPULSE.

ACE

1958-62: Black label, silver print.

1962: Dark blue label, white at top, "ACE" in blue oval.

1971 (2020-21): Yellow label, black print.

1975 (2022): Red label, black print.

Custom labels were used on 1007 and 1008.

APPLE

1968-75: Green "Granny Smith" apple label on one side, sliced apple on the other. Some, though not all, albums from 1968-70 had a line of small white print on the sliced side with "A Subsidiary of Capitol Industries, Inc." along the bottom and a tiny Capitol logo. The small print appears only to have been used at one Capitol pressing plant, so two albums could both be originals, yet one will have the "Capitol logo" and the other won't.

1975: "All Rights Reserved" disclaimer added to the label print.

Apple 34001 was originally issued with a red apple label. Custom labels exist on many numbers.

ARGO

Early mono editions had a greenish label, some with gold print, some with silver print, with "ULTRA HIGH FIDELITY" adjacent to the vertical "ARGO." Later mono editions are known to have a silver label with black print or a black label with silver print, also with "ULTRA HIGH FIDELITY."

Early stereo editions have dark blue labels with silver print.

The next label was silver with black print, but without the words "ULTRA HIGH FIDELITY."

The final Argo label (to the end of 1965) was a brown label with a pink and white "ARGO" in an oval at left. The Argo label was replaced by Cadet in 1965.

ARISTA

1975-76 (AL 4001 to 4105?): Light blue label, white Arista logo with "Arista Records" beneath.

1976-77: Light blue label, white Arista logo with "Arista" beneath.

1977-79: Black label, light blue Arista logo, "Arista" underneath.

1979-84: Fading blue label, three-dimensional Arista logo at top, "Arista" at left side of logo slanting upward.

1984-90: Black label, "ARISTA" above multicolor mountain skyline.

1990-end: Black label, "ARISTA" above white mountain skyline.

Custom labels were used on some releases.

ATCO

1958-61 (33-101 to 33-138): Yellow label with a harp at the upper left.

1961-68 mono: Gold and gray label, "AT" to left of center hole, "CO" to right of center hole in white background.

1961-68 stereo (SD 33-139 to SD 33-256): Purple and brown label, "AT" to left of center hole, "CO" to right of center hole in white background.

1969-77: Yellow label, "Atco" logo at left. Earlier labels have a "1841 Broadway" address, later ones have a "75 Rockefeller Plaza" address and add a small "W" (Warner Communications) logo in the small print.

1978-84: Gray label, logo at top.

1985-end: Whitish label, "ATCO" in different colored letters at an angle at top with many smaller "ATCO"s in the background.

ATLANTIC

1950-60 mono: Black label, silver print.

1959-60 stereo: Green label, silver print.

1960: So-called "bullseye" label. Monos have orange, purple and black fan around the center hole and "Atlantic" in orange and purple band at top; stereos have blue and green fan around the center hole and "Atlantic" in blue and green band at top.

1960-61: "White fan logo" issues. Monos were orange and purple, stereos were green and blue. Through the center hole is a white strip; on the right side of the center hole, a white "fan" in a black background can be found.

1961-68: "Black fan logo" issues. The "fan" at right switches to a black logo inside a white box.

1969-end: Red and green label with Atlantic logo at top. Early editions have an "1841 Broadway" address along the lower rim; later on, the address was changed and a small "W" (Warner Communications) logo was added.

Custom labels were used for some releases.

AUDIO LAB

A budget label created by Syd Nathan of King Records, all Audio Lab LPs have blue labels with silver print.

BELL

1965-69: Blue label, silver print.

1970-74: Silver label, black print.

BETHLEHEM

Original Bethlehem labels were maroon with silver print, with the word "Bethlehem" in an arc at the top of the label and a treble clef with ornamentation below. Later labels were maroon with silver print and "BETHLEHEM" in a silver box at the top and the words "HIGH FIDELITY" underneath.

It went through several distributors. In 1959, King Records acquired a half-interest in the label, then in 1962 took full ownership. Around this time, the back covers began to have the King Records address on them.

After a dormant period, Bethlehem returned in the 1970s with a series of reissues; these can be identified easily because there is information on the cover that they were distributed by RCA Victor.

BLUE NOTE

No other label inspires such passion among jazz album collectors as Blue Note. In some cases, even the most minute of label differences can mean a lot.

Lexington Ave. issues:

1951-57 (all original 10-inch LPs, and 12-inch LPs numbered 1200 and 1501 to about 1543): White label with blue print, "33 1/3 Microgroove Long Playing" in large print along the edge of the label from about 11 o'clock to about 4 o'clock, with "Blue Note Records 767 Lexington Ave. NYC" underneath that. All Blue Note LPs with this label are in mono.

The earliest of these records, especially in the 10-inch series, do not have a so-called "groove guard" along the edge of the LP, as later pressings do. The highly collectible issues that *do* have the raised edge also have what is known as a "deep groove" in both sides of the record, visible on the label between the words "33 1/3 Microgroove Long Playing" and "Blue Note Records 767 Lexington Ave. NYC."

West 63rd issues:

1958-62 (from 1544 to the end of the 1500s and the 4000 series to about 4100): White label with blue print, "33 1/3 Microgroove Long Playing" in large print along the edge of the label from about 11 o'clock to about 4 o'clock, with any of three different variations of the address, in approximate order of release:

"Blue Note Records – 47 West 63rd – New York 23"

"Blue Note Records – 47 West 63rd – NYC"

"Blue Note Records Inc. – 47 West 63rd – NYC"

Stereo records also exist on this label; these say "33 1/3 Stereo Long Playing" in large print along the edge of the label from 11 o'clock to 4 o'clock.

Most West 63rd issues, like the earlier Lexington Ave. editions, feature the "deep groove" in the label area.

Known anomalies: Some records exist with the Lexington Ave. address on one label and the West 63rd address on the other; these get the West 63rd prices.

West 61st issues:

As best as can be ascertained, *no* Blue Note labels ever used the "43 West 61st St., New York" on them, though covers did. Copies of this cover address have been found with records containing West 63rd labels, "New York, USA" labels, even "A Division of Liberty Records, Inc." labels.

New York, USA issues:

1962-66 (from about 4101 to about 4252, including stereo equivalents in the 84000 series): White label with blue print, "33 1/3 Microgroove Long Playing" or "33 1/3 Stereo Long Playing" in large print along the edge of the label from about 11 o'clock to about 4 o'clock, with "Blue Note Records Inc. – New York, USA" underneath that.

Most "New York, USA" issues, like the earlier Lexington Ave. and West 63rd editions, feature the

"deep groove" in the label area. But because many of these are first re-pressings of Lexington Ave. or West 63rd editions, these versions do not bring as much as their earlier counterparts.

Known anomalies: Some later editions with this label have a small registered trademark symbol ® under the letter "E" of the word "NOTE" on the label. These are not common, but they seem to bring less than copies that don't have the ® on the label.

Liberty issues:

1966-70 (from about 84253 to somewhere in the early 84300s): White label with blue print, "33 1/3 Microgroove Long Playing" or "33 1/3 Stereo Long Playing" in large print along the edge of the label from about 11 o'clock to about 4 o'clock, with "Blue Note Records – A Division of Liberty Records, Inc." underneath that.

All of these have the ® symbol under the final "E" of "NOTE."

With the sale of Blue Note to Liberty in 1966, there may still be a groove in the label area, but it is no longer the "deep groove" of the 1950s and earlier 1960s.

Many reissues of earlier albums exist with this label.

Liberty/UA issues:

1970 (possibly only in 84330s and 84340s): Black label, with a light blue area covering the far left area of the label. Centered atop this blue area is a rectangular "Blue Note" logo similar to the logo that appeared on covers before this. At the bottom of the label in white are the words "Liberty/UA Inc. Los Angeles, California."

Reissues exist on this label. Jazz discographers have had a difficult time placing this label, because few of the known records on this label are original editions. But Transamerica, the owners of the Liberty/UA labels at this time, folded the Liberty label in early 1971. Therefore this label cannot be any later than that. Also, this label must come before the "United Artists" labels (see next entry).

United Artists issues:

1971-73 (from about 84349 until the 84000s were discontinued): White label with blue print restored, "33 1/3 Stereo Long Playing" in large print along the edge of the label from about 11 o'clock to about 4 o'clock, with "Blue Note Records – A Division of United Artists Records, Inc." underneath that. All of these have the ® symbol under the final "E" of "NOTE." Unlike earlier versions of this label, however, the album title, artist, number, song titles and personnel information are often printed in *black*. Reissues exist with this label.

1973-76 (original Blue Notes of this period were integrated into the new United Artists numbering system; new Blue Notes had numbers such as "BN-LA000-G"): Dark blue label, stylized black "b" in the upper right corner of the label with a blue eighth note forming the hole of the "b," with the words "Blue Note" underneath, in black, to the right of the center hole. Artist, title and number information is in silver print. At the bottom of this label in black are the words "Blue Note Records – A Division of United Artists Records Inc. – Made in U.S.A. – All Rights Reserved." Reissues exist with this label.

1977-78: (original Blue Notes of this period were integrated into the United Artists numbering system; new Blue Notes had numbers such as "BN-LA000-G"): Dark blue label, stylized white "b" in the upper right corner of the label with a blue eighth note forming the hole of the "b," with the words "Blue Note" underneath, in white, to the right of the center hole. Artist, title and number information is in silver print. At the bottom of this label in black are the words "Blue Note Records – Manufactured by United Artists Music and Records Group Inc. – Los Angeles, California – Made in U.S.A." Reissues exist with this label.

Mid 1970s (dates vary): Dark blue label, stylized white "b" inside a black circle in the upper *left* corner of the label with a blue eighth note forming the hole of the "b," with the words "The Blue Note" above the black circle and "Re-Issue Series" below the black circle. Artist, title and number information is in silver print. At the bottom of this label in black are the words "Blue Note Records – Manufactured by United Artists Music and Records Group Inc. – Los Angeles, California – Made in U.S.A."

Capitol/EMI issues:

1986-present: White label with blue print, "The Finest in Jazz Since 1939" in large print along the edge of the label from about 11 o'clock to about 4 o'clock. Both new issues and reissues exist with this label.

Classic Records issues:

1999-present: These attempt to duplicate, as closely as possible, the original issues of the LPs. But all of these do have a Classic Records disclaimer on the back cover amid the legalese.

Japanese reissues:

We don't cover these specifically in the price guide; on average, they seem to bring around $30 in near-mint condition, so they have value. They are made to look almost identical to original pressings, just as the Classic re-releases are. But the best way to identify these is the word "JASRAC" on the label and-or the trail-off wax.

BLUE THUMB

1969 (first four LPs): Black label.

1969-74 (Gulf & Western distribution): Off-white, almost gray label, with blue thumb print at upper left.

1974-end: Multicolored (yellow, orange, purple) "target" label with "abc Blue Thumb" at top of label between two lines and a blue thumb print at upper left.

BLUESVILLE
1960-63: Bright blue label with silver print.
1964-end: Lighter blue label with Prestige trident logo at right side.

BLUESWAY
1967-68: Blue label.
1968-74: Black label, blue rim around outside.

BRUNSWICK
1950-63: Black label, silver print.
1963-72: Black label, color band through center, "A Division of Decca Records" in fine print.
1972-end: Black label, color band through center, "Manufactured by Brunswick Record Corp." along rim.

BUDDAH
1967-72: Multicolor kaleidoscope label with black drawing of Buddha at bottom and "BUDDAH RECORDS" on either side of drawing.
1972-76: Maroon label with smiling Buddha figure, "BUDDAH RECORDS" in white at top.
1977-end: Black label with Arista logo added at bottom.

BUENA VISTA
Best known as the label of Annette, it actually predates her hits slightly.
The first series was BV-1300; these have turquoise labels with silver print.
The BV-3300 series, where the Annette records are, were first issued with a black label and silver print. Later ones were issued with a half black, half mostly yellow label with a slight rainbow effect, "Buena Vista" in black over the yellow section.
The BV-4000 series was a continuation of the Disneyland WDL-4000 series (see Disneyland listing for more detail). 4022-4025 were originally issued on black labels, silver print; 4026-4048 first came out on the half black, half yellow label mentioned in the BV-3300 series.
The 1980s issues in the 62000 series have a blue and red label with a white strip just above the center hole that goes through the middle of the center hole. The "Buena Vista" logo is in red at the upper left.

CADENCE
(Not to be confused with the 1980s label "Cadence Jazz," this is the 1950s and early 1960s label.)
1954-61 (1000 series, 3000-3051?, 4000s, 5000s, 25000 series to 25051?): Maroon lower two-thirds of label; upper third is silver with "cadence" in lowercase and a metronome logo.
1961-64 (3052?-3068, 25052?-25068): Red label, black rim with "CADENCE RECORDS" inside in white.

CADET
Cadet replaced the Argo label in 1965. Many Argo titles were reissued in Argo covers with Cadet labels.

The first label was an all light blue label with "CADET" across the top in black.
The second label was a fading blue label with "CADET" across the top in fading red, white and blue letters.
1971-end (50000 and 60000 series, GRT distribution): Yellow label, red rim, horizontal red stripe through center hole, "CADET" at left.

CADET CONCEPT
All issues have a gray label with black print, "CADET" in pink, "CONCEPT" in orange (red).

CAMDEN – See RCA CAMDEN.

CAMEO
1958 (1001): Black label, brown print, cameo at top.
1958-60 (1002-1007?): Orange label, black print, cameo at top.
1960-68: Red and black label, white cameo in yellow border at left.
1968 (20,000): Purple label, white at top, "Cameo" across the top in an arc, cameo logo inside "o."

CANADIAN-AMERICAN
1959-61 (1001-1005?): Black label, silver print.
1961-65 (1006?-1018): Black label, five color bars across top of label.

CAPITOL
Capitol is at times a confusing label. For now, we're sticking to the regular pop series in this label roundup. Especially in the 1980s, the budget labels used different color schemes; for now, we're ignoring them, but we would appreciate more information.
1949-54 (10-inch albums, most with "H" prefix): Purple label with silver print. Some labels have a silver ring near the outer rim, some do not. Also, some exist with a red label and gold print and/or an "L" prefix.
1954-58 (12-inch mono albums): On albums with a "T" prefix, turquoise label, with or without silver ring near outer rim. Some albums, those with a "W" prefix, were issued with a gray label.
1958-59 (mono and stereo, approx. 1021-1225): Black label, rainbow ring around outside rim (usually called the "black colorband label") with white Capitol logo and "Long Playing High Fidelity" at the left of the label.
1959-62 (mono and stereo, approx. 1226-1660?): Same as 1958-59, except a white line replaces the words "Long Playing High Fidelity."
1962-68 (approx. 1660-2999): Black colorband label, Capitol logo moved to top of label.
1968-69 (approx. 101-200s in new numbering system): Black colorband label, Capitol logo at top, with extra print along the edge of the colorband "A Subsidiary of Capitol Industries, Inc." added to "Mfd. By Capitol Records Inc."

1969-71 (200s into the 700s?): Lime green label, "Capitol" at upper left, new Capitol "target" logo at top.

1971-72 (700s into early 11000s): Red label, "Capitol" at upper left, purple Capitol "target" logo at top. Sometimes assumed to be a country label only, it was used on all Capitol releases for this short period.

1972-78 (Early 11000s into 11800s): Orange label, "Capitol" in greenish letters across bottom of label. Some issues geared toward the R&B market have a red label with "Capitol" in black letters across the bottom.

1978-83 (11800s into 12200s): Purple label with huge white "Capitol" logo dominating the top third of the label.

1983-88: The black colorband label with the logo at the top returns, except that the perimeter print is in black, inside the color ring, instead of outside it in white as in the 1960s.

1988-present: Purple label with much smaller Capitol logo at top of label and a long ring of unbroken type around the outer rim.

Custom labels were used on many titles, and especially from 1978 to the present, older labels were often used out of sequence to create a nostalgic feel.

CARLTON

All labels are tan with a black "C" around the center ring and a white strip to the right with a black "Carlton" in it.

CASABLANCA

1974 (9000 series): Dark blue label with Bogart mug and "Manufactured and Distributed by Warner Bros. Records Inc." in white along the bottom.

1974-76 (7000-7020s): Dark blue label with Bogart mug, "Manufactured and Distributed by Casablanca Records Inc." in white along the bottom.

1976-77 (7020s-7050?): Tan label, desert scene at top, "Casablanca" at top.

1977-81 (7050?-7100s): Tan label, desert scene at top, "Casablanca Record and FilmWorks" at top.

1981-end (7100s into six-digit numbers): "Manufactured and Distributed by Polygram" at bottom.

CHALLENGE

1958-63 mono (600-617): Blue label, silver print, "Challenge" logo in oval at top.

1960-65 stereo (2500-2521): Black label, silver print, "Challenge" logo in oval at top.

1963-65 mono (618-621): Blue-green label, silver print, "Challenge" logo in oval at top.

1966-67 (622-624, 2522-2524): Black label, silver print, "CHALLENGE" in block letters across the top.

1969-end (2000 series): Black label, white coat of arms logo at top, "Challenge" in red.

CHANCELLOR

1958-59 (5001-5003): Pink label, black print.

1959-63 (5004-5032): Black label, silver print, "Chancellor" in red across top of label.

CHECKER

1957-65 (1400s and 2971-2995): Black label, silver print, "CHECKER" at left of center hole in vertical block letters. Some issues have maroon label with silver print that are otherwise identical to the black label versions.

1965-66 (2996-3001): Light blue label with alternating red and black checkers at top of label.

1966-71 (3002-3017): Fading blue label with "CHECKER" across the top in fading red, white and blue letters.

1971-end (reissues): Blue label, purple rim, purple stripe through center hole, "CHECKER" at left.

CHESS

1956-1963 (1425-1482): Black label, silver print, "CHESS" at left of center hole in vertical block letters. Some issues have blue label with silver print that are otherwise identical to the black label versions. Those few stereo releases in this time had gold labels with black print.

1963-65 (1483?-1500?): Black label, "CHESS" across the top in gold with a four-color knight chess piece in back. This basic label design also exists on a blue label with all-silver print and no four-color graphics.

1965 (1490s): Fading blue label, "CHESS" across the top in all white letters.

1965-71 (1500-1553 and 400 series): Fading blue label with "CHESS" across the top in fading red, white and blue letters.

1971-76 (50000 and 60000 series, later 200, 400 and 700 series): Orange label, light blue rim, light blue stripe through center hole, "CHESS" at left.

1982-89 (8200, 8300, 8400, 8500, 9000 series): Dark blue label, silver print, "CHESS RECORDS" in arc at top, checkerboard motif around lower edge.

CHRYSALIS

1972-77: Green label, red butterfly at lower left, "Chrysalis" in red along bottom.

1977-87: White label fading to blue at bottom, white butterfly at lower left, "Chrysalis" in white along bottom. During this time, distribution changed from independent to the CBS family of labels; reissues of 1300-series albums have a new prefix, usually "PV," and the number "4" before the four digits.

1987-89: White label, colored butterfly at left.

1989-end: Off-white label, different butterfly logo.

CIRCLE

Early to mid 1950s: White label, "Circle" in script lettering.

Late 1950s: White label, "Circle" in block lettering.

CLASS
1957-58 (5001-5002): Black label, silver print.
1959 (5003-5004): Maroon label, silver print.

CLEF
Before 1956: Black label, drawing of trumpet player at upper left, "Clef Records, Inc." at bottom.
1956 and later: The label was incorporated into Verve; "Clef Series" appears under "Verve Records" on reissues of some Clef titles and some new releases as well.

COED
1960 (901): Yellow label, black print.
1960 (902): Black label, silver print.
1961-63 (903-906): Red label, black and white print.

COLGEMS
1966-67: Red label, white area at top in which "COLGEMS" appears in red, "TM of Colgems Records" appears underneath the top logo.
1967-70: Same as above, "TM of Colgems Records" is deleted.

COLPIX
1958-62?: Gold label, "COLPIX" in red curving around top of label with line drawing of Statue of Liberty underneath.
1962?-64?: Gold label, strip of movie film with "COLPIX RECORDS" in white background within.
1964?-66?: Light blue label, strip of movie film with "COLPIX RECORDS" in light blue background within.
1966 (4001, stereo only): Dark blue label, silver print, no strip of movie film.

COLUMBIA (pop)
The below apply only to pop (GL, CL, CS series before 1970, prefixes ending in "C" after 1970) releases.

10-Inch LPs:
1948-54 (6000 series): Maroon label, gold print, "Long Playing" at bottom.
1955 (10-inch LPs, 2500 House Party Series): Red and black label with six white "eye" logos, three at left, three at right.

12-Inch Mono LPs:
1951-53 (501-525): Black label, silver print, "Long Playing" at bottom. Originals have a "GL" prefix.
1953-55 (525-600s): Maroon label, gold print, "Long Playing" at bottom.
1955-62 (600s-no earlier than 1779): Red and black label with six white "eye" logos, three at left, three at right.
(See below.)
1962-65 (1780?-2300s): Red label, "COLUMBIA" in white along the top, "GUARANTEED HIGH FIDELITY" in black along bottom.
1965-68 (2300s-2800s): Red label, "COLUMBIA" in white along the top, "360 SOUND MONO 360 SOUND" in white along the bottom. Some of the 1968 issues simply say "MONO" along the bottom.

12-Inch Stereo LPs:
1958-62 (8000-no earlier than 8579): Red and black label with six white "eye" logos, three at left, three at right, "STEREO FIDELITY" in white along the bottom.
1962-63 (8580?-unknown): Red label, "COLUMBIA" in white along the top, "360 SOUND STEREO 360 SOUND" in black along bottom, no arrows.
1963-65 (range unknown): Red label, "COLUMBIA" in white along the top, "360 SOUND STEREO 360 SOUND" in black along bottom, arrows added to left of first "360" and right of second "SOUND."
1965-70 (9100s-9999, CS 1000 series, 30000-30050?): Red label, "COLUMBIA" in white along the top, "360 SOUND STEREO 360 SOUND" in white along the bottom.
1970-90: Orange label, gold "COLUMBIA" six times in ring along outer edge.
1990-present: Red label, "COLUMBIA" in white along top, all other label print in black.
Custom labels were used for some releases.

COLUMBIA SPECIAL PRODUCTS (CSP)
Late 1950s-1970: Red label, black strip curving along the top of the label, "COLUMBIA SPECIAL PRODUCTS" in white over the black.
1971-82?: Orange label, "CSP" in yellow at top of label, "COLUMBIA SPECIAL PRODUCTS" in smaller print beneath.
1982?-early 1990s: Orange label, "CBS SPECIAL PRODUCTS" in three lines to the left of the center hole.
Early 1990s: Orange label, "Sony Music Special Products" in two lines to the left of the center hole.

CONTEMPORARY
Mono editions from the 1950s and early 1960s have yellow labels with black print. There are three subtly different versions of this label; we don't know if this is the order in which they were issued or not. One

has the words "RECORDS" along the bottom with no ornamentation. A second label variant has a small interlocking "CR" inside the "O" of "RECORDS," and a third has the letters "CR" in yellow in a black box above the "O" of "RECORDS."

The earliest stereo records on Contemporary actually used the designation "Stereo Records" instead of Contemporary. These have gold labels with black print. All of these eventually were reissued on Contemporary, again with gold labels and black print.

1970s: Green label.

1980s: Orange-gold label.

Fantasyhas reissued some Contemporary LPs with original-style labels; these are distinguished from originals by their "OJC" prefixes.

CORAL

1950s-1963: Maroon label, silver print.

1963-68: Black label, rainbow ring near center, "A Subsidiary of Decca Records" in fine print.

1968-70: Black label, rainbow ring near center, "A Division of MCA Records" in fine print.

COTILLION

1969-72: Grayish label, "Cotillion" in box at top.

1976-80s: Reactivated label; purple with a round "C" logo at top.

CROWN

This was a budget label. It began by putting some rare R&B and blues sides on LP, but eventually its issues became cheesier and cheesier.

1950s-60: Black label, gold or silver print. Some of the early Crown titles also exist on red vinyl.

1960-mid 60s: Black label, each letter of "CROWN" in a different color.

Mid 60s-late 60s: Gray label, black print.

DAKAR

1969-70 (9000s): Black label with wide rainbow colorband along the edge.

1972-76 (76900s): White label, black print.

DECCA

1949-54 (10-inch LPs in the 5000 series plus 12-inch LPs in the 8000 series): Black label, gold print. Earliest pressings have a "DLP" prefix, which was quickly replaced by "DL."

1954-60 (later 10-inch LPs and 12-inch LPs from around 8100 to 8981): Black label, silver print. Stereo pressings, which added a "7" to the mono number, had maroon labels with silver print.

1960-66 (4000-4830s, 74000-74830s): Black label with rainbow stripe through center hole and "Mfrd. By Decca Records" in the fine print.

1967-71 (4830s to end of mono, 74830 into some 75000s and 79000s): Black label with rainbow stripe through center hole and "A Division of MCA" in the fine print.

1972-73: Black label with rainbow stripe through

center hole and "Mfrd. By MCA" in the fine print.

In addition to the regular series, Decca had a "Gold Label Series" of classical music; these have gold labels with black print.

MCA merged Decca, Uni and Kapp in January 1973 and closed down all three.

DEL-FI

1959 (1201): Light blue, black printing, blue circles on a black background around the outside of the label.

1959 (1202-1204): Light blue label, gold and black diamonds around the outside of the label.

1959-64 (1205-1249): Black label, blue and gold diamonds around the outside of the label.

DERAM

The basic label is white at the bottom, brown at the top with "DERAM" in white letters over the brown background.

Some U.S. pressings have the word "DERAM" in a smaller brown box, with the word "LONDON" in script underneath; these are not easy to find.

DISNEYLAND

One of the most confusing labels, albums were issued in several numerical series, sometimes simultaneously.

The first LPs on the label were in the WDL-4000 series. Early pressings have yellow labels and black print with "A Disneyland Record" underneath the center hole. Later editions have red labels with silver print and "Disneyland" in an arc above the center hole.

The WDL-3000 series came next. 3001 was issued with the above yellow label; it was reissued, and all others had their original issue, with a purple label, silver print, and "Disneyland" along the upper edge of the label.

Next were the ST-3900 series. Original editions were issued with purple labels, silver print. Some were reissued in the 1970s with a yellow label, a rainbow band curving along the top edge and "Disneyland" in white on the rainbow.

The next series was in the ST-1900 range. Original editions of these have light blue labels with black print; some later originals and first reissues have a darker blue label; the final reissues have green labels.

The next, and most common, series was the DQ-1200 and 1300 series. Original issues have yellow labels with black print, "Disneyland" curving along the top. Reissues from the 1970s and 1980s have the yellow rainbow label and usually omit the "DQ."

A 1970s and 1980s line was the 2500 series; all of these come with the yellow rainbow label.

Further clarifications are welcome.

DOLTON

1959-62: Light blue label, dark blue print with fish logos at left of center hole.

1962-65: Darker blue label, multicolor fish logo to the left of the center hole.

1966-68: Mostly black label, blue section to left of center hole with stylized red-and-black "D" in white background.

DORE

1960s: Light blue label, feather at top.

1970s: Dark blue label, larger feather on top.

1970s: Black label, multicolor logo.

DOT

1954-56: Maroon label with "Gallatin, Tennessee" in fine print. A possible transition label, maroon with "Hollywood, Cal." in fine print, may exist. (45s exist with this label.)

1956-68: Black label, multicolored cursive "Dot" logo at top.

1968-70: Black label, both "DOT" and Paramount logos appear at top of label.

1971-74: Purple and orange label, "DOT" in box at top of label.

1974-75: Multicolored (yellow, orange, purple) "target" label with "abc Dot Records" at top of label between two lines.

1976-77: Multicolored (yellow, orange, purple) "target" label with "abc Dot" at top of label between two lines.

DUNHILL

1965-68 (50000-50030s): Black label, "DUNHILL" in white with gold border at top.

1968-72 (50030s-50170s): Black label, "DUNHILL" and "abc" in multicolored boxes at top.

1973: "DUNHILL" in a white rectangle spelled out in children's blocks. Very short-lived label. Quickly replaced by 1968-72 label again until another new label was created.

1974-75: Multicolored (yellow, orange, purple) "target" label with "abc Dunhill" at top of label between two lines.

ELEKTRA

1950s: White label with "electron" logo.

Late 1950s-1961?: Gray label, small guitar player at top.

1961?-1966?: Gold label, large guitar player at top.

1966-69: Gold (tan) label with large stylized "E" at top.

1969-70: Red label with large stylized "E" at top.

1971-74: Dark greenish label with butterfly holding white stylized "E" at left, "13 Columbus Circle" address along outer edge.

1975-79: Lighter greenish label with butterfly holding white stylized "E" at left, "W" (Warner Communications) logo added to the fine print.

1980-83: Red label, small white stylized "E" logo at top.

1984-89: Black and red label, "ELEKTRA" across top.

1989-91: Gray label.

1991-present: Tan label.

Custom labels were used for some releases.

EMARCY

"EmArcy" is a phonetic spelling of "MRC" or "Mercury Record Corporation." The label was used off and on in the 1950s, 1960s and beyond.

1954-58: Blue label, silver print, "EmArcy" logo at upper left, line drawing of a drummer at right.

Early 1960s: Blue label, silver print, "Mercury" logo in double oval, "Emarcy Jazz" under the word "Mercury" sandwiched between the two ovals.

Later 1960s: Gray label.

1970s and 1980s reissues: Brownish label with brown border; line drawing of drummer at top.

EMBER

1958 (100, 200, 300, 400): Red label, black print.

1959 (401, reissues of earlier titles): White label, black print, eight circles around the outside of the label. The word "EMBER" is depicted in burning logs.

1960s (reissues): Black label, silver print.

1960s (800 series): Black label, "EMBER" logo at left with red flames emanating from it.

END

All End LPs (301-316) were issued with a gray label, a front end of a dog at top left, the back end of a dog at top right, and "end" in red letters. The words "A Product of End Music Inc., New York, N.Y." is at the bottom.

Reissues have the same basic label design, but "A Division of Roulette Records, Inc." is the new fine print.

Still later reissues have a light blue label with an orange band through the center hole and the word "END" in blue on either end of the band.

ENJOY

The only album issued on this label has a gold label with blue print.

ENTERPRISE

1967-68 (13-100 series): Blue label, rainbow at top with "Enterprise" in black over the rainbow. These were distributed by Atlantic.

1968-72 (1001-1024, 5000-5002): Black label, "ENTERPRISE" in yellow at top.

1972-74 (1025-1038, 5003-5007, 7501-7510): Black label, "ENTERPRISE" in white directly above center hole, large rainbow-colored stylized "E" above that.

EPIC

1955-62: Yellow label with series of short black lines around the perimeter and "Epic" on top. Some early labels also are gold with a similar design. Stereo issues (1959-62) have the same label but with "Stereorama" above the word "Epic" on the top of the label.

1962-63: Yellow label with "Epic" appearing eight times around the perimeter (mono); yellow label

with "Epic Stereo" appearing three times around the perimeter (stereo)

1963-65 (24040s-24160s mono, 26040s-26160s stereo): Yellow label, "A Product of CBS" as part of the fine print.

1965-73 (all later monos, stereos into the 31000s): Yellow label, no "A Product of CBS" at bottom.

1973-79: Orange label with white concentric circles, Epic logo in white at top.

1979-present: Dark blue label, "Epic" in cursive letters across top.

EXCELLO

1960-mid 1960s (8000-8005?): Orange label, blue print.

Mid 1960s-early 1970s: White label, black print, pink and green arrows at top of label.

Early 1970s-1976: Light blue label, "excello" in white background in box.

FANTASY

10-Inch LPs

All of these have maroon labels with gold print. All were pressed on various shades of vinyl as well as black vinyl. Versions exist on red, blue, green, purple and even combinations of more than one color.

12-Inch LPs (mono)

Mono albums originally were numbered with a 3-prefix and starting at 200. Eventually, the dash was dropped and these became the 3200 series. All of these should have red labels with gold print, though some near the end of the mono series may have red labels with silver print.

The below dates are approximate; we don't know at what numbers the changeovers occurred.

1955-57: Records are deep red vinyl, almost maroon.

1957-58: Original pressings are on black vinyl; it is unknown how many records first issued on red vinyl between 1955 and 1957 were reissued at this time.

1958-63: Original pressings are on bright red vinyl.

1963-67: Original pressings are on black vinyl.

12-Inch LPs (stereo)

Stereo albums were numbered in the 8000s originally; with a change in list price of LPs in the early 1970s, the "8" was changed to "9" on new issues.

Early 1960s-1963: Original pressings have a blue label with gold print, and the records are on bright blue vinyl.

1963-72: Original pressings have a blue label with gold print and are on black vinyl. Some later pressings have blue labels with silver print. Also, the vinyl itself began to get flimsier.

1972-74: Brown label with circular stylized "F" logo at top. Lighter brown horizontal and vertical bars form the same "F" logo on the entire label.

1974-78: Brown label with circular stylized "F" logo at top, with no lighter brown bars.

1978-early 1980s: Blue fading to white label with lightning bolts around the circular stylized "F" logo at top.

Early 1980s on: Blue label with purple stylized "F" logo at top.

Some reissues in the "OJC" series use the label that was contemporary at the time the record was first issued. The prefix and new number give away their reissue status.

Colored vinyl note

When Fantasy was doing red vinyl mono LPs and blue vinyl stereo LPs at the same time, sometimes the signals got crossed. We know of examples with blue labels and red vinyl, and we also know of records with red labels and blue vinyl. We do not yet know if the sound matches the label or the vinyl color; in other words, we don't know if the red vinyl records play mono despite having stereo labels, or if they play stereo, to match the label information. These are uncommon, and are quite collectible, unlike most "error pressings."

FEDERAL

Early 10-inch albums have all-green labels, "Federal" in silver across the top.

Albums in the 500 series have black labels with silver print and the word "Federal" straight across the top of the label. These are among the rarest and most valuable albums in all of record collecting. Federal albums with green labels and silver top appear to be bootlegs.

FELSTED

All Felsted albums have orange labels with black print.

FIRE

1959-60 (100-101): White label, red print.

1960-62 (102-105): Red label, black print.

FORUM/FORUM CIRCLE

This budget label reissued material that first appeared on the Roulette label.

1960 (16000 series): Black label, gold print.

1961-63 (9000 series): Mono issues have maroon labels; stereo issues have red labels.

1964 (Forum Circle series): Mono issues have light blue labels, stereo issues have yellow labels.

FRATERNITY

1950s (1001-1012?): Light blue label.

Early 1960s (1013?-1018?): Red label, black print.

Mid to late 1960s and beyond (1019?-1028): Maroon label, silver print.

GEE

1956-59 (701-704): Red label, black print, "GEE" in large red letters in a black background at top.

1961-62 (705-707): Gray label, "GEE RECORDS" across the bottom.

GEFFEN

1980-85: White label with horizontal pinstripes.
1985-1990s: Black label.

GONE

All albums on this label, which had LP releases from 1958-61, have pink and tan labels.

GORDY

1962-67 (901-927?): Purple label, "Gordy" in cursive yellow letters at top superimposed over an oval with the slogan "IT'S WHAT'S IN THE GROOVES THAT COUNT."
1968-1980s (928? forward): Purple label, "GORDY" in purple to left of center hole, yellow wedge going through center hole from left to right.

HARMONY

This was Columbia's budget label from the mid 1950s until the early 1970s.
1957-early 1960s: Maroon label, silver print.
Early 1960s-late 1960s: Black label, silver print.
Late 1960s-early 1970s: Brown label.
Early 1970s: Gold label, Harmony logo in red.

HERALD

1955-58 (0100-0111): "Spokes label": Multicolored spokes emanate from the center hole to the outside. Above the center hole is a yellow trumpet with a yellow banner and "HERALD" in black print.
1960 (1012): Black label, silver print.
1960-62 (1013-1015): Yellow label, silver print.

HICKORY

1960-62 (100-110?): Black label, silver print, "Hickory" slants upward at top of label.
1963-73 (111?-168): Black label, rainbow at upper left.
1973-75 (4501-4524): Brown label, rainbow at upper left, "MGM Records" lion at right of center hole.
1976-77 (44001-44009?): Multicolored (yellow, orange, purple) "target" label with "abc Records" at top of label between two lines and the "Hickory" logo at left of center hole.
1977-79 (44010?-44017): Multicolored (yellow, orange, purple) "target" label with "abc" in an eighth note at top of label, and "Hickory" logo to the right of the note.

HIFI

Standard issues have silver labels with "HIFIRECORD" three times around the perimeter. The word "HIFI" is in silver, "RECORD" is in red.
Jazz records have silver labels with 'HIFIJAZZ" four times around the perimeter. The word "HIFI" is in silver, "JAZZ" is in red.
Also see LIFE.

HIP

Four albums came out on this label from 1969-72. The label is red and pink with "Hip" in blue print bordered in black.

IMPERIAL

1950-56 (10-inch LPs; 12-inch LPs in the 100 series): Blue label, "IMPERIAL" in script print at top.
1956-57 (9001-9041?): Maroon label, "IMPERIAL" in silver block letters at top.
1957-64 (9042?-9267?, mono): Black label with colored rays emanating from Imperial logo at top.
1959-64 (12001-12267?, stereo): Black label, silver print, with "IMPERIAL STEREO" directly above the center hole. Some of the later 12250-12267 issues had the mono "colored rays" label with the word "Stereo" added.
1964-66 (9268?-9320s?, 12268?-12320s?): Black label, "IR/Imperial" to left of center hole, white area above logo, pink area below logo.
1966-70 (9320s? to end of monos, 12320s?-12457): Black label, "IR/Imperial" logo to left of center hole in white with red background; green areas above and below logo, which has been enlarged.

IMPULSE!

1961-68 (1-100 and at least to 9124): Orange label, wide black ring around outside of label, with the word "impulse!" appearing four times in the black area.
1968-72: Black label, red border "impulse!" and "abc" in multicolored boxes at top.
1973-74: Black label, no red border, "impulse" in multicolored letters, "impulse" and "abc" in boxes at top.
1974-77: Multicolored (green, blue, purple) "target" label with "abc Impulse" at top of label between two lines.
1978-79: Multicolored (yellow, red, purple) "target" label with "abc" musical note standing alone and "Impulse" at top of label between two lines.
1980s reissues I: Records in the MCA-29000 series had MCA blue labels with a rainbow, with a small "impulse!" logo above "MCA RECORDS."
1980s reissues II: Some reissues have a black and red label with "MCA impulse!" in white just under the 9 o'clock position.
1990s reissues: Orange label, narrow black ring around outside, "impulse!" in black at 3 o'clock.

ISLAND

Since the label was first set up as a U.S. entity in 1972, it's been distributed by Capitol, independently, by Warner Bros. and Atco (at the same time for different artists!) and PolyGram. The labels have changed even more often than the distribution, and it's possible we missed a variation or two.
1972-74: Sunray label, "ISLAND" along bottom of label in stylized letters.
1974-75: Yellow background on label, "water skier" offshore, "island" along top.
1975-77: Black label with "I" logo at bottom and "Island Records" underneath.
1977-80: Orange and blue label.

1981-82: Light blue label with darker blue ring around the outside.

1982-83: Dark purple label with skyscraper at left and "Island" slanting upward.

1983-84: Light blue label, "Island" in red across top.

1985-90: Black label.

Custom labels were used for some issues.

JAMIE

1958: Yellow label.

1959-67: White and gold label.

1970 (3034): Orange and black label.

JANUS

1970-76 (3000s, early 7000s): Brownish gold label.

1977-78 (later 7000s): Reddish orange label.

JAZZLAND

Mono labels are yellow with black print. Stereo labels are black with silver print.

JOSIE

The first label was cream colored with blue print and "josie" at the top of the label in a blue oval.

The second label was tan with black print with the "josie" logo in a black oval. The logo sits atop a group of multicolored stripes emanating vertically from a horizontal white line that goes through the center hole.

The third label was tan with black print, "JOSIE" spelled in five different colors vertically to the left of the center hole.

JUBILEE

1950s (10-inch LPs from 1-25, 12-inch LPs from 1000-1014?): Pink label, black print.

1956-59 (1015?-1104?): Blue label, silver print.

1959-61 (1105?-1121?): Flat black label, silver print, "jubilee" in silver spiked oval at top of label.

1961-64 (5001-5055): Glossy black label, silver print, "jubilee" in large colored spiked oval at top of label.

1965-69 (8001-8031): Glossy black label, silver print, "jubilee" in much smaller colored spiked oval at top of label.

KAMA SUTRA

1965-69: Yellow label.

1970-71: Pink label.

1972-74: Light blue label, Garden of Eden scene at top.

KAPP

1955-59: Maroon label, silver print. Some issues have a blue label, silver print.

1959-62: Black and blue label with red "K" at top of label and "KAPP" underneath.

1962-64: Black and blue label with white major's hat and "KAPP" underneath.

1964-71: Black label with major's hat and "KAPP" underneath.

1971-73: Orange and purple label.

MCA merged Decca, Uni and Kapp in January 1973

and closed down all three.

Custom labels were used on some issues. For example, there are some early Christmas releases with silver labels and red and green holly leaves adorning the label.

KEEN

1958-59 (2000 series): Colored vertical stripes with letters of "KEEN" in individual gray circles.

1959-60 (86100 series): Black label, "KEEN" to left of center hole, five-color vertical stripe next to it.

KING

One of the most confusing labels at first glance, it's made even more so because of the often wide disparity in asking prices for what appear to be insignificant differences in the size and style of logo.

Early to mid 1950s (10-inch LPs): Maroon label, silver print. "KING" is in a straight line at the top of the label.

1955-early 1960s (500-late 600s): Black label, silver print, "KING" curves along the outside and is about two inches wide at the top of the label.

Early 1960s-mid 1960s (late 600s-unknown): Black label, silver print, "KING" curves along the outside and is about three inches wide at the top of the label (the letters are thicker and more stretched out than the earlier version).

Late 1950s-mid 1960s (stereo releases): Blue label, silver print, "KING" curves along the outside and is about three inches wide at the top of the label.

Mid 1960s-early 1970s: Blue label, silver print, "KING" straight across the top with a crown centered above the "I" and "N."

Late 1960s: James Brown LPs had a custom brown and orange label with his face on it.

Early 1970s (1146-1154): Yellow label with a sitting king right of the center hole.

Mid 1970s (16000 series): Yellow label with "KING" vertically at top of label and two protrusions to form a stylized letter "K" coming from it.

Late 1970s (5000 series): Restores blue crowned King label of the mid- to late-1960s.

KIRSHNER

Successor to Calendar Records.

1969-mid 1970s: Orange label, "KIRSHNER" in individual boxes across the top.

Mid 1970s-early 1980s (CBS distribution): White label with multicolor top.

Custom labels were used on some CBS albums.

LAURIE

1959 (1000-1002): Gold label, black print.

1960-1980s (1003-1010, 2002-2052, 4000 series): Gold "pentagram" in center of label with black background surrounding it. Early pressings tend to be quite firm and substantial, and some seem to be almost brittle; later pressings tend to have glossier labels and flimsier wax.

LIBERTY

1956-60 (3001-3140? mono): Turquoise label, silver print, "LIBERTY" at top of label with drawing of Statue of Liberty above.

1958-60 (early 7000s stereo to 7140?): Black label, silver print, "LIBERTY" at top of label with drawing of Statue of Liberty above, huge word "STEREO" just below the logo.

1960-66 (3141?-3420?, 7141?-7420?): Black label, rainbow colored area left of center hole, "LIBERTY" in white over a gold crest left of center hole.

1960-69 (12000 and 14000 "Premier Series"): Gold label, black print, design similar to above except that black lines replace the rainbow area.

1966-69 (3421?-end of mono, 7421?-7620?): Black label, rainbow colored area left of center hole, white vertical line abutting rainbow area, "LIBERTY" in black inside a rounded white box with a Statue of Liberty graphic.

1970-71 (7620?-end of original series): Black label, rainbow colored area left of center hole, white vertical line abutting rainbow area, "LIBERTY" in black inside a squared-off white box with a Statue of Liberty graphic, "Liberty/UA Inc." at bottom of label.

1980-86 (reactivated label, 1000-51100 series and 10000 reissue series): Gray label, multicolored "Liberty" across top.

Custom labels were used for some issues, most notably 1960s issues by the Chipmunks, which have black labels with cartoon renditions of Alvin, Theodore, Simon and David Seville.

LIFE (HIFI)

Actually the "Hifi Life Series," but because of the prominence of the word "Life" on the label, most collectors call this the Life label.

Original issues have a red label with the word "Life" in cursive white letters. Later issues have either yellow or gold labels with a smaller "Life" in black letters.

LIMELIGHT

Original labels are dark green and black with silver print, with multiple images of a spotlight in the background. Later labels are pink with greenish rays emanating from the bottom of the label.LONDON (pop)

London releases can be quite confusing. At times, its records for release in the U.S. were pressed both in the U.S. and in England, and different labels were used in each country. The following applies to pop issues only – classical releases are another ballgame entirely. By the 1980s, almost all, if not all, London classical releases were being pressed in Europe, even those meant for sale in the U.S.

10-Inch Albums

Early to mid 1950s: Some have deep blue labels with gold print; some have red labels with gold print.

12-Inch Mono Albums

Mid 1950s-1964 ("LL" prefix until about 3380): Deep red label, silver print, "LONDON" in cursive capital letters across the top with an "ffrr" ear above the "LONDON." Two horizontal silver lines go through the center hole; between these lines are the words "Full Frequency Range Recording."

1964-65 (about 3380-3430): Deep red label, silver print, "LONDON" in a box with the "ffrr" ear logo to the right of this. All of these pressings have print that says "Made in England by the Decca Record Co., Ltd." and will have upside-down matrix numbers on the label.

1964-65 (about 3380-3460): Deep red label, silver print, "LONDON" stands alone, unboxed, above the center hole. All these labels have print that says "Made in U.S.A." Both the above two series ran at the same time, and neither is more "original" than the other, but the "ffrr" pressings are much more rare.

1966-68 (about 3460 to end): Varying shades of red labels (1966s tend to be bright red, 1967s almost maroon) with "LONDON" in a box at the top of the label.

Stereo Albums

1959-64 (PS series to about 379): Deep blue label, silver print, "LONDON" in cursive capital letters across the top with an "ffss" ear above the "LONDON." Underneath this, in a silver box with blue type, are the words "Full Frequency Stereophonic Sound." The earliest stereos have blue shaded back covers; these are known among audiophiles as "blue backs" and demand a premium.

1964-65 (about 380-430): Deep blue label, silver print, "LONDON" in a box with the "ffss" ear logo to the right of this. All of these pressings have print that says "Made in England by the Decca Record Co., Ltd." and will have upside-down matrix numbers on the label.

1964-65 (about 380-460): Deep blue label, silver print, "LONDON" stands alone, unboxed, above the center hole. All these labels have print that says "Made in U.S.A." Both the above two series ran at the same time, and neither is more "original" than the other, but the "ffss" pressings are much more rare.

1966-78 (about 460-early 700s): Varying shades of blue labels (earlier ones are much richer blue than later ones) with "LONDON" in a box at the top of the label.

A "sunrise" label was used on 45s starting around 1976 until about 1983; it's unknown if this was used on LPs, but if it was, it certainly wasn't used until after 1978. Later London pop labels are white with red trim and "LONDON" in white inside a black upside-down triangle.

MAINSTREAM
1960s: Silvery-blue label.

1970s: Red and black label, "Red Lion Productions" at upper right, "Mainstream" at upper left.

MCA
1973 (2100): All-black label, white print; appears to have been used only on this number.

1973-77: Black label, silver print, rainbow at upper left.

1977-79: Tan label, darker tan ring around rim.

1980-late 1990s: Blue label, black print, rainbow at upper left.

Late 1990s: White label, new "MCA/Music Corporation of America" logo left of center hole.

Custom labels were used on some releases.

MERCURY (pop)
1949-1955 (25000 series, all 10-inch LPs): Black label, silver print, "MERCURY" curving around outside of top of label.

1955-early 1960s (12-inch mono, 20000-20700s, also stereo from 60000 to 60700s): Black label, silver print, "MERCURY" stands alone at top, no print along lower edge of label.

Early 1960s-1965 (20700s-20900s; 60700s-60900s): Black label, silver print, "Mercury" in an oval. Some of these issues add "Vendor: Mercury Record Corporation" along lower edge of label. Stereo editions have the "Vendor: Mercury Record Corporation" under the word "STEREO" at the top.

1965-68 (20900s-end, 60900s-61200?): Red label, "MERCURY" in all capital letters across top with Mercury head at upper left.

1968-72 (61200?-61300s? and early SRM-1 series to 670 or so): Bright red label, twelve "Mercury" logos along the outer rim of the label.

1973-74 (SRM-1-670 to 999?): Bright red label, seven "Mercury" logos along the outer rim of the label.

1974-83: Chicago skyline label.

1983-90s: Black label, "Mercury" in glowing red letters across the top.

1990s: Black label, "Mercury" logo in white inside a red diamond at top of label.

Custom labels exist for some issues.

METROJAZZ
All issues have red labels.

MGM
1949-59 (10-inch LPs and 12-inch LPs to approximately 3770): Yellow label, black trim and print.

1960-68 (3771?-4515?): Black label, multicolor letters across top.

1968-76 (4516? into 5000s): Blue and gold swirl label.

Except for a very few releases, MGM ceased to exist as a record label in 1976; its material became part of the growing PolyGram empire.

MILESTONE
There are several label variations, but we have not yet established the exact chronology. The first one for sure is a white label with red and black print and the outline of an "M" at the top. Probably the second is a blue label with silver print, also with an "M" outline.

In the early 1970s, Milestone became part of the Fantasy family of labels. Albums exist with brown labels (mid 1970s) and red-orange labels (mid to late 1970s). These have a colored-in, stylized "M" at the top.

MINIT
1961-63 (0001-0004): Orange label, black print.

1964-68 (24005-24023?, 40005-40023?): Black label, silver print, "MINIT" logo to left of center hole, "A Product of Liberty Records" along bottom.

1968-89 (40024?-40028): Same as above, but "Liberty/UA Records" is the new perimeter print.

MONUMENT
1959 (4000 and 14000 only): White label, gray to black vertical stripes, "MONUMENT" above center hole in black with gold trim.

1960-62 (4001-4009, 14001-14009): White and copper swirl label, "Monument" at top, Washington Monument right of center hole.

1963 (8000-8004?, 18000-18004?): White and multicolor swirl label, "Monument" at top, Washington Monument right of center hole.

1963-71 (8005?-end, 18005?-18147): Light green label, gold band around rim, stylized blue, pink and yellow Washington monument above "monument" at top of label.

1971-76 (30000 series, CBS distribution): Dark orange, almost brown, label.

1977-81 (6600, 7600, 8600 series): Black label with "MONUMENT" spelled out in simulated stone-carved letters across the top.

1982-83 (38000 series): Silver label.

MOODSVILLE
Originals have green labels with "PRESTIGE" in lighter silver print above the word "MOODSVILLE," also in silver print. Reissues used the Prestige "trident" logo at the right on a blue label.

MOTOWN
1961 (1000): White label, blue print, large blue "M" at top center that serves to turn the two O's in "MOTOWN" on their sides.

1961-62 (1001-1006): Blue label with map on upper half of the label. The original map stretches from western Kansas to the Atlantic coast with a red star over Detroit.

1962-1980s (1007 on): Blue label with map on upper half of the label. This map stretches only from mid-Indiana to mid-Pennsylvania. This design remained basically unchanged into the 1980s, with only changes in perimeter print. There is also more yellow in the word "MOTOWN" in 1970s and 1980s

pressings than in 1960s pressings, where the letters fade from red to yellow to blue. Later pressings never make it all the way to the same rich blue as earlier versions.

MOWEST

A short-lived Motown label of the early 1970s, all of its LPs have a beach-at-sunset label with the top and bottom parts in orange and the middle in light blue.

MUSICOR

1962: Brown label.
1962-69: Black label.
1970-75?: Tan label.
1976?-end: Green and yellow label.

NEW JAZZ

In the 12-inch LP series, 8201 through 8204 were issued originally on the yellow Prestige label. All other original 12-inch LPs, plus reissues of 8201-8204, have purple labels. Later reissues have blue labels with the Prestige "trident" logo at the right side.

NORGRAN

This Norman Granz label is, both on 10-inch and 12-inch LPs, yellow with black print with a drawing at the upper left of two dancers. Later labels are yellow with black print and the "trumpet player" logo (the same one that appears on Clef and Verve) at the upper left.

ODE

1967-70: Yellow label, "Ode" logo in black print left of the center hole.
1970-71: White and silver label, "Ode 70" at upper right.
1971-75: White and silver label, "Ode Records Inc." at upper right.
1975-78: Tan label with both Ode and Epic logos.

OKEH

Although active for a long time, Okeh LPs were only issued from 1962 through 1969. All labels are purple with the familiar "Okeh" logo in gold above the center hole.

PACIFIC JAZZ / WORLD PACIFIC

10-Inch LPs

These have a prefix of "PJ LP-" and have a black label with silver print, "Pacific" on one line toward the upper left, "Jazz" on a second line toward the upper right.

12-Inch LPs

Mid 1950s-1957: Black label, silver print, "Pacific" on one line toward the upper left, "Jazz" on a second line toward the upper right. These have a "PJ" prefix and a number in the 1200s and "PJM" for numbers in the 400s.
Late 1957-60: *Name changed to World Pacific.* These have a black label with silver print. There are two versions of this label; the earlier one has "WORLD PACIFIC RECORDS" on three lines inside a rectangle, with "PACIFIC" much larger than the other two words, with a circle next to it inside the rectangle. The later one has "WORLD PACIFIC RECORDS" on three lines inside a rectangle at the upper left, and an oval inside a rectangle is adjacent to the right. These have a "WP" prefix for numbers in the 1200s and "WPM" for numbers in the 400s. Stereo editions used the same label, but they had an "ST" prefix and were numbered in the 1000s.
1960-65: *Name restored to Pacific Jazz.* Mono records have a black label with silver print, with the words "high fidelity" above the words "PACIFIC JAZZ" on one line at the top; stereo records have a blue label with silver print, with the word "stereo" above the words "PACIFIC JAZZ" on one line at the top.
1965-70: *Two different labels, Pacific Jazz and World Pacific.* The label designs were similar; both were black with a color area at the left of the label. On Pacific Jazz LPs, this colored area is orange and yellow with a "PJ Pacific Jazz" logo in a rectangle. On World Pacific LPs, this area is light blue in the upper half and darker blue in the lower half, with a globe and "World Pacific" in a rectangle.
Around 1970, some LPs were issued with the merged label "World Pacific Jazz."
Later issues on Pacific Jazz are blue and green.

PARAMOUNT

Not to be confused with ABC-Paramount, this was an entirely different label established around 1969.
Most, if not all, original issues have a gray label with Paramount logo to the left of the center hole in black. Some 1970s reissues, after ABC bought the rights to the label, have a blue label with a white "Paramount" logo at the top.

PARKWAY

1960-61 (7001-7005?): Orange label, "PARKWAY" in uneven black letters across the top.
1961-67 (7006?-7057): Orange and yellow label, "PARKWAY" in white letters straight across the top.
1967 (50,000): Gold label.

PARROT (Chicago label)

One LP was issued on this label; it has a maroon label with silver print.

PARROT (London subsidiary)

Except for some subtle perimeter print changes, this label was the same from 1964-76: Black with a colored bird left of center hole and the word "parrot" in yellow at the upper right.

PEACOCK

Almost entirely a gospel label, it had three distinct label designs. The first label was black with silver print, "PEACOCK" in silver above the center hole, a drawing of a peacock in black over the logo. The second label, after ABC picked up distribution, was

also black with silver print, but "PEACOCK" was now in white and the peacock drawing was in color.

In 1974, the label changed to an unknown design with "abc Peacock" at top of label between two lines.

PHILIPS (pop)

The below does not apply to classical LPs issued on the Philips label in the 1980s. Most of those were pressed overseas, usually in The Netherlands, then exported to the U.S. for sale.

The basic label stayed the same from 1962 through the early 1970s: It was black with the "PHILIPS" shield above the center hole. The changes all had to do with the perimeter print, as follows:

1962-63: "Chicago 1, Illinois" at the bottom

1963-66: "Vendor: Mercury Record Corporation" at the bottom.

1966-70: No perimeter print at bottom.

1970-74: "Manufactured and Distributed by Mercury" at the bottom.

PHILLES

1962-63 (4001-4005): Light blue label with black print.

1964-66 (4006-4011): Yellow and red label, black print.

PHILLIPS INTERNATIONAL

All the LPs issued on this label have a blue world map with a red, white and blue banner across the top. Over the banner it says "Sam C. Phillips International Corp."

PICKWICK

A budget label, most of the albums on this label are common and rarely fetch more than single digits or low double digits in any condition.

From the mid-1960s to about 1976, the label was silver with black print. Starting around 1976 into the early 1980s, the label was black with a multicolored Pickwick logo.

POLYDOR

Labels are red from 1969 into the 1990s, with the only changes taking place in the perimeter print.

PORTRAIT

1976-early 80s: Gray label.

1980s: Black label.

Custom labels were used on some releases.

PRESTIGE

10-inch LPs: Red label, silver print, "446 W. 50th St., N.Y.C." address on label.

12-inch LPs, early 1950s-1956 (7000 to approximately 7141): Yellow label, black print, "446 W. 50th St., N.Y.C." address on label.

1956-64 (7142 to approximately 7320): Yellow label, black print, "203 South Washington Ave., Bergenfield, N.J." address on label.

1964-67 (late 7320s to somewhere in the 7400s): Blue label, "trident" logo on the right, with "203 S. Washington Ave., Bergenfield, N.J." address on label.

1967-69: Blue label, "trident" logo in a circle on top.

1969-71: Purple label, "trident" logo in a circle on top.

1972-early 1980s: Green label.

Reissues exist on most of these labels. Also, in the 1980s, Fantasy established its "Original Jazz Classics" series, and those in the series that had been on Prestige used yellow Prestige labels. These are easily distinguished from originals by the "OJC" prefix and references either to Fantasy or to Berkeley, California, or both.

RAMA

Labels are dark blue with silver print.

RARE EARTH

1969 (505-509): The lower half of the label is white. The upper half has an orange background, a drawing of a tree and the words "RARE EARTH" in white. This label was later used as the promo label, but for the

first editions of these early LPs, it also was the stock label.

1970-76 (511-550): All-orange label with a drawing of a tree and the words "RARE EARTH" in white.

RCA CAMDEN

This was RCA Victor's budget label.

1954-57: Pink label.

1957-64: Blue label, purple perimeter.

1964-68: Light blue label, dark blue perimeter.

1969-75: All-blue label with "RCA" turned on its side at left and "Camden" right of the center hole.

Most Camden titles still in print in 1975 were reissued with the same number on Pickwick.

RCA SPECIAL PRODUCTS

Before 1973, there was no label with this official name. Special-products issues on RCA were easily identifiable by the prefix "PR," "PRM" or "PRS" and a three-digit number.

The earliest of these (early 1960s-1968) have a flat black label and silver print, "RCA VICTOR" in silver and an outline of the Nipper logo in silver underneath.

The next series of these (1968-73) have a tan, almost maize, label, with "RCA" on its side at the left of the center hole, "Victor" to the right of the center hole, and no dog.

When the entire RCA catalog began using alphanumeric prefixes in 1973, RCA Special Products got its own series beginning, for the most part, with "DPL1." Early label colors vary; some are green, some are light blue. By 1977 the label was black with the dog near top, "RCA Special Products" on two lines in white to the left of the dog.

RCA VICTOR (pop)

Another long and involved label with sometimes overlapping label designs, the below apply only to pop albums.

10-Inch Albums

1951-55: Most pop albums have black labels with silver print. A silver ring goes all the way around the label. The words "RCA VICTOR" are along the upper edge above the silver ring. An outline of Nipper is under the silver ring at top. Some albums of this period also had green labels with silver print; reissues of older material had silver-gray labels with red print.

Mono 12-Inch Albums

Before 1955 (early 1000s): Black labels with silver print; silver ring all the way around the label; "RCA VICTOR" along upper edge above the ring; outline of Nipper at top under ring.

1955-63 (mid 1000s-2700s): Shiny black label, "RCA VICTOR" in silver with full-bodied Nipper logo underneath. The bottom of the label says "LONG 33 1/3 PLAY."

1963-64 (2700s-2999): Shiny black label, "RCA VICTOR" in white with full Nipper logo. The bottom of the label says "MONO" in some cases; others have an extra-bold "DYNAGROOVE" across the bottom with the word "MONO" in much smaller print on either side.

1965-68 (3300-3900s): Shiny black label, "RCA VICTOR" is much larger along top of label, the Nipper logo is slightly smaller underneath. Along the bottom is either "MONAURAL" or "MONO DYNAGROOVE."

Stereo 12-Inch Albums

1958-63 (2000s-2700s): Shiny black label, "RCA VICTOR" in silver with full-bodied Nipper logo underneath. The bottom of the label says "LIVING STEREO."

1963-64 (2700s-2999): Shiny black label, "RCA VICTOR" in white with full-bodied Nipper logo underneath. The bottom of the label says "STEREO" in some cases; others have an extra-bold "DYNAGROOVE" across the bottom with the word "STEREO" in much smaller print on either side. This series also had the first rechanneled stereo releases, all of which had numbers before 2000; these have the extra bold word "STEREO" at the bottom with "Electronically Reprocessed" underneath.

1965-68 (3300s-early 4000s): Shiny black label, "RCA VICTOR" is much larger along top of label, the Nipper logo is slightly smaller underneath. Along the bottom is either "STEREO," "STEREO DYNAGROOVE" or "STEREO Electronically Reprocessed."

1969-71 (early 4000s-about 4460): Orange label on rigid, non-flexible vinyl, "RCA" on its side to left of center hole, "Victor" to right of center hole, no dog logo.

1971-76 (4460?-APL1-1000 or so): Orange label on so-called "Dynaflex" vinyl, "RCA" on its side to left of center hole, "Victor" to right of center hole, no dog logo.

1974-76 (early APL1 series): Tan label, released simultaneously with above orange label. Tan labels were used in Indianapolis, which explains why more of these are found in the East, and the orange labels were used in Hollywood, which explains why more of these are found in the West.

1976-late 1980s: Black label, Nipper logo is restored and added to upper right. "RCA" is now above the center hole to the left of Nipper, "Victor" is on its side to the left of the center hole.

Late 1980s-1990s: Mostly red label with circular "RCA" logo in black background at top. There are other variations of this label as well. It was not until this label that the word "Victor" was dropped from pop LPs.

RENDEZVOUS

1958-60 (1301-1310?): Brown label, silver print.
1960-end (1311?-1314): Black label, silver print, "rendezvous records" in white above center hole.

REPRISE

1961-67 (6001-6280?, 1000-1022?; 2000-2015?): Pink, gold and green label with a large steamboat at the upper left corner and the word "reprise:" on the label at upper right. Albums in the 1000 series, which were Frank Sinatra issues, had his photo on the label instead of the steamboat.
1968-70 (6281?-6400s; 1024-1029; 2016?-2025?): Two-tone orange label (rich orange at top, duller orange on bottom) with a smaller steamboat, an "r:" logo in a red circle with a "W7" logo overlapping it at its left.
1970-early 1980s (6400s on, 2026?-2200s): All-tan (dull orange) label with steamboat, the "W7" logo is gone, though the "r:" remains, this time in a box rather than a circle.
Mid 1980s: Black and red label.
Late 1980s-present: Light blue and maize label.

RIVERSIDE

Early 1950s-1956 (all 10-inch LPs, and 12-inch LPs into the 250s): White label; "RIVERSIDE" is in white inside a light blue rectangle; one horizontal and two vertical lines, all of which are light blue, form a box; artist, title and number information is in black. These say "Released by Bill Grauer Productions, New York City" at the bottom.
1956-63 (250s to approximately 476): Mono records have blue labels with the "microphone and two reels of tape" logo at top; stereo copies (adding a "9" to the mono catalog number) have black labels with the "microphone and two reels" logo at top. These say "Bill Grauer Productions, New York City" at the bottom.

1964-67: Turquoise label, just the word "RIVERSIDE" at top and "Orpheum Productions Inc., New York" at the bottom.
Late 1960s reissues: Black label, wide red ring around outside, new Riverside logo in black inside a white box, "Distributed by ABC Records, Inc. New York, N.Y. 10019 - Made in U.S.A." at bottom.
Many titles have been reissued with facsimile Riverside labels on the Fantasy "OJC" prefix series.

ROLLING STONES

1971 (59100): Earliest stock copies of the first album on the label have white labels.
1971-84 (all others): Yellow label with red "lips and tongue" logo left of the center hole.
Custom labels exist for some releases.

ROULETTE

1957 (25001-25003): Black label, silver print, "ROULETTE" in silver along top, silver roulette wheel underneath label name.
1957-59 (25004-25045?): Black label, silver print, "ROULETTE" in white along top, red roulette wheel underneath label name.
1959-62 (25046?-25180s? and 52000 to about 52050): White label, black print, "ROULETTE" in black along top, blue, red, yellow and green "spokes" through center hole.
1962-63 (25180s?-25230s?): Left side of label is orange, right side is pink, black print, "ROULETTE" in white to left of center hole between two white lines.
1963-1970s (25230-25361; 42000 and 3000 series): Alternating orange and yellow label in the pattern of a roulette wheel, "ROULETTE" in black near the top of the label.
1980s (59000 series): Alternating orange and yellow label in the pattern of a roulette wheel, "ROULETTE" in green near the top of the label.
Roulette had many other numbering systems, most notably the 52000 series for jazz. We'd appreciate help in placing those series within the above time frame.

RSO

1973-75: Peach label, distributed by Atco.
1976-78: Tan label, distributed by Polydor (has Polydor logo in fine print).
1978-81: Tan label, distributed by Polygram (no Polydor logo in fine print).
1981-83: Silver label.

SAVOY

1950-1960s: Maroon label.
1970s (reissues): Brown label, "Distributed by Arista."

SCEPTER

1961 (501): Red label, "Scepter" in black script and a silver outline.
1962-71: Red label, black wedge through center hole, "SCEPTER RECORDS" in white in two lines at the left of the center hole.

Late 1960s-1973: Kaleidoscopic label, "SCEPTER RECORDS" in black inside white oval at top of label. There may be some overlap between this label and the earlier one, as there also was in 45s.

1974-76: Dark blue label, "SCEPTER" in white.

SCORE

A reissue label for Aladdin material, many of these are quite rare, though not nearly as rare as the Aladdin originals. All of these have maroon labels with "SCORE" above the center hole in an oval.

SHELTER

1971-72 (8900-8910?): Red label with an upside-down Superman logo at left.

1972-73: Red label with blacked-out upside-down Superman logo on top.

1974-76 (MCA distribution): Yellow label.

1977-78 (ABC distribution): Orange label with crescent moon at left.

SIRE

1968-70 (97000 series): White label, both Sire and London logos at top of label.

1970-71: Yellow label, blue stylized "S" at top, "Distributed by Polydor Records" in fine print.

1972-74: Yellow label, blue stylized "S" at top, "Distributed by Famous Music, A G+W Company" in fine print.

1974-76: Yellow label, blue stylized "S" at top, "Distributed by ABC Records Inc." in fine print.

1977-1980s: Yellow label, blue stylized "S" at top, makes reference to distribution by Warner Bros.

SMASH

1961-68: Flat red label, "SMASH" at top of label.

1968-71: Red label, both "SMASH" and Mercury logos at top of label.

SOUL

1965-66 (701-702): White label, black print, "SOUL" printed vertically in purple to the left of the center hole in a light purple background.

1966-78 (703-751): Label has three circles with three shades of purple. The "SOUL" logo is in white, centered at the top of the label.

SOUND STAGE 7

1963-66 (5000-5003?, 15000-15003?): Red label, black print, "SOUND 7 STAGE" above center hole.

1968-70 (15004?-15009): Black label, "SOUND STAGE" in two rows in white print over a blue "7."

1972-75 (30000 series): Gold label.

SPECIALTY

1957 (100): White label with wide black ring around the outside and a narrow yellow ring between the white and black areas. "Specialty" is in cursive letters in yellow over the black ring at the top of the label.

1957-70 (2100-2140s?): Gold label, black print, "Specialty" in gold letters across the top over a

black background.

1971-89 (2140s-end): Black and white label, "Specialty" in large yellow letters over the black part of the label. Similar in spirit to the design of 1950s 45 rpm labels.

STAX

1962-68 (701-726): Mono releases have light blue labels with black "Stax" logo at top and stack of records over it. Stereo releases have yellow labels with the same "Stax" records logo.

1968-72 (2000-2045, 3001): Yellow label with "finger-snapping" logo in blue tint at the left of center hole.

1972-75 (2046-2047; 3002-3024, 5500 series): Yellow label with "finger-snapping" logo in brown at left of center hole.

1976-late 1980s (4100 and 8500 series): Purple fading to white label, "finger-snapping" logo in black at left of center hole.

STEREO RECORDS – See CONTEMPORARY.

STRAND

Mostly a budget label, its labels were orange with black print.

SUE

Early 1960s: Orange label, black print, "Sue RECORDS" in white print left of center hole.

Mid 1960s: Orange label, black print, "Sue RECORDS" in black print left of center hole.

1969 (8801): Red label, black print.

SUN

1956-65 (1220-1275): Yellow label, brown print. Musical notes ring the outer edge of the label. Alternating brown and yellow rays emanate from the center hole area. The letters "SUN" are in yellow over the rays. At the bottom of the label, in yellow print with brown background, are the words "Memphis, Tennessee."

1969-86 (100-148, 1000-1035): Yellow label, brown print. Four "targets" are visible in the lower half of the label. The music notes only go around half the label instead of nearly all of it, and at the bottom is "Sun International Corp., A Division of the Shelby Singleton Corp., Nashville, U.S.A."

SUNSET

This was Liberty Records' budget label. It has a black label with a light blue area at the left of the label; the "SUNSET" logo is to the left of the center hole.

SWAN

1959-63 (501-512?): White label, red print.

1964-end (513?-517): Black label, silver print.

SWINGVILLE

Mono records have red or maroon labels with silver print, and with "PRESTIGE" in lighter silver print above the word "SWINGVILLE," also in silver print. Stereo records are purple with silver print, with only

the word "SWINGVILLE" in silver between two solid horizontal lines.

Reissues from the mid-1960s have blue labels with the Prestige "trident" logo at the right.

TAMLA

1961-62 (220-231?): White label, black print. Above the center hole is an overlapping globe-record logo with "TAMLA" in an arc above the globe. The oceans of the world and center hole of the record are colored purple.

1962 (229?-233?): Yellow label, black print, same as above except that the oceans and record hole are colored brown.

1963-67 (236?-280?): Yellow label, black print, side-by-side record and globe at top of label, "TAMLA" in yellow over the globe.

1968-1980s (281?-end): Yellow label, black print, brown areas at upper left and upper right of label, "TAMLA" logo, with flattened globe above, in box centered at top.

TEEM

Ace imprint; purple label with silver print.

THRESHOLD

1970-73 (1-10?): White label, purple logo.
1974-83 (11?-end): Dark blue label.

TOP RANK

On mono labels, the upper left quadrant of the label is white with a drawing in gold of a man hitting a gong; the other three quadrants of the label are red.

On stereo labels, the upper left quadrant of the label is white with a drawing in red of a man hitting a gong; the other three quadrants of the label are gold.

TOWER

1965-68: Orange label.
1968-69: Multicolored, striped label.

TRACK

1970-71: Black label, distributed by Atlantic.
1972: Silver label with Decca logo.
1973-75: Brown label, distributed by MCA.

20TH CENTURY/20TH FOX

1958-early 1960s: Light blue "clouds" label, "20th Fox" logo in red at top of label.

Mid 1960s-early 1970s: Black label with gold border, "20th Century Fox Records" logo at top of label. Most of these issues were distributed by ABC.

1972-77: Light blue label, "20th Century" logo in white at top of label.

1978-early 1980s: Light brown label with added spotlights, logo again changes to "20th Century Fox."

UNITED ARTISTS

1958-59: Red and black label, "UNITED" to left of center hole, "ARTISTS" to right of center hole.

1959: Mono albums had an all-red label; stereo albums had blue labels.

1960: Black label, large "UA" logo on top.

1960-68: Black label, blue, gold, white and red circles along upper edge of label, "UNITED" in gold, "ARTISTS" underneath in white, both words in a rounded-off rectangle.

1968-70: Pink and orange label.

1970-71: Black label, orange area at left of center hole, "UA/United Artists" logo in box directly left of center hole.

1971-77: Tan label with "UA" in brown at top.

1977-80: Multicolored "sunrise" label.

Note: United Artists had a jazz series for several years starting in 1962. These were numbered in the UAJ-14000 series for mono and UAJS-15000 for stereo. Original labels on both mono and stereo are gray with a silhouette of a saxophonist.

V.I.P.

This Motown label had a brown, tan, orange, yellow and white label. The "V.I.P." logo is printed vertically to the left of the center hole, inside an oval with an orange background.

VALIANT

Early 1960s: Purple label.
Mid 1960s: Red and black label.

VANGUARD

Early years through 1963: Mono issues were maroon with silver print.

Late 1958s-mid 1960s: Stereo issues were black with silver print.

Mid 1960s-early 1970s: Silvery gray to bronze label with white horseman logo on bottom.

Other labels also existed; we appreciate more information, as many Vanguard releases stayed in print for two decades or more.

VEE JAY

Pre-bankruptcy issues:

1957-60 (1001-1016; 1022; 5001-5005?): Maroon label, silver print with a squiggly line under the words "Vee-Jay RECORDS." A silver band is around the outside of the label. In this number range, stereo issues were gray with black print with otherwise identical graphics.

1960-64 (1019-21; 1023-1070s?, 5006?-5053?, 3004-3037): Black label, silver print, "Vee Jay" logo in white with a treble clef between the two words, surrounded by a red oval. The outer rim of the label has a rainbow band.

1964-65 (1070s-1154; 5054?-5083; 2501-2509): Black label, silver print, "VJ" in white, "VEE-JAY RECORDS" underneath that in two lines in white, all surrounded by two white brackets. The outer rim of the label has a rainbow band.

1964-65 (various, as needed): Black label, silver print, no rainbow band. The letters "VJ" stand alone with "VEE JAY RECORDS" underneath, all in silver print, no brackets.

Post-bankruptcy issues:

Late 1960s-early 1970s: Black label, silver print. Most have the "VJ" and "VEE-JAY RECORDS" in brackets, all in silver print. Some have "VJ" on one line and "RECORDS" on another with no brackets, still all in silver print. Although these records were issued in stereo jackets, they generally play mono!

(This may be the source and time period of most of the "best" illegitimate *Introducing The Beatles* albums, as they match this description. The Beatles albums are considered "counterfeits" because Vee-Jay did not have the rights to reproduce them after 1964. The material Vee-Jay actually owned and reissued at this time, such as *Duke Of Earl* by Gene Chandler, is considered legitimate product, though less valuable than the originals.)

1972-74 (1001-1011 and 2-1000 to 2-1008): Red label, silver print, similar to original maroon Vee-Jay label. At least one of these (1002) was issued on a pink label with black print.

1977 (VJ International): Orange label, black "VJ International" logo in white circle.

VERVE

1956-60 (8000 series mono, 6000 series stereo): Black label, silver print, "Verve Records, Inc." at bottom, "MGV" prefix. Early copies have the famous "trumpet player" logo at the left; these command a premium over those with the large "T" logo.

1961-early 1970s (8000 series): Black label, silver print, "MGM Records" at bottom, "V" prefix for mono, "V6" for stereo.

1966-early 1970s (5000 series): Dark blue label, silver print, "V" prefix for mono, "V6" for stereo.

Early 1970s-1975: White label with both "Verve" and "MGM" logos at top of label.

Various labels were used after Verve was reactivated in the early 1980s.

VIK

A 1950s RCA subsidiary, its issues were black with a multicolor "Vik" logo across the top.

VOLT

1965-68 (411-419): Yellow label, black print, "VOLT RECORDS" above center hole, yellow lightning bolt in black background beneath that.

1969-72 (6001-6017): Dark blue label, black print.

1972-74 (6018-6023 and 9500 series): Orange label, black print.

WAND

1960s: White with black top.

Early 1970s: Kaleidoscope label, "Wand" in black across top of label.

WARNER BROS.

Mono Albums

1958-62 (1200-1470?): Gray label, black "WB" shield at top, "WB" letters in shield are in gold print.

1962-66 (1470?-1620?): Gray label, black "WB" shield at top, "WB" letters in shield are in white print.

1966-67 (1620?-1700s): Gold label.

Stereo Albums

1958-67 (1200-1730?): Gold label.

1968-70 (1730?-1840?): Green label, "Warner Bros.-Seven Arts Records" along top edge, "W7" logo boxed underneath that.

1970-73 (1840?-1890?; 2500-2700?): Green label, "Warner Bros. Records" along top edge, "WB" shield logo underneath that.

1973-78 (2700?-3150?): So-called "Burbank palm trees" label. "Burbank, Home of Warner Bros. Records" along top edge, black "WB" shield underneath that, lined boulevard of palm trees comprises the label design.

1978-83? (3150?-25000?): Tan label, narrow horizontal lines every quarter inch or so, large "WB" shield at top of label.

1983?-present (25000?-on): White label, no horizontal lines, large "WB" shield remains at top.

WARWICK

Original mono labels were white with a green filled-in circle in the middle of the label. Four yellow circles are on the left of the label; four blue circles tend toward the right of the label. At the top is a Warwick crest logo with a green shield. Original stereo labels were also white, but instead of the green filled-in circle, a blue dot is to the right of the center hole and a yellow dot to the left of the center hole. Concentric like-colored circles surround each dot.

The second version of the mono label was plain white with black print and the Warwick logo in black. Stereo labels were purple with silver print and the Warwick logo in silver.

WHITE WHALE

1965-67 (100-120?, 7100-7120?): Dark blue label.

1967-70 (7120?-end): Lighter blue label with concentric white circles.

WORLD PACIFIC – See PACIFIC JAZZ.

"X"

This subsidiary of RCA Victor released albums from 1954 through 1956. The label is white with red print and a big red "X" at the top of the label.

DATING RCA ALBUMS

On all albums pressed by RCA Victor from the early 1950s through 1972, there is an eight-digit master number, four of which are to the left of a hyphen, four of which are to the right.

For albums first released before 1955, you can tell what year the record was mastered by looking at the first two digits. For albums mastered from 1955-72, you can tell the year by looking at the first digit, which will always be a letter.

This list won't tell you what year the album was actually pressed; for that, you still need to see the label guide.

The following works on all RCA family albums, including Red Seal, Camden, Bluebird and Victrola. It also works on non-RCA albums that were pressed at the RCA plants, including custom pressings. So you might want to check some albums on such labels as 20th Fox, Cadence and Motown, just to name three, to see if they have RCA-style master numbers.

Here is the RCA code.

1951-54: The first two digits of the master number correspond to the following years.
E1: 1951
E2: 1952
E3: 1953
E4: 1954

1955-72: RCA altered the code so that only the first digit corresponded to the year.
F: 1955
G: 1956
H: 1957
J: 1958
K: 1959
L: 1960
M: 1961
N: 1962
P: 1963
R: 1964
S: 1965
T: 1966
U: 1967
W: 1968
X: 1969
Z: 1970
A: 1971
B: 1972

After 1972: RCA changed its published master numbers to the same number as the record number, with an added "A" for side 1 and a "B" for side 2. You can no longer tell the year based on the master number.

A

Number	Title	Yr	NM

ABDUL-MALIK, AHMED
Bassist and composer, a pioneer of "world music."

Albums
NEW JAZZ

Number	Title	Yr	NM
❑ NJLP-8282 [M]	Sounds of Africa	1962	$200

—Purple label

Number	Title	Yr	NM
❑ NJLP-8282 [M]	Sounds of Africa	1965	$150

—Blue label, trident logo at right

Number	Title	Yr	NM
❑ NJLP-8266 [M]	The Music of Ahmed Abdul-Malik	1961	$200

—Purple label

Number	Title	Yr	NM
❑ NJLP-8266 [M]	The Music of Ahmed Abdul-Malik	1965	$150

—Blue label, trident logo at right

PRESTIGE

Number	Title	Yr	NM
❑ PRLP-16003 [M]	Eastern Moods	1963	$300

RCA VICTOR

Number	Title	Yr	NM
❑ LPM-2015 [M]	East Meets West	1959	$200
❑ LSP-2015 [S]	East Meets West	1959	$200

RIVERSIDE

Number	Title	Yr	NM
❑ RLP 12-287 [M]	Jazz Sahara	1958	$300
❑ RLP-1121 [S]	Jazz Sahara	1959	$250

STATUS

Number	Title	Yr	NM
❑ ST-8303 [M]	Spellbound	1965	$80

ABERCROMBIE, JOHN, AND RALPH TOWNER
Also see each artist's individual listings.

Albums
ECM

Number	Title	Yr	NM
❑ 1207	Five Years Later	1981	$25
❑ 1080	Sargasso Sea	1976	$25

ABERCROMBIE, JOHN
Guitarist, sometimes mandolin player. Also see RICHIE BEIRACH.

Albums
ECM

Number	Title	Yr	NM
❑ 1133	Arcade	1979	$25
❑ 1117	Characters	1978	$25
❑ 1061	Gateway	1975	$25
❑ 1105	Gateway 2	1977	$25
❑ 1164	John Abercrombie Quartet	1980	$25
❑ 1191	M	1981	$25
❑ 25009	Night	1984	$20
❑ 1047	Timeless	1974	$25

JAM

Number	Title	Yr	NM
❑ 5001	Straight Flight	198?	$25

ABRAMS, MUHAL RICHARD
Piano and synthesizer player, also a composer and a co-founder of the Association for the Advancement of Creative Musicians. Also see ANTHONY BRAXTON; LEROY JENKINS.

Albums
ARISTA/NOVUS

Number	Title	Yr	NM
❑ 3000	Lifea Blinec	1978	$25
❑ 3007	Spiral/Live	1979	$25

BLACK SAINT

Number	Title	Yr	NM
❑ BSR 0017	1-OQA + 19	1978	$30
❑ BSR 0061	Blues Forever	1981	$25
❑ BSR 0091	Colors in Thirty-Third	1987	$25
❑ BSR 0051	Duet	1981	$25

—With Amina Claudine Myers

Number	Title	Yr	NM
❑ BSR 0033	Lifelong Ambitions	1980	$25

—With Leroy Jenkins

Number	Title	Yr	NM
❑ BSR 0041	Mama and Daddy	1981	$25
❑ BSR 0071	Rejoicing with the Light	1983	$25
❑ BSR 0003	Sightsong	1975	$30

—Featuring Malachi Favors

Number	Title	Yr	NM
❑ BSR 0032	Spihumonesty	1980	$25
❑ 120103	The Hearinga Suite	1989	$30
❑ BSR 0081	View From Within	1984	$25

DELMARK

Number	Title	Yr	NM
❑ DS-413	Levels and Degrees of Light	1968	$25
❑ DS-430	Things to Come From Those Now Gone	1972	$35
❑ DS-423	Young at Heart, Wise in Time	1970	$50

INDIA NAVIGATION

Number	Title	Yr	NM
❑ IN-1058	Afrisong	1975	$35

ACOUSTIC ALCHEMY
Group led by acoustic guitarists Nick Webb and Greg Carmichael.

Albums
MCA

Number	Title	Yr	NM
❑ 6291	Blue Chip	1989	$25
❑ 42125	Natural Elements	1988	$25
❑ 5816	Red Dust and Spanish Lace	1987	$25

ADAMS, GEORGE-DANNIE RICHMOND QUARTET
Also see each artist's individual listings.

Albums
SOUL NOTE

Number	Title	Yr	NM
❑ SN-1057	Gentleman's Agreement	1983	$30
❑ SN-1007	Hand to Hand	1980	$30

ADAMS, GEORGE-DON PULLEN QUARTET
Also see each artist's individual listings.

Albums
BLUE NOTE

Number	Title	Yr	NM
❑ BLJ-46907	A Song Everlasting	1987	$25
❑ BT-85122	Breakthrough	1986	$25

SOUL NOTE

Number	Title	Yr	NM
❑ SN-1004	Don't Lose Control	198?	$30
❑ SN-1094	Live at the Village Vanguard	1985	$30
❑ 121144-1	Live at the Village Vanguard 2	199?	$25

TIMELESS

Number	Title	Yr	NM
❑ LPSJP-147	Earth Beams	1990	$30

ADAMS, GEORGE
Tenor saxophone player.

Albums
BLUE NOTE

Number	Title	Yr	NM
❑ B1-91984	Nightingale	1989	$25

—Tenor sax

ECM

Number	Title	Yr	NM
❑ 1141	Sound Suggestions	1979	$30

TIMELESS

Number	Title	Yr	NM
❑ 322	Paradise Space Shuttle	1981	$30

ADAMS, JERRI
Female singer.

Albums
COLUMBIA

Number	Title	Yr	NM
❑ CL916 [M]	It's Cool Inside	1956	$40
❑ CL1258 [M]	Play for Keeps	1958	$40

ADAMS, PEPPER, AND FRANK FOSTER
Also see each artist's individual listings.

Albums
MUSE

Number	Title	Yr	NM
❑ MR-5313 [B]	Generations	1986	$35

ADAMS, PEPPER, AND JIMMY KNEPPER
Also see each artist's individual listings.

Albums
METROJAZZ

Number	Title	Yr	NM
❑ E-1004 [M]	The Pepper-Knepper Quintet	1958	$350
❑ SE-1004 [S]	The Pepper-Knepper Quintet	1959	$350

ADAMS, PEPPER
Baritone saxophone player.

Albums
BETHLEHEM

Number	Title	Yr	NM
❑ BCP-6056 [M]	Motor City Scene	1961	$200
❑ 6056 [B]	Motor City Scene	19--	$500

—red label

ENJA

Number	Title	Yr	NM
❑ 2060	Julian	1976	$35
❑ 2074	Twelfth and Pingree	1976	$50

FANTASY

Number	Title	Yr	NM
❑ OJC-031 [M]	10 to 4 at the 5 Spot	198?	$30

—Reissue of Riverside 12-265

INNER CITY

Number	Title	Yr	NM
❑ IC-3014	Julian	1976	$30

INTERLUDE

Number	Title	Yr	NM
❑ MO-502 [M]	Pepper Adams 5	1959	$100

—Reissue of Mode 112

Number	Title	Yr	NM
❑ ST-1002 [S]	Pepper Adams 5	1959	$60

—Reissue of Mode 112; remixed into stereo; black vinyl

Number	Title	Yr	NM
❑ ST-1002 [S]	Pepper Adams 5	1959	$150

—Orange vinyl

MODE

Number	Title	Yr	NM
❑ LP-112 [M]	Pepper Adams 5	1957	$250

—With Mel Lewis

MUSE

Number	Title	Yr	NM
❑ MR-5182	Reflectory	1979	$50
❑ MR-5213	The Master	1980	$35

PALO ALTO

Number	Title	Yr	NM
❑ PA-8009	Urban Dreams	1981	$35

PRESTIGE

Number	Title	Yr	NM
❑ PRST-7677 [B]	Encounter	1969	$150

—With Zoot Sims

REGENT

Number	Title	Yr	NM
❑ MG-6066 [M]	The Cool Sound of Pepper Adams	1958	$180

SAVOY

Number	Title	Yr	NM
❑ MG-12211 [M]	The Cool Sound of Pepper Adams	196?	$40

—Reissue of Regent 6066

SAVOY JAZZ

Number	Title	Yr	NM
❑ SJL-1142	Pure Pepper	198?	$30

—Reissue of Savoy 12211

WARWICK

Number	Title	Yr	NM
❑ W-2041 [M]	Out of This World	1961	$200

—With Donald Byrd

WORKSHOP JAZZ

Number	Title	Yr	NM
❑ WSJ-219 [M]	Pepper Adams Plays the Compositions of Charles Mingus	1964	$150
❑ WSJS-219 [S]	Pepper Adams Plays the Compositions of Charles Mingus	1964	$140

WORLD PACIFIC

Number	Title	Yr	NM
❑ PJM-407 [M]	Critic's Choice	1957	$400

—With Mel Lewis

Number	Title	Yr	NM
❑ WPM-407 [M]	Critic's Choice	1958	$400

—With Mel Lewis; reissue with new prefix

ZIM

Number	Title	Yr	NM
❑ ZLS2000 [B]	Ephemera	197?	$100

ADDERLEY, CANNONBALL
Alto sax player and bandleader. Member of MILES DAVIS' group during the Kind Of Blue era. His band's recording of the JOE ZAWINUL composition "Mercy, Mercy, Mercy," when released as an edited 45, was one of the biggest jazz hits of the 1960s. Also see NAT ADDERLEY; RAY BROWN; ERIC DOLPHY; GIL EVANS; THE NUTTY SQUIRRELS; NANCY WILSON.

Albums
AMBASSADOR

Number	Title	Yr	NM
❑ S-98053	The Love Album	197?	$35

BLUE NOTE

Number	Title	Yr	NM
❑ BLP-1595 [M]	Somethin' Else	1958	$1200

—Deep groove" version; W. 63rd St. address on label

Number	Title	Yr	NM
❑ BLP-1595 [M]	Somethin' Else	1958	$200

—Regular version; W. 63rd St. address on label

Number	Title	Yr	NM
❑ BST-1595 [S]	Somethin' Else	1959	$150

—Deep groove" version; W. 63rd St. address on label

Number	Title	Yr	NM
❑ BST-1595 [S]	Somethin' Else	1959	$175

—Regular version; W. 63rd St. address on label

Number	Title	Yr	NM
❑ BST-81595 [S]	Somethin' Else	1963	$60

—New York, USA" address on label

| ❑ BST-81595 [S] | Somethin' Else | 1966 | $50 |

—With "A Division of Liberty Records" on label

| ❑ BN-LA169-F | Somethin' Else | 1973 | $30 |

—Reissue

| ❑ LT-169 | Somethin' Else | 1981 | $25 |

—Another reissue

| ❑ BST-81595 | Somethin' Else | 1984 | $25 |

—The Finest in Jazz Since 1939" label

| ❑ ST-46338 | Somethin' Else | 1997 | $50 |

—Audiophile reissue

| ❑ BST-81595 | Somethin' Else | 199? | $60 |

—Classic Records reissue on 180-gram vinyl

| ❑ BST-1595 [S] | Somethin' Else | 2002 | $60 |

—Classic Records reissue on 200-gram vinyl

| ❑ BLP-1595 [M] | Somethin' Else | 2002 | $100 |

—Classic Records reissue on 200-gram vinyl

| ❑ BLP-1595C | Somethin' Else | 2002 | $200 |

—Comparison Pack"; contains both the mono and stereo versions of the LP; Classic Records issue on 200-gram vinyl

CAPITOL

Number	Title	Yr	NM
❑ T2822 [M]	74 Miles Away -- Walk Tall	1967	$75
❑ ST2822 [S]	74 Miles Away -- Walk Tall	1967	$80
❑ ST2987	Accent on Africa	1968	$80
❑ SWBO-812	Cannonball Adderley and Friends	1971	$80
❑ SVBB-11233	Cannonball Adderley and Friends	1974	$35

—Reissue of 812

❑ SM-11817	Cannonball Adderley and Friends, Vol. 1	1978	$25
❑ SM-11838	Cannonball Adderley and Friends, Vol. 2	1978	$25
❑ ST-2877	Cannonball Adderley and the Bossa Rio Sextet with Sergio Mendes	1968	$150

—Reissue of 8 of the 10 tracks from Riverside 9455

❑ T2399 [M]	Cannonball Adderley -- Live!	1965	$80
❑ ST2399 [S]	Cannonball Adderley -- Live!	1965	$100
❑ SM-2399	Cannonball Adderley -- Live!	1976	$25
❑ ST-162	Cannonball in Person	1968	$80
❑ SKAO-404	Country Preacher	1970	$100
❑ SKAO-80404	Country Preacher	1970	$100

—Capitol Record Club edition

❑ T2203 [M]	Domination	1964	$80
❑ ST2203 [S]	Domination	1964	$100
❑ ST-484	Experience in E, Tensity, Dialogues	1970	$60
❑ T2216 [M]	Fiddler on the Roof	1965	$80
❑ ST2216 [S]	Fiddler on the Roof	1965	$100
❑ ST-11008	Fiddler on the Roof	1972	$35

—Reissue of 2216

❑ T2531 [M]	Great Love Themes	1966	$80
❑ ST2531 [S]	Great Love Themes	1966	$100
❑ ST-11121	Happy People	1973	$40
❑ T2284 [M]	Live Session	1965	$80
❑ ST2284 [S]	Live Session	1965	$100
❑ T2663 [M]	Mercy, Mercy, Mercy!	1967	$80
❑ ST2663 [S]	Mercy, Mercy, Mercy!	1967	$75
❑ SM-2663	Mercy, Mercy, Mercy!	1976	$25
❑ SN-16153	Mercy, Mercy, Mercy!	1981	$20

—Budget-line reissue

| ❑ ST-8-2663 [S] | Mercy, Mercy, Mercy! | 1969 | $80 |

—Capitol Record Club edition

❑ ST-11484	Music, You All	1975	$75
❑ SN-16002	The Best of Cannonball Adderley	1979	$20
❑ SKAO2939	The Best of Cannonball Adderley	1968	$75

—Black label with colorband

| ❑ SKAO-502939 | The Best of Cannonball Adderley | 1976 | $35 |

—Columbia House edition; orange labels

❑ SWBO-846	The Black Messiah	1972	$250
❑ SWBB-636	The Price You Got to Pay to Be Free	1971	$250
❑ SABB-11120	The Soul of the Bible	1973	$300

—Reproductions exist

❑ STBB-697	Walk Tall/Quiet Nights	1971	$80
❑ T2617 [M]	Why Am I Treated So Bad?	1966	$60
❑ ST2617 [S]	Why Am I Treated So Bad?	1966	$80

DOBRE

Number	Title	Yr	NM
❑ 1008	Cannonball, Volume 1	1977	$30

EMARCY

Number	Title	Yr	NM
❑ EMS-2-404	Beginnings	1976	$50
❑ MG-36135 [M]	Cannonball's Sharpshooters	1958	$200
❑ MG-36043 [M]	Julian "Cannonball" Adderley	1955	$150
❑ MG-36063 [M]	Julian "Cannonball" Adderley and Strings	1956	$200
❑ MG-36146 [M]	Jump for Joy	1958	$150

Number	Title	Yr	NM
❑ SR-80017 [S]	Jump for Joy	1958	$120

EVEREST ARCHIVE OF FOLK & JAZZ

Number	Title	Yr	NM
❑ FS-261	Cannonball Adderley and John Coltrane	1973	$30

—Abridged reissue of Limelight 86009

FANTASY

Number	Title	Yr	NM
❑ OJC-258	African Waltz	1987	$25
❑ F-79006	Big Man	1976	$50
❑ OJC-035	Cannonball Adderley Quintet in San Francisco	1982	$25
❑ OJC-142	Cannonball Adderley Sextet in New York	1985	$25
❑ F-9435	Inside Straight	1973	$50
❑ OJC-105	Know What I Mean?	1984	$25
❑ F-9445	Love, Sex and the Zodiac	1974	$175
❑ F-9505	Lovers	1975	$40
❑ FSP2 [DJ]	Musical Highlights from Big Man	1975	$60
❑ OJC-435	Nippon Soul	1990	$35
❑ F-79004	Phenix	1975	$60
❑ OJC-361	Portrait of Cannonball	1989	$25
❑ F-9455	Pyramid	1974	$40
❑ OJC-306	The Cannonball Adderley Quintet Plus	1988	$25
❑ OJC-032	Things Are Getting Better	1982	$25

LIMELIGHT

Number	Title	Yr	NM
❑ LM82009 [M]	Cannonball and Coltrane	1964	$100

—Reissue of Mercury 20449

| ❑ LS86009 [S] | Cannonball and Coltrane | 1964 | $100 |

—Reissue of Mercury 60134

MERCURY

Number	Title	Yr	NM
❑ SR-60134 [S]	Cannonball Adderley Quintet in Chicago	1960	$100
❑ MG-20616 [M]	Cannonball En Route	1961	$150
❑ SR-60616 [S]	Cannonball En Route	1961	$100
❑ MG-20531 [M]	Cannonball's Sharpshooters	1960	$150

—Reissue of EmArcy 36135

❑ SR-60531 [S]	Cannonball's Sharpshooters	1960	$100
❑ SR-60530 [S]	Jump for Joy	1960	$100
❑ MG-20530 [M]	Jump for Joy	1960	$150

—Reissue of EmArcy 36146

| ❑ MG-20652 [M] | The Lush Side of Cannonball Adderley | 1961 | $150 |

—Reissue of EmArcy 36063

| ❑ SR-60652 [R] | The Lush Side of Cannonball Adderley | 1961 | $100 |

MILESTONE

Number	Title	Yr	NM
❑ M-47059	Alabama/Africa	1982	$35
❑ M-9030	Cannonball Adderley in New Orleans	197?	$50
❑ M-47039	Coast to Coast	1976	$60
❑ M-47001	Eight Giants	1973	$35
❑ M-47029	The Japanese Concerts	1975	$60
❑ M-9106	The Sextet	198?	$35
❑ M-47053	What I Mean	1979	$35

PABLO LIVE

Number	Title	Yr	NM
❑ 2308238	What Is This Thing Called Soul	1984	$30

PICKWICK

Number	Title	Yr	NM
❑ SPC-3128	I Got It Bad and That Ain't Good	196?	$25
❑ SPC-3255	Quiet Nights of Quiet Stars	196?	$25

—Reissue of eight of the 10 tracks on Riverside 9455; co-credited to Sergio Mendes

RIVERSIDE

Number	Title	Yr	NM
❑ RLP377 [M]	African Waltz	1961	$200
❑ RS9377 [S]	African Waltz	1961	$200
❑ RLP355 [M]	Cannonball Adderley and the Poll-Winners	1960	$200
❑ RS9355 [S]	Cannonball Adderley and the Poll-Winners	1960	$200
❑ RLP344 [M]	Cannonball Adderley Quintet at the Lighthouse	1960	$200
❑ RS9344 [S]	Cannonball Adderley Quintet at the Lighthouse	1960	$200
❑ RLP 12-311 [M]	Cannonball Adderley Quintet in San Francisco	1959	$300
❑ RLP1157 [S]	Cannonball Adderley Quintet in San Francisco	1959	$300
❑ 6062	Cannonball Adderley Quintet in San Francisco	197?	$35

—Reissue of 1157

❑ RLP388 [M]	Cannonball Adderley Quintet Plus	1961	$200
❑ RS9388 [S]	Cannonball Adderley Quintet Plus	1961	$200
❑ RS9404 [S]	Cannonball Adderley Sextet in New York	1962	$200
❑ 6108	Cannonball Adderley Sextet in New York	197?	$35

—Reissue of 9404

❑ RM499 [M]	Cannonball in Europe	1964	$150
❑ RS9499 [S]	Cannonball in Europe	1964	$150
❑ RLP455 [M]	Cannonball's Bossa Nova	1963	$150

Number	Title	Yr	NM
❑ RS9455 [S]	Cannonball's Bossa Nova	1963	$150
❑ RS9416 [S]	Cannonball's Greatest Hits	1962	$200
❑ RLP416 [M]	Cannonball's Greatest Hits	1962	$200
❑ RLP 12-303 [M]	Cannonball Takes Charge	1959	$300
❑ RLP1148 [S]	Cannonball Takes Charge	1959	$300
❑ RLP444 [M]	Jazz Workshop Revisited	1963	$150
❑ RS9444 [S]	Jazz Workshop Revisited	1963	$150
❑ 6051	Know What I Mean?	197?	$35

—Reissue of 9433

❑ RLP477 [M]	Nippon Soul -- Recorded in Concert in Tokyo	1964	$150
❑ RS9477 [S]	Nippon Soul -- Recorded in Concert in Tokyo	1964	$150
❑ RS3041	Planet Earth	1969	$100
❑ RLP 12-269 [M]	Portrait of Cannonball	1958	$300
❑ RS3038	The Best of Cannonball Adderley	1968	$100
❑ RLP 12-322 [M]	Them Dirty Blues	1960	$200
❑ RLP1170 [S]	Them Dirty Blues	1960	$200
❑ RLP1128 [S]	Things Are Getting Better	1959	$200
❑ 6122	Things Are Getting Better	197?	$35

—Reissue of 1128

SAVOY

Number	Title	Yr	NM
❑ MG-12018 [M]	Presenting Cannonball	196?	$150

—Cannonballs pictured on cover with band members merely listed

SAVOY JAZZ

Number	Title	Yr	NM
❑ SJL-1195	Discoveries	1987	$35
❑ SJC-401	Presenting Cannonball	1985	$30

—Reissue of Savoy 12018

| ❑ SJL-2206 | Spontaneous Combustion | 1976 | $35 |

SEARS

Number	Title	Yr	NM
❑ SPS-460	Jump for Joy	196?	$35

TRIP

Number	Title	Yr	NM
❑ TLP-5573 [M]	In the Land of Hi-Fi	197?	$35

WING

Number	Title	Yr	NM
❑ SRW-16362 [S]	Cannonball Adderley Quintet	196?	$50

WONDERLAND/RIVERSIDE

Number	Title	Yr	NM
❑ RLP1435 [M]	A Child's Introduction to Jazz	196?	$100

—Adderley narrates an album introducing the works of such artists as Armstrong, Monk, Waller, etc.

ADDERLEY, CANNONBALL AND NAT

Also see each artist's individual listings.

Albums

LIMELIGHT

Number	Title	Yr	NM
❑ LM82032 [M]	Them Adderleys	1966	$100
❑ LS86032 [S]	Them Adderleys	1966	$100

ADDERLEY, NAT

Cornet player who also played trumpet, mellophone and fluegel horn. Best known as a sideman in the band of his brother, CANNONBALL ADDERLEY.

Albums

A&M

Number	Title	Yr	NM
❑ SP-3017	Calling Out Loud	1969	$35
❑ LP-2005 [M]	You, Baby	1968	$60

—Mono is promo only

| ❑ SP-3005 [S] | You, Baby | 1968 | $35 |
| ❑ SP9-3005 | You, Baby | 1983 | $35 |

—Audio Master Plus" reissue

ATLANTIC

Number	Title	Yr	NM
❑ 1439 [M]	Autobiography	1965	$35
❑ SD1439 [S]	Autobiography	1965	$50
❑ 1475 [M]	Live at Memory Lane	1967	$50
❑ SD1475 [S]	Live at Memory Lane	1967	$35
❑ 1460 [M]	Sayin' Something	1966	$35
❑ SD1460 [S]	Sayin' Something	1966	$50

CAPITOL

Number	Title	Yr	NM
❑ SVBB-11025	Cannonball Adderley Presents Soul Zodiac	1972	$250

EMARCY

Number	Title	Yr	NM
❑ MG-36091 [M]	Introducing Nat Adderley	1955	$250
❑ MG-36100 [M]	To the Ivy League from Nat	1956	$200

FANTASY

Number	Title	Yr	NM
❑ OJC-255	Branching Out	1987	$25

—Reissue of Riverside 12-285

| ❑ OJC-648 | In the Bag | 1991 | $30 |

—Reissue of Jazzland 975

| ❑ OJC-363 | The Work Song | 198? | $25 |

—Reissue of Riverside 1167

GALAXY

Number	Title	Yr	NM
❑ 5120	Little New York Midtown Music	197?	$25

JAZZLAND

Number	Title	Yr	NM
❑ JLP-75 [M]	In the Bag	1962	$60

Acoustic Alchemy, *Blue Chip*, MCA 6291, **$25.**

Pepper Adams, *Critic's Choice*, World Pacific PJM-407, **$400.**

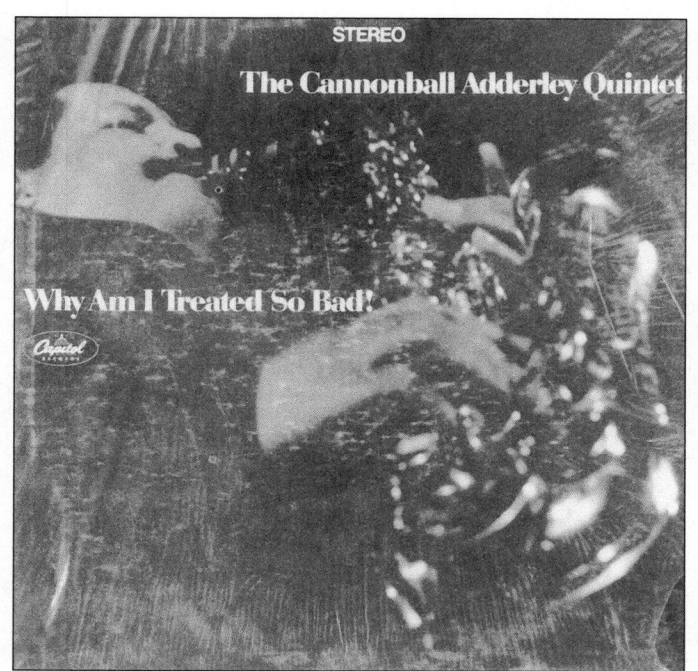

Cannonball Adderley, *Why Am I Treated So Bad?*, Capitol ST 2617, **$80.**

Cannonball Adderley, *The Sextet*, Milestone M-9106, **$35.**

Number	Title	Yr	NM
❏ JLP-975 [S]	In the Bag	1962	$40
❏ JLP-47 [M]	Naturally!	1961	$60
❏ JLP-947 [S]	Naturally!	1961	$40

LITTLE DAVID

Number	Title	Yr	NM
❏ LD1012	Hummin'	1975	$30

MILESTONE

❏ MSP-9009	Natural Soul	1968	$35
❏ MSP-9016	The Scavenger	1968	$35
❏ 47047	Work Songs	197?	$30

PRESTIGE

| ❏ 10090 | Double Exposure | 1974 | $30 |

RIVERSIDE

❏ RLP 12-285 [M]	Branching Out	1958	$300
❏ RM-474 [M]	Little Big Horn!	1964	$150
❏ RS-9474 [S]	Little Big Horn!	1964	$150
❏ RLP 12-301 [M]	Much Brass	1959	$250
❏ RLP-1143 [S]	Much Brass	1959	$250
❏ RLP-330 [M]	That's Right!	1960	$200
❏ RS-9330 [S]	That's Right!	1960	$200
❏ RLP 12-318 [M]	The Work Song	1960	$200
❏ RLP-1167 [S]	The Work Song	1960	$200
❏ 6041	The Work Song	197?	$30
— Reissue			

SAVOY

| ❏ MG-12021 [M] | That's Nat | 1955 | $150 |

SAVOY JAZZ

| ❏ SJL-1128 | That's Nat | 198? | $25 |
| *— Reissue of Savoy 12021* | | | |

STEEPLECHASE

| ❏ SCS-1059 | Don't Look Back | 198? | $25 |

THERESA

| ❏ TR-122 | Blue Autumn | 1987 | $25 |
| ❏ TR-117 | On the Move | 198? | $25 |

WING

| ❏ MGW-60000 [M] | Introducing Nat Adderley | 1956 | $100 |

AIR
Trio with Henry Threadgill on saxes and horns, Fred Hopkins on bass, and Steve McCall on drums and percussion. New Air featured Threadgill and Hopkins with Pheeroan Ak Laff on percussion.

Albums

ANTILLES

Number	Title	Yr	NM
❏ 1007	80 Degrees Below '82	1982	$25

ARISTA/NOVUS

❏ 3014	Air Lore	1980	$15
❏ 3008	Montreux	1979	$15
❏ 3002	Open Air Suit	1978	$15

BLACK SAINT

❏ BSR-0049	Air Mail	198?	$15
❏ BSR-0032	Live Air	198?	$15
❏ BSR-0084	Live at Montreal International Jazz Festival	198?	$12
— As "New Air			

INDIA NAVIGATION

| ❏ IN-1064 | Air Raid | 1976 | $18 |
| ❏ IN-1057 | Air Song | 1975 | $18 |

NESSA

| ❏ 12 | Time | 1978 | $18 |

AIRTO
Full name: Airto Moreira. Percussionist who was with MILES DAVIS' Bitches Brew-era band and CHICK COREA'S original Return To Forever. Also see DEODATO/AIRTO; FLORA PURIM.

Albums

ACCORD

Number	Title	Yr	NM
❏ SN-7184	Brazilian Heatwave	1982	$25

ARISTA

| ❏ AL4068 | Identity | 1975 | $25 |
| ❏ AL4116 | Promises of the Sun | 1976 | $25 |

BUDDAH

❏ BDS-21-SK	Natural Feelings	1970	$35
❏ BDS-5085	Seeds on the Ground	1971	$35
❏ BDA-5668	The Essential ... Airto	197?	$35

CTI

❏ 6028	Fingers	1973	$30
❏ CTSQ-6028 [Q]	Fingers	1974	$30
❏ 6020	Free	1972	$30
❏ 8000	Free	197?	$25
— Reissue of 6020			

SALVATION

| ❏ 701 | Virgin Land | 1974 | $30 |

WARNER BROS.

| ❏ BS3084 | I'm Fine, How Are You? | 1977 | $25 |
| ❏ BSK3279 | Touching You, Touching Me | 1979 | $25 |

Number	Title	Yr	NM

AKIYOSHI, TOSHIKO, AND LEON SASH
Also see each artist's individual listings.

Albums

VERVE

| ❏ MGV-8236 [M] | Toshiko and Leon Sash at Newport | 1958 | $150 |
| ❏ V-8236 [M] | Toshiko and Leon Sash at Newport | 1961 | $30 |

AKIYOSHI, TOSHIKO-LEW TABACKIN BIG BAND
Lew Tabackin is Akiyoshi's second husband. Also see each artist's individual listings.

Albums

JAM

| ❏ 03 | Farewell to Mingus | 1981 | $25 |
| ❏ 06 | Tanuki's Night Out | 1982 | $25 |

RCA VICTOR

❏ AFL1-2678	Insights	1978	$30
❏ AFL1-3019	Kogun	1979	$30
— Recorded in 1974			
❏ JPL1-1350	Long Yellow Road	1976	$35
❏ AFL1-1350	Long Yellow Road	1978	$25
— Reissue with new prefix			
❏ CPL2-2242	Road Time	1977	$25
❏ JPL1-0723	Tales of a Courtesan	1976	$35
❏ AFL1-0723	Tales of a Courtesan	1978	$25
— Reissue with new prefix			

AKIYOSHI, TOSHIKO
Piano player and bandleader. She also recorded as Toshiko Mariano when she was married to Charlie Mariano.

Albums

CANDID

❏ CD-8015 [M]	Toshiko Mariano	1960	$40
❏ CS-9015 [S]	Toshiko Mariano	1960	$50
❏ CD-8012 [M]	Toshiko Mariano Quartet	1960	$40
❏ CS-9012 [S]	Toshiko Mariano Quartet	1960	$50

CONCORD JAZZ

| ❏ CJ-69 | Finesse | 1978 | $25 |
| ❏ CJ-324 | Interlude | 1987 | $25 |

DAUNTLESS

| ❏ DM-4308 [M] | The Country and Western Sounds of Jazz | 1963 | $40 |
| ❏ DS-6308 [S] | The Country and Western Sounds of Jazz | 1963 | $50 |

INNER CITY

| ❏ 6046 | Dedications | 1977 | $30 |
| ❏ 6066 | Notorious Tourist from the East | 1978 | $30 |

METROJAZZ

| ❏ E-1001 [M] | United Notions | 1958 | $120 |
| ❏ SE-1001 [S] | United Notions | 1959 | $120 |

NORGRAN

| ❏ MGN-22 [10] | Toshiko's Piano | 1954 | $250 |

STORYVILLE

| ❏ STLP-918 [M] | Toshiko Akiyoshi, Her Trio, Her Quartet | 1957 | $60 |

VEE JAY

| ❏ LP-2505 [M] | Jazz in Japan | 1964 | $30 |
| *— As "Toshiko Mariano and Her Big Band* | | | |

VERVE

| ❏ MGV-8273 [M] | The Many Sides of Toshiko | 1958 | $120 |
| ❏ V-8273 [M] | The Many Sides of Toshiko | 1961 | $30 |

ALBAM, MANNY
Arranger and composer, also a baritone and tenor saxophone player. Also see STEVE ALLEN AND MANNY ALBAM.

Albums

ABC IMPULSE!

| ❏ AS-19 [S] | Jazz Goes to the Movies | 196? | $30 |
| *— Reissue of Impulse! AS-19* | | | |

CORAL

❏ CRL59102 [M]	A Gallery of Gershwin	1958	$40
❏ CRL57231 [M]	Sophisticated Lady -- The Songs of Duke Ellington	1958	$40
❏ CRL59101 [M]	The Blues Is Everybody's Business	195?	$40
❏ CRL57142 [M]	The Jazz Greats of Our Time	1957	$40
❏ CRL57173 [M]	The Jazz Greats of Our Time, Volume 2	1957	$40
❏ CRL57207 [M]	West Side Story	1958	$40

DECCA

| ❏ DL4517 [M] | Music from West Side Story | 1964 | $35 |
| ❏ DL74517 [S] | Music from West Side Story | 1964 | $25 |

Number	Title	Yr	NM

DOT

| ❏ DLP-9004 [M] | Jazz New York | 1958 | $80 |
| ❏ DLP-9008 [M] | Steve's Song | 1958 | $80 |

IMPULSE!

| ❏ A-19 [M] | Jazz Goes to the Movies | 1962 | $120 |
| ❏ AS-19 [S] | Jazz Goes to the Movies | 1962 | $120 |

MCA

| ❏ 1376 | The Jazz Greats of Our Time | 198? | $30 |

MERCURY

| ❏ MG-20325 [M] | With All My Love | 1958 | $100 |

RCA VICTOR

❏ LPM-2508 [M]	I Had the Craziest Dream	1962	$25
❏ LSA-2508 [S]	I Had the Craziest Dream	1962	$30
❏ LPM-2432 [M]	More Double Exposure	1961	$25
❏ LSA-2432 [S]	More Double Exposure	1961	$30
❏ LPM-1279 [M]	The Drum Suite	1956	$50
❏ LPM-1211 [M]	The RCA Victor Jazz Workshop	1956	$50

SOLID STATE

❏ SM-17000 [M]	Brass on Fire	1966	$35
❏ SS-18000 [S]	Brass on Fire	1966	$25
❏ SM-17009 [M]	The Soul of the City	1966	$25
❏ SS-18009 [S]	The Soul of the City	1966	$35

TOP RANK

| ❏ RM-313 [M] | Double Exposure | 1960 | $40 |

UNITED ARTISTS

| ❏ UAL-3079 [M] | Drum Feast | 1959 | $30 |
| ❏ UAS-6079 [S] | Drum Feast | 1959 | $40 |

VOCALION

| ❏ VL3678 [M] | West Side Story | 196? | $35 |

ALBANY, JOE, AND NIELS-HENNING ORSTED PEDERSEN
Also see each artist's individual listings.

Albums

INNER CITY

| ❏ IC-2019 | Two's Company | 1976 | $35 |

STEEPLECHASE

| ❏ SCS-1019 | Two's Company | 198? | $35 |
| *— Reissue of Inner City 2019* | | | |

ALBANY, JOE, AND WARNE MARSH
Also see each artist's individual listings.

Albums

FANTASY

| ❏ OJC-1749 [M] | The Right Combination | 1990 | $35 |
| *— Reissue of Riverside 12-270* | | | |

RIVERSIDE

| ❏ RLP 12-270 [M] | The Right Combination | 1958 | $300 |

ALBANY, JOE
Pianist.

Albums

ELEKTRA/MUSICIAN

| ❏ 60161 | Portrait of an Artist | 1983 | $30 |

INNER CITY

| ❏ IC-2003 | Birdtown Birds | 1976 | $60 |

INTERPLAY

| ❏ IP-7723 | Bird Lives! | 1979 | $50 |

REVELATION

| ❏ 25 | At Home Alone | 197? | $60 |
| ❏ 16 | Proto-Bopper | 197? | $60 |

RIVERSIDE

| ❏ RS-3023 | The Legendary Jazz Pianist | 1968 | $100 |

SEABREEZE

| ❏ SB-1004 | The Albany Touch | 1977 | $60 |

STEEPLECHASE

| ❏ SCS-1003 | Birdtown Birds | 198? | $35 |
| *— Reissue of Inner City 2003* | | | |

ALBRIGHT, LOLA
Female singer.

Albums

COLUMBIA

| ❏ CL1327 [M] | Dreamsville | 1959 | $40 |
| ❏ CS8133 [S] | Dreamsville | 1959 | $50 |

ALBRIGHT, MAX
Drummer.

Albums

Number	Title	Yr	NM
MOTIF			
❑ 502 [M]	Mood for Max	1956	$60

ALDEN, HOWARD-DAN BARRETT QUINTET
Also see each artist's individual listings.
Albums

Number	Title	Yr	NM
CONCORD JAZZ			
❑ CJ-349	Swing Street	1988	$25

ALDEN, HOWARD
Guitarist, both of the six- and seven-string varieties.
Albums

Number	Title	Yr	NM
CONCORD JAZZ			
❑ CJ-378	The Howard Alden Trio	1988	$25
FAMOUS DOOR			
❑ HL-154	Swinging Into Prominence	1988	$25
STOMP OFF			
❑ SOS-1200	Howard Alden Plays the Music of Harry Reser	1991	$30

ALESS, TONY
Pianist.
Albums

Number	Title	Yr	NM
ROOST			
❑ RST-2202 [M]	Tony Aless and His Long Island Suite	1955	$80

ALEXANDER, BOB
See AL KLINK AND BOB ALEXANDER.

ALEXANDER, JOE, AND TIMMONS, BOBBY
Alexander plays tenor saxophone. Also see BOBBY TIMMONS.
Albums

Number	Title	Yr	NM
JAZZLAND			
❑ JLP-923 [S]	Blue Jubilee	1960	$40

ALEXANDER, MONTY, AND ERNEST RANGLIN
Also see each artist's individual listings.
Albums

Number	Title	Yr	NM
PAUSA			
❑ 7110	Just Friends	198?	$25

ALEXANDER, MONTY
Pianist.
Albums

Number	Title	Yr	NM
BASF			
❑ 20913	Here Comes the Sun	197?	$30
❑ 25352	Rass!	197?	$30
❑ 25103	We've Only Just Begun	1972	$30
CONCORD JAZZ			
❑ CJ-108	Facets	1980	$25
❑ CJ-287	Full Steam Ahead	1985	$25
❑ CJ-231	Reunion in Europe	1984	$25
— With John Clayton and Jeff Hamilton			
CONCORD PICANTE			
❑ CJP-124	Ivory and Steel	1981	$25
❑ CJP-359	Jamboree	1988	$25
MGM			
❑ SE-4736	Taste of Freedom	1971	$35
PABLO			
❑ 2310826	Jamento	1978	$30
❑ 2310836	Monty Alexander in Tokyo	1979	$30
PACIFIC JAZZ			
❑ PJ-86 [M]	Alexander the Great	1966	$25
❑ ST-86 [S]	Alexander the Great	1966	$30
❑ PJ-10094 [M]	Spooky	1966	$25
❑ ST-20094 [S]	Spooky	1966	$30
PAUSA			
❑ 7083	Montreux Alexander Live	197?	$30
❑ 7032	Now Is the Time	197?	$30
❑ 7129	With Love	198?	$25
RCA VICTOR			
❑ LPM-3930 [M]	Zing	1968	$60
❑ LSP-3930 [S]	Zing	1968	$35
VERVE			
❑ V6-8790	This Is Monty Alexander	1970	$35
VERVE/MPS			
❑ 821151-1	The Duke Ellington Songbook	1984	$25

ALEXANDER, MONTY / NIELS-HENNING ORSTED PEDERSEN / GRADY TATE
Also see each artist's individual listings.
Albums

Number	Title	Yr	NM
SOUL NOTE			
❑ 121152-1	Threesome	198?	$30

ALEXANDER, MONTY / RAY BROWN / HERB ELLIS
Also see each artist's individual listings.
Albums

Number	Title	Yr	NM
CONCORD JAZZ			
❑ CJ-253	Overseas Special	1983	$25
❑ CJ-136	Trio	1981	$25
❑ CJ-193	Triple Treat	1982	$25
❑ CJ-338	Triple Treat II	1988	$25
❑ CJ-394	Triple Treat III	1989	$25

ALEXANDER, ROLAND
Tenor saxophone player and sometimes a pianist.
Albums

Number	Title	Yr	NM
NEW JAZZ			
❑ NJLP-8267 [M]	Pleasure Bent	1962	$150
—Purple label			
❑ NJLP-8267 [M]	Pleasure Bent	1965	$150
— Blue label, trident at right			

ALEXANDRIA, LOREZ
Female singer.
Albums

Number	Title	Yr	NM
ABC IMPULSE!			
❑ AS-62	Alexandria the Great	1968	$200
—Reissue of Impulse! AS-62			
ARGO			
❑ LP-694 [M]	Deep Roots	1962	$140
❑ LPS-694 [S]	Deep Roots	1962	$175
❑ LP-663 [M]	Early in the Morning	1960	$140
❑ LPS-663 [S]	Early in the Morning	1960	$175
— With the Ramsey Lewis Trio			
❑ LP-720 [M]	For Swingers Only	1963	$140
❑ LPS-720 [S]	For Swingers Only	1963	$175
❑ LP-682 [M]	Sing No Sad Songs for Me	1961	$140
❑ LPS-682 [S]	Sing No Sad Songs for Me	1961	$175
CADET			
❑ LPS-682	Sing No Sad Songs for Me	1966	$60
— Reissue of Argo 682			
DISCOVERY			
❑ DS-800	A Woman Knows	1979	$100
❑ DS-905	Harlem Butterfly (Sings the Songs of Johnny Mercer Vol. 2)	1984	$50
❑ DS-782	How Will I Remember You?	1978	$120
❑ DS-826	Lorez Alexandria Sings Johnny Mercer	1981	$60
IMPULSE!			
❑ A-62 [M]	Alexandria the Great	1964	$160
❑ AS-62 [S]	Alexandria the Great	1964	$200
❑ A-76 [M]	More of the Great Lorez Alexandria	1965	$160
KING			
❑ 565 [M]	Lorez Sings Prez	1956	$200
— Black label, crownless "King			
❑ 676 [M]	Singing Songs Everyone Knows	1959	$200
— Black label, crownless "King			
❑ 657 [M]	The Band Swings, Lorez Sings	1959	$200
— Black label, crownless "King			
❑ S-657 [S]	The Band Swings, Lorez Sings	1959	$300
— Dark blue label, crownless "King			
❑ 542 [M]	This Is Lorez	1956	$200
— Black label, crownless "King			
MCA			
❑ 29000	Alexandria the Great	198?	$25
— Reissue of ABC Impulse! AS-62			
PZAZZ			
❑ LP-320	Didn't We	1968	$100
❑ LP-324	In a Different Bag	1969	$60
TREND			
❑ TR-547	Dear to My Heart	1988	$35
❑ TR-538	Tangerine (Sings the Songs of Johnny Mercer Vol. 3)	1986	$35

ALFRED, CHUZ
Saxophone player.
Albums

Number	Title	Yr	NM
SAVOY			
❑ MG-12030 [M]	Jazz Young Blood	1955	$75
— With Ola Hanson and Chuck Lee			

ALLEN, BYRON, TRIO
The other members of his trio were Ted Robinson and Maceo Gilchrist.
Albums

Number	Title	Yr	NM
ESP-DISK'			
❑ 1005 [M]	The Byron Allen Trio	1965	$325
❑ S-1005 [S]	The Byron Allen Trio	1965	$325

ALLEN, DAVID
Male singer. Also includes releases as "David Allyn."
Albums

Number	Title	Yr	NM
EVEREST			
❑ LP-5224 [M]	David Allen	1964	$35
❑ SD-1224 [S]	David Allen	1964	$25
PACIFIC JAZZ			
❑ PJM-408 [M]	A Sure Thing	1957	$60
❑ ST-1006 [S]	A Sure Thing	1959	$60
WORLD PACIFIC			
❑ WP-1295 [M]	David Allen Sings the Jerome Kern Songbook	1960	$100
❑ ST-1295 [S]	David Allen Sings the Jerome Kern Songbook	1960	$100
❑ WP-1250 [M]	Let's Face the Music and Dance	1958	$150

ALLEN, HENRY "RED", AND KID ORY
Also see each artist's individual listings.
Albums

Number	Title	Yr	NM
VERVE			
❑ MGV-1018 [M]	Henry "Red" Allen Meets Kid Ory	1957	$150
❑ V-1018 [M]	Henry "Red" Allen Meets Kid Ory	1961	$25
❑ MGVS-6076 [S]	Henry "Red" Allen Meets Kid Ory	1959	$150
❑ V6-1018 [S]	Henry "Red" Allen Meets Kid Ory	1961	$25
❑ MGV-1020 [M]	We've Got Rhythm	1958	$150
❑ V-1020 [M]	We've Got Rhythm	1961	$25
❑ MGVS-6121 [S]	We've Got Rhythm	1959	$150
❑ V6-1020 [S]	We've Got Rhythm	1961	$25

ALLEN, HENRY "RED", AND RED NORVO
Also see each artist's individual listings.
Albums

Number	Title	Yr	NM
BRUNSWICK			
❑ BL58044 [10]	Battle of Jazz, Vol. 6	1953	$60

ALLEN, HENRY "RED"; JACK TEAGARDEN; KID ORY
Also see each artist's individual listings.
Albums

Number	Title	Yr	NM
VERVE			
❑ MGV-8233 [M]	Red Allen, Jack Teagarden & Kid Ory at Newport	1958	$100
❑ V-8233 [M]	Red Allen, Jack Teagarden & Kid Ory at Newport	1961	$25
❑ UMV-2624	Verve at Newport	198?	$25

ALLEN, HENRY "RED"
Highly influential trumpet player of the Dixieland and swing eras, also a singer and composer.
Albums

Number	Title	Yr	NM
AMERICAN RECORDING SOCIETY			
❑ G-436 [M]	Traditional Jazz	195?	$40
COLUMBIA			
❑ CL2447 [M]	Feelin' Good	1966	$35
❑ CS9247 [S]	Feelin' Good	1966	$25
PRESTIGE			
❑ PRST-7755	Memorial Album	1968	$35
RCA VICTOR			

Number	Title	Yr	NM
❏ LPV-556 [M]	Henry "Red" Allen	1965	$50
❏ LPM-1509 [M]	Ride, Red, Ride in Hi-Fi	1957	$50

SWINGVILLE

❏ SWLP-2034 [M]	Mr. Allen	1962	$40
—Purple label			
❏ SWLP-2034 [M]	Mr. Allen	1965	$25
—Blue label, trident logo at right			
❏ SWST-2034 [M]	Mr. Allen	1962	$50
—Red label			
❏ SWST-2034 [S]	Mr. Allen	1965	$30
—Blue label, trident logo at right			

TIME-LIFE

❏ STL-J-16	Giants of Jazz	1981	$50

VERVE

❏ MGV-1025 [M]	Red Allen Plays King Oliver	1959	$100
❏ V-1025 [M]	Red Allen Plays King Oliver	1961	$25
❏ V6-1025 [S]	Red Allen Plays King Oliver	1961	$30

X

❏ LVA-3033 [M]	Ridin' with Red	1955	$60

ALLEN, STEVE, AND MANNY ALBAM
Also see each artist's individual listings.

Albums

DOT

❏ DLP3194 [M]	…And All That Jazz	1959	$75
❏ DLP25194 [S]	…And All That Jazz	1959	$75

ALLEN, STEVE
Pianist, composer and comedian in many different styles. The below list includes only his jazz-oriented work. See the Standard Catalog of American Records for other LPs. Also see MARY ANNE JACKSON; JACK KEROUAC.

Albums

CORAL

❏ CRL57018 [M]	Jazz for Tonight	1956	$30
❏ CRL57028 [M]	Let's Dance	1956	$30

DECCA

❏ DL8151 [M]	Steve Allen's All Star Jazz Concert, Vol. 1	1955	$150
❏ DL8152 [M]	Steve Allen's All Star Jazz Concert, Vol. 2	1955	$150

DOT

❏ DLP3480 [M]	Bossa Nova Jazz	1963	$60
❏ DLP25380 [S]	Bossa Nova Jazz	1963	$75
❏ DLP3515 [M]	Gravy Waltz and 11 Current Hits!	1963	$60
❏ DLP25515 [S]	Gravy Waltz and 11 Current Hits!	1963	$75

ALLISON, MOSE
Male singer and pianist. Also see THE MANHATTAN ALL STARS.

Albums

ATLANTIC

❏ SD1550	Hello There, Universe	1971	$50
❏ 1389 [M]	I Don't Worry About a Thing	1962	$150
❏ SD1389 [S]	I Don't Worry About a Thing	1962	$150
❏ SD1511	I've Been Doin' Some Thinkin'	1969	$60
—1841 Broadway" address on label			
❏ SD1511	I've Been Doin' Some Thinkin'	1976	$30
—75 Rockefeller Plaza" address on label			
❏ 1450 [M]	Mose Alive!	1966	$60
❏ SD1450 [S]	Mose Alive!	1966	$40
—Blue and green label			
❏ SD1450 [S]	Mose Alive!	1969	$50
—Red and green label with "1841 Broadway" address			
❏ SD1627	Mose in Your Ear	1973	$50
—1841 Broadway" address on label			
❏ SD1627	Mose in Your Ear	1976	$30
—75 Rockefeller Plaza" address on label			
❏ 1398 [M]	Swingin' Machine	1963	$50
❏ SD1398 [S]	Swingin' Machine	1963	$30
❏ SD1542	The Best of Mose Allison	1970	$35
❏ 1424 [M]	The Word from Mose	1964	$50
❏ SD1424 [S]	The Word from Mose	1964	$60
❏ SD1584	Western Man	1972	$35
❏ 1456 [M]	Wild Man on the Loose	1966	$60
❏ SD1456 [S]	Wild Man on the Loose	1966	$40
❏ SD1691	Your Mind Is on Vacation	1976	$35

BLUE NOTE

❏ BLJ-48015	Ever Since the World Ended	1988	$35
❏ B1-93840	My Backyard	1990	$50

COLUMBIA

Number	Title	Yr	NM
❏ CL1565 [M]	I Love the Life I Live	1960	$30
—Red and black label with six "eye" logos			
❏ CS8365 [S]	I Love the Life I Live	1960	$30
—Red and black label with six "eye" logos			
❏ C30564	Retrospective	1971	$35
❏ CL1444 [M]	The Transfiguration of Hiram Brown	1960	$30
❏ CS8240 [S]	The Transfiguration of Hiram Brown	1960	$30

COLUMBIA SPECIAL PRODUCTS

❏ P13518	V-8 Ford Blues	197?	$35

ELEKTRA/MUSICIAN

❏ 60237	Lessons in Living	1984	$30
❏ E1-60125	Middle Class White Boy	1983	$30

EPIC

❏ LA16031 [M]	Take to the Hills	1962	$100
❏ BA17031 [S]	Take to the Hills	1962	$80
❏ LN24183 [M]	V-8 Ford Blues	1966	$100
❏ BN26183 [S]	V-8 Ford Blues	1966	$100

FANTASY

❏ OJC-075	Back Country Suite	198?	$30
—Reissue of Prestige 7091			
❏ OJC-6004	Greatest Hits	1988	$30
❏ OJC-457	Local Color	1990	$30
—Reissue of Prestige 7121			

ODYSSEY

❏ 32160294	Mose Goes	1968	$35

PRESTIGE

❏ PRLP-7189 [M]	Autumn Song	1960	$200
—Yellow label with Bergenfield, NJ address on label			
❏ PRLP-7189 [M]	Autumn Song	196?	$25
—Blue label, trident logo			
❏ PRLP-7091 [M]	Back Country Suite	1957	$300
—With "W. 50th St., NYC" address on label			
❏ PRLP-7152 [M]	Creek Bank	1959	$200
—Yellow label with Bergenfield, NJ address on label			
❏ P-24055	Creek Bank	1975	$60
❏ PRLP-7152 [M]	Creek Bank	196?	$30
—Blue label, trident logo			
❏ PRLP-7423 [M]	Down Home Piano	1966	$25
—Blue label, trident logo at right			
❏ PRST-7423 [S]	Down Home Piano	1966	$30
—Blue label, trident logo at right			
❏ PRLP-7121 [M]	Local Color	1958	$300
—With "W. 50th St., NYC" address on label			
❏ PR-24002	Mose Allison	1972	$60
❏ PRLP-7446 [M]	Mose Allison Plays for Lovers	1967	$30
❏ PRST-7446 [S]	Mose Allison Plays for Lovers	1967	$25
❏ PRLP-7279 [M]	Mose Allison Sings (The Seventh Son)	1963	$40
—Yellow label with Bergenfield, NJ address on label			
❏ PRST-7279 [S]	Mose Allison Sings (The Seventh Son)	1963	$50
—Silver label			
❏ P-10052	Mose Allison Sings (The Seventh Son)	1973	$35
—Reissue of PRST-7279			
❏ PRST-7279 [S]	Mose Allison Sings (The Seventh Son)	196?	$30
—Blue label, trident logo at right			
❏ P-24089	Ol' Devil Mose	1980	$60
❏ PRLP-7215 [M]	Ramblin' with Mose	1961	$200
—Yellow label with Bergenfield, NJ address on label			
❏ PRLP-7215 [M]	Ramblin' with Mose	196?	$30
—Blue label, trident logo			
❏ PRLP-7137 [M]	Young Man Blues	1958	$200
—With "W. 50th St., NYC" address on label			

ALMEIDA, LAURINDO, AND CHARLIE BYRD
Also see each artist's individual listings.

Albums

CONCORD PICANTE

❏ CJP-150	Brazilian Soul	1981	$25
❏ CJP-211	Latin Odyssey	1983	$35
❏ CP-290	Tango	1985	$25

ALMEIDA, LAURINDO
Guitarist, composer, arranger, bossa nova pioneer, he also has recorded and composed in the classical vein. As it can be difficult to separate them, all his known LPs are listed below. Also see HERB ELLIS; STAN GETZ AND LAURINDO ALMEIDA; THE MODERN JAZZ QUARTET.

Albums

ANGEL

Number	Title	Yr	NM
❏ S-36064	Clair de Lune	197?	$30
❏ S-36050	Duets with the Spanish Guitar	197?	$30
❏ S-36051	Duets with the Spanish Guitar, Vol. 2	197?	$30
❏ S-36076	Duets with the Spanish Guitar, Vol. 3	197?	$30
❏ S-37322	Prelude	197?	$35

CAPITOL

❏ T2701 [M]	A Man and a Woman	1967	$75
❏ ST2701 [S]	A Man and a Woman	1967	$75
❏ SM-2701	A Man and a Woman	1976	$25
—Reissue			
❏ T2063 [M]	Broadway Solo Guitar	1964	$60
❏ ST2063 [S]	Broadway Solo Guitar	1964	$75
❏ H-193 [10]	Concert Creations for Guitar	1950	$150
❏ P8625 [M]	Concerto de Copacabana	196?	$60
❏ SP8625 [S]	Concerto de Copacabana	196?	$35
❏ SP8636	Concerto for Guitar and Small Orchestra	196?	$35
❏ P8447 [M]	Contemporary Creations for Spanish Guitar	195?	$100
❏ P8532 [M]	Conversations with the Guitar	196?	$80
❏ SP8532 [S]	Conversations with the Guitar	196?	$100
❏ P8467 [M]	Danzas!	196?	$80
❏ PAO8406 [M]	Duets with the Spanish Guitar	1958	$100
—Gatefold cover			
❏ P8406 [M]	Duets with the Spanish Guitar	196?	$80
—Regular cover			
❏ DP8406 [R]	Duets with the Spanish Guitar	196?	$60
❏ P8461 [M]	For My True Love	1959	$80
❏ SP8461 [S]	For My True Love	1959	$100
❏ T2197 [M]	Guitar from Ipanema	1964	$75
❏ ST2197 [S]	Guitar from Ipanema	1964	$80
❏ P8341 [M]	Guitar Music from the Romantic Era	195?	$100
❏ DP8601 [R]	Guitar Music from the Romantic Era	196?	$60
❏ P8601 [M]	Guitar Music from the Romantic Era	196?	$75
—Reissue of 8341			
❏ P8321 [M]	Guitar Music of Latin America	195?	$100
❏ P8295 [M]	Guitar Music of Spain	195?	$100
❏ T1263 [M]	Happy Cha Cha Cha	1959	$80
❏ P8381 [M]	Impressaoes do Brasil	195?	$75
❏ T1946 [M]	It's a Bossa Nova World	1963	$75
❏ ST1946 [S]	It's a Bossa Nova World	1963	$25
❏ SP8497 [S]	Music of the Spanish Guitar	196?	$80
❏ T2419 [M]	New Broadway-Hollywood Hits	1965	$60
❏ ST2419 [S]	New Broadway-Hollywood Hits	1965	$50
❏ T1872 [M]	Ole! Bossa Nova	1963	$50
❏ ST1872 [S]	Ole! Bossa Nova	1963	$25
❏ P8571 [M]	Reverie for Spanish Guitars	196?	$80
❏ SP8571 [S]	Reverie for Spanish Guitars	196?	$100
❏ P8482 [M]	Songs of Enchantment	196?	$50
❏ SP8482 [S]	Songs of Enchantment	196?	$25
❏ T2345 [M]	Suenos (Dreams)	1965	$50
❏ DP8686 [R]	The Best of Laurindo Almeida	1969	$60
❏ STER-291	The Guitar of Laurindo Almeida	1969	$40
❏ P8546 [M]	The Guitar Worlds of Laurindo Almeida	196?	$75
❏ SP8546 [S]	The Guitar Worlds of Laurindo Almeida	196?	$80
❏ P8582 [M]	The Intimate Bach: Duets with the Spanish Guitar Vol. 2	196?	$75
❏ SP8582 [S]	The Intimate Bach: Duets with the Spanish Guitar Vol. 2	196?	$80
❏ ST2866	The Look of Love	1968	$80
❏ P8392 [M]	The New World of the Guitar	195?	$100
❏ P8521 [M]	The Spanish Guitars of Laurindo Almeida	196?	$50
❏ SP8521 [S]	The Spanish Guitars of Laurindo Almeida	196?	$80
❏ P8497 [M]	Villa-Lobos: Music for the Spanish Guitar	196?	$50
❏ P8367 [M]	Vistas d'Espana	195?	$100
❏ T1759 [M]	Viva Bossa Nova!	1962	$50
❏ ST1759 [S]	Viva Bossa Nova!	1962	$25

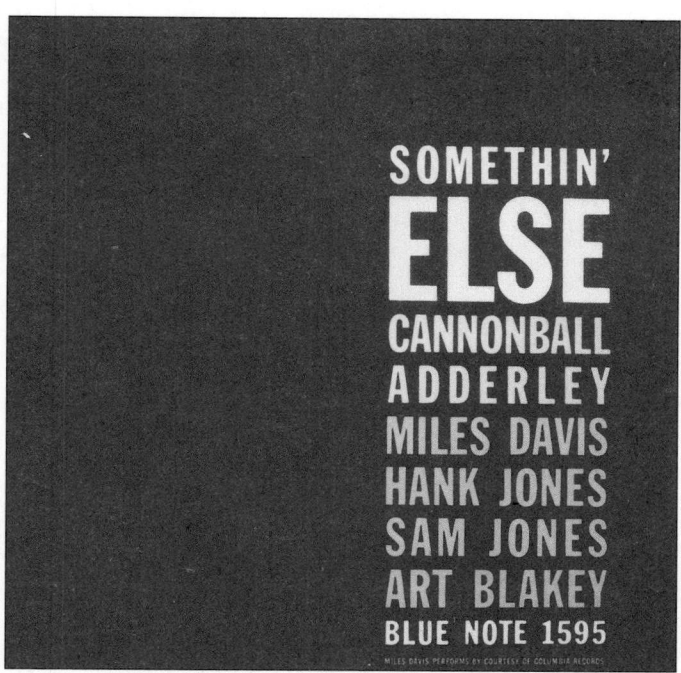

Cannonball Adderley, *Somethin' Else*, Blue Note BLP-1595, "deep groove" edition with W. 63rd St. address on label, **$200**.

Joe Albany with Warne Marsh, *The Right Combination*, Riverside RLP 12-270, **$300**.

Lorez Alexandria, *This Is Lorez*, King 542, black label, no crown, **$200**.

Mose Allison, *Mose Alive!*, Atlantic SD 1450, blue and green label, **$40**.

Number	Title	Yr	NM
❏ SM-1759	Viva Bossa Nova!	197?	$25
CONCORD CONCERTO			
❏ CC-2001	First Concerto for Guitar and Orchestra	1980	$25
❏ CC-2003	Laurindo Almeida with Bud Shank	198?	$25
CONCORD JAZZ			
❏ CJ-238	Artistry in Rhythm	1984	$25
❏ CJ-84	Chamber Jazz	1979	$35
CORAL			
❏ CRL56049 [10]	A Guitar Recital of Famous Serenades	1952	$80
❏ CRL57056 [M]	A Guitar Recital of Famous Serenades	1956	$50
—Maroon label original			
❏ CRL57056 [M]	A Guitar Recital of Famous Serenades	196?	$30
—Black label with color bars			
❏ CRL56086 [10]	Latin Melodies	1952	$80
CRYSTAL CLEAR			
❏ CCS-8007	New Directions	1979	$40
—Direct-to-disc recording			
❏ CCS-8001	Virtuoso Guitar	1978	$40
—Direct-to-disc recording; plays at 45 rpm; white vinyl			
❏ CCS-8001	Virtuoso Guitar	1978	$30
—Direct-to-disc recording; plays at 45 rpm; black vinyl			
DAYBREAK			
❏ DR-2013	The Best of Everything	1972	$35
DOBRE			
❏ DR1000	Latin Guitar	1977	$50
❏ 1024	Trio	197?	$25
EVEREST			
❏ SDBR-3287 [R]	Spanish Guitar Recital	196?	$25
INNER CITY			
❏ IC6031	Concierto de Aranjuez	1979	$35
ORION			
❏ ORS7259	The Art of Laurindo Almeida	197?	$35
PACIFIC JAZZ			
❏ PJLP-7 [10]	Laurindo Almeida Quartet	1953	$200
❏ PJLP-13 [10]	Laurindo Almeida Quartet, Vol. 2	1954	$200
❏ PJ-1204 [M]	Laurindo Almeida Quartet Featuring Bud Shank	1955	$120
—Reissue of 10-inch Pacific Jazz LPs; red vinyl			
❏ PJ-1204 [M]	Laurindo Almeida Quartet Featuring Bud Shank	1955	$80
—Reissue of 10-inch Pacific Jazz LPs; black vinyl			
PAUSA			
❏ PR9009	Brazilliance	1983	$25
—Reissue			
PICKWICK			
❏ SPC-3172	I Left My Heart in San Francisco	197?	$20
PRO ARTE			
❏ PAD-235	3 Guitars 3	1985	$25
—With Sharon Isbin and Larry Coryell			
SUTTON			
❏ SU247 [M]	Flamenco	196?	$25
TOWER			
❏ T5060 [M]	Acapulco '22	1967	$60
❏ DT5060 [R]	Acapulco '22	1967	$50
WARNER BROS.			
❏ WS1803	Classical Current: Electronic Excursions	1969	$60
—Original U.S. edition is on a green "W7" label			
❏ ST-92083	Classical Current: Electronic Excursions	1969	$100
—Capitol Record Club edition			
WORLD PACIFIC			
❏ WP-1412 [M]	Brazilliance, Vol. 1	1962	$30
—Reissue of World Pacific 1204			
❏ WPS-21412 [S]	Brazilliance, Vol. 1	196?	$100
❏ T90078 [M]	Brazilliance, Vol. 1	196?	$150
—Capitol Record Club edition			
❏ WP-1419 [M]	Brazilliance, Vol. 2	1962	$30
❏ ST-1419 [S]	Brazilliance, Vol. 2	1962	$30
❏ WP-1425 [M]	Brazilliance, Vol. 3	1962	$30
❏ ST-1425 [S]	Brazilliance, Vol. 3	1962	$30
❏ PJ-1204 [M]	Laurindo Almeida Quartet Featuring Bud Shank	1958	$150
—Reissue of Pacific Jazz 1204			

ALMERICO, TONY
New Orleans-style trumpeter and bandleader.

Albums

Number	Title	Yr	NM
IMPERIAL			
❏ LP-9151 [M]	French Quarter Jazz	1961	$150
❏ LP-12072 [S]	French Quarter Jazz	1961	$150

ALMOND, JOHNNY
Baritone saxophone player.

Albums

Number	Title	Yr	NM
DERAM			
❏ DES18030	Music Machine	1969	$35

ALPERT, HERB
Trumpet player. Best known for his 1960s pop material with the Tijuana Brass, his 1970s and 1980s material is more adventurous and often touches on jazz, thus it is included here.

Albums

Number	Title	Yr	NM
A&M			
❏ SP-3717	Beyond	1980	$20
❏ SP-4949	Blow Your Own Horn	1983	$20
❏ SP-3731	Fandango	1982	$20
❏ SP-4591	Just You and Me	1976	$25
❏ SP-5125	Keep Your Eye on Me	1987	$20
❏ SP-3728	Magic Man	1981	$20
❏ SP-5273	My Abstract Heart	1989	$20
❏ 7502153451	North on South Street	1991	$30
❏ SP-4790	Rise	1979	$25
❏ SP-3714	Rise	1980	$20
—Reissue of 4790			
❏ SP-5209	Under a Spanish Moon	1988	$20
❏ SP-5082	Wild Romance	1985	$20
MOBILE FIDELITY			
❏ Jan-0053	Rise	1981	$60
—Audiophile vinyl			

ALPERT, HERB/HUGH MASEKELA
Also see each artist's individual listings.

Albums

Number	Title	Yr	NM
A&M			
❏ SP-3150	Herb Alpert/Hugh Masekela	198?	$20
❏ SP-4727	Main Event	1978	$25
HORIZON			
❏ 728	Herb Alpert/Hugh Masekela	1978	$25

ALPERT, TRIGGER
Bass player.

Albums

Number	Title	Yr	NM
RIVERSIDE			
❏ RLP 12-225 [M]	Trigger Happy!	1956	$350
—White label, blue print			
❏ RLP 12-225 [M]	Trigger Happy!	195?	$40
—Blue label with microphone logo			

ALVIN, DANNY
Drummer and bandleader.

Albums

Number	Title	Yr	NM
JAZZOLOGY			
❏ 8 [M]	Danny Alvin and the Kings of Dixieland	1964	$50
❏ S-8 [S]	Danny Alvin and the Kings of Dixieland	1964	$50
STEPHENY			
❏ MF-4002 [M]	Club Basin Street	1957	$100

AMERICAN JAZZ ENSEMBLE, THE

Albums

Number	Title	Yr	NM
EPIC			
❏ LA16040 [M]	New Dimensions	1962	$50
❏ BA17040 [S]	New Dimensions	1962	$60
RCA VICTOR			
❏ LPM-2557 [M]	The American Jazz Ensemble in Rome	1962	$25
❏ LSP-2557 [S]	The American Jazz Ensemble in Rome	1962	$30

AMMONS, ALBERT, AND PETE JOHNSON
Also see each artist's individual listings.

Albums

Number	Title	Yr	NM
RCA VICTOR			
❏ LPT-9 [10]	8 to the Bar	1952	$175

AMMONS, ALBERT
Boogie-woogie pianist and father of GENE AMMONS.

Albums

Number	Title	Yr	NM
BLUE NOTE			
❏ BLP-7017 [10]	Boogie Woogie Classics	1951	$300
COMMODORE			
❏ XFL-15357 [M]	The Boogie Woogie and the Blues	198?	$30
MERCURY			
❏ MG-25012 [10]	Boogie Woogie Piano	1950	$250

AMMONS, ALBERT / MEADE LUX LEWIS
Also see each artist's individual listings.

Albums

Number	Title	Yr	NM
MOSAIC			
❏ MR3-103	The Complete Blue Note Recordings of Albert Ammons and Meade Lux Lewis	198?	$50
—Limited edition of 5,000			

AMMONS, GENE, AND JAMES MOODY
Also see each artist's individual listings.

Albums

Number	Title	Yr	NM
PRESTIGE			
❏ P-10065	Chicago Concert	1973	$60

AMMONS, GENE, AND RICHARD "GROOVE" HOLMES
Also see each artist's individual listings.

Albums

Number	Title	Yr	NM
PACIFIC JAZZ			
❏ PJ-32 [M]	Groovin' with Jug	1961	$150
❏ ST-32 [S]	Groovin' with Jug	1961	$120

AMMONS, GENE, AND SONNY STITT
Also see each artist's individual listings.

Albums

Number	Title	Yr	NM
CADET			
❏ LP-785 [M]	Jug and Sonny	1967	$40
❏ LPS-785 [S]	Jug and Sonny	1967	$60
—Fading blue label			
❏ LPS-785 [S]	Jug and Sonny	197?	$35
—Yellow and pink label (reissue)			
CHESS			
❏ LP1445 [M]	Jug and Sonny	1960	$150
❏ CH-91549	Jug and Sonny	198?	$25
PRESTIGE			
❏ PRST-7823	Blues Up and Down Vol. 1	1969	$50
❏ PRLP-107 [10]	Gene Ammons vs. Sonny Stitt: Battle of the Saxes	1951	$250
❏ PRLP-7234 [M]	Soul Summit	1962	$150
❏ PRST-7234 [S]	Soul Summit	1962	$150
❏ PRLP-7454 [M]	Soul Summit	1967	$50
❏ PRST-7454 [S]	Soul Summit	1967	$35
❏ P-10100	Together Again for the Last Time	197?	$50
❏ PRST-7606	We'll Be Together Again	1969	$40
❏ PRST-10019	You Talk That Talk!	1970	$40
VERVE			
❏ V-8426 [M]	Boss Tenors	1962	$60
❏ V6-8426 [S]	Boss Tenors	1962	$60
❏ V-8468 [M]	Boss Tenors in Orbit	1962	$60
❏ V6-8468 [S]	Boss Tenors in Orbit	1962	$60
❏ 2V6S-8812 [S]	Prime Cuts	1972	$50

AMMONS, GENE
Nicknamed "Jug." Tenor saxophone player.

Albums

Number	Title	Yr	NM
ANALOGUE PRODUCTIONS			
❏ AP 038 [M]	The Soulful Moods of Gene Ammons	199?	$60
—180-gram reissue of Moodsville 28			
ARGO			

Number	Title	Yr	NM
❑ 697 [M]	Dig Him	1962	$120
❑ S-697 [S]	Dig Him	1962	$100
❑ S-698 [S]	Just Jug	1962	$40

CADET

Number	Title	Yr	NM
❑ 2CA-60038	Early Visions	1975	$35
❑ LP-783 [M]	Makes It Happen	1967	$40
❑ LPS-783 [S]	Makes It Happen	1967	$50

—Fading blue label (original)

Number	Title	Yr	NM
❑ CA-783 [S]	Makes It Happen	197?	$35

—Yellow and pink label (reissue)

CHESS

Number	Title	Yr	NM
❑ CH2-92514	Early Visions	198?	$30

—Reissue of Cadet 60038

Number	Title	Yr	NM
❑ LP1442 [M]	Soulful Saxophone	1959	$140

—Black vinyl

Number	Title	Yr	NM
❑ LP1442 [DJ]	Soulful Saxophone	1959	$150

—White label promo; multicolor swirl vinyl

EMARCY

Number	Title	Yr	NM
❑ EMS-2-400	The "Jug" Sessions	1976	$50
❑ MG-26031 [10]	With or Without	1954	$300

ENJA

Number	Title	Yr	NM
❑ 3093	Gene Ammons in Sweden	1981	$35

FANTASY

Number	Title	Yr	NM
❑ OJC-014	All-Star Sessions	1982	$25
❑ OJC-351	Bad! Bossa Nova	198?	$25
❑ OJC-192	Blue Gene	1985	$25
❑ OJC-297	Boss Tenor	1988	$25
❑ OJC-244	Funky	1987	$25
❑ OJC-6005	Gene Ammons' Greatest Hits, Vol. 1: The Sixties	1988	$30
❑ OJC-129	Jammin' in Hi-Fi	198?	$25
❑ OJC-211	Jammin' with Gene	1986	$25
❑ OJC-395	Live in Chicago	198?	$25
❑ OJC-651	The Big Sound	1991	$30
❑ OJC-013	The Happy Blues	198?	$25

MOODSVILLE

Number	Title	Yr	NM
❑ MVLP-18 [M]	Nice and Cool	1961	$150

—Originals have green label

Number	Title	Yr	NM
❑ MVLP-18 [M]	Nice and Cool	1965	$40

—Second editions have blue label with trident at right

Number	Title	Yr	NM
❑ MVLP-28 [M]	The Soulful Moods of Gene Ammons	1963	$150

—Originals have green label

Number	Title	Yr	NM
❑ MVLP-28 [M]	The Soulful Moods of Gene Ammons	1965	$40

—Second editions have blue label with trident at right

Number	Title	Yr	NM
❑ MVST-28 [S]	The Soulful Moods of Gene Ammons	1963	$150

PRESTIGE

Number	Title	Yr	NM
❑ PRLP-7369 [M]	Angel Eyes	1965	$100

—Originals have blue label with trident at right

Number	Title	Yr	NM
❑ PRST-7369 [S]	Angel Eyes	1965	$120

—Originals have blue label with trident at right

Number	Title	Yr	NM
❑ PRLP-7257 [M]	Bad! Bossa Nova	1962	$150

—Originals have yellow label, Bergenfield, N.J. address; some copies have a cover calling this "Jungle Soul! (ca' purange)

Number	Title	Yr	NM
❑ P-10070	Big Bad Jug	1973	$40
❑ PRST-10006	Black Cat	1970	$60

—Original on purple label

Number	Title	Yr	NM
❑ PRST-10006	Black Cat	1973	$60

—Second edition on green label

Number	Title	Yr	NM
❑ MPP-2514	Blue Groove	1982	$30
❑ PRLP-7445 [M]	Boss Soul!	1967	$100

—Originals have blue label with trident at right

Number	Title	Yr	NM
❑ PRST-7445 [S]	Boss Soul!	1967	$100

—Originals have blue label with trident at right

Number	Title	Yr	NM
❑ PRLP-7180 [M]	Boss Tenor	1960	$200

—Originals have yellow label, Bergenfield, N.J. address

Number	Title	Yr	NM
❑ PRST-7180 [S]	Boss Tenor	1960	$200

—Originals have silver label

Number	Title	Yr	NM
❑ PRLP-7534 [M]	Boss Tenor	1967	$100

—Reissue of 7180; originals have blue label with trident at right

Number	Title	Yr	NM
❑ PRST-7534 [S]	Boss Tenor	1967	$60

—Reissue of 7180; originals have blue label with trident at right

Number	Title	Yr	NM
❑ P-10080	Brasswind	1974	$60
❑ P-10021	Brother Jug	1970	$40
❑ PRST-10010	Chase!	1970	$60
❑ P-10040	Free Again	1972	$60
❑ PRLP-107 [10]	Gene Ammons	1951	$300
❑ P-10078	Gene Ammons and Friends at Montreux	1973	$35
❑ PRLP-127 [10]	Gene Ammons Favorites, Volume 2	1952	$300
❑ PRLP-149 [10]	Gene Ammons Favorites, Volume 3	1953	$300
❑ PRLP-211 [10]	Gene Ammons Jazz Session	1955	$300
❑ PRLP-7495 [M]	Gene Ammons Live in Chicago	1967	$100

—Originals have blue label with trident at right

Number	Title	Yr	NM
❑ PRST-7495 [S]	Gene Ammons Live in Chicago	1967	$40

—Originals have blue label with trident at right

Number	Title	Yr	NM
❑ P-10093	Goodbye	1975	$50
❑ PRST-10058	Got My Own	1973	$60
❑ P-10084	Greatest Hits	1974	$60
❑ PRLP-7039 [M]	Hi Fidelity Jam Session	1956	$300
❑ PRST-7192 [S]	Jug	1960	$200

—Originals have silver label

Number	Title	Yr	NM
❑ PRLP-7192 [M]	Jug	1960	$200

—Originals have yellow label, Bergenfield, N.J. address

Number	Title	Yr	NM
❑ PRST-7192 [S]	Jug	1972	$60

—Reissue; trident logo at top

Number	Title	Yr	NM
❑ P-24021	Jug and Dodo	1972	$50
❑ P-24036	Juganthology	197?	$50
❑ PRST-7552	Jungle Soul	1968	$40

—Reissue of 7257

Number	Title	Yr	NM
❑ PRLP-7287 [M]	Late Hour Special	1964	$40

—Originals have yellow label, Bergenfield, N.J. address

Number	Title	Yr	NM
❑ PRST-7287 [S]	Late Hour Special	1964	$100

—Originals have silver label

Number	Title	Yr	NM
❑ P-10022	My Way	197?	$50
❑ P-7862	Night Lights	1985	$30
❑ PRLP-7060 [M]	Not Really the Blues	1960	$200

—Retitled version of "Jammin' with Gene

Number	Title	Yr	NM
❑ PRLP-7270 [M]	Preachin'	1963	$120

—Originals have yellow label, Bergenfield, N.J. address

Number	Title	Yr	NM
❑ PRST-7270 [S]	Preachin'	1963	$140

—Originals have silver label

Number	Title	Yr	NM
❑ PRLP-7400 [M]	Sock!	1966	$100

—Originals have blue label with trident at right

Number	Title	Yr	NM
❑ PRST-7400 [S]	Sock!	1966	$120

—Originals have blue label with trident at right

Number	Title	Yr	NM
❑ PRLP-7275 [M]	Soul Summit, Volume 2	1963	$120

—Originals have yellow label, Bergenfield, N.J. address

Number	Title	Yr	NM
❑ PRST-7275 [S]	Soul Summit, Volume 2	1963	$140

—Originals have silver label

Number	Title	Yr	NM
❑ PRLP-112 [10]	Tenor Sax Favorites, Volume 1	1951	$300
❑ PRST-7774	The Best of Gene Ammons	1970	$50
❑ PRST-7708	The Best of Gene Ammons for Beautiful People	1969	$50
❑ P-24098	The Big Sound of Gene Ammons	1981	$50
❑ P-10023	The Boss Is Back	197?	$50

—Reissue of 7739

Number	Title	Yr	NM
❑ PRST-7739	The Boss Is Back!	1970	$60
❑ P-24079	The Gene Ammons Story: Gentle Jug	197?	$50
❑ P-24071	The Gene Ammons Story: Organ Combos	197?	$60
❑ P-24058	The Gene Ammons Story: The 78 Era	197?	$50
❑ PRLP-7039 [M]	The Happy Blues	1960	$200

—Retitled version of "Hi Fidelity Jam Session

Number	Title	Yr	NM
❑ PRST-7654	The Happy Blues -- Jam Session, Vol. 1	1969	$60

—Second reissue of 7039

Number	Title	Yr	NM
❑ PRLP-7176 [M]	The Twister	1960	$200

—Originals have yellow label, Bergenfield, N.J. address; reissue of 7110

Number	Title	Yr	NM
❑ PRLP-7238 [M]	Twistin' the Jug	1962	$200

—Originals have yellow label, Bergenfield, N.J. address

Number	Title	Yr	NM
❑ PRST-7238 [S]	Twistin' the Jug	1962	$120

—Originals have silver label

Number	Title	Yr	NM
❑ PRLP-7208 [M]	Up Tight!	1961	$150

—Originals have yellow label, Bergenfield, N.J. address

Number	Title	Yr	NM
❑ PRST-7208 [S]	Up Tight!	1961	$150

—Originals have silver label

Number	Title	Yr	NM
❑ PRLP-7320 [M]	Velvet Soul	1964	$120

—Originals have yellow label, Bergenfield, N.J. address

Number	Title	Yr	NM
❑ PRST-7320 [S]	Velvet Soul	1964	$150

—Originals have silver label

Number	Title	Yr	NM
❑ PRLP-7320 [M]	Velvet Soul	1965	$40

—Blue label with tridenr at right

Number	Title	Yr	NM
❑ PRST-7320 [S]	Velvet Soul	1965	$100

—Blue label with tridenr at right

Number	Title	Yr	NM
❑ PRLP-7050 [M]	Woofin' and Tweetin'	1960	$200

—Retitled version of "Gene Ammons All Star Session

ROOTS

Number	Title	Yr	NM
❑ 1002	Swinging the Jugg	1976	$50

SAVOY

Number	Title	Yr	NM
❑ MG-14033 [M]	Golden Saxophone	1961	$100
❑ SJL-1103	Red Top	1976	$30

STATUS

Number	Title	Yr	NM
❑ 18	Nice & Cool	197?	$35

TRIP

Number	Title	Yr	NM
❑ TLP-5578 [M]	Light, Bluesy and Moody	197?	$30

UPFRONT

Number	Title	Yr	NM
❑ UPF-116	Nothing But Soul	1968	$35

—Reissue of Vee-Jay material

VEE JAY

Number	Title	Yr	NM
❑ LP-3024 [M]	Juggin' Around	1961	$150
❑ LPS-3024 [S]	Juggin' Around	1961	$150

WING

Number	Title	Yr	NM
❑ MGW-12156 [M]	Light, Bluesy and Moody	1963	$150

—Reissue of EmArcy 10-inch LP

Number	Title	Yr	NM
❑ SRW-16156 [R]	Light, Bluesy and Moody	1963	$35

AMRAM, DAVID

French horn player and composer; also dabbles in piano, guitar, flute and whistle. Also has written operas and classical orchestral works.

Albums

ELEKTRA/MUSICIAN

Number	Title	Yr	NM
❑ 60195	Latin Jazz Celebration	1983	$25

FLYING FISH

Number	Title	Yr	NM
❑ FC-27753	Autobiography	198?	$25
❑ FF-094	Friends, At Home/Around the World	1979	$25
❑ FF-057	Havana/New York	1978	$30
❑ FC-27752	No More Walls	198?	$25

AMRAM-BARROW QUARTET, THE

Also see DAVID AMRAM.

Albums

DECCA

Number	Title	Yr	NM
❑ DL8558 [M]	Jazz Studio No. 6	1957	$120

AMY, CURTIS, AND DUPREE BOLTON

Bolton's instrument is the trumpet. Also see CURTIS AMY.

Albums

PACIFIC JAZZ

Number	Title	Yr	NM
❑ PJ-70 [M]	Katanga!	1963	$30
❑ ST-70 [S]	Katanga!	1963	$60

—Red vinyl

Number	Title	Yr	NM
❑ ST-70 [S]	Katanga!	1963	$30

—Black vinyl

AMY, CURTIS, AND FRANK BUTLER

Also see each artist's individual listings.

Albums

PACIFIC JAZZ

Number	Title	Yr	NM
❑ PJ-19 [M]	Groovin' Blue	1961	$30
❑ ST-19 [S]	Groovin' Blue	1961	$40

AMY, CURTIS, AND PAUL BRYANT

Also see each artist's individual listings.

Albums

KIMBERLY

Number	Title	Yr	NM
❑ 2020 [M]	This Is the Blues	1963	$25
❑ 11020 [S]	This Is the Blues	1963	$30

PACIFIC JAZZ

Number	Title	Yr	NM
❑ PJ-26 [M]	Meetin' Here	1961	$30
❑ ST-26 [S]	Meetin' Here	1961	$40
❑ PJ-9 [M]	The Blues Message	1960	$30
❑ ST-9 [S]	The Blues Message	1960	$40

AMY, CURTIS, AND VICTOR FELDMAN

Also see each artist's individual listings.

Albums

PACIFIC JAZZ

Number	Title	Yr	NM
❑ PJ-46 [M]	Way Down	1962	$30
❑ ST-46 [S]	Way Down	1962	$30

AMY, CURTIS

Saxophone player (soprano, alto, tenor and baritone) and occasional flutist as well. He played the sax solo on the Doors' hit single "Touch Me."

Albums

Number	Title	Yr	NM

PACIFIC JAZZ

Number	Title	Yr	NM
❏ PJ-62 [M]	Tippin' On Through -- Recorded "Live" at the Lighthouse	1962	$30
❏ ST-62 [S]	Tippin' On Through -- Recorded "Live" at the Lighthouse	1962	$30

PALOMAR

❏ G-24003 [M]	Sounds of Hollywood and Broadway	1965	$35
❏ GS-34003 [S]	Sounds of Hollywood and Broadway	1965	$25

VERVE

❏ V-8684 [M]	Mustang	1966	$35
❏ V6-8684 [S]	Mustang	1966	$25

ANDERSEN, ARLID
Bass player.

Albums

ECM

❏ 1236	A Molde Concert	1981	$30
❏ 1127	Green Shading Into Blue	1978	$30
❏ 1082	Shimri	1976	$30

ANDERSON, CAT
Trumpeter, mostly with the DUKE ELLINGTON orchestra.

Albums

CLASSIC JAZZ

❏ CJ-142	Cat Speaks	1979	$30

EMARCY

❏ MG-36142 [M]	Cat on a Hot Tin Roof	1958	$200

INNER CITY

❏ 1143	Cat Anderson	198?	$25

MERCURY

❏ MG-20522 [M]	Cat on a Hot Tin Roof	1959	$100
❏ SR-60199 [S]	Cat on a Hot Tin Roof	1959	$100

ANDERSON, CHRIS
Pianist..

Albums

JAZZLAND

❏ JLP-57 [M]	Inverted Images	1961	$30
❏ JLP-957 [S]	Inverted Images	1961	$40

ANDERSON, ERNESTINE
Female singer.

Albums

CONCORD JAZZ

❏ CJ-319	Be Mine Tonight	1987	$50
❏ CJ-214	Big City	1983	$50
❏ CJ-31	Hello Like Before	1977	$50
❏ CJ-54	Live from Concord to London	1978	$60
❏ CJ-147	Never Make Your Move Too Soon	1982	$50
❏ CJ-109	Sunshine	1980	$50
❏ CJ-263	When the Sun Goes Down	1985	$50

MERCURY

❏ MG-20400 [M]	Ernestine Anderson	1959	$100
❏ SR-60074 [S]	Ernestine Anderson	1959	$300
❏ MG-20492 [M]	Fascinating Ernestine	1959	$150
❏ SR-60171 [S]	Fascinating Ernestine	1959	$250
❏ MG-20354 [M]	Hot Cargo	1958	$200
❏ MG-20582 [M]	Moanin'	1960	$100
❏ SR-60242 [S]	Moanin'	1960	$150
❏ MG-20496 [M]	My Kinda Swing	1959	$200
❏ SR-60175 [S]	My Kinda Swing	1959	$250

SUE

❏ LP1015 [M]	The New Sound of Ernestine Anderson	1963	$50

WING

❏ MGW-12281 [M]	My Kinda Swing	1964	$35
❏ SRW-16281 [S]	My Kinda Swing	1964	$50

ANDERSON, IVIE, AND LENA HORNE
Female singer. One of the first featured solo singers with a jazz band, Anderson sang on the original version of the DUKE ELLINGTON classic "It Don't Mean A Thing (If It Ain't Got That Swing)." Also see LENA HORNE.

Albums

JAZZTONE

❏ J-1262 [M]	Lena and Ivie	1956	$40

ANDERSON, RAY
Trombone player.

Albums

GRAMAVISION

❏ R1-79453	What Because	1990	$30

MINOR MUSIC

❏ MM-007	You Be	1986	$30

SOUL NOTE

❏ SN-1087	Right Down Your Alley	1985	$30

ANDERZA, EARL
Alto saxophone player.

Albums

PACIFIC JAZZ

❏ PJ-65 [M]	Outa Sight	1963	$30
❏ ST-65 [S]	Outa Sight	1963	$30

ANDRE'S CUBAN ALL-STARS

Albums

CLEF

❏ MGC-515 [10]	Cubano	1954	$250

— This was reissued on 12-inch as part of a JACK COSTANZO album.

ANDREWS, ERNIE
Male singer.

Albums

DISCOVERY

❏ 825	From the Heart	198?	$30

GENE NORMAN PRESENTS

❏ GNP-42 [M]	Ernie Andrews	1959	$40
❏ GNP-28 [M]	In the Dark	1957	$40
❏ GNP-43 [M]	Travelin' Light	1959	$40
❏ GNPS-10008 [S]	Travelin' Light	1959	$40

GNP CRESCENDO

❏ GNPS-10008 [S]	Travelin' Light	196?	$35

ANDREWS, GAYLE
Female singer?

Albums

HI-LIFE

❏ HL-54 [M]	Love's a Snap	195?	$30

ANDY AND THE BEY SISTERS
Vocal group. Andy Bey also is a pianist.

Albums

PRESTIGE

❏ PRLP-7346 [M]	Now! Hear!	1964	$40
❏ PRST-7346 [S]	Now! Hear!	1964	$50
❏ PRLP-7411 [M]	'Round About Midnight	1965	$40
❏ PRST-7411 [S]	'Round About Midnight	1965	$50

ANNA MARIE
Female singer, possibly Anna Marie Wooldridge, who later recorded as ABBEY LINCOLN.

Albums

VESTA

❏ LP-101 [10]	Anna Marie	1955	$80

ANTHONY, RAY
Trumpeter and bandleader. Member of the GLENN MILLER orchestra before starting his own band after World War II. Most of his albums are in an easy-listening vein.

Albums

AERO SPACE

❏ RA1007	Around the World	197?	$25
❏ RA1028	Let's Go Dancing	197?	$30

— Green vinyl; Arthur Murray promotional item; add 25 percent if certificate for a free dance lesson is included

CAPITOL

❏ T1371 [M]	Arthur Murray Favorites -- Fox Trots	1960	$60
❏ H362 [10]	Campus Rumpus	195?	$80
❏ T2043 [M]	Charade and Other Top Themes	1964	$60
❏ ST2043 [S]	Charade and Other Top Themes	1964	$75
❏ T1420 [M]	Dancing Alone Together	1960	$60

Number	Title	Yr	NM
—Black colorband label, Capitol logo at left			
❏ ST1420 [S]	Dancing Alone Together	1960	$75
—Black colorband label, Capitol logo at left			
❏ T1420 [M]	Dancing Alone Together	1962	$40
—Black colorband label, Capitol logo at top			
❏ ST1420 [S]	Dancing Alone Together	1962	$60
—Black colorband label, Capitol logo at top			
❏ T1028 [M]	Dancing Over the Waves	1958	$75
❏ T723 [M]	Dream Dancing	1956	$75
❏ T1608 [M]	Dream Dancing Medley	1961	$60
❏ ST1608 [S]	Dream Dancing Medley	1961	$75
❏ T2457 [M]	Dream Dancing Today	1966	$60
❏ ST2457 [S]	Dream Dancing Today	1966	$75
❏ M-11978	Fox Trots	1979	$25
❏ H258 [10]	Fox Trots	195?	$60
❏ T563 [M]	Golden Horn	1955	$75
❏ T2530 [M]	Hit Songs to Remember	1966	$60
❏ ST2530 [S]	Hit Songs to Remember	1966	$75
❏ H292 [10]	Houseparty Hop	195?	$75

— Reissue of L 292; purple label; "This Album Contains 8 Selections" on upper right back cover

❏ L292 [10]	Houseparty Hop	195?	$80

— Original issue; maroon label; "In addition to the selections listed, this long playing record contains: PERDIDO - WAGON WHEELS" under the title on back cover

❏ T1783 [M]	I Almost Lost My Mind	1962	$60
❏ ST1783 [S]	I Almost Lost My Mind	1962	$75
❏ H476 [10]	I Remember Glenn Miller	1954	$75
❏ T749 [M]	Jam Session at the Tower	1956	$75
❏ T1304 [M]	Like Wild!	1959	$60
❏ ST1304 [S]	Like Wild!	1959	$75
❏ T917 [M]	Moments Together	1958	$75
❏ T1252 [M]	More Dream Dancing	1959	$60
❏ ST1252 [S]	More Dream Dancing	1959	$75
❏ T2150 [M]	My Love, Forgive Me	1964	$60
❏ ST2150 [S]	My Love, Forgive Me	1964	$50
❏ T1066 [M]	Ray Anthony Plays Steve Allen	1958	$50
❏ T1917 [M]	Smash Hits of '63	1963	$60
❏ ST1917 [S]	Smash Hits of '63	1963	$50
❏ T1200 [M]	Sound Spectacular	1959	$50
❏ T831 [M]	Star Dancing	1957	$50
❏ T2188 [M]	Swim, Swim, C'mon, Let's Swim	1964	$60
❏ ST2188 [S]	Swim, Swim, C'mon, Let's Swim	1964	$50
❏ T969 [M]	The Dream Girl	1958	$75
❏ T1477 [M]	The Hits of Ray Anthony	1960	$60
❏ T1421 [M]	The New Ray Anthony Show	1960	$60
❏ ST1421 [S]	The New Ray Anthony Show	1960	$50
❏ T1668 [M]	Twist with Ray Anthony	1961	$60
❏ ST1668 [S]	Twist with Ray Anthony	1961	$50
❏ T1752 [M]	Worried Mind	1962	$60
❏ ST1752 [S]	Worried Mind	1962	$60
❏ T866 [M]	Young Ideas	1957	$60

CIRCLE

❏ CLP-96	Sweet and Swingin' 1949-1953	1987	$25

HINDSIGHT

❏ HSR-240	Young Man with a Horn	1988	$25

RANWOOD

❏ 8153	Golden Hits	197?	$25
❏ 8083	I Get the Blues When It Rains	197?	$25
❏ 8059	Love Is for the Two of Us	197?	$25
❏ R.8033	Now	197?	$25

— Cover uses "R." prefix, label uses "RLP" prefix

APPLEYARD, PETER
Vibraphone player.

Albums

AUDIO FIDELITY

❏ AFLP-1901 [M]	The Vibe Sound of Peter Appleyard	1958	$40
❏ AFSD-5901 [S]	The Vibe Sound of Peter Appleyard	1958	$40

ARGO, TONY

Albums

SAVOY

❏ MG-12157 [M]	Jazz Argosy	1960	$40

ARISTOCRATS OF DIXIELAND, THE
Members: Joe Perkins; George Palmer; Bob Bruce; Bob Eastman; Jim Morton; Bill Seabrook.

Albums

AUDIOPHILE

❏ AP-129	Florida Blues	1979	$25

Number	Title	Yr	NM

ARMSTRONG, LIL HARDIN

Pianist, female singer, composer, arranger and bandleader. The second wife of LOUIS ARMSTRONG, she played on many Hot Five and Hot Seven sessions.

Albums

RIVERSIDE

Number	Title	Yr	NM
❏ RLP-401 [M]	Lil Armstrong and Her Orchestra	1962	$150
❏ RLP-9401 [R]	Lil Armstrong and Her Orchestra	1962	$150
❏ RLP 12-120 [M]	Satchmo and Me	1956	$250

—*White label, blue print*

| ❏ RLP 12-120 [M] | Satchmo and Me | 195? | $40 |

—*Blue label with microphone logo at top*

ARMSTRONG, LOUIS, AND DUKE ELLINGTON

Also see each artist's individual listings. (SC1)
Also see each artist's individual listings.

Albums

MOBILE FIDELITY

❏ 2-155	The Great Reunion	1984	$150

—*Audiophile vinyl*

PICKWICK

❏ PC-3033	Louis Armstrong and Duke Ellington	196?	$25

ROULETTE

❏ RE-108	The Duke Ellington-Louis Armstrong Era	1973	$35
❏ R52103 [M]	The Great Reunion	1963	$50
❏ SR52103 [S]	The Great Reunion	1963	$60
❏ R52074 [M]	Together for the First Time	1961	$60
❏ SR52074 [S]	Together for the First Time	1961	$50

ARMSTRONG, LOUIS, AND OSCAR PETERSON

Also see each artist's individual listings. (SC1)
Also see each artist's individual listings.

Albums

VERVE

❏ MGV-8322 [M]	Louis Armstrong Meets Oscar Peterson	1959	$100
❏ MGVS-6062 [S]	Louis Armstrong Meets Oscar Peterson	1960	$100
❏ V-8322 [M]	Louis Armstrong Meets Oscar Peterson	1961	$50
❏ V6-8322 [S]	Louis Armstrong Meets Oscar Peterson	1961	$35

ARMSTRONG, LOUIS, AND SIDNEY BECHET

Also see each artist's individual listings.

Albums

JOLLY ROGER

❏ 5029 [M]	Louis Armstrong and Sidney Bechet	195?	$40

ARMSTRONG, LOUIS, AND THE MILLS BROTHERS

Also see each artist's individual listings.

Albums

DECCA

❏ DL5509 [10]	Louis Armstrong and the Mills Brothers	1954	$150

ARMSTRONG, LOUIS

Nickname: "Satchmo." Cornet and trumpet player, male singer, certainly the most influential jazz musician of the first half of the 20th century, if not of all time. Also see BING CROSBY AND LOUIS ARMSTRONG; ELLA FITZGERALD AND LOUIS ARMSTRONG; KING OLIVER.

Albums

ABC

❏ S-650	What a Wonderful World	1968	$60

ACCORD

❏ SN-7161	Mr. Music	1982	$25

AMSTERDAM

❏ AMS12009	Louis Armstrong and His Friends	1970	$35

AUDIO FIDELITY

❏ AFLP-2128 [M]	Ain't Gonna Give Nobody None of My Jelly Roll	1964	$35
❏ AFSD-6128 [S]	Ain't Gonna Give Nobody None of My Jelly Roll	1964	$50

Number	Title	Yr	NM
❏ AFLP-1924 [M]	Louie and the Dukes of Dixieland	1960	$60
❏ AFSD-5924 [S]	Louie and the Dukes of Dixieland	1960	$40
❏ AFSD-6241	Louis Armstrong	196?	$35
❏ AFLP-1930 [M]	Louis Armstrong Plays King Oliver	1960	$60
❏ AFSD-5930 [S]	Louis Armstrong Plays King Oliver	1960	$40
❏ AFLP-2132 [M]	The Best of Louis Armstrong	1964	$35
❏ AFSD-6132 [S]	The Best of Louis Armstrong	1964	$50

BIOGRAPH

❏ C-5	Great Soloists	1973	$30
❏ C-6	Louis Armstrong Plays the Blues	1973	$30

BLUEBIRD

❏ 9759-1-RB	Louis Armstrong & His Orchestra 1932-33: Laughin' Louie	1989	$30
❏ 5920-1-RB	Pops: The 1940s Small Band Sides	1987	$35
❏ 8310-1-RB	What a Wonderful World	1988	$25
❏ AXM2-5519	Young Louis (1932-1933)	1984	$30

BRUNSWICK

❏ BL58004 [10]	Armstrong Classics	1950	$175
❏ BL754136	I Will Wait for You	1968	$35

BUENA VISTA

❏ BV-4044	Disney Swings the Satchmo Way	1968	$40

CHIAROSCURO

❏ 2003	Great Alternatives	1977	$30
❏ 2002	Snake Rag	1977	$30
❏ 2006	Sweetheart	1977	$30

COLUMBIA

❏ CL840 [M]	Ambassador Satch	1956	$40
❏ CL591 [M]	Louis Armstrong Plays W.C. Handy	1954	$120

—*Maroon label, gold print (original)*

| ❏ CL591 [M] | Louis Armstrong Plays W.C. Handy | 1955 | $50 |

—*Red and black label with six "eye" logos*

❏ CL6335 [10]	Louis Armstrong Plays W.C. Handy, Volume 2	1955	$50
❏ CL2638 [M]	Louis Armstrong's Greatest Hits	1967	$50
❏ CS9438 [R]	Louis Armstrong's Greatest Hits	1967	$30
❏ PC9438 [R]	Louis Armstrong's Greatest Hits	198?	$20

—*Budget-line reissue*

| ❏ CL1077 [M] | Satchmo the Great | 1957 | $60 |
| ❏ CL708 [M] | Satch Plays Fats | 1955 | $50 |

—*Red and black label with six "eye" logos*

| ❏ G30416 | The Genius of Louis Armstrong, Vol. 1 | 1971 | $35 |
| ❏ ML4383 [M] | The Louis Armstrong Story, Volume 1: Louis Armstrong and His Hot Five | 1951 | $100 |

—*Green label, gold or silver print*

| ❏ CL851 [M] | The Louis Armstrong Story, Volume 1: Louis Armstrong and His Hot Five | 1956 | $60 |

—*Red and black label with six "eye" logos; reissue of 4383*

| ❏ CL851 [M] | The Louis Armstrong Story, Volume 1: Louis Armstrong and His Hot Five | 197? | $30 |

—*Orange label*

| ❏ ML4384 [M] | The Louis Armstrong Story, Volume 2: Louis Armstrong and His Hot Seven | 1951 | $100 |

—*Green label, gold or silver print*

| ❏ CL852 [M] | The Louis Armstrong Story, Volume 2: Louis Armstrong and His Hot Seven | 1956 | $60 |

—*Red and black label with six "eye" logos; reissue of 5484*

| ❏ ML4385 [M] | The Louis Armstrong Story, Volume 3: Louis Armstrong and Earl Hines | 1951 | $100 |

—*Green label, gold or silver print*

| ❏ CL853 [M] | The Louis Armstrong Story, Volume 3: Louis Armstrong and Earl Hines | 1956 | $60 |

—*Red and black label with six "eye" logos; reissue of 4385*

| ❏ CL853 [M] | The Louis Armstrong Story, Volume 3: Louis Armstrong and Earl Hines | 197? | $30 |

—*Orange label reissue*

| ❏ ML4386 [M] | The Louis Armstrong Story, Volume 4: Louis Armstrong Favorites | 1951 | $100 |

—*Green label, gold or silver print*

| ❏ CL854 [M] | The Louis Armstrong Story, Volume 4: Louis Armstrong Favorites | 1956 | $60 |

—*Red and black label with six "eye" logos; reissue of 4386*

COLUMBIA JAZZ MASTERPIECES

❏ CJ40242	Louis Armstrong Plays W.C. Handy	1986	$25
❏ CJ40378	Satch Plays Fats	1986	$25

COLUMBIA MUSICAL TREASURIES

❏ P4M5676	40 Greatest Hits	197?	$50

COLUMBIA SPECIAL PRODUCTS

❏ JCL708 [M]	Satch Plays Fats	196?	$30

—*"Special Collector's Series" reissue*

DECCA

❏ DL74330 [R]	A Musical Autobiography, 1928-1930	1962	$30
❏ DL4227 [M]	I Love Jazz	1962	$50
❏ DL74227 [R]	I Love Jazz	1962	$30
❏ DL8284 [M]	Jazz Classics	1956	$150

—*Black label, silver print*

| ❏ DL8284 [M] | Jazz Classics | 1960 | $35 |

—*Black label with color bars*

❏ DL5280 [10]	Jazz Concert	1950	$150
❏ DL4245 [M]	King Louis	1962	$50
❏ DL74245 [R]	King Louis	1962	$30
❏ DL5532 [10]	Latter-Day Louis	1954	$150
❏ DL8488 [M]	Louis and the Angels	1957	$120

—*Black label, silver print*

| ❏ DL8488 [M] | Louis and the Angels | 1960 | $35 |

—*Black label with color bars*

| ❏ DL8781 [M] | Louis and the Good Book | 1958 | $100 |

—*Black label, silver print*

| ❏ DL8741 [M] | Louis and the Good Book | 1960 | $35 |

—*Black label with color bars*

| ❏ DL8168 [M] | Louis Armstrong at the Crescendo, Volume 1 | 1955 | $150 |

—*Black label, silver print*

❏ DL5536 [10]	Louis Armstrong-Gordon Jenkins	1954	$150
❏ DL5279 [10]	New Orleans Days	1950	$200
❏ DL8283 [M]	New Orleans Jazz	1956	$120

—*Black label, silver print*

| ❏ DL8283 [M] | New Orleans Jazz | 1960 | $35 |

—*Black label with color bars*

| ❏ DL8329 [M] | New Orleans Nights | 1957 | $120 |

—*Black label, silver print*

| ❏ DL8329 [M] | New Orleans Nights | 1960 | $35 |

—*Black label with color bars*

| ❏ DL8329 [M] | New Orleans Nights | 1960 | $35 |

—*Black label with color bars*

❏ DL5225 [10]	New Orleans to New York	1950	$200
❏ DL9225 [M]	Rare Items (1935-1944)	196?	$50
❏ DL79225 [R]	Rare Items (1935-1944)	196?	$30
❏ DX155 [M]	Satchmo, A Musical Autobiography	1956	$175

—*Black labels, silver print*

| ❏ DXM155 [M] | Satchmo, A Musical Autobiography | 1960 | $40 |

—*Black labels with color bars*

❏ DL8963 [M]	Satchmo, A Musical Autobiography, 1923-1925	1960	$60
❏ DL78963 [R]	Satchmo, A Musical Autobiography, 1923-1925	196?	$30
❏ DL4230 [M]	Satchmo, A Musical Autobiography, 1926-1927	1962	$60
❏ DL4330 [M]	Satchmo, A Musical Autobiography, 1928-1930	1962	$60
❏ DL4331 [M]	Satchmo, A Musical Autobiography, 1930-1934	1962	$60
❏ DL8041 [M]	Satchmo at Pasadena	1954	$150

—*Black label, silver print*

| ❏ DL8041 [M] | Satchmo at Pasadena | 1960 | $35 |

—*Black label with color bars*

| ❏ DX108 [M] | Satchmo at Symphony Hall | 1954 | $150 |

—*Black labels, silver print*

| ❏ DL8037 [M] | Satchmo at Symphony Hall, Volume 1 | 1954 | $150 |

—*Black label, silver print*

| ❏ DL8037 [M] | Satchmo at Symphony Hall, Volume 1 | 1960 | $35 |

—*Black label with color bars*

| ❏ DL8038 [M] | Satchmo at Symphony Hall, Volume 2 | 1954 | $150 |

—*Black label, silver print*

| ❏ DL8038 [M] | Satchmo at Symphony Hall, Volume 2 | 1960 | $35 |

Number	Title	Yr	NM
—Black label with color bars			
❏ DL8840 [M]	Satchmo in Style	1958	$100
—Black label, silver print			
❏ DL8840 [M]	Satchmo in Style	1960	$35
—Black label with color bars			
❏ DL8330 [M]	Satchmo on Stage	1957	$120
—Black label, silver print			
❏ DL8330 [M]	Satchmo on Stage	1960	$35
—Black label with color bars			
❏ DL8327 [M]	Satchmo's Collector's Items	1957	$120
—Black label, silver print			
❏ DL8327 [M]	Satchmo's Collector's Items	1960	$35
—Black label with color bars			
❏ DL5401 [10]	Satchmo Serenades	1952	$150
❏ DL8211 [M]	Satchmo Serenades	1956	$150
—Black label, silver print			
❏ DL8211 [M]	Satchmo Serenades	1960	$35
—Black label with color bars			
❏ DL4137 [M]	Satchmo's Golden Favorites	1961	$50
❏ DL74137 [R]	Satchmo's Golden Favorites	1961	$30
❏ DL8126 [M]	Satchmo Sings	1955	$150
—Black label, silver print			
❏ DL8126 [M]	Satchmo Sings	1960	$35
—Black label with color bars			
❏ DXB183 [M]	The Best of Louis Armstrong	196?	$60
❏ DXSB7183 [R]	The Best of Louis Armstrong	196?	$35
❏ DL9233 [M]	Young Louis the Sideman (1924-1927)	196?	$50
❏ DL79233 [R]	Young Louis the Sideman (1924-1927)	196?	$30
DISNEYLAND			
❏ STER-1341	The Wonderful World of Walt Disney	1971	$50
—Reissue of Buena Vista 4044			
EVEREST			
❏ 3312 [R]	In Memoriam	1971	$25
EVEREST ARCHIVE OF FOLK & JAZZ			
❏ 258	Louis "Satchmo" Armstrong	197?	$30
❏ 312	Louis Armstrong, Vol. 2	197?	$25
GNP CRESCENDO			
❏ 11001	An Evening with Louis Armstrong	1977	$35
❏ 9050	Pasadena Concert, Vol. II	1987	$25
HARMONY			
❏ HS11316	Louis Armstrong	197?	$30
❏ KH31236	The Louis Armstrong Saga	1971	$30
IAJRC			
❏ LP-29	Oregon State Fair, 1960	198?	$25
JOLLY ROGER			
❏ 5009 [10]	Louis Armstrong	1954	$100
KAPP			
❏ KL-1364 [M]	Hello, Dolly!	1964	$30
MCA			
❏ 1304	Back in New York	197?	$25
❏ 538	Hello, Dolly!	197?	$25
—Reissue of Kapp LP			
❏ 1300	Louis and the Good Book	197?	$25
—Reissue of Decca 8741			
❏ 2-4013	Louis Armstrong at the Crescendo	197?	$30
—Reissue of Decca 8168/8169 in one sleeve			
❏ 42328	Louis Armstrong of New Orleans	1990	$30
❏ 1306	Louis with Guest Stars	197?	$25
❏ 1335	Old Favorites	197?	$25
❏ 10006	Satchmo, A Musical Autobiography	197?	$60
—Reissue of Decca 155			
❏ 2-4057	Satchmo at Symphony Hall	197?	$30
—Reissue of Decca 108			
❏ 1334	Satchmo For Ever!	197?	$25
❏ 1322	Satchmo's Collector's Items	197?	$25
—Reissue of Decca 8327			
❏ 1316	Satchmo Serenades	197?	$25
—Reissue of Decca 8211			
❏ 1312	Swing That Music!	197?	$25
❏ 2-4035	The Best of Louis Armstrong	197?	$30
—Reissue of Decca 7183			
❏ 25204	What a Wonderful World	1988	$25
—Reissue of ABC 650			
❏ 1301	Young Louis the Sideman	197?	$25
—Reissue of Decca 9233			
MERCURY			
❏ MG-21081 [M]	Louis Armstrong Sings Louis Armstrong	1965	$100

Number	Title	Yr	NM
❏ SR-61081 [S]	Louis Armstrong Sings Louis Armstrong	1965	$100
METRO			
❏ M-510 [M]	Hello, Louis	1965	$150
❏ MS-510 [S]	Hello, Louis	1965	$250
MILESTONE			
❏ 2010	Early Portrait	1969	$25
❏ 47017	Louis Armstrong and King Oliver	197?	$30
MOSAIC			
❏ MQ8-146	The Complete Decca Studio Recordings of Louis Armstrong and the All-Stars	199?	$150
PABLO			
❏ 2310941	Mack the Knife	1990	$30
PAIR			
❏ PDL2-1042	The Jazz Legend	1986	$30
PAUSA			
❏ 9018	The Greatest of Louis Armstrong	1983	$25
RCA VICTOR			
❏ LPM-2322 [M]	A Rare Batch of Satch	1961	$60
❏ VPM-6044	July 4, 1900/July 6, 1971	1971	$50
❏ LPM-2971 [M]	Louis Armstrong in the '30s/ in the '40s	1964	$50
❏ LSP-2971(e) [R]	Louis Armstrong in the '30s/ in the '40s	1964	$30
❏ LJM-1005 [M]	Louis Armstrong Sings the Blues	1954	$100
❏ LPT7 [10]	Louis Armstrong Town Hall Concert	1951	$150
❏ LPM-1443 [M]	Town Hall Concert Plus	1957	$100
RIVERSIDE			
❏ RLP 12-122 [M]	Louis Armstrong 1923	1956	$250
—White label, blue print			
❏ RLP 12-122 [M]	Louis Armstrong 1923	195?	$40
—Blue label			
❏ RLP-1001 [10]	Louis Armstrong Plays the Blues	1953	$300
❏ RLP-1029 [10]	Louis Armstrong with King Oliver's Creole Jazz Band 1923	1953	$300
❏ RLP 12-101 [M]	The Young Louis Armstrong	1956	$250
—White label, blue print			
❏ RLP 12-101 [M]	The Young Louis Armstrong	195?	$40
—Blue label			
SEAGULL			
❏ LG-8206	Greatest Hits: Live in Concert	198?	$30
STORYVILLE			
❏ 4012	Louis Armstrong and His All-Stars	1980	$25
SWING			
❏ SW-8450	Louis and the Big Bands	1984	$25
TIME-LIFE			
❏ STBB-22	Big Bands: Louis Armstrong	1985	$35
❏ STL-J-01	Giants of Jazz	1978	$50
VANGUARD			
❏ VSD91/92	Essential Louis Armstrong	1977	$35
❏ VMS73129	Essential Louis Armstrong, Vol. 1	1986	$20
VERVE			
❏ MGV-4035 [M]	I've Got the World on a String	1959	$100
❏ MGVS-6101 [S]	I've Got the World on a String	1960	$100
❏ V-4035 [M]	I've Got the World on a String	1961	$50
❏ V6-4035 [S]	I've Got the World on a String	1961	$35
❏ MGVS-4035	I've Got the World on a String	199?	$60
—Classic Records reissue			
❏ MGV-4012 [M]	Louis Under the Stars	1957	$150
❏ MGVS-6044 [S]	Louis Under the Stars	1960	$100
❏ V-4012 [M]	Louis Under the Stars	1961	$50
❏ V6-4012 [S]	Louis Under the Stars	1961	$35
❏ MGV-4012 [S]	Louis Under the Stars	199?	$60
—180-gram reissue; distributed by Classic Records			
❏ V-8595 [M]	The Best of Louis Armstrong	1964	$35
❏ V6-8595 [S]	The Best of Louis Armstrong	1964	$35
❏ SW-90658 [S]	The Best of Louis Armstrong	1964	$80
—Capitol Record Club edition			
❏ V-8569 [M]	The Essential Louis A.	1963	$30
❏ V6-8569 [S]	The Essential Louis A.	1963	$35
VOCALION			
❏ VL73851 [R]	Here's Louis Armstrong	196?	$25
❏ VL3851 [R]	Here's Louis Armstrong	196?	$35
❏ VL73871 [R]	The One and Only Louis Armstrong	1968	$25

Number	Title	Yr	NM
WING			
❏ SR-16381	Great Louis	196?	$25

ARMSTRONG, LOUIS/AL HIRT
Also see each artist's individual listings.

Albums

MURRAY HILL			
❏ 930633	Louis Armstrong and Al Hirt Play Dixieland Trumpet	197?	$50

ARNOLD, BUDDY
Tenor saxophonist. Also plays clarinet and oboe. Played in the STAN KENTON band.

Albums

ABC-PARAMOUNT			
❏ ABC-114 [M]	Wailing	1956	$60

ARNOLD, HARRY
Alto saxophone player, clarinet player, bandleader, composer.

Albums

ATCO			
❏ 33-120 [M]	I Love Harry Arnold (And All That Jazz)	1960	$40
EMARCY			
❏ MG-36139 [M]	Harry Arnold and His Orchestra	1958	$150
❏ SR-80006 [S]	Harry Arnold and His Orchestra	1958	$150
JAZZLAND			
❏ JLP-65 [M]	Harry Arnold's Great Big Band and Friends	1962	$30
❏ JLP-965 [S]	Harry Arnold's Great Big Band and Friends	1962	$30
JAZZTONE			
❏ J-1270 [M]	The Jazztone Mystery Band	1957	$40
RIVERSIDE			
❏ RM-7536 [M]	Dancing on Broadway to the Music of Cole Porter	196?	$25
❏ RS-97536 [S]	Dancing on Broadway to the Music of Cole Porter	196?	$30
❏ RM-7526 [M]	Let's Dance on Broadway	196?	$25
❏ RS-97526 [S]	Let's Dance on Broadway	196?	$30

ART ENSEMBLE OF CHICAGO
Also see LESTER BOWIE; ROSCOE MITCHELL. (LP)
Influential quintet: LESTER BOWIE (horns), Malachi Favors (bass and strings), Joseph Jarman (reeds), ROSCOE MITCHELL (reeds) and Don Moye (percussion, post-1973). Fontella Bass ("Rescue Me") was an early female singer.

Albums

AECO			
❏ 04	Kabalaba	1978	$35
ARISTA/FREEDOM			
❏ AL1903	The Paris Session	197?	$35
ATLANTIC			
❏ SD1639	Bap-Tizum	1973	$35
❏ SD1651	Fanfare for the Warriors	1974	$35
❏ 90046	Fanfare for the Warriors	1983	$25
—Reissue of 1651			
DELMARK			
❏ DS-432/433	Live at Mandel Hall	1974	$35
DIW			
❏ 8014	Ancient to the Future	1987	$25
❏ 8038	Art Ensemble of Soweto	1990	$30
❏ 8005	Live in Japan	1986	$25
❏ 8011	Naked	1987	$25
❏ 8033	The Alternate Express	1989	$30
❏ 8021/22	The Complete Live in Japan	198?	$35
ECM			
❏ 1167	Full Force	1980	$30
❏ 1126	Nice Guys	1979	$30
❏ 25014	The Third Decade	1985	$25
❏ 1211	Urban Bushmen	1982	$35
INNER CITY			
❏ 1004	Certain Blacks	197?	$30
NESSA			
❏ N-4	Les Stances a Sophie	1970	$35
—With Fontella Bass			
❏ N-5	Old/Quartet	1975	$25
❏ N-3	People in Sorrow	1969	$30
PAULA			
❏ LPS-4001	Chi-Congo	197?	$35
PRESTIGE			

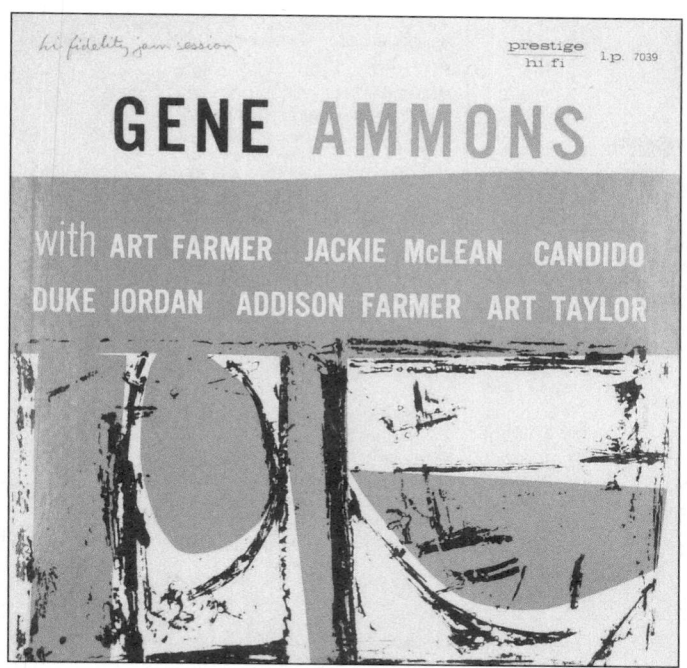

Gene Ammons, *Hi-Fidelity Jam Session*, Prestige PRLP-7039, **$300**.

Gene Ammons, *Funky*, Prestige PRLP-7083, original issue, **$200**.

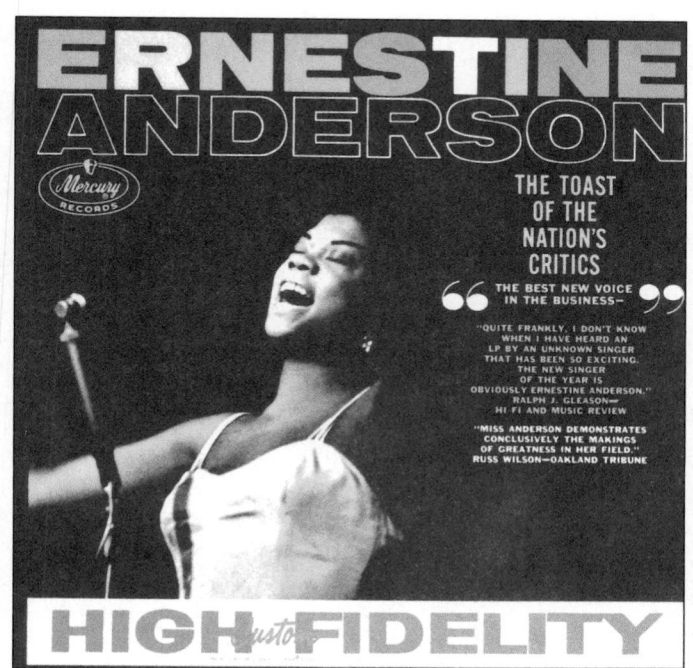

Ernestine Anderson, *Ernestine Anderson*, Mercury MG 20400, mono, **$100**.

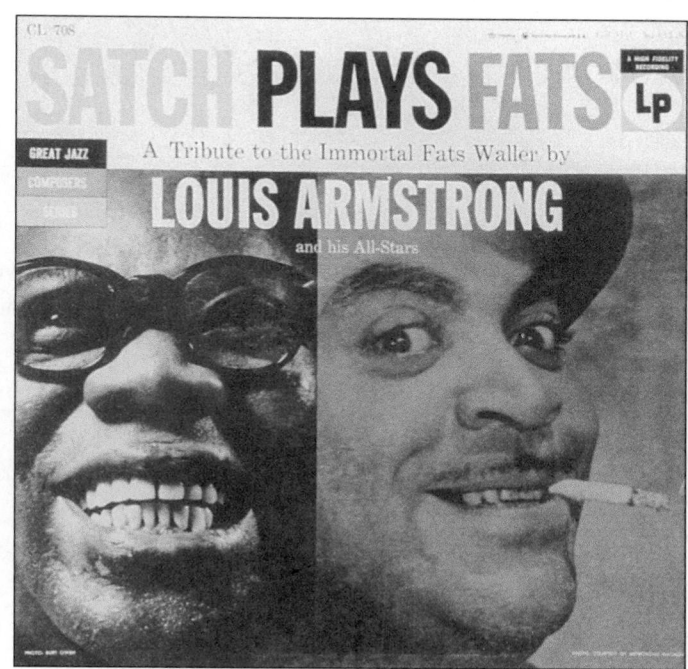

Louis Armstrong, *Satch Plays Fats*, Columbia CL 708, original edition, **$50**.

Number	Title	Yr	NM
❏ 10049	Art Ensemble of Chicago with Fontella Bass	1972	$35
❏ 10064	Phase One	197?	$35

ARTER, CARL
Pianist.
Albums
EARWIG
| ❏ LPS-4905 | Song from Far Away | 1986 | $25 |

ARTHUR, BROOKS
Albums
VERVE
❏ V-8650 [M]	Sole Forms	1966	$35
❏ V6-8650 [S]	Sole Forms	1966	$35
❏ V6-8779	Traces	1969	$35

ASH, MARVIN
Pianist.
Albums
CAPITOL
| ❏ H188 [10] | Honky Tonk Piano | 1950 | $100 |
JAZZ MAN
| ❏ LPJM-335 [10] | Marvin Ash | 1954 | $50 |
JUMP
| ❏ JL-4 [10] | Marvin Ash | 1954 | $50 |

ASHBY, DOROTHY
Harp player.
Albums
ARGO
| ❏ LP-690 [M] | Dorothy Ashby | 1962 | $30 |
| ❏ LPS-690 [S] | Dorothy Ashby | 1962 | $30 |
ATLANTIC
| ❏ 1447 [M] | The Fantastic Jazz Harp of Dorothy Ashby | 1966 | $35 |
| ❏ SD1447 [S] | The Fantastic Jazz Harp of Dorothy Ashby | 1966 | $25 |
CADET
| ❏ LPS-809 | Afro-Harping | 1968 | $35 |
| ❏ LP-690 [M] | Dorothy Ashby | 1966 | $30 |
— Reissue of Argo LP-690
| ❏ LPS-690 [S] | Dorothy Ashby | 1966 | $35 |
— Reissue of Argo LPS-690
| ❏ LPS-825 | Dorothy's Harp | 1969 | $35 |
| ❏ LPS-841 | Rubaiyat | 1970 | $35 |
CHESS
| ❏ CH-91555 | Afro-Harping | 198? | $25 |
— Reissue of Cadet 809
JAZZLAND
| ❏ JLP-61 [M] | Soft Winds | 1961 | $30 |
| ❏ JLP-961 [S] | Soft Winds | 1961 | $30 |
NEW JAZZ
| ❏ NJLP-8209 [M] | In a Minor Groove | 1965 | $150 |
— Blue label, trident logo at right
PRESTIGE
| ❏ PRLP-7639 | Dorothy Plays for Beautiful People | 1969 | $35 |
— Reissue of New Jazz 8209
| ❏ PRLP-7638 | The Best of Dorothy Ashby | 1969 | $35 |
— Reissue of 7140
REGENT
| ❏ MG-6039 [M] | Dorothy Ashby -- Jazz Harpist | 1957 | $60 |
SAVOY
| ❏ MG-12212 [M] | Dorothy Ashby -- Jazz Harpist | 196? | $35 |
— Reissue of Regent 6039

ASHBY, HAROLD
Tenor saxophone player.
Albums
GEMINI
| ❏ GMLP-60-1 | The Viking | 1988 | $25 |
PROGRESSIVE
| ❏ PRO-7040 | Presenting Harold Ashby | 1979 | $25 |

ASHBY, IRVING
Guitarist. Member of NAT KING COLE's trio in the late 1940s.
Albums
AUDIOPHILE
| ❏ AP-133 | Memoirs | 1980 | $25 |

ASMUSSEN, SVEND
Violinist.
Albums
ANGEL
| ❏ ANG.60010 [10] | Rhythm Is Our Business | 1955 | $75 |
| ❏ ANG.60000 [10] | Svend Asmussen and His Unmelancholy Danes | 1955 | $75 |
BRUNSWICK
| ❏ BL58051 [10] | Hot Fiddle | 1953 | $80 |
DOCTOR JAZZ
| ❏ FW39150 | June Night | 1983 | $30 |
EPIC
| ❏ LN3210 [M] | Skol! | 1955 | $100 |

ASMUSSEN, SVEND / STEPHANE GRAPPELLI
Also see each artist's individual listings.
Albums
STORYVILLE
| ❏ SLP-4088 | Two of a Kind | 198? | $30 |

ASTAIRE, FRED
Male singer.
Albums
CHOREO
| ❏ A-1 [M] | Three Evenings with Fred Astaire | 1961 | $40 |
CLEF
| ❏ MGC-662 [M] | The Fred Astaire Story, Volume 1 | 1955 | $300 |
— Reissue of Mercury 1001
| ❏ MGC-663 [M] | The Fred Astaire Story, Volume 2 | 1955 | $300 |
— Reissue of Mercury 1002
| ❏ MGC-664 [M] | The Fred Astaire Story, Volume 3 | 1955 | $300 |
— Reissue of Mercury 1003
| ❏ MGC-665 [M] | The Fred Astaire Story, Volume 4 | 1955 | $300 |
— Reissue of Mercury 1004
DRG
| ❏ DARC-3-1102 | The Astaire Story | 197? | $60 |
EPIC
| ❏ LN3103 [M] | Nothing Thrilled Us Half As Much | 1955 | $200 |
| ❏ FLM13103 [M] | Nothing Thrilled Us Half As Much | 196? | $100 |
— Reissue of 3103
| ❏ FLS15103 [R] | Nothing Thrilled Us Half As Much | 196? | $75 |
| ❏ LN3137 [M] | The Best of Fred Astaire | 1955 | $200 |
KAPP
| ❏ KL-1165 [M] | Fred Astaire Now | 1959 | $60 |
| ❏ KS-3165 [S] | Fred Astaire Now | 1959 | $60 |
MCA
| ❏ 1552 | Fred Astaire Sings | 198? | $30 |
MERCURY
| ❏ MGC-1001/4 [M] | The Fred Astaire Story | 1953 | $1000 |
— Spiral-bound four-record set, pressed on blue vinyl, autographed by Fred Astaire
❏ MGC-1001 [M]	The Fred Astaire Story, Volume 1	1954	$600
❏ MGC-1002 [M]	The Fred Astaire Story, Volume 2	1954	$300
❏ MGC-1003 [M]	The Fred Astaire Story, Volume 3	1954	$300
❏ MGC-1004 [M]	The Fred Astaire Story, Volume 4	1954	$300
VERVE
❏ MGV-2114 [M]	Easy to Dance With	1958	$150
❏ MGV-2010 [M]	Mr. Top Hat	1956	$200
VOCALION
❏ VL3716 [M]	Fred Astaire	1964	$35

AULD, GEORGIE
Tenor saxophone player, also plays alto and soprano saxes as well as clarinet.
Albums
ABC-PARAMOUNT
| ❏ ABC-287 [M] | Georgie Auld Plays for Melancholy Babies | 1958 | $40 |
| ❏ ABCS-287 [S] | Georgie Auld Plays for Melancholy Babies | 1959 | $30 |
ALLEGRO
| ❏ 3102 [M] | Jazz Concert | 1953 | $40 |
APOLLO
| ❏ LAP-102 [10] | Concert in Jazz | 1951 | $80 |
CORAL
❏ CRL57029 [M]	Lullaby of Broadway	1956	$40
❏ CRL56085 [10]	Manhattan	1953	$80
❏ CRL57032 [M]	Misty	1956	$40
❏ CRL56060 [10]	Tenderly	1952	$80
DISCOVERY
❏ DL3007 [10]	That's Auld	1950	$300
EMARCY
❏ MG-36090 [M]	Dancing in the Land of Hi-Fi	1956	$200
JARO
❏ JAM-5003 [M]	Hawaii on the Rocks	1959	$30
MUSICRAFT
❏ 501	Georgie Auld and His Orchestra, Vol. 1	197?	$25
❏ 509	Georgie Auld and His Orchestra, Vol. 2	197?	$25
PHILIPS
❏ PHM200096 [M]	Georgie Auld Plays to the Winners	1963	$35
❏ PHS600096 [S]	Georgie Auld Plays to the Winners	1963	$25
❏ PHM200116 [M]	Here's to the Losers	1963	$35
❏ PHS600116 [S]	Here's to the Losers	1963	$25
ROOST
❏ RST-403 [10]	Georgie Auld Quintet	1951	$80
TOP RANK
❏ RM-333 [M]	Good Enough to Keep	1960	$40
❏ RM-306 [M]	The Melody Lingers On	1959	$40
UNITED ARTISTS
❏ UAL-3068 [M]	Manhattan with Strings	1959	$40
❏ UAS-6068 [S]	Manhattan with Strings	1959	$30
XANADU
❏ 190	Homage	197?	$25

AUSTIN, CLAIRE
Female singer.
Albums
CONTEMPORARY
| ❏ C-5002 [M] | When Your Lover Has Gone | 1956 | $200 |
FANTASY
| ❏ OJC-1711 | When Your Lover Has Gone | 198? | $30 |
— Reissue of Contemporary 5002
GHB
| ❏ S-22 | Claire Austin and the Great Excelsior Band | 197? | $35 |
GOOD TIME JAZZ
| ❏ L-24 [10] | Claire Austin Sings the Blues | 1954 | $120 |
JAZZOLOGY
| ❏ 52 | Goin' Crazy | 197? | $35 |

AUSTRALIAN ALL STARS, THE
Albums
BETHLEHEM
| ❏ BCP-6070 [M] | Jazz for Beach-Niks | 1963 | $200 |
| ❏ BCP-6073 [M] | Jazz for Surf-Niks | 1963 | $200 |

AUSTRALIAN JAZZ QUARTET, THE
Members were Bryce Rohde, Errol Buddle and JACK BROKENSHA - all from Down Under - with American Dick Healy.
Albums
BETHLEHEM
❏ BCP-1031 [10]	The Australian Jazz Quartet	195?	$60
❏ BCP-6003	The Australian Jazz Quartet	1955	$250
❏ BCP-6002	The Australian Jazz Quartet	197?	$35
— Reissue distributed by RCA Victor
| ❏ BCP-6012 [M] | The Australian Jazz Quartet at the Varsity Drag | 1956 | $200 |
| ❏ BCP-6029 [M] | The Australian Jazz Quartet In Free Style | 1959 | $200 |

Number	Title	Yr	NM
❑ BCP-6022 [M]	The Australian Jazz Quartet	1957	$250
	Plays the Best of Broadway		
	Musical Hits		
❑ BCP-6015 [M]	The Australian Jazz Quartet	1957	$250
	Plus One		
❑ BCP-6002 [M]	The Australian Jazz Quartet/	1955	$250
	Quintet		
❑ BCP-6030 [M]	Three Penny Opera	1959	$200

AYERS, ROY, AND WAYNE HENDERSON
Also see each artist's individual listings.

Albums

POLYDOR
❑ PD-1-6276	Prime Time	1980	$25
❑ PD-1-6179	Step Into Our Life	1978	$25

AYERS, ROY
Includes "Roy Ayers Ubiquity." (SC1)
Earlier material appears in the Goldmine Standard Catalog of
American Records 1950-1975. Includes material as "Roy Ayers
Ubiquity." (SC2)
Vibraphone player. Fronted a jazz-funk (fusion) band called Roy
Ayers' Ubiquity, the releases of which are included below.

Albums

ATLANTIC
❑ SD1692	Daddy Bug & Friends	1976	$30
❑ SD1538	Daddy Bug	1969	$50
❑ SD1514	Stoned Soul Picnic	1968	$50
❑ 1488 [M]	Virgo Vibes	1967	$50

COLUMBIA
❑ FC39422	In the Dark	1984	$25

ICHIBAN
❑ ICH-1028	Drive	198?	$25
❑ ICH-1040	Wake Up	198?	$25

POLYDOR
❑ PD-1-6327	Africa, Center of the World	1981	$25
❑ PD6046	A Tear to a Smile	1975	$25
❑ PD6032	Change Up the Groove	1974	$25
❑ PD-1-6070	Everybody Loves the	1976	$25
	Sunshine		
❑ PD-1-6348	Feeling Good	1982	$25
❑ PD-1-6204	Fever	1979	$25
❑ PD5022	He's Coming	1972	$30
❑ PD-1-6126	Let's Do It	1978	$25
❑ PD-1-6108	Lifeline	1977	$25
❑ PD-1-6301	Love Fantasy	1980	$25
❑ PD6057	Mystic Voyage	1976	$25
❑ PD-1-6246	No Stranger to Love	1979	$25
❑ PD5045	Red, Black and Green	1973	$30
❑ PD-1-6078	Red, Black and Green	1976	$25
—Reissue of 5045			
❑ PD-1-6091	Vibrations	1977	$25
❑ PD6016	Virgo Red	1973	$30
❑ PD-1-6159	You Send Me	1978	$25

UNITED ARTISTS
❑ UAL-3325 [M]	West Coast Vibes	1964	$50
❑ UAS-6325 [S]	West Coast Vibes	1964	$60

AYLER, ALBERT
Tenor and alto sax player.

Albums

ABC IMPULSE!
❑ AS-9155 [S]	Live at the Village Vanguard	1968	$160
❑ IA-9336	Live at the Village Vanguard	1978	$35
❑ AS-9165	Love Cry	1968	$200
❑ AS-9191	Music Is the Healing Force	1969	$200
	of the Universe		
❑ AS-9257	Re-evaluations: The Impulse	1974	$35
	Years		
❑ AS-9208	The Last Album	1971	$200

ARISTA/FREEDOM
❑ AL1000	Vibrations	1976	$35
❑ AL1018	Witches and Devils	1977	$35

ESP-DISK'
❑ 1010 [M]	Bells	1965	$300
—Black vinyl			
❑ 1010 [M]	Bells	1965	$400
—Yellow vinyl			
❑ S-1010 [S]	Bells	1965	$250
❑ ESP-3030	Prophecy	1975	$40
❑ 1020 [M]	Spirits Rejoice	1966	$700
❑ S-1020 [S]	Spirits Rejoice	1966	$350
❑ 1002 [M]	Spiritual Unity	1965	$1000

FANTASY
❑ 6016 [M]	My Name Is Albert Ayler	196?	$25
❑ 86016 [S]	My Name Is Albert Ayler	196?	$30

GNP CRESCENDO
❑ GNPS-9022	The First Recordings	1973	$30

IMPULSE!

Number	Title	Yr	NM
❑ A-9155 [M]	Live at the Village Vanguard	1967	$160
❑ AS-9155 [S]	Live at the Village Vanguard	1967	$160

MCA
❑ 4129	Live at the Village Vanguard	198?	$30
—Reissue of ABC Impulse 9336			

AZAMA, ETHEL
Female singer.

Albums

LIBERTY
❑ LRP-3142 [M]	Cool Heat	1960	$40
❑ LST-7142 [S]	Cool Heat	1960	$50
❑ LRP-3104 [M]	Exotic Dreams	1959	$25
❑ LST-7104 [S]	Exotic Dreams	1959	$30

AZIMUTH
John Taylor; Norma Winstone; Kenny Wheeler.

Albums

ECM
❑ 1099	Azimuth	1977	$12
❑ 1289	Azimuth '85	1985	$12
❑ 1163	Depart	1979	$12
❑ 1130	The Touchstone	1978	$12

AZYMUTH
Jose Roberto Bertrami, Alex Malheiros and Ivan Conti.

Albums

INTIMA
❑ D1-73517	Tudo Bem	1989	$15

MILESTONE
❑ M-9109	Cascades	1982	$12
❑ M-9156	Crazy Rhythm	1988	$12
❑ M-9128	Flame	1984	$12
❑ M-9089	Light as a Feather	1979	$15
❑ M-9097	Outubro	1980	$15
❑ M-9134	Spectrum	1985	$12
❑ M-9101	Telecommunication	1982	$12
❑ M-9143	Tightrope Walker	1987	$12

B

BABASIN, HARRY
Bass player and celloist. Also see THE JAZZPICKERS.

Albums

MODE
❑ LP-119 [M]	Jazz Pickers	1957	$100

NOCTURNE
❑ NLP-3 [10]	Harry Babasin Quartet	1954	$150

BABASIN, HARRY/TERRY GIBBS
Also see each artist's individual listings.

Albums

PREMIER
❑ PM-2010 [M]	Pick 'n' Pat	1963	$35
❑ PS-2010 [R]	Pick 'n' Pat	1963	$25

BACH, STEVE
Keyboard player.

Albums

CAFÉ
❑ 59-00733	Holiday	1986	$30
❑ 59-00736	Zero Gravity	1987	$30

EAGLE
❑ SM-4220	Child's Play	1986	$30

SOUNDWINGS
❑ SW-2112	More Than a Dream	1989	$30

BAGLEY, DON
Bass player.

Albums

DOT
❑ DLP-25070 [S]	Basically Bagley	1959	$80
❑ DLP-9007 [M]	The Soft Sell	1959	$100
❑ DLP-29007 [S]	The Soft Sell	1959	$80

REGENT
❑ MG-6061 [M]	Jazz on the Rocks	1957	$60

SAVOY
❑ MG-12210 [M]	Jazz on the Rocks	196?	$25

Number	Title	Yr	NM

BAILEY, BENNY
Trumpeter. Played in the group led by QUINCY JONES.

Albums

ARGO
❑ LP-668 [M]	The Music of Quincy Jones	1961	$30
❑ LPS-668 [S]	The Music of Quincy Jones	1961	$30

CANDID
❑ CD-8011 [M]	Big Brass	1960	$30
❑ CS-9011 [S]	Big Brass	1960	$40

GEMINI
❑ GMLP-69-1	While My Lady Sleeps	1990	$30

BAILEY, BUSTER
Clarinet player, sometimes played saxophone.

Albums

FELSTED
❑ FAJ-7003 [M]	All About Memphis	1959	$40
❑ SJA-2003 [S]	All About Memphis	1959	$40

BAILEY, DAVE
Drummer.

Albums

EPIC
❑ LA16011 [M]	Gettin' Into Something	1960	$150
❑ BA17011 [S]	Gettin' Into Something	1960	$200
—yellow label			
❑ LA16008 [M]	One Foot in the Gutter	1960	$150
❑ BA17008 [S]	One Foot in the Gutter	1960	$200
❑ BA17008 [S]	One Foot in the Gutter	199?	$60
—Classic Records reissue			
❑ LA16021 [M]	Two Feet in the Gutter	1961	$150

❑ BA17021 [S]	Two Feet in the Gutter	1961	$150

JAZZ LINE
❑ 33-01 [M]	Bash!	1961	$350

JAZZTIME
❑ JT-003 [M]	Reaching Out	1961	$350
❑ JS-003 [S]	Reaching Out	1961	$150
—Reissued under GRANT GREEN's name			

BAILEY, MILDRED
Female singer. One of the very first featured vocalists with a jazz
band when she filled that role for PAUL WHITEMAN.

Albums

ALLEGRO
❑ 4009 [10]	Mildred Bailey Songs	1952	$80
❑ 4040 [10]	Mildred Bailey Songs	1954	$80

COLUMBIA
❑ C3L22	Her Greatest Performances	1962	$50
—With booklet; originals have red labels with "Guaranteed			
High Fidelity" at bottom			
❑ CL6094 [10]	Serenade	1950	$60

DECCA
❑ DL5133 [10]	Mildred Bailey Memorial	1950	$120
	Album		
❑ DL5387 [10]	The Rockin' Chair Lady	195?	$60

EVEREST ARCHIVE OF FOLK & JAZZ
❑ 269	Mildred Bailey	197?	$30

HINDSIGHT
❑ HSR-133	Mildred Bailey 1944	198?	$25

MONMOUTH-EVERGREEN
❑ 6814	All of Me	196?	$35

REGENT
❑ MG-6032 [M]	Me and the Blues	1957	$50

ROYALE

Number	Title	Yr	NM
❑ VLP6078 [10]	Mildred Bailey Sings	195?	$80

SAVOY

❑ MG-12219 [M]	Me and the Blues	196?	$25

SAVOY JAZZ

❑ SJL-1151	The Majestic Mildred Bailey	198?	$30

SUNBEAM

❑ 209	Radio Show 1944-45	197?	$30

BAILEY, PEARL, AND LOUIS BELLSON
Also see each artist's individual listings.

Albums

EVEREST ARCHIVE OF FOLK & JAZZ

❑ FS284 [R]	Pearl Bailey and Louis Bellson	197?	$25

BAILEY, PEARL
Female singer.

Albums

COLUMBIA

❑ CL6099 [10]	Pearl Bailey Entertains	1950	$100
❑ CL985 [M]	The Definitive Pearl Bailey	1957	$60

CORAL

❑ CRL57162 [M]	Cultured Pearl	1958	$40
❑ CRL56078 [10]	I'm with You	1954	$100
❑ CRL57037 [M]	Pearl Bailey	1957	$40
❑ CRL56068 [10]	Say Si Si	1953	$100

MERCURY

❑ MG-20277 [M]	The Intoxicating Pearl Bailey	1957	$100

PROJECT 3

❑ PR5022SD	The Real Pearl	1968	$35

RCA VICTOR

❑ LSP-4529	Pearl's Pearls	1971	$35

ROULETTE

❑ R-25195 [M]	All About Good Little Girls and Bad Little Boys	1963	$50

— Originals have a pink and orange label

❑ SR-25195 [S]	All About Good Little Girls and Bad Little Boys	1963	$60

— Originals have a pink and orange label

❑ R-25222 [M]	C'est La Vie	1963	$50

— Originals have a pink and orange label

❑ SR-25222 [S]	C'est La Vie	1963	$60

— Originals have a pink and orange label

❑ R-25181 [M]	Come On, Let's Play with Pearlie Mae	1962	$50

— Originals have a white label with colored spokes

❑ SR-25181 [S]	Come On, Let's Play with Pearlie Mae	1962	$60

— Originals have a white label with colored spokes

❑ R-25300 [M]	For Women Only	1965	$35
❑ SR-25300 [S]	For Women Only	1965	$50
❑ R-25167 [M]	Happy Sounds	1962	$50

— Originals have a white label with colored spokes

❑ SR-25167 [S]	Happy Sounds	1962	$60

— Originals have a white label with colored spokes

❑ R-25101 [M]	More Songs for Adults Only	1960	$50

— Originals have a white label with colored spokes

❑ SR-25101 [S]	More Songs for Adults Only	1960	$60

— Originals have a white label with colored spokes

❑ R-25125 [M]	Naughty But Nice	1960	$50

— Originals have a white label with colored spokes

❑ SR-25125 [S]	Naughty But Nice	1960	$60

— Originals have a white label with colored spokes

❑ R-25012 [M]	Pearl Bailey A Broad	1957	$60

— Black label original

❑ SR-25012 [R]	Pearl Bailey A Broad	196?	$30
❑ R-25016 [M]	Pearl Bailey Sings for Adults Only	1959	$50

— Originals have a white label with colored spokes

❑ SR-25016 [S]	Pearl Bailey Sings for Adults Only	1959	$60

— Originals have a white label with colored spokes

❑ R-25063 [M]	Pearl Bailey Sings Porgy and Bess and Other Gershwin Melodies	1959	$50

— Originals have a white label with colored spokes

❑ SR-25063 [S]	Pearl Bailey Sings Porgy and Bess and Other Gershwin Melodies	1959	$60

— Originals have a white label with colored spokes

❑ R-25155 [M]	Pearl Bailey Sings Songs of Harold Arlen	1961	$50

— Originals have a white label with colored spokes

❑ SR-25155 [S]	Pearl Bailey Sings Songs of Harold Arlen	1961	$60

— Originals have a white label with colored spokes

❑ R-25271 [M]	Songs by James Van Heusen	1964	$35
❑ SR-25271 [S]	Songs by James Van Heusen	1964	$50
❑ R-25116 [M]	Songs of the Bad Old Days	1960	$50

— Originals have a white label with colored spokes

❑ SR-25116 [S]	Songs of the Bad Old Days	1960	$60

— Originals have a white label with colored spokes

❑ SR5004	Songs of the Bad Old Days	1976	$30
❑ R-25037 [M]	St. Louis Blues	1958	$60

— Black label original

❑ SR-25037 [S]	St. Louis Blues	1959	$60

— Originals have a white label with colored spokes

❑ R-25144 [M]	The Best of Pearl Bailey	1961	$50

— Originals have a white label with colored spokes

❑ SR-25144 [S]	The Best of Pearl Bailey	1961	$60

— Originals have a white label with colored spokes

❑ SR-25144 [S]	The Best of Pearl Bailey	1964	$35

— Orange and yellow "roulette wheel" label

❑ R-25259 [M]	The Risque World of Pearl Bailey	1964	$35
❑ SR-25259 [S]	The Risque World of Pearl Bailey	1964	$50

VOCALION

❑ VL3621 [M]	Gems by Pearl Bailey	1958	$60

BAILEY, VICTOR
Bass player.

Albums

ATLANTIC

❑ 81978	Bottoms Up	1989	$30

BAKER, BUDDY
Trombone player.

Albums

VERVE

❑ MGV-2006 [M]	Two in Love	1956	$200
❑ V-2006 [M]	Two in Love	1961	$25

BAKER, CHET, AND ART PEPPER
Also see each artist's individual listings.

Albums

PACIFIC JAZZ

❑ PJ-18 [M]	Picture of Health	1961	$50

WORLD PACIFIC

❑ WP-1234 [M]	Playboys	1958	$150
❑ PJ-1234 [M]	Playboys	1958	$250

BAKER, CHET, AND LEE KONITZ
Also see each artist's individual listings.

Albums

INDIA NAVIGATION

❑ IN-1052	In Concert	198?	$30

BAKER, CHET, AND PAUL BLEY
Also see each artist's individual listings.

Albums

STEEPLECHASE

❑ SCS-1207	Diane	198?	$25

BAKER, CHET, JIM HALL; HUBERT LAWS
Also see each artist's individual listings.

Albums

CTI

❑ 9007	Studio Trieste	1983	$25

BAKER, CHET
Trumpeter, fluegel horn player and occasional singer. Also see RUSS FREEMAN; STAN GETZ; THE MARIACHI BRASS; GERRY MULLIGAN.

7-Inch Extended Plays

PACIFIC JAZZ

❑ 1222 [B]	Sings	1954	$400

Albums

Number	Title	Yr	NM
ANALOGUE PRODUCTIONS			
❑ AAPJ-016	Chet	199?	$30

— Audiophile reissue

ARTISTS HOUSE

❑ 9411	Once Upon a Summertime	1978	$30

BAINBRIDGE

❑ 1040	Albert's House	198?	$25

BLUEBIRD

❑ 2001-1-RB	The Italian Sessions	1990	$30

BLUE NOTE

❑ B1-92932	Let's Get Lost/The Best of Chet Baker	1989	$30

BOPLICITY

❑ BOP-13	Cool Out	198?	$25

CADENCE JAZZ

❑ CJ-1019	Improviser	198?	$25

COLPIX

❑ CP-476 [M]	Chet Baker Sings and Plays	1964	$40
❑ SCP-476 [S]	Chet Baker Sings and Plays	1964	$50

COLUMBIA

❑ CL549 [M]	Chet Baker and Strings	1954	$80

— Maroon label, gold print

❑ CL549 [M]	Chet Baker and Strings	1955	$60

— Red and black label with six "eye" logos

CROWN

❑ CLP-5317 [M]	Chet Baker Quintette	196?	$25
❑ CST-317 [R]	Chet Baker Quintette	196?	$35

CTI

❑ 6050	She Was Too Good to Me	1974	$30

ENJA

❑ 4016	Peace	1982	$25
❑ R1-79600	The Last Great Concert: My Favorite Songs Vol. 1	1989	$30
❑ R1-79624	The Last Great Concert: My Favorite Songs Vol. 2	1989	$30

FANTASY

❑ OJC-087	Chet	198?	$30

— Reissue of Riverside 1135

❑ OJC-370	Chet Baker in Milan	198?	$30

— Reissue of Jazzland 18

❑ OJC-207	Chet Baker in New York	1985	$50

— Reissue of Riverside 1119

❑ OJC-137	Chet Baker Plays the Best of Lerner and Loewe	198?	$30

— Reissue of Riverside 1152

❑ OJC-492	Chet Baker with Fifty Italian Strings	1991	$30

— Reissue of Jazzland 921

❑ OJC-303	It Could Happen to You -- Chet Baker Sings	1988	$25

— Reissue of Riverside 1120

❑ OJC-405	Once Upon a Summertime	1989	$25

— Reissue of Galaxy 5150

GALAXY

❑ 5150	Once Upon a Summertime	1977	$35

HARMONY

❑ HL7320 [M]	Love Walked In	1962	$25

HORIZON

❑ 726	You Can't Go Home Again	1977	$30

INNER CITY

❑ 1120	Broken Wing	198?	$25

JAZZLAND

❑ JLP-11 [M]	Chet Baker and Orchestra	1960	$40
❑ JLP-911 [S]	Chet Baker and Orchestra	1960	$40
❑ JLP-18 [M]	Chet Baker in Milan	1960	$40
❑ JLP-918 [S]	Chet Baker in Milan	1960	$40
❑ JLP-21 [M]	Chet Baker with Fifty Italian Strings	1960	$40
❑ JLP-921 [S]	Chet Baker with Fifty Italian Strings	1960	$40

LIMELIGHT

❑ LM-82003 [M]	Baby Breeze	1964	$30
❑ LS-86003 [S]	Baby Breeze	1964	$30
❑ LM-82019 [M]	Baker's Holiday	1965	$30
❑ LS-86019 [S]	Baker's Holiday	1965	$30

MOSAIC

❑ MR4-113	The Complete Pacific Jazz Live Recordings of the Chet Baker Quartet with Russ Freeman	199?	$80
❑ MR4-122	The Complete Pacific Jazz Studio Recordings of the Chet Baker Quartet with Russ Freeman	199?	$120

PACIFIC JAZZ

❑ PJ-1224 [M]	Chet Baker and Crew	1956	$120

Louis Armstrong, *A Rare Batch of Satch*, RCA Victor LPM-2322, **$60**.

Louis Armstrong, *The Best of Louis Armstrong*, Audio Fidelity AFSD 6132, **$60**.

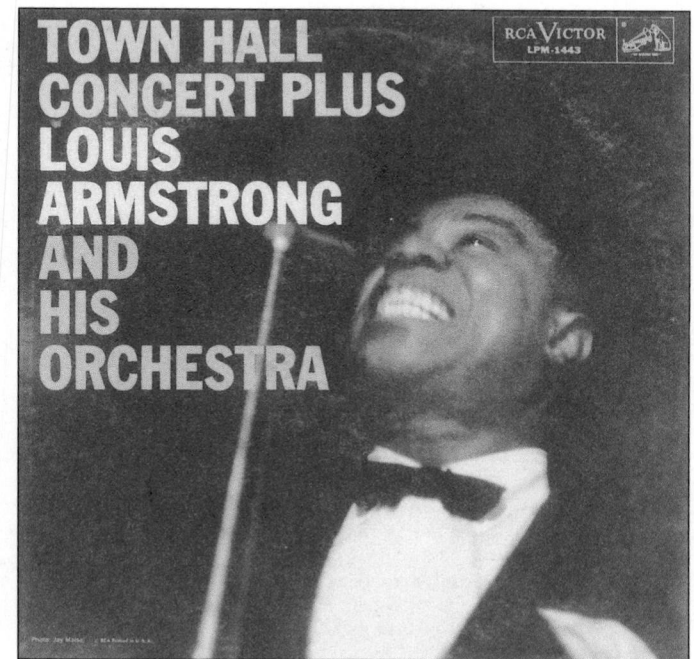

Louis Armstrong, Town Hall Concert Plus, RCA Victor LPM-1443, **$100**.

Louis Armstrong, *Louis Armstrong Plays W.C. Handy*, Columbia CL 591, maroon label with gold print, **$120**.

Number	Title	Yr	NM
❏ PJ-1229 [M]	Chet Baker Big Band	1957	$120
❏ PJLP-9 [10]	Chet Baker Ensemble	1954	$200
❏ PJLP-3 [10]	Chet Baker Quartet	1953	$200
❏ PJLP-6 [10]	Chet Baker Quartet Featuring Russ Freeman	1953	$200
❏ PJLP-15 [10]	Chet Baker Sextet	1954	$200
❏ PJLP-11 [10]	Chet Baker Sings	1954	$200
❏ PJ-1222 [M]	Chet Baker Sings	1956	$400
❏ PJ-1202 [M]	Chet Baker Sings and Plays with Bud Shank, Russ Freeman and Strings	1955	$120
❏ PJ-1206 [M]	The Trumpet Artistry of Chet Baker	1955	$120

PAUSA

❏ 9011	The Trumpet Artistry of Chet Baker	198?	$25

PRESTIGE

❏ PRLP-7512 [M]	Boppin' with the Chet Baker Quintet	1967	$30
❏ PRST-7512 [S]	Boppin' with the Chet Baker Quintet	1967	$25
❏ PRLP-7478 [M]	Comin' On with the Chet Baker Quintet	1967	$30
❏ PRST-7478 [S]	Comin' On with the Chet Baker Quintet	1967	$25
❏ PRLP-7496 [M]	Cool Burnin' with the Chet Baker Quintet	1967	$30
❏ PRST-7496 [S]	Cool Burnin' with the Chet Baker Quintet	1967	$25
❏ PRLP-7460 [M]	Groovin' with the Chet Baker Quintet	1966	$25
❏ PRST-7460 [S]	Groovin' with the Chet Baker Quintet	1966	$30
❏ PRLP-7449 [M]	Smokin' with the Chet Baker Quintet	1966	$25
❏ PRST-7449 [S]	Smokin' with the Chet Baker Quintet	1966	$30

RIVERSIDE

❏ RLP-1135 [S]	Chet	1959	$300
❏ RLP-1119 [S]	Chet Baker in New York	1959	$300
❏ 6095	Chet Baker in New York	197?	$30
—Reissue			
❏ RLP-1152 [S]	Chet Baker Plays Lerner and Loewe	1959	$300

SCEPTER

❏ 540 [M]	Angel Eyes	1966	$25
❏ S-540 [S]	Angel Eyes	1966	$30

STEEPLECHASE

❏ SCS-1142	Daybreak	1981	$30
❏ SCS-1131	No Problem	198?	$30
❏ SCS-1180	Someday My Prince Will Come	198?	$25
❏ SCS-1122	The Touch of Your Lips	1980	$30
❏ SCS-1168	This Is Always	198?	$25

TIMELESS

❏ LPSJP-251	As Time Goes By	1990	$30
❏ LPSJP-252	Cool Cat: Chet Baker Plays, Chet Baker Sings	1990	$30
❏ LPSJP-192	Mr. B.	1990	$30

TRIP

❏ 5569	Chet Baker Sings and Plays Billie Holiday	197?	$25

VERVE

❏ V6-8798	Blood, Chet and Tears	1969	$35

WORLD PACIFIC

❏ WP-1224 [M]	Chet Baker and Crew	1958	$150
—Reissue of Pacific Jazz 1224			
❏ ST-1004 [S]	Chet Baker and Crew	1959	$150
❏ WP-1229 [M]	Chet Baker Big Band	1958	$150
—Reissue of Pacific Jazz 1229			
❏ WP-1218 [M]	Chet Baker in Europe	1958	$150
—Reissue of Pacific Jazz 1218			
❏ WP-1826 [M]	Chet Baker Sings	1964	$100
—Reissue of World Pacific 1222			
❏ ST-1826 [R]	Chet Baker Sings	1964	$100
❏ WP-1202 [M]	Chet Baker Sings and Plays with Bud Shank, Russ Freeman and Strings	1958	$150
—Reissue of Pacific Jazz 1202			
❏ WP-1852 [M]	Double Shot	1967	$100
❏ WPS-21852 [S]	Double Shot	1967	$100
❏ WP-1842 [M]	Hat's Off	1966	$100
❏ WPS-21842 [S]	Hat's Off	1966	$100
❏ WPS-21859 [S]	In the Mood	1968	$100
❏ WP-1858 [M]	Into My Life	1967	$100
❏ WPS-21858 [S]	Into My Life	1967	$100
❏ WP-1203 [M]	Jazz at Ann Arbor	1958	$150
—Reissue of Pacific Jazz 1203			
❏ WP-1249 [M]	Pretty/Groovy	1958	$200
❏ WP-1847 [M]	Quietly, There	1966	$100
❏ WPS-21847 [S]	Quietly, There	1966	$100
❏ WP-1206 [M]	The Trumpet Artistry of Chet Baker	1958	$150
—Reissue of Pacific Jazz 1206			

WORLD PACIFIC JAZZ

❏ ST-20138 [R]	Chet Baker Plays and Sings	1968	$100
—Compilation of 1950s Pacific Jazz material			

BAKER, DAVID, AND HIS 21ST CENTURY BEBOP BAND

Baker is a trombone player.

Albums

LAUREL

❏ LR-503	David Baker and His 21st Century Bebop Band	1984	$30
❏ LR-504	RSVP	1985	$30
❏ LR-505	Struttin'	1986	$30

BAKER, JOSEPHINE

Female singer.

Albums

COLUMBIA

❏ FL9533 [10]	Chansons Americaines	1951	$100
❏ FL9532 [10]	Josephine Baker	1951	$100

COLUMBIA MASTERWORKS

❏ ML2609 [10]	Chansons Americaines	1952	$80
❏ ML2613 [10]	Encores Americaines	1952	$80
❏ ML2608 [10]	Josephine Baker Sings	1952	$80

JOLLY ROGER

❏ 5015 [10]	Josephine Baker	1951	$50

MERCURY

❏ MG-25151 [10]	Avec Josephine Baker	1952	$150
❏ MG-25105 [10]	The Inimitable Josephine Baker	1952	$150

RCA VICTOR RED SEAL

❏ LSC-2427 [S]	The Fabulous Josephine Baker	1960	$50
—Original with "shaded dog" label			
❏ LM-2427 [M]	The Fabulous Josephine Baker	1960	$25
—Original with "shaded dog" label			

BAKER, LAVERN

Mostly a rhythm and blues singer, Baker did do one jazz album, listed below.

Albums

ATLANTIC

❏ 1281 [M]	LaVern Baker Sings Bessie Smith	1958	$250
—Black label			
❏ 1281 [M]	LaVern Baker Sings Bessie Smith	1960	$250
—Red and purple label, "fan" logo in white			
❏ 1281 [M]	LaVern Baker Sings Bessie Smith	1963	$50
—Red and purple label, "fan" logo in black			
❏ SD1281 [S]	LaVern Baker Sings Bessie Smith	1959	$300
—Green label			
❏ SD1281 [S]	LaVern Baker Sings Bessie Smith	1960	$250
—Green and blue label, "fan" logo in white			
❏ SD1281 [S]	LaVern Baker Sings Bessie Smith	1963	$60
—Green and blue label, "fan" logo in black			
❏ 90980	LaVern Baker Sings Bessie Smith	1989	$30
—Reissue of SD 1281			

BAKER, SHORTY, AND DOC CHEATHAM

Also see each artist's individual listings.

Albums

SWINGVILLE

❏ SVLP-2021 [M]	Shorty & Doc	1961	$50
—Purple label			
❏ SVLP-2021 [M]	Shorty & Doc	1965	$30
—Blue label with trident logo at right			

BAKER, SHORTY

Trumpeter.

Albums

KING

❏ 608 [M]	Broadway Beat	1958	$80

BALDWIN, BOB

Keyboard player and pianist.

Albums

ATLANTIC

❏ 82098	Rejoice	1990	$30

MALACO

❏ MJ-1501	I've Got a Long Way to Go	1988	$25

BALES, BURT

Pianist.

Albums

ABC-PARAMOUNT

❏ ABC-181 [M]	Jazz from the San Francisco Waterfront	1957	$40

CAVALIER

❏ 5007 [10]	On the Waterfront	195?	$60

EUPHONIC

❏ ESR-1210 [M]	New Orleans Ragtime	196?	$30

GOOD TIME JAZZ

❏ L-19 [10]	New Orleans Joys	1954	$50

BALES & LINGLE

BURT BALES and PAUL LINGLE, both pianists.

Albums

GOOD TIME JAZZ

❏ L-12025 [M]	They Tore My Playhouse Down	1955	$50

BALL, KENNY

Trumpeter and bandleader. His "Midnight in Moscow" was a hit single in 1962.

Albums

JAZZOLOGY

❏ 65	In Concert in the USA, Volume 1	1979	$25
❏ 66	In Concert in the USA, Volume 2	1979	$25

KAPP

❏ KL-1340 [M]	Big Ones	1963	$35
❏ KS-3340 [S]	Big Ones	1963	$50
❏ KL-1392 [M]	For the Jet Set	1964	$35
❏ KS-3392 [S]	For the Jet Set	1964	$50
❏ KL-1285 [M]	It's Trad	1962	$50
❏ KS-3285 [S]	It's Trad	1962	$50
❏ KL-1276 [M]	Midnight in Moscow	1962	$50
❏ KS-3276 [S]	Midnight in Moscow	1962	$50
❏ KL-1314 [M]	More	1963	$35
❏ KS-3314 [S]	More	1963	$50
❏ KL-1294 [M]	Recorded Live	1962	$50
❏ KS-3294 [S]	Recorded Live	1962	$50
❏ KL-1348 [M]	Washington Square and the Best of Kenny Ball	1964	$35
❏ KS-3348 [S]	Washington Square and the Best of Kenny Ball	1964	$50

BALL, ROCKY, AND THE RAZ'MATAZ JAZZ BAND

Banjo player.

Albums

BONFIRE

❏ 502	For Your Listening Pleasure	198?	$25
❏ 501	Hot Dixieland Jazz	198?	$25
❏ 503	Salute to Li'l Wally	198?	$25

BALL, RONNIE

Pianist.

Albums

SAVOY

❏ MG-12075 [M]	All About Ronnie	1956	$40

BALLOU, MONTE, AND HIS NEW CASTLE JAZZ BAND

Banjo player and bandleader. Also see THE FAMOUS CASTLE JAZZ BAND.

Albums

GHB

❏ GHB-155	They're Moving Willie's Grave to Dig a Sewer	1986	$25

Number	Title	Yr	NM

BALMER, DAN
Guitarist. Formerly a member of TOM GRANT's band.
Albums
CMG
| ❏ CML-8013 | Becoming Became | 1989 | $30 |

BANG, BILLY
Violinist. Also see STRING TRIO OF NEW YORK.
Albums
CELLULOID
| ❏ CELL-5004 | Outline #12 | 198? | $30 |

SOUL NOTE
❏ SN-1036	Invitation	1982	$30
❏ 121136	Live at Carlos 1	1987	$30
❏ SN-1016	Rainbow Gladiator	1981	$30
❏ SN-1086	The Fire from Within	1985	$30

BANJO KINGS, THE
Banjo players Dick Roberts and Red Roundtree with a revolving cast of backing musicians.
Albums
GOOD TIME JAZZ
❏ L-12029 [M]	Nostalgia Revisited	1956	$40
❏ L-15 [10]	The Banjo Kings	1953	$50
❏ L-12015 [M]	The Banjo Kings	1955	$50
❏ L-12015 [M]	The Banjo Kings, Vol. 1	198?	$25
— Reissue with revised title and thinner vinyl			
❏ L-25 [10]	The Banjo Kings, Vol. 2	1954	$50
❏ L-12047 [M]	The Banjo Kings Enjoy the Good Old Days	1958	$40
❏ S-12047 [S]	The Banjo Kings Enjoy the Good Old Days	1959	$30
❏ L-12036 [M]	The Banjo Kings Go West	1957	$40

BARBARIN, PAUL, AND PUNCH MILLER
Also see each artist's individual listings.
Albums
ATLANTIC
| ❏ 1410 [M] | Paul Barbarin and Punch Miller | 1963 | $25 |
| ❏ SD1410 [S] | Paul Barbarin and Punch Miller | 1963 | $30 |

BARBARIN, PAUL
Drummer and bandleader.
Albums
ATLANTIC
❏ 1215 [M]	New Orleans Jazz	1955	$300
— Black label			
❏ 1215 [M]	New Orleans Jazz	1961	$150
— Multi-color label, white "fan" logo at right			
❏ 1215 [M]	New Orleans Jazz	1963	$35
— Multi-color label, black "fan" logo at right			
❏ SD1215 [S]	New Orleans Jazz	1959	$300
— Green label			
❏ SD1215 [S]	New Orleans Jazz	1961	$150
— Multi-color label, white "fan" logo at right			
❏ SD1215 [S]	New Orleans Jazz	1963	$35
— Multi-color label, black "fan" logo at right			

CIRCLE
| ❏ 408 [10] | Paul Barbarin's New Orleans Band | 1951 | $150 |

CONCERT HALL JAZZ
| ❏ 1006 [10] | New Orleans Jamboree | 1954 | $50 |

GHB
❏ GHB-140 [M]	Bourbon St. Beat	197?	$30
— Reissue of Southland LP			
❏ GHB-2 [M]	Paul Barbarin and His New Orleans Jazz Band	1962	$25

JAZZTONE
| ❏ J-1205 [M] | New Orleans Jamboree | 1955 | $50 |

NOBILITY
| ❏ 708 | Last Journey of a Jazzman | 196? | $25 |

SOUTHLAND
| ❏ SLP-237 [M] | Bourbon St. Beat | 195? | $40 |

STORYVILLE
| ❏ 4049 [M] | Jazz from New Orleans | 198? | $25 |

BARBARIN, PAUL / JOHNNY ST. CYR
St. Cyr played guitar and banjo. Also see PAUL BARBARIN.
Albums
SOUTHLAND
| ❏ SLP-212 [M] | Paul Barbarin and His Jazz Band/Johnny St. Cyr and His Hot Five | 1955 | $50 |

BARBARIN, PAUL / SHARKEY BONANO
Also see each artist's individual listings.
Albums
RIVERSIDE
❏ RLP 12-217 [M]	New Orleans Contrasts	1955	$300
— White label, blue print			
❏ RLP 12-217 [M]	New Orleans Contrasts	195?	$40
— Blue label with microphone logo			

BARBARY, RICHARD
Male singer.
Albums
A&M
| ❏ SP-3010 | Soul Machine | 1969 | $50 |

BARBER, CHRIS
Trombonist and bandleader. His version of "Petite Fleur" was a top-five pop hit in 1959.
Albums
ATLANTIC
| ❏ 1292 [M] | Here Is Chris Barber | 1959 | $300 |

COLPIX
| ❏ CP-404 [M] | Chris Barber Plays "Trad | 1959 | $60 |

GHB
| ❏ GHB-40 [M] | Collaboration | 1967 | $35 |

LAURIE
❏ LLP-1009 [M]	Chris Barber's "American" Jazz Band	1962	$60
❏ 1001 [M]	Petite Fleur	1959	$40
❏ LLP-1003 [M]	Trad Jazz Volume 1	1960	$60

BARBER, PATRICIA
Pianist and female singer.
Albums
PREMONITION
❏ PREM737-1	Café Blue	199?	$30
— Audiophile vinyl			
❏ 90747	Companion	1999	$30
— Audiophile vinyl			
❏ PREM747-1	Modern Cool	1998	$30
— Audiophile vinyl			
❏ 27290	Nightclub	2000	$30
— Audiophile vinyl			

BARBIERI, GATO & DOLLAR BRAND
Also see each artist's individual listings.
Albums
ARISTA FREEDOM
| ❏ AL1003 | Confluence | 1975 | $35 |

BARBIERI, GATO
Earlier material appears in the Goldmine Standard Catalog of American Records 1950-1975. (SC2)
Tenor saxophone player.
Albums
A&M
❏ SP-4597	Caliente!	1976	$25
❏ SP-3247	Caliente!	198?	$20
— Reissue of 4597			
❏ SP-4774	Euphoria	1979	$25
❏ SP-3188	Euphoria	198?	$20
— Reissue of 4774			
❏ SP-3029	Fire and Passion	1970	$60
❏ SP-9-3029	Fire and Passion	1984	$35
— Audio Master Plus" reissue			
❏ SP-4655	Ruby, Ruby	1977	$25
❏ SP-4710	Tropico	1978	$25

ABC IMPULSE!
❏ ASD-9303	Chapter Four -- Alive in New York	1975	$200
❏ AS-9248	Chapter One -- Latin America	1973	$200
❏ ASD-9279	Chapter Three -- Viva Emiliano Zapata	1974	$200
❏ AS-9263	Chapter Two -- Hasta Siempre	1974	$200

BLUEBIRD
| ❏ 6995-1-RB | Third World Revisited | 1988 | $30 |

DOCTOR JAZZ
| ❏ FW40183 | Apasionado | 1986 | $25 |
| ❏ W2X39204 | Gato...Para Los Amigos | 1985 | $30 |

ESP-DISK'
| ❏ 1049 | In Search of the Mystery | 1968 | $100 |

FANIA
| ❏ JM608 | Gato = Bahia | 1982 | $30 |

FLYING DUTCHMAN
❏ FD10117	3rd World	1970	$50
❏ BXL1-2826	3rd World	1978	$25
— Reissue of 10117			
❏ AYL1-3815	3rd World	1980	$20
— Budget-line reissue			
❏ FD10158	Bolivia	1973	$60
❏ BXL1-2830	Bolivia	1978	$25
— Reissue of 10158			
❏ BDL1-1147	El Gato	1976	$30
❏ AYL1-3817	El Gato	1980	$20
— Budget-line reissue			
❏ FD10151	El Pampero	1973	$50
❏ BXL1-2828	El Pampero	1978	$25
— Reissue of 10151			
❏ FD10144	Fenix	1972	$50
❏ BXL1-2827	Fenix	1978	$25
— Reissue of 10144			
❏ FD10165	The Legend of Gato Barbieri	1974	$50
❏ FD10156	Under Fire	1973	$50
❏ BXL1-2829	Under Fire	1978	$25
— Reissue of 10156			
❏ BDL1-0550	Yesterdays	1974	$30
❏ AYL1-3816	Yesterdays	1980	$20
— Budget-line reissue			

MCA
❏ 29003	Chapter Four -- Alive in New York	1981	$25
— Reissue of Impulse 9303			
❏ 29002	Chapter Two -- Hasta Siempre	1981	$20
— Reissue of Impulse 9263			

QUINTESSENCE
| ❏ QJ-25281 | Gato Barbieri | 1979 | $25 |
| *— Reissue of 1974 recordings* | | | |

UNITED ARTISTS
| ❏ UA-LA045-F | Last Tango in Paris | 1973 | $35 |

BARBOSA-LIMA, CARLOS, AND SHARON ISBIN
Sharon Isbin is an acoustic guitarist usually associated with classical music.
Albums
CONCORD CONCERTO
| ❏ CC-2012 | Rhapsody in Blue/West Side Story | 1988 | $25 |

CONCORD PICANTE
| ❏ CJP-320 | Brazil, With Love | 1987 | $25 |

BARBOSA-LIMA, CARLOS
Acoustic guitarist who also plays classical music.
Albums
CONCORD CONCERTO
❏ CC-2008	Carlos Barbosa-Lima Plays The Entertainer and Other Works by Scott Joplin	1985	$25
❏ CC-2005	Carlos Barbosa-Lima Plays the Music of Jobim and Gershwin	1983	$25
❏ CC-2006	Carlos Barbosa-Lima Plays the Music of Luiz Bonfa and Cole Porter	1984	$25
❏ CC-2009	Impressions	1991	$30

BARKER, WARREN
Composer and conductor.
Albums
WARNER BROS.

Number	Title	Yr	NM
❏ W1205 [M]	The King and I" for Orchestra	1958	$30
❏ WS1205 [S]	The King and I" for Orchestra	1958	$30
❏ W1290 [M]	TV Guide -- Top TV Themes	1959	$30
❏ WS1290 [S]	TV Guide -- Top TV Themes	1959	$40
❏ B1308 [M]	William Holden Presents a Musical Touch of Far Away Places	1959	$60
❏ BS1308 [S]	William Holden Presents a Musical Touch of Far Away Places	1959	$40

BARNES, CHERYL
Female singer.
Albums
OPTIMISM

Number	Title	Yr	NM
❏ OP-3105	Cheryl	198?	$30

BARNES, EMIL
Clarinet player.
Albums
AMERICAN MUSIC

Number	Title	Yr	NM
❏ LP-641 [10]	New Orleans Trad Jazz	1952	$50

JAZZOLOGY

Number	Title	Yr	NM
❏ JCE-34 [M]	Emil Barnes and His New Orleans Music	197?	$30
❏ JCE-23 [M]	Too Well Thou Lov'st	1967	$30

BARNES, GEORGE, AND KARL KRESS
Also see each artist's individual listings.
Albums
STASH

Number	Title	Yr	NM
❏ ST-222	Two Guitars	198?	$25
❏ ST-228	Two Guitars and a Horn	198?	$25

UNITED ARTISTS

Number	Title	Yr	NM
❏ UAL3335 [M]	Town Hall Concert	1963	$60
❏ UAS6335 [S]	Town Hall Concert	1963	$60

BARNES, GEORGE
Guitarist. Also see RUBY BRAFF AND GEORGE BARNES.
Albums
DECCA

Number	Title	Yr	NM
❏ DL8658 [M]	Guitars -- By George	1957	$120

—Black label, silver print

GRAND AWARD

Number	Title	Yr	NM
❏ GA 33-358 [M]	Guitar in Velvet	195?	$30

MERCURY

Number	Title	Yr	NM
❏ MG-20956 [M]	Guitar Galaxies	1962	$100
❏ SR-60956 [S]	Guitar Galaxies	1962	$100
❏ PPS-2011 [M]	Guitar Galaxies	196?	$100
❏ PPS-6011 [S]	Guitar Galaxies	196?	$100

BARNES, MAE
Female singer.
Albums
ATLANTIC

Number	Title	Yr	NM
❏ ALS-404 [10]	Fun with Mae Barnes	1953	$400

VANGUARD

Number	Title	Yr	NM
❏ VRS-9036 [M]	Meet Mae Barnes	1958	$100

BARNET, CHARLIE
Saxophone player (alto, tenor, baritone), male singer, bandleader.
Albums
AIRCHECK

Number	Title	Yr	NM
❏ 5	Charlie Barnet and His Orchestra 1945	197?	$25
❏ 30	Charlie Barnet On the Air Vol. 2	198?	$25

ALAMAC

Number	Title	Yr	NM
❏ QSR2446	Charlie Barnet & His Orchestra 1949	198?	$25

AVA

Number	Title	Yr	NM
❏ A-10 [M]	Charlie Barnet !?!?!?!?!?!?!	1962	$30
❏ AS-10 [S]	Charlie Barnet !?!?!?!?!?!?!	1962	$30

BLUEBIRD

Number	Title	Yr	NM
❏ AXM2-5526	The Complete Charlie Barnet Vol. 1, 1935-37	197?	$35
❏ AXM2-5577	The Complete Charlie Barnet Vol. 2, 1939	197?	$35

Number	Title	Yr	NM
❏ AXM2-5581	The Complete Charlie Barnet Vol. 3, 1939-40	197?	$35
❏ AXM2-5585	The Complete Charlie Barnet Vol. 4, 1940	197?	$35
❏ AXM2-5587	The Complete Charlie Barnet Vol. 5, 1940-41	197?	$35
❏ AXM2-5590	The Complete Charlie Barnet Vol. 6, 1940-41	197?	$35

BRIGHT ORANGE

Number	Title	Yr	NM
❏ XBO-706 [S]	The Stereophonic Sound of the Charlie Barnet Orchestra	196?	$35

CAPITOL

Number	Title	Yr	NM
❏ H235 [10]	Big Bands	195?	$100
❏ T624 [M]	Classics in Jazz	1955	$80
❏ T1403 [M]	Jazz Oasis	1960	$50
❏ ST1403 [S]	Jazz Oasis	1960	$60
❏ H325 [10]	The Modern Idiom	1952	$300

CHOREO

Number	Title	Yr	NM
❏ A-10 [M]	Charlie Barnet !?!?!?!?!?!?!	196?	$25
❏ AS-10 [S]	Charlie Barnet !?!?!?!?!?!?!	196?	$30

—Some copies have Choreo logo on front cover, but Ava labels and back cover

CIRCLE

Number	Title	Yr	NM
❏ CLP-65	Charlie Barnet and His Orchestra 1941	198?	$25

CLEF

Number	Title	Yr	NM
❏ MGC-164 [10]	Charlie Barnet Dance Session, Vol. 1	1954	$250
❏ MGC-165 [10]	Charlie Barnet Dance Session, Vol. 2	1954	$250
❏ MGC-114 [10]	Charlie Barnet Plays Charlie Barnet	1953	$250
❏ MGC-139 [10]	Dance with Charlie Barnet	1953	$250
❏ MGC-638 [M]	One Night Stand	1955	$200

COLUMBIA

Number	Title	Yr	NM
❏ CL639 [M]	Town Hall Jazz Concert	1955	$60

—Maroon label, gold print

Number	Title	Yr	NM
❏ CL639 [M]	Town Hall Jazz Concert	195?	$40

—Black and red label with six "eye" logos

CREATIVE WORLD

Number	Title	Yr	NM
❏ ST1056	Charlie Barnet Big Band 1967	197?	$30

—Reissue of Vault LPS-9004

CROWN

Number	Title	Yr	NM
❏ CLP-5114 [M]	A Tribute to Harry James	195?	$25
❏ CLP-5127 [M]	Charlie Barnet Presents a Salute to Harry James	195?	$25
❏ CLP-5134 [M]	On Stage with Charlie Barnet	1959	$25

DECCA

Number	Title	Yr	NM
❏ DL8098 [M]	Hop on the Skyliner	195?	$50

EVEREST

Number	Title	Yr	NM
❏ LPBR-5008 [M]	Cherokee	1958	$30
❏ SDBR-1008 [S]	Cherokee	1959	$25
❏ LPBR-5059 [M]	More Charlie Barnet	196?	$25
❏ SDBR-5059 [S]	More Charlie Barnet	196?	$30

HEP

Number	Title	Yr	NM
❏ 2005	Live at Basin Street East	198?	$25

MCA

Number	Title	Yr	NM
❏ 2-4069	The Best of Charlie Barnet	1975	$30

—Black rainbow labels

Number	Title	Yr	NM
❏ 2-4069	The Best of Charlie Barnet	1980	$25

—Blue rainbow labels

MERCURY

Number	Title	Yr	NM
❏ MGC-114 [10]	Charlie Barnet Plays Charlie Barnet	1952	$250

RCA VICTOR

Number	Title	Yr	NM
❏ LPV-551 [M]	Charlie Barnet (Volume 1)	1968	$25
❏ LPV-567 [M]	Charlie Barnet (Volume 2)	1969	$25
❏ LPM-1091 [M]	Redskin Romp	1955	$60
❏ LPT-3062 [10]	Rockin' in Rhythm	195?	$80
❏ LPM-2081 [M]	The Great Dance Bands	1960	$25

SUNSET

Number	Title	Yr	NM
❏ SUS-5150	Cherokee	1967	$30

SWING

Number	Title	Yr	NM
❏ 103 [M]	Charlie Barnet and His Orchestra	195?	$40

TIME-LIFE

Number	Title	Yr	NM
❏ STBB-07	Big Bands: Charlie Barnet	1983	$35

VAULT

Number	Title	Yr	NM
❏ LP-9004 [M]	Charlie Barnet Big Band 1967	1967	$25
❏ LPS-9004 [S]	Charlie Barnet Big Band 1967	1967	$35

VERVE

Number	Title	Yr	NM
❏ MGV-2007 [M]	Dance Bash	1956	$150
❏ V-2007 [M]	Dance Bash	1961	$25
❏ MGV-2027 [M]	Dancing Party	1956	$150
❏ V-2027 [M]	Dancing Party	1961	$25

Number	Title	Yr	NM
❏ MGV-2031 [M]	For Dancing Lovers	1956	$150
❏ V-2031 [M]	For Dancing Lovers	1961	$25
❏ MGV-2040 [M]	Lonely Street	1957	$150
❏ V-2040 [M]	Lonely Street	1961	$25

BARR, WALT
Guitarist.
Albums
MUSE

Number	Title	Yr	NM
❏ 5238	Artful Dancer	1980	$35
❏ 5210	East Winds	1979	$35
❏ 5172	First Visit	1978	$35

BARRETT, DAN
Trombone player, both slide and valve.
Albums
CONCORD JAZZ

Number	Title	Yr	NM
❏ CJ-331	Strictly Instrumental	1988	$25

BARRETT, EMMA
Known as "Sweet Emma." Pianist and female singer.
Albums
GHB

Number	Title	Yr	NM
❏ 142 [M]	Emma Barrett at Disneyland	1969	$30

—Reissue of Southland 242

Number	Title	Yr	NM
❏ 141 [M]	Sweet Emma Barrett and Her New Orleans Music	1969	$30

—Reissue of Southland 241

NOBILITY

Number	Title	Yr	NM
❏ 711 [M]	The Bell Gal and Her New Orleans Jazz	196?	$25

RIVERSIDE

Number	Title	Yr	NM
❏ RLP-364 [M]	Sweet Emma	1960	$200
❏ RS-9364 [R]	Sweet Emma	196?	$25

SOUTHLAND

Number	Title	Yr	NM
❏ 242 [M]	Emma Barrett at Disneyland	1967	$25
❏ 241 [M]	Sweet Emma Barrett and Her New Orleans Music	1964	$25

BARRETTO, RAY
Percussionist (mostly congas) and bandleader. Also a legendary figure in Latin samba music. Had a hit single in 1963 with "El Watusi."
Albums
ATLANTIC

Number	Title	Yr	NM
❏ SD19198	Can You	1978	$30
❏ SD19140	Eye of the Beholder	1977	$30
❏ SD 2-509	Tomorrow: Ray Barretto Live	197?	$35

CTI

Number	Title	Yr	NM
❏ 9002	La Cuna	198?	$25

FANIA

Number	Title	Yr	NM
❏ SLP-388	Barretto Head Sounds	197?	$25
❏ SLP-410	From the Beginning	197?	$25
❏ SLP-362	Hard Hands	1970	$25
❏ SLP-391	Power	197?	$25
❏ SLP-403	The Message	197?	$25
❏ SLP-378	Together	197?	$25

FANTASY

Number	Title	Yr	NM
❏ 24713	Carnaval	197?	$35

TICO

Number	Title	Yr	NM
❏ LP-1087 [M]	Charanga Moderna	1962	$25
❏ SLP-1087 [S]	Charanga Moderna	1962	$30
❏ LP-1114 [M]	Guajira y Guaguanco	1964	$25
❏ SLP-1114 [S]	Guajira y Guaguanco	1964	$30
❏ LP-1102 [M]	La Moderna De Siempre	1963	$25
❏ SLP-1102 [S]	La Moderna De Siempre	1963	$30
❏ CLP-1314	Lo Mejor De Ray Barretto	1973	$35
❏ SLP-1205	Something to Remember	1969	$35
❏ LP-1099 [M]	The Hit Latin Style of Ray Barretto	1963	$25
❏ SLP-1099 [S]	The Hit Latin Style of Ray Barretto	1963	$30

BARRON, BILL
Tenor saxophone player. Also a soprano saxophone player and flutist.
Albums
AUDIO FIDELITY

Number	Title	Yr	NM
❏ AFLP-2123 [M]	Now Hear This!	1964	$25
❏ AFSD-6123 [S]	Now Hear This!	1964	$30

DAUNTLESS

Number	Title	Yr	NM
❏ DM-4312 [M]	West Side Story Bossa Nova	1963	$30
❏ DS-6312 [S]	West Side Story Bossa Nova	1963	$30

Number	Title	Yr	NM

MUSE
❏ 5235	Jazz Caper	1978	$30
❏ 5306	Variations in Blue	1983	$30

SAVOY
❏ MG-12183 [M]	Hot Line	1965	$150
❏ MG-12163 [M]	Modern Windows	1962	$150
❏ MG-12303	Motivation	197?	$35
❏ MG-12160 [M]	The Tenor Stylings of Bill Barron	1961	$40

SAVOY JAZZ
❏ SJL-1184	Nebulae	1987	$25
❏ SJL-1160	The Hot Line	1986	$25

BARRON, KENNY, AND TED DUNBAR
Also see each artist's individual listings.

Albums
MUSE
❏ MR-5140	In Tandem	1975	$30

BARRON, KENNY
Pianist.

Albums
BLACK HAWK
❏ 50601	1 + 1 + 1	1986	$30

CRISS CROSS
❏ 3008	Green Chimneys	1984	$30

EASTWIND
❏ 709	Spiral	1982	$30

LIMETREE
❏ 20	Landscape	1984	$30

MUSE
❏ MR-5220	Golden Lotus	1980	$30
❏ MR-5080	Lucifer	1975	$30
❏ MR-5044	Peruvian Blue	1974	$30
❏ MR-5014	Sunset to Dawn	1973	$30

WHY NOT
❏ 25032	Imo Live	1982	$30

WOLF
❏ 1203	Innocence	1978	$35

XANADU
❏ 188	Kenny Barron at the Piano	1981	$30

BARTLEY, CHARLENE
Female singer.

Albums
RCA VICTOR
❏ LPM-1478 [M]	Weekend of a Private Secretary	1957	$50

BARTZ, GARY
Alto and soprano saxophone player and composer.

Albums
ARISTA
❏ AL4263	Bartz	1979	$15

CAPITOL
❏ SW-11789	Love Affair	1978	$15
❏ ST-11647	My Sanctuary	1977	$15

CATALYST
❏ 7610	Ju Ju Man	1976	$15

MILESTONE
❏ 9018	Another Earth	1969	$25
❏ 9031	Harlem Bush Music -- Taifa	1971	$25
❏ 9032	Harlem Bush Music -- Uhuru	1972	$25
❏ 9027	Home!	1970	$25
❏ 9006	Libra	1968	$25

PRESTIGE
❏ 10068	Follow the Medicine Man	197?	$35
❏ 66001	I've Known Rivers	197?	$25
❏ 10057	Juju St. Songs	197?	$35
❏ 10083	Singerella -- A Ghetto Fairy Tale	197?	$35
❏ 10092	The Shadow 'Do	1975	$35

VEE JAY
❏ VJS-3068	Love Song	1977	$30

BASIE, COUNT, AND BILLY ECKSTINE
Also see each artist's individual listings.

Albums
ROULETTE
❏ R52029 [M]	Basie/Eckstine, Incorporated	1959	$60
❏ SR52029 [S]	Basie/Eckstine, Incorporated	1959	$40
❏ SR42017	Count Basie and Billy Eckstine	1968	$35

— Reissue

BASIE, COUNT, AND DIZZY GILLESPIE
Also see each artist's individual listings.

Albums
PABLO
❏ 2310833	The Gifted Ones	1979	$25

VERVE
❏ V-8560 [M]	The Count Basie Band and the Dizzy Gillespie Band at Newport	1963	$50
❏ V6-8560 [S]	The Count Basie Band and the Dizzy Gillespie Band at Newport	1963	$60

BASIE, COUNT, AND DUKE ELLINGTON
Also see each artist's individual listings.

Albums
ACCORD
❏ SN-7200	Heads of State	1982	$25

BASIE, COUNT, AND JOE WILLIAMS
Also see each artist's individual listings.

Albums
CLEF
❏ MGC-678 [M]	Count Basie Swings/Joe Williams Sings	1955	$250

ROULETTE
❏ R52093 [M]	Back to Basie and Blues	1963	$60
❏ SR52093 [S]	Back to Basie and Blues	1963	$60
❏ R52033 [M]	Everyday I Have the Blues	1959	$60
❏ SR52033 [S]	Everyday I Have the Blues	1959	$40
❏ R52054 [M]	Just the Blues	1960	$60
❏ SR52054 [S]	Just the Blues	1960	$40
❏ R52021 [M]	Memories Ad Lib	1959	$60
❏ SR52021 [S]	Memories Ad Lib	1959	$40

VANGUARD
❏ VRS-8508 [M]	A Night at Count Basie's	1955	$175

VERVE
❏ MGV-8063 [M]	Count Basie Swings/Joe Williams Sings	1957	$250

— Reissue of Clef 678
❏ V-8488 [M]	Count Basie Swings/Joe Williams Sings	1962	$60

— Reissue of 8063
❏ V6-8488 [R]	Count Basie Swings/Joe Williams Sings	1962	$30
❏ UMV-2650	The Greatest	1981	$25
❏ MGV-2016 [M]	The Greatest! Count Basie Swings/Joe Williams Sings Standards	1956	$100
❏ MGVS-6006 [S]	The Greatest! Count Basie Swings/Joe Williams Sings Standards	1960	$100

BASIE, COUNT, AND MAYNARD FERGUSON
Also see each artist's individual listings.

Albums
ROULETTE
❏ R52117 [M]	Big Band Scene '65	1965	$50
❏ SR52117 [S]	Big Band Scene '65	1965	$60

BASIE, COUNT, AND OSCAR PETERSON
Also see each artist's individual listings.

Albums
PABLO
❏ 2310843	Night Rider	1979	$25
❏ 2310722	Satch" and "Josh	1975	$30
❏ 2310802	Satch and Josh Again	1978	$25
❏ 2310896	The Timekeepers	198?	$30
❏ 2310923	Yessir, That's My Baby	1987	$25

BASIE, COUNT, AND SAMMY DAVIS, JR.
Also see each artist's individual listings.

Albums
VERVE
❏ V-8605 [M]	Our Shining Hour	1965	$35
❏ V6-8605 [S]	Our Shining Hour	1965	$50

BASIE, COUNT, AND THE MILLS BROTHERS
Also see each artist's individual listings.

Albums
DOT
❏ DLP-25838	The Board of Directors	1968	$75

BASIE, COUNT; JOE WILLIAMS; LAMBERT, HENDRICKS AND ROSS
Also see each artist's individual listings.

Albums
ROULETTE
❏ R52018 [M]	Sing Along with Basie	1959	$50
❏ SR52018 [S]	Sing Along with Basie	1959	$60

BASIE, COUNT
Pianist, organist and bandleader. Also see TONY BENNETT; TERESA BREWER; EDDIE DAVIS; ELLA FITZGERALD; ARTHUR PRYSOCK; FRANK SINATRA; SARAH VAUGHAN; JACKIE WILSON.

Albums
ABC
❏ 4001	16 Great Performances	1974	$30
❏ AC-30004	The ABC Collection	1976	$30

ABC IMPULSE!
❏ AS-15 [S]	Count Basie and the Kansas City Seven	1968	$30
❏ IA-9351	Retrospective Sessions	1978	$30

ABC-PARAMOUNT
❏ ABC-570 [M]	Basie's Swingin' -- Voices Singin'	1966	$50
❏ ABCS-570 [S]	Basie's Swingin' -- Voices Singin'	1966	$60

ACCORD
❏ SN-7183	Command Performance	1981	$25

ALAMAC
❏ QSR-2412	Count Basie and His Orchestra 1937	198?	$25

AMERICAN RECORDING SOCIETY
❏ G-422 [M]	Basie's Best	1957	$40
❏ G-401 [M]	Count Basie	1956	$40
❏ G-435 [M]	Mainstream Jazz Swing	1957	$40
❏ G-402 [M]	The Band That Swings the Blues	1956	$40

BASF
❏ 25111	Basic Basie	1973	$35

BOOK-OF-THE-MONTH CLUB
❏ 91-6545	The Early Years	1982	$60

— Alternate number: P3-16389

BRIGHT ORANGE
❏ XBO-702	Count Basie Featuring B.B. King	196?	$50

BRUNSWICK
❏ BL58019 [10]	Basie's Best	195?	$100
❏ BL754127	Basie's in the Bag	196?	$35
❏ BL54012 [M]	Count Basie	1957	$40

BULLDOG
❏ BDL-2020	20 Golden Pieces of Count Basie	1980	$30

CLEF
❏ MGC-666 [M]	Basie	1955	$350
❏ MGC-749 [M]	Basie in Europe	1956	---

— Canceled; released as Verve 8199
❏ MGC-633 [M]	Basie Jazz	1954	$350
❏ MGC-729 [M]	Basie Rides Again!	1956	$300
❏ MGC-723 [M]	Basie Roars Again	1956	$300
❏ MCG-120 [10]	Count Basie and His Orchestra Collates	1953	$350
❏ MGC-148 [10]	Count Basie Big Band	1954	$350
❏ MGC-626 [M]	Count Basie Dance Session #1	1954	$350
❏ MGC-647 [M]	Count Basie Jazz Session #2	1955	$350
❏ MCG-146 [10]	Count Basie Sextet	1954	$350
❏ MGC-722 [M]	The Band of Distinction	1956	$300
❏ MGC-685 [M]	The Count	1956	$300
❏ MGC-706 [M]	The Swinging Count	1956	$300

COLISEUM
❏ 51003 [M]	The Happiest Millionaire	1968	$35
❏ 41003 [M]	The Happiest Millionaire	1968	$40

COLUMBIA
❏ CL2560 [10]	Basie Bash	1956	$150
❏ CL901 [M]	Blues By Basie	1956	$40
❏ CL754 [M]	Classics	1955	$120
❏ CL6079 [10]	Dance Parade	1949	$175
❏ CL997 [M]	One O'Clock Jump	1956	$40
❏ G31224	Super Chief	1972	$35

COLUMBIA JAZZ MASTERPIECES
❏ CJ40608	The Essential Count Basie, Volume 1	1987	$25
❏ CJ40835	The Essential Count Basie, Volume 2	1987	$25
❏ CJ44150	The Essential Count Basie, Volume 3	1988	$25

COLUMBIA JAZZ ODYSSEY
❏ PC36824	Blues By Basie	1981	$20

Number	Title	Yr	NM
COLUMBIA SPECIAL PRODUCTS			
❏ P14355	The Count	198?	$20
COMMAND			
❏ 33-905 [M]	Broadway Basie's...Way	1966	$30
❏ RS905SD [S]	Broadway Basie's...Way	1966	$35
❏ CQ-40004 [Q]	Broadway Basie's...Way	1972	$60
❏ 33-912 [M]	Hollywood... Basie's Way	1967	$35
❏ RS912SD [S]	Hollywood... Basie's Way	1967	$30
DAYBREAK			
❏ 2005	Have a Nice Day	1971	$30
DECCA			
❏ DL8049 [M]	Count Basie and His Orchestra	1954	$150
❏ DL78049 [R]	Count Basie and His Orchestra	196?	$30
❏ DL5111 [10]	Count Basie at the Piano	1950	$250
❏ DXB170 [M]	The Best of Count Basie	196?	$60
❏ DXSB7170 [R]	The Best of Count Basie	196?	$35
DOCTOR JAZZ			
❏ FW39520	Afrique	1985	$25
—Reissue of Flying Dutchman 10138			
DOT			
❏ DLP-25938	Standing Ovation	1969	$75
❏ DLP-25902	Straight Ahead	1969	$75
EMARCY			
❏ MG-26023 [10]	Jazz Royalty	1954	$200
EMUS			
❏ ES12011	Basie at Birdland	197?	$25
EPIC			
❏ LN3169 [M]	Basie's Back in Town	1955	$200
❏ LN3107 [M]	Lester Leaps In	1955	$200
—With Lester Young			
❏ LN3168 [M]	Let's Go to Prez	1955	$200
—With Lester Young			
❏ LN1117 [10]	Rock the Blues	1955	$300
❏ LG1021 [10]	The Old Count and the New Count -- Basie	1954	$300
EVEREST ARCHIVE OF FOLK & JAZZ			
❏ FS-318	Savoy Ballroom 1937	197?	$25
FANTASY			
❏ OJC-416	88 Basie Street	198?	$30
❏ OJC-379	Basie Big Band Montreux '77	1989	$25
—Reissue of Pablo Live 2308 209			
❏ OJC-600	Kansas City 3/For the Second Time	1991	$30
—Reissue of Pablo 2310 878			
❏ OJC-449	Kansas City 6	1990	$30
—Reissue of Pablo 2310 871			
FLYING DUTCHMAN			
❏ FD10138	Afrique	1972	$60
FORUM			
❏ F-9032 [M]	Kansas City Suite	196?	$30
❏ SF-9032 [S]	Kansas City Suite	196?	$35
—Reissue of Roulette 52056			
❏ F-9063 [M]	Not Now -- I'll Tell You When	196?	$30
❏ SF-9063 [S]	Not Now -- I'll Tell You When	196?	$35
—Reissue of Roulette 52044			
❏ F-9060 [M]	One More Time	196?	$30
❏ SF-9060 [S]	One More Time	196?	$35
—Reissue of Roulette 52024			
GROOVE MERCHANT			
❏ 2001	Evergreens	1972	$30
HAPPY TIGER			
❏ 1007	Basie on the Beatles	196?	$60
HARMONY			
❏ HL7229 [M]	Basie's Best	1960	$35
❏ HS11371	Just in Time	1970	$30
IMPULSE!			
❏ A-15 [M]	Count Basie and the Kansas City Seven	1962	$200
❏ AS-15 [S]	Count Basie and the Kansas City Seven	1962	$160
INTERMEDIA			
❏ QS-5039	The Classic Count	198?	$25
❏ QS-5028	The Deacon	198?	$25
JAZZ ARCHIVES			
❏ JA-41	At the Famous Door, 1938-1939	198?	$25
❏ JA-16	The Count at the Chatterbox, 1937	198?	$25
JAZZ MAN			
❏ 5006	Ain't It the Truth	198?	$25
JAZZ PANORAMA			
❏ 1803 [10]	Count Basie and Lester Young	1951	$175
MCA			

Number	Title	Yr	NM
❏ 718	16 Greatest Performances	198?	$20
❏ 29003	Count Basie and the Kansas City Seven	198?	$20
❏ 4108	Good Morning Blues	197?	$30
❏ 42324	One O'Clock Jump	1990	$30
❏ 4130	Retrospective Sessions	198?	$25
❏ 4163	Showtime	198?	$25
❏ 29005	Standing Ovation	198?	$20
❏ 29004	Straight Ahead	198?	$20
❏ 4050	The Best of Count Basie	197?	$30
MCA/IMPULSE!			
❏ 5656	Count Basie and the Kansas City Seven	1986	$20
MERCURY			
❏ MG-25105 [10]	Count Basie and His Kansas City Seven	1952	$300
❏ MGC-120 [10]	Count Basie and His Orchestra Collates	1952	$300
METRO			
❏ M-516 [M]	Count Basie	1965	$250
❏ MS-516 [S]	Count Basie	1965	$150
MGM			
❏ GAS-126	Count Basie (Golden Archive Series)	1970	$35
MOBILE FIDELITY			
❏ 1-237	April in Paris	1995	$120
—Audiophile vinyl			
❏ 1-129	Basie Plays Hefti	1985	$150
—Audiophile vinyl			
MOSAIC			
❏ MR12-135	The Complete Roulette Live Recordings of Count Basie and His Orchestra	199?	$200
❏ MQ15-149	The Complete Roulette Studio Recordings of Count Basie and His Orchestra	199?	$250
PABLO			
❏ 2310901	88 Basie Street	1984	$50
❏ 2310925	Basie and His Friends	1988	$30
❏ 2310745	Basie and Zoot	1976	$50
❏ 2310756	Basie Big Band	1975	$50
❏ 2310786	Basie Jam #2	1977	$35
❏ 2310840	Basie Jam #3	1979	$30
❏ 2310718	Basie Jam	1975	$35
❏ 2310750	Basie Jam/Montreux '75	1976	$30
❏ 2310924	Count Basie Get Together	1987	$25
❏ 2310920	Fancy Pants	1987	$25
❏ 2310874	Farmers Market Barbecue	1982	$25
❏ 2310712	For the First Time	1974	$30
❏ 2310767	I Told You So	1976	$30
❏ 2310871	Kansas City 6	198?	$30
❏ 2310859	Kansas City Shout	1980	$30
—With Joe Turner and Eddie "Cleanhead" Vinson			
❏ 2310891	Me & You	1983	$25
❏ 2310919	Mostly Blues...And Some Others	1987	$25
❏ 2310797	Prime Time	1977	$30
❏ 2310852	The Best of Basie	1980	$25
❏ 2405408	The Best of the Count Basie Band	198?	$25
❏ 2310709	The Bosses	1974	$30
PABLO LIVE			
❏ 2308207	Basie Big Band Montreux '77	1977	$30
❏ 2308209	Basie Jam/Montreux '77	1977	$30
❏ 2308246	Live in Japan, 1978	198?	$25
PABLO TODAY			
❏ 2312126	Kansas City 5	198?	$25
❏ 2312112	On the Road	1980	$25
❏ 2312131	Warm Breeze	198?	$25
PAIR			
❏ PDL2-1045	Basic Basie	1986	$30
PAUSA			
❏ 7105	High Voltage	198?	$25
PICKWICK			
❏ SPC-3500	Everything's Coming Up Roses	197?	$25
❏ SPC-3028 [S]	His Hits of the 60's	196?	$30
❏ PC-3028 [M]	His Hits of the 60's	196?	$35
PRESTIGE			
❏ 24109	Reunions	197?	$30
QUINTESSENCE			
❏ 25151	Everything's Coming Up Roses	197?	$25
RCA CAMDEN			
❏ CAL-497 [M]	Basie's Basement	1959	$60
❏ CAL-514 [M]	Count Basie in Kansas City	1959	$60
❏ CAL-395 [M]	The Count	1958	$60
RCA VICTOR			
❏ LPV-514 [M]	Count Basie in Kansas City	1965	$60
❏ AFM1-5180	Kansas City Style	1985	$25
REPRISE			
❏ R-6153 [M]	Pop Goes the Basie	1965	$35

Number	Title	Yr	NM
❏ RS-6153 [S]	Pop Goes the Basie	1965	$50
❏ R-6070 [M]	This Time by Basie! Hits of the 50's and 60's	1963	$50
❏ R9-6070 [S]	This Time by Basie! Hits of the 50's and 60's	1963	$60
ROULETTE			
❏ R52113 [M]	Back with Basie	1964	$50
❏ SR52113 [S]	Back with Basie	1964	$60
❏ R52003 [M]	Basie	1958	$100
—White label with colored "spokes			
❏ SR52003 [S]	Basie	1958	$120
—Black vinyl; white label with colored "spokes			
❏ SR52003 [S]	Basie	1958	$300
—Red vinyl; white label with colored "spokes			
❏ R52003 [M]	Basie	1964	$60
—Orange and yellow "roulette wheel" label			
❏ R52003 [M]	Basie	2003	$60
—200-gram vinyl reissue; distributed by Classic Records			
❏ SR52003 [S]	Basie	1964	$40
—Orange and yellow "roulette wheel" label			
❏ R52065 [M]	Basie at Birdland	1961	$60
❏ SR52065 [S]	Basie at Birdland	1961	$60
❏ R52011 [M]	Basie Plays Hefti	1958	$60
❏ SR52011 [S]	Basie Plays Hefti	1958	$60
❏ R52056 [M]	Benny Carter's Kansas City Suite	1960	$60
❏ SR52056 [S]	Benny Carter's Kansas City Suite	1960	$60
❏ R52028 [M]	Breakfast, Dance & Barbeque	1959	$60
❏ SR52028 [S]	Breakfast, Dance & Barbeque	1959	$60
❏ R52032 [M]	Chairman of the Board	1959	$60
❏ SR52032 [S]	Chairman of the Board	1959	$60
❏ R52099 [M]	Count Basie in Sweden	1963	$50
❏ SR52099 [S]	Count Basie in Sweden	1963	$60
❏ R52036 [M]	Dance Along with Basie	1959	$60
❏ SR52036 [S]	Dance Along with Basie	1959	$60
❏ R52106 [M]	Easin' It	1963	$50
❏ SR52106 [S]	Easin' It	1963	$60
❏ RE-102	Echoes of an Era (The Count Basie Years)	1971	$35
❏ RE-107	Echoes of an Era (The Vocal Years)	1971	$35
❏ SR42009	Fantail	1968	$35
❏ RE-124	Kansas City Suite/Easin' It	1973	$35
❏ R52044 [M]	Not Now -- I'll Tell You When	1960	$60
❏ SR52044 [S]	Not Now -- I'll Tell You When	1960	$60
❏ R52024 [M]	One More Time	1959	$60
❏ SR52024 [S]	One More Time	1959	$60
❏ R52051 [M]	String Along with Basie	1960	$60
❏ SR52051 [S]	String Along with Basie	1960	$60
❏ R52081 [M]	The Best of Basie	1962	$35
❏ SR52081 [S]	The Best of Basie	1962	$50
❏ R52089 [M]	The Best of Basie, Volume 2	1962	$35
❏ SR52089 [S]	The Best of Basie, Volume 2	1962	$50
❏ RE-118	The Best of Count Basie	1971	$35
❏ RB-1 [M]	The Count Basie Story	1960	$40
❏ SRB-1 [S]	The Count Basie Story	1960	$100
❏ SR42015	The Kid from Red Bank	1968	$35
❏ R52086 [M]	The Legend	1962	$50
❏ SR52086 [S]	The Legend	1962	$60
❏ R52111/3 [M]	The World of Count Basie	1964	$40
❏ SR52111/3 [S]	The World of Count Basie	1964	$100
SOLID STATE			
❏ SS-18032	Basie Meets Bond	1968	$35
—Reissue of United Artists LP			
TIME-LIFE			
❏ STBB-08	Big Bands: Count Basie	1983	$35
❏ STL-J-22	Giants of Jazz	1982	$50
UNITED ARTISTS			
❏ UAL-3480 [M]	Basie Meets Bond	1966	$60
❏ UAS-6480 [S]	Basie Meets Bond	1966	$60
UPFRONT			
❏ UPF-142	Count Basie and His Orchestra	1969	$30
VEE JAY			
❏ VJS-3054	I Got Rhythm	198?	$30
VERVE			
❏ VE-2-2517	16 Men Swinging	197?	$30
❏ MGV-8012 [M]	April in Paris	1957	$150
❏ V-8012 [M]	April in Paris	1961	$60
❏ UMV-1-2641	April in Paris	198?	$25
❏ 821291-1	Basic Basie	198?	$30
❏ V6-8783	Basie	1969	$35
❏ MGV-8199 [M]	Basie in London	1957	$100
❏ V-8199 [M]	Basie in London	1961	$50
❏ V-8597 [M]	Basie Land	1964	$35
❏ V6-8597 [S]	Basie Land	1964	$50
❏ V-8616 [M]	Basie Picks the Winners	1965	$35
❏ V6-8616 [S]	Basie Picks the Winners	1965	$50
❏ MGV-8108 [M]	Basie Rides Again!	1957	$250
—Reissue of Clef 729			
❏ V-8108 [M]	Basie Rides Again!	1961	$50
❏ MGV-8018 [M]	Basie Roars Again	1957	$250
—Reissue of Clef 723			

Louis Armstrong, *The Louis Armstrong Story Volume 3: Louis Armstrong and Earl Hines*, Columbia CL 853, red and black label with six "eye" logos, **$60**.

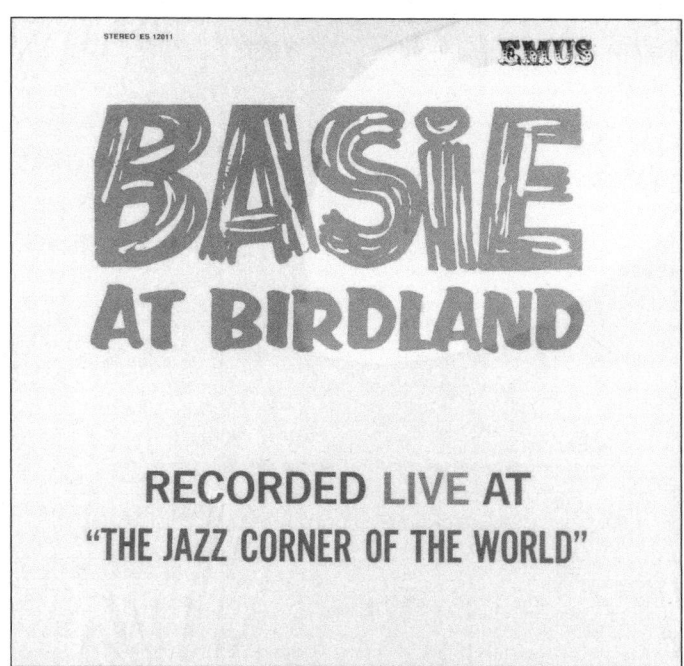

Count Basie, *Basie at Birdland*, Emus ES 12011, **$25**.

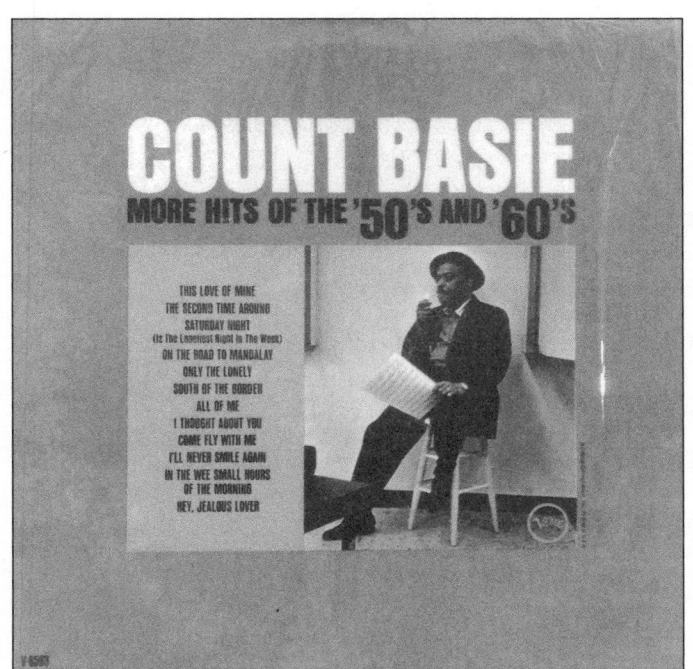

Count Basie, *More Hits of the '50s and '60s*, Verve V-8563, **$60**.

Count Basie, *Li'l Ol' Groovemaker ... Basie!*, Verve V-8549, **S60**.

Number	Title	Yr	NM
❏ V-8018 [M]	Basie Roars Again	1961	$50
❏ V-8687 [M]	Basie's Beat	1967	$50
❏ V6-8687 [S]	Basie's Beat	1967	$35
❏ V-8659 [M]	Basie's Beatle Bag	1966	$60
❏ V6-8659 [S]	Basie's Beatle Bag	1966	$40
❏ MGV-8243 [M]	Count Basie at Newport	1958	$150
❏ MGVS-6024 [S]	Count Basie at Newport	1960	$100
❏ V-8243 [M]	Count Basie at Newport	1961	$50
❏ V6-8243 [S]	Count Basie at Newport	1961	$50
❏ UMV-1-2619	Count Basie at Newport	198?	$25
❏ MGV-8291 [M]	Hall of Fame	1958	$100
❏ V-8291 [M]	Hall of Fame	1961	$50
❏ 825194-1	High Voltage (Basic Basie Vol. 2)	198?	$25
❏ VSP-12 [M]	Inside Basie, Outside	1966	$35
❏ VSPS-12 [S]	Inside Basie, Outside	1966	$50
❏ V-8549 [M]	Li'l Ol' Groovemaker…Basie!	1963	$50
❏ V6-8549 [S]	Li'l Ol' Groovemaker…Basie!	1963	$60
❏ V-8563 [M]	More Hits of the 50's and 60's	1963	$50
❏ V6-8563 [S]	More Hits of the 50's and 60's	1963	$60
❏ V-8511 [M]	On My Way and Shoutin' Again!	1963	$35
❏ V6-8511 [S]	On My Way and Shoutin' Again!	1963	$50
❏ VE-2-2542	Paradise Squat	197?	$30
❏ MGV-8103 [M]	The Band of Distinction	1957	$250
—Reissue of Clef 722			
❏ V-8103 [M]	The Band of Distinction	1961	$50
❏ MGV-8070 [M]	The Count	1957	$250
—Reissue of Clef 120			
❏ V-8070 [M]	The Count	1961	$50
❏ V-8407 [M]	The Essential Count Basie	1961	$35
❏ V6-8407 [S]	The Essential Count Basie	1961	$50
❏ MGV-8104 [M]	The King of Swing	1957	$300
—Reissue of Clef 724			
❏ V-8104 [M]	The King of Swing	1961	$50
❏ V6-8831	The Newport Years	1973	$30
❏ MGV-8090 [M]	The Swinging Count!	1957	$300
—Reissue of Clef 706			
❏ V-8090 [M]	The Swinging Count!	1961	$50
❏ V-8596 [M]	Verve's Choice -- Best of Count Basie	1964	$35
❏ V6-8596 [S]	Verve's Choice -- Best of Count Basie	1964	$50

BASIN STREET SIX, THE
New Orleans Dixieland band that served to introduce PETE FOUNTAIN.

Albums
CIRCLE

❏ L-403 [10]	Dixieland from New Orleans	1951	$50

EMARCY

❏ MG-26012 [10]	The Basin Street Six	1954	$250

MERCURY

❏ MG-20151 [M]	Strictly Dixie	195?	$100
❏ MG-25111 [10]	The Basin Street Six	1951	$100

BASS, MARTHA AND FONTELLA
Female singers. Fontella Bass also appeared with ART ENSEMBLE OF CHICAGO.

Albums
SOUL NOTE

❏ SN-1006	From the Root to the Source	197?	$30

BASSO-VALDAMBRINI OCTET, THE

Albums
VERVE

❏ MGV-20009 [M]	Jazz Festival, Milan	1960	$100
❏ V-20009 [M]	Jazz Festival, Milan	1961	$25
❏ MGV-20011 [M]	The New Sound from Italy	1960	$100
❏ MGVS-6152 [S]	The New Sound from Italy	1960	$100
❏ V-20011 [M]	The New Sound from Italy	1961	$25
❏ V6-20011 [S]	The New Sound from Italy	1961	$25

BAUDUC, RAY, AND NAPPY LAMARE
Ray Bauduc is a drummer, male singer and bandleader; Nappy LaMare is a guitarist and male singer.

Albums
CAPITOL

❏ T877 [M]	Riverboat Dandies	1957	$75

MERCURY

❏ SR-60186 [S]	On a Swinging Date	1960	$100
❏ MG- (unknown) [M]	On a Swinging Date	1960	$100

BAUER, BILLY
Guitarist.

Albums
AD LIB

❏ AAL-5501 [10]	Let's Have a Session	1955	$200

INTERPLAY

❏ IP-8603	Anthology	198?	$30

NORGRAN

❏ MGN-1082 [M]	Billy Bauer Plectrist	1956	$80

VERVE

❏ V-8172 [M]	Billy Bauer Plectrist	1961	$25

BAXTER, LES
Bandleader; earlier a male singer and saxophone player. Best known for his pioneering work in what has become known as "exotica" music, this album seemed to fit within the scope of this book.

Albums
CAPITOL

❏ T1117 [M]	African Jazz	1958	$60

BAY CITY JAZZ BAND, THE
San Francisco-based group. Those who appear on both albums are Sanford Newbauer, Everett Farey, Walt Yost, Roy Giomi, Don Keeler and Lloyd Byassee.

Albums
GOOD TIME JAZZ

❏ S-10053 [S]	Golden Days	1969	$35
❏ L-12017 [M]	The Bay City Jazz Band	1955	$40

BAYARD, EDDIE, AND THE NEW ORLEANS CLASSIC JAZZ ORCHESTRA
Bayard is a cornet player and bandleader.

Albums
STOMP OFF

❏ SOS-1145	The Owls' Hoot	1987	$30

BAYETE
Also see TODD COCHRAN.

Albums
PRESTIGE

❏ 10062	Seeking Other Beauty	1973	$30
❏ 10045	Worlds Around the Sun	1972	$60

BEAL, JEFF
Trumpeter and composer.

Albums
ANTILLES

❏ 90625	Liberation	1987	$25
❏ 91237	Perpetual Motion	1989	$25

BEAN, BILLY
Guitarist. Also see JOHNNY PISANO AND BILLY BEAN.

Albums
RIVERSIDE

❏ RLP-380 [M]	The Trio	1961	$200
❏ RS-9380 [S]	The Trio	1961	$200

BEBOP AND BEYOND
Non-profit all-star band formed by saxophone player Mel Martin.

Albums
CONCORD JAZZ

❏ CJ-244	Bebop and Beyond	1984	$35

BECHET, SIDNEY, AND BOB WILBER
Also see each artist's individual listings.

Albums
COMMODORE

❏ 15774	New Orleans Style Old and New	198?	$25

BECHET, SIDNEY, AND BUNK JOHNSON
Also see each artist's individual listings.

Albums
JAZZ ARCHIVES

❏ JA-48	Bechet, Bunk and Boston 1945	198?	$25

BECHET, SIDNEY, AND EDDIE CONDON
Also see each artist's individual listings.

Albums
SAVOY

❏ MG-12208 [M]	We Dig Dixieland	196?	$25

BECHET, SIDNEY, AND MARTIAL SOLAL
Also see each artist's individual listings.

Albums
WORLD PACIFIC

❏ PJ-1236 [M]	Young Ideas	1957	$300
❏ WP-1236 [M]	Young Ideas	1957	$250
—Reissue with new prefix			

BECHET, SIDNEY, AND MARTY MARSALA
Marty Marsala is a trumpeter. Also see SIDNEY BECHET.

Albums
JAZZ ARCHIVES

❏ JA-44	Jazz from California	198?	$25

BECHET, SIDNEY, AND MEZZ MEZZROW
Also see each artist's individual listings.

Albums
CLASSIC JAZZ

❏ 28	Sidney Bechet and Mezz Mezzrow	198?	$30

JAZZ ARCHIVES

❏ JA-39	Really the Blues Concert	198?	$25

BECHET, SIDNEY, AND MUGGSY SPANIER
Also see each artist's individual listings.

Albums
ALLEGRO ELITE

❏ 4123 [10]	Bechet-Spanier Quartet	1956	$40

BECHET, SIDNEY, AND WINGY MANONE
Also see each artist's individual listings.

Albums
JAZZ ARCHIVES

❏ JA-29	Together at Town Hall, 1947	198?	$25

BECHET, SIDNEY
Soprano saxophone player and sometimes clarinetist. Also see ALBERT NICHOLAS.

Albums
ATLANTIC

❏ 1206 [M]	Sidney Bechet Duets	1956	$300
—With Muggsy Spanier			
❏ ALS-118 [10]	Sidney Bechet Solos	1952	$350

BLUEBIRD

❏ AXM2-5516	Master Musician	1976	$50
❏ 6590-1-RB	The Legendary Sidney Bechet	198?	$25

BLUE NOTE

❏ BLP-7008 [10]	Days Beyond Recall	1951	$500
❏ BLP-7026 [10]	Dixie by the Fabulous Sidney Bechet	1953	$500
❏ BLP-1203 [M]	Giant of Jazz, Volume 1	1955	$1200
—Deep groove" version; Lexington Ave. address on label			
❏ BLP-1203 [M]	Giant of Jazz, Volume 1	1955	$500
—Deep groove" edition, W. 63rd St. address on label			
❏ BST-81203 [R]	Giant of Jazz, Volume 1	1968	$50
—With "A Division of Liberty Records" on label			
❏ BLP-1203 [M]	Giant of Jazz, Volume 1	1963	$200
—New York, USA" on label			
❏ BLP-1204 [M]	Giant of Jazz, Volume 2	1955	$1500
—Deep groove" version (deep indentation under label on both sides)			
❏ BLP-1204 [M]	Giant of Jazz, Volume 2	1955	$1000
—Regular edition, Lexington Ave. address on label			
❏ BST-81204 [R]	Giant of Jazz, Volume 2	1968	$50
—With "A Division of Liberty Records" on label			
❏ BST-81204 [R]	Giant of Jazz, Volume 2	1971	$35
—With "A Division of United Artists Records" on label			
❏ BLP-7002 [10]	Jazz Classics, Volume 1	1950	$500
❏ BLP-1201 [M]	Jazz Classics, Volume 1	1955	$800
—Deep groove" version; Lexington Ave. address on label			
❏ BLP-1201 [M]	Jazz Classics, Volume 1	1958	$200

Number	Title	Yr	NM
—Deep groove" edition, W. 63rd St. address on label			
❑ BST-81201 [R]	Jazz Classics, Volume 1	1968	$50
—With "A Division of Liberty Records" on label			
❑ BLP-1201 [M]	Jazz Classics, Volume 1	1963	$150
—New York, USA" on label			
❑ BLP-7003 [10]	Jazz Classics, Volume 2	1950	$500
❑ BLP-1202 [M]	Jazz Classics, Volume 2	1955	$1000
—Deep groove" version; Lexington Ave. address on label			
❑ BLP-1202 [M]	Jazz Classics, Volume 2	1958	$800
—Deep groove" edition, W. 63rd St. address on label			
❑ BST-81202 [R]	Jazz Classics, Volume 2	1968	$50
—With "A Division of Liberty Records" on label			
❑ BLP-1202 [M]	Jazz Classics, Volume 2	1963	$200
—New York, USA" on label			
❑ BLP-7024 [10]	Jazz Festival Concert, Paris 1952 -- Volume 1	1953	$500
❑ BLP-7025 [10]	Jazz Festival Concert, Paris 1952 -- Volume 2	1953	$500
❑ BLP-7029 [10]	Olympia Concert, Paris 1954 -- Volume 1	1954	$500
❑ BLP-7030 [10]	Olympia Concert, Paris 1954 -- Volume 2	1954	$500
❑ BLP-7001 [10]	Sidney Bechet's Blue Note Jazz Men	1950	$1000
❑ BLP-7014 [10]	Sidney Bechet's Blue Note Jazz Men, Volume 2	1951	$500
❑ BLP-7009 [10]	Sidney Bechet with the Blue Note Jazz Men	1951	$500
❑ BLP-1207 [M]	The Fabulous Sidney Bechet	1956	$1500
—Deep groove" version; Lexington Ave. address on label			
❑ BLP-1207 [M]	The Fabulous Sidney Bechet	1956	$800
—Deep groove" edition, W. 63rd St. address on label			
❑ BST-81207 [R]	The Fabulous Sidney Bechet	1968	$30
—With "A Division of Liberty Records" on label			
❑ BLP-7020 [10]	The Fabulous Sidney Bechet and His Hot Six	1952	$500
❑ BLP-7022 [10]	The Port of Harlem Six	1952	$500
BRUNSWICK			
❑ BL54037 [M]	Sidney Bechet in Paris	1958	$80
❑ BL54048 [M]	The Sidney Bechet Story	1959	$60
COLUMBIA			
❑ CL836 [M]	Grand Master of the Soprano Sax and Clarinet	1956	$60
—Red and black label with six "eye" logos			
❑ CL1410 [M]	Sidney Bechet In Concert at the Brussels Fair	1960	$40
—Red and black label with six "eye" logos			
COMMODORE			
❑ FL-20020 [10]	New Orleans Style, Old and New	1952	$250
DIAL			
❑ LP-301 [10]	Black Stick	195?	$600
❑ LP-302 [10]	Sidney Bechet with Wally Bishop's Orchestra	195?	$600
EVEREST ARCHIVE OF FOLK & JAZZ			
❑ FS-323	Sidney Bechet Volume 2	197?	$30
❑ FS-228	Sidney Bechet with Guest Artist Lionel Hampton	1969	$30
GNP CRESCENDO			
❑ GNP-9012	Sidney Bechet	197?	$30
❑ GNP-9037	The Legendary Sidney Bechet	1976	$30
GOOD TIME JAZZ			
❑ L-12013 [M]	King of the Soprano Saxophone	1955	$60
JAZZOLOGY			
❑ J-35	The Genius of Sidney Bechet	197?	$30
JAZZ PANORAMA			
❑ 1801 [10]	Sidney Bechet, Vol. 1	1951	$200
❑ 1809 [10]	Sidney Bechet, Vol. 2	1951	$200
JOLLY ROGER			
❑ 5028 [10]	Sidney Bechet	1954	$80
LONDON			
❑ WV91050 [10]	La Nuit Est Une Sorciere	1955	$80
MCA			
❑ 1330	Blackstick	198?	$25
MOSAIC			
❑ MR6-110	The Complete Blue Note Recordings of Sidney Bechet	198?	$250
—Limited edition of 7,500			
RCA VICTOR			
❑ LPV-510 [M]	Bechet of New Orleans	1965	$30

Number	Title	Yr	NM
—Purple label original			
❑ LPV-510 [M]	Bechet of New Orleans	1969	$25
—Orange label reissue			
❑ LPV-535 [M]	Blue Bechet	1966	$30
❑ LPT-22 [10]	Sidney Bechet	1951	$300
❑ LPT-31 [10]	Treasury of Immortal Performances	1951	$300
REPRISE			
❑ R-6076 [M]	The Immortal Sidney Bechet	1963	$30
❑ R9-6076 [R]	The Immortal Sidney Bechet	1963	$25
RIVERSIDE			
❑ RLP-2516 [10]	Sidney Bechet and His Soprano Sax	1955	$300
RONDO-LETTE			
❑ A24 [M]	Jam Session Vintage 1946	1953	$40
SAVOY			
❑ MG-15013 [10]	Sidney Bechet	1952	$250
STINSON			
❑ 46 [R]	Haitian Moods	196?	$30
STORYVILLE			
❑ 4028	Sessions	198?	$25
❑ STLP-902 [M]	Sidney Bechet at Storyville	1955	$60
❑ STLP-301 [10]	Sidney Bechet at Storyville, Vol. 1	1954	$200
❑ STLP-306 [10]	Sidney Bechet at Storyville, Vol. 2	1954	$200
TIME-LIFE			
❑ STL-J-09	Giants of Jazz	1980	$50
X			
❑ LVA-3024 [10]	Sidney Bechet and His New Orleans Feetwarmers	1954	$120

BECHET, SIDNEY / OMER SIMEON

Also see each artist's individual listings.

Albums

JAZZTONE			
❑ J-1213 [M]	Jazz A La Creole	1955	$50

BECK, JOE

Electric guitarist. DAVID SANBORN was in his band on the Kudu album, before the latter became famous; when reissued in 1979, both artists were credited equally.

Albums

CTI			
❑ 8002	Beck & Sanborn	1979	$25
—Reissue of Kudu 21 with new title			
CTI/CBS ASSOCIATED			
❑ FZ40805	Beck & Sanborn	1987	$25
KUDU			
❑ 21	Beck	1975	$30
POLYDOR			
❑ PD-1-6092	Watch the Time	1976	$25

BECK, PIA

Pianist and female singer.

Albums

EPIC			
❑ LN3269 [M]	Dutch Treat	1956	$80

BEE, DAVID

Alto saxophone player.

Albums

BALLY			
❑ BAL-12005 [M]	Belgian Jazz	1956	$30
JUBILEE			
❑ JLP-1076 [M]	Dixieland at the World's Fair	1958	$30

BEEBE, JIM, 'S CHICAGO JAZZ

Trombone player and bandleader.

Albums

DELMARK			
❑ DS-219	Cornet Chop Suey	1980	$25
— With Tommy Bridges			
❑ DS-218	Saturday Night Function	1979	$25

BEIDERBECKE, BIX

Cornet player, bandleader and occasional pianist. Also see JEAN GOLDKETTE; PAUL WHITEMAN.

Albums

Number	Title	Yr	NM
BLUEBIRD			
❑ 6845-1-R	Bix Lives!	1989	$30
COLUMBIA			
❑ GL507 [M]	The Bix Beiderbecke Story, Volume 1: Bix and His Gang	1952	$50
—Black label, silver print			
❑ CL507 [M]	The Bix Beiderbecke Story, Volume 1: Bix and His Gang	1953	$40
—Maroon label, gold print			
❑ CL844 [M]	The Bix Beiderbecke Story, Volume 1: Bix and His Gang	1963	$25
—Guaranteed High Fidelity" label			
❑ CL844 [M]	The Bix Beiderbecke Story, Volume 1: Bix and His Gang	1966	$35
—360 Sound" label			
❑ CL844 [M]	The Bix Beiderbecke Story, Volume 1: Bix and His Gang	1970	$30
—Orange label			
❑ GL508 [M]	The Bix Beiderbecke Story, Volume 2: Bix and Tram	1952	$50
—Black label, silver print			
❑ CL508 [M]	The Bix Beiderbecke Story, Volume 2: Bix and Tram	1953	$40
—Maroon label, gold print			
❑ CL845 [M]	The Bix Beiderbecke Story, Volume 2: Bix and Tram	1956	$30
—Red and black label with six "eye" logos			
❑ CL845 [M]	The Bix Beiderbecke Story, Volume 2: Bix and Tram	1963	$25
—Guaranteed High Fidelity" label			
❑ CL845 [M]	The Bix Beiderbecke Story, Volume 2: Bix and Tram	1966	$35
—360 Sound" label			
❑ CL845 [M]	The Bix Beiderbecke Story, Volume 2: Bix and Tram	1970	$30
—Orange label			
❑ GL509 [M]	The Bix Beiderbecke Story, Volume 3: The Whiteman Years	1952	$50
—Black label, silver print			
❑ CL509 [M]	The Bix Beiderbecke Story, Volume 3: The Whiteman Years	1953	$40
—Maroon label, gold print			
❑ CL846 [M]	The Bix Beiderbecke Story, Volume 3: The Whiteman Years	1956	$30
—Red and black label with six "eye" logos			
❑ CL846 [M]	The Bix Beiderbecke Story, Volume 3: The Whiteman Years	1963	$25
—Guaranteed High Fidelity" label			
❑ CL846 [M]	The Bix Beiderbecke Story, Volume 3: The Whiteman Years	1966	$35
—360 Sound" label			
❑ CL846 [M]	The Bix Beiderbecke Story, Volume 3: The Whiteman Years	1970	$30
—Orange label			
COLUMBIA MASTERWORKS			
❑ ML4811 [M]	The Bix Beiderbecke Story, Volume 1	1950	$125
❑ ML4812 [M]	The Bix Beiderbecke Story, Volume 2	1950	$125
❑ ML4813 [M]	The Bix Beiderbecke Story, Volume 3	1950	$125
EVEREST ARCHIVE OF FOLK & JAZZ			
❑ 317	Bix Beiderbecke	197?	$25
JAZZ TREASURY			
❑ S-1003	Bix Beiderbecke with the Wolverines	197?	$30
JOLLY ROGER			
❑ 5010 [10]	Bix Beiderbecke	1954	$50
MILESTONE			
❑ 47019	Bix Beiderbecke and the Chicago Cornets	197?	$35
OLYMPIC			
❑ 7130	Bix Beiderbecke and the Wolverines 1924	198?	$25
RCA VICTOR			
❑ LPM-2323 [M]	The Bix Beiderbecke Legend	1961	$30
—Long Play" on label			

Number	Title	Yr	NM
❑ LPM-2323 [M]	The Bix Beiderbecke Legend	1963	$35

—Mono" or "Monaural" on label

RIVERSIDE

❑ RLP-1050 [10]	Bix Beiderbecke and the Wolverines	1954	$300
❑ RLP 12-123 [M]	Bix Beiderbecke and the Wolverines	1956	$250

—White label, blue print

❑ RLP 12-123 [M]	Bix Beiderbecke and the Wolverines	195?	$30

—Blue label with microphone logo

❑ RLP-1023 [10]	Early Bix	1954	$300

TIME-LIFE

❑ STL-J-04	Giants of Jazz	1979	$50

BEIRACH, RICHIE, AND JOHN ABERCROMBIE
Also see each artist's individual listings.

Albums

PATHFINDER

❑ PTF-8701	Emerald City	1988	$25

BEIRACH, RICHIE
Pianist.

Albums

ECM

❑ 1142	Elm	1979	$30
❑ 1054	Eon	197?	$35
❑ 1104	Hubris	1977	$30

MAGENTA

❑ MA-0202	Breathing of Statues	1985	$25

PATHFINDER

❑ PTF-8617	Antarctica	1987	$25

BELGRAVE, MARCUS
Trumpeter and flugel horn player.

Albums

TRIBE

❑ 2228	Gemini II	1975	$35

BELL, AARON
Mostly a bass player, though also plays piano, trumpet and tuba. Also see THE MANHATTAN ALL STARS.

Albums

HERALD

❑ HLP-0100 [M]	Three Swinging Bells	1955	$75

LION

❑ L-70111 [M]	Music from "77 Sunset Strip"	1959	$30
❑ L-70112 [M]	Music from "Peter Gunn"	1959	$30
❑ L-70113 [M]	Music from "Victory at Sea"	1959	$30

RCA VICTOR

❑ LPM-1876 [M]	After the Party's Over	1958	$50

BELL, CHARLES
Pianist.

Albums

ATLANTIC

❑ 1400 [M]	Another Dimension	1963	$150
❑ SD1400 [S]	Another Dimension	1963	$150

COLUMBIA

❑ CL1582 [M]	The Charles Bell Contemporary Jazz Quartet	1961	$200
❑ CS8382 [S]	The Charles Bell Contemporary Jazz Quartet	1961	$200

GATEWAY

❑ 7012 [M]	Charles Bell in Concert	1964	$35
❑ S-7012 [S]	Charles Bell in Concert	1964	$25

BELL, DEE
Female singer.

Albums

CONCORD JAZZ

❑ CJ-206	Let There Be Love	1982	$25

BELL, GRAEME
Pianist and bandleader.

Albums

ANGEL

❑ ANG.60002 [10]	Inside Jazz Down Under	1954	$60

JAZZOLOGY

❑ J-75	Graeme Bell Jazz	197?	$30

BELL, MARTY
Male singer. He is backed on the below album by DON ELLIOTT.

Albums

RIVERSIDE

❑ RLP 12-206 [M]	The Voice of Marty Bell	1956	$250

—White label, blue print

❑ RLP 12-206 [M]	The Voice of Marty Bell	1957	$300

—Blue label, microphone logo

BELLETTO, AL
Mostly an alto saxophone player, he also plays baritone sax and clarinet.

Albums

CAPITOL

❑ T751 [M]	Half and Half	1956	$80
❑ T6514 [M]	Sounds and Songs	1955	$100
❑ T6506 [M]	The Al Belletto Sextette	1955	$100
❑ T901 [M]	Whisper Not	1957	$150

KING

❑ 716 [M]	The Big Sound	1961	$50

BELLSON, LOUIS, AND GENE KRUPA
Also see each artist's individual listings.

Albums

ROULETTE

❑ R-52098 [M]	The Mighty Two	1962	$25
❑ SR-52098 [S]	The Mighty Two	1962	$30

BELLSON, LOUIS, AND LALO SCHIFRIN
Also see each artist's individual listings.

Albums

ROULETTE

❑ R-52120 [M]	Explorations	1964	$35
❑ SR-52120 [S]	Explorations	1964	$25

BELLSON, LOUIS, AND WALFREDO DE LOS REYES
Reyes is a drummer and percussionist most often associated with Cuban and Puerto Rican music. Also see LOUIS BELLSON.

Albums

FANTASY

❑ OJC-632	Edue Ritmos Cubanos	1991	$30

—Reissue of Pablo 2310 807

PABLO

❑ 2310807	Edue Ritmos Cubanos	1978	$30

BELLSON, LOUIS
Drummer, bandleader, arranger and composer.

Albums

ABC IMPULSE!

❑ AS-9107 [S]	Thunderbird	1968	$30

—Reissue of Impulse AS-9107

CAPITOL

❑ H348 [10]	Just Jazz All-Stars	1952	$300

CONCORD JAZZ

❑ CJ-36	150 M P H	1977	$30
❑ CJ-105	Dynamite!	1979	$30
❑ CJ-350	Live at the Jazz Showcase	1988	$30
❑ CJ-157	London Scene	198?	$30
❑ CJ-64	Prime Time	1978	$30
❑ CJ-73	Raincheck	1978	$30
❑ CJ-141	Side Track	198?	$30
❑ CJ-20	The Louis Bellson 7 Live at the Concord Festival	1977	$30

DISCWASHER

❑ 002	Note Smoking	1979	$30

—Direct-to-disc recording

IMPULSE!

❑ A-9107 [M]	Thunderbird	1966	$120
❑ AS-9107 [S]	Thunderbird	1966	$120

NORGRAN

❑ MGN-1085 [M]	Concerto for Drums	1956	$0

—Canceled

❑ MGN-1007 [M]	Journey Into Love	1954	$300
❑ MGN-1011 [M]	Louis Bellson and His Drums	1954	$300
❑ MGN-7 [10]	The Amazing Artistry of Louis Bellson	1954	$200
❑ MGN-1020 [M]	The Driving Louis Bellson	1955	$200
❑ MGN-14 [10]	The Exciting Mr. Bellson (And His Big Band)	1954	$200

PABLO

❑ 2310899	Cool, Cool Blue	198?	$30
❑ 2310755	Explosion	1975	$35
❑ 2310838	Jam	1979	$30
❑ 2310880	London Gig	198?	$30
❑ 2310834	Matterhorn	1979	$30
❑ 2310813	Sunshine Rock	1978	$30
❑ 2405407	The Best of Louis Bellson	198?	$30

PROJECT 3

❑ PR5029SD	Breakthrough!	1968	$35

ROULETTE

❑ R-65002 [M]	Around the World in Percussion	1962	$25
❑ SR-65002 [S]	Around the World in Percussion	1962	$30
❑ R-52087 [M]	Big Band Jazz from the Summit	1962	$25
❑ SR-52087 [S]	Big Band Jazz from the Summit	1962	$30

SEAGULL

❑ LG-8208	Louis Bellson and Orchestra	198?	$25

VERVE

❑ V-8016 [M]	Concerto for Drums	1961	$25
❑ MGV-8354 [M]	Drummer's Holiday	1959	$100
❑ V-8354 [M]	Drummer's Holiday	1959	$100
❑ MGV-8193 [M]	Drumorama!	1957	$125
❑ V-8193 [M]	Drumorama!	1957	$125
❑ MGV-8258 [M]	Let's Call It Swing	1958	$150
❑ V-8258 [M]	Let's Call It Swing	1958	$150
❑ MGV-8256 [M]	Louis Bellson at the Flamingo	1958	$120
❑ V-8256 [M]	Louis Bellson at the Flamingo	1958	$120
❑ MGV-2131 [M]	Louis Bellson Swings Jules Styne	1960	$100
❑ MGVS-6138 [S]	Louis Bellson Swings Jules Styne	1960	$100
❑ V-2131 [M]	Louis Bellson Swings Jules Styne	1960	$100
❑ V6-2131 [S]	Louis Bellson Swings Jules Styne	1960	$100
❑ MGV-8280 [M]	Music, Romance and Especially Love	1958	$120
❑ V-8280 [M]	Music, Romance and Especially Love	1958	$120
❑ MGV-8137 [M]	Skin Deep	1957	$50

—Reissue of Norgran 1046

❑ V-8137 [M]	Skin Deep	1957	$100
❑ MGV-2123 [M]	The Brilliant Bellson Sound	1960	$120
❑ MGVS-6093 [S]	The Brilliant Bellson Sound	1960	$120
❑ V-2123 [M]	The Brilliant Bellson Sound	1960	$120
❑ V6-2123 [S]	The Brilliant Bellson Sound	1960	$120
❑ MGV-8186 [M]	The Hawk Talks	1957	$300

—Reissue of Norgran 1099

❑ V-8186 [M]	The Hawk Talks	1957	$150

VOSS

❑ VLP1-42936	Note Smoking	1988	$25

—Reissue of Discwasher 002

BELLSON, LOUIS/ RAY BROWN/PAUL SMITH
Also see each artist's individual listings.

Albums

PAUSA

❑ 7167	Intensive Care	1978	$30

VOSS

❑ VLP1-42933	Intensive Care	1988	$25

—Reissue

BELVIN, JESSE
Primarily a rhythm and blues singer, the below album is in a jazz vein.

Albums

RCA VICTOR

❑ LSP-2105 [S]	Mr. Easy	1960	$40

BENNETT, BETTY

Albums

ATLANTIC

❑ 1226 [M]	Nobody Else But Me	1956	$300

—Black label

❑ 1226 [M]	Nobody Else But Me	1961	$150

Number	Title	Yr	NM

— Multicolor label, white "fan" logo

TREND
| ❏ TL-1006 [10] | Betty Bennett Sings Previn Arrangements | 1954 | $120 |

UNITED ARTISTS
| ❏ UAL-3070 [M] | I Love to Sing | 1959 | $40 |
| ❏ UAS-6070 [S] | I Love to Sing | 1959 | $50 |

BENNETT, BOBBY
Female singer.

BENNETT, MAX
Bass player. Was a member of TOM SCOTT's L.A. Express in the 1970s.

Albums
BETHLEHEM
| ❏ BCP-48 [M] | Johnny Jaguar | 1957 | $250 |
| ❏ BCP-1028 [10] | Max Bennett Quintet | 1955 | $250 |

PALO ALTO
| ❏ TBA-216 | The Drifter | 1986 | $25 |

BENNETT, RICHARD RODNEY
Pianist and composer. Also has worked in the classical realm.

Albums
AUDIOPHILE
| ❏ AP-168 | Harold Arlen's Songs | 1982 | $25 |
| ❏ AP-206 | Take Love Easy | 1985 | $25 |

DRG
| ❏ SL-5182 | A Different Side of Sondheim | 1978 | $25 |
| ❏ DRG-6102 | Special Occasions | 1979 | $25 |

BENNETT, TONY, AND BILL EVANS

Albums
DRG
| ❏ MRS-901 | Together Again | 1985 | $20 |

FANTASY
| ❏ F-9489 | The Tony Bennett/Bill Evans Album | 1975 | $30 |

IMPROV
| ❏ 7117 | Together Again | 1978 | $30 |

MOBILE FIDELITY
| ❏ 1-117 | The Tony Bennett/Bill Evans Album | 1981 | $40 |

— Audiophile vinyl

BENNETT, TONY, AND COUNT BASIE
Also see each artist's individual listings.

Albums
COLUMBIA
| ❏ CL1294 [M] | Tony Bennett In Person | 1959 | $60 |
| ❏ CS8104 [S] | Tony Bennett In Person | 1959 | $40 |

COLUMBIA LIMITED EDITION
| ❏ LE10125 | Tony Bennett In Person | 197? | $30 |

ROULETTE
❏ R25231 [M]	Bennett and Basie Strike Up the Band	1963	$50
❏ SR25231 [S]	Bennett and Basie Strike Up the Band	1963	$60
❏ R25072 [M]	Count Basie Swings/Tony Bennett Sings	1961	$60
❏ SR25072 [S]	Count Basie Swings/Tony Bennett Sings	1961	$60

BENNETT, TONY
Male singer. Mostly a pop singer in the 1950s and 1960s ("Because of You," "Cold, Cold Heart" and "I Left My Heart In San Francisco" are among his hits), he turned to the jazz repertoire in the 1970s and beyond. For a more complete discography, see the Standard Catalog of American Records.

Albums
COLUMBIA
❏ FC44029	Bennett/Berlin	1987	$25
❏ C63668	Bennett Sings Ellington -- Hot and Cool	1999	$30
❏ FC40344	The Art of Excellence	1986	$25
❏ CG40424	Tony Bennett Jazz	1987	$30

DRG
| ❏ MRS-910 | Make Magnificent Music | 1985 | $25 |
| ❏ DARC-2-2102 | The Rodgers and Hart Songbook | 1986 | $35 |

IMPROV
❏ 7123	Beautiful Music	1979	$30
❏ 7112	Life Is Beautiful	1975	$30
❏ 7120	Tony Bennett Sings More Rodgers and Hart	1978	$30
❏ 7113	Tony Bennett Sings Rodgers and Hart	197?	$30

BENOIT, DAVID
Pianist and composer.

Albums
AVI
❏ AV-6074	Can You Imagine	1980	$15
❏ AV-8620	Christmastime	1985	$15
❏ AV-6138	Digits	1984	$15
❏ AV-6025	Heavier Than Yesterday	1977	$20
❏ AV-6214	Stages	1983	$15
❏ AV-8712	Waves of Raves	1986	$15

GRP
❏ 1047	Every Step of the Way	1987	$15
❏ 1035	Freedom at Midnight	1986	$15
❏ 9621	Inner Motion	1990	$15
❏ 9587	Urban Daydreams	1989	$15
❏ 9595	Waiting for Spring	1989	$15

SPINDLETOP
| ❏ STP-104 | This Side Up | 1986 | $15 |

BENSON, GEORGE
Guitarist and male singer who had many hit singles as a vocalist from the mid-1970s into the early 1980s.

Albums
A&M
| ❏ SP-3014 | Shape of Things to Come | 1969 | $50 |

— Brown label
| ❏ SP-3014 | Shape of Things to Come | 1976 | $30 |

— Silvery label with fading "A&M" logo
| ❏ SP9-3014 | Shape of Things to Come | 1983 | $35 |

— Audio Master Plus" reissue
| ❏ SP-3020 | Tell It Like It Is | 1969 | $50 |

— Brown label
| ❏ SP-3020 | Tell It Like It Is | 1976 | $30 |

— Silvery label with fading "A&M" logo
| ❏ SP9-3020 | Tell It Like It Is | 1984 | $35 |

— Audio Master Plus" reissue
| ❏ SP-3203 | The Best of George Benson | 1983 | $25 |
| ❏ SP-3028 | The Other Side of Abbey Road | 1970 | $60 |

— Brown label
| ❏ SP-3028 | The Other Side of Abbey Road | 1976 | $30 |

— Silvery label with fading "A&M" logo
| ❏ SP9-3028 | The Other Side of Abbey Road | 1984 | $35 |

— Audio Master Plus" reissue

COLUMBIA
❏ CG33569	Benson Burner	1976	$30
❏ CL2613 [M]	The George Benson Cook Book	1967	$50
❏ CS9413 [S]	The George Benson Cook Book	1967	$50

— Red "360 Sound" label
| ❏ CS9413 | The George Benson Cook Book | 1976 | $25 |

— Orange label
| ❏ PC9413 | The George Benson Cook Book | 198? | $20 |

— Reissue with new prefix
| ❏ CL2525 [M] | The Most Exciting New Guitarist on the Jazz Scene Today -- It's Uptown | 1966 | $50 |
| ❏ CS9325 [S] | The Most Exciting New Guitarist on the Jazz Scene Today -- It's Uptown | 1966 | $50 |

— Red "360 Sound" label
| ❏ CS9325 | The Most Exciting New Guitarist on the Jazz Scene Today -- It's Uptown | 1976 | $25 |

— Orange label
| ❏ PC9325 | The Most Exciting New Guitarist on the Jazz Scene Today -- It's Uptown | 198? | $20 |

— Reissue with new prefix

CTI
❏ 6045	Bad Benson	1974	$30
❏ 6069	Benson & Farrell	1976	$30
❏ 6009	Beyond the Blue Horizon	1971	$30
❏ 6033	Body Talk	1973	$30
❏ CTSQ-6033 [Q]	Body Talk	1973	$60
❏ 8030	Cast Your Fate to the Wind	1982	$25
❏ 6072	George Benson In Concert -- Carnegie Hall	1976	$30
❏ 6062	Good King Bad	1976	$30
❏ 8031	Summertime: In Concert	198?	$25
❏ 8014	Take Five	198?	$25
❏ 6015	White Rabbit	1972	$30
❏ 8009	White Rabbit	198?	$25

FANTASY
| ❏ OJC-461 | The New Boss Guitar of George Benson | 1990 | $30 |

— Reissue of Prestige 7310

MOBILE FIDELITY
| ❏ Jan-0011 | Breezin' | 1979 | $120 |

— Audiophile vinyl

POLYDOR
| ❏ PD-1-6084 | Blue Benson | 1976 | $25 |

PRESTIGE
❏ 24072	George Benson & Jack McDuff	1976	$35
❏ PRLP-7310 [M]	The New Boss Guitar of George Benson	1964	$60
❏ PRST-7310 [S]	The New Boss Guitar of George Benson	1964	$40

VERVE
| ❏ V6-8771 | Goodies | 1969 | $50 |

WARNER BROS.
❏ 25178	20/20	1985	$25
❏ 26295	Big Boss Band	1990	$35
❏ BS2919	Breezin'	1976	$35

— With no mention of "This Masquerade" on front cover
| ❏ BS2919 | Breezin' | 1976 | $25 |

— With "Contains This Masquerade" on front cover
| ❏ BSK3111 | Breezin' | 1977 | $20 |

— Reissue of 2919
❏ HS3453	Give Me the Night	1980	$25
❏ BSK2983	In Flight	1977	$25
❏ 23744	In Your Eyes	1983	$25
❏ 2BSK3277	Livin' Inside Your Love	1979	$30
❏ 25907	Tenderly	1989	$30
❏ 2HS3577	The George Benson Collection	1981	$30
❏ 25705	Twice the Love	1988	$25
❏ 2WS3139	Weekend in L.A.	1978	$30
❏ 25475	While the City Sleeps…	1986	$25

BENTON, WALTER
Tenor saxophone player.

BERG, BOB
Tenor saxophone player, also sometimes heard on soprano sax.

Albums
RED
| ❏ VPA-178 | Steppin' -- Live in Europe | 1985 | $30 |

XANADU
| ❏ 159 | New Birth | 1978 | $35 |

BERGAMO, JOHN
Percussionist and composer.

Albums
CMP
| ❏ CMP-27-ST | On the Edge | 1987 | $25 |

BERGER, BENGT
Drummer, percussionist and bandleader.

Albums
ECM
| ❏ 1179 | Bitter Funeral Beer | 1981 | $30 |

BERGER, KARL
Vibraphone and pianist.

Albums
CMC
| ❏ 00101 | Peace Church | 197? | $25 |

ENJA
| ❏ 2022 | With Silence | 1974 | $35 |

ESP-DISK'
| ❏ 1041 [M] | Karl Berger | 1967 | $250 |
| ❏ S-1041 [S] | Karl Berger | 1967 | $250 |

MILESTONE
| ❏ MSP-9026 | Tune In | 1969 | $35 |

Number	Title	Yr	NM

BERGMAN, BORAH
Pianist.
Albums
CHIAROSCURO

Number	Title	Yr	NM
❏ 158	Bursts of Joy	1979	$30
❏ 125	Discovery	1973	$35
❏ 118	Solo	1972	$35

SOUL NOTE

| ❏ SN-1030 | New Frontier | 1984 | $30 |
| ❏ SN-1080 | Upside Down Visions | 1985 | $30 |

BERIGAN, BUNNY, AND WINGY MANONE
Also see each artist's individual listings.
Albums
X

| ❏ LVA-3034 [10] | Swing Session 1934 | 1954 | $80 |

BERIGAN, BUNNY
Trumpeter and male singer.
Albums
BIOGRAPH

| ❏ C-10 | Bunny Berigan 1932-37 | 197? | $30 |

BLUEBIRD

❏ AXM2-5584	The Complete Bunny Berigan, Volume 1	197?	$35
❏ 5657-1-RB[(2)]	The Complete Bunny Berigan, Volume 2	1987	$35
❏ 9953-1-RB[(2)]	The Complete Bunny Berigan, Volume 3	1990	$35

EPIC

| ❏ LA16004 [M] | Bunny Berigan and His Boys | 196? | $25 |
| ❏ LN3109 [M] | Take It, Bunny! | 1955 | $100 |

HINDSIGHT

| ❏ HSR-239 | Bunny Berigan 1937-38 | 1988 | $25 |

JAZZ ARCHIVES

| ❏ JA-11 | Down by the Old Mill Stream | 198? | $25 |

MCA

| ❏ 1362 | Decca/Champion Sessions | 198? | $30 |

RCA CAMDEN

| ❏ CAL-550 [M] | Bunny | 195? | $25 |

RCA VICTOR

❏ LPV-550 [M]	Bunny	1966	$25
❏ LPT-10 [10]	Bunny Berigan 1937-38	1951	$80
❏ LPT-1003 [M]	Bunny Berigan Plays Again	1952	$50
❏ LPM-2078 [M]	Great Dance Bands of the 30s and 40s	1959	$40

TIME-LIFE

| ❏ STL-J-25 | Giants of Jazz | 1982 | $50 |

BERIGAN, BUNNY/JACK TEAGARDEN
Also see each artist's individual listings.
Albums
FOLKWAYS

| ❏ FJ-2819 | The Big Band Sound of Bunny Berigan and Jack Teagarden | 1982 | $30 |

BERK, DICK, AND THE JAZZ ADOPTION AGENCY
Drummer and bandleader.
Albums
DISCOVERY

❏ DS-890	Big Jake	1986	$25
❏ DS-922	More Birds Less Feathers	1987	$25
❏ DS-877	The Rare One	1985	$25

TREND

| ❏ 550 | Lover | 198? | $25 |

BERLINER, JAY
Acoustic guitarist.
Albums
MAINSTREAM

| ❏ 384 | Bananas Not Equal | 1973 | $35 |

BERLINER, PAUL, AND KUDU
Ethnomusicologist and occasional male singer who plays a variety of traditional African instruments.
Albums
FLYING FISH

| ❏ FF-092 | The Sun Rises Later Here | 1979 | $35 |

Number	Title	Yr	NM

BERMAN, SONNY
Trumpeter.
Albums
ESOTERIC

| ❏ ES-532 [M] | Sonny Berman 1946 | 1954 | $120 |

BERNE, TIM, AND BILL FRISELL
Also see each artist's individual listings.
Albums
EMPIRE

| ❏ EPC72K | ...Theoretically | 1984 | $50 |

MINOR MUSIC

| ❏ 08 | …Theoretically | 1986 | $35 |

BERNE, TIM
Alto saxophone player.
Albums
COLUMBIA

| ❏ FC40530 | Fulton Street Maul | 1987 | $30 |
| ❏ FC44073 | Sanctified Dreams | 1987 | $30 |

EMPIRE

❏ EPC36K	7X	1980	$50
❏ EPC60K-2	Songs and Rituals in Real Time	1982	$60
❏ EPC48K	Spectres	1981	$50
❏ EPC24K	The Five Year Plan	1979	$50

JMT

| ❏ 834431-1 | Fractured Fairy Tales | 1989 | $35 |

SOUL NOTE

| ❏ SN-1091 | Mutant Variations | 1984 | $30 |
| ❏ SN-1061 | The Ancestors | 1983 | $30 |

BERNHARDT, WARREN
Pianist.
Albums
ARISTA/NOVUS

❏ AN3011	Floating	1979	$30
❏ AN3020	Manhattan Update	1980	$30
❏ AN3001	Solo Piano	1978	$30

BERNHART, MILT
Trombonist.
Albums
DECCA

| ❏ DL9214 [M] | The Sounds of Bernhart | 1959 | $80 |
| ❏ DL79214 [S] | The Sounds of Bernhart | 1959 | $80 |

RCA VICTOR

| ❏ LPM-1123 [M] | Modern Brass | 1955 | $250 |

BERNSTEIN, LEONARD
Composer and conductor, mostly in the classical realm. The below album features the first Columbia recordings of MILES DAVIS.
Albums
COLUMBIA

| ❏ CL919 [M] | What Is Jazz? | 1956 | $100 |

—Red and black label with six "eye" logos

BERRY, BILL
Trumpeter and fluegel horn player.
Albums
CONCORD JAZZ

| ❏ CJ-27 | Hello Rev | 1977 | $30 |
| ❏ CJ-75 | Shortcake | 1978 | $30 |

DIRECTIONAL SOUND

| ❏ 5002 [M] | Jazz and Swinging Percussion | 1963 | $25 |
| ❏ S-5002 [S] | Jazz and Swinging Percussion | 1963 | $30 |

PARADE

| ❏ SP-353 [M] | Broadway Escapades | 196? | $25 |

BERRY, CHU
Tenor saxophone player.
Albums
COMMODORE

❏ XFL15353	A Giant of the Tenor Sax	198?	$25
❏ DL-30017 [M]	Chu Berry	1959	$80
❏ FL-20024 [10]	Chu Berry Memorial	1952	$250

Number	Title	Yr	NM

ENCORE

| ❏ EE22007 | Chu (1936-1940) | 1968 | $35 |

EPIC

| ❏ LG3124 [M] | Chu | 1955 | $150 |

MAINSTREAM

| ❏ 56038 [M] | Sittin' In | 1965 | $30 |
| ❏ S-6038 [R] | Sittin' In | 1965 | $35 |

BERT, EDDIE
Trombonist.
Albums
DISCOVERY

| ❏ DL-3020 [M] | Eddie Bert Quintet | 1953 | $300 |

JAZZTONE

| ❏ J-1223 [M] | Modern Moods | 1956 | $200 |

SAVOY

| ❏ MG-12015 [M] | Musician of the Year | 1955 | $75 |

SAVOY JAZZ

| ❏ SJL-1186 | Kaleidoscope | 198? | $25 |

SOMERSET

| ❏ SF-5200 [M] | Like Cool | 1958 | $40 |

—Reissue of Trans World LP

TRANS WORLD

| ❏ TWLP-208 [M] | Let's Dig Bert | 1955 | $100 |

BERTONCINI, GENE, AND MICHAEL MOORE
Michael Moore is a bass player. Also see GENE BERTONCINI.
Albums
OMNISOUND

| ❏ GJB-3333 | Bridges | 198? | $30 |
| ❏ GJB-3334 | Close Ties | 198? | $30 |

STASH

| ❏ ST-258 | O Grande Amor: A Bossa Nova Collection | 1986 | $25 |
| ❏ ST-272 | Strollin' | 1987 | $25 |

BERTONCINI, GENE
Acoustic guitarist.
Albums
EVOLUTION

| ❏ 3001 | Evolution | 1969 | $35 |

BEST, JOHNNY/DICK CATHCART
Best was a trumpeter and occasional bandleader. Also see DICK CATHCART.
Albums
MERCURY

| ❏ PPM-2009 [M] | Dixieland | 1961 | $100 |
| ❏ PPS-6009 [S] | Dixieland (Left and Right) | 1961 | $100 |

—Odd record with Best's band in the left channel and Cathcart's in the right!

BETTERS, HAROLD
Trombonist.
Albums
GATEWAY

❏ GLP-7014 [M]	Do Anything You Wanna	1966	$25
❏ GS-7014 [S]	Do Anything You Wanna	1966	$35
❏ GLP-7008 [M]	Even Better	1966	$25
❏ GS-7008 [S]	Even Better	1966	$35
❏ GLP-7001 [M]	Harold Betters at the Encore	1964	$25
❏ GS-7001 [S]	Harold Betters at the Encore	1964	$35
❏ GLP-7009 [M]	Harold Betters Meets Slide Hampton	1966	$25
❏ GS-7009 [S]	Harold Betters Meets Slide Hampton	1966	$35
❏ 7021	Jazz Showcase	197?	$30
❏ GLP-7015 [M]	Swingin' on the Railroad	1966	$25
❏ GS-7015 [S]	Swingin' on the Railroad	1966	$35
❏ GLP-7004 [M]	Take Off	1964	$25
❏ GS-7004 [S]	Take Off	1964	$35
❏ 7017	The Best of Betters	197?	$30

REPRISE

❏ R-6241 [M]	Funk City Express	1966	$35
❏ RS-6241 [S]	Funk City Express	1966	$25
❏ R-6208 [M]	Out of Sight and Sound	1966	$35
❏ RS-6208 [S]	Out of Sight and Sound	1966	$25
❏ R-6195 [M]	Ram-Bunk-Shush	1965	$35
❏ RS-6195 [S]	Ram-Bunk-Shush	1965	$25

Sidney Bechet, *Sidney Bechet and His New Orleans Feetwarmers*, "X" LVA-3024, **$60**.

George Benson and Earl Klugh, Collaboration, Warner Bros. 25580, **$20**.

Art Blakey, *Blakey*, EmArcy MG 26030, 10-inch LP, **$500**.

Art Blakey, *Drum Suite*, Columbia CL1002, red and black label with six "eye" logos, **$60**.

BICKERT, ED, AND DON THOMPSON
Also see each artist's individual listings.

Albums

SACKVILLE

Number	Title	Yr	NM
4010	Dance to the Lady	198?	$25
4005	Ed Bickert & Don Thompson	198?	$25

BICKERT, ED
Guitarist.

Albums

CONCORD JAZZ

Number	Title	Yr	NM
CJ-232	Bye Bye Baby	1983	$25
CJ-216	Ed Bickert at Toronto's Bourbon Street	1982	$25
CJ-284	I Wished on the Moon	1985	$25
CJ-380	Third Floor Richard	1989	$25

PM

Number	Title	Yr	NM
PMR-010	Ed Bickert	1976	$30

BIGARD, BARNEY, AND ART HODES
Also see each artist's individual listings.

Albums

DELMARK

Number	Title	Yr	NM
DS-211	Bucket's Got a Hole In It	1969	$35

BIGARD, BARNEY
Clarinetist and tenor saxophone player.

Albums

LIBERTY

Number	Title	Yr	NM
LRP-3072 [M]	Jazz Hall of Fame	1957	$40

BIGARD, BARNEY/ALBERT NICHOLAS
Also see each artist's individual listings.

Albums

RCA VICTOR

Number	Title	Yr	NM
LPV-566 [M]	Barney Bigard/Albert Nicholas	1966	$25

BILK, ACKER, AND BENT FABRIC
Also see each artist's individual listings.

Albums

ATCO

Number	Title	Yr	NM
33-175 [M]	Together	1965	$30
SD 33-175 [S]	Together	1965	$35

BILK, ACKER, AND KEN COLYER
Also see each artist's individual listings.

Albums

STOMP OFF

Number	Title	Yr	NM
SOS-1119	It Looks Like a Big Time Tonight	198?	$25

BILK, ACKER
Clarinetist and bandleader. His rendition of "Stranger on the Shore" was a chart-topper in both the United States and his native Great Britain.

Albums

ATCO

Number	Title	Yr	NM
33-144 [M]	Above the Stars	1962	$35
SD 33-144 [S]	Above the Stars	1962	$50
33-181 [M]	Acker Bilk in Paris	1966	$30
SD 33-181 [S]	Acker Bilk in Paris	1966	$35
33-168 [M]	A Touch of Latin	1964	$30
SD 33-168 [S]	A Touch of Latin	1964	$35
33-158 [M]	Call Me Mister	1963	$35
SD 33-158 [S]	Call Me Mister	1963	$50
33-170 [M]	Great Themes from Great Foreign Films	1965	$30
SD 33-170 [S]	Great Themes from Great Foreign Films	1965	$35
33-197 [M]	Mood for Love	1966	$30
SD 33-197 [S]	Mood for Love	1966	$35
33-150 [M]	Only You	1963	$35
SD 33-150 [S]	Only You	1963	$50
33-129 [M]	Stranger on the Shore	1961	$35
SD 33-129 [S]	Stranger on the Shore	1961	$50

GNP CRESCENDO

Number	Title	Yr	NM
GNPS-2191	Acker Bilk Plays Lennon and McCartney	1988	$30
GNPS-2116	The Best of Acker Bilk: His Clarinet and Strings	198?	$25
GNPS-2171	The Best of Acker Bilk: His Clarinet and Strings, Volume 2	198?	$25

REPRISE

Number	Title	Yr	NM
R-6031 [M]	A Stranger No More	1962	$50
RS-6031 [R]	A Stranger No More	1962	$35

BISHOP, JOHN
Guitarist.

Albums

TANGERINE

Number	Title	Yr	NM
TRCS-1508	Bishop's Whirl	1969	$35
TRCS-1513	John Bishop Plays His Guitar	1970	$35

BISHOP, WALTER, JR.
Pianist.

Albums

BLACK JAZZ

Number	Title	Yr	NM
2	Coral Keys	1972	$35
QD-14 [Q]	Keeper of My Soul	1974	$40

INTERPLAY

Number	Title	Yr	NM
IP-8605	Just in Time	1988	$25

JAZZTIME

Number	Title	Yr	NM
JS-002 [S]	Speak Low	1961	$250

MUSE

Number	Title	Yr	NM
5151	Cubicle	1978	$30
5183	Hot House	1979	$30
5142	Soul Village	1977	$30
5066	Speak Low	1976	$30

— Reissue of Jazztime JS-002

Number	Title	Yr	NM
5060	Valley Land	1976	$30

PRESTIGE

Number	Title	Yr	NM
PRST-7730	The Walter Bishop Trio 1965	1969	$25

SEABREEZE

Number	Title	Yr	NM
1002	Soliloquy	1975	$30

XANADU

Number	Title	Yr	NM
114	Bish Bash	1977	$30

BLACK BOTTOM STOMPERS (ENGLAND)
Named after one of the great early jazz bands, this group plays traditional Dixieland-style material. Many changes of personnel over the years, with John Goddard (trombone) appearing to have been a constant.

Albums

STOMP OFF

Number	Title	Yr	NM
SOS-1045	Stomp Off, Let's Go	1982	$25

BLACK BOTTOM STOMPERS (SWITZERLAND)
Similar to its UK namesake, this group plays traditional Dixieland-style material.

Albums

STOMP OFF

Number	Title	Yr	NM
SOS-1130	Four O'Clock Blues	1987	$25

BLACK EAGLE JAZZ BAND
See NEW BLACK EAGLE JAZZ BAND.

BLACKBYRDS, THE
Mostly vocal group founded by DONALD BYRD, though he is not a member.

Albums

FANTASY

Number	Title	Yr	NM
F-9535	Action	1977	$30
F-9602	Better Days	1980	$30
F-9490	City Life	1975	$35
F-9472	Flying Start	1974	$35
FPM-4004 [Q]	Flying Start	1975	$40
F-9570	Night Grooves	1978	$30
F-9444	The Blackbyrds	1974	$35
F-9518	Unfinished Business	1976	$35

BLACKMAN, CINDY
Drummer.

Albums

MUSE

Number	Title	Yr	NM
MR-5341	Arcane	1988	$30

BLAIR, SALLIE

Albums

BETHLEHEM

Number	Title	Yr	NM
BCP-6009 [M]	Squeeze Me	1957	$250

MGM

Number	Title	Yr	NM
E-3723 [M]	Hello, Tiger!	1959	$40
SE-3723 [S]	Hello, Tiger!	1959	$50

BLAIR, TOM
Female singer.

BLAKE, BETTY
Female singer.

BLAKE, EUBIE
Pianist and composer.

Albums

BIOGRAPH

Number	Title	Yr	NM
1011	Blues & Ragtime	1972	$30
1012	Blues & Spirituals	1972	$30

COLUMBIA

Number	Title	Yr	NM
C2S847	The Eighty-Six Years of Eubie Blake	1969	$25

— Red "360 Sound" labels

Number	Title	Yr	NM
C2S847	The Eighty-Six Years of Eubie Blake	1970	$35

— Orange labels

EUBIE BLAKE MUSIC

Number	Title	Yr	NM
EBM-4	Early Rare Recordings	197?	$30
EBM-7	Early Rare Recordings, Vol. 2	197?	$30
EBM-8	Eubie Blake and His Proteges	197?	$30
EBM-1	Eubie Blake Featuring Ivan Harold Browning	197?	$30
EBM-3	Eubie Blake with Edith Wilson and Ivan Harold Browning	197?	$30
EBM-6	Introducing Jim Hession	197?	$30
EBM-5	Live Concert	197?	$30
EBM-2	Rags to Classics: Charlestown Rag	197?	$30
EBM-9	Song Hits	197?	$30

QUICKSILVER

Number	Title	Yr	NM
QS-9003	Tricky Fingers	198?	$25

BLAKE, RAN
Pianist. Also see JAKI BYARD.

Albums

ARISTA/NOVUS

Number	Title	Yr	NM
AN3019	Film Noir	1980	$30
AN3006	Rapport	1978	$30

ESP-DISK'

Number	Title	Yr	NM
1011 [M]	Ran Blake Plays Solo Piano	1965	$250
S-1011 [S]	Ran Blake Plays Solo Piano	1965	$250

GC

Number	Title	Yr	NM
4176	Take One	197?	$30
4177	Take Two	197?	$30

GM RECORDINGS

Number	Title	Yr	NM
GM-3007	Painted Rhythms: The Compleat Ran Blake, Vol. 1	1987	$30
GM-3008	Painted Rhythms: The Compleat Ran Blake, Vol. 2	1989	$30

IAI

Number	Title	Yr	NM
373842	Breakthru	1976	$30

MILESTONE

Number	Title	Yr	NM
MSP-9021	The Blue Potato	1969	$35

OWL

Number	Title	Yr	NM
029	Portrait of Doktor Mabuse	1978	$35
012	The Realization of a Dream	1978	$35
017	Third Stream Recompositions	1977	$35
041	Vertigo	1986	$35

SOUL NOTE

Number	Title	Yr	NM
SN-1027	Duke Dreams	198?	$30
SN-1077	Suffield Gothic	1983	$30

BLAKEY, ART, AND THE JAZZ MESSENGERS
Blakey was a drummer and bandleader. The Jazz Messengers were a somewhat fluid organization of musicians. Some of the below albums credit only Art Blakey; others only the Jazz Messengers; others credit both.

Albums

ABC IMPULSE!

Number	Title	Yr	NM
❑ AS-45 [S]	A Jazz Message	1968	$30
—Reissue of Impulse AS-45			
❑ AS-7 [S]	Art Blakey!!!! Jazz Messengers!!!!	1968	$30
—Reissue of Impulse AS-7			
BETHLEHEM			
❑ BCP-6027 [M]	Art Blakey's Big Band	1958	$250
❑ BCPS-6027 [S]	Art Blakey's Big Band	1959	$200
❑ BCP-6037	Hard Drive	197?	$30
—Reissue of 6023, distributed by RCA Victor			
❑ BCP-6015	The Finest of Art Blakey	197?	$30
—Reissue of 6027, distributed by RCA Victor			
BLUEBIRD			
❑ 6286-1-RB	Theory of Art	1987	$25
BLUE NOTE			
❑ BLP-1521 [M]	A Night at Birdland, Volume 1	1956	$800
—Regular version, Lexington Ave. address on label			
❑ BLP-1521 [M]	A Night at Birdland, Volume 1	1957	$350
—With W. 63rd St. address on label			
❑ BLP-1521 [M]	A Night at Birdland, Volume 1	1963	$200
—With "New York, USA" address on label			
❑ BST-81521 [R]	A Night at Birdland, Volume 1	1968	$60
—With "A Division of Liberty Records" on label			
❑ BLP-1521 [M]	A Night at Birdland, Volume 1	1967	$100
—A Division of Liberty Records" on label			
❑ BLP-5038 [10]	A Night at Birdland, Volume 2	1954	$800
❑ BLP-1522 [M]	A Night at Birdland, Volume 2	1956	$1000
—Regular version, Lexington Ave. address on label			
❑ BLP-1522 [M]	A Night at Birdland, Volume 2	1957	$750
—With W. 63rd St. address on label			
❑ BLP-1522 [M]	A Night at Birdland, Volume 2	1963	$500
—With "New York, USA" address on label			
❑ BST-81522 [R]	A Night at Birdland, Volume 2	1968	$25
—With "A Division of Liberty Records" on label			
❑ BLP-5039 [10]	A Night at Birdland, Volume 3	1954	$300
❑ BLP-4049 [M]	A Night in Tunisia	1960	$150
—Regular version, with W. 63rd St. address on label			
❑ BLP-4049 [M]	A Night in Tunisia	1963	$60
—With "New York, USA" address on label			
❑ BST-84049 [S]	A Night in Tunisia	1960	$60
—With W. 63rd St. address on label			
❑ BST-84049 [S]	A Night in Tunisia	1963	$25
—With "New York, USA" address on label			
❑ BST-84049 [S]	A Night in Tunisia	196?	$30
—With "A Division of Liberty Records" on label			
❑ B1-84049	A Night in Tunisia	1989	$25
—The Finest in Jazz Since 1939" reissue			
❑ BLP-4003 [M]	Art Blakey and the Jazz Messengers	1958	$200
—Regular version, with W. 63rd St. address on label			
❑ BST-4003 [S]	Art Blakey and the Jazz Messengers	1959	$80
—Regular version, with W. 63rd St. address on label			
❑ BST-4003 [S]	Art Blakey and the Jazz Messengers	1963	$25
—With "New York, USA" address on label			
❑ BST-84003 [S]	Art Blakey and the Jazz Messengers	196?	$30
—With "A Division of Liberty Records" on label			
❑ BLP-1507 [M]	At the Café Bohemia, Volume 1	1956	$200
—Regular version, Lexington Ave. address on label			
❑ BLP-1507 [M]	At the Café Bohemia, Volume 1	1957	$100
—With W. 63rd St. address on label			
❑ BLP-1507 [M]	At the Café Bohemia, Volume 1	1963	$60
—With "New York, USA" address on label			
❑ BST-81507 [R]	At the Café Bohemia, Volume 1	1968	$25
—With "A Division of Liberty Records" on label			
❑ BST-81507 [M]	At the Café Bohemia, Volume 1	1985	$25
—The Finest in Jazz Since 1939" reissue			
❑ BLP-1508 [M]	At the Café Bohemia, Volume 2	1956	$200
—Regular version, Lexington Ave. address on label			
❑ BLP-1508 [M]	At the Café Bohemia, Volume 2	1957	$100
—With W. 63rd St. address on label			
❑ BLP-1508 [M]	At the Café Bohemia, Volume 2	1963	$60
—With "New York, USA" address on label			
❑ BST-81508 [R]	At the Café Bohemia, Volume 2	1968	$25
—With "A Division of Liberty Records" on label			
❑ B1-81508	At the Café Bohemia, Volume 2	1987	$25
—The Finest in Jazz Since 1939" reissue			
❑ BLP-4015 [M]	At the Jazz Corner of the World, Volume 1	1958	$150
—Regular version, with W. 63rd St. address on label			
❑ BLP-4015 [M]	At the Jazz Corner of the World, Volume 1	1963	$60
—With "New York, USA" address on label			
❑ BST-84015 [S]	At the Jazz Corner of the World, Volume 1	1959	$350
—Deep groove" version (deep indentation under label on both sides)			
❑ BST-84015 [S]	At the Jazz Corner of the World, Volume 1	1959	$60
—Regular version, with W. 63rd St. address on label			
❑ BST-84015 [S]	At the Jazz Corner of the World, Volume 1	1963	$25
—With "New York, USA" address on label			
❑ BST-84015 [S]	At the Jazz Corner of the World, Volume 1	196?	$30
—With "A Division of Liberty Records" on label			
❑ BLP-4016 [M]	At the Jazz Corner of the World, Volume 2	1958	$150
—Regular version, with W. 63rd St. address on label			
❑ BLP-4016 [M]	At the Jazz Corner of the World, Volume 2	1963	$60
—With "New York, USA" address on label			
❑ BST-84016 [S]	At the Jazz Corner of the World, Volume 2	1959	$60
—Regular version, with W. 63rd St. address on label			
❑ BST-84016 [S]	At the Jazz Corner of the World, Volume 2	1963	$25
—With "New York, USA" address on label			
❑ BST-84016 [S]	At the Jazz Corner of the World, Volume 2	196?	$30
—With "A Division of Liberty Records" on label			
❑ BST-84016 [S]	At the Jazz Corner of the World, Volume 2	197?	$25
—New darker label; with "United Artists Music and Records Group" on label			
❑ BLP-4104 [M]	Buhaina's Delight	1962	$60
—With "New York, USA" on label			
❑ BST-84104 [S]	Buhaina's Delight	1962	$40
—With "New York, USA" address on label			
❑ BST-84104 [S]	Buhaina's Delight	196?	$30
—With "A Division of Liberty Records" on label			
❑ BLP-4170 [M]	Free for All	1965	$60
❑ BST-84170 [S]	Free for All	1965	$40
—With "New York, USA" address on label			

Number	Title	Yr	NM
❑ BST-84170 [S]	Free for All	196?	$30
—With "A Division of Liberty Records" on label			
❑ BLP-4004 [M]	Holiday for Skins, Volume 1	1958	$200
—Deep groove" version (deep indentation under label on both sides)			
❑ BLP-4004 [M]	Holiday for Skins, Volume 1	1958	$150
—Regular version, with W. 63rd St. address on label			
❑ BLP-4004 [M]	Holiday for Skins, Volume 1	1963	$60
—With "New York, USA" address on label			
❑ BST-4004 [S]	Holiday for Skins, Volume 1	1959	$150
—Deep groove" version (deep indentation under label on both sides)			
❑ BST-4004 [S]	Holiday for Skins, Volume 1	1959	$120
—Regular version, with W. 63rd St. address on label			
❑ BST-4004 [S]	Holiday for Skins, Volume 1	1963	$25
—With "New York, USA" address on label			
❑ BST-84004 [S]	Holiday for Skins, Volume 1	196?	$30
—With "A Division of Liberty Records" on label			
❑ BLP-4005 [M]	Holiday for Skins, Volume 2	1958	$200
—Deep groove" version (deep indentation under label on both sides)			
❑ BLP-4005 [M]	Holiday for Skins, Volume 2	1958	$150
—Regular version, with W. 63rd St. address on label			
❑ BLP-4005 [M]	Holiday for Skins, Volume 2	1963	$60
—With "New York, USA" address on label			
❑ BST-4005 [S]	Holiday for Skins, Volume 2	1959	$150
—Deep groove" version (deep indentation under label on both sides)			
❑ BST-4005 [S]	Holiday for Skins, Volume 2	1959	$120
—Regular version, with W. 63rd St. address on label			
❑ BST-4005 [S]	Holiday for Skins, Volume 2	1963	$25
—With "New York, USA" address on label			
❑ BST-84005 [S]	Holiday for Skins, Volume 2	196?	$30
—With "A Division of Liberty Records" on label			
❑ BLP-4193 [M]	Indestructible	1966	$60
❑ BST-84193 [S]	Indestructible	1966	$40
—With "New York, USA" address on label			
❑ BST-84193 [S]	Indestructible	196?	$30
—With "A Division of Liberty Records" on label			
❑ BST-84193 [S]	Indestructible	1986	$25
—The Finest in Jazz Since 1939" reissue			
❑ BLP-4245 [M]	Like Someone in Love	1967	$80
❑ BST-84245 [S]	Like Someone in Love	1967	$40
—With "New York, USA" address on label			
❑ BST-84245 [S]	Like Someone in Love	196?	$30
—With "A Division of Liberty Records" on label			
❑ B1-84245	Like Someone in Love	1989	$25
—The Finest in Jazz Since 1939" reissue			
❑ BN-LA473-4047	Live Messengers	1975	$35
❑ BLP-4054 [M]	Meet You at the Jazz Corner of the World, Volume 1	1960	$125
—With W. 63rd St. address on label			
❑ BLP-4054 [M]	Meet You at the Jazz Corner of the World, Volume 1	1963	$60
—With "New York, USA" address on label			
❑ BST-84054 [S]	Meet You at the Jazz Corner of the World, Volume 1	1960	$60
—With W. 63rd St. address on label			
❑ BST-84054 [S]	Meet You at the Jazz Corner of the World, Volume 1	1963	$25
—With "New York, USA" address on label			
❑ BST-84054 [S]	Meet You at the Jazz Corner of the World, Volume 1	196?	$30
—With "A Division of Liberty Records" on label			
❑ BLP-4055 [M]	Meet You at the Jazz Corner of the World, Volume 2	1960	$125
—With W. 63rd St. address on label			
❑ BLP-4055 [M]	Meet You at the Jazz Corner of the World, Volume 2	1963	$60
—With "New York, USA" address on label			
❑ BST-84055 [S]	Meet You at the Jazz Corner of the World, Volume 2	1960	$60
—With W. 63rd St. address on label			
❑ BST-84055 [S]	Meet You at the Jazz Corner of the World, Volume 2	1963	$25
—With "New York, USA" address on label			
❑ BST-84055 [S]	Meet You at the Jazz Corner of the World, Volume 2	196?	$30
—With "A Division of Liberty Records" on label			
❑ B1-46516	Moanin'	199?	$35
—Audiophile reissue of 84003			
❑ BLP-4090 [M]	Mosaic	1961	$150
—With 61st St. address on label			
❑ BLP-4090 [M]	Mosaic	1963	$60

Number	Title	Yr	NM
— With "New York, USA" address on label			
❏ BST-84090 [S]	Mosaic	1961	$120
— With 61st St. address on label			
❏ BST-84090 [S]	Mosaic	1963	$25
— With "New York, USA" address on label			
❏ BST-84090 [S]	Mosaic	196?	$30
— With "A Division of Liberty Records" on label			
❏ B1-46523	Mosaic	199?	$35
— Audiophile reissue			
❏ LT-1065	Once Upon a Groove	1980	$25
❏ BLP-1554 [M]	Orgy in Rhythm, Volume 1	1957	$750
— Deep groove" version (deep indentation under label on both sides)			
❏ BLP-1554 [M]	Orgy in Rhythm, Volume 1	1957	$200
— Regular version, with W. 63rd St. address on label			
❏ BLP-1554 [M]	Orgy in Rhythm, Volume 1	1963	$150
— With "New York, USA" address on label			
❏ BST-81554 [R]	Orgy in Rhythm, Volume 1	1968	$25
— With "A Division of Liberty Records" on label			
❏ BLP-1555 [M]	Orgy in Rhythm, Volume 2	1957	$300
— Regular version, with W. 63rd St. address on label			
❏ BLP-1555 [M]	Orgy in Rhythm, Volume 2	1957	$850
— Deep groove" version (deep indentation under label on both sides)			
❏ BLP-1555 [M]	Orgy in Rhythm, Volume 2	1963	$150
— With "New York, USA" address on label			
❏ BST-81555 [R]	Orgy in Rhythm, Volume 2	1968	$25
— With "A Division of Liberty Records" on label			
❏ BST-84347	Roots and Herbs	1970	$30
— With "Liberty/UA" on label			
❏ BLP-4097 [M]	The African Beat	1961	$150
— With 61st St. address on label			
❏ BLP-4097 [M]	The African Beat	1963	$60
— With "New York, USA" address on label			
❏ BST-84097 [S]	The African Beat	1961	$60
— With 61st St. address on label			
❏ BST-84097 [S]	The African Beat	1963	$30
— With "New York, USA" address on label			
❏ BST-84097 [S]	The African Beat	196?	$30
— With "A Division of Liberty Records" on label			
❏ B1-93205	The Best of Art Blakey and the Jazz Messengers	1989	$30
❏ BLP-4029 [M]	The Big Beat	1960	$300
— Deep groove" version (deep indentation under label on both sides)			
❏ BLP-4029 [M]	The Big Beat	1960	$150
— Regular version, with W. 63rd St. address on label			
❏ BLP-4029 [M]	The Big Beat	1963	$60
— With "New York, USA" address on label			
❏ BST-84029 [S]	The Big Beat	1960	$60
— With W. 63rd St. address on label			
❏ BST-84029 [S]	The Big Beat	1963	$25
— With "New York, USA" address on label			
❏ BST-84029 [S]	The Big Beat	196?	$30
— With "A Division of Liberty Records" on label			
❏ BST-84029 [S]	The Big Beat	1985	$25
— The Finest in Jazz Since 1939" reissue			
❏ BLP-4156 [M]	The Freedom Rider	1964	$60
❏ BST-84156 [S]	The Freedom Rider	1964	$40
— With "New York, USA" address on label			
❏ BST-84156 [S]	The Freedom Rider	196?	$30
— With "A Division of Liberty Records" on label			
❏ BST-84258 [S]	The Witch Doctor	1969	$25
— With "A Division of Liberty Records" on label			
CADET			
❏ LP-4049 [M]	Tough!	1966	$30
❏ LPS-4049 [S]	Tough!	1966	$30
CATALYST			
❏ 7902	Jazz Messengers '70	197?	$30
COLUMBIA			
❏ CL1002 [M]	Drum Suite	1957	$60
— Red and black label with six "eye" logos			

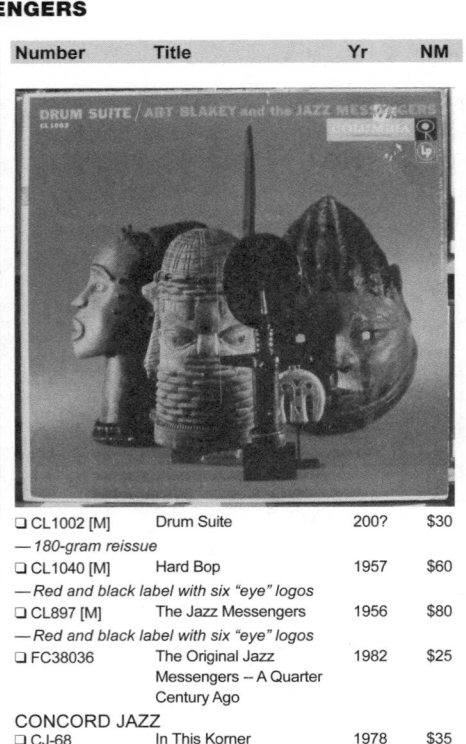

Number	Title	Yr	NM
❏ CL1002 [M]	Drum Suite	200?	$30
— 180-gram reissue			
❏ CL1040 [M]	Hard Bop	1957	$60
— Red and black label with six "eye" logos			
❏ CL897 [M]	The Jazz Messengers	1956	$80
— Red and black label with six "eye" logos			
❏ FC38036	The Original Jazz Messengers -- A Quarter Century Ago	1982	$25
CONCORD JAZZ			
❏ CJ-68	In This Korner	1978	$35
❏ CJ-196	Keystone 3	1982	$25
❏ CJ-307	Live at Kimball's	1986	$25
❏ CJ-256	New York Scene	1984	$25
❏ CJ-168	Straight Ahead	1981	$25
ELEKTRA			
❏ EKL-120 [M]	A Midnight Session with the Jazz Messengers	1957	$80
EMARCY			
❏ MG-26030 [10]	Blakey	1954	$500
EPIC			
❏ LA16017 [M]	Art Blakey in Paris	1961	$60
❏ BA17017 [S]	Art Blakey in Paris	1961	$80
❏ LA16009 [M]	Paris Concert	1960	$60
❏ BA17009 [S]	Paris Concert	1960	$80
EVEREST ARCHIVE OF FOLK & JAZZ			
❏ 332	Jazz Messengers	197?	$25
FANTASY			
❏ OJC-038	Caravan	198?	$25
❏ OJC-145	Kyoto	198?	$25
❏ OJC-090	Ugetsu	198?	$25
GNP CRESCENDO			
❏ GNPS-2182	Live at Sweet Basil	1986	$25
IMPULSE!			
❏ A-45 [M]	A Jazz Message	1963	$200
❏ AS-45 [S]	A Jazz Message	1963	$160
❏ A-7 [M]	Art Blakey!!!! Jazz Messengers!!!!	1961	$120
❏ AS-7 [S]	Art Blakey!!!! Jazz Messengers!!!!	1961	$160
JOSIE			
❏ JOZ-3501 [M]	Cu-Bop	1962	$40
— Reissue of Jubilee LP			
❏ JS-3501 [S]	Cu-Bop	1962	$30
JUBILEE			
❏ JLP-1049 [M]	Cu-Bop	1958	$80
LIMELIGHT			
❏ LM-82034 [M]	Buttercorn Lady	1966	$25
❏ LS-86034 [S]	Buttercorn Lady	1966	$30
❏ LM-82038 [M]	Hold On, I'm Coming	1966	$25
❏ LS-86038 [S]	Hold On, I'm Coming	1966	$30
❏ LM-82001 [M]	'S Make It	1965	$25
❏ LS-86001 [S]	'S Make It	1965	$30
❏ LM-82019 [M]	Soul Finger	1965	$25
❏ LS-86019 [S]	Soul Finger	1965	$30
MCA IMPULSE!			
❏ MCA-5648	A Jazz Message	1986	$20
— Reissue			
MILESTONE			
❏ 47008	Thermo	197?	$35
MOSAIC			
❏ MR10-141	The Complete Blue Note Recordings of Art Blakey's 1960 Jazz Messengers	199?	$150
ODYSSEY			
❏ PC36809	Hard Bop	1981	$25
❏ PC37021	The Jazz Messengers	1981	$25
PACIFIC JAZZ			

Number	Title	Yr	NM
❏ PJM-402 [M]	Ritual	1957	$80
❏ PJ-15 [M]	Ritual	1961	$40
— Reissue of 402			
PRESTIGE			
❏ 10076	Anthenagin	197?	$30
❏ 10067	Buhaina	197?	$30
❏ 10047	Child's Dance	197?	$15
RCA VICTOR			
❏ LPM-2654 [M]	A Night in Tunisia	1963	$40
— Reissue of Vik 1115			
❏ LSP-2654 [R]	A Night in Tunisia	1963	$25
RIVERSIDE			
❏ RS-438 [M]	Caravan	1962	$200
❏ RS-9438 [S]	Caravan	1962	$200
❏ 6074	Caravan	197?	$30
❏ RS-493 [M]	Kyoto	1966	$100
❏ RS-9493 [S]	Kyoto	1966	$100
❏ RS-464 [M]	Ugetsu	1963	$150
❏ RS-9464 [S]	Ugetsu	1963	$150
❏ RS-3022	Ugetsu	1968	$100
ROULETTE			
❏ SR-5003	Backgammon	1976	$30
❏ SR-5008	Gypsy Folk Tales	1977	$30
SAVOY			
❏ MG-12171 [M]	Art Blakey and the Jazz Messengers	1960	$30
SAVOY JAZZ			
❏ SJL-1112	Mirage	1977	$35
SOLID STATE			
❏ SS-18033	Three Blind Mice	1969	$30
SOUL NOTE			
❏ 121155-1	I Get a Kick Out of You	1990	$30
❏ 121105-1	Not Yet	1989	$30
TIMELESS			
❏ SJP-307	Feel the Wind	1990	$30
❏ 301	In My Prime, Vol. 1	1979	$30
❏ 317	Reflections in Blue	1980	$30
TRIP			
❏ 5019	Art Blakey and the Jazz Messengers	197?	$25
❏ 5034	Art Blakey and the Jazz Messengers Live	197?	$25
❏ 5505	Buttercorn Lady	197?	$25
UNITED ARTISTS			
❏ UAJ-14002 [M]	Three Blind Mice	1962	$40
❏ UAJS-15002 [S]	Three Blind Mice	1962	$50
❏ UAS-5633	Three Blind Mice	197?	$25
VEE JAY			
❏ VJS-3066	Bag of Blues Featuring Buddy DeFranco	1977	$30
VIK			
❏ LX-1115 [M]	A Night in Tunisia	1958	$100
❏ LX-1103 [M]	Art Blakey and the Jazz Messengers Play Selections from Lerner and Loewe	1957	$100

BLAKEY, ART, AND THE JAZZ MESSENGERS/ ELMO HOPE

Albums

PACIFIC JAZZ

❏ PJ-33 [M]	The Jazz Messengers and Elmo Hope	1962	$40

BLAKEY, ART, AND THE JAZZ MESSENGERS/ MAX ROACH

Also see each artist's individual listings.

Albums

CHESS

❏ CH2-92511	Percussion Discussion	198?	$35

BLAKEY, ART, AND THE JAZZ MESSENGERS WITH THELONIOUS MONK

Also see each artist's individual listings.

Albums

ATLANTIC

❏ 1278 [M]	Art Blakey's Jazz Messengers with Thelonious Monk	1958	$300
— Black label			
❏ 1278 [M]	Art Blakey's Jazz Messengers with Thelonious Monk	1960	$300
— Multicolor label, white "fan" logo			

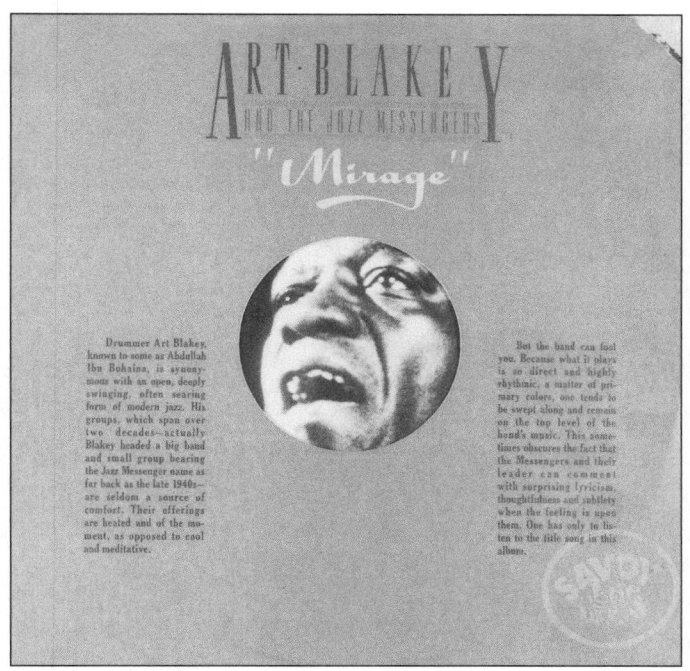

Art Blakey, *Mirage*, Savoy Jazz SJL-1112, **$35**.

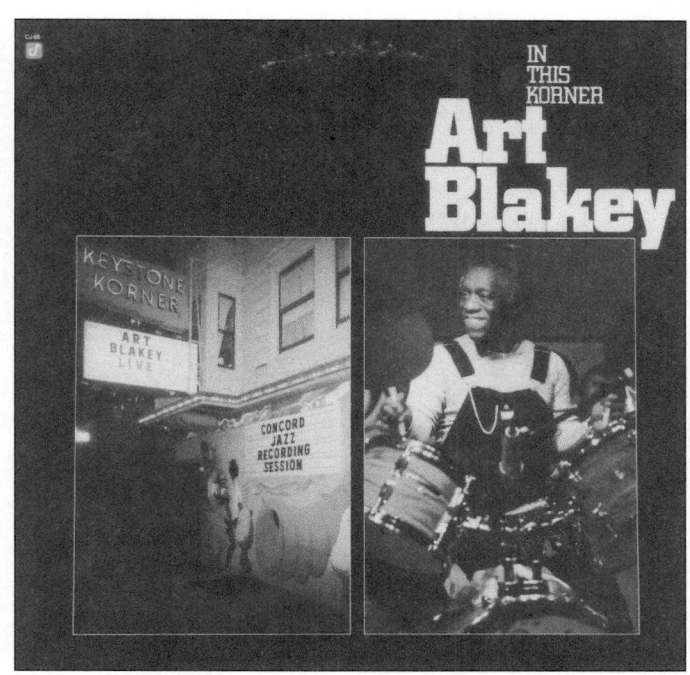

Art Blakey, *In This Korner* – Concord Jazz CJ-68, **S35**.

Paul Bley, *Introducing Paul Bley*, Debut DLP-7, **$600**.

Ronnell Bright, *Bright's Spot*, Regent MG 6041, **$100**.

Number	Title	Yr	NM
❑ 1278 [M]	Art Blakey's Jazz Messengers with Thelonious Monk	1963	$150
—Multicolor label, black "fan" logo			
❑ SD1278 [S]	Art Blakey's Jazz Messengers with Thelonious Monk	1959	$300
—Green label			
❑ SD1278 [S]	Art Blakey's Jazz Messengers with Thelonious Monk	1960	$300
—Multicolor label, white "fan" logo			
❑ SD1278 [S]	Art Blakey's Jazz Messengers with Thelonious Monk	1963	$150
—Multicolor label, black "fan" logo			
ODYSSEY			
❑ 32160246	Art Blakey with the Original Jazz Messengers	1968	$35

BLANCHARD, PIERRE
Violinist. Also see LEE KONITZ.

Albums
SUNNYSIDE
| ❑ SSC-1023 | Music for String Quartet, Jazz Trio, Violin and Lee Konitz | 1988 | $25 |

BLANCHARD, TERENCE, AND DONALD HARRISON
Harrison is an alto saxophone player. Both are alumni of ART BLAKEY AND HIS JAZZ MESSENGERS.

Albums
COLUMBIA
❑ FC44216	Black Pearl	1988	$25
❑ FC40830	Crystal Star	1987	$25
❑ BFC40335	Nascence	1986	$25
GEORGE WEIN COLLECTION
❑ GW-3008	Discernment	1986	$30
❑ GW-3002	New York Second Line	1984	$30

BLAZING REDHEADS
Quartet consisting of Danielle Dowers, drums; Michaelle Goerlitz, timbales/congas/percussion; Klaudia Promessi, saxophone/flute; and Donna Viscuso, saxophone/flute/piccolo/harmonica.

Albums
REFERENCE RECORDINGS
| ❑ RR-26 | Blazing Redheads | 1988 | $25 |
| ❑ RR-41 | Crazed Women | 1991 | $25 |

BLEY, CARLA
Pianist, composer and conductor.

Albums
ECM
| ❑ 25003 | Heavy Heart | 1984 | $25 |
ECM/WATT
❑ ECM W-14	Heavy Heart	1983	$30
❑ ECM W-122-Jan	I Hate to Sing	1982	$30
❑ ECM W-12	Live!	1982	$30
❑ ECM W-11	Social Studies	1980	$30
JCOA
❑ 3-LP-EOTH	Escalator Over the Hill	1971	$30
WATT
❑ 6	Dinner Music	1976	$35
❑ 8	European Tour 1977	1978	$35
❑ 9	Musique Mecanique	1979	$35
❑ 1	Tropic Appetites	1974	$35

BLEY, PAUL, AND GARY PEACOCK
Also see each artist's individual listings.

Albums
ECM
| ❑ 1003ST | Paul Bley with Gary Peacock | 1973 | $35 |
| *—Original issue, made in Germany?* | | | |

BLEY, PAUL, AND NIELS-HENNING ORSTED PEDERSEN
Also see each artist's individual listings.

Albums
INNER CITY
| ❑ IC-2005 | Paul Bley and Niels-Henning Orsted Pedersen | 1973 | $35 |
STEEPLECHASE
| ❑ SCS-1005 | Paul Bley and Niels-Henning Orsted Pedersen | 198? | $30 |

BLEY, PAUL; GARY PEACOCK; BARRY ALTSCHUL
Barry Altschul is a drummer. Also see PAUL BLEY; GARY PEACOCK.

Albums
IAI
| ❑ 373849 | Japan Suite | 1977 | $35 |
| ❑ 373844 | Virtuosi | 1976 | $35 |

BLEY, PAUL
Pianist and synthesizer player. Also see CHET BAKER AND PAUL BLEY.

Albums
ARISTA/FREEDOM
| ❑ AL1901 | Copenhagen and Haarlem | 197? | $50 |
DEBUT
| ❑ DLP-7 [10] | Introducing Paul Bley | 1954 | $600 |
ECM
❑ 1010ST	Ballads	1973	$50
—Original issue, made in Germany?			
❑ 1320	Fragments	198?	$35
—Made in Germany			
❑ 1023ST	Open to Love	1974	$35
—Original issue, made in Germany?			
❑ ECM-1-1023	Open to Love	197?	$30
—Distributed by Polydor			
EMARCY
❑ MG-36092 [M]	Paul Bley	1955	$200
ESP-DISK'
❑ 1008 [M]	Barrage	1965	$250
❑ S-1008 [S]	Barrage	1965	$250
❑ 1021 [M]	Closer	1966	$250
❑ S-1021 [S]	Closer	1966	$250
FANTASY
❑ OJC-201	Introducing Paul Bley	198?	$150
—Reissue of Debut 7			
GENE NORMAN
❑ GNP-31 [M]	Solemn Meditation	1957	$80
GNP CRESCENDO
❑ GNPS-31 [R]	Solemn Meditation	197?	$35
❑ GT-3002	Solemn Meditation	198?	$35
IAI
❑ 373840	Alone Again	1975	$35
❑ 373853	Axis	1978	$50
❑ 373839	Quiet Song	1975	$35
—With Jimmy Giuffre and Bill Connors			
❑ 373841	Turning Point	1975	$30
—With John Gilmore			
INNER CITY
❑ IC-1007	Live at the Hillcrest 1958	197?	$35
LIMELIGHT
❑ LS-86060	Mr. Joy	1968	$175
MILESTONE
❑ MSP-9046	Paul Bley and Scorpio	1973	$120
—Reproductions exist			
❑ MSP-9033	Synthesizer Show	1970	$150
OWL
❑ 034	Tears	1984	$40
SAVOY
❑ MG-12182 [M]	Footloose!	1964	$80
SAVOY JAZZ
❑ SJL-1148	Floater	1984	$35
❑ SJL-1175	Syndrome	1987	$35
❑ SJL-1192	Turns	1988	$35
SOUL NOTE
❑ SN-1140	Paul Bley Group	1986	$35
❑ SN-1085	Sonor	1984	$35
❑ SN-1090	Tango Palace	1985	$35
STEEPLECHASE
❑ SCS-1214	My Standard	198?	$35
❑ SCS-1205	Questions	198?	$50
❑ SCS-1236	Solo Piano	198?	$50
❑ SCS-1246	The Nearness of You	198?	$35
TRIP
❑ TLP-5587	Mr. Joy	197?	$35
WING
❑ MGW-60001 [M]	Paul Bley	1956	$120

BLOOD, SWEAT AND TEARS
Jazz-rock band formed by Al Kooper, who appeared only on Child Is Father to the Man. He was replaced by lead singer David Clayton-Thomas. The group's jazz quotient varied from album to album.

Albums
ABC
| ❑ 1015 | Brand New Day | 1977 | $25 |
CBS SPECIAL PRODUCTS
| ❑ P16660 | Musically Speaking | 1982 | $25 |
COLUMBIA
❑ CS9720	Blood, Sweat and Tears	1969	$35
—Red "360 Sound" label			
❑ CS9720	Blood, Sweat and Tears	1970	$25
—Orange label			
❑ PC9720	Blood, Sweat and Tears	1980	$20
❑ KC30090	Blood, Sweat and Tears 3	1970	$25
❑ PC30090	Blood, Sweat and Tears 3	1986	$20
❑ KC31170	Blood, Sweat and Tears' Greatest Hits	1972	$25
—With the single versions of "You've Made Me So Very Happy," "Spinning Wheel," and "And When I Die" (all in mono)			
❑ PC31170	Blood, Sweat and Tears' Greatest Hits	1980	$20
❑ PCQ31170 [Q]	Blood, Sweat and Tears' Greatest Hits	1976	$60
—Reissue with new prefix			
❑ KC30590	BS&T: 4	1971	$25
❑ CS9616 [S]	Child Is Father to the Man	1968	$35
—Red "360 Sound" label			
❑ CS9616	Child Is Father to the Man	1970	$25
—Orange label			
❑ PC9619	Child Is Father to the Man	1980	$20
❑ HC49619	Child Is Father to the Man	1981	$100
—Half-speed mastered edition			
❑ CS9616 [M]	Child Is Father to the Man	1968	$350
—White label promo only, "Special Mono Radio Station Copy" sticker on cover, with same number as stereo edition			
❑ PC32929	Mirror Image	1974	$25
❑ PC34233	More Than Ever	1976	$25
❑ KC31780	New Blood	1972	$25
❑ PC33484	New City	1975	$25
❑ KC32180	No Sweat	1973	$25
DIRECT DISK
❑ SD-16605	Blood, Sweat and Tears	1981	$120
MCA
❑ 3227	Blood, Sweat and Tears	1981	$0
—Canceled?			
❑ L33-1865 [DJ]	Nuclear Blues	1980	$35
—Promo only on gold vinyl			
❑ 3061	Nuclear Blues	1980	$25
MOBILE FIDELITY
❑ 1-251	Blood, Sweat and Tears	1996	$100
—Audiophile vinyl; fewer than 2,000 pressed			

BLUE BIRD SOCIETY ORCHESTRA, THE

Albums
STASH
| ❑ ST-268 | The Blue Bird Society Orchestra | 1987 | $25 |

BLUE STARS
Vocal group from France, formed by American BLOSSOM DEARIE. Their version of "Lullaby of Birdland" was a top-20 U.S. pop hit in early 1956. Some members of the group later were in THE DOUBLE SIX OF PARIS and THE SWINGLE SINGERS.

Albums
EMARCY
| ❑ MG-36067 [M] | Lullaby of Birdland | 1956 | $200 |

BLUIETT, HAMIET
Baritone saxophone player, sometimes a flutist. Also see WORLD SAXOPHONE QUARTET.

Albums
BLACK SAINT

Number	Title	Yr	NM
❏ BSR-0014	Resolution	198?	$30
CHIAROSCURO			
❏ CH-182	Orchestra, Duo and Sextet	1978	$30
INDIA NAVIGATION			
❏ IN-1030	Birthright	1977	$30
❏ IN-1025	Endangered Species	1976	$30
❏ IN-1039	S.O.S.	1979	$30
SOUL NOTE			
❏ SN-1018	Dangerously Suite	198?	$30
❏ SN-1088	Ebu	1985	$30

BLYTHE, ARTHUR
Alto saxophone player and bandleader.
Albums

Number	Title	Yr	NM
ADELPHI			
❏ 5008	Bush Baby	1978	$30
COLUMBIA			
❏ FC37427	Blythe Spirit	1981	$25
❏ FC40237	Da-Da	1986	$25
❏ FC38163	Elaborations	1982	$25
❏ JC36583	Illusions	1980	$25
❏ PC36583	Illusions	198?	$20
— Budget-line reissue			
❏ JC36300	In the Tradition	1979	$25
❏ JC35638	Lenox Avenue Breakdown	1979	$25
❏ FC38661	Light Blue	1983	$25
❏ FC39411	Put Sunshine In It	1984	$25
INDIA NAVIGATION			
❏ IN-1038	Metamorphosis	1979	$30
❏ IN-1029	The Grip	1977	$30

BLYTHE, JIMMY
Pianist; pioneer in the "boogie-woogie" style.
Albums

Number	Title	Yr	NM
EUPHORIA			
❏ EES-101	Messin' Around	198?	$30
❏ EES-102	Messin' Around, Vol. 2	198?	$30
RIVERSIDE			
❏ RLP-1031 [10]	Chicago Stomps and the Dixie Four	1954	$300
❏ RLP-1036 [10]	Jimmy Blythe's State Street Ramblers	1954	$300

BOBO, WILLIE
Percussionist (generally congas, timbales and drums) and occasional male singer.
Albums

Number	Title	Yr	NM
BLUE NOTE			
❏ BN-LA711-G	Tomorrow Is Here	1977	$40
COLUMBIA			
❏ JC36108	Bobo	1979	$60
— Reproductions exist			
❏ JC35734	Hell of an Act to Follow	1978	$40
— Reproductions exist			
MGM			
❏ LAT-10012	Spanish Blues Band	197?	$40
❏ LAT-10007	Spanish Grease	197?	$40
❏ LAT-10011	Uno, Dos, Tres	197?	$40
ROULETTE			
❏ R-52097 [M]	Bobo's Beat	1962	$120
❏ SR-52097 [S]	Bobo's Beat	1962	$150
SUSSEX			
❏ SXBS-7003	Do What You Want to Do	1971	$40
— Reproductions exist			
TICO			
❏ T-1108 [M]	Do That Thing	1963	$120
❏ ST-1108 [S]	Do That Thing	1963	$150
— Reproductions exist			
TRIP			
❏ 5013	Latin Beat	1974	$25
VERVE			
❏ V6-8772	A New Dimension	1969	$100
❏ V-8699 [M]	Bobo Motion	1967	$40
❏ V6-8699 [S]	Bobo Motion	1967	$40
❏ V6-8781	Evil Ways	1969	$40
❏ V-8669 [M]	Feelin' So Good	1966	$40
❏ V6-8669 [S]	Feelin' So Good	1966	$100
❏ V-8685 [M]	Juicy	1967	$40
❏ V6-8685 [S]	Juicy	1967	$40
❏ V6-8736 [S]	Spanish Blues Band	1968	$40
❏ V-8736 [M]	Spanish Blues Band	1968	$120
— May be promo only			
❏ V-8631 [M]	Spanish Grease	1965	$60
❏ V6-8631 [S]	Spanish Grease	1965	$40
❏ V-8648 [M]	Uno, Dos, Tres	1966	$60
❏ V6-8648 [S]	Uno, Dos, Tres	1966	$40

BOCAGE, PETER
His most prominent instruments were the violin and trumpet, though he also played banjo, xylophone, mandolin, guitar, trombone and baritone horn.
Albums

Number	Title	Yr	NM
JAZZOLOGY			
❏ JCE-32	Peter Bocage with His Creole Serenaders	1979	$25
❏ JCE-29	San Jacinto Hall	1978	$25
RIVERSIDE			
❏ RLP-379 [M]	Peter Bocage with His Creole Serenaders	1961	$200
❏ RLP-9379 [S]	Peter Bocage with His Creole Serenaders	1961	$200

BOCIAN, MICHAEL
Guitarist and composer.
Albums

Number	Title	Yr	NM
GM RECORDINGS			
❏ GM-3002	For This Gift	1982	$25

BOFILL, ANGELA
Female singer.
Albums

Number	Title	Yr	NM
ARISTA			
❏ AL8-8258	Let Me Be the One	1984	$12
❏ AL9576	Something About You	1981	$12
❏ AL8-8125	Something About You	198?	$10
— Reissue of 9576			
❏ AL8-8198	Teaser	1983	$12
❏ AL8-8396	Tell Me Tomorrow	1985	$12
❏ AL8-8425	The Best of Angela Bofill	1986	$12
❏ AL9616	Too Tough	1983	$12
❏ AL8-8000	Too Tough	198?	$10
— Reissue of 9616			
ARISTA/GRP			
❏ GL5501	Angel of the Night	1979	$15
❏ GL8-8060	Angel of the Night	198?	$10
— Reissue of 5501			
❏ GL5000	Angie	1978	$15
❏ GLB-8302	Angie	198?	$10
— Reissue of 5000			
CAPITOL			
❏ C1-48335	Intuition	1988	$12

BOHANNON, GEORGE
Trombonist. Also has played tenor sax, flute, piano and bass.
Albums

Number	Title	Yr	NM
WORKSHOP JAZZ			
❏ WSJ-214 [M]	Bold Bohannon	1964	$0
— Canceled?			
❏ WSJ-207 [M]	Boss Bossa Nova	1963	$80

BOLCOM, WILLIAM
Pianist and composer.
Albums

Number	Title	Yr	NM
JAZZOLOGY			
❏ JCE-72	William Bolcom Plays His Own Rags	198?	$25
NONESUCH			
❏ N-71257	Heliotrope Bouquet (Piano Rags, 1900-70)	1971	$30
❏ N-71299	Pastimes and Piano Rags	1972	$30

BOLL WEEVIL JAZZ BAND
Albums

Number	Title	Yr	NM
GHB			
❏ 89	Red Hot in Memphis	197?	$25
❏ 31 [M]	Volume 1	1966	$30
❏ 32 [M]	Volume 2: Just a Little While	1966	$30
❏ 33 [M]	Volume 3: One More Time	1966	$30
❏ 34 [M]	Volume 4: One More Time Again	1966	$30
❏ 48	Volume 5: A Hot Band Is Hard to Find	1968	$25

BOLLING, CLAUDE
Pianist and composer.
Albums

Number	Title	Yr	NM
BALLY			
❏ BAL-12003 [M]	French Jazz	1956	$40

Number	Title	Yr	NM
CBS			
❏ FM42474	Bolling Plays Ellington, Vol. 1	1988	$25
❏ FM42476	Bolling Plays Ellington, Vol. 2	1988	$25
❏ FM42318	Suite No. 2 for Flute and Jazz Piano Trio	1987	$25
CBS MASTERWORKS			
❏ FM39245	Big Band	1985	$25
❏ M336845	Bolling	1981	$30
— Combines 33233, 35128, and 35864 in one box			
❏ FM36691	California Suite	1980	$25
— With Hubert Laws and Shelly Manne; not the same as the original soundtrack recording			
❏ FM37264	Concerto for Classic Guitar and Jazz Piano	1981	$25
— With Alexandre Lagoya; reissue of RCA Red Seal 0149			
❏ FM39244	Jazz A La Francaise	1985	$25
❏ FM39059	Suite for Cello and Jazz Piano Trio	1984	$25
— With Yo-Yo Ma, others			
❏ FM37798	Suite for Chamber Orchestra and Jazz Piano Trio	1982	$25
❏ FM36731	Toot Suite for Trumpet and Jazz Piano	1980	$25
— With Maurice Andre			
COLUMBIA			
❏ PC33277	Original Ragtime	1975	$25
❏ FM39009	Original Ragtime	1984	$20
— Reissue of 33277			
COLUMBIA MASTERWORKS			
❏ M35864	Picnic Suite for Flute, Guitar and Jazz Piano	1979	$25
— With Jean-Pierre Rampal and Alexandre Lagoya			
❏ M33233	Suite for Flute and Jazz Piano	1975	$25
— With Jean-Pierre Rampal			
❏ M35128	Suite for Violin and Jazz Piano	1978	$25
— With Pinchas Zuckerman			
DRG			
❏ SL-5201	Nuances	1986	$25
JAZZ MAN			
❏ 5018	Rolling with Bolling	198?	$25
— Reissue of Omega OSL-6			
MERCURY			
❏ 812569-1	Bolling Blues	1983	$25
OMEGA			
❏ OKL-6 [M]	Rolling with Bolling	1960	$30
❏ OSL-6 [S]	Rolling with Bolling	1960	$30
PHILIPS			
❏ PHM200204 [M]	Two-Beat Mozart	1966	$35
❏ PHS600204 [S]	Two-Beat Mozart	1966	$25
RCA RED SEAL			
❏ FRL1-0149	Concerto for Classic Guitar and Jazz Piano	1973	$30
— With Alexandre Lagoya			

BONANO, SHARKEY, AND LIZZIE MILES
Also see each artist's individual listings.
Albums

Number	Title	Yr	NM
CAPITOL			
❏ T792 [M]	A Night in Old New Orleans	1956	$75
❏ H367 [10]	Midnight on Bourbon Street	1952	$80
❏ T367 [M]	Midnight on Bourbon Street	1954	$75

BONANO, SHARKEY
Trumpeter. Also see PAUL BARBARIN.
Albums

Number	Title	Yr	NM
CAPITOL			
❏ T266 [M]	Kings of Dixieland	1954	$75
❏ H266 [10]	Sharkey's Southern Comfort	1951	$80
CIRCLE			
❏ LP-422 [10]	Sharkey Bonano	1951	$50
GMB			
❏ 122	Sharkey Bonano and His Kings of Dixieland	198?	$25
ROULETTE			
❏ R-25112 [M]	Dixieland at the Roundtable	1960	$30
SOUTHLAND			
❏ 222 [M]	Kings of Dixieland	1959	$30
❏ SLP-205 [10]	New Orleans Dixieland Session	1954	$50
❏ 205 [M]	New Orleans Jam Session	1961	$30

BOND, JAMES, SEXTETTE

Albums

Number	Title	Yr	NM
MIRWOOD			
❏ M-7001 [M]	The James Bond Songbook	1966	$30
❏ S-7001 [S]	The James Bond Songbook	1966	$30

BONFA, LUIZ
Guitarist and composer. Also see STAN GETZ; PAUL WINTER.

Albums

Number	Title	Yr	NM
ATLANTIC			
❏ 8028 [M]	The Fabulous Guitar of Luiz Bonfa/Amor!	1959	$300
—Black label			
❏ 8028 [M]	The Fabulous Guitar of Luiz Bonfa/Amor!	1960	$250
— White "bullseye" label			
❏ 8028 [M]	The Fabulous Guitar of Luiz Bonfa/Amor!	1961	$150
—Multicolor label, white "fan" logo at right			
❏ 8028 [M]	The Fabulous Guitar of Luiz Bonfa/Amor!	1963	$50
— Multicolor label, black "fan" logo at right			
❏ SD8028 [S]	The Fabulous Guitar of Luiz Bonfa/Amor!	1959	$300
— Green label			
❏ SD8028 [S]	The Fabulous Guitar of Luiz Bonfa/Amor!	1960	$250
— White "bullseye" label			
❏ SD8028 [S]	The Fabulous Guitar of Luiz Bonfa/Amor!	1961	$150
— Multicolor label, white "fan" logo at right			
❏ SD8028 [S]	The Fabulous Guitar of Luiz Bonfa/Amor!	1963	$50
— Multicolor label, black "fan" logo at right			
CAPITOL			
❏ T10134 [M]	Brazilian Guitar	1958	$60
— Turquoise label			
DOT			
❏ DLP-25848	Black Orpheus Impressions	1969	$75
❏ DLP-25881	Bonfa	1969	$75
❏ DLP-3804 [M]	Luiz Bonfa	1967	$75
❏ DLP-25804 [S]	Luiz Bonfa	1967	$75
❏ DLP-25825	Luiz Bonfa Plays Great Songs	1968	$75
EPIC			
❏ LN24124 [M]	Softly	1964	$75
❏ BN26124 [S]	Softly	1964	$50
PHILIPS			
❏ PHM200199 [M]	Braziliana	1965	$30
❏ PHS600199 [S]	Braziliana	1965	$35
❏ PHM200087 [M]	Brazil's King of the Bossa Nova and Guitar	1963	$35
❏ PHS600087 [S]	Brazil's King of the Bossa Nova and Guitar	1963	$25
❏ PHM200208 [M]	The Brazilian Scene	1966	$30
❏ PHS600208 [S]	The Brazilian Scene	1966	$35
RCA VICTOR			
❏ LSP-4376	The New Face of Bonfa	1970	$35
VERVE			
❏ V-8522 [M]	Luiz Bonfa Plays and Sings Bossa Nova	1963	$35
❏ V6-8522 [S]	Luiz Bonfa Plays and Sings Bossa Nova	1963	$25

BONNEMERE, EDDIE
Pianist.

Albums

Number	Title	Yr	NM
PRESTIGE			
❏ PRLP-7354 [M]	Jazz Oriented	1965	$25
❏ PRST-7354 [S]	Jazz Oriented	1965	$30
ROOST			
❏ RST-2236 [M]	Piano Bon Bons	1959	$30
❏ SLP-2236 [S]	Piano Bon Bons	1959	$40
❏ RST-419 [10]	Piano Mambo with Bonnemere	1954	$50
❏ RST-2241 [M]	The Sound of Memory	1960	$30
❏ SLP-2241 [S]	The Sound of Memory	1960	$40

BOSTIC, EARL
Alto saxophone player and bandleader.

Albums

Number	Title	Yr	NM
GRAND PRIX			
❏ K-404 [M]	The Earl of Bostic	196?	$35
❏ KS-404 [R]	The Earl of Bostic	196?	$30
❏ K-416 [M]	Wild Man	196?	$35
❏ KS-416 [R]	Wild Man	196?	$30
KING			
❏ K-5010X	14 Original Greatest Hits	1977	$30
❏ 947 [M]	24 Songs That Earl Loved the Most	1966	$40
❏ 597 [M]	Alto Magic in Hi-Fi	1958	$150
❏ KS-597 [S]	Alto Magic in Hi-Fi	1959	$300
❏ 395-515 [M]	Alto-Tude	1956	$175
❏ 395-503 [M]	Bostic for You	1956	$175
❏ 613 [M]	Bostic Workshop	1959	$100
❏ KS-613 [S]	Bostic Workshop	1959	$175
❏ 786 [M]	By Popular Demand	1961	$100
❏ 558 [M]	C'mon and Dance with Earl Bostic	1956	$150
❏ KS-558 [S]	C'mon and Dance with Earl Bostic	1959	$300
❏ 395-525 [M]	Dance Time	1956	$150
❏ 395-500 [M]	Dance to the Best of Bostic	195?	$80
— Second cover with girl in a swimsuit pictured			
❏ 395-500 [M]	Dance to the Best of Bostic	1956	$175
— Original cover with Earl Bostic pictured			
❏ 295-64 [10]	Earl Bostic and His Alto Sax	1951	$200
—Black vinyl			
❏ 295-64 [10]	Earl Bostic and His Alto Sax	1951	$400
— Red vinyl			
❏ 295-65 [10]	Earl Bostic and His Alto Sax	1951	$200
—Black vinyl			
❏ 295-65 [10]	Earl Bostic and His Alto Sax	1951	$400
— Red vinyl			
❏ 295-66 [10]	Earl Bostic and His Alto Sax	1951	$200
—Black vinyl			
❏ 295-66 [10]	Earl Bostic and His Alto Sax	1951	$400
— Red vinyl			
❏ 295-72 [10]	Earl Bostic and His Alto Sax	1952	$200
❏ 295-76 [10]	Earl Bostic and His Alto Sax	1952	$200
❏ 295-77 [10]	Earl Bostic and His Alto Sax	1952	$200
❏ 295-78 [10]	Earl Bostic and His Alto Sax	1952	$200
❏ 295-79 [10]	Earl Bostic and His Alto Sax	1952	$200
❏ 295-103 [10]	Earl Bostic and His Alto Sax	1954	$200
❏ 827 [M]	Earl Bostic Plays Bossa Nova	1963	$100
❏ 295-95 [10]	Earl Bostic Plays the Old Standards	1954	$200
❏ KS-1048 [S]	Harlem Nocturne	1969	$60
❏ 571 [M]	Hits of the Swing Age	1957	$150
❏ 705 [M]	Hit Tunes of Big Broadway Shows	1960	$100
❏ KS-705 [S]	Hit Tunes of Big Broadway Shows	1960	150
❏ 395-547 [M]	Invitation to Dance	1956	$150
❏ 846 [M]	Jazz As I Feel It	1963	$100
❏ 395-529 [M]	Let's Dance with Earl Bostic	1956	$150
❏ 662 [M]	Musical Pearls	1960	$100
❏ KS-662 [S]	Musical Pearls	1960	$150
❏ 583 [M]	Showcase of Swinging	1958	$150
❏ 838 [M]	Dance Hits Songs of the Fantastic Fifties, Volume 2	1963	$100
❏ 620 [M]	Sweet Tunes from the Roaring Twenties	1959	$100
❏ KS-620 [S]	Sweet Tunes from the Roaring Twenties	1959	$175
❏ 602 [M]	Sweet Tunes of the Fantastic Fifties	1959	$100
❏ 640 [M]	Sweet Tunes of the Sentimental Forties	1960	$100
❏ KS-640 [S]	Sweet Tunes of the Sentimental Forties	1960	$150
❏ 632 [M]	Sweet Tunes of the Swinging Thirties	1959	$100
❏ KS-632 [S]	Sweet Tunes of the Swinging Thirties	1959	$175
❏ 881 [M]	The Best of Earl Bostic, Volume 2	1964	$100
❏ 921 [M]	The Great Hits of 1964	1964	$100
❏ 900 [M]	The New Sound	1964	$100
PHILIPS			
❏ PHM200262 [M]	The Song Is Not Ended	1967	$60
❏ PHS600262 [S]	The Song Is Not Ended	1967	$60

BOSTIC, EARL/JIMMY LUNCEFORD
Also see each artist's individual listings.

Albums

Number	Title	Yr	NM
ALLEGRO ELITE			
❏ 4053 [10]	Earl Bostic/Jimmy Lunceford Orchestras	195?	$40

BOSWELL, CONNEE
Female singer. Also a pianist, saxophone player, violinist and cellist.

Albums

Number	Title	Yr	NM
DECCA			
❏ DL8356 [M]	Connee	1956	$150
❏ DL5390 [10]	Connee Boswell	1951	$200
❏ DL5445 [10]	Singing the Blues	1952	$150
DESIGN			
❏ DLP-68 [M]	Connee Boswell Sings Irving Berlin	196?	$30
❏ DLPS-68 [R]	Connee Boswell Sings Irving Berlin	196?	$20
❏ DLP-101 [M]	The New Sound of Connee Boswell	196?	$30
❏ DLPS-101 [R]	The New Sound of Connee Boswell	196?	$20
RCA VICTOR			
❏ LPM-1426 [M]	Connee Boswell and the Original Memphis Five	1957	$40

BOTHWELL, JOHNNY
Alto saxophone player and bandleader.

Albums

Number	Title	Yr	NM
BRUNSWICK			
❏ BL58033 [10]	Presenting Johnny Bothwell	1953	$100

BOULOU
See BOULOU FERRE.

BOURBON STREET STOMPERS, THE

Albums

Number	Title	Yr	NM
TIME			
❏ 52118 [M]	We Like Dixieland	196?	$35
❏ S-2118 [S]	We Like Dixieland	196?	$25

BOWIE, LESTER, AND PHILIP WILSON
Also see each artist's individual listings.

Albums

Number	Title	Yr	NM
IAI			
❏ 373854	Duet	1978	$30

BOWIE, LESTER
Trumpeter and fluegel horn player. Also see ART ENSEMBLE OF CHICAGO.

Albums

Number	Title	Yr	NM
BLACK SAINT			
❏ BSR-0020	Fifth Power	197?	$30
ECM			
❏ 23789	All the Magic	1984	$25
❏ 25034	I Only Have Eyes for You	1985	$25
❏ 1209	The Great Pretender	1981	$30
MUSE			
❏ MR-5055	Fast Last!	1975	$30
❏ MR-5337	Hello Dolly	1987	$25
❏ MR-5081	Rope-a-Dope	1975	$30
NESSA			
❏ N-1	Numbers 1 and 2	1968	$30
VENTURE			
❏ 90650	Twilight Dreams	1988	$25

BOWIE, PAT
Female singer.

Albums

Number	Title	Yr	NM
PRESTIGE			
❏ PRLP-7437 [M]	Feelin' Good	1967	$30
❏ PRST-7437 [S]	Feelin' Good	1967	$30
❏ PRLP-7385 [M]	Out of Sight	1965	$30
❏ PRST-7385 [S]	Out of Sight	1965	$30

BOWN, PATTI
Pianist.

Albums

Number	Title	Yr	NM
COLUMBIA			
❏ CL1379 [M]	Patti Bown Plays Big Piano	1959	$30

BOYD, ROCKY
Tenor saxophone player.

Albums

Number	Title	Yr	NM
JAZZTIME			
❏ JS-001 [S]	Ease It	1961	$250

Number	Title	Yr	NM

BRACE, JANET
Female singer.
Albums
ABC-PARAMOUNT
| ❏ ABC-116 [M] | Special Delivery | 1956 | $50 |

BRACKEEN, CHARLES
Tenor and soprano saxophone player.
Albums
SILKHEART
❏ SH-110	Attainment	198?	$30
❏ SH-105	Bannar	198?	$30
❏ SH-111	Worshippers Come Nigh	198?	$30
STRATA-EAST
❏ 19736	Rhythm X	1974	$30

BRACKEEN, JOANNE
Albums
ANTILLES
| ❏ 1001 | Special Identity | 198? | $25 |
CHOICE
❏ CRS1024	Prism	1978	$30
❏ CRS1009	Snooze	1976	$30
❏ CRS1016	Tring-a-Ling	1977	$30
COLUMBIA
❏ JC36593	Ancient Dynasty	1980	$25
❏ JC36075	Keyed In	1979	$25
CONCORD JAZZ
❏ CJ-316	Fi-Fi Goes to Heaven	1987	$25
❏ CJ-280	Havin' Fun	1985	$25
PAUSA
❏ 7045	Mythical Magic	1979	$30
TIMELESS
❏ TI-302	Aft	1980	$30

BRADFORD, BOBBY
Trumpeter. Also see JOHN CARTER AND BOBBY BRADFORD.
Albums
EMANEM
| ❏ 3302 | Love's Dream | 1976 | $25 |
NESSA
| ❏ N-17 | Bobby Bradford with John Stevens and the Spontaneous Music Ensemble, Vol. 1 | 198? | $25 |
| ❏ N-18 | Bobby Bradford with John Stevens and the Spontaneous Music Ensemble, Vol. 2 | 198? | $25 |
SOUL NOTE
| ❏ 121168-1 | One Night Stand | 1990 | $30 |

BRADFORD, CLEA
Female singer.
Albums
CADET
| ❏ LPS-810 | Her Point of View | 1969 | $35 |
MAINSTREAM
| ❏ 56042 [M] | Clea Bradford Now | 1965 | $30 |
| ❏ S-6042 [S] | Clea Bradford Now | 1965 | $30 |
NEW JAZZ
| ❏ NJLP-8320 [M] | Clea Bradford with Clark Terry | 1963 | $0 |
—Canceled
STATUS
| ❏ ST-8320 [M] | Clea Bradford with Clark Terry | 1965 | $40 |
TRU-SOUND
| ❏ TRU-15005 [M] | These Dues | 1962 | $50 |

BRADFORD, PERRY
Male singer, composer and pianist.
Albums
CRISPUS ATTUCKS
| ❏ 101 [M] | The Perry Bradford Story | 1957 | $60 |

BRADLEY, WILL
Trombonist and bandleader.
Albums

EPIC
❏ LG1005 [10]	Boogie Woogie	1954	$250
❏ LN3115 [M]	Boogie Woogie	1955	$100
❏ LN3199 [M]	The House of Bradley	1955	$100
❏ LN1127 [10]	The House of Bradley	1954	$250
RCA VICTOR
❏ LPM-2098 [M]	Big Band Boogie	1960	$40
❏ LSP-2098 [S]	Big Band Boogie	1960	$50
WALDORF MUSIC HALL
❏ MH 33-132 [10]	Jazz -- Dixieland and Chicago Style	195?	$40
❏ MH 33-122 [10]	Jazz Encounter	195?	$40

BRADSHAW, EVANS
Pianist.
Albums
RIVERSIDE
| ❏ RLP 12-296 [M] | Pieces of Eighty-Eight | 1959 | $250 |
| ❏ RLP-1136 [S] | Pieces of Eighty-Eight | 1959 | $250 |

BRAFF, RUBY, AND DICK HYMAN
Also see each artist's individual listings.
Albums
CONCORD JAZZ
| ❏ CJ-393 | Music from My Fair Lady | 1989 | $30 |
GEORGE WEIN COLLECTION
| ❏ GW-3003 | America the Beautiful | 198? | $25 |

BRAFF, RUBY, AND ELLIS LARKINS
Also see each artist's individual listings.
Albums
CHIAROSCURO
| ❏ 117 | The Grand Reunion | 1972 | $35 |
VANGUARD
❏ VRS-8019 [10]	Inventions in Jazz -- Volume 1	1955	$160
❏ VRS-8020 [10]	Inventions in Jazz -- Volume 2	1955	$160
❏ VRS-8516 [M]	Pocketful of Dreams	1957	$80
❏ VRS-8507 [M]	Two By Two	1956	$80

BRAFF, RUBY, AND GEORGE BARNES
Also see each artist's individual listings.
Albums
CHIAROSCURO
| ❏ 126 | Live at the New School | 1975 | $35 |
| ❏ 121 | The Ruby Braff-George Barnes Quartet | 1973 | $35 |
CONCORD JAZZ
| ❏ CJ-5 | The Ruby Braff-George Barnes Quartet Plays Gershwin | 1975 | $30 |
| ❏ CJ-7 | The Ruby Braff-George Barnes Quartet Salutes Rodgers and Hart | 1976 | $30 |

BRAFF, RUBY, AND SCOTT HAMILTON
Also see each artist's individual listings.
Albums
CONCORD JAZZ
| ❏ CJ-274 | A First | 1985 | $25 |
| ❏ CJ-296 | A Sailboat in the Moonlight | 1986 | $25 |

BRAFF, RUBY; PEE WEE RUSSELL; BOBBY HENDERSON
Also see each artist's individual listings.
Albums
VERVE
| ❏ MGV-8241 [M] | The Ruby Braff Octet with Pee Wee Russell and Bobby Henderson at Newport | 1958 | $100 |
| ❏ V-8241 [M] | The Ruby Braff Octet with Pee Wee Russell and Bobby Henderson at Newport | 1961 | $30 |

BRAFF, RUBY
Cornet player and trumpeter.
Albums
ABC-PARAMOUNT
| ❏ ABC-141 [M] | Ruby Braff Featuring Dave McKenna | 1956 | $40 |

AMERICAN RECORDING SOCIETY
| ❏ G-445 [M] | Hey, Ruby | 1957 | $40 |
BETHLEHEM
| ❏ BCP-6043 | Adoration of the Melody | 197? | $35 |
—Reissue material, distributed by RCA Victor
❏ BCP-1034 [10]	Ball at Bethlehem	1955	$250
❏ BCP-82 [M]	Handful of Cool Jazz	1958	$200
❏ BCP-1032 [10]	Holiday in Braff	1955	$250
❏ BCP-5 [M]	Omnibus	1955	$250
❏ BCP-1005 [10]	Ruby Braff Quartet	1954	$250
❏ BCP-6043 [M]	The Best of Braff	1960	$200
BLACK LION
❏ 127	Hear Me Talkin'	197?	$30
CHIAROSCURO
❏ 115	International Quartet Plus Three	1972	$35
CONCERT HALL JAZZ
❏ 1210 [M]	Little Big Horn	1955	$60
CONCORD JAZZ
❏ CJ-381	Me, Myself and I	1989	$30
EPIC
❏ LN3377 [M]	Braff!	1957	$100
FINESSE
❏ FW37988	Very Sinatra	1983	$30
JAZZTONE
❏ J-1210 [M]	Little Big Horn	1955	$50
RCA VICTOR
❏ LPM-1966 [M]	Easy Now	1959	$30
❏ LSP-1966 [S]	Easy Now	1959	$40
❏ LPM-1510 [M]	Hi-Fi Salute to Bunny	1957	$40
❏ LPM-1332 [M]	The Magic Horn of Ruby Braff	1956	$40
❏ LPM-1008 [M]	To Fred Astaire with Love	1955	$60
SACKVILLE
❏ 3022	Ruby Braff with the Ed Brickert Trio	198?	$25
STEREO-CRAFT
❏ RTN-507 [M]	You're Getting to Be a Habit with Me	1959	$60
❏ RTS-507 [S]	You're Getting to Be a Habit with Me	1959	$40
STORYVILLE
❏ STLP-320 [10]	Hustlin' and Bustlin'	1955	$80
❏ STLP-908 [M]	Hustlin' and Bustlin'	1956	$50
UNITED ARTISTS
❏ UAL-3045 [M]	Blowing Around the Around	1959	$30
❏ UAS-6045 [S]	Blowing Around the Around	1959	$40
❏ UAL-4093 [M]	Ruby Braff-Marshall Brown Sextet	1960	$30
❏ UAS-5093 [S]	Ruby Braff-Marshall Brown Sextet	1960	$40
VANGUARD
❏ VRS-8504 [M]	The Ruby Braff Special	1955	$125
WARNER BROS.
❏ W1273 [M]	Ruby Braff Goes Girl Crazy	1959	$30
❏ WS1273 [S]	Ruby Braff Goes Girl Crazy	1959	$40

BRAITH, GEORGE
Tenor and soprano saxophone player.
Albums
BLUE NOTE
| ❏ BST-84171 [S] | Extension | 1966 | $25 |
—With "A Division of Liberty Records" on label
| ❏ BLP-4148 [M] | Two Souls in One | 1963 | $80 |
—With "New York, USA" on label
| ❏ BST-84148 [S] | Two Souls in One | 1963 | $50 |
—With "New York, USA" on label
| ❏ BST-84148 [S] | Two Souls in One | 1966 | $25 |
—With "A Division of Liberty Records" on label
PRESTIGE
❏ PRLP-7474 [M]	Laughing Soul	1967	$30
❏ PRST-7474 [S]	Laughing Soul	1967	$25
❏ PRLP-7515 [M]	Musart	1967	$30

BRAND, DOLLAR
See ABDULLAH IBRAHIM.

BRASS COMPANY, THE
Group led by BILL HARDMAN.
Albums
SACKVILLE
| ❏ 3006 | Sangoma | 198? | $25 |
STRATA-EAST
| ❏ 19752 | Colors | 1974 | $25 |

BRASS ENSEMBLE OF THE JAZZ AND CLASSICAL MUSIC SOCIETY, THE

Members: MILES DAVIS; URBIE GREEN; J.J. JOHNSON; OSIE JOHNSON.

Albums

COLUMBIA

Number	Title	Yr	NM
☐ CL941 [M]	Music for Brass	1956	$120

BRAUFMAN, ALAN

Alto saxophone player, clarinetist and flutist.

Albums

INDIA NAVIGATION

Number	Title	Yr	NM
☐ IN-1024	Valley of Search	197?	$30

BRAXTON, ANTHONY, AND DEREK BAILEY

Derek Bailey is a guitarist. Also see ANTHONY BRAXTON.

Albums

EMANEM

Number	Title	Yr	NM
☐ 3313	Duo 1	197?	$35
☐ 3314	Duo 2	197?	$35

INNER CITY

Number	Title	Yr	NM
☐ 1041	Live at Wigmor	198?	$30

BRAXTON, ANTHONY, AND MUHAL RICHARD ABRAMS

Also see each artist's individual listings.

Albums

ARISTA

Number	Title	Yr	NM
☐ AL4101	Duets	1976	$35

BRAXTON, ANTHONY

Alto saxophone player and composer. Also plays other saxes, clarinet, flute, piano and percussion.

Albums

ANTILLES

Number	Title	Yr	NM
☐ 1005	Six Compositions: Quartet	1981	$30

ARISTA

Number	Title	Yr	NM
☐ AL4064	5 Pieces 1975	1975	$35
☐ A2L8602	Alto Sax Improvisations '79	1979	$35
☐ AL4080	Creative Orchestra Music 1976	1976	$35
☐ AL4181	For Trio	1978	$35
☐ AL4032	New York, Fall 1974	1975	$35
☐ AL5002	The Montreux/Berlin Concerts	1977	$25

ARISTA FREEDOM

Number	Title	Yr	NM
☐ AL1902	The Complete Braxton 1971	1978	$25

BLACK SAINT

Number	Title	Yr	NM
☐ BSR-0066	Four Compositions: Quartet 1983	1983	$30
☐ BSR-0086	Four Compositions: Quartet 1984	1985	$30
☐ 120116-1	Six Monk Compositions	1987	$30

BLUEBIRD

Number	Title	Yr	NM
☐ 6626-1-RB	Anthony Braxton Live	1988	$25

CONCORD JAZZ

Number	Title	Yr	NM
☐ CJ-213	A Ray Brown 3	1982	$30

DELMARK

Number	Title	Yr	NM
☐ DS-420/1	For Alto	1971	$30
☐ DS-415	Three Compositions of New Jazz	1969	$25
☐ DS-428	Together Alone	1973	$25

— With Joseph Jarman

HAT HUT

Number	Title	Yr	NM
☐ 1984	Composition 98	1981	$35
☐ 1995/96	Open Aspects '82	1982	$35
☐ 2019	Performance	1983	$35

INNER CITY

Number	Title	Yr	NM
☐ 2015	In the Tradition	197?	$35
☐ IC2045	In the Tradition, Vol. 2	1976	$35
☐ 1008	Saxophone Improvisations -- Series F	197?	$35

MAGENTA

Number	Title	Yr	NM
☐ MA-0203	Seven Standards 1985	1986	$30
☐ MA-0205	Seven Standards 1985, Volume 2	1986	$30

SACKVILLE

Number	Title	Yr	NM
☐ 3007	Trio and Duet	198?	$25

SOUND ASPECTS

Number	Title	Yr	NM
☐ SAS-009	Anthony Braxton with the Robert Schumann Quartet	1986	$30

STEEPLECHASE

Number	Title	Yr	NM
☐ SCS-1015	In the Tradition	198?	$25
☐ SCS-1045	In the Tradition, Volume 2	198?	$25

BREAKSTONE, JOSHUA

Guitarist and composer.

Albums

CONTEMPORARY

Number	Title	Yr	NM
☐ C-14025	Echoes	1987	$25
☐ C-14040	Evening Star	1988	$25
☐ C-14050	Self-Portrait in Swing	1989	$25

BRECKER, MICHAEL

Tenor saxophone player. Also see THE BRECKER BROTHERS; DREAMS.

Albums

GRP

Number	Title	Yr	NM
☐ GR-9622	Now You See It (Now You Don't)	1990	$20

MCA IMPULSE!

Number	Title	Yr	NM
☐ 42229	Don't Try This at Home	1989	$20
☐ 5980	Michael Brecker	1987	$15

BRECKER, RANDY, AND ELIANE ELIAS

Also see each artist's individual listings.

Albums

PASSPORT

Number	Title	Yr	NM
☐ PJ-88013	Amanda	1987	$12

BRECKER, RANDY

Trumpeter. Also see THE BRECKER BROTHERS; DREAMS.

Albums

MCA

Number	Title	Yr	NM
☐ 6334	Toe to Toe	1990	$20

PASSPORT

Number	Title	Yr	NM
☐ PJ-88039	In the Idiom	1988	$20

SOLID STATE

Number	Title	Yr	NM
☐ SS-18051	Score	1969	$30

BRECKER BROTHERS, THE

Also see MICHAEL BRECKER; RANDY BRECKER.

Albums

ARISTA

Number	Title	Yr	NM
☐ AL4061	Back to Back	1976	$25
☐ AQ4061 [Q]	Back to Back	1976	$60
☐ AB4272	Détente	1979	$25
☐ AL4122	Don't Stop the Music	1977	$25
☐ AB4185	Heavy Metal Be-Bop	1978	$25
☐ AL9550	Straphangin'	1981	$30
☐ AL4037	The Brecker Brothers	1975	$30

BREGMAN, BUDDY

Pianist, composer and conductor. Also see BING CROSBY.

Albums

VERVE

Number	Title	Yr	NM
☐ MGV-2094 [M]	Dig Buddy Bregman in Hi-Fi	1959	$100
☐ V-2094 [M]	Dig Buddy Bregman in Hi-Fi	1961	$25
☐ MGV-2064 [M]	Funny Face	1958	$150
☐ V-2064 [M]	Funny Face	1961	$25
☐ MGV-2042 [M]	Swingin' Kicks	1957	$150
☐ MGVS-6013 [S]	Swingin' Kicks	1960	$80
☐ V-2042 [M]	Swingin' Kicks	1961	$25
☐ V6-2042 [S]	Swingin' Kicks	1961	$35
☐ MGV-2093 [M]	The Gershwin Anniversary Album	1959	$100
☐ V-2093 [M]	The Gershwin Anniversary Album	1961	$25

WORLD PACIFIC

Number	Title	Yr	NM
☐ WP-1263 [M]	Swingin' Standards	1959	$100
☐ ST-1024 [S]	Swingin' Standards	1959	$100

BREWER, TERESA, AND COUNT BASIE

Also see each artist's individual listings.

Albums

DOCTOR JAZZ

Number	Title	Yr	NM
☐ FW38836	Songs of Bessie Smith	1984	$20

FLYING DUTCHMAN

Number	Title	Yr	NM
☐ FD10161	Songs of Bessie Smith	1973	$30

BREWER, TERESA, AND MERCER ELLINGTON

Also see each artist's individual listings.

Albums

DOCTOR JAZZ

Number	Title	Yr	NM
☐ FW40031	The Cotton Connection	1985	$25

BREWER, TERESA, AND STEPHANE GRAPPELLI

Also see each artist's individual listings.

Albums

DOCTOR JAZZ

Number	Title	Yr	NM
☐ FW38448	On the Road Again	198?	$25

BREWER, TERESA, AND SVEND ASMUSSEN

Also see each artist's individual listings.

Albums

DOCTOR JAZZ

Number	Title	Yr	NM
☐ FW40233	On the Good Ship Lollipop	1987	$25

BREWER, TERESA

Female singer. Her 1950s and 1960s material was pop-oriented and is not listed here. It can be found in the Standard Catalog of American Records.

Albums

DOCTOR JAZZ

Number	Title	Yr	NM
☐ ASLP804	Good News	198?	$12
☐ FW40951	Good News	198?	$10
☐ FW38534	I Dig Big Band Singers	1983	$12
☐ W2X39521	Live at Carnegie Hall and Montreux, Switzerland	1984	$15
☐ FW40232	Midnight Café	1986	$12

FLYING DUTCHMAN

Number	Title	Yr	NM
☐ BSL1-0577	Good News	1974	$15

PROJECT 3

Number	Title	Yr	NM
☐ 5108	Come Follow the Band	1982	$12

BRIDGEWATER, DEE DEE

Female singer.

Albums

ATLANTIC

Number	Title	Yr	NM
☐ SD18188	Dee Dee Bridgewater	1976	$15

ELEKTRA

Number	Title	Yr	NM
☐ 6E-188	Bad for Me	1979	$12
☐ 6E-306	Dee Dee Bridgewater	1980	$12
☐ 6E-119	Just Family	1978	$12

MCA/IMPULSE

Number	Title	Yr	NM
☐ MCA-6331	Live in Paris	1989	$15

BRIGGS, KAREN

Violinist.

Albums

VITAL

Number	Title	Yr	NM
☐ VTL-009	Karen	1996	$25

BRIGHT, RONNELL

Pianist, bandleader and composer.

Albums

REGENT

Number	Title	Yr	NM
☐ MG-6041 [M]	Bright's Spot	1957	$100

SAVOY

Number	Title	Yr	NM
☐ MG-12206 [M]	Bright's Spot	196?	$60

— Reissue of Regent LP

VANGUARD

Number	Title	Yr	NM
☐ VRS-8512 [M]	Bright's Flight	1957	$150

BRIGNOLA, NICK

Baritone saxophone player. Also has played most of the other saxes, clarinet, flute and piccolo on record.

Albums

BEE HIVE

Number	Title	Yr	NM
☐ BH-7000	Baritone Madness	1977	$30
☐ BH-7010	Burn Brigade	1979	$30

DISCOVERY

Number	Title	Yr	NM
☐ DS-917	Northern Lights	1986	$25

INTERPLAY

Number	Title	Yr	NM
☐ IP-7719	New York Bound	198?	$30

SEA BREEZE

Number	Title	Yr	NM
☐ SB-2003	L.A. Bound	198?	$30

BRISKER, GORDON

Tenor saxophone player, also an occasional flute and piano player.

Albums

DISCOVERY

Number	Title	Yr	NM
☐ DS-923	About Charlie	1987	$25

Number	Title	Yr	NM
❏ DS-938	New Beginning	1987	$25
SEA BREEZE			
❏ SB-2016	Cornerstone	1985	$25

BRITT, PAT
Saxophone player.

Albums

CATALYST
| ❏ 7612 | Starsong | 1976 | $30 |

CRESTVIEW
| ❏ CR-3075 [M] | Jazz from San Francisco | 1967 | $25 |
| ❏ CRS-3075 [S] | Jazz from San Francisco | 1967 | $35 |

VEE JAY
| ❏ VJS-3064 | Jazz from San Francisco | 1975 | $30 |
| ❏ VJS-3070 | Jazzman | 1975 | $30 |

BROADBENT, ALAN
Pianist.

Albums

DISCOVERY
| ❏ DS-929 | Everything I Love | 1987 | $25 |

GRANITE
| ❏ 7901 | Palette | 1979 | $30 |

TREND
| ❏ TR-546 | Another Time | 1988 | $25 |

BROCK, HERBIE
Pianist.

Albums

SAVOY
| ❏ MG-12069 [M] | Brock's Tops | 1956 | $40 |
| ❏ MG-12066 [M] | Herbie Brock Solo | 1956 | $40 |

BROCK, JIM
Percussionist.

Albums

REFERENCE RECORDINGS
| ❏ RR-31 | Tropic Affair | 198? | $35 |

BRODIE, HUGH, AND IMPULSE
Brodie is a tenor and soprano saxophone player.

Albums

CADENCE JAZZ
| ❏ CJ-1004 | Live and Cooking at the Wild Oat | 1981 | $20 |

BROKENSHA, JACK
Vibraphone player. Also see THE AUSTRALIAN JAZZ QUARTET.

Albums

SAVOY
| ❏ MG-12180 | And Then I Said | 1962 | $30 |

BROOKMEYER, BOB, AND BILL EVANS
Also see each artist's individual listings.

Albums

UNITED ARTISTS
| ❏ UAL-3044 [M] | The Ivory Hunters -- Double Barreled Piano | 1959 | $50 |
| ❏ UAS-6044 [S] | The Ivory Hunters -- Double Barreled Piano | 1959 | $40 |

BROOKMEYER, BOB, AND MEL LEWIS
Also see each artist's individual listings.

Albums

GRYPHON
| ❏ 912 | Live at the Village Vanguard | 1980 | $30 |

BROOKMEYER, BOB, AND ZOOT SIMS
Also see each artist's individual listings.

Albums

JAZZTONE
| ❏ J-1239 [M] | Bob Brookmeyer and Zoot Sims | 1956 | $40 |

STORYVILLE
| ❏ STLP-907 [M] | Tonight's Jazz Today | 1956 | $80 |
| ❏ STLP-914 [M] | Whoo-eeee! | 1956 | $150 |

BROOKMEYER, BOB; JIM HALL; JIMMY RANEY
Also see each artist's individual listings.

Albums

KIMBERLY
| ❏ 2021 [M] | Brookmeyer and Guitars | 1963 | $30 |
| ❏ 11021 [S] | Brookmeyer and Guitars | 1963 | $25 |

WORLD PACIFIC
❏ PJ-1239 [M]	The Street Swingers	1957	$350
❏ WP-1239 [M]	The Street Swingers	1958	$250
—*Reissue with new prefix*			

BROOKMEYER, BOB
Valve trombonist, arranger, composer and sometimes piano player. Also see THE MANHATTAN JAZZ ALL STARS; GERRY MULLIGAN; JIMMY RANEY; BUD SHANK; PHIL URSO.

Albums

ATLANTIC
❏ 1320 [M]	Portrait of the Artist	1960	$250
—*Black label*			
❏ 1320 [M]	Portrait of the Artist	1961	$150
—*Multicolor label, white "fan" logo at right*			
❏ SD1320 [S]	Portrait of the Artist	1960	$250
—*Green label*			
❏ SD1320 [S]	Portrait of the Artist	1961	$150
—*Multicolor label, white "fan" logo at right*			

CLEF
| ❏ MGC-644 [M] | Bob Brookmeyer Plays Bob Brookmeyer and Some Others | 1955 | $250 |
| ❏ MGC-732 [M] | The Modernity of Bob Brookmeyer | 1956 | $300 |

COLUMBIA
| ❏ CL2237 [M] | Bob Brookmeyer and Friends | 1965 | $35 |
| ❏ CS9037 [S] | Bob Brookmeyer and Friends | 1965 | $25 |

CROWN
| ❏ CLP-5318 [M] | Bob Brookmeyer | 196? | $35 |

FANTASY
| ❏ OJC-1729 | The Dual Role of Bob Brookmeyer | 1990 | $30 |
| —*Reissue of Prestige 7066* | | | |

FINESSE
| ❏ FW37488 | Through a Looking Glass | 198? | $25 |

GRYPHON
| ❏ 785 | Bob Brookmeyer's Small Band | 1978 | $35 |

MERCURY
| ❏ MG-20600 [M] | Jazz Is a Kick | 1960 | $100 |
| ❏ SR-60600 [S] | Jazz Is a Kick | 1960 | $100 |

NEW JAZZ
❏ NJLP-8294 [M]	Revelation	1963	$150
—*Purple label*			
❏ NJLP-8294 [M]	Revelation	1965	$150
—*Blue label, trident logo at right*			

ODYSSEY
| ❏ PC36804 | Bob Brookmeyer and Friends | 1980 | $25 |
| —*Reissue of Columbia 9037* | | | |

PACIFIC JAZZ
| ❏ PJLP-16 [10] | Bob Brookmeyer Quartet | 1954 | $150 |

PRESTIGE
| ❏ PRLP-214 [10] | Bob Brookmeyer with Jimmy Raney | 1955 | $300 |
| ❏ PRLP-7066 [M] | The Dual Role of Bob Brookmeyer | 1956 | $300 |

SONET
| ❏ 778 | Back Again | 1979 | $30 |

STORYVILLE
| ❏ STLP-305 [10] | Bob Brookmeyer Featuring Al Cohn | 1954 | $300 |

TODAY'S JAZZ
| ❏ J-1239 [M] | Bob Brookmeyer and Zoot Sims | 196? | $30 |

TRIP
| ❏ 5568 | Jazz Is a Kick | 197? | $25 |

UNITED ARTISTS
| ❏ UAL-4008 [M] | Kansas City Revisited | 1959 | $50 |
| ❏ UAS-5008 [S] | Kansas City Revisited | 1959 | $40 |

VERVE
❏ V-8413 [M]	7 X Wilder	1961	$100
❏ V6-8413 [S]	7 X Wilder	1961	$100
❏ V-8455 [M]	Gloomy Sunday and Other Bright Moments	1962	$30
❏ V6-8455 [S]	Gloomy Sunday and Other Bright Moments	1962	$30
❏ V-8385 [M]	The Blues, Hot and Cold	1961	$30
❏ V6-8385 [S]	The Blues, Hot and Cold	1961	$30
❏ MGV-8111 [M]	The Modernity of Bob Brookmeyer	1957	$250
❏ V-8111 [M]	The Modernity of Bob Brookmeyer	1961	$150
❏ V-8498 [M]	Trombone Jazz Samba	1962	$30
❏ V6-8498 [S]	Trombone Jazz Samba	1962	$30

VIK
| ❏ LX-1071 [M] | Brookmeyer | 1957 | $50 |

WORLD PACIFIC
| ❏ PJ-1233 [M] | Traditionalism Revisited | 1958 | $150 |

BROOKS, CECIL, III
Drummer.

Albums

MUSE
| ❏ MR-5377 | The Collective | 1989 | $30 |

BROOKS, DONNA
Female singer.

Albums

DAWN
| ❏ DLP-1105 [M] | I'll Take Romance | 1956 | $120 |

BROOKS, JOHN BENSON
Pianist, bandleader, arranger and composer.

Albums

DECCA
❏ DL5018 [M]	Avant Slant	1968	$40
—*White label promo only; in stereo cover with "Monaural" sticker on front*			
❏ DL75018 [S]	Avant Slant	1968	$25

RIVERSIDE
| ❏ RLP 12-276 [M] | The Alabama Concerto | 1958 | $300 |
| ❏ RLP-1123 [S] | The Alabama Concerto | 1959 | $300 |

VIK
| ❏ LX-1083 [M] | Folk Jazz U.S.A. | 1957 | $40 |

BROOKS, RANDY
Trumpeter and bandleader.

Albums

CIRCLE
| ❏ CLP-035 | Randy Brooks and His Orchestra 1945-47 | 198? | $25 |

DECCA
| ❏ DL8201 [M] | Trumpet Moods | 195? | $30 |

BROOKS, ROY

Albums

IM-HOTEP
| ❏ CS-030 | Ethnic Expressions | 197? | $35 |

MUSE
| ❏ MR-5003 | Free Slave | 197? | $35 |

WORKSHOP JAZZ
| ❏ WSJ-220 [M] | Roy Brooks Beat | 1964 | $50 |
| ❏ WSJS-220 [S] | Roy Brooks Beat | 1964 | $60 |

BROOKS, TINA
Real name: Harold Floyd Brooks. Tenor saxophone player.

Albums

BLUE NOTE
❏ BLP-4052 [M]	Back to the Tracks	1960	$3500
—*Released canceled, test pressings exist*			
❏ BST-84052 [S]	Back to the Tracks	1960	$0
—*Canceled*			
❏ BST-84052 [S]	Back to the Tracks	199?	$40
—*Classic Records reissue; first U.S. vinyl issue*			
❏ BST-84041 [S]	True Blue	1960	$0
—*Canceled*			
❏ B1-28975	True Blue	1994	$25

MOSAIC
| ❏ MR4-106 | The Complete Blue Note Recordings of the Tina Brooks Quintets | 1984 | $150 |

BROOM, BOBBY
Guitarist.
Albums
Number	Title	Yr	NM
ARISTA			
❏ AL-8-8253	Bobby Broom	1984	$12
ARISTA/GRP			
❏ GL5504	Clean Sweep	1981	$12

BROTHER MATTHEW
Alto saxophone player.
Albums
Number	Title	Yr	NM
ABC-PARAMOUNT			
❏ ABC-121	Brother Matthew	1956	$50

BROUSSARD, JULES
Saxophone player and flutist.
Albums
Number	Title	Yr	NM
HEADFIRST			
❏ 796	Jules Broussard	198?	$30

BROWN, BOOTS / DAN DREW
Boots Brown and His Blockbusters are Shorty Rogers, Milt Bernhart, Bud Shank, Jimmy Giuffre, Gerry Mulligan, Marty Paich, Jimmy Wyble, Howard Rumsey, Roy Harte and J. J. Johnson. Dan Drew and His Daredevils are Eddie Bert, Al Cohn, Osie Johnson, Buddy Jones, Elliott Lawrence, Charlie O'Kane and Nick Travis.
Albums
Number	Title	Yr	NM
GROOVE			
❏ LG-1000 [M]	Rock That Boat	1955	$300

BROWN, CHARLES
Earlier material appears in the Goldmine Standard Catalog of American Records 1950-1975. (SC2)
Male singer and pianist, an R&B/blues musician with jazz roots.
Albums
Number	Title	Yr	NM
ALADDIN			
❏ LP-702 [10]	Mood Music	1952	$7500
—Red vinyl; VG value 3000; VG+ value 5250			
❏ LP-702 [10]	Mood Music	1952	$4000
—Black vinyl; VG value 1500; VG+ value 2750			
❏ LP-809 [M]	Mood Music	1956	——
—Unreleased?			
ALLIGATOR			
❏ AL-4771	One More for the Road	1989	$30
BIG TOWN			
❏ 1003	Merry Christmas Baby	1977	$30
❏ 1005	Music Maestro Please	1978	$25
BLUESWAY			
❏ BLS-6039	Charles Brown -- Legend	1970	$60
BULLSEYE BLUES			
❏ BB-9501	All My Life	1990	$50
IMPERIAL			
❏ LP-9178 [M]	Charles Brown Sings Million Sellers	1961	$400
JEWEL			
❏ 5006	Blues 'N' Brown	1972	$30
KING			
❏ 775 [M]	Charles Brown Sings Christmas Songs	1961	$300
❏ KS-775 [S]	Charles Brown Sings Christmas Songs	1963	$300
—Stereo copies (whether true stereo or rechanneled, we don't know) exist on blue labels with "King" in block letters (no crown)			
❏ 878 [M]	The Great Charles Brown	1963	$200
MAINSTREAM			
❏ 56035 [M]	Ballads My Way	1965	$50
❏ S-6035 [S]	Ballads My Way	1965	$60
❏ 56007 [M]	Boss of the Blues	1965	$50
❏ S-6007 [S]	Boss of the Blues	1965	$60
MOSAIC			
❏ MQ7-153	The Complete Aladdin Recordings of Charles Brown	1994	$150
SCORE			
❏ SLP-4011 [M]	Driftin' Blues	1958	$400
❏ SLP-4036 [M]	More Blues with Charles Brown	1959	——
—Unreleased			

BROWN, CLIFFORD, AND ART FARMER
Also see each artist's individual listings.
Albums
Number	Title	Yr	NM
PRESTIGE			
❏ PRLP-167 [10]	Clifford Brown and Art Farmer with the Swedish All Stars	1953	$300

BROWN, CLIFFORD, AND MAX ROACH
Also see each artist's individual listings.
Albums
Number	Title	Yr	NM
ELEKTRA/MUSICIAN			
❏ 60026	Pure Genius	1982	$30
EMARCY			
❏ MG-36008 [M]	Brown and Roach Incorporated	1955	$250
❏ MG-26043 [10]	Clifford Brown and Max Roach	1954	$600
❏ MG-36036 [M]	Clifford Brown and Max Roach	1955	$650
GENE NORMAN			
❏ GNP-5 [10]	Clifford Brown and Max Roach, Vol. 1	1954	$300
❏ GNP-7 [10]	Clifford Brown and Max Roach, Vol. 2	1954	$300
❏ GNP-125 [10]	Gene Norman Presents Max Roach and Clifford Brown	1954	$400
❏ GNP-18 [M]	The Best of Max Roach and Clifford Brown In Concert	1955	$250
MAINSTREAM			
❏ MRL-386 [M]	Daahoud	197?	$30
TRIP			
❏ 5550	All Stars	197?	$25
❏ 5530	A Study in Brown	197?	$25
❏ 5537	Best Coast Jazz	197?	$25
❏ 5520	Brown and Roach Incorporated	197?	$25
❏ 5511 [B]	Clifford Brown and Max Roach at Basin Street	197?	$25
❏ 5540	Jordu	197?	$25

BROWN, CLIFFORD
Trumpeter. Considered to be among the greatest of bebop trumpet players, he died at age 26 in an auto accident. Also see TADD DAMERON; BOB GORDON; GIGI GRYCE; SONNY ROLLINS.
Albums
Number	Title	Yr	NM
BLUE NOTE			
❏ BST-84428	Alternate Takes	198?	$30
❏ BN-LA267-G	Brownie Eyes	1974	$30
❏ BLP-1526 [M]	Clifford Brown Memorial Album	1956	$150
—Regular edition, Lexington Ave. address on label			
❏ BLP-1526 [M]	Clifford Brown Memorial Album	196?	$150
—With W. 63rd St. address on label			
❏ BLP-1526 [M]	Clifford Brown Memorial Album	196?	$60
—With "New York, USA" address on label			
❏ BST-81526 [R]	Clifford Brown Memorial Album	1967	$30
—With "A Division of Liberty Records" on label			
❏ BST-81526	Clifford Brown Memorial Album	1985	$25
—The Finest in Jazz Since 1939" reissue			
❏ BLP-5047 [10]	Clifford Brown Quartet	1954	$500
❏ BLP-5032 [10]	New Star on the Horizon	1953	$500
COLUMBIA			
❏ KC32284	The Beginning and the End	1973	$35
❏ C32284	The Beginning and the End	197?	$30
—Reissue with new prefix			
EMARCY			
❏ MG-36102 [M]	Clifford Brown All Stars	1956	$200
FANTASY			
❏ OJC-359	Clifford Brown Big Band in Paris	198?	$25
❏ OJC-017	Clifford Brown Memorial	198?	$25
❏ OJC-357	Clifford Brown Quartet in Paris	198?	$25
❏ OJC-358	Clifford Brown Sextet in Paris	198?	$25
JAZZTONE			
❏ J-1281 [M]	Jazz Messages	195?	$40
LIMELIGHT			
❏ 2-8201 [M]	The Immortal Clifford Brown	1965	$40
❏ 2-8601 [R]	The Immortal Clifford Brown	1965	$30
MERCURY			
❏ MG-20827 [M]	Remember Clifford	1963	$100
❏ SR-60827 [R]	Remember Clifford	1963	$100
MOSAIC			
❏ MR5-104	The Complete Blue Note and Pacific Jazz Recordings of Clifford Brown	198?	$80
NEW JAZZ			
❏ NJLP-8301 [M]	Clifford Brown	1963	$0
—Canceled			
PACIFIC JAZZ			
❏ LN-10126	Jazz Immortal	198?	$25
❏ PJLP-19 [10]	The Clifford Brown Ensemble	1955	$300
PRESTIGE			
❏ PRLP-16008 [M]	Clifford Brown	1964	$40
❏ PRST-7840	Clifford Brown Big Band in Paris	1970	$30
❏ 24020	Clifford Brown in Paris	1971	$35
❏ PRLP-7055 [M]	Clifford Brown Memorial	1956	$300
❏ PRST-7662 [R]	Clifford Brown Memorial Album	1969	$30
❏ PRST-7761	Clifford Brown Quartet in Paris	1969	$30
❏ PRST-7794	Clifford Brown Sextet in Paris	1970	$30
TRIP			
❏ 5502	Clifford Brown with Strings	197?	$25

BROWN, DONALD
Best known as a pianist, Brown also is a bass player, trumpeter, drummer and composer.
Albums
Number	Title	Yr	NM
MUSE			
❏ MR-5385	Sources of Inspiration	198?	$25
SUNNYSIDE			
❏ SSC-1025	Early Bird	1988	$25

BROWN, LAWRENCE
Trombonist.
Albums
Number	Title	Yr	NM
ABC IMPULSE!			
❏ AS-89	Inspired Abandon	1968	$30
CLEF			
❏ MGC-682 [M]	Slide Trombone	1955	$300
IMPULSE!			
❏ A-89 [M]	Inspired Abandon	1965	$120
❏ AS-89 [S]	Inspired Abandon	1965	$120
VERVE			
❏ MGV-8067 [M]	Slide Trombone	1957	$100
❏ V-8067 [M]	Slide Trombone	1961	$25

BROWN, LES, AND VIC SCHOEN
Also see each artist's individual listings.
Albums
Number	Title	Yr	NM
KAPP			
❏ KRL-4504 [M]	Impact! Band Meets Band	196?	$50
—Reissue of KDL-7003			
❏ KRS-4504 [S]	Impact! Band Meets Band	196?	$60
—Reissue of KDS-7003			
❏ KDL-7003 [M]	Stereophonic Suite for Two Bands	195?	$60
❏ KDS-7003 [S]	Stereophonic Suite for Two Bands	195?	$40
MCA			
❏ 1548	Stereophonic Suite for Two Bands	198?	$30

BROWN, LES
Saxophone player and bandleader.
Albums
Number	Title	Yr	NM
CAPITOL			
❏ T657 [M]	College Classics	1955	$75
—Turquoise or gray label			
❏ T886 [M]	Composer's Holiday	1957	$60
—Turquoise or gray label			
❏ T959 [M]	Concert Modern	1958	$60
—Turquoise or gray label			
❏ T746 [M]	Les Brown's in Town	1956	$60
—Turquoise or gray label			
❏ T659 [M]	The Les Brown All Stars	1955	$75
—Turquoise or gray label			

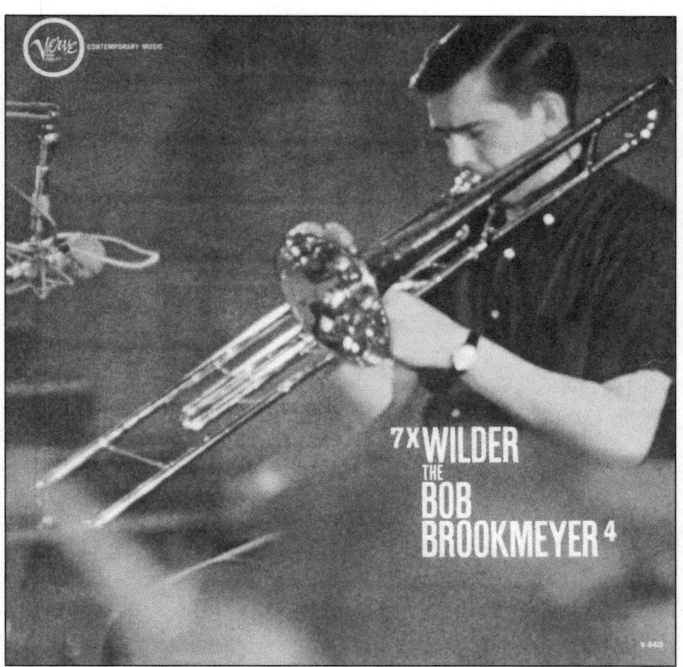

Bob Brookmeyer, *7 X Wilder*, Verve V-8413, **$100**.

Bob Brookmeyer, Jim Hall, Jimmy Raney, *The Street Swingers*, World Pacific PJ-1239, $350.

Dave Brubeck, *Re-Union*, Fantasy 3268, red vinyl, **$120**.

Dave Brubeck, *Dave Brubeck Plays and Plays and Plays and … ,* Fantasy 3259, red vinyl, **$120**.

Number	Title	Yr	NM
☐ T1174 [M]	The Les Brown Story	1959	$60
—Black colorband label, logo at left			
☐ ST1174 [S]	The Les Brown Story	1959	$60
—Black colorband label, logo at left			
☐ SM-1174	The Les Brown Story	1976	$20
—Reissue with new prefix			

CIRCLE

Number	Title	Yr	NM
☐ CLP-90	Les Brown and His Orchestra 1946	1986	$25

COLUMBIA

Number	Title	Yr	NM
☐ CL1497 [M]	Bandland	1960	$35
—Red and black label with six "eye" logos			
☐ CS8288 [S]	Bandland	1960	$25
—Red and black label with six "eye" logos			
☐ CL6159 [10]	Classics in Rhythm	195?	$40
☐ CL6060 [10]	Dance Parade	1949	$40
☐ CL539 [M]	Dance with Les Brown	1954	$40
—Maroon label, gold print			
☐ CL2030 [M]	Explosive Sound	1964	$35
—Guaranteed High Fidelity" on label			
☐ CS8830 [S]	Explosive Sound	1964	$25
—360 Sound Stereo" in black on label			
☐ CL2512 [10]	I've Got My Love to Keep Me Warm	1955	$50
☐ CL1818 [M]	Revolution in Sound	1962	$35
—Red and black label with six "eye" logos			
☐ CS8618 [S]	Revolution in Sound	1962	$25
—Red and black label with six "eye" logos			
☐ CL649 [M]	Sentimental Journey	1955	$40
—Maroon label, gold print			
☐ CL649 [M]	Sentimental Journey	1955	$40
—Red and black label with six "eye" logos			
☐ CL2561 [10]	The Cool Classics	1955	$50
☐ CS8394 [S]	The Lerner and Loewe Bandbook	1960	$25
—Red and black label with six "eye" logos			
☐ CL(# unk) [M]	The Lerner and Loewe Bandbook	1960	$35
—Red and black label with six "eye" logos			
☐ CL2119 [M]	The Young Beat	1964	$35
—Guaranteed High Fidelity" on label			
☐ CS8919 [S]	The Young Beat	1964	$25
—360 Sound Stereo" in black on label			
☐ CL6123 [10]	Your Dance Date with Les Brown	1950	$40

COLUMBIA SPECIAL PRODUCTS

Number	Title	Yr	NM
☐ P14361	Sentimental Journey	198?	$25

CORAL

Number	Title	Yr	NM
☐ CRL56108 [10]	Invitation	1954	$50
☐ CRL57311 [M]	Jazz Song Book	1959	$30
☐ CRL757311 [S]	Jazz Song Book	1959	$30
☐ CX-1 [M]	Les Brown Concert at the Palladium	1953	$60
☐ CRL57000 [M]	Les Brown Concert at the Palladium, Part 1	1954	$40
☐ CRL57001 [M]	Les Brown Concert at the Palladium, Part 1	1954	$40
☐ CRL56094 [10]	Les Dance	1953	$50
☐ CRL56116 [10]	Les Dream	1954	$50
☐ CRL57165 [10]	Love Letters in the Sand	1957	$30
☐ CRL57058 [M]	More from Les	1956	$30
☐ CRL56077 [10]	Musical Weather Vane	1953	$50
☐ CRL57051 [M]	Open House	1956	$30
☐ CRL56026 [10]	Over the Rainbow	1951	$50
☐ CRL57300 [M]	Swing Song Book	1959	$30
☐ CRL757300 [S]	Swing Song Book	1959	$30
☐ CRL56030 [10]	The Sound of Renown	1951	$50
☐ CRL57030 [M]	The Sound of Renown	1955	$40
☐ CRL56109 [10]	Time to Dance	1954	$50
☐ CRL56046 [10]	You're My Everything	1952	$100

DAYBREAK

Number	Title	Yr	NM
☐ 2007	New Horizons	1972	$30

DECCA

Number	Title	Yr	NM
☐ DL4768 [M]	A Sign of the Times	1966	$30
☐ DL74768 [S]	A Sign of the Times	1966	$35
☐ DL4607 [M]	In Town	1965	$30
☐ DL74607 [S]	In Town	1965	$35
☐ DL4965 [M]	The World of the Young	1968	$25
☐ DL74965 [S]	The World of the Young	1968	$30

FANTASY

Number	Title	Yr	NM
☐ F-9650	Digital Swing	1987	$30

GREAT AMERICAN

Number	Title	Yr	NM
☐ 1010	Les Brown Goes Direct to Disc	1981	$25

HARMONY

Number	Title	Yr	NM
☐ HL7335 [M]	Hits from The Sound of Music, My Fair Lady, Camelot and Others	1965	$30

Number	Title	Yr	NM
☐ HS11135 [S]	Hits from The Sound of Music, My Fair Lady, Camelot and Others	1965	$30
☐ HL7100 [M]	Les Brown's Greatest	196?	$30
☐ HL7211 [M]	Sentimental Journey	196?	$30
☐ KH32015	The Beat of the Bands	1972	$25

HINDSIGHT

Number	Title	Yr	NM
☐ HSR-103	Les Brown and His Orchestra 1944-45	198?	$25
☐ HSR-131	Les Brown and His Orchestra 1949	198?	$25
☐ HSR-199	Les Brown and His Orchestra 1956-57	198?	$25
☐ HSR-132	Les Brown and His Orchestra Vol. 3	198?	$25

INSIGHT

Number	Title	Yr	NM
☐ 213	Les Brown and His Orchestra, 1949	198?	$25

MCA

Number	Title	Yr	NM
☐ 4070	The Best of Les Brown	1974	$30

TIME-LIFE

Number	Title	Yr	NM
☐ STBB-11	Big Bands: Les Brown	1984	$35

VOCALION

Number	Title	Yr	NM
☐ VL3618 [M]	Les Dance	196?	$30

BROWN, MARION, AND ELLIOTT SCHWARTZ
Schwartz is a pianist and composer. Also see MARION BROWN.

Albums

CENTURY

Number	Title	Yr	NM
☐ 41746	Soundways	1973	$35

BROWN, MARION, AND GUNTER HAMPEL
Also see each artist's individual listings.

Albums

IAI

Number	Title	Yr	NM
☐ 373855	Reeds 'n Vibes	1978	$30

BROWN, MARION
Alto saxophone player.

Albums

ABC IMPULSE!

Number	Title	Yr	NM
☐ AS-9252	Geechee Recollections	1973	$30
☐ AS-9275	Sweet Earth Flying	1974	$30
☐ AS-9139	Three for Shepp	1968	$30
☐ ASD-9304	Vista	1975	$30

ARISTA FREEDOM

Number	Title	Yr	NM
☐ AL1904	Duets	1975	$35
☐ AL1001	Porto Novo	1975	$30

ECM

Number	Title	Yr	NM
☐ 1004	Afternoon of a Georgia Faun	197?	$35

ESP-DISK'

Number	Title	Yr	NM
☐ 1022 [M]	Marion Brown Quartet	1966	$25
☐ S-1022 [S]	Marion Brown Quartet	1966	$35
☐ 1040 [M]	Why Not?	1967	$100
☐ S-1040 [S]	Why Not?	1967	$100

IMPULSE!

Number	Title	Yr	NM
☐ A-9139 [M]	Three for Shepp	1967	$120
☐ AS-9139 [S]	Three for Shepp	1967	$200

SWEET EARTH

Number	Title	Yr	NM
☐ SER-1001	Solo Saxophone	1978	$30

TIMELESS

Number	Title	Yr	NM
☐ TI-314	La Placita -- Live in Willisau	197?	$30

BROWN, MEL
Drummer.

Albums

ABC

Number	Title	Yr	NM
☐ AA-1103	Actor of Music	1978	$30

ABC IMPULSE!

Number	Title	Yr	NM
☐ AS-9249 [Q]	Big Foot Country Girl	1974	$40
☐ A-9180 [M]	Blues for We	1969	$200
☐ AS-9180 [S]	Blues for We	1969	$200
☐ A-9152 [M]	Chicken Fat	1967	$120
☐ AS-9152 [S]	Chicken Fat	1967	$200
☐ AS-9209	Fifth	1971	$200
☐ AS-9186	I'd Rather Suck My Thumb	1970	$200
☐ A-9169 [M]	The Wizard	1968	$160
☐ AS-9169 [S]	The Wizard	1968	$200

BLUESWAY

Number	Title	Yr	NM
☐ 6064	18 Pounds of Uncleaned Chittlins	1973	$35

BROWN, MILTON
Bandleader and male singer. Along with BOB WILLS, he was one of the pioneers in the mixture of jazz and country music known as "Western swing."

Albums

MCA

Number	Title	Yr	NM
☐ 1509	Milton Brown and His Brownies: Pioneer Western Swing Band	198?	$30

BROWN, ODELL
Organist.

Albums

CADET

Number	Title	Yr	NM
☐ LP-800 [M]	Ducky	1967	$50
☐ LPS-800 [S]	Ducky	1967	$35
☐ LPS-838	Free Delivery	1970	$35
☐ LP-788 [M]	Mellow Yellow	1967	$50
☐ LPS-788 [S]	Mellow Yellow	1967	$35
☐ LPS-823	Odell Brown Plays Otis Redding	1969	$35
☐ LP-775 [M]	Raising the Roof	1966	$35
☐ LPS-775 [S]	Raising the Roof	1966	$50

PAULA

Number	Title	Yr	NM
☐ 4005	Odell Brown	1974	$30

BROWN, OSCAR, JR.
Male singer, poet and composer.

Albums

ATLANTIC

Number	Title	Yr	NM
☐ SD1649	Brother Where Are You	1973	$35
☐ SD18106	Fresh	1974	$30
☐ SD1629	Movin' On	1972	$35

COLUMBIA

Number	Title	Yr	NM
☐ CL1774 [M]	Between Heaven and Hell	1962	$30
—Red and black label with six "eye" logos			
☐ CS8574 [S]	Between Heaven and Hell	1962	$30
—Red and black label with six "eye" logos			
☐ CL1873 [M]	In a New Mood	1963	$25
—Red label, "Guaranteed High Fidelity" in black			
☐ CS8673 [S]	In a New Mood	1963	$30
—Red label, "360 Sound Stereo" in black			
☐ CL2025 [M]	Oscar Brown Jr. Tells It Like It Is	1964	$25
—Red label, "Guaranteed High Fidelity" in black			
☐ CS8825 [S]	Oscar Brown Jr. Tells It Like It Is	1964	$30
—Red label, "360 Sound Stereo" in black			
☐ CL1577 [M]	Sin and Soul	1960	$30
—Red and black label with six "eye" logos			
☐ CS8377 [S]	Sin and Soul	1960	$30
—Red and black label with six "eye" logos			

FONTANA

Number	Title	Yr	NM
☐ MGF-27549 [M]	Finding a New Friend	1966	$35
☐ SRF-67549 [S]	Finding a New Friend	1966	$25
☐ MGF-27540 [M]	Mr. Oscar Brown Goes to Washington	1965	$35
☐ SRF-67540 [S]	Mr. Oscar Brown Goes to Washington	1965	$25

BROWN, PETE
Alto and tenor saxophone player; also has played trumpet and violin.

Albums

BETHLEHEM

Number	Title	Yr	NM
☐ BCP-1011 [10]	Peter the Great	1954	$250

VERVE

Number	Title	Yr	NM
☐ MGV-8365 [M]	From the Heart	1958	$150
☐ MGVS-6133 [S]	From the Heart	1960	$120
☐ V-8365 [M]	From the Heart	1962	$25
☐ V6-8365 [S]	From the Heart	1962	$35

BROWN, PETE/JONAH JONES
Also see each artist's individual listings.

Albums

BETHLEHEM

Number	Title	Yr	NM
☐ BCP-4 [M]	Jazz Kaleidoscope	1957	$250

Number	Title	Yr	NM

BROWN, PUD, AND EDDIE MILLER
Also see each artist's individual listings.

Albums

NEW ORLEANS JAZZ

| ❑ NORJC-001 | Jazz for Two | 198? | $25 |

BROWN, PUD
Tenor saxophone player and clarinetist.

Albums

JAZZOLOGY

| ❑ J-166 | Pud Brown Plays Clarinet | 198? | $25 |

BROWN, RAY, AND JIMMIE ROWLES
Also see each artist's individual listings.

Albums

CONCORD JAZZ

| ❑ CJ-66 | As Good As Gold | 1977 | $30 |
| ❑ CJ-122 | Tasty | 1979 | $30 |

BROWN, RAY
Bass player. Also see THE POLL WINNERS; ANDRE PREVIN.

Albums

BLUESWAY

| ❑ BLS-6056 | Hard Times | 1971 | $35 |

CONCORD JAZZ

❑ CJ-375	Bam Bam Bam	1989	$30
❑ CJ-19	Brown's Bag	1976	$30
❑ CJ-293	Don't Forget the Blues	1986	$25
❑ CJ-213	Ray Brown 3	1982	$25
❑ CJ-268	Soular Energy	1985	$25
❑ CJ-102	The Ray Brown Trio Live at the Concord Jazz Festival	1979	$30
❑ CJ-315	The Red Hot Ray Brown Trio	1987	$25

CONTEMPORARY

| ❑ C-7641 | Something for Lester | 1978 | $25 |

FANTASY

| ❑ OJC-412 | Something for Lester | 1990 | $30 |

NORGRAN

| ❑ MGN-1105 [M] | Bass Hit! | 1956 | $0 |

—Canceled; released on Verve 8022

VERVE

❑ V-8022 [M]	Bass Hit!	1961	$25
❑ MGV-8390 [M]	Jazz Cello	1960	$100
❑ V-8390 [M]	Jazz Cello	1961	$25
❑ V-8580 [M]	Much in Common	1964	$30
❑ V6-8580 [S]	Much in Common	1964	$30

—With Milt Jackson

❑ V-8615 [M]	Ray Brown/Milt Jackson	1965	$30
❑ V6-8615 [S]	Ray Brown/Milt Jackson	1965	$30
❑ V-8444 [M]	Ray Brown with the All Star Big Band Featuring Cannonball Adderley	1962	$30
❑ V6-8444 [S]	Ray Brown with the All Star Big Band Featuring Cannonball Adderley	1962	$30
❑ UMV-2117	This Is Ray Brown	198?	$25
❑ VSP-10 [M]	Two for the Blues	1966	$30
❑ VSPS-10 [S]	Two for the Blues	1966	$35

BROWN, REUBEN, AND RICHIE COLE
Brown is a pianist. Also see RICHIE COLE.

Albums

ADELPHIA

| ❑ AD-5001 | Starburst | 1976 | $30 |

BROWN, RONNIE
Pianist.

Albums

PHILIPS

| ❑ PHM200130 [M] | Jazz for Everyone | 1964 | $35 |
| ❑ PHS600130 [S] | Jazz for Everyone | 1964 | $25 |

BROWN, RUTH
Earlier material appears in the Goldmine Standard Catalog of American Records 1950-1975. (SC2)
Female singer. Most of her recordings are in the rhythm and blues field and are located in the Standard Catalog of American Records 1950-1975.

Albums

ATLANTIC

| ❑ 1308 [M] | Last Date with Ruth Brown | 1959 | $300 |

Number	Title	Yr	NM

—Black label

| ❑ SD1308 [S] | Last Date with Ruth Brown | 1959 | $300 |

—Green label

| ❑ SD1308 [S] | Last Date with Ruth Brown | 1961 | $150 |

—Blue and green label, "fan" logo in white

DOBRE

| ❑ 1041 | You Don't Know Me | 1978 | $30 |

FANTASY

| ❑ F-9662 | Blues on Broadway | 1989 | $30 |
| ❑ F-9661 | Have a Good Time | 1988 | $30 |

ICHIBAN

| ❑ SPEG-4023 | Brown, Black and Beautiful | 198? | $30 |

MAINSTREAM

❑ 56034 [M]	Ruth Brown '65	1965	$60
❑ S-6034 [S]	Ruth Brown '65	1965	$60
❑ 369	Softly	1972	$30

SKYE

| ❑ SK-13 | Black Is Brown and Brown Is Beautiful | 1970 | $35 |

BROWN, TED
Tenor saxophone player.

Albums

CRISS CROSS

| ❑ 1031 | Free Spirit | 1988 | $30 |

VANGUARD

| ❑ VRS-8515 [M] | Free Wheeling | 1956 | $1000 |

BROWN, WINI
Female singer.

Albums

SAVOY JAZZ

| ❑ SJL-1163 [M] | Miss Brown for You | 1986 | $25 |

BROWNE, BRIAN
Pianist.

Albums

JAZZIMAGE

| ❑ JZ-105 | Beatles | 198? | $35 |

BROWNE, TOM
Trumpeter.

Albums

ARISTA

| ❑ AL8107 | Rockin' Radio | 1983 | $10 |
| ❑ AL8-8249 | Tommy Gun | 1984 | $10 |

ARISTA/GRP

❑ GL5003	Browne Sugar	1979	$12
❑ GL5008	Love Approach	1980	$12
❑ GL5502	Love Approach	1981	$10

—Reissue of 5008

| ❑ GL5503 | Magic | 1981 | $12 |
| ❑ GL5507 | Yours Truly | 1981 | $25 |

MALACO

| ❑ MJ-1500 | No Longer I | 1989 | $15 |

BRUBECK, DAVE
Pianist, composer and bandleader. His quartet was one of the most popular and influential jazz groups of the late 1950s and early 1960s. Also see PAUL DESMOND.

7-Inch Extended Plays

COLUMBIA

| ❑ B-435 [PS] | Jazz Goes to College Vol. I | 1955 | $40 |

—Dual-pocket sleeve for 1940 and 1941

| ❑ B-436 [PS] | Jazz Goes to College Vol. II | 1955 | $40 |

—Dual-pocket sleeve for 1942 and 1943

Albums

ATLANTIC

❑ SD1684	All the Things We Are	1976	$30
❑ SD1660	Brother, The Great Spirit Made Us All	1974	$30
❑ SD 2-317	The Art of Dave Brubeck: The Fantasy Years	1975	$35
❑ SD1607	The Last Set at Newport	1972	$30
❑ SD1606	Truth Is Fallen	1972	$30
❑ SD1645	Two Generations of Brubeck	1974	$30
❑ SD1641	We're All Together Again for the First Time	1973	$30

BOOK-OF-THE-MONTH

| ❑ 80-5547 | Early Fantasies | 1980 | $50 |

COLUMBIA

Number	Title	Yr	NM

❑ G30625	Adventures in Time	1971	$35
❑ KG32761	All-Time Greatest Hits	1974	$35
❑ CL932 [M]	American Jazz Festival at Newport '56	1956	$100

—Red/black label with six "eye" logos

| ❑ CL932 [M] | American Jazz Festival at Newport '56 | 1962 | $50 |

—Red "Guaranteed High Fidelity" label

| ❑ CL2348 [M] | Angel Eyes | 1965 | $50 |

—Red "Guaranteed High Fidelity" label

| ❑ CL2348 [M] | Angel Eyes | 1966 | $30 |

—Red "360 Sound" label

| ❑ CS9148 [S] | Angel Eyes | 1965 | $60 |

—Red label, "360 Sound" in black

| ❑ CS9148 [S] | Angel Eyes | 1966 | $35 |

—Red label, "360 Sound" in white

| ❑ CL2602 [M] | Anything Goes! Dave Brubeck Quartet Plays Cole Porter | 1966 | $35 |
| ❑ CS9402 [S] | Anything Goes! Dave Brubeck Quartet Plays Cole Porter | 1966 | $50 |

—Red "360 Sound" label

| ❑ CS9402 | Anything Goes! Dave Brubeck Quartet Plays Cole Porter | 1971 | $30 |

—Orange label

| ❑ PC9402 | Anything Goes! Dave Brubeck Quartet Plays Cole Porter | 1981 | $20 |

—Reissue with new prefix

| ❑ PC37022 | A Place in Time | 1981 | $25 |

—Reissue of Odyssey LP

| ❑ CL1466 [M] | Bernstein Plays Brubeck Plays Bernstein | 1960 | $60 |

—Red/black label with six "eye" logos

| ❑ CL1466 [M] | Bernstein Plays Brubeck Plays Bernstein | 1962 | $35 |

—Red "Guaranteed High Fidelity" label

| ❑ CL1466 [M] | Bernstein Plays Brubeck Plays Bernstein | 1966 | $30 |

—Red "360 Sound" label

| ❑ CS9749 | Blues Roots | 1969 | $35 |

—Red "360 Sound" label

| ❑ CS9749 | Blues Roots | 1971 | $30 |

—Orange label

| ❑ CL1998 [M] | Bossa Nova U.S.A. | 1963 | $50 |

—Red "Guaranteed High Fidelity" label

| ❑ CL1998 [M] | Bossa Nova U.S.A. | 1966 | $30 |

—Red "360 Sound" label

| ❑ CS8798 [S] | Bossa Nova U.S.A. | 1963 | $60 |

—Red label, "360 Sound" in black

| ❑ CS8798 [S] | Bossa Nova U.S.A. | 1966 | $35 |

—Red label, "360 Sound" in white

| ❑ CL1963 [M] | Brandenburg Gate Revisited | 1963 | $50 |

—Red "Guaranteed High Fidelity" label

| ❑ CL1963 [M] | Brandenburg Gate Revisited | 1966 | $30 |

—Red "360 Sound" label

| ❑ CS8763 [S] | Brandenburg Gate Revisited | 1963 | $60 |

—Red label, "360 Sound" in black

| ❑ CS8763 [S] | Brandenburg Gate Revisited | 1966 | $35 |

—Red label, "360 Sound" in white

| ❑ CL2695 [M] | Bravo Brubeck! | 1967 | $50 |
| ❑ CS9495 [S] | Bravo Brubeck! | 1967 | $35 |

—Red "360 Sound" label

| ❑ CS9495 | Bravo Brubeck! | 1971 | $30 |

—Orange label

| ❑ CL1553 [M] | Brubeck and Rushing | 1961 | $60 |

—Red/black label with six "eye" logos

| ❑ CL1553 [M] | Brubeck and Rushing | 1962 | $35 |

—Red "Guaranteed High Fidelity" label

| ❑ CL1553 [M] | Brubeck and Rushing | 1966 | $30 |

—Red "360 Sound" label

| ❑ CS8353 [S] | Brubeck and Rushing | 1961 | $60 |

—Red/black label with six "eye" logos

| ❑ CS8353 [S] | Brubeck and Rushing | 1962 | $50 |

—Red label, "360 Sound" in black

| ❑ CS8353 [S] | Brubeck and Rushing | 1966 | $35 |

—Red label, "360 Sound" in white

| ❑ KC32143 | Brubeck at the Berlin Philharmonic | 1973 | $30 |
| ❑ CS9897 | Brubeck in Amsterdam | 1969 | $35 |

—Red "360 Sound" label

Number	Title	Yr	NM
❑ CS9897	Brubeck in Amsterdam	1971	$30
—Orange label			
❑ KG31298	Brubeck On Campus	1972	$35
❑ CS8257 [S]	Brubeck Plays Bernstein Plays Brubeck	1960	$60
—Red/black label with six "eye" logos			
❑ CS8257 [S]	Brubeck Plays Bernstein Plays Brubeck	1962	$50
—Red label, "360 Sound" in black			
❑ CS8257 [S]	Brubeck Plays Bernstein Plays Brubeck	1966	$35
—Red label, "360 Sound" in white			
❑ CS8257	Brubeck Plays Bernstein Plays Brubeck	1971	$30
—Orange label			
❑ CL878 [M]	Brubeck Plays Brubeck	1956	$120
—Red/black label with six "eye" logos			
❑ CL878 [M]	Brubeck Plays Brubeck	1962	$50
—Red "Guaranteed High Fidelity" label			
❑ CL878 [M]	Brubeck Plays Brubeck	1966	$30
—Red "360 Sound" label			
❑ CL622 [M]	Brubeck Time	1955	$120
—Red/black label with six "eye" logos			
❑ CL622 [M]	Brubeck Time	1962	$50
—Red "Guaranteed High Fidelity" label			
❑ CL622 [M]	Brubeck Time	1966	$30
—Red "360 Sound" label			
❑ CS9704	Compadres	1968	$35
—Red "360 Sound" label			
❑ CS9704	Compadres	1971	$30
—Orange label			
❑ CL1775 [M]	Countdown -- Time in Outer Space	1962	$60
—Red/black label with six "eye" logos			
❑ CL1775 [M]	Countdown -- Time in Outer Space	1962	$35
—Red "Guaranteed High Fidelity" label			
❑ CL1775 [M]	Countdown -- Time in Outer Space	1966	$30
—Red "360 Sound" label			
❑ CS8575 [S]	Countdown -- Time in Outer Space	1962	$40
—Red/black label with six "eye" logos			
❑ CS8575 [S]	Countdown -- Time in Outer Space	1962	$50
—Red label, "360 Sound" in black			
❑ CS8575 [S]	Countdown -- Time in Outer Space	1966	$35
—Red label, "360 Sound" in white			
❑ CL590 [M]	Dave Brubeck at Storyville: 1954	1954	$150
—Dark red label, gold print; released at the same time as 6330 and 6331			
❑ CL590 [M]	Dave Brubeck at Storyville: 1954	1955	$100
—Red/black label with six "eye" logos			
❑ CL590 [M]	Dave Brubeck at Storyville: 1954	1962	$50
—Red "Guaranteed High Fidelity" label			
❑ CL590 [M]	Dave Brubeck at Storyville: 1954	1966	$30
—Red "360 Sound" label			
❑ CL6330 [10]	Dave Brubeck at Storyville: 1954, Volume 1	1954	$150
❑ CL6331 [10]	Dave Brubeck at Storyville: 1954, Volume 2	1954	$150
❑ CL2484 [M]	Dave Brubeck's Greatest Hits	1966	$35
❑ CS9284 [S]	Dave Brubeck's Greatest Hits	1966	$50
—Red "360 Sound" label			
❑ CS9284	Dave Brubeck's Greatest Hits	1971	$30
—Orange label			
❑ PC9284	Dave Brubeck's Greatest Hits	1981	$20
—Reissue with new prefix			
❑ CL1059 [M]	Dave Digs Disney	1957	$40
—Red/black label with six "eye" logos			
❑ CL1059 [M]	Dave Digs Disney	1962	$50
—Red "Guaranteed High Fidelity" label			
❑ CL1059 [M]	Dave Digs Disney	1966	$30
—Red "360 Sound" label			
❑ CS8090 [S]	Dave Digs Disney	1959	$100
—Red/black label with six "eye" logos			
❑ CS8090 [S]	Dave Digs Disney	1962	$60
—Red label, "360 Sound" in black			
❑ CS8090 [S]	Dave Digs Disney	1966	$35
—Red label, "360 Sound" in white			
❑ CL1347 [M]	Gone with the Wind	1959	$40
—Red/black label with six "eye" logos			
❑ CL1347 [M]	Gone with the Wind	1962	$50
—Red "Guaranteed High Fidelity" label			
❑ CL1347 [M]	Gone with the Wind	1966	$30
—Red "360 Sound" label			
❑ CS8156 [S]	Gone with the Wind	1959	$100
—Red/black label with six "eye" logos			
❑ CS8156 [S]	Gone with the Wind	1962	$60
—Red label, "360 Sound" in black			
❑ CS8156 [S]	Gone with the Wind	1966	$35
—Red label, "360 Sound" in white			
❑ CS8156	Gone with the Wind	1971	$30
—Orange label			
❑ CG33666	Gone with the Wind/Time Out	1975	$35
❑ CL2712 [M]	Jackpot	1967	$50
❑ CS9512 [S]	Jackpot	1967	$35
—Red "360 Sound" label			
❑ CL699 [M]	Jazz: Red Hot and Cool	1955	$120
—Red/black label with six "eye" logos			
❑ CL699 [M]	Jazz: Red Hot and Cool	1962	$50
—Red "Guaranteed High Fidelity" label			
❑ CL699 [M]	Jazz: Red Hot and Cool	1966	$30
—Red "360 Sound" label			
❑ CS8645 [R]	Jazz: Red Hot and Cool	1963	$35
—Red label, "360 Sound" in black			
❑ CS8645 [R]	Jazz: Red Hot and Cool	1966	$30
—Red label, "360 Sound" in white			
❑ CL566 [M]	Jazz Goes to College	1954	$150
—Dark red label, gold print; released at the same time as 6321 and 6322			
❑ CL566 [M]	Jazz Goes to College	1955	$100
—Red/black label with six "eye" logos			
❑ CL566 [M]	Jazz Goes to College	1962	$50
—Red "Guaranteed High Fidelity" label			
❑ CL566 [M]	Jazz Goes to College	1966	$30
—Red "360 Sound" label			
❑ CL6321 [10]	Jazz Goes to College, Volume 1	1954	$175
❑ CL6322 [10]	Jazz Goes to College, Volume 2	1954	$175
❑ CL1034 [M]	Jazz Goes to Junior College	1957	$40
—Red/black label with six "eye" logos			
❑ CL1034 [M]	Jazz Goes to Junior College	1962	$50
—Red "Guaranteed High Fidelity" label			
❑ CL1034 [M]	Jazz Goes to Junior College	1966	$30
—Red "360 Sound" label			
❑ CL1251 [M]	Jazz Impressions of Eurasia	1958	$40
—Red/black label with six "eye" logos			
❑ CL1251 [M]	Jazz Impressions of Eurasia	1962	$50
—Red "Guaranteed High Fidelity" label			
❑ CL1251 [M]	Jazz Impressions of Eurasia	1966	$30
—Red "360 Sound" label			
❑ CS8058 [S]	Jazz Impressions of Eurasia	1959	$100
—Red/black label with six "eye" logos			
❑ CS8058 [S]	Jazz Impressions of Eurasia	1962	$60
—Red label, "360 Sound" in black			
❑ CS8058 [S]	Jazz Impressions of Eurasia	1966	$35
—Red label, "360 Sound" in white			
❑ CL2212 [M]	Jazz Impressions of Japan	1964	$50
—Red "Guaranteed High Fidelity" label			
❑ CL2212 [M]	Jazz Impressions of Japan	1966	$30
—Red "360 Sound" label			
❑ CS9012 [S]	Jazz Impressions of Japan	1964	$60
—Red label, "360 Sound" in black			
❑ CS9012 [S]	Jazz Impressions of Japan	1966	$35
—Red label, "360 Sound" in white			
❑ CS9012	Jazz Impressions of Japan	1971	$30
—Orange label			
❑ PC9012	Jazz Impressions of Japan	1981	$20
—Reissue with new prefix			
❑ CL2275 [M]	Jazz Impressions of New York	1965	$50
—Red "Guaranteed High Fidelity" label			
❑ CL2275 [M]	Jazz Impressions of New York	1966	$30
—Red "360 Sound" label			
❑ CS9075 [S]	Jazz Impressions of New York	1965	$60
—Red label, "360 Sound" in black			
❑ CS9075 [S]	Jazz Impressions of New York	1966	$35
—Red label, "360 Sound" in white			
❑ CS9075	Jazz Impressions of New York	1971	$30
—Orange label			
❑ PC9075	Jazz Impressions of New York	1981	$20
—Reissue with new prefix			
❑ CL984 [M]	Jazz Impressions of the U.S.A.	1957	$100
—Red/black label with six "eye" logos			
❑ CL984 [M]	Jazz Impressions of the U.S.A.	1962	$50
—Red "Guaranteed High Fidelity" label			
❑ CL984 [M]	Jazz Impressions of the U.S.A.	1966	$30
—Red "360 Sound" label			
❑ CL2437 [M]	My Favorite Things	1966	$35
❑ CS9237 [S]	My Favorite Things	1966	$50
—Red "360 Sound" label			
❑ CL1249 [M]	Newport 1958	1958	$40
—Red/black label with six "eye" logos			
❑ CL1249 [M]	Newport 1958	1962	$50
—Red "Guaranteed High Fidelity" label			
❑ CL1249 [M]	Newport 1958	1966	$30
—Red "360 Sound" label			
❑ CS8082 [S]	Newport 1958	1959	$100
—Red/black label with six "eye" logos			
❑ CS8082 [S]	Newport 1958	1962	$60
—Red label, "360 Sound" in black			
❑ CS8082 [S]	Newport 1958	1966	$35
—Red label, "360 Sound" in white			
❑ CL1439 [M]	Southern Scene	1960	$60
—Red/black label with six "eye" logos			
❑ CL1439 [M]	Southern Scene	1962	$35
—Red "Guaranteed High Fidelity" label			
❑ CL1439 [M]	Southern Scene	1966	$30
—Red "360 Sound" label			
❑ CS8235 [S]	Southern Scene	1960	$60
—Red/black label with six "eye" logos			
❑ CS8235 [S]	Southern Scene	1962	$50
—Red label, "360 Sound" in black			
❑ CS8235 [S]	Southern Scene	1966	$35
—Red label, "360 Sound" in white			
❑ CL2316 [M]	Take Five	1965	$50
—Red "Guaranteed High Fidelity" label			
❑ CL2316 [M]	Take Five	1966	$30
—Red "360 Sound" label			
❑ CS9116 [S]	Take Five	1965	$60
—Red label, "360 Sound" in black			
❑ CS9116 [S]	Take Five	1966	$35
—Red label, "360 Sound" in white			
❑ C2L26 [M]	The Dave Brubeck Quartet at Carnegie Hall	1963	$60
—Red "Guaranteed High Fidelity" label			
❑ C2L26 [M]	The Dave Brubeck Quartet at Carnegie Hall	1966	$35
—Red "360 Sound" label			
❑ C2S826 [S]	The Dave Brubeck Quartet at Carnegie Hall	1963	$60
—Red label, "360 Sound" in black			
❑ C2S826 [S]	The Dave Brubeck Quartet at Carnegie Hall	1966	$50
—Red label, "360 Sound" in white			
❑ C2S826	The Dave Brubeck Quartet at Carnegie Hall	1971	$35
—Orange label			
❑ CL1168 [M]	The Dave Brubeck Quartet in Europe	1958	$40
—Red/black label with six "eye" logos			
❑ CL1168 [M]	The Dave Brubeck Quartet in Europe	1962	$50
—Red "Guaranteed High Fidelity" label			
❑ CL1168 [M]	The Dave Brubeck Quartet in Europe	1966	$30
—Red "360 Sound" label			
❑ CS9672	The Last Time We Saw Paris	1968	$35

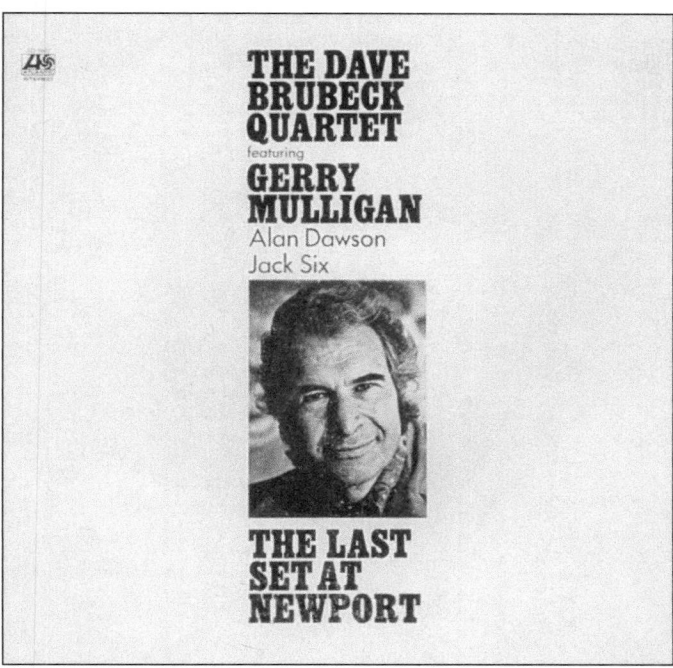

Dave Brubeck, *The Last Set at Newport*, Atlantic SD 1607, **$30**.

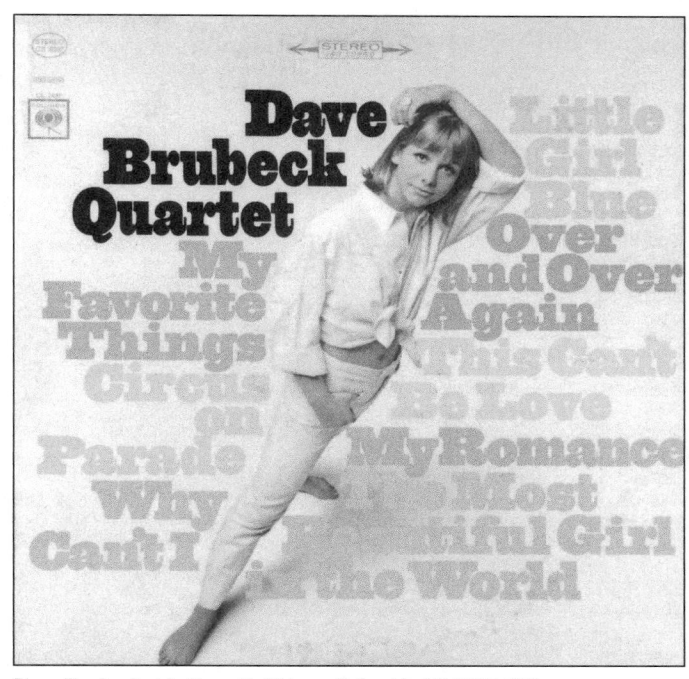

Dave Brubeck, *My Favorite Things*, Columbia CS 9237, **$50**.

Dave Brubeck, *Old Sounds from San Francisco*, Fantasy 3-16, 10-inch LP, red or purple vinyl, **$250**.

Lord Buckley, *Hipsters, Flipsters and Finger Poppin' Daddies, Knock Me Your Lobes*, RCA Victor LPM-3246, 10-inch LP, **$600**.

Number	Title	Yr	NM
—Red "360 Sound" label			
❏ CS9572	The Last Time We Saw Paris	1971	$30
— Orange label			
❏ CL1454 [M]	The Riddle	1960	$60
— Red/black label with six "eye" logos			
❏ CL1454 [M]	The Riddle	1962	$35
— Red "Guaranteed High Fidelity" label			
❏ CL1454 [M]	The Riddle	1966	$30
— Red "360 Sound" label			
❏ CS8248 [S]	The Riddle	1960	$60
— Red/black label with six "eye" logos			
❏ CS8248 [S]	The Riddle	1962	$50
— Red label, "360 Sound" in black			
❏ CS8248 [S]	The Riddle	1966	$35
— Red label, "360 Sound" in white			
❏ C30522	The Summit Sessions	1971	$30
❏ CL2127 [M]	Time Changes	1964	$50
— Red "Guaranteed High Fidelity" label			
❏ CL2127 [M]	Time Changes	1966	$30
— Red "360 Sound" label			
❏ CS8927 [S]	Time Changes	1964	$60
— Red label, "360 Sound" in black			
❏ CS8927 [S]	Time Changes	1966	$35
— Red label, "360 Sound" in white			
❏ CL1690 [M]	Time Further Out	1961	$60
— Red/black label with six "eye" logos			
❏ CL1690 [M]	Time Further Out	1962	$35
— Red "Guaranteed High Fidelity" label			
❏ CL1690 [M]	Time Further Out	1966	$30
— Red "360 Sound" label			
❏ CS8490 [S]	Time Further Out	1961	$60
— Red/black label with six "eye" logos			
❏ CS8490 [S]	Time Further Out	1962	$50
— Red label, "360 Sound" in black			
❏ CS8490 [S]	Time Further Out	1966	$35
— Red label, "360 Sound" in white			
❏ CS8490	Time Further Out	1971	$30
— Orange label			
❏ PC8490	Time Further Out	1981	$20
— Reissue with new prefix			
❏ CL2512 [M]	Time In	1966	$35
❏ CS9312 [S]	Time In	1966	$50
— Red "360 Sound" label			
❏ CS9312	Time In	1971	$30
— Orange label			
❏ PC9312	Time In	1981	$20
— Reissue with new prefix			
❏ CL1397 [M]	Time Out	1960	$60
— Red/black label with six "eye" logos			
❏ PC8192	Time Out	1981	$20
— Reissue with new prefix			
❏ CS8192	Time Out	1995	$60
— Audiophile vinyl, distributed by Classic Records			
❏ CL1397 [M]	Time Out Featuring "Take Five	1962	$35
— Red "Guaranteed High Fidelity" label; beginning with this issue, the cover was altered to emphasize the hit			
❏ CL1397 [M]	Time Out Featuring "Take Five	1966	$30
— Red "360 Sound" label			
❏ CS8192 [S]	Time Out Featuring "Take Five	1962	$50
— Red label, "360 Sound" in black; beginning with this issue, the cover was altered to emphasize the hit			
❏ CS8192 [S]	Time Out Featuring "Take Five	1966	$35
— Red label, "360 Sound" in white			
❏ CS8192	Time Out Featuring "Take Five	1971	$30
— Orange label			
❏ CL1609 [M]	Tonight Only!	1961	$60
— Red/black label with six "eye" logos			
❏ CL1609 [M]	Tonight Only!	1962	$35
— Red "Guaranteed High Fidelity" label			
❏ CL1609 [M]	Tonight Only!	1966	$30
— Red "360 Sound" label			
❏ CS8409 [S]	Tonight Only!	1961	$60
— Red/black label with six "eye" logos			
❏ CS8409 [S]	Tonight Only!	1962	$50
— Red label, "360 Sound" in black			
❏ CS8409 [S]	Tonight Only!	1966	$35

Number	Title	Yr	NM
— Red label, "360 Sound" in white			
COLUMBIA JAZZ MASTERPIECES			
❏ CJ40627	Gone with the Wind	1987	$25
❏ CJ45149	Jazz Goes to College	1989	$25
❏ CJ40455	The Dave Brubeck Quartet Plays Music from West Side Story and Other Shows and Films	1987	$25
❏ CJ40585	Time Out	1987	$25
COLUMBIA LIMITED EDITION			
❏ LE10013	Gone with the Wind	197?	$25
CONCORD JAZZ			
❏ CJ-103	Back Home	1979	$25
❏ CJ-317	Blue Rondo	1987	$25
❏ CJ-198	Concord on a Summer Night	1982	$25
❏ CJ-259	For Iola	1985	$25
❏ CJ-353	Moscow Night	1988	$25
❏ CJ-178	Paper Moon	1982	$25
❏ CJ-299	Reflections	1986	$25
❏ CJ-129	Tritonis	1980	$25
CROWN			
❏ CLP5470 [M]	Dave Brubeck and the George Nielson Quartet	196?	$35
❏ CLP-5406 [M]	The Greats	196?	$35
DECCA			
❏ DL710181	Brubeck/Mulligan/Cincinnati	1971	$30
❏ DL710175	The Gates of Justice	1969	$30
❏ DXSA7202	The Light in the Wilderness	1968	$35
— Records are individually numbered "DL 710,155" and "DL 710,156			
DIRECT DISK			
❏ 106	A Cut Above	1979	$60
FANTASY			
❏ 3249 [M]	Brubeck & Desmond at Wilshire-Ebell	1957	$175
— Dark red vinyl			
❏ 3249 [M]	Brubeck & Desmond at Wilshire-Ebell	195?	$60
— Black vinyl, red label, non-flexible vinyl			
❏ 3249 [M]	Brubeck & Desmond at Wilshire-Ebell	196?	$40
— Black vinyl, red label, flexible vinyl			
❏ 3301 [M]	Brubeck A La Mode	1960	$120
— Red vinyl			
❏ 3301 [M]	Brubeck A La Mode	1960	$40
— Black vinyl, red label, non-flexible vinyl			
❏ 3301 [M]	Brubeck A La Mode	196?	$60
— Black vinyl, red label, flexible vinyl			
❏ 8047 [S]	Brubeck A La Mode	1962	$100
— Blue vinyl			
❏ 8047 [S]	Brubeck A La Mode	196?	$60
— Black vinyl, blue label, non-flexible vinyl			
❏ 8047 [S]	Brubeck A La Mode	196?	$50
— Black vinyl, blue label, flexible vinyl			
❏ OJC-200	Brubeck A La Mode	1985	$25
❏ 8095 [S]	Brubeck and Desmond at Wilshire-Ebell	1962	$100
— Blue vinyl			
❏ 8095 [S]	Brubeck and Desmond at Wilshire-Ebell	1962	$60
— Black vinyl, blue label, non-flexible vinyl			
❏ 8095 [S]	Brubeck and Desmond at Wilshire-Ebell	196?	$50
— Black vinyl, blue label, flexible vinyl			
❏ 3229 [M]	Brubeck-Desmond	1956	$175
— Dark red vinyl; reissue of 3-5			
❏ 3229 [M]	Brubeck-Desmond	195?	$60
— Black vinyl, red label, non-flexible vinyl			
❏ 3229 [M]	Brubeck-Desmond	196?	$40
— Black vinyl, red label, flexible vinyl			
❏ 8092 [R]	Brubeck-Desmond	1962	$40
— Blue vinyl			
❏ 8092 [R]	Brubeck-Desmond	1962	$50
— Black vinyl, blue label, non-flexible vinyl			
❏ 8092 [R]	Brubeck-Desmond	196?	$35
— Black vinyl, blue label, flexible vinyl			
❏ 24727	Brubeck-Desmond	1982	$35
❏ 3240 [M]	Brubeck Desmond: Jazz at Storyville	1957	$175
— Dark red vinyl; reissue of 3-8			
❏ 3240 [M]	Brubeck Desmond: Jazz at Storyville	195?	$60
— Black vinyl, red label, non-flexible vinyl			
❏ 3240 [M]	Brubeck Desmond: Jazz at Storyville	196?	$40
— Black vinyl, red label, flexible vinyl			

Number	Title	Yr	NM
❏ 3332 [M]	Brubeck Tjader	1962	$120
— Red vinyl			
❏ 3332 [M]	Brubeck Tjader	1962	$40
— Black vinyl, red label, non-flexible vinyl			
❏ 3332 [M]	Brubeck Tjader	196?	$60
— Black vinyl, red label, flexible vinyl			
❏ 8074 [R]	Brubeck Tjader	1962	$40
— Blue vinyl			
❏ 8074 [R]	Brubeck Tjader	1962	$50
— Black vinyl, blue label, non-flexible vinyl			
❏ 8074 [R]	Brubeck Tjader	196?	$35
— Black vinyl, blue label, flexible vinyl			
❏ 3-3 [10]	Dave Brubeck Octet	1951	$150
❏ 3239 [M]	Dave Brubeck Octet	1956	$175
— Dark red vinyl; reissue of 3-3			
❏ 3239 [M]	Dave Brubeck Octet	195?	$60
— Black vinyl, red label, non-flexible vinyl			
❏ 3239 [M]	Dave Brubeck Octet	196?	$40
— Black vinyl, red label, flexible vinyl			
❏ 8094 [R]	Dave Brubeck Octet	1962	$40
— Blue vinyl			
❏ 8094 [R]	Dave Brubeck Octet	1962	$50
— Black vinyl, blue label, non-flexible vinyl			
❏ 8094 [R]	Dave Brubeck Octet	196?	$35
— Black vinyl, blue label, flexible vinyl			
❏ 3259 [M]	Dave Brubeck Plays and Plays and Plays and Plays and…	1958	$120
— Red vinyl			
❏ 3259 [M]	Dave Brubeck Plays and Plays and Plays and Plays and…	195?	$40
— Black vinyl, red label, non-flexible vinyl			
❏ 3259 [M]	Dave Brubeck Plays and Plays and Plays and Plays and…	196?	$60
— Black vinyl, red label, flexible vinyl			
❏ 3230 [M]	Dave Brubeck Quartet	1956	$175
— Dark red vinyl; reissue of 3-7			
❏ 3230 [M]	Dave Brubeck Quartet	195?	$60
— Black vinyl, red label, non-flexible vinyl			
❏ 3230 [M]	Dave Brubeck Quartet	196?	$40
— Black vinyl, red label, flexible vinyl			
❏ 8093 [R]	Dave Brubeck Quartet	1962	$40
— Blue vinyl			
❏ 8093 [R]	Dave Brubeck Quartet	1962	$50
— Black vinyl, blue label, non-flexible vinyl			
❏ 8093 [R]	Dave Brubeck Quartet	196?	$35
— Black vinyl, blue label, flexible vinyl			
❏ 3-5 [10]	Dave Brubeck Quartet with Paul Desmond	1952	$150
❏ 3-7 [10]	Dave Brubeck Quartet with Paul Desmond	1952	$150
❏ 3-1 [10]	Dave Brubeck Trio	1951	$150
❏ 3-2 [10]	Dave Brubeck Trio	1951	$150
❏ 3-4 [10]	Dave Brubeck Trio	1952	$150
❏ 3204 [M]	Dave Brubeck Trio	1956	$175
— Dark red vinyl; reissue of 3-1			
❏ 3204 [M]	Dave Brubeck Trio	195?	$60
— Black vinyl, red label, non-flexible vinyl			
❏ 3204 [M]	Dave Brubeck Trio	196?	$40
— Black vinyl, red label, flexible vinyl			
❏ 3205 [M]	Dave Brubeck Trio: Distinctive Rhythm Instrumentals	1956	$175
— Dark red vinyl; reissue of 3-2			
❏ 3205 [M]	Dave Brubeck Trio: Distinctive Rhythm Instrumentals	195?	$60
— Black vinyl, red label, non-flexible vinyl			
❏ 3205 [M]	Dave Brubeck Trio: Distinctive Rhythm Instrumentals	196?	$40
— Black vinyl, red label, flexible vinyl			
❏ 3331 [M]	Dave Brubeck Trio Featuring Cal Tjader	1962	$120
— Red vinyl			
❏ 3331 [M]	Dave Brubeck Trio Featuring Cal Tjader	1962	$40
— Black vinyl, red label, non-flexible vinyl			
❏ 3331 [M]	Dave Brubeck Trio Featuring Cal Tjader	196?	$60
— Black vinyl, red label, flexible vinyl			

Number	Title	Yr	NM
❑ 8073 [R]	Dave Brubeck Trio Featuring Cal Tjader	1962	$40
—Blue vinyl			
❑ 8073 [R]	Dave Brubeck Trio Featuring Cal Tjader	1962	$50
—Black vinyl, blue label, non-flexible vinyl			
❑ 8073 [R]	Dave Brubeck Trio Featuring Cal Tjader	196?	$35
—Black vinyl, blue label, flexible vinyl			
❑ MPF-4528	Greatest Hits from the Fantasy Years	1987	$25
❑ 3-11 [10]	Jazz at Oberlin	1953	$200
—Red vinyl			
❑ 3245 [M]	Jazz at Oberlin	1957	$175
—Dark red vinyl; reissue of 3-11			
❑ 3245 [M]	Jazz at Oberlin	195?	$60
—Black vinyl, red label, non-flexible vinyl			
❑ 3245 [M]	Jazz at Oberlin	196?	$40
—Black vinyl, red label, flexible vinyl			
❑ 8069 [R]	Jazz at Oberlin	1962	$40
—Blue vinyl			
❑ 8069 [R]	Jazz at Oberlin	196?	$50
—Black vinyl, blue label, non-flexible vinyl			
❑ 8069 [R]	Jazz at Oberlin	196?	$35
—Black vinyl, blue label, flexible vinyl			
❑ OJC-046	Jazz at Oberlin	198?	$25
—Reissue of 3245			
❑ 3-11 [10]	Jazz at Oberlin	1953	$175
—Black vinyl			
❑ 3-8 [10]	Jazz at Storyville	1953	$150
❑ 8080 [R]	Jazz at Storyville	1962	$40
—Blue vinyl			
❑ 8080 [R]	Jazz at Storyville	1962	$50
—Black vinyl, blue label, non-flexible vinyl			
❑ 8080 [R]	Jazz at Storyville	196?	$35
—Black vinyl, blue label, flexible vinyl			
❑ 3-10 [10]	Jazz at the Blackhawk	1953	$150
❑ 3210 [M]	Jazz at the Blackhawk	1956	$175
—Dark red vinyl; reissue of 3-10			
❑ 3210 [M]	Jazz at the Blackhawk	195?	$60
—Black vinyl, red label, non-flexible vinyl			
❑ 3210 [M]	Jazz at the Blackhawk	196?	$40
—Black vinyl, red label, flexible vinyl			
❑ 3-13 [10]	Jazz at the College of the Pacific	1954	$150
❑ 3223 [M]	Jazz at the College of the Pacific	1956	$175
—Dark red vinyl; reissue of 3-13			
❑ 3223 [M]	Jazz at the College of the Pacific	195?	$60
—Black vinyl, red label, non-flexible vinyl			
❑ 3223 [M]	Jazz at the College of the Pacific	196?	$40
—Black vinyl, red label, flexible vinyl			
❑ 8078 [R]	Jazz at the College of the Pacific	1962	$40
—Blue vinyl			
❑ 8078 [R]	Jazz at the College of the Pacific	196?	$50
—Black vinyl, blue label, non-flexible vinyl			
❑ 8078 [R]	Jazz at the College of the Pacific	196?	$35
—Black vinyl, blue label, flexible vinyl			
❑ OJC-047	Jazz at the College of the Pacific	198?	$25
—Reissue of 3223			
❑ OJC-236	Near Myth	1986	$25
—Reissue of Fantasy 3319			
❑ 3319 [M]	Near-Myth	1961	$120
—Red vinyl			
❑ 3319 [M]	Near-Myth	1961	$40
—Black vinyl, red label, non-flexible vinyl			
❑ 3319 [M]	Near-Myth	196?	$60
—Black vinyl, red label, flexible vinyl			
❑ 8063 [S]	Near-Myth	1962	$100
—Blue vinyl			
❑ 8063 [S]	Near-Myth	196?	$60
—Black vinyl, blue label, non-flexible vinyl			
❑ 8063 [S]	Near-Myth	196?	$50
—Black vinyl, blue label, flexible vinyl			
❑ 3-16 [10]	Old Sounds from San Francisco	1954	$250
—Red or purple vinyl			

Number	Title	Yr	NM
❑ 3-20 [10]	Paul and Dave's Jazz Interwoven	1955	$150
❑ 3268 [M]	Re-Union	1958	$120
—Red vinyl			
❑ 3268 [M]	Re-Union	195?	$40
—Black vinyl, red label, non-flexible vinyl			
❑ 3268 [M]	Re-Union	196?	$60
—Black vinyl, red label, flexible vinyl			
❑ 8007 [S]	Re-Union	1962	$100
—Blue vinyl			
❑ 8007 [S]	Re-Union	196?	$60
—Black vinyl, blue label, non-flexible vinyl			
❑ 8007 [S]	Re-Union	196?	$50
—Black vinyl, blue label, flexible vinyl			
❑ OJC-150	Re-Union	198?	$25
❑ 24728	Stardust	198?	$35
❑ OJC-101	The Dave Brubeck Octet	198?	$25
—Reissue of Fantasy 3239			
❑ 24726	The Dave Brubeck Trio	198?	$35
❑ 3298 [M]	Two Knights at the Black Hawk	1959	$120
—Red vinyl			
❑ 3298 [M]	Two Knights at the Black Hawk	1959	$40
—Black vinyl, red label, non-flexible vinyl			
❑ 3298 [M]	Two Knights at the Black Hawk	196?	$60
—Black vinyl, red label, flexible vinyl			
❑ 8081 [R]	Two Knights at the Blackhawk	1962	$40
—Blue vinyl			
❑ 8081 [R]	Two Knights at the Blackhawk	1962	$50
—Black vinyl, blue label, non-flexible vinyl			
❑ 8081 [R]	Two Knights at the Blackhawk	196?	$35
—Black vinyl, blue label, flexible vinyl			

HARMONY

Number	Title	Yr	NM
❑ HS11336	Gone with the Wind	1969	$30
❑ HS11253	Instant Brubeck	1968	$30

HORIZON

Number	Title	Yr	NM
❑ SP-703	1975: The Duets	1975	$30
❑ SP-714	The Dave Brubeck Quartet 25th Anniversary	1976	$30

JAZZTONE

Number	Title	Yr	NM
❑ J-1272 [M]	Best of Brubeck	195?	$40

MOBILE FIDELITY

Number	Title	Yr	NM
❑ 1-216	We're All Together Again for the First Time	1994	$120
—Audiophile vinyl			

MOON

Number	Title	Yr	NM
❑ 028	St. Louis Blues	1992	$50

ODYSSEY

Number	Title	Yr	NM
❑ 32160248	A Place in Time	1968	$30

TOMATO

Number	Title	Yr	NM
❑ 7018	The New Brubeck Quartet at Montreux	1978	$30

BRUCE, LENNY

Stand-up comedian who was highly influenced by 1950s jazz life.

Albums

BIZARRE

Number	Title	Yr	NM
❑ 2XS6329	The Berkeley Concert	1969	$60

DOUGLAS

Number	Title	Yr	NM
❑ Z30872	What I Was Arrested For	1971	$35
—Reissue of 2			

FANTASY

Number	Title	Yr	NM
❑ 7007 [M]	I Am Not a Nut, Elect Me	1960	$175
—Opaque, non-flexible red vinyl			
❑ 7007 [M]	I Am Not a Nut, Elect Me	1960	$40
—Non-flexible black vinyl			
❑ 7007 [M]	I Am Not a Nut, Elect Me	1962	$40
—Translucent, flexible red vinyl			
❑ 7007 [M]	I Am Not a Nut, Elect Me	1962	$50
—Flexible black vinyl			
❑ 7001 [M]	Interviews of Our Times	1959	$175
—Opaque, non-flexible red vinyl; tan cover with Lenny Bruce's name blacked out throughout the back			
❑ 7001 [M]	Interviews of Our Times	1959	$40
—Non-flexible black vinyl; cover changed to blue tint			
❑ 7001 [M]	Interviews of Our Times	1962	$40
—Translucent, flexible red vinyl			

Number	Title	Yr	NM
❑ 7001 [M]	Interviews of Our Times	1962	$50
—Flexible black vinyl			
❑ 7011 [M]	Lenny Bruce, American	1961	$175
—Opaque, non-flexible red vinyl			
❑ 7011 [M]	Lenny Bruce, American	1961	$40
—Non-flexible black vinyl			
❑ 7011 [M]	Lenny Bruce, American	1962	$40
—Translucent, flexible red vinyl			
❑ 7011 [M]	Lenny Bruce, American	1962	$50
—Flexible black vinyl			
❑ 34201	Lenny Bruce at the Curran Theater	1971	$40
❑ 7017	Thank You Masked Man	1971	$35
❑ 7012 [M]	The Best of Lenny Bruce	1962	$100
—Red vinyl			
❑ FP-1 [DJ]	The Promo Album	196?	$200
—Promo-only compilation of material from albums 7001, 7003, 7007 and 7011			
❑ 79003	The Real Lenny Bruce	1975	$50
❑ 7003 [M]	The Sick Humor of Lenny Bruce	1959	$175
—Opaque, non-flexible red vinyl			
❑ 7003 [M]	The Sick Humor of Lenny Bruce	1959	$40
—Non-flexible black vinyl			
❑ 7003 [M]	The Sick Humor of Lenny Bruce	1962	$40
—Translucent, flexible red vinyl			

LENNY BRUCE

Number	Title	Yr	NM
❑ LB-3001/2 [M]	Lenny Bruce Is Out Again	196?	$300
—Privately pressed version with white labels and Lenny's address on cover			
❑ LB-9001/2 [10]	Warning: Sale of This Album...	1962	$500
—Privately pressed LP with routines used as evidence in Lenny's obscenity trial			

PHILLIES

Number	Title	Yr	NM
❑ PHLP-4010 [M]	Lenny Bruce Is Out Again	1966	$175
—Reissue of Lenny Bruce 3001/2			

UNITED ARTISTS

Number	Title	Yr	NM
❑ UAS9800	Lenny Bruce/Carnegie Hall	1972	$60
❑ UAL3580 [M]	The Midnight Concert	1967	$60
❑ UAS6794	The Midnight Concert	1972	$35
—Reissue of 6580			
❑ UAS6580	The Midnight Concert	1967	$50

WARNER/SPECTOR

Number	Title	Yr	NM
❑ SP9101	The Law, the Language and Lenny Bruce	1975	$35

BRUEL, MAX

Baritone saxophone player.

Albums

EMARCY

Number	Title	Yr	NM
❑ MG-36062 [M]	Cool Bruel	1955	$200

BRUNEL, BUNNY

Bass player.

Albums

INNER CITY

Number	Title	Yr	NM
❑ 1162	Ivanhoe	198?	$25
❑ 1102	Touch	198?	$25

BRUNIOUS, WENDELL

Albums

GHB

Number	Title	Yr	NM
❑ GHB-194	Wendell Brunious and His New Orleans Jazz Band in the Tradition	198?	$25

BRUNIS, GEORG

Trombonist. Member of NEW ORLEANS RHYTHM KINGS.

Albums

COMMODORE

Number	Title	Yr	NM
❑ FL-20008 [10]	King of the Tailgate Trombone	1950	$80
❑ DL30015 [M]	King of the Tailgate Trombone	1959	$40

JAZZOLOGY

Number	Title	Yr	NM
❑ J-012	Georg Brunis and His Rhythm Kings	1965	$35

Number	Title	Yr	NM
JOLLY ROGER			
❏ 5024 [10]	Georg Brunis and the New Orleans Rhythm Kings	1954	$50
RIVERSIDE			
❏ RLP-1024 [10]	Georg Brunis and the Original New Orleans Rhythm Kings	1954	$300

BRYAN, JOY
Female singer.
Albums

Number	Title	Yr	NM
CONTEMPORARY			
❏ M-3604 [M]	Make the Man Love Me	1961	$200
❏ S-7604 [S]	Make the Man Love Me	1961	$200
MODE			
❏ LP-108 [M]	Joy Bryan Sings	1957	$80

BRYANT, BOBBY
Trumpeter.
Albums

Number	Title	Yr	NM
CADET			
❏ LP-795 [M]	Ain't Doing Too B-A-D, Bad	1967	$25
❏ LPS-795 [S]	Ain't Doing Too B-A-D, Bad	1967	$35
❏ CA-50011	Swahili Strut	1972	$30
VEE JAY			
❏ VJS-3059	Big Band Blues	1974	$25
WORLD PACIFIC			
❏ ST-20159	The Jazz Excursion Into "Hair	1969	$100

BRYANT, CLORA
Trumpeter and female singer.
Albums

Number	Title	Yr	NM
MODE			
❏ LP-106 [M]	Gal with a Horn	1957	$150

BRYANT, PAUL
Organist. Also see CURTIS AMY AND PAUL BRYANT.
Albums

Number	Title	Yr	NM
FANTASY			
❏ 3363 [M]	Groove Time	1964	$25
❏ 8363 [S]	Groove Time	1964	$30
❏ 3357 [M]	Something's Happening	1963	$25
❏ 8357 [S]	Something's Happening	1963	$30
PACIFIC JAZZ			
❏ PJ-12 [M]	Burnin'	1961	$40

BRYANT, RAY
Pianist and composer. Also see THE PRESTIGE BLUES SWINGERS.
Albums

Number	Title	Yr	NM
ATLANTIC			
❏ SD1626	Alone at Montreux	1972	$30
❏ SD1564	MCMLXX	1970	$35
CADET			
❏ LP-767 [M]	Gotta Travel On	1966	$35
❏ LPS-767 [S]	Gotta Travel On	1966	$50
❏ 50052	In the Cut	1974	$30
❏ 50038	It Was a Very Good Year	1973	$35
❏ LP-778 [M]	Lonesome Traveler	1966	$35
❏ LPS-778 [S]	Lonesome Traveler	1966	$50
❏ LP-781 [M]	Slow Freight	1967	$35
❏ LPS-781 [S]	Slow Freight	1967	$50
❏ LPS-830	Sound Ray	1969	$35
❏ LP-801 [M]	Take a Bryant Step	1967	$50
❏ LPS-801 [S]	Take a Bryant Step	1967	$35
❏ LP-793 [M]	The Ray Bryant Touch	1967	$50
❏ LPS-793 [S]	The Ray Bryant Touch	1967	$35
❏ LPS-818	Up Above the Rock	1968	$35
CLASSIC JAZZ			
❏ 130	Hot Turkey	198?	$25
COLUMBIA			
❏ CL1633 [M]	Con Alma	1961	$50
❏ CS8433 [S]	Con Alma	1961	$60
❏ CL1746 [M]	Dancing the Big Twist	1962	$50
❏ CS8546 [S]	Dancing the Big Twist	1962	$60
❏ CL1867 [M]	Hollywood Jazz Beat	1962	$50
❏ CS8667 [S]	Hollywood Jazz Beat	1962	$60
❏ CL1449 [M]	Little Susie	1960	$50
❏ CS8244 [S]	Little Susie	1960	$60
❏ CL1476 [M]	The Madison Time	1960	$60
❏ CS8276 [S]	The Madison Time	1960	$60
COLUMBIA JAZZ MASTERPIECES			
❏ CJ44058	Con Alma	1988	$25
EMARCY			
❏ 836368-1	Golden Earrings	1989	$30

Number	Title	Yr	NM
❏ 832235-1	Ray Bryant Plays Basie and Ellington	1987	$30
❏ 832589-1	The Ray Bryant Trio Today	1988	$30
EPIC			
❏ LN3279 [M]	Ray Bryant Trio	1956	$300
FANTASY			
❏ OJC-213	Alone with the Blues	1987	$25
—Reissue			
❏ OJC-371	Montreux '77	1989	$25
—Reissue of Pablo Live 2308 201			
NEW JAZZ			
❏ NJLP-8213 [M]	Alone with the Blues	1959	$200
—Purple label			
❏ NJLP-8213 [M]	Alone with the Blues	1965	$150
—Blue label with trident logo			
❏ NJLP-8227 [M]	Ray Bryant Trio	1965	$150
—Blue label with trident logo			
PABLO			
❏ 2310820	All Blues	1978	$25
❏ 2310764	Here's Ray Bryant	1976	$25
❏ 2310860	Potpourri	1981	$25
❏ 2310798	Solo Flight	1977	$25
❏ 2405402	The Best of Ray Bryant	198?	$25
PABLO LIVE			
❏ 2308201	Montreux '77	1977	$25
PRESTIGE			
❏ PRLP-7837	Alone with the Blues	1971	$35
—Reissue of New Jazz 8213			
❏ PRT-7837	Alone with the Blues	1973	$30
—Reissue; "Distributed by Fantasy Records, Berkeley, California" on label			
❏ 24038	Me and the Blues	1973	$35
SIGNATURE			
❏ SS-6008 [S]	Ray Bryant Plays	1960	$250
SUE			
❏ LP-1032 [M]	Cold Turkey	1964	$40
❏ LPS-1032 [S]	Cold Turkey	1964	$100
❏ LP-1016 [M]	Groove House	1963	$40
❏ LPS-1016 [S]	Groove House	1963	$100
❏ LP-1019 [M]	Live at Basin Street	1964	$40
❏ LPS-1019 [S]	Live at Basin Street	1964	$100
❏ STLP-1036 [M]	Ray Bryant Soul	1965	$40
❏ STLPS-1036 [S]	Ray Bryant Soul	1965	$100

BRYANT, RUSTY
Tenor and alto saxophone player.
Albums

Number	Title	Yr	NM
DOT			
❏ DLP-3006 [M]	All Night Long	1956	$80
—Maroon label			
❏ DLP-3353 [M]	America's Greatest Jazz	1961	$75
❏ DLP-25353 [S]	America's Greatest Jazz	1961	$75
❏ DLP-3079 [M]	Rusty Bryant Plays Jazz	1957	$80
FANTASY			
❏ OJC-331	Rusty Bryant Returns	1988	$25
—Reissue of Prestige 7626			
PRESTIGE			
❏ 10013	Fire Eater	1972	$30
❏ 10073	For the Good Times	1974	$30
❏ 10053	Friday Night Funk	1973	$30
❏ PRST-7735	Night Train Now!	1970	$30
❏ PRST-7626	Rusty Bryant Returns	1969	$30
❏ PRST-7798	Soul Liberation	1971	$30
❏ 10085	Until It's Time for You to Go	1974	$30
❏ 10037	Wild Fire	1972	$30

BUCCI, JOE
Organist.
Albums

Number	Title	Yr	NM
CAPITOL			
❏ T1840 [M]	Wild About Basie	1963	$60
❏ ST1840 [S]	Wild About Basie	1963	$80

BUCKLEY, LORD
Stand-up comedian and MC popular in jazz circles in the 1950s.
Albums

Number	Title	Yr	NM
CRESTVIEW			
❏ CRV-801 [M]	The Best of Lord Buckley	1963	$100
❏ CRV7-801 [S]	The Best of Lord Buckley	1963	$120
ELEKTRA			
❏ EKS-74047	The Best of Lord Buckley	1969	$60
—Reissue of Crestview 7-801			
RCA VICTOR			

Number	Title	Yr	NM
❏ LPM-3246 [10]	Hipsters, Flipsters and Finger Poppin' Daddies, Knock Me Your Lobes	1955	$600
REPRISE			
❏ RS6389	A Most Immaculately Hip Aristocrat	1970	$100
—Reissue of Straight 1054			
STRAIGHT			
❏ STS-1054	A Most Immaculately Hip Aristocrat	1970	$150
VAYA			
❏ 1715 [10]	Euphoria	195?	$600
—Red vinyl			
❏ 101/2 [M]	Euphoria, Volume 1	1955	$300
❏ 107/8 [M]	Euphoria, Volume 2	1955	$400
WORLD PACIFIC			
❏ WPS-21889	Bad Rapping of the Marquis de Sade	1969	$300
❏ WP-1849 [M]	Blowing His Mind (and Yours, Too)	1966	$300
❏ WPS-21879	Buckley's Best	1968	$150
❏ WP-1815 [M]	Lord Buckley in Concert	1964	$200
—Reissue of 1279			
❏ WP-1279 [M]	The Way Out Humor of Lord Buckley	1959	$350
—With "Far Out Humor" on the back cover			
❏ WP-1279 [M]	The Way Out Humor of Lord Buckley	1959	$350
—With correct "Way Out Humor" on the back cover			

BUCKNER, MILT
Organist; sometimes a piano and vibraphone player.
Albums

Number	Title	Yr	NM
ARGO			
❏ LP-702 [M]	Midnight Mood	1962	$35
❏ LPS-702 [S]	Midnight Mood	1962	$25
❏ LP-660 [M]	Mighty High	1960	$35
❏ LPS-660 [S]	Mighty High	1960	$25
❏ LP-670 [M]	Please Mr. Organ Player	1960	$35
❏ LPS-670 [S]	Please Mr. Organ Player	1960	$25
BASF			
❏ 20631	Chords	1972	$35
BETHLEHEM			
❏ BCP-6072 [M]	The New World of Milt Buckner	1963	$200
CAPITOL			
❏ T722 [M]	Rockin' Hammond	1956	$80
—Turquoise or gray label			
❏ T642 [M]	Rockin' with Milt	1955	$80
—Turquoise or gray label			
❏ T938 [M]	Send Me Softly	1958	$80
—Turquoise or gray label			
CLASSIC JAZZ			
❏ 141	Green Onions	198?	$25
JAZZ MAN			
❏ 5012	Rockin' Again	198?	$30
PRESTIGE			
❏ PRST-7668	Milt Buckner in Europe '66	1969	$35
REGENT			
❏ MG-6004 [M]	Organ -- Sweet 'n' Swing	195?	$30
SAVOY			
❏ MG-15023 [10]	Milt Buckner Piano	1953	$120

BUCKNER, TEDDY
Trumpeter, bandleader, sometimes a fluegel horn player.
Albums

Number	Title	Yr	NM
AIRCHECK			
❏ 10	Teddy Buckner and His Orchestra 1955	198?	$25
DIXIELAND JUBILEE			
❏ DJ-505 [M]	A Salute to Louis Armstrong	1959	$25
❏ DJS-505 [S]	A Salute to Louis Armstrong	1959	$35
❏ DJ-503 [M]	In Concert at the Dixieland Jubilee	195?	$25
❏ DJS-503 [R]	In Concert at the Dixieland Jubilee	196?	$30
❏ DJ-504 [M]	Teddy Buckner and His Dixieland Band	195?	$25
❏ DJS-504 [R]	Teddy Buckner and His Dixieland Band	195?	$30
❏ DJ-507 [M]	Teddy Buckner and the All Stars	1959	$25
❏ DJS-507 [S]	Teddy Buckner and the All Stars	1959	$35

Number	Title	Yr	NM
❏ DJS-516	Teddy Buckner at the Crescendo	196?	$35
❏ DJ-510 [M]	Teddy Buckner on the Sunset Strip	1960	$25
❏ DJS-510 [S]	Teddy Buckner on the Sunset Strip	1960	$35

GENE NORMAN

Number	Title	Yr	NM
❏ GNP-(# unk) [10]	Dixieland Jubilee	195?	$50

—Red vinyl

❏ GNP-11 [M]	Teddy Buckner	1955	$50

GNP CRESCENDO

❏ GNP-68 [M]	Midnight in Moscow	1962	$30
❏ GNPS-68 [S]	Midnight in Moscow	1962	$35

BUCKSHOT LEFONQUE

Jazz/funk/hip-hop group led by BRANFORD MARSALIS.

Albums

COLUMBIA

Number	Title	Yr	NM
❏ C257322	Buckshot LeFonque	1994	$20
❏ C67584	Music Evolution	1997	$15
❏ CAS8780 [EP]	Music Evolution (Sampler)	1997	$12

—Promo only; five songs

❏ CAS6566 [EP]	Selections from Buckshot Lefonque	1995	$12

—Promo only; five songs

BUDIMIR, DENNIS

Guitarist. Also a session musician who, among other jobs, played on most of the Partridge Family's albums!

Albums

MAINSTREAM

Number	Title	Yr	NM
❏ 56059 [M]	Creeper	1966	$25
❏ S-6059 [S]	Creeper	1966	$30

REVELATION

❏ REV-M-1 [M]	Alone Together	1967	$30
❏ REV-1 [S]	Alone Together	1967	$25
❏ REV-4	A Second Coming	1968	$25
❏ REV-14	Session with Albert	1971	$25
❏ REV-8	Sprung Free!	1969	$25

BUDWIG, MONTY

Bass player.

Albums

CONCORD JAZZ

Number	Title	Yr	NM
❏ CJ-79	Dig	198?	$25

BUG ALLEY

Canadian vocal and instrumental group featuring Karen Young.

Albums

P.M.

Number	Title	Yr	NM
❏ PMR-019	Bug Alley	1980	$35

BUNCH, JOHN

Pianist.

Albums

AUDIOPHILE

Number	Title	Yr	NM
❏ AP-184	Jubilee	1982	$25

CHIAROSCURO

❏ 144	John Bunch Plays Music of Kurt Weill	1975	$30

CONCORD JAZZ

❏ CJ-328	The Best Thing for You	1987	$25

FAMOUS DOOR

❏ 107	John's Bunch	1976	$30
❏ 114	John's Other Bunch	1977	$30
❏ 118	Slick Funk	1978	$30

BUNKER, LARRY

Drummer, percussionist and vibraphone player.

Albums

VAULT

Number	Title	Yr	NM
❏ LP-9005 [M]	Live at Shelly's Manne-Hole	1966	$25
❏ LPS-9005 [S]	Live at Shelly's Manne-Hole	1966	$35

BURGER, JACK

Drummer, most notably on bongos.

Albums

HIFI

Number	Title	Yr	NM
❏ R-803 [M]	Let's Play Bongos!	1957	$40
❏ R-809 [M]	Let's Play Congas	1958	$30

Number	Title	Yr	NM
❏ RS-809 [S]	Let's Play Congas	1959	$40
❏ R-804 [M]	The End on Bongos!	1957	$40

BURKE, CHRIS, AND HIS NEW ORLEANS MUSIC

Clarinet player.

Albums

GHB

Number	Title	Yr	NM
❏ 175	True to New Orleans	1985	$25

BURKE, RAY

Clarinet and saxophone player. Also see JOHNNY WIGGS.

Albums

NEW ORLEANS

Number	Title	Yr	NM
❏ 7202	Speakeasy Boys (1937-49)	198?	$25

SOUTHLAND

❏ SLP-209 [10]	Contemporary New Orleans Jazz	1955	$200

BURKE, VINNIE

Bass player. Also see OSCAR PETTIFORD; BUCKY PIZZARELLI.

Albums

ABC-PARAMOUNT

Number	Title	Yr	NM
❏ ABC-139 [M]	The Vinnie Burke All Stars	1956	$50
❏ ABC-170 [M]	The Vinnie Burke String Jazz Quartet	1957	$50

BETHLEHEM

❏ BCP-1010 [10]	East Coast Jazz 2	1954	$250

BURNETT, CARL

Drummer.

Albums

DISCOVERY

Number	Title	Yr	NM
❏ 819	Carl Burnett Plays the Music of Richard Rodgers	198?	$25

BURNS, RALPH

Pianist, arranger and composer.

Albums

BETHLEHEM

Number	Title	Yr	NM
❏ BCP-68 [M]	Bijou	1957	$250

CLEF

❏ MGC-115 [10]	Free Forms	1953	$300

DECCA

❏ DL8235 [M]	Jazz Studio 5	1956	$150
❏ DL9068 [M]	New York's a Song	1959	$80
❏ DL79068 [S]	New York's a Song	1959	$80
❏ DL9215 [M]	Porgy and Bess	1959	$80
❏ DL79215 [S]	Porgy and Bess	1959	$80
❏ DL8555 [M]	The Masters Revisited	1957	$120
❏ DL9207 [M]	Very Warm for Jazz	1959	$80
❏ DL79207 [S]	Very Warm for Jazz	1959	$125

EPIC

❏ LN24015 [M]	Swingin' Down the Lane	1962	$60
❏ BN26015 [S]	Swingin' Down the Lane	1962	$80

JAZZTONE

❏ J-1228 [M]	Spring Sequence	1956	$50

MERCURY

❏ MGC-115 [10]	Free Forms	1952	$300

MGM

❏ E-3616 [M]	The Swinging Seasons	1958	$50
❏ SE-3616 [S]	The Swinging Seasons	1959	$40

NORGRAN

❏ MGN-1028 [M]	Ralph Burns Among the JATP's	1955	$120

PERIOD

❏ SPL-1109 [10]	Bijou	1955	$120
❏ SPL-1105 [10]	Spring Sequence	1955	$120

VERVE

❏ MGV-8121 [M]	Ralph Burns Among the JATP's	1957	$100
❏ V-8121 [M]	Ralph Burns Among the JATP's	1961	$25

WARWICK

❏ W-5001 [M]	Where There's Burns There's Fire	1961	$100
❏ W-5001ST [S]	Where There's Burns There's Fire	1961	$140

BURNS, RALPH/BILLIE HOLIDAY

Also see each artist's individual listings.

Albums

CLEF

Number	Title	Yr	NM
❏ MGC-718 [M]	The Free Forms of Ralph Burns/The Songs of Billie Holiday	1956	$300

VERVE

❏ MGV-8098 [M]	Jazz Recital	1957	$150
❏ V-8098 [M]	Jazz Recital	1961	$25

BURNS, RON

Drummer.

Albums

ROULETTE

Number	Title	Yr	NM
❏ R-52095 [M]	Skin Burns	1963	$25
❏ SR-52095 [S]	Skin Burns	1963	$30

BURRELL, DAVE

Pianist. Also see BEAVER HARRIS 360 DEGREE MUSIC EXPERIENCE.

Albums

ARISTA FREEDOM

Number	Title	Yr	NM
❏ AL1906	High Won/High Two	1975	$35

DOUGLAS

❏ SD798	High	1969	$25

HAT ART

❏ 2025	Windward Passages	1987	$35

—Reissue of Hat Hut 05

HAT HUT

❏ 05	Windward Passages	1979	$50

BURRELL, KENNY, AND GROVER WASHINGTON. JR.

Also see each artist's individual listings.

Albums

BLUE NOTE

Number	Title	Yr	NM
❏ BT-85106	Togethering	1985	$25

BURRELL, KENNY, AND JIMMY RANEY

Also see each artist's individual listings.

Albums

PRESTIGE

Number	Title	Yr	NM
❏ PRLP-7119 [M]	Two Guitars	1957	$250

BURRELL, KENNY, AND JOHN COLTRANE

Also see each artist's individual listings.

Albums

FANTASY

Number	Title	Yr	NM
❏ OJC-300	Kenny Burrell and John Coltrane	1987	$25
❏ OJC-079	The Cats	198?	$25

—Reissue of New Jazz 8217

NEW JAZZ

❏ NJLP-8276 [M]	Kenny Burrell with John Coltrane	1962	$200

—Purple label

❏ NJLP-8276 [M]	Kenny Burrell with John Coltrane	1965	$150

—Blue label with trident logo

❏ NJLP-8217 [M]	The Cats	1959	$1500

—Purple label

❏ NJLP-8217 [M]	The Cats	1965	$150

—Blue label with trident logo

PRESTIGE

❏ 24059	Kenny Burrell & John Coltrane	197?	$35

—Reissue of New Jazz and Prestige LPs in one package

❏ PRLP-7532 [M]	Kenny Burrell Quintet with John Coltrane	1967	$60
❏ PRST-7532 [S]	Kenny Burrell Quintet with John Coltrane	1967	$50

BURRELL, KENNY; TINY GRIMES; BILL JENNINGS

Also see each artist's individual listings.

Albums

STATUS

Number	Title	Yr	NM
❏ ST-8318 [M]	Guitar Soul	1965	$40

BURRELL, KENNY

Guitarist. Also see CHARLIE BYRD; JOHN JENKINS; FRANK WESS.

Albums

ARGO

Number	Title	Yr	NM
❏ LP-655 [M]	A Night at the Vanguard	1959	$100
❏ LPS-655 [S]	A Night at the Vanguard	1959	$120

BLUE NOTE

Number	Title	Yr	NM
❏ BST-1596 [S]	Blue Lights, Volume 1	1959	$140
—Regular version, W. 63rd St., NYC address on label			
❏ BLP-1596 [M]	Blue Lights, Volume 1	1963	$100
—New York, USA address on label			
❏ BST-1596 [S]	Blue Lights, Volume 1	1963	$60
—New York, USA address on label			
❏ BST-81596 [S]	Blue Lights, Volume 1	1967	$35
—A Division of Liberty Records" on label			
❏ BLP-1597 [M]	Blue Lights, Volume 2	1958	$140
—Regular version, W. 63rd St., NYC address on label			
❏ BST-1597 [S]	Blue Lights, Volume 2	1959	$140
—Regular version, W. 63rd St., NYC address on label			
❏ BLP-1597 [M]	Blue Lights, Volume 2	1963	$100
—New York, USA address on label			
❏ BST-1597 [S]	Blue Lights, Volume 2	1963	$60
—New York, USA address on label			
❏ BST-81597 [S]	Blue Lights, Volume 2	1967	$35
—A Division of Liberty Records" on label			
❏ B1-85137	Generation	1987	$25
❏ BLP-1523 [M]	Introducing Kenny Burrell	1956	$1500
—Regular version, Lexington Ave. address on label			
❏ BLP-1523 [M]	Introducing Kenny Burrell	1957	$800
—W. 63rd St., NYC address on label			
❏ BLP-1523 [M]	Introducing Kenny Burrell	1963	$200
—New York, USA address on label			
❏ BST-81523 [R]	Introducing Kenny Burrell	1967	$30
—A Division of Liberty Records" on label			
❏ BST-81543 [R]	Kenny Burrell, Volume 2	1967	$30
—A Division of Liberty Records" on label			
❏ BLP-4123 [M]	Midnight Blue	1963	$100
—New York, USA address on label			
❏ BST-84123 [S]	Midnight Blue	1963	$40
—New York, USA address on label			
❏ BST-84123 [S]	Midnight Blue	1967	$35
—A Division of Liberty Records" on label			
❏ BST-84123	Midnight Blue	1985	$25
—The Finest in Jazz Since 1939" reissue			
❏ BLP-4021 [M]	On View at the Five Spot Café	1960	$140
—Regular version, W. 63rd St., NYC address on label			
❏ BST-84021 [S]	On View at the Five Spot Café	1960	$120
—W. 63rd St., NYC address on label			
❏ BLP-4021 [M]	On View at the Five Spot Café	1963	$100
—New York, USA address on label			
❏ BST-84021 [S]	On View at the Five Spot Café	1963	$60
—New York, USA address on label			
❏ BST-84021 [S]	On View at the Five Spot Café	1967	$35
—A Division of Liberty Records" on label			
❏ B1-90260	Pieces of Blue and the Blues	1988	$25

CADET

Number	Title	Yr	NM
❏ LP-779 [M]	Have Yourself a Soulful Little Christmas	1966	$35
❏ LPS-779 [S]	Have Yourself a Soulful Little Christmas	1966	$50
❏ LP-769 [M]	Men at Work	1965	$35
—Reissue of Argo 655			
❏ LPS-769 [S]	Men at Work	1965	$50
—Reissue of Argo 655			
❏ LP-798 [M]	Ode to 52nd Street	1967	$50
❏ LPS-798 [S]	Ode to 52nd Street	1967	$35
❏ LP-772 [M]	The Tender Gender	1966	$35
❏ LPS-772 [S]	The Tender Gender	1966	$50

CHESS

Number	Title	Yr	NM
❏ CH-9316	A Night at the Vanguard	1990	$30
—Reissue of Argo 655			
❏ CH-60019	Cool Cookin'	1973	$35
❏ CH2-92509	Recapitulation	198?	$30

COLUMBIA

Number	Title	Yr	NM
❏ CL1703 [M]	Weaver of Dreams	1961	$50
❏ CS8503 [S]	Weaver of Dreams	1961	$60

CONCORD JAZZ

Number	Title	Yr	NM
❏ CJ-121	Moon and Sand	1980	$25
❏ CJ-45	Tin Tin Deo	1978	$25
❏ CJ-83	When Lights Are Low	1978	$25

CONTEMPORARY

Number	Title	Yr	NM
❏ C-14058	Guiding Spirit	1990	$30

CTI

Number	Title	Yr	NM
❏ 6011	God Bless the Child	1970	$30

DENON

Number	Title	Yr	NM
❏ 7533	Lush Life	1979	$35
❏ 7541	'Round Midnight	1979	$35

FANTASY

Number	Title	Yr	NM
❏ OJC-456	All Day Long	1990	$30
❏ OJC-427	All Night Long	1990	$30
❏ F-9427	Both Feet on the Ground	1973	$30
❏ 79005	Ellington Is Forever	1975	$35
❏ 79008	Ellington Is Forever, Vol. 2	197?	$35
❏ MPF-4506	For Duke	1981	$25
❏ OJC-019	Kenny Burrell	198?	$25
—Reissue of Prestige 7088			
❏ F-9417	'Round Midnight	1972	$30
❏ F-9514	Sky Street	1975	$30
❏ F-9558	Stormy Monday	1978	$30
❏ OJC-216	Two Guitars	198?	$25
❏ F-9458	Up the Street	1974	$30

KAPP

Number	Title	Yr	NM
❏ KL-1326 [M]	Lotta Bossa Nova	1962	$50
❏ KS-3326 [S]	Lotta Bossa Nova	1962	$60

MOODSVILLE

Number	Title	Yr	NM
❏ MVLP-29 [M]	Bluesy Burrell	1963	$40
—Green label			
❏ MVST-29 [S]	Bluesy Burrell	1963	$40
—Green label			
❏ MVLP-29 [M]	Bluesy Burrell	1965	$50
—Blue label with trident logo			
❏ MVST-29 [S]	Bluesy Burrell	1965	$60
—Blue label with trident logo			

MUSE

Number	Title	Yr	NM
❏ 5317	A La Carte	1984	$25
❏ 5281	Groovin' High	1983	$25
❏ 5144	Handcrafted	1979	$25
❏ 5241	Kenny Burrell in New York	1982	$25
❏ 5264	Listen to the Dawn	1982	$25
❏ 5216	Live at the Village Vanguard	1979	$25

PAUSA

Number	Title	Yr	NM
❏ 9000	Midnight	198?	$25

PRESTIGE

Number	Title	Yr	NM
❏ 24025	All Day Long & All Night Long	197?	$35
—Reissue of both albums in one package			
❏ PRLP-7277 [M]	All Day Long	1963	$100
—Reissue of 7081			
❏ PRST-7277 [R]	All Day Long	1963	$50
❏ PRLP-7073 [M]	All Night Long	1957	$300
—Actually an all-star session; reissued as a Kenny Burrell album, thus it is listed here			
❏ PRLP-7289 [M]	All Night Long	1964	$100
—Reissue of 7073			
❏ PRST-7289 [R]	All Night Long	1964	$50
❏ PRLP-7308 [M]	Blue Moods	1964	$60
—Reissue of 7088			
❏ PRST-7308 [R]	Blue Moods	1964	$50
❏ PRLP-7347 [M]	Crash	1964	$60
❏ PRST-7347 [S]	Crash	1964	$60
❏ PRLP-7088 [M]	Kenny Burrell	1957	$300
❏ PRST-7578	Out of This World	1968	$35
—Reissue of Moodsville 29			
❏ PRLP-7315 [M]	Soul Call	1964	$60
❏ PRST-7315 [S]	Soul Call	1964	$60
❏ PRLP-7448 [M]	The Best of Kenny Burrell	1967	$60
❏ PRST-7448 [S]	The Best of Kenny Burrell	1967	$50

SAVOY JAZZ

Number	Title	Yr	NM
❏ SJL-1120	Monday Stroll	1978	$25
—Reissue			

VERVE

Number	Title	Yr	NM
❏ V-8656 [M]	A Generation Ago Today	1966	$35
❏ V6-8656 [S]	A Generation Ago Today	1966	$50
❏ V6-8773	Asphalt Canyon Suite	1969	$35
❏ V-8553 [M]	Blue Bash!	1963	$50
❏ V6-8553 [S]	Blue Bash!	1963	$60
❏ V-8746 [M]	Blues-- The Common Ground	1968	$50
❏ V6-8746 [S]	Blues-- The Common Ground	1968	$35
❏ V-8612 [M]	Guitar Forms	1965	$35
❏ V6-8612 [S]	Guitar Forms	1965	$50
❏ UMV-2070	Guitar Forms	198?	$25
—Reissue of 8612			
❏ V6-8751	Night Song	1968	$35

VOSS

Number	Title	Yr	NM
❏ VLP1-42930	Heritage	1988	$25

BURROUGH, ROSLYN

Female singer.

Albums

SUNNYSIDE

Number	Title	Yr	NM
❏ SSC-1009	Love Is Here	1985	$25

BURTON, ANN

Female singer.

Albums

INNER CITY

Number	Title	Yr	NM
❏ 6026	By Myself Alone	1974	$30

BURTON, GARY, AND CHICK COREA

Also see each artist's individual listings.

Albums

ECM

Number	Title	Yr	NM
❏ 1024ST	Crystal Silence	1973	$30
—Original edition; made in Germany?			
❏ 1140	Duet	1978	$30
❏ ECM2-1182	Gary Burton and Chick Corea In Concert	1979	$35
—Distributed by Warner Bros.			
❏ 23797	Lyric Suite for Sextet	1983	$25
—Distributed by Warner Bros.			
❏ 1260	Lyric Suite for Sextet	1983	$30
—Made in Germany			

BURTON, GARY; SONNY ROLLINS; CLARK TERRY

Also see each artist's individual listings.

Albums

RCA VICTOR

Number	Title	Yr	NM
❏ LPM-2725 [M]	Three in Jazz	1963	$35
❏ LSP-2725 [S]	Three in Jazz	1963	$25

BURTON, GARY

Vibraphone player.

Albums

ATLANTIC

Number	Title	Yr	NM
❏ SD1598	Alone at Last	1971	$30
❏ SD1577	Gary Burton with Keith Jarrett	1971	$30
❏ SD1560	Good Vibes	1970	$30
❏ SD1597	Paris Encounter	1972	$30
❏ SD1531	Throb	1969	$30
❏ SD 2-321	Turn of the Century	1976	$35

BLUEBIRD

Number	Title	Yr	NM
❏ 6280-1-RB	Artist's Choice	1987	$25

ECM

Number	Title	Yr	NM
❏ 1072	Dreams So Real	1976	$30
❏ 1184	Easy As Pie	1979	$30
❏ 1055	Hotel Hello	1974	$30
❏ 1092	Passengers	1977	$30
❏ 1226	Picture This	1980	$30
❏ 25024	Real Life Hits	1985	$25
❏ 1051	Ring	1975	$30
❏ 1040	Seven Songs for Quartet and Chamber Orchestra	1974	$30
❏ 1030	The New Quartet	1973	$30
❏ 1111	Times Square	1978	$30

GRP

Number	Title	Yr	NM
❏ GR-9598	Reunion	1990	$30
❏ GR-9569	Times Like These	1988	$25

RCA CAMDEN

Number	Title	Yr	NM
❏ ACL1-0200	Norwegian Wood	1973	$25

RCA VICTOR

Number	Title	Yr	NM
❏ LSP-3988	A Genuine Tong Funeral	1968	$35
❏ LSP-4098	Country Roads and Other Places	1969	$35
❏ LPM-3835 [M]	Duster	1967	$25
❏ LSP-3835 [S]	Duster	1967	$35
❏ LPM-3985 [M]	Gary Burton Quartet In Concert	1968	$30

Clora Bryant, *Gal with a Horn*, Mode LP-106, **$150**.

Ralph Burns, *Free Forms*, Mercury MG C-115, 10-inch LP, **$300**.

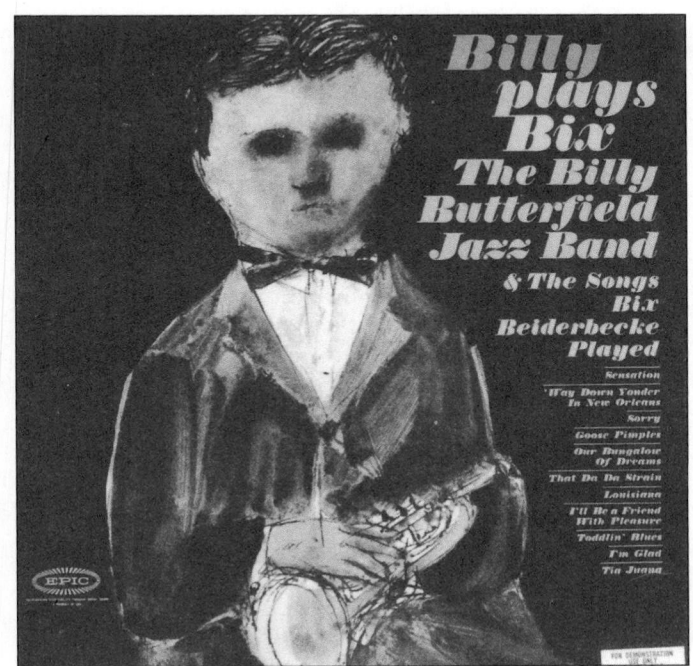

Billy Butterfield, *Billy Plays Bix*, Epic LA 16026, **$60**.

Billy Byers, Joe Newman, Eddie Bert, *East Coast Sounds*, Jazztone J-1276, **$60**.

Number	Title	Yr	NM
❏ LSP-3985 [S]	Gary Burton Quartet In Concert	1968	$35
❏ LPM-3901 [M]	Lofty Fake Anagram	1967	$25
❏ LSP-3901 [S]	Lofty Fake Anagram	1967	$35
❏ LPM-2420 [M]	New Vibe Man in Town	1961	$25
❏ LSP-2420 [S]	New Vibe Man in Town	1961	$30
❏ LPM-2880 [M]	Something's Coming	1964	$25
❏ LSP-2880 [S]	Something's Coming	1964	$30
❏ LPM-3719 [M]	Tennessee Firebird	1966	$35
❏ LSP-3719 [S]	Tennessee Firebird	1966	$25
❏ LPM-3360 [M]	The Groovy Sound of Music	1965	$35
❏ LSP-3360 [S]	The Groovy Sound of Music	1965	$25
❏ LPM-3642 [M]	The Time Machine	1966	$35
❏ LSP-3642 [S]	The Time Machine	1966	$25
❏ LPM-2665 [M]	Who Is Gary Burton?	1963	$50
❏ LSP-2665 [S]	Who Is Gary Burton?	1963	$60

BURTON, JOE
Pianist.
Albums
ACE
| ❏ LP-1002 [M] | Joe Burton Plays | 1959 | $0 |

—Canceled?

CORAL
❏ CRL57175 [M]	Here I Am in Love Again	1958	$40
❏ CRL757175 [S]	Here I Am in Love Again	1959	$30
❏ CRL57098 [M]	Joe Burton Session	1957	$40

JODAY
| ❏ J-1000 [M] | The Subtle Sound of Joe Burton | 1963 | $35 |
| ❏ JS-1000 [S] | The Subtle Sound of Joe Burton | 1963 | $25 |

REGENT
| ❏ MG-6036 [M] | Jazz Pretty | 1957 | $50 |

BUSH, CHARLIE
Guitarist.
Albums
REVELATION
| ❏ REV-33 | Local Living Legend | 1979 | $30 |

BUSHKIN, JOE
Pianist and composer.
Albums
ATLANTIC
| ❏ ALR-108 [10] | I Love a Piano | 1950 | $250 |
| ❏ 81621 | Play It Again, Joe | 1985 | $25 |

CAPITOL
| ❏ T832 [M] | A Fellow Needs a Girl | 1957 | $60 |

—Turquoise or gray label

| ❏ T1094 [M] | Blue Angels | 1959 | $40 |

—Black colorband label, logo at left

| ❏ ST1094 [S] | Blue Angels | 1959 | $60 |

—Black colorband label, logo at left

| ❏ T911 [M] | Bushkin Spotlights Berlin | 1958 | $60 |

—Turquoise or gray label

| ❏ T711 [M] | Midnight Rhapsody | 1956 | $60 |

—Turquoise or gray label

| ❏ T759 [M] | Skylight Rhapsody | 1956 | $60 |

—Turquoise or gray label

COLUMBIA
❏ CL6201 [10]	After Hours	195?	$50
❏ CS9615	Doctor Dolittle	1968	$30
❏ CL6152 [10]	Piano Moods	195?	$50

DECCA
| ❏ DL4731 [M] | Night Sounds of San Francisco | 1965 | $30 |
| ❏ DL74731 [S] | Night Sounds of San Francisco | 1965 | $35 |

EPIC
| ❏ LN3345 [M] | Piano After Midnight | 1956 | $60 |

REPRISE
| ❏ R-6119 [M] | In Concert, Town Hall | 1964 | $35 |
| ❏ RS-6119 [S] | In Concert, Town Hall | 1964 | $25 |

ROYALE
| ❏ 18118 [10] | Joe Bushkin | 195? | $50 |

BUSSE, HENRY
Albums
HINDSIGHT
| ❏ HSR-122 | The Uncollected Henry Busse and His Orchestra, 1935 | 1978 | $25 |

BUTLER, ARTIE
Organist, better known as an arranger, mostly for pop singers.
Albums
A&M
| ❏ SP-2007 [M] | Have You Met Miss Jones? | 1968 | $50 |

—Mono appears to be promo only, in stereo cover with "Monaural" sticker

| ❏ SP-3007 [S] | Have You Met Miss Jones? | 1968 | $30 |

BUTLER, BILLY
Guitarist.
Albums
FANTASY
| ❏ OJC-334 | Guitar Soul | 1988 | $30 |

—Reissue of Prestige 7734

OKEH
| ❏ OKM12115 [M] | Right Track | 1966 | $50 |
| ❏ OKS14115 [S] | Right Track | 1966 | $60 |

PRESTIGE
❏ PRST-7734	Guitar Soul	1969	$30
❏ PRST-7854	Night Life	1971	$30
❏ PRST-7622	This Is Billy Butler	1968	$30
❏ PRST-7797	Yesterday, Today and Tomorrow	1970	$60

BUTLER, FRANK
Drummer. Also see CURTIS AMY.
Albums
XANADU
| ❏ 152 | The Stepper | 1977 | $25 |
| ❏ 169 | Wheelin' and Dealin' | 1978 | $25 |

BUTTERFIELD, BILLY
Trumpeter. Also see BOBBY HACKETT.
Albums
CAPITOL
| ❏ H424 [10] | Classics in Jazz | 195? | $80 |
| ❏ H201 [10] | Stardusting | 1950 | $80 |

CIRCLE
| ❏ CLP-037 | Billy Butterfield with Ted Easton's Jazz Band | 1977 | $35 |

COLUMBIA
❏ CL1514 [M]	Billy Blows His Horn	1960	$25
❏ CS8314 [S]	Billy Blows His Horn	1960	$30
❏ CL1673 [M]	The Golden Horn	1961	$25

—Red and black label with six "eye" logos

| ❏ CS8473 [S] | The Golden Horn | 1961 | $30 |

—Red and black label with six "eye" logos

| ❏ CS8473 [S] | The Golden Horn | 196? | $25 |

—360 Sound Stereo" on label

EPIC
| ❏ LA16026 [M] | Billy Plays Bix | 1962 | $60 |
| ❏ BA17026 [S] | Billy Plays Bix | 1962 | $80 |

ESSEX
❏ 403 [M]	Billy Butterfield at Amherst	1955	$50
❏ 401 [M]	Billy Butterfield at Princeton	1955	$50
❏ 404 [M]	Billy Butterfield at Rutgers	1955	$50
❏ 402 [M]	Billy Butterfield Goes to NYU	1955	$50
❏ ESLP-111 [10]	Far Away Places	195?	$50

HINDSIGHT
| ❏ HSR-173 | Billy Butterfield 1946 | 198? | $25 |

JAZZOLOGY
| ❏ J-117 | Just Friends | 1984 | $30 |
| ❏ J-93 | Watch What Happens | 198? | $25 |

JOY
| ❏ JL-1003 [M] | The New Dance Sound of Billy Butterfield | 196? | $40 |

RCA VICTOR
❏ LPM-1699 [M]	A Lovely Way to Spend an Evening	1958	$30
❏ LSP-1699 [S]	A Lovely Way to Spend an Evening	1958	$40
❏ LPM-1566 [M]	A Touch of the Blues	1958	$40
❏ LPM-1212 [M]	New York Land Dixie	1956	$40
❏ LPM-1590 [M]	Thank You for a Lovely Evening	1958	$30
❏ LPM-1441 [M]	They're Playing Our Song	1957	$40

SOMERSET
| ❏ P-2200 [M] | I'm In the Mood for the Magic Trumpet of Billy Butterfield and His Orchestra | 196? | $35 |

WESTMINSTER
| ❏ WL-3020 [10] | Billy Butterfield | 1954 | $50 |
| ❏ WL-6006 [M] | Dancing for Two in Love | 1955 | $50 |

BUTTERFIELD, ERSKINE
Pianist, male singer and composer.
Albums
CIRCLE
| ❏ CLP-062 | Tuesday and Ten | 198? | $25 |

DAVIS
| ❏ JD-104 [M] | Piano Cocktail | 1951 | $40 |

BYARD, JAKI, AND RAN BLAKE
Also see each artist's individual listings.
Albums
SOUL NOTE
| ❏ SN-1022 | Improvisations | 198? | $30 |

BYARD, JAKI
Pianist.
Albums
MUSE
| ❏ 5173 | Family Man | 1978 | $35 |
| ❏ 5007 | There'll Be Some Changes Made | 1974 | $25 |

NEW JAZZ
| ❏ NJLP-8256 [M] | Here's Jaki | 1965 | $150 |

—Blue label with trident logo at right

| ❏ NJLP-8273 [M] | Hi-Fly | 1962 | $150 |

—Purple label

| ❏ NJLP-8273 [M] | Hi-Fly | 1965 | $150 |

—Blue label with trident logo at right

PRESTIGE
| ❏ PRLP-7463 [M] | Freedom Together | 1967 | $40 |

—Blue label with trident logo at right

| ❏ PRST-7463 [S] | Freedom Together | 1967 | $40 |

—Blue label with trident logo at right

| ❏ PRST-7463 [S] | Freedom Together | 1968 | $30 |

—Blue label with trident logo in circle at top

❏ 24086	Giant Steps	197?	$25
❏ PRST-7573	Jaki Byard with Strings!	1968	$30
❏ PRLP-7419 [M]	Live!	1966	$30

—Blue label with trident logo at right

| ❏ PRST-7419 [S] | Live! | 1966 | $40 |

—Blue label with trident logo at right

| ❏ PRST-7419 [S] | Live! | 1968 | $30 |

—Blue label with trident logo in circle at top

| ❏ PRLP-7477 [M] | Live! Volume 2 | 1967 | $40 |

—Blue label with trident logo at right

| ❏ PRST-7477 [S] | Live! Volume 2 | 1967 | $40 |

—Blue label with trident logo at right

| ❏ PRST-7477 [S] | Live! Volume 2 | 1968 | $30 |

—Blue label with trident logo in circle at top

| ❏ PRLP-7524 [M] | On the Spot | 1967 | $50 |

—Blue label with trident logo at right

| ❏ PRST-7524 [S] | On the Spot | 1967 | $40 |

—Blue label with trident logo at right

| ❏ PRST-7524 [S] | On the Spot | 1968 | $30 |

—Blue label with trident logo in circle at top

| ❏ PRLP-7397 [M] | Out Front | 1965 | $30 |

—Blue label with trident logo at right

| ❏ PRST-7397 [S] | Out Front | 1965 | $40 |

—Blue label with trident logo at right

| ❏ PRST-7397 [S] | Out Front | 1968 | $30 |

—Blue label with trident logo in circle at top

❏ PRST-7686	Solo Piano	1969	$30
❏ PRST-7615	The Jaki Byard Experience	1969	$30
❏ PRST-7550	The Sunshine of My Soul	1968	$30

SOUL NOTE
❏ 121125	Foolin' Myself	199?	$30
❏ SN-1075	Phantasies	1985	$30
❏ 121175	Phantasies II	199?	$30
❏ SN-1031	To Them -- To Us	198?	$30

BYAS, DON, AND BUD POWELL
Also see each artist's individual listings.
Albums
COLUMBIA
| ❏ JC35755 | A Tribute to Cannonball | 1979 | $30 |

Number	Title	Yr	NM

BYAS, DON
Tenor saxophone player. Also see MARY LOU WILLIAMS.

Albums

ATLANTIC
| ❏ ALR-117 [10] | Don Byas Solos | 1952 | $350 |

BATTLE
| ❏ B-6121 [M] | April in Paris | 1963 | $30 |
| ❏ BS-6121 [S] | April in Paris | 1963 | $40 |

BLACK LION
| ❏ 160 | Anthropology | 1973 | $35 |

DIAL
| ❏ LP-216 [10] | Tenor Saxophone Concerto | 1951 | $400 |

DISCOVERY
| ❏ 3022 [10] | Don Byas with Beryl Booker | 1954 | $250 |

EMARCY
| ❏ MG-26026 [10] | Don Byas Sax | 1954 | $200 |

GNP CRESCENDO
| ❏ GNP-9027 | Don Byas | 197? | $30 |

NORGRAN
| ❏ MGN-12 [10] | In France "Don Byas Et Ses Rhythmes" | 1954 | $300 |

ONYX
| ❏ 208 | Midnight at Minton's | 197? | $35 |

PRESTIGE
| ❏ PRST-7598 | Don Byas In Paris | 1969 | $25 |
| ❏ PRST-7692 [B] | Don Byas Meets Ben Webster | 1969 | $100 |

—aka Ben Webster Meets Don Byas

REGENT
| ❏ MG-6044 [M] | Jazz Free and Easy | 1957 | $80 |

SAVOY
❏ MG-9007 [10]	Don Byas Sax	1952	$150
❏ MG-12203	Jazz Free and Easy	196?	$50
❏ SJL-2213	Savoy Jam Party	197?	$35
❏ MG-15043 [10]	Tenor Sax Solos	1955	$120

SEECO
| ❏ SLP-35 [10] | Don Byas Favorites | 1955 | $150 |

BYAS, DON/ BERNARD PEIFFER
Also see each artist's individual listings.

Albums

CLEF
| ❏ MGC-748 [M] | Jazz from Saint-Germain Des Pres | 1956 | $0 |

—Canceled

VERVE
| ❏ MGV-8119 [M] | Jazz from Saint-Germain Des Pres | 1957 | $150 |
| ❏ V-8119 [M] | Jazz from Saint-Germain Des Pres | 1961 | $25 |

BYAS, DON/BUDDY TATE
Also see each artist's individual listings.

Albums

ALLEGRO
| ❏ 1741 [M] | All Star Jazz | 1956 | $40 |

BYERS, BILLY; JOE NEWMAN; EDDIE BERT
Also see each artist's individual listings.

Albums

JAZZTONE
| ❏ J-1276 [M] | East Coast Sounds | 1959 | $60 |

BYERS, BILLY
Trombonist and arranger.

Albums

CONCERT HALL JAZZ
| ❏ 1217 [M] | Byers' Guide | 1955 | $80 |

MERCURY
| ❏ PPM-2028 [M] | Impressions of Duke Ellington | 196? | $25 |
| ❏ PPS-6028 [S] | Impressions of Duke Ellington | 196? | $100 |

RCA VICTOR
| ❏ LPM-1269 [M] | The Jazz Workshop | 1956 | $80 |

WING
| ❏ SRW-16398 [S] | Impressions of Duke Ellington | 196? | $20 |

BYRD, CHARLIE, AND FATHER MALCOLM BOYD
Boyd, a priest popular in the Summer of Love era, reads excerpts from his works with Byrd's guitar accompaniment.

Albums

COLUMBIA
❏ CL2548 [M]	Are You Running With Me, Jesus?	1966	$35
❏ CS9348 [S]	Are You Running With Me, Jesus?	1966	$50
❏ CL2657 [M]	Happening Prayers for Now	1967	$35
❏ CS9457 [S]	Happening Prayers for Now	1967	$35

BYRD, CHARLIE, HERB ELLIS & BARNEY KESSEL
Also see each artist's individual listings.

Albums

CONCORD JAZZ
| ❏ CJD-1002 | Straight Tracks | 1986 | $50 |

—Direct-to-disc recording
❏ C-4	The Great Guitars	197?	$30
❏ C-23	The Great Guitars	197?	$30
❏ CJ-209	The Great Guitars at Charlie's Georgetown	1982	$25
❏ CJ-131	The Great Guitars at the Winery	1981	$25

BYRD, CHARLIE
Guitarist and composer. Also see STAN GETZ.

Albums

COLUMBIA
❏ CS9841	Aquarius	1969	$35
❏ C30380	A Stroke of Genius	1971	$30
❏ CL2504 [M]	A Touch of Gold	1966	$30
❏ CS9304 [S]	A Touch of Gold	1966	$35
❏ CL2337 [M]	Brazilian Byrd	1965	$35

—Guaranteed High Fidelity" on label
| ❏ CL2337 [M] | Brazilian Byrd | 1965 | $30 |

—360 Sound Mono" on label
| ❏ CS9137 [S] | Brazilian Byrd | 1965 | $50 |

—Red label, "360 Sound" in black
| ❏ CS9137 [S] | Brazilian Byrd | 1965 | $35 |

—Red label, "360 Sound" in white
| ❏ PC9137 | Brazilian Byrd | 198? | $20 |

—Reissue with new prefix
| ❏ CS9137 | Brazilian Byrd | 1971 | $25 |

—Orange label
❏ CL2592 [M]	Byrdland	1967	$50
❏ CS9392 [S]	Byrdland	1967	$35
❏ CL2555 [M]	Christmas Carols for Solo Guitar	1966	$35
❏ CS9355 [S]	Christmas Carols for Solo Guitar	1966	$50
❏ CS9667	Delicately	1968	$35
❏ G30622	For All We Know	1971	$35
❏ CS9627	Hit Trip	1968	$60

—Special Mono Radio Station Copy" with white label
❏ CS9627 [M]	Hit Trip	1968	$35
❏ CL2652 [M]	Hollywood Byrd	1967	$50
❏ CS9452 [S]	Hollywood Byrd	1967	$35
❏ CS9869	Let Go	1969	$35
❏ CS1053	Let It Be	1970	$30
❏ CL2692 [M]	More Brazilian Byrd	1967	$50
❏ CS9492 [S]	More Brazilian Byrd	1967	$35
❏ C31025	Onda Nuevo	1972	$30
❏ CS9582	Sketches of Brazil (Music of Villa Lobos)	1968	$35
❏ CS9747	The Great Byrd	1968	$35
❏ CS9970	The Greatest Hits of the 60's	1970	$30
❏ CG31967	The World of Charlie Byrd	1972	$35
❏ CL2435 [M]	Travellin' Man Recorded Live	1966	$30
❏ CS9235 [S]	Travellin' Man Recorded Live	1966	$35

CONCORD JAZZ
❏ CJ-82	Blue Byrd	1979	$25
❏ CJ-304	Byrd & Brass	1986	$25
❏ CJ-252	Isn't It Romantic	1984	$25
❏ CJ-374	It's a Wonderful World	1989	$30

CONCORD PICANTE
| ❏ P-173 | Brazilville | 1981 | $25 |
| ❏ P-114 | Sugarloaf Suite | 1980 | $25 |

CRYSTAL CLEAR
| ❏ 8002 | Charlie Byrd | 1979 | $60 |

—Direct-to-disc recording; plays at 45 rpm

FANTASY
| ❏ OJC-107 | Bossa Nova Pelos Passaros | 198? | $25 |

—Reissue of Riverside 436
| ❏ OJC-262 | Byrd at the Gate | 1987 | $25 |

—Reissue of Riverside 9467

❏ F-9466	Byrd by the Sea	1974	$30
❏ F-9429	Crystal Silence	1973	$30
❏ F-9496	Top Hat	1975	$30

IMPROV
| ❏ 7116 | Charlie Byrd Swings Downtown | 1977 | $30 |

MILESTONE
| ❏ 47049 | Charlie Byrd in Greenwich Village | 1978 | $35 |
| ❏ 47005 | Latin Byrd | 1973 | $35 |

MOBILE FIDELITY
| ❏ 1-515 | Byrd at the Gate | 1982 | $100 |

—Audiophile vinyl

OFFBEAT
❏ OLP-3009 [M]	Blues Sonata	1960	$60
❏ OS-93009 [S]	Blues Sonata	1960	$60
❏ OJ-3007 [M]	Charlie's Choice	1960	$60
❏ OS-93007 [S]	Charlie's Choice	1960	$60
❏ OJ-3001 [M]	Jazz at the Show Boat, Volume 1	1959	$60
❏ OS-93001 [S]	Jazz at the Show Boat, Volume 1	1959	$60
❏ OJ-3005 [M]	Jazz at the Show Boat, Volume 2	1959	$60
❏ OS-93005 [S]	Jazz at the Show Boat, Volume 2	1959	$60
❏ OJ-3006 [M]	Jazz at the Show Boat, Volume 3	1959	$60
❏ OS-93006 [S]	Jazz at the Show Boat, Volume 3	1959	$60

PICKWICK
| ❏ SPC-3042 | Byrd and the Herd | 196? | $30 |

RIVERSIDE
❏ RM-453 [M]	Blues Sonata	1963	$150
❏ RS-9453 [S]	Blues Sonata	1963	$150
❏ 6054	Blues Sonata	197?	$25
❏ RM-436 [M]	Bossa Nova Pelos Passaros	1962	$200
❏ RS-9436 [S]	Bossa Nova Pelos Passaros	1962	$200
❏ RM-467 [M]	Byrd at the Gate	1964	$150
❏ RS-9467 [S]	Byrd at the Gate	1964	$150
❏ RM-449 [M]	Byrd in the Wind	1963	$150
❏ RS-9449 [S]	Byrd in the Wind	1963	$150
❏ RS-3044	Byrd Man with Strings	1969	$100
❏ RM-481 [M]	Byrd Song	1966	$100
❏ RM-448 [M]	Byrd's Word	1963	$150
❏ RS-9448 [S]	Byrd's Word	1963	$150
❏ RM-452 [M]	Charlie Byrd at the Village Vanguard	1963	$150
❏ RS-9452 [S]	Charlie Byrd at the Village Vanguard	1963	$150
❏ RM-427 [M]	Latin Impressions	1962	$150
❏ RS-9427 [S]	Latin Impressions	1962	$150
❏ RM-450 [M]	Mr. Guitar	1963	$150
❏ RS-9450 [S]	Mr. Guitar	1963	$150
❏ RM-454 [M]	Once More! Bossa Nova	1963	$150
❏ RS-9454 [S]	Once More! Bossa Nova	1963	$150
❏ RM-498 [M]	Solo Flight	1967	$100
❏ RS-9498 [S]	Solo Flight	1967	$100
❏ RM-451 [M]	The Guitar Artistry of Charlie Byrd	1963	$150
❏ RS-9451 [S]	The Guitar Artistry of Charlie Byrd	1963	$150
❏ RS-3005	The Guitar Artistry of Charlie Byrd	1968	$100

SAVOY
| ❏ MG-12116 [M] | Blues for Night People | 1957 | $40 |
| ❏ MG-12099 [M] | Jazz Recital | 1957 | $40 |

SAVOY JAZZ
| ❏ SJL-1131 | First Flight | 1980 | $25 |
| ❏ SJL-1121 | Midnight Guitar | 1980 | $25 |

BYRD, DONALD; HANY MOBLEY; KENNY BURRELL
Also see each artist's individual listings.

Albums

STATUS
| ❏ ST-8317 [M] | Donald Byrd, Hank Mobley & Kenny Burrell | 1965 | $40 |

BYRD, DONALD
Earlier material appears in the Goldmine Standard Catalog of American Records 1950-1975. (SC2)
Trumpeter and flugel horn player. Discovered the vocal group THE BLACKBYRDS. Also see PEPPER ADAMS; KENNY DREW; ART FARMER; RED GARLAND; THE JAZZ LAB; HANK MOBLEY.

Albums

AMERICAN RECORDING SOCIETY
| ❏ G-437 [M] | Modern Jazz | 1957 | $300 |

BLUE NOTE
| ❏ BLP-4124 [M] | A New Perspective | 1964 | $200 |
| ❏ BST-84124 [S] | A New Perspective | 1964 | $150 |

Number	Title	Yr	NM

— New York, USA" address on label

| BST-84124 [S] | A New Perspective | 1967 | $60 |

— A Division of Liberty Records" on label

| BST-84124 | A New Perspective | 198? | $30 |

— The Finest in Jazz Since 1939" reissue

| BN-LA047-F | Black Byrd | 1973 | $35 |
| LO-047 | Black Byrd | 1981 | $20 |

— Reissue of LA047

BLP-4259 [M]	Blackjack	1967	$100
BST-84259 [S]	Blackjack	1967	$50
BLP-4048 [M]	Byrd in Flight	1960	$150

— W. 63rd St., NYC address on label

| BLP-4048 [M] | Byrd in Flight | 1963 | $100 |

— New York, USA" address on label

| BST-84048 [S] | Byrd in Flight | 1960 | $120 |

— W. 63rd St., NYC address on label

| BST-84048 [S] | Byrd in Flight | 1963 | $60 |

— New York, USA" address on label

| BST-84048 [S] | Byrd in Flight | 1967 | $30 |

— A Division of Liberty Records" on label

| BLP-4019 [M] | Byrd in Hand | 1959 | $150 |

— W. 63rd St., NYC address on label

| BLP-4019 [M] | Byrd in Hand | 1963 | $100 |

— New York, USA" address on label

| BST-84019 [S] | Byrd in Hand | 1959 | $120 |

— W. 63rd St., NYC address on label

| BST-84019 [S] | Byrd in Hand | 1963 | $60 |

— New York, USA" address on label

| BST-84019 [S] | Byrd in Hand | 1967 | $30 |

— A Division of Liberty Records" on label

| BST-84007 [S] | Byrd in Hand | 1967 | $30 |

— A Division of Liberty Records" on label

| BST-84019 | Byrd in Hand | 198? | $25 |

— The Finest in Jazz Since 1939" reissue

BN-LA633-G	Caricatures	1976	$35
LT-991	Chant	1980	$30
LT-1096	Creeper	1981	$30
BLP-4060 [M]	Donald Byrd at the Half Note Café, Volume 1	1961	$150

— W. 63rd St., NYC address on label

| BLP-4060 [M] | Donald Byrd at the Half Note Café, Volume 1 | 1963 | $100 |

— New York, USA" address on label

| BST-84060 [S] | Donald Byrd at the Half Note Café, Volume 1 | 1961 | $120 |

— W. 63rd St., NYC address on label

| BST-84060 [S] | Donald Byrd at the Half Note Café, Volume 1 | 1963 | $60 |

— New York, USA" address on label

| BST-84060 [S] | Donald Byrd at the Half Note Café, Volume 1 | 1967 | $30 |

— A Division of Liberty Records" on label

| BLP-4061 [M] | Donald Byrd at the Half Note Café, Volume 2 | 1961 | $150 |

— W. 63rd St., NYC address on label

| BLP-4061 [M] | Donald Byrd at the Half Note Café, Volume 2 | 1963 | $100 |

— New York, USA" address on label

| BST-84061 [S] | Donald Byrd at the Half Note Café, Volume 2 | 1961 | $120 |

— W. 63rd St., NYC address on label

| BST-84061 [S] | Donald Byrd at the Half Note Café, Volume 2 | 1963 | $60 |

— New York, USA" address on label

| BST-84061 [S] | Donald Byrd at the Half Note Café, Volume 2 | 1967 | $30 |

— A Division of Liberty Records" on label

BN-LA700-G	Donald Byrd's Best	1976	$35
BST-84349	Electric	1970	$50
B1-36195	Electric Byrd	1996	$35
BST-84380	Ethiopian Nights	1972	$50
BST-84319	Fancy Free	1969	$50
B1-89796	Fancy Free	1993	$35
BLP-4118 [M]	Free Form	1963	$100
BST-84118 [S]	Free Form	1963	$60

— New York, USA" address on label

| BST-84118 [S] | Free Form | 1967 | $30 |

— A Division of Liberty Records" on label

| BST-84118 | Free Form | 1986 | $25 |

— The Finest in Jazz Since 1939" reissue

| BLP-4026 [M] | Fuego | 1960 | $150 |

— W. 63rd St., NYC address on label

| BLP-4026 [M] | Fuego | 1963 | $100 |

— New York, USA" address on label

| BST-84026 [S] | Fuego | 1959 | $120 |

— W. 63rd St., NYC address on label

| BST-84026 [S] | Fuego | 1963 | $60 |

— New York, USA" address on label

| BST-84026 [S] | Fuego | 1967 | $30 |

— A Division of Liberty Records" on label

| BLP-4188 [M] | I'm Tryin' to Get Home | 1965 | $100 |
| BST-84188 [S] | I'm Tryin' to Get Home | 1965 | $60 |

— New York, USA" address on label

| BST-84188 [S] | I'm Tryin' to Get Home | 1967 | $30 |

— A Division of Liberty Records" on label

| BST-84188 | I'm Tryin' to Get Home | 1986 | $25 |

— The Finest in Jazz Since 1939" reissue

B1-31875	Kofi	1995	$35
BLP-4238 [M]	Mustang!	1966	$100
BST-84238 [S]	Mustang!	1966	$60

— New York, USA" address on label

| BST-84238 [S] | Mustang! | 1967 | $30 |

— A Division of Liberty Records" on label

| BLP-4007 [M] | Off to the Races | 1959 | $200 |

— Deep groove" version (deep indentation under label on both sides)

| BLP-4007 [M] | Off to the Races | 1959 | $150 |

— W. 63rd St., NYC address on label

| BLP-4007 [M] | Off to the Races | 1963 | $100 |

— New York, USA" address on label

| BST-4007 [S] | Off to the Races | 1959 | $150 |

— Deep groove" version (deep indentation under label on both sides)

| BST-4007 [S] | Off to the Races | 1959 | $120 |

— W. 63rd St., NYC address on label

| BST-4007 [S] | Off to the Races | 1963 | $60 |

— New York, USA" address on label

| BN-LA549-G | Places and Spaces | 1975 | $35 |
| LW-549 | Places and Spaces | 1981 | $20 |

— Reissue of LA549

| BLP-4101 [M] | Royal Flush | 1962 | $100 |
| BST-84101 [S] | Royal Flush | 1962 | $60 |

— New York, USA" address on label

| BST-84101 [S] | Royal Flush | 1967 | $30 |

— A Division of Liberty Records" on label

BN-LA368--G	Sleeping Into Tomorrow	1975	$35
BN-LA140-G	Street Lady	1974	$35
LN-10054	Street Lady	1981	$20

— Budget-line reissue

| BLP-4075 [M] | The Cat Walk | 1961 | $150 |

— 61st St, New York address on label

| BLP-4075 [M] | The Cat Walk | 1963 | $100 |

— New York, USA" address on label

| BST-84075 [S] | The Cat Walk | 1961 | $120 |

— 61st St, New York address on label

| BST-84075 [S] | The Cat Walk | 1963 | $60 |

— New York, USA" address on label

| BST-84075 [S] | The Cat Walk | 1967 | $30 |

— A Division of Liberty Records" on label

DELMARK

| DS-407 | First Flight | 1990 | $30 |

DISCOVERY

| 869 | September Afternoon | 198? | $25 |

ELEKTRA

6E-247	Donald Byrd and 125th St., N.Y.C.	1980	$25
5E-531	Love Byrd	1981	$25
6E-144	Thank You for F.U.M.L. (Funking Up My Life)	1978	$25
60188	Words, Sounds, Colors and Shapes	1982	$25

LANDMARK

| LLP-1523 | Getting Down to Business | 1990 | $30 |
| LLP-1516 | Harlem Blues | 1988 | $25 |

SAVOY

| MG-12032 [M] | Byrd's Word | 1956 | $175 |
| MG-12064 [M] | The Jazz Message of Donald Byrd | 1956 | $200 |

SAVOY JAZZ

| SJL-1101 | Long Green | 198? | $25 |
| SJL-1114 | Star Eyes | 198? | $25 |

TRANSITION

TRLP-17 [M]	Byrd Blows on Beacon Hill	1956	$2500
TRLP-5 [M]	Byrd Jazz	1956	$1400
TRLP-4 [M]	Byrd's Eye View	1956	$1400

TRIP

| 5000 | Two Sides of Donald Byrd | 1974 | $35 |

VERVE

| V-8609 [M] | Up with Donald Byrd | 1965 | $50 |
| V6-8609 [S] | Up with Donald Byrd | 1965 | $60 |

BYRNE, BOBBY; WILL BRADLEY; BUD FREEMAN

Also see each artist's individual listings.

Albums

GRAND AWARD

| GA 33-313 [M] | Jazz, Dixieland-Chicago | 1955 | $50 |

BYRNE, BOBBY

Trombonist and bandleader.

Albums

COMMAND

RS 33-894 [M]	1966 -- Magnificent Movie Themes	1966	$30
RS894SD [S]	1966 -- Magnificent Movie Themes	1966	$35
RS928SD [S]	Sound in the 8th Dimension	1968	$80

GRAND AWARD

GA 33-381 [M]	Great Song Hits of the Glenn Miller Orchestra	1958	$30
GA207SD [S]	Great Song Hits of the Glenn Miller Orchestra	1958	$40
GA 33-382 [M]	Great Song Hits of the Tommy and Jimmy Dorsey Orchestras	1958	$30
GA206SD [S]	Great Song Hits of the Tommy and Jimmy Dorsey Orchestras	1958	$40
GA 33-392 [M]	Great Themes of America's Greatest Bands	1958	$30
GA225SD [S]	Great Themes of America's Greatest Bands	1959	$40
GA 33-416 [M]	The Jazzbone's Connected to the Trombone	1959	$40
GA248SD [S]	The Jazzbone's Connected to the Trombone	1959	$50

WALDORF MUSIC HALL

| MH 33-121 [10] | Dixieland Jazz | 195? | $50 |

BYRON, GEORGE

Male singer.

Albums

ATLANTIC

| 1293 [M] | Premiere Performance | 1958 | $300 |

— Black label

C

CABLES, GEORGE

Pianist.

Albums

CONTEMPORARY

| C-14030 | By George: The Music of George Gershwin | 1987 | $25 |
| C-14001 | Cables' Vision | 1979 | $35 |

— Pianist.

| C-14015 | Circle | 198? | $30 |
| C-14014 | Phantom of the City | 198? | $30 |

CABO FRIO

Fusion band from New York.

Albums

ZEBRA

ZEB-5990	Cabo Frio	198?	$25
ZR-5002	Just Having Fun	198?	$30
ZEB-5685	Right On the Money	1986	$25

CACIA, PAUL

Trumpeter and bandleader.

Albums

HAPPY HOUR

| HH6001 | Paul Cacia Presents The Alumni Tribute to Stan Kenton | 198? | $25 |
| HH5004 | Quantum Leap | 198? | $25 |

— Trumpeter and bandleader.

OUTSTANDING

| OUTS-056 | Quantum Leap | 1986 | $30 |

Bobby Byrne, *The Jazzbone's Connected to the Trombone*, Grand Award GA 33-416, **$40**.

Barbara Carroll, *Lullabies in Rhythm*, RCA Victor LJM-1023, **$60**.

Benny Carter, *Benny Carter Plays Pretty*, Norgran MGN-1015, **$200**.

Ron Carter, Blues Farm, CTI 6027, **$50**.

Number	Title	Yr	NM

CAFÉ NOIR
So-called "gypsy jazz" quartet: Randy Erwin (vocals); Gail Hess (violin); Lyle West (guitar), Jason Bucklin (guitar).
Albums
GAJO
| ❑ GR-1001 | Café Noir | 1988 | $25 |

CAHEN, FRANCOIS
Pianist, former member of French progressive rock band Magma.
Albums
INNER CITY
| ❑ 1118 | Great Winds | 1979 | $35 |

—*Pianist, former member of French progressive rock band Magma.*

CAIN, JACKIE, AND ROY KRAL
Wife-and-husband vocal duo. Kral also is a pianist.
Albums
ABC-PARAMOUNT
❑ ABC-163 [M]	Bits and Pieces	1957	$50
❑ ABC-207 [M]	Free and Easy	1958	$50
❑ ABC-267 [M]	In the Spotlight	1959	$40
❑ ABCS-267 [S]	In the Spotlight	1959	$50
❑ ABC-120 [M]	The Glory of Love	1956	$50
AUDIOPHILE
❑ AP-230	One More Rose (A Tribute to the Lyrics of Alan Jay Lerner)	1988	$25
BRUNSWICK
❑ BL54026 [M]	Jackie Cain and Roy Kral	1957	$50
CAPITOL
❑ ST2936	Grass	1968	$75
COLUMBIA
❑ CL1704 [M]	Double Take	1961	$30
❑ CS8504 [S]	Double Take	1961	$30
❑ CS8260 [S]	Sweet and Low Down	1960	$30
CONCORD JAZZ
❑ CJ-149	East of Suez	1981	$30
❑ CJ-186	High Standards	198?	$30
❑ CJ-115	Star Sounds	1979	$30
CONTEMPORARY
❑ C-14046	Full Circle	1989	$30
CTI
❑ 6040	A Wilder Alias	1974	$35
❑ 6019	Time and Love	1972	$35
DISCOVERY
❑ 907	We've Got It: The Music of Cy Coleman	1986	$25
FANTASY
❑ F-9643	Bogie	1986	$25
FINESSE
❑ FW38324	A Stephen Sondheim Collection	1983	$25
MCA
❑ 4169	Jackie & Roy	198?	$30
REGENT
❑ MG-6057 [M]	Jackie & Roy	1957	$50
ROULETTE
❑ R-25278 [M]	By Jupiter & Girl Crazy	1964	$25
❑ SR-25278 [S]	By Jupiter & Girl Crazy	1964	$30
SAVOY
❑ MG-12198 [M]	Jackie and Roy	196?	$25
STORYVILLE
❑ STLP-322 [10]	Jackie & Roy	1955	$120
❑ STLP-915 [M]	Sing Baby, Sing!	1956	$60
❑ STLP-904 [M]	Storyville Presents Jackie & Roy	1955	$75
STUDIO 7
❑ 402	By the Sea	1978	$30
VERVE
❑ V-8668 [M]	Changes	1966	$25
❑ V6-8668 [S]	Changes	1966	$30
❑ V-8688 [M]	Lovesick	1967	$30
❑ V6-8688 [S]	Lovesick	1967	$25

CAIOLA, AL
Guitarist. Most of his work is in a more pop vein; for a more complete listing, see the Standard Catalog of American Records.
Albums
CHANCELLOR
| ❑ CHL-5008 [M] | Great Pickin' | 1960 | $60 |
| ❑ CHS-5008 [S] | Great Pickin' | 1960 | $60 |
SAVOY
| ❑ MG-12033 [M] | Deep in a Dream | 1955 | $50 |
| ❑ MG-12057 [M] | Serenade in Blue | 1956 | $40 |
UNITED ARTISTS
| ❑ UAL-3299 [M] | Cleopatra and All That Jazz | 1963 | $60 |
| ❑ UAS-6299 [S] | Cleopatra and All That Jazz | 1963 | $60 |

CALIFORNIA RAMBLERS, THE
Early white jazz band, none of whom were from California.
Albums
BIOGRAPH
| ❑ 12021 | Hallelujah, Vol. 2 1925-29 | 197? | $25 |
| ❑ 12020 | Miss Annabelle Lee 1925-27 | 197? | $25 |

CALIMAN, HADLEY
Tenor and soprano saxophone player and sometimes flutist.
Albums
CATALYST
| ❑ 0(# unknown) | Celebration | 1977 | $30 |
| ❑ 7604 | Projecting | 1976 | $30 |
MAINSTREAM
| ❑ MRL-318 | Hadley Caliman | 1971 | $25 |
| ❑ MRL-342 | Iapetus | 1972 | $25 |

CALLENDER, RED
Bass player and sometimes tuba player.
Albums
CROWN
| ❑ CLP-5012 [M] | Callender Speaks Low | 1957 | $50 |
| ❑ CLP-5025 [M] | Swingin' Suite | 1957 | $40 |
LEGEND
| ❑ 1005 | Basin Street Bass | 197? | $30 |
METROJAZZ
| ❑ E-1007 [M] | The Lowest | 1958 | $120 |
| ❑ SE-1007 [S] | The Lowest | 1959 | $120 |
MODERN
| ❑ MLP-1201 [M] | Swingin' Suite | 1956 | $80 |
RED
| ❑ KM2248 | Red Callender Speaks Low | 1978 | $35 |

CALLOWAY, CAB
Male singer and bandleader. Best known for the "hi-de-ho" chorus of the song "Minnie the Moocher."
Albums
BRUNSWICK
| ❑ BL58101 [10] | Cab Calloway | 1954 | $100 |
COLUMBIA
| ❑ CG32593 | The Hi De Ho Man | 1973 | $25 |
CORAL
| ❑ CRL57408 [M] | Blues Make Me Happy | 1962 | $30 |
| ❑ CRL757408 [S] | Blues Make Me Happy | 1962 | $30 |
EPIC
| ❑ LN3265 [M] | Swing Showman | 1957 | $100 |
GLENDALE
| ❑ GLS9007 | Cab Calloway | 1984 | $25 |
GONE
| ❑ LP-101 [M] | Cotton Club Revue '58 | 1958 | $80 |
MCA
| ❑ 1344 | Mr. Hi-De-Ho | 198? | $25 |
P.I.P.
| ❑ 6801 | Cab Calloway '68 | 1968 | $50 |
RCA VICTOR
| ❑ LPM-2021 [M] | Hi De Hi De Ho | 1958 | $30 |
VOCALION
| ❑ VL73820 | The Blues | 196? | $30 |

CAMERON, BRUCE
Cornet player.
Albums
DISCOVERY
| ❑ 793 | With All My Love | 198? | $25 |
SEA BREEZE
| ❑ 9801 | Jet Away | 198? | $25 |

CAMERON, DOUG
Violinist.
Albums
SPINDLETOP
| ❑ STP-103 | Freeway Mentality | 1986 | $30 |

CAMERON, JOHN
Pianist, keyboard player, arranger and composer.
Albums
DERAM
| ❑ DES18033 | Off Centre | 1969 | $25 |

CAMILO, MICHEL
Pianist.
Albums
EPIC
| ❑ OE45295 | On Fire | 1989 | $60 |
PORTRAIT
| ❑ OR44482 | Michael Camilo | 1988 | $25 |

CAMP, RED
Pianist.
Albums
COOK
❑ LP-5005 [M]	Camp Has a Ball	1957	$50
❑ LP-1087 [10]	Camp Inventions: Bold New Design for Jazz Piano	1955	$60
❑ LP-1089 [10]	Red Camp	1955	$60

CAMPBELL, JOHN
Pianist.
Albums
CONTEMPORARY
| ❑ C-14053 | After Hours | 1989 | $30 |
| ❑ C-14061 | Turning Point | 1991 | $35 |

CANADIAN ALL STARS, THE
Albums
DISCOVERY
| ❑ DL-3025 [10] | The Canadian All Stars | 1954 | $250 |

CANAL STREET RAGTIMERS
Members: Roy Bower, Tony Smith, Martin Rodger, Chris Brown, John Featherhouse, Derek Gracie, Colin Knight, Derek Hamer.
Albums
GHB
| ❑ 4 [M] | Canal Street Ragtimers | 196? | $30 |

—*Members: Roy Bower, Tony Smith, Martin Rodger, Chris Brown, John Featherhouse, Derek Gracie, Colin Knight, Derek Hamer*

CANDIDO
Drummer, especially prominent on congas and bongos.
Albums
ABC-PARAMOUNT
❑ ABC-125 [M]	Candido Featuring Al Cohn	1956	$50
❑ ABC-453 [M]	Candido's Comparsa	1963	$25
❑ ABCS-453 [S]	Candido's Comparsa	1963	$30
❑ ABC-236 [M]	In Indigo	1958	$50
❑ ABCS-236 [S]	In Indigo	1959	$40
❑ ABC-286 [M]	Latin Fire	1959	$40
❑ ABCS-286 [S]	Latin Fire	1959	$50
❑ ABC-180 [M]	The Volcanic Candido	1957	$50
BLUE NOTE
❑ BST-84357	Beautiful	1970	$35
POLYDOR
❑ PD-5063	Drum Fever	1973	$30
RCA VICTOR
❑ LPM-2027 [M]	Beautiful	1959	$30
❑ LSP-2027 [S]	Beautiful	1959	$40
ROULETTE
❑ R-52078 [M]	Conga Soul	1962	$25
❑ SR-52078 [S]	Conga Soul	1962	$30
SOLID STATE
❑ SS-18066	The Thousand Finger Man	1969	$35

CANDOLI, CONTE, AND FRANK ROSOLINO
Also see each artist's individual listings.

Albums

RCA VICTOR

Number	Title	Yr	NM
❏ TPL1-1509	Conversation	197?	$30

CANDOLI, CONTE, AND PHIL WOODS
Also see each artist's individual listings.

Albums

PAUSA

Number	Title	Yr	NM
❏ PR-7189	Old Acquaintance	1986	$25

CANDOLI, CONTE, AND STAN LEVEY
Also see each artist's individual listings.

Albums

BETHLEHEM

Number	Title	Yr	NM
❏ BCP-9 [M]	West Coasting	1956	$250

CANDOLI, CONTE
Trumpeter. Also see THE CANDOLI BROTHERS.

Albums

Number	Title	Yr	NM
ANDEX			
❏ A-3002 [M]	Mucho Calor	1958	$50
❏ AS-3002 [S]	Mucho Calor	1959	$40
BETHLEHEM			
❏ BCP-1016 [10]	Sincerely, Conte Candoli	1954	$250
❏ BCP-30 [M]	Toots Sweet	1956	$250
CROWN			
❏ CLP-5162 [M]	Little Band, Big Jazz	1960	$25
❏ CST-190 [R]	Little Band, Big Jazz	196?	$30
—Black vinyl			
❏ CST-190 [R]	Little Band, Big Jazz	196?	$30
—Red vinyl			

CANDOLI, PETE
Trumpeter. Also see THE CANDOLI BROTHERS.

Albums

Number	Title	Yr	NM
DECCA			
❏ DL4761 [M]	Moscow Mule (And Many More Kicks)	1966	$35
❏ DL74761 [S]	Moscow Mule (And Many More Kicks)	1966	$25
KAPP			
❏ KL-1230 [M]	For Pete's Sake	1960	$25
❏ KS-3230 [S]	For Pete's Sake	1960	$30
SOMERSET			
❏ SF-17200 [M]	Blues, When Your Lover Has Gone	1963	$25
❏ SFS-17200 [S]	Blues, When Your Lover Has Gone	1963	$30

CANDOLI BROTHERS, THE
Also see CONTE CANDOLI; PETE CANDOLI.

Albums

Number	Title	Yr	NM
DOT			
❏ DLP-3168 [M]	Bell, Book and Candoli	1959	$75
❏ DLP-25168 [S]	Bell, Book and Candoli	1959	$75
❏ DLP-3062 [M]	The Brothers Candoli	1957	$100
IMPULSE!			
❏ 29064	The Brothers Candoli	198?	$25
MERCURY			
❏ MG-20515 [M]	Two for the Money	1959	$100
❏ SR-60191 [S]	Two for the Money	1959	$100
WARNER BROS.			
❏ W1462 [M]	The Brothers Candoli	1962	$25
❏ WS1462 [S]	The Brothers Candoli	1962	$30

CAPERS, VALERIE
Pianist, arranger and composer.

Albums

ATLANTIC

Number	Title	Yr	NM
❏ SD3003	Portrait in Soul	1970	$35

CAPP-PIERCE JUGGERNAUT, THE
Big band: Frank Capp (drummer) and Nat Pierce (pianist), leaders.

Albums

CONCORD JAZZ

Number	Title	Yr	NM
❏ CJ-40	Juggernaut	1979	$30

—*Frank Capp and Nat Pierce, leaders*

Number	Title	Yr	NM
❏ CJ-336	Live at the Alley Cat	1988	$25
❏ CJ-72	Live at the Century Plaza	1980	$30
❏ CJ-183	The Juggernaut Orchestra Strikes Again	1981	$30

CAPRARO, JOE
Banjo player.

Albums

SOUTHLAND

Number	Title	Yr	NM
❏ 220 [M]	Dixieland	1959	$25

CARAM, ANA
Female singer.

Albums

CHESKY

Number	Title	Yr	NM
❏ JR-28	Rio After Dark	199?	$30

—*Audiophile vinyl*

CARAMIA, TONY
Pianist.

Albums

STOMP OFF

Number	Title	Yr	NM
❏ SOS-1209	Hot Ivories	1991	$35

CARBO, GLADYS
Female singer.

Albums

SOUL NOTE

Number	Title	Yr	NM
❏ 121197	Street Cries	1990	$30

CAREY, DAVE
British bandleader.

Albums

LAURIE

Number	Title	Yr	NM
❏ LLP-1004 [M]	Bandwagon Plus 2	1959	$30

CAREY, MUTT, AND PUNCH MILLER
Punch Miller is a trumpeter and male singer. Also see MUTT CAREY.

Albums

Number	Title	Yr	NM
SAVOY			
❏ MG-12038 [M]	Jazz -- New Orleans	1955	$100
❏ MG-12050 [M]	Jazz -- New Orleans, Vol. 2	1955	$100
SAVOY JAZZ			
❏ SJC-415	New Orleans Jazz	1985	$25

CAREY, MUTT
Trumpeter. Member of "Spike's Seven Pods of Pepper Orchestra," the KID ORY-led group that made the first jazz record released by black musicians (1922).

Albums

RIVERSIDE

Number	Title	Yr	NM
❏ RLP-1042 [10]	Mutt Carey Plays the Blues	1954	$300

CARISI, JOHN
Trumpeter.

Albums

COLUMBIA

Number	Title	Yr	NM
❏ CL1419 [M]	The New Jazz Sound of "Show Boat"	1960	$30
❏ CS(# unk) [S]	The New Jazz Sound of "Show Boat"	1960	$30

CARLTON, LARRY
Guitarist. Also see THE CRUSADERS.

Albums

Number	Title	Yr	NM
BLUE THUMB			
❏ BTS-46	Singing/Playing	1972	$35
GRP			
❏ 9611	Collection	1990	$30
MCA			
❏ 5689	Alone/But Never Alone	1986	$20
❏ 6322	Christmas at Our House	1989	$25
❏ 42003	Discovery	1987	$20
❏ 6237	On Solid Ground	1989	$20

Number	Title	Yr	NM
UNI			
❏ 73036	With a Little Help from My Friends	1968	$50
WARNER BROS.			
❏ 23834	Friends	1983	$20
❏ BSK3221	Larry Carlton	1978	$25
❏ BSK3635	Sleepwalk	1981	$25
❏ BSK3380	Strikes Twice	1980	$25

CARMICHAEL, HOAGY
Pianist, male singer and composer. He co-wrote "Star Dust," one of the most recorded songs in music history.

Albums

Number	Title	Yr	NM
BIOGRAPH			
❏ 37	Stardust (1927-30)	198?	$25
BLUEBIRD			
❏ 8333-1-RB	Stardust, And Much More	1989	$30
BOOK-OF-THE-MONTH			
❏ 61-5450	Hoagy Carmichael	1984	$30
DECCA			
❏ DL5068 [10]	Stardust Road	1950	$150
❏ DL8588 [M]	Stardust Road	1958	$100
GOLDEN			
❏ LP-198-18 [M]	Havin' a Party	1958	$30
JAZZTONE			
❏ J-1266 [M]	Hoagy Sings Carmichael	1957	$30
KIMBERLY			
❏ 2023 [M]	The Legend of Hoagy Carmichael	1962	$30
❏ 11023 [R]	The Legend of Hoagy Carmichael	196?	$25
MCA			
❏ 20196	Hong Kong Blues	198?	$25
❏ 1507	Stardust Road	198?	$25
PACIFIC JAZZ			
❏ PJ-1223 [M]	Hoagy Sings Carmichael	1956	$60
PAUSA			
❏ 9006	Hoagy Sings Carmichael	1982	$25
RCA VICTOR			
❏ CPL1-3370(e)	A Legendary Performer and Composer	1979	$35
❏ LPT-3072 [10]	Old Rockin' Chair	1953	$80
TOTEM			
❏ 1039	The 1944-45 V-Disc Sessions	198?	$25

CARMICHAEL, JUDY
Pianist.

Albums

STATIRAS

Number	Title	Yr	NM
❏ SLP-8074	Jazz Piano	1985	$30
❏ SLP-8078	Pearls	1986	$30
❏ SLP-8072	Two-Handed Stride	1985	$30

CARN, DOUG, AND JEAN CARN
Jean Carn, Doug's then-wife, is a female singer. Also see DOUG CARN.

Albums

Number	Title	Yr	NM
BLACK JAZZ			
❏ 3	Infant Eyes	1971	$35
❏ QT-16 [Q]	Revelation	1973	$40
❏ QD-8 [Q]	Spirit of the New Land	1972	$40
OVATION			
❏ 1702	Higher Ground	197?	$30

CARN, DOUG
Keyboard player (mostly organ).

Albums

Number	Title	Yr	NM
SAVOY			
❏ MG-12195	The Doug Carn Trio	1969	$25
TABLIGHI			
❏ 100	Ah Rahman!	1978	$30

CARNEY, HARRY
Baritone saxophone player. Also played clarinet and bass clarinet.

Albums

Number	Title	Yr	NM
VERVE			
❏ MGV-2028 [M]	Moods for Girl and Boy	1957	$300
—Reissue of Clef 640			
❏ V-2028 [M]	Moods for Girl and Boy	1957	$150

CARPENTER, IKE

Albums

Number	Title	Yr	NM
ALADDIN			
❏ LP-811 [M]	Lights Out	1957	$0
—Unreleased			
DISCOVERY			
❏ DL3003 [10]	Dancers in Love	1949	$300
INTRO			
❏ 950 [10]	Lights Out	1952	$300
SCORE			
❏ SLP-4010 [M]	Lights Out	1957	$150

CARR, GEORGIA
Female singer.

Albums

Number	Title	Yr	NM
TOPS			
❏ L-1617 [M]	Songs by a Moody Miss	195?	$30
VEE JAY			
❏ LP-1105 [M]	Rocks in My Bed	1964	$25
❏ VJS-1105 [S]	Rocks in My Bed	1964	$30

CARR, HELEN
Female singer.

Albums

Number	Title	Yr	NM
BETHLEHEM			
❏ BCP-1027 [10]	Down in the Depths on the 90th Floor	1955	$250
❏ BCP-45 [M]	Why Do I Love You	1956	$250

CARR, IAN, AND NUCLEUS
Carr is a trumpet and fluegel horn player. On the below albums, the other members of Nucleus included Brian Smith (tenor sax, soprano sax, percussion); Geoff Castle (electric piano, synthesizer); Billy Kristian (bass) and Roger Sellers (drums).

Albums

Number	Title	Yr	NM
CAPITOL			
❏ ST-11771	In Flagrante Delicto	1978	$30
❏ ST-11916	Out of the Long Dark	1979	$30

CARR, JOYCE
Female singer.

Albums

Number	Title	Yr	NM
AUDIOPHILE			
❏ AP-148	Joyce Carr	198?	$30
SEECO			
❏ 440 [M]	Make The Man Love Me	1960	$325

CARR, LARRY
Pianist.

Albums

Number	Title	Yr	NM
AUDIOPHILE			
❏ AP-223	Fit as a Fiddle	198?	$30

CARR, LODI
Female singer.

Albums

Number	Title	Yr	NM
LAURIE			
❏ LLP-1007 [M]	Lady Bird	1960	$30

CARR, RICHARD
Violinist.

Albums

Number	Title	Yr	NM
AUDIOPHILE			
❏ AP-194	Afternoon in New York	1984	$30
PROGRESSIVE			
❏ P-7047	String Vibrations	1986	$30

CARRINGTON, TERRI LYNN
Drummer.

Albums

Number	Title	Yr	NM
VERVE			
❏ 837697-1	Real Life Story	1989	$35

CARROLL, BAIKIDA
Trumpeter and composer.

Albums

Number	Title	Yr	NM
HAT HUT			
❏ 0M/N	The Spoken Word	197?	$25
SOUL NOTE			
❏ SN-1023	Shadows & Reflections	198?	$30

CARROLL, BARBARA
Pianist.

Albums

Number	Title	Yr	NM
ATLANTIC			
❏ ALR-132 [10]	Piano Panorama	195?	$80
BLUE NOTE			
❏ BN-LA645-G	Barbara Carroll	1976	$35
DISCOVERY			
❏ DS-847	Barbara Carrol at the Piano	1980	$35
KAPP			
❏ KL-1113 [M]	Flower Drum Song	1958	$30
❏ KS-(# unk) [S]	Flower Drum Song	1958	$30
❏ KL-1193 [M]	Satin Doll	1959	$30
LIVINGSTON			
❏ 1081 [10]	Barbara Carroll Trio	1953	$100
RCA VICTOR			
❏ LJM-1001 [M]	Barbara Carroll Trio	1954	$50
❏ LPM-1137 [M]	Have You Met Miss Carroll?	1956	$50
❏ LPM-1396 [M]	It's a Wonderful World	1957	$50
❏ LJM-1023 [M]	Lullabies in Rhythm	1955	$60
❏ LPM-1296 [M]	We Just Couldn't Say Goodbye	1956	$50
SESAC			
❏ N-3201 [M]	Why Not?	1959	$60
❏ SN-3201 [S]	Why Not?	1959	$40
UNITED ARTISTS			
❏ UA-LA778-H	From the Beginning	1978	$20
VERVE			
❏ MGV-2095 [M]	Barbara	1958	$150
❏ V-2095 [M]	Barbara	1961	$25
❏ MGV-2063 [M]	Funny Face	1957	$150
—Orange label			
❏ MGV-2063 [M]	Funny Face	1957	$150
—Black label			
❏ MGV-2092 [M]	The Best of George and Ira Gershwin	1958	$120
❏ V-2092 [M]	The Best of George and Ira Gershwin	1961	$25
WARNER BROS.			
❏ W1710 [M]	Barbara Carroll Live! Her Piano and Trio	1967	$50
❏ WS1710 [S]	Barbara Carroll Live! Her Piano and Trio	1967	$50
❏ W1543 [M]	Hello Dolly" and "What Makes Sammy Run	1964	$35
❏ WS1543 [S]	Hello Dolly" and "What Makes Sammy Run	1964	$50

CARROLL, BARBARA/MARY LOU WILLIAMS
Also see each artist's individual listings.

Albums

Number	Title	Yr	NM
ATLANTIC			
❏ 1271 [M]	Ladies in Jazz	1958	$250
—Black label			
❏ 1271 [M]	Ladies in Jazz	1961	$150
—Multi-color label, white "fan" logo			

CARROLL, JOE
Male singer.

Albums

Number	Title	Yr	NM
CHARLIE PARKER			
❏ PLP-802 [M]	The Man with the Happy Sound	1962	$30
❏ PLP-802S [S]	The Man with the Happy Sound	1962	$30
EPIC			
❏ LN3272 [M]	Joe Carroll	1956	$100

CARSON, ERNIE, AND BOB GREEN

Albums

Number	Title	Yr	NM
GHB			
❏ 56	Strutters, Volume 1	197?	$25
❏ 57	Strutters, Volume 2	197?	$25

CARSON, ERNIE
Cornet player, pianist and bandleader.

Albums

Number	Title	Yr	NM
GHB			
❏ 95	Brother Lowdown	197?	$25
❏ 125	Ernie Carson and the Original Cottonmouth Jazz Band at the Hookers' Ball	1980	$25
❏ 162	Southern Comfort	198?	$25
JAZZOLOGY			
❏ JCE-5	Eleanor Buck, A Celebration Service, Sept. 18, 1983	1984	$25
❏ J-89	Ernie Carson and Rhythm	1983	$25
❏ 54	Ernie Carson and the Capitol City Jazz Band	198?	$25
❏ J-45	The Carson-Bornemann All Stars	198?	$25

CARTER, BENNY; BEN WEBSTER; BARNEY BIGARD
Also see each artist's individual listings.

Albums

Number	Title	Yr	NM
SWINGVILLE			
❏ SVLP-2032 [M]	B.B.B. & Co.	1962	$40
—Purple label			
❏ SVST-2032 [S]	B.B.B. & Co.	1962	$50
—Red label			
❏ SVLP-2032 [M]	B.B.B. & Co.	1965	$25
—Blue label, trident logo at right			
❏ SVST-2032 [S]	B.B.B. & Co.	1965	$30
—Blue label, trident logo at right			

CARTER, BENNY; COLEMAN HAWKINS; BEN WEBSTER
Also see each artist's individual listings.

Albums

Number	Title	Yr	NM
BLUEBIRD			
❏ 9683-1-RB	Three Great Swing Saxophonists	1989	$30

CARTER, BENNY
Jazz multi-instrumentalist and bandleader. Of his hundreds of recordings, only the following single made the country charts. Alto and tenor saxophone player, clarinetist, trombone player, pianist, arranger, composer and bandleader.

Albums

Number	Title	Yr	NM
20TH CENTURY-FOX			
❏ TFM-3134 [M]	Benny Carter in Paris	1963	$25
❏ TFS-4134 [S]	Benny Carter in Paris	1963	$30
ABC IMPULSE!			
❏ AS-9116 [S]	Additions to Further Definitions	1968	$30
❏ AS-12 [S]	Further Definitions	1968	$30
ANALOGUE PRODUCTIONS			
❏ AP-13	Jazz Giant	199?	$30
—Audiophile reissue			
AUDIO LAB			
❏ AL-1505 [M]	The Fabulous Benny Carter	1959	$150
CLEF			
❏ MGC-141 [10]	Cosmopolite	1953	$350
CONCORD JAZZ			
❏ CJ-285	A Gentleman and His Music	1985	$25
CONTEMPORARY			
❏ C-3555 [M]	Jazz Giant	1958	$250
❏ S-7028 [S]	Jazz Giant	1960	$250
—Reissue of Stereo Records 7028			
❏ S-7555 [S]	Jazz Giant	197?	$30
—Reissue of 7028			
❏ M-3561 [M]	Swingin' the Twenties	1959	$250
❏ S-7561 [S]	Swingin' the Twenties	1959	$250
FANTASY			
❏ OJC-167	Jazz Giant	198?	$25
—Reissue of Contemporary 7555			
❏ OJC-374	Montreux '77	1988	$25
—Reissue of Pablo Live 2308 204			
❏ OJC-339	Swingin' the Twenties	198?	$25
—Reissue of Contemporary 7561			
HINDSIGHT			
❏ HSR-218	Benny Carter and His Orchestra 1944	1985	$25
IMPULSE!			

Number	Title	Yr	NM
❏ A-9116 [M]	Additions to Further Definitions	1966	$120
❏ AS-9116 [S]	Additions to Further Definitions	1966	$160
❏ A-12 [M]	Further Definitions	1962	$120
❏ AS-12 [S]	Further Definitions	1962	$120
MCA			
❏ 29066	Additions to Further Definitions	198?	$20
❏ 29006	Further Definitions	198?	$20
MCA IMPULSE!			
❏ MCA-5651	Further Definitions	1986	$25
MOVIETONE			
❏ 1020 [M]	Autumn Leaves	1967	$25
❏ 72020 [S]	Autumn Leaves	1967	$35
MUSICAL HERITAGE SOCIETY			
❏ MHS912375Z	In the Mood for Swing	1989	$30
NORGRAN			
❏ MGN-1058 [M]	Alone Together	1956	$300
— With Oscar Peterson			
❏ MGN-1025 [M]	Benny Carter	1955	$0
— Canceled			
❏ MGN-1015 [M]	Benny Carter Plays Pretty	1955	$200
❏ MGN-1070 [M]	Cosmopolite	1956	$250
❏ MGN-1044 [M]	New Jazz Sounds	1955	$300
— With Dizzy Gillespie, Bill Harris			
❏ MGN-21 [10]	The Formidable Benny Carter	1954	$300
❏ MGN-10 [10]	The Urbane Mr. Carter	1954	$250
PABLO			
❏ 2310926	Benny Carter Meets Oscar Peterson	1987	$25
❏ 2310781	Cater, Gillespie, Inc.	1976	$30
— With Dizzy Gillespie			
❏ 2310935	My Kind of Trouble	1989	$30
❏ 2405409	The Best of Benny Carter	198?	$25
❏ 2310768	The King	1975	$30
❏ 2310922	Wonderland	1987	$25
PABLO LIVE			
❏ 2308216	Live and Well in Japan	1979	$30
❏ 2308204	Montreux '77	1978	$30
PRESTIGE			
❏ PR-7643	Benny Carter 1933	1969	$35
❏ 2513	Opening Blues	198?	$25
STEREO RECORDS			
❏ S-7028 [S]	Jazz Giant	1959	$40
STORYVILLE			
❏ 4047	Summer Serenade	1981	$25
SWING			
❏ SW-8403	Benny Carter and His Orchestra 1938 and 1946	1985	$25
TIME-LIFE			
❏ STL-J-10	Giants of Jazz	1980	$50
UNITED ARTISTS			
❏ UAL-4017 [M]	Aspects	1960	$30
❏ UAS-5017 [S]	Aspects	1960	$40
❏ UAL-3055 [M]	Can Can" and "Anything Goes	1959	$30
❏ UAS-6055 [S]	Can Can" and "Anything Goes	1959	$40
❏ UAL-4073 [M]	Can Can" and "Anything Goes	1960	$25
❏ UAS-5073 [S]	Can Can" and "Anything Goes	1960	$30
❏ UAL-4080 [M]	Jazz Calendar	1960	$25
❏ UAS-5080 [S]	Jazz Calendar	1960	$30
❏ UAL-4094 [M]	Sax A La Carter	1961	$25
❏ UAS-5094 [S]	Sax A La Carter	1961	$30
VERVE			
❏ MGV-8148 [M]	Alone Together	1957	$300
— Reissue of Norgran 1058			
❏ V-8148 [M]	Alone Together	1961	$60
❏ MGV-8160 [M]	Cosmopolite	1957	$200
— Reissue of Norgran 1070			
❏ V-8160 [M]	Cosmopolite	1961	$25
❏ MGV-2025 [M]	Moonglow -- Love Songs by Benny Carter	1957	$200
— Reissue of Norgran 1015			
❏ V-2025 [M]	Moonglow -- Love Songs by Benny Carter	1961	$25
❏ MGV-8135 [M]	New Jazz Sounds	1957	$300
— Reissue of Norgran 1044			
❏ V-8135 [M]	New Jazz Sounds	1961	$25

CARTER, BETTY

Female singer. Also see RAY CHARLES AND BETTY CARTER.

Albums

Number	Title	Yr	NM
ABC IMPULSE!			
❏ AS-9321	What a Little Moonlight	197?	$200

Number	Title	Yr	NM
ABC-PARAMOUNT			
❏ ABC-363 [M]	The Modern Sound of Betty Carter	1960	$200
❏ ABCS-363 [S]	The Modern Sound of Betty Carter	1960	$200
ATCO			
❏ 33-152 [M]	'Round Midnight	1963	$50
❏ SD 33-152 [S]	'Round Midnight	1963	$60
BET-CAR			
❏ 1001	Betty Carter	1970	$30
❏ MK1003	The Audience with Betty Carter	1980	$25
❏ 1002	The Betty Carter Album	197?	$30
PEACOCK			
❏ PLP-90 [M]	Out There with Betty Carter	1958	$120
ROULETTE			
❏ SR-5000	Finally	1969	$30
❏ SR-5005	Now It's My Turn	1976	$25
UNITED ARTISTS			
❏ UAL3379 [M]	Inside Betty Carter	1964	$50
❏ UAS6379 [S]	Inside Betty Carter	1964	$60
❏ UAS-5639	Inside Betty Carter	1971	$25
— Reissue of 6379			
VERVE			
❏ 843991-1	Droppin' Things	1990	$35
❏ 835661-1	Look What I Got	1988	$30
❏ 835684-1	The Audience with Betty Carter	1988	$35
— Reissue of Bet-Car 1003			
❏ 835682-1	The Betty Carter Album	1988	$30
— Reissue of Bet-Car 1002			

CARTER, JOHN, AND BOBBY BRADFORD

Also see each artist's individual listings.

Albums

Number	Title	Yr	NM
FLYING DUTCHMAN			
❏ FDS-108	Flight for Four	1969	$25
❏ FD-10108	Flight for Four	1971	$35
— Reissue of 108			
❏ FDS-128	Self Determination Music	1970	$25
❏ FD-10128	Self Determination Music	1971	$35
— Reissue of 128			
REVELATION			
❏ 18	Secrets	1978	$35
❏ 9	The New Art Ensemble	1977	$35

CARTER, JOHN

Clarinetist. Also an alto and tenor saxophone player and flutist. Also see CLARINET SUMMIT.

Albums

Number	Title	Yr	NM
BLACK SAINT			
❏ BSR-0057	Dauwhe	1983	$30
❏ BSR-0047	Night Fire	1982	$30
FLYING DUTCHMAN			
❏ FDS-109	John Carter	1969	$25
GRAMAVISION			
❏ 18-8603	Castles of Ghana	1986	$30
❏ 18-8704	Dance of the Love Ghosts	1987	$30
❏ 18-8809	Ghosts	1988	$30
❏ 79422	Shadows on the Wall	1989	$30

CARTER, RON, AND JIM HALL

Also see each artist's individual listings.

Albums

Number	Title	Yr	NM
CONCORD JAZZ			
❏ CJ-245	Live at Village West	1983	$35
❏ CJ-270	Telephone	1985	$35

CARTER, RON; HERBIE HANCOCK; TONY WILLIAMS

Also see each artist's individual listings.

Albums

Number	Title	Yr	NM
MILESTONE			
❏ M-9105	Third Plane	1981	$30

CARTER, RON

Bass player.

Albums

Number	Title	Yr	NM
CTI			
❏ 6037	All Blues	1974	$50
❏ 6027	Blues Farm	1973	$50
❏ 8001	Blues Farm	1979	$35

Number	Title	Yr	NM
— Reissue of 6027			
❏ 6051	Spanish Blue	1975	$50
❏ 6064	Yellow and Green	1976	$50
ELEKTRA/MUSICIAN			
❏ 60214	Etudes	1984	$30
EMARCY			
❏ 836366-1	All Alone	1988	$30
EMBRYO			
❏ SD521	Uptown Conversation	1970	$25
FANTASY			
❏ OJC-432	Where?	1990	$30
KUDU			
❏ 25	Anything Goes	1976	$35
MILESTONE			
❏ M-9086	A Song for You	1978	$30
❏ M-9096	New York Slick	1979	$35
❏ M-9088	Parade	1978	$30
❏ M-9107	Parfait	1981	$30
❏ M-9073	Pastels	1976	$30
❏ M-9099	Patrao	1980	$35
❏ M-9082	Peg Leg	1977	$30
❏ M-55004	Piccolo	1977	$50
❏ M-9092	Pick 'Em	1979	$30
❏ M-9100	Super Strings	1981	$30
NEW JAZZ			
❏ NJLP-8265 [M]	Where?	1961	$200
— With Eric Dolphy and Mal Waldron; purple label			
❏ NJLP-8265 [M]	Where?	1965	$150
— With Eric Dolphy and Mal Waldron;; blue label, trident logo at right			
RSO			
❏ RS-1-3085	Empire Jazz	1980	$50

CARVIN, MICHAEL

Drummer and bandleader.

Albums

Number	Title	Yr	NM
INNER CITY			
❏ 2038	The Camel	1975	$35
MUSE			
❏ MR-5370	Between You and Me	1989	$30
❏ MR-5352	First Time	1988	$25
STEEPLECHASE			
❏ SCS-1038	The Camel	198?	$25

CARY, DICK

Pianist. Also a trumpeter and alto horn player.

Albums

Number	Title	Yr	NM
BELL			
❏ BLP-44 [M]	Hot and Cool	1961	$60
CIRCLE			
❏ CLP-018	The Amazing Dick Cary	198?	$25
FAMOUS DOOR			
❏ HL-140	California Doings	1980	$30
GOLDEN CREST			
❏ GC-3024 [M]	Dixieland Goes Progressive	1958	$50
STEREOCRAFT			
❏ RTN-106 [S]	Hot and Cool	196?	$30

CASEY, AL (2)

Guitarist. Not the same Al Casey who was involved in the careers of Duane Eddy and Lee Hazlewood, among others.

Albums

Number	Title	Yr	NM
MOODSVILLE			
❏ MVLP-12 [M]	The Al Casey Quartet	1960	$100
— Green label			
❏ MVLP-12 [M]	The Al Casey Quartet	1965	$60
— Blue label, trident logo at right			
SWINGVILLE			
❏ SVLP-2007 [M]	Buck Jumpin'	1960	$100
— Purple label			
❏ SVLP-2007 [M]	Buck Jumpin'	1965	$60
— Blue label, trident logo at right			

CASIMIR, JOHN

Clarinet player and bandleader.

Albums

Number	Title	Yr	NM
JAZZOLOGY			
❏ JCE-5	Casimir's Paragon Jazz Band	1967	$35
❏ JCE-21	Tomorrow Tomorrow	1967	$35

Number	Title	Yr	NM

CASIOPEA
Japanese fusion band.
Albums
ALFA
❏ AAA10002	Eyes of the Mind	1981	$35

MILESTONE
❏ M-9133	Zoom	1985	$30

CASTLE, LEE
Trumpeter and bandleader.
Albums
CELEBRITY
❏ CEL-203 [M]	World Famous Dixieland Favorites	1952	$40

DAVIS
❏ JD-105 [M]	Dixieland Heaven	1951	$60

CASTLE, PAULA
Female singer.
Albums
BETHLEHEM
❏ BCP-1036 [10]	Paula Castle	1955	$500

CASTLE JAZZ BAND, THE
See THE FAMOUS CASTLE JAZZ BAND.

CASTRO, JOE
Pianist.
Albums
ATLANTIC
❏ 1324 [M]	Groove Funk Soul	1960	$250
— Black label			
❏ SD1324 [S]	Groove Funk Soul	1960	$250
— Green label			
❏ 1264 [M]	Mood Jazz	1957	$300
— Black label			
❏ 1264 [M]	Mood Jazz	1961	$150
— Multicolor label with white "fan" logo			
❏ SD1264 [S]	Mood Jazz	1959	$300
— Green label			
❏ SD1264 [S]	Mood Jazz	1961	$150
— Multicolor label with white "fan" logo			

CATALYST
Jazz-funk band: Eddie Green (keyboards), Odean Pope (tenor sax), Sherman Ferguson (drums) and Alphonso Johnson and Tyrone Brown (bass players).
Albums
COBBLESTONE
❏ 9018	Catalyst	1972	$25

MUSE
❏ MR-5069	A Tear and a Smile	1975	$35
❏ MR-5170	Catalyst	198?	$30
❏ MR-5025	Perception	1973	$35
❏ MR-5042	Unity	1974	$35

CATHCART, DICK
Trumpeter and arranger. Also see JOHNNY BEST.
Albums
WARNER BROS.
❏ W1275 [M]	Bix/MCMLIX	1959	$30
❏ WS1275 [S]	Bix/MCMLIX	1959	$30

CATHERINE, PHILIP
Guitarist. Also see LARRY CORYELL.
Albums
WARNER BROS.
❏ BS2950	Nairam	1977	$35

CATINGUB, MATT
Alto saxophone player, pianist, bandleader, arranger and composer.
Albums
REFERENCE RECORDINGS
❏ RR-14	Your Friendly Neighborhood Big Band	1985	$50
— Plays at 45 rpm			

Number	Title	Yr	NM

SEA BREEZE
❏ SB-2025	Hi-Tech Big Band	1985	$25
❏ SB-3006	In the Land of the Long White Cloud	1990	$30
❏ SB-2013	My Mommy and Me	1983	$25

CAVANAUGH, PAGE
Pianist and male singer.
Albums
CAPITOL
❏ T879 [M]	Fats Sent Me	1957	$60
❏ T1001 [M]	Swingin' Down the Road from Paris to Rome	1958	$75

X
❏ LX-3027 [10]	Page Cavanaugh Trio	1954	$50

CELESTIN, OSCAR
Cornet player and bandleader.
Albums
FOLKLYRIC
❏ 9030	Oscar "Papa" Celestin and His New Orleans Jazz Band	198?	$25

IMPERIAL
❏ LP-9149 [M]	Birth of the Blues	1961	$150
❏ LP-9125 [M]	Dixieland King	1961	$150
❏ LP-12062 [S]	Dixieland King	1961	$150
❏ LP-9199 [M]	Oscar "Papa" Celestin's New Orleans Jazz Band	1962	$150
❏ LP-12199 [S]	Oscar "Papa" Celestin's New Orleans Jazz Band	1962	$150

JAZZOLOGY
❏ JCE-28	Ragtime Band	1968	$25

SOUTHLAND
❏ SLP-206 [10]	Papa's Golden Wedding	1955	$100

CELL BLOCK SEVEN
Albums
DIXIELAND JUBILEE
❏ DJ-506 [M]	A Dixieland Riot	195?	$50
❏ DJS-506 [R]	A Dixieland Riot	196?	$30

CENTIPEDE
55-piece band of British progressive rock and jazz musicians. This is the American issue of an album originally issued on Neon in the UK in 1971.
Albums
RCA VICTOR
❏ CPL2-5042	Septober Energy	1974	$40

CENTURY 22 FEATURING GEORGE SHAW
Albums
TBA
❏ TB-209	Flight 2201	198?	$25

CHALLIS, BILL
Arranger and bandleader.
Albums
CIRCLE
❏ CLP-71	Bill Challis and His Orchestra: 1936	198?	$25
❏ CLP-72	Bill Challis and His Orchestra: More 1936	198?	$25

CHALOFF, SERGE
Baritone saxophone player. Also see THE FOUR BROTHERS.
Albums
CAPITOL
❏ M-11032	Blue Serge	1972	$35
— Capitol Jazz Classics, Vol. 7			
❏ T742 [M]	Blue Serge	1959	$100
— Black colorband label, logo at left			
❏ T6510 [M]	Boston Blow-Up	1955	$250

MOSAIC
❏ MQ5-147	The Complete Serge Chaloff Sessions	1993	$120

STORYVILLE
❏ STLP-350 [10]	Serge & Boots	1955	$300
❏ STLP-317 [10]	The Fable of Mable	1954	$300

Number	Title	Yr	NM

CHALOFF, SERGE/OSCAR PETTIFORD
Also see each artist's individual listings.
Albums
MERCER
❏ LP-1003 [10]	New Stars, New Sounds, Volume 2	1951	$300

CHAMBERLAND, LINC
Guitarist.
Albums
MUSE
❏ MR-5064	A Place Within	1976	$30
❏ MR-5263	Yet to Come	1981	$25

CHAMBERS, JOE, AND LARRY YOUNG
Also see each artist's individual listings.

CHAMBERS, JOE
Drummer and sometime vibraphone player.
Albums
MUSE
❏ MR-5035	The Almoravid	197?	$30

CHAMBERS, PAUL, AND JOHN COLTRANE
Also see each artist's individual listings.
Albums
BLUE NOTE
❏ BN-LA451-H2 [(2)]	High Step	1975	$60
— Reissue of Blue Note 1534 plus other material			

CHAMBERS, PAUL
Bass player. Also see KENNY DREW; ROY HAYNES; THE JAZZ MODES.
Albums
BLUE NOTE
❏ BLP-1569 [M]	Bass on Top	1957	$400
— Regular version, W. 63rd St. address on label			
❏ BLP-1569 [M]	Bass on Top	1963	$200
— New York, USA" address on label			
❏ BST-1569 [S]	Bass on Top	1959	$400
— Regular version, W. 63rd St. address on label			
❏ BST-1569 [S]	Bass on Top	1963	$130
— New York, USA" address on label			
❏ BST-81569 [S]	Bass on Top	196?	$50
— A Division of Liberty Records" on label			
❏ BLP-1564 [M]	Paul Chambers Quintet	1957	$400
— Deep groove" version, W. 63rd St. address on label			
❏ BLP-1564 [M]	Paul Chambers Quintet	1957	$200
— Regular version, W. 63rd St. address on label			
❏ BLP-1564 [M]	Paul Chambers Quintet	1963	$80
— New York, USA" address on label			
❏ BST-1564 [S]	Paul Chambers Quintet	1959	$250
— Deep groove" version, W. 63rd St. address on label			
❏ BST-1564 [S]	Paul Chambers Quintet	1959	$150
— Regular version, W. 63rd St. address on label			
❏ BST-1564 [S]	Paul Chambers Quintet	1963	$30
— New York, USA" address on label			
❏ BST-81564 [S]	Paul Chambers Quintet	196?	$50
— A Division of Liberty Records" on label			
❏ BLP-1534 [M]	Whims of Chambers	1956	$1200
— Deep groove" version, Lexington Ave. address on label			
❏ BLP-1534 [M]	Whims of Chambers	1958	$750
— Deep groove" version, W, 63rd St. address on label			
❏ BLP-1534 [M]	Whims of Chambers	1963	$150
— New York, USA" address on label			
❏ BST-81534 [R]	Whims of Chambers	196?	$50
— A Division of Liberty Records" on label			

EPITAPH
❏ E-4001	Paul Chambers 1935-1969	1975	$50

IMPERIAL
❏ LP-9182 [M]	A Jazz Delegation from the East: Chambers' Music	1961	$150
❏ LP-12182 [S]	A Jazz Delegation from the East: Chambers' Music	1961	$150

JAZZ WEST
❏ JWLP-7 [M]	A Jazz Delegation from the East: Chambers' Music	1956	$600

Serge Chaloff, *Boston Blow-Up!*, Capitol T 6510, **$250**.

Paul Chambers, *Go*, Vee-Jay SR-1014, **$100**.

Ray Charles and Betty Carter, *Ray Charles and Betty Carter*,
ABC-Paramount ABC 385, **$120**.

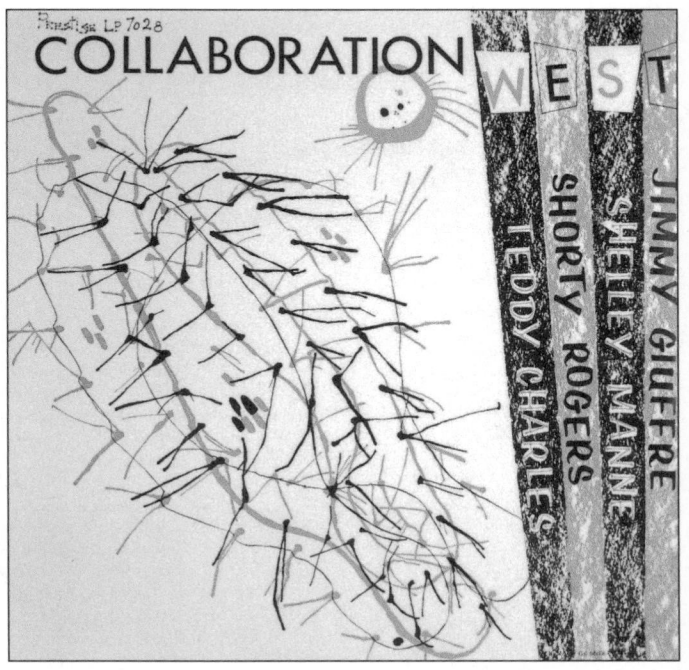

Teddy Charles et al., *Collaboration West*, Prestige PRLP-7028, yellow
label with W. 50th St. address, **$300**.

Number	Title	Yr	NM
SCORE			
❏ SLP-4033 [M]	A Jazz Delegation from the East: Chambers' Music	1958	$80
TRIP			
❏ 5026	Just Friends	197?	$35
VEE JAY			
❏ LP-3012 [M]	First Bassman	1960	$50
❏ SR-3012 [S]	First Bassman	1960	$80
❏ VJS-3012 [S]	First Bassman	198?	$35
—Reissue on thinner vinyl			
❏ SR-1014 [S]	Go	1959	$100
❏ VJS-1014 [S]	Go	198?	$35
—Reissue on thinner vinyl			

CHAMBLEE, EDDIE
Tenor saxophone player.

Albums

Number	Title	Yr	NM
EMARCY			
❏ MG-36124 [M]	Chamblee Music	1958	$200
❏ MG-36131 [M]	Doodlin'	1958	$200
❏ SR-80007 [S]	Doodlin'	1959	$200
MERCURY			
❏ SR-60127 [S]	Chamblee Music	1960	$100
PRESTIGE			
❏ PRLP-7321 [M]	The Rocking Tenor Sax of Eddie Chamblee	1964	$30
—Yellow label			
❏ PRST-7321 [S]	The Rocking Tenor Sax of Eddie Chamblee	1964	$30
—Silver label			

CHANCLER, NDUGU
Drummer.

Albums

Number	Title	Yr	NM
MCA			
❏ 6302	Old Friends, New Friends	1989	$30

CHAPIN, JIM
Drummer.

Albums

Number	Title	Yr	NM
CLASSIC JAZZ			
❏ 6 [M]	Jim Chapin Sextet	197?	$25
❏ 7 [M]	Skin Tight	197?	$25
PRESTIGE			
❏ PRLP-213 [10]	Jim Chapin Sextet	1955	$250

CHARLES, RAY, AND BETTY CARTER
Earlier material appears in the Goldmine Standard Catalog of American Records. Also see each artist's individual listings.

Albums

Number	Title	Yr	NM
ABC			
❏ S-385 [S]	Ray Charles and Betty Carter	1967	$50
—Reissue of ABC-Paramount ABCS-385			
ABC-PARAMOUNT			
❏ ABC-385 [M]	Ray Charles and Betty Carter	1961	$120
❏ ABCS-385 [S]	Ray Charles and Betty Carter	1961	$150
DCC COMPACT CLASSICS			
❏ LPZ-2005	Ray Charles and Betty Carter	1995	$150
—Audiophile vinyl			
DUNHILL COMPACT CLASSICS			
❏ DZL-039	Ray Charles and Betty Carter	1988	$35
—Clear vinyl reissue			

CHARLES, RAY, AND CLEO LAINE
Also see each artist's individual listings.

Albums

Number	Title	Yr	NM
RCA VICTOR			
❏ CPL2-1831	Porgy & Bess	1976	$35
❏ DJL1-2163	Porgy & Bess	1976	$50
—Promo-only excerpts from 2-record set			

CHARLES, RAY, AND MILT JACKSON
Also see each artist's individual listings.

Number	Title	Yr	NM
Albums			
ATLANTIC			
❏ 1279 [M]	Soul Brothers	1958	$300
—Black label			
❏ 1279 [M]	Soul Brothers	1960	$250
—Red and white label, white fan logo on right			
❏ 1279 [M]	Soul Brothers	1962	$150
—Red and white label, black fan logo on right			
❏ SD1279 [S]	Soul Brothers	1959	$300
—Green label			
❏ SD1279 [S]	Soul Brothers	1960	$250
—Blue and green label, white fan logo on right			
❏ SD1279 [S]	Soul Brothers	1962	$150
—Blue and green label, black fan logo on right			
❏ 1360 [M]	Soul Meeting	1961	$150
—Red and white label, white fan logo on right			
❏ 1360 [M]	Soul Meeting	1962	$150
—Red and white label, black fan logo on right			
❏ SD1360 [S]	Soul Meeting	1961	$150
—Blue and green label, white fan logo on right			
❏ SD1360 [S]	Soul Meeting	1962	$150
—Blue and green label, black fan logo on right			

CHARLES, RAY
Impossible to classify, Charles recorded all kinds of music during his long career; the below are his most jazz-oriented. For a more complete listing, see the Standard Catalog of American Records. Also see DAVID NEWMAN.

Albums

Number	Title	Yr	NM
ABC IMPULSE!			
❏ AS-2 [S]	Genius + Soul = Jazz	1968	$30
ATLANTIC			
❏ 1289 [M]	Ray Charles at Newport	1958	$300
—Black label			
❏ 1289 [M]	Ray Charles at Newport	1960	$250
—Red and white label, white fan logo on right			
❏ 1289 [M]	Ray Charles at Newport	1962	$150
—Red and white label, black fan logo on right			
❏ SD1289 [S]	Ray Charles at Newport	1959	$300
—Green label			
❏ SD1289 [S]	Ray Charles at Newport	1960	$250
—Blue and green label, white fan logo on right			
❏ SD1289 [S]	Ray Charles at Newport	1962	$150
—Blue and green label, black fan logo on right			
❏ SD1543	The Best of Ray Charles	1970	$30
❏ 1369 [M]	The Genius After Hours	1961	$150
—Red and white label, white fan logo on right			
❏ 1369 [M]	The Genius After Hours	1962	$150
—Red and white label, black fan logo on right			
❏ SD1369 [S]	The Genius After Hours	1961	$150
—Blue and green label, white fan logo on right			
❏ SD1369 [S]	The Genius After Hours	1962	$150
—Blue and green label, black fan logo on right			
❏ 90464	The Genius After Hours	1986	$25
—Reissue			
❏ 1312 [M]	The Genius of Ray Charles	1960	$250
—Black label			
❏ 1312 [M]	The Genius of Ray Charles	1960	$250
—White "bullseye" label			
❏ 1312 [M]	The Genius of Ray Charles	1960	$250
—Red and white label, white fan logo on right			
❏ SD1312 [S]	The Genius of Ray Charles	1960	$250
—Green label			
❏ SD1312 [S]	The Genius of Ray Charles	1960	$250
—White "bullseye" label			
❏ SD1312 [S]	The Genius of Ray Charles	1960	$250
—Blue and green label, white fan logo on right			
❏ SD1312 [S]	The Genius of Ray Charles	1962	$150
—Blue and green label, black fan logo on right			
❏ SD1312 [S]	The Genius of Ray Charles	1968	$50
—Brown and purple label			
❏ 1259 [M]	The Great Ray Charles	1957	$300
—Black label			
❏ 1259 [M]	The Great Ray Charles	1960	$250
—Red and white label, white fan logo on right			
❏ 1259 [M]	The Great Ray Charles	1962	$150
—Red and white label, black fan logo on right			
❏ SD1259 [S]	The Great Ray Charles	1959	$300
—Green label			
❏ SD1259 [S]	The Great Ray Charles	1960	$250
—Blue and green label, white fan logo on right			
❏ SD1259 [S]	The Great Ray Charles	1962	$150
—Blue and green label, black fan logo on right			
BARONET			
❏ B-111 [M]	The Artistry of Ray Charles	196?	$30
❏ BS-111 [R]	The Artistry of Ray Charles	196?	$25
❏ B-117 [M]	The Great Ray Charles	196?	$30
❏ BS-117 [R]	The Great Ray Charles	196?	$25
CORONET			
❏ CX-173 [M]	Ray Charles	196?	$30
❏ CXS-173 [R]	Ray Charles	196?	$25
CROSSOVER			
❏ 9007	My Kind of Jazz, Part 3	1976	$30
DUNHILL COMPACT CLASSICS			
❏ DZL-038	Genius + Soul = Jazz	1988	$35
—Clear vinyl reissue			
HOLLYWOOD			
❏ 505 [M]	The Fabuolus Ray Charles	1959	$150
❏ 504 [M]	The Original Ray Charles	1959	$150
IMPULSE!			
❏ A-2 [M]	Genius + Soul = Jazz	1961	$200
PREMIER			
❏ PS-6001 [R]	Fantastic Ray Charles	196?	$25
❏ PM2004 [M]	The Great Ray Charles	196?	$30
❏ PS2004 [R]	The Great Ray Charles	196?	$25
TANGERINE			
❏ 1512	My Kind of Jazz	1970	$30
❏ 1516	My Kind of Jazz No. II	1973	$30

CHARLES, TEDDY
Vibraphone player. Also see LEE KONITZ; MANHATTAN ALL STARS; PRESTIGE JAZZ QUARTET.

Albums

Number	Title	Yr	NM
ATLANTIC			
❏ 1229 [M]	The Teddy Charles Tentet	1956	$300
—Black label			
❏ 1229 [M]	The Teddy Charles Tentet	1961	$150
—Multicolor label with white "fan" logo			
❏ 1274 [M]	Word from Bird	1956	$300
—Black label			
❏ 1274 [M]	Word from Bird	1961	$150
—Multicolor label with white "fan" logo			
BETHLEHEM			
❏ BCP-6032 [M]	Salute to Hamp	1959	$200
FANTASY			
❏ OJC-122	Collaboration: West	198?	$25
—Reissue of Prestige 7028			
JOSIE			
❏ JOZ-3505 [M]	Teddy Charles Trio Plays Duke Ellington	1963	$30
❏ JJS-3505 [S]	Teddy Charles Trio Plays Duke Ellington	1963	$30
JUBILEE			
❏ JLP-1047 [M]	Three for Duke	1957	$50
❏ JGS-1047 [S]	Three for Duke	1959	$40
NEW JAZZ			
❏ NJLP-1106 [10]	Teddy Charles New Directions Quartet	1955	$600
PRESTIGE			
❏ PRLP-7028 [M]	Collaboration: West	1956	$300
—Yellow label with 446 W. 50th St. address			
❏ PRLP-7028 [M]	Collaboration: West	196?	$30
—Blue label, trident logo on right			
❏ PRLP-7078 [M]	Evolution	1957	$300
—Yellow label			
❏ PRLP-7078 [M]	Evolution	196?	$30
—Blue label, trident logo on right			
❏ PRLP-143 [10]	New Directions Vol. 1	1953	$300
❏ PRLP-150 [10]	New Directions Vol. 2	1953	$300
❏ PRLP-164 [10]	New Directions Vol. 3	1953	$300
❏ PRLP-169 [10]	New Directions Vol. 4	1954	$300
❏ PRLP-178 [10]	New Directions Vol. 5	1954	$300
—With Bob Brookmeyer			
❏ PRLP-132 [10]	Teddy Charles and His Trio	1952	$400
❏ PRLP-206 [10]	Teddy Charles New Directions Quartet	1955	$300
—Reissue of New Jazz 1106			
SAVOY			
❏ MG-12174 [M]	The Vibe-Rant Quintet	1961	$30
—Reissue of Elektra LP			
SOUL NOTE			
❏ 121183	Live at the Verona Jazz Festival, 1988	1990	$30

UNITED ARTISTS

Number	Title	Yr	NM
❏ UAL-3365 [M]	Russia Goes Jazz	1964	$30
❏ UAS-6365 [S]	Russia Goes Jazz	1964	$30

WARWICK
Number	Title	Yr	NM
❏ W-2033 [M]	Jazz in the Garden of the Museum of Modern Art	1960	$50

CHARLESTON CITY ALL-STARS
Studio group composed of members of Enoch Light's Light Brigade.

Albums

ABC WESTMINSTER GOLD
❏ WGAS-68004	The Roaring 20's, Volume 2	197?	$30

GRAND AWARD
❏ GA 33-411 [M]	Dixieland	1959	$30
❏ GA243SD [S]	Dixieland	1959	$35
❏ GA 33-327 [M]	The Roaring 20's	1957	$35
❏ GA201SD [S]	The Roaring 20's	1958	$30
❏ GA 33-340 [M]	The Roaring 20's, Volume 2	1957	$35
❏ GA211SD [S]	The Roaring 20's, Volume 2	1958	$30
❏ GA 33-353 [M]	The Roaring 20's, Volume 3	1957	$35
❏ GA229SD [S]	The Roaring 20's, Volume 3	1958	$30
❏ GA 33-370 [M]	The Roaring 20's, Volume 4	1958	$35

WALDORF MUSIC HALL
❏ MH 33-142 [M]	The Roaring Twenties	195?	$50

CHARQUET & CO.

Albums

STOMP OFF
❏ SOS-1008	Crazy Quilt	197?	$30
❏ SOS-1053	Everybody Stomp	198?	$25
❏ SOS-1076	Jungle Jamboree	198?	$25
❏ SOS-1039	Live at Joseph Lam Club	198?	$25
❏ SOS-1195	You'll Long for Me	198?	$25

CHARTERS, ANN
Pianist.

Albums

GNP CRESCENDO
❏ GNPS-9021	A Joplin Bouquet	197?	$25
❏ GNPS-9032	The Genius of Scott Joplin	197?	$25

KICKING MULE
❏ 101	Scott Joplin and His Friends	198?	$25

CHASE
Jazz-rock nonet (four horns, four-piece rhythm section, lead vocalist). Fronted by Bill Chase (trumpet), who had played in the MAYNARD FERGUSON, WOODY HERMAN and STAN KENTON bands.

Albums

EPIC
❏ E30472	Chase	1971	$25
❏ EQ30472 [Q]	Chase	1973	$60
❏ EG33737	Chase/Ennea	1976	$25
❏ KE31097	Ennea	1972	$25
❏ KE32572	Pure Music	1974	$25
❏ EQ32572 [Q]	Pure Music	1974	$60

CHEATHAM, DOC, AND SAMMY PRICE
Also see each artist's individual listings.

Albums

SACKVILLE
❏ 3029	Black Beauty	198?	$30
❏ 3013	Doc & Sammy	198?	$30
❏ 3024	Sweet Substitute	198?	$30

CHEATHAM, DOC
Trumpeter and male singer.

Albums

CLASSIC JAZZ
❏ 113	Good for What Ails Ya	1977	$30

CHEATHAM, JEANNIE AND JIMMY
Jeannie is a pianist and female singer. Jimmy is a trombone player.

Albums

CONCORD JAZZ
❏ CJ-373	Back to the Neighborhood	1989	$30
❏ CJ-321	Homeward Bound	1987	$25
❏ CJ-297	Midnight Mama	1986	$25
❏ CJ-258	Sweet Baby Blues	1985	$25

CHERRY, DON (2)
Jazz trumpeter, also father of 1980s hitmaker Neneh Cherry and 1990s hitmaker Eagle-Eye Cherry. Also see JOHN COLTRANE; JAZZ COMPOSERS ORCHESTRA; STEVE LACY.

Albums

A&M
❏ SP-5258	Art Deco	1989	$50

ANTILLES
❏ AN7034	The Eternal Now	197?	$100

ATLANTIC
❏ SD18217	Hear and Now	1977	$100

BASF
❏ 20680	Eternal Rhythm	1972	$60

BLUE NOTE
❏ BLP-4226 [M]	Complete Communion	1966	$200
— "New York, USA" address on label			
❏ BST-84226 [S]	Complete Communion	1966	$120
— "New York, USA" address on label			
❏ BST-84226 [S]	Complete Communion	1968	$40
— "A Division of Liberty Records" on label			
❏ BLP-4247 [M]	Symphony for Improvisers	1966	$200
— "New York, USA" address on label			
❏ BST-84247 [S]	Symphony for Improvisers	1966	$120
— "New York, USA" address on label			
❏ BST-84247 [S]	Symphony for Improvisers	1968	$40
— "A Division of Liberty Records" on label			
❏ BST-84311	Where Is Brooklyn?	1969	$120
— "A Division of Liberty Records" on label			

ECM
❏ ECM1-1230	El Corazon	1982	$35
— With Ed Blackwell; distributed by Warner Bros.			

HORIZON
❏ SP-717	Don Cherry	1976	$60

INNER CITY
❏ IC1009	Togetherness	197?	$50

JCOA
❏ 1006	Relativity Suite	1974	$100

MOSAIC
❏ MQ3-145	The Complete Blue Note Recordings of Don Cherry	199?	$120

PICCADILLY
❏ PIC-3515	Tibet	1981	$60

CHESKY, DAVID, BAND

Albums

COLUMBIA
❏ JC36799	Rush Hour	1980	$25

CHESTER, BOB
Bandleader and arranger.

Albums

CIRCLE
❏ 44	Bob Chester and His Orchestra: 1940-41	198?	$25
❏ 74	Bob Chester and His Orchestra: More 1940-41	198?	$25

CHICAGO
Mostly a rock band with some jazz elements. By 1972, most of its jazz tendencies had been superseded. For a more complete listing, see the Standard Catalog of American Records.

Albums

ACCORD
❏ SN-7140	Toronto Rock 'n Roll Revival, 1982 Part I		$30
— Reissue of Magnum LP			

COLUMBIA
❏ KGP24	Chicago	1970	$40
— Red labels with "360 Sound" at bottom; label and spine call the album "Chicago"			
❏ C4X30865	Chicago at Carnegie Hall	1971	$60
— With box, 4 posters and program; deduct for missing items			
❏ C4Q30865 [Q]	Chicago at Carnegie Hall	1971	$0
— Scheduled but never released			
❏ KG30863	Chicago at Carnegie Hall, Vol. 1 & 2	1971	$35
— First half of the 4-LP box, possibly for Columbia Record Club only			
❏ KG30864	Chicago at Carnegie Hall, Vol. 3 & 4	1971	$35
— Second half of the 4-LP box, possibly for Columbia Record Club only			
❏ KGP24	Chicago II	1970	$35
— Orange labels			
❏ KGP24	Chicago II	1970	$60
— Red labels with "360 Sound" at bottom; label and spine call the album "Chicago II"			
❏ C230110	Chicago III	1971	$35
❏ C2Q30110 [Q]	Chicago III	1974	$40
❏ GP8	Chicago Transit Authority	1969	$60
— Red labels with "360 Sound" at bottom			
❏ GP8	Chicago Transit Authority	1970	$35
— Orange labels; most copies add a Roman numeral "I" to the title on spine			

MAGNUM
❏ MR604	Chicago Transit Authority Live in Concert	1978	$50
— Taken from their 1969 Toronto Rock 'n Roll Revival performance			

MOBILE FIDELITY
❏ 2-128	Chicago Transit Authority	1983	$150
— Audiophile vinyl			

CHICAGO HOT SIX
Led by Roy Rubenstein.

Albums

GHB
❏ 176	Stompin' at the Good Time	1982	$25

CHICAGO RHYTHM

Albums

JAZZOLOGY
❏ J-157	Caution Blues	198?	$25
❏ J-127	'Round Evening	198?	$25

STOMP OFF
❏ SOS-1026	Chicago Rhythm	198?	$25
❏ SOS-1164	Made in Chicago	1989	$30
❏ SOS-1059	One in a Million	1982	$25

CHILDERS, BUDDY
Trumpeter.

Albums

LIBERTY
❏ LJH-6013 [M]	Buddy Childers Quartet	1957	$100
❏ LJH-6009 [M]	Sam Songs	1956	$100

TREND
❏ TR-539	Just Buddy's	1986	$50

CHILDS, BILLY
Pianist.

Albums

WINDHAM HILL
❏ WH-0113	Take For Example This	1988	$30
❏ WH-0118	Twilight Is Upon Us	1989	$30

CHILES AND PETTIFORD
Walter Chiles (piano, vocal) and Clarence Pettiford (bass, vocal).

Albums

ATLANTIC
❏ 8111 [M]	Live at Jilly's	1965	$40
❏ SD8111 [S]	Live at Jilly's	1965	$50

CHITTISON, HERMAN
Pianist.

Albums

AUDIOPHILE
❏ AP-39 [M]	The Melody Lingers On	1986	$25

COLUMBIA
❏ CL6134 [10]	Herman Chittison	1950	$50
❏ CL6182 [10]	Herman Chittison Trio	1951	$50

ROYALE
❏ 1824 [10]	Cocktail Time	195?	$40

Number	Title	Yr	NM

CHRIST GABRIEL JAZZ MISSIONARY GROUP

Albums

MUSICMASTER RECORDS

☐ no number [B]	Christ Gabriel Jazz Missionary Group	1974	$1500

CHRISTIAN, CHARLIE
Guitarist. Also see BENNY GOODMAN.

Albums

COLUMBIA

☐ G30779	Solo Flight -- The Genius of Charlie Christian	1972	$25

COLUMBIA JAZZ MASTERPIECES

☐ CJ40846	Charlie Christian -- The Genius of the Electric Guitar	1986	$35

COUNTERPOINT

☐ 548 [M]	The Harlem Jazz Scene 1941	195?	$60

ESOTERIC

☐ ESJ-1 [10]	Jazz Immortal	1951	$200

—*Red vinyl*

☐ ES-548 [M]	The Harlem Jazz Scene 1941	1956	$80

EVEREST ARCHIVE OF FOLK & JAZZ

☐ 219	Charlie Christian	197?	$25

CHRISTY, JUNE
Female singer.

Albums

CAPITOL

☐ T1308 [M]	Ballads for Night People	1959	$100

—*Black label with colorband, Capitol logo at left*

☐ ST1308 [S]	Ballads for Night People	1959	$60

—*Black label with colorband, Capitol logo at left*

☐ T1845 [M]	Big Band Specials	1962	$80
☐ ST1845 [S]	Big Band Specials	1962	$100
☐ T1586 [M]	Do-Re-Mi	1961	$60

—*Black label with colorband, Capitol logo at left*

☐ ST1586 [S]	Do-Re-Mi	1961	$150

—*Black label with colorband, Capitol logo at left*

☐ T656 [M]	Duets	1955	$75

—*Turquoise label*

☐ T902 [M]	Gone for the Day	1957	$60

—*Turquoise label*

☐ T1202 [M]	June Christy Recalls Those Kenton Days	1959	$100

—*Black label with colorband, Capitol logo at left*

☐ ST1202 [S]	June Christy Recalls Those Kenton Days	1959	$75

—*Black label with colorband, Capitol logo at left*

☐ T833 [M]	June -- Fair and Warmer!	1957	$75

—*Turquoise label*

☐ T1076 [M]	June's Got Rhythm	1958	$100

—*Black label with colorband, Capitol logo at left*

☐ ST1076 [S]	June's Got Rhythm	1958	$75

—*Black label with colorband, Capitol logo at left*

☐ T1498 [M]	Off Beat	1961	$75

—*Black label with colorband, Capitol logo at left*

☐ ST1498 [S]	Off Beat	1961	$150

—*Black label with colorband, Capitol logo at left*

☐ TBO1327 [M]	Road Show	1960	$100

—*Black label with colorband, Capitol logo at left*

☐ STBO1327 [S]	Road Show	1960	$75

—*Black label with colorband, Capitol logo at left*

☐ T2410 [M]	Something Broadway, Something Latin	1965	$100
☐ ST2410 [S]	Something Broadway, Something Latin	1965	$100
☐ H516 [10]	Something Cool	1954	$250
☐ T516 [M]	Something Cool	1955	$150

—*Turquoise label; blue-green cover with June's eyes closed*

☐ T516 [M]	Something Cool	1959	$100

—*Black label with colorband, logo at left; with original blue-green cover with June's eyes closed*

☐ SM-516 [S]	Something Cool	197?	$25
☐ ST516 [S]	Something Cool	1960	$50

—*Re-recording of the original mono LP; issued with different cover than original mono LP, in color with June's eyes open; black label, Capitol logo at left*

☐ T516 [M]	Something Cool	1962	$50

—*Black label with colorband, logo at top; issued with different cover than original mono LP, in color with June's eyes open*

☐ T1605 [M]	That Time of Year	1961	$75
☐ ST1605 [S]	That Time of Year	1961	$150

—*Black label with colorband, Capitol logo at left*

☐ T1693 [M]	The Best of June Christy	1962	$100

—*Black label with colorband*

☐ ST1693 [S]	The Best of June Christy	1962	$100

—*Black logo with colorband*

☐ SM-11961	The Best of June Christy	1979	$25
☐ T1398 [M]	The Cool School	1960	$100

—*Black label with colorband, Capitol logo at left*

☐ ST1398 [S]	The Cool School	1960	$60

—*Black label with colorband, Capitol logo at left*

☐ T1953 [M]	The Intimate June Christy	1963	$80
☐ ST1953 [S]	The Intimate June Christy	1963	$100
☐ T725 [M]	The Misty Miss Christy	1956	$75

—*Turquoise label*

☐ T1114 [M]	The Song Is June!	1959	$100

—*Black label with colorband, Capitol logo at left*

☐ ST1114 [S]	The Song Is June!	1959	$75

—*Black label with colorband, Capitol logo at left*

☐ T1006 [M]	This Is June Christy!	1958	$75

—*Turquoise label*

DISCOVERY

☐ DS-836	Impromptu	1982	$30
☐ DS-911	Interlude	1986	$25
☐ DS-919	The Misty Miss Christy	1986	$25

HINDSIGHT

☐ HSR-219	June Christy, Vol. 1	1986	$25
☐ HSR-235	June Christy, Vol. 2	1988	$25

PAUSA

☐ 9039	Big Band Specials	198?	$25

CHRYSANTHEMUM RAGTIME BAND

Albums

STOMP OFF

☐ SOS-1047	Bringin' 'Em Back Alive!	1983	$25
☐ SOS-1079	Come On and Hear	1984	$25
☐ SOS-1168	Dancing on the Edge of the World	1988	$25
☐ SOS-1196	Joy Rag	1989	$25
☐ SOS-1123	Preserves	1987	$25

CIRCLE
Barry Altschul (drums); ANTHONY BRAXTON; CHICK COREA; DAVE HOLLAND.

Albums

ECM

☐ 1018/19 ST	Paris Concert	197?	$25

—*Original issue, made in Germany?*

☐ ECM2-1018	Paris Concert	1972	$20

—*Distributed by Polydor*

CIRILLO, WALLY/BOBBY SCOTT
Cirillo is a pianist and composer. Also see BOBBY SCOTT.

Albums

SAVOY

☐ MG-15055 [10]	Cirillo and Scott	1955	$80

CLARINET SUMMIT
Alvin Batiste; JOHN CARTER; JIMMY HAMILTON; DAVID MURRAY.

Albums

INDIA NAVIGATION

☐ IN-1062	In Concert at the Public Theater, Vol. 1	1985	$30
☐ IN-1067	In Concert at the Public Theater, Vol. 2	1985	$30

CLARK, ALICE
Female singer.

Albums

MAINSTREAM

☐ MRL-362	Alice Clark	1972	$25

CLARK, DOTTIE
Female singer.

Albums

MAINSTREAM

☐ 56006 [M]	I'm Lost	1966	$25
☐ S-6006 [S]	I'm Lost	1966	$30

CLARK, JOHN
French horn player and occasional guitarist.

Albums

ECM

☐ 1176	Faces	1981	$30

CLARK, SONNY
Pianist and composer.

Albums

BLUE NOTE

☐ BLP-1588 [M]	Cool Struttin'	1958	$5000

—*Deep groove" version (deep indentation under label on both sides)*

☐ BLP-1588 [M]	Cool Struttin'	1958	$800

—*Regular version, W. 63rd St. address on label*

☐ BLP-1588 [M]	Cool Struttin'	1963	$300

—*New York, USA" address on label*

☐ BST-1588 [S]	Cool Struttin'	1959	$1000

—*Deep groove" version (deep indentation under label on both sides)*

☐ BST-1588 [S]	Cool Struttin'	1959	$200

—*Regular version, W. 63rd St. address on label*

☐ BST-1588 [S]	Cool Struttin'	1963	$125

—*New York, USA" address on label*

☐ BST-81588 [S]	Cool Struttin'	1967	$60

—*A Division of Liberty Records" on label*

☐ BST-81588 [S]	Cool Struttin'	1970	$50

—*Mostly black label, "Liberty/UA" at bottom*

☐ BLJ-81588	Cool Struttin'	1987	$30

—*The Finest in Jazz Since 1939" reissue*

☐ BST-1588-45 [S]	Cool Struttin'	200?	$200

—*Classic Records box set of four 45 rpm 12-inch records*

☐ BST-1588 [S]	Cool Struttin'	1997	$150

—*180-gram reissue; distributed by Classic Records*

☐ BLP-1592 [M]	Cool Struttin' -- Volume 2	1959	$0

—*Canceled*

☐ BST-1592 [S]	Cool Struttin' -- Volume 2	1959	$0

—*Canceled*

☐ BLP-1570 [M]	Dial "S" for Sonny	1957	$3500

—*Deep groove" version; W. 63rd St. address on label*

☐ BLP-1570 [M]	Dial "S" for Sonny	1957	$200

—*Regular version, W. 63rd St. address on label*

☐ BLP-1570 [M]	Dial "S" for Sonny	1963	$150

—*New York, USA" address on label*

☐ BST-1570 [S]	Dial "S" for Sonny	1959	$200

—*Regular version, W. 63rd St. address on label*

☐ BST-1570 [S]	Dial "S" for Sonny	1963	$100

—*New York, USA" address on label*

☐ BST-81570 [S]	Dial "S" for Sonny	1967	$60

—*A Division of Liberty Records" on label*

☐ BLP-4091 [M]	Leapin' and Lopin'	1961	$200

—*W. 63rd St. address on label*

☐ BLP-4091 [M]	Leapin' and Lopin'	1963	$200

—*New York, USA" address on label*

☐ BST-84091 [S]	Leapin' and Lopin'	1961	$150

—*W. 63rd St. address on label*

☐ BST-84091 [S]	Leapin' and Lopin'	1963	$50

—*New York, USA" address on label*

☐ BST-84091 [S]	Leapin' and Lopin'	1967	$60

—*A Division of Liberty Records" on label*

☐ BLP-1579 [M]	Sonny Clark Trio	1958	$300

—*Regular version, W. 63rd St. address on label*

☐ BST-1579 [S]	Sonny Clark Trio	1959	$500

—*Deep groove" version; W. 63rd St. address on label*

☐ BST-1579 [S]	Sonny Clark Trio	1959	$250

—*Regular version, W. 63rd St. address on label*

☐ BST-1579 [S]	Sonny Clark Trio	1963	$80

—*New York, USA" address on label*

☐ BST-81579 [S]	Sonny Clark Trio	1967	$60

—*A Division of Liberty Records" on label*

☐ BLP-1576 [M]	Sonny's Crib	1957	$300

—*Regular version, W. 63rd St. address on label*

☐ BLP-1576 [M]	Sonny's Crib	1963	$250

—*New York, USA" address on label*

☐ BST-1576 [S]	Sonny's Crib	1959	$1250

—*Deep groove" version; W. 63rd St. address on label*

☐ BST-1576 [S]	Sonny's Crib	1959	$300

—*Regular version, W. 63rd St. address on label*

☐ BST-1576 [S]	Sonny's Crib	1963	$200

—*New York, USA" address on label*

Buddy Childers, *Sam Songs*, Liberty LJH 6009, **$100**.

June Christy, *This Is June Christy!*, Capitol T 1006, turquoise label, **$75**.

Sonny Clark, *Sonny's Crib*, Blue Note BLP-1576, mono, deep groove version, W. 63rd St. address on label, **$1,250**.

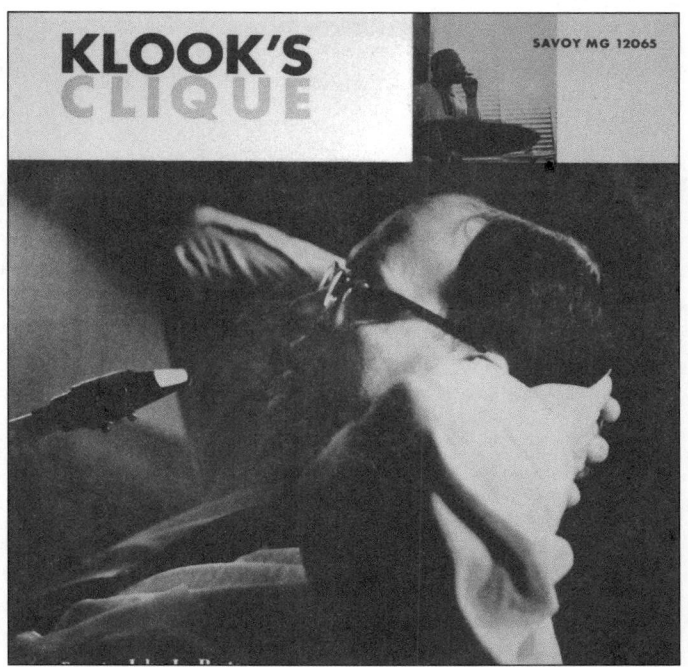

Kenny Clarke, *Klook's Clique*, Savoy MG 12065, **S100**.

Number	Title	Yr	NM
❏ BST-81576 [S]	Sonny's Crib	1967	$60
—A Division of Liberty Records" on label			
TIME			
❏ T-70010 [M]	Sonny Clark Trio	1960	$1200
❏ 52101 [M]	Sonny Clark Trio	1962	$30
❏ S-2101 [S]	Sonny Clark Trio	1962	$30
XANADU			
❏ 121	Memorial Album	1975	$35

CLARK, SPENCER
Bass saxophone player.

Albums

Number	Title	Yr	NM
AUDIOPHILE			
❏ 131	Spencer Clark and His Bass Sax Play Sweet & Hot	1978	$30

CLARKE, BUCK
Drummer, mostly on congas and bongos.

Albums

Number	Title	Yr	NM
ARGO			
❏ LP-4007 [M]	Drum Sum	1961	$30
❏ LPS-4007 [S]	Drum Sum	1961	$30
❏ LP-4021 [M]	The Buck Clarke Sound	1963	$30
❏ LPS-4021 [S]	The Buck Clarke Sound	1963	$30
OFFBEAT			
❏ OLP-3003 [M]	Cool Hands	1960	$30
❏ OS-93003 [S]	Cool Hands	1960	$40

CLARKE, KEN
Pianist.

Albums

Number	Title	Yr	NM
MGM			
❏ E-205 [10]	Jazz Piano	1953	$50

CLARKE, KENNY, AND ERNIE WILKINS
Also see each artist's individual listings.

Albums

Number	Title	Yr	NM
SAVOY			
❏ MG-12007 [M]	Plenty for Kenny	1955	$80

CLARKE, KENNY
Drummer. An early member of THE MODERN JAZZ QUARTET. Also see THE CLARKE-BOLAND BIG BAND.

Albums

Number	Title	Yr	NM
EPIC			
❏ LN3376 [M]	Kenny Clarke Plays Andre Hodeir	1957	$80
PRESTIGE			
❏ PRST-7605	Paris Bebop Sessions	1969	$35
SAVOY			
❏ MG-12017 [M]	Bohemia After Dark	1955	$80
❏ MG-15051 [10]	Kenny Clarke, Vol. 1	195?	$200
❏ MG-15053 [10]	Kenny Clarke, Vol. 2	195?	$200
❏ MG-12065 [M]	Klook's Clique	1956	$100
❏ MG-12006 [M]	Telefunken Blues	1955	$80
SAVOY JAZZ			
❏ SJL-1111	Kenny Clarke Meets the Detroit Jazzmen	198?	$25
SOUL NOTE			
❏ SN-1078	Pieces of Time	1983	$30
SWING			
❏ SW-8411	Kenny Clarke in Paris Vol. 1	1986	$25

CLARKE, STANLEY, AND GEORGE DUKE
Also see each artist's individual listings.

Albums

Number	Title	Yr	NM
EPIC			
❏ FE36918	The Clarke/Duke Project	1981	$60
❏ PE36918	The Clarke/Duke Project	198?	$20
—Budget-line reissue			
❏ FE38934	The Clarke/Duke Project II	1983	$25

CLARKE, STANLEY
Bassist. Also see RETURN TO FOREVER.

Albums

Number	Title	Yr	NM
EPIC			
❏ FE40040	Find Out!	1985	$25
❏ FE40275	Hideaway	1986	$25
❏ PE36974	Journey to Love	1981	$20

Number	Title	Yr	NM
—Reissue of Nemperor 433			
❏ FE38086	Let Me Know You	1982	$60
❏ JE36506	Rocks, Pebbles and Sand	1980	$25
❏ PE36975	School Days	1981	$20
—Reissue of Nemperor 900			
❏ PE36973	Stanley Clarke	1981	$20
—Reissue of Nemperor 431			
❏ FE38688	Time Exposure	1984	$25
NEMPEROR			
❏ KZ235680	I Wanna Play for You	1979	$35
❏ NE433	Journey to Love	1975	$30
❏ JZ35303	Modern Man	1978	$25
—Original issue			
❏ PZ35303	Modern Man	1985	$20
—Reissue with new prefix and bar code			
❏ NE439	School Days	1976	$30
❏ SD900	School Days	1978	$25
—Reissue of 439			
❏ NE431	Stanley Clarke	1974	$30
POLYDOR			
❏ PD-5531	Children of Forever	1973	$35
❏ 827559-1	Children of Forever	1985	$20
—Reissue			
PORTRAIT			
❏ FR40923	If This Bass Could Only Talk	1988	$25

CLARKE-BOLAND BIG BAND, THE
KENNY CLARKE and Francy Boland (pianist).

Albums

Number	Title	Yr	NM
ATLANTIC			
❏ 1401 [M]	Jazz Is Universal	1963	$50
❏ SD1401 [S]	Jazz Is Universal	1963	$50
❏ 1404 [M]	The Clarke-Boland Big Band	1963	$50
❏ SD1404 [S]	The Clarke-Boland Big Band	1963	$50
BASF			
❏ 29686	All Smiles	1972	$35
❏ 25102	The Big Band Sound	1971	$25
BLACK LION			
❏ 131	At Her Majesty's Pleasure	1974	$35
BLUE NOTE			
❏ BLP-4092 [M]	The Golden Eight	1961	$200
—As "Kenny Clarke-Francy Boland & Co."; W. 63rd St. address on label			
❏ BLP-4092 [M]	The Golden Eight	1963	$200
—As "Kenny Clarke-Francy Boland & Co."; "New York, USA" address on label			
❏ BST-84092 [S]	The Golden Eight	1961	$150
—As "Kenny Clarke-Francy Boland & Co."; W. 63rd St. address on label			
❏ BST-84092 [S]	The Golden Eight	1963	$80
—As "Kenny Clarke-Francy Boland & Co."; "New York, USA" address on label			
❏ BST-84092 [S]	The Golden Eight	1967	$60
—As "Kenny Clarke-Francy Boland & Co."; "A Division of Liberty Records" on label			
COLUMBIA			
❏ CL2314 [M]	Now Hear Our Meanin'	1965	$35
❏ CS9114 [S]	Now Hear Our Meanin'	1965	$25
MUSE			
❏ MR-5056	Open Door	197?	$30
PAUSA			
❏ 7097	Sax No End	198?	$25
POLYDOR			
❏ 24-4501	Volcano	1970	$35
PRESTIGE			
❏ PRST-7634	Fire, Heat, Soul and Guts	1969	$35
❏ PRST-7760	Latin Kaleidoscope	1970	$35
❏ PRST-7699	Let's Face the Music	1969	$35

CLASSIC JAZZ ENSEMBLE
With Armin Von der Heydt (clarinet), Steve Jensen (trumpet, cornet) and others.

Albums

Number	Title	Yr	NM
DELMARK			
❏ DE-221	Classic Blues	1989	$25

CLASSIC JAZZ QUARTET, THE
Dick Sudhalter (cornet); Joe Muranyi (clarinet and alto sax); Dick Wellstood (piano); Marty Grotz (guitar, vocals).

Albums

JAZZOLOGY

Number	Title	Yr	NM
❏ J-139	The Classic Jazz Quartet	1985	$25
STOMP OFF			
❏ SOS-1125	MCMLXXXVI	1986	$25

CLAY, JAMES, AND DAVID "FATHEAD" NEWMAN
Also see each artist's individual listings.

Albums

Number	Title	Yr	NM
FANTASY			
❏ OJC-257	The Sound of the Wide Open Spaces!!!	1987	$30
RIVERSIDE			
❏ RLP 12-327 [M]	The Sound of the Wide Open Spaces!!!	1960	$200
—Blue label			
❏ RLP-1178 [S]	The Sound of the Wide Open Spaces!!!	1960	$200
—Black label			

CLAY, JAMES
Flutist and tenor saxophone player.

Albums

Number	Title	Yr	NM
RIVERSIDE			
❏ RS-9349 [S]	A Double Dose of Soul	1961	$200
—Black label			

CLAYTON, BUCK, AND BUDDY TATE
Also see each artist's individual listings.

Albums

Number	Title	Yr	NM
PRESTIGE			
❏ 24040	Kansas City Nights	1974	$35
SWINGVILLE			
❏ SVLP-2017 [M]	Buck and Buddy	1961	$50
—Purple label			
❏ SVLP-2017 [M]	Buck and Buddy	1965	$30
—Blue label, trident logo at right			
❏ SVLP-2030 [M]	Buck and Buddy Blow the Blues	1962	$40
—Purple label			
❏ SVLP-2030 [M]	Buck and Buddy Blow the Blues	1965	$25
—Blue label, trident logo at right			
❏ SVST-2030 [S]	Buck and Buddy Blow the Blues	1962	$50
—Red label			
❏ SVST-2030 [S]	Buck and Buddy Blow the Blues	1965	$30
—Blue label, trident logo at right			

CLAYTON, BUCK; RUBY BRAFF; MEL POWELL
Also see each artist's individual listings.

Albums

Number	Title	Yr	NM
VANGUARD			
❏ VRS-8514 [M]	Buckin' the Blues	1957	$80
❏ VRS-8008 [10]	Buck Meets Ruby	1954	$100
❏ VRS-8517 [M]	Buck Meets Ruby and Mel	1957	$80

CLAYTON, BUCK
Trumpeter.

Albums

Number	Title	Yr	NM
ALLEGRO ELITE			
❏ 4121 [10]	Buck Clayton All Stars	195?	$40
CHIAROSCURO			
❏ 132	A Buck Clayton Jam Session	1974	$30
❏ 143	A Buck Clayton Jam Session, Vol. II	1975	$30
❏ 152	A Buck Clayton Jam Session, Vol. III: Jazz Party Time	1976	$30
❏ 163	A Buck Clayton Jam Session, Vol. IV: Jay Hawk	1977	$30
COLUMBIA			
❏ CL882 [M]	All the Cats Join In	1956	$40
—Red and black label with six "eye" logos			
❏ CL614 [M]	Buck Clayton Jams Benny Goodman	1955	$60
—Maroon label, gold print			
❏ CL614 [M]	Buck Clayton Jams Benny Goodman	1955	$40
—Red and black label with six "eye" logos			

Number	Title	Yr	NM
❑ CL567 [M]	How Hi the Fi: A Jam Session	1954	$50
—Maroon label, gold print			
❑ CL6326 [10]	How Hi the Fi: A Jam Session	1954	$60
❑ CL567 [M]	How Hi the Fi: A Jam Session	1955	$40
—Red and black label with six "eye" logos			
❑ CL808 [M]	Jazz Spectacular	1956	$40
—Red and black label with six "eye" logos			
❑ CL701 [M]	Jumpin' at the Woodside	1955	$50
—Red and black label with six "eye" logos			
❑ CL6325 [10]	Moten Swing -- Sentimental Journey	1954	$60
❑ CL1320 [M]	Songs for Swingers	1959	$30
—Red and black label with six "eye" logos			
❑ CS8123 [S]	Songs for Swingers	1959	$30
—Red and black label with six "eye" logos			
❑ CL548 [M]	The Huckle-Buck and Robbins' Nest: A Jam Session	1954	$50
—Maroon label, gold print			
❑ CL548 [M]	The Huckle-Buck and Robbins' Nest: A Jam Session	1955	$40
—Red and black label with six "eye" logos			

COLUMBIA JAZZ MASTERPIECES

Number	Title	Yr	NM
❑ CJ44291	Jam Sessions from the Vaults	1988	$30

FANTASY

❑ OJC-1709	The Classic Swing of Buck Clayton	1985	$30

INNER CITY

❑ 7009	Passport to Paradise	1980	$25

JAZZTONE

❑ J-1225 [M]	Meet Buck Clayton	1956	$40

STASH

❑ ST-281	A Swingin' Dream	1989	$30

STEEPLECHASE

❑ SCC-6006/7	Copenhagen Concert	198?	$35

VANGUARD

❑ 103/104	Essential Buck Clayton	197?	$35

CLAYTON, BUCK/WILD BILL DAVISON
Also see each artist's individual listings.

Albums

JAZZTONE

❑ J-1267 [M]	Singing Trumpets	1957	$40

CLAYTON, KID
Trumpeter.

Albums

FOLKWAYS

❑ FJ-2859	The First Kid Clayton Session (1952)	1983	$30

JAZZOLOGY

❑ JCE-22	Exit Stares	1967	$30

CLAYTON, STEVE

Albums

SOVEREIGN

❑ SOV-501	All Aglow Again	1986	$25
❑ SOV-500	Inner Spark	1985	$25

CLAYTON BROTHERS, THE
Jeff Clayton (saxophone, flute) and John Clayton (bass).

Albums

CONCORD JAZZ

❑ CJ-138	It's All in the Family	1980	$25
❑ CJ-89	The Clayton Brothers	1978	$25

CLEVELAND, JIMMY
Trombone player. Also see SONNY ROLLINS.

Albums

EMARCY

❑ MG-36126 [M]	Cleveland Style	1958	$200
❑ MG-26003 [M]	Rhythm Crazy	1964	$100

MERCURY

❑ MG-20442 [M]	A Map of Jimmy Cleveland	1959	$100
❑ SR-60117 [S]	A Map of Jimmy Cleveland	1959	$100

Number	Title	Yr	NM
❑ MG-20553 [M]	Cleveland Style	1960	$100
❑ SR-60121 [S]	Cleveland Style	1959	$150

CLIFTON, BILL
Pianist.

Albums

COLUMBIA

❑ CL6166 [10]	Piano Moods	1951	$50

CLINTON, LARRY
Bandleader, composer and arranger.

Albums

CIRCLE

❑ 58	Larry Clinton and His Orchestra 1941 and 1949	198?	$25

EVEREST

❑ LPBR-5096 [M]	My Million Sellers	196?	$25
❑ SDBR-1096 [S]	My Million Sellers	196?	$30

HINDSIGHT

❑ HSR-109	Larry Clinton and His Orchestra 1937-38	198?	$25

RCA CAMDEN

❑ CAL-434 [M]	Dance Date	1958	$50

SUNBEAM

❑ 208	Larry Clinton and His Orchestra 1937-41	198?	$25

CLOONEY, ROSEMARY, AND BING CROSBY
Also see each artist's individual listings.

Albums

CAPITOL

❑ T2300 [M]	That Travelin' Two-Beat	1965	$25
❑ ST2300 [S]	That Travelin' Two-Beat	1965	$60

RCA CAMDEN

❑ CAS-2330	Rendezvous	1968	$18

RCA VICTOR

❑ LPM-1854 [M]	Fancy Meeting You Here	1958	$25
❑ LSP-1854 [S]	Fancy Meeting You Here	1958	$30

CLOONEY, ROSEMARY
Female singer. More pop-oriented on her Columbia recordings, after a retirement she started a second successful career as a jazz singer on the Concord Jazz label.

Albums

COLUMBIA

❑ CL2572 [10]	A Date with the King	1956	$50
❑ CL872 [M]	Blue Rose	1956	$40
❑ CL2569 [10]	Children's Favorites	1955	$60
❑ CL969 [M]	Clooney Tunes	1957	$80
❑ CL6224 [10]	Hollywood's Best	1952	$60
❑ CL585 [M]	Hollywood's Best	1955	$60
❑ CL2597 [10]	My Fair Lady	1956	$50
❑ CL2581 [10]	On Stage	1956	$50
❑ CL1006 [M]	Ring Around the Rosie	1957	$40
—With the Hi-Lo's			
❑ CL6297 [10]	Rosemary Clooney (While We're Young)	1954	$60
❑ CL1230 [M]	Rosie's Greatest Hits	1958	$40
—Six "eye" logos on label			
❑ CL1230 [M]	Rosie's Greatest Hits	1962	$30
—Guaranteed High Fidelity" on label			
❑ CL1230 [M]	Rosie's Greatest Hits	1965	$25
—360 Sound Mono" on label			
❑ CL2525 [10]	Tenderly	1955	$60
❑ CL6338 [10]	White Christmas	1954	$120

COLUMBIA SPECIAL PRODUCTS

❑ P13085	Blue Rose	197?	$15
❑ P14382	Come On-a My House	197?	$15
❑ P13083	Hollywood's Best	197?	$15

CONCORD JAZZ

❑ CJ-47	Everything's Coming Up Rosie	1978	$15
❑ CJ-81	Here's to My Lady	1979	$15
❑ CJ-226	My Buddy	1984	$15
—With Woody Herman			
❑ CJ-282	Rosemary Clooney Sings Ballads	1985	$15
❑ CJ-185	Rosemary Clooney Sings Cole Porter	1982	$15
❑ CJ-210	Rosemary Clooney Sings Harold Arlen	1983	$15
❑ CJ-112	Rosemary Clooney Sings Ira Gershwin	1980	$15
❑ CJ-333	Rosemary Clooney Sings the Lyrics of Johnny Mercer	1988	$15

Number	Title	Yr	NM
❑ CJ-255	Rosemary Clooney Sings the Music of Irving Berlin	1985	$15
❑ CJ-308	Rosemary Clooney Sings the Music of Jimmy Van Heusen	1987	$15
❑ CJ-60	Rosie Sings Bing	1979	$15
❑ CJ-364	Show Tunes	1989	$15
❑ CJ-144	With Love	1981	$30

CORAL

❑ CRL57266 [M]	Swing Around Rosie	1959	$30
❑ CRL757266 [S]	Swing Around Rosie	1959	$40

HARMONY

❑ HL7454 [M]	Mixed Emotions	1968	$25
❑ HS11124 [R]	Mixed Emotions	1968	$15
❑ HL7123 [M]	Rosemary Clooney in High Fidelity	195?	$30
❑ HL9501 [M]	Rosemary Clooney Sings for Children	196?	$25

HINDSIGHT

❑ HSR-234	Rosemary Clooney 1951-1952	1988	$12

HOLIDAY

❑ 1946	Christmas with Rosemary Clooney	1981	$12

MGM

❑ E-3782 [M]	Hymns from the Heart	1959	$30
❑ SE-3782 [S]	Hymns from the Heart	1959	$40
❑ E-3687 [M]	Oh, Captain!	1958	$40
❑ E-3834 [M]	Rosie Clooney Swings Softly	1960	$30
❑ SE-3834 [S]	Rosie Clooney Swings Softly	1960	$40

MISTLETOE

❑ MLP-1234	Christmas with Rosemary Clooney	1978	$15

RCA VICTOR

❑ LPM-2133 [M]	A Touch of Tabasco	1960	$25
❑ LPM-2212 [M]	Clap Hands, Here Comes Rosie	1960	$25
❑ LSP-2212 [S]	Clap Hands, Here Comes Rosie	1960	$30
❑ LPM-2565 [M]	Country Hits from the Heart	1963	$25
❑ LSP-2565 [S]	Country Hits from the Heart	1963	$30
❑ LPM-2265 [M]	Rosie Solves the Swingin' Riddle	1961	$25
❑ LSP-2265 [S]	Rosie Solves the Swingin' Riddle	1961	$30

REPRISE

❑ R-6088 [M]	Love	1963	$30
❑ R9-6088 [S]	Love	1963	$40
❑ R-6108 [M]	Thanks for Nothing	1964	$30
❑ RS-6108 [S]	Thanks for Nothing	1964	$40

TIME-LIFE

❑ SLGD-16	Legendary Singers: Rosemary Clooney	1986	$20

CLOONEY SISTERS, THE
Also see ROSEMARY CLOONEY.

COATES, JOHN, JR.
Pianist.

Albums

OMNISOUND

❑ 1021	After the Before	1978	$30
❑ 1015	Alone and Live at the Deer Head	1977	$30
❑ 1022	In the Open Space	1979	$35
❑ 1038	Pocono Friends	1981	$35
❑ 1045	Pocono Friends Encore	1982	$30
❑ 1024	Rainbow Road	1979	$30
❑ 1004	The Jazz Piano of John Coates, Jr.	197?	$30
❑ 1032	Tokyo Concert	1980	$30

SAVOY

❑ MG-12082 [M]	Portrait	1956	$40

COBB, ARNETT; DIZZY GILLESPIE; JEWEL BROWN
Brown is a pianist and female singer. Also see ARNETT COBB; DIZZY GILLESPIE.

Albums

FANTASY

❑ F-9659	Show Time	1987	$30

COBB, ARNETT
Tenor saxophone player.

Albums

APOLLO

❑ LAP-105 [10]	Swingin' with Arnett Cobb	1952	$250

BEE HIVE

Number	Title	Yr	NM
❏ BH-7017	Keep On Pushin'	1985	$30

CLASSIC JAZZ

❏ 102	The Wild Man from Texas	1976	$35

FANTASY

❏ OJC-219	Party Time	198?	$25
❏ OJC-323	Smooth Sailing	1988	$25

HOME COOKING

❏ HCS-114	The Wild Man from Texas	1990	$30

— *Reissue of Classic Jazz 102*

MOODSVILLE

❏ MVLP-14 [M]	Ballads by Cobb	1961	$50

— *Green label*

❏ MVLP-14 [M]	Ballads by Cobb	1965	$30

— *Blue label, trident logo at right*

MUSE

❏ MR-5191	Live at Sandy's	1977	$30
❏ MR-5236	More Live at Sandy's	1979	$30

PRESTIGE

❏ PRLP-7151 [M]	Blow, Arnett, Blow	1959	$200

— *Yellow label*

❏ PRLP-7151 [M]	Blow, Arnett, Blow	1963	$30

— *Blue label, trident logo at right*

❏ PRST-7151 [R]	Blow, Arnett, Blow	196?	$30
❏ PRST-7835	Go Power!	1970	$35
❏ PRLP-7175 [M]	More Party Time	1960	$200

— *Yellow label*

❏ PRLP-7175 [M]	More Party Time	1963	$30

— *Blue label, trident logo at right*

❏ PRLP-7216 [M]	Movin' Right Along	1963	$30

— *Blue label, trident logo at right*

❏ PRLP-7165 [M]	Party Time	1959	$200

— *Yellow label*

❏ PRLP-7227 [M]	Sizzlin'	1962	$150

— *Yellow label*

❏ PRST-7227 [S]	Sizzlin'	1962	$150

— *Silver label*

❏ PRST-7227 [S]	Sizzlin'	1963	$30

— *Blue label, trident logo at right*

❏ PRLP-7184 [M]	Smooth Sailing	1960	$200

— *Yellow label*

❏ PRST-7711	The Best of Arnett Cobb	1969	$35

PROGRESSIVE

❏ 7037	Arnett Cobb Is Back!	1978	$30
❏ 7054	Funky Butt	1981	$30

COBB, JUNIE C.
Pianist. On other recordings, he played clarinet, alto saxophone and tenor sax.

Albums

RIVERSIDE

❏ RLP-415 [M]	Junie C. Cobb and His New Hometown Band	1962	$150
❏ RS-9415 [S]	Junie C. Cobb and His New Hometown Band	1962	$150

COBHAM, BILLY, AND GEORGE DUKE
Also see each artist's individual listings.

Albums

ATLANTIC

❏ SD18194	Live On Tour in Europe	1976	$25

COBHAM, BILLY
Drummer. Also see MAHAVISHNU ORCHESTRA.

Albums

ATLANTIC

❏ SD18149	A Funky Thide of Sings	1975	$30
❏ SD7300	Crosswinds	1974	$35

— *Original pressings have "1841 Broadway" address on label*

❏ SD19174	Inner Conflicts	1978	$30
❏ SD18166	Life & Times	1976	$30
❏ SD18139	Shabazz (Recorded Live in Europe)	1975	$35
❏ SD7268	Spectrum	1973	$35

— *Original pressings have "1841 Broadway" address on label*

❏ SD19238	The Best of Billy Cobham	1979	$30
❏ SD18121	Total Eclipse	1974	$35

COLUMBIA

❏ JC35993	B.C.	1979	$30
❏ JC34939	Magic	1977	$30
❏ JC35457	Simplicity of Expression – Depth of Thought	1978	$30
❏ JC36400	The Best of Billy Cobham	1980	$30

ELEKTRA/MUSICIAN

❏ 60123	Observations &	1982	$35
❏ 60233	Smokin'	1983	$35

GRP

❏ GR-9575	Billy's Best Hits	1988	$25
❏ GR-1040	Picture This	1987	$25
❏ GR-1027	Power Play	1986	$25
❏ GR-1020	Warning	1986	$30

COCHRAN, CHARLES
Male singer.

Albums

AUDIOPHILE

❏ AP-177	Haunted Heart	1982	$30

COCHRAN, TODD
Pianist and keyboard player.

Albums

VITAL

❏ VTL-001	Todd	1991	$25

COCHRANE, MICHAEL
Pianist.

Albums

SOUL NOTE

❏ SN-1151	Elements	198?	$30

CODONA
Trio whose name comes from the first two letters of each participant — COLLIN WALCOTT; DON CHERRY; NANA VASCONCELOS.

Albums

ECM

❏ 1132	Codona	1979	$30
❏ 1177	Codona 2	1980	$30
❏ 23785	Codona 3	1983	$30

COE, JIMMY
Baritone, alto and tenor saxophone player and bandleader.

Albums

DELMARK

❏ DL-443	After Hours Joint	1989	$25

COHN, AL, AND BILLY MITCHELL
Also see each artist's individual listings.

Albums

XANADU

❏ 185	Night Flight to Dakar	1980	$25
❏ 180	Xanadu in Africa	1979	$25

COHN, AL, AND JIMMY ROWLES
Also see each artist's individual listings.

Albums

XANADU

❏ 145	Heavy Love	1978	$25

COHN, AL, AND ZOOT SIMS
Also see each artist's individual listings.

Albums

ABUNDANT SOUNDS

❏ 1 [M]	Either Way	1960	$175

CORAL

❏ CRL57171 [M]	Al and Zoot	1958	$175

MCA

❏ 1377	Al Cohn Quintet Featuring Zoot Sims	198?	$30

MERCURY

❏ MG-20606 [M]	You 'n Me	1960	$100
❏ SR-60606 [S]	You 'n Me	1960	$150

MUSE

❏ MR-5016	Body and Soul	1974	$35
❏ MR-5356	Body and Soul	1988	$25

— *Reissue of 5016*

RCA VICTOR

❏ LPM-1282 [M]	From A to Z	1956	$150

SONET

❏ 684	Motoring Along	197?	$30

TRIP

❏ 5548	You 'n Me	197?	$25

ZIM

❏ 2002	Either Way	197?	$30

COHN, AL; RICH KAMUCA; BILL PERKINS
Also see each artist's individual listings.

Albums

RCA VICTOR

❏ LPM-1162 [M]	The Brothers	1955	$150

COHN, AL; SCOTT HAMILTON; BUDDY TATE
Also see each artist's individual listings.

Albums

CONCORD JAZZ

❏ CJ-172	Tour de Force	198?	$25

COHN, AL
Tenor saxophone player and arranger. Also see BOOTS BROWN; CANDIDO; THE FOUR BROTHERS; THE FOUR MOST; ZOOT SIMS.

Albums

BIOGRAPH

❏ 12063	Be Loose	197?	$25

CONCORD JAZZ

❏ CJ-155	Nonpareil	1981	$25
❏ CJ-194	Overtures	1982	$25
❏ CJ-241	Standards of Excellence	1983	$25

CORAL

❏ CRL57118 [M]	Al Cohn Quintet	1957	$50

DAWN

❏ DLP-1110 [M]	Cohn on the Saxophone	1956	$120

PRESTIGE

❏ PRST-7819	Broadway 1954	1970	$30

PROGRESSIVE

❏ PLP-3002 [10]	Al Cohn Quartet	1953	$300
❏ PLP-3004 [10]	Al Cohn Quintet	1953	$300

RCA VICTOR

❏ LPM-1161 [M]	Four Brass, One Tenor	1956	$80
❏ LJM-1024 [M]	Mr. Music	1955	$80
❏ LPM-2312 [M]	Son of Drum Suite	1960	$40
❏ LSP-2312 [S]	Son of Drum Suite	1960	$50
❏ LPM-1207 [M]	That Old Feeling	1956	$80
❏ LPM-1116 [M]	The Natural Seven	1955	$80

SAVOY

❏ MG-12048 [M]	Cohn's Tones	1956	$80

SAVOY JAZZ

❏ SJL-1126	The Progressive	197?	$25

TIMELESS

❏ LPSJP-259	Rifftide	1990	$30

XANADU

❏ 138	America	1976	$25
❏ 179	No Problem	1979	$25
❏ 110	Play It Now	1975	$25

COHN, AL/SHORTY ROGERS
Also see each artist's individual listings.

Albums

RCA VICTOR

❏ LJM-1020 [M]	East Coast -- West Coast Scene	1954	$200

COHN, STEVE
Pianist.

Albums

CADENCE JAZZ

❏ CJ-1020	Shapes Sounds Theories	198?	$20

COIL, PAT
Pianist, composer and arranger.

Albums

SHEFFIELD LABS

❏ TLP-34	Just Ahead	1993	$60

— *Audiophile vinyl*

❏ TLP-31	Steps	1991	$40

— *Audiophile vinyl*

Number	Title	Yr	NM

COKER, DOLO
Pianist.
Albums
XANADU

❏ 178	All Alone	1979	$25
❏ 142	California Hard	1976	$25
❏ 139	Dolo!	1976	$25
❏ 153	Third Down	1977	$25

COKER, JERRY
Tenor saxophone player and arranger.
Albums
FANTASY

❏ 3214 [M]	Modern Music from Indiana University	1956	$200

—Red vinyl

❏ 3214 [M]	Modern Music from Indiana University	1957	$250

—Black vinyl

REVELATION

❏ 45	A Re-Emergence	1983	$30
❏ 47	Rebirth	1984	$30

COLA, GEORGE "KID SHEIK
Trumpeter and male singer.
Albums
GHB

❏ GHB-187	Kid Sheik in England	1986	$25
❏ GHB-47	Kid Sheik Plays Blues and Standards	197?	$25
❏ GHB-76	Stompers	197?	$25

JAZZOLOGY

❏ JCE-31	Kid Sheik and Sheik's Swingers	1967	$30

COLBY, MARK
Tenor and soprano saxophone player.
Albums
COLUMBIA

❏ JC35725	One Good Turn	1979	$25
❏ JC35298	Serpentine Fire	1978	$25

COLD SWEAT
Craig Harris, David Murray, George Adams and Arthur Blythe are in this group.
Albums
JMT

❏ 834426-1	Cold Sweat Plays J.B.	1989	$35

COLE, COZY
Drummer. Had an unexpected pop hit in 1958 with the instrumental "Topsy II."
Albums
AUDITION

❏ 33-5943 [M]	Cozy Cole	1955	$100

BETHLEHEM

❏ BCP-21 [M]	Jazz at the Metropole Café	1955	$250

CHARLIE PARKER

❏ PLP-403 [M]	A Cozy Conaption of Carmen	1962	$50
❏ PLP-403S [S]	A Cozy Conaption of Carmen	1962	$60

COLUMBIA

❏ CL2553 [M]	It's a Rockin' Thing	1965	$35
❏ CS9353 [S]	It's a Rockin' Thing	1965	$50

CORAL

❏ CRL57423 [M]	Drum Beat Dancing Feet	1962	$35
❏ CRL57457 [M]	It's a Cozy World	1964	$35
❏ CRL757457 [S]	It's a Cozy World	1964	$50

FELSTED

❏ 7002 [M]	Cozy's Caravan/Earl's Backroom	1958	$100
❏ 2002 [S]	Cozy's Caravan/Earl's Backroom	1958	$40

GRAND AWARD

❏ GA 33-334 [M]	After Hours	1956	$40

KING

❏ 673 [M]	Cozy Cole	1959	$120
❏ KS-673 [S]	Cozy Cole	1959	$300

LOVE

❏ 500M [M]	Topsy	1959	$175
❏ 500S [S]	Topsy	1959	$200

PARIS

❏ 122 [M]	Cozy Cole and His All-Stars	1958	$100

PLYMOUTH

❏ P 12-155 [M]	Cozy Cole and His All Stars	195?	$30

SAVOY

❏ MG-12197 [M]	Concerto for Cozy	196?	$50

WHO'S WHO IN JAZZ

❏ 21003	Lionel Hampton Presents Cozy Cole & Marty Napoleon	1977	$25

COLE, COZY/JIMMY MCPARTLAND
Also see each artist's individual listings.
Albums
WALDORF MUSIC HALL

❏ MH 33-162 [10]	After Hours	195?	$50

COLE, HOLLY
Albums
BLUE NOTE JAZZ

❏ JP-5003	Temptation	2001	$40

—Audiophile edition issued by Classic Records (CD was issued in 1995)

COLE, IKE
Male singer, brother of Nat.
Albums
DEE GEE

❏ LPM-4001 [M]	Ike Cole's Tribute to His Brother Nat	1966	$40
❏ ST-4001 [S]	Ike Cole's Tribute to His Brother Nat	1966	$50

DOT

❏ DLP-25943	Picture This!	1969	$30

GUEST STAR

❏ G-1502 [M]	Ike Cole -- The Brother of Nat King Cole	196?	$18
❏ GS-1502 [S]	Ike Cole -- The Brother of Nat King Cole	196?	$18

PROMENADE

❏ 2099 [M]	Ike Cole Sings	196?	$18

UNITED ARTISTS

❏ UAL-3569 [M]	Same Old You	1967	$30
❏ UAS-6569 [S]	Same Old You	1967	$30

COLE, NAT KING
lFirst renowned as a piano player in The King Cole Trio, then as a male singer. The other members of the Trio were Oscar Moore (guitar) and Wesley Prince (bass). For a more complete listing, including his pop material, see the Standard Catalog of American Records.
Albums
CAPITOL

❏ W782 [M]	After Midnight	1956	$60

—Turquoise label

❏ W782 [M]	After Midnight	1958	$100

—Black label with colorband, "Capitol" at left

❏ W782 [M]	After Midnight	1962	$80

—Black label with colorband, "Capitol" at top

❏ H213 [10]	Harvest of Hits	1950	$250

—Original; purple label

❏ L213 [10]	Harvest of Hits	195?	$60

—Reissue; maroon label, "H" mechanically crossed out on back cover with "L" stamped next to it

❏ T592 [M]	Instrumental Classics	1955	$75
❏ H156 [10]	Nat King Cole at the Piano	1950	$250
❏ H420 [10]	Nat King Cole Sings for Two in Love	1953	$150

—Original; purple label

❏ T420 [M]	Nat King Cole Sings for Two in Love	1955	$75

—Turquoise label

❏ T420 [M]	Nat King Cole Sings for Two in Love	1958	$100

—Black label with colorband, "Capitol" at left

❏ T420 [M]	Nat King Cole Sings for Two in Love	1962	$80

—Black label with colorband, "Capitol" at top

❏ DT420 [R]	Nat King Cole Sings for Two in Love	1963	$50
❏ L420 [10]	Nat King Cole Sings for Two in Love	195?	$50

—Reissue; maroon label, back cover probably has "H" mechanically crossed out with "L" stamped next to it

❏ W1675 [M]	Nat King Cole Sings/George Shearing Plays	1962	$100

—Black label with colorband, "Capitol" at left

❏ W1675 [M]	Nat King Cole Sings/George Shearing Plays	1963	$50

—Black label with colorband, "Capitol" at top

❏ SW1675 [S]	Nat King Cole Sings/George Shearing Plays	1962	$100

—Black label with colorband, "Capitol" at left

❏ SW1675 [S]	Nat King Cole Sings/George Shearing Plays	1963	$80

—Black label with colorband, "Capitol" at top

❏ SM-1675	Nat King Cole Sings/George Shearing Plays	197?	$20

—Reissue with new prefix

❏ W1713 [M]	Nat King Cole Sings the Blues	1962	$80

—Black label with colorband, "Capitol" at left

❏ SW1713 [S]	Nat King Cole Sings the Blues	1962	$100

—Black label with colorband, "Capitol" at left

❏ W1929 [M]	Nat King Cole Sings the Blues, Volume 2	1963	$50
❏ SW1929 [S]	Nat King Cole Sings the Blues, Volume 2	1963	$80
❏ H332 [10]	Penthouse Serenade	1951	$200

—Original; purple label

❏ L332 [10]	Penthouse Serenade	195?	$50

—Reissue; maroon label, "H" mechanically crossed out on back cover with "L" stamped next to it

❏ W514 [M]	Tenth Anniversary Album	1955	$75

—Gray label; released simultaneously with H1-514 and H2-514

❏ H1-514 [10]	Tenth Anniversary Album, Part 1	1954	$150

—Contains Side 1 of W 514

❏ H2-514 [10]	Tenth Anniversary Album, Part 2	1954	$150

—Contains Side 2 of W 514

❏ N-16260	The Best of the King Cole Trio -- Volume 1	1982	$20
❏ N-16281	The Best of the King Cole Trio -- Volume 2	1982	$20
❏ H8 [10]	The King Cole Trio	1950	$250
❏ H29 [10]	The King Cole Trio, Volume 2	1950	$250
❏ H59 [10]	The King Cole Trio, Volume 3	1950	$250
❏ H177 [10]	The King Cole Trio, Volume 4	1950	$250
❏ H220 [10]	The Nat King Cole Trio	1950	$200
❏ T2311 [M]	The Nat King Cole Trio	1965	$60
❏ W689 [M]	The Piano Style of Nat King Cole	1956	$75

—Turquoise label

❏ W689 [M]	The Piano Style of Nat King Cole	1958	$100

—Black label with colorband, "Capitol" at left

❏ W689 [M]	The Piano Style of Nat King Cole	1962	$80

—Black label with colorband, "Capitol" at top

❏ SQBO91278	The Swingin' Moods of Nat King Cole	1967	$100

—Capitol Record Club exclusive

❏ M-11033 [M]	Trio Days	1972	$50

DECCA

❏ DL8260 [M]	In the Beginning	1956	$150

—Black label, silver print

❏ DL8260 [M]	In the Beginning	1960	$60

—Black label with color bars

EVEREST ARCHIVE OF FOLK & JAZZ

❏ 290	Nature Boy	197?	$25

MARK 56

❏ 739	Early 1940s	197?	$35

MCA

❏ 4020	From the Very Beginning	1973	$30

MOBILE FIDELITY

❏ Jan-0081	Nat King Cole Sings/George Shearing Plays	1981	$100

—Audiophile vinyl

MOSAIC

Number	Title	Yr	NM
❑ MR27-138	The Complete Capitol Recordings of the Nat King Cole Trio	1991	$800
SAVOY JAZZ			
❑ SJL-1205	Nat King Cole & The King Cole Trio	1989	$30
SCORE			
❑ SLP-4019 [M]	The King Cole Trio and Lester Young	1957	$150
TIME-LIFE			
❑ SLGD-01	Legendary Singers: Nat King Cole	1985	$35
❑ SLGD-15	Legendary Singers: Nat King Cole: Take Two	1986	$35
TRIP			
❑ 7	The Nat "King" Cole Trio	197?	$30
VERVE			
❑ VSP-14 [M]	Nat Cole at JATP	1966	$35
❑ VSPS-14 [R]	Nat Cole at JATP	1966	$30
❑ VSP-25 [M]	Nat Cole at JATP 2	1966	$35
❑ VSPS-25 [R]	Nat Cole at JATP 2	1966	$30

COLE, RICHIE, AND BOOTS RANDOLPH
Randolph is a pop, rock and country saxophone player whose solo recordings are outside the scope of this book. Also see RICHIE COLE.

Albums

Number	Title	Yr	NM
PALO ALTO			
❑ PA-8041	Yakety Madness	1983	$25

COLE, RICHIE, AND ERIC KLOSS
Also see each artist's individual listings.

Albums

Number	Title	Yr	NM
MUSE			
❑ MR-5082	Battle of the Saxes	1976	$25

COLE, RICHIE, AND HANK CRAWFORD
Also see each artist's individual listings.

Albums

Number	Title	Yr	NM
MILESTONE			
❑ M-9180	Bossa International	1990	$30

COLE, RICHIE, AND PHIL WOODS
Also see each artist's individual listings.

Albums

Number	Title	Yr	NM
MUSE			
❑ MR-5237	Side by Side	1980	$25

COLE, RICHIE
Alto saxophone player.

Albums

Number	Title	Yr	NM
ADELPHI			
❑ AD5001	Starburst	1976	$25
CONCORD JAZZ			
❑ CJ-314	Pure Imagination	1987	$25
MILESTONE			
❑ M-9152	Popbop	1987	$25
❑ M-9162	Signature	1988	$25
MUSE			
❑ MR-5270	Alive at the Village Vanguard	1981	$25
❑ MR-5155	Alto Madness	1977	$25
❑ MR-5245	Cool "C	1981	$25
❑ MR-5207	Hollywood Madness	1979	$25
❑ MR-5192	Keeper of the Flame	1978	$25
❑ MR-5119	New York Afternoon	1976	$25
❑ MR-5295	Some Things Speak for Themselves	1982	$25
PALO ALTO			
❑ PA-8036	Alto Annie's Theme	1983	$25
❑ PA-8070	Bossa Nova Eyes	1985	$25
❑ PA-8023	Return to Alto Acres	1982	$25

COLEMAN, BILL
Trumpeter, sometimes a fluegel horn player and male singer.

Albums

Number	Title	Yr	NM
BLACK LION			
❑ 128	London!	197?	$30
❑ 212	Mainstream at Montreux	1974	$30
DRG			
❑ SL-5200	Blowing for the Cats: The Final Big Band Sessions	198?	$25
SWING			
❑ SW-8410	Bill Coleman with George Duvivier & Co.	198?	$25
❑ SW-8402	Paris 1936-38	198?	$25

COLEMAN, CY
Pianist.

Albums

Number	Title	Yr	NM
BENIDA			
❑ LP-1023A [10]	Cy Coleman	1955	$60
CAPITOL			
❑ T1952 [M]	Piano Witchcraft	1963	$50
❑ ST1952 [S]	Piano Witchcraft	1963	$60
❑ T2355 [M]	The Art of Love	1965	$75
❑ ST2355 [S]	The Art of Love	1965	$50
COLUMBIA			
❑ C32804	Broadway Tunesmith	1973	$25
❑ CL2578 [M]	If My Friends Could See Me Now	1966	$30
❑ CS9378 [S]	If My Friends Could See Me Now	1966	$35
DRG			
❑ SL-5205	Comin' Home	1988	$25
EVEREST			
❑ LPBR-5092 [M]	Playboy's Penthouse	196?	$30
❑ SDBR-1092 [S]	Playboy's Penthouse	196?	$30
MGM			
❑ SE-4501	Ages of Rock	1968	$30
WESTMINSTER			
❑ WLP-15001 [M]	Cool Coleman	195?	$40

COLEMAN, EARL
Male singer.

Albums

Number	Title	Yr	NM
ATLANTIC			
❑ SD8172	Love Songs	1968	$35
FANTASY			
❑ OJC-187	Earl Coleman Returns	1986	$25
PRESTIGE			
❑ PRLP-7045 [M]	Earl Coleman Returns	1956	$300
—Yellow label			
❑ PRLP-7045 [M]	Earl Coleman Returns	196?	$30
—Blue label, trident logo at right			
STASH			
❑ 243	Stardust	1984	$25
XANADU			
❑ 147	A Song for You	1978	$30
❑ 175	There's Something About an Old Love	1979	$30

COLEMAN, ERNIE
The front cover spells his name "Colman," but the back cover says "Coleman."

Albums

Number	Title	Yr	NM
WARNER BROS.			
❑ W1261 [M]	Be Gentle, Please	1959	$60
❑ WS1261 [S]	Be Gentle, Please	1959	$60

COLEMAN, GEORGE
Alto and tenor saxophone player.

Albums

Number	Title	Yr	NM
THERESA			
❑ TR-126	George Coleman at Yoshi's	1989	$30
❑ TR-120	Manhattan Panorama	1986	$25
TIMELESS			
❑ 312	Meditation	197?	$30

COLEMAN, GLORIA
Organist.

Albums

Number	Title	Yr	NM
ABC IMPULSE!			
❑ AS-47	Soul Sisters	1968	$30
IMPULSE!			
❑ A-47 [M]	Soul Sisters	1963	$120
❑ AS-47 [S]	Soul Sisters	1963	$120
MAINSTREAM			
❑ MRL-322	Gloria Coleman Sings and Swings -- Organ	1972	$30

COLEMAN, ORNETTE
Alto saxophone player, composer, tenor saxophone player, trumpeter, violinist. Gave birth to "free jazz," named after his Atlantic album of the same name.

Albums

Number	Title	Yr	NM
ABC IMPULSE!			
❑ AS-9187	Crisis	1969	$120
❑ AS-9178	Ornette at 12	1968	$120
ANTILLES			
❑ AN-2001	Of Human Feelings	198?	$35
ARISTA FREEDOM			
❑ AL1900	The Great London Concert	1978	$25
ARTISTS HOUSE			
❑ 1	Body Meta	1977	$25
❑ 6	Soapsuds	1978	$25
ATLANTIC			
❑ 1327 [M]	Change of the Century	1960	$250
—Multicolor label, white "fan" logo			
❑ 1327 [M]	Change of the Century	1963	$50
—Multicolor label, black "fan" logo			
❑ SD1327 [S]	Change of the Century	1960	$250
—Multicolor label, white "fan" logo			
❑ SD1327 [S]	Change of the Century	1963	$50
—Multicolor label, black "fan" logo			
❑ SD1327 [S]	Change of the Century	1969	$30
—Red and green label, "1841 Broadway" on label			
❑ 1327 [M]	Change of the Century	1960	$250
—Black label			
❑ SD1327 [S]	Change of the Century	1960	$250
—Green label			
❑ SD1327 [S]	Change of the Century	1976	$25
❑ 1364 [M]	Free Jazz	1961	$150
—Multicolor label, white "fan" logo			
❑ SD1364 [S]	Free Jazz	1961	$150
—Multicolor label, white "fan" logo			
❑ SD1364 [S]	Free Jazz	1963	$50
—Multicolor label, black "fan" logo			
❑ SD1364 [S]	Free Jazz	1969	$30
—Red and green label			
❑ 1378 [M]	Ornette	1961	$150
—Multicolor label, white "fan" logo			
❑ 1378 [M]	Ornette	1963	$35
—Multicolor label, black "fan" logo			
❑ SD1378 [S]	Ornette	1961	$150
—Multicolor label, white "fan" logo			
❑ SD1378 [S]	Ornette	1963	$25
—Multicolor label, black "fan" logo			
❑ SD1378 [S]	Ornette	1969	$30
—Red and green label			
❑ 90530	Ornette	198?	$25
—Reissue of 1378			
❑ 1394 [M]	Ornette on Tenor	1962	$150
—Multicolor label, black "fan" logo			
❑ SD1394 [S]	Ornette on Tenor	1962	$150
—Multicolor label, black "fan" logo			
❑ SD1394 [S]	Ornette on Tenor	1969	$30
—Red and green label			
❑ SD1572	The Art of Improvisors	1971	$35
❑ SD1558	The Best of Ornette Coleman	1970	$35
❑ 1317 [M]	The Shape of Jazz to Come	1960	$250
—Multicolor label, white "fan" logo			
❑ 1317 [M]	The Shape of Jazz to Come	1963	$35
—Multicolor label, black "fan" logo			
❑ SD1317 [S]	The Shape of Jazz to Come	1959	$300
—Bullseye" label			
❑ SD1317 [S]	The Shape of Jazz to Come	1960	$250
—Multicolor label, white "fan" logo			
❑ SD1317 [S]	The Shape of Jazz to Come	1963	$25
—Multicolor label, black "fan" logo			
❑ SD1317 [S]	The Shape of Jazz to Come	1969	$30
—Red and green label			
❑ 1353 [M]	This Is Our Music	1960	$250
—Multicolor label, white "fan" logo			
❑ 1353 [M]	This Is Our Music	1963	$35
—Multicolor label, black "fan" logo			
❑ SD1353 [S]	This Is Our Music	1960	$250
—Multicolor label, white "fan" logo			
❑ SD1353 [S]	This Is Our Music	1963	$25
—Multicolor label, black "fan" logo			
❑ SD1353 [S]	This Is Our Music	1969	$30
—Red and green label			

James Clay and David "Fathead" Newman, *The Sound of the Wide Open Spaces!!!!*, Riverside RLP-1178, **$200**.

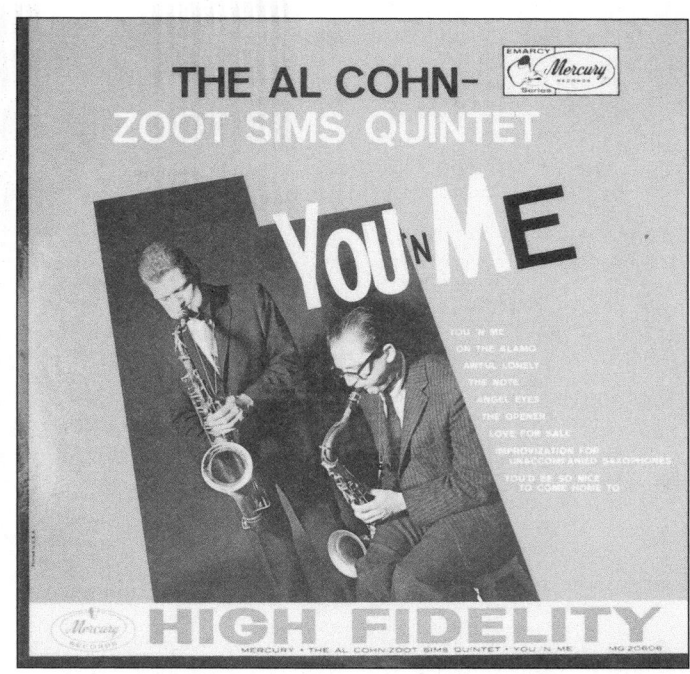

Al Cohn-Zoot Sims Quintet, *You 'n Me*, Mercury MG 20606, **$100**.

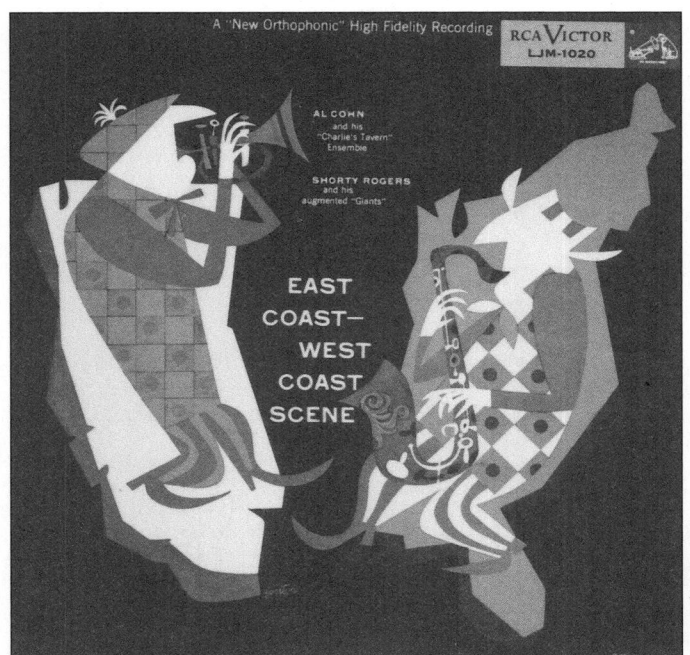

Al Cohn/Shorty Rogers, *East Coast-West Coast Scene*, RCA Victor LJM-1020, **$200**.

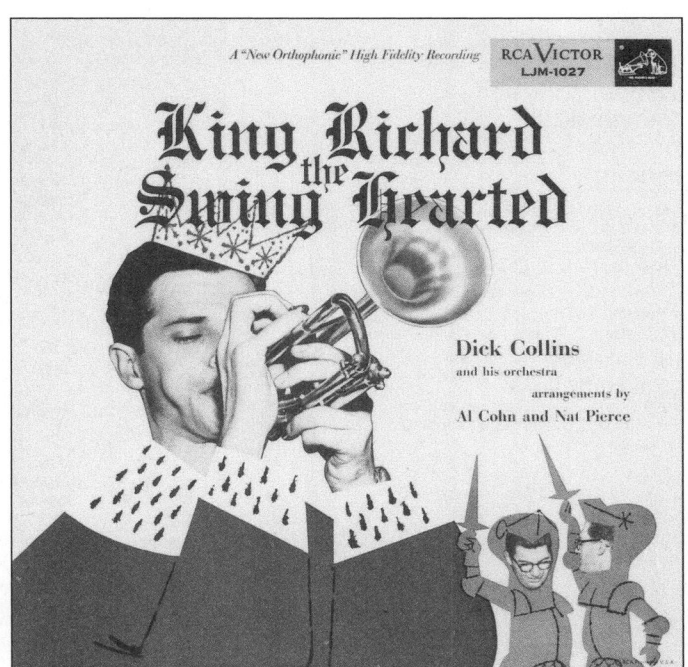

Dick Collins, *King Richard the Swing Hearted*, RCA Victor LJM-1027, **$100**.

Number	Title	Yr	NM
❏ SD1588	Twins	1972	$35
❏ SD8810	Twins	198?	$30
BLUE NOTE			
❏ BST-84356	Love Call	1970	$25
❏ BST-84287	New York Is Now!	1968	$30
❏ BLP-4224 [M]	Ornette Coleman at the Golden Circle, Stockholm, Volume 1	1965	$60
❏ BST-84224 [S]	Ornette Coleman at the Golden Circle, Stockholm, Volume 1	1965	$40
—*New York, USA" on label*			
❏ BST-84224 [S]	Ornette Coleman at the Golden Circle, Stockholm, Volume 1	1967	$35
—*A Division of Liberty Records" on label*			
❏ BLP-4225 [M]	Ornette Coleman at the Golden Circle, Stockholm, Volume 2	1965	$60
❏ BST-84225 [S]	Ornette Coleman at the Golden Circle, Stockholm, Volume 2	1965	$40
—*New York, USA" on label*			
❏ BST-84225 [S]	Ornette Coleman at the Golden Circle, Stockholm, Volume 2	1967	$35
—*A Division of Liberty Records" on label*			
❏ BLP-4246 [M]	The Empty Foxhole	1966	$60
❏ BST-84246 [S]	The Empty Foxhole	1966	$40
—*New York, USA" on label*			
❏ BST-84246 [S]	The Empty Foxhole	1967	$30
—*A Division of Liberty Records" on label*			
❏ B1-28982	The Empty Foxhole	1994	$35
❏ BLP-4210 [M]	Town Hall Concert, Volume 1	1965	$0
—*Canceled*			
❏ BST-84210 [S]	Town Hall Concert, Volume 1	1965	$0
—*Canceled*			
❏ BLP-4211 [M]	Town Hall Concert, Volume 2	1965	$0
—*Canceled*			
❏ BST-84211 [S]	Town Hall Concert, Volume 2	1965	$0
—*Canceled*			
COLUMBIA			
❏ FC38029	Broken Shadows	198?	$30
❏ KC31061	Science Fiction	1972	$25
❏ CG33669	Science Fiction/Skies of America	1976	$25
❏ KC31562	Skies of America	1972	$25
CONTEMPORARY			
❏ C-3551 [M]	The Music of Ornette Coleman -- Something Else!	1958	$250
❏ S-7551 [S]	The Music of Ornette Coleman -- Something Else!	1959	$250
❏ M-3569 [M]	Tomorrow Is the Question	1959	$250
❏ S-7569 [S]	Tomorrow Is the Question	1959	$250
FANTASY			
❏ OJC-163	The Music of Ornette Coleman -- Something Else!	198?	$30
—*Reissue of Contemporary 7551*			
❏ OJC-342	Tomorrow Is the Question	198?	$30
—*Reissue of Contemporary 7569*			
FLYING DUTCHMAN			
❏ 123	Friends and Neighbors	1970	$25
❏ FD-10123	Friends and Neighbors	1972	$35
—*Reissue of 123*			
HORIZON			
❏ 722	Dancing in Your Head	1977	$35
IAI			
❏ 373852	Classics, Volume 1	197?	$25
INNER CITY			
❏ 1001	Live at the Hillcrest Club 1958	197?	$25
MOON			
❏ MLP-022	Broken Shadows	1992	$35
PORTRAIT			
❏ OR44301	Virgin Beauty	1988	$35
RCA VICTOR			
❏ LPM-2982 [M]	The Music of Ornette Coleman	1964	$30
❏ LSP-2982 [S]	The Music of Ornette Coleman	1964	$30

Number	Title	Yr	NM
COLEMAN, STEVE			
Alto saxophone player.			
Albums			
JMT			
❏ 850001	Motherland Pulse	1985	$35
❏ 860005	On the Edge of Tomorrow	1986	$35
❏ 834425-1	Strata Institute Cipher Syntax	1988	$30
❏ 870010	World Expansion	1987	$35
NOVUS			
❏ 63180-1 [EP]	A Tale of 3 Cities The EP	1995	$30
COLES, JOHNNY			
Trumpeter.			
Albums			
BLUE NOTE			
❏ BST-84144 [S]	Little Johnny C	1963	$50
—*New York, USA" on label*			
❏ BST-84144 [S]	Little Johnny C	1967	$35
—*A Division of Liberty Records" on label*			
EPIC			
❏ BA17015 [S]	The Warm Sound	1961	$300
MAINSTREAM			
❏ MRL-346	Katumbo (Dance)	1972	$25
COLIANNI, JOHN			
Pianist.			
Albums			
CONCORD JAZZ			
❏ CJ-367	Blues-O-Matic	1989	$30
❏ CJ-309	John Colianni	1987	$25
COLINA, MICHAEL			
Keyboard player, composer and producer.			
Albums			
PRIVATE MUSIC			
❏ 2041-1-P	The Shadow of Urbano	1988	$25
COLLETTE, BUDDY			
Saxophone player (alto, tenor), clarinet player, flutist, composer.			
Albums			
ABC-PARAMOUNT			
❏ ABC-179 [M]	Calm, Cool and Collette	1957	$60
CHALLENGE			
❏ CHL-603 [M]	Everybody's Buddy	1958	$50
CONTEMPORARY			
❏ C-3522 [M]	Man of Many Parts	1956	$200
❏ S-7522 [S]	Man of Many Parts	1959	$250
❏ C-3531 [M]	Nice Day with Buddy Collette	1957	$250
❏ S-7531 [S]	Nice Day with Buddy Collette	1959	$250
CROWN			
❏ CLP-5019 [M]	Bongo Madness	195?	$30
DIG			
❏ LP-101 [M]	Tanganyika	1956	$100
DOOTO			
❏ DTL-245 [M]	Buddy's Best	1957	$100
—*Red vinyl*			
❏ DTL-245 [M]	Buddy's Best	1957	$60
—*Black vinyl*			
EMARCY			
❏ MG-36133 [M]	Swingin' Shepherds	1958	$200
❏ SR-80005 [S]	Swingin' Shepherds	1959	$200
FANTASY			
❏ OJC-239	Man of Many Parts	198?	$25
INTERLUDE			
❏ MO-505 [M]	Modern Interpretations of Porgy & Bess	196?	$30
❏ ST-1005 [S]	Modern Interpretations of Porgy & Bess	196?	$40
LEGEND			
❏ 1004	Now and Then	1974	$30
MERCURY			
❏ MG-20447 [M]	At the Cinema	1959	$100
❏ SR-60132 [S]	At the Cinema	1959	$100
MUSIC & SOUND			
❏ 1001 [M]	Polynesia	196?	$30
❏ S-1001 [S]	Polynesia	196?	$40
RGB			
❏ 2001	Block Buster	1975	$30

Number	Title	Yr	NM
SOUL NOTE			
❏ 121165	Flute Talk	1990	$35
SPECIALTY			
❏ SP-5002 [M]	Jazz Loves Paris	1960	$50
SURREY			
❏ S-1009 [M]	Buddy Collette on Broadway	1965	$35
❏ SS-1009 [S]	Buddy Collette on Broadway	1965	$25
TAMPA			
❏ TP-34 [M]	Star Studded Cast	1959	$150
WORLD PACIFIC			
❏ WP-1823 [M]	Warm Winds	1964	$100
❏ ST-1823 [S]	Warm Winds	1964	$100
COLLIE, MAX, AND HIS RHYTHM ACES			
Trombonist and bandleader.			
Albums			
GHB			
❏ GHB-63	On Tour in the U.S.A.	198?	$25
COLLINS, AL "JAZZBO			
Famous jazz radio announcer who lent his name to the below recordings.			
Albums			
ABC IMPULSE!			
❏ AS-9150 [S]	A Lovely Bunch of Al "Jazzbo" Collins	1968	$35
CORAL			
❏ CRL57035 [M]	East Coast Jazz Scene	1956	$80
EVEREST			
❏ LPBR-5097 [M]	Swingin' at the Opera	1960	$30
❏ SDBR-1097 [S]	Swingin' at the Opera	1960	$40
IMPULSE!			
❏ A-9150 [M]	A Lovely Bunch of Al "Jazzbo" Collins	1967	$160
❏ AS-9150 [S]	A Lovely Bunch of Al "Jazzbo" Collins	1967	$120
OLD TOWN			
❏ LP-2001 [M]	In the Purple Grotto	1961	$30
COLLINS, CAL			
Guitarist.			
Albums			
CONCORD JAZZ			
❏ CJ-95	Blues on My Mind	1979	$25
❏ CJ-119	By Myself	1980	$25
❏ CJ-71	Cal Collins In San Francisco	1978	$25
❏ CJ-59	Cincinnati to L.A.	1977	$25
❏ CJ-166	Cross Country	1981	$25
❏ CJ-137	Interplay	1981	$25
FAMOUS DOOR			
❏ HL-123	Ohio Boss Guitar	198?	$25
PAUSA			
❏ 7159	Milestones	198?	$25
COLLINS, DICK			
Trumpeter and composer.			
Albums			
RCA VICTOR			
❏ LJM-1019 [M]	Horn of Plenty	1955	$100
❏ LJM-1027 [M]	King Richard the Swing Hearted	1955	$100
COLLINS, JOYCE			
Pianist.			
Albums			
DISCOVERY			
❏ 828	Moment to Moment	198?	$25
JAZZLAND			
❏ JLP-24 [M]	The Girl Here Plays Mean Piano	1960	$30
❏ JLP-924 [S]	The Girl Here Plays Mean Piano	1960	$30
COLLINS, LEE			
Trumpeter.			
Albums			
NEW ORLEANS			
❏ 7203 [M]	Night at Victory Club	198?	$25

Number	Title	Yr	NM

COLONNA, JERRY
Trombone player.

Albums

DECCA
| ❏ DL5540 [10] | Music? For Screaming!!! | 1955 | $150 |

LIBERTY
| ❏ SL-9004 [M] | Along the Dixieland Hi-Fi Way | 1957 | $40 |
| ❏ LRP-3046 [M] | Let's All Sing with Jerry Colonna | 1957 | $40 |

COLTRANE, ALICE, AND CARLOS SANTANA
Also see ALICE COLTRANE; SANTANA. (SC1)
Also see ALICE COLTRANE; SANTANA. (LP)
Also see each artist's individual entries.

Albums

COLUMBIA
| ❏ PC32900 | Illuminations | 1974 | $50 |
— No bar code on cover

COLTRANE, ALICE
Piantis, organist and harp player. Widow of JOHN COLTRANE. She played in his group for a time.

Albums

ABC IMPULSE!
❏ AS-9156	A Monastic Trio	1968	$160
❏ AS-9185	Huntington Ashram Monastery	1969	$200
❏ AS-9203	Journey in Satchidananda	1970	$200
❏ AS-9224	Lord of Lords	1972	$160
❏ AS-9196	Ptah the El Daoud	1969	$200
❏ AS-9232	Reflection On Creation and Space	1973	$200
❏ AS-9210	Universal Consciousness	1971	$200
❏ AS-9218	World Galaxy	1972	$160

GRP/IMPULSE!
| ❏ IMP-228 | Journey in Satchidanada | 1997 | $35 |
— 180-gram reissue

WARNER BROS.
❏ BS2916	Eternity	1975	$50
❏ BS2986	Radha-Krsna Nama Sankirtana	1976	$60
❏ BS3077	Transcendence	1977	$50
❏ 2WB3218	Transfiguration	1978	$40

COLTRANE, JOHN
Tenor and soprano saxophone player. One of the most important and influential figures in jazz history. Also see CANNONBALL ADDERLEY; KENNY BURRELL; TADD DAMERON; MILES DAVIS; RAY DRAPER; WILBUR HARDEN; MILT JACKSON; THELONIOUS MONK; CECIL TAYLOR.

Albums

ABC IMPULSE!
❏ AS-6 [S]	Africa/Brass	1968	$200
❏ AS-9273	Africa/Brass, Volume 2	1974	$160
❏ AS-77 [S]	A Love Supreme	1968	$200
— Black label with red border
| ❏ AS-77 [S] | A Love Supreme | 1978 | $30 |
— abc" musical note at top of yellow, red, purple "target" label
| ❏ AS-77 [S] | A Love Supreme | 1974 | $35 |
— Green, blue, purple "target" label
| ❏ AS-95 [S] | Ascension | 1968 | $200 |
— With "Edition II" in dead wax; black label with red ring
| ❏ AS-95 [S] | Ascension | 1978 | $30 |
— abc" musical note at top of yellow, red, purple "target" label
| ❏ AS-32 [S] | Ballads | 1968 | $200 |
— Black label with red ring
| ❏ AS-32 [S] | Ballads | 1973 | $100 |
— All-black label
| ❏ AS-21 [S] | Coltrane | 1968 | $200 |
— Black label with red ring
| ❏ AS-50 [S] | Coltrane Live at Birdland | 1968 | $200 |
— Black label with red ring
| ❏ AS-50 [S] | Coltrane Live at Birdland | 1975 | $35 |
— Green blue, purple "target" label
| ❏ IA-9246 | Concert Japan | 1973 | $35 |
| ❏ AS-66 [S] | Crescent | 1968 | $200 |
— Black label with red ring
| ❏ AS-30 [S] | Duke Ellington and John Coltrane | 1968 | $200 |
— Black label with red ring
| ❏ AS-30 [S] | Duke Ellington and John Coltrane | 1973 | $120 |
— All-black label
| ❏ AS-9120 [S] | Expression | 1968 | $200 |
— Black label with red ring
❏ IA-9332	First Meditations	1978	$30
❏ AS-9200	Greatest Years	1971	$200
❏ AS-9223	Greatest Years, Volume 2	1973	$35
❏ IA-9278	Greatest Years, Volume 3	1974	$35
❏ AS-42 [S]	Impressions	1968	$200
— Black label with red ring
❏ AS-9225	Infinity	1973	$30
❏ IA-9277	Interstellar Space	1974	$30
❏ AS-40 [S]	John Coltrane + Johnny Hartman	1968	$200
— Black label with red ring
| ❏ AS-40 [S] | John Coltrane + Johnny Hartman | 1975 | $35 |
— Green blue, purple "target" label
| ❏ AS-9106 [S] | Kulu Se Mama | 1968 | $200 |
— Black label with red ring
| ❏ AS-10 [S] | Live at the Village Vanguard | 1968 | $200 |
| ❏ AS-9124 [S] | Live at the Village Vanguard Again! | 1968 | $200 |
— Black label with red ring
| ❏ AS-9124 [S] | Live at the Village Vanguard Again! | 1975 | $35 |
— Green, blue and purple "target" label
| ❏ AS-9202 | Live in Seattle | 1971 | $200 |
| ❏ AS-9110 [S] | Meditations | 1968 | $200 |
— Black label with red ring
| ❏ AS-9110 [S] | Meditations | 1975 | $35 |
— Green, blue and purple "target" label
| ❏ AS-9110 [S] | Meditations | 1978 | $30 |
— abc" musical note at top of yellow, red, purple "target" label
| ❏ AS-94 [S] | New Thing at Newport | 1968 | $200 |
— Black label with red ring
| ❏ AS-9140 [S] | Om | 1968 | $200 |
— Black label with red ring
❏ AS-9161	Selflessness	1969	$200
❏ AS-9211	Sun Ship	1971	$200
❏ IA-9306	The Gentle Side of John Coltrane	1976	$35
❏ AS-85 [S]	The John Coltrane Quartet Plays	1968	$200
— Black label with red ring
❏ IZ-9345	The Mastery of John Coltrane Vol. 1: Feelin' Good	1978	$30
❏ IZ-9346	The Mastery of John Coltrane Vol. 2: Different Drum	1978	$30
❏ IA-9360	The Mastery of John Coltrane Vol. 3: Jupiter Variation	1978	$30
❏ IZ-9361	The Mastery of John Coltrane Vol. 4: Trane's Moods	1978	$30
❏ IA-9325	The Other Village Vanguard Tapes	1977	$35
❏ AS-9195	Transition	1969	$200

ATLANTIC
| ❏ 90462 | Countdown | 1986 | $25 |
| ❏ SD1311 [S] | Giant Steps | 1959 | $300 |
— Green label
| ❏ SD1311 [S] | Giant Steps | 1960 | $250 |
— Green and blue label, white fan logo
| ❏ SD1311 [S] | Giant Steps | 1959 | $300 |
— Bullseye" label
| ❏ 1361 [M] | My Favorite Things | 1962 | $150 |
— Orange and purple label, black fan logo
| ❏ SD1361 [S] | My Favorite Things | 1961 | $150 |
— Green and blue label, white fan logo
❏ SD 2-313	The Art of John Coltrane	1973	$35
❏ 90041	The Avant-Garde	1983	$25
❏ SD1541	The Best of John Coltrane	1970	$30
❏ SD1553	The Coltrane Legacy	1971	$30

ATLANTIC/RHINO
| ❏ R1-71984 | The Heavyweight Champion: The Complete Atlantic Recordings | 1995 | $250 |
— Box set with liner notes; albums pressed on 150-gram vinyl

ATLANTIC/RHINO HANDMADE
| ❏ RHM1-7784 | The Heavyweight Champion: The Complete Atlantic Recordings (Year 2000 Second Edition) | 2000 | $200 |
— Year 2000 Second Edition" at lower right back cover; limited, numbered edition of 1,500 copies on 180-gram vinyl

| ❏ RHM1-7784 | The Heavyweight Champion: The Complete Atlantic Recordings (Year 2000 Second Edition) | 2000 | $200 |
— Year 2000 Second Edition" on lower left back cover; limited edition of 1,500, un-numbered, on 180-gram vinyl; pressed in the U.S. for export

BLUE NOTE
| ❏ BLP-1577 [M] | Blue Train | 1957 | $250 |
— Regular version, W. 63rd St., NYC address on label
| ❏ BST-1577 [S] | Blue Train | 1959 | $200 |
— Regular version, W. 63rd St., NYC address on label
| ❏ BLP-1577 [M] | Blue Train | 1965 | $400 |
— New York, USA" address on label
| ❏ BST-1577 [S] | Blue Train | 1965 | $300 |
— New York, USA" address on label
| ❏ BST-81577 | Blue Train | 1967 | $60 |
— A Division of Liberty Records" on label
| ❏ BST-81577 | Blue Train | 198? | $30 |
— The Finest in Jazz Since 1939" reissue
| ❏ B1-81577 | Blue Train | 1988 | $30 |
— Reissue with new prefix
| ❏ B1-46095 | Blue Train | 1997 | $35 |
— 180-gram reissue

COLTRANE
| ❏ AU-4950 | Cosmic Music | 1966 | $300 |
| ❏ AU-5000 | Cosmic Music | 1966 | $200 |

DCC COMPACT CLASSICS
| ❏ LPZ-2032 | Lush Life | 1997 | $120 |
— Audiophile vinyl

FANTASY
❏ OJC-415	Bahia	1990	$30
❏ OJC-352	Black Pearls	1989	$25
❏ OJC-460	Cattin' with Coltrane and Quinichette	1990	$30
❏ OJC-020	Coltrane	198?	$25
❏ OJC-393	Dakar	1989	$25
❏ OJC-394	Last Trane	1989	$25
❏ OJC-131	Lush Life	198?	$25
❏ OJC-078	Settin' the Pace	198?	$25
❏ OJC-021	Soultrane	198?	$25
❏ OJC-246	Standard Coltrane	1987	$25
❏ OJC-127	Tenor Conclave	1991	$30
❏ OJC-189	Traneing In	1986	$25

GRP/IMPULSE!
❏ GR-155	A Love Supreme	1995	$35
❏ GR-156	Ballads	1995	$35
❏ IMP-215	Coltrane	1997	$35
❏ IMP-198	Coltrane Live at Birdland	1997	$35
❏ IMP-200	Crescent	1997	$35
❏ IMP-166	Duke Ellington and John Coltrane	1997	$35
❏ GR-157	John Coltrane + Johnny Hartman	1995	$35
❏ IMP-213	Live at the Village Vanguard Again!	1997	$35
❏ IMP-169	Stellar Regions	1995	$35
❏ IMP-167	Sun Ship	1997	$35
❏ IMP-214	The John Coltrane Quartet Plays	1997	$35

IMPULSE!
❏ A-6 [M]	Africa/Brass	1961	$500
❏ AS-6 [S]	Africa/Brass	1961	$200
❏ A-77 [M]	A Love Supreme	1965	$200
❏ AS-77 [S]	A Love Supreme	1965	$300
❏ A-95 [M]	Ascension	1965	$300
— Without "Edition II" in dead wax
| ❏ A-95 [M] | Ascension | 1966 | $200 |
— With "Edition II" in dead wax
| ❏ AS-95 [S] | Ascension | 1965 | $180 |
— Without "Edition II" in dead wax
| ❏ AS-95 [S] | Ascension | 1966 | $200 |
— With "Edition II" in dead wax
❏ A-32 [M]	Ballads	1963	$160
❏ AS-32 [S]	Ballads	1963	$200
❏ A-21 [M]	Coltrane	1962	$160
❏ AS-21 [S]	Coltrane	1962	$200
❏ A-50 [M]	Coltrane Live at Birdland	1963	$160
❏ AS-50 [S]	Coltrane Live at Birdland	1963	$200
❏ SMAS-90232 [S]	Coltrane Live at Birdland	1964	$250
— Capitol Record Club edition
❏ A-66 [M]	Crescent	1964	$160
❏ AS-66 [S]	Crescent	1964	$200
❏ A-30 [M]	Duke Ellington and John Coltrane	1963	$200
❏ A-9120 [M]	Expression	1967	$200
❏ AS-9120 [S]	Expression	1967	$160
❏ SMAS-91288 [S]	Expression	1967	$300
— Capitol Record Club edition
| ❏ A-42 [M] | Impressions | 1963 | $200 |
| ❏ AS-42 [S] | Impressions | 1963 | $160 |

Number	Title	Yr	NM
❏ A-40 [M]	John Coltrane + Johnny Hartman	1963	$200
❏ AS-40 [S]	John Coltrane + Johnny Hartman	1963	$200
❏ A-9106 [M]	Kulu Se Mama	1966	$200
❏ AS-9106 [S]	Kulu Se Mama	1966	$200
❏ A-10 [M]	Live at the Village Vanguard	1962	$200
❏ AS-10 [S]	Live at the Village Vanguard	1962	$1200
❏ A-9124 [M]	Live at the Village Vanguard Again!	1967	$300
❏ AS-9124 [S]	Live at the Village Vanguard Again!	1967	$200
❏ A-9110 [M]	Meditations	1966	$160
❏ AS-9110 [S]	Meditations	1966	$200
❏ A-94 [M]	New Thing at Newport	1965	$200
❏ AS-94 [S]	New Thing at Newport	1965	$160
❏ A-85 [M]	The John Coltrane Quartet Plays	1965	$200
❏ AS-85 [S]	The John Coltrane Quartet Plays	1965	$160

MCA

Number	Title	Yr	NM
❏ 29007	Africa/Brass	1981	$20
❏ 29008	Africa/Brass, Volume 2	1981	$20
❏ 29017	A Love Supreme	1981	$20
❏ 29020	Ascension	1981	$20
❏ 29012	Ballads	1981	$20
❏ 29011	Coltrane	1981	$20
❏ 29015	Coltrane Live at Birdland	1981	$20
❏ 4135	Concert Japan	1981	$25
❏ 29025	Cosmic Music	1981	$20
❏ 29016	Crescent	1981	$20
❏ 29032	Duke Ellington and John Coltrane	1981	$20
❏ 29023	Expression	1981	$20
❏ 29030	First Meditations	1981	$20
❏ 4131	Greatest Years	1981	$25
❏ 4132	Greatest Years, Volume 2	1981	$25
❏ 4133	Greatest Years, Volume 3	1981	$25
❏ 29014	Impressions	1981	$20
❏ 29029	Interstellar Space	1981	$20
❏ 29013	John Coltrane + Johnny Hartman	1981	$20
❏ 29021	Kulu Se Mama	1981	$20
❏ 29009	Live at the Village Vanguard	1981	$20
❏ 29010	Live at the Village Vanguard Again!	1981	$20
❏ 4134	Live in Seattle	1981	$25
❏ 29022	Meditations	1981	$20
❏ 29019	New Thing at Newport	1981	$20
❏ 29024	Om	1981	$20
❏ 29026	Selflessness	1981	$20
❏ 29028	Sun Ship	1981	$20
❏ 4136	The Gentle Side of John Coltrane	1981	$25
❏ 29018	The John Coltrane Quartet Plays	1981	$20
❏ 4138	The Mastery of John Coltrane Vol. 1: Feelin' Good	1981	$25
❏ 4139	The Mastery of John Coltrane Vol. 2: Different Drum	1981	$25
❏ 29031	The Mastery of John Coltrane Vol. 3: Jupiter Variation	1981	$20
❏ 4140	The Mastery of John Coltrane Vol. 4: Trane's Moods	1981	$25
❏ 4137	The Other Village Vanguard Tapes	1981	$25
❏ 29027	Transition	1981	$20

MCA/IMPULSE!

Number	Title	Yr	NM
❏ 42231	Africa/Brass	1988	$25
❏ 5660	A Love Supreme	1986	$25
❏ 5885	Ballads	1987	$25
❏ 5883	Coltrane	1987	$25
❏ 33109	Coltrane Live at Birdland	198?	$25
❏ 5889	Crescent	1987	$25
❏ 39103	Duke Ellington and John Coltrane	1988	$25
❏ 5887	Impressions	1987	$25
❏ 5661	John Coltrane + Johnny Hartman	1986	$25
❏ 39136	Live at the Village Vanguard	1988	$25
❏ 39118	Om	1988	$25
❏ 33110	The John Coltrane Quartet Plays	198?	$25

PABLO

Number	Title	Yr	NM
❏ 2405417	The Best of John Coltrane	198?	$25

PABLO LIVE

Number	Title	Yr	NM
❏ 2620101	Afro Blue Impressions	198?	$30
❏ 2308227	Bye Bye Blackbird	1981	$30
❏ 2308222	European Tour	1981	$30
❏ 2308217	The Paris Concert	1980	$30

PRESTIGE

Number	Title	Yr	NM
❏ PRLP-7353 [M]	Bahia	1965	$60
❏ PRST-7353 [S]	Bahia	1965	$60
❏ 24110	Bahia	198?	$30
❏ PRLP-7316 [M]	Black Pearls	1964	$40

— Yellow label

Number	Title	Yr	NM
❏ PRST-7316 [S]	Black Pearls	1964	$40

— Silver label

Number	Title	Yr	NM
❏ PRLP-7316 [M]	Black Pearls	1964	$60

— Blue label with trident logo

Number	Title	Yr	NM
❏ PRST-7316 [S]	Black Pearls	1964	$60

— Blue label with trident logo

Number	Title	Yr	NM
❏ 24037	Black Pearls	1974	$35
❏ PRLP-7158 [M]	Cattin' with Coltrane and Quinichette	1959	$450

— Yellow label

Number	Title	Yr	NM
❏ PRLP-7105 [M]	Coltrane	1957	$1200

— Yellow label

Number	Title	Yr	NM
❏ PRLP-7105 [M]	Coltrane	1964	$60

— Blue label with trident logo

Number	Title	Yr	NM
❏ PRLP-7280 [M]	Dakar	1963	$40

— Yellow label

Number	Title	Yr	NM
❏ PRST-7280 [S]	Dakar	1963	$40

— Silver label

Number	Title	Yr	NM
❏ PRLP-7280 [M]	Dakar	1964	$60

— Blue label with trident logo

Number	Title	Yr	NM
❏ PRST-7280 [S]	Dakar	1964	$60

— Blue label with trident logo

Number	Title	Yr	NM
❏ 24104	Dakar	198?	$30
❏ 24003	John Coltrane	1972	$35
❏ PRLP-7123 [M]	John Coltrane and the Red Garland Trio	1957	$650

— Yellow label

Number	Title	Yr	NM
❏ PRLP-7426 [M]	John Coltrane Plays for Lovers	1966	$60
❏ PRST-7426 [S]	John Coltrane Plays for Lovers	1966	$60
❏ PRLP-7188 [M]	Lush Life	1960	$200

— Yellow label

Number	Title	Yr	NM
❏ PRLP-7188 [M]	Lush Life	1964	$60

— Blue label with trident logo

Number	Title	Yr	NM
❏ PRST-7581 [R]	Lush Life	1968	$30
❏ PRLP-7247 [M]	Mating Call	1962	$150

— Yellow label

Number	Title	Yr	NM
❏ PRST-7247 [R]	Mating Call	196?	$60

— Silver label

Number	Title	Yr	NM
❏ PRLP-7247 [M]	Mating Call	1964	$60

— Blue label with trident logo

Number	Title	Yr	NM
❏ PRST-7247 [R]	Mating Call	1964	$50

— Blue label with trident logo

Number	Title	Yr	NM
❏ PRST-7725	Mating Call	1970	$30
❏ 24014	More Lasting Than Bronze	1973	$35
❏ 24084	On a Misty Night	198?	$30
❏ 24094	Rain or Shine	198?	$30
❏ PRLP-7213 [M]	Settin' the Pace	1961	$200

— Yellow label

Number	Title	Yr	NM
❏ PRLP-7213 [M]	Settin' the Pace	1964	$60

— Blue label with trident logo

Number	Title	Yr	NM
❏ PRLP-7142 [M]	Soultrane	1958	$500

— Yellow label

Number	Title	Yr	NM
❏ PRLP-7531 [M]	Soultrane	1967	$60
❏ PRLP-7142 [M]	Soultrane	1964	$60

— Blue label with trident logo

Number	Title	Yr	NM
❏ PRST-7531 [R]	Soultrane	1967	$30
❏ PRLP-7243 [M]	Standard Coltrane	1962	$150

— Yellow label

Number	Title	Yr	NM
❏ PRST-7243 [S]	Standard Coltrane	1962	$150

— Silver label

Number	Title	Yr	NM
❏ PRLP-7243 [M]	Standard Coltrane	1964	$60

— Blue label with trident logo

Number	Title	Yr	NM
❏ PRST-7243 [S]	Standard Coltrane	1964	$60

— Blue label with trident logo

Number	Title	Yr	NM
❏ PRLP-7268 [M]	Stardust	1963	$40

— Yellow label

Number	Title	Yr	NM
❏ PRST-7268 [S]	Stardust	1963	$40

— Silver label

Number	Title	Yr	NM
❏ PRLP-7268 [M]	Stardust	1964	$60

— Blue label with trident logo

Number	Title	Yr	NM
❏ PRST-7268 [S]	Stardust	1964	$60

— Blue label with trident logo

Number	Title	Yr	NM
❏ PRLP-7249 [M]	Tenor Conclave	1962	$150

— Yellow label

Number	Title	Yr	NM
❏ PRST-7249 [R]	Tenor Conclave	196?	$60

— Silver label

Number	Title	Yr	NM
❏ PRLP-7249 [M]	Tenor Conclave	1964	$60

— Blue label with trident logo

Number	Title	Yr	NM
❏ PRST-7249 [R]	Tenor Conclave	1964	$50

— Blue label with trident logo

Number	Title	Yr	NM
❏ PRLP-7292 [M]	The Believer	1964	$40

— Yellow label

Number	Title	Yr	NM
❏ PRST-7292 [S]	The Believer	1964	$40

— Silver label

Number	Title	Yr	NM
❏ PRLP-7292 [M]	The Believer	1964	$60

— Blue label with trident logo

Number	Title	Yr	NM
❏ PRST-7292 [S]	The Believer	1964	$60

— Blue label with trident logo

Number	Title	Yr	NM
❏ PRST-7609 [R]	The First Trane	1969	$30
❏ PRLP-7378 [M]	The Last Trane	1965	$60
❏ PRST-7378 [S]	The Last Trane	1965	$60
❏ PRST-7825	The Master	1971	$30
❏ 24056	The Stardust Session	197?	$35
❏ PRLP-7123 [M]	Traneing In	1964	$60

— Blue label with trident logo; reissue with new title

Number	Title	Yr	NM
❏ PRST-7651 [R]	Traneing In	1969	$30
❏ PRST-7746	Trane's Reign	1970	$30
❏ PRST-7670 [R]	Two Tenors	1969	$30
❏ 24069	Wheelin'	197?	$30

RHINO

Number	Title	Yr	NM
❏ R1-75203	Giant Steps	2003	$35

— Reissue on 180-gram vinyl

SOLID STATE

Number	Title	Yr	NM
❏ SM-17025 [M]	Coltrane Time	1968	$60
❏ SS-18025 [S]	Coltrane Time	1968	$35

TRIP

Number	Title	Yr	NM
❏ 5001	Trane Tracks	1974	$35

UNITED ARTISTS

Number	Title	Yr	NM
❏ UAJ-14001 [M]	Coltrane Time	1962	$40
❏ UAJS-15001 [S]	Coltrane Time	1962	$100
❏ UAS-5638	Coltrane Time	1972	$30

— Reissue of 15001

COLUMBO, CHRIS

Drummer.

Albums

STRAND

Number	Title	Yr	NM
❏ SL-1044 [M]	Jazz Rediscovered	1962	$30
❏ SLS-1044 [S]	Jazz Rediscovered	1962	$40
❏ SL-1095 [M]	Summertime	1963	$30
❏ SLS-1095 [S]	Summertime	1963	$40

COLYER, KEN

British trumpeter, cornet player, guitarist, male singer and bandleader.

Albums

GHB

Number	Title	Yr	NM
❏ 161	Live at the 100 Club	198?	$25

LONDON

Number	Title	Yr	NM
❏ LL1340 [M]	Back to the Delta	1956	$40
❏ LL1618 [M]	Club Session with Colyer	1957	$40
❏ PB904 [10]	New Orleans to London	1954	$100

STORYVILLE

Number	Title	Yr	NM
❏ SLP-144	Ken's Early Days	197?	$30

COMMANDERS, THE

Led by Eddie Grady.

Albums

DECCA

Number	Title	Yr	NM
❏ DL8117 [M]	Dance Party	1955	$150

— Led by Eddie Grady

COMPOSER'S WORKSHOP ENSEMBLE, THE

Led by WARREN SMITH.

Albums

STRATA-EAST

Number	Title	Yr	NM
❏ 1972-3	The Composer's Workshop Ensemble	197?	$30
❏ 7422	(We've Been) Around	1974	$30

CON BRIO

Albums

PLUG

Number	Title	Yr	NM
❏ PLUG-4	Con Brio	1986	$30

CONCORD ALL STARS, THE

Collection of artists, all of whom are or were signed to the Concord Jazz label.

Albums

CONCORD JAZZ

Number	Title	Yr	NM
❏ CJ-348	Ow!	1988	$25
❏ CJ-347	Take 8	1988	$25

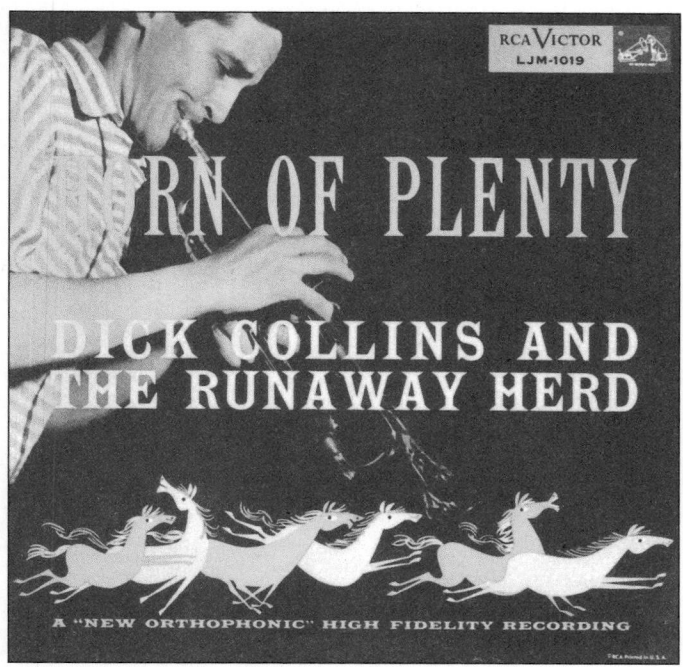

Dick Collins, *Horn of Plenty*, RCA Victor LJM-1019, **$100**.

John Coltrane, *Coltrane*, Prestige PRLP-7105, yellow label, **$1,200**.

John Coltrane, *The Last Trane*, Prestige PRLP-7378, **$60**.

John Coltrane with Tadd Dameron, *Mating Call*, Prestige PRLP-7247, yellow label, **$150**.

Number	Title	Yr	NM

CONCORD FESTIVAL ALL STARS, THE

Collection of artists, all of whom are or were signed to the Concord Jazz label.

Albums

CONCORD JAZZ
❏ CJ-366	20th Anniversary	1989	$30

CONCORD JAZZ ALL STARS, THE

Collection of artists, all of whom are or were signed to the Concord Jazz label.

Albums

CONCORD JAZZ
❏ CJ-182	The Concord Jazz All Stars at Northsea Jazz Festival	1982	$30
❏ CJ-205	The Concord Jazz All Stars at Northsea Jazz Festival, Vol. 2	1982	$30

CONCORD SUPER BAND, THE

Collection of artists, all of whom are or were signed to the Concord Jazz label.

Albums

CONCORD JAZZ
❏ CJ-120	CSB II	1980	$35
❏ CJ-80	The Concord Super Band in Tokyo	1979	$35

CONDON, EDDIE

Guitarist, banjo player, vocalist and bandleader. Also see SIDNEY BECHET.

Albums

ATLANTIC
❏ 90461	That Toddlin' Town: Chicago Jazz Revisited	1986	$25

CHIAROSCURO
❏ 154	Eddie Condon in Japan	1978	$30
❏ 108	Town Hall Concerts, Volume 1	197?	$30
❏ 113	Town Hall Concerts, Volume 2	197?	$30

COLUMBIA
❏ CL719 [M]	Bixieland	1955	$50
—Red and black label with six "eye" logos			
❏ CL632 [M]	Chicago Style Jazz	1955	$50
—Red and black label with six "eye" logos			
❏ CL881 [M]	Eddie Condon's Treasury of Jazz	1956	$40
—Red and black label with six "eye" logos			
❏ CL616 [M]	Jammin' at Condon's	1955	$60
—Maroon label, gold print			
❏ CL616 [M]	Jammin' at Condon's	1955	$50
—Red and black label with six "eye" logos			
❏ CL1089 [M]	The Roaring Twenties	1958	$40
—Red and black label with six "eye" logos			
❏ KG31564	The World of Eddie Condon	1972	$50
❏ PG31564	The World of Eddie Condon	197?	$35
—Reissue with new prefix			

COMMODORE
❏ XFL-16568	A Good Band Is Hard to Find	198?	$25
❏ FL20022 [M]	Ballin' the Jack	195?	$50
❏ FL30010 [M]	Condon A La Carte	195?	$60
❏ XFL-15355	The Liederkranz Sessions	198?	$25
❏ XFL-14427	Windy City Seven/Jam Sessions at Commodore	198?	$25

DECCA
❏ DL8281 [M]	A Night at Eddie Condon's	1956	$120
❏ DL5137 [10]	George Gershwin Jazz Concert	1950	$150
❏ DL9234 [M]	Gershwin Program (1941-1945)	1968	$30
❏ DL79234 [R]	Gershwin Program (1941-1945)	1968	$30
❏ DL8282 [M]	Ivy League Jazz	195?	$40
❏ DL5195 [10]	Jazz Band Ball (Volume 1)	1951	$200
❏ DL5203 [10]	Jazz Concert at Eddie Condon's	1951	$200
❏ DL5218 [10]	Jazz Concert at Eddie Condon's	1950	$150
❏ DL5246 [10]	We Call It Music	1951	$200

DESIGN
❏ DLP-47 [M]	Confidentially…It's Condon	196?	$30
❏ DLP-148 [M]	Eddie Condon & Dixieland All Stars	196?	$30

DOT
❏ DLP-3141 [M]	Dixieland Dance Party	1958	$80

EPIC
❏ LA16024 [M]	Midnight in Moscow	1962	$75
❏ BA17024 [S]	Midnight in Moscow	1962	$50

JAZZOLOGY
❏ J-101/2	1944 Jam Sessions	198?	$35
❏ JCE-10	Eddie Condon Concert	196?	$35
❏ J-50	Eddie Condon Jazz	197?	$35
❏ J-73	The Spirit of Condon	1979	$30
❏ JCE-1001/2	Town Hall Concerts, Volume 1	1988	$35
❏ JCE-1003/4	Town Hall Concerts, Volume 2	1988	$35
❏ JCE-1005/6	Town Hall Concerts, Volume 3	1988	$35
❏ JCE-1007/8	Town Hall Concerts, Volume 4	1990	$35
❏ JCE-1009/10	Town Hall Concerts, Volume 5	1990	$35
❏ JCE-1011/12	Town Hall Concerts, Volume 6	1990	$35
❏ JCE-1013/14	Town Hall Concerts, Volume 7	1992	$35

JAZZ PANORAMA
❏ 1805 [10]	Eddie Condon	1951	$40

JOLLY ROGER
❏ 5025 [10]	Eddie Condon	1954	$60
❏ 5018 [10]	Eddie Condon and His Orchestra Featuring Pee Wee Russell	1954	$60

MAINSTREAM
❏ 56024 [M]	Eddie Condon: A Legend	1965	$30
❏ S-6024 [R]	Eddie Condon: A Legend	1965	$35

MCA
❏ 4071	The Best of Eddie Condon	197?	$35
—Black rainbow labels			

MCA CORAL
❏ 20013	Sunny Day	198?	$25

MGM
❏ E-3651 [M]	Eddie Condon Is Uptown Now	1960	$30
❏ SE-3651 [S]	Eddie Condon Is Uptown Now	1960	$30

MOSAIC
❏ MQ7-152	The Complete CBS Recordings of Eddie Condon and His All-Stars	199?	$120

TRIP
❏ 5800	Eddie Condon and His Jazz Concert Orchestra	197?	$35

WARNER BROS.
❏ W1315 [M]	That Toddlin' Town	1959	$60
❏ WS1315 [S]	That Toddlin' Town	1959	$40

X
❏ LX-3005 [M]	Eddie Condon's Hot Shots	1954	$50

CONNELLY, PEGGY

Female singer.

Albums

BETHLEHEM
❏ BCP-53 [M]	That Old Black Magic	1957	$250

CONNICK, HARRY, JR.

Pianist, male singer and guitarist.

Albums

COLUMBIA
❏ FC44369	20	1988	$30
❏ C269794	30	2001	$35
❏ BFC40702	Harry Connick, Jr.	1987	$15
❏ C46223	Lofty's Roach Souffle	1990	$20
❏ C86077	Songs I Heard	2001	$20
❏ C46146	We Are in Love	1990	$20
❏ SC45319	When Harry Met Sally… (soundtrack)	1989	$30

CONNOR, CHRIS, AND MAYNARD FERGUSON

Also see each artist's individual listings.

Albums

ATLANTIC
❏ 8049 [M]	Double Exposure	1961	$150
—Multi-color label, white "fan" logo			
❏ 8049 [M]	Double Exposure	196?	$30
—Multi-color label, black "fan" logo			
❏ SD8049 [S]	Double Exposure	1961	$150
—Multi-color label, white "fan" logo			
❏ SD8049 [S]	Double Exposure	196?	$35
—Multi-color label, black "fan" logo			

❏ 90143	Double Exposure	198?	$25
—Reissue			

ROULETTE
❏ R52068 [M]	Two's Company	1961	$30
—White label with colored spokes			
❏ SR52068 [S]	Two's Company	1961	$40
—White label with colored spokes			

CONNOR, CHRIS

Female singer.

Albums

ABC
❏ ABC-585 [M]	Chris Connor Now	1966	$25
❏ ABCS-585 [S]	Chris Connor Now	1966	$30

ABC-PARAMOUNT
❏ ABC-529 [M]	Gentle Bossa Nova	1965	$25
❏ ABCS-529 [S]	Gentle Bossa Nova	1965	$30

APPLAUSE
❏ APLP-1020	Chris Connor Live	1982	$20

ATLANTIC
❏ 1286 [M]	A Jazz Date with Chris Connor	1958	$300
—Black label			
❏ 1286 [M]	A Jazz Date with Chris Connor	196?	$25
—Multi-color label, white "fan" logo			
❏ 1286 [M]	A Jazz Date with Chris Connor	196?	$30
—Multi-color label, black "fan" logo			
❏ 8046 [M]	A Portrait of Chris	1960	$250
—Multi-color label, white "fan" logo			
❏ 8046 [M]	A Portrait of Chris	196?	$30
—Multi-color label, black "fan" logo			
❏ SD8046 [S]	A Portrait of Chris	1960	$250
—Multi-color label, white "fan" logo			
❏ SD8046 [S]	A Portrait of Chris	196?	$35
—Multi-color label, black "fan" logo			
❏ 1307 [M]	Ballads of the Sad Café	1959	$300
—Black label			
❏ 1307 [M]	Ballads of the Sad Café	196?	$25
—Multi-color label, white "fan" logo			
❏ 1307 [M]	Ballads of the Sad Café	196?	$30
—Multi-color label, black "fan" logo			
❏ SD1307 [S]	Ballads of the Sad Café	1959	$300
—Green label			
❏ SD1307 [S]	Ballads of the Sad Café	196?	$30
—Multi-color label, white "fan" logo			
❏ SD1307 [S]	Ballads of the Sad Café	196?	$35
—Multi-color label, black "fan" logo			
❏ 1228 [M]	Chris Connor	1956	$300
—Black label			
❏ 1228 [M]	Chris Connor	196?	$25
—Multi-color label, white "fan" logo			
❏ 1228 [M]	Chris Connor	196?	$30
—Multi-color label, black "fan" logo			
❏ SD1228 [S]	Chris Connor	1958	$300
—Green label			
❏ SD1228 [S]	Chris Connor	196?	$30
—Multi-color label, white "fan" logo			
❏ SD1228 [S]	Chris Connor	196?	$35
—Multi-color label, black "fan" logo			
❏ 2-601 [M]	Chris Connor Sings the George Gershwin Almanac of Song	1957	$300
—Black label			
❏ 2-601 [M]	Chris Connor Sings the George Gershwin Almanac of Song	196?	$40
—Multi-color label, white "fan" logo			
❏ 2-601 [M]	Chris Connor Sings the George Gershwin Almanac of Song	196?	$25
—Multi-color label, black "fan" logo			
❏ 1309 [M]	Chris Connor Sings the George Gershwin Almanac of Song, Vol. 1	1959	$300
—Black label			
❏ 1309 [M]	Chris Connor Sings the George Gershwin Almanac of Song, Vol. 1	196?	$25
—Multi-color label, white "fan" logo			

Number	Title	Yr	NM
❏ 1309 [M]	Chris Connor Sings the George Gershwin Almanac of Song, Vol. 1	196?	$30
—Multi-color label, black "fan" logo			
❏ 1310 [M]	Chris Connor Sings the George Gershwin Almanac of Song, Vol. 2	1959	$300
—Black label			
❏ 1310 [M]	Chris Connor Sings the George Gershwin Almanac of Song, Vol. 2	196?	$25
—Multi-color label, white "fan" logo			
❏ 1310 [M]	Chris Connor Sings the George Gershwin Almanac of Song, Vol. 2	196?	$30
—Multi-color label, black "fan" logo			
❏ 1290 [M]	Chris Craft	1958	$300
—Black label			
❏ 1290 [M]	Chris Craft	196?	$25
—Multi-color label, white "fan" logo			
❏ 1290 [M]	Chris Craft	196?	$30
—Multi-color label, black "fan" logo			
❏ 8040 [M]	Chris In Person	1959	$300
—Black label			
❏ 8040 [M]	Chris In Person	196?	$25
—Multi-color label, white "fan" logo			
❏ 8040 [M]	Chris In Person	196?	$30
—Multi-color label, black "fan" logo			
❏ SD8040 [S]	Chris In Person	1959	$300
—Green label			
❏ SD8040 [S]	Chris In Person	196?	$30
—Multi-color label, white "fan" logo			
❏ SD8040 [S]	Chris In Person	196?	$35
—Multi-color label, black "fan" logo			
❏ 8061 [M]	Free Spirits	1962	$150
—Multi-color label, black "fan" logo			
❏ SD8061 [S]	Free Spirits	1962	$150
—Multi-color label, black "fan" logo			
❏ 1240 [M]	He Loves Me, He Loves Me Not	1956	$300
—Black label			
❏ 1240 [M]	He Loves Me, He Loves Me Not	196?	$25
—Multi-color label, white "fan" logo			
❏ 1240 [M]	He Loves Me, He Loves Me Not	196?	$30
—Multi-color label, black "fan" logo			
❏ SD1240 [S]	He Loves Me, He Loves Me Not	1958	$300
—Green label			
❏ SD1240 [S]	He Loves Me, He Loves Me Not	196?	$30
—Multi-color label, white "fan" logo			
❏ SD1240 [S]	He Loves Me, He Loves Me Not	196?	$35
—Multi-color label, black "fan" logo			
❏ 1240 [M]	He Loves Me, He Loves Me Not	1960	$250
—White "bullseye" label			
❏ SD1240 [S]	He Loves Me, He Loves Me Not	1960	$250
—White "bullseye" label			
❏ 8014 [M]	I Miss You So	1957	$300
—Black label			
❏ 8014 [M]	I Miss You So	196?	$25
—Multi-color label, white "fan" logo			
❏ 8014 [M]	I Miss You So	196?	$30
—Multi-color label, black "fan" logo			
❏ 8014 [M]	I Miss You So	1960	$250
—White "bullseye" label			
❏ 8032 [M]	Witchcraft	1959	$300
—Black label			
❏ 8032 [M]	Witchcraft	196?	$50
—Multi-color label, white "fan" logo			
❏ 8032 [M]	Witchcraft	196?	$30
❏ SD8032 [S]	Witchcraft	1959	$300
—Green label			
❏ SD8032 [S]	Witchcraft	196?	$60
—Multi-color label, white "fan" logo			
❏ SD8032 [S]	Witchcraft	196?	$35
—Multi-color label, black "fan" logo			
❏ 8032 [M]	Witchcraft	1960	$250
—White "bullseye" label			

AUDIOPHILE

Number	Title	Yr	NM
❏ AP-208	Sweet and Swinging	199?	$35

BAINBRIDGE

| ❏ 6230 | Sketches | 198? | $25 |
| *—Reissue of Stanyan 10029* | | | |

BETHLEHEM

❏ BCP-56 [M]	Chris	1957	$250
❏ BCP-1002 [10]	Chris Connor Sings Lullabys for Lovers	1954	$250
❏ BCP-1001 [10]	Chris Connor Sings Lullabys of Birdland	1954	$250
❏ BCP-6004 [M]	Chris Connor Sings Lullabys of Birdland	1955	$250
❏ BCP-6004 [M]	Chris Connor Sings Lullabys of Birdland	1984	$15
—Reissue			
❏ BCP-6010	Cocktails and Dusk	197?	$30
❏ 2BP-1001	The Finest	197?	$35
❏ BCP-20 [M]	This Is Chris	1955	$250

CLARION

❏ 611 [M]	Chris Connor Sings George Gershwin	1966	$20
—Abbreviated version of Atlantic 2-601			
❏ SD611 [R]	Chris Connor Sings George Gershwin	1966	$12

CONTEMPORARY

| ❏ C-14023 | Classic | 1987 | $30 |
| ❏ C-14038 | New Again | 1988 | $30 |

FM

❏ 312 [M]	A Weekend in Paris	1964	$50
❏ S-312 [S]	A Weekend in Paris	1964	$60
❏ 300 [M]	Chris Connor at the Village Gate	1963	$50
❏ S-300 [S]	Chris Connor at the Village Gate	1963	$60

PROGRESSIVE

| ❏ 7028 | Sweet and Singing | 1979 | $30 |

STANYAN

| ❏ 10029 | Sketches | 1972 | $35 |

STASH

| ❏ 232 | Love Being Here with You | 1984 | $30 |

CONNORS, BILL
Guitarist.

Albums

ECM

Number	Title	Yr	NM
❏ 1120	Of Mist and Melting	1977	$35
❏ 1158	Swimming with a Hole in My Body	1979	$30
❏ 1057	Theme to the Gaurdian	197?	$35

PATHFINDER

❏ PTF-8707	Assembler	1987	$25
❏ PTF-8620	Double Up	1986	$25
❏ PTF-8503	Step It	1985	$25

CONNORS, NORMAN
Drummer and bandleader.

Albums

ACCORD

Number	Title	Yr	NM
❏ SN-7210	Just Imagine	1982	$20

ARISTA

❏ AB4216	Invitation	1979	$25
❏ AL9575	Mr. C.	1981	$25
❏ AL9534	Take It to the Limit	1980	$25
❏ AB4177	This Is Your Life	1978	$25

BUDDAH

❏ BDS-5674	Dance of Magic	1977	$50
—Reissue of Cobblestone 9024			
❏ BDS-5675	Dark of Light	1977	$50
—Reissue of Cobblestone 9035			
❏ BDS-5142	Love from the Sun	1973	$30
❏ BDS-5682	Romantic Journey	1977	$25
❏ BDS-5643	Saturday Night Special	1975	$25
❏ BDS-5611	Slewfoot	1974	$30
❏ BDS-5716	The Best of Norman Connors & Friends	1978	$25
❏ BDS-5655	You Are My Starship	1976	$25

CAPITOL

| ❏ C1-48515 | Passion | 1988 | $25 |

COBBLESTONE

| ❏ 9024 | Dance of Magic | 1972 | $60 |
| ❏ 9035 | Dark of Light | 1973 | $60 |

CONTEMPORARY JAZZ ENSEMBLE, THE

Albums

PRESTIGE

Number	Title	Yr	NM
❏ PRLP-163 [10]	New Sounds from Rochester	1953	$350

CONTI, ROBERT
Guitarist. Also see JOE PASS.

Albums

DISCOVERY

| ❏ 834 | Robert Conti Jazz Quintet | 1981 | $30 |

TREND

❏ TR-540	Laura	1986	$30
❏ TR-519	Solo Guitar	198?	$25
—Direct-to-disc recording			

CONTINENTAL OCTETTE, THE

Albums

CROWN

| ❏ CLP-5220 [M] | Modern Jazz Greats | 196? | $25 |

COOK, JUNIOR
Tenor saxophone player.

Albums

MUSE

| ❏ MR-5159 | Good Cookin' | 1979 | $30 |
| ❏ MR-5218 | Something's Cookin' | 1981 | $30 |

COOL BRITONS, THE
Also see THE SWINGING SWEDES.

Albums

BLUE NOTE

| ❏ BLP-5052 [10] | New Sounds from Olde England | 1954 | $300 |

COON, JACKIE
Cornet and fluegel horn player.

Albums

SEA BREEZE

| ❏ SB-1009 | Jazzin' Around | 1987 | $25 |

COOPER, BOB
Tenor saxophone player and composer. Also played oboe.

Albums

CAPITOL

❏ H6501 [10]	Bob Cooper	1954	$150
❏ T6501 [M]	Bob Cooper	1955	$80
❏ T1586 [M]	Do Re Mi	1961	$60
❏ ST1586 [S]	Do Re Mi	1961	$60
❏ H6513 [10]	Shifting Winds	1955	$100
❏ T6513 [M]	Shifting Winds	1955	$80

CONTEMPORARY

❏ C-3544 [M]	Coop!	1958	$250
❏ S-7012 [S]	Coop!	1959	$250
—Reissue of Stereo Records 7012			
❏ C-14017	In a Mellotone	1986	$25

DISCOVERY

| ❏ 822 | Bob Cooper Plays the Music of Michel Legrand | 1981 | $30 |

FANTASY

| ❏ OJC-161 | Coop! | 198? | $25 |

STEREO RECORDS

| ❏ S-7012 [S] | Coop! | 1958 | $50 |

TREND

| ❏ TR-518 | Tenor Sax Impressions | 198? | $25 |
| *—Direct-to-disc recording* | | | |

WORLD PACIFIC

| ❏ WPM-411 [M] | Bob Cooper Swings TV | 1958 | $150 |

COOPER, JEROME
Drummer.

Albums

ABOUT TIME

| ❏ 1008 | Outer and Interactions | 1988 | $25 |
| ❏ 1002 | The Unpredictability of Predictability | 1979 | $25 |

HAT HUT

| ❏ 07 | For the People | 1980 | $30 |

Number	Title	Yr	NM

CORBIN, HAROLD

Albums

ROULETTE
❏ R-52079 [M]	Soul Brother	1961	$30
❏ SR-52079 [S]	Soul Brother	1961	$30

CORCORAN, CORKY
Tenor saxophone player.

Albums

C.C. PRODUCTION
❏ 4012 [M]	Corky Corcoran Plays Everywhere	1974	$15

CELESTIAL
❏ Vol.1 [M]	Sounds of Jazz	1958	$300
— Red vinyl			
❏ Vol.1 [M]	Sounds of Jazz	1958	$200
— Black vinyl			

EPIC
❏ LN3319 [M]	The Sound of Love	1956	$150

RCS
❏ 2555 [M]	Corky Corcoran Plays Something	197?	$30

COREA, CHICK, AND LIONEL HAMPTON
Also see each artist's individual listings.

Albums

WHO'S WHO IN JAZZ
❏ WWLP21016	Live at Midem	1980	$35

COREA, CHICK; HERBIE HANCOCK; KEITH JARRETT; MCCOY TYNER
Also see each artist's individual listings.

Albums

ATLANTIC
❏ SD1696	Corea/Hancock/Jarrett/Tyner	1976	$30

COREA, CHICK
Pianist, keyboard and synthesizer player, composer and bandleader. Also see CIRCLE; RETURN TO FOREVER.

Albums

51 WEST
❏ Q16078	Jazzman	1979	$35

ATLANTIC
❏ SD 2-305	Inner Space	1973	$35

BLUE NOTE
❏ BN-LA395-H2[(2)]	Chick Corea	1975	$35
— The Blue Note Reissue Series" labels			
❏ LWB-395	Chick Corea	1981	$25
— Reissue with new prefix			
❏ BN-LA472-H2[(2)]	Circling In	1976	$50
— The Blue Note Reissue Series" labels			
❏ BN-LA882-4047	Circulus	1978	$50
❏ B1-90055	Now He Sings, Now He Sobs	1988	$30
— Reissue; "The Finest in Jazz Since 1939" on label			
❏ BST-84353	Song of Singing	1970	$40
— A Division of Liberty Records" on label			
❏ BST-84353	Song of Singing	1984	$50
— Reissue, "The Finest in Jazz Since 1939" on label			

ECM
❏ 1009ST	A.R.C.	197?	$35
— Original issue, made in Germany?			
❏ ECM1-1009	A.R.C.	1977	$30
— Distributed by Polydor			
❏ 25005	Children's Songs	1984	$25
— Distributed by Warner Bros.			
❏ 1267	Children's Songs	1984	$30
— Made in Germany			
❏ 1014ST	Piano Improvisations, Vol. 1	1974	$35
— Original edition; made in Germany?			
❏ ECM-1-1014	Piano Improvisations, Vol. 1	1977	$30
— Distributed by Polydor			
❏ 1020ST	Piano Improvisations, Vol. 2	197?	$35
— Original edition; made in Germany?			
❏ ECM1-1020	Piano Improvisations, Vol. 2	1977	$30
— Distributed by Polydor			
❏ 25035	Septet	1985	$25
— Distributed by Warner Bros.			

❏ 1297	Septet	1985	$30
— Made in Germany			
❏ 1232	Trio Music	198?	$30
❏ 25013	Voyage	1985	$25
— Distributed by Warner Bros.			
❏ 1282	Voyage	1985	$30
— Made in Germany			

ELEKTRA/MUSICIAN
❏ 60167	Again & Again	1984	$25

GROOVE MERCHANT
❏ 4406	Piano Giants	197?	$50
❏ 2202	Sundance	1972	$60
❏ GM530	Sundance	1974	$35
— Reissue of 2202			

GRP
❏ GR-1053	Eye of the Beholder	1988	$25
❏ GR-9601	Inside Out	1991	$35
❏ GR-1036	Light Years	1987	$25
❏ GR-9582	The Chick Corea Akoustic Band	1989	$30
❏ GRP-A-1026	The Chick Corea Elektric Band	1987	$25

MUSE
❏ MR5011	Bliss!	1973	$50

PACIFIC JAZZ
❏ LN-10057	Now He Sings, Now He Sobs	1981	$25
— Reissue of Solid State 18039			

POLYDOR
❏ PD-1-6208	Delphi I	1979	$25
❏ PD-2-6334	Delphi II & III	1982	$35
❏ PD-1-6160	Friends	1978	$25
❏ PD-2-9003	My Spanish Heart	1976	$35
❏ PD-1-6176	Secret Agent	1979	$25
❏ PD-6062	The Leprechaun	1976	$25
❏ PD-1-6130	The Mad Hatter	1978	$25

QUINTESSENCE
❏ QJ-25011	Before Forever	1978	$30

SOLID STATE
❏ SS-18055	Chick Corea "Is	1969	$50
❏ SS-18039	Now He Sings, Now He Sobs	1969	$50

VORTEX
❏ 2004	Tones for Joan's Bones	1971	$60

WARNER BROS.
❏ BSK3425	Tap Step	1980	$25
❏ BSK3552	Three Quartets	1981	$25
❏ 23699	Touchstone	1983	$25

COREY, JILL

Albums

COLUMBIA
❏ CL1095 [M]	Sometimes I'm Happy, Sometimes I'm Blue	1957	$60

CORWIN, BOB
Pianist.

Albums

RIVERSIDE
❏ RLP 12-220 [M]	Bob Corwin Quartet with Don Elliott	1956	$250
— White label, blue print			
❏ RLP 12-220 [M]	Bob Corwin Quartet with Don Elliott	1957	$250
— Blue label with microphone logo			

CORYELL, LARRY, AND ALPHONSE MOUZON
Also see each artist's individual listings.

Albums

ATLANTIC
❏ SD18220	Back Together Again	1977	$30

CORYELL, LARRY, AND BRIAN KEANE
Also see each artist's individual listings.

Albums

FLYING FISH
❏ FF-337	Just Like Being Born	1985	$30

CORYELL, LARRY, AND PHILIP CATHERINE
Also see each artist's individual listings.

Albums

ELEKTRA
❏ 6E-153	Splendid	1978	$30
❏ 6E-123	Twin House	1977	$30

CORYELL, LARRY, AND STEVE KAHN
Also see each artist's individual listings.

Albums

ARISTA
❏ AB4156	Two for the Road	1978	$30

CORYELL, LARRY
Guitarist. Also see JAZZ COMPOSERS ORCHESTRA.

Albums

ARISTA
❏ AL4077	Aspects	1976	$35
❏ AL4052	Level One	1975	$35
❏ AL4108	The Lion and the Ram	1977	$35

ARISTA/NOVUS
❏ AN3005	European Imperssions	1978	$30
❏ AN3017	Tributaries	1979	$30

CONCORD JAZZ
❏ CJ-289	Together	1986	$25

FLYING DUTCHMAN
❏ FD-10139	Barefoot Boy	1971	$35
❏ 51-1000	Fairyland	1971	$25

MEGA
❏ 607	Fairyland	197?	$35
— Reissue of Flying Dutchman 51-1000			

MUSE
❏ MR-5303	Comin' Home	1985	$25
❏ MR-5319	Equipoise	1986	$25
❏ MR-5350	Toku Do	1988	$30

RCA VICTOR
❏ AYL1-3961	Barefoot Boy	198?	$20
— Reissue of Flying Dutchman 10139			

SHANACHIE
❏ 97005	The Dragon Gate	1990	$35

STEEPLECHASE
❏ SCS-1187	A Quiet Day in Spring	1983	$25

VANGUARD
❏ VSD-79360	Another Side of Larry Coryell	1975	$35
❏ VSD-79375	Basics	1976	$30
❏ VSD-6547	Coryell	1969	$60
❏ VSD-79342	Introducing the Eleventh House	1974	$35
❏ VSQ-40036 [Q]	Introducing the Eleventh House	1974	$30
❏ VSD-6509	Lady Coryell	1969	$40
❏ VSD-79410	Larry Coryell and the Eleventh House at Montreux	1978	$30
❏ VSD-6573	Larry Coryell at the Village Gate	1971	$35
❏ VSQ-40006 [Q]	Larry Coryell at the Village Gate	197?	$30
❏ VSD-79319	Offering	1972	$35
❏ VSQ-40013 [Q]	Offering	197?	$30
❏ VSD-79367	Planet End	1975	$30
❏ VSD-79426	Return	1979	$30
❏ VSD-6558	Spaces	1970	$35
❏ VSD-79345	Spaces	1974	$30
— Reissue of 6558 with new cover			
❏ VSD-75/76	The Essential Larry Coryell	1975	$35
❏ VSD-79329	The Real Great Escape	1973	$35
❏ VSQ-40023 [Q]	The Real Great Escape	197?	$30
❏ VSD-79353	The Restful Mind	1975	$30

COSMIC, MICHAEL

Albums

COSMIC RECORDS
❏ 85 [B]	Peace In The World		$2000
— handmade cover			

COSMIC TWINS, THE
Ron Burton and John Lewis.

Albums

STRATA-EAST
❏ SES-7410	The Waterbearers	1974	$30

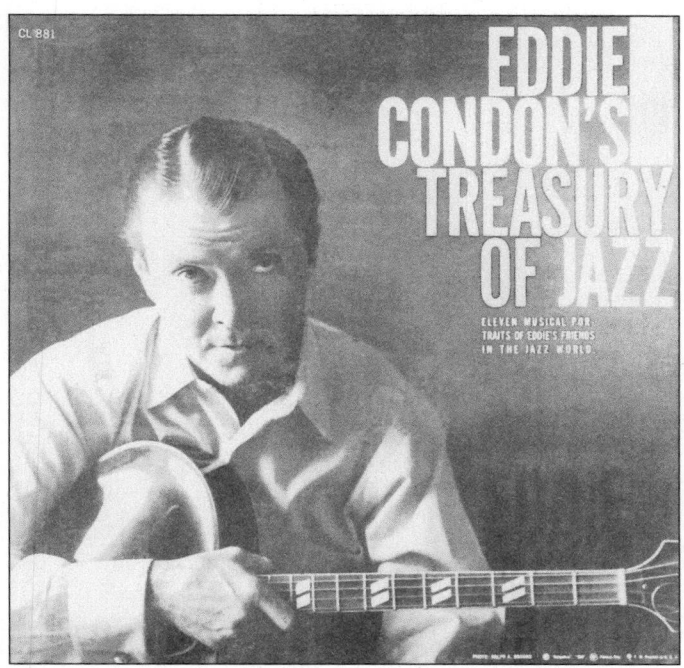

Eddie Condon, *Eddie Condon's Treasury of Jazz*, Columbia CL 881, **$40**.

Eddie Condon, *A Night at Eddie Condon's*, Decca DL 8281, **$120**.

Eddie Condon, *Eddie Condon & Dixieland All Stars*, Design DLP-148, **$30**.

Corky Corcoran, *Sounds of Jazz*, Celestial Vol. 1, black vinyl, **$200**.

Number	Title	Yr	NM

COSTA, EDDIE, AND ART FARMER
Also see each artist's individual listings.

Albums

PREMIER
| ❑ PM-2002 [M] | In Their Own Sweet Way | 1962 | $50 |
| ❑ PMS-2002 [R] | In Their Own Sweet Way | 196? | $30 |

COSTA, EDDIE
Vibraphone player and pianist. Also see THE MANHATTAN JAZZ SEPTETTE; JOHN MEHEGAN.

Albums

CORAL
| ❑ CRL57230 [M] | Guys and Dolls Like Vibes | 1958 | $200 |

DOT
| ❑ DLP-3206 [M] | The House of Blue Lights | 1959 | $600 |
| ❑ DLP-25206 [S] | The House of Blue Lights | 1959 | $500 |

INTERLUDE
❑ MO-508 [M]	Eddie Costa Quintet	1959	$100
—Reissue of Mode 118			
❑ ST-1008 [S]	Eddie Costa Quintet	1959	$60

JOSIE
| ❑ JOZ-3509 [M] | Eddie Costa with the Burke Trio | 1963 | $25 |
| ❑ JSS-2509 [S] | Eddie Costa with the Burke Trio | 1963 | $30 |

JUBILEE
| ❑ JLP-1025 [M] | Eddie Costa Quintet with the Vinnie Burke Trio | 1956 | $60 |

MODE
| ❑ LP-118 [M] | Eddie Costa Quintet | 1957 | $250 |

COSTA, EDDIE/MAT MATTHEWS AND DON ELLIOTT
Also see each artist's individual listings.

Albums

VERVE
| ❑ MGV-8237 [M] | Eddie Costa with Rolf Kuhn and Dick Johnson/Mat Matthews and Don Elliott at Newport | 1958 | $150 |
| ❑ V-8237 [M] | Eddie Costa with Rolf Kuhn and Dick Johnson/Mat Matthews and Don Elliott at Newport | 1961 | $30 |

COSTA, JOHNNY
Pianist and composer.

Albums

CORAL
| ❑ CRL57117 [M] | The Most Beautiful Girl in the World | 1957 | $30 |

SAVOY
| ❑ MG-15056 [10] | Johnny Costa | 1955 | $80 |
| ❑ MG-12052 [M] | The Amazing Johnny Costa | 1956 | $50 |

SAVOY JAZZ
| ❑ SJL-1190 | Neighborhood | 198? | $25 |

COSTANZO, JACK
Bongo player.

Albums

GENE NORMAN
| ❑ GNP-19 [M] | Mr. Bongo | 1955 | $60 |

LIBERTY
❑ LRP-3137 [M]	Afro Can-Can	1960	$30
❑ LST-7137 [S]	Afro Can-Can	1960	$30
❑ LRP-3109 [M]	Bongo Fever	1959	$30
❑ LST-7109 [S]	Bongo Fever	1959	$30
❑ LRP-3093 [M]	Latin Fever	1958	$30
❑ LST-7020 [S]	Latin Fever	1958	$30
❑ LRP-3177 [M]	Learn-Play Bongos	1960	$30
❑ LRP-3195 [M]	Naked City	1961	$30
❑ LST-7195 [S]	Naked City	1961	$30

NORGRAN
| ❑ MGN-32 [10] | Afro-Cubano | 1954 | $300 |

SUNSET
| ❑ SUM-1134 [M] | Bongo Fever | 196? | $30 |
| ❑ SUS-5134 [S] | Bongo Fever | 196? | $30 |

COSTANZO, JACK/ANDRE'S CUBAN ALL STARS
Also see each artist's individual listings.

Albums

NORGRAN

Number	Title	Yr	NM
❑ MGN-1067 [M]	Afro-Cubano	1956	$350

—Combined reissue of Norgran 32 (by the former) and Clef 515 (by the latter)

VERVE
| ❑ MGV-8157 [M] | Afro-Cubano | 1957 | $200 |
| ❑ V-8157 [M] | Afro-Cubano | 1961 | $60 |

COTTRELL, LOUIS
Clarinetist and saxophone player.

Albums

NOBILITY
| ❑ LP-703 | Dixieland Hall Presents Louis Cottrell and His New Orleans Jazz | 197? | $35 |

RIVERSIDE
| ❑ RLP-385 [M] | Bourbon Street | 1961 | $200 |
| ❑ RS-9385 [S] | Bourbon Street | 1961 | $200 |

COTTRELL, LOUIS/'HERB HALL
Hall played clarinet and saxophone. Also see LOUIS COTTRELL.

Albums

GHB
| ❑ 156 | Clarinet Legends | 198? | $25 |

COULTER, CLIFF
Pianist (mostly electric).

Albums

ABC IMPULSE!
| ❑ AS-9216 | Do It Now! | 1972 | $200 |
| ❑ AS-9197 | Eastside San Jose | 1971 | $200 |

COUNCE, CURTIS
Bass player.

Albums

ANALOGUE PRODUCTIONS
| ❑ AP-3006 | You Get More Bounce with Curtis Counce | 199? | $35 |

BOPLICITY
| ❑ BOP-7 | Exploring the Future | 198? | $30 |
| —Reissue of Dooto LP | | | |

CONTEMPORARY
❑ C-7539	Counceltation	197?	$25
—Retitled version of "You Get More Bounce with Curtis Counce			
❑ S-7526 [S]	Curtis Counce Group	1959	$250
❑ S-7526 [S]	Landslide	196?	$30
—Retitled version of "Curtis Counce Group			
❑ C-7655	Sonority	198?	$25
❑ M-3539 [M]	You Get More Bounce with Curtis Counce	1957	$250
❑ S-7539 [S]	You Get More Bounce with Curtis Counce	1959	$250

DOOTO
| ❑ DTL-247 [M] | Exploring the Future | 1958 | $50 |

FANTASY
❑ OJC-423	Carl's Blues	1990	$30
—Reissue of Contemporary 7574			
❑ OJC-159	You Get More Bounce with Curtis Counce	198?	$25
—Reissue of Contemporary 7539			

COWELL, STANLEY
Pianist.

Albums

ARISTA FREEDOM
| ❑ AL1009 | Beautiful Circles | 197? | $30 |
| ❑ AL1032 | Blues for the Viet Cong | 197? | $30 |

ECM
| ❑ 1026 | Illusion Suite | 1973 | $30 |

GALAXY
❑ 5125	Equipoise	1979	$30
❑ 5131	New World	1979	$30
❑ 5111	Talkin' Bout Love	1978	$30
❑ 5104	Waiting for ...	1977	$30

STRATA-EAST
| ❑ SES-19743 | Musa-Ancestral Streams | 1974 | $25 |
| ❑ SES-19765 | Regeneration | 1976 | $25 |

Number	Title	Yr	NM

COX, IDA
Female singer.

Albums

FANTASY
| ❑ OJC-1758 | Blues for Rampart Street | 198? | $35 |
| —Reissue of Riverside 9374 | | | |

RIVERSIDE
| ❑ RLP-374 [M] | Blues for Rampart Street | 1961 | $200 |
| ❑ RS-9374 [S] | Blues for Rampart Street | 1961 | $200 |

COX, KENNY, CONTEMPORARY JAZZ QUINTET
Cox is a pianist.

Albums

BLUE NOTE
| ❑ BST-84302 | Introducing Kenny Cox | 1969 | $75 |
| ❑ BST-84339 | Multidirection | 1970 | $75 |

COX, SONNY

Albums

CADET
| ❑ LP-765 [M] | The Wailer | 1966 | $35 |
| ❑ LPS-765 [S] | The Wailer | 1966 | $25 |

CRAM, PAUL
Tenor saxophone player, composer and arranger.

Albums

ONARI/A&M
| ❑ 06 | Blue Tales in Time | 1982 | $30 |

CRAWFORD, HANK, AND JIMMY MCGRIFF
Also see each artist's individual listings.

Albums

MILESTONE
❑ M-9177	On the Blue Side	1990	$30
❑ M-9142	Soul Survivors	1986	$25
❑ M-9153	Steppin' Up	1988	$25

CRAWFORD, HANK
Saxophone player (tenor, alto and baritone), pianist and composer.

Albums

ATLANTIC
❑ 1455 [M]	After Hours	1966	$35
❑ SD1455 [S]	After Hours	1966	$50
❑ 1436 [M]	Dig These Blues	1965	$35
❑ SD1436 [S]	Dig These Blues	1965	$50
❑ SD1503	Double Cross	1968	$60
❑ 1387 [M]	From the Heart	1962	$150
❑ SD1387 [S]	From the Heart	1962	$150
❑ 1356 [M]	More Soul	1960	$250
—Purple and red label, white fan logo			
❑ SD1356 [S]	More Soul	1960	$250
—Green and blue label, white fan logo			
❑ 1356 [M]	More Soul	1962	$150
—Purple and red label, black fan logo			
❑ SD1356 [S]	More Soul	1962	$150
—Green and blue label, black fan logo			
❑ 1470 [M]	Mr. Blues	1967	$50
❑ SD1470 [S]	Mr. Blues	1967	$35
❑ SD1523	Mr. Blues Plays Lady Soul	1969	$35
❑ 1405 [M]	Soul of the Ballad	1963	$35
❑ SD1405 [S]	Soul of the Ballad	1963	$50
❑ SD 2-315	The Art of Hank Crawford	1973	$35
❑ SD1557	The Best of Hank Crawford	1970	$35
❑ 1372 [M]	The Soul Clinic	1961	$150
—Purple and red label, white fan logo			
❑ SD1372 [S]	The Soul Clinic	1961	$150
—Green and blue label, white fan logo			
❑ 1372 [M]	The Soul Clinic	1962	$150
—Purple and red label, black fan logo			
❑ SD1372 [S]	The Soul Clinic	1962	$150
—Green and blue label, black fan logo			
❑ 1423 [M]	True Blue	1964	$35
❑ SD1423 [S]	True Blue	1964	$50

COTILLION
| ❑ SD18003 | It's a Funky Thing to Do | 1971 | $50 |

KUDU
❑ KU-39	Cajun Sunrise	1979	$35
❑ KU-19	Don't You Worry 'Bout a Thing	1975	$50
❑ KU-33	Hank Crawford's Back	1977	$35

Number	Title	Yr	NM
❏ KU-06	Help Me Make It Through the Night	1972	$50
❏ KU-26	I Hear a Symphony	1976	$50
❏ KU-35	Tico Rico	1977	$35
❏ KU-08	We've Got a Good Thing	1973	$50
❏ KU-15	Wildflower	1974	$50

MILESTONE

❏ M-9129	Down on the Deuce	1985	$25
❏ M-9182	Groove Master	1990	$30
❏ M-9119	Indigo Blue	1984	$25
❏ M-9112	Midnight Ramble	1983	$25
❏ M-9149	Mr. Chips	1987	$25
❏ M-9168	Night Beat	1988	$25
❏ M-9140	Roadhouse Symphony	1986	$25

MOBILE FIDELITY

❏ 1-224	Soul of the Ballad	1995	$60

— Audiophile vinyl

CRAWFORD, RAY
Guitarist.

Albums

CANDID

❏ CJM-8028 [M]	Smooth Groove	1963	$30
❏ CJS-9028 [S]	Smooth Groove	1963	$30

DOBRE

❏ 1021	One Step at a Time	1978	$30

CREATIVE CONSTRUCTION COMPANY
ANTHONY BRAXTON, LEO SMITH, LEROY JENKINS and Steve McCall.

Albums

MUSE

❏ MR-5071	Volume 1	1975	$35
❏ MR-5097	Volume 2	1976	$35

CREEKMORE, TOM

Albums

DISCOVERY

❏ DS-791	She Is It	198?	$25

CREQUE, NEAL
Keyboard player (electric piano and organ).

Albums

COBBLESTONE

❏ 9023	Contrast!	1972	$30
❏ 9005	Creque	1971	$35

MUSE

❏ MR-5226	Black Velvet Rose	1980	$25
❏ MR-5029	Neal Creque and the Hands of Time	1973	$30

CREVELING, CAROLE

Albums

EUTERPE

❏ ETP-101 [M]	Carole Creveling	1955	$60

CRINER, CLYDE
Pianist and synthesizer player.

Albums

NOVUS

❏ 3029-1-N	Behind the Sun	1988	$25
❏ 3066-1-N	The Color of Dark	1989	$30

TERRA

❏ T-4	New England	1985	$30

CRISPELL, MARILYN
Pianist.

Albums

BLACK SAINT

❏ BSR-0069	Live in Berlin	1984	$30
❏ 120069	Live in Berlin	198?	$25

— Reissue of 0069

CADENCE JAZZ

❏ CJR-1015	Spirit Music	1983	$25

CRISS, SONNY, AND KENNY DORHAM
Also see each artist's individual listings.

Albums

ABC IMPULSE!

❏ IA-9337	Bopmasters	197?	$200

MCA

❏ 4141	Bopmasters	198?	$30

— Reissue of ABC Impulse! 9337

CRISS, SONNY
Alto saxophone player.

Albums

ABC IMPULSE!

❏ AS-9326	The Joy of Sax	197?	$35
❏ AS-9312	Warm and Sonny	197?	$35

CLEF

❏ MGC-122 [10]	Sonny Criss Collates	1953	$350

FANTASY

❏ OJC-655	Portrait of Sonny Criss	1991	$30

— Reissue of Prestige 7526

❏ OJC-430	This Is Sonny Criss!	1990	$30

— Reissue of Prestige 7511

IMPERIAL

❏ LP-12205 [R]	Criss Cross	1963	$150
❏ LP-9006 [M]	Jazz U.S.A.	1956	$250

MERCURY

❏ MGC-122 [10]	Sonny Criss Collates	1953	$0

— Cover exists, but all known copies contain Clef labels

MUSE

❏ MR-5068	Crisscraft	1975	$35
❏ MR-5089	Out of Nowhere	1976	$35

PABLO

❏ 2310929	Intermission Riff	1988	$25

PRESTIGE

❏ PRST-7742	Hits of the 60s	1970	$35
❏ PRST-7628	I'll Catch the Sun	1969	$25
❏ PRLP-7526 [M]	Portrait of Sonny Criss	1967	$30
❏ PRST-7526 [S]	Portrait of Sonny Criss	1967	$30
❏ PRST-7610	Rockin' in Rhythm	1969	$25
❏ PRST-7576	Sonny's Dream	1968	$25
❏ PRST-7558	The Beat Goes On	1968	$25
❏ PRLP-7511 [M]	This Is Sonny Criss!	1966	$30
❏ PRST-7511 [S]	This Is Sonny Criss!	1966	$30
❏ PRLP-7530 [M]	Up, Up and Away	1967	$40
❏ PRST-7530 [S]	Up, Up and Away	1967	$30

XANADU

❏ 200	Memorial Album	198?	$25
❏ 105	Saturday Morning	197?	$35

CROOK, HAL
Trombone player.

Albums

OMNISOUND

❏ 1039	Hello Heaven	198?	$25

CROSBY, BING, AND FRED ASTAIRE

Albums

UNITED ARTISTS

❏ UA-LA588-G	A Couple of Song and Dance Men	1976	$30

CROSBY, BING, AND LOUIS ARMSTRONG
Also see each artist's individual listings.

Albums

CAPITOL

❏ SM-11735	Bing Crosby and Louis Armstrong	1977	$25

MGM

❏ E-3882 [M]	Bing and Satchmo	1960	$35
❏ SE-3882 [S]	Bing and Satchmo	1960	$50

CROSBY, BING
IMale singer. Not only was he the most popular singer of the first half of the 20th century, he was one of the most influential. While most of his vocals were influenced by jazz, the below covers only his "jazziest," mostly his pre-Decca material. For a more complete listing of Bing's hundreds of albums, see the Standard Catalog of American Records.

Albums

BIOGRAPH

❏ C-13	Bing Crosby 1929-33	1973	$30
❏ M-1	When the Blue of the Night Meets the Gold of the Day	197?	$25

BRUNSWICK

❏ BL58000 [10]	Bing Crosby, Volume 1	1950	$100
❏ BL58001 [10]	Bing Crosby, Volume 2	1950	$100
❏ BL54005 [M]	The Voice of Bing in the 1930s	1957	$60

COLUMBIA

❏ C35093	Bing Crosby Collection, Vol. 1	1977	$25
❏ C35094	Bing Crosby Collection, Vol. 2	1977	$25
❏ C2L43	Bing in Hollywood 1930-1934	196?	$35

— Red "360 Sound" labels

❏ C2L43	Bing in Hollywood 1930-1934	1971	$30

— Orange labels

❏ CL6027 [10]	Crosby Classics	1949	$100
❏ CL6105 [10]	Crosby Classics, Volume 2	1950	$100
❏ CL2502 [10]	Der Bingle	1955	$50
❏ C4X44229	The Crooner: The Columbia Years	1988	$40

COLUMBIA SPECIAL PRODUCTS

❏ P14369	Bing	197?	$25

DAYBREAK

❏ 2014	Bing and Basie	1972	$30

DECCA

❏ DL5390 [10]	Bing and Connee	1953	$150

— With Connee Boswell

❏ DL5323 [10]	Bing and the Dixieland Bands	1951	$200
❏ DL5064 [10]	Cole Porter Songs	1950	$150
❏ DL5126 [10]	Stardust	1950	$200

HARMONY

❏ HL7094 [M]	Crosby Classics	1958	$35
❏ HS11313 [R]	Crosby Classics	196?	$25

MCA

❏ 1502	Rare 1930-31 Brunswick Recordings	198?	$25

MOBILE FIDELITY

❏ 1-260	Bing Sings Whilst Bregman Swings	1996	$40

— Audiophile vinyl

RCA VICTOR

❏ LPM-1473 [M]	Bing with a Beat	1957	$60

VERVE

❏ MGV2020 [M]	Bing Sings Whilst Bregman Swings	1956	$200
❏ V-2020 [M]	Bing Sings Whilst Bregman Swings	1961	$60

X

❏ XLVA-4250 [M]	Young Bing Crosby	1955	$100

CROSBY, BOB
Male singer and bandleader.

Albums

AIRCHECK

❏ 17	Bob Crosby and His Orchestra 1940	197?	$25

CAPITOL

❏ H293 [10]	Bob Crosby and His Bobcats	1952	$80
❏ T293 [M]	Bob Crosby and His Bobcats	1955	$75
❏ T1556 [M]	The Hits of Bob Crosby's Bobcats	1961	$50

CIRCLE

❏ 1	Bob Crosby and His Orchestra 1938	198?	$25
❏ 34	Bob Crosby and His Orchestra 1938-39	198?	$25

COLUMBIA

❏ CL766 [M]	The Bob Crosby Show	1956	$30

CORAL

❏ CRL57060 [M]	Bobcats' Blues	1956	$40
❏ CRL57061 [M]	Bobcats On Parade	1956	$40
❏ CRL57089 [M]	Bob Crosby 1936-1956	1957	$40
❏ CRL57062 [M]	Bob Crosby in Hi-Fi	1956	$40
❏ CRL56003 [10]	Dixieland Jazz 1	1950	$50
❏ CRL56018 [10]	Marches in Dixieland Style	1950	$50
❏ CRL56039 [10]	St. Louis Blues	1950	$50
❏ CRL56000 [10]	Swinging at the Sugar Bowl	1950	$50
❏ CRL57005 [M]	The Bobcats' Ball	1955	$50
❏ CRL57170 [M]	The Bobcats in Hi-Fi	1958	$40

DECCA

❏ DL8061 [M]	Bob Crosby's Bobcats	1954	$150
❏ DL4856 [M]	Bob Crosby's Bobcats -- Their Greatest Hits	1967	$25

Number	Title	Yr	NM
❏ DL74856 [R]	Bob Crosby's Bobcats -- Their Greatest Hits	1967	$30
❏ DL8042 [M]	Five Feet of Swing	1954	$150
DOT			
❏ DLP-3278 [M]	Bob Crosby's Great Hits	196?	$75
❏ DLP-25278 [S]	Bob Crosby's Great Hits	196?	$75
❏ DLP-3382 [M]	C'est Si Bon	196?	$75
❏ DLP-25382 [S]	C'est Si Bon	196?	$75
❏ DLP-3170 [M]	Petite Fleur	1959	$75
❏ DLP-3136 [M]	South Pacific Blows Warm	1958	$75
❏ DLP-25136 [S]	South Pacific Blows Warm	1959	$75
HINDSIGHT			
❏ HSR-192	Bob Crosby and His Orchestra 1941-42	198?	$20
❏ HSR-209	Bob Crosby and His Orchestra 1952-53	1985	$20
MCA			
❏ 253	Bob Crosby's Bobcats -- Their Greatest Hits	1974	$25
❏ 4083	The Best of Bob Crosby	1974	$30
MONMOUTH-EVERGREEN			
❏ 7026	Mardi Gras Parade	1970	$35
❏ 6815	The Bob Crosby Orchestra Live	1968	$35
PAUSA			
❏ 9034	This Hits of Bob Crosby's Bobcats	198?	$25
—Reissue of Capitol 1556			
SUNBEAM			
❏ 216	The Bob Crosby Orchestra 1938-39	197?	$25
TIME-LIFE			
❏ STBB-14	Big Bands: Bob Crosby	1984	$35

CROSSE, JON
Tenor saxophone player.
Albums

Number	Title	Yr	NM
JAZZ CAT			
❏ JCR-101	Lullabies Go Jazz	1986	$25

CROSSFIRE
Australian fusion band.
Albums

Number	Title	Yr	NM
HEADFIRST			
❏ HF9704	East of Where	198?	$25

CROSSING POINT
Albums

Number	Title	Yr	NM
CLAY PIGEON			
❏ CP-1027	Listener Friendly	1986	$35
OPTIMISM			
❏ OP-5001	Listener Friendly	1988	$25
❏ OP-5002	Point of No Return	1988	$25

CROSSINGS
Dan Carillo (guitar) and Marc Irwin with guests.
Albums

Number	Title	Yr	NM
IRIS			
❏ IL-1001	Child's Play	198?	$25
❏ IL-1000	Crossings of the Spirit	198?	$25

CROTHERS, CONNIE, AND RICHARD TABNICK
Tabnick is an alto saxophone player. Also see CONNIE CROTHERS.
Albums

Number	Title	Yr	NM
NEW ARTISTS			
❏ NA-1003	Duo Dimension	1987	$25

CROTHERS, CONNIE
Pianist.
Albums

Number	Title	Yr	NM
INNER CITY			
❏ IC-2022	Perception	1974	$35
JAZZ			
❏ JR-4	Solo	1980	$35
NEW ARTISTS			
❏ NA-1002	Concert at Cooper Union	198?	$25
STEEPLECHASE			
❏ SCS-1022	Perception	1986	$30

CROTHERS, CONNIE/LENNY POPKIN QUARTET
Also see each artist's individual listings.
Albums

Number	Title	Yr	NM
NEW ARTISTS			
❏ NA-1005	Love Energy	1989	$30

CRUSADERS, THE (1)
Originally known as the Jazz Crusaders, whose records are included below. Members included Wilton Felder (tenor saxophone), Wayne Henderson (trombone), JOE SAMPLE (piano) and Nesbit "Stix" Hooper (drums).
Albums

Number	Title	Yr	NM
ABC BLUE THUMB			
❏ 6022	Chain Reaction	1975	$25
❏ BT-6001	Crusaders 1	1975	$30
❏ SPMK-42 [DJ]	Crusaders In-Store Sampler Album	1978	$50
—Promo-only issue			
❏ 6029	Free As the Wind	1977	$25
❏ BA-6030	Images	1978	$25
❏ BT-6010	Scratch	1975	$25
—Reissue			
❏ BTSY-9002	Southern Comfort	1974	$30
❏ 6027	The Best of the Crusaders	1976	$30
❏ 6024	Those Southern Knights	1976	$25
APPLAUSE			
❏ APBL-2313	Powerhouse	197?	$30
—Reissue of Pacific Jazz 20136			
BLUE NOTE			
❏ LT-1046	Live Sides	1980	$25
❏ BN-LA170-G [(2)]	Tough Talk	1974	$30
❏ BN-LA530-H2[(2)]	Young Rabbits	1977	$30
❏ LWB-530	Young Rabbits	1981	$25
—Reissue of BN-LA530-H2			
BLUE THUMB			
❏ BT-6001	Crusaders 1	1972	$35
❏ BT-6010	Scratch	1974	$30
❏ BT-7000	The 2nd Crusade	1973	$35
❏ BTSA1 [DJ]	The Crusaders Promotional Album	1973	$50
—Promo-only album contains one side of material from "Crusaders 1" and one side from "The 2nd Crusade			
❏ BT-6007	Unsung Heroes	1973	$30
CHISA			
❏ 804	Old Socks, New Shoes… New Socks, Old Shoes	1970	$30
—As "Jazz Crusaders			
❏ 807	Pass the Plate	1971	$30
CRUSADERS			
❏ 16002	Ongaku-Kai: Live in Japan	1982	$60
—Audiophile vinyl			
❏ 16000	Street Life	1982	$60
—Audiophile vinyl			
LIBERTY			
❏ LST-11005	Give Peace a Chance	1970	$35
—As "Jazz Crusaders			
MCA			
❏ 6015	2nd Crusade	198?	$25
—Reissue of Blue Thumb 7000			
❏ 37146	Chain Reaction	198?	$20
—Reissue of Blue Thumb 6022			
❏ 6014	Crusaders 1	198?	$25
—Reissue of Blue Thumb 6001			
❏ 37073	Free As the Wind	198?	$20
—Reissue of Blue Thumb 6029			
❏ 5429	Ghetto Blaster	1984	$25
❏ 37074	Images	198?	$20
—Reissue of Blue Thumb 6030			
❏ 42168	Life in the Modern World	1988	$25
❏ 5124	Rhapsody and Blues	1980	$25
❏ 37174	Rhapsody and Blues	198?	$20
—Reissue of 5124			
❏ 8017	Royal Jam	1982	$30
❏ 37072	Scratch	198?	$20
—Reissue of Blue Thumb 6010			
❏ 6016	Southern Comfort	198?	$25
—Reissue of Blue Thumb 9002			
❏ 5254	Standing Tall	1981	$25
❏ 37240	Standing Tall	1985	$20
—Reissue of 5254			
❏ 3094	Street Life	1979	$25
❏ 6006	The Best of the Crusaders	1980	$25
—Reissue of Blue Thumb 6027			
❏ 5781	The Good and Bad Times	1987	$25
❏ 42087	The Vocal Album	1988	$25
❏ 37147	Those Southern Knights	198?	$20
—Reissue of Blue Thumb 6024			
MOBILE FIDELITY			
❏ Jan-0010	Chain Reaction	1979	$40
—Audiophile vinyl			
MOTOWN			
❏ M796	The Crusaders At Their Best	1973	$30
❏ M5-195V1	The Crusaders At Their Best	1981	$25
MOWEST			
❏ 118	Hollywood	1972	$30
PACIFIC JAZZ			
❏ PJ-10092 [M]	Chili Con Soul	1965	$50
❏ ST-20092 [S]	Chili Con Soul	1965	$60
❏ T-90598 [M]	Chili Con Soul	1965	$100
—Capitol Record Club edition			
❏ PJ-27 [M]	Freedom Sound	1961	$60
❏ ST-27 [S]	Freedom Sound	1961	$60
❏ PJ-76 [M]	Heat Wave	1963	$60
❏ ST-76 [S]	Heat Wave	1963	$60
❏ ST-20131	Lighthouse '68	1968	$50
❏ PJ-10098 [M]	Live at the Lighthouse '66	1966	$50
❏ ST-20098 [S]	Live at the Lighthouse '66	1966	$60
❏ PJ-43 [M]	Lookin' Ahead	1962	$60
❏ ST-43 [S]	Lookin' Ahead	1962	$60
—Black vinyl			
❏ ST-43 [S]	Lookin' Ahead	1962	$120
—Yellow vinyl			
❏ ST-20136	Powerhouse	1968	$50
❏ PJ-83 [M]	Stretchin' Out	1964	$60
❏ ST-83 [S]	Stretchin' Out	1964	$60
❏ PJ-10106 [M]	Talk That Talk	1966	$50
❏ ST-20106 [S]	Talk That Talk	1966	$60
❏ ST-20175	The Best of the Jazz Crusaders	1969	$50
❏ PJ-10115 [M]	The Festival Album	1967	$60
❏ ST-20115 [S]	The Festival Album	1967	$50
❏ PJ-57 [M]	The Jazz Crusaders at the Lighthouse	1962	$60
❏ ST-57 [S]	The Jazz Crusaders at the Lighthouse	1962	$60
❏ ST-90481 [S]	The Jazz Crusaders at the Lighthouse	1965	$100
—Capitol Record Club edition			
❏ ST-20165	The Jazz Crusaders at the Lighthouse '69	1969	$50
❏ PJ-87 [M]	The Thing	1964	$60
❏ ST-87 [S]	The Thing	1964	$60
❏ PJ-68 [M]	Tough Talk	1963	$60
❏ ST-68 [S]	Tough Talk	1963	$60
❏ PJ-10124	Uh Huh	1967	$60
❏ ST-20124	Uh Huh	1967	$50
PAUSA			
❏ 9005	The Best of the Jazz Crusaders	1979	$25
—As "Jazz Crusaders			
WORLD PACIFIC JAZZ			
❏ ST-20098 [S]	Live at the Lighthouse '66	1970	$100
—Reissue with "Liberty/UA" on label			

CRYSTAL
Among the members were Charlie Camorata (keyboards), Jim Lucas (bass) and Peter Cardarelli (saxophone).
Albums

Number	Title	Yr	NM
BLACKHAWK			
❏ BKH-51501	Clear	1986	$25

CUBER, RONNIE
Baritone saxophone player.
Albums

Number	Title	Yr	NM
XANADU			
❏ 135	Cuber Libre	1976	$35
❏ 156	The Eleventh Day of Aquarius	1978	$35

CULLUM, JIM (JR.)
Cornet player and bandleader. Son of the below Jim Cullum.
Albums

Number	Title	Yr	NM
JAZZOLOGY			
❏ 132	Life in Memphis	198?	$25
STOMP OFF			
❏ SOS-1148	Super Satch	1987	$25

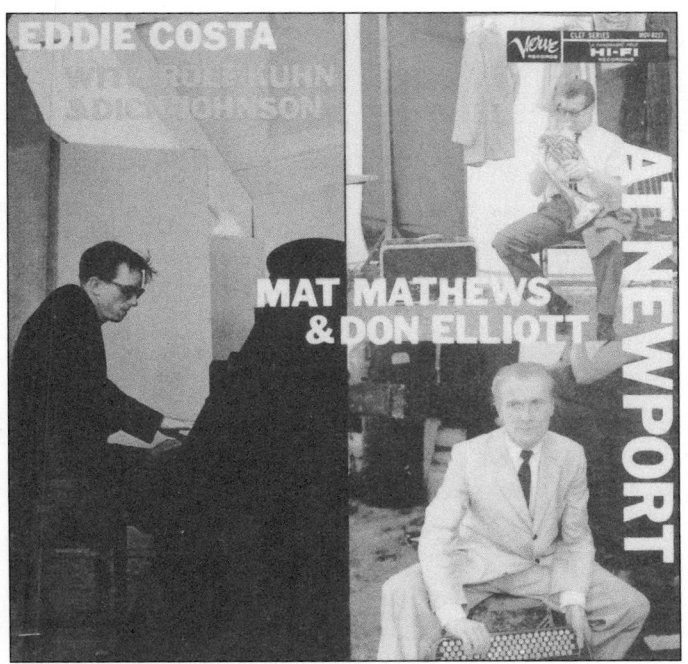

Eddie Costa, *Eddie Costa with Rolf Kuhn and Dick Johnson/Mat Matthews and Don Elliott at Newport*, Verve MGV 8237, **$150**.

Hank Crawford, *Indigo Blue*, Milestone M-9119, **$25**.

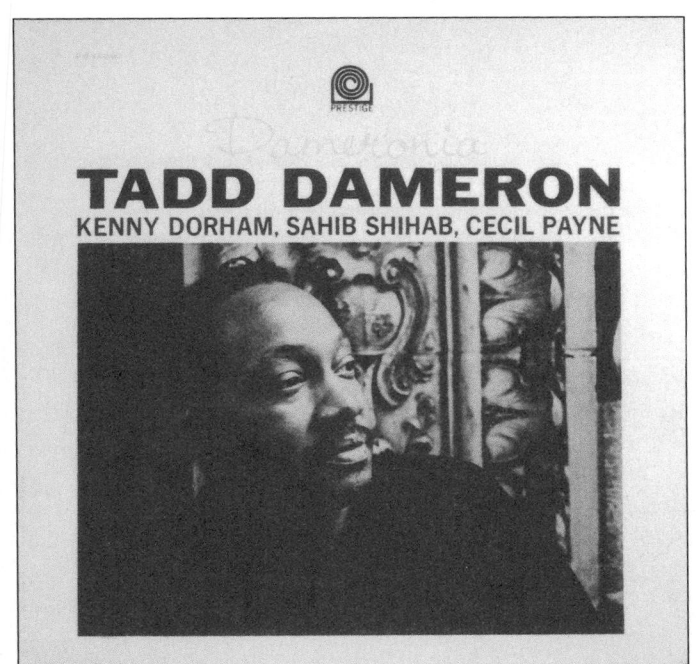

Tadd Dameron, *Dameronia*, Prestige PRLP-16007, **$100**.

Tadd Dameron, *Fontainebleu*, Prestige PRLP-7037, **$300**.

Number	Title	Yr	NM

CULLUM, JIM (SR.)
Clarinet player and bandleader.

Albums

AUDIOPHILE
❑ 107 [B]	Eloquent Clarinet	1972	$35
❑ 117	Jazz -- The Music of Jim Cullum, Sr.	1972	$30

CUNIMONDO, FRANK
Pianist, keyboard player and occasional vocalist.

Albums

MONDO
❑ M-101	Communication	197?	$25
❑ M-104	Echoes	197?	$25
❑ M-103	Introducing Lynn Marino	197?	$25
❑ M-105	Sagittarius	197?	$25
❑ M-102	The Lamp Is Low	197?	$25
❑ S1-90175	The Top Shelf Collection	197?	$25

CUOZZO, MIKE
Tenor saxophone player.

CURRAN, ED

Albums

SAVOY
❑ MG-12191 [M]	Elysa	1967	$25

CURRENT EVENTS
Among the members was pianist Darrell Grant.

Albums

VERVE FORECAST
❑ 839388-1	Current Events	1989	$35

CURSON, TED
Trumpeter, fluegel horn player and piccolo trumpet player.

Albums

ARISTA FREEDOM
❑ AL1030	Flip Top	197?	$35
❑ AL1021	Tears	197?	$35

ATLANTIC
❑ 1441 [M]	The New Thing and the Blue Thing	1965	$25
❑ SD1441 [S]	The New Thing and the Blue Thing	1965	$30

AUDIO FIDELITY
❑ AFLP-2123 [M]	Now Hear This	1964	$25
❑ AFSD-6123 [S]	Now Hear This	1964	$30

FANTASY
❑ OJC-1744	Fire Down Below	1990	$30

INDIA NAVIGATION
❑ IN-1054	Blue Piccolo	1976	$35

INNER CITY
❑ IC1017	Jubilant Power	1976	$30

INTERPLAY
❑ 7716	Blowin' Away	1978	$30
❑ 7726	I Heard Mingus	1980	$30
❑ 7722	The Trio	1979	$30

PRESTIGE
❑ PRLP-7263 [M]	Fire Down Below	1963	$30
—Yellow label, Bergenfield, N.J. address			
❑ PRLP-7263 [M]	Fire Down Below	1965	$25
—Blue label with trident logo at right			
❑ PRST-7263 [S]	Fire Down Below	1963	$40
—Silver label, Bergenfield, N.J. address			
❑ PRST-7263 [S]	Fire Down Below	1965	$30
—Blue label with trident logo at right			

CYRILLE, ANDREW, AND MILFORD GRAVES
Also see each artist's individual listings.

Albums

IPS
❑ 001	Dialogue of the Drums	1974	$25

CYRILLE, ANDREW; JEANNE LEE; JIMMY LYONS
Also see each artist's individual listings.

Albums

BLACK SAINT
❑ BSR-0030	Nuba	198?	$30

CYRILLE, ANDREW
Drummer and percussionist.

Albums

ICTUS
❑ 09	The Loop	197?	$35

IPS
❑ 02	Celebration	1977	$35
❑ 03	Junction	1978	$35

SOUL NOTE
❑ SN-1078	Pieces of Time	198?	$30
❑ SN-1012	Special People	1981	$30
❑ SN-1062	The Navigator	1982	$30

D

DA COSTA, PAULINHO
Percussionist. Regularly used as a session musician by other jazz and rock artists.

Albums

FANTASY
❑ OJC-630	Agora	1991	$30

PABLO
❑ 2310785	Agora	1976	$35

PABLO TODAY
❑ 2312102	Happy People	1979	$30

DAGRADI, TONY
Saxophone player, primarily tenor sax.

Albums

GRAMAVISION
❑ 8103	Lunar Eclipse	1982	$30
❑ 8001	Oasis	1981	$30

ROUNDER
❑ 2071	Dreams of Love	1988	$25

DAHLANDER, NILS-BERTIL "BERT
Drummer.

Albums

EVERYDAY
❑ EDLP528	Talkin' Jazz: Untitled #1	1990	$35
—As "Bert Dahlander"			

VERVE
❑ MGV-8253 [M]	Skol	1958	$100
❑ V-8253 [M]	Skol	1961	$25

DAILEY, ALBERT
Pianist. Also see STAN GETZ.

Albums

COLUMBIA
❑ KC31278	Day After the Dawn	1973	$35

MUSE
❑ MR-5256	Textures	198?	$25

STEEPLECHASE
❑ SCS-1107	That Old Feeling	198?	$25

DAILY, PETE
Cornet player and bandleader.

Albums

CAPITOL
❑ H385 [10]	Dixie by Daily	1953	$80
❑ T385 [M]	Dixie by Daily	1954	$60
❑ H183 [10]	Dixieland Band	1950	$80
❑ T183 [M]	Dixieland Band	1954	$60

DAILY, PETE/PHIL NAPOLEON
Also see each artist's individual listings.

Albums

DECCA
❑ DL5261 [10]	Pete Daily/Phil Napoleon	195?	$50

DALEY, JOE
Tenor saxophone player. Also a clarinet player, flutist and composer.

Albums

RCA VICTOR
❑ LPM-2763 [M]	Joe Daley at Newport '63	1963	$25
❑ LSP-2763 [S]	Joe Daley at Newport '63	1963	$30

DALINE
See DALINE JONES.

DALLWITZ, DAVE
Australian trombonist, pianist, composer and bandleader.

Albums

STOMP OFF
❑ SOS-1112	Elephant Stomp	1987	$25
❑ SOS-1098	Nostalgia	1985	$25

DALTO, JORGE
Pianist and keyboard player.

Albums

CONCORD PICANTE
❑ CJP-275	Urban Oasis	1985	$25

D'AMBROSIO, MEREDITH
Pianist and female singer.

Albums

PALO ALTO
❑ 8019	Little Jazz Bird	1982	$30

SHIAH
❑ SR-109	Another Time	198?	$35

SPRING INC.
❑ 0SPR	Lost in His Arms	1978	$35

SUNNYSIDE
❑ SSC-1017	Another Time	1987	$25
❑ SSC-1011	It's Your Dance	1985	$25
❑ SSC-1018	Lost in His Arms	1987	$25
❑ SSC-1039	South to a Warmer Place	1989	$30
❑ SSC-1028	The Cove	1988	$25

DAMERON, TADD
Pianist, arranger, composer and bandleader.

Albums

FANTASY
❑ OJC-055	Fontainebleu	198?	$30
—Reissue of Prestige 7037			
❑ OJC-212	Mating Call	198?	$30
—Reissue of Prestige 7070			
❑ OJC-143	The Magic Touch of Tadd Dameron	198?	$30
—Reissue of Riverside 9419			

JAZZLAND
❑ JLP-50 [M]	Fats Navarro Featured with the Tadd Dameron Quintet	1962	$150
❑ JLP-68 [M]	The Tadd Dameron Band	1962	$150

MILESTONE
❑ M-47041	Fats Navarro Featured with the Tadd Dameron Band	1977	$50

NEW JAZZ
❑ NJLP-8300 [M]	Dameronia	1963	$0
—Canceled; reassigned to Prestige 16007			

PRESTIGE
❑ PRLP-159 [10]	A Study in Dameronia	1953	$600
❑ PRLP-16007 [M]	Dameronia	1964	$100
❑ PRLP-7037 [M]	Fontainebleu	1956	$300
❑ PRLP-7070 [M]	Mating Call	1956	$300
—Reissued as 7247 and 7725 as a John Coltrane LP; see his listings			
❑ PRST-7842	Memorial Album	1970	$35

RIVERSIDE
❑ RS-3019	Good Bait	1968	$100
❑ RLP-419 [M]	The Magic Touch of Tadd Dameron	1962	$150
❑ RS-9419 [S]	The Magic Touch of Tadd Dameron	1962	$150

D'AMICO, HANK
Clarinet and saxophone player. Also see AARON SACHS.

Albums

BETHLEHEM
❑ BCP-1006 [10]	Hank's Holiday	1954	$250

DANCY, MEL

Albums

Number	Title	Yr	NM
MAINSTREAM			
❑ MRL-378	A Little Lovin'	1972	$30

D'ANDREA, FRANCO

Pianist.

Albums

Number	Title	Yr	NM
RED			
❑ NS-201	My One and Only Love	198?	$30
❑ NS-202	No Idea of Time	1985	$30

DANE, BARBARA

Female singer and guitarist.

Albums

Number	Title	Yr	NM
BARBARY COAST			
❑ 33014 [M]	Trouble in Mind	1959	$40
— Reissue of San Francisco LP			
CAPITOL			
❑ T1758 [M]	On My Way	1962	$100
❑ ST1758 [S]	On My Way	1962	$75
DOT			
❑ DLP-3177 [M]	Living with the Blues	1959	$150
❑ DLP-25177 [S]	Living with the Blues	1959	$80
FOLKWAYS			
❑ FA-2468	Barbara Dane and the Chambers Brothers	1966	$150
❑ FA-2471	Folk Songs	1966	$60
HORIZON			
❑ WP-1602 [M]	When I Was a Young Girl	1962	$60
❑ WPS-1602 [S]	When I Was a Young Girl	1962	$40
— Black vinyl			
❑ WPS-1602 [S]	When I Was a Young Girl	1962	$120
— Gold vinyl			
PAREDON			
❑ 1003	FTA! Songs of the GI Resistance	1970	$35
❑ 1014	I Hate the Capitalist System	1973	$35
❑ 1046	When We Make It Through	1982	$35
SAN FRANCISCO			
❑ 33014 [M]	Trouble in Mind	1957	$120

DANIEL, TED

Trumpeter.

Albums

Number	Title	Yr	NM
UJAMAA			
❑ 1001	Ted Daniel	197?	$30

DANIELS, EDDIE

Clarinet and tenor saxophone player; also a composer.

Albums

Number	Title	Yr	NM
CHOICE			
❑ 1002	A Flower for All Seasons	1974	$30
COLUMBIA			
❑ JC36290	Morning Thunder	1980	$25
GRP			
❑ GR-9584	Blackwood	1989	$30
❑ GR-1024	Breakthrough	198?	$25
❑ GR-1050	Memos from Paradise: The Music of Roger Kellaway	1988	$25
❑ GR-1034	To Bird with Love	1987	$25
MUSE			
❑ MR-5154	Brief Encounter	1978	$30
PRESTIGE			
❑ PRLP-7506 [M]	First Prize	1967	$40
❑ PRST-7506 [S]	First Prize	1967	$30

DANIELS, HALL

Albums

Number	Title	Yr	NM
JUMP			
❑ JL-9 [10]	Hall Daniels Septet	1955	$80
— Issued on blue vinyl			

DANIELS, MIKE, AND HIS DELTA JAZZMEN

Daniels is a trumpeter and bandleader.

Albums

Number	Title	Yr	NM
STOMP OFF			
❑ SOS-1203	Together Again -- Thirty Years On!	1991	$30

DANKO, HAROLD, AND KIRK LIGHTSEY

Also see each artist's individual listings.

Albums

Number	Title	Yr	NM
SUNNYSIDE			
❑ SSC-1004	Shorter by Two	1985	$25

DANKO, HAROLD, AND RUFUS REID

Also see each artist's individual listings.

Albums

Number	Title	Yr	NM
SUNNYSIDE			
❑ SSC-1001	Mirth Song	1985	$25

DANKO, HAROLD

Pianist.

Albums

Number	Title	Yr	NM
DREAMSTREET			
❑ 104	Coincidence	1980	$30
INNER CITY			
❑ IC-1069	Chasin' Bad Guys	1979	$30
❑ IC-1029	Harold Danko Quartet Featuring Gregory Herbert	1978	$30
SUNNYSIDE			
❑ SSC-1033	Alone But Not Forgotten	1989	$30
❑ SSC-1008	Ink and Water	1985	$25

DANKWORTH, JOHN

British saxophone and clarinet player, bandleader and composer.

Albums

Number	Title	Yr	NM
DRG			
❑ MRS-507	Movies 'N' Me	198?	$25
FONTANA			
❑ SRF-67603	The Sophisticated Johnnie Dankworth	1969	$25
❑ MGF-27543 [M]	Zodiac Variations	1966	$35
❑ SRF-67543 [S]	Zodiac Variations	1966	$50
IAJRC			
❑ LP39	Johnny Dankworth's Big Band In the Fifties	198?	$25
MCA CLASSICS			
❑ 25932	Crossing Over the Bridge	1987	$25
ROULETTE			
❑ R-52059 [M]	Collaboration	1961	$25
❑ SR-52059 [S]	Collaboration	1961	$30
❑ R-52040 [M]	England's Ambassador of Jazz	1960	$25
❑ SR-52040 [S]	England's Ambassador of Jazz	1960	$30
❑ R-52096 [M]	Jazz from Abroad	1963	$25
❑ SR-52096 [S]	Jazz from Abroad	1963	$30
VERVE			
❑ MG V-20006 [M]	5 Steps to Dankworth	1957	$150
— Also contains several tracks by others who are performing songs Dankworth wrote			

DANKWORTH, JOHN/BILLY STRAYHORN

Also see each artist's individual listings.

Albums

Number	Title	Yr	NM
ROULETTE			
❑ RE-121	Echoes of an Era	1973	$35

DAPOGNY, JIM, AND BUTCH THOMPSON

Also see each artist's individual listings.

Albums

Number	Title	Yr	NM
STOMP OFF			
❑ SOS-1183	How Could We Be So Blue?	1988	$25

DAPOGNY, JIM

Pianist and bandleader.

Albums

Number	Title	Yr	NM
JAZZOLOGY			
❑ J-140	Back Home in Illinois	1984	$25
❑ J-120	Jim Dapogny's Chicago Jazz Band	1983	$25

DARCH, BOB

Pianist.

Albums

Number	Title	Yr	NM
UNITED ARTISTS			
❑ UAL-3120 [M]	Ragtime Piano	1960	$25
❑ UAS-6120 [S]	Ragtime Piano	1960	$30

DARDANELLE

Female singer.

Albums

Number	Title	Yr	NM
AUDIOPHILE			
❑ AP-191	A Woman's Intuition	198?	$25
❑ AP-214	Down Home	1985	$25
❑ AP-145	Echoes Singing Ladies	1982	$25
❑ AP-32	Gold Braid	1983	$25
STASH			
❑ ST-202	Songs for New Lovers	1978	$25
❑ ST-217	The Colors of My Life	198?	$25

DARDANELLE AND VIVIAN LORD

Also see each artist's individual listings.

Albums

Number	Title	Yr	NM
STASH			
❑ ST-231	The Two of Us	1983	$25

DARENSBOURG, JOE

Clarinet player.

Albums

Number	Title	Yr	NM
GHB			
❑ 90	Barrelhousin' with Joe	197?	$25
GNP CRESCENDO			
❑ GNP-515	Petite Fleur	197?	$25
❑ GNP-514	Yellow Dog Blues	197?	$25

DARK

Jazz/fusion/world music band: Mark Nauseef (drums, percussion), Leonice Shinneman (percussion), Mark London Sims (bass), Miroslav Tadic (guitar).

Albums

Number	Title	Yr	NM
CMP			
❑ 28	Dark	1987	$30

DARLING, DAVID

Cellist.

Albums

Number	Title	Yr	NM
ECM			
❑ 1219	Cycles	198?	$25
❑ 1161	Journal October	1980	$30

DARR, ALICE

Female singer.

Albums

Number	Title	Yr	NM
CHARLIE PARKER			
❑ PLP-611 [M]	I Only Know How to Cry	1962	$30
❑ PLP-611S [S]	I Only Know How to Cry	1962	$40

DARTMOUTH INDIAN CHIEFS

Albums

Number	Title	Yr	NM
TRANSITION			
❑ TRLP-23 [M]	Chiefly Jazz	1956	$120

DASH, JULIAN

Tenor saxophone player and composer. Co-writer of "Tuxedo Junction."

Albums

Number	Title	Yr	NM
MASTER JAZZ			
❑ 8106	Portrait	1970	$25

DAUGHERTY, JACK

Trumpeter, conductor, composer and arranger. Best known as the producer of the early hits by the Carpenters!

Albums

Number	Title	Yr	NM
A&M			
❑ SP-3038	Jack Daugherty and the Class of '71	1971	$25
MONTEREY			
❑ 100	Carmel by the Sea	1976	$35

DAVENPORT, WALLACE

Trumpeter.

Albums

Number	Title	Yr	NM
GHB			
❑ 146	Darkness on the Delta	198?	$25

Number	Title	Yr	NM

DAVIDSON, LOWELL
Pianist and composer.

Albums

ESP-DISK'
| ❏ 1012 [M] | Lowell Davidson Trio | 1965 | $100 |
| ❏ S-1012 [S] | Lowell Davidson Trio | 1965 | $100 |

DAVIS, ANTHONY
Pianist and composer.

Albums

GRAMAVISION
❏ 8101	Episteme	1981	$30
❏ 8303	Hemispheres	1983	$30
❏ 8201	I've Known Rivers	1982	$30
❏ 8401	Middle Passage	1984	$30
❏ R1-79441	Trio Squared	1989	$30
❏ 8612	Undine	1986	$30

INDIA NAVIGATION
❏ IN-1041	Hidden Voices	1979	$35
❏ IN-1047	Lady in the Mirror	1980	$35
❏ IN-1036	Songs for the Old World	1978	$35
❏ IN-1056	Variations in Dream-Time	1981	$35

PAUSA
| ❏ 7120 | Under the Double Moon | 198? | $25 |

SACKVILLE
| ❏ 3020 | Of Blues and Dreams | 198? | $25 |

DAVIS, ART
Bass player.

Albums

INTERPLAY
| ❏ 7728 | Reemergence | 197? | $30 |

SOUL NOTE
| ❏ 121143 | Life | 198? | $30 |

DAVIS, BOB
Pianist.

Albums

STEPHENY
| ❏ MF-4000 [M] | Jazz in Orbit | 1958 | $60 |
| ❏ MFS-8003 [S] | Jazz in Orbit | 1960 | $50 |

ZEPHYR
| ❏ 12001 [M] | Jazz from the North Coast | 1959 | $50 |

DAVIS, CHARLES
Baritone saxophone player. Also has played tenor and alto saxes.

Albums

STRATA-EAST
| ❏ 7425 | Ingia! | 1974 | $35 |

WEST 54
| ❏ 8006 | Dedicated to Tadd | 1979 | $30 |

DAVIS, EDDIE "LOCKJAW", AND HARRY "SWEETS" EDISON
Also see each artist's individual listings.

Albums

PABLO
| ❏ 2310882 | Jazz at the Philharmonic 1983 | 1983 | $30 |

STORYVILLE
| ❏ 4004 | Eddie "Lockjaw" Davis and Harry "Sweets" Edison | 197? | $30 |

DAVIS, EDDIE "LOCKJAW", AND JOHNNY GRIFFIN
Also see each artist's individual listings.

Albums

FANTASY
| ❏ OJC-264 | Griff & Lock | 1987 | $25 |

JAZZLAND
❏ JLP-60 [M]	Blues Up and Down	1961	$40
❏ JLP-960 [S]	Blues Up and Down	1961	$50
❏ JLP-42 [M]	Griff & Lock	1961	$40
❏ JLP-942 [S]	Griff & Lock	1961	$50
❏ JLP-39 [M]	Lookin' at Monk	1961	$40
❏ JLP-939 [S]	Lookin' at Monk	1961	$50
❏ JLP-76 [M]	Tough Tenor Favorites	1962	$40
❏ JLP-976 [S]	Tough Tenor Favorites	1962	$50
❏ JLP-31 [M]	Tough Tenors	1960	$40
❏ JLP-931 [S]	Tough Tenors	1960	$50

MILESTONE
| ❏ 47035 | The Toughest Tenors | 198? | $35 |

PAUSA
| ❏ 7062 | The Tough Tenors Again 'n' Again | 197? | $25 |

PRESTIGE
❏ PRLP-7282 [M]	Battle Stations	1963	$30
❏ PRST-7282 [S]	Battle Stations	1963	$40
❏ 24099	Live at Minton's	197?	$35
❏ PRLP-7407 [M]	The Breakfast Show	1965	$30
—Reissue of 7191			
❏ PRST-7407 [S]	The Breakfast Show	1965	$30
❏ PRLP-7309 [M]	The First Set -- Recorded Live at Minton's	1964	$30
❏ PRST-7309 [S]	The First Set -- Recorded Live at Minton's	1964	$40
❏ PRLP-7357 [M]	The Late Show -- Recorded Live!	1965	$30
❏ PRST-7357 [S]	The Late Show -- Recorded Live!	1965	$30
❏ PRLP-7330 [M]	The Midnight Show at Minton's Playhouse	1964	$30
❏ PRST-7330 [S]	The Midnight Show at Minton's Playhouse	1964	$30
❏ PRLP-7191	The Tenor Scene	1961	$150

DAVIS, EDDIE "LOCKJAW", AND SHIRLEY SCOTT
Also see each artist's individual listings.

Albums

FANTASY
| ❏ OJC-216 | Jaws | 198? | $25 |
| ❏ OJC-322 | Jaws in Orbit | 1988 | $25 |

MOODSVILLE
❏ MVLP-4 [M]	Eddie "Lockjaw" Davis with Shirley Scott	1960	$50
—Green label			
❏ MVLP-4 [M]	Eddie "Lockjaw" Davis with Shirley Scott	1965	$30
—Blue label, trident logo on right			
❏ MVLP-30 [M]	Misty	1963	$50
—Green label			
❏ MVLP-30 [M]	Misty	1965	$30
—Blue label, trident logo on right			
❏ MVST-30 [S]	Misty	1963	$50
—Green label			
❏ MVST-30 [S]	Misty	1965	$30
—Blue label, trident logo on right			

PRESTIGE
❏ PRLP-7154 [M]	Jaws	1959	$200
❏ PRLP-7171 [M]	Jaws in Orbit	1959	$200
❏ PRLP-7301 [M]	Smokin'	1964	$40
❏ PRST-7301 [S]	Smokin'	1964	$30
❏ PRST-7710	The Best of Eddie "Lockjaw" Davis with Shirley Scott	1970	$35

DAVIS, EDDIE "LOCKJAW
Tenor saxophone player.

Albums

BETHLEHEM
❏ BCP-6035 [M]	Eddie's Function	197?	$35
—Reissue material, distributed by RCA Victor			
❏ BCP-6069 [M]	The Best of Eddie "Lockjaw" Davis	1963	$200
❏ BCPS-6069 [R]	The Best of Eddie "Lockjaw" Davis	196?	$25

CLASSIC JAZZ
| ❏ 116 | Sweet and Lovely | 197? | $30 |

ENJA
| ❏ 3097 | Jaws' Blues | 1981 | $30 |

FANTASY
❏ OJC-403	Afro-Jaws	1989	$30
❏ OJC-384	Montreux '77	1989	$30
❏ OJC-629	Straight Ahead	1991	$30
❏ OJC-652	The Eddie "Lockjaw" Davis Cookbook, Vol. 1	1991	$30
❏ OJC-653	The Eddie "Lockjaw" Davis Cookbook, Vol. 2	1991	$30
❏ OJC-429	Trane Whistle	1990	$30

INNER CITY
| ❏ IC-2058 | Swingin' Till the Girls Come Home | 1976 | $35 |

JAZZLAND
| ❏ JLP-97 [M] | Alma Alegre | 1962 | $30 |
| ❏ JLP-997 [S] | Alma Alegre | 1962 | $30 |

KING
❏ 599 [M]	Big Beat Jazz	1958	$100
❏ 566 [M]	Jazz with a Beat	1957	$100
❏ 395-526 [M]	Jazz with a Horn	1957	$100
❏ 395-506 [M]	Modern Jazz Expression	1956	$300
❏ 637 [M]	This and That	1959	$100
❏ 606 [M]	Uptown	1958	$100

MUSE
| ❏ MR-5202 | Heavy Hitter | 1979 | $30 |

PABLO
| ❏ 2310778 | Straight Ahead | 197? | $35 |
| ❏ 2405414 | The Best of Eddie "Lockjaw" Davis | 198? | $25 |

PABLO LIVE
| ❏ 2308214 | Montreux '77 | 1978 | $30 |

PRESTIGE
❏ PRLP-7242 [M]	Goin' to the Meeting	1962	$150
❏ PRST-7242 [S]	Goin' to the Meeting	1962	$150
❏ PRST-7660	In the Kitchen	1969	$35
—Reissue of 7141 in (rechanneled?) stereo			
❏ PRLP-7261 [M]	I Only Have Eyes for You	1963	$40
❏ PRST-7261 [S]	I Only Have Eyes for You	1963	$50
❏ PRST-7834	Stolen Moments	197?	$35
—Reissue of 7206 in (rechanneled?) stereo			
❏ PRLP-7141 [M]	The Eddie "Lockjaw" Davis Cookbook	1958	$200
—Cover photo features Davis with no hat			
❏ 24039	The Eddie "Lockjaw" Davis Cookbook	197?	$50
❏ PRLP-7219 [M]	The Eddie "Lockjaw" Davis Cookbook, Vol. 3	1961	$150
❏ PRST-7219 [S]	The Eddie "Lockjaw" Davis Cookbook, Vol. 3	1961	$150
❏ PRST-7782	The Rev.	197?	$35
—Reissue of 7161 in (rechanneled?) stereo			
❏ PRLP-7271 [M]	Trackin'	1963	$40
❏ PRST-7271 [S]	Trackin'	1963	$50
❏ PRLP-7206 [M]	Trane Whistle	1961	$150

RCA VICTOR
❏ LPM-3652 [M]	Lock the Fox	1966	$25
❏ LSP-3652 [S]	Lock the Fox	1966	$30
❏ LPM-3882 [M]	Love Calls	1967	$30
❏ LSP-3882 [S]	Love Calls	1967	$25
❏ LPM-3741 [M]	The Fox and the Hounds	1967	$30
❏ LSP-3741 [S]	The Fox and the Hounds	1967	$25

RIVERSIDE
❏ RLP-373 [M]	Afro-Jaws	1961	$200
❏ RS-9373 [S]	Afro-Jaws	1961	$200
❏ RLP-430 [M]	Jawbreakers	1962	$150
❏ RS-9430 [S]	Jawbreakers	1962	$150

ROOST
| ❏ RST-2227 [M] | Eddie Davis Trio | 1957 | $100 |
| ❏ LP-422 [10] | Goodies | 1954 | $150 |

ROULETTE
❏ R-52007 [M]	Count Basie Presents Eddie Davis	1958	$60
—White label with color spokes			
❏ R-52007 [M]	Count Basie Presents Eddie Davis	1963	$30
—Orange and yellow "roulette wheel" label			
❏ SR-52007 [S]	Count Basie Presents Eddie Davis	1959	$50
—White label with color spokes			
❏ SR-52007 [S]	Count Basie Presents Eddie Davis	1963	$25
—Orange and yellow "roulette wheel" label			
❏ R-52019 [M]	Eddie Davis Trio	1959	$60
—White label with color spokes			
❏ R-52019 [M]	Eddie Davis Trio	1963	$30
—Orange and yellow "roulette wheel" label			
❏ SR-52019 [S]	Eddie Davis Trio	1959	$50
—White label with color spokes			
❏ SR-52019 [S]	Eddie Davis Trio	1963	$25
—Orange and yellow "roulette wheel" label			

STEEPLECHASE
| ❏ SCS-1181 | All of Me | 198? | $25 |
| ❏ SCS-1058 | Swingin' Till the Girls Come Home | 198? | $25 |

DAVIS, EDDY
Banjo player and bandleader.

Albums

JAZZOLOGY
| ❏ J-67 | Eddy Davis and His Hot Jazz Orchestra | 1979 | $25 |
| ❏ J-88 | Eddy Davis and His Hot Jazz Orchestra | 1982 | $25 |

Tadd Dameron, *Fats Navarro Featured with the Tadd Dameron Quintet*, Jazzland JLP-50, **$150**.

Tadd Dameron, *The Magic Touch*, Riverside RS-9419, **$150**.

Miles Davis, *Sketches of Spain*, Columbia CS 8271, original red and black label with six "eye" logos, **$150**

Miles Davis, *Miles Ahead*, Columbia PC 8633, later reissue, **$20**.

Number	Title	Yr	NM

DAVIS, JACKIE
Organist.
Albums
CAPITOL
| ❏ T815 [M] | Chasing Shadows | 1957 | $60 |

—Turquoise or gray label
| ❏ T1180 [M] | Jackie Davis Meets the Trombones | 1959 | $60 |

—Black colorband label, logo at left

DAVIS, JOHNNY "SCAT
Male singer.
Albums
KING
| ❏ 626 [M] | Here's Lookin' Atcha | 1959 | $80 |

DAVIS, MEL
Trumpeter.
Albums
EPIC
| ❏ LN3268 [M] | Trumpet with a Soul | 1956 | $80 |

RCA CAMDEN
| ❏ CAL-2127 [M] | The Big Ones of '66 | 1966 | $30 |
| ❏ CAS-2127 [S] | The Big Ones of '66 | 1966 | $35 |

TIME
❏ 52087 [M]	Shoot the Trumpet Player	1962	$25
❏ S-2087 [S]	Shoot the Trumpet Player	1962	$30
❏ 52117 [M]	We Like Broadway	1963	$25
❏ S-2117 [S]	We Like Broadway	1963	$30

DAVIS, MILES, AND JOHN COLTRANE
Also see each artist's individual listings.
Albums
MOODSVILLE
| ❏ MVLP-32 [M] | Miles Davis and John Coltrane Play Richard Rodgers | 1963 | $100 |

—Green label
| ❏ MVLP-32 [M] | Miles Davis and John Coltrane Play Richard Rodgers | 1965 | $60 |

—Blue label, trident logo at right

PRESTIGE
| ❏ PRLP-7322 [M] | Miles Davis and John Coltrane Play Rodgers and Hart | 1964 | $40 |
| ❏ PRST-7322 [R] | Miles Davis and John Coltrane Play Rodgers and Hart | 1964 | $50 |

DAVIS, MILES, AND MARCUS MILLER
Also see each artist's individual listings.
Albums
WARNER BROS.
| ❏ 25655 | Music from Siesta | 1987 | $35 |

DAVIS, MILES, AND TADD DAMERON
Also see each artist's individual listings.
Albums
COLUMBIA
| ❏ JC34804 | Paris Festival International, May 1949 | 1978 | $50 |

DAVIS, MILES, AND THELONIOUS MONK
Also see each artist's individual listings.
Albums
COLUMBIA
| ❏ CL2178 [M] | Miles and Monk at Newport | 1964 | $40 |

—Guaranteed High Fidelity" on label
| ❏ CL2178 [M] | Miles and Monk at Newport | 1965 | $60 |

—360 Sound Mono" on label
| ❏ CS8978 [S] | Miles and Monk at Newport | 1964 | $120 |

—360 Sound Stereo" in black on label
| ❏ CS8978 [S] | Miles and Monk at Newport | 1965 | $60 |

—360 Sound Stereo" in white on label
| ❏ KCS8978 | Miles and Monk at Newport | 1974 | $25 |

—Orange label, new prefix
| ❏ PC8978 | Miles and Monk at Newport | 1977 | $20 |

—Orange label, new prefix; some have bar codes
| ❏ PC8978 | Miles and Monk at Newport | 199? | $30 |

—180-gram reissue

DAVIS, MILES
Trumpeter, bandleader and composer. The most significant post-World War II jazz musician, he experimented in everything from bebop to hip-hop, alternately enthralling and/or infuriating his fans. The number of prominent soloists and bandleaders who passed through his groups is enormous. Also see LEONARD BERNSTEIN; THE BRASS ENSEMBLE; LEE KONITZ.

Albums
ALA
| ❏ AJ-503 | Archives of Jazz, Vol. 3 | 198? | $30 |

BLUE NOTE
❏ BLP-5022 [10]	Miles Davis, Vol. 2	1953	$1000
❏ BLP-5040 [10]	Miles Davis, Vol. 3	1954	$1000
❏ BLP-1501 [M]	Miles Davis, Volume 1	1955	$800

—Deep groove" version; Lexington Ave. address on label
| ❏ BLP-1501 [M] | Miles Davis, Volume 1 | 1958 | $800 |

—Deep groove" version, W. 63rd St. address on label
| ❏ BLP-1501 [M] | Miles Davis, Volume 1 | 1958 | $175 |

—Regular version, W. 63rd St. address on label
| ❏ BLP-1501 [M] | Miles Davis, Volume 1 | 1963 | $80 |

—New York, USA" address on label
| ❏ BLP-1501 [M] | Miles Davis, Volume 1 | 1966 | $100 |

—With "A Division of Liberty Records" on label
| ❏ BLP-81501 [B] | Miles Davis, Volume 1 | 1968 | $60 |

—Rechanneled stereo version of 1501
| ❏ BST-81501 | Miles Davis, Volume 1 | 1985 | $30 |

—The Finest in Jazz Since 1939" reissue label
| ❏ BLP-1502 [M] | Miles Davis, Volume 2 | 1955 | $500 |

—Deep groove" version; Lexington Ave. address on label
| ❏ BLP-1502 [M] | Miles Davis, Volume 2 | 1955 | $550 |

—Deep groove" version; W. 63rd St. address on label
| ❏ BLP-1502 [M] | Miles Davis, Volume 2 | 1958 | $175 |

—Regular version, W. 63rd St. address on label
| ❏ BLP-1502 [M] | Miles Davis, Volume 2 | 1963 | $80 |

—With New York, USA address on label
| ❏ BLP-1502 [M] | Miles Davis, Volume 2 | 1966 | $100 |

—With "A Division of Liberty Records" on label
| ❏ BLP-81502 [B] | Miles Davis, Volume 2 | 1968 | $60 |

—Rechanneled stereo version of 1502
| ❏ BST-81502 | Miles Davis, Volume 2 | 1985 | $30 |

—The Finest in Jazz Since 1939" reissue label
| ❏ BLP-5013 [10] | Miles Davis (Young Man with a Horn) | 1952 | $1000 |

BOOK-OF-THE-MONTH CLUB
| ❏ 91-7725 | Master of Styles | 198? | $40 |

CAPITOL
| ❏ T762 [M] | Birth of the Cool | 1956 | $300 |

—Turquoise label
| ❏ T1974 [M] | Birth of the Cool | 1963 | $60 |

—Reissue of 762; black label with rainbow ring, Capitol logo at top
| ❏ DT1974 [R] | Birth of the Cool | 1963 | $75 |
| ❏ T762 [M] | Birth of the Cool | 1958 | $250 |

—Black label wirh rainbow ring, Capitol logo at left
| ❏ T762 [M] | Birth of the Cool | 2003 | $40 |

—Classic Records reissue on 200-gram vinyl
| ❏ H459 [10] | Classics in Jazz | 1954 | $300 |

—First 33 1/3 rpm issue of some of the "Birth of the Cool" sessions
| ❏ M-11026 [M] | The Complete Birth of the Cool | 1972 | $80 |
| ❏ N-16168 [M] | The Complete Birth of the Cool | 198? | $25 |

—Budget-line reissue

CHARLIE PARKER
| ❏ PLP-824 | Many Miles of Davis | 196? | $100 |

COLUMBIA
| ❏ PG33967 | Agharta | 1976 | $40 |
| ❏ KC30455 | A Tribute to Jack Johnson | 1971 | $50 |

—Original issue
| ❏ PC30455 | A Tribute to Jack Johnson | 1977 | $20 |

—Orange label, new prefix; some with bar codes
| ❏ PC30455 | A Tribute to Jack Johnson | 199? | $30 |

—180-gram reissue
| ❏ C2X45332 | Aura | 1989 | $60 |
| ❏ C32025 | Basic Miles -- The Classic Performances of Miles Davis | 1973 | $50 |

—Original prefix

| ❏ PC32025 | Basic Miles -- The Classic Performances of Miles Davis | 198? | $20 |

—Budget-line reissue; bar code on cover
| ❏ PC32025 | Basic Miles -- The Classic Performances of Miles Davis | 199? | $30 |

—180-gram reissue
| ❏ CG32866 | Big Fun | 1974 | $60 |

—Original prefix
| ❏ PG32866 | Big Fun | 1977 | $35 |

—Orange labels, new prefix
| ❏ GP26 | Bitches Brew | 1970 | $120 |

—360 Sound Stereo" on red labels
| ❏ GP26 | Bitches Brew | 1970 | $60 |

—Orange labels; no bar code on cover
| ❏ GQ30997 [Q] | Bitches Brew | 1972 | $150 |
| ❏ PG26 | Bitches Brew | 1977 | $35 |

—Orange labels, new prefix; some have bar code on cover
| ❏ KC236278 | Circle in the Round | 1980 | $50 |
| ❏ FC38991 | Decoy | 1984 | $30 |

—Original issue
| ❏ FC38991 | Decoy | 199? | $30 |

—180-gram reissue
| ❏ KC236472 | Directions | 1981 | $50 |
| ❏ CL2350 [M] | E.S.P. | 1965 | $60 |

—Guaranteed High Fidelity" on label
| ❏ CL2350 [M] | E.S.P. | 1965 | $50 |

—360 Sound Mono" on label
| ❏ CS9150 [S] | E.S.P. | 1965 | $120 |

—360 Sound Stereo" in black on label
| ❏ CS9150 [S] | E.S.P. | 1965 | $100 |

—360 Sound Stereo" in white on label
| ❏ CS9150 | E.S.P. | 1971 | $50 |

—Orange label
| ❏ KCS9150 | E.S.P. | 1974 | $35 |

—Orange label, new prefix
| ❏ PC9150 | E.S.P. | 1977 | $20 |

—Orange label, new prefix; some have bar code on back
| ❏ PC9150 | E.S.P. | 199? | $30 |

—180-gram reissue
| ❏ J1 | Facets | 1973 | $30 |
| ❏ CS9750 | Filles de Kilimanjaro | 1969 | $50 |

—360 Sound Stereo" on red label
| ❏ CS9750 | Filles de Kilimanjaro | 1971 | $30 |

—Orange label
| ❏ KCS9750 | Filles de Kilimanjaro | 1974 | $25 |

—Orange label, new prefix
| ❏ PC9750 | Filles de Kilimanjaro | 1977 | $20 |

—Orange label, new prefix; some have bar codes
| ❏ PC9750 | Filles de Kilimanjaro | 199? | $30 |

—180-gram reissue
| ❏ CL2453 [M] | Four" & More -- Recorded Live in Concert | 1966 | $60 |
| ❏ CS9253 [S] | Four" & More -- Recorded Live in Concert | 1966 | $60 |

—360 Sound Stereo" on red label
| ❏ CS9253 | Four" & More -- Recorded Live in Concert | 1971 | $35 |

—Orange label
| ❏ KCS9253 | Four" & More -- Recorded Live in Concert | 1974 | $30 |

—Orange label, new prefix
| ❏ PC9253 | Four" & More -- Recorded Live in Concert | 1977 | $20 |

—Orange label, new prefix; some have bar codes
| ❏ PC9253 | Four" & More -- Recorded Live in Concert | 199? | $30 |

—180-gram reissue
| ❏ KG33236 | Get Up With It | 1974 | $60 |

—Original prefix
| ❏ PG33236 | Get Up With It | 1977 | $50 |

—Orange labels, new prefix
| ❏ C238506 | Heard 'Round the World | 1983 | $50 |
| ❏ CS9875 | In a Silent Way | 1969 | $40 |

—360 Sound Stereo" on red label
| ❏ CS9875 | In a Silent Way | 1971 | $50 |

—Orange label
| ❏ KCS9875 | In a Silent Way | 1974 | $30 |

—Orange label, new prefix
| ❏ PC9875 | In a Silent Way | 1977 | $20 |

—Orange label, new prefix; some have bar codes
| ❏ KG32092 | In Concert | 1973 | $60 |
| ❏ PG32092 | In Concert | 1977 | $35 |

—Orange labels, new prefix

Number	Title	Yr	NM
❏ S30455	Jack Johnson	1971	$100

—Original issue on gray "Masterworks" label

Number	Title	Yr	NM
❏ C32470	Jazz at the Plaza, Vol. 1	1973	$50

—Original prefix

| ❏ PC32470 | Jazz at the Plaza, Vol. 1 | 1977 | $20 |

—Reissue with new prefix; some have bar codes

| ❏ PC32470 | Jazz at the Plaza, Vol. 1 | 199? | $30 |

—180-gram reissue

| ❏ CL1268 [M] | Jazz Track | 1958 | $175 |

—Red and black label with six "eye" logos; with abstract drawing on cover

| ❏ CL1268 [M] | Jazz Track | 1958 | $140 |

—Red and black label with six "eye" logos; with Miles and a woman on cover

| ❏ CL1355 [M] | Kind of Blue | 1959 | $600 |

—Red and black label with six "eye" logos

| ❏ CL1355 [M] | Kind of Blue | 1963 | $100 |

—Guaranteed High Fidelity" on label

| ❏ CL1355 [M] | Kind of Blue | 1965 | $60 |

—360 Sound Mono" on label

| ❏ CS8163 [S] | Kind of Blue | 1959 | $250 |

—Black and red label with "Stereo Fidelity" at top and "Columbia" in white at bottom; six white "eye" logos on label

| ❏ CS8163 [S] | Kind of Blue | 1963 | $120 |

—360 Sound Stereo" in black on label

| ❏ CS8163 [S] | Kind of Blue | 1965 | $40 |

—360 Sound Stereo" in white on label

| ❏ CS8163 | Kind of Blue | 1971 | $50 |

—Orange label

| ❏ KCS8163 | Kind of Blue | 1974 | $30 |

—Orange label, new prefix

| ❏ PC8163 | Kind of Blue | 1977 | $20 |

—Orange label, new prefix; some have bar codes

| ❏ CS8163 | Kind of Blue | 1997 | $150 |

—Contains both the original Side 1, which was mastered slightly fast, and the "correct" Side 1 (as Side 3), with an alternate take of "Flamenco Sketches" on Side 4 (at 45 rpm); distributed by Classic Records

| ❏ CS8163 | Kind of Blue | 2002 | $300 |

—Blue vinyl; 200-gram edition; distributed by Classic Records; approximately 100 copies were pressed

| ❏ CS8163 | Kind of Blue | 2002 | $200 |

—Blue vinyl; 180-gram edition; distributed by Classic Records; 500 copies were pressed

| ❏ CS8163-45 | Kind of Blue | 1999 | $175 |

—Distributed by Classic Records; pressed on four single-sided 12-inch 45 rpm records

| ❏ CS8163 | Kind of Blue | 2001 | $60 |

—200-gram pressing; distributed by Classic Records; contains Side 1 at its "correct" speed

| ❏ C238266 | Live at the Plugged Nickel | 1982 | $50 |
| ❏ G30954 | Live-Evil | 1971 | $60 |

—Original edition

| ❏ GQ30954 [Q] | Live-Evil | 1973 | $150 |
| ❏ CL1041 [M] | Miles Ahead | 1957 | $200 |

—Red and black label with six "eye" logos; cover has a white woman and her child on a sailboat

| ❏ CL1041 [M] | Miles Ahead | 1957 | $175 |

—Red and black label with six "eye" logos; cover has Miles Davis blowing his trumpet

| ❏ CL1041 [M] | Miles Ahead | 1963 | $40 |

—Guaranteed High Fidelity" on label

| ❏ CL1041 [M] | Miles Ahead | 1965 | $60 |

—360 Sound Mono" on label

| ❏ CS8633 [R] | Miles Ahead | 1963 | $50 |

—Rechanneled stereo version of 1041; "360 Sound Stereo" in black on label

| ❏ CS8633 | Miles Ahead | 1971 | $30 |

—Orange label

| ❏ KCS8633 | Miles Ahead | 1974 | $25 |

—Orange label, new prefix

| ❏ PC8633 | Miles Ahead | 1977 | $20 |

—Orange label, new prefix; some have bar codes

| ❏ CS8633 [R] | Miles Ahead | 1963 | $35 |

—360 Sound Stereo" in white on label

| ❏ CL1812 [M] | Miles Davis at Carnegie Hall | 1962 | $100 |

—Red and black label with six "eye" logos

| ❏ CL1812 [M] | Miles Davis at Carnegie Hall | 1963 | $60 |

—Guaranteed High Fidelity" on label

| ❏ CL1812 [M] | Miles Davis at Carnegie Hall | 1965 | $50 |

—Mono" on label

| ❏ CS8612 [S] | Miles Davis at Carnegie Hall | 1962 | $120 |

Number	Title	Yr	NM

—Red and black label with six "eye" logos

| ❏ CS8612 [S] | Miles Davis at Carnegie Hall | 1962 | $60 |

—360 Sound Stereo" in black on label

| ❏ CS8612 [S] | Miles Davis at Carnegie Hall | 1965 | $60 |

—360 Sound Stereo" in white on label

| ❏ CS8612 | Miles Davis at Carnegie Hall | 1971 | $35 |

—Orange label

| ❏ KCS8612 | Miles Davis at Carnegie Hall | 1974 | $30 |

—Orange label, new prefix

| ❏ PC8612 | Miles Davis at Carnegie Hall | 1977 | $20 |

—Orange label, new prefix; may have bar code on back cover

| ❏ PC8612 | Miles Davis at Carnegie Hall | 199? | $30 |

—180-gram vinyl reissue

| ❏ G30038 | Miles Davis at Fillmore | 1970 | $60 |

—Original prefix

| ❏ CG30038 | Miles Davis at Fillmore | 197? | $35 |

—Later prefix

| ❏ J17 | Miles Davis at Newport | 1973 | $30 |
| ❏ CS9808 | Miles Davis' Greatest Hits | 1969 | $50 |

—360 Sound Stereo" on red label

| ❏ CS9808 | Miles Davis' Greatest Hits | 1971 | $30 |

—Orange label

| ❏ KCS9808 | Miles Davis' Greatest Hits | 1974 | $25 |

—Orange label, new prefix

| ❏ PC9808 | Miles Davis' Greatest Hits | 1977 | $20 |

—Orange label, new prefix; some have bar codes

| ❏ PC9808 | Miles Davis' Greatest Hits | 199? | $30 |

—180-gram reissue

| ❏ CL2183 [M] | Miles Davis in Europe | 1964 | $40 |

—Guaranteed High Fidelity" on label

| ❏ CL2183 [M] | Miles Davis in Europe | 1965 | $60 |

—360 Sound Mono" on label

| ❏ CS8983 [S] | Miles Davis in Europe | 1964 | $40 |

—360 Sound Stereo" in black on label

| ❏ CS8983 [S] | Miles Davis in Europe | 1965 | $60 |

—360 Sound Stereo" in white on label

| ❏ CS8983 | Miles Davis in Europe | 1971 | $35 |

—Orange label

| ❏ KCS8983 | Miles Davis in Europe | 1974 | $30 |

—Orange label, new prefix

| ❏ PC8983 | Miles Davis in Europe | 1977 | $20 |

—Orange label, new prefix; some have bar codes

| ❏ PC8983 | Miles Davis in Europe | 199? | $30 |

—180-gram reissue

| ❏ CL1669 [M] | Miles Davis in Person, Vol. 1 (Friday Nights at the Blackhawk, San Francisco) | 1961 | $60 |

—Red and black label with six "eye" logos; later pressings may exist

| ❏ CS8469 [S] | Miles Davis in Person, Vol. 1 (Friday Nights at the Blackhawk, San Francisco) | 1961 | $60 |

—Red and black label with six "eye" logos; later pressings may exist

| ❏ CL1670 [M] | Miles Davis in Person, Vol. 2 (Saturday Nights at the Blackhawk, San Francisco) | 1961 | $60 |

—Six "eye" logos on label; later pressings may exist

| ❏ CS8470 [S] | Miles Davis in Person, Vol. 2 (Saturday Nights at the Blackhawk, San Francisco) | 1961 | $60 |

—Six "eye" logos on label; later pressings may exist

| ❏ C2L20 [M] | Miles Davis in Person (Friday & Saturday Nights at the Blackhawk, San Francisco) | 1961 | $100 |

—Six "eye" logos on label

| ❏ C2L20 [M] | Miles Davis in Person (Friday & Saturday Nights at the Blackhawk, San Francisco) | 1963 | $60 |

—Guaranteed High Fidelity" on label

| ❏ C2L20 [M] | Miles Davis in Person (Friday & Saturday Nights at the Blackhawk, San Francisco) | 1965 | $60 |

—Mono" on label

| ❏ C2S820 [S] | Miles Davis in Person (Friday & Saturday Nights at the Blackhawk, San Francisco) | 1961 | $120 |

—Red and black label with six "eye" logos

Number	Title	Yr	NM
❏ C2S820 [S]	Miles Davis in Person (Friday & Saturday Nights at the Blackhawk, San Francisco)	1963	$60

—360 Sound Stereo" in black on label

| ❏ C2S820 [S] | Miles Davis in Person (Friday & Saturday Nights at the Blackhawk, San Francisco) | 1965 | $60 |

—360 Sound Stereo" in white on label

| ❏ C2S820 | Miles Davis in Person (Friday & Saturday Nights at the Blackhawk, San Francisco) | 1971 | $35 |

—Orange labels

| ❏ CL2828 [M] | Miles in the Sky | 1968 | $150 |
| ❏ CS9628 [S] | Miles in the Sky | 1968 | $60 |

—360 Sound Stereo" on red label

| ❏ CS9628 | Miles in the Sky | 1971 | $35 |

—Orange label

| ❏ KCS9628 | Miles in the Sky | 1974 | $30 |

—Orange label, new prefix

| ❏ PC9628 | Miles in the Sky | 1977 | $20 |

—Orange label, new prefix; some have bar codes

| ❏ PC9628 | Miles in the Sky | 199? | $30 |

—180-gram reissue

| ❏ CL2601 [M] | Miles Smiles | 1966 | $40 |
| ❏ CS9401 [S] | Miles Smiles | 1966 | $60 |

—360 Sound Stereo" on red label

| ❏ CS9401 | Miles Smiles | 1971 | $35 |

—Orange label

| ❏ KCS9401 | Miles Smiles | 1974 | $30 |

—Orange label, new prefix

| ❏ PC9401 | Miles Smiles | 1977 | $20 |

—Orange label, new prefix; some have bar codes

| ❏ PC9401 | Miles Smiles | 199? | $30 |

—180-gram reissue

| ❏ A2S1374 [DJ] | Miles to Go | 1982 | $40 |

—Promo-only compilation

| ❏ CL1193 [M] | Milestones | 1958 | $150 |

—Red and black label with six "eye" logos

| ❏ CL1193 [M] | Milestones | 1963 | $40 |

—Guaranteed High Fidelity" on label

| ❏ CL1193 [M] | Milestones | 1965 | $60 |

—360 Sound Mono" on label

| ❏ CL2628 [M] | Milestones | 1967 | $60 |

—Reissue of 1193?

| ❏ CS8021 [S] | Milestones | 1959 | $200 |

—Red and black label with six "eye" logos

| ❏ CS8021 [S] | Milestones | 1963 | $175 |

—360 Sound Stereo" in black on label

| ❏ CS8021 [S] | Milestones | 1965 | $120 |

—360 Sound Stereo" in white on label

| ❏ CS9428 [R] | Milestones | 1967 | $60 |

—360 Sound Stereo" on red label; reissue of 8021

| ❏ KCS9428 | Milestones | 1974 | $30 |

—Orange label, new prefix

| ❏ PC9428 | Milestones | 1977 | $20 |

—Orange label, new prefix; some have bar codes

| ❏ CS9428 | Milestones | 1971 | $35 |

—Orange label

| ❏ CL2306 [M] | My Funny Valentine | 1965 | $60 |

—Guaranteed High Fidelity" on label

| ❏ CL2306 [M] | My Funny Valentine | 1965 | $50 |

—Mono" on label

| ❏ CS9106 [S] | My Funny Valentine | 1965 | $60 |

—360 Sound Stereo" in black on label

| ❏ CS9106 [S] | My Funny Valentine | 1965 | $50 |

—360 Sound Stereo" in white on label

| ❏ CS9106 | My Funny Valentine | 1971 | $30 |

—Orange label

| ❏ KCS9106 | My Funny Valentine | 1974 | $25 |

—Orange label, new prefix

| ❏ PC9106 | My Funny Valentine | 1977 | $20 |

—Orange label, new prefix

| ❏ CL2794 [M] | Nefertiti | 1968 | $100 |
| ❏ CS9594 [S] | Nefertiti | 1968 | $50 |

—360 Sound Stereo" on red label

| ❏ CS9594 | Nefertiti | 1971 | $30 |

—Orange label

| ❏ KCS9594 | Nefertiti | 1974 | $25 |

—Orange label, new prefix

Number	Title	Yr	NM
❏ PC9594	Nefertiti	1977	$20
—Orange label, new prefix			
❏ KC31906	On the Corner	1972	$30
❏ PC31906	On the Corner	1977	$20
—Orange label, new prefix			
❏ CL1274 [M]	Porgy and Bess	1958	$100
—Six "eye" logos on label			
❏ CL1274 [M]	Porgy and Bess	1963	$60
—Guaranteed High Fidelity" on label			
❏ CL1274 [M]	Porgy and Bess	1965	$50
—Mono" on label			
❏ CS8085 [S]	Porgy and Bess	1959	$100
—Six "eye" logos on label			
❏ CS8085 [S]	Porgy and Bess	1963	$60
—360 Sound Stereo" in black on label			
❏ CS8085 [S]	Porgy and Bess	1965	$50
—360 Sound Stereo" in white on label			
❏ CS8085	Porgy and Bess	1971	$30
—Orange label			
❏ KCS8085	Porgy and Bess	1974	$25
—Orange label, new prefix			
❏ PC8085	Porgy and Bess	1977	$20
—Orange label, new prefix			
❏ CL2106 [M]	Quiet Nights	1964	$60
—Guaranteed High Fidelity" on label			
❏ CL2106 [M]	Quiet Nights	1965	$50
—Mono" on label			
❏ CS8906 [S]	Quiet Nights	1964	$60
—360 Sound Stereo" in black on label			
❏ CS8906 [S]	Quiet Nights	1965	$50
—360 Sound Stereo" in white on label			
❏ CS8906	Quiet Nights	1971	$30
—Orange label			
❏ KCS8906	Quiet Nights	1974	$25
—Orange label, new prefix			
❏ PC8906	Quiet Nights	1977	$20
—Orange label, new prefix			
❏ CL949 [M]	'Round About Midnight	1957	$100
—Six "eye" logos on label			
❏ CL949 [M]	'Round About Midnight	1963	$60
—Guaranteed High Fidelity" on label			
❏ CL949 [M]	'Round About Midnight	1965	$50
—Mono" on label			
❏ CS8649 [R]	'Round About Midnight	1963	$30
—Rechanneled stereo version of 949			
❏ CS8649	'Round About Midnight	1971	$30
—Orange label			
❏ KCS8649	'Round About Midnight	1974	$25
—Orange label, new prefix			
❏ PC8649	'Round About Midnight	1977	$20
—Orange label, new prefix			
❏ CL2051 [M]	Seven Steps to Heaven	1963	$60
—Guaranteed High Fidelity" on label			
❏ CL2051 [M]	Seven Steps to Heaven	1965	$50
—Mono" on label			
❏ CS8851 [S]	Seven Steps to Heaven	1963	$60
—360 Sound Stereo" in black on label			
❏ CS8851 [S]	Seven Steps to Heaven	1965	$50
—360 Sound Stereo" in white on label			
❏ CS8851	Seven Steps to Heaven	1971	$30
—Orange label			
❏ KCS8851	Seven Steps to Heaven	1974	$25
—Orange label, new prefix			
❏ PC8851	Seven Steps to Heaven	1977	$20
—Orange label, new prefix			
❏ CL1480 [M]	Sketches of Spain	1960	$100
—Six "eye" logos on label			
❏ CL1480 [M]	Sketches of Spain	1963	$60
—Guaranteed High Fidelity" on label			
❏ CS8271 [S]	Sketches of Spain	1960	$150
—Red and black label with six "eye" logos			
❏ CS8271 [S]	Sketches of Spain	1963	$60
—360 Sound Stereo" in black on label			
❏ CS8271 [S]	Sketches of Spain	1965	$50
—360 Sound Stereo" in white on label			
❏ CS8271	Sketches of Spain	1971	$30
—Orange label			
❏ KCS8271	Sketches of Spain	1974	$25
—Orange label, new prefix			
❏ PC8271	Sketches of Spain	1977	$20
—Orange label, new prefix			

Number	Title	Yr	NM
❏ CS8271 [S]	Sketckes of Spain	1999	$60
—Audiophile reissue; distributed by Classic Records			
❏ CL1656 [M]	Someday My Prince Will Come	1961	$40
—Six "eye" logos on label			
❏ CL1656 [M]	Someday My Prince Will Come	1963	$60
—Guaranteed High Fidelity" on label			
❏ CL1656 [M]	Someday My Prince Will Come	1965	$50
—Mono" on label			
❏ CS8456 [S]	Someday My Prince Will Come	1961	$40
—Six "eye" logos on label			
❏ CS8456 [S]	Someday My Prince Will Come	1963	$60
—360 Sound Stereo" in black on label			
❏ CS8456 [S]	Someday My Prince Will Come	1965	$50
—360 Sound Stereo" in white on label			
❏ KCS8456	Someday My Prince Will Come	1974	$25
—Orange label, new prefix			
❏ PC8456	Someday My Prince Will Come	1977	$20
—Orange label, new prefix			
❏ CL2732 [M]	Sorcerer	1967	$60
❏ CS9532 [S]	Sorcerer	1967	$50
—360 Sound Stereo" on red label			
❏ CS9532	Sorcerer	1971	$30
—Orange label			
❏ KCS9532	Sorcerer	1974	$25
—Orange label, new prefix			
❏ PC9532	Sorcerer	1977	$20
—Orange label, new prefix			
❏ FC38657	Star People	1983	$25
❏ C5X45000	The Columbia Years 1955-1985	1988	$120
❏ FC36790	The Man with the Horn	1981	$30
—Original edition			
❏ HC46790	The Man with the Horn	1982	$100
—Half-Speed Mastered" on cover			
❏ PC36790	The Man with the Horn	198?	$20
—Budget-line reissue with new prefix			
❏ PC36790	The Man with the Horn	199?	$30
—180-gram reissue			
❏ C6X36976	The Miles Davis Collection Vol. 1: 12 Sides of Miles	1980	$175
❏ PC34396	Water Babies	1977	$30
—Original has no bar code			
❏ PC34396	Water Babies	198?	$20
—Reissue with bar code			
❏ C238005	We Want Miles	1982	$30
❏ FC40023	You're Under Arrest	1985	$25
COLUMBIA JAZZ MASTERPIECES			
❏ CJ44151	Ballads	1988	$25
❏ CJ44151	Ballads	199?	$30
—180-gram reissue			
❏ C2J40577	Bitches Brew	1987	$35
❏ CJ40645	Cookin' at the Plugged Nickel	1987	$35
❏ CJ40580	In a Silent Way	1987	$25
❏ CJ40580	In a Silent Way	199?	$30
—180-gram reissue			
❏ CJ40579	Kind of Blue	1987	$35
—Reissue; when this version of the album was prepared, Columbia discovered that all of Side 1 on the original LP was mastered at the wrong speed; this album was the first time it was mastered "correctly			
❏ CJ40609	Live Miles: More Music from the Legendary Carnegie Hall Concert	1987	$25
❏ CJ40609	Live Miles: More Music from the Legendary Carnegie Hall Concert	199?	$30
—180-gram reissue			
❏ CJ40784	Miles Ahead	1987	$25
❏ CJ40784	Miles Ahead	199?	$30
—180-gram reissue			
❏ CJ44052	Miles and Coltrane	1988	$25
❏ CJ44052	Miles and Coltrane	199?	$30
—180-gram reissue			
❏ CJ44257	Miles Davis in Person, Vol. 1 (Friday Nights at the Blackhawk, San Francisco)	1988	$25

Number	Title	Yr	NM
❏ CJ44257	Miles Davis in Person, Vol. 1 (Friday Nights at the Blackhawk, San Francisco)	199?	$30
—180-gram reissue			
❏ CJ44425	Miles Davis in Person, Vol. 2 (Saturday Nights at the Blackhawk, San Francisco)	1989	$25
❏ CJ40837	Milestones	1987	$25
❏ CJ40837	Milestones	199?	$30
—180-gram reissue			
❏ CJ40647	Porgy and Bess	1987	$25
❏ CJ40610	'Round About Midnight	1987	$25
❏ CJ40578	Sketches of Spain	1987	$25
❏ CJ40947	Someday My Prince Will Come	1987	$25
COLUMBIA LIMITED EDITION			
❏ LE10018	Miles Davis in Person, Vol. 1 (Friday Nights at the Blackhawk, San Francisco)	197?	$35
❏ LE10076	Miles Davis in Person, Vol. 2 (Saturday Nights at the Blackhawk, San Francisco)	197?	$35
COLUMBIA SPECIAL PRODUCTS			
❏ P13811	Facets	1977	$30
CONTEMPORARY			
❏ C-7645	Miles Davis and the Lighthouse All-Stars At Last!	1985	$35
DEBUT			
❏ DEB120 [M]	Blue Moods	1955	$400
EVEREST ARCHIVE OF FOLK & JAZZ			
❏ FS-283	Miles Davis	197?	$25
FANTASY			
❏ OJC-245	Bags Groove	1987	$30
—Reissue of Prestige 7109			
❏ OJC-093	Blue Haze	198?	$30
—Reissue of Prestige 7054			
❏ 6001 [M]	Blue Moods	1962	$350
—Reissue of Debut album; red vinyl			
❏ 6001 [M]	Blue Moods	1963	$140
—Black vinyl, red label			
❏ 86001 [R]	Blue Moods	1962	$120
—Blue vinyl			
❏ 86001 [R]	Blue Moods	1963	$60
—Black vinyl, blue label			
❏ OJC-043	Blue Moods	198?	$30
—Reissue of Fantasy 6001			
❏ OJC-071	Collectors' Item	198?	$30
—Reissue of Prestige 7044			
❏ OJC-128	Cookin' with the Miles Davis Quintet	198?	$30
—Reissue of Prestige 7094			
❏ OJC-005	Dig Miles Davis/Sonny Rollins	198?	$30
—Reissue of Prestige 7012			
❏ OJC-053	Miles Davis and Horns	198?	$30
—Reissue of Prestige 7025			
❏ OJC-480	Miles Davis and the Lighthouse All-Stars At Last!	1991	$30
—Reissue of Contemporary 7645			
❏ OJC-012	Miles Davis and the Milt Jackson Quintet/Sextet	198?	$25
—Reissue of Prestige 7034			
❏ OJC-347	Miles Davis and the Modern Jazz Giants	198?	$30
—Reissue of Prestige 7150			
❏ OJC-006	Miles -- The New Miles Davis Quintet	198?	$30
—Reissue of Prestige 7014			
❏ OJC-190	Relaxin' with the Miles Davis Quintet	1985	$25
—Reissue of Prestige 7129			
❏ OJC-391	Steamin' with the Miles Davis Quintet	1989	$25
—Reissue of Prestige 7200			
❏ OJC-004	The Musings of Miles	198?	$30
—Reissue of Prestige 7007			
❏ OJC-213	Walkin'	1987	$25
—Reissue of Prestige 7076			
❏ OJC-296	Workin' with the Miles Davis Quintet	1987	$25
—Reissue of Prestige 7166			
FONTANA			
❏ MGF-27532 [M]	Jazz on the Screen	1965	$40
—With Art Blakey and the Jazz Messengers			

Miles Davis, *Miles Davis, Vol. 2*, Blue Note BLP-5022, 10-inch LP, **$1,000**.

Miles Davis featuring Sonny Rollins, *Dig*, Prestige PRLP-7012, color cover, yellow label with W. 50th St. address, **$300**.

Miles Davis, *Miles Davis and Horns*, Prestige PRLP-7025, yellow label with W. 50th St. address, **$400**.

Miles Davis, *In Person* (Friday and Saturday Nights at the Blackhawk, San Francisco), Columbia C2S 820, original with "360 Sound Stereo" in black on label, **$40**.

Number	Title	Yr	NM
❑ SRF-67532 [S]	Jazz on the Screen	1965	$40
JAZZ HERITAGE			
❑ 913427F [M]	Dig Miles Davis/Sonny Rollins	198?	$35
—Mail-order reissue			
MOBILE FIDELITY			
❑ 1-177	Someday My Prince Will Come	1985	$150
—Audiophile vinyl			
MOSAIC			
❑ MQ11-164	Miles Davis & Gil Evans: The Complete Columbia Studio Recordings	1996	$400
❑ MQ6-183	The Complete Bitches Brew Sessions	1999	$175
❑ MQ6-220	The Complete Blackhawk Sessions	2003	$175
❑ MQ9-191	The Complete Columbia Recordings of Miles Davis with John Coltrane	2000	$170
❑ MQ5-209	The Complete In a Silent Way Sessions (September 1968-February 1969)	2002	$150
❑ MQ10-158	The Complete Plugged Nickel Sessions	1995	$300
❑ MQ10-177	The Complete Studio Recordings of the Miles Davis Quintet 1965-June 1968	1998	$150
PAIR			
❑ PDL2-1095	Best of Miles Davis	1986	$30
PHILIPS			
❑ 836305-1	Elevator to the Scaffold (L'Ancenseur Pour L'Echafaud)	198?	$30
—Reissue of Columbia 1268			
PRESTIGE			
❑ PRLP-7076 [M]	All Stars	1957	$500
—With W. 50th St. address on yellow label			
❑ PRLP-7076 [M]	All Stars	196?	$40
—With trident on blue label			
❑ PRLP-7076 [M]	All Stars	1958	$300
—With Bergenfield, N.J. address on yellow label			
❑ PRLP-7109 [M]	Bags Groove	1957	$300
—With W. 50th St. address on yellow label			
❑ PRLP-7109 [M]	Bags Groove	196?	$40
—With trident on blue label			
❑ PRLP-7109 [M]	Bags Groove	1958	$300
—With Bergenfield, N.J. address on yellow label			
❑ PRLP-7054 [M]	Blue Haze	1956	$300
—With W. 50th St. address on yellow label			
❑ PRLP-7054 [M]	Blue Haze	196?	$40
—With trident on blue label			
❑ PRLP-140 [10]	Blue Period	1953	$300
❑ P-12	Chronicle: The Complete Prestige Recordings	1980	$300
❑ PRLP-7044 [M]	Collectors' Item	1956	$300
—With W. 50th St. address on yellow label			
❑ PRLP-7044 [M]	Collectors' Item	196?	$40
—With trident on blue label			
❑ P-24022	Collector's Items	1973	$50
❑ PRST-7744 [R]	Conception	1970	$50
❑ PRLP-7094 [M]	Cookin' with the Miles Davis Quintet	1957	$500
—With W. 50th St. address on yellow label			
❑ PRLP-7094 [M]	Cookin' with the Miles Davis Quintet	196?	$40
—With trident on blue label			
❑ PRLP-7094 [M]	Cookin' with the Miles Davis Quintet	1958	$300
—With Bergenfield, N.J. address on yellow label			
❑ P-24054	Dig	197?	$35
❑ PRLP-7281 [M]	Diggin'	1963	$175
—Reissue of 7012; with Bergenfield, NJ address on yellow label			
❑ PRLP-7281 [M]	Diggin'	196?	$40
—With trident on blue label			
❑ PRST-7281 [R]	Diggin'	1963	$60
❑ PRLP-7012 [M]	Dig Miles Davis/Sonny Rollins	1956	$1250
—Gray cover			
❑ PRLP-7012 [M]	Dig Miles Davis/Sonny Rollins	1957	$300
—Color cover; yellow label with W. 50th St. address			
❑ PRLP-7168 [M]	Early Miles	1959	$200
—Reissue of 7025; with Bergenfield, NJ address on yellow label			

Number	Title	Yr	NM
❑ PRLP-7168 [M]	Early Miles	196?	$40
—With trident on blue label			
❑ PRST-7674 [R]	Early Miles	1969	$35
—Reissue of 7168			
❑ P-24064	Green Haze	1976	$50
❑ PRLP-7373 [M]	Jazz Classics	1965	$60
❑ PRST-7373 [R]	Jazz Classics	1965	$50
❑ PRST-7822 [R]	Miles Ahead!	1971	$35
❑ PR-24001	Miles Davis	1972	$50
❑ PRLP-196 [10]	Miles Davis All Stars, Volume 1	1955	$350
❑ PRLP-200 [10]	Miles Davis All Stars, Volume 2	1955	$350
❑ PRLP-7025 [M]	Miles Davis and Horns	1956	$400
—Yellow label with W. 50th St. address			
❑ PRLP-7025 [M]	Miles Davis and Horns	1958	$250
—Yellow label, Bergenfield, N.J. address			
❑ PRLP-7034 [M]	Miles Davis and the Milt Jackson Quintet/Sextet	1956	$400
—With W. 50th St. address on yellow label			
❑ PRLP-7034 [M]	Miles Davis and the Milt Jackson Quintet/Sextet	196?	$40
—With trident on blue label			
❑ PRLP-7034 [M]	Miles Davis and the Milt Jackson Quintet/Sextet	1958	$250
—Yellow label with Bergenfield, N.J. address			
❑ PRLP-7150 [M]	Miles Davis and the Modern Jazz Giants	1958	$250
—With Bergenfield, NJ address on yellow label			
❑ PRLP-7150 [M]	Miles Davis and the Modern Jazz Giants	196?	$40
—With trident on blue label			
❑ PRST-7650 [R]	Miles Davis and the Modern Jazz Giants	1969	$50
—Reissue of 7150			
❑ 16-3 [M]	Miles Davis and the Modern Jazz Giants	1957	$1000
—This album plays at 16 2/3 rpm and is marked as such; white label			
❑ PRLP-161 [10]	Miles Davis Featuring Sonny Rollins	1953	$350
❑ PRLP-7457 [M]	Miles Davis' Greatest Hits	1967	$60
❑ PRST-7457 [R]	Miles Davis' Greatest Hits	1967	$35
❑ PRLP-154 [10]	Miles Davis Plays Al Cohn Compositions	1953	$350
❑ PRLP-7352 [M]	Miles Davis Plays for Lovers	1965	$60
❑ PRST-7352 [R]	Miles Davis Plays for Lovers	1965	$50
❑ PRLP-7322 [M]	Miles Davis Plays Richard Rodgers	1964	$60
❑ PRST-7322 [R]	Miles Davis Plays Richard Rodgers	1964	$50
❑ PRLP-185 [10]	Miles Davis Quintet	1954	$250
❑ PRLP-187 [10]	Miles Davis Quintet Featuring Sonny Rollins	1954	$250
❑ PRLP-182 [10]	Miles Davis Sextet	1954	$250
❑ PRLP-7014 [M]	Miles -- The New Miles Davis Quintet	1956	$300
—Yellow label with W. 50th St. address			
❑ PRST-7540 [R]	Odyssey	1968	$30
—Reissue of 7034			
❑ PRST-7847	Oleo	1972	$30
❑ PRLP-7129 [M]	Relaxin' with the Miles Davis Quintet	1957	$600
—With W. 50th St. address on yellow label			
❑ PRLP-7129 [M]	Relaxin' with the Miles Davis Quintet	196?	$40
—With trident on blue label			
❑ PRLP-7129 [M]	Relaxin' with the Miles Davis Quintet	1957	$250
—With Bergenfield, NJ address on yellow label			
❑ PRST-7580 [R]	Steamin'	1968	$30
—Reissue of 7200			
❑ PRLP-7200 [M]	Steamin' with the Miles Davis Quintet	1961	$750
—With Bergenfield, NJ address on yellow label			
❑ PRLP-7200 [M]	Steamin' with the Miles Davis Quintet	196?	$60
—With trident on blue label			
❑ PRLP-7221 [M]	The Beginning	1962	$150
—Reissue of 7007; with Bergenfield, NJ address on yellow label			
❑ PRLP-7221 [M]	The Beginning	196?	$60
—With trident on blue label			
❑ PRLP-7007 [M]	The Musings of Miles	1955	$400
—Yellow label with W. 50th St. address			
❑ PRLP-124 [10]	The New Sounds of Miles Davis	1952	$350
❑ PRLP-7254 [M]	The Original Quintet	1963	$100

Number	Title	Yr	NM
—Reissue of 7014; with Bergenfield, NJ address on yellow label			
❑ PRLP-7254 [M]	The Original Quintet	196?	$60
—With trident on blue label			
❑ PRST-7254 [R]	The Original Quintet	1963	$50
❑ 24012	The Tallest Trees	1972	$35
❑ 24077	Tune Up	197?	$30
❑ PRST-7608 [R]	Walkin'	1969	$30
—Reissue of 7076			
❑ 24034	Workin' and Steamin'	1973	$35
❑ PRLP-7166 [M]	Workin' with the Miles Davis Quintet	1959	$200
—With Bergenfield, NJ address on yellow label			
❑ PRLP-7166 [M]	Workin' with the Miles Davis Quintet	196?	$60
—With trident on blue label			
SAVOY JAZZ			
❑ SJL-1196	First Miles	1989	$30
TRIP			
❑ 5015	Miles of Jazz	1974	$25
UNITED ARTISTS			
❑ UAS-9952	Miles Davis	1972	$50
—Reissue of Blue Note material			
WARNER BROS.			
❑ 25873	Amandla	1989	$50
❑ 26938	Doo-Bop	1992	$35
❑ 25490	Tutu	1986	$25

DAVIS, RICHARD

Bass player.

Albums

Number	Title	Yr	NM
BASF			
❑ 20725	Muses for Richard Davis	1973	$35
COBBLESTONE			
❑ 9003	Philosophy of the Spiritual	1972	$35
GALAXY			
❑ 5102	Fancy Free	1978	$25
MUSE			
❑ MR-5093	As One	1977	$30
❑ MR-5027	Dealin'	1974	$30
❑ MR-5002	Epistrophy & Now's the Time	1973	$30
❑ MR-5115	Harvest	1978	$30
❑ MR-5180	Way Out West	198?	$25
❑ MR-5083	With Understanding	1976	$30
PAUSA			
❑ 7022	Jazz Wave	197?	$25

DAVIS, SAMMY, JR., AND CARMEN MCRAE

Also see each artist's individual listings.

Albums

Number	Title	Yr	NM
DECCA			
❑ DL8490 [M]	Boy Meets Girl	1957	$150

DAVIS, SAMMY, JR., AND COUNT BASIE

Also see each artist's individual listings.

Albums

Number	Title	Yr	NM
MGM			
❑ SE-4825	Sammy Davis Jr. and Count Basie	1972	$25
—Reissue of Verve LP?			
VERVE			
❑ V-8605 [M]	Our Shining Hour	1965	$30
❑ V6-8605 [S]	Our Shining Hour	1965	$35

DAVIS, SAMMY, JR.

Mostly a pop singer, he dabbled in jazz occasionally. For a more complete listing of his releases, see the Standard Catalog of American Records.

Albums

Number	Title	Yr	NM
DECCA			
❑ DL8981 [M]	I Got a Right to Swing	1960	$50
❑ DL78981 [S]	I Got a Right to Swing	1960	$60
❑ DL8676 [M]	Mood to Be Wooed	1958	$100
REPRISE			
❑ R-6236 [M]	Sammy Davis. Jr., Sings/ Laurindo Almeida Plays	1966	$30
❑ RS-6236 [S]	Sammy Davis. Jr., Sings/ Laurindo Almeida Plays	1966	$35

Number	Title	Yr	NM

DAVIS, STANTON
Trumpeter and flugel horn player.

Albums

OUTRAGEOUS

❏ 2	Better Days	1977	$35

DAVIS, WALTER, JR.

Albums

BLUE NOTE

❏ BLP-4018 [M]	Davis Cup	1959	$150

—Regular version with W. 63rd St. address on label

❏ BLP-4018 [M]	Davis Cup	1964	$60

—With New York, USA address on label

❏ BST-84018 [S]	Davis Cup	1959	$60

—Regular version with W. 63rd St. address on label

❏ BST-84018 [S]	Davis Cup	1964	$25

—With New York, USA address on label

❏ BST-84018 [S]	Davis Cup	1967	$35

—With "A Division of Liberty Records" on label

❏ B1-32098	Davis Cup	1995	$35

RED

❏ VPA-150	A Being Such As You	198?	$30
❏ VPA-153	Blues Walk	198?	$30

DAVIS, WILD BILL
Organist. Also see JOHNNY HODGES AND WILD BILL DAVIS.

Albums

CORAL

❏ CRL57427 [M]	Lover	1962	$25
❏ CRL757427 [S]	Lover	1962	$30
❏ CRL57417 [M]	One More Time	1962	$25
❏ CRL757417 [S]	One More Time	1962	$30

EPIC

❏ LN3308 [M]	Evening Concerto	1956	$100
❏ LN1004 [10]	Here's Wild Bill Davis	1954	$200
❏ LN1121 [M]	On the Loose	1955	$100
❏ LN3118 [M]	Wild Bill Davis at Birdland	1955	$250

EVEREST

❏ LPBR-5094 [M]	Dance the Madison	1960	$30
❏ SDBR-1094 [S]	Dance the Madison	1960	$30
❏ LPBR-5125 [M]	Dis Heah	1961	$30
❏ SDBR-1125 [S]	Dis Heah	1961	$30
❏ LPBR-5052 [M]	Flying High	1959	$30
❏ SDBR-1052 [S]	Flying High	1959	$30
❏ LPBR-5014 [M]	My Fair Lady	1958	$30
❏ SDBR-1014 [S]	My Fair Lady	1959	$30
❏ LPBR-5116 [M]	Organ Grinder's Swing	1960	$30
❏ SDBR-1116 [S]	Organ Grinder's Swing	1960	$30
❏ LPBR-5133 [M]	The Music from "Milk and Honey"	1961	$30
❏ SDBR-1133 [S]	The Music from "Milk and Honey"	1961	$30

IMPERIAL

❏ LP-9015 [M]	Wild Bill Davis in Hollywood	1956	$200
❏ LP-9010 [M]	Wild Bill Davis on Broadway	1956	$200
❏ LP-9201 [M]	Wild Wild Wild Wild	1963	$150
❏ LP-12201 [R]	Wild Wild Wild Wild Wild Wild Wild Wild Wild	1963	$175

RCA VICTOR

❏ LSP-4139	Doin' His Thing	1969	$35
❏ LPM-3314 [M]	Free, Frantic and Funky	1965	$35
❏ LSP-3314 [S]	Free, Frantic and Funky	1965	$25
❏ LPM-3578 [M]	Live at Count Basie's	1966	$35
❏ LSP-3578 [S]	Live at Count Basie's	1966	$25
❏ LPM-3799 [M]	Midnight to Dawn	1967	$25
❏ LSP-3799 [S]	Midnight to Dawn	1967	$35

SUNSET

❏ SUS-5191	Flying Home	196?	$35

TANGERINE

❏ 1509	Wonderful World	197?	$35

DAVISON, WILD BILL, AND EDDIE MILLER
Also see each artist's individual listings.

Albums

REALTIME

❏ 306	Wild Bill Davison and Eddie Miller Play Hoagy Carmichael	198?	$25

DAVISON, WILD BILL, AND RALPH SUTTON
Also see each artist's individual listings.

Albums

STORYVILLE

❏ 4027	Together Again	197?	$25

DAVISON, WILD BILL
Trumpeter, cornet player and bandleader.

Albums

AIRCHECK

❏ 31	Wild Bill Davison	198?	$25

AUDIOPHILE

❏ AP-149	Beautifully Wild	197?	$30

CHIAROSCURO

❏ 124	Live at the Rainbow Room	197?	$35

CIRCLE

❏ LP-405 [10]	Showcase	1951	$80

COLUMBIA

❏ CL871 [M]	Pretty Wild: Wild Bill Davison with Strings	1956	$40
❏ CL983 [M]	Wild Bill Davison with Strings Attached	1957	$40

COMMODORE

❏ FL-20000 [10]	Dixieland Jazz Jamboree	1950	$100
❏ FL-30009 [M]	Mild and Wild	1959	$60
❏ XFL-14939	That's a-Plenty	198?	$25

DIXIELAND JUBILEE

❏ DJ-508 [M]	Greatest of the Greats	1958	$30
❏ DJS-508 [S]	Greatest of the Greats	1958	$30

JAZZOLOGY

❏ J-22	After Hours	196?	$35
❏ J-18	Blowin' Wild	1966	$25
❏ J-37	Jazz on a Saturday Afternoon, Vol. 1	197?	$30
❏ J-38	Jazz on a Saturday Afternoon, Vol. 2	197?	$30
❏ J-39	Jazz on a Saturday Afternoon, Vol. 3	197?	$30
❏ J-128	Lady of the Evening	1986	$25
❏ J-133	Live in Memphis	1986	$25
❏ J-14 [M]	Rompin' and Stompin'	196?	$25
❏ JCE-14 [S]	Rompin' and Stompin'	196?	$30
❏ J-25	Surfside Jazz	196?	$35
❏ J-151	Wild Bill Davison and His 75th Anniversary Jazz Band	1986	$25
❏ J-103	Wild Bill Davison and His Jazz Band	198?	$25
❏ J-70	Wild Bill Davison and the Classic Jazz Collegium	197?	$30
❏ J-30	Wild Bill Davison at Bull Run	1968	$35
❏ J-121	Wild Bill Davison In London	1987	$25
❏ J-2 [M]	Wild Bill Davison's Jazzologists	1962	$50
❏ JCE-2 [S]	Wild Bill Davison's Jazzologists	1962	$30
❏ J-160	Wild Bill Davison with Freddy Randall and His Band	198?	$25

REGENT

❏ MG-6026 [M]	When the Saints Go Marching In	196?	$50

RIVERSIDE

❏ RLP 12-211 [M]	Sweet and Hot	1956	$250

—White label, blue print

❏ RLP 12-211 [M]	Sweet and Hot	195?	$30

—Blue label, microphone logo at top

SACKVILLE

❏ 3002	The Jazz Giants	198?	$25

SAVOY

❏ MG-12214 [M]	Dixieland	1969	$35
❏ MG-12035 [M]	Jazz at Storyville	1955	$75
❏ MG-12055 [M]	Ringside at Condon's	1955	$75

—Reissue of two 10-inch LPs (15029 and 15030) that are listed in the Various Artists Collection area

SAVOY JAZZ

❏ SJL-2229	Individualism	198?	$35
❏ SJC-403	Ringside at Condon's	198?	$25

STORYVILLE

❏ 4048	But Beautiful	197?	$25
❏ 4029	Papa Bue's Viking Jazz Band	197?	$25
❏ 4005	Wild Bill Davison with Eddie Condon's All Stars	197?	$25

DAWSON, SID
Trombonist and bandleader.

Albums

DELMAR

❏ DL-109 [10]	Sid Dawson's Riverboat Gamblers	195?	$60

DAY, CORA LEE
Female singer.

Albums

ROULETTE

❏ R-52048 [M]	My Crying Hour	1960	$30
❏ SR-52048 [S]	My Crying Hour	1960	$40

DAY, DORIS
Female singer. Sang with both the HARRY JAMES and LES BROWN orchestras; she sang on one of the latter's best-remembered songs, "Sentimental Journey."

Albums

COLUMBIA

❏ CL1614 [M]	Bright and Shiny	1960	$25
❏ CS8414 [S]	Bright and Shiny	1960	$30
❏ CL6248 [10]	By the Light of the Silvery Moon	1953	$60
❏ CL6273 [10]	Calamity Jane	1953	$60
❏ CL1232 [M]	Cuttin' Capers	1959	$25
❏ CS8078 [S]	Cuttin' Capers	1959	$30
❏ CL1053 [M]	Day By Night	1958	$30
❏ CS8089 [S]	Day By Night	1959	$30
❏ CL624 [M]	Day Dreams	1955	$50

—Red label, gold print

❏ CL624 [M]	Day Dreams	1956	$30

—Six "eye" logos on label

❏ CL749 [M]	Day in Hollywood	1956	$30
❏ CL1210 [M]	Doris Day's Greatest Hits	1958	$30

—Six "eye" logos on label

❏ CS8635 [P]	Doris Day's Greatest Hits	1962	$25

—360 Sound Stereo" in black at bottom

❏ PC8635	Doris Day's Greatest Hits	198?	$10

—Budget-line reissue

❏ CL1752 [M]	Duet	1962	$25

—With Andre Previn

❏ CS8552 [S]	Duet	1962	$30

—With Andre Previn

❏ C2L5 [M]	Hooray for Hollywood	1959	$40
❏ C2S805 [S]	Hooray for Hollywood	1959	$50
❏ CL1366 [M]	Hooray for Hollywood, Volume 1	1959	$25
❏ CS8066 [S]	Hooray for Hollywood, Volume 1	1959	$30
❏ CL1367 [M]	Hooray for Hollywood, Volume 2	1959	$25
❏ CS8067 [S]	Hooray for Hollywood, Volume 2	1959	$30
❏ CL1660 [M]	I Have Dreamed	1961	$25
❏ CS8460 [S]	I Have Dreamed	1961	$30
❏ CL6198 [10]	I'll See You in My Dreams	1951	$60
❏ CL2310 [M]	Latin for Lovers	1965	$15
❏ CS9110 [S]	Latin for Lovers	1965	$25
❏ CL2518 [10]	Lights, Camera, Action	1955	$60
❏ DD1 [M]	Listen to Day	1960	$25
❏ DDS1 [S]	Listen to Day	1960	$30
❏ CL2131 [M]	Love Him!	1964	$25
❏ CS8931 [S]	Love Him!	1964	$25
❏ CL710 [M]	Love Me or Leave Me	1955	$60

—Red label, gold print

❏ CL710 [M]	Love Me or Leave Me	1956	$30

—Six "eye" logos on label

❏ CL710 [M]	Love Me or Leave Me	1962	$25

—Guaranteed High Fidelity" or "Mono" on label

❏ CS8773 [R]	Love Me or Leave Me	1963	$15
❏ CL6168 [10]	Lullaby of Broadway	1951	$60
❏ CL6186 [10]	On Moonlight Bay	1951	$60
❏ CL2360 [M]	Sentimental Journey	1965	$15
❏ CS9160 [S]	Sentimental Journey	1965	$20
❏ CL1470 [M]	Show Time	1960	$25
❏ CS8261 [S]	Show Time	1960	$25
❏ CL6149 [10]	Tea for Two	1950	$60
❏ CS9026 [S]	The Doris Day Christmas Album	1964	$25
❏ CL1438 [M]	What Every Girl Should Know	1960	$25
❏ CS8234 [S]	What Every Girl Should Know	1960	$30
❏ CL2266 [M]	With a Smile and a Song	1965	$30
❏ CS9066 [S]	With a Smile and a Song	1965	$35
❏ CL1904 [M]	You'll Never Walk Alone	1962	$35
❏ CS8704 [S]	You'll Never Walk Alone	1962	$50
❏ CL6339 [10]	Young at Heart	1954	$120

—Six songs by Doris Day, two by Frank Sinatra

❏ CL6106 [10]	Young Man with a Horn	1950	$175
❏ CL582 [M]	Young Man with a Horn	1954	$40

—Reissue of 6106; red label, gold print

❏ CL6071 [10]	You're My Thrill	1949	$120

COLUMBIA LIMITED EDITION

❏ LE10197	The Doris Day Christmas Album	197?	$12

COLUMBIA SPECIAL PRODUCTS

Number	Title	Yr	NM
❑ P13346	The Doris Day Christmas Album	197?	$12
—Reissue of CS 9026			
❑ C10988	The Doris Day Christmas Album	197?	$12
—Reissue of CS 9026			
❑ P213231	The Magic of Doris Day	1976	$20
❑ XTV82021/2 [M]	Wonderful Day	1961	$40
HARMONY			
❑ HL9559 [M]	Do Re Mi (And Other Children's Favorites)	196?	$15
❑ HS14559 [S]	Do Re Mi (And Other Children's Favorites)	196?	$15
❑ HL7392 [M]	Great Movie Hits	1966	$15
❑ HS11192 [R]	Great Movie Hits	1966	$15
❑ KH31498	Softly, As I Leave You	1972	$12
❑ HS11382	The Magic of Doris Day	1970	$15
❑ HS11282	Whatever Will Be, Will Be (Que Sera, Sera)	1968	$15
HEARTLAND			
❑ HL1102/3	The Best of Doris Day	1990	$20
—Mail-order offer; alternate number is CBS Special Products P2 22031			
HINDSIGHT			
❑ HSR-200	Doris Day with Van Alexander's Orchestra	198?	$12

DEAN, PETER

Albums

AUDIO FIDELITY			
❑ AFSD-6280	Peter Dean in Fun City	197?	$35
BUDDAH			
❑ BDS-5613	Four or Five Times	1974	$35
INNER CITY			
❑ IC-4002	Only Time Will Tell	1979	$30
MONMOUTH-EVERGREEN			
❑ 7092	Where Did the Magic Go	198?	$30
PROJECT 3			
❑ PR5075SD	Ding Dong Daddy!	196?	$35

DEAN, SUZANNE
Female singer.

Albums

NOVA			
❑ 8808-1	Dreams Come True	198?	$25
❑ 9028-1	I Wonder	1988	$25

DEANGELIS, JIM, AND TONY SIGNA
DeAngelis is a guitarist; Signa is a flutist.

Albums

STATIRAS			
❑ SLP-8075	Gridlock	1985	$25

DEARANGO, BILL
Guitarist.

Albums

EMARCY			
❑ MG-26020 [10]	Bill DeArango	1954	$250

DEARIE, BLOSSOM
Female singer and pianist. Known to some as one of the singers on the "Schoolhouse Rock" ABC cartoon series ("Figure Eight" and "Unpack Your Adjectives"). Also see THE BLUE STARS.

Albums

CAPITOL			
❑ T2086 [M]	May I Come In	1964	$75
❑ ST2086 [S]	May I Come In	1964	$40
❑ SM-2086	May I Come In	1976	$25
—Reissue with new prefix			
DAFFODIL			
❑ BMD-102	1975	1975	$35
❑ BMD-101	Blossom Dearie Sings	197?	$35
❑ BMD-109	Chez Wahlberg, Part I	198?	$30
❑ BMD-108	Et Tu Bruce (Volume VIII)	198?	$25
❑ BMD-103	My New Celebrity Is You	197?	$25
❑ BMD-105	Needlepoint Magic	198?	$30
❑ BMD-107	Positively Volume VII	198?	$25
❑ BMD-106	Simply Volume VI	1983	$25
❑ BMD-110	Songs of Chelsea	1987	$25
❑ BMD-104	Winchester in Apple Blossom Time	197?	$50

Number	Title	Yr	NM
DRG			
❑ DARC-1105	Blossom Dearie On Broadway	1980	$35
FONTANA			
❑ MGF-27562 [M]	Blossom Time	1966	$35
❑ SRF-67562 [S]	Blossom Time	1966	$25
VERVE			
❑ MGV-2037 [M]	Blossom Dearie	1957	$150
❑ V-2037 [M]	Blossom Dearie	1961	$25
❑ UMV-2639	Blossom Dearie	198?	$25
❑ MGV-2109 [M]	Blossom Dearie Sings Comden & Green	1959	$150
❑ MGVS-6050 [S]	Blossom Dearie Sings Comden & Green	1960	$150
❑ V-2109 [M]	Blossom Dearie Sings Comden & Green	1961	$25
❑ V6-2109 [S]	Blossom Dearie Sings Comden & Green	1961	$30
❑ MGV-2133 [M]	Broadway Song Hits	1960	$120
❑ MGVS-6139 [S]	Broadway Song Hits	1960	$120
❑ V-2133 [M]	Broadway Song Hits	1961	$25
❑ V6-2133 [S]	Broadway Song Hits	1961	$30
❑ MGV-2081 [M]	Give Him the Ooh-La-La	1958	$100
❑ V-2081 [M]	Give Him the Ooh-La-La	1961	$25
❑ MGV-2125 [M]	My Gentleman Friend	1959	$100
❑ MGVS-6112 [S]	My Gentleman Friend	1960	$100
❑ V-2125 [M]	My Gentleman Friend	1961	$25
❑ V6-2125 [S]	My Gentleman Friend	1961	$30
❑ MGV-2111 [M]	Once Upon a Summertime	1958	$120
❑ MGVS-6020 [S]	Once Upon a Summertime	1960	$100
❑ V-2111 [M]	Once Upon a Summertime	1961	$25
❑ V6-2111 [S]	Once Upon a Summertime	1961	$30
❑ 827757-1	Once Upon a Summertime	1986	$25

DECAUTER, KOEN, AND ORANGE KELLIN
DeCauter is a reed player (often on soprano saxophone). Kellin plays clarinet.

Albums

GHB			
❑ GHB-242	New Orleans Swing with Koen DeCauter and Orange Kellin: A Little Piece of Paradise	1990	$30

DECEMBER BAND, THE

Albums

GHB			
❑ GHB-197	The December Band, Volume 1	1986	$25
❑ GHB-198	The December Band, Volume 2	1986	$25

DEDRICK, RUSTY
Trumpeter, arranger and composer.

Albums

4 CORNERS OF THE WORLD			
❑ FC-4207 [M]	The Big Band Sound	1964	$35
❑ FCS-4207 [S]	The Big Band Sound	1964	$25
COUNTERPOINT			
❑ 552 [M]	Salute to Bunny	1957	$50
ESOTERIC			
❑ ESJ-9 [10]	Rhythm and Winds	1955	$100
KEYNOTE			
❑ 1103 [M]	Rusty Dedrick	1955	$75
MONMOUTH-EVERGREEN			
❑ 6918	Harold Arlen in Hollywood	1969	$35
❑ 7035	Many Facets, Many Friends	1970	$35
MONUMENT			
❑ MLP-6502 [M]	A Jazz Journey	1965	$35
❑ SLP-16502 [S]	A Jazz Journey	1965	$25

DEFRANCESCO, JOEY
Organist.

Albums

COLUMBIA			
❑ FC44463	All of Me	1989	$35

DEFRANCO, BUDDY, AND TOMMY GUMINA
Also see each artist's individual listings.

Albums

MERCURY			
❑ MG-20743 [M]	Kaleidoscope	1962	$100
❑ SR-60743 [S]	Kaleidoscope	1962	$100
❑ MG-20833 [M]	Polytones	1963	$100
❑ SR-60833 [S]	Polytones	1963	$100

Number	Title	Yr	NM
❑ MG-20685 [M]	Presenting the Buddy DeFranco-Tommy Gumina Quintet	1962	$100
❑ SR-60685 [S]	Presenting the Buddy DeFranco-Tommy Gumina Quintet	1962	$100
❑ MG-20900 [M]	The Girl from Ipanema	1964	$100
❑ SR-60900 [S]	The Girl from Ipanema	1964	$100

DEFRANCO, BUDDY
Clarinet player. Also see TERRY GIBBS; GLENN MILLER ORCHESTRA; GERRY MULLIGAN.

Albums

CHOICE			
❑ 1008	Free Sail	1974	$35
❑ 1017	Waterbed	1977	$30
CLASSIC JAZZ			
❑ 33	Buddy DeFranco and Jim Gillis	1978	$30
DECCA			
❑ DL4031 [M]	Pacific Standard Swingin' Time	1961	$25
❑ DL74031 [S]	Pacific Standard Swingin' Time	1961	$30
DOT			
❑ DLP-9006 [M]	Cross-Country Suite	1958	$80
GENE NORMAN			
❑ GNP-2 [10]	Buddy DeFranco Takes You to the Stars	1954	$120
HAMILTON			
❑ HL-133 [M]	Cross-Country Suite	1964	$25
❑ HS-12133 [R]	Cross-Country Suite	1964	$30
MGM			
❑ E-3396 [M]	Buddy DeFranco	1956	$80
❑ E-253 [10]	Buddy DeFranco with Strings	1954	$100
❑ E-177 [10]	King of the Clarinet	1952	$120
MOSAIC			
❑ MR5-117	The Complete Recordings of the Buddy DeFranco Quartet/Quintet with Sonny Clark	199?	$100
NORGRAN			
❑ MGN-1096 [M]	Autumn Leaves	1956	$200
❑ MGN-1105 [M]	Broadway Showcase	1956	$0
—Canceled; reassigned to Verve 2033			
❑ MGN-1012 [M]	Buddy DeFranco and His Clarinet	1954	$200
❑ MGN-1016 [M]	Buddy DeFranco and Oscar Peterson Play George Gershwin	1955	$200
❑ MGN-1026 [M]	Buddy DeFranco Quartet	1955	$200
❑ MGN-1079 [M]	In a Mellow Mood	1956	$150
❑ MGN-1068 [M]	Jazz Tones	1956	$150
❑ MGN-1069 [M]	Mr. Clarinet	1956	$150
❑ MGN-1094 [M]	Odalisque	1956	$150
❑ MGN-16 [10]	Pretty Moods by Buddy DeFranco	1954	$150
❑ MGN-3 [10]	The Buddy DeFranco Quartet	1954	$300
❑ MGN-1085 [M]	The Buddy DeFranco Wailers	1956	$150
❑ MGN-1006 [M]	The Progressive Mr. DeFranco	1954	$120
PABLO			
❑ 2310906	Mr. Lucky	198?	$30
PROGRESSIVE			
❑ 7014	Like Someone in Love	1979	$30
SONET			
❑ 724	Boronquin	197?	$30
VERVE			
❑ MGV-8183 [M]	Autumn Leaves	1957	$200
—Reissue of Norgran 1096			
❑ V-8183 [M]	Autumn Leaves	1961	$60
❑ MGV-8315 [M]	Bravura	1959	$150
❑ MGVS-6051 [S]	Bravura	1960	$120
❑ V-8315 [M]	Bravura	1961	$25
❑ V6-8315 [S]	Bravura	1961	$25
❑ MGV-2033 [M]	Broadway Showcase	1957	$150
❑ V-2033 [M]	Broadway Showcase	1961	$25
❑ MGV-8384 [M]	Buddy DeFranco	1960	$0
—Canceled			
❑ MGVS-6167 [S]	Buddy DeFranco	1960	$0
—Canceled			
❑ MGV-8210 [M]	Buddy DeFranco and the Oscar Peterson Quartet	1958	$150
❑ V-8210 [M]	Buddy DeFranco and the Oscar Peterson Quartet	1961	$25
❑ MGV-2090 [M]	Buddy DeFranco Plays Artie Shaw	1958	$150

Number	Title	Yr	NM
❑ V-2090 [M]	Buddy DeFranco Plays Artie Shaw	1961	$25
❑ MGV-2089 [M]	Buddy DeFranco Plays Benny Goodman	1958	$150
❑ V-2089 [M]	Buddy DeFranco Plays Benny Goodman	1961	$25
❑ MGV-8382 [M]	Closed Session	1960	$100
❑ MGVS-6165 [S]	Closed Session	1960	$100
❑ V-8382 [M]	Closed Session	1961	$25
❑ V6-8382 [S]	Closed Session	1961	$25
❑ UMV-2632	Closed Session	198?	$25
❑ MGV-8221 [M]	Cooking the Blues	1958	$150
❑ V-8221 [M]	Cooking the Blues	1961	$25
❑ MGV-8363 [M]	Generalissimo	1960	$150
❑ MGVS-6132 [S]	Generalissimo	1960	$150
❑ V-8363 [M]	Generalissimo	1961	$25
❑ V6-8363 [S]	Generalissimo	1961	$25
❑ MGV-2108 [M]	I Hear Benny Goodman and Artie Shaw	1958	$150
❑ MGVS-6032 [S]	I Hear Benny Goodman and Artie Shaw	1960	$100
❑ MGV-8279 [M]	I Hear Benny Goodman and Artie Shaw	1958	$0

—Canceled; issued as 2108

❑ V-2108 [M]	I Hear Benny Goodman and Artie Shaw	1961	$25
❑ V6-2108 [S]	I Hear Benny Goodman and Artie Shaw	1961	$25
❑ MGV-8169 [M]	In a Mellow Mood	1957	$300

—Reissue of Norgran 1079

❑ V-8169 [M]	In a Mellow Mood	1961	$25
❑ MGV-8158 [M]	Jazz Tones	1957	$300

—Reissue of Norgran 1068

❑ V-8158 [M]	Jazz Tones	1961	$25
❑ MGV-8383 [M]	Live Date!	1960	$100
❑ MGVS-6166 [S]	Live Date!	1960	$100
❑ V-8383 [M]	Live Date!	1961	$25
❑ V6-8383 [S]	Live Date!	1961	$25
❑ MGV-8159 [M]	Mr. Clarinet	1957	$150

—Reissue of Norgran 1069

❑ V-8159 [M]	Mr. Clarinet	1961	$25
❑ MGV-8182 [M]	Odalisque	1957	$150

—Reissue of Norgran 1094

❑ V-8182 [M]	Odalisque	1961	$25
❑ MGV-8224 [M]	Sweet and Lovely	1958	$150
❑ V-8224 [M]	Sweet and Lovely	1961	$25
❑ MGV-8175 [M]	The Buddy DeFranco Wailers	1957	$200

—Reissue of Norgran 1085

❑ V-8175 [M]	The Buddy DeFranco Wailers	1961	$25
❑ MGV-2022 [M]	The George Gershwin Songbook	1956	$200

—Reissue of Norgran 1016

❑ MGV-8375 [M]	Wholly Cats	1960	$60
❑ MGVS-6150 [S]	Wholly Cats	1960	$60
❑ V-8375 [M]	Wholly Cats	1961	$50
❑ V6-8375 [S]	Wholly Cats	1961	$50

DEGEN, BOB
Pianist.

Albums

ENJA

Number	Title	Yr	NM
❑ 3015	Chartreuse	198?	$25

INNER CITY

Number	Title	Yr	NM
❑ IC-3027	Children of the Night	1978	$30

DEHAVEN, DOC
Trumpeter and bandleader.

Albums

CUCA

Number	Title	Yr	NM
❑ K-3000 [M]	Dixieland Treasure	1962	$25
❑ K-3100 [M]	Doc DeHaven On Location	1963	$25
❑ K-3200 [M]	Doc Swings a Little	1964	$25
❑ K-3400 [M]	Erle of Madison	1967	$25
❑ K-3300 [M]	Just Off State Street	1966	$25
❑ KS-3300 [S]	Just Off State Street	1966	$30

DEJOHNETTE, JACK
Drummer and percussionist. Also a pianist and keyboard player.

Albums

COLUMBIA

Number	Title	Yr	NM
❑ C31176	Compost (Take Off Your Body)	1971	$25

ECM

Number	Title	Yr	NM
❑ 25010	Album Album	1984	$25
❑ 23790	Inflation Blues	1983	$25
❑ 1128	New Directions	1978	$30
❑ 1157	New Directions in Europe	1980	$30
❑ 1103	New Rags	1977	$30
❑ 1079	Pictures	1976	$30

Number	Title	Yr	NM
❑ 1152	Special Edition	1980	$30
❑ 1189	Tin Can Alley	1981	$30
❑ 1074	Untitled	1976	$30

IMPULSE!/MCA

Number	Title	Yr	NM
❑ 5992	Irresistible Force	1987	$25

LANDMARK

Number	Title	Yr	NM
❑ LLP-1504	The Piano Album	1985	$25

MCA

Number	Title	Yr	NM
❑ 42313	Parallel Realities	1990	$35
❑ 42160	Zebra	1986	$25

MILESTONE

Number	Title	Yr	NM
❑ MSP-9029	Have You Heard?	1970	$35
❑ MSP-9022	The DeJohnette Complex	1969	$25

PRESTIGE

Number	Title	Yr	NM
❑ 10094	Cosmic Chicken	1975	$35
❑ 10081	Sorcery	1974	$35

DELANEY, JACK
Trombone player and bandleader.

Albums

SOUTHLAND

Number	Title	Yr	NM
❑ LP-201 [10]	Jack Delaney and George Girard in New Orleans	1954	$50
❑ LP-214 [10]	Jack Delaney with Lee Collins	1954	$50

DELEGATES, THE (2)
See BILLY LARKIN.

DELIRIUM TREMOLO
Members: Tom Stuip (plectrum banjo, tenor banjo); Ronald Jansen Heijtmajer (bass saxophone, alto saxophone, C-melody saxophone); Guido Nielsen (violin, piano).

Albums

STOMP OFF

Number	Title	Yr	NM
❑ SOS-1177	Banjophobia	1987	$25

DEMANO, HANK
Trumpeter.

Albums

FREEWAY

Number	Title	Yr	NM
❑ FLJP-1 [M]	Hank DeMano Quartet	1955	$60

DEMERLE, LES
Drummer.

Albums

DOBRE

Number	Title	Yr	NM
❑ 1020	Transfusion	1978	$30

PALO ALTO

Number	Title	Yr	NM
❑ 8008	On Fire	1981	$30

DENNIS, JOHN
Pianist.

Albums

DEBUT

Number	Title	Yr	NM
❑ DEB-121 [M]	New Piano Expressions	1955	$150

DENNIS, MATT
Pianist, male singer, composer and arranger. Worked with several big bands, most notably with TOMMY DORSEY.

Albums

JUBILEE

Number	Title	Yr	NM
❑ JLP-1105 [M]	Welcome Matt Dennis	1959	$50
❑ JGS-1105 [S]	Welcome Matt Dennis	1959	$60

KAPP

Number	Title	Yr	NM
❑ KL-1024 [M]	Matt Dennis Plays and Sings Matt Dennis	1956	$60

MCA

Number	Title	Yr	NM
❑ 1547	Matt Dennis Plays and Sings Matt Dennis	198?	$30

RCA VICTOR

Number	Title	Yr	NM
❑ LPM-1134 [M]	Dennis, Anyone?	1955	$50
❑ LPM-1322 [M]	Play Melancholy Baby	1956	$60
❑ LPM-1065 [M]	She Dances Overhead	1954	$40

DENNY, DOTTY

Albums

A440

Number	Title	Yr	NM
❑ AJ-506 [M]	Dotty Digs Duke	1954	$125
❑ AJ-505 [M]	Tribute to Edgar Sampson	1954	$125

DEODATO
Full name: Eumir Deodato. Keyboard player, pianist and arranger. His version of "Also Sprach Zarathustra (2001)" was a left-field pop hit in 1973.

Albums

ATLANTIC

Number	Title	Yr	NM
❑ 82048	Somewhere Out There	1989	$30

CTI

Number	Title	Yr	NM
❑ 7081	2001	1977	$25
❑ CTS-6029	Deodato 2	1973	$30
❑ CTSQ-6029 [Q]	Deodato 2	1973	$60
❑ CTS-6021	Prelude	1972	$30
❑ CTSQ-6021 [Q]	Prelude	1973	$60
❑ 8021	Prelude	198?	$20

—Reissue of 6021

MCA

Number	Title	Yr	NM
❑ 457	Artistry	1974	$25
❑ 491	First Cuckoo	1975	$25
❑ 2219	Very Together	1976	$25
❑ 697	Very Together	198?	$20

—Reissue of 2219

❑ 410	Whirlwinds	1974	$25

WARNER BROS.

Number	Title	Yr	NM
❑ BSK3649	Happy Hour	1981	$25
❑ BSK3321	Knights of Fantasy	1979	$25
❑ BSK3132	Love Island	1978	$25
❑ 25175	Motion	1984	$25
❑ BSK3467	Night Cruiser	1980	$30

DEODATO/AIRTO
Also see each artist's individual listings.

Albums

CTI

Number	Title	Yr	NM
❑ CTS-6041	In Concert	1974	$30
❑ CTSQ-6041 [Q]	In Concert	1974	$60

DEPARIS, SIDNEY
Trumpeter and bandleader. Also a tuba player and male singer. WILBUR DePARIS is his brother.

Albums

BLUE NOTE

Number	Title	Yr	NM
❑ B-6501	DeParis Dixie	1969	$25
❑ BLP-7016 [10]	Sidney DeParis' Blue Note Stompers	1951	$300

DEPARIS, SIDNEY/JAMES P. JOHNSON
Also see each artist's individual listings.

Albums

BLUE NOTE

Number	Title	Yr	NM
❑ B-6506	Original Blue Note Jazz, Volume 3	1969	$25

DEPARIS, WILBUR, AND JIMMY WITHERSPOON
Also see each artist's individual listings.

Albums

ATLANTIC

Number	Title	Yr	NM
❑ 1266 [M]	New Orleans Blues	1957	$300

—Black label

❑ 1266 [M]	New Orleans Blues	1961	$150

—Multicolor label, white "fan" logo

❑ 1266 [M]	New Orleans Blues	1964	$30

—Multicolor label, black "fan" logo

DEPARIS, WILBUR
Trombone player and bandleader. Brother of SIDNEY DePARIS.

Albums

A440

Number	Title	Yr	NM
❑ AJ-503 [10]	New New Orleans Jazz	1954	$60

ATLANTIC

Number	Title	Yr	NM
❑ 1233 [M]	Marchin' and Swingin'	1956	$300

—Black label

❑ 1233 [M]	Marchin' and Swingin'	1961	$150

—Multicolor label, white "fan" logo

❑ 1233 [M]	Marchin' and Swingin'	1964	$35

Number	Title	Yr	NM
—Multicolor label, black "fan" logo			
❏ SD1233 [S]	Marchin' and Swingin'	1958	$250
—Green label			
❏ SD1233 [S]	Marchin' and Swingin'	1961	$150
—Multicolor label, white "fan" logo			
❏ SD1233 [S]	Marchin' and Swingin'	1964	$35
—Multicolor label, black "fan" logo			
❏ 1219 [M]	New New Orleans Jazz	1956	$300
—Black label			
❏ 1219 [M]	New New Orleans Jazz	1961	$150
—Multicolor label, white "fan" logo			
❏ 1219 [M]	New New Orleans Jazz	1964	$35
—Multicolor label, black "fan" logo			
❏ SD1219 [S]	New New Orleans Jazz	1958	$250
—Green label			
❏ SD1219 [S]	New New Orleans Jazz	1961	$150
—Multicolor label, white "fan" logo			
❏ SD1219 [S]	New New Orleans Jazz	1964	$35
—Multicolor label, black "fan" logo			
❏ SD1552	Over and Over Again	1970	$35
❏ 1300 [M]	Something Old, New, Gay, Blue	1958	$300
—Black label			
❏ 1300 [M]	Something Old, New, Gay, Blue	1961	$150
—Multicolor label, white "fan" logo			
❏ 1300 [M]	Something Old, New, Gay, Blue	1964	$35
—Multicolor label, black "fan" logo			
❏ SD1300 [S]	Something Old, New, Gay, Blue	1958	$300
—Green label			
❏ SD1300 [S]	Something Old, New, Gay, Blue	1961	$150
—Multicolor label, white "fan" logo			
❏ SD1300 [S]	Something Old, New, Gay, Blue	1964	$35
—Multicolor label, black "fan" logo			
❏ 1318 [M]	That's a-Plenty	1959	$300
—Black label			
❏ 1318 [M]	That's a-Plenty	1961	$150
—Multicolor label, white "fan" logo			
❏ 1318 [M]	That's a-Plenty	1964	$35
—Multicolor label, black "fan" logo			
❏ SD1318 [S]	That's a-Plenty	1959	$300
—Green label			
❏ SD1318 [S]	That's a-Plenty	1961	$150
—Multicolor label, white "fan" logo			
❏ SD1318 [S]	That's a-Plenty	1964	$35
—Multicolor label, black "fan" logo			
❏ 1336 [M]	The Wild Jazz Age	1960	$250
—Multicolor label, white "fan" logo			
❏ 1336 [M]	The Wild Jazz Age	1964	$35
—Multicolor label, black "fan" logo			
❏ SD1336 [S]	The Wild Jazz Age	1960	$250
—Multicolor label, white "fan" logo			
❏ SD1336 [S]	The Wild Jazz Age	1964	$25
—Multicolor label, black "fan" logo			
❏ ALS-143 [10]	Wilbur DeParis, Volume 2	1953	$300
❏ ALS-141 [10]	Wilbur DeParis and His Rampart Street Ramblers	1952	$350
❏ 1253 [M]	Wilbur DeParis at Symphony Hall	1957	$300
—Black label			
❏ 1253 [M]	Wilbur DeParis at Symphony Hall	1961	$150
—Multicolor label, white "fan" logo			
❏ 1253 [M]	Wilbur DeParis at Symphony Hall	1964	$35
—Multicolor label, black "fan" logo			
❏ SD1253 [S]	Wilbur DeParis at Symphony Hall	1958	$300
—Green label			
❏ SD1253 [S]	Wilbur DeParis at Symphony Hall	1961	$150
—Multicolor label, white "fan" logo			
❏ SD1253 [S]	Wilbur DeParis at Symphony Hall	1964	$35
—Multicolor label, black "fan" logo			
❏ 1363 [M]	Wilbur DeParis on the Riviera	1961	$150
—Multicolor label, white "fan" logo			

Number	Title	Yr	NM
❏ 1363 [M]	Wilbur DeParis on the Riviera	1964	$35
—Multicolor label, black "fan" logo			
❏ SD1363 [S]	Wilbur DeParis on the Riviera	1961	$150
—Multicolor label, white "fan" logo			

Number	Title	Yr	NM
❏ SD1363 [S]	Wilbur DeParis on the Riviera	1964	$50
—Multicolor label, black "fan" logo			
❏ 1288 [M]	Wilbur DeParis Plays Cole Porter	1958	$300
—Black label			
❏ 1288 [M]	Wilbur DeParis Plays Cole Porter	1961	$150
—Multicolor label, white "fan" logo			
❏ 1288 [M]	Wilbur DeParis Plays Cole Porter	1964	$35
—Multicolor label, black "fan" logo			
HERITAGE			
❏ SS-1207 [M]	Wilbur DeParis	1956	$100

DERISE, JOE
Pianist and male singer.

Albums

AUDIOPHILE			
❏ AP-153	House of Flowers	1981	$30
❏ AP-231	Joe DeRise Sings and Plays the Jimmy Van Heusen Anthology, Vol. 1	1989	$25
❏ AP-232	Joe DeRise Sings and Plays the Jimmy Van Heusen Anthology, Vol. 2	1989	$25
❏ AP-233	Joe DeRise Sings and Plays the Jimmy Van Heusen Anthology, Vol. 3	1989	$25
❏ AP-174	The Blues Are Out of Town	1982	$30
❏ AP-215	The Joe DeRise Tentette Is Mad About You	1986	$25
BETHLEHEM			
❏ BCP-1039 [10]	Joe DeRise Sings	1955	$250
❏ BCP-51 [M]	Joe DeRise with the Australian Jazz Quintet	1956	$250
INNER CITY			
❏ IC-4003	I'll Remember Suzanne	1979	$30

DES PLANTES, TED
Pianist and bandleader.

Albums

JAZZOLOGY			
❏ J-125	Ted Des Plantes and His Buddies	1983	$25
STOMP OFF			
❏ SOS-1136	Swedish-American Hot Jazz Collaboration	1987	$25

DESCENDANTS OF MIKE & PHOEBE, THE

Albums

STRATA-EAST			
❏ SES-19744	A Spirit Speaks	1973	$60

DESMARAIS, LORRAINE
Pianist.

Albums

JAZZIMAGE			
❏ JZ-106	Andiamo	1985	$30
❏ JZ-100	Lorraine Desmarais Trio	1984	$30

DESMOND, PAUL
Alto saxophone player. Long-time member of DAVE BRUBECK's classic quartet. Wrote the hit "Take Five." Also see GERRY MULLIGAN.

Albums

A&M			
❏ SP-3032	Bridge Over Troubled Water	1970	$50
❏ SP-3024	From the Hot Afternoon	1969	$35
❏ SP9-3024	From the Hot Afternoon	198?	$50
—Audio Master Plus" reissue			
❏ SP-3015	Summertime	1969	$35
ARTISTS HOUSE			
❏ AH2	Paul Desmond	1978	$25
CTI			
❏ CTS-6059	Pure Desmond	1975	$25
❏ CTS-6039	Skylark	1974	$25
CTI/CBS ASSOCIATED			
❏ FZ40806	Pure Desmond	1987	$25
—Reissue of CTI 6059			
❏ FZ44170	Skylark	1988	$25
—Reissue of CTI 6039			
DISCOVERY			
❏ 840	East of the Sun	198?	$25
FANTASY			
❏ 3-21 [10]	Paul Desmond	1955	$175
❏ 3235 [M]	Paul Desmond Quartet Featuring Don Elliott	1956	$150
—Red vinyl			
❏ 3235 [M]	Paul Desmond Quartet Featuring Don Elliott	1957	$40
—Black vinyl, red label, non-flexible vinyl			
❏ 3235 [M]	Paul Desmond Quartet Featuring Don Elliott	1962	$50
—Black vinyl, red label, flexible vinyl			
❏ OJC-119	Paul Desmond Quartet Featuring Don Elliott	198?	$25
—Reissue of Fantasy 3235			
FINESSE			
❏ FW37487	Paul Desmond and the Modern Jazz Quartet	1981	$25
HORIZON			
❏ 850	Paul Desmond Live	1976	$35
MOSAIC			
❏ MR6-120	The Complete Recordings of the Paul Desmond Quartet with Jim Hall	199?	$300
RCA CAMDEN			
❏ ACL1-0201	Samba de Orfeo	1973	$25
RCA VICTOR			
❏ LPM-3320 [M]	Boss Antigua	1965	$50
❏ LSP-3320 [S]	Boss Antigua	1965	$60
❏ LPM-2438 [M]	Desmond Blue	1961	$60
❏ LSP-2438 [S]	Desmond Blue	1961	$60
❏ LPM-3480 [M]	Easy Living	1965	$50
❏ LSP-3480 [S]	Easy Living	1965	$60
❏ LPM-3407 [M]	Glad to Be Unhappy	1965	$50
❏ LSP-3407 [S]	Glad to Be Unhappy	1965	$60
❏ ANL1-2807	Pure Gold	1978	$25
❏ LPM-2569 [M]	Take Ten	1962	$60
❏ LSP-2569 [S]	Take Ten	1962	$60
❏ LPM-2654 [M]	Two of a Mind	1963	$60
❏ LSP-2654 [S]	Two of a Mind	1963	$60
WARNER BROS.			
❏ W1356 [M]	First Place Again	1960	$60
❏ WS1356 [S]	First Place Again	1960	$60

DESOUZA, RAUL
Trombonist.

Albums

CAPITOL			
❏ SW-11774	Don't Ask My Neighbors	1978	$30
❏ ST-11648	Sweet Lucy	1977	$60
❏ ST-11918	'Til Tomorrow Comes	1979	$30
MILESTONE			
❏ 9061	Colors	1975	$35

Miles Davis, *Blue Moods*, Debut DEB-120, **$400**.

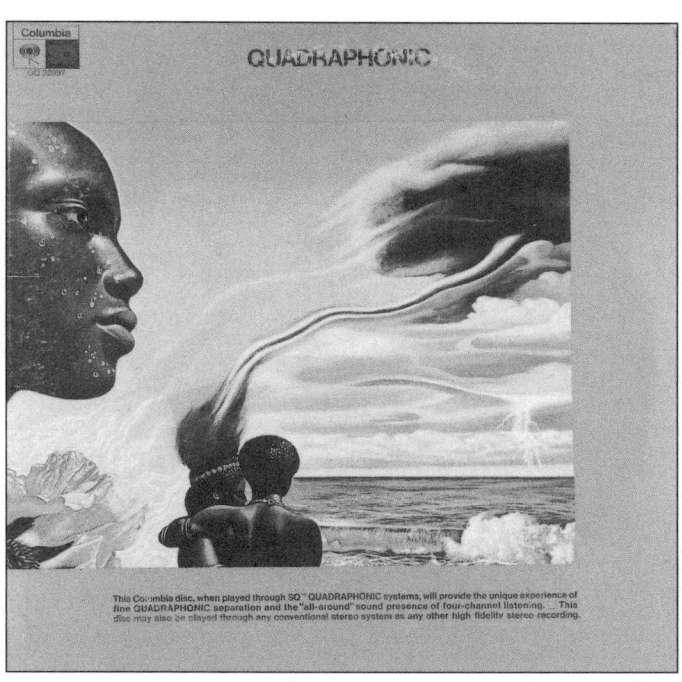

Miles Davis, *Bitches Brew*, Columbia GQ 30997, quadraphonic version, **$150**.

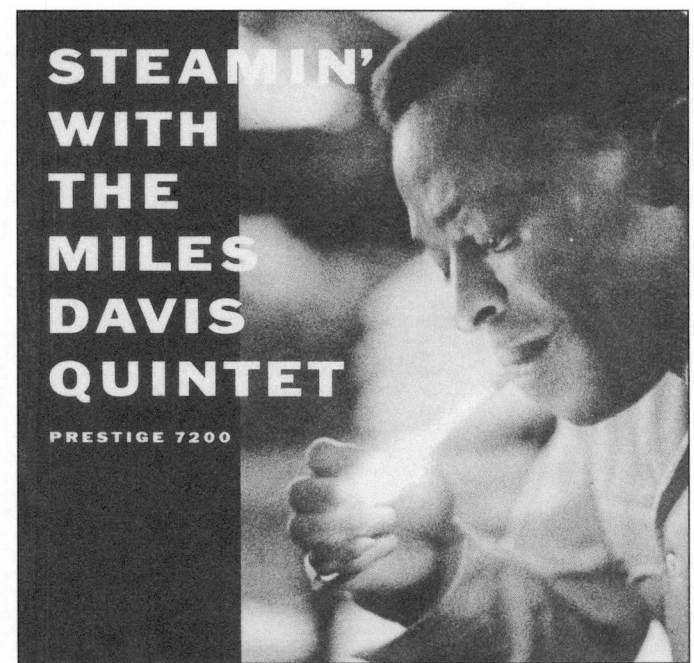

Miles Davis, *Steamin' with the Miles Davis Quintet*, Prestige PRLP 7200, yellow label, **$750**.

Eric Dolphy, *Outward Bound*, New Jazz NJLP-8236, **$450**.

Number	Title	Yr	NM

DEUCE
Jean Fineberg (saxophone, flute) and Ellen Seeling (trumpet).

Albums

REDWOOD
| ❏ R-8602 | Deuce | 1986 | $30 |

—*Jean Fineberg and Ellen Seeling*

DEUCHAR, JIMMY
Trumpeter and mellophone player.

Albums

CONTEMPORARY
| ❏ C-3529 [M] | Pub Crawling | 1957 | $250 |

DIAZ MENA, ANTONIO
Conga player.

Albums

AUDIO FIDELITY
| ❏ AFLP-2117 [M] | Eso Es En Latin Jazz Man | 1963 | $35 |
| ❏ AFSD-6117 [S] | Eso Es En Latin Jazz Man | 1963 | $25 |

DICKENSON, VIC, AND JOE THOMAS
Thomas played trumpet. Also see VIC DICKENSON.

Albums

ATLANTIC
| ❏ 1303 [M] | Mainstream | 1958 | $250 |

—*Black label*
| ❏ 1303 [M] | Mainstream | 1961 | $150 |

—*Multicolor label, white "fan" logo*
| ❏ SD1303 [S] | Mainstream | 1958 | $250 |

—*Green label*
| ❏ SD1303 [S] | Mainstream | 1961 | $150 |

—*Multicolor label, white "fan" logo*

DICKENSON, VIC
Trombone player and occasional male singer.

Albums

JAZZTONE
| ❏ J-1259 [M] | Slidin' Swing | 1956 | $40 |

SACKVILLE
| ❏ 2015 | Just Friends | 198? | $30 |

SONET
| ❏ 720 | Trombone Cholly | 197? | $25 |

STORYVILLE
| ❏ STLP-920 [M] | Vic's Boston Story | 1957 | $40 |

VANGUARD
❏ VRS-99/100	The Essential Vic Dickenson	197?	$35
❏ VRS-8001 [10]	Vic Dickenson Septet, Volume 1	1953	$50
❏ VRS-8002 [10]	Vic Dickenson Septet, Volume 2	1953	$50
❏ VRS-8012 [10]	Vic Dickenson Septet, Volume 3	1954	$50
❏ VRS-8013 [10]	Vic Dickenson Septet, Volume 4	1954	$50
❏ VRS-8520 [M]	Vic Dickenson Showcase, Volume 1	1958	$80
❏ VRS-8521 [M]	Vic Dickenson Showcase, Volume 2	1958	$80

DICKERSON, DWIGHT
Pianist.

Albums

DISCOVERY
| ❏ DS-792 | Sooner or Later | 1978 | $30 |

DICKERSON, WALT
Vibraphone player, composer and arranger. Also see PIERRE DORGE.

Albums

AUDIO FIDELITY
❏ AFLP-2131 [M]	Unity	1963	$25
❏ AFSD-6131 [S]	Unity	1963	$30
❏ AFLP-2217 [M]	Vibes in Motion	1968	$30

—*Reissue of Dauntless 4313*
| ❏ AFSD-6217 [S] | Vibes in Motion | 1968 | $35 |

—*Reissue of Dauntless 6313*

DAUNTLESS
| ❏ DM-4313 [M] | Jazz Impressions of "Lawrence of Arabia | 1963 | $30 |

Number	Title	Yr	NM
❏ DS-6313 [S]	Jazz Impressions of "Lawrence of Arabia	1963	$30

INNER CITY
| ❏ IC-2042 | Peace | 1976 | $35 |

MGM
| ❏ E-4358 [M] | Impressions of "A Patch of Blue | 1965 | $25 |
| ❏ SE-4358 [S] | Impressions of "A Patch of Blue | 1965 | $30 |

NEW JAZZ
| ❏ NJLP-8268 [M] | A Sense of Direction | 1962 | $150 |

—*Purple label*
| ❏ NJLP-8268 [M] | A Sense of Direction | 1965 | $150 |

—*Blue label, trident logo at right*
| ❏ NJLP-8275 [M] | Relativity | 1962 | $150 |

—*Purple label*
| ❏ NJLP-8275 [M] | Relativity | 1965 | $150 |

—*Blue label, trident logo at right*
| ❏ NJLP-8254 [M] | This Is Walt Dickerson | 1965 | $150 |

—*Blue label, trident logo at right*
| ❏ NJLP-8283 [M] | To My Queen | 1962 | $150 |

—*Purple label*
| ❏ NJLP-8283 [M] | To My Queen | 1965 | $150 |

—*Blue label, trident logo at right*

SOUL NOTE
| ❏ SN-1028 | Life Rays | 1982 | $30 |

STEEPLECHASE
❏ SCS-1089	Divine Gemini	197?	$30
❏ SCS-1146	I Hear You John	198?	$30
❏ SCS-1115	Landscape with Open Door	1978	$30
❏ SCS-1042	Peace	197?	$25

—*Reissue of Inner City 2042*
| ❏ SCS-1070 | Serendipity | 197? | $30 |
| ❏ SCD-17002 | Shades of Love | 198? | $30 |

—*Direct-to-disc recording*
❏ SCS-1213	Tenderness	198?	$30
❏ SCS-1112	To My Queen Revisited	1978	$30
❏ SCS-1130	To My Son	1979	$30
❏ SCS-1126	Visions	1979	$30

DICKIE, NEVILLE
Pianist.

Albums

STOMP OFF
❏ SOS-1052	Eye Openers	1982	$25
❏ SOS-1176 [B]	Neville Dickie Meets Fats, the Lion and the Lamb	1988	$25
❏ SOS-1096	Taken in Stride	1986	$25

DIGABLE PLANETS
Hip-hop group; most of its samples and influences came from jazz. Its biggest hit single, "Rebirth of Slick (Cool Like Dat)," samples Art Blakey.

Albums

PENDULUM
| ❏ E1-30654 | Blowout Comb | 1994 | $15 |
| ❏ 61414 | Reachin' (A New Refutation of Time and Space) | 1993 | $15 |

DIGGS, DAVID
Keyboard player, composer, arranger and producer.

Albums

INSTANT JOY
| ❏ 1002 | Supercook! | 198? | $25 |

PALO ALTO
| ❏ 8037 | Realworld | 198? | $25 |

PBR
| ❏ 12 | Elusion | 1979 | $30 |
| ❏ 9 | Out on a Limb | 197? | $30 |

TBA
| ❏ TB-213 | Right Before Your Eyes | 1986 | $25 |
| ❏ TB-207 | Streetshadows | 1985 | $25 |

DIMEOLA, AL
Guitarist. Sometimes a keyboard player and percussionist. Also see RETURN TO FOREVER.

Albums

COLUMBIA
| ❏ JC35277 | Casino | 1978 | $25 |
| ❏ PC35277 | Casino | 1980 | $20 |

—*Budget-line reissue*
| ❏ HC46454 | Electric Rendezvous | 198? | $50 |

Number	Title	Yr	NM
	—*Half-speed mastered edition*		
❏ FC37654	Electric Rendezvous	1982	$25
❏ PC37654	Electric Rendezvous	198?	$20
	—*Budget-line reissue*		
❏ HC44461	Elegant Gypsy	198?	$40
	—*Half-speed mastered edition*		
❏ PC34461	Elegant Gypsy	1976	$25
	—*Original issue with no bar code*		
❏ JC35561	Elegant Gypsy	197?	$20
	—*Reissue with new prefix*		
❏ PC35561	Elegant Gypsy	198?	$20
	—*Budget-line reissue with bar code*		
❏ HC47152	Friday Night in San Francisco	198?	$50
	—*Half-speed mastered edition*		
❏ PC34074	Land of the Midnight Sun	1976	$25
	—*Original issue with no bar code*		
❏ PC34074	Land of the Midnight Sun	1980	$20
	—*Budget-line reissue with bar code*		
❏ FC38944	Scenario	1983	$25
❏ C2X36270	Splendido Hotel	1980	$30
❏ FC38373	Tour de Force -- "Live	1982	$25

EMI-MANHATTAN
| ❏ MLT-46995 | Tirami Su | 1987 | $25 |

MANHATTAN
| ❏ ST-53002 | Cielo E Terra | 1985 | $25 |
| ❏ ST-53011 | Soaring Through a Dream | 1987 | $25 |

DIRECT FLIGHT

Albums

DIRECT DISC
| ❏ DD-104 | Spectrum | 1980 | $60 |

—*Direct-to-disc recording*

DIRTY DOZEN JAZZ BAND, THE

Albums

COLUMBIA
| ❏ FC45042 | Voodoo | 1989 | $35 |

GEORGE WEIN COLLECTION
| ❏ GW-3005 | My Feet Can't Fail Me Now | 1984 | $30 |

ROUNDER
| ❏ 2052 | Live: Mardi Gras in Montreux | 1986 | $30 |

DITMAS, BRUCE
Drummer.

Albums

CHIAROSCURO
| ❏ 195 | Aeray Dust | 1977 | $35 |

DIXIE SMALL FRY, THE
The five members were all between the ages of 11 and 13 when this was recorded.

Albums

LIBERTY
| ❏ LRP-3057 [M] | The Dixie Small Fry in Hi-Fi | 1957 | $40 |
| ❏ LST-7010 [S] | The Dixie Small Fry in Hi-Fi | 1958 | $40 |

DIXIE STOMPERS, THE

Albums

DELMAR
| ❏ DL-204 [M] | Jazz at Westminster College | 195? | $60 |

—*Blue vinyl; label says "DL-201" though cover says "204*
| ❏ DL-112 [10] | The Dixie Stompers Play New Orleans Jazz | 195? | $80 |
| ❏ DL-113 [10] | Wake the Levee | 195? | $80 |

RCA VICTOR
| ❏ LPM-1212 [M] | New York Land Dixie | 1956 | $80 |

DIXIELAND RHYTHM KINGS, THE
Also see TONY PARENTI.

Albums

BLACKBIRD
| ❏ 12006 | A Trip to Waukesha | 197? | $35 |

EMPIRICAL
| ❏ LP-102 [10] | The Dixieland Rhythm Kings | 1954 | $80 |

GHB
| ❏ GHB-7 | The Dixieland Rhythm Kings | 1963 | $35 |

Number	Title	Yr	NM
RIVERSIDE			
❏ RLP 12-210 [M]	Dixieland in Hi-Fi	1956	$250
— White label, blue print			
❏ RLP 12-210 [M]	Dixieland in Hi-Fi	1957	$250
— Blue label, microphone logo			
❏ RLP 12-289 [M]	Jazz in Retrospect	1959	$250
❏ RLP-2505 [10]	New Orleans Jazz Party	1954	$300
❏ RLP 12-259 [M]	The Dixieland Rhythm Kings at the Hi-Fi Jazz Band Ball	1958	$300

DIXON, BILL

Trumpeter, flugel horn player, pianist and composer. Also see ARCHIE SHEPP.

Albums

Number	Title	Yr	NM
CADENCE JAZZ			
❏ CJ-1024/25	Collection	1985	$25
RCA VICTOR			
❏ LPM-3844 [M]	Intents and Purposes	1967	$30
❏ LSP-3844 [S]	Intents and Purposes	1967	$25
SAVOY			
❏ MG-12184	The Bill Dixon 7-Tette	1964	$25
SOUL NOTE			
❏ SN-1008	Bill Dixon in Italy, Volume 1	1980	$30
❏ SN-1011	Bill Dixon in Italy, Volume 2	1981	$30
❏ SN-1037/38	Nov-81	1982	$35
❏ 121138	Son of Sisyphus	1990	$35
❏ 121111	Thoughts	1987	$30

DIXON, ERIC

Tenor saxophone player and flutist.

Albums

Number	Title	Yr	NM
MASTER JAZZ			
❏ 8124	Eric's Edge	197?	$35

DIZRHYTHMIA

Members: Jakko Jakszyck (guitar, sitar, piano, synthesizers, vocals); Gavin Harrison (drums, percussion); Danny Thompson (bass); Pandit Dinesh (tabla, percussion); Sultan Khan (sarangi).

Albums

Number	Title	Yr	NM
ANTILLES			
❏ 91026	Disrhythmia	1988	$25

DJAVAN

Male singer and composer.

Albums

Number	Title	Yr	NM
COLUMBIA			
❏ FC44276	Bird of Paradise	1988	$25

DOBBINS, BILL

Pianist, composer and arranger.

Albums

Number	Title	Yr	NM
ADVENT			
❏ 5003	Textures	1974	$35
OMNISOUND			
❏ 1036	Dedications	1980	$25
❏ 1041	Where One Relaxes	1981	$25
TELARC			
❏ 5003	Textures	198?	$25
— Reissue of Advent LP			

DODD, BILLY

Albums

Number	Title	Yr	NM
JAZZOLOGY			
❏ J-161	Billy Dodd's Swing All-Stars, Volume One	198?	$25
❏ J-162	Billy Dodd's Swing All-Stars, Volume Two	198?	$25
❏ J-130	Doctor Billy Dodd and Friends	1985	$25

DODDS, BABY

Drummer. Brother of JOHNNY DODDS.

Albums

Number	Title	Yr	NM
AMERICAN MUSIC			
❏ 1 [M]	Baby Dodds No. 1	1951	$50
❏ 2 [M]	Baby Dodds No. 2	1951	$50
❏ 3 [M]	Baby Dodds No. 3	1951	$50
FOLKWAYS			
❏ FP-30 [10]	Footnotes to Jazz, Vol. 1 -- Baby Dodds' Drum Solos	1951	$80
GHB			
❏ GHB-50	Jazz A La Creole	1969	$35

DODDS, JOHNNY, AND KID ORY

Also see each artist's individual listings.

Albums

Number	Title	Yr	NM
EPIC			
❏ LN3207 [M]	Johnny Dodds and Kid Ory	1956	$200
❏ LA16004 [M]	Johnny Dodds and Kid Ory	1960	$100

DODDS, JOHNNY

Clarinetist and sometimes saxophone player.

Albums

Number	Title	Yr	NM
BIOGRAPH			
❏ 12024	Johnny Dodds and Tommy Ladner, 1923-28	198?	$25
BRUNSWICK			
❏ BL58016 [10]	The King of New Orleans Clarinets	1951	$100
HERWIN			
❏ 115	Paramount Recordings Vol. 1: 1926-1929	198?	$30
JOLLY ROGER			
❏ 5012 [10]	Johnny Dodds	1954	$50
MCA			
❏ 42326	South Side Chicago Jazz	1990	$35
❏ 1328	Spirit of New Orleans	198?	$25
MILESTONE			
❏ M-2011	Chicago Mess Around	1968	$25
❏ M-2002 [M]	The Immortal Johnny Dodds	1967	$25
RCA VICTOR			
❏ LPV-558 [M]	Sixteen Rare Recordings	1965	$30
RIVERSIDE			
❏ RLP 12-135 [M]	In the Alley: Johnny Dodds, Volume 2	1961	$200
❏ RLP-1002 [10]	Johnny Dodds, Volume 1	1953	$300
❏ RLP-1015 [10]	Johnny Dodds, Volume 2	1953	$300
❏ RLP 12-104 [M]	Johnny Dodds' New Orleans Clarinet	1956	$250
— White label, blue print			
❏ RLP 12-104 [M]	Johnny Dodds' New Orleans Clarinet	195?	$40
— Blue label with microphone logo			
TIME-LIFE			
❏ STL-J-26	Giants of Jazz	1982	$25
X			
❏ LX-3006 [10]	Johnny Dodds' Washboard Band	1954	$60

DODDS, JOHNNY/JIMMY NOONE

Also see each artist's individual listings.

Albums

Number	Title	Yr	NM
BRUNSWICK			
❏ BL58046 [10]	Battle of Jazz, Volume 8	1953	$150

DODSON, MARGE

Female singer.

Albums

Number	Title	Yr	NM
COLUMBIA			
❏ CL1309 [M]	In the Still of the Night	1959	$30
❏ CL1458 [M]	New Voice in Town	1960	$30
❏ CS8258 [S]	New Voice in Town	1960	$40

DOGGETT, BILL

Pianist, organist and arranger. As much rhythm & blues as he was jazz, he's best known for his 1956 hit record "Honky Tonk."

Albums

Number	Title	Yr	NM
ABC-PARAMOUNT			
❏ 507 [M]	Wow!	1965	$50
❏ S-507 [S]	Wow!	1965	$60
AFTER HOURS			
❏ AFT-4112	The Right Choice	1991	$35
COLUMBIA			
❏ CL2082 [M]	Fingertips	1963	$50
❏ CS8882 [S]	Fingertips	1963	$60
❏ CL1814 [M]	Oops!	1962	$50
❏ CS8614 [S]	Oops!	1962	$60
❏ CL1942 [M]	Prelude to the Blues	1963	$50
❏ CS8742 [S]	Prelude to the Blues	1963	$60
KING			
❏ K-5009	14 Original Greatest Hits	1977	$25
❏ 395-600 [M]	A Bill Doggett Christmas	1959	$40
❏ 295-89 [10]	All-Time Christmas Favorites	1955	$200
❏ 830 [M]	American Songs in the Bossa Nova Style	1963	$40
❏ 395-533 [M]	A Salute to Ellington	1958	$120
❏ 395-523 [M]	As You Desire	1957	$120
❏ KLP-523 [M]	As You Desire	1987	$25
— Reissue with "Highland Records" on label			
❏ 723 [M]	Back Again with More	1960	$100
❏ 641 [M]	Big City Dance Party	1959	$100
❏ 295-82 [10]	Bill Doggett -- His Organ and Combo	1955	$300
❏ 295-83 [10]	Bill Doggett -- His Organ and Combo, Volume 2	1955	$300
❏ 667 [M]	Bill Doggett On Tour	1959	$100
❏ 959 [M]	Bonanza of 24 Hit Songs	1966	$60
❏ 759 [M]	Bonanza of 24 Songs	1960	$100
❏ 395-563 [M]	Candle Glow	1958	$120
❏ 395-532 [M]	Dame Dreaming	1958	$120
❏ KLP-532 [M]	Dame Dreaming	1987	$25
— Reissue with "Highland Records" on label			
❏ 395-585 [M]	Dance Awhile	1959	$120
❏ KLP-585 [M]	Dance Awhile	1987	$25
— Reissue with "Highland Records" on label			
❏ 395-531 [M]	Everybody Dance to the Honky Tonk	1958	$120
❏ 706 [M]	For Reminiscent Lovers, Romantic Songs	1960	$100
❏ 633 [M]	High and Wide	1959	$100
❏ 395-609 [M]	Hold It	1959	$120
❏ KS-1078	Honky Tonk Popcorn	1969	$100
❏ 395-514 [M]	Hot Doggett	1957	$120
❏ 868 [M]	Impressions	1964	$40
❏ 395-502 [M]	Moondust	1957	$120
❏ KS-1101	Ram-Bunk-Shush	1970	$60
❏ KS-1104	Sentimental Journey	1970	$60
❏ 295-102 [10]	Sentimentally Yours	1956	$150
❏ KS-1108	Soft	1970	$60
❏ 395-582 [M]	Swingin' Easy	1959	$120
❏ 908 [M]	The Best of Bill Doggett	1964	$40
❏ 395-557 [M]	The Doggett Beat for Dancing Feet	1958	$120
❏ KLP-557 [M]	The Doggett Beat for Dancing Feet	1987	$25
— Reissue with "Highland Records" on label			
❏ 778 [M]	The Many Moods of Bill Doggett	1960	$100
❏ KLP-778 [M]	The Many Moods of Bill Doggett	1987	$25
— Reissue with "Highland Records" on label			
❏ KS-1097	The Nearness of You	1970	$60
POWER PAK			
❏ 269	Hold It!	197?	$25
ROULETTE			
❏ R25330 [M]	Honky Tonk A La Mod	1966	$50
❏ SR25330 [S]	Honky Tonk A La Mod	1966	$60
STARDAY			
❏ 3023	16 Bandstand Favorites	197?	$25
WARNER BROS.			
❏ W1404 [M]	3,046 People Danced 'Til 4 AM	1960	$50
❏ WS1404 [S]	3,046 People Danced 'Til 4 AM	1960	$60
❏ W1452 [M]	Bill Doggett Swings	1962	$50
❏ WS1452 [S]	Bill Doggett Swings	1962	$60
❏ W1421 [M]	The Band with the Beat	1961	$50
❏ WS1421 [S]	The Band with the Beat	1961	$60
WHO'S WHO IN JAZZ			
❏ 21002	Lionel Hampton Presents Bill Doggett	1977	$30

DOKY, NIELS LAN

Pianist.

Albums

Number	Title	Yr	NM
MILESTONE			
❏ M-9178	Dreams	1990	$35
STORYVILLE			
❏ SLP-4160	Daybreak	1989	$30
❏ SLP-4117	Here or There	1986	$25
❏ SLP-4140	The Target	1987	$25
❏ SLP-4144	The Truth	1988	$25

DOLDINGER, KLAUS

Tenor saxophone player, clarinetist, soprano saxophone player and composer. Also see PASSPORT.

Albums

Number	Title	Yr	NM
PHILIPS			
❏ PHM200125 [M]	Dig Doldinger	1966	$25
❏ PHS600125 [S]	Dig Doldinger	1966	$30
WORLD PACIFIC			
❏ WPS-20176	Blues Happening	1969	$100

Number	Title	Yr	NM

DOLPHY, ERIC

Alto saxophone player, flutist, clarinetist and bass clarinetist. Also see THE JAZZ ARTISTS GUILD; THE LATIN JAZZ QUINTET; ORCHESTRA USA.

Albums

BLUE NOTE

Number	Title	Yr	NM
❏ BT-85131	Other Aspects	1987	$25
❏ BLP-4163 [M]	Out to Lunch!	1964	$150
❏ BST-84163 [S]	Out to Lunch!	1964	$80

—*"New York, USA" on label*

❏ BST-84163 [S]	Out to Lunch!	1966	$60

—*"A Division of Liberty Records" on label*

❏ BST-84163 [S]	Out to Lunch!	1970	$50

—*Mostly black label with "Liberty/UA" at bottom*

❏ BST-84163 [S]	Out to Lunch!	1971	$35

—*A Division of United Artists" on label*

❏ BST-84163 [S]	Out to Lunch!	1985	$30

—*The Finest in Jazz Since 1939" reissue*

❏ B1-46524	Out to Lunch!	199?	$35

—*Reissue of 84163*

❏ BST-84163 [S]	Out to Lunch!	1973	$30

—*Dark blue label with black stylized "b" at upper right*

CELLULOID

Number	Title	Yr	NM
❏ CELL-5014	Conversations	198?	$25
❏ CELL-5015	Iron Man	198?	$25

DOUGLAS

❏ SD785	Iron Man	1969	$30
❏ KZ30873	Iron Man	1971	$25
❏ 6002	Jitterbug Waltz	197?	$35

EPITAPH

❏ E-4010	Eric Dolphy 1928-1964	1975	$35

EVEREST ARCHIVE OF FOLK & JAZZ

❏ FS-227	Eric Dolphy and Cannonball Adderley	1968	$30

EXODUS

❏ EX-6005 [M]	The Memorial Album	1966	$25

—*Reissue of Vee Jay LP-2503*

❏ EXS-6005 [S]	The Memorial Album	1966	$25

—*Reissue of Vee Jay LPS-2503*

FANTASY

❏ OJC-133	Eric Dolphy at the Five Spot	198?	$25

—*Reissue of New Jazz 8260*

❏ OJC-247	Eric Dolphy at the Five Spot, Volume 2	198?	$25

—*Reissue of Prestige 7294*

❏ OJC-413	Eric Dolphy in Europe, Volume 1	1990	$30

—*Reissue of Prestige 7304*

❏ OJC-414	Eric Dolphy in Europe, Volume 2	1990	$30

—*Reissue of Prestige 7350*

❏ OJC-415	Eric Dolphy in Europe, Volume 3	1990	$30

—*Reissue of Prestige 7366*

❏ OJC-353	Eric Dolphy Memorial Album	198?	$25

—*Reissue of Prestige 7334*

❏ OJC-400	Far Cry	1989	$30

—*Reissue of New Jazz 8270*

❏ OJC-023	Out There	198?	$25

—*Reissue of New Jazz 8252*

❏ OJC-022	Outward Bound	198?	$25

—*Reissue of New Jazz 8236*

FM

❏ 308 [M]	Conversations	1963	$40
❏ S-308 [S]	Conversations	1963	$50

FONTANA

❏ 822226-1	Last Date	1986	$25

GM

❏ GM-3005	Vintage Dolphy	1986	$35

INNER CITY

❏ IC-3017	The Berlin Concerts	1978	$35

LIMELIGHT

❏ LM-82013 [M]	Last Date	1964	$30
❏ LS-86013 [S]	Last Date	1964	$40

NEW JAZZ

❏ NJLP-8260 [M]	Eric Dolphy at the Five Spot	1961	$650

—*Purple label*

❏ NJLP-8260 [M]	Eric Dolphy at the Five Spot	1965	$150

—*Blue label, trident logo at right*

❏ NJLP-8270 [M]	Far Cry	1962	$400

—*Purple label*

❏ NJLP-8270 [M]	Far Cry	1965	$150

—*Blue label, trident logo at right*

Number	Title	Yr	NM
❏ NJLP-8252 [M]	Out There	1960	$300

—*Purple label*

❏ NJLP-8252 [M]	Out There	1965	$150

—*Blue label, trident logo at right*

❏ NJLP-8236 [M]	Outward Bound	1960	$450

PRESTIGE

❏ 24027	Copenhagen Concert	197?	$25
❏ MPP-2517	Dash One	198?	$25
❏ 24008	Eric Dolphy	197?	$25
❏ PRLP-7294	Eric Dolphy at the Five Spot, Volume 2	1964	$400

—*Yellow label*

❏ PRLP-7294 [M]	Eric Dolphy at the Five Spot, Volume 2	1965	$25

—*Blue label, trident logo at right*

❏ PRST-7294 [S]	Eric Dolphy at the Five Spot, Volume 2	1964	$50

—*Silver label*

❏ PRST-7294 [S]	Eric Dolphy at the Five Spot, Volume 2	1965	$30

—*Blue label, trident logo at right*

❏ PRLP-7304 [M]	Eric Dolphy in Europe, Volume 1	1964	$40

—*Yellow label*

❏ PRLP-7304 [M]	Eric Dolphy in Europe, Volume 1	1965	$25

—*Blue label, trident logo at right*

❏ PRST-7304 [S]	Eric Dolphy in Europe, Volume 1	1964	$50

—*Silver label*

❏ PRST-7304 [S]	Eric Dolphy in Europe, Volume 1	1965	$30

—*Blue label, trident logo at right*

❏ PRLP-7350 [M]	Eric Dolphy in Europe, Volume 2	1965	$25
❏ PRST-7350 [S]	Eric Dolphy in Europe, Volume 2	1965	$30
❏ PRLP-7366 [M]	Eric Dolphy in Europe, Volume 3	1965	$25
❏ PRST-7366 [S]	Eric Dolphy in Europe, Volume 3	1965	$30
❏ PRLP-7334 [M]	Eric Dolphy Memorial Album	1964	$25
❏ PRST-7334 [S]	Eric Dolphy Memorial Album	1964	$30
❏ PRST-7747	Far Cry	1970	$35
❏ 34002	Great Concert	1974	$30
❏ PRLP-7382 [M]	Here and There	1965	$25
❏ PRST-7382 [S]	Here and There	1965	$30
❏ PRST-7611	Live at the Five Spot, Volume 1	1969	$35
❏ PRST-7826	Live at the Five Spot, Volume 2	1971	$35
❏ 24053	Magic	197?	$35
❏ PRST-7652	Out There	1969	$35
❏ PRLP-7311 [M]	Outward Bound	1964	$50

—*Yellow label*

❏ PRLP-7311 [M]	Outward Bound	1965	$30

—*Blue label, trident logo at right*

❏ PRST-7311 [S]	Outward Bound	1964	$40

—*Silver label*

❏ PRST-7311 [S]	Outward Bound	1965	$25

—*Blue label, trident logo at right*

❏ P-24070	Status	1977	$35
❏ PRST-7843	Where?	1971	$35

TRIP

❏ 5506	Last Date	197?	$30
❏ 5012	The Greatness of Eric Dolphy	197?	$30

VEE JAY

❏ LP-2503 [M]	The Memorial Album	1964	$30
❏ LPS-2503 [S]	The Memorial Album	1964	$40

DOMNERUS, ARNE

Alto saxophone player and clarinetist. Also see BENGT HALLBERG.

Albums

PRESTIGE

❏ PRLP-134 [10]	New Sounds from Sweden, Volume 4	1952	$350

RCA CAMDEN

❏ CAL-417 [M]	Swedish Modern Jazz	1958	$60

RCA VICTOR

❏ LPT-3032 [10]	Around the World in Jazz	1953	$250

DOMNERUS, ARNE/LARS GULLIN

Also see each artist's individual listings.

Albums

PRESTIGE

Number	Title	Yr	NM
❏ PRLP-133 [10]	New Sounds from Sweden, Volume 3	1952	$350

DONAHUE, SAM

Tenor saxophone player and trumpeter.

Albums

CAPITOL

❏ H626 [10]	Classics in Jazz	1955	$80
❏ H613 [10]	For Young Moderns in Love	1955	$100
❏ T613 [M]	For Young Moderns in Love	1956	$60

DONALD, BARBARA

Trumpeter.

Albums

CADENCE JAZZ

❏ CJ-1011	Olympia Live	198?	$25
❏ CJ-1017	Past & Tomorrows	198?	$25

DONALDSON, BOBBY

Drummer and bandleader.

Albums

GOLDEN CREST

❏ GC-1003	Unlimited	196?	$25

SAVOY

❏ MG-12128 [M]	Dixieland Jazz Party	1958	$40
❏ SST-13003 [S]	Dixieland Jazz Party	1959	$30

WORLD WIDE

❏ 20005	Bobby Donaldson and the 7th Avenue Stompers	196?	$25

DONALDSON, LOU

Alto saxophone player.

Albums

ARGO

❏ LP-747 [M]	Cole Slaw	1965	$60
❏ LPS-747 [S]	Cole Slaw	1965	$60
❏ LP-734 [M]	Possum Head	1964	$60
❏ LPS-734 [S]	Possum Head	1964	$60
❏ LP-724 [M]	Signifyin'	1963	$60
❏ LPS-724 [S]	Signifyin'	1963	$60

BLUE NOTE

❏ BLP-4263 [M]	Alligator Boogaloo	1967	$150
❏ BST-84263 [S]	Alligator Boogaloo	1967	$100

—*With "A Division of Liberty Records" on label*

❏ BLP-1593 [M]	Blues Walk	1958	$300

—*Regular version with W. 63rd St. address on label*

❏ BLP-1593 [M]	Blues Walk	1963	$80

—*With New York, USA address on label*

❏ BST-1593 [S]	Blues Walk	1959	$100

—*Regular version with W. 63rd St. address on label*

❏ BST-1593 [S]	Blues Walk	1963	$50

—*With New York, USA address on label*

❏ BST-81593 [S]	Blues Walk	1967	$30

—*With "A Division of Liberty Records" on label*

❏ BST-81593	Blues Walk	1985	$30

—*The Finest in Jazz Since 1939" reissue*

❏ BST-84370	Cosmos	1971	$35
❏ BST-84337	Everything I Play Is Funky	1970	$100

—*With "A Division of Liberty Records" on label*

❏ B1-31248	Everything I Play Is Funky	1995	$35

—*Reissue of 84337*

❏ BLP-4125 [M]	Good Gracious	1963	$150
❏ BST-84125 [S]	Good Gracious	1963	$100

—*With "New York, USA" on label*

❏ BST-84125 [S]	Good Gracious	1967	$50

—*With "A Division of Liberty Records" on label*

❏ BLP-4079 [M]	Gravy Train	1962	$200

—*With W. 63rd St. address on label*

❏ BLP-4079 [M]	Gravy Train	1963	$175

—*With New York, USA address on label*

❏ BST-84079 [S]	Gravy Train	1962	$175

—*With W. 63rd St. address on label*

❏ BST-84079 [S]	Gravy Train	1963	$100

—*With New York, USA address on label*

❏ BST-84079 [S]	Gravy Train	1967	$60

—*With "A Division of Liberty Records" on label*

❏ BLP-4066 [M]	Here 'Tis	1961	$200

Lou Donaldson, *Good Gracious*, Blue Note BLP-4125, **$150**.

Kenny Dorham, *Jazz Contemporary*, Time S/2004, **$250**.

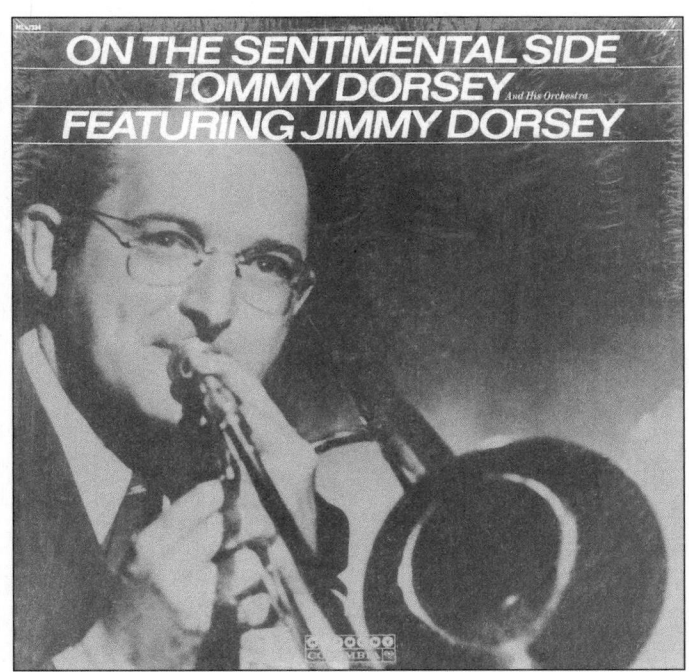

Tommy Dorsey featuring Jimmy Dorsey, *On the Sentimental Side*, Harmony HL 7334, **$35**.

Tommy Dorsey, *The Best of Tommy Dorsey*, RCA Victor LSP-3674(e), **$30**.

Number	Title	Yr	NM
—With W. 63rd St. address on label			
❏ BLP-4066 [M]	Here 'Tis	1963	$150
—With New York, USA address on label			
❏ BST-84066 [S]	Here 'Tis	1961	$175
—With W. 63rd St. address on label			
❏ BST-84066 [S]	Here 'Tis	1963	$100
—With New York, USA address on label			
❏ BST-84318	Hot Dog	1969	$100
—With "A Division of Liberty Records" on label			
❏ B1-28267	Hot Dog	1994	$35
—Reissue of 84318			
❏ BLP-4012 [M]	LD + 3	1959	$200
—Regular version with W. 63rd St. address on label			
❏ BLP-4012 [M]	LD + 3	1963	$80
—With New York, USA address on label			
❏ BST-4012 [S]	LD + 3	1960	$150
—Regular version with W. 63rd St. address on label			
❏ BST-4012 [S]	LD + 3	1963	$60
—With New York, USA address on label			
❏ BLP-4053 [M]	Light Foot	1960	$120
—With W. 63rd St. address on label			
❏ BLP-4053 [M]	Light Foot	1963	$200
—With New York, USA address on label			
❏ BST-84053 [S]	Light Foot	1960	$175
—With W. 63rd St. address on label			
❏ BST-84053 [S]	Light Foot	1963	$100
—With New York, USA address on label			
❏ BLP-5030 [10]	Lou Donaldson-Clifford Brown	1954	$500
❏ BLP-1537 [M]	Lou Donaldson Quartet/ Quintet/Sextet	1957	$1200
—Deep groove" version; Lexington Ave. address on label			
❏ BLP-1537 [M]	Lou Donaldson Quartet/ Quintet/Sextet	1958	$800
—Deep groove" version; W. 63rd St. address on label			
❏ BLP-1537 [M]	Lou Donaldson Quartet/ Quintet/Sextet	1958	$175
—Regular version with W. 63rd St. address on label			
❏ BLP-1537 [M]	Lou Donaldson Quartet/ Quintet/Sextet	1963	$80
—With New York, USA address on label			
❏ B1-81537	Lou Donaldson Quartet/ Quintet/Sextet	1989	$30
—Reissue of 1537			
❏ BLP-5021 [10]	Lou Donaldson Quintet/ Quartet	1953	$500
❏ BLP-5055 [10]	Lou Donaldson Sextet, Volume 2	1955	$500
❏ BLP-1591 [M]	Lou Takes Off	1958	$850
—Deep groove" version; W. 63rd St. address on label			
❏ BLP-1591 [M]	Lou Takes Off	1958	$250
—Regular version with W. 63rd St. address on label			
❏ BLP-1591 [M]	Lou Takes Off	1963	$140
—With New York, USA address on label			
❏ BST-1591 [S]	Lou Takes Off	1959	$300
—Regular version with W. 63rd St. address on label			
❏ BST-1591 [S]	Lou Takes Off	1963	$200
—With New York, USA address on label			
❏ BST-81591 [S]	Lou Takes Off	1966	$50
—With "A Division of Liberty Records" on label			
❏ BST-84254	Lush Life	1986	$35
—The Finest in Jazz Since 1939" label; first issue of this LP			
❏ BST-84280	Midnight Creeper	1968	$120
—A Division of Liberty Records" on label			
❏ LT-1028	Midnight Sun	1980	$60
❏ BLP-4271 [M]	Mr. Shing-a-Ling	1968	$200
❏ BST-84271 [S]	Mr. Shing-a-Ling	1968	$100
—With "A Division of Liberty Records" on label			
❏ B1-89794	Pretty Thing	1993	$35
—Reissue of 84359			
❏ BST-84359	Pretty Things	1970	$35
❏ BN-LA109-F	Sassy Soul Strut	1973	$60
❏ BST-84299	Say It Loud!	1969	$100
—With "A Division of Liberty Records" on label			
❏ BN-LA024-F	Sophisticated Lou	1972	$60
❏ BLP-4036 [M]	Sunny Side Up	1960	$400
—Deep groove" version; W. 63rd St. address on label			
❏ BLP-4036 [M]	Sunny Side Up	1960	$200
—Regular version with W. 63rd St. address on label			
❏ BLP-4036 [M]	Sunny Side Up	1963	$80
—With New York, USA address on label			
❏ BST-84036 [S]	Sunny Side Up	1960	$175
—With W. 63rd St. address on label			
❏ BST-84036 [S]	Sunny Side Up	1963	$100

Number	Title	Yr	NM
—With New York, USA address on label			
❏ B1-32095	Sunny Side Up	1995	$35
—Reissue of 84036			
❏ BN-LA259-G	Sweet Lou	1974	$60
❏ 4254/84254	Sweet Slumber	1967	$0
—Canceled			
❏ BLP-1566 [M]	Swing and Soul	1957	$250
—Deep groove" version; W. 63rd St. address on label			
❏ BLP-1566 [M]	Swing and Soul	1957	$150
—Regular version with W. 63rd St. address on label			
❏ BLP-1566 [M]	Swing and Soul	1963	$80
—With New York, USA address on label			
❏ BST-1566 [S]	Swing and Soul	1959	$150
—Deep groove" version; W. 63rd St. address on label			
❏ BST-1566 [S]	Swing and Soul	1959	$175
—Regular version with W. 63rd St. address on label			
❏ BST-1566 [S]	Swing and Soul	1963	$60
—With New York, USA address on label			
❏ BLP-4108 [M]	The Natural Soul	1963	$150
❏ BST-84108 [S]	The Natural Soul	1963	$120
—With "New York, USA" on label			
❏ BST-84108 [S]	The Natural Soul	1967	$50
—With "A Division of Liberty Records" on label			
❏ BST-84108	The Natural Soul	1987	$30
—The Finest in Jazz Since 1939" reissue			
❏ B1-31876	The Scorpion: Live at the Cadillac Club	1995	$35
❏ BLP-4025 [M]	The Time Is Right	1960	$800
—Deep groove" version (deep indentation under label on both sides)			
❏ BLP-4025 [M]	The Time Is Right	1960	$150
—Regular version with W. 63rd St. address on label			
❏ BLP-4025 [M]	The Time Is Right	1963	$100
—With New York, USA address on label			
❏ BST-84025 [S]	The Time Is Right	1960	$175
—With W. 63rd St. address on label			
❏ BST-84025 [S]	The Time Is Right	1963	$100
—With New York, USA address on label			
❏ BLP-1545 [M]	Wailing with Lou	1957	$1250
—Deep groove" version; W. 63rd St. address on label			
❏ BLP-1545 [M]	Wailing with Lou	1957	$300
—Regular version with W. 63rd St. address on label			
❏ BLP-1545 [M]	Wailing with Lou	1963	$140
—With New York, USA address on label			
CADET			
❏ LP-789 [M]	Blowin' in the Wind	1967	$60
❏ LPS-789 [S]	Blowin' in the Wind	1967	$50
❏ LP-747 [M]	Cole Slaw	1966	$50
—Reissue of Argo 747			
❏ LPS-747 [S]	Cole Slaw	1966	$35
—Reissue of Argo 747			
❏ LPS-842	Fried Buzzard — Lou Donaldson Live	1970	$50
❏ LPS-815	Lou Donaldson At His Best	1969	$50
❏ LP-759 [M]	Musty Rusty	1966	$60
❏ LPS-759 [S]	Musty Rusty	1966	$60
❏ LP-734 [M]	Possum Head	1966	$50
—Reissue of Argo 734			
❏ LPS-734 [S]	Possum Head	1966	$35
—Reissue of Argo 734			
❏ LP-768 [M]	Rough House Blues	1966	$60
❏ LPS-768 [S]	Rough House Blues	1966	$60
❏ LP-724 [M]	Signifyin'	1966	$50
—Reissue of Argo 724			
❏ LPS-724 [S]	Signifyin'	1966	$35
—Reissue of Argo 724			
CHESS			
❏ 2CA60007	Ha' Mercy	1972	$30
COTILLION			
❏ SD9905	A Different Scene	1976	$35
❏ SD9915	Color As a Way of Life	1977	$35
MUSE			
❏ MR-5292	Back Street	1983	$30
❏ MR-5247	Sweet Poppa Lou	1982	$30
SUNSET			
❏ SUS-5258	Down Home	1969	$30
❏ SUS-5318	I Won't Cry Anymore	1970	$30
TIMELESS			
❏ SJP-153	Forgotten Man	198?	$25

Number	Title	Yr	NM
DONALDSON, WALTER			
Composer ("Makin' Whoopee," "Carolina in the Morning" and dozens of others).			
Albums			
MONMOUTH-EVERGREEN			
❏ 7059	The Greatest Song Hits	197?	$30
DONATO, JOAO			
Pianist, organist and sometimes trombone player.			
Albums			
BLUE THUMB			
❏ BT-21	A Bad Donato	1972	$35
—Distributed by Famous Music			
❏ BT-8821	A Bad Donato	1970	$25
—Distributed by Capitol			
MUSE			
❏ MR-5017	Joao Donato	197?	$30
RCA VICTOR			
❏ LPM-3473 [M]	The New Sound of Brazil	1966	$35
❏ LSP-3473 [S]	The New Sound of Brazil	1966	$25
DONEGAN, DOROTHY			
Pianist.			
Albums			
AUDIOPHILE			
❏ AP-209	The Explosive Dorothy Donegan	198?	$25
CAPITOL			
❏ T1226 [M]	Donnybrook with Dorothy	1960	$60
❏ ST1226 [S]	Donnybrook with Dorothy	1960	$60
❏ T1135 [M]	Dorothy Donegan Live!	1959	$60
❏ ST1135 [S]	Dorothy Donegan Live!	1959	$60
FORUM			
❏ F-9003 [M]	Dorothy Donegan at the Embers	196?	$35
—Reissue of Roulette R-25010			
❏ SF-9003 [R]	Dorothy Donegan at the Embers	196?	$30
JUBILEE			
❏ LP-11 [10]	Dorothy Donegan Trio	1955	$80
❏ JLP-1013 [M]	September Song	1956	$60
MGM			
❏ E-278 [10]	Dorothy Donegan Piano	1954	$80
PROGRESSIVE			
❏ PRO-7056	The Explosive Dorothy Donegan	198?	$30
ROULETTE			
❏ R-25010 [M]	Dorothy Donegan at the Embers	1957	$50
❏ R-25154 [M]	It Happened One Night	1961	$30
❏ SR-25154 [S]	It Happened One Night	1961	$40
DONELIAN, ARMEN			
Pianist.			
Albums			
SUNNYSIDE			
❏ SSC-1019	A Reverie	1987	$25
❏ SSC-1031	Secrets	1988	$25
DORGE, PIERRE, AND WALT DICKERSON			
Also see each artist's individual entries.			
Albums			
STEEPLECHASE			
❏ SCS-1115	Landscape with Open Door	1978	$30
DORGE, PIERRE			
Danish guitarist, bandleader, composer and arranger.			
Albums			
STEEPLECHASE			
❏ SCS-1132	Ballad Round Left Corner	1979	$30
❏ SCS-1188	Brikama	198?	$25
❏ SCS-1208	Even the Moon Is Dancing	198?	$25
❏ SCS-1228	Johnny Lives	198?	$25
❏ SCS-1162	Pierre Dorge and the New Jungle Orchestra	1982	$30
DORHAM, KENNY			
Trumpeter, composer and arranger. Also see THE JAZZ ARTISTS GUILD.			
Albums			

Number	Title	Yr	NM
BAINBRIDGE			
❑ 1048	Kenny Dorham	198?	$25
❑ 1043	Show Boat	198?	$25
BLUE NOTE			
❑ BLP-1535 [M]	Kenny Dorham Octet/Sextet	1956	$150
—Regular version with Lexington Ave. address on label			
❑ BLP-1535 [M]	Kenny Dorham Octet/Sextet	1963	$3500
—New York, USA" address on label			
❑ BLP-1524 [M]	'Round About Midnight at the Café Bohemia	1956	$1000
—Deep groove" version (deep indentation under label on both sides)			
❑ BLP-1524 [M]	'Round About Midnight at the Café Bohemia	1956	$750
—Regular version with Lexington Ave. address on label			
❑ BLP-1524 [M]	'Round About Midnight at the Café Bohemia	1963	$60
—New York, USA" address on label			
❑ BLP-4181 [M]	Trompeta Toccata	1964	$60
—New York, USA" address on label			
❑ BST-84181 [S]	Trompeta Toccata	1964	$40
—New York, USA" address on label			
❑ BST-84181 [S]	Trompeta Toccata	1966	$35
—A Division of Liberty Records" on label			
❑ BST-84181	Trompeta Toccata	1985	$25
—The Finest in Jazz Since 1939" reissue			
❑ BLP-4127 [M]	Una Mas	1963	$60
—New York, USA" address on label			
❑ BST-84127 [S]	Una Mas	1963	$40
—New York, USA" address on label			
❑ BST-84127 [S]	Una Mas	1966	$35
—A Division of Liberty Records" on label			
❑ BST-84127 [S]	Una Mas	197?	$30
—United Artists" on label			
❑ BLP-4063 [M]	Whistle Stop	1961	$150
—W. 63rd St. address on label			
❑ BLP-4063 [M]	Whistle Stop	1963	$100
—New York, USA" address on label			
❑ BST-84063 [S]	Whistle Stop	1961	$120
—W. 63rd St. address on label			
❑ BST-84063 [S]	Whistle Stop	1963	$60
—New York, USA" address on label			
❑ BST-84063 [S]	Whistle Stop	1966	$35
—A Division of Liberty Records" on label			
❑ BST-84063 [S]	Whistle Stop	197?	$30
—United Artists" on label			
❑ B1-28978	Whistle Stop	1994	$35
DEBUT			
❑ DLP-9 [10]	Kenny Dorham Quintet	1954	$1000
FANTASY			
❑ OJC-463	2 Horns 2 Rhythm	1990	$30
—Reissue of Riverside 255			
❑ OJC-134	Blue Spring	198?	$25
❑ OJC-028	Jazz Contrasts	198?	$25
❑ OJC-113	Kenny Dorham Quintet	198?	$25
—Reissue of Debut 9			
❑ OJC-250	Quiet Kenny	1987	$25
—Reissue of New Jazz 8225			
JARO			
❑ JAM-5007 [M]	The Arrival of Kenny Dorham	1960	$400
❑ JAS-8007 [S]	The Arrival of Kenny Dorham	1960	$400
JAZZLAND			
❑ JLP-14 [M]	Kenny Dorham and Friends	1960	$40
❑ JLP-914 [S]	Kenny Dorham and Friends	1960	$50
❑ JLP-82 [M]	Kenny Dorham and Friends	1962	$25
❑ JLP-982 [S]	Kenny Dorham and Friends	1962	$30
❑ JLP-3 [M]	The Swingers	1960	$40
❑ JLP-903 [S]	The Swingers	1960	$50
MILESTONE			
❑ 47036	But Beautiful	197?	$35
MUSE			
❑ MR-5053	Ease It	1974	$35
NEW JAZZ			
❑ NJLP-8225 [M]	Quiet Kenny	1965	$150
—Blue label, trident logo at right			
PACIFIC JAZZ			
❑ PJ-41 [M]	Inta Somethin' -- Recorded Live at the Jazz Workshop	1962	$700
❑ ST-41 [S]	Inta Somethin' -- Recorded Live at the Jazz Workshop	1962	$40
PRESTIGE			
❑ PRST-7754	Kenny Dorham 1959	1970	$25

Number	Title	Yr	NM
RIVERSIDE			
❑ RLP 12-255 [M]	2 Horns 2 Rhythm	1957	$300
❑ RLP 12-297 [M]	Blue Spring	1959	$300
❑ RLP-1139 [S]	Blue Spring	1959	$300
❑ RLP 12-239 [M]	Jazz Contrasts	1957	$400
—White label, blue print			
❑ RLP 12-239 [M]	Jazz Contrasts	1959	$250
—Blue label, microphone logo			
❑ RLP-1105 [S]	Jazz Contrasts	1959	$250
—Black label, microphone logo			
❑ 6075	Jazz Contrasts	197?	$35
❑ RLP 12-275 [M]	This Is the Moment!	1958	$300
STEEPLECHASE			
❑ SCC-6011	Scandia Skies	198?	$30
❑ SCC-6010	Short Story	198?	$30
TIME			
❑ 52004 [M]	Jazz Contemporary	1960	$250
❑ S-2004 [S]	Jazz Contemporary	1960	$250
❑ 52024 [M]	Show Boat	1960	$40
❑ S-2024 [S]	Show Boat	1960	$50
UNITED ARTISTS			
❑ UAJ-14007 [M]	Matador	1962	$30
❑ UAJS-15007 [S]	Matador	1962	$40
❑ UAS-5631	Matador	1971	$25
—Reissue of 15007			
XANADU			
❑ 125	Memorial Album	197?	$35

DORHAM, KENNY/CLARK TERRY
Also see each artist's individual listings.

Albums

Number	Title	Yr	NM
JAZZLAND			
❑ JLP-10 [M]	Top Trumpets	1960	$40
❑ JLP-910 [S]	Top Trumpets	1960	$50

DOROUGH, BOB
Pianist and male singer. Best known as the musical director of the ABC cartoon series "Schoolhouse Rock."

Albums

Number	Title	Yr	NM
BETHLEHEM			
❑ BCP-11 [M]	Devil May Care	1955	$250
❑ BCP-6023	Yardbird Suite	197?	$50
—Reissue of 11, distributed by RCA Victor			
CLASSIC JAZZ			
❑ 18	An Excursion Through Oliver	197?	$35
❑ 19	The Medieval Jazz Quartet Plus 3	197?	$35
FOCUS			
❑ FL-336 [M]	Better Than Anything	1967	$30
❑ FS-336 [S]	Better Than Anything	1967	$25
INNER CITY			
❑ IC-1023	Just About Everything	197?	$35
LAISSEZ-FAIRE			
❑ 02	Beginning to See the Light	1976	$25
MUSIC MINUS ONE			
❑ 225 [M]	Oliver	1963	$30

DORSEY, JIMMY
Clarinetist, alto saxophone player, trumpeter, cornet player and bandleader. Also see THE DORSEY BROTHERS.

Albums

Number	Title	Yr	NM
ATLANTIC			
❑ 81801	Dorsey, Then and Now	1988	$25
CIRCLE			
❑ 30	Jimmy Dorsey and His Orchestra 1939-40	198?	$25
❑ 46	Jimmy Dorsey and His Orchestra Mostly 1940	198?	$25
COLUMBIA			
❑ CL6095 [10]	Dixie by Dorsey	1950	$100
❑ CL608 [M]	Dixie by Dorsey	1955	$50
—Maroon label with gold print			
❑ CL608 [M]	Dixie by Dorsey	1955	$75
—Red and black label with six "eye" logos			
❑ CL6114 [10]	Dorseyland Band	1950	$100
CORAL			
❑ CRL56004 [10]	Contrasting Music, Volume 1	1950	$50
❑ CRL56008 [10]	Contrasting Music, Volume 2	1950	$50
❑ CRL56033 [10]	Gershwin Music	1950	$50
DECCA			
❑ DL4853 [M]	Jimmy Dorsey's Greatest Hits	1967	$25
❑ DL74853 [R]	Jimmy Dorsey's Greatest Hits	1967	$30
❑ DL5091 [10]	Latin American Favorites	1950	$150

Number	Title	Yr	NM
❑ DL8153 [M]	Latin American Favorites	1955	$150
—Black label, silver print			
❑ DL8609 [M]	The Great Jimmy Dorsey	1957	$120
—Black label, silver print			
DOT			
❑ DLP-3437 [M]	So Rare	1962	$75
—Reissue of Fraternity LP			
❑ DLP-25437 [R]	So Rare	196?	$75
FRATERNITY			
❑ F-1008 [M]	Fabulous Jimmy Dorsey	1957	$30
HINDSIGHT			
❑ HSR-101	Jimmy Dorsey and His Orchestra 1939-40	198?	$25
❑ HSR-153	Jimmy Dorsey and His Orchestra 1942-44	198?	$25
❑ HSR-203	Jimmy Dorsey and His Orchestra 1948	198?	$25
❑ HSR-165	Jimmy Dorsey and His Orchestra 1949, 1951	198?	$25
❑ HSR-178	Jimmy Dorsey and His Orchestra 1950	198?	$25
INSIGHT			
❑ 210	Jimmy Dorsey and His Orchestra 1939-42	198?	$25
LION			
❑ L-70063 [M]	Jimmy Dorsey and His Orchestra	1958	$50
MCA			
❑ 252	Jimmy Dorsey's Greatest Hits	197?	$30
—Reissue of Decca 74853; black label with rainbow			
❑ 252	Jimmy Dorsey's Greatest Hits	198?	$20
—Reissue; blue label with rainbow			
❑ 4073	The Best of Jimmy Dorsey	1975	$30
—Original edition has a gatefold cover and black labels with rainbow			
POWER PAK			
❑ 244	Jimmy Dorsey Plays His Biggest Hits	197?	$25
TIME-LIFE			
❑ STBB-10	Big Bands: Jimmy Dorsey	1984	$35
TRIP			
❑ 5815	So Rare!	197?	$25

DORSEY, TOMMY, ORCHESTRA (WARREN COVINGTON, DIRECTOR)
Covington, a trombonist, became leader of the Dorsey band after Tommy's death. This version of the band had a hit single in 1958 with "Tea for Two Cha Cha."

Albums

Number	Title	Yr	NM
DECCA			
❑ DL8904 [M]	Dance and Romance	1959	$80
❑ DL78904 [S]	Dance and Romance	1959	$80
❑ DL4120 [M]	Dance to the Songs Everybody Knows	1960	$35
❑ DL74120 [S]	Dance to the Songs Everybody Knows	1960	$25
❑ DL8996 [M]	It Takes Two to Bunny Hop..	1960	$35
❑ DL78996 [S]	It Takes Two to Bunny Hop..	1960	$25
❑ DL8980 [M]	It Takes Two to Cha-Cha…	1959	$80
❑ DL78980 [S]	It Takes Two to Cha-Cha…	1959	$80
❑ DL8943 [M]	More Tea for Two Cha Chas	1959	$80
❑ DL78943 [S]	More Tea for Two Cha Chas	1959	$80
❑ DL8842 [M]	Tea for Two Cha Cha	1958	$100
❑ DL78842 [S]	Tea for Two Cha Cha	1958	$100
❑ DL8802 [M]	The Fabulous Arrangements of Tommy Dorsey	1958	$120
❑ DL78802 [S]	The Fabulous Arrangements of Tommy Dorsey	1958	$120
❑ DL4130 [M]	Tricky Trombones	1961	$35
❑ DL74130 [S]	Tricky Trombones	1961	$25
MCA			
❑ 185	It Takes Two to Bunny Hop..	197?	$25
❑ 534	It Takes Two to Cha-Cha…	197?	$25
—Reissue of Decca 78996			
❑ 180	More Tea for Two Cha Chas	197?	$25
—Reissue of Decca 78943			
❑ 178	Tea for Two Cha Chas	197?	$25
—Reissue of Decca 78842			

DORSEY, TOMMY
Trombonist, trumpet player and bandleader. Starred items (*) include one or more tracks with FRANK SINATRA as vocalist. Also see THE DORSEY BROTHERS.

Albums

Number	Title	Yr	NM
20TH CENTURY FOX			
❏ TFM-3157 [M]	This Is Tommy Dorsey and His Greatest Band, Vol. 1	196?	$25
❏ TFS-4157 [R]	This Is Tommy Dorsey and His Greatest Band, Vol. 1	196?	$30
❏ TFM-3158 [M]	This Is Tommy Dorsey and His Greatest Band, Vol. 2	196?	$25
❏ TFS-4158 [R]	This Is Tommy Dorsey and His Greatest Band, Vol. 2	196?	$30
❏ FOX1005 [M]	Tommy Dorsey and His Orchestra: His Greatest Arrangements -- His Greatest Band	196?	$25

— Million Seller Hits" reissue series

Number	Title	Yr	NM
❏ TCF101/102 [M]	Tommy Dorsey's Greatest Band	1959	$30
BLUEBIRD			
❏ AXM2-5521	The Complete Tommy Dorsey, Volume 1	197?	$35
❏ AXM2-5549	The Complete Tommy Dorsey, Volume 2	197?	$35
❏ AXM2-5560	The Complete Tommy Dorsey, Volume 3	197?	$35
❏ AXM2-5564	The Complete Tommy Dorsey, Volume 4	197?	$35
❏ AXM2-5573	The Complete Tommy Dorsey, Volume 5	197?	$35
❏ AXM2-5578	The Complete Tommy Dorsey, Volume 6	197?	$35
❏ AXM2-5582	The Complete Tommy Dorsey, Volume 7	197?	$35
❏ AXM2-5586	The Complete Tommy Dorsey, Volume 8	197?	$35
❏ 9987-1-RB	Yes, Indeed!	1990	$35
COLPIX			
❏ CP401 [M]	The Great T.D.	1958	$50
❏ CP436 [M]	Tommy Dorsey & His Orchestra Volume 4	1962	$50
❏ CP498 [M]	Tommy Dorsey -- A Man and His Trombone	196?	$50
DECCA			
❏ DL5448 [10]	In a Sentimental Mood	1952	$150
❏ DL5449 [10]	Tenderly	1952	$150
❏ DL5317 [10]	Tommy Dorsey Plays Howard Dietz	1951	$200
❏ DL5452 [10]	Your Invitation to Dance	1952	$150
HARMONY			
❏ HL7334 [M]	On the Sentimental Side	196?	$35
❏ KH32014	The Beat of the Big Bands	1972	$25
MCA			
❏ 732	Sentimental	198?	$20
❏ 4074	The Best of Tommy Dorsey	197?	$30
MOVIETONE			
❏ MTM-1019 [M]	The Tommy Dorsey Years	1967	$35
❏ MTS-72019 [R]	The Tommy Dorsey Years	1967	$30
❏ MTM-1004 [M]	Tommy Dorsey's Hullaballoo	196?	$35
❏ MTS-72004 [R]	Tommy Dorsey's Hullaballoo	196?	$30
PICKWICK			
❏ PTP-2035	I'm Getting Sentimental*	197?	$30
RCA CAMDEN			
❏ CAL-800 [M]	Dedicated to You*	1964	$35
❏ CAS-800(e) [R]	Dedicated to You*	1964	$25
❏ ADL2-0178	I'll See You in My Dreams*	1973	$35
❏ CXS-9027	I'm Getting Sentimental*	1972	$35
❏ CAL-650 [M]	The One and Only Tommy Dorsey*	1961	$35
❏ CAS-650(e) [R]	The One and Only Tommy Dorsey*	196?	$25
RCA VICTOR			
❏ ALPT-15 [M]	All Time Hits*	1951	$80
❏ LPT-10 [M]	Getting Sentimental with Tommy Dorsey*	1951	$80
❏ LPM-1643 [M]	Having a Wonderful Time*	1958	$40
❏ ANL1-2162(e)	On the Sunny Side of the Street	1977	$25
❏ ANL1-1586	Pure Gold*	1976	$25
❏ LPM-6003 [M]	That Sentimental Gentleman*	1957	$80

— Box set

Number	Title	Yr	NM
❏ LPM-3674 [M]	The Best of Tommy Dorsey*	1966	$25
❏ LSP-3674 [R]	The Best of Tommy Dorsey*	1966	$30
❏ ANL1-1087	The Best of Tommy Dorsey	1976	$25
❏ LPT-3005 [M]	This Is Tommy Dorsey*	1952	$80
❏ VPM-6038	This Is Tommy Dorsey*	1971	$30
❏ LPT-3018 [10]	This Is Tommy Dorsey	1952	$50
❏ VPM-6064	This Is Tommy Dorsey, Volume 2*	197?	$30
❏ VPM-6087	This Is Tommy Dorsey and His Clambake Seven	1973	$25

— Orange labels

Number	Title	Yr	NM
❏ VPM-6087	This Is Tommy Dorsey and His Clambake Seven	1977	$20

— Black labels, dog near top

Number	Title	Yr	NM
❏ LPM-1425 [M]	Tommy Dorsey Plays Cole Porter and Jerome Kern	1956	$30

Number	Title	Yr	NM
❏ LPM-22 [10]	Tommy Dorsey Plays Cole Porter for Dancing	1951	$50
❏ LPM-1432 [M]	Tribute to Dorsey, Volume 1*	1956	$40
❏ LPM-1433 [M]	Tribute to Dorsey, Volume 2*	1956	$40
❏ LPM-1229 [M]	Yes Indeed*	1956	$100
SUNBEAM			
❏ 201	Tommy Dorsey and His Orchestra 1935-39	197?	$25
❏ 220	Tommy Dorsey and His Orchestra 1944-46	197?	$25
TIME-LIFE			
❏ STBB-19	Big Bands: Sentimental Genrtleman*	1985	$25
❏ STBB-02	Big Bands: Tommy Dorsey*	1983	$25
VOCALION			
❏ VL3613 [M]	Dance Party	196?	$35
❏ VL73613 [R]	Dance Party	196?	$25

DORSEY BROTHERS, THE

Big bands in which both JIMMY DORSEY and TOMMY DORSEY appeared.

Albums

Number	Title	Yr	NM
CIRCLE			
❏ 20	The Dorsey Brothers Orchestra 1935	198?	$25
COLUMBIA			
❏ CL1240 [M]	Sentimental and Swinging	1958	$30

— Red and black label with six "eye" logos

Number	Title	Yr	NM
❏ C2L8	The Fabulous Dorseys in Hi-Fi	1958	$40

— Red and black labels with six "eye" logos

Number	Title	Yr	NM
❏ CL1190 [M]	The Fabulous Dorseys in Hi Fi, Volume I	1957	$30

— Red and black label with six "eye" logos

Number	Title	Yr	NM
DECCA			
❏ DL8631 [M]	Dixieland Jazz	1958	$120

— Black label, silver print

Number	Title	Yr	NM
❏ DL8631 [M]	Dixieland Jazz	1961	$35

— Black label with color bars

Number	Title	Yr	NM
❏ DL8654 [M]	The Swinging Dorseys	1958	$100

— Black label, silver print

Number	Title	Yr	NM
❏ DL8654 [M]	The Swinging Dorseys	1961	$35

— Black label with color bars

Number	Title	Yr	NM
DESIGN			
❏ DLP-20 [M]	Their Shining Hour	196?	$30
❏ DLPS-20 [R]	Their Shining Hour	196?	$25
MCA			
❏ 1505	The 1934-35 Decca Sessions	198?	$25
RIVERSIDE			
❏ RLP 12-811 [M]	A Backward Glance	1958	$300
❏ RLP-1008 [10]	Jazz of the Roaring Twenties	1953	$300
❏ RLP-1051 [10]	The Dorsey Brothers with the California Ramblers	1955	$300
SUNBEAM			
❏ 301	The Dorsey Brothers 1934	197?	$25
❏ 210	The Fabulous Dorsey Brothers	197?	$25
❏ 224	The Fabulous Dorsey Brothers, Volume 2	197?	$25

DOUBLE IMAGE

DAVE SAMUELS and DAVID FRIEDMAN form the core of this group.

Albums

Number	Title	Yr	NM
CELESTIAL HARMONIES			
❏ CEL-015	In Lands I Never Saw	1986	$25
ECM			
❏ 1146	Dawn	1978	$30
ENJA			
❏ 2096	Double Image	198?	$30
INNER CITY			
❏ IC-3013	Double Image	1978	$35

DOUBLE SIX OF PARIS, THE

Vocal group formed in France, also known as "Les Double Six": Jacques Danjean, Jeannine "Mimi" Perrin, Claude Germain, Ward Swingle, Christine Legrand, Jean-Claude Briodin. Several were ex-members of THE BLUE STARS. Also see DIZZY GILLESPIE; THE SWINGLE SINGERS.

Albums

Number	Title	Yr	NM
CAPITOL			
❏ T10259 [M]	The Double Six of Paris	1961	$250

Number	Title	Yr	NM
❏ ST10259 [S]	The Double Six of Paris	1961	$250
PHILIPS			
❏ PHM200026 [M]	Swingin' Singin'	1962	$40
❏ PHS600026 [S]	Swingin' Singin'	1962	$120
❏ PHM200141 [M]	The Double Six of Paris Sings Ray Charles	1964	$175
❏ PHS600141 [S]	The Double Six of Paris Sings Ray Charles	1964	$150

DOWN HOME JAZZ BAND, THE

Albums

Number	Title	Yr	NM
STOMP OFF			
❏ SOS-1171	Hambone Kelly's Favorites	1987	$25
❏ SOS-1217	The Down Home Jazz Band in New Orleans	1990	$25
❏ SOS-1199	The San Francisco Jazz Tradition	1989	$25
❏ SOS-1190	Yerba Buena Style	1988	$25

DOYLE, ARTHUR

Tenor saxophone player.

Albums

Number	Title	Yr	NM
AUDIBLE HISS			
❏ AHS-004	Arthur Doyle Plays and Sings from the Songbook, Volume One	1995	$30
ECSTATIC PEACE			
❏ 29	Arthur Doyle Plays More Alabama Feeling	1990	$30

DRAKE, DONNA

Female singer.

Albums

Number	Title	Yr	NM
LUXOR			
❏ LP-1 [M]	The Wynton Kelly Trio Introduces Donna Drake -- Donna Sings Dinah	1968	$30
❏ LPS-1 [S]	The Wynton Kelly Trio Introduces Donna Drake -- Donna Sings Dinah	1968	$25

DRAPER, RAY

Tuba player and composer.

Albums

Number	Title	Yr	NM
JOSIE			
❏ JOZ-3004 [M]	Tuba Jazz	1963	$30
❏ JLPS-3004 [S]	Tuba Jazz	1963	$25
JUBILEE			
❏ JLP-1090 [M]	Tuba Jazz	1959	$50
NEW JAZZ			
❏ NJLP-8228 [M]	Ray Draper Quintet Featuring John Coltrane	1965	$150

— Blue label, trident logo at right

DREAMS

Jazz-rock group. Among its members were MICHAEL BRECKER, RANDY BRECKER and BILLY COBHAM.

Albums

Number	Title	Yr	NM
COLUMBIA			
❏ C30225	Dreams	1970	$35

DREW, DAN

See BOOTS BROWN. (LP)
See BOOTS BROWN.

DREW, DORIS

Albums

Number	Title	Yr	NM
MODE			
❏ MOD-126 [M]	The Delightful Doris Drew	1957	$80

DREW, KENNY, AND NIELS-HENNING ORSTED PEDERSEN

Also see each artist's individual listings.

Albums

Number	Title	Yr	NM
INNER CITY			
❏ IC-2002	Duo	1973	$35
❏ IC-2010	Duo 2	1974	$35
❏ IC-2031	Duo Live in Concert	1974	$35
❏ SCS-1031	Duo Live in Concert	198?	$30

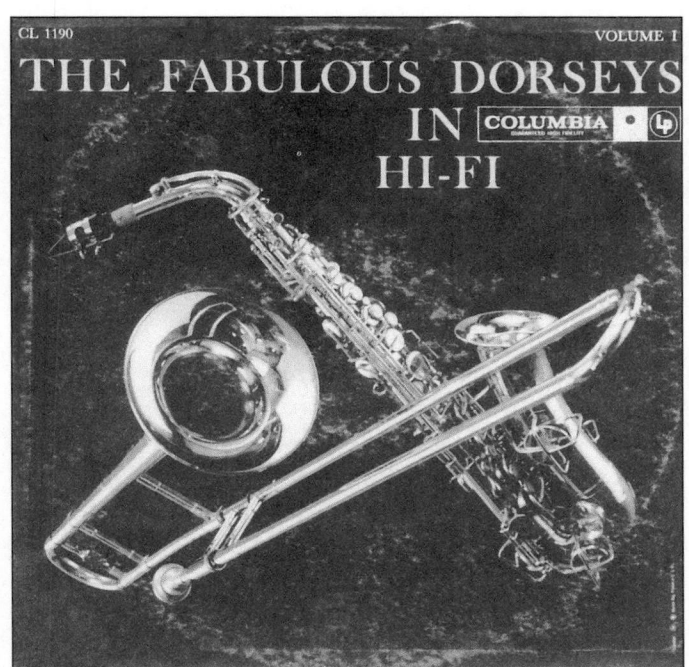

Tommy and Jimmy Dorsey, *The Fabulous Dorseys in Hi-Fi, Volume I*, Columbia CL 1190, red and black label with six "eye" logos, **$90**.

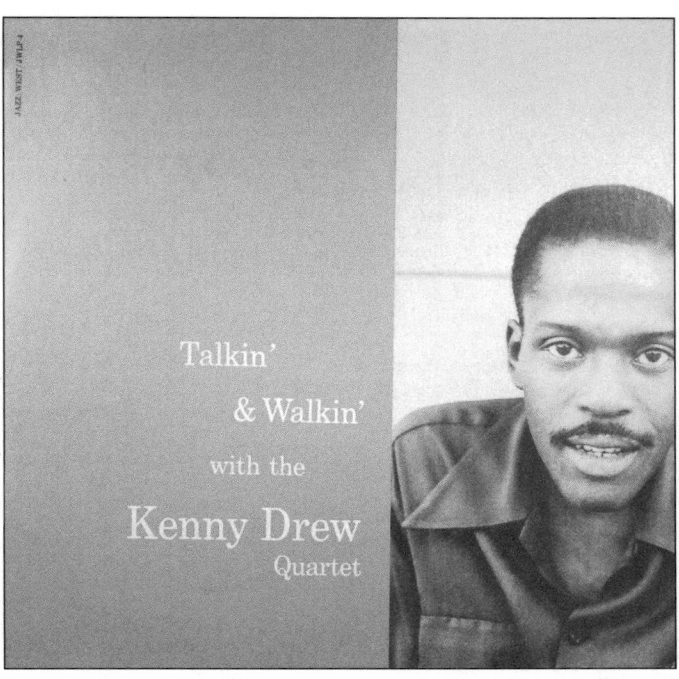

Kenny Drew, *Talkin' & Walkin' with the Kenny Drew Quartet*, Jazz West JWLP-4, **$700**.

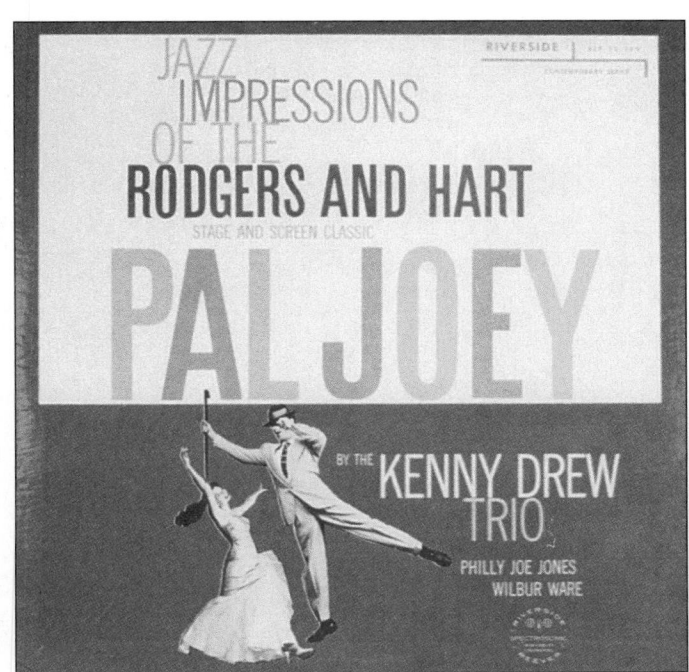

Kenny Drew, *Pal Joey*, Riverside RLP 12-249, **$350**.

Duke Ellington, *Sophisticated Ellington*, RCA Victor CPL2-4098(e), two-record set, **$30**.

Number	Title	Yr	NM

— Reissue of Inner City 2031

STEEPLECHASE

| ❑ SCS-1002 | Duo | 198? | $30 |

— Reissue of Inner City 2002

| ❑ SCS-1010 | Duo 2 | 198? | $30 |

— Reissue of Inner City 2010

DREW, KENNY; DONALD BYRD; HANK MOBLEY
Also see each artist's individual listings.

Albums

JAZZLAND

| ❑ JLP-6 [M] | Hard Bop | 1960 | $50 |

— Reissue of Riverside 236

| ❑ JLP-906 [S] | Hard Bop | 1960 | $40 |

DREW, KENNY; PAUL CHAMBERS; PHILLY JOE JONES
Also see each artist's individual listings.

Albums

JAZZLAND

| ❑ JLP-909 [S] | The Tough Piano Trio | 1960 | $40 |
| ❑ JLP-9 [M] | The Tough Piano Trio | 1960 | $200 |

— Reissue of Riverside 224

DREW, KENNY
Pianist.

Albums

BLUE NOTE

| ❑ BLP-5023 [10] | Introducing the Kenny Drew Trio | 1953 | $400 |
| ❑ BLP-4059 [M] | Undercurrent | 1964 | $60 |

— New York, USA" address on label

| ❑ BST-84059 [S] | Undercurrent | 1961 | $80 |

— W. 63rd St." address on label

| ❑ BST-84059 [S] | Undercurrent | 1964 | $30 |

— New York, USA" address on label

| ❑ BST-84059 [S] | Undercurrent | 1966 | $35 |

— A Division of Liberty Records" on label

FANTASY

❑ OJC-065	Kenny Drew Trio	198?	$25
❑ OJC-6007	Kenny Drew Trio/Quartet/Quintet	198?	$30
❑ OJC-483	This Is New	1991	$30

INNER CITY

❑ IC-2007	Everything I Love	1973	$35
❑ IC-2034	If You Could See Me Now	1974	$35
❑ IC-2048	Morning	1975	$35

JAZZ WEST

| ❑ JWLP-4 [M] | Talkin' and Walkin' with the Kenny Drew Quartet | 1955 | $700 |

JUDSON

| ❑ L-3005 [M] | Harold Arlen Showcase | 1957 | $50 |
| ❑ L-3004 [M] | Harry Warren Showcase | 1957 | $50 |

NORGRAN

| ❑ MGN-1002 [M] | Progressive Piano | 1954 | $200 |
| ❑ MGN-29 [10] | The Ideation of Kenny Drew | 1954 | $400 |

RIVERSIDE

| ❑ RLP 12-811 [M] | I Love Jerome Kern | 1956 | $250 |
| ❑ RLP 12-224 [M] | Kenny Drew Trio | 1956 | $2000 |

— White label, blue print

| ❑ RLP 12-224 [M] | Kenny Drew Trio | 195? | $50 |

— Blue labe, microphone logo at top

❑ 6037	Kenny Drew Trio	197?	$30
❑ RLP 12-249 [M]	Pal Joey	1957	$350
❑ RLP-1112 [S]	Pal Joey	1959	$250
❑ 6106	Pal Joey	197?	$30
❑ RLP 12-236 [M]	This Is New	1957	$300

— White label, blue print

| ❑ RLP 12-236 [M] | This Is New | 195? | $50 |

— Blue labe, microphone logo at top

| ❑ 6066 | This Is New | 197? | $30 |

SOUL NOTE

❑ SN-1040	It Might As Well Be Spring	1981	$30
❑ SN-1081	Kenny Drew and Far Away	1983	$30
❑ 121081	Kenny Drew and Far Away	198?	$25

— Reissue of 1081

| ❑ SN-1031 | Your Soft Eyes | 1980 | $30 |
| ❑ 121031 | Your Soft Eyes | 198? | $25 |

— Reissue of 1031

STEEPLECHASE

| ❑ SCS-1016 | Dark Beauty | 198? | $30 |
| ❑ SCS-1007 | Everything I Love | 198? | $30 |

— Reissue of Inner City 2007

| ❑ SCS-1034 | If You Could See Me Now | 198? | $30 |

— Reissue of Inner City 2034

❑ SCS-1106	In Concert	198?	$30
❑ SCS-1077	Lite Flite	198?	$30
❑ SCS-1048	Morning	198?	$30
❑ SCS-1129	Ruby, My Dear	1977	$30

XANADU

| ❑ 167 | For Sure | 197? | $30 |
| ❑ 166 | Home Is Where the Soul Is | 197? | $30 |

D'RIVERA, PAQUITO
Saxophone player and clarinetist, originally from Cuba. Also see IRAKERE.

Albums

COLUMBIA

❑ FC44077	Celebration	1988	$25
❑ FC40156	Explosion	1985	$25
❑ FC38899	Live at the Keystone Korner	1983	$25
❑ FC40583	Manhattan Burn	1987	$25
❑ FC38177	Mariel	1982	$25
❑ FC37374	Paquito Blowin'	1981	$25
❑ FC39584	Why Not!	1984	$25

D'RONE, FRANK

Albums

CADET

| ❑ LPS-806 | Brand New Morning | 1968 | $35 |

MERCURY

❑ MG-20586 [M]	After the Ball	1960	$100
❑ SR-60246 [S]	After the Ball	1960	$150
❑ SR-60721 [S]	Frank D'Rone In Person	196?	$100
❑ MG-20721 [M]	Frank D'Rone In Person	196?	$100
❑ MG-20418 [M]	Frank D'Rone Sings	1959	$100
❑ SR-90064 [S]	Frank D'Rone Sings	1959	$100

DRY JACK
Fusion band formed by Chuck Lamb (keyboards) and Rich Lamb (bass).

Albums

INNER CITY

| ❑ IC-1063 | Magical Elements | 1978 | $35 |
| ❑ IC-1075 | Whale City | 1979 | $35 |

DRY THROAT FIVE, THE
Members: Bertrand Neyroud (clarinet, melodica); René Hagmann (alto saxophone, clarinet, trombone, cornet, trumpet, tuba); Raymond Graisier (washboard, drums, metallophone); Pierre-Alain Maret (banjo); Michel Rudaz (tuba)

Albums

STOMP OFF

| ❑ SOS-1151 | My Melancholy Baby | 1989 | $25 |
| ❑ SOS-1114 | Who's Blue? | 1986 | $25 |

DUDZIAK, URSZULA
Female singer.

Albums

ARISTA

| ❑ AL4132 | Midnight Rain | 1976 | $35 |
| ❑ AL4065 | Urszula | 1975 | $35 |

COLUMBIA

| ❑ KC32902 | Newborn Light | 1972 | $25 |

INNER CITY

| ❑ IC-1066 | Future Talk | 1979 | $35 |

DUGGAN, LAR
Pianist.

Albums

PHILO

| ❑ PH-9002 | From the Lake Studies | 198? | $30 |

DUKE, DOUGLAS
Organist.

Albums

HERALD

| ❑ HLP-0102 [M] | Sounds Impossible | 1956 | $50 |

REGENT

| ❑ MG-6013 [M] | Jazz Organist | 196? | $30 |

DUKE, GEORGE
Pianist, keyboard player and male singer. Also see STANLEY CLARKE.

Albums

ELEKTRA

❑ 60480	George Duke	1986	$30
❑ 60778	Night After Night	1989	$30
❑ 60398	Thief in the Night	1985	$35

EPIC

❑ FE38208	1976 Solo Keyboard Album	1983	$100
❑ FE36483	A Brazilian Love Affair	1980	$35
❑ JE35366	Don't Let Go	1978	$60
❑ PE35366	Don't Let Go	198?	$20

— Budget-line reissue with new prefix and bar code

❑ FE37532	Dream On	1982	$60
❑ JE35701	Follow the Rainbow	1979	$75
❑ PE34469	From Me to You	1977	$60

— Orange label, no bar code on cover

| ❑ PE34469 | From Me to You | 198? | $20 |

— Budget-line reissue; dark blue label, bar code on cover

❑ FE38513	Guardian of the Light	1983	$60
❑ JE36263	Master of the Game	1979	$75
❑ PE36263	Master of the Game	198?	$25

— Budget-line reissue with new prefix

| ❑ JE34883 | Reach For It | 1977 | $75 |

— Orange label; no bar code on cover

| ❑ PE34883 | Reach For It | 198? | $20 |

— Budget-line reissue; dark blue label, bar code on back

| ❑ FE39262 | Rendezvous | 1984 | $75 |

LIBERTY

| ❑ ST-11004 | Save the Country | 1970 | $60 |

— Original issue

MPS/BASF

❑ 22018	Faces in Reflection	1974	$35
❑ 25355	Feel	1974	$50
❑ 25671	I Love the Blues, She Heard My Cry	1975	$50
❑ 22835	Liberated Fantasies	1976	$35
❑ 25613	The Aura Will Prevail	1975	$50

PACIFIC JAZZ

| ❑ PJ-LA891-H | George Duke | 1978 | $35 |
| ❑ LN-10127 | Save the Country | 198? | $30 |

— Reissue

PAUSA

| ❑ PR7070 | I Love the Blues | 1980 | $25 |
| ❑ PR7042 | The Aura Will Prevail | 198? | $25 |

— Reissue of MPS/BASF 25613

PICKWICK

| ❑ SPC-3588 | Save the Country | 1978 | $35 |

— Reissue of Liberty 11004

VERVE/MPS

| ❑ 821665-1 | Feel | 1984 | $25 |

— Reissue of MPS/BASF 25355

| ❑ 821837-1 | The Aura Will Prevail | 1984 | $25 |

— Reissue of Pausa 7042

DUKE, KENO
Drummer.

Albums

STRATA-EAST

| ❑ SES-7416 | Sense of Values | 1974 | $30 |

TRIDENT

| ❑ 501 | Crest of the Wave | 197? | $25 |

DUKES, JOE, AND JACK McDUFF
Drummer. Also see JACK McDUFF.

Albums

PRESTIGE

| ❑ PRLP-7324 [M] | Soulful Drums | 1964 | $30 |
| ❑ PRST-7324 [S] | Soulful Drums | 1964 | $30 |

DUKE'S MEN, THE
Small groups from DUKE ELLINGTON's orchestra, many of which contain The Duke.

Albums

EPIC

| ❑ LN3237 [M] | Ellington's Sidekicks | 1956 | $100 |
| ❑ LG3108 [M] | The Duke's Men | 1955 | $100 |

Number	Title	Yr	NM

DUKES OF DIXIELAND, THE
Founded by Frank Assunto (trumpet) and Fred Assunto (trombone) in the late 1940s.
Albums
AUDIO FIDELITY

Number	Title	Yr	NM
❏ AFLP-1918 [M]	Carnegie Hall Concert	1959	$35
❏ AFSD-5918 [S]	Carnegie Hall Concert	1959	$35
❏ AFLP-1924 [M]	Louie and the Dukes of Dixieland	1960	$35
❏ AFSD-5924 [S]	Louie and the Dukes of Dixieland	1960	$35
❏ AFLP-1851 [M]	Marching Along with the Dukes of Dixieland, Vol. 3	1957	$35
❏ AFSD-5851 [S]	Marching Along with the Dukes of Dixieland, Vol. 3	1958	$50
❏ AFLP-1862 [M]	Mardi Gras Time	1958	$35
❏ AFSD-5862 [S]	Mardi Gras Time	1958	$50
❏ AFLP-1861 [M]	Minstrel Time with the Phenomenal Dukes of Dixieland, Volume 5	1957	$35
❏ AFSD-5861 [S]	Minstrel Time with the Phenomenal Dukes of Dixieland, Volume 5	1958	$50
❏ AFLP-1976 [M]	More of the Best of the Dukes of Dixieland	1962	$35
❏ AFSD-5976 [S]	More of the Best of the Dukes of Dixieland	1962	$35
❏ AFLP-1928 [M]	Piano Ragtime (Vol. 11)	1960	$35
❏ AFSD-5928 [S]	Piano Ragtime (Vol. 11)	1960	$35
❏ AFSD-6172	Tailgating	1967	$30
❏ AFLP-1956 [M]	The Best of the Dukes of Dixieland	1961	$35
❏ AFSD-5956 [S]	The Best of the Dukes of Dixieland	1961	$35
❏ AFLP-1860 [M]	The Dukes of Dixieland On Bourbon Street, Vol. 4	1958	$35
❏ AFSD-5860 [S]	The Dukes of Dixieland On Bourbon Street, Vol. 4	1958	$50
❏ AFLP-1891 [M]	The Dukes of Dixieland On Campus	1959	$35
❏ AFSD-5891 [S]	The Dukes of Dixieland On Campus	1959	$50
❏ AFSD-6174	The Dukes of Dixieland On Parade	1967	$30
❏ AFLP-1892 [M]	Up the Mississippi	1959	$35
❏ AFSD-5892 [S]	Up the Mississippi	1959	$50
❏ AFLP-1823 [M]	You Have to Hear It to Believe It -- The Dukes of Dixieland, Vol. 1	1956	$35
❏ AFSD-5823 [S]	You Have to Hear It to Believe It -- The Dukes of Dixieland, Vol. 1	196?	$50
❏ AFLP-1840 [M]	You Have to Hear It to Believe It -- The Dukes of Dixieland, Vol. 2	1957	$35
❏ AFSD-5840 [S]	You Have to Hear It to Believe It -- The Dukes of Dixieland, Vol. 2	196?	$50

COLUMBIA

Number	Title	Yr	NM
❏ CL1728 [M]	Breakin' It Up on Broadway	1962	$30
❏ CS8528 [S]	Breakin' It Up on Broadway	1962	$35
❏ CL1871 [M]	Dixieland Hootenanny!	1963	$30
❏ CS8671 [S]	Dixieland Hootenanny!	1963	$35
❏ CL2194 [M]	Struttin' at the World's Fair	1964	$30
❏ CS8994 [S]	Struttin' at the World's Fair	1964	$35
❏ CL1966 [M]	The Dukes at Disneyland, Volume 1	1963	$30
❏ CS8766 [S]	The Dukes at Disneyland, Volume 1	1963	$35

DECCA

Number	Title	Yr	NM
❏ DL4708 [M]	Come On and Hear	1966	$30
❏ DL74708 [S]	Come On and Hear	1966	$35
❏ DL4863 [M]	Come to the Cabaret	1967	$35
❏ DL74863 [S]	Come to the Cabaret	1967	$30
❏ DL74975	Dixieland's Greatest Hits	1968	$30
❏ DL4653 [M]	Live" At Bourbon Street, Chicago	1965	$30
❏ DL74653 [S]	Live" At Bourbon Street, Chicago	1965	$35
❏ DL4807 [M]	Sunrise, Sunset	1966	$30
❏ DL74807 [S]	Sunrise, Sunset	1966	$35
❏ DL4864 [M]	Thoroughly Modern Millie	1967	$35
❏ DL74864 [S]	Thoroughly Modern Millie	1967	$30

HARMONY

Number	Title	Yr	NM
❏ HL7349 [M]	Best of the Dukes of Dixieland	1965	$30
❏ HS11149 [S]	Best of the Dukes of Dixieland	1965	$30

MCA

Number	Title	Yr	NM
❏ 268	Dixieland's Greatest Hits	1973	$25

— Reissue of Decca 74975

RCA VICTOR

Number	Title	Yr	NM
❏ LPM-2097 [M]	The Dukes of Dixieland at the Jazz Band Ball	1960	$30
❏ LSP-2097(e) [R]	The Dukes of Dixieland at the Jazz Band Ball	1960	$35

ROULETTE

Number	Title	Yr	NM
❏ R-25029 [M]	Curtain Going Up	1958	$50

VIK

Number	Title	Yr	NM
❏ LX-1025 [M]	The Dukes of Dixieland at the Jazz Band Ball	1956	$60

VOCALION

Number	Title	Yr	NM
❏ VL73846	Hello, Dolly!	1968	$25

DUNBAR, TED
Guitarist and composer. Also see KENNY BARRON.
Albums
XANADU

Number	Title	Yr	NM
❏ 196	Jazz Guitarist	1982	$30
❏ 155	Opening Remarks	1978	$35
❏ 181	Secundum Artem	1980	$30

DUNCAN, DANNY
Albums
X

Number	Title	Yr	NM
❏ LVA-3040 [10]	Ragtime Jamboree	1955	$60

DUNCAN, SAMMY
Albums
JAZZOLOGY

Number	Title	Yr	NM
❏ J-77	Jazz and Blues	1979	$25
❏ J-64	Sammy Duncan and His Underground All Stars	197?	$25
❏ J-84	Swingin' Jazz	1980	$25
❏ J-118	When the Saints Go Marching In	1987	$25
❏ J-119	When You're Swingin'	1987	$25

NATIONAL RECORDING CO.

Number	Title	Yr	NM
❏ NRC-LPA1	Cool Dixieland Jazz from Out of the South	197?	$30

DUNN, DOROTHY
See ANNIE ROSS.

DUPREE, CORNELL
Guitarist.
Albums
ANTILLES

Number	Title	Yr	NM
❏ 90984	Coast to Coast	1988	$25

ATLANTIC

Number	Title	Yr	NM
❏ SD7311	Teasin'	1975	$30

DURAN, EDDIE
Guitarist.
Albums
CONCORD JAZZ

Number	Title	Yr	NM
❏ CJ-94	Ginza	1979	$30
❏ CJ-271	One By One	1985	$25

FANTASY

Number	Title	Yr	NM
❏ 3247 [M]	Jazz Guitarist	1957	$80
— Red vinyl			
❏ 3247 [M]	Jazz Guitarist	195?	$40
— Black vinyl			
❏ OJC-120	Jazz Guitarist	198?	$25

DUSHON, JEAN
Female singer. Early in her career (1961), she had a one-off 45 rpm single on Atco produced by Phil Spector. Also see RAMSEY LEWIS.
Albums
ARGO

Number	Title	Yr	NM
❏ LP-4039 [M]	Make Way for Jean DuShon	1964	$30
❏ LPS-4039 [S]	Make Way for Jean DuShon	1964	$30

DUTCH SWING COLLEGE BAND, THE
Founded by Peter Schilperoort, Frans Vink and Joost van Os on May 5, 1945 (Liberation Day, the end of the German occupation of the Netherlands).
Albums
EPIC

Number	Title	Yr	NM
❏ LN3211 [M]	Dixieland Goes Dutch	1955	$80

EVEREST ARCHIVE OF FOLK & JAZZ

Number	Title	Yr	NM
❏ 341	The Dutch Swing College Band	1979	$25

PHILIPS

Number	Title	Yr	NM
❏ PHM200010 [M]	Dixie Goes Dutch	1962	$35
❏ PHS600010 [S]	Dixie Goes Dutch	1962	$25

TIMELESS

Number	Title	Yr	NM
❏ 525	The Dutch Swing College Band	198?	$25
❏ 516	The Dutch Swing College Band At Its Best	198?	$25

DYANI, JOHNNY; OKAY TEMIZ; MONGEZI FEZA
Temiz is a percussionist; Feza played trumpet. Also see JOHNNY DYANI.

DYANI, JOHNNY
Bass player, pianist and male singer. Also see THREE.
Albums
STEEPLECHASE

Number	Title	Yr	NM
❏ SCS-1186	Afrika	198?	$30
❏ SCS-1209	Angolan City	198?	$30
❏ SCS-1163	Mbizo	1982	$30
❏ SCS-1109	Song for Biko	1978	$30
❏ SCS-1098	Witchdoctor's Son	197?	$30

E

EAGER, ALLAN
Alto and tenor saxophone player.
Albums
SAVOY

Number	Title	Yr	NM
❏ MG-9015 [10]	New Trends in Modern Music, Volume 2	1952	$250
❏ MG-15044 [10]	Tenor Sax	1954	$200

EAGLE BRASS BAND, THE
Members: John Ewing, Alex Less (trombones); Benny Booker (tuba); Joe Darensbourg (clarinet); Floyd Turnham (alto sax); Sam Lee (tenor sax); Teddy Edwards (snare drum); Barry Martyn (bass drum); Wendell Eugene, Mike Owen (trombones); Chris Burke (clarinet).
Albums
GHB

Number	Title	Yr	NM
❏ GHB-60	The Eagle Brass Band	1978	$25
❏ GHB-170	The Last of the Line	1986	$25

EARDLEY, JON
Trumpeter.
Albums
FANTASY

Number	Title	Yr	NM
❏ OJC-1746	From Hollywood to New York	1988	$25
❏ OJC-123	Jon Eardley Seven	198?	$25

NEW JAZZ

Number	Title	Yr	NM
❏ NJLP-1105 [10]	Jon Eardley in Hollywood	1954	$300

PRESTIGE

Number	Title	Yr	NM
❏ PRLP-205 [10]	Jon Eardley in Hollywood	1955	$400

EARLAND, CHARLES
Organist.
Albums
COLUMBIA

Number	Title	Yr	NM
❏ JC36449	Coming to You Live	1980	$25
❏ FC37573	Earland's Jam	1982	$25
❏ FC38547	Earland's Street Themes	1983	$25

FANTASY

Number	Title	Yr	NM
❏ OJC-335	Black Talk!	1988	$25

— Reissue of Prestige 7758

MERCURY

Number	Title	Yr	NM
❏ SRM-1-1049	Odyssey	1976	$25
❏ SRM-1-3720	Perception	1978	$25
❏ SRM-1-1149	Revelation	1977	$25
❏ SRM-1-1139	The Great Pyramid	1976	$25

MILESTONE

Number	Title	Yr	NM
❏ M-9165	Front Burner	1988	$25
❏ M-9175	Third Degree Burn	1989	$25

MUSE

Number	Title	Yr	NM
❏ MR-5181	Infant Eyes	1980	$25
❏ MR-5240	In the Pocket	1984	$25
❏ MR-5156	Mama Roots	1979	$25
❏ MR-5201	Pleasant Afternoon	1981	$25
❏ MR-5126	Smokin'	1978	$25

PRESTIGE

Number	Title	Yr	NM
PRST-7815	Black Drops	1970	$35
10029	Black Drops	1971	$25
—Reissue of 7815			
PRST-7758	Black Talk!	1970	$50
10024	Black Talk!	1971	$25
—Reissue of 7758			
2501	Burners	1982	$25
10061	Charles III	1973	$30
10041	Intensity	1972	$30
10095	Kharma	1975	$30
66002	Leaving This Planet	1974	$35
10051	Live at the Lighthouse	1972	$30
10009	Living Black!	1971	$30
10018	Soul Story	1971	$30

TRIP

Number	Title	Yr	NM
5004	Charles Earland	1974	$25

EASLEY, BILL

Tenor saxophone player and clarinetist.

Albums

SUNNYSIDE

Number	Title	Yr	NM
SSC-1022	Wind Inventions	1988	$25

EAST NEW YORK ENSEMBLE DE PARIS, THE

Albums

FOLKWAYS

Number	Title	Yr	NM
F-33867	At the Helm	1974	$40

EASTERN REBELLION

The core of the group on these recordings was Cedar Walton (piano), Sam Jones (bass) and Billy Higgins (drums).

Albums

TIMELESS

Number	Title	Yr	NM
306	Eastern Rebellion	1976	$35
318	Eastern Rebellion II	1977	$35

EASTON, TED

Drummer and bandleader.

Albums

CIRCLE

Number	Title	Yr	NM
12	A Salute to Satchmo	198?	$25

EASY RIDERS JAZZ BAND, THE

Led by Big Bill Bissonette.

Albums

JAZZ CRUSADE

Number	Title	Yr	NM
1002	My Life Will Be Sweeter Someday	1963	$40

EATON, CLEVELAND

Bass player. Formerly in the RAMSEY LEWIS Trio.

Albums

OVATION

Number	Title	Yr	NM
OV-1703	Instant Hip	1974	$25
OV-1742	Keep Love Alive	197?	$35

EATON, JOHN

Pianist. May or may not be the same person as below.

Albums

CHIAROSCURO

Number	Title	Yr	NM
CH-174	Like Old Times	1977	$30
CH-137	Solo Piano	1975	$30

EATON, JOHNNY

Pianist. May or may not be the same person as below.

Albums

COLUMBIA

Number	Title	Yr	NM
CL737 [M]	College Jazz: Modern	1956	$40
CL996 [M]	Far Out, Far In	1957	$40

EAVES, HUBERT

Keyboard player.

Albums

INNER CITY

Number	Title	Yr	NM
IC-6012	Esteric Funk	1976	$25

ECHOES OF HARLEM

This is the title of this jazz album - no artist is listed, but it's all by the same band.

Albums

ROYALE

Number	Title	Yr	NM
LP-18128 [10]	Echoes of Harlem	195?	$80

ECKSTINE, BILLY, AND SARAH VAUGHAN

See SARAH VAUGHAN AND BILLY ECKSTINE. (SC1) Male singer and bandleader. Also an occasional trumpeter and valve trombone player. Also see COUNT BASIE; EARL "FATHA" HINES.

ECKSTINE, BILLY

Albums

AUDIO LAB

Number	Title	Yr	NM
AL-1549 [M]	Mr. B	1960	$200

DELUXE

Number	Title	Yr	NM
FA-2010 [M]	Billy Eckstine and His Orchestra	195?	$80

EMARCY

Number	Title	Yr	NM
MG-36129 [M]	Billy Eckstine's Imagination	1958	$200
MG-26025 [10]	Blues for Sale	1954	$300
MG-36029 [M]	Blues for Sale	1955	$350
MG-36010 [M]	I Surrender, Dear	1955	$250
MG-26027 [M]	The Love Songs of Mr. B	1954	$300
MG-36030 [M]	The Love Songs of Mr. B	1955	$200

ENTERPRISE

Number	Title	Yr	NM
ENS-1017	Feel the Warm	1971	$35
ENS-5004	Senior Soul	1972	$35
ENS-1013	Stormy	1971	$35

FORUM

Number	Title	Yr	NM
F-9027 [M]	Once More with Feeling	196?	$35
SF-9027 [S]	Once More with Feeling	196?	$35

KING

Number	Title	Yr	NM
295-12 [10]	The Great Mr. B	1953	$300

LION

Number	Title	Yr	NM
L-70057 [M]	The Best of Billy Eckstine	1958	$60

MERCURY

Number	Title	Yr	NM
MG-20674 [M]	Billy Eckstine and Quincy Jones at Basin St. East	1962	$100
SR-60674 [S]	Billy Eckstine and Quincy Jones at Basin St. East	1962	$100
MG-20333 [M]	Billy's Best	1958	$100
SR-60086 [S]	Billy's Best	1958	$150
MG-20637 [M]	Broadway, Bongos and Mr. B	1961	$100
SR-60637 [S]	Broadway, Bongos and Mr. B	1961	$100
MG-20736 [M]	Don't Worry 'Bout Me	1962	$100
SR-60736 [S]	Don't Worry 'Bout Me	1962	$100
MG-20796 [M]	The Golden Hits of Billy Eckstine	1963	$100
SR-60796 [S]	The Golden Hits of Billy Eckstine	1963	$100

METRO

Number	Title	Yr	NM
M-537 [M]	Everything I Have Is Yours	1965	$250
MS-537 [R]	Everything I Have Is Yours	1965	$150

MGM

Number	Title	Yr	NM
E-153 [10]	Billy Eckstine Sings Rodgers & Hammerstein Favorites	1952	$300
E-548 [10]	I Let a Song Go Out of My Heart	1951	$160
E-257 [10]	Mr. B with a Beat	1954	$150
E-3176 [M]	Mr. B with a Beat	1955	$100
E-3209 [M]	Rendezvous	1955	$100
E-523 [10]	Songs by Billy Eckstine	1951	$160
E-219 [10]	Tenderly	1953	$300
E-3275 [M]	That Old Feeling	1956	$100

MOTOWN

Number	Title	Yr	NM
MS677	For Love of Ivy	1969	$60
M646 [M]	My Way	1966	$50
MS646 [S]	My Way	1966	$60
M632 [M]	Prime of My Life	1965	$50
MS632 [S]	Prime of My Life	1965	$60

NATIONAL

Number	Title	Yr	NM
NLP-2001 [10]	Billy Eckstine Sings	1949	$200

REGENT

Number	Title	Yr	NM
MG-6054 [M]	My Deep Blue Dream	1957	$100
MG-6052 [M]	Prisoner of Love	1957	$100
MG-6053 [M]	The Duke, the Blues and Me	1957	$100
MG-6058 [M]	You Call It Madness	1957	$100

ROULETTE

Number	Title	Yr	NM
R-25052 [M]	No Cover, No Minimum	1961	$60
SR-25052 [S]	No Cover, No Minimum	1961	$60
R-25104 [M]	Once More with Feeling	1962	$60
SR-25104 [S]	Once More with Feeling	1962	$60

SAVOY

Number	Title	Yr	NM
1127	Billy Eckstine Sings	1979	$30
SJL-2214	Mr. B and the Band/The Savoy Sessions	1976	$35

TRIP

Number	Title	Yr	NM
5567	The Modern Sound of Mr. B	197?	$25

VERVE

Number	Title	Yr	NM
819442-1	Everything I Have Is Yours: The MGM Years	1986	$35

XANADU

Number	Title	Yr	NM
207	I Want to Talk About You	1987	$25

EDDIE AND BETTY

Piano and vocal duo: Eddie and Betty Cole. Eddie was the older brother of NAT KING COLE.

Albums

WARNER BROS.

Number	Title	Yr	NM
W1350 [M]	Nightlife for Daydreamers	1959	$60
WS1350 [S]	Nightlife for Daydreamers	1959	$60

EDISON, HARRY "SWEETS

Trumpeter. Also see EDDIE "LOCKJAW" DAVIS; ROY ELDREDGE; BUDDY RICH; BEN WEBSTER; LESTER YOUNG.

Albums

AMERICAN RECORDING SOCIETY

Number	Title	Yr	NM
G-430 [M]	Sweets	1957	$40

LIBERTY

Number	Title	Yr	NM
LRP-3484 [M]	When Lights Are Low	1966	$50
LST-7484 [S]	When Lights Are Low	1966	$60

PABLO

Number	Title	Yr	NM
2310934	For My Pals	198?	$30
2310934	Lights	1976	$35
2310806	Simply Sweets	1977	$35

PABLO LIVE

Number	Title	Yr	NM
2308237	'S Wonderful	198?	$30

PACIFIC JAZZ

Number	Title	Yr	NM
PJLP-4 [10]	Harry Edison Quartet	1953	$150
PJ-11 [M]	The Inventive Harry Edison	1960	$50

ROULETTE

Number	Title	Yr	NM
R-52041 [M]	Patented by Edison	1960	$30
SR-52041 [S]	Patented by Edison	1960	$40
R-52023 [M]	Sweetenings	1960	$40
SR-52023 [S]	Sweetenings	1960	$40

SUE

Number	Title	Yr	NM
LP-1030 [M]	Sweets for the Sweet	1964	$40
STLP-1030 [S]	Sweets for the Sweet	1964	$50

VEE JAY

Number	Title	Yr	NM
LP-1104 [M]	For the Sweet Taste of Love	1964	$30
LPS-1104 [S]	For the Sweet Taste of Love	1964	$40
VJS-3065	Home with Sweets	1975	$25

VERVE

Number	Title	Yr	NM
MGV-8211 [M]	Gee Baby, Ain't I Good to You?	1958	$150
V-8211 [M]	Gee Baby, Ain't I Good to You?	1961	$25
MGV-8293 [M]	Harry Edison Swings Buck Clayton, And Vice Versa	1958	$100
V-8293 [M]	Harry Edison Swings Buck Clayton, And Vice Versa	1961	$25
MGVS-6016 [S]	Harry Edison Swings Buck Clayton, And Vice Versa	1959	$100
V6-8293 [S]	Harry Edison Swings Buck Clayton, And Vice Versa	1961	$25
MGV-8353 [M]	Mr. Swing	1959	$100
V-8353 [M]	Mr. Swing	1961	$25
MGVS-6118 [S]	Mr. Swing	1960	$100
V6-8358 [S]	Mr. Swing	1961	$25
MGV-8097 [M]	Sweets	1957	$150
V-8097 [M]	Sweets	1961	$25
MGV-8295 [M]	The Swinger	1959	$100
V-8295 [M]	The Swinger	1961	$25
MGVS-6037 [S]	The Swinger	1960	$80
V6-8295 [S]	The Swinger	1961	$25

EDWARDS, EDDIE

Trombone player and violinist.

Albums

COMMODORE

Number	Title	Yr	NM
FL-20003 [10]	Eddie Edwards' Original Dixieland Jazz Band	1950	$60

EDWARDS, TEDDY

Tenor saxophone player.

Albums

CONTEMPORARY

Number	Title	Yr	NM
S-7592 [S]	Good Gravy	1961	$200
S-7606 [S]	Heart and Soul	1962	$200
M-3583 [M]	Teddy's Ready	1960	$200

Number	Title	Yr	NM
☐ S-7583 [S]	Teddy's Ready	1960	$200
☐ S-7588 [S]	Together Again	1961	$200
FANTASY			
☐ OJC-177	Heart and Soul	198?	$25
☐ OJC-424	Together Again	1990	$30
MUSE			
☐ MR-5045	Feelin's	1974	$30
PACIFIC JAZZ			
☐ ST-6 [S]	It's About Time	1960	$40
PRESTIGE			
☐ PRLP-7522 [M]	It's Alright	1967	$30
☐ PRST-7522 [S]	It's Alright	1967	$30
☐ PRLP-7518 [M]	Nothin' But the Truth	1967	$30
☐ PRST-7518 [S]	Nothin' But the Truth	1967	$30
STEEPLECHASE			
☐ SCS-1147	Out of This World	1980	$30
XANADU			
☐ 134	Inimitable	1976	$30

EGAN, MARK
Bass player. Also see ELEMENTS.

Albums

Number	Title	Yr	NM
GRP			
☐ GR-9572	A Touch of Light	1988	$25
HIPPOCKET			
☐ HP-104	Mosaic	1985	$25
WINDHAM HILL			
☐ WH-0104	Mosaic	1987	$25
—Reissue of HipPocket 104			

EGILSSON, ARNI
Bass player.

Albums

Number	Title	Yr	NM
INNER CITY			
☐ IC-1103	Bassus Erectus	1981	$30

EITHER/ORCHESTRA, THE
Ten-piece band led by saxophone player and composer Russ Gershon.

Albums

Number	Title	Yr	NM
ACCURATE			
☐ AC-2222	Dial "E" for Either/Orchestra	1987	$30
☐ AC-3232	Radium	1989	$30

ELDRIDGE, ROY, AND BENNY CARTER
Also see each artist's individual listings.

Albums

Number	Title	Yr	NM
AMERICAN RECORDING SOCIETY			
☐ G-413 [M]	The Urbane Jazz of Roy Eldridge and Benny Carter	1957	$40
VERVE			
☐ MGV-8202 [M]	The Urbane Jazz of Roy Eldridge and Benny Carter	1957	$100
☐ V-8202 [M]	The Urbane Jazz of Roy Eldridge and Benny Carter	1961	$25

ELDRIDGE, ROY, AND DIZZY GILLESPIE
Also see each artist's individual listings.

Albums

Number	Title	Yr	NM
CLEF			
☐ MGC-641 [M]	Roy and Diz	1955	$300
☐ MGC-671 [M]	Roy and Diz, Volume 2	1955	$300
☐ MGC-731 [M]	The Trumpet Kings	1956	$250
☐ MGC-730 [M]	Trumpet Battle	1956	$250
PABLO			
☐ 2310816	Jazz Maturity	1977	$35
VERVE			
☐ VSP-28 [M]	Soul Mates	1966	$35
☐ VSPS-28 [R]	Soul Mates	1966	$30
☐ MGV-8110 [M]	The Trumpet Kings	1957	$100
☐ V-8110 [M]	The Trumpet Kings	1961	$25
☐ MGV-8109 [M]	Trumpet Battle	1957	$100
☐ V-8109 [M]	Trumpet Battle	1961	$25

ELDRIDGE, ROY; DIZZY GILLESPIE; HARRY "SWEETS" EDISON
Also see each artist's individual listings.

Albums

Number	Title	Yr	NM
VERVE			
☐ MGV-8212 [M]	Tour de Force	1958	$150
☐ V-8212 [M]	Tour de Force	1961	$25

ELDRIDGE, ROY
Best known as a trumpeter, he also played fluegel horn and piano. Also see COLEMAN HAWKINS; EARL "FATHA" HINES; THE JAZZ ARTISTS GUILD; OSCAR PETERSON; ART TATUM; LESTER YOUNG.

Albums

Number	Title	Yr	NM
AMERICAN RECORDING SOCIETY			
☐ G-420 [M]	Swing Goes Dixie	1956	$40
CLEF			
☐ MGC-705 [M]	Dale's Wail	1956	$250
☐ MGC-683 [M]	Little Jazz	1956	$250
☐ MGC-716 [M]	Mr. Jazz	1956	$0
—Canceled			
☐ MGC-704 [M]	Rockin' Chair	1956	$250
☐ MGC-113 [10]	Roy Eldridge Collates	1953	$300
☐ MGC-150 [10]	The Roy Eldridge Quintet	1954	$300
☐ MGC-162 [10]	The Strolling Mr. Eldridge	1954	$300
COLUMBIA			
☐ C238033	Early Years	1983	$30
DIAL			
☐ LP-304 [10]	Little Jazz Four: Trumpet Fantasy	1953	$400
DISCOVERY			
☐ DL-2009 [10]	Roy Eldridge with Zoot Sims	1954	$250
FANTASY			
☐ OJC-628	Happy Time	1991	$30
☐ OJC-373	Montreux '77	1989	$30
GNP CRESCENDO			
☐ GNP-9009	Roy Eldridge	197?	$30
JAZZ ARCHIVES			
☐ JA-14	Arcadia Shuffle	198?	$25
LONDON			
☐ PB375 [10]	Roy Eldridge Quartet	1954	$120
MASTER JAZZ			
☐ 8110	The Nifty Cat	1970	$25
☐ 8121	The Nifty Cat Strikes West	197?	$25
MCA			
☐ 1355	All the Cats Join In	198?	$25
MERCURY			
☐ MGC-113 [10]	Roy Eldridge Collates	1952	$300
METRO			
☐ M-513 [M]	Roy Eldridge	1965	$150
☐ MS-513 [R]	Roy Eldridge	1965	$150
PABLO			
☐ 2310746	Happy Time	1975	$35
☐ 2310869	Little Jazz	198?	$30
☐ 2310928	Loose Walk	198?	$25
☐ 2405413	The Best of Roy Eldridge	198?	$25
☐ 2310766	What It's All About	1976	$35
PABLO LIVE			
☐ 2308203	Montreux '77	1978	$30
PRESTIGE			
☐ PRLP-114 [10]	Roy Eldridge in Sweden	1951	$250
VERVE			
☐ MGV-8089 [M]	Dale's Wail	1957	$250
—Reissue of Clef 705			
☐ V-8089 [M]	Dale's Wail	1961	$250
☐ VE-2-2531	Dale's Wail	198?	$35
☐ MGV-8068 [M]	Little Jazz	1957	$300
—Reissue of Clef 683			
☐ V-8068 [M]	Little Jazz	1961	$25
☐ MGV-8088 [M]	Rockin' Chair	1957	$200
—Reissue of Clef 704			
☐ V-8088 [M]	Rockin' Chair	1961	$25
☐ UMV-2686	Rockin' Chair	198?	$25
☐ V-1010 [M]	Swing Goes Dixie	1961	$25
☐ MGV-8389 [M]	Swingin' on the Town	1960	$80
☐ V-8389 [M]	Swingin' on the Town	1961	$25
XANADU			
☐ 140	Roy Eldridge at Jerry Newman's	198?	$25

ELDRIDGE, ROY/SAMMY PRICE
Also see each artist's individual listings.

Albums

Number	Title	Yr	NM
BRUNSWICK			
☐ BL58045 [10]	Battle of Jazz, Volume 7	1953	$60

ELEMENTS
Fusion band led by MARK EGAN and drummer Danny Gottlieb.

Albums

Number	Title	Yr	NM
ANTILLES			
☐ AN-1021	Forward Motion	198?	$25
☐ AN-1017	The Elements	198?	$25
—Reissue of Philo album			

Number	Title	Yr	NM
NOVUS			
☐ 3031-1-N	Illumination	1988	$25
☐ 3058-1-N	Liberal Arts	1989	$30
PHILO			
☐ 9011	The Elements	198?	$35

ELEVENTH HOUSE, THE
See LARRY CORYELL.

ELGART, BILL
Drummer.

Albums

Number	Title	Yr	NM
MARK LEVINSON			
☐ 3	A Life	1980	$30

ELGART, CHARLIE

Albums

Number	Title	Yr	NM
NOVUS			
☐ 3068-1-N	Balance	1989	$30
☐ 3045-1-N	Signs of Life	1988	$25

ELGART, LARRY
Alto saxophone player and bandleader. Also see LES AND LARRY ELGART.

Albums

Number	Title	Yr	NM
BRUNSWICK			
☐ BL58054 [10]	Impressions of Outer Space	1954	$120
DECCA			
☐ DL8034 [M]	Music for Barefoot Ballerinas	1955	$150
☐ DL5526 [10]	The Larry Elgart Band with Strings	1954	$175
MGM			
☐ E-4080 [M]	More Music in Motion!	1962	$35
☐ SE-4080 [S]	More Music in Motion!	1962	$50
☐ E-4028 [M]	Music in Motion!	1962	$35
☐ SE-4028 [S]	Music in Motion!	1962	$50
☐ E-3891 [M]	Sophisticated Sixties	1960	$35
☐ SE-3891 [S]	Sophisticated Sixties	1960	$50
☐ E-4007 [M]	The City	1961	$35
☐ SE-4007 [S]	The City	1961	$50
☐ E-3896 [M]	The Shape of Sounds to Come	1961	$35
☐ SE-3896 [S]	The Shape of Sounds to Come	1961	$50
☐ E-3961 [M]	Visions	1961	$35
☐ SE-3961 [S]	Visions	1961	$50
PROJECT 3			
☐ PR5102	The Larry Elgart Dance Band	1979	$25
RCA CAMDEN			
☐ CAL-575 [M]	Easy Goin' Swing	1960	$30
☐ CAS-575 [S]	Easy Goin' Swing	1960	$35
☐ CXS-9036	That Old Feeling	1972	$30
RCA VICTOR			
☐ AFL1-4095	Flight of the Condor	1981	$25
☐ AFL1-4343	Hooked on Swing	1982	$25
☐ AYL1-5025	Hooked on Swing	1984	$20
—Budget-line reissue			
☐ AFL1-4589	Hooked on Swing, Volume 2	1983	$25
☐ AYL1-5026	Hooked on Swing, Volume 2	1984	$20
—Budget-line reissue			
☐ AFL1-4850	Larry Elgart and His Manhattan Swing Orchestra	1984	$25
☐ LPM-1961 [M]	Larry Elgart and His Orchestra	1959	$35
☐ LSP-1961 [S]	Larry Elgart and His Orchestra	1959	$50
☐ LPM-2045 [M]	New Sounds at the Roosevelt	1959	$35
☐ LSP-2045 [S]	New Sounds at the Roosevelt	1959	$50
☐ LPM-2166 [M]	Saratoga	1960	$35
☐ LSP-2166 [S]	Saratoga	1960	$50
☐ AYL1-7178	(The Theme from) La Cage Aux Folles	1986	$20

ELGART, LES
Trumpeter and bandleader. Also see LES AND LARRY ELGART.

Albums

Number	Title	Yr	NM
CIRCLE			
☐ CLP-126	Les Elgart and His Orchestra	198?	$25
COLUMBIA			
☐ CS8690 [S]	Best Band on Campus	1963	$30
☐ CL1890 [M]	Best Band on Campus	1963	$25
☐ CL2578 [10]	Campus Hop	1955	$50
☐ CL1500 [M]	Designs for Dancing	1960	$25
☐ CS8291 [S]	Designs for Dancing	1960	$30

Number	Title	Yr	NM
❏ CL1008 [M]	For Dancers Also	1957	$30
❏ CL803 [M]	For Dancers Only	1956	$30
❏ CL1567 [M]	Half Satin - Half Latin	1961	$25
❏ CS8367 [S]	Half Satin - Half Latin	1961	$30
❏ CL1659 [M]	It's De-Lovely	1961	$25
❏ CS8459 [S]	It's De-Lovely	1961	$30
❏ CL6287 [10]	Just One More Dance	195?	$40
❏ CL594 [M]	Just One More Dance	1954	$40

—Maroon label, gold print

Number	Title	Yr	NM
❏ CL594 [M]	Just One More Dance	1955	$40

—Red and black label with six "eye" logos

Number	Title	Yr	NM
❏ CL1052 [M]	Les and Larry Elgart and Their Orchestra	1957	$30
❏ CS8092 [S]	Les and Larry Elgart and Their Orchestra	1959	$30
❏ CL1291 [M]	Les Elgart On Tour	1959	$25
❏ CS8103 [S]	Les Elgart On Tour	1959	$30
❏ CL2590 [10]	More of Les	1955	$50
❏ CL2503 [10]	Prom Date	1954	$40
❏ CL536 [M]	Sophisticated Swing	1953	$40

—Maroon label, gold print

Number	Title	Yr	NM
❏ CS8002 [S]	Sound Ideas	1958	$30
❏ CL619 [M]	The Band of the Year	1955	$50

—Maroon label, gold print; first LP appearance of "Bandstand Boogie

Number	Title	Yr	NM
❏ CS8245 [S]	The Band with That Sound	1960	$30
❏ CL1450 [M]	The Band with That Sound	1960	$25
❏ CL684 [M]	The Dancing Sound	1955	$40
❏ CL875 [M]	The Elgart Touch	1956	$30

—Red and black label, six "eye" logos

Number	Title	Yr	NM
❏ CL1350 [M]	The Great Sound of Les Elgart	1959	$25
❏ CS8159 [S]	The Great Sound of Les Elgart	1959	$30
❏ CS8585 [S]	The Twist Goes to College	1962	$30
❏ CL1785 [M]	The Twist Goes to College	1962	$25

COLUMBIA SPECIAL PRODUCTS

Number	Title	Yr	NM
❏ P13168	The Greatest Dance Band in the Land	197?	$25

HARMONY

Number	Title	Yr	NM
❏ HL7374 [M]	The Greatest Dance Band in the Land	196?	$30
❏ HS11174 [R]	The Greatest Dance Band in the Land	196?	$25

SUTTON

Number	Title	Yr	NM
❏ SU283 [M]	Les Elgart and Blazing Brass	196?	$25

ELGART, LES AND LARRY

Twice the Elgart brothers joined in a big band. The first time, from 1953-59, is included in the LES ELGART listings. The second time, from 1963-70, is listed below. Also see LARRY ELGART.

Albums

COLUMBIA

Number	Title	Yr	NM
❏ CL2112 [M]	Big Band Hootenanny	1963	$35
❏ CS8912 [S]	Big Band Hootenanny	1963	$25
❏ CL2221 [M]	Command Performance! Les & Larry Elgart Play the Great Dance Hits	1964	$35
❏ CS9021 [S]	Command Performance! Les & Larry Elgart Play the Great Dance Hits	1964	$25
❏ CL2355 [M]	Elgart Au-Go-Go	1965	$35
❏ CS9155 [S]	Elgart Au-Go-Go	1965	$25
❏ CL2633 [M]	Girl Watchers	1967	$25
❏ CS9433 [S]	Girl Watchers	1967	$35
❏ CS9722	Les & Larry Elgart's Greatest Hits	1968	$35
❏ CL1123 [M]	Sound Ideas	1958	$30
❏ CL2511 [M]	Sound of the Times	1966	$35
❏ CS9311 [S]	Sound of the Times	1966	$25
❏ PC38341	Swingtime	1982	$25
❏ CL2301 [M]	The New Elgart Touch	1965	$35
❏ CS9101 [S]	The New Elgart Touch	1965	$25
❏ CL2780 [M]	The Wonderful World of Today's Hits	1968	$30
❏ CS9580 [S]	The Wonderful World of Today's Hits	1968	$35
❏ CL2591 [M]	Warm and Sensuous	1966	$35
❏ CS9391 [S]	Warm and Sensuous	1966	$25

HARMONY

Number	Title	Yr	NM
❏ KH32053	Wonderful World	1972	$25

SWAMPFIRE

Number	Title	Yr	NM
❏ 207	Bridge Over Troubled Water	1971	$30
❏ 202	Nashville Country Brass	196?	$30
❏ 203	Nashville Country Guitars	196?	$30
❏ 201	Nashville Country Piano	196?	$30

ELIAS, ELIANE

Pianist and female singer.

Albums

BLUE NOTE

Number	Title	Yr	NM
❏ B1-48785	Cross Currents	1988	$25
❏ BST-46994	Illusions	1987	$25
❏ B1-91411	So Far So Close	1989	$30

ELIOVSON, STEVE

Guitarist.

Albums

ECM

Number	Title	Yr	NM
❏ 1198	Dawn Dance	198?	$25

ELLIAS, RODDY

Guitarist and composer.

Albums

INNER CITY

Number	Title	Yr	NM
❏ IC-1081	A Night for Stars	1980	$25

ELLINGSON, PAUL

Pianist.

Albums

IVY JAZZ

Number	Title	Yr	NM
❏ IJ1-E-1-2	Solo Piano Jazz	198?	$35

ELLINGTON, DUKE, ORCHESTRA (MERCER ELLINGTON, DIRECTOR)

Recordings made after Duke's son Mercer took over the orchestra in 1974.

Albums

DOCTOR JAZZ

Number	Title	Yr	NM
❏ FW40029	Hot and Bothered: A Re-Creation	1986	$25
❏ FW40359	New Mood Indigo	1987	$25

FANTASY

Number	Title	Yr	NM
❏ F-9481	Continuum	1975	$30

GRP

Number	Title	Yr	NM
❏ GR-1038	Digital Duke	1987	$25

HOLIDAY

Number	Title	Yr	NM
❏ HDY1916	Take the Holiday Train	1980	$20

ELLINGTON, DUKE

Pianist, composer, arranger and bandleader - simply, one of America's greatest musical figures. Also see LOUIS ARMSTRONG; JOHN COLTRANE; THE DUKE'S MEN; THE ELLINGTONIANS; ELLA FITZGERALD; COLEMAN HAWKINS; JOHNNY HODGES; FRANK SINATRA.

Albums

AAMCO

Number	Title	Yr	NM
❏ ALP-301 [M]	The Royal Concert of Duke Ellington, Vol. 1	196?	$60

— Reissue of Bethlehem material

Number	Title	Yr	NM
❏ ALP-313 [M]	The Royal Concert of Duke Ellington, Vol. 2	196?	$60

— Reissue of Bethlehem material

ABC IMPULSE!

Number	Title	Yr	NM
❏ 9285	Ellingtonia, Volume 2	1974	$35
❏ 9256	Ellingtonia: Reevaluations, The Impulse Years	1973	$35
❏ IA-9350	Great Tenor Encounters	1978	$35

AIRCHECK

Number	Title	Yr	NM
❏ 4	Duke on the Air	197?	$25
❏ 29	Duke on the Air, Vol. 2	198?	$25

ALLEGRO

Number	Title	Yr	NM
❏ 3082 [M]	Duke Ellington	1953	$100
❏ 1591 [M]	Duke Ellington and His Orchestra Play	1955	$100
❏ 4014 [10]	Duke Ellington and His Orchestra Play	1954	$175
❏ 4038 [10]	Duke Ellington and His Orchestra Play	1954	$175

ATLANTIC

Number	Title	Yr	NM
❏ SD1688	Jazz Violin Session	1976	$30
❏ SD1580	New Orleans Suite	1971	$30
❏ QD1580 [Q]	New Orleans Suite	1974	$40
❏ SD1665	Recollections of the Big Band Era	1974	$30
❏ 90043	Recollections of the Big Band Era	1982	$25
❏ SD 2-304	The Great Paris Concert	1972	$35

BASF

Number	Title	Yr	NM
❏ 21704	Collages	1973	$30

BETHLEHEM

Number	Title	Yr	NM
❏ BCP-6005 [M]	Duke Ellington Presents	1956	$300
❏ BCP-60 [M]	Historically Speaking, The Duke	1956	$250

Number	Title	Yr	NM
❏ 6013	The Bethlehem Years, Vol. 1	197?	$25

BIOGRAPH

Number	Title	Yr	NM
❏ M-2	Band Shorts (1929-1935)	1978	$25

BLUEBIRD

Number	Title	Yr	NM
❏ 6287-1-RB	And His Mother Called Him Bill	1987	$20

—Reissue of RCA Victor 3906

Number	Title	Yr	NM
❏ 6641-1-RB [(4)]	Black, Brown and Beige	1988	$60
❏ 5659-1-RB [(4)]	Duke Ellington: The Blanton-Webster Band	1986	$60
❏ 6852-1-RB	Early Ellington	1989	$25

BLUE NOTE

Number	Title	Yr	NM
❏ BT-85129	Money Jungle	1986	$25

—Reissue of United Artists 15017

BOOK-OF-THE-MONTH

Number	Title	Yr	NM
❏ 30-5622	At Fargo, 1940	1978	$50

BRIGHT ORANGE

Number	Title	Yr	NM
❏ 709	The Stereophonic Sound of Duke Ellington	1973	$30

BRUNSWICK

Number	Title	Yr	NM
❏ BL54007 [M]	Early Ellington	1954	$100
❏ BL58002 [10]	Ellingtonia, Volume 1	1950	$175
❏ BL58012 [10]	Ellingtonia, Volume 2	1950	$175

BULLDOG

Number	Title	Yr	NM
❏ BDL-2021	20 Golden Pieces of Duke Ellington	198?	$25

CAPITOL

Number	Title	Yr	NM
❏ T637 [M]	Dance to the Duke	1955	$75

— Turquoise label

Number	Title	Yr	NM
❏ T637 [M]	Dance to the Duke	1958	$80

— Black label with colorband, logo at left

Number	Title	Yr	NM
❏ T521 [M]	Ellington '55	1955	$75

— Turquoise label

Number	Title	Yr	NM
❏ T521 [M]	Ellington '55	1958	$80

— Black label with colorband, logo at left

Number	Title	Yr	NM
❏ M-11674	Ellington '55	1977	$25
❏ T679 [M]	Ellington Showcase	1956	$60

— Turquoise label

Number	Title	Yr	NM
❏ T679 [M]	Ellington Showcase	1958	$80

— Black label with colorband, logo at left

Number	Title	Yr	NM
❏ M-11058	Piano Reflections	1972	$30
❏ H440 [10]	Premiered by Ellington	1953	$250
❏ T1602 [M]	The Best of Duke Ellington	1961	$80
❏ DT1602 [R]	The Best of Duke Ellington	1961	$60
❏ SM-1602	The Best of Duke Ellington	197?	$25

— Reissue with new prefix

Number	Title	Yr	NM
❏ N-16172	The Best of Duke Ellington	198?	$20

— Budget-line reissue

Number	Title	Yr	NM
❏ H477 [10]	The Duke Plays Ellington	1954	$250
❏ T477 [M]	The Duke Plays Ellington	1954	$60

— Turquoise label

Number	Title	Yr	NM
❏ T477 [M]	The Duke Plays Ellington	1958	$80

— Black label with colorband, logo at left

CIRCLE

Number	Title	Yr	NM
❏ CLP-101	Duke Ellington World Broadcasting Series, Vol. 1	1986	$25
❏ CLP-102	Duke Ellington World Broadcasting Series, Vol. 2	1986	$25
❏ CLP-103	Duke Ellington World Broadcasting Series, Vol. 3	1986	$25
❏ CLP-104	Duke Ellington World Broadcasting Series, Vol. 4	199?	$25
❏ CLP-105	Duke Ellington World Broadcasting Series, Vol. 5 (1943)	199?	$25
❏ CLP-106	Duke Ellington World Broadcasting Series, Vol. 6 (1945)	1988	$25
❏ CLP-108	Duke Ellington World Broadcasting Series, Vol. 8 (1945)	1988	$25
❏ CLP-109	Duke Ellington World Broadcasting Series, Vol. 9 (1945)	1988	$25

COLUMBIA

Number	Title	Yr	NM
❏ CL951 [M]	A Drum Is a Woman	1957	$40
❏ CL2593 [10]	Al Hibbler with the Duke	1956	$150
❏ CL1790 [M]	All American	1962	$50
❏ CS8590 [S]	All American	1962	$60
❏ CL663 [M]	Blue Light	1955	$50
❏ CL1445 [M]	Blues in Orbit	1960	$60
❏ CL1162 [M]	Brown, Black and Beige	1958	$60
❏ CS8015 [S]	Brown, Black and Beige	1958	$60
❏ CL1282 [M]	Duke Ellington at the Bal Masque	1959	$60
❏ CS8098 [S]	Duke Ellington at the Bal Masque	1959	$60
❏ CL1323 [M]	Duke Ellington Jazz Party	1959	$60
❏ CS8127 [S]	Duke Ellington Jazz Party	1959	$60

Duke Ellington, *Ellington Indigos*, Columbia CS 8053, red and black label with six "eye" logos, **$60**.

Duke Ellington, *Jumpin' Punkins*, RCA Victor LPV-517, purple label, **$50**.

Duke Ellington, *Liberian Suite*, Columbia CL 6073, 10-inch LP, **$175**.

Duke Ellington, *Ellington Showcase*, Capitol T 679, turquoise label, **$60**.

Number	Title	Yr	NM
❑ KG32064	Duke Ellington Presents Ivie Anderson	1973	$35
❑ CS9629	Duke Ellington's Greatest Hits	1969	$35
❑ CL2522 [10]	Duke's Mixture	1955	$150
❑ CS8648 [R]	Ellington at Newport	1963	$30
❑ PC8648	Ellington at Newport	198?	$20
—Budget-line reissue			
❑ CL934 [M]	Ellington at Newport '56	1957	$40
—Red and black label with six "eye" logos			
❑ CL934 [M]	Ellington at Newport '56	1963	$35
—Red label with "Guaranteed High Fidelity" or "360 Sound Mono			
❑ CL1085 [M]	Ellington Indigos	1958	$60
❑ CS8053 [S]	Ellington Indigos	1958	$60
—Red and black label with six "eye" logos			
❑ CL1085 [M]	Ellington Indigos	1963	$35
—Red label with "Guaranteed High Fidelity" or "360 Sound Mono			
❑ CS8053 [S]	Ellington Indigos	1963	$35
—Red label with "360 Sound Stereo			
❑ PC8053	Ellington Indigos	198?	$20
—Budget-line reissue			
❑ CL1400 [M]	Festival Session	1960	$60
❑ CL1715 [M]	First Time	1962	$60
❑ CS8515 [S]	First Time	1962	$60
❑ CL2562 [10]	Here's the Duke	1955	$150
❑ CL830 [M]	Hi-Fi Ellington Uptown	1956	$40
❑ CL830 [M]	Hi-Fi Ellington Uptown	1963	$35
—Red label with "Guaranteed High Fidelity" or "360 Sound Mono			
❑ PC37340	It Don't Mean a Thing	1981	$20
—Reissue			
❑ C32471	Jazz at the Plaza -- Vol. II	1973	$30
❑ CL6073 [10]	Liberian Suite	1949	$175
❑ CL848 [M]	Liberian Suite	1956	$40
—Reissue of Columbia 6073			
❑ CL825 [M]	Masterpieces by Ellington	1956	$40
—Reissue of Columbia Masterworks 4418			
❑ CL825 [M]	Masterpieces by Ellington	1963	$35
—Red label with "Guaranteed High Fidelity" or "360 Sound Mono			
❑ CL1907 [M]	Midnight in Paris	1963	$50
❑ CS8829 [S]	Midnight in Paris	1963	$60
❑ CL6024 [10]	Mood Ellington	1949	$175
❑ CL1245 [M]	Newport 1958	1959	$60
❑ CS8072 [S]	Newport 1958	1959	$60
❑ CL1597 [M]	Peer Gynt Suite/Suite Thursday	1961	$60
❑ CS8397 [S]	Peer Gynt Suite/Suite Thursday	1961	$60
❑ CL1546 [M]	Piano in the Background	1960	$60
❑ CS8346 [S]	Piano in the Background	1960	$40
❑ CL1546 [M]	Piano in the Background	1963	$35
—Red label with "Guaranteed High Fidelity" or "360 Sound Mono			
❑ CS8346 [S]	Piano in the Background	1963	$35
—Red label with "360 Sound Stereo			
❑ CL1033 [M]	Such Sweet Thunder	1957	$40
❑ CL1198 [M]	The Cosmic Scene	1959	$150
❑ C3L27 [M]	The Ellington Era, Vol. 1	1963	$40
❑ C3L39 [M]	The Ellington Era, Vol. 2	1964	$40
❑ FC38028	The Girl's Suite & Perfume Suite	1982	$25
❑ CL558 [M]	The Music of Duke Ellington	1954	$100
—Maroon label with gold print			
❑ CL558 [M]	The Music of Duke Ellington	1956	$40
—Red and black label with six "eye" logos			
❑ CL558 [M]	The Music of Duke Ellington	1963	$35
—Red label with "Guaranteed High Fidelity" or "360 Sound Mono			
❑ CL1541 [M]	The Nutcracker Suite	1960	$60
❑ CS8341 [S]	The Nutcracker Suite	1960	$40
❑ G32471	The World of Duke Ellington	1974	$35
❑ KG33341	The World of Duke Ellington, Volume 2	1975	$35
❑ CG33961	The World of Duke Ellington, Volume 3	1975	$35

COLUMBIA JAZZ MASTERPIECES
Number	Title	Yr	NM
❑ CJ44051	Blues in Orbit	1988	$25
—Reissue of Columbia 8241			
❑ CJ40712	Duke Ellington Jazz Party	1987	$25
—Reissue of Columbia 8127			
❑ CJ40587	Ellington at Newport	1987	$25
—Reissue of Columbia 934			
❑ CJ44444	Ellington Indigos	1989	$25
—Reissue of Columbia 8053			
❑ CJ40586	First Time	1987	$25
—Reissue of Columbia 8515			
❑ CJ40836	Uptown	1987	$25

COLUMBIA JAZZ ODYSSEY
Number	Title	Yr	NM
❑ PC36979	The Festival Session	1981	$25

COLUMBIA MASTERWORKS
Number	Title	Yr	NM
❑ ML4639 [M]	Ellington Uptown	1951	$175
—Blue or green label, gold print			
❑ ML4639 [M]	Ellington Uptown	195?	$50
—Oddly, this exists as a reissue on the red and black "6 eye" label			
❑ ML4418 [M]	Masterpieces by Ellington	1951	$175

COLUMBIA SPECIAL PRODUCTS
Number	Title	Yr	NM
❑ P13291	Duke Ellington's Greatest Hits (Recorded Live in Concert)	1976	$25
❑ P13500	Festival Session	1976	$25
❑ P14359	Suite Thursday/Controversial Suite/Harlem Suite	198?	$25

DAYBREAK
Number	Title	Yr	NM
❑ DR2017	The Symphonic Ellington	1973	$30

DECCA
Number	Title	Yr	NM
❑ DL9224 [M]	Duke Ellington, Volume 1 -- In the Beginning	1958	$120
—Black label, silver print			
❑ DL9224 [M]	Duke Ellington, Volume 1 -- In the Beginning	1961	$60
—Black label with color bars			
❑ DL79224 [R]	Duke Ellington, Volume 1 -- In the Beginning	1958	$120
—Black label, silver print			
❑ DL79224 [R]	Duke Ellington, Volume 1 -- In the Beginning	1961	$35
—Black label with color bars			
❑ DL9241 [M]	Duke Ellington, Volume 2 -- Hot in Harlem	1959	$80
—Black label, silver print			
❑ DL9241 [M]	Duke Ellington, Volume 2 -- Hot in Harlem	1961	$60
—Black label with color bars			
❑ DL79241 [R]	Duke Ellington, Volume 2 -- Hot in Harlem	1959	$80
—Black label, silver print			
❑ DL79241 [R]	Duke Ellington, Volume 2 -- Hot in Harlem	1961	$35
—Black label with color bars			
❑ DL9247 [M]	Duke Ellington, Volume 3 -- Rockin' in Rhythm	1959	$80
—Black label, silver print			
❑ DL9247 [M]	Duke Ellington, Volume 3 -- Rockin' in Rhythm	1961	$60
—Black label with color bars			
❑ DL79247 [R]	Duke Ellington, Volume 3 -- Rockin' in Rhythm	1959	$80
—Black label, silver print			
❑ DL79247 [R]	Duke Ellington, Volume 3 -- Rockin' in Rhythm	1961	$35
—Black label with color bars			
❑ DL75069	Duke Ellington in Canada	1969	$35

DISCOVERY
Number	Title	Yr	NM
❑ 871	Afro Bossa	198?	$25
—Reissue of Reprise 6069			
❑ 841	Concert in the Virgin Islands	198?	$25
—Reissue of Reprise 6185			

DOCTOR JAZZ
Number	Title	Yr	NM
❑ W2X39137	All-Star Road Band	1984	$30
❑ W2X40012	All-Star Road Band, Vol. 2	1985	$30
❑ FW40030	Happy Reunion	1985	$25
❑ FW40359	New Mood Indigo	1986	$25

DO YOU LIKE JAZZ
Number	Title	Yr	NM
❑ P13293	Monologue	1973	$30

EVEREST ARCHIVE OF FOLK & JAZZ
Number	Title	Yr	NM
❑ 327	Duke Ellington at Carnegie Hall	197?	$30
❑ 221	Early Duke Ellington	1968	$30
❑ 249	Early Duke Ellington Vol. 2	1970	$30
❑ 266	Early Duke Ellington Vol. 3	1972	$30

FANTASY
Number	Title	Yr	NM
❑ F-9498	Afro-American Eclipse	1976	$30
❑ F-9636	Duke Ellington Featuring Paul Gonsalves	198?	$25
❑ OJC-623	Duke Ellington Featuring Paul Gonsalves	1991	$30
—Reissue of 9636			
❑ F-8407/8	Duke Ellington's Second Sacred Concert	1971	$35
❑ OJC-108	Great Times!	198?	$25
—Reissue of Riverside 9475			

Number	Title	Yr	NM
❑ F-8419	Latin American Suite	1971	$30
❑ OJC-469	Latin American Suite	1990	$25
—Reissue of 8419			
❑ OJC-645	The Afro-Eurasian Eclipse	1991	$30
—Reissue of 9498			
❑ OJC-446	The Ellington Suites	1990	$25
—Reissue of Pablo 2310 762			
❑ F-9640	The Intimacy of the Blues	1986	$25
❑ OJC-624	The Intimacy of the Blues	1991	$30
—Reissue of 9640			
❑ F-9462	The Pianist	1974	$30
❑ OJC-633	Up in Duke's Workshop	1991	$30
—Reissue of Pablo 2310 815			
❑ F-9433	Yale Concert	1974	$30

FLYING DUTCHMAN
Number	Title	Yr	NM
❑ 10166	It Don't Mean a Thing	1973	$30
❑ BXL1-2832	It Don't Mean a Thing	1978	$25
—Reissue			
❑ 10112	My People	1969	$35

FOLKWAYS
Number	Title	Yr	NM
❑ FJ-2968	First Annual Tour of the Pacific Northwest, Spring, 1952	198?	$40

GALAXY
Number	Title	Yr	NM
❑ 4807	Duke Ellington and His Famous Orchestra and Soloists	197?	$35

GNP CRESCENDO
Number	Title	Yr	NM
❑ GNP-9045	The 1953 Pasadena Concert	1986	$25
❑ GNP-9049	The 1954 Los Angeles Concert	1987	$25

HALL OF FAME
Number	Title	Yr	NM
❑ 625/6/7	The Immortal Duke Ellington	197?	$50

HARMONY
Number	Title	Yr	NM
❑ H30566	Duke Ellington's Greatest Hits Live	1971	$30
❑ HL7436 [M]	Fantasies	1967	$60
❑ HS11236 [R]	Fantasies	1967	$30
❑ HS11323	In My Solitude	1969	$30

HINDSIGHT
Number	Title	Yr	NM
❑ HSR-125	Duke Ellington 1946	198?	$25
❑ HSR-126	Duke Ellington 1946, Volume 2	198?	$25
❑ HSR-127	Duke Ellington 1946, Volume 3	198?	$25
❑ HSR-128	Duke Ellington 1947	198?	$25
❑ HSR-129	Duke Ellington 1947, Volume 2	198?	$25

IAJRC
Number	Title	Yr	NM
❑ LP-45	Fairfield, Connecticut Jazz Fest 1956	198?	$20

INTERMEDIA
Number	Title	Yr	NM
❑ QS-5021	Do Nothin' Till You Hear from Me	198?	$25
❑ QS-5020	Lullaby of Birdland	198?	$25
❑ QS-5063	Satin Doll	198?	$25
❑ QS-5002	Sophisticated Duke	198?	$25

JAZZBIRD
Number	Title	Yr	NM
❑ 2009	Meadowbrook to Manhattan	1980	$25

JAZZ ODYSSEY
Number	Title	Yr	NM
❑ 32160252	Nutcracker and Peer Gynt Suites	196?	$30

JAZZ PANORAMA
Number	Title	Yr	NM
❑ 1802 [10]	Duke Ellington -- Vol. 1	1951	$175
❑ 1811 [10]	Duke Ellington -- Vol. 2	1951	$175
❑ 1816 [10]	Duke Ellington -- Vol. 3	1951	$175

LONDON
Number	Title	Yr	NM
❑ AL-3551 [10]	The Duke -- 1926	195?	$100

MCA
Number	Title	Yr	NM
❑ 1374	Brunswick-Vocalion Rarities	198?	$25
❑ 2075	Duke Ellington, Volume 1 -- In the Beginning	197?	$25
—Reissue of Decca 79224			
❑ 1358	Duke Ellington, Volume 1 -- In the Beginning	198?	$20
—Reissue of 2075			
❑ 2076	Duke Ellington, Volume 2 -- Hot in Harlem	197?	$25
—Reissue of Decca 79241			
❑ 1359	Duke Ellington, Volume 2 -- Hot in Harlem	198?	$20
—Reissue of 2076			
❑ 2077	Duke Ellington, Volume 3 -- Rockin' in Rhythm	197?	$25
—Reissue of Decca 79247			
❑ 1360	Duke Ellington, Volume 3 -- Rockin' in Rhythm	198?	$20

Number	Title	Yr	NM
—Reissue of 2077			
❏ 4142	Great Tenor Encounters	198?	$30
—Reissue of Impulse! 9350			
❏ 42325	The Brunswick Era, Vol. 1	1990	$30

MOBILE FIDELITY
| ❏ 1-214 | Anatomy of a Murder | 1995 | $120 |
| *—Audiophile vinyl* | | | |

MOSAIC
| ❏ MQ8-160 | The Complete Capitol Recordings of Duke Ellington | 199? | $250 |

MUSICRAFT
| ❏ 2002 | Carnegie Hall Concert | 1986 | $25 |

PABLO
❏ 2310703	Duke's Big 4	1974	$30
❏ 2310787	Intimate	197?	$30
❏ 2405401	The Best of Duke Ellington	198?	$25
❏ 2310762	The Ellington Suites	197?	$30
❏ 2310721	This One's for Blanton	197?	$30
❏ 2310815	Up in Duke's Workshop	1980	$25

PABLO LIVE
| ❏ 2308245 | Harlem | 198? | $25 |
| ❏ 2308247 | In the Uncommon Market | 198? | $25 |

PAIR
| ❏ PDL2-1011 | Original Recordings by Duke Ellington | 1986 | $30 |

PICCADILLY
| ❏ 3524 | Classic Ellington | 198? | $25 |

PICKWICK
| ❏ SPC-3390 | We Love You Madly | 197? | $25 |

PRESTIGE
❏ 24045	Duke Ellington's Second Sacred Concert	1974	$30
—Reissue of Fantasy 8407/8			
❏ 24073	The Carnegie Hall Concerts: December 1944	1977	$35
❏ 24075	The Carnegie Hall Concerts: December 1947	1977	$35
❏ 34003	The Carnegie Hall Concerts: January 1943	197?	$50
❏ 24074	The Carnegie Hall Concerts: January 1946	1977	$35
❏ 24029	The Golden Duke	1973	$35

RCA CAMDEN
❏ CAL-394 [M]	Duke Ellington at Tanglewood	1958	$50
❏ CAL-459 [M]	Duke Ellington at the Cotton Club	1959	$50
❏ ACL2-0152	Mood Indigo	1973	$35
❏ ACL-7052	The Duke at Tanglewood	197?	$25
—Reissue of RCA Red Seal LSC-2857			

RCA VICTOR
❏ LPM-3906 [M]	And His Mother Called Him Bill	1968	$100
❏ LSP-3906 [S]	And His Mother Called Him Bill	1968	$35
❏ LPM-3582 [M]	Concert of Sacred Music	1966	$35
❏ LSP-3582 [S]	Concert of Sacred Music	1966	$50
❏ LPV-506 [M]	Daybreak Express	1964	$50
❏ LPM-1092 [M]	Duke and His Men	1955	$50
❏ WPT-11 [10]	Duke Ellington	1951	$175
❏ LPM-1715 [M]	Duke Ellington at His Very Best	1958	$40
❏ LPT-3067 [10]	Duke Ellington Plays the Blues	1952	$175
❏ APL1-1023	Eastbourne Performance	1974	$30
❏ LPT-1004 [M]	Ellington's Greatest	1954	$40
❏ LPM-3782 [M]	Far East Suite	1967	$60
❏ LSP-3782 [S]	Far East Suite	1967	$35
❏ LPV-568 [M]	Flaming Youth	1969	$50
❏ LPM-1364 [M]	In a Mellotone	1957	$40
—Black label, dog at top, "Long Play" at bottom			
❏ LPM-1364 [M]	In a Mellotone	196?	$60
—Black label, dog at top, "Mono" at bottom			
❏ LPM-1364 [M]	In a Mellotone	1969	$50
—Orange label			
❏ LPV-541 [M]	Johnny Come Lately	1967	$150
❏ LPV-517 [M]	Jumpin' Punkins	1965	$50
❏ LPV-553 [M]	Pretty Woman	1968	$50
❏ ANL1-2811	Pure Gold	1978	$25
❏ LJM-1002 [M]	Seattle Concert	1954	$100
❏ CPL2-4098	Sophisticated Ellington	1983	$30
❏ SP-33-394 [M]	The Duke at Tanglewood	1966	$60
—Special Interview Recording for Radio Station Programming			
❏ LPM-6009 [M]	The Indispensible Duke Ellington	1961	$100
❏ LPM-3576 [M]	The Popular Duke Ellington	1966	$35
❏ LSP-3576 [S]	The Popular Duke Ellington	1966	$50
❏ VPM-6042	This Is Duke Ellington	1972	$35
❏ LPT-3017 [10]	This Is Duke Ellington and His Orchestra	1952	$175

RCA VICTOR RED SEAL

Number	Title	Yr	NM
❏ LM-2857 [M]	The Duke at Tanglewood	1966	$35
❏ LSC-2857 [S]	The Duke at Tanglewood	1966	$50

REPRISE
❏ R-6069 [M]	Afro-Bossa	1962	$50
❏ R9-6069 [S]	Afro-Bossa	1962	$50
❏ R-6185 [M]	Concert in the Virgin Islands	1965	$50
❏ RS-6185 [S]	Concert in the Virgin Islands	1965	$35
❏ R-6234 [M]	Duke Ellington's Greatest Hits	1967	$50
❏ RS-6234 [S]	Duke Ellington's Greatest Hits	1967	$35
❏ R-6122 [M]	Ellington '65: Hits of the '60s/ This Time by Ellington	1964	$50
❏ RS-6122 [S]	Ellington '65: Hits of the '60s/ This Time by Ellington	1964	$50
❏ R-6154 [M]	Ellington '66	1965	$50
❏ RS-6154 [S]	Ellington '66	1965	$35
❏ R-6141 [M]	Mary Poppins	1964	$50
❏ RS-6141 [S]	Mary Poppins	1964	$50
❏ R-6097 [M]	The Symphonic Ellington	1963	$50
❏ R9-6097 [S]	The Symphonic Ellington	1963	$50
❏ R-6168 [M]	Will Big Bands Ever Come Back?	1965	$50
❏ RS-6168 [S]	Will Big Bands Ever Come Back?	1965	$35

RIVERSIDE
❏ RLP 12-129 [M]	Birth of Big Band Jazz	1956	$350
—White label, blue print			
❏ RLP 12-129 [M]	Birth of Big Band Jazz	195?	$30
—Blue label with mike logo			
❏ RLP-475 [M]	Great Times!	1963	$150
❏ RS-9475 [S]	Great Times!	1963	$150

RONDO-LETTE
| ❏ A-7 [M] | Duke Ellington and Orchestra | 1958 | $60 |

ROULETTE
| ❏ 108 | Echoes of an Era | 1971 | $35 |

ROYALE
| ❏ 18143 [10] | Duke Ellington and His Orchestra | 195? | $50 |
| ❏ 18152 [10] | Duke Ellington Plays Ellington | 195? | $50 |

SMITHSONIAN COLLECTION
| ❏ P6-15079 | An Explosion of Genius 1938-1940 | 1976 | $100 |
| *—Produced in association with Columbia Special Products* | | | |

SOLID STATE
❏ SS-19000	75th Birthday	1970	$50
❏ SM-18022	Money Jungle	1968	$35
—Reissue of United Artists 15017			

STANYAN
| ❏ 10105 | For Always | 197? | $30 |

STARDUST
| ❏ SD-124 [M] | Duke | 196? | $30 |
| ❏ SDS-124 [R] | Duke | 196? | $30 |

STORYVILLE
| ❏ SLP-4003 | Duke Ellington and His Orchestra | 198? | $25 |

SUPER MAJESTIC
| ❏ 2000 | Duke Ellington | 197? | $30 |

SUTTON
| ❏ SU-276 [M] | Duke Meets Leonard Feather | 196? | $30 |

TIME-LIFE
❏ STBB-16	Big Bands: Cotton Club Nights	1983	$35
❏ STBB-05	Big Bands: Duke Ellington	1983	$35
❏ STL-J-02	Giants of Jazz	1978	$50

TREND
| ❏ 2004 | Carnegie Hall Concert | 198? | $25 |
| ❏ 529 | The Symphonic Ellington | 1982 | $50 |

UNITED ARTISTS
❏ UAJ-14017 [M]	Money Jungle	1962	$40
❏ UAJS-15017 [S]	Money Jungle	1962	$40
❏ UAS-5632	Money Jungle	1972	$30
—Reissue			
❏ UXS-92	Togo Bravo Suite	1972	$35

VEE JAY
| ❏ VJS-3061 | Love You Madly | 198? | $25 |

VERVE
| ❏ V-8701 [M] | Soul Call | 1967 | $35 |
| ❏ V6-8701 [S] | Soul Call | 1967 | $30 |

X
| ❏ LVA-3037 [10] | Duke Ellington Plays | 1955 | $175 |

ELLINGTON, MERCER
Trumpet player, bandleader and composer; took over the DUKE ELLINGTON ORCHESTRA after his father's death.

Albums

Number	Title	Yr	NM

CORAL
❏ CRL0(????) [M]	Black and Tan Fantasy	1958	$30
❏ CRL0(????) [S]	Black and Tan Fantasy	1958	$40
❏ CRL57293 [M]	Colors in Rhythm	1959	$30
❏ CRL757293 [S]	Colors in Rhythm	1959	$40
❏ CRL57225 [M]	Stepping Into Swing Society	1958	$30
❏ CRL757225 [S]	Stepping Into Swing Society	1958	$40

MCA
| ❏ 349 | Black and Tan Fantasy | 197? | $30 |

ELLINGTONIANS, THE
Assorted members of DUKE ELLINGTON's orchestra. Also see THE DUKE'S MEN.

Albums

MERCER
| ❏ LP-1004 [10] | The Ellingtonians with Al Hibbler | 1951 | $250 |

ELLIOT, MIKE
Guitarist.

Albums

ASI
❏ 5003	Atrio	197?	$25
❏ 5007	City Traffic	197?	$25
❏ 5001	Natural Life	197?	$25

PAUSA
| ❏ 7139 | Diffusion | 1981 | $25 |

ELLIOT, RICHARD
Tenor saxophone player.

Albums

INTIMA
❏ SJE-73283	Initial Approach	1987	$25
—Reissue of ITI album			
❏ D1-73348	Take to the Skies	1989	$30
❏ D1-73321	The Power of Suggestion	1988	$30
❏ SJ-73233	Trolltown	1987	$30

ITI
| ❏ JL-030 | Initial Approach | 198? | $35 |

ELLIOTT, DON
Mellophone player, male singer, and occasional trumpeter and vibraphone player. Also see BOB CORWIN; PAUL DESMOND; THE NUTTY SQUIRRELS; CAL TJADER.

Albums

ABC-PARAMOUNT
❏ ABC-142 [M]	Don Elliott at the Modern Jazz Room	1956	$40
❏ ABC-228 [M]	Jamaica Jazz	1958	$40
❏ ABCS-228 [S]	Jamaica Jazz	1959	$30
❏ ABC-106 [M]	Musical Offering	1956	$40
❏ ABC-190 [M]	The Voices of Don Elliott	1957	$50

BETHLEHEM
| ❏ BCP-15 [M] | Don Elliott Sings | 1955 | $250 |
| ❏ BCP-12 [M] | Mellophone | 1955 | $250 |

COLUMBIA
| ❏ PC33799 | Rejuvenation | 1975 | $30 |

DECCA
| ❏ DL9208 [M] | The Mello Sound | 1958 | $100 |
| ❏ DL79208 [S] | The Mello Sound | 1958 | $100 |

DESIGN
| ❏ DLP-69 [M] | Music for the Sensational 60's | 196? | $35 |
| ❏ DLPS-69 [S] | Music for the Sensational 60's | 196? | $30 |

HALLMARK
| ❏ 317 [M] | Pal Joey | 1957 | $50 |

JAZZLAND
| ❏ JLP-15 [M] | Double Trumpet Doings | 1960 | $40 |
| ❏ JLP-915 [S] | Double Trumpet Doings | 1960 | $30 |

RCA VICTOR
| ❏ LJM-1007 [M] | Don Elliott Quintet | 1954 | $60 |

RIVERSIDE
❏ RLP 12-218 [M]	Counterpoint for Six Valves	1956	$250
—White label, blue print			
❏ RLP 12-218 [M]	Counterpoint for Six Valves	195?	$40
—Blue label, microphone logo			
❏ RLP-2517 [10]	Six Valves	1955	$300

SAVOY
| ❏ MG-9033 [10] | The Versatile Don Elliott | 1953 | $120 |

VANGUARD
| ❏ VRS-8016 [10] | Doubles in Brass | 1954 | $100 |

Number	Title	Yr	NM

ELLIOTT, DON/SAM MOST
Also see each artist's individual listings.

Albums

JAZZTONE

❏ J-1256 [M]	Doubles in Jazz	1957	$40

VANGUARD

❏ VRS-8522 [M]	Doubles in Jazz	1957	$100

—*Partial reissue of 8016 and 8014*

ELLIS, ANITA
Female singer.

Albums

ELEKTRA

❏ EKL-179 [M]	The World in My Arms	1959	$40

EPIC

❏ LN3419 [M]	Him	1958	$80
❏ LN3280 [M]	I Wonder What Became of Me	1956	$80

ELLIS, DON
Trumpeter, composer and bandleader.

Albums

ATLANTIC

❏ SD19178	Live at Montreux	1977	$30
❏ SD18227	Survival/Music from Other Galaxies and Planets	1977	$30

BARNABY

❏ BR-5020	How Time Passes	197?	$30

—*Reissue of Candid LP*

BASF

❏ 25341	Haiku	1974	$35
❏ 25123	Soaring	1973	$35

CANDID

❏ CJM-8004 [M]	How Time Passes	1961	$50
❏ CJS-9004 [S]	How Time Passes	1961	$60

COLUMBIA

❏ CS9721	Autumn	1969	$35
❏ KC31766	Connection	1972	$35
❏ G30243	Don Ellis at the Fillmore	1970	$25
❏ CG30243	Don Ellis at the Fillmore	197?	$35

—*Reissue with new prefix*

❏ CL2785 [M]	Electric Bath	1968	$30
❏ CS9585 [S]	Electric Bath	1968	$35
❏ CS9668	Shock Treatment	1968	$35
❏ G30927	Tears of Joy	1971	$25
❏ CG30927	Tears of Joy	197?	$35

—*Reissue with new prefix*

❏ CS9889	The New Don Ellis Band Goes Underground	1969	$25

FANTASY

❏ OJC-431	New Ideas	1990	$30

NEW JAZZ

❏ NJLP-8257 [M]	New Ideas	1961	$150

—*Purple label*

❏ NJLP-8257 [M]	New Ideas	1965	$150

—*Blue label, trident logo at right*

PACIFIC JAZZ

❏ PJ-10112 [M]	Don Ellis "Live" At Monterey	1967	$25
❏ ST-20112 [S]	Don Ellis "Live" At Monterey	1967	$35
❏ PJ-55 [M]	Essence	1962	$30
❏ ST-55 [S]	Essence	1962	$40
❏ PJ-10123 [M]	Live in 3/2 3/4 Time	1967	$25
❏ ST-20123 [S]	Live in 3/2 3/4 Time	1967	$35

PAUSA

❏ 7028	Soaring	1979	$25

—*Reissue of BASF 25123*

PRESTIGE

❏ PRST-7607	New Ideas	1969	$35

ELLIS, HERB, AND JOE PASS
Also see each artist's individual listings.

Albums

CONCORD JAZZ

❏ CJ-1	Jazz/Concord	197?	$35
❏ CJ-2	Seven Come Eleven	197?	$35

PABLO

❏ 2310714	Two for the Road	1974	$35

ELLIS, HERB, AND RAY BROWN
Also see each artist's individual listings.

Albums

CONCORD JAZZ

❏ CJ-6	After You've Gone	197?	$30
❏ CJ-12	Hot Tracks	1977	$30
❏ CJ-10	Rhythm Willie	197?	$30
❏ CJ-3	Soft Shoe	197?	$30

ELLIS, HERB, AND RED MITCHELL
Also see each artist's individual listings.

Albums

CONCORD JAZZ

❏ CJ-372	Doggin' Around	1989	$30

ELLIS, HERB, AND REMO PALMIER
Also see each artist's individual listings.

Albums

CONCORD JAZZ

❏ CJ-56	Windflower	1978	$30

ELLIS, HERB, AND ROSS TOMPKINS
Also see each artist's individual listings.

Albums

CONCORD JAZZ

❏ CJ-17	A Pair to Draw On	1977	$30

ELLIS, HERB
Guitarist.

Albums

COLUMBIA

❏ CL2330 [M]	Herb Ellis Guitar	1965	$35
❏ CS9130 [S]	Herb Ellis Guitar	1965	$25

CONCORD JAZZ

❏ CJ-116	Herb Ellis at Montreux, Summer 1979	1980	$25
❏ CJ-181	Herb Mix	1982	$25
❏ CJ-77	Soft and Mellow	1979	$25

DOT

❏ DLP-3678 [M]	The Man with the Guitar	1965	$75
❏ DLP-25678 [S]	The Man with the Guitar	1965	$75

EPIC

❏ LA16039 [M]	Herb Ellis and "Stuff" Smith Together	1963	$50
❏ BA17039 [S]	Herb Ellis and "Stuff" Smith Together	1963	$60
❏ LA16034 [M]	The Midnight Roll	1962	$60
❏ BA17034 [S]	The Midnight Roll	1962	$60
❏ LA16036 [M]	Three Guitars in Bossa Nova Time	1963	$50
❏ BA17036 [S]	Three Guitars in Bossa Nova Time	1963	$60

NORGRAN

❏ MGN-1081 [M]	Ellis in Wonderland	1956	$200

VERVE

❏ MGV-8171 [M]	Ellis in Wonderland	1957	$200

—*Reissue of Norgran 1081*

❏ V-8171 [M]	Ellis in Wonderland	1961	$25
❏ MGV-8278 [M]	Herb Ellis	1958	$0

—*Canceled*

❏ MGVS-6045 [S]	Herb Ellis Meets Jimmy Giuffre	1960	$100
❏ V-8311 [M]	Herb Ellis Meets Jimmy Giuffre	1961	$25
❏ V6-8311 [S]	Herb Ellis Meets Jimmy Giuffre	1961	$25
❏ V-8252 [M]	Nothing But the Blues	1961	$25
❏ V-8448 [M]	Softly…But With That Feeling	1962	$25
❏ V6-8448 [S]	Softly…But With That Feeling	1962	$30
❏ MGV-8381 [M]	Thank You, Charlie Christian	1960	$80
❏ MGVS-6164 [S]	Thank You, Charlie Christian	1960	$80
❏ V-8381 [M]	Thank You, Charlie Christian	1961	$25
❏ V6-8381 [S]	Thank You, Charlie Christian	1961	$25

ELLIS, LLOYD
Guitarist.

Albums

CARLTON

❏ LP 12-104 [M]	Fastest Guitar in the World	1958	$100

FAMOUS DOOR

❏ HL-100	Las Vegas 3 AM	197?	$30

TREY

❏ TLP-902 [M]	So Tall, So Cool, So There!	1960	$60

ELLIS, PEE WEE
Tenor saxophone player.

Albums

SAVOY

❏ SJL-3301	Home in the Country	1976	$25

ELMAN, ZIGGY
Trumpeter and bandleader.

Albums

CIRCLE

❏ 70	Ziggy Elman and His Orchestra 1947	198?	$25

MGM

❏ E-163 [10]	Dancing with Zig	1952	$50
❏ E-3389 [M]	Sentimental Trumpet	1956	$40
❏ E-535 [10]	Ziggy Elman and His Orchestra	195?	$100

SUNBEAM

❏ 202	Angels Sing 1938-39	198?	$25

ELSTAK, NEDLEY
Trumpeter.

Albums

ESP-DISK'

❏ 1076	The Machine	1969	$100

ELY, CHET

Albums

GHB

❏ 67	Til Times Get Better	197?	$25

EMMONS, BUDDY
Steel guitar player, better known in the country-western realm.

Albums

MERCURY

❏ MG-20843 [M]	Steel Guitar Jazz	1963	$150
❏ SR-60843 [S]	Steel Guitar Jazz	1963	$150

ENEVOLDSEN, BOB
Trombone player (both slide and valve), bass clarinet player, and tenor saxophone player.

Albums

LIBERTY

❏ LJH-6008 [M]	Smorgasboard	1956	$50

NOCTURNE

❏ NLP-6 [M]	Bob Enevoldsen Quintet	1954	$150

TAMPA

❏ TP-14 [M]	Reflections in Jazz	1957	$200

—*Colored vinyl*

❏ TP-14 [M]	Reflections in Jazz	1958	$150

—*Black vinyl*

ENNIS, ETHEL
Female singer.

Albums

BASF

❏ 25121	10 Sides of Ethel Ennis	1973	$35

CAPITOL

❏ T941	Change of Scenery	1957	$60
❏ T1078 [M]	Have You Forgotten?	1959	$75

JUBILEE

❏ JLP-5024 [M]	Ethel Ennis Sings	1963	$25
❏ SJLP-5024 [S]	Ethel Ennis Sings	1963	$30
❏ JLP-1021 [M]	Lullabies for Losers	1956	$50

PICKWICK

❏ PC-3021 [M]	Ethel Ennis	196?	$30
❏ SPC-3021 [S]	Ethel Ennis	196?	$30

RCA CAMDEN

❏ ACL1-0157	God Bless the Child	1973	$25

RCA VICTOR

❏ LPM-2984 [M]	Eyes for You	1964	$25
❏ LSP-2984 [S]	Eyes for You	1964	$30
❏ LSP-2862 [S]	Once Again, Ethel Ennis	1964	$30
❏ LPM-2862 [M]	Once Again, Ethel Ennis	1964	$25
❏ LPM-2786 [M]	This Is Ethel Ennis	1964	$25
❏ LSP-2786 [S]	This Is Ethel Ennis	1964	$30

Number	Title	Yr	NM

ENNIS, SKINNAY
Male singer.
Albums
HINDSIGHT
| ❏ HSR-164 | Skinnay Ennis 1947-48 | 198? | $25 |

ENRIQUEZ, BOBBY
Pianist.
Albums
GNP CRESCENDO
❏ GNPS-2155	Espana	1983	$25
❏ GNPS-2179	Live at Concerts by the Sea	1985	$20
❏ GNPS-2183	Live at Concerts by the Sea, Volume II	1986	$20
❏ GNPS-2161	Live in Tokyo	198?	$20
❏ GNPS-2168	Live in Tokyo, Volume II	198?	$20
❏ GNPS-2151	Prodigious Piano	198?	$20
❏ GNPS-2144	The Wildman	198?	$20
❏ GNPS-2148	The Wildman Meets the Madman	198?	$20

PORTRAIT
| ❏ FR44160 | Wild Piano | 1988 | $30 |

ENSEMBLE AL-SALAAM, THE
Albums
STRATA-EAST
| ❏ SES-7418 | The Sojourner | 1974 | $40 |

ENYARD, RON, AND PAULA OWEN
Enyard is a drummer. Owen is a female singer.
Albums
CADENCE JAZZ
| ❏ CJR-1031 | Red, Green and Blues (In Living Black and White) | 1987 | $25 |

ERICSON, ROLF
Trumpeter.
Albums
EMARCY
| ❏ MG-36106 [M] | Rolf Ericson and His All American Stars | 1957 | $200 |

ERNEY, DEWEY
Male vocalist.
Albums
DISCOVERY
| ❏ DS-881 | A Beautiful Friendship | 1982 | $25 |

ERSKINE, PETER
Drummer.
Albums
CONTEMPORARY
| ❏ C-14010 | Peter Erskine | 1983 | $30 |
FANTASY
| ❏ OJC-610 | Peter Erskine | 1991 | $30 |
PASSPORT
| ❏ 88032 | Transition | 198? | $25 |

ERVIN, BOOKER
Tenor saxophone player. Also see BOOKER LITTLE.
Albums
BARNABY
| ❏ Z30560 | That's It! | 1971 | $35 |
— Reissue of Candid 9014
BETHLEHEM
| ❏ BCP-6048 [M] | The Book Cooks | 1961 | $250 |
| ❏ BCP-6025 | The Book Cooks | 197? | $35 |
— Reissue with RCA Victor distrbution
BLUE NOTE
| ❏ 4134/84134 | Back from the Gig | 1963 | $0 |
— Canceled
| ❏ BN-LA488-H2 | Back from the Gig | 1975 | $25 |
| ❏ BST-84314 | Booker Ervin | 1969 | $0 |
— Canceled
| ❏ BST-84283 | The In Between | 1969 | $30 |
CANDID
| ❏ CJS-9014 [S] | That's It! | 1961 | $50 |

ERVIN, BOOKER/HORACE PARLAN
Also see each artist's individual listings.
Albums
INNER CITY
| ❏ IC-3006 | Lament | 1977 | $35 |

ERWIN, PEE WEE
Trumpeter.
Albums
BRUNSWICK
| ❏ BL54011 [M] | The Land of Dixie | 1956 | $40 |
CADENCE
| ❏ CLP-1011 [M] | Dixieland at Grandview Inn | 1956 | $40 |
JAZZOLOGY
| ❏ J-80 | Swingin' That Music | 1981 | $25 |
STRAND
| ❏ SL-1001 [M] | Peter Meets the Wolf in Dixieland | 1959 | $50 |
| ❏ SLS-1001 [S] | Peter Meets the Wolf in Dixieland | 1959 | $60 |
URANIA
| ❏ UJLP-1202 [M] | Accent on Dixieland | 1955 | $250 |

ESCHETE, RON
Seven-string guitarist.
Albums
BAINBRIDGE
| ❏ BT-6267 | Christmas Impressions | 1986 | $25 |
| ❏ BT-6264 | Stump Jumper | 1986 | $25 |
MUSE
| ❏ MR-5246 | Line-Up | 1980 | $30 |
| ❏ MR-5186 | To Let You Know I Care | 1979 | $30 |
MUSIC IS MEDICINE
| ❏ 9055 | Christmas Impressions | 1982 | $35 |

ESCOVEDO, PETE
Percussionist, male vocalist and bandleader.
Albums
CROSSOVER
| ❏ CR-5005 | Mister E. | 1988 | $30 |
| ❏ CR-5002 | Yesterday's Memories, Tomorrow's Dreams | 1987 | $30 |

ESCOVEDO, PETE AND SHEILA
Sheila Escovedo, Pete's daughter, is a drummer, percussionist and female vocalist. She is better known to pop and R&B fans as Prince protégé "Sheila E."
Albums
FANTASY
| ❏ F-9545 | Happy Together | 1977 | $35 |
| ❏ F-9524 | Solo Two | 1976 | $35 |

ESHELMAN, DAVE, JAZZ GARDEN BIG BAND
Eshelman is a trombonist, bandleader, arranger and composer.
Albums
SEA BREEZE
| ❏ SB-2039 | Deep Voices | 1989 | $30 |

PACIFIC JAZZ
| ❏ PJ-10199 [M] | Structurally Sound | 1968 | $40 |
| ❏ ST-20199 [S] | Structurally Sound | 1968 | $25 |
PRESTIGE
| ❏ PRST-7293 [S] | Exultation! | 1964 | $30 |
| ❏ PRST-7844 | Exultation! | 197? | $35 |
— Reissue of 7293
❏ 24091	Freedom and the Space Sessions	1979	$35
❏ PRST-7417 [S]	Groovin' High	1966	$30
❏ PRST-7499 [S]	Heavy!	1968	$25
❏ PRLP-7435 [M]	Settin' the Pace	1967	$30
❏ PRST-7435 [S]	Settin' the Pace	1967	$25
❏ PRST-7340 [S]	The Blues Book	1965	$30
❏ PRST-7295 [S]	The Freedom Book	1964	$30
❏ PRST-7318 [S]	The Song Book	1964	$30
❏ PRLP-7386 [M]	The Space Book	1965	$30
❏ PRST-7386 [S]	The Space Book	1965	$30
❏ PRST-7462 [S]	The Trance	1967	$25
SAVOY
❏ MG-12154 [M]	Cookin'	1960	$50
SAVOY JAZZ
❏ SJL-1119	Down in the Dumps	198?	$25

ETHNIC HERITAGE ENSEMBLE, THE
Led by drummer and percussionist Kahil El'Zabar, other members include Joe Bowie (trombone), Harold Atu Murray (flute, thumb piano and various percussion instruments) and Ed Wilkerson (tenor sax).
Albums
RED
| ❏ VPA-156 | Impressions | 198? | $35 |
SILKHEART
| ❏ SH-108 | Ancestral Song | 198? | $30 |

ETHRIDGE, KELLIS
Albums
INNER CITY
| ❏ IC-1109 | Tomorrow Sky | 1980 | $25 |

EUBANKS, KEVIN
Guitarist.
Albums
ELEKTRA/MUSICIAN
| ❏ 60213 | Guitarist | 1983 | $35 |
GRP
❏ GR-1029	Face to Face	1985	$25
❏ GR-1041	Heat of Heat	1986	$25
❏ GR-1031	Opening Night	1985	$25
❏ GR-1054	Shadow Prophets	1988	$25
❏ GR-1008	Sundance	1984	$25
❏ GR-9580	The Searcher	1989	$30

EUBANKS, ROBIN
Trombone player. KEVIN EUBANKS is his brother.
Albums
JMT
| ❏ 834433-1 | Dedication | 1989 | $30 |
| ❏ 834424-1 | Different Perspectives | 1988 | $25 |

EUREKA BRASS BAND, THE
The leader was trumpeter Percy Humphrey.
Albums
ATLANTIC
| ❏ 1408 [M] | The Eureka Brass Band | 1963 | $50 |
| ❏ SD1408 [S] | The Eureka Brass Band | 1963 | $50 |
— Multicolor label with black "fan" logo at right
| ❏ SD1408 [S] | The Eureka Brass Band | 1969 | $25 |
— Red and green label with "1841 Broadway" address
| ❏ SD1408 [S] | The Eureka Brass Band | 1975 | $20 |
— Red and green label with "75 Rockefeller Plaza" address and "W" logo in perimeter print
FOLKWAYS
| ❏ FA-2642 [M] | Music of New Orleans | 195? | $50 |
PAX
| ❏ LP-9001 [10] | New Orleans Parade | 1954 | $60 |

EUROPEAN CLASSIC JAZZ BAND, THE
Albums
STOMP OFF
| ❏ SOS-1070 | Whip Me with Plenty of Love | 1984 | $25 |

EUROPEAN CLASSIC JAZZ TRIO, THE
Albums
STOMP OFF
| ❏ SOS-1142 | That's Like It Ought to Be | 1988 | $25 |

EUROPEAN JAZZ QUARTET, THE
Albums
PULSE
| ❏ 3001 [M] | New Jazz from the Old World | 1957 | $50 |

EVANS, BILL (1), AND JIM HALL
Also see each artist's individual listings.
Albums
BLUE NOTE
| ❏ B1-90583 | Undercurrent | 1988 | $25 |
SOLID STATE

Number	Title	Yr	NM
❑ SS-18018	Undercurrent	1968	$25

UNITED ARTISTS

Number	Title	Yr	NM
❑ UAJ-14003 [M]	Undercurrent	1962	$40
❑ UAJS-15003 [S]	Undercurrent	1962	$50
❑ UAS-5640	Undercurrent	197?	$35

EVANS, BILL (1)

Pianist. Also see BOB BROOKMEYER; GARY McFARLAND.

Albums

COLUMBIA

Number	Title	Yr	NM
❑ KC31490	Living Time: Events I-VIII	1972	$35
❑ C30855	The Bill Evans Album	1971	$35
❑ PC30855	The Bill Evans Album	198?	$20

—Budget-line reissue

Number	Title	Yr	NM
❑ CG33672	The Bill Evans Album/Living Time	1976	$35

CTI

Number	Title	Yr	NM
❑ 6004	Montreux II	1971	$35

ELEKTRA/MUSICIAN

Number	Title	Yr	NM
❑ 60164	The Paris Concert, Volume 1	1984	$30
❑ 60311	The Paris Concert, Volume 2	1986	$30

FANTASY

Number	Title	Yr	NM
❑ F-9542	Alone (Again)	1977	$30
❑ OJC-263	Bill Evans at Shelly's Manne-Hole	1987	$25
❑ F-9568	Crosscurrents	1978	$30
❑ F-9618	Eloquence	1982	$25
❑ OJC-068	Everybody Digs Bill Evans	198?	$25
❑ OJC-037	Explorations	198?	$25
❑ F-9630	From the 70s	198?	$25
❑ OJC-369	How My Heart Sings	198?	$25
❑ OJC-308	Interplay	198?	$25
❑ F-9475	Intuition	1975	$30
❑ OJC-470	Intuition	1990	$30
❑ F-9593	I Will Say Goodbye	1980	$30
❑ F-9510	Montreux III	1976	$30
❑ OJC-434	Moonbeams	1990	$30
❑ OJC-025	New Jazz Conceptions	1982	$25
❑ OJC-088	Portrait in Jazz	198?	$25
❑ F-9529	Quintessence	1976	$30
❑ F-9608	Re: The Person I Knew	198?	$25
❑ F-9501	Since We Met	1975	$30
❑ OJC-622	Since We Met	1991	$30
❑ OJC-140	Sunday at the Village Vanguard	198?	$25
❑ F-9457	The Tokyo Concert	1974	$30
❑ OJC-345	The Tokyo Concert	1990	$30
❑ OJC-210	Waltz for Debby	198?	$25

MGM

Number	Title	Yr	NM
❑ SE-4723	From Left to Right	1970	$35

MILESTONE

Number	Title	Yr	NM
❑ 47063	Conception	198?	$35
❑ 9151	Jazzhouse	1988	$25
❑ 9125	More from the Vanguard	198?	$25
❑ 47024	Peace Piece & Others	197?	$35
❑ 47034	Spring Leaves	197?	$35
❑ 47066	The Interplay Sessions	198?	$30
❑ 47046	The Second Trio	197?	$35
❑ 9170	The Solo Sessions, Volume 1	1989	$30
❑ 47002	The Village Vanguard Sessions	197?	$35
❑ 47068	Time Remembered	198?	$30
❑ 9164	You're Gonna Hear from Me	198?	$25

MOSAIC

Number	Title	Yr	NM
❑ MQ10-171	The Final Village Vanguard Sessions -- June 1980	1996	$200

PAUSA

Number	Title	Yr	NM
❑ 7050	Symbiosis	1979	$25

RIVERSIDE

Number	Title	Yr	NM
❑ 6197	Bill Evans at Shelly's Manne-Hole	198?	$25
❑ RLP-487 [M]	Bill Evans at Shelly's Manne-Hole, Hollywood, California	1965	$150
❑ RS-9487 [S]	Bill Evans at Shelly's Manne-Hole, Hollywood, California	1965	$150
❑ RLP1129 [S]	Everybody Digs Bill Evans	1959	$300
❑ 6090	Everybody Digs Bill Evans	197?	$30
❑ 6038	Explorations	197?	$30
❑ RLP-473 [M]	How My Heart Sings!	1964	$150
❑ RS-9473 [S]	How My Heart Sings!	1964	$150
❑ RS-9445 [S]	Interplay	1963	$150
❑ RS-3013	Live at Shelly's Manne-Hole	1968	$100
❑ RM-3006 [M]	Live at the Village Vanguard	1967	$100
❑ RS-3006 [S]	Live at the Village Vanguard	1967	$100
❑ RS-9428 [S]	Moonbeams	1962	$150
❑ 6175	Moonbeams	198?	$25
❑ RLP 12-223 [M]	New Jazz Conceptions	1956	$1200

—Photo on cover, label is white with blue print

Number	Title	Yr	NM
❑ RLP 12-223 [M]	New Jazz Conceptions	1958	$300

—New cover, label is blue with microphone logo at top

Number	Title	Yr	NM
❑ RS-3042	Peace Pieces	1969	$100
❑ RM-3001 [M]	Polka Dots and Moonbeams	1967	$100
❑ RS-3001 [S]	Polka Dots and Moonbeams	1967	$100
❑ RLP1162 [S]	Portrait in Jazz	1959	$250
❑ RS-9376 [S]	Sunday at the Village Vanguard	1961	$200
❑ R-018	The Complete Riverside Recordings	1985	$200
❑ 6118	Waltz for Debby	197?	$30

TIMELESS

Number	Title	Yr	NM
❑ LPSJP-331	Consecration I	1990	$35
❑ LPSJP-332	Consecration II	1990	$35

VERVE

Number	Title	Yr	NM
❑ V-8675 [M]	A Simple Matter of Conviction	1966	$35
❑ V6-8675 [S]	A Simple Matter of Conviction	1966	$25
❑ UMV-2107	A Simple Matter of Conviction	198?	$25
❑ V6-8792	Bill Evans Alone	1969	$35
❑ V6-8762	Bill Evans at the Montreux Jazz Festival	1968	$35
❑ 827844-1	Bill Evans at the Montreux Jazz Festival	1986	$25
❑ V6-8762	Bill Evans at the Montreux Jazz Festival	199?	$30

—Classic Records reissue on audiophile vinyl

Number	Title	Yr	NM
❑ V-8683 [M]	Bill Evans at Town Hall	1966	$35
❑ V6-8683 [S]	Bill Evans at Town Hall	1966	$25
❑ V-8578 [M]	Bill Evans Trio '64	1964	$35
❑ V6-8578 [S]	Bill Evans Trio '64	1964	$25
❑ V-8613 [M]	Bill Evans Trio '65	1965	$35
❑ V6-8613 [S]	Bill Evans Trio '65	1965	$25
❑ V-8640 [M]	Bill Evans Trio with Symphony Orchestra	1965	$35
❑ V6-8640 [S]	Bill Evans Trio with Symphony Orchestra	1965	$25
❑ VE-2-2545	California Here I Come	198?	$30
❑ V-8526 [M]	Conversations with Myself	1963	$25
❑ V6-8526 [S]	Conversations with Myself	1963	$30
❑ V-8497 [M]	Empathy	1962	$30
❑ V6-8497 [S]	Empathy	1962	$30
❑ V-8727 [M]	Further Conversations with Myself	1967	$25
❑ V6-8727 [S]	Further Conversations with Myself	1967	$35
❑ V-8655 [M]	Intermodulation	1966	$175
❑ V6-8655 [S]	Intermodulation	1966	$25
❑ UMV-2106	Intermodulation	198?	$25
❑ V3HB-8841	Return Engagement	1973	$25
❑ V-8747 [M]	The Best of Bill Evans	1967	$25
❑ V6-8747 [S]	The Best of Bill Evans	1967	$35
❑ UMV-2053	The Bill Evans Trio at Town Hall	198?	$25
❑ VE-2-2509	Trios and Duos	197?	$35
❑ V6-8777	What's New	1968	$35

WARNER BROS.

Number	Title	Yr	NM
❑ BSK3293	Affinity	1978	$30
❑ BSK3177	New Conversations	1977	$30
❑ HS3411	We Will Meet Again	1979	$30
❑ HS3504	You Must Believe in Spring	1981	$30

EVANS, BILL (2)

No relation to the more prominent man above, he is a saxophone player; he also plays flute and keyboards and is a composer.

Albums

BLUE NOTE

Number	Title	Yr	NM
❑ BT-85111	The Alternative Man	1985	$25

ELEKTRA/MUSICIAN

Number	Title	Yr	NM
❑ 60349	Living in the Crest of a Wave	1986	$25

EVANS, DOC

Cornet player and bandleader.

Albums

AUDIOPHILE

Number	Title	Yr	NM
❑ AP-50 [M]	Classics of the 20's	195?	$40

—Red vinyl

Number	Title	Yr	NM
❑ AP-29 [M]	Dixieland Session	195?	$40
❑ AP-11 [M]	Doc Evans and His Band, Volume 1	195?	$40
❑ AP-12 [M]	Doc Evans and His Band, Volume 2	195?	$40
❑ AP-95	Doc Evans at the Gas Light	1989	$25

—Reissue with same number

Number	Title	Yr	NM
❑ AP-95 [M]	Doc Evans at the Gas Light	196?	$25
❑ AS-95 [S]	Doc Evans at the Gas Light	196?	$30
❑ AP-4	Down in Jungle Town	1987	$25
❑ APS-5968	Reminiscing in Dixieland	196?	$30

—Red vinyl

Number	Title	Yr	NM
❑ AP-31 [M]	The Cornet Artistry of Doc Evans	195?	$40
❑ AP-34 [M]	Traditional Jazz	195?	$40

—Red vinyl

Number	Title	Yr	NM
❑ AP-44 [M]	Traditional Jazz	195?	$40

—Red vinyl

Number	Title	Yr	NM
❑ AP-45 [M]	Traditional Jazz	195?	$40

—Red vinyl

Number	Title	Yr	NM
❑ AP-33 [M]	Traditional Jazz	195?	$40

—Red vinyl

Number	Title	Yr	NM
❑ XL-328 [M]	Traditional Jazz	195?	$40
❑ XL-329 [M]	Traditional Jazz	195?	$40

CONCERT DISC

Number	Title	Yr	NM
❑ CS-47	Doc Evans + 4 = Dixie	1961	$30
❑ CS-48	Muskrat Ramble	196?	$30

FOLKWAYS

Number	Title	Yr	NM
❑ FA-2855	Doc Evans and His Dixieland Jazz Band	195?	$30

JAZZOLOGY

Number	Title	Yr	NM
❑ J-86	Blues in Dixieland	197?	$25
❑ J-87	Command Performance	197?	$25
❑ J-85	Jazz Heritage, Volume 1	197?	$25

SOMA

Number	Title	Yr	NM
❑ MG-1201 [M]	Classic Jazz at Carleton	1954	$40
❑ MG-100 [M]	Dixieland Concert	1953	$50
❑ MG-101 [10]	Dixieland Concert	1953	$50

EVANS, GIL

Pianist, keyboard player, arranger and composer.

Albums

ABC IMPULSE!

Number	Title	Yr	NM
❑ AS-9 [S]	Into the Hot	1968	$35
❑ AS-4 [S]	Out of the Cool	1968	$35
❑ IA-9340	The Great Arrangers	1978	$35

AMPEX

Number	Title	Yr	NM
❑ A-10102	Gil Evans	1971	$35

ANTILLES

Number	Title	Yr	NM
❑ AN-1010	Priestess	198?	$25

ARTISTS HOUSE

Number	Title	Yr	NM
❑ 14	Where Flamingoes Fly	198?	$25

ATLANTIC

Number	Title	Yr	NM
❑ SD1643	Svengali	1973	$30
❑ QD1643 [Q]	Svengali	1973	$30
❑ 90048	Svengali	1983	$20

BLUE NOTE

Number	Title	Yr	NM
❑ BN-LA461-H2	Pacific Standard Time	1975	$35

EMARCY

Number	Title	Yr	NM
❑ 836401-1	Rhythm-A-Ning	1989	$30

FANTASY

Number	Title	Yr	NM
❑ OJC-346	Gil Evans Plus Ten	198?	$25

IMPULSE!

Number	Title	Yr	NM
❑ A-9 [M]	Into the Hot	1962	$120
❑ AS-9 [S]	Into the Hot	1962	$120
❑ A-4 [M]	Out of the Cool	1961	$120
❑ AS-4 [S]	Out of the Cool	1961	$120

INNER CITY

Number	Title	Yr	NM
❑ IC-1110	Little Wing	198?	$30

MCA

Number	Title	Yr	NM
❑ 29034	Into the Hot	198?	$20
❑ 29033	Out of the Cool	198?	$20
❑ 4143	The Great Arrangers	198?	$25

MCA IMPULSE!

Number	Title	Yr	NM
❑ 5653	Out of the Cool	1986	$25

NEW JAZZ

Number	Title	Yr	NM
❑ NJLP-8215 [M]	Big Stuff	1959	$150

—Purple label

Number	Title	Yr	NM
❑ NJLP-8215 [M]	Big Stuff	1965	$150

—Blue label, trident logo at right

PACIFIC JAZZ

Number	Title	Yr	NM
❑ PJ-28 [M]	America's #1 Arranger	1961	$30
❑ PJ-40 [M]	Cannonball Adderley/Gil Evans	1962	$30
❑ ST-40 [S]	Cannonball Adderley/Gil Evans	1962	$30

PRESTIGE

Number	Title	Yr	NM
❑ 24049	An Arranger's Touch	197?	$35
❑ PRST-7756	Big Stuff	1970	$35

RCA VICTOR

Number	Title	Yr	NM
❑ CPL1-0667	Gil Evans Plays Jimi Hendrix	1974	$25
❑ LPM-1057 [M]	There Comes a Time	1955	$80
❑ APL1-1057	There Comes a Time	1976	$30

VERVE

Number	Title	Yr	NM
❑ V6-8838	Previously Unreleased Recordings	1974	$30
❑ V-8555 [M]	The Individualism of Gil Evans	1963	$25
❑ V6-8555 [S]	The Individualism of Gil Evans	1963	$30

WORLD PACIFIC

Number	Title	Yr	NM
❑ WP-1270 [M]	Great Jazz Standards	1959	$150
❑ ST-1027 [S]	Great Jazz Standards	1959	$150
❑ WP-1246 [M]	New Bottle, Old Wine	1958	$150
❑ ST-1011 [S]	New Bottle, Old Wine	1959	$150

Duke Ellington, *The Cosmic Scene*, Columbia CL 1198, red and black label with six "eye" logos, **$150**.

Duke Ellington Orchestra, *Digital Duke*, GRP GR-1038, **$25**.

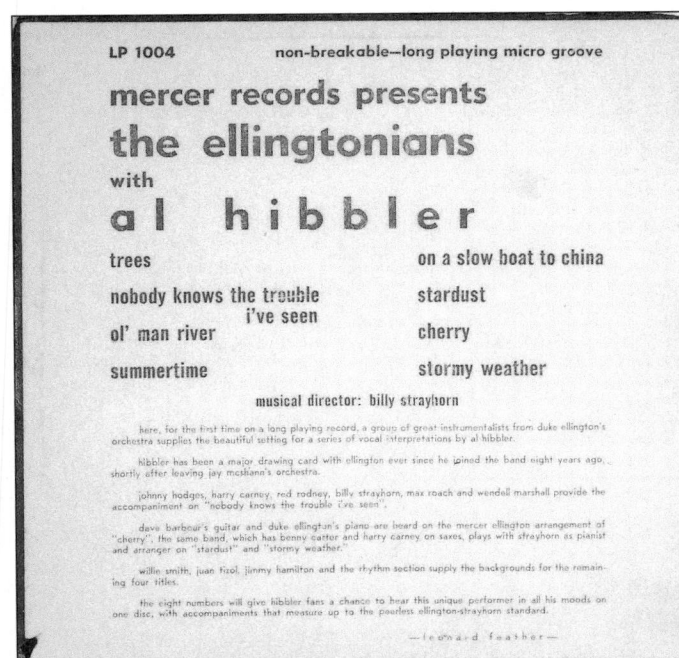

The Ellingtonians with Al Hibbler, *The Ellingtonians with Al Hibbler*, Mercer LP 1004, 10-inch LP, **$250**.

Art Farmer, *When Farmer Met Gryce*, Prestige PRLP-7085, yellow label, **$500**.

EVANS, JOHN
Pianist.

Albums

OMEGA

Number	Title	Yr	NM
❏ OL-49 [M]	Mainstream Jazz Piano	1960	$25
❏ OSL-49 [S]	Mainstream Jazz Piano	1960	$25

EVANS, LEE
Pianist.

Albums

CAPITOL

Number	Title	Yr	NM
❏ T1625 [M]	Big Piano/Big Band/Big Sound	1962	$75
❏ ST1625 [S]	Big Piano/Big Band/Big Sound	1962	$40
❏ T1847 [M]	The Lee Evans Trio	1963	$75
❏ ST1847 [S]	The Lee Evans Trio	1963	$40

EVANS, RICHARD
Bass player.

Albums

ARGO

Number	Title	Yr	NM
❏ LP-675 [M]	Home Cookin'	1961	$30
❏ LPS-675 [S]	Home Cookin'	1961	$30
❏ LP-658 [M]	Richard's Almanac	1960	$30
❏ LPS-658 [S]	Richard's Almanac	1960	$40

EVERGREEN CLASSIC JAZZ BAND

Albums

STOMP OFF

Number	Title	Yr	NM
❏ SOS-1202	Trust Me… I'm a Musician	1991	$25

EVERYMAN BAND
Members: Michael Suchorsky (drums); DAVID TORN (guitar); Bruce Yaw (bass); MARTY FOGEL (saxophones).

Albums

ECM

Number	Title	Yr	NM
❏ 1234	Everyman Band	1983	$30
❏ 1290	Without Warning	1985	$25

EWELL, DON
Pianist.

Albums

ANALOGUE PRODUCTIONS

Number	Title	Yr	NM
❏ APJ-19	Yellow Dog Blues	199?	$60

—*Audiophile reissue on red vinyl*

AUDIOPHILE

Number	Title	Yr	NM
❏ APS-5966	Yellow Dog Blues	196?	$50

CHIAROSCURO

Number	Title	Yr	NM
❏ 130	Don Ewell	1974	$35
❏ 106	Jazz Portrait of the Artist	1972	$35
❏ 127	Take It in Stride	1973	$35

GHB

Number	Title	Yr	NM
❏ 30	Don Ewell in New Orleans	196?	$25

GOOD TIME JAZZ

Number	Title	Yr	NM
❏ L-12046 [M]	Free 'N Easy	1956	$40
❏ S-10046 [S]	Free 'N Easy	1960	$30
❏ L-12021 [M]	Music to Listen to Don Ewell By	1955	$50
❏ L-12043 [M]	The Man Here Plays Fine Piano	1956	$40
❏ S-10043 [S]	The Man Here Plays Fine Piano	1960	$30

JAZZOLOGY

Number	Title	Yr	NM
❏ JCE-84	Don Ewell and Bob Greene Together!	198?	$25
❏ J-29	Don Ewell and the All-Stars	197?	$25
❏ J-69	Don Ewell Quintet	198?	$25

NEW ORLEANS

Number	Title	Yr	NM
❏ NOR-7209	Don Ewell and Herb Hall in New Orleans	198?	$25

STOMP OFF

Number	Title	Yr	NM
❏ SOS-1077	Chicago '57	198?	$25

WINDIN' BALL

Number	Title	Yr	NM
❏ LP-101 [10]	Don Ewell	1953	$50
❏ LP-102 [10]	Don Ewell and Mama Yancey	1953	$50
❏ LP-103 [10]	Don Ewell Plays Tunes Played by the King Oliver Band	1953	$50
❏ LP-103 [M]	Don Ewell Plays Tunes Played by the King Oliver Band	195?	$30

EX-HERMANITES, THE
See TERRY GIBBS AND BILL HARRIS.

EYEBALL
Fusion band led by Dutch pianist and composer Jasper van't Hof.

Albums

CMP

Number	Title	Yr	NM
❏ CMP-11-ST	Eyeball	198?	$30

EYERMANN, TIM, AND EAST COAST OFFERING
Eyermann is a soprano, alto and tenor saxophone player and clarinetist.

Albums

BLUEMOON

Number	Title	Yr	NM
❏ R1-79151	Jazz on L	1989	$30
❏ R1-79163	Outside/Inside	1990	$30

INNER CITY

Number	Title	Yr	NM
❏ IC-1095	Aloha	198?	$30

MCA

Number	Title	Yr	NM
❏ 5494	East Coast Offering	1985	$25
❏ 5589	Walkin' With You	1986	$25

EYGES, DAVID
Cello player.

Albums

MUSIC UNLIMITED

Number	Title	Yr	NM
❏ 7432	Crossroads	1982	$30
❏ 7431	The Arrow	1981	$30

F

FABRIC, BENT
Danish pianist. Also see ACKER BILK.

Albums

ATCO

Number	Title	Yr	NM
❏ 33-148 [M]	Alley Cat	1962	$35
❏ SD 33-148 [S]	Alley Cat	1962	$50
❏ 33-185 [M]	Never Tease Tigers	1966	$30
❏ SD 33-185 [S]	Never Tease Tigers	1966	$35
❏ 33-202 [M]	Operation Lovebirds	1967	$30
❏ SD 33-202 [S]	Operation Lovebirds	1967	$35
❏ 33-164 [M]	Organ Grinder's Swing	1964	$30
❏ SD 33-164 [S]	Organ Grinder's Swing	1964	$35
❏ 33-221 [M]	Relax	1967	$35
❏ SD 33-221 [S]	Relax	1967	$30
❏ 33-173 [M]	The Drunken Penguin	1965	$30
❏ SD 33-173 [S]	The Drunken Penguin	1965	$35
❏ 33-155 [M]	The Happy Puppy	1963	$30
❏ SD 33-155 [S]	The Happy Puppy	1963	$35

FADDIS, JON
Trumpeter.

Albums

BUDDAH

Number	Title	Yr	NM
❏ BDS-5727	Good and Plenty	1979	$30

CONCORD JAZZ

Number	Title	Yr	NM
❏ CJ-291	Legacy	1986	$25

EPIC

Number	Title	Yr	NM
❏ OE45266	Into the FaddisPhere	1989	$75

PABLO

Number	Title	Yr	NM
❏ 2310765	Youngblood	1977	$35

FAGERQUIST, DON
Trumpeter.

Albums

MODE

Number	Title	Yr	NM
❏ LP-124 [M]	Music to Fill a Void	1957	$100

FAME, GEORGIE, AND ANNIE ROSS
Also see each artist's individual listings.

Albums

DRG

Number	Title	Yr	NM
❏ 5197	Georgie Fame and Annie Ross in Hoagland	198?	$30

FAME, GEORGIE
British organist, keyboard player and male vocalist.

Albums

EPIC

Number	Title	Yr	NM
❏ BN26563	Shorty Featuring Georgie Fame	1968	$100
❏ BN26368	The Ballad of Bonnie and Clyde	1968	$100

IMPERIAL

Number	Title	Yr	NM
❏ LP-9331 [M]	Get Away	1966	$175
❏ LP-12331 [R]	Get Away	1966	$150
❏ LP-9282 [M]	Yeh, Yeh	1965	$175
❏ LP-12282 [P]	Yeh, Yeh	1965	$175

—*Entire album is stereo except "Yeh, Yeh" (rechanneled)*

ISLAND

Number	Title	Yr	NM
❏ ILPS9293	Georgie Fame	1975	$25

FAMOUS CASTLE JAZZ BAND, THE

Albums

GOOD TIME JAZZ

Number	Title	Yr	NM
❏ L-12030 [M]	The Famous Castle Jazz Band in Hi-Fi	1957	$40
❏ S-7021 [S]	The Famous Castle Jazz Band in Stereo	1959	$30
❏ S-10030 [S]	The Famous Castle Jazz Band in Stereo	197?	$25
❏ L-12037 [M]	The Famous Castle Jazz Band Plays the Five Pennies	1959	$40
❏ S-10037 [S]	The Famous Castle Jazz Band Plays the Five Pennies	1959	$30

STEREO RECORDS

Number	Title	Yr	NM
❏ S-7021 [S]	The Famous Castle Jazz Band in Stereo	1958	$40

FARLOW, TAL
Guitarist.

Albums

AMERICAN RECORDING SOCIETY

Number	Title	Yr	NM
❏ G-418 [M]	The Swinging Guitar of Tal Farlow	1957	$40

BLUE NOTE

Number	Title	Yr	NM
❏ BLP-5042 [10]	Tal Farlow Quartet	1954	$300

CONCORD JAZZ

Number	Title	Yr	NM
❏ CJ-154	Chromatic Palette	1981	$30
❏ CJ-204	Cookin' on All Burners	1982	$30
❏ CJ-26	Sign of the Times	1976	$30
❏ CJ-57	Tal Farlow '78	1978	$30
❏ CJ-266	The Legendary Tal Farlow	1986	$25

FANTASY

Number	Title	Yr	NM
❏ OJC-356	The Return of Tal Farlow/1969	198?	$25

INNER CITY

Number	Title	Yr	NM
❏ IC-1099	Trilogy	197?	$30

NORGRAN

Number	Title	Yr	NM
❏ MGN-1097 [M]	Autumn in New York	1956	$200
❏ MGN-1101 [M]	Fascinating Rhythm	1956	$200
❏ MGN-1102 [M]	Tal	1956	$100
❏ MGN-1014 [M]	The Artistry of Tal Farlow	1955	$300
❏ MGN-19 [10]	The Tal Farlow Album	1954	$150
❏ MGN-1047 [M]	The Tal Farlow Album	1955	$100

PRESTIGE

Number	Title	Yr	NM
❏ 24042	Guitar Player	197?	$25
❏ PRST-7732	The Return of Tal Farlow/1969	1969	$25

VERVE

Number	Title	Yr	NM
❏ MGV-8123 [M]	A Recital by Tal Farlow	1957	$50

—*Reissue of Norgran 1030*

Number	Title	Yr	NM
❏ V-8123 [M]	A Recital by Tal Farlow	1961	$25
❏ MGV-8184 [M]	Autumn in New York	1957	$200

—*Reissue of Norgran 1097*

Number	Title	Yr	NM
❏ V-8184 [M]	Autumn in New York	1961	$60
❏ 815236-1	Poppin' and Burnin'	198?	$30
❏ MGV-8021 [M]	Tal	1957	$50

—*Reissue of Norgran 1102*

Number	Title	Yr	NM
❏ V-8021 [M]	Tal	1961	$25
❏ UMV-2565	Tal	198?	$25
❏ MGV-8371 [M]	Tal Farlow Plays the Music of Harold Arlen	1960	$80
❏ MGVS-6144 [S]	Tal Farlow Plays the Music of Harold Arlen	1960	$0

—*Canceled*

Number	Title	Yr	NM
❏ V-8371 [M]	Tal Farlow Plays the Music of Harold Arlen	1961	$25
❏ MGV-8370 [M]	The Guitar Artistry of Tal Farlow	1960	$100
❏ MGVS-6143 [S]	The Guitar Artistry of Tal Farlow	1960	$100

Number	Title	Yr	NM
❏ V-8370 [M]	The Guitar Artistry of Tal Farlow	1961	$25
❏ V6-8370 [S]	The Guitar Artistry of Tal Farlow	1961	$35
❏ MGV-8011 [M]	The Interpretations of Tal Farlow	1957	$300
—Reissue of Norgran 1027			
❏ V-8011 [M]	The Interpretations of Tal Farlow	1961	$25
❏ MGV-8138 [M]	The Tal Farlow Album	1957	$100
—Reissue of Norgran 1047			
❏ V-8138 [M]	The Tal Farlow Album	1961	$25
❏ UMV-2584	The Tal Farlow Album	198?	$25
❏ MGV-8289 [M]	This Is Tal Farlow	1958	$150
❏ V-8289 [M]	This Is Tal Farlow	1961	$25
XANADU			
❏ 109	The Fuerst Set	197?	$30
❏ 119	The Second Set	197?	$30

FARMER, ART

Trumpeter and fluegel horn player. Also played something called the "flumpet," a hybrid of the two instruments, starting in 1989. Also see CLIFFORD BROWN; EDDIE COSTA; BENNIE GREEN; THE JAZZTET; THE PRESTIGE BLUES SWINGERS.

Albums

Number	Title	Yr	NM
ABC-PARAMOUNT			
❏ ABC-200 [M]	Last Night When We Were Young	1958	$60
ARGO			
❏ LP-678 [M]	Art	1961	$30
❏ LPS-678 [S]	Art	1961	$30
❏ LP-738 [M]	Perception	1964	$30
❏ LPS-738 [S]	Perception	1964	$30
ATLANTIC			
❏ 1412 [M]	Interaction	1963	$50
❏ SD1412 [S]	Interaction	1963	$50
❏ 1421 [M]	Live at the Half Note	1964	$30
❏ SD1421 [S]	Live at the Half Note	1964	$30
❏ 1442 [M]	Sing Me Softly of the Blues	1965	$25
❏ SD1442 [S]	Sing Me Softly of the Blues	1965	$30
❏ 1430 [M]	To Sweden with Love	1964	$25
❏ SD1430 [S]	To Sweden with Love	1964	$30
COLUMBIA			
❏ CL2746 [M]	Art Farmer Plays the Great Jazz Hits	1967	$30
❏ CS9546 [S]	Art Farmer Plays the Great Jazz Hits	1967	$25
❏ CL2588 [M]	Baroque Sketches	1966	$25
❏ CS9388 [S]	Baroque Sketches	1966	$25
❏ CL2649 [M]	The Time and the Place	1967	$30
❏ CS9449 [S]	The Time and the Place	1967	$25
❏ C238232	Time and Place	198?	$30
COLUMBIA JAZZ ODYSSEY			
❏ PC36826	Art Farmer Plays the Great Jazz Hits	1980	$25
CONCORD JAZZ			
❏ CJ-212	Warm Valley	1982	$30
❏ CJ-179	Work of Art	198?	$30
CONTEMPORARY			
❏ C-14042	Blame It on My Youth	198?	$25
❏ S-7636	On the Road	197?	$35
❏ C-14055	Ph. D.	1989	$30
❏ C-3554 [M]	Portrait of Art Farmer	1958	$250
❏ S-7027 [S]	Portrait of Art Farmer	1959	$250
❏ S-7554	Portrait of Art Farmer	197?	$35
❏ C-14029	Something to Live For: The Music of Billy Strayhorn	1987	$25
CTI			
❏ 7083	Big Blues	1978	$35
❏ 7073	Crawl	1977	$35
❏ 7080	Something You Got	1977	$35
❏ 9000	Yama	198?	$30
FANTASY			
❏ OJC-241	Art Farmer Quintet	1987	$25
❏ OJC-398	Farmer's Market	1989	$30
❏ OJC-478	On the Road	1990	$30
❏ OJC-166	Portrait of Art	198?	$25
❏ OJC-054	The Art Farmer Septet	198?	$25
❏ OJC-018	Two Trumpets	198?	$25
❏ OJC-072	When Farmer Met Gryce	198?	$25
INNER CITY			
❏ IC-6024	Live at Boomer's	197?	$35
❏ IC-6004	The Summer Knows	197?	$35
❏ IC-6014	To Duke with Love	197?	$35
MAINSTREAM			
❏ MRL-371	Gentle Eyes	1972	$25
❏ MRL-332	Homecoming	1971	$25
MERCURY			
❏ MG-20786 [M]	Listen to Art Farmer and the Orchestra	1963	$100
❏ SR-60786 [S]	Listen to Art Farmer and the Orchestra	1963	$100
MOON			

Number	Title	Yr	NM
❏ MLP-014	Art Worker	199?	$35
NEW JAZZ			
❏ NJLP-8258 [M]	Early Art	1961	$150
—Purple label			
❏ NJLP-8258 [M]	Early Art	1965	$150
—Blue label, trident logo at right			
❏ NJLP-8289 [M]	Evening in Casablanca	1962	$150
—Purple label			
❏ NJLP-8289 [M]	Evening in Casablanca	1965	$150
—Blue label, trident logo at right			
❏ NJLP-8203 [M]	Farmer's Market	1958	$150
—Purple label			
❏ NJLP-8203 [M]	Farmer's Market	1965	$150
—Blue label, trident logo at right			
❏ NJLP-8278 [M]	Work of Art	1962	$150
—Purple label			
❏ NJLP-8278 [M]	Work of Art	1965	$150
—Blue label, trident logo at right			
PAUSA			
❏ 7133	From Vienna with Art	198?	$30
❏ 9025	Modern Art	198?	$25
PRESTIGE			
❏ PRLP-193 [10]	Art Farmer Quartet	1954	$300
❏ PRLP-181 [10]	Art Farmer Quintet	1954	$300
❏ PRLP-209 [10]	Art Farmer Quintet	1955	$300
❏ PRLP-7017 [M]	Art Farmer Quintet Featuring Gigi Gryce	1956	$300
—Yellow label with W. 50th St. address			
❏ PRLP-177 [10]	Art Farmer Quintet Featuring Sonny Rollins	1954	$400
❏ PRLP-162 [10]	Art Farmer Septet	1953	$300
❏ PRLP-7031 [M]	Art Farmer Septet	1956	$300
—Yellow label with W. 50th St. address			
❏ PRST-7665	Early Art	1969	$35
❏ 24032	Farmer's Market	197?	$35
❏ PRLP-7344 [M]	Trumpets All Out	1964	$50
❏ PRST-7344 [R]	Trumpets All Out	1964	$30
❏ PRLP-7085 [M]	When Farmer Met Gryce	1957	$500
SCEPTER			
❏ S-521 [M]	The Many Faces of Art Farmer	1964	$25
❏ SS-521 [S]	The Many Faces of Art Farmer	1964	$30
SOUL NOTE			
❏ SN-1026	I'll Take Manhattan	198?	$30
❏ SN-1046	Mirage	1983	$30
❏ SN-1076	You Make Me Smile	1985	$30
STEREO RECORDS			
❏ S-7027 [S]	Portrait of Art Farmer	1958	$40
UNITED ARTISTS			
❏ UAL-4062 [M]	Aztec Suite	1959	$50
❏ UAS-5062 [S]	Aztec Suite	1959	$40
❏ UAL-4047 [M]	Brass Shout	1959	$50
❏ UAS-5047 [S]	Brass Shout	1959	$40
❏ UAL-4007 [M]	Modern Art	1958	$250
❏ UAS-5007 [S]	Modern Art	1959	$250

FARMER, ART/ART TAYLOR

Also see each artist's individual listings.

Albums

Number	Title	Yr	NM
PRESTIGE			
❏ PRLP-7342 [M]	Hard Cookin'	1964	$50
❏ PRST-7342 [R]	Hard Cookin'	1964	$30

FARR, JIMMY

Albums

Number	Title	Yr	NM
CIRCLE			
❏ CLP-26	Best by Farr	197?	$25

FARRAH, SHAMEK

Alto saxophone player.

Albums

Number	Title	Yr	NM
STRATA-EAST			
❏ SES-7412	First Impressions	1974	$40

FARRELL, JOE; FLORA PURIM; AIRTO MOREIRA

Also see each artist's individual listings (for Moreira, see AIRTO).

Albums

Number	Title	Yr	NM
REFERENCE RECORDINGS			
❏ RR-24	Three-Way Mirror	1989	$25

FARRELL, JOE

Tenor and soprano saxophone player, flutist and clarinetist. Also see FUSE ONE.

Albums

Number	Title	Yr	NM
CONTEMPORARY			
❏ C-14002	Sonic Text	1980	$30
CTI			
❏ 6053	Canned Funk	1975	$35
❏ 6003	Joe Farrell Quartet	1970	$25
❏ 6023	Moon Germs	1972	$25
❏ 8003	Moon Germs	197?	$25
—Reissue of 6023			
❏ 6014	Outback	1971	$25
❏ 8005	Outback	197?	$25
—Reissue of 6014			
❏ 6034	Penny Arcade	1973	$35
❏ 6065	Song of the Wind	1976	$35
❏ 6042	Upon This Rock	1974	$35
JAZZ A LA CARTE			
❏ 4	Farrell's Inferno	1979	$35
WARNER BROS.			
❏ BS3121	La Cathedral y El Toro	1977	$30
❏ BSK3225	Night Dancing	1978	$30
XANADU			
❏ 174	Skateboard Park	1979	$35

FASCIANI, GUY

Albums

Number	Title	Yr	NM
INNER CITY			
❏ IC-1161	The Stairway Caper	198?	$35

FASOLI, CLAUDIO

Tenor and soprano saxophone player.

Albums

Number	Title	Yr	NM
SOUL NOTE			
❏ SN-1071	Lido	1983	$35

FATOOL, NICK

Drummer and bandleader.

Albums

Number	Title	Yr	NM
JAZZOLOGY			
❏ J-158	Nick Fatool's Jazz Band -- Spring of '87	1987	$25

FATTBURGER

Members in the 1980s: Tom Aros (percussion); Carl Evans Jr. (keyboards); Mark Hunter (bass); Kevin Koch (drums); Steve Laury (guitar).

Albums

Number	Title	Yr	NM
INTIMA			
❏ SJ-73287	Good News	1987	$25
❏ D1-73334	Living in Paradise	1988	$25
❏ D1-73503	Time Will Tell	1989	$30
OPTIMISM			
❏ OP-2001	One of a Kind	198?	$30

FAVERO, ALBERTO

Argentinean saxophone player, composer and conductor.

Albums

Number	Title	Yr	NM
CATALYST			
❏ 7914	Suite Trane	197?	$30

FAVRE, PIERRE

Drummer and percussionist.

Albums

Number	Title	Yr	NM
ECM			
❏ 1274	Singing Drums	1985	$30

FAWKES, WALLY

Clarinetist and bandleader.

Albums

Number	Title	Yr	NM
STOMP OFF			
❏ SOS-1060	That's the Blues, Old Man	198?	$25
❏ SOS-1144	Whatever Next!	1988	$25

Number	Title	Yr	NM

FAYE, FRANCES
Pianist and female singer.

Albums

BETHLEHEM

| ❏ BCP-6006 | Bad, Bad, Frances Faye | 1976 | $35 |

—Reissue of 23, distributed by RCA Victor

❏ BCP-6017 [M]	Frances Faye Sings Folk Songs	1957	$250
❏ BCP-23 [M]	I'm Wild Again	1955	$250
❏ BCP-62 [M]	Relaxin' with Frances Faye	1957	$250

CAPITOL

| ❏ H512 [10] | No Reservations | 1954 | $150 |
| ❏ T512 [M] | No Reservations | 1955 | $80 |

—Turquoise or gray label

| ❏ T512 [M] | No Reservations | 1958 | $60 |

—Black label with colorband, logo at left

GENE NORMAN

| ❏ GNP-41 [M] | Caught in the Act | 1958 | $40 |
| ❏ GNP-92 [M] | Caught in the Act, Volume 2 | 1959 | $40 |

GNP CRESCENDO

❏ GNP-41 [M]	Caught in the Act	196?	$35
❏ GNPS-41 [S]	Caught in the Act	196?	$30
❏ GNP-92 [M]	Caught in the Act, Volume 2	196?	$35
❏ GNPS-92 [S]	Caught in the Act, Volume 2	196?	$30

IMPERIAL

| ❏ LP-9063 [M] | Frances Faye | 1959 | $0 |

—Canceled

❏ LP-9158 [M]	Frances Faye Sings the Blues	1961	$150
❏ LP-9059 [M]	Frances Faye Swings Fats Domino	1958	$150
❏ LP-12007 [M]	Frances Faye Swings Fats Domino	1959	$150

REGINA

| ❏ R-315 [M] | You Gotta Go! Go! Go! | 1964 | $60 |
| ❏ RS-315 [S] | You Gotta Go! Go! Go! | 1964 | $60 |

VERVE

❏ MGV-2147 [M]	Frances Faye in Frenzy	1961	$40
❏ V-2147 [M]	Frances Faye in Frenzy	1961	$25
❏ V-8434 [M]	Swinging All the Way with Frances Faye	1962	$25
❏ V6-8434 [S]	Swinging All the Way with Frances Faye	1962	$30

FAZOLA, IRVING
Clarinetist and saxophone player.

Albums

MERCURY

| ❏ MG-25016 [10] | Irving Fazola and His Dixielanders | 1950 | $100 |

FAZOLA, IRVING/GEORGE HARTMANN
Also see IRVING FAZOLA.

Albums

EMARCY

| ❏ MG-36022 [M] | New Orleans Express | 1954 | $200 |

FEATHER, LEONARD
Best known as a jazz critic and author, Feather didn't merely write on the subject; he also was a pianist, arranger and composer.

Albums

ABC-PARAMOUNT

| ❏ ABC-110 [M] | Swingin' on the Vibories | 1956 | $60 |

INTERLUDE

| ❏ MO-511 [M] | Leonard Feather Presents 52nd Street | 1959 | $40 |
| ❏ ST-1011 [S] | Leonard Feather Presents 52nd Street | 1959 | $30 |

MAINSTREAM

| ❏ MRL-388 | Freedom Jazz Dance | 1974 | $25 |
| ❏ MRL-348 | Night Blooming Jazzmen | 1972 | $25 |

MGM

❏ E-3494 [M]	Hi-Fi Suite	1957	$50
❏ E-3650 [M]	Oh, Captain!	1958	$50
❏ E-270 [10]	Winter Sequence	1954	$200

MODE

| ❏ LP-127 [M] | Leonard Feather Presents Bop | 1957 | $60 |

FEATHER, LORRAINE
Female singer and composer. Also see FULL SWING.

Albums

CONCORD JAZZ

| ❏ CJ-78 | Sweet Lorraine | 1979 | $30 |

FEATHER (2)
Vocal group.

Albums

DISCOVERY

❏ DS-867	ChenYu Lips	198?	$25
❏ DS-821	Goin' Through Changes	198?	$25
❏ DS-903	Zanzibar	1986	$25

FELDER, WILTON
Bass player and composer. Also see THE CRUSADERS.

Albums

ABC

| ❏ AA-1109 | We All Have a Star | 1978 | $35 |

MCA

❏ 5406	Gentle Fire	1983	$25
❏ 5144	Inherit the Wind	1980	$25
❏ 27031	Inherit the Wind	198?	$20

—Reissue

❏ 42096	Love Is a Rush	1987	$25
❏ 5510	Secrets	1985	$25
❏ AA-1109	We All Have a Star	1979	$25

—Reissue of ABC 1109

| ❏ 700 | We All Have a Star | 198? | $20 |

—Budget-line reissue of MCA 1109

WORLD PACIFIC

| ❏ ST-20152 | Bullitt | 196? | $150 |

FELDMAN, VICTOR
Vibraphone player and pianist. Also see CURTIS AMY.

Albums

AVA

| ❏ A-19 [M] | Soviet Jazz Themes | 1963 | $60 |
| ❏ AS-19 [S] | Soviet Jazz Themes | 1963 | $60 |

CHOICE

| ❏ CRS1005 [M] | Your Smile | 1974 | $35 |

COHEARANT

| ❏ CSR1001 | In My Pocket | 1977 | $40 |

CONCORD JAZZ

| ❏ CJ-38 | The Artful Dodger | 1977 | $30 |

CONTEMPORARY

❏ M-5005 [M]	Latinsville	1960	$350
❏ S-9005 [S]	Latinsville	1960	$300
❏ S-7541 [S]	Suite Sixteen	1959	$250
❏ C-3549 [M]	The Arrival of Victor Feldman	1958	$250
❏ S-7549 [S]	The Arrival of Victor Feldman	1959	$250

FANTASY

| ❏ OJC-402 | Merry Olde Soul | 1989 | $30 |
| ❏ OJC-268 | The Arrival of Victor Feldman | 1987 | $25 |

INFINITY

| ❏ 5000 [M] | A Taste of Honey and a Taste of Bossa Nova | 1962 | $60 |

INTERLUDE

| ❏ MO-510 [M] | With Mallets Aforethought | 1959 | $40 |

—Reissue of Mode LP

MODE

| ❏ LP-120 [M] | Victor Feldman on Vibes | 1957 | $120 |

NAUTILUS

| ❏ NR-50 | The Secret of the Andes | 1982 | $50 |

—Audiophile vinyl

PACIFIC JAZZ

❏ ST-20128 [S]	Venezuela Joropo	196?	$60
❏ PJ-20128 [M]	Venezuela Joropo	196?	$60
❏ PJ-10121 [M]	Victor Feldman Plays Everything in Sight	196?	$50
❏ ST-20121 [S]	Victor Feldman Plays Everything in Sight	196?	$60

PALO ALTO

❏ PA-8066	Fiesta	1984	$25
❏ PA-8053	The Secret of the Andes	1982	$25
❏ PA-8056	To Chopin with Love	1983	$25

RIVERSIDE

| ❏ RLP-366 [M] | Merry Ole Soul | 1961 | $200 |
| ❏ RS-9366 [S] | Merry Ole Soul | 1961 | $200 |

VEE JAY

| ❏ LP-2507 [M] | It's a Wonderful World | 1965 | $50 |

| ❏ LP-1096 [M] | Love Me with All Your Heart | 1964 | $60 |

WORLD PACIFIC

| ❏ WP-1807 [M] | Stop the World, I Want to Get Off | 1962 | $100 |
| ❏ ST-1807 [S] | Stop the World, I Want to Get Off | 1962 | $150 |

—Black vinyl

| ❏ ST-1807 [S] | Stop the World, I Want to Get Off | 1962 | $200 |

—Yellow vinyl

FELICE, DEE
Produced by James Brown.

Albums

BETHLEHEM

| ❏ B-10000 | In Heat | 1969 | $50 |

—Produced by JAMES BROWN.

FELICE, ERNICE
Accordion player.

Albums

CAPITOL

| ❏ H192 [10] | Ernice Felice Quartet | 1950 | $100 |

FENIX JAZZ BAND OF ARGENTINA, THE

Albums

STOMP OFF

| ❏ SOS-1129 | Grandpa's Spells | 1987 | $25 |

FERGUSON, ALLYN
Composer and arranger.

Albums

AVA

| ❏ A-32 [M] | Pictures at an Exhibition Framed in Jazz | 1963 | $30 |
| ❏ AS-32 [S] | Pictures at an Exhibition Framed in Jazz | 1963 | $30 |

DISCOVERY

| ❏ DS-810 | Pictures at an Exhibition Framed in Jazz | 1980 | $30 |

—Reissue of AS-32

FERGUSON, MAYNARD
Trumpeter and bandleader. Also see CHRIS CONNOR.

Albums

BASF

| ❏ 20662 | Trumpet Rhapsody | 1973 | $30 |

BLACK HAWK

| ❏ BKH-50101 | Body and Soul | 1986 | $25 |

BLUEBIRD

| ❏ 6455-1-RB | The Bluebird Dreamband | 1987 | $25 |

CAMEO

❏ C-1066 [M]	Come Blow Your Horn	1964	$50
❏ SC-1066 [S]	Come Blow Your Horn	1964	$60
❏ C-1046 [M]	The New Sounds of Maynard Ferguson	1963	$50
❏ SC-1046 [S]	The New Sounds of Maynard Ferguson	1963	$60

COLUMBIA

| ❏ C31117 | Alive and Well in London | 1972 | $30 |
| ❏ PC31117 | Alive and Well in London | 198? | $20 |

—Budget-line reissue

| ❏ JC35480 | Carnival | 1978 | $25 |
| ❏ PC35480 | Carnival | 1980 | $20 |

—Budget-line reissue

| ❏ KC33007 | Chameleon | 1974 | $30 |
| ❏ PC33007 | Chameleon | 1975 | $25 |

—Early reissue of KC 33007; no bar code

| ❏ PC33007 | Chameleon | 1980 | $20 |

—Budget-line reissue with bar code

| ❏ PC34457 | Conquistador | 1977 | $25 |

—No bar code

| ❏ PCQ34457 [Q] | Conquistador | 1977 | $60 |
| ❏ PC34457 | Conquistador | 1980 | $20 |

—Budget-line reissue with bar code

| ❏ HC44457 | Conquistador | 1982 | $100 |

—Half-speed mastered edition

❏ FC37713	Hollywood	1982	$25
❏ JC36124	Hot	1979	$25
❏ JC36766	It's My Time	1980	$25

Number	Title	Yr	NM
❏ PC36978	Maynard Ferguson	1981	$25
❏ C30466	M.F. Horn	1971	$30
❏ PC30466	M.F. Horn	198?	$20
—Budget-line reissue			
❏ KC32403	M.F. Horn/3	1973	$30
❏ PC32403	M.F. Horn/3	198?	$20
—Budget-line reissue			
❏ KG32732	M.F. Horn 4 & 5/Live at	1973	$35
	Jimmy's		
❏ PG32732	M.F. Horn 4 & 5/Live at	198?	$25
	Jimmy's		
—Budget-line reissue			
❏ CG33660	M.F. Horn/M.F. Horn Two	1975	$35
❏ KC31709	M.F. Horn Two	1972	$30
❏ PC31709	M.F. Horn Two	198?	$20
—Budget-line reissue			
❏ JC34971	New Vintage	1977	$25
❏ PC33953	Primal Scream	1976	$25
—No bar code			
❏ JC36361	The Best of Maynard	1980	$25
	Ferguson		
❏ PC36361	The Best of Maynard	1986	$20
	Ferguson		
—Budget-line reissue			
EMARCY			
❏ MG-36076 [M]	Around the Horn with	1956	$200
	Maynard Ferguson		
❏ MG-36114 [M]	Boy with Lots of Brass	1957	$200
❏ MG-26024 [10]	Dimensions	1954	$300
❏ MG-36044 [M]	Dimensions	1956	$200
❏ MG-36009 [M]	Jam Session Featuring	1955	$250
	Maynard Ferguson		
❏ MG-36021 [M]	Maynard Ferguson Octet	1955	$200
❏ MG-26017 [10]	Maynard Ferguson's	1954	$300
	Hollywood Party		
❏ MG-36046 [M]	Maynard Ferguson's	1956	$200
	Hollywood Party		
❏ EMS-2-406	Stratospheric	1976	$30
EMUS			
❏ ES-12024 [S]	Maynard	197?	$25
—Reissue of Roulette material			
ENTERPRISE			
❏ S-13-101	Ridin' High	1968	$35
FORUM			
❏ F-9035 [M]	Jazz for Dancing	196?	$30
❏ SF-9035 [S]	Jazz for Dancing	196?	$35
INTIMA			
❏ D1-73390	Big Bop Nouveau	1990	$30
❏ SJ-73279	High Voltage	1987	$30
MAINSTREAM			
❏ MRL-372	6 By 6	1973	$30
❏ 805	Big "F"	1974	$35
❏ 56031 [M]	Color Him Wild	1965	$35
❏ S-6031 [S]	Color Him Wild	1965	$50
❏ MRL-359	Dues	1972	$30
❏ 56060 [M]	Maynard Ferguson Sextet	1966	$35
❏ S-6060 [S]	Maynard Ferguson Sextet	1966	$50
❏ MRL-316	Screamin' Blue	1971	$30
❏ 56045 [M]	The Blues Roar	1965	$35
❏ S-6045 [S]	The Blues Roar	1965	$50
MERCURY			
❏ MG-20556 [M]	Boy with Lots of Brass	1960	$100
❏ SR-60124 [S]	Boy with Lots of Brass	1960	$100
MOSAIC			
❏ MQ14-156	The Complete Roulette	1994	$250
	Recordings of the Maynard		
	Ferguson Orchestra		
NAUTILUS			
❏ NR-57	Storm	1983	$40
—Audiophile vinyl			
PALO ALTO			
❏ PA-8077	Live from San Francisco	1985	$25
❏ PA-8052	Storm	1983	$25
PAUSA			
❏ 7037	Trumpet Rhapsody	1980	$25
—Reissue of BASF LP			
PRESTIGE			
❏ PRLP-7636	Maynard Ferguson 1969	1969	$35
ROULETTE			
❏ R52027 [M]	A Message from Birdland	1959	$60
❏ SR52027 [S]	A Message from Birdland	1959	$60
❏ R52012 [M]	A Message from Newport	1958	$60
❏ SR52012 [S]	A Message from Newport	1958	$60
❏ RE-116	A Message from Newport/	1972	$35
	Newport Suite		
—Reissue of 52012 and 52047 in one package			
❏ R52055 [M]	Let's Face the Music and	1960	$60
	Dance		
❏ SR52055 [S]	Let's Face the Music and	1960	$60
	Dance		
❏ R52064 [M]	Maynard '61	1961	$60

Number	Title	Yr	NM
❏ SR52064 [S]	Maynard '61	1961	$60
❏ RE-122	Maynard '61/Si! Si! M.F.	1973	$35
—Reissue of 52064 and 52084 in one package			
❏ R52083 [M]	Maynard '62	1962	$35
❏ SR52083 [S]	Maynard '62	1962	$50
❏ R52097 [M]	Maynard '63	1963	$35
❏ SR52097 [S]	Maynard '63	1963	$50
❏ R52107 [M]	Maynard '64	1964	$35
❏ SR52107 [S]	Maynard '64	1964	$50
❏ R52038 [M]	Maynard Ferguson Plays	1959	$60
	Jazz for Dancing		
❏ SR52038 [S]	Maynard Ferguson Plays	1959	$60
	Jazz for Dancing		
❏ R52047 [M]	Newport Suite	1960	$60
❏ SR52047 [S]	Newport Suite	1960	$60
❏ R52084 [M]	Si! Si! M.F.	1962	$35
❏ SR52084 [S]	Si! Si! M.F.	1962	$50
❏ R52058 [M]	Swingin' My Way Through	1960	$60
	College		
❏ SR52058 [S]	Swingin' My Way Through	1960	$60
	College		
❏ SK-101	The Ferguson Years	197?	$35
❏ R52110 [M]	The World of Maynard	1964	$35
	Ferguson		
❏ SR52110 [S]	The World of Maynard	1964	$50
	Ferguson		
TRIP			
❏ 5558	Around the Horn with	197?	$20
	Maynard Ferguson		
❏ 5507	Dimensions	197?	$20
❏ 5525	Jam Session Featuring	197?	$20
	Maynard Ferguson		
VIK			
❏ LX-1070 [M]	Birdland Dream Band, Vol. 1	1957	$75
❏ LX-1077 [M]	Birdland Dream Band, Vol. 2	1957	$75

FERLINGHETTI, LAWRENCE

Jazz-influenced beat poet.

Albums

FANTASY			
❏ 7004 [M]	The Impeachment of	1958	$200
	Eisenhower		
—Red vinyl			

FERRE, BOULOU

Guitarist.

Albums

4 CORNERS OF THE WORLD			
❏ FCL-4211 [M]	Boulou with the Paris All	1966	$25
	Stars		
❏ FCS-4211 [S]	Boulou with the Paris All	1966	$30
	Stars		
❏ FCL-4234 [M]	Jazz/Left Bank	1967	$30
❏ FCS-4234 [S]	Jazz/Left Bank	1967	$25
—As "Boulou with the Paris All Stars"			
STEEPLECHASE			
❏ SCS-1222	Nuages	198?	$30
❏ SCS-1210	Relax and Enjoy	198?	$30

FERRE, BOULOU AND ELOIS

Elois Ferre is a guitarist. Also see BOULOU FERRE.

Albums

STEEPLECHASE			
❏ SCS-1140	Gypsy Dreams	198?	$30
❏ SCS-1120	Pour Django	198?	$30

FERRE, BOULOU/NIELS-HENNING ORSTED PEDERSEN/ELOIS FERRE

Also see BOULOU AND ELOIS FERRE; NIELS-HENNING ORSTED PEDERSEN.

Albums

STEEPLECHASE			
❏ SCS-1171	Trinity	1982	$30

FETTIG, MARY

Alto and soprano saxophone player and flutist.

Albums

CONCORD JAZZ			
❏ CJ-273	In Good Company	1985	$25

Number	Title	Yr	NM
FIELDING, JANE			

Female singer.

Albums

JAZZ WEST			
❏ LP-5 [M]	Embers Glow	1956	$300
❏ LP-3 [M]	Jazz Trio for Voice, Piano	1955	$300
	and Bass		

FIELDING, JERRY

Bandleader, arranger and composer. Also see THE HI-LO'S.

Albums

ABC-PARAMOUNT			
❏ ABC-542 [M]	Hollywood Brass	1966	$35
❏ ABCS-542 [S]	Hollywood Brass	1966	$25
COMMAND			
❏ RS 33-921 [M]	Near East Brass	1967	$30
❏ RS921SD [S]	Near East Brass	1967	$35
DECCA			
❏ DL8450 [M]	Fielding's Formula	1957	$120
❏ DL8669 [M]	Hollywood Wind Jazztet	1958	$120
❏ DL8100 [M]	Sweet with a Beat	1955	$150
❏ DL8371 [M]	Swingin' in Hi-Fi	1956	$150
KAPP			
❏ KL-1026 [M]	Dance Concert	1956	$50
SIGNATURE			
❏ SM-1028 [M]	Favorite Christmas Music	1960	$25
❏ SS-1028 [S]	Favorite Christmas Music	1960	$30
TIME			
❏ 52059 [M]	A Bit of Ireland	196?	$35
❏ S-2059 [S]	A Bit of Ireland	196?	$25
❏ 52042 [M]	Magnificence in Brass	196?	$35
❏ S-2042 [S]	Magnificence in Brass	196?	$25
❏ 52119 [M]	We Like Brass	196?	$35
❏ S-2119 [S]	We Like Brass	196?	$25
TREND			
❏ TL-1000 [10]	Jerry Fielding and His Great	1953	$120
	New Orchestra		
❏ TL-1004 [10]	Jerry Fielding Plays a Dance	1954	$100
	Concert		

FIELDS, BRANDON

Tenor saxophone player.

Albums

NOVA			
❏ 8602	The Other Side of the Story	1986	$25
❏ 8811	The Traveler	1988	$25

FIELDS, HERBIE

Tenor saxophone player and clarinetist.

Albums

DECCA			
❏ DL8130 [M]	Blow Hot -- Blow Cool	1956	$150
FRATERNITY			
❏ F-1011 [M]	Fields in Clover	1959	$60
RKO UNIQUE			
❏ ULP-146 [M]	A Night at Kitty's	1957	$50

FIELDS, SHEP

Bandleader and arranger.

Albums

CIRCLE			
❏ 133	Shep Fields and His	199?	$25
	Orchestra 1947-51		
❏ 38	Shep Fields and His	198?	$25
	Rippling Rhythm Orchestra		
	1947-50		
DOT			
❏ DLP-3348 [M]	The Rippling Rhythm of	1960	$75
	Shep Fields		
❏ DLP-25348 [S]	The Rippling Rhythm of	1960	$75
	Shep Fields		
GOLDEN CREST			
❏ S-3037 [R]	Rippling Rhythms	196?	$30
❏ 3037 [M]	Rippling Rhythms	196?	$25
❏ S-3061 [R]	Shep Fields at the	196?	$30
	Shamrock Hilton		
❏ 3061 [M]	Shep Fields at the	196?	$25
	Shamrock Hilton		
HINDSIGHT			
❏ HSR-179	Shep Fields and His	198?	$25
	Orchestra 1942		
❏ HSR-160	Shep Fields' New Music,	198?	$25
	1942-44		
JUBILEE			

Number	Title	Yr	NM
❏ JLP-1056 [M]	Cocktails, Dinner and Dancing	1958	$30

SUNBEAM

❏ 316	Shep Fields and His Rippling Rhythm Orchestra 1936-38	198?	$25

FINE, MILO

Albums

FUSETRON

❏ 010	Another Outbreak of Iconoclasm (Two Eggs, Slightly Beaten)	1995	$35

HAT ART

❏ 2033	Old Eyes	1983	$30

HAT HUT

❏ 0E	Hah!	1977	$35
❏ 0S/T	MFG in Minnesota	1978	$25
❏ 1RO-1	Old Eyes	1980	$35
❏ 0H	The Constant Extension of Inescapable Tradition	1978	$35

SHIH SHIH WU AI

❏ 3	Against the Betrayers	1980	$25
❏ 6	April/October 1991	1992	$35
❏ 5	Get Down! Shove It! It's Tango Time!	1986	$25
❏ 2	Improvisations (Being Free)	1975	$25
❏ 4	Lucid Anarchists (Meat with Two Potatoes)	1981	$25

FIREHOUSE FIVE PLUS TWO, THE

Jazz band comprising employees of the Walt Disney Company, led by trombonist Ward Kimball. The personnel changed frequently over the years.

Albums

GOOD TIME JAZZ

❏ L-12044 [M]	Around the World	1961	$30
❏ S-10044 [S]	Around the World	1961	$30
❏ L-12040 [M]	Dixieland Favorites	1960	$30
❏ S-10040 [S]	Dixieland Favorites	1960	$30
❏ L-1 [10]	The Firehouse Five Plus Two, Volume 1	1953	$50
❏ L-2 [10]	The Firehouse Five Plus Two, Volume 2	1953	$50
❏ L-6 [10]	The Firehouse Five Plus Two, Volume 3	1953	$50
❏ L-16 [10]	The Firehouse Five Plus Two, Volume 4	1953	$50
❏ L-12049 [M]	The Firehouse Five Plus Two at Disneyland	1962	$30
❏ S-10049 [S]	The Firehouse Five Plus Two at Disneyland	1962	$30
❏ L-12038 [M]	The Firehouse Five Plus Two Crashes a Party	1960	$30
❏ S-10038 [S]	The Firehouse Five Plus Two Crashes a Party	1960	$30
❏ L-12018 [M]	The Firehouse Five Plus Two Goes South!	1955	$40
❏ L-23 [10]	The Firehouse Five Plus Two Goes South!, Volume 5	1954	$60
❏ L-12052 [M]	The Firehouse Five Plus Two Goes to a Fire	1964	$30
❏ S-10052 [S]	The Firehouse Five Plus Two Goes to a Fire	1964	$30
❏ L-12028 [M]	The Firehouse Five Plus Two Goes to Sea	1957	$30
❏ S-10028 [S]	The Firehouse Five Plus Two Goes to Sea	1960	$30
❏ L-12014 [M]	The Firehouse Five Plus Two Plays for Lovers	1955	$40
❏ L-12010 [M]	The Firehouse Five Story, Volume 1	1955	$40
❏ L-12011 [M]	The Firehouse Five Story, Volume 2	1955	$40
❏ L-12012 [M]	The Firehouse Five Story, Volume 3	1955	$40
❏ L-12054 [M]	Twenty Years Later	196?	$30
❏ S-10054 [S]	Twenty Years Later	1969	$30

STEREO RECORDS

❏ S-7005 [S]	The Firehouse Five Plus Two Goes to Sea	1959	$40

FIRST HOUSE

Members: Ken Stubbs (alto saxophone); Django Bates (piano, tenor horn); Mick Hutton (bass); Martin France (drums).

Albums

ECM

❏ 1393	Cantilena	1990	$30
❏ 1307	Erendira	1987	$25

FIRST JAZZ PIANO QUARTET, THE

Members: Irving Joseph; Bernie Leighton; Morris Nanton; Moe Weschler.

Albums

WARNER BROS.

❏ W1274 [M]	The First Jazz Piano Quartet	1959	$30
❏ WS1274 [S]	The First Jazz Piano Quartet	1959	$30

FISCHER, CLARE

Pianist, organist, keyboard player and composer.

Albums

ATLANTIC

❏ SD1520	Thesaurus	1969	$35

COLUMBIA

❏ CL2691 [M]	Songs for Rainy Day Lovers	1967	$30
❏ CS9491 [S]	Songs for Rainy Day Lovers	1967	$35

DISCOVERY

❏ DS-820	Alone Together	198?	$25
❏ DS-786	America	1978	$30
❏ DS-934	By and With Himself	1987	$25
❏ DS-852	Clare Fischer and the Sometimes Voices	1982	$25
❏ DS-914	Crazy Bird	1984	$25
❏ DS-807	Duality	1979	$30
❏ DS-921	Free Fall	1986	$25
❏ DS-835	Machacha	198?	$25
❏ DS-817	Salsa Picante	1979	$30
❏ DS-798	'Twas Only Yesterday	1978	$30

LIGHT

❏ 5544	Love Is Surrender	197?	$30

PACIFIC JAZZ

❏ PJ-77 [M]	Extension	1963	$30
❏ ST-77 [S]	Extension	1963	$30
❏ PJ-52 [M]	First Time Out	1962	$30
❏ ST-52 [S]	First Time Out	1962	$30
❏ PJ-10096 [M]	Manteca	1966	$35
❏ ST-20096 [S]	Manteca	1966	$25
❏ PJ-67 [M]	Surging Ahead	1963	$30
❏ ST-67 [S]	Surging Ahead	1963	$30

PAUSA

❏ 7086	2 Plus 2	198?	$25

REVELATION

❏ REV-2	Easy Living	1968	$35
❏ REV-37	Head, Heart and Hands	198?	$25
❏ REV-31	Jazz Song	1979	$30
❏ REV-6	One to Get Ready, Four to Go	1968	$35
❏ REV-15	Reclamation Act of 1972	1972	$35
❏ REV-23	T'Da-a-a!	1976	$35
❏ REV-13	The Great White Hope	1969	$35
❏ REV-26	The State of His Art	1976	$30

WORLD PACIFIC

❏ WP-1830 [M]	So Danco Samba	1964	$100
❏ ST-21830 [S]	So Danco Samba	1964	$100

FISCHER, LOU

Bassist. Also see THE CRUSADERS.

Albums

SEA BREEZE

❏ SB-2012	Royal St.	198?	$25

FISCHER, WILLIAM S.

Moog synthesizer player, composer and arranger.

Albums

EMBRYO

❏ 529	Circles	1970	$30

FISELE, JERRY

Albums

DELMAR

❏ DL-101 [10]	Jerry Fisele and the Fabulous Windy City Six	1954	$50

FISHER, EDDIE, QUINTET

Guitarist and occasional male singer, this is not the pop singer of the 1950s.

Albums

CADET

❏ CA-848	The Next Hundred Years	1971	$35
❏ LPS-828	The Third Cup	1969	$35

STANG

❏ 1032	Hot Lunch	1977	$35

FISHER, ELLIOT

Violinist (regular and electronic).

Albums

DOBRE

❏ 1003	In the Land of Make Believe	1976	$50

FISHER, KING

Trumpeter and bandleader.

Albums

JAZZOLOGY

❏ J-13	King Fisher and His All Stars	196?	$30

FITCH, MAL

Male singer, pianist and composer.

Albums

EMARCY

❏ MG-36041 [M]	Mal Fitch	1956	$200

FITE, BUDDY

Guitarist.

Albums

BELL

❏ 6058	Buddy Fite and Friend	1970	$35

CYCLONE

❏ CY4100	Buddy Fite	1971	$30
❏ CY4110	Changes	1972	$30

DIFFERENT DRUMMER

❏ 1001	Buddy Fite Plays for Satin Dolls	1975	$35

FITZGERALD, ELLA, AND BILLIE HOLIDAY

Also see each artist's individual listings.

Albums

AMERICAN RECORDING SOCIETY

❏ G-433 [M]	Ella Fitzgerald and Billie Holiday at Newport	1957	$40

VERVE

❏ MGV-8234 [M]	Ella Fitzgerald and Billie Holiday at Newport	1958	$150
❏ MGVS-6022 [S]	Ella Fitzgerald and Billie Holiday at Newport	1960	$100
❏ V-8234 [M]	Ella Fitzgerald and Billie Holiday at Newport	1961	$50
❏ V6-8234 [S]	Ella Fitzgerald and Billie Holiday at Newport	1961	$50
❏ V-8826	Newport Years	1973	$30

FITZGERALD, ELLA, AND COUNT BASIE

Also see each artist's individual listings.

Albums

PABLO TODAY

❏ 2312110	A Perfect Match	1980	$30

— *Red vinyl*

VERVE

❏ V-4061 [M]	Ella and Basie!	1963	$60
❏ V6-4061 [S]	Ella and Basie!	1963	$60
❏ ST-90028 [S]	Ella and Basie!	1964	$100

— *Capitol Record Club edition*

❏ T-90028 [M]	Ella and Basie!	1964	$100

— *Capitol Record Club edition*

FITZGERALD, ELLA, AND DUKE ELLINGTON

Also see each artist's individual listings.

Albums

PABLO LIVE

❏ 2308242	The Stockholm Concert 1966	1984	$25

FITZGERALD, ELLA, AND LOUIS ARMSTRONG

Also see each artist's individual listings.

Albums

METRO

❏ M-601 [M]	Louis and Ella	1967	$150
❏ MS-601 [S]	Louis and Ella	1967	$150

MOBILE FIDELITY

❏ 2-248	Ella and Louis Again	1996	$150

— *Audiophile vinyl*

VERVE

Ella Fitzgerald, *The Best of Ella Fitzgerald Vol. II*, MCA 2-4016, two-record set, black labels with rainbow, **$35**.

Ella Fitzgerald, *Mack the Knife/Ella in Berlin*, Verve MGV-4041, **$50**.

Ella Fitzgerald, *Ella Fitzgerald Sings the Gershwin Song Book Vol. 1*, Verve MGV-4013, **$100**.

Helen Forrest, *Voice of the Name Bands*, Capitol T 704, **$80**.

Number	Title	Yr	NM
❏ V-4003 [M]	Ella and Louis	1961	$50
❏ V6-8811	Ella and Louis	1972	$35
❏ MGV-4006-2 [M]	Ella and Louis Again	1956	$150
❏ V-4006-2 [M]	Ella and Louis Again	1961	$60
❏ MGV-4017 [M]	Ella and Louis Again, Vol. 1	1958	$150
❏ V-4017 [M]	Ella and Louis Again, Vol. 1	1961	$50
❏ MGV-4018 [M]	Ella and Louis Again, Vol. 2	1958	$150
❏ V-4018 [M]	Ella and Louis Again, Vol. 2	1961	$50
❏ MGV-4011-2 [M]	Porgy and Bess	1957	$250
❏ MGVS-6040-2 [S]	Porgy and Bess	1960	$120
❏ V-4011-2 [M]	Porgy and Bess	1961	$60
❏ V6-4011-2 [S]	Porgy and Bess	1961	$60
❏ VE-1-2507	Porgy and Bess	197?	$25
❏ 827475-1	Porgy and Bess	198?	$30

FITZGERALD, ELLA
Female singer, one of the giants of jazz.
Albums
AMERICAN RECORDING SOCIETY

❏ G-433 [M]	Ella Fitzgerald At Newport	195?	$40

ATLANTIC
| ❏ SD1631 | Ella Loves Cole | 1972 | $30 |

BAINBRIDGE
| ❏ 6223 | Things Ain't What They Used to Be | 1982 | $25 |

— *Reissue of Reprise 6432*

BASF
| ❏ 20712 | Watch What Happens | 1972 | $30 |

CAPITOL
❏ T2685 [M]	Brighten the Corner	1967	$80
❏ ST2685 [S]	Brighten the Corner	1967	$75
❏ SM-11793	Brighten the Corner	1978	$25
❏ T2805 [M]	Ella Fitzgerald's Christmas	1967	$80
❏ ST2805 [S]	Ella Fitzgerald's Christmas	1967	$60

— *Same as above, but in stereo*
❏ ST2888	Misty Blue	1968	$75
❏ ST2960	Thirty by Ella	1968	$50
❏ SN-16276	Thirty by Ella	1983	$25

— *Budget-line reissue*

CLASSICS RECORD LIBRARY/VERVE
| ❏ 80-55713 | Ella Fitzgerald Sings the George and Ira Gershwin Songbook | 1978 | $40 |

— *Reissue of the entire set for Book-of-the-Month Club*

COLUMBIA
| ❏ KG32557 | Carnegie Hall & Newport Jazz Festival 1973 | 1973 | $35 |

DECCA
❏ DL4447 [M]	Early Ella	1964	$35
❏ DL74447 [R]	Early Ella	1964	$30
❏ DL8477 [M]	Ella and Her Fellas	1957	$150
❏ DL5300 [10]	Ella Fitzgerald Sings Gershwin Songs	1951	$200
❏ DL8378 [M]	Ella Sings Gershwin	1957	$150
❏ DL4451 [M]	Ella Sings Gershwin	1964	$35
❏ DL74451 [R]	Ella Sings Gershwin	1964	$30
❏ DL8832 [M]	For Sentimental Reasons	1958	$120
❏ DL4129 [M]	Golden Favorites	1961	$50
❏ DL74129 [R]	Golden Favorites	1961	$30
❏ DL8149 [M]	Lullabies of Birdland	1955	$150
❏ DL8696 [M]	Miss Ella Fitzgerald and Mr. Nelson Riddle Invite You to Listen and Relax	1958	$100
❏ DL4887 [M]	Smooth Sailing	1967	$35
❏ DL74887 [R]	Smooth Sailing	1967	$30
❏ DL8068 [M]	Songs in a Mellow Mood	1954	$150
❏ DL5084 [10]	Souvenir Album	1950	$250
❏ DL4446 [M]	Stairway to the Stars	1964	$35
❏ DL74446 [R]	Stairway to the Stars	1964	$30
❏ DL8155 [M]	Sweet and Hot	1955	$100
❏ DXB156 [M]	The Best of Ella	1959	$200

— *Black labels, silver print*
| ❏ DXB156 [M] | The Best of Ella | 1961 | $60 |

— *Black labels with color bars*
| ❏ DXSB7156 [R] | The Best of Ella | 196? | $50 |
| ❏ DL8695 [M] | The First Lady of Song | 1958 | $120 |

EVEREST ARCHIVE OF FOLK & JAZZ
| ❏ 276 | Ella Fitzgerald | 1973 | $30 |

FANTASY
| ❏ OJC-442 | Ella & Nice | 1990 | $30 |

— *Reissue of Pablo Live 2308 234*
| ❏ OJC-376 | Montreux '77 | 1989 | $30 |

— *Reissue of Pablo Live 2308 206*

INTERMEDIA
| ❏ QS-5049 | Ella by Starlight | 198? | $25 |

MCA
❏ 215	Ella Sings Gershwin	1973	$25
❏ 734	Memories	198?	$25
❏ 4047	The Best of Ella	197?	$35
❏ 4016	The Best of Ella Fitzgerald, Vol. II	1973	$35

Number	Title	Yr	NM
METRO			
❏ M-500 [M]	Ella Fitzgerald	1965	$150
❏ MS-500 [S]	Ella Fitzgerald	1965	$150
❏ M-567 [M]	The World of Ella Fitzgerald	1966	$150
❏ MS-567 [S]	The World of Ella Fitzgerald	1966	$150
MGM			
❏ GAS-130	Ella Fitzgerald (Golden Archive Series)	1970	$35
PABLO			
❏ 2310772	Again	1977	$30
❏ 2310938	All That Jazz	1990	$30
❏ 2310814	Dream Dancing	1978	$30
❏ 2310921	Easy Living	1987	$25
❏ 2310759	Ella and Oscar	1976	$30
❏ 2310711	Ella in London	1974	$30
❏ 2310829	Fine and Mellow	1979	$30
❏ 2310825	Lady Time	1978	$30
❏ 2310751	Montreux '75	1976	$30
❏ 2310888	Speak Love	1983	$25
❏ 2310702	Take Love Easy	1974	$30
❏ 2405421	The Best of Ella Fitzgerald	198?	$25
PABLO LIVE			
❏ 2308234	Ella & Nice	197?	$35
❏ 2308206	Montreux '77	1978	$30
PABLO TODAY			
❏ 2312132	A Classy Pair	1983	$25
❏ 2630201	Ella Abraca Jobim: Ella Fitzgerald Sings the Antonio Carlos Jobim Song Book	1981	$35
❏ 2312140	Nice Work If You Can Get It	198?	$25
❏ 2312138	The Best Is Yet to Come	1982	$25
PAUSA			
❏ 7130	Love You Madly	198?	$25
PICKWICK			
❏ SPC-3259	Misty Blues	1974	$25
PRESTIGE			
❏ PRLP-7685	Sunshine of Your Love	1970	$35
REPRISE			
❏ RS-6354	Ella	1969	$35
❏ RS-6432	Things Ain't What They Used to Be	1971	$30
SUNBEAM			
❏ 205	Ella Fitzgerald and Her Orchestra, 1940	197?	$25
TIME-LIFE			
❏ SLGD-03	Legendary Singers: Ella Fitzgerald	1985	$35
VERVE			
❏ V-4066 [M]	A Tribute to Cole Porter	1964	$60
❏ V6-4066 [S]	A Tribute to Cole Porter	1964	$60
❏ V-4053 [M]	Clap Hands, Here Comes Charley	1962	$40
❏ V6-4053 [S]	Clap Hands, Here Comes Charley	1962	$300
❏ V-8745 [M]	Ella "Live	1968	$60
❏ V6-8745 [S]	Ella "Live	1968	$35
❏ V-4072 [M]	Ella & Duke at Cote d'Azur	1967	$40
❏ V6-4072 [S]	Ella & Duke at Cote d'Azur	1967	$60
❏ V-4070 [M]	Ella at Duke's Place	1966	$50
❏ V6-4070 [S]	Ella at Duke's Place	1966	$50
❏ SMAS-90644 [S]	Ella at Duke's Place	1966	$100
— *Capitol Record Club edition*			
❏ V-4065 [M]	Ella at Juan Les Pins	1964	$60
❏ V6-4065 [S]	Ella at Juan Les Pins	1964	$60
❏ MGV-8264 [M]	Ella Fitzgerald at the Opera House	1958	$150
❏ MGVS-6026 [S]	Ella Fitzgerald at the Opera House	1960	$100
❏ V-8264 [M]	Ella Fitzgerald at the Opera House	1961	$50
❏ V6-8264 [S]	Ella Fitzgerald at the Opera House	1961	$50
❏ MGV-4049 [M]	Ella Fitzgerald Sings Cole Porter	1961	$40
❏ V-4049 [M]	Ella Fitzgerald Sings Cole Porter	1961	$50
❏ MGV-4050 [M]	Ella Fitzgerald Sings More Cole Porter	1961	$40
❏ V-4050 [M]	Ella Fitzgerald Sings More Cole Porter	1961	$50
❏ MGV-4001-2 [M]	Ella Fitzgerald Sings the Cole Porter Song Book	1956	$150
❏ V-4001-2 [M]	Ella Fitzgerald Sings the Cole Porter Song Book	1961	$60
❏ MGV-4010-4 [M]	Ella Fitzgerald Sings the Duke Ellington Song Book	1957	$150
— *Combines 4008 and 4009 into one package*			
❏ V-10-4 [M]	Ella Fitzgerald Sings the Duke Ellington Song Book	196?	$100
❏ MGV-4008-2 [M]	Ella Fitzgerald Sings the Duke Ellington Song Book, Vol. 1	1957	$150
❏ V-4008-2 [M]	Ella Fitzgerald Sings the Duke Ellington Song Book, Vol. 1	1961	$60

Number	Title	Yr	NM
❏ MGV-4009-2 [M]	Ella Fitzgerald Sings the Duke Ellington Song Book, Vol. 2	1957	$150
❏ V-4009-2 [M]	Ella Fitzgerald Sings the Duke Ellington Song Book, Vol. 2	1961	$60
❏ MGV-4029-5 [M]	Ella Fitzgerald Sings the George and Ira Gershwin Song Book	1959	$250
— *Box set with 4024 through 4028 plus bonus 10-inch LP*			
❏ MGV-4029-5 [M]	Ella Fitzgerald Sings the George and Ira Gershwin Song Book	1959	$500
— *Box set with 4024 through 4028 plus bonus 10-inch LP, all in walnut box with leather pockets*			
❏ MGVS-6082-5 [S]	Ella Fitzgerald Sings the George and Ira Gershwin Song Book	1960	$200
— *Box set with 6077 through 6081 plus bonus 10-inch LP*			
❏ V-29-5 [M]	Ella Fitzgerald Sings the George and Ira Gershwin Song Book	196?	$175
— *Reissue of MGV-4029*			
❏ V6-29-5 [S]	Ella Fitzgerald Sings the George and Ira Gershwin Song Book	196?	$175
— *Reissue of MGVS-6082*			
❏ MGV-4024 [M]	Ella Fitzgerald Sings the George and Ira Gershwin Song Book, Vol. 1	1959	$100
❏ MGVS-6077 [S]	Ella Fitzgerald Sings the George and Ira Gershwin Song Book, Vol. 1	1960	$100
❏ V-4024 [M]	Ella Fitzgerald Sings the George and Ira Gershwin Song Book, Vol. 1	1961	$50
❏ V6-4024 [S]	Ella Fitzgerald Sings the George and Ira Gershwin Song Book, Vol. 1	1961	$50
❏ MGV-4025 [M]	Ella Fitzgerald Sings the George and Ira Gershwin Song Book, Vol. 2	1959	$100
❏ MGVS-6078 [S]	Ella Fitzgerald Sings the George and Ira Gershwin Song Book, Vol. 2	1960	$100
❏ V-4025 [M]	Ella Fitzgerald Sings the George and Ira Gershwin Song Book, Vol. 2	1961	$50
❏ V6-4025 [S]	Ella Fitzgerald Sings the George and Ira Gershwin Song Book, Vol. 2	1961	$50
❏ MGV-4026 [M]	Ella Fitzgerald Sings the George and Ira Gershwin Song Book, Vol. 3	1959	$100
❏ MGVS-6079 [S]	Ella Fitzgerald Sings the George and Ira Gershwin Song Book, Vol. 3	1960	$100
❏ V-4026 [M]	Ella Fitzgerald Sings the George and Ira Gershwin Song Book, Vol. 3	1961	$50
❏ V6-4026 [S]	Ella Fitzgerald Sings the George and Ira Gershwin Song Book, Vol. 3	1961	$50
❏ MGV-4027 [M]	Ella Fitzgerald Sings the George and Ira Gershwin Song Book, Vol. 4	1959	$100
❏ MGVS-6080 [S]	Ella Fitzgerald Sings the George and Ira Gershwin Song Book, Vol. 4	1960	$100
❏ V-4027 [M]	Ella Fitzgerald Sings the George and Ira Gershwin Song Book, Vol. 4	1961	$50
❏ V6-4027 [S]	Ella Fitzgerald Sings the George and Ira Gershwin Song Book, Vol. 4	1961	$50
❏ MGV-4028 [M]	Ella Fitzgerald Sings the George and Ira Gershwin Song Book, Vol. 5	1959	$100
❏ MGVS-6081 [S]	Ella Fitzgerald Sings the George and Ira Gershwin Song Book, Vol. 5	1960	$100
❏ V-4028 [M]	Ella Fitzgerald Sings the George and Ira Gershwin Song Book, Vol. 5	1961	$50
❏ V6-4028 [S]	Ella Fitzgerald Sings the George and Ira Gershwin Song Book, Vol. 5	1961	$50
❏ MGV-4013 [M]	Ella Fitzgerald Sings the Gershwin Song Book	1957	$100
❏ MGVS-7000 [S]	Ella Fitzgerald Sings the Gershwin Song Book	1959	$100
❏ MGV-4046-2 [M]	Ella Fitzgerald Sings the Harold Arlen Song Book	1961	$120

Number	Title	Yr	NM
❑ V-4057 [M]	Ella Fitzgerald Sings the Harold Arlen Song Book, Vol. 1	1962	$60
❑ V6-4057 [S]	Ella Fitzgerald Sings the Harold Arlen Song Book, Vol. 1	1962	$60
❑ V-4058 [M]	Ella Fitzgerald Sings the Harold Arlen Song Book, Vol. 2	1962	$60
❑ V6-4058 [S]	Ella Fitzgerald Sings the Harold Arlen Song Book, Vol. 2	1962	$60
❑ MGV-4019-2 [M]	Ella Fitzgerald Sings the Irving Berlin Song Book	1958	$250
❑ MGVS-6005-2 [S]	Ella Fitzgerald Sings the Irving Berlin Song Book	1960	$120
❑ V-4019-2 [M]	Ella Fitzgerald Sings the Irving Berlin Song Book	1961	$60
❑ V6-4019-2 [S]	Ella Fitzgerald Sings the Irving Berlin Song Book	1961	$60
❑ MGV-4030 [M]	Ella Fitzgerald Sings the Irving Berlin Song Book, Vol. 1	1959	$100
❑ MGVS-6052 [S]	Ella Fitzgerald Sings the Irving Berlin Song Book, Vol. 1	1960	$120
❑ V-4030 [M]	Ella Fitzgerald Sings the Irving Berlin Song Book, Vol. 1	1961	$50
❑ V6-4030 [S]	Ella Fitzgerald Sings the Irving Berlin Song Book, Vol. 1	1961	$50
❑ MGV-4031 [M]	Ella Fitzgerald Sings the Irving Berlin Song Book, Vol. 2	1959	$100
❑ MGVS-6053 [S]	Ella Fitzgerald Sings the Irving Berlin Song Book, Vol. 2	1960	$120
❑ V-4031 [M]	Ella Fitzgerald Sings the Irving Berlin Song Book, Vol. 2	1961	$50
❑ V6-4031 [S]	Ella Fitzgerald Sings the Irving Berlin Song Book, Vol. 2	1961	$50
❑ V-4060 [M]	Ella Fitzgerald Sings the Jerome Kern Song Book	1963	$60
❑ V6-4060 [S]	Ella Fitzgerald Sings the Jerome Kern Song Book	1963	$60
❑ V-8670 [M]	Ella Fitzgerald Sings the Jerome Kern Song Book	1967	$0
—Canceled reissue			
❑ V-4067 [M]	Ella Fitzgerald Sings the Johnny Mercer Song Book	1965	$50
❑ V6-4067 [S]	Ella Fitzgerald Sings the Johnny Mercer Song Book	1965	$50
❑ MGV-4002-2 [M]	Ella Fitzgerald Sings the Rodgers & Hart Song Book	1956	$150
❑ MGV-4022 [M]	Ella Fitzgerald Sings the Rodgers & Hart Song Book, Vol. 1	1959	$100
❑ MGVS-6009 [S]	Ella Fitzgerald Sings the Rodgers & Hart Song Book, Vol. 1	1960	$100
❑ V-4022 [M]	Ella Fitzgerald Sings the Rodgers & Hart Song Book, Vol. 1	1961	$50
❑ V6-4022 [S]	Ella Fitzgerald Sings the Rodgers & Hart Song Book, Vol. 1	1961	$50
❑ MGV-4023 [M]	Ella Fitzgerald Sings the Rodgers & Hart Song Book, Vol. 2	1959	$100
❑ MGVS-6010 [S]	Ella Fitzgerald Sings the Rodgers & Hart Song Book, Vol. 2	1960	$100
❑ V-4023 [M]	Ella Fitzgerald Sings the Rodgers & Hart Song Book, Vol. 2	1961	$50
❑ V6-4023 [S]	Ella Fitzgerald Sings the Rodgers & Hart Song Book, Vol. 2	1961	$50
❑ V-4002-2 [M]	Ella Fitzgerald Sings the Rodgers and Hart Song Book	1961	$60
❑ V-4069 [M]	Ella in Hamburg	1966	$50
❑ V6-4069 [S]	Ella in Hamburg	1966	$50
❑ MGV-4052 [M]	Ella in Hollywood	1961	$40
❑ V6-4052 [S]	Ella in Hollywood	1961	$50
❑ 835454-1	Ella in Rome: The Birthday Concert	1988	$25
❑ V-4059 [M]	Ella Sings Broadway	1963	$60
❑ V6-4059 [S]	Ella Sings Broadway	1963	$60
❑ V-4054 [M]	Ella Swings Brightly with Nelson	1962	$60
❑ V6-4054 [S]	Ella Swings Brightly with Nelson	1962	$60

Number	Title	Yr	NM
❑ V-4055 [M]	Ella Swings Gently with Nelson	1962	$60
❑ V6-4055 [S]	Ella Swings Gently with Nelson	1962	$60
❑ MGV-4021 [M]	Ella Swings Lightly	1958	$150
❑ MGVS-6019 [S]	Ella Swings Lightly	1960	$100
❑ V-4021 [M]	Ella Swings Lightly	1961	$50
❑ V6-4021 [S]	Ella Swings Lightly	1961	$50
❑ MGV-4042 [M]	Ella Wishes You a Swinging Christmas	1960	$100
❑ MGVS-64042 [S]	Ella Wishes You a Swinging Christmas	1960	$120
❑ V-4042 [M]	Ella Wishes You a Swinging Christmas	1961	$40
❑ V6-4042 [S]	Ella Wishes You a Swinging Christmas	1961	$100
❑ VE-1-2539	Ella Wishes You a Swinging Christmas	198?	$30
—Reissue			
❑ 827150-1	Ella Wishes You a Swinging Christmas	198?	$25
❑ MGV-4036 [M]	Get Happy!	1960	$100
❑ MGVS-6102 [S]	Get Happy!	1960	$100
❑ V6-4036 [S]	Get Happy!	1961	$50
❑ V-4064 [M]	Hello, Dolly!	1964	$60
❑ V6-4064 [S]	Hello, Dolly!	1964	$60
❑ MGV-4034 [M]	Hello, Love	1959	$100
❑ MGVS-6100 [S]	Hello, Love	1960	$100
❑ V-4034 [M]	Hello, Love	1961	$50
❑ V6-4034 [S]	Hello, Love	1961	$50
❑ V6-8817	History	1973	$35
❑ 825098-1	Lady Be Good	1985	$25
❑ MGV-4043 [M]	Let No Man Write My Epitaph	1961	$40
❑ V-4043 [M]	Let No Man Write My Epitaph	1961	$50
❑ V6-4043 [S]	Let No Man Write My Epitaph	1961	$50
❑ MGV-4004 [M]	Like Someone in Love	1957	$150
❑ MGVS-6000 [S]	Like Someone in Love	1960	$100
❑ V-4004 [M]	Like Someone in Love	1961	$50
❑ V6-4004 [S]	Like Someone in Love	1961	$50
❑ MGVS-6163 [S]	Mack the Knife -- Ella in Berlin	1960	$100
❑ V-4041 [M]	Mack the Knife -- Ella in Berlin	1961	$50
❑ V6-4041 [S]	Mack the Knife -- Ella in Berlin	1961	$50
❑ 825670-1	Mack the Knife -- Ella in Berlin	1985	$25
❑ MGVS-64041 [S]	Mack the Knife -- Ella in Berlin	1960	$100
❑ MGV-8288 [M]	One O'Clock Jump	1958	$100
❑ V-8288 [M]	One O'Clock Jump	1961	$50
❑ V-4068 [M]	Porgy & Bess	1965	$50
❑ V6-4068 [M]	Porgy & Bess	1965	$50
❑ V-4056 [M]	Rhythm Is My Business	1962	$60
❑ V6-4056 [S]	Rhythm Is My Business	1962	$60
❑ MGV-4032 [M]	Sweet Songs for Swingers	1959	$100
❑ MGVS-6072 [S]	Sweet Songs for Swingers	1960	$80
❑ V-4032 [M]	Sweet Songs for Swingers	1961	$50
❑ V6-4032 [S]	Sweet Songs for Swingers	1961	$50
❑ V-4063 [M]	The Best of Ella Fitzgerald	1964	$35
❑ V6-4063 [S]	The Best of Ella Fitzgerald	1964	$35
❑ V-8720 [M]	The Best of Ella Fitzgerald	1967	$35
❑ V6-8720 [S]	The Best of Ella Fitzgerald	1967	$30
❑ V6-8795	The Best of Ella Fitzgerald, Vol. 2	1969	$30
❑ VE-2-2511	The Cole Porter Song Book	197?	$35
❑ 823278-1	The Cole Porter Song Book	198?	$30
❑ VE-2-2535	The Duke Ellington Song Book	1979	$35
❑ 827163-1	The Duke Ellington Song Book, Vol. 1	198?	$30
❑ VE-2-2540	The Duke Ellington Song Book, Vol. 2	1982	$35
❑ 827169-1	The Duke Ellington Song Book, Vol. 2	198?	$30
❑ 825024-1	The George and Ira Gershwin Songbook (Complete)	198?	$60
❑ 823279-1	The George and Ira Gershwin Songbook (Highlights)	198?	$30
❑ VE-2-2525	The George Gershwin Song Book	1978	$35
❑ 817526-1	The Harold Arlen Song Book	1984	$35
❑ 829533-1	The Irving Berlin Song Book	1988	$30
❑ 825669-1	The Jerome Kern Song Book	1985	$25
❑ 823247-1	The Johnny Mercer Song Book	1985	$25
❑ VE-2-2519	The Rodgers and Hart Song Book	197?	$35
❑ 821693-1	The Rodgers and Hart Song Book	198?	$30
❑ V-4062 [M]	These Are the Blues	1963	$60
❑ V6-4062 [S]	These Are the Blues	1963	$60
❑ V-4071 [M]	Whisper Not	1966	$50
❑ V6-4071 [S]	Whisper Not	1966	$50

VOCALION

Number	Title	Yr	NM
❑ VL3797 [M]	Ella Fitzgerald	1967	$30
❑ VL73797 [R]	Ella Fitzgerald	1967	$30

FIVE, THE

Members: CONTE CANDOLI; BUDDY CLARK; PETE JOLLY; MEL LEWIS; BILL PERKINS.

Albums

Number	Title	Yr	NM
RCA VICTOR			
❑ LPM-1121 [M]	The Five	1955	$80

FIVE-A-SLIDE

Albums

Number	Title	Yr	NM
AUDIOPHILE			
❑ AP-180	Five-a-Slide	198?	$30

FIVE BROTHERS

Members: Frank Capp; BOB ENEVOLDSEN; HERBIE HARPER; RED MITCHELL; Don Overburg.

Albums

Number	Title	Yr	NM
TAMPA			
❑ TP-25 [M]	Five Brothers	1957	$250
—Red vinyl			
❑ TP-25 [M]	Five Brothers	1958	$150
—Black vinyl			

FLAHIVE, LARRY

Pianist.

Albums

Number	Title	Yr	NM
SEA BREEZE			
❑ SB-2020	Standard Flay	1983	$25

FLANAGAN, TOMMY, AND HANK JONES

Also see each artist's individual listings.

Albums

Number	Title	Yr	NM
GALAXY			
❑ 5152	More Delights	1985	$25
❑ 5113	Our Delights	1978	$30

FLANAGAN, TOMMY

Pianist. Also see THE NEW YORK JAZZ SEPTET.

Albums

Number	Title	Yr	NM
ENJA			
❑ 4014	Confirmation	1982	$30
❑ 4022	Giant Steps	1983	$30
FANTASY			
❑ OJC-372	Montreux '77	1989	$30
❑ OJC-473	Something Borrowed, Something Blue	1990	$30
❑ OJC-182	The Tommy Flanagan Trio	198?	$25
GALAXY			
❑ 5110	Something Borrowed, Something Blue	1978	$30
INNER CITY			
❑ IC-3029	Ballads and Blues	1979	$35
❑ IC-3009	Eclypso	1977	$35
❑ IC-1071	Tommy Flanagan Plays the Music of Harold Arlen	1980	$30
❑ IC-1084	Trinity	198?	$25
MOODSVILLE			
❑ MVLP-9 [M]	The Tommy Flanagan Trio	1960	$50
—Green label			
❑ MVLP-9 [M]	The Tommy Flanagan Trio	1965	$30
—Blue label, trident logo at right			
ONYX			
❑ 206	The Tommy Flanagan Trio and Sextet	197?	$35
PABLO			
❑ 2405410	The Best of Tommy Flanagan	198?	$25
❑ 2310724	Tokyo Recital	1975	$35
PABLO LIVE			
❑ 2308202	Montreux '77	1978	$35
PRESTIGE			
❑ PRLP-7134 [M]	Overseas	1958	$3500
❑ PRST-7632	Overseas	1969	$35
REGENT			
❑ MG-6055 [M]	Jazz... It's Magic	1958	$80
SAVOY JAZZ			
❑ SJL-1158	Jazz... It's Magic	1986	$25
STATIRAS			
❑ SLP-8073	The Magnificent	1985	$25
TIMELESS			
❑ SJP-301	Jazz Poet	1990	$30

Number	Title	Yr	NM

FLEMING, KING
Pianist and composer.
Albums

ARGO
❏ LP-4004 [M]	Misty Night	1961	$30
❏ LPS-4004 [S]	Misty Night	1961	$30
❏ LP-4019 [M]	Stand By!	1962	$30
❏ LPS-4019 [S]	Stand By!	1962	$30

CADET
❏ LP-4053 [M]	Weary Traveler	1966	$35
❏ LPS-4053 [S]	Weary Traveler	1966	$25

FLINT, SHELBY
Female singer. Best known as a pop-folk singer in the early 1960s ("Angel on My Shoulder" was her hit), years later she returned as a jazz vocalist.
Albums

MAD SATYR
❏ MSR-101	You've Been On My Mind	1982	$60

FLORENCE, BOB
Pianist, male singer and composer.
Albums

CARLTON
❏ LP 12-115 [M]	Name Band: 1959	1959	$40
❏ STLP 12-115 [S]	Name Band: 1959	1959	$60

DISCOVERY
❏ DS-832	Westlake	1982	$25

ERA
❏ EL-20003 [M]	Bob Florence and Trio	1956	$100

TREND
❏ TR-523	Live at Concerts by the Sea	1980	$25
❏ TR-536	Magic Time	1984	$25
❏ TR-545	Trash Can City	1987	$25

WORLD PACIFIC
❏ WPS-21860 [S]	Pet Project: The Bob Florence Big Band Plays Petula Clark Hits	196?	$100
❏ WP-1860 [M]	Pet Project: The Bob Florence Big Band Plays Petula Clark Hits	196?	$100

FLORES, CHUCK
Drummer.
Albums

CONCORD JAZZ
❏ CJ-49	Drum Flower	1978	$30

DONRE
❏ 1001	Flores Azules	1976	$30

FLORY, MED
Alto, tenor and baritone saxophone player. Also an arranger and composer.
Albums

JOSIE
❏ JOZ-3506 [M]	Med Flory Big Band	1963	$30
❏ JJS-3506 [S]	Med Flory Big Band	1963	$25

JUBILEE
❏ JLP-1066 [M]	Jazzwave	1958	$50
❏ SDJLP-1066 [S]	Jazzwave	1959	$40

FLYING ISLAND
Members: Bill Baron (drums, percussion); Jeff Bova (keyboards, trumpet); Faith Fraioli (violin); Thom Preli (bass); Ray Smith (guitar).
Albums

VANGUARD
❏ VSD-79368	Another Kind of Space	197?	$35
❏ VSD-79359	Flying Island	197?	$35

FOGEL, MARTY
Tenor saxophone player. Also see EVERYMAN BAND.
Albums

CMP
❏ CMP-37-ST	Many Bobbing Heads, At Last	1990	$30

FOL, RAYMOND
Pianist.
Albums

PHILIPS
❏ PHM200198 [M]	Vivaldi's Four Seasons in Jazz	1966	$30
❏ PHS600198 [S]	Vivaldi's Four Seasons in Jazz	1966	$35

FOLEY, GEORGE
Pianist.
Albums

STOMP OFF
❏ SOS-1085	I Like It	1985	$25
❏ SOS-1187	Smiles and Kisses	1991	$30

FORD, RICKY
Tenor saxophone player.
Albums

MUSE
❏ MR-5227	Flying Colors	1981	$25
❏ MR-5296	Future's Gold	198?	$25
❏ MR-5275	Interpretations	198?	$25
❏ MR-5322	Looking Ahead	1987	$25
❏ MR-5188	Manhattan Plaza	1979	$30
❏ MR-5349	Saxotic Stomp	1988	$25
❏ MR-5314	Shorter Ideas	1985	$25
❏ MR-5250	Tenor for the Times	1982	$25

NEW WORLD
❏ 204	Loxodonta Africana	1977	$35

FOREFRONT, THE
Group of four trumpets, bass and drums founded by Bobby Lewis.
Albums

AFI
❏ 21557	Incantation	197?	$25

FORETICH, HERMAN
Clarinetist.
Albums

AUDIOPHILE
❏ AP-124	Herman Foretich and His Atlanta Swing Quartet	196?	$35

JAZZOLOGY
❏ J-144	The Foretich Four	1987	$25

FORMAN, BRUCE, AND GEORGE CABLES
Also see each artist's individual listings.
Albums

CONCORD JAZZ
❏ CJ-279	Dynamics	1985	$25

FORMAN, BRUCE
Guitarist.
Albums

CHOICE
❏ 1026	Coast to Coast	1980	$30

CONCORD JAZZ
❏ CJ-251	Full Circle	1984	$25
❏ CJ-368	Pardon Me!	1989	$30
❏ CJ-332	There Are Times	1988	$25

MUSE
❏ MR-5273	20/20	1982	$25
❏ MR-5299	In Transit	1982	$25
❏ MR-5251	River Journey	1981	$25
❏ MR-5315	The Bash	1985	$25

FORMAN, MITCHELL
Keyboard player.
Albums

MAGENTA
❏ MA-0201	Train of Thought	198?	$30

SOUL NOTE
❏ SN-1050	Childhood Dreams	198?	$30
❏ SN-1070	Only a Memory	198?	$30

FORREST, EUGENE "FLIP
Albums

SAVOY
❏ MG-14392	I Heard It on the Radio	197?	$25

FORREST, HELEN, AND DICK HAYMES
Haymes is a male singer not otherwise listed in this book. Also see HELEN FORREST.
Albums

MCA
❏ 1546	Long Ago and Far Away	198?	$30

FORREST, HELEN
Female singer.
Albums

AUDIOPHILE
❏ AP-47	On the Sunny Side of the Street	1958	$60

CAPITOL
❏ T704 [M]	Voice of the Name Bands	1956	$80
— Turquoise label			

JOYCE
❏ 6008	Big Bands' Greatest Vocalists, Vol. 2	197?	$20
❏ 6012	Big Bands' Greatest Vocalists, Vol. 4	197?	$20
❏ 6019	Big Bands' Greatest Vocalists, Vol. 7	197?	$20
❏ 6021	Big Bands' Greatest Vocalists, Vol. 8	197?	$20

STASH
❏ ST-225	Now and Forever	198?	$35

FORREST, JIMMY, AND MILES DAVIS
Also see each artist's individual listings.
Albums

PRESTIGE
❏ PRST-7858	Live at the Barrel	197?	$35
❏ PRST-7860	Live at the Barrel, Volume 2	197?	$35

FORREST, JIMMY
Tenor saxophone player. Also see OLIVER NELSON.
Albums

DELMARK
❏ DL-404	All the Gin Is Gone	196?	$50
❏ DL-427	Black Forrest	1972	$35
❏ DL-435	Night Train	197?	$35

FANTASY
❏ OJC-199	Forrest Fire	1985	$30
❏ OJC-350	Most Much!	198?	$30
❏ OJC-097	Out of the Forrest	198?	$30

NEW JAZZ
❏ NJLP-8250 [M]	Forrest Fire	1960	$200
— Purple label			
❏ NJLP-8250 [M]	Forrest Fire	1965	$150
— Blue label with trident logo at right			
❏ NJLP-8293 [M]	Soul Street	1962	$200
— Purple label			
❏ NJLP-8293 [M]	Soul Street	1965	$150
— Blue label with trident logo at right			

PALO ALTO
❏ 8021	Heart of the Forrest	1982	$30

PRESTIGE
❏ PRLP-7218 [M]	Most Much!	1961	$200
— Yellow label			
❏ PRLP-7218 [M]	Most Much!	1965	$40
— Blue label with trident logo at right			
❏ PRLP-7202 [M]	Out of the Forrest	1961	$200
— Yellow label			
❏ PRLP-7202 [M]	Out of the Forrest	1965	$40
— Blue label with trident logo at right			
❏ PRLP-7235 [M]	Sit Down and Relax with Jimmy Forrest	1962	$150
— Yellow label			
❏ PRLP-7235 [M]	Sit Down and Relax with Jimmy Forrest	1965	$40
— Blue label with trident logo at right			
❏ PRST-7235 [S]	Sit Down and Relax with Jimmy Forrest	1962	$150
— Silver label			

Jimmy Forrest, *Most Much*!, Prestige PRLP-7218, yellow label, **$200**.

Bud Freeman, *Something Tender*, United Artists UAJ 14033, **$40**.

Slim Gaillard/Meade Lux Lewis, *Boogie Woogie at the Philharmonic*, Clef MGC-506, **$300**.

Red Garland, *A Garland of Red*, Prestige PRLP-7064, yellow label with W. 50th St. address, **$300**.

Number	Title	Yr	NM
❑ PRST-7235 [S]	Sit Down and Relax with Jimmy Forrest	1965	$50
—Blue label with trident logo at right			
❑ PRST-7235 [S]	Sit Down and Relax with Jimmy Forrest	1973	$30
—Green label reissue			
❑ PRST-7712	The Best of Jimmy Forrest	196?	$30
UNITED			
❑ 02 [10]	Night Train	1955	$120

FORRESTER, BOBBY
Organist.
Albums
Number	Title	Yr	NM
DOBRE			
❑ 1012	Organist	197?	$30

FORTUNE, SONNY
Alto and tenor saxophone player, clarinetist and flutist. Also see STAN HUNTER.
Albums
Number	Title	Yr	NM
ATLANTIC			
❑ SD19187	Infinity Is	1978	$30
❑ SD18225	Serengeti Minstrel	1977	$30
❑ SD19239	With Sound Reason	1979	$30
HORIZON			
❑ 704	Awakening	1975	$35
❑ 711	Waves	1976	$35
STRATA-EAST			
❑ SES-7423	Long Before Our Mothers Cried	1974	$25

FOSTER, CHUCK
Bandleader, reeds player and male singer.
Albums
Number	Title	Yr	NM
CIRCLE			
❑ 68	Chuck Foster and His Orchestra 1945-46	198?	$25
HINDSIGHT			
❑ HSR-171	Chuck Foster and His Orchestra 1938-39	198?	$25
❑ HSR-115	Chuck Foster and His Orchestra 1940	198?	$25
PHILLIPS INTERNATIONAL			
❑ PLP-1965 [M]	Chuck Foster at the Hotel Peabody	1961	$200
SEA BREEZE			
❑ SB-2023	Long Overdue	1985	$25

FOSTER, FRANK, AND FRANK WESS
Also see each artist's individual listings.
Albums
Number	Title	Yr	NM
CONCORD JAZZ			
❑ CJ-276	Frankly Speaking	1986	$25
PABLO			
❑ 2310905	Two for the Blues	198?	$30
SAVOY JAZZ			
❑ SJL-2249	Two Franks Please!	198?	$30

FOSTER, FRANK
Tenor saxophone player and composer. Also see ELMO HOPE; PAUL QUINICHETTE.
Albums
Number	Title	Yr	NM
ARGO			
❑ LP-717 [M]	Basie Is Our Boss	1963	$30
❑ LPS-717 [S]	Basie Is Our Boss	1963	$30
BLUE NOTE			
❑ BST-84316	Frank Foster	1969	$0
—Canceled			
❑ BLP-5043 [10]	Frank Foster Quintet	1954	$400
❑ BST-84278	Manhattan Fever	1968	$30
MAINSTREAM			
❑ MRL-349	The Loud Minority	1972	$25
PRESTIGE			
❑ PRLP-7461 [M]	Fearless	1966	$30
❑ PRST-7461 [S]	Fearless	1966	$30
❑ PRLP-7479 [M]	Soul Outing!	1967	$30
❑ PRST-7479 [S]	Soul Outing!	1967	$30
STEEPLECHASE			
❑ SCS-1170	A House That Love Built	1982	$30

FOSTER, GARY
Saxophone player, clarinetist and flutist.
Albums
Number	Title	Yr	NM
REVELATION			
❑ REV-19	Grand Clu Classe	197?	$25
❑ REV-5	Subconsciously	1968	$25

FOSTER, HERMAN
Pianist.
Albums
Number	Title	Yr	NM
ARGO			
❑ LPS-727 [S]	Ready and Willing	1964	$30
EPIC			
❑ LA16010 [M]	Have You Heard?	1960	$50
❑ BA17010 [S]	Have You Heard?	1960	$60
❑ BA17016 [S]	The Explosive Piano of Herman Foster	1961	$60

FOSTER, RONNIE
Organist and keyboard player. Also see FUSE ONE.
Albums
Number	Title	Yr	NM
BLUE NOTE			
❑ BN-LA425-G	Cheshire Cat	1975	$35
❑ BN-LA261-G	On the Avenue	1974	$35
❑ BN-LA098-G	Sweet Revival	1973	$35
❑ BST-84382	Two Headed Freap	1972	$25
❑ B1-32082	Two Headed Freap	1995	$35
—Reissue of 84382			
COLUMBIA			
❑ JC36019	Delight	1979	$30
❑ JC35373	Love Satellite	1978	$30

FOUGERAT, TONY
Albums
Number	Title	Yr	NM
GHB			
❑ GHB-89	Every Man a King	197?	$25
❑ GHB-147	Live at the Maple Leaf Bar	198?	$25

FOUNTAIN, PETE, AND "BIG" TINY LITTLE
Albums
Number	Title	Yr	NM
CORAL			
❑ CRL57334 [M]	Mr. New Orleans Meets Mr. Honky Tonk	1961	$35
❑ CRL757334 [S]	Mr. New Orleans Meets Mr. Honky Tonk	1961	$50

FOUNTAIN, PETE, AND AL HIRT
Also see each artist's individual listings.
Albums
Number	Title	Yr	NM
CORAL			
❑ CRL57389 [M]	Bourbon Street	1962	$35
❑ CRL757389 [S]	Bourbon Street	1962	$50
MGM			
❑ E-4216 [M]	The Very Best of Al Hirt and Pete Fountain	1964	$30
❑ SE-4216 [S]	The Very Best of Al Hirt and Pete Fountain	1964	$35
MONUMENT			
❑ 8602	Super I	1975	$25

FOUNTAIN, PETE
Clarinetist.
Albums
Number	Title	Yr	NM
CAPITOL			
❑ SN-16224	Pete Fountain and Friends	1982	$20
❑ SN-16225	Way Down Yonder in New Orleans	1982	$20
CORAL			
❑ CRL57486 [M]	A Taste of Honey	1966	$30
❑ CRL757486 [S]	A Taste of Honey	1966	$35
❑ CRL757507	Both Sides Now	1969	$30
❑ CRL57487 [M]	Candy Clarinet -- Merry Christmas from Pete Fountain	1966	$30
❑ CRL757487 [S]	Candy Clarinet -- Merry Christmas from Pete Fountain	1966	$35
❑ CRL757513	Dr. Fountain's Magical Licorice Stick	1971	$30
❑ CRL757511	Golden Favorites	1970	$30
❑ CRL57378 [M]	I Love Paris	1961	$35
❑ CRL757378 [S]	I Love Paris	1961	$50

Number	Title	Yr	NM
❑ CRL57488 [M]	I've Got You Under My Skin	1967	$30
❑ CRL757488 [S]	I've Got You Under My Skin	1967	$35
❑ CRL57200 [M]	Lawrence Welk Presents Pete Fountain	1958	$50
❑ CRL57460 [M]	Licorice Stick	1964	$30
❑ CRL757460 [S]	Licorice Stick	1964	$35
❑ CRL757510	Make Your Own Kind of Music	1970	$30
❑ CRL57484 [M]	Mood Indigo	1966	$30
❑ CRL757484 [S]	Mood Indigo	1966	$35
❑ CRL57473 [M]	Mr. Stick Man	1965	$30
❑ CRL757473 [S]	Mr. Stick Man	1965	$35
❑ CRL57496 [M]	Music to Turn You On	1967	$35
❑ CRL757496 [S]	Music to Turn You On	1967	$30
❑ CRL57429 [M]	New Orleans at Midnight	1964	$30
❑ CRL757429 [S]	New Orleans at Midnight	1964	$35
❑ CRL57419 [M]	New Orleans Scene	1963	$35
❑ CRL757419 [S]	New Orleans Scene	1963	$50
❑ CRL57517	New Orleans Tennessee	1971	$30
❑ CRL57314 [M]	Pete Fountain at the Bateau Lounge	1960	$35
❑ CRL757314 [S]	Pete Fountain at the Bateau Lounge	1960	$50
❑ CRL57313 [M]	Pete Fountain Day	1960	$35
❑ CRL757313 [S]	Pete Fountain Day	1960	$50
❑ CRL57357 [M]	Pete Fountain On Tour	1961	$35
❑ CRL757357 [S]	Pete Fountain On Tour	1961	$50
❑ CRL57499 [M]	Pete Fountain Plays Bert Kaempfert	1968	$35
❑ CRL757499 [S]	Pete Fountain Plays Bert Kaempfert	1968	$30
❑ CRL57333 [M]	Pete Fountain Salutes the Great Clarinetists	1960	$35
❑ CRL757333 [S]	Pete Fountain Salutes the Great Clarinetists	1960	$50
❑ CRL57359 [M]	Pete Fountain's French Quarter	1961	$35
❑ CRL757359 [S]	Pete Fountain's French Quarter	1961	$50
❑ CRL57401 [M]	Pete Fountain's Music from Dixie	1962	$35
❑ CRL757401 [S]	Pete Fountain's Music from Dixie	1962	$50
❑ CRL57282 [M]	Pete Fountain's New Orleans	1959	$35
❑ CRL757282 [S]	Pete Fountain's New Orleans	1959	$50
❑ CRL57453 [M]	Pete's Place	1964	$30
❑ CRL757453 [S]	Pete's Place	1964	$35
❑ CRL57424 [M]	Plenty of Pete	1963	$30
❑ CRL757424 [M]	Plenty of Pete	1963	$35
❑ CRL757516	Something/Misty	1971	$30
❑ CRL57440 [M]	South Rampart Street Parade	1963	$30
❑ CRL757440 [S]	South Rampart Street Parade	1963	$35
❑ CRL57474 [M]	Standing Room Only	1965	$30
❑ CRL757474 [S]	Standing Room Only	1965	$35
❑ CRL57394 [M]	Swing Low Sweet Chariot	1962	$35
❑ CRL757394 [S]	Swing Low Sweet Chariot	1962	$50
❑ CXS-710	The Best of Pete Fountain	1969	$35
❑ CRL57284 [M]	The Blues	1959	$35
❑ CRL757284 [M]	The Blues	1959	$50
❑ CRL757505	Those Were the Days	1969	$30
❑ CRL757503	Walking Through New Orleans	1968	$30
DECCA			
❑ DL75378	Dr. Fountain's Magical Licorice Stick	1972	$25
—Reissue of Coral 757513			
❑ DL75377	Mr. New Orleans	1972	$30
❑ DL75380	New Orleans Tennessee	1972	$30
—Reissue of Coral 757517			
❑ DL75374	Pete Fountain's New Orleans	1972	$30
—Reissue of Coral 757282			
❑ DL75379	Something/Misty	1972	$25
—Reissue of Coral 757516			
❑ DL75375	The Blues	1972	$30
—Reissue of Coral 757284			
EVEREST ARCHIVE OF FOLK & JAZZ			
❑ 257	New Orleans All-Stars	197?	$25
FIRST AMERICAN			
❑ 7706	New Orleans Jazz	1978	$25
INTERMEDIA			
❑ QS-5038	Down on Rampart Street	198?	$20
JUCU			
❑ JMK-12S	Pete Fountain's Jazz Reunion	1976	$30
MCA			
❑ 336	Crescent City	1974	$25
❑ 507	Dr. Fountain's Magical Licorice Stick	1974	$25
—Reissue of Decca 75378			
❑ 165	Mr. New Orleans	1973	$25
—Reissue of Decca 75377			

Number	Title	Yr	NM
❑ 508	New Orleans Tennessee	1974	$25

— *Reissue of Decca 75380*

Number	Title	Yr	NM
❑ 505	Pete Fountain's New Orleans	1974	$25

— *Reissue of Decca 75374*

Number	Title	Yr	NM
❑ 176	Something/Misty	1973	$25

— *Reissue of Decca 75379*

Number	Title	Yr	NM
❑ 2-4032	The Best of Pete Fountain	1974	$30

— *Reissue of Coral 710*

Number	Title	Yr	NM
❑ 2-4095	The Best of Pete Fountain, Vol. 2	1976	$30

— *Black labels with rainbow*

Number	Title	Yr	NM
❑ 2-4095	The Best of Pete Fountain, Vol. 2	1977	$25

— *Tan labels*

Number	Title	Yr	NM
❑ 506	The Blues	1974	$25

— *Reissue of Decca 75375*

PICKWICK

Number	Title	Yr	NM
❑ SPC-3201	High Society	1971	$25
❑ SPC-3024	Pete Fountain	196?	$30

RCA CAMDEN

Number	Title	Yr	NM
❑ CAL-727 [M]	Dixieland	1962	$30
❑ CAS-727 [R]	Dixieland	1962	$25

RCA VICTOR

Number	Title	Yr	NM
❑ LPM-2097 [M]	Pete Fountain at the Jazz Band Ball	1960	$35
❑ LSP-2097 [S]	Pete Fountain at the Jazz Band Ball	1960	$50

VOCALION

Number	Title	Yr	NM
❑ VL3803 [M]	And the Angels Sing	1967	$30
❑ VL73803 [S]	And the Angels Sing	1967	$30

FOUR BROTHERS, THE

Members: SERGE CHALOFF; AL COHN; ZOOT SIMS; HERBIE STEWARD.

Albums

VIK

Number	Title	Yr	NM
❑ LX-1096 [M]	The Four Brothers -- Together Again	1957	$80

FOUR FRESHMEN, THE

Male vocal group and multi-instrumentalists. The original lineup was Bob Flanigan, Don Barbour, Ross Barbour and Hal Kratsch (1948-53), then the first three plus Ken Errair (1953-56), then the first three plus Ken Albers (1956-60). Bill Comstock replaced Don Barbour in 1960; that lineup remained stable until 1973. Many members have come and gone since; 22 different lineups have sung under the name.

Albums

CAPITOL

Number	Title	Yr	NM
❑ T763 [M]	4 Freshmen and 5 Trumpets	1957	$60
❑ SM-11965	Best of the Four Freshmen	1978	$25
❑ T1378 [M]	First Affair	1960	$80
❑ ST1378 [S]	First Affair	1960	$100
❑ T844 [M]	Four Freshmen and Five Saxes	1957	$60
❑ T683 [M]	Four Freshmen and Five Trombones	1956	$60
❑ SM-11639	Four Freshmen and Five Trombones	1977	$25
❑ T743 [M]	Freshmen Favorites	1956	$60
❑ DT743 [R]	Freshmen Favorites	196?	$60
❑ SM-743	Freshmen Favorites	197?	$25
❑ T1103 [M]	Freshmen Favorites, Vol. 2	1959	$80
❑ ST1103 [S]	Freshmen Favorites, Vol. 2	1959	$100
❑ T1485 [M]	Freshmen Year	1961	$80
❑ ST1485 [S]	Freshmen Year	1961	$100
❑ T2067 [M]	Funny How Time Slips Away	1964	$75
❑ ST2067 [S]	Funny How Time Slips Away	1964	$80
❑ T1950 [M]	Got That Feelin'	1963	$75
❑ ST1950 [S]	Got That Feelin'	1963	$80
❑ T1189 [M]	Love Lost	1959	$80
❑ ST1189 [S]	Love Lost	1959	$100
❑ T2168 [M]	More Four Freshmen and Five Trombones	1964	$75
❑ ST2168 [S]	More Four Freshmen and Five Trombones	1964	$80
❑ T1682 [M]	Stars in Our Eyes	1962	$80
❑ ST1682 [S]	Stars in Our Eyes	1962	$100
❑ T1753 [M]	Swingers	1963	$50
❑ ST1753 [S]	Swingers	1963	$80
❑ T1640 [M]	The Best of the Four Freshmen	1962	$80
❑ ST1640 [S]	The Best of the Four Freshmen	1962	$100
❑ T1255 [M]	The Four Freshmen and Five Guitars	1959	$80
❑ ST1255 [S]	The Four Freshmen and Five Guitars	1959	$100

Number	Title	Yr	NM
❑ T1008 [M]	The Four Freshmen In Person	1958	$100
❑ ST1008 [S]	The Four Freshmen In Person	1958	$60
❑ T1860 [M]	The Four Freshmen In Person, Volume 2	1963	$75
❑ ST1860 [S]	The Four Freshmen In Person, Volume 2	1963	$80
❑ T1295 [M]	Voices and Brass	1960	$80
❑ ST1295 [S]	Voices and Brass	1960	$100
❑ T1543 [M]	Voices in Fun	1961	$80
❑ ST1543 [S]	Voices in Fun	1961	$100
❑ T992 [M]	Voices in Latin	1958	$100
❑ T1074 [M]	Voices in Love	1958	$80
❑ ST1074 [S]	Voices in Love	1958	$100
❑ H522 [10]	Voices in Modern	1955	$150
❑ T522 [M]	Voices in Modern	1955	$75

CREATIVE WORLD

Number	Title	Yr	NM
❑ ST-1059	Stan Kenton and the Four Freshmen at Butler University	1972	$50

LIBERTY

Number	Title	Yr	NM
❑ LST-7630	Different Strokes	1969	$35
❑ LST-7590	In a Class By Themselves	1969	$35
❑ LN-10181	In a Class By Themselves	198?	$20
❑ LST-7563	Today Is Tomorrow	1968	$35

PAUSA

Number	Title	Yr	NM
❑ PR-9040	4 Freshmen and 5 Trumpets	1985	$25
❑ PR-7193	Fresh!	1986	$25
❑ PR-9029	The Four Freshmen and Five Guitars	198?	$25

PICKWICK

Number	Title	Yr	NM
❑ SPC-3563	A Taste of Honey	1977	$25
❑ SPC-3080	The Fabulous Four Freshmen	196?	$30

SUNSET

Number	Title	Yr	NM
❑ SUS-5289	My Special Angel	1970	$30

FOUR MOST, THE

Members: AL COHN; HANK JONES; MUNDELL LOWE; MAT MATHEWS; OSCAR PETTIFORD; JOE PUMA; GENE QUILL.

Albums

DAWN

Number	Title	Yr	NM
❑ DLP-1111 [M]	The Four Most	1956	$80

FOURTH WAY, THE

Early electric jazz group: MIKE NOCK (keyboards); RON McCLURE (bass), Michael White (violin); Eddie Marshall (drums).

Albums

CAPITOL

Number	Title	Yr	NM
❑ ST-317	The Fourth Way	1969	$100

HARVEST

Number	Title	Yr	NM
❑ SKAO-423	The Sun and Moon Have Come Together	1970	$50
❑ ST-666	Werewolf	1971	$50

FRANCIS, PANAMA

Drummer and bandleader.

Albums

20TH CENTURY FOX

Number	Title	Yr	NM
❑ TFS-6101 [S]	Tough Talk	196?	$30
❑ TFM-6101 [M]	Tough Talk	196?	$30

CLASSIC JAZZ

Number	Title	Yr	NM
❑ 149	Panama Francis and His Savoy Sultans, Volume 1	197?	$25
❑ 150	Panama Francis and His Savoy Sultans, Volume 2	197?	$25

EPIC

Number	Title	Yr	NM
❑ LN3839 [M]	Exploding Drums	1959	$60
❑ BN629 [S]	Exploding Drums	1959	$60

STASH

Number	Title	Yr	NM
❑ ST-223	Everything Swings	198?	$25
❑ ST-218	Grooving	198?	$25

FRANKLIN, ARETHA

Female singer and pianist. In her pre-Atlantic days, "The Queen of Soul" was anything but. Much of her Columbia output was jazzy or pop-oriented. For a more complete listing, see the Standard Catalog of American Records 1950-1975.

Albums

COLUMBIA

Number	Title	Yr	NM
❑ CL1612 [M]	Aretha	1961	$100

— *Red and black label with six "eye" logos*

Number	Title	Yr	NM
❑ CL1612 [M]	Aretha	1963	$50

— *Guaranteed High Fidelity" on label*

Number	Title	Yr	NM
❑ CL1612 [M]	Aretha	1965	$35

— *360 Sound Mono" on label*

Number	Title	Yr	NM
❑ CS8412 [S]	Aretha	1961	$150

— *Red and black label with six "eye" logos*

Number	Title	Yr	NM
❑ CS8412 [S]	Aretha	1963	$60

— *360 Sound Stereo" on label*

Number	Title	Yr	NM
❑ FC40708	Aretha After Hours	1987	$25
❑ CL2673 [M]	Aretha Franklin's Greatest Hits	1967	$60
❑ CS9473 [S]	Aretha Franklin's Greatest Hits	1967	$50

— *360 Sound Stereo" on label*

Number	Title	Yr	NM
❑ CS9601	Aretha Franklin's Greatest Hits, Volume 2	1968	$50

— *360 Sound Stereo" on label*

Number	Title	Yr	NM
❑ FC40105	Aretha Franklin Sings the Blues	1985	$25
❑ KG31355	In the Beginning/The World of Aretha Franklin 1960-1967	1972	$50
❑ CL2079 [M]	Laughing on the Outside	1963	$50

— *Guaranteed High Fidelity" on label*

Number	Title	Yr	NM
❑ CL2079 [M]	Laughing on the Outside	1965	$35

— *360 Sound Mono" on label*

Number	Title	Yr	NM
❑ CS8879 [S]	Laughing on the Outside	1963	$60

— *360 Sound Stereo" on label*

Number	Title	Yr	NM
❑ CL2281 [M]	Runnin' Out of Fools	1964	$50

— *Guaranteed High Fidelity" on label*

Number	Title	Yr	NM
❑ CL2281 [M]	Runnin' Out of Fools	1965	$35

— *360 Sound Mono" on label*

Number	Title	Yr	NM
❑ CS9081 [S]	Runnin' Out of Fools	1964	$60

— *360 Sound Stereo" on label*

Number	Title	Yr	NM
❑ CS9776	Soft and Beautiful	1969	$50

— *360 Sound Stereo" on label*

Number	Title	Yr	NM
❑ CL2521 [M]	Soul Sister	1966	$50
❑ CS9321 [S]	Soul Sister	1966	$60

— *360 Sound Stereo" on label*

Number	Title	Yr	NM
❑ PC38042	Sweet Bitter Love	1982	$25
❑ CL2754 [M]	Take a Look	1967	$60
❑ CS9554 [S]	Take a Look	1967	$50

— *360 Sound Stereo" on label*

Number	Title	Yr	NM
❑ CL2629 [M]	Take It Like You Give It	1967	$60
❑ CS9429 [S]	Take It Like You Give It	1967	$50

— *360 Sound Stereo" on label*

Number	Title	Yr	NM
❑ CL1761 [M]	The Electrifying Aretha Franklin	1962	$40

— *Red and black label with six "eye" logos*

Number	Title	Yr	NM
❑ CL1761 [M]	The Electrifying Aretha Franklin	1963	$50

— *Guaranteed High Fidelity" on label*

Number	Title	Yr	NM
❑ CL1761 [M]	The Electrifying Aretha Franklin	1965	$35

— *360 Sound Mono" on label*

Number	Title	Yr	NM
❑ CS8561 [S]	The Electrifying Aretha Franklin	1962	$100

— *Red and black label with six "eye" logos*

Number	Title	Yr	NM
❑ KC31953	The First 12 Sides	1973	$30
❑ C237377	The Legendary Queen of Soul	1981	$30
❑ CL1876 [M]	The Tender, The Moving, The Swinging Aretha Franklin	1962	$40

— *Red and black label with six "eye" logos*

Number	Title	Yr	NM
❑ CL1876 [M]	The Tender, The Moving, The Swinging Aretha Franklin	1963	$50

— *Guaranteed High Fidelity" on label*

Number	Title	Yr	NM
❑ CL1876 [M]	The Tender, The Moving, The Swinging Aretha Franklin	1965	$35

— *360 Sound Mono" on label*

Number	Title	Yr	NM
❑ CS8676 [S]	The Tender, The Moving, The Swinging Aretha Franklin	1963	$60

— *360 Sound Stereo" on label*

Number	Title	Yr	NM
❑ CS8676 [S]	The Tender, The Moving, The Swinging Aretha Franklin	1962	$100

— *Red and black label with six "eye" logos*

Number	Title	Yr	NM
❑ CS9956	Today I Sing the Blues	1970	$35

— *360 Sound Stereo" on label*

Number	Title	Yr	NM
❑ GP4	Two All-Time Great Albums in One Great Package	196?	$60

— *Contains CS 9081 and CS 9429*

Number	Title	Yr	NM
❑ CL2163 [M]	Unforgettable	1964	$50

— *Guaranteed High Fidelity" on label*

Number	Title	Yr	NM
❏ CL2163 [M]	Unforgettable	1965	$35
—360 Sound Mono" on label			
❏ CS8963 [S]	Unforgettable	1964	$60
—360 Sound Stereo" on label			
❏ CL2351 [M]	Yeah!!!	1965	$50
—Guaranteed High Fidelity" on label			
❏ CL2351 [M]	Yeah!!!	1966	$35
—360 Sound Mono" on label			
❏ CS9151 [S]	Yeah!!!	1965	$60
—360 Sound Stereo" on label			
COLUMBIA SPECIAL PRODUCTS			
❏ C11282	Runnin' Out of Fools	1972	$30
❏ C10589	Take a Look	1971	$30
HARMONY			
❏ KH30606	Greatest Hits 1960-1965	1971	$30
❏ KH30606	Greatest Hits 1960-1966	1972	$30
❏ HS11349	Once in a Lifetime	1969	$30
❏ HS11418	Two Sides of Love	1970	$30

FRANKLIN, HENRY
Bass player.

Albums

Number	Title	Yr	NM
BLACK JAZZ			
❏ QD-7	The Skipper	1972	$25
❏ QD-17	The Skipper At Home	1974	$25
CATALYST			
❏ 7618	Tribal Dance	1976	$30
OVATION			
❏ OV-1801	Blue Lights	197?	$35

FRANKLIN, RODNEY
Keyboard player.

Albums

Number	Title	Yr	NM
COLUMBIA			
❏ FC37154	Endless Flight	1982	$25
❏ JC35558	In the Center	1978	$25
❏ FC40307	It Takes Two	1986	$25
❏ FC38198	Learning to Love	1983	$25
❏ FC38953	Marathon	1984	$25
❏ JC36747	Rodney Franklin	1980	$25
❏ FC39962	Sky Dance	1985	$25
❏ JC36122	You'll Never Know	1979	$25
NOVUS			
❏ 3038-1-N	King of Diamonds	1988	$25

FRANKS, MICHAEL
Male singer.

Albums

Number	Title	Yr	NM
BRUT			
❏ 6005	Michael Franks	1973	$50
DIRECT DISK			
❏ SD-16611	Tiger in the Rain	1980	$60
—Audiophile vinyl			
DRG			
❏ SL-5210	Previously Unavailable	1989	$30
—Reissue of John Hammond LP			
JOHN HAMMOND			
❏ BFW38664	Previously Unavailable	1983	$35
REPRISE			
❏ 26183	Blue Pacific	1990	$15
❏ MS2230	The Art of Tea	1975	$25
WARNER BROS.			
❏ BSK3167	Burchfield Nines	1978	$25
❏ BSK3648	Objects of Desire	1981	$25
❏ BSK3427	One Bad Habit	1980	$25
❏ 23962	Passion Fruit	1983	$20
❏ 25275	Skin Dive	1985	$20
❏ BS3004	Sleeping Gypsy	1977	$25
❏ 25570	The Camera Never Lies	1987	$20
❏ BSK3294	Tiger in the Rain	1979	$25

FRANZETTI, CARLOS
Pianist, composer and arranger.

Albums

Number	Title	Yr	NM
INNER CITY			
❏ IC-1113	Galaxy Dust	1980	$30
PROGRESSIVE			
❏ PRO-7030	Prometheus	198?	$30

FRASER, HUGH
Trombonist and pianist.

Albums

Number	Title	Yr	NM
JAZZIMAGE			
❏ JZ-115	Looking Up	1988	$25

FRAZIER, CAESAR
Organist and male singer. Some of these may spell his first name "Ceasar."

Albums

Number	Title	Yr	NM
EASTBOUND			
❏ 9009	Caesar Frazier '74	1974	$40
❏ 9002	Hail Caesar!	1973	$50
WESTBOUND			
❏ WT6103	Another Life	1978	$30
❏ 206	Caesar Frazier '75	1975	$30

FREE FLIGHT
Founded by flutist Jim Walker; MIKE GARSON has been a near-permanent member also. The rest of the group varies from year to year.

Albums

Number	Title	Yr	NM
ARABESQUE			
❏ 8130	Free Flight	1981	$30
CBS			
❏ BFM42143	Illumination	1986	$25
PALO ALTO			
❏ PA-8075	Beyond the Clouds	1984	$25
❏ PA-8050	Soaring	1983	$25
❏ PA-8024	The Jazz/Classical Union	1982	$25
VOSS			
❏ VLP1-42932	Free Flight	1988	$25
—Reissue of Arabesque LP			

FREE MUSIC QUARTET, THE

Albums

Number	Title	Yr	NM
ESP-DISK'			
❏ 1083	Free Music One and Two	1969	$100

FREEDMAN, BOB
Pianist. Also a saxophone player and composer.

Albums

Number	Title	Yr	NM
COBBLESTONE			
❏ 9009	Journeys of Odysseus	1972	$25
SAVOY			
❏ MG-15040 [10]	Piano Moods	1954	$50

FREEMAN, BUD, AND BUDDY TATE
Also see each artist's individual listings.

Albums

Number	Title	Yr	NM
CIRCLE			
❏ 69	Two Beautiful	198?	$25

FREEMAN, BUD
Tenor saxophone player, clarinetist and composer. Also see BOBBY BYRNE; JOE MARSALA.

Albums

Number	Title	Yr	NM
BETHLEHEM			
❏ BCP-29 [M]	Newport News	1955	$250
❏ BCP-6033	Test of Time	197?	$30
—Reissue, distributed by RCA Victor			
CAPITOL			
❏ H625 [10]	Classics in Jazz	1955	$150
❏ T625 [M]	Classics in Jazz	1955	$80
CHIAROSCURO			
❏ 135	The Joy of Sax	1975	$35
CIRCLE			
❏ 10	Bud Freeman and Jimmy McPartland Meet the Ted Easton Jazz Band	198?	$25
COLUMBIA			
❏ CL6107 [10]	Comes Jazz	1950	$100
❏ CL2558 [10]	Jazz -- Chicago Style	1955	$80
COMMODORE			
❏ XFL-14941	Three's No Crowd	198?	$30
DECCA			
❏ DL5213 [10]	Wolverine Jazz	1950	$200
DOT			

Number	Title	Yr	NM
❏ DLP-3166 [M]	Bud Freeman and His Summa Cum Laude Trio	1959	$80
❏ DLP-25166 [S]	Bud Freeman and His Summa Cum Laude Trio	1959	$75
❏ DLP-3254 [M]	Midnight Session	1960	$75
❏ DLP-25254 [S]	Midnight Session	1960	$80
EMARCY			
❏ MG-36013 [M]	Midnight at Eddie Condon's	1955	$200
FANTASY			
❏ OJC-183	Bud Freeman All Stars	198?	$25
—Reissue of Swingville 2012			
HALO			
❏ 50275 [M]	Bud Freeman	195?	$35
HARMONY			
❏ HL7046 [M]	Bud Freeman and His All-Star Jazz	1957	$30
IAJRC			
❏ LP-53	See What the Boys in the Back Room Will Have	198?	$25
JAZZ ARCHIVES			
❏ JA-38	Summer Concert 1960	198?	$25
JAZZOLOGY			
❏ J-165	The Compleat Bud Freeman	198?	$25
MONMOUTH-EVERGREEN			
❏ 7022	The Compleat Bud Freeman	1970	$25
PARAMOUNT			
❏ CJS-105 [10]	Bud Freeman and the Chicagoans	195?	$80
PROMENADE			
❏ 2134 [M]	Dixieland U.S.A.	196?	$30
RCA VICTOR			
❏ LPM-1508 [M]	Chicago Austin High School Jazz in Hi-Fi	1957	$50
SWINGVILLE			
❏ SVLP-2012 [M]	Bud Freeman All Stars	1960	$50
—Purple label			
❏ SVLP-2012 [M]	Bud Freeman All Stars	1965	$30
—Blue label with trident logo at right			
TRIP			
❏ 5529	Midnight at Eddie Condon's	197?	$25
UNITED ARTISTS			
❏ UAJ-14033 [M]	Something Tender -- Bud Freeman and Two Guitars	1963	$40
❏ UAJS-15033 [S]	Something Tender -- Bud Freeman and Two Guitars	1963	$50

FREEMAN, CHICO
Tenor saxophone player. Also a trumpeter, keyboard player and composer. Also see THE YOUNG LIONS.

Albums

Number	Title	Yr	NM
BLACKHAWK			
❏ BKH-50801	The Pied Piper	1986	$25
BLACK SAINT			
❏ BSR-0036	No Time Left	1977	$30
CONTEMPORARY			
❏ C-7640	Beyond the Rain	1978	$30
❏ C-14008	Destiny's Dance	1981	$30
❏ C-14005	Peaceful Heart, Gentle Spirit	1980	$30
ELEKTRA/MUSICIAN			
❏ 60361	Tangents	1984	$25
❏ 60163	Tradition in Transition	1983	$25
FANTASY			
❏ OJC-479	Beyond the Rain	1991	$25
INDIA NAVIGATION			
❏ IN-1031	Chico	1977	$35
❏ IN-1035	Kings of Mali	1978	$35
❏ IN-1063	Morning Prayer	198?	$30
❏ IN-1045	Spirit Sensitive	1979	$35
❏ IN-1042	The Outside Within	1981	$30
❏ IN-1059	The Search	1981	$30

FREEMAN, GEORGE
Guitarist.

Albums

Number	Title	Yr	NM
DELMARK			
❏ DS-424	Birth Sign	197?	$30
GROOVE MERCHANT			
❏ 3305	Man and Woman	1975	$35
❏ 519	New Improved Funk	1973	$35

FREEMAN, RUSS
Pianist. Not the same Russ Freeman who is with THE RIPPINGTONS.

Red Garland, All Mornin' Long, Prestige PRLP-7130, yellow label with W. 50th St. address, **$300**.

Red Garland, *Manteca*, Prestige PRLP-7139, yellow label with W. 50th St. address, **$300**.

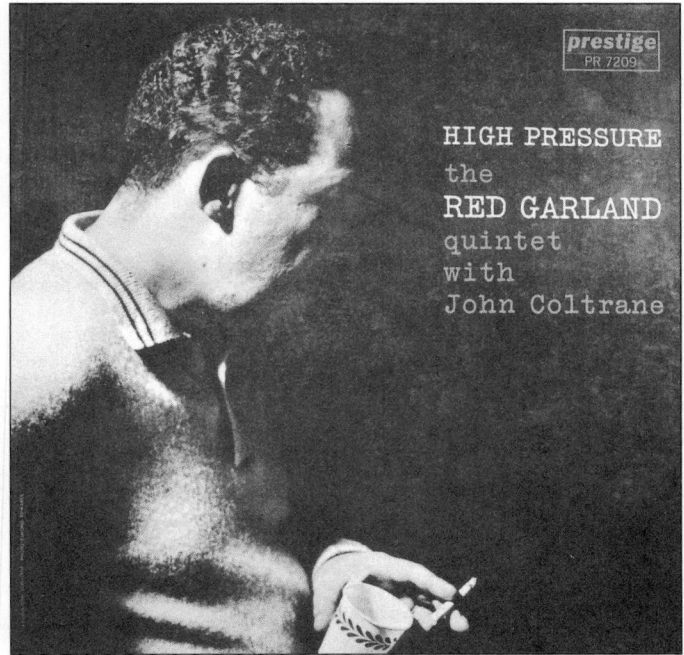

Red Garland, *High Pressure*, Prestige PRLP-7209, yellow label with Bergenfield, N.J., address, **$200**.

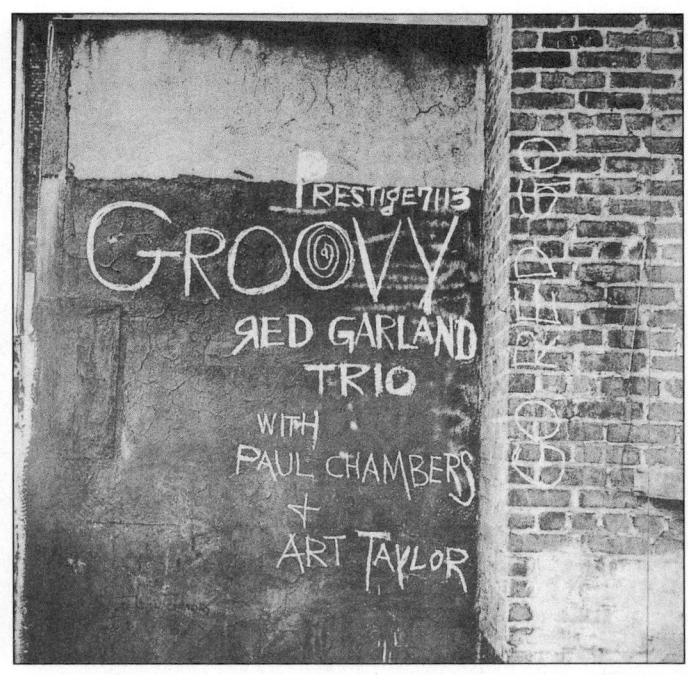

Red Garland, *Groovy*, Prestige PRLP-7113, yellow label with W. 50th St. address, **$300**.

Number	Title	Yr	NM

Albums

PACIFIC JAZZ
| ❏ PJ-1232 [M] | Quartet: Russ Freeman/ Chet Baker | 1957 | $200 |

—Label says Pacific Jazz, but cover is on World Pacific

| ❏ PJLP-8 [10] | The Russ Freeman Trio | 1953 | $120 |
| ❏ PJ-1212 [M] | Trio: Russ Freeman/Richard Twardzik | 1956 | $100 |

WORLD PACIFIC
| ❏ WP-1232 [M] | Quartet: Russ Freeman/ Chet Baker | 1958 | $150 |

—Both label and cover are on World Pacific

| ❏ WP-1212 [M] | Trio: Russ Freeman/Richard Twardzik | 1958 | $150 |

FREEMAN, STAN

Pianist, harpsichordist and composer. Best known for his harpsichord work on the ROSEMARY CLOONEY hit "Come On-a My House."

Albums

AUDIOPHILE
| ❏ AP-202 | Not a Care in the World | 1986 | $25 |

COLUMBIA
❏ CL6193 [10]	Come On-a Stan's House	1951	$60
❏ CL6158 [10]	Piano Moods	1951	$50
❏ CL1120 [M]	Stan Freeman Swings "The Music Man	1958	$30

HARMONY
| ❏ HL7067 [M] | Stan Freeman Plays 30 All-Time Hits | 195? | $25 |

FREEMAN, VON

Tenor saxophone player.

Albums

ATLANTIC
| ❏ SD1628 | Doin' It Right Now | 1972 | $30 |

NESSA
| ❏ 6 | Have No Fear | 1975 | $35 |
| ❏ 11 | Serenade and Blues | 197? | $35 |

FRENCH, ALBERT "PAPA

Banjo player and bandleader.

Albums

NOBILITY
| ❏ LP-702 [M] | A Night at Dixieland Hall | 195? | $40 |

FRENCH MARKET JAZZ BAND, THE

Albums

FLYING DUTCHMAN
| ❏ BDL1-1239 | The French Market Jazz Band | 1976 | $25 |

FRIEDMAN, DAVID

Vibraphone player.

Albums

ENJA
| ❏ 3089 | Of the Wind's Eye | 1982 | $30 |

INNER CITY
| ❏ IC-3004 | Futures Passed | 1976 | $30 |
| ❏ IC-6005 | Winter Love April Joy | 1979 | $30 |

FRIEDMAN, DON

Pianist.

Albums

PRESTIGE
| ❏ PRLP-7488 [M] | Metamorphosis | 1966 | $30 |
| ❏ PRST-7488 [S] | Metamorphosis | 1966 | $30 |

PROGRESSIVE
| ❏ PRO-7036 | Hot Knepper and Pepper | 198? | $30 |

RIVERSIDE
❏ RLP-384 [M]	A Day in the City	1961	$200
❏ RS-9384 [S]	A Day in the City	1961	$200
❏ RS-9431 [S]	Circle Waltz	1962	$200
❏ 6082	Circle Waltz	197?	$35

—Reissue of 9431

❏ RLP-485 [M]	Dreams and Explorations	1965	$150
❏ RS-9485 [S]	Dreams and Explorations	1965	$150
❏ RLP-463 [M]	Flashback	1963	$150
❏ RS-9463 [S]	Flashback	1963	$150
❏ 6094	Flashback	197?	$35

—Reissue of 9463

FRIENDS

Jazz-rock band featuring JOHN ABERCROMBIE and Marc Cohen.

Albums

OBLIVION
| ❏ OD-3 | Friends | 1974 | $25 |

—Jazz-rock band with John Abercrombie and Marc Cohen

FRIESEN, DAVID, AND JOHN STOWELL

Stowell is a guitarist. Also see DAVID FRIESEN.

Albums

INNER CITY
| ❏ IC-1061 | Through the Listening Glass | 1979 | $30 |

FRIESEN, DAVID

Bass player.

Albums

GLOBAL PACIFIC
| ❏ OW40718 | Inner Voices | 1987 | $25 |

INNER CITY
❏ IC-1086	Other Mansions	1980	$30
❏ IC-1019	Star Dance	1977	$30
❏ IC-1027	Waterfall Rainbow	1978	$30

MUSE
| ❏ MR-5109 | Color Pool | 197? | $30 |
| ❏ MR-5255 | Storyteller | 1981 | $25 |

STEEPLECHASE
| ❏ SCS-1138 | Paths Beyond Tracing | 1980 | $30 |

FRIESEN, EUGENE

Cellist. Member of the PAUL WINTER Consort.

Albums

LIVING MUSIC
| ❏ LM-0007 | New Friend | 1986 | $25 |

FRIGO, JOHNNY

Violinist.

Albums

MERCURY
| ❏ MG-20285 [M] | I Love Johnny Frigo, He Swings | 1957 | $100 |

FRISELL, BILL, AND VERNON REID

Reid, a guitarist, was later with the rock band Living Colour. Also see BILL FRISELL.

Albums

MINOR MUSIC
| ❏ MM-005 | Smash and Scatteration | 1984 | $35 |

FRISELL, BILL

Guitarist.

Albums

ECM
| ❏ 1241 | In Line | 198? | $25 |
| ❏ 25026 | Rambler | 1985 | $25 |

ELEKTRA/MUSICIAN
| ❏ 60843 | Before We Were Born | 1988 | $25 |

FRISHBERG, DAVE

Pianist, male singer and composer.

Albums

CONCORD JAZZ
| ❏ CJ-37 | Getting Some Fun Out | 197? | $30 |
| ❏ CJ-74 | You're a Lucky Guy | 1978 | $30 |

FANTASY
| ❏ F-9651 | Can't Take You Nowhere | 1987 | $25 |
| ❏ F-9638 | Live at Vine Street | 1985 | $25 |

OMNISOUND
| ❏ 1040 | Songbook | 198? | $25 |
| ❏ 1051 | Songbook, Volume 2 | 198? | $25 |

FROEBA, FRANK

Pianist.

Albums

DECCA
| ❏ DL5043 [10] | Back Room Piano | 1950 | $150 |

| ❏ DL5048 [10] | Old Time Piano | 1950 | $150 |

ROYALE
| ❏ 1818 [10] | Old Time Piano | 1954 | $40 |

VARSITY
| ❏ 6031 [10] | Boys in the Backroom | 1950 | $50 |

FROM THE OTHER SIDE JAZZ BAND

Among the members: Mike Greenblatt.

Albums

SOUL NOTE
| ❏ 121106 | From the Other Side | 1990 | $30 |

FRONTIERE, DOMINIC

Accordion player, bandleader and composer.

Albums

COLUMBIA
❏ CL1427 [M]	Love Eyes: The Moods of Romance	1960	$30
❏ CS8224 [S]	Love Eyes: The Moods of Romance	1960	$40
❏ CL1273 [M]	Pagan Festival	1958	$40

LIBERTY
❏ LRP-3032 [M]	Dom Frontiere Plays the Classics	1957	$40
❏ LRP-3015 [M]	Fabulous!	1956	$40
❏ LST-7008 [S]	Mr. Accordion	1958	$40

—Evidently not issued in mono

| ❏ LJH-6002 [M] | The Dom Frontiere Sextet | 1956 | $50 |

FRUSCELLA, TONY

Trumpeter.

FUKUMURA, HIROSHI

Trombone player.

Albums

INNER CITY
| ❏ IC-6067 | Hunt Up Wind | 198? | $30 |

FULL CIRCLE

Among this fusion band's members are Karl Lundberg (keyboards, vocals); Anders Bostrom (flute, piccolo) and Philip Hamilton (vocals, percussion).

Albums

COLUMBIA
| ❏ FC40966 | Full Circle | 1988 | $25 |
| ❏ FC44474 | Myth America | 1989 | $30 |

FULL FAITH AND CREDIT BIG BAND, THE

Albums

PALO ALTO
| ❏ PA-8001 | Debut | 198? | $25 |
| ❏ PA-8003 | JazzFaire | 198? | $25 |

FULL MOON

Albums

DOUGLAS
| ❏ KZ31904 | Full Moon | 1972 | $35 |

FULL SWING

Female vocal trio. Also see LORRAINE FEATHER.

Albums

CYPRESS
| ❏ YL 0109 | In Full Swing | 1988 | $25 |
| ❏ YL 0128 | The End of the Sky | 1989 | $30 |

PLANET
| ❏ BXL1-4426 | Good Times Are Back! | 1982 | $25 |

FULLER, CURTIS

Trombone player.

Albums

ABC IMPULSE!
| ❏ AS-22 [S] | Cabin in the Sky | 1968 | $30 |

BEE HIVE
| ❏ BH-7007 | Fire and Filigree | 197? | $30 |

BLUE NOTE
| ❏ BLP-1572 [M] | Bone and Bari | 1957 | $200 |

Number	Title	Yr	NM
—Regular version with W. 63rd St. address on label			
❏ BLP-1572 [M]	Bone and Bari	1963	$130
—New York, USA" address on label			
❏ BST-1572 [S]	Bone and Bari	1959	$150
—Regular version with W. 63rd St. address on label			
❏ BST-1572 [S]	Bone and Bari	1963	$100
—New York, USA" address on label			
❏ BST-81572 [S]	Bone and Bari	1967	$35
—A Division of Liberty Records" on label			
❏ BLP-1583 [M]	Curtis Fuller, Volume 3	1958	$180
—Regular version with W. 63rd St. address on label			
❏ BLP-1583 [M]	Curtis Fuller, Volume 3	1963	$200
—New York, USA" address on label			
❏ BST-1583 [S]	Curtis Fuller, Volume 3	1959	$150
—Regular version with W. 63rd St. address on label			
❏ BST-1583 [S]	Curtis Fuller, Volume 3	1963	$100
—New York, USA" address on label			
❏ BST-81583 [S]	Curtis Fuller, Volume 3	1967	$35
❏ BLP-1567 [M]	The Opener	1957	$3000
—Deep groove" version (deep indentation under label on both sides)			
❏ BLP-1567 [M]	The Opener	1957	$150
—Regular version with W. 63rd St. address on label			
❏ BLP-1567 [M]	The Opener	1963	$60
—New York, USA" address on label			
❏ BST-1567 [S]	The Opener	1959	$50
—Regular version with W. 63rd St. address on label			
❏ BST-1567 [S]	The Opener	1963	$25
—New York, USA" address on label			
❏ BST-81567 [S]	The Opener	1967	$35
—A Division of Liberty Records" on label			
EPIC			
❏ BA17020 [S]	South American Cookin'	1961	$100
❏ LA16013 [M]	The Magnificent Trombone	1961	$60
❏ BA17013 [M]	The Magnificent Trombone	1961	$80
FANTASY			
❏ OJC-077	New Trombone	198?	$25
IMPULSE!			
❏ A-22 [M]	Cabin in the Sky	1962	$120
❏ AS-22 [S]	Cabin in the Sky	1962	$120
❏ A-13 [M]	Soul Trombone	1962	$120
❏ AS-13 [S]	Soul Trombone	1962	$120
MAINSTREAM			
❏ MRL-333	Crankin'	1971	$25
❏ MRL-370	Smokin'	1972	$25
NEW JAZZ			
❏ NJLP-8305 [M]	Curtis Fuller and Hampton Hawes with French Horns	1963	$0
—Canceled; re-assigned to Status label			
❏ NJLP-8277 [M]	Curtis Fuller with Red Garland	1962	$150
—Purple label			
❏ NJLP-8277 [M]	Curtis Fuller with Red Garland	1965	$150
—Blue label, trident logo at right			
REGENT			
❏ MG-6055 [M]	Jazz...It's Magic	1957	$80
SAVOY			
❏ MG-12141 [M]	Blues-Ette	1959	$50
❏ ST-13006 [S]	Blues-Ette	1959	$40
❏ MG-12151 [M]	Curtis Fuller	1960	$40
❏ MG-12164 [M]	Images of Curts Fuller	1960	$40
❏ MG-12144 [M]	Imagination	1959	$40
❏ MG-12209 [M]	Jazz...It's Magic	196?	$25
SAVOY JAZZ			
❏ SJL-2239	All-Star Sextets	197?	$30
❏ SJL-1135	Blues-Ette	198?	$25
SMASH			
❏ MGS-27034 [M]	Jazz Conference Abroad	1962	$30
❏ SRS-67034 [S]	Jazz Conference Abroad	1962	$30
STATUS			
❏ ST-8305 [M]	Curtis Fuller and Hampton Hawes with French Horns	1965	$40
UNITED ARTISTS			
❏ UAS-5051 [S]	Sliding Easy	1959	$40
WARWICK			
❏ W-2038ST [S]	Boss of the Soul Stream Trombone	1961	$50

FULLER, GIL
Bandleader and composer.

Albums

PACIFIC JAZZ

Number	Title	Yr	NM
❏ PJ-93 [M]	Gil Fuller and the Monterey Jazz Orchestra with Dizzy Gillespie	1965	$30
❏ ST-93 [S]	Gil Fuller and the Monterey Jazz Orchestra with Dizzy Gillespie	1965	$30
❏ LN-10060	Gil Fuller and the Monterey Jazz Orchestra with Dizzy Gillespie	198?	$20
—Budget-line reissue			
❏ PJ-10101 [M]	Night Flight	1966	$25
❏ ST-20101 [S]	Night Flight	1966	$30
❏ LN-10128	Night Flight	198?	$20
—Budget-line reissue			

FULLER, JERRY (2)
Clarinetist.

Albums

ANDEX

Number	Title	Yr	NM
❏ A-3008 [M]	Clarinet Portrait	1958	$40
❏ AS-3008 [S]	Clarinet Portrait	1959	$30

FUNK INC.
Members in the 1970s: Eugene Barr (tenor saxophone); Bobby Watley (organ); Steve Weakley; Jimmy Munford; Cecil Hunt (percussion).

Albums

PRESTIGE

Number	Title	Yr	NM
❏ 10043	Chicken Lickin'	1972	$35
❏ 10031	Funk Inc.	1971	$35
❏ 10059	Hangin' Out	1973	$35
❏ 10087	Priced to Sell	1974	$35
❏ 10071	Superfunk	1973	$35

FUSE ONE
All-star group: JOE FARRELL; JOHN McLAUGHLIN; RONNIE FOSTER; STANLEY CLARKE; Ndugu; PAULINHO DA COSTA,; Lenny White (drums); Marcus Miller (bass); WYNTON MARSALIS; DAVE VALENTIN; GEORGE BENSON.

Albums

CTI

Number	Title	Yr	NM
❏ 9003	Fuse One	1980	$30
❏ 9006	Silk	1981	$30

FUTTERMAN, JOEL
Pianist, curved soprano saxophone player and Indian flutist.

Albums

SILKHEART

Number	Title	Yr	NM
❏ SH-125	Vision in Time	1991	$30

G

GADD GANG, THE
Drummer and percussionist Steve Gadd with CORNELL DUPREE, EDDIE GOMEZ, Richard Tee (keyboards) and guests.

Albums

COLUMBIA

Number	Title	Yr	NM
❏ FC44327	Here and Now	1988	$30
❏ FC40864	The Gadd Gang	1987	$25

GAFA, AL
Guitarist.

Albums

PABLO

Number	Title	Yr	NM
❏ 2310782	Leblon Beach	1976	$30

GAILLARD, SLIM
Best known as a guitarist and male singer. Also a pianist, vibraphone player, tenor saxophone player and composer; he co-wrote "Flat Foot Floogie" and "Cement Mixer (Put-ti Put-ti)," among others.

Albums

ALLEGRO ELITE

Number	Title	Yr	NM
❏ 4050 [10]	Slim Gaillard Plays	195?	$30
CLEF			
❏ MGC-126 [10]	Mish Mash	1953	$250
❏ MGC-138 [10]	Slim Cavorts	1953	$250
DISC			
❏ DLP-505 [10]	Opera in Vout	195?	$200

Number	Title	Yr	NM
DOT			
❏ DLP-25190 [S]	Slim Gaillard Rides Again	1959	$80
❏ DLP-3190 [M]	Slim Gaillard Rides Again	1959	$75
KING			
❏ 295-80 [10]	Slim Gaillard/Boogie	195?	$100
MCA			
❏ 1508	The Dot Sessions	198?	$75
MERCURY			
❏ MGC-126 [10]	Mish Mash	1953	$0
—Canceled; reassigned to Clef 126			
NORGRAN			
❏ MGN-13 [10]	Slim Gaillard and His Musical Aggregation Wherever They May Be	1954	$100
VERVE			
❏ MGV-2013 [M]	Smorgasbord, Help Yourself	1956	$200
❏ V-2013 [M]	Smorgasbord, Help Yourself	1961	$25

GAILLARD, SLIM/DIZZY GILLESPIE
Also see each artist's individual listings.

Albums

ULTRAPHONIC

Number	Title	Yr	NM
❏ ULP-50273 [M]	Gaillard and Gillespie	1958	$40

GAILLARD, SLIM/MEADE LUX LEWIS
Also see each artist's individual listings.

Albums

CLEF

Number	Title	Yr	NM
❏ MGC-506 [10]	Boogie Woogie at the Philharmonic	1954	$300
MERCURY			
❏ MGC-506 [10]	Boogie Woogie at the Philharmonic	1951	$300

GAINEN, MAURY
Violinist.

Albums

DISCOVERY

Number	Title	Yr	NM
❏ DS-855	Jazz Sunrise	198?	$25

GALASSO, MICHAEL

Albums

ECM

Number	Title	Yr	NM
❏ 1245	Scenes	198?	$30

GALAXY ALL-STARS, THE

Albums

GALAXY

Number	Title	Yr	NM
❏ GXY-95001	Live Under the Sky	1979	$35

GALBRAITH, BARRY
Guitarist. Also see THE MANHATTAN JAZZ SEPTETTE.

Albums

DECCA

Number	Title	Yr	NM
❏ DL9200 [M]	Guitar and the Wind	1958	$120
❏ DL79200 [S]	Guitar and the Wind	1959	$80

GALE, EDDIE
Trumpeter.

Albums

BLUE NOTE

Number	Title	Yr	NM
❏ BST-84320	Black Rhythm Happening	1969	$30
❏ BST-84294	Eddie Gale's Ghetto Music	1968	$30

GALE, ERIC
Guitarist.

Albums

COLUMBIA

Number	Title	Yr	NM
❏ PC34421	Ginseng	1977	$25
—Original edition with no bar code			
❏ JC34938	Multiplication	1978	$25
❏ JC35715	Part of You	1979	$25
❏ JC36363	The Best of Eric Gale	1980	$25
❏ JC36570	Touch of Silk	1981	$25
ELEKTRA/MUSICIAN			
❏ 60022	Blue Horizon	1982	$25
❏ 60198	Island Breeze	1984	$25

Number	Title	Yr	NM
EMARCY			
❑ 836369-1	In a Jazz Tradition	1989	$30
KUDU			
❑ 11	Forecast	1973	$35

GALLAGHER, BRIAN
Saxophone player, flutist and male singer.

Albums

CYPRESS			
❑ 0126	Coming Home	1989	$30

GALLERY (2)
Members: David Samuels (vibraharp, marimba); Michael DiPasqua (drums, percussion); Paul McCandless (soprano saxophone, oboe, English horn); David Darling (cello); Ratzo Harris (bass). No relation to the pop group of the 1970s.

Albums

ECM			
❑ 1206	Gallery	1982	$30

GALLODORO, AL
Clarinetist and saxophone player. Also see FREDDIE GARDNER.

Albums

ARCO			
❑ AL-3 [10]	Al Gallodoro Concert	1950	$50
COLUMBIA			
❑ CL6188 [10]	Al Gallodoro	1951	$50

GALLOWAY, JIM
Soprano, baritone and tenor saxophone player and clarinetist.

Albums

SACKVILLE			
❑ 4002	The Metro Stompers	198?	$150
❑ 4011	Thou Swell	198?	$25
❑ 2007	Three Is Company	198?	$25

GALPER, HAL
Pianist.

Albums

BLACKHAWK			
❑ BKH529	Naturally	1987	$35
CENTURY			
❑ 1120	Speak with a Single Voice	1978	$35
CONCORD JAZZ			
❑ CJ-383	Portrait	1988	$25
ENJA			
❑ 4006	Speak with a Single Voice	198?	$30
INNER CITY			
❑ IC-3012	Now Hear This	1977	$35
❑ IC-2067	Reach Out	1978	$35
MAINSTREAM			
❑ MRL-337	The Guerrilla Band	1971	$25
❑ MRL-354	Wild Bird	1972	$50
STEEPLECHASE			
❑ SCS-1067	Reach Out	198?	$30
— *Reissue of Inner City 2067*			

GAMALON
Fusion band led by guitarists Bruce Brucato and George Puleo.

Albums

AMHERST			
❑ AMH-3318	Gamalon	1988	$35

GAMBRELL, FREDDIE, AND PAUL HORN
Also see each artist's individual lstings.

Albums

WORLD PACIFIC			
❑ WP-1262 [M]	Mikado	1959	$150
❑ ST-1023 [S]	Mikado	1959	$100

GAMBRELL, FREDDIE
Pianist. Also see CHICO HAMILTON.

Albums

WORLD PACIFIC			
❑ WP-1256 [M]	Freddie Gambrell	1959	$150

Number	Title	Yr	NM
GANDELMAN, LEO			

Tenor saxophone player.

Albums

VERVE FORECAST			
❑ 836424-1	Western World	1989	$30

GANELIN TRIO, THE
From the former Soviet Union: Vyacheslav Ganelin (piano, guitar, percussion); Vladimir Tarasov (drums, percussion); Vladimir Chekasin (reeds).

Albums

HAT ART			
❑ 2027	Non Troppo	1986	$35

GANG STARR
Hip-hop duo influenced by jazz. Also see GURU.

Albums

CHRYSALIS			
❑ F1-21910	Daily Operation	1992	$20
❑ F1-28435	Hard to Earn	1994	$20
❑ F1-21798	Step In the Arena	1991	$20
VIRGIN			
❑ 47279	Full Clip -- A Decade of Gang Starr	1999	$25
❑ 45585	Moment of Truth	1998	$20
WILD PITCH			
❑ E1-98709	No More Mr. Nice Guy	1992	$15
❑ 2001	No More Mr. Nice Guy	1989	$20

GANNON, JIM
Guitarist.

Albums

CATALYST			
❑ 7605	Gannon's Back in Town	1976	$35

GARBAREK, JAN, AND BOBO STENSON
Stenson is a pianist. Also see JAN GARBAREK.

Albums

ECM			
❑ 1075	Dansere	1976	$30
❑ 1041	Witchi-Tai-To	1973	$30

GARBAREK, JAN, AND KJELL JOHNSEN
Johnsen is a pipe organ player. Also see JAN GARBAREK.

Albums

ECM			
❑ 1169	Aftenland	1980	$25

GARBAREK, JAN, AND TERJE RYPDAL
Also see each artist's individual listings.

Albums

ARISTA FREEDOM			
❑ AL1031	Esoteric	197?	$30

GARBAREK, JAN
Saxophone (soprano, tenor, bass) player. Also a clarinetist, flutist and percussionist.

Albums

ECM			
❑ 1093	Dis	1977	$30
❑ 1200	Eventyr	1981	$25
❑ 25033	It's OK to Listen to the Gray Voice	1985	$25
❑ 1151	Magico	1979	$25
❑ 1223	Paths, Prints	1982	$25
❑ 1135	Photo With…	1978	$25
❑ 1118	Places	1978	$25
❑ 23798	Wayfarer	1984	$25
FLYING DUTCHMAN			
❑ FD-10125	The Esoteric Circle	1971	$25

GARCIA, DICK
Guitarist.

Albums

SEECO			
❑ SLP-428 [M]	A Message from Dick Garcia	1958	$150

Number	Title	Yr	NM
GARCIA, RUSS, AND MARTY PAICH			

Also see each artist's individual listings.

Albums

BETHLEHEM			
❑ BCP-6039 [M]	Jazz Music for Birds and Hep Cats	1960	$300
❑ SBCP-6039 [S]	Jazz Music for Birds and Hep Cats	1960	$300

GARCIA, RUSS
Guitarist, arranger and composer.

Albums

ABC-PARAMOUNT			
❑ ABC-147 [M]	The Johnny Evergreens	1956	$50
BETHLEHEM			
❑ BCP-46 [M]	Four Horns and a Lush Life	1956	$250
❑ BCP-6044	I'll Never Forget What's Her Name	1978	$30
— *Reissue, distributed by RCA Victor*			
❑ BCP-1040 [10]	Wigville	1955	$250
DISCOVERY			
❑ DS-814	I Lead a Charmed Life	1980	$30
KAPP			
❑ KL-1050 [M]	Listen to the Music of Russell Garcia	1957	$50
LIBERTY			
❑ LRP-3062 [M]	Enchantment (The Music of Joe Greene)	1958	$30
❑ LRP-3084 [M]	Fantastica	1958	$30
VERVE			
❑ MGV-2088 [M]	The Warm Feeling	1957	$100
❑ V-2088 [M]	The Warm Feeling	1961	$25

GARDNER, FREDDY, AND AL GALLODORO
Also see each artist's individual listings.

Albums

COLUMBIA			
❑ CL623 [M]	The Immortal Freddy Gardner and Al Gallodoro	1954	$40
— *Maroon label, gold print*			

GARDNER, FREDDY
Clarinetist and tenor, alto and baritone saxophone player.

Albums

COLUMBIA			
❑ CL6187 [10]	Freddy Gardner	195?	$50

GARDONY, LASZLO
Pianist.

Albums

ANTILLES			
❑ 91250	The Legend of Tsumi	1989	$30
❑ 90694	The Secret	1988	$30

GARI, RALPH
Clarinetist. Also played alto saxophone, flute, piccolo and English horn.

Albums

EMARCY			
❑ MG-36019 [M]	Ralph Gari	1955	$200

GARLAND, HANK
Guitarist. Also known as a session musician for country artists.

Albums

COLUMBIA			
❑ CL1572 [M]	Jazz Winds from a New Direction	1961	$30
❑ CS8372 [S]	Jazz Winds from a New Direction	1961	$40
❑ CL1913 [M]	The Unforgettable Guitar of Hank Garland	1962	$30
❑ CS8713 [S]	The Unforgettable Guitar of Hank Garland	1962	$40
HARMONY			
❑ HL7231 [M]	Velvet Guitar	196?	$25
❑ HS11028 [S]	Velvet Guitar	196?	$30
SESAC			
❑ SN-2301/2 [M]	Subtle Swing	196?	$100

Erroll Garner, *Feeling Is Believing*, Mercury SR 61308, newer Mercury logo on cover, **$30**.

Erroll Garner, *Now Playing: Erroll Garner*, MGM E-4335, **$35**.

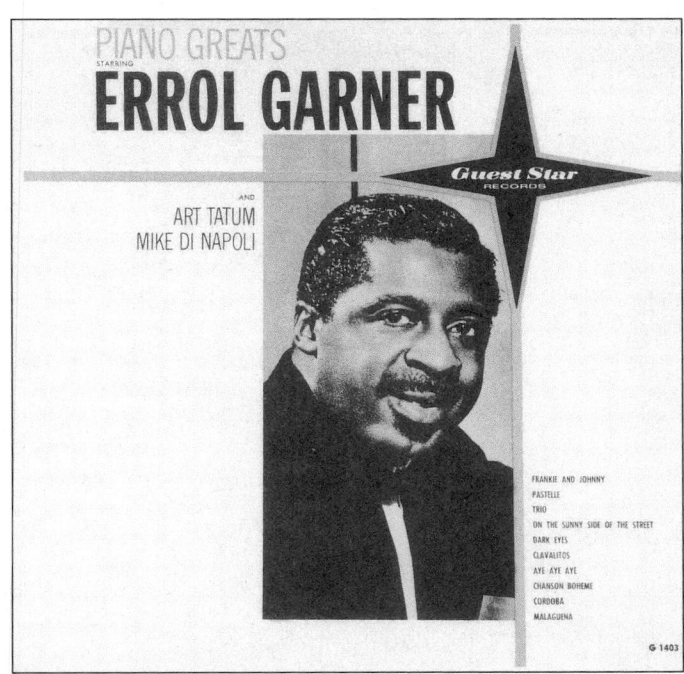

Erroll Garner, *Piano Greats*, Guest Star G 1403, **$30**.

Erroll Garner, *Other Voices*, Columbia CL 1014, red and black label with six "eye" logos, **$60**.

Number	Title	Yr	NM

GARLAND, RED

Pianist. Also see JOHN COLTRANE; CURTIS FULLER; COLEMAN HAWKINS.

Albums

FANTASY

Number	Title	Yr	NM
❑ OJC-126	A Garland of Red	198?	$25
— Reissue of Prestige 7064			
❑ OJC-193	All Kinds of Weather	1985	$25
— Reissue of Prestige 7148			
❑ OJC-293	All Morning Long	1988	$25
— Reissue of Prestige 7130			
❑ OJC-265	Bright and Breezy	1987	$25
— Reissue of Jazzland 948			
❑ OJC-472	Crossings	1990	$30
— Reissue of Galaxy 5106			
❑ OJC-392	Dig It!	1989	$30
— Reissue of Prestige 7229			
❑ OJC-061	Groovy	198?	$25
— Reissue of Prestige 7113			
❑ OJC-349	High Pressure	198?	$25
— Reissue of Prestige 7209			
❑ OJC-428	Manteca	1990	$30
— Reissue of Prestige 7139			
❑ OJC-647	Red Alert	1991	$25
— Reissue of Galaxy 5109			
❑ OJC-360	Red Garland & Eddie "Lockjaw" Davis	198?	$25
— Reissue of Moodsville 1			
❑ OJC-073	Red Garland's Piano	198?	$25
— Reissue of Prestige 7086			
❑ OJC-295	Red in Bluesville	198?	$25
— Reissue of Prestige 7157			
❑ OJC-481	Soul Junction	1991	$30
— Reissue of Prestige 7181			
❑ OJC-224	The Red Garland Trio	198?	$25
— Reissue of Moodsville 6			

GALAXY

❑ 5106	Crossings	1978	$30
❑ 5115	Equinox	1979	$30
❑ 5109	Red Alert	1978	$30
❑ 5129	Stepping Out	198?	$25
❑ 5135	Strike Up the Band	198?	$25

JAZZLAND

❑ JLP-48 [M]	Bright and Breezy	1961	$100
❑ JLP-948 [S]	Bright and Breezy	1961	$120
❑ JLP-87 [M]	Red's Good Groove!	1963	$120
❑ JLP-987 [S]	Red's Good Groove!	1963	$120
❑ JLP-73 [M]	Solar	1962	$100
❑ JLP-973 [S]	Solar	1962	$120
❑ JLP-62 [M]	The Nearness of You -- Ballads Played by Red Garland	1962	$100
❑ JLP-962 [S]	The Nearness of You -- Ballads Played by Red Garland	1962	$120

MOODSVILLE

❑ MVLP-10 [M]	Alone with the Blues	1960	$100
— Green label			
❑ MVLP-10 [M]	Alone with the Blues	1965	$50
— Blue label, trident logo at right			
❑ MVLP-3 [M]	Red Alone -- Vol. 3	1960	$100
— Green label			
❑ MVLP-3 [M]	Red Alone -- Vol. 3	1965	$50
— Blue label, trident logo at right			
❑ MVLP-1 [M]	Red Garland & Eddie "Lockjaw" Davis	1960	$100
— Green label			
❑ MVLP-1 [M]	Red Garland & Eddie "Lockjaw" Davis	1965	$50
— Blue label, trident logo at right			
❑ MVLP-6 [M]	The Red Garland Trio	1960	$100
— Green label			
❑ MVLP-6 [M]	The Red Garland Trio	1965	$50
— Blue label, trident logo at right			

MUSE

❑ MR-5130	Feelin' Red	1980	$30
❑ MR-5311	I Left My Heart	1985	$25

NEW JAZZ

❑ NJLP-8325 [M]	High Pressure	1963	$0
— Canceled; reassigned to Status			
❑ NJLP-8314 [M]	Li'l Darlin'	1963	$0
— Canceled; reassigned to Status			
❑ NJLP-8326 [M]	Red Garland Live!	1963	$0
— Canceled; reassigned to Status			

PRESTIGE

❑ PRLP-7064 [M]	A Garland of Red	1958	$300
— Yellow label with Bergenfield, N.J. address			
❑ PRLP-7130 [M]	All Morning Long	1958	$300
— Yellow label with Bergenfield, N.J. address			
❑ PRLP-7276 [M]	Can't See for Lookin'	1963	$60
❑ PRST-7276 [S]	Can't See for Lookin'	1963	$60
❑ PRLP-7229 [M]	Dig It!	1962	$150
❑ PRST-7229 [S]	Dig It!	1962	$150
❑ PRLP-7113 [M]	Groovy	1958	$300
— Yellow label with Bergenfield, N.J. address			
❑ PRLP-7288 [M]	Halleloo-Y'all	1964	$60
❑ PRST-7288 [S]	Halleloo-Y'all	1964	$80
❑ PRST-7838	It's a Blue World	1971	$50
❑ 24023	Jazz Junction	1972	$35
❑ PRLP-7139 [M]	Manteca	1958	$300
— Yellow label with Bergenfield, N.J. address			
❑ PRLP-7139 [M]	Manteca	1958	$200
— Yellow label, W. 50th St. NYC address on label			
❑ PRST-7752	P.C. Blues	1970	$50
❑ PRLP-7170 [M]	Red Garland at the Prelude	1959	$200
— Yellow label with Bergenfield, N.J. address			
❑ PRST-7658	Red Garland Revisited!	1969	$50
❑ PRLP-7086 [M]	Red Garland's Piano	1957	$250
— Yellow label, W. 50th St., New York address on label			
❑ PRLP-7086 [M]	Red Garland's Piano	1958	$200
— Yellow label with Bergenfield, N.J. address			
❑ PRLP-7157 [M]	Red in Bluesville	1959	$200
— Yellow label with Bergenfield, N.J. address			
❑ 24078	Rediscovered Masters	1979	$35
❑ PRLP-7193 [M]	Rojo	1961	$200
— Yellow label with Bergenfield, N.J. address			
❑ 24090	Saying Something	1980	$35
❑ PRLP-7307 [M]	Soul Burnin'	1964	$50
❑ PRST-7307 [S]	Soul Burnin'	1964	$60
❑ PRLP-7181 [M]	Soul Junction	1960	$200
— Yellow label with Bergenfield, N.J. address			
❑ PRLP-7258 [M]	When There Are Grey Skies	1963	$250
❑ PRST-7258 [S]	When There Are Grey Skies	1963	$120

RIVERSIDE

❑ 6099	Bright and Breezy	197?	$35

STATUS

❑ ST-8325 [M]	High Pressure	1965	$60
❑ ST-8314 [M]	Li'l Darlin'	1965	$60
❑ ST-8326 [M]	Red Garland Live!	1965	$60

GARNER, ERROLL

Pianist and composer; wrote the standard "Misty." Also see DODO MARMAROSA; KAY STARR; ART TATUM.

Albums

ABC-PARAMOUNT

❑ 395 [M]	Closeup in Swing	1961	$50
❑ S-395 [S]	Closeup in Swing	1961	$60
❑ 365 [M]	Dreamstreet	1961	$50
❑ S-365 [S]	Dreamstreet	1961	$60

ATLANTIC

❑ ALR-112 [10]	Erroll Garner at the Piano	1951	$250
❑ ALR-128 [10]	Passport to Fame	1952	$350
❑ 1315 [M]	Perpetual Motion	1959	$300
— Black label			
❑ ALR-135 [10]	Piano Solos, Volume 2	1952	$350
❑ ALR-109 [10]	Rhapsody	1950	$250
❑ 1227 [M]	The Greatest Garner	1956	$300
— Black label			
❑ 1227 [M]	The Greatest Garner	1961	$150
— Multi-color label with white "fan" logo			
❑ 1227 [M]	The Greatest Garner	196?	$30
— Multi-color label with black "fan" logo			

BARONET

❑ B-109 [M]	Informal Piano Improvisations	1962	$30
❑ BS-109 [R]	Informal Piano Improvisations	1962	$25

BLUE NOTE

❑ BLP-5007 [10]	Overture to Dawn, Volume 1	1952	$500
❑ BLP-5008 [10]	Overture to Dawn, Volume 2	1952	$500
❑ BLP-5014 [10]	Overture to Dawn, Volume 3	1953	$500
❑ BLP-5015 [10]	Overture to Dawn, Volume 4	1953	$500
❑ BLP-5016 [10]	Overture to Dawn, Volume 5	1953	$500

CLARION

❑ 610 [M]	Serenade in Blue	1966	$30
❑ SD610 [S]	Serenade in Blue	1966	$30

COLUMBIA

❑ CL883 [M]	Concert by the Sea	1956	$60
❑ CS9821 [R]	Concert by the Sea	1970	$30
❑ CL1141 [M]	Encores in Hi-Fi	1958	$60
❑ CL535 [M]	Erroll Garner	1953	$120
— Red label with gold print			
❑ CL535 [M]	Erroll Garner	1956	$60
— Red and black label with six "eye" logos			
❑ CL6259 [10]	Erroll Garner Plays for Dancing	1953	$150
❑ CL667 [M]	Erroll Garner Plays for Dancing	1956	$60
❑ CL2540 [10]	Garnerland	1955	$120
❑ CL6173 [10]	Gems	1951	$150
❑ CL583 [M]	Gems	1954	$120
— Red label with gold print			
❑ CL583 [M]	Gems	1956	$60
— Red and black label with six "eye" logos			
❑ CL617 [M]	Gone Garner Gonest	1955	$120
— Red label with gold print			
❑ CL617 [M]	Gone Garner Gonest	1956	$60
— Red and black label with six "eye" logos			
❑ CL2606 [10]	He's Here! He's Gone! He's Garner!	1956	$120
❑ CL1014 [M]	Other Voices	1957	$60
— Red and black label wirh six "eye" logos			
❑ CS9820 [R]	Other Voices	1970	$30
❑ C2L9 [M]	Paris Impressions	1958	$40
❑ CL1216 [M]	Paris Impressions, Volume 1	1958	$50
❑ CS8131 [S]	Paris Impressions, Volume 1	1958	$60
❑ CL1217 [M]	Paris Impressions, Volume 2	1958	$50
❑ CL6139 [10]	Piano Moods	1950	$150
❑ PG33424	Play It Again, Erroll!	1975	$30
❑ CL1060 [M]	Soliloquy	1957	$60
❑ CL6209 [10]	Solo Flight	1952	$150.00
❑ CL1512 [M]	Swinging Solos	1960	$50
❑ CS8312 [S]	Swinging Solos	1960	$60
❑ CL939 [M]	The Most Happy Piano	1957	$60
❑ CL1452 [M]	The One and Only Erroll Garner	1960	$50
❑ CS8252 [S]	The One and Only Erroll Garner	1960	$60
❑ CL1587 [M]	The Provocative Erroll Garner	1961	$50
❑ CS8387 [S]	The Provocative Erroll Garner	1961	$60

COLUMBIA JAZZ MASTERPIECES

❑ CJ40863	Long Ago and Far Away	1987	$30

COLUMBIA SPECIAL PRODUCTS

❑ P14386	Dreamy	1978	$25

DIAL

❑ LP-205 [10]	Erroll Garner, Volume 1	1950	$200
❑ LP-902 [M]	Free Piano Improvisations Recorded by Baron Timme Rosenkranz at One of His Famous Gaslight Jazz Sessions	1949	$300

EMARCY

❑ MG-36069 [M]	Erroll!	1956	$200
❑ 826224-1	Erroll Garner Plays Gershwin and Kern	1986	$25
❑ MG-26016 [10]	Garnering	1954	$200
❑ MG-36026 [M]	Garnering	1955	$200
❑ MG-26042 [10]	Gone with Garner	1954	$200
❑ 832994-1	The Erroll Garner Collection Vol. 1: Easy to Love	1988	$25
❑ 834935-1	The Erroll Garner Collection Vol. 2: Dancing on the Ceiling	1989	$25

EVEREST ARCHIVE OF FOLK & JAZZ

❑ 245	Erroll Garner	1970	$25

GUEST STAR

❑ G1403 [M]	Piano Greats	196?	$30
— With tracks by Art Tatum and Mike Di Napoli			
❑ GS1403 [S]	Piano Greats	196?	$25
— With tracks by Art Tatum and Mike Di Napoli			

HALL OF FAME

❑ 610	Early Erroll	198?	$25

HARMONY

❑ HS11268	One More Time	1968	$30

JAZZTONE

❑ J-1269 [M]	Early Erroll	1957	$40

KING

❑ 295-17 [10]	Piano Stylist	1952	$150
❑ 395-540 [M]	Piano Variations	1958	$150

LONDON

❑ XPS617	Gemini	1972	$30
❑ APS640	Magician	1973	$30

MERCURY

❑ MG-20090 [M]	Afternoon of an Elf	1955	$150
❑ 826457-1	Afternoon of an Elf	1986	$25
— Reissue			
❑ MG-25117 [10]	Erroll Garner at the Piano	1951	$250
❑ MG-20009 [M]	Erroll Garner at the Piano	1953	$150
❑ MG-20662 [M]	Erroll Garner Plays Misty	1962	$100
❑ SR-60662 [S]	Erroll Garner Plays Misty	1962	$100
— Black label, all-silver print			
❑ SR-60662 [S]	Erroll Garner Plays Misty	1965	$150

Number	Title	Yr	NM

—Red label, "MERCURY" in all caps at top

| SR-60662 | Erroll Garner Plays Misty | 1975 | $25 |

—Chicago skyline label

| SR-60662 | Erroll Garner Plays Misty | 1983 | $20 |

—Black label, neon-style "mercury" logo

MG-21308 [M]	Feeling Is Believing	1964	$100
SR-61308 [S]	Feeling Is Believing	1964	$100
SR-61308 [S]	Feeling Is Believing	1970	$30

—Newer Mercury logo on cover

MG-25157 [10]	Gone with Garner	1951	$250
MG-20055 [M]	Mambo Moves Garner	1954	$150
MG-20859 [M]	New Kind of Love	1963	$100
SR-60859 [S]	New Kind of Love	1963	$100
MG-20063 [M]	Solitaire	1954	$150
MG-20803 [M]	The Best of Erroll Garner	1963	$100
SR-60803 [S]	The Best of Erroll Garner	1963	$100

MGM

E-4361 [M]	Campus Concert	1966	$30
SE-4361 [S]	Campus Concert	1966	$35
E-4335 [M]	Now Playing: Erroll Garner	1966	$30
SE-4335 [S]	Now Playing: Erroll Garner	1966	$35
E-4463 [M]	That's My Kick	1967	$35
SE-4463 [S]	That's My Kick	1967	$30
E-4520 [M]	Up in Erroll's Room	1967	$35
SE-4520 [S]	Up in Erroll's Room	1967	$30

PICKWICK

| SPC-3254 | Deep Purple | 197? | $25 |

REPRISE

R6080 [M]	One World Concert	1963	$50
RS6080 [S]	One World Concert	1963	$60
R6080 [DJ]	One World Concert	1963	$40

—Six-song sampler -- three on each side -- on a 12-inch record that plays at 45 rpm. This comes in a different cover than the stock copy; this is clearly marked "Special 45 RPM Preview Record" on the top front.

RONDO-LETTE

| A-15 [M] | Erroll Garner | 1958 | $60 |

SAVOY

SJL-2207	Elf	198?	$30
MG-15026 [10]	Erroll Garner at the Piano	1953	$150
MG-15000 [10]	Erroll Garner Plays Piano Solos	1950	$150
MG-15001 [10]	Erroll Garner Plays Piano Solos, Volume 2	1950	$150
MG-15002 [10]	Erroll Garner Plays Piano Solos, Volume 3	1950	$150
MG-15003 [10]	Erroll Garner Plays Piano Solos, Volume 4	1950	$1500
MG-12002 [M]	Penthouse Serenade	1955	$75
SJC-411	Penthouse Serenade	1985	$25
MG-12003 [M]	Serenade to "Laura	1955	$75
SJL-1118	Yesterdays	198?	$25

TRIP

| 5519 | Garnering | 197? | $25 |

WING

| MGW12134 | Erroll Garner Moods | 196? | $30 |

GARNER, ERROLL/BILLY TAYLOR

Also see each artist's individual listings.

Albums

SAVOY

| MG-12008 [M] | Erroll Garner/Billy Taylor | 1955 | $100 |

GARNER, ERROLL/OSCAR PETERSON/ ART TATUM

Also see each artist's individual listings.

Albums

RCA CAMDEN

| CAL-882 [M] | Great Jazz Pianists of Our Time | 196? | $35 |
| CAS-882 [R] | Great Jazz Pianists of Our Time | 196? | $30 |

GARNER, ERROLL/PETE JOHNSON

Also see each artist's individual listings.

Albums

GRAND AWARD

| GA 33-321 [M] | Jazz Piano | 1956 | $60 |

—Without removable cover

GARNER, MORRIS

Albums

THUNDERBIRD

| TH-1958 [M] | The Worst of Morris Garner | 196? | $30 |

GARNETT, CARLOS

Saxophone player and male singer.

Albums

MUSE

MR-5040	Black Love	1973	$35
MR-5104	Cosmos Nucleus	1976	$40
MR-5057	Journey to Enlightenment	1974	$25
MR-5079	Let the Melody Ring On	1975	$30
MR-5133	New Love	1977	$40

GARRETT, KENNY

Alto saxophone player.

Albums

ATLANTIC

| 82046 | Prisoner of Love | 1989 | $30 |

GARSON, MIKE, AND JIM WALKER

Walker is a flutist. Also see MIKE GARSON.

Albums

REFERENCE RECORDINGS

| RR-18 | Reflections | 1987 | $35 |

GARSON, MIKE

Pianist and composer.

Albums

JAZZ HOUNDS

| 05 | Jazzical | 1982 | $30 |

REFERENCE RECORDINGS

RR-20	Serendipity	1987	$35
RR-37	The Oxnard Sessions	1991	$50
RR-53	The Oxnard Sessions, Volume Two	1993	$60

GASCA, LUIS

Trumpeter. Also a session musician for rock artists such as Van Morrison.

Albums

ATLANTIC

| SD1527 | Little Giants | 1970 | $60 |

BLUE THUMB

| BTS-37 | Luis Gasca | 1972 | $60 |

FANTASY

| F-9461 | Born to Love You | 1974 | $60 |
| F-9504 | Collage | 1976 | $60 |

—Brown label (original)

GASKIN, LEONARD

Bass player.

Albums

SWINGVILLE

| SVLP-2033 [M] | At the Darktown Strutters' Ball | 1962 | $40 |

—Purple label

| SVLP-2033 [M] | At the Darktown Strutters' Ball | 1965 | $25 |

—Blue label, trident logo at right

| SVST-2033 [S] | At the Darktown Strutters' Ball | 1962 | $50 |

—Red label

| SVST-2033 [S] | At the Darktown Strutters' Ball | 1965 | $30 |

—Blue label, trident logo at right

| SVLP-2031 [M] | At the Jazz Band Ball | 1962 | $40 |

—Purple label

| SVLP-2031 [M] | At the Jazz Band Ball | 1965 | $25 |

—Blue label, trident logo at right

| SVST-2031 [S] | At the Jazz Band Ball | 1962 | $50 |

—Red label

| SVST-2031 [S] | At the Jazz Band Ball | 1965 | $30 |

—Blue label, trident logo at right

GASLINI, GIORGIO

Pianist, composer and conductor.

Albums

SOUL NOTE

121270	Ayler's Wings	1991	$30
SN-1020	Gaslini Plays Monk	1981	$30
121020	Gaslini Plays Monk	199?	$25

—Reissue of 1020

121220	Multipli	199?	$30
SN-1120	Schumann Reflections	1984	$30
121120	Schumann Reflections	199?	$25

—Reissue of 1120

GATEWAY

See JOHN ABERCROMBIE.

GAULT, BILLY

Pianist.

Albums

INNER CITY

| IC-2027 | When Destiny Calls | 197? | $35 |

STEEPLECHASE

| SCS-1027 | When Destiny Calls | 198? | $25 |

GAUTHE, JACQUES

Clarinetist and soprano saxophone player.

Albums

GHB

| GHB-179 | Riz A La Creole | 1987 | $25 |

STOMP OFF

| SOS-1170 | Cassoulet Stomp | 1989 | $25 |

GAVIN, KEVIN

Male singer.

Albums

CHARLIE PARKER

| PLP-810 [M] | Hey! This Is Kevin Gavin | 1962 | $30 |
| PLP-810S [S] | Hey! This Is Kevin Gavin | 1962 | $40 |

GAYLE, CHARLES

Tenor saxophone player, bass clarinetist, keyboard player, pianist and violist.

Albums

SILKHEART

SH-115	Always Born	1988	$25
SH-116	Homeless	1988	$25
SH-117	Spirits Before	1988	$25

GAYLE, ROZELLE

Albums

MERCURY

| MG-20374 [M] | Like, Be My Guest | 1958 | $100 |

GEE, MATTHEW

Trombonist. Also see JOHNNY GRIFFIN.

Albums

RIVERSIDE

| RLP 12-221 [M] | Jazz by Gee! | 1956 | $250 |

—White label, blue print

| RLP 12-221 [M] | Jazz by Gee! | 1958 | $300 |

—Blue label, microphone logo at top

GEISSMAN, GRANT

Guitarist and composer.

Albums

BLUEMOON

| R1-79152 | Take Another Look | 1990 | $30 |

CONCORD JAZZ

| CJ-62 | Good Stuff | 1978 | $30 |

PAUSA

| 7150 | Put Away Childish Toys | 198? | $30 |

TBA

TB-241	All My Tomorrows	1989	$30
TB-217	Drinkin' from the Money River	198?	$30
TB-224	Snapshots	198?	$30

GELB, LARRY

Pianist.

Albums

CADENCE JAZZ

| 1012 | The Language of Blue | 198? | $25 |

Number	Title	Yr	NM

GELLER, HERB
Alto saxophone player. Also a soprano sax player, flutist and male singer.

Albums

ATCO

Number	Title	Yr	NM
□ 33-109 [M]	Gypsy	1959	$40

ATLANTIC

| □ SD1681 | Rhyme and Reason | 1975 | $30 |

EMARCY

□ MG-26045 [10]	Herb Geller Plays	1954	$200
□ MG-36024 [M]	The Gellers	1955	$250
□ MG-36040 [M]	The Herb Geller Sextette	1955	$250

JOSIE

| □ JOZ-3502 [M] | Alto Saxophone | 1962 | $30 |
| □ JLPS-3502 [S] | Alto Saxophone | 1962 | $25 |

JUBILEE

□ JLP-1044 [M]	Fire in the West	1957	$50
□ SDJLP-1044 [S]	Fire in the West	1959	$40
□ JG-1094 [M]	Stax of Sax	1959	$50

GELLER, LORRAINE
Pianist.

Albums

DOT

| □ DLP-3174 [M] | Lorraine Geller at the Piano | 1959 | $1500 |

GENERATION BAND, THE
All-star group led by VICTOR FELDMAN. Other members have included LEE RITENOUR and TOM SCOTT.

Albums

NAUTILUS

| □ NR-62 | Soft Shoulder | 198? | $40 |
—Audiophile vinyl

PALO ALTO

| □ PA-8054 | Soft Shoulder | 198? | $30 |

TBA

| □ TB-202 | Call of the Wild | 198? | $25 |
| □ TB-208 | High Visibility | 1985 | $25 |

GEORGIA GRINDERS, THE

Albums

STOMP OFF

| □ SOS-1068 | A Tribute to Roy Palmer | 1984 | $25 |

GETZ, EDDIE
Alto saxophone player.

Albums

MGM

| □ E-3462 [M] | The Eddie Getz Quintette | 1957 | $50 |

GETZ, STAN, AND ALBERT DAILEY
Also see each artist's individual listings.

Albums

ELEKTRA/MUSICIAN

| □ 60370 | Poetry | 1985 | $25 |

GETZ, STAN, AND BILL EVANS
Also see each artist's individual listings.

Albums

VERVE

| □ V3G-8833 | Previously Unreleased Recordings | 1974 | $30 |

GETZ, STAN, AND BOB BROOKMEYER
Also see each artist's individual listings.

Albums

VERVE

| □ V-8418 [M] | Stan Getz and Bob Brookmeyer (Recorded Fall 1961) | 1961 | $50 |
| □ V6-8418 [S] | Stan Getz and Bob Brookmeyer (Recorded Fall 1961) | 1961 | $50 |

GETZ, STAN, AND CHARLIE BYRD
Also see each artist's individual listings.

Albums

DCC COMPACT CLASSICS

Number	Title	Yr	NM
□ LPZ-2011	Jazz Samba	1995	$60
—Audiophile vinyl

VERVE

| □ V-8432 [M] | Jazz Samba | 1962 | $50 |
| □ V6-8432 [S] | Jazz Samba | 1962 | $60 |
—With "MGM Records" on label print

| □ UMJ-3158 | Jazz Samba | 198? | $25 |
| □ 810061-1 | Jazz Samba | 198? | $25 |
—Reissue

| □ V6-8432 [S] | Jazz Samba | 1976 | $30 |
—"Manufactured and Marketed by Polydor Incorporated" on label

GETZ, STAN, AND CHET BAKER
Also see each artist's individual listings.

Albums

STORYVILLE

| □ 4090 | Line for Lyons | 1984 | $25 |

GETZ, STAN, AND GERRY MULLIGAN
Also see each artist's individual listings.

Albums

MAINSTREAM

| □ MRL364 | Yesterday | 1972 | $35 |

GETZ, STAN, AND HORACE SILVER
Also see each artist's individual listings.

Albums

BARONET

| □ B-102 [M] | A Pair of Kings | 1962 | $35 |
| □ BS-102 [R] | A Pair of Kings | 196? | $25 |

GETZ, STAN, AND J.J. JOHNSON
Also see each artist's individual listings.

Albums

VERVE

| □ MGV-8405 [M] | Stan Getz and J.J. Johnson | 1961 | $0 |
—Unreleased

□ MGV-8265 [M]	Stan Getz and J.J. Johnson at the Opera House	1958	$100
□ MGVS-6027 [S]	Stan Getz and J.J. Johnson at the Opera House	1960	$80
□ V-8265 [M]	Stan Getz and J.J. Johnson at the Opera House	1961	$50
□ V6-8265 [S]	Stan Getz and J.J. Johnson at the Opera House	1961	$35
□ V6-8490 [S]	Stan Getz and J.J. Johnson at the Opera House	1962	$35
□ V-8490 [M]	Stan Getz and J.J. Johnson at the Opera House	1962	$35

GETZ, STAN, AND JOAO GILBERTO
Also see each artist's individual listings.

Albums

MOBILE FIDELITY

| □ 1-208 | Getz/Gilberto | 1994 | $100 |
—Audiophile vinyl

VERVE

□ V-8623 [M]	Getz/Gilberto #2	1965	$35
□ V6-8623 [S]	Getz/Gilberto #2	1965	$50
□ V-8545 [M]	Getz/Gilberto	1964	$35
□ V6-8545 [S]	Getz/Gilberto	1964	$50
□ UMV-2099	Getz/Gilberto	198?	$25
—Reissue

| □ 810048-1 | Getz/Gilberto | 198? | $25 |
—Reissue

GETZ, STAN, AND LAURINDO ALMEIDA
Also see each artist's individual listings.

Albums

VERVE

| □ V-8665 [M] | Stan Getz with Guest Artist Laurindo Almeida | 1965 | $35 |
| □ V6-8665 [S] | Stan Getz with Guest Artist Laurindo Almeida | 1965 | $50 |

GETZ, STAN, AND OSCAR PETERSON
Also see each artist's individual listings.

Albums

VERVE

Number	Title	Yr	NM
□ MGV-8251 [M]	Stan Getz and the Oscar Peterson Trio	1958	$100
□ V-8251 [M]	Stan Getz and the Oscar Peterson Trio	1961	$50
—Reissue of MGV-8251

| □ V6-8251 [R] | Stan Getz and the Oscar Peterson Trio | 196? | $30 |
| □ UMV-2665 | Stan Getz and the Oscar Peterson Trio | 198? | $25 |
—Reissue

| □ MGV-8348 [M] | Stan Getz with Gerry Mulligan and the Oscar Peterson Trio | 1959 | $100 |
| □ V-8348 [M] | Stan Getz with Gerry Mulligan and the Oscar Peterson Trio | 1961 | $50 |
—Reissue of MGV-8348

| □ V6-8348 [R] | Stan Getz with Gerry Mulligan and the Oscar Peterson Trio | 1961 | $30 |

GETZ, STAN, AND WARDELL GRAY
Also see each artist's individual listings.

Albums

DAWN

| □ DLP-1126 [M] | Tenors Anyone? | 1958 | $200 |

SEECO

| □ SLP-7 [10] | Highlights in Modern Jazz | 1954 | $300 |

GETZ, STAN, AND ZOOT SIMS
Also see each artist's individual listings.

Albums

FANTASY

| □ OJC-008 | The Brothers | 1982 | $30 |

PRESTIGE

| □ PRLP-7022 [M] | The Brothers | 1956 | $400 |
—Yellow label with W. 50th St. address

| □ PRLP-7252 [M] | The Brothers | 1963 | $175 |
—Yellow label with Bergenfield, N.J. address

GETZ, STAN; DIZZY GILLESPIE; SONNY STITT
Also see each artist's individual listings.

Albums

VERVE

| □ MGV-8198 [M] | For Musicians Only | 1958 | $150 |
| □ V-8198 [M] | For Musicians Only | 1961 | $60 |

GETZ, STAN
Influential and popular tenor saxophone player and bandleader. Also see DIZZY GILLESPIE; LIONEL HAMPTON; BILLIE HOLIDAY; MODERN JAZZ SOCIETY; GERRY MULLIGAN; CAL TJADER.

Albums

A&M

| □ SP-5297 | Apasionado | 1990 | $35 |

AMERICAN RECORDING SOCIETY

□ G-407 [M]	Cool Jazz of Stan Getz	1956	$40
□ G-428 [M]	Intimate Portrait	1957	$40
□ G-443 [M]	Stan Getz '57	1957	$40

BLACKHAWK

| □ BKH-51101 | Voyage | 1986 | $25 |

BLUE RIBBON

| □ BR-8012 [M] | Rhythms | 1961 | $50 |
| □ BS-8012 [R] | Rhythms | 1961 | $25 |

CLEF

| □ MGC-137 [10] | Stan Getz Plays | 1953 | $350 |
| □ MGC-143 [10] | The Artistry of Stan Getz | 1953 | $350 |

COLUMBIA

□ PC33703	Best of Two Worlds	1975	$35
□ PC32706	Captain Marvel	1974	$35
□ JC35992	Children of the World	1979	$30
□ JC36403	The Best of Stan Getz	1980	$30
□ CJ44047	The Lyrical Stan Getz	1988	$30
□ FC38272	The Master	1983	$25
□ JC34873	The Peacocks	1977	$30

CONCORD JAZZ

| □ CJ-188 | Pure Getz | 1983 | $30 |
| □ CJ-158 | The Dolphin | 198? | $30 |

CROWN

Stan Getz, *Big Band Bossa Nova*, Verve V-8494, **$50**.

Stan Getz, *Cool Velvet – Stan Getz and Strings*, Verve MG VS-68379, stereo, **$100**.

Stan Getz, *Opus de Bop*, Savoy SJL 1105, **$30**.

Stan Getz, *Getz Au Go Go*, Verve V6-8600, **$50**.

Number	Title	Yr	NM
CLP-5002 [M]	Groovin' High	1957	$40
—Reissue of Modern 1202			
DALE			
21 [10]	In Retrospect	1951	$400
EMARCY			
838771-1	Billy Highstreet Samba	1990	$30
FANTASY			
OJC-121	Stan Getz Quartets	198?	$25
—Reissue of Prestige 7002			
HALL OF FAME			
606	Stan Getz and His Tenor Sax	197?	$30
INNER CITY			
1040	Gold	1977	$30
INTERMEDIA			
QS-5057	Stella by Starlight	198?	$25
JAZZ MAN			
5014	Forrest Eyes	1982	$30
JAZZTONE			
J-1230 [M]	Stan Getz	1956	$40
J-1240 [M]	Stan Getz '57	1957	$40
METRO			
M-501 [M]	The Melodic Stan Getz	1965	$150
MS-501 [S]	The Melodic Stan Getz	1965	$250
METRONOME			
BLP-6 [M]	The Sound	1956	$200
MGM			
SE-4696	Marrakesh Express	1970	$35
MODERN			
MLP-1202 [M]	Groovin' High	1956	$150
MOSAIC			
MR4-131	The Complete Recordings of the Stan Getz Quintet with Jimmy Raney	199?	$120
NEW JAZZ			
NJLP-8214 [M]	Long Island Sound	1959	$300
—Reissue of Prestige 7002; purple label			
NJLP-8214 [M]	Long Island Sound	1965	$150
—Blue label with trident logo on right			
NORGRAN			
MGN-1008 [M]	Interpretations by the Stan Getz Quintet #2	1954	$300
MGN-1029 [M]	Interpretations by the Stan Getz Quintet #3	1955	$300
MGN-1000 [M]	Interpretations by the Stan Getz Quintet	1954	$300
MGN-1088 [M]	More West Coast Jazz with Stan Getz	1956	$300
MGN-1087 [M]	Stan Getz '56	1956	$175
MGN-2000-2 [M]	Stan Getz at the Shrine	1955	$300
—Boxed set with booklet			
MGN-1042 [M]	Stan Getz Plays	1955	$700
—Reissue of Clef 137 and 143 on one 12-inch LP			
MGN-1032 [M]	West Coast Jazz	1955	$300
PICKWICK			
SPC-3031	Stan Getz In Concert	197?	$25
PRESTIGE			
24088	Early Getz	197?	$30
PRLP-7255 [M]	Early Stan	1963	$40
PRST-7255 [R]	Early Stan	1963	$50
PRLP-7434 [M]	Getz Plays Jazz Classics	1967	$60
—Reissue of PRLP 7255			
PRST-7434 [R]	Getz Plays Jazz Classics	1967	$35
—Reissue of PRST 7255			
PRLP-7516 [M]	Preservation	1967	$60
PRST-7516 [R]	Preservation	1967	$35
24019	Stan Getz	197?	$35
PRLP-104 [10]	Stan Getz, Volume 2	1951	$250
PRLP-102 [10]	Stan Getz and the Tenor Sax Stars	1951	$250
PRLP-7256 [M]	Stan Getz' Greatest Hits	1963	$40
PRST-7256 [R]	Stan Getz' Greatest Hits	1963	$50
PRLP-7337 [M]	Stan Getz' Greatest Hits	1967	$60
—Reissue of PRLP 7256			
PRST-7337 [R]	Stan Getz' Greatest Hits	1967	$35
—Reissue of PRST 7256			
PRLP-108 [10]	Stan Getz-Lee Konitz	1951	$250
PRLP-7002 [M]	Stan Getz Quartets	1955	$300
ROOST			
R-417 [10]	Chamber Music	1953	$300
LP-2258 [M]	Getz Age	1963	$60
SLP-2258 [R]	Getz Age	1963	$35
R-407 [10]	Jazz at Storyville	1952	$150
R-411 [10]	Jazz at Storyville, Volume 2	1952	$150
R-420 [10]	Jazz at Storyville, Volume 3	1954	$150
LP-2255 [M]	Modern World	1963	$150
SLP-2255 [R]	Modern World	1963	$150
LP-2251 [M]	Moonlight in Vermont	1963	$60
SLP-2251 [R]	Moonlight in Vermont	1963	$35
R-423 [10]	Split Kick	1954	$150
R-402 [10]	Stan Getz	1950	$200
R-404 [10]	Stan Getz and the Swedish All Stars	1951	$200
LP-2209 [M]	Storyville	1956	$150
—Reissue of R-407 and half of R-411			
LP-2225 [M]	Storyville, Volume 2	1957	$150
—Reissue of R-423 and the other half of R-411			
LP-2249 [M]	The Greatest of Stan Getz	1963	$60
LP-2207 [M]	The Sounds of Stan Getz	1956	$150
—Reissue of R-402			
RK-103 [M]	The Stan Getz Years	1964	$40
SRK-103 [R]	The Stan Getz Years	1964	$60
ROULETTE			
RE-123	Stan Getz/Sonny Stitt	1973	$35
RE-119	The Best of Stan Getz	1972	$35
SAVOY			
MG-9004 [10]	New Sounds in Modern Music	1951	$300
SJL-1105	Opus de Bop	1977	$30
STEEPLECHASE			
SCS-1073/4	Live at Montmartre	1986	$30
VERVE			
VS-200 [M]	An Introduction to the World of Stan Getz	1964	$35
V6S-200 [S]	An Introduction to the World of Stan Getz	1964	$50
—Sampler of material from five LPs plus one single-only track			
VSP-22 [M]	Another Time, Another Place	1966	$35
VSPS-22 [R]	Another Time, Another Place	1966	$25
MGV-8296 [M]	Award Winner	1959	$150
V-8296 [M]	Award Winner	1961	$50
—Reissue of MGV-8296			
V6-8296 [R]	Award Winner	196?	$30
V-8494 [M]	Big Band Bossa Nova	1962	$50
V6-8494 [S]	Big Band Bossa Nova	1962	$60
V6-8807	Communications '72	1972	$35
MGV-8379 [M]	Cool Velvet -- Stan Getz and Strings	1960	$100
MGVS-6160 [S]	Cool Velvet -- Stan Getz and Strings	1960	$0
—Unreleased			
V-8379 [M]	Cool Velvet -- Stan Getz and Strings	1961	$50
—Reissue of MGV-8379			
V6-8379 [S]	Cool Velvet -- Stan Getz and Strings	1961	$50
MGVS-68379 [S]	Cool Velvet -- Stan Getz and Strings	1960	$100
V6-8780	Didn't We	1969	$35
V6-8802-2	Dynasty	1971	$50
VSP-2 [M]	Eloquence	1966	$35
VSPS-2 [R]	Eloquence	1966	$25
V-8412 [M]	Focus	1961	$60
V6-8412 [S]	Focus	1961	$50
VR-1-2528	Focus	1977	$25
—Reissue of 8412			
UMV-2071	Focus	198?	$25
—Reissue			
V-8600 [M]	Getz Au Go Go	1964	$35
V6-8600 [S]	Getz Au Go Go	1964	$50
UMV-2075	Getz Au Go Go	198?	$25
—Reissue			
821725-1	Getz Au Go Go	198?	$25
—Reissue			
V6-8815-2	History of Stan Getz	1973	$35
MGV-8331 [M]	Imported from Europe	1959	$150
V-8331 [M]	Imported from Europe	1961	$50
—Reissue of MGV-8331			
V6-8331 [R]	Imported from Europe	196?	$30
MGV-8122 [M]	Interpretations by the Stan Getz Quintet #3	1957	$300
—Reissue of Norgran 1029			
V-8122 [M]	Interpretations by the Stan Getz Quintet #3	1961	$50
—Reissue of MGV-8122			
UMV-2100	Jazz Samba Encore	198?	$25
—Reissue			
823613-1	Jazz Samba Encore	198?	$25
—Reissue			
V-8523 [M]	Jazz Samba Encore!	1963	$50
—With Luiz Bonfa			
V6-8523 [S]	Jazz Samba Encore!	1963	$60
—With Luiz Bonfa			
MGV-8177 [M]	More West Coast Jazz with Stan Getz	1957	$300
—Reissue of Norgran 1088			
V-8177 [M]	More West Coast Jazz with Stan Getz	1961	$50
—Reissue of MGV-8177			
V6-8177 [R]	More West Coast Jazz with Stan Getz	196?	$30
V-8554 [M]	Reflections	1964	$35
V6-8554 [S]	Reflections	1964	$50
V3HB-8844	Return Engagement	1974	$35
MGV-8029 [M]	Stan Getz '57	1957	$100
—Reissue of Norgran 1087 with revised title			
V-8029 [M]	Stan Getz '57	1961	$50
—Reissue of MGV-8029			
MGV-8200 [M]	Stan Getz and the Cool Sounds	1957	$100
—Reissue of American Recording Society 407 with new name			
V-8200 [M]	Stan Getz and the Cool Sounds	1961	$50
—Reissue of MGV-8200			
V6-8200 [R]	Stan Getz and the Cool Sounds	196?	$30
MGV-8393-2 [M]	Stan Getz At Large	1960	$120
V-8393-2 [M]	Stan Getz At Large	1961	$60
—Reissue of MGV-8393-2			
V6-8393-2 [R]	Stan Getz At Large	1961	$35
MGV-8401 [M]	Stan Getz At Large, Volume 1	1960	$0
—Unreleased			
MGV-8402 [M]	Stan Getz At Large, Volume 2	1960	$0
—Unreleased			
MGV-8188-2	Stan Getz at the Shrine	1957	$175
—Reissue of Norgran 2000-2			
V-8188-2 [M]	Stan Getz at the Shrine	1961	$60
—Reissue of MGV-8188-2			
V6-8188-2 [R]	Stan Getz at the Shrine	196?	$35
MGV-8213 [M]	Stan Getz in Stockholm	1958	$100
—Reissue of American Recording Society 428 with new name			
V-8213 [M]	Stan Getz in Stockholm	1961	$50
—Reissue of MGV-8213			
V6-8213 [R]	Stan Getz in Stockholm	196?	$30
UMV-2614	Stan Getz in Stockholm	198?	$25
—Reissue			
MGV-8133 [M]	Stan Getz Plays	1957	$100
—Reissue of Norgran 1042			
V-8133 [M]	Stan Getz Plays	1961	$50
—Reissue of MGV-8133			
V6-8133 [R]	Stan Getz Plays	196?	$30
VSP-31 [M]	Stan Getz Plays Blues	1966	$35
VSPS-31 [R]	Stan Getz Plays Blues	1966	$25
MGV-8356 [M]	Stan Getz Quintet	1960	$0
—Unreleased			
MGV-8263 [M]	Stan Meets Chet	1958	$120
—With Chet Baker			
V-8263 [M]	Stan Meets Chet	1961	$50
—Reissue of MGV-8263			
V6-8263 [R]	Stan Meets Chet	196?	$30
815239-1	Stan the Man	1983	$25
V-8693 [M]	Sweet Rain	1967	$60
V6-8693 [S]	Sweet Rain	1967	$35
V-8719 [M]	The Best of Stan Getz	1967	$60
V6-8719 [R]	The Best of Stan Getz	1967	$35
VE-2-2510	The Corea/Evans Sessions	1976	$35
823242-1	The Corea/Evans Sessions	198?	$30
—Reissue			
823611-1	The Girl from Ipanema: The Bossa Nova Years	1984	$100
MGV-8321 [M]	The Soft Swing	1959	$100
V-8321 [M]	The Soft Swing	1961	$50
—Reissue of MGV-8321			
V6-8321 [R]	The Soft Swing	196?	$30
MGV-8294 [M]	The Steamer	1959	$100
V-8294 [M]	The Steamer	1961	$50
—Reissue of MGV-8294			
V6-8294 [R]	The Steamer	196?	$30
V-8707 [M]	Voices	1967	$60
V6-8707 [S]	Voices	1967	$35
MGV-8028 [M]	West Coast Jazz	1957	$200
—Reissue of Norgran 1032			
V-8028 [M]	West Coast Jazz	1961	$50
—Reissue of MGV-8028			
V6-8028 [R]	West Coast Jazz	196?	$30
V-8752 [M]	What the World Needs Now -- Stan Getz Plays Bacharach and David	1968	$60
V6-8752 [S]	What the World Needs Now -- Stan Getz Plays Bacharach and David	1968	$35

GHIGLIONI, TIZIANA
Female singer.

Albums

Number	Title	Yr	NM
SOUL NOTE			
❏ 121156	Somebody Special	198?	$30
❏ SN-1056	Sounds of Love	1984	$30
❏ 121056	Sounds of Love	198?	$25

GIBBONS, SHANNON
Female singer.

Albums

Number	Title	Yr	NM
SOUL NOTE			
❏ 121163	Shannon Gibbons	1987	$30

GIBBS, GEORGIA
Female singer. Nicknamed "Her Nibs," she was a veteran of several big bands.

Albums

Number	Title	Yr	NM
BELL			
❏ 6000S [S]	Call Me Georgia Gibbs	1966	$25
CORAL			
❏ CRL56037 [10]	Ballin' the Jack	1951	$50
EMARCY			
❏ MG-36103 [M]	Swingin' with Gibbs	1957	$200
EPIC			
❏ LN24059 [M]	Georgia Gibbs' Greatest Hits	1963	$40
❏ BN26059 [S]	Georgia Gibbs' Greatest Hits	1963	$40
GOLDEN TONE			
❏ 14093 [R]	Her Nibs!! Miss Georgia Gibbs	1962	$12
— Cover misspells it "Nibbs			
❏ 4093 [M]	Her Nibs!! Miss Georgia Gibbs	1962	$15
IMPERIAL			
❏ LP-9107 [M]	Something's Gotta Give	1960	$150
❏ LP-12064 [S]	Something's Gotta Give	1960	$150
MERCURY			
❏ MG-25175 [10]	Georgia Gibbs Sings Oldies	1953	$100
❏ MG-20071 [M]	Music and Memories	1955	$100
❏ MG-20114 [M]	Song Favorites	1956	$100
❏ MG-20170 [M]	Swingin' with Her Nibs	1956	$100
❏ MG-25199 [10]	The Man That Got Away	1954	$100
ROYALE			
❏ 18126 [10]	Georgia Gibbs and Orchestra	195?	$40
SUNSET			
❏ SUM-1113 [M]	Her Nibs, Miss Georgia Gibbs	196?	$20
❏ SUS-5113 [S]	Her Nibs, Miss Georgia Gibbs	196?	$20

GIBBS, MICHAEL, AND GARY BURTON
Also see each artist's individual listings.

Albums

Number	Title	Yr	NM
POLYDOR			
❏ PD-6503	In the Public Interest	197?	$35

GIBBS, MICHAEL
Trombonist, pianist, arranger, bandleader and composer.

Albums

Number	Title	Yr	NM
DERAM			
❏ DES18048	Michael Gibbs	1970	$25

GIBBS, TERRY, AND BILL HARRIS
Also see each artist's individual listings.

Albums

Number	Title	Yr	NM
MODE			
❏ LP-129 [M]	The Ex-Hermanites	1957	$80
PREMIER			
❏ PM-2006 [M]	Woodchoppers' Ball	1963	$35
❏ PS-2006 [R]	Woodchoppers' Ball	1963	$25

GIBBS, TERRY, AND BUDDY DEFRANCO
Also see each artist's individual listings.

Albums

Number	Title	Yr	NM
CONTEMPORARY			
❏ C-14056	Air Mail Special	1990	$30
❏ C-14036	Chicago Fire	1987	$25
PALO ALTO			
❏ PA-8011	Jazz Party -- First Time Together	1982	$25

GIBBS, TERRY
Vibraphone player and percussionist. Also see HARRY BABASIN.

Albums

Number	Title	Yr	NM
ABC IMPULSE!			
❏ AS-58 [S]	Take It from Me	1968	$35
BRUNSWICK			
❏ BL54009 [M]	Terry	1955	$60
❏ BL56055 [10]	Terry Gibbs Quartet	1954	$100
CONTEMPORARY			
❏ C-7647	Dream Band	1986	$25
❏ C-14022	The Latin Connection	1986	$25
❏ C-7652	Volume 2: The Sundown Sessions	1987	$25
❏ C-7654	Volume 3: Flying Home	1988	$25
❏ C-7656	Volume 4: Main Stem	1990	$30
DOT			
❏ DLP-3726 [M]	Reza	1966	$75
❏ DLP-25726 [S]	Reza	1966	$75
EMARCY			
❏ MG-36075 [M]	Mallets A-Plenty	1956	$200
❏ MG-36148 [M]	More Vibes on Velvet	1959	$200
❏ MG-36138 [M]	Steve Allen's All Stars	1958	$200
❏ SR-80004 [S]	Steve Allen's All Stars	1959	$200
❏ MG-36047 [M]	Terry Gibbs	1956	$200
❏ MG-36128 [M]	Terry Plays the Duke	1958	$200
❏ MG-36064 [M]	Vibes on Velvet	1956	$200
IMPULSE!			
❏ A-58 [M]	Take It from Me	1964	$120
❏ AS-58 [S]	Take It from Me	1964	$120
INTERLUDE			
❏ MO-506 [M]	Vibrations	1959	$40
❏ ST-1006 [S]	Vibrations	1959	$30
JAZZ A LA CARTE			
❏ 1	Live at the Lord	1978	$35
❏ 2	Smoke 'Em Up	1978	$30
LIMELIGHT			
❏ LM-82005 [M]	El Nutto	1964	$25
❏ LS-86005 [S]	El Nutto	1964	$30
MAINSTREAM			
❏ 56048 [M]	It's Time We Met	1965	$35
❏ S-6048 [S]	It's Time We Met	1965	$25
MCA			
❏ 29035	Take It from Me	198?	$20
MERCURY			
❏ MG-20704 [M]	Explosion!	1962	$100
❏ SR-60704 [S]	Explosion!	1962	$100
❏ MG-20812 [M]	Jewish Melodies in Jazztime	1963	$250
❏ SR-60812 [S]	Jewish Melodies in Jazztime	1963	$250
❏ MG-20440 [M]	Launching a New Sound in Music	1959	$100
❏ SR-60112 [S]	Launching a New Sound in Music	1959	$100
❏ MG-20518 [M]	Steve Allen's All Stars	1960	$100
❏ SR-60195 [S]	Steve Allen's All Stars	1960	$100
MODE			
❏ LP-123 [M]	A Jazz Band Ball	1957	$80
ROOST			
❏ LP-2260 [M]	El Latino	1965	$35
❏ RS-2260 [S]	Latino	1965	$25
TIME			
❏ 52105 [M]	Hootenanny My Way	1963	$30
❏ S-2105 [S]	Hootenanny My Way	1963	$30
❏ 52120 [M]	Terry Gibbs with Sal Nistico	196?	$25
❏ S-2120 [S]	Terry Gibbs with Sal Nistico	196?	$30
TRIP			
❏ 5545	Launching a New Band	197?	$25
VERVE			
❏ MGV-2136 [M]	Music from Cole Porter's "Can-Can"	1960	$100
❏ V-2136 [M]	Music from Cole Porter's "Can-Can"	1961	$25
❏ MGVS-6145 [S]	Music from Cole Porter's "Can-Can"	1960	$100
❏ V6-2136 [S]	Music from Cole Porter's "Can-Can"	1961	$25
❏ V-8496 [M]	Straight Ahead	1962	$25
❏ V6-8496 [S]	Straight Ahead	1962	$30
❏ MGV-2134 [M]	Swing Is Here!	1960	$80
❏ V-2134 [M]	Swing Is Here!	1961	$25
❏ MGVS-6140 [S]	Swing Is Here!	1960	$80
❏ V6-2134 [S]	Swing Is Here!	1961	$25
❏ V-8447 [M]	That Swing Thing	1962	$25
❏ V6-8447 [S]	That Swing Thing	1962	$30
❏ MGV-2151 [M]	The Exciting Terry Gibbs Big Band	1960	$120
❏ V-2151 [M]	The Exciting Terry Gibbs Big Band	1961	$25
❏ V6-2151 [S]	The Exciting Terry Gibbs Big Band	1961	$30
WING			
❏ MGW-12255 [M]	Terry Plays the Duke	196?	$35
❏ SRW-16255 [R]	Terry Plays the Duke	196?	$25
XANADU			
❏ 210	Bopstacle Course	198?	$25

GIBSON, DON (2)
Pianist; not to be confused with the country singer of the same name.

Albums

Number	Title	Yr	NM
JAZZOLOGY			
❏ J-40	The Al Capone Memorial Jazz Band	197?	$30

GIFFORD, WALT

Albums

Number	Title	Yr	NM
DELMARK			
❏ DS-204 [M]	Walt Gifford's New Yorkers	1959	$30

GIL, GILBERTO
Guitarist and male singer.

Albums

Number	Title	Yr	NM
BRAZILOID			
❏ BR-4009	Ao Vivo Em Toquio	1989	$30
❏ BR-4000	Soy Loco Por Ti America	1988	$30
ELEKTRA			
❏ 6E-167	Nightingale	1979	$30
PHILIPS			
❏ 832216-1	Gilberto Gil	1988	$25

GILBERT, ANN
Female singer.

Albums

Number	Title	Yr	NM
GROOVE			
❏ LG-1004 [M]	The Many Moods of Ann	1956	$50

GILBERT, RONNIE
Female singer. Best known as a member of the folk group The Weavers, the below LP has a backing band of jazz musicians.

Albums

Number	Title	Yr	NM
RCA VICTOR			
❏ LPM-1591 [M]	In Hi-Fi, The Legend of Bessie Smith	1958	$40

GILBERT & SULLIVAN JAZZ WORKSHOP, THE
Members: MEL LEWIS (gong, drums); Bobby Gibbons (guitar); Milt Bernhart (trombone); JOHN GRAAS (French horn) Frank Flynn (vibes); Red Mandel (flute, clarinet); Cappy Lewis (trumpet); Morty Cobb (bass); John Rotella (baritone and alto saxophones).

Albums

Number	Title	Yr	NM
ANDEX			
❏ A-27101 [M]	The Coolest Mikado	1961	$25
❏ AS-27101 [S]	The Coolest Mikado	1961	$30

GILBERTO, ASTRUD
Female singer. Also see STAN GETZ.

Albums

Number	Title	Yr	NM
CTI			
❏ CTS-6008	Astrud Gilberto with Stanley Turrentine	1970	$30
ELEKTRA/MUSICIAN			
❏ 60760	Live in Montreux	1988	$25
PERCEPTION			
❏ 29	Now	1973	$25
VERVE			
❏ V6-8793	17-Sep-69	1969	$30
❏ V-8673 [M]	A Certain Smile, A Certain Sadness	1966	$30
❏ V6-8673 [S]	A Certain Smile, A Certain Sadness	1966	$35
❏ V-8708 [M]	Beach Samba	1967	$30
❏ V6-8708 [S]	Beach Samba	1967	$35
❏ V6-8776	I Haven't Got Anything Better to Do	1969	$30
❏ V-8643 [M]	Look to the Rainbow	1966	$30
❏ V6-8643 [S]	Look to the Rainbow	1966	$35
❏ 821566-1	Look to the Rainbow	1986	$25
— Reissue of V6-8643			
❏ V-8608 [M]	The Astrud Gilberto Album	1965	$30
❏ V6-8608 [S]	The Astrud Gilberto Album	1965	$35
❏ V-8629 [M]	The Shadow of Your Smile	1965	$30
❏ V6-8629 [S]	The Shadow of Your Smile	1965	$35
❏ SW-90649 [S]	The Shadow of Your Smile	1965	$80
— Capitol Record Club edition			
❏ V6-8754	Windy	1968	$30

Number	Title	Yr	NM

GILBERTO, JOAO
Guitarist and male singer. Also see STAN GETZ.

Albums

ATLANTIC

☐ 8070 [M]	The Boss of the Bossa Nova	1963	$50
☐ SD8070 [S]	The Boss of the Bossa Nova	1963	$50
☐ 8076 [M]	The Warm World of Joao Gilberto	1964	$35
☐ SD8076 [S]	The Warm World of Joao Gilberto	1964	$25

CAPITOL

☐ T2160 [M]	Joao Gilberto and Antonio Carlos Jobim	1964	$75
☐ ST2160 [S]	Joao Gilberto and Antonio Carlos Jobim	1964	$40
☐ ST2160 [S]	Joao Gilberto and Antonio Carlos Jobim	1978	$12
—Purple label, large Capitol logo			
☐ T10280 [M]	Pops in Portuguese	196?	$50
☐ ST10280 [S]	Pops in Portuguese	196?	$60

WARNER BROS.

☐ BS3053	Amoroso	1978	$25
☐ BSK3613	Brasel	1981	$25

GILL, JOHN
Pianist.

Albums

STOMP OFF

☐ SOS-1157	Big City Blues	1988	$25
☐ SOS-1126	Down Home Blues	1987	$25
☐ SOS-1066	Finger Buster	1984	$25
☐ SOS-1094	I Lost My Heart in Dixie Land	1986	$25
☐ SOS-1156	Some Sweet Day	1988	$25

GILLESPIE, DIZZY, AND CHARLIE PARKER
Also see each artist's individual listings.

Albums

ROOST

☐ LP-2234 [M]	Diz 'n' Bird In Concert	1959	$80
☐ SK-106 [M]	The Beginning: Diz and Bird	1960	$100

GILLESPIE, DIZZY, AND DJANGO REINHARDT
Also see each artist's individual listings.

Albums

CLEF

☐ MGC-747 [M]	Jazz from Paris	1956	$350
—Canceled; reassigned to Verve			

VERVE

☐ MGV-8015 [M]	Jazz from Paris	1957	$150
☐ V-8015 [M]	Jazz from Paris	1961	$30

GILLESPIE, DIZZY, AND STAN GETZ
Also see each artist's individual listings.

Albums

NORGRAN

☐ MGN-1050 [M]	Diz and Getz	1956	$200
☐ MGN-2 [10]	The Dizzy Gillespie-Stan Getz Sextet #1	1954	$300
☐ MGN-18 [10]	The Dizzy Gillespie-Stan Getz Sextet #2	1954	$300

VERVE

☐ MGV-8141 [M]	Diz and Getz	1957	$150
—Reissue of Norgran 1050			
☐ V-8141 [M]	Diz and Getz	1961	$60
☐ VE-2-2521	Diz and Getz	197?	$35

GILLESPIE, DIZZY
Trumpeter, male singer and composer; one of the most important figures in jazz history. His visual trademarks were the upturned bell on his instrument and his puffed-out cheeks as he played. Also see COUNT BASIE; ROY ELDRIDGE; GIL FULLER; SLIM GAILLARD; STAN GETZ; THE MODERN JAZZ SEXTET; CHARLIE PARKER; THE QUINTET.

Albums

ALLEGRO

☐ 3083 [M]	Dizzy Gillespie	195?	$120
☐ 4023 [10]	Dizzy Gillespie	195?	$200
☐ 3017 [M]	Dizzy Gillespie Plays	195?	$120
☐ 4108 [10]	Dizzy Gillespie Plays	195?	$200

AMERICAN RECORDING SOCIETY

☐ G-423 [M]	Big Band Jazz	1955	$100
☐ G-405 [M]	Jazz Creations/Dizzy Gillespie	1955	$100

ATLANTIC

☐ 81646	Closer to the Source	1986	$25
☐ 1257 [M]	Dizzy at Home and Abroad	1957	$300
—Black label			
☐ 1257 [M]	Dizzy at Home and Abroad	1961	$150
—Multi-color label with white "fan" logo			
☐ ALR-138 [10]	Dizzy Gillespie	1952	$400
☐ ALR-142 [10]	Dizzy Gillespie, Vol. 2	1952	$400

BANDSTAND

☐ BDLP-1513	Groovin' High	1992	$35

BARONET

☐ 105 [M]	A Handful of Modern Jazz	1961	$40

BLUEBIRD

☐ 5785-1-RB [(2)]	Dizziest	1987	$35

BLUE NOTE

☐ BLP-5017 [10]	Horn of Plenty	1953	$300

BULLDOG

☐ BDL-2006	20 Golden Pieces of Dizzy Gillespie	198?	$25

CLEF

☐ MGC-136 [10]	Dizzy Gillespie with Strings	1953	$350

CONTEMPORARY

☐ C-2504 [10]	Dizzy in Paris	1953	$250

COUNTERPOINT

☐ C-5548	Dizzy Gillespie, 1941	197?	$30

DEE GEE

☐ LP-1000 [10]	Dizzy Gillespie	1950	$300

DIAL

☐ 212 [10]	Modern Trumpets	1952	$400

DISCOVERY

☐ DL-3013 [10]	Dizzy Gillespie Plays, Johnny Richards Conducts	1950	$300

ELEKTRA/MUSICIAN

☐ 60300	One Night in Washington	1984	$25

EMARCY

☐ EMS-2-410	Composer's Concepts	197?	$35

EVEREST ARCHIVE OF FOLK & JAZZ

☐ 237	Dizzy Gillespie	1970	$25
☐ 272	Dizzy Gillespie, Volume 2	197?	$25
☐ 301	Dizzy Gillespie, Volume 3	197?	$25
☐ 346	The King of Bop	198?	$25

FANTASY

☐ OJC-447	Afro-Cuban Jazz Moods	1990	$30
☐ OJC-381	Dizzy Gillespie Jam: Montreux '77	1989	$25
☐ OJC-443	Dizzy's Big Four	1990	$25

GATEWAY

☐ 7025	Sweet Soul	198?	$30

GENE NORMAN

☐ GNP-23 [M]	Dizzy Gillespie and His Big Band	1957	$80
☐ GNP-4 [10]	Dizzy Gillespie with His Original Big Band	195?	$200

GNP CRESCENDO

☐ GNP-9028	Dizzy!	197?	$25
☐ GNP-23 [M]	Dizzy Gillespie and His Big Band	196?	$25
☐ GNPS-23 [R]	Dizzy Gillespie and His Big Band	196?	$30
☐ GNP-9006	Paris Concert	197?	$25

GRP

☐ GR-1012	New Faces	198?	$25

GWP

☐ 2023	Souled Out	197?	$35

IMPULSE!

☐ AS-9149	Swing Low, Sweet Cadillac!	1967	$200

INTERMEDIA

☐ QS-5033	Body & Soul Featuring Sarah Vaughan	198?	$25

JAZZ MAN

☐ 5017	The Giant	198?	$30
☐ 5021	The Source	198?	$30

LIMELIGHT

☐ LM-82007 [M]	Jambo Caribe	1964	$25
☐ LS-86007 [S]	Jambo Caribe	1964	$30
☐ LM-82042 [M]	The Melody Lingers On	1967	$25
☐ LS-86042 [S]	The Melody Lingers On	1967	$30
☐ LM-82022 [M]	The New Continent	1965	$25
☐ LS-86022 [S]	The New Continent	1965	$30

MAINSTREAM

☐ MRL-325	Dizzy Gillespie with the Mitchell-Ruff Duo	1972	$35

MCA

☐ 29036	Swing Low, Sweet Cadillac	198?	$20

MOON

☐ MLP-035	Angel City	1992	$35

MUSICRAFT

☐ MVS-2009	Groovin' High	1986	$25

☐ MVS-2010	One Bass Hit	1986	$25

NORGRAN

☐ MGN-1003 [M]	Afro Dizzy	1954	$400
☐ MGN-1090 [M]	Diz Big Band	1956	$250
☐ MGN-1023 [M]	Dizzy and Strings	1955	$250
☐ MGN-1083 [M]	Jazz Recital	1956	$300
☐ MGN-1084 [M]	World Statesman	1956	$200

PABLO

☐ 2310771	Afro-Cuban Jazz Moods	1976	$30
☐ 2625708	Bahiana	1976	$35
☐ 2310719	Dizzy's Big Four	1975	$30
☐ 2310749	Dizzy's Big Seven: Montreux '75	1976	$30
☐ 2310794	Free Ride	1977	$30
☐ 2310889	In Helsinki: To a Finland Station	198?	$25
☐ 2310784	Party	1977	$30
☐ 2312136	The Alternate Blues	198?	$25
☐ 2310885	The Best of Dizzy Gillespie	198?	$25
☐ 2405411	The Best of Dizzy Gillespie	198?	$25

PABLO LIVE

☐ 2308226	Digital Dizzy at Montreux 1980	1980	$30
☐ 2308211	Dizzy Gillespie Jam: Montreux '77	1977	$30
☐ 2308229	Sumemrtime	1980	$30

PERCEPTION

☐ 13	Portrait of Jenny	1971	$35
☐ 2	The Real Thing	197?	$35

PHILIPS

☐ PHM200048 [M]	Dizzy at the French Riviera	1962	$25
☐ PHS600048 [S]	Dizzy at the French Riviera	1962	$30
☐ PHM200106 [M]	Dizzy Gillespie and the Double Six of Paris	1963	$100
☐ PHS600106 [S]	Dizzy Gillespie and the Double Six of Paris	1963	$150
☐ PHM200123 [M]	Dizzy Gillespie Goes Hollywood	1964	$25
☐ PHS600123 [S]	Dizzy Gillespie Goes Hollywood	1964	$30
☐ 822897-1	Dizzy Gillespie on the Frence Riviera	1986	$25
☐ PHM200070 [M]	New Wave!	1962	$25
☐ PHS600070 [S]	New Wave!	1962	$30
☐ PHM200091 [M]	Something Old, Something New	1963	$25
☐ PHS600091 [S]	Something Old, Something New	1963	$30
☐ PHM200138 [M]	The Cool World	1964	$100
☐ PHS600138 [S]	The Cool World	1964	$150

PHOENIX

☐ 4	The Big Bands	197?	$25
☐ 2	The Small Groups	197?	$25

PRESTIGE

☐ PRST-7818	Dizzy Gillespie at Salle Plevel '48	1970	$30
☐ 24030	In the Beginning	197?	$35
☐ P-24047	The Giant	1975	$35

RCA VICTOR

☐ LJM-1009 [M]	Dizzier and Dizzier	1954	$120
☐ LPV-530 [M]	Dizzy Gillespie	1966	$30

REGENT

☐ MG-6043 [M]	School Days	1957	$100

REPRISE

☐ R-6072 [M]	Dateline: Europe	1963	$25
☐ R9-6072 [S]	Dateline: Europe	1963	$30

RONDO-LETTE

☐ A-11 [M]	Dizzy Gillespie	195?	$30

ROOST

☐ LP-2214 [M]	Concert in Paris	1957	$120
☐ R-414 [10]	Dizzy Over Paris	1953	$250

SAVOY

☐ MG-12020 [M]	Groovin' High	1955	$75
☐ MG-12047 [M]	The Champ	1956	$60
☐ MG-12110 [M]	The Dizzy Gillespie Story	1957	$60

SAVOY JAZZ

☐ SJL-2209	Dee Gee Days	197?	$35
☐ SJC-402	The Dizzy Gillespie Story	1985	$25

SOLID STATE

☐ SS-18061	Cornucopia	1969	$25
☐ SS-18034	Live at the Village Vanguard	1968	$60
☐ SS-18054	My Way	1969	$25

SUTTON

☐ SU-287 [M]	Featuring Dizzy Gillespie	196?	$20
☐ SSU-287 [S]	Featuring Dizzy Gillespie	196?	$15

TIMELESS

☐ LPSJP-250	Dizzy Gillespie Meets the Phil Woods Quintet	1990	$30

TRIP

☐ 5566	Something Old, Something New	197?	$25

VERNON

☐ 506 [M]	The Everlivin' "Diz	196?	$35
☐ 506 [S]	The Everlivin' "Diz	196?	$30

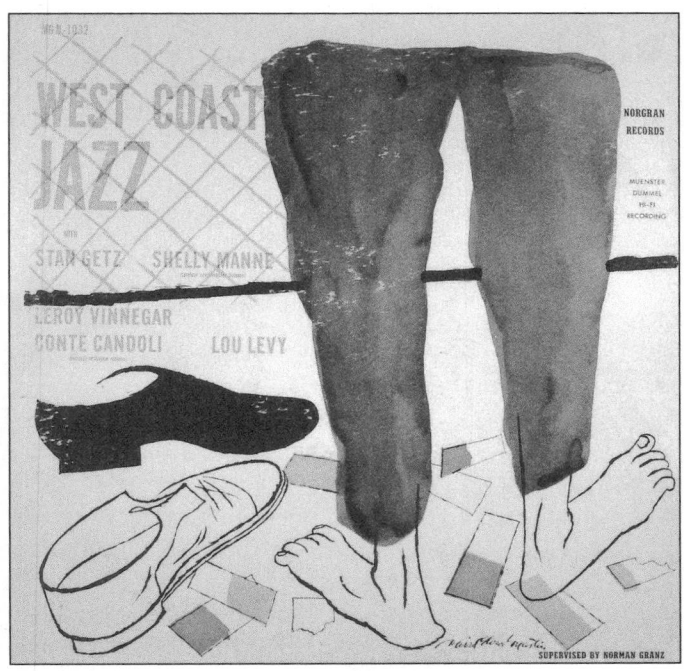

Stan Getz, *West Coast Jazz*, Norgran MGN-1032, **$300**.

Stan Getz and Zoot Sims, *The Brothers*, Prestige PRLP-7022, yellow label with W. 50th St. address, **$400**.

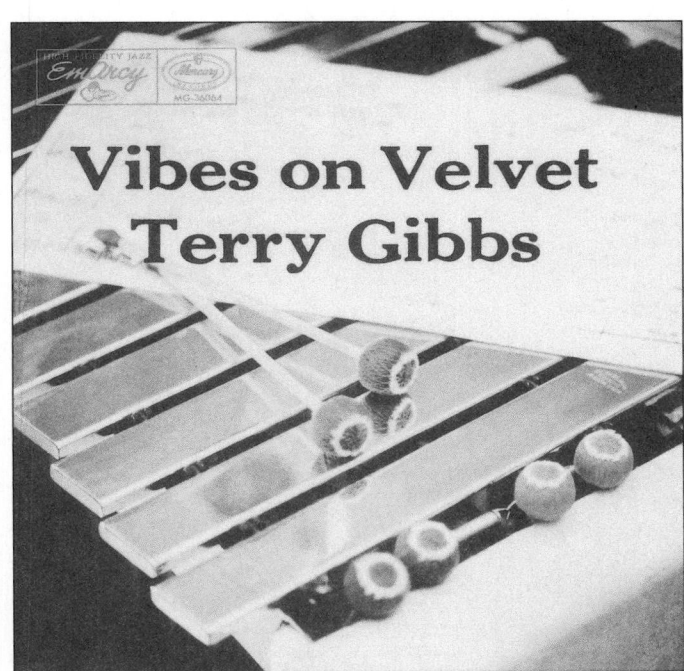

Terry Gibbs, *Vibes on Velvet*, EmArcy MG 36064, **$200**.

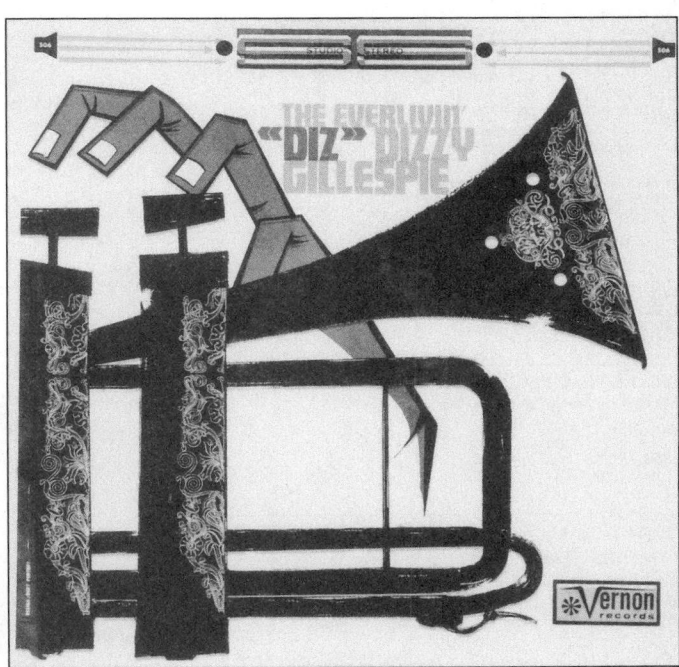

Dizzy Gillespie, *The Everlivin' "Diz,"* Vernon 506, stereo, **$30**.

Number	Title	Yr	NM

VERVE

Number	Title	Yr	NM
MGV-8191 [M]	Afro Dizzy	1957	$200
V-8401 [M]	An Electrifying Evening with the Dizzy Gillespie Quintet	1961	$25
V6-8401 [S]	An Electrifying Evening with the Dizzy Gillespie Quintet	1961	$30
UMV-2605	An Electrifying Evening with the Dizzy Gillespie Quintet	198?	$25
V-8423 [M]	Carnegie Hall Concert	1962	$25
V6-8423 [S]	Carnegie Hall Concert	1962	$30
VE-2-2524	Diz and Roy	197?	$35
MGV-8178 [M]	Diz Big Band	1957	$125
V-8178 [M]	Diz Big Band	1961	$30
V-8477 [M]	Dizzy, Rollins & Stitt	1962	$25
—Reissue of MGV-8260			
V6-8477 [M]	Dizzy, Rollins & Stitt	1962	$30
V-8560 [M]	Dizzy at Newport	1964	$25
V6-8560 [S]	Dizzy at Newport	1964	$30
MGV-8214 [M]	Dizzy Gillespie and Stuff Smith	1958	$150
V-8214 [M]	Dizzy Gillespie and Stuff Smith	1961	$30
MGV-8242 [M]	Dizzy Gillespie at Newport	1958	$150
V-8242 [M]	Dizzy Gillespie at Newport	1961	$30
MGVS-6023 [S]	Dizzy Gillespie at Newport	1960	$100
V6-8242 [S]	Dizzy Gillespie at Newport	1961	$30
MGV-8017 [M]	Dizzy in Greece	1957	$125
V-8017 [M]	Dizzy in Greece	1961	$30
MGV-8260 [M]	Duets	1958	$150
—With Sonny Rollins and Sonny Stitt			
MGV-8394 [M]	Gillespiana	1960	$100
V-8394 [M]	Gillespiana	1961	$30
V6-8394 [S]	Gillespiana	1961	$30
MGV-8352 [M]	Greatest Trumpet of Them All	1959	$100
V6-8352 [S]	Greatest Trumpet of Them All	1961	$30
V-8352 [M]	Greatest Trumpet of Them All	1961	$30
MGVS-6117 [S]	Greatest Trumpet of Them All	1960	$100
MGV-8313 [M]	Have Trumpet, Will Excite	1959	$100
V-8313 [M]	Have Trumpet, Will Excite	1961	$30
MGVS-6047 [S]	Have Trumpet, Will Excite	1960	$100
V6-8313 [S]	Have Trumpet, Will Excite	1961	$30
UMV-2692	Have Trumpet, Will Excite	198?	$25
MGV-8173 [M]	Jazz Recital	1957	$150
V-8173 [M]	Jazz Recital	1961	$30
MGV-8208 [M]	Manteca	1958	$120
V-8208 [M]	Manteca	1961	$30
VSP-7 [M]	Night in Tunisia	1966	$35
VSPS-7 [S]	Night in Tunisia	1966	$35
V-8411 [M]	Perceptions	1961	$25
V6-8411 [S]	Perceptions	1961	$30
MGV-8386 [M]	Portrait of Duke	1960	$150
V-8386 [M]	Portrait of Duke	1961	$30
MGV-8328 [M]	The Ebullient Mr. Gillespie	1959	$100
V6-8328 [S]	The Ebullient Mr. Gillespie	1961	$30
V-8328 [M]	The Ebullient Mr. Gillespie	1961	$30
MGVS-6068 [S]	The Ebullient Mr. Gillespie	1960	$100
V-8566 [M]	The Essential Dizzy Gillespie	1964	$25
V6-8566 [S]	The Essential Dizzy Gillespie	1964	$30
V6-8830	The Newport Years	197?	$30
821662-1	The Reunion Big Band	198?	$25
VE-2-2505	The Sonny Rollins/Sonny Stitt Sessions	1976	$35
MGV-8174 [M]	World Statesman	1957	$120
V-8174 [M]	World Statesman	1961	$60

WING

Number	Title	Yr	NM
MGW-12318 [M]	The New Wave!	1966	$30
SRW-16318 [S]	The New Wave!	1966	$30

GILLESPIE, DIZZY/JIMMY MCPARTLAND
Also see each artist's individual listings.

Albums

MGM

Number	Title	Yr	NM
E-3286 [M]	Hot vs. Cool	1955	$80

GINSBERG, ALLEN
Jazz-influenced beat poet.

Albums

ATLANTIC

Number	Title	Yr	NM
4001 [M]	Allen Ginsburg Reads Kaddish	1966	$60

GIRARD, GEORGE
Trumpeter and bandleader.

Albums

VIK

Number	Title	Yr	NM
LX-1058 [M]	Jam Session on Bourbon Street	1957	$40
LX-1063 [M]	Stompin' at the Famous Door	1957	$40

GISMONTI, EGBERTO, AND NANA VASCONCELOS
Also see each artist's individual listings.

Albums

ECM

Number	Title	Yr	NM
25015	Duas Vozes	1985	$25

GISMONTI, EGBERTO
Pianist, guitarist, flutist and male singer.

Albums

ECM

Number	Title	Yr	NM
1089	Danca Das Cabecas	1976	$30
1203	Sanfona	1981	$35
1116	Sol Do Meio Dia	1978	$30
1136	Solo	1979	$25

GIUFFRE, JIMMY, AND MARTY PAICH
Also see each artist's individual listings.

Albums

GNP CRESCENDO

Number	Title	Yr	NM
GNPS-9040	Tenors West	197?	$30

GIUFFRE, JIMMY
Clarinetist, saxophone player (tenor and baritone) and flutist.
Also see HERB ELLIS; LEE KONITZ.

Albums

ATLANTIC

Number	Title	Yr	NM
1295 [M]	Four Brothers Sound	1959	$300
—Black label			
1295 [M]	Four Brothers Sound	1960	$250
—Multicolor label, white "fan" logo at right			
SD1295 [S]	Four Brothers Sound	1959	$300
—Green label			
SD1295 [S]	Four Brothers Sound	1960	$250
—Multicolor label, white "fan" logo at right			
90144	Jimmy Giuffre Clarinet	198?	$25
1276 [M]	Music Man	1958	$250
—Black label			
1276 [M]	Music Man	1960	$250
—Multicolor label, white "fan" logo at right			
1276 [M]	Music Man	1963	$35
—Multicolor label, black "fan" logo at right			
SD1276 [S]	Music Man	1959	$300
—Green label			
SD1276 [S]	Music Man	1960	$250
—Multicolor label, white "fan" logo at right			
SD1276 [S]	Music Man	1963	$35
—Multicolor label, black "fan" logo at right			
1238 [M]	The Jimmy Giuffre Clarinet	1956	$300
—Black label			
1238 [M]	The Jimmy Giuffre Clarinet	1960	$250
—Multicolor label, white "fan" logo at right			
1238 [M]	The Jimmy Giuffre Clarinet	1963	$50
—Multicolor label, black "fan" logo at right			
1254 [M]	The Jimmy Giuffre Three	1957	$300
—Black label			
1254 [M]	The Jimmy Giuffre Three	1960	$250
—Multicolor label, white "fan" logo at right			

1254 [M]	The Jimmy Giuffre Three	1963	$50
—Multicolor label, black "fan" logo at right			

Number	Title	Yr	NM
1282 [M]	Trav'lin' Light	1958	$300
—Black label			
1282 [M]	Trav'lin' Light	1960	$250
—Multicolor label, white "fan" logo at right			
1282 [M]	Trav'lin' Light	1963	$35
—Multicolor label, black "fan" logo at right			
SD1282 [S]	Trav'lin' Light	1959	$300
—Green label			
SD1282 [S]	Trav'lin' Light	1960	$250
—Multicolor label, white "fan" logo at right			
SD1282 [S]	Trav'lin' Light	1963	$35
—Multicolor label, black "fan" logo at right			
1330 [M]	Western Suite	1963	$35
—Multicolor label, black "fan" logo at right			
SD1330 [S]	Western Suite	1963	$35
—Multicolor label, black "fan" logo at right			

CAPITOL

Number	Title	Yr	NM
H549 [10]	Jimmy Giuffre	1954	$300
T549 [M]	Jimmy Giuffre	1955	$200
T634 [M]	Tangents in Jazz	1955	$200

CHOICE

Number	Title	Yr	NM
1001	Music for People, Birds, Butterflies and Mosquitos	1974	$50
1011	River Chant	1975	$50

COLUMBIA

Number	Title	Yr	NM
CL1964 [M]	Free Fall	1963	$35
CS8764 [S]	Free Fall	1963	$25

IAI

Number	Title	Yr	NM
373859	Jimmy Giuffre at the IAI Festival	1978	$30

MOSAIC

Number	Title	Yr	NM
MQ10-176	The Complete Capitol & Atlantic Recordings of Jimmy Giuffre	1998	$300
—Limited edition of 5,000			

SOUL NOTE

Number	Title	Yr	NM
SN-1058	Dragonfly	1983	$35
121058	Dragonfly	199?	$30
121158	Liquid Dancers	1991	$35
SN-1108	Quasar	1986	$50
121108	Quasar	199?	$30

VERVE

Number	Title	Yr	NM
MGV-8361 [M]	Ad Lib	1960	$150
V-8361 [M]	Ad Lib	1961	$60
MGVS-6130 [S]	Ad Lib	1960	$150
V6-8361 [S]	Ad Lib	1961	$60
MGV-8397 [M]	Fusion	1961	$40
V-8397 [M]	Fusion	1961	$25
V6-8397 [S]	Fusion	1961	$30
MGV-8395 [M]	Piece for Clarinet and String Orchestra	1961	$40
V-8395 [M]	Piece for Clarinet and String Orchestra	1961	$25
V6-8395 [S]	Piece for Clarinet and String Orchestra	1961	$30
MGV-8307 [M]	Seven Pieces	1959	$100
V-8307 [M]	Seven Pieces	1961	$25
MGVS-6039 [S]	Seven Pieces	1960	$100
V6-8307 [S]	Seven Pieces	1961	$35
MGV-8337 [M]	The Easy Way	1960	$100
V-8337 [M]	The Easy Way	1961	$25
MGVS-6095 [S]	The Easy Way	1960	$100
V6-8337 [S]	The Easy Way	1961	$35
MGV-8387 [M]	The Jimmy Giuffre Quartet In Person	1961	$40
V-8387 [M]	The Jimmy Giuffre Quartet In Person	1961	$25
V6-8387 [S]	The Jimmy Giuffre Quartet In Person	1961	$30
MGV-8402 [M]	Thesis	1961	$40
V-8402 [M]	Thesis	1961	$25
V6-8402 [S]	Thesis	1961	$30

GLASEL, JOHN
Trumpeter.

Albums

ABC-PARAMOUNT

Number	Title	Yr	NM
ABC-165 [M]	Jazz Session	1957	$50

GOLDEN CREST

Number	Title	Yr	NM
1002 [M]	Jazz Unlimited	1960	$30

GLEASON, JACKIE

Albums

CAPITOL

Number	Title	Yr	NM
W1020 [M]	Riff Jazz	1958	$50
SW1020 [S]	Riff Jazz	1959	$60

Number	Title	Yr	NM

GLENN, ROGER
Flutist, vibraphone player and percussionist.
Albums
FANTASY
| ❑ F-9516 | Reachin' | 197? | $30 |

GLENN, TYREE
Trombonist and vibraphone player.
Albums
ROULETTE
❑ R-25115 [M]	Let's Have a Ball	1960	$30
❑ SR-25115 [S]	Let's Have a Ball	1960	$30
❑ R-25184 [M]	The Trombone Artistry of Tyree Glenn	1962	$25
❑ SR-25184 [S]	The Trombone Artistry of Tyree Glenn	1962	$30
❑ R-25075 [M]	Try a Little Tenderness	1959	$40
❑ SR-25075 [S]	Try a Little Tenderness	1959	$30
❑ R-25138 [M]	Tyree Glenn at London House in Chicago	1961	$25
❑ SR-25138 [S]	Tyree Glenn at London House in Chicago	1961	$30
❑ R-25009 [M]	Tyree Glenn at the Embers	1957	$40
❑ R-25050 [M]	Tyree Glenn at the Roundtable	1959	$40
❑ SR-25050 [S]	Tyree Glenn at the Roundtable	1959	$30

GOLD, SANFORD
Pianist.
Albums
PRESTIGE
| ❑ PRLP-7019 [M] | Piano d'Or | 1956 | $300 |

GOLDBERG, STU
Pianist.
Albums
PAUSA
❑ 7123	Eye of the Beholder	1981	$25
❑ 7036	Solos, Duos, Trio	1978	$25
❑ 7095	Variations by Goldberg	1980	$25

GOLDEN AGE JAZZ BAND
Led by banjo player Dick Oxtot.
Albums
ARHOOLIE
| ❑ 4007 | Golden Age Jazz Band | 197? | $35 |

GOLDEN EAGLE JAZZ BAND
Albums
STOMP OFF
| ❑ SOS-1080 | Oh My Babe | 1985 | $25 |
| ❑ SOS-1100 | Young Woman's Blues | 1986 | $25 |

GOLDEN STATE JAZZ BAND
Albums
STOMP OFF
| ❑ SOS-1006 | Alive and At Bay | 1983 | $25 |

GOLDIE, DON
Trumpeter.
Albums
ARGO
❑ LP-4010 [M]	Brilliant!	1961	$30
❑ LPS-4010 [S]	Brilliant!	1961	$30
❑ LP-708 [M]	Trumpet Caliente	1963	$30
❑ LPS-708 [S]	Trumpet Caliente	1963	$30
JAZZOLOGY
❑ J-135	Don Goldie's Jazz Express	1986	$25
VERVE
❑ V-8475 [M]	Trumpet Exodus	1962	$30
❑ V6-8475 [S]	Trumpet Exodus	1962	$30

GOLDKETTE, JEAN
Pianist and bandleader.
Albums
X
| ❑ LVA-3017 [10] | Jean Goldkette and His Orchestra Featuring Bix Beiderbecke | 1954 | $60 |

GOLDSBURY, MACK
Saxophone player.
Albums
MUSE
| ❑ MR-5194 | Anthropo-logic | 1979 | $25 |

GOLDSTEIN, GIL
Pianist, accordion player and arranger.
Albums
CHIAROSCURO
| ❑ 201 | Pure As Rain | 1978 | $30 |
MUSE
| ❑ MR-5229 | Wrapped in a Cloud | 1980 | $25 |

GOLIA, VINNY
Multi-instrumentalist credited with playing 19 different woodwind instruments.
Albums
NINE WINDS
❑ NW 0110	Compositions for Large Ensemble	1984	$25
❑ NW 0120	Facts of Their Own Lives	1986	$35
❑ NW 0117	Goin' Ahead	1985	$30
❑ NW 0103	... In the Right Order ...	1979	$35
❑ NW 0102	Openhearted	1978	$30
❑ NW 0127	Out for Blood	1989	$30
❑ NW 0108	Slice of Life	1981	$30
❑ NW 0104	Solo	1980	$30
❑ NW 0101	Spirits in Fellowship	1977	$30
❑ NW 0109	The Gift of Fury	1982	$30

GOLSON, BENNY
Tenor saxophone player and composer. Also see CURTIS FULLER; THE JAZZTET; RAHSAAN ROLAND KIRK.
Albums
ARGO
❑ LP-716 [M]	Free	1963	$50
❑ LPS-716 [S]	Free	1963	$60
❑ LP-681 [M]	Take a Number from 1 to 10	1961	$30
❑ LPS-681 [S]	Take a Number from 1 to 10	1961	$40
AUDIO FIDELITY
❑ AFLP-2150 [M]	Just Jazz	1966	$60
❑ AFSD-6150 [S]	Just Jazz	1966	$40
❑ AFLP-1978 [M]	Pop + Jazz = Swing	1962	$60
❑ AFSD-5978 [S]	Pop + Jazz = Swing	1962	$40
COLUMBIA
❑ JC35359	I'm Always Dancin' to the Music	1978	$50
❑ PC34678	Killer Joe	1977	$50
CONTEMPORARY
❑ C-3552 [M]	Benny Golson's New York Scene	1958	$250
FANTASY
❑ OJC-164	Benny Golson's New York Scene	198?	$30
—Reissue of Contemporary 3552			
❑ OJC-226	Groovin' with Golson	198?	$30
—Reissue of New Jazz 8220			
❑ OJC-1750	The Other Side of Benny Golson	1990	$35
—Reissue of Riverside 290			
JAZZLAND
❑ JLP-85 [M]	Reunion	1962	$60
❑ JLP-985 [S]	Reunion	1962	$50
MERCURY
❑ MG-20801 [M]	Turning Point	1963	$100
❑ SR-60801 [S]	Turning Point	1963	$100
MILESTONE
❑ M-47048	Blues On Down	1978	$50
NEW JAZZ
❑ NJLP-8248 [M]	Gettin' With It	1960	$200
—Purple label			
❑ NJLP-8248 [M]	Gettin' With It	1965	$150
—Blue label, trident logo at right			
❑ NJLP-8235	Gone with Golson	1965	$150
—Blue label, trident logo at right			
❑ NJLP-8220 [M]	Groovin' with Golson	1959	$200
—Purple label			
❑ NJLP-8220 [M]	Groovin' with Golson	1965	$150
—Blue label, trident logo at right			
PRESTIGE
❑ PRLP-7361 [M]	Stockholm Sojourn	1965	$30
❑ PRST-7361 [S]	Stockholm Sojourn	1965	$40
RIVERSIDE
❑ 6070	The Modern Touch	197?	$30
❑ RLP 12-256 [M]	The Modern Touch of Benny Golson	1957	$250
❑ RLP 12-290 [M]	The Other Side of Benny Golson	1958	$300
SWING
❑ SW-8418	Benny Golson in Paris	1987	$30
TIMELESS
❑ LPSJP-177	California Message	1980	$35
❑ LPSJP-235	This Is for You, John	1983	$35
UNITED ARTISTS
❑ UAL-4020 [M]	Benny Golson and the Philadelphians	1959	$100
❑ UAS-5020 [S]	Benny Golson and the Philadelphians	1959	$80
VERVE
❑ V-8710 [M]	Tune In, Turn On	1967	$40
❑ V6-8710 [S]	Tune In, Turn On	1967	$60

GOMEZ, EDDIE
Bass player.
Albums
COLUMBIA
| ❑ FC44214 | Power Play | 1988 | $25 |

GONSALVES, PAUL, AND ROY ELDREDGE
Also see each artist's individual listings.
Albums
FANTASY
| ❑ F-9646 | Mexican Bandit Meets Pittsburgh Pirate | 1986 | $25 |

GONSALVES, PAUL
Tenor saxophone player.
Albums
ABC IMPULSE!
❑ AS-41 [S]	Cleopatra Feelin' Jazzy	1967	$35
❑ AS-52 [S]	Salt and Pepper	1967	$35
❑ AS-55 [S]	Tell It the Way It Is	1967	$35
ARGO
❑ LPS-626 [S]	Cookin'	1959	$40
BLACK LION
❑ 191	Just a Sittin' and a Rockin'	197?	$35
CATALYST
❑ 7913	Buenos Aires	197?	$35
FANTASY
❑ OJC-203	Gettin' Together	198?	$25
IMPULSE!
❑ A-41 [M]	Cleopatra Feelin' Jazzy	1963	$120
❑ AS-41 [S]	Cleopatra Feelin' Jazzy	1963	$120
❑ A-52 [M]	Salt and Pepper	1963	$120
❑ AS-52 [S]	Salt and Pepper	1963	$120
❑ A-55 [M]	Tell It the Way It Is	1963	$120
❑ AS-55 [S]	Tell It the Way It Is	1963	$120

GONSALVES, VIRGIL
Baritone saxophone player, clarinetist and male singer.
Albums
LIBERTY
| ❑ LJH-6010 [M] | Jazz San Francisco Style | 1956 | $50 |
NOCTURNE
| ❑ NLP-8 [10] | Virgil Gonsalves | 1954 | $80 |
OMEGA
| ❑ OML-1047 [M] | Jazz at Monterey | 1959 | $40 |

GONZALES, BABS
Female singer.
Albums
CHIAROSCURO
| ❑ 2025 | Live at Small's Paradise | 197? | $35 |
DAUNTLESS
| ❑ DM-4311 [M] | Sunday Afternoon at Small's Paradise | 1963 | $40 |

Number	Title	Yr	NM
❑ DS-6311 [S]	Sunday Afternoon at Small's Paradise	1963	$50

HOPE

Number	Title	Yr	NM
❑ 01 [M]	Voila!	1958	$150

JARO

Number	Title	Yr	NM
❑ JAS-8000 [S]	Cool Philosophy	1959	$100

GONZALES, JERRY

Trumpeter and fluegel horn player.

Albums

AMERICAN CLAVE

Number	Title	Yr	NM
❑ 1001	Ya Yo Me Cure	198?	$30

ENJA

Number	Title	Yr	NM
❑ R1-79609	Obatala	1990	$30
❑ 4040	The River Is Deep	1982	$30

GOODE, BRAD

Trumpeter.

Albums

DELMARK

Number	Title	Yr	NM
❑ DS-440	Shock of the New	1989	$30

GOODMAN, BENNY

Clarinet player and bandleader known as "The King of Swing."
Also see BEN POLLACK.

Albums

ABC

Number	Title	Yr	NM
❑ AC-30014	The ABC Collection	1976	$30

AIRCHECK

Number	Title	Yr	NM
❑ 16	Benny Goodman and His Orchestra	197?	$30
❑ 16	Benny Goodman and His Orchestra On the Air, Vol. 1	1986	$25

—*Reissue of above with revised title*

Number	Title	Yr	NM
❑ 32	Benny Goodman and His Orchestra On the Air, Vol. 2	1986	$25
❑ 34	Benny Goodman and His Orchestra On the Air, Vol. 3	1986	$25

BIOGRAPH

Number	Title	Yr	NM
❑ C-1	Great Soloists 1929-33	1972	$25

BLUEBIRD

Number	Title	Yr	NM
❑ AXM2-5505	The Complete Benny Goodman, Vol. 1 (1935)	197?	$30
❑ AXM2-5515	The Complete Benny Goodman, Vol. 2 (1935-36)	197?	$30
❑ AXM2-5532	The Complete Benny Goodman, Vol. 3 (1936)	197?	$30
❑ AXM2-5537	The Complete Benny Goodman, Vol. 4 (1936-37)	197?	$30
❑ AXM2-5557	The Complete Benny Goodman, Vol. 5 (1937-38)	197?	$30
❑ AXM2-5566	The Complete Benny Goodman, Vol. 6 (1938)	197?	$30
❑ AXM2-5567	The Complete Benny Goodman, Vol. 7 (1938-39)	197?	$30
❑ AXM2-5568	The Complete Benny Goodman, Vol. 8 (1936-39)	197?	$30

BRUNSWICK

Number	Title	Yr	NM
❑ BL54010 [M]	Benny Goodman 1927-34	1954	$40
❑ BL58015 [10]	Chicago Jazz Classics	1950	$50

CAPITOL

Number	Title	Yr	NM
❑ T669 [M]	Benny Goodman Combos	1956	$60

—*Turquoise label*

Number	Title	Yr	NM
❑ T669 [M]	Benny Goodman Combos	1958	$40

—*Black label with colorband, Capitol logo on left*

Number	Title	Yr	NM
❑ W565 [M]	B.G. in Hi-Fi	1955	$75

—*Gray label*

Number	Title	Yr	NM
❑ W565 [M]	B.G. in Hi-Fi	1958	$30

—*Black label with colorband, Capitol logo on left*

Number	Title	Yr	NM
❑ H1-565 [10]	B.G. in Hi-Fi (Volume 1)	1955	$75
❑ H2-565 [10]	B.G. in Hi-Fi (Volume 2)	1955	$75
❑ H295 [10]	Easy Does It	1952	$80
❑ T2157 [M]	Hello Benny!	1964	$60
❑ ST2157 [S]	Hello Benny!	1964	$75
❑ T2282 [M]	Made in Japan	1965	$60
❑ ST2282 [S]	Made in Japan	1965	$75
❑ T668 [M]	Mostly Sextets	1956	$60

—*Turquoise label*

Number	Title	Yr	NM
❑ T668 [M]	Mostly Sextets	1958	$40

—*Black label with colorband, Capitol logo on left*

Number	Title	Yr	NM
❑ S706 [M]	Selections Featured in "The Benny Goodman Story	1956	$60

—*Turquoise label*

Number	Title	Yr	NM
❑ S706 [M]	Selections Featured in "The Benny Goodman Story	1958	$50

—*Black label with colorband, Capitol logo on left*

Number	Title	Yr	NM
❑ SM-706	Selections Featured in "The Benny Goodman Story	197?	$25

—*Reissue of S 706*

Number	Title	Yr	NM
❑ H202 [10]	Session for Six	1950	$80
❑ T395 [M]	Session for Six	1953	$75

—*Turquoise label*

Number	Title	Yr	NM
❑ T395 [M]	Session for Six	1958	$50

—*Black label with colorband, Capitol logo on left*

Number	Title	Yr	NM
❑ H479 [10]	Small Combo 1947	1954	$80
❑ H409 [10]	The Benny Goodman Band	1953	$80
❑ T409 [M]	The Benny Goodman Band	1953	$60

—*Turquoise label*

Number	Title	Yr	NM
❑ T409 [M]	The Benny Goodman Band	1958	$40

—*Black label with colorband, Capitol logo on left*

Number	Title	Yr	NM
❑ H343 [10]	The Benny Goodman Trio	1952	$80
❑ H441 [10]	The Goodman Touch	1953	$80
❑ T441 [M]	The Goodman Touch	1953	$60

—*Turquoise label*

Number	Title	Yr	NM
❑ T441 [M]	The Goodman Touch	1958	$50

—*Black label with colorband, Capitol logo on left*

Number	Title	Yr	NM
❑ T1514 [M]	The Hits of Benny Goodman	1961	$50

—*Black label with colorband, Capitol logo on left*

Number	Title	Yr	NM
❑ T1514 [M]	The Hits of Benny Goodman	1963	$75

—*Black label with colorband, Capitol logo on top*

Number	Title	Yr	NM
❑ DT1514 [R]	The Hits of Benny Goodman	1961	$60
❑ SM-1514	The Hits of Benny Goodman	197?	$25

—*Reissue of DT 1514*

CBS MASTERWORKS

Number	Title	Yr	NM
❑ OSL160 [M]	The Famous 1938 Carnegie Hall Jazz Concert	198?	$35

—*Late reissue; grayish labels with "CBS Masterworks" circling the edge*

CENTURY

Number	Title	Yr	NM
❑ 1150	The King of Swing Direct to Disc	1979	$30

—*Direct-to-disc audiophile recording*

CHESS

Number	Title	Yr	NM
❑ LP-1440 [DJ]	Benny Rides Again	1960	$100

—*Multi-color swirl vinyl*

Number	Title	Yr	NM
❑ LP-1440 [M]	Benny Rides Again	1960	$50
❑ LPS-1440 [S]	Benny Rides Again	1960	$30
❑ CH-9161	Benny Rides Again	1984	$25

—*Reissue*

CLASSICS RECORD LIBRARY

Number	Title	Yr	NM
❑ RL-7673 [M]	An Album of Swing Classics	1967	$50
❑ SRL-7673 [S]	An Album of Swing Classics	1967	$40

—*Above two were compiled for Book-of-the-Month Club*

COLUMBIA

Number	Title	Yr	NM
❑ CL2533 [10]	Benny at the Ballroom	1955	$50

—*Retitled reissue of 6100*

Number	Title	Yr	NM
❑ CL534 [M]	Benny Goodman and His Orchestra	1953	$40

—*Maroon label with gold print*

Number	Title	Yr	NM
❑ CL534 [M]	Benny Goodman and His Orchestra	1955	$40

—*Red and black label with six "eye" logos*

Number	Title	Yr	NM
❑ CL6033 [10]	Benny Goodman and Peggy Lee	1949	$80
❑ CL523 [M]	Benny Goodman Presents Eddie Sauter Arrangements	1953	$40

—*Maroon label with gold print*

Number	Title	Yr	NM
❑ CL523 [M]	Benny Goodman Presents Eddie Sauter Arrangements	1955	$40

—*Red and black label with six "eye" logos*

Number	Title	Yr	NM
❑ GL523 [M]	Benny Goodman Presents Eddie Sauter Arrangements	1953	$50

—*Black label, silver print*

Number	Title	Yr	NM
❑ CL524 [M]	Benny Goodman Presents Fletcher Henderson Arrangements	1954	$40

—*Maroon label with gold print*

Number	Title	Yr	NM
❑ CL524 [M]	Benny Goodman Presents Fletcher Henderson Arrangements	1953	$40

—*Red and black label with six "eye" logos*

Number	Title	Yr	NM
❑ GL524 [M]	Benny Goodman Presents Fletcher Henderson Arrangements	1953	$50

—*Black label, silver print*

Number	Title	Yr	NM
❑ CL2483 [M]	Benny Goodman's Greatest Hits	1966	$35
❑ CS9283 [S]	Benny Goodman's Greatest Hits	1966	$30

—*360 Sound Stereo" on label*

Number	Title	Yr	NM
❑ PC9283	Benny Goodman's Greatest Hits	198?	$20

—*Reissue*

Number	Title	Yr	NM
❑ CL1579 [M]	Benny Goodman Swings Again	1960	$30
❑ CS8379 [S]	Benny Goodman Swings Again	1960	$30
❑ C2L16 [M]	Benny in Brussels	195?	$40

—*Red and black label with six white "eye" logos*

Number	Title	Yr	NM
❑ CL1247 [M]	Benny in Brussels, Vol. I	1958	$30
❑ CS8075 [S]	Benny in Brussels, Vol. I	1959	$40
❑ CL1248 [M]	Benny in Brussels, Vol. II	1958	$30
❑ CS8076 [S]	Benny in Brussels, Vol. II	1959	$40
❑ CL814 [M]	Carnegie Hall Jazz Concert, Volume 1	1956	$30

—*Red and black label with six "eye" logos*

Number	Title	Yr	NM
❑ CL814 [M]	Carnegie Hall Jazz Concert, Volume 1	1963	$25

—*Red label with "Guaranteed High Fidelity" or "Mono" at bottom*

Number	Title	Yr	NM
❑ CL815 [M]	Carnegie Hall Jazz Concert, Volume 2	1956	$30

—*Red and black label with six "eye" logos*

Number	Title	Yr	NM
❑ CL815 [M]	Carnegie Hall Jazz Concert, Volume 2	1963	$25

—*Red label with "Guaranteed High Fidelity" or "Mono" at bottom*

Number	Title	Yr	NM
❑ CL815 [M]	Carnegie Hall Jazz Concert, Volume 2	197?	$15

—*Orange label with "Mono" under "CL 815" at left*

Number	Title	Yr	NM
❑ CL816 [M]	Carnegie Hall Jazz Concert, Volume 3	1956	$30

—*Red and black label with six "eye" logos*

Number	Title	Yr	NM
❑ CL816 [M]	Carnegie Hall Jazz Concert, Volume 3	1963	$25

—*Red label with "Guaranteed High Fidelity" or "Mono" at bottom*

Number	Title	Yr	NM
❑ CL500 [M]	Combos	1952	$40

—*Maroon label with gold print*

Number	Title	Yr	NM
❑ CL500 [M]	Combos	1955	$40

—*Red and black label with six "eye" logos*

Number	Title	Yr	NM
❑ GL500 [M]	Combos	1951	$50

—*Black label, silver print*

Number	Title	Yr	NM
❑ CL6048 [10]	Dance Parade	1949	$50
❑ CL6100 [10]	Dance Parade, Volume 2	1950	$50
❑ CL6052 [10]	Goodman Sextet Session	1949	$50
❑ GL102 [10]	Let's Hear the Melody	1950	$60
❑ CL6302 [10]	Let's Hear the Melody	1951	$50

—*Reissue of GL 102*

Number	Title	Yr	NM
❑ FC38265	Seven Come Eleven	1983	$25
❑ PG33405	Solid Gold Instrumental Hits	1975	$30
❑ KG31547	The All-Time Greatest Hits of Benny Goodman	1972	$35
❑ PG31547	The All-Time Greatest Hits of Benny Goodman	197?	$30

—*Reissue*

Number	Title	Yr	NM
❑ CL652 [M]	The Benny Goodman Sextet and Orchestra with Charlie Christian	1955	$40

—*Red and black label with six "eye" logos*

Number	Title	Yr	NM
❑ CL652 [M]	The Benny Goodman Sextet and Orchestra with Charlie Christian	1963	$25

—*Red label with "Guaranteed High Fidelity" or "Mono" at bottom*

Number	Title	Yr	NM
❑ CL516 [M]	The Benny Goodman Trio Plays for the Fletcher Henderson Fund	1953	$40

—*Maroon label with gold print*

Number	Title	Yr	NM
❑ CL516 [M]	The Benny Goodman Trio Plays for the Fletcher Henderson Fund	1955	$40

—*Red and black label with six "eye" logos*

Number	Title	Yr	NM
❑ GL516 [M]	The Benny Goodman Trio Plays for the Fletcher Henderson Fund	1952	$50

—*Reissue of Martin Block 1000; black label, silver print*

Number	Title	Yr	NM
❑ CL2564 [10]	The B.G. Six	1955	$50

—*Retitled reissue of 6052*

Number	Title	Yr	NM
❑ CL501 [M]	The Golden Era Series Presents Benny Goodman and His Orchestra	1952	$40

—*Maroon label with gold print*

Number	Title	Yr	NM
❑ CL501 [M]	The Golden Era Series Presents Benny Goodman and His Orchestra	1955	$40

—*Red and black label with six "eye" logos*

Dizzy Gillespie, The Cool World, Philips PHS 600-138, **$150**.

Dizzy Gillespie, *Featuring Dizzy Gillespie*, Sutton SSU 287, **$20**.

Jimmy Giuffre, *Tangents in Jazz*, Capitol T 634, **$200**.

Benny Golson, *Turning Point*, Mercury MG 20801, **$100**.

Number	Title	Yr	NM
❑ GL501 [M]	The Golden Era Series Presents Benny Goodman and His Orchestra	1951	$50
—Black label, silver print			
❑ CL820 [M]	The Great Benny Goodman	1956	$30
—Red and black label with six "eye" logos			
❑ CL820 [M]	The Great Benny Goodman	1963	$25
—Red label with "Guaranteed High Fidelity" or "Mono" at bottom			
❑ CS8643 [R]	The Great Benny Goodman	1962	$30
—Red label, "360 Sound Stereo" at bottom			
❑ PC8643	The Great Benny Goodman	198?	$20
—Reissue			
❑ CS8643 [R]	The Great Benny Goodman	1970	$25
—Orange label			
❑ CL1324 [M]	The Happy Session	1959	$30
❑ CS8129 [S]	The Happy Session	1959	$30
❑ CL817 [M]	The King of Swing, Volume 1	1956	$30
❑ CL818 [M]	The King of Swing, Volume 2	1956	$30
❑ CL819 [M]	The King of Swing, Volume 3	1956	$30
❑ CL552 [M]	The New Benny Goodman Sextet	1954	$40
—Maroon label with gold print			
❑ CL552 [M]	The New Benny Goodman Sextet	1955	$40
—Red and black label with six "eye" logos			
❑ CL821 [M]	Vintage Goodman	1956	$30
COLUMBIA JAZZ MASTERPIECES			
❑ CJ44292	Slipped Disc, 1945-1946	1988	$25
COLUMBIA MASTERWORKS			
❑ SL180 [M]	1937-38 Jazz Concert No. 2	1950	$150
❑ ML4590 [M]	1937-38 Jazz Concert No. 2, Volume 1	1950	$40
❑ ML4591 [M]	1937-38 Jazz Concert No. 2, Volume 2	1950	$40
❑ ML4358 [M]	Carnegie Hall Jazz Concert, Volume 1	1950	$40
❑ ML4359 [M]	Carnegie Hall Jazz Concert, Volume 2	1950	$40
❑ SL176 [M]	King of Swing	1950	$150
❑ ML4613 [M]	King of Swing, Volume 1	1950	$40
❑ ML4614 [M]	King of Swing, Volume 2	1950	$40
❑ ML6205 [M]	Meeting at the Summit	1961	$35
— With the Columbia Jazz Combo and the Columbia Orchestra			
❑ MS6805 [S]	Meeting at the Summit	1961	$25
— With the Columbia Jazz Combo and the Columbia Orchestra			
❑ SL160 [M]	The Famous 1938 Carnegie Hall Jazz Concert	1950	$100
— Green labels			
❑ OSL160 [M]	The Famous 1938 Carnegie Hall Jazz Concert	1963	$40
— Gray labels with "Columbia" at top			
❑ OSL160 [M]	The Famous 1938 Carnegie Hall Jazz Concert	1956	$150
— Gray and black labels with six "eye" logos			
❑ OSL160 [M]	The Famous 1938 Carnegie Hall Jazz Concert	1970	$25
— Olive labels with "Columbia" circling edge			
❑ OSL180 [M]	The King of Swing	1956	$150
— Gray and black labels with six "eye" logos			
❑ OSL180 [M]	The King of Swing	1963	$40
— Gray labels with "Columbia" at top			
COLUMBIA MUSICAL TREASURY			
❑ P4M5678	The Best of Benny Goodman	197?	$30
— Issued by Columbia House			
COMMAND			
❑ RS-921	Benny Goodman & Paris: Listen to the Magic	1967	$35
DECCA			
❑ DXB188 [M]	The Benny Goodman Story	1956	$250
— Black label, silver print			
❑ DXB188 [M]	The Benny Goodman Story	1961	$40
— Black label with color bars			
❑ DXSB7188 [R]	The Benny Goodman Story	196?	$35
❑ DL8252 [M]	The Benny Goodman Story, Volume 1	1956	$250
— Black label, silver print			
❑ DL8252 [M]	The Benny Goodman Story, Volume 1	1961	$25
— Black label with color bars			

Number	Title	Yr	NM
❑ DL78252 [R]	The Benny Goodman Story, Volume 1	1961	$25
❑ DL8253 [M]	The Benny Goodman Story, Volume 2	1956	$250
— Black label, silver print			
❑ DL8253 [M]	The Benny Goodman Story, Volume 2	1961	$25
— Black label with color bars			
❑ DL78253 [R]	The Benny Goodman Story, Volume 2	1961	$25
DOCTOR JAZZ			
❑ W2X40350	Airplay	1986	$30
EVEREST ARCHIVE OF FOLK & JAZZ			
❑ 277	Benny Goodman	1973	$30
GIANTS OF JAZZ			
❑ 1030	The Benny Goodman Caravans -- Big Band Broadcasts Vol. 1: Ciribiribin	1983	$25
❑ 1033	The Benny Goodman Caravans -- Big Band Broadcasts Vol. 2: Swingin' Down the Lane	1985	$25
❑ 1036	The Benny Goodman Caravans -- Big Band Broadcasts Vol. 3: One O'Clock Jump	1985	$25
❑ 1039	The Benny Goodman Caravans -- Big Band Broadcasts Vol. 4: Sing, Sing, Sing	1985	$25
❑ 1034	The Benny Goodman Caravans -- The Small Groups, Vol. 1	1985	$25
HARMONY			
❑ HL7005 [M]	Peggy Lee Sings with Benny Goodman	1957	$30
❑ HS11271 [R]	Sing, Sing, Sing	1968	$25
❑ HL7278 [M]	Swingin' Benny Goodman Sextet	196?	$35
❑ HL7225 [M]	Swing Time	196?	$35
❑ HL7190 [M]	Swing with Benny Goodman in High Fidelity	196?	$35
❑ HS11090 [R]	Swing with Benny Goodman in High Fidelity	196?	$25
INTERMEDIA			
❑ QS-5046	All the Cats Join In	198?	$25
LONDON			
❑ PS918/9	Live at Carnegie Hall 1978	1979	$35
LONDON PHASE 4			
❑ SP-44182/83	Benny Goodman On Stage	1972	$35
❑ SPB-21	Benny Goodman Today	1971	$35
MARTIN BLOCK			
❑ MB-1000 [M]	The Benny Goodman Trio Plays for the Fletcher Henderson Fund	1951	$60
MCA			
❑ 4018	Jazz Holiday	197?	$30
MEGA			
❑ 51-5002	Let's Dance Again	1971	$30
❑ 606	Let's Dance Again	1974	$25
— Reissue of 51-5002			
MGM			
❑ E-3788 [M]	Performance Recordings, Volume 1	1959	$30
❑ E-3789 [M]	Performance Recordings, Volume 2	1959	$30
❑ E-3790 [M]	Performance Recordings, Volume 3	1959	$30
❑ 3E-9 [M]	The Benny Goodman Treasure Chest	1959	$150
❑ E-3788 [M]	The Benny Goodman Treasure Chest, Volume 1	198?	$20
— Reissue on blue and gold label			
❑ E-3789 [M]	The Benny Goodman Treasure Chest, Volume 2	198?	$20
— Reissue on blue and gold label			
❑ E-3790 [M]	The Benny Goodman Treasure Chest, Volume 3	198?	$20
— Reissue on blue and gold label			
❑ E-3810 [M]	The Sound of Music	1960	$25
❑ SE-3810 [S]	The Sound of Music	1960	$30
MOSAIC			
❑ MQ6-148	The Complete Capitol Small Group Recordings of Benny Goodman 1944-1955	199?	$150
MUSICMASTERS			
❑ MM-20112Z	Let's Dance	1986	$25
— From the PBS TV special of 1985			
PAIR			

Number	Title	Yr	NM
❑ PDL2-1014	Original Recordings by Benny Goodman	1986	$30
❑ PDL2-1054	Original Recordings by Benny Goodman, Volume 2	1986	$30
❑ PDL2-1093	Original Recordings by Benny Goodman, Volume 3	1986	$30
PAUSA			
❑ 9031	The Benny Goodman Trios (and One Duet)	198?	$25
PICKWICK			
❑ SPC-3529	Francaise	197?	$25
❑ SPC-3270	Let's Dance	197?	$25
PRESTIGE			
❑ PRST-7644	Benny Goodman and the Giants of Swing	1969	$35
RCA CAMDEN			
❑ CAL-872 [M]	Benny Goodman and His Orchestra Featuring Great Vocalists of Our Times	1965	$35
❑ CAS-872 [S]	Benny Goodman and His Orchestra Featuring Great Vocalists of Our Times	1965	$30
❑ CAL-624 [M]	Swing, Swing, Swing	1960	$35
❑ CAS-624(e) [R]	Swing, Swing, Swing	1960	$25
RCA VICTOR			
❑ CPL1-2470	A Legendary Performer	1977	$25
❑ LPT-17 [10]	A Treasury of Immortal Performances	1951	$50
❑ WPT12 [10]	Benny Goodman	1951	$50
❑ LPT-1005 [M]	Benny Goodman	1954	$40
❑ LOC-6008 [M]	Benny Goodman in Moscow	1962	$25
❑ LSO-6008 [S]	Benny Goodman in Moscow	1962	$30
❑ LPT-3004 [10]	Benny Goodman Quartet	1952	$50
❑ LPV-521 [M]	B.G. The Small Groups	1965	$35
❑ WPT26 [10]	Immortal Performances	1952	$50
❑ ANL1-0973(e)	Pure Gold	1974	$25
— Reissue of LPS-4005(e)			
❑ LPM-1226 [M]	The Benny Goodman Trio/Quartet/Quintet	1956	$40
❑ LSP-4005(e)	The Best of Benny Goodman	1968	$35
❑ AFL1-4005(e)	The Best of Benny Goodman	1977	$25
— Reissue of LSP-4005			
❑ LPM-1099 [M]	The Golden Age of Benny Goodman	1956	$40
❑ LPT-6703 [M]	The Golden Age of Swing	1956	$600
— Five-record set in white vinyl binder with bound-in booklet			
❑ LPM-2247 [M]	The Kingdom of Swing	1960	$25
❑ LSP-2247 [S]	The Kingdom of Swing	1960	$30
❑ LPM-1239 [M]	This Is Benny Goodman	1956	$40
❑ VPM-6040 [PS]	This Is Benny Goodman	1971	$35
❑ VPM-6063	This Is Benny Goodman, Vol. 2	1972	$35
❑ LPT-3056 [10]	This Is Benny Goodman and His Orchestra	1954	$50
❑ LPM-2698 [M]	Together Again	1964	$35
❑ LSP-2698 [S]	Together Again	1964	$25
SUNBEAM			
❑ 126	At the Madhattan Room Dec. 18, 1937	197?	$30
❑ 123	At the Madhattan Room Nov. 4, 1937	197?	$30
❑ 116	At the Madhattan Room Oct. 13, 1937	197?	$15
❑ 117	At the Madhattan Room Oct. 16, 1937	197?	$30
❑ 118	At the Madhattan Room Oct. 20, 1937	197?	$30
❑ 133	Benny Goodman 1933	197?	$25
❑ 148	Benny Goodman 1934	197?	$25
❑ 158	Benny Goodman 1941-42	1984	$25
❑ 154	Benny Goodman 1946	197?	$25
❑ 111	Benny Goodman Accompanies Girls 1931-33	197?	$25
❑ 138	Benny Goodman and His Orchestra 1931-33, Volume 1	197?	$25
❑ 139	Benny Goodman and His Orchestra 1931-33, Volume 2	197?	$25
❑ 140	Benny Goodman and His Orchestra 1931-33, Volume 3	197?	$25
❑ 152	Benny Goodman and His Orchestra 1937-38	197?	$30
❑ 135	Benny Goodman and the Modernists 1934-35	197?	$25
❑ 106	Benny Goodman In a Mellotone Manner 1930-31	197?	$25
❑ 105	Benny Goodman On the Air 1935-36, Volume 1	197?	$25
❑ 153	Benny Goodman On the Air 1935-36, Volume 2	197?	$25
❑ 107	Benny Goodman On the Side 1929-31	197?	$25

Number	Title	Yr	NM
❑ 142	Benny Goodman On V-Disc 1939-48, Volume 1	197?	$25
❑ 143	Benny Goodman On V-Disc 1939-48, Volume 2	197?	$25
❑ 144	Benny Goodman On V-Disc 1939-48, Volume 3	197?	$25
❑ 156	Broadcasts from Hollywood 1946-47	197?	$25
❑ 146	Camel Caravan 1937, Volume 1	197?	$25
❑ 147	Camel Caravan 1937, Volume 2	197?	$25
❑ 145	Fitch Bandwagon 1945	197?	$25
❑ 128/32	From the Congress Hotel, Chicago, 1935-36	197?	$30
❑ 149	Jam Session 1935-37	197?	$25
❑ 112	Rare Benny Goodman 1927-29	197?	$25
❑ 141	The Benny Goodman Boys 1928-29	197?	$25
❑ 151	The Benny Goodman Show 1946	197?	$25
❑ 113	The Hotsy Totsy Gang 1928-29	197?	$25
❑ 100	The Let's Dance Broadcasts 1934-35, Volume 1	197?	$25
❑ 104	The Let's Dance Broadcasts 1934-35, Volume 2	197?	$25
❑ 150	The Let's Dance Broadcasts 1934-35, Volume 3	197?	$25
❑ 114	Whoopee Makers 1928-29	197?	$25

TIME-LIFE

❑ STBB-03	Big Bands: Benny Goodman	1983	$35
❑ STBB-23	Big Bands: King of Swing	1986	$35
❑ STL-J-05	Giants of Jazz	1979	$50

VERVE

❑ V-8582 [M]	The Essential Benny Goodman	1964	$35
❑ V6-8582 [S]	The Essential Benny Goodman	1964	$35

WESTINGHOUSE

❑ XTV27713/4 [M]	Benny Goodman Plays World Favorites in High Fidelity	1958	$30

— *No number on cover or label; these numbers come from the trail-off wax*

❑ 0(no cat #) [M]	Benny in Brussels	1958	$100

GOODMAN, BENNY/CHARLIE BARNET

Also see each artist's individual listings.

Albums

CAPITOL

❑ M-11061	BeBop Spoken Here	197?	$30

GOODMAN, JERRY, AND JAN HAMMER

Goodman, a violinist, was a member of the first MAHAVISHNU ORCHESTRA, as was Hammer. Also see JAN HAMMER.

Albums

NEMPEROR

❑ SD430	Like Children	1975	$25

GOODRICK, MICK

Guitarist.

Albums

ECM

❑ 1139	In Pas(s)ing	1979	$30

GOODWIN, BILL

Drummer.

Albums

OMNISOUND

❑ 1029	Bill Goodwin's Solar Energy	1981	$25
❑ 1050	Network	1983	$25

GORDON, BOB

Baritone saxophone player. Also see JACK MONTROSE.

Albums

PACIFIC JAZZ

❑ PJLP-12 [10]	Meet Mr. Gordon	1954	$200

TAMPA

❑ TP-26 [M]	Jazz Impressions	1957	$250

— *Red vinyl*

❑ TP-26 [M]	Jazz Impressions	1958	$150

— *Black vinyl*

GORDON, BOBBY

Clarinetist.

Albums

DECCA

Number	Title	Yr	NM
❑ DL4726 [M]	The Lamp Is Low	1966	$30
❑ DL74726 [S]	The Lamp Is Low	1966	$35
❑ DL4394 [M]	Warm and Sentimental	1963	$30
❑ DL74394 [S]	Warm and Sentimental	1963	$35
❑ DL4507 [M]	Young Man's Fancy	1964	$30
❑ DL74507 [S]	Young Man's Fancy	1964	$35

GORDON, BOB/CLIFFORD BROWN

Also see each artist's individual listings.

Albums

PACIFIC JAZZ

❑ PJ-3 [M]	Jazz Immortal	1960	$50
❑ PJ-1214 [M]	The Bob Gordon Quintet/ The Clifford Brown Ensemble	1956	$100

GORDON, DEXTER

Tenor saxophone player. Also see WARDELL GRAY.

Albums

BASF

❑ 20698	A Day in Copenhagen	197?	$35

BETHLEHEM

❑ BCP-36 [M]	Daddy Plays the Horn	1956	$1400
❑ BCP-6008	The Bethlehem Years	197?	$30

— *Reissue, distributed by RCA Victor*

BLACK LION

❑ 108	The Montmartre Collection	197?	$35

BLUE NOTE

❑ BLP-4133 [M]	A Swingin' Affair	1963	$120

— *With "New York, USA" address on label*

❑ BST-84133 [S]	A Swingin' Affair	1963	$150

— *With "New York, USA" address on label*

❑ BST-84133 [S]	A Swingin' Affair	1967	$40

— *With "A Division of Liberty Records" on label*

❑ BST-84133	A Swingin' Affair	199?	$30

— *Classic Records 180-gram audiophile reissue*

❑ LT-989	Clubhouse	1980	$30
❑ BLP-4083 [M]	Dexter Calling	1961	$200

— *With W. 63rd St. address on label*

❑ BLP-4083 [M]	Dexter Calling	1963	$150

— *With "New York, USA" address on label*

❑ BST-84083 [S]	Dexter Calling	1961	$200

— *With W. 63rd St. address on label*

❑ BST-84083 [S]	Dexter Calling	1963	$150

— *With "New York, USA" address on label*

❑ BST-84083 [S]	Dexter Calling	1967	$40

— *With "A Division of Liberty Records" on label*

❑ BN-LA393-H2	Dexter Gordon	1975	$60
❑ BLP-4077 [M]	Doin' Allright	1961	$250

— *With W. 63rd St. addresss on label*

❑ BLP-4077 [M]	Doin' Allright	1963	$150

— *With "New York, USA" address on label*

❑ BST-84077 [S]	Doin' Allright	1961	$300

— *With W. 63rd St. addresss on label*

❑ BST-84077 [S]	Doin' Allright	1963	$200

— *With "New York, USA" address on label*

❑ BST-84077 [S]	Doin' Allright	1967	$40

— *With "A Division of Liberty Records" on label*

❑ BST-84077	Doin' Allright	1985	$30

— *The Finest in Jazz Since 1939" reissue*

❑ BST-84077 [S]	Doin' Allright	1970	$60

— *Mostly black label with "Liberty/UA" at bottom*

❑ BLP-4204 [M]	Gettin' Around	1965	$7000

— *With "New York, USA" address on label*

❑ BST-84204 [S]	Gettin' Around	1965	$80

— *With "New York, USA" address on label*

❑ BST-84204 [S]	Gettin' Around	1967	$60

— *With "A Division of Liberty Records" on label*

❑ BLP-4112 [M]	Go	1962	$150

— *With "New York, USA" address on label*

❑ BST-84112 [S]	Go	1962	$120

— *With "New York, USA" address on label*

❑ BST-84112 [S]	Go	1967	$40

— *With "A Division of Liberty Records" on label*

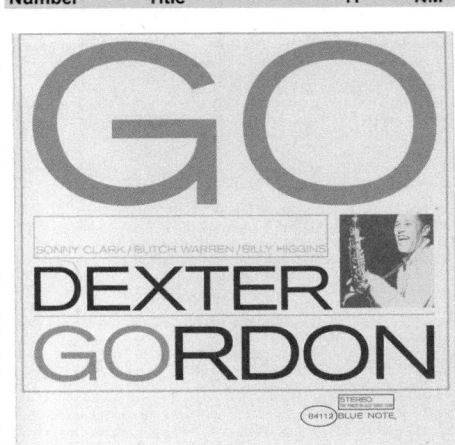

Number	Title	Yr	NM
❑ BST-84112 [B]	Go	1985	$30

— *The Finest in Jazz Since 1939" reissue*

❑ LT-1051	Landslide	1980	$30
❑ BABB-85112	Nights at the Keystone	198?	$30
❑ BLP-4176 [M]	One Flight Up	1964	$150

— *With "New York, USA" address on label*

❑ BST-84176 [S]	One Flight Up	1964	$80

— *With "New York, USA" address on label*

❑ BST-84176 [S]	One Flight Up	1967	$60

— *With "A Division of Liberty Records" on label*

❑ BST-84176	One Flight Up	1986	$30

— *The Finest in Jazz Since 1939" reissue*

❑ BLP-4146 [M]	Our Man in Paris	1963	$150

— *With "New York, USA" address on label*

❑ BST-84146 [S]	Our Man in Paris	1963	$100

— *With "New York, USA" address on label*

❑ BST-84146 [S]	Our Man in Paris	1967	$60

— *With "A Division of Liberty Records" on label*

❑ BST-84146	Our Man in Paris	1987	$30

— *The Finest in Jazz Since 1939" reissue*

❑ B1-91139	The Best of Dexter Gordon	1988	$30
❑ BT-85135	The Other Side of 'Round Midnight	1986	$30

BOPLICITY

❑ BOP-6	Dexter Blows Hot and Cool	198?	$25

COLUMBIA

❑ JC36853	Gotham City	1981	$25
❑ JC36853	Gotham City	2000	$30

— *180-gram reissue*

❑ JC35987	Great Encounters	1979	$25
❑ PG34650	Homecoming	1977	$35
❑ JC35608	Manhattan Symphonie	1978	$30
❑ PC35608	Manhattan Symphonie	198?	$20

— *Budget-line reissue*

❑ JC34989	Sophisticated Giant	1977	$30
❑ JC36356	The Best of Dexter Gordon	1979	$25

DIAL

❑ LP-204 [10]	Dexter Gordon Quintet	1950	$400

DISCOVERY

❑ 79005	American Classic	1995	$35

DOOTO

❑ DL-207 [M]	Dexter Blows Hot and Cool	196?	$400

— *Maroon label with "Dooto*

DOOTONE

❑ DL-207 [M]	Dexter Blows Hot and Cool	1956	$3000

— *Red vinyl*

❑ DL-207 [M]	Dexter Blows Hot and Cool	1957	$1200

— *Black vinyl; "Dootone" label with no zip code*

❑ DL-207 [M]	Dexter Blows Hot and Cool	197?	$100

— *Maroon label with zip code*

ELEKTRA/MUSICIAN

❑ 60126	American Classic	1983	$25

FANTASY

❑ OJC-299	Tower of Power	198?	$25

INNER CITY

❑ IC-2080	Biting the Apple	1977	$30
❑ IC-2060	Bouncin'	197?	$35
❑ IC-2030	More Than You Know	197?	$35
❑ IC-2040	Stable Mable	1975	$35
❑ IC-2050	Swiss Nights	1975	$35
❑ IC-2025	The Apartment	197?	$35
❑ IC-2006	The Meeting	1973	$35
❑ IC-2020	The Source	1973	$35

JAZZLAND

❑ JLP-29 [M]	The Resurgence of Dexter Gordon	1960	$50

Number	Title	Yr	NM
❏ JLP-929 [S]	The Resurgence of Dexter Gordon	1960	$60
JAZZ MAN			
❏ 5023	Dexter Gordon at Montmartre	198?	$25
PAUSA			
❏ 7058	A Day in Copenhagen	1980	$25
PRESTIGE			
❏ PRST-7763	A Day in Copenhagen	1970	$25
❏ 10079	Blues A La Suisse	1973	$35
❏ 10051	Ca' Purange	197?	$35
❏ 10069	Generation	197?	$35
❏ 10020	Jumpin' Blues	197?	$35
❏ PRST-7680	More Power	1969	$25
❏ PRST-7829	Panther!	1971	$25
❏ 2511	Resurgence	198?	$25
❏ 10091	Tangerine	197?	$35
❏ 2502	The Ballad Album	198?	$25
❏ PRST-7623	The Tower of Power	1969	$25
SAVOY			
❏ MG-9003 [10]	All Star Series -- Dexter Gordon	1951	$250
❏ MG-12130 [M]	Dexter Rides Again	1958	$100
❏ MG-9016 [10]	New Trends in Modern Jazz, Volume 3	1952	$250
SAVOY JAZZ			
❏ SJC-407	Jazz Concert, West Coast	1985	$25
❏ SJL-2211	Long Tall Dexter	197?	$35
❏ SJL-1154	Master Takes: The Savoy Recordings	198?	$25
❏ SJL-2222	The Hunt	197?	$35
STEEPLECHASE			
❏ SCC-6028	Billie's Bounce	198?	$30
❏ SCC-1080	Biting the Apple	198?	$25
❏ SCS-1060	Bouncin'	198?	$25
❏ SCC-6008	Cheese Cake	198?	$30
❏ SCC-6004	Cry Me a River	198?	$30
❏ SCC-6022	It's You or No One	198?	$30
❏ SCC-6015	I Want More	198?	$30
❏ SCS-1156	Lullaby for a Monster	198?	$25
❏ SCS-1030	More Than You Know	198?	$25
❏ SCS-1136	Something Different	1980	$30
❏ SCS-1040	Stable Mable	198?	$25
❏ SCS-1145	Strings & Things	198?	$30
❏ SCS-1050	Swiss Nights, Volume 1	198?	$35
❏ SCS-1090	Swiss Nights, Volume 2	198?	$25
❏ SCS-1110	Swiss Nights, Volume 3	198?	$25
❏ SCS-1025	The Apartment	198?	$25
❏ SCS-1206	The Shadow of Your Smile	198?	$30
WHO'S WHO IN JAZZ			
❏ 21011	Who's Who Presents Dexter Gordon and Lionel Hampton	1977	$30

GORDON, DEXTER/HOWARD MCGHEE
Also see each artist's individual listings.
Albums
JAZZTONE			
❏ J-1235 [M]	The Chase	1956	$40

GORDON, FRANK
Trumpeter.
Albums
SOUL NOTE			
❏ SN-1096	Clarion Echoes	1986	$25

GORDON, GRAY
Saxophone player and bandleader.
Albums
HINDSIGHT			
❏ HSR-206	Gray Gordon and His Tic Toc Rhythm 1939	198?	$25

GORDON, HONI
Female singer.
Albums
PRESTIGE			
❏ PRLP-7230 [M]	Honi Gordon Sings	1962	$150
❏ PRST-7230 [S]	Honi Gordon Sings	1962	$150

GORDON, JOE
Trumpeter.
Albums
CONTEMPORARY			
❏ M-3597 [M]	Lookin' Good	1961	$200
❏ S-7597 [S]	Lookin' Good	1961	$200
EMARCY			
❏ MG-26046 [10]	Introducing Joe Gordon	1954	$200

Number	Title	Yr	NM
❏ MG-36025 [M]	Introducing Joe Gordon	1955	$250
FANTASY			
❏ OJC-174	Lookin' Good	198?	$25
TRIP			
❏ 5535	Introducing Joe Gordon	197?	$25

GORDON, JOHN
Albums
STRATA-EAST			
❏ SES-19760	Step by Step	197?	$25

GORDON, JON
Trombone player.
Albums
GEMINI TAURUS			
❏ TRLP-827	Beginning and Endings	1989	$30

GORRILL, LIZ, AND ANDY FITE
Fite is a guitarist. Also see LIZ GORRILL.
Albums
NEW ARTISTS			
❏ NA-1004	Phantasmagoria	1988	$25

GORRILL, LIZ
Pianist and female singer.
Albums
JAZZ RECORDS			
❏ JR-2	I Feel Like I'm Home	198?	$35
❏ JR-7	True Fun	198?	$30

GOSSEZ, PIERRE
Clarinetist and saxophone player.
Albums
VANGUARD CARDINAL			
❏ C-10061	Bach Takes a Trip	1969	$25

GOTTLIEB, DANNY
Drummer. Also see ELEMENTS.
Albums
ATLANTIC			
❏ 81806	Aquamarine	1988	$25
❏ 81958	Whirlwind	1989	$30

GOULD, CHUCK
Bandleader and male singer.
Albums
VIK			
❏ LX-1123 [M]	Chuck Gould Plays A La Fletcher Henderson	1957	$50

GOWANS, BRAD
Trombone player, arranger and bandleader.
Albums
RCA VICTOR			
❏ LJM-3000 [10]	Brad Gowans' New York Nine	1954	$50

GOYKOVICH, DUSKO
Trumpeter and fluegel horn player.
Albums
ENJA			
❏ 2020	After Hours	197?	$30

GOZZO, CONRAD
Trumpeter.
Albums
RCA VICTOR			
❏ LPM-1124 [M]	Goz the Great	1955	$60

GRAAS, JOHN
French horn player. Also see THE GILBERT & SULLIVAN JAZZ WORKSHOP.
Albums

Number	Title	Yr	NM
ANDEX			
❏ A-3003 [M]	Premiere in Jazz	1958	$50
❏ AS-3003 [S]	Premiere in Jazz	1959	$40
DECCA			
❏ DL8343 [M]	Jazz Lab 1	1956	$150
❏ DL8478 [M]	Jazz Lab 2	1957	$120
❏ DL8677 [M]	Jazzmantics	1958	$120
❏ DL8079 [M]	Jazz Studio 2	1954	$150
❏ DL8104 [M]	Jazz Studio 3	1955	$150
EMARCY			
❏ MG-36117 [M]	Coup de Graas	1958	$200
KAPP			
❏ KL-1046 [M]	French Horn Jazz	1957	$50
MERCURY			
❏ SR-80020 [S]	Coup de Graas	1959	$100
TREND			
❏ TL-1005 [10]	French Horn Jazz	1954	$120

GRACEN, THELMA
Female singer.
Albums
EMARCY			
❏ MG-36096 [M]	Thelma Gracen	1956	$350
WING			
❏ MGW-60005 [M]	Thelma Gracen	1956	$150

GRAHAM, ED
Drummer.
Albums
M&K REALTIME			
❏ 106	Hot Stix	1980	$40

—Direct-to-disc recording; plays at 45 rpm

GRAMERCY SIX, THE
No relation to the ARTIE SHAW Gramercy Five. Among the members: Nick Fatool, Al Henderson, Jud DeNaut, Shorty Sherrock, Eddie Rosa.
Albums
EDISON INTERNATIONAL			
❏ P-502 [M]	Great Swinging Sounds Vol. 1	1959	$30

GRAND DOMINION JAZZ BAND
Organized by Michael Cox (banjo). Other members: Bob Pelland (piano); Bob Jackson (trumpet); Jim Armstrong (trombone); Greey Green (clarinet, alto saxophone); Mike Duffy (bass); Stephen Joseph (drums).
Albums
GHB			
❏ GHB-174	Grand Dominion Jazz Band	1984	$25
STOMP OFF			
❏ SOS-1189	Ain't Nobody Got the Blues Like Me	1988	$25
❏ SOS-1139	Don't Give Up the Ship	1987	$25

GRANT, TOM
Pianist, keyboard player and male singer.
Albums
CMG			
❏ CML-8007	Heart of the City	198?	$20
❏ CML-8009	Just the Right Moment	198?	$20
❏ CML-8010	Take Me to Your Dream	198?	$20
❏ CML-8008	Tom Grant	198?	$20
PAUSA			
❏ 7174	Just the Right Moment	1985	$25
❏ 7199	Take Me to Your Dream	1986	$25
❏ 7145	Tom Grant	198?	$25

GRAPPELLI, STEPHANE, AND BARNEY KESSEL
Also see each artist's individual listings.
Albums
BLACK LION			
❏ 105	I Remember Django	197?	$35
JAZZ MAN			
❏ 5008	I Remember Django	198?	$25
MOBILE FIDELITY			
❏ 1-111	I Remember Django	1984	$50

—Audiophile vinyl

Benny Golson, *Free*, Argo 716, mono, **$50**.

Benny Goodman, *The Famous 1938 Carnegie Hall Jazz Concert, Vol. 3*, Columbia CL 816, red and black label with six "eye" logos, **$30**.

Benny Goodman, *Meeting at the Summit*, Columbia Masterworks MS 6805, gray label with "360 Sound Stereo," **$25**.

Bob Gordon, *Meet Mr. Gordon*, Pacific Jazz PJ-12, 10-inch LP, **$200**.

Number	Title	Yr	NM

GRAPPELLI, STEPHANE, AND DAVID GRISMAN
Also see each artist's individual listings.

Albums

WARNER BROS.
| ❏ BSK3550 | Live | 1981 | $25 |

GRAPPELLI, STEPHANE, AND GEORGE SHEARING
Also see each artist's individual listings.

Albums

VERVE
| ❏ 821868-1 | The Reunion | 1985 | $25 |

GRAPPELLI, STEPHANE, AND HANK JONES
Also see each artist's individual listings.

Albums

MUSE
| ❏ MR-5287 | A Two-fer | 198? | $25 |

GRAPPELLI, STEPHANE, AND JEAN-LUC PONTY
Also see each artist's individual listings.

Albums

EVEREST ARCHIVE OF FOLK & JAZZ
| ❏ FS-355 | Violin Summit | 1979 | $25 |

PAUSA
| ❏ 7074 | Giants | 1979 | $25 |

GRAPPELLI, STEPHANE, AND MCCOY TYNER
Also see each artist's individual listings.

Albums

MILESTONE
| ❏ M-9181 | One on One | 1990 | $30 |

GRAPPELLI, STEPHANE, AND TERESA BREWER
Also see each artist's individual listings.

Albums

DOCTOR JAZZ
| ❏ FW38448 | On the Road Again | 1983 | $25 |

GRAPPELLI, STEPHANE, AND VASSAR CLEMENTS
Clements is a fiddler/violinist best known for his bluegrass music; he does not have an entry in this book. Also see STEPHANE GRAPPELLI.

Albums

FLYING FISH
| ❏ FF-421 | Together at Last | 1987 | $25 |

GRAPPELLI, STEPHANE, AND YO-YO MA
Ma is a cellist best known in the classical realm; he does not have an entry in this book. Also see STEPHANE GRAPPELLI.

Albums

CBS
| ❏ FM45574 | Anything Goes: The Music of Cole Porter | 1989 | $30 |

GRAPPELLI, STEPHANE
Violinist.

Albums

ANGEL
❏ DS-37790	Brandenberg Boogie (Music of Bach)	1980	$30
❏ DS-38063	Just One of Those Things	198?	$30
❏ DS-37886	We've Got the World on a String	198?	$30

ARSITA FREEDOM
| ❏ AL1033 | The Parisian | 197? | $30 |

ATLANTIC
❏ 1391 [M]	Feeling + Finesse = Jazz	1962	$150
❏ SD1391 [S]	Feeling + Finesse = Jazz	1962	$150
❏ 90140	Feeling + Finesse = Jazz	198?	$25
❏ 82095	Olympia '88	1990	$30

BARCLAY
| ❏ 820007 | Music to Pass the Time | 196? | $25 |

BASF
| ❏ 20876 | Afternoon in Paris | 1972 | $35 |

BLACK LION
❏ 047	I Got Rhythm	1974	$25
❏ 211	Just One of the Things	1974	$35
❏ 313	Talk of the Town	1975	$30

CLASSIC JAZZ
| ❏ 23 | Homage to Django | 197? | $25 |
| ❏ 24 | Stephane Grappelli and Bill Coleman | 197? | $35 |

COLUMBIA
| ❏ JC35415 | Uptown Dance | 1978 | $25 |

CONCORD JAZZ
❏ CJ-139	Stephane Grappelli at the Winery	1980	$25
❏ CJ-225	Stephanova	1983	$25
❏ CJ-169	Vintage 1981	1981	$25

DOCTOR JAZZ
| ❏ FW38727 | Live at Carnegie Hall | 1983 | $25 |

EMARCY
| ❏ MG-36120 [M] | Improvisations | 1957 | $200 |

EVEREST ARCHIVE OF FOLK & JAZZ
| ❏ 311 | Stephane Grappelli | 197? | $30 |

FANTASY
| ❏ OJC-441 | Tivoli Gardens | 1990 | $25 |

GRP
| ❏ GR-1032 | Stephane Grappelli Plays Jerome Kern | 1987 | $25 |

PABLO LIVE
| ❏ 2308220 | Tivoli Gardens | 1979 | $30 |

PAUSA
❏ 7071	Afternoon in Paris	1979	$25
❏ 7098	Violinspiration	198?	$25
❏ 7041	Young Django	1979	$25

VANGUARD
| ❏ VSD-81/82 | Satin Doll | 197? | $35 |
| ❏ VMS-73130 | Satin Doll, Volume 1 | 198? | $25 |

VERVE
| ❏ MGV-20001 [M] | Musique Pour Arreter Le Temps (Music to Stop the Clock By) | 195? | $60 |

— As "Stephane Grappelly"
| ❏ 815672-1 | Young Django | 198? | $25 |

GRAVES, CONLEY
Pianist.

Albums

DECCA
❏ DL8220 [M]	Genius at Work	1956	$150
❏ DL8412 [M]	Piano Dynamics	1957	$120
❏ DL8475 [M]	Rendezvous in Paris	1957	$120

LIBERTY
| ❏ LRP-3007 [M] | V.I.P. (Very Important Pianist) | 1956 | $40 |

NOCTURNE
| ❏ NLP-4 [10] | Piano Artistry | 1954 | $100 |

GRAVES, JOE
Trumpeter.

Albums

CAPITOL
| ❏ T1977 [M] | The Great New Swingers | 1963 | $60 |
| ❏ ST1977 [S] | The Great New Swingers | 1963 | $60 |

GRAVES, MILFORD
Drummer. Also see THE NEW YORK ART QUINTET.

Albums

ESP-DISK'
| ❏ 1015 [M] | Milford Graves Percussion Ensemble | 1966 | $100 |
| ❏ S-1015 [S] | Milford Graves Percussion Ensemble | 1966 | $100 |

IPS
| ❏ 04 | Babi | 197? | $35 |
| ❏ 290 | Nommo | 197? | $35 |

GRAVINE, ANITA
Female singer.

Albums

STASH
| ❏ ST-256 | I Always Knew | 1985 | $25 |

GRAY, GLEN
Saxophone player and bandleader. Also see JONAH JONES.

45s

CAPITOL
| ❏ SXE-1739 [S] | Blowin' Up a Storm/Farewell Blues | 196? | $20 |

— Small hole, plays at 33 1/3 rpm

Albums

| ❏ T856 [M] | Casa Loma Caravan | 1957 | $80 |

— Turquoise label
❏ W747 [M]	Casa Loma in Hi-Fi!	1956	$100
❏ T1506 [M]	Please Mr. Gray...More Sounds of the Great Bands	1961	$60
❏ ST1506 [S]	Please Mr. Gray...More Sounds of the Great Bands	1961	$50
❏ T1615 [M]	Shall We Swing?	1961	$60
❏ ST1615 [S]	Shall We Swing?	1961	$50
❏ T1234 [M]	Solo Spotlight	1960	$60
❏ ST1234 [S]	Solo Spotlight	1960	$50
❏ W1022 [M]	Sounds of the Great Bands!	1959	$60
❏ SW1022 [S]	Sounds of the Great Bands!	1959	$50
❏ SM-1022	Sounds of the Great Bands!	197?	$25

— Reissue
❏ T2131 [M]	Sounds of the Great Bands in Latin	1964	$50
❏ ST2131 [S]	Sounds of the Great Bands in Latin	1964	$60
❏ T1067 [M]	Sounds of the Great Bands Volume 2	1959	$60
❏ ST1067 [S]	Sounds of the Great Bands Volume 2	1959	$50
❏ SM-1067	Sounds of the Great Bands Volume 2	197?	$25

— Reissue
❏ T1739 [M]	Sounds of the Great Bands Volume 5: They All Swung the Blues	1962	$60
❏ ST1739 [S]	Sounds of the Great Bands Volume 5: They All Swung the Blues	1962	$50
❏ T1938 [M]	Sounds of the Great Bands Volume 7: Today's Best	1963	$50
❏ ST1938 [S]	Sounds of the Great Bands Volume 7: Today's Best	1963	$60
❏ T2014 [M]	Sounds of the Great Bands Volume 8: More of Today's Best	1964	$50
❏ ST2014 [S]	Sounds of the Great Bands Volume 8: More of Today's Best	1964	$60
❏ T1588 [M]	Sounds of the Great Casa Loma Band	1961	$50
❏ DT1588 [R]	Sounds of the Great Casa Loma Band	1961	$60
❏ SM-1588	Sounds of the Great Casa Loma Band	197?	$25

— Reissue
❏ T1289 [M]	Swingin' Decade	1960	$60
❏ ST1289 [S]	Swingin' Decade	1960	$50
❏ T1400 [M]	Swingin' Southern Style	1961	$60
❏ ST1400 [S]	Swingin' Southern Style	1961	$50
❏ T1812 [M]	Themes of the Great Bands	1963	$60
❏ ST1812 [S]	Themes of the Great Bands	1963	$50
❏ SM-1812	Themes of the Great Bands	197?	$25

— Reissue

CIRCLE
| ❏ 16 | Glen Gray and the Casa Loma Orchestra | 198? | $25 |

CORAL
| ❏ CRL56009 [10] | Glen Gray Souvenirs | 1950 | $100 |
| ❏ CRL56006 [10] | Hoagy Carmichael Songs | 1950 | $100 |

CREATIVE WORLD
| ❏ ST-1055 | Shall We Swing? | 197? | $25 |

DECCA
❏ DL75016 [R]	Greatest Hits	1968	$30
❏ DL5089 [10]	Musical Smoke Rings	1950	$120
❏ DL5397 [10]	No-Name Jive	1953	$150
❏ DL8570 [M]	Smoke Rings	1957	$120

HARMONY
| ❏ HL7045 [M] | The Great Recordings of Glen Gray | 1957 | $50 |

HINDSIGHT
| ❏ HSR-104 | Glen Gray and the Casa Loma Orchestra, 1939-1940 | 198? | $25 |
| ❏ HSR-120 | Glen Gray and the Casa Loma Orchestra, 1943-1946 | 198? | $25 |

INSIGHT
| ❏ 214 | Glen Gray and the Casa Loma Orchestra, 1939-1946 | 198? | $25 |

MCA
| ❏ 122 | Greatest Hits | 1973 | $25 |

— Reissue of Decca 75016

Number	Title	Yr	NM
❏ 20199	Smoke Rings	198?	$20
❏ 4076	The Best of Glen Gray	197?	$30

GRAY, JERRY

Arranger and composer best known for his work with the GLENN MILLER band; he, in fact, took over its reins following Miller's death.

Albums

CRAFTSMAN

❏ 8035 [M]	More Miller Hits	195?	$25

DECCA

❏ DL5375 [10]	A Tribute to Glenn Miller	1951	$200
❏ DL5478 [10]	Dance Time	1952	$150
❏ DL5266 [10]	Dance to the Music of Gray	1950	$150
❏ DL5312 [10]	In the Mood ...	1951	$200
❏ DL8101 [M]	Jerry Gray and His Orchestra	1955	$150

DOT

❏ DLP-3741 [M]	This Is Jerry Gray	1966	$75
❏ DLP-25741 [S]	This Is Jerry Gray	1966	$75

GOLDEN TONE

❏ C-4005 [M]	Glenn Miller Favorites	196?	$30

HINDSIGHT

❏ HSR-212	Jerry Gray and His Orchestra 1952	198?	$25

LIBERTY

❏ LRP-3038 [M]	Hi-Fi Shades of Gray	1956	$40
❏ LST-7002 [S]	Hi-Fi Shades of Gray	1958	$40
❏ LRP-3089 [M]	Jerry Gray at the Hollywood Palladium	1958	$40
❏ LST-7013 [S]	Jerry Gray at the Hollywood Palladium	1958	$40

TOPS

❏ L-1627 [M]	A Salute to Glenn Miller	1958	$30
❏ L-1640 [M]	Glenn Miller Greats	1958	$30

VOCALION

❏ VL3602 [M]	A Tribute to Glenn Miller	196?	$25

WARNER BROS.

❏ W1446 [M]	Singin' and Swingin'	1962	$25
❏ WS1446 [S]	Singin' and Swingin'	1962	$30

GRAY, WARDELL, AND DEXTER GORDON

Also see each artist's individual listings.

Albums

DECCA

❏ DL7025 [10]	The Chase and the Steeple Chase	1952	$250

JAZZTONE

❏ J-1235 [M]	The Chase and the Steeple Chase	1956	$50

MCA

❏ 1336	The Chase and the Steeple Chase	198?	$25

GRAY, WARDELL

Tenor saxophone player. Also see LOUIS BELLSON; STAN GETZ.

Albums

CROWN

❏ CLP-5293 [M]	Wardell Gray	196?	$35

— Gray label

❏ CST-293 [R]	Wardell Gray	196?	$30
❏ CLP-5004 [M]	Way Out Wardell	1957	$40

— Originals have a black label with the word "crown" in small letters at top

❏ CLP-5278 [M]	Way Out Wardell	1962	$25
❏ CST-278 [R]	Way Out Wardell	1962	$15

CUSTOM

❏ CS-1060 [R]	Shades of Gray	196?	$30
❏ CM-2060 [M]	Shades of Gray	196?	$35

FANTASY

❏ OJC-050	Wardell Gray Memorial, Volume 1	1982	$25

— Reissue of Prestige 7008

❏ OJC-051	Wardell Gray Memorial, Volume 2	1982	$25

— Reissue of Prestige 7009

MODERN

❏ MLP-1204 [M]	Way Out Wardell	1956	$300

PHILOLOGY/SPHERE

❏ W-14	Light Gray, Vol. 1	198?	$25
❏ W-36	Light Gray, Vol. 2	198?	$25

PRESTIGE

❏ P-24062	Central Ave.	1976	$50

Number	Title	Yr	NM
❏ PRLP-128 [10]	Jazz Concert	1952	$300
❏ PRLP-7008 [M]	Wardell Gray Memorial, Volume 1	1955	$300
❏ PRLP-7009 [M]	Wardell Gray Memorial, Volume 2	1955	$300
❏ PRLP-7343 [M]	Wardell Gray Memorial Album	1964	$50
❏ PRST-7343 [R]	Wardell Gray Memorial Album	1964	$30
❏ PRLP-147 [10]	Wardell Gray's Los Angeles Stars	1953	$350
❏ PRLP-115 [10]	Wardell Gray Tenor Sax	1951	$350

UNITED

❏ US-7722 [R]	Shades of Gray	197?	$30

XANADU

❏ 146	Live in Hollywood	197?	$35

GRAYE, TONY

Albums

FUTURA

❏ 55514	Let's Swing Away	197?	$35
❏ 55515	The Blue Horn of Tony Graye	197?	$35

ZIM

❏ ZMS-2001	Oh Gee!	1975	$35

GREAT EXCELSIOR JAZZ BAND

Led by pianist Ray Skjelbred.

Albums

VOYAGER

❏ VRLP-202	Hot Jazz from the Territory	198?	$25
❏ VRLP-204	Remembering Joe	198?	$25
❏ VRLP-203	Roast Chestnuts	198?	$25

GREAT GUITARS, THE

See CHARLIE BYRD, HERB ELLIS & BARNEY KESSEL.

GREAT JAZZ TRIO, THE

Members: RON CARTER; HANK JONES; TONY WILLIAMS.

Albums

EAST WIND

❏ 10005	Direct from L.A.	1978	$60

— Direct-to-disc recording

INNER CITY

❏ IC-6023	Kindness, Joy, Love and Happiness	1978	$30
❏ IC-6003	Love for Sale	1976	$30
❏ IC-6030	Milestones	1979	$30
❏ IC-6013	The Great Jazz Trio at the Village Vanguard	1977	$30

GRECO, BUDDY

Male singer, pianist, arranger and bandleader.

Albums

APPLAUSE

❏ APLP-1004	Hot Nights	1982	$25

BAINBRIDGE

❏ 8004	Greatest Hits	198?	$35

CORAL

❏ CRL57022 [M]	Buddy Greco at Mister Kelly's	1956	$60

EPIC

❏ LN24010 [M]	Buddy and Soul	1962	$60
❏ BN26010 [S]	Buddy and Soul	1962	$75
❏ LN24043 [M]	Buddy Greco's Greatest Hits	1963	$60
❏ BN26043 [S]	Buddy Greco's Greatest Hits	1963	$75
❏ LN24057 [M]	Buddy Greco Sings for Intimate Moments	1963	$60
❏ BN26057 [S]	Buddy Greco Sings for Intimate Moments	1963	$75
❏ LN3771 [M]	Buddy's Back in Town	1961	$60
❏ BN593 [S]	Buddy's Back in Town	1961	$75
❏ LN24181 [M]	From the Wrists Down	1965	$60
❏ BN26181 [S]	From the Wrists Down	1965	$75
❏ LN3793 [M]	I Like It Swinging	1961	$60
❏ BN602 [S]	I Like It Swinging	1961	$75
❏ LN3820 [M]	Let's Love	1961	$60
❏ BN615 [S]	Let's Love	1961	$75
❏ LN24130 [M]	Modern Sounds of Hank Williams	1965	$60
❏ BN26130 [S]	Modern Sounds of Hank Williams	1965	$75
❏ LN3660 [M]	My Buddy	1960	$60
❏ BN557 [S]	My Buddy	1960	$75
❏ LN24088 [M]	My Last Night in Rome	1964	$60
❏ BN26088 [S]	My Last Night in Rome	1964	$75
❏ LN24116 [M]	On Stage	1964	$60

Number	Title	Yr	NM
❏ BN26116 [S]	On Stage	1964	$75
❏ LN24032 [M]	Soft and Gentle	1962	$60
❏ BN26032 [S]	Soft and Gentle	1962	$75
❏ LN3746 [M]	Songs for Swinging Losers	1960	$60
❏ BN585 [S]	Songs for Swinging Losers	1960	$75

HARMONY

❏ HL7448 [M]	You're Something Else	196?	$25
❏ HS11248 [S]	You're Something Else	196?	$30

KAPP

❏ KL-1033 [M]	Broadway Melodies	1956	$50
❏ KL-1107 [M]	Buddy	1958	$50
❏ KL-1231 [M]	The Best of Buddy Greco	1961	$35

PROJECT 3

❏ PR5105	For Once in My Life: In Concert	1980	$25

REPRISE

❏ RS-6256 [S]	Away We Go!	1967	$30
❏ R-6256 [M]	Away We Go!	1967	$35
❏ R-6220 [M]	Big Band and Ballads	1966	$30
❏ RS-6220 [S]	Big Band and Ballads	1966	$35
❏ RS-6230 [S]	Buddy's in a Brand New Bag	1966	$35
❏ R-6230 [M]	Buddy's in a Brand New Bag	1966	$30

SCEPTER

❏ SPS-579	Let the Sunshine In	1969	$30

SUTTON

❏ SSU282 [M]	All Time Favorites Featuring Buddy Greco	196?	$25

VOCALION

❏ VL3706 [M]	Here's Buddy Greco	1964	$30
❏ VL73706 [R]	Here's Buddy Greco	1964	$25

GREEN, BENNIE

Trombonist. Also see J.J. JOHNSON.

Albums

BAINBRIDGE

❏ 1048	Bennie Green	198?	$25

BARBARY

❏ M33015 [M]	Play More Than You Can Stand	196?	$30

BETHLEHEM

❏ BCP-6018	Cat Walk	197?	$35

— Reissue of 6054, distributed by RCA Victor

❏ BCP-6054 [M]	Hornful of Soul	1961	$250
❏ BCP-4019 [M]	Hornful of Soul	196?	$25

— Reissue of 6054

BLUE NOTE

❏ BLP-1587 [M]	Back on the Scene	1958	$200

— Regular version with W. 63rd St. addresss on label

❏ BLP-1587 [M]	Back on the Scene	1963	$150

— With "New York, USA" address on label

❏ BST-1587 [S]	Back on the Scene	1959	$100

— Regular version with W. 63rd St. addresss on label

❏ BST-81587 [S]	Back on the Scene	1963	$25

— With "New York, USA" address on label

❏ BST-81587 [S]	Back on the Scene	1967	$35

— With "A Division of Liberty Records" on label

❏ BLP-1599 [M]	Soul Stirrin'	1958	$120

— Deep groove" version (deep indentation under label on both sides)

❏ BLP-1599 [M]	Soul Stirrin'	1958	$150

— Regular version with W. 63rd St. addresss on label

❏ BLP-1599 [M]	Soul Stirrin'	1963	$60

— With "New York, USA" address on label

❏ BST-1599 [S]	Soul Stirrin'	1959	$80

— Deep groove" version (deep indentation under label on both sides)

❏ BST-1599 [S]	Soul Stirrin'	1959	$60

— Regular version with W. 63rd St. addresss on label

❏ BST-81599 [S]	Soul Stirrin'	1963	$25

— With "New York, USA" address on label

❏ BST-81599 [S]	Soul Stirrin'	1967	$35

— With "A Division of Liberty Records" on label

❏ BLP-4010 [M]	Walkin' and Talkin'	1959	$300

— Deep groove" version (deep indentation under label on both sides)

❏ BLP-4010 [M]	Walkin' and Talkin'	1959	$150

— Regular version with W. 63rd St. addresss on label

❏ BLP-4010 [M]	Walkin' and Talkin'	1963	$60

— With "New York, USA" address on label

❏ BST-4010 [S]	Walkin' and Talkin'	1959	$300

— Deep groove" version (deep indentation under label on both sides)

❏ BST-4010 [S]	Walkin' and Talkin'	1959	$60

— Regular version with W. 63rd St. addresss on label

Number	Title	Yr	NM
❏ BST-84010 [S]	Walkin' and Talkin'	1963	$25

—*With "New York, USA" address on label*

Number	Title	Yr	NM
❏ BST-84010 [S]	Walkin' and Talkin'	1967	$35

—*With "A Division of Liberty Records" on label*

ENRICA

| ❏ 2002 [M] | Bennie Green Swings the Blues | 1960 | $30 |
| ❏ S-2002 [S] | Bennie Green Swings the Blues | 1960 | $40 |

FANTASY

| ❏ OJC-1728 | Bennie Green Blows His Horn | 198? | $25 |
| ❏ OJC-1752 | Walkin' Down | 198? | $25 |

JAZZLAND

| ❏ JLP-43 [M] | Glidin' Along | 1961 | $30 |
| ❏ JLP-943 [S] | Glidin' Along | 1961 | $30 |

PRESTIGE

❏ PRLP-210 [10]	Bennie Blows His Horn	1955	$300
❏ PRLP-7041 [M]	Bennie Green and Art Farmer	1956	$400
❏ PRLP-7052 [M]	Bennie Green Blows His Horn	1956	$300
❏ PRLP-7160 [M]	Bennie Green Blows His Horn	1959	$200
❏ PRST-7776	The Best of Bennie Green	1970	$35
❏ PRLP-7049	Walking Down	1956	$300

RCA VICTOR

| ❏ LPM-2376 [M] | Futura | 1961 | $30 |
| ❏ LSP-2376 [S] | Futura | 1961 | $30 |

TIME

| ❏ 52021 [M] | Bennie Green | 1960 | $40 |
| ❏ S-2021 [S] | Bennie Green | 1960 | $50 |

VEE JAY

| ❏ LP-1005 [M] | The Swingin'est | 1959 | $50 |
| ❏ SR-1005 [S] | The Swingin'est | 1959 | $50 |

—*This LP was reissued as "Juggin' Around" by GENE AMMONS on Vee Jay 3024*

| ❏ VJS-1005 [S] | The Swingin'est | 198? | $25 |

—*Reissue on thinner vinyl*

GREEN, BENNIE/PAUL QUINICHETTE

Also see each artist's individual listings.

Albums

DECCA

| ❏ DL8176 [M] | Blow Your Horn | 1955 | $150 |

GREEN, BERNIE

Albums

BARBARY COAST

| ❏ 33015-S [S] | Bernie Green Plays More Than You Can Stand in Hi-Fi | 1958 | $100 |

RCA VICTOR

| ❏ LSA-2376 [S] | Futura | 1961 | $100 |
| ❏ LSP-1929 [S] | Musically Mad | 1959 | $175 |

SAN FRANCISCO

| ❏ M-33015 [M] | Bernie Green Plays More Than You Can Stand in Hi-Fi | 1957 | $100 |

GREEN, BUNKY

Alto saxophone player (sometimes tenor) and bandleader.

Albums

ARGO

| ❏ LP-753 [M] | Testifyin' Time | 1965 | $30 |
| ❏ LPS-753 [S] | Testifyin' Time | 1965 | $30 |

CADET

❏ LP-766 [M]	Playin' for Keeps	1966	$30
❏ LPS-766 [S]	Playin' for Keeps	1966	$30
❏ LP-753 [M]	Testifyin' Time	1966	$35
❏ LPS-753 [S]	Testifyin' Time	1966	$25
❏ LP-780 [M]	The Latinization of Bunky Green	1967	$30
❏ LPS-780 [S]	The Latinization of Bunky Green	1967	$30

VANGUARD

❏ VSD-79425	Places We've Never Been	1979	$30
❏ VSD-79387	Transformations	197?	$30
❏ VSD-79413	Visions	1978	$30

GREEN, BYRDIE

Female singer.

Albums

PRESTIGE

| ❏ PRLP-7509 [M] | I Got It Bad | 1967 | $25 |
| ❏ PRST-7509 [S] | I Got It Bad | 1967 | $35 |

Number	Title	Yr	NM
❏ PRST-7574	Sister Byrdie	1968	$35
❏ PRLP-7503 [M]	The Golden Thrush Speaks	1967	$25
❏ PRST-7503 [S]	The Golden Thrush Speaks	1967	$35

GREEN, FREDDIE

Guitarist.

Albums

RCA VICTOR

| ❏ LPM-1210 [M] | Mr. Rhythm | 1956 | $50 |

GREEN, GRANT

Guitarist.

Albums

BLUE NOTE

| ❏ BLP-84360 | Alive! | 1970 | $120 |

—*We're not sure what the original label is; it could be the blue and white label with "A Division of Liberty Records," the mostly black label with "Liberty/UA," or the blue and white label with "A Division of United Artists Records*

| ❏ BLP-84360 | Alive! | 1973 | $100 |

—*Dark blue label with black stylized "b" at upper right*

| ❏ BLP-4139 [M] | Am I Blue | 1963 | $175 |

—*With "New York, USA" on label*

| ❏ BLP-84139 [S] | Am I Blue | 1963 | $175 |

—*With New York, USA address on label*

| ❏ BLP-84139 [S] | Am I Blue | 1968 | $100 |

—*With "A Division of Liberty Records" on label*

| ❏ BLP-84432 | Born to Be Blue | 1985 | $200 |
| ❏ BLP-84327 | Carryin' On | 1969 | $175 |

—*A Division of Liberty Records" on label*

| ❏ BLP-4132 [M] | Feelin' the Spirit | 1963 | $80 |
| ❏ BLP-84132 [S] | Feelin' the Spirit | 1963 | $175 |

—*With New York, USA address on label*

| ❏ BLP-84132 [S] | Feelin' the Spirit | 1968 | $100 |

—*With "A Division of Liberty Records" on label*

| ❏ BLP-84310 | Goin' West | 1969 | $175 |

—*A Division of Liberty Records" on label*

| ❏ BLP-4064 [M] | Grant's First Stand | 1961 | $200 |

—*With W. 63rd St. addresss on label*

| ❏ BLP-4064 [M] | Grant's First Stand | 1963 | $200 |

—*With New York, USA address on label*

| ❏ BLP-84064 [S] | Grant's First Stand | 1961 | $150 |

—*With W. 63rd St. addresss on label*

| ❏ BLP-84064 [S] | Grant's First Stand | 1963 | $150 |

—*With New York, USA address on label*

| ❏ BLP-84064 [S] | Grant's First Stand | 1968 | $100 |

—*With "A Division of Liberty Records" on label*

| ❏ BLP-4086 [M] | Grant Stand | 1962 | $200 |

—*With W. 63rd St. address on label*

| ❏ BLP-4086 [M] | Grant Stand | 1963 | $175 |

—*With New York, USA address on label*

| ❏ BLP-84086 [S] | Grant Stand | 1962 | $150 |

—*With W. 63rd St. address on label*

| ❏ BLP-84086 [S] | Grant Stand | 1963 | $175 |

—*With New York, USA address on label*

| ❏ BLP-84086 [S] | Grant Stand | 1968 | $100 |

—*With "A Division of Liberty Records" on label*

| ❏ BLP-84086 [S] | Grant Stand | 197? | $100 |

—*Dark blue label with white stylized "b" at upper right*

| ❏ BLP-84342 | Green Is Beautiful | 1970 | $120 |

—*A Division of Liberty Records" on label*

| ❏ BLP-4071 [M] | Green Street | 1961 | $200 |

—*With W. 63rd St. addresss on label*

| ❏ BLP-4071 [M] | Green Street | 1963 | $120 |

—*With New York, USA address on label*

| ❏ BLP-84071 [S] | Green Street | 1961 | $150 |

—*With W. 63rd St. addresss on label*

| ❏ BLP-84071 [S] | Green Street | 1963 | $120 |

—*With New York, USA address on label*

| ❏ BLP-84071 [S] | Green Street | 1968 | $100 |

—*With "A Division of Liberty Records" on label*

| ❏ BLP-4154 [M] | Idle Moments | 1964 | $800 |
| ❏ BLP-84154 [S] | Idle Moments | 1964 | $175 |

—*With New York, USA address on label*

| ❏ BLP-84154 [S] | Idle Moments | 1968 | $100 |

—*With "A Division of Liberty Records" on label*

| ❏ BLP-4202 [M] | I Want to Hold Your Hand | 1964 | $80 |
| ❏ BLP-84202 [S] | I Want to Hold Your Hand | 1964 | $175 |

—*With New York, USA address on label*

| ❏ BLP-84202 [S] | I Want to Hold Your Hand | 1968 | $100 |

—*With "A Division of Liberty Records" on label*

Number	Title	Yr	NM
❏ BN-LA037-G2	Live at the Lighthouse	1973	$100
❏ LT-1032	Nigeria	1980	$100
❏ BLP-84413	Shades of Green	1972	$150

—*A Division of United Artists Records" on blue and white label*

| ❏ LT-990 | Solid | 1980 | $40 |
| ❏ BLP-4253 [M] | Street of Dreams | 1967 | $175 |

—*A Division of Liberty Records" on label*

| ❏ BLP-84253 [S] | Street of Dreams | 1967 | $150 |

—*A Division of Liberty Records" on label*

| ❏ BLP-4099 [M] | Sunday Mornin' | 1962 | $200 |

—*With W. 63rd St. address on label*

| ❏ BLP-4099 [M] | Sunday Mornin' | 1963 | $150 |

—*With New York, USA address on label*

| ❏ BLP-84099 [S] | Sunday Mornin' | 1962 | $150 |

—*With W. 63rd St. address on label*

| ❏ BLP-84099 [S] | Sunday Mornin' | 1963 | $200 |

—*With New York, USA address on label*

| ❏ BLP-84099 [S] | Sunday Mornin' | 1968 | $100 |

—*With "A Division of Liberty Records" on label*

| ❏ BLP-4183 [M] | Talkin' About! | 1964 | $80 |
| ❏ BLP-84183 [S] | Talkin' About! | 1964 | $175 |

—*With New York, USA address on label*

| ❏ BLP-84183 [S] | Talkin' About! | 1968 | $100 |

—*With "A Division of Liberty Records" on label*

| ❏ BLP-84415 | The Final Comedown | 1972 | $150 |

—*A Division of United Artists Records" on blue and white label*

| ❏ BLP-4111 [M] | The Latin Bit | 1962 | $175 |

—*With "New York, USA" on label*

| ❏ BLP-84111 [S] | The Latin Bit | 1962 | $175 |

—*With New York, USA address on label; reproductions exist*

| ❏ BLP-84111 [S] | The Latin Bit | 1968 | $100 |

—*With "A Division of Liberty Records" on label*

| ❏ BLP-84373 | Visions | 1971 | $150 |

COBBLESTONE

| ❏ CST-9002 | Iron City | 1972 | $175 |

—*Reproductions exist*

DELMARK

❏ DL-404 [M]	All the Gin Is Gone	1966	$60
❏ DS-404 [S]	All the Gin Is Gone	1966	$60
❏ DL-427 [M]	Black Forrest	1966	$60
❏ DS-427 [S]	Black Forrest	1966	$60

KUDU

| ❏ KU-29 | The Main Attraction | 1976 | $60 |

MOSAIC

| ❏ MR5-133 | The Complete Blue Note Recordings of Grant Green with Sonny Clark | 199? | $300 |

MUSE

| ❏ MR-5014 | Green Blues | 1973 | $60 |
| ❏ MR-5120 | Iron City | 197? | $60 |

VERSATILE

| ❏ MSG-6002 | Easy | 1978 | $50 |

VERVE

| ❏ V-8627 [M] | His Majesty, King Funk | 1965 | $175 |
| ❏ V6-8627 [S] | His Majesty, King Funk | 1965 | $120 |

GREEN, PHIL

Albums

LONDON

| ❏ LPB-17 [10] | Rhythm on Reeds | 1950 | $50 |

GREEN, URBIE

Trombonist. Also see THE BRASS ENSEMBLE OF THE JAZZ & CLASSICAL MUSIC SOCIETY; THE MANHATTAN JAZZ SEPTETTE.

Albums

ABC-PARAMOUNT

| ❏ ABC-137 [M] | All About Urbie Green | 1956 | $50 |
| ❏ ABC-101 [M] | Blues and Other Shades of Green | 1955 | $75 |

BETHLEHEM

| ❏ BCP-14 [M] | East Coast Jazz, Volume 6 | 1955 | $250 |
| ❏ BCP-6041 | The Lyrical Language of Urbie Green | 197? | $30 |

—*Reissue of 14, distributed by RCA Victor*

BLUE NOTE

| ❏ BLP-5036 [10] | Urbie Green Septet | 1954 | $250 |

COMMAND

| ❏ RS 33-815 [M] | The Persuasive Trombone of Urbie Green | 1960 | $30 |
| ❏ RS815SD [S] | The Persuasive Trombone of Urbie Green | 1960 | $35 |

Dexter Gordon, *Doin' Allright*, Blue Note BLP-4077, mono, with W. 63rd St. address on label, **$250**.

Dexter Gordon, *Go*, Blue Note BLP-4112, mono, **$150**.

John Graas, *French Horn Jazz*, Kapp KL-1046, **$50**.

John Graas, *Jazzmantics*, Decca DL 8677, **$120**.

Number	Title	Yr	NM
❏ RS 33-838 [M]	The Persuasive Trombone of Urbie Green, Volume 2	1962	$30
❏ RS838SD [S]	The Persuasive Trombone of Urbie Green, Volume 2	1962	$35
❏ RS 33-857 [M]	Urbie Green and His 6-Tet	1963	$30
❏ RS857SD [S]	Urbie Green and His 6-Tet	1963	$35
CTI			
❏ 7079	Senor Blues	1977	$30
❏ 7070	The Fox	1976	$30
PROJECT 3			
❏ PR5014SD	21 Trombones	1967	$30
❏ PR5024SD	21 Trombones, Volume 2	1968	$30
❏ PR5066SD	Bein' Green	1972	$30
❏ PR5087SD	Big Beautiful Band	1974	$25
❏ PR5052SD	Green Power	1970	$30
RCA VICTOR			
❏ LPM-1969 [M]	Best of the New Broadway Show Hits	1959	$40
❏ LSP-1969 [S]	Best of the New Broadway Show Hits	1959	$40
❏ LPM-1741 [M]	Jimmy McHugh in Hi-Fi	1958	$50
❏ LSP-1741 [S]	Jimmy McHugh in Hi-Fi	1958	$60
❏ LPM-1667 [M]	Let's Face the Music and Dance	1958	$40
❏ LSP-1667 [S]	Let's Face the Music and Dance	1958	$40
VANGUARD			
❏ VRS-8010 [10]	Urbie Green and His Band	1954	$120
X			
❏ LXA-3026 [10]	A Cool Yuletide	1954	$120

GREEN, URBIE/VIC DICKENSON
Also see each artist's individual listings.

Albums

Number	Title	Yr	NM
JAZZTONE			
❏ J-1259 [M]	Urbie Green Octet/Slidin' Swing	1957	$40

GREEN, WILLIAM
Saxophone player and flutist.

Albums

Number	Title	Yr	NM
EVEREST			
❏ LPBR-5213 [M]	Shades of Green	1963	$35
❏ SDBR-1213 [S]	Shades of Green	1963	$25

GREENE, BOB
Pianist and bandleader.

GREENE, BURTON, AND ALAN SILVA
Silva is a pianist. Also see BURTON GREENE.

Albums

Number	Title	Yr	NM
HAT HUT			
❏ 15	Ongoing Strings	198?	$35

GREENE, BURTON
Pianist.

Albums

Number	Title	Yr	NM
COLUMBIA			
❏ CS9784	Presenting Burton Greene	1969	$35
ESP-DISK'			
❏ 1024 [M]	Burton Greene	1966	$100
❏ S-1024 [S]	Burton Greene	1966	$100
❏ S-1074	Burton Greene Concert Tour	1968	$100

GREENE, DODO
Female singer.

Albums

Number	Title	Yr	NM
BLUE NOTE			
❏ BLP-9001 [M]	My Hour of Need	1962	$100
—With W. 63rd St. addresss on label			
❏ BLP-9001 [M]	My Hour of Need	1963	$60
—With "New York, USA" address on label			
❏ BST-89001 [S]	My Hour of Need	1967	$25
—With "A Division of Liberty Records" on label			

GREENIDGE, ROBERT, AND MICHAEL UTLEY
Greenidge plays steel drums; Utley is a keyboard player, composer and producer. Both are also members of Jimmy Buffett's Coral Reefer Band.

Albums

MCA MASTER SERIES

Number	Title	Yr	NM
❏ 6258	Heat	1989	$30
❏ 42045	Jubilee	1987	$25
❏ 5695	Mad Music	1985	$25

GREENWICH, SONNY
Guitarist.

Albums

Number	Title	Yr	NM
PM			
❏ PMR-016	Evol-ution: Love's Opposite	1978	$35

GREY, AL, AND WILD BILL DAVIS
Also see each artist's individual listings.

Albums

Number	Title	Yr	NM
CLASSIC JAZZ			
❏ 103	Keybone	197?	$35

GREY, AL
Trombonist.

Albums

Number	Title	Yr	NM
ARGO			
❏ LP-689 [M]	Al Grey and the Billy Mitchell Sextet	1962	$25
❏ LPS-689 [S]	Al Grey and the Billy Mitchell Sextet	1962	$30
❏ LP-731 [M]	Boss Bones	1964	$25
❏ LPS-731 [S]	Boss Bones	1964	$30
❏ LP-718 [M]	Having a Ball	1963	$25
❏ LPS-718 [S]	Having a Ball	1963	$30
❏ LP-711 [M]	Night Song	1963	$25
❏ LPS-711 [S]	Night Song	1963	$30
❏ LP-700 [M]	Snap Your Fingers	1962	$25
❏ LPS-700 [S]	Snap Your Fingers	1962	$30
❏ LP-653 [M]	The Last of the Big Plungers	1960	$30
❏ LPS-653 [S]	The Last of the Big Plungers	1960	$30
❏ LP-677 [M]	The Thinking Man's Trombone	1961	$25
❏ LPS-677 [S]	The Thinking Man's Trombone	1961	$30
CHESS			
❏ 2-ACMJ-409	Basic Grey	1976	$35
CLASSIC JAZZ			
❏ 118	Grey's Mood	197?	$35
COLUMBIA			
❏ FC38505	Struttin' and Shoutin'	1983	$25
TANGERINE			
❏ TRC-1504 [M]	Shades of Grey	1965	$35
❏ TRCS-1504 [S]	Shades of Grey	1965	$25

GRICE, JANET
Bassoonist. Also has played the recorder.

Albums

Number	Title	Yr	NM
OPTIMISM			
❏ OP-3203	Song for Andy	1988	$25

GRIER, JIMMY
Clarinetist, saxophone player and bandleader.

Albums

Number	Title	Yr	NM
HINDSIGHT			
❏ HSR-177	Jimmy Grier and His Orchestra 1935-36	198?	$25

GRIFFIN, DELLA
Female singer.

Albums

Number	Title	Yr	NM
DOBRE			
❏ 1009	Della Griffin Sings	1978	$30

GRIFFIN, DICK
Trombonist.

Albums

Number	Title	Yr	NM
STRATA-EAST			
❏ SES-19747	The Eighth Wonder	1975	$25

GRIFFIN, JOHNNY, AND MATTHEW GEE
Also see each artist's individual listings.

Albums

Number	Title	Yr	NM
ATLANTIC			
❏ 1431 [M]	Soul Groove	1965	$25
❏ SD1431 [S]	Soul Groove	1965	$30

GRIFFIN, JOHNNY
Tenor saxophone player. Also see THELONIOUS MONK; WILBUR WARE.

Albums

Number	Title	Yr	NM
ARGO			
❏ LP-624 [M]	Johnny Griffin Quartet	1958	$50
BLACK LION			
❏ 304	You Leave Me Breathless	197?	$35
BLUE NOTE			
❏ BLP-1559 [M]	A Blowing Session	1957	$1000
—Regular version, "W. 63rd St." address on label			
❏ BLP-1559 [M]	A Blowing Session	1963	$130
—With "New York, USA" address on label			
❏ BST-85133	Introducing Johnny Griffin	1985	$25
—The Finest in Jazz Since 1939" reissue			
❏ BT-46536	Introducing Johnny Griffin	198?	$25
—Another "The Finest in Jazz Since 1939" reissue			
❏ BST-81580 [S]	The Congregation	1967	$35
—With "A Division of Liberty Records" on label			
❏ B1-89383	The Congregation	1994	$35
—The Finest in Jazz Since 1939" reissue			
EMARCY			
❏ MG-26001 [M]	Night Lady	1967	$100
❏ SR-66001 [S]	Night Lady	1967	$100
FANTASY			
❏ OJC-485	The Big Soul-Band	1990	$30
❏ OJC-136	The Little Giant	198?	$25
GALAXY			
❏ 5126	Bush Dance	1979	$30
❏ 5146	Call It Whatchawaana	1984	$30
❏ 5132	NYC Underground	1980	$30
❏ 5117	Return of the Griffin	1979	$30
❏ 5139	To the Ladies	1981	$30
INNER CITY			
❏ IC-2004	Blues for Harvey	1973	$35
❏ IC-6042	Live Tokyo	197?	$25
JAZZLAND			
❏ JLP-93 [M]	The Little Giant	1961	$40
❏ JLP-993 [S]	The Little Giant	1961	$30
MILESTONE			
❏ 47014	Big Soul	197?	$25
❏ 47054	Little Giant	197?	$35
MOON			
❏ MLP-004	Body and Soul	1992	$35
RIVERSIDE			
❏ RLP-368 [M]	Change of Pace	1961	$200
❏ RS-9368 [S]	Change of Pace	1961	$200
❏ RLP-462 [M]	Do Nothing 'Til You Hear from Me	1963	$150
❏ RS-9462 [S]	Do Nothing 'Til You Hear from Me	1963	$150
❏ RLP-437 [M]	Grab This!	1962	$150
❏ RS-9437 [S]	Grab This!	1962	$150
❏ 6145	Studio Jazz Party	198?	$30
❏ RLP-338 [M]	Studio Jazz Party	1960	$200
❏ RS-9338 [S]	Studio Jazz Party	1960	$200
❏ RLP 12-331 [M]	The Big Soul-Band	1960	$200
❏ RLP-1171 [S]	The Big Soul-Band	1960	$200
❏ RLP-420 [M]	The Kerry Dancers	1962	$350
❏ RS-9420 [S]	The Kerry Dancers	1962	$150
❏ RLP 12-304 [M]	The Little Giant	1959	$250
❏ RLP-1149 [S]	The Little Giant	1959	$250
❏ RLP-479 [M]	Wade in the Water	1964	$150
❏ RS-9479 [S]	Wade in the Water	1964	$150
❏ RLP 12-274 [M]	Way Out!	1958	$300
❏ RLP-387 [M]	White Gardenia	1961	$200

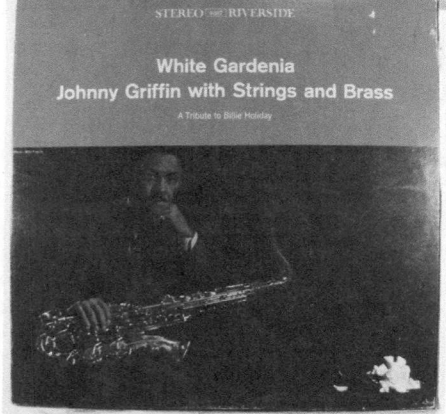

Number	Title	Yr	NM
❏ RS-9387 [S]	White Gardenia	1961	$200
STEEPLECHASE			
❏ SCS-1004	Blues for Harvey	198?	$30

Number	Title	Yr	NM

TIMELESS
❏ 311	The Jamfs Are Coming	198?	$30
❏ LPSJP-121	The Jamfs Are Coming	1990	$25

— Reissue of 311

GRIFFITH, JOHNNY, TRIO
Keyboard player; a member of the Motown studio band.

Albums

WORKSHOP JAZZ
❏ WSJ205 [M]	Jazz	1963	$200

GRIMES, HENRY
Bass player.

Albums

ESP-DISK'
❏ 1027 [M]	Henry Grimes Trio	1966	$100
❏ S-1027 [S]	Henry Grimes Trio	1966	$100

GRIMES, TINY
Guitarist (four- and six-string) and male singer. Also see KENNY BURRELL; THE PRESTIGE BLUES SWINGERS.

Albums

CLASSIC JAZZ
❏ 114	Some Groovy Fours	197?	$30

COLLECTABLES
❏ COL-5321	Tiny Grimes and Friends	198?	$25
❏ COL-5317	Tiny Grimes and His Rocking Highlanders, Volume 2	198?	$25
❏ COL-5304	Tiny Grimes Featuring Screamin' Jay Hawkins	198?	$25

FANTASY
❏ OJC-191	Callin' the Blues	1985	$25

MUSE
❏ MR-5012	Profoundly Blue	1974	$30

PRESTIGE
❏ PRLP-7138 [M]	Blues Grooves	1958	$300

— Yellow label

SWINGVILLE
❏ SVLP-2004 [M]	Callin' the Blues	1960	$50

— Purple label
❏ SVLP-2004 [M]	Callin' the Blues	1965	$30

— Blue label, trident logo at right
❏ SVLP-2002 [M]	Tiny in Swingville	1960	$50

— Purple label
❏ SVLP-2002 [M]	Tiny in Swingville	1965	$30

— Blue label, trident logo at right

UNITED ARTISTS
❏ UAL-3232 [M]	Big Time Guitar	1962	$30
❏ UAS-6232 [S]	Big Time Guitar	1962	$30

GRISMAN, DAVID
Mandolin player. Also see STEPHANE GRAPPELLI; GRATEFUL DEAD related.

Albums

HORIZON
❏ SP-731	Hot Dawg	1979	$16

ROUNDER
❏ 0190	Acoustic Christmas	1983	$30
❏ 0169	Here Today	198?	$25
❏ 0251/2	Home Is Where the Heart Is	1988	$30
❏ 0069	The Rounder Album	1976	$16

SUGAR HILL
❏ SH-3713	Early Dawg	1980	$25

WARNER BROS.
❏ BSK3469	David Grisman Quintet '80	1980	$25
❏ 23804	Dawg Jazz	1983	$25
❏ BSK3618	Mondo Mando	1982	$25

ZEBRA/ACOUSTIC
❏ ZEA-6153	Acousticity	1986	$25

GRISMAN QUINTET, DAVID

Albums

KALEIDOSCOPE
❏ 5	David Grisman Quintet	1977	$25

Number	Title	Yr	NM

GRISSOM, JIMMY
Male singer.

Albums

ARGO
❏ LP-729 [M]	World of Trouble	1963	$60
❏ LPS-729 [S]	World of Trouble	1963	$60

GROLNICK, DON, AND MICHAEL BRECKER
Grolnick was a pianist, producer and composer. Also see MICHAEL BRECKER.

Albums

HIPPOCKET
❏ HP-106	Hearts and Numbers	1985	$30

WINDHAM HILL
❏ WH-0106	Hearts and Numbers	1987	$25

— Reissue of HipPocket 106

GROOVE, MAX
Pianist and keyboard player.

Albums

OPTIMISM
❏ OP-3108	Center of Gravity	198?	$25

GROOVE COLLECTIVE, THE
Members: Gordon Clay aka Nappy G (timbales, vocals); Jay Rodriguez (saxophone, flute, vocals); Genji Siriasi (drums); Richard Worth (flute, vocals); Christopher Theberge (percussion); Jonathan Maron (guitar); William Ware III (vibes); David Jenson (tenor sax); Josh Roseman (trombone); Fabio Morgera (trumpet).

Albums

REPRISE
❏ 45541	The Groove Collective	1994	$25

GROSSMAN, STEVE
Soprano and tenor saxophone player.

Albums

ATLANTIC
❏ SD19230	Perspective	1979	$25

PM
❏ PMR-002	Some Shapes to Come	1974	$30
❏ PMR-012	Terra Firma	1977	$30

RED
❏ VPA189	Love Is the Thing	1986	$30
❏ VPA176	Way Out East	1985	$30

GROSZ, MARTY
Guitarist.

Albums

RIVERSIDE
❏ RLP 12-268 [M]	Hurrah for Bix	1958	$300
❏ RLP-1109 [S]	Hurrah for Bix	1959	$250

STOMP OFF
❏ SOS-1158	Marty Grosz and the Keepers of the Flame	1988	$25
❏ SOS-1214	Unsaturated Fats	1991	$25

GROUP, THE
Vocal group: Larry Benson, Anne Gable, Tom Kampman.

Albums

RCA VICTOR
❏ LPM-2663 [M]	The Group	1963	$50
❏ LSP-2663 [S]	The Group	1963	$60

GROVE, DICK
Pianist, arranger and composer.

Albums

PACIFIC JAZZ
❏ PJ-74 [M]	Little Bird Suite	1963	$25
❏ ST-74 [S]	Little Bird Suite	1963	$30

GRUNING, TOM

Albums

INNER CITY
❏ IC-1119	Midnight Lullaby	198?	$30

Number	Title	Yr	NM

GRUNTZ, GEORGE
Pianist, composer and bandleader.

Albums

PHILIPS
❏ PHM200162 [M]	Bach Humbug	1964	$35
❏ PHS600162 [S]	Bach Humbug	1964	$25

GRUSIN, DAVE, AND LEE RITENOUR
Also see each artist's individual listings.

Albums

GRP
❏ GRPA-1015	Harlequin	1985	$25

GRUSIN, DAVE
Pianist, composer and arranger also known for his many film and television scores, not included below.

Albums

COLUMBIA
❏ CL2344 [M]	Kaleidoscope	1965	$25
❏ CS9144 [S]	Kaleidoscope	1965	$30

EPIC
❏ LN24023 [M]	Piano Strings and Moonlight	1962	$80
❏ BN26023 [S]	Piano Strings and Moonlight	1962	$100
❏ LN3829 [M]	Subways Are for Sleeping	1962	$80
❏ BN622 [S]	Subways Are for Sleeping	1962	$100

GRP
❏ GR-1037	Cinemagic	1987	$25
❏ GRP-A-1001	Dave Grusin and the NY/LA Dream Band	1982	$25
❏ GR-9592	Migration	1989	$30
❏ GRP-A-1018	Mountain Dance	198?	$20

— Another reissue of GRP/Arista 5010
❏ GRP-A-1006	Night-Lines	1984	$25
❏ GR-1011	One of a Kind	198?	$25
❏ GR-1051	Sticks and Stones	1988	$25
❏ GR-9579	The Dave Grusin Collection	1989	$30

GRP/ARISTA
❏ GL5506	Live in Japan	1981	$25
❏ GRP-5010	Mountain Dance	1980	$25
❏ GL8-8058	Mountain Dance	198?	$20

— Budget-line reissue
❏ GRP-5900	Mountain Dance	1981	$25

— Limiteed edition special pressing
❏ GRP-5510	Out of the Shadows	1982	$25
❏ GL8-8139	Out of the Shadows	198?	$20

— Budget-line reissue

POLYDOR
❏ PD-1-6118	One of a Kind	1977	$35

SHEFFIELD LABS
❏ SL-5	Discovered Again!	1976	$30

— Direct-to-disc recording

SHEFFIELD TREASURY
❏ ST-500	Discovered Again!	198?	$25

— Reissue of Sheffield Labs 5

VERSATILE
❏ NED1135	Don't Touch	1977	$25

GRYCE, GIGI, AND CLIFFORD BROWN
Also see each artist's individual listings.

Albums

BLUE NOTE
❏ BLP-5048 [10]	Gigi Gryce-Clifford Brown Sextet	1954	$400

GRYCE, GIGI, AND DONALD BYRD
See THE JAZZ LAB.

GRYCE, GIGI
Alto saxophone player and flutist. Also see ART FARMER.

Albums

BLUE NOTE
❏ BLP-5050 [10]	Gigi Gryce and His Little Band, Volume 2	1954	$300
❏ BLP-5051 [10]	Gigi Gryce Qunitet/Sextet, Volume 3	1954	$300
❏ BLP-5049 [10]	Gigi Gryce's Jazztime Paris	1954	$300

FANTASY
❏ OJC-081	The Rat Race Blues	198?	$25

MERCURY
❏ MG-20628 [M]	Reminiscin'	1961	$100
❏ SR-60628 [S]	Reminiscin'	1961	$100

METROJAZZ

Number	Title	Yr	NM
❏ SE-1006 [S]	Gigi Gryce	1959	$350

NEW JAZZ

Number	Title	Yr	NM
❏ NJLP-8230 [M]	Sayin' Somethin'!	1965	$150
—Blue label, trident logo at right			
❏ NJLP-8246 [M]	The Hap'nin's	1965	$150
—Blue label, trident logo at right			
❏ NJLP-8262 [M]	The Rat Race Blues	1961	$150
—Purple label			
❏ NJLP-8262 [M]	The Rat Race Blues	1965	$150
—Blue label, trident logo at right			

SAVOY

Number	Title	Yr	NM
❏ MG-12137 [M]	Nica's Tempo	1958	$80

SIGNAL

Number	Title	Yr	NM
❏ S-1201 [M]	Gigi Gryce Quartet	1955	$300

GUARALDI, VINCE

Pianist and composer. Best known for his music for the early "Peanuts" TV specials and for the hit tune "Cast Your Fate to the Wind."

Albums

FANTASY

Number	Title	Yr	NM
❏ 8431	A Charlie Brown Christmas	1971	$30
—Reissue of 85019; dark blue label			
❏ 8431	A Charlie Brown Christmas	1988	$35
—Remastered version with "1988" on back cover. Lighter blue label. Also has a bonus track!			
❏ 5019 [M]	A Charlie Brown Christmas	1964	$30
❏ 3257 [M]	A Flower Is a Lovesome Thing	1958	$40
—Red vinyl			
❏ 3257 [M]	A Flower Is a Lovesome Thing	195?	$30
—Black vinyl, red label, non-flexible vinyl			
❏ 3257 [M]	A Flower Is a Lovesome Thing	196?	$35
—Black vinyl, red label, flexible vinyl			
❏ OJC-235	A Flower Is a Lovesome Thing	198?	$25
—Reissue of 3257			
❏ 3362 [M]	From All Sides	1966	$25
❏ 8362 [S]	From All Sides	1966	$25
❏ 3359 [M]	Jazz Impressions	1965	$30
❏ 8359 [S]	Jazz Impressions	1965	$30
❏ OJC-287	Jazz Impressions	1987	$25
—Reissue of 8359			
❏ 3337 [M]	Jazz Impressions of Black Orpheus (Cast Your Fate to the Wind)	1962	$40
—Red vinyl			
❏ 3337 [M]	Jazz Impressions of Black Orpheus (Cast Your Fate to the Wind)	1962	$30
—Black vinyl, red label, non-flexible vinyl			
❏ 3337 [M]	Jazz Impressions of Black Orpheus (Cast Your Fate to the Wind)	1962	$35
—Black vinyl, red label, flexible vinyl			
❏ 8089 [S]	Jazz Impressions of Black Orpheus (Cast Your Fate to the Wind)	1962	$40
—Blue vinyl			
❏ 8089 [S]	Jazz Impressions of Black Orpheus (Cast Your Fate to the Wind)	1962	$35
—Black vinyl, blue label, flexible vinyl			
❏ 8089 [S]	Jazz Impressions of Black Orpheus (Cast Your Fate to the Wind)	1962	$30
—Black vinyl, blue label, non-flexible vinyl			
❏ OJC-437	Jazz Impressions of Black Orpheus (Cast Your Fate to the Wind)	198?	$25
—Reissue of 8089			
❏ 3371 [M]	Live at the El Matador	1967	$25
❏ 8371 [S]	Live at the El Matador	1967	$25
❏ OJC-289	Live at the El Matador	1987	$25
—Reissue of 8371			
❏ 8377	Live-Live-Live	1968	$25
❏ 3213 [M]	Modern Music from San Francisco	1956	$200
—Red vinyl			
❏ 3213 [M]	Modern Music from San Francisco	195?	$30
—Black vinyl, red label, non-flexible vinyl			

Number	Title	Yr	NM
❏ OJC-272	Modern Music from San Francisco	1987	$25
—Reissue of 3213			
❏ 3360 [M]	The Latin Side of Vince Guaraldi	1965	$30
❏ 8360 [S]	The Latin Side of Vince Guaraldi	1965	$30
❏ 3358 [M]	Tour de Force	1964	$30
❏ 8358 [S]	Tour de Force	1964	$30
❏ 3356 [M]	Vince Guaraldi and Bola Sete and Friends	1964	$30
❏ 8356 [S]	Vince Guaraldi and Bola Sete and Friends	1964	$30
❏ 3367 [M]	Vince Guaraldi at Grace Cathedral	1967	$25
❏ 8367 [S]	Vince Guaraldi at Grace Cathedral	1967	$25
❏ 3352 [M]	Vince Guaraldi in Person	1963	$30
❏ 8352 [S]	Vince Guaraldi in Person	1963	$60
❏ MPF-4505	Vince Guaraldi's Greatest Hits	1981	$30
❏ 3225 [M]	Vince Guaraldi Trio	1956	$50
—Red vinyl			
❏ 3225 [M]	Vince Guaraldi Trio	195?	$30
—Black vinyl, red label, non-flexible vinyl			
❏ 3225 [M]	Vince Guaraldi Trio	196?	$35
—Black vinyl, red label, flexible vinyl			
❏ OJC-149	Vince Guaraldi Trio	198?	$25
—Reissue of 3225			

MOBILE FIDELITY

Number	Title	Yr	NM
❏ 1-112	Jazz Impressions of Black Orpheus (Cast Your Fate to the Wind)	1983	$50
—Audiophile vinyl			

WARNER BROS.

Number	Title	Yr	NM
❏ WS1828	Alma-Ville	1970	$35
❏ WS1775	Eclectic	1969	$35
❏ WS1747	Oh Good Grief!	1968	$25

GUARALDI, VINCE/CONTE CANDOLI

Also see each artist's individual listings.

Albums

CROWN

Number	Title	Yr	NM
❏ CLP-5417 [M]	Vince Guaraldi and the Conte Candoli All Stars	1963	$30
❏ CST-417 [R]	Vince Guaraldi and the Conte Candoli All Stars	1963	$25

PREMIER

Number	Title	Yr	NM
❏ PM-2009 [M]	Vince Guaraldi-Conte Candoli Quartet	1963	$30
❏ PS-2009 [R]	Vince Guaraldi-Conte Candoli Quartet	1963	$25

GUARALDI, VINCE/FRANK ROSOLINO

Also see each artist's individual listings.

Albums

PREMIER

Number	Title	Yr	NM
❏ PM-2014 [M]	Vince Guaraldi-Frank Rosolino Quintet	1963	$30
❏ PS-2014 [R]	Vince Guaraldi-Frank Rosolino Quintet	1963	$25

GUARNIERI, JOHNNY

Pianist and composer. Also see BERNIE LEIGHTON.

Albums

CLASSIC JAZZ

Number	Title	Yr	NM
❏ 105	Gliss Me Again	197?	$30

CORAL

Number	Title	Yr	NM
❏ CRL57085 [M]	Songs of Hudson and DeLange	1957	$40
❏ CRL57086 [M]	The Duke Again	1957	$40

DOBRE

Number	Title	Yr	NM
❏ 1017	Johnny Guarnieri Plays Walter Donaldson	197?	$30

DOT

Number	Title	Yr	NM
❏ DLP-3647 [M]	Piano Dimensions	1965	$75
❏ DLP-25647 [S]	Piano Dimensions	1965	$75

GOLDEN CREST

Number	Title	Yr	NM
❏ GC-3020 [M]	Johnny Guarnieri Plays Johnny Guarnieri	1958	$40

JIM TAYLOR PRESENTS

Number	Title	Yr	NM
❏ 102	Johnny Guarnieri Plays Harry Warren	197?	$30

RCA CAMDEN

Number	Title	Yr	NM
❏ CAL-345 [M]	Cheerful Little Earful	1958	$35
❏ CAL-391 [M]	Side by Side	1958	$35

ROYALE

Number	Title	Yr	NM
❏ 1296 [M]	An Hour of Modern Music	1952	$40
❏ VLP6047 [10]	Johnny Guarnieri/Tony Mottola/Bob Haggart/Cozy Cole	195?	$50

SAVOY

Number	Title	Yr	NM
❏ MG-15007 [10]	Hot Piano	1951	$80

SOUNDS GREAT

Number	Title	Yr	NM
❏ SG-5001	Echoes of Ellington	198?	$25

TAZ-JAZ

Number	Title	Yr	NM
❏ 1002	Stealin' Apples	1977	$30
❏ 1001	Superstride	1976	$30

GUESNON, GEORGE

Guitarist, banjo player and male singer.

Albums

JAZZ CRUSADE

Number	Title	Yr	NM
❏ 2011	Echoes from New Orleans	196?	$35

JAZZOLOGY

Number	Title	Yr	NM
❏ JCE-11	Creole Blues	1967	$35

GULDA, FRIEDRICH

Pianist also known for his straight classical work.

Albums

COLUMBIA

Number	Title	Yr	NM
❏ CL2251 [M]	From Vienna with Jazz	1964	$30
❏ CS9051 [S]	From Vienna with Jazz	1964	$35
❏ CL2346 [M]	The Ineffable Friedrich Gulda	1965	$30
❏ CS9146 [S]	The Ineffable Friedrich Gulda	1965	$35

RCA VICTOR

Number	Title	Yr	NM
❏ LPM-1355 [M]	Friedrich Gulda at Birdland	1957	$50

GULLIN, LARS

Baritone saxophone player. Also see ARNE DOMNERUS; BENGT HALLBERG.

Albums

ATLANTIC

Number	Title	Yr	NM
❏ 1246 [M]	Baritone Sax	1956	$300
—Black label			
❏ 1246 [M]	Baritone Sax	1960	$300
—Multicolor label, white "fan" logo at right			

CONTEMPORARY

Number	Title	Yr	NM
❏ C-2505 [10]	Modern Sounds	1953	$250

EMARCY

Number	Title	Yr	NM
❏ MG-26044 [10]	Gullin's Garden	1954	$300
❏ MG-26041 [10]	Lars Gullin Quartet	1954	$300
❏ MG-36059 [M]	Lars Gullin with the Moretone Singers	1955	$200

PRESTIGE

Number	Title	Yr	NM
❏ PRLP-144 [10]	New Sounds from Sweden, Volume 5	1953	$300
❏ PRLP-151 [10]	New Sounds from Sweden, Volume 7	1953	$300

GULLY LOW JAZZ BAND

Led by David Ostwald.

Albums

GHB

Number	Title	Yr	NM
❏ GHB-163	In Dreamland	1984	$25

GUMBS, ONAJE ALLAN

Pianist.

Albums

STEEPLECHASE

Number	Title	Yr	NM
❏ SCS-1069	Onaje	198?	$30

ZEBRA/MCA

Number	Title	Yr	NM
❏ ZEB-42120	That Special Part of Me	1988	$25

GURU

Jazz-influenced rapper, one-half of GANG STARR.

Albums

CHRYSALIS

Number	Title	Yr	NM
❏ F1-21998	Jazzmatazz Vol. 1	1993	$25
❏ F1-34290	Jazzmatazz Vol. 2: The New Reality	1995	$20

VIRGIN

Number	Title	Yr	NM
❏ 50188	Jazzmatazz Vol. 3: Streetsoul	2000	$20

Wardell Gray, *Way Out Wardell*, Crown CLP-5004, black label with the word "crown" in all lowercase letters, **$40**.

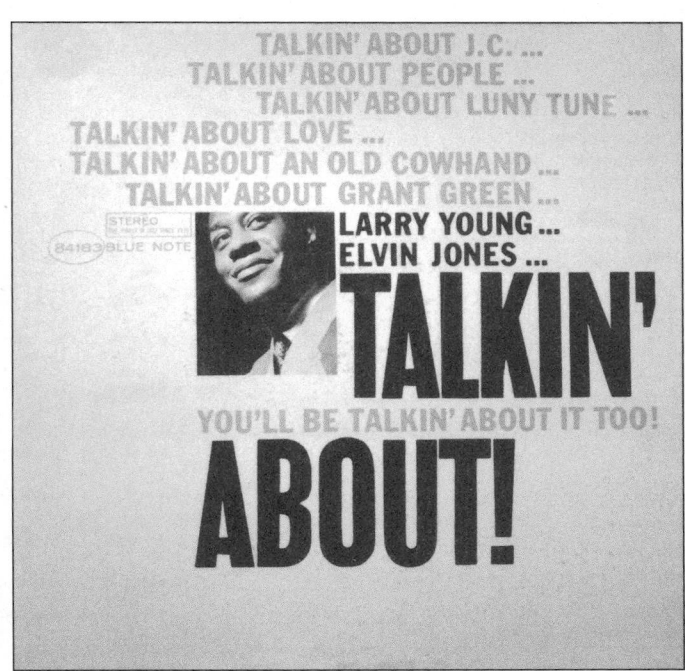

Grant Green, *Talkin' About!*, Blue Note BLP-84183, stereo, "New York USA" on label, **$175**.

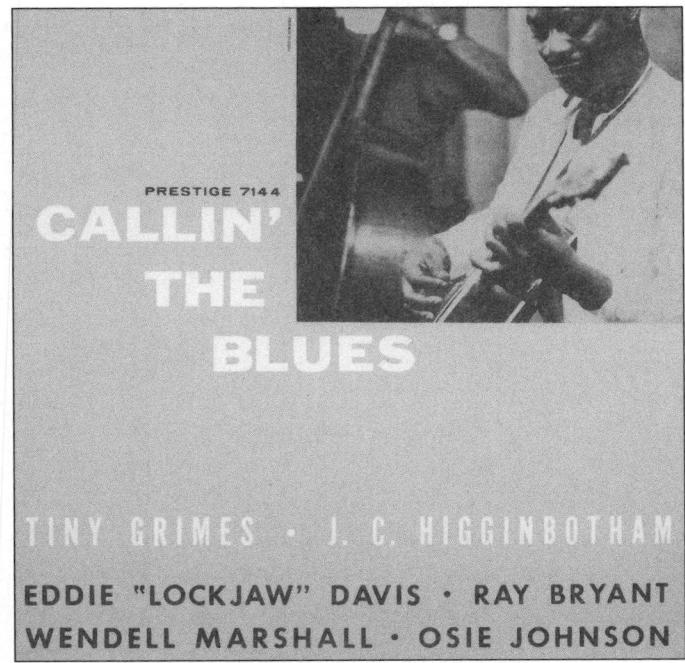

Tiny Grimes, *Callin' the Blues*, Prestige PRLP-7144, yellow label, **$300**.

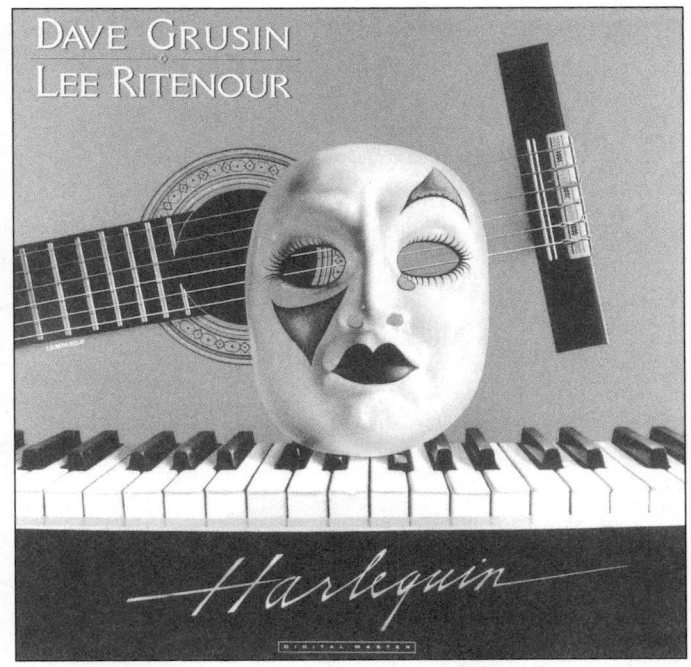

Dave Grusin/Lee Ritenour, *Harlequin*, GRP A-1015, **$25**.

Number	Title	Yr	NM

GUSTAFSSON, RUNE
Guitarist.

Albums

ATLANTIC
| SD8234 | Rune at the Top | 1969 | $30 |

GNP CRESCENDO
| GNPS-2118 | Move | 1976 | $25 |

PABLO TODAY
| 2312106 | The Sweetest Sounds | 1979 | $30 |

GWALTNEY, TOMMY
Clarinetist and alto saxophone player.

Albums

RIVERSIDE
| RLP-353 [M] | Goin' to Kansas City | 1960 | $200 |

H

HACKETT, BOBBY, AND BILLY BUTTERFIELD
Also see each artist's individual listings.

Albums

VERVE
| V-8723 [M] | Bobby/Billy/Brazil | 1967 | $35 |
| V6-8723 [S] | Bobby/Billy/Brazil | 1967 | $30 |

HACKETT, BOBBY
Cornet player, trumpeter and guitarist. Also see JACK TEAGARDEN.

Albums

BRUNSWICK
| BL56014 [10] | Trumpet Solos | 1950 | $50 |

CAPITOL
T1172 [M]	Blues with a Kick	1959	$60
ST1172 [S]	Blues with a Kick	1959	$60
T1077 [M]	Bobby Hackett at the Embers	1958	$60
—Black colorband label, logo at left			
ST1077 [S]	Bobby Hackett at the Embers	1958	$60
—Black colorband label, logo at left			
T1077 [M]	Bobby Hackett at the Embers	1962	$40
—Black colorband label, logo at top			
ST1077 [S]	Bobby Hackett at the Embers	1962	$40
—Black colorband label, logo at top			
T1235 [M]	Bobby Hackett Quartet	1959	$60
ST1235 [S]	Bobby Hackett Quartet	1959	$60
T692 [M]	Coast Concert	1956	$60
—Turquoise or gray label			
T1002 [M]	Don't Take Your Love from Me	1958	$60
—Turquoise or gray label			
T1002 [M]	Don't Take Your Love from Me	1958	$60
—Black colorband label, logo at left			
T1413 [M]	Easy Beat	1960	$50
ST1413 [S]	Easy Beat	1960	$60
T857 [M]	Gotham Jazz Scene	1957	$60
—Turquoise or gray label			
T857 [M]	Gotham Jazz Scene	1957	$60
—Black colorband label, logo at left			
T575 [M]	In a Mellow Mood	1955	$75
—Turquoise or gray label			
T575 [M]	In a Mellow Mood	1955	$75
—Black colorband label, logo at left			
T933 [M]	Jazz Ultimate	1958	$75
—Turquoise or gray label			
T933 [M]	Jazz Ultimate	1958	$60
—Black colorband label, logo at left			
ST933 [S]	Jazz Ultimate	1959	$60
—Black colorband label, logo at left			
SM-933	Jazz Ultimate	1976	$25
—Reissue with new prefix			
T719 [M]	Rendezvous	1956	$75
—Turquoise or gray label			
T719 [M]	Rendezvous	1956	$60
—Black colorband label, logo at left			
H458 [10]	Soft Lights	1954	$80

T458 [M]	Soft Lights	1955	$75
—Turquoise or gray label			
T458 [M]	Soft Lights	1955	$75
—Black colorband label, logo at left			

CHIAROSCURO
105	Live at Roosevelt Grill	1972	$30
138	Live at Roosevelt Grill, Volume 2	197?	$30
161	Live at Roosevelt Grill, Volume 3	197?	$30

COLUMBIA
CL1602 [M]	Dream Awhile	1961	$25
CS8402 [S]	Dream Awhile	1961	$30
CL6156 [10]	Jazz Session	1951	$50
CL1895 [M]	Night Love	1962	$35
CS8695 [S]	Night Love	1962	$25
CL2566 [10]	The Bobby Hackett Horn	1955	$60
CL1729 [M]	The Most Beautiful Horn in the World	1962	$25
CS8529 [S]	The Most Beautiful Horn in the World	1962	$30

COMMODORE
| FL-20016 [10] | Horn A Plenty | 1951 | $50 |

DOBRE
| 1004 | Thanks Bobby | 197? | $25 |

ENCORE
| EE22003 [M] | The Bobby Hackett Horn | 1968 | $30 |

EPIC
LN24174 [M]	A String of Pearls	1966	$60
BN26174 [S]	A String of Pearls	1966	$75
LN24099 [M]	Hello, Louis!	1964	$60
BN26099 [S]	Hello, Louis!	1964	$75
LA16037 [M]	Oliver!	1963	$60
BA17037 [S]	Oliver!	1963	$75
LN3106 [M]	The Hackett Horn	1956	$80
LN24080 [M]	The Music of Bert Kaempfert	1964	$60
BN26080 [S]	The Music of Bert Kaempfert	1964	$75
LN24061 [M]	The Music of Mancini	1963	$60
BN26061 [S]	The Music of Mancini	1963	$75
FLM13107 [M]	The Swingin'est Gals in Town	196?	$75
FLS15107 [S]	The Swingin'est Gals in Town	196?	$25
LN24155 [M]	The Trumpet's Greatest Hits	1965	$60
BN26155 [S]	The Trumpet's Greatest Hits	1965	$75
LN24220 [M]	Tony Bennett's Greatest Hits	1966	$60
BN26220 [S]	Tony Bennett's Greatest Hits	1966	$75

FLYING DUTCHMAN
| BDL1-0829 | Strike Up the Band | 1975 | $30 |
| FD-10159 | What a Wonderful World | 1973 | $30 |

JAZZOLOGY
| J-111 | Bobby Hackett and His Orchestra, 1943 | 198? | $25 |
| JCE-76 | Live from Manassas | 1979 | $25 |

PAUSA
| 9038 | Coast Concert | 198? | $25 |

PICKWICK
| PC-3012 [M] | Bobby Hackett with Strings | 1966 | $30 |
| SPC-3012 [S] | Bobby Hackett with Strings | 1966 | $25 |

PROJECT 3
PR5016SD	A Time for Love	1968	$30
PR26033	Memorable and Mellow	1979	$30
PR5006SD	That Midnight Touch	1967	$30
PR5034SD	This Is My Bag	1969	$30

SEAGULL
| LG-8201 | Goodnight My Love | 198? | $25 |

SESAC
N-4105 [M]	Candlelight and Romance	1960	$30
SN-4105 [S]	Candlelight and Romance	1960	$30
N-4101 [M]	The Spirit Swings Me	1960	$30
SN-4101 [S]	The Spirit Swings Me	1960	$30

STORYVILLE
| 4059 | Sextet Recordings | 198? | $25 |

VERVE
| V-8698 [M] | Creole Cookin' | 1967 | $40 |
| V6-8698 [S] | Creole Cookin' | 1967 | $30 |

HACKETT, BOBBY/MAX KAMINSKY
Also see each artist's individual listings.

Albums

BRUNSWICK
| BL58043 [10] | Battle of Jazz, Vol. 5 | 1953 | $50 |

HADEN, CHARLIE, AND HAMPTON HAWES
Also see each artist's individual listings.

Albums

ARTISTS HOUSE
| 4 | As Long As There's Music | 1979 | $30 |

HADEN, CHARLIE; JAN GARBAREK; EGBERTO GISMONTI
Also see each artist's individual listings.

Albums

ECM
| 1170 | Folk Songs | 1979 | $30 |

HADEN, CHARLIE
Bass player and occasional male singer.

Albums

ABC IMPULSE!
| AS-9183 | Liberation Music Orchestra | 1973 | $200 |

ECM
| 23794 | Ballad of the Fallen | 1982 | $25 |

HORIZON
| SP-710 | Closeness | 197? | $35 |
| SP-727 | The Golden Number | 1978 | $35 |

SOUL NOTE
| 121172 | Silence | 1990 | $30 |

VERVE
| 831673-1 | Quartet West | 1987 | $25 |
| 837031-1 | Quartet West in Angel City | 1988 | $25 |

HAGGART, BOB
Bass player, composer and bandleader. Also see YANK LAWSON.

Albums

COMMAND
| RS 33-849 [M] | Big Noise from Winnetka | 1963 | $30 |
| RS849SD [S] | Big Noise from Winnetka | 1963 | $35 |

JAZZOLOGY
J-149	A Portrait of Bix	1986	$25
J-94	Bob Haggart Enjoys Carolina in the Morning	1982	$25
J-74	Sentimental Journey	1980	$25

HAHN, JERRY
Guitarist.

Albums

ARHOOLIE
| 8006 | Jerry Hahn Quintet | 197? | $35 |

CHANGES
| LP-7001 | Arabein | 1968 | $25 |

FANTASY
| F-9426 | Moses | 1974 | $35 |

HAIG, AL, AND JIMMY RANEY
Also see each artist's individual listings.

Albums

CHOICE
| 1010 | Strings Attached | 197? | $30 |

HAIG, AL
Pianist.

Albums

COUNTERPOINT
| C-551 [M] | Jazz Will o' the Wisp | 1957 | $100 |

ESOTERIC
| ESJ-7 [10] | Al Haig Trio | 1954 | $200 |

EVEREST ARCHIVE OF FOLK & JAZZ
| 293 | Jazz Will o' the Wisp | 197? | $25 |

INNER CITY
| IC-1073 | Al Haig Plays Music of Jerome Kern | 197? | $30 |

INTERPLAY
| 7707 | Portrait of Bud Powell | 1978 | $30 |
| 7713 | Serendipity | 1978 | $30 |

MINT
| AL-711 [M] | Al Haig Today | 1964 | $150 |

PACIFIC JAZZ
| PJLP-18 [10] | Al Haig Trio | 1955 | $150 |

PERIOD
| SPL-1104 [10] | Al Haig Quartet | 1954 | $150 |

PRESTIGE
| PRST-7841 | Al Haig Trio and Quartet | 1970 | $35 |

SEABREEZE
1005	Interplay	1977	$30
1008	Manhattan Memories	1978	$30
1001	Piano Interpretation	1976	$30
1006	Piano Time	1977	$30

Number	Title	Yr	NM
SEECO			
❏ SLP-7 [10]	Highlights in Modern Jazz	195?	$250
XANADU			
❏ 206	Live in Hollywood	198?	$25

HAIG, AL/MARY LOU WILLIAMS
Also see each artist's individual listings.

Albums

Number	Title	Yr	NM
PRESTIGE			
❏ PRLP-175 [10]	Piano Moderns	1953	$300

HAKIM, OMAR
Drummer. Also an occasional guitarist and male singer.

Albums

Number	Title	Yr	NM
GRP			
❏ GR-9585	Rhythm Deep	1989	$30

HAKIM, SADIK
Pianist.

Albums

Number	Title	Yr	NM
STEEPLECHASE			
❏ SCS-1091	Witches, Goblins	198?	$30

HALE, CORKY
Pianist, harpist and female singer.

Albums

Number	Title	Yr	NM
GENE NORMAN			
❏ GNP-17 [M]	Corky Hale	1956	$50
GNP CRESCENDO			
❏ GNP-17 [M]	Corky Hale	196?	$35
❏ GNP-9035	Corky Hale Plays Gershwin and Duke	197?	$30
STASH			
❏ ST-245	Harp Beat	198?	$30

HALEN, CARL
Cornet player and trumpeter.

Albums

Number	Title	Yr	NM
EMPIRICAL			
❏ LP-101 [10]	Gin Bottle Seven	1957	$50
RIVERSIDE			
❏ RLP 12-231 [M]	Gin Bottle Jazz	1958	$300
—White label, blue print			
❏ RLP 12-231 [M]	Gin Bottle Jazz	1959	$250
—Blue label, microphone logo at top			
❏ RLP 12-261 [M]	Whoopee Makers' Jazz	1958	$300
❏ RLP-1103 [S]	Whoopee Makers' Jazz	1958	$300

HALL, ADELAIDE
Female singer.

Albums

Number	Title	Yr	NM
MONMOUTH-EVERGREEN			
❏ 7080	That Wonderful...	1970	$25

HALL, BECKY
Female singer.

Albums

Number	Title	Yr	NM
AAMCO			
❏ ALP-324 [M]	A Tribute to Bessie Smith	1958	$30

HALL, EDMOND
Clarinetist. Also a baritone saxophone player. Also see MIFF MOLE.

Albums

Number	Title	Yr	NM
CIRCLE			
❏ C-52	Rompin' in '44	198?	$25
MOSAIC			
❏ MR6-109	The Complete Edmond Hall/ James P. Johnson/Sidney De Paris/Vic Dickenson Blue Note Sessions	199?	$100
MOUNT VERNON			
❏ MVM-124	Rumpus on Rampart St.	197?	$30
STORYVILLE			

Number	Title	Yr	NM
❏ 4009	Live at Club Hangover, Volume 4	198?	$25
UNITED ARTISTS			
❏ UAL-4028 [M]	Petite Fleur	1959	$40
❏ UAS-5028 [S]	Petite Fleur	1959	$30

HALL, EDMOND/ART HODES
Also see each artist's individual listings.

Albums

Number	Title	Yr	NM
BLUE NOTE			
❏ B-6504 [M]	Original Blue Note Jazz, Volume 1	1969	$25

HALL, EDMOND/SIDNEY DEPARIS
Also see each artist's individual listings.

Albums

Number	Title	Yr	NM
BLUE NOTE			
❏ BLP-7007 [10]	Jamming in Jazz Hall	1951	$200

HALL, GEORGE
Violinist and bandleader.

Albums

Number	Title	Yr	NM
BLUEBIRD			
❏ AXM2-5504	George Hall and His Taft Hotel Orchestra (1933-1937)	1975	$35
HINDSIGHT			
❏ HSR-144	George Hall and His Orchestra 1937	198?	$25

HALL, HERB
Alto and baritone saxophone player.

Albums

Number	Title	Yr	NM
BIOGRAPH			
❏ 3003	Herb Hall Quartet	196?	$35

HALL, JIM, AND RED MITCHELL
Also see each artist's individual listings.

Albums

Number	Title	Yr	NM
ARTISTS HOUSE			
❏ 5	Jim Hall and Red Mitchell	1979	$30

HALL, JIM, AND RON CARTER
Also see each artist's individual listings.

Albums

Number	Title	Yr	NM
FANTASY			
❏ OJC-467	Alone Together	1990	$30
MILESTONE			
❏ 9045	Alone Together	1974	$35

HALL, JIM
Guitarist. Also see BOB BROOKMEYER; BILL EVANS; ZOOT SIMS.

Albums

Number	Title	Yr	NM
BASF			
❏ 20708	It's Nice to Be with You	1972	$35
CONCORD JAZZ			
❏ CJ-384	All Across the City	1989	$30
❏ CJ-161	Circles	1982	$25
❏ CJ-298	Jim Hall's Three	1986	$25
CTI			
❏ 6060	Concierto	1977	$30
FANTASY			
❏ OJC-649	Where Would I Be	1991	$30
HORIZON			
❏ SP-715	Commitment	1976	$30
❏ SP-705	Live	1975	$30
MILESTONE			
❏ 9037	Where Would I Be	1973	$35
PACIFIC JAZZ			
❏ PJ-10 [M]	Good Friday Blues	1960	$40
❏ PJ-79 [M]	Jazz Guitar	1963	$30
❏ ST-79 [S]	Jazz Guitar	1963	$30
PAUSA			
❏ 7112	In a Sentimental Mood	198?	$25
WORLD PACIFIC			
❏ WP-1227 [M]	Jazz Guitar	1958	$150

HALL BROTHERS JAZZ BAND, THE
Led by pianist Mike Polad. Also see KID THOMAS.

HALLBERG, BENGT
Pianist. Also see REINHOLD SVENSSON.

Albums

Number	Title	Yr	NM
EPIC			
❏ LN3375 [M]	Bengt Hallberg	1957	$250
PRESTIGE			
❏ PRLP-176 [10]	Bengt Hallberg's Swedish All-Stars	1953	$350

HALLBERG, BENGT/ARNE DOMNERUS
Also see each artist's individual listings.

Albums

Number	Title	Yr	NM
PRESTIGE			
❏ PRLP-145 [10]	New Sounds from Sweden, Volume 6	1953	$400

HALLBERG, BENGT/LARS GULLIN
Also see each artist's individual listings.

Albums

Number	Title	Yr	NM
PRESTIGE			
❏ PRLP-121 [10]	New Sounds from Sweden, Volume 2	1952	$400

HALLEY, PAUL
Pianist, organist and composer.

Albums

Number	Title	Yr	NM
GRAMAVISION			
❏ 7704	Nightwatch	198?	$25
LIVING MUSIC			
❏ LM-0009	Pianosong	1986	$25

HAMBRO, LENNY
Alto saxophone player.

Albums

Number	Title	Yr	NM
COLUMBIA			
❏ CL757 [M]	Message from Hambro	1956	$40
EPIC			
❏ LN3361 [M]	The Nature of Things	1956	$80
SAVOY			
❏ MG-15031 [10]	Mambo Hambro	1954	$50

HAMILTON, CHICO
Drummer and bandleader. Also see LAURINDO ALMEIDA

Albums

Number	Title	Yr	NM
ABC IMPULSE!			
❏ AS-82 [S]	Chi Chi Chico	1968	$35
❏ AS-9102 [S]	El Chico	1968	$35
❏ AS-9213	His Great Hits	1971	$200
❏ AS-59 [S]	Man from Two Worlds	1968	$35
❏ AS-29 [S]	Passin' Thru	1968	$35
❏ AS-9174	The Best of Chico Hamilton	1969	$35
❏ AS-9130 [S]	The Dealer	1968	$35
❏ AS-9114 [S]	The Further Adventures of El Chico	1968	$35
BLUE NOTE			
❏ BN-LA622-G	Chico Hamilton & Players	1976	$30
❏ BN-LA520-G	Peregrinations	1975	$30
COLUMBIA			
❏ CS8419 [S]	Chico Hamilton Special	1961	$60
❏ CS8607 [S]	Drumfusion	1962	$60
DECCA			
❏ DL8614 [M]	Jazz from the Sweet Smell of Success	1957	$120
DISCOVERY			
❏ 831	Gongs East	1981	$25
—Reissue of Warner Bros. 1271			
ELEKTRA			
❏ 6E-257	Nomad	1980	$25
ENTERPRISE			
❏ SD7501	The Master	1974	$30
FLYING DUTCHMAN			
❏ 10135	Exigente	1971	$35
IMPULSE!			
❏ A-82 [M]	Chi Chi Chico	1965	$200
❏ AS-82 [S]	Chi Chi Chico	1965	$200
❏ A-9102 [M]	El Chico	1965	$200
❏ AS-9102 [S]	El Chico	1965	$120
❏ A-59 [M]	Man from Two Worlds	1964	$200

Number	Title	Yr	NM
❑ AS-59 [S]	Man from Two Worlds	1964	$200
❑ A-29 [M]	Passin' Thru	1963	$200
❑ AS-29 [S]	Passin' Thru	1963	$200
❑ A-9130 [M]	The Dealer	1966	$200
❑ SMAS-91138 [S]	The Dealer	1966	$300
—Capitol Record Club edition			
❑ A-9114 [M]	The Further Adventures of El Chico	1966	$200
❑ AS-9114 [S]	The Further Adventures of El Chico	1966	$200
JAZZTONE			
❑ J-1264 [M]	Delightfully Modern	1957	$40
MCA			
❑ 638	El Chico	198?	$20
—Reissue of Impulse! 9102			
❑ 637	Man from Two Worlds	198?	$20
—Reissue of Impulse! 59			
❑ 29037	Passin' Thru	198?	$25
—Reissue of Impulse! 29			
❑ 29038	The Best of Chico Hamilton	198?	$25
—Reissue of Impulse! 9174			
MERCURY			
❑ SRM-1-1163	Catwalk	1977	$30
NAUTILUS			
❑ NR-13	Reaching for the Top	1981	$60
—Audiophile vinyl			
PACIFIC JAZZ			
❑ PJ-1231 [M]	Chico Hamilton Plays the Music of Fred Katz	1957	$150
❑ PJ-1209 [M]	Chico Hamilton Quintet	1955	$150
❑ PJ-1225 [M]	Chico Hamilton Quintet	1957	$150
❑ PJ-1216 [M]	Chico Hamilton Quintet In Hi-Fi	1956	$150
❑ PJLP-17 [10]	Chico Hamilton Trio	1955	$175
❑ PJ-1220 [M]	Chico Hamilton Trio	1956	$150
❑ PJ-39 [M]	Spectacular	1962	$60
—Reissue of 1209			
REPRISE			
❑ R-6078 [M]	A Different Journey	1963	$60
❑ R9-6078 [S]	A Different Journey	1963	$40
SOLID STATE			
❑ SS-18050	Headhunters	1969	$35
❑ SS-18043	The Gamut	1969	$35
SOUL NOTE			
❑ 121191	Reunion	1989	$30
SUNSET			
❑ SUS-5215	Easy Livin'	196?	$30
WARNER BROS.			
❑ W1245 [M]	Chico Hamilton Quintet with Strings Attached	1958	$100
❑ WS1245 [S]	Chico Hamilton Quintet with Strings Attached	1958	$120
❑ WS1271 [S]	Gongs East	1958	$120
WORLD PACIFIC			
❑ WP-1231 [M]	Chico Hamilton Plays the Music of Fred Katz	1958	$200
❑ WP-1225 [M]	Chico Hamilton Quintet	1958	$200
❑ ST-1005 [S]	Chico Hamilton Quintet	1958	$150
❑ WP-1216 [M]	Chico Hamilton Quintet In Hi-Fi	1958	$200
❑ WP-1258 [M]	Ellington Suite	1959	$200
❑ ST-1016 [S]	Ellington Suite	1959	$150
❑ PJ-1238 [M]	South Pacific in Hi-Fi	1957	$200
❑ WP-1238 [M]	South Pacific in Hi-Fi	1958	$150
❑ ST-1003 [S]	South Pacific in Hi-Fi	1958	$150
❑ PJ-1242 [M]	The Chico Hamilton Trio Featuring Freddie Gambrell	1957	$200
❑ WP-1242 [M]	The Chico Hamilton Trio Featuring Freddie Gambrell	1958	$150
❑ ST-1008 [S]	The Chico Hamilton Trio Featuring Freddie Gambrell	1958	$150
❑ WP-1287 [M]	The Original Hamilton Quintet	1960	$200

HAMILTON, DAVE
Vibraphone player.

Albums

WORKSHOP JAZZ

Number	Title	Yr	NM
❑ WSJ-206 [M]	Blue Vibrations	1963	$80

HAMILTON, JEFF
Drummer.

Albums

CONCORD JAZZ

Number	Title	Yr	NM
❑ CJ-187	Indiana	1982	$25

HAMILTON, JIMMY
Clarinetist and tenor saxophone player. Also see BENNY MORTON / JIMMY HAMILTON.

Albums

EVEREST

Number	Title	Yr	NM
❑ LPBR-5100 [M]	Swing Low, Sweet Chariot	1960	$30
❑ SDBR-1100 [S]	Swing Low, Sweet Chariot	1960	$30
SWINGVILLE			
❑ SVLP-2028 [M]	Can't Help Swingin'	1961	$50
—Purple label			
❑ SVLP-2028 [M]	Can't Help Swingin'	1965	$30
—Blue label, trident logo at right			
URANIA			
❑ UJLP-1204 [M]	Accent on Clarinet	1955	$250
❑ UJLP-1003 [10]	Clarinet in Hi-Fi	1954	$350
❑ UJLP-1208 [M]	Clarinet in Hi-Fi	1955	$150

HAMILTON, SCOTT, AND BUDDY TATE
Also see each artist's individual listings.

Albums

CONCORD JAZZ

Number	Title	Yr	NM
❑ CJ-85	Back to Back	1979	$30
❑ CJ-148	Scott's Buddy	1981	$25

HAMILTON, SCOTT, AND WARREN VACHE
Also see each artist's individual listings.

Albums

CONCORD JAZZ

Number	Title	Yr	NM
❑ CJ-111	Skyscrapers	1980	$25
❑ CJ-70	With Scott's Band in New York	1978	$30

HAMILTON, SCOTT; JAKE HANNA; DAVE MCKENNA
Also see each artist's individual listings.

Albums

CONCORD JAZZ

Number	Title	Yr	NM
❑ CJ-305	Major League	1986	$25

HAMILTON, SCOTT
Tenor saxophone player.

Albums

CONCORD JAZZ

Number	Title	Yr	NM
❑ CJ-165	Apples and Oranges	1981	$25
❑ CJ-197	Close Up	1982	$25
❑ CJ-233	In Concert	1984	$25
❑ CJ-61	Scott Hamilton 2	1978	$30
❑ CJ-42	Scott Hamilton Is a Good Wind Who Is Blowing Us No Ill	1977	$30
❑ CJ-127	Tenorshoes	1980	$25
❑ CJ-311	The Right Time	1987	$25
❑ CJ-254	The Second Set	1984	$25
FAMOUS DOOR			
❑ 119	The Swinging Young Scott	197?	$25
PROGRESSIVE			
❑ 7026	Grand Appearance	1979	$25

HAMLIN, JOHNNY
Accordion player.

Albums

ARGO

Number	Title	Yr	NM
❑ LP-4001 [M]	Johnny Hamiln Quintet	1961	$30
❑ LPS-4001 [S]	Johnny Hamiln Quintet	1961	$30

HAMMACK, BOBBY
Pianist.

Albums

LIBERTY

Number	Title	Yr	NM
❑ LRP-3016 [M]	Power House	1956	$40

HAMMER, ATLE
Trombonist.

Albums

GEMINI TAURUS

Number	Title	Yr	NM
❑ GMLP-65	Arizona Blue	1991	$35

HAMMER, BOB
Pianist, composer and arranger.

Albums

ABC-PARAMOUNT

Number	Title	Yr	NM
❑ ABC-497 [M]	Beatle Jazz	1964	$30
❑ ABCS-497 [S]	Beatle Jazz	1964	$40

HAMMER, JAN
Keyboard player, composer and bandleader. A onetime member of MAHAVISHNU ORCHESTRA, he is best known for his television theme from Miami Vice.

Albums

ASYLUM

Number	Title	Yr	NM
❑ 6E-173	Black Sheep	1979	$12
❑ 6E-232	Hammer	1979	$12
BASF			
❑ MC20688	Make Love	1976	$15
—Recorded in 1968			
MCA			
❑ 42103	Escape from Television	1988	$12
NEMPEROR			
❑ JZ35003	Melodies	1977	$12
❑ PZ35003	Melodies	198?	$10
—Budget-line reissue			
❑ NE437	Oh, Yeah?	1976	$20
❑ BZ40382	The Early Years (1974-1977)	1986	$12
❑ NE432	The First Seven Days	1975	$15
❑ AS424 [DJ]	The Jan Hammer Group Live	1978	$30
—Promo-only album			
PASSPORT			
❑ PB6051	City Slicker	1985	$15
—With James Young			

HAMMOND, JOHNNY
Organist and occasional pianist. He also recorded as Johnny "Hammond" Smith; the below listings include those albums as well as the Johnny Hammond ones.

Albums

KUDU

Number	Title	Yr	NM
❑ 01	Breakout	1971	$30
❑ 16	Higher Ground	1974	$30
❑ KSQX-16 [Q]	Higher Ground	1974	$60
❑ 10	The Prophet	1973	$30
❑ 04	Wild Horses/Rock Steady	1972	$30
MILESTONE			
❑ 9083	Don't Let the System Get You	1978	$35
❑ 9068	Forever Taurus	1976	$35
❑ 9062	Gears	1975	$35
❑ 9076	Storm Warning	1977	$35
NEW JAZZ			
❑ NJLP-8221 [M]	All Soul	1959	$200
—Purple label			
❑ NJLP-8221 [M]	All Soul	1965	$150
—Blue label with trident logo			
❑ NJLP-8288 [M]	Look Out!	1962	$200
—Purple label			
❑ NJLP-8288 [M]	Look Out!	1965	$150
—Blue label with trident logo			
❑ NJLP-8241 [M]	Talk That Talk	1960	$200
—Purple label			
❑ NJLP-8241 [M]	Talk That Talk	1965	$150
—Blue label with trident logo			
❑ NJLP-8229 [M]	That Good Feelin'	1959	$200
—Purple label			
❑ NJLP-8229 [M]	That Good Feelin'	1965	$150
—Blue label with trident logo			
PRESTIGE			
❑ PRST-7777	Best for Lovers	1970	$35
❑ PRST-7736	Black Feeling	1969	$35
❑ PRST-7564	Dirty Grape	1968	$50
❑ PRLP-7494 [M]	Ebb Tide	1967	$60
❑ PRST-7494 [S]	Ebb Tide	1967	$50
❑ PRLP-7217 [M]	Gettin' the Message	1961	$200
—Yellow label			
❑ PRLP-7217 [M]	Gettin' the Message	1965	$60
—Blue label with trident logo			
❑ PRST-7846	Good 'Nuff	1970	$35
❑ 10002	Here It 'Tis	1971	$35
❑ PRLP-7482 [M]	Love Potion #9	1967	$60
❑ PRST-7482 [S]	Love Potion #9	1967	$50
❑ PRST-7588	Nasty	1968	$50
❑ PRLP-7420 [M]	Opus de Funk	1966	$60
❑ PRST-7420 [S]	Opus de Funk	1966	$60

Bengt Hallberg, *Bengt Hallberg*, Epic LN 3375, **$250**.

Toni Harper, *Night Mood*, RCA Victor LPM-2253, **$30**.

Hampton Hawes, For Real!, Contemporary S-7589, **$250**.

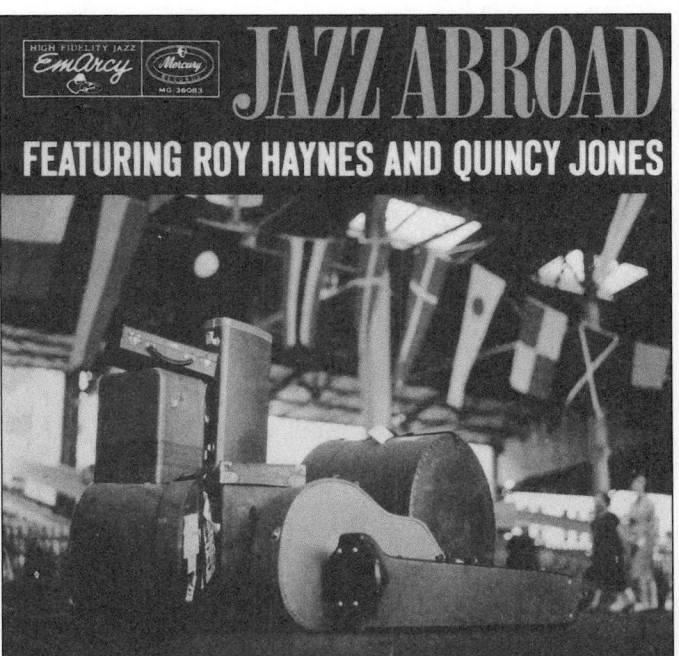

Roy Haynes & Quincy Jones, *Jazz Abroad*, EmArcy MG 36083, **$200**.

Number	Title	Yr	NM
❏ PRST-7549	Soul Flowers	1968	$50
❏ PRST-7681	Soul Talk	1969	$50
❏ PRLP-7203 [M]	Stimulation	1965	$60
—Blue label with trident logo			
❏ PRST-7786	Stimulation	1970	$35
❏ PRST-7705	The Best of Johnny	1969	$35
	"Hammond" Smith		
❏ PRLP-7408 [M]	The Stinger	1965	$50
❏ PRST-7408 [S]	The Stinger	1965	$60
❏ PRLP-7464 [M]	The Stinger Meets the	1966	$50
	Golden Thrush		
❏ PRST-7464 [S]	The Stinger Meets the	1966	$60
	Golden Thrush		
❏ 10015	What's Going On	1971	$35
RIVERSIDE			
❏ RLP-496 [M]	A Little Taste	1965	$150
❏ RS-9496 [S]	A Little Taste	1965	$150
❏ RLP-442 [M]	Black Coffee	1963	$150
❏ RS-9442 [S]	Black Coffee	1963	$150
❏ RLP-466 [M]	Mr. Wonderful	1963	$150
❏ RS-9466 [S]	Mr. Wonderful	1963	$150
❏ RLP-482 [M]	Open House!	1965	$150
❏ RS-9482 [S]	Open House!	1965	$150
SALVATION			
❏ 702	A Gambler's Life	1974	$30

HAMPEL, GUNTER, AND BOULOU FERRE

Also see each artist's individual listings.

Albums

BIRTH

❏ 006	Espace	1970	$30

HAMPEL, GUNTER

Vibraphone player, flutist, bass clarinetist, baritone saxophone player and occasional male singer, percussionist and pianist.

Albums

BIRTH

❏ 0028	All Is Real	1978	$25
❏ 0031	All the Things You Could Be	1980	$25
	If Charles Mingus Was Your		
	Daddy		
❏ 009	Angel	1972	$25
❏ 0032	A Place to Be with Us	1981	$25
❏ 0011	Broadway/Folksong	1972	$25
❏ 0034	Cavana	1982	$25
❏ 0021/0022	Celebrations	1974	$30
❏ 0036	Companion	1983	$25
❏ 0024	Cosmic Dancer	1975	$25
❏ 002	Dances	1970	$30
❏ 0025	Enfant Terrible	1976	$25
❏ 008	Familie	1972	$25
❏ 0030	Freedom of the Universe	1978	$25
❏ 0039	Fresh Heat	1985	$25
❏ 0035	Generator	1982	$25
❏ 0012	I Love Being with You	1972	$25
❏ 0017	Journey to the Song Within	1974	$25
❏ 0038	Jubilation	1984	$25
❏ 0033	Life on This Planet 1981	1981	$25
❏ 0016	Out from Under	1974	$25
❏ 005	People Symphony	1970	$30
❏ 0023	Ruomi	1975	$25
❏ 007	Spirits	1971	$25
❏ 003	Symphony No. 5 and 6	1970	$30
❏ 0027	That Came Down on Me	1978	$25
❏ 001	The 8th of July, 1969	1969	$40
❏ 0026	Transformation	1976	$25
❏ 0013	Unity Dance	1973	$25
❏ 0029	Vogelfrei	1978	$25
❏ 0010	Waltz for 3 Universes in a	1972	$25
	Corridor		
ESP-DISK'			
❏ 1042 [M]	Music from Europe	1967	$100
❏ S-1042 [S]	Music from Europe	1967	$100
FLYING DUTCHMAN			
❏ 126	The 8th of July, 1969	1970	$40
❏ FD-10126	The 8th of July, 1969	1971	$25
FMP			
❏ 0770	Wellen/Waves	1980	$35
HORO			
❏ 33/34	Oasis	1978	$30
KHARMA			
❏ PK8	Flying Carpet	1978	$30

HAMPTON, LIONEL, AND CHARLIE TEAGARDEN

Also see each artist's individual listings.

Albums

CORAL

❏ CRL57438 [M]	The Great Hamp and Little T.	1963	$15
❏ CRL757438 [S]	The Great Hamp and Little T.	1963	$25

HAMPTON, LIONEL, AND STAN GETZ

Also see each artist's individual listings.

Albums

NORGRAN

❏ MGN-1037 [M]	Hamp and Getz	1955	$1002
VERVE			
❏ MGV-8128 [M]	Hamp and Getz	1957	$150
❏ V-8128 [M]	Hamp and Getz	1961	$25

HAMPTON, LIONEL, AND SVEND ASMUSSEN

Also see each artist's individual listings.

Albums

SONET

❏ 779	As Time Goes By	1979	$30

HAMPTON, LIONEL; ART TATUM; BUDDY RICH

Also see each artist's individual listings.

Albums

CLEF

❏ MGC-709 [M]	The Hampton-Tatum-Rich Trio	1956	$200
VERVE			
❏ MGV-8093 [M]	The Hampton-Tatum-Rich Trio	1957	$150
❏ V-8093 [M]	The Hampton-Tatum-Rich Trio	1961	$25

HAMPTON, LIONEL

Vibraphone player (essentially the father of jazz vibes), he also was a drummer, pianist, male singer and bandleader. Also see CHICK COREA; BENNY GOODMAN.

Albums

ABC IMPULSE!

❏ AS-78 [S]	You Better Know It	1968	$35
AMERICAN RECORDING SOCIETY			
❏ G-403 [M]	The Swinging Jazz of Lionel	1956	$40
	Hampton		
ATLANTIC			
❏ 81644	Sentimental Journey	1986	$25
AUDIO FIDELITY			
❏ AFLP-1913 [M]	Hamp's Big Band	1958	$30
❏ AFSD-5913 [S]	Hamp's Big Band	1958	$40
❏ AFSD-5849 [S]	Lionel	1958	$40
BLUEBIRD			
❏ 6458-1-RB	Hot Mallets	1987	$25
❏ AXM6-5536	The Complete Lionel	1976	$50
	Hampton 1937-1941		
BLUE NOTE			
❏ BLP-5046 [10]	Rockin' and Groovin'	1954	$300
BRUNSWICK			
❏ BL754213	Off Into a Black Thing	1977	$30
❏ BL754190	Please Sunrise	1973	$35
❏ BL754203	Stop! I Don't Need No	1974	$35
	Sympathy		
❏ BL754182	Them Changes	1972	$35
❏ BL754198	There It Is!	1974	$35
CLASSIC JAZZ			
❏ 136	Jazz Giants '77	198?	$25
CLEF			
❏ MGC-727 [M]	Air Mail Special	1956	$300
❏ MGC-735 [M]	Flying Home	1956	$300
❏ MGC-738 [M]	Hamp!	1956	$300
❏ MGC-737 [M]	Hamp Roars Again	1956	$0
—Canceled			
❏ MGC-744 [M]	Hamp's Big Four	1956	$300
❏ MGC-726 [M]	King of the Vibes	1956	$300
❏ MGC-670 [M]	Lionel Hampton Big Band	1955	$250
❏ MGC-714 [M]	Lionel Hampton Plays Love	1956	$300
	Songs		
❏ MGC-736 [M]	Swingin' with Hamp	1956	$300
❏ MGC-142 [10]	The Lionel Hampton Quartet	1953	$300
❏ MGC-611 [M]	The Lionel Hampton Quartet	1954	$200
❏ MGC-673 [M]	The Lionel Hampton Quartet	1954	$200
❏ MGC-667 [M]	The Lionel Hampton Quartet	1955	$250
	and Quintet		
❏ MGC-628 [M]	The Lionel Hampton Quintet	1954	$200
❏ MGC-642 [M]	The Lionel Hampton Quintet,	1955	$250
	Volume 2		
COLUMBIA			
❏ CL1304 [M]	Golden Vibes	1959	$30
❏ CS8110 [S]	Golden Vibes	1959	$25
❏ CL1486 [M]	Silver Vibes	1960	$30
❏ CS8277 [S]	Silver Vibes	1960	$25
❏ CL1661 [M]	Soft Vibes	1961	$25
❏ CS8461 [S]	Soft Vibes	1961	$25
❏ CL711 [M]	Wailin' at the Trianon	1956	$40
CONTEMPORARY			

Number	Title	Yr	NM
❏ C-3502 [M]	Hampton in Paris	1955	$200
CORONET			
❏ CX-159 [M]	Lionel Hampton	196?	$15
❏ CXS-159 [S]	Lionel Hampton	196?	$15
DECCA			
❏ DL8088 [M]	All American Award Concert	1955	$150
	at Carnegie Hall		
—Black label, silver print			
❏ DL8088 [M]	All American Award Concert	196?	$25
	at Carnegie Hall		
—Black label with color bars			
❏ DL5230 [10]	Boogie Woogie	1950	$150
❏ DL4296 [M]	Hamp's Golden Favorites	1962	$35
❏ DL74296 [S]	Hamp's Golden Favorites	1962	$25
❏ DL7013 [10]	Just Jazz	1962	$80
❏ DL9055 [M]	Just Jazz	1958	$120
❏ DL5297 [10]	Moonglow	1951	$200
❏ DL8230 [M]	Moonglow	1956	$120
—Black label, silver print			
❏ DL8230 [M]	Moonglow	196?	$25
—Black label with color bars			
❏ DL79244 [R]	Stepping Out Volume 1	197?	$15
	1942-1945		
❏ DL4194 [M]	The Original Star Dust	1962	$35
❏ DL74194 [S]	The Original Star Dust	1962	$25
EMARCY			
❏ MG-27538 [10]	Crazy Hamp	1954	$300
❏ MG-36034 [M]	Crazy Rhythm	1955	$200
❏ MG-27537 [10]	Hamp in Paris	1954	$200
❏ MG-36032 [M]	Hamp in Paris	1955	$250
❏ MG-36035 [M]	Jam Session in Paris	1955	$250
EPIC			
❏ LN3190 [M]	Apollo Hall Concert 1954	1955	$100
❏ LA16027 [M]	Many Splendored Vibes	1962	$50
❏ BA17027 [S]	Many Splendored Vibes	1962	$60
EVEREST ARCHIVE OF FOLK & JAZZ			
❏ 348	Hamp in Paris	197?	$25
FOLKWAYS			
❏ FJ-2871	A Jazz Man for All Seasons	196?	$50
GATEWAY			
❏ 7020	Jazz Showcase	197?	$30
GENE NORMAN			
❏ GNP-15 [M]	Lionel Hampton with the	1956	$50
	Just Jazz All-Stars		
GLAD HAMP			
❏ GH-3050 [M]	All That Twistin' Jazz	1962	$30
❏ GHS-3050 [S]	All That Twistin' Jazz	1962	$30
❏ GH-1024	Ambassador at Large	198?	$25
❏ GH-1009 [M]	A Taste of Hamp	1965	$25
❏ GHS-1009 [S]	A Taste of Hamp	1965	$25
❏ GH-1004 [M]	Bossa Nova Jazz	1963	$25
❏ GHS-1004 [S]	Bossa Nova Jazz	1963	$25
❏ GH-1021	Chameleon	198?	$25
❏ GH-1007 [M]	East Meets West	1965	$150
❏ GHS-1007 [S]	East Meets West	1965	$150
❏ GH-1006 [M]	Hamp in Japan	1964	$25
❏ GHS-1006 [S]	Hamp in Japan	1964	$25
❏ GHS-1011	Hamp Stamps	1967	$35
❏ GH-1005 [M]	Lionel Hampton on Tour	1963	$25
❏ GHS-1005 [S]	Lionel Hampton on Tour	1963	$25
❏ GH-1020	Lionel Hampton's Big Band	198?	$25
	Live		
❏ GH-1023	Made in Japan	198?	$25
❏ GH-1026	One of a Kind	1988	$25
❏ GH-1022	Outrageous	198?	$25
❏ GH-1003 [M]	The Exciting Hamp in	1962	$25
	Europe		
❏ GHS-1003 [S]	The Exciting Hamp in	1962	$25
	Europe		
❏ GH-1001 [M]	The Many Sides of Lionel	1961	$25
	Hampton		
❏ GHS-1001 [S]	The Many Sides of Lionel	1961	$25
	Hampton		
GNP CRESCENDO			
❏ GNP-15 [M]	Lionel Hampton with the	196?	$25
	Just Jazz All-Stars		
❏ GNPS-15 [R]	Lionel Hampton with the	196?	$30
	Just Jazz All-Stars		
GROOVE MERCHANT			
❏ 4400	The Works!	197?	$35
HARMONY			
❏ KH32165	Good Vibes	1972	$25
❏ HL7115 [M]	Hamp in Hi-Fi	1958	$30
❏ HL7281 [M]	The One and Only Lionel	1961	$25
	Hampton		
HINDSIGHT			
❏ HSR-237	Lionel Hampton Septet 1962	1988	$25
IMPULSE!			
❏ A-78 [M]	You Better Know It	1965	$200
❏ AS-78 [S]	You Better Know It	1965	$200
JAZZ MAN			
❏ 5011	Lionel Hampton and His	198?	$25
	Giants		
JAZZTONE			

Number	Title	Yr	NM
❏ J-1246 [M]	Lionel Hampton's All Star Groups	1957	$40
❏ J-1238 [M]	The Fabulous Lionel Hampton and His All-Stars	1957	$40
❏ J-1040 [10]	Visit on a Skyscraper	195?	$50

LION

❏ L-70064 [M]	Lionel Hampton and His Orchestra	1958	$30

MCA

❏ 42329	Gene Norman Presents Just Jazz	1990	$30
❏ 204	Golden Favorites	197?	$25
❏ 1351	Rarities	198?	$25
❏ 1315	Steppin' Out	198?	$25
❏ 1331	Sweatin' with Hamp	198?	$25
❏ 4057	The Best of Lionel Hampton	197?	$30

MGM

❏ E-285 [10]	Oh, Rock	1954	$120
❏ E-3386 [M]	Oh, Rock	1956	$50

NORGRAN

❏ MGN-1080 [M]	Lionel Hampton and His Giants	1956	$200

PERFECT

❏ 12002 [M]	Lionel Hampton Swings	1959	$30
❏ 14002 [S]	Lionel Hampton Swings	1959	$40

QUINTESSENCE

❏ 25031	Flyin'	197?	$30

RCA CAMDEN

❏ CAL-402 [M]	Jivin' the Vibes	1958	$30
❏ CAL-317 [M]	Open House	1957	$30

RCA VICTOR

❏ LPT-18 [10]	A Treasury of Immortal Performances	1951	$100
❏ LJM-1000 [M]	Hot Mallets	1954	$50
❏ LPM-1422 [M]	Jazz Flamenco	1957	$50
❏ LPM-3917 [M]	Lionel Hampton Plays Bert Kaempfert	1968	$30
❏ LSP-3917 [S]	Lionel Hampton Plays Bert Kaempfert	1968	$35
❏ LPM-2318 [M]	Swing Classics	1961	$30
❏ LSP-2318 [R]	Swing Classics	196?	$35

SPIN-O-RAMA

❏ M-3077 [M]	Lionel Hampton at the Vibes	196?	$30

SWING

❏ SW-8415	Lionel Hampton in Paris	1987	$25

TIMELESS

❏ LPSJP-142	Lionel Hampton's All Star Band at Newport '78	1990	$30
❏ 303	Live in Emmen, Holland	197?	$30

TIME-LIFE

❏ STBB-24	Big Bands: Lionel Hampton	1986	$35

UPFRONT

❏ UPF-153	Jammin'	197?	$30

VERVE

❏ MGV-8106 [M]	Air Mail Special	1957	$200
❏ V-8106 [M]	Air Mail Special	1961	$60
❏ MGV-8112 [M]	Flying Home	1957	$150
❏ V-8112 [M]	Flying Home	1961	$25
❏ MGV-8226 [M]	Hallelujah Hamp	1958	$100
❏ V-8226 [M]	Hallelujah Hamp	1961	$25
❏ MGV-8114 [M]	Hamp!	1957	$150
❏ V-8114 [M]	Hamp!	1961	$25
❏ MGV-8117 [M]	Hamp's Big Four	1957	$150
❏ V-8117 [M]	Hamp's Big Four	1961	$25
❏ MGV-8105 [M]	King of the Vibes	1957	$150
❏ V-8105 [M]	King of the Vibes	1961	$25
❏ MGV-8275 [M]	Lionel Hampton	1958	$0
—Canceled			
❏ MGV-8223 [M]	Lionel Hampton '58	1958	$120
❏ V-8223 [M]	Lionel Hampton '58	1961	$25
❏ MGV-8170 [M]	Lionel Hampton and His Giants	1957	$150
❏ V-8170 [M]	Lionel Hampton and His Giants	1961	$25
❏ MGV-2018 [M]	Lionel Hampton Plays Love Songs	1957	$150
❏ V-2018 [M]	Lionel Hampton Plays Love Songs	1961	$25
❏ MGV-8113 [M]	Swingin' with Hamp	1957	$150
❏ V-8113 [M]	Swingin' with Hamp	1961	$25
❏ VE-2-2543	The Blues Ain't News to Me	1982	$35
❏ MGV-8215 [M]	The Genius of Lionel Hampton	1958	$100
❏ V-8215 [M]	The Genius of Lionel Hampton	1961	$25
❏ MGV-8228 [M]	The High and the Mighty	1958	$150
❏ V-8228 [M]	The High and the Mighty	1961	$25
❏ MGV-8019 [M]	Travelin' Band	1957	$100
❏ V-8019 [M]	Travelin' Band	1961	$25

WHO'S WHO IN JAZZ

❏ 21017	Blackout	1978	$30
❏ 21008	Who's Who Presents Lionel Hampton	1977	$30

HAMPTON, SLIDE

Trombonist, thus the nickname "Slide." Also has played tuba. Also see HAROLD BETTERS.

Albums

ATLANTIC

Number	Title	Yr	NM
❏ 1396 [M]	Explosion!	1962	$150
❏ SD1396 [S]	Explosion!	1962	$150
❏ SD1379 [S]	Jazz with a Twist	1962	$150
❏ 1339 [M]	Sister Salvation	1960	$250
—Multicolor label, white "fan" logo at right			
❏ 1339 [M]	Sister Salvation	1962	$150
—Multicolor label, black "fan" logo at right			
❏ SD1339 [S]	Sister Salvation	1960	$250
—Multicolor label, white "fan" logo at right			
❏ SD1339 [S]	Sister Salvation	1962	$150
—Multicolor label, black "fan" logo at right			
❏ 1362 [M]	Somethin' Sanctified	1961	$150
—Multicolor label, white "fan" logo at right			
❏ 1362 [M]	Somethin' Sanctified	1962	$150
—Multicolor label, black "fan" logo at right			
❏ SD1362 [S]	Somethin' Sanctified	1961	$150
—Multicolor label, white "fan" logo at right			
❏ SD1362 [S]	Somethin' Sanctified	1962	$150
—Multicolor label, black "fan" logo at right			

CHARLIE PARKER

❏ PLP-803 [M]	Two Sides of Slide	1962	$30
❏ PLP-803S [S]	Two Sides of Slide	1962	$30

EPIC

❏ LA16030 [M]	Drum Suite	1963	$40
❏ BA17030 [S]	Drum Suite	1963	$60

STRAND

❏ SL-1006 [M]	Slide Hampton and His Horn of Plenty	1959	$40
❏ SLS-1006 [S]	Slide Hampton and His Horn of Plenty	1959	$40

HANCOCK, HERBIE, AND CHICK COREA

Also see each artist's individual listings.

Albums

COLUMBIA

❏ PC235663	An Evening with Herbie Hancock and Chick Corea	1979	$30

POLYDOR

❏ PD-2-6238	An Evening with Chick Corea and Herbie Hancock	1979	$35

HANCOCK, HERBIE

Pianist, keyboard player and composer. Also see HEADHUNTERS.

Albums

BLUE NOTE

❏ BST-84175 [S]	Empyrean Isles	1967	$35
—With "A Division of Liberty Records" on label			
❏ BST-84175	Empyrean Isles	1985	$25
—The Finest in Jazz Since 1939" reissue			
❏ BN-LA399-H2[(2)]	Herbie Hancock	1975	$35
❏ BST-84147 [S]	Inventions and Dimensions	1967	$35
—With "A Division of Liberty Records" on label			
❏ BST-84147	Inventions and Dimensions	1987	$25
—The Finest in Jazz Since 1939" reissue			
❏ BLP-4195 [M]	Maiden Voyage	1965	$150
❏ BST-84195 [S]	Maiden Voyage	1967	$35
—With "A Division of Liberty Records" on label			
❏ BST-84195 [S]	Maiden Voyage	197?	$30
—A Division of United Artists" on label			
❏ B1-46339	Maiden Voyage	1997	$50
—Audiophile reissue			
❏ BST-84195 [S]	Maiden Voyage	1985	$25
—The Finest in Jazz Since 1939" reissue			
❏ BST-84126 [S]	My Point of View	1967	$35
—With "A Division of Liberty Records" on label			
❏ BST-84126	My Point of View	1987	$25
—The Finest in Jazz Since 1939" reissue			
❏ BST-84279	Speak Like a Child	1968	$35
❏ BST-84279	Speak Like a Child	1986	$25
—The Finest in Jazz Since 1939" reissue			
❏ BN-LA152-F	Succotash	1974	$30
❏ BLP-4109 [M]	Takin' Off	1962	$200
❏ BST-84109 [S]	Takin' Off	1967	$35
—With "A Division of Liberty Records" on label			
❏ BST-84109	Takin' Off	1987	$25
—The Finest in Jazz Since 1939" reissue			

Number	Title	Yr	NM
❏ BST-84407	The Best of Herbie Hancock	1971	$35
❏ B1-91142	The Best of Herbie Hancock	1988	$25
❏ BST-84321	The Prisoner	1969	$35
❏ BST-84321	The Prisoner	1987	$25
—The Finest in Jazz Since 1939" reissue			

COLUMBIA

❏ JC35764	Feets Don't Fail Me Now	1979	$30
❏ PC35764	Feets Don't Fail Me Now	198?	$20
—Budget-line reissue			
❏ FC38814	Future Shock	1983	$25
❏ 8C839913 [EP]	Hardrock	1984	$30
—Picture disc			
❏ KC32371	Head Hunters	1973	$30
❏ CQ32371 [Q]	Head Hunters	1973	$40
❏ PC32371	Head Hunters	197?	$20
—Reissue (with or without bar code)			
❏ FC37928	Lite Me Up	1982	$25
❏ PC37928	Lite Me Up	198?	$20
—Budget-line reissue			
❏ FC37387	Magic Windows	1981	$25
❏ PC37387	Magic Windows	198?	$20
—Budget-line reissue			
❏ PC33812	Man-Child	1975	$30
—No bar code on cover			
❏ PC33812	Man-Child	198?	$20
—Budget-line reissue with bar code			
❏ JC36415	Monster	1980	$25
❏ PC36415	Monster	198?	$20
—Budget-line reissue			
❏ JC36578	Mr. Hands	1980	$25
❏ PC36578	Mr. Hands	198?	$20
—Budget-line reissue			
❏ FC40025	Perfect Machine	1988	$25
❏ SC40464	'Round Midnight	1986	$25
❏ PC34280	Secrets	1976	$30
—No bar code on cover			
❏ PCQ34280 [Q]	Secrets	1976	$40
❏ PC34280	Secrets	198?	$20
—Budget-line reissue with bar code			
❏ KC32212	Sextant	1973	$30
❏ PC32212	Sextant	198?	$20
—Budget-line reissue			
❏ PCQ32212 [Q]	Sextant	197?	$60
❏ FC39478	Sound-System	1984	$25
❏ PC39478	Sound-System	1985	$20
—Budget-line reissue			
❏ JC34907	Sunlight	1978	$30
❏ JC36309	The Best of Herbie Hancock	1979	$30
❏ PC32965	Thrust	1974	$30
—No bar code on cover			
❏ PCQ32965 [Q]	Thrust	1974	$40
❏ PC32965	Thrust	198?	$20
—Budget-line reissue with bar code			
❏ FC39870	Village Life	1985	$25
❏ PG34688	V.S.O.P.	1977	$35
❏ C234976	V.S.O.P. Quintet	1978	$35

MGM

❏ E-4447 [M]	Blow-Up	1967	$40
❏ SE-4447 [S]	Blow-Up	1967	$100
—Also includes one track by the Yardbirds			

PAUSA

❏ 9002	Succotash	198?	$25

TRIP

❏ UPF-194	Traces	197?	$30

WARNER BROS.

❏ BS2617	Crossings	1972	$35
❏ WS1834	Fat Albert Rotunda	1970	$35
❏ WS1898	Mwandishi	1971	$35
❏ 2WS2807	Treasure Chest	1974	$35

HANDY, CAP'N JOHN

Alto saxophone player. Not the same person as the JOHN HANDY below.

Albums

GHB

❏ GHBS-41	All Aboard, Volume 1	1967	$50
❏ GHBS-42	All Aboard, Volume 2	1967	$50
❏ GHBS-43	All Aboard, Volume 3	1967	$50
❏ GHB-166	Cap'n John Handy with Geoff Bull and Bary Martyn's Band	1986	$25
❏ GHB-38	Everybody's Talking	1967	$50

RCA VICTOR

❏ LPM-3762 [M]	Introducing Cap'n John Handy	1967	$30
❏ LSP-3762 [S]	Introducing Cap'n John Handy	1967	$35
❏ LSP-3929	New Orleans and the Blues	1968	$50

Number	Title	Yr	NM

HANDY, GEORGE
Pianist.
Albums
X
| LXA-1032 [M] | By George! Handy, Of Course | 1954 | $80 |
| LXA-1004 [M] | Handyland, U.S.A. | 1954 | $100 |

HANDY, JOHN
Saxophone (soprano, alto, tenor, baritone) player and bandleader. Best known in pop and R&B circles for his 1976 hit single "Hard Work," he is not the same person as the CAP'N JOHN HANDY above.
Albums
ABC IMPULSE!
| AS-9324 | Carnival | 1977 | $25 |
| ASD-9314 | Hard Work | 1976 | $35 |
COLUMBIA
CL2697 [M]	New View	1967	$60
CS9497 [S]	New View	1967	$60
CS9689	Projections	1968	$60
CL2462 [M]	Recorded Live at the Monterey Jazz Festival	1966	$35
CS9262 [S]	Recorded Live at the Monterey Jazz Festival	1966	$50
CL2567 [M]	The Second John Handy Album	1966	$50
CS9367 [S]	The Second John Handy Album	1966	$60
MILESTONE
M-9173	Centerpiece: John Handy with Class	1989	$30
QUARTET
Q-1005	Excursion in Blue	1988	$60
ROULETTE
RE-132	In the Vernacular	197?	$50
—Compilation of earlier material
R52042 [M]	In the Ver-nac'-u-lar	1960	$50
SR52042 [S]	In the Ver-nac'-u-lar	1960	$50
R52121 [M]	John Handy Jazz	1964	$50
SR52121 [S]	John Handy Jazz	1964	$60
R52088 [M]	No Coast Jazz	1962	$50
SR52088 [S]	No Coast Jazz	1962	$60
R52124 [M]	Quote, Unquote	1964	$50
SR52124 [S]	Quote, Unquote	1964	$60
WARNER BROS.
BSK3242	Handy Dandy Man	1978	$30
BSK3170	Where Go the Boats	1978	$30

HANDY, W.C.
Cornet player and bandleader, but far more influential as a composer ("St. Louis Blues" is a jazz standard, and "Beale Street Blues" and "Memphis Blues" helped spread the music).
Albums
DRG
| SL-5192 | Father of the Blues | 1980 | $25 |
HERITAGE
| 0052 [10] | Blues Revisited | 195? | $120 |

HANNA, JAKE
Drummer.
Albums
CONCORD JAZZ
CJ-11	Jake Hanna and Carl Fontana Live	1975	$30
CJ-35	Jake Hanna Takes Manhattan	1977	$30
CJ-22	Kansas City Express	1976	$30

HANNA, KEN
Trumpeter, composer, arranger and conductor.
Albums
CAPITOL
| T6512 [M] | Jazz for Dancers | 1955 | $75 |

HANNA, ROLAND, AND GEORGE MRAZ
Also see each artist's individual listings.
Albums
CHOICE
| 1018 | Sir Elf Plus One | 1978 | $35 |

HANNA, ROLAND
Pianist.
Albums
ARISTA FREEDOM
| AL1010 | Perugia | 1975 | $30 |
ATCO
33-108 [M]	Destry Rides Again	1959	$40
SD 33-108 [S]	Destry Rides Again	1959	$40
33-121 [M]	Easy to Love	1960	$30
SD 33-121 [S]	Easy to Love	1960	$40
AUDIOPHILE
AP-157	This Must Be Love	198?	$25
BASF
20875	Child of Gemini	1972	$30
BEE HIVE
BH-7013	Roland Hanna and the New York Jazz Quartet in Chicago	198?	$25
CHOICE
1003	Sir Elf	1974	$35
INNER CITY
IC-1072	Roland Hanna Plays Music of Alec Wilder	197?	$30
PROGRESSIVE
7012	Time for the Dancers	1978	$30
STORYVILLE
4018	Swing Me No Waltzes	198?	$25
WEST 54TH
8003	A Gift from the Magi	1979	$30

HANNIBAL
Full name: Hannibal Marvin Peterson. Trumpeter and percussionist.
Albums
ATLANTIC
| 81973 | Visions of a New World | 1989 | $30 |

HANRAHAN, KIP
Percussionist, composer and arranger.
Albums
AMERICAN CLAVE
1011 [EP]	A Few Short Notes at the End of the Run	1987	$30
1007	Coup De Tete	198?	$30
1008/9	Desire Develops an Edge	1984	$35
1010	Vertical's Currency	1985	$30
PANGAEA
42137	Days & Nights of Blue Luck Inverted	1988	$12

HANSON, OLA
See CHUZ ALFRED.

HAPPY JAZZ BAND, THE
Members: Cliff Brewton, piano; Benny Valfre, banjo; Harvey Kindervater, drums; Willson Davis, sousaphone; Gene McKinney, trombone; Jim Cullum Jr.., cornet; Jim Cullum Sr., clarinet.
Albums
AUDIOPHILE
AP-114	College Street Caper	196?	$30
AP-96 [M]	Goose Pimples	196?	$30
APS-96 [S]	Goose Pimples	196?	$35
AP-200	High Society	196?	$30
AP-86 [M]	Jazz from the San Antonio River	196?	$30
APS-86 [S]	Jazz from the San Antonio River	196?	$35
AP-93 [M]	Jim Cullum's Happy Jazz Band	196?	$30
APS-93 [S]	Jim Cullum's Happy Jazz Band	196?	$35
AP-87 [M]	Real Stuff	196?	$30
APS-87 [S]	Real Stuff	196?	$35
HAPPY JAZZ
HJ-202	We've Had Mighty Good Weather	1970	$30
HJ-201	Zacatecas	1969	$30
—Cliff Brewton, piano; Benny Valfre,banjo; Harvey Kindervater,drums; Willson Davis, sousaphone; Gene McKinney, trombone; Jim Cullum Jr.,cornet; Jim Cullum Sr., clarinet.

HAQUE, FAREED
Guitarist.
Albums
PANGAEA
| 82012 | Manresa | 1989 | $30 |
| 42156 | Voices Rising | 1988 | $25 |

HARDAWAY, BOB
Tenor saxophone player. Also see EDDIE SHU.

HARDEN, WILBUR
Fluegel horn player and trumpeter.
Albums
SAVOY
MG-12131 [M]	Jazz Way Out	1958	$50
SST-13004 [S]	Jazz Way Out	1959	$40
MG-12127 [M]	Mainstream 1958/The East Coast Jazz Scene Featuring John Coltrane	1958	$60
MG-12136 [M]	Tanganyika Suite	1958	$50
SST-13005 [S]	Tanganyika Suite	1959	$40
MG-12134 [M]	The King and I	1958	$50
SST-13002 [S]	The King and I	1959	$40

HARDIMAN, DAVID
Trumpeter and bandleader.
Albums
THERESA
| 104 | It'll Be Alright | 197? | $25 |

HARDING, ELLERINE
Female singer.
Albums
MAINSTREAM
| MRL-377 | Ellerine Harding | 1972 | $25 |

HARDMAN, BILL
Trumpeter. Also see JACKIE McLEAN.
Albums
MUSE
MR-5259	Focus	198?	$25
MR-5152	Home	1978	$30
MR-5184	Politely	1981	$30
SAVOY JAZZ
SJL-1164	Saying Something	1986	$25

HARDY, HAGOOD
Vibraphone player and composer.
Albums
CAPITOL
ST-11552	Maybe Tomorrow	1976	$25
ST-11488	The Homecoming	1975	$25
SN-16300	The Homecoming	198?	$20
—Budget-line reissue

HARGROVE, ROY
Trumpeter.
Albums
NOVUS
| 3082-1-N | Diamond in the Rough | 1990 | $30 |

HARIAN, KENT
Bandleader.
Albums
CARAVAN
| LP-15611 [M] | Echoes of Joy | 1956 | $250 |

HARLEY, RUFUS
Perhaps the world's only jazz bagpipes player.
Albums
ATLANTIC
SD3001 [S]	Bagpipe Blues	1967	$35
3001 [M]	Bagpipe Blues	1967	$25
SD1539	King/Queens	1970	$35
SD3006	Scotch & Soul	1968	$35
SD1504	Tribute to Courage	1969	$35

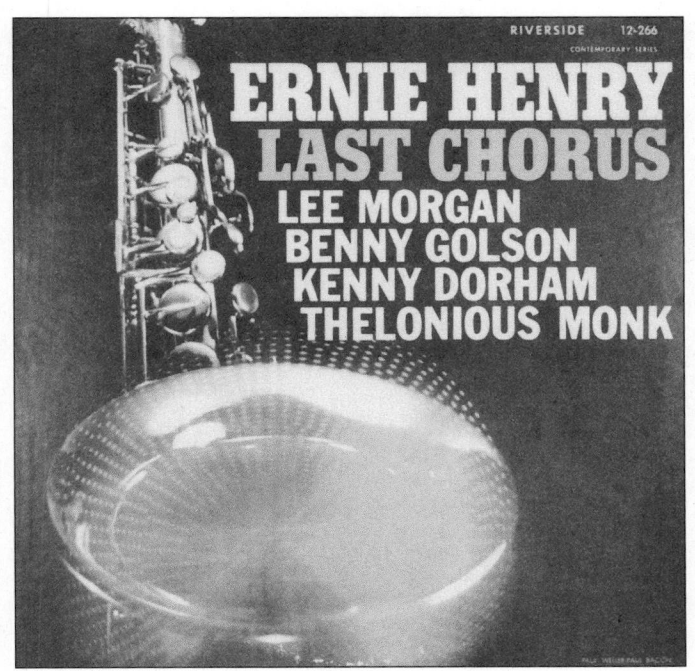

Ernie Henry, *Last Chorus*, Riverside RLP 12-266, **$300**.

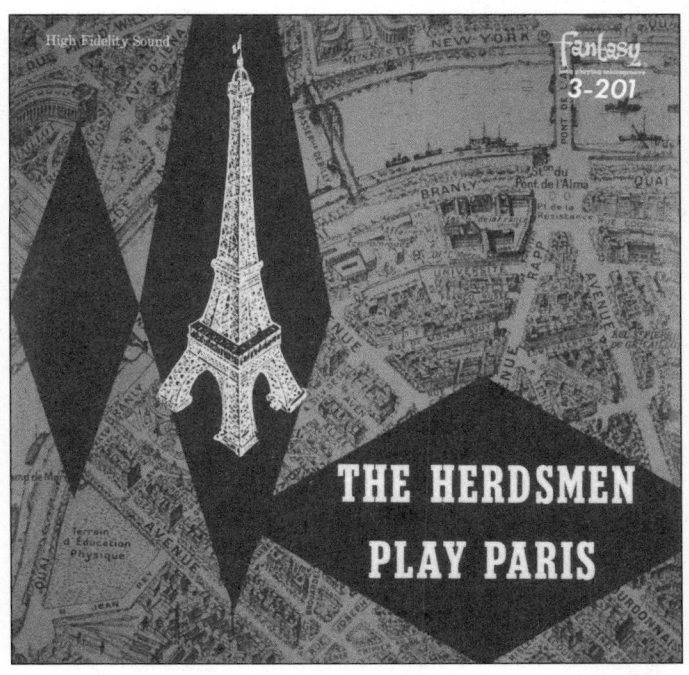

The Herdsmen, *The Herdsmen Play Paris*, Fantasy 3-201, green vinyl, **$80**.

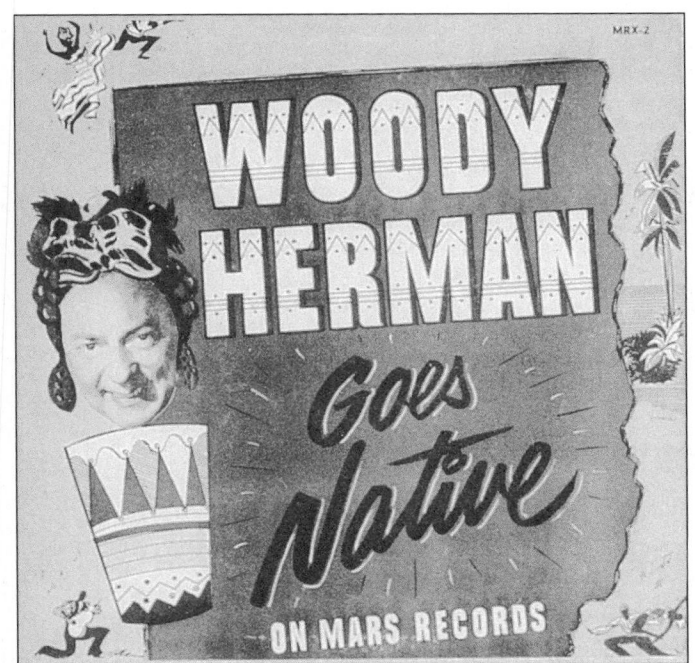

Woody Herman, *Woody Herman Goes Native*, Mars MRX-2, 10-inch LP, **$250**.

Milt Hinton, Wendell Marshall, Bull Ruther, *Basses Loaded!*, RCA Victor LPM-1107, **$80**.

Number	Title	Yr	NM

HARNELL, JOE
Pianist, most of whose recordings are more in a pop vein.

Albums

JUBILEE
❏ JGM-5020 [M]	Joe Harnell and His Trio	1963	$35

—Reissue of 1015

❏ JLP-1015 [M]	Piano Inventions of Jo Harnell	1956	$100

HARPER, BILLY
Tenor saxophone player.

Albums

BLACK SAINT
❏ BSR-0001	Black Saint	198?	$18

SOUL NOTE
❏ SN-1001	Billy Harper In Europe	198?	$18

STRATA-EAST
❏ SES-19739	Capra Black	1973	$40

HARPER, HERBIE
Trombonist.

Albums

LIBERTY
❏ LRP-6003 [M]	Herbie Harper	1956	$80

NOCTURNE
❏ NLP-7 [10]	Herbie Harper	1954	$150
❏ NLP-1 [10]	Herbie Harper Quintet	1954	$150

SEABREEZE
❏ SBD-101	Herbie Harper Revisited	1981	$30

TAMPA
❏ TP-11 [M]	Herbie Harper Quintet	1957	$200

—Red vinyl

❏ TP-11 [M]	Herbie Harper Quintet	1958	$150

—Black vinyl

HARPER, TONI
Female singer.

Albums

RCA VICTOR
❏ LPM-2092 [M]	Lady Lonely	1960	$30
❏ LSP-2092 [S]	Lady Lonely	1960	$40
❏ LPM-2253 [M]	Night Mood	1960	$30
❏ LSP-2253 [S]	Night Mood	1960	$40

VERVE
❏ MGV-2001 [M]	Toni Harper Sings	1956	$200
❏ V-2001 [M]	Toni Harper Sings	1961	$50

HARPER, WALT
Pianist.

Albums

GATEWAY
❏ 7005 [M]	Harper's Ferry	1964	$35
❏ 7016 [M]	On the Road	1966	$25
❏ S-7016 [S]	On the Road	1966	$35

HARPER BROTHERS, THE
Led by Winard Harper (drums) and Phillip Harper (trumpet).

Albums

VERVE
❏ 837033-1	The Harper Brothers	1988	$25

HARRELL, TOM
Trumpeter, fluegel horn player and composer.

Albums

BLACKHAWK
❏ BKH-50901	The Play of Light	1986	$25

CONTEMPORARY
❏ C-14059	Form	1990	$30
❏ C-14054	Sail Away	1989	$30
❏ C-14043	Stories	1988	$25

HARRIOTT, JOE
Alto saxophone player, also played baritone and tenor saxes.

Albums

ATLANTIC
❏ 1482 [M]	Indo-Jazz Fusions	1967	$35
❏ SD1482 [S]	Indo-Jazz Fusions	1967	$30
❏ 1465 [M]	Indo-Jazz Suite	1966	$30
❏ SD1465 [S]	Indo-Jazz Suite	1966	$35

CAPITOL

Number	Title	Yr	NM
❏ T10351 [M]	Abstract	1962	$50
❏ DT10351 [R]	Abstract	1962	$50

JAZZLAND
❏ JLP-49 [M]	Free Form	1961	$30
❏ JLP-949 [S]	Free Form	1961	$30
❏ JLP-37 [M]	Southern Horizons	1961	$30
❏ JLP-937 [S]	Southern Horizons	1961	$30

HARRIS, ART, AND MITCH LEIGH
Leigh is a bassoonist and composer (co-writer of "The Impossible Dream"). Also see ART HARRIS.

Albums

EPIC
❏ LG1010 [10]	Modern Woodwind Expressions	1954	$100
❏ LN3200 [M]	New Jazz in Hi-Fi	1956	$80

KAPP
❏ KL-1011 [M]	Baroque Band and Brass Choir -- Jazz 1775	1956	$40

HARRIS, ART
Pianist and composer.

Albums

KAPP
❏ KL-1015 [M]	Jazz Goes to Post-Graduate School	1956	$40

HARRIS, BARRY
Pianist.

Albums

ARGO
❏ LP-644 [M]	Breakin' It Up	1959	$40
❏ LPS-644 [S]	Breakin' It Up	1959	$30

CADET
❏ LP-644 [M]	Breakin' It Up	1966	$25
❏ LPS-644 [S]	Breakin' It Up	1966	$35

FANTASY
❏ OJC-208	Barry Harris at the Jazz Workshop	1986	$25
❏ OJC-486	Preminado	1991	$30

MILESTONE
❏ 47050	Stay Right With It	197?	$35

PRESTIGE
❏ PRST-7600	Bull's Eye	1969	$25
❏ PRLP-7498 [M]	Luminescence	1967	$30
❏ PRST-7498 [S]	Luminescence	1967	$25
❏ PRST-7733	Magnificent!	1970	$25

RIVERSIDE
❏ 6123	Barry Harris at the Jazz Workshop	197?	$30
❏ RLP-435 [M]	Chasin' the Bird	1962	$200
❏ RS-9435 [S]	Chasin' the Bird	1962	$200
❏ RLP-392 [M]	Listen to Barry Harris	1961	$200
❏ RS-9392 [S]	Listen to Barry Harris	1961	$200
❏ RLP-413 [M]	Newer Than New	1962	$150
❏ RS-9413 [S]	Newer Than New	1962	$150
❏ RS-9354 [S]	Preminado	1961	$200
❏ 6047	Preminado	197?	$30

XANADU
❏ 154	Barry Harris Plays Barry Harris	1978	$30
❏ 113	Barry Harris Plays Tadd Dameron	1975	$30
❏ 130	Live in Tokyo	1976	$30
❏ 213	The Bird of Red and Gold	1990	$35
❏ 177	Tokyo: 1976	1980	$30

HARRIS, BEAVER, AND DON PULLEN
Also see each artist's individual listings.

Albums

HANNIBAL
❏ HNBL-2701	A Well Kept Secret	198?	$25

HARRIS, BEAVER
Drummer.

Albums

BLACK SAINT
❏ BSR-0006/7	In-Sanity	198?	$50

CADENCE JAZZ
❏ 1002	Live at Nyon	198?	$30
❏ 1003	Negcaumongus	198?	$25

RED
❏ VPA-146	360 Degree Aeutopia	198?	$30
❏ VPA-151	Safe	198?	$30

SOUL NOTE
❏ SN-1002	Beautiful Africa	198?	$35

Number	Title	Yr	NM

HARRIS, BILL (1), AND CHARLIE VENTURA
Also see each artist's individual listings.

Albums

PHOENIX
❏ 14	Aces	197?	$25
❏ 11	Live at the Three Deuces	197?	$25

HARRIS, BILL (1)
This Bill Harris is a trombonist. Also see TERRY GIBBS; CHUBBY JACKSON.

Albums

CLEF
❏ MGC-125 [10]	Bill Harris Collates	1953	$300

FANTASY
❏ 3263 [M]	Bill Harris and Friends	1958	$40

—Red vinyl

❏ 3263 [M]	Bill Harris and Friends	1959	$30

—Black vinyl

❏ OJC-083	Bill Harris and Friends	198?	$25

MERCURY
❏ MGC-125 [10]	Bill Harris Collates	1953	$0

—Canceled

NORGRAN
❏ MGN-1062 [M]	The Bill Harris Herd	1956	$200

VERVE
❏ MGV-8152 [M]	The Bill Harris Herd	1957	$150

XANADU
❏ 191	Memorial Album	198?	$30

HARRIS, BILL (2)
This Bill Harris is a guitarist.

Albums

EMARCY
❏ MG-36097 [M]	Bill Harris	1956	$200
❏ MG-36113 [M]	The Harris Touch	1957	$200

MERCURY
❏ MG-20552 [M]	The Harris Touch	1960	$100
❏ SR-60552 [S]	The Harris Touch	1960	$100

WING
❏ MGW-12220 [M]	Great Guitar Sounds	1963	$25
❏ SRW-16220 [S]	Great Guitar Sounds	1963	$35

HARRIS, CRAIG
Trombonist.

Albums

INDIA NAVIGATION
❏ IN-1060	Aboriginal Affairs	198?	$30

JMT
❏ 834415-1	Blackout in the Square Root of Soul	1988	$30
❏ 834408-1	Shelter	1987	$30

SOUL NOTE
❏ SN-1055	Black Bone	198?	$30

HARRIS, DON "SUGARCANE"
Violinist, male singer and composer who also worked in R&B (The Squires, Don & Dewey) and rock (Frank Zappa, Pure Food & Drug Act).

Albums

BASF
❏ 21792	Cup Full of Dreams	1973	$35
❏ 20878	Fiddler on the Rock	1972	$35
❏ 21912	I'm On Your Case	1974	$35
❏ 21293	Sugarcane's Got the Blues	1972	$35

EPIC
❏ E30027	Sugarcane	1971	$75

HARRIS, EDDIE
Tenor saxophone player and composer.

Albums

ANGELACO
❏ AN3002	Sounds Incredible	1980	$30

ATLANTIC
❏ SD1675	Bad Luck Is All I Have	1975	$30
❏ SD1554	Come On Down!	1970	$35
❏ SD1595	Eddie Harris Live at Newport	1971	$30
❏ SD1625	Eddie Harris Sings the Blues	1973	$30
❏ SD1647	E.H. in the U.K.	1974	$30
❏ SD 2-311	Excursions	1973	$35
❏ SD1573	Free Speech	1971	$35
❏ SD1529	High Voltage	1969	$35

Number	Title	Yr	NM
❏ SD1698	How Can You Live Like That	1977	$30
❏ SD1669	I Need Some Money	1975	$30
❏ SD1611	Instant Death	1972	$30
❏ SW-94771	Instant Death	1972	$35

— Capitol Record Club edition

❏ SD1659	Is It In	1974	$30
❏ 1453 [M]	Mean Greens	1966	$30
❏ SD1453 [S]	Mean Greens	1966	$35
❏ SD1506	Plug Me In	1968	$35
❏ SD1517	Silver Cycles	1969	$35
❏ SD1545	The Best of Eddie Harris	1970	$35
❏ 1545 [M]	The Best of Eddie Harris	1970	$60

— Promo-only white label mono pressing

❏ SD1495	The Electrifying Eddie Harris	1968	$35
❏ 1448 [M]	The In Sound	1966	$30
❏ SD1448 [S]	The In Sound	1966	$35
❏ 1478 [M]	The Tender Storm	1967	$35
❏ SD1478 [S]	The Tender Storm	1967	$35
❏ SD8807	The Versatile Eddie Harris	1982	$25
❏ SD1683	Why You're Overweight	1976	$30

BUDDAH

| ❏ BDS4004 | Sculpture | 1969 | $30 |

COLUMBIA

❏ CL2168 [M]	Cool Sax, Warm Heart	1964	$35
❏ CS8968 [S]	Cool Sax, Warm Heart	1964	$50
❏ CL2295 [M]	Cool Sax from Hollywood to Broadway	1965	$35
❏ CS9095 [S]	Cool Sax from Hollywood to Broadway	1965	$50
❏ CS9681 [S]	Here Comes the Judge	1968	$35
❏ CS9681 [M]	Here Comes the Judge	1968	$60

— Mono copies are promo only

EXODUS

| ❏ EX-6002 [M] | For Bird and Bags | 1966 | $35 |

GNP CRESCENDO

| ❏ GNPS-2073 | Black Sax | 1973 | $35 |

JANUS

| ❏ 3020 | Smokin' | 1970 | $30 |

MUTT & JEFF

| ❏ 5018 | The Real Electrifying Eddie Harris | 1982 | $30 |

RCA VICTOR

| ❏ APL1-2942 | I'm Tired | 1978 | $25 |
| ❏ AFL1-3402 | Playin' With Myself | 1980 | $25 |

STEEPLECHASE

| ❏ 1151 | Eddie Harris Steps Up | 1981 | $25 |

SUNSET

| ❏ SUS-5234 | The Explosive Eddie Harris | 1969 | $30 |

TRADITION

| ❏ 2067 | Genius | 1969 | $30 |

TRIP

| ❏ 5005 | Shades of Eddie Harris | 1974 | $30 |

UPFRONT

| ❏ UPF-106 | The Soul of Eddie Harris | 197? | $25 |

VEE JAY

❏ LP3028 [M]	A Study in Jazz	1962	$50
❏ SR3028 [S]	A Study in Jazz	1962	$60
❏ LP3034 [M]	Bossa Nova	1963	$50
❏ LP3031 [M]	Eddie Harris Goes to the Movies	1962	$50
❏ SR3031 [S]	Eddie Harris Goes to the Movies	1962	$60
❏ LP3016 [M]	Exodus to Jazz	1961	$60
❏ SR3016 [S]	Exodus to Jazz	1961	$40
❏ VJS-3016	Exodus to Jazz	198?	$25

— Reissue with thinner vinyl

❏ VJS-3058	For Bird and Bags	198?	$25
❏ LP3037 [M]	Half and Half	1963	$60
❏ SR3037 [S]	Half and Half	1963	$60
❏ LP3027 [M]	Jazz for "Breakfast at Tiffany's	1961	$60
❏ SR3027 [S]	Jazz for "Breakfast at Tiffany's	1961	$40
❏ LP3025 [M]	Mighty Like a Rose	1961	$60
❏ SR3025 [S]	Mighty Like a Rose	1961	$40
❏ VJLP1081 [M]	The Theme from Exodus and Other Film Spectaculars	1964	$35
❏ VJLPS1081 [S]	The Theme from Exodus and Other Film Spectaculars	1964	$50

HARRIS, GENE

Pianist. Also see THE THREE SOUNDS.

Albums

BLUE NOTE

❏ BN-LA313-G	Astral Signal	1974	$25
❏ BST-84423	Gene Harris of the Three Sounds	1972	$25
❏ BN-LA519-G	Nexus	1975	$35
❏ BN-LA634-G	Special Way	1976	$35
❏ BST-84378	The Three Sounds	1971	$25
❏ BN-LA760-H	Tone Tantrum	1977	$35
❏ BN-LA141-G [(2)]	Yesterday, Today and Tomorrow	1973	$60

Number	Title	Yr	NM

CONCORD JAZZ

| ❏ CJ-303 | The Gene Harris Trio Plus One | 1986 | $25 |

JAM

| ❏ 08 | Hot Lips | 198? | $30 |

JUBILEE

| ❏ JGM-1115 [M] | Genie in My Soul | 1959 | $40 |
| ❏ JLP-1005 [M] | Our Love Is Here to Stay | 1955 | $60 |

HARRIS, HAROLD

Pianist.

Albums

VEE JAY

❏ LP-3036 [M]	Harold Harris at the Playboy Club	1963	$30
❏ SR-3036 [S]	Harold Harris at the Playboy Club	1963	$30
❏ LP-3018 [M]	Here's Harold	1962	$30
❏ SR-3018 [S]	Here's Harold	1962	$30

HARRISON, CASS

Albums

MGM

| ❏ E-3388 [M] | The Duke and I | 1956 | $40 |
| ❏ E-3495 [M] | Wrappin' It Up | 1957 | $40 |

HARRISON, WENDELL

Clarinetist and tenor saxophone player.

Albums

REBIRTH

❏ WHR-140	Birth of a Fossil	1986	$25
❏ WHR-160	Carnivorous Lady	1988	$30
❏ WHR-015	Dreams of a Love Supreme	1985	$25
❏ WHR-016	Organic Dream	1985	$25
❏ WHR-040	Reawakening	1985	$25
❏ WHR-150	Wait" Broke the Wagon Down	1987	$25

TRIBE

| ❏ PRSD-2212 | Evening with the Devil | 197? | $100 |
| ❏ PRSD-4002 | Message from the Tribe, Vol. 3 | 197? | $100 |

WENHA

| ❏ 015 | Dreams of a Love Supreme | 198? | $50 |
| ❏ 2212 | Evening with the Devil | 198? | $25 |

— Reissue of Tribe 2212

| ❏ 4002 | Message from the Tribe | 198? | $25 |

— Reissue of Tribe 4002

| ❏ 016 | Organic Dream | 198? | $40 |

HARROW, NANCY

Female singer.

Albums

ATLANTIC

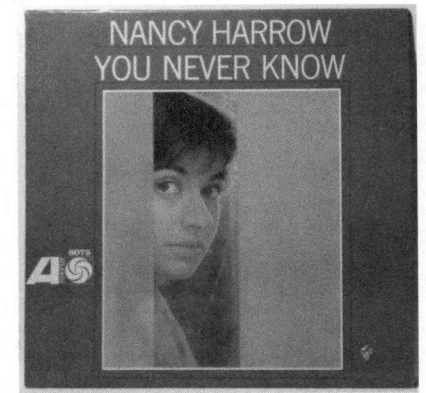

| ❏ 8075 [M] | You Never Know | 1963 | $60 |
| ❏ SD8075 [S] | You Never Know | 1963 | $60 |

AUDIOPHILE

| ❏ AP-142 | Anything Goes | 1979 | $30 |

CANDID

| ❏ CD-8008 [M] | Wild Women Don't Have the Blues | 1962 | $60 |
| ❏ CD-9008 [S] | Wild Women Don't Have the Blues | 1962 | $40 |

HART, BILLY

Drummer.

Albums

GRAMAVISION

| ❏ 18-8502 | Oshumare | 1986 | $30 |

HORIZON

| ❏ SP-725 | Enchance | 1978 | $30 |

HART, JOHN

Guitarist.

Albums

BLUE NOTE

| ❏ B1-93476 | One Down | 1990 | $35 |

HARTH, ALFRED

Multi-instrumentalist (tenor sax; alto sax; baritone sax; trumpet; trombone; clarinet; bass clarinet; cello; male singer).

Albums

ECM

| ❏ 1264 | This Earth | 198? | $25 |

HARTMAN, GEORGE

See IRVING FAZOLA.

HARTMAN, JOHNNY

Male singer.

Albums

ABC IMPULSE!

| ❏ AS-57 [S] | I Just Dropped By to Say Hello | 1968 | $30 |

Number	Title	Yr	NM

THE VOICE THAT IS! JOHNNY HARTMAN

Number	Title	Yr	NM
❏ AS-74 [S]	The Voice That Is	1968	$30

ABC-PARAMOUNT

❏ ABC-574 [M]	The Unforgettable Johnny Hartman	1966	$30
❏ ABCS-574 [S]	The Unforgettable Johnny Hartman	1966	$40

AUDIOPHILE

❏ AP-181	This One's for Tedi	1981	$30

BEE HIVE

❏ BH-7012	Once in Every Life	198?	$25

BETHLEHEM

❏ BCP-6045	All of Me	197?	$30

—Reissue, distributed by RCA Victor

❏ BCP-6014 [M]	All of Me: The Debonair Mr. Hartman	1957	$250
❏ BCP-43 [M]	Songs from the Heart	1956	$250

IMPULSE!

❏ A-57 [M]	I Just Dropped By to Say Hello	1964	$200
❏ AS-57 [S]	I Just Dropped By to Say Hello	1964	$200
❏ A-74 [M]	The Voice That Is	1965	$200
❏ AS-74 [S]	The Voice That Is	1965	$200

MCA

❏ 29039	I Just Dropped By to Say Hello	1980	$25
❏ 29040	The Voice That Is	1980	$25

MUSICOR

❏ 2502	Johnny Hartman, Johnny Hartman	1976	$30

PERCEPTION

❏ PLP-41	I've Been There	1973	$35

REGENT

❏ MG-6014 [M]	Just You, Just Me	1956	$80

SAVOY JAZZ

❏ SJL-1134	First, Lasting and Always	198?	$25

HARVEY, LAURENCE

The below are spoken-word recordings with a jazz background. Harvey is much better known as an actor (The Manchurian Candidate, among others).

Albums

ATLANTIC

❏ 1367 [M]	This Is My Beloved	1962	$150
❏ SD1367 [S]	This Is My Beloved	1962	$150

HASHIM, MICHAEL

Alto and soprano saxophone player.

Albums

STASH

❏ 227	Peacocks	1983	$25

HASSELBACH, MARK

Best known as a trumpeter, but also plays fluegel horn, flute, trombone and keyboards, with an occasional turn as drummer or bass player.

Albums

JAZZIMAGE

❏ JZ-104	Hasselblast	198?	$30

Number	Title	Yr	NM

HASSELL, JON

Trumpeter. A pioneer in ambient music, he has collaborated with Brian Eno.

Albums

ECM

❏ 1327	Power Spot	1987	$30

INTUITION

❏ C1-91186	Flash of the Spirit	1989	$30
❏ C1-46880	The Surgeon of the Nightsky Restores Dead Things by the Power of Sound	1988	$30

LOVELY

❏ 1021	Vernal Equinox	1978	$35

OPAL/WARNER BROS.

❏ 26153	City: Works of Fiction	1990	$35

TOMATO

❏ TOM-7019	Earthquake Island	1979	$35

HATZA, GREG

Organist.

Albums

CORAL

❏ CRL57495 [M]	Organized Jazz	1963	$35
❏ CRL757495 [S]	Organized Jazz	1963	$25
❏ CRL57493 [M]	The Wizardry of Greg Hatza	1962	$30
❏ CRL757493 [S]	The Wizardry of Greg Hatza	1962	$35

HAUSER, FRITZ

Drummer.

Albums

HAT ART

❏ 2023	Solodrumming	1986	$35

HAVENS, BOB

Trombonist and bandleader.

Albums

GHB

❏ GHB-143 [M]	Bob Havens' New Orleans All-Stars	1969	$100

SOUTHLAND

❏ 226 [M]	Bob Havens in New Orleans	1961	$35
❏ 243 [M]	Bob Havens' New Orleans All-Stars	1966	$30

HAWES, HAMPTON

Pianist. Also see CURTIS FULLER; FREDDIE REDD.

Albums

ARISTA FREEDOM

❏ AL1043	Copenhagen Night Music	1977	$50
❏ AL1020	Live at the Montmartre	1976	$50

BLACK LION

❏ 122	Spanish Steps	197?	$50

CONCORD JAZZ

❏ CJ-222	Recorded Live at the Great American Music Hall	198?	$35

CONTEMPORARY

❏ C-3545 [M]	All Night Session! Volume 1	1958	$250
❏ S-7545 [S]	All Night Session! Volume 1	1960	$250
❏ C-3546 [M]	All Night Session! Volume 2	1958	$250
❏ S-7546 [S]	All Night Session! Volume 2	1960	$250
❏ C-3547 [M]	All Night Session! Volume 3	1958	$250
❏ S-7547 [S]	All Night Session! Volume 3	1960	$250
❏ C-3523 [M]	Everybody Likes Hampton Hawes	1956	$200
❏ M-3589 [M]	For Real!	1959	$250
❏ S-7589 [S]	For Real!	1959	$250
❏ C-3553 [M]	Four! Hampton Hawes!!!	1958	$250
❏ S-7553 [S]	Four! Hampton Hawes!!!	1960	$250
❏ C-3505 [M]	Hampton Hawes	1955	$200
❏ M-3616 [M]	Here and Now	1965	$150
❏ S-7616 [S]	Here and Now	1965	$150
❏ M-3631 [M]	I'm All Smiles	1967	$150
❏ S-7631 [S]	I'm All Smiles	1967	$150
❏ M-3614 [M]	The Green Leaves of Summer	1964	$200
❏ S-7614 [S]	The Green Leaves of Summer	1964	$200
❏ M-3621 [M]	The Seance	1966	$150
❏ S-7621 [S]	The Seance	1966	$150
❏ C-3515 [M]	This Is Hampton Hawes	1956	$200

ENJA

❏ 3099	Live at Jazz Showcase in Chicago, Vol. 1	198?	$35

FANTASY

❏ OJC-638	All Night Session! Volume 1	1991	$35
❏ OJC-639	All Night Session! Volume 2	1991	$35

Number	Title	Yr	NM
❏ OJC-640	All Night Session! Volume 3	1991	$35
❏ OJC-421	Everybody Likes Hampton Hawes	1990	$35
❏ OJC-165	Four! Hampton Hawes!!!	198?	$30
❏ OJC-316	Hampton Hawes	198?	$30
❏ OJC-178	I'm All Smiles	198?	$30
❏ OJC-455	Seance	1990	$35
❏ OJC-476	The Green Leaves of Summer	1991	$35
❏ OJC-318	This Is Hampton Hawes	198?	$30

JAS

❏ JAS-4002	Hampton Hawes Trio at Montreux	1976	$35
❏ JAS-4004	The Two Sides of Hampton Hawes	1977	$50

JAZZ MAN

❏ 5022	Spanish Steps	198?	$25

MOON

❏ MLP-005	Autumn Leaves in Paris	1990	$60

PRESTIGE

❏ PR-10060	Blues for Walls	1973	$60
❏ PRST-7695	Hampton Hawes in Europe	1969	$60
❏ PRLP-212 [10]	Hampton Hawes Quartet	1955	$300
❏ 10088	Northern Windows	1974	$40
❏ P-10077	Playin' in the Yard	1974	$60
❏ PR-10046	The Universe	1972	$60

RCA VICTOR

❏ JPL1-1508	Challenge	1976	$50

STEREO RECORDS

❏ S-7026 [S]	Four! Hampton Hawes!!!	1959	$100

VANTAGE

❏ VLP-1 [10]	Hamp Hawes	1954	$300

VAULT

❏ LPS-9009	Hampton Hawes Plays Movie Musicals	1969	$25
❏ LPS-9010	High in the Sky	1970	$30

XANADU

❏ 161	Memorial Album	198?	$35

HAWES, HAMPTON/PAUL CHAMBERS

Also see each artist's individual listings.

Albums

XANADU

❏ 104	The East/West Controversy	1975	$60

HAWKINS, COLEMAN, AND BENNY CARTER

Also see each artist's individual listings.

Albums

MOON

❏ MLP-001	Jammin' the Blues	199?	$35

SWING

❏ 8403	Coleman Hawkins and Benny Carter	1985	$25

HAWKINS, COLEMAN, AND BUD POWELL

Also see each artist's individual listings.

Albums

BLACK LION

❏ 159	Hawk in Germany	197?	$30

HAWKINS, COLEMAN, AND CLARK TERRY

Also see each artist's individual listings.

Albums

COLUMBIA

❏ CL1991 [M]	Back in Bean's Bag	1963	$35
❏ CS8791 [S]	Back in Bean's Bag	1963	$25
❏ CS8791 [S]	Back in Bean's Bag	1999	$30

— Classic Records reissue on audiophile vinyl

HAWKINS, COLEMAN, AND FRANK HUNTER

Also see each artist's individual listings.

Albums

MIRA

❏ M-3003 [M]	The Hawk and the Hunter	1965	$25
❏ MS-3003 [S]	The Hawk and the Hunter	1965	$30

HAWKINS, COLEMAN, AND LESTER YOUNG

Also see each artist's individual listings.

Albums

DOCTOR JAZZ

❏ FW38446	Classic Tenors	1983	$25

FLYING DUTCHMAN

Number	Title	Yr	NM
❏ BXM1-2823	Classic Tenors	1978	$30
ZIM			
❏ 1000	Coleman Hawkins and Lester Young	197?	$25

HAWKINS, COLEMAN, AND PEE WEE RUSSELL
Also see each artist's individual listings.

Albums

CANDID			
❏ CD-8020 [M]	Jazz Reunion	1960	$40
❏ CS-9020 [S]	Jazz Reunion	1960	$40

HAWKINS, COLEMAN, AND ROY ELDREDGE
Also see each artist's individual listings.

Albums

PHOENIX			
❏ 3	Coleman Hawkins and Roy Eldredge 1939	197?	$25
VERVE			
❏ MGV-8266 [M]	At the Opera House	1958	$150
❏ V-8266 [M]	At the Opera House	1961	$60
❏ MGVS-6028 [S]	At the Opera House	1960	$150
❏ V6-8266 [S]	At the Opera House	1961	$60

HAWKINS, COLEMAN; ROY ELDREDGE; JOHNNY HODGES
Also see each artist's individual listings.

Albums

VERVE			
❏ V-8509 [M]	Alive at the Village Gate	1963	$25
❏ V6-8509 [S]	Alive at the Village Gate	1963	$30
❏ V6-8509 [S]	Alive at the Village Gate	199?	$30
—Classic Records reissue on audiophile vinyl			

HAWKINS, COLEMAN; ROY ELDREDGE; PETE BROWN; JO JONES
Also see each artist's individual listings.

Albums

VERVE			
❏ MGV-8240 [M]	All Stars at Newport	1958	$150
❏ V-8240 [M]	All Stars at Newport	1961	$60

HAWKINS, COLEMAN
Tenor saxophone player. A favorite among audiophiles, his "Body and Soul" is a standard. Also see EARL "FATHA" HINES; SONNY ROLLINS; CLARK TERRY.

Albums

ABC IMPULSE!			
❏ AS-28 [S]	Desafinado	1968	$35
❏ AS-26 [S]	Duke Ellington Meets Coleman Hawkins	1968	$35
❏ AS-9258	Reevaluations: The Impulse Years	197?	$35
❏ AS-34 [S]	Today and Now	1968	$35
❏ AS-87 [S]	Wrapped Tight	1968	$35
ADVANCE			
❏ LSP-9 [10]	Coleman Hawkins Favorites	1951	$300
AMERICAN RECORDING SOCIETY			
❏ G-316 [M]	Coleman Hawkins and His Orchestra	1956	$50
APOLLO			
❏ LAP-101 [10]	Coleman Hawkins All Stars	1951	$300
BLUEBIRD			
❏ 5658-1-RB [(2)]	Body and Soul	1986	$35
BRUNSWICK			
❏ BL58030 [10]	Tenor Sax	1952	$200
CAPITOL			
❏ H327 [10]	Classics in Jazz	1952	$300
❏ T819 [M]	Gilded Hawk	1957	$150
❏ M-11030	Hollywood Stampede	1973	$35
COMMODORE			
❏ XFL-14936	Coleman Hawkins	198?	$25
❏ FL-20025 [10]	King of the Tenor Sax	1952	$300
CONCERT HALL JAZZ			
❏ J-1201 [M]	Improvisations Unlimited	1955	$75
CONTINENTAL			
❏ 16006 [M]	On the Bean	1962	$30
❏ S-16006 [S]	On the Bean	1962	$30
CROWN			
❏ CLP-5181 [M]	Coleman Hawkins and His Orchestra	1960	$25

Number	Title	Yr	NM
❏ CST-206 [R]	Coleman Hawkins and His Orchestra	196?	$25
❏ CLP-5207 [M]	The Hawk Swing	1961	$25
❏ CST-224 [R]	The Hawk Swing	196?	$25
DECCA			
❏ DL4081 [M]	The Hawk Blows at Midnight	1961	$30
❏ DL74081 [S]	The Hawk Blows at Midnight	1961	$40
❏ DL8127 [M]	The Hawk Talks	1955	$150
EMARCY			
❏ MG-26013 [10]	The Bean	1954	$250
EVEREST ARCHIVE OF FOLK & JAZZ			
❏ 252	Coleman Hawkins	197?	$25
FANTASY			
❏ OJC-181	At Ease with Coleman Hawkins	1985	$25
❏ OJC-418	Coleman Hawkins Plus the Red Garland Trio	1990	$30
❏ OJC-294	Hawk Eyes	1988	$25
❏ OJC-6001	In a Mellow Tone	1988	$25
❏ OJC-420	Night Hawk	1990	$30
❏ OJC-096	Soul	198?	$25
❏ OJC-225	The Coleman Hawkins All Stars	198?	$25
❏ OJC-027	The Hawk Flies High	1982	$25
FELSTED			
❏ FAJ-7005 [M]	The High and Mighty Hawk	1959	$60
❏ SJA-2005 [S]	The High and Mighty Hawk	1959	$80
GNP CRESCENDO			
❏ GNP-9003	Coleman Hawkins in Holland	197?	$25
GRP IMPULSE!			
❏ 227 [S]	Desafinado	199?	$35
—Reissue on audiophile vinyl			
IMPULSE!			
❏ A-28 [M]	Desafinado	1963	$120
❏ AS-28 [S]	Desafinado	1963	$120
❏ A-26 [M]	Duke Ellington Meets Coleman Hawkins	1962	$120
❏ AS-26 [S]	Duke Ellington Meets Coleman Hawkins	1962	$120
❏ AS-34 [S]	Today and Now	1963	$120
❏ A-87 [M]	Wrapped Tight	1965	$200
❏ AS-87 [S]	Wrapped Tight	1965	$200
JAZZ MAN			
❏ 5042	Jazz Reunion	198?	$25
JAZZTONE			
❏ J-1201 [M]	Timeless Jazz	1955	$60
—Reissue of Concert Hall Jazz 1201			
MAINSTREAM			
❏ 56037 [M]	Meditations	1965	$30
❏ S-6037 [R]	Meditations	1965	$35
MASTER JAZZ			
❏ 8115	The High and Mighty Hawk	197?	$30
MILESTONE			
❏ M-47015	The Hawk Flies	1973	$35
MOODSVILLE			
❏ MVLP-7 [M]	At Ease with Coleman Hawkins	1960	$50
—Green label			
❏ MVLP-7 [M]	At Ease with Coleman Hawkins	1965	$30
—Blue label, trident logo at right			
❏ MVLP-23 [M]	Good Old Broadway	1962	$40
—Gren label			
❏ MVLP-23 [M]	Good Old Broadway	1965	$25
—Blue label, trident logo at right			
❏ MVST-23 [S]	Good Old Broadway	1962	$50
—Green label			
❏ MVST-23 [S]	Good Old Broadway	1965	$30
—Blue label, trident logo at right			
❏ MVLP-31 [M]	Make Someone Happy	1963	$40
—Green label			
❏ MVLP-31 [M]	Make Someone Happy	1965	$25
—Blue label, trident logo at right			
❏ MVST-31 [S]	Make Someone Happy	1963	$50
—Green label			
❏ MVST-31 [S]	Make Someone Happy	1965	$30
—Blue label, trident logo at right			
❏ MVLP-15 [M]	The Hawk Relaxes	1961	$50
—Green label			
❏ MVLP-15 [M]	The Hawk Relaxes	1965	$30
—Blue label, trident logo at right			
❏ MVLP-25 [M]	The Jazz Version of No Strings	1962	$40
—Green label			
❏ MVLP-25 [M]	The Jazz Version of No Strings	1965	$25
—Blue label, trident logo at right			

Number	Title	Yr	NM
❏ MVST-25 [S]	The Jazz Version of No Strings	1962	$50
—Green label			
❏ MVST-25 [S]	The Jazz Version of No Strings	1965	$30
—Blue label, trident logo at right			
MOON			
❏ MLP-018	Coleman Hawkins Vs. Oscar Peterson	199?	$35
PABLO			
❏ 2310933	Bean Stalkin'	198?	$30
❏ 2310707	Sirius	197?	$35
PHILIPS			
❏ PHM200022 [M]	Jazz at the Metropole	1962	$25
❏ PHS600022 [S]	Jazz at the Metropole	1962	$30
PHOENIX			
❏ 13	Centerpiece	197?	$25
❏ 8	In Concert	197?	$25
PRESTIGE			
❏ PRST-7824	Bean and the Boys	1970	$35
❏ PRST-7753	Blues Groove	1970	$35
❏ PRST-7824	Coleman Hawkins and the Boys	1971	$30
❏ PRLP-7156 [M]	Hawk Eyes	1958	$300
❏ PRST-7857	Hawk Eyes!	1971	$35
❏ 24051	Jam Session in Swingville	198?	$30
❏ P-24106	Moonglow	1981	$30
❏ PRST-7671	Night Hawk	1969	$35
❏ PRST-7647	Pioneers	1969	$35
❏ PRLP-7149 [M]	Soul	1958	$200
❏ 24083	The Real Thing	198?	$30
QUINTESSENCE			
❏ 25371	Golden Hawk	1979	$25
RCA VICTOR			
❏ LPV-501 [M]	Body and Soul	1965	$25
❏ LJM-1017 [M]	Hawk In Flight	1955	$80
RIVERSIDE			
❏ RLP 12-117/8 [M]	Coleman Hawkins: A Documentary	1956	$250
❏ RLP 12-233 [M]	The Hawk Flies High	1959	$250
—Blue label, microphone logo at top			
❏ 3049	Think Deep	1970	$100
SAVOY			
❏ MG-12013 [M]	The Hawk Returns	1955	$120
❏ MG-15039 [10]	The Hawk Talks	1954	$200
SAVOY JAZZ			
❏ SJL-1123	Coleman Hawkins Meets the Big Sax Section	1979	$25
STINSON			
❏ SLP-22 [10]	Originals with Hawkins	1950	$300
❏ SLP-22 [M]	Originals with Hawkins	195?	$40
SUNBEAM			
❏ 204	Coleman Hawkins at the Savoy 1940	197?	$25
SWINGVILLE			
❏ SVLP-2035 [M]	Blues Groove	1962	$50
—Purple label			
❏ SVLP-2035 [M]	Blues Groove	1965	$30
—Blue label, trident logo at right			
❏ SVST-2035 [S]	Blues Groove	1962	$40
—Red label			
❏ SVST-2035 [S]	Blues Groove	1965	$25
—Blue label, trident logo at right			
❏ SVLP-2001 [M]	Coleman Hawkins Plus the Red Garland Trio	1960	$50
—Purple label			
❏ SVLP-2001 [M]	Coleman Hawkins Plus the Red Garland Trio	1965	$30
—Blue label, trident logo at right			
❏ SVLP-2039 [M]	Hawk Eyes	1962	$50
—Purple label			
❏ SVLP-2039 [M]	Hawk Eyes	1965	$30
—Blue label, trident logo at right			
❏ SVST-2039 [S]	Hawk Eyes	1962	$40
—Red label			
❏ SVST-2039 [S]	Hawk Eyes	1965	$25
—Blue label, trident logo at right			
❏ SVLP-2016 [M]	Night Hawk	1961	$50
—Purple label			
❏ SVLP-2016 [M]	Night Hawk	1965	$30
—Blue label, trident logo at right			
❏ SVLP-2038 [M]	Soul	1962	$50
—Purple label			
❏ SVLP-2038 [M]	Soul	1965	$30
—Blue label, trident logo at right			
❏ SVST-2038 [S]	Soul	1962	$40

Number	Title	Yr	NM
—Red label			
❏ SVST-2038 [S]	Soul	1965	$25
—Blue label, trident logo at right			
❏ SVLP-2005 [M]	The Coleman Hawkins All Stars	1960	$50
—Purple label			
❏ SVLP-2005 [M]	The Coleman Hawkins All Stars	1965	$30
—Blue label, trident logo at right			
❏ SVLP-2024 [M]	Things Ain't What They Used to Be	1961	$40
—Purple label			
❏ SVLP-2024 [M]	Things Ain't What They Used to Be	1965	$25
—Blue label, trident logo at right			
❏ SVST-2024 [S]	Things Ain't What They Used to Be	1961	$50
—Red label			
❏ SVST-2024 [S]	Things Ain't What They Used to Be	1965	$30
—Blue label, trident logo at right			
❏ SVLP-2025 [M]	Years Ago	1961	$40
—Purple label			
❏ SVLP-2025 [M]	Years Ago	1965	$50
—Blue label, trident logo at right			
❏ SVST-2025 [S]	Years Ago	1961	$100
—Red label			
❏ SVST-2025 [S]	Years Ago	1965	$60
—Blue label, trident logo at right			
TIME-LIFE			
❏ STL-J-06	Giants of Jazz	1979	$50
TRIP			
❏ 5515	Coleman Hawkins and the Trumpet Kings	197?	$25
URANIA			
❏ UJLP-41201 [R]	Accent on Tenor Sax	196?	$150
VERVE			
❏ MGV-8346 [M]	Coleman Hawkins and His Confreres with the Oscar Peterson Trio	1959	$150
❏ MGVS-6110 [S]	Coleman Hawkins and His Confreres with the Oscar Peterson Trio	1960	$100
❏ V-8346 [M]	Coleman Hawkins and His Confreres with the Oscar Peterson Trio	1961	$30
❏ V6-8346 [S]	Coleman Hawkins and His Confreres with the Oscar Peterson Trio	1961	$25
❏ UMV-2623	Coleman Hawkins at Newport	198?	$25
❏ MGV-8327 [M]	Coleman Hawkins Encounters Ben Webster	1959	$150
❏ MGVS-6066 [S]	Coleman Hawkins Encounters Ben Webster	1960	$100
❏ V-8327 [M]	Coleman Hawkins Encounters Ben Webster	1961	$30
❏ V6-8327 [S]	Coleman Hawkins Encounters Ben Webster	1961	$25
❏ UMV-2532	Coleman Hawkins Encounters Ben Webster	198?	$25
❏ MGVS-6066 [S]	Coleman Hawkins Encounters Ben Webster	199?	$30
—Classic Records reissue on audiophile vinyl			
❏ V-8509 [M]	Hawkins! Alive! At the Village Gate	1963	$30
❏ V6-8509 [S]	Hawkins! Alive! At the Village Gate	1963	$30
❏ V-8568 [M]	The Essential Coleman Hawkins	1964	$25
❏ V6-8568 [S]	The Essential Coleman Hawkins	1964	$30
❏ MGV-8261 [M]	The Genius of Coleman Hawkins	1958	$100
❏ MGVS-6033 [S]	The Genius of Coleman Hawkins	1960	$150
❏ V-8261 [M]	The Genius of Coleman Hawkins	1961	$30
❏ V6-8261 [S]	The Genius of Coleman Hawkins	1961	$25
❏ 825673-1	The Genius of Coleman Hawkins	1986	$25
❏ V6-8829	The Newport Years	197?	$35
VIK			
❏ LX-1059 [M]	The Hawk in Paris	1957	$80
WORLD WIDE			
❏ MGS-20001 [S]	Coleman Hawkins with the Basie Saxophone Section	1958	$50
XANADU			
❏ 189	Dutch Treat	198?	$25

Number	Title	Yr	NM
❏ 195	Jazz Tones	198?	$25
❏ 111	Thanks for the Memory	198?	$25

HAWKINS, COLEMAN/BEN WEBSTER
Also see each artist's individual listings.

Albums

Number	Title	Yr	NM
BRUNSWICK			
❏ BL54016 [M]	The Big Sounds of Coleman Hawkins and Ben Webster	1956	$80

HAWKINS, COLEMAN/GEORGIE AULD
Also see each artist's individual listings.

Albums

Number	Title	Yr	NM
GRAND AWARD			
❏ GA 33-316 [M]	Jazz Concert	1955	$100
—With wrap-around cover intact			
❏ GA 33-316 [M]	Jazz Concert	1955	$60
—Without wrap-around cover			

HAWKINS, ERSKINE
Trumpeter, bandleader and composer. Wrote "Tuxedo Junction."

Albums

Number	Title	Yr	NM
CORAL			
❏ CRL56051 [10]	After Hours	1954	$120
DECCA			
❏ DL4081 [M]	The Hawk Blows at Midnight	1960	$30
❏ DL74081 [S]	The Hawk Blows at Midnight	1960	$40
IMPERIAL			
❏ LP-9191 [M]	25 Golden Years of Jazz, Volume 1	1962	$150
❏ LP-12191 [S]	25 Golden Years of Jazz, Volume 1	1962	$150
❏ LP-9197 [M]	25 Golden Years of Jazz, Volume 2	1962	$150
❏ LP-12197 [S]	25 Golden Years of Jazz, Volume 2	1962	$150
MCA			
❏ 1361	Tuxedo Junction	198?	$25
RCA VICTOR			
❏ LPM-2227 [M]	After Hours	1960	$40

HAWKS, BILLY
Organist and male singer.

Albums

Number	Title	Yr	NM
PRESTIGE			
❏ PRST-7556	More Heavy Soul	1968	$25
❏ PRLP-7501 [M]	New Genius of the Blues	1967	$30
❏ PRST-7501 [S]	New Genius of the Blues	1967	$25

HAYES, ALVIN
Trombone player.

Albums

Number	Title	Yr	NM
PALO ALTO/TBA			
❏ TBA-221	Star Gaze	1987	$25

HAYES, CLANCY
Banjo player and male singer.

Albums

Number	Title	Yr	NM
DELMARK			
❏ DS-9210 [S]	Oh By Jingo	1965	$30
DOWN HOME			
❏ MGD-3 [M]	Clancy Hayes Sings	1956	$60
GOOD TIME JAZZ			
❏ L-12050 [M]	Swingin' Minstrel	1963	$25
❏ S-10050 [S]	Swingin' Minstrel	1963	$30
VERVE			
❏ MGV-1003 [M]	Clancy Hayes Sings	1957	$150

HAYES, LOUIS, AND JUNIOR COOK
Also see each artist's individual listings.

Albums

Number	Title	Yr	NM
TIMELESS			
❏ 307	Ichi-Ban	1979	$50

HAYES, LOUIS
Drummer and bandleader. Also see YUSEF LATEEF.

Albums

Number	Title	Yr	NM
GRYPHON			
❏ G-787	Variety Is the Spice of Life	1979	$50
MUSE			
❏ MR-5052	Breath of Life	1974	$60
❏ MR-5125	Real Thing	1977	$35
VEE JAY			
❏ LP-3010 [M]	Louis Hayes	1960	$80
❏ SR-3010 [S]	Louis Hayes	1960	$150

HAYES, MARTHA
Female singer.

Albums

Number	Title	Yr	NM
JUBILEE			
❏ JLP-1023 [M]	A Hayes Named Martha	1956	$50

HAYES, TUBBY
Tenor and soprano saxophone player, flutist and vibraphone player. Also see THE JAZZ COURIERS; DIZZY REECE.

Albums

Number	Title	Yr	NM
EPIC			
❏ LA16019 [M]	Introducing Tubby	1961	$80
❏ BA17019 [S]	Introducing Tubby	1961	$100
❏ LA16023 [M]	Tubby the Tenor	1962	$80
❏ BA17023 [S]	Tubby the Tenor	1962	$100
❏ BA17023 [S]	Tubby the Tenor	199?	$60
—Classic Records reissue on audiophile vinyl			
SMASH			
❏ MGS-27026 [M]	Tubby's Back in Town	1963	$40
❏ SRS-67026 [S]	Tubby's Back in Town	1963	$50

HAYNES, GRAHAM
Cornet player.

Albums

Number	Title	Yr	NM
MUSE			
❏ MR-5402	What Time It Be!	1991	$30

HAYNES, ROY; PHINEAS NEWBORN; PAUL CHAMBERS
Also see each artist's individual listings.

Albums

Number	Title	Yr	NM
FANTASY			
❏ OJC-196	We Three	1986	$25
NEW JAZZ			
❏ NJLP-8210 [M]	We Three	1958	$200

HAYNES, ROY
Drummer.

Albums

Number	Title	Yr	NM
ABC IMPULSE!			
❏ AS-23	Out of the Afternoon	1968	$200
—Black label with red ring			
EMARCY			
❏ MG-26048 [10]	Bushman's Holiday	1954	$250
GALAXY			
❏ 5103	Thank You	1978	$30
❏ 5116	Vistalite	1979	$30
IMPULSE!			
❏ AS-23 [S]	Out of the Afternoon	1962	$160
MAINSTREAM			
❏ MRL-313	Hip Ensemble	1971	$25
❏ MRL-351	Senyah	1972	$25
MCA			
❏ 639	Out of the Afternoon	1980	$25
NEW JAZZ			
❏ NJLP-8286 [M]	Cracklin'	1962	$150
—Purple label			
❏ NJLP-8286 [M]	Cracklin'	1965	$150
—Blue label, trident logo at right			
❏ NJLP-8287 [M]	Cymbalism	1962	$150
—Purple label			
❏ NJLP-8287 [M]	Cymbalism	1965	$150
—Blue label, trident logo at right			
❏ NJLP-8245 [M]	Just Us	1965	$150
—Blue label, trident logo at right			
PACIFIC JAZZ			
❏ PJ-82 [M]	People	1964	$30
❏ ST-82 [S]	People	1964	$40
PRESTIGE			
❏ 2504	Bad News	198?	$30

Jutta Hipp, Jutta – New Faces, New Sounds from Germany, Blue Note BLP-5056, 10-inch LP, **$800**.

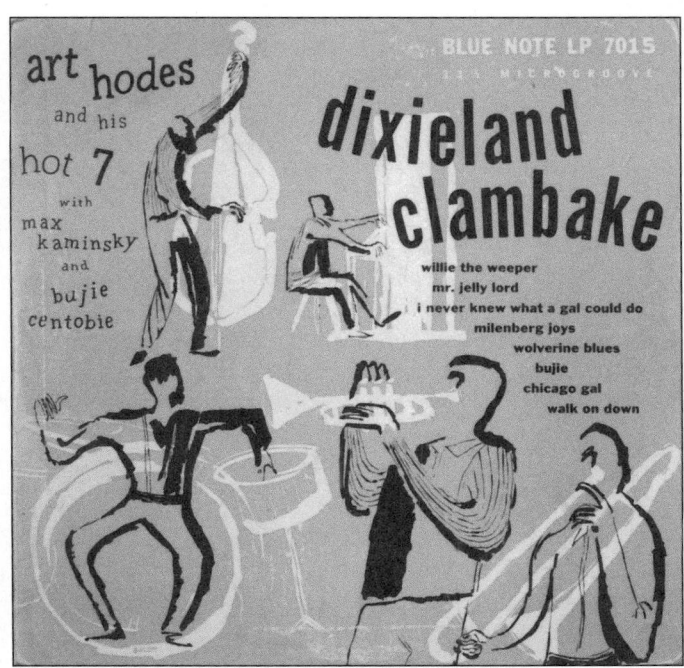

Art Hodes, *Dixieland Clambake*, Blue Note BLP-7015, 10-inch LP, **$500**.

Billie Holiday, *The Blues Are Brewin'*, Decca DL 8701, black label with silver print, **$120**.

Billie Holiday, *Billie Holiday*, Commodore FL-30008, **$100**.

HAYNES, ROY/QUINCY JONES
Also see each artist's individual listings.

Albums

Number	Title	Yr	NM
EMARCY			
❏ MG-36083 [M]	Jazz Abroad	1956	$200

HAZEL, MONK
Drummer and occasional cornet and mellophone player.

Albums

Number	Title	Yr	NM
SOUTHLAND			
❏ SLP-217 [M]	Monk Hazel	1956	$40

HAZELL, EDDIE
Guitarist and male singer.

Albums

Number	Title	Yr	NM
AUDIOPHILE			
❏ AP-179	Live at Gulliver's -- I Go for That!	1984	$25
❏ AP-137	Sugar, Don't You Know	1979	$30
MONMOUTH-EVERGREEN			
❏ 7075	Take Your Shoes Off, Baby	197?	$30

HAZILLA, JON
Drummer.

Albums

Number	Title	Yr	NM
CADENCE JAZZ			
❏ CJR-1035	Chicplacity	1988	$25

HEADHUNTERS
HERBIE HANCOCK's backing band on his classic album of the same name: Blackbird McKnight (guitar); Bennie Maupin (saxophones, clarinet); Paul Jackson (bass); Bill Summers (percussion); Mike Clark (bass).

Albums

Number	Title	Yr	NM
ARISTA			
❏ AB4146	Straight from the Gate	1978	$40
❏ AL4038	Survival of the Fittest	1975	$120
— Reproductions exist			

HEALY, PAT
Female singer.

Albums

Number	Title	Yr	NM
WORLD PACIFIC			
❏ WP-409 [M]	Just Before Dawn	1958	$150

HEARD, J.C.
Drummer and male singer.

Albums

Number	Title	Yr	NM
ARGO			
❏ LP-633 [M]	This Is Me, J.C.	1958	$40
❏ LPS-633 [S]	This Is Me, J.C.	1959	$30

HEATH, ALBERT
Drummer. Also see THE HEATH BROTHERS.

Albums

Number	Title	Yr	NM
MUSE			
❏ MR-5031	Kwanza (The First)	1974	$25
O'BE			
❏ LP-301	Kawaida	1969	$40
TRIP			
❏ 5032	Kawaida	1974	$30
— As "Kuumba Toudie Heath			

HEATH, JIMMY
Tenor and alto saxophone player and composer. Also see THE RIVERSIDE JAZZ STARS.

Albums

Number	Title	Yr	NM
COBBLESTONE			
❏ CST-9012	The Gap Sealer	197?	$35
FANTASY			
❏ OJC-6006	Nice People	198?	$25
LANDMARK			
❏ LLP-1506	New Picture	1986	$25
❏ LLP-1514	Peer Pleasure	1987	$25
MILESTONE			
❏ 47025	Fast Company	197?	$35

Number	Title	Yr	NM
MUSE			
❏ MR-5138	Jimmy	197?	$35
❏ MR-5028	Love and Understanding	1974	$35
RIVERSIDE			
❏ RLP-486 [M]	On the Trail	1965	$150
❏ RS-9486 [S]	On the Trail	1965	$150
❏ RLP 12-333 [M]	Really Big	1960	$200
❏ 6060	Swamp Seed	197?	$30
❏ RLP-465 [M]	Swamp Soul	1963	$150
❏ RS-9465 [S]	Swamp Soul	1963	$150
❏ RLP-372 [M]	The Quota	1961	$200
❏ RS-9372 [S]	The Quota	1961	$200
❏ RLP 12-314 [M]	The Thumper	1960	$200
❏ RLP-1160 [S]	The Thumper	1960	$200
❏ RLP-400 [M]	Triple Threat	1962	$150
❏ RS-9400 [S]	Triple Threat	1962	$150
XANADU			
❏ 118	Picture of Heath	1976	$30

HEATH, TED, BAND
Recorded after Heath's retirement, the group was led by trombonist Don Lusher.

Albums

Number	Title	Yr	NM
LONDON PHASE 4			
❏ SP44186	A Salute to Glenn Miller	1972	$25
❏ SP44148	Beatles, Bach and Bacharach	1971	$35
❏ SP44177	Big Band Themes Revisited	197?	$25
❏ SP44178	Big Band Themes Revisited, Volume 2	197?	$25
❏ SP44140	Big Ones	1970	$30
❏ SP44284	Coast to Coast	1977	$25
❏ SP44104	Swing Is King	1968	$30
❏ SP44113	Swing Is King, Volume 2	1969	$30
❏ SP44220	The Ted Heath Band Salutes the Duke	197?	$25
❏ SP44228	The Ted Heath Band Salutes Tommy Dorsey	197?	$25
❏ SP44164	Those Were the Days	1971	$30

HEATH, TED
British trombone player and bandleader.

Albums

Number	Title	Yr	NM
EVEREST ARCHIVE OF FOLK & JAZZ			
❏ 215	Ted Heath's Big Band	1970	$25
LONDON			
❏ PS535	21st Anniversary Album	1968	$30
❏ LL1716 [M]	All Time Top Twelve	1957	$50
❏ PS117 [S]	All Time Top Twelve	1958	$60
— Re-recorded version of LL 1716			
❏ LL1676 [M]	A Yank in Europe	1956	$50
❏ LL3125 [M]	Big Band Blues	1959	$50
❏ PS172 [S]	Big Band Blues	1959	$60
❏ LL3325 [M]	Big Band Spirituals	1963	$30
❏ LB-732 [10]	Black and White Magic	195?	$40
❏ LL1217 [M]	Gershwin for Moderns	1956	$50
❏ LL3106 [M]	Great Film Hits	1959	$50
❏ PS159 [S]	Great Film Hits	1959	$60
❏ LL3057 [M]	Hits I Missed	1958	$50
❏ PS116 [S]	Hits I Missed	1958	$60
❏ LL1211 [M]	Jazz Concert at the London Palladium, Vol. 3	1955	$60
❏ LL1379 [M]	Jazz Concert at the London Palladium, Vol. 4	1956	$50
❏ LL1279 [M]	Kern for Moderns	1956	$50
❏ LL3195 [M]	Latin Swingers	1961	$35
❏ LB-511 [10]	Listen to My Music	195?	$40
❏ LL3127 [M]	My Very Good Friends The Bandleaders	1959	$50
❏ PS174 [S]	My Very Good Friends The Bandleaders	1959	$60
❏ LL3367 [M]	New Palladium Performances	1964	$30
❏ LL3058 [M]	Old English	1958	$50
❏ LL3124 [M]	Pop Hits from the Classics	1959	$50
❏ PS171 [S]	Pop Hits from the Classics	1959	$60
❏ LL1749 [M]	Rhapsody in Blue	1957	$50
❏ LL1500 [M]	Rodgers for Moderns	1956	$50
❏ LL3062 [M]	Shall We Dance	1959	$50
❏ PS148 [S]	Shall We Dance	1959	$60
❏ LL1737 [M]	Showcase	1957	$50
❏ LL3146 [M]	Songs for the Young at Heart	1960	$35
❏ PS190 [S]	Songs for the Young at Heart	1960	$50
❏ LL1721 [M]	Spotlight on Sidemen	1957	$50
❏ PS138 [S]	Swing Session	1958	$60
— New stereo recordings of the same material as appears on LL 802			
❏ LPB-374 [10]	Ted Heath and His Orchestra	195?	$40
❏ LL1566 [M]	Ted Heath at Carnegie Hall	1956	$50
❏ LL802 [M]	Ted Heath at the London Palladium	1953	$50
❏ LL3143 [M]	Ted Heath in Concert	1960	$35
❏ PS187 [S]	Ted Heath in Concert	1960	$50

Number	Title	Yr	NM
❏ LL978 [M]	Ted Heath Plays the Music of Fats Waller	1954	$50
❏ LL1564 [M]	Ted Heath's First American Tour	1956	$50
❏ LL750 [M]	Ted Heath Strikes Up the Band	1953	$50
❏ PS140 [S]	Ted Heath Swings in High Stereo	1958	$60
❏ LPB-340 [10]	Tempo for Dancing	195?	$40
❏ LL3138 [M]	The Big Band Dixie Sound	1960	$35
❏ PS184 [S]	The Big Band Dixie Sound	1960	$50
❏ LL3192 [M]	The Hits of the Thirties	1961	$35
❏ PS216 [S]	The Hits of the Thirties	1961	$50
❏ LL3128 [M]	The Hits of the Twenties	1960	$35
❏ PS175 [S]	The Hits of the Twenties	1960	$50
❏ LL3047 [M]	Things to Come	1958	$50
❏ LL1743 [M]	Tribute to the Fabulous Dorseys	1957	$50
LONDON PHASE 4			
❏ SP44017	Big Band Bash	1962	$35
❏ P54002 [M]	Big Band Percussion	1961	$30
❏ SP44002 [S]	Big Band Percussion	1961	$35
❏ SP44036 [S]	Big Band Spirituals	1963	$35
❏ SP44074	Chartbusters	1966	$30
❏ SP44046 [S]	New Palladium Performances	1964	$30
❏ SP44079	Pow!	1966	$30
❏ SP44023	Satin Strings and Bouncing Brass	1963	$35
❏ SP44038	Swing vs. Latin	1964	$35
❏ SP44063	The Sound of Music	1965	$30
RICHMOND			
❏ B20034 [M]	Big Band Beat	196?	$30
❏ B20096 [M]	Big Band Gershwin	196?	$30
❏ B20097 [M]	Big Band Kern	196?	$30
❏ B20098 [M]	Big Band Rodgers	196?	$30
❏ B20037 [M]	Ted Heath Plays Gershwin	196?	$30
❏ B20082 [M]	Ted Heath Plays the Music of Fats Waller	196?	$30

HEATH BROTHERS, THE
Led by ALBERT HEATH and Percy Heath (bass).

Albums

Number	Title	Yr	NM
ANTILLES			
❏ AN-1003	Brotherly Love	1982	$30
❏ AN-1016	Brothers and Others	198?	$30
COLUMBIA			
❏ FC37126	Expressions of Life	1981	$30
❏ JC35816	In Motion: The Heath Brothers and Brass Choir	1979	$30
❏ FC36374	Live at the Public Theatre	1980	$30
❏ JC35573	Passin' Thru	1978	$30

HECKMAN, DON
Clarinetist and bandleader.

HEFTI, NEAL

Albums

Number	Title	Yr	NM
COLUMBIA			
❏ CL1516 [M]	Light and Right	1960	$25
❏ CS8316 [S]	Light and Right	1960	$30
CORAL			
❏ CX2 [M]	Hollywood Song Book	1959	$40
❏ 7CX2 [S]	Hollywood Song Book	1959	$60
❏ CRL57241 [M]	Hollywood Song Book, Volume 1	1958	$30
❏ CRL757241 [S]	Hollywood Song Book, Volume 1	1959	$30
❏ CRL57242 [M]	Hollywood Song Book, Volume 2	1958	$30
❏ CRL757242 [S]	Hollywood Song Book, Volume 2	1959	$30
❏ CRL57256 [M]	Music U.S.A.	1959	$25
❏ CRL56083 [10]	Swingin' on a Coral Reef	1953	$50
EPIC			
❏ LN3481 [M]	Pardon My Do-Wah	1958	$60
❏ LN3113 [M]	Singing Instrumentals	1956	$100
❏ LG1013 [10]	Singing Instrumentals	1955	$100
RCA VICTOR			
❏ LPM-3573 [M]	Batman Theme (and 11 Other Bat-Songs)	1966	$50
❏ LSP-3573 [S]	Batman Theme (and 11 Other Bat-Songs)	1966	$60
❏ LPM-3621 [M]	Hefti in Gotham City	1966	$50
❏ LSP-3621 [S]	Hefti in Gotham City	1966	$60
REPRISE			
❏ R-6039 [M]	Jazz Pops	1962	$25
❏ R9-6039 [S]	Jazz Pops	1962	$30
❏ R-6018 [M]	Themes from TV's Top 12	1962	$25
❏ R9-6018 [S]	Themes from TV's Top 12	1962	$30
VIK			
❏ LX-1092 [M]	Concert Miniatures	1957	$60
X			
❏ LXA-3021 [10]	Music of Rudolf Frimi	1954	$50

Number	Title	Yr	NM
HEIDT, HORACE			

Bandleader.

Albums

HINDSIGHT

Number	Title	Yr	NM
❏ HSR-194	Horace Heidt and His Musical Knights 1939	198?	$25
❏ HSR-202	The Uncollected Horace Heidt and His Orchestra Vol. 2	1984	$25

SUNBEAM

❏ 4	Horace Heidt and His Orchestra 1927-29	198?	$25

HELIOCENTRIC

Members: Norn Scutti; Al von Seggern; Jeff Pressing; John Leftwich.

Albums

DISCOVERY

❏ 806	Heliocentric	1979	$30

HELLBORG, JONAS

Bass player.

Albums

DAY EIGHT

❏ DEM 002	All Our Steps	1983	$35
❏ DEM 006	Axis	1986	$30
❏ DEM 009	Bass	1988	$30
❏ DEM 004	Elegant Punk	1984	$30
❏ DEM0 (????)	Jonas Hellborg Group	1988	$30
❏ DEM 001	The Bassic Thing	1982	$50

HELM, BOB

Clarinetist.

Albums

RIVERSIDE

❏ RLP-2510 [10]	Bob Helm	1954	$300

HELM, BOB/LU WATTERS

Also see each artist's individual listings.

Albums

RIVERSIDE

❏ RLP 12-213 [M]	San Francisco Style	1956	$250

HEMPHILL, JULIUS

Alto and tenor saxophone player, flutist and male singer.

Albums

BLACK SAINT

❏ BSR-0040	Flat-Out Jump Suite	198?	$35
❏ BSR-0015	Raw Material and Residuals	197?	$35

ELEKTRA/MUSICIAN

❏ 60831	Julius Hemphill's Big Band	1988	$25

MBARI

❏ 0(????)	Blue Boye	1977	$60
❏ 0(????)	'Coon Bid'ness	1974	$40
❏ 5001	Dogon A.D.	1972	$50

MINOR MUSIC

❏ MM-003	Georgia Blue	1985	$30

RED

❏ VPA-138	Live in New York	1976	$35

SACKVILLE

❏ 3018	Buster Bee	198?	$30

HENDERSON, BILL

Male singer.

Albums

DISCOVERY

❏ 779	Live at the Times	1978	$30
❏ 802	Street of Dreams	1979	$30
❏ 846	Tribute to Johnny Mercer	1982	$30

MGM

❏ E-4128 [M]	Bill Henderson with the Oscar Peterson Trio	1963	$30
❏ SE-4128 [S]	Bill Henderson with the Oscar Peterson Trio	1963	$30

VEE JAY

❏ LP-1031 [M]	Bill Henderson	1961	$30
❏ SR-1031 [S]	Bill Henderson	1961	$40
❏ LP-1015 [M]	Bill Henderson Sings	1959	$30
❏ SR-1015 [S]	Bill Henderson Sings	1959	$40

VERVE

Number	Title	Yr	NM
❏ V-8619 [M]	When My Dreamboat Comes Home	1965	$50
❏ V6-8619 [S]	When My Dreamboat Comes Home	1965	$60

HENDERSON, BOBBY

Pianist. Also a trumpeter and male singer. Also see RUBY BRAFF.

Albums

CHIAROSCURO

❏ 102 [B]	Home in the Clouds	1971	$35

— *Reissue of Halcyon 102*

❏ 122	Last Recordings	1973	$35

HALCYON

❏ 102	Home in the Clouds	1970	$25

VANGUARD

❏ VRS-8511 [M]	Handful of Keys	1955	$80

HENDERSON, EDDIE

Trumpeter.

Albums

BLUE NOTE

❏ BN-LA636-G	Heritage	1976	$25
❏ BN-LA464-G	Sunburst	1975	$25

CAPITOL

❏ ST-11761	Comin' Through	1977	$35
❏ SW-11846	Mahal	1978	$30
❏ ST-11984	Runnin' To Your Love	1979	$30

CAPRICORN

❏ CP 0122	Inside Out	1974	$35
❏ CP 0118	Realization	1973	$35

HENDERSON, FLETCHER

Pianist, bandleader, arranger. His band was a precursor to, and a heavy influence on, the Swing Era.

Albums

BIOGRAPH

❏ 12039	Fletcher Henderson 1923-27	197?	$30
❏ C-12	Fletcher Henderson 1924-41	197?	$30

BLUEBIRD

❏ AXM2-5507	The Complete Fletcher Henderson	197?	$35

COLUMBIA

❏ C4L19 [M]	The Fletcher Henderson Story	1961	$100

— *Box set with booklet; red and black labels with six "eye" logos*

❏ C4L19 [M]	The Fletcher Henderson Story	1963	$50

— *Red "Guaranteed High Fidelity" labels*

❏ C4L19 [M]	The Fletcher Henderson Story	1966	$30

— *Red "360 Sound Mono" labels*

DECCA

❏ DL9227 [M]	Fletcher Henderson: First Impression (Vol. 1 1924-1931)	1958	$120

— *Black label, silver print*

❏ DL9227 [M]	Fletcher Henderson: First Impression (Vol. 1 1924-1931)	1961	$30

Number	Title	Yr	NM
— *Black label with color bars*			
❏ DL79227 [R]	Fletcher Henderson: First Impression (Vol. 1 1924-1931)	196?	$35
❏ DL9228 [M]	Fletcher Henderson: The Swing's the Thing (Vol. 2 1931-1934)	1958	$120
— *Black label, silver print*			
❏ DL9228 [M]	Fletcher Henderson: The Swing's the Thing (Vol. 2 1931-1934)	1961	$30
— *Black label with color bars*			
❏ DL79228 [R]	Fletcher Henderson: The Swing's the Thing (Vol. 2 1931-1934)	196?	$35
❏ DL6025 [10]	Fletcher Henderson Memorial Album	1952	$150

HISTORICAL

❏ 13	Fletcher Henderson 1923-24	1967	$25
❏ 18	Fletcher Henderson Volume 2: 1923-25	1967	$25

JAZZTONE

❏ J-1285 [M]	The Big Reunion	1958	$30

MCA

❏ 1310	First Impressions	198?	$25
❏ 1346	The Rarest Fletcher	198?	$25
❏ 1318	The Swing's the Thing	198?	$25

MILESTONE

❏ M-2005	The Immortal Fletcher Henderson	196?	$30

RIVERSIDE

❏ RLP-1055 [10]	Fletcher Henderson	1954	$300

SAVOY JAZZ

❏ SJL-1152	The Crown King of Swing	198?	$25

SUTTON

❏ SSL-286 [M]	Fletcher Henderson with Slam Stewart	195?	$30

SWING

❏ SW-8445/6	Fletcher Henderson and His Dixie Stompers 1925-1928	198?	$35

X

❏ LVA-3013 [10]	Fletcher Henderson and His Connie's Inn Orchestra	1954	$150

HENDERSON, JOE

Primarily a tenor saxophone player, he also has played soprano sax and flute.

Albums

BLUE NOTE

❏ BST-84189 [S]	Inner Urge	1967	$35
— *A Division of Liberty Records" on label*			
❏ BST-84166 [S]	In 'n Out	1967	$35
— *A Division of Liberty Records" on label*			
❏ BST-84227 [S]	Mode for Joe	1967	$35
— *A Division of Liberty Records" on label*			

❏ BST-84152 [S]	Our Thing	1967	$35
— *A Division of Liberty Records" on label*			

Number	Title	Yr	NM

Number	Title	Yr	NM
❏ BST-84140 [S]	Page One	1967	$35

—A Division of Liberty Records" on label

❏ BT-85123	State of the Tenor	1987	$25
❏ BT-85126	State of the Tenor Vol. 2: Live at the Village Vanguard	1987	$25

CONTEMPORARY
| ❏ C-14006 | Relaxin' at Camarillo | 198? | $30 |

FANTASY
| ❏ OJC-465 | The Kicker | 1990 | $30 |

FONTANA
| ❏ SRF-67590 | Hits, Hits, Hits! | 1969 | $60 |

MILESTONE
❏ M-9040	Black Is the Color	1972	$25
❏ M-9066	Black Miracle	1976	$35
❏ M-9071	Black Narcissus	1976	$35
❏ M-9057	Canyon Lady	1974	$35
❏ M-9053	Elements	1974	$35
❏ 47058	Foresight	198?	$35
❏ M-9028	If You're Not Part	1970	$25
❏ M-9034	In Pursuit of Blackness	1971	$25
❏ M-9047	Joe Henderson In Japan	1972	$25
❏ M-9050	Multiple	1973	$35
❏ M-9008	The Kicker	1968	$25

PAUSA
| ❏ 7075 | Mirror, Mirror | 1980 | $25 |

TODD
| ❏ MT-2701 [M] | Snap Your Fingers | 1962 | $100 |
| ❏ ST-2701 [S] | Snap Your Fingers | 1962 | $140 |

HENDERSON, WAYNE
Trombonist. Also see THE CRUSADERS.
Albums

ABC
| ❏ AB-1020 | Big Daddy's Place | 1977 | $25 |

POLYDOR
| ❏ PD-1-6227 | Emphasized | 1980 | $25 |
| ❏ PD-1-6145 | Living on a Dream | 1978 | $25 |

HENDRICKS, JON
Male singer. Also see LAMBERT, HENDRICKS & BAVAN; LAMBERT, HENDRICKS & ROSS.
Albums

COLUMBIA
❏ CL1583 [M]	Evolution of the Blues	1961	$30
❏ CS8383 [S]	Evolution of the Blues	1961	$40
❏ CL1805 [M]	Fast Livin' Blues	1962	$30
❏ CS8605 [S]	Fast Livin' Blues	1962	$40

ENJA
| ❏ 4032 | Cloudburst | 198? | $30 |

MUSE
| ❏ MR-5258 | Love | 1982 | $25 |

REPRISE
| ❏ R-6089 [M] | Salud! | 1964 | $30 |
| ❏ R9-6089 [S] | Salud! | 1964 | $30 |

SMASH
| ❏ MGS-27069 [M] | Recorded In Person at the Trident | 1963 | $30 |
| ❏ SRS-67069 [S] | Recorded In Person at the Trident | 1963 | $30 |

STANYAN
| ❏ 10132 | September Songs | 197? | $30 |

WORLD PACIFIC
| ❏ WP-1283 [M] | A Good Git-Together | 1959 | $150 |

HENDRICKS, MICHELE
Female singer.
Albums

MUSE
| ❏ MR-5336 | Carryin' On | 1988 | $25 |
| ❏ MR-5363 | Keepin' Me Satisfied | 1989 | $30 |

HENKE, MEL
Pianist and composer.
Albums

CONTEMPORARY
| ❏ C-5001 [M] | Dig Mel Henke | 1955 | $200 |
| ❏ C-5003 [M] | Now Spin This | 1956 | $200 |

DOBRE
| ❏ 1031 | Love Touch | 197? | $30 |

WARNER BROS.
| ❏ WS1472 [S] | La Dolce Henke | 1962 | $50 |

HENRIQUE, LUIZ
Male singer.
Albums

FONTANA
| ❏ MGF-27553 [M] | Listen to Me | 1966 | $25 |
| ❏ SRF-67553 [S] | Listen to Me | 1966 | $30 |

VERVE
| ❏ V-8697 [M] | Barra Limpa | 1967 | $30 |
| ❏ V6-8697 [S] | Barra Limpa | 1967 | $25 |

HENRY, ERNIE
Alto saxophone player.
Albums

FANTASY
❏ OJC-086	Last Chorus	198?	$25
❏ OJC-102	Presenting Ernie Henry	198?	$30
❏ OJC-1722	Seven Standards and a Blues	198?	$30

RIVERSIDE
❏ RLP 12-266 [M]	Last Chorus	1958	$300
❏ 6040	Presenting Ernie Henry	197?	$60
❏ RLP 12-248 [M]	Seven Standards and a Blues	1957	$500

HENRY'S BOOTBLACKS
Albums

STOMP OFF
| ❏ SOS-1149 | Hullabaloo | 1988 | $25 |

HENSON-CONANT, DEBORAH
Harpist and female singer.
Albums

GRP
| ❏ GR-9578 | On the Rise | 1989 | $20 |

HERBECK, RAY
Saxophone player, clarinetist and bandleader.
Albums

CIRCLE
| ❏ CLP-78 | Modern Music with Romance | 198? | $25 |

GLENDALE
| ❏ 6025 | Live and Romantic | 1985 | $25 |

HERBERT, MORT
Bass player and composer.
Albums

SAVOY
| ❏ MG-12073 [M] | Night People | 1956 | $40 |

HERBIG, GARY
Saxophone, bass clarinet and flute player.
Albums

HEADFIRST
| ❏ A-723 | Gary Herbig | 198? | $25 |

HERDSMEN, THE
Various members of WOODY HERMAN's band: Ralph Burns; Jerry Coker; Dick Collins; Chuck Flores; Dick Haffner; Red Kelly; Bill Perkins; Cy Touff.
Albums

FANTASY
| ❏ 3201 [M] | The Herdsmen Play Paris | 1955 | $80 |

—Green vinyl

HERMAN, WOODY
Bandleader, saxophone player and clarinetist. Also see THE EX-HERMANITES; THE FOUR BROTHERS; THE HERDSMEN; THE SMALL HERD.
Albums

ACCORD
| ❏ SN-7185 | All Star Session | 1981 | $25 |

AMERICAN RECORDING SOCIETY
| ❏ G-410 [M] | The Progressive Big Band Sound | 1956 | $40 |

ATLANTIC
❏ 1328 [M]	Woody Herman at the Monterey Jazz Festival	1960	$250
❏ SD1328 [S]	Woody Herman at the Monterey Jazz Festival	1960	$250
❏ 90044	Woody Herman at the Monterey Jazz Festival	1982	$25

—Reissue of 1328

BRUNSWICK
| ❏ BL54024 [M] | The Swinging Herman Herd | 1957 | $40 |

BULLDOG
| ❏ 2005 | 20 Golden Pieces of Woody Herman | 198? | $25 |

CADET
❏ LPS-835	Heavy Exposure	1969	$30
❏ LPS-819	Light My Fire	1969	$30
❏ LPS-845	Woody	1970	$30

CAPITOL
❏ T784 [M]	Blues Groove	1956	$60
❏ H324 [10]	Classics in Jazz	1952	$250
❏ T324 [M]	Classics in Jazz	1955	$75
❏ M-11034	Early Autumn	1972	$25
❏ T658 [M]	Road Band	1955	$75
❏ T1554 [M]	The Hits of Woody Herman	1961	$80
❏ DT1554 [R]	The Hits of Woody Herman	1961	$60
❏ SM-1554	The Hits of Woody Herman	197?	$20
❏ T560 [M]	The Woody Herman Band	1955	$75

CENTURY
| ❏ CR-1110 | Chick, Donald, Walter and Woodrow | 1978 | $30 |
| ❏ CRDD-1080 | Road Father | 1979 | $60 |

—Direct-to-disc recording

CHESS
| ❏ 402 | Double Exposure | 197? | $35 |

CLEF
| ❏ MGC-745 [M] | Jazz, the Utmost! | 1956 | $300 |

COLUMBIA
❏ CL6049 [10]	Dance Parade	1949	$140
❏ C32530	Jazz Hoot	1974	$30
❏ CL651 [M]	Music for Tired Lovers	1955	$50
❏ CL2357 [M]	My Kind of Broadway	1965	$30
❏ CS9157 [S]	My Kind of Broadway	1965	$35
❏ CL2509 [10]	Ridin' Herd	1955	$120
❏ CL6026 [10]	Sequence in Jazz	1949	$140
❏ CL2552 [M]	The Jazz S(w)inger	1966	$30
❏ CS9352 [S]	The Jazz S(w)inger	1966	$35
❏ CL592 [M]	The Three Herds	1955	$100

—Maroon label with gold print

| ❏ CL592 [M] | The Three Herds | 1956 | $60 |

—Red and black label with six "eye" logos

❏ C3L25 [M]	The Thundering Herds	1963	$100
❏ CL683 [M]	Twelve Shades of Blue	1956	$60
❏ CL2563 [10]	Woody!	1955	$120
❏ CL6092 [10]	Woody Herman and His Woodchoppers	1950	$140
❏ CL2491 [M]	Woody Herman's Greatest Hits	1966	$30
❏ CS9291 [S]	Woody Herman's Greatest Hits	1966	$35
❏ PC9291	Woody Herman's Greatest Hits	198?	$20

—Reissue with new prefix

❏ CL2693 [M]	Woody Live -- East & West	1967	$250
❏ CS9493 [S]	Woody Live -- East & West	1967	$250
❏ CL2436 [M]	Woody's Winners	1965	$30
❏ CS9236 [S]	Woody's Winners	1965	$35

CONCORD JAZZ
| ❏ CJ-302 | 50th Anniversary Tour | 1986 | $30 |
| ❏ CJ-191 | Live at the Concord Jazz Festival | 1982 | $30 |

Helen Humes, *Songs I Like to Sing!*, Contemporary S-7582, **$200**.

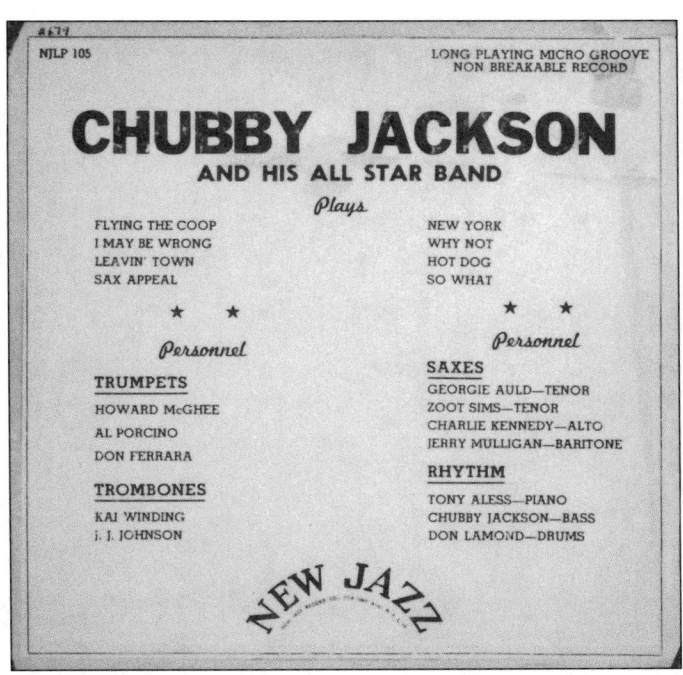

Chubby Jackson, *Chubby Jackson and His All Star Band*, New Jazz NJLP-105, 10-inch LP, **$800**.

Chubby Jackson and Bill Harris, *The Small Herd*, EmArcy MG 26003, 10-inch LP, **$200**.

Illinois Jacquet, *Illinois Jacquet Septet*, Clef MGC-676, **$350**.

Number	Title	Yr	NM
❏ CJ-170	Woody Herman and Friends at the Monterey Jazz Festival 1979	198?	$30
❏ CJ-330	Woody's Gold Star	1987	$30
❏ CJ-240	World Class	1983	$30
CORAL			
❏ CRL56005 [10]	Blue Prelude	1950	$140
❏ CRL56010 [10]	Woody Herman Souvenirs	1950	$140
❏ CRL56090 [10]	Woody's Best	1953	$140
CROWN			
❏ CLP5180 [M]	The New Swingin' Herman Band	1960	$50
❏ CST205 [S]	The New Swingin' Herman Herd	1960	$50
DECCA			
❏ DL9229 [M]	The Turning Point -- 1943-44	1967	$35
❏ DL79229 [R]	The Turning Point -- 1943-44	1967	$25
❏ DL8133 [M]	Woodchopper's Ball	1955	$150
❏ DL4484 [M]	Woody Herman's Golden Hits	1964	$35
❏ DL74484 [R]	Woody Herman's Golden Hits	1964	$25
DIAL			
❏ LP-210 [10]	Swinging with the Woodchoppers	1950	$150
DISCOVERY			
❏ 815	The Third Herd	198?	$25
❏ 845	The Third Herd, Volume 2	198?	$25
EVEREST			
❏ SDBR-1032 [S]	Moody Woody	1958	$40
❏ LPBR-5032 [M]	Moody Woody	1958	$60
❏ EV-1222 [M]	The Best of Woody Herman	1963	$35
❏ EV-5222 [S]	The Best of Woody Herman	1963	$50
❏ LPBR-5003 [M]	The Herd Rides Again	1958	$60
❏ SDBR-1003 [S]	The Herd Rides Again… In Stereo	1958	$40
EVEREST ARCHIVE OF FOLK & JAZZ			
❏ 281	Woody Herman	197?	$25
❏ 316	Woody Herman, Vol. 2	197?	$25
❏ 338	Woody Herman, Vol. 3	197?	$25
FANTASY			
❏ 8414	Brand New	1971	$30
❏ F-9477	Children of Lima	1975	$30
❏ FPM-4003 [Q]	Children of Lima	1975	$60
❏ F-9609	Feelin' So Blue	1982	$25
❏ F-9432	Giant Steps	1973	$30
❏ OJC-344	Giant Steps	198?	$25
—Reissue of 9432			
❏ F-9499	King Cobra	1976	$30
❏ F-9470	The Herd at Montreux	1974	$30
❏ 9416	The Raven Speaks	1972	$30
❏ F-9452	The Thundering Herd	1973	$30
FORUM			
❏ F-9016 [M]	Woody Herman Sextet at the Round Table	196?	$50
❏ FS-9016 [S]	Woody Herman Sextet at the Round Table	196?	$60
HARMONY			
❏ HL7013 [M]	Bijou	1957	$50
❏ HL7093 [M]	Summer Sequence	1957	$50
HINDSIGHT			
❏ HSR-116	Woody Herman and His Orchestra 1937	198?	$25
❏ HSR-134	Woody Herman and His Orchestra 1944	198?	$25
INSIGHT			
❏ 208	Woody Herman and His Orchestra 1937-44	198?	$25
JAZZLAND			
❏ JLP-17 [M]	The Fourth Herd	1960	$60
❏ JLP-917 [S]	The Fourth Herd	1960	$60
LION			
❏ L-70059 [M]	The Herman Herd at Carnegie Hall	1958	$60
MARS			
❏ MRX-1 [10]	Dance Date on Mars	1952	$250
❏ MRX-2 [10]	Woody Herman Goes Native	1953	$250
MCA			
❏ 219	Golden Favorites	1973	$25
❏ 4077	The Best of Woody Herman	197?	$35
METRO			
❏ M-514 [M]	Woody Herman	1966	$250
❏ MS-514 [R]	Woody Herman	1966	$150
MGM			
❏ E-284 [10]	Blue Flame	1955	$140
❏ E-3043 [M]	Carnegie Hall 1946	1953	$100
—Compiles 158 and 159 on one 12-inch LP			
❏ E-192 [10]	The Third Herd	1953	$140
❏ E-158 [10]	Woody Herman at Carnegie Hall, 1946, Vol. 1	1952	$140
❏ E-159 [10]	Woody Herman at Carnegie Hall, 1946, Vol. 2	1952	$140

Number	Title	Yr	NM
MOBILE FIDELITY			
❏ 1-219	The Fourth Herd	1994	$60
—Audiophile vinyl			
PHILIPS			
❏ PHM200092 [M]	Encore: Woody Herman 1963	1963	$35
❏ PHS600092 [S]	Encore: Woody Herman 1963	1963	$50
❏ PHM200004 [M]	Swing Low, Sweet Chariot	1962	$35
❏ PHS600004 [S]	Swing Low, Sweet Chariot	1962	$50
❏ PHM200131 [M]	The Swinging Herman Herd Recorded Live	1964	$35
❏ PHS600131 [S]	The Swinging Herman Herd Recorded Live	1964	$50
❏ PHM200118 [M]	Woody Herman: 1964	1964	$35
❏ PHS600118 [S]	Woody Herman: 1964	1964	$50
❏ PHM200065 [M]	Woody Herman 1963	1963	$35
❏ PHS600065 [S]	Woody Herman 1963	1963	$50
❏ PHM200171 [M]	Woody's Big Band Goodies	1965	$35
❏ PHS600171 [S]	Woody's Big Band Goodies	1965	$50
PICCADILY			
❏ 3333	It's Coolin' Time	198?	$25
PICKWICK			
❏ SPC-3591	Blowin' Up a Storm	1978	$25
RCA VICTOR			
❏ BGL2-2203	40th Anniversary Carnegie Hall Concert	1977	$35
ROULETTE			
❏ R25067 [M]	Woody Herman Sextet at the Round Table	1959	$60
❏ SR25067 [S]	Woody Herman Sextet at the Round Table	1959	$40
SUNBEAM			
❏ 206	Woody Herman and His Orchestra 1936	198?	$25
SUNSET			
❏ SUM-1139 [M]	Blowin' Up a Storm	1966	$25
❏ SUS-5139 [S]	Blowin' Up a Storm	1966	$30
TIME-LIFE			
❏ STBB-09	Big Bands: Woody Herman	1984	$35
TRIP			
❏ 5547	Woody 1963	1974	$25
VERVE			
❏ V6-8764	Concerto for Herd	1968	$50
❏ MGV-2030 [M]	Early Autumn	1957	$125
❏ V-2030 [M]	Early Autumn	1963	$35
❏ V-8558 [M]	Hey! Heard the Herd?	1963	$50
—Reissue of Verve 8216			
❏ V6-8558 [S]	Hey! Heard the Herd?	1963	$35
❏ MGV-8014 [M]	Jazz, the Utmost!	1957	$300
—Reissue of Clef LP			
❏ V-8014 [M]	Jazz, the Utmost!	1963	$35
❏ MGV-2096 [M]	Love Is the Sweetest Thing -- Sometimes	1958	$120
❏ V-2096 [M]	Love Is the Sweetest Thing -- Sometimes	1963	$35
❏ MGV-8216 [M]	Men from Mars	1958	$120
❏ MGV-2069 [M]	Songs for Hip Lovers	1957	$150
❏ V-2069 [M]	Songs for Hip Lovers	1963	$35
❏ VSP-1 [M]	The First Herd at Carnegie Hall	1966	$35
❏ VSPS-1 [R]	The First Herd at Carnegie Hall	1966	$25
❏ MGV-8255 [M]	Woody Herman '58	1958	$150
❏ V-8255 [M]	Woody Herman '58	1963	$35
❏ VSP-26 [M]	Woody Herman's Woodchoppers & The First Herd Live at Carnegie Hall	1966	$35
❏ VSPS-26 [R]	Woody Herman's Woodchoppers & The First Herd Live at Carnegie Hall	1966	$25
WHO'S WHO IN JAZZ			
❏ 21013	Lionel Hampton Presents Woody Herman	1979	$30
WING			
❏ MGW-12329 [M]	Woody's Big Band Goodies	1966	$25
❏ SRW-16329 [S]	Woody's Big Band Goodies	1966	$30

HERMAN, WOODY/TITO PUENTE
Also see each artist's individual listings.

Albums

Number	Title	Yr	NM
EVEREST			
❏ LPBR-5010 [M]	Herman's Beat of Puente	1958	$40
❏ SDBR-1010 [S]	Herman's Beat of Puente	1958	$40

Number	Title	Yr	NM
HERMETO			

Brazilian multi-instrumentalist.

Albums

Number	Title	Yr	NM
MUSE			
❏ MR-5086	Hermeto	197?	$30
WARNER BROS.			
❏ BS2980	Slaves Mass	1976	$35

HERSCH, FRED
Pianist.

Albums

Number	Title	Yr	NM
CHESKY			
❏ 90	Dancing in the Dark	1993	$25
CONCORD JAZZ			
❏ CJ-267	Horizons	1985	$25

HERSEY, BAIRD
Guitarist, synthesizer player and bandleader.

Albums

Number	Title	Yr	NM
ARISTA NOVUS			
❏ AN3016	Have You Heard	1979	$30
❏ AN3004	Lookin' for That Groove	1977	$30

HERWIG, CONRAD
Trombonist.

Albums

Number	Title	Yr	NM
SEA BREEZE			
❏ SB-2034	With Every Breath	1987	$25

HEYWOOD, EDDIE
Pianist, composer, bandleader and arranger. Best known for his piano solo on the hit version of "Canadian Sunset" with Hugo Winterhalter's orchestra.

Albums

Number	Title	Yr	NM
BRUNSWICK			
❏ BL58036 [10]	Eddie Heywood '45	1953	$100
CAPITOL			
❏ ST-163	Soft Summer Breeze	1969	$60
❏ ST2833	With Love and Strings	1968	$60
COLUMBIA			
❏ CL6157 [10]	Piano Moods	1951	$100
COMMODORE			
❏ FL-20007 [10]	Eight Selections	1950	$150
❏ XFL-15876	The Biggest Little Band of the Forties	198?	$30
CORAL			
❏ CRL57095 [M]	Featuring Eddie Heywood	1957	$40
DECCA			
❏ DL8202 [M]	Lightly and Politely	1956	$120
❏ DL8270 [M]	Swing Low Sweet Heywood	1956	$150
EMARCY			
❏ MG-36042 [M]	Eddie Heywood	1955	$200
EPIC			
❏ LN3327 [M]	Eddie Heywood at Twilight	1956	$100
LIBERTY			
❏ LRP-3313 [M]	Canadian Sunset Bossa Nova	1963	$30
❏ LST-7313 [S]	Canadian Sunset Bossa Nova	1963	$35
❏ LRP-3250 [M]	Eddie Heywood's Golden Encores	1962	$30
❏ LST-7250 [S]	Eddie Heywood's Golden Encores	1962	$35
❏ LST-7279 [S]	Manhattan Beat	1963	$35
❏ LRP-3279 [M]	Manhattan Beat	1963	$30
MAINSTREAM			
❏ S-6001 [S]	Begin the Beguine	1964	$35
❏ 96001 [M]	Begin the Beguine	1964	$30
MERCURY			
❏ MG-20445 [M]	Breezin' Along with the Breeze	1959	$100
❏ SR-60115 [S]	Breezin' Along with the Breeze	1959	$100
❏ MG-20590 [M]	Eddie Heywood at the Piano	1960	$100
❏ SR-60248 [S]	Eddie Heywood at the Piano	1960	$100
❏ MG-20632 [M]	One for My Baby	1960	$100
❏ SR-60632 [S]	One for My Baby	1960	$100
MGM			
❏ E-3260 [M]	Eddie Heywood	1956	$40
❏ E-135 [10]	It's Easy to Remember	1952	$100
❏ E-3093 [M]	Pianorama	1955	$50
RCA VICTOR			
❏ LPM-1529 [M]	Canadian Sunset	1957	$60
❏ LSP-1529 [S]	Canadian Sunset	1958	$40

Number	Title	Yr	NM
❏ LPM-1900 [M]	The Keys and I	1958	$60
❏ LPM-1466 [M]	The Touch of Eddie Heywood	1957	$60

SUNSET

❏ SUM-1121 [M]	An Affair to Remember	196?	$30
❏ SUS-5121 [S]	An Affair to Remember	196?	$30

VOCALION

❏ VL3748 [M]	The Piano Stylings of Eddie Heywood	1966	$35
❏ VL73748 [R]	The Piano Stylings of Eddie Heywood	1966	$30

WING

❏ MGW-12287 [M]	Breezin' Along	196?	$35
❏ SRW-16287 [S]	Breezin' Along	196?	$30
❏ MGW-12137 [M]	Eddie Heywood	196?	$35
❏ SRW-16137 [S]	Eddie Heywood	196?	$30

HI-LO'S, THE
Vocal group: Gene Puerling; Bob Strassen (replaced by Don Shelton in 1959); Clark Burroughs; Bob Morse.

Albums

COLUMBIA

❏ CS8300 [S]	All Over the Place	1960	$60
❏ CL1416 [M]	Broadway Playbill	1959	$60
❏ CS8213 [S]	Broadway Playbill	1959	$40
❏ CL1023 [M]	Now Hear This	1957	$60
❏ CL952 [M]	Suddenly It's the Hi-Lo's	1957	$60
❏ CL1259 [M]	The Hi-Lo's and All That Jazz	1958	$60
❏ CS8077 [S]	The Hi-Lo's and All That Jazz	1958	$40
❏ CL1723 [M]	This Time It's Love	1962	$60
❏ CS8523 [S]	This Time It's Love	1962	$60

COLUMBIA SPECIAL PRODUCTS

❏ P14387	Harmony in Jazz	1978	$30

DRG

❏ SL5184	Clap Yo' Hands	198?	$30

KAPP

❏ KL1194 [M]	On Hand	1960	$60

— Reissue of Starlite 7008

❏ KL1027 [M]	The Hi-Lo's and the Jerry Fielding Band	1956	$60
❏ KL1184 [M]	Under Glass	1959	$60

— Reissue of Starlite 7005

MCA

❏ 4171	The Hi-Lo's Collection	197?	$35

OMEGA

❏ OSL-11 [S]	The Hi-Lo's in Stereo	195?	$30

PAUSA

❏ 7040	Back Again	198?	$30
❏ 7093	Now	198?	$30

REPRISE

❏ R-6066 [M]	The Hi-Lo's Happen to Bossa Nova	1963	$50
❏ R9-6066 [S]	The Hi-Lo's Happen to Bossa Nova	1963	$60

STARLITE

❏ 6004 [10]	Listen!	1955	$120
❏ 7006 [M]	Listen!	1956	$40

— Reissue of 6004

❏ 7008 [M]	On Hand	1956	$40
❏ 6005 [10]	The Hi-Lo's, I Presume	1955	$120
❏ 7007 [M]	The Hi-Lo's. I Presume	1956	$40

— Reissue of 6005

❏ 7005 [M]	Under Glass	1956	$40

HIBBLER, AL
Male singer, best known for his 1955 hit version of "Unchained Melody."

Albums

ARGO

❏ LP-601 [M]	Melodies by Al Hibbler	1956	$40

— Reissue of Marterry LP

ATLANTIC

❏ 1251 [M]	After the Lights Go Down Low	1957	$300

— Black label

❏ 1251 [M]	After the Lights Go Down Low	1961	$250

— Mostly red label, white fan logo

❏ 1251 [M]	After the Lights Go Down Low	1963	$150

— Mostly red label, black fan logo

BRUNSWICK

❏ BL54036 [M]	Al Hibbler with the Ellingtonians	1957	$50

DECCA

Number	Title	Yr	NM
❏ DL8862 [M]	Al Hibbler Remembers the Big Songs of the Big Bands	1959	$100
❏ DL78862 [S]	Al Hibbler Remembers the Big Songs of the Big Bands	1959	$100
❏ DL8420 [M]	Here's Hibbler	1957	$120
❏ DL8757 [M]	Hits by Hibbler	1958	$120
❏ DL8328 [M]	Starring Al Hibbler	1956	$150
❏ DL8697 [M]	Torchy and Blue	1958	$100

DISCOVERY

❏ 842	It's Monday Every Day	198?	$15

— Reissue of Reprise LP

LMI

❏ 10001 [M]	Early One Morning	1964	$30

MCA

❏ 4098	The Best of Al Hibbler	197?	$20

NORGRAN

❏ MGN-4 [10]	Al Hibbler Favorites	1954	$300
❏ MGN-15 [10]	Al Hibbler Sings Duke Ellington	1954	$300

OPEN SKY

❏ OSR-3126	For Sentimental Reasons	1986	$15

REPRISE

❏ R-2005 [M]	It's Monday Every Day	1961	$30
❏ R9-2005 [S]	It's Monday Every Day	1961	$40

SCORE

❏ SLP-4013 [M]	I Surrender, Dear	1957	$100

VERVE

❏ MGV-4000 [M]	Al Hibbler Sings Love Songs	1956	$150
❏ V-4000 [M]	Al Hibbler Sings Love Songs	1961	$60

HICKS, JOHN
Pianist.

Albums

STRATA-EAST

❏ SES-8002	Hells Bells	1979	$35

THERESA

❏ TR-119	John Hicks	1986	$30
❏ TR-123	John Hicks In Concert	1987	$30
❏ TR-115	Some Other Time	1983	$30

WEST 54TH

❏ 8004	After the Morning	1980	$30

HIGGINBOTHAM, J.C.
Trombonist.

Albums

JAZZOLOGY

❏ J-28	J.C. Higginbotham Comes Home!	1968	$30

HIGGINS, BILLY
Drummer and composer.

Albums

CONTEMPORARY

❏ C-14024	Bridgework	1987	$25

RED

❏ VPA-164	Once More	198?	$30
❏ VPA-141	Soweto	1979	$30

HIGGINS, EDDIE
Pianist, clarinetist and bass player.

Albums

ATLANTIC

❏ 1446 [M]	Soulero	1966	$35
❏ SD1446 [S]	Soulero	1966	$25

VEE JAY

❏ LP-3017 [M]	Eddie Higgins	1961	$30
❏ SR-3017 [S]	Eddie Higgins	1961	$40

HIGH SOCIETY JAZZ BAND, THE

Albums

STOMP OFF

❏ SOS-1166	'Lasses Candy	1989	$25
❏ SOS-1010	Shake It and Break It	1981	$30

HIGHER PRIMATES
Members: Glenn Davis, Peter LeMaitre, Ron Glick (percussion); Ed Schuller, Roy Cumming, Ratso Harris (bass); Mark Reboul (saxophone); Herb Robertson (trumpet).

Albums

GM

❏ 3003	Environmental Impressions	1985	$25

HIGHTOWER, DONNA
Female singer.

Albums

CAPITOL

Number	Title	Yr	NM
❏ T1273 [M]	Gee Baby…Ain't I Good to You	1959	$60
❏ ST1273 [S]	Gee Baby…Ain't I Good to You	1959	$80
❏ T1133 [M]	Take One	1959	$75
❏ ST1133 [S]	Take One	1959	$80

HILDINGER, DAVE
Pianist and vibraphone player.

Albums

BATON

❏ 1204 [M]	The Young Moderns	1957	$40

HILL, ANDREW
Pianist.

Albums

ARISTA FREEDOM

❏ AL1023	Montreux	1976	$35
❏ AL1007	Spiral	1975	$35

ARTISTS HOUSE

❏ 9	From California with Love	1979	$30

BLUE NOTE

❏ BLP4203 [M]	Andrew!!! -- The Music of Andrew Hill	1965	$0

— not known to exist

❏ BST-84151 [S]	Black Fire	1967	$35

— With "A Division of Liberty Records" on label

❏ BLP-4217 [M]	Compulsion	1965	$60
❏ BST-84217 [S]	Compulsion	1965	$30

— With "New York, USA" address on label

❏ BST-84217 [S]	Compulsion	1967	$35

— With "A Division of Liberty Records" on label

❏ LN-1030	Dance with Andrew Hill	1980	$30
❏ BST-84303	Grass Roots	1968	$25
❏ B1-92051	Internal Spirit	198?	$25
❏ BST-84159 [S]	Judgment!	1964	$40

— With "New York, USA" address on label

❏ BST-84159 [S]	Judgment!	1967	$35

— With "A Division of Liberty Records" on label

❏ B1-28981	Judgment!	1994	$35
❏ BST-84330	Lift Every Voice	1969	$25
❏ BLP-4233 [M]	One for One	1966	$0

— Canceled

❏ BST-84233 [S]	One for One	1966	$0

— Canceled

❏ BN-LA459-H2	One for One	1975	$25
❏ BLP-4167 [M]	Point of Departure	1964	$60
❏ BST-84167 [S]	Point of Departure	1964	$40

— With "New York, USA" address on label

❏ BST-84167 [S]	Point of Departure	1967	$35

— With "A Division of Liberty Records" on label

❏ B1-32097	Smokestack	1995	$35
❏ BST-84160 [S]	Smoke Stack	1964	$40

— With "New York, USA" address on label

❏ BST-84160 [S]	Smoke Stack	1967	$35

— With "A Division of Liberty Records" on label

INNER CITY

❏ IC-2044	Divine Revelation	1976	$35
❏ IC-2026	Invitation	1975	$35
❏ IC-6022	Nefertiti	1977	$35

SOUL NOTE

❏ SN-1010	Faces of Hope	198?	$30
❏ 121113	Shades	199?	$30
❏ SN-1013	Strange Serenade	198?	$30
❏ 121110	Verona Rag	199?	$30

STEEPLECHASE

❏ SCS-1044	Divine Revelation	198?	$30
❏ SCS-1026	Invitation	198?	$30

WARWICK

❏ W-2002 [M]	So in Love	1960	$60
❏ W-2002ST [S]	So in Love	1960	$80

HILL, BUCK
Tenor saxophone player.

Albums

STEEPLECHASE

❏ SCS-1160	Easy to Love	198?	$35
❏ SCS-1173	Impressions	198?	$35
❏ SCS-1123	Scope	1980	$35
❏ SCS-1095	This Is Buck Hill	1979	$35

Number	Title	Yr	NM

HILL, TINY
Bandleader, male singer, banjo player and drummer. Curiously, after World War II he had four Top 10 hits on the country charts!

Albums

HINDSIGHT
| ❑ HSR-159 | The Uncollected Tiny Hill and His Orchestra, 1944 | 1980 | $12 |

MERCURY
❑ MG-20630 [M]	Dancin' and Singin' with Tiny Hill	195?	$150
❑ SR-60631 [R]	Golden Hits	196?	$20
❑ MG-25126 [10]	Tiny Hill	1952	$100

HILL, VINSON
Pianist.

Albums

SAVOY
| ❑ MG-12187 [M] | The Vinson Hill Trio | 1966 | $30 |

HIMBER, RICHARD
Bandleader.

Albums

CIRCLE
| ❑ 7 | Richard Himber and His Orchestra: 1939-1940 | 198? | $25 |

HINES, EARL "FATHA," AND BUDD JOHNSON
Also see each artist's individual listings.

Albums

CLASSIC JAZZ
| ❑ 129 | Linger Awhile | 197? | $30 |

HINES, EARL "FATHA," AND COLEMAN HAWKINS
Also see each artist's individual listings.

Albums

LIMELIGHT
| ❑ LM-82020 [M] | The Grand Reunion | 1965 | $25 |
| ❑ LS-86020 [S] | The Grand Reunion | 1965 | $30 |

TRIP
| ❑ 5557 | The Grand Reunion | 197? | $25 |

HINES, EARL "FATHA," AND JAKI BYARD
Also see each artist's individual listings.

Albums

VERVE/MPS
| ❑ 825195-1 | Duet | 1985 | $25 |

HINES, EARL "FATHA," AND MARVA JOSIE
Josie is a female singer. Also see EARL "FATHA" HINES.

Albums

CATALYST
| ❑ 7622 | His Old Lady and Me | 197? | $30 |

HINES, EARL "FATHA," AND MAXINE SULLIVAN
Also see each artist's individual listings.

Albums

CHIAROSCURO
| ❑ 107 | Live at the Overseas Press Club | 1971 | $35 |

HINES, EARL "FATHA," AND PAUL GONSALVES
Also see each artist's individual listings.

Albums

BLACK LION
| ❑ 306 | It Don't Mean a Thing | 197? | $30 |

HINES, EARL "FATHA," AND ROY ELDRIDGE
Also see each artist's individual listings.

Albums

LIMELIGHT
| ❑ LM-82028 [M] | The Grand Reunion, Volume 2 | 1965 | $25 |
| ❑ LS-86028 [S] | The Grand Reunion, Volume 2 | 1965 | $30 |

XANADU
| ❑ 106 | At the Village Vanguard | 197? | $30 |

HINES, EARL "FATHA," AND TERESA BREWER
Also see each artist's individual listings.

Albums

DOCTOR JAZZ
| ❑ FW38810 | We Love You Fats | 1983 | $25 |

HINES, EARL "FATHA"
Pianist, male singer and composer. Also see COZY COLE; JOHNNY HODGES.

Albums

ABC IMPULSE!
| ❑ AS-9108 [S] | Once Upon a Time | 1968 | $35 |

ADVANCE
| ❑ 4 [10] | Fats Waller Memorial Set | 1951 | $150 |

ATLANTIC
| ❑ ALS-120 [10] | Earl Hines: QRS Solos | 1952 | $350 |

AUDIOPHILE
❑ APS-112	Earl Hines Comes In Handy	197?	$35
❑ APS-113	Hines Does Hoagy	197?	$35
❑ APS-111	My Tribute to Louis	1971	$35

BASF
| ❑ 20749 | Fatha and His Flock On Tour | 1972 | $35 |

BIOGRAPH
| ❑ 12056 | Earl Hines in New Orleans | 197? | $25 |
| ❑ 12055 | Solo Walk in Tokyo | 197? | $25 |

BLACK LION
| ❑ 112 | Tea for Two | 1973 | $30 |
| ❑ 200 | Tour de Force | 1974 | $30 |

BLUEBIRD
| ❑ AXM2-5508 | Fatha Jumps | 197? | $35 |

BRAVO
| ❑ K-134 | Earl Fatha Hines and His Orchestra | 196? | $25 |

BRUNSWICK
| ❑ BL58035 [10] | Earl Hines Plays Fats Waller | 1953 | $120 |

CAPITOL
| ❑ T1971 [M] | Earl "Fatha" Hines | 1963 | $60 |
| ❑ ST1971 [S] | Earl "Fatha" Hines | 1963 | $60 |

CHIAROSCURO
❑ 116	An Evening with Hines	1972	$25
❑ 200	Earl Hines in New Orleans	1978	$30
❑ 157	Live at the New School	1974	$30
❑ 180	Live at the New School, Volume 2	1977	$30
❑ 131	Quintessential 1974	1974	$35
❑ 120	Quintessential Continued	1973	$35
❑ 101	Quintessential Recording Session	1971	$35
—Reissue of Halcyon 101			

CLASSIC JAZZ
| ❑ 144 | Earl Hines at Sundown | 198? | $30 |
| ❑ 31 | Earl Hines Plays Gershwin | 1974 | $35 |

COLUMBIA
❑ CL6171 [10]	Piano Moods	1951	$120
❑ CL2320 [M]	The New Earl Hines Trio	1965	$25
❑ CS9120 [S]	The New Earl Hines Trio	1965	$30

COLUMBIA JAZZ MASTERPIECES
| ❑ CJ44197 | Live at the Village Vanguard | 1988 | $25 |

CONTACT
| ❑ 2 [M] | Spontaneous Explorations | 1964 | $30 |
| ❑ S-2 [S] | Spontaneous Explorations | 1964 | $30 |

CRAFTSMEN
| ❑ 8041 [M] | Swingin' and Singin' | 1960 | $30 |

DECCA
❑ DL79235 [R]	Earl Hines at the Apex Club	1968	$30
❑ DL9235 [M]	Earl Hines at the Apex Club	1968	$30
❑ DL75048	Fatha Blows Best	1969	$35
❑ DL79221 [R]	Southside Swing (1934-35)	1967	$30

DELMARK
| ❑ DS-212 | Earl Hines At Home | 1969 | $30 |

DIAL
| ❑ LP-306 [10] | Earl Hines All Stars | 1953 | $250 |
| ❑ LP-303 [10] | Earl Hines Trio | 1952 | $250 |

ENSIGN
| ❑ 22021 | Earl Hines Rhythm | 1969 | $25 |

EPIC
| ❑ LN3501 [M] | Earl "Fatha" Hines | 1958 | $100 |
| ❑ LN3223 [M] | Oh, Fatha! | 1956 | $100 |

EVEREST ARCHIVE OF FOLK & JAZZ
| ❑ 246 | Earl "Fatha" Hines | 1970 | $30 |
| ❑ 322 | Earl "Fatha" Hines, Volume 2 | 197? | $25 |

FANTASY
❑ OJC-1740	A Monday Date	198?	$25
❑ 3238 [M]	Earl "Fatha" Hines Solo	1956	$100
—Red vinyl			
❑ 3238 [M]	Earl "Fatha" Hines Solo	195?	$50

—Black vinyl			
❑ 3217 [M]	Fatha" Plays "Fats	1956	$100
—Red vinyl			
❑ 3217 [M]	Fatha" Plays "Fats	195?	$50
—Black vinyl			
❑ 8381	Incomparable	1968	$30

FLYING DUTCHMAN
| ❑ FD-10147 | The Mighty Fatha | 1973 | $35 |

FOCUS
| ❑ FM-335 [M] | The Real Earl Hines In Concert | 1965 | $30 |
| ❑ FS-335 [S] | The Real Earl Hines In Concert | 1965 | $30 |

GNP CRESCENDO
❑ GNP-9042	Earl "Fatha" Hines All-Stars	197?	$25
❑ GNP-9043	Earl "Fatha" Hines All-Stars, Vol. 2	197?	$25
❑ GNP-9010	Earl "Fatha" Hines in Paris	197?	$25
❑ GNPS-9054	Live at the Crescendo	1992	$30

HALCYON
| ❑ 101 | The Quintessential Recording Session | 196? | $25 |

HALL OF FAME
| ❑ 609 | Earl "Fatha" Hines All-Stars | 197? | $25 |

IMPROV
| ❑ 7114 | Live at the Downtown Club | 1976 | $30 |

IMPULSE!
| ❑ A-9108 [M] | Once Upon a Time | 1966 | $120 |
| ❑ AS-9108 [S] | Once Upon a Time | 1966 | $120 |

INNER CITY
| ❑ IC-1142 | Paris Session | 198? | $30 |

JAZZ PANORAMA
| ❑ 7 [M] | All Stars | 1961 | $40 |

M&K
| ❑ 105 | Fatha | 1979 | $30 |
| —Direct-to-disc recording | | | |

MASTER JAZZ
❑ 8101	Blues and Things	1970	$35
❑ 8114	Earl Hines Plays Duke Ellington	1971	$35
❑ 8132	Earl Hines Plays Duke Ellington, Volume 4	1975	$30
❑ 8126	Earl Hines Plays Duke Ellington, Volumes 2 and 3	1973	$25
❑ 8109	Hines '65	1971	$35

MCA
❑ 29070	Once Upon a Time	198?	$25
❑ 1373	Rhythm Sundae	198?	$25
❑ 1311	South Side Swing	198?	$25

MERCURY
| ❑ MG-25018 [10] | Earl Hines and the All Stars | 1950 | $300 |

MGM
| ❑ E-3832 [M] | Earl's Pearls | 1960 | $30 |
| ❑ SE-3832 [S] | Earl's Pearls | 1960 | $30 |

MILESTONE
| ❑ 2012 | Monday Date 1928 | 197? | $30 |

MUSE
| ❑ MR-2001/2 | The Legendary Little Theatre Concert of 1964 | 198? | $35 |
| ❑ DE-602 | The Legendary Little Theatre Concert of 1964, Volume 1 | 198? | $25 |

NOCTURNE
| ❑ NLP-5 [10] | Earl "Fatha" Hines | 1954 | $150 |

PRESTIGE
| ❑ 24043 | Another Monday Date | 197? | $35 |
| ❑ 2515 | Boogie Woogie on St. Louis Blues | 198? | $30 |

QUICKSILVER
| ❑ QS-9001 | Fatha | 198? | $25 |
| ❑ QS-9000 | Live and in Living Jazz | 198? | $25 |

RCA VICTOR
❑ LPT-20 [10]	Earl Hines with Billy Eckstine	1953	$120
❑ LPV-512 [M]	The Grand Terrace Band	1965	$30
❑ LPM-3380 [M]	Up to Date	1965	$25
❑ LSP-3380 [S]	Up to Date	1965	$30

RIVERSIDE
| ❑ RLP-398 [M] | A Monday Date | 1961 | $200 |
| ❑ RS-9398 [R] | A Monday Date | 196? | $25 |

ROYALE
| ❑ 18166 [10] | Eal "Fatha" Hines -- Great Piano Solos | 195? | $120 |

STORYVILLE
| ❑ 4063 | Earl Hines at the Club Hangover | 198? | $25 |

TIARA
| ❑ TMT-7524 [M] | Earl "Fatha" Hines with Buck Clayton | 195? | $25 |

TIME-LIFE

Number	Title	Yr	NM
❏ STL-J-11	Giants of Jazz	1980	$60

TOPS

Number	Title	Yr	NM
❏ L-1599 [M]	Fatha	195?	$30

TRIP

❏ J-3	All-Star Session	1970	$30

VERVE

❏ VSP-35 [M]	Life with Fatha	1966	$25
❏ VSPS-35 [R]	Life with Fatha	1966	$30

WHO'S WHO IN JAZZ

❏ 21004	Lionel Hampton Presents Earl Hines	1978	$30

X

❏ LVA-3023 [10]	Piano Solos	1954	$120

XANADU

❏ 203	Varieties!	1985	$25

HINO, TERUMASA
Trumpeter.

Albums

CATALYST

❏ 7910	At the Berlin Jazz Festival '71	197?	$30
❏ 7901	Fuji	197?	$30

EMJA

❏ 2028	Taro's Mood	197?	$35

INNER CITY

❏ IC-6068	City Connection	198?	$30
❏ IC-6069	Daydream	198?	$30
❏ IC-6065	May Dance	197?	$30
❏ IC-6027	Speak to Loneliness	197?	$30

HINTON, MILT; WENDELL MARSHALL; BULL RUTHER
All of the above are bass players. Also see MILT HINTON.

Albums

RCA VICTOR

❏ LPM-1107 [M]	Basses Loaded!	1955	$80

HINTON, MILT
Bass player.

Albums

BETHLEHEM

❏ BCP-10 [M]	East Coast Jazz Series #5	1957	$250
❏ BCP-1020 [10]	Milt Hinton Quartet	1955	$250

CHIAROSCURO

❏ 188	Trio	1978	$30

EPIC

❏ LN3271 [M]	The Rhythm Section	1956	$100

EXPOSURE

❏ 6231910	The Judge's Decision	198?	$30

FAMOUS DOOR

❏ 104	Here Swings The Judge	197?	$35

HINZE, CHRIS
Flutist and composer.

Albums

ATLANTIC

❏ SD19185	Bamboo	1978	$30

COLUMBIA

❏ KC33363	Sister Slick	1975	$30

HIPP, JUTTA
Pianist.

Albums

BLUE NOTE

❏ BLP-1515 [M]	Jutta Hipp at the Hickory House, Volume 1	1956	$1000

—Deep groove" version, Lexington Ave. address on label

❏ BLP-1515 [M]	Jutta Hipp at the Hickory House, Volume 1	1956	$800

—Deep groove" version, W. 63rd St. address on label

❏ BLP-1515 [M]	Jutta Hipp at the Hickory House, Volume 1	1963	$200

—With "New York, USA" address on label

❏ BLP-1516 [B]	Jutta Hipp at the Hickory House, Volume 2	1956	$1000

—Lexington Ave address

❏ BLP-1530 [M]	Jutta Hipp with Zoot Sims	1956	$5000

—Deep groove" version; Lexington Ave. address on label

❏ BLP-1530 [M]	Jutta Hipp with Zoot Sims	1956	$2000

—Deep groove" version, W. 63sr St. address on label

Number	Title	Yr	NM
❏ BLP-1530 [M]	Jutta Hipp with Zoot Sims	1963	$150

— With "New York, USA" address on label

❏ BLP-1530 [M]	Jutta Hipp with Zoot Sims	2003	$100

—200-gram reissue; distributed by Classic Records

❏ BLP-5056 [10]	Jutta -- New Faces, New Sounds from Germany	1955	$800

MGM

❏ E-3157 [M]	Cool Europe	1955	$150

HIROTA, JOJI
Percussionist and singer.

Albums

INNER CITY

❏ IC-1127	Wheel of Fortune	198?	$30

HIRT, AL, AND ANN-MARGRET
Ann-Margret is a female singer whose solo recordings are outside the jazz realm. Also see AL HIRT.

Albums

RCA VICTOR

❏ LPM-2690 [M]	Beauty and the Beard	1964	$25
❏ LSP-2690 [S]	Beauty and the Beard	1964	$25

HIRT, AL, AND PETE FOUNTAIN
See PETE FOUNTAIN AND AL HIRT.

HIRT, AL
Trumpeter and occasional male singer. One of the most popular musicians of the 1960s Dixieland revival.

Albums

ACCORD

❏ SN-7187	Java	1981	$10

ALLEGIANCE

❏ AV-5032	Blues Line	1986	$10
❏ AV-5018	Showtime	1985	$10

AUDIO FIDELITY

❏ AF-6282	Hirt…So Good!	1978	$25
❏ AFLP-1878 [M]	Swingin' Dixie	1959	$35
❏ AFSD-5878 [S]	Swingin' Dixie	1959	$25
❏ AFLP-1877 [M]	Swingin' Dixie (At Dan's Pier 600 in New Orleans)	1959	$35
❏ AFSD-5877 [S]	Swingin' Dixie (At Dan's Pier 600 in New Orleans)	1959	$25
❏ AFLP-1926 [M]	Swingin' Dixie (Vol. 3)	1961	$35
❏ AFSD-5926 [S]	Swingin' Dixie (Vol. 3)	1961	$25
❏ T-90284 [M]	Swingin' Dixie (Vol. 3)	196?	$80

— Capitol Record Club edition

❏ ST-90284 [S]	Swingin' Dixie (Vol. 3)	196?	$80

— Capitol Record Club edition

❏ AFLP-1927 [M]	Swingin' Dixie (Vol. 4)	1961	$35
❏ AFSD-5927 [S]	Swingin' Dixie (Vol. 4)	1961	$25

CORAL

❏ CRL57402 [M]	Al Hirt in New Orleans	1962	$30
❏ CRL757402 [S]	Al Hirt in New Orleans	1962	$35

CROWN

❏ CLP-5457 [M]	The Dawn Busters	196?	$30
❏ CST-457 [S]	The Dawn Busters	196?	$30

GHB

❏ 107	Mardi Gras Parade Music	197?	$25

GWP

❏ 2005	Al Hirt Country	1971	$25
❏ 2004	Al Hirt Gold	1971	$25
❏ 2002	Paint Your Wagon	1970	$25

LONGINES SYMPHONETTE

❏ LWCP1	The Best of Dixieland Jazz	196?	$30

METRO

❏ M-517 [M]	Al Hirt	1965	$150
❏ MS-517 [S]	Al Hirt	1965	$150

MONUMENT

❏ 7603	Jumbo's Gumbo	1977	$10

— Reissue of 33885

❏ PZ33885	Jumbo's Gumbo	1975	$25
❏ KZ32913	Raw Sugar/Sweet Sauce/ Banana Puddin'	1974	$25
❏ 6642	Raw Sugar/Sweet Sauce/ Banana Puddin'	1976	$10

— Reissue of 32913

PAIR

❏ PDL2-1048	New Orleans By Night	1986	$15

RCA CAMDEN

❏ CXS-9015	Al Hirt Blows His Own Horn	1972	$30
❏ CAS-2316	Al's Place	1970	$25
❏ CAS-2573	Have a Merry Little	1971	$25

Number	Title	Yr	NM
❏ CAL-2138 [M]	Struttin' Down Royal Street	1967	$30
❏ CAS-2138 [S]	Struttin' Down Royal Street	1967	$25

RCA VICTOR

❏ LPM-2354 [M]	Al (He's the King) Hirt and His Band	1961	$30
❏ LSP-2354 [S]	Al (He's the King) Hirt and His Band	1961	$35
❏ LSP-4247	Al Hirt	1970	$30
❏ LPM-2497 [M]	Al Hirt at the Mardi Gras	1962	$30
❏ LSP-2497 [S]	Al Hirt at the Mardi Gras	1962	$35
❏ LSP-4101	Al Hirt Now	1969	$30
❏ LPM-3917 [M]	Al Hirt Plays Bert Kaempfert	1968	$20
❏ LSP-3917 [S]	Al Hirt Plays Bert Kaempfert	1968	$35
❏ LPM-2917 [M]	Cotton Candy	1964	$30
❏ LSP-2917 [S]	Cotton Candy	1964	$35
❏ LSP-4161	Here in My Heart	1969	$30
❏ LPM-2733 [M]	Honey in the Horn	1963	$30
❏ LSP-2733 [S]	Honey in the Horn	1963	$35
❏ LPM-2446 [M]	Horn A-Plenty	1962	$30
❏ LSP-2446 [S]	Horn A-Plenty	1962	$35
❏ LSP-4020	In Love with You	1968	$30
❏ LPM-3653 [M]	Latin in the Horn	1966	$30
❏ LSP-3653 [S]	Latin in the Horn	1966	$35
❏ LPM-3416 [M]	Live at Carnegie Hall	1965	$30
❏ LSP-3416 [S]	Live at Carnegie Hall	1965	$35
❏ LPM-3773 [M]	Music to Watch Girls By	1967	$30
❏ LSP-3773 [S]	Music to Watch Girls By	1967	$35
❏ LPM-2607 [M]	Our Man in New Orleans	1963	$30
❏ LSP-2607 [S]	Our Man in New Orleans	1963	$35
❏ LM-2729 [M]	Pops" Goes the Trumpet	1964	$35
❏ LSC-2729 [S]	Pops" Goes the Trumpet	1964	$35

— With the Boston Pops Orchestra conducted by Arthur Fiedler

❏ LPM-3878 [M]	Soul in the Horn	1967	$35
❏ LSP-3878 [S]	Soul in the Horn	1967	$35
❏ LPM-2965 [M]	Sugar Lips	1964	$30
❏ LSP-2965 [S]	Sugar Lips	1964	$35
❏ LPM-3337 [M]	That Honey Horn Sound	1965	$30
❏ LSP-3337 [S]	That Honey Horn Sound	1965	$35
❏ LPM-3309 [M]	The Best of Al Hirt	1965	$30
❏ LSP-3309 [S]	The Best of Al Hirt	1965	$35
❏ ANL1-1034	The Best of Al Hirt	1975	$25
❏ LPM-3556 [M]	The Best of Al Hirt, Volume 2	1966	$30
❏ LSP-3556 [S]	The Best of Al Hirt, Volume 2	1966	$35
❏ LPM-2366 [M]	The Greatest Horn in the World	1961	$30
❏ LSP-2366 [S]	The Greatest Horn in the World	1961	$35
❏ LPM-3579 [M]	The Happy Trumpet	1966	$30
❏ LSP-3579 [S]	The Happy Trumpet	1966	$35
❏ LPM-3716 [M]	The Horn Meets the Hornet	1967	$30
❏ LSP-3716 [S]	The Horn Meets the Hornet	1967	$35
❏ LPM-3417 [M]	The Sound of Christmas	1965	$25
❏ LSP-3417 [S]	The Sound of Christmas	1965	$30
❏ LPM-3492 [M]	They're Playing Our Song	1966	$30
❏ LSP-3492 [S]	They're Playing Our Song	1966	$35
❏ VPS-6046	This Is Al Hirt	1970	$35
❏ VPS-6057	This Is Al Hirt, Volume 2	1972	$35
❏ LPM-2584 [M]	Trumpet and Strings	1962	$30
❏ LSP-2584 [S]	Trumpet and Strings	1962	$35
❏ LPM-3979 [M]	Unforgettable	1968	$20
❏ LSP-3979 [S]	Unforgettable	1968	$30

VERVE

❏ MGV-1027 [M]	Blockbustin' Dixie!	195?	$25
❏ V-1027 [M]	Blockbustin' Dixie!	1961	$25
❏ MGV-1012 [M]	Swinging Dixie from Dan's Pier 600	1957	$150

VOCALION

❏ VL73907	Floatin' Down to Cotton Town	1970	$25

WYNCOTE

❏ 9089	The Dawn Busters	196?	$25

HITTMAN, JEFF, AND YOSHITAKA UEMATSU
Hittman plays tenor saxophone; Uematsu is a drummer.

Albums

SOUL NOTE

❏ 121137	Mosaic	1990	$35

HODEIR, ANDRE
Composer and conductor.

Albums

EMARCY

❏ SR-66005	Plain Old Blues	1967	$100

JAZZOLOGY

❏ J-7	Summit Meeting	1965	$35

PHILIPS

❏ PHM200073 [M]	Jazz Et Al	1963	$30
❏ PHS600073 [S]	Jazz Et Al	1963	$30

SAVOY

❏ MG-12104 [M]	American Jazzmen Play Andre Hodeir	1957	$40
❏ MG-12113 [M]	Andre Hodeir Presents the Paris Scene	1957	$40

SAVOY JAZZ

❏ SJL-1194	Essais	198?	$25

HODES, ART
Pianist. Also see EDMOND HALL.

Albums

Number	Title	Yr	NM
AUDIOPHILE			
❏ AP-54	Mostly Blues	196?	$35
❏ AP-54	Some Legendary Art	1986	$25
—Retitled reissue			
BLUE NOTE			
❏ BLP-7005 [10]	Art Hodes' Hot Five	1950	$500
❏ BLP-7015 [10]	Dixieland Clambake	1951	$500
❏ BLP-7006 [10]	Dixieland Jubilee	1950	$500
❏ BLP-7021 [10]	Out of the Backroom	1952	$500
❏ B-6508 [M]	Sittin' In	1969	$30
❏ BLP-7004 [10]	The Best in Two-Beat	1950	$500
❏ B-6502 [M]	The Funky Piano of Art Hodes	1969	$30
—A Division of Liberty Records" on label			
CAPITOL			
❏ M-11030	Hollywood Stampede	1973	$80
DELMARK			
❏ DS-215	Friar's Inn Revisited	197?	$35
❏ DS-213	Hodes' Art	197?	$35
❏ DS-211	My Bucket's Got a Hole In It	1969	$50
DOTTED EIGHTH			
❏ 1000 [M]	Art for Art's Sake	195?	$50
EMARCY			
❏ MG-26104 [10]	Jazz Chicago Style	1954	$200
❏ SRE-66005	Plain Old Blues	196?	$25
EUPHONIC			
❏ 1213	I Remember Bessie	198?	$25
❏ 1207	The Art of Hodes	198?	$25
❏ 1218	When Music Was Music	198?	$25
GHB			
❏ 171	Art Hodes and the Magolia Jazz Band, Vol. 1	1984	$35
❏ 172	Art Hodes and the Magolia Jazz Band, Vol. 2	1984	$35
JAZZOLOGY			
❏ J-20	Andre Hodeir with the All-Star Stompers	1966	$50
❏ J-104	Apex Blues	198?	$30
❏ J-155	Art Hodes and His Blues Six-Blues Groove	198?	$30
❏ J-74	Down Home Blues	197?	$30
❏ J-79	Echoes of Chicago	1979	$35
❏ J-46 [M]	For Art's Sake	196?	$25
❏ J-58	Home Cookin'	1974	$35
❏ J-83	The Jazz Record Story, Vol. 2	1979	$30
❏ J-113	The Trios	198?	$30
MERCURY			
❏ MG-20185 [M]	Chicago Style Jazz	1957	$100
MOSAIC			
❏ MR5-114	The Complete Art Hodes Blue Note Sessions	199?	$200
—Limited edition of 7,500			
MUSE			
❏ MR-5279	Just the Two of Us	1982	$25
❏ MR-5252	Someone to Watch Over Me	1981	$25
PARAMOUNT			
❏ LP-113 [M]	The Trios	1955	$150
PRESTIGE			
❏ 24083	The Real Thing	198?	$35
RIVERSIDE			
❏ RLP-1012 [10]	Chicago Rhythm Kings	1953	$300
SACKVILLE			
❏ 3039	Blues in the Night	198?	$25
STOMP OFF			
❏ SOS-1184	The Music of Lovie Austin	1988	$25
STORYVILLE			
❏ 4057	Selections from the Gutter	198?	$25

HODES, JOHNNY, AND EARL "FATHA" HINES
Also see each artist's individual listings.

Albums

Number	Title	Yr	NM
VERVE			
❏ V-8647 [M]	Stride Right	1966	$25
❏ V-8732 [M]	Swing's Our Thing	1967	$30
❏ V6-8732 [S]	Swing's Our Thing	1967	$35

HODES, JOHNNY, AND WILD BILL DAVIS
Also see each artist's individual listings.

Albums

Number	Title	Yr	NM
RCA VICTOR			
❏ LPM-3393 [M]	Con-Soul and Sax	1965	$25
❏ LSP-3393 [S]	Con-Soul and Sax	1965	$30

Number	Title	Yr	NM
❏ LPM-3706 [M]	Eddie Hodges and Wild Bill Davis In Atlantic City	1966	$35
❏ LSP-3706 [S]	Eddie Hodges and Wild Bill Davis In Atlantic City	1966	$25
VERVE			
❏ V-8570 [M]	A Mess of Blues	1964	$25
❏ V6-8570 [S]	A Mess of Blues	1964	$30
❏ V-8406 [M]	Blue Hodges	1961	$25
❏ V6-8406 [S]	Blue Hodges	1961	$30
❏ V-8635 [M]	Blue Pyramid	1965	$25
❏ V6-8635 [S]	Blue Pyramid	1965	$30
❏ V-8599 [M]	Blue Rabbit	1964	$25
❏ V6-8599 [S]	Blue Rabbit	1964	$30
❏ V-8617 [M]	Joe's Blues	1965	$25
❏ V6-8617 [S]	Joe's Blues	1965	$30
❏ V-8630 [M]	Wings and Things	1965	$50
❏ V6-8630 [S]	Wings and Things	1965	$60

HODGES, JOHNNY
Alto saxophone, and occasional soprano saxophone, player. Also see GERRY MULLIGAN.

Albums

Number	Title	Yr	NM
ABC IMPULSE!			
❏ AS-61 [S]	Everybody Knows	1968	$35
AMERICAN RECORDING SOCIETY			
❏ G-421 [M]	Johnny Hodges and the Ellington All-Stars	195?	$40
BLUEBIRD			
❏ 5903-1-RB	Triple Play	1987	$25
CLEF			
❏ MGC-128 [10]	Johnny Hodges Collates #2	1953	$350
❏ MGC-111 [10]	Johnny Hodges Collates	1953	$300
❏ MGC-151 [10]	Swing with Johnny Hodges	1954	$0
—Canceled; reassigned to Norgran			
DOT			
❏ DLP-3682 [M]	Johnny Hodges with Lawrence Welk's Orchestra	1966	$75
❏ DLP-25682 [S]	Johnny Hodges with Lawrence Welk's Orchestra	1966	$100
ENCORE			
❏ EE-22001 [M]	Hodge Podge	1968	$35
EPIC			
❏ LN3105 [M]	Hodge Podge	1955	$100
FLYING DUTCHMAN			
❏ FD-10120	Three Shades of Blue	1972	$35
❏ 120	Three Shades of Blue	1971	$25
IMPULSE!			
❏ A-61 [M]	Everybody Knows	1964	$120
❏ AS-61 [S]	Everybody Knows	1964	$120
JAZZ PANORAMA			
❏ 1806 [10]	Johnny Hodges	1951	$150
MASTER JAZZ			
❏ 8107	Memory	1970	$35
MCA			
❏ 29071	Everybody Knows	198?	$25
MERCER			
❏ LP-1000 [10]	Johnny Hodges, Vol. 1	1951	$150
❏ LP-1006 [10]	Johnny Hodges, Vol. 2	1951	$150
MERCURY			
❏ MGC-128 [10]	Johnny Hodges Collates #2	1953	$0
—Canceled; reassigned to Clef			
❏ MGC-111 [10]	Johnny Hodges Collates	1952	$350
MGM			
❏ SE-4715	Tribute	1970	$35
MOSAIC			
❏ MR6-126	The Complete Johnny Hodges Sessions 1951-1955	199?	$150
NORGRAN			
❏ MGN-1048 [M]	Castle Rock	1955	$200
❏ MGN-1045 [M]	Creamy	1955	$300
❏ MGN-1055 [M]	Ellingtonia '56	1956	$200
❏ MGN-1092 [M]	In a Mellow Tone	1956	$200
❏ MGN-1059 [M]	In a Tender Mood	1956	$200
❏ MGN-1024 [M]	Johnny Hodges Dance Bash	1955	$300
❏ MGN-1004 [M]	Memories of Ellington	1954	$300
❏ MGN-1009 [M]	More of Johnny Hodges	1954	$300
❏ MGN-1091 [M]	Perdido	1956	$200
❏ MGN-1 [10]	Swing with Johnny Hodges	1954	$200
❏ MGN-1061 [M]	The Blues	1956	$80
❏ MGN-1060 [M]	Used to Be Duke	1956	$200
ONYX			
❏ 216	Ellingtonia	197?	$30
PABLO LIVE			
❏ 2620102	Sportpalast, Berlin	1978	$35
PRESTIGE			
❏ 24103	Caravan	198?	$35
RCA VICTOR			
❏ LPT-3000 [10]	Alto Sax	1952	$150

Number	Title	Yr	NM
❏ LPV-533 [M]	Things Ain't What They Used to Be	1966	$25
❏ LPM-3867 [M]	Triple Play	1967	$30
❏ LSP-3867 [S]	Triple Play	1967	$25
STORYVILLE			
❏ 4073	A Man and His Music	198?	$30
TIME-LIFE			
❏ STL-J-19	Giants of Jazz	1981	$50
VERVE			
❏ VSP-20 [M]	Alto Blues	1966	$30
❏ VSPS-20 [R]	Alto Blues	1966	$25
❏ MGV-8317 [M]	Back to Back -- Duke Ellington and Johnny Hodges Play the Blues	1959	$150
❏ MGVS-6055 [S]	Back to Back -- Duke Ellington and Johnny Hodges Play the Blues	1960	$150
❏ V-8317 [M]	Back to Back -- Duke Ellington and Johnny Hodges Play the Blues	1961	$25
❏ V6-8317 [S]	Back to Back -- Duke Ellington and Johnny Hodges Play the Blues	1961	$25
❏ V-8680 [M]	Blue Notes	1966	$60
❏ V6-8680 [S]	Blue Notes	1966	$40
❏ MGV-8358 [M]	Blues-a-Plenty	1960	$150
❏ MGVS-6123 [S]	Blues-a-Plenty	1960	$25
—Unreleased			
❏ V-8358 [M]	Blues-a-Plenty	1961	$25
❏ V6-8358 [S]	Blues-a-Plenty	1961	$25
❏ V6-8358 [S]	Blues-a-Plenty	199?	$30
—Classic Records reissue on audiophile vinyl			
❏ MGV-8139 [M]	Castle Rock	1957	$200
—Reissue of Norgran 1048			
❏ V-8139 [M]	Castle Rock	1961	$25
❏ 827758-1	Castle Rock	1986	$25
❏ MGV-8136 [M]	Creamy	1957	$200
—Reissue of Norgran 1045			
❏ V-8136 [M]	Creamy	1961	$25
❏ V-8726 [M]	Don't Sleep in the Subway	1967	$25
❏ V6-8726 [S]	Don't Sleep in the Subway	1967	$35
❏ MGV-8203 [M]	Duke's in Bed	1957	$125
❏ V-8203 [M]	Duke's in Bed	1961	$25
❏ MGV-8145 [M]	Ellingtonia '56	1957	$200
—Reissue of Norgran 1055			
❏ V-8145 [M]	Ellingtonia '56	1961	$25
❏ MGV-8180 [M]	In a Mellow Tone	1957	$300
—Reissue of Norgran 1092			
❏ V-8180 [M]	In a Mellow Tone	1961	$25
❏ MGV-8149 [M]	In a Tender Mood	1957	$300
—Reissue of Norgran 1059			
❏ V-8149 [M]	In a Tender Mood	1961	$25
❏ MGV-8391 [M]	Johnny Hodges	1961	$0
—Canceled			
❏ V/V6-8546	Johnny Hodges	1963	$0
—Canceled			
❏ VSP-3 [M]	Johnny Hodges and All the Duke's Men	1966	$30
❏ VSPS-3 [R]	Johnny Hodges and All the Duke's Men	1966	$25
❏ V-8452 [M]	Johnny Hodges with Billy Strayhorn	1962	$30
❏ V6-8452 [S]	Johnny Hodges with Billy Strayhorn	1962	$30
❏ MGV-8355 [M]	Not So Dukish	1960	$150
❏ MGVS-6120 [S]	Not So Dukish	1960	$0
—Canceled			
❏ V-8355 [M]	Not So Dukish	1961	$25
❏ MGV-8179 [M]	Perdido	1957	$150
—Reissue of Norgran 1091			
❏ V-8179 [M]	Perdido	1961	$25
❏ V6-8834	Previously Unreleased Recordings	1973	$35
❏ V6-8753	Rippin' and Runnin'	1968	$35
❏ V-8561 [M]	Sandy's Gone	1963	$30
❏ V6-8561 [S]	Sandy's Gone	1963	$30
❏ MGV-8345 [M]	Side by Side	1959	$100
❏ MGVS-6109 [S]	Side by Side	1960	$100
❏ V-8345 [M]	Side by Side	1961	$25
❏ V6-8345 [S]	Side by Side	1961	$25
❏ MGVS-6109 [S]	Side by Side	199?	$30
—Classic Records reissue on audiophile vinyl			
❏ MGV-8271 [M]	The Big Sound	1958	$150
❏ MGVS-6017 [S]	The Big Sound	1960	$150
❏ V-8271 [M]	The Big Sound	1961	$25
❏ V6-8271 [S]	The Big Sound	1961	$25
❏ UMV-2525	The Big Sound	198?	$25
❏ V-8151 [M]	The Blues	1961	$25
❏ V-8492 [M]	The Eleventh Hour	1962	$30
❏ V6-8492 [S]	The Eleventh Hour	1962	$30
❏ MGV-8314 [M]	The Prettiest Gershwin	1959	$100
❏ MGVS-6048 [S]	The Prettiest Gershwin	1960	$100
❏ V-8314 [M]	The Prettiest Gershwin	1961	$25
❏ V6-8314 [S]	The Prettiest Gershwin	1961	$25
❏ VE2-2532	The Smooth One	1979	$35

Illinois Jacquet and Lester Young, Battle of the Saxes, Aladdin LP-701, 10-inch LP, **$1,200**.

Ahmad Jamal, *Portfolio of Ahmad Jamal*, Argo LP 2638, two-record set with limited edition number and raised image on front, **$40**.

Bobby Jaspar, *Bobby Jaspar and His All Stars*, EmArcy MG 36105, **$200**.

Jazz Lab (Don Byrd-Gigi Gryce), *Jazz Lab*, Columbia CL 998, **$150**.

Number	Title	Yr	NM
❏ MGV-8150 [M]	Used to Be Duke	1957	$200
—Reissue of Norgran 1060			
❏ V-8150 [M]	Used to Be Duke	1961	$25

HOFMANN, HOLLY
Flutist.
Albums
CAPRI
❏ 74011	Take Note	1989	$30

HOGGARD, JAY
Vibraphone player.
Albums
CONTEMPORARY
❏ C-14007	Rain Forest	1980	$30

GRAMAVISION
❏ GR-8204	Love Survives	1983	$25

GRP/ARISTA
❏ GL5004	Days Like These	1979	$30

INDIA NAVIGATION
❏ IN-1049	Mystic Winds, Tropic Breezes	1981	$30
❏ IN-1068	Riverside Dance	1985	$30
❏ IN-1040	Solo Vibes Concert	1979	$35

MUSE
❏ MR-5383	Overview	1989	$30
❏ MR-5410	The Little Tiger	1991	$35

HOLDSWORTH, ALLAN
Guitarist of BRUFORD and UK fame.
Albums
CTI
❏ 6068	Velvet	197?	$18

ENIGMA
❏ ST-73203	Atavachron	1986	$15
❏ 72031-1	I.O.U.	1985	$18
—Reissue			

LUNA CRACK
❏ AH-100	I.O.U.	1982	$25

HOLIDAY, BILLIE, AND STAN GETZ
Also see each artist's individual listings.
Albums
DALE
❏ 25 [10]	Billie and Stan	1951	$400

HOLIDAY, BILLIE
Female singer, one of the greatest jazz vocalists ever. Also see RALPH BURNS; ELLA FITZGERALD; TEDDY WILSON.
Albums
AMERICAN RECORDING SOCIETY
❏ G-409 [M]	Billie Holiday Sings	1956	$300
—Reissue of Clef 713			
❏ G-431 [M]	Lady Sings the Blues	1957	$300
—Reissue of Clef 721			

ATLANTIC
❏ 1614	Strange Fruit	1972	$35

BLACKHAWK
❏ BKH-50701	Billie Holiday at Monterey	1986	$25

BOOK-OF-THE-MONTH CLUB
❏ 90-5652	Ain't Nobody's Business If I Do	1975	$60
—Box set with booklet; pressed on CSP labels; alternate number is "P4 12969			

BULLDOG
❏ 1007	Billie's Blues	198?	$25

CLEF
❏ MGC-686 [M]	A Recital by Billie Holiday	1956	$350
—Reissue of 144 and 161 as one 12-inch LP			
❏ MGC-169 [10]	Billie Holiday at Jazz at the Philharmonic	1955	$600
❏ MGC-161 [10]	Billie Holiday Favorites	1954	$350
❏ MGC-721 [M]	Lady Sings the Blues	1956	$350
❏ MGC-690 [M]	Solitude -- Songs by Billie Holiday	1956	$350
—Reissue of 118			

COLLECTABLES
❏ COL-5142	Fine and Mellow	198?	$30

COLUMBIA

Number	Title	Yr	NM
❏ CL6163 [10]	Billie Holiday Favorites	1951	$200
❏ CL2666 [M]	Billie Holiday's Greatest Hits	1967	$35
❏ CL6129 [10]	Billie Holiday Sings	1950	$200
❏ C32080	Billie's Blues/The Original Recordings by Billie Holiday	1973	$35
❏ PC32080	Billie's Blues/The Original Recordings by Billie Holiday	198?	$20
—Reissue of Harmony LP			
❏ G30782	God Bless the Child	1972	$50
❏ CL637 [M]	Lady Day	1954	$140
—Maroon label, gold print			
❏ CL637 [M]	Lady Day	1956	$40
—Red and black label with six "eye" logos			
❏ CL637 [M]	Lady Day	1962	$35
—Red "Guaranteed High Fidelity" or "360 Sound" label			
❏ CL637 [M]	Lady Day	197?	$30
—Orange label			
❏ CL1157 [M]	Lady in Satin	1958	$40
—Red and black label with six "eye" logos			
❏ CS8048 [S]	Lady in Satin	1958	$40
—Red and black label with six "eye" logos			
❏ CL1157 [M]	Lady in Satin	1962	$35
—Red "Guaranteed High Fidelity" or "360 Sound" label			
❏ CS8048 [S]	Lady in Satin	1962	$35
—Red "Guaranteed High Fidelity" or "360 Sound" label			
❏ CS8048 [S]	Lady in Satin	1999	$60
—Classic Records reissue on audiophile vinyl			
❏ CG32121	The Billie Holiday Story, Volume 1	1973	$35
❏ CG32124	The Billie Holiday Story, Volume 2	1973	$35
❏ CG32127	The Billie Holiday Story, Volume 3	1973	$35
❏ C3L21 [M]	The Golden Years	1962	$100
—Red and black label with six "eye" logos			
❏ C3L21 [M]	The Golden Years	1963	$60
—Red "Guaranteed High Fidelity" or "360 Sound" label			
❏ C3L40 [M]	The Golden Years, Volume 2	1966	$60
—Red label, "Mono" at bottom			
❏ C3L40 [M]	The Golden Years, Volume 2	197?	$50
—Orange labels			

COLUMBIA JAZZ MASTERPIECES
❏ CJ40247	Lady in Satin	1987	$25
❏ CJ40646	The Quintessential Billie Holiday, Vol. 1	1987	$25
❏ CJ40790	The Quintessential Billie Holiday, Vol. 2	1987	$25
❏ CJ44048	The Quintessential Billie Holiday, Vol. 3	1988	$25
❏ CJ44252	The Quintessential Billie Holiday, Vol. 4	1988	$25
❏ CJ44423	The Quintessential Billie Holiday, Vol. 5	1989	$25
❏ C45449	The Quintessential Billie Holiday, Vol. 6	1990	$25
❏ C46180	The Quintessential Billie Holiday, Vol. 7	1990	$25

COLUMBIA MUSICAL TREASURY
❏ P3M5869	The Golden Years	197?	$50

COLUMBIA SPECIAL PRODUCTS
❏ P14338	Swing, Brother, Swing	198?	$25

COMMODORE
❏ FL-30008 [M]	Billie Holiday	1959	$100
—Reissue of 20006			
❏ FL-30011 [M]	Billie Holiday with Eddie Heywood and His Orchestra	1959	$100
—Reissue of 20005			

CROWN
❏ CLP-5380 [M]	Billie Holiday & Vivian Fears	196?	$50
❏ CST-380 [R]	Billie Holiday & Vivian Fears	196?	$30

DECCA
❏ DL75040 [R]	Billie Holiday's Greatest Hits	1968	$30
❏ DL5040 [M]	Billie Holiday's Greatest Hits	1968	$60
—Mono is white label promo only; "Monaural" sticker covers the word "Stereo" on cover			
❏ DL5345 [10]	Lover Man	1951	$200
❏ DL8702 [M]	Lover Man	1958	$120
❏ DXB-161 [M]	The Billie Holiday Story	1959	$200
❏ DXSB-7161 [R]	The Billie Holiday Story	1959	$200
❏ DL8701 [M]	The Blues Are Brewin'	1958	$120
❏ DL8215 [M]	The Lady Sings	1956	$120

ESP-DISK'
❏ 3002	The Lady Lives, Vol. 1	1973	$100
❏ 3003	The Lady Lives, Vol. 2	1973	$100

EVEREST ARCHIVE OF FOLK & JAZZ
❏ 265	Billie Holiday	197?	$30
❏ FS-310	Billie Holiday, Vol. 2	1976	$30

HALL

Number	Title	Yr	NM
❏ 622	I've Gotta Right to Sing	197?	$30

HARMONY
❏ KH32080	Billie's Blues	1973	$25

INTERMEDIA
❏ QS-5076	Billie Holiday Talks and Sings	198?	$25

JAZZ MAN
❏ 5005	Billie Holiday at Storyville	198?	$25

JAZZTONE
❏ J-1209 [M]	Billie Holiday Sings	1955	$100
—Reissue of Commodore 20005			

JOLLY ROGER
❏ 5020 [10]	Billie Holiday, Volume 1	1954	$175
❏ 5021 [10]	Billie Holiday, Volume 2	1954	$175
❏ 5022 [10]	Billie Holiday, Volume 3	1954	$175

KENT GOSPEL
❏ KST600	Billie Holiday Sings	197?	$35

MAINSTREAM
❏ 56022 [M]	Once Upon a Time	1965	$60
❏ S-6022 [R]	Once Upon a Time	1965	$30
❏ 56000 [M]	The Commodore Recordings	1965	$60
❏ S-6000 [R]	The Commodore Recordings	1965	$30

MCA
❏ 275	Billie Holiday's Greatest Hits	1973	$25
—Reissue of Decca 75040			
❏ 4006	The Billie Holiday Story	1973	$30
—Reissue of Decca 7161			

METRO
❏ M-515 [M]	Billie Holiday	1965	$250
❏ MS-515 [R]	Billie Holiday	1965	$150

MGM
❏ M3G-4948	Archetypes	1974	$30
❏ E-3764 [M]	Billie Holiday	1959	$40
❏ SE-3764 [S]	Billie Holiday	1959	$100
❏ GAS-122	Billie Holiday (Golden Archive Series)	1970	$30

MOBILE FIDELITY
❏ 1-247	Body and Soul	1996	$200
—Audiophile vinyl			

MONMOUTH/EVERGREEN
❏ 7046	Gallant Lady	1973	$30

PARAMOUNT
❏ PA-6059	Songs and Conversations	1973	$30

PHOENIX 10
❏ PHX-312	Billie Holiday Live	1981	$20

PICKWICK
❏ PC-3335	Billie Holiday Sings the Blues	197?	$25

RIC
❏ M-2001 [M]	Rare Live Recording	1964	$60

SCORE
❏ SLP-4014 [M]	Billie Holiday Sings the Blues	1957	$200

SOLID STATE
❏ SS-18040	Lady Love	1969	$30

SUNSET
❏ SUM-1147 [M]	Shades of Blue	1967	$30
❏ SUS-5147 [R]	Shades of Blue	1967	$25

TIME-LIFE
❏ STL-J-03	Giants of Jazz	1979	$60
—Alternate number is Columbia Special Products P3 14786			

TOTEM
❏ 1037	Billie Holiday On the Air	198?	$25

TRIP
❏ 5024	Billie Holiday Live	1974	$25

UNITED ARTISTS
❏ UAJ-14014 [M]	Lady Love	1962	$40
❏ UASJ-15014 [S]	Lady Love	1962	$100
❏ UAS-5625	Lady Love	1972	$25
—Reissue of 15014			

VERVE
❏ MGV-8329 [M]	All or Nothing at All	1959	$150
❏ V-8329 [M]	All or Nothing at All	1959	$150
❏ V6-8329 [R]	All or Nothing at All	196?	$30
❏ VE-2-2529	All or Nothing at All	198?	$35
❏ 827160-1	All or Nothing at All	1987	$25
❏ MGV-8027 [M]	A Recital by Billie Holiday	1957	$200
—Reissue of Clef 686			
❏ V-8027 [M]	A Recital by Billie Holiday	1961	$50
❏ MGV-8197 [M]	Body and Soul	1957	$150
❏ V-8197 [M]	Body and Soul	1961	$50
❏ 817359-1	Embraceable You	198?	$30
❏ 2V6S-8816	History of the Real Billie Holiday	1973	$35

Number	Title	Yr	NM
❑ 823233-1	History of the Real Billie Holiday	198?	$30
❑ VSP-5 [M]	Lady	1966	$35
❑ VSPS-5 [R]	Lady	1966	$30
❑ MGV-8099 [M]	Lady Sings the Blues	1957	$300
— Reissue of Clef 721			
❑ MGV-8026 [M]	Music for Torching	1957	$300
— Reissue of Clef 669			
❑ V-8026 [M]	Music for Torching	1961	$50
❑ MGV-8074 [M]	Solitude -- Songs by Billie Holiday	1957	$200
— Reissue of Clef 690			
❑ V-8074 [M]	Solitude -- Songs by Billie Holiday	1961	$50
❑ V6-8074 [R]	Solitude -- Songs by Billie Holiday	196?	$30
❑ MGV-8257 [M]	Songs for Distingue Lovers	1958	$120
❑ MGVS-6021 [S]	Songs for Distingue Lovers	1960	$120
❑ V-8257 [M]	Songs for Distingue Lovers	1961	$50
❑ V6-8257 [S]	Songs for Distingue Lovers	1961	$60
❑ MGVS-6021-45 [S]	Songs for Distingue Lovers	1999	$50
— Classic Records reissue on two 12-inch 45-rpm records			
❑ MGVS-6021 [S]	Songs for Distingue Lovers	199?	$60
— Classic Records reissue on audiophile vinyl			
❑ MGV-8302 [M]	Stay with Me	1959	$100
❑ V-8302 [M]	Stay with Me	1961	$50
❑ VE-2-2515	Stormy Blues	1976	$35
❑ 823230-1	Stormy Blues	198?	$30
❑ V6-8808 [R]	The Best of Billie Holiday	1973	$25
❑ 823246-1	The Billie Holiday Songbook	198?	$25
❑ V-8410 [M]	The Essential Billie Holiday	1961	$50
❑ V6-8410 [R]	The Essential Billie Holiday	1961	$30
❑ V-8505 [M]	The Essential Jazz Vocals	1963	$50
❑ V6-8505 [R]	The Essential Jazz Vocals	1963	$30
❑ VE-2-2503	The First Verve Sessions	1976	$35
❑ MGV-8338-2 [M]	The Unforgettable Lady Day	1959	$150
❑ V-8338-2 [M]	The Unforgettable Lady Day	1961	$60

HOLIDAY, BILLIE/AL HIBBLER
Also see each artist's individual listings.

Albums

IMPERIAL			
❑ LP-9185 [M]	Billie Holiday, Al Hibbler and the Blues	1962	$200
❑ LP-12185 [R]	Billie Holiday, Al Hibbler and the Blues	196?	$175

HOLIDAY, JOE
Tenor saxophone player.

Albums

DECCA			
❑ DL8487 [M]	Holiday for Jazz	1957	$120
PRESTIGE			
❑ PRLP-131 [10]	Joe Holiday	1952	$300

HOLIDAY, JOE/BILLY TAYLOR
Also see each artist's individual listings.

Albums

PRESTIGE			
❑ PRLP-171 [10]	Mambo Jazz	1953	$350

HOLLAND, DAVE
Bass player. The first album below was as "David Holland." Also see CIRCLE.

Albums

ECM			
❑ 1027	Conference of the Birds	1974	$35
— As "David Holland			
❑ 1109	Emerald Tears	1978	$30
❑ 25001	Jumpin' In	1984	$25
❑ 23787	Life Cycle	1983	$25
❑ 25032	Seeds of Time	1985	$25

HOLLIDAY, JUDY, AND GERRY MULLIGAN
Also see each artist's individual listings.

Albums

DRG			
❑ SL-5191	Holliday with Mulligan	1979	$30

HOLLIDAY, JUDY
Female singer. Best known as an actress, she won an Oscar for her performance in Born Yesterday.

Albums

Number	Title	Yr	NM
COLUMBIA			
❑ CL1153 [M]	Trouble Is a Man	1958	$30
❑ CS8041 [S]	Trouble Is a Man	1959	$40
DRG			
❑ MRS-602	Trouble Is a Man	198?	$25

HOLLOWAY, RED, AND CLARK TERRY
Also see each artist's individual listings.

Albums

CONCORD JAZZ			
❑ CJ-390	Locksmith Blues	1989	$30

HOLLOWAY, RED
Tenor saxophone player.

Albums

CONCORD JAZZ			
❑ CJ-322	Red Holloway & Company	1987	$25
FANTASY			
❑ OJC-327	Cookin' Together	1988	$25
JAM			
❑ 014	Hittin' the Road Again	198?	$30
PRESTIGE			
❑ PRST-7778	Best of the Soul Organ Giants	1970	$35
❑ PRLP-7299 [M]	Burner	1964	$50
— Yellow label, Bergenfield, N.J. address			
❑ PRLP-7299 [M]	Burner	1965	$30
— Blue label, trident logo at right			
❑ PRST-7299 [S]	Burner	1964	$50
— Yellow label, Bergenfield, N.J. address			
❑ PRST-7299 [S]	Burner	1965	$30
— Blue label, trident logo at right			
❑ PRLP-7325 [M]	Cookin' Together	1964	$30
❑ PRST-7325 [S]	Cookin' Together	1964	$40
❑ PRLP-7473 [M]	Red Soul	1966	$25
❑ PRST-7473 [S]	Red Soul	1966	$30
❑ PRLP-7390 [M]	Sax, Strings and Soul	1965	$25
❑ PRST-7390 [S]	Sax, Strings and Soul	1965	$30
STEEPLECHASE			
❑ SCS-1192	Nica's Dream	198?	$30

HOLLYDAY, CHRISTOPHER
Alto saxophone player.

Albums

JAZZ BEAT			
❑ 102	Oh Brother!	198?	$35
NOVUS			
❑ 3055-1-N	Christopher Hollyday	1989	$30
❑ 3087-1-N	On Course	1990	$35
RBI			
❑ 402	Reverence	1988	$35

HOLLYWOOD JAZZ QUINTET, THE

Albums

GATEWAY			
❑ 7018	Neon	1979	$30
❑ 7019	Nuances	1980	$30

HOLLYWOOD SAXOPHONE QUARTET, THE

Albums

LIBERTY			
❑ LRP-3047 [M]	Gold Rush Suite	1957	$40
❑ LRP-3080 [M]	Sax Appeal	1958	$30
❑ LRP-6005 [M]	The Hollywood Saxophone Quartet	1955	$50

HOLMAN, BILL
Tenor saxophone player, arranger and composer.

Albums

ANDEX			
❑ A-3004 [M]	In a Jazz Orbit	1958	$40
❑ AS-3004 [S]	In a Jazz Orbit	1959	$30
❑ A-3005 [M]	Jive for Five	1958	$40
❑ AS-3005 [S]	Jive for Five	1959	$30
CAPITOL			
❑ T1464 [M]	Great Big Band	1960	$60
❑ ST1464 [S]	Great Big Band	1960	$60
❑ H6500 [10]	The Bill Holman Octet	1954	$200
CORAL			
❑ CRL57188 [M]	The Fabulous Bill Holman	1958	$80
CREATIVE WORLD			
❑ ST-1053	Great Big Band	197?	$35

Number	Title	Yr	NM
HOLMES, RICHARD "GROOVE"			
Organist. Also see JIMMY WITHERSPOON.			

Albums

BLUE NOTE			
❑ BST-84372	Comin' On Home	1971	$30
FANTASY			
❑ OJC-329	Soul Message	1988	$25
— Reissue of Prestige 7435			
FLYING DUTCHMAN			
❑ BDL1-1537	I'm in the Mood for Love	1976	$30
GROOVE MERCHANT			
❑ 505	American Pie	1972	$30
❑ 527	New Groove	1973	$30
❑ 512	Night Glider	1972	$30
MUSE			
❑ 5358	Blues All Day Long	1989	$25
❑ 5239	Broadway	1981	$25
❑ 5167	Good Vibrations	1979	$25
❑ 5134	Shippin' Out	1978	$25
PACIFIC JAZZ			
❑ PJ-59 [M]	After Hours	1962	$50
❑ ST-59 [S]	After Hours	1962	$60
❑ ST-20171	Come Together	1970	$35
❑ PJ-32 [M]	Groovin' with Jug	1961	$60
❑ ST-32 [S]	Groovin' with Jug	1961	$40
❑ LN-10130	Groovin' with Jug	198?	$20
— Busget-line reissue			
❑ PJ-23 [M]	Richard "Groove" Holmes	1961	$60
❑ ST-23 [S]	Richard "Groove" Holmes	1961	$60
❑ PJ-51 [M]	Somethin' Special	1962	$50
❑ ST-51 [S]	Somethin' Special	1962	$60
❑ PJ-10105 [M]	Tell It Like It Tis	1966	$35
❑ ST-20105 [S]	Tell It Like It Tis	1966	$50
❑ ST-20153	Workin' on a Groovy Thing	1969	$35
❑ ST-20163	X-77	1969	$35
PRESTIGE			
❑ PRST-7514 [S]	Get Up and Get It	1967	$35
❑ PRLP-7468 [M]	Living Soul	1966	$35
❑ PRST-7468 [S]	Living Soul	1966	$50
❑ PRLP-7485 [M]	Misty	1966	$35
❑ PRST-7485 [S]	Misty	1966	$50
❑ PRST-7435 [M]	Soul Message	1966	$35
❑ PRST-7435 [S]	Soul Message	1966	$50
❑ PRST-7741	Soul Mist	1970	$35
❑ PRST-7543	Soul Power	1968	$35
❑ PRLP-7493 [M]	Spicy	1967	$50
❑ PRST-7493 [S]	Spicy	1967	$35
❑ PRLP-7497 [M]	Super Cool	1967	$50
❑ PRST-7497 [S]	Super Cool	1967	$35
❑ PRST-7601	That Healin' Feelin'	1969	$35
❑ PRST-7768	The Best for Beautiful People	1971	$35
❑ PRST-7700	The Best of Richard "Groove" Holmes	1969	$35
❑ PRST-7778	The Best of Soul Organ Giants	1972	$30
❑ PRST-7570	The Groover	1968	$35
VERSATILE			
❑ MSG6003	Dancing in the Sun	1977	$35
WARNER BROS.			
❑ W1553 [M]	Book of the Blues	1964	$50
❑ WS1553 [S]	Book of the Blues	1964	$60
WORLD PACIFIC			
❑ ST-20147	Welcome Home	1968	$150

HOLT, RED
Drummer, formerly with the RAMSEY LEWIS Trio. Also see YOUNG-HOLT UNLIMITED.

Albums

ARGO			
❑ LP-696 [M]	Look Out! Look Out!	1962	$25
❑ LPS-696 [S]	Look Out! Look Out!	1962	$30
PAULA			
❑ 4006	Isaac, Isaac, Isaac	197?	$35
❑ 4007	The Other Side of the Moon	197?	$35

HOMI & JARVIS
Also see JOHN JARVIS.

Albums

GRP			
❑ GR-1005	Friend of a Friend	198?	$25

HONEY DREAMERS, THE

Albums

FANTASY			
❑ 3207 [M]	The Honey Dreamers Sing Gershwin	1956	$80
— Red vinyl			

Number	Title	Yr	NM
❑ 3207 [M]	The Honey Dreamers Sing Gershwin	195?	$40

—Black vinyl

HOOPER, LES

Composer, arranger and conductor. Also a male singer and keyboard player.

Albums

CHURCHILL

Number	Title	Yr	NM
❑ 67234	Dorian Blue	1977	$30
❑ 67235	Hoopla	1978	$30

CREATIVE WORLD

❑ ST-3002	Look What They've Done	197?	$35

JAZZ HOUNDS

❑ 04	Raisin' the Roof	1982	$30

PAUSA

❑ 7185	Hoopla	1986	$25

HOOPER, STIX

Drummer. Also see THE CRUSADERS.

Albums

ARTFUL BALANCE

❑ ABI-7214	Lay It on the Line	1989	$15

MCA

❑ 3180	The World Within	1980	$12
❑ 5374	Touch the Feeling	1982	$12

HOOPES, RONNIE

Pianist.

Albums

REVELATION

❑ 21	Respect for a Great Tradition	197?	$35

HOPE, ELMO

Pianist and composer. Also see ART BLAKEY.

Albums

BEACON

❑ BS-401 [S]	High Hopes	1961	$350

BLUE NOTE

❑ BLP-5044 [10]	Elmo Hope Quintet	1954	$300
❑ BLP-5029 [10]	Elmo Hope Trio	1953	$300

CELEBRITY

❑ 209 [M]	Elmo Hope Trio	1962	$30
❑ S-209 [S]	Elmo Hope Trio	1962	$30

CONTEMPORARY

❑ M-3620 [M]	The Elmo Hope Trio	1966	$150

FANTASY

❑ OJC-477	Elmo Hope Trio	1991	$30
❑ OJC-1703	Hope Meets Foster	1985	$25
❑ OJC-1751	Meditations	198?	$25

HIFI

❑ J-616 [M]	Elmo Hope	1960	$40
❑ JS-616 [S]	Elmo Hope	1960	$50

INNER CITY

❑ IC-1018	Last Sessions	197?	$35
❑ IC-1037	Last Sessions, Volume 2	1978	$35

MILESTONE

❑ 47037	All Star Sessions	197?	$35

PRESTIGE

❑ PRST-7675	Elmo Hope Memorial Album	1969	$35
❑ PRLP-7021 [M]	Hope Meets Foster	1956	$600
❑ PRLP-7021 [M]	Wail, Frank, Wail	1957	$250

—Retitled reissue of above album

RIVERSIDE

❑ RLP-381 [M]	Homecoming!	1961	$200
❑ RS-9381 [S]	Homecoming!	1961	$200
❑ 6161	Homecoming!	198?	$30
❑ RLP-408 [M]	Hope-Full	1962	$150
❑ RS-9408 [S]	Hope-Full	1962	$150

HOPE, STAN

Pianist.

Albums

MAINSTREAM

❑ MRL-327	Stan Hope	1972	$35

HOPKINS, CLAUDE

Pianist, composer and bandleader.

Albums

CHIAROSCURO

Number	Title	Yr	NM
❑ 114	Crazy Fingers	1972	$35

DESIGN

❑ DLP-30 [M]	Golden Era of Dixieland Jazz 1887-1937	1957	$30

JAZZ ARCHIVES

❑ JA-27	Singin' in the Rain	198?	$25

SWINGVILLE

❑ SVLP-2020 [M]	Let's Jam	1961	$50

—Purple label

❑ SVLP-2020 [M]	Let's Jam	1965	$30

—Blue label, trident logo at right

❑ SVLP-2041 [M]	Swing Time	1962	$50

—Purple label

❑ SVLP-2041 [M]	Swing Time	1965	$30

—Blue label, trident logo at right

❑ SVLP-2009 [M]	Yes Indeed	1960	$100

—Purple label

❑ SVLP-2009 [M]	Yes Indeed	1965	$60

—Blue label, trident logo at right

HOPKINS, KENYON

Composer.

Albums

VERVE

❑ V-8694 [M]	Dream Songs	1967	$25
❑ V6-8694 [S]	Dream Songs	1967	$30

HOPKINS, LINDA

Female singer.

Albums

PALO ALTO

❑ PA-8034	How Blue Can You Get	1982	$12

HORENSTEIN, STEPHEN

Baritone and tenor saxophone player and composer.

Albums

SOUL NOTE

❑ SN-1099	Collages: Jerusalem '85	1986	$30

HORN, PAUL

Flutist, also has played clarinet and alto saxophone. His 1968 Epic album Inside is considered one of the first "New Age" recordings.

Albums

ABC IMPULSE!

❑ IA-9356	Plenty of Horn	1978	$35

BLUE NOTE

❑ BN-LA529-H2	Paul Horn in India	1975	$35

COLUMBIA

❑ CL2050 [M]	Impressions of "Cleopatra	1963	$35
❑ CS8850 [S]	Impressions of "Cleopatra	1963	$15
❑ CL1922 [M]	Profile of a Jazz Musician	1962	$30
❑ CS8722 [S]	Profile of a Jazz Musician	1962	$15
❑ CL1677 [M]	The Sound of Paul Horn	1961	$12
❑ CS8477 [S]	The Sound of Paul Horn	1961	$30

DOT

❑ DLP-3091 [M]	House of Horn	1957	$100
❑ DLP-9002 [M]	Plenty of Horn	1958	$100
❑ DLP-29002 [S]	Plenty of Horn	1959	$80

EPIC

❑ PE34231	Altura do Sol	1976	$60
❑ BXN26466	Inside	1969	$75
❑ PE26466	Inside	198?	$20

—Budget-line reissue with new prefix

❑ KE31600	Inside II	1971	$75
❑ KE33561	Paul Horn + Nexus	1975	$60
❑ KE32837	Visions	1973	$60

EVEREST ARCHIVE OF FOLK & JAZZ

❑ 308	Paul Horn	197?	$25

HIFI

❑ J-615 [M]	Something Blue	1960	$30
❑ JS-615 [S]	Something Blue	1960	$40

ISLAND

❑ ILSD6	Special Edition	197?	$15

KUCKUCK

❑ 11075	Inside the Cathedral	198?	$30
❑ KU-060/061	Inside the Great Pyramid	198?	$25
❑ 12060	Inside the Great Pyramid	198?	$35

—Reissue with new number

❑ 11062	Inside the Taj Mahal	198?	$30
❑ 11083	The Peace Album	1988	$30

LOST LAKE

Number	Title	Yr	NM
❑ LL-0091	Sketches: A Collection	1986	$30

MCA

❑ 4144	Plenty of Horn	198?	$30

OVATION

❑ OV-1405	Concert Ensemble	1970	$35

RCA VICTOR

❑ LPM-3386 [M]	Cycle	1965	$25
❑ LSP-3386 [S]	Cycle	1965	$12
❑ LPM-3519 [M]	Here's That Rainy Day	1966	$35
❑ LSP-3519 [S]	Here's That Rainy Day	1966	$25
❑ LPM-3414 [M]	Jazz Suite on the Mass Texts	1965	$25
❑ LSP-3414 [S]	Jazz Suite on the Mass Texts	1965	$12
❑ LPM-3613 [M]	Monday, Monday	1966	$25
❑ LSP-3613 [S]	Monday, Monday	1966	$25

WORLD PACIFIC

❑ WP-1266 [M]	Impressions	1959	$150

HORN, SHIRLEY

Pianist and female singer.

Albums

ABC-PARAMOUNT

❑ ABC-538 [M]	Travelin' Light	1965	$40
❑ ABCS-538 [S]	Travelin' Light	1965	$50

MERCURY

❑ MG-20761 [M]	Loads of Love	1963	$100
❑ MG-20835 [M]	Shirley Horn with Horns	1963	$100
❑ SR-60835 [S]	Shirley Horn with Horns	1963	$100
❑ SR-60835 [S]	Shirley Horn with Horns	199?	$30

—Classic Records reissue on audiophile vinyl

STEEPLECHASE

❑ SCS-1111	A Lazy Afternoon	1979	$30
❑ SCS-1157	All Night Long	1981	$30
❑ SCS-1023	Garden of the Blues	198?	$30
❑ SCS-1164	Violets for Your Furs	1982	$30

STEREO-CRAFT

❑ RTN-16 [M]	Embers and Ashes	1961	$60
❑ RTS-16 [S]	Embers and Ashes	1961	$80

VERVE

❑ 837933-1	Close Enough for Love	1989	$30
❑ 832235-1	I Thought About You	1987	$25

HORNE, LENA, AND HARRY BELAFONTE

Belafonte is a male singer not otherwise listed in this book. Also see LENA HORNE.

Albums

RCA VICTOR

❑ LOC-1507 [M]	Porgy and Bess	1959	$60
❑ LSO-1507 [S]	Porgy and Bess	1959	$40

HORNE, LENA

Female singer. Earlier material appears in the Goldmine Standard Catalog of American Records .

Albums

20TH CENTURY FOX

❑ TF-4115 [M]	Here's Lena Now	1964	$35
❑ TFS-4115 [S]	Here's Lena Now	1964	$50

ACCORD

❑ SN-7190	Standing Room Only	198?	$25

BLUEBIRD

❑ 9985-1-RB	Stormy Weather: The Legendary Lena	1990	$30

BUDDAH

❑ BDS-5084	Nature's Baby	1971	$30
❑ BDS-5669	The Essential Lena Horne	197?	$30

BULLDOG

❑ BDL-2000	20 Golden Pieces of Lena Horne	198?	$25

CHARTER

❑ CLP-101 [M]	Lena Sings Your Requests	1963	$35
❑ CLS-101 [S]	Lena Sings Your Requests	1963	$50
❑ CLP-106 [M]	Like Latin	1964	$35
❑ CLS-106 [S]	Like Latin	1964	$50

DRG

❑ MRS-510	Lena Goes Latin	1986	$25
❑ MRS-501	Lena Horne With Lennie Hayton & the Marty Paich Orchestra	1985	$25

JAZZTONE

❑ J-1262 [M]	Lena and Ivie	1957	$100

LIBERTY

❑ LN-10194	Lena in Hollywood	198?	$20

LION

❑ L-70050 [M]	I Feel So Smoochie	1959	$50

MGM

Number	Title	Yr	NM
❏ E-545 [10]	Lena Horne Sings	1952	$100
❏ M3G-5409	The One and Only	197?	$25

MOBILE FIDELITY

Number	Title	Yr	NM
❏ Feb-0094	Lena Horne: The Lady and Her Music	1982	$100

— *Audiophile vinyl*

MOVIETONE

Number	Title	Yr	NM
❏ MTM71005 [M]	Once in a Lifetime	196?	$35
❏ MTS72005 [S]	Once in a Lifetime	196?	$50

PAIR

Number	Title	Yr	NM
❏ PDL2-1055	Lena	1986	$30

QWEST

Number	Title	Yr	NM
❏ 2QW3597	Lena Horne: The Lady and Her Music	1981	$30

RCA VICTOR

Number	Title	Yr	NM
❏ LPM-1879 [M]	Give the Lady What She Wants	1958	$60
❏ LSP-1879 [S]	Give the Lady What She Wants	1958	$40
❏ LPM-1148 [M]	It's Love	1955	$100
❏ BGL1-1799	Lena	1976	$30
❏ AYL1-4389	Lena, A New Album	1983	$20

— *"Best Buy Series" reissue*

Number	Title	Yr	NM
❏ BGL1-1026	Lena and Michel	1975	$30

— *With Michel Legrand*

Number	Title	Yr	NM
❏ LPM-2364 [M]	Lena Horne at the Sands	1961	$60
❏ LSP-2364 [S]	Lena Horne at the Sands	1961	$60
❏ LSO-1028 [S]	Lena Horne at the Waldorf Astoria	1957	$40
❏ LPM-2587 [M]	Lena…Lovely and Alive	1963	$60
❏ LSP-2587 [S]	Lena…Lovely and Alive	1963	$60
❏ LPM-2465 [M]	Lena on the Blue Side	1962	$60
❏ LSP-2465 [S]	Lena on the Blue Side	1962	$60
❏ LPM-1895 [M]	Songs of Burke and Van Heusen	1959	$60
❏ LSP-1895 [S]	Songs of Burke and Van Heusen	1959	$40
❏ LPM-1375 [M]	Stormy Weather	1956	$100
❏ LPT-3061 [10]	This Is Lena Horne	1952	$100

SKYE

Number	Title	Yr	NM
❏ 15	Lena & Gabor	1970	$35

— *With Gabor Szabo*

STANYAN

Number	Title	Yr	NM
❏ POW-3006	Stormy Weather	198?	$25

— *Reissue of 10126*

Number	Title	Yr	NM
❏ 10126	Stormy Weather	197?	$30

SUNBEAM

Number	Title	Yr	NM
❏ 212	A Date with Lena Horne	198?	$25

— *With Fletcher Henderson and His Orchestra*

THREE CHERRIES

Number	Title	Yr	NM
❏ TC-44411	The Men in My Life	1989	$25

TIME-LIFE

Number	Title	Yr	NM
❏ SLGD-05	Legendary Singers: Lena Horne	1985	$35

TOPS

Number	Title	Yr	NM
❏ L-1502 [M]	Lena Horne	1958	$50
❏ L-931 [10]	Lena Horne Sings	195?	$40
❏ L-910 [10]	Moanin' Low	195?	$40

UNITED ARTISTS

Number	Title	Yr	NM
❏ UAL3433 [M]	Feelin' Good	1965	$35
❏ UAS6433 [S]	Feelin' Good	1965	$50
❏ UAL3470 [M]	Lena in Hollywood	1966	$35
❏ UAS6470 [S]	Lena in Hollywood	1966	$50
❏ UAL3546 [M]	Merry from Lena	1966	$35
❏ UAS6546 [S]	Merry from Lena	1966	$50

— *Black label, "United Artists" in rounded box at top*

Number	Title	Yr	NM
❏ UAS6546 [S]	Merry from Lena	1972	$30

— *Tan label*

Number	Title	Yr	NM
❏ UAL3496 [M]	Soul	1966	$35
❏ UAS6496 [S]	Soul	1966	$50

HORTA, TONINHO
Guitarist, pianist and male singer.

Albums

VERVE FORECAST

Number	Title	Yr	NM
❏ 835183-1	Diamond Land	1988	$25
❏ 839734-1	Moonstone	1989	$30

HORVITZ, WAYNE
Pianist, organist, keyboard player and composer.

Albums

BLACK SAINT

Number	Title	Yr	NM
❏ BSR-0059	Some Order, Long Understood	1982	$30

ELEKTRA/MUSICIAN

Number	Title	Yr	NM
❏ 60759	This New Generation	1988	$25

HOT ANTIC JAZZ BAND, THE
Members include: Michel Bastide (cornet, trombone, vocals); Jean-François Bonnel (clarinet, cornet, saxophones, vocals); Bernard Antherieu (clarinet, alto saxophone, banjo, vocals); Philippe Raspail (tenor sax, clarinet, alto sax, vocals); Martin Seck (piano, vocals); Jean-Pierre Dubois (banjo, clarinet, kazoo, vocals); Christian Lefevre (tuba, trombone, vocals).

Albums

STOMP OFF

Number	Title	Yr	NM
❏ SOS-1044	I Got the Stinger	1982	$25
❏ SOS-1099	Jazz Battle	1985	$25
❏ SOS-1154	Puttin' On the Ritz	1988	$25
❏ SOS-1058	We Love You Jabbo	1983	$25

HOT COTTON JAZZ BAND, THE
Members include Gene Rush (piano) and Bob Baker (clarinet).

Albums

GHB

Number	Title	Yr	NM
❏ 168	Stompin' Room Only, Vol. 1	1984	$25
❏ 169	Stompin' Room Only, Vol. 2	1984	$25
❏ 188	Take Your Tomorrow	1986	$25

HOT JAZZ ORCHESTRA

Albums

REVELATION

Number	Title	Yr	NM
❏ 28	Hot Jazz Orchestra	1979	$25

HOTEL EDISON ROOF ORCHESTRA, THE

Albums

STOMP OFF

Number	Title	Yr	NM
❏ SOS-1169	Breakaway	1988	$25

HOUGHTON, STEVE
Drummer and percussionist.

Albums

SEABREEZE

Number	Title	Yr	NM
❏ SB-2018	The Steve Houghton Album	198?	$25

HOUN, FRED, AND THE AFRO-ASIAN MUSIC ENSEMBLE
Houn is a baritone saxophone player and bandleader.

Albums

SOUL NOTE

Number	Title	Yr	NM
❏ SN-1117	Tomorrow Is Now!	1986	$30
❏ 121117	Tomorrow Is Now!	198?	$30

— *Reissue of 1117*

Number	Title	Yr	NM
❏ 121167	We Refuse to Be Used and Abused	1990	$35

HOWARD, DAVE
Male singer.

Albums

CHOREO

Number	Title	Yr	NM
❏ C-5 [M]	I Love Everybody	1961	$30
❏ CS-5 [S]	I Love Everybody	1961	$30

HOWARD, EDDY
Male singer, guitarist, trombonist and bandleader. His biggest hit was "(It's No) Sin" in 1951.

Albums

COLUMBIA

Number	Title	Yr	NM
❏ CL6067 [10]	Eddy Howard	1949	$120

HINDSIGHT

Number	Title	Yr	NM
❏ HSR-156	Eddy Howard 1945-1948	198?	$25
❏ HSR-119	Eddy Howard 1946-1951	198?	$25
❏ HSR-405	Eddy Howard and His Orchestra Play 22 Original Big Band Favorites	198?	$30

INSIGHT

Number	Title	Yr	NM
❏ 205	Eddy Howard and His Orchestra 1945-1951	198?	$25

MERCURY

Number	Title	Yr	NM
❏ MG-20562 [M]	Eddy Howard's Golden Hits	1961	$100
❏ SR-60562 [S]	Eddy Howard's Golden Hits	1961	$100
❏ MG-20817 [M]	Eddy Howard Sings and Plays the Great Band Hits	196?	$100
❏ SR-60817 [S]	Eddy Howard Sings and Plays the Great Band Hits	196?	$100

Number	Title	Yr	NM
❏ MG-20665 [M]	Eddy Howard Sings and Plays the Great Old Waltzes	1962	$100
❏ SR-60665 [S]	Eddy Howard Sings and Plays the Great Old Waltzes	1962	$100
❏ MG-20432 [M]	Great for Dancing	1958	$100
❏ SR-60104 [S]	Great for Dancing	1959	$100
❏ MG-20910 [M]	Intimately Yours	1965	$100
❏ SR-60910 [S]	Intimately Yours	1965	$100
❏ MG-20593 [M]	More Eddy Howard's Golden Hits	1962	$100
❏ SR-60593 [S]	More Eddy Howard's Golden Hits	1962	$100
❏ MG-20312 [M]	Paradise Isle	195?	$100
❏ MG-25011 [10]	Selected Song Favorites	1949	$150

— *Title appears only on label; cover simply states "Eddy Howard and His Orchestra"*

Number	Title	Yr	NM
❏ MG-20112 [M]	Singing in the Rain	195?	$100
❏ MG-21014 [M]	Softly and Sincerely	196?	$100
❏ SR-61014 [S]	Softly and Sincerely	196?	$100

WING

Number	Title	Yr	NM
❏ MGW-12171 [M]	Eddy Howard Sings Words of Love	196?	$30
❏ SRW-16171 [S]	Eddy Howard Sings Words of Love	196?	$30
❏ MGW-12104 [M]	Saturday Night Dance Date	196?	$30
❏ SRW-16104 [S]	Saturday Night Dance Date	196?	$30
❏ MGW-12194 [M]	Sleepy Serenade	196?	$30
❏ SRW-16194 [S]	Sleepy Serenade	196?	$30
❏ MGW-12249 [M]	The Velvet Voice	196?	$30
❏ SRW-16249 [S]	The Velvet Voice	196?	$30
❏ MGW-12171 [M]	Words of Love	196?	$30
❏ SRW-16171 [S]	Words of Love	196?	$30

HOWARD, GEORGE
Soprano and alto saxophone player.

Albums

GRP

Number	Title	Yr	NM
❏ GR-9629	Love and Understanding	1991	$35

MCA

Number	Title	Yr	NM
❏ 5855	A Nice Place to Be	1987	$25
❏ 6335	Personal	1990	$30
❏ 42145	Reflections	1988	$25

PALO ALTO

Number	Title	Yr	NM
❏ PA-8035	Asphalt Garden	1982	$30
❏ TB-205	Dancing in the Sun	198?	$25
❏ TB-210	Love Will Follow	1987	$25
❏ TB-201	Steppin' Out	198?	$25

HOWARD, JIM
Guitarist.

Albums

SEABREEZE

Number	Title	Yr	NM
❏ SB-2005	No Compromise	1983	$25

HOWARD, JOE
Trombonist.

Albums

KING

Number	Title	Yr	NM
❏ 661 [M]	The Golden Sound	1959	$50

SUNSET

Number	Title	Yr	NM
❏ SU-3001 [M]	Patterns for Trombone	1955	$50

HOWARD, KID
Trumpeter and bandleader.

Albums

GHB

Number	Title	Yr	NM
❏ 23	Kid Howard at San Jacinto Hall	1966	$30

JAZZOLOGY

Number	Title	Yr	NM
❏ JCE-14	Kid Howard and the Vida Jazz Band	1967	$30
❏ JCE-18	Kid Howard's Olympia Band	1967	$30

HOWARD, NOAH
Alto saxophone player.

Albums

ALTOSAX

Number	Title	Yr	NM
❏ 1001	Patterns	197?	$35
❏ 25055	Quartetto	197?	$35

CHIAROSCURO

Number	Title	Yr	NM
❏ 2016	Oie	1979	$30

ESP-DISK'

Number	Title	Yr	NM
❏ S-1064 [S]	Live at Judson Hall	1969	$100
❏ 1073	Noah Howard	1968	$0

— *Canceled*

Number	Title	Yr	NM
❏ 1031 [M]	Noah Howard Quartet	1966	$150
❏ S-1031 [S]	Noah Howard Quartet	1966	$150

Number	Title	Yr	NM

HOWELL, MICHAEL
Guitarist.

Albums

CATALYST
| 7615 | Alone | 1976 | $30 |

MILESTONE
| M-9054 | In the Silence | 1974 | $30 |
| M-9048 | Looking Glass | 1973 | $30 |

HOWELL, REUBEN

Albums

MOTOWN
| M771L | Reuben Howell | 1973 | $50 |

HUBBARD, DAVE
Tenor saxophone player.

Albums

MAINSTREAM
| MRL-317 | Dave Hubbard | 1971 | $35 |

HUBBARD, FREDDIE, AND OSCAR PETERSON
Also see each artist's individual listings.

Albums

PABLO
| 2310876 | Face to Face | 198? | $25 |

HUBBARD, FREDDIE, AND STANLEY TURRENTINE
Also see each artist's individual listings.

Albums

CTI
| CTS-6044 | In Concert, Volume 1 | 1974 | $25 |
| CTS-6049 | In Concert, Volume 2 | 1975 | $25 |

HUBBARD, FREDDIE
Trumpeter, fluegel horn player and composer.

Albums

ABC IMPULSE!
AS-9237	Re-Evaluation: The Impulse Years	1973	$35
AS-27 [S]	The Artistry of Freddie Hubbard	1968	$30
AS-38 [S]	The Body and Soul of Freddie Hubbard	1968	$30

ATLANTIC
1477 [M]	Backlash	1967	$60
SD1477 [S]	Backlash	1967	$35
90466	Backlash	1986	$20
—Reissue of SD 1477
SD1549	Black Angel	1971	$30
SD1501	High Pressure Blues	1969	$35
SD1526	Soul Experiment	1970	$30
80108	Sweet Return	1983	$25
SD 2-314	The Art of Freddie Hubbard	1974	$35

BASF
| 10726 | The Hub of Hubbard | 1972 | $30 |

BLUE NOTE
| BST-84196 [S] | Blue Spirits | 1967 | $35 |
— With "A Division of Liberty Records" on label
| BST-84196 | Blue Spirits | 1987 | $25 |
— The Finest in Jazz Since 1939" reissue
| BST-84172 [S] | Breaking Point | 1967 | $35 |
— With "A Division of Liberty Records" on label
B1-85121	Doubletake	1987	$25
BN-LA356-H [(2)]	Freddie Hubbard	1975	$35
BLP-4056 [M]	Goin' Up	1960	$700
— With W. 63rd St. address on label
| BLP-4056 [M] | Goin' Up | 1963 | $100 |
— With New York, USA address on label
| BST-84056 [S] | Goin' Up | 1963 | $60 |
— With New York, USA address on label
| BST-84056 [S] | Goin' Up | 1967 | $35 |
— With "A Division of Liberty Records" on label
| 4135/84135 | Here to Stay | 1963 | $0 |
— Scheduled, but unreleased until 1985
| BST-84135 | Here to Stay | 1985 | $30 |
| BST-84073 [S] | Hub Cap | 1963 | $60 |
— With New York, USA address on label
| BST-84073 [S] | Hub Cap | 1967 | $35 |
— With "A Division of Liberty Records" on label

| BST-84073 | Hub Cap | 198? | $25 |
— The Finest in Jazz Since 1939" reissue
| BST-84115 [S] | Hub-Tones | 1962 | $60 |
— With New York, USA address on label
| BST-84115 [S] | Hub-Tones | 1967 | $35 |
— With "A Division of Liberty Records" on label
| BST-84115 | Hub-Tones | 1985 | $25 |
— The Finest in Jazz Since 1939" reissue
| B1-85139 | Life-Flight | 1987 | $25 |
| BLP-4040 [M] | Open Sesame | 1960 | $1200 |
— Deep groove" version (deep indentation under label on both sides)
| BLP-4040 [M] | Open Sesame | 1963 | $100 |
— With New York, USA address on label
| BST-84040 [S] | Open Sesame | 1960 | $120 |
— With W. 63rd St. addresss on label
| BST-84040 [S] | Open Sesame | 1963 | $60 |
— With New York, USA address on label
| BST-84040 [S] | Open Sesame | 1967 | $35 |
— With "A Division of Liberty Records" on label
| BST-84040 | Open Sesame | 1989 | $25 |
— The Finest in Jazz Since 1939" reissue
| BST-84040 [S] | Open Sesame | 199? | $60 |
— Classic Records reissue on audiophile vinyl
| BLP-4085 [M] | Ready for Freddie | 1963 | $100 |
— With New York, USA address on label
| BST-84085 [S] | Ready for Freddie | 1963 | $60 |
— With New York, USA address on label
| BST-84085 [S] | Ready for Freddie | 1967 | $35 |
— With "A Division of Liberty Records" on label
| B1-32094 | Ready for Freddie | 1995 | $30 |
— The Finest in Jazz Since 1939" reissue
B1-93202	The Best of Freddie Hubbard	1989	$30
BJT-48017	The Eternal Triangle	1988	$30
BLP-4207 [M]	The Night of the Cookers – Live at Club Le Marchal, Vol. 1	1965	$100
BST-84207 [S]	The Night of the Cookers – Live at Club Le Marchal, Vol. 1	1965	$60
— With New York, USA address on label
| BST-84207 [S] | The Night of the Cookers – Live at Club Le Marchal, Vol. 1 | 1967 | $35 |
— With "A Division of Liberty Records" on label
| BLP-4208 [M] | The Night of the Cookers – Live at Club Le Marchal, Vol. 2 | 1965 | $100 |
| BST-84208 [S] | The Night of the Cookers – Live at Club Le Marchal, Vol. 2 | 1965 | $60 |
— With New York, USA address on label
| BST-84208 [S] | The Night of the Cookers – Live at Club Le Marchal, Vol. 2 | 1967 | $35 |
— With "A Division of Liberty Records" on label
| B1-90905 | Times 'R Changin' | 1989 | $30 |

COLUMBIA
PC34902	Bundle of Joy	1977	$25
KC33048	High Energy	1974	$25
PC33556	Liquid Love	1975	$25
JC36015	Love Connection	1979	$25
FC36418	Skagly	1980	$25
JC35386	Super Blue	1978	$25
JC36358	The Best of Freddie Hubbard	1979	$25
PC34166	Windjammer	1976	$25

CTI
| CTS-6013 | First Light | 1972 | $30 |
| 8017 | First Light | 198? | $20 |
— Reissue of 6013
CTS-6044	Freddie Hubbard In Concert	1974	$25
CTS-6036	Keep Your Soul Together	1974	$25
CTS-6056	Polar AC	1975	$25
CTS-6001	Red Clay	1970	$30
8016	Red Clay	198?	$20
— Reissue of 6001
CTS-6018	Sky Dive	1973	$25
CTS-6047	The Baddest Hubbard	1974	$25
CTS-6007	The Straight Life	1971	$30
8022	The Straight Life	198?	$20
— Reissue of 6007

CTI/CBS ASSOCIATED
| FZ40687 | First Light | 1987 | $25 |

ELEKTRA/MUSICIAN
| 60029 | Ride Like the Wind | 1982 | $25 |

ENJA
| 3095 | Outpost | 1981 | $25 |

FANTASY
9626	A Little Night Music	1983	$25
9635	Classics	1984	$25
9615	Keystone Bop	1982	$25
9610	Splash	1981	$25

IMPULSE!
A-27 [M]	The Artistry of Freddie Hubbard	1962	$200
AS-27 [S]	The Artistry of Freddie Hubbard	1962	$200
A-38 [M]	The Body and Soul of Freddie Hubbard	1963	$200
AS-38 [S]	The Body and Soul of Freddie Hubbard	1963	$200

LIBERTY
| LT-1110 | Mistral | 1981 | $25 |

PABLO
| 2312134 | Born to Be Blue | 1982 | $25 |
| 2310884 | The Best of Freddie Hubbard | 1983 | $25 |

PABLO LIVE
| 2620113 | Live at the Northsea Jazz Festival, The Hague, 1980 | 1983 | $30 |

PABLO TODAY
| 2312134 | Born to Be Blue | 198? | $25 |

PAUSA
| 7122 | Rollin' | 1982 | $25 |

PHOENIX 10
| PHX318 | Extended | 1981 | $20 |

PICCADILLY
| 3467 | Intrepid Fox | 198? | $25 |

QUINTESSENCE
| 25161 | Skylark | 1978 | $25 |

REAL TIME
| 305 | Back to Birdland | 198? | $25 |

HUBBELL, FRANK

Albums

PHILIPS
| PHS600293 | Frank Hubbell and the Stompers | 1969 | $35 |

HUBNER, ABBI, AND HIS LOW DOWN WIZARDS

Albums

STOMP OFF
| SOS-1093 | Twenty Years, Live in Concert | 1986 | $25 |

HUCKO, PEANUTS, AND RALPH SUTTON
Also see each artist's individual listings.

Albums

CHIAROSCURO
| 167 | Live at Condon's | 1978 | $30 |

HUCKO, PEANUTS
Clarinetist and tenor saxophone player. Also see REX STEWART.

Albums

CIRCLE
| C-21 | Peanuts | 198? | $25 |

GRAND AWARD
| GA 33-331 [M] | Tribute to Benny Goodman | 1956 | $40 |

HUCKO, PEANUTS/RAY MCKINLEY
Also see each artist's individual listings.

Albums

GRAND AWARD
| GA 33-333 [M] | The Swingin' 30s | 1956 | $40 |

HUDSON, DEAN
There was no Dean Hudson; it was a fictitious name used by various groups of University of Florida big-band musicians to imply continuity.

Albums

CIRCLE
| C-13 | Dean Hudson and His Orchestra 1942-1948 | 198? | $25 |

The Jazztet (Art Farmer-Benny Golson), *Another Git Together*, Mercury SR 60737, **$100**.

The Jazztet (Art Farmer-Benny Golson), *Meet the Jazztet*, Argo LP-664, **$50**.

John Jenkins, *John Jenkins with Kenny Burrell*, Blue Note BLP-1573, "deep groove" edition with W. 63rd St. address on label, **$1,000**.

Dick Johnson, *Music for Swinging Moderns*, EmArcy MG 36081, **$200**.

Number	Title	Yr	NM
❑ CLP-136	Dean Hudson and His Orchestra 1943-1944	198?	$25
❑ C-40	Dean Hudson and His Orchestra -- Now!	1982	$25
❑ C-86	More Dean Hudson and His Orchestra 1941 and 1948`	198?	$25

HUG, ARMAND
Pianist.
Albums
CIRCLE
| ❑ L-411 [10] | New Orleans 88 | 1951 | $60 |

GHB
| ❑ 144 | Armand Hug | 1988 | $25 |

GOLDEN CREST
| ❑ GC-3045 [M] | New Orleans Piano | 196? | $35 |
| ❑ GC-3064 | Rags and Blues | 196? | $35 |

JAZZOLOGY
| ❑ J-83 | Armand Hug Plays Bix | 197? | $30 |

LAND O' JAZZ
| ❑ 3475 | Autobiography in Jazz | 197? | $30 |

PARAMOUNT
| ❑ LP-114 [10] | Armand Hug Plays Armand Piron | 1954 | $50 |

SOUTHLAND
| ❑ 228 [M] | Dixieland | 1961 | $35 |
| ❑ 244 [M] | Piano in New Orleans | 196? | $35 |

HUG, ARMAND/EDDIE MILLER
Also see each artist's individual listings.
Albums
GHB
| ❑ 121 | Armand Hug and His New Orleans Dixielanders/Eddie Miller and His New Orleans Rhythm Pals | 198? | $25 |

LAND O' JAZZ
| ❑ 5876 | Just Friends | 198? | $25 |

HUGHES, LANGSTON
The below are spoken-word recordings.
Albums
VERVE
| ❑ VSP-36 [M] | The Weary Blues | 1966 | $25 |
| ❑ VSPS-36 [R] | The Weary Blues | 1966 | $15 |

HUGHES, RHETA
Female singer.
Albums
COLUMBIA
| ❑ CL2385 [M] | Introducing An Electrifying New Star | 1965 | $30 |
| ❑ CS9185 [S] | Introducing An Electrifying New Star | 1965 | $40 |

HUMAN ARTS ENSEMBLE
Membership included Charles "Bobo" Shaw (drums, bugle); Joseph Bowie (trombone); Luther Thomas (alto saxophone); James Emery (guitar); John Lindberg (bass).
Albums
ARISTA FREEDOM
| ❑ AF1022 | Under the Sun | 1975 | $30 |
| ❑ AF1039 | Whisper of Dharma | 1977 | $30 |

HUMES, HELEN
Female singer.
Albums
AUDIOPHILE
| ❑ AP-107 | Helen Humes | 1980 | $50 |

CLASSIC JAZZ
| ❑ 120 | Let the Good Times Roll | 197? | $30 |
| ❑ 110 | Sneakin' Around | 197? | $30 |

COLUMBIA
| ❑ PC33488 | The Talk of the Town | 1975 | $35 |

CONTEMPORARY
❑ M-3582 [M]	Songs I Like to Sing	1960	$200
❑ S-7582 [S]	Songs I Like to Sing	1960	$200
❑ M-3598 [M]	Swingin' with Humes	1961	$200
❑ S-7598 [S]	Swingin' with Humes	1961	$200
❑ M-3571 [M]	'Tain't Nobody's Biz-Ness If I Do	1960	$200

Number	Title	Yr	NM
❑ S-7571 [S]	'Tain't Nobody's Biz-Ness If I Do	1960	$200

FANTASY
❑ OJC-171	Songs I Like to Sing	198?	$30
❑ OJC-608	Swingin' with Humes	1991	$35
❑ OJC-453	'Tain't Nobody's Biz-Ness If I Do	1990	$35

JAZZ MAN
| ❑ 5003 | On the Sunny Side of the Street | 1981 | $35 |

JAZZOLOGY
| ❑ J-55 | Incomparable | 197? | $30 |

MUSE
| ❑ MR-5233 | Helen | 1980 | $30 |
| ❑ MR-5217 | Helen Humes with the Muse All Stars | 197? | $30 |

SAVOY JAZZ
| ❑ SJL-1159 | E-Baba-Le-Ba": The Rhythm & Blues Years | 1986 | $30 |

HUMPHREY, BOBBI
Flutist and female singer.
Albums
BLUE NOTE
❑ BN-LA142-G	Blacks and Blues	1974	$25
❑ BST-84421	Dig This	1972	$30
❑ BN-LA550-G	Fancy Dancer	1975	$25
❑ BST-84379	Flute-In	1971	$30
❑ BN-LA344-G	Satin Doll	1974	$25
❑ BN-LA699-G	The Best of Bobbi Humphrey	1976	$25

EPIC
❑ JE35338	Freestyle	1978	$25
❑ PE34704	Tailor Made	1977	$25
❑ JE36368	The Best of Bobbi Humphrey	1980	$25
❑ JE35607	The Good Life	1979	$25

HUMPHREY, EARL
Trombonist and bandleader. Percy and Willie were his brothers.
Albums
BIOGRAPH
| ❑ CEN-11 | Earl Humphrey and His Footwarmers | 197? | $30 |

HUMPHREY, PAUL
Drummer. Had a pop and R&B hit with "Cool Aid" in 1971.
Albums
BLUE THUMB
| ❑ BTS66 | America, Wake Up! | 1974 | $30 |
| ❑ BTS47 | Supermellow | 1973 | $30 |

DISCOVERY
| ❑ DS-850 | Paul Humphrey Sextet | 1981 | $25 |

LIZARD
| ❑ 20106 | Paul Humphrey & the Cool Aid Chemists | 1971 | $35 |

HUMPHREY, PERCY
Trumpeter. He, Earl and Willie were brothers.
Albums
BIOGRAPH
| ❑ CEN-13 | Percy Humphrey at Manny's Tavern | 197? | $30 |

GHB
| ❑ 85 | Percy Humphrey and the Crescent City Joymakers | 197? | $25 |

JAZZOLOGY
| ❑ JCE-26 | Percy Humphrey and the Crescent City Joymakers | 197? | $30 |

PEARL
| ❑ PS-3 | Climax Rag | 197? | $35 |

RIVERSIDE
| ❑ RLP-378 [M] | Percy Humphrey's Crescent City Joymakers | 1961 | $200 |
| ❑ RS-9378 [R] | Percy Humphrey's Crescent City Joymakers | 196? | $35 |

Number	Title	Yr	NM

HUMPHREY, WILLIE
Clarinetist, brother of Earl and Percy.
Albums
GHB
| ❑ 248 | New Orleans Jazz from Willie Humphrey | 198? | $25 |

HUNDLEY, CRAIG
Keyboard player.
Albums
WORLD PACIFIC
| ❑ WPS-21900 | Rhapsody in Blue | 1970 | $100 |
| ❑ WPS-21896 | The Craig Hundley Trio Plays with the Big Boys | 1969 | $100 |

HUNT, PEE WEE
Trombonist, male singer and bandleader.
Albums
ALLEGRO
| ❑ 1633 [M] | Dixieland | 1956 | $30 |

CAPITOL
❑ T984 [M]	Cole Porter Ala Dixie	1957	$60
— Turquoise label			
❑ H312 [10]	Dixieland Detour	1952	$80
❑ T1265 [M]	Dixieland Kickoff	1959	$60
❑ T783 [M]	Pee Wee and Fingers	1956	$60
❑ T1362 [M]	Pee Wee Hunt's Dance Party	1960	$40
❑ ST1362 [S]	Pee Wee Hunt's Dance Party	1960	$80
❑ H203 [10]	Straight from Dixie	1950	$75
❑ T203 [M]	Straight from Dixie	195?	$60
❑ H492 [10]	Swingin' Around	1954	$75
❑ T1853 [M]	The Best of Pee Wee Hunt	1962	$75
❑ DT1853 [R]	The Best of Pee Wee Hunt	1962	$60
❑ T1144 [M]	The Blues A La Dixie	1958	$60

ROYALE
| ❑ 18153 [10] | Pee Wee Hunt and His Dixieland Band | 195? | $40 |

SOLITAIRE
| ❑ 507 [10] | Dixieland Capers | 195? | $30 |

HUNT, PEE WEE/PEE WEE RUSSELL
Also see each artist's individual listings.
Albums
RONDO-LETTE
| ❑ A2 [M] | Dixieland: Pee Wee Hunt and Pee Wee Russell | 195? | $30 |

HUNTER, ALBERTA
Female singer.
Albums
COLUMBIA
❑ JC36430	Amtrak Blues	1980	$25
❑ FC38970	Look for the Silver Lining	1983	$25
❑ FC37691	The Glory of Alberta Hunter	1982	$30
❑ PC37691	The Glory of Alberta Hunter	1985	$20
—Budget-line reissue			

DRG
| ❑ SL-5195 | Legendary Alberta Hunter | 198? | $25 |

FANTASY
| ❑ OBC-510 | Alberta Hunter with Lovie Austin's Blues Serenaders | 198? | $25 |

RIVERSIDE
| ❑ RLP-418 [M] | Alberta Hunter with Lovie Austin's Blues Serenaders | 1962 | $200 |
| ❑ RS-9418 [R] | Alberta Hunter with Lovie Austin's Blues Serenaders | 196? | $35 |

STASH
| ❑ ST-115 | Classic Alberta Hunter: The Thirties | 1978 | $25 |
| ❑ ST-123 | Young Alberta Hunter: The Twenties | 1984 | $25 |

HUNTER, FRANK
Arranger and composer.
Albums
JUBILEE
| ❑ JLP-1020 [M] | Sounds of Hunter | 1956 | $50 |

Number	Title	Yr	NM

HUNTER, LURLEAN
Female singer.
Albums

ATLANTIC
| 1344 [M] | Blue and Sentimental | 1960 | $300 |
| SD1344 [S] | Blue and Sentimental | 1960 | $300 |

VIK
| LX-1061 [M] | Night Life | 1956 | $80 |

HUNTER, STAN, AND SONNY FORTUNE
Hunter is a keyboard player, Also see SONNY FORTUNE.
Albums

PRESTIGE
| PRLP-7458 [M] | Trip on the Strip | 1967 | $30 |
| PRST-7458 [S] | Trip on the Strip | 1967 | $25 |

HUSSAIN, ZAKIR
Tabla (Indian drum) player.
Albums

ECM
| 1349 | Making Music | 1987 | $25 |

HUTCHERSON, BOBBY
Vibraphone and marimba player.
Albums

BLUE NOTE
| BST-84333 | Bobby Hutcherson Now | 1969 | $25 |
— *With "A Division of Liberty Records" on label*
| BN-LA257-G | Cirrus | 1973 | $30 |
| BST-84213 [S] | Components | 1967 | $35 |
— *With "A Division of Liberty Records" on label*
| B1-29027 | Components | 1994 | $35 |
— *Reissue*
| BST-84198 [S] | Dialogue | 1967 | $35 |
— *With "A Division of Liberty Records" on label*
| BST-84198 | Dialogue | 198? | $25 |
— *The Finest in Jazz Since 1939" reissue*
| BST-84231 [S] | Happenings | 1967 | $60 |
— *With "A Division of Liberty Records" on label*
BST-84376	Head On	1971	$35
BN-LA789-H	Knucklebean	1977	$30
BN-LA396-G	Linger Lane	1974	$30
LT-1086	Medina	1980	$25
BN-LA551-G	Montara	1975	$30
BST-84416	Natural Illusions	1972	$35
LT-1044	Patterns	1980	$25
B1-33583	Patterns	1995	$35
— *Reissue*
| BST-84362 | San Francisco | 1970 | $25 |
| B1-28268 | San Francisco | 1994 | $35 |
— *Reissue*
| LT-996 | Spiral | 1979 | $25 |
| BLP-4244 [M] | Stick-Up! | 1968 | $300 |
— *Scheduled for release in mono, but evidently never came out*
| BST-84291 | Total Eclipse | 1969 | $25 |
— *With "A Division of Liberty Records" on label*
| BST-84291 | Total Eclipse | 1985 | $25 |
— *The Finest in Jazz Since 1939" reissue*
| BN-LA710-G | View from Inside | 1977 | $30 |
| BN-LA615-G | Waiting | 1976 | $30 |

COLUMBIA
JC35814	Conception: The Gift of Love	1979	$25
JC35550	Highway 1	1978	$25
FC36402	Un Poco Loco	1980	$25

CONTEMPORARY
| C-14009 | Solo/Quartet | 1982 | $30 |

FANTASY
| OJC-425 | Solo/Quartet | 1990 | $30 |

LANDMARK
LLP-1522	Ambos Mundos	1989	$35
LLP-1508	Color Schemes	1986	$30
LLP-1517	Cruisin' the 'Bird	1988	$30
LLP-501	Good Bait	1985	$30
LLP-1513	In the Vanguard	1987	$30

THERESA
| TR-124 | Farewell Keystone | 1989 | $30 |

HYLTON, JACK
British pianist, organist, male singer and bandleader.
Albums

FLAPPER

Number	Title	Yr	NM
702	Jack Hylton and His Orchestra 1925-28: Light Music from the Variety Stage	198?	$25

HYMAN, DICK
Pianist, harpsichord player, organist, Moog synthesizer pioneer, bandleader, arranger and composer. His version of "Moritat (Mack the Knife)" was second only to Bobby Darin's in sales.
Albums

ATLANTIC
| SD1671 | Satchmo Remembered | 1975 | $25 |

CHIAROSCURO
| 198 | Themes and Variations on "A Child Is Born | 1978 | $25 |

COLUMBIA MASTERWORKS
| M32587 | Ferdinand "Jelly Roll" Morton -- Transcriptions for Orchestra | 1974 | $30 |

COMMAND
RS 33-911 [M]	Brazilian Impressions	1966	$35
RS911SD [S]	Brazilian Impressions	1966	$50
RS951SD	Concerto Electro	1970	$60
RS 33-856 [M]	Electrodynamics	1963	$35
RS856SD [S]	Electrodynamics	1963	$50
RS 33-862 [M]	Fabulous	1963	$35
RS862SD [S]	Fabulous	1963	$50
RS 33-899 [M]	Happening!	1966	$35
RS899SD [S]	Happening!	1966	$50
RS 33-875 [M]	Keyboard Kaleidoscope	1964	$35
RS875SD [S]	Keyboard Kaleidoscope	1964	$50
RS924SD	Mirrors	1967	$50
RS938SD	Moog -- The Electric Eclectics of Dick Hyman	1968	$60
RSSD980/2	Organ Antics	1974	$50
RS 33-811 [M]	Provocative Piano	1960	$35
RS811SD [S]	Provocative Piano	1960	$50
RS 33-824 [M]	Provocative Piano Volume 2	1961	$35
RS824SD [S]	Provocative Piano Volume 2	1961	$50
RS933SD	Sweet Sweet Soul	1968	$60
RS 33-832 [M]	The Dick Hyman Trio	1961	$35
RSSD973/2	The Kaleidoscopic Keyboard	1974	$50
RS 33-891 [M]	The Man from O.R.G.A.N.	1965	$40
RS891SD [S]	The Man from O.R.G.A.N.	1965	$100
RSSD968/2	The Synthesizer	1973	$40
— *Reissue of "Electric Eclectics" and "Age of Electronicus"*

GRAPEVINE
| 3309 | Waltz Dressed in Blue | 1978 | $30 |

LION
| L-70067 [M] | Swingin' Double Date | 1958 | $35 |

MGM
| E-3535 [M] | 60 Great All-Time Songs, Vol. 1 | 1957 | $50 |
— *Yellow label*
| E-3536 [M] | 60 Great All-Time Songs, Vol. 2 | 1957 | $50 |
— *Yellow label*
| E-3537 [M] | 60 Great All-Time Songs, Vol. 3 | 1957 | $50 |
— *Yellow label*
| E-3586 [M] | 60 Great All-Time Songs, Vol. 4 | 1958 | $50 |
— *Yellow label*
| E-3587 [M] | 60 Great All-Time Songs, Vol. 5 | 1958 | $50 |
— *Yellow label*
| E-3588 [M] | 60 Great All-Time Songs, Vol. 6 | 1958 | $50 |
— *Yellow label*
| E-3726 [M] | 60 Great Continental and Classical Favorites | 1959 | $50 |
| E-3725 [M] | 60 Great Songs from Broadway Musicals | 1959 | $50 |
— *Yellow label*
| E-3724 [M] | 60 Great Songs That Say "I Love You | 1959 | $50 |
— *Yellow label*
E-3821 [M]	After Six	1960	$50
SE-3821 [S]	After Six	1960	$60
E-3379 [M]	Behind a Shady Nook	1956	$60
— *Yellow label*
| E-3606 [M] | Dick Hyman and Harpsichord in Hi-Fi | 1958 | $50 |
— *Yellow label*
| E-3642 [M] | Gigi | 1958 | $50 |
— *Yellow label*
| E-3494 [M] | Hi-Fi Suite | 1957 | $60 |
— *Yellow label*
| E-4119 [M] | Moon Gas | 1963 | $50 |
| SE-4119 [S] | Moon Gas | 1963 | $60 |

Number	Title	Yr	NM
E-3483 [M]	Red Sails in the Sunset	1957	$60
— *Yellow label*
| E-3553 [M] | Rockin' Sax and Rollin' Organ | 1958 | $60 |
— *Yellow label*
SE-4649	Space Reflex	1969	$35
E-3808 [M]	Strictly Organic	1960	$50
SE-3808 [S]	Strictly Organic	1960	$60
E-3329 [M]	The "Unforgettable" Sound of the Dick Hyman Trio	1955	$75
— *Yellow label*
| E-289 [10] | The "Unforgettable" Sound of the Dick Hyman Trio | 1955 | $50 |
| E-3280 [M] | The Dick Hyman Trio Swings | 1954 | $60 |
— *Yellow label*
| E-3747 [M] | Whoop-Up! | 1959 | $50 |
— *Yellow label*
| SE-3747 [S] | Whoop-Up! | 1959 | $60 |

MONMOUTH-EVERGREEN
| MES7065 | Genius at Play | 1974 | $35 |

MUSICAL HERITAGE SOCIETY
| MHS912213K | Face the Music: Irving Berlin | 198? | $25 |

PROJECT 3
PR5057SD	Fantomfingers	1971	$60
PR5070SD	Piano Solos	1972	$35
PR5054SD	The Sensuous Piano of "D	1970	$35
PR5080SD	Traditional Jazz Piano	1973	$35

RCA VICTOR GOLD SEAL
| AGL1-3651 | Scott Joplin: 16 Classic Rags | 1980 | $20 |
— *Reissue*

RCA VICTOR RED SEAL
| XRL1-4746 | Kitten on the Keys: Music of Zez Confrey | 1983 | $25 |
| ARL1-1257 | Scott Joplin: 16 Classic Rags | 1976 | $25 |

REFERENCE RECORDINGS
| RR-33 | Dick Hyman Plays Fats Waller | 1991 | $60 |

SEAGULL
| LG-8209 | Love Story | 198? | $25 |

STOMP OFF
| SOS-1141 | Gulf Coast Blues: The Music of Clarence Williams | 1987 | $25 |

SUNSET
| SUM-1140 [M] | I'll Never Be the Same | 1966 | $30 |
| SUS-5140 [S] | I'll Never Be the Same | 1966 | $35 |

I

IBRAHIM, ABDULLAH
Pianist, male singer, cellist, flutist and soprano saxophone player. Originally recorded under the name "Dollar Brand"; those albums are also listed below.
Albums

BLACKHAWK
| BKH-50207 | Water from an Ancient Well | 1986 | $25 |

BLACK LION
| 192 | This Is Dollar Brand | 197? | $30 |

CHIAROSCURO
2004	Cape Town Fringe	197?	$30
187	Journey	1978	$30
2012	Soweto	197?	$30

DENON
| 7537 | Anthems for the New Nations | 1978 | $30 |

ELEKTRA
| 6E-252 | African Marketplace | 1980 | $25 |

ENJA
R1-79617	African River	1990	$35
2026	African Sketchbook	197?	$35
2032	African Space Program	197?	$35
2048	Good News from Africa	1976	$35
R1-79601	Mindif (Original Soundtrack Recording for the Film "Chocolat")	1989	$35

INNER CITY
IC-3003	Children of Africa	197?	$30
IC-6049	Ode to Duke Ellington	198?	$25
IC-3031	Tears and Laughter	1979	$30

REPRISE
| R-6111 [M] | Duke Ellington Presents the Dollar Brand Trio | 1965 | $25 |

Number	Title	Yr	NM
❏ RS-6111 [S]	Duke Ellington Presents the Dollar Brand Trio	1965	$30

SACKVILLE

❏ 3009	African Portraits	198?	$25

WEST 54

❏ 8011	Memories	1979	$30

ILORI, SOLOMON
Guitarist, percussionist and male singer.

Albums

BLUE NOTE

❏ BLP-4136 [M]	African High Life	1963	$100
❏ BST-84136 [S]	African High Life	1963	$80

— With "New York, USA" address on label

❏ BST-84136 [S]	African High Life	1967	$30

— With "A Division of Liberty Records" on label

IND, PETER
Bass player.

Albums

WAVE

❏ W-1 [M]	Looking Out	1961	$30
❏ WS-1 [S]	Looking Out	1961	$30

INSTANT COMPOSERS POOL (ICP ORCHESTRA)
A fluid organization with MISHA MENGELBERG as the constant.

Albums

ICP

❏ 022	Live Soncino	1980	$30
❏ 020	Tetterettet	1977	$30
❏ 026	The ICP Orchestra Performs Nichols-Monk	1987	$35

INTERNATIONAL JAZZ BAND
Members: Kid Thomas Valentine, BILL BISSONETTE, Sammy Rimington, Emanuel Paul, Bill Sinclair, Dick Griffith, Dick McCarthy, Barry Martyn.

Albums

GHB

❏ 20	International Jazz Band Volume 1	1966	$35
❏ 21	International Jazz Band Volume 2	1966	$35

INTERNATIONAL JAZZ GROUP
Led by Andre Persiany.

Albums

SWING

❏ SW-8407	International Jazz Group, Volume 1	198?	$25
❏ SW-8416	International Jazz Group, Volume 2	1987	$25

IRAKERE
Cuban jazz band founded by Chucho Valdes (piano), ARTURO SANDOVAL, PAQUITO D'RIVERA and Oscar Valdes. Many membership changes in its history.

Albums

COLUMBIA

❏ JC35655	Irakere	1979	$30
❏ JC36107	Irakere II	1980	$30

MILESTONE

❏ M-9103	Chekere Son	198?	$30
❏ M-9111	El Coco	198?	$30

IRVIN, BOOKER
See BOOKER ERVIN.

IRVIN, TINY
Female singer.

Albums

EARWIG

❏ LPS-4903	You Don't Know What Love Is	1986	$30

IRVINE, WELDON
Organist, pianist and keyboard player.

Albums

BMG SPECIAL PRODUCTS

❏ DRL1-1794	Cosmic Vortex	199?	$20

—Reissue

❏ DRL1-1795	Sinbad	199?	$20

—Reissue

❏ DRL1-1796	Spirit Man	199?	$20

—Reissue

NODLEW

❏ 1001	Liberated Brother	1972	$300
❏ 1002	Time Capsule	1973	$300

—Reproductions exist

RCA VICTOR

❏ APL1-0703	Cosmic Vortex	1974	$120
❏ APL1-1363	Sinbad	1976	$150
❏ APL1-0909	Spirit Man	1975	$120

STRATA-EAST

❏ SES-19479	In Harmony	1974	$120

ISAACS, IKE
Guitarist.

Albums

RGB

❏ 2000	Ike Isaccs at the Pied Piper	197?	$30

ISHAM, MARK
Trumpeter, keyboard player and composer.

Albums

VIRGIN

❏ 90900	Castalia	1988	$25

WINDHAM HILL

❏ WH-1041	Film Music of Mark Isham	1985	$25
❏ WH-1080	Tibet	1989	$30
❏ WH-1027	Vapor Drawings	1983	$25

ITOH, KIMIKO
Female singer.

Albums

COLUMBIA

❏ FC45214	Follow Me	1989	$30
❏ FC44203	For Lovers Only	1988	$25

J

J.F.K. QUINTET, THE
Among the members of this group were Andrew White on alto saxophone and Walter Booker on bass.

Albums

RIVERSIDE

❏ RLP-396 [M]	New Frontiers from Washington	1961	$200
❏ RS-9396 [S]	New Frontiers from Washington	1961	$200
❏ RLP-424 [M]	Young Ideas	1962	$150
❏ RS-9424 [S]	Young Ideas	1962	$150

J.J. & KAI
See J.J. JOHNSON AND KAI WINDING.

JACINTHA
Female singer.

Albums

GROOVE NOTE

❏ 2001	Here's to Ben	1999	$30

—Audiophile vinyl

JACK PINE SAVAGES, THE

Albums

JIM TAYLOR PRESENTS

❏ 104	The Beiderbecke Legend Is Alive and Well	197?	$35

JACKIE AND ROY
See JACKIE CAIN AND ROY KRAL.

JACKSON, CALVIN
Pianist and composer.

Albums

COLUMBIA

❏ CL756 [M]	Calvin Jackson and the All Stars Quartet	1956	$50
❏ CL824 [M]	Rave Notice	1956	$50

LIBERTY

❏ LRP-3071 [M]	Jazz Variations	1957	$40

X

❏ LXA-1005 [M]	Calvin Jackson at the Plaza	1954	$50

JACKSON, CHUBBY, AND BILL HARRIS
Also see each artist's individual listings.

Albums

EMARCY

❏ MG-26012 [M]	Out of the Herd	1965	$100
❏ SR-66012 [R]	Out of the Herd	1965	$100
❏ MG-26003 [10]	The Small Herd	1954	$200

MERCURY

❏ MG-25076 [10]	Jazz Journey	1950	$300

JACKSON, CHUBBY
Bass player.

Albums

ARGO

❏ LP-614 [M]	Chubby's Back	1957	$80
❏ LPS-614 [S]	Chubby's Back	1959	$125
❏ LP-625 [M]	I'm Entitled to You	1958	$80

EVEREST

❏ LPBR-5009 [M]	Chubby Takes Over	1959	$30
❏ SDBR-1009 [S]	Chubby Takes Over	1959	$40
❏ LPBR-5041 [M]	Jazz Then Till Now	1960	$30
❏ SDBR-1041 [S]	Jazz Then Till Now	1960	$40
❏ LPBR-5029 [M]	The Big Three	1959	$30
❏ SDBR-1029 [S]	The Big Three	1959	$40

LAURIE

❏ LLP-2011 [M]	Twist Calling	1962	$30

NEW JAZZ

❏ NJLP-105 [10]	Chubby Jackson and His All Star Band	1950	$800

— Original; reissued as Prestige 105

PRESTIGE

❏ PRLP-105 [10]	Chubby Jackson and His All Star Band	1951	$600
❏ PRST-7641	Chubby Jackson Sextet and Big Band	1969	$25

RAINBOW

❏ 708 [10]	Chubby Jackson	1951	$400

STEREO-CRAFT

❏ RTN-108 [M]	The Big Three	195?	$50
❏ RTS-108 [S]	The Big Three	195?	$50

JACKSON, FRANZ
Tenor saxophone player, clarinetist, male singer and arranger.

Albums

PINNACLE

❏ 109 [M]	Franz Jackson	1966	$25
❏ S-104 [S]	Night at Red Arrow	196?	$25
❏ 104 [M]	Night at Red Arrow	196?	$35
❏ 102 [M]	No Saints	1961	$25

RIVERSIDE

❏ RLP-406 [M]	Franz Jackson and the Original Jass All-Stars	1962	$200
❏ RS-9406 [R]	Franz Jackson and the Original Jass All-Stars	196?	$35

JACKSON, FRED
Tenor saxophone player.

Albums

BLUE NOTE

❏ BST-84094 [S]	Hootin' 'N Tootin'	1967	$25

— With "A Division of Liberty Records" on label

JACKSON, MARY ANNE

Albums

HANOVER

❏ HM-8009 [M]	The Wild Piano of Mary Anne Jackson	1959	$80

Number	Title	Yr	NM

JACKSON, MICHAEL GREGORY

Guitarist.

Albums

ARISTA/NOVUS
❏ AN3015	Heart & Center	1979	$35

BIJA
❏ 1000	Clarity	1976	$30

ENJA
❏ 4026	Cowboys, Cartoons and Assorted Candy	1982	$35

IAI
❏ 373857	Karmonic Suite	1978	$25

JACKSON, MILT, AND JOHN COLTRANE

Also see each artist's individual listings.

JACKSON, MILT, AND MONTY ALEXANDER

Also see each artist's individual listings.

Albums

PABLO
❏ 2310804	Soul Fusion	1978	$30

JACKSON, MILT, AND WES MONTGOMERY

Also see each artist's individual listings.

Albums

FANTASY
❏ OJC-234	Bags Meets Wes	198?	$25

RIVERSIDE
❏ RLP-407 [M]	Bags Meets Wes	1962	$200
❏ RS-9407 [S]	Bags Meets Wes	1962	$200
❏ 6058	Bags Meets Wes	197?	$30

JACKSON, MILT

Vibraphone player, occasional pianist and male singer. He was the co-founder of THE MODERN JAZZ QUARTET. Also see RAY BROWN; MILES DAVIS; HOWARD McGHEE.

Albums

ABC IMPULSE!
❏ AS-70 [S]	Jazz n' Samba	1968	$35
❏ AS-9193	Memphis Jackson	1969	$200
❏ AS-9230	Milt Jackson Quartet	1973	$30
❏ AS-14 [S]	Statements	1968	$35
❏ AS-9189	That's the Way It Is	1969	$200
❏ AS-9282	The Impulse Years	1974	$35

ATLANTIC
❏ 1294 [M]	Bags & Flutes	1958	$300
—Black label			
❏ 1294 [M]	Bags & Flutes	1961	$250
—Multicolor label, white "fan" logo at right			
❏ 1294 [M]	Bags & Flutes	1963	$50
—Multicolor label, black "fan" logo at right			
❏ SD1294 [S]	Bags & Flutes	1959	$300
—Green label			
❏ SD1294 [S]	Bags & Flutes	1961	$250
—Multicolor label, white "fan" logo at right			
❏ SD1294 [S]	Bags & Flutes	1963	$50
—Multicolor label, black "fan" logo at right			
❏ 1342 [M]	Ballad Artistry	1960	$300
—Multicolor label, white "fan" logo at right			
❏ 1342 [M]	Ballad Artistry	1963	$50
—Multicolor label, black "fan" logo at right			
❏ SD1342 [S]	Ballad Artistry	1960	$300
—Multicolor label, white "fan" logo at right			
❏ SD1342 [S]	Ballad Artistry	1963	$50
—Multicolor label, black "fan" logo at right			
❏ 1242 [M]	Ballads and Blues	1956	$300
—Black label			
❏ 1242 [M]	Ballads and Blues	1961	$250
—Multicolor label, white "fan" logo at right			
❏ 1242 [M]	Ballads and Blues	1963	$50
—Multicolor label, black "fan" logo at right			
❏ 1316 [M]	Bean Bags	1959	$300
—Black label			
❏ 1316 [M]	Bean Bags	1961	$250
—Multicolor label, white "fan" logo at right			
❏ 1316 [M]	Bean Bags	1963	$50
—Multicolor label, black "fan" logo at right			
❏ SD1316 [S]	Bean Bags	1959	$300
—Green label			

Number	Title	Yr	NM
❏ SD1316 [S]	Bean Bags	1961	$250
—Multicolor label, white "fan" logo at right			
❏ SD1316 [S]	Bean Bags	1963	$50
—Multicolor label, black "fan" logo at right			
❏ 90465	Bean Bags	1986	$25
❏ 1269 [M]	Plenty, Plenty Soul	1957	$300
—Black label			
❏ SD1269 [S]	Plenty, Plenty Soul	1959	$300
—Green label			
❏ 1269 [M]	Plenty, Plenty Soul	1961	$150
—Multicolor label, white "fan" logo at right			
❏ 1269 [M]	Plenty, Plenty Soul	1963	$35
—Multicolor label, black "fan" logo at right			
❏ SD1269 [S]	Plenty, Plenty Soul	1961	$150
—Multicolor label, white "fan" logo at right			
❏ SD1269 [S]	Plenty, Plenty Soul	1963	$35
—Multicolor label, black "fan" logo at right			
❏ SD8811	Plenty, Plenty Soul	198?	$25
❏ SD 2-319	The Art of Milt Jackson	197?	$35
❏ 1417 [M]	Vibrations	1964	$35
❏ SD1417 [S]	Vibrations	1964	$25

BLUE NOTE
❏ BN-LA590-H2	All Star Bags	1976	$35
❏ BLP-1509 [M]	Milt Jackson	1956	$200
—Regular version with Lexington Ave. address on label			
❏ BLP-1509 [M]	Milt Jackson	1963	$60
—With "New York, USA" address on label			
❏ BST-81509 [R]	Milt Jackson	196?	$35
—With "A Division of Liberty Records" on label			
❏ B1-81509	Milt Jackson	1987	$25
—The Finest in Jazz Since 1939" reissue			
❏ BLP-5011 [10]	Wizard of the Vibes	1952	$300

CTI
❏ 6038	Goodbye	1974	$35
❏ 6046	Olinga	1974	$35
❏ 6024	Sunflower	1973	$35
❏ 8004	Sunflower	197?	$25
—Reissue of 6024			

DEE GEE
❏ 1002 [10]	Milt Jackson	1952	$300

EASTWEST
❏ 90991	Bebop	1988	$30

FANTASY
❏ OJC-366	Big Bags	198?	$25
❏ OJC-448	Feelings	1990	$25
❏ OJC-404	For Someone I Love	1989	$30
❏ OJC-260	Invitation	1987	$25
❏ OJC-601	It Don't Mean a Thing If You Can't Tap Your Foot to It	1991	$35
❏ OJC-309	Live" at the Village Gate	1988	$25
❏ OJC-001	Milt Jackson Quartet	1982	$35
❏ OJC-375	Montreux '77	198?	$25

GNP CRESCENDO
❏ GNP-9007	Milt Jackson	197?	$25

IMPULSE!
❏ A-70 [M]	Jazz n' Samba	1964	$120
❏ AS-70 [S]	Jazz n' Samba	1964	$120
❏ A-14 [M]	Statements	1962	$120
❏ AS-14 [S]	Statements	1962	$120

LIMELIGHT
❏ LM-82024 [M]	At the Museum of Modern Art	1965	$25
❏ LS-86024 [S]	At the Museum of Modern Art	1965	$30
❏ LM-82045 [M]	Born Free	1966	$25
❏ LS-86045 [S]	Born Free	1966	$30
❏ LM-82006 [M]	In a New Setting	1964	$25
❏ LS-86006 [S]	In a New Setting	1964	$30

MILESTONE
❏ 47006	Big Band Bags	1972	$35

PABLO
❏ 2310873	Ain't But a Few of Us Left	198?	$30
❏ 2310932	A London Bridge	1988	$30
❏ 2310842	Bag's Bag	1979	$30
❏ 2310867	Big Mouth	198?	$30
❏ 2310916	Brother Jim	1987	$25
❏ 2310774	Feelings	1976	$30
❏ 2310909	It Don't Mean a Thing If You Can't Tap Your Foot to It	1986	$35
❏ 2310897	Milt Jackson & Co.	198?	$30
❏ 2310822	Milt Jackson with Count Basie and the Big Band, Volume 1	1978	$30
❏ 2310823	Milt Jackson with Count Basie and the Big Band, Volume 2	1978	$30
❏ 2310832	Soul Believer	1979	$30
❏ 2405405	The Best of Milt Jackson	198?	$25
❏ 2310757	The Big 3	1976	$30
❏ 2310753	The Big 4 at Montreux '75	1976	$30

PABLO LIVE

Number	Title	Yr	NM
❏ 2620103	Kosei Nenkin	197?	$35
❏ 2308235	Live in London: Memories of Thelonious Monk	198?	$30
❏ 2308205	Montreux '77	1977	$30

PABLO TODAY
❏ 2312124	Nightmist	198?	$30

PRESTIGE
❏ PRLP-7003 [M]	Milt Jackson	1955	$350
❏ PRLP-183 [10]	Milt Jackson Quintet	1954	$300
❏ 24048	Opus de Funk	197?	$35
❏ PRLP-7224 [M]	Soul Pioneers	1962	$150
❏ PRST-7655	The Complete Milt Jackson	1969	$35

QUINTESSENCE
❏ 25391	Milt Jackson (1961-69)	1980	$25

RIVERSIDE
❏ 3021	Bags and Brass	1968	$100
❏ RLP-429 [M]	Big Bags	1962	$200
❏ RS-9429 [S]	Big Bags	1962	$200
❏ RLP-478 [M]	For Someone I Love	1966	$100
❏ RS-9478 [S]	For Someone I Love	1966	$100
❏ RLP-446 [M]	Invitation	1963	$150
❏ RS-9446 [S]	Invitation	1963	$150
❏ RLP-495 [M]	Live" at the Village Gate	1967	$100
❏ RS-9495 [S]	Live" at the Village Gate	1967	$100

SAVOY
❏ MG-12080 [M]	Jackson's Ville	1956	$50
❏ MG-12070 [M]	Jazz Skyline	1956	$50
❏ MG-12061 [M]	Meet Milt	1956	$50
❏ MG-15058 [10]	Milt Jackson	1954	$150
❏ MG-12046 [M]	Milt Jackson Quartette	1955	$60
❏ MG-12042 [M]	Roll 'Em Bags	1955	$60

SAVOY JAZZ
❏ SJL-1130	Bluesology	198?	$25
❏ SJL-2204	Second Nature	197?	$30
❏ SJL-1106	The First Q	197?	$25
❏ SJC-410	The Jazz Skyline	1985	$25

TRIP
❏ 5553	At the Museum of Modern Art	197?	$25

UNITED ARTISTS
❏ UAL-4022 [M]	Bags' Opus	1959	$40
❏ UAS-5022 [S]	Bags' Opus	1959	$30

VERVE
❏ V6-8761	Milt Jackson and the Hip String Quartet	1969	$35

JACKSON, MUNYUNGO

Percussionist.

Albums

VITAL MUSIC
❏ VTL-002	Munyungo	199?	$35

JACKSON, PAUL, JR.

Guitarist.

Albums

ATLANTIC
❏ 81841	I Came to Play	1988	$25
❏ 82065	Out of the Shadows	1990	$30

JACKSON, RONALD SHANNON

Drummer and percussionist; has also played flute on record.

Albums

ABOUT TIME
❏ AT-1003	Eye on You	1980	$25

ANTILLES
❏ AN-1015	Barbeque Dog	1983	$35
❏ AN-1008	Man Dance	1982	$35

CARAVAN OF DREAMS
❏ 85005	Live at the Caravan of Dreams	1986	$35
❏ 012	Texas	1988	$35
❏ 09	When Colors Play	1987	$35

ISLAND
❏ 90247	Decode Yourself	1985	$25

MOERS
❏ 01086	Nasty	1981	$25
❏ 01081	Street Priest	1981	$25

OAO/CELLULOID
❏ 5011	Pulse	1984	$35

JACKSON, WILLIS

Tenor saxophone player.

Albums

ATLANTIC
❏ SD18145	The Way We Were	1975	$30

CADET

Number	Title	Yr	NM
❏ LP-763 [M]	Smoking with Willis	1966	$35
❏ LPS-763 [S]	Smoking with Willis	1966	$50

COTILLION
❏ SD9908	Willis Jackson Plays with Feeling	1977	$35

CTI
❏ 6024	Sunflower	1972	$35

FANTASY
❏ OJC-220	Cool Gator	198?	$25
❏ OJC-321	Please, Mr. Jackson	1988	$25

MOODSVILLE
❏ MVLP-17 [M]	In My Solitude	1961	$100

— Green label

❏ MVLP-17 [M]	In My Solitude	1965	$60

— Blue label, trident logo at right

MUSE
❏ MR-5162	Bar Wars	1978	$30
❏ MR-5048	Headed and Gutted	1975	$30
❏ MR-5100	In the Valley	1976	$30
❏ MR-5200	Lockin' Horns	1979	$30
❏ MR-5294	Nothing Butt	198?	$25
❏ MR-5146	The Gator Horn	1978	$30
❏ MR-5036	West Africa	1974	$30
❏ MR-5316	Ya Understand Me?	198?	$25

PRESTIGE
❏ PRLP-7183 [M]	Blue Gator	1960	$200
❏ PRST-7850	Blue Gator	197?	$35
❏ PRLP-7260 [M]	Bossa Nova Plus	1962	$150
❏ PRST-7260 [S]	Bossa Nova Plus	1962	$150
❏ PRLP-7329 [M]	Boss Shoutin'	1964	$60
❏ PRST-7329 [S]	Boss Shoutin'	1964	$60
❏ PRLP-7211 [M]	Cookin' Sherry	1961	$200
❏ PRST-7211 [S]	Cookin' Sherry	1961	$200
❏ PRLP-7172 [M]	Cool Gator	1959	$200
❏ 2516	Gatorade	198?	$30
❏ PRST-7648	Gator's Groove	1969	$50
❏ PRLP-7285 [M]	Grease 'n' Gravy	1963	$60
❏ PRST-7285 [S]	Grease 'n' Gravy	1963	$40
❏ PRST-7830	Keep On a-Blowing	1971	$50
❏ PRLP-7380 [M]	Live! Action	1965	$60
❏ PRST-7380 [S]	Live! Action	1965	$60
❏ PRLP-7348 [M]	Live! Jackson's Action	1965	$60
❏ PRST-7348 [S]	Live! Jackson's Action	1965	$60
❏ PRLP-7273 [M]	Loose...	1963	$60
❏ PRST-7273 [S]	Loose...	1963	$40
❏ PRLP-7317 [M]	More Gravy	1964	$60
❏ PRST-7317 [S]	More Gravy	1964	$40
❏ PRLP-7264 [M]	Neapolitan Nights	1963	$60
❏ PRST-7264 [S]	Neapolitan Nights	1963	$40
❏ PRLP-7162 [M]	Please, Mr. Jackson	1959	$200
❏ PRST-7783	Please Mr. Jackson	1970	$50
❏ PRLP-7196 [M]	Really Groovin'	1961	$200
❏ PRST-7551	Soul Grabber	1968	$50
❏ PRLP-7396 [M]	Soul Night -- Live!	1965	$60
❏ PRST-7396 [S]	Soul Night -- Live!	1965	$60
❏ PRST-7571	Star Bag	1968	$50
❏ PRST-7602	Swivel Hips	1969	$50
❏ PRLP-7412 [M]	Tell It...	1966	$50
❏ PRST-7412 [S]	Tell It...	1966	$60
❏ PRST-7702	The Best of Willis Jackson with Brother Jack McDuff	1969	$35
❏ PRST-7770	The Best -- Soul Stompin'	1971	$35
❏ PRLP-7296 [M]	The Good Life	1964	$60
❏ PRST-7296 [S]	The Good Life	1964	$40
❏ PRLP-7232 [M]	Thunderbird	1962	$150
❏ PRST-7232 [S]	Thunderbird	1962	$150
❏ PRLP-7364 [M]	Together Again	1965	$60
❏ PRST-7364 [S]	Together Again	1965	$60
❏ PRLP-7428 [M]	Together Again...Again	1966	$50
❏ PRST-7428 [S]	Together Again...Again	1966	$60

TRIP
❏ 5028	Funky Reggae	197?	$25
❏ 5007	Mellow Blues	197?	$30
❏ 5030	Willis Jackson Plays Around with the Hits	197?	$25

VERVE
❏ V-8589 [M]	'Gator Tails	1964	$35
❏ V6-8589 [S]	'Gator Tails	1964	$50
❏ V6-8782	Willis Jackson	1969	$35

JACOBY, DON
Trumpeter.

Albums

DECCA
❏ DL4241 [M]	The Swinging Big Sound	1963	$35
❏ DL74241 [S]	The Swinging Big Sound	1963	$25

JACQUET, ILLINOIS, AND BEN WEBSTER
Also see each artist's individual listings.

Albums

CLEF
❏ MGC-680 [M]	The Kid" and "The Brute	1955	$350

VERVE
❏ MGV-8065 [M]	The Kid" and "The Brute	1957	$300

— Reissue of Clef 680

❏ V-8065 [M]	The Kid" and "The Brute	1961	$25

JACQUET, ILLINOIS, AND LESTER YOUNG
Also see each artist's individual listings.

Albums

ALADDIN
❏ LP-701 [10]	Battle of the Saxes	1953	$1200

JACQUET, ILLINOIS
Tenor saxophone player. Also see REX STEWART; LESTER YOUNG.

Albums

ALADDIN
❏ LP-708 [10]	Illinois Jacquet and His Tenor Sax	1954	$500
❏ LP-803 [M]	Illinois Jacquet and His Tenor Sax	1956	$300

APOLLO
❏ LP-104 [10]	Illinois Jacquet Jam Session	1951	$600

ARGO
❏ LP-746 [M]	Bosses of the Ballad	1964	$40
❏ LP-735 [M]	Desert Winds	1964	$40
❏ LPS-735 [S]	Desert Winds	1964	$50
❏ LPS-746 [S]	Illinois Jacquet Plays Cole Porter	1964	$50
❏ LP-722 [M]	The Message	1963	$40
❏ LPS-722 [S]	The Message	1963	$50

ATLANTIC
❏ 81816	Jacquet's Got It!	1988	$30

BLACK LION
❏ 146	Genius at Work	197?	$50

CADET
❏ LP-746 [M]	Bosses of the Ballad	1966	$50

— Reissue of Argo 746; fading blue label

❏ LPS-746 [S]	Bosses of the Ballad	1966	$30

— Reissue of Argo 746; fading blue label

❏ LP-735 [M]	Desert Winds	1966	$50

— Reissue of Argo 735; fading blue label

❏ LPS-735 [S]	Desert Winds	1966	$30

— Reissue of Argo 735; fading blue label

❏ LPS-773 [S]	Go Power!	1966	$50
❏ LP-754 [M]	Spectrum	1965	$40
❏ LPS-754 [S]	Spectrum	1965	$50
❏ LP-722 [M]	The Message	1966	$50

— Reissue of Argo 722; fading blue label

❏ LPS-722 [S]	The Message	1966	$30

— Reissue of Argo 722; fading blue label

❏ CA-722 [S]	The Message	197?	$25

— Yellow and red label

CHESS
❏ CH-91554	The Message	1984	$25

— Reissue

CLASSIC JAZZ
❏ 112	Illinois Jacquet with Wild Bill Davis	1978	$50
❏ 146	Jacquet's Street	1981	$50

CLEF
❏ MGC-702 [M]	Groovin' with Jacquet	1956	$350
❏ MGC-129 [10]	Illinois Jacquet Collates #2	1953	$350
❏ MGC-112 [10]	Illinois Jacquet Collates	1953	$350
❏ MGC-676 [M]	Illinois Jacquet Septet	1955	$350
❏ MGC-167 [10]	Jazz by Jacquet	1954	$350
❏ MGC-622 [M]	Jazz Moods	1955	$350
❏ MGC-700 [M]	Jazz Moods by Illinois Jacquet	1956	$300
❏ MGC-701 [M]	Port of Rico	1956	$300
❏ MGC-750 [M]	Swing's the Thing	1956	$300

EPIC
❏ LA16033 [M]	Illinois Jacquet	1963	$80
❏ BA17033 [S]	Illinois Jacquet	1963	$100
❏ BA17033 [S]	Illinois Jacquet	199?	$30

— Classic Records reissue on audiophile vinyl

FANTASY
❏ OJC-417	Bottoms Up!	1990	$30
❏ OJC-614	The Blues -- That's Me	1991	$35

GROOVE NOTE
❏ 2003	Birthday Party	1999	$50

— Audiophile vinyl; one record has the entire album, the other has two tracks at 45 rpm

IMPERIAL
❏ LP-9184 [M]	Flying Home	1962	$150
❏ LP-12184 [S]	Flying Home	1962	$150

JAZZ MAN
❏ 5034	Genius at Work	198?	$30

JRC
❏ 11434	Birthday Party	197?	$60

MERCURY
❏ MGC-129 [10]	Illinois Jacquet Collates #2	1953	$0

— Canceled; issued on Clef

❏ MGC-112 [10]	Illinois Jacquet Collates	1952	$500

MOSAIC
❏ MQ6-165	The Complete Illinois Jacquet Sessions 1945-50	199?	$100

PRESTIGE
❏ PRST-7575	Bottoms Up!	1968	$40
❏ P-24057	How High the Moon	1975	$60
❏ PRST-7731	The Blues -- That's Me	1969	$40
❏ PRST-7597	The King!	1968	$40
❏ PRST-7629	The Soul Explosion	1969	$40

RCA VICTOR
❏ LPM-3236 [10]	Black Velvet	1954	$500

ROULETTE
❏ R-52035 [M]	Illinois Jacquet Flies Again	1959	$125
❏ SR-52035 [S]	Illinois Jacquet Flies Again	1959	$60

SAVOY
❏ MG-15024 [10]	Tenor Sax	1953	$400

VERVE
❏ MGV-8086 [M]	Groovin' with Jacquet	1957	$300

— Reissue of Clef 702

❏ V-8086 [M]	Groovin' with Jacquet	1961	$30
❏ MGV-8061 [M]	Illinois Jacquet and His Orchestra	1957	$300

— Reissue of Clef 676

❏ V-8061 [M]	Illinois Jacquet and His Orchestra	1961	$30
❏ MGV-8084 [M]	Jazz Moods by Illinois Jacquet	1957	$300

— Reissue of Clef 700

❏ V-8084 [M]	Jazz Moods by Illinois Jacquet	1961	$30
❏ MGV-8085 [M]	Port of Rico	1957	$200

— Reissue of Clef 701

❏ V-8085 [M]	Port of Rico	1961	$30
❏ MGV-8023 [M]	Swing's the Thing	1957	$200

— Reissue of Clef 750

❏ V-8023 [M]	Swing's the Thing	1961	$30
❏ VE-2-2544	The Cool Rage	198?	$50

JACQUET, RUSSELL
Trumpeter and occasional male singer.

Albums

KING
❏ 295-81 [10]	Russell Jacquet and His All Stars	1954	$250

JAFFE, ANDY
Pianist.

Albums

STASH
❏ ST-247	Manhattan Projections	1985	$25

JAMAL, AHMAD
Pianist. His most popular recordings were on Argo/Cadet and featured a trio with Israel Crosby (bass) and Vernell Fournier (drums).

Albums

20TH CENTURY
❏ T-417	Ahmad Jamal '73	1973	$25
❏ T-600	Genetic Walk	1980	$25
❏ T-631	Greatest Hits	1981	$25
❏ T-622	Intervals	1980	$25
❏ T-432	Jamaica	1974	$25

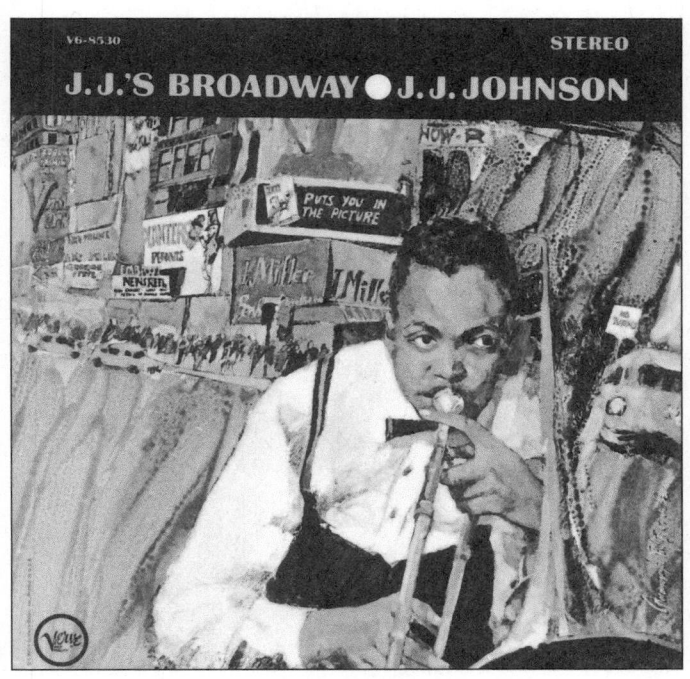

J.J. Johnson, *J.J.'s Broadway*, Verve V6-8530, **$25**.

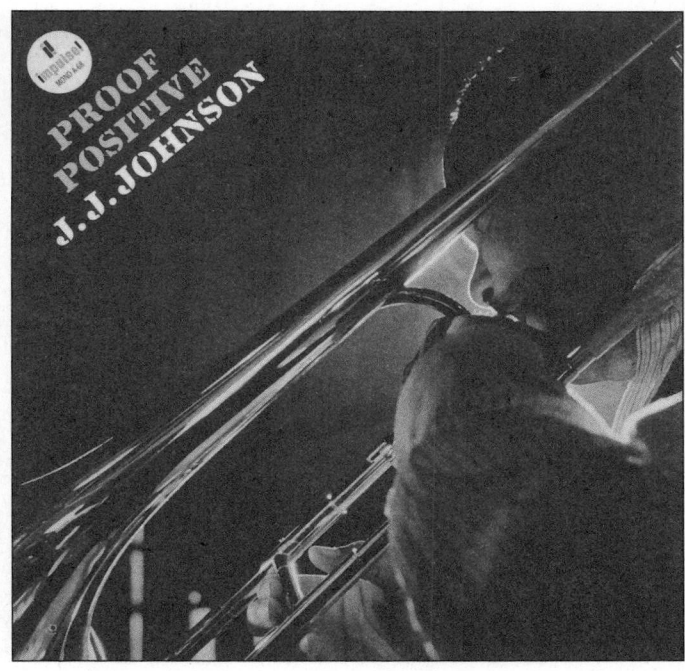

J.J. Johnson, *Proof Positive*, Impulse! A-68, mono, **$160**.

J.J. Johnson, *First Place*, Columbia CL 1030, red and black label with six "eye" logos, **$50**.

J.J. Johnson and Kai Winding, *The Great Kai & J.J.,* Impulse! A-1, mono, **$160**.

Number	Title	Yr	NM
❏ T-459	Jamal Plays Jamal	1975	$25
❏ T-555	One	1978	$25
❏ T-515	Steppin' Out with a Dream	1977	$25

ABC

❏ S-660	Tranquility	1968	$30

ABC IMPULSE!

❏ AS-9176	At the Top -- Poinciana Revisited	1969	$35
❏ SMAS-92005	At the Top -- Poinciana Revisited	1969	$150

— Capitol Record Club edition

❏ AS-9217	Freeflight	1971	$30
❏ AS-9226	Outertimeinnerspace	1972	$30
❏ AS-9260	Re-evaluations: The Impulse Years	1975	$30
❏ AS-9194	The Awakening	1970	$35
❏ AS-9238	Tranquility	1973	$30

ARGO

❏ LP-636 [M]	Ahmad Jamal, Volume IV	1958	$60
❏ LPS-636 [S]	Ahmad Jamal, Volume IV	1958	$40
❏ LP-703 [M]	Ahmad Jamal at the Blackhawk	1962	$50
❏ LPS-703 [S]	Ahmad Jamal at the Blackhawk	1962	$60
❏ LP-667 [M]	Ahmad Jamal at the Pershing Volume 2	1961	$50
❏ LPS-667 [S]	Ahmad Jamal at the Pershing Volume 2	1961	$60
❏ LP-685 [M]	Alhambra	1961	$50
❏ LPS-685 [S]	Alhambra	1961	$60
❏ LP-691 [M]	All of You	1962	$50
❏ LPS-691 [S]	All of You	1962	$60
❏ LP-628 [M]	But Not for Me/Ahmad Jamal at the Pershing	1958	$60
❏ LPS-628 [S]	But Not for Me/Ahmad Jamal at the Pershing	1958	$40
❏ LP-602 [M]	Chamber Music of the New Jazz	1956	$100

— With "Creative Hi-Fidelity Modern Music" on cover; "ship" label; reissue of Parrot LP

❏ LP-602 [M]	Chamber Music of the New Jazz	1956	$60

— Dark green label, gold or silver print

❏ LP-610 [M]	Count 'Em 88	1957	$60
❏ LP-758 [M]	Extensions	1965	$50
❏ LPS-758 [S]	Extensions	1965	$60
❏ LP-662 [M]	Happy Moods	1960	$50
❏ LPS-662 [S]	Happy Moods	1960	$60
❏ LP-646 [M]	Jamal at the Penthouse	1959	$60
❏ LPS-646 [S]	Jamal at the Penthouse	1959	$40
❏ LP-673 [M]	Listen to Ahmad Jamal	1961	$50
❏ LPS-673 [S]	Listen to Ahmad Jamal	1961	$60
❏ LP-712 [M]	Macanudo	1963	$50
❏ LPS-712 [S]	Macanudo	1963	$60
❏ LP-733 [M]	Naked City" Theme	1964	$50
❏ LPS-733 [S]	Naked City" Theme	1964	$60
❏ LP-719 [M]	Poin'-ci-an'a	1963	$50
❏ LPS-719 [S]	Poin'-ci-an'a	1963	$60
❏ LP-2638 [M]	Portfolio of Ahmad Jamal	1959	$40

— Textured cover with raised image of Jamal; limited, numbered edition

❏ LPS-2638 [S]	Portfolio of Ahmad Jamal	1959	$100
❏ LP-751 [M]	The Roar of the Greasepaint	1965	$50
❏ LPS-751 [S]	The Roar of the Greasepaint	1965	$60

ATLANTIC

❏ 81793	Crystal	1987	$25
❏ 81258	Digital Works	1985	$30
❏ 81699	Live at the Montreal Jazz Festival 1985	1986	$30
❏ 81645	Rossiter Road	1986	$25

CADET

❏ LP-636 [M]	Ahmad Jamal, Volume IV	1966	$30
❏ LPS-636 [S]	Ahmad Jamal, Volume IV	1966	$35
❏ LP-703 [M]	Ahmad Jamal at the Blackhawk	1966	$30
❏ LPS-703 [S]	Ahmad Jamal at the Blackhawk	1966	$35
❏ LP-667 [M]	Ahmad Jamal at the Pershing Volume 2	1966	$30
❏ LPS-667 [S]	Ahmad Jamal at the Pershing Volume 2	1966	$35
❏ LP-685 [M]	Alhambra	1966	$30
❏ LPS-685 [S]	Alhambra	1966	$35
❏ LP-691 [M]	All of You	1966	$30
❏ LPS-691 [S]	All of You	1966	$35
❏ LP-628 [M]	But Not for Me/Ahmad Jamal at the Pershing	1966	$30
❏ LPS-628 [S]	But Not for Me/Ahmad Jamal at the Pershing	1966	$35
❏ LP-792 [M]	Cry Young	1967	$50
❏ LPS-792 [S]	Cry Young	1967	$35
❏ LP-758 [M]	Extensions	1966	$30
❏ LPS-758 [S]	Extensions	1965	$35
❏ CA-758 [S]	Extensions	197?	$30

— Reissue; yellow and red label with "A Division of All Platinum Record Group" on label

❏ LP-662 [M]	Happy Moods	1966	$30
❏ LPS-662 [S]	Happy Moods	1966	$35
❏ LP-777 [M]	Heat Wave	1966	$35
❏ LPS-777 [S]	Heat Wave	1966	$50

— Original with fading blue label

❏ LPS-777 [S]	Heat Wave	1977	$30

— Reissue, "a division of All Platinum Record Group" on back cover

❏ 50035	Inspiration	1974	$35
❏ LP-646 [M]	Jamal at the Penthouse	1966	$30
❏ LPS-646 [S]	Jamal at the Penthouse	1966	$35
❏ LP-673 [M]	Listen to Ahmad Jamal	1966	$30
❏ LPS-673 [S]	Listen to Ahmad Jamal	1966	$35
❏ LP-712 [M]	Macanudo	1966	$30
❏ LPS-712 [S]	Macanudo	1966	$35
❏ LP-733 [M]	Naked City" Theme	1966	$30
❏ LPS-733 [S]	Naked City" Theme	1966	$35
❏ LP-719 [M]	Poin'-ci-an'a	1966	$30
❏ LPS-719 [S]	Poin'-ci-an'a	1966	$35
❏ LP-2638 [M]	Portfolio of Ahmad Jamal	1966	$35

— Cadet issues generally did not have embossed covers

❏ LPS-2638 [S]	Portfolio of Ahmad Jamal	1966	$50

— Cadet issues generally did not have embossed covers

❏ LP-764 [M]	Rhapsody	1966	$35
❏ LPS-764 [S]	Rhapsody	1966	$50
❏ LP-786 [M]	Standard Eyes	1967	$35
❏ LPS-786 [S]	Standard Eyes	1967	$50
❏ LPS-807	The Bright, the Blue and the Beautiful	1968	$35
❏ LP-751 [M]	The Roar of the Greasepaint	1966	$30
❏ LPS-751 [S]	The Roar of the Greasepaint	1966	$35

CATALYST

❏ 7606	Live at Oil Can Harry's	1978	$30

CHESS

❏ CH-91553	Poinciana	198?	$25
❏ CH-2-9223	Sun Set	1984	$30

EPIC

❏ LN3212 [M]	Ahmad Jamal Trio	1956	$300

— Yellow label with lines around rim

❏ BN627 [R]	Ahmad Jamal Trio	196?	$100
❏ LN3212 [M]	Ahmad Jamal Trio	1963	$300

— Yellow label, no lines around rim

❏ LN3631 [M]	The Piano Scene of Ahmad Jamal	1959	$100
❏ BN634 [S]	The Piano Scene of Ahmad Jamal	1959	$100

GRP/IMPULSE!

❏ 226	The Awakening	199?	$35

— Reissue on audiophile vinyl

MCA

❏ 29041	At the Top -- Poinciana Revisited	198?	$20

— Reissue of Impulse! 9178

❏ 29043	Freelight	198?	$20

— Reissue of Impulse! 9217

❏ 29042	The Awakening	198?	$20

— Reissue of Impulse! 9194

MCA/IMPULSE!

❏ 5644	The Awakening	1986	$25

— Another reissue of Impulse! 9194

MOTOWN

❏ M8-945	Night Song	1981	$25

PARROT

❏ 55-245/6 [M]	Ahmad Jamal Plays	1955	$1500

— VG value 500; VG+ value 1000

JAMAL, KHAN

Vibraphone and marimbas player.

Albums

DOGTOWN

❏ no number [B]	Drum Dance to the Motherland		$1500

STASH

❏ ST-278	Infinity	1988	$25

STEEPLECHASE

❏ SCS-1196	Dark Warrior	198?	$30

JAMES, BOB, AND DAVID SANBORN

Also see each artist's individual listings.

Albums

WARNER BROS.

❏ 25393	Double Vision	1986	$25

JAMES, BOB, AND EARL KLUGH

Also see each artist's individual listings.

Albums

CAPITOL

Number	Title	Yr	NM
❏ SMAS-12244	Two of a Kind	1982	$30

MOBILE FIDELITY

❏ 1-124	Two of a Kind	1984	$40

— Original Master Recording" banner across top of front cover

TAPPAN ZEE

❏ HC46241	One on One	198?	$60

— Half-speed mastered edition

❏ FC36241	One on One	1979	$25

JAMES, BOB

Pianist, keyboard player, composer and arranger.

Albums

CBS MASTERWORKS

❏ IM39540	Rameau	1985	$30

COLUMBIA

❏ FC38678	The Genie (Themes & Variations from the TV Series "Taxi")	1983	$25

CTI

❏ 7074	BJ4	1977	$35
❏ CTS-6043	One	1974	$50
❏ CTS-6063	Three	1976	$35
❏ CTS-6057	Two	1975	$60

ESP-DISK'

❏ 1009 [M]	Explosions	1965	$150
❏ S-1009 [S]	Explosions	1965	$175

MERCURY

❏ MG-20768 [M]	Bold Conceptions	1963	$100
❏ SR-60768 [S]	Bold Conceptions	1963	$150

TAPPAN ZEE

❏ FC39580	12	1985	$25
❏ C2X36786	All Around the Town	1981	$30
❏ FC36838	BJ4	1981	$25

— Reissue of CTI 7074

❏ PC36838	BJ4	1985	$10

— Budget-line reissue

❏ AS1299 [DJ]	Bob James/Dave Herman Interview	1981	$35

— Promo-only radio program

❏ FC38801	Foxie	1983	$25
❏ JC36422	H	1980	$25
❏ FC38067	Hands Down	1982	$25
❏ JC34896	Heads	1977	$25
❏ PC34896	Heads	1985	$10

— Budget-line reissue

❏ JC36056	Lucky Seven	1979	$25
❏ PC36056	Lucky Seven	1985	$10

— Budget-line reissue

❏ AS699 [DJ]	Lucky Seven/One on One Sampler	1979	$60

— Edited selections from both of the above albums; promo only

❏ FC36835	One	1981	$25

— Reissue of CTI 6043

❏ PC36835	One	1985	$10

— Budget-line reissue

❏ FC37495	Sign of the Times	1981	$25
❏ HC47495	Sign of the Times	1982	$60

— Half-speed mastered edition

❏ FC36837	Three	1981	$30

— Reissue of CTI 6063

❏ PC36837	Three	1985	$10

— Budget-line reissue

❏ JC35594	Touchdown	1978	$25
❏ HC45594	Touchdown	1982	$60

— Half-speed mastered edition

❏ PC35594	Touchdown	1985	$10

— Budget-line reissue

❏ FC36836	Two	1981	$30

— Reissue of CTI 6057

❏ PC36836	Two	1985	$20

— Budget-line reissue

WARNER BROS.

❏ 26256	Grand Piano Canyon	1990	$35
❏ 25757	Ivory Coast	1988	$25
❏ 25495	Obsession	1986	$25

Number	Title	Yr	NM

JAMES, DWIGHT

Albums

CADENCE JAZZ
| ❏ CJ-1014 | Inner Heat | 198? | $25 |

JAMES, GREGORY
Guitarist.

Albums

INNER CITY
| ❏ IC-1050 | Alicia | 1978 | $35 |

JAMES, HARRY
Trumpeter and bandleader. Items with an asterisk (*) feature at least one track with FRANK SINATRA on vocals.

Albums

AIRCHECK
| ❏ 18 | Harry James On the Air | 197? | $25 |
| ❏ 33 | Harry James On the Air, Vol. 2 | 1986 | $25 |

BAINBRIDGE
| ❏ BT-6252 | Ciribiribin | 1982 | $25 |

CAPITOL
❏ W654 [M]	Harry James in Hi-Fi	1955	$75
❏ T1093 [M]	Harry's Choice	1958	$60
❏ W712 [M]	More Harry James in Hi-Fi	1956	$60
❏ T1515 [M]	The Hits of Harry James	1961	$50

—Black colorband label, logo at left
| ❏ DT1515 [R] | The Hits of Harry James | 1961 | $60 |
| ❏ T1515 [M] | The Hits of Harry James | 1962 | $75 |

—Black colorband label, logo at top
| ❏ M-1515 | The Hits of Harry James | 197? | $30 |

—Mono reissue
| ❏ T1037 [M] | The New James | 1958 | $60 |
| ❏ T874 [M] | Wild About Harry | 1957 | $100 |

CIRCLE
| ❏ 39 | Harry James and His Orchestra 1954 | 198? | $25 |
| ❏ 5 | Harry James and His Orchestra with Dick Haymes | 198? | $25 |

COLUMBIA
| ❏ CL655 [M] | *All Time Favorites | 1955 | $50 |

—Maroon label, gold print
❏ CL6009 [10]	*All Time Favorites	1949	$100
❏ CL2630 [M]	*Harry James' Greatest Hits	1967	$50
❏ CS9430 [R]	*Harry James' Greatest Hits	1967	$30

—Red "360 Sound" label
| ❏ CS9430 [R] | *Harry James' Greatest Hits | 1970 | $25 |

—Orange label
| ❏ PC9430 | *Harry James' Greatest Hits | 198? | $20 |

—Budget-line reissue
| ❏ CL6088 [10] | Dance Parade | 1950 | $50 |
| ❏ CL562 [M] | Dancing in Person with Harry James at the Hollywood Palladium | 1954 | $40 |

—Maroon label, gold print
| ❏ CL669 [M] | Jazz Session | 1955 | $50 |
| ❏ CL615 [M] | Juke Box Jamboree | 1955 | $50 |

—Maroon label, gold print
| ❏ GL522 [M] | One Night Stand | 1953 | $50 |

—Black label, silver print
| ❏ CL522 [M] | One Night Stand | 1953 | $40 |

—Maroon label, gold print
| ❏ CL581 [M] | Soft Lights, Sweet Trumpet | 1954 | $40 |

—Maroon label, gold print
❏ CL6207 [10]	Soft Lights, Sweet Trumpet	1952	$50
❏ CL2527 [10]	The Man with the Horn	1955	$60
❏ CL553 [M]	Trumpet After Midnight	1954	$40

—Maroon label, gold print
| ❏ CL6044 [10] | Trumpet Time | 1950 | $50 |
| ❏ CL6138 [10] | Your Dance Date | 1951 | $100 |

DOT
❏ DLP-3735 [M]	Harry James and His Western Friends	1966	$75
❏ DLP-25735 [S]	Harry James and His Western Friends	1966	$75
❏ DLP-3728 [M]	Live at the Riverboat	1966	$75
❏ DLP-25728 [S]	Live at the Riverboat	1966	$75
❏ DLP-3801 [M]	Our Leader	1967	$75
❏ DLP-25801 [S]	Our Leader	1967	$75

HARMONY
❏ KH32018	Best of the Big Bands	1972	$25
❏ HL7159 [M]	Harry James and His Great Vocalists	196?	$35
❏ HL7191 [M]	Harry James Plays the Songs That Sold a Million	196?	$35
❏ HS11245 [R]	Harry James Plays the Songs That Sold a Million	196?	$25
❏ HL7162 [M]	Harry James Plays Trumpet Rhapsody	196?	$35
❏ HS11326	Laura	1969	$25
❏ HL7269 [M]	Strictly Instrumental	196?	$35

HINDSIGHT
❏ HSR-102	Harry James and His Orchestra 1943-46	198?	$25
❏ HSR-123	Harry James and His Orchestra 1943-46	198?	$25
❏ HSR-141	Harry James and His Orchestra 1943-46, Vol. 4	198?	$25
❏ HSR-142	Harry James and His Orchestra 1943-53	198?	$25
❏ HSR-150	Harry James and His Orchestra 1947-49	198?	$25
❏ HSR-135	Harry James and His Orchestra 1948-49	198?	$25
❏ HSR-406	Harry James and His Orchestra Play 22 Original Big Band Recordings	198?	$30

INSIGHT
| ❏ 203 | Harry James and His Orchestra 1943-53 | 198? | $25 |

JAZZ ARCHIVES
| ❏ JA-31 | Young Harry James | 198? | $25 |

LONDON PHASE 4
| ❏ SP-44109 | Golden Trumpet | 1968 | $35 |

LONGINES SYMPHONETTE
| ❏ LS-217 | Harry James Dance Band Spectacular | 196? | $30 |

METRO
| ❏ M-536 [M] | Harry Not Jesse | 1966 | $150 |
| ❏ MS-536 [S] | Harry Not Jesse | 1966 | $150 |

MGM
❏ E-4214 [M]	25th Anniversary Album	1964	$30
❏ SE-4214 [S]	25th Anniversary Album	1964	$35
❏ E-4137 [M]	Double Dixie	1963	$35
❏ SE-4137 [S]	Double Dixie	1963	$25
❏ E-3778 [M]	Harry James and His New Swingin' Band	1959	$25
❏ SE-3778 [S]	Harry James and His New Swingin' Band	1959	$30
❏ E-3848 [M]	Harry James Today	1960	$25
❏ SE-3848 [S]	Harry James Today	1960	$30
❏ E-4274 [M]	In a Relaxed Mood	1965	$30
❏ SE-4274 [S]	In a Relaxed Mood	1965	$35
❏ E-4265 [M]	New Versions of Down Beat Favorites	1965	$30
❏ SE-4265 [S]	New Versions of Down Beat Favorites	1965	$35
❏ E-4003 [M]	Requests on the Road	1961	$25
❏ SE-4003 [S]	Requests on the Road	1961	$30
❏ E-4058 [M]	The Solid Gold Trumpet	1962	$35
❏ SE-4058 [S]	The Solid Gold Trumpet	1962	$25

PAIR
| ❏ PDL2-1158 | Big Band Favorites | 1986 | $30 |

PAUSA
| ❏ 9037 | More Harry James in Hi-Fi | 198? | $25 |

PICKWICK
❏ PC-3006 [M]	Mr. Trumpet	196?	$35
❏ SPC-3006 [R]	Mr. Trumpet	196?	$25
❏ SPC-3126	The Shadow of Your Smile	196?	$25
❏ PC-3044 [M]	You Made Me Love You	196?	$35
❏ SPC-3044 [R]	You Made Me Love You	196?	$25

SAVOY JAZZ
| ❏ SJL-2262 | First Team Player on the Jazz Varsity | 198? | $30 |

SHEFFIELD LABS
| ❏ 6 | Comin' From a Good Place | 1978 | $35 |

—Direct-to-disc recording
| ❏ 11 | Still Harry After All These Years | 1979 | $25 |

—Direct-to-disc recording; comes in box with booklet
| ❏ 3 | The King James Version | 1976 | $35 |

—Direct-to-disc recording

SUNBEAM
| ❏ 203 | Harry James and His Orchestra 1940 | 197? | $25 |
| ❏ 217 | Harry James and His Orchestra 1954 | 197? | $25 |

TIME-LIFE
| ❏ STBB-04 | Big Bands: Harry James | 1983 | $35 |

JAMES, WOODY; SHELLY MANNE; FRANK STRAZZARI

Albums

PAUSA
| ❏ 7020 | Crystallizations | 198? | $25 |

JAMES, WOODY

Albums

SEA BREEZE
| ❏ SB-2011 | Hardcore Jazz | 198? | $25 |
| ❏ SB-2015 | Zinger | 1985 | $25 |

JANIS, CONRAD
Trombonist and bandleader.

Albums

CIRCLE
| ❏ L-404 [10] | Conrad Janis' Tailgate Jazz Band | 1951 | $50 |

JUBILEE
| ❏ JLP-1010 [M] | Conrad Janis and His Tailgate Five | 1955 | $50 |
| ❏ JLP-7 [10] | Conrad Janis and His Tailgaters | 1954 | $50 |

RIVERSIDE
| ❏ RLP 12-215 [M] | Dixieland Jam Session | 1956 | $250 |

—White label, blue print

JARMAN, JOSEPH, AND DON MOYE
Moye is a drummer and percussionist. Also see ART ENSEMBLE OF CHICAGO; JOSEPH JARMAN.

Albums

BLACK SAINT
| ❏ BSR-0042 | Black Paladins | 198? | $30 |
| ❏ BSR-0052 | Earth Passage | 198? | $30 |

INDIA NAVIGATION
| ❏ IN-1033 | Egwu-Anwu | 1978 | $25 |

JARMAN, JOSEPH
Tenor saxophone player and a founder of ART ENSEMBLE OF CHICAGO.

Albums

AECO
| ❏ 02 | Sunbound | 1979 | $35 |

DELMARK
| ❏ DS-417 | As If It Were the Seasons | 1969 | $25 |
| ❏ DS-410 | Song for | 1968 | $25 |

JAROSLAV
Keyboard player and male vocalist.

Albums

COLUMBIA
| ❏ JC35537 | Checkin' In | 1978 | $30 |

JARRE, JEAN-MICHEL
Synthesizer and keyboard player, a pioneer in what has become known as "electronica."

Albums

DREYFUS/POLYDOR
❏ 833170-1	Concerts Houston/Lyon	1987	$25
❏ 829456-1	Equinoxe	1987	$20
❏ 829457-1	Magnetic Fields	1987	$20
❏ 827885-1	Oxygene	1987	$20
❏ 829125-1	Rendez-Vous	1986	$20
❏ 811551-1	The Concerts in China	1983	$30
❏ 823763-1	Zoolook	1984	$20

MOBILE FIDELITY
| ❏ 1-227 | Equinoxe | 1995 | $50 |

—Audiophile vinyl
| ❏ 1-212 | Oxygene | 1995 | $50 |

—Audiophile vinyl

POLYDOR
❏ PD-1-6175	Equinoxe	1979	$25
❏ PD-1-6225	Magnetic Fields	1981	$25
❏ PD-1-6112	Oxygene	1977	$25

JARREAU, AL
Male singer.

Albums

Number	Title	Yr	NM

BAINBRIDGE
| ❑ BT-6237 | Al Jarreau 1965 | 1982 | $10 |

MOBILE FIDELITY
| ❑ Jan-0019 | All Fly Home | 1980 | $40 |
—Audiophile vinyl

REPRISE
❑ MS2248	Glow	1976	$12
❑ 25778	Heart's Horizon	1988	$12
❑ MS2224	We Got By	1975	$12

WARNER BROS.
❑ 25331	Al Jarreau in London	1985	$10
❑ BSK3229	All Fly Home	1978	$12
❑ BSK3576	Breakin' Away	1981	$10
❑ 25106	High Crime	1984	$10
❑ 23801	Jarreau	1983	$10
❑ 25477	L Is for Lover	1986	$10
❑ 2WS3052	Look to the Rainbow/Live in Europe	1977	$15
❑ BSK3434	This Time	1980	$10

JARRETT, KEITH, AND JACK DEJOHNETTE
Also see each artist's individual listings.

Albums

ECM
| ❑ 1021ST | Ruta & Daitya | 1973 | $35 |
—Original issue; made in Germany?
| ❑ ECM-1-1021 | Ruta & Daitya | 197? | $30 |
—Manufactured by Polydor

JARRETT, KEITH
Pianist, organist and keyboard player. Also an occasional flutist and soprano saxophone player.

Albums

ABC IMPULSE!
❑ ASH-9305	Backhand	1975	$200
❑ IA-9334	Bop-Be	1977	$30
❑ AS-9331	Byablue	1977	$30
❑ ASD-9301	Death and the Flower	1974	$35
❑ AS-9240	Fort Yawuh	1973	$35
❑ ASD-9315	Mysteries	1976	$30
❑ ASD-9322	Shades	1976	$30
❑ IA-9348	The Best of Keith Jarrett	1978	$25
❑ AS-9274	Treasure Island	1974	$35

ATLANTIC
❑ SD1612	Birth	1972	$35
❑ SD1673	El Juicio (The Judgment)	1975	$30
❑ SD1596	Mourning of a Star	1971	$50
❑ SD8808	Somewhere Before	1981	$30
—Reissue of Vortex 2012

COLUMBIA
| ❑ KG31580 | Expectations | 1972 | $50 |
—Original edition
| ❑ PG31580 | Expectations | 198? | $30 |
—Reissue with new prefix; some with bar code on cover

ECM
| ❑ ECM-1-1070 | Arbour Zena | 1976 | $30 |
—Distribuited by Polydor
| ❑ ECM1-1070 | Arbour Zena | 197? | $25 |
—Distributed by Warner Bros. (reissue)
| ❑ 1050ST | Belonging | 1974 | $35 |
—Original, made in Germany?
| ❑ 1344/5 | Book of Ways | 1986 | $30 |
—Made in Germany
| ❑ ECM1-1175 | Celestial Hawk | 1981 | $25 |
—Distributed by Warner Bros.
| ❑ 1392 | Changeless | 1990 | $60 |
—Made in Germany
| ❑ 25007 | Changes | 1984 | $25 |
—Distributed by Warner Bros.
| ❑ 1276 | Changes | 1984 | $35 |
—Made in Germany (U.S. version issued on 25007)
| ❑ ECM1-1228 | Concerts | 1982 | $25 |
—Abridged version of 1227; distributed by Warner Bros.
| ❑ ECM3-1227 | Concerts | 1982 | $50 |
—Distributed by Warner Bros.; box set
| ❑ 1379 | Dark Intervals | 1988 | $35 |
—Made in Germany
| ❑ ECM-T-1150 | Eyes of the Heart | 1979 | $35 |
—Distributed by Warner Bros.
| ❑ 1017ST | Facing You | 1973 | $35 |
—Original edition, made in Germany?
| ❑ ECM 1-1017 | Facing You | 197? | $30 |
—U.S. pressing, distributed by Polydor
| ❑ ECM1-1174 | G.I. Gurdjieff Sacred Hymns | 1981 | $25 |

—Distributed by Warner Bros.
| ❑ ECM-2-1086 | Hymns/Spheres | 1977 | $35 |
—Distributed by Polydor
| ❑ 1033/4 ST | In the Light | 1976 | $50 |
—Original edition
| ❑ ECM 2-1033 | In the Light | 197? | $35 |
—Reissue with new prefix, distributed by Polydor
| ❑ ECM-D-1201 | Invocations/The Moth and the Flame | 1981 | $30 |
—Distributed by Warner Bros.
| ❑ 1049ST | Luminessence | 1974 | $35 |
—Original, made in Germany
| ❑ ECM1-1049 | Luminessence | 197? | $30 |
—Distributed by Warner Bros.
| ❑ ECM1-1115 | My Song | 1978 | $30 |
—Distributed by Warner Bros.
| ❑ ECM2-1171 | Nude Ants | 1980 | $35 |
—Distributed by Warner Bros.
| ❑ 1382 | Personal Mountains | 1989 | $35 |
—Made in Germany
| ❑ 1035/6/7 ST | Solo Concerts | 1974 | $60 |
—Original issue, made in Germany?
| ❑ ECM-3-1035 | Solo Concerts | 197? | $50 |
—Distributed by Polydor
| ❑ 1333/4 | Spirits | 1986 | $50 |
—Made in Germany
| ❑ ECM-2-1090 | Staircase | 1977 | $35 |
—Distributed by Polydor
| ❑ 23793 | Standards, Volume 1 | 1983 | $30 |
—Distributed by Warner Bros.
| ❑ 1255 | Standards, Volume 1 | 1983 | $35 |
—Made in Germany
| ❑ 25023 | Standards, Volume 2 | 1985 | $30 |
—Distributed by Warner Bros.
| ❑ 1289 | Standards, Volume 2 | 1985 | $35 |
—Made in Germany
| ❑ 25041 | Standards Live | 1986 | $30 |
—Distributed by Warner Bros.
| ❑ 1317 | Standards Live | 1986 | $35 |
—Made in Germany
| ❑ 1360/1 | Still Live | 1988 | $60 |
—Made in Germany
| ❑ ECM-1-1085 | Survivors' Suite | 1977 | $30 |
—Distributed by Polydor
| ❑ ECM-2-1064 | The Koln Concert | 1976 | $35 |
—Distributed by Polydor
| ❑ 1100 | The Sun Bear Concerts | 1977 | $150 |
—Made in Germany

MCA
| ❑ 29048 | Bop-Be | 1980 | $25 |
—Reissue of Impulse 9334
| ❑ 29047 | Byablue | 1980 | $25 |
—Reissue of Impulse 9331
| ❑ 29046 | Death and the Flower | 1980 | $25 |
—Reissue of Impulse 9301
| ❑ 29044 | Fort Yawuh | 1980 | $25 |
—Reissue of Impulse 9240
| ❑ 2-4125 | Great Moments with Keith Jarrett | 1981 | $50 |
| ❑ 29045 | Treasure Island | 1980 | $25 |
—Reissue of Impulse 9274
| ❑ 39106 | Treasure Island | 198? | $200 |
—Another reissue of Impulse 9274

VORTEX
❑ 2006	Life Between the Exit Signs	1969	$60
❑ 2008	Restoration Ruin	1969	$60
❑ 2012	Somewhere Before	1970	$60

JARRETT, KEITH/MCCOY TYNER

Albums

AT EASE
| ❑ MD-11119 | Masters of the Piano | 1978 | $50 |
—Record made for sale at military bases

JARRETT, SCOTT
Pianist and male singer.

Albums

GRP/ARISTA
| ❑ GL5007 | Without Rhyme or Reason | 1979 | $30 |

JARVIS, JOHN
Pianist and composer.

Albums

CRYSTAL CLEAR
| ❑ 8004 | Evolutions | 1980 | $50 |
—Direct-to-disc recording

MCA
❑ 5690	So Far So Good	1986	$25
❑ 5963	Something Constructive	1987	$25
❑ 6263	Whatever Works	1988	$25

JASEN, DAVE
Pianist.

Albums

BLUE GOOSE
| ❑ 3001 | Fingerbustin' Ragtime | 197? | $30 |
| ❑ 3002 | Rompin', Stompin' Ragtime | 197? | $30 |

EUPHONIC
| ❑ 1206 | Creative Ragtime | 196? | $30 |

FOLKWAYS
| ❑ FC-3561 | Rip-Roarin' Ragtime | 1977 | $25 |

JASMINE
Members: Roger Rosenberg; Bill O'Connell; Carmen Lundy.

Albums

WEST 54
| ❑ 8007 | Jasmine | 1980 | $30 |

JASPAR, BOBBY
Tenor saxophone player and flutist. Also see THE NUTTY SQUIRRELS.

Albums

EMARCY
| ❑ MG-36105 [M] | Bobby Jaspar and His All Stars | 1957 | $200 |

RIVERSIDE
| ❑ RLP 12-240 [M] | Bobby Jaspar | 1957 | $250 |
—White label, blue print
| ❑ RLP 12-240 [M] | Bobby Jaspar | 1959 | $300 |
—Blue label, microphone label at top
| ❑ 6156 | Tenor and Flute | 198? | $30 |

SWING
| ❑ SW-8413 | Bobby Jaspar In Paris | 1986 | $25 |

JAUME, ANDRE, AND JOE MCPHEE
Also see each artist's individual listings.

Albums

HAT HUT
| ❑ 12 | Tales and Prophecies | 1980 | $50 |

JAUME, ANDRE
Reeds player.

Albums

HAT ART
| ❑ 2003 | Musique Pour 3 & 8: Errance | 1986 | $35 |

HAT HUT
| ❑ 1989/90 | Musique Pour 8: L'oc | 1981 | $50 |
| ❑ 0R | Saxanimalier | 1979 | $30 |

JAZZ ARTISTS GUILD, THE
Members: ERIC DOLPHY; KENNT DORHAM; ROY ELDRIDGE; JO JONES; ABBEY LINCLON; CHARLES MINGUS; MAX ROACH.

Albums

CANDID
| ❑ CD-8022 [M] | Newport Rebels | 1960 | $40 |
| ❑ CS-9022 [S] | Newport Rebels | 1960 | $50 |

JAZZ BROTHERS, THE
Led by CHUCK MANGIONE and his brother GAP MANGIONE.

Albums

RIVERSIDE
❑ RLP-371 [M]	Hey, Baby!	1961	$200
❑ RS-9371 [S]	Hey, Baby!	1961	$200
❑ RLP-335 [M]	Jazz Brothers	1960	$200
❑ RS-9335 [S]	Jazz Brothers	1960	$200
❑ RLP-405 [M]	Spring Fever	1962	$150
❑ RS-9405 [S]	Spring Fever	1962	$150

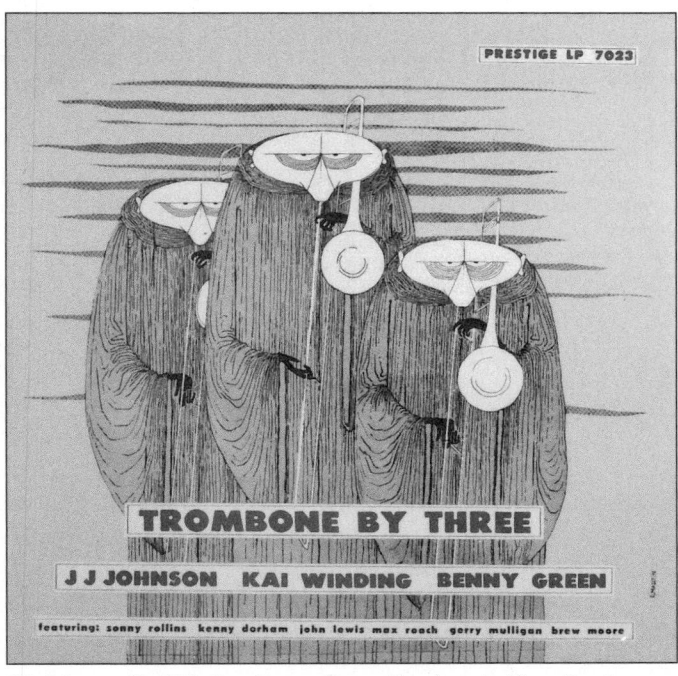

J.J. Johnson, Kai Winding, Benny Green, *Trombone by Three*, Prestige PRLP-7023, **$300**.

Carmell Jones, *The Remarkable Carmell Jones*, Pacific Jazz ST-29, **$50**.

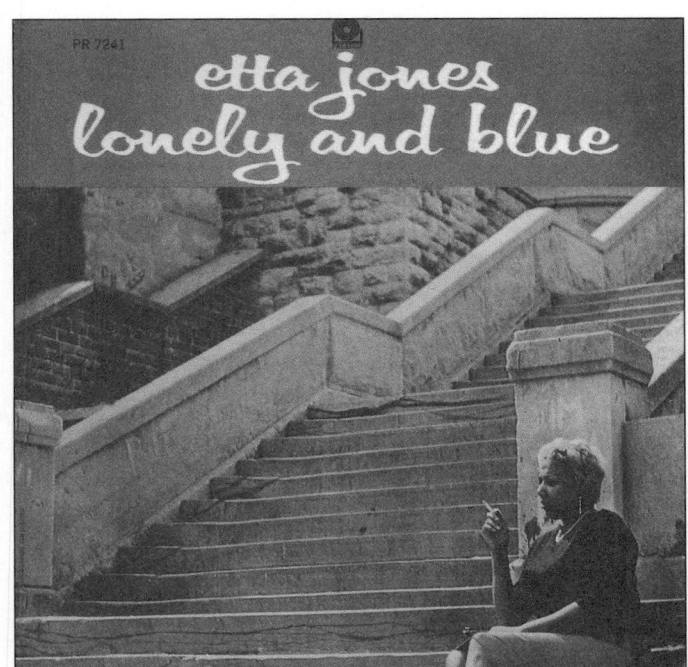

Etta Jones, *Lonely and Blue*, Prestige PRLP-7241, yellow label, **$150**.

Etta Jones, *The Jones Girl ... Etta*, King 544, **$150**.

Number	Title	Yr	NM

JAZZ CITY
Members include Pete Christlieb (tenor sax) and Harry Kevis Jr. (drums).

Albums

RAHMP
| ❏ 2 | Jazz City | 197? | $25 |

JAZZ CITY ALL-STARS, THE

Albums

BETHLEHEM
| ❏ BCP-79 [M] | Jazz City Presents the Jazz City All-Stars | 1957 | $250 |

JAZZ COMPOSERS ORCHESTRA

Albums

JCOA
| ❏ LP-1001/2 | Jazz Composers Orchestra | 1968 | $40 |

JAZZ CONTEMPORARIES

Albums

STRATA-EAST
| ❏ SES1972-2 | Reasons in Tonality | 1972 | $35 |

JAZZ CORPS, THE
Members: Tommy Peltier (cornet, fleugel horn); [RAHSAAN] ROLAND KIRK (tenor sax, flute, baritone sax); Fred Rodriguez (tenor and alto saxes, flute); Lynn Blessing (vibes); Bill Plummer (bass); Maurice Miller (drums).

Albums

PACIFIC JAZZ
❏ PJ-10116 [M]	The Jazz Corps Under the Direction of Tommy Peltier	1967	$30
❏ ST-20116 [S]	The Jazz Corps Under the Direction of Tommy Peltier	1967	$35
❏ LN-10131	The Jazz Corps Under the Direction of Tommy Peltier	198?	$25
— *Budget-line reissue*

JAZZ COURIERS, THE
British group whose members included TUBBY HAYES; Kenny Nepper; Ronnie Scott; Phil Seamen; Terry Shannon.

Albums

CARLTON
| ❏ LP 12-116 [M] | The Couriers of Jazz | 1959 | $50 |
| ❏ ST 12-116 [S] | The Couriers of Jazz | 1959 | $40 |
JAZZLAND
| ❏ JLP-34 [M] | Message from Britain | 1961 | $30 |
| ❏ JLP-934 [S] | Message from Britain | 1961 | $30 |
WHIPPET
| ❏ WLP-700 [M] | The Jazz Couriers | 1956 | $120 |

JAZZ CRUSADERS, THE
See THE CRUSADERS.

JAZZ EXPONENTS, THE
Members: Norm Diamond; Bill Elliott; Jack Gridley; Dick Rionda.

Albums

ARGO
| ❏ LP-622 [M] | The Jazz Exponents | 1958 | $40 |

JAZZ FIVE, THE
Members: Vic Arch; Malcolm Cecil; Brian Dee; Bill Eyden; Barry Klein.

Albums

RIVERSIDE
| ❏ RLP-361 [M] | The Hooter | 1961 | $200 |
| ❏ RS-9361 [S] | The Hooter | 1961 | $200 |

JAZZ INTERACTIONS ORCHESTRA, THE
Members: Joe Newman (trumpet, conductor); Ernie Royal, Ray Copeland, Burt Collins, Marvin Stamm (trumpets); Benny Powell, Paul Faulise, Wayne Andre, Jimmy Cleveland (trombones); Jimmy Buffington, Ray Alonge (French horns); Don Butterfield (tuba); Phil Woods, George Marge (alto sax, flute); Jerry Dodgion, Zoot Sims (tenor sax); Danny Bank (bass, bass clarinet, flute); Patti Bown (piano); Ron Carter, George Duvivier (bass); Ed Shaughnessy (drums); Bobby Rosengarden (percussion); Oliver Nelson (composer, arranger, conductor).

Albums

VERVE
| ❏ V-8731 [M] | Jazzhattan Suite | 1967 | $25 |
| ❏ V6-8731 [S] | Jazzhattan Suite | 1967 | $30 |

JAZZ LAB, THE
Led by CHARLIE BYRD and GIGI GRYCE.

Albums

COLUMBIA
| ❏ CL998 [M] | Jazz Lab | 1957 | $150 |
| ❏ CL998 [M] | Jazz Lab | 199? | $30 |
— *180-gram reissue*
| ❏ CL1058 [M] | Modern Jazz Perspective/ Jazz Lab, Volume 2 | 1957 | $300 |
JAZZLAND
| ❏ JLP-1 [M] | Jazz Lab | 1960 | $50 |
| ❏ JLP-901 [S] | Jazz Lab | 1960 | $60 |
JOSIE
| ❏ JOZ-3500 [M] | Gigi Gryce and Donald Byrd | 1962 | $40 |
— *Reissue of Jubilee album*
| ❏ JS-3500 [R] | Gigi Gryce and Donald Byrd | 196? | $25 |
JUBILEE
| ❏ JLP-1059 [M] | Jazz Lab | 1958 | $100 |
RIVERSIDE
| ❏ RLP 12-229 [M] | Gigi Gryce and the Jazz Lab Quintet | 1957 | $250 |
— *White label, blue print*
| ❏ RLP 12-229 [M] | Gigi Gryce and the Jazz Lab Quintet | 1959 | $250 |
— *Blue label, microphone logo at top*
| ❏ RLP-1110 [S] | Gigi Gryce and the Jazz Lab Quintet | 1959 | $250 |

JAZZ MEMBERS BIG BAND

Albums

SEA BREEZE
| ❏ SB-2028 | Live at Fitzgerald | 1986 | $25 |
| ❏ SB-2014 | May Day | 1985 | $25 |

JAZZ MESSENGERS, THE
See ART BLAKEY.

JAZZ MODES, THE
See LES JAZZ MODES.

JAZZ O'MANIACS, THE

Albums

STOMP OFF
| ❏ SOS-1046 | Have You Ever Felt This Way | 198? | $25 |
| ❏ SOS-1071 | Sweet Mumtaz | 1984 | $25 |

JAZZ PIANO QUARTET, THE
Members: ROLAND HANNA; DICK HYMAN; HANK JONES; MARIAN McPARTLAND.

Albums

RCA VICTOR
| ❏ CPL1-0680 | Let It Happen | 1974 | $35 |

JAZZ SYMPHONICS

Albums

RENFRO
| ❏ LP-12369 | The Beginning | 1968 | $60 |

JAZZ WARRIORS
Led by COURTNEY PINE with a constantly changing membership.

Albums

ANTILLES
| ❏ 90681 | Out of Many, One People | 1987 | $25 |

JAZZ WAVE, LTD., THE
See THAD JONES AND MEL LEWIS.

JAZZMOBILE ALL-STARS, THE
Led by BILLY TAYLOR. Other members: Jimmy Owens (trumpet, fluegel horn); FRANK WESS; TED DUNBAR; Victor Gaskin (bass); Bobby Thomas (drums).

Albums

TAYLOR-MADE
| ❏ TL-1003 | The Jazzmobile All Stars | 1989 | $30 |

JAZZPICKERS, THE
Led by HARRY BABASIN. Other members at different times included BUDDY COLLETTE; TERRY GIBBS; and RED NORVO.

Albums

EMARCY
| ❏ MG-36123 [M] | Command Performance | 1958 | $200 |
| ❏ MG-36111 [M] | The Jazzpickers | 1957 | $200 |
MERCURY
| ❏ SR-80013 [S] | For Moderns Only | 1959 | $100 |

JAZZTET, THE
Featuring ART FARMER and BENNY GOLSON.

Albums

ARGO
❏ LP-672 [M]	Big City Sounds	1961	$40
❏ LPS-672 [S]	Big City Sounds	1961	$50
❏ LP-664 [M]	Meet the Jazztet	1960	$50
❏ LPS-664 [S]	Meet the Jazztet	1960	$60
❏ LP-684 [M]	The Jazztet and John Lewis	1961	$40
❏ LPS-684 [S]	The Jazztet and John Lewis	1961	$50
❏ LPS-688 [S]	The Jazztet at Birdhouse	1961	$50
CADET
❏ LP-664 [M]	Meet the Jazztet	1966	$60
❏ LPS-664 [S]	Meet the Jazztet	1966	$30
— *Fading blue label*
| ❏ CA-664 [S] | Meet the Jazztet | 197? | $25 |
— *Yellow and red label*
CHESS
| ❏ CH-9159 | Meet the Jazztet | 198? | $15 |
— *Reissue*
CONTEMPORARY
| ❏ C-14020 | Back to the City | 1987 | $30 |
| ❏ C-14034 | Real Time | 1988 | $30 |
MERCURY
❏ MG-20737 [M]	Another Git-Together	1962	$100
❏ SR-60737 [S]	Another Git-Together	1962	$100
❏ MG-20698 [M]	Here and Now	1962	$100
❏ SR-60698 [S]	Here and Now	1962	$100
SOUL NOTE
❏ SN-1066	Moment to Moment	1984	$35

JEANNEAU, FRANCOIS
Saxophone player, arranger and composer.

Albums

INNER CITY
| ❏ IC-1022 | Techniques Douces | 197? | $35 |

JEFFERSON, CARTER
Saxophone player.

Albums

TIMELESS
| ❏ 309 | The Rise of Atlantis | 1979 | $30 |

JEFFERSON, EDDIE
Male singer; popularized "vocalese," the art of putting lyrics to jazz solos.

Albums

FANTASY
| ❏ OJC-396 | Body and Soul | 1989 | $30 |
| ❏ OJC-613 | Come Along with Me | 1991 | $30 |

Number	Title	Yr	NM
❑ OJC-307	Letter from Home	1988	$25
INNER CITY			
❑ IC-1016	Jazz Singer	197?	$35
❑ IC-1033	Main Man	1978	$35
MUSE			
❑ MR-5063	Still On the Planet	1976	$30
❑ MR-5127	The Live-Liest	197?	$30
❑ MR-5043	Things Are Getting Better	1974	$30
PRESTIGE			
❑ PRST-7619	Body and Soul	1969	$25
❑ PRST-7698	Come Along with Me	1969	$25
❑ 24095	There I Go Again	198?	$35
RIVERSIDE			
❑ RLP-411 [M]	Letter from Home	1962	$150
❑ RS-9411 [S]	Letter from Home	1962	$150

JEFFERSON, RON
Drummer. Also see LES JAZZ MODES.

Albums

Number	Title	Yr	NM
CATALYST			
❑ 7601	Vous Etes Swing	1976	$30
PACIFIC JAZZ			
❑ PJ-36 [M]	Love Lifted Me	1962	$30
❑ ST-36 [S]	Love Lifted Me	1962	$40

JEFFREY, PAUL
Tenor saxophone player.

Albums

Number	Title	Yr	NM
MAINSTREAM			
❑ MRL-376	Family	1972	$35
❑ MRL-406	Paul Jeffrey	1973	$35
❑ MRL-390	Watershed	1973	$35
SAVOY			
❑ MG-12192 [M]	Electrifying Sounds	1968	$25

JEFFRIES, FRAN
Female singer.

Albums

Number	Title	Yr	NM
MONUMENT			
❑ MLP-8069 [M]	This Is Fran Jeffries	1967	$25
❑ SLP-18069 [S]	This Is Fran Jeffries	1967	$25
WARWICK			
❑ W-2020 [M]	Fran Can Really Hang You Up the Most	1960	$25

JEFFRIES, HERB
Male singer.

Albums

Number	Title	Yr	NM
BETHLEHEM			
❑ BCP-72 [M]	Say It Isn't So	1957	$250
CORAL			
❑ CRL56066 [10]	Herb Jeffries Sings Flamingo and Other Songs in a Mellow Mood	1952	$200
❑ CRL56044 [10]	Time on My Hands	1951	$175
DOBRE			
❑ DR-1047	I Remember the Bing	1978	$35
GOLDEN TONE			
❑ 14066 [S]	The Devil Is a Woman	196?	$30
❑ C-4066 [M]	The Devil Is a Woman	196?	$30
HARMONY			
❑ HL7048 [M]	Herb Jeffries	195?	$20
MERCURY			
❑ MG-25090 [10]	Herb Jeffries Sings	1950	$300
❑ MG-25091 [10]	Just Jeffries	1950	$300
❑ MG-25089 [10]	Magenta Moods	1950	$300
RCA VICTOR			
❑ LPM-1608 [M]	Senor Flamingo	1957	$40
RKO UNIQUE			
❑ ULP-128 [M]	Jamaica	1956	$60

JENKINS, JOHN; CLIFF JORDAN; BOBBY TIMMONS
Also see each artist's individual listings.

Albums

Number	Title	Yr	NM
FANTASY			
❑ OJC-251	Jenkins, Jordan & Timmons	1987	$30
NEW JAZZ			
❑ NJLP-8232 [M]	Jenkins, Jordan and Timmons	1960	$200

—Purple label

Number	Title	Yr	NM
❑ NJLP-8232 [M]	Jenkins, Jordan and Timmons	1965	$150

—Blue label with trident logo

JENKINS, JOHN
Alto saxophone player. Also see PHIL WOODS.

Albums

Number	Title	Yr	NM
BLUE NOTE			
❑ BLP-1573 [M]	John Jenkins with Kenny Burrell	1958	$1000

—Regular version with W. 63rd St., New York address on label

Number	Title	Yr	NM
❑ BLP-1573 [M]	John Jenkins with Kenny Burrell	1963	$140

—With "New York, USA" address on label

Number	Title	Yr	NM
❑ BST-1573 [S]	John Jenkins with Kenny Burrell	1959	$250

—Regular version with W. 63rd St., New York address on label

Number	Title	Yr	NM
❑ BST-1573 [S]	John Jenkins with Kenny Burrell	1963	$140

—With "New York, USA" address on label

Number	Title	Yr	NM
❑ BST-81573 [S]	John Jenkins with Kenny Burrell	1967	$60

—With "A Division of Liberty Records" on label

Number	Title	Yr	NM
REGENT			
❑ MG-6056 [M]	Jazz Eyes	1957	$150
SAVOY			
❑ MG-12201 [M]	Jazz Eyes	196?	$40

JENKINS, LEROY, AND MUHAL RICHARD ABRAMS
Also see each artist's individual listings.

Albums

Number	Title	Yr	NM
BLACK SAINT			
❑ BSR-0033	Duo	198?	$30

JENKINS, LEROY
Violinist.

Albums

Number	Title	Yr	NM
BLACK SAINT			
❑ BSR-0060	Mixed Quartet	198?	$30
❑ BSR-0022	The Legend of Ai Glatson	198?	$30
❑ BSR-0083	Urban Blues	1985	$30
INDIA NAVIGATION			
❑ IN-1028	Solo Concert	1977	$30
JCOA			
❑ LP-1010	For Players Only	1975	$35
TOMATO			
❑ TOM-8001	Space Minds, New Worlds	1979	$35

JENKINS, MARV

Albums

Number	Title	Yr	NM
OROVOX			
❑ 1001 [M]	Marv Jenkins Arrives	196?	$40
❑ S-1001 [S]	Marv Jenkins Arrives	196?	$40
REPRISE			
❑ R-6077 [M]	Good Little Man at the Rubaiyat Room	1963	$25
❑ R9-6077 [S]	Good Little Man at the Rubaiyat Room	1963	$30

JENKS, GLENN
Pianist.

Albums

Number	Title	Yr	NM
STOMP OFF			
❑ SOS-1179	Ragtime Alchemy	1989	$25

JENNEY, JACK
Trombonist.

Albums

Number	Title	Yr	NM
COLUMBIA			
❑ GL100 [10]	The Golden Era	1949	$50
COLUMBIA MASTERWORKS			
❑ ML4803 [M]	Jack Jenney	195?	$80

JENNINGS, BILL
Guitarist. Also see KENNY BURRELL.

Albums

Number	Title	Yr	NM
AUDIO LAB			
❑ AL-1514 [M]	Guitar/Vibes	1959	$100
KING			
❑ 398-508 [M]	Mood Indigo	1955	$100
❑ 295-106 [10]	The Fabulous Guitar of Bill Jennings	195?	$250
PRESTIGE			
❑ PRST-7788	Enough Said	1970	$30
❑ PRLP-7177 [M]	Glide On	1960	$200
❑ PRST-7836	Glide On	1971	$30

JERNIGAN, DOUG, AND BUCKY PIZZARELLI
Jernigan is a pedal steel guitar player. Also see BUCKY PIZZARELLI.

Albums

Number	Title	Yr	NM
FLYING FISH			
❑ 043	Doug and Bucky	1977	$30

JETSTREAM
Also see GEORGE SHAW.

Albums

Number	Title	Yr	NM
PALO ALTO			
❑ TB-211	Around the World	198?	$25

JEWKES, NOEL
Saxophone player and flutist.

Albums

Number	Title	Yr	NM
REVELATION			
❑ 30	Just Passin' Thru	1980	$30

JOBIM, ANTONIO CARLOS
Guitarist, pianist, composer and arranger. Also see STAN GETZ; HERBIE MANN; FRANK SINATRA.

Albums

Number	Title	Yr	NM
A&M			
❑ SP-3031	Tide	1970	$35
❑ SP9-3031	Tide	1984	$50

—Audio Master Plus" reissue

Number	Title	Yr	NM
❑ SP-3002	Wave	1968	$35
❑ SP9-3002	Wave	1983	$50

—Audio Master Plus" reissue

Number	Title	Yr	NM
CTI			
❑ 6002	Stone Flower	1973	$30
DISCOVERY			
❑ DS-848	A Certain Mr. Jobim	198?	$25
PHILIPS			
❑ 832766-1	Personalidade Series	1988	$25
VERSATILE			
❑ NED1132	Jobim	1977	$30
VERVE			
❑ 833234-1	Passarim	1988	$25
❑ V-8547 [M]	The Composer of "Desafinado" Plays	1963	$30
❑ V6-8547 [S]	The Composer of "Desafinado" Plays	1963	$35
WARNER BROS.			
❑ W1636 [M]	Love, Strings	1966	$25
❑ WS1636 [S]	Love, Strings	1966	$25

—Gold label

Number	Title	Yr	NM
❑ 2BS3409	Terra Brasilis	1981	$30
❑ W1611 [M]	The Wonderful World of Antonio Carlos Jobim	1966	$25
❑ WS1611 [S]	The Wonderful World of Antonio Carlos Jobim	1966	$25
❑ BS2928	Urubu	1976	$25

JOHANSSON, JAN
Pianist.

Albums

Number	Title	Yr	NM
DOT			
❑ DLP-3416 [M]	Sweden Non-Stop	1962	$75
❑ DLP-25416 [S]	Sweden Non-Stop	1962	$75

Number	Title	Yr	NM

JOHANSSON, LASSE
Guitarist.
Albums
KICKING MULE
| ❏ KM-170 | King Porter Stomp -- The Music of Jelly Roll Morton | 198? | $30 |

JOHNSON, ALPHONSO
Bass player.
Albums
EPIC
❏ PE34118	Moonshadows	1975	$25
❏ JE34869	Spellbound	1977	$25
❏ JE36521	The Best of Alphonso Johnson	1979	$25
❏ PE34364	Yesterday's Dreams	1976	$25

JOHNSON, ARNOLD
Bandleader.
Albums
CIRCLE
| ❏ 32 | Swinging the Classics | 198? | $25 |

JOHNSON, BUDD
Saxophone player (mostly tenor), occasional male singer, composer and arranger. Also see THE JPJ QUARTET.
Albums
ARGO
❏ LP-721 [M]	French Cookin'	1963	$30
❏ LPS-721 [S]	French Cookin'	1963	$30
❏ LP-748 [M]	Off the Wall	1965	$30
❏ LPS-748 [S]	Off the Wall	1965	$30
❏ LP-736 [M]	Ya! Ya!	1964	$60
❏ LPS-736 [S]	Ya! Ya!	1964	$60
FANTASY
❏ OJC-209	Budd Johnson and the Four Brass Giants	1985	$25
❏ OJC-1720	Let's Swing	198?	$25
FELSTED
❏ FAJ-7007 [M]	Blues A La Mode	1959	$60
❏ SJA-2007 [S]	Blues A La Mode	1959	$80
MASTER JAZZ
❏ 8119	Blues A La Mode	197?	$30
RIVERSIDE
❏ RLP-343 [M]	Budd Johnson and the Four Brass Giants	1960	$200
❏ RS-9343 [S]	Budd Johnson and the Four Brass Giants	1960	$200
SWINGVILLE
❏ SVLP-2015 [M]	Let's Swing	1961	$50
—Purple label			
❏ SVLP-2015 [M]	Let's Swing	1965	$30
—Blue label, trident logo at right			

JOHNSON, BUDDY & ELLA
Ella is a female singer. Also see BUDDY JOHNSON.
Albums
MERCURY
| ❏ MG-20347 [M] | Swing Me | 195? | $150 |
ROULETTE
| ❏ R25085 [M] | Go Ahead and Rock and Roll | 1959 | $150 |
| ❏ SR25085 [S] | Go Ahead and Rock and Roll | 1959 | $200 |

JOHNSON, BUDDY
Pianist, male singer, arranger, composer and bandleader.
Albums
MCA
| ❏ 1356 | Fine Brown Frame | 198? | $25 |
MERCURY
❏ MG-20330 [M]	Buddy Johnson Wails	195?	$150
❏ SR-60072 [S]	Buddy Johnson Wails	195?	$150
❏ MG-20209 [M]	Rock 'N' Roll	195?	$150
❏ MG-20347 [M]	Swing Me	195?	$150
❏ MG-20322 [M]	Walkin'	195?	$150
WING
❏ MGW-12234 [M]	Buddy Johnson Wails	196?	$60
❏ MGW-12005 [M]	Rock 'N' Roll	1956	$150
❏ MGW-12111 [M]	Rock 'n' Roll Stage Show	1963	$40

JOHNSON, BUNK, AND LU WATTERS
Also see each artist's individual listings.
Albums
GOOD TIME JAZZ
| ❏ L-12024 [M] | Bunk and Lu | 195? | $40 |

JOHNSON, BUNK
Trumpeter. One of the earliest known jazz musicians, he had a second go-round after being rediscovered in the 1940s. Also see ERNESTINE WASHINGTON.
Albums
AMERICAN MUSIC
| ❏ 644 [10] | Bunk Johnson Talking | 1952 | $60 |
| ❏ 638 [10] | Bunk Plays the Blues -- The Spirituals | 1951 | $60 |
COLUMBIA
❏ CL829 [M]	Bunk Johnson	1955	$50
—Red and black label with six "eye" logos			
❏ GL520 [M]	Bunk Johnson and His Band	1952	$60
—Black label, silver print			
❏ CL520 [M]	Bunk Johnson and His Band	1953	$50
—Maroon label, gold print			
❏ CL520 [M]	Bunk Johnson and His Band	1955	$50
—Red and black label with six "eye" logos			
COLUMBIA MASTERWORKS
❏ ML4802 [M]	The Last Testament of a Great New Orleans Jazzman	1950	$80
COMMODORE
❏ DL-30007 [M]	The Bunk Johnson Band	1952	$50
FOLKLYRIC
❏ 9047	Bunk Johnson and His New Orleans Jazz Band	1986	$25
GHB
❏ 101	Spicy Advice	198?	$25
GOOD TIME JAZZ
❏ L-12048 [M]	Bunk Johnson and His Superior Jazz Band	1962	$30
❏ L-17 [10]	Bunk Johnson and the Yerba Buena Jazz Band	1953	$50
MAINSTREAM
❏ 56039 [M]	Bunk Johnson -- A Legend	1965	$25
❏ S-6039 [R]	Bunk Johnson -- A Legend	1965	$30
TRIP
❏ J-2	Bunk Johnson	1970	$30

JOHNSON, CHARLIE
Pianist and bandleader.
Albums
X
| ❏ LVA-3026 [10] | Harlem in the Twenties, Vol. 2 | 1954 | $60 |

JOHNSON, DAVID EARLE; JAN HAMMER; JOHN ABERCROMBIE
Also see each artist's individual listings.
Albums
PLUG
| ❏ 1 | The Midweek Blues | 1986 | $30 |

JOHNSON, DAVID EARLE
Drummer, percussionist and male singer.
Albums
CMP
| ❏ CMP-14-ST | Hip Address | 1980 | $30 |
| ❏ CMP-20-ST | Skin Deep – Yeah! | 1981 | $30 |
VANGUARD
| ❏ VSD-79401 | Time Free | 197? | $25 |

JOHNSON, DICK
Clarinetist, saxophone player (soprano, alto and tenor) and flutist. Also see EDDIE COSTA.
Albums
CONCORD JAZZ
❏ CJ-107	Dick Johnson Plays Alto Sax & Flute & Soprano Sax & Clarinet	1979	$30
❏ CJ-146	Piano Mover	1980	$30
❏ CJ-135	Spider's Blues	1980	$30
❏ CJ-167	Swing Shift	1981	$30

EMARCY
| ❏ MG-36081 [M] | Music for Swinging Moderns | 1956 | $200 |

JOHNSON, EDDIE
Tenor saxophone player.
Albums
NESSA
| ❏ N-22 | Indian Summer | 1981 | $30 |

JOHNSON, HENRY
Guitarist.
Albums
MCA
| ❏ 6329 | Never Too Much | 1990 | $30 |

JOHNSON, J.J., AND JOE PASS
Also see each artist's individual listings.
Albums
PABLO
| ❏ 2310911 | We'll Be Together Again | 198? | $25 |

JOHNSON, J.J., AND KAI WINDING
Also see each artist's individual listings.
Albums
A&M
❏ SP-3016	Betwixt and Between	1969	$25
—As "J & K			
❏ SP-3008	Israel	1968	$25
—As "K. & J.J."			
❏ SP9-3008	Israel	1983	$20
—As "K. & J.J."; "Audio Master Plus" reissue			
❏ SP-3027	Stonebone	1970	$0
—Canceled			
ABC IMPULSE!
❏ AS-1 [S]	The Great Kai & J.J.	1968	$30
BETHLEHEM
❏ BCP-6001 [M]	K + J.J. (East Coast Jazz/7)	1955	$250
—With the number "BCP 13" on the upper right corner of the front cover and "BCP 6001" stickers on the back cover and "BCP 6001" on the labels			
❏ BCP-13 [M]	K + J.J. (East Coast Jazz/7)	1955	$250
—With "BCP 13" on the label as well as the cover			
❏ BCP-6001 [M]	The Finest Kai Winding and J.J. Johnson	197?	$30
—Reissue with new title, distributed by RCA Victor			
COLUMBIA
❏ CL973 [M]	Jay and Kai	1957	$50
—Red and black label with six "eye" logos			
❏ CL973 [M]	Jay and Kai	1963	$25
—Red label with "Guaranteed High Fidelity" or "360 Sound Mono" at bottom			
❏ CL892 [M]	J.J. Johnson, Kai Winding + 6	1956	$50
—Red and black "6-eye" label			
❏ CL892 [M]	J.J. Johnson, Kai Winding + 6	1963	$25
—Red label with "Guaranteed High Fidelity" or "360 Sound Mono" at bottom			
❏ CL2573 [10]	Kai + J.J.	1955	$80
❏ CL742 [M]	Trombone for Two	1956	$50
—Red label with "360 Sound Stereo" in black or white at bottom			
❏ CL742 [M]	Trombone for Two	1963	$25
—Red label with "Guaranteed High Fidelity" or "360 Sound Mono" at bottom			
COLUMBIA JAZZ ODYSSEY
❏ PC37001 [M]	J.J. Johnson, Kai Winding + 6	198?	$25
IMPULSE!
❏ A-1 [M]	The Great Kai & J.J.	1961	$160
❏ AS-1 [S]	The Great Kai & J.J.	1961	$200
MCA
❏ 29061	The Great Kai & J.J.	1980	$25
PRESTIGE
❏ PRLP-195 [10]	Jay and Kai	1954	$300
❏ PRLP-7253 [M]	Looking Back	1963	$50
❏ PRST-7253 [R]	Looking Back	1963	$30
❏ PRLP-109 [10]	Modern Jazz Trombones	1951	$250
SAVOY
❏ MG-15038 [10]	Jay and Kai	1954	$120

Quincy Jones, *Go West, Man*!, ABC-Paramount ABC-186, **$150**.

Thad Jones, *The Magnificent Thad Jones*, *Volume 3*, Blue Note BLP-1546, "deep groove" edition with W. 63rd St. address on label, **$800**.

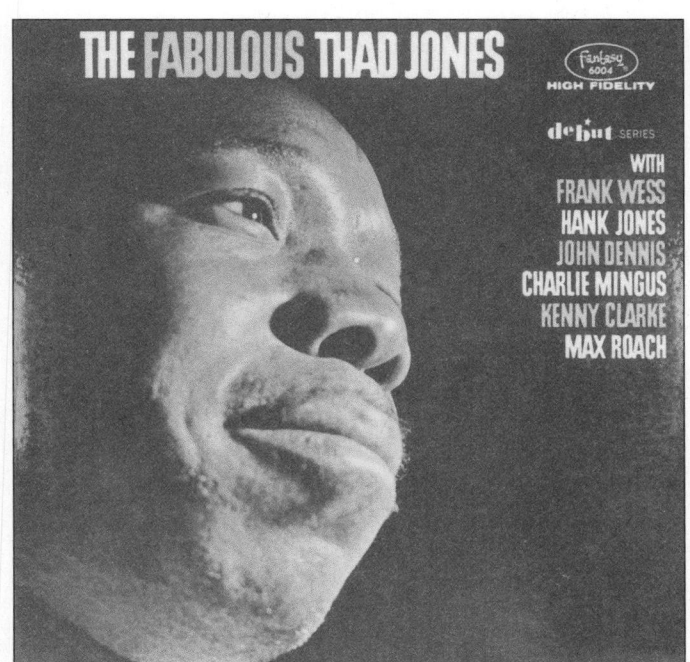

Thad Jones, *The Fabulous Thad Jones*, Fantasy 6004, mono, red vinyl, **$50**.

Thad Jones, *The Fabulous Thad Jones*, Debut DLP-12, 10-inch LP, **$600**.

Number	Title	Yr	NM
☐ MG-12010 [M]	Jay and Kai	1955	$80
☐ MG-15048 [10]	Jay and Kai, Volume 2	1955	$100
☐ MG-15049 [10]	Jay and Kai, Volume 3	1955	$100
☐ MG-12106 [M]	J.J. Johnson's Jazz Quintets	1957	$80
X			
☐ LXA-1040 [M]	An Afternoon at Birdland	1956	$80

JOHNSON, J.J., AND NAT ADDERLEY
Also see each artist's individual listings.

Albums

PABLO LIVE

Number	Title	Yr	NM
☐ 2620109	Yokohama Concert	1977	$35

JOHNSON, J.J.; KAI WINDING; BENNIE GREEN
Also see each artist's individual listings.

Albums

DEBUT

Number	Title	Yr	NM
☐ DEB-126 [M]	Four Trombones	1958	$150
☐ DLP-5 [10]	Jazz Workshop, Volume 1	1953	$300
☐ DLP-14 [10]	Jazz Workshop, Volume 2	1955	$300

FANTASY

☐ 6005 [M]	Four Trombones	1963	$50
—Red vinyl			
☐ 6005 [M]	Four Trombones	1963	$30
—Black vinyl			
☐ 86005 [R]	Four Trombones	1963	$40
—Blue vinyl			
☐ 86005 [R]	Four Trombones	1963	$25
—Black vinyl			
☐ OJC-091	Trombones by Three	198?	$25

PRESTIGE

☐ PRLP-7030 [M]	J.J. Johnson, Kai Winding, Bennie Green	1956	$350
— Yellow label with W. 50th St. address			
☐ 16-4 [M]	Trombone by Three	1956	$2000
— This album plays at 16 2/3 rpm and is marked as such; white label			

JOHNSON, J.J.
Trombonist, arranger and composer. Also see THE BRASS ENSEMBLE OF THE JAZZ & CLASSICAL MUSIC SOCIETY; STAN GETZ; SONNY STITT.

Albums

ABC IMPULSE!

Number	Title	Yr	NM
☐ AS-68 [S]	Proof Positive	1968	$200
—Black label with red ring			
☐ AS-68 [S]	Proof Positive	1975	$30
— Green, blue, purple "target" label			

BLUE NOTE

☐ BLP-5057 [10]	Jay Jay Johnson, Volume 2	1955	$700
☐ BLP-5070 [10]	Jay Jay Johnson, Volume 3	1955	$700
☐ BLP-5028 [10]	Jay Jay Johnson All Stars	1953	$700
☐ BLP-1505 [M]	The Eminent Jay Jay Johnson, Volume 1	1955	$1000
—Deep groove" version; Lexington Ave. address on label			
☐ BLP-1505 [M]	The Eminent Jay Jay Johnson, Volume 1	1958	$1000
—Deep groove" version, W. 63rd St. address on label			
☐ BLP-1505 [M]	The Eminent Jay Jay Johnson, Volume 1	1963	$100
—New York, USA" address on label			
☐ BST-81505 [R]	The Eminent Jay Jay Johnson, Volume 1	1967	$50
—A Division of Liberty Records" on label			
☐ BLP-1506 [M]	The Eminent Jay Jay Johnson, Volume 2	1958	$1500
—Deep groove" version, W. 63rd St. address on label			
☐ BLP-1506 [M]	The Eminent Jay Jay Johnson, Volume 2	1955	$1500
—Deep groove" version; Lexington Ave. address on label			
☐ BLP-1506 [M]	The Eminent Jay Jay Johnson, Volume 2	1963	$100
—New York, USA" address on label			
☐ BST-81506 [R]	The Eminent Jay Jay Johnson, Volume 2	1967	$50
—A Division of Liberty Records" on label			
☐ B1-81505	The Eminent J.J. Johnson, Volume 1	1989	$35
—The Finest in Jazz Since 1939" reissue			
☐ B1-81506	The Eminent J.J. Johnson, Volume 2	1989	$35
—The Finest in Jazz Since 1939" reissue			

COLUMBIA

Number	Title	Yr	NM
☐ CL1737 [M]	A Touch of Satin	1962	$40
—Red and black label with six "eye" logos			
☐ CL1737 [M]	A Touch of Satin	1963	$35
—Red label with "Guaranteed High Fidelity" or "360 Sound Mono" at bottom			
☐ CS8537 [S]	A Touch of Satin	1962	$50
—Red and black label with six "eye" logos			
☐ CS8537 [S]	A Touch of Satin	1963	$25
—Red label with "360 Sound Stereo" in black or white at bottom			
☐ CL1303 [M]	Blue Trombone	1959	$40
—Red and black label with six "eye" logos			
☐ CL1303 [M]	Blue Trombone	1963	$30
—Red label with "Guaranteed High Fidelity" or "360 Sound Mono" at bottom			
☐ CS8109 [S]	Blue Trombone	1959	$50
—Red and black label with six "eye" logos			
☐ CS8109 [S]	Blue Trombone	1963	$35
—Red label with "360 Sound Stereo" in black or white at bottom			
☐ CL1084 [M]	Dial J.J. 5	1957	$50
—Red and black label with six "eye" logos			
☐ CL1084 [M]	Dial J.J. 5	1963	$35
—Red label with "Guaranteed High Fidelity" or "360 Sound Mono" at bottom			
☐ CL1030 [M]	First Place	1957	$50
—Red and black label with six "eye" logos			
☐ CL1030 [M]	First Place	1963	$35
—Red label with "Guaranteed High Fidelity" or "360 Sound Mono" at bottom			
☐ CL935 [M]	J" Is for Jazz	1956	$50
—Red and black label with six "eye" logos			
☐ CL935 [M]	J" Is for Jazz	1963	$35
—Red label with "Guaranteed High Fidelity" or "360 Sound Mono" at bottom			
☐ CL1606 [M]	J.J. Inc	1961	$30
—Red and black label with six "eye" logos			
☐ CL1606 [M]	J.J. Inc	1963	$30
—Red label with "Guaranteed High Fidelity" or "360 Sound Mono" at bottom			
☐ CS8406 [S]	J.J. Inc	1961	$40
—Red and black label with six "eye" logos			
☐ CS8406 [S]	J.J. Inc	1963	$35
—Red label with "360 Sound Stereo" in black or white at bottom			
☐ CL1161 [M]	J.J. In Person	1958	$50
—Red and black label with six "eye" logos			
☐ CL1161 [M]	J.J. In Person	1963	$35
—Red label with "Guaranteed High Fidelity" or "360 Sound Mono" at bottom			
☐ CS8009 [S]	J.J. In Person	1959	$40
—Red and black label with six "eye" logos			
☐ CS8009 [S]	J.J. In Person	1963	$30
—Red label with "360 Sound Stereo" in black or white at bottom			
☐ CL1383 [M]	Really Livin'	1959	$40
—Red and black label with six "eye" logos			
☐ CL1383 [M]	Really Livin'	1963	$30
—Red label with "Guaranteed High Fidelity" or "360 Sound Mono" at bottom			
☐ CS8178 [S]	Really Livin'	1959	$50
—Red and black label with six "eye" logos			
☐ CS8178 [S]	Really Livin'	1963	$35
—Red label with "360 Sound Stereo" in black or white at bottom			
☐ CL1547 [M]	Trombones and Voices	1960	$30
—Red and black label with six "eye" logos			
☐ CL1547 [M]	Trombones and Voices	1963	$30
—Red label with "Guaranteed High Fidelity" or "360 Sound Mono" at bottom			
☐ CS8347 [S]	Trombones and Voices	1960	$40
—Red and black label with six "eye" logos			
☐ CS8347 [S]	Trombones and Voices	1963	$35
—Red label with "360 Sound Stereo" in black or white at bottom			

COLUMBIA JAZZ ODYSSEY

| ☐ PC36808 | J.J. Inc. | 1979 | $25 |

IMPULSE!

| ☐ A-68 [M] | Proof Positive | 1965 | $160 |
| ☐ AS-68 [S] | Proof Positive | 1965 | $200 |

MCA

Number	Title	Yr	NM
☐ 29072	Proof Positive	1980	$25

MILESTONE

| ☐ M-9093 | Pinnacles | 1979 | $30 |

MOSAIC

| ☐ MQ11-169 | The Complete Columbia J.J. Johnson Small Group Sessions | 199? | $300 |

PABLO TODAY

| ☐ 2312123 | Concepts in Blue | 1980 | $30 |

PRESTIGE

| ☐ 24067 | Early Bones | 197? | $35 |

RCA VICTOR

☐ LPM-3544 [M]	Broadway Express	1966	$25
☐ LSP-3544 [S]	Broadway Express	1966	$30
☐ LPM-3458 [M]	Goodies	1965	$25
☐ LSP-3458 [S]	Goodies	1965	$30
☐ LPM-3350 [M]	J.J.!	1965	$25
☐ LSP-3350 [S]	J.J.!	1965	$30
☐ LPM-3833 [M]	The Total J.J. Johnson	1967	$30
☐ LSP-3833 [S]	The Total J.J. Johnson	1967	$25

REGENT

| ☐ MG-6001 [M] | Jazz South Pacific | 1956 | $50 |

SAVOY

| ☐ MG-12205 [M] | Jazz South Pacific | 196? | $50 |
| *—Reissue of Regent 6001* | | | |

SAVOY JAZZ

| ☐ SJL-2232 | Mad Bebop | 198? | $30 |

VERVE

| ☐ V-8530 [M] | J.J.'s Broadway | 1963 | $25 |
| ☐ V6-8530 [S] | J.J.'s Broadway | 1963 | $30 |

JOHNSON, J.J./BENNIE GREEN
Also see each artist's individual listings.

Albums

PRESTIGE

Number	Title	Yr	NM
☐ PRLP-123 [10]	Modern Jazz Trombones, Volume 2	1952	$300

JOHNSON, JAMES P.
Pianist, composer and arranger, he was a pioneer in what became known as "stride piano." Also see SIDNEY DePARIS; OMER SIMEON.

Albums

BIOGRAPH

| ☐ 1003 | Rare Piano Rolls | 1972 | $30 |
| ☐ 1009 | Rare Piano Rolls, Volume 2 | 1972 | $30 |

BLUE NOTE

| ☐ BLP-7012 [10] | Jazz Band Ball | 1951 | $300 |
| ☐ BLP-7011 [10] | Stomps, Rags and Blues | 1951 | $300 |

COLUMBIA

☐ CL1780 [M]	Father of the Stride Piano	1961	$30
—Red and black label with six "eye" logos			
☐ CL1780 [M]	Father of the Stride Piano	1963	$35
—All-red label, "Guaranteed High Fidelity" or "360 Sound Mono" at bottom			

DECCA

| ☐ DL5228 [10] | James P. Johnson Plays Fats Waller Favorites | 1951 | $200 |
| ☐ DL5190 [10] | The Daddy of the Piano | 1950 | $150 |

FOLKWAYS

☐ FJ-2816	Striding in Dixieland	196?	$25
☐ FJ-2850	The Original James P. Johnson	196?	$30
☐ FJ-2842 [M]	Yamekraw	1962	$60

RIVERSIDE

☐ RLP 12-151 [M]	Backwater Blues	1955	$300
—White label, blue print			
☐ RLP 12-151 [M]	Backwater Blues	1959	$300
—Blue label, microphone logo at top			
☐ RLP-1046 [10]	Early Harlem Piano, Vol. 2	1954	$300
☐ RLP-1056 [10]	Harlem Rent Party	1955	$300
☐ RLP 12-105 [M]	Rediscovered Early Solos	1955	$300
—White label, blue print			
☐ RLP 12-105 [M]	Rediscovered Early Solos	1959	$250
—Blue label, microphone logo at top			
☐ RLP-1011 [10]	Rent Party	1953	$300

SOUNDS

| ☐ 1204 | Father of the Stride Piano | 196? | $35 |

STINSON

| ☐ SLP-21 [10] | New York Jazz | 1950 | $120 |
| ☐ SLP-21 [M] | New York Jazz | 195? | $50 |

TIME-LIFE

| ☐ STL-J-18 | Giants of Jazz | 1981 | $50 |

Number	Title	Yr	NM

JOHNSON, LAMONT
Pianist, composer and arranger.
Albums
MAINSTREAM

| ❏ MRL-328 | Sun, Moon and Stars | 1972 | $35 |

JOHNSON, MARC
Bass player.
Albums
ECM

| ❏ 25040 | Bass Desires | 1986 | $25 |

JOHNSON, OSIE
Drummer, male singer and arranger. Also see THE BRASS ENSEMBLE OF THE JAZZ & CLASSICAL MUSIC SOCIETY; THE MANHATTAN JAZZ SEPTETTE.
Albums
BETHLEHEM

| ❏ BCP-66 [M] | The Happy Jazz of Osie Johnson | 1957 | $250 |

PERIOD

| ❏ SPL-1112 [10] | Johnson's Whacks | 1955 | $80 |
| ❏ SPL-1108 [10] | Osie's Oasis | 1955 | $80 |

RCA VICTOR

| ❏ LPM-1369 [M] | A Bit of the Blues | 1957 | $40 |

JOHNSON, PETE
Pianist. Also see ALBERT AMMONS; ERROLL GARNER; JOE TURNER.
Albums
BLUE NOTE

| ❏ BLP-7019 [10] | Boogie Woogie Blues and Skiffle | 1952 | $300 |

BRUNSWICK

| ❏ BL58041 [10] | Boogie Woogie Mood | 1953 | $80 |

MCA

| ❏ 1333 | Boogie Woogie Mood | 198? | $25 |

RIVERSIDE

| ❏ RLP-1056 [10] | Jumpin' with Pete Johnson | 1955 | $300 |

SAVOY

| ❏ MG-14018 [M] | Pete's Blues | 1958 | $120 |

SAVOY JAZZ

| ❏ SJL-414 | Pete's Blues | 1985 | $25 |

JOHNSON, PETE/HADDA BROOKS
Also see each artist's individual listings.
Albums
CROWN

| ❏ CLP-5058 [M] | Boogie | 195? | $25 |

JOHNSON, PLAS
Tenor saxophone player. He is the soloist on the original soundtrack version of the theme from The Pink Panther.
Albums
CAPITOL

❏ T1503 [M]	Mood for the Blues	1961	$60
❏ ST1503 [S]	Mood for the Blues	1961	$60
❏ T1281 [M]	This Must Be the Plas!	1960	$60
❏ ST1281 [S]	This Must Be the Plas!	1960	$60

CONCORD JAZZ

| ❏ CJ-15 | Blues | 1975 | $25 |
| ❏ CJ-24 | Positively | 1976 | $25 |

TAMPA

❏ TP-24 [M]	Bop Me, Daddy	1957	$200
—Colored vinyl			
❏ TP-24 [M]	Bop Me, Daddy	1958	$150
—Black vinyl			

JOHNSON, RUDOLPH
Saxophone player.
Albums
BLACK JAZZ

| ❏ 11 | Second Coming | 1972 | $30 |
| ❏ 4 | Spring Rain | 1971 | $30 |

OVATION

| ❏ OV-1805 | Time and Space | 1977 | $35 |

JOHNSON, WAYNE
Guitarist.
Albums
INNER CITY

| ❏ IC-1098 | Arrowhead | 198? | $30 |

ZEBRA

| ❏ ZR-5003 | Everybody's Painting Pictures | 1984 | $30 |

ZEBRA/MCA

| ❏ 42228 | Spirit of the Dancer | 1988 | $25 |

JOLLY, PETE
Pianist. Also see THE FIVE.
Albums
A&M

❏ SP-4184	Give a Damn	1970	$30
❏ SP-4145	Herb Alpert Presents Pete Jolly	1968	$30
❏ SP-3033	Seasons	1969	$30

AVA

❏ A-51 [M]	Hello Jolly	1964	$50
❏ AS-51 [S]	Hello Jolly	1964	$60
❏ A-22 [M]	Little Bird	1963	$50
❏ AS-22 [S]	Little Bird	1963	$60
❏ A-39 [M]	Sweet September	1963	$50
❏ AS-39 [S]	Sweet September	1963	$60

CHARLIE PARKER

| ❏ PLP-825 [M] | Pete Jolly Gasses Everybody | 1962 | $50 |
| ❏ PLP-825S [S] | Pete Jolly Gasses Everybody | 1962 | $60 |

COLUMBIA

| ❏ CL2397 [M] | Too Much, Baby | 1965 | $50 |
| ❏ CS9197 [S] | Too Much, Baby | 1965 | $60 |

MAINSTREAM

| ❏ S-6114 | The Best of Pete Jolly | 196? | $35 |

METROJAZZ

| ❏ E-1014 [M] | Impossible | 1958 | $300 |
| ❏ SE-1014 [S] | Impossible | 1958 | $300 |

MGM

| ❏ E-4127 [M] | 5 O'Clock Shadows | 1963 | $50 |
| ❏ SE-4127 [S] | 5 O'Clock Shadows | 1963 | $60 |

RCA VICTOR

❏ LPM-1125 [M]	Duo, Trio, Quartet	1955	$100
❏ LPM-1105 [M]	Jolly Jumps In	1955	$100
❏ LPM-1367 [M]	When Lights Are Low	1957	$100

STEREO FIDELITY

| ❏ SFS-11000 [S] | Continental Jazz | 1960 | $60 |

TRIP

| ❏ TLP-5817 | A Touch of Jazz | 197? | $25 |

JONES, BOBBY
Clarinetist and tenor saxophone player.
Albums
ENJA

| ❏ 2046 | Hill Country Suite | 1975 | $35 |

JONES, BOOGALOO JOE
Guitarist.
Albums
PRESTIGE

❏ 10072	Black Whip	1973	$30
❏ PRST-7697	Boogaloo Joe	1969	$25
❏ PRST-7557	Mind Bender	1968	$25
❏ PRST-7617	My Fire! More of the Psychedelic Soul Jazz Guitar of Joe Jones	1968	$25
—As "Joe Jones"			
❏ 10004	No Way!	1971	$30
❏ PRST-7766	Right On Brother!	1970	$25
❏ 10056	Snake Rhythm Rock	1972	$30
❏ 10035	What It Is	1971	$30

JONES, CARMELL
Trumpeter, composer and arranger. Also see TRICKY LOFTON.
Albums
PACIFIC JAZZ

❏ PJ-53 [M]	Business Meetin'	1962	$40
❏ ST-53 [S]	Business Meetin'	1962	$50
—Black vinyl			
❏ ST-53 [S]	Business Meetin'	1962	$80
—Yellow vinyl			

| ❏ PJ-29 [M] | The Remarkable Carmell Jones | 1961 | $40 |
| ❏ ST-29 [S] | The Remarkable Carmell Jones | 1961 | $50 |

PRESTIGE

❏ PRST-7669	Carmell Jones in Europe	1969	$25
❏ PRLP-7401 [M]	Jay Hawk Talk	1965	$30
❏ PRST-7401 [S]	Jay Hawk Talk	1965	$40

JONES, CONNIE
Trumpeter.
Albums
JAZZOLOGY

| ❏ J-49 | Connie Jones with the Crescent City Jazz Band | 197? | $25 |

JONES, DALINE
Female singer.
Albums
TBA

| ❏ TBA-220 | Secret Fantasy | 1986 | $30 |
| ❏ TBA-231 | Share the Love | 1987 | $30 |

JONES, DILL
Pianist.
Albums
CHIAROSCURO

| ❏ 112 | The Music of Bix Beiderbecke | 197? | $35 |

PALO ALTO

| ❏ PA-8016 | Earth Jones | 1982 | $30 |

JONES, ELVIN, AND THE JIMMY GARRISON SEXTETTE
Garrison is a bass player. Also see ELVIN JONES.
Albums
IMPULSE!

| ❏ A-49 [M] | Illumination | 1963 | $120 |
| ❏ AS-49 [S] | Illumination | 1963 | $120 |

JONES, ELVIN
Drummer. Also see THE JONES BROTHERS; PHILLY JOE JONES.
Albums
ABC IMPULSE!

❏ AS-88 [S]	Dear John C.	1968	$35
❏ AS-9160	Heavy Sounds	1968	$200
❏ AS-9283	The Impulse Years	197?	$35

ATLANTIC

❏ 1443 [M]	And Then Again	1965	$25
❏ SD1443 [S]	And Then Again	1965	$30
❏ 1485 [M]	Midnight Walk	1967	$25
❏ SD1485 [S]	Midnight Walk	1967	$30

BLUE NOTE

❏ BST-84361	Coalition	1970	$30
❏ BST-84414	Elvin Jones	1972	$25
❏ BST-84369	Genesis	1971	$25
❏ BN-LA015-G [(2)]	Live at the Lighthouse	1973	$25
❏ BN-LA110-F	Mr. Jones	1973	$35
❏ BST-84331	Poly-Currents	1969	$30
❏ BST-84331	Poly-Currents	1986	$25
—The Finest in Jazz Since 1939" reissue			
❏ BN-LA506-H2	Prime Element	1976	$25
❏ BST-84282	Puttin' It Together	1968	$30
❏ BST-84305	The Ultimate Elvin Jones	1969	$30

ENJA

| ❏ 2036 | Live at the Vanguard | 1974 | $35 |

FANTASY

| ❏ OJC-259 | Elvin! | 1987 | $25 |

IMPULSE!

| ❏ A-88 [M] | Dear John C. | 1965 | $120 |
| ❏ AS-88 [S] | Dear John C. | 1965 | $120 |

MCA

| ❏ 29068 | Dear John C. | 1980 | $25 |

PAUSA

| ❏ 7052 | Rememberance | 1979 | $25 |

PM

| ❏ 04 | Live at Town Hall | 197? | $35 |
| ❏ 05 | On the Mountain | 197? | $35 |

QUICKSILVER

| ❏ QS-4001 | Brother John | 198? | $25 |

RIVERSIDE

Number	Title	Yr	NM
❏ RLP-409 [M]	Elvin!	1962	$200
❏ RS-9409 [S]	Elvin!	1962	$200
❏ 6192	Elvin!	198?	$30
VANGUARD			
❏ VSD-79372	Main Force	1976	$35
❏ VSD-79362	New Agenda	1975	$35
❏ VSD-79389	Time Capsule	1977	$35

JONES, ETTA
Female singer.

Albums

Number	Title	Yr	NM
FANTASY			
❏ OJC-298	Don't Go to Strangers	198?	$25
❏ OJC-221	Something Nice	198?	$25
KING			
❏ 707 [M]	Etta Jones Sings	1960	$80
❏ 544 [M]	The Jones Girl...Etta	1956	$150
MUSE			
❏ MR-5411	Christmas with Etta Jones	1989	$30
❏ MR-5333	Fine and Mellow	1987	$25
❏ MR-5175	If You Could See Me Now	1979	$30
❏ MR-5351	I'll Be Seeing You	1989	$30
❏ MR-5262	Love Me with All of Your Heart	198?	$25
❏ MR-5145	Mother's Eyes	1977	$30
❏ MR-5099	Ms. Jones to You	197?	$30
❏ MR-5214	Save Your Love for Me	1981	$25
❏ MR-5379	Sugar	1989	$30
PRESTIGE			
❏ PRLP-7186 [M]	Don't Go to Strangers	1960	$200
—Yellow label			
❏ PRLP-7186 [M]	Don't Go to Strangers	1964	$25
—Blue label, trident logo at right			
❏ PRST-7186 [S]	Don't Go to Strangers	1960	$200
—Silver label			
❏ PRST-7186 [S]	Don't Go to Strangers	1964	$30
—Blue label, trident logo at right			
❏ PRLP-7443 [M]	Etta Jones' Greatest Hits	1967	$30
❏ PRST-7443 [S]	Etta Jones' Greatest Hits	1967	$25
❏ PRLP-7214 [M]	From the Heart	1961	$200
—Yellow label			
❏ PRLP-7214 [M]	From the Heart	1964	$25
—Blue label, trident logo at right			
❏ PRST-7214 [S]	From the Heart	1961	$200
—Silver label			
❏ PRST-7214 [S]	From the Heart	1964	$30
—Blue label, trident logo at right			
❏ PRLP-7284 [M]	Holler!	1963	$40
—Yellow label			
❏ PRLP-7284 [M]	Holler!	1964	$25
—Blue label, trident logo at right			
❏ PRST-7284 [S]	Holler!	1963	$50
—Silver label			
❏ PRST-7284 [S]	Holler!	1964	$30
—Blue label, trident logo at right			
❏ PRLP-7241 [M]	Lonely and Blue	1962	$150
—Yellow label			
❏ PRLP-7241 [M]	Lonely and Blue	1964	$25
—Blue label, trident logo at right			
❏ PRST-7241 [S]	Lonely and Blue	1962	$150
—Silver label			
❏ PRST-7241 [S]	Lonely and Blue	1964	$30
—Blue label, trident logo at right			
❏ PRLP-7272 [M]	Love Shout	1963	$40
—Yellow label			
❏ PRLP-7272 [M]	Love Shout	1964	$25
—Blue label, trident logo at right			
❏ PRST-7272 [S]	Love Shout	1963	$50
—Silver label			
❏ PRST-7272 [S]	Love Shout	1964	$30
—Blue label, trident logo at right			
❏ PRLP-7194 [M]	Something Nice	1961	$200
—Yellow label			
❏ PRLP-7194 [M]	Something Nice	1964	$30
—Blue label, trident logo at right			
❏ PRLP-7204 [M]	So Warm -- Etta Jones and Strings	1961	$200
—Yellow label			
❏ PRLP-7204 [M]	So Warm -- Etta Jones and Strings	1964	$25
—Blue label, trident logo at right			
❏ PRST-7204 [S]	So Warm -- Etta Jones and Strings	1961	$200
—Silver label			

Number	Title	Yr	NM
❏ PRST-7204 [S]	So Warm -- Etta Jones and Strings	1964	$30
—Blue label, trident logo at right			
ROULETTE			
❏ R-25329 [M]	Etta Jones Sings	1965	$25
❏ SR-25329 [S]	Etta Jones Sings	1965	$30
WESTBOUND			
❏ 203	Etta Jones '75	1975	$25

JONES, HANK, AND RED MITCHELL
Also see each artist's individual listings.

Albums

Number	Title	Yr	NM
TIMELESS			
❏ SJP-283	Duo	1990	$35

JONES, HANK; RAY BROWN; JIMMIE SMITH
Also see each artist's individual listings.

Albums

Number	Title	Yr	NM
CONCORD JAZZ			
❏ CJ-32	Hank Jones/Ray Brown/ Jimmie Smith	197?	$30

JONES, HANK
Pianist. Also see THE FOUR MOST; THE JONES BROTHERS; JOHN LEWIS; THE TRIO.

Albums

Number	Title	Yr	NM
ABC-PARAMOUNT			
❏ ABC-496 [M]	This Is Ragtime Now	1964	$25
❏ ABCS-496 [S]	This Is Ragtime Now	1964	$30
ARGO			
❏ LP-728 [M]	Here's Love	1963	$25
❏ LPS-728 [S]	Here's Love	1963	$30
CAPITOL			
❏ T1175 [M]	Porgy and Bess	1959	$75
❏ ST1175 [S]	Porgy and Bess	1959	$60
❏ T1044 [M]	The Talented Touch of Hank Jones	1958	$75
❏ ST1044 [S]	The Talented Touch of Hank Jones	1958	$60
CLEF			
❏ MGC-100 [10]	Hank Jones Piano	1953	$300
❏ MGC-707 [M]	Urbanity -- Piano Solos by Hank Jones	1956	$250
CONCORD JAZZ			
❏ CJ-391	Lazy Afternoon	1989	$30
FANTASY			
❏ OJC-471	Just for Fun	1990	$30
GALAXY			
❏ 5123	Ain't Misbehavin'	1979	$30
❏ 5105	Just for	1977	$30
❏ 5108	Tiptoe Tapdance	1978	$30
GOLDEN CREST			
❏ GC-3042 [M]	Hank Jones Swings "Gigi	1958	$50
❏ GC-5002 [S]	Hank Jones Swings "Gigi	1959	$40
❏ GCS-3042 [S]	Hank Jones Swings "Gigi	196?	$25
INNER CITY			
❏ IC-6020	Hanky Panky	197?	$30
MERCURY			
❏ MG-25022 [10]	Hank Jones Piano	1950	$300
❏ MG-35014 [10]	Hank Jones Piano	1950	$300
❏ MGC-100 [10]	Hank Jones Piano	195?	$250
MUSE			
❏ MR-5123	Bop Redux	1977	$30
❏ MR-5169	Grovin' High	1979	$30
PAUSA			
❏ 7051	Have You Met This Jones?	1979	$25
PROGRESSIVE			
❏ 7004	Arigato	1976	$30
RCA VICTOR			
❏ LPM-2570 [M]	Arrival Time	1962	$30
❏ LSP-2570 [S]	Arrival Time	1962	$30
SAVOY			
❏ MG-12037 [M]	Hank Jones Quartet-Quintet	1955	$80
❏ MG-12087 [M]	Hank Jones Trio	1956	$80
❏ MG-12084 [M]	Have You Met Hank Jones	1956	$80
❏ MG-12053 [M]	The Trio	1956	$80
SAVOY JAZZ			
❏ SJL-1193	Bluebird	198?	$25
❏ SJL-1124	Hank Jones	198?	$25
❏ SJL-1138	Relaxin' at Camarillo	198?	$25
VERVE			
❏ MGV-8091 [M]	Urbanity -- Piano Solos by Hank Jones	1957	$100
❏ V-8091 [M]	Urbanity -- Piano Solos by Hank Jones	1961	$30

JONES, HOWARD

Albums

Number	Title	Yr	NM
ELEKTRA			
❏ R133246 [EP]	Action Replay	1986	$10
—RCA Music Service edition			
❏ 60466 [EP]	Action Replay	1986	$10
❏ 60794	Cross That Line	1989	$12
❏ 60794 [DJ]	Cross That Line	1989	$15
—Promo-only white label audiophile vinyl			
❏ R143992	Dream into Action	1985	$12
—RCA Music Service edition			
❏ 60390	Dream into Action	1985	$10
❏ 60346	Human's Lib	1984	$10
❏ R134013	One to One	1986	$12
—RCA Music Service edition			
❏ 60499	One to One	1986	$12

JONES, ISHAM
Bandleader and composer.

Albums

Number	Title	Yr	NM
RCA VICTOR			
❏ LPV-504 [M]	The Great Isham Jones and His Orchestra	1966	$25

JONES, JO
Drummer. Also see COLEMAN HAWKINS; JAZZ ARTISTS GUILD; THE JONES BOYS.

Albums

Number	Title	Yr	NM
EVEREST			
❏ LPBR-5023 [M]	Jo Jones Trio	1959	$30
❏ SDBR-1023 [S]	Jo Jones Trio	1959	$30
❏ LPBR-5110 [M]	Percussion and Bass	1960	$30
❏ SDBR-1110 [S]	Percussion and Bass	1960	$30
❏ LPBR-5099 [M]	Vamp Till Ready	1960	$30
❏ SDBR-1099 [S]	Vamp Till Ready	1960	$30
EVEREST ARCHIVE OF FOLK & JAZZ			
❏ 329	Jo Jones	197?	$25
JAZZTONE			
❏ J-1242 [M]	Jo Jones Special	1956	$50
PABLO			
❏ 2310799	Main Man	1976	$35
VANGUARD			
❏ VRS-8525 [M]	Jo Jones Plus Two	1959	$60
❏ VSD-2031 [S]	Jo Jones Plus Two	1959	$50
❏ VRS-8503 [M]	Jo Jones Special	1955	$100

JONES, JONAH, AND EARL "FATHA" HINES
Also see each artist's individual listings.

Albums

Number	Title	Yr	NM
CHIAROSCURO			
❏ 118	Back on the Street	1973	$30

JONES, JONAH
Trumpeter and male singer. Also see PETE BROWN; JACK TEAGARDEN.

Albums

Number	Title	Yr	NM
ANGEL			
❏ ANG.60005 [10]	Jonah Wails -- 1st Blast	1954	$150
❏ ANG.60006 [10]	Jonah Wails -- 2nd Blast	1954	$150
BETHLEHEM			
❏ BCP-1014 [10]	Jonah Jones Sextet	1954	$250
CAPITOL			
❏ T1948 [M]	And Now, In Person -- Jonah Jones	1963	$75
❏ ST1948 [S]	And Now, In Person -- Jonah Jones	1963	$80
❏ T1405 [M]	A Touch of Blue	1960	$80
❏ ST1405 [S]	A Touch of Blue	1960	$100
❏ T2087 [M]	Blowin' Up a Storm	1964	$75
❏ ST2087 [S]	Blowin' Up a Storm	1964	$80
❏ T1641 [M]	Broadway Swings Again	1961	$80
❏ ST1641 [S]	Broadway Swings Again	1961	$100
❏ T1557 [M]	Great Instrumental Hits Styled by Jonah Jones	1961	$80
❏ ST1557 [S]	Great Instrumental Hits Styled by Jonah Jones	1961	$100
❏ T1375 [M]	Hit Me Again!	1960	$80
❏ ST1375 [S]	Hit Me Again!	1960	$100
❏ T1193 [M]	I Dig Chicks	1959	$80
❏ ST1193 [S]	I Dig Chicks	1959	$100
❏ T1773 [M]	Jazz Bonus	1962	$75
❏ ST1773 [S]	Jazz Bonus	1962	$80
❏ T1660 [M]	Jonah Jones/Glenn Gray	1961	$80
❏ ST1660 [S]	Jonah Jones/Glenn Gray	1961	$100
❏ SM-1660	Jonah Jones/Glenn Gray	197?	$25
❏ T1115 [M]	Jonah Jumps Again	1959	$100

Stanley Jordan, *Flying Home*, EMI-Manhattan E1-48682, **$25**.

Richie Kamuca, *Richie Kamuca Quartet*, Mode LP-102, **$200**.

Richie Kamuca, *West Coast Jazz in Hi-Fi*, Hifijazz JS-609, stereo, **$50**.

Wynton Kelly, *Kelly Blue*, Riverside RLP-1142, **$250**.

Number	Title	Yr	NM
☐ ST1115 [S]	Jonah Jumps Again	1959	$100
☐ T1404 [M]	Jumpin' with a Shuffle	1960	$80
☐ ST1404 [S]	Jumpin' with a Shuffle	1960	$100
☐ T1039 [M]	Jumpin' with Jonah	1958	$100
☐ ST1039 [S]	Jumpin' with Jonah	1958	$100
☐ T839 [M]	Muted Jazz	1957	$75
☐ T1083 [M]	Swingin' at the Cinema	1958	$100
☐ ST1083 [S]	Swingin' at the Cinema	1958	$100
☐ T963 [M]	Swingin' On Broadway	1958	$75
☐ T1237 [M]	Swingin' 'Round the World	1959	$80
☐ ST1237 [S]	Swingin' 'Round the World	1959	$100
☐ T2594 [M]	The Best of Jonah Jones	1966	$75
☐ ST2594 [S]	The Best of Jonah Jones	1966	$60
☐ T1532 [M]	The Unsinkable Molly Brown	1961	$80
☐ ST1532 [S]	The Unsinkable Molly Brown	1961	$100

CIRCLE

Number	Title	Yr	NM
☐ CLP-83	1944: Butterflies in the Rain	198?	$25

DECCA

Number	Title	Yr	NM
☐ DL4638 [M]	Hello Broadway	1965	$30
☐ DL74638 [S]	Hello Broadway	1965	$35
☐ DL74918	Jazz Tropical!	1968	$30
☐ DL4688 [M]	On the Sunny Side of the Street	1966	$30
☐ DL74688 [S]	On the Sunny Side of the Street	1966	$35
☐ DL4800 [M]	Sweet with a Beat	1967	$35
☐ DL74800 [S]	Sweet with a Beat	1967	$30
☐ DL4765 [M]	Tijuana Taxi	1966	$30
☐ DL74765 [S]	Tijuana Taxi	1966	$35

GROOVE

Number	Title	Yr	NM
☐ LG-1001 [M]	Jonah Jones at the Embers	1956	$100

HALL OF FAME

Number	Title	Yr	NM
☐ 613	After Hours Jazz	198?	$25

JAZZ MAN

Number	Title	Yr	NM
☐ 5009	Confessin'	1981	$25

MOTOWN

Number	Title	Yr	NM
☐ M-683	Along Came Jonah	1969	$40
☐ M-690	Little Dis, Little Dat	1970	$40

PICKWICK

Number	Title	Yr	NM
☐ SPC-3008	Swing Along	196?	$30

RCA CAMDEN

Number	Title	Yr	NM
☐ CAS-2328	Jonah Jones Quartet	1969	$30

RCA VICTOR

Number	Title	Yr	NM
☐ LPM-2004 [M]	Jonah Jones at the Embers	1959	$40

—Reissue of Groove and Vik LP

SWING

Number	Title	Yr	NM
☐ 8408	Paris 1954	198?	$25

VIK

Number	Title	Yr	NM
☐ LXA-1135 [M]	Jonah Jones at the Embers	1958	$40

—Reissue of Groove LP

JONES, JONAH/CHARLIE SHAVERS
Also see each artist's individual listings.

Albums

BETHLEHEM

Number	Title	Yr	NM
☐ BCP-6034 [M]	Sounds of the Trumpets	1959	$200

JONES, NORAH
Female singer and pianist.

Albums

BLUE NOTE

Number	Title	Yr	NM
☐ BTE32088	Come Away with Me	2004	$20

—Standard-weight issue with lyrics on back cover; "Manufactured by Caroline Distribution" on back

Number	Title	Yr	NM
☐ BTE84800	Feels Like Home	2004	$20

—Standard-weight edition; "Manufactured by Caroline Distribution" on back cover

CLASSICRECORDS.COM

Number	Title	Yr	NM
☐ JP-5004	Come Away with Me	2002	$30

—Audiophile pressing; heavyweight vinyl with gatefold cover

JONES, PHILLY JOE, AND ELVIN JONES
Also see each artist's individual listings.

Albums

ATLANTIC

Number	Title	Yr	NM
☐ 1428 [M]	Together	1964	$30
☐ SD1428 [S]	Together	1964	$30

JONES, PHILLY JOE
Drummer. Also see KENNY DREW.

Albums

ATLANTIC

Number	Title	Yr	NM
☐ 1340 [M]	Philly Joe's Beat	1960	$250

—Multicolor label, white "fan" logo on right

Number	Title	Yr	NM
☐ 1340 [M]	Philly Joe's Beat	1963	$35

—Multicolor label, black "fan" logo on right

Number	Title	Yr	NM
☐ SD1340 [S]	Philly Joe's Beat	1960	$250

—Multicolor label, white "fan" logo on right

Number	Title	Yr	NM
☐ SD1340 [S]	Philly Joe's Beat	1963	$35

—Multicolor label, black "fan" logo on right

BLACK LION

Number	Title	Yr	NM
☐ 142	Trailways Express	197?	$30

FANTASY

Number	Title	Yr	NM
☐ OJC-230	Blues for Dracula	198?	$25
☐ OJC-484	Showcase	1991	$30

GALAXY

Number	Title	Yr	NM
☐ 5122	Advance!	1980	$30
☐ 5153	Drum Song	1985	$25
☐ 5112	Philly Mignon	1978	$30

RIVERSIDE

Number	Title	Yr	NM
☐ RLP 12-282 [M]	Blues for Dracula	1958	$300
☐ 6055	Blues for Dracula	197?	$35
☐ RLP 12-302 [M]	Drums Around the World	1959	$300
☐ RLP-1147 [S]	Drums Around the World	1959	$300
☐ RLP 12-313 [M]	Showcase	1959	$250
☐ RLP-1159 [S]	Showcase	1959	$250
☐ 6193	Showcase	198?	$30

UPTOWN

Number	Title	Yr	NM
☐ 2715	Look, Stop, Listen	198?	$30
☐ 2711	To Tadd with Love	198?	$30

JONES, QUINCY
Bandleader, producer, composer, arranger, record company executive, and a trumpeter, too. The below list includes some of his soundtrack work. Also see BILLY ECKSTINE; ROY HAYNES; THE JONES BOYS.

Albums

A&M

Number	Title	Yr	NM
☐ SP-3617	Body Heat	1974	$25
☐ QU-53617 [Q]	Body Heat	1974	$30
☐ SP-3191	Body Heat	1982	$20

—Budget-line reissue

Number	Title	Yr	NM
☐ SP-3030	Gula Matari	1970	$30
☐ SP-3705	I Heard That!!	1976	$30
☐ SP-6507	I Heard That!!	198?	$25

—Budget-line reissue

Number	Title	Yr	NM
☐ SP-4526	Mellow Madness	1975	$25
☐ QU-54526 [Q]	Mellow Madness	1975	$30
☐ SP-4626	Roots	1977	$25
☐ SP-3037	Smackwater Jack	1971	$30
☐ SP-4685	Sounds…And Stuff Like That!	1978	$25
☐ SP-3249	Sounds…And Stuff Like That!	198?	$20

—Budget-line reissue

Number	Title	Yr	NM
☐ SP-3200	The Best	1982	$20
☐ SP-3278	The Best, Vol. 2	1985	$20
☐ SP-3721	The Dude	1981	$25
☐ SP-3248	The Dude	198?	$20

—Budget-line reissue

Number	Title	Yr	NM
☐ SP-3023	Walking in Space	1969	$30
☐ SP-3041	You've Got It Bad Girl	1973	$30
☐ QU-53041 [Q]	You've Got It Bad Girl	1974	$30

ABC

Number	Title	Yr	NM
☐ D-782	Mode	1973	$30

ABC IMPULSE!

Number	Title	Yr	NM
☐ IA-9342	Quintessential Charts	1978	$30
☐ AS-11 [S]	The Quintessence	1968	$35

ABC-PARAMOUNT

Number	Title	Yr	NM
☐ 186 [M]	Go West, Man!	1957	$175
☐ 149 [M]	This Is How I Feel About Jazz	1956	$175

CHESS

Number	Title	Yr	NM
☐ CH-91562	The Music of Quincy Jones	198?	$25

COLGEMS

Number	Title	Yr	NM
☐ COM-107 [M]	In Cold Blood	1967	$50

EMARCY

Number	Title	Yr	NM
☐ MG-36083 [M]	Jazz Abroad	1956	$200
☐ 818177-1	The Birth of a Band	1984	$30

GRP/IMPULSE!

Number	Title	Yr	NM
☐ 222	The Quintessence	199?	$35

—Reissue on audiophile vinyl

IMPULSE!

Number	Title	Yr	NM
☐ A-11 [M]	The Quintessence	1962	$200
☐ AS-11 [S]	The Quintessence	1962	$200

LIBERTY

Number	Title	Yr	NM
☐ LOM-16004 [M]	Enter Laughing	1967	$60
☐ LOS-17004 [S]	Enter Laughing	1967	$60

MCA

Number	Title	Yr	NM
☐ 4145	Quintessential Charts	198?	$25

—Reissue of ABC Impulse 9342

Number	Title	Yr	NM
☐ 5578	The Slugger's Wife	1985	$30

MCA/IMPULSE!

Number	Title	Yr	NM
☐ 5728	The Quintessence	1986	$20

MERCURY

Number	Title	Yr	NM
☐ PPS-2014 [M]	Around the World	1961	$100
☐ PPS-6014 [S]	Around the World	1961	$100
☐ MG-20751 [M]	Big Band Bossa Nova	1962	$100
☐ SR-60751 [S]	Big Band Bossa Nova	1962	$100
☐ MG-20444 [M]	Birth of a Band	1959	$150
☐ SR-60129 [S]	Birth of a Band	1959	$200
☐ MG-20938 [M]	Golden Boy	1964	$100
☐ SR-60938 [S]	Golden Boy	1964	$100
☐ MG-20612 [M]	I Dig Dancers	1960	$100
☐ SR-60612 [S]	I Dig Dancers	1960	$150
☐ MG-21025 [M]	Mirage	1965	$100
☐ SR-61025 [S]	Mirage	1965	$100
☐ SRM-2-612	Ndeda	1972	$35
☐ MG-20653 [M]	Quincy Jones at Newport '61	1961	$100
☐ SR-60653 [S]	Quincy Jones at Newport '61	1961	$100
☐ MG-20863 [M]	Quincy Jones Explores the Music of Henry Mancini	1964	$100
☐ SR-60863 [S]	Quincy Jones Explores the Music of Henry Mancini	1964	$100
☐ MG-21050 [M]	Quincy Jones Plays for Pussycats	1965	$100
☐ SR-61050 [S]	Quincy Jones Plays for Pussycats	1965	$100
☐ MG-20799 [M]	Quincy Jones Plays Hip Hits	1963	$100
☐ SR-60799 [S]	Quincy Jones Plays Hip Hits	1963	$100
☐ MG-21063 [M]	Quincy's Got a Brand New Bag	1965	$100
☐ SR-61063 [S]	Quincy's Got a Brand New Bag	1965	$100
☐ MG-21070 [M]	Slender Thread	1966	$100
☐ SR-61070 [S]	Slender Thread	1966	$100
☐ MG-20561 [M]	The Great, Wide World of Quincy Jones	1960	$150
☐ SR-60221 [S]	The Great, Wide World of Quincy Jones	1960	$200
☐ MG-21011 [M]	The Pawnbroker	1964	$100
☐ SR-61011 [S]	The Pawnbroker	1964	$100

MOBILE FIDELITY

Number	Title	Yr	NM
☐ Jan-0078	You've Got It Bad Girl	1981	$60

—Audiophile vinyl

NAUTILUS

Number	Title	Yr	NM
☐ NR-52	The Dude	198?	$40

—Audiophile vinyl

PRESTIGE

Number	Title	Yr	NM
☐ PRLP-172 [10]	Quincy Jones with the Swedish-American All Stars	1953	$300

QWEST

Number	Title	Yr	NM
☐ 26020	Back on the Block	1989	$30
☐ 25356	The Color Purple	1985	$50

—Boxed set on purple vinyl

Number	Title	Yr	NM
☐ 25389	The Color Purple	1985	$35

—Gatefold package on purple vinyl

TRIP

Number	Title	Yr	NM
☐ 5554	Live at Newport '61	197?	$20
☐ 5514	The Great Wide World of Quincy Jones	1974	$20

UNITED ARTISTS

Number	Title	Yr	NM
☐ UAS-5214	They Call Me Mister Tibbs	1970	$60

WING

Number	Title	Yr	NM
☐ SRW-16398	Around the World	1969	$30

JONES, RICHARD M.
Pianist.

Albums

FOLKWAYS

Number	Title	Yr	NM
☐ FJ-2817	Chicago Dixieland in the Forties	198?	$30

JONES, RODNEY
Guitarist.

Albums

TIMELESS

Number	Title	Yr	NM
☐ 323	Articulation	1979	$30

JONES, RUFUS
Drummer.

Albums

CAMEO

Number	Title	Yr	NM
☐ C-1076 [M]	Five on Eight	1964	$30
☐ SC-1076 [S]	Five on Eight	1964	$30

JONES, SAM
Bass player.

Albums

Number	Title	Yr	NM
FANTASY			
❏ OJC-6008	Right Down in Front	198?	$25
INTERPLAY			
❏ 7720	The Bassist	1979	$30
MUSE			
❏ MR-5149	Something in Common	1977	$35
RIVERSIDE			
❏ RLP-432 [M]	Down Home	1962	$200
❏ RS-9432 [S]	Down Home	1962	$200
❏ 6079	Soul Society	197?	$35
❏ RLP-358 [M]	The Chant!	1961	$200
❏ RS-9358 [S]	The Chant!	1961	$200
❏ RLP 12-324 [M]	The Soul Society	1960	$200
❏ RLP-1172 [S]	The Soul Society	1960	$200
SEA BREEZE			
❏ 2004	Something New	1979	$30
STEEPLECHASE			
❏ SCS-1097	Visitation	198?	$30
XANADU			
❏ 129	Cello Again	197?	$30
❏ 150	Changes and Things	1978	$30

JONES, SPIKE, AND THE CITY SLICKERS

Drummer and bandleader, best known as a master parodist of both classical and popular music of his day.

Albums

Number	Title	Yr	NM
CORNOGRAPHIC			
❏ 1001	King of Corn	197?	$25
GOLDBERG & O'REILY			
❏ MF205/4	The Craziest Show on Earth	1977	$50
— Collection of radio show performances			
HINDSIGHT			
❏ HSR-185	The Uncollected Spike Jones 1946	198?	$25
LIBERTY			
❏ LRP-3154 [M]	60 Years of Music America Hates Best	1960	$100
❏ LST-7154 [S]	60 Years of Music America Hates Best	1960	$150
❏ LRP-3370 [M]	My Man	1964	$50
❏ LST-7370 [S]	My Man	1964	$60
❏ LRP-3140 [M]	Omnibust	1959	$100
❏ LST-7140 [S]	Omnibust	1959	$150
— Black vinyl			
❏ LST-7140 [S]	Omnibust	1959	$150
— Red vinyl			
❏ LRP-3349 [M]	Spike Jones' New Band	1964	$60
❏ LST-7349 [S]	Spike Jones' New Band	1964	$40
❏ LRP-3401 [M]	Spike Jones Plays Hank Williams Hits	1965	$50
❏ LST-7401 [S]	Spike Jones Plays Hank Williams Hits	1965	$60
❏ LRP-3338 [M]	Washington Square	1963	$50
❏ LST-7338 [S]	Washington Square	1963	$60
RCA GOLD SEAL			
❏ AGL1-4142	Spike Jones Is Murdering the Classics!	1982	$20
— Reissue			
RCA RED SEAL			
❏ LSC-3235 [R]	Spike Jones Is Murdering the Classics!	1971	$50
RCA VICTOR			
❏ LPM-3054 [10]	Bottoms Up	1952	$200
❏ LPM-3128 [10]	Spike Jones Murders Carmen and Kids the Classics	1953	$200
❏ LPT-18 [10]	Spike Jones Plays the Charleston	1952	$200
❏ LPM-2224 [M]	Thank You Music Lovers	1960	$100
— RCA Victor" in silver above dog, "Long 33 1/3 Play" at bottom of label			
❏ LPM-2224 [M]	Thank You Music Lovers	1965	$60
— RCA Victor" in white above dog, "Monaural" at bottom of label			
❏ LPM-3849 [M]	The Best of Spike Jones	1967	$60
❏ LSP-3849 [R]	The Best of Spike Jones	1967	$50
❏ ANL1-1035	The Best of Spike Jones	1975	$25
— Reissue			
❏ AYL1-3748	The Best of Spike Jones, Volume 1	1980	$20
— Best Buy Series" reissue			
❏ AYL1-3870	The Best of Spike Jones, Volume 2	1981	$20
— Best Buy Series" reissue			
❏ ANL1-2312	The Best of Spike Jones, Volume 2	1977	$25
— Reissue			

Number	Title	Yr	NM
RHINO			
❏ R170261	Dinner Music…For People Who Aren't Very Hungry	1988	$30
❏ R170196	It's a Spike Jones Christmas	1988	$30
UNITED ARTISTS			
❏ UA-LA439-E	The Very Best of Spike Jones	1975	$30
VERVE			
❏ MGV-4005 [M]	Dinner Music…For People Who Aren't Very Hungry	1957	$150
❏ V-4005 [M]	Dinner Music…For People Who Aren't Very Hungry	1961	$60
❏ MGV-2021 [M]	Let's Sing a Song for Christmas	1956	$200
❏ V-2021 [M]	Let's Sing a Song for Christmas	1961	$60
WARNER BROS.			
❏ W1332 [M]	Spike Jones in Hi-Fi	1959	$40
❏ WS1332 [S]	Spike Jones in Hi-Fi	1959	$100
— This is the title on the front of the LP cover, but the spine says "Spike Jones in Stereo"			

JONES, TAMIKO

Female singer. Also see HERBIE MANN.

Albums

Number	Title	Yr	NM
A&M			
❏ SP-3011	I'll Be Anything for You	1969	$60
ARISTA			
❏ AL-4040	Love Trip	1975	$60
DECEMBER			
❏ DR-8500	Tamiko	1968	$60
METROMEDIA			
❏ MD1030	Tamiko Jones in Muscle Shoals	1970	$60

JONES, THAD, AND MEL LEWIS

Also see each artist's individual listings.

Albums

Number	Title	Yr	NM
ARTISTS HOUSE			
❏ 3	Quartet	1980	$30
BLUE NOTE			
❏ BST-84346	Consummation	1970	$30
❏ BN-LA392-H [(2)]	Thad Jones/Mel Lewis	1975	$35
❏ BST-89905	The Jazz Wave Ltd. On Tour (Volume 1)	1970	$30
HORIZON			
❏ SP-724	Live in Munich	1978	$30
❏ SP-707	New Life	1976	$30
❏ SP-701	Suite for Pops	1975	$30
MOSAIC			
❏ MQ7-151	The Complete Solid State Recordings of the Thad Jones-Mel Lewis Orchestra	199?	$150
PAUSA			
❏ 7012	Thad Jones-Mel Lewis Orchestra and Manuel De Sica	198?	$25
PHILADELPHIA INT'L.			
❏ KZ33152 [B]	Potpourri	1974	$150
RCA VICTOR			
❏ AFL1-3423	Thad Jones/Mel Lewis and Umo	1980	$50
SOLID STATE			
❏ SS-18058	Central Park North	1969	$35
❏ SM-17016 [M]	Live at the Village Vanguard	1967	$40
❏ SS-18016 [S]	Live at the Village Vanguard	1967	$40
❏ SS-18048	Monday Night	1969	$35
❏ SM-17003 [M]	Presenting Thad Jones, Mel Lewis and the Jazz Orchestra	1966	$25
❏ SS-18003 [S]	Presenting Thad Jones, Mel Lewis and the Jazz Orchestra	1966	$25
❏ SS-18041	Thad Jones and Mel Lewis Featuring Miss Ruth Brown	1968	$35

JONES, THAD, AND PEPPER ADAMS

Also see each artist's individual listings.

Albums

Number	Title	Yr	NM
MILESTONE			
❏ MLP-1001 [M]	Mean What You Say	1966	$150
❏ MSP-9001 [S]	Mean What You Say	1966	$60

JONES, THAD

Trumpeter, cornet player, arranger and composer. Also see THE JONES BOYS; THE JONES BROTHERS; SONNY ROLLINS; FRANK WESS.

Albums

Number	Title	Yr	NM
BIOGRAPH			
❏ 12059	Greetings and Salutations	197?	$30
BLUE NOTE			
❏ BLP-1513 [M]	Detroit-New York Junction	1956	$1500
— Deep groove" version; Lexington Ave. address on label			
❏ BLP-1513 [M]	Detroit-New York Junction	1963	$500
— With "New York, USA" address on label			
❏ BST-81513 [R]	Detroit-New York Junction	1967	$50
— With "A Division of Liberty Records" on label			
❏ BLP-1527 [M]	The Magnificent Thad Jones	1956	$1000
— Deep groove" version; Lexington Ave. address on label			
❏ BLP-1527 [M]	The Magnificent Thad Jones	1956	$750
— Deep groove" version, W. 63rd St. address on label			
❏ BLP-1527 [M]	The Magnificent Thad Jones	1963	$100
— With "New York, USA" address on label			
❏ BST-81527 [R]	The Magnificent Thad Jones	1967	$50
— With "A Division of Liberty Records" on label			
❏ BLP-1546 [M]	The Magnificent Thad Jones, Volume 3	1957	$800
— Deep groove" version; W. 63rd St. address on label			
❏ BLP-1546 [M]	The Magnificent Thad Jones, Volume 3	1957	$400
— Regular version, W. 63rd St., NY address on label			
❏ BLP-1546 [M]	The Magnificent Thad Jones, Volume 3	1963	$150
— With "New York, USA" address on label			
❏ BST-81546 [R]	The Magnificent Thad Jones, Volume 3	1967	$50
— With "A Division of Liberty Records" on label			
DEBUT			
❏ DLP-17 [10]	Jazz Collaborations	1954	$600
❏ DEB-127 [10]	Thad Jones	1958	$400
❏ DLP-12 [10]	The Fabulous Thad Jones	1954	$600
FANTASY			
❏ 6004 [M]	The Fabulous Thad Jones	1962	$50
— Red vinyl			
❏ 6004 [M]	The Fabulous Thad Jones	1962	$30
— Black vinyl			
❏ 86004 [R]	The Fabulous Thad Jones	1962	$30
— Blue vinyl			
❏ 86004 [R]	The Fabulous Thad Jones	1962	$35
— Black vinyl			
❏ OJC-625	The Fabulous Thad Jones	1991	$35
MOSAIC			
❏ MQ5-172	The Complete Blue Note/ UA/Roulette Recordings of Thad Jones	199?	$100
PERIOD			
❏ SPL-1208 [M]	Mad Thad	1956	$650
PRESTIGE			
❏ P-24017	After Hours	197?	$50
❏ MPP-2506	Thad Jones and Charles Mingus	1980	$35
STEEPLECHASE			
❏ SCS-1197	Three and One	198?	$30
UNITED ARTISTS			
❏ UAL-4025 [M]	Motor City Scene	1959	$500
— red label			
❏ UAS-5025 [S]	Motor City Scene	1959	$60

JONES BOYS, THE (2)

A collaboration of unrelated musicians, all with the last name of Jones: Eddie, Jimmy, Jo, Quincy, Renauld and Thad.

Albums

Number	Title	Yr	NM
PERIOD			
❏ SPL-1210 [M]	The Jones Bash	1954	$80

JONES BROTHERS, THE

A collaboration of Joneses who really were brothers: Elvin, Hank and Thad.

Albums

Number	Title	Yr	NM
METROJAZZ			
❏ E-1003 [M]	Keepin' Up with the Joneses	1958	$120
❏ SE-1003 [S]	Keepin' Up with the Joneses	1958	$120

Number	Title	Yr	NM

JOPLIN, SCOTT
Pianist and composer. He was a pioneer in ragtime music, a precursor to jazz piano.

Albums

BIOGRAPH

❏ 1008	Ragtime, Vol. 2	197?	$25
❏ 1010	Ragtime, Vol. 3	197?	$25
❏ 1006	Scott Joplin 1916: Classic Solos	197?	$25

JORDAN, CLIFFORD
Tenor saxophone player. Also see JOHN JENKINS.

Albums

ATLANTIC

❏ 1444 [M]	These Are My Roots	1965	$30
❏ SD1444 [S]	These Are My Roots	1965	$30

BEE HIVE

❏ BH-7018	Dr. Chicago	1986	$25

BLUE NOTE

❏ BLP-1549 [M]	Blowing In from Chicago	1957	$800
— Regular version, W. 63rd St., NY address on label			
❏ BLP-1549 [M]	Blowing In from Chicago	1963	$150
— With "New York, USA" address on label			
❏ BST-81549 [R]	Blowing In from Chicago	1967	$30
— With "A Division of Liberty Records" on label			
❏ BLP-1582 [M]	Cliff Craft	1963	$150
— With "New York, USA" address on label			
❏ BST-1582 [S]	Cliff Craft	1959	$200
— Regular version, W. 63rd St., NY address on label			
❏ BST-1582 [S]	Cliff Craft	1963	$100
— With "New York, USA" address on label			
❏ BST-81582 [S]	Cliff Craft	1967	$35
— With "A Division of Liberty Records" on label			
❏ BST-81582 [S]	Cliff Craft	199?	$30
— Classic Records reissue on audiophile vinyl			
❏ BLP-1565 [M]	Clifford Jordan	1957	$150
— Regular version, W. 63rd St., NY address on label			
❏ BLP-1565 [M]	Clifford Jordan	1963	$60
— With "New York, USA" address on label			
❏ BST-1565 [S]	Clifford Jordan	1959	$60
— Regular version, W. 63rd St., NY address on label			
❏ BST-1565 [S]	Clifford Jordan	1963	$25
— With "New York, USA" address on label			
❏ BST-81565 [S]	Clifford Jordan	1967	$35
— With "A Division of Liberty Records" on label			

FANTASY

❏ OJC-494	Bearcat	1991	$35
❏ OJC-147	Starting Time	198?	$25

INNER CITY

❏ IC-2033	Firm Roots	197?	$35
❏ IC-2047	The Highest Mountain	197?	$35

JAZZLAND

❏ JLP-40 [M]	A Story Tale	1961	$30
❏ JLP-940 [S]	A Story Tale	1961	$40
❏ JLP-69 [M]	Bearcat	1962	$30
❏ JLP-969 [S]	Bearcat	1962	$40
❏ JLP-52 [M]	Starting Time	1961	$30
❏ JLP-952 [S]	Starting Time	1961	$40

MUSE

❏ MR-5128	Inward Fire	197?	$30
❏ MR-5076	Night of the Mark VII	197?	$30
❏ MR-5105	Remembering Me-Me	197?	$30
❏ MR-5163	The Adventurer	197?	$30

RIVERSIDE

❏ RLP-340 [M]	Spellbound	1960	$200
❏ RS-9340 [S]	Spellbound	1960	$200

SOUL NOTE

❏ SN-1084	Repetition	1984	$30

STEEPLECHASE

❏ SCS-1033	Film Roots	198?	$30
❏ SCS-1198	Half Note	198?	$30
❏ SCS-1071	On Stage, Volume 1	197?	$30
❏ SCS-1092	On Stage, Volume 2	198?	$30
❏ SCS-1104	On Stage, Volume 3	198?	$30
❏ SCS-1047	The Highest Mountain	198?	$30

STRATA-EAST

❏ SES19737/8	Glass Bead Games	1974	$30
❏ SES1972-1	In the World	1972	$25

VORTEX

❏ 2010	Soul Fountain	1970	$25

JORDAN, DUKE
Pianist.

Albums

BLUE NOTE

❏ BLP-4046 [M]	Flight to Jordan	1963	$60
— With "New York, USA" address on label			
❏ BST-84046 [S]	Flight to Jordan	1960	$60
— With W. 63rd St., NY address on label			
❏ BST-84046 [S]	Flight to Jordan	1963	$25
— With "New York, USA" address on label			

❏ BST-84046 [S]	Flight to Jordan	1967	$35
— With "A Division of Liberty Records" on label			

CHARLIE PARKER

❏ PLP-805 [M]	East and West of Jazz	1962	$200
❏ PLP-805S [S]	East and West of Jazz	1962	$200

INNER CITY

❏ IC-2046	Duke's Delight	197?	$35
❏ IC-2011	Flight to Denmark	197?	$35
❏ IC-2024	Two Loves	197?	$35

NEW JAZZ

❏ NJ-810 [10]	Jordu	195?	$200

PRESTIGE

❏ PRST-7849	Jordu	1970	$30

SAVOY

❏ MG-12149 [M]	Duke Jordan	1959	$80

SAVOY JAZZ

❏ SJL-1169	Flight to Jordan	1986	$25

SIGNAL

❏ S-1202 [M]	Duke Jordan	1955	$250

STEEPLECHASE

❏ SCS-1135	Change of Pace	1979	$30
❏ SCS-1103	Duke's Artistry	1978	$30
❏ SCS-1046	Duke's Delight	198?	$30
❏ SCS-1011	Flight to Denmark	198?	$30
❏ SCS-1088	Flight to Japan	198?	$30
❏ SCS-1150	Great Session	198?	$30
❏ SCS-1063/4	Live in Japan	198?	$35
❏ SCS-1127	Lover Man	198?	$30
❏ SCS-1143	Midnight Moonlight	198?	$30
❏ SCS-1053	Misty Thursday	198?	$30
❏ SCS-1165	Thinking of You	198?	$30
❏ SCS-1189	Tivol One	198?	$30
❏ SCS-1193	Tivol Two	198?	$30
❏ SCS-1175	Truth	198?	$30
❏ SCS-1024	Two Loves	198?	$30
❏ SCS-1211	Wait and See	198?	$30

JORDAN, DUKE/HALL OVERTON
Overton is a pianist. Also see DUKE JORDAN.

Albums

SAVOY

❏ MG-12145 [M]	Do It Yourself Jazz	1959	$100
❏ MG-12146 [M]	Jazz Laboratory Series	1959	$100

SIGNAL

❏ S-101/2 [M]	Jazz Laboratory Series	1955	$250
— Deduct 20 percent if book is missing			

JORDAN, KENT
Flutist.

Albums

COLUMBIA

❏ FC39325	No Question About It	1984	$25

JORDAN, LOUIS
Alto saxophone player, male singer, bandleader and composer. Considered to be a major influence on rhythm 'n' blues and rock 'n' roll.

Albums

CIRCLE

❏ 53	Louis Jordan and the Tympany Five: 1944-45	198?	$12
❏ 97	More Louis Jordan and His Tympany Five	198?	$12

CLASSIC JAZZ

❏ 148	I Believe in Music	198?	$15

DECCA

❏ DL5035 [M]	Greatest Hits	1968	$30
❏ DL75035 [R]	Greatest Hits	1968	$20
❏ DL8551 [M]	Let the Good Times Roll	1958	$100
— Black label, silver print			

MCA

❏ 274	Greatest Hits	197?	$12
❏ 1337	Greatest Hits, Vol. 2	1980	$12
❏ 4079	The Best of Louis Jordan	197?	$15

MERCURY

❏ MG-20331 [M]	Man, We're Wailin'	1958	$200
❏ MG-20242 [M]	Somebody Up There Digs Me	1957	$200

SCORE

❏ SLP-4007 [M]	Go Blow Your Horn	1957	$200

TANGERINE

❏ 1503 [M]	Hallelujah	1964	$25
❏ S-1503 [S]	Hallelujah	1964	$30

WING

❏ MGW-12126 [M]	Somebody Up There Digs Me	1962	$30

JORDAN, SHEILA
Female singer.

Albums

BLACKHAWK

❏ BKH-50501	The Crossing	1986	$25

BLUE NOTE

❏ BLP-9002 [M]	Portrait of Sheila Jordan	1962	$150
— With W. 63rd St., NY address on label			
❏ BLP-9002 [M]	Portrait of Sheila Jordan	1963	$60
— With "New York, USA" address on label			
❏ BST-89002 [R]	Portrait of Sheila Jordan	1967	$30
— With "A Division of Liberty Records" on label			

MUSE

❏ MR-5390	Lost and Found	1990	$35
❏ MR-5366	Old Time Feeling	1989	$30

PALO ALTO

❏ PA-8038	Old Time Feeling	1982	$30

STEEPLECHASE

❏ SCS-1081	Sheila	1978	$30

WAVE

❏ W-1 [M]	Looking Out	1961	$60
❏ WS-1 [S]	Looking Out	1961	$80

JORDAN, STANLEY
Guitarist.

Albums

BLUE NOTE

❏ B1-92356	Cornucopia	1990	$35
❏ BT-85101	Magic Touch	1985	$25
❏ BT-85130	Standards Volume 1	1986	$25
❏ SPRO-9434/5 [DJ]	Stanley Jordan	1985	$50
— Promo-only live recordings			

EMI MANHATTAN

❏ E1-48682	Flying Home	1988	$25

TANGENT

❏ 1001	Touch Sensitive	1982	$175

JORDAN, TAFT
Trumpeter and male singer.

Albums

MERCURY

❏ MG-20429 [M]	The Moods of Taft Jordan	1959	$100
❏ SR-60101 [S]	The Moods of Taft Jordan	1959	$100

MOODSVILLE

❏ MVLP-21 [M]	Mood Indigo -- Taft Jordan Plays Duke Ellington	1961	$50
— Green label			

Beverly Kenney, *Born to Be Blue*, Decca DL 8850, **$300**.

Stan Kenton, *Kenton Showcase – The Music of Bill Holman*, Capitol H 526, 10-inch LP, **$200**.

Morgana King, *Folk Songs A La King*, United Artists UAS 6026, **$175**.

Morgana King, For You, For Me, For Evermore, EmArcy MG 36079, **$200**.

Number	Title	Yr	NM
❑ MVLP-21 [M]	Mood Indigo -- Taft Jordan Plays Duke Ellington	1965	$30

—Blue label, trident logo at right

STATUS

❑ 21 [M]	Mood Indigo -- Taft Jordan Plays Duke Ellington	196?	$30

—Reissue of Moodsville 21

JORGENSMANN, THEO

Clarinetist.

Albums

CMP

Number	Title	Yr	NM
❑ CMP-4-ST	Go Ahead Clarinet	198?	$25
❑ CMP-19-ST	Laterna Magica	198?	$25
❑ CMP-15-ST	Next Adventure	198?	$25
❑ CMP-6-ST	Song of BoWaGe	198?	$25

JOYRIDE

Ten-member all-star band.

Albums

NOVA

❑ 8705	Joyride	1987	$25

JPJ QUARTET, THE

Members: BUDD JOHNSON; DILL JONES; Bill Pemberton (bass); Oliver Jackson (drums).

Albums

MASTER JAZZ

❑ 8111	Montreux '71	1972	$35

JUJU

See ONENESS OF JUJU.

JUNGLE CRAWLERS, THE

Albums

STOMP OFF

❑ SOS-1084	Stompin' On Down	1985	$25

JURGENS, DICK

Trumpeter and bandleader.

Albums

HINDSIGHT

Number	Title	Yr	NM
❑ HSR-138	Dick Jurgens and His Orchestra 1937-38	198?	$25
❑ HSR-111	Dick Jurgens and His Orchestra 1937-39	198?	$25
❑ HSR-191	Dick Jurgens and His Orchestra 1938	198?	$25

JURIS, VIC

Guitarist.

Albums

MUSE

Number	Title	Yr	NM
❑ MR-5265	Bleecker Street	1982	$30
❑ MR-5206	Horizon Drive	1979	$35
❑ MR-5150	Road Song	1978	$35

K

KALAPARUSHA

See KALAPARUSHA MAURICE McINTYRE.

KALLAO, ALEX

Pianist.

Albums

BATON

Number	Title	Yr	NM
❑ BL-1205 [M]	Alex Kallao in Concert, University of Ottawa	1957	$60

RCA VICTOR

❑ LJM-1011 [M]	Evening at the Embers	1954	$50

KAMINSKY, MAX

Trumpeter. Also see BOBBY HACKETT.

Albums

Number	Title	Yr	NM

CHIAROSCURO

❑ 176	When Summer Is Gone	1977	$30

COMMODORE

❑ FL-20019 [10]	Max Kaminsky	1952	$50

CONCERT HALL JAZZ

❑ 1009 [10]	Windy City Jazz	1955	$100

MGM

❑ E-261 [10]	When the Saints Go Marching In	1954	$100

RCA VICTOR

❑ LJM-3003 [10]	Jazz on the Campus, Ltd.	1954	$50

UNITED ARTISTS

❑ UAL-3174 [M]	Max Goes East	1961	$25
❑ UAS-6174 [S]	Max Goes East	1961	$30

KAMUCA, RICHIE

Tenor saxophone player. Also see AL COHN; BILL PERKINS.

Albums

CONCORD JAZZ

Number	Title	Yr	NM
❑ CJ-96	Charlie	1979	$60
❑ CJ-39	Drop Me Off in Harlem	1977	$35
❑ CJ-41	Richie	1977	$50

FANTASY

❑ OJC-1760	West Coast Jazz in Hi-Fi	198?	$30

HIFI

❑ R-604 [M]	Jazz Erotica	1957	$200
❑ J-609 [M]	West Coast Jazz in Hi-Fi	1959	$60
❑ JS-609 [S]	West Coast Jazz in Hi-Fi	1959	$50

JAZZZ

❑ 104	Richie Kamuca 1976	1976	$30

KAPLAN, ARTIE

Baritone saxophone player, producer and arranger.

Albums

HOPI

Number	Title	Yr	NM
❑ VHS901	Confessions of a Male Chauvinist Pig	1971	$30

KAPLAN, LEIGH

Pianist.

Albums

CAMBRIA

Number	Title	Yr	NM
❑ C-1019	Dizzy Fingers	1987	$25
❑ C-1016	Shades of Dring	198?	$25

KARMA

Albums

HORIZON

Number	Title	Yr	NM
❑ SP-713	Celebration	1976	$35
❑ SP-723	For Everybody	1977	$35

KARUKAS

Full name: Gregg Karukas. Keyboard player and pianist.

Albums

OPTIMISM

❑ OP-3101	The Nightowl	1988	$25

KASAI, KIMIKO

Female singer.

Albums

CATALYST

❑ 7900	One for the Lady	1977	$30

KASSEL, ART

Bandleader.

Albums

HINDSIGHT

Number	Title	Yr	NM
❑ HSR-162	Kassels In The Air Orchestra 1944	198?	$25
❑ HSR-170	Kassels In The Air Orchestra 1945	198?	$25

KAPP

❑ KL-1248 [M]	Dance to the Music of Art Kassel	1962	$25

KATINDIG, BOY

Keyboard player and composer.

Albums

Number	Title	Yr	NM

PAUSA

❑ 7137	Midnight Lady	198?	$25

KATZ, BRUCE

Keyboard player and pianist.

Albums

AUDIOQUEST

Number	Title	Yr	NM
❑ AQ-1012	Crescent Crawl	199?	$30
❑ AQ-1026	Transformation	1994	$30

KATZ, DICK; DEREK SMITH; RENE URTREGER

All three are pianists. Also see DICK KATZ; DEREK SMITH.

Albums

ATLANTIC

Number	Title	Yr	NM
❑ 1287 [M]	John Lewis Presents Jazz Piano International	1958	$300

—Black label

❑ 1287 [M]	John Lewis Presents Jazz Piano International	1961	$150

—Multicolor label, white "fan" logo at right

KATZ, DICK

Pianist and composer.

Albums

ATLANTIC

Number	Title	Yr	NM
❑ 1314 [M]	Piano and Pin	1959	$300

—Black label

❑ 1314 [M]	Piano and Pin	1961	$150

—Multicolor label, white "fan" logo at right

❑ SD1314 [S]	Piano and Pin	1959	$300

—Green label

❑ SD1314 [S]	Piano and Pin	1961	$150

—Multicolor label, white "fan" logo at right

KATZ, FRED

Pianist and cellist.

Albums

DECCA

Number	Title	Yr	NM
❑ DL9213 [M]	4-5-6 Trio	1958	$120
❑ DL79213 [S]	4-5-6 Trio	1958	$120
❑ DL9217 [M]	Fred Katz and Jammers	1958	$120
❑ DL9202 [M]	Soulo Cello	1958	$100
❑ DL79202 [S]	Soulo Cello	1958	$100

WARNER BROS.

❑ W1277 [M]	Folk Songs for Far Out Folks	1959	$30
❑ WS1277 [S]	Folk Songs for Far Out Folks	1959	$30

KAWAGUCHI, GEORGE, AND ART BLAKEY

Kawaguchi is a drummer. Also see ART BLAKEY.

Albums

STORYVILLE

❑ 4100	Killer Joe	1982	$30

KAWASAKI, RYO

Guitarist.

Albums

INNER CITY

Number	Title	Yr	NM
❑ IC-6006	Eight Mile Road	197?	$35
❑ IC-6016	Prism	197?	$35

RCA VICTOR

❑ APL1-1855	Juice	1977	$35

KAYE, MILTON

Pianist.

Albums

GOLDEN CREST

Number	Title	Yr	NM
❑ GC-31032	Ragtime at the Rosebud	197?	$30
❑ CRS-4127	The Classic Rags of Joe Lamb	197?	$30

—Single-sided LP in gatefold sleeve (B-side is blank)

KAYE, SAMMY

Clarinet player, more famous as a bandleader.

Albums

COLUMBIA

❑ CL2541 [10]	Christmas Serenade	1955	$50

—House Party Series" issue

Number	Title	Yr	NM
❑ CL1571 [M]	Dancing on a Silken Cloud	1960	$35
❑ CS8371 [S]	Dancing on a Silken Cloud	1960	$50
❑ CL668 [M]	Music, Maestro, Please!	195?	$30
❑ CL885 [M]	My Fair Lady (For Dancing)	1956	$50
❑ CL1018 [M]	Popular American Waltzes	1957	$50
❑ CL1236 [M]	Strauss Waltzes for Dancing	1959	$35
❑ CL6155 [10]	Sunday Serenade	1953	$40
❑ CL964 [M]	Sunday Serenade	1957	$50
❑ CL561 [M]	Swing and Sway with Sammy Kaye	195?	$30

DECCA

Number	Title	Yr	NM
❑ DL4070 [M]	Christmas Day with Sammy Kaye	1960	$30
❑ DL74070 [S]	Christmas Day with Sammy Kaye	1960	$35
❑ DL4502 [M]	Come Dance to the Hits	1964	$30
❑ DL74502 [S]	Come Dance to the Hits	1964	$35
❑ DL4357 [M]	Come Dance with Me	1963	$30
❑ DL74357 [S]	Come Dance with Me	1963	$35
❑ DL4590 [M]	Come Dance with Me (Vol. 2)	1965	$30
❑ DL74590 [S]	Come Dance with Me (Vol. 2)	1965	$35
❑ DL4924 [M]	Dance and Be Happy	1967	$35
❑ DL74924 [S]	Dance and Be Happy	1967	$30
❑ DL4655 [M]	Dancetime	1965	$30
❑ DL74655 [S]	Dancetime	1965	$35
❑ DL4121 [M]	Dance to My Golden Favorites	1961	$30
❑ DL74121 [S]	Dance to My Golden Favorites	1961	$35
❑ DL4424 [M]	Dreamy Serenades	1963	$30
❑ DL74424 [S]	Dreamy Serenades	1963	$35
❑ DL4306 [M]	For Your Dancing Pleasure	1962	$30
❑ DL74306 [S]	For Your Dancing Pleasure	1962	$35
❑ DL4970 [M]	Glory of Love	1967	$35
❑ DL74970 [S]	Glory of Love	1967	$30
❑ DL4823 [M]	Let's Face the Music	1967	$30
❑ DL74823 [S]	Let's Face the Music	1967	$35
❑ DL4247 [M]	New Twists on Old Favorites	1962	$30
❑ DL74247 [S]	New Twists on Old Favorites	1962	$35
❑ DL4215 [M]	Sexy Strings and Subtle Saxes	1962	$30
❑ DL74215 [S]	Sexy Strings and Subtle Saxes	1962	$35
❑ DL4754 [M]	Shall We Dance	1966	$30
❑ DL74754 [S]	Shall We Dance	1966	$35
❑ DL4071 [M]	Sing and Sway with Sammy Kaye	1960	$30
❑ DL74071 [S]	Sing and Sway with Sammy Kaye	1960	$35
❑ DL4154 [M]	Songs I Wish I Had Played…The First Time Around	1961	$30
❑ DL74154 [S]	Songs I Wish I Had Played…The First Time Around	1961	$35
❑ DL4862 [M]	Swing & Sway in Hawaii	1967	$35
❑ DL74862 [S]	Swing & Sway in Hawaii	1967	$30
❑ DL4687 [M]	Swing and Sway Au-Go-Go	1965	$30
❑ DL74687 [S]	Swing and Sway Au-Go-Go	1965	$35
❑ DL75106	The 30's Are Here to Stay	1968	$30

HARMONY

Number	Title	Yr	NM
❑ HS11261	All-Time Waltz Favorites	1968	$30
❑ HL7357 [M]	Beautiful Waltzes for Dancing	196?	$35
❑ HS11157 [R]	Beautiful Waltzes for Dancing	196?	$30
❑ KH32013	Best of the Big Bands	1971	$25
❑ HL7187 [M]	Dancing with Sammy Kaye in Hi-Fi	196?	$35
❑ HS11087 [R]	Dancing with Sammy Kaye in Hi-Fi	196?	$30
❑ HS11377	Harbor Lights	1970	$25
❑ HL7230 [M]	In a Dancing Mood	196?	$35
❑ HS11121 [R]	My Fair Lady	1964	$30
❑ HL7321 [M]	My Fair Lady	1964	$35

HINDSIGHT

Number	Title	Yr	NM
❑ HSR-402	22 Original Big Band Recordings	198?	$30
❑ HSR-158	1940-41	198?	$25
❑ HSR-163	1942-43	198?	$25
❑ HSR-207	1944-46	198?	$25

MCA

Number	Title	Yr	NM
❑ 191	Dance to My Golden Favorites	1973	$25
—Reissue of Decca 74121			
❑ 205	Plays Swing & Sway	1973	$25
—Reissue of Decca 74306			
❑ 278	The 30's Are Here to Stay	197?	$25
—Reissue of Decca material			
❑ 4027	The Best of Sammy Kaye	197?	$30

PROJECT 3

Number	Title	Yr	NM
❑ PR-5065SD	If You've Got the Time	1972	$25
❑ PR-5065QD [Q]	If You've Got the Time	1972	$30

RCA CAMDEN

Number	Title	Yr	NM
❑ CAL-261 [M]	Music for Dancing	1956	$50
❑ CAL-355 [M]	Swing and Sway with Sammy Kaye	1957	$50

RCA VICTOR

Number	Title	Yr	NM
❑ LPM15 [10]	Sammy Kaye Plays Irving Berlin for Dancing	1950	$100
❑ LPM-3966 [M]	The Best of Sammy Kaye	1967	$50
❑ LSP-3966 [R]	The Best of Sammy Kaye	1967	$30
❑ VPM-6070	This Is Sammy Kaye	1972	$30

VOCALION

Number	Title	Yr	NM
❑ VL73919	Theme from "Love Story"	1971	$25

KAZ, FRED

Pianist.

Albums

ATLANTIC

Number	Title	Yr	NM
❑ 1335 [M]	Eastern Exposure	1960	$250
—Multicolor label, white "fan" logo at right			
❑ SD1335 [S]	Eastern Exposure	1960	$250
—Multicolor label, white "fan" logo at right			

KEATING, JOHNNY

Trombonist, pianist, arranger and composer.

Albums

BALLY

Number	Title	Yr	NM
❑ BAL-12001 [M]	English Jazz	1956	$50

DOT

Number	Title	Yr	NM
❑ DLP-3066 [M]	Swinging Scots	1957	$80

KEENE, BOB

Clarinet player and bandleader, best known as the founder of the Del-Fi record label.

Albums

ANDEX

Number	Title	Yr	NM
❑ S-4001 [M]	Solo for 7	1958	$50

DEL-FI

Number	Title	Yr	NM
❑ DFLP-1222 [M]	Twist to Radio KRLA	1962	$30
❑ DFLP-1202 [M]	Unforgettable Love Songs of the 50's	1959	$40

GENE NORMAN

Number	Title	Yr	NM
❑ GNP-149 [10]	Bob Keene	1954	$50

KEISER TWINS, THE

Peter Keiser (bass) and Walter Keiser (drums).

Albums

CBS

Number	Title	Yr	NM
❑ FM44737	The Keiser Twins	1988	$25

KELLAWAY, ROGER, AND RED MITCHELL

Also see each artist's individual listings.

Albums

STASH

Number	Title	Yr	NM
❑ ST-271	Fifty/Fifty	1988	$25

KELLAWAY, ROGER

Pianist, bass player, arranger and composer.

Albums

A&M

Number	Title	Yr	NM
❑ SP-3034	Cello Quartet	1970	$30
❑ SP-3040	Center of the Circle	1972	$35
❑ SP-3618	Come to the Meadow	1974	$25

CHOICE

Number	Title	Yr	NM
❑ CRS-6833	Ain't Misbehavin'	1989	$25

DISCWASHER

Number	Title	Yr	NM
❑ 003	Nostalgia Suite	1979	$25

DOBRE

Number	Title	Yr	NM
❑ 1045	Say That Again	1978	$25

PACIFIC JAZZ

Number	Title	Yr	NM
❑ PJ-10122 [M]	Spirit Feel	196?	$25
❑ ST-20122 [S]	Spirit Feel	196?	$35
❑ LN-10070	Spirit Feel	198?	$20
—Budget-line reissue			

PRESTIGE

Number	Title	Yr	NM
❑ PRST-7399 [S]	The Roger Kellaway Trio	1965	$30

REGINA

Number	Title	Yr	NM
❑ R-298 [M]	Portraits	1964	$25
❑ RS-298 [S]	Portraits	1964	$30

VOSS

Number	Title	Yr	NM
❑ VLP1-42935	Nostalgia Suite	1988	$25

WORLD PACIFIC

Number	Title	Yr	NM
❑ WP-21861 [M]	Stride	1967	$100
❑ WPS-21861 [S]	Stride	1967	$100

KELLER, ALLEN

Male singer.

Albums

CHARLIE PARKER

Number	Title	Yr	NM
❑ PLP-817 [M]	A New Look at the World	1962	$30
❑ PLP-817S [S]	A New Look at the World	1962	$30

KELLER, HAL

Pianist.

Albums

SAND

Number	Title	Yr	NM
❑ 7 [M]	Hal Keller Debut	1957	$150

SOUND

Number	Title	Yr	NM
❑ 602 [M]	Hal Keller Debut	1959	$150

KELLEY, PAT

Guitarist.

Albums

NOVA

Number	Title	Yr	NM
❑ 8704-1	Views of the Future	1988	$25

KELLEY, PECK

Pianist and bandleader.

Albums

COMMODORE

Number	Title	Yr	NM
❑ XF2-17017	Peck Kelley Jam	198?	$30

KELLIN, ORANGE

Clarinetist.

Albums

BIOGRAPH

Number	Title	Yr	NM
❑ CEN-7	Orange Kellin in New Orleans	197?	$25

KELLY, BEVERLY

Female singer.

Albums

AUDIO FIDELITY

Number	Title	Yr	NM
❑ AFLP-1874 [M]	Beverly Kelly Sings	1958	$30
❑ AFSD-5874 [S]	Beverly Kelly Sings	1958	$40

RIVERSIDE

Number	Title	Yr	NM
❑ RS-9345 [S]	Bev Kelly In Person	1960	$200
❑ 6042	Bev Kelly In Person	197?	$30
❑ RLP-328 [M]	Love Locked Out	1960	$200
❑ RS-9328 [S]	Love Locked Out	1960	$200
❑ 6052	Love Locked Out	197?	$30

KELLY, ED

Pianist, organist, arranger and composer.

Albums

THERESA

Number	Title	Yr	NM
❑ 106	Ed Kelly and Friend	197?	$35
❑ 103	Music from the Black Museum	197?	$30

KELLY, GEORGE

Tenor saxophone player.

Albums

STASH

Number	Title	Yr	NM
❑ 240	George Kelly Plays Music of Don Redman	198?	$25

KELLY, JACK

Albums

JUBILEE

Number	Title	Yr	NM
❑ JLP-21 [10]	Jack Kelly's Badinage	1955	$60

KELLY, JOE

Albums

BLACKBIRD

Number	Title	Yr	NM
❑ 4001	Blackbird Presents Joe Kelly	197?	$30

Number	Title	Yr	NM

KELLY, JULIE, AND TOM GARVIN
Garvin is a pianist. Also see JULIE KELLY.

Albums

CMG

| ❏ CML-8017 | Some Other Time | 1989 | $30 |

KELLY, JULIE
Female singer.

Albums

PAUSA

| ❏ 7186 | Never Let Me Go | 1986 | $25 |
| ❏ 7154 | We're On Our Way | 198? | $25 |

KELLY, NANCY
Female singer and arranger.

Albums

AMHERST

| ❏ AMH-3317 | Live Jazz | 1988 | $25 |

KELLY, WYNTON
Pianist and composer. Also see DONNA DRAKE; STEVE LACY.

Albums

BLUE NOTE

| ❏ BLP-5025 [10] | Piano Interpretations by Wynton Kelly | 1953 | $400 |

DELMARK

| ❏ DS-441 | The Last Trio Session | 1989 | $50 |

EPITAPH

| ❏ E-4007 | Wynton Kelly 1931-1971 | 1975 | $50 |

FANTASY

| ❏ OJC-033 | Kelly Blue | 198? | $30 |
| ❏ OJC-401 | Wynton Kelly Piano | 1989 | $35 |

JAZZLAND

| ❏ JLP-83 [M] | Whisper Not | 1962 | $40 |
| ❏ JLP-983 [S] | Whisper Not | 1962 | $100 |

MILESTONE

| ❏ MSP-9004 | Full View | 1968 | $60 |
| ❏ M-47026 | Keep It Moving | 1975 | $60 |

RIVERSIDE

❏ RLP 12-298 [M]	Kelly Blue	1959	$400
❏ RLP-1142 [S]	Kelly Blue	1959	$250
❏ 6114	Kelly Blue	197?	$35
❏ 6043	Whisper Not	197?	$35

| ❏ RLP 12-254 [M] | Wynton Kelly Piano | 1957 | $350 |

TRIP

| ❏ TLX-5010 | Smokin' | 197? | $35 |

VEE JAY

❏ VJ-1086 [M]	Best of Wynton Kelly	1964	$40
❏ VJS-1086 [S]	Best of Wynton Kelly	1964	$50
❏ VJS-3072-2	Final Notes	1977	$30
❏ LP-3011 [M]	Kelly at Midnite	1960	$80
❏ SR-3011 [S]	Kelly at Midnite	1960	$500
❏ LP-1016 [M]	Kelly Great	1960	$80
❏ SR-1016 [S]	Kelly Great	1960	$100
❏ LP-3004 [M]	Kelly Great	1960	$60
—Reissue of LP-1016			
❏ VJS-3038	Someday My Prince Will Come	1977	$50
❏ LP-3022 [M]	Wynton Kelly	1961	$100
❏ SR-3022 [S]	Wynton Kelly	1961	$120
❏ VJS-3071	Wynton Kelly In Concert	1977	$50

VERVE

❏ V-8576 [M]	Comin' In the Back Door	1964	$60
❏ V6-8576 [S]	Comin' In the Back Door	1964	$40
❏ V-8588 [M]	It's All Right	1964	$60

Number	Title	Yr	NM

❏ V6-8588 [S]	It's All Right	1964	$30
❏ V-8633 [M]	Smokin' at the Half Note	1965	$50
❏ V6-8633 [S]	Smokin' at the Half Note	1965	$30
❏ V-8622 [M]	Undiluted	1965	$40
❏ V6-8622 [S]	Undiluted	1965	$50

XANADU

| ❏ 198 | Blues On Purpose | 198? | $25 |

KEMP, HAL
Bandleader.

Albums

CIRCLE

| ❏ C-25 | Hal Kemp and His Orchestra 198? 1934 | | $25 |

HINDSIGHT

❏ HSR-143	Hal Kemp and His Orchestra 198? 1934		$25
❏ HSR-161	Hal Kemp and His Orchestra 198? 1934, Volume 2		$25
❏ HSR-222	Hal Kemp and His Orchestra 198? 1936		$25

KENIA
Female singer.

Albums

ZEBRA

| ❏ ZEB-42149 | Distant Horizon: Rio/New York | 1988 | $30 |
| ❏ ZEB-5967 | Initial Thrill | 1987 | $30 |

KENNEDY, CHARLIE
See CHARLIE VENTURA.

KENNEY, BEVERLY
Female singer.

Albums

DECCA

❏ DL8850 [M]	Born to Be Blue	1959	$300
❏ DL8948 [M]	Like Yesterday	1960	$200
❏ DL78948 [S]	Like Yesterday	1960	$300

ROOST

❏ RST-2206 [M]	Beverly Kenney Sings for Johnny Smith	1956	$300
❏ RST-2218 [M]	Beverly Kenney with Jimmy Jones and the Basie-ites	1957	$300
❏ RST-2212 [M]	Come Swing with Me	1956	$300

KENNY G
Saxophone player, mostly soprano and alto.

Albums

ARISTA

❏ AL8-8427	Duotones	1986	$20
❏ AL8-8192	G Force	1984	$20
❏ AL8-8282	Gravity	1985	$20
❏ AL9608	Kenny G	1982	$25
❏ ALB6-8299	Kenny G	1985	$20
—Reissue of 9608			
❏ A2L-8613	Kenny G Live	1989	$30
❏ AL-8457	Silhouette	1988	$20

KENT, MARSHALL

Albums

HERWIN

| ❏ 301 | Pallet on the Floor | 197? | $35 |

KENTON, STAN, AND TEX RITTER
Ritter is a male country-western singer not otherwise listed in this book. Also see STAN KENTON.

Albums

CAPITOL

| ❏ T1757 [M] | Stan Kenton/Tex Ritter | 1962 | $200 |
| ❏ ST1757 [S] | Stan Kenton/Tex Ritter | 1962 | $250 |

KENTON, STAN
Pianist, bandleader, composer and arranger. He pioneered what became known as "progressive jazz."

Albums

CAPITOL

| ❏ T1985 [M] | Adventures in Blues | 1963 | $50 |
| —Black label with colorband, Capitol logo at top | | | |

Number	Title	Yr	NM

❏ ST1985 [S]	Adventures in Blues	1963	$75
—Black label with colorband, Capitol logo at top			
❏ T1796 [M]	Adventures in Jazz	1962	$50
—Black label with colorband, Capitol logo at top			
❏ ST1796 [S]	Adventures in Jazz	1962	$75
—Black label with colorband, Capitol logo at top			
❏ T1844 [M]	Adventures in Time	1963	$50
—Black label with colorband, Capitol logo at top			
❏ ST1844 [S]	Adventures in Time	1963	$75
—Black label with colorband, Capitol logo at top			
❏ T1621 [M]	A Merry Christmas	1961	$75
❏ ST1621 [S]	A Merry Christmas	1961	$80
❏ H172 [10]	A Presentation of Progressive Jazz	1950	$200
❏ T172 [M]	A Presentation of Progressive Jazz	195?	$75
❏ T1931 [M]	Artistry in Bossa Nova	1963	$60
❏ ST1931 [S]	Artistry in Bossa Nova	1963	$75
❏ M-11027	Artistry in Jazz	1972	$25
❏ H167 [10]	Artistry in Rhythm	1950	$200
❏ T167 [M]	Artistry in Rhythm	195?	$60
—Turquoise label			
❏ T167 [M]	Artistry in Rhythm	1959	$75
—Black label with colorband, Capitol logo at left			
❏ T167 [M]	Artistry in Rhythm	1962	$60
—Black label with colorband, Capitol logo at top			
❏ DT167 [R]	Artistry in Rhythm	1969	$40
❏ SM-167 [R]	Artistry in Rhythm	1975	$20
—Reissue with new prefix			
❏ T2132 [M]	Artistry in Voices and Brass	1964	$60
—Black label with colorband, Capitol logo at top			
❏ ST2132 [S]	Artistry in Voices and Brass	1964	$75
—Black label with colorband, Capitol logo at top			
❏ T995 [M]	Back to Balboa	1958	$60
—Turquoise label			
❏ H353 [10]	City of Glass	1952	$200
❏ T736 [M]	City of Glass/This Modern World	1956	$60
—Combination of 353 and 460 onto one 12-inch LP, turquoise label			
❏ H358 [10]	Classics	1952	$200
❏ T358 [M]	Classics	195?	$60
—Turquoise label			
❏ T666 [M]	Contemporary Concepts	1955	$200
—Turquoise label			
❏ T731 [M]	Cuban Fire!	1956	$60
—Turquoise label			
❏ T731 [M]	Cuban Fire!	1959	$80
—Black label with colorband, Capitol logo at left			
❏ SM-11794 [M]	Cuban Fire!	1978	$25
—Reissue of Capitol T 731			
❏ T656 [M]	Duet	1955	$75
—With June Christy; turquoise label			
❏ H155 [10]	Encores	1950	$200
❏ T155 [M]	Encores	195?	$60
—Turquoise label			
❏ ST2974	Finian's Rainbow	1968	$60
❏ P189 [10]	Innovations in Modern Music	1950	$200
❏ ST2932	Jazz Compositions of Dee Barton	1968	$60
❏ T1460 [M]	Kenton at the Las Vegas Tropicana	1961	$100
—Black label with colorband, Capitol logo at left			
❏ ST1460 [S]	Kenton at the Las Vegas Tropicana	1961	$80
—Black label with colorband, Capitol logo at left			
❏ W724 [M]	Kenton in Hi-Fi	1956	$75
—Gray label			
❏ W724 [M]	Kenton in Hi-Fi	1959	$80
—Black label with colorband, logo at left			
❏ SW724 [S]	Kenton in Hi-Fi	1959	$150
—Black label with colorband, logo at left; one fewer track than mono version			
❏ SW724 [S]	Kenton in Hi-Fi	1962	$100
—Black label with colorband, logo at top; one fewer track than mono version			
❏ T2655 [M]	Kenton Plays for Today	1966	$60
—Black label with colorband, Capitol logo at top			
❏ ST2655 [S]	Kenton Plays for Today	1966	$75
—Black label with colorband, Capitol logo at top			
❏ TAO2217 [M]	Kenton Plays Wagner	1964	$60
—Black label with colorband, Capitol logo at top			
❏ STAO2217 [S]	Kenton Plays Wagner	1964	$75
—Black label with colorband, Capitol logo at top			
❏ W524 [M]	Kenton Showcase	1954	$75

Morgana King, *Let Me Love You*, United Artists UAL 30020-S, **$175**.

Teddi King, *To You from Teddi King*, RCA Victor LPM-1313, **$175**.

King Pleasure/Annie Ross, *King Pleasure Sings/Annie Ross Sings*, Prestige PRLP-7128, yellow label with W. 50th St. address, **$300**.

Rahsaan Roland Kirk and Al Hibbler, *A Meeting of the Times*, Atlantic SD 1630, **$35**.

Number	Title	Yr	NM
❑ H526 [10]	Kenton Showcase -- The Music of Bill Holman	1954	$200
❑ H525 [10]	Kenton Showcase -- The Music of Bill Russo	1954	$200
❑ T1609 [M]	Kenton's West Side Story	1961	$100
—Black label with colorband, Capitol logo at left			
❑ ST1609 [S]	Kenton's West Side Story	1961	$80
—Black label with colorband, Capitol logo at left			
❑ T1609 [M]	Kenton's West Side Story	1961	$75
—Black label with colorband, Capitol logo at top			
❑ ST1609 [S]	Kenton's West Side Story	1961	$60
—Black label with colorband, Capitol logo at top			
❑ SM-12037	Kenton's West Side Story	1979	$25
—Reissue of Capitol ST 1609			
❑ T810 [M]	Kenton with Voices	1957	$75
—Turquoise label			
❑ T1130 [M]	Lush Interlude	1959	$100
—Black label with colorband, Capitol logo at left			
❑ ST1130 [S]	Lush Interlude	1959	$80
—Black label with colorband, Capitol logo at left			
❑ H190 [10]	Milestones	1950	$200
❑ T190 [M]	Milestones	195?	$75
—Turquoise label			
❑ T190 [M]	Milestones	196?	$100
—Black colorband label, logo at left			
❑ ST-305	Music from "Hair	1969	$50
❑ H383 [10]	New Concepts of Artistry in Rhythm	1953	$200
❑ T383 [M]	New Concepts of Artistry in Rhythm	195?	$75
—Turquoise label			
❑ H421 [10]	Popular Favorites	1953	$200
❑ T421 [M]	Popular Favorites	195?	$75
—Turquoise label			
❑ H462 [10]	Portraits on Standards	1953	$200
❑ T462 [M]	Portraits on Standards	195?	$75
—Turquoise label			
❑ T462 [M]	Portraits on Standards	196?	$100
—Black colorband label, logo at left			
❑ H386 [10]	Prologue: This Is an Orchestra	1953	$200
❑ T932 [M]	Rendezvous with Kenton	1957	$75
—Turquoise label			
❑ TBO1327 [M]	Road Show	1960	$75
—Black label with colorband, Capitol logo at left			
❑ STBO1327 [S]	Road Show	1960	$100
—Black label with colorband, Capitol logo at left			
❑ TBO1327 [M]	Road Show	1962	$80
—Black label with colorband, Capitol logo at top			
❑ STBO1327 [S]	Road Show	1962	$50
—Black label with colorband, Capitol logo at top			
❑ H426 [10]	Sketches on Standards	1953	$200
❑ T426 [M]	Sketches on Standards	195?	$75
—Turquoise label			
❑ T1394 [M]	Standards in Silhouette	1960	$100
—Black label with colorband, Capitol logo at left			
❑ ST1394 [S]	Standards in Silhouette	1960	$80
—Black label with colorband, Capitol logo at left			
❑ T1394 [M]	Standards in Silhouette	1962	$50
—Black label with colorband, Capitol logo at top			
❑ ST1394 [S]	Standards in Silhouette	1962	$60
—Black label with colorband, Capitol logo at top			
❑ STCL-575	Stan Kenton	1970	$80
❑ MAS2424 [M]	Stan Kenton Conducts the Los Angeles Neophonic Orchestra	1966	$60
—Black label with colorband, Capitol logo at top			
❑ SMAS2424 [S]	Stan Kenton Conducts the Los Angeles Neophonic Orchestra	1966	$50
—Black label with colorband, Capitol logo at top			
❑ L248 [10]	Stan Kenton Presents	1951	$200
❑ T248 [M]	Stan Kenton Presents	195?	$75
—Turquoise label			
❑ T248 [M]	Stan Kenton Presents	196?	$100
—Black colorband label, logo at left			
❑ T248 [M]	Stan Kenton Presents	196?	$50
—Black colorband label, logo at top			
❑ T2327 [M]	Stan Kenton's Greatest Hits	1965	$60
—Black label with colorband, Capitol logo at top			
❑ DT2327 [R]	Stan Kenton's Greatest Hits	1965	$50
—Black label with colorband, Capitol logo at top			
❑ SM-2327	Stan Kenton's Greatest Hits	197?	$20
—Reissue with new prefix			
❑ N-16182	Stan Kenton's Greatest Hits	1984	$20
—Budget-line reissue			
❑ T1068 [M]	The Ballad Style of Stan Kenton	1959	$100
—Black label with colorband, Capitol logo at left			
❑ ST1068 [S]	The Ballad Style of Stan Kenton	1959	$80
—Black label with colorband, Capitol logo at left			
❑ T1068 [M]	The Ballad Style of Stan Kenton	1962	$75
—Black label with colorband, Capitol logo at top			
❑ ST1068 [S]	The Ballad Style of Stan Kenton	1962	$60
—Black label with colorband, Capitol logo at top			
❑ STB-12016	The Comprehensive Kenton	1979	$35
❑ TDB569 [M]	The Kenton Era	1955	$250
—Box set with 44-page book			
❑ WDX569 [M]	The Kenton Era	196?	$250
—Box set with 44-page book; limited edition reissue with black label, Capitol logo at left			
❑ PRO-206/7 [DJ]	The Kenton Era (Excerpts)	1955	$75
❑ T1276 [M]	The Kenton Touch	1960	$100
—Black label with colorband, Capitol logo at left			
❑ ST1276 [S]	The Kenton Touch	1960	$80
—Black label with colorband, Capitol logo at left			
❑ T1533 [M]	The Romantic Approach	1961	$100
—Black label with colorband, Capitol logo at left			
❑ ST1533 [S]	The Romantic Approach	1961	$80
—Black label with colorband, Capitol logo at left			
❑ T1533 [M]	The Romantic Approach	1961	$50
—Black label with colorband, Capitol logo at top			
❑ ST1533 [S]	The Romantic Approach	1961	$60
—Black label with colorband, Capitol logo at top			
❑ T1674 [M]	The Sophisticated Approach	1962	$60
—Black label with colorband, Capitol logo at top			
❑ ST1674 [S]	The Sophisticated Approach	1962	$50
—Black label with colorband, Capitol logo at top			
❑ T1166 [M]	The Stage Door Swings	1959	$100
—Black label with colorband, Capitol logo at left			
❑ ST1166 [S]	The Stage Door Swings	1959	$80
—Black label with colorband, Capitol logo at left			
❑ STCL2989	The Stan Kenton Deluxe Set	1968	$80
❑ ST2810	The World We Know	1968	$60
❑ H460 [10]	This Modern World	1953	$200
❑ W1305 [M]	Viva Kenton!	1960	$100
—Black label with colorband, Capitol logo at left			
❑ SW1305 [S]	Viva Kenton!	1960	$80
—Black label with colorband, Capitol logo at left			

CREATIVE WORLD

Number	Title	Yr	NM
❑ ST1070	7.5 on the Richter Scale	1973	$25
❑ ST1037 [R]	A Concert in Progessive Jazz	197?	$20
—Reissue of Capitol T 172			
❑ ST1012	Adventures in Blues	197?	$25
—Reissue of Capitol ST 1985			
❑ ST1010	Adventures in Jazz	197?	$25
—Reissue of Capitol ST 1796			
❑ ST1025	Adventures in Standards	197?	$25
❑ ST1011	Adventures in Time	197?	$25
—Reissue of Capitol ST 1844			
❑ ST1045	Artistry in Bossa Nova	197?	$25
❑ ST1043 [R]	Artistry in Rhythm	197?	$20
—Reissue of Capitol DT 167			
❑ ST1038	Artistry in Voices and Brass	197?	$25
—Reissue of Capitol ST 2132			
❑ ST1031	Back to Balboa	197?	$25
—Reissue of Capitol T 995			
❑ ST1065	Birthday in Britain	1973	$25
❑ ST1006 [R]	City of Glass/This Modern World	197?	$20
—Reissue of Capitol T 736			
❑ ST1027 [R]	Collector's Choice	197?	$20
❑ ST1003 [R]	Contemporary Concepts	197?	$20
—Reissue of Capitol T 666			
❑ ST1008 [R]	Cuban Fire!	197?	$20
—Reissue of Capitol T 731			
❑ ST1048 [R]	Duet	197?	$20
—Reissue of Capitol T 656			
❑ ST1034 [R]	Encores	197?	$20
—Reissue of Capitol T 155			
❑ ST1073	Fire, Fury and Fun	1974	$25
❑ ST1074	Hits in Concert	197?	$25
❑ ST1009 [R]	Innovations in Modern Music	197?	$20
—Reissue of Capitol P 189			
❑ ST1022	Jazz Compositions of Dee Barton	197?	$25
—Reissue of Capitol ST 2932			
❑ ST1077	Journey Into Capricorn	1977	$25
❑ ST1076	Kenton '76	1976	$25
❑ ST1032	Kenton at the Las Vegas Tropicana	197?	$25
—Reissue of Capitol ST 1460			
❑ ST1036 [R]	Kenton By Request, Vol. I	197?	$20
❑ ST1040 [R]	Kenton By Request, Vol. II	197?	$20
❑ ST1062 [R]	Kenton By Request, Vol. III	197?	$20
❑ ST1064 [R]	Kenton By Request, Vol. IV	197?	$20
❑ ST1066 [R]	Kenton By Request, Vol. V	197?	$20
❑ ST1069	Kenton By Request, Vol. VI	197?	$25
❑ ST1004 [R]	Kenton in Stereo	197?	$25
—Reissue of Capitol W 724			
❑ ST1072	Kenton Plays Chicago	1974	$25
❑ ST1024	Kenton Plays Wagner	197?	$25
—Reissue of Capitol STAO 2217			
❑ ST1001	Kenton's Christmas	1970	$30
❑ ST1026 [R]	Kenton Showcase	197?	$20
—Reissue of Capitol W 524			
❑ ST1007	Kenton's West Side Story	197?	$25
—Reissue of Capitol ST 1609			
❑ ST1039 [Q]	Live at Brigham Young	1971	$40
❑ ST1058 [Q]	Live at Butler University	1972	$60
❑ ST1015	Live at Redlands University	1971	$25
❑ ST1005	Lush Interlude	197?	$25
—Reissue of Capitol ST 1130			
❑ ST1047 [R]	Milestones	197?	$20
—Reissue of Capitol T 190			
❑ ST1060 [Q]	National Anthems of the World	1972	$60
❑ ST1002 [R]	New Concepts of Artistry in Rhythm	197?	$25
—Reissue of Capitol T 383			
❑ ST1042 [R]	Portraits on Standards	197?	$20
—Reissue of Capitol T 462			
❑ ST1057	Rendezvous with Kenton	197?	$25
—Reissue of Capitol T 932			
❑ ST1019	Road Show, Volume 1	197?	$25
—Partial reissue of Capitol STBO 1327			
❑ ST1020	Road Show, Volume 2	197?	$25
—Partial reissue of Capitol STBO 1327			
❑ ST1041 [R]	Sketches on Standards	197?	$20
—Reissue of Capitol T 426			
❑ ST1071	Solo	1973	$25
❑ ST1029 [R]	Some Women I've Known	197?	$20
❑ ST1049	Standards in Silhouette	197?	$25
—Reissue of Capitol ST 1394			
❑ ST1013	Stan Kenton Conducts the Los Angeles Neophonic Orchestra	197?	$25
—Reissue of Capitol SMAS 2424			
❑ ST1061 [R]	Stan Kenton -- Formative Years	197?	$20
—Reissue of Decca DL 8259			
❑ ST1023 [R]	Stan Kenton Presents	197?	$20
—Reissue of Capitol T 248			
❑ CW-3005	Stan Kenton Presents Gabe Baltazar	1979	$25
❑ ST1046	Stan Kenton with Jean Turner	197?	$25
❑ ST1059 [Q]	Stan Kenton with the Four Freshmen at Butler University	1972	$60
❑ ST1079	Street of Dreams	197?	$25
❑ ST1068	The Ballad Style of Stan Kenton	197?	$20
—Reissue of Capitol ST 1068			
❑ ST1035 [R]	The Christy Years	197?	$20
❑ ST1080	The Exciting Stan Kenton	197?	$25
❑ ST1028 [R]	The Fabulous Alumni of Stan Kenton	197?	$20
❑ ST1078 [R]	The Jazz Compositions of Stan Kenton	197?	$20
❑ ST1030 [R]	The Kenton Era	197?	$80
—Reissue of Capitol TDB 569			
❑ ST1033	The Kenton Touch	197?	$25
—Reissue of Capitol ST 1276			
❑ ST1050 [R]	The Lighter Side of Stan Kenton	197?	$20
❑ ST1017	The Romantic Approach	197?	$20
—Reissue of Capitol ST 1533			
❑ ST1018	The Sophisticated Approach	197?	$25
—Reissue of Capitol ST 1674			
❑ ST1044	The Stage Door Swings	197?	$25
—Reissue of Capitol ST 1166			
❑ ST1067	Too Much	197?	$25

Number	Title	Yr	NM
❏ ST1063	Viva Kenton!	197?	$25

— Reissue of Capitol SW 1305

DECCA

Number	Title	Yr	NM
❏ DL8259 [M]	Stan Kenton -- Formative Years	195?	$30

— All-black label with silver print

| ❏ DL8259 [M] | Stan Kenton -- Formative Years | 1960 | $35 |

— Black label with color bars

HINDSIGHT

❏ HSR-118	Stan Kenton 1941	1984	$20
❏ HSR-124	Stan Kenton 1941, Volume 2	1984	$20
❏ HSR-136	Stan Kenton 1943-44	1984	$20
❏ HSR-147	Stan Kenton 1944-45	1984	$20
❏ HSR-157	Stan Kenton 1945-47	1984	$20
❏ HSR-195	Stan Kenton 1962	1984	$20

INSIGHT

| ❏ 206 | Stan Kenton and His Orchestra, Volume 1 | 197? | $25 |
| ❏ 217 | Stan Kenton and His Orchestra, Volume 2 | 197? | $25 |

LONDON PHASE 4

| ❏ ST-44276 | Live in Europe | 1976 | $25 |
| ❏ BP44179/80 | Stan Kenton Today | 1972 | $40 |

MOBILE FIDELITY

| ❏ Jan-0091 | Kenton Plays Wagner | 1982 | $60 |

— Audiophile vinyl

MOSAIC

| ❏ MR6-136 | The Complete Capitol Recordings of the Holman and Russo Charts | 199? | $300 |
| ❏ MQ10-163 | The Complete Capitol Studio Recordings of Stan Kenton 1943-47 | 199? | $300 |

SUNBEAM

| ❏ 213 | Artistry in Rhythm, 1944-45 | 197? | $25 |

TIME-LIFE

| ❏ STBB-13 | Big Bands: Stan Kenton | 1984 | $35 |

KENTON, STAN/JUNE CHRISTY/ THE FOUR FRESHMEN

Also see each artist's individual listings.

Albums

CAPITOL

| ❏ STCL-575 | Stan Kenton/June Christy/ The Four Freshmen | 1970 | $100 |

— Reissue of an album by each artist in a 3-LP box -- ST 1796 (Kenton), ST 516 (Christy), ST 1008 (Four Freshmen)

KENYATTA, ROBIN

Alto saxophone player and flutist.

Albums

ATLANTIC

❏ SD1633	Gypsy Man	1972	$25
❏ SD1656	Stompin' at the Savoy	1974	$35
❏ SD1644	Terra Nova	1973	$35

MUSE

| ❏ MR-5095 | Beggars | 1979 | $30 |
| ❏ MR-5062 | Nomusa | 1975 | $30 |

VORTEX

| ❏ 2005 | Until | 1969 | $25 |

KEPPARD, FREDDIE

Cornet player and bandleader.

Albums

HERWIN

| ❏ 101 | Freddie Keppard 1926 | 197? | $30 |

MILESTONE

| ❏ 2014 | Freddie Keppard and Tommy Ladnier | 197? | $30 |

KEROUAC, JACK

Jazz-influenced beat poet and author.

Albums

DOT

| ❏ DLP-3154 [M] | Poetry for the Beat Generation | 1959 | $10000 |

— Acknowledged to be extremely rare; approximately 130 copies were distributed and only a small handful are known to exist today; the same performance is on Hanover 5000; VG value 5000; VG+ value 7500

HANOVER

Number	Title	Yr	NM
❏ HML-5006 [M]	Blues and Haikus	1959	$250

— AL COHN and ZOOT SIMS play saxophones behind Kerouac on this album

RHINO

| ❏ R1-70939 | The Jack Kerouac Collection | 1990 | $120 |

— Box set compiling the Hanover and Verve LPs plus an LP of unreleased material

VERVE

| ❏ MGV-15005 [M] | Readings on the Beat Generation | 1960 | $250 |

KERR, BROOKS, AND PAUL QUINICHETTE

Also see each artist's individual listings.

Albums

FAMOUS DOOR

| ❏ 106 | Preview | 197? | $35 |

KERR, BROOKS

Pianist.

Albums

CHIAROSCURO

| ❏ 2001 | Soda Fountain Rag | 197? | $30 |

KESL, LENNIE

Male singer.

Albums

REVELATION

| ❏ 29 | Walkin' On Air | 1978 | $30 |

KESSEL, BARNEY, AND HERB ELLIS

Also see each artist's individual listings.

Albums

CONCORD JAZZ

| ❏ CJ-34 | Butterfly | 1976 | $30 |

KESSEL, BARNEY, AND RED MITCHELL

Also see each artist's individual listings.

Albums

JAZZ MAN

| ❏ 5025 | Two Way Conversation | 198? | $25 |

KESSEL, BARNEY, AND STEPHANE GRAPPELLI

Also see each artist's individual listings.

Albums

BLACK LION

| ❏ 173 | Limehouse Blues | 197? | $35 |

KESSEL, BARNEY

Guitarist. Also see THE POLL WINNERS.

Albums

BLACK LION

❏ 310	Blue Soul	197?	$35
❏ 210	Summertime in Montreux	197?	$30
❏ 130	Swinging Easy	197?	$30

CONCORD JAZZ

❏ CJ-9	Barney Plays Kessel	197?	$30
❏ CJ-164	Jellybeans	1981	$25
❏ CJ-33	Soaring	1976	$30
❏ CJ-221	Solo	1982	$25

CONTEMPORARY

❏ C-2508 [10]	Barney Kessel, Volume 1	1953	$250
❏ C-2514 [10]	Barney Kessel, Volume 2	1954	$250
❏ M-3563 [M]	Barney Kessel Plays "Carmen"	1959	$250
❏ S-7563 [S]	Barney Kessel Plays "Carmen"	1959	$250
❏ C-3511 [M]	Easy Like	1956	$200
❏ M-3618 [M]	Feeling Free	1965	$150
❏ S-7618 [S]	Feeling Free	1965	$150
❏ C-3512 [M]	Kessel Plays Standards	1956	$200
❏ M-3603 [M]	Let's Cook!	1962	$200
❏ S-7603 [S]	Let's Cook!	1962	$200
❏ C-3521 [M]	Music to Listen to Barney Kessel By	1956	$200
❏ S-7521 [S]	Music to Listen to Barney Kessel By	1959	$250
❏ C-14044	Red Hot and Blues	198?	$25
❏ M-3565 [M]	Some Like It Hot	1959	$250
❏ S-7565 [S]	Some Like It Hot	1959	$250
❏ C-14033	Spontaneous Combustion	1987	$25
❏ M-3613 [M]	Swingin' Party	1963	$200

Number	Title	Yr	NM
❏ S-7613 [S]	Swingin' Party	1963	$200
❏ C-3513 [M]	To Swing or Not to Swing	1956	$200
❏ M-3585 [M]	Workin' Out!	1960	$200
❏ S-7585 [S]	Workin' Out!	1960	$200

EMERALD

| ❏ 1401 [M] | On Fire | 1965 | $35 |
| ❏ 2401 [S] | On Fire | 1965 | $25 |

FANTASY

❏ OJC-269	Barney Kessel Plays "Carmen"	198?	$25
❏ OJC-153	Easy Like	198?	$25
❏ OJC-179	Feeling Free	198?	$25
❏ OJC-238	Kessel Plays Standards	198?	$25
❏ OJC-168	Some Like It Hot	198?	$25
❏ OJC-317	To Swing or Not to Swing	1987	$25

RCA CAMDEN

| ❏ CAS-2404 | Guitarra | 1970 | $25 |

REPRISE

❏ R-6049 [M]	Bossa Nova	1962	$35
❏ R9-6049 [S]	Bossa Nova	1962	$25
❏ R-6019 [M]	Breakfast at Tiffany's	1961	$35
❏ R-6073 [M]	Kessel/Jazz	1963	$35
❏ R9-6073 [S]	Kessel/Jazz	1963	$25

STEREO RECORDS

| ❏ S-7001 [S] | Music to Listen to Barney Kessel By | 1958 | $50 |

KESSLER, SIEGFRIED, AND DAUNIK LAZRO

Kessler is a pianist. Also see DAUNIK LAZRO.

Albums

HAT HUT

| ❏ 3502 | Aeros | 1982 | $30 |

KEYS, CALVIN

Guitarist.

Albums

OVATION

| ❏ OV-1804 | Criss Cross | 1978 | $30 |

KHAN, STEVE

Guitarist.

Albums

ANTILLES

| ❏ AN-1020 | Casa Loco | 198? | $25 |
| ❏ AN-1018 | Eyewitness | 198? | $25 |

ARISTA/NOVUS

| ❏ AN3023 | Evidence | 1980 | $30 |

COLUMBIA

❏ JC36129	Arrows	1979	$25
❏ JC36406	The Best of Steve Khan	1980	$25
❏ JC35539	The Blue Man	1978	$25
❏ JC34857	Tightrope	1977	$25

KICKLIGHTER, RICHY

Guitarist.

Albums

ICHIBAN

| ❏ ICH-1051 | In the Night | 198? | $25 |
| ❏ ICH-1019 | Just for Kicks | 198? | $25 |

KID SHEIK

See GEORGE "KID SHEIK" COLA.

KID THOMAS

Real name: Thomas Valentine. Trumpeter and bandleader.

Albums

AMERICAN MUSIC

| ❏ 642 [10] | Kid Thomas | 1952 | $50 |

ARHOOLIE

| ❏ 1016 | New Orleans Jazz | 1967 | $30 |

GHB

❏ GHB-80	Kid Thomas and His Algiers Stompers	197?	$30
❏ GHB-291	Kid Thomas in England	198?	$25
❏ GHB-24 [M]	Kid Thomas + The Hall Brothers Jazz Band	196?	$25

JAZZOLOGY

| ❏ JCE-13 | Sonnets from Algiers | 1967 | $30 |

NEW ORLEANS

| ❏ NOR7201 | Kid Thomas at Kohlman's Tavern | 1972 | $30 |

— Label calls this "Thomas Valentine at Kohlman's Tavern"

RIVERSIDE

Number	Title	Yr	NM
❏ RLP-365 [M]	Kid Thomas and His Algiers Stompers	1961	$200
❏ RS-9365 [R]	Kid Thomas and His Algiers Stompers	1961	$200
❏ RLP-386 [M]	Kid Thomas and His Algiers Stompers	1961	$200
❏ RS-9386 [R]	Kid Thomas and His Algiers Stompers	1961	$200

KIKUCHI, MASABUMI
Pianist.

Albums

CATALYST
| ❏ 7916 | Matrix | 197? | $30 |

INNER CITY
| ❏ IC-6021 | Wishes/Kochi | 1979 | $35 |

KILIMANJARO
Members: Paul Asbell (various guitars); Bill Kinzie (drums, percussion); Tony Markellis (basses); Chas Eller (keyboards, pianos); ,Rafael Cruz (congas, percussion).

Albums

PHILO
| ❏ 9001 | Kilimanjaro | 1979 | $30 |
| ❏ 9005 | Kilimanjaro 2 | 1981 | $30 |

KIMBALL, JEANETTE
Pianist.

Albums

NEW ORLEANS
| ❏ 7208 | Sophisticated Lady | 198? | $25 |

KIMURA, YOSHIKO

Albums

INNER CITY
| ❏ IC-6043 | Memories | 1978 | $35 |

KINCAIDE, DEAN
Saxophone player, bandleader, arranger and composer.

Albums

WEATHERS
| ❏ 5610 [M] | Arranged for You | 1954 | $50 |

KINESIS

Albums

HEADFIRST
| ❏ 9705 | New Life | 198? | $25 |

KING, MORGANA
Female singer.

Albums

ASCOT
❏ AS16020 [S]	Everybody Loves Saturday Night	1965	$60
❏ AM13025 [M]	More Morgana	1965	$60
❏ AS16025 [S]	More Morgana	1965	$60
❏ AM13019 [M]	The End of a Love Affair	1965	$60

—Reissue of United Artists 30020

| ❏ AM13014 [M] | The Winter of My Discontent | 1964 | $60 |
| ❏ AS16014 [S] | The Winter of My Discontent | 1964 | $60 |

EMARCY
| ❏ MG-36079 [M] | For You, For Me, For Evermore | 1956 | $200 |

MAINSTREAM
❏ MRL-355	Cuore di Mama	1974	$35
❏ 56052 [M]	Miss Morgana King	1965	$50
❏ S-6052 [S]	Miss Morgana King	1965	$60
❏ MRL-321	Taste of Honey	1972	$35
❏ 56015 [M]	With a Taste of Honey	1964	$50

Number	Title	Yr	NM
❏ S-6015 [S]	With a Taste of Honey	1964	$60

MERCURY
| ❏ MG-20231 [M] | Morgana King Sings the Blues | 1958 | $250 |

MUSE
❏ MR-5339	Another Time, Another Space	1988	$25
❏ MR-5190	Everything Must Change	1978	$25
❏ MR-5224	Higher Ground	1979	$25
❏ MR-5257	Looking Through the Eyes of Love	1981	$25
❏ MR-5301	Portraits	1983	$25
❏ MR-5326	Simply Eloquent	1986	$25
❏ MR-5166	Stretchin' Out	1977	$25

PARAMOUNT
| ❏ PAS-6067 | New Beginnings | 1973 | $30 |

RCA CAMDEN
| ❏ CAL-543 [M] | The Greatest Songs Ever Swung | 1959 | $50 |
| ❏ CAS-543 [S] | The Greatest Songs Ever Swung | 1959 | $60 |

REPRISE
❏ R6257 [M]	Gemini Changes	1967	$50
❏ RS6257 [S]	Gemini Changes	1967	$60
❏ R6192 [M]	It's a Quiet Thing	1966	$50
❏ RS6192 [S]	It's a Quiet Thing	1966	$60

Number	Title	Yr	NM
❏ R6205 [M]	Wild Is Love	1966	$50
❏ RS6205 [S]	Wild Is Love	1966	$60

TRIP
| ❏ 5533 | Morgana King Sings | 197? | $25 |

UNITED ARTISTS
❏ UAL3028 [M]	Folk Songs A La King	1960	$150
❏ UAS6028 [S]	Folk Songs A La King	1960	$175
❏ UAL30020 [M]	Let Me Love You	1960	$175
❏ UAS30020-S [S]	Let Me Love You	1960	$120

VERVE
| ❏ V-5061 [M] | I Know How It Feels | 1968 | $60 |
| ❏ V6-5061 [S] | I Know How It Feels | 1968 | $60 |

WING
| ❏ MGW-12307 [M] | More Morgana King | 1965 | $35 |
| ❏ SRW-16307 [S] | More Morgana King | 1965 | $50 |

KING, SANDRA
Female singer and pianist.

Albums

AUDIOPHILE
| ❏ AP-197 | Songs by Vernon Duke | 1984 | $30 |

KING, TEDDI, AND DAVE MCKENNA
Also see each artist's individual listings.

Albums

INNER CITY
| ❏ IC-1044 | This Is New | 1977 | $50 |

KING, TEDDI
Female singer.

Albums

AUDIOPHILE
| ❏ AP-117 | Lovers and Losers | 1976 | $35 |
| ❏ AP-150 | Someone to Light Up Your Life | 1979 | $30 |

CORAL
| ❏ CRL757278 [S] | All the King's Songs | 1959 | $150 |

RCA VICTOR
❏ LPM-1454 [M]	A Girl and Her Songs	1957	$150
❏ LPM-1147 [M]	Bidin' My Time	1956	$150
❏ LPM-1313 [M]	To You from Teddi King	1957	$175

STORYVILLE
❏ STLP-903 [M]	Now In Vogue	1956	$150
❏ STLP-302 [10]	'Round Midnight	1954	$250
❏ STLP-314 [10]	Storyville Presents Teddi King	1954	$200

KING CURTIS
Tenor saxophone player, best known for his session work with legendary early R&B and rock 'n' roll artists.

7-Inch Extended Plays

ATLANTIC
| ❏ SD 7-33-338 [PS] | Get Ready | 197? | $30 |

—Part of "Little LP" series (#217)

| ❏ SD 7-33-338 | Let It Be/Get Ready/ Something//Sugar Foot/ Soulin'/Someday We'll Be Together | 197? | $20 |

—Stereo jukebox issue; small hole, plays at 33 1/3 rpm

Albums

ATCO
❏ SD 33-385	Everybody's Talkin'	1972	$50
❏ SD 33-338	Get Ready	1970	$50
❏ 33-113 [M]	Have Tenor Sax, Will Blow	1959	$40
❏ SD 33-113 [S]	Have Tenor Sax, Will Blow	1959	$120
❏ SD 33-293	Instant Groove	1969	$50
❏ 33-231 [M]	King Size Soul	1967	$60
❏ SD 33-231 [S]	King Size Soul	1967	$50
❏ SD 33-359	Live at Fillmore West	1971	$50
❏ 33-198 [M]	Live at Small's Paradise	1966	$50
❏ SD 33-198 [S]	Live at Small's Paradise	1966	$60
❏ 33-247 [M]	Sweet Soul	1968	$60
❏ SD 33-247 [S]	Sweet Soul	1968	$50
❏ 33-189 [M]	That Lovin' Feeling	1966	$50
❏ SD 33-189 [S]	That Lovin' Feeling	1966	$60
❏ SD 33-266	The Best of King Curtis	1968	$50
❏ 33-211 [M]	The Great Memphis Hits	1967	$50
❏ SD 33-211 [S]	The Great Memphis Hits	1967	$60

ATLANTIC
| ❏ SD1637 | Blues Montreux | 1973 | $30 |

CAPITOL
❏ T1756 [M]	Country Soul	1963	$100
❏ ST1756 [S]	Country Soul	1963	$60
❏ T2341 [M]	King Curtis Plays the Hits Made Famous by Sam Cooke	1965	$100
❏ ST2341 [S]	King Curtis Plays the Hits Made Famous by Sam Cooke	1965	$100
❏ T2095 [M]	Soul Serenade	1964	$100
❏ ST2095 [S]	Soul Serenade	1964	$100
❏ SM-11798	Soul Serenade	1978	$25

—Reissue

| ❏ T2858 [M] | The Best of King Curtis | 1968 | $150 |

—Red and white "Starline" label; may be promo only

| ❏ SM-11963 | The Best of King Curtis | 1979 | $25 |

—Reissue

| ❏ ST2858 [S] | The Best of King Curtis | 1968 | $100 |

CLARION
| ❏ 615 [M] | The Great "K" Curtis | 1966 | $50 |
| ❏ SD615 [S] | The Great "K" Curtis | 1966 | $60 |

COLLECTABLES
| ❏ COL-5156 | Golden Classics: Enjoy… The Best of King Curtis | 198? | $25 |
| ❏ COL-5119 | Soul Twist | 198? | $25 |

EVEREST
| ❏ LPBR-5121 [M] | Azure | 1961 | $100 |

FANTASY

Number	Title	Yr	NM
❏ OJC-198	The New Scene of King Curtis	1985	$25
— Reissue of New Jazz 8237			
❏ OBC-512	Trouble in Mind	1988	$25
— Reissue of Tru-Sound 15001			

NEW JAZZ

Number	Title	Yr	NM
❏ NJLP-8237 [M]	The New Scene of King Curtis	1960	$200
— Purple label			
❏ NJLP-8237 [M]	The New Scene of King Curtis	1965	$150
— Blue label with trident logo on right			

PRESTIGE

Number	Title	Yr	NM
❏ 24033	Jazz Groove	198?	$35
❏ PRST-7789	King Soul	1970	$35
❏ PRLP-7222 [M]	Soul Meeting	1962	$150
❏ PRST-7222 [S]	Soul Meeting	1962	$150
❏ PRST-7833	Soul Meeting	1971	$35
— Reissue of 7222			
❏ PRST-7709	The Best of King Curtis	1969	$35
❏ PRST-7775	The Best of King Curtis -- One More Time	1970	$35

RCA CAMDEN

Number	Title	Yr	NM
❏ CAS-2242	Sax in Motion	1968	$35

RCA VICTOR

Number	Title	Yr	NM
❏ LPM-2494 [M]	Arthur Murray's Music for Dancing: The Twist!	1962	$60
❏ LSP-2494 [S]	Arthur Murray's Music for Dancing: The Twist!	1962	$60

TRU-SOUND

Number	Title	Yr	NM
❏ TS-15009 [M]	Doin' the Dixie Twist	1962	$100
❏ TS-15008 [M]	It's Party Time	1962	$100
❏ TS-15001 [M]	Trouble in Mind	1961	$100

KING PLEASURE

Male singer; the acknowledged inventor of "vocalese" (basically, putting words to jazz solos).

Albums

EVEREST ARCHIVE OF FOLK AND JAZZ

Number	Title	Yr	NM
❏ FS-262 [M]	King Pleasure	197?	$15

FANTASY

Number	Title	Yr	NM
❏ OJC-1771 [S]	Golden Days	1991	$20

HIFI

Number	Title	Yr	NM
❏ J-425 [M]	Golden Days	1960	$40
❏ JS-425 [S]	Golden Days	1960	$50

PRESTIGE

Number	Title	Yr	NM
❏ PRLP-208 [10]	King Pleasure Sings	1955	$500
❏ PRLP-7586	Original Moody's Mood	1968	$30
❏ PR-24017	The Source	1972	$30

SOLID STATE

Number	Title	Yr	NM
❏ SS-18021 [S]	Mr. Jazz	1968	$30
— Reissue of United Artists 15031			

UNITED ARTISTS

Number	Title	Yr	NM
❏ UAS-5634 [S]	Moody's Mood for Love	1972	$25
❏ UAJ-14031 [M]	Mr. Jazz	1962	$40
❏ UAJS-15031 [S]	Mr. Jazz	1962	$50

KING PLEASURE/ANNIE ROSS

Also see each artist's individual listings.

Albums

FANTASY

Number	Title	Yr	NM
❏ OJC-217 [M]	King Pleasure Sings/Annie Ross Sings	198?	$15

PRESTIGE

Number	Title	Yr	NM
❏ PRLP-7128 [M]	King Pleasure Sings/Annie Ross Sings	1957	$300
— Yellow label, W. 50th Street address on label			
❏ PRLP-7128 [M]	King Pleasure Sings/Annie Ross Sings	1958	$300
— Yellow label, Bergenfield, N.J. address on label			
❏ PRLP-7128 [M]	King Pleasure Sings/Annie Ross Sings	1965	$40
— Blue label, trident logo at right			

KING'S MEN FIVE, THE

Albums

CUCA

Number	Title	Yr	NM
❏ 1130 [M]	The King's Men Five	1965	$25

KINSEY, TONY

Drummer and occasional pianist.

Albums

LONDON

Number	Title	Yr	NM
❏ LL1672 [M]	Kinsey Come On	1957	$50

KIRBY, JOHN

Bass player, bandleader and arranger. Also see SARAH VAUGHAN.

Albums

CIRCLE

Number	Title	Yr	NM
❏ 14	John Kirby and His Orchestra 1941	198?	$25
❏ 64	John Kirby and His Orchestra 1941-42	198?	$25

CLASSIC JAZZ

Number	Title	Yr	NM
❏ 22	The Biggest Little Band in the Land	197?	$25

COLUMBIA

Number	Title	Yr	NM
❏ CG33557	Boss of the Bass	1975	$35
❏ GL502 [M]	John Kirby and His Orchestra	1951	$50
— Black label, silver print			
❏ CL502 [M]	John Kirby and His Orchestra	1953	$40
— Maroon label, gold print			

COLUMBIA MASTERWORKS

Number	Title	Yr	NM
❏ ML4801 [10]	John Kirby and His Orchestra	195?	$60

EPITAPH

Number	Title	Yr	NM
❏ E-4004	John Kirby 1908-1952	1975	$30

HARMONY

Number	Title	Yr	NM
❏ HL7124 [M]	Intimate Swing	1958	$30

TRIP

Number	Title	Yr	NM
❏ 5802	The Biggest Little Band	197?	$25

KIRCHNER, BILL

Saxophone player, arranger, composer and jazz historian. (He won a Grammy for his liner notes for a Miles Davis boxed set.)

Albums

SEA BREEZE

Number	Title	Yr	NM
❏ SB-2017	Infant Eyes	1983	$25
❏ SB-2010	What It Is to Be Frank	1982	$25

KIRK, ANDY

Bass saxophone and tuba player, also a bandleader.

Albums

CORAL

Number	Title	Yr	NM
❏ CRL56019 [10]	Andy Kirk Souvenir Album – Vol. 1	1951	$100

DECCA

Number	Title	Yr	NM
❏ DL79232	Instrumentally	1968	$35

MAINSTREAM

Number	Title	Yr	NM
❏ MRL-399	Mar-36	1975	$30

MCA

Number	Title	Yr	NM
❏ 1308	Instrumentally Speaking	198?	$25
❏ 4105	The Best of Andy Kirk and the Clouds of Joy	197?	$30
❏ 1343	The Lady Who Swings the Band	198?	$25

RCA VICTOR

Number	Title	Yr	NM
❏ LPM-1302 [M]	A Mellow Bit of Rhythm	1956	$40

KIRK, RAHSAAN ROLAND

Versatile musician who played tenor, baritone and bass saxophones, stritch, manzello, clarinet, flute, piccolo, trumpet, English horn, pipes, harmonica, whistle, harmonium, percussion, et al. - sometimes more than one at a time - and even sang once in a while. Also see THE JAZZ CORDS.

Albums

ABC

Number	Title	Yr	NM
❏ AA-1106	Cry	1978	$30

ARGO

Number	Title	Yr	NM
❏ LP-669 [M]	Introducing Roland Kirk	1960	$60
❏ LPS-669 [S]	Introducing Roland Kirk	1960	$80

ATLANTIC

Number	Title	Yr	NM
❏ SD1630	A Meeting of the Times	1973	$35
— With Al Hibbler			
❏ SD1601	Blacknuss	1972	$35
❏ SD 2-907	Bright Moments	1974	$25

Number	Title	Yr	NM
❏ 3007 [M]	Here Comes the Whistle Man	1967	$30
❏ SD3007 [S]	Here Comes the Whistle Man	1967	$35
❏ SD1518	Left and Right	1969	$35
❏ SD1578	Natural Black Inventions	1971	$35
❏ SD1686	Other Folks' Music	1976	$30
❏ SD1640	Prepare Thyself to Deal with a Miracle	1974	$35
❏ SD1575	Rahsaan Rahsaan	1970	$35
❏ SD 2-303	The Art of Rahsaan Roland Kirk	1973	$25
❏ SD1592	The Best of Rahsaan Roland Kirk	1972	$35
❏ SD1674	The Case of the 3-Sided Dream in Audio Color	1975	$35
❏ 1502 [M]	The Inflated Tear	1968	$30
❏ SD1502 [S]	The Inflated Tear	1968	$35
❏ 90045	The Inflated Tear	1983	$25
❏ SD 2-1003	Vibration	1978	$35
❏ SD1534	Volunteered Slavery	1969	$35

BETHLEHEM

Number	Title	Yr	NM
❏ BCP-6016	Early Roots	197?	$50
— Reissue of 6064, distributed by RCA Victor			
❏ BCP-6064 [M]	Third Dimension	1962	$250

EMARCY

Number	Title	Yr	NM
❏ EMS-2-411	Kirk's Works	1975	$50

FANTASY

Number	Title	Yr	NM
❏ OJC-459	Kirk's Work	1990	$35

KING

Number	Title	Yr	NM
❏ 539 [M]	Triple Threat	1956	$1750

LIMELIGHT

Number	Title	Yr	NM
❏ LM-82008 [M]	I Talk with the Spirits	1964	$120
❏ LS-86008 [S]	I Talk with the Spirits	1964	$150
— Reproductions exist			
❏ LM-82027 [M]	Rip, Rig and Panic	1965	$100
❏ LS-86027 [S]	Rip, Rig and Panic	1965	$120
❏ LM-82033 [M]	Slightly Latin	1966	$100
❏ LS-86033 [S]	Slightly Latin	1966	$120

MERCURY

Number	Title	Yr	NM
❏ MG-20748 [M]	Domino	1962	$100
❏ SR-60748 [S]	Domino	1962	$100
❏ MG-20939 [M]	Gifts and Messages	1964	$100
❏ SR-60939 [S]	Gifts and Messages	1964	$100
❏ MG-20894 [M]	Kirk in Copenhagen	1963	$100
❏ SR-60894 [S]	Kirk in Copenhagen	1963	$100
❏ MG-20800 [M]	Reeds and Deeds	1963	$100
❏ SR-60800 [S]	Reeds and Deeds	1963	$100
❏ MG-20844 [M]	Roland Kirk Meets the Benny Golson Orchestra	1963	$100
❏ SR-60844 [S]	Roland Kirk Meets the Benny Golson Orchestra	1963	$100
❏ MG-20679 [M]	We Free Kings	1962	$100
❏ SR-60679 [S]	We Free Kings	1962	$100
❏ 826455-1	We Free Kings	1986	$30

PRESTIGE

Number	Title	Yr	NM
❏ PRLP-7450 [M]	Funk Underneath	1967	$50
❏ PRST-7450 [R]	Funk Underneath	1967	$60
❏ PRLP-7210 [M]	Kirk's Work	1961	$200
❏ 24080	Pre-Rahsaan	1978	$35

TRIP

Number	Title	Yr	NM
❏ TLP-5503	Domino	197?	$50
❏ TLP-5512	Kirk in Copenhagen	197?	$50
❏ TLP-5541	We Free Kings	197?	$50

VERVE

Number	Title	Yr	NM
❏ V-8709 [M]	Now Please Don't You Cry, Beautiful Edith	1967	$100
❏ V6-8709 [S]	Now Please Don't You Cry, Beautiful Edith	1967	$80

WARNER BROS.

Number	Title	Yr	NM
❏ BSK3035	Boogie-Woogie String Along for Real	1977	$25
❏ BS2982	Kirkatron	1977	$25
❏ BS2918	The Return of the 5,000 Pound Man	1976	$25

KIRKLAND, LEROY

Guitarist.

Albums

IMPERIAL

Number	Title	Yr	NM
❏ LP-9198 [M]	Twistin', Mashin' and All That Jazz	1962	$150
❏ LP-12198 [S]	Twistin', Mashin' and All That Jazz	1962	$150

KITAEV, ANDREI, AND BILL DOUGLASS

Kitaev is a pianist, Douglass plays bass.

Albums

REFERENCE RECORDINGS

Number	Title	Yr	NM
❏ RR-6	First Takes	198?	$25

Number	Title	Yr	NM

KITAJIMA, OSANU
Keyboard and synthesizer player. Also plays koto, guitar and percussion.

Albums
ARISTA
| ❏ AL9570 | Dragon King | 1982 | $25 |

HEADFIRST
| ❏ HF-9706 | Masterless Samurai | 1981 | $25 |

KITAMURA, ELJI
Clarinetist.

Albums
CONCORD JAZZ
| ❏ CJ-217 | Seven Stars | 198? | $25 |
| ❏ CJ-152 | Swing Elji | 198? | $25 |

KITTRELL, JEAN
Female singer and bandleader.

Albums
GHB
| ❏ 51 | 'Tain't Nobody's Bizness | 197? | $30 |

KITTYHAWK
Featuring Paul Edwards, Dan Bortz (on the first EMI America LP) and Randy Strom (on the other two LPs), who play the Chapman Stick, a 10- or 12-stringed instrument that combines guitar and bass but is tapped like a piano (rather than strummed or plucked) to make sounds.

Albums
EMI AMERICA
| ❏ SW-17029 | Kittyhawk | 1980 | $30 |
| ❏ ST-17053 | Race for the Oasis | 1981 | $30 |

ZEBRA
| ❏ ZR-5001 | Fanfare | 198? | $30 |

KLEMMER, JOHN, AND EDDIE HARRIS
Also see each artist's individual listings.

Albums
CRUSADERS
| ❏ 16015 | Two Tone | 1982 | $60 |
—Part of MCA's "Audiophile Series

KLEMMER, JOHN
Earlier material appears in the Goldmine Standard Catalog of American Records 1950-1975. (SC2)
Tenor and soprano saxophone player.

Albums
ABC
❏ AA-1068	Arabesque	1978	$25
❏ ABCD-950	Barefoot Ballet	1976	$25
❏ AA-1116	Brazilia	1979	$25
❏ AA-1106	Cry	1978	$25
❏ ABCD-836	Fresh Feathers	1974	$35
❏ AB-1007	LifeStyle (Living & Loving)	1977	$25
❏ ABCD-922	Touch	1975	$25

ABC IMPULSE!
❏ AS-9214	Constant Throb	1973	$35
❏ AS-9244	Intensity	1974	$200
❏ AS-9269	Magic and Movement	1974	$200
❏ AS-9220	Waterfalls	1973	$35

ARISTA/NOVUS
| ❏ AN2-3500 | Nexus | 1979 | $35 |

BLUEBIRD
| ❏ 6577-1-RB | Nexus One | 1987 | $25 |

CADET
❏ LPS808	And We Were Lovers	1968	$50
❏ LP797 [M]	Involvement	1967	$40
❏ LPS797 [S]	Involvement	1967	$50
—Fading blue label
| ❏ CA-797 [S] | Involvement | 197? | $35 |
—Pink and yellow label reissue

CADET CONCEPT
❏ LPS326	All the Children Cried	1970	$50
❏ LPS321	Blowin' Gold	1969	$60
❏ LPS330	Eruptions	1971	$50

CHESS
| ❏ CH2-92501 | Blowin' Gold | 1984 | $30 |
—Reissue of CH-8300
| ❏ CH-8300 | Blowin' Gold | 1982 | $30 |
—Compilation of tracks from three Cadet Concept LPs
| ❏ 2ACMJ-401 | Magic Moments | 1976 | $35 |

ELEKTRA
❏ 5E-527	Hush	1981	$25
❏ 6E-284	Magnificent Madness	1980	$25
❏ 5E-566	Solo Saxophone II: Life	1982	$25

ELEKTRA/MUSICIAN
| ❏ 60197 | Finesse | 1983 | $25 |

MCA
| ❏ 37015 | Arabesque | 1980 | $20 |
—Reissue of ABC 1068
| ❏ 1585 | Arabesque | 198? | $20 |
—Reissue of MCA 37015
| ❏ 37013 | Barefoot Ballet | 1980 | $20 |
—Reissue of ABC 950
| ❏ AA-1116 | Brazilia | 1979 | $20 |
—Reissue of ABC 1116
| ❏ 37115 | Brazilia | 1980 | $20 |
—Reissue of MCA 1116
| ❏ 1639 | Brazilia | 198? | $20 |
—Reissue of MCA 37115
| ❏ 37017 | Constant Throb | 1980 | $20 |
—Reissue of ABC Impulse 9214
| ❏ 37016 | Cry | 1980 | $20 |
—Reissue of ABC 1106
| ❏ 37012 | Fresh Feathers | 1980 | $25 |
—Reissue of ABC 836
| ❏ 37019 | Intensity | 1980 | $25 |
—Reissue of ABC Impulse 9244
| ❏ 37014 | LifeStyle (Living & Loving) | 1980 | $20 |
—Reissue of ABC 1007
| ❏ 37020 | Magic and Movement | 1980 | $25 |
—Reissue of ABC Impulse 9269
❏ 6246	Music	1989	$30
❏ 8014	The Best of John Klemmer, Volume One/Mosaic	1979	$30
❏ 6007	The Best of John Klemmer, Volume One/Mosaic	198?	$25
—Reissue of MCA 8014
| ❏ 6017 | The Best of John Klemmer, Volume Two/The Impulse Years | 1982 | $30 |
| ❏ 37152 | Touch | 198? | $20 |
—Reissue of ABC 922
| ❏ 1654 | Touch | 198? | $20 |
—Reissue of MCA 37152
| ❏ 37018 | Waterfalls | 1980 | $25 |
—Reissue of ABC Impulse 9220

MOBILE FIDELITY
| ❏ Jan-006 | Touch | 1979 | $60 |
—Original Master Recording" at top of front cover; audiophile vinyl

NAUTILUS
| ❏ NR-22 | Finesse | 1981 | $150 |
—SuperDisc" audiophile vinyl
| ❏ NR-4 | Straight from the Heart | 1980 | $150 |
—Super Disc" audiophile vinyl

KLINK, AL/BOB ALEXANDER
Klink is an alto and tenor saxophone player. Alexander is a trombonist.

Albums
GRAND AWARD
| ❏ GA 33-525 [M] | Progressive Jazz | 1956 | $80 |
—With removable outer cover
| ❏ GA 33-525 [M] | Progressive Jazz | 1956 | $30 |
—Without removable outer cover

KLOSS, ERIC, AND BARRY MILES
Also see each artist's individual listings.

Albums
MUSE
| ❏ MR-5112 | Together | 1976 | $35 |

KLOSS, ERIC, AND GIL GOLDSTEIN
Also see each artist's individual listings.

Albums
OMNISOUND
| ❏ 1044 | Sharing | 1981 | $30 |

KLOSS, ERIC
Alto and tenor saxophone player.

Albums
COBBLESTONE
| ❏ 9006 | Doors | 1972 | $25 |

MUSE
❏ MR-5077	Bodies' Warmth	1975	$35
❏ MR-5196	Celebration	1979	$30
❏ MR-5291	Doors	198?	$30
—Reissue of Cobblestone 9006
❏ MR-5038	Essence	1974	$35
❏ MR-5147	Now	1978	$30
❏ MR-5019	One, Two, Free	1973	$35

PRESTIGE
❏ PRST-7793	Consciousness!	1970	$35
❏ PRLP-7520 [M]	First Class Kloss	1967	$30
❏ PRST-7520 [S]	First Class Kloss	1967	$25
❏ PRLP-7486 [M]	Grits & Gravy	1967	$30
❏ PRST-7486 [S]	Grits & Gravy	1967	$25
❏ PRST-7627	In the Land of the Giants	1969	$35
❏ PRLP-7442 [M]	Introducing Eric Kloss	1966	$25
❏ PRST-7442 [S]	Introducing Eric Kloss	1966	$30
❏ PRST-7535	Life Force	1968	$25
❏ PRLP-7469 [M]	Love and All That Jazz	1966	$25
❏ PRST-7469 [S]	Love and All That Jazz	1966	$30
❏ PRST-7594	Sky Shadows	1969	$35
❏ PRST-7689	To Hear Is to See!	1970	$35
❏ PRST-7565	We're Goin' Up	1968	$35

KLUGH, EARL
Guitarist and keyboard player. Also see GEORGE BENSON; BOB JAMES.

Albums
BLUE NOTE
| ❏ BN-LA596-G | Earl Klugh | 1976 | $25 |
| ❏ LN-10163 | Earl Klugh | 198? | $20 |
—Budget-line reissue
| ❏ BN-LA737-H | Finger Paintings | 1977 | $25 |
| ❏ LO-737 | Finger Paintings | 198? | $20 |
—Reissue with new prefix
| ❏ BN-LA667-G | Living Inside Your Love | 1976 | $25 |
| ❏ LO-667 | Living Inside Your Love | 198? | $20 |
—Reissue with new prefix

CAPITOL
❏ ST-12405	Key Notes (Greatest Hits)	1985	$25
❏ ST-12253	Low Ride	1983	$25
❏ ST-12372	Nightsongs	1984	$25
❏ ST-12323	Wishful Thinking	1984	$25

LIBERTY
| ❏ LT-51113 | Crazy for You | 1981 | $25 |
| ❏ LN-10308 | Crazy for You | 1986 | $20 |
—Budget-line reissue
| ❏ LN-10257 | Finger Paintings | 198? | $20 |
—Budget-line reissue
| ❏ LO-942 | Heart String | 198? | $20 |
—Reissue of United Artists 942
| ❏ LN-10231 | Heart String | 198? | $20 |
—Budget-line reissue
| ❏ LT-1079 | Late Night Guitar | 1980 | $25 |
| ❏ LN-10233 | Living Inside Your Love | 198? | $20 |
—Budget-line reissue
| ❏ LMAS-877 | Magic in Your Eyes | 198? | $20 |
—Reissue of United Artists 877

MOBILE FIDELITY
| ❏ Jan-0025 | Finger Paintings | 1979 | $100 |
—Audiophile vinyl
| ❏ UHQR 1-025 | Finger Paintings | 1982 | $200 |
—Ultra High Quality" audiophile vinyl in box
| ❏ Jan-0076 | Late Night Guitar | 1981 | $100 |
—Audiophile vinyl

UNITED ARTISTS
❏ LT-1026	Dream Come True	1980	$25
❏ UA-LA942-H	Heart String	1979	$25
❏ UA-LA877-H	Magic in Your Eyes	1978	$25

WARNER BROS.
❏ 25478	Life Stories	1986	$25
❏ 25262	Soda Fountain Shuffle	1985	$25
❏ 26018	Solo Guitar	1989	$30
❏ 25902	Whispers and Promises	1989	$30

Moe Koffman Quintet Featuring Dizzy Gillespie, *Oop-Pop-a-Da*,
Soundwings/Duke Street SW-2108, **$30**.

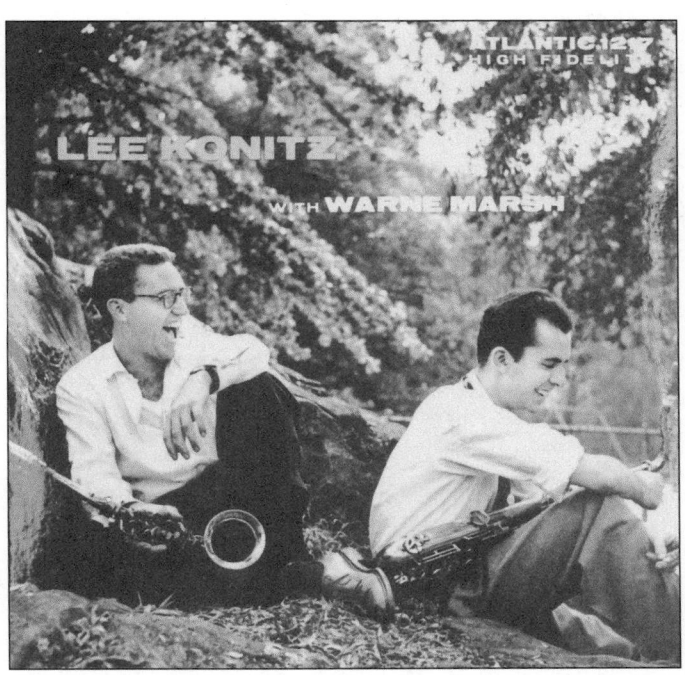

Lee Konitz, *Lee Konitz with Warne Marsh*, Atlantic 1217, black label, **$300**.

Lee Konitz, *The Lee Konitz Duets*, Milestone MSP-9013, **$25**.

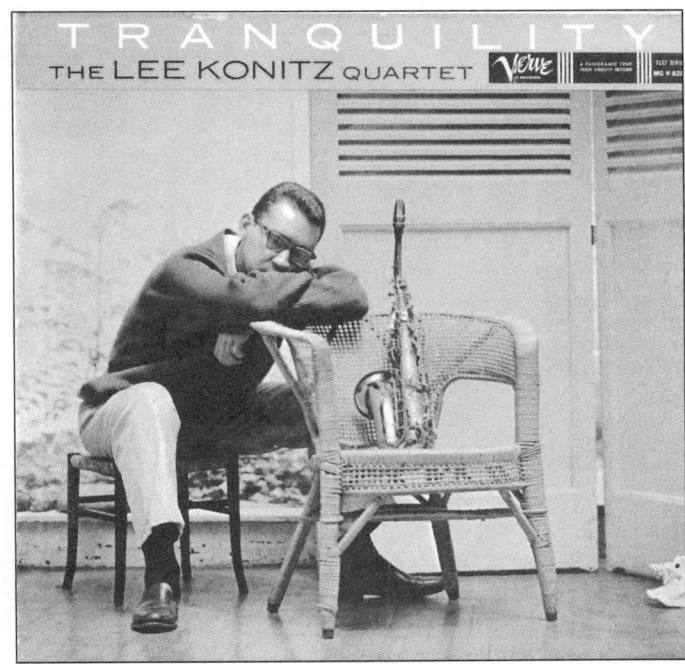

Lee Konitz, *Tranquility*, Verve MGV-8281, **$150**.

Number	Title	Yr	NM

KNAPP, JAMES
Trumpeter and composer.
Albums
ECM

Number	Title	Yr	NM
❏ 1194	First Avenue	198?	$30

KNEE, BERNIE
Male singer, best known for his work in advertising jingles.
Albums
AUDIOPHILE

Number	Title	Yr	NM
❏ AP-144	Bernie Knee	198?	$30

KNEPPER, JIMMY
Trombonist. Also see PEPPER ADAMS; TONY SCOTT.
Albums
BETHLEHEM

Number	Title	Yr	NM
❏ BCP-77 [M]	A Swinging Introduction to Jimmy Knepper	1957	$250
❏ BCP-6031	Idol of the Flies	197?	$30

— Reissue, distributed by RCA Victor

DEBUT

Number	Title	Yr	NM
❏ DEB-129 [M]	New Faces	1956	$0

— Canceled

INNER CITY

Number	Title	Yr	NM
❏ IC-6047	Knepper in L.A.	197?	$30

SOUL NOTE

Number	Title	Yr	NM
❏ SN-1092	I Dream Too Much	1984	$30

STEEPLECHASE

Number	Title	Yr	NM
❏ SCS-1061	Cunningbird	1977	$30

KNIGHT, BOBBY, AND THE GREAT AMERICAN TROMBONE CO.
Knight, a bass and tenor trombonist and arranger, is joined by Carl Fontana, Charles Loper, Lew McCreary and Frank Rosolino on trombones and Phil Teele on bass trombone, with additional backing musicians.
Albums
SEA BREEZE

Number	Title	Yr	NM
❏ SB-2009	Cream of the Crop	198?	$25

KNIGHTS OF DIXIELAND, THE
Albums
JAZZOLOGY

Number	Title	Yr	NM
❏ J-4 [M]	A Night with the Knights of Dixieland	1964	$35

KNOPF, PAUL
Pianist.
Albums
PLAYBACK

Number	Title	Yr	NM
❏ PLP-502 [M]	And the Walls Came Tumbling Down	1960	$40
❏ PLP-502ST [S]	And the Walls Came Tumbling Down	1960	$50
❏ PLP-501 [M]	Enigma of a Day	1959	$40
❏ PLP-501ST [S]	Enigma of a Day	1959	$50
❏ PLP-600 [M]	Music from the Morgue	1961	$40
❏ PLP-600ST [S]	Music from the Morgue	1961	$50
❏ PLP-503 [M]	Paul Knoft Trio	1960	$40
❏ PLP-503ST [S]	Paul Knoft Trio	1960	$50
❏ PLP-500 [M]	The Outcat	1959	$40
❏ PLP-500ST [S]	The Outcat	1959	$50

KOCH, MERLE
Pianist.
Albums
AUDIOPHILE

Number	Title	Yr	NM
❏ AP-135	Merle Koch and Eddie Miller at Michele's	1979	$25
❏ AP-126	The Polite Jazz Quartet	1978	$25

JAZZOLOGY

Number	Title	Yr	NM
❏ J-80	Jazz Piano	197?	$25

KOFFMAN, MOE
Flutist , saxophone player and composer, best known for "The Swingin' Shepherd Blues."
Albums
ASCOT

Number	Title	Yr	NM
❏ AM13001 [M]	Moe Koffman Plays for the Teens	1962	$50

JANUS

Number	Title	Yr	NM
❏ 7037	Museum Pieces	1978	$25

JUBILEE

Number	Title	Yr	NM
❏ JLP-1037 [M]	Cool and Hot Sax	1957	$40
❏ JGS-8009	Moe Koffman Goes Electric	1968	$60
❏ JLP-1074 [M]	The Shepherd Swings Again	1958	$40
❏ JGS-8016	Turned On	1968	$60

SOUNDWINGS/DUKE STREET

Number	Title	Yr	NM
❏ SW2108	Oop-Pop-A-Da	1988	$30

— With Dizzy Gillespie

UNITED ARTISTS

Number	Title	Yr	NM
❏ UAJ-14029 [M]	Tales of Koffman	1963	$60
❏ UAJS-15029 [S]	Tales of Koffman	1963	$60

KOHANNA, DEE
Albums
ROCK CREEK

Number	Title	Yr	NM
❏ 01	Eclipse	1979	$35

KOHLMAN, FREDDIE
Drummer.
Albums
MGM

Number	Title	Yr	NM
❏ E-297 [10]	New Orleans Now -- New Orleans Then	1955	$80

KOINONIA
Members: Abraham Laboriel (bass, acoustic guitar); Justo Almario (saxophone); Bill Maxwell (drums); Lou Pardini (keyboards, vocals); Harlan Rogers (keyboards).
Albums
BREAKER

Number	Title	Yr	NM
❏ 9970	Celebration	1984	$25
❏ 9946	More Than a Feeling	1983	$25

KOLLER, HANS
Tenor and baritone saxophone player.
Albums
DISCOVERY

Number	Title	Yr	NM
❏ DL-2005 [10]	Hans Koller	1954	$250

VANGUARD

Number	Title	Yr	NM
❏ VRS-8509 [M]	Hans Across the Sea	1956	$100

KONITZ, LEE, AND HAL GALPER
Also see each artist's individual listings.
Albums
INNER CITY

Number	Title	Yr	NM
❏ IC-2057	Windows	1976	$35

STEEPLECHASE

Number	Title	Yr	NM
❏ SCS-1057	Windows	198?	$30

KONITZ, LEE, AND MARTIAL SOLAL
Also see each artist's individual listings.
Albums
PAUSA

Number	Title	Yr	NM
❏ 7138	Duo: Live at Berlin Jazz Days 1980	198?	$25

KONITZ, LEE, AND RED MITCHELL
Also see each artist's individual listings.
Albums
INNER CITY

Number	Title	Yr	NM
❏ IC-2018	I Concentrate on You	1975	$35

STEEPLECHASE

Number	Title	Yr	NM
❏ SCS-1018	I Concentrate on You	198?	$30

KONITZ, LEE
Alto saxophone player. Also see STAN GETZ; GERRY MULLIGAN; LENNY TRISTANO.
Albums
ATLANTIC

Number	Title	Yr	NM
❏ SD8235	Duets	1969	$35
❏ 1258 [M]	Inside Hi-Fi	1957	$300

— Black label

Number	Title	Yr	NM
❏ 1258 [M]	Inside Hi-Fi	1961	$150

— Multicolor label, white "fan" logo at right

Number	Title	Yr	NM
❏ SD1258 [S]	Inside Hi-Fi	1958	$300

— Green label

Number	Title	Yr	NM
❏ SD1258 [S]	Inside Hi-Fi	1961	$150

— Multicolor label, white "fan" logo at right

Number	Title	Yr	NM
❏ 1217 [M]	Lee Konitz with Warne Marsh	1955	$300

— Black label

Number	Title	Yr	NM
❏ 1217 [M]	Lee Konitz with Warne Marsh	1961	$150

— Multicolor label, white "fan" logo at right

Number	Title	Yr	NM
❏ 90050	Lee Konitz with Warne Marsh	198?	$25
❏ 1273 [M]	The Real Lee Konitz	1958	$300

— Black label

Number	Title	Yr	NM
❏ 1273 [M]	The Real Lee Konitz	1961	$150

— Multicolor label, white "fan" logo at right

CHIAROSCURO

Number	Title	Yr	NM
❏ 186	The Nonet	1977	$30
❏ 166	The Quartet	1976	$30

CHOICE

Number	Title	Yr	NM
❏ 1019	Tenorlee	1977	$30

FANTASY

Number	Title	Yr	NM
❏ OJC-466	Duets	1990	$30
❏ OJC-186	Subconscious-Lee	198?	$25

IAI

Number	Title	Yr	NM
❏ 373845	Pyramid	1977	$35

INNER CITY

Number	Title	Yr	NM
❏ IC-2035	Lone-Lee	1975	$35

JAZZTONE

Number	Title	Yr	NM
❏ J-1275 [M]	Jazz at Storyville / Jazz at Storyville	1957	$40

MILESTONE

Number	Title	Yr	NM
❏ MSP-9025	Peacemeal	1968	$25
❏ MSP-9060	Satori	1975	$25
❏ MSP-9038	Spirits	1969	$25
❏ MSP-9013	The Lee Konitz Duets	1968	$25

PAUSA

Number	Title	Yr	NM
❏ 7019	Lee Konitz Meets Warne Marsh Again	198?	$25

PRESTIGE

Number	Title	Yr	NM
❏ 24081	First Sessions 1949-50	198?	$35
❏ PRLP-7004 [M]	Lee Konitz Groups	1955	$350
❏ PRLP-116 [10]	Lee Konitz -- The New Sounds	1951	$400
❏ PRLP-7250 [M]	Subconscious-Lee	1962	$150

PROGRESSIVE

Number	Title	Yr	NM
❏ 7003	Figure and Spirit	1977	$35

ROOST

Number	Title	Yr	NM
❏ LP-416 [10]	Originalee	1953	$200

ROULETTE

Number	Title	Yr	NM
❏ SR-5006	The Nonet	1976	$35

SOUL NOTE

Number	Title	Yr	NM
❏ 121119	Ideal Scene	198?	$30
❏ SN-1069	Live at Laren	198?	$30
❏ 121169	The New York Album	1990	$30

STEEPLECHASE

Number	Title	Yr	NM
❏ SCS-1072	Jazz & Juan	198?	$30
❏ SCS-1035	Lone-Lee	198?	$30
❏ SCS-1119	Yes, Yes Nonet	1979	$30

STORYVILLE

Number	Title	Yr	NM
❏ STLP-313 [10]	Konitz	1954	$250
❏ STLP-304 [10]	Lee Konitz at Storyville	1954	$250
❏ STLP-901 [M]	Lee Konitz at Storyville	1956	$120
❏ STLP-323 [10]	Lee Konitz in Harvard Square	1955	$200

SUNNYSIDE

Number	Title	Yr	NM
❏ SSC-1003	Dovetail	1985	$25

VERVE

Number	Title	Yr	NM
❏ MGV-8286 [M]	An Image -- Lee Konitz with Strings	1958	$120
❏ V-8286 [M]	An Image -- Lee Konitz with Strings	1961	$30
❏ MGVS-6035 [S]	An Image -- Lee Konitz with Strings	1959	$150
❏ V6-8286 [S]	An Image -- Lee Konitz with Strings	1961	$25
❏ MGV-8335 [M]	Lee Konitz Meets Jimmy Giuffre	1959	$100
❏ V-8335 [M]	Lee Konitz Meets Jimmy Giuffre	1961	$25
❏ MGVS-6073 [S]	Lee Konitz Meets Jimmy Giuffre	1959	$100
❏ V6-8335 [S]	Lee Konitz Meets Jimmy Giuffre	1961	$35
❏ V-8399 [M]	Motion	1961	$25
❏ V6-8399 [S]	Motion	1961	$30
❏ UMV-2563	Motion	198?	$25
❏ MGV-8281 [M]	Tranquility	1958	$150
❏ V-8281 [M]	Tranquility	1961	$30
❏ MGV-8209 [M]	Very Cool	1958	$150

Number	Title	Yr	NM
❏ V-8209 [M]	Very Cool	1961	$30
❏ MGV-8362 [M]	You and Lee	1960	$60
❏ V-8362 [M]	You and Lee	1961	$50
❏ MGVS-6131 [S]	You and Lee	1960	$60
❏ V6-8362 [S]	You and Lee	1961	$35

KONITZ, LEE/MILES DAVIS/TEDDY CHARLES
Also see each artist's individual listings.

Albums

NEW JAZZ
| ❏ NJLP-8295 [M] | Ezz-Thetic | 1962 | $150 |

— Purple label
| ❏ NJLP-8295 [M] | Ezz-Thetic | 1965 | $150 |

— Blue label, trident logo at right

PRESTIGE
| ❏ PRST-7827 | Ezz-Thetic | 1970 | $30 |

KONRAD, BERNT
Soprano, alto, tenor, baritone and bass saxophone player and bass clarinetist.

Albums

HAT HUT
| ❏ 3509 | Traumtanzer | 198? | $30 |

KOONSE, DAVE AND LARRY
Both are guitarists.

Albums

DOBRE
| ❏ 1035 | Father and Son | 197? | $30 |

KRAL, IRENE
Female singer.

Albums

AVA
| ❏ A-33 [M] | Better Than Anything | 1963 | $40 |
| ❏ AS-33 [S] | Better Than Anything | 1963 | $50 |

CATALYST
| ❏ 7625 | Kral Space | 1977 | $30 |

CHOICE
| ❏ CRS1020 | Gentle Rain | 197? | $30 |
| ❏ CRS1012 | Where Is Love? | 197? | $30 |

DRG
| ❏ MRS-505 | Irene Kral and the Junior Mance Trio | 198? | $25 |

MAINSTREAM
| ❏ 56058 [M] | Wonderful Life | 1965 | $60 |
| ❏ S-6058 [S] | Wonderful Life | 1965 | $40 |

UNITED ARTISTS
❏ UAL-3052 [M]	Steve Irene O!	1959	$120
❏ UAS-6052 [S]	Steve Irene O!	1959	$150
❏ UAL-4016 [M]	The Band and I	1959	$120
❏ UAS-5016 [S]	The Band and I	1959	$150

KRAUSS, ALISON, AND UNION STATION

Albums

MOBILE FIDELITY
| ❏ MFSL 2-276 | So Long, So Wrong | 2004 | $100 |

— Original Master Recording" at top of cover

KRESS, CARL, AND GEORGE BARNES
See GEORGE BARNES.

KRESS, CARL
Guitarist; one of the first jazz guitarists.

Albums

CAPITOL
| ❏ H368 [10] | Classics in Jazz | 1953 | $80 |

KRESTON, JUDY, AND DAVID LAHM
Kreston is a female singer; Lahm is a pianist.

Albums

PLUG
| ❏ PLUG-6 | Here In Love Lies the Answer | 1986 | $30 |

KRIVDA, ERNIE
Tenor saxophone player.

Albums

CADENCE JAZZ
| ❏ CJR-1028 | Tough Tenor Red Hot | 1987 | $25 |

INNER CITY
❏ IC-1043	Alchemist	1978	$35
❏ IC-1083	Glory Strut	198?	$30
❏ IC-1031	Satanic	1977	$35

KROG, KARIN, AND DEXTER GORDON
Krog is a female singer and sometimes percussionist. Also see DEXTER GORDON.

Albums

STORYVILLE
| ❏ 4045 | Some Other Spring | 198? | $30 |

KRONOS QUARTET
Jazz and classical string quartet: David Hurrington (violin); John Sherba (violin); Hank Dutt (viola); Joan Jeanrenaud (cello).

Albums

LANDMARK
| ❏ LLP-1505 | Monk Suite (Music of Monk & Ellington) | 1985 | $30 |
| ❏ LLP-1510 | Music of Bill Evans | 1986 | $30 |

REFERENCE RECORDINGS
| ❏ RR-9 | In Formation | 198? | $30 |

— Audiophile vinyl

KRUPA, GENE, AND CHARLIE VENTURA
Also see each artist's individual listings.

Albums

COMMODORE
| ❏ FL-20028 [10] | The Krupa-Ventura Trio | 1950 | $100 |

KRUPA, GENE; LIONEL HAMPTON; TEDDY WILSON
Also see each artist's individual listings.

Albums

CLEF
| ❏ MGC-681 [M] | Selections from "The Benny Goodman Story | 1956 | $200 |

VERVE
| ❏ MGV-8066 [M] | Gene Krupa-Lionel Hampton-Teddy Wilson with Red Callender | 1957 | $300 |

— Reissue of Clef 681 with new title
| ❏ V-8066 [M] | Gene Krupa-Lionel Hampton-Teddy Wilson with Red Callender | 1961 | $30 |

KRUPA, GENE
Drummer and bandleader.

Albums

AIRCHECK
| ❏ 35 | Gene Krupa on the Air, 1944-46 | 198? | $25 |

AMERICAN RECORDING SOCIETY
| ❏ L-427 [M] | Drummer Man | 1957 | $40 |
| ❏ L-411 [M] | Gene Krupa Quartet | 1956 | $40 |

CLEF
| ❏ MGC-703 [M] | Drum Boogie | 1956 | $200 |
| ❏ MGC-607 [M] | Gene Krupa | 1954 | $0 |

— Canceled
❏ MGC-514 [10]	Gene Krupa Trio	1953	$200
❏ MGC-684 [M]	Krupa and Rich	1955	$200
❏ MGC-710 [M]	Krupa's Wail	1956	$0

— Canceled
❏ MGC-627 [M]	Sing, Sing, Sing -- The Rocking Mr. Krupa and His Orchestra	1954	$200
❏ MGC-728 [M]	The Driving Gene Krupa Plays with His Sextet	1956	$200
❏ MGC-687 [M]	The Exciting Gene Krupa and His Quartet	1956	$200
❏ MGC-668 [M]	The Gene Krupa Quartet	1955	$200
❏ MGC-147 [10]	The Gene Krupa Sextet #1	1954	$200
❏ MGC-152 [10]	The Gene Krupa Sextet #2	1954	$200
❏ MGC-631 [M]	The Gene Krupa Sextet #3	1954	$200
❏ MGC-500 [M]	The Gene Krupa Trio at Jazz at the Philharmonic	1953	$200
❏ MGC-121 [10]	The Gene Krupa Trio Collates	1953	$300

— With either Clef or Mercury cover

COLUMBIA
❏ CL6066 [10]	Dance Parade	1949	$100
❏ CL2515 [10]	Drummin' Man	1955	$60
❏ C2L29 [M]	Drummin' Man	1962	$50

— Red and black labels with six "eye" logos; box set with booklet; deduct 20 percent if book is missing
| ❏ C2L29 [M] | Drummin' Man | 1963 | $25 |

— Red labels, "Guaranteed High Fidelity" or "360 Sound Mono" on label
| ❏ CL6017 [10] | Gene Krupa | 1949 | $100 |
| ❏ CL735 [M] | Gene Krupa | 1956 | $30 |

— Red and black label with six "eye" logos
| ❏ CL735 [M] | Gene Krupa | 1963 | $35 |

— Red label, "Guaranteed High Fidelity" or "360 Sound Mono" on label
| ❏ KG32663 | Gene Krupa, His Orchestra and Anita O'Day | 1974 | $35 |
| ❏ CL641 [M] | Gene Krupa's Sidekicks | 1955 | $50 |

— Maroon label, gold print
| ❏ CL641 [M] | Gene Krupa's Sidekicks | 1955 | $40 |

— Red and black label with six "eye" logos

COLUMBIA SPECIAL PRODUCTS
| ❏ P14379 | Krupa Swings | 197? | $25 |

ENCORE
| ❏ EE22027 | That Drummer's Band | 196? | $35 |

HARMONY
| ❏ HL7252 [M] | The Gene Krupa Story in Music | 1960 | $35 |

INTERMEDIA
| ❏ QS-5050 | Hot Drums | 198? | $25 |

MERCURY
❏ MGC-514 [10]	Gene Krupa Trio	1953	$200
❏ MGC-500 [M]	The Gene Krupa Trio at Jazz at the Philharmonic	1953	$150
❏ MGC-121 [10]	The Gene Krupa Trio Collates	1953	$300

— With Mercury cover and Mercury labels

METRO
| ❏ M-518 [M] | Gene Krupa | 1965 | $250 |
| ❏ MS-518 [R] | Gene Krupa | 1965 | $150 |

MGM
| ❏ GAS-132 | Gene Krupa (Golden Archive Series) | 1970 | $30 |

RCA CAMDEN
| ❏ CAL-340 [M] | Mutiny in the Parlor | 1958 | $30 |

SUNBEAM
| ❏ 225 | The World's Greatest Drummer | 197? | $25 |

TIME-LIFE
| ❏ STBB-12 | Big Bands: Gene Krupa | 1984 | $35 |

VERVE
❏ MGVS-6042 [S]	Big Noise from Winnetka -- Gene Krupa at the London House	1960	$150
❏ V-8310 [M]	Big Noise from Winnetka -- Gene Krupa at the London House	1961	$30
❏ V6-8310 [S]	Big Noise from Winnetka -- Gene Krupa at the London House	1961	$25
❏ V-8450 [M]	Classics in Percussion	1962	$35
❏ V6-8450 [S]	Classics in Percussion	1962	$25
❏ MGV-8087 [M]	Drum Boogie	1957	$125
❏ V-8087 [M]	Drum Boogie	1961	$30
❏ 827843-1	Drummer Man	1986	$25
❏ MGV-2008 [M]	Drummer Man -- Gene Krupa in Highest-Fi	1956	$150

— Orange label
| ❏ MGV-2008 [M] | Drummer Man -- Gene Krupa in Highest-Fi | 1957 | $125 |

— Black label
| ❏ V-2008 [M] | Drummer Man -- Gene Krupa in Highest-Fi | 1961 | $30 |
| ❏ MGV-8373 [M] | Gene Krupa | 1960 | $0 |

— Canceled
| ❏ MGVS-6148 [S] | Gene Krupa | 1960 | $0 |

— Canceled
❏ MGV-8292 [M]	Gene Krupa Plays Gerry Mulligan Arrangements	1958	$150
❏ MGVS-6008 [S]	Gene Krupa Plays Gerry Mulligan Arrangements	1959	$100
❏ V-8292 [M]	Gene Krupa Plays Gerry Mulligan Arrangements	1961	$30
❏ V6-8292 [S]	Gene Krupa Plays Gerry Mulligan Arrangements	1961	$25

Number	Title	Yr	NM
❑ MGV-4016 [M]	Gene Krupa Plays the Classics	1958	$0
—Canceled			
❑ MGV-8300 [M]	Hey! Here's Gene Krupa	1959	$150
❑ V-8300 [M]	Hey! Here's Gene Krupa	1961	$30
❑ MGV-8069 [M]	Krupa and Rich	1957	$150
❑ V-8069 [M]	Krupa and Rich	1961	$30
❑ V-8400 [M]	Krupa and Rich	1961	$30
❑ V6-8400 [S]	Krupa and Rich	1961	$25
❑ MGV-8276 [M]	Krupa Rocks	1958	$150
❑ V-8276 [M]	Krupa Rocks	1961	$30
❑ V-8571 [M]	Let Me Off Uptown -- The Essential Gene Krupa	1964	$35
❑ V6-8571 [S]	Let Me Off Uptown -- The Essential Gene Krupa	1964	$25
❑ V-8414 [M]	Percussion King	1961	$35
❑ V6-8414 [S]	Percussion King	1961	$25
❑ MGV-8190 [M]	Sing, Sing, Sing	1957	$80
❑ V-8190 [M]	Sing, Sing, Sing	1961	$30
❑ VSP-4 [M]	That Drummer's Band	1966	$35
❑ VSPS-4 [R]	That Drummer's Band	1966	$30
❑ MGV-8107 [M]	The Driving Gene Krupa	1957	$125
❑ V-8107 [M]	The Driving Gene Krupa	1961	$30
❑ MGV-8369 [M]	The Drum Battle	1960	$100
❑ UMV-2594	The Exciting Gene Krupa	198?	$25
❑ MGV-8071 [M]	The Exciting Gene Krupa and His Quartet	1957	$100
❑ V-8071 [M]	The Exciting Gene Krupa and His Quartet	1961	$30
❑ MGV-8031 [M]	The Gene Krupa Trio	1957	$150
❑ V-8031 [M]	The Gene Krupa Trio	1961	$30
❑ V-8584 [M]	The Great New Gene Krupa Quartet Featuring Charlie Ventura	1964	$35
❑ MGV-8204	The Jazz Rhythms of Gene Krupa	1957	$150
❑ V-8204 [M]	The Jazz Rhythms of Gene Krupa	1961	$30
❑ V-8484 [M]	The Original Drum Battle	1962	$35
❑ V6-8484 [R]	The Original Drum Battle	196?	$30
❑ V-8594 [M]	Verve's Choice -- The Best of Gene Krupa	1964	$35
❑ V6-8594 [S]	Verve's Choice -- The Best of Gene Krupa	1964	$30

KUHN, JOACHIM
Pianist. Also see ROLF KUHN.

Albums

ATLANTIC			
❑ SD1695	Springfever	1976	$30
❑ SD19193	Sunshower	1978	$25
CMP			
❑ CMP-26-ST	Distance	1987	$25
❑ CMP-22-ST	I'm Not Dreaming	1986	$25
❑ CMP-29-ST	Wandlungen/ Transformations	1987	$25

KUHN, PETER
Clarinetist and bass clarinetist.

Albums

HAT HUT			
❑ 09	Ghost of a Trance	1980	$35
SOUL NOTE			
❑ SN-1043	The Kill	1981	$30

KUHN, ROLF
Clarinetist.

Albums

URANIA			
❑ US-1220 [M]	Sound of Jazz	1962	$100
❑ US-41220 [S]	Sound of Jazz	1962	$100
VANGUARD			
❑ VRS-8510 [M]	Streamline	1955	$125

KUHN, ROLF AND JOACHIM
Also see each artist's individual listings.

Albums

ABC IMPULSE!			
❑ AS-9150	Impressions of New York	1968	$200

KUHN, STEVE, AND SHEILA JORDAN
Also see each artist's individual listings.

Albums

ECM			
❑ 1159	Playground	1979	$30

KUHN, STEVE, AND TOSHIKO AKIYOSHI
Also see each artist's individual listings.

Albums

DAUNTLESS			
❑ DM-4308 [M]	The Country & Western Sound for Jazz Pianos	1963	$25
❑ DS-6308 [S]	The Country & Western Sound for Jazz Pianos	1963	$30

Pianist.

Albums

ABC IMPULSE!			
❑ AS-9136 [S]	The October Suite	1968	$30
BUDDAH			
❑ BDS-5098	Steve Kuhn	1972	$35
CONTACT			
❑ CM-5 [M]	Steve Kuhn Trio Featuring Steve Swallow and Pete LaRoca	1965	$25
❑ CS-5 [S]	Steve Kuhn Trio Featuring Steve Swallow and Pete LaRoca	1965	$30
ECM			
❑ ECM-1-1058	Ecstasy	1975	$30
❑ 1213	Last Year's Waltz	1982	$25
❑ 1094	Motility	1977	$30
❑ 1124	Non-Fiction	1978	$30
❑ 1052	Trance	197?	$30
IMPULSE!			
❑ A-9136 [M]	The October Suite	1967	$160
❑ AS-9136 [S]	The October Suite	1967	$120
MUSE			
❑ MR-5106	Raindrops/Live in New York	1978	$30
PRESTIGE			
❑ PRST-7694	Steve Kuhn in Europe	1969	$35

KUSTBANDET
New Orleans-style Dixieland music from a band based in Stockholm, Sweden.

Albums

STOMP OFF			
❑ SOS-1178	The New Call of the Freaks	1989	$30

KYNARD, CHARLES
Organist, pianist and composer.

Albums

FANTASY			
❑ OJC-333	Reelin' with the Feelin'	1988	$25
MAINSTREAM			
❑ MRL-331	Charles Kynard	1972	$25

❑ MRL-366 [B]	Woga	1973	$50
❑ MRL-389	Your Mama Don't Dance	1973	$50
PACIFIC JAZZ			
❑ PJ-72 [M]	Where It's At!	1963	$60
❑ ST-72 [S]	Where It's At!	1963	$40
PRESTIGE			
❑ PRST-7796	Afro-disiac	1970	$25
❑ PRST-7599	Professor Soul	1968	$25
❑ PRST-7688	Reelin' with the Feelin'	1969	$25
❑ PRST-7630	The Soul Brotherhood	1969	$25
❑ 10008	Wa-tu-wa-zui	1971	$25
WORLD PACIFIC			
❑ WP-1823 [M]	Warm Winds	1964	$100
❑ ST-1823 [S]	Warm Winds	1964	$100

KYSER, KAY
Bandleader. He was immensely popular in the 1940s.

Albums

CAPITOL			
❑ T1692 [M]	Kay Kyser's Greatest Hits	196?	$50
❑ ST1692 [S]	Kay Kyser's Greatest Hits	196?	$40
COLUMBIA			
❑ CL6012 [10]	Campus Favorites	1948	$80
❑ CG33572	The World of Kay Kyser	1976	$20
HARMONY			
❑ HL7136 [M]	Campus Rally	196?	$20
SUNBEAM			
❑ SB-218 [M]	Kay Kyser and His Orchestra 1935-39	198?	$15

L

L.A. 4
Members: LAURINDO ALMEIDA; RAY BROWN; SHELLY MANNE; BUD SHANK.

Albums

CONCORD JAZZ			
❑ CJ-215	Executive Suite	1982	$25
❑ CJ-1001 [B]	Just Friends	1980	$100
—Direct-to-disc recording			
❑ CJ-199	Just Friends	1981	$25
—Regular version			
❑ CJ-100	Live at Montreux, 1979	1980	$25
❑ CJ-156	Montage	1981	$25
❑ CJ-8	Scores	197?	$35
❑ CJ-18	The L.A. 4	197?	$30
❑ CJ-63	Watch What Happens	1978	$30
❑ CJ-130	Zaca	1980	$25
EAST WIND			
❑ 10004	Going Home	197?	$30
—Audiophile issue			
❑ 10003	Pavanne Pour Une Infante Defunte	197?	$30
—Audiophile issue			

L.A. JAZZ CHOIR, THE
Founded and directed by Gerald Eskelin.

Albums

MOBILE FIDELITY			
❑ Jan-0096	Listen	1982	$150
—Audiophile vinyl			
PAUSA			
❑ 7184	From All Sides	1986	$30

L.A. JAZZ ENSEMBLE, THE
Led by ROLAND VAZQUEZ.

Albums

PBR			
❑ 8	Urantia	197?	$30

L.A. JAZZ WORKSHOP, THE

Albums

AM-PM			
❑ 16	The Shopwork Shuffle	1986	$25
SEA BREEZE			
❑ SB-2021	Stan's Donuts	198?	$25

LABARBERA, PAT
Saxophone player.

Albums

PM			
❑ 09	Pass It On	197?	$30

LACY, STEVE, AND MAL WALDRON
Also see each artist's individual listings.

Albums

HAT ART			
❑ 2015	Herbe de L'Oubli & Snake-Out	1986	$35
HAT HUT			
❑ 3501	Snake-Out	198?	$30

Number	Title	Yr	NM

LACY, STEVE, AND MICHAEL SMITH
Also see each artist's individual listings.

Albums
IAI
| ❏ 373847 | Sidelines | 197? | $35 |

LACY, STEVE
Soprano saxophone player.

Albums
ADELPHI
| ❏ 5004 | Raps | 1977 | $30 |

BARNABY
| ❏ BR-5013 | The Straight Horn of Steve Lacy | 1977 | $30 |

BLACK SAINT
| ❏ BSR-0008 | Trickles | 198? | $30 |
| ❏ BSR-0035 | Troubles | 198? | $30 |

CANDID
| ❏ CD-8007 [M] | The Straight Horn of Steve Lacy | 1960 | $40 |
| ❏ CS-9007 [S] | The Straight Horn of Steve Lacy | 1960 | $50 |

EMANEM
❏ 3310	Saxophone Special	1975	$35
❏ 3316	School Days	1975	$35
❏ 301	Steve Lacy Solo	1973	$35
❏ 304	The Crust	1974	$35

ESP-DISK'
| ❏ 1060 [M] | The Forest and the Zoo | 1967 | $200 |
| ❏ S-1060 [S] | The Forest and the Zoo | 1967 | $200 |

FANTASY
❏ OJC-1755	Evidence	198?	$30
❏ OJC-063	Reflections: Steve Lacy Plays Thelonious Monk	198?	$30
❏ OJC-130	Steve Lacy Soprano Sax	198?	$30

HAT ART
❏ 2006	Blinks	1986	$35
❏ 2022	Futurities	1986	$35
❏ 2014	N.Y. Capers	1986	$35
❏ 2029	The Way	1987	$35

HAT HUT
❏ 1982/3	Ballets	1982	$35
❏ 14	Capers	1980	$35
❏ 0F	Clinkers	1977	$35
❏ 2001	Prospectus	198?	$35
❏ 1985/86	Songs	1982	$35
❏ 0K/L	Stamps	1978	$25
❏ 03	The Way	1979	$25
❏ 20	Tips	1980	$30

NEW JAZZ
| ❏ NJLP-8271 [M] | Evidence | 1962 | $200 |
—Purple label
| ❏ NJLP-8271 [M] | Evidence | 1965 | $150 |
—Blue label, trident logo at right
| ❏ NJLP-8206 [M] | Reflections: Steve Lacy Plays Thelonious Monk | 1958 | $300 |
—Purple label
| ❏ NJLP-8206 [M] | Reflections: Steve Lacy Plays Thelonious Monk | 1965 | $150 |
—Blue label, trident logo at right
| ❏ NJLP-8308 [M] | Wynton Kelly with Steve Lacy | 1963 | $0 |
—Canceled; issued on Status

NOVUS
❏ 3079-1-N	Anthem	1990	$30
❏ 3021-1-N	Momentum	1988	$25
❏ 3049-1-N	The Door	1989	$30

PRESTIGE
| ❏ 2505 | Evidence | 198? | $30 |
| ❏ PRLP-7125 [M] | Steve Lacy Soprano Sax | 1956 | $500 |

QED
| ❏ 997 | School Days | 197? | $30 |

RED
| ❏ VPA-120 | Axieme Vol. 1 | 198? | $30 |
| ❏ VPA-121 | Axieme Vol. 2 | 198? | $30 |

SILKHEART
| ❏ SH-103 | One Fell Swoop | 198? | $25 |
| ❏ SH-102 | The Gleam | 198? | $25 |

SOUL NOE
| ❏ SN-1035 | The Flame | 198? | $30 |

SOUL NOTE
❏ 121210	More Monk	199?	$35
❏ 121160	Only Monk	199?	$35
❏ 121135	The Condor	1990	$35
❏ 121185	The Window	199?	$35

STATUS
| ❏ ST-8308 [M] | Wynton Kelly with Steve Lacy | 1965 | $120 |

LADNIER, TOMMY
Trumpeter.

Albums
RIVERSIDE
❏ RLP-1026 [10]	Early Ladnier	1954	$300
❏ RLP-1019 [10]	Ida Cox with Tommy Ladnier	1953	$300
❏ RLP-1044 [10]	Tommy Ladnier Plays the Blues	1954	$300

X
| ❏ LVA-3027 [M] | Tommy Ladnier | 1954 | $60 |

LAFORGE, JACK
Male singer.

Albums
AUDIO FIDELITY
| ❏ AFLP-2161 [M] | Hit the Road Jack | 196? | $35 |
| ❏ AFSD-6161 [S] | Hit the Road Jack | 196? | $25 |

REGINA
❏ R-309 [M]	Comin' Home Baby	196?	$25
❏ RS-309 [S]	Comin' Home Baby	196?	$30
❏ R-319 [M]	Goldfinger	1965	$25
❏ RS-319 [S]	Goldfinger	1965	$30
❏ R-716 [M]	Hawaii and I	196?	$25
❏ RS-716 [S]	Hawaii and I	196?	$30
❏ R-282 [M]	I Remember You	196?	$25
❏ RS-282 [S]	I Remember You	196?	$30
❏ R-314 [M]	Jazz Portrait of Jack LaForge	196?	$25
❏ RS-314 [S]	Jazz Portrait of Jack LaForge	196?	$30
❏ R-327 [M]	Our Crazy Affair	196?	$25
❏ RS-327 [S]	Our Crazy Affair	196?	$30
❏ R-313 [M]	Promise Her Anything	196?	$25
❏ RS-313 [S]	Promise Her Anything	196?	$30
❏ R-288 [M]	Unchain My Heart	196?	$25
❏ RS-288 [S]	Unchain My Heart	196?	$30
❏ R-301 [M]	You Fascinate Me So	196?	$50
❏ RS-301 [S]	You Fascinate Me So	196?	$60

LAGGERS, MAX, AND THE STOMPERS

Albums
GHB
| ❏ GHB-157 | In the New Orleans Tradition | 198? | $25 |

LAGRENE, BIRELI
Guitarist.

Albums
ANTILLES
| ❏ AN-1009 | 15 | 198? | $25 |
| ❏ AN-1002 | Routes to Django | 1981 | $30 |

BLUE NOTE
| ❏ B1-90967 | Foreign Affairs | 1988 | $25 |
| ❏ BT-48016 | Inferno | 1987 | $25 |

LAHM, DAVID
Pianist.

Albums
PALO ALTO
| ❏ PA-8027 | Real Jazz for Folks Who Feel Jazz | 198? | $30 |

PLUG
| ❏ PLUG-7 | The Highest Standards | 1986 | $25 |

LAINE, CLEO, AND DUDLEY MOORE
Also see each artist's individual listings.

Albums
FINESSE
| ❏ FW38091 | Smilin' Through | 1983 | $30 |

LAINE, CLEO, AND JAMES GALWAY
Galway is a mostly classical flutist whose solo work is outside the scope of this book.

Albums
RCA RED SEAL
| ❏ ARL1-3628 | Sometimes When We Touch | 198? | $25 |

LAINE, CLEO
Female singer.

Albums
BUDDAH
| ❏ BDS-5607 | Day By Day | 1972 | $35 |

CBS
| ❏ FM39211 | Let the Music Take You | 1984 | $25 |
| ❏ FM39736 | That Old Feeling | 1985 | $25 |

DRG
❏ MR2S-608	An Evening with Cleo Lane and the John Dankworth Quartet	198?	$30
❏ DARC2-2101	Cleo at Carnegie: The 10th Anniversary Concert	198?	$30
❏ MRS-502	Cleo Lane with John Dankworth's Orchestra	198?	$25
❏ SL-5198	One More Day	198?	$25

FONTANA
❏ MGF-27531 [M]	Shakespeare and All That Jazz	1966	$35
❏ SRF-67531 [S]	Shakespeare and All That Jazz	1966	$25
❏ MGF-27552 [M]	Woman to Woman	1967	$50
❏ SRF-67552 [S]	Woman to Woman	1967	$35

GNP CRESCENDO
| ❏ GNPS-9024 | Cleo's Choice | 197? | $25 |

JAZZ MAN
| ❏ 5033 | Live at Wavendon Festival | 198? | $25 |

RCA
| ❏ 7702-1-R | Cleo Sings Sondheim | 1988 | $25 |

RCA VICTOR
| ❏ CPL1-5059 | A Beautiful Thing | 1974 | $35 |
| ❏ AFL1-5059 | A Beautiful Thing | 1978 | $25 |
—Reissue with new prefix
| ❏ AYL1-3805 | A Beautiful Thing | 1980 | $20 |
—Budget-line reissue
| ❏ APL1-1937 | Best Friends | 1976 | $30 |
| ❏ AFL1-1937 | Best Friends | 1978 | $25 |
—Reissue with new prefix
| ❏ LPL1-5113 | Born Friday | 197? | $30 |
| ❏ AFL1-5113 | Born Friday | 1978 | $25 |
—Reissue with new prefix
❏ AFL1-2926	Gonna Get Through	1978	$25
❏ LPL1-5000	I Am a Song	1973	$35
❏ AFL1-5000	I Am a Song	1978	$25
—Reissue with new prefix
| ❏ LPL1-5015 | Live at Carnegie Hall | 1973 | $35 |
| ❏ AFL1-5015 | Live at Carnegie Hall | 1978 | $25 |
—Reissue with new prefix
| ❏ AYL1-3751 | Live at Carnegie Hall | 1980 | $20 |
—Budget-line reissue
| ❏ APL1-2407 | Return to Carnegie Hall | 1977 | $30 |
| ❏ AFL1-2407 | Return to Carnegie Hall | 1978 | $25 |
—Reissue with new prefix

STANYAN
| ❏ 10067 | Day By Day | 197? | $30 |
| ❏ 10122 | Easy Livin' | 197? | $30 |

LAINE, FRANKIE
Mostly a male pop singer, Laine made some forays into jazzy music as listed below.

Albums
COLUMBIA
❏ CL808 [M]	Jazz Spectacular	1956	$30
❏ CS8087 [S]	Reunion in Rhythm	1959	$30
❏ CL1317 [M]	You Are My Love	1960	$50

HINDSIGHT
| ❏ HSR-216 | Frankie Laine with Carl Fischer and His Orchestra, 1947 | 1985 | $12 |

LAIRD, RICK
Bass player.

Albums
TIMELESS
| ❏ 308 | Soft Focus | 197? | $30 |

LAKE, OLIVER
Saxophone player. Also see WORLD SAXOPHONE QUARTET.

Albums
ARISTA/FREEDOM
| ❏ AF1008 | Heavy Spirits | 1975 | $35 |
| ❏ AF1024 | Ntu | 1976 | $35 |

ARISTA/NOVUS
| ❏ AN3010 | Focus | 1979 | $30 |
| ❏ AN3003 | Life Dance Of Is | 1978 | $30 |

BLACK SAINT
| ❏ BSR-0054 | Clevont Fitzhubert | 198? | $30 |
| ❏ BSR-0044 | Prophet | 198? | $30 |

GRAMAVISION

Number	Title	Yr	NM
❑ 8106	Oliver Lake & Jump Up	198?	$25
❑ 8206	Plug It	198?	$25

LALA, MIKE

Albums

GHB

Number	Title	Yr	NM
❑ GHB-120	Mike Lala and His Dixie Six	198?	$25

LAMARCH, SUSAN

Albums

STOMP OFF

Number	Title	Yr	NM
❑ SOS-1032	Vamp 'Til Ready	198?	$25

LAMB, JOSEPH
Pianist.

Albums

FOLKWAYS

Number	Title	Yr	NM
❑ FJ-3562 [M]	Classic Ragtime	1960	$30

LAMB, NATALIE, AND SAMMY PRICE
Lamb is a female singer. Also see SAMMY PRICE.

Albums

GHB

Number	Title	Yr	NM
❑ GHB-84	Natalie Lamb and Sammy Price and the Blues	198?	$25

LAMBERT, DAVE
Male singer. Also see LAMBERT, HENDRICKS AND BAVAN; LAMBERT, HENDRICKS AND ROSS.

Albums

UNITED ARTISTS

Number	Title	Yr	NM
❑ UAL-3084 [M]	Dave Lambert Sings and Swings Alone	1959	$40
❑ UAS-6084 [S]	Dave Lambert Sings and Swings Alone	1959	$50

LAMBERT, DONALD
Pianist.

Albums

JAZZOLOGY

Number	Title	Yr	NM
❑ JCE-59	Giant Stride	197?	$25

LAMBERT, HENDRICKS AND BAVAN
Successor vocal trio to LAMBERT, HENDRICKS AND ROSS consisting of DAVE LAMBERT; JON HENDRICKS; Yolanda Bavan.

Albums

BLUEBIRD

Number	Title	Yr	NM
❑ 6282-1-RB	Swingin' Til the Girls Come Home	1987	$25

RCA VICTOR

Number	Title	Yr	NM
❑ LPM-2747 [M]	Lambert, Hendricks and Bavan at Newport	1963	$30
❑ LSP-2747 [S]	Lambert, Hendricks and Bavan at Newport	1963	$40
❑ LPM-2861 [M]	Lambert, Hendricks and Bavan at the Village Gate	1964	$30
❑ LSP-2861 [S]	Lambert, Hendricks and Bavan at the Village Gate	1964	$40
❑ LPM-2635 [M]	Live at Basin Street East	1963	$30
❑ LSP-2635 [S]	Live at Basin Street East	1963	$40

LAMBERT, HENDRICKS AND ROSS
Vocal trio: DAVE LAMBERT; JON HENDRICKS; ANNIE ROSS.

Albums

ABC IMPULSE!

Number	Title	Yr	NM
❑ AS-83 [S]	Sing a Song of Basie	1968	$35

ABC-PARAMOUNT

Number	Title	Yr	NM
❑ ABC-223 [M]	Sing a Song of Basie	1958	$50
❑ ABCS-223 [S]	Sing a Song of Basie	1958	$50

COLUMBIA

Number	Title	Yr	NM
❑ CL1675 [M]	High Flying	1961	$30
—Black and red label with six "eye" logos			
❑ CS8475 [S]	High Flying	1961	$40
—Black and red label with six "eye" logos			
❑ CL1675 [M]	High Flying	1963	$35
—Red label with "Guaranteed High Fidelity" or "360 Sound Mono" at bottom			
❑ CS8475 [S]	High Flying	1963	$25
—Red label with "360 Sound Stereo" at bottom			
❑ CL1510 [M]	Lambert, Hendricks and Ross Sing Ellington	1960	$30
—Black and red label with six "eye" logos			
❑ CS8310 [S]	Lambert, Hendricks and Ross Sing Ellington	1960	$40
—Black and red label with six "eye" logos			
❑ CL1510 [M]	Lambert, Hendricks and Ross Sing Ellington	1963	$35
—Red label with "Guaranteed High Fidelity" or "360 Sound Mono" at bottom			
❑ CS8310 [S]	Lambert, Hendricks and Ross Sing Ellington	1963	$25
—Red label with "360 Sound Stereo" at bottom			
❑ KC32911	The Best of Lambert, Hendricks and Ross	1974	$35
❑ C32911	The Best of Lambert, Hendricks and Ross	197?	$25
—First reissue with new prefix			
❑ PC32911	The Best of Lambert, Hendricks and Ross	198?	$20
—Second reissue with new prefix and bar code			
❑ CL1403 [M]	The Hottest New Group in Jazz	1959	$30
—Black and red label with six "eye" logos			
❑ CL1403 [M]	The Hottest New Group in Jazz	1963	$35
—Red label with "Guaranteed High Fidelity" or "360 Sound Mono" at bottom			
❑ CS8198 [S]	The Hottest New Group in Jazz	1959	$40
—Black and red label with six "eye" logos			
❑ CS8198 [S]	The Hottest New Group in Jazz	1963	$25
—Red label with "360 Sound Stereo" at bottom			

COLUMBIA JAZZ ODYSSEY

Number	Title	Yr	NM
❑ PC37020	Lambert, Hendricks and Ross with the Ike Isaacs Trio	1983	$25

IMPULSE!

Number	Title	Yr	NM
❑ A-83 [M]	Sing a Song of Basie	1965	$120
—Reissue of ABC-Paramount ABC-223			
❑ AS-83 [S]	Sing a Song of Basie	1965	$120
—Reissue of ABC-Paramount ABCS-223			

MCA

Number	Title	Yr	NM
❑ 29049	Sing a Song of Basie	1980	$20

ODYSSEY

Number	Title	Yr	NM
❑ 32160292	Way-Out Voices	1968	$35

ROULETTE

Number	Title	Yr	NM
❑ R-52018 [M]	Sing Along with Basie	1959	$40
❑ SR-52018 [S]	Sing Along with Basie	1959	$50

WORLD PACIFIC

Number	Title	Yr	NM
❑ WP-1264 [M]	The Swingers!	1959	$150
❑ ST-1025 [S]	The Swingers!	1959	$150

LAMBSON, ROGER
Saxophone player.

Albums

SEA BREEZE

Number	Title	Yr	NM
❑ SB-2035	Dreams of Mexico	198?	$25

LAMOND, DON
Drummer.

Albums

COMMAND

Number	Title	Yr	NM
❑ RS 33-842 [M]	Off Beat Percussion	1962	$35
❑ RS832SD [S]	Off Beat Percussion	1962	$25

PROGRESSIVE

Number	Title	Yr	NM
❑ PRO-7067	Extraordinary	198?	$25

LANCASTER, BYARD
Alto and soprano saxophone player, flutist and bass clarinetist.

Albums

VORTEX

Number	Title	Yr	NM
❑ 2003	It's Not Up to Us	1968	$30

LAND, HAROLD, AND BLUE MITCHELL
Also see each artist's individual listings.

Albums

CONCORD JAZZ

Number	Title	Yr	NM
❑ CJ-44	Mapenzi	1977	$30

LAND, HAROLD
Tenor saxophone player. Also see RED MITCHELL.

Albums

BLUE NOTE

Number	Title	Yr	NM
❑ LT-1057	Take Aim	1980	$25

CADET

Number	Title	Yr	NM
❑ LPS-813	The Peace-Maker	1968	$35

CONTEMPORARY

Number	Title	Yr	NM
❑ M-3550 [M]	Grooveyard	1959	$250
—Reissue with new title			
❑ S-7550 [S]	Grooveyard	1959	$250
❑ C-3550 [M]	Harold in the Land of Hi-Fi	1958	$250
❑ M-3619 [M]	The Fox	1965	$150
❑ S-7619 [S]	The Fox	1965	$150

FANTASY

Number	Title	Yr	NM
❑ OJC-493	Eastward Ho! Harold Land in New York	1991	$30
❑ OJC-162 [B]	In the Land of Jazz	1984	$200
❑ OJC-343	The Fox	198?	$25
❑ OJC-146	West Coast Blues!	198?	$25

HIFI

Number	Title	Yr	NM
❑ SJ-612 [S]	The Fox	1960	$80

IMPERIAL

Number	Title	Yr	NM
❑ LP-9247 [M]	Jazz Impressions of Folk Music	1963	$150
❑ LP-12247 [S]	Jazz Impressions of Folk Music	1963	$150

JAZZLAND

Number	Title	Yr	NM
❑ JLP-33 [M]	Eastward Ho! Harold Land in New York	1961	$40
❑ JLP-933 [S]	Eastward Ho! Harold Land in New York	1961	$50
❑ JLP-20 [M]	West Coast Blues!	1960	$40
❑ JLP-920 [S]	West Coast Blues!	1960	$50

MAINSTREAM

Number	Title	Yr	NM
❑ MRL-344	Choma (Burn)	1972	$35
❑ MRL-367	Damisi	1973	$35
❑ MRL-314	New Shade of Blue	1971	$35

MUSE

Number	Title	Yr	NM
❑ MR-5272	Xocia's Dance	198?	$25

LANDE, ART, AND JAN GARBAREK
Also see each artist's individual listings.

Albums

ECM

Number	Title	Yr	NM
❑ 1038	Red Lanta	197?	$35

LANDE, ART; DAVE SAMUELA; PAUL MCCANDLESS
Also see each artist's individual listings.

Albums

ECM

Number	Title	Yr	NM
❑ 1208	Skylight	1982	$30

LANDE, ART
Pianist.

Albums

1750 ARCH

Number	Title	Yr	NM
❑ 1769	The Eccentricities of Earl Dant	1978	$35
❑ 1778	The Story of Ba-Ku	1979	$35

ECM

Number	Title	Yr	NM
❑ 1106	Desert	197?	$35
❑ 1081	Rubisa Patrol	197?	$35

LANE, STEVE, AND THE SOUTHERN STOMPERS
Lane is a cornet player and bandleader.

Albums

STOMP OFF

Number	Title	Yr	NM
❑ SOS-1040	Snake Rag	198?	$25

Lee Konitz, *Inside Hi-Fi*, Atlantic 1258, black label, **$300**.

Steve Lacy, *Reflections: Steve Lacy Plays Thelonious Monk*, New Jazz NJLP-8206, purple label, **$300**.

John La Porta, *The Most Minor*, Everest SDBR-1037, **$60**.

Elliot Lawrence, *Elliot Lawrence Plays for Swinging Dancers*, Fantasy 3246, red vinyl, **$40**.

Number	Title	Yr	NM

LANG, EDDIE
Guitarist, considered the first jazz guitar virtuoso.
Albums
YAZOO

Number	Title	Yr	NM
❏ 1059	Virtuoso	198?	$25

LANG, RONNIE
Alto saxophone player.
Albums
TOPS

| ❏ L-1521 [M] | Modern Jazz | 1958 | $250 |

LANGDON, JIM
Albums
CUCA

| ❏ 1100 [M] | Jim Langdon Trio | 1965 | $25 |

LANGFORD, BILL
Organist.
Albums
FANTASY

| ❏ 8396 | Gangbusters and Lollipops | 197? | $25 |

LAPORTA, JOHN
Clarinetist.
Albums
DEBUT

| ❏ DLP-10 [10] | The John LaPorta Quintet | 1954 | $400 |
| ❏ DEB-122 [M] | Three Moods | 1955 | $350 |

EVEREST

| ❏ LPBR-5037 [M] | The Most Minor | 1959 | $50 |
| ❏ SDBR-1037 [S] | The Most Minor | 1959 | $60 |

FANTASY

❏ 3228 [M]	Conceptions	1956	$80
— Red vinyl			
❏ 3228 [M]	Conceptions	1956	$40
— Black vinyl			
❏ 3237 [M]	South American Brothers	1956	$80
— Red vinyl			
❏ 3237 [M]	South American Brothers	1956	$40
— Black vinyl			
❏ 3248 [M]	The Clarinet Artistry of John LaPorta	1957	$80
— Red vinyl			
❏ 3248 [M]	The Clarinet Artistry of John LaPorta	1957	$40
— Black vinyl			

MUSIC MINUS ONE

| ❏ 4003 [M] | Eight Men In Search of a Drummer | 1961 | $30 |

LARKIN, BILLY
lPianist. Includes records by "The Delegates" and "Billy Larkin and the Delegates."
Albums
AURA

❏ AR83003 [M]	Blue Lights	196?	$50
❏ ARS23003 [S]	Blue Lights	196?	$60
❏ 23002 [S]	Pigmy	1964	$30
— As "The Delegates			
❏ 83002 [M]	Pigmy	1964	$25
— As "The Delegates			

BRYAN

| ❏ 105 | Billy Larkin | 1975 | $20 |

SUNBIRD

| ❏ SN50107 | All My Best | 1981 | $12 |

WORLD PACIFIC

❏ WP-1843 [M]	Ain't That a Groove	1966	$100
❏ WPS-21843 [S]	Ain't That a Groove	1966	$100
❏ WP-1863 [M]	Don't Stop!	1967	$100
❏ WPS-21863 [S]	Don't Stop!	1967	$100
❏ WP-1850 [M]	Hold On	1967	$100
❏ WPS-21850 [S]	Hold On	1967	$100
❏ WP-1837 [M]	Hole in the Wall	1966	$100
❏ WPS-21837 [S]	Hole in the Wall	1966	$100
❏ WPS-21883	The Best of Billy Larkin & the Delegates	1968	$100

LARKINS, ELLIS, AND TONY MIDDLETON
Middleton is a male singer. Also see ELLIS LARKINS.
Albums
CONCORD JAZZ

| ❏ CJ-134 | Swingin' for Hamp | 1979 | $25 |

LARKINS, ELLIS
Pianist. Also see RUBY BRAFF.
Albums
ANTILLES

| ❏ DGTL-101 | Ellis Larkins | 198? | $35 |

CLASSIC JAZZ

| ❏ 145 | Smooth One | 1977 | $30 |

DECCA

❏ DL9211 [M]	Blue and Sentimental	1958	$120
❏ DL79211 [S]	Blue and Sentimental	1958	$120
❏ DL5391 [10]	Blues in the Night	1952	$200
❏ DL8303 [M]	Manhattan at Midnight	1956	$120
❏ DL9205 [M]	The Soft Touch	1958	$100
❏ DL79205 [S]	The Soft Touch	1958	$100

STANYAN

❏ 10074	Ellis Larkins Plays Bacharach and McKuen	197?	$35
❏ 10011	Hair	1969	$30
❏ 10024	Lost in the Wood	197?	$30

STORYVILLE

| ❏ STLP-913 [M] | Do Nothin' Till You Hear from Me | 1956 | $50 |
| ❏ STLP-316 [10] | Perfume and Rain | 1955 | $80 |

LARKINS, ELLIS/LEE WILEY
Also see each artist's individual listings.
Albums
STORYVILLE

| ❏ STLP-911 [M] | Duologue | 1956 | $60 |

LAROCA, PETE
Drummer and composer.
Albums
BLUE NOTE

❏ B1-32091	Basra	1995	$35
— The Finest in Jazz Since 1939" reissue			
❏ BLP-4205 [M]	Basra	1965	$60
❏ BST-84205 [S]	Basra	1965	$40
— With "New York, USA" address on label			
❏ BST-84205 [S]	Basra	1967	$35
— With "A Division of Liberty Records" on label			

DOUGLAS

| ❏ SD782 | Turkish Woman at the Bath | 1969 | $35 |

MUSE

| ❏ MR-5011 | Bliss | 197? | $30 |

LAROCCA, NICK
Cornet player. Also see ORIGINAL DIXIELAND JASS (JAZZ) BAND.
Albums
SOUTHLAND

| ❏ 230 [M] | Nick LaRocca and His Dixieland Band | 196? | $25 |

LARSEN, MORTON G.
Pianist.
Albums
STOMP OFF

| ❏ SOS-1009 | Morton G. Larsen Plays Robert Clemente | 198? | $25 |

LARSEN, NEIL
Keyboard player.
Albums
A&M

❏ SP-3117	High Gear	1980	$25
❏ SP-3116	Jungle Fever	1980	$25
— Reissue of Horizon 733			

HORIZON

| ❏ SP-738 | High Gear | 1979 | $35 |
| ❏ SP-733 | Jungle Fever | 1978 | $35 |

LASHA, PRINCE
Flutist and composer.
Albums
CONTEMPORARY

❏ S-7617	Firebirds	1968	$75
❏ M-3610 [M]	The Cry	1963	$200
❏ S-7610 [S]	The Cry	1963	$200

LASHLEY, BARBARA, AND RAY SKJELBRED
Lashley is a female singer. Also see RAY SKJELBRED.
Albums
STOMP OFF

| ❏ SOS-1152 | Sweet and Lowdown | 1988 | $25 |

LASK, ULRICH
Saxophone player.
Albums
ECM

| ❏ 1217 | Lask | 198? | $30 |
| ❏ 1268 | Sucht und Ordnung | 1985 | $30 |

LAST EXIT
Members: Peter Brotzmann (reeds); Sonny Sharrock (guitar); BILL LASWELL (bass); RONALD SHANNON JACKSON (drums, vocals).
Albums
CELLULOID

| ❏ CELL-8140 | Cassette Recordings '87 | 1988 | $15 |

ENEMY

| ❏ 88561-8176-1 | Last Exit | 1986 | $25 |
| ❏ 88561-8178-1 | The Noise of Trouble | 1987 | $18 |

VENTURE

| ❏ 91015 | Iron Path | 1988 | $15 |

LAST POETS, THE
Proto-rap group highly influenced by jazz.
Albums
BLUE THUMB

| ❏ BT-52 | At Last | 1973 | $60 |
| ❏ BT-39 | Chastisement | 1972 | $60 |

CASABLANCA

| ❏ NBLP7051 | Delights of the Garden | 1977 | $60 |

CELLULOID

| ❏ 6136 | Delights of the Garden | 198? | $25 |
| ❏ 6108 | Oh My People | 198? | $25 |

COLLECTABLES

| ❏ COL-6500 | Right On! | 198? | $25 |

JUGGERNAUT

| ❏ 8802 | Right On! | 1971 | $100 |
| — As "The Original Last Poets" | | | |

LASWELL, BILL, AND PETER BROTZMANN
One-half of LAST EXIT. Also see BILL LASWELL.
Albums
CELLULOID

| ❏ CELL-5016 | Low Life | 198? | $15 |

LASWELL, BILL
Bass player. Also see LAST EXIT.
Albums
ELEKTRA/MUSICIAN

| ❏ 60221 | Basslines | 1984 | $12 |

VENTURE

| ❏ 90888 | Hear No Evil | 1988 | $12 |

LATARSKI, DON
Guitarist.
Albums
INNER CITY

| ❏ IC-1114 | Haven | 198? | $30 |

PAUSA

| ❏ 7146 | Lifeline | 1983 | $25 |

Number	Title	Yr	NM

LATEEF, YUSEF

Flutist, tenor saxophone player, oboist, occasional bassoonist and player of more exotic reed instruments as well.

Albums

ABC IMPULSE!

Number	Title	Yr	NM
❑ AS-84 [S]	1984	1968	$200
❑ AS-9117 [S]	A Flat, G Flat and C	1968	$200
❑ ASD-9310	Club Date	1976	$160
❑ AS-56 [S]	Jazz Around the World	1968	$200
❑ AS-69 [S]	Live at Pep's	1968	$200
❑ AS-92 [S]	Psychicemotus	1968	$200
❑ AS-9259	Re-evaluations: The Impulse Years	1974	$200
❑ AS-9125 [S]	The Golden Flute	1968	$200
❑ IA-9353	The Live Session	1978	$200

ALA

| ❑ AJ-502 | Archives of Jazz, Vol. 2 | 198? | $25 |

ARGO

| ❑ LP-634 [M] | Live at Cranbrook | 1959 | $150 |

ATLANTIC

❑ SD 2-1000	10 Years Hence	1977	$60
❑ 81663	Concerto for Yusef Lateef	1988	$30
❑ SD1635	Hush 'n' Thunder	1973	$50
❑ 81977	Nocturnes	1989	$35
❑ SD1650	Part of the Search	1974	$35
❑ SD1563	Suite 16	1970	$60
❑ SD1591	The Best of Yusef Lateef	1971	$50

—1841 Broadway" address on label

| ❑ SD1591 | The Best of Yusef Lateef | 1976 | $30 |

—75 Rockefeller Plaza" address on label

| ❑ SD1508 | The Blue Lateef | 1968 | $60 |

—Blue and green label

| ❑ SD1508 | The Blue Lateef | 1969 | $50 |

—Red and green label

| ❑ SD1499 | The Complete Lateef | 1968 | $40 |

—Blue and green label

| ❑ SD1499 | The Complete Lateef | 1969 | $50 |

—Red and green label

❑ SD1548	The Diverse Lateef	1970	$60
❑ SD1685	The Doctor Is In... And Out	1976	$50
❑ SD1602	The Gentle Giant	1972	$60
❑ SD1525	Yusef Lateef's Detroit	1969	$175

—Reproductions exist

| ❑ 81717 | Yusef Lateef's Little Symphony | 1987 | $35 |

CADET

| ❑ LPS-816 | Live at Cranbrook | 1969 | $60 |
| ❑ LP-634 [M] | Live at Cranbrook | 1966 | $40 |

CHARLIE PARKER

| ❑ PLP-814 [M] | Lost in Sound | 1962 | $100 |
| ❑ PLP-814S [S] | Lost in Sound | 1962 | $120 |

CTI

| ❑ 7082 | Autophysiopsychic | 1977 | $50 |
| ❑ 7088 | In a Temple Garden | 1979 | $50 |

DELMARK

| ❑ DL-407 [M] | Yusef! | 1965 | $40 |
| ❑ DS-407 [M] | Yusef! | 1965 | $100 |

EVEREST ARCHIVE OF FOLK & JAZZ

| ❑ FS-285 | Yusef Lateef | 197? | $25 |

FANTASY

| ❑ OJC-482 | Cry! Tender | 1991 | $30 |

—Reissue of Prestige 7748

| ❑ OJC-612 | Eastern Sounds | 1991 | $35 |

—Reissue of Prestige 7139

| ❑ OJC-399 | Other Sounds | 1989 | $25 |

IMPULSE!

❑ A-84 [M]	1984	1965	$200
❑ AS-84 [S]	1984	1965	$160
❑ A-9117 [M]	A Flat, G Flat and C	1966	$200
❑ AS-9117 [S]	A Flat, G Flat and C	1966	$200
❑ A-56 [M]	Jazz Around the World	1963	$160
❑ AS-56 [S]	Jazz Around the World	1963	$200
❑ A-69 [M]	Live at Pep's	1964	$200
❑ AS-69 [S]	Live at Pep's	1964	$200
❑ MAS-90216 [M]	Live at Pep's	1964	$300

—Capitol Record Club edition

❑ A-92 [M]	Psychicemotus	1966	$200
❑ AS-92 [S]	Psychicemotus	1966	$200
❑ A-9125 [M]	The Golden Flute	1966	$200
❑ AS-9125 [S]	The Golden Flute	1966	$200

LANDMARK

| ❑ LLP-502 | Yusef Lateef in Nigeria | 1985 | $50 |

MCA

| ❑ 4146 | Live Session | 198? | $35 |

—Reissue of ABC Impulse! 9353

MILESTONE

| ❑ M-47009 | The Many Faces of Yusef Lateef | 1973 | $60 |

MOODSVILLE

| ❑ MVLP-22 [M] | Eastern Sounds | 1961 | $175 |

—Green label, silver print

| ❑ MVST-22 [S] | Eastern Sounds | 1961 | $200 |

—Green label, silver print

NEW JAZZ

| ❑ NJLP-8234 [M] | Cry! Tender | 1960 | $300 |

—Purple label

| ❑ NJLP-8234 [M] | Cry! Tender | 1965 | $200 |

—Blue label, trident logo at right

| ❑ NJLP-8272 [M] | Into Something | 1962 | $300 |

—Purple label

| ❑ NJLP-8272 [M] | Into Something | 1965 | $200 |

—Blue label, trident logo at right

| ❑ NJLP-8218 [M] | Other Sounds | 1959 | $300 |

—Purple label

| ❑ NJLP-8218 [M] | Other Sounds | 1965 | $200 |

—Blue label, trident logo at right

| ❑ NJLP-8261 [M] | The Sounds of Yusef | 1961 | $300 |

—Reissue of Prestige 7122; purple label

| ❑ NJLP-8261 [M] | The Sounds of Yusef | 1965 | $200 |

—Blue label, trident logo at right

PRESTIGE

❑ P-24035	Blues for the Orient	1974	$35
❑ PRST-7748	Cry! Tender	1970	$50
❑ PRLP-7319 [M]	Eastern Sounds	1964	$120
❑ PRST-7319 [S]	Eastern Sounds	1964	$140

—Reissue of Moodsville 22

❑ PRST-7653	Expressions	1969	$40
❑ PRST-7832	Imagination	1971	$60
❑ PRST-7637	Into Something	1968	$35
❑ PR-24007	Lateef	1972	$60
❑ PRLP-7122 [M]	The Sounds of Yusef	1957	$200

—Yellow label

❑ PRLP-7398 [M]	The Sounds of Yusef	1966	$60
❑ PRST-7398 [S]	The Sounds of Yusef Lateef	1966	$40
❑ PRLP-7447 [M]	Yusef Lateef Plays for Lovers	1967	$60
❑ PRST-7447 [S]	Yusef Lateef Plays for Lovers	1967	$60
❑ P-24105	Yusef's Bag	1981	$60

RIVERSIDE

❑ RLP-337 [M]	The Centaur and the Phoenix	1960	$200
❑ RLP-9337 [S]	The Centaur and the Phoenix	1960	$200
❑ RS-3011	This Is Yusef Lateef	1968	$100
❑ RLP 12-325 [M]	Three Faces of Yusef Lateef	1960	$200
❑ RLP-1176 [S]	Three Faces of Yusef Lateef	1960	$300

SAVOY

❑ MG-12120 [M]	Jazz and the Sounds of Nature	1958	$175
❑ MG-12109 [M]	Jazz for the Thinker	1957	$175
❑ MG-12103 [M]	Jazz Mood	1957	$175
❑ MG-12117 [M]	Prayer to the East	1957	$175
❑ MG-12139 [M]	The Dreamer	1958	$175
❑ SR-13007 [S]	The Dreamer	1959	$175
❑ MG-12140 [M]	The Fabric of Jazz	1958	$175
❑ SR-13008 [S]	The Fabric of Jazz	1959	$175

SAVOY JAZZ

❑ SJL-2238	Angel Eyes	1979	$60
❑ SJL-2226	Gong!	1978	$60
❑ SJL-2205	Morning: The Savoy Sessions	1976	$50

TRIP

| ❑ 5018 | Outside Blues | 1973 | $30 |

UPFRONT

| ❑ UPF-183 | Dexterity | 197? | $25 |

VERVE

| ❑ MGV-8217 [M] | Before Dawn | 1958 | $200 |
| ❑ V-8217 [M] | Before Dawn | 1961 | $40 |

VJ INTERNATIONAL

| ❑ VJS-3052 [M] | Contemplation | 1974 | $100 |

—Reissue of Vee-Jay 3010, which was originally credited to LOUIS HAYES.

LATIN ALL-STARS, THE

Albums

CROWN

| ❑ CLP5159 [M] | Jazz Heat-Bongo Beat | 1959 | $30 |

LATIN JAZZ QUINTET, THE

Members: Charles Simons (vibraphone); Gene Casey (piano); Bill Ellington (bass); Manuel Ramos (drums, timbales); Juan Amalbert (congas).

Albums

NEW JAZZ

| ❑ NJLP-8251 [M] | Caribe | 1960 | $200 |

—Purple label

| ❑ NJLP-8251 [M] | Caribe | 1965 | $200 |

—Blue label, trident logo at right

| ❑ NJLP-8321 [M] | Latin Soul | 1963 | $0 |

—Reassigned to Status

PRESTIGE

| ❑ MPP-2503 [B] | Caribe | 1980 | $25 |
| ❑ NJLP8251 [M] | Caribe | 1960 | $300 |

—Purple label

TRIP

| ❑ 8008 | Oh! Pharaoh Speak | 197? | $30 |

TRU-SOUND

| ❑ TRU-15003 [M] | Hot Sauce | 1962 | $40 |
| ❑ TRU-15012 [M] | The Latin Jazz Quintet | 1962 | $40 |

LAUER, CHRISTOF

Tenor saxophone player.

Albums

CMP

| ❑ CMP-39-ST | Christof Lauer | 1990 | $30 |

LAURENCE, BABY

Tap dancer. Laurence dances to the music of a jazz band on the below LP.

Albums

CLASSIC JAZZ

| ❑ 30 | Dancemaster | 197? | $25 |

LAVERNE, ANDY

Pianist.

Albums

STEEPLECHASE

| ❑ SCS-1086 | Another World | 198? | $30 |

LAVITZ, T.

Piano and keyboard player. Member of The Dixie Dregs (not included in this book).

Albums

INTIMA

| ❑ D1-73512 | T. Lavitz and the Bad Habits | 1989 | $30 |

LAWRENCE, ARNIE

Alto saxophone (and other reed instruments) player.

Albums

DOCTOR JAZZ

| ❑ FW38445 | Arnie Lawrence and Treasure Island | 1983 | $25 |

EMBRYO

| ❑ SD525 | Inside an Hour Glass | 1970 | $25 |

PROJECT 3

| ❑ PR-5028 | Look Toward a Dream | 1968 | $25 |
| ❑ PR-5011 | You're Gonna Hear From Me | 1967 | $50 |

LAWRENCE, AZAR

Alto saxophone player.

Albums

PRESTIGE

❑ 10086	Bridge Into a New Age	1973	$35
❑ 10099	People Moving	1976	$35
❑ 10097	Summer Solstice	1975	$35

LAWRENCE, ELLIOT

Pianist, bandleader and composer.

Albums

DECCA

| ❑ DL5274 [10] | College Prom | 1950 | $150 |
| ❑ DL5353 [10] | Moonlight on the Campus | 1951 | $200 |

FANTASY

| ❑ 3290 [M] | Big Band Sound | 1959 | $40 |

—Red vinyl

| ❑ 3290 [M] | Big Band Sound | 1959 | $30 |

—Black vinyl, red label, non-flexible vinyl

| ❑ 3290 [M] | Big Band Sound | 196? | $35 |

—Black vinyl, red label, flexible vinyl

| ❑ 8031 [S] | Big Band Sound | 196? | $30 |

—Blue vinyl

Number	Title	Yr	NM
❏ 8031 [S]	Big Band Sound	196?	$25
—Black vinyl, blue label, non-flexible vinyl			
❏ 8031 [S]	Big Band Sound	196?	$30
—Black vinyl, blue label, flexible vinyl			
❏ 3226 [M]	Dream	1956	$50
—Red vinyl			
❏ 3226 [M]	Dream	1956	$30
—Black vinyl, red label, non-flexible vinyl			
❏ 3226 [M]	Dream	196?	$25
—Black vinyl, red label, flexible vinyl			
❏ 3261 [M]	Dream On -- Dance On	1958	$40
—Red vinyl			
❏ 3261 [M]	Dream On -- Dance On	1958	$30
—Black vinyl, red label, non-flexible vinyl			
❏ 3261 [M]	Dream On -- Dance On	196?	$35
—Black vinyl, red label, flexible vinyl			
❏ 8002 [S]	Dream On -- Dance On	196?	$30
—Blue vinyl			
❏ 8002 [S]	Dream On -- Dance On	196?	$25
—Black vinyl, blue label, non-flexible vinyl			
❏ 8002 [S]	Dream On -- Dance On	196?	$30
—Black vinyl, blue label, flexible vinyl			
❏ 3246 [M]	Elliot Lawrence Plays for Swinging Dancers	1957	$40
—Red vinyl			
❏ 3246 [M]	Elliot Lawrence Plays for Swinging Dancers	1957	$30
—Black vinyl, red label, non-flexible vinyl			
❏ 3246 [M]	Elliot Lawrence Plays for Swinging Dancers	196?	$35
—Black vinyl, red label, flexible vinyl			
❏ 8021 [S]	Elliot Lawrence Plays for Swinging Dancers	196?	$30
—Blue vinyl			
❏ 8021 [S]	Elliot Lawrence Plays for Swinging Dancers	196?	$25
—Black vinyl, blue label, non-flexible vinyl			
❏ 8021 [S]	Elliot Lawrence Plays for Swinging Dancers	196?	$30
—Black vinyl, blue label, flexible vinyl			
❏ 3206 [M]	Elliot Lawrence Plays Gerry Mulligan Arrangements	1956	$50
—Red vinyl			
❏ 3206 [M]	Elliot Lawrence Plays Gerry Mulligan Arrangements	1956	$30
—Black vinyl, red label, non-flexible vinyl			
❏ 3206 [M]	Elliot Lawrence Plays Gerry Mulligan Arrangements	196?	$25
—Black vinyl, red label, flexible vinyl			
❏ OJC-117	Elliot Lawrence Plays Gerry Mulligan Arrangements	198?	$25
❏ 3219 [M]	Elliot Lawrence Plays Tiny Kahn and Johnny Mandel Arrangements	1956	$50
—Red vinyl			
❏ 3219 [M]	Elliot Lawrence Plays Tiny Kahn and Johnny Mandel Arrangements	1956	$30
—Black vinyl, red label, non-flexible vinyl			
❏ 3219 [M]	Elliot Lawrence Plays Tiny Kahn and Johnny Mandel Arrangements	196?	$25
—Black vinyl, red label, flexible vinyl			
❏ 3236 [M]	Swinging at the Steel Pier	1956	$50
—Red vinyl			
❏ 3236 [M]	Swinging at the Steel Pier	1956	$30
—Black vinyl, red label, non-flexible vinyl			
❏ 3236 [M]	Swinging at the Steel Pier	196?	$25
—Black vinyl, red label, flexible vinyl			
HINDSIGHT			
❏ HSR-182	Elliot Lawrence and His Orchestra 1946	1982	$25
JAZZTONE			
❏ J-1279 [M]	Big Band Modern	1958	$60
MOBILE FIDELITY			
❏ 2-229	The Music of Elliot Lawrence	1995	$40
—"Original Master Recording" at top of cover			
SESAC			
❏ N-1153 [M]	Jump Steady	1960	$30
❏ SN-1153 [S]	Jump Steady	1960	$40
SURREY			
❏ S-1019 [M]	Winds on Velvet	196?	$30
❏ SS-1019 [S]	Winds on Velvet	196?	$35

Number	Title	Yr	NM
TOP RANK			
❏ RM-304 [M]	Music for Trapping (Tender, That Is)	1959	$60
VIK			
❏ LX-1124 [M]	Hi-Fi-ing Winds	1958	$40
❏ LX-1113 [M]	Jazz Goes Broadway	1958	$60

LAWRENCE, GARY
Pianist and bandleader.
Albums
BLUE GOOSE			
❏ 2020	Gary Lawrence and His Sizzling Syncopators	1979	$25

LAWRENCE, MARK
Flugel horn player, trumpeter, bass player and synthesizer player.

LAWRENCE, MIKE
Albums
OPTIMISM			
❏ OP-3104	Nightwind	198?	$25

LAWRENCE, T.J.
Albums
EAGLE			
❏ SM-4194	Illuminations	1985	$25

LAWS, HUBERT
Flutist, pianist, saxophone player and composer.
Albums
Number	Title	Yr	NM
ATLANTIC			
❏ 1452 [M]	Flute By-Laws	1966	$50
❏ SD1452 [S]	Flute By-Laws	1966	$50
❏ SD1509	Laws Cause	1970	$60
❏ 1432 [M]	The Laws of Jazz	1965	$50
❏ SD1432 [S]	The Laws of Jazz	1965	$60
—Red and purple label			
❏ SD8813	The Laws of Jazz	1981	$20
—Reissue of 1432			
❏ SD1432 [S]	The Laws of Jazz	1969	$35
—Red and green label			
❏ SD1624	Wild Flower	1973	$35
CBS			
❏ M39858	Blanchard: New Earth Sonata; Telemann: Suite in A; Amazing Grace	1985	$25
COLUMBIA			
❏ JC36396	Family	1980	$35
❏ JC35708	Land of Passion	1979	$25
❏ FC38850	Make It Last	1983	$25
❏ PC34330	Romeo and Juliet	1976	$30
❏ JC35022	Say It with Silence	1978	$25
❏ FC36365	The Best of Hubert Laws	1981	$25
CTI			
❏ 6006	Afro-Classic	1971	$50
❏ 8019	Afro-Classic	198?	$25
—Reissue of 6006			
❏ 6025	Carnegie Hall	1973	$35
❏ 1002	Crying Song	1970	$60
—Original issue			
❏ 6000	Crying Song	1970	$35
—Reissue of 1002			
❏ CTX-33	In the Beginning	1974	$50
❏ 6022	Morning Star	1972	$35
❏ 6012	Rite of Spring	1972	$35
❏ 8020	Rite of Spring	198?	$25
—Reissue of 6012			
❏ 6058	The Chicago Theme	1975	$35
❏ 8015	The Chicago Theme	198?	$25
—Reissue of 6058			
❏ 6065	Then There Was Light, Vol. 1	1976	$30
—Half of "In the Beginning," originally issued as part of CTX 3+3			
❏ 6066	Then There Was Light, Vol. 2	1976	$30
—Half of "In the Beginning," originally issued as part of CTX 3+3			
❏ 7071	The San Francisco Concert	1977	$35

LAWS, RONNIE
Soprano saxophone player.
Albums
Number	Title	Yr	NM
BLUE NOTE			
❏ BN-LA628-G	Fever	1976	$30
❏ BN-LA730-H	Friends and Strangers	1977	$25
❏ BN-LA452-G	Pressure Sensitive	1975	$35
CAPITOL			
❏ ST-12375	Classic Masters	1984	$25
❏ ST-512375	Classic Masters	1984	$30
—Columbia House edition			
❏ ST-12261	Mr. Nice Guy	1983	$25
COLUMBIA			
❏ FC40902	All Day Rhythm	1987	$25
❏ BFC40089	Mirror Town	1986	$25
LIBERTY			
❏ LT-1001	Every Generation	1981	$20
—Reissue of United Artists 1001			
❏ LO-628	Fever	198?	$20
—Reissue of Blue Note 628			
❏ LN-10255	Fever	198?	$20
—Budget-line reissue			
❏ LO-881	Flame	198?	$20
—Reissue of United Artists 881			
❏ LN-10232	Flame	198?	$20
—Budget-line reissue			
❏ LW-730	Friends and Strangers	198?	$20
—Reissue of Blue Note 730			
❏ LN-10164	Pressure Sensitive	198?	$20
—Reissue of Blue Note 452			
❏ LO-51087	Solid Ground	1981	$25
❏ LN-10307	Solid Ground	1986	$20
—Budget-line reissue			
UNITED ARTISTS			
❏ LT-1001	Every Generation	1980	$30
❏ UA-LA881-H	Flame	1978	$25

LAWSON, DEE
Albums
ROULETTE			
❏ R-52017 [M]	'Round Midnight	1958	$30
❏ SR-52017 [S]	'Round Midnight	1958	$40

LAWSON, HUGH
Pianist.
Albums
SOUL NOTE			
❏ SN-1052	Colour	1983	$30
STORYVILLE			
❏ 4078	Prime Time	198?	$25

LAWSON, JANET
Female singer.
Albums
INNER CITY			
❏ IC-1118	Janet Lawson Quintet	1981	$30
OMNISOUND			
❏ 1052	Dreams Can Be	1983	$30

LAWSON, STELLA
Albums
STASH			
❏ 235	Goin' For It	198?	$25

LAWSON, YANK, AND BOB HAGGART
Also known as the Lawson-Haggart Jazz Band and the World's Greatest Jazz Band, both of which are covered below. Also see each artist's individual listings.
Albums
Number	Title	Yr	NM
ATLANTIC			
❏ SD1570	Live at the Roosevelt Grill	1970	$35
❏ SD1582	What's New?	1971	$35
DECCA			
❏ DL5456 [10]	Blues on the River	1952	$200
❏ DL8196 [M]	Blues on the River	1955	$150
❏ DL8801 [M]	Boppin' at the Hop	1959	$100
❏ DL78801 [S]	Boppin' at the Hop	1959	$100
❏ DL5427 [10]	College Fight Songs	1952	$150
❏ DL8453 [M]	Hold That Tiger	1956	$150
❏ DL5439 [10]	Lawson-Haggart Band	1952	$150

Elliot Lawrence, *Elliot Lawrence Plays Gerry Mulligan Arrangements*, Fantasy 3206, red vinyl, **$50**.

Elliot Lawrence, *Music for Trapping (Tender, That Is)*, Top Rank RM-304, **$60**.

Peggy Lee, *Black Coffee*, Decca DL 8358, black label with silver print, **$30-$60**.

Peggy Lee, *Rendezvous with Peggy Lee*, Capitol T 151, 12-inch version, turquoise label, **$80**.

Number	Title	Yr	NM
❏ DL5368 [10]	Lawson-Haggart Band Play Jelly Roll's Jazz	1952	$150
❏ DL8182 [M]	Lawson-Haggart Band Play Jelly Roll's Jazz	1955	$150
❏ DL5437 [10]	Lawson-Haggart Band Play King Oliver's Jazz	1952	$150
❏ DL8195 [M]	Lawson-Haggart Band Play King Oliver's Jazz	1955	$150
❏ DL5533 [10]	Louis' Hot Fives and Sevens	1954	$150
❏ DL8200 [M]	Louis' Hot Fives and Sevens	1955	$150
❏ DL5529 [10]	South of the Mason-Dixon Line	1954	$200
❏ DL8197 [M]	South of the Mason-Dixon Line	1955	$200
❏ DL5502 [10]	Windy City Jazz	1953	$150
❏ DL8198 [M]	Windy City Jazz	1955	$150
EVEREST			
❏ LPBR-5084 [M]	Dixieland Goes West	1960	$25
❏ SDBR-1084 [S]	Dixieland Goes West	1960	$30
❏ LPBR-5040 [M]	Junior Prom	1959	$30
❏ SDBR-1040 [S]	Junior Prom	1959	$25
PROJECT 3			
❏ PR-5039	Extra	1969	$25
❏ PR-5033	The World's Greatest Jazz Band	1968	$25
STINSON			
❏ SLP-59 [10]	Lawson-Haggart with Jerry Jerome and His Orchestra	1957	$30

LAWSON, YANK

Trumpeter and bandleader.

Albums

Number	Title	Yr	NM
ABC-PARAMOUNT			
❏ ABC-518 [M]	Big Yank Is Here	1965	$35
❏ ABCS-518 [S]	Big Yank Is Here	1965	$25
❏ ABC-567 [M]	Ole Dixie	1965	$35
❏ ABCS-567 [S]	Ole Dixie	1965	$25
AUDIOPHILE			
❏ AP-221	Yank Lawson Plays Mostly Blues	1986	$25
BRUNSWICK			
❏ BL58035 [10]	Yank Lawson	1953	$120
DOCTOR JAZZ			
❏ FW40064	That's a Plenty	1985	$25
RIVERSIDE			
❏ RLP-2509 [10]	Yank Lawson's Dixieland Jazz	1954	$300

LAZAR, SAM

Organist.

Albums

Number	Title	Yr	NM
ARGO			
❏ LP-4015 [M]	Playback	1962	$30
❏ LPS-4015 [S]	Playback	1962	$40
❏ LP-714 [M]	Soul Merchant	1963	$30
❏ LPS-714 [S]	Soul Merchant	1963	$30
❏ LP-4002 [M]	Space Flight	1961	$30
❏ LPS-4002 [S]	Space Flight	1961	$40

LAZRO, DAUNIK

Baritone and alto saxophone player.

Albums

Number	Title	Yr	NM
HAT ART			
❏ 2010	Sweet Zee	1986	$35
HAT HUT			
❏ 11	Entrance Gates Tshee Park	198?	$35

LEA, BARBARA, AND BOB DOROUGH

Also see each artist's individual listings.

Albums

Number	Title	Yr	NM
AUDIOPHILE			
❏ AP-165	Hoagy's Children	1981	$30

LEA, BARBARA

Female singer.

Albums

Number	Title	Yr	NM
AUDIOPHILE			
❏ AP-86	A Woman in Love	197?	$30
❏ AP-175	Do It Again	1984	$25
❏ AP-125	Remembering Lee Wiley	197?	$30
❏ AP-119	The Devil Is Afraid of Music	197?	$30
FANTASY			
❏ OJC-1713	Barbara Lea	198?	$25
❏ OJC-1742	Lea in Love	1990	$30
PRESTIGE			
❏ PRLP-7065 [M]	Barbara Lea	1956	$300

Number	Title	Yr	NM
❏ PRLP-7100 [M]	Lea in Love	1957	$300
RIVERSIDE			
❏ RLP-2518 [10]	A Woman in Love	1955	$300

LEADBELLY

One of America's greatest folk singers, the below is "jazz" in name only.

Albums

Number	Title	Yr	NM
CAPITOL			
❏ H369 [10]	Classics in Jazz	1953	$300

LEADERS, THE

Collaboration of bandleaders and composers: CHICO FREEMAN; CECIL McBEE; KIRK LIGHTSEY; LESTER BOWIE; ARTHUR BLYTHE; and Famadou Don Moye.

Albums

Number	Title	Yr	NM
BLACK SAINT			
❏ 120119	Out Here Like This	1989	$35
❏ 120129	Unforeseen Blessings	1990	$35

LEAHEY, HARRY

Guitarist.

Albums

Number	Title	Yr	NM
OMNISOUND			
❏ 1042	Silver Threads	198?	$25
❏ 1031	Still Waters	198?	$25

LEAPER, BOB

British trumpeter and bandleader.

Albums

Number	Title	Yr	NM
LONDON			
❏ LL3391 [M]	Big Band Beatle Songs	1964	$60
❏ SP44056 [S]	Big Band Beatle Songs	1964	$40

LEARY, JAMES

Bass player.

Albums

Number	Title	Yr	NM
VITAL MUSIC			
❏ VTL-003	James	199?	$35
❏ VTL-005	James II	199?	$35

LEE, CHUCK

See CHUZ ALFRED; HOWARD RUMSEY.

LEE, EDDIE

Pianist and vibraphone player.

Albums

Number	Title	Yr	NM
GEORGIAN			
❏ GR2001 [M]	Windy City Profile	1958	$40

LEE, JEANNE, AND RAN BLAKE

Lee is a female singer. Also see RAN BLAKE.

Albums

Number	Title	Yr	NM
BLUEBIRD			
❏ 6461-1-RB	The Legendary Duets	1987	$30
RCA VICTOR			
❏ LPM-2500 [M]	The Newest Sound Around	1962	$30
❏ LSP-2500 [S]	The Newest Sound Around	1962	$40

LEE, JEANNE

Albums

Number	Title	Yr	NM
EARTHFORM RECORDS			
❏ 814 [B]	Conspiracy	1975	$350
SEEDS			
❏ no cat [B]	Conspiracy		$500

LEE, JOHN, AND GERRY BROWN

Lee plays bass and synthesizers; Brown is a drummer and percussionist.

Albums

Number	Title	Yr	NM
BLUE NOTE			
❏ BN-LA541-G	Mango Sunrise	1976	$30
❏ BN-LA701-G	Still Can't Say Enough	1977	$30

LEE, JULIA

Female singer, pianist and composer.

Albums

Number	Title	Yr	NM
CAPITOL			
❏ H228 [10]	Party Time	1950	$300
PAUSA			
❏ 9020	Julia Lee and Her Boyfriends	198?	$25

LEE, PEGGY

Female singer. Earlier material appears in the Goldmine Standard Catalog of American Records.

Albums

Number	Title	Yr	NM
A&M			
❏ SP-4547	Mirrors	1975	$15
ATLANTIC			
❏ SD18108	Let's Love	1974	$15
CAPITOL			
❏ T1366 [M]	All Aglow Again	1960	$50
—Black label with colorband, Capitol logo at left			
❏ T1366 [M]	All Aglow Again	1962	$80
—Black label with colorband, Capitol logo at top			
❏ ST1366 [S]	All Aglow Again	1960	$50
—Black label with colorband, Capitol logo at left			
❏ ST1366 [S]	All Aglow Again	1962	$40
—Black label with colorband, Capitol logo at top			
❏ T1213 [M]	Alright, Okay, You Win	1959	$60
❏ ST1213 [S]	Alright, Okay, You Win	1959	$60
❏ ST-183	A Natural Woman	1969	$40
❏ T1520 [M]	Basin Street East	1961	$40
—Black label with colorband, Capitol logo at left			
❏ T1520 [M]	Basin Street East	1962	$80
—Black label with colorband, Capitol logo at top			
❏ ST1520 [S]	Basin Street East	1961	$60
—Black label with colorband, Capitol logo at left			
❏ ST1520 [S]	Basin Street East	1962	$40
—Black label with colorband, Capitol logo at top			
❏ SM-1520	Basin Street East	1977	$12
—Reissue with new prefix			
❏ T1219 [M]	Beauty and the Beat	1959	$60
—With George Shearing; black label with colorband, Capitol logo at left			
❏ ST1219 [S]	Beauty and the Beat	1959	$60
—With George Shearing; black label with colorband, Capitol logo at left			
❏ T1219 [M]	Beauty and the Beat	1962	$40
—With George Shearing; black label with colorband, Capitol logo at top			
❏ ST1219 [S]	Beauty and the Beat	1962	$40
—With George Shearing; black label with colorband, Capitol logo at top			
❏ T1743 [M]	Bewitching-Lee!	1962	$250
—Black "The Star Line" label			
❏ DT1743 [R]	Bewitching-Lee!	1962	$40
❏ T2475 [M]	Big $pender	1966	$40
❏ ST2475 [S]	Big $pender	1966	$40
❏ T1671 [M]	Blue Cross Country	1962	$40
❏ ST1671 [S]	Blue Cross Country	1962	$60
❏ ST-463	Bridge Over Troubled Water	1970	$15
❏ T1423 [M]	Christmas Carousel	1960	$25
❏ ST1423 [S]	Christmas Carousel	1960	$60
❏ T2732 [M]	Extra Special	1967	$40
❏ ST2732 [S]	Extra Special	1967	$25
❏ STBB-517	Folks Who Live on the Hill/ Broadway Ala Lee	1970	$20
❏ T2469 [M]	Guitars Ala Lee	1966	$40
❏ ST2469 [S]	Guitars Ala Lee	1966	$50
❏ T2390 [M]	Happy Holiday	1965	$50
❏ ST2390 [S]	Happy Holiday	1965	$40
❏ T1630 [M]	If You Go	1962	$50
❏ ST1630 [S]	If You Go	1962	$60
❏ T1131 [M]	I Like Men	1959	$60
❏ ST1131 [S]	I Like Men	1959	$60
❏ T1857 [M]	I'm a Woman	1963	$50
❏ SM-1857	I'm a Woman	1977	$12
—Reissue with new prefix			
❏ T1969 [M]	In Love Again	1963	$50
❏ ST1969 [S]	In Love Again	1963	$60
❏ T2096 [M]	In the Name of Love	1964	$40
❏ ST2096 [S]	In the Name of Love	1964	$25
❏ ST-386	Is That All There Is?	1969	$50
❏ SM-386	Is That All There Is?	197?	$12
—Reissue with new prefix			
❏ T979 [M]	Jump for Joy	1958	$75
—Turquoise or gray label			
❏ T979 [M]	Jump for Joy	1959	$60
—Black label with colorband, Capitol logo at left			
❏ ST979 [S]	Jump for Joy	1959	$60
❏ T1290 [M]	Latin Ala Lee!	1960	$40

Number	Title	Yr	NM
— Black label with colorband, Capitol logo at left			
❏ T1290 [M]	Latin Ala Lee!	1962	$50
— Black label with colorband, Capitol logo at top			
❏ ST1290 [S]	Latin Ala Lee!	1960	$60
— Black label with colorband, Capitol logo at left			
❏ ST1290 [S]	Latin Ala Lee!	1962	$40
— Black label with colorband, Capitol logo at top			
❏ SM-1290	Latin Ala Lee!	1977	$12
— Reissue with new prefix			
❏ ST-622	Make It with You	1970	$15
❏ T1850 [M]	Mink Jazz	1963	$40
❏ ST1850 [S]	Mink Jazz	1963	$60
❏ H204 [10]	My Best to You	1952	$150
❏ T204 [M]	My Best to You	1954	$80
— Turquoise or gray label			
❏ T204 [M]	My Best to You	1959	$60
— Black label with colorband, Capitol logo at left			
❏ ST-11077	Norma Deloris Egstrom from Jamestown, North Dakota	1972	$15
❏ T1475 [M]	Ole Ala Lee!	1961	$25
❏ ST1475 [S]	Ole Ala Lee!	1961	$60
❏ T2320 [M]	Pass Me By	1965	$40
❏ ST2320 [S]	Pass Me By	1965	$50
❏ STCL-576	Peggy Lee	1970	$30
❏ DKAO-377	Peggy Lee's Greatest	1969	$15
❏ SN-16140	Peggy Lee Sings Songs of Cy Coleman	198?	$10
❏ T1401 [M]	Pretty Eyes	1960	$50
— Black label with colorband, Capitol logo at left			
❏ T1401 [M]	Pretty Eyes	1962	$40
— Black label with colorband, Capitol logo at top			
❏ ST1401 [S]	Pretty Eyes	1960	$60
— Black label with colorband, Capitol logo at left			
❏ ST1401 [S]	Pretty Eyes	1962	$40
— Black label with colorband, Capitol logo at top			
❏ H151 [10]	Rendezvous with Peggy Lee	1952	$150
❏ T151 [M]	Rendezvous with Peggy Lee	1954	$80
— Turquoise or gray label			
❏ T151 [M]	Rendezvous with Peggy Lee	1959	$60
— Black label with colorband, Capitol logo at left			
❏ ST2781	Somethin' Groovy	1968	$40
❏ T1772 [M]	Sugar 'n' Spice	1962	$50
❏ ST1772 [S]	Sugar 'n' Spice	1962	$60
❏ T2388 [M]	That Was Then, Now Is Now	1965	$40
❏ ST2388 [S]	That Was Then, Now Is Now	1965	$50
❏ ST2887	The Hits of Peggy Lee	1968	$25
❏ T864 [M]	The Man I Love	1957	$80
— Turquoise label			
❏ ST864 [S]	The Man I Love	1959	$60
❏ T1049 [M]	Things Are Swingin'	1958	$60
❏ ST1049 [S]	Things Are Swingin'	1959	$60
❏ ST-810	Where Did They Go	1971	$30
COLUMBIA			
❏ CL6033 [10]	Benny Goodman and Peggy Lee	1949	$60
DECCA			
❏ DL5482 [10]	Black Coffee	1953	$150
❏ DL4458 [M]	Lover	1964	$30
❏ DL74458 [R]	Lover	1964	$25
❏ DL8816 [M]	Miss Wonderful	1959	$80
❏ DL8591 [M]	Sea Shells	1958	$100
❏ DL5539 [10]	Songs in an Intimate Style	1953	$150
❏ DXB164 [M]	The Best of Peggy Lee	1964	$30
❏ DXSB7164 [R]	The Best of Peggy Lee	1964	$25
❏ DL4461 [M]	The Fabulous Peggy Lee	1964	$30
❏ DL74461 [R]	The Fabulous Peggy Lee	1964	$25
DRG			
❏ SL-5190	Close Enough for Love	1979	$15
EVEREST ARCHIVE OF FOLK & JAZZ			
❏ 294	Peggy Lee	197?	$12
GLENDALE			
❏ 6023	You Can Depend on Me	1982	$25
HARMONY			
❏ H30024	Miss Peggy Lee	1970	$12
❏ HL7005 [M]	Peggy Lee Sings with Benny Goodman	195?	$30
HINDSIGHT			
❏ HSR-220	Peggy Lee with the David Barbour and Billy May Bands, 1948	1985	$12
MCA			
❏ 4049	The Best of Peggy Lee	197?	$15
MERCURY			
❏ SRM-1-1172	Live in London	1977	$15
MUSICMASTERS			
❏ 5005	Peggy Sings the Blues	1988	$15
PAUSA			
❏ PR-9043	Sugar 'n' Spice	1985	$12
PICKWICK			
❏ SPC-3192	I've Got the World	1971	$12

Number	Title	Yr	NM
❏ SPC-3090	Once More with Feeling	196?	$12
S&P			
❏ 502	Bewitching-Lee!	2003	$30
— Reissue on 180-gram vinyl			
❏ 504	Latin Ala Lee!	2004	$30
— Reissue on 180-gram vinyl			
TIME-LIFE			
❏ SLGD-07	Legendary Singers: Peggy Lee	1985	$20
VOCALION			
❏ VL73903	Crazy in the Heart	1969	$12
❏ VL3776 [M]	So Blue	1966	$20
❏ VL73776 [R]	So Blue	1966	$12

LEE, PERRY
Organist.

Albums
ROULETTE

Number	Title	Yr	NM
❏ R-52080 [M]	A Night at Count Basie's	1962	$25
❏ SR-52080 [S]	A Night at Count Basie's	1962	$25

LEE, THOMAS OBOE
Flutist (despite his name) and composer of both jazz and classical works.

Albums
GM RECORDINGS

Number	Title	Yr	NM
❏ GM-3004	Departed Feathers	1986	$25

LEEDS, ERIC
Flutist and saxophone player; also a member of Prince's live backing group.

Albums
PAISLEY PARK

Number	Title	Yr	NM
❏ 27499	Times Square	1991	$35

LEES, GENE, AND ROGER KELLAWAY
Also see each artist's individual listings.

Albums
CHOICE

Number	Title	Yr	NM
❏ CRS-6832	Leaves on the Water	1986	$25

LEES, GENE
Male singer. Better known as a composer, lyricist and author.

Albums
STASH

Number	Title	Yr	NM
❏ ST-269	Gene Lees Sings the Gene Lees Songbook	1987	$25

LEESE, TIM

Albums
MUSIC IS MEDICINE

Number	Title	Yr	NM
❏ 9036	After Hours	198?	$30

LEFEBVRE, DAVE
Woodwinds player.

Albums
JAZZ HOUNDS

Number	Title	Yr	NM
❏ 01	Marble Dust	198?	$30

LEFEBVRE, GARY
Tenor and alto saxophone player.

Albums
DISCOVERY

Number	Title	Yr	NM
❏ DS-849	Gary LeFebvre Quartet	1981	$30

LEGGE, WADE
Pianist.

Albums
BLUE NOTE

Number	Title	Yr	NM
❏ BLP-5031 [10]	New Faces New Sounds	1953	$600

LEGGIO, CARMEN
Tenor saxophone player.

Albums

Number	Title	Yr	NM
DREAMSTREET			
❏ 103	Aerial View	1979	$30
FAMOUS DOOR			
❏ 125	Tarytown Tenor	1978	$30
GOLDEN CREST			
❏ GCS-1000	Jazz	196?	$25
PROGRESSIVE			
❏ PRO-7010	Smile	1980	$25

LEGRAND, MICHEL
Pianist and composer; best known for his film scores.

Albums

Number	Title	Yr	NM
BELL			
❏ 6071	Brian's Song Themes & Variations	1972	$25
❏ 4200	Twenty Songs of the Century	1974	$30
COLUMBIA			
❏ CL888 [M]	Castles in Spain	1956	$60
❏ CL647 [M]	Holiday in Rome	1955	$75
❏ CL555 [M]	I Love Paris	1954	$40
❏ CL1437 [M]	I Love Paris	1960	$60
❏ CS8237 [S]	I Love Paris	1960	$50
❏ PC9237	I Love Paris	1987	$20
— Reissue with new prefix			
❏ CL1139 [M]	Legrand in Rio	1957	$60
❏ CL1250 [M]	Legrand Jazz	1958	$40
— Miles Davis appears on this record			
❏ CS8079 [S]	Legrand Jazz	1959	$40
— Miles Davis appears on this record			
❏ CL1115 [M]	Michel Legrand Plays Cole Porter	1957	$60
❏ CL706 [M]	Vienna Holiday	1955	$75
GRYPHON			
❏ 786	Jazz Grand	1978	$25
HARMONY			
❏ KH31549	Cole Porter, Volume I	1972	$25
❏ KH31540	Cole Porter, Volume II	1972	$25
❏ HL7331 [M]	I Love Paris	196?	$30
❏ HS11131 [S]	I Love Paris	196?	$30
MERCURY			
❏ MG20342 [M]	C'est Magnifique	1958	$100
MGM			
❏ SE-4491	Cinema La Grand	1967	$35
MOBILE FIDELITY			
❏ 1-504	Jazz Grand	198?	$100
— Audiophile vinyl			
PABLO TODAY			
❏ 2312139	After the Rain	198?	$25
PHILIPS			
❏ PHM200143 [M]	Michel Legrand Sings	1964	$60
❏ PHS600143 [S]	Michel Legrand Sings	1964	$60
❏ PHM200074 [M]	The Michel Legrand Big Band Plays Richard Rogers	1963	$50
❏ PHS600074 [S]	The Michel Legrand Big Band Plays Richard Rogers	1963	$60
RCA VICTOR			
❏ BGL1-1028	Concert	1976	$25
❏ BXL1-1028	Concert	1978	$20
— Reissue with new prefix			
❏ BGL1-0850	Jimmy's	1975	$25
❏ BXL1-0850	Jimmy's	1978	$20
— Reissue with new prefix			
❏ BGL1-1392	Michel Legrand and Friends	1976	$25
❏ BXL1-1392	Michel Legrand and Friends	1978	$20
— Reissue with new prefix			
VERVE			
❏ V6-8760	Michel Legrand at Shelly's Mann-Hole	1969	$30

LEIGH, CAROL
Female singer.

Albums

Number	Title	Yr	NM
GHB			
❏ 152	Blame It on the Blues	198?	$30
❏ 167	Go Back Where You Stayed Last Night	198?	$30
❏ GHB-88	Wild Women Don't Have the Blues	197?	$30
❏ 136	You've Got to Give Me Some	1980	$30
STOMP OFF			
❏ SOS-1064	If You Don't Know, I Know Who Will	1983	$25
❏ SOS-1087	I'm Busy and You Can't Come In	1985	$25

Number	Title	Yr	NM

LEIGHTON, BERNIE
Pianist.

Albums

CAMEO
| ❑ C-1005 [M] | Dizzy Fingers | 1959 | $60 |

COLUMBIA
| ❑ CL6112 [10] | East Side Rendezvous | 1950 | $80 |

MONMOUTH-EVERGREEN
| ❑ 7068 | Bernie Leighton Plays Duke Ellington Live at Jimmy Weston's | 197? | $30 |

LEIGHTON, BERNIE/JOHNNY GUARNIERI
Also see each artist's individual listings.

Albums

EMARCY
| ❑ MG-26018 [10] | Piano Stylings | 1954 | $250 |

LEITCH, PETER
Guitarist.

Albums

PAUSA
| ❑ 7132 | Jump Street | 1981 | $25 |

LELLIS, TOM
Male singer.

Albums

INNER CITY
| ❑ IC-1090 | And In This Corner | 198? | $35 |

LEMER, PETER
Pianist.

Albums

ESP-DISK'
| ❑ 1057 | Local Colour | 1968 | $200 |

LEONARD, HARLAN
Alto saxophone player and bandleader.

Albums

RCA VICTOR
| ❑ LPV-531 [M] | Harlan Leonard and His Rockets | 1965 | $30 |

LEONARD, HARVEY
Pianist.

Albums

KEYNOTE
| ❑ 1102 [M] | Jazz Ecstasy | 1955 | $60 |

LEONHART, JAY
Bass player, male singer and composer.

Albums

SUNNYSIDE
| ❑ SSC-1032 | The Double Cross | 1989 | $30 |
| ❑ SSC-1006 | There's Gonna Be Trouble | 1985 | $25 |

LES JAZZ MODES
Members: JULIUS WATKINS (French horn), CHARLIE ROUSE (tenor sax), GILDO MAHONES (piano), Martin Rivera (bass) and RON JEFFERSON (drums).

Albums

ATLANTIC
❑ 1306 [M]	Les Jazz Modes	1959	$300
—Black label			
❑ 1306 [M]	Les Jazz Modes	1961	$150
—Multicolor label, white "fan" logo at right			
❑ SD-1306 [S]	Les Jazz Modes	1959	$300
—Green label			
❑ SD-1306 [S]	Les Jazz Modes	1961	$150
—Multicolor label, white "fan" logo at right			
❑ 1280 [M]	The Most Happy Fella	1958	$250
—Black label			
❑ 1280 [M]	The Most Happy Fella	1961	$150
—Multicolor label, white "fan" logo at right			

DAWN

❑ DLP-1101 [M]	Jazzville	1956	$100
❑ DLP-1108 [M]	Les Jazz Modes	1956	$100
❑ DLP-1117 [M]	Mood in Scarlet	1957	$100

SEECO
| ❑ CELP-466 [M] | Smart Jazz for the Smart Set | 1960 | $100 |

LESBERG, JACK
Bass player.

Albums

FAMOUS DOOR
| ❑ 120 | Hollywood | 1977 | $30 |

LESLIE, BILL
Tenor saxophone player.

Albums

ARGO
| ❑ LP-710 [M] | Diggin' the Chicks | 1962 | $30 |
| ❑ LPS-710 [S] | Diggin' the Chicks | 1962 | $30 |

LESMANA, INDRA
Pianist.

Albums

ZEBRA
| ❑ ZEB-5709 | For Earth and Heaven | 1986 | $25 |
| ❑ ZR-5005 | Indra Lesmana and Nebula | 1984 | $30 |

LETMAN, JOHN
Trumpeter.

Albums

BETHLEHEM
| ❑ BCP-6053 [M] | The Many Angles of John Letman | 1961 | $200 |
| ❑ SBCP-6053 [S] | The Many Angles of John Letman | 1961 | $200 |

LEVEY, STAN
Drummer. Also see CONTE CANDOLI; MAX ROACH.

Albums

BETHLEHEM
❑ BCP-71 [M]	Grand Stan	1957	$250
❑ BCP-1017 [10]	Stan Levey Plays	1954	$250
❑ BCP-6030 [M]	Stanley the Steamer	197?	$35
—Reissue of 37, distributed by RCA Victor			
❑ BCP-37 [M]	This Time the Dream's On Me	1956	$250

MODE
| ❑ LP-101 [M] | Stan Levey Quartet | 1957 | $80 |

LEVIEV, MILCHO
Pianist.

Albums

DOBRE
| ❑ 1025 | Piano Lesson | 197? | $30 |

OPTIMISM
| ❑ OP-2004 | Destination | 198? | $25 |

TREND
| ❑ 530 | Music for Big Band and Symphony Orchestra | 1982 | $25 |

LEVIN, MARC
Cornet player.

Albums

SAVOY
| ❑ MG-12190 [M] | The Dragon Suite | 1967 | $30 |

SWEET DRAGON
| ❑ 1 | Songs, Dances and Prayers | 197? | $25 |

LEVIN, PETE
Pianist, organist, keyboard player, banjo player and composer.

Albums

GRAMAVISION
| ❑ R1-79456 | Party in the Basement | 1990 | $35 |

LEVINE, HENRY
Trumpeter.

Albums

RCA CAMDEN
| ❑ CAL-321 [M] | Lower Basin Street | 1958 | $30 |

RCA VICTOR
| ❑ LPM-1283 [M] | Dixieland Jazz Band | 1956 | $50 |

LEVINE, MARK
Pianist.

Albums

CATALYST
| ❑ 7614 | Up 'Til Now | 1976 | $30 |

CONCORD JAZZ
| ❑ CJ-234 | Concepts | 1984 | $25 |
| ❑ CJ-352 | Smiley and Me | 1988 | $25 |

LEVINSON, MARK
Bass player.

Albums

MARK LEVINSON
| ❑ 7 | Jazz at Long Wharf | 1979 | $60 |
| —Audiophile edition pressed at 45 rpm | | | |

LEVISTER, ALONZO
Pianist, composer and arranger.

Albums

DEBUT
| ❑ DEB-125 [M] | Manhattan Moondrama | 1956 | $250 |

LEVITT, ROD
Trombonist, composer and bandleader.

Albums

RCA VICTOR
❑ LPM-3615 [M]	42nd Street	1966	$35
❑ LSP-3615 [S]	42nd Street	1966	$25
❑ LPM-3372 [M]	Insight	1965	$35
❑ LSP-3372 [S]	Insight	1965	$25
❑ LPM-3448 [M]	Solid Ground	1965	$35
❑ LSP-3448 [S]	Solid Ground	1965	$25

RIVERSIDE
| ❑ RLP-471 [M] | The Dynamic Sound Patterns of the Rod Levitt Orchestra | 1964 | $150 |
| ❑ RS-9471 [S] | The Dynamic Sound Patterns of the Rod Levitt Orchestra | 1964 | $150 |

LEVITTS, THE
Family group: Al Levitt (drums); Sean Levitt (guitar); Stella Levitt, Michele Levitt, Miron Levitt, Teresa Levitt (vocals). One of the backing musicians is CHICK COREA.

Albums

ESP-DISK'
| ❑ S-1095 | We Are the Levitts | 1970 | $200 |

LEVY, LOU
Pianist.

Albums

DOBRE
| ❑ 1042 | A Touch of Class | 1978 | $30 |

INTERPLAY
| ❑ 7711 | Tempus Fugue It | 197? | $25 |

JUBILEE
| ❑ JLP-1101 [M] | Lou Levy Plays Baby Grand Jazz | 1959 | $40 |
| ❑ SDJLP-1101 [S] | Lou Levy Plays Baby Grand Jazz | 1959 | $40 |

NOCTURNE
| ❑ NLP-10 [10] | Lou Levy Trio | 1954 | $100 |

PHILIPS
| ❑ PHM200056 [M] | The Hymn | 1962 | $35 |
| ❑ PHS600056 [S] | The Hymn | 1962 | $25 |

RCA VICTOR
| ❑ LPM-1319 [M] | Jazz in Four Colors | 1956 | $50 |
| ❑ LPM-1267 [M] | Solo Scene | 1956 | $50 |

John Lewis and Bill Perkins, *Grand Encounter: 2° East, 3° West*, Pacific Jazz PJ-1217, **$300**.

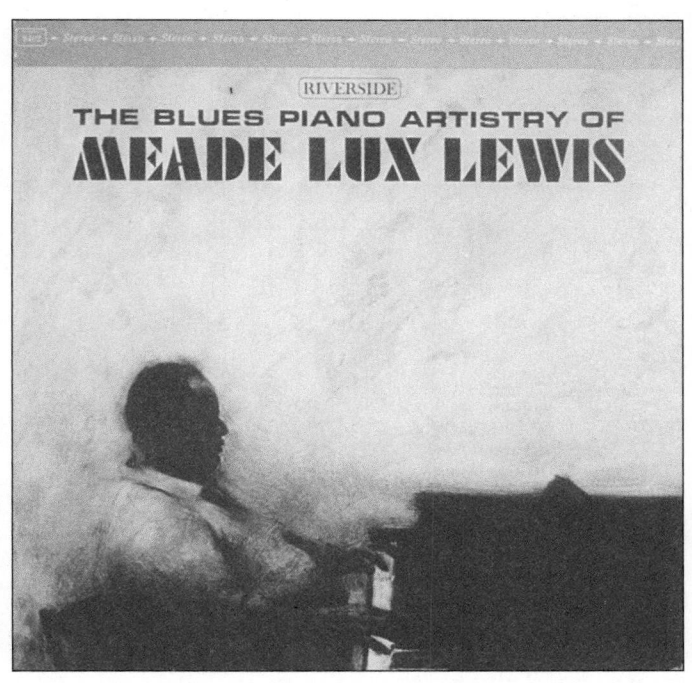

Meade Lux Lewis, *The Blues Piano Artistry of Meade Lux Lewis*, Riverside RS-9402, **$200**.

Mel Lewis Sextet, *Mel Lewis Sextet*, Mode LP-103, **$120**.

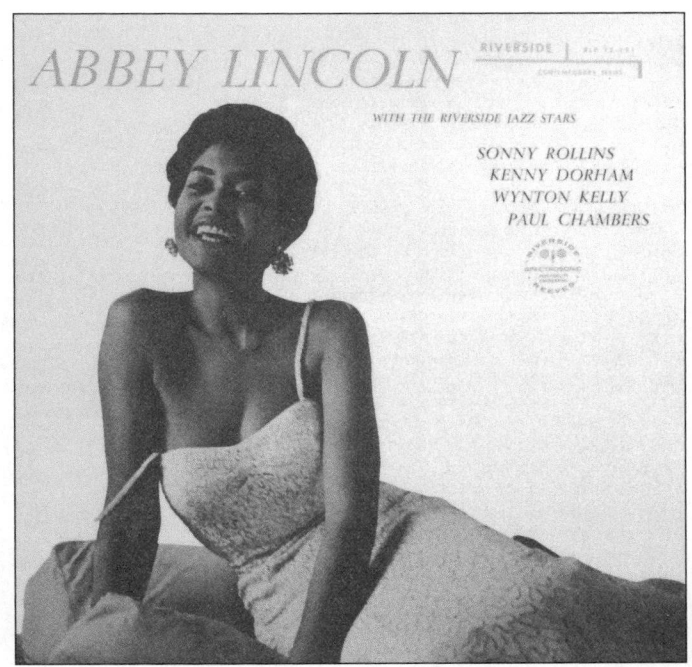

Abbey Lincoln, *That's Him* (Abbey Lincoln with the Riverside Jazz Stars), Riverside RLP-1107, **$300**.

LEVY, LOU/CONTE CANDOLI

Also see each artist's individual listings.

Albums

Number	Title	Yr	NM
ATLANTIC			
❏ 1268 [M]	West Coast Wailers	1957	$300
—Black label			
❏ 1268 [M]	West Coast Wailers	1961	$150
—Multicolor label, white "fan" logo at right			

LEVY, O'DONEL

Guitarist and male singer.

Albums

Number	Title	Yr	NM
GROOVE MERCHANT			
❏ 501	Black Velvet	1971	$30
❏ 507	Breeding of Mind	1972	$30
❏ 518	Dawn of a New Day	1973	$30
❏ 535	Everything I Do Gonna Be Funky	1975	$30
❏ 4408	Hands of Fire	197?	$30
❏ 526	Simba	1974	$30
❏ 3313	Windows	197?	$50

LEWES, WILSON

Albums

Number	Title	Yr	NM
DIPLOMAT			
❏ D-2369 [M]	The "In" Crowd	1965	$25
❏ DS-2369 [S]	The "In" Crowd	1965	$30
❏ D-2378 [M]	The Shadow of Your Smile	1966	$25
❏ DS-2378 [S]	The Shadow of Your Smile	1966	$30

LEWIS, GEORGE (1)

Clarinetist and occasional alto saxophone player.

Albums

Number	Title	Yr	NM
AMERICAN MUSIC			
❏ 645 [10]	George Lewis with Kid Shots Madison	1952	$80
❏ 639 [10]	The George Lewis Band in the French Quarter	1951	$80
ATLANTIC			
❏ 1411 [M]	The George Lewis Band	1963	$50
❏ SD1411 [S]	The George Lewis Band	1963	$50
BIOGRAPH			
❏ CEN-1	George Lewis and His Mustache Stompers	197?	$25
BLUE NOTE			
❏ BLP-1205 [M]	George Lewis and His New Orleans Stompers, Volume 1	1955	$1000
—Regular version, Lexington Ave. address on label			
❏ BLP-1205 [M]	George Lewis and His New Orleans Stompers, Volume 1	1963	$150
—With "New York, USA" address on label			
❏ BST-81205 [R]	George Lewis and His New Orleans Stompers, Volume 1	1967	$30
—With "A Division of Liberty Records" on label			
❏ BLP-1206 [M]	George Lewis and His New Orleans Stompers, Volume 2	1955	$1000
—Regular version, Lexington Ave. address on label			
❏ BLP-1206 [M]	George Lewis and His New Orleans Stompers, Volume 2	1963	$150
—With "New York, USA" address on label			
❏ BST-81206 [R]	George Lewis and His New Orleans Stompers, Volume 2	1967	$30
—With "A Division of Liberty Records" on label			
❏ BLP-1208 [M]	George Lewis Concert!	1955	$800
—Regular version, Lexington Ave. address on label			
❏ BLP-1208 [M]	George Lewis Concert!	1963	$100
—With "New York, USA" address on label			
❏ BST-81208 [R]	George Lewis Concert!	1967	$30
—With "A Division of Liberty Records" on label			
❏ BLP-7010 [10]	George Lewis' New Orleans Stompers, Volume 1	1951	$250
❏ BLP-7013 [10]	George Lewis' New Orleans Stompers, Volume 2	1951	$250
❏ BLP-7027 [10]	George Lewis' New Orleans Stompers, Volume 3	1954	$250
❏ BLP-7028 [10]	George Lewis' New Orleans Stompers, Volume 4	1954	$250
CAVALIER			
❏ CVLP-6004 [M]	George Lewis in Hi-Fi	1956	$60
CIRCLE			
❏ L-421 [10]	George Lewis and His New Orleans All-Stars	1951	$80
DELMAR			

Number	Title	Yr	NM
❏ DL-201 [M]	Doctor Jazz	195?	$50
❏ DL-202 [M]	On Parade	195?	$50
DELMARK			
❏ DL-203	George Lewis Memorial Album	196?	$25
❏ DL-202	George Lewis' New Orleans Stompers	196?	$30
DISC JOCKEY			
❏ DDL-100 [M]	Jazz at Ohio Union	195?	$1200
—Box set with booklet			
EMPIRICAL			
❏ EM-107 [10]	Spirituals in Ragtime	1956	$80
EVEREST ARCHIVE OF FOLK & JAZZ			
❏ 240	George Lewis	197?	$25
FANTASY			
❏ OJC-1739	George Lewis of New Orleans	198?	$25
❏ OJC-1736	Jazz at Vespers	198?	$25
FOLKLYRIC			
❏ 9030	George Lewis and His New Orleans Ragtime Jazz Band	198?	$25
GHB			
❏ GHB-10	City of a Million Dreams	1964	$30
❏ GHB-29	Easy Riders Jazz Band	1965	$30
❏ GHB-39	Easy Riders Jazz Band	1968	$30
❏ GHB-37	For Dancers Only	1968	$30
❏ GHB-5	George Lewis and His Ragtime Stompers	196?	$30
❏ GHB-14	George Lewis in Japan, Volume 1	1965	$30
❏ GHB-15	George Lewis in Japan, Volume 2	1965	$30
❏ GHB-16	George Lewis in Japan, Volume 3	1965	$30
❏ GHB-68	The Big Four	1970	$30
JAZZ CRUSADE			
❏ 2004	Jazzology Poll	1965	$30
JAZZ MAN			
❏ LP-1 [10]	George Lewis' Ragtime Band	1953	$80
—Limited First Pressing Dec. 25, 1953" on label at left			
❏ LJ-331 [10]	New Orleans Music	1954	$80
JAZZOLOGY			
❏ JCE-19	Endless the Trek	1967	$30
❏ JCE-3 [M]	George Lewis and His Ragtime Stompers	196?	$35
❏ SJCE-3 [S]	George Lewis and His Ragtime Stompers	196?	$30
❏ JCE-27	George Lewis at Congo Square	196?	$30
MOSAIC			
❏ MR5-132	The Complete Blue Note Recordings of George Lewis	199?	$100
PARADOX			
❏ LP-6001 [10]	George Lewis	1951	$80
RIVERSIDE			
❏ RLP-2507 [10]	George Lewis	1954	$300
❏ RLP 12-283 [M]	George Lewis of New Orleans	1958	$300
❏ RLP-2512 [10]	George Lewis with Guest Artist Red Allen	1955	$300
❏ RLP 12-230 [M]	Jazz at Vespers	1957	$250
—White label, blue print			
❏ RLP 12-230 [M]	Jazz at Vespers	1959	$250
—Blue label, microphone logo at top			
❏ RLP 12-207 [M]	Jazz in the Classic New Orleans Tradition	1956	$250
—White label, blue print			
❏ RLP 12-207 [M]	Jazz in the Classic New Orleans Tradition	1959	$250
—Blue label, microphone logo at top			
SOUTHLAND			
❏ SLP-208 [10]	George Lewis	1955	$80
STORYVILLE			
❏ 4022	George Lewis and His Ragtime Band In Concert	197?	$30
❏ 4055	George Lewis at Club Hangover, Volume 1	198?	$25
❏ 4061	George Lewis at Club Hangover, Volume 3	198?	$25
❏ 4049	Jazz from New Orleans	198?	$25
VERVE			
❏ MGV-1019 [M]	Blues from the Bayou	1957	$150
❏ V-1019 [M]	Blues from the Bayou	1961	$25
❏ MGVS-6113 [S]	Blues from the Bayou	1960	$120
❏ V6-1019 [S]	Blues from the Bayou	1961	$35
❏ MGV-1021 [M]	Doctor Jazz	1957	$125
❏ V-1021 [M]	Doctor Jazz	1961	$25
❏ MGVS-6122 [S]	Doctor Jazz	1960	$100
❏ V6-1021 [S]	Doctor Jazz	1961	$35

Number	Title	Yr	NM
❏ MGV-8232 [M]	George Lewis and Turk Murphy at Newport	1958	$100
❏ V-8232 [M]	George Lewis and Turk Murphy at Newport	1961	$25
❏ MGV-1027 [M]	George Lewis' Dixieland Band	1957	$150
❏ V-1027 [M]	George Lewis' Dixieland Band	1961	$25
❏ MGV-1024 [M]	Hot Time in the Old Town Tonight	1957	$150
❏ V-1024 [M]	Hot Time in the Old Town Tonight	1961	$25
❏ V6-1024 [S]	Hot Time in the Old Town Tonight	1961	$25
❏ MGV-8325 [M]	Oh, Didn't He Ramble	1959	$100
❏ MGVS-6064 [S]	Oh, Didn't He Ramble	1960	$100
❏ V-8325 [M]	Oh, Didn't He Ramble	1961	$25
❏ V6-8325 [S]	Oh, Didn't He Ramble	1961	$35
❏ MGV-8303 [M]	On Stage: George Lewis Concert, Volume 1	1959	$100
❏ V-8303 [M]	On Stage: George Lewis Concert, Volume 1	1961	$25
❏ MGV-8304 [M]	On Stage: George Lewis Concert, Volume 2	1959	$100
❏ V-8304 [M]	On Stage: George Lewis Concert, Volume 2	1961	$25
❏ MGV-8277 [M]	The Perennial George Lewis	1958	$100
❏ V-8277 [M]	The Perennial George Lewis	1961	$25
❏ UMV-2621	Verve at Newport	198?	$30

LEWIS, GEORGE (2), AND DOUGLAS EWART

Ewart plays many different reed instruments. Also see GEORGE LEWIS (2).

Albums

Number	Title	Yr	NM
BLACK SAINT			
❏ BSR-0026	The Imaginary Suite	198?	$30

LEWIS, GEORGE (2)

Trombonist and composer.

Albums

Number	Title	Yr	NM
BLACK SAINT			
❏ BSR-0029	Homage to Charles Parker	198?	$30
❏ BSR-0016	Monads	198?	$30
LOVELY			
❏ VR-1101	Chicago Slow Dance	198?	$35

LEWIS, JOHN, AND BILL PERKINS

Also see each artist's individual listings.

Albums

Number	Title	Yr	NM
PACIFIC JAZZ			
❏ PJ-1217 [M]	Grand Encounter: 2' East, 3' West	1956	$300
❏ PJ-44 [M]	Grand Encounter: 2' East, 3' West	1962	$60
—Reissue with new number			
PAUSA			
❏ 9019	Grand Encounter: 2' East, 3' West	198?	$30
WORLD PACIFIC			
❏ WP-1217 [M]	Grand Encounter: 2' East, 3' West	1959	$250

LEWIS, JOHN, AND HANK JONES

Also see each artist's individual listings.

Albums

Number	Title	Yr	NM
LITTLE DAVID			
❏ LD1079	An Evening with Two Grand Pianos	1979	$30

LEWIS, JOHN, AND SACHA DISTEL

Distel is a male singer and guitarist not otherwise listed in this book. Also see JOHN LEWIS.

Albums

Number	Title	Yr	NM
ATLANTIC			
❏ 1267 [M]	Afternoon in Paris	1964	$25
—Multicolor label, black "fan" logo at right			
❏ 1267 [M]	Afternoon in Paris	1957	$300
—Black label			
❏ 1267 [M]	Afternoon in Paris	1961	$250
—Multicolor label, white "fan" logo at right			

Number	Title	Yr	NM

LEWIS, JOHN

Pianist and composer. Also see THE MODERN JAZZ QUARTET; THE MODERN JAZZ SEXTET; ORCHESTRA U.S.A.

Albums

ATLANTIC

Number	Title	Yr	NM
❏ 1402 [M]	Animal Dance	1963	$150
❏ SD1402 [S]	Animal Dance	1963	$150
❏ 1425 [M]	Essence	1964	$35
❏ SD1425 [S]	Essence	1964	$25
❏ 1392 [M]	European Encounter	1963	$50
❏ SD1392 [S]	European Encounter	1963	$50
❏ 90533	European Encounter	1986	$25
❏ 1313 [M]	Improvised Meditations and Excursions	1959	$300

—Black label

| ❏ 1313 [M] | Improvised Meditations and Excursions | 1961 | $150 |

—Multicolor label, white "fan" logo at right

| ❏ 1313 [M] | Improvised Meditations and Excursions | 1964 | $35 |

—Multicolor label, black "fan" logo at right

| ❏ SD1313 [S] | Improvised Meditations and Excursions | 1959 | $300 |

—Green label

| ❏ SD1313 [S] | Improvised Meditations and Excursions | 1961 | $150 |

—Multicolor label, white "fan" logo at right

| ❏ SD1313 [S] | Improvised Meditations and Excursions | 1964 | $35 |

—Multicolor label, black "fan" logo at right

| ❏ 1365 [M] | John Lewis Presents Jazz Abstractions | 1961 | $150 |

—Multicolor label, white "fan" logo at right

| ❏ 1365 [M] | John Lewis Presents Jazz Abstractions | 1964 | $35 |

—Multicolor label, black "fan" logo at right

| ❏ SD1365 [S] | John Lewis Presents Jazz Abstractions | 1961 | $150 |

—Multicolor label, white "fan" logo at right

| ❏ SD1365 [S] | John Lewis Presents Jazz Abstractions | 1964 | $25 |

—Multicolor label, black "fan" logo at right

| ❏ 1370 [M] | Original Sin | 1961 | $150 |

—Multicolor label, white "fan" logo at right

| ❏ 1370 [M] | Original Sin | 1964 | $35 |

—Multicolor label, black "fan" logo at right

| ❏ SD1370 [S] | Original Sin | 1961 | $150 |

—Multicolor label, white "fan" logo at right

| ❏ SD1370 [S] | Original Sin | 1964 | $25 |

—Multicolor label, black "fan" logo at right

| ❏ 1334 [M] | The Golden Striker | 1960 | $250 |

—Multicolor label, white "fan" logo at right

| ❏ 1334 [M] | The Golden Striker | 1964 | $35 |

—Multicolor label, black "fan" logo at right

| ❏ SD1334 [S] | The Golden Striker | 1960 | $250 |

—Multicolor label, white "fan" logo at right

| ❏ SD1334 [S] | The Golden Striker | 1964 | $50 |

—Multicolor label, black "fan" logo at right

| ❏ 1272 [M] | The John Lewis Piano | 1958 | $300 |

—Black label

| ❏ 1272 [M] | The John Lewis Piano | 1961 | $150 |

—Multicolor label, white "fan" logo at right

| ❏ 1272 [M] | The John Lewis Piano | 1964 | $35 |

—Multicolor label, black "fan" logo at right

| ❏ 1375 [M] | The Wonderful World of Jazz | 1961 | $150 |

—Multicolor label, white "fan" logo at right

| ❏ SD1375 [S] | The Wonderful World of Jazz | 1961 | $150 |

—Multicolor label, white "fan" logo at right

| ❏ 1375 [M] | The Wonderful World of Jazz | 1964 | $35 |

—Multicolor label, black "fan" logo at right

| ❏ SD1375 [S] | The Wonderful World of Jazz | 1964 | $25 |

—Multicolor label, black "fan" logo at right

| ❏ 90979 | The Wonderful World of Jazz | 1989 | $30 |

COLUMBIA

| ❏ PC33534 | P.O.V. | 1976 | $25 |

EMARCY

| ❏ 838036-1 | Midnight in Paris | 1990 | $30 |
| ❏ 834478-1 | The Garden of Delight: Delaunay's Dilemma | 1989 | $30 |

FINESSE

Number	Title	Yr	NM
❏ FW37681	Album for Nancy Harrow	1982	$25
❏ FW38187	Kansas City Breaks	1983	$25

PHILIPS

❏ 836821-1	Bach: Preludes and Fugues, Vol. 3	1989	$30
❏ 824381-1	John Lewis Plays Bach's "Well-Tempered Clavier"	1985	$25
❏ 826698-1	The Bridge Game	1986	$25
❏ 832015-1	The Chess Game	1987	$30
❏ 832588-1	The Chess Game, Volume 2	1988	$30

RCA VICTOR

| ❏ LPM-1742 [M] | European Windows | 1958 | $50 |

LEWIS, KATHARINE HANDY

Female singer, daughter of W.C. HANDY.

Albums

FOLKWAYS

| ❏ FJ-3540 [M] | W.C. Handy Blues | 1958 | $30 |

LEWIS, MEADE LUX, AND LOUIS BELLSON

Also see each artist's individual listings.

Albums

CLEF

| ❏ MGC-632 [M] | Boogie Woogie Piano and Drums | 1954 | $200 |

LEWIS, MEADE LUX

Pianist; one of the most popular boogie-woogie style pianists. Also see ALBERT AMMONS; SLIM GAILLARD.

Albums

ABC-PARAMOUNT

| ❏ ABC-164 [M] | Out of the Roaring 20's | 1956 | $50 |

ATLANTIC

| ❏ ALS-133 [10] | Boogie-Woogie Interpretations | 1952 | $250 |

BLUE NOTE

| ❏ BLP-7018 [10] | Boogie-Woogie Classics | 1952 | $600 |

DISC

| ❏ DLP-352 [10] | Meade Lux Lewis at the Philharmonic | 195? | $400 |

DOWN HOME

| ❏ MGD-6 [M] | Cat House Piano | 1955 | $0 |

—Canceled

| ❏ MGD-7 [M] | Yancey's Last Ride | 1956 | $120 |

FANTASY

| ❏ OJC-1759 | The Blues Piano Artistry of Meade Lux Lewis | 198? | $30 |

MERCURY

| ❏ MG-25158 [10] | Meade Lux Lewis | 1951 | $300 |

MUSE

| ❏ MR-5063 | Still On the Planet | 1976 | $50 |

PHILIPS

| ❏ PHM200044 [M] | Boogie Woogie House Party | 196? | $25 |
| ❏ PHS600044 [S] | Boogie Woogie House Party | 196? | $30 |

RIVERSIDE

| ❏ RLP-402 [M] | The Blues Piano Artistry of Meade Lux Lewis | 1962 | $200 |
| ❏ RS-9402 [S] | The Blues Piano Artistry of Meade Lux Lewis | 1962 | $200 |

STINSON

| ❏ 25 [M] | Meade Lux Lewis | 196? | $30 |

TOPS

| ❏ L-1533 [M] | Barrelhouse Piano | 195? | $40 |

VERVE

❏ MGV-1006 [M]	Cat House Piano	1957	$200
❏ V-1006 [M]	Cat House Piano	1961	$40
❏ MGV-1007 [M]	Meade Lux Lewis	1957	$150
❏ V-1007 [M]	Meade Lux Lewis	1961	$30

LEWIS, MEL

Drummer. Also see THE FIVE; THAD JONES-MEL LEWIS ORCHESTRA.

Albums

ATLANTIC

| ❏ 81655 | 20th Anniversary | 1986 | $25 |

FINESSE

| ❏ FW37987 | Make Me Smile | 1984 | $25 |

HORIZON

| ❏ SP-716 | Mel Lewis and Friends | 1976 | $30 |

MODE

| ❏ LP-103 [M] | Mel Lewis Sextet | 1957 | $120 |

PAUSA

Number	Title	Yr	NM
❏ 7115	Live in Montreux	1981	$25

SAN FRANCISCO

| ❏ 2 [M] | Got 'Cha | 1957 | $150 |

TELARC

| ❏ DG-10044 | Naturally | 1980 | $30 |

VEE JAY

| ❏ VJS-3062 | Gettin' Together | 1974 | $25 |

LEWIS, RAMSEY, AND JEAN DUSHON

Also see each artist's individual listings.

Albums

ARGO

| ❏ 750 [M] | You Better Believe Me | 1965 | $60 |
| ❏ 750S [S] | You Better Believe Me | 1965 | $60 |

LEWIS, RAMSEY, AND NANCY WILSON

Also see each artist's individual listings.

Albums

COLUMBIA

| ❏ FC39326 | The Two of Us | 1984 | $25 |

LEWIS, RAMSEY

Pianist and keyboard player. Most of his Argo and Chess albums were released under the moniker "Ramsey Lewis Trio." The other two members of the classic trio were ELDEE YOUNG (bass) and RED HOLT (drums), who later formed their own groups.

Albums

ARGO

❏ LP-645 [M]	An Hour with the Ramsey Lewis Trio	1959	$40
❏ LPS-645 [S]	An Hour with the Ramsey Lewis Trio	1959	$100
❏ LP-732 [M]	Bach to the Blues	1964	$60
❏ LPS-732 [S]	Bach to the Blues	1964	$60
❏ LP-723 [M]	Barefoot Sunday Blues	1963	$60
❏ LPS-723 [S]	Barefoot Sunday Blues	1963	$60
❏ LP-705 [M]	Bossa Nova	1962	$60
❏ LPS-705 [S]	Bossa Nova	1962	$60
❏ LP-755 [M]	Choice! The Best of the Ramsey Lewis Trio	1965	$60
❏ LPS-755 [S]	Choice! The Best of the Ramsey Lewis Trio	1965	$40
❏ LP-701 [M]	Country Meets the Blues	1962	$60
❏ LPS-701 [S]	Country Meets the Blues	1962	$60
❏ LP-627 [M]	Gentleman of Jazz	1958	$100
❏ LPS-627 [S]	Gentleman of Jazz	1959	$120
❏ LP-611 [M]	Gentleman of Swing	1958	$100
❏ LPS-611 [S]	Gentleman of Swing	1959	$120
❏ LP-680 [M]	More Music from the Soil	1961	$40
❏ LPS-680 [S]	More Music from the Soil	1961	$100
❏ LP-745 [M]	More Sounds of Christmas	1964	$60
❏ LPS-745 [S]	More Sounds of Christmas	1964	$60
❏ LP-715 [M]	Pot Luck	1963	$60
❏ LPS-715 [S]	Pot Luck	1963	$60
❏ LP-687 [M]	Sound of Christmas	1961	$40
❏ LPS-687 [S]	Sound of Christmas	1961	$100
❏ LP-665 [M]	Stretching Out	1960	$40
❏ LPS-665 [S]	Stretching Out	1960	$100
❏ LP-757 [M]	The In Crowd	1965	$60
❏ LPS-757 [S]	The In Crowd	1965	$60
❏ LP-741 [M]	The Ramsey Lewis Trio at the Bohemian Caverns	1964	$60
❏ LPS-741 [S]	The Ramsey Lewis Trio at the Bohemian Caverns	1964	$60
❏ LP-671 [M]	The Ramsey Lewis Trio in Chicago	1961	$40
❏ LPS-671 [S]	The Ramsey Lewis Trio in Chicago	1961	$100
❏ LP-642 [M]	The Ramsey Lewis Trio with Lee Winchester	1959	$40
❏ LPS-642 [S]	The Ramsey Lewis Trio with Lee Winchester	1959	$100
❏ LP-693 [M]	The Sound of Spring	1962	$60
❏ LPS-693 [S]	The Sound of Spring	1962	$60

CADET

❏ LP-645 [M]	An Hour with the Ramsey Lewis Trio	1966	$30
❏ LPS-645 [S]	An Hour with the Ramsey Lewis Trio	1966	$35
❏ LPS-827	Another Voyage	1969	$35
❏ LP-732 [M]	Bach to the Blues	1966	$30
❏ LPS-732 [S]	Bach to the Blues	1966	$35
❏ 60001	Back to the Roots	1971	$30
❏ LP-723 [M]	Barefoot Sunday Blues	1966	$30
❏ LPS-723 [S]	Barefoot Sunday Blues	1966	$35
❏ LP-705 [M]	Bossa Nova	1966	$30
❏ LPS-705 [S]	Bossa Nova	1966	$35
❏ LP-755 [M]	Choice! The Best of the Ramsey Lewis Trio	1965	$35
❏ LPS-755 [S]	Choice! The Best of the Ramsey Lewis Trio	1965	$50
❏ LP-701 [M]	Country Meets the Blues	1966	$30
❏ LPS-701 [S]	Country Meets the Blues	1966	$35
❏ LP-794 [M]	Dancing in the Street	1967	$50

LEWIS, RAMSEY (continued)

Number	Title	Yr	NM
☐ LPS-794 [S]	Dancing in the Street	1967	$35
☐ LP-627 [M]	Gentleman of Jazz	1966	$30
☐ LPS-627 [S]	Gentleman of Jazz	1966	$35
☐ LP-611 [M]	Gentleman of Swing	1966	$30
☐ LPS-611 [S]	Gentleman of Swing	1966	$35
☐ LP-790 [M]	Goin' Latin	1967	$50
☐ LPS-790 [S]	Goin' Latin	1967	$35
☐ 50020	Groover	1973	$30
☐ LP-761 [M]	Hang On Ramsey!	1966	$30
☐ LPS-761 [S]	Hang On Ramsey!	1966	$50
☐ 60018	Inside Ramsey Lewis	1972	$35
☐ LPS-811	Maiden Voyage	1968	$35
☐ LP-680 [M]	More Music from the Soil	1966	$30
☐ LPS-680 [S]	More Music from the Soil	1966	$35
☐ LPS-680 [S]	More Music from the Soil	197?	$30

—Reissue with "A Division of All Platinum Record Group" on label

Number	Title	Yr	NM
☐ LP-745 [M]	More Sounds of Christmas	1966	$35
☐ LPS-745 [S]	More Sounds of Christmas	1966	$50
☐ LPS-821	Mother Nature's Son	1969	$35
☐ LP-715 [M]	Pot Luck	1966	$30
☐ LPS-715 [S]	Pot Luck	1966	$35
☐ LPS-836	Ramsey Lewis, The Piano Player	1970	$35
☐ 50058	Solid Ivory	1974	$35
☐ LP-687X [M]	Sound of Christmas	1966	$50

—Reissue of Argo 687

Number	Title	Yr	NM
☐ LPS-687X [S]	Sound of Christmas	1966	$50

—Reissue of Argo 687-S

Number	Title	Yr	NM
☐ LP-665 [M]	Stretching Out	1966	$30
☐ LPS-665 [S]	Stretching Out	1966	$35
☐ LP-771 [M]	Swingin'	1966	$35
☐ LPS-771 [S]	Swingin'	1966	$50
☐ LPS-839	The Best of Ramsey Lewis	1970	$35
☐ LP-757 [M]	The In Crowd	1965	$30
☐ LPS-757 [S]	The In Crowd	1965	$35
☐ LPS-844	Them Changes	1970	$35
☐ LP-782 [M]	The Movie Album	1967	$50
☐ LPS-782 [S]	The Movie Album	1967	$35
☐ LP-741 [M]	The Ramsey Lewis Trio at the Bohemian Caverns	1966	$30
☐ LPS-741 [S]	The Ramsey Lewis Trio at the Bohemian Caverns	1966	$35
☐ LP-671 [M]	The Ramsey Lewis Trio in Chicago	1966	$30
☐ LPS-671 [S]	The Ramsey Lewis Trio in Chicago	1966	$35
☐ LP-693 [M]	The Sound of Spring	1966	$30
☐ LPS-693 [S]	The Sound of Spring	1966	$35
☐ LPS-799	Up Pops Ramsey Lewis	1968	$35
☐ LP-774 [M]	Wade in the Water	1966	$35
☐ LPS-774 [S]	Wade in the Water	1966	$50
☐ LP-750 [M]	You Better Believe It	1966	$30
☐ LPS-750 [S]	You Better Believe It	1966	$35

CBS

Number	Title	Yr	NM
☐ FM42661	A Classic Encounter	1988	$25

CHESS

Number	Title	Yr	NM
☐ 9001	Solid Ivory	197?	$30

—Reissue of Cadet 50058

Number	Title	Yr	NM
☐ CH9716	Sound of Christmas	1984	$25

—Reissue of Argo 687-S

COLUMBIA

Number	Title	Yr	NM
☐ FC38294	Chance Encounter	1983	$25
☐ PC33800	Don't It Feel Good	1975	$25

—Originals have no bar code

Number	Title	Yr	NM
☐ PC33800	Don't It Feel Good	198?	$20

—Budget-line reissue with bar code

Number	Title	Yr	NM
☐ FC40108	Fantasy	1985	$25
☐ KC32030	Funky Serenity	1973	$30
☐ FC40677	Keys to the City	1987	$25
☐ JC35483	Legacy	1978	$25
☐ PC35483	Legacy	198?	$20

—Budget-line reissue

Number	Title	Yr	NM
☐ FC38787	Les Fleurs	1983	$25
☐ FC37687	Live at the Savoy	1982	$25
☐ PC37687	Live at the Savoy	198?	$20

—Budget-line reissue

Number	Title	Yr	NM
☐ HC47687	Live at the Savoy	1982	$150

—Half-speed mastered edition

Number	Title	Yr	NM
☐ PC34696	Love Notes	1977	$25
☐ JC35815	Ramsey	1979	$25
☐ KC32490	Ramsey Lewis' Newly Recorded All-Time, Non-Stop Golden Hits	1973	$30
☐ PC32490	Ramsey Lewis' Newly Recorded All-Time, Non-Stop Golden Hits	197?	$20

—Reissue with new prefix

Number	Title	Yr	NM
☐ FC39158	Reunion	1983	$25
☐ JC36423	Routes	1980	$25
☐ PC36423	Routes	198?	$20

—Budget-line reissue

Number	Title	Yr	NM
☐ PC34173	Salongo	1976	$25

—Originals have no bar code

Number	Title	Yr	NM
☐ PC34173	Salongo	198?	$20

—Budget-line reissue with bar code

Number	Title	Yr	NM
☐ KC32897	Solar Wind	1974	$30
☐ KC33194	Sun Goddess	1974	$25
☐ PC33194	Sun Goddess	197?	$20

—Reissue with new prefix

Number	Title	Yr	NM
☐ HC43194	Sun Goddess	1982	$100

—Half-speed mastered edition

Number	Title	Yr	NM
☐ JC35018	Tequila Mockingbird	1977	$25
☐ FC36364	The Best of Ramsey Lewis	1980	$25
☐ FC37153	Three Piece Suite	1981	$25
☐ KC31096	Upendo Ni Pamoja	1972	$30
☐ CQ31096 [Q]	Upendo Ni Pamoja	1972	$60
☐ CG33663	Upendo Ni Pamoja/Funky Serenity	1975	$30
☐ FC44190	Urban Renewal	1989	$35

COLUMBIA JAZZ ODYSSEY

Number	Title	Yr	NM
☐ PC37019	Blues for the Night Owl	1981	$25

EMARCY

Number	Title	Yr	NM
☐ MG-36150 [M]	Down to Earth	1958	$200
☐ SR-80029 [S]	Down to Earth	1958	$100

MERCURY

Number	Title	Yr	NM
☐ MG-20536 [M]	Down to Earth	1965	$100
☐ SR-60536 [S]	Down to Earth	1965	$100

LEWIS, TED

Clarinetist, male singer and bandleader.

Albums

BIOGRAPH

Number	Title	Yr	NM
☐ C-7	Ted Lewis' Orchestra, Volume 1	198?	$25
☐ C-8	Ted Lewis' Orchestra, Volume 2	198?	$25

COLUMBIA

Number	Title	Yr	NM
☐ CL6127 [10]	Classic Jazz	1950	$50

DECCA

Number	Title	Yr	NM
☐ DL8321 [M]	Is Everybody Happy?	1956	$150
☐ DL5114 [10]	Ted Lewis and His Orchestra	195?	$50
☐ DL4905 [M]	Ted Lewis' Greatest Hits	1967	$30
☐ DL74905 [R]	Ted Lewis' Greatest Hits	1967	$35
☐ DL8322 [M]	The Medicine Man for the Blues	1956	$120

EPIC

Number	Title	Yr	NM
☐ LN3170 [M]	Everybody's Happy!	1955	$80

MCA

Number	Title	Yr	NM
☐ 2-4101	The Best of Ted Lewis	1976	$35

—Black rainbow labels

OLYMPIC

Number	Title	Yr	NM
☐ OL-7127	Me and My Shadow	1974	$25

RKO

Number	Title	Yr	NM
☐ ULP-108 [M]	Me and My Shadow	195?	$50

LEWIS, WILLIE

Alto saxophone player and bandleader.

Albums

SWING

Number	Title	Yr	NM
☐ 8400/1	Willie Lewis and His Entertainers	198?	$30

LIBBY, JERRY

Albums

SABRINA

Number	Title	Yr	NM
☐ SA-100 [M]	Live? At Wilkins	1964	$25

LIDSTROM, JACK

Trumpeter.

Albums

WORLD PACIFIC

Number	Title	Yr	NM
☐ PJ-1235 [M]	Look, Dad! They're Comin' Down the Street in Hi-Fi	1957	$150

LIEBMAN, DAVE

Soprano and tenor saxophone player.

Albums

ARTISTS HOUSE

Number	Title	Yr	NM
☐ 8	Pendulum	1978	$30

CMP

Number	Title	Yr	NM
☐ CMP-40-ST	Chant	1990	$35
☐ CMP-9-ST	Dedications	198?	$30
☐ CMP-24-ST	The Loneliness of a Long-Distance Runner	1987	$30

COLUMBIA

Number	Title	Yr	NM
☐ JC36581	What It Is	1979	$25

ECM

Number	Title	Yr	NM
☐ 1046	Drum Ode	1975	$35
☐ 1039	Lookout Farm	197?	$35

—As "David Liebman

HEADS UP

Number	Title	Yr	NM
☐ HUP-3005	The Energy of the Chance	1989	$35

HORIZON

Number	Title	Yr	NM
☐ SP-709	Fantasies	1976	$30
☐ SP-721	Light'n Up, Please!	1977	$30
☐ SP-702	Sweet Hands	1976	$30

PM

Number	Title	Yr	NM
☐ PMR-022	Memories, Dreams and Reflections	1986	$30
☐ PMR-023	Picture Show	1986	$30

WEST 54

Number	Title	Yr	NM
☐ 8012	First Visit	1979	$30

LIGHTHOUSE ALL-STARS, THE

See HOWARD RUMSEY.

LIGHTSEY, KIRK

Pianist.

Albums

SUNNYSIDE

Number	Title	Yr	NM
☐ SSC-1020	Everything Is Changed	198?	$30
☐ SSC-1002	Lightsey 1	1985	$30
☐ SSC-1005	Lightsey 2	1985	$30
☐ SSC-1014	Lightsey Live	1987	$30

LIGON, BERT

Pianist, bandleader, arranger and composer.

Albums

INNER CITY

Number	Title	Yr	NM
☐ IC-1107	The Condor	198?	$30

SEA BREEZE

Number	Title	Yr	NM
☐ SB-3002	Dancing Bare	198?	$30

LIMEHOUSE JAZZ BAND, THE

Albums

STOMP OFF

Number	Title	Yr	NM
☐ SOS-1014	Rhythm Is Our Business	1981	$25

LINCOLN, ABBEY

Female singer.

Albums

BARMABY

Number	Title	Yr	NM
☐ KZ31037	Straight Ahead	1972	$60

CANDID

Number	Title	Yr	NM
☐ CD-8015 [M]	Straight Ahead	1960	$80
☐ CS-9015 [S]	Straight Ahead	1960	$100

ENJA

Number	Title	Yr	NM
☐ 4060	Talking to the Sun	1983	$50

FANTASY

Number	Title	Yr	NM
☐ OJC-069	Abbey Is Blue	1983	$30
☐ OJC-205	It's Magic	1985	$30
☐ OJC-085	That's Him!	198?	$30

INNER CITY

Number	Title	Yr	NM
☐ IC-1117	Golden Lady	198?	$60
☐ IC-6040	The People in Me	1978	$50

JAZZ MAN

Number	Title	Yr	NM
☐ 5043	Straight Ahead	198?	$35

—Reissue of Barnaby 31037

LIBERTY

Number	Title	Yr	NM
☐ LRP-3025 [M]	Abbey Lincoln's Affair	1957	$125

RIVERSIDE

Number	Title	Yr	NM
☐ RLP 12-308 [M]	Abbey Is Blue	1959	$300
☐ RLP-1153 [S]	Abbey Is Blue	1959	$300
☐ 6088	Abbey Is Blue	197?	$50
☐ RLP 12-277 [M]	It's Magic	1958	$300
☐ RLP-1107 [S]	That's Him!	1958	$300

LINDBERG, JOHN

Bass player and composer.

Albums

BLACK SAINT

Number	Title	Yr	NM
☐ BSR-0062	Dimension 5	1982	$30
☐ BSR-0072	Give and Take	1983	$30
☐ BSR-0082	Trilogy of Works for Eleven Instrumentalists	1985	$30

SOUND ASPECTS

Number	Title	Yr	NM
☐ SAS-001	The East Side Suite	1985	$30

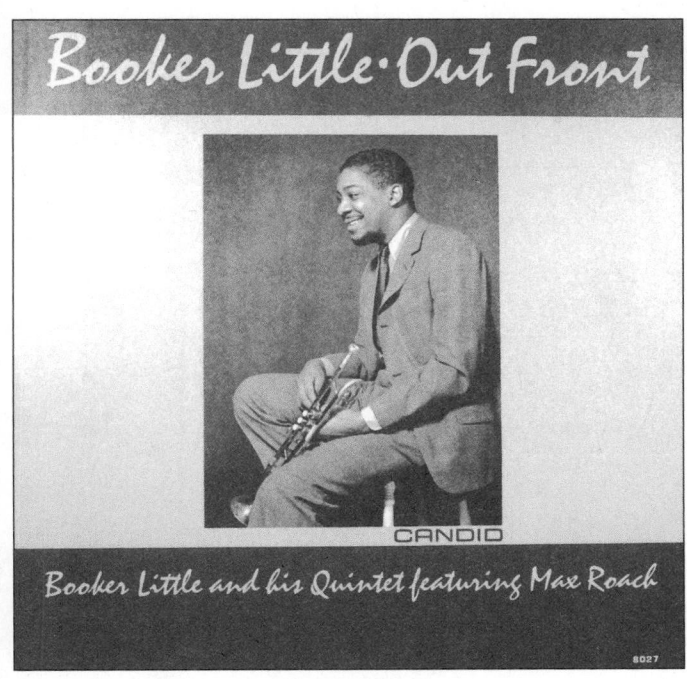

Booker Little, *Out Front*, Candid CD-9027, **$80**.

Mundell Lowe, *Tacet for Neurotics*, Offbeat OLP-3010, **$80**.

Mundell Lowe, *The Mundell Lowe Quartet*, Riverside RLP 12-204, white label with blue print, **$250**.

Teo Macero, *Teo*, Prestige PRLP-7104, **$250**.

Number	Title	Yr	NM

LINDBERG, NILS
Pianist and composer.

Albums
CAPITOL

❏ T10363 [M]	Trisection	196?	$25
❏ ST10363 [S]	Trisection	196?	$60

LINDH, JAYSON
Flutist. Also recorded under the name "Bjorn J-Son Lindh"; these are included below.

Albums
JAS

❏ JAS-4000	Second Carneval	1975	$25

METRONOME

❏ DIX-3001	Cous-Cous	1973	$30
❏ DIX-3000	Ramadan	1972	$30
❏ DIX-3002	Sissel	1974	$30

STORYVILLE

❏ 4132	Atlantis	1983	$30

—As "Bjorn J-Son Lindh"

VANGUARD

❏ VSD-79434	A Day at the Surface	1979	$30

—As "Bjorn J-Son Lindh"

LINGLE, PAUL
Pianist.

Albums
EUPHONIC

❏ 1217	Dance of the Witch Hazels	198?	$25
❏ 1220	The Legend of Lingle	198?	$25

LINN, RAY
Trumpeter.

Albums
DISCOVERY

❏ DS-823	Empty Suit Blues	1981	$25

TREND

❏ 515	Chicago Jazz	1980	$50

—Direct-to-disc recording

LINS, IVAN
Male singer and composer.

Albums
PHILIPS

❏ 822672-1	Juntos (Together)	1986	$25

LINSKY, JEFF
Guitarist.

Albums
CONCORD PICANTE

❏ CJP-363	Up Late	1988	$25

LIPSKIN, MIKE
Pianist, arranger and composer.

Albums
FLYING DUTCHMAN

❏ FD-10140	California	1972	$35

LIPSKY, HELMUT
Violinist.

Albums
JAZZIMAGE

❏ JZ-101	Melosphere	198?	$30

LIST, GARRETT
Trombonist and composer.

Albums
LOVELY

❏ VR-1201	Fire and Ice	198?	$30

LISTEN (2)
Group led by saxophone player Mel Martin.

Albums
INNER CITY

❏ IC-1055	Growing	1978	$35
❏ IC-1025	Listen	1977	$35

LISTON, MELBA
Trombonist, composer and arranger.

Albums
METROJAZZ

❏ E-1013 [M]	Melba Liston and Her Bones	1958	$120
❏ SE-1013 [S]	Melba Liston and Her Bones	1958	$120

LITTLE, BOOKER, AND BOOKER ERVIN
Also see each artist's individual listings.

Albums
TCB

❏ 1003	Sounds of Inner City	197?	$40

LITTLE, BOOKER
Trumpeter. Also see YOUNG MEN FROM MEMPHIS.

Albums
BAINBRIDGE

❏ BT-1041	Booker Little	1981	$25

BARNABY

❏ BR-5019	Out Front	1977	$35

BETHLEHEM

❏ BCP-6034	Victory and Sorrow	197?	$60

—Reissue of 6061, distributed by RCA Victor

CANDID

❏ CS-9027 [S]	Out Front	1961	$80

UNITED ARTISTS

❏ UAL-4034 [M]	The Booker Little Four	1959	$120
❏ UAS-5034 [S]	The Booker Little Four	1959	$100

LIVING JAZZ
Studio group featuring woodwinds player Phil Bodner.

Albums
RCA CAMDEN

❏ CAL-985 [M]	A Lover's Concerto	1966	$25
❏ CAS-985 [S]	A Lover's Concerto	1966	$30
❏ CAL-878 [M]	Dear Heart and Other Favorites	1965	$25
❏ CAS-878 [S]	Dear Heart and Other Favorites	1965	$30
❏ CAS-2298	Fool on the Hill	1969	$25
❏ CAS-2436	Hot Butter and Soul	1970	$25
❏ ACL1-0202	Manha de Carnival	1973	$25
❏ CAL-2196 [M]	Ode to Young Lovers	1968	$30
❏ CAS-2196 [S]	Ode to Young Lovers	1968	$25
❏ CAL-914 [M]	Quiet Nights	1965	$25
❏ CAS-914 [S]	Quiet Nights	1965	$30
❏ CAL-848 [M]	The Girl from Ipanema and Other Hits	1964	$25
❏ CAS-848 [S]	The Girl from Ipanema and Other Hits	1964	$30
❏ CAL-2135 [M]	The Soul of Brazil	1967	$30
❏ CAS-2135 [S]	The Soul of Brazil	1967	$25

RCA VICTOR

❏ APL1-2386	Hello Young Lovers	1977	$25

LLOYD, CHARLES
Tenor saxophone player and flutist.

Albums
4 MEN WITH BEARDS

❏ 4M-119	Love-In	2003	$35

—180-gram audiophile reissue

A&M

❏ SP-3046	Geeta	1973	$50
❏ SP-3044	Waves	1973	$35

ATLANTIC

❏ SD1500	Charles Lloyd in Europe	1969	$50
❏ SD1571	Charles Lloyd in the Soviet Union	1971	$50
❏ 1459 [M]	Dream Weaver	1966	$35
❏ SD1459 [S]	Dream Weaver	1966	$50

—Blue and green label

❏ SD1459 [S]	Dream Weaver	1969	$30

—Red and green label, white stripe through center hole

❏ SD1586	Flowering of the Original Charles Lloyd Quintet	1972	$50
❏ 1473 [M]	Forest Flower	1967	$60
❏ SD1473 [S]	Forest Flower	1967	$60
❏ SD1493	Journey Within	1968	$60
❏ 1481 [M]	Love-In	1967	$40
❏ SD1481 [S]	Love-In	1967	$40
❏ SD1519	Soundtrack	1970	$50
❏ SD1556	The Best of Charles Lloyd	1970	$35

BLUE NOTE

❏ BT-85104	A Night in Copenhagen	1985	$35

COLUMBIA

❏ CL2267 [M]	Discovery!	1965	$200
❏ CS9067 [S]	Discovery!	1965	$200
❏ CS9609 [M]	Nirvana	1968	$100

—White label promo; "Special Mono Radio Station Copy" sticker on stereo cover

❏ CS9609 [S]	Nirvana	1968	$60
❏ CL2412 [M]	Of Course, Of Course	1966	$60
❏ CS9212 [S]	Of Course, Of Course	1966	$60
❏ PC36981 [S]	Of Course, Of Course	1980	$25

—Reissue of CS 9212

DESTINY

❏ 10003	Autumn in New York Volume 1	1979	$35

ECM

❏ 1398	Fish Out of Water	1990	$50

—Made in Germany

ELEKTRA/MUSICIAN

❏ 60220	Montreux '82	1983	$30

KAPP

❏ KS-3634	Moon Man	1971	$35
❏ KS-3647	Warm Waters	1971	$60

PACIFIC ARTS

❏ 7-139	Big Sur Tapestry	1979	$30
❏ 7-123	Weavings	1978	$30

LOBO (2)
Full name: Edu Lobo. Guitarist, male singer and composer - and unrelated to the pop singer of the early 70s who called himself "Lobo."

Albums
A&M

❏ SP-3035	Sergio Mendes Presents Lobo	1970	$30

LOCASCIO, JOE
Pianist.

Albums
CMG

❏ CML-8002	Gliders	1988	$25
❏ CML-8015	Marionette	1989	$30

LOCKE, JOE
Vibraphone player.

Albums
CADENCE JAZZ

❏ CJR-1034	Scenario	1988	$25

LOCKWOOD, DIDIER
Violinist.

Albums
GRAMAVISION

❏ 18-8412	Didier Lockwood Group	1984	$25
❏ 18-8504	Out of the Blue	1985	$25

INNER CITY

❏ IC-1092	Surya	1982	$30

PAUSA

❏ 7125	Fasten Seat Belts	1981	$25
❏ 7094	Live in Montreux	1981	$25
❏ 7046	New World	1979	$25

LOCO, JOE

Albums
FANTASY

❏ 3277 [M]	Cha-Cha-Cha	1958	$30

—Red vinyl

❏ 3277 [M]	Cha-Cha-Cha	1958	$30

—Black vinyl, red label, non-flexible vinyl

❏ 3277 [M]	Cha-Cha-Cha	196?	$20

—Black vinyl, red label, flexible vinyl

❏ 8022 [S]	Cha-Cha-Cha	1962	$30

—Blue vinyl

❏ 8022 [S]	Cha-Cha-Cha	1962	$25

—Black vinyl, blue label, non-flexible vinyl

❏ 8022 [S]	Cha-Cha-Cha	196?	$20

—Black vinyl, blue label, flexible vinyl

❏ 3280 [M]	Going Loco	1958	$30

—Red vinyl

❏ 3280 [M]	Going Loco	1958	$30

—Black vinyl, red label, non-flexible vinyl

❏ 3280 [M]	Going Loco	196?	$20

Number	Title	Yr	NM
—Black vinyl, red label, flexible vinyl			
❏ 8042 [S]	Going Loco	1962	$30
—Blue vinyl			
❏ 8042 [S]	Going Loco	1962	$25
—Black vinyl, blue label, non-flexible vinyl			
❏ 8042 [S]	Going Loco	196?	$20
—Black vinyl, blue label, flexible vinyl			
❏ 3215 [M]	Invitation to the Mambo	1956	$30
—Red vinyl			
❏ 3215 [M]	Invitation to the Mambo	1956	$30
—Black vinyl, red label, non-flexible vinyl			
❏ 3215 [M]	Invitation to the Mambo	196?	$20
—Black vinyl, red label, flexible vinyl			
❏ 3294 [M]	Latin Jewels	1959	$30
—Red vinyl			
❏ 3294 [M]	Latin Jewels	1959	$25
—Black vinyl, red label, non-flexible vinyl			
❏ 3294 [M]	Latin Jewels	196?	$25
—Black vinyl, red label, flexible vinyl			
❏ 8041 [S]	Latin Jewels	1962	$30
—Blue vinyl			
❏ 8041 [S]	Latin Jewels	1962	$25
—Black vinyl, blue label, non-flexible vinyl			
❏ 8041 [S]	Latin Jewels	196?	$25
—Black vinyl, blue label, flexible vinyl			
❏ 3285 [M]	Ole, Ole, Ole	1959	$30
—Red vinyl			
❏ 3285 [M]	Ole, Ole, Ole	1959	$25
—Black vinyl, red label, non-flexible vinyl			
❏ 3285 [M]	Ole, Ole, Ole	196?	$25
—Black vinyl, red label, flexible vinyl			
❏ 8028 [S]	Ole, Ole, Ole	1962	$30
—Blue vinyl			
❏ 8028 [S]	Ole, Ole, Ole	1962	$25
—Black vinyl, blue label, non-flexible vinyl			
❏ 8028 [S]	Ole, Ole, Ole	196?	$25
—Black vinyl, blue label, flexible vinyl			
❏ 3321 [M]	Pachanga with Joe Loco	1961	$30
—Red vinyl			
❏ 3321 [M]	Pachanga with Joe Loco	1961	$25
—Black vinyl, red label, non-flexible vinyl			
❏ 3321 [M]	Pachanga with Joe Loco	196?	$25
—Black vinyl, red label, flexible vinyl			
❏ 8064 [S]	Pachanga with Joe Loco	1962	$30
—Blue vinyl			
❏ 8064 [S]	Pachanga with Joe Loco	1962	$25
—Black vinyl, blue label, non-flexible vinyl			
❏ 8064 [S]	Pachanga with Joe Loco	196?	$25
—Black vinyl, blue label, flexible vinyl			
❏ 3303 [M]	The Best of Joe Loco	1960	$30
—Red vinyl			
❏ 3303 [M]	The Best of Joe Loco	1960	$25
—Black vinyl, red label, non-flexible vinyl			
❏ 3303 [M]	The Best of Joe Loco	196?	$20
—Black vinyl, red label, flexible vinyl			
❏ 8048 [S]	The Best of Joe Loco	1962	$30
—Blue vinyl			
❏ 8048 [S]	The Best of Joe Loco	1962	$25
—Black vinyl, blue label, non-flexible vinyl			
❏ 8048 [S]	The Best of Joe Loco	196?	$20
—Black vinyl, blue label, flexible vinyl			

IMPERIAL

Number	Title	Yr	NM
❏ LP-12019 [S]	Happy Go Loco	1959	$150
❏ LP-9073 [M]	Happy Go Loco	1959	$150
❏ LP-12014 [S]	Let's Go Loco	1959	$150
❏ LP-9070 [M]	Let's Go Loco	1959	$150
❏ LP-9166 [M]	Pachanga Twist	1962	$150
❏ LP-12079 [S]	Pachanga Twist	1962	$150

TICO

Number	Title	Yr	NM
❏ LP-132 [10]	Instrumental Mambos (Vol. 7)	1955	$50
❏ LP-123 [10]	Mambo Dance Favorites, Vol. 5	195?	$40
❏ LP-1012 [M]	Mambo Fantasy	1956	$30
❏ LP-1006 [M]	Mambo Moods	1955	$40
❏ LP-109 [10]	Mambos, Vol. 1	195?	$40
❏ LP-111 [10]	Mambos, Vol. 2	195?	$40
❏ LP-121 [10]	Mambos, Vol. 3	195?	$40
❏ LP-122 [10]	Mambos, Vol. 4	195?	$40
❏ LP-129 [10]	Mambo U.S.A.	1954	$40
❏ LP-1013 [M]	Viva Mambo!	1956	$30

LOFSKY, LORNE

Guitarist.

Albums

PABLO TODAY

Number	Title	Yr	NM
❏ 2312122	It Could Happen to You	1979	$30

LOFTON, CLARENCE

Pianist. Nicknamed "Cripple."

Albums

RIVERSIDE

Number	Title	Yr	NM
❏ RLP-1037 [10]	Honky-Tonk and Boogie-Woogie Piano	1954	$300

LOFTON, TRICKY, AND CARMELL JONES

Lofton plays trombone. Also see CARMELL JONES.

Albums

PACIFIC JAZZ

Number	Title	Yr	NM
❏ PJ-49 [M]	Brass Bag	1962	$40
❏ ST-49 [S]	Brass Bag	1962	$50

LOGAN, GIUSEPPI

Alto and tenor saxophone player.

Albums

ESP-DISK'

Number	Title	Yr	NM
❏ 1007 [M]	Giuseppi Logan Quartet	1965	$200
❏ S-1007 [S]	Giuseppi Logan Quartet	1965	$200
❏ 1013 [M]	More Giuseppi Logan	1965	$200
❏ S-1013 [S]	More Giuseppi Logan	1965	$200

LOMBARDO, GUY

Bandleader and violinist; his Royal Canadians were the most popular of the "sweet" bands, and he helped make "Auld Lang Syne" a New Year's Eve staple.

Albums

CAPITOL

Number	Title	Yr	NM
❏ T916 [M]	A Decade on Broadway 1935-45	1958	$80
—Turquoise label			
❏ T916 [M]	A Decade on Broadway 1935-45	1958	$75
—Black colorband label, logo at left			
❏ T916 [M]	A Decade on Broadway 1935-45	1962	$60
—Black colorband label, logo at top			
❏ DT916 [R]	A Decade on Broadway 1935-45	196?	$40
—Black colorband label, logo at top			
❏ T788 [M]	A Decade on Broadway 1946-56	1956	$80
—Turquoise label			
❏ T788 [M]	A Decade on Broadway 1946-56	1958	$75
—Black colorband label, logo at left			
❏ T788 [M]	A Decade on Broadway 1946-56	1962	$60
—Black colorband label, logo at top			
❏ DT788 [R]	A Decade on Broadway 1946-56	196?	$40
—Black colorband label, logo at top			
❏ T2481 [M]	A Wonderful Year	1966	$60
❏ ST2481 [S]	A Wonderful Year	1966	$60
❏ T1019 [M]	Berlin by Lombardo	1958	$80
—Turquoise or gray label			
❏ ST1019 [S]	Berlin by Lombardo	1959	$100
—Black colorband label, logo at left			
❏ T1019 [M]	Berlin by Lombardo	1959	$75
—Black colorband label, logo at left			
❏ T1019 [M]	Berlin by Lombardo	1962	$40
—Black colorband label, logo at top			
❏ ST1019 [S]	Berlin by Lombardo	1962	$60
—Black colorband label, logo at top			
❏ T1121 [M]	Dancing Room Only	1959	$75
—Black colorband label, logo at left			
❏ ST1121 [S]	Dancing Room Only	1959	$80
—Black colorband label, logo at left			
❏ ST1121 [S]	Dancing Room Only	1962	$60
—Black colorband label, logo at top			
❏ T1121 [M]	Dancing Room Only	1962	$40
—Black colorband label, logo at top			
❏ SN-16192	Dancing Room Only	198?	$20
—Budget-line reissue			
❏ T1593 [M]	Drifting and Dreaming	1961	$75
—Black colorband label, logo at left			
❏ ST1593 [S]	Drifting and Dreaming	1961	$80
—Black colorband label, logo at left			
❏ ST1593 [S]	Drifting and Dreaming	1962	$60
—Black colorband label, logo at top			
❏ T1593 [M]	Drifting and Dreaming	1962	$40
—Black colorband label, logo at top			
❏ SM-1593	Drifting and Dreaming	1976	$20
—Reissue with new prefix			
❏ STCL-578	Guy Lombardo	1970	$100
❏ T2350 [M]	Guy Lombardo and His Royal Canadians Play Songs of Carmen Lombardo	1965	$60
❏ DT2350 [R]	Guy Lombardo and His Royal Canadians Play Songs of Carmen Lombardo	1965	$50
❏ ST1393 [S]	Guy Lombardo at Harrah's Club	1960	$80
❏ T1393 [M]	Guy Lombardo at Harrah's Club	1960	$75
❏ T2298 [M]	Guy Lombardo Presents Kenny Gardner	1965	$60
❏ ST2298 [S]	Guy Lombardo Presents Kenny Gardner	1965	$75
❏ T2559 [M]	Guy Lombardo's Broadway	1966	$60
❏ ST2559 [S]	Guy Lombardo's Broadway	1966	$75
❏ ST-340	Is That All There Is?	1969	$25
❏ SM-340	Is That All There Is?	1976	$20
—Reissue with new prefix			
❏ T892 [M]	Lively Guy	1957	$80
—Turquoise label			
❏ T892 [M]	Lively Guy	1958	$75
—Black colorband label, logo at left			
❏ T892 [M]	Lively Guy	1962	$60
—Black colorband label, logo at top			
❏ DT892 [R]	Lively Guy	196?	$25
❏ T2777 [M]	Lombardo Country	1967	$75
❏ ST2777 [S]	Lombardo Country	1967	$60
❏ W738 [M]	Lombardo in Hi-Fi	1956	$80
—Gray label			
❏ W738 [M]	Lombardo in Hi-Fi	1958	$75
—Black colorband label, logo at left			
❏ W738 [M]	Lombardo in Hi-Fi	1962	$60
—Black colorband label, logo at top			
❏ ST2825	Medleys on Parade	1968	$40
❏ KAO1443 [M]	Sing the Songs of Christmas	1960	$50
—Black colorband label, logo at left			
❏ SKAO1443 [S]	Sing the Songs of Christmas	1960	$80
—Black colorband label, logo at left			
❏ TAO1443 [M]	Sing the Songs of Christmas	1962	$60
—Black colorband label, logo at top			
❏ STAO1443 [S]	Sing the Songs of Christmas	1962	$50
—Black colorband label, logo at top			
❏ T1461 [M]	The Best of Guy Lombardo	1961	$80
—Black colorband label, logo at left			
❏ DT1461 [R]	The Best of Guy Lombardo	1961	$40
—Black colorband label, logo at top			
❏ T1461 [M]	The Best of Guy Lombardo	1962	$60
—Black colorband label, logo at top			
❏ SKAO2940	The Best of Guy Lombardo, Vol. 2	1968	$25
❏ T2052 [M]	The Lombardo Touch	1964	$60
❏ ST2052 [S]	The Lombardo Touch	1964	$75
❏ TDL2181 [M]	The Lombardo Years	1964	$100
❏ STDL2181 [S]	The Lombardo Years	1964	$100
❏ ST-128	The New Songs -- The New Sounds	1969	$25
❏ T1947 [M]	The Sweetest Medleys This Side of Heaven	1963	$60
❏ DT1947 [R]	The Sweetest Medleys This Side of Heaven	1963	$50
❏ T2639 [M]	The Sweetest Sounds Today	1967	$50
❏ ST2639 [S]	The Sweetest Sounds Today	1967	$60
❏ T1306 [M]	The Sweetest Waltzes This Side of Heaven	1960	$50
—Black colorband label, logo at left			
❏ ST1306 [S]	The Sweetest Waltzes This Side of Heaven	1960	$80
—Black colorband label, logo at left			
❏ ST1306 [S]	The Sweetest Waltzes This Side of Heaven	1962	$60
—Black colorband label, logo at top			
❏ T1306 [M]	The Sweetest Waltzes This Side of Heaven	1962	$50
—Black colorband label, logo at top			
❏ SN-16193	The Sweetest Waltzes This Side of Heaven	198?	$20

Number	Title	Yr	NM
—Budget-line reissue			
❏ ST2829	They're Playing Our Songs	1968	$25
❏ T1738 [M]	Waltzing with Guy Lombardo	1962	$60
❏ ST1738 [S]	Waltzing with Guy Lombardo	1962	$60
❏ T739 [M]	Your Guy Lombardo Medley	1956	$100
—Turquoise label			
❏ T739 [M]	Your Guy Lombardo Medley	1958	$60
—Black colorband label, logo at left			
❏ T739 [M]	Your Guy Lombardo Medley	1962	$60
—Black colorband label, logo at top			
❏ DT739 [R]	Your Guy Lombardo Medley	196?	$50
❏ SM-739	Your Guy Lombardo Medley	1976	$20
—Reissue with new prefix			
❏ T1244 [M]	Your Guy Lombardo Medley, 1960 Vol. 2	1960	$60
—Black colorband label, logo at left			
❏ ST1244 [S]	Your Guy Lombardo Medley, 1960 Vol. 2	1960	$80
—Black colorband label, logo at left			
❏ T1244 [M]	Your Guy Lombardo Medley, 1962 Vol. 2	1962	$50
—Black colorband label, logo at top			
❏ ST1244 [S]	Your Guy Lombardo Medley, 1962 Vol. 2	1962	$60
—Black colorband label, logo at top			
❏ T1598 [M]	Your Guy Lombardo Medley, 1961 Vol. 3	1961	$60
—Black colorband label, logo at left			
❏ ST1598 [S]	Your Guy Lombardo Medley, 1961 Vol. 3	1961	$80
—Black colorband label, logo at left			
❏ ST1598 [S]	Your Guy Lombardo Medley, 1962 Vol. 3	1962	$60
—Black colorband label, logo at top			
❏ T1598 [M]	Your Guy Lombardo Medley, 1962 Vol. 3	1962	$50
—Black colorband label, logo at top			

DECCA

Number	Title	Yr	NM
❏ DL8070 [M]	A Night at the Roosevelt	195?	$50
—Black label, silver print			
❏ DL8070 [M]	A Night at the Roosevelt	1961	$30
—Black label with color bars			
❏ DL4280 [M]	By Special Request	1962	$30
❏ DL74280 [S]	By Special Request	1962	$35
❏ DL4735 [M]	Dance Medley Time	1966	$25
❏ DL74735 [S]	Dance Medley Time	1966	$30
❏ DL4180 [M]	Dance to the Songs Everybody Knows	1961	$30
❏ DL74180 [S]	Dance to the Songs Everybody Knows	1961	$35
❏ DL4288 [M]	Dancing Piano	1962	$30
❏ DL74288 [S]	Dancing Piano	1962	$35
❏ DL8136 [M]	Enjoy Yourself	1955	$150
—Black label, silver print			
❏ DL8136 [M]	Enjoy Yourself	1961	$30
—Black label with color bars			
❏ DL5329 [10]	Enjoy Yourself	195?	$60
❏ DL8254 [M]	Everybody Dance	1956	$150
—Black label, silver print			
❏ DL8254 [M]	Everybody Dance	1961	$30
—Black label with color bars			
❏ DL5442 [10]	Everybody Dance, Vol. 2	1952	$150
❏ DL5434 [10]	Everybody Dance to the Music of Guy Lombardo	1952	$150
❏ DL4149 [M]	Far Away Places	1961	$30
❏ DL74149 [S]	Far Away Places	1961	$35
❏ DL4430 [M]	Golden Folk Songs	1964	$25
❏ DL74430 [S]	Golden Folk Songs	1964	$30
❏ DL4593 [M]	Golden Medleys	1965	$25
❏ DL74593 [S]	Golden Medleys	1965	$30
❏ DL4380 [M]	Golden Minstrel Songs for Dancing	1963	$30
❏ DL74380 [S]	Golden Minstrel Songs for Dancing	1963	$35
❏ DL4812 [M]	Guy Lombardo's Greatest Hits	1966	$25
❏ DL74812 [S]	Guy Lombardo's Greatest Hits	1966	$30
❏ DL5156 [10]	Hawaiian Songs	1950	$150
❏ DL8843 [M]	Instrumentally Yours	1959	$80
—Black label, silver print			
❏ DL8843 [M]	Instrumentally Yours	1961	$30
—Black label with color bars			
❏ DL4516 [M]	Italian Songs Everybody Knows	1964	$25
❏ DL74516 [S]	Italian Songs Everybody Knows	1964	$30
❏ DL8354 [M]	Jingle Bells	1956	$150
—Black label, silver print			
❏ DL78354 [R]	Jingle Bells	196?	$25

Number	Title	Yr	NM
❏ DL8354 [M]	Jingle Bells	1961	$30
—Black label with color bars			
❏ DL5430 [10]	Jingle Bells	1952	$150
❏ DL5127 [10]	Latin Rhythms	195?	$60
❏ DL8249 [M]	Lombardoland	1956	$120
—Black label, silver print			
❏ DL8249 [M]	Lombardoland	1961	$30
—Black label with color bars			
❏ DL5041 [10]	Lombardoland	1949	$150
❏ DL8097 [M]	Lombardoland, U.S.A.	195?	$50
—Black label, silver print			
❏ DL8097 [M]	Lombardoland, U.S.A.	1961	$30
—Black label with color bars			
❏ DL5328 [10]	Lombardoland, Vol. 2	195?	$60
❏ DL4177 [M]	New Year's Eve with Guy Lombardo	1961	$30
❏ DL74177 [S]	New Year's Eve with Guy Lombardo	1961	$35
❏ DL8255 [M]	Oh! How We Danced	1956	$120
—Black label, silver print			
❏ DL8255 [M]	Oh! How We Danced	1961	$30
—Black label with color bars			
❏ DL4371 [M]	Play a Happy Song	1963	$30
❏ DL74371 [S]	Play a Happy Song	1963	$35
❏ DL5024 [10]	Sidewalks of New York	1949	$150
❏ DL8333 [M]	Silver Jubilee	1956	$150
—Black label, silver print			
❏ DL8333 [M]	Silver Jubilee	1961	$30
—Black label with color bars			
❏ DL5235 [10]	Silver Jubilee -- 1925-1950	1950	$150
❏ DL4567 [M]	Snuggled on Your Shoulder	1965	$25
❏ DL74567 [S]	Snuggled on Your Shoulder	1965	$30
❏ DL8135 [M]	Soft and Sweet	1955	$150
—Black label, silver print			
❏ DL8135 [M]	Soft and Sweet	1961	$30
—Black label with color bars			
❏ DL5097 [10]	Song Hits from Broadway Shows	1949	$150
❏ DL5322 [10]	Souvenirs	195?	$60
❏ DL5277 [10]	Square Dances (Without Calls)	195?	$60
❏ DL8208 [M]	The Band Played On	1955	$150
—Black label, silver print			
❏ DL8208 [M]	The Band Played On	1961	$30
—Black label with color bars			
❏ DXB185 [M]	The Best of Guy Lombardo	1964	$50
❏ DXSB7185 [R]	The Best of Guy Lombardo	1964	$35
❏ DL4268 [M]	The Best Songs Are the Old Songs	1962	$35
❏ DL74268 [S]	The Best Songs Are the Old Songs	196?	$30
❏ DL8894 [M]	The Sidewalks of New York	1959	$80
—Black label, silver print			
❏ DL8894 [M]	The Sidewalks of New York	1961	$30
—Black label with color bars			
❏ DL5330 [10]	The Sweetest Music This Side of Heaven	195?	$60
❏ DL8962 [M]	The Sweetest Music This Side of Heaven (A Musical Biography 1926-1932)	1960	$35
—Black label, silver print			
❏ DL8962 [M]	The Sweetest Music This Side of Heaven (A Musical Biography 1926-1932)	1960	$25
—Black label with color bars			
❏ DL78962 [S]	The Sweetest Music This Side of Heaven (A Musical Biography 1926-1932)	1960	$50
—Black label, silver print			
❏ DL78962 [S]	The Sweetest Music This Side of Heaven (A Musical Biography 1926-1932)	1960	$30
—Black label with color bars			
❏ DL4229 [M]	The Sweetest Music This Side of Heaven (A Musical Biography 1932-1939)	1962	$30
❏ DL74229 [S]	The Sweetest Music This Side of Heaven (A Musical Biography 1932-1939)	1962	$35
❏ DL4328 [M]	The Sweetest Music This Side of Heaven (A Musical Biography 1944-1948)	1962	$30
❏ DL74328 [S]	The Sweetest Music This Side of Heaven (A Musical Biography 1944-1948)	1962	$35
❏ DL4329 [M]	The Sweetest Music This Side of Heaven (A Musical Biography 1949-1954)	1962	$30

Number	Title	Yr	NM
❏ DL74329 [S]	The Sweetest Music This Side of Heaven (A Musical Biography 1949-1954)	1962	$35
❏ DL4123 [M]	The Sweetest Pianos This Side of Heaven	1961	$30
❏ DL74123 [S]	The Sweetest Pianos This Side of Heaven	1961	$35
❏ DLP5002 [10]	The Twin Pianos -- Vol. 1	1949	$150
—Both record and sleeve have "DLP" prefix			
❏ DL5002 [10]	The Twin Pianos -- Vol. 1	195?	$60
—Record has "DL" prefix; sleeve may or may not have "DL			
❏ DLP5003 [10]	The Twin Pianos -- Vol. 2	1949	$150
—Both record and sleeve have "DLP" prefix			
❏ DL5003 [10]	The Twin Pianos -- Vol. 2	195?	$60
—Record has "DL" prefix; sleeve may or may not have "DL			
❏ DL8251 [M]	Twin Piano Magic	1956	$150
—Black label, silver print			
❏ DL8251 [M]	Twin Piano Magic	1961	$30
—Black label with color bars			
❏ DL5447 [10]	Twin Piano Magic	195?	$60
❏ DL8119 [M]	Twin Pianos	195?	$50
—Black label, silver print			
❏ DL8119 [M]	Twin Pianos	1961	$30
—Black label with color bars			
❏ DL5193 [10]	Waltzes	195?	$60
❏ DL8256 [M]	Waltzland	1956	$150
—Black label, silver print			
❏ DL8256 [M]	Waltzland	1961	$30
—Black label with color bars			
❏ DL5325 [10]	Waltzland	1951	$200
❏ DL8205 [M]	Waltz Time	1955	$150
—Black label, silver print			
❏ DL8205 [M]	Waltz Time	1961	$30
—Black label with color bars			

HINDSIGHT

Number	Title	Yr	NM
❏ HSR-187	Guy Lombardo and His Royal Canadians 1950	198?	$25

LONDON

Number	Title	Yr	NM
❏ XPS904	Every Night Is New Year's Eve	1973	$25

MCA

Number	Title	Yr	NM
❏ 15031	Auld Lang Syne	198?	$25
❏ 242	Dance Medley Time	197?	$20
—Reissue of Decca 74735			
❏ 197	Dance to the Songs Everybody Knows	1973	$20
—Reissue of Decca 74180			
❏ 103	Golden Medleys	1973	$20
—Reissue of Decca 74593			
❏ 245	Guy Lombardo's Greatest Hits	197?	$20
—Reissue of Decca 74812			
❏ 15035	I Saw Mommy Kissing Santa Claus	198?	$25
❏ 15012	Jingle Bells	197?	$25
—Reissue of Decca 78354; black rainbow label			
❏ 15012	Jingle Bells	1977	$20
—Tan label			
❏ 15012	Jingle Bells	1980	$20
—Blue rainbow label			
❏ 15000	New Year's Eve with Guy Lombardo	1974	$25
—Reissue of MCA 195; black rainbow label			
❏ 195	New Year's Eve with Guy Lombardo	1973	$30
—Reissue of Decca 74177			
❏ 15000	New Year's Eve with Guy Lombardo	1977	$20
—Tan label			
❏ 15000	New Year's Eve with Guy Lombardo	1980	$20
—Blue rainbow label			
❏ 4041	The Best of Guy Lombardo	197?	$30
—Black rainbow labels			
❏ 4041	The Best of Guy Lombardo	1977	$25
—Tan labels			
❏ 4041	The Best of Guy Lombardo	1980	$25
—Blue rainbow labels			
❏ 4082	The Best of Guy Lombardo, Vol. 2	197?	$30
—Black rainbow labels			
❏ 4082	The Best of Guy Lombardo, Vol. 2	1977	$25
—Tan labels			

Machito, *Afro-Cuban Jazz*, Mercury MGC-505, 10-inch LP with Mercury (not Clef) label, **$300**.

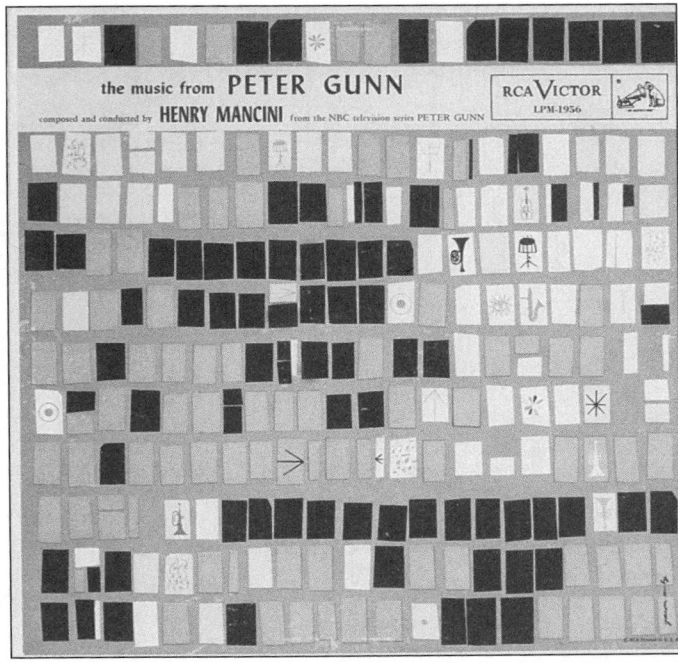

Henry Mancini, *The Music from Peter Gunn*, RCA Victor LPM-1956, original "block" cover design, **$40**.

Herbie Mann, *East Coast Jazz 4*, Bethlehem BCP 1018, 10-inch LP, **$250**.

Herbie Mann, *Sultry Serenade*, Riverside RLP 12-234, white label, blue print, **$300**.

Number	Title	Yr	NM
❑ 4082	The Best of Guy Lombardo, Vol. 2	1980	$25
—Blue rainbow labels			
❑ 89	The Best Songs Are the Old Songs	1973	$20
—Reissue of Decca 74268			
❑ 201	The Sweetest Music This Side of Heaven	1973	$20
—Reissue of Decca 78962?			

MCA CORAL

❑ CR20105	Here's Guy Lombardo	197?	$25

PAIR

❑ PDL2-1046	Guy Lombardo	1986	$30

PICKWICK

❑ SPC-3358	Alley Cat	197?	$20
❑ SPC1011	Deck the Halls	196?	$25
—Silver label			
❑ SPC1011	Deck the Halls	197?	$20
—Reissue on black label			
❑ SPC-3193	Enjoy Yourself	196?	$25
❑ SPC-3257	Red Roses for a Blue Lady	197?	$20
❑ SPC-3530	Seems Like Old Times	197?	$20
❑ SPC-3530	Seems Like Old Times	197?	$20
❑ SPC-3073	Sweet and Heavenly	196?	$25
❑ SPC-3312	The Impossible Dream	197?	$20
❑ PTP-2009	The Sweet Sounds	197?	$25

RCA CAMDEN

❑ CAL-445 [M]	An Evening with Guy Lombardo	195?	$35
❑ CAS-445 [R]	An Evening with Guy Lombardo	196?	$25
❑ CAL-255 [M]	Guy Lombardo Plays	195?	$35
❑ CAS-255 [R]	Guy Lombardo Plays	196?	$25
❑ CAL-578 [M]	He's My Guy	195?	$35

RCA VICTOR

❑ CPL1-2047(e)	A Legendary Performer	1977	$25
❑ VPM-6071	This Is Guy Lombardo	197?	$30
❑ LPT-3059 [10]	This Is Guy Lombardo and His Orchestra	1954	$40

SUNBEAM

❑ 308	On the Air 1935	197?	$25

VOCALION

❑ VL3605 [M]	Dance in the Moonlight	1958	$35
❑ VL73605 [R]	Dance in the Moonlight	196?	$25
❑ VL73833	Here's Guy Lombardo	1968	$25

LONDON, JULIE

Female singer.

Albums

LIBERTY

❑ LRP-3043 [M]	About the Blues	1957	$40
—Green label			
❑ LST-7012 [S]	About the Blues	1958	$140
—Black label, silver print			
❑ LRP-3043 [M]	About the Blues	1960	$50
—Black label, colorband and logo at left			
❑ LST-7012 [S]	About the Blues	1960	$60
—Black label, colorband and logo at left			
❑ LRP-3434 [M]	All Through the Night	1965	$60
❑ LST-7434 [S]	All Through the Night	1965	$60
❑ LRP-3164 [M]	Around Midnight	1960	$60
❑ LST-7164 [S]	Around Midnight	1960	$40
❑ SCR-1 [S]	By Myself	196?	$60
—Columbia Record Club exclusive			
❑ MCR-1 [M]	By Myself	196?	$60
—Columbia Record Club exclusive			
❑ SL-9002 [M]	Calendar Girl	1956	$175
❑ LST-7546	Easy Does It	1968	$50
❑ LRP-3416 [M]	Feeling Good	1965	$60
❑ LST-7416 [S]	Feeling Good	1965	$60
❑ LRP-3478 [M]	For the Night People	1966	$60
❑ LST-7478 [S]	For the Night People	1966	$60
❑ LRP-3096 [M]	Julie	1957	$40
—Green label			
❑ LST-7004 [S]	Julie	1958	$140
—Black label, silver print			
❑ LRP-3152 [M]	Julie…At Home	1960	$60
❑ LST-7152 [S]	Julie…At Home	1960	$175
—Blue vinyl			
❑ LST-7152 [S]	Julie…At Home	1960	$40
—Black vinyl			
❑ LST-7027 [S]	Julie Is Her Name	1958	$175
—Blue vinyl			
❑ LST-7027 [S]	Julie Is Her Name	1958	$175
—Red vinyl			
❑ LST-7027 [S]	Julie Is Her Name	1958	$40
—Black label, silver print			

Number	Title	Yr	NM
❑ LRP-3006 [M]	Julie Is Her Name	1960	$50
—Black label, colorband and logo at left			
❑ LST-7027 [S]	Julie Is Her Name	1960	$60
—Black label, colorband and logo at left			
❑ LRP-3100 [M]	Julie Is Her Name, Volume 2	1958	$40
—Green label			
❑ LST-7100 [S]	Julie Is Her Name, Volume 2	1958	$40
—Black label, silver print			
❑ LRP-3100 [M]	Julie Is Her Name, Volume 2	1960	$50
—Black label, colorband and logo at left			
❑ LST-7100 [S]	Julie Is Her Name, Volume 2	1960	$60
—Black label, colorband and logo at left			
❑ LRP-3342 [M]	Julie London	1964	$60
❑ LST-7342 [S]	Julie London	1964	$60
❑ LRP-3375 [M]	Julie London In Person at the Americana	1964	$60
❑ LST-7375 [S]	Julie London In Person at the Americana	1964	$60
❑ LRP-3291 [M]	Julie's Golden Greats	1963	$60
—White cover			
❑ LRP-3291 [M]	Julie's Golden Greats	1963	$60
—Black cover			
❑ LST-7291 [S]	Julie's Golden Greats	1963	$60
—White cover			
❑ LST-7291 [S]	Julie's Golden Greats	1963	$60
—Black cover			
❑ LRP-3278 [M]	Latin in a Satin Mood	1963	$60
❑ LST-7278 [S]	Latin in a Satin Mood	1963	$60
❑ LRP-3105 [M]	London By Night	1958	$60
—Green label			
❑ LST-7105 [S]	London By Night	1958	$40
—Black label, silver print			
❑ LRP-3012 [M]	Lonely Girl	1956	$100
—Green label			
❑ LST-7029 [S]	Lonely Girl	1958	$40
—Black label, silver print			
❑ LRP-3012 [M]	Lonely Girl	1960	$50
—Black label, colorband and logo at left			
❑ LST-7029 [S]	Lonely Girl	1960	$60
—Black label, colorband and logo at left			
❑ LRP-3231 [M]	Love Letters	1962	$60
❑ LST-7231 [S]	Love Letters	1962	$60
❑ LRP-3249 [M]	Love on the Rocks	1963	$60
❑ LST-7249 [S]	Love on the Rocks	1963	$60
❑ LRP-3060 [M]	Make Love to Me	1957	$40
—Green label			
❑ LST-7060 [S]	Make Love to Me	1958	$40
—Black label, silver print			
❑ LRP-3060 [M]	Make Love to Me	1960	$50
—Black label, colorband and logo at left			
❑ LST-7060 [S]	Make Love to Me	1960	$60
—Black label, colorband and logo at left			
❑ LRP-3493 [M]	Nice Girls Don't Stay for Breakfast	1967	$60
❑ LST-7493 [S]	Nice Girls Don't Stay for Breakfast	1967	$60
❑ LRP-3392 [M]	Our Fair Lady	1965	$60
❑ LST-7392 [S]	Our Fair Lady	1965	$60
❑ LRP-3171 [M]	Send for Me	1961	$60
❑ LST-7171 [S]	Send for Me	1961	$40
❑ LRP-3203 [M]	Sophisticated Lady	1962	$60
❑ LST-7203 [S]	Sophisticated Lady	1962	$60
❑ LRP-3119 [M]	Swing Me an Old Song	1959	$60
—Green label			
❑ LST-7119 [S]	Swing Me an Old Song	1959	$40
—Black label, silver print			
❑ S-6601 [S]	The Best of Julie London	1962	$40
❑ LRP-3300 [M]	The End of the World	1963	$60
❑ LST-7300 [S]	The End of the World	1963	$60
❑ LRP-3324 [M]	The Wonderful World of Julie London	1963	$60
❑ LST-7324 [S]	The Wonderful World of Julie London	1963	$60
❑ LRP-3192 [M]	Whatever Julie Wants	1961	$60
❑ LST-7192 [S]	Whatever Julie Wants	1961	$40
❑ LRP-3514 [M]	With Body and Soul	1967	$60
❑ LST-7514 [S]	With Body and Soul	1967	$60
❑ LRP-3130 [M]	Your Number Please	1959	$60
—Green label			
❑ LST-7130 [S]	Your Number Please	1959	$40
—Black label, silver print			
❑ LRP-3130 [M]	Your Number Please	1960	$50
—Black label, colorband and logo at left			
❑ LST-7130 [S]	Your Number Please	1960	$60
—Black label, colorband and logo at left			
❑ LST-7609	Yummy, Yummy, Yummy	1969	$50

SUNSET

❑ SUS-5207	Gone with the Wind	196?	$30
❑ SUM-1104 [M]	Julie London	196?	$30
❑ SUS-5104 [S]	Julie London	196?	$35
❑ SUM-1161 [M]	Soft and Sweet	196?	$30
❑ SUS-5161 [S]	Soft and Sweet	196?	$35

UNITED ARTISTS

❑ UA-LA437-E	The Very Best of Julie London	1975	$30

LONDON RAGTIME ORCHESTRA, THE

Albums

STOMP OFF

❑ SOS-1081	Bouncing Around	1985	$25

LONG, BARBARA

Female singer.

Albums

SAVOY

❑ MG-12161 [M]	Soul	1961	$30

LONG, DANNY

Pianist.

Albums

CAPITOL

❑ T1988 [M]	Jazz Furlough	1963	$75
❑ ST1988 [S]	Jazz Furlough	1963	$50

LONG, JOHNNY

Violinist and bandleader.

Albums

CIRCLE

❑ 56	Johnny Long and His Orchestra 1941-1942	198?	$25

LONGMIRE, WILBERT

Guitarist.

Albums

COLUMBIA

❑ JC35754	Champagne	1979	$25
❑ JC35365	Sunny Side Up	1978	$25

PACIFIC JAZZ

❑ ST-20161	Revolution	1969	$25

LONGNON, JEAN-LOUP

Trumpeter, composer and bandleader.

Albums

ATLANTIC

❑ 81829	Jean-Loup Longnon and His New Your Orchestra	1988	$25

LONGO, MIKE

Pianist.

Albums

GROOVE MERCHANT

❑ 525	Funkia	1974	$25

MAINSTREAM

❑ MRL-334	Matrix	1972	$35
❑ MRL-357	The Awakening	1972	$35

PABLO

❑ 2310769	Talk with Spirits	197?	$35

LONGO, PAT

Alto saxophone player and bandleader.

Albums

TOWN HALL

❑ 33	Billy May for President	198?	$25
❑ 25	Chain Reaction	1980	$25
❑ 30	Crocodile Tears	1981	$25

LOOKOFSKY, HARRY

Violinist and violist. Played the string parts on the Left Banke's hit single "Walk Away Renee." (His son, Mike Brown, wrote the song and was part of the group.)

Albums

ATLANTIC

❑ 1319 [M]	Stringville	1959	$300
—Black label			
❑ 1319 [M]	Stringville	1961	$150

Number	Title	Yr	NM
— Multicolor label, white "fan" logo at right			
1319 [M]	Stringville	1964	$35
— Multicolor label, black "fan" logo at right			
SD1319 [S]	Stringville	1959	$300
— Green label			
SD1319 [S]	Stringville	1961	$150
— Multicolor label, white "fan" logo at right			
SD1319 [S]	Stringville	1964	$30
— Multicolor label, black "fan" logo at right			

LORBER, JEFF
Keyboard player, arranger and composer.
Albums
ARISTA

Number	Title	Yr	NM
AL9545	Galaxian	1981	$12
AL8119	Galaxian	198?	$10
— Reissue of 9545			
AL8-8025	In the Heat of the Night	1984	$12
AL9583	It's a Fact	1982	$12
AL8218	It's a Fact	198?	$10
— Reissue of 9583			
AL8393	Lift Off	1986	$12
AL8-8269	Step by Step	1985	$12
AB4234	Water Sign	1979	$12
AL8360	Water Sign	198?	$10
— Reissue of 4234			
AL9516	Wizard Island	1980	$25
AL8340	Wizard Island	198?	$20
— Reissue of 9516			

INNER CITY

Number	Title	Yr	NM
IC-1026	Jeff Lorber Fusion	1977	$18
IC-1056	Soft Space	1978	$18

WARNER BROS.

Number	Title	Yr	NM
25492	Private Passion	1986	$12

LORD, VIVIAN
Pianist and female singer.
Albums
STASH

Number	Title	Yr	NM
ST-241	Love Dance	198?	$25

LORIMER, MICHAEL
Guitarist.
Albums
DANCING CAT

Number	Title	Yr	NM
DC-3002	Remembranza	198?	$30

LOTTRIDGE, RICHARD, AND JOAN WILDMAN
Lottridge plays bassoon; Wildman plays piano and keyboards.
Albums
UNIVERSITY OF WISCONSIN

Number	Title	Yr	NM
UW-102	Something New: The Unique Sounds of Jazz Bassoon	1986	$35

LOUISIANA REPERTORY JAZZ BAND
Albums
STOMP OFF

Number	Title	Yr	NM
SOS-1140	Hot and Sweet Sounds of Lost New Orleans	1987	$25
SOS-1029	New Orleans	198?	$25
SOS-1055	Uptown Jazz	198?	$25

LOUNGE LIZARDS, THE
Founded by JOHN LURIE. Revolving membership over the years.
Albums
EDITIONS EG

Number	Title	Yr	NM
EGS-108	The Lounge Lizards	1981	$30

EUROPA

Number	Title	Yr	NM
JP-2012	Live from the Drunken Boat	1983	$35

ISLAND

Number	Title	Yr	NM
90529	Live in Tokyo -- Big Heart	1986	$25
90592	No Pain for Cakes	1987	$25

LOUSSIER, JACQUES
Pianist.
Albums
LONDON

Number	Title	Yr	NM
LL3454/5 [M]	Bach Jazz	1965	$35
PS454/5 [S]	Bach Jazz	1965	$25
820245-1 [S]	Bach Jazz, Vol. 1	1985	$25
820246-1 [S]	Bach Jazz, Vol. 2	1985	$25
PS524	Bach Jazz, Vol. 5	1968	$30
LL3144 [M]	Play Bach	196?	$35
LL3287 [M]	Play Bach, Vol. 1	1964	$30
PS287 [S]	Play Bach, Vol. 1	1964	$35
LL3288 [M]	Play Bach, Vol. 2	1964	$30
PS288 [S]	Play Bach, Vol. 2	1964	$35
LL3289 [M]	Play Bach, Vol. 3	1964	$30
PS289 [S]	Play Bach, Vol. 3	1964	$35
LL3365 [M]	Play Bach, Vol. 4	1964	$30
PS365 [S]	Play Bach, Vol. 4	1964	$35

LOVANO, JOE
Alto saxophone player and composer.
Albums
SOUL NOTE

Number	Title	Yr	NM
121132	Tones, Shapes and Colors	1985	$30
121182	Village Rhythm	1988	$30

LOVETT, LEE
Pianist.
Albums
STRAND

Number	Title	Yr	NM
SL-1055 [M]	Jazz Dance Party	1962	$50
SLS-1055 [S]	Jazz Dance Party	1962	$60
SL-1059 [M]	Misty	1962	$50
SLS-1059 [S]	Misty	1962	$60

WYNNE

Number	Title	Yr	NM
WLP-108 [M]	Jazz Dance Party	195?	$30

LOWE, FRANK, AND EUGENE CHADBOURNE
Chadbourne is a guitarist. Also see FRANK LOWE.
Albums
QED

Number	Title	Yr	NM
995	Don't Punk Out	1977	$30

LOWE, FRANK
Tenor saxophone player.
Albums
ARISTA/FREEDOM

Number	Title	Yr	NM
AF1015	Fresh	1976	$30

BLACK SAINT

Number	Title	Yr	NM
BSR-0005	The Flam	198?	$30

CADENCE JAZZ

Number	Title	Yr	NM
CJR-1007	Skizoke	198?	$25

ESP-DISK'

Number	Title	Yr	NM
3013	Black Beings	197?	$200

SOUL NOTE

Number	Title	Yr	NM
SN-1082	Decision in Paradise	1985	$30
SN-1032	Erotic Heartbreak	198?	$30

LOWE, MUNDELL
Guitarist. Also see THE FOUR MOST.
Albums
CHARLIE PARKER

Number	Title	Yr	NM
PLP-822 [M]	Blues for a Stripper	1962	$40
PLP-822S [S]	Blues for a Stripper	1962	$50

DOBRE

Number	Title	Yr	NM
1018	Incomparable	1978	$35

FAMOUS DOOR

Number	Title	Yr	NM
HL-102	California Guitar	1974	$30

JAZZLAND

Number	Title	Yr	NM
JLP-8 [M]	Low-Down Guitar	1960	$60

OFFBEAT

Number	Title	Yr	NM
OLP-3010 [M]	Tacet for Neurotics	1960	$80
OS-93010 [S]	Tacet for Neurotics	1960	$100

PAUSA

Number	Title	Yr	NM
7152	Mundell Lowe Presents Transit West	1983	$35

RCA CAMDEN

Number	Title	Yr	NM
CAL-490 [M]	Porgy and Bess	1959	$25
CAS-490 [S]	Porgy and Bess	1959	$25
CAL-522 [M]	TV Action Jazz!	1959	$25
CAS-522 [S]	TV Action Jazz!	1959	$25
CAL-627 [M]	TV Action Jazz! -- Volume 2	1960	$30
CAS-627 [S]	TV Action Jazz! -- Volume 2	1960	$30

RCA VICTOR

Number	Title	Yr	NM
LJM-3002 [10]	The Mundell Lowe Quintet	1954	$120

RIVERSIDE

Number	Title	Yr	NM
RLP 12-238 [M]	A Grand Night for Swinging	1957	$250
— White label, blue print			
RLP 12-238 [M]	A Grand Night for Swinging	1959	$250
— Blue label, microphone logo at top			
RLP 12-208 [M]	Guitar Moods	1956	$250
— White label, blue print			
6089	Mundell Lowe Quintet	197?	$35
RLP 12-219 [M]	New Music of Alec Wilder	1956	$250
— White label, blue print			
RLP 12-219 [M]	New Music of Alec Wilder	1959	$250
— Blue label, microphone logo at top			
RLP 12-204 [M]	The Mundell Lowe Quartet	1956	$250
— White label, blue print			
RLP 12-204 [M]	The Mundell Lowe Quartet	1959	$250
— Blue label, microphone logo at top			

LUCAS, DOUG
Albums
SHADY BROOK

Number	Title	Yr	NM
SB 33-004	Niara	1975	$30

LUCAS, REGGIE
Guitarist and composer. Wrote several of Madonna's early hit singles.
Albums
INNER CITY

Number	Title	Yr	NM
IC-6010	Survival Themes	197?	$35

LUCIE, LAWRENCE
Guitarist.
Albums
TOY

Number	Title	Yr	NM
1001	Cool and Warm Guitar	197?	$35
1006	Mixed Emotions	1980	$30
1003	Sophisticated Lady/After Sundown	1978	$30
1005	This Is It	1979	$30

LUCRAFT, HOWARD
Guitarist and composer.
Albums
DECCA

Number	Title	Yr	NM
DL8679 [M]	Showcase for Modern Jazz	1958	$100

LUDI, WERNER
Saxophone player.
Albums
HAT ART

Number	Title	Yr	NM
2018	Lunatico	1986	$35

LUDWIG, GENE
Organist.
Albums
MUSE

Number	Title	Yr	NM
MR-5164	Now's the Time	1979	$30

LUNA
Albums
ARHOOLIE

Number	Title	Yr	NM
ST-8001	Space Swell	1968	$25

LUNCEFORD, JIMMIE
Multi-instrumentalist., bandleader and composer.
Albums
AIRCHECK

Number	Title	Yr	NM
8	Victory	197?	$25

ALLEGRO ELITE

Number	Title	Yr	NM
0(????) [10]	Jimmie Lunceford Plays	195?	$40

CIRCLE

Number	Title	Yr	NM
11	Jimmie Lunceford and His Orchestra 1940	198?	$25
CLP-92	Jimmie Lunceford and His Orchestra 1944	198?	$25

COLUMBIA

Number	Title	Yr	NM
GL104 [10]	Lunceford Special	1950	$80
CL2715 [M]	Lunceford Special	1967	$30
CS9515 [R]	Lunceford Special	1967	$35
— Red "360 Sound" label			

Number	Title	Yr	NM
❏ CL634 [M]	Lunceford Special	1955	$60

—Maroon label, gold print

❏ CL634 [M]	Lunceford Special	1956	$40

—Red and black label with six "eye" logos

COLUMBIA MASTERWORKS

❏ ML4804 [M]	Lunceford Special	195?	$60

DECCA

❏ DL5393 [10]	For Dancers Only	1952	$150
❏ DL9238 [M]	Harlem Shout	1968	$40
❏ DL79238 [R]	Harlem Shout	1968	$25
❏ DL8050 [M]	Jimmie Lunceford and His Orchestra	1954	$150
❏ DL9237 [M]	Rhythm Is Our Business	1968	$40
❏ DL79237 [R]	Rhythm Is Our Business	1968	$25

MCA

❏ 1314	Blues in the Night	198?	$25
❏ 1307	For Dancers Only	198?	$25
❏ 1305	Harlem Shout	198?	$25
❏ 1320	Jimmie's Legacy	198?	$25
❏ 1321	Last Sparks	198?	$25
❏ 1302	Rhythm Is Our Business	198?	$25

PICKWICK

❏ SPC-3531	Blues in the Night	197?	$25

SUNBEAM

❏ 221	Jimmie Lunceford and Band 1939-42	197?	$25

TIME-LIFE

❏ STBB-27	Big Bands: Jimmie Lunceford	1986	$35

X

❏ LX-3002 [M]	Jimmie Lunceford and His Chickasaw Syncopators	1954	$60

LURIE, JOHN
Soprano and alto saxophone player and male singer. Also see THE LOUNGE LIZARDS.

Albums

ENIGMA

❏ SJ-73213	Stranger Than Paradise	1986	$25

LYLE, BOBBY
Pianist.

Albums

ATLANTIC

❏ 81938	Ivory Dreams	1989	$30

CAPITOL

❏ ST-11627	Genie	1976	$25
❏ SW-11809	New Warrior	1978	$25

LYMAN, ABE
Bandleader and drummer.

Albums

HINDSIGHT

❏ HSR-184	Abe Lyman and His Orchestra 1941	198?	$25

LYMAN, ARTHUR
Vibraphone and marimba player. Best known for his long line of exotica LPs, the below is his only jazz offering.

Albums

HIFI

❏ R-607 [M]	Leis of Jazz	1958	$50
❏ SR-607 [S]	Leis of Jazz	1958	$60

LYNNE, GLORIA
Female singer. Earlier material appears in the Goldmine Standard Catalog of American Records.

Albums

ABC IMPULSE!

❏ ASD-9311	I Don't Know How to Love Him	1976	$30

CANYON

❏ 7709	Happy and In Love	1970	$35

COLLECTABLES

❏ COL-5138	Golden Classics	198?	$25

DESIGN

❏ D-177 [M]	My Funny Valentine	196?	$25
❏ DS-177 [S]	My Funny Valentine	196?	$30

EVEREST

❏ EV-5230 [M]	After Hours	1965	$50
❏ EV-1230 [S]	After Hours	1965	$60
❏ LPBR-5101 [M]	Day In, Day Out	1961	$50

Number	Title	Yr	NM
❏ SDBR-1101 [S]	Day In, Day Out	1961	$60
❏ EV-5220 [M]	Gloria, Marty & Strings	1963	$50
❏ EV-1220 [S]	Gloria, Marty & Strings	1963	$60
❏ LPBR-5203 [M]	Gloria Blue	1962	$50
❏ SDBR-1203 [S]	Gloria Blue	1962	$60
❏ EV-5238 [M]	Gloria Lynne '66	1966	$35
❏ EV-1238 [S]	Gloria Lynne '66	1966	$50
❏ LPBR-5132 [M]	Gloria Lynne at Basin Street East	1962	$50
❏ SDBR-1132 [S]	Gloria Lynne at Basin Street East	1962	$60
❏ LPBR-5208 [M]	Gloria Lynne at the Las Vegas Thunderbird	1963	$50
❏ SDBR-1208 [S]	Gloria Lynne at the Las Vegas Thunderbird	1963	$60
❏ E-5001 [M]	Gloria Lynne Live! Take 1	1959	$60
❏ ES-1001 [S]	Gloria Lynne Live! Take 1	1959	$40
❏ EV-5228 [M]	Glorious Gloria Lynne	1964	$50
❏ EV-1228 [S]	Glorious Gloria Lynne	1964	$60
❏ EV-5237 [M]	Go! Go! Go!	1965	$35
❏ EV-1237 [S]	Go! Go! Go!	1965	$50
❏ LPBR-5128 [M]	He Needs Me	1961	$50
❏ SDBR-1128 [S]	He Needs Me	1961	$60
❏ LPBR-5126 [M]	I'm Glad There Is You	1961	$50
❏ SDBR-1126 [S]	I'm Glad There Is You	1961	$60
❏ EV-5226 [M]	I Wish You Love	1964	$50
❏ EV-1226 [S]	I Wish You Love	1964	$60
❏ ST-90057 [M]	I Wish You Love	196?	$100

—Capitol Record Club edition

❏ LPBR-5063 [M]	Lonely and Sentimental	1960	$50
❏ SDBR-1063 [S]	Lonely and Sentimental	1960	$60
❏ LPBR-5022 [M]	Miss Gloria Lynne	1959	$50
❏ SDBR-1022 [S]	Miss Gloria Lynne	1959	$60
❏ EV-5231 [M]	The Best of Gloria Lynne	1965	$35
❏ EV-1231 [S]	The Best of Gloria Lynne	1965	$50
❏ LPBR-5131 [M]	This Little Boy of Mine	1961	$50
❏ SDBR-1131 [S]	This Little Boy of Mine	1961	$60
❏ LPBR-5090 [M]	Try a Little Tenderness	1960	$50
❏ SDBR-1090 [S]	Try a Little Tenderness	1960	$60

FONTANA

❏ MGF-27561 [M]	Gloria	1966	$35
❏ SRF-67561 [S]	Gloria	1966	$50
❏ SRF-67577	Here, There and Everywhere	1968	$35
❏ MGF-27528 [M]	Intimate Moments	1964	$35
❏ SRF-67528 [S]	Intimate Moments	1964	$50
❏ MGF-27546 [M]	Love and a Woman	1965	$35
❏ SRF-67546 [S]	Love and a Woman	1965	$50
❏ MGF-27541 [M]	Soul Serenade	1965	$35
❏ SRF-67541 [S]	Soul Serenade	1965	$50
❏ MGF-27571 [M]	The Other Side of Gloria Lynne	1967	$50
❏ SRF-67571 [S]	The Other Side of Gloria Lynne	1967	$35
❏ MGF-27555 [M]	Where It's At	1966	$35
❏ SRF-67555 [S]	Where It's At	1966	$50

HIFI

❏ SR-441	Greatest Hits	1969	$35
❏ L-440 [M]	The Gloria Lynne Calendar	1966	$35
❏ SL-440 [S]	The Gloria Lynne Calendar	1966	$50

INTERMEDIA

❏ QS-5069	Classics	198?	$25

MERCURY

❏ SRM-1-633	A Very Gentle Sound	1972	$35

MUSE

❏ MR-5381	A Time for Love	198?	$25

SUNSET

❏ SUM-1145 [M]	Gloria Lynne	1966	$30
❏ SUS-5145 [S]	Gloria Lynne	1966	$30
❏ SUS-5221	Golden Greats	1968	$30
❏ SUM-1171 [M]	I Wish You Love	1967	$30
❏ SUS-5171 [S]	I Wish You Love	1967	$30

UPFRONT

❏ 146	Gloria Lynne	197?	$30

LYON, JIMMY
Pianist.

Albums

FINNADAR

❏ 9034	Johnny Lyon Plays Cole Porter's Steinway and Music	198?	$35

LYONS, JIMMY
Tenor saxophone player.

Albums

BLACK SAINT

❏ BSR-0087	Give It Up	1986	$30
❏ 120125	Something in Return	1990	$35

HAT ART

❏ 2028	Jump Up/What to Do About	1986	$35

—Reissue of Hat Hut 21

HAT HUT

❏ 21	Jump Up/What to Do About	198?	$25
❏ 0Y/Z/Z	Push	1979	$30
❏ 3503	Riffs	198?	$30

LYTLE, JOHNNY
Vibraphone player.

Albums

FANTASY

❏ OJC-110	The Village Caller	198?	$25

JAZZLAND

❏ JLP-22 [M]	Blue Vibes	1960	$30
❏ JLP-922 [S]	Blue Vibes	1960	$30
❏ JLP-44 [M]	Happy Ground	1961	$30
❏ JLP-944 [S]	Happy Ground	1961	$30
❏ JLP-81 [M]	Moon Child	1962	$30
❏ JLP-981 [S]	Moon Child	1962	$30
❏ JLP-67 [M]	Nice and Easy	1962	$30
❏ JLP-967 [S]	Nice and Easy	1962	$30

MILESTONE

❏ 9043	People and Love	197?	$35
❏ 9036	Soulful Rebel	197?	$35

MUSE

❏ MR-5158	Everything Must Change	1978	$30
❏ MR-5185	Fast Hands	1981	$25
❏ MR-5271	Good Vibes	1982	$25
❏ MR-5387	Happy Ground	1991	$35

RIVERSIDE

❏ RM-3003 [M]	A Groove	1967	$100
❏ RS-3003 [S]	A Groove	1967	$100
❏ RLP-456 [M]	Got That Feeling	1963	$150
❏ RS-9456 [S]	Got That Feeling	1963	$150
❏ RLP-470 [M]	Happy Ground	1964	$150
❏ RS-9470 [S]	Happy Ground	1964	$150
❏ RS-3017	Moon Child	1968	$100
❏ RLP-480 [M]	The Village Caller	1965	$100

SOLID STATE

❏ SS-18014	A Man and a Woman	1967	$25
❏ SS-18044	Be Proud	1969	$25
❏ SS-18056	Close Enough	1969	$25

LYTTELTON, HUMPHREY
Trumpeter and bandleader.

Albums

ANGEL

❏ ANG.60008 [10]	Some Like It Hot	1955	$75

BETHLEHEM

❏ BCP-6063 [M]	Humph Plays Standards	1961	$250

LONDON

❏ LL3132 [M]	Humph Dedicates	195?	$30
❏ PS178 [S]	Humph Dedicates	1959	$30
❏ LL3101 [M]	I Play As I Please	195?	$30

SACKVILLE

❏ 3033	Humphrey Lyttelton in Canada	198?	$30

STOMP OFF

❏ SOS-1160	Delving Back and Forth with Humph	1989	$25
❏ SOS-1111	Scatterbrains	1986	$25

M

MABERN, HAROLD
Pianist. Also see THE MODERN JAZZ TRIO.

Albums

FANTASY

❏ OJC-330	Rakin' and Scrapin'	1988	$25

PRESTIGE

❏ PRST-7687 [B]	Workin' and Wailin'	1969	$100

SACKVILLE

❏ 2016	Live at Café Des Copains	198?	$30

MACDONALD, KEITH

Albums

LANDMARK

❏ LLP-1503	This Is Keith MacDonald	1985	$25
❏ LLP-1509	Waiting	1986	$25

MACDOWELL, AL
Bass player.

Albums

GRAMAVISION

❏ R1-79450	Time Peace	1990	$30

MACERO, TEO
Tenor saxophone player and composer. Also see THE MANHATTAN JAZZ ALL-STARS.

Albums

Number	Title	Yr	NM
AMERICAN CLAVE			
❑ 1002	Teo	198?	$35
COLUMBIA			
❑ CL842 [M]	What's New?	1956	$80
—Red and black label with six "eye" logos			
DEBUT			
❑ DLP-6 [10]	Explorations by Teo Macero	1954	$500
DOCTOR JAZZ			
❑ FW40111	Acoustical Suspension	1986	$35
FANTASY			
❑ OJC-1715	Teo -- Teo Macero with the Prestige Jazz Quartet	198?	$30
FINNADAR			
❑ SR9024	Time Plus 7	1979	$50
PALO ALTO			
❑ PA-8046	Impressions of Charles Mingus	1984	$50
PRESTIGE			
❑ PRLP-7104 [M]	Teo -- Teo Macero with the Prestige Jazz Quartet	1957	$250

MACHITO
Bandleader, male singer and percussionist.

Albums

Number	Title	Yr	NM
CLEF			
❑ MGC-505 [10]	Afro-Cuban Jazz	1953	$300
❑ MGC-689 [M]	Afro-Cuban Jazz	1956	$250
❑ MGC-511 [10]	Machito Jazz with Flip and Bird	1953	$300
CORAL			
❑ CRL757258 [S]	Vacation at the Concord	1959	$30
DECCA			
❑ DL5157 [10]	Machito's Afro-Cuban	1950	$250
FORUM			
❑ F-9043 [M]	Asia Minor	196?	$30
—Reissue of Tico 1033			
❑ SF-9043 [S]	Asia Minor	196?	$30
❑ F-9038 [M]	Mi Amigo, Machito	196?	$30
—Reissue of Tico 1053			
❑ SF-9038 [S]	Mi Amigo, Machito	196?	$30
GNP CRESCENDO			
❑ GNPS-58 [R]	Machito at the Crescendo	198?	$20
❑ GNPS-72 [R]	The World's Greatest Latin Band	198?	$20
MERCURY			
❑ MGC-505 [10]	Afro-Cuban Jazz	1951	$300
❑ MG-25009 [10]	Jungle Drums	1950	$300
❑ MGC-511 [10]	Machito Jazz with Flip and Bird	1952	$300
❑ MG-25020 [10]	Rhumbas	1950	$300
RCA VICTOR			
❑ LPM-3944 [M]	Machito Goes Memphis	1968	$40
❑ LSP-3944 [S]	Machito Goes Memphis	1968	$25
ROULETTE			
❑ R-52006 [M]	Kenya	1958	$40
❑ SR-52006 [S]	Kenya	1958	$30
❑ R-52026 [M]	With Flute to Boot	1959	$40
❑ SR-52026 [S]	With Flute to Boot	1959	$60
TICO			
❑ LP-1074 [M]	A Night with Machito	1960	$50
❑ LPS-1074 [S]	A Night with Machito	1960	$60
❑ LP-1029 [M]	Asia Minor Cha Cha Cha	1956	$80
❑ LP-1002 [M]	Cha Cha Cha at the Palladium	1955	$80
❑ LP-138 [10]	El Niche	1956	$150
❑ LP-1045 [M]	Inspired by "The Sun Also Rises	1957	$80
❑ LP-1062 [M]	Irving Berlin in Latin America	1959	$60
❑ CLP-1314	Latin Soul Plus Jazz	1973	$25
❑ CLP-1328	Lo Mejor De Machito Y Sus AfroCubans Con Graciela	1974	$25
❑ LP-1053 [M]	Mi Amigo, Machito	1959	$60
❑ LP-1033 [M]	Si Si, No No	1957	$80
❑ LP-1084 [M]	The New Sound of Machito (El Sonido Nuevo de Machito)	1962	$40
❑ LPS-1084 [S]	The New Sound of Machito (El Sonido Nuevo de Machito)	1962	$50
❑ LP-1094 [M]	Tremendo Cumban!	1963	$40
❑ LPS-1094 [S]	Tremendo Cumban!	1963	$50
❑ LP-1090 [M]	Variedades	1963	$40
❑ LPS-1090 [S]	Variedades	1963	$50
TIMELESS			

Number	Title	Yr	NM
❑ LPSJP-183	Machito and His Salsa Big Band	1990	$30
VERVE			
❑ MGV-8073 [M]	Afro-Cuban Jazz	1957	$200
❑ V-8073 [M]	Afro-Cuban Jazz	1961	$60
❑ VSP-19 [M]	Soul Source	1966	$25
❑ VSPS-19 [R]	Soul Source	1966	$30

MACK, DAVID

Albums

Number	Title	Yr	NM
SEREMUS			
❑ SRE-1009 [M]	New Directions	1965	$25
❑ SRS-12009 [S]	New Directions	1965	$30

MACKAY, BRUCE

Albums

Number	Title	Yr	NM
ORO			
❑ 1	Bruce Mackay	196?	$25

MACKAY, DAVID, AND VICKI HAMILTON
MacKay is a pianist; Hamilton is a female singer.

Albums

Number	Title	Yr	NM
ABC IMPULSE!			
❑ AS-9184	David MacKay and Vicki Hamilton	1969	$200
DISCOVERY			
❑ 868	Hands	1982	$25

MACPHERSON, FRASER
Tenor saxophone player.

Albums

Number	Title	Yr	NM
CONCORD JAZZ			
❑ CJ-224	Indian Summer	1983	$25
❑ CJ-269	Jazz Prose	1985	$25
❑ CJ-92	Live at the Planetarium	1976	$25

MADIGAN, BETTY
Female singer.

Albums

Number	Title	Yr	NM
MGM			
❑ E-3448 [M]	Am I Blue?	1956	$40

MADISON, AL

Albums

Number	Title	Yr	NM
GOLDEN CREST			
❑ GC-3048 [M]	Meet Al Madison	196?	$30

MADISON, JIMMY
Drummer.

Albums

Number	Title	Yr	NM
ADELPHI			
❑ 5007	Bumps	1978	$30

MAGNOLIA JAZZ BAND
Core members: Robbie Schlosser, cornet and string bass; Bill Napier, clarinet; Paul Mehling, guitar and banjo.

Albums

Number	Title	Yr	NM
STOMP OFF			
❑ SOS-1016	Red Onion Blues	198?	$25
❑ SOS-1137	Shake That Thing	1987	$25

MAGNUSSON, BOB
Bass player.

Albums

Number	Title	Yr	NM
DISCOVERY			
❑ 804	Revelation	1979	$30
❑ 824	Road Work Ahead	1980	$30
❑ 912	Song for Janet Lee	1984	$25
TREND			
❑ 528	Two Generations of Music	1981	$35
—Direct-to-disc recording			

MAGNUSSON, JAKOB
Bass player.

Albums

Number	Title	Yr	NM
OPTIMISM			
❑ OP-2002	Time Zone	198?	$25

MAHAVISHNU ORCHESTRA
Highly influential fusion group: BILLY COBHAM; JERRY GOODMAN; JAN HAMMER; RICK LAIRD; JOHN McLAUGHLIN.

Albums

Number	Title	Yr	NM
COLUMBIA			
❑ KC32957	Apocalypse	1974	$35
❑ PC32957	Apocalypse	197?	$20
—Reissue with new prefix			
❑ KC32766	Between Nothingness and Eternity	1973	$35
❑ PC32766	Between Nothingness and Eternity	197?	$20
—Reissue with new prefix; with or without bar code on cover			
❑ KC31996	Birds of Fire	1973	$25
❑ CQ31996 [Q]	Birds of Fire	1973	$60
❑ PC31996	Birds of Fire	197?	$20
—Reissue with new prefix; with or without bar code			
❑ PC33908	Inner Worlds	1976	$25
—Original with no bar code			
❑ PC33908	Inner Worlds	198?	$20
—Reissue with bar code			
❑ JC36394	The Best of Mahavishnu Orchestra	1980	$25
❑ PC31067	The Inner Mounting Flame	197?	$20
—Reissue with new prefix; with or without bar code			
❑ PC33411	Visions of the Emerald Beyond	1975	$25
—Original with no bar code			
❑ PC33411	Visions of the Emerald Beyond	198?	$20
—Reissue with bar code			

MAHONES, GILDO
Pianist. Also see LES JAZZ MODES.

Albums

Number	Title	Yr	NM
NEW JAZZ			
❑ NJLP-8299 [M]	Shooting High	1963	$0
—Canceled			
PRESTIGE			
❑ PRLP-16004 [M]	Shooting High	1964	$40
❑ PRLP-7339 [M]	The Soulful Piano of Gildo Mahones	1964	$30
❑ PRST-7339 [S]	The Soulful Piano of Gildo Mahones	1964	$40

MAINIERI, MIKE, AND WARREN BERNHARDT
Also see each artist's individual listings.

Albums

Number	Title	Yr	NM
ARISTA/NOVUS			
❑ AN3009	Free	1978	$30

MAINIERI, MIKE
Vibraphone player, producer and composer. Also see STEPS AHEAD.

Albums

Number	Title	Yr	NM
ARGO			
❑ LP-706 [M]	Blues on the Other Side	1963	$30
❑ LPS-706 [S]	Blues on the Other Side	1963	$30
ARISTA			
❑ AL4133	Love	1976	$25
SOLID STATE			
❑ SS-18029	Insight	1968	$20
❑ SS-18049	Journey Thru an Electric Tube	1969	$20
WARNER BROS.			
❑ BSK3586	Wanderlust	1982	$25

MAKOWICZ, ADAM, AND GEORGE MRAZ
Mraz is a bass player. Also see ADAM MAKOWICZ.

Albums

Number	Title	Yr	NM
STASH			
❑ ST-216	Classic Jazz Duets	198?	$25

MAKOWICZ, ADAM
Pianist.

Albums

Number	Title	Yr	NM
CHOICE			
❑ 1028	From My Window	198?	$30
COLUMBIA			

Number	Title	Yr	NM
❏ JC35320	Adam	1978	$25

NOVUS

Number	Title	Yr	NM
❏ 3003-1-N	Moonray	1986	$25
❏ 3022-1-N	Naughty Baby	1988	$25

SHEFFIELD LABS

Number	Title	Yr	NM
❏ 21	The Name Is Makowicz (ma-ko-vitch)	1984	$50

—Audiophile vinyl

MALHEIROS, ALEX
Bass player, occasional guitarist and male singer. Also see AZYMUTH.

Albums

MILESTONE

Number	Title	Yr	NM
❏ M-9131	Atlantic Forest	1985	$25

MALINVERNI, PETE
Pianist, bandleader and composer.

Albums

SEA BREEZE

Number	Title	Yr	NM
❏ SB-2037	Don't Be Shy	198?	$25

MALLET BUSTERS
Arnold Faber and Allan Molnar.

Albums

JAZZIMAGE

Number	Title	Yr	NM
❏ JZ-103	Mallet Busters	198?	$25

MANCE, JUNIOR
Pianist. Also see WILBUR WARE.

Albums

ATLANTIC

Number	Title	Yr	NM
❏ SD1521	At the Top	1969	$35
❏ 1479 [M]	Harlem Lullaby	1967	$25
❏ SD1479 [S]	Harlem Lullaby	1967	$35
❏ 1496 [M]	I Believe to My Soul	1968	$30
❏ SD1496 [S]	I Believe to My Soul	1968	$35
❏ SD1562	With a Lotta Help from My Friends	1970	$35

BEE HIVE

Number	Title	Yr	NM
❏ BH-7015	Truckin' and Trakin'	198?	$30

CAPITOL

Number	Title	Yr	NM
❏ T2092 [M]	Get Ready, Set, Jump!	1964	$50
❏ ST2092 [S]	Get Ready, Set, Jump!	1964	$60

Number	Title	Yr	NM
❏ T2218 [M]	Straight Ahead	1965	$50
❏ ST2218 [S]	Straight Ahead	1965	$50
❏ T2393 [M]	That's Where It Is	1965	$50
❏ ST2393 [S]	That's Where It Is	1965	$50

FANTASY

Number	Title	Yr	NM
❏ OJC-204	Junior Mance Trio at the Village Vanguard	198?	$25

INNER CITY

Number	Title	Yr	NM
❏ IC-6018	Holy Mama	197?	$35

JAZZLAND

Number	Title	Yr	NM
❏ JLP-53 [M]	Big Chief!	1961	$30
❏ JLP-953 [S]	Big Chief!	1961	$30
❏ JLP-77 [M]	Happy Time	1962	$30
❏ JLP-977 [S]	Happy Time	1962	$30
❏ JLP-41 [M]	Junior Mance Trio at the Village Vanguard	1961	$40
❏ JLP-941 [S]	Junior Mance Trio at the Village Vanguard	1961	$40
❏ JLP-63 [M]	The Jazz Soul of Hollywood	1961	$30

Number	Title	Yr	NM
❏ JLP-963 [S]	The Jazz Soul of Hollywood	1961	$30
❏ JLP-30 [M]	The Soulful Piano of Junior Mance	1960	$30
❏ JLP-930 [S]	The Soulful Piano of Junior Mance	1960	$30

MILESTONE

Number	Title	Yr	NM
❏ M-9041	That Lovin' Feelin'	197?	$35

POLYDOR

Number	Title	Yr	NM
❏ PD-5051	Touch	1974	$35

RIVERSIDE

Number	Title	Yr	NM
❏ RLP-447 [M]	Junior's Blues	1963	$150
❏ RS-9447 [S]	Junior's Blues	1963	$150
❏ 6059	Soulful Piano	197?	$30

SACKVILLE

Number	Title	Yr	NM
❏ 3031	For Dancers Only	198?	$25

VERVE

Number	Title	Yr	NM
❏ MGV-8319 [M]	Junior	1959	$100
❏ MGVS-6057 [S]	Junior	1960	$100
❏ V-8319 [M]	Junior	1961	$25
❏ V6-8319 [S]	Junior	1961	$35

MANCINI, HENRY
Pianist, bandleader and composer. Most of his music is in the pop or easy-listening vein, but the below albums - including several soundtracks - are definitely jazz. For a more complete listing, see the Standard Catalog of American Records.

Albums

LIBERTY

Number	Title	Yr	NM
❏ LT-51135	Trail of the Pink Panther	1982	$25

RCA VICTOR

Number	Title	Yr	NM
❏ LPM-2258 [M]	Combo!	1960	$50
❏ LSP-2258 [S]	Combo!	1960	$60
❏ LPM-3694 [M]	Mancini '67	1967	$35
❏ LSP-3694 [S]	Mancini '67	1967	$35
❏ LPM-2040 [M]	More Music from Peter Gunn	1959	$50
❏ LSP-2040 [S]	More Music from Peter Gunn	1959	$60
❏ LPM-2360 [M]	Mr. Lucky Goes Latin	1961	$50
❏ LSP-2360 [S]	Mr. Lucky Goes Latin	1961	$60
❏ LPM-2198 [M]	Music from Mr. Lucky	1960	$50
❏ LSP-2198 [S]	Music from Mr. Lucky	1960	$60
❏ ABL1-0968	Return of the Pink Panther	1975	$30
❏ ABD1-0968 [Q]	Return of the Pink Panther	1975	$60
❏ LPM-1956 [M]	The Music from Peter Gunn	1959	$40

—Original cover is a "block" design with "Peter Gunn" at top

Number	Title	Yr	NM
❏ LPM-1956 [M]	The Music from Peter Gunn	1959	$50

—First reissue cover is green/blue on front with huge "Peter Gunn" in center; back cover has a figure with a gun and a small photo of Henry Mancini at the lower left positioned so that it appears the gun is aimed at his head; catalog number on back cover is followed by "RE"

Number	Title	Yr	NM
❏ LSP-1956 [S]	The Music from Peter Gunn	1959	$100

—Original cover is a "block" design with "Peter Gunn" at top

Number	Title	Yr	NM
❏ LSP-1956 [S]	The Music from Peter Gunn	1959	$60

—First reissue cover is green/blue on front with huge "Peter Gunn" in center; back cover has a figure with a gun and a small photo of Henry Mancini at the lower left positioned so that it appears the gun is aimed at his head; catalog number on back cover is followed by "RE"

Number	Title	Yr	NM
❏ LPM-1956 [M]	The Music from Peter Gunn	1959	$30

—Second reissue cover is green/blue on front with huge "Peter Gunn" in center; back cover has a figure with a gun and a large photo of Henry Mancini at the upper left; catalog number on back is followed by "RE 2"

Number	Title	Yr	NM
❏ LSP-1956 [S]	The Music from Peter Gunn	1959	$35

—Second reissue cover is green/blue on front with huge "Peter Gunn" in center; back cover has a figure with a gun and a large photo of Henry Mancini at the upper left; catalog number on back is followed by "RE 2"

Number	Title	Yr	NM
❏ LPM-2795 [M]	The Pink Panther	1964	$35
❏ LSP-2795 [S]	The Pink Panther	1964	$50

UNITED ARTISTS

Number	Title	Yr	NM
❏ UA-LA694-G	The Pink Panther Strikes Again	1976	$20

MANCUSO, GUS
Baritone horn player and trombonist.

Albums

FANTASY

Number	Title	Yr	NM
❏ 3223 [M]	Introducing Gus Mancuso	1956	$60

—Red vinyl

Number	Title	Yr	NM
❏ 3223 [M]	Introducing Gus Mancuso	1956	$40

—Black vinyl

Number	Title	Yr	NM
❏ 3282 [M]	Music from New Faces	1958	$40

—Red vinyl

Number	Title	Yr	NM
❏ 3282 [M]	Music from New Faces	1958	$30

—Black vinyl

Number	Title	Yr	NM
❏ 8025 [S]	Music from New Faces	1960	$30

—Blue vinyl

Number	Title	Yr	NM
❏ 8025 [S]	Music from New Faces	1960	$35

—Black vinyl

MANDEL, MIKE
Keyboard player.

Albums

VANGUARD

Number	Title	Yr	NM
❏ VSD-79409	Sky Music	1978	$30
❏ VSD-79437	Utopia Parkway	1979	$30

MANETTA, FESS
Pianist.

Albums

JAZZOLOGY

Number	Title	Yr	NM
❏ JCE-6	Whorehouse Piano	198?	$25

MANGELSDORF, ALBERT
Trombonist and composer.

Albums

ENJA

Number	Title	Yr	NM
❏ 2006	Live in Tokyo	1974	$35

PACIFIC JAZZ

Number	Title	Yr	NM
❏ PJ-10095 [M]	Now, Jazz Ramwong	1966	$30
❏ ST-20095 [S]	Now, Jazz Ramwong	1966	$35

PAUSA

Number	Title	Yr	NM
❏ 7091	Hamburger Idylle	198?	$25
❏ 7055	Triologue	197?	$25

MANGIONE, CHUCK
Fluegel horn and trumpet player; had pop success in the late 1970s with the single "Feels So Good" and several followups. Also see THE JAZZ BROTHERS.

Albums

A&M

Number	Title	Yr	NM
❏ SP-4911	70 Miles Young	1982	$25
❏ SP-3237	70 Miles Young	198?	$10

—Budget-line reissue

Number	Title	Yr	NM
❏ SP-6701	An Evening of Magic -- Chuck Mangione Live at the Hollywood Bowl	1979	$30
❏ SP-4557	Bellavia	1975	$25
❏ QU-54557 [Q]	Bellavia	1975	$60
❏ SP-3172	Bellavia	198?	$10

—Budget-line reissue

Number	Title	Yr	NM
❏ SP-4518	Chase the Clouds Away	1975	$25
❏ QU-54518 [Q]	Chase the Clouds Away	1975	$60
❏ SP-3115	Chase the Clouds Away	198?	$10

—Budget-line reissue

Number	Title	Yr	NM
❏ SP-6700	Children of Sanchez	1978	$30
❏ SP-4658	Feels So Good	1977	$25
❏ SP-3219	Feels So Good	198?	$10

—Budget-line reissue

Number	Title	Yr	NM
❏ SP-3715	Fun and Games	1980	$25
❏ SP-3193	Fun and Games	1983	$10

—Budget-line reissue

Number	Title	Yr	NM
❏ SP-4612	Main Squeeze	1976	$25
❏ SP-3220	Main Squeeze	198?	$10

—Budget-line reissue

Number	Title	Yr	NM
❏ SP-6513	Tarantella	1981	$30
❏ SP-3282	The Best of Chuck Mangione	1985	$25

COLUMBIA

Number	Title	Yr	NM
❏ FC39479	Disguise	1984	$25
❏ FC40984	Eyes of the Veiled Temptress	1988	$25
❏ FC38686	Journey to a Rainbow	1983	$25
❏ PC38686	Journey to a Rainbow	1986	$10

—Budget-line reissue

Number	Title	Yr	NM
❏ FC38101	Love Notes	1982	$25
❏ PC38101	Love Notes	198?	$10

—Budget-line reissue

Number	Title	Yr	NM
❏ FC40254	Save Tonight for Me	1986	$25

FANTASY

Number	Title	Yr	NM
❏ OJC-495	Recuerdo	1991	$30

—Reissue of Jazzland 984

JAZZLAND

Number	Title	Yr	NM
❏ JLP-84 [M]	Recuerdo	1962	$40
❏ JLP-984 [S]	Recuerdo	1962	$100

MERCURY

Shelly Manne, *More Swinging Sounds Vol. 5*, Contemporary C 3519, **$300**.

Shelly Manne, *Swinging Sounds in Stereo*, Stereo Records S 7007, **$80**.

Manteca, *No Heroes*, Soundwings/Duke Street SW 2111, **$30**.

Harpo Marx, *Harp by Harpo*, RCA Victor LPM-27, 10-inch LP, **$250**.

Number	Title	Yr	NM
❏ SRM-1-650	Alive!	1973	$30
❏ 824301-1	Alive!	198?	$20
—Reissue of 650			
❏ SRM-1-1050	Encore/The Chuck Mangione Concerts	1975	$25
❏ SRM-2-800	Friends & Love -- A Chuck Mangione Concert	1971	$35
❏ SRM-1-681	Friends & Love/Highlights	1973	$30
❏ SRM-1-684	Land of Make Believe	1973	$30
❏ SRM-2-8601	The Best of Chuck Mangione	1978	$30
❏ SRM-1-631	The Chuck Mangione Quartet	1972	$30
❏ SRM-2-7501	Together: A New Chuck Mangione Concert	1971	$35
MILESTONE			
❏ 47042	Jazz Brother	1977	$30
—Reissue of material issued by "The Jazz Brothers"			

MANGIONE, GAP
Pianist, organist and keyboard player. Also see THE JAZZ BROTHERS.

Albums
Number	Title	Yr	NM
A&M			
❏ SP-4762	Dancin' Is Makin' Love	1979	$25
❏ SP-4621	Gap Mangione!	197?	$25
❏ SP-3407	She and I	1974	$25
❏ SP-4694	Suite Lady	1978	$25
FEELS SO GOOD			
❏ FSG9002	The Boys from Rochester	1987	$30
GRC			
❏ 9001	Diana in the Autumn Wind	1968	$30
MERCURY			
❏ SRM-1-647	Sing Along Junk	1972	$30

MANHATTAN JAZZ ALL-STARS, THE
Members: MOSE ALLISON; AARON BELL; BOB BROOKMEYER; TEDDY CHARLES; Addison Farmer (bass); TEO MACERO; DAVE McKENNA; JIMMY RANEY; Ed Shaughnessy (drums); ZOOT SIMS; SIR CHARLES THOMPSON; NICK TRAVIS; JULIUS WATKINS; PHIL WOODS.

Albums
Number	Title	Yr	NM
COLUMBIA			
❏ CL1426 [M]	Swinging Guys and Dolls	1960	$30
❏ CS8223 [S]	Swinging Guys and Dolls	1960	$30

MANHATTAN JAZZ SEPTETTE, THE
Members: EDDIE COSTA, BARRY GALBRAITH, URBIE GREEN, OSIE JOHNSON, HERBIE MANN, HAL McKUSICK, OSCAR PETTIFORD.

Albums
Number	Title	Yr	NM
CORAL			
❏ CRL57090 [M]	The Manhattan Jazz Septette	1956	$80

MANHATTAN RHYTHM KINGS
Vocal and instrumental trio: Tripp Hanson; Brian Nalepka; Hal Shane.

Albums
Number	Title	Yr	NM
INNER CITY			
❏ IC-1124	Manhattan Rhythm Kings	198?	$30

MANHATTAN TRANSFER
Vocal quartet: Laurel Masse (soprano, replaced by Cheryl Bentine in 1979); Janis Siegel (alto); Alan Paul (tenor); Tim Hauser (bass).

Albums
Number	Title	Yr	NM
ATLANTIC			
❏ 80104	Bodies and Souls	1983	$25
❏ 81233	Bop Doo-Wopp	1984	$30
❏ 81803	Brasil	1987	$25
❏ SD18183	Coming Out	1976	$25
❏ SD19258	Extensions	1979	$25
❏ 81723	Live	1987	$25
❏ SD16036	Mecca for Moderns	1981	$25
❏ SD19163	Pastiche	1978	$25
❏ SD19319	The Best of the Manhattan Transfer	1981	$25
❏ SD18133	The Manhattan Transfer	1975	$25
❏ 81266	Vocalese	1985	$25
CAPITOL			
❏ ST-778	Jukin'	1971	$35
—With Gene Pistilli			
❏ ST-11405	Jukin'	1975	$25

Number	Title	Yr	NM
—With Gene Pistilli; reissue of 778			
❏ SN-16223	Jukin'	198?	$20
—With Gene Pistilli; budget-line reissue			
COLUMBIA			
❏ C47079	The Offbeat of Avenues	1991	$35
MOBILE FIDELITY			
❏ 1-199	Extensions	1994	$100
—Audiophile vinyl			

MANN, DAVID
Tenor saxophone player.

Albums
Number	Title	Yr	NM
ANTILLES			
❏ 90628	Games	1988	$25
❏ 91050	Insight	1989	$30

MANN, ED
Percussionist.

Albums
Number	Title	Yr	NM
CMP			
❏ CMP-38-ST	Get Up	1988	$25

MANN, HERBIE, AND BUDDY COLLETTE
Also see each artist's individual listings.

Albums
Number	Title	Yr	NM
INTERLUDE			
❏ MO-503 [M]	Flute Fraternity	1959	$40
—Reissue of Mode 114			
❏ ST-1103 [S]	Flute Fraternity	1959	$60
MODE			
❏ LP-114 [M]	Flute Fraternity	1957	$140

MANN, HERBIE, AND JOAO GILBERTO
Also see each artist's individual listings.

Albums
Number	Title	Yr	NM
ATLANTIC			
❏ SD8105 [S]	Herbie Mann and Joao Gilberto with Antonio Carlos Jobim	1965	$50

MANN, HERBIE, AND MACHITO
Also see each artist's individual listings.

Albums
Number	Title	Yr	NM
ROULETTE			
❏ R-52122 [M]	Afro-Jazziac	1963	$35
❏ SR-52122 [S]	Afro-Jazziac	1963	$50

MANN, HERBIE
Best known as a flutist, he also plays tenor saxophone. Also see LaVERN BAKER; THE MANHATTAN JAZZ SEPTETTE; NEW YORK JAZZ QUARTET; SAHIB SHIHAB.

Albums
Number	Title	Yr	NM
A&M			
❏ LP-2003 [M]	Glory of Love	1967	$60
❏ SP-3003 [S]	Glory of Love	1967	$35
❏ SP9-3003	Glory of Love	1983	$50
—Audio Master Plus" reissue			
ATLANTIC			
❏ 80077	Astral Island	1983	$25
❏ SD18209	Bird in a Silver Cage	1977	$25
❏ SD19169	Brazil -- Once Again	1978	$25
❏ SD1540	Concerto Grosso in D Blues	1969	$30
❏ SD1670	Discotheque	1975	$25
❏ 1397 [M]	Do the Bossa Nova with Herbie Mann	1962	$150
❏ SD1397 [S]	Do the Bossa Nova with Herbie Mann	1962	$150
❏ SD1658	First Light	1974	$30
❏ SD19112	Herbie Mann & Fire Island	1977	$25
❏ 1380 [M]	Herbie Mann at the Village Gate	1962	$150
❏ SD1380 [S]	Herbie Mann at the Village Gate	1962	$150
❏ 1413 [M]	Herbie Mann Live at Newport	1963	$50
❏ SD1413 [S]	Herbie Mann Live at Newport	1963	$50
❏ 1407 [M]	Herbie Mann Returns to the Village Gate	1963	$50
❏ SD1407 [S]	Herbie Mann Returns to the Village Gate	1963	$50
❏ 1454 [M]	Herbie Mann Today	1966	$35

Number	Title	Yr	NM
❏ SD1454 [S]	Herbie Mann Today	1966	$50
❏ SD1632	Hold On, I'm Comin'	1973	$30
❏ QD1632 [Q]	Hold On, I'm Comin'	1973	$60
❏ 1475 [M]	Impressions of the Middle East	1967	$50
❏ SD1475 [S]	Impressions of the Middle East	1967	$35
❏ 1422 [M]	Latin Fever	1964	$35
❏ SD1422 [S]	Latin Fever	1964	$50
❏ SD1536	Live at the Whisky A-Go-Go	1969	$30
❏ SD1648	London Underground	1974	$30
❏ 8141 [M]	Mann and a Woman	1967	$50
❏ SD8141 [S]	Mann and a Woman	1967	$35
❏ SD16046	Mellow	1981	$25
❏ SD1522	Memphis Underground	1969	$30
❏ SD1610	Mississippi Gambler	1972	$30
❏ 1462 [M]	Monday Night at the Village Gate	1966	$35
❏ SD1462 [S]	Monday Night at the Village Gate	1966	$50
❏ 1433 [M]	My Kinda Groove	1965	$35
❏ SD1433 [S]	My Kinda Groove	1965	$50
❏ 1471 [M]	New Mann at Newport	1967	$50
❏ SD1471 [S]	New Mann at Newport	1967	$35
❏ 1426 [M]	Nirvana	1964	$35
❏ 90141	Nirvana	1984	$25
❏ 1464 [M]	Our Mann Flute	1966	$35
❏ SD1464 [S]	Our Mann Flute	1966	$50
❏ SD1655	Reggae	1974	$30
❏ 1384 [M]	Right Now	1962	$150
❏ SD1384 [S]	Right Now	1962	$150
❏ 81285	See Through Spirits	1986	$25
❏ 1445 [M]	Standing Ovation at Newport	1965	$35
❏ SD1445 [S]	Standing Ovation at Newport	1965	$50
❏ SD19221	Super Mann	1979	$25
❏ SD1682	Surprises	1976	$30
❏ 1483 [M]	The Beat Goes On	1967	$50
❏ SD1483 [S]	The Beat Goes On	1967	$35
❏ SD1544	The Best of Herbie Mann	1970	$30
❏ 1343 [M]	The Common Ground	1960	$250
❏ SD1343 [S]	The Common Ground	1960	$250
❏ SD 2-300 [S]	The Evolution of Mann	1972	$35
❏ 2-300 [M]	The Evolution of Mann	1972	$40
—Mono is white label promo only with "d/j copy monaural" sticker on front cover			
❏ 1371 [M]	The Family of Mann	1961	$150
❏ SD1371 [S]	The Family of Mann	1961	$150
❏ 1490 [M]	The Herbie Mann String Album	1968	$60
❏ SD1490 [S]	The Herbie Mann String Album	1968	$35
❏ 1513 [M]	The Inspiration I Feel	1969	$60
—Mono is promo only			
❏ SD1513 [S]	The Inspiration I Feel	1969	$35
❏ 1437 [M]	The Roar of the Greasepaint, The Smell of the Crowd	1965	$35
❏ SD1437 [S]	The Roar of the Greasepaint, The Smell of the Crowd	1965	$50
❏ SD1642	Turtle Bay	1973	$30
❏ SD1497	Wailing Dervishes	1968	$35
❏ SD1676	Waterbed	1975	$30
❏ SD1507	Windows Open	1969	$30
❏ SD19252	Yellow Fever	1980	$25
BETHLEHEM			
❏ BCP-6011	Early Mann	1976	$25
—Reissue of older material; distributed by Caytronics			
❏ BCP-1018 [10]	East Coast Jazz 4	1954	$250
❏ BCP-24 [M]	Flamingo, My Goodness -- Four Flutes, Vol. 2	1955	$250
❏ BCP-58 [M]	Herbie Mann Plays	1956	$250
❏ BCP-6067 [M]	The Epitome of Jazz	1963	$200
❏ BCP-40 [M]	The Herbie Mann-Sam Most Quintet	1956	$250
❏ BCP-6020 [M]	The Mann with the Most	1960	$250
COLUMBIA			
❏ CS1068	Big Boss	1970	$30
❏ CL2388 [M]	Latin Mann	1965	$35
❏ CS9188 [S]	Latin Mann	1965	$50
COLUMBIA SPECIAL PRODUCTS			
❏ JCS9188	Latin Mann	197?	$30
—Part of "Jazz Greats" Collectors' Series			
EMBRYO			
❏ 531	Memphis Two-Step	1971	$30
❏ 526	Muscle Shoals Nitty Gritty	1970	$30
❏ 532	Push Push	1971	$30
❏ 520	Stone Flute	1970	$30
EPIC			
❏ LN3499 [M]	Herbie Mann with the Ilcken Trio	1958	$250
❏ LN3395 [M]	Salute to the Flute	1957	$250
FINNADAR			
❏ 9014	Gagaku and Beyond	197?	$25
HERBIE MANN MUSIC			
❏ HMM-1	Herbie Mann Music	1981	$60
—Direct-to-disc recording			
JAZZLAND			

Number	Title	Yr	NM
❑ JLP-5 [M]	Herbie Mann Quintet	1960	$60
— Reissue of Riverside 245			
MILESTONE			
❑ 47010	Let Me Tell You	1973	$30
NEW JAZZ			
❑ NJLP-8211 [M]	Just Walkin'	1958	$200
— Purple label			
❑ NJLP-8211 [M]	Just Walkin'	1964	$150
— Blue label with trident logo			
PRESTIGE			
❑ PRST-7659	Herbie Mann in Sweden	1969	$30
❑ PRLP-7136 [M]	Mann in the Morning	1958	$300
❑ PRLP-7432 [M]	The Best of Herbie Mann	1965	$35
❑ PRST-7432 [R]	The Best of Herbie Mann	1965	$30
RIVERSIDE			
❑ RLP 12-245 [M]	Great Ideas of Western Mann	1957	$250
❑ 6084	Great Ideas of Western Mann	197?	$25
❑ S-3029	Moody Mann	1969	$100
❑ RLP 12-234 [M]	Sultry Serenade	1957	$300
— Blue on white label			
❑ RLP 12-234 [M]	Sultry Serenade	1958	$300
— Blue label with reel and microphone logo			
SAVOY			
❑ MG-12102 [M]	Flute Suite	1957	$100
❑ MG-12107 [M]	Mann Alone	1957	$100
❑ MG-12108 [M]	Yardbird Suite	1957	$100
SAVOY JAZZ			
❑ SJL-1102	Be Bop Synthesis	197?	$25
SOLID STATE			
❑ SS-18020	Jazz Impressions of Brazil	1968	$30
❑ SS-18023	St. Thomas	1968	$30
SURREY			
❑ S-1015 [M]	Big Band	1965	$35
❑ SS-1015 [S]	Big Band	1965	$50
TRIP			
❑ 5031	Super Mann	1974	$25
UNITED ARTISTS			
❑ UAL-4042 [M]	African Suite	1959	$60
❑ UAS-5042 [S]	African Suite	1959	$40
❑ UAJ-14009 [M]	Brasil, Bossa Nova and Blue	1962	$60
❑ UAJS-15009 [S]	Brasil, Bossa Nova and Blue	1962	$40
❑ UAS-5638	Brazil Blues	1972	$30
❑ UAJ-14022 [M]	St. Thomas	1962	$60
❑ UAJS-15022 [S]	St. Thomas	1962	$40
VERVE			
❑ VSP-19 [M]	Big Band Mann	1966	$35
❑ VSPS-19 [R]	Big Band Mann	1966	$30
❑ VSP-8 [M]	Bongo, Conga and Flute	1966	$35
❑ VSPS-8 [R]	Bongo, Conga and Flute	1966	$30
❑ V6-8821	Et Tu Flute	1973	$35
❑ MGV-8336 [M]	Flautista! -- Herbie Mann Plays Afro-Cuban Jazz	1959	$100
❑ MGVS-6074 [S]	Flautista! -- Herbie Mann Plays Afro-Cuban Jazz	1960	$120
❑ V-8336 [M]	Flautista! -- Herbie Mann Plays Afro-Cuban Jazz	1961	$50
❑ V6-8336 [S]	Flautista! -- Herbie Mann Plays Afro-Cuban Jazz	1961	$35
❑ MGV-8392 [M]	Flute, Brass, Vibes and Percussion	1960	$120
❑ V-8392 [M]	Flute, Brass, Vibes and Percussion	1961	$50
❑ MGV-8247 [M]	The Magic Flute of Herbie Mann	1958	$120
❑ V-8247 [M]	The Magic Flute of Herbie Mann	1961	$50
❑ V-8527 [M]	The Sound of Mann	1963	$50
❑ V6-8527 [S]	The Sound of Mann	1963	$35

MANNE, SHELLY

Drummer and male singer. Also see BOOTS BROWN; ART PEPPER; THE POLL WINNERS; ANDRE PREVIN; RUTH PRICE.

Albums

Number	Title	Yr	NM
ABC IMPULSE!			
❑ AS-20 [S]	2 3 4	1968	$200
— Black label with red ring			
ATLANTIC			
❑ 1469 [M]	Boss Sounds!	1967	$35
❑ SD1469 [S]	Boss Sounds!	1967	$30
❑ 8157 [M]	Daktari	1968	$30
❑ SD8157 [S]	Daktari	1968	$30
❑ 1487 [M]	Jazz Gunn	1967	$25
❑ SD1487 [S]	Jazz Gunn	1967	$30
CAPITOL			
❑ T2313 [M]	Manne, That's Gershwin	1965	$75
❑ ST2313 [S]	Manne, That's Gershwin	1965	$40
❑ T2173 [M]	My Fair Lady" with Un-Original Cast	1964	$50

Number	Title	Yr	NM
❑ ST2173 [S]	My Fair Lady" with Un-Original Cast	1964	$40
❑ SM-2173	My Fair Lady" with Un-Original Cast	1976	$25
— Reissue with new prefix			
❑ T2610 [M]	Shelly Manne Sounds	1966	$60
❑ ST2610 [S]	Shelly Manne Sounds	1966	$50
CONCORD JAZZ			
❑ CJ-21	Perk Up	1976	$30
CONTEMPORARY			
❑ C-3559 [M]	Bells Are Ringing	1958	$250
❑ S-7559 [S]	Bells Are Ringing	1959	$250
❑ M-3599 [M]	Checkmate	1961	$200
❑ S-7599 [S]	Checkmate	1961	$200
❑ C-3536 [M]	Concerto for Clarinet and Combo	1957	$250
❑ C-3533 [M]	Li'l Abner	1957	$250
❑ S-7533 [S]	Li'l Abner	1959	$250
❑ M-3593/4 [M]	Live! Shelly Manne and His Men at the Manne-Hole	1961	$200
❑ S-7593/4 [S]	Live! Shelly Manne and His Men at the Manne-Hole	1961	$200
❑ C-3527 [M]	Modern Jazz Performance of Songs from "My Fair Lady	1957	$300
❑ S-7527 [S]	Modern Jazz Performance of Songs from "My Fair Lady	1959	$350
❑ C-3519 [M]	More Swinging Sounds, Vol. 5	1957	$300
❑ M-3609 [M]	My Son, the Jazz Drummer!	1962	$200
❑ S-7609 [S]	My Son, the Jazz Drummer!	1962	$200
❑ M-3624 [M]	Outside	1966	$150
❑ S-7624 [S]	Outside	1966	$150
❑ C-3525 [M]	Shelly Manne and His Friends	1957	$250
❑ C-2503 [10]	Shelly Manne and His Men	1953	$250
❑ C-2511 [10]	Shelly Manne and His Men, Volume 2	1954	$250
❑ M-3577 [M]	Shelly Manne and His Men at the Black Hawk, Vol. 1	1960	$200
❑ S-7577 [S]	Shelly Manne and His Men at the Black Hawk, Vol. 1	1960	$200
❑ M-3578 [M]	Shelly Manne and His Men at the Black Hawk, Vol. 2	1960	$200
❑ S-7578 [S]	Shelly Manne and His Men at the Black Hawk, Vol. 2	1960	$200
❑ M-3579 [M]	Shelly Manne and His Men at the Black Hawk, Vol. 3	1960	$200
❑ S-7579 [S]	Shelly Manne and His Men at the Black Hawk, Vol. 3	1960	$200
❑ M-3580 [M]	Shelly Manne and His Men at the Black Hawk, Vol. 4	1960	$200
❑ S-7580 [S]	Shelly Manne and His Men at the Black Hawk, Vol. 4	1960	$200
❑ C-14018	Shelly Manne in Zurich	1986	$25
❑ C-3560 [M]	Shelly Manne Plays "Peter Gunn	1958	$250
❑ S-7025 [S]	Shelly Manne Plays "Peter Gunn	1959	$250
❑ M-3566 [M]	Son of Gunn	1959	$250
❑ S-7566 [S]	Son of Gunn	1959	$250
❑ M-5006 [M]	Sounds Unheard Of	1962	$200
❑ S-9006 [S]	Sounds Unheard Of	1962	$200
❑ C-3516 [M]	Swinging Sounds, Vol. 4	1956	$200
❑ S-7519 [S]	Swinging Sounds in Stereo	1959	$250
❑ C-3557 [M]	The Gambit	1958	$250
❑ S-7557 [S]	The Gambit	1959	$250
❑ C-2516 [10]	The Three	1954	$250
❑ M-3584 [M]	The Three and The Two	1960	$200
❑ C-2518 [10]	The Two	1954	$250
❑ C-3507 [M]	The West Coast Sound	1955	$200
DEE GEE			
❑ 1003 [10]	Here's That Manne	1952	$300
DISCOVERY			
❑ 909	Manne, That's Gershwin!	1986	$25
— Reissue of Capitol ST 2313			
❑ 783	Rex	1976	$35
DOCTOR JAZZ			
❑ FW38728	Shelly Manne and His Friends	1983	$25
FANTASY			
❑ OJC-336	Modern Jazz Performance of Songs from "My Fair Lady	198?	$25
❑ OJC-320	More Swinging Sounds, Vol. 5	198?	$25
❑ OJC-240	Shelly Manne and His Men at the Black Hawk, Vol. 1	198?	$25
❑ OJC-267	Swinging Sounds, Vol. 4	1987	$25
❑ OJC-176	The Three and The Two	198?	$25
❑ OJC-152	The West Coast Sound	198?	$25
FLYING DUTCHMAN			
❑ FD-10150	Signature: Shelly Manne & Co.	1973	$35
— Reissue of 1940s recordings in mono			
GALAXY			
❑ 5101	Essence	1978	$30
❑ 5124	French Concert	1979	$30
IMPULSE!			

Number	Title	Yr	NM
❑ A-20 [M]	2 3 4	1962	$160
❑ AS-20 [S]	2 3 4	1962	$200
MAINSTREAM			
❑ MRL-375	Mannekind	1972	$35
MCA			
❑ 29073	2 3 4	1980	$20
STEREO RECORDS			
❑ S-7019 [S]	Li'l Abner	1958	$50
❑ S-7002 [S]	Modern Jazz Performance of Songs from "My Fair Lady	1958	$250
❑ S-7025 [S]	Shelly Manne Plays "Peter Gunn	1958	$50
❑ S-7007 [S]	Swinging Sounds in Stereo	1958	$80
❑ S-7030 [S]	The Gambit	1958	$50
TREND			
❑ 526	Double Piano Jazz Quartet	1980	$30
❑ 527	Double Piano Jazz Quartet, Volume 2	1980	$30
❑ 525	Interpretations of Bach and Mozart	1980	$30

MANNE, SHELLY/BILL RUSSO

Also see each artist's individual listings.

Albums

Number	Title	Yr	NM
SAVOY			
❑ MG-12045 [M]	Deep Purple	1955	$60

MANONE, WINGY

Trumpeter, bandleader, male singer and composer. Also see BUNNY BERIGAN.

Albums

Number	Title	Yr	NM
DECCA			
❑ DL8473 [M]	Trumpet on the Wing	1957	$120
IMPERIAL			
❑ LP-9190 [M]	Wingy Manone on the Jazzband Bus	1962	$175
❑ LP-12190 [S]	Wingy Manone on the Jazzband Bus	1962	$150
MCA			
❑ 1364	Jam and Jive	1983	$15
RCA VICTOR			
❑ LPV-563 [M]	Wingy Manone, Volume 1	1969	$50
STORYVILLE			
❑ 4066	Wingy Manone with Papa Bue's Viking Jazzband	198?	$25
X			
❑ LVA-3014 [10]	Wingy Manone, Vol. 1	1954	$100

MANTECA

Canadian fusion group led by Aaron Davis (keyboards) and Matt Zimbel (percussion).

Albums

Number	Title	Yr	NM
DUKE STREET			
❑ DSR31038	Fire Me Up	1987	$30
— Made in Canada			
❑ DSR31027	No Heroes	1986	$30
— Made in Canada			
❑ DSR31055	Perfect Foot	1989	$35
— Made in Canada			
READY			
❑ LR 017	Manteca	198?	$35
— Made in Canada			
❑ LR 050	Strength in Numbers	1985	$35
— Made in Canada			
SOUNDWINGS/DUKE STREET			
❑ SW2111	No Heroes	1986	$30

MANTILLA, RAY

Percussionist.

Albums

Number	Title	Yr	NM
INNER CITY			
❑ IC-1052	Mantilla	1978	$35
RED RECORD			
❑ VPA-174	Hands of Fire	198?	$30

MANTLER, MICHAEL

Trumpeter.

Albums

Number	Title	Yr	NM
ECM			
❑ 23786	Something There	1984	$25

Number	Title	Yr	NM

WATT
❏ 3	13 & 3/4	197?	$25
❏ 7	Movies	1978	$35
❏ 2	No Answer	197?	$25
❏ 5	Silence	197?	$25

MARABLE, LAWRENCE
Drummer.

MARCUS, LEW
Pianist.
Albums
SAVOY
❏ MG-15006 [10]	Back Room Piano	1951	$50

MARCUS, STEVE
Tenor saxophone player.
Albums
FLYING DUTCHMAN
❏ BDL1-1461	Sometime Other Than Now	1976	$30

VORTEX
❏ 2009	The Count's Rock Band	1969	$25
❏ 2013	The Lord's Prayer	1969	$25
❏ 2001	Tomorrow Never Knows	1968	$25

MARCUS, WADE
Arranger and composer.
Albums
ABC IMPULSE!
❏ AS-9318	Metamorphosis	197?	$30

MARDIN, ARIF
Composer, arranger and producer.
Albums
ATLANTIC
❏ SD1661	Journey	1974	$30

MARGITZA, RICK
Tenor saxophone player and composer.
Albums
BLUE NOTE
❏ B1-92279	Color	1989	$30

MARIA, TANIA
Pianist and female singer.
Albums
CAPITOL
❏ C1-90966	Forbidden Colors	1988	$25

CONCORD PICANTE
❏ CJP-200	Come with Me	1982	$25
❏ CJP-230	Love Explosion	1984	$25
❏ CJP-151	Piquant	1981	$25
❏ CJP-175	Taurus	1982	$25
❏ CJP-264	The Real Tania Maria: Wild!	1985	$25

MANHATTAN
❏ ST-53045	Lady from Barzil	1986	$25
❏ ST-53000	Made in New York	1985	$25

MARIACHI BRASS, THE
Studio group modeled after the Tijuana Brass and featuring CHET BAKER. This group also did the original version of the theme from "The Dating Game."
Albums
WORLD PACIFIC
❏ WP-1839 [M]	A Taste of Tequila	1966	$100
❏ WPS-21839 [S]	A Taste of Tequila	1966	$100
❏ WP-1852 [M]	Double Shot	1966	$100
❏ WPS-21852 [S]	Double Shot	1966	$100
❏ WP-1842 [M]	Hats Off!!!	1966	$100
❏ WPS-21842 [S]	Hats Off!!!	1966	$100
❏ WP-1859 [M]	In the Mood	1967	$100
❏ WPS-21859 [S]	In the Mood	1967	$100

MARIANO, CHARLIE, AND JERRY DODGION
Dodgion is a flute and alto saxophone player. Also see CHARLIE MARIANO.
Albums
WORLD PACIFIC
❏ WP-1245 [M]	Beauties of 1918	1958	$150

MARIANO, CHARLIE
Alto saxophone player. Also has played soprano sax and flute. Also see TOSHIKO AKIYOSHI; NAT PIERCE.
Albums
ATLANTIC
❏ SD1608	The Mirror	197?	$35

BETHLEHEM
❏ BCP-25 [M]	Alto Sax for Young Moderns	1956	$500
❏ BCP-1022 [10]	Charlie Mariano Sextet	1955	$350

CATALYST
❏ 7915	Reflections	197?	$35

CMP
❏ CMP-10-ST	Crystal Balls	198?	$25
❏ CMP-2-ST	October	198?	$25

ECM
❏ 1256	Charlie Mariano with the Kamataka College of Percussion	1985	$30

FANTASY
❏ OJC-1745	Charlie Mariano Boston All Stars	1990	$30
❏ 3-10 [10]	Charlie Mariano Sextet	1953	$180

IMPERIAL
❏ IMP-3006 [10]	Charlie Mariano Quintet Volume 1	1955	$400
❏ IMP-3007 [10]	Charlie Mariano Quintet Volume 2	1955	$200

INNER CITY
❏ IC-1024	October	1977	$35

INTUITION
❏ C1-90787	Mariano	1988	$25

PRESTIGE
❏ PRLP-130 [10]	Charlie Mariano	1952	$300
❏ PRLP-153 [10]	Charlie Mariano Boston All Stars	1953	$300

REGINA
❏ R-286 [M]	A Jazz Portrait of Charlie Mariano	1963	$30
❏ RS-286 [S]	A Jazz Portrait of Charlie Mariano	1963	$30

MARIANO, TOSHIKO
See TOSHIKO AKIYOSHI. (LP)
See TOSHIKO AKIYOSHI.

MARIENTHAL, ERIC
Saxophone player (alto, tenor and soprano).
Albums
GRP
❏ GR-9586	Round Trip	1989	$30
❏ GR-1052	Voices of the Heart	1988	$25

MARK-ALMOND
The constants in this British band were Jon Mark (guitar, bass, percussion, vocals) and Johnny Almond (saxophones, vibes, vocals, percussion, flute).
Albums
ABC
❏ D-945	To the Heart	1976	$25

BLUE THUMB
❏ BTS27	Mark-Almond	1971	$30
—Reissue of 8827			
❏ BTS-8827	Mark-Almond	1971	$35
❏ BTS32	Mark-Almond II	1971	$30
❏ BTS50	The Best of Mark-Almond	1973	$30

COLUMBIA
❏ KC32486	Mark-Almond 73	1973	$30
❏ KC31917	Rising	1972	$30
❏ PC31917	Rising	198?	$20
—Budget-line reissue			
❏ CG33648	Rising/Mark-Almond 73	1976	$35

HORIZON
❏ SP-730	Other People's Rooms	1978	$25

MCA
❏ 711	Mark-Almond II	198?	$20
—Reissue of Blue Thumb 32			
❏ 792	The Best of Mark-Almond	198?	$20
—Reissue of Blue Thumb 50			
❏ 793	To the Heart	198?	$20
—Reissue of ABC 945			

PACIFIC ARTS
❏ 7-142	The Best of the Mark-Almond Band…Live	1980	$25

MARKEWICH, REESE
Albums
MODERN AGE
❏ MA-134 [M]	New Designs in Jazz	1958	$50

MARKHAM, JOHN
Drummer.
Albums
FAMOUS DOOR
❏ 121	San Francisco Jazz	1977	$30

MARKOWITZ, MARKIE
Trumpeter.
Albums
FAMOUS DOOR
❏ 111	Marky's Vibes	197?	$35

MARLENE
See MARLENE VER PLANCK.

MARLOW, JANET
10-string guitarist, female singer and composer.
Albums
CMG
❏ CML-8003	Outside the City	198?	$25

MARMAROSA, DODO
Pianist.
Albums
ARGO
❏ LPS-4012 [S]	Dodo's Back	1961	$30

PHOENIX
❏ 20	Piano Man	197?	$30

SPOTLITE
❏ 108	Dodo Marmarosa Trio	197?	$25

MARMAROSA, DODO/ERROLL GARNER
Also see each artist's individual listings.
Albums
CONCERT HALL JAZZ
❏ 1001 [10]	Piano Contrasts	1955	$60

DIAL
❏ LP-208 [10]	Piano Contrasts	1950	$250

MAROCCO, FRANK
Accordion player.
Albums
DISCOVERY
❏ 797	Jazz Accordion	1979	$30
❏ 854	Road to Marocco	198?	$25
❏ 838	The Trio	198?	$25

TREND
❏ 516	New Colors	1980	$35
—Direct-to-disc recording			

MAROHNIC, CHUCK
Pianist.
Albums
STEEPLECHASE
❏ SCS-4002	Copenhagen Suite	198?	$30
❏ SCS-1155	Permutations	198?	$30

MARR, HANK
Pianist and organist.
Albums
KING
❏ KSD-1061	Greasy Spoon	1969	$25
❏ 1011 [M]	Hank Marr Plays 24 Originals	1966	$25
❏ 899 [M]	Live at Club 502	1964	$40
❏ 933 [M]	On and Off Stage	1965	$30
❏ 1025 [M]	Sounds from the Marr-Ket Place	1968	$25
❏ 829 [M]	Teentime Dance Steps	1963	$30

Mat Mathews, *The Modern Art of Jazz*, Dawn DLP 1104, **$300**.

Mary Ann McCall, *Melancholy Baby*, Coral CRL 757276, **$80**.

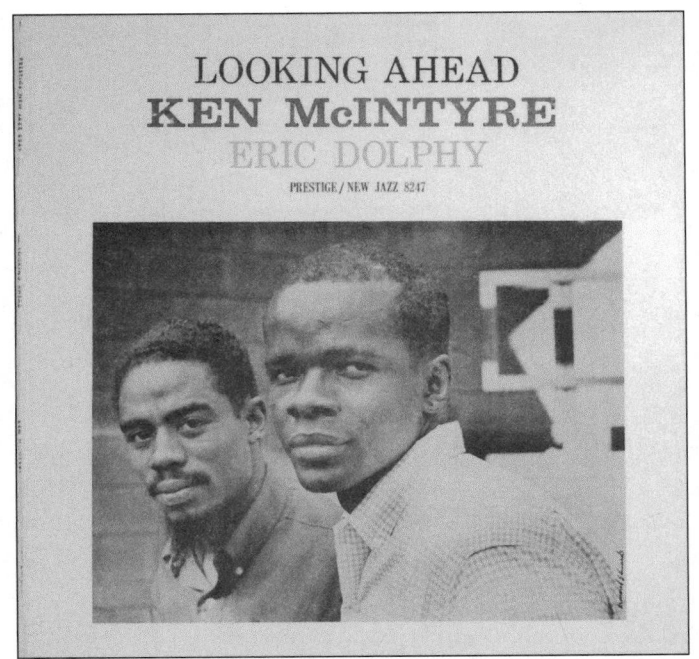

Ken McIntyre, *Looking Ahead*, New Jazz NJLP-8247, purple label, **$150**.

Hal McKusick, *Cross Section – Saxes*, Decca DL 9209, **$50**.

Number	Title	Yr	NM

MARROW, ESTHER
Female singer better known in the gospel realm.
Albums
FANTASY
❏ 9414 — Sister Woman — 1972 — $35

MARSALA, JOE
Clarinetist, saxophone player, bandleader and composer. Also see RAY McKINLEY.
Albums
JAZZOLOGY
❏ J-106 — Joe Marsala and His Jazz Band, 1944 — 198? — $25

MARSALA, JOE/BUD FREEMAN
Also see each artist's individual listings.
Albums
BRUNSWICK
❏ BL58037 [10] — Battle of Jazz, Vol. 1 — 1953 — $50

MARSALIS, BRANFORD
Tenor and soprano saxophone player and male singer. Also see BUCKSHOT LEFONQUE.
Albums
CBS MASTERWORKS
❏ M42122 — Romances for Saxophone — 1986 — $15
COLUMBIA
❏ OC44055 — Random Abstract — 1988 — $12
❏ FC40711 — Renaissance — 1987 — $12
❏ FC40363 — Royal Garden Blues — 1986 — $12
❏ FC38951 — Scenes in the City — 1984 — $12
❏ CX244199 — Trio Jeepy — 1989 — $20
❏ CAS1628 [DJ] — Trio Jeepy Interchords Special — 1989 — $20
JAZZ PLANET
❏ JP-5004 — The Dark Keys — 1996 — $30

MARSALIS, ELLIS
Pianist and male singer; father of Branford and Wynton.
Albums
SPINDLETOP
❏ ST-105 — Homecoming — 1986 — $12

MARSALIS, WYNTON
Trumpeter and composer.
Albums
CBS
❏ IM42137 — Carnaval — 1987 — $12
COLUMBIA
❏ FC40009 — Black Codes (From the Underground) — 1985 — $12
❏ FC45287 — Crescent City Christmas Card — 1989 — $12
❏ FC39530 — Hot House Flowers — 1984 — $12
❏ FC40308 — J Mood — 1986 — $12
❏ PC240675 — Live at Blues Alley — 1988 — $15
❏ FC40461 — Marsalis Standard Time — 1987 — $12
❏ C47346 — Standard Time Vol. 2 -- Intimacy Calling — 1991 — $20
❏ C46143 — Standard Time Vol. 3 -- The Resolution of Romance — 1990 — $15
❏ OC45091 — The Majesty of the Blues — 1989 — $15
❏ FC38641 — Think of One — 1983 — $12
❏ HC47574 — Wynton Marsalis — 198? — $60
— Half-speed mastered edition
❏ FC37574 — Wynton Marsalis — 1982 — $25
WHO'S WHO IN JAZZ
❏ 21024 — Wynton Marsalis with Art Blakey and His Jazz Messengers — 1981 — $35

MARSH, GEORGE, AND JOHN ABERCROMBIE
Also see each artist's individual listings.
Albums
1750 ARCH
❏ 1804 — Drum Strum — 198? — $30

MARSH, GEORGE
Drummer.
Albums
1750 ARCH
❏ 1791 — Marshland — 1982 — $30

MARSH, HUGH
Violinist.
Albums
SOUNDWINGS/DUKE STREET
❏ SW-210 — Shaking the Pumpkin — 1988 — $30

MARSH, MILTON
Composer, conductor and male vocalist.
Albums
STRATA-EAST
❏ SES-19758 — Monism — 1975 — $25

MARSH, WARNE, AND SAL MOSCA
Also see each artist's individual listings.
Albums
INTERPLAY
❏ 7725 — How Deep/How High — 1980 — $30

MARSH, WARNE; CLARE FISCHER; GARY FOSTER
Also see each artist's individual listings.
Albums
REVELATION
❏ 17 — First Symposium on Relaxed Improvisation — 197? — $35

MARSH, WARNE
Tenor saxophone player. Also see LEE KONITZ.
Albums
ATLANTIC
❏ 1291 [M] — Warne Marsh — 1961 — $150
— Multicolor label, white "fan" logo at right
❏ SD1291 [S] — Warne Marsh — 1961 — $150
— Multicolor label, white "fan" logo at right
DISCOVERY
❏ 863 — How Deep/How High — 198? — $25
IMPERIAL
❏ LP-9027 [M] — Jazz of Two Cities — 1957 — $175
❏ LP-12013 [S] — The Winds of Warne Marsh — 1959 — $175
— Retitled version in stereo?
INTERPLAY
❏ 8604 — Posthumous — 1986 — $30
❏ 8602 — Two Days in the Life of Warne Marsh — 1986 — $30
❏ 7709 — Warne Out — 197? — $30
NESSA
❏ N-7 — All Music — 1977 — $30
REVELATION
❏ R-12 — Ne Plus Ultra — 1970 — $25
❏ 22 — The Art of Improvising — 197? — $30
❏ 27 — The Art of Improvising, Vol. 3 — 197? — $30
STORYVILLE
❏ 4001 — Jazz Exchange, Vol. 1 — 197? — $30
❏ 4026 — Jazz Exchange, Vol. 2: Live at the Montmartre Club — 198? — $30
XANADU
❏ 151 — Live in Hollywood — 197? — $30

MARSHALL, EDDIE
Drummer and recorder player.
Albums
TIMELESS
❏ 315 — Dance of the Sun — 1977 — $30

MARSHALL, JACK
Guitarist, composer and arranger. Wrote the theme to the TV show The Munsters.
Albums
CAPITOL
❏ T1108 [M] — 18th Century Jazz — 1959 — $50
❏ ST1108 [S] — 18th Century Jazz — 1959 — $60

Number	Title	Yr	NM

❏ T1939 [M] — My Son the Surf Nut — 1963 — $60
❏ ST1939 [S] — My Son the Surf Nut — 1963 — $75
❏ T1601 [M] — Songs Without Words — 1961 — $50
❏ ST1601 [S] — Songs Without Words — 1961 — $60
❏ T1194 [M] — Soundsville! — 1959 — $50
❏ ST1194 [S] — Soundsville! — 1959 — $60
❏ T1351 [M] — The Marshall Swings — 1960 — $40
❏ ST1351 [S] — The Marshall Swings — 1960 — $60
❏ T1727 [M] — The Twangy, Shoutin', Fantastic Big-Band Sounds of Tuff Jack — 1962 — $60
❏ ST1727 [S] — The Twangy, Shoutin', Fantastic Big-Band Sounds of Tuff Jack — 1962 — $75

MARSHALL, WENDELL
See MILT HINTON.

MARTIN, ARCH
Trombonist.
Albums
ZEPHYR
❏ 12009 [M] — Arch Martin Quintet — 1959 — $30

MARTIN, FREDDY
Saxophone player and bandleader.
Albums
CAPITOL
❏ T2347 [M] — As Time Goes By — 1965 — $40
❏ ST2347 [S] — As Time Goes By — 1965 — $60
❏ T2098 [M] — Best of the New Favorites — 1964 — $40
❏ ST2098 [S] — Best of the New Favorites — 1964 — $60
❏ T1269 [M] — C'mon, Let's Dance — 1960 — $60
— Black colorband label, logo at left
❏ T1269 [M] — C'mon, Let's Dance — 1962 — $40
— Black colorband label, logo at top
❏ ST1269 [S] — C'mon, Let's Dance — 1960 — $75
— Black colorband label, logo at left
❏ ST1269 [S] — C'mon, Let's Dance — 1962 — $60
— Black colorband label, logo at top
❏ T2028 [M] — Freddy Martin Plays the Hits — 1964 — $50
❏ ST2028 [S] — Freddy Martin Plays the Hits — 1964 — $60
❏ T2163 [M] — Freddy Martin Plays the Hits, Vol, 2 — 1964 — $50
❏ ST2163 [S] — Freddy Martin Plays the Hits, Vol, 2 — 1964 — $60
❏ T1889 [M] — In a Sentimental Mood — 1963 — $50
❏ ST1889 [S] — In a Sentimental Mood — 1963 — $60
❏ T1486 [M] — Seems Like Old Times — 1961 — $60
— Black colorband label, logo at left
❏ T1486 [M] — Seems Like Old Times — 1962 — $50
— Black colorband label, logo at top
❏ ST1486 [S] — Seems Like Old Times — 1961 — $50
— Black colorband label, logo at left
❏ ST1486 [S] — Seems Like Old Times — 1962 — $60
— Black colorband label, logo at top
❏ T1582 [M] — The Hits of Freddie Martin — 1962 — $50
❏ ST1582 [M] — The Hits of Freddie Martin — 1962 — $60
❏ T2018 [M] — Tonight We Love — 1964 — $50
❏ ST2018 [S] — Tonight We Love — 1964 — $60
DECCA
❏ DL74908 [R] — Freddy Martin's Greatest Hits — 1967 — $25
❏ DL4908 [M] — Freddy Martin's Greatest Hits — 1967 — $35
❏ DL4839 [M] — The Most Requested — 1967 — $35
❏ DL74839 [R] — The Most Requested — 1967 — $25
HINDSIGHT
❏ HSR-151 — Freddy Martin and His Orchestra 1940 — 198? — $25
❏ HSR-169 — Freddy Martin and His Orchestra 1944-46 — 198? — $25
❏ HSR-205 — Freddy Martin and His Orchestra 1948, 1952 — 198? — $25
❏ HSR-190 — Freddy Martin and His Orchestra 1952 — 198? — $25
KAPP
❏ KL-1286 [M] — Dancing Tonight — 1963 — $30
❏ KS-3286 [S] — Dancing Tonight — 1963 — $35
❏ KL-1261 [M] — Great Waltzes of the World — 1962 — $30
❏ KS-3261 [S] — Great Waltzes of the World — 1962 — $35
❏ KL-1271 [M] — Great Waltzes of the World, Volume 2 — 1962 — $30
❏ KS-3271 [S] — Great Waltzes of the World, Volume 2 — 1962 — $35
❏ KL-1490 [M] — The Most Beautiful Girl in the World — 1966 — $25
❏ KS-3490 [S] — The Most Beautiful Girl in the World — 1966 — $30
MCA

Number	Title	Yr	NM
❑ 4021	54 Great Waltzes	197?	$30
❑ 258	Freddy Martin's Greatest Hits	197?	$20
❑ 4080	The Best of Freddy Martin	197?	$30
RCA VICTOR			
❑ LPM-1414 [M]	Freddy Martin at the Cocoanut Grove	1957	$30
❑ LSP-4044 [R]	The Best of Freddy Martin	1969	$25
❑ VPM-6072	This Is Freddy Martin	197?	$35
SUNBEAM			
❑ 313	Music in the Martin Manner 1933-39	197?	$25

MARTIN, JUAN
Guitarist.

Albums

Number	Title	Yr	NM
NOVUS			
❑ 3005-1-N	Painter in Sound	1986	$25
❑ 3036-1-N	Through the Moving Window	1988	$25

MARTIN, RONEE
Female singer.

Albums

Number	Title	Yr	NM
SOUNDWINGS			
❑ SW-2105	Sensation	1987	$25

MARTIN, SPIDER
Saxophone player.

Albums

Number	Title	Yr	NM
IMPROV			
❑ 7118	Absolutely	197?	$30

MARTINO, PAT
Guitarist. Also see THE PHILADELPHIA EXPERIMENT.

Albums

Number	Title	Yr	NM
COBBLESTONE			
❑ 9015	The Visit	1972	$25
FANTASY			
❑ OJC-355	Baiyina (The Clear Evidence)	198?	$25
❑ OJC-397	Desperado	1989	$30
❑ OJC-248	East!	198?	$25
❑ OJC-195	El Hombre	198?	$25
❑ OJC-223	Strings!	198?	$25
MUSE			
❑ MR-5039	Consciousness	1975	$30
❑ MR-5075	Exit	1976	$30
❑ MR-5096	Footprints	1977	$30
❑ MR-5026	Live!	1974	$30
❑ MR-5328	The Return	198?	$25
❑ MR-5090	We'll Be Together Again	1977	$30
PRESTIGE			
❑ PRST-7589	Baiyina (The Clear Evidence)	1968	$35
❑ PRST-7795	Desperado	1970	$35
❑ PRST-7562	East!	1968	$35
❑ PRST-7513 [S]	El Hombre	1967	$35
❑ PRLP-7513 [M]	El Hombre	1967	$30
❑ PRLP-7547 [M]	Strings!	1967	$30
❑ PRST-7547 [S]	Strings!	1967	$35
WARNER BROS.			
❑ BS2977	Joyous Lake	1977	$25
❑ BS2921	Starbright	1976	$25

MARX, BILL
Pianist.

Albums

Number	Title	Yr	NM
VEE JAY			
❑ LP-3032 [M]	Jazz Kaleidoscope	1962	$25
❑ SR-3032 [S]	Jazz Kaleidoscope	1962	$30
❑ LP-3035 [M]	My Son, the Folk Swinger	1963	$25
❑ SR-3035 [S]	My Son, the Folk Swinger	1963	$30

MARX, DICK, AND JOHN FRIGO
Also see each artist's individual listings.

Albums

Number	Title	Yr	NM
BRUNSWICK			
❑ BL54006 [M]	Two Much Piano	1955	$50

MARX, DICK
Pianist.

Albums

Number	Title	Yr	NM
OMEGA			
❑ OML-1002 [M]	Marx Makes Broadway	1958	$40
❑ OSL-2 [S]	Marx Makes Broadway	1959	$30

— *The front cover of the above LP spells his last name "Marks," though it is spelled correctly on the label and back cover*

MARX, HARPO
Harpist.

Albums

Number	Title	Yr	NM
MERCURY			
❑ MG-20363 [M]	Harpo at Work!	1959	$150
❑ SR-60016 [S]	Harpo at Work!	1959	$150
❑ MG-20232 [M]	Harpo in Hi-Fi	1957	$150
RCA VICTOR			
❑ LPM-27 [10]	Harp by Harpo	1952	$250
WING			
❑ MGW-12164 [M]	Harpo	1960	$40

MARYLAND JAZZ BAND

Albums

Number	Title	Yr	NM
GHB			
❑ GHB-178	25 Years of Jazz with the Maryland Jazz Band	1987	$25

MAS, JEAN-PIERRE, AND CESARIUS ALVIM
Mas is a pianist; Alvim is a bass player.

Albums

Number	Title	Yr	NM
INNER CITY			
❑ IC-1014	Lourmel	197?	$35

MASEKELA, HUGH
Cornet player, fluegel horn player, trumpeter, occasional percussionist and male singer, best known for his hit song "Grazing in the Grass." Also see HERB ALPERT.

Albums

Number	Title	Yr	NM
ABC IMPULSE!			
❑ IA-9343	African Connection	1978	$30
BLUE THUMB			
❑ BT-6003	Home Is Where the Music Is	1973	$25
❑ BT-6015	I Am Not Afraid	1974	$25
❑ BT-62	Introducing Hedzoleh Sounds	1972	$25
CASABLANCA			
❑ NBLP7023	Colonial Man	1976	$25
❑ NBLP7036	Melody Maker	1977	$25
❑ NBLP7017	The Boy's Doin' It	1975	$25
❑ NBLP7079	You Told Your Mama	1978	$25
CHISA			
❑ CS-803	Reconstruction	1970	$30
❑ CS-808	Union of South Africa	1971	$30
JIVE			
❑ JL-8210	Techno Bush	1984	$25
❑ JL-8382	Waiting for the Rain	1985	$25
MERCURY			
❑ SR-61109	Grr	1969	$30
❑ MG-20797 [M]	The Trumpet of Hugh Masekela	1963	$100
❑ SR-60797 [S]	The Trumpet of Hugh Masekela	1963	$100
MGM			
❑ GAS-116	Hugh Masekela (Golden Archive Series)	1970	$30
❑ E-4415 [M]	Hugh Masekela's Next Album	1966	$30
❑ SE-4415 [S]	Hugh Masekela's Next Album	1966	$35
❑ E-4372 [M]	The Americanization of Ooga Booga	1966	$30
❑ SE-4372 [S]	The Americanization of Ooga Booga	1966	$35
❑ E-4468 [M]	The Lasting Impression of Hugh Masekela	1967	$35
❑ SE-4468 [S]	The Lasting Impression of Hugh Masekela	1967	$30
NOVUS			
❑ 3070-1-R	Uptownship	1990	$30
UNI			
❑ 3015 [M]	Hugh Masekela Is Alive and Well at the Whisky	1967	$50
❑ 73015 [S]	Hugh Masekela Is Alive and Well at the Whisky	1967	$30
❑ 3010 [M]	Hugh Masekela's Latest	1967	$35
❑ 73010 [S]	Hugh Masekela's Latest	1967	$30
❑ 73041	Masekela	1969	$30
❑ 73051	Masekela -- Vol. 2	1970	$30
❑ 73028	The Promise of a Future	1968	$30
VERVE			
❑ V6-8651	24 Karat Hits	1968	$35
WARNER BROS.			
❑ 25566	Tomorrow	1987	$25

MASLAK, KESHAVAN
Saxophone player, clarinetist, occasional guitarist and drummer.

Albums

Number	Title	Yr	NM
BLACK SAINT			
❑ BSR-0079	Blaster Master	198?	$30

MASON, CHRISTOPHER
Alto saxophone player.

Albums

Number	Title	Yr	NM
OPTIMISM			
❑ OP-3218	Something Beautiful	198?	$25

MASON, HARVEY
Drummer. Also see HEADHUNTERS.

Albums

Number	Title	Yr	NM
ARISTA			
❑ AL4096	Earthmover	1976	$30
❑ AL4157	Funk in a Mason Jar	1978	$30
❑ AL4054	Marching in the Street	1975	$30

MASON, JAMES
Guitarist.

MASSO, GEORGE
Trombonist, pianist and vibraphone player.

Albums

Number	Title	Yr	NM
DREAMSTREET			
❑ DR-108	Pieces of Eight	1986	$25
FAMOUS DOOR			
❑ 129	Choice N.Y.C.	197?	$30
❑ 148	No Frills, Just Music	198?	$25
❑ 138	Swinging Case of Masso-ism	1981	$30

MASTER CYLINDER
Texas-based fusion band.

Albums

Number	Title	Yr	NM
INNER CITY			
❑ IC-1112	Elsewhere	198?	$30

MASTERS, FRANKIE
Bandleader and male singer.

Albums

Number	Title	Yr	NM
CIRCLE			
❑ 62	Frankie Masters and His Orchestra 1945-46	198?	$25

MASTERS, JOE
Pianist and composer.

Albums

Number	Title	Yr	NM
COLUMBIA			
❑ CS9398 [S]	The Jazz Mass	1967	$25
❑ CL2598 [M]	The Jazz Mass	1967	$30
DISCOVERY			
❑ 785	The Jazz Mass	197?	$35

MASTERS, MARK
Composer and arranger.

Albums

Number	Title	Yr	NM
SEA BREEZE			
❑ SB-2022	Early Start	198?	$30
❑ SB-2033	Silver Threads Among the Blues	1987	$30

MASTERSOUNDS, THE

Members: Benny Barth (drums); Richie Crabtree (piano); BUDDY MONTGOMERY; MONK MONTGOMERY. Also see THE MONTGOMERY BROTHERS.

Albums

Number	Title	Yr	NM
FANTASY			
❏ 3316 [M]	A Date with the Mastersounds	1961	$40
—Red vinyl			
❏ 3316 [M]	A Date with the Mastersounds	1962	$30
—Black vinyl			
❏ 8062 [S]	A Date with the Mastersounds	1961	$30
—Blue vinyl			
❏ 8062 [S]	A Date with the Mastersounds	1962	$25
—Black vinyl			
❏ OJC-282	A Date with the Mastersounds	1987	$25
❏ OJC-280	Swinging with the Mastersounds	1987	$25
❏ 3305 [M]	Swingin' with the Mastersounds	1960	$40
—Red vinyl			
❏ 3305 [M]	Swingin' with the Mastersounds	1962	$30
—Black vinyl			
❏ 8050 [S]	Swingin' with the Mastersounds	1961	$30
—Blue vinyl			
❏ 3327 [M]	The Mastersounds on Tour	1961	$40
—Red vinyl			
❏ 3327 [M]	The Mastersounds on Tour	1962	$30
—Black vinyl			
❏ 8066 [S]	The Mastersounds on Tour	1961	$30
—Blue vinyl			
❏ 8066 [S]	The Mastersounds on Tour	1962	$25
—Black vinyl			
PACIFIC JAZZ			
❏ PJM-403 [M]	Introducing the Mastersounds	1957	$50
❏ PJM-405 [M]	The King and I	1958	$50
WORLD PACIFIC			
❏ WP-1260 [M]	Ballads and Blues	1959	$150
❏ ST-1019 [S]	Ballads and Blues	1959	$100
❏ WP-1252 [M]	Flower Drum Song	1958	$150
❏ ST-1012 [S]	Flower Drum Song	1958	$100
❏ WP-1280 [M]	Happy Holidays from Many Lands	1959	$150
❏ ST-1030 [S]	Happy Holidays from Many Lands	1959	$100
❏ WP-1271 [M]	Jazz Showcase	1959	$100
—Reissue of Pacific Jazz 403			
❏ WP-1243 [M]	Kismet	1958	$150
❏ ST-1010 [S]	Kismet	1958	$100
❏ WP-1272 [M]	The King and I	1959	$100
—Reissue of Pacific Jazz 405			
❏ ST-1017 [S]	The King and I	1959	$100
❏ WP-1269 [M]	The Mastersounds in Concert	1959	$150
❏ ST-1026 [S]	The Mastersounds in Concert	1959	$100
❏ WP-1284 [M]	The Mastersounds Play Horace Silver	1960	$150
❏ ST-1284 [S]	The Mastersounds Play Horace Silver	1960	$100

MATERIAL

Group led by BILL LASWELL and Michael Beinhorn (synthesizers) with a flexible supporting cast.

Albums

Number	Title	Yr	NM
ELEKTRA/MUSICIAN			
❏ 60042	Memory Serves	1982	$12
❏ 60206	One Down	1984	$12

MATHEWS, MAT

Accordion player. Also see EDDIE COSTA; THE FOUR MOST; THE NEW YORK JAZZ QUARTET.

Albums

Number	Title	Yr	NM
AUDIOPHILE			
❏ AP-219	Mat Mathews and Friends	1987	$25
BRUNSWICK			
❏ BL54013 [M]	Bag's Groove	1956	$80
DAWN			
❏ DLP-1104 [M]	The Modern Art of Jazz	1956	$300

MATHEWS, RONNIE

Pianist.

Albums

Number	Title	Yr	NM
BEE HIVE			
❏ 7011	Legacy	197?	$30
❏ 7008	Roots, Branches and Dances	197?	$30
PRESTIGE			
❏ PRLP-7303 [M]	Doin' the Thang	1964	$30
❏ PRST-7303 [S]	Doin' the Thang	1964	$40
TIMELESS			
❏ LPSJP-304	Selena's Dance	1990	$30

MATHIS, JOHNNY

Male singer. Known for his pop and easy listening hits, he is backed by a jazz combo on this, his debut album. For the rest of his discography, see the Standard Catalog of American Records.

Albums

Number	Title	Yr	NM
COLUMBIA			
❏ CL887 [M]	Johnny Mathis	1957	$100

MATLOCK, MATTY

Clarinetist and arranger.

Albums

Number	Title	Yr	NM
RCA VICTOR			
❏ LPM-1413 [M]	Pete Kelly at Home	1957	$40
WARNER BROS.			
❏ WS1280 [S]	Four Button Dixie	1958	$40
X			
❏ LXA-3035 [10]	Sports Parade	1955	$60

MATRIX

Nonet co-founded by pianist-composer John Harmon in Appleton, Wisconsin. Among the other musicians were Mike Hale (trumpet).

Albums

Number	Title	Yr	NM
PABLO TODAY			
❏ 2312121	Harvest	1980	$30

MATTHEWS, DAVID

Pianist.

Albums

Number	Title	Yr	NM
CTI			
❏ 5005	Dune	1977	$30
GNP CRESCENDO			
❏ GNP-2153	Delta Lady	198?	$25
❏ GNP-2162	Grand Connection	198?	$25
❏ GNP-2157	Grand Cross	198?	$25
❏ GNP-2174	Ice Fuse One	198?	$25
❏ GNP-2185	Speed Demon	1986	$25
❏ GNP-2169	Super Funky Sax	198?	$25
KUDU			
❏ 30	Shoogie Wanna Boogie	1976	$35
MUSE			
❏ MR-5073	David Matthews' Big Band at the 5 Spot	1976	$25
❏ MR-5096	Flight	1977	$25

MATTHEWS, ONZY

Bandleader, composer and arranger.

Albums

Number	Title	Yr	NM
CAPITOL			
❏ T2099 [M]	Blues with a Touch of Elegance	1964	$75
❏ ST2099 [S]	Blues with a Touch of Elegance	1964	$40

MATTHEWS, WALT

Albums

Number	Title	Yr	NM
FRETLESS			
❏ 158	The Dance in Your Eye	198?	$30

MATTSON, PHIL

Male singer.

Albums

Number	Title	Yr	NM
DOCTOR JAZZ			
❏ FW40349	Setting Standards	1986	$25

MATZ, PETER

Composer, arranger and bandleader.

Albums

Number	Title	Yr	NM
PROJECT 3			
❏ PR5007SD	Peter Matz Brings 'Em Back	1967	$35

MAULAWI

Albums

Number	Title	Yr	NM
STRATA-EAST			
❏ SES104-74	Maulawi	1974	$30

MAUPIN, BENNIE

Tenor and soprano saxophone player and bass clarinetist.

Albums

Number	Title	Yr	NM
ECM			
❏ 1043	The Jewel in the Lotus	197?	$35
MERCURY			
❏ SRM-1-3717	Moonscapes	1978	$25
❏ SRM-1-1148	Slow Traffic	1976	$25

MAURO, TURK

Albums

Number	Title	Yr	NM
STORYVILLE			
❏ 4076	The Underdog	198?	$25

MAXTED, BILLY

Albums

Number	Title	Yr	NM
BRUNSWICK			
❏ BL58052 [10]	Honky Tonk Piano	1953	$60
CADENCE			
❏ CLP-1005 [M]	Billy Maxted Plays Hi-Fi Keyboard	1955	$50
❏ CLP-1013 [M]	Dixieland Manhattan Style	1955	$50
❏ CLP-3013 [M]	Dixieland Manhattan Style	1958	$30
❏ CLP-1012 [M]	Jazz at Nick's	1955	$50
LIBERTY			
❏ LRP-3474 [M]	Maxted Makes It	1966	$30
❏ LST-7474 [S]	Maxted Makes It	1966	$35
❏ LRP-3492 [M]	Satin Doll	1967	$35
❏ LST-7492 [S]	Satin Doll	1967	$30
SEECO			
❏ CELP-458 [M]	Art of Jazz	1960	$125
❏ CELP-4580 [S]	Art of Jazz	1960	$125
❏ CELP-438 [M]	Bourbon St. Billy and the Blues	1960	$125
❏ CELP-4380 [S]	Bourbon St. Billy and the Blues	1960	$125

MAXWELL, JIMMIE

Trumpeter and fluegel horn player.

Albums

Number	Title	Yr	NM
CIRCLE			
❏ 50	Let's Fall in Love	198?	$25

MAY, BILLY

Albums

Number	Title	Yr	NM
BAINBRIDGE			
❏ ST1001	I Believe in You	197?	$30
CAPITOL			
❏ H349 [10]	A Band Is Born!	1952	$60
❏ T349 [M]	A Band Is Born!	195?	$60
—Turquoise label original			
❏ H374 [10]	Bacchanalia!	1953	$60
❏ T374 [M]	Bacchanalia!	195?	$60
—Turquoise label original			
❏ L329 [10]	Big Band Bash	1952	$60
❏ T329 [M]	Big Band Bash	195?	$60
—Turquoise label original			
❏ T1043 [M]	Big Fat Brass	1958	$80
—Black colorband label, Capitol logo at left			
❏ ST1043 [S]	Big Fat Brass	1958	$100
—Black colorband label, Capitol logo at left			
❏ T1888 [M]	Bill's Bag	1963	$75
❏ ST1888 [S]	Bill's Bag	1963	$80
❏ T771 [M]	Billy May Plays for Fancy Dancin'	1956	$100
—Turquoise label original			
❏ H487 [10]	Billy May's Naughty Operetta!	1953	$60
❏ T487 [M]	Billy May's Naughty Operetta!	195?	$60

Jackie McLean, *One Step Beyond*, Blue Note BLP-4137, **$120**.

Jackie McLean, *A Fickle Sonance*, Blue Note BLP-4089, with W. 63rd St. address on label, **$800**.

Gil Melle, *Melle Plays Primitive Modern*, Prestige PRLP-7040, yellow label with W. 50th St. address, **$300**.

Helen Merrill, *Dream of You*, EmArcy MG-36078, blue label with drummer logo, **$80**.

Number	Title	Yr	NM
— Turquoise label original			
❑ T2560 [M]	Billy May Today	1965	$60
❑ ST1329 [S]	Cha Cha!	1959	$100
— Black colorband label, Capitol logo at left			
❑ T1329 [M]	Cha Cha!	1959	$80
— Black colorband label, Capitol logo at left			
❑ T1367 [M]	Cha Cha Mambos	1959	$80
— Black colorband label, logo at left			
❑ TAO924 [M]	Jimmie Lunceford in Hi-Fi: Authentic Re-Creations of the Lunceford Style	1958	$100
— Turquoise label original			
❑ STAO924 [S]	Jimmie Lunceford in Hi-Fi: Authentic Re-Creations of the Lunceford Style	1958	$75
— Black colorband label, Capitol logo at left			
❑ H237 [10]	Join the Band	1951	$75
❑ T1377 [M]	Pow!	1959	$300
— Gold "The Star Line" label			
❑ T677 [M]	Sorta-Dixie!	195?	$60
— Turquoise label original			
❑ M11885 [M]	Sorta-Dixie!	197?	$25
— Reissue of Capitol 677			
❑ T562 [M]	Sorta-May	195?	$60
— Turquoise label original			
❑ M562 [M]	Sorta-May	197?	$25
— Reissue with new prefix			
❑ T1417 [M]	The Girls and Boys on Broadway	1960	$75
— Black colorband label, Capitol logo at left			
❑ ST1417 [S]	The Girls and Boys on Broadway	1960	$80
— Black colorband label, Capitol logo at left			
❑ T1581 [M]	The Great Jimmie Lunceford: Authentic Re-Creations of the Lunceford Style by Billy May	1961	$250
— Gold "The Star Line" label			
❑ ST1581 [S]	The Great Jimmie Lunceford: Authentic Re-Creations of the Lunceford Style by Billy May	1961	$250
— Gold "The Star Line" label			
❑ T1709 [M]	The Sweetest Swingin' Sounds of No Strings	196?	$50
❑ ST1709 [S]	The Sweetest Swingin' Sounds of No Strings	196?	$80
CREATIVE WORLD			
❑ ST-1054	Sorta-Dixie!	197?	$30
❑ ST-1051 [M]	Sorta-May	197?	$30
IMPERIAL			
❑ LP-9042 [M]	Fuzzy Pink Nightgown	1957	$200
— Movie soundtrack			
PAUSA			
❑ PR9035	A Band Is Born!	198?	$25
— Reissue of Capitol T 349			
PICKWICK			
❑ PC-3010 [M]	Hey It's May	196?	$35
❑ SPC-3010 [R]	Hey It's May	196?	$20
STEREO SOUNDS			
❑ SA-12	Music for Uptight Guys	196?	$35
TIME			
❑ 52064 [M]	Billy May and His Orchestra	1962	$35
❑ S-2064 [S]	Billy May and His Orchestra	1962	$50
TIME-LIFE			
❑ STL-340	The Swing Era: 1930-1936	197?	$50
— Box set with hardcover book; re-creations of original big-band charts, with some contributions by the Glenn Gray Orchestra			
❑ STL-341	The Swing Era: 1936-1937	197?	$50
— Box set with hardcover book; re-creations of original big-band charts, with some contributions by the Glenn Gray Orchestra			
❑ STL-342	The Swing Era: 1937-1938	197?	$50
— Box set with hardcover book; re-creations of original big-band charts, with some contributions by the Glenn Gray Orchestra			
❑ STL-343	The Swing Era: 1938-1939	197?	$50
— Box set with hardcover book; re-creations of original big-band charts, with some contributions by the Glenn Gray Orchestra			
❑ STL-344	The Swing Era: 1939-1940	197?	$50
— Box set with hardcover book; re-creations of original big-band charts, with some contributions by the Glenn Gray Orchestra			
❑ STL-345	The Swing Era: 1940-1941	197?	$50
— Box set with hardcover book; re-creations of original big-band charts, with some contributions by the Glenn Gray Orchestra			
❑ STL-346	The Swing Era: 1941-1942	197?	$50
— Box set with hardcover book; re-creations of original big-band charts, with some contributions by the Glenn Gray Orchestra			
❑ STL-347	The Swing Era: 1942-1944	197?	$50
— Box set with hardcover book; re-creations of original big-band charts, with some contributions by the Glenn Gray Orchestra			
❑ STL-348	The Swing Era: 1944-1945	197?	$50
— Box set with hardcover book; re-creations of original big-band charts, with some contributions by the Glenn Gray Orchestra			
❑ STL-352	The Swing Era: Curtain Call	197?	$50
— Box set with hardcover book; re-creations of original big-band charts, with some contributions by the Glenn Gray Orchestra			
❑ STL-351	The Swing Era: Encore!	197?	$50
— Box set with hardcover book; re-creations of original big-band charts, with some contributions by the Glenn Gray Orchestra			
❑ STL-350	The Swing Era: Into the '50s	197?	$50
— Box set with hardcover book; re-creations of original big-band charts, with some contributions by the Glenn Gray Orchestra			
❑ STL-353	The Swing Era: One More Time	197?	$50
— Box set with hardcover book; re-creations of original big-band charts, with some contributions by the Glenn Gray Orchestra			
❑ STL-349	The Swing Era: The Postwar Years	197?	$50
— Box set with hardcover book; re-creations of original big-band charts, with some contributions by the Glenn Gray Orchestra			

MAYERL, BILLY

Pianist, bandleader and composer.

Albums

Number	Title	Yr	NM
FLAPPER			
❑ 704/5	The Versatility of Billy Mayerl	198?	$35

MAYL, GENE

Bass player and bandleader.

Albums

Number	Title	Yr	NM
BLACKBIRD			
❑ 12006	A Trip to Waukesha	1969	$35
JAZZOLOGY			
❑ J-6 [M]	Gene Mayl's Dixieland Rhythm Kings	1964	$35

MAYS, BILL

Pianist and composer.

Albums

Number	Title	Yr	NM
TREND			
❑ TR-532	Tha's Delights	1984	$30

MAYS, LYLE

Pianist.

Albums

Number	Title	Yr	NM
GEFFEN			
❑ GHS24097	Lyle Mays	1986	$25
❑ GHS24204	Street Dreams	1988	$25

M'BOOM

Percussion group led by MAX ROACH.

Albums

Number	Title	Yr	NM
COLUMBIA			
❑ JC37066	M'Boom	1981	$30
SOUL NOTE			
❑ SN-1059	Collage	198?	$30

MCBEE, CECIL

Bass player.

Albums

Number	Title	Yr	NM
ENJA			
❑ 3041	Compassion	198?	$30
INDIA NAVIGATION			
❑ IN-1043	Alternate Spaces	197?	$35
❑ IN-1053	Flying Out	198?	$35
INNER CITY			
❑ IC-3023	Music from the Source	197?	$35
STRATA-EAST			
❑ SES-7417	Mutima	1975	$30

MCBROWNE, LENNY

Drummer.

Albums

Number	Title	Yr	NM
PACIFIC JAZZ			
❑ PJ-1 [M]	The Four Souls	1960	$30
❑ ST-1 [S]	The Four Souls	1960	$40
RIVERSIDE			
❑ RLP-346 [M]	Eastern Lights	1960	$200
❑ RS-9346 [S]	Eastern Lights	1960	$200

MCCALL, MARY ANN

Female singer. Also see CHARLIE VENTURA.

Albums

Number	Title	Yr	NM
CORAL			
❑ CRL57276 [M]	Melancholy Baby	1959	$60
❑ CRL757276 [S]	Melancholy Baby	1959	$80
DISCOVERY			
❑ 3011 [10]	Mary Ann McCall Sings	1950	$300
JUBILEE			
❑ JLP-1078 [M]	Detour to the Moon	1958	$60
SAVOY JAZZ			
❑ SJL-1178	Easy Living	198?	$35

MCCANN, HOOPS

Not a real person, but a character from the Steely Dan song "Glamour Profession." All the band members had played on Steely Dan records.

Albums

Number	Title	Yr	NM
MCA			
❑ 42202	The Hoops McCann Band Plays the Music of Steely Dan	1988	$25

MCCANN, LES, AND EDDIE HARRIS

Also see each artist's individual listings.

Albums

Number	Title	Yr	NM
ATLANTIC			
❑ SD1583	Second Movement	1971	$35
❑ SD1537	Swiss Movement	1969	$35

MCCANN, LES

Pianist, male singer and composer. Also see CLIFFORD SCOTT.

Albums

Number	Title	Yr	NM
A&M			
❑ SP-4780	Tall, Dark and Handsome	1979	$25
❑ SP-4718	The Man	1978	$25
ABC IMPULSE!			
❑ AS-9333	Live at the Roxy	1978	$25
❑ AS-9329	The Music Lets Me Be	1977	$25
ATLANTIC			
❑ SD1666	Another Beginning	1974	$30
❑ SD1547	Comment	1970	$35
❑ SD1679	Hustle to Survive	1975	$30
❑ SD1603 [S]	Invitation to Openness	1972	$30
❑ 1603 [M]	Invitation to Openness	1972	$60
— Mono is white label promo only with "d/j copy monaural" sticker on front cover			
❑ SD1646	Layers	1973	$30
❑ SD 2-312	Live at Montreux	1974	$35
❑ SD1516	Much Les	1969	$35
❑ SD1690	River High, River Low	1976	$30
❑ SD1619	Talk to the People	1972	$30
JAM			
❑ 019	Les McCann's Music Box	1984	$25
❑ 012	The Longer You Wait	1984	$25
LIMELIGHT			
❑ LM-82031 [M]	Beaux J. Pooboo	1966	$35
❑ LS-86031 [S]	Beaux J. Pooboo	1966	$50
❑ LM-82043 [M]	Bucket O' Grease	1967	$50
❑ LS-86043 [S]	Bucket O' Grease	1967	$35
❑ LM-82016 [M]	But Not Really	1965	$35
❑ LS-86016 [S]	But Not Really	1965	$50
❑ LM-82041 [M]	Les McCann Plays the Hits	1966	$35

Number	Title	Yr	NM
❑ LS-86041 [S]	Les McCann Plays the Hits	1966	$50
❑ LM-82036 [M]	Live at Shelly's Manne-Hole	1966	$35
❑ LS-86036 [S]	Live at Shelly's Manne-Hole	1966	$50
❑ LM-82046 [M]	Live at the Bohemian	1967	$50
	Caverns, Washington, D.C.		
❑ LS-86046 [S]	Live at the Bohemian	1967	$35
	Caverns, Washington, D.C.		
❑ LM-82025 [M]	Poo Boo	1965	$35
❑ LS-86025 [S]	Poo Boo	1965	$50

PACIFIC JAZZ

❑ PJ-10107 [M]	A Bag of Gold	1966	$35
❑ ST-20107 [S]	A Bag of Gold	1966	$50
❑ PJ-81 [M]	Jazz Waltz	1964	$35
❑ ST-81 [S]	Jazz Waltz	1964	$50
❑ PJ-45 [M]	Les McCann in New York	1962	$50
❑ ST-45 [S]	Les McCann in New York	1962	$60
❑ LN-10078	Les McCann in New York	1980	$20

— Budget-line reissue

❑ PJ-16 [M]	Les McCann in San	1961	$60
	Francisco		
❑ ST-16 [S]	Les McCann in San	1961	$60
	Francisco		
❑ LN-10077	Les McCann in San	1980	$20
	Francisco		

— Budget-line reissue

❑ PJ-31 [M]	Les McCann Sings	1961	$50
❑ ST-31 [S]	Les McCann Sings	1961	$60
❑ PJ-84 [M]	McCanna	1964	$35
❑ ST-84 [S]	McCanna	1964	$50
❑ PJ-91 [M]	McCann/Wilson	1965	$35

— With Gerald Wilson

❑ ST-91 [S]	McCann/Wilson	1965	$50

— With Gerald Wilson

❑ PJ-56 [M]	On Time	1962	$40

— Yellow vinyl

❑ PJ-56 [M]	On Time	1962	$50

— Black vinyl

❑ ST-56 [S]	On Time	1962	$100

— Yellow vinyl

❑ ST-56 [S]	On Time	1962	$60

— Black vinyl

❑ PJ-25 [M]	Pretty Lady	1961	$50
❑ ST-25 [S]	Pretty Lady	1961	$60
❑ PJ-63 [M]	Shampoo	1962	$35
❑ ST-63 [S]	Shampoo	1962	$50
❑ PJ-78 [M]	Soul Hits	1963	$35
❑ ST-78 [S]	Soul Hits	1963	$50
❑ LN-10079	Soul Hits	1980	$20

— Budget-line reissue

❑ PJ-10097 [M]	Spanish Onions	1966	$35
❑ ST-20097 [S]	Spanish Onions	1966	$50
❑ PJ-69 [M]	The Gospel Truth	1963	$35
❑ ST-69 [S]	The Gospel Truth	1963	$50
❑ PJ-7 [M]	The Shout	1960	$50
❑ ST-7 [S]	The Shout	1960	$60
❑ LN-10083	The Shout	1980	$20

— Budget-line reissue

❑ PJ-2 [M]	The Truth	1960	$60
❑ ST-2 [S]	The Truth	1960	$60

STONE

❑ 1906	Butterfly	1988	$25

SUNSET

❑ SUS-5214	Django	1969	$25
❑ SUS-5296	Unlimited	1970	$25

WORLD PACIFIC

❑ ST-20173	Les McCann Sings & Plays	1970	$100
	in the Big City		
❑ ST-20166	More Or Les McCann	1969	$100

MCCLURE, RON

Bass player, composer and arranger.

Albums

ODE/NEW ZEALAND

❑ SODE-160	Home Base	1985	$30

MCCONNELL, ROB

Trombonist (both slide and valve) and composer.

Albums

PAUSA

❑ 7148	Again, Vol. 1	1983	$25
❑ 7140	Big Band Jazz Vol. 1	198?	$25
❑ 7141	Big Band Jazz Vol. 2	198?	$25
❑ 7067	Present Perfect	1980	$25
❑ 7031	The Rob McConnell and	1979	$25
	Boss Brass Jazz Album		
❑ 7106	Tribute	198?	$25

MCCORKLE, SUSANNAH

Female singer.

Albums

CONCORD JAZZ

❑ CJ-370	No More Blues	1989	$30

INNER CITY

❑ IC-1141	Music of Harry Warren	198?	$30
❑ IC-1151	People You Never Get to	1984	$30
	Love		
❑ IC-1101	Songs of Johnny Mercer	198?	$30
❑ IC-1131	Songs of Yip Harburg	198?	$30

PAUSA

❑ 7195	How Do You Keep the Music	1986	$25
	Playing?		
❑ 7175	Thanks for the Memory	1985	$25

MCCOY, CLYDE

Trumpeter and bandleader.

Albums

CAPITOL

❑ H311 [10]	Sugar Blues	195?	$150
❑ T311 [M]	Sugar Blues	1955	$80

— Turquoise or gray label

❑ T311 [M]	Sugar Blues	1959	$75

— Black colorband label, logo at left

❑ T311 [M]	Sugar Blues	1963	$60

— Black colorband label, logo at top

❑ DT311 [R]	Sugar Blues	196?	$60
❑ SM-311 [R]	Sugar Blues	197?	$25

CIRCLE

❑ CLP-82	Sugar Blues, 1951	198?	$25

DESIGN

❑ DLP-28 [M]	The Golden Era of the Sugar	196?	$30
	Blues		

HINDSIGHT

❑ HSR-180	Clyde McCoy and His	198?	$25
	Orchestra 1936		

MERCURY

❑ MG-20730 [M]	Blue Prelude	1962	$100
❑ SR-60730 [S]	Blue Prelude	1962	$100
❑ SR-60677 [S]	Really McCoy	1961	$100
❑ MG-20677 [M]	Really McCoy	1961	$100
❑ MG-20110 [M]	The Blues	195?	$100

TOP RANK

❑ RM-350 [M]	Dixieland's Best Friend	1961	$30
❑ RS-650 [S]	Dixieland's Best Friend	1961	$40

WING

❑ MGW-12260 [M]	Dancing to the Blues	196?	$30
❑ SRW-16260 [S]	Dancing to the Blues	196?	$30

MCCOY, FREDDIE

Vibraphone player.

Albums

COBBLESTONE

❑ 9004	Gimme Some	1972	$25

PRESTIGE

❑ PRST-7542	Beans and Greens	1968	$30
❑ PRLP-7470 [M]	Funk Drops	1967	$30
❑ PRST-7470 [S]	Funk Drops	1967	$30
❑ PRST-7582	Listen Here	1968	$30
❑ PRLP-7395 [M]	Lonely Avenue	1965	$25
❑ PRST-7395 [S]	Lonely Avenue	1965	$30
❑ PRLP-7487 [M]	Peas 'N' Rice	1967	$30
❑ PRST-7487 [S]	Peas 'N' Rice	1967	$30
❑ PRST-7561	Soul Yogi	1968	$30
❑ PRST-7706	The Best of Freddie McCoy	1969	$25

MCCROBY, RON

Jazz whistler.

Albums

CONCORD JAZZ

❑ CJ-208	Ron McCroby Plays Puccolo	1982	$25
❑ CJ-257	The Other Whistler	1984	$25

PRO ARTE

❑ PAD-258	Breezin' the Classics	1985	$25

MCDERMOT, TOM

Albums

STOMP OFF

❑ SOS-1024	New Rags	198?	$25

MCDONOUGH, DICK, AND CARL KRESS

McDonough was one of the first jazz guitarists. Also see CARL KRESS.

Albums

JAZZ ARCHIVES

❑ JA-32	The Guitar Genius of Dick	198?	$25
	McDonough and Carl Kress		

MCDUFF, JACK

Organist and composer; also known as "Brother Jack McDuff." Also see JOE DUKES.

Albums

ATLANTIC

❑ 1463 [M]	A Change Is Gonna Come	1966	$35
❑ SD1463 [S]	A Change Is Gonna Come	1966	$50
❑ SD1498	Double Barreled Soul	1968	$35
❑ SD1472 [S]	Tobacco Road	1967	$35

BLUE NOTE

❑ BST-84322	Down Home Style	1969	$35
❑ BST-84334	Moon Rappin'	1970	$35
❑ BST-84348	To Seek a New Home	1970	$35
❑ BST-84358	Who Knows	1971	$35

CADET

❑ CH-50024	Check This Out	1973	$30
❑ CH-50051	Fourth Dimension	1974	$30
❑ LPS-817	Getting Our Thing Together	1969	$35
❑ LPS-831	Gin and Orange	1970	$35
❑ CH-60031	Magnetic Feel	1975	$30
❑ LPS-812	Natural Thing	1968	$35
❑ CH-60017	The Healin' System	1972	$30

CHESS

❑ 19004	Sophisticated Funk	1976	$30

FANTASY

❑ OJC-326	Brother Jack Meets the Boss	1988	$25

— Reissue of Prestige 7228

❑ OJC-222	The Honeydripper	198?	$25

— Reissue of Prestige 7199

❑ OJC-324	Tough 'Duff	1988	$25

— Reissue of Prestige 7185

MUSE

❑ MR-5361	The Re-Entry	1989	$30

PRESTIGE

❑ PRST-7771	Best of the Big Soul Band	1970	$35
❑ PRLP-7174 [M]	Brother Jack	1960	$200
❑ PRST-7785	Brother Jack	1970	$35
❑ PRLP-7481 [M]	Brother Jack McDuff's	1967	$60
	Greatest Hits		
❑ PRST-7481 [S]	Brother Jack McDuff's	1967	$50
	Greatest Hits		
❑ PRLP-7220 [M]	Goodnight, It's Time to Go	1961	$200
❑ PRST-7220 [S]	Goodnight, It's Time to Go	1961	$200
❑ PRLP-7492 [M]	Hallelujah Time!	1967	$60
❑ PRST-7492 [S]	Hallelujah Time!	1967	$50
❑ PRST-7422 [M]	Hot Barbeque	1966	$60
❑ PRST-7642	I Got a Woman	1969	$50
❑ PRST-7596	Jack McDuff Plays for	1969	$50
	Beautiful People		
❑ PRLP-7274 [M]	Live!	1963	$40
❑ PRST-7274 [S]	Live!	1963	$40
❑ PRLP-7286 [M]	Live! At the Jazz Workshop	1964	$40
❑ PRST-7286 [S]	Live! At the Jazz Workshop	1964	$40
❑ PRST-7703	Live! The Best of Brother	1969	$50
	Jack McDuff		
❑ PRLP-7228 [M]	Mellow Gravy -- Brother	1962	$150
	Jack Meets the Boss		
❑ PRST-7228 [S]	Mellow Gravy -- Brother	1962	$150
	Jack Meets the Boss		
❑ PRST-7851	On With It	1973	$30
❑ PRLP-7333 [M]	Prelude	1964	$60
❑ PRST-7333 [S]	Prelude	1964	$60
❑ 24013	Rock Candy	1972	$35
❑ PRLP-7259 [M]	Screamin'	1963	$40
❑ PRST-7259 [S]	Screamin'	1963	$40
❑ PRLP-7404 [M]	Silk and Soul	1965	$60
❑ PRST-7404 [S]	Silk and Soul	1965	$60
❑ PRLP-7265 [M]	Somethin' Slick!	1963	$40
❑ PRST-7265 [S]	Somethin' Slick!	1963	$40
❑ PRST-7567	Soul Circle	1968	$50
❑ PRST-7666	Steppin' Out	1969	$50
❑ PRLP-7362 [M]	The Concert McDuff	1965	$60
	Recorded Live!		
❑ PRST-7362 [S]	The Concert McDuff	1965	$60
	Recorded Live!		
❑ PRLP-7323 [M]	The Dynamic Jack McDuff	1964	$40
❑ PRST-7323 [S]	The Dynamic Jack McDuff	1964	$40
❑ PRLP-7199 [M]	The Honeydripper	1961	$200
❑ PRST-7529	The Midnight Sun	1968	$50
❑ PRST-7814	Tough Duff	1971	$35
❑ PRLP-7185 [M]	Tough 'Duff	1960	$200
❑ PRLP-7476 [M]	Walk On By	1967	$60
❑ PRST-7476 [S]	Walk On By	1967	$50

MCFARLAND, GARY

Vibraphone player, percussionist, composer, bandleader and arranger. Also see ORCHESTRA USA.

Albums

Number	Title	Yr	NM
ABC IMPULSE!			
❏ AS-46 [S]	Points of Departure	1968	$35
❏ AS-9112 [S]	Profiles	1968	$35
❏ AS-9122 [S]	Simpatico	1968	$35
❏ AS-9104 [S]	Tijuana Jazz	1968	$35
BUDDAH			
❏ BDS95001	Butterscotch Rum	1967	$50
COBBLESTONE			
❏ CST9019	Requiem for Gary McFarland	1972	$50
IMPULSE!			
❏ A-46 [M]	Point of Departure	1963	$200
❏ AS-46 [S]	Points of Departure	1963	$160
❏ A-9112 [M]	Profiles	1966	$200
❏ AS-9112 [S]	Profiles	1966	$160
❏ A-9122 [M]	Simpatico	1966	$200
❏ AS-9122 [S]	Simpatico	1966	$160
❏ A-9104 [M]	Tijuana Jazz	1966	$200
❏ AS-9104 [S]	Tijuana Jazz	1966	$200
SKYE			
❏ SK-8	America the Beautiful	1969	$50
❏ SK-2	Does the Sun Really Shine on the Moon?	1968	$50
❏ SK-11	Slaves	1970	$60
❏ SK-14	Today	1970	$60
VERVE			
❏ V/V6-8674	Gary McFarland	1965	$0
—*Canceled*			
❏ V-8443 [M]	How to Succeed in Business Without Really Trying	1962	$50
❏ V6-8443 [S]	How to Succeed in Business Without Really Trying	1962	$60
❏ V-8738 [M]	Scorpio and Other Signs	1967	$100
❏ V6-8738 [S]	Scorpio and Other Signs	1967	$40
❏ V-8603 [M]	Soft Samba	1964	$60
❏ V6-8603 [S]	Soft Samba	1964	$60
❏ V-8682 [M]	Soft Samba Strings	1966	$60
❏ V6-8682 [S]	Soft Samba Strings	1966	$60
❏ V-8786	Sympathetic Vibrations	1969	$60
❏ V-8632 [M]	The "In" Sound	1965	$40
❏ V6-8632 [S]	The "In" Sound	1965	$100
❏ V-8518 [M]	The Gary McFarland Orchestra with Special Guest Soloist Bill Evans	1963	$60
❏ V6-8518 [S]	The Gary McFarland Orchestra with Special Guest Soloist Bill Evans	1963	$60

MCFERRIN, BOBBY

Male singer. Best known for the 1988 hit "Don't Worry Be Happy."

Albums

Number	Title	Yr	NM
BLUE NOTE			
❏ BT-85110	Spontaneous Inventions	1986	$15
ELEKTRA/MUSICIAN			
❏ E1-60023	Bobby McFerrin	1982	$12
❏ 60366	The Voice	1985	$12
EMI MANHATTAN			
❏ E1-48059	Simple Pleasures	1988	$10
❏ E1-548059	Simple Pleasures	1988	$12
—*Columbia House edition*			

MCGARITY, LOU

Trombonist and male singer.

Albums

Number	Title	Yr	NM
ARGO			
❏ LP-654 [M]	Blue Lou	1960	$30
❏ LPS-654 [S]	Blue Lou	1960	$40
JUBILEE			
❏ JGM-1108 [M]	Some Like It Hot	1959	$50

MCGHEE, HOWARD

Trumpeter and composer. Also see DEXTER GORDON; COLEMAN HAWKINS.

Albums

Number	Title	Yr	NM
ARGO			
❏ LP-4020 [M]	House Warmin'	1963	$30
❏ LPS-4020 [S]	House Warmin'	1963	$30
BETHLEHEM			
❏ BCP-6055 [M]	Dusty Blue	1961	$250
❏ BCPS-6055 [S]	Dusty Blue	1961	$250
❏ BCP-61 [M]	Life Is Just a Bowl of Cherries	1957	$250
❏ BCP-6039	That Bop Thing	197?	$30
—*Reissue of 42, distributed by RCA Victor*			

Number	Title	Yr	NM
❏ BCP-42 [M]	The Return of Howard McGhee	1956	$650
BLACK LION			
❏ 305	Shades of Blue	197?	$30
BLUE NOTE			
❏ BLP-5024 [10]	Howard McGhee, Volume 2	1953	$300
❏ BLP-5012 [10]	Howard McGhee's All Stars/ Howard McGhee-Fats Navarro Sextet	1952	$300
CADET			
❏ LP-4020 [M]	House Warmin'	1966	$30
❏ LPS-4020 [S]	House Warmin'	1966	$35
CONTEMPORARY			
❏ M-3596 [M]	Maggie's Back in Town	1961	$200
❏ S-7596 [S]	Maggie's Back in Town	1961	$200
DIAL			
❏ LP-217 [10]	Night Music	1951	$300
HI-LO			
❏ HL-6001 [10]	Jazz Goes to the Battlefront, Vol. 1	1952	$250
❏ HL-6002 [10]	Jazz Goes to the Battlefront, Vol. 2	1952	$250
SAVOY			
❏ MG-12026 [M]	Howard McGhee and Milt Jackson	1955	$80
SAVOY JAZZ			
❏ SJL-2219	Maggie	197?	$35
STEEPLECHASE			
❏ SCS-1024	Just Be There	198?	$30
STORYVILLE			
❏ 4077	Jazzbrothers	198?	$30
❏ 4080	Young at Heart	198?	$30
UNITED ARTISTS			
❏ UAJ-14028 [M]	Nobody Knows You When You're Down and Out	1963	$30
❏ UAJS-15028 [S]	Nobody Knows You When You're Down and Out	1963	$40
ZIM			
❏ 2004	Cookin' Time	197?	$30
❏ 2006	Live at Emerson's	197?	$30

MCGLOHON, LOONIS

Pianist and composer.

Albums

Number	Title	Yr	NM
AUDIOPHILE			
❏ AP-166	Loonis in London	1982	$25

MCGOVERN, PATTY, AND THOMAS TALBERT

McGovern is a female singer. Also see THOMAS TALBERT.

Albums

Number	Title	Yr	NM
ATLANTIC			
❏ 1245 [M]	Wednesday's Child	1956	$300
—*Black label*			
❏ 1245 [M]	Wednesday's Child	1961	$150
—*Multicolor label, white "fan" logo at right*			

MCGREGOR, CHRIS, BROTHERHOOD OF BREATH

McGregor is a pianist, composer and bandleader.

Albums

Number	Title	Yr	NM
VENTURE			
❏ 90988	Country Cooking	1988	$25

MCGRIFF, JIMMY, AND JUNIOR PARKER

Albums

Number	Title	Yr	NM
CAPITOL			
❏ ST-569	Dudes Doin' Business	1971	$35

MCGRIFF, JIMMY

Organist.

Albums

Number	Title	Yr	NM
BLUE NOTE			
❏ BST-84374	Black Pearl	1971	$35
❏ BST-84350	Electric Funk	1970	$35
❏ BST-84364	Something to Listen To	1971	$35
CAPITOL			
❏ ST-616	Soul Sugar	1970	$50
COLLECTABLES			
❏ COL-5147	Blues for Mr. Jimmy	198?	$25
GROOVE MERCHANT			

Number	Title	Yr	NM
❏ 2203	Black and Blues	1971	$35
❏ 520	Come Together	1973	$30
❏ 509	Fly Dude	1973	$35
❏ 3300	Giants of the Organ In Concert	1974	$35
❏ 2205	Good Things Don't Happen Every Day	1971	$35
❏ 503	Groove Grease	1972	$35
❏ 529	If You're Ready Come Go with Me	1974	$30
❏ 506	Let's Stay Together	1972	$35
❏ 534	Main Squeeze	1975	$30
❏ 3311	Mean Machine	1976	$30
❏ 3309	Stump Juice	1976	$30
JAM			
❏ 02	City Lights	1982	$30
❏ 05	Movin' Upside the Blues	1983	$30
LRC			
❏ 9320	Outside Looking In	1978	$35
❏ 9316	Tailgunner	1977	$35
MILESTONE			
❏ M-9163	Blue to the 'Bone	1988	$25
❏ M-9116	Countdown	1984	$25
❏ M-9126	Skywalk	1985	$25
❏ M-9135	State of the Art	1986	$25
❏ M-9148	The Starting Five	1987	$25
QUINTESSENCE			
❏ 25061	Soul	1978	$30
SOLID STATE			
❏ SS-18017	A Bag Full of Blues	1968	$50
❏ SM-17002 [M]	A Bag Full of Soul	1966	$35
❏ SS-18002 [S]	A Bag Full of Soul	1966	$50
❏ SS-18060	A Thing to Come By	1969	$50
❏ SM-17006 [M]	Cherry	1967	$50
❏ SS-18006 [S]	Cherry	1967	$50
❏ SS-18036	Honey	1968	$50
❏ SS-18030	I've Got a New Woman	1968	$50
❏ SS-18053	Step I	1969	$50
❏ SM-17001 [M]	The Big Band of Jimmy McGriff	1966	$35
❏ SS-18001 [S]	The Big Band of Jimmy McGriff	1966	$50
❏ SS-18063	The Way You Look Tonight	1970	$50
❏ SS-18045	The Worm	1968	$50
SUE			
❏ LP-1039 [M]	Blues for Mister Jimmy	1965	$60
❏ STLP-1039 [S]	Blues for Mister Jimmy	1965	$40
❏ LP-1018 [M]	Christmas with McGriff	1963	$60
❏ STLP-1018 [S]	Christmas with McGriff	1963	$40
❏ LP-1012 [M]	I've Got a Woman	1962	$60
❏ STLP-1012 [S]	I've Got a Woman	1962	$40
❏ LP-1017 [M]	Jimmy McGriff at the Apollo	1963	$60
❏ STLP-1017 [S]	Jimmy McGriff at the Apollo	1963	$40
❏ LP-1020 [M]	Jimmy McGriff at the Organ	1963	$60
❏ STLP-1020 [S]	Jimmy McGriff at the Organ	1963	$40
❏ LP-1013 [M]	One of Mine	1963	$60
❏ STLP-1013 [S]	One of Mine	1963	$40
❏ LP-1043 [M]	Toast to Greatest Hits	1966	$50
❏ STLP-1043 [S]	Toast to Greatest Hits	1966	$60
❏ LP-1033 [M]	Topkapi	1964	$60
SUNSET			
❏ SUS-5264	The Great Jimmy McGriff	1969	$25
VEEP			
❏ VP-13522 [M]	Greatest Organ Hits	1967	$60
❏ VPS-16522 [S]	Greatest Organ Hits	1967	$50
❏ VP-13515 [M]	Live Where the Action Is	1966	$50

MCHARGUE, ROSY

Clarinetist, saxophone player, male singer and composer.

Albums

Number	Title	Yr	NM
JUMP			
❏ JL-8 [10]	Dixie Combo	1955	$60

MCINTOSH, LADD

Bandleader and composer.

Albums

Number	Title	Yr	NM
SEA BREEZE			
❏ 2007	Energy	198?	$25

MCINTYRE, HAL

Alto saxophone player and bandleader.

Albums

Number	Title	Yr	NM
COLUMBIA			
❏ CL6124 [10]	Dance Date	1950	$50
FORUM			
❏ F-9018 [M]	It Seems Like Only Yesterday	196?	$30
❏ SF-9018 [S]	It Seems Like Only Yesterday	196?	$35
HINDSIGHT			
❏ HSR-172	Hal McIntyre and His Orchestra 1943-45	198?	$25

Helen Merrill, *Helen Merrill with Strings*, EmArcy MG-36057, blue label with drummer logo, **$80**.

Helen Merrill, *The Nearness of You*, EmArcy MG 36134, **$350**.

Pat Metheny, *Letter from Home*, Geffen GHS 24245, **$35**.

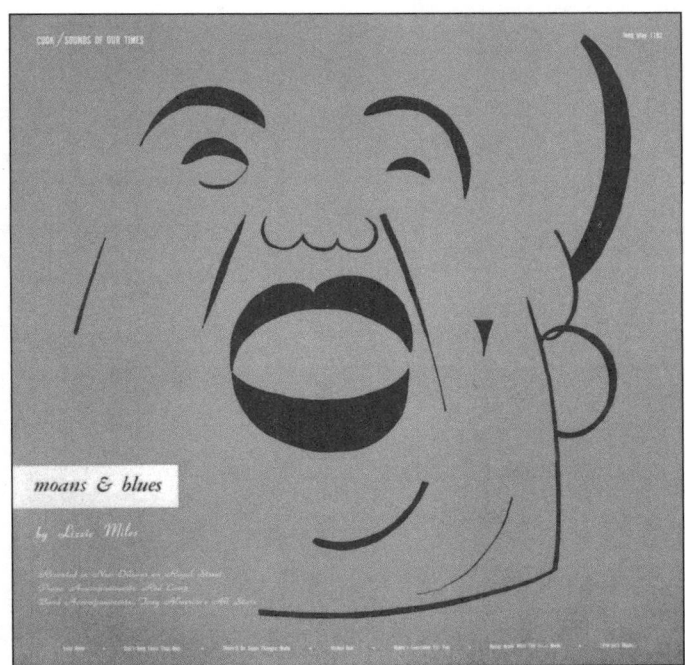

Lizzie Miles, *Moans and Blues*, Cook 1182, **$60**.

Number	Title	Yr	NM

ROULETTE

❏ R-25079 [M]	It Seems Like Only Yesterday	1959	$25
❏ SR-25079 [S]	It Seems Like Only Yesterday	1959	$30

MCINTYRE, KALAPARUSHA MAURICE
Tenor saxophone player, clarinetist, flutist and percussionist.

Albums

BLACK SAINT
❏ BSR-0037	Peace and Blessings	198?	$30

DELMARK
❏ DS-425	Forces and Feelings	197?	$25
❏ DS-419	Humility	1969	$25

MCINTYRE, KEN
Alto saxophone player, bass clarinetist, oboist, bassoonist, flutist.

Albums

FANTASY
❏ OJC-252	Looking Ahead	1987	$30

INNER CITY
❏ IC-2014	Hindsight	1976	$40
❏ IC-2039	Home	197?	$60
❏ IC-2065	Introducing the Vibrations	1977	$60
❏ IC-2049	Open Horizon	1976	$50

NEW JAZZ
❏ NJLP-8247 [M]	Looking Ahead	1965	$150
—Blue label, trident logo at right			
❏ NJLP-8259 [M]	Stone Blues	1961	$150
—Purple label			
❏ NJLP-8259 [M]	Stone Blues	1965	$150
—Blue label, trident logo at right			

STEEPLECHASE
❏ SCS-1114	Chasing the Sun	198?	$35
❏ SCS-1014	Hindsight	198?	$50
❏ SCS-1039	Home	198?	$35
❏ SCS-1065	Introducing the Vibrations	198?	$35
❏ SCS-1049	Open Horizon	198?	$35

UNITED ARTISTS
❏ UAJ-14015 [M]	Year of the Iron Sheep	1962	$100
❏ UAJS-15015 [S]	Year of the Iron Sheep	1962	$120

MCKAY, STUART

Albums

RCA VICTOR
❏ LJM-1021 [M]	Stuart McKay and His Woods	1955	$50

MCKENNA, DAVE, AND HALL OVERTON
Overton is an arrangers and composer. Also see DAVE McKENNA.

Albums

BETHLEHEM
❏ BCP-6049 [M]	Dual Piano Jazz	1960	$300
❏ BCPS-6049 [S]	Dual Piano Jazz	1960	$300

MCKENNA, DAVE; SCOTT HAMILTON; JAKE HANNA
Also see each artist's individual listings.

Albums

CONCORD JAZZ
❏ CJ-97	No Bass Hit	1979	$30

MCKENNA, DAVE
Pianist. Also see THE MANHATTAN JAZZ ALL-STARS.

Albums

ABC-PARAMOUNT
❏ ABC-104 [M]	Solo Piano	1956	$40

CHIAROSCURO
❏ 175	Dave "Fingers" McKenna	197?	$30
❏ 136	Dave McKenna Quartet Featuring Zoot Sims	197?	$35
❏ 202	McKenna	1978	$30
❏ 119	Piano Solos	197?	$35

CONCORD JAZZ
❏ CJ-227	Celebration of Hoagy Carmichael	1984	$25
❏ CJ-292	Dancing in the Dark	1986	$25
❏ CJ-174	Dave McKenna Plays Music of Harry Warren	198?	$25
❏ CJ-99	Giant Strides	1979	$30
❏ CJ-123	Left Handed Complement	1980	$30

❏ CJ-313	My Friend the Piano	1987	$25
❏ CJ-365	No More Ouzo for Puzo	1989	$30
❏ CJ-261	The Key Man	1985	$25

EPIC
❏ LN3558 [M]	Dave McKenna	1959	$60
❏ BN527 [S]	Dave McKenna	1959	$60

FAMOUS DOOR
❏ 122	No Holds Barred	1978	$30

HALCYON
❏ 108	Cookin' at Michael's Pub	197?	$35

SHIAH
❏ MK-1	By Myself	198?	$30

MCKENZIE, RED, AND EDDIE CONDON
McKenzie was a male singer, comb and kazoo player, and bandleader. Also see EDDIE CONDON.

Albums

JAZZOLOGY
❏ J-110	Chicagoans (1944)	198?	$25

MCKINLEY, RAY, AND EDDIE SAUTER
Eddie Sauter was half of SAUTER-FINEGAN. Also see RAY McKINLEY.

Albums

SAVOY
❏ MG-12024 [M]	Borderline	1955	$60

MCKINLEY, RAY
Drummer, male singer and bandleader. Also see PEANUTS HUCKO; GLENN MILLER ORCHESTRA.

Albums

ALLEGRO ELITE
❏ 4129 [10]	Ray McKinley and His Famous Orchestra	195?	$100
❏ 4015 [10]	Ray McKinley Plays Sauter and Others	195?	$50

SAVOY JAZZ
❏ SJK-2261	The Most Versatile Band in the World	198?	$30

MCKINLEY, RAY/JOE MARSALA
Also see each artist's individual listings.

Albums

DECCA
❏ DL5262 [10]	Dixieland Jazz Battle, Vol. 2	1950	$150

MCKINLEY, TOM, AND ED SCHULLER
McKinley is a pianst; Schuller is a bass player.

Albums

GM
❏ 3001	Life Cycle	1982	$25

MCKINNEY, HAROLD
Pianist.

Albums

TRIBE
❏ 2233	Voices and Rhythms	197?	$40

MCKINNEY'S COTTON PICKERS
Led by drummer Bill McKinney, they were an important early big band.

Albums

RCA VICTOR
❏ LPT-24 [10]	McKinney's Cotton Pickers	1952	$60

X
❏ LVA-3031 [10]	McKinney's Cotton Pickers	1954	$50

MCKUSICK, HAL
Alto saxophone player, clarinetist, bass clarinetist and flutist. Also see THE MANHATTAN JAZZ SEPTETTE; THE NUTTY SQUIRRELS; BETTY ST. CLAIRE; PHIL WOODS.

Albums

BETHLEHEM
❏ BCP-16 [M]	East Coast Jazz/8	1955	$250

CORAL
❏ CRL57116 [M]	Jazz at the Academy	1957	$80

MCA

❏ 1379	Hal McKusick Quintet Featuring Art Farmer 1957	198?	$15

RCA VICTOR
❏ LPM-1164 [M]	Hal McKusick in the 20th Century Drawing Room	1956	$80
❏ LPM-1366 [M]	The Jazz Workshop	1957	$120

MCLAUGHLIN, JOHN
Guitarist. Also see MAHAVISHNU ORCHESTRA; CARLOS SANTANA.

Albums

CBS
❏ FM45578	Mediterranean Concerto	1989	$35

CELLULOID
❏ CEL-5010	Devotion	198?	$25
—Reissue of Douglas 31568			

COLUMBIA
❏ PC34372	A Handful of Beauty	1977	$30
—No bar code on cover			
❏ JC35785	Electric Dreams	1979	$25
❏ JC35326	Electric Guitarist	1978	$30
—No bar code on cover			
❏ FC37152	Friday Night in San Francisco	1981	$25
—With Al DiMeola and Paco De Lucia			
❏ JC34980	Natural Elements	1977	$30
—No bar code on cover			
❏ FC38645	Passion, Grace & Fire	1983	$25
—With Al DiMeola and Paco De Lucia			
❏ PC34162	Shakti with John McLaughlin	1976	$30
—No bar code on cover			
❏ JC36355	The Best of John McLaughlin	1980	$30
❏ PC36355	The Best of John McLaughlin	198?	$20
—Reissue with new prefix			

DOUGLAS
❏ KZ31568	Devotion	1972	$35
—Reissue of 4			
❏ 4	Devotion	1970	$50
❏ KZ30766	My Goals Beyond	1971	$35
—Original issue			

DOUGLAS CASABLANCA
❏ ADLP-6003	My Goals Beyond	1976	$30
—Reissue of Douglas 30766; second issue of this album			

ELEKTRA/MUSICIAN
❏ E1-60031	My Goals Beyond	1982	$30
—Third issue of this album			

POLYDOR
❏ PD-5510	Extrapolation	1972	$50
❏ PD-1-6074	Extrapolation	1972	$30
—Reissue of 5510			

PYE
❏ 12103	Where Fortune Smiles	1975	$50
—Recorded in 1970; this was the first U.S. issue of this material			

RELATIVITY
❏ 88561-8061-1	Adventures in Radioland	1986	$30

RYKO ANALOGUE
❏ RALP-0051	My Goals Beyond	1987	$50
—Clear vinyl; fourth issue of this album			

WARNER BROS.
❏ BSK3619	Belo Horizonte	1981	$35
❏ 25190	Mahavishnu	1985	$25
❏ 23723	Music Spoken Here	1982	$25

MCLEAN, JACKIE, AND MICHAEL CARVIN
Also see each artist's individual listings.

Albums

INNER CITY
❏ IC-2028	Antiquity	197?	$35

STEEPLECHASE
❏ SCS-1028	Antiquity	198?	$30

MCLEAN, JACKIE
Alto saxophone player. Also see PHIL WOODS.

Albums

BLUE NOTE
❏ BLP-4218 [M]	Action Action Action	1965	$120
—With "New York, USA" address on label			

Number	Title	Yr	NM
❑ BST-84218 [S]	Action Action Action	1965	$100
— With "New York, USA" address on label			
❑ BST-84218 [S]	Action Action Action	1967	$30
— With "A Division of Liberty Records" on label			
❑ BLP-4089 [M]	A Fickle Sonance	1961	$800
— With W. 63rd St. address on label			
❑ BLP-4089 [M]	A Fickle Sonance	1963	$250
— With "New York, USA" address on label			
❑ BST-84089 [S]	A Fickle Sonance	1961	$350
— With W. 63rd St. address on label			
❑ BST-84089 [S]	A Fickle Sonance	1963	$300
— With "New York, USA" address on label			
❑ BST-84089 [S]	A Fickle Sonance	1967	$150
— With "A Division of Liberty Records" on label			
❑ BLP-4067 [M]	Bluesnik	1961	$400
— With W. 63rd St. address on label			
❑ BLP-4067 [M]	Bluesnik	1963	$80
— With "New York, USA" address on label			
❑ BST-84067 [S]	Bluesnik	1961	$200
— With W. 63rd St. address on label			
❑ BST-84067 [S]	Bluesnik	1963	$60
— With "New York, USA" address on label			
❑ BST-84067 [S]	Bluesnik	1967	$60
— With "A Division of Liberty Records" on label			
❑ B1-84067 [S]	Bluesnik	1989	$30
— The Finest in Jazz Since 1939" reissue			
❑ BST-84284	'Bout Soul	1968	$80
— With "A Division of Liberty Records" on label			
❑ BLP-4038 [M]	Capuchin Swing	1963	$80
— With "New York, USA" address on label			
❑ BST-84038 [S]	Capuchin Swing	1960	$250
— With W. 63rd St. address on label			
❑ BST-84038 [S]	Capuchin Swing	1963	$60
— With "New York, USA" address on label			

Number	Title	Yr	NM
❑ BST-84038 [S]	Capuchin Swing	1967	$60
— With "A Division of Liberty Records" on label			
❑ LT-994	Consequences	1979	$25
❑ BST-84345	Demon's Dance	1969	$80
— With "A Division of Liberty Records" on label			
❑ BST-84345	Demon's Dance	198?	$25
— The Finest in Jazz Since 1939" reissu			
❑ BLP-4165 [M]	Destination... Out!	1964	$120
— With "New York, USA" address on label			
❑ BST-84165 [S]	Destination... Out!	197?	$20
— Dark blue label with white stylized "B			
❑ BST-84165 [S]	Destination... Out!	1964	$100
— With "New York, USA" address on label			
❑ BST-84165 [S]	Destination... Out!	1967	$40
— With "A Division of Liberty Records" on label			
❑ BN-LA483-4047	Hipnosis	1975	$60
❑ BLP-4179 [M]	It's Time!	1964	$100
— With "New York, USA" address on label			
❑ BST-84179 [S]	It's Time!	1964	$100
— With "New York, USA" address on label			
❑ BST-84179 [S]	It's Time!	1967	$30
— With "A Division of Liberty Records" on label			
❑ BLP-4116 [M]	Jackie McLean Quintet	1962	$0
— Canceled			
❑ BST-84116 [S]	Jackie McLean Quintet	1962	$0
— Canceled			
❑ BST-84051 [S]	Jackie's Bag	1960	$250

Number	Title	Yr	NM
— With W. 63rd St. address on label			
❑ BST-84051 [S]	Jackie's Bag	1963	$60
— With "New York, USA" address on label			
❑ BST-84051 [S]	Jackie's Bag	1967	$60
— With "A Division of Liberty Records" on label			
❑ BST-84051 [S]	Jackie's Bag	1985	$30
— The Finest in Jazz Since 1939" reissue			
❑ BLP-4223 [M]	Jackknife	1965	$0
— Canceled			
❑ BST-84223 [S]	Jackknife	1965	$0
— Canceled			
❑ BN-LA457-H2	Jackknife	1975	$60
— First issue of unreleased material from 1960s			
❑ BLP-4106 [M]	Let Freedom Ring	1962	$300
— With "New York, USA" address on label			
❑ BST-84106 [S]	Let Freedom Ring	1962	$200
— With "New York, USA" address on label			
❑ BST-84106 [S]	Let Freedom Ring	1967	$40
— With "A Division of Liberty Records" on label			
❑ BST-84106 [S]	Let Freedom Ring	198?	$30
— The Finest in Jazz Since 1939" reissue			
❑ BLP-4262 [M]	New and Old Gospel	1967	$250
— With "A Division of Liberty Records" on label			
❑ BST-84262 [S]	New and Old Gospel	1967	$120
— With "A Division of Liberty Records" on label			
❑ BLP-4236 [M]	New Frequency	1966	$0
— Canceled			
❑ BST-84236 [S]	New Frequency	1966	$0
— Canceled			
❑ BLP-4013 [M]	New Soil	1959	$500
— Deep groove" version; W. 63rd St. address on label			
❑ BLP-4013 [M]	New Soil	1959	$300
— Regular version, W. 63rd St. address on label			
❑ BLP-4013 [M]	New Soil	1963	$100
— With "New York, USA" address on label			
❑ BST-4013 [S]	New Soil	1959	$300
— Deep groove" version; W. 63rd St. address on label			
❑ BST-4013 [S]	New Soil	1959	$200
— Regular version, W. 63rd St. address on label			
❑ BST-4013 [S]	New Soil	1963	$40
— With "New York, USA" address on label			
❑ BST-84013 [S]	New Soil	1967	$60
— With "A Division of Liberty Records" on label			
❑ B1-84013 [S]	New Soil	1989	$30
— The Finest in Jazz Since 1939" reissue			
❑ BLP-4137 [M]	One Step Beyond	1963	$120
— With "New York, USA" address on label			
❑ BST-84137 [S]	One Step Beyond	1963	$100
— With "New York, USA" address on label			
❑ BST-84137 [S]	One Step Beyond	1967	$40
— With "A Division of Liberty Records" on label			
❑ BST-84137 [S]	One Step Beyond	198?	$30
— The Finest in Jazz Since 1939" reissue			
❑ BST-84137 [S]	One Step Beyond	197?	$20
— Dark blue label with black stylized "B			
❑ BLP-4215 [M]	Right Now!	1965	$150
— With "New York, USA" address on label			
❑ BST-84215 [S]	Right Now!	1965	$100
— With "New York, USA" address on label			
❑ BST-84215 [S]	Right Now!	1967	$30
— With "A Division of Liberty Records" on label			
❑ BLP-4024 [M]	Swing, Swang, Swingin'	1959	$1200
— Deep groove" version; W. 63rd St. address on label			
❑ BLP-4024 [M]	Swing, Swang, Swingin'	1959	$500
— Regular version, W. 63rd St. address on label			
❑ BLP-4024 [M]	Swing, Swang, Swingin'	1963	$100
— With "New York, USA" address on label			
❑ BST-84024 [S]	Swing, Swang, Swingin'	1959	$400
— With W. 63rd St. address on label			
❑ BST-84024 [S]	Swing, Swang, Swingin'	1963	$80
— With "New York, USA" address on label			
❑ BST-84024 [S]	Swing, Swang, Swingin'	1967	$60
— With "A Division of Liberty Records" on label			
❑ BST-84427	Tippin' the Scales	198?	$35
❑ LT-1085	Vertigo	1980	$25

BOPLICITY
Number	Title	Yr	NM
❑ BOP-2	Swing, Swang, Swingin'	198?	$25

FANTASY
Number	Title	Yr	NM
❑ OJC-056	4, 5 and 6	198?	$30
❑ OJC-253	A Long Drink of the Blues	1987	$30
❑ OJC-074	Jackie McLean & Co.	198?	$30

Number	Title	Yr	NM
❑ OJC-1717	Jackie's Pal -- Introducing Bill Hardman	198?	$30
❑ OJC-426	Lights Out!	1990	$35
❑ OJC-197	Makin' the Changes	1985	$30
❑ OJC-098	McLean's Scene	198?	$30
❑ OJC-354	Strange Blues	198?	$30

INNER CITY
Number	Title	Yr	NM
❑ IC-2013	Ghetto Lullaby	197?	$35
❑ IC-2001	Live at Montmartre	197?	$35
❑ IC-6029	New Wine	1978	$35
❑ IC-2023	New York Calling	197?	$35
❑ IC-2009	Ode to Super	197?	$35

JOSIE
Number	Title	Yr	NM
❑ JJM-3503 [M]	Jackie McLean Sextet	1963	$60
❑ JJM-3507 [M]	Jackie McLean Sextet	1963	$60
❑ JLPS-3503 [S]	Jackie McLean Sextet	1963	$40
❑ JLPS-3507 [S]	Jackie McLean Sextet	1963	$40

JUBILEE
Number	Title	Yr	NM
❑ JLP-1093 [M]	Jackie McLean Plays Fat Jazz	1959	$200
❑ JLP-1064 [M]	The Jackie McLean Quintet	1958	$150

MOSAIC
Number	Title	Yr	NM
❑ MQ6-150	The Complete Blue Note 1964-66 Jackie McLean Sessions	1993	$200
— Limited edition of 5,000			

NEW JAZZ
Number	Title	Yr	NM
❑ NJLP-8279 [M]	4, 5 and 6	1962	$200
— Purple label			
❑ NJLP-8279 [M]	4, 5 and 6	1965	$150
— Blue label, trident logo at right			
❑ NJLP-8253 [M]	A Long Drink of the Blues	1961	$500
— Purple label			
❑ NJLP-8253 [M]	A Long Drink of the Blues	1965	$150
— Blue label, trident logo at right			
❑ NJLP-8312 [M]	Alto Madness	1963	$0
— Canceled; reassigned to Status			
❑ NJLP-8323 [M]	Jackie McLean & Co.	1963	$0
— Canceled; reassigned to Status			
❑ NJLP-8263 [M]	Lights Out!	1961	$200
— Purple label			
❑ NJLP-8263 [M]	Lights Out!	1965	$150
— Blue label, trident logo at right			
❑ NJLP-8231 [M]	Makin' the Changes	1960	$600
— Purple label			
❑ NJLP-8231 [M]	Makin' the Changes	1965	$150
— Blue label, trident logo at right			
❑ NJLP-8212 [M]	McLean's Scene	1958	$400
— Purple label			
❑ NJLP-8212 [M]	McLean's Scene	1965	$150
— Blue label, trident logo at right			
❑ NJLP-8290 [M]	Steeplechase	1962	$200
— Purple label			
❑ NJLP-8290 [M]	Steeplechase	1965	$150
— Blue label, trident logo at right			

PRESTIGE
Number	Title	Yr	NM
❑ PRLP-7048 [M]	4, 5 and 6	1956	$1500
— 446 W. 50th St., N.Y.C." address on yellow label			
❑ PRLP-7114 [M]	Alto Madness	1957	$1000
— Yellow label			
❑ MPP-2512	Alto Madness	198?	$30
❑ P-24076	Contour	1977	$50
❑ PRLP-7068 [M]	Jackie's Pal -- Introducing Bill Hardman	1956	$2000
— 446 W. 50th St., N.Y.C." address on yellow label			
❑ PRLP-7035 [M]	Lights Out!	1956	$1000
— 446 W. 50th St., N.Y.C." address on yellow label			
❑ PRST-7757	Lights Out!	1970	$60
❑ PRLP-7500 [M]	Strange Blues	1967	$40
❑ PRST-7500 [R]	Strange Blues	1967	$60

RCA VICTOR
Number	Title	Yr	NM
❑ AFL1-3230 [S]	Monuments	1979	$30

ROULETTE
Number	Title	Yr	NM
❑ RE-129	Echoes of an Era (Tune-Up)	1976	$35

STATUS
Number	Title	Yr	NM
❑ ST-8312 [M]	Alto Madness	1965	$60
❑ ST-8323 [M]	Jackie McLean & Co.	1965	$60

STEEPLECHASE
Number	Title	Yr	NM
❑ SCS-1013	A Ghetto Lullaby	198?	$30
❑ SCC-6005	Dr. Jackie	198?	$30
❑ SCS-1001	Live at Montmartre	198?	$30
❑ SCS-1023	New York Calling	198?	$30
❑ SCS-1009	Ode to Super	198?	$30
❑ SCS-1006	The Meeting	198?	$30
❑ SCS-1020	The Source	198?	$30

TRIP
Number	Title	Yr	NM
❑ TLX-5027	Two Sides of Jackie McLean	197?	$50

MCLEAN, RENE
Tenor and soprano saxophone player.

Albums

Number	Title	Yr	NM
INNER CITY			
❏ IC-2037	Watch Out	197?	$35
STEEPLECHASE			
❏ SCS-1037	Watch Out!	198?	$30

MCMANUS, JILL

Albums

Number	Title	Yr	NM
CONCORD JAZZ			
❏ CJ-242	Symbols of Hopi	1984	$25

MCNABB, TED
Bandleader.

Albums

Number	Title	Yr	NM
EPIC			
❏ LN3663 [M]	Ted McNabb and Company	1959	$100
❏ BN558 [S]	Ted McNabb and Company	1959	$80

MCNEELY, JIM
Pianist, keyboard player, bandleader and composer.

Albums

Number	Title	Yr	NM
GATEMOUTH			
❏ 1001	The Plot Thickens	1980	$30
MUSE			
❏ MR-5378	The Plot Thickens	198?	$25
STEEPLECHASE			
❏ SCS-4001	Rain's Dance	198?	$30

MCNEIL, JOHN
Trumpeter.

Albums

Number	Title	Yr	NM
STEEPLECHASE			
❏ SCS-1154	Clean Sweep	198?	$30
❏ SCS-1099	Embarkation	1978	$30
❏ SCS-1117	Faun	198?	$30
❏ SCS-1183	I've Got the World on a String	198?	$30
❏ SCS-1128	Look to the Sky	198?	$30
❏ SCS-1133	The Glass Room	1979	$30

MCNEILL, LLOYD
Flutist.

Albums

Number	Title	Yr	NM
ASHA			
❏ 3	Washington Suite	1976	$35

MCPARTLAND, JIMMY
Cornet player and trumpeter. Also see DIZZY GILLESPIE.

Albums

Number	Title	Yr	NM
BRUNSWICK			
❏ BL54018 [M]	Dixieland Band	1955	$60
❏ BL58049 [10]	Shades of Bix	1953	$80
EPIC			
❏ LN3371 [M]	Jimmy McPartland's Dixieland	1956	$80
❏ LN3463 [M]	The Music Man" Goes Dixieland, The	1958	$80
❏ BN506 [S]	The Music Man" Goes Dixieland, The	1958	$60
HARMONY			
❏ HS11264	Dixieland	1968	$30
JAZZOLOGY			
❏ J-16 [M]	Jimmy McPartland On Stage	196?	$35
❏ J-137	One Night Stand	1986	$25
JAZZTONE			
❏ J-1227 [M]	The Middle Road	1956	$40
MCA			
❏ 4110	Shades of Bix	197?	$30
MERCURY			
❏ MG-20460 [M]	Meet Me in Chicago	1959	$100
❏ SR-60143 [S]	Meet Me in Chicago	1959	$100
PALACE			
❏ M-708 [M]	Dixieland Vol. 1	196?	$35
RCA CAMDEN			
❏ CAL-549 [M]	That Happy Dixieland Jazz	1960	$30
RCA VICTOR			
❏ LPV-549 [M]	That Happy Dixieland Jazz	1966	$25

MCPARTLAND, JIMMY/PAUL BARBARIN
Also see each artist's individual listings.

Albums

Number	Title	Yr	NM
JAZZTONE			
❏ J-1241 [M]	Dixieland Now and Then	195?	$30

MCPARTLAND, MARIAN, AND GEORGE SHEARING
Also see each artist's individual listings.

Albums

Number	Title	Yr	NM
SAVOY			
❏ MG-12016 [M]	Great Britain's Marion McPartland and George Shearing	1955	$50

MCPARTLAND, MARIAN
Pianist.

Albums

Number	Title	Yr	NM
ARGO			
❏ LP-640 [M]	Marion McPartland at the London House	1959	$40
❏ LPS-640 [S]	Marion McPartland at the London House	1959	$30
BAINBRIDGE			
❏ 1045	Marian McPartland with Ben Tucker	198?	$25
CAPITOL			
❏ T699 [M]	After Dark	1956	$60
❏ T574 [M]	Marion McPartland at the Hickory House	1955	$75
❏ T785 [M]	Marion McPartland Trio	1957	$75
CONCORD JAZZ			
❏ CJ-86	From This Moment On	1979	$25
❏ CJ-118	Marian McPartland at the Festival	1981	$25
❏ CJ-326	Marian McPartland Plays the Music of Billy Strayhorn	1987	$25
❏ CJ-202	Personal Choice	1982	$25
❏ CJ-101	Portrait of Marian McPartland	1980	$25
❏ CJ-272	Willow Creek and Other Ballads	1985	$25
DOT			
❏ DLP-25907	My Old Flame	1969	$75
HALCYON			
❏ 103	Ambience	1971	$35
❏ 105	Delicate Balance	1972	$35
❏ 100	Interplay	1970	$35
❏ 117	Live at the Carlyle	1979	$30
❏ 109	Marian McPartland Plays Alec Wilder	197?	$35
❏ 115	Now's the Time	1978	$30
❏ 111	Solo Concert at Haverford	197?	$30
IMPROV			
❏ 7115	A Fine Romance	1976	$30
SAVOY			
❏ MG-15019 [10]	Jazz at Storyville, Volume 3	1952	$80
❏ MG-15032 [10]	Jazz at the Hickory House	1953	$80
❏ MG-12005 [M]	Lullaby of Birdland	1955	$60
❏ MG-15027 [10]	Marion McPartland	1953	$80
❏ MG-12004 [M]	Marion McPartland in Concert	1955	$60
❏ MG-15021 [10]	Piano Moods	1952	$80
SAVOY JAZZ			
❏ SJL-2248	Marian McPartland at the Hickory House	198?	$35
TIME			
❏ 52073 [M]	Bossa Nova Plus Soul	1963	$30
❏ S-2073 [S]	Bossa Nova Plus Soul	1963	$30
❏ 52189 [M]	West Side Story	196?	$30
❏ S-2189 [S]	West Side Story	196?	$30

MCPARTLAND, MARIAN AND JIMMY
Also see each artist's individual listings.

Albums

Number	Title	Yr	NM
HALCYON			
❏ 116	Goin' Back a Ways	198?	$30
❏ 107	Live at the Monticello	197?	$35
❏ 114	Swingin'	197?	$30
IMPROV			
❏ 7122	Wanted!	1977	$30

MCPHEE, JOE
Tenor saxophone player, trumpeter, valve trombonist, clarinetist, pianist and keyboard player.

Albums

Number	Title	Yr	NM
CJR			
❏ 2	Nation Time	197?	$30
❏ 4	Pieces of Light	197?	$30
❏ 3	Trinity	197?	$30
HAT ART			
❏ 2033	Po Music: A Future Retrospective	1987	$35
HAT HUT			
❏ 0A	Black Magic Man	1974	$30
❏ 0P	Glasses	1978	$25
❏ 0I/J	Graphics	1977	$30
❏ 01	Old Eyes	1979	$25
❏ 0D	Rotation	1977	$25
❏ 0C	Tenor	1976	$25
❏ 1987/8	Topology	1981	$30
❏ 0O	Variations on a Blue Line/Round Midnight	1978	$25

MCPHERSON, CHARLES
Alto saxophone player.

Albums

Number	Title	Yr	NM
MAINSTREAM			
❏ MRL-329	Charles McPherson	1972	$35
❏ MRL-365	Siku Ya Bibi	1973	$35
❏ MRL-395	Today's Man	1974	$35
PRESTIGE			
❏ PRLP-7359 [M]	Bebop Revisited	1965	$30
❏ PRST-7359 [S]	Bebop Revisited	1965	$40
❏ PRLP-7427 [M]	Con Alma!	1966	$30
❏ PRST-7427 [S]	Con Alma!	1966	$40
❏ PRST-7559	From This Moment On	1968	$30
❏ PRST-7603	Horizons	1969	$30
❏ PRST-7743	McPherson's Mood	1970	$25
❏ PRLP-7480 [M]	The Charles McPherson Quintet Live!	1967	$40
❏ PRST-7480 [S]	The Charles McPherson Quintet Live!	1967	$30
XANADU			
❏ 115	Beautiful	1976	$30
❏ 170	Free Bop	1979	$30
❏ 131	Live in Tokyo	1977	$30
❏ 149	New Horizons	1978	$30

MCRAE, CARMEN
Female singer and pianist.

Albums

Number	Title	Yr	NM
ACCORD			
❏ SN-7152	Love Songs	1981	$25
ATLANTIC			
❏ 8143 [M]	For Once in My Life	1967	$50
❏ SD8143 [S]	For Once in My Life	1967	$35
❏ SD1568	Just a Little Lovin'	1971	$30
❏ 8165 [M]	Portrait of Carmen	1968	$60
❏ SD8165 [S]	Portrait of Carmen	1968	$35
❏ SD 2-904	The Great American Songbook	1971	$50
❏ SD8200 [S]	The Sound of Silence	1968	$35
❏ 8200 [M]	The Sound of Silence	1968	$60

—Mono is white label promo only; "d/j copy monaural" sticker on front cover

Number	Title	Yr	NM
BAINBRIDGE			
❏ 6221	The Sound of Silence	198?	$25
BETHLEHEM			
❏ BCP-1023 [10]	Carmen McRae	1955	$250
BLUE NOTE			
❏ BN-LA635-G	Can't Hide Love	1976	$30
❏ BN-LA462-G	I Am Music	1975	$30
❏ BN-LA709-H2	The Great Music Hall	1977	$35
❏ LWB-709	The Great Music Hall	1981	$30

—Reissue of BN-LA709-H2

Number	Title	Yr	NM
BUDDAH			
❏ B2D-6501	I'm Coming Home Again	1980	$35
CATALYST			
❏ 7904	As Time Goes By	197?	$30
COLUMBIA			
❏ CL1730 [M]	Lover Man	1962	$50
❏ CS8530 [S]	Lover Man	1962	$60
❏ CL1943 [M]	Something Wonderful	1962	$50
❏ CS8743 [S]	Something Wonderful	1962	$60
CONCORD JAZZ			
❏ CJ-342	Fine and Mellow	1988	$25
❏ CJ-128	Two for the Road	1980	$25
❏ CJ-235	You're Looking at Me: A Collection of Nat King Cole Songs	1984	$25
DECCA			
❏ DL8583 [M]	After Glow	1957	$150

—Black label, silver print

Number	Title	Yr	NM
❏ DL8583 [M]	After Glow	1960	$50

—Black label with color bars

Lizzy Miles, *Hot Songs My Mother Taught Me*, Cook 1183, **$60**.

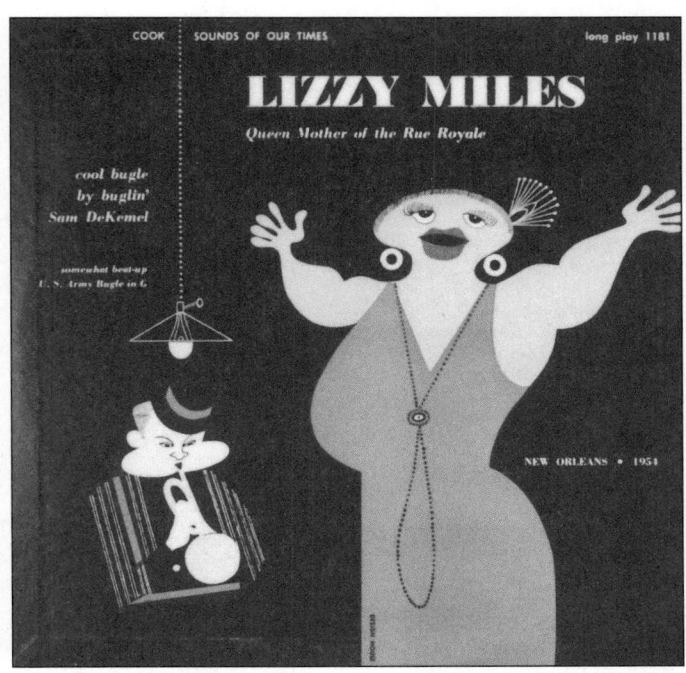

Lizzy Miles, *Queen Mother of the Rue Royale*, Cook 1181, 10-inch LP, **$80**.

Glenn Miller, *Selections from "The Glenn Miller Story" and Other Hits*, RCA Victor LSP-1192 (e), rechanneled stereo, black label, dog on top, **$35**.

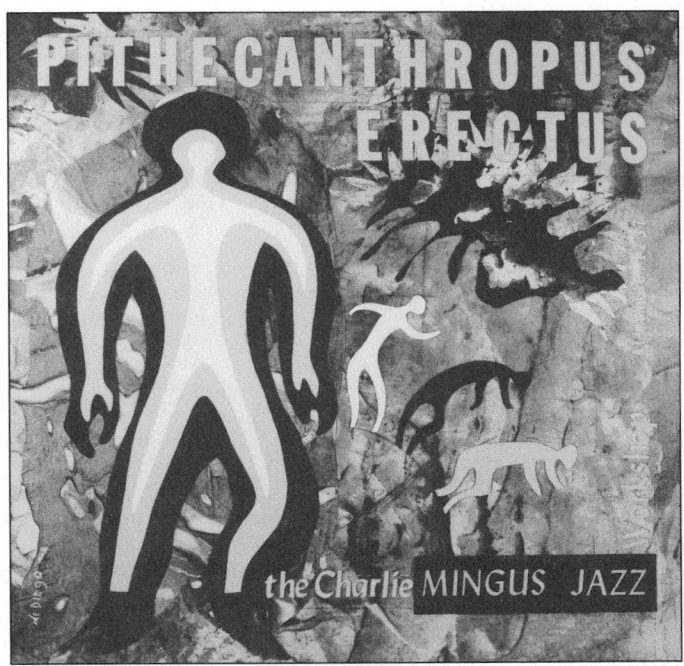

Charles Mingus, *Pithecanthropus Erectus*, Atlantic 1237, black label, **$300**.

Number	Title	Yr	NM
❏ DL8815 [M]	Birds of a Feather	1959	$100
—Black label, silver print			
❏ DL8815 [M]	Birds of a Feather	1960	$50
—Black label with color bars			
❏ DL8347 [M]	Blue Moon	1960	$50
—Black label with color bars			
❏ DL8173 [M]	By Special Request	1955	$150
—Black label, silver print			
❏ DL8173 [M]	By Special Request	1960	$50
—Black label with color bars			
❏ DL8738 [M]	Carmen for Cool Ones	1958	$120
—Black label, silver print			
❏ DL8738 [M]	Carmen for Cool Ones	1960	$50
—Black label with color bars			
❏ DL8662 [M]	Mad About the Man	1958	$100
—Black label, silver print			
❏ DL8662 [M]	Mad About the Man	1960	$50
—Black label with color bars			
❏ DL8267 [M]	Torchy!	1956	$150
—Black label, silver print			
❏ DL8267 [M]	Torchy!	1960	$50
—Black label with color bars			

FOCUS
| ❏ FL-334 [M] | Bittersweet | 1964 | $35 |
| ❏ FS-334 [S] | Bittersweet | 1964 | $50 |

GROOVE MERCHANT
❏ 522	A Whole Lot of Human Feeling	1973	$30
❏ 531	Ms. Jazz	1974	$30
❏ 4401	Velvet Soul	197?	$35

HARMONY
❏ KH32177	Carmen McRae Sings Billie Holiday	1972	$25
❏ HL7452 [M]	Yesterdays	1968	$50
❏ HS11252 [S]	Yesterdays	1968	$30

JAZZ MAN
| ❏ 5004 | Carmen McRae and the Kenny Clarke/Francy Boland Big Band | 198? | $25 |

KAPP
❏ KL-1117 [M]	Book of Ballads	1958	$60
❏ KS-3000 [S]	Book of Ballads	1958	$60
❏ KL-1169 [M]	Something to Swing About	1960	$60
❏ KS-3053 [S]	Something to Swing About	1960	$60
❏ KL-1541 [M]	This Is Carmen McRae	1967	$50
❏ KS-3541 [S]	This Is Carmen McRae	1967	$35
❏ KL-1135 [M]	When You're Away	1959	$60
❏ KS-3018 [S]	When You're Away	1959	$60

MAINSTREAM
❏ 56084 [M]	Alfie	1966	$35
❏ S-6084 [S]	Alfie	1966	$50
❏ 800	Alive!	1974	$35
❏ 309	Carmen McRae	1971	$30
❏ 352	Carmen McRae In Person	1972	$30
❏ 338	Carmen's Gold	1972	$30
❏ 56044 [M]	Haven't We Met?	1965	$35
❏ S-6044 [S]	Haven't We Met?	1965	$50
❏ S-6091 [S]	In Person/San Francisco	1967	$35
❏ 387	I Want You	1972	$30
❏ S-6110	Live & Wailin'	1968	$35
❏ 403	Live and Doin' It	1974	$30
❏ 56028 [M]	Second to None	1965	$35
❏ S-6028 [S]	Second to None	1965	$50
❏ 56065 [M]	Woman Talk	1966	$35
❏ S-6065 [S]	Woman Talk	1966	$50

MCA
| ❏ 4111 | The Greatest of Carmen McRae | 197? | $30 |

NOVUS
| ❏ 3086-1-N | Carmen Sings Monk | 1990 | $30 |

PAUSA
| ❏ 9003 | Can't Hide Love | 198? | $25 |

QUINTESSENCE
| ❏ 25021 | Ms. Jazz | 1978 | $25 |
| —Reissue of Groove Merchant 531 | | | |

STANYAN
| ❏ 10115 | Mad About the Man | 197? | $30 |

TEMPONIC
| ❏ 29562 | Carmen | 1972 | $30 |

TIME
| ❏ 52104 [M] | Live at Sugar Hill | 1960 | $50 |
| ❏ S-2104 [S] | Live at Sugar Hill | 1960 | $60 |

VOCALION
| ❏ VL3697 [M] | Carmen McRae | 1963 | $35 |
| ❏ VL73828 | My Foolish Heart | 1969 | $30 |

MCRITCHIE, GREG
Arranger and composer.

Albums

CADET
| ❏ LP-4058 [M] | Fighting Back | 1967 | $30 |
| ❏ LPS-4058 [S] | Fighting Back | 1967 | $35 |

ZEPHYR
| ❏ 12005 [M] | Easy Jazz on a Fish Beat Bass | 1959 | $250 |

MCSHANN, JAY
Pianist, male singer and bandleader.

Albums

ATLANTIC
❏ SD8804	The Big Apple Bash	1979	$30
❏ 90047	The Big Apple Bash	198?	$25
—Reissue of 8804			
❏ SD8800	The Last of Jay McShann	197?	$30

CAPITOL
| ❏ T2645 [M] | McShann's Piano | 1967 | $40 |
| ❏ ST2645 [S] | McShann's Piano | 1967 | $40 |

CLASSIC JAZZ
| ❏ 128 | Confessin' the Blues | 197? | $30 |

DECCA
❏ DL5503 [10]	Kansas City Memories	1954	$500
—CHARLIE PARKER appears on this LP			
❏ DL9236 [M]	Kansas City Memories	1958	$250
❏ DL79236 [R]	Kansas City Memories	196?	$35

MASTER JAZZ
| ❏ 8113 | Going to Kansas City | 197? | $35 |

MCA
| ❏ 1338 | The Early Bird | 198? | $25 |

SACKVILLE
❏ 3040	Airmail Special	198?	$25
❏ 3019	A Tribute to Fats Waller	198?	$25
❏ 3011	Crazy Legs and Friday Strut	1977	$25
❏ 3035	Just a Little So and So	198?	$25
❏ 3021	Kansas City Hustle	198?	$25
❏ 3006	The Man from Muskogee	198?	$25
❏ 3025	Tuxedo Junction	1980	$25

MECCA, LOU
Guitarist.

Albums

BLUE NOTE
| ❏ BLP-5067 [10] | Lou Mecca Quartet | 1955 | $300 |

MEHEGAN, JOHN, AND EDDIE COSTA
Also see each artist's individual listings.

Albums

SAVOY
| ❏ MG-12049 [M] | A Pair of Pianos | 1956 | $40 |

MEHEGAN, JOHN
Pianist and composer.

Albums

EPIC
| ❏ LA16007 [M] | Act of Jazz | 1960 | $40 |
| ❏ BA17007 [S] | Act of Jazz | 1960 | $60 |

PERSPECTIVE
| ❏ PR-1 [M] | From Barrelhouse to Bop | 195? | $50 |

SAVOY
| ❏ MG-12028 [M] | Reflections | 1956 | $40 |
| ❏ MG-15054 [10] | The Last Mehegan | 1955 | $75 |

TJ
| ❏ LP-1 [M] | Casual Affair | 1959 | $40 |

MELDONIAN, DICK
Alto and tenor saxophone player.

Albums

PROGRESSIVE
❏ 7062	Plays Gene Roland Music	198?	$25
❏ 7033	Some of These Days	1979	$30
❏ 7058	The Jersey Swing Concerts	198?	$25

STATINAS
| ❏ SLP-8076 | It's a Wonderful World | 1985 | $25 |

MELILLO, MIKE
Pianist.

Albums

RED RECORD
| ❏ VPA-188 | 'Live and Well | 1986 | $30 |
| ❏ VPA-170 | Piano Solo | 198? | $30 |

MELIS, MARCELLO
Bass player.

Albums

BLACK SAINT
❏ BSR-0073	Angedras	1983	$30
❏ BSR-0023	Free to Dance	198?	$30
❏ BSR-0012	New Village on the Left	198?	$30

MELLE, GIL
Saxophone player and composer who later created many electronic instruments.

Albums

BLUE NOTE
❏ BLP-5033 [10]	Gil Melle Quintet, Volume 2	1953	$800
❏ BLP-5054 [10]	Gil Melle Quintet, Volume 3	1954	$800
❏ BLP-5063 [10]	Gil Melle Quintet, Volume 4	1954	$800
	– Five Impressions of Color		
❏ BLP-5020 [10]	Gil Melle Quintet/Sextet	1953	$800
❏ B1-92168	Mindscape	1989	$35

GIL MELLE

| ❏ BLP-1517 [M] | Patterns in Jazz | 1956 | $800 |
| —Regular version, Lexington Ave. address on label | | | |

FANTASY
| ❏ OJC-1753 | Gil's Guests | 198? | $35 |
| ❏ OJC-1712 | Melle Plays Primitive Modern | 198? | $35 |

PRESTIGE
❏ PRLP-7063 [M]	Gil's Guests	1956	$300
—Yellow label with W. 50th St. address			
❏ PRLP-7040 [M]	Melle Plays Primitive Modern	1956	$300
—Yellow label with W. 50th St. address			
❏ PRLP-7097 [M]	Quadrama	1957	$250
—Yellow label			

VERVE
| ❏ V6-8744 | Tome VI | 1968 | $40 |

MELLO-LARKS, THE
Vocal group: Adele Castle; Joseph Eich; Thomas Hamm; Robert Wolter.

Albums

RCA CAMDEN
| ❏ CAL-530 [M] | Just for a Lark | 1959 | $40 |

MELROSE, FRANK
Pianist and composer.

Albums

ABC-PARAMOUNT
| ❏ 0(????) [M] | Kansas City Frank Melrose | 1956 | $50 |

MEMBERS ONLY
Group led by NELSON RANGELL.

Albums

MUSE
| ❏ MR-5332 | Members Only | 1987 | $25 |
| ❏ MR-5348 | Members Only...Too: The Way You Make Me Feel | 1989 | $30 |

MEMPHIS NIGHTHAWKS, THE

Albums

Number	Title	Yr	NM
DELMARK			
❏ DS-216	The Memphis Nighthawks	197?	$35
GOLDEN CREST			
❏ GC-4162	Stabilizer	1977	$30

MENDELSON, STAN
Pianist.
Albums

Number	Title	Yr	NM
LAND O' JAZZ			
❏ 2674	Storyville Piano	1978	$25

MENDES, SERGIO
Pianist and bandleader best known for the jazzy pop sounds of Brasil '66. Also see CANNONBALL ADDERLEY.
Albums

Number	Title	Yr	NM
A&M			
❏ SP-5250	Arara	1989	$30
❏ SP-4984	Confetti	1984	$25
❏ SP-4197	Crystal Illusions	1969	$35
❏ LP-122 [M]	Equinox	1967	$35
❏ SP-4122 [S]	Equinox	1967	$35
❏ SP-4160	Fool on the Hill	1968	$35
❏ SP-3108	Fool on the Hill	198?	$20
—Budget-line reissue			
❏ SP-4252	Greatest Hits	1970	$35
❏ SP-3258	Greatest Hits	198?	$20
—Budget-line reissue			
❏ SP-4137	Look Around	1968	$35
❏ SP-4315	Pais Tropical	1971	$30
❏ SP-4353	Primal Roots	1972	$30
❏ SP-4937	Sergio Mendes	1983	$30
❏ LP-116 [M]	Sergio Mendes and Brasil '66	1966	$30
❏ SP-4116 [S]	Sergio Mendes and Brasil '66	1966	$35
❏ SP-5135	Sergio Mendes and Brasil '86	1986	$25
❏ SP-4284	Stillness	1970	$35
❏ SP-3522	The Sergio Mendes Foursider	1973	$35
❏ SP-6012	The Sergio Mendes Foursider	198?	$25
—Budget-line reissue			
❏ SP-4236	Ye-Me-Le	1969	$35
ATLANTIC			
❏ 1466 [M]	Great Arrival	1966	$35
❏ SD1466 [S]	Great Arrival	1966	$50
❏ 8177 [M]	Sergio Mendes' Favorite Things	1968	$40
—White label promo only			
❏ SD8177 [S]	Sergio Mendes' Favorite Things	1968	$50
❏ 8112 [M]	Sergio Mendes In Person at the El Matador	1967	$50
❏ SD8112 [S]	Sergio Mendes In Person at the El Matador	1967	$35
❏ 1480 [M]	The Beat of Brazil	1967	$50
❏ SD1480 [S]	The Beat of Brazil	1967	$35
❏ 1434 [M]	The Swinger from Rio	1965	$35
❏ SD1434 [S]	The Swinger from Rio	1965	$50
BELL			
❏ 1119	Love Music	1973	$25
❏ 1305	Vintage 74	1974	$25
CAPITOL			
❏ T2294 [M]	In a Brazilan Bag	1965	$150
❏ ST2294 [S]	In a Brazilan Bag	1965	$200
ELEKTRA			
❏ 7E-1055	Homecooking	1976	$25
❏ 6E-214	Magic Lady	1980	$25
❏ 7E-1027	Sergio Mendes	1975	$25
❏ EQ-1027 [Q]	Sergio Mendes	1975	$40
❏ 6E-134	Sergio Mendes and Brasil '88	1978	$25
❏ 7E-1102	Sergio Mendes and the New Brasil '77	1977	$25
MOBILE FIDELITY			
❏ 1-118	Sergio Mendes and Brasil '66	1984	$100
—Audiophile vinyl			
PHILIPS			
❏ PHM200263 [M]	Quiet Nights	1968	$50
❏ PHS600263 [S]	Quiet Nights	1968	$35
PICKWICK			
❏ SPC-3149	So Nice	1972	$25
TOWER			
❏ T5052 [M]	In a Brazilan Bag	1966	$75
—Reissue of Capitol 2294			
❏ ST5052 [S]	In a Brazilan Bag	1966	$150
—Reissue of Capitol 2294			

MENGELBERG, MISHA
Pianist.
Albums

Number	Title	Yr	NM
SOUL NOTE			
❏ SN-1104	Change of Season	1985	$30

MENZA, DON
Tenor and alto saxophone player, clarinetist and flutist.
Albums

Number	Title	Yr	NM
CATALYST			
❏ 7617	First Flight	1976	$35
PALO ALTO			
❏ PA-8010	Flip Pocket	1981	$30
PAUSA			
❏ 7170	Horn of Plenty	1985	$25
REAL TIME			
❏ RT-301	Burnin'	198?	$35
VOSS			
❏ VLP1-42931	Horn of Plenty	1988	$25

MENZLES, HAMISH
Albums

Number	Title	Yr	NM
MUSIC IS MEDICINE			
❏ 9028	Jazz Tracks	1979	$30

MERCER, JOHNNY
Male singer; far better known as a composer.
Albums

Number	Title	Yr	NM
CAPITOL			
❏ T907 [M]	Ac-Cent-Tchu-Ate the Positive	1957	$150
❏ H214 [10]	Johnny Mercer Sings	1950	$250
❏ H210 [10]	Music of Jerome Kern	1950	$250
JUPITER			
❏ JLP-1001 [M]	Johnny Mercer Sings Just for Fun	1956	$100
PAUSA			
❏ PR9062	Jonny Mercer Sings Jonny Mercer	1986	$25
—Name is indeed misspelled on the label as "Jonny			

MERCER, MABEL, AND BOBBY SHORT
Also see each artist's individual listings.
Albums

Number	Title	Yr	NM
ATLANTIC			
❏ SD 2-604	Mabel Mercer and Bobby Short at Town Hall	1968	$25

MERCER, MABEL
Female singer.
Albums

Number	Title	Yr	NM
ATLANTIC			
❏ 1213 [M]	Mabel Mercer Sings Cole Porter	1955	$300
—Black label			
❏ 1213 [M]	Mabel Mercer Sings Cole Porter	1961	$150
—Multicolor label, white "fan" logo at right			
❏ 1213 [M]	Mabel Mercer Sings Cole Porter	1963	$35
—Multicolor label, black "fan" logo at right			
❏ 81264	Mabel Mercer Sings Cole Porter	1985	$25
❏ 1322 [M]	Merely Marvelous Mabel Mercer	1960	$250
—Black label			
❏ SD1322 [S]	Merely Marvelous Mabel Mercer	1960	$250
—Green label			
❏ 1322 [M]	Merely Marvelous Mabel Mercer	1961	$150
—Multicolor label, white "fan" logo at right			
❏ 1322 [M]	Merely Marvelous Mabel Mercer	1963	$35
—Multicolor label, black "fan" logo at right			
❏ SD1322 [S]	Merely Marvelous Mabel Mercer	1961	$150
—Multicolor labels, white "fan" logo at right			

Number	Title	Yr	NM
❏ SD1322 [S]	Merely Marvelous Mabel Mercer	1963	$25
—Multicolor labels, black "fan" logo at right			
❏ 1244 [M]	Midnight at Mabel Mercer's	1956	$300
—Black label			
❏ 1244 [M]	Midnight at Mabel Mercer's	1961	$150
—Multicolor label, white "fan" logo at right			
❏ 1244 [M]	Midnight at Mabel Mercer's	1963	$35
—Multicolor label, black "fan" logo at right			
❏ 1301 [M]	Once in a Blue Moon	1959	$300
—Black label			
❏ SD1301 [S]	Once in a Blue Moon	1959	$300
—Green label			
❏ 1301 [M]	Once in a Blue Moon	1961	$150
—Multicolor label, white "fan" logo at right			
❏ 1301 [M]	Once in a Blue Moon	1963	$35
—Multicolor label, black "fan" logo at right			
❏ SD1301 [S]	Once in a Blue Moon	1961	$150
—Multicolor labels, white "fan" logo at right			
❏ SD1301 [S]	Once in a Blue Moon	1963	$25
—Multicolor labels, black "fan" logo at right			
❏ ALS-402 [10]	Songs by Mabel Mercer, Volume 1	1954	$300
❏ ALS-403 [10]	Songs by Mabel Mercer, Volume 2	1954	$300
❏ 2-602 [M]	The Art of Mabel Mercer	1959	$300
—Black labels			
❏ 2-602 [M]	The Art of Mabel Mercer	1961	$250
—Multicolor labels, white "fan" logo at right			
❏ 2-602 [M]	The Art of Mabel Mercer	1963	$50
—Multicolor labels, black "fan" logo at right			
❏ SD 2-605	The Second Town Hall Concert	1969	$25
—Red and green label with "1841 Broadway" address			
❏ SD 2-605	The Second Town Hall Concert	1975	$15
—Red and green label with "75 Rockefeller Plaza" address			
AUDIOPHILE			
❏ AP-161/2	Echoes of My Life	197?	$35
DECCA			
❏ DL4472 [M]	Mabel Mercer Sings	1964	$35
❏ DL74472 [S]	Mabel Mercer Sings	1964	$25
STANYAN			
❏ SR10108 [M]	For Always	1974	$30

MERIAN, LEON
Trumpeter.
Albums

Number	Title	Yr	NM
SEECO			
❏ CELP-459 [M]	Fiorello!	1960	$150
❏ CELP-4590 [S]	Fiorello!	1960	$150
❏ CELP-447 [M]	This Time the Swing's On Me	1960	$100
❏ CELP-4470 [S]	This Time the Swing's On Me	1960	$100

MERIWETHER, ROY
Albums

Number	Title	Yr	NM
CAPITOL			
❏ ST-102	Soul Knight	1969	$60
COLUMBIA			
❏ CL2498 [M]	Popcorn and Soul Groovin' at the Movies	1966	$35
❏ CS9298 [S]	Popcorn and Soul Groovin' at the Movies	1966	$25
❏ CL2744 [M]	Soul Invader	1968	$30
❏ CS9544 [S]	Soul Invader	1968	$35
❏ CL2433 [M]	Soup and Onions (Soul Cookin')	1966	$35
❏ CS9233 [S]	Soup and Onions (Soul Cookin')	1966	$25
❏ CL2584 [M]	Stone Truth	1967	$25
❏ CS9384 [S]	Stone Truth	1967	$35

MERRILL, HELEN, AND JOHN LEWIS
Also see each artist's individual listings.
Albums

Number	Title	Yr	NM
MERCURY			
❏ SRM-1-1150	Helen Merrill and John Lewis	197?	$30

MERRILL, HELEN
Female singer.
Albums

Number	Title	Yr	NM
CATALYST			
❏ 7912	Autumn Love	197?	$60
❏ 7903	Helen Sings, Teddy Swings	197?	$60
DRG			
❏ SL-5204	The Rodgers & Hammerstein Album	1987	$30
EMARCY			
❏ MG-36107 [M]	Merrill at Midnight	1958	$300
—Blue label, double oval at top, "Emarcy Jazz" between the two ovals under "Mercury			
❏ MG-36134 [M]	The Nearness of You	1958	$350
INNER CITY			
❏ IC-1125	Casa Forte	198?	$35
❏ IC-1080	Chasin' the Bird	198?	$35
❏ IC-1060	Something Special	1978	$35
LANDMARK			
❏ LLP-1308	A Shade of Difference	1986	$30
MAINSTREAM			
❏ 56014 [M]	The Artistry of Helen Merrill	1965	$30
❏ S-6014 [S]	The Artistry of Helen Merrill	1965	$30
MERCURY			
❏ 826340-1	The Complete Helen Merrill on Mercury	1985	$80
METROJAZZ			
❏ E-1010 [M]	You've Got a Date with the Blues	1958	$120
❏ SE-1010 [S]	You've Got a Date with the Blues	1958	$150
MILESTONE			
❏ M-9019	Shade of Difference	1969	$25
❏ MLP-1003 [M]	The Feeling Is Mutual	1967	$40
❏ MLS-9003 [S]	The Feeling Is Mutual	1967	$30
OWL			
❏ 044	Music Makers	1986	$60
TRIP			
❏ TLP-5526	Helen Merrill Sings	197?	$35
❏ TLP-5552	Helen Merrill with Strings	197?	$35

MERRIWETHER, ROY, TRIO
Meriwether is a pianist and composer. The other members of his trio varied.

MESSNER, JOHNNY
Saxophone player, clarinetist and bandleader.

Albums

Number	Title	Yr	NM
HINDSIGHT			
❏ HSR-186	Johnny Messner and His Hotel McAlpin Orchestra 1939-40	198?	$25

METHENY, MIKE
Trumpeter.

Albums

Number	Title	Yr	NM
HEADFIRST			
❏ 9712	Blue Jay Sessions	198?	$25
MCA/IMPULSE!			
❏ 5755	Day In, Night Out	1986	$25

METHENY, PAT, AND LYLE MAYS
Also see each artist's individual listings.

Albums

Number	Title	Yr	NM
ECM			
❏ ECM1-1190	As Falls Wichita, So Falls Wichita Falls	1981	$25
—Distributed by Warner Bros.			

METHENY, PAT, AND ORNETTE COLEMAN
Also see each artist's individual listings.

Albums

Number	Title	Yr	NM
GEFFEN			
❏ GHS24096	Song X	1986	$25

METHENY, PAT
Guitarist (electric, acoustic and hybrids thereof).

Albums

Number	Title	Yr	NM
ECM			
❏ ECM2-1180	80/81	1980	$35
—Distributed by Warner Bros.			
❏ ECM1-1155	American Garage	1979	$25
—Distributed by Warner Bros.			
❏ PRO-A-810 [DJ]	An Hour with Pat Metheny	1979	$120

Number	Title	Yr	NM
—Promo-only music and interviews			
❏ ECM-1-1073	Bright Size Life	1976	$30
—Distributed by Polydor			
❏ ECM-1-1073	Bright Size Life	1979	$25
—Reissue, distributed by Warner Bros.			
❏ 25008	First Circle	1984	$25
❏ 1278	First Circle	1984	$30
—Made in Germany			
❏ PRO 030 [DJ]	Live in Concert	1977	$120
—Promo-only release			
❏ ECM1-1131	New Chautauqua	1979	$25
—Distributed by Warner Bros.			
❏ ECM1-1216	Offramp	1982	$25
—Distributed by Warner Bros.			
❏ ECM1-1114	Pat Metheny Group	1978	$25
—Distributed by Warner Bros.			
❏ 25006	Rejoicing	1984	$25
❏ 1271	Rejoicing	1984	$30
—Made in Germany			
❏ 23791	Travels	1983	$35
❏ 1252/3	Travels	1983	$50
—Made in Germany			
❏ ECM1-1097	Watercolors	1977	$30
—Distributed by Warner Bros.			
❏ 823270-1	Works	1984	$30
—Made in West Germany (not issued in U.S.)			
GEFFEN			
❏ GHS24245	Letter from Home	1989	$35
❏ GHS24293	Question and Answer	1990	$50
❏ GHS24145	Still Life (Talking)	1987	$25
WARNER BROS.			
❏ WBMS-106 [DJ]	Live on Tour	1979	$60
—Part of "The Warner Bros. Music Show" series; promo only			

METROPOLITAN JAZZ OCTET

Albums

Number	Title	Yr	NM
ARGO			
❏ LP-659 [M]	The Legend of Bix	1960	$30

MEZZROW, MEZZ
Clarinetist and bandleader.

Albums

Number	Title	Yr	NM
BLUE NOTE			
❏ BLP-7023 [10]	Mezz Mezzrow and His Band	1952	$300
LONDON			
❏ TKL-93092 [10]	A La Schola Cantorum	195?	$60
RCA VICTOR			
❏ LJM-1006 [M]	Mezzin' Around	1954	$50
SWING			
❏ SW-8409	Paris 1955, Volume 1	1986	$25
X			
❏ LVA-3027 [10]	Mezz Mezzrow	1954	$100
❏ LVA-3015 [10]	Mezz Mezzrow's Swing Session	1954	$100

MFG
From the initials of its members: JOE McPHEE; MILO FINE; Steve Gnitka (guitar).

Albums

Number	Title	Yr	NM
HAT HUT			
❏ 0S/T	MFG in Minnesota	1978	$30

MICROSCOPIC SEPTET, THE
Led by Phillip Johnston (soprano saxophone). Other members: Joel Forrester (piano); Paul Shapiro (tenor sax); Don Davis (alto sax); Dave Sewelson (baritone sax); David Hofstra (bass and tuba); Richard Dworkin (drums).

Albums

Number	Title	Yr	NM
OSMOSIS			
❏ 0(????)	Off Beat Glory	198?	$30
STASH			
❏ ST-276	Beauty Based on Science	1988	$25

MIGLIORI, JAY
Tenor and baritone saxophone player; also has played alto sax and flute.

Albums

DISCOVERY

Number	Title	Yr	NM
❏ DS-859	The Courage	198?	$25
PBR			
❏ 5	Count the Nights and Times	197?	$35
TRANSITION			
❏ TRLP-18 [M]	Jay Migliori Quintet	1956	$0
—Canceled			

MIL-COMBO, THE
Among the members are Don Mamblow, Connie Milano and Ziggi Milonzi.

Albums

Number	Title	Yr	NM
CAPITOL			
❏ T579 [M]	The Mil-Combo	1955	$80

MILBURN, AMOS
Pianist and male singer; one of the links between boogie-woogie and R&B piano styles.

Albums

Number	Title	Yr	NM
ALADDIN			
❏ LP-704 [10]	Rockin' the Boogie	1952	$8000
—Red vinyl, blue cover			
❏ LP-704 [10]	Rockin' the Boogie	1952	$4000
—Black vinyl			
❏ LP-810 [M]	Rockin' the Boogie	1957	$0
—Canceled			
IMPERIAL			
❏ LP-9176 [M]	Million Sellers	1962	$500
MOSAIC			
❏ MQ10-155	The Complete Aladdin Recordings of Amos Milburn	199?	$180
—Limited editon of 3,500			
MOTOWN			
❏ 608 [M]	The Return of Amos Milburn, "The" Blues Boss	1963	$900
SCORE			
❏ LP-4035 [M]	Amos Milburn Sings the Blues	1958	$0
—Canceled			
❏ LP-4012 [M]	Let's Have a Party	1957	$800

MILBURN, AMOS/WYNONIE HARRIS/ETC.

Albums

Number	Title	Yr	NM
ALADDIN			
❏ LP-703 [10]	Party After Hours	1952	$8000
—Red vinyl, blue cover			
❏ LP-703 [10]	Party After Hours	1952	$4000
—Black vinyl			

MILES, BARRY
Keyboard player and drummer.

Albums

Number	Title	Yr	NM
CENTURY			
❏ 1070	Fusion Is…	1979	$25
—Audiophile edition			
CHARLIE PARKER			
❏ PLP-804 [M]	Miles of Genius	1962	$30
❏ PLP-804S [S]	Miles of Genius	1962	$30
GRYPHON			
❏ 783	Fusion Is…	1978	$30
LONDON			
❏ XPS661	Magic Theatre	1975	$30
❏ XPS651	Silverlight	1975	$30
MAINSTREAM			
❏ MRL-382	Scatbird	1974	$35
❏ MRL-353	White Heat	1973	$35
POPPY			
❏ PY-40009	Barry Miles	1970	$25
RCA VICTOR			
❏ BGL1-2200	Sky Train	1977	$30

MILES, BOB

Albums

Number	Title	Yr	NM
OPTIMISM			
❏ OP-2003	Windstorm	198?	$25

Charles Mingus, *Blues & Roots*, Atlantic SD 1305, mostly white label with "bullseye" in middle, **$300**.

Charles Mingus, *Oh Yeah*, Atlantic 1377, mono, white "fan" logo on label, **$150**.

Blue Mitchell, *Big 6*, Riverside RLP 12-273, **$300**.

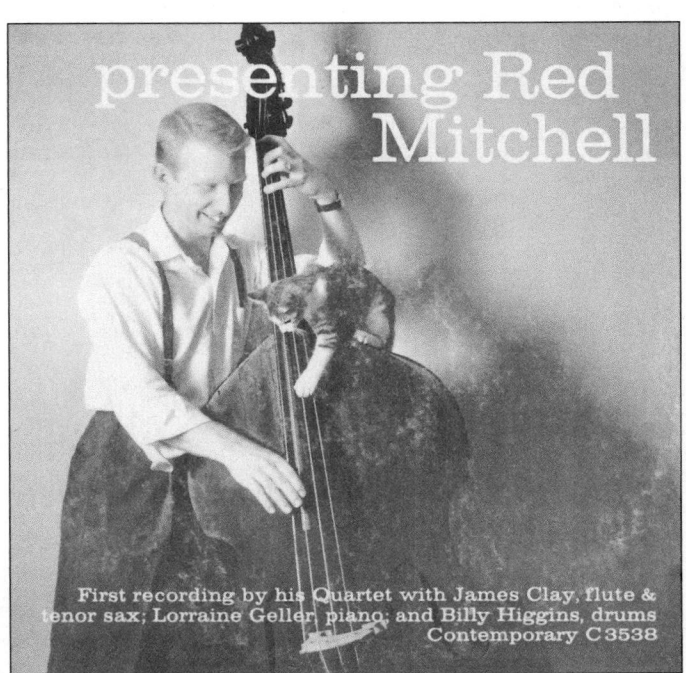

Red Mitchell, *Presenting Red Mitchell*, Contemporary C-3538, **$350**.

Number	Title	Yr	NM

MILES, BUTCH
Drummer.
Albums
DREAMSTREET
| ❏ 102 | Lady Be Good | 1980 | $30 |

FAMOUS DOOR
❏ 132	Butch Miles Salutes Chick Webb	1979	$30
❏ 142	Butch Miles Salutes Gene Krupa	1982	$25
❏ 135	Butch Miles Swings Some Standards	1981	$25
❏ 124	Encore	1978	$30
❏ 145	Hail to the Chief	1982	$25
❏ 117	Miles of Swing	1977	$30
❏ 150	More Miles… More Standards	1985	$25

MILES, LIZZIE
Female singer.
Albums
COOK
❏ 1183 [M]	Hot Songs My Mother Taught Me	195?	$60
❏ 1182 [M]	Moans and Blues	195?	$60
❏ 1181 [10]	Queen Mother of the Rue Royale	1955	$80
❏ 1184 [M]	Torchy Lullabies My Mother Taught Me	195?	$60

—Black vinyl
| ❏ 1184 [M] | Torchy Lullabies My Mother Taught Me | 195? | $200 |

—Rose-colored vinyl

MILESTONE JAZZSTARS, THE
Members: RON CARTER; SONNY ROLLINS; McCOY TYNER.
Albums
MILESTONE
| ❏ 55006 | Milestone Jazzstars In Concert | 1978 | $35 |

MILL CITY SEVEN, THE
Albums
JAZZOLOGY
| ❏ J-19 | The Mill City Seven | 1974 | $25 |

MILLER, CLARENCE "BIG"
Male singer.
Albums
COLUMBIA
❏ CL1808 [M]	Big Miller Sings, Twists, Shouts and Preaches	1962	$30
❏ CS8608 [S]	Big Miller Sings, Twists, Shouts and Preaches	1962	$30
❏ CL1611 [M]	Revelation and the Blues	1961	$30
❏ CS8411 [S]	Revelation and the Blues	1961	$30

UNITED ARTISTS
| ❏ UAL-3047 [M] | Did You Ever Hear the Blues? | 1959 | $40 |
| ❏ UAS-6047 [S] | Did You Ever Hear the Blues? | 1959 | $60 |

MILLER, DON
Guitarist.
Albums
KING
| ❏ 712 [M] | The Don Miller Quartet | 1960 | $60 |

MILLER, EDDIE, AND ARMAND HUG
Also see each artist's individual listings.
Albums
LAND O' JAZZ
| ❏ 5876 | Just Friends | 1979 | $30 |

MILLER, EDDIE
Tenor saxophone player, clarinetist and male singer.
Albums
CAPITOL
| ❏ T614 [M] | Classics in Jazz | 1955 | $80 |

FAMOUS DOOR
| ❏ 131 | It's Miller Time | 1979 | $30 |

MILLER, EDDIE/GEORGE VAN EPS
Also see each artist's individual listings.
Albums
JUMP
| ❏ JL-5 [10] | Eddie Miller/George Van Eps | 1953 | $50 |

MILLER, GARY
Albums
CIRCLE
| ❏ 2 | Gary Miller and the Celebration Road Show Live On Stage | 197? | $25 |

MILLER, GLENN, ORCHESTRA
Albums
GRP
| ❏ GRP-A-1002 | In the Digital Mood | 1983 | $25 |

MILLER, GLENN, ORCHESTRA (BUDDY DEFRANCO, DIRECTOR)
Also see BUDDY DeFRANCO.
Albums
EPIC
| ❏ LN24206 [M] | Something New | 1966 | $60 |
| ❏ BN26206 [S] | Something New | 1966 | $75 |

PARAMOUNT
| ❏ PAS-5034 | The Glenn Miller Orchestra | 1970 | $30 |

RCA VICTOR
❏ LPM-3819 [M]	In the Mod	1967	$35
❏ LSP-3819 [S]	In the Mod	1967	$30
❏ LPM-3971 [M]	The Glenn Miller Orchestra Makes the Goin' Great	1968	$40
❏ LSP-3971 [S]	The Glenn Miller Orchestra Makes the Goin' Great	1968	$30
❏ LPM-3880 [M]	The Glenn Miller Orchestra Returns to the Glen Island Casino	1968	$25
❏ LSP-3880 [S]	The Glenn Miller Orchestra Returns to the Glen Island Casino	1968	$30

MILLER, GLENN, ORCHESTRA (RAY MCKINLEY, DIRECTOR)
Also see RAY McKINLEY.
Albums
EPIC
❏ LN24133 [M]	Glenn Miller Time -- 1965	1965	$75
❏ BN26133 [S]	Glenn Miller Time -- 1965	1965	$40
❏ LN24157 [M]	Great Songs of the 60's	1965	$75
❏ BN26157 [S]	Great Songs of the 60's	1965	$50

RCA VICTOR
❏ LPM-2193 [M]	Dance, Anyone?	1960	$30
❏ LSP-2193 [S]	Dance, Anyone?	1960	$30
❏ LPM-2519 [M]	Echoes of Glenn Miller	1962	$30
❏ LSP-2519 [S]	Echoes of Glenn Miller	1962	$30
❏ LPM-2436 [M]	Glenn Miller Time	1961	$30
❏ LSP-2436 [S]	Glenn Miller Time	1961	$30
❏ LPM-1948 [M]	On Tour with the New Glenn Miller Orchestra	1959	$30
❏ LSP-1948 [S]	On Tour with the New Glenn Miller Orchestra	1959	$40
❏ LPM-1678 [M]	Something Old, New, Borrowed and Blue	1958	$30
❏ LSP-1678 [S]	Something Old, New, Borrowed and Blue	1958	$40
❏ LPM-2270 [M]	The Authentic Sound of the New Glenn Miller Orchestra -- Today	1961	$30
❏ LSP-2270 [S]	The Authentic Sound of the New Glenn Miller Orchestra -- Today	1961	$30
❏ LPM-2080 [M]	The Great Dance Bands of the 30's and 40's	1960	$30
❏ LSP-2080 [S]	The Great Dance Bands of the 30's and 40's	1960	$30
❏ ANL1-2975(e) [S]	The Great Dance Bands of the 30's and 40's	1978	$10

—Reissue of LSP-2080
❏ LPM-1852 [M]	The Miller Sound	1959	$30
❏ LSP-1852 [S]	The Miller Sound	1959	$40
❏ LPM-1522 [M]	The New Glenn Miller Orchestra in Hi-Fi	1957	$30
❏ LSP-1522 [S]	The New Glenn Miller Orchestra in Hi-Fi	1958	$40

MILLER, GLENN
Trombonist, bandleader, arranger and composer. Led the most popular of all the big bands; it was so popular that six decades after his death, there is still a GLENN MILLER ORCHESTRA that tours regularly.
Albums
20TH CENTURY
| ❏ T2-904 | Remember Glenn | 197? | $35 |

20TH CENTURY FOX
❏ TFM-3159 [M]	This Is Glenn Miller and His Greatest Orchestra, Volume 1	1964	$35
❏ TFS-4159 [R]	This Is Glenn Miller and His Greatest Orchestra, Volume 1	1964	$25
❏ TFM-3160 [M]	This Is Glenn Miller and His Greatest Orchestra, Volume 2	1964	$35
❏ TFS-4160 [R]	This Is Glenn Miller and His Greatest Orchestra, Volume 2	1964	$25

20TH FOX
❏ TCF-100-2 [M]	Glenn Miller and His Orchestra Original Film Sound Tracks	1958	$30
❏ TCF-100-2S [R]	Glenn Miller and His Orchestra Original Film Sound Tracks	1961	$25
❏ FOX3020 [M]	Glenn Miller's Original Film Soundtracks, Volume 1	1958	$50

—Half of 101
| ❏ FOX3021 [M] | Glenn Miller's Original Film Soundtracks, Volume 2 | 1958 | $50 |

—Half of 101

BANDSTAND
| ❏ BS-7136 | A Million Dreams Ago | 198? | $25 |

BLUEBIRD
❏ 6360-1-RB	Maj. Glenn Miller and the Army Air Force Band	1987	$25
❏ AXM2-5512	The Complete Glenn Miller Volume 1, 1938-39	1975	$30
❏ AXM2-5514	The Complete Glenn Miller Volume 2, 1939	1976	$30
❏ AXM2-5534	The Complete Glenn Miller Volume 3, 1939-40	1976	$30
❏ AXM2-5558	The Complete Glenn Miller Volume 4, 1940	1978	$30
❏ AXM2-5565	The Complete Glenn Miller Volume 5, 1940	1979	$30
❏ AXM2-5569	The Complete Glenn Miller Volume 6, 1940-41	1980	$30
❏ AXM2-5570	The Complete Glenn Miller Volume 7, 1941	1980	$30
❏ AXM2-5571	The Complete Glenn Miller Volume 8, 1941-42	1980	$30
❏ AXM2-5574	The Complete Glenn Miller Volume 9, 1939-42	1980	$30
❏ 9785-1-RB	The Popular Recordings 1938-1942	1989	$30

EPIC
| ❏ LA16002 [M] | Glenn Miller | 1960 | $40 |

EVEREST
| ❏ 4005/5 | His Complete Recordings on Columbia (1928-1938) As Player and Conductor | 1982 | $30 |

—Box set with 8-page booklet

HARMONY
| ❏ HS11393 [R] | Collector's Choice | 1970 | $30 |

INTERMEDIA
| ❏ QS-5045 | A String of Pearls | 198? | $20 |

KOALA
| ❏ AW14186 | Chattanooga Choo Choo | 1979 | $30 |

MERCURY
| ❏ 826635-1 | Glenn Miller In Hollywood | 1986 | $30 |

—Reissue of material formerly on 20th Century

MOVIETONE
❏ MTM-1003 [M]	Glenn Miller's Shindig	1965	$35
❏ MTS-72003 [R]	Glenn Miller's Shindig	1965	$25
❏ MTS-72018 [R]	The Glenn Miller Years	1967	$30

PAIR
| ❏ PDL2-1003 | Original Recordings, Volume 1 | 1986 | $30 |
| ❏ PDL2-1036 | Original Recordings, Volume 2 | 1986 | $30 |

PICKWICK
| ❏ DL2-0168 | A String of Pearls | 197? | $25 |

—Reissue of RCA Camden ACL2-0168
| ❏ ACL-7009 | Parade of Hits | 1976 | $20 |

Number	Title	Yr	NM
RCA			
7648-1-R	Pure Gold	1988	$10
7652-1-R	The Best of Glenn Miller	1988	$10
RCA CAMDEN			
ACL2-0168	A String of Pearls	1973	$30
CXS-9004	Sunrise Serenade	197?	$30
CAL-751 [M]	The Great Glenn Miller	1963	$35
CAS-751(e) [R]	The Great Glenn Miller	1963	$30
CAL-2128 [M]	The Nearness of You and Others	1967	$35
CAS-2128 [R]	The Nearness of You and Others	1967	$30
CAS-2267	The One and Only Glenn Miller	1968	$25
CAL-829 [M]	The Original Recordings	1964	$35
CAS-829(e) [R]	The Original Recordings	1964	$30
ACL-0503	This Time the Dream's On Me	1974	$20
RCA SPECIAL PRODUCTS			
DMM4-0322	Glenn Miller	1978	$25

—Box set; mail-order offer

Number	Title	Yr	NM
RCA VICTOR			
CPM2-0693	A Legendary Performer	1974	$30
CPL1-2080	A Legendary Performer, Volume 2	1976	$25
CPL1-2495	A Legendary Performer, Volume 3	1977	$25
LPM-3657 [M]	Blue Moonlight	1966	$35
LSP-3657 [R]	Blue Moonlight	1966	$25
LPM-6100 [M]	For the Very First Time…	195?	$50

—Black "Long Play" labels in leatherette spiral-bound binder

Number	Title	Yr	NM
LPT-31 [10]	Glenn Miller	1951	$60
VPM-6019	Glenn Miller: A Memorial 1944-1969	1969	$35
LPT-6700	Glenn Miller and His Orchestra Limited Edition	1953	$150

—Silver labels with red print in leatherette spiral-bound binder

Number	Title	Yr	NM
LPT-6700 [M]	Glenn Miller and His Orchestra Limited Edition -- Second Pressing	195?	$60

—Black "Long Play" labels in leatherette spiral-bound binder

Number	Title	Yr	NM
LPT-6701 [M]	Glenn Miller and His Orchestra Limited Edition Volume Two	1954	$120

—Black "Long Play" labels in leatherette spiral-bound binder

Number	Title	Yr	NM
LPT-6701 [M]	Glenn Miller and His Orchestra Limited Edition Volume Two -- Second Pressing	195?	$60

—Black "Long Play" labels in leatherette spiral-bound binder; identified as "Second Pressing" throughout

Number	Title	Yr	NM
LPT-6702 [M]	Glenn Miller Army Air Force Band	1955	$120

—Black "Long Play" labels in leatherette spiral-bound binder

Number	Title	Yr	NM
LPT-6702 [M]	Glenn Miller Army Air Force Band	195?	$60

—Same as above, but in box rather than in binder

Number	Title	Yr	NM
LPM-1193 [M]	Glenn Miller Concert	1956	$40
LPT-16 [10]	Glenn Miller Concert -- Volume 1	1951	$60
LPT-30 [10]	Glenn Miller Concert -- Volume 2	1951	$60
LPT-3001 [10]	Glenn Miller Concert -- Volume 3	195?	$60
LPM-6101 [M]	Glenn Miller On the Air	1963	$40
LSP-6101 [R]	Glenn Miller On the Air	1963	$30
LPM-2767 [M]	Glenn Miller On the Air Volume 1	1963	$35
LSP-2767 [R]	Glenn Miller On the Air Volume 1	1963	$25
LPM-2768 [M]	Glenn Miller On the Air Volume 2	1963	$35
LSP-2768 [R]	Glenn Miller On the Air Volume 2	1963	$25
LPM-2769 [M]	Glenn Miller On the Air Volume 3	1963	$35
LSP-2769 [R]	Glenn Miller On the Air Volume 3	1963	$25
PR-114	Glenn Miller Originals	1962	$25

—Promotional item for Salada Foods Inc.

Number	Title	Yr	NM
LPT-1016 [M]	Juke Box Saturday Night	1955	$50
LPM-1494 [M]	Marvelous Miller Moods	1957	$40
PRM-181 [M]	Moonlight Serenade	1965	$35
ANL1-0974	Pure Gold	1975	$20
AYL1-3666	Pure Gold	1980	$10
LPM-1192 [M]	Selections from "The Glenn Miller Story" and Other Hits	1956	$40
LSP-1192(e) [R]	Selections from "The Glenn Miller Story" and Other Hits	196?	$35

—Black label, dog on top

Number	Title	Yr	NM
AFL1-1192	Selections from "The Glenn Miller Story" and Other Hits	1977	$20
AYL1-3759	Selections from "The Glenn Miller Story" and Other Hits	1981	$10

Number	Title	Yr	NM
LPT-3057 [10]	Selections from the Film "The Glenn Miller Story"	1954	$60
LPT-3067 [10]	Sunrise Serenade	1954	$60
LPM-3377 [M]	The Best of Glenn Miller	1965	$35
LSP-3377(e) [R]	The Best of Glenn Miller	1965	$25

—Black label

Number	Title	Yr	NM
AYL1-3871	The Best of Glenn Miller	1981	$10
LSP-3377(e) [R]	The Best of Glenn Miller	1969	$20

—Orange label

Number	Title	Yr	NM
LPM-3564 [M]	The Best of Glenn Miller Volume 2	1966	$35
LSP-3564 [R]	The Best of Glenn Miller Volume 2	1966	$25
AYL1-3809	The Best of Glenn Miller Volume 2	1981	$10
LSP-4125 [R]	The Best of Glenn Miller Volume 3	1969	$30
AFL1-2825	The Best of Glenn Miller Volume 3	1978	$20
AYL1-3810	The Best of Glenn Miller Volume 3	1981	$10
LPM-3873 [M]	The Chesterfield Broadcasts, Volume 1	1967	$35
LSP-3873 [R]	The Chesterfield Broadcasts, Volume 1	1967	$25
ANL1-1139	The Chesterfield Broadcasts, Volume 1	1975	$20
LSP-3981 [R]	The Chesterfield Broadcasts, Volume 2	1968	$30
LPM-1506 [M]	The Glenn Miller Carnegie Hall Concert	1957	$40
LOP-1005 [M]	The Marvelous Miller Medleys	1958	$40
LPM-1973 [M]	The Marvelous Miller Medleys	1959	$30
LSP-1973 [R]	The Marvelous Miller Medleys	196?	$35
LPT-1031 [M]	The Nearness of You	1955	$50
LPM-1189 [M]	The Sound of Glenn Miller	1956	$40
LPT-3002 [10]	This Is Glenn Miller	195?	$60
LPM-1190 [M]	This Is Glenn Miller	1956	$40
VPM-6080	This Is Glenn Miller's Army Air Force Band	1972	$35
LPT-3036 [10]	This Is Glenn Miller -- Volume 2	195?	$60
READER'S DIGEST			
RD4-64 [R]	The Unforgettable Glenn Miller	1968	$25
SANDY HOOK			
SH2055	Uncle Sam Presents the Band of the Army Air Forces Training Command	1981	$25
SPRINGBOARD			
SPX-6013	Remember Glenn	1973	$30
SUNBEAM			
SB-232	Glenn Miller and His Chesterfield Orchestra	1984	$25
TIME-LIFE			
STBB-01	Big Bands: Glenn Miller	1983	$35
STBB-29	Big Bands: Glenn Miller: Take Two	1986	$35
STBB-17	Big Bands: Major Glenn Miller	1985	$35

MILLER, MARCUS

Bassist. Also see MILES DAVIS.

Albums

Number	Title	Yr	NM
WARNER BROS.			
25074	Marcus Miller	1984	$30
23806	Suddenly	1983	$35

MILLER, MULGREW

Pianist.

Albums

Number	Title	Yr	NM
LANDMARK			
LLP-1525	From Day to Day	1990	$30
LLP-1507	Keys to the City	198?	$25
LLP-1519	The Countdown	1989	$30
LLP-1515	Wingspan	1988	$25
LLP-1511	Work!	1986	$25

MILLER, PUNCH

Trumpeter and male singer. Also see PAUL BARBARIN.

Albums

Number	Title	Yr	NM
HERWIN			
108	Jazz Rarities 1929-30	197?	$25
IMPERIAL			
LP-9160 [M]	Hongo Fongo	1962	$150
JAZZ CRUSADE			

Number	Title	Yr	NM
2016	Oh Lady Be Good	196?	$35
JAZZOLOGY			
JCE-12	Kid Punch	1967	$35
J-17	River's in Mourning	197?	$25

MILLER, STEVEN

Guitarist and keyboard player.

Albums

Number	Title	Yr	NM
HIPPOCKET			
HP-102	Singing Whale Songs in a Low Voice	1983	$15
WINDHAM HILL			
WH-0102	Singing Whale Songs in a Low Voice	1987	$12

—Reissue of HipPocket 102

MILLINDER, LUCKY

Bandleader and occasional male singer. A transitional figure between jazz (swing) and R among those who passed through his band were DIZZY GILLESPIE and BILL DOGGETT.

Albums

Number	Title	Yr	NM
ALAMAC			
QSR-2425	Lucky Millinder and His Orchestra 1941-43	198?	$25
HINDSIGHT			
HSR-233	The Uncollected Lucky Millinder and His Orchestra 1942	198?	$25
MCA			
1357	Let It Roll	198?	$30

MILLMAN, JACK

Trumpet and fluegel horn player.

Albums

Number	Title	Yr	NM
DECCA			
DL8156 [M]	Jazz Studio 4	1955	$150
ERA			
EL-20005 [M]	Blowing Up a Storm	1956	$60

—Red vinyl

Number	Title	Yr	NM
EL-20005 [M]	Blowing Up a Storm	1956	$40

—Black vinyl

Number	Title	Yr	NM
LIBERTY			
LJH-6007 [M]	Shades of Things to Come	1956	$50

MILLS BROTHERS, THE

Vocal group also known for its uncanny ability to imitate musical instruments with its voices: John Mills, Jr. (bass, also played guitar), Herbert Mills (tenor), Harry Mills (baritone), Donald Mills (tenor). When John Jr. died in 1936, John Mills, Sr., took his place and Norman Brown became guitarist. Also see LOUIS ARMSTRONG; COUNT BASIE.

Albums

Number	Title	Yr	NM
ABC			
4004	16 Great Performances	1975	$12
1027	The Best of the Mills Brothers, Volume 2	1978	$15
ABC SONGBIRD			
SBDP-255	Inspiration	1974	$12
DECCA			
DL5050 [10]	Barber Shop Ballads	1950	$150
DL5051 [10]	Barber Shop Ballads	1950	$150
DL8890 [M]	Barber Shop Harmony	1959	$100
DL5516 [10]	Four Boys and a Guitar	1954	$150
DL8827 [M]	Glow with the Mills Brothers	1958	$120
DL75174 [R]	Golden Favorites, Volume 2	1970	$12
DL8892 [M]	Harmonizin' with the Mills Brothers	1959	$80
DL5506 [10]	Meet the Mills Brothers	1954	$150
DL8219 [M]	Memory Lane	1956	$120
DL8491 [M]	One Dozen Roses	1957	$120
DL4084 [M]	Our Golden Favorites	1960	$25
DL74084 [R]	Our Golden Favorites	196?	$15
DL8209 [M]	Singin' and Swingin'	1956	$150
DL5102 [10]	Souvenir Album	1950	$150
DL8148 [M]	Souvenir Album	1955	$150
DXB193 [M]	The Best of the Mills Brothers	1965	$25
DXSB7193 [R]	The Best of the Mills Brothers	1965	$25
DL8664 [M]	The Mills Brothers in Hi-Fi	1958	$100
DL5337 [10]	Wonderful Words	1951	$200
DOT			
DLP-3465 [M]	Beer Barrel Polka and Other Hits	1962	$60

Number	Title	Yr	NM
❑ DLP-25465 [S]	Beer Barrel Polka and Other Hits	1962	$60
❑ DLP-25927	Dream	1969	$60
❑ DLP-25809	Fortuosity	1968	$60
❑ DLP-3565 [M]	Gems by the Mills Brothers	1964	$60
❑ DLP-25565 [S]	Gems by the Mills Brothers	1964	$60
❑ DLP-3208 [M]	Great Barbershop Hits	1959	$75
❑ DLP-25208 [S]	Great Barbershop Hits	1959	$75
❑ DLP-3368 [M]	Great Hawaiian Hits	1961	$60
❑ DLP-25368 [S]	Great Hawaiian Hits	1961	$75
❑ DLP-3568 [M]	Hymns We Love	1964	$60
❑ DLP-25568 [S]	Hymns We Love	1964	$60
❑ DLP-25232 [S]	Merry Christmas	1959	$75

— Same as above, but in stereo; with cursive "Dot" logo

Number	Title	Yr	NM
❑ DLP-3232 [M]	Merry Christmas	1959	$75
❑ DLP-25232 [S]	Merry Christmas	1968	$60

— With "Dot"/"Paramount" logo

Number	Title	Yr	NM
❑ DLP-25103 [S]	Mmmm, The Mills Brothers	1958	$75
❑ DLP-25872	My Shy Violet	1968	$60
❑ DLP-3363 [M]	San Antonio Rose	1961	$60
❑ DLP-25363 [S]	San Antonio Rose	1961	$75
❑ DLP-3592 [M]	Say Si Si and Other Great Latin Hits	1964	$60
❑ DLP-25592 [S]	Say Si Si and Other Great Latin Hits	1964	$60
❑ DLP-3652 [M]	Ten Years of Hits 1954-1964	1965	$60
❑ DLP-25652 [S]	Ten Years of Hits 1954-1964	1965	$60
❑ DLP-3744 [M]	That Country Feeling	1966	$60
❑ DLP-25744 [S]	That Country Feeling	1966	$60
❑ DLP-3508 [M]	The End of the World	1963	$60
❑ DLP-25508 [S]	The End of the World	1963	$60
❑ DLP-3157 [M]	The Mills Brothers' Great Hits	1958	$75
❑ DLP-25157 [S]	The Mills Brothers' Great Hits	1958	$75

— Black vinyl

Number	Title	Yr	NM
❑ DLP-25157 [S]	The Mills Brothers' Great Hits	195?	$200

— Blue vinyl

Number	Title	Yr	NM
❑ DLP-3308 [M]	The Mills Brothers' Great Hits, Volume 2	1960	$60
❑ DLP-25308 [S]	The Mills Brothers' Great Hits, Volume 2	1960	$75
❑ DLP-25960	The Mills Brothers In Motion	1970	$60
❑ DLP-3783 [M]	The Mills Brothers Live	1967	$60
❑ DLP-25783 [S]	The Mills Brothers Live	1967	$60
❑ DLP-3237 [M]	The Mills Brothers Sing	1960	$75
❑ DLP-25237 [S]	The Mills Brothers Sing	1960	$75
❑ DL-3766 [M]	The Mills Brothers Today	1966	$60
❑ DLP-25766 [S]	The Mills Brothers Today	1966	$60
❑ DLP-3699 [M]	These Are the Mills Brothers	1966	$60
❑ DLP-25699 [S]	These Are the Mills Brothers	1966	$60
❑ DLP-3338 [M]	Yellow Bird	1960	$75
❑ DLP-25338 [S]	Yellow Bird	1960	$100

EVEREST ARCHIVE OF FOLK & JAZZ

Number	Title	Yr	NM
❑ 300	The Mills Brothers	197?	$12
❑ 328	The Mills Brothers, Volume 2	197?	$12

GNP CRESCENDO

Number	Title	Yr	NM
❑ GNP-9106	Four Boys and a Guitar	197?	$12

HAMILTON

Number	Title	Yr	NM
❑ HL-116 [M]	The Mills Brothers Sing for You	1964	$15
❑ HS-12116 [S]	The Mills Brothers Sing for You	1964	$15

MARK 56

Number	Title	Yr	NM
❑ 709	Original Radio Broadcasts	197?	$12

MCA

Number	Title	Yr	NM
❑ 717	16 Great Performances	1980	$10
❑ 132	Golden Favorites, Volume 2	1973	$12
❑ 15029	Merry Christmas	198?	$12
❑ 188	Old Golden Favorites	1973	$12
❑ 4039	The Best of the Mills Brothers	197?	$15
❑ 1556	The Mills Brothers	198?	$12
❑ 27083	The Mills Brothers Great Hits	1980	$10
❑ 28116	Were You There	198?	$10

MCA SPECIAL MARKETS

Number	Title	Yr	NM
❑ MSM2-35067	Classic Mills Brothers	198?	$12

PARAMOUNT

Number	Title	Yr	NM
❑ PAS-6038	A Donut and a Dream	1973	$15
❑ PAS-5025	No Turnin' Back	1971	$15
❑ PAS-1010	The Best of the Mills Brothers	1973	$15
❑ PAS-1027	The Best of the Mills Brothers, Volume 2	1974	$20
❑ PAS-6024	What a Wonderful World	1972	$15

PICKWICK

Number	Title	Yr	NM
❑ SPC-3076	14 Karat Gold	196?	$12
❑ SPC-3107	Anytime	197?	$12
❑ SPC-3220	Cab Driver	197?	$12
❑ SPC-3137	Dream a Little Dream	197?	$12
❑ SPC-1025	Merry Christmas	1979	$12

— Reissue of Dot album with one fewer track

Number	Title	Yr	NM
❑ 2008	Songs You Remember	197?	$12
❑ 2030	The Mills Brothers	1973	$12
❑ SPC-3556	The Mills Brothers	1976	$10
❑ SPC-3158	Till We Meet Again	197?	$12

RANWOOD

Number	Title	Yr	NM
❑ 7035	22 Great Hits	1985	$12
❑ 8152	50th Anniversary	197?	$12
❑ 8123	Cab Driver	197?	$12
❑ 8198	Command Performance	198?	$10
❑ 8139	Country's Greatest Hits	197?	$12
❑ 8133	The Mills Brothers Story	197?	$12

SUNNYVALE

Number	Title	Yr	NM
❑ 1023	Timeless	1978	$12

VOCALION

Number	Title	Yr	NM
❑ VL3607 [M]	In a Mellow Tone	196?	$15
❑ VL73607 [R]	In a Mellow Tone	196?	$12
❑ VL73859 [R]	Such Sweet Singing	1969	$12

MINASI, DOM

Guitarist.

Albums

BLUE NOTE

Number	Title	Yr	NM
❑ BN-LA426-G	I Have the Feeling I've Been Here	1975	$35
❑ BN-LA258-G	When Joanna Loved Me	1974	$35

MINCE, JOHNNY

Saxophone player and clarinetist.

Albums

JAZZOLOGY

Number	Title	Yr	NM
❑ J-163	Summer of '79	1989	$25
❑ J-126	The Master Comes Home	1985	$25

MONMOUTH-EVERGREEN

Number	Title	Yr	NM
❑ 7090	Summer of '79	1979	$30

MINERVA JAZZ BAND

Albums

STOMP OFF

Number	Title	Yr	NM
❑ SOS-1117	A Pile of Logs and Stone Called Home	1986	$25

MINGUS, CHARLES

Bass player, composer, bandleader and arranger. Also see DUKE ELLINGTON; JAZZ ARTISTS GUILD; JONI MITCHELL; THE QUINTET.

Albums

ABC IMPULSE!

Number	Title	Yr	NM
❑ AS-35 [S]	Black Saint and Sinner Lady	1968	$200

— Black label with red ring

Number	Title	Yr	NM
❑ AS-60 [S]	Charlie Mingus Plays Piano	1968	$200

— Black label with red ring

Number	Title	Yr	NM
❑ AS-54 [S]	Mingus, Mingus, Mingus, Mingus, Mingus	1968	$200

— Black label with red ring

Number	Title	Yr	NM
❑ AS-9234	Reevaluation -- The Impulse Years	1973	$35

ATLANTIC

Number	Title	Yr	NM
❑ SD1700	3 or 4 Shades	1977	$30
❑ 1305 [M]	Blues & Roots	1959	$300

— White "bullseye" label

Number	Title	Yr	NM
❑ 1305 [M]	Blues & Roots	1961	$250

— Multicolor label, white "fan" logo at right

Number	Title	Yr	NM
❑ 1305 [M]	Blues & Roots	1964	$30

— Multicolor label, black "fan" logo at right

Number	Title	Yr	NM
❑ SD1305 [S]	Blues & Roots	1959	$300

— White "bullseye" label

Number	Title	Yr	NM
❑ SD1305 [S]	Blues & Roots	1961	$250

— Multicolor label, white "fan" logo at right

Number	Title	Yr	NM
❑ SD1305 [S]	Blues & Roots	1964	$25

— Multicolor label, black "fan" logo at right

Number	Title	Yr	NM
❑ SD1677	Changes 1	1975	$30
❑ SD1678	Changes 2	1975	$30
❑ SD3001	Charles Mingus at Antibes	1979	$35
❑ SD8801	Cumbia & Jazz Fusion	197?	$30
❑ SD8803	Me, Myself An Eye	1979	$30
❑ SD1667	Mingus at Carnegie Hall	1974	$30
❑ SD1653	Mingus Moves	1974	$30
❑ 1377 [M]	Oh, Yeah	1961	$150

— Multicolor label, white "fan" logo at right

Number	Title	Yr	NM
❑ 1377 [M]	Oh, Yeah	1964	$25

— Multicolor label, black "fan" logo at right

Number	Title	Yr	NM
❑ SD1377 [S]	Oh, Yeah	1961	$150

— Multicolor label, white "fan" logo at right

Number	Title	Yr	NM
❑ SD1377 [S]	Oh, Yeah	1964	$30

— Multicolor label, black "fan" logo at right

Number	Title	Yr	NM
❑ SD 3-600	Passions of a Man: The Charles Mingus Anthology	1980	$25
❑ 1237 [M]	Pithecanthropus Erectus	1956	$300

— Black label

Number	Title	Yr	NM
❑ 1237 [M]	Pithecanthropus Erectus	1961	$150

— Multicolor label, white "fan" logo at right

Number	Title	Yr	NM
❑ 1237 [M]	Pithecanthropus Erectus	1964	$25

— Multicolor label, black "fan" logo at right

Number	Title	Yr	NM
❑ SD8809	Pithecanthropus Erectus	1981	$30
❑ SD8805	Something Like a Bird	1979	$30
❑ SD 2-302	The Art of Charles Mingus	1973	$35
❑ SD1555	The Best of Charles Mingus	1970	$35
❑ 1260 [M]	The Clown	1957	$300

— Black label

Number	Title	Yr	NM
❑ 1260 [M]	The Clown	1961	$150

— Multicolor label, white "fan" logo at right

Number	Title	Yr	NM
❑ 1260 [M]	The Clown	1964	$25

— Multicolor label, black "fan" logo at right

Number	Title	Yr	NM
❑ 90142	The Clown	198?	$25
❑ 1417 [M]	Tonight at Noon	1964	$30
❑ SD1417 [S]	Tonight at Noon	1964	$30

BARNABY

Number	Title	Yr	NM
❑ BR-5012	Charles Mingus Presents	1978	$30
❑ Z30561	Charles Mingus Presents the Quartet	1971	$35
❑ BR-6015	Stormy Weather	1976	$30
❑ KZ31034	The Candid Recordings	1972	$35

BETHLEHEM

Number	Title	Yr	NM
❑ BCP-6026 [M]	A Modern Jazz Symposium of Jazz and Poetry	1958	$250
❑ BCP-6019 [M]	East Coasting	1957	$250
❑ BCP-6019	East Coasting	197?	$35

— Reissue, distributed by RCA Victor

Number	Title	Yr	NM
❑ BCP-65 [M]	The Jazz Experiment of Charlie Mingus	1956	$250

BLUEBIRD

Number	Title	Yr	NM
❑ 5644-1-RB [(2)]	New Tijuana Moods	1986	$35

CANDID

Number	Title	Yr	NM
❑ CD-8005 [M]	Charles Mingus Presents Charles Mingus	1960	$40
❑ CD-8021 [M]	Mingus	1960	$40
❑ CS-9021 [S]	Mingus	1960	$50

CHARLES MINGUS

Number	Title	Yr	NM
❑ JWS-001/2	Mingus at Monterey	1966	$700

— Single-pocket jacket with sepia-tone photo on front

Number	Title	Yr	NM
❑ JWS-001/2	Mingus at Monterey	1966	$300

— Gatefold jacket with color photo on front; "This album can be purchased only by mail" on back cover

Number	Title	Yr	NM
❑ JWS-001/2	Mingus at Monterey	1968	$60

— Gatefold jacket with color photo on front; distributed by Fantasy

Number	Title	Yr	NM
❑ JWS-005	My Favorite Quintet	1966	$300

— This album can be purchased only by mail" on back cover

Number	Title	Yr	NM
❑ JWS-013/14	Special Music Written For (But Not Heard At) Monterey	1966	$1000

— Single-pocket jacket; "This album can be purchased only by mail" on back cover

Number	Title	Yr	NM
❑ JWS-009	Town Hall Concert 1964, Vol. 1	1966	$300

— This album can be purchased only by mail" on back cover

COLUMBIA

Number	Title	Yr	NM
❑ G30628	Better Git It in Your Soul	1971	$25
❑ CG30628	Better Git It in Your Soul	197?	$30

— Reissue with new prefix

Number	Title	Yr	NM
❑ KG31814	Charles Mingus and Friends	1973	$25
❑ KC31039	Let My Children Hear Music	1972	$35
❑ PC31039	Let My Children Hear Music	198?	$20

— Reissue with new prefix

Number	Title	Yr	NM
❑ CL1370 [M]	Mingus Ah Um	1959	$80

— Red and black label with six "eye" logos

Number	Title	Yr	NM
❑ CL1370 [M]	Mingus Ah Um	1963	$40

— Red label with "Guaranteed High Fidelity" at bottom

Number	Title	Yr	NM
❑ CL1370 [M]	Mingus Ah Um	1966	$30

— Red label with "360 Sound Mono" at bottom

Number	Title	Yr	NM
❑ CS8171 [S]	Mingus Ah Um	1959	$120

— Red and black label with six "eye" logos

Number	Title	Yr	NM
❑ CS8171 [S]	Mingus Ah Um	1963	$50

— Red label with "360 Sound Stereo" in black at bottom

Number	Title	Yr	NM
❑ CS8171 [S]	Mingus Ah Um	1966	$40

— Red label with "360 Sound Stereo" in white at bottom

Number	Title	Yr	NM
❑ CS8171 [S]	Mingus Ah Um	1971	$35

— Orange label, "Columbia" repeated along edge

Number	Title	Yr	NM
❑ PC8171	Mingus Ah Um	198?	$20

— Budget-line reissue with new prefix

Number	Title	Yr	NM
❑ CS8171 [S]	Mingus Ah Um	199?	$30

— Classic Records reissue on audiophile vinyl

Number	Title	Yr	NM
❑ CL1440 [M]	Mingus Dynasty	1960	$30

— Red and black label with six "eye" logos

The Mitchells, Get Those Elephants Out'a Here, Metrojazz SE-1012, **$150**.

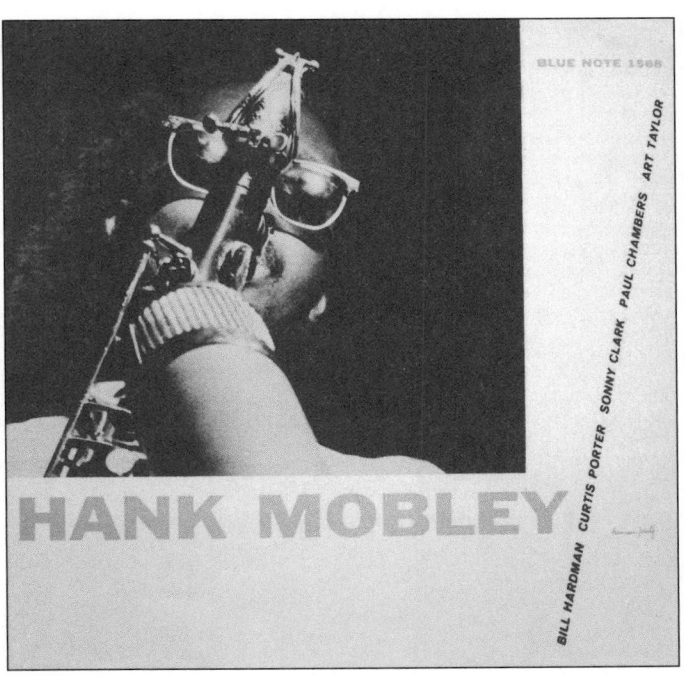

Hank Mobley, *Hank Mobley*, Blue Note BST-1568, "deep groove" version with W. 63rd St. address, **$400**.

Hank Mobley, *Hank Mobley Quartet*, Blue Note BLP-5066, 10-inch LP, **$1,500**.

Modern Jazz Quartet, *No Sun in Venice*, Atlantic SD 1284, all-green label, **$300**.

Number	Title	Yr	NM
❑ CL1440 [M]	Mingus Dynasty	1963	$25
—Red label with "Guaranteed High Fidelity" at bottom			
❑ CL1440 [M]	Mingus Dynasty	1966	$35
—Red label with "360 Sound Mono" at bottom			
❑ CS8236 [S]	Mingus Dynasty	1960	$40
—Red and black label with six "eye" logos			
❑ CS8236 [S]	Mingus Dynasty	1963	$30
—Red label with "360 Sound Stereo" in black at bottom			
❑ CS8236 [S]	Mingus Dynasty	1966	$25
—Red label with "360 Sound Stereo" in white at bottom			
❑ CS8236 [S]	Mingus Dynasty	1971	$30
—Orange label, "Columbia" repeated along edge			
❑ JG35717	Nostalgia in Times Square	1979	$35
COLUMBIA JAZZ MASTERPIECES			
❑ CJ40648	Mingus Ah Um	1987	$25
❑ CJ44050	Shoes of the Fisherman's Wife	1988	$25
DEBUT			
❑ DEB-123 [M]	Mingus at the Bohemia	1956	$500
❑ DLP-1 [10]	Strings and Keys	1953	$500
ENJA			
❑ 3077	Mingus in Europe	198?	$30
EVEREST ARCHIVE OF FOLK & JAZZ			
❑ 235	Charlie Mingus	1969	$30
FANTASY			
❑ 6002 [M]	Chazz!	1962	$50
—Red vinyl			
❑ 6002 [M]	Chazz!	1962	$30
—Black vinyl			
❑ 86002 [R]	Chazz!	196?	$30
—Blue vinyl			
❑ 86002 [R]	Chazz!	196?	$35
—Black vinyl			
❑ JWS-001/2	Mingus at Monterey	1969	$25
—Reissue of Charles Mingus 001/2			
❑ OJC-045	Mingus at the Bohemia	198?	$25
❑ JWS-005	My Favorite Quintet	1969	$35
—Reissue of Charles Mingus 005			
❑ 6017 [M]	Right Now -- Live at the Jazz Workshop	1966	$30
❑ 86017 [S]	Right Now -- Live at the Jazz Workshop	1966	$30
❑ OJC-237	Right Now -- Live at the Jazz Workshop	198?	$25
❑ 6009 [M]	The Charlie Mingus Quartet + Max Roach	1963	$30
❑ 86009 [R]	The Charlie Mingus Quartet + Max Roach	196?	$35
❑ OJC-440	The Charlie Mingus Quartet + Max Roach	1990	$30
❑ OJC-042	Town Hall Concert 1964	198?	$25
❑ JWS-009	Town Hall Concert 1964, Vol. 1	1969	$35
—Reissue of Charles Mingus 009			
GATEWAY			
❑ 7026	His Final Work	1979	$30
GRP/IMPULSE!			
❑ 217	Charlie Mingus Plays Piano	1997	$200
—Reissue on audiophile vinyl			
IMPULSE!			
❑ A-35 [M]	Black Saint and Sinner Lady	1963	$120
❑ AS-35 [S]	Black Saint and Sinner Lady	1963	$160
❑ A-60 [M]	Charlie Mingus Plays Piano	1964	$120
❑ AS-60 [S]	Charlie Mingus Plays Piano	1964	$160
❑ A-54 [M]	Mingus, Mingus, Mingus, Mingus, Mingus	1963	$120
❑ AS-54 [S]	Mingus, Mingus, Mingus, Mingus, Mingus	1963	$160
JAZZ MAN			
❑ 5002	Mingus	198?	$30
❑ 5048	Mingus Presents	198?	$30
JAZZTONE			
❑ J-1226 [M]	Jazz Experiment	1956	$60
❑ J-1271 [M]	The Jazz Experiments of Charlie Mingus	1957	$50
JOSIE			
❑ JOZ-3508 [M]	Mingus Three	1963	$30
❑ JLPS-3508 [R]	Mingus Three	1963	$25
JUBILEE			
❑ JLP-1054 [M]	Mingus Trio	1958	$80
LIMELIGHT			
❑ LM-82015 [M]	Mingus Revisited	1965	$30
❑ LS-86105 [S]	Mingus Revisited	1965	$30
MCA IMPULSE!			
❑ MCA-39119	Mingus, Mingus, Mingus, Mingus, Mingus	198?	$25
❑ MCA-5649	The Black Saint and the Sinner Lady	1986	$25

Number	Title	Yr	NM
MERCURY			
❑ MG-20627 [M]	Pre-Bird	1961	$100
❑ SR-60627 [S]	Pre-Bird	1961	$100
MOSAIC			
❑ MQ4-143	The Complete 1959 CBS Charles Mingus Sessions	199?	$150
❑ MR4-111	The Complete Candid Recordings of Charles Mingus	199?	$200
—Limited edition of 7,500			
PERIOD			
❑ SPL-1107 [10]	Jazzical Moods, Volume 1	1955	$200
❑ SLP-1111 [10]	Jazzical Moods, Volume 2	1955	$200
PRESTIGE			
❑ 24010	Charles Mingus	197?	$35
❑ 24100	Mingus at Monterey	198?	$35
❑ 24092	Portrait	1980	$35
❑ 24028	Reincarnation of a Lovebird	197?	$35
❑ 34001	The Great Concert	197?	$25
QUINTESSENCE			
❑ 25171	Soul Fusion	197?	$30
RCA VICTOR			
❑ LPM-2533 [M]	Tijuana Moods	1962	$40
❑ LSP-2533 [S]	Tijuana Moods	1962	$50
❑ APL1-0939	Tijuana Moods	1974	$30
—Reissue of 2533			
❑ LSP-2533 [S]	Tijuana Moods	199?	$30
—Classic Records reissue on audiophile vinyl			
SAVOY			
❑ MG-15050 [10]	Charlie Mingus	1955	$200
❑ MG-12059 [M]	Jazz Composers Workshop	1956	$100
SAVOY JAZZ			
❑ SJL-1113	Jazz Workshop	197?	$25
SOLID STATE			
❑ SS-18024	Town Hall Concert	1968	$25
❑ SS-18019	Wonderland	1968	$50
TRIP			
❑ 5040	Charles Mingus Trio and Sextet	197?	$25
❑ 5017	Mingus Moods	197?	$25
❑ 5513	Mingus Revisited	197?	$25
UNITED ARTISTS			
❑ UAL-4036 [M]	Jazz Portraits	1959	$40
❑ UAS-5036 [S]	Jazz Portraits	1959	$50
❑ UAJ-14024 [M]	Town Hall Concert	1963	$40
❑ UAJS-15024 [S]	Town Hall Concert	1963	$50
❑ UAJ-14005 [M]	Wonderland	1962	$40
❑ UAJS-15005 [S]	Wonderland	1962	$100
❑ UAS-5637	Wonderland	1972	$30
WHO'S WHO IN JAZZ			
❑ 21005	Lionel Hampton Presents Charles Mingus	1978	$35

MINGUS DYNASTY

Loose aggregation of musicians, most of whom had played in various CHARLES MINGUS bands, formed after Mingus' death.

Albums

Number	Title	Yr	NM
ELEKTRA			
❑ 6E-248	Chair in the Sky	1980	$25
SOUL NOTE			
❑ SN-1142	Mingus' Sound of Love	1988	$30
❑ SN-1042	Reincarnation	1982	$30

MINIMAL KIDDS

German group featuring Gebhard Ullmann (reeds) and Andreas Willers (guitar).

Albums

Number	Title	Yr	NM
INTUITION			
❑ C1-46879	No Age	1989	$30

MINION, FRANK

Albums

Number	Title	Yr	NM
BETHLEHEM			
❑ BCP-6033 [M]	Forward Sound	1959	$200
❑ BCP-6052 [M]	The Soft Land of Make Believe	1961	$200
❑ BCPS-6052 [S]	The Soft Land of Make Believe	1961	$200

MISSOURIANS, THE

Members: William Blue (clarinet, alto saxophone); Andrew Brown (clarinet, tenor saxophone); R.Q. Dickerson (trumpet); Lockwood Lewis (vocals, leader); Leroy Maxey (drums); Earres Prince (piano); George Scott (clarinet, alto saxophone); Jimmy Smith (tuba); De Priest Wheeler (trumpet); Morris White (violin).

Number	Title	Yr	NM
Albums			
X			
❑ LVA-3020 [10]	Harlem in the Twenties, Volume 1	1954	$50

MISTER SPATS

Members included Richard Shulman (piano) and Steve Evans.

Albums

Number	Title	Yr	NM
PAUSA			
❑ 7194	Love Speaks	1986	$25

MIT

Albums

Number	Title	Yr	NM
HAT HUT			
❑ 18	MIT	198?	$35

MITCHELL, BILLY

Tenor saxophone player. Also see AL GREY.

Albums

Number	Title	Yr	NM
CATALYST			
❑ 7611	Now's the Time	1976	$30
OPTIMISM			
❑ OP-2501	Faces	1987	$25
❑ OP-2502	In Focus	1988	$25
PAUSA			
❑ 7158	Blue City Jam	198?	$25
❑ 7192	Night Theme	1986	$25
SMASH			
❑ MGS-27042 [M]	A Little Juicy	1962	$30
❑ SRS-67042 [S]	A Little Juicy	1962	$30
❑ MGS-27027 [M]	This Is Billy Mitchell	1962	$30
❑ SRS-67027 [S]	This Is Billy Mitchell	1962	$30
TRIP			
❑ 5534	Billy Mitchell with Bobby Hutcherson	197?	$25
XANADU			
❑ 158	Colossus of Detroit	1978	$30
❑ 182	De Lawd's Blues	198?	$25

MITCHELL, BLUE

Trumpeter. Also see THE MITCHELLS; THE RIVERSIDE JAZZ STARS.

Albums

Number	Title	Yr	NM
ABC IMPULSE!			
❑ AS-9328	African Violet	1977	$35
❑ IA-9347	Summer Soft	1978	$35
BLUE NOTE			
❑ BST-84324	Bantu Village	1969	$40
—With "A Division of Liberty Records" on label			
❑ BLP-4257 [M]	Boss Horn	1967	$100
—With "A Division of Liberty Records" on label			
❑ BST-84257 [S]	Boss Horn	1967	$30
—With "A Division of Liberty Records" on label			
❑ BLP-4228 [M]	Bring It Home to Me	1966	$100
—New York, USA" on label			
❑ BST-84228 [S]	Bring It Home to Me	1966	$50
—With "New York, USA" address on label			
❑ BST-84228 [S]	Bring It Home to Me	1967	$60
—With "A Division of Liberty Records" on label			
❑ BST-84300	Collision in Black	1968	$30
—With "A Division of Liberty Records" on label			
❑ BLP-4214 [M]	Down With It	1965	$100
—New York, USA" on label			
❑ BST-84214 [S]	Down With It	1965	$50
—With "New York, USA" address on label			
❑ BST-84214 [S]	Down With It	1967	$60
—With "A Division of Liberty Records" on label			
❑ BST-84272	Heads Up!	1968	$30
—With "A Division of Liberty Records" on label			
❑ BLP-4142 [M]	Step Lightly	1963	$0
—Cancelled			
❑ BST-84142 [S]	Step Lightly	1963	$0
—Cancelled			
❑ LT-1082	Step Lightly	1980	$50
❑ BLP-4178 [M]	The Thing to Do	1964	$150
—New York, USA" on label			
❑ BST-84178 [S]	The Thing to Do	1964	$80
—With "New York, USA" address on label			
❑ BST-84178 [S]	The Thing to Do	1967	$60
—With "A Division of Liberty Records" on label			

Number	Title	Yr	NM
❏ BST-84178 [S]	The Thing to Do	1985	$30

— The Finest in Jazz Since 1939" reissue

FANTASY

❏ OJC-6009	Blues on My Mind	198?	$30
❏ OJC-615	The Big Six	1991	$35

FORTISSIMO

❏ XK8006	Brasses and Strings	1961	$150

— Red vinyl; record plays from the inside out

JAM

❏ 5002	Last Dance	1977	$50

MAINSTREAM

❏ MRL-315	Blue Mitchell	1971	$100
❏ MRL-374	Blue's Blues	1973	$40
❏ MRL-413	Booty	1974	$60
❏ MRL-400	Graffiti Blues	1974	$40
❏ MRL-392	Last Tango = Blues	1973	$150

— Reproductions exist

❏ MRL-402	Many Shades of Blue Mitchell	1974	$40
❏ MRL-343	Vital	1972	$100

MCA

❏ 29050	African Violet	1980	$25
❏ 29051	Summer Soft	1980	$25

MILESTONE

❏ M-47055	A Blue Time	1979	$60

MOSAIC

❏ MQ6-178	The Complete Blue Note Sessions	199?	$100

RCA VICTOR

❏ APL1-1493	Funktion Junction	1976	$50
❏ APL1-1109	Stratosonic Nuances	1975	$60

RIVERSIDE

❏ RLP-414 [M]	A Sure Thing	1962	$150
❏ RS-9414 [S]	A Sure Thing	1962	$150
❏ RLP-336 [M]	Blue's Moods	1960	$200
❏ RS-9336 [S]	Blue's Moods	1960	$200
❏ 6045	Blue's Moods	197?	$35
❏ RLP 12-309 [M]	Blue Soul	1959	$300
❏ RLP-1155 [M]	Blue Soul	1959	$300
❏ RLP 12-293 [M]	Out of the Blue	1958	$300
❏ RLP-1131 [S]	Out of the Blue	1959	$250
❏ RLP-367 [M]	Smooth as the Wind	1961	$200
❏ RS-9367 [S]	Smooth as the Wind	1961	$200
❏ RLP 12-273 [M]	The Big Six	1958	$300
❏ RLP-439 [M]	The Cup Bearers	1963	$150
❏ RS-9439 [S]	The Cup Bearers	1963	$150

MITCHELL, GROVER

Trombonist.

Albums

STASH

❏ ST-277	Truckin' with Grover Mitchell and His Orchestra	1988	$25

MITCHELL, JONI

Female singer. Best known in the folk, pop and rock realms, the below LPs feature backing and inspiration by jazz musicians.

Albums

ASYLUM

❏ 5E-505	Mingus	1979	$25
❏ BB-704	Shadows and Light	1980	$30

MITCHELL, OLLIE

Trumpeter.

Albums

PAUSA

❏ 7128	Blast Off	198?	$25

MITCHELL, PAUL

Pianist.

Albums

VERVE

❏ V-8713 [M]	Live at the Atlanta Playboy Club	1967	$25
❏ V6-8713 [S]	Live at the Atlanta Playboy Club	1967	$30

MITCHELL, RED, AND HAROLD LAND

Also see each artist's individual listings.

Albums

ATLANTIC

❏ 1376 [M]	Hear Ye!	1961	$150

— Multicolor label, white "fan" logo at right

Number	Title	Yr	NM
❏ 1376 [M]	Hear Ye!	1964	$25

— Multicolor label, black "fan" logo at right

❏ SD1376 [S]	Hear Ye!	1961	$150

— Multicolor label, white "fan" logo at right

❏ SD1376 [S]	Hear Ye!	1964	$30

— Multicolor label, black "fan" logo at right

MITCHELL, RED

Bass player. Also see THE MITCHELLS; OSCAR PETTIFORD; THE VIDEO ALL-STARS.

Albums

BETHLEHEM

❏ BCP-1033 [10]	Happy Minors	1955	$400
❏ BCP-38 [M]	Jam for Your Bread	1956	$250

CONTEMPORARY

❏ C-3538 [M]	Presenting Red Mitchell	1957	$250

FANTASY

❏ OJC-158	Presenting Red Mitchell	198?	$30

PACIFIC JAZZ

❏ PJ-22 [M]	Rejoice	1961	$30
❏ ST-22 [S]	Rejoice	1961	$40

PAUSA

❏ 7018	Red Mitchell Meets Manusardi	198?	$25

STEEPLECHASE

❏ SCS-1161	Chocolate Cadillac	198?	$30

MITCHELL, ROSCOE

Reeds player. Also see ART ENSEMBLE OF CHICAGO.

Albums

BLACK SAINT

❏ BSR-0050	3 X 4 Eye	198?	$30
❏ BSR-0070	Roscoe Mitchell and Sound and Space Ensembles	198?	$30

DELMARK

❏ D-408 [M]	Roscoe Mitchell Sextet	1966	$30
❏ DS-408 [S]	Roscoe Mitchell Sextet	1966	$25

NESSA

❏ N-2	Congliptious	1968	$30
❏ N-14/15	L-R-G/The Maze/S II Examples	1980	$25
❏ N-9/10	Nonaah	1977	$30
❏ N-5	Old/Quartet	197?	$35
❏ N-20	Snurdy McGurdy and Her Dancin' Shoes	1981	$35

MITCHELL, WHITEY

Bass player. Also see THE MITCHELLS; THE NEW YORK JAZZ QUARTET.

Albums

ABC-PARAMOUNT

❏ ABC-126 [M]	Whitey Mitchell Sextette	1956	$100

MITCHELL-RUFF DUO, THE

Featuring Dwike Mitchell (piano) and Willie Ruff (bass, French horn).

Albums

ATLANTIC

❏ 1458 [M]	After This Message	1966	$25
❏ SD1458 [S]	After This Message	1966	$30
❏ 1374 [M]	The Catbird Seat	1961	$150

— Multicolor label, white "fan" logo at right

❏ 1374 [M]	The Catbird Seat	1964	$35

— Multicolor label, black "fan" logo at right

❏ SD1374 [S]	The Catbird Seat	1961	$150

— Multicolor label, white "fan" logo at right

❏ SD1374 [S]	The Catbird Seat	1964	$50

— Multicolor label, black "fan" logo at right

EPIC

❏ LN3318 [M]	Campus Concert	1956	$80
❏ LN3221 [M]	The Mitchell-Ruff Duo	1956	$80

FORUM

❏ F-9031 [M]	Jazz Mission to Moscow	196?	$30

— Reissue of Roulette R-52034

❏ SF-9031 [S]	Jazz Mission to Moscow	196?	$35

— Reissue of Roulette SR-52034

MAINSTREAM

❏ MRL-335	Strayhorn	1972	$35

ROULETTE

❏ R-52002 [M]	Appearing Nightly	1958	$40
❏ SR-52002 [S]	Appearing Nightly	1959	$30

Number	Title	Yr	NM
❏ R-52025 [M]	Jazz for Juniors	1959	$30
❏ SR-52025 [S]	Jazz for Juniors	1959	$30
❏ R-52034 [M]	Jazz Mission to Moscow	1959	$30
❏ SR-52034 [S]	Jazz Mission to Moscow	1959	$30
❏ R-52013 [M]	The Mitchell-Ruff Duo Plus Strings and Brass	1958	$40
❏ SR-52013 [S]	The Mitchell-Ruff Duo Plus Strings and Brass	1959	$30
❏ R-52037 [M]	The Sound of Music	1960	$30
❏ SR-52037 [S]	The Sound of Music	1960	$30

MITCHELLS, THE

Members: BLUE MITCHELL; RED MITCHELL; WHITEY MITCHELL.

Albums

METROJAZZ

❏ E-1012 [M]	Get Those Elephants Out'a Here	1958	$175
❏ SE-1012 [S]	Get Those Elephants Out'a Here	1958	$150

MJT + 3

Members: Bob Cranshaw (bass); HAROLD MABERN (piano); Walter Perkins (drums); FRANK STROZIER (alto sax); Willie Thomas (trumpet).

Albums

ARGO

❏ LP-621 [M]	Daddy-O Presents MJT + 3	1957	$40

TRIP

❏ 5025	Branching Out	197?	$30

VEE JAY

❏ LP-3008 [M]	Make Everybody Happy	1960	$30
❏ SR-3008 [S]	Make Everybody Happy	1960	$30
❏ LP-3014 [M]	MJT + 3	1961	$30
❏ SR-3014 [S]	MJT + 3	1961	$30
❏ LP-1013 [M]	Walter Perkins' MJT + 3	1959	$30
❏ SR-1013 [S]	Walter Perkins' MJT + 3	1959	$40

MOBLEY, HANK

Tenor saxophone player. Also see DONALD BYRD; KENNY DREW.

Albums

BLUE NOTE

❏ BLP-4230 [M]	A Caddy for Daddy	1966	$1000

— With "New York, USA" address on label

❏ BST-84230 [S]	A Caddy for Daddy	1966	$400

— With "New York, USA" address on label

❏ BST-84230 [S]	A Caddy for Daddy	1967	$40

— With "A Division of Liberty Records" on label

❏ BST-84431	Another Workout	1986	$50
❏ B1-33582	A Slice Off the Top	1995	$35

— The Finest in Jazz Since 1939" reissue

❏ BLP-4209 [M]	Dippin'	1965	$150

— With "New York, USA" address on label

❏ BST-84209 [S]	Dippin'	1965	$100

— With "New York, USA" address on label

❏ BST-84209 [S]	Dippin'	1967	$40

— With "A Division of Liberty Records" on label

❏ BST-84425	Far Away Lands	1985	$50
❏ BLP-1560 [M]	Hank	1957	$1500

— Regular version, W. 63rd St. address on label

❏ BLP-1560 [M]	Hank	1963	$140

— With "New York, USA" address on label

❏ BST-81560 [R]	Hank	1967	$25

— With "A Division of Liberty Records" on label

❏ BLP-1550 [M]	Hank Mobley	1957	$1200

— Deep groove" version; W. 63rd St. address on label

❏ BLP-1550 [M]	Hank Mobley	1957	$300

— Regular version, W. 63rd St. address on label

❏ BLP-1550 [M]	Hank Mobley	1963	$150

— With "New York, USA" address on label

❏ BST-81550 [R]	Hank Mobley	1967	$25

— With "A Division of Liberty Records" on label

❏ BLP-1568 [M]	Hank Mobley	1963	$80

— With "New York, USA" address on label

❏ BST-1568 [S]	Hank Mobley	1959	$400

— Deep groove" version; W. 63rd St. address on label

❏ BST-1568 [S]	Hank Mobley	1959	$200

— Regular version, W. 63rd St. address on label

❏ BST-1568 [S]	Hank Mobley	1963	$40

— With "New York, USA" address on label

❏ BST-81568 [S]	Hank Mobley	1967	$25

— With "A Division of Liberty Records" on label

Number	Title	Yr	NM
❏ BLP-4241 [M]	Hank Mobley	1966	$0
—Canceled			
❏ BST-84241 [S]	Hank Mobley	1966	$0
—Canceled			
❏ BLP-1568 [M]	Hank Mobley	200?	$60
—200-gram reissue, distributed by Classic Records			
❏ BLP-1544 [M]	Hank Mobley and His All Stars	1957	$800
—Deep groove" version; W. 63rd St. address on label			
❏ BLP-1544 [M]	Hank Mobley and His All Stars	1957	$300
—Regular version, W. 63rd St. address on label			
❏ BLP-1544 [M]	Hank Mobley and His All Stars	1963	$200
—With "New York, USA" address on label			
❏ BST-81544 [R]	Hank Mobley and His All Stars	1967	$25
—With "A Division of Liberty Records" on label			
❏ BLP-5066 [10]	Hank Mobley Quartet	1955	$1500
❏ BLP-1540 [M]	Hank Mobley with Donald Byrd and Lee Morgan	1957	$1000
—Deep groove" version, Lexington Ave. address on label			
❏ BLP-1540 [M]	Hank Mobley with Donald Byrd and Lee Morgan	1963	$850
—With "New York, USA" address on label			
❏ BST-81540 [R]	Hank Mobley with Donald Byrd and Lee Morgan	1967	$25
—With "A Division of Liberty Records" on label			
❏ BST-84273	High Voltage	1986	$30
—The Finest in Jazz Since 1939" reissue			
❏ BLP-4273 [M]	Hi Voltage	1968	$500
—With "A Division of Liberty Records" address on label			
❏ BST-84273 [S]	Hi Voltage	1968	$100
—With "A Division of Liberty Records" on label			
❏ BLP-4149 [M]	No Room for Squares	1963	$200
—With "New York, USA" address on label			
❏ BST-84149 [S]	No Room for Squares	1963	$100
—With "New York, USA" address on label			
❏ BST-84149 [S]	No Room for Squares	1967	$40
—With "A Division of Liberty Records" on label			
❏ B1-84149	No Room for Squares	1989	$35
—The Finest in Jazz Since 1939" reissue			
❏ BLP-1574 [M]	Peckin' Time	1958	$1500
—Deep groove" version; W. 63rd St. address on label			
❏ BLP-1574 [M]	Peckin' Time	1958	$300
—Regular version, W. 63rd St. address on label			
❏ BLP-1574 [M]	Peckin' Time	1963	$200
—With "New York, USA" address on label			
❏ BST-81574 [R]	Peckin' Time	1967	$25
—With "A Division of Liberty Records" on label			
❏ B1-84288	Peckin' Time	1988	$30
—The Finest in Jazz Since 1939" reissue			
❏ BST-84288	Reach Out!	1968	$80
—With "A Division of Liberty Records" on label			
❏ BLP-4058 [M]	Roll Call	1963	$100
—With "New York, USA" address on label			
❏ BST-84058 [S]	Roll Call	1961	$200
—With W. 63rd St. address on label			
❏ BST-84058 [S]	Roll Call	1963	$40
—With "New York, USA" address on label			
❏ BST-84058 [S]	Roll Call	1967	$60
—With "A Division of Liberty Records" on label			
❏ BST-84058	Roll Call	199?	$30
—180-gram reissue; distributed by Classic Records			
❏ LT-995	Slice Off the Top	1979	$50
❏ BLP-4031 [M]	Soul Station	1960	$1000
—Deep groove" version; W. 63rd St. address on label			
❏ BLP-4031 [M]	Soul Station	1960	$200
—Regular version, W. 63rd St. address on label			
❏ BLP-4031 [M]	Soul Station	1963	$80
—With "New York, USA" address on label			
❏ BST-84031 [S]	Soul Station	1960	$200
—With W. 63rd St. address on label			
❏ BST-84031 [S]	Soul Station	1963	$40
—With "New York, USA" address on label			
❏ BST-84031 [S]	Soul Station	1967	$60
—With "A Division of Liberty Records" on label			
❏ BST-84031	Soul Station	1987	$35
—The Finest in Jazz Since 1939" reissue			
❏ BST-84435	Straight No Filter	1986	$60
❏ BST-84329	The Flip	1969	$80
—With "A Division of Liberty Records" on label			

Number	Title	Yr	NM
❏ BLP-4186 [M]	The Turnaround!	1964	$200
—With "New York, USA" address on label			
❏ BST-84186 [S]	The Turnaround!	1964	$100
—With "New York, USA" address on label			
❏ BST-84186 [S]	The Turnaround!	1967	$40
—With "A Division of Liberty Records" on label			
❏ B1-84186	The Turnaround!	1989	$35
—The Finest in Jazz Since 1939" reissue			
❏ LT-1045	Thinking of Home	1980	$60
❏ LT-1081	Third Season	1981	$60
❏ BLP-4080 [M]	Workout	1961	$1000
—With W. 63rd St. address on label			

Number	Title	Yr	NM
❏ BLP-4080 [M]	Workout	1963	$600
—With "New York, USA" address on label			
❏ BST-84080 [S]	Workout	1961	$200
—With W. 63rd St. address on label			
❏ BST-84080 [S]	Workout	1963	$300
—With "New York, USA" address on label			
❏ BST-84080 [S]	Workout	1967	$60
—With "A Division of Liberty Records" on label			
❏ B1-84080	Workout	1988	$30
—The Finest in Jazz Since 1939" reissue			
PRESTIGE			
❏ PRST-7661	Hank Mobley's Message	1969	$60
❏ P-24063	Messages	1976	$60
❏ PRLP-7061 [M]	Mobley's Message	1956	$800
—Yellow label with W. 50th St. address			
❏ PRLP-7082 [M]	Mobley's Second Message	1957	$650
—Yellow label with W. 50th St. address			
❏ PRST-7667	Mobley's Second Message	1969	$60
SAVOY			
❏ MG-12092 [M]	Jazz Message #2	1956	$400
STATUS			
❏ ST-8311 [M]	52nd Street Theme	1965	$80

MODERN JAZZ DISCIPLES, THE
Members: Bill Brown; Wilbur Jackson; Mike Kelly; Roy McCurdy; Curtis Peagler; Lee Tucker.

Albums
NEW JAZZ

Number	Title	Yr	NM
❏ NJLP-8222 [M]	Modern Jazz Disciples	1959	$250
—Purple label			
❏ NJLP-8222 [M]	Modern Jazz Disciples	1965	$150
—Blue label, trident logo at right			
❏ NJLP-8240 [M]	Right Down Front	1960	$150
—Purple label			
❏ NJLP-8240 [M]	Right Down Front	1965	$150
—Blue label, trident logo at right			

MODERN JAZZ ENSEMBLE, THE
See THE MODERN JAZZ SOCIETY.

MODERN JAZZ QUARTET, THE
The classic lineup was Percy Heath (bass); MILT JACKSON (vibes); Connie Kay (drums and percussion); JOHN LEWIS (piano). KENNY CLARKE was the original drummer. Also see OSCAR PETERSON; SONNY ROLLINS.

Albums
APPLE

Number	Title	Yr	NM
❏ STAO-3360	Space	1970	$30

Number	Title	Yr	NM
❏ STAO-5-3360	Space	1970	$80
—Capitol Record Club edition			
❏ ST-3353	Under the Jasmine Tree	1969	$30
❏ ST-5-3353	Under the Jasmine Tree	1969	$80
—Capitol Record Club edition			
ATLANTIC			
❏ 1420 [M]	A Quartet Is a Quartet Is a Quartet	1964	$35
❏ SD1420 [S]	A Quartet Is a Quartet Is a Quartet	1964	$25
—Multicolor label, black "fan" logo at right			
❏ SD1420 [S]	A Quartet Is a Quartet Is a Quartet	1969	$25
—Red and green label			
❏ 1468 [M]	Blues at Carnegie Hall	1967	$35
❏ SD1468 [S]	Blues at Carnegie Hall	1967	$35
—Blue and green label, black "fan" logo at right			
❏ SD1468 [S]	Blues at Carnegie Hall	1969	$30
—Red and green label			
❏ SD1652	Blues on Bach	1974	$30
❏ SQ1652 [Q]	Blues on Bach	1974	$30
❏ 1429 [M]	Collaboration -- The Modern Jazz Quartet with Laurindo Almeida	1964	$30
❏ SD1429 [S]	Collaboration -- The Modern Jazz Quartet with Laurindo Almeida	1969	$25
—Red and green label			
❏ SD1429 [S]	Collaboration -- The Modern Jazz Quartet with Laurindo Almeida	1964	$35
—Multicolor label, black "fan" logo at right			
❏ 1231 [M]	Fontessa	1956	$300
—Black label			
❏ 1231 [M]	Fontessa	1960	$250
—Multicolor label, white "fan" logo at right			
❏ 1231 [M]	Fontessa	1963	$50
—Multicolor label, black "fan" logo at right			
❏ SD1231 [S]	Fontessa	1958	$300
—Green label			
❏ SD1231 [S]	Fontessa	1960	$250
—Multicolor label, white "fan" logo at right			
❏ SD1231 [S]	Fontessa	1963	$50
—Multicolor label, black "fan" logo at right			
❏ SD1231 [S]	Fontessa	1969	$25
—Red and green label			
❏ 1449 [M]	Jazz Dialogue	1966	$30
❏ SD1449 [S]	Jazz Dialogue	1966	$35
—Multicolor label, black "fan" logo at right			
❏ SD1449 [S]	Jazz Dialogue	1969	$25
—Red and green label			
❏ SD1623	Legendary Profile	1973	$30
❏ 1486 [M]	Live at the Lighthouse	1967	$25
❏ SD1486 [S]	Live at the Lighthouse	1967	$30
—Multicolor label, black "fan" logo at right			
❏ SD1486 [S]	Live at the Lighthouse	1969	$25
—Red and green label			
❏ 1381 [M]	Lonely Woman	1962	$150
❏ SD1381 [S]	Lonely Woman	1962	$150
—Multicolor label, black "fan" logo at right			
❏ SD1381 [S]	Lonely Woman	1969	$25
—Red and green label			
❏ SD8806	More from the Last Concert	198?	$25
❏ 1284 [M]	No Sun in Venice	1958	$250
—Black label			
❏ 1284 [M]	No Sun in Venice	1960	$250
—Multicolor label, white "fan" logo at right			
❏ 1284 [M]	No Sun in Venice	1963	$35
—Multicolor label, black "fan" logo at right			
❏ SD1284 [S]	No Sun in Venice	1958	$300
—Green label			
❏ SD1284 [S]	No Sun in Venice	1960	$250
—Multicolor label, white "fan" logo at right			
❏ SD1284 [S]	No Sun in Venice	1963	$30
—Multicolor label, black "fan" logo at right			
❏ SD1284 [S]	No Sun in Venice	1969	$25
—Red and green label			
❏ SD1589	Plastic Dreams	1972	$30
❏ 1325 [M]	Pyramid	1960	$250
—Black label			
❏ 1325 [M]	Pyramid	1961	$150
—Multicolor label, white "fan" logo at right			
❏ 1325 [M]	Pyramid	1963	$35
—Multicolor label, black "fan" logo at right			

Modern Jazz Quartet, *Blues at Carnegie Hall*, Atlantic SD 1488, blue
and green label, **$35**.

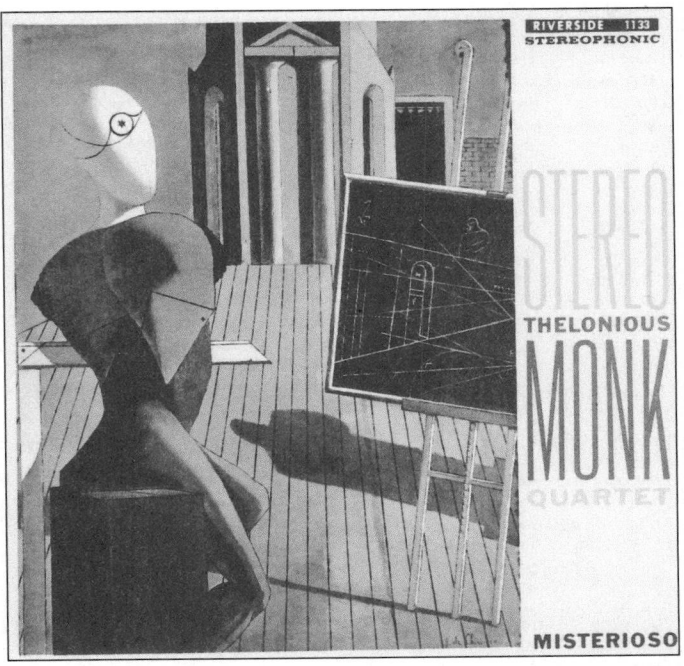

Thelonious Monk, *Misterioso*, Riverside RLP-1133, stereo, black label, **$300**.

Thelonious Monk and John Coltrane, *Thelonious Monk with John
Coltrane*, Jazzland JLP-946, **$150**.

Thelonious Monk, *Thelonious in Action Recorded at the Five Spot Café*,
New York, With Johnny Griffin, Riverside RLP-1190, stereo, black label,
$200.

Number	Title	Yr	NM
❑ SD1325 [S]	Pyramid	1960	$250
—Green label			
❑ SD1325 [S]	Pyramid	1961	$150
—Multicolor label, white "fan" logo at right			
❑ SD1325 [S]	Pyramid	1963	$30
—Multicolor label, black "fan" logo at right			
❑ SD1325 [S]	Pyramid	1969	$25
—Red and green label			
❑ SD 2-301	The Art of the Modern Jazz Quartet	1973	$35
❑ SD1546	The Best of the Modern Jazz Quartet	1970	$30
❑ 1390 [M]	The Comedy	1963	$50
❑ SD1390 [S]	The Comedy	1963	$50
—Multicolor label, black "fan" logo at right			
❑ SD1390 [S]	The Comedy	1969	$25
—Red and green label			
❑ 2-603 [M]	The European Concert	1961	$150
—Multicolor labels, white "fan" logo at right			
❑ 2-603 [M]	The European Concert	1963	$50
—Multicolor labels, black "fan" logo at right			
❑ SD 2-603 [S]	The European Concert	1961	$150
—Multicolor labels, white "fan" logo at right			
❑ SD 2-603 [S]	The European Concert	1963	$50
—Multicolor labels, black "fan" logo at right			
❑ SD 2-603 [S]	The European Concert	1969	$35
—Red and green labels			
❑ 1385 [M]	The European Concert, Volume 1	1962	$150
❑ SD1385 [S]	The European Concert, Volume 1	1962	$150
—Multicolor label, black "fan" logo at right			
❑ SD1385 [S]	The European Concert, Volume 1	1969	$25
—Red and green label			
❑ 1386 [M]	The European Concert, Volume 2	1962	$150
❑ SD1386 [S]	The European Concert, Volume 2	1962	$150
—Multicolor label, black "fan" logo at right			
❑ SD1386 [S]	The European Concert, Volume 2	1969	$25
—Red and green label			
❑ SD 2-909	The Last Concert	1975	$35
❑ SQ 2-909 [Q]	The Last Concert	1975	$40
❑ 1265 [M]	The Modern Jazz Quartet	1957	$300
—Black label			
❑ 1265 [M]	The Modern Jazz Quartet	1960	$150
—Multicolor label, white "fan" logo at right			
❑ 1265 [M]	The Modern Jazz Quartet	1963	$150
—Multicolor label, black "fan" logo at right			
❑ 1359 [M]	The Modern Jazz Quartet and Orchestra	1961	$300
—Multicolor label, white "fan" logo at right			
❑ 1359 [M]	The Modern Jazz Quartet and Orchestra	1963	$150
—Multicolor label, black "fan" logo at right			
❑ SD1359 [S]	The Modern Jazz Quartet and Orchestra	1961	$200
—Multicolor label, white "fan" logo at right			
❑ SD1359 [S]	The Modern Jazz Quartet and Orchestra	1963	$150
—Multicolor label, black "fan" logo at right			
❑ SD1359 [S]	The Modern Jazz Quartet and Orchestra	1969	$25
—Red and green label			
❑ 1247 [M]	The Modern Jazz Quartet at the Music Inn	1956	$300
—Black label			
❑ 1247 [M]	The Modern Jazz Quartet at the Music Inn	1960	$150
—Multicolor label, white "fan" logo at right			
❑ 1247 [M]	The Modern Jazz Quartet at the Music Inn	1963	$150
—Multicolor label, black "fan" logo at right			
❑ 90049	The Modern Jazz Quartet at the Music Inn	1983	$25
❑ 1299 [M]	The Modern Jazz Quartet at the Music Inn, Volume 2	1958	$250
—Black label			
❑ 1299 [M]	The Modern Jazz Quartet at the Music Inn, Volume 2	1960	$150
—Multicolor label, white "fan" logo at right			
❑ 1299 [M]	The Modern Jazz Quartet at the Music Inn, Volume 2	1963	$150

Number	Title	Yr	NM
—Multicolor label, black "fan" logo at right			
❑ SD 1299 [S]	The Modern Jazz Quartet at the Music Inn, Volume 2	1958	$250
—Green label			
❑ SD 1299 [S]	The Modern Jazz Quartet at the Music Inn, Volume 2	1960	$150
—Multicolor label, white "fan" logo at right			
❑ SD 1299 [S]	The Modern Jazz Quartet at the Music Inn, Volume 2	1963	$150
—Multicolor label, black "fan" logo at right			
❑ SD 1299 [S]	The Modern Jazz Quartet at the Music Inn, Volume 2	1969	$25
—Red and green label			
❑ 1440 [M]	The Modern Jazz Quartet Plays Gershwin's "Porgy and Bess"	1965	$30
❑ SD1440 [S]	The Modern Jazz Quartet Plays Gershwin's "Porgy and Bess"	1965	$35
—Multicolor label, black "fan" logo at right			
❑ SD1440 [S]	The Modern Jazz Quartet Plays Gershwin's "Porgy and Bess"	1969	$25
—Red and green label			
❑ 1414 [M]	The Sheriff	1964	$35
❑ SD1414 [S]	The Sheriff	1964	$25
—Multicolor label, black "fan" logo at right			
❑ SD1414 [S]	The Sheriff	1969	$25
—Red and green label			
❑ 1345 [M]	Third Stream Music	1960	$250
—Multicolor label, white "fan" logo at right			
❑ 1345 [M]	Third Stream Music	1963	$30
—Multicolor label, black "fan" logo at right			
❑ SD1345 [S]	Third Stream Music	1960	$250
—Multicolor label, white "fan" logo at right			
❑ SD1345 [S]	Third Stream Music	1963	$35
—Multicolor label, black "fan" logo at right			
❑ SD1345 [S]	Third Stream Music	1969	$25
—Red and green label			
❑ 81761	Three Windows	1987	$25
EASTWEST			
❑ 90826	For Ellington	1988	$25
FANTASY			
❑ OJC-002	Concorde	1982	$25
❑ OJC-057	Django	198?	$25
❑ OJC-125	Modern Jazz Quartet/Milt Jackson Quintet	198?	$25
LITTLE DAVID			
❑ LD3001	In Memoriam	1975	$30
❑ 90130	In Memoriam	198?	$25
MOBILE FIDELITY			
❑ 1-206	Blues at Carnegie Hall	1994	$40
—Audiophile vinyl			
❑ Jan-0090	Live at the Lighthouse	1982	$50
—Audiophile vinyl			
❑ 1-205	The Modern Jazz Quartet	1994	$40
—Audiophile vinyl			
❑ 1-228	The Modern Jazz Quartet at the Music Inn, Volume 2	1995	$60
—Audiophile vinyl			
PABLO			
❑ 2405423	The Best of the Modern Jazz Quartet	198?	$25
❑ 2310917	Topsy: This One's for Basie	198?	$25
PABLO LIVE			
❑ 2308243	Reunion at Budokan	198?	$25
❑ 2308244	Together Again... At Montreux Jazz Festival	198?	$25
PABLO TODAY			
❑ 2312142	Together Again	1984	$25
PRESTIGE			
❑ PRLP-7005 [M]	Concorde	1955	$300
—Yellow label originals			
❑ 16-1 [M]	Concorde	1955	$500
—This album plays at 16 2/3 rpm and is marked as such; white label; one side has the Modern Jazz Quartet, the other side has Milt Jackson			
❑ PRLP-7057 [M]	Django	1956	$325
—Yellow label originals			
❑ PRST-7749	First Recordings	1970	$30
❑ PRLP-7059 [M]	Modern Jazz Quartet/Milt Jackson Quintet	1956	$300
—Yellow label originals			
❑ 24005	The Modern Jazz Quartet	197?	$35

Number	Title	Yr	NM
❑ PRLP-170 [10]	The Modern Jazz Quartet, Volume 2	1953	$350
❑ PRLP-7421 [M]	The Modern Jazz Quartet Play for Lovers	1966	$25
❑ PRST-7421 [R]	The Modern Jazz Quartet Play for Lovers	1966	$30
❑ PRLP-7425 [M]	The Modern Jazz Quartet Plays Jazz Classics	1966	$25
❑ PRST-7425 [R]	The Modern Jazz Quartet Plays Jazz Classics	1966	$30
❑ PRLP-160 [10]	The Modern Jazz Quartet with Milt Jackson	1953	$350
SAVOY			
❑ MG-12046 [M]	Modern Jazz Quartet	1955	$250
SOLID STATE			
❑ SS-18035	The Modern Jazz Quartet on Tour	1968	$30
UNITED ARTISTS			
❑ UAL-4072 [M]	Patterns	1960	$30
❑ UAS-5072 [S]	Patterns	1960	$30

MODERN JAZZ QUINTET, THE

Albums

Number	Title	Yr	NM
SURREY			
❑ S-1030 [M]	Q.T. Hush	1966	$30
❑ SS-1030 [S]	Q.T. Hush	1966	$30

MODERN JAZZ SEXTET, THE

Members: Skeeter Best (guitar); DIZZY GILLESPIE (trumpet); Percy Heath (bass); JOHN LEWIS (piano); CHARLIE PERSIP (drums); SONNY STITT (alto & tenor sax).

Albums

Number	Title	Yr	NM
AMERICAN RECORDING SOCIETY			
❑ G-429 [M]	The Modern Jazz Sextet	1957	$300
NORGRAN			
❑ MGN-1076 [M]	The Modern Jazz Sextet	1956	$200
VERVE			
❑ VE-1-2533	Dizzy Meets Sonny	197?	$30
❑ MGV-8166 [M]	The Modern Jazz Sextet	1957	$300
❑ V-8166 [M]	The Modern Jazz Sextet	1961	$150

MODERN JAZZ SOCIETY, THE

Members: STAN GETZ; Percy Heath; J.J. JOHNSON; Connie Kay; James Politis; Jim Poole; Janet Putnam; AARON SACHS; Gunther Schuller; TONY SCOTT; LUCKY THOMPSON; Manny Ziegler.

Albums

Number	Title	Yr	NM
AMERICAN RECORDING SOCIETY			
❑ G-432 [M]	A Concert of Contemporary Music	1957	$250
NORGRAN			
❑ MGN-1040 [M]	A Concert of Contemporary Music	1955	$250
VERVE			
❑ MGV-8131 [M]	A Concert of Contemporary Music	1957	$250
❑ V-8131 [M]	A Concert of Contemporary Music	1961	$200
❑ VSP-18 [M]	Little David's Fugue	1966	$25
—As "The Modern Jazz Ensemble			
❑ VSPS-18 [R]	Little David's Fugue	1966	$30
—As "The Modern Jazz Ensemble			

MODERN JAZZ STARS, THE

Collections of mostly late 1940s and early 1950s masters from the Modern Records archives. Among those known to be on at least one of the songs on these two records are TEDDY EDWARDS; JIMMY GIUFFRE; WARDELL GRAY; SHELLY MANNE; VIDO MUSSO; HOWARD McGHEE; ART PEPPER; BEN WEBSTER, and others.

Albums

Number	Title	Yr	NM
CROWN			
❑ CLP-5009 [M]	Jazz Masquerade	1957	$30
—Original edition has black label with silver print			
❑ CLP-5008 [M]	Jazz Surprise	1957	$30

MODERN JAZZ TRIO

See MJT + 3.

Number	Title	Yr	NM

MODERN MANDOLIN QUARTET, THE
Members: Paul Binkley; John Imholtz; David Peters; Dana Rath.

Albums

LOST LAKE ARTS

| ❏ LL-0095 | Modern Mandolin Quartet | 1988 | $30 |

MOER, PAUL
Pianist.

Albums

DEL-FI

| ❏ DFLP-1212 [M] | Contemporary Jazz Classics | 1961 | $200 |
| ❏ DFST-1212 [S] | Contemporary Jazz Classics | 1961 | $200 |

MOFFETT, CHARLES
Drummer.

Albums

SAVOY

| ❏ MG-12194 | The Gift | 1969 | $25 |

MOFFETT, CHARNETT
Bass player.

Albums

BLUE NOTE

| ❏ B1-91650 | Beauty Within | 1989 | $35 |
| ❏ BT-46993 | Nett Man | 1987 | $25 |

MOFFITT, PETER
Cello player and flutist.

Albums

NOVUS

| ❏ 3059-1-N | Riverdance | 1989 | $30 |
| ❏ 3020-1-N | Zoe's Song | 1987 | $25 |

MOJO JAZZIN' FIVE

Albums

STOMP OFF

| ❏ SOS-1086 | South Side Chicago Style | 1985 | $25 |

MOLE, MIFF
Trombonist.

Albums

JAZZOLOGY

| ❏ J-105 | Milt Mole and His World Jam Session Band, 1944 | 198? | $25 |
| ❏ JCE-5 [M] | The Immortal Miff Mole | 1964 | $35 |

MOLE, MIFF/EDMUND HALL
Also see each artist's individual listings.

Albums

BRUNSWICK

| ❏ BL58042 [10] | Battle of Jazz, Volume 4 | 1953 | $60 |

MOLENAT, CLAUDE

Albums

VANGUARD

| ❏ VSD-319 | Trumpet/Organ/Rhythm | 197? | $30 |

MONCUR, GRACHAN, III
Trombonist.

Albums

BLUE NOTE

❏ BLP-4153 [M]	Evolution	1963	$60
❏ BST-84153 [S]	Evolution	1963	$30
— With "New York, USA" address on label			
❏ BST-84153 [S]	Evolution	1967	$35
— With "A Division of Liberty Records" on label			
❏ BST-84153 [S]	Evolution	1986	$25
— The Finest in Jazz Since 1939" reissue			
❏ BLP-4177 [M]	Some Other Stuff	1964	$60
❏ BST-84177 [S]	Some Other Stuff	1964	$30
— With "New York, USA" address on label			
❏ BST-84177 [S]	Some Other Stuff	1967	$35
— With "A Division of Liberty Records" on label			

JCOA

| ❏ 1009 | Echoes of Prayer | 197? | $35 |

PICCADILLY

| ❏ 3520 | African Concepts | 198? | $25 |

MONK, MEREDITH
Female singer and composer.

Albums

ECM

| ❏ 1197 | Dolmen Music | 198? | $25 |
| ❏ 23792 | Turtle Dreams | 1983 | $25 |

LOVELY

| ❏ 1051 | Key | 198? | $25 |

MONK, THELONIOUS, AND JOHN COLTRANE
Also see each artist's individual listings.

Albums

FANTASY

| ❏ OJC-039 | Thelonious Monk with John Coltrane | 198? | $30 |

JAZZLAND

| ❏ JLP-46 [M] | Thelonious Monk with John Coltrane | 1961 | $175 |
| ❏ JLP-946 [S] | Thelonious Monk with John Coltrane | 1961 | $150 |

MILESTONE

| ❏ M-47011 | Monk/Trane | 1973 | $50 |

RIVERSIDE

❏ RLP-490 [M]	Thelonious Monk with John Coltrane	1965	$100
— Reissue of Jazzland 46			
❏ RS-9490 [S]	Thelonious Monk with John Coltrane	1965	$40
— Reissue of Jazzland 946			

MONK, THELONIOUS
Pianist and composer; one of the most influential and important post-World War II jazz figures. Also see ART BLAKEY; MILES DAVIS.

Albums

ANALOGUE PRODUCTIONS

| ❏ AP-37 | The Riverside Tenor Sessions | 1999 | $250 |

BANDSTAND

| ❏ BDLP-1516 | April in Paris | 1992 | $30 |
| ❏ BDLP-1505 | Blue Monk | 1992 | $30 |

BLACK LION

| ❏ 152 | Something in Blue | 1972 | $50 |
| ❏ 197 | The Man I Love | 1973 | $50 |

BLUE NOTE

❏ BLP-5002 [10]	Genius of Modern Music, Vol. 1	1952	$800
❏ BLP-1510 [M]	Genius of Modern Music, Vol. 1	1956	$400
— Deep groove" version; Lexington Ave. address on label			
❏ BLP-1510 [M]	Genius of Modern Music, Vol. 1	1958	$200
— Deep groove" edition, W. 63rd St. address on label			
❏ BLP-1510 [M]	Genius of Modern Music, Vol. 1	1963	$80
— New York, USA" address on label			
❏ BLP-81510 [R]	Genius of Modern Music, Vol. 1	1968	$100
— A Division of Liberty Records" on label			
❏ BST-81510	Genius of Modern Music, Vol. 1	1985	$30
— The Finest in Jazz Since 1939" reissue			
❏ BLP-5009 [10]	Genius of Modern Music, Vol. 2	1952	$800
❏ BLP-1511 [M]	Genius of Modern Music, Vol. 2	1956	$800
— Deep groove" version; Lexington Ave. address on label			
❏ BLP-1511 [M]	Genius of Modern Music, Vol. 2	1958	$400
— Deep groove" edition, W. 63rd St. address on label			
❏ BLP-1511 [M]	Genius of Modern Music, Vol. 2	1963	$150
— New York, USA" address on label			
❏ BLP-81511 [R]	Genius of Modern Music, Vol. 2	1968	$100
— A Division of Liberty Records" on label			
❏ BST-81511	Genius of Modern Music, Vol. 2	1985	$30
— The Finest in Jazz Since 1939" reissue			
❏ BN-LA579-H2	The Complete Genius	1976	$50

| ❏ LWB-579 | The Complete Genius | 1981 | $35 |
| — Reissue of BN-LA579-H2 | | | |

COLUMBIA

❏ JG35720	Always Know	1979	$50
❏ CL2038 [M]	Criss-Cross	1963	$60
— Guaranteed High Fidelity" on label			
❏ CS8838 [S]	Criss-Cross	1963	$120
— 360 Sound Stereo" in black on label			
❏ CL2038 [M]	Criss-Cross	1966	$50
— 360 Sound Mono" on label			
❏ CL2038 [M]	Criss-Cross	199?	$30
— 180-gram reissue			
❏ CS8838 [S]	Criss-Cross	1966	$60
— 360 Sound Stereo" in white on label			
❏ CS9775	Greatest Hits	1969	$50
— Red "360 Sound" label			
❏ CS9775	Greatest Hits	1971	$30
— Orange label			
❏ PC9775	Greatest Hits	198?	$20
— Reissue with new prefix			
❏ CL2184 [M]	It's Monk's Time	1964	$60
— Guaranteed High Fidelity" on label			
❏ CS8984 [S]	It's Monk's Time	1964	$140
— 360 Sound Stereo" in black on label			
❏ CL2184 [M]	It's Monk's Time	1966	$50
— 360 Sound Mono" on label			
❏ CS8984 [S]	It's Monk's Time	1966	$60
— 360 Sound Stereo" in white on label			
❏ CS8984 [S]	It's Monk's Time	199?	$30
— 180-gram reissue			
❏ C238030	Live at the It Club	1983	$60
— Original edition			
❏ C238030	Live at the It Club	199?	$35
— 180-gram reissue			
❏ C238269	Live at the Jazz Workshop	1983	$60
❏ CL2416 [M]	Misterioso	1966	$60
— 360 Sound Mono" on label			
❏ CS9216 [S]	Misterioso	1966	$60
— 360 Sound Stereo" on red label			
❏ CL2416 [M]	Misterioso	199?	$30
— 180-gram reissue			
❏ CL2291 [M]	Monk	1965	$60
— Guaranteed High Fideilty" on label			
❏ CS9091 [S]	Monk	1965	$100
— 360 Sound Stereo" in black on label			
❏ CS9091 [S]	Monk	1966	$60
— 360 Sound Stereo" in white on label			
❏ CS9091 [S]	Monk	199?	$30
— 180-gram reissue			
❏ CL2291 [M]	Monk	1966	$50
— 360 Sound Mono" on label			
❏ CL2164 [M]	Monk Big Band and Quartet In Concert	1964	$60
— Guaranteed High Fidelity" on label			
❏ CS8964 [S]	Monk Big Band and Quartet In Concert	1964	$150
— 360 Sound Stereo" in black on label			
❏ CL2164 [M]	Monk Big Band and Quartet In Concert	1966	$50
— 360 Sound Mono" on label			
❏ CS8964 [S]	Monk Big Band and Quartet In Concert	1966	$60
— 360 Sound Stereo" in white on label			
❏ CS8964 [S]	Monk Big Band and Quartet In Concert	199?	$30
— 180-gram reissue			
❏ CS9806	Monk's Blues	1969	$150
— Red "360 Sound" label			
❏ CS9806	Monk's Blues	1971	$35
— Orange label			
❏ PC9806	Monk's Blues	198?	$20
— Reissue with new prefix; most have bar codes on back cover			
❏ PC9806	Monk's Blues	199?	$30
— 180-gram reissue			
❏ CL1965 [M]	Monk's Dream	1963	$60
— Guaranteed High Fideilty" on label			
❏ CS8765 [S]	Monk's Dream	1963	$140
— 360 Sound Stereo" in black on label			
❏ CL1965 [M]	Monk's Dream	1966	$50
— 360 Sound Mono" on label			

Number	Title	Yr	NM
❏ CS8765 [S]	Monk's Dream	1966	$60

—*360 Sound Stereo" in white on label*

Number	Title	Yr	NM
❏ CS8765 [S]	Monk's Dream	199?	$30

—*180-gram reissue*

❏ CL2349 [M]	Solo Monk	1965	$60

—*360 Sound Mono" on label*

❏ CS9149 [S]	Solo Monk	1965	$40

—*Red "360 Sound" label*

❏ CS9149	Solo Monk	1971	$30

—*Orange label*

❏ PC9149	Solo Monk	198?	$20

—*Reissue with new prefix; most have bar codes*

❏ PC9149	Solo Monk	199?	$30

—*180-gram reissue*

❏ CL2651 [M]	Straight No Chaser	1967	$100

—*Red label with "Mono*

❏ CS9451 [S]	Straight No Chaser	1967	$40

—*Red "360 Sound" label*

❏ CS9451	Straight No Chaser	1971	$30

—*Orange label*

❏ PC9451	Straight No Chaser	198?	$20

—*Reissue with new prefix*

❏ PC9451	Straight No Chaser	199?	$30

—*180-gram reissue*

❏ C238510	The Tokyo Concerts	1984	$50

—*Original edition*

❏ C238510	The Tokyo Concerts	199?	$35

—*180-gram reissue*

❏ CS9632 [S]	Underground	1968	$60

—*Red "360 Sound" label*

❏ CS9632	Underground	1971	$30

—*Orange label*

❏ PC9632	Underground	198?	$20

—*Reissue with new prefix*

❏ CS9632 [M]	Underground	1968	$100

—*White label promo only with stereo number; "Special Mono Radio Station Copy" sticker on stereo cover*

❏ PC9632	Underground	199?	$30

—*180-gram reissue*

❏ KG32892	Who's Afraid of the Big Band Monk	1974	$60
❏ KG32892	Who's Afraid of the Big Band Monk	199?	$35

—*180-gram reissue*

COLUMBIA JAZZ MASTERPIECES

❏ CJ40786	Monk's Dream	1987	$25
❏ CJ44297	The Composer	1988	$30
❏ CJ40785	Underground	1987	$25

COLUMBIA LIMITED EDITION

❏ LE10122	Criss-Cross	197?	$30

COLUMBIA MUSICAL TREASURY

❏ DS338	Monk's Miracles	1967	$60

—*Columbia Record Club exclusive*

EVEREST ARCHIVE OF FOLK & JAZZ

❏ FS-336	Piano Solos	1978	$30

FANTASY

❏ OJC-362	5 By Monk By 5	1989	$30
❏ OJC-231	Alone in San Francisco	1987	$30
❏ OJC-026	Brilliant Corners	198?	$30
❏ OJC-206	Misterioso	1985	$30
❏ OJC-016	Monk	198?	$30
❏ OJC-488	Monk in Italy	1991	$30
❏ OJC-084	Monk's Music	198?	$30
❏ OJC-301	Mulligan Meets Monk	1988	$30
❏ OJC-254	Thelonious Himself	1987	$30
❏ OJC-103	Thelonious in Action	198?	$30
❏ OJC-305	Thelonious Monk at the Blackhawk	1988	$30
❏ OJC-135	Thelonious Monk at Town Hall	1984	$30
❏ OJC-024	Thelonious Monk Plays Duke Ellington	198?	$30
❏ OJC-059	Thelonious Monk/Sonny Rollins	198?	$30
❏ OJC-010	Thelonious Monk Trio	198?	$30
❏ OJC-064	The Unique Thelonious Monk	198?	$30

GATEWAY

❏ GSLP-7023	Monk's Music	197?	$35

GNP CRESCENDO

❏ 9008	Thelonious Monk	197?	$35

JAZZ MAN

❏ 5017	Something in Blue	1980	$30

MILESTONE

❏ M-47060	April in Paris/Live	198?	$50
❏ M-9124	Blues Five Spot	1984	$35
❏ M-47023	Brilliance	1975	$60
❏ M-9115	Evidence	1983	$30
❏ M-47064	Memorial Album	1982	$50
❏ M-47004	Pure Monk	1972	$50
❏ M-47067	'Round Midnight	198?	$50
❏ M-47043	Thelonious Monk at the Five Spot	1978	$50
❏ M-47033	Thelonious Monk In Person	1976	$60
❏ M-47052	The Riverside Trios	1980	$50

MOSAIC

❏ MR4-112	The Complete Black Lion and Vogue Recordings	199?	$250

—*Limited edition of 7,500*

❏ MR4-101	The Complete Blue Note Recordings of Thelonious Monk	198?	$200

—*Limited edition of 7,500*

PICCADILLY

❏ 3521	Monkisms	198?	$30

PRESTIGE

❏ PRST-7848	Blue Monk, Volume 2	197?	$35
❏ PRLP-7159 [M]	Monk's Moods	1959	$200

—*Reissue of 7027; yellow label with Bergenfield, N.J. address*

❏ PRST-7751	Reflections, Volume 1	1970	$50
❏ PRST-7656	The Genius of Thelonious Monk	1969	$50
❏ PRLP-7363 [M]	The Golden Monk	1965	$60

—*Reissue of 7245*

❏ PRST-7363 [R]	The Golden Monk	1965	$50
❏ PRLP-7508 [M]	The High Priest	1967	$100

—*Reissue of 7159*

❏ PRST-7508 [R]	The High Priest	1967	$50
❏ PRLP-7027 [M]	Thelonious Monk	1956	$700

—*Reissue of 142 and 189 on one 12-inch record; yellow label with W. 50th St. address; label calls this "Thelonious Monk Trio"*

❏ PR-24006	Thelonious Monk	1971	$50
❏ PRLP-180 [10]	Thelonious Monk Quintet	1954	$800
❏ PRLP-166 [10]	Thelonious Monk Quintet with Sonny Rollins and Julius Watkins	1953	$800
❏ PRLP-7075 [M]	Thelonious Monk/Sonny Rollins	1957	$500

—*Reissue of 166; yellow label with W. 50th St. address*

❏ PRLP-142 [10]	Thelonious Monk Trio	1953	$800
❏ PRLP-189 [10]	Thelonious Monk Trio	1954	$800
❏ PRLP-7245 [M]	We See	1962	$300

—*Reissue of 7053*

❏ PRLP-7169 [M]	Work	1959	$200

—*Reissue of 7075*

RIVERSIDE

❏ RLP 12-305 [M]	5 By Monk By 5	1959	$300

—*Blue label with reel and microphone logo*

❏ RLP1150 [S]	5 By Monk By 5	1959	$350

—*Black label with reel and microphone logo*

❏ 6086	5 By Monk By 5	197?	$30
❏ 6163	Alone in San Francisco	198?	$30
❏ RS-3037	Best of Thelonious Monk	1969	$100
❏ RLP 12-226 [M]	Brilliant Corners	1957	$1000

—*White label with blue print*

❏ RLP 12-226 [M]	Brilliant Corners	1958	$300

—*Blue label with reel and microphone logo*

❏ RS-3009 [R]	CT Meets Monk	1968	$100
❏ 6107	Meet Thelonious Monk and Gerry Mulligan	197?	$30
❏ RM-3000 [M]	Mighty Monk	1967	$100
❏ RS-3000 [S]	Mighty Monk	1967	$100
❏ RLP 12-279 [M]	Misterioso	1958	$300

—*Blue label with reel-and-microphone logo*

❏ RLP1133 [S]	Misterioso	1958	$300

—*Black label with reel and microphone logo*

❏ 6119	Misterioso	197?	$30
❏ RLP-491 [M]	Monk in France	1965	$150
❏ RS-9491 [S]	Monk in France	1965	$150
❏ RS-3015 [R]	Monk Plays Duke	1968	$100
❏ RLP 12-242 [M]	Monk's Music	1957	$700

—*White label with blue print*

❏ RLP 12-242 [M]	Monk's Music	1958	$300

—*Blue label with reel and microphone logo*

❏ RLP1101 [S]	Monk's Music	1959	$250

—*Black label with reel and microphone logo*

❏ RM-3004 [M]	Monk's Music	1967	$100
❏ RS-3004 [S]	Monk's Music	1967	$100
❏ 6207	Monk's Music	1983	$50
❏ RLP 12-247 [M]	Mulligan Meets Monk	1957	$400

—*White label with blue print*

❏ RLP 12-247 [M]	Mulligan Meets Monk	1958	$300

—*Blue label with reel and microphone logo*

❏ RLP1106 [S]	Mulligan Meets Monk	1959	$250

—*Black label with reel and microphone logo*

❏ RS-3047	Panorama!	1970	$100

❏ R-022	The Complete Riverside Recordings	1987	$500
❏ RLP 12-312 [M]	Thelonious Alone in San Francisco	1959	$200

—*Blue label with reel and microphone logo*

❏ RLP1158 [S]	Thelonious Alone in San Francisco	1959	$200

—*Black label with reel and microphone logo*

❏ RLP 12-235 [M]	Thelonious Himself	1957	$400

—*White label with blue print*

❏ RLP 12-235 [M]	Thelonious Himself	1958	$300

—*Blue label with reel and microphone logo*

❏ 6053 [M]	Thelonious Himself	197?	$30
❏ 6102	Thelonious in Action	197?	$30
❏ RLP 12-262 [M]	Thelonious in Action Recorded at the Five Spot Café, New York, With Johnny Griffin	1958	$300

—*Blue label with reel and microphone logo*

❏ RLP1190 [S]	Thelonious in Action Recorded at the Five Spot Café, New York, With Johnny Griffin	1960	$200

—*Black label with reel and microphone logo*

❏ 6198	Thelonious Monk at the Blackhawk	198?	$30
❏ 6183	Thelonious Monk at Town Hall	198?	$30
❏ RLP-443 [M]	Thelonious Monk in Italy	1963	$150
❏ RS-9443 [S]	Thelonious Monk in Italy	1963	$150
❏ RLP 12-201 [M]	Thelonious Monk Plays Duke Ellington	1955	$900

—*White label with blue print*

❏ 6039 [M]	Thelonious Monk Plays Duke Ellington	197?	$30
❏ RLP 12-323 [M]	Thelonious Monk Quartet Plus Two at the Blackhawk	1960	$200

—*Blue label with reel and microphone logo*

❏ RLP1171 [S]	Thelonious Monk Quartet Plus Two at the Blackhawk	1960	$200

—*Black label with reel and microphone logo*

❏ RLP-421 [M]	Thelonious Monk's Greatest Hits	1962	$150
❏ RS-9421 [S]	Thelonious Monk's Greatest Hits	1962	$150
❏ RLP 12-300 [M]	The Thelonious Monk Orchestra at Town Hall	1959	$200

—*Blue label with reel and microphone logo*

❏ RLP1138 [S]	The Thelonious Monk Orchestra at Town Hall	1959	$200

—*Black label with reel and microphone logo*

❏ RS-9483/4 [S]	The Thelonious Monk Story	1965	$120
❏ RLP-483/4 [M]	The Thelonious Monk Story	1965	$140
❏ RLP-483 [M]	The Thelonious Monk Story, Volume 1	1965	$150
❏ RS-9483 [S]	The Thelonious Monk Story, Volume 1	1965	$150
❏ RLP-484 [M]	The Thelonious Monk Story, Volume 2	1965	$150
❏ RS-9484 [S]	The Thelonious Monk Story, Volume 2	1965	$150
❏ RLP 12-209 [M]	The Unique Thelonious Monk	1956	$500

—*White label with blue print*

❏ RLP 12-209 [M]	The Unique Thelonious Monk	1958	$300

—*Blue label with reel and microphone logo*

❏ 6068 [M]	The Unique Thelonious Monk	197?	$30
❏ RLP-460/1 [M]	Two Hours with Thelonious Monk	1963	$150
❏ RS-9460/1 [S]	Two Hours with Thelonious Monk	1963	$150
❏ RS-3020X [R]	Two Hours with Thelonious Monk	1969	$100

TRIP

❏ 5022	Pure Monk	1974	$30

XANADU

❏ 202	Live at the Village Gate	1985	$35

MONNIER, ALAIN

Albums

HAT HUT

❏ 3505	Tribulat	198?	$35

J.R. Monterose, *The Message*, Jaro JAS-8004, **$1,000**.

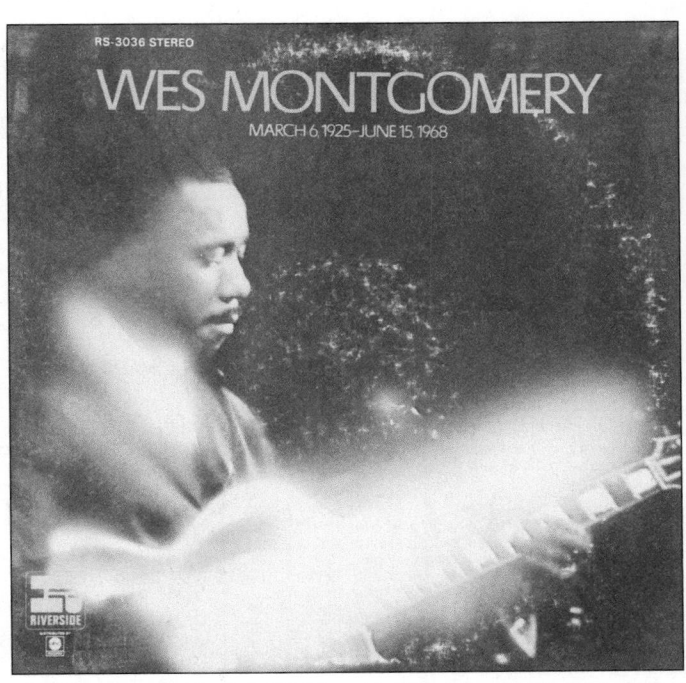

Wes Montgomery, March 6, 1925-June 15, 1968, Riverside RS-3036, **$100**.

Wes Montgomery, *California Dreaming*, Verve V6-8672, mono, **$50**.

Wes Montgomery, *A Day in the Life*, A&M SP-3001, **$30**.

MONROE, VAUGHN

Male singer, bandleader and occasional trumpeter.

Albums

DOT

Number	Title	Yr	NM
DLP-3548 [M]	Great Gospels -- Great Hymns	1963	$60
DLP-25548 [S]	Great Gospels -- Great Hymns	1963	$60
DLP-3470 [M]	Great Themes of Famous Bands and Famous Singers	1962	$60
DLP-25470 [S]	Great Themes of Famous Bands and Famous Singers	1962	$60
DLP-3431 [M]	His Greatest Hits	1962	$60
DLP-25431 [S]	His Greatest Hits	1962	$60
DLP-3584 [M]	His Greatest Hits, Volume 2	1964	$60
DLP-25584 [S]	His Greatest Hits, Volume 2	1964	$60
DLP-3419 [M]	Surfer's Stomp	1962	$75
DLP-25419 [S]	Surfer's Stomp	1962	$80

HAMILTON

Number	Title	Yr	NM
HLP-137 [M]	Racing with the Moon	1965	$12
HLP-12137 [S]	Racing with the Moon	1965	$15

RCA CAMDEN

Number	Title	Yr	NM
CAL-329 [M]	Dance with Me	1956	$30
CAL-354 [M]	Dreamland Special	1956	$30

RCA VICTOR

Number	Title	Yr	NM
LPM-1493 [M]	House Party	1957	$30
LPM-3817 [M]	The Best of Vaughn Monroe	1967	$25
LSP-3817 [R]	The Best of Vaughn Monroe	1967	$15
ANL1-1140	The Best of Vaughn Monroe	1976	$10
LPM-1799 [M]	There I Sing, Swing It Again	1958	$30
LSP-1799 [S]	There I Sing, Swing It Again	1958	$30
VPM-6073	This Is Vaughn Monroe	1972	$20
LPM-3048 [10]	Vaughn Monroe Caravan	1952	$40
LPM-13 [10]	Vaughn Monroe Plays Victor Herbert for Dancing	1952	$40

MONTANA

Albums

LABOR

Number	Title	Yr	NM
5	Montana	198?	$30

MONTARROYOS, MARCIO

Trumpeter.

Albums

BLACK SUN

Number	Title	Yr	NM
15001	Samba Solstice	1987	$30

COLUMBIA

Number	Title	Yr	NM
FC38952	Carioca	1983	$25

LORIMAR

Number	Title	Yr	NM
FC37929	Magic Moment	1982	$25

PM

Number	Title	Yr	NM
014	Marcio Montarroyos and Stone Alliance	1977	$35

MONTEGO JOE

Percussionist.

Albums

ESP-DISK'

Number	Title	Yr	NM
S-1067	Montego Joe's HARYOU Percussion Ensemble	1968	$200

PRESTIGE

Number	Title	Yr	NM
PRLP-7336 [M]	Arriba Con Montego Joe	1964	$30
PRST-7336 [S]	Arriba Con Montego Joe	1964	$30
PRLP-7413 [M]	Wild and Warm	1966	$60
PRST-7413 [S]	Wild and Warm	1966	$60

MONTEROSE, J.R.

Tenor saxophone player.

Albums

BLUE NOTE

Number	Title	Yr	NM
BST-81536 [R]	J.R. Monterose	1967	$35

— *With "A Division of Liberty Records" on label*

Number	Title	Yr	NM
BLP-1536 [M]	J.R. Monterose	2003	$100

— *200-gram reissue; distributed by Classic Records*

CADENCE JAZZ

Number	Title	Yr	NM
CJ-1013	Bebop Loose and Live	198?	$50

JARO

Number	Title	Yr	NM
JAM-5004 [M]	The Message	1959	$1000
JAS-8004 [S]	The Message	1959	$1000

PROGRESSIVE

Number	Title	Yr	NM
PRO7049	Lush Life	1979	$60

STUDIO 4

Number	Title	Yr	NM
100 [M]	J.R. Monterose in Action	195?	$2000

UPTOWN

Number	Title	Yr	NM
272	J.R. Monterose in Albany	1980	$35
276	J.R. Monterose in Duo with Tommy Flanagan….And a Little Pleasure	198?	$35

XANADU

Number	Title	Yr	NM
126	Straight Ahead	197?	$50

MONTGOMERY, BUDDY

Vibraphone player, pianist and composer. Also see THE MASTERSOUNDS; THE MONTGOMERY BROTHERS.

Albums

ABC IMPULSE!

Number	Title	Yr	NM
AS-9192	This Rather Than That	1970	$200

BEAN

Number	Title	Yr	NM
102	Ties	197?	$35

LANDMARK

Number	Title	Yr	NM
LLP-1518	So Why Not?	1989	$30
LLP-1512	Ties of Love	1987	$25

MILESTONE

Number	Title	Yr	NM
M-9015	Two-Sided Album	1969	$25

MONTGOMERY, DAVID, AND CECIL LYTLE

Both are pianists.

Albums

KLAVIER

Number	Title	Yr	NM
533	Rags and Blues	197?	$30

SONIC ARTS

Number	Title	Yr	NM
6	Ragtime Piano for Four Hands	197?	$25

— *Direct-to-disc recording*

MONTGOMERY, MARIAN

Female singer.

Albums

CAPITOL

Number	Title	Yr	NM
T1962 [M]	Let There Be Love, Let There Be Swing, Let There Be Marian Montgomery	1963	$60
ST1962 [S]	Let There Be Love, Let There Be Swing, Let There Be Marian Montgomery	1963	$60
T2185 [M]	Lovin' Is Livin'	1964	$60
ST2185 [S]	Lovin' Is Livin'	1964	$60
T1884 [M]	Marian Montgomery Swings for Winners and Losers	1963	$60
ST1884 [S]	Marian Montgomery Swings for Winners and Losers	1963	$60

DECCA

Number	Title	Yr	NM
DL4773 [M]	What's New?	1965	$25
DL74773 [S]	What's New?	1965	$30

MONTGOMERY, MONK

Bass player. Also see THE MASTERSOUNDS; THE MONTGOMERY BROTHERS.

Albums

CHISA

Number	Title	Yr	NM
CS-806	Bass Odyssey	1971	$25
CS-801	It's Never Too Late	1970	$25

PHILADELPHIA INT'L.

Number	Title	Yr	NM
KZ33153 [B]	Reality	1974	$60

MONTGOMERY, WES

Guitarist. Also see MILT JACKSON; THE MONTGOMERY BROTHERS; JIMMY SMITH.

Albums

A&M

Number	Title	Yr	NM
LP-2001 [M]	A Day in the Life	1967	$50
SP-3001 [S]	A Day in the Life	1967	$30
SP9-3001	A Day in the Life	1983	$35

— *Audio Master Plus" reissue*

Number	Title	Yr	NM
SP-3006	Down Here on the Ground	1968	$35
SP9-3006	Down Here on the Ground	1983	$35

— *Audio Master Plus" reissue*

Number	Title	Yr	NM
SP-4247	Greatest Hits	1970	$35
SP-3012	Road Song	1968	$35
SP9-3012	Road Song	1984	$35

— *Audio Master Plus" reissue*

ACCORD

Number	Title	Yr	NM
SN-7170	The Classic Sound of Wes Montgomery	1981	$25

BLUE NOTE

Number	Title	Yr	NM
BN-LA531-H2	Beginnings	1976	$60
LWB-531	Beginnings	1981	$60

— *Reissue of BN-LA531-H2*

DCC COMPACT CLASSICS

Number	Title	Yr	NM
LPZ-2014	Goin' Out of My Head	1996	$40

— *Audiophile vinyl*

FANTASY

Number	Title	Yr	NM
OJC-034	A Dynamic New Sound	198?	$30
OJC-261	Boss Guitar	1987	$30
OJC-106	Full House	198?	$30
OJC-368	Fusion! Wes Montgomery with Strings	198?	$30
OJC-489	Guitar on the Go	1991	$35
OJC-089	Movin' Along	198?	$30
OJC-144	Portrait of Wes	198?	$30
OJC-233	So Much Guitar!	198?	$30
OJC-036	The Incredible Jazz Guitar of Wes Montgomery	198?	$30

MGM

Number	Title	Yr	NM
GAS-120	Wes Montgomery (Golden Archive Series)	1970	$35

MILESTONE

Number	Title	Yr	NM
9110	Encores	1983	$25
47051	Groove Brothers	1979	$30
47040	Movin'	197?	$30
47030	Pretty Blue	197?	$30
47065	The Alternative Wes Montgomery	1982	$30
47013	Wes Montgomery and Friends	1973	$35
47003	While We're Young	1972	$35
47057	Yesterdays	198?	$30

MOBILE FIDELITY

Number	Title	Yr	NM
MFSL-508	Bumpin'	198?	$100

— *Original Master Recording" at top of cover*

PACIFIC JAZZ

Number	Title	Yr	NM
PJ-10104 [M]	Easy Groove	1966	$35
ST-20104 [S]	Easy Groove	1966	$50
PJ-10130 [M]	Kismet	1967	$50
ST-20130 [S]	Kismet	1967	$35
PJ-5 [M]	Montgomeryland	1960	$60
ST-5 [S]	Montgomeryland	1960	$40
ST-20137	Portrait of Wes Montgomery	1968	$35

PICCADILLY

Number	Title	Yr	NM
3584	Jazz Guitar	198?	$25

RIVERSIDE

Number	Title	Yr	NM
RLP 12-310 [M]	A Dynamic New Sound	1959	$300
RLP-459 [M]	Boss Guitar	1963	$150
RS-9459 [S]	Boss Guitar	1963	$150
6111	Boss Guitar	197?	$25
RLP-434 [M]	Full House	1962	$700
RS-9434 [S]	Full House	1962	$150
6069	Full House	197?	$25
RLP-472 [M]	Fusion! Wes Montgomery with Strings	1964	$150
RS-9472 [S]	Fusion! Wes Montgomery with Strings	1964	$150
6210	Fusion! Wes Montgomery with Strings	198?	$25
RLP-494 [M]	Guitar on the Go	1965	$150
RS-9494 [S]	Guitar on the Go	1965	$150
6168	Guitar on the Go	198?	$25
RM-3002 [M]	In the Wee Small Hours	1967	$100

— *Reissue of 472*

Number	Title	Yr	NM
RS-3002 [S]	In the Wee Small Hours	1967	$100

— *Reissue of 9472*

Number	Title	Yr	NM
RS-3036	March 6, 1925-June 15, 1968	1968	$100
RLP-342 [M]	Movin' Along	1960	$200
RS-9342 [S]	Movin' Along	1960	$200
6199	Movin' Along	198?	$25
RLP1156 [S]	New Concepts in Jazz Guitar	1959	$250
RS-3046	Panorama	1969	$100
RLP-492 [M]	Portrait of Wes	1965	$150
RS-9492 [S]	Portrait of Wes	1965	$150
6202	Portrait of Wes	198?	$25
RS-3014	'Round Midnight	1968	$100

— *Reissue of 1156*

Number	Title	Yr	NM
RLP-382 [M]	So Much Guitar!	1961	$200
RS-9382 [S]	So Much Guitar!	1961	$200
6100	So Much Guitar!	197?	$25
RS-3039	The Best of Wes Montgomery	1968	$100
6080	The Dynamic New Jazz Sound of Wes Montgomery	197?	$25
RLP 12-320 [M]	The Incredible Jazz Guitar of Wes Montgomery	1960	$600
RLP1169 [S]	The Incredible Jazz Guitar of Wes Montgomery	1960	$200
6046	The Incredible Jazz Guitar of Wes Montgomery	197?	$25
RS-3012	This Is Wes Montgomery	1968	$100

— *Reissue of 9459*

VERVE

Number	Title	Yr	NM
V-8625 [M]	Bumpin'	1965	$35

Number	Title	Yr	NM
❏ V6-8625 [S]	Bumpin'	1965	$50
❏ V-8672 [M]	California Dreaming	1967	$50
❏ V6-8672 [S]	California Dreaming	1967	$35
❏ V6-8796	Eulogy	1970	$35
❏ V-8642 [M]	Goin' Out of My Head	1966	$35
❏ V6-8642 [S]	Goin' Out of My Head	1966	$50
❏ V6-8804	Just Walkin'	1971	$30
❏ V6-8610 [M]	Movin' Wes	1965	$35
❏ V6-8610 [S]	Movin' Wes	1965	$50
❏ V3HB-8839	Return Engagement	1974	$35
❏ VE-2-2513	Small Group Recording	197?	$35
❏ V-8653 [M]	Tequila	1966	$35
❏ V-8714 [M]	The Best of Wes Montgomery	1967	$50
❏ V6-8714 [S]	The Best of Wes Montgomery	1967	$35
❏ V6-8757	The Best of Wes Montgomery, Vol. 2	1968	$35
❏ V6-8813	The History of Wes Montgomery	1972	$35
❏ V6-8765	Willow Weep for Me	1969	$35

MONTGOMERY BROTHERS, THE

BUDDY MONTGOMERY, MONK MONTGOMERY and WES MONTGOMERY. Also see THE MASTERSOUNDS; GEORGE SHEARING.

Albums

FANTASY
Number	Title	Yr	NM
❏ OJC-138	Groove Yard	198?	$25
❏ 3308 [M]	The Montgomery Brothers	1960	$50
— Red vinyl			
❏ 3308 [M]	The Montgomery Brothers	1960	$30
— Black vinyl			
❏ 8052 [S]	The Montgomery Brothers	1960	$40
— Blue vinyl			
❏ 8052 [S]	The Montgomery Brothers	1960	$30
— Black vinyl			
❏ 3323 [M]	The Montgomery Brothers in Canada	1961	$50
— Red vinyl			
❏ 3323 [M]	The Montgomery Brothers in Canada	1961	$30
— Black vinyl			
❏ 8066 [S]	The Montgomery Brothers in Canada	1961	$40
— Blue vinyl			
❏ 8066 [S]	The Montgomery Brothers in Canada	1961	$30
— Black vinyl			
❏ OJC-283	The Montgomery Brothers in Canada	1987	$25
❏ 3376 [M]	Wes' Best	1967	$25
❏ 8376 [S]	Wes' Best	1967	$35

PACIFIC JAZZ
Number	Title	Yr	NM
❏ PJ-17 [M]	Wes, Buddy and Monk Montgomery	1961	$30

RIVERSIDE
Number	Title	Yr	NM
❏ RLP-362 [M]	Groove Yard	1961	$200
❏ RS-9362 [S]	Groove Yard	1961	$200
❏ 6141	Groove Yard	198?	$30

WORLD PACIFIC
Number	Title	Yr	NM
❏ PJ-1240 [M]	The Montgomery Brothers and Five Others	1957	$150
❏ WP-1240 [M]	The Montgomery Brothers and Five Others	1958	$150

— Reissue with new prefix

MONTOLIU, TETE

Pianist.

Albums

CONTEMPORARY
Number	Title	Yr	NM
❏ C-14004	Lunch in L.A.	1980	$30

ENJA
Number	Title	Yr	NM
❏ 2040	Songs for Love	197?	$35

INNER CITY
Number	Title	Yr	NM
❏ IC-2017	Catalonian Fire	197?	$35
❏ IC-2021	Music for Perla	197?	$35
❏ IC-2029	Tete!	197?	$35

PAUSA
Number	Title	Yr	NM
❏ 7057	Piano for Nuria	1979	$25

STEEPLECHASE
Number	Title	Yr	NM
❏ SCS-1152/3	Boston Concert	1981	$50
❏ SCS-1148	Catalonian Nights Vol. 1	1980	$30
❏ SCS-1185	Face to Face	198?	$30
❏ SCS-1137	I Wanna Talk About You	1980	$30
❏ SCS-1054	Tete-a-Tete	197?	$30
❏ SCS-1199	That's All	198?	$30
❏ SCS-1108	Tootie's Tempo	198?	$30

TIMELESS

Number	Title	Yr	NM
❏ 304	Catalonian Folksongs	1979	$30

MONTROSE, JACK

Tenor saxophone player, arranger and composer.

Albums

ATLANTIC
Number	Title	Yr	NM
❏ 1223 [M]	Arranged, Played, Composed by Jack Montrose with Bob Gordon	1956	$300
— Black label			
❏ 1223 [M]	Arranged, Played, Composed by Jack Montrose with Bob Gordon	1961	$250
— Multicolor label, white "fan" logo at right			
❏ 1223 [M]	Arranged, Played, Composed by Jack Montrose with Bob Gordon	1964	$35
— Multicolor label, black "fan" logo at right			

PACIFIC JAZZ
Number	Title	Yr	NM
❏ PJ-1208 [M]	Jack Montrose Sextet	1955	$150
— Red vinyl			
❏ PJ-1208 [M]	Jack Montrose Sextet	1955	$80
— Black vinyl			

RCA VICTOR
Number	Title	Yr	NM
❏ LPM-1451 [M]	Blues and Vanilla	1957	$50
❏ LPM-1572 [M]	The Horns Full	1957	$50

WORLD PACIFIC
Number	Title	Yr	NM
❏ WP-1208 [M]	Jack Montrose Sextet	1958	$150

MOODY, JAMES

Tenor and alto saxophone player and flutist. Also see ART BLAKEY; THE NEW YORK JAZZ SEXTET.

Albums

ARGO
Number	Title	Yr	NM
❏ LP-695 [M]	Another Bag	1962	$30
❏ LPS-695 [S]	Another Bag	1962	$40
❏ LP-740 [M]	Comin' On Strong	1964	$30
❏ LPS-740 [S]	Comin' On Strong	1964	$40
❏ LP-603 [M]	Flute 'n the Blues	1956	$40
— Reissue of Creative 603			
❏ LP-725 [M]	Great Day	1963	$30
❏ LPS-725 [S]	Great Day	1963	$30
❏ LP-666 [M]	Hey! It's James Moody	1960	$30
❏ LPS-666 [S]	Hey! It's James Moody	1960	$40
❏ LP-648 [M]	James Moody	1959	$40
❏ LPS-648 [S]	James Moody	1959	$30
❏ LP-637 [M]	Last Train from Overbrook	1959	$40
❏ LPS-637 [S]	Last Train from Overbrook	1959	$30
❏ LP-613 [M]	Moody's Mood for Love	1957	$40
❏ LP-679 [M]	Moody with Strings	1961	$30
❏ LPS-679 [S]	Moody with Strings	1961	$40

BLUE NOTE
Number	Title	Yr	NM
❏ BLP-5006 [10]	James Moody and His Modernists	1952	$300
❏ BLP-5005 [10]	James Moody with Strings	1952	$300

CADET
Number	Title	Yr	NM
❏ LP-695 [M]	Another Bag	1966	$30
❏ LPS-695 [S]	Another Bag	1966	$35
❏ LP-740 [M]	Comin' On Strong	1966	$30
❏ LPS-740 [S]	Comin' On Strong	1966	$35
❏ LP-756 [M]	Cookin' the Blues	1965	$25
❏ LPS-756 [S]	Cookin' the Blues	1965	$30
❏ 2CA-60010	Everything About Sax and Flute	1972	$25
❏ LP-603 [M]	Flute 'n the Blues	1966	$35
❏ LP-725 [M]	Great Day	1966	$30
❏ LPS-725 [S]	Great Day	1966	$35
❏ LP-666 [M]	Hey! It's James Moody	1966	$30
❏ LPS-666 [S]	Hey! It's James Moody	1966	$35
❏ LP-648 [M]	James Moody	1966	$30
❏ LPS-648 [S]	James Moody	1966	$35
❏ LP-637 [M]	Last Train from Overbrook	1966	$30
❏ LPS-637 [S]	Last Train from Overbrook	1966	$35
❏ LP-613 [M]	Moody's Mood for Love	1966	$35
❏ LP-679 [M]	Moody with Strings	1966	$30
❏ LPS-679 [S]	Moody with Strings	1966	$35

CHESS
Number	Title	Yr	NM
❏ CH-91548	Flute 'n' the Blues	198?	$25
❏ 2ACMJ-403	Moody's Mood	1976	$35
❏ CH-91522	The Great Day	198?	$25

CREATIVE
Number	Title	Yr	NM
❏ LP-603 [M]	Flute 'n Blues	1956	$150

DIAL
Number	Title	Yr	NM
❏ LP-209 [10]	James Moody, His Saxophone and His Band	1950	$400

EMARCY
Number	Title	Yr	NM
❏ MG-26040 [10]	Moodsville	1954	$300
❏ MG-26004 [10]	The Moody Story	1954	$300
❏ MG-36031 [M]	The Moody Story	1955	$200

FANTASY

Number	Title	Yr	NM
❏ OJC-188	James Moody's Moods	1985	$25

MILESTONE
Number	Title	Yr	NM
❏ M-9023	Blues and Other Colors	1970	$25
❏ M-9005	Brass Figures	1968	$25

MUSE
Number	Title	Yr	NM
❏ MR-5020	Feelin' It Together	1974	$30
❏ MR-5001	Never Again!	1973	$30

NOVUS
Number	Title	Yr	NM
❏ 3026-1-N	Moving Forward	1988	$25
❏ 3004-1-N	Something Special	1986	$25
❏ 3063-1-N	Sweet and Lovely	1989	$30

PAULA
Number	Title	Yr	NM
❏ LPS-4003	Sax and Flute Man	197?	$30

PAUSA
Number	Title	Yr	NM
❏ 7029	Too Heavy for Words	1979	$25

PRESTIGE
Number	Title	Yr	NM
❏ PRST-7625	Don't Look Away Now!	1969	$35
❏ PRLP-7011 [M]	Hi-Fi Party	1955	$300
❏ PRST-7740	Hi-Fi Party, Volume 2	1970	$35
❏ 24015	James Moody	197?	$35
❏ PRLP-198 [10]	James Moody and His Band	1954	$300
❏ PRLP-110 [10]	James Moody Favorites, No. 1	1951	$250
❏ PRLP-125 [10]	James Moody Favorites, No. 2	1952	$300
❏ PRLP-146 [10]	James Moody Favorites, No. 3	1953	$300
❏ PRLP-7431 [M]	James Moody's Greatest Hits	1967	$30
❏ PRST-7431 [R]	James Moody's Greatest Hits	1967	$35
❏ PRLP-7441 [M]	James Moody's Greatest Hits, Volume 2	1967	$30
❏ PRST-7441 [R]	James Moody's Greatest Hits, Volume 2	1967	$35
❏ PRLP-7056 [M]	James Moody's Moods	1956	$300
❏ PRLP-7072 [M]	Moody	1956	$300
❏ PRLP-157 [10]	Moody in France	1953	$350
❏ PRLP-192 [10]	Moody's Mood	1954	$300
❏ PRST-7554	Moody's Moods	1968	$35
❏ PRLP-7179 [10]	Moody's Workshop	1960	$200
❏ PRST-7663	Moody's Workshop	1969	$35
❏ PRLP-7036 [M]	Wail, Moody, Wail	1956	$300
❏ PRST-7853	Wail Moody Wail, Volume 3	1971	$35

ROOST
Number	Title	Yr	NM
❏ RST-405 [10]	James Moody in France	1951	$250

SCEPTER
Number	Title	Yr	NM
❏ SRM-525 [M]	Running the Gamut	1965	$25
❏ SPS-525 [S]	Running the Gamut	1965	$30

TRIP
Number	Title	Yr	NM
❏ 5521	The Moody Story (1951-52)	197?	$25

VANGUARD
Number	Title	Yr	NM
❏ VSD-79404	Beyond	1978	$30
❏ VSD-79381	Sun Journey	1976	$30
❏ VSD-79366	Timeless	1975	$30

MOODY, JAMES/GEORGE WALLINGTON

Also see each artist's individual listings.

Albums

BLUE NOTE
Number	Title	Yr	NM
❏ B-6503 [M]	The Beginning and End of Bop	1969	$30

MOODY, PHIL

Pianist.

Albums

SOMERSET
Number	Title	Yr	NM
❏ P-10400 [M]	Intimate Jazz	1959	$30

MOONDOC, JEMEEL

Alto saxophone player.

Albums

CADENCE JAZZ
Number	Title	Yr	NM
❏ CJ-1006	New York Live	198?	$25

SOUL NOTE
Number	Title	Yr	NM
❏ SN-1051	Judy's Bounce	1981	$30
❏ SN-1041	Konstanze's Delight	1981	$30

MOONDOG

Percussionist, male singer and composer.

Albums

COLUMBIA
Number	Title	Yr	NM
❏ KC30897	Moondog 2	1971	$50

— With booklet (deduct 20 percent if missing)

COLUMBIA MASTERWORKS
Number	Title	Yr	NM
❏ MS7335	Moondog	1969	$30

Number	Title	Yr	NM
— Gray label with "360 Sound Stereo" at bottom			
❏ MS7335	Moondog	2001	$15
— 180-gram reissue			
EPIC			
❏ LG1002 [10]	Moondog and His Friends	1954	$300
FANTASY			
❏ OJC-1741	Moondog	1990	$20
MOONDOG			
❏ 1	Snaketime Series by Moondog	1956	$800
— With paper insert; deduct 25 percent if it is missing			
MUSICAL HERITAGE SOCIETY			
❏ MHS3803	Moondog	1978	$40
PRESTIGE			
❏ PRLP-7042 [M]	Moondog	1956	$300
— Yellow label with W. 50th St. address			
❏ PRLP-7069 [M]	More Moondog	1957	$300
— Yellow label with W. 50th St. address			

MOONEY, JOE
Accordion player, pianist, organist and male singer.
Albums
ATLANTIC			
❏ 1255 [M]	Lush Life	1958	$250
— Black label			
❏ 1255 [M]	Lush Life	1961	$150
— Multicolor label, white "fan" logo at right			
COLUMBIA			
❏ CL2186 [M]	The Greatness of Joe Mooney	1964	$35
❏ CS8986 [S]	The Greatness of Joe Mooney	1964	$25
❏ CL2345 [M]	The Happiness of Joe Mooney	1965	$30
❏ CS9145 [S]	The Happiness of Joe Mooney	1965	$35
DECCA			
❏ DL8468 [M]	On the Rocks	1957	$120
❏ DL5555 [10]	You Go to My Head	1955	$350

MOONLIGHT BROADCASTERS, THE
Albums
STOMP OFF			
❏ SOS-1193	Radio Nights	1991	$25

MOOR, DET
Albums
GALLANT			
❏ GT4001 [M]	Great Jazz from Great TV	1962	$40

MOORE, ADA
Female singer.
Albums
DEBUT			
❏ DLP-15 [10]	Jazz Workshop	1955	$300
FANTASY			
❏ OJC-1701	Ada Moore	1985	$25

MOORE, BREW
Tenor saxophone player. Also see FATS NAVARRO.
Albums
FANTASY			
❏ 3264 [M]	Brew Moore	1958	$50
— Red vinyl			
❏ 3264 [M]	Brew Moore	1958	$30
— Black vinyl			
❏ OJC-049	Brew Moore	198?	$25
❏ 86013 [S]	Brew Moore in Europe	1962	$25
— Black vinyl			
❏ 3222 [M]	The Brew Moore Quintet	1956	$80
— Red vinyl			
❏ 3222 [M]	The Brew Moore Quintet	1956	$40
— Black vinyl			
❏ OJC-100	The Brew Moore Quintet	198?	$25
SAVOY			
❏ MG-9028 [10]	Tenor Sax	1953	$150
STEEPLECHASE			
❏ SCS-6016	If I Had You	198?	$30
❏ SCS-6019	I Should Care	198?	$30
STORYVILLE			
❏ 4019	No More Brew	198?	$25

MOORE, DEBBY
Guitarist and female singer.
Albums
TOP RANK			
❏ RM-12-301 [M]	My Kind of Blues	1959	$40

MOORE, DUDLEY
Pianist; best known as an actor.
Albums
ATLANTIC			
❏ SD1403 [S]	Beyond the Fringe and All That Jazz	1963	$60
LONDON			
❏ PS558	Dudley Moore Trio	1969	$60

MOORE, GLEN, AND DAVID FRIESEN
Moore is a bass player. Also see DAVID FRIESEN.
Albums
VANGUARD			
❏ VSD-79383	Glen Moore and David Friesen In Concert	1976	$30

MOORE, JERRY
Male singer.
Albums
ESP-DISK'			
❏ 1061	Life Is a Constant Journey Home	1968	$200

MOORE, MARILYN
Female singer.
Albums
BETHLEHEM			
❏ BCP-73 [M]	Moody	1957	$250

MOORE, OSCAR
Guitarist; member of the King Cole Trio.
Albums
CHARLIE PARKER			
❏ PLP-830 [M]	The Fabulous Oscar Moore Guitar	1962	$30
❏ PLP-830S [S]	The Fabulous Oscar Moore Guitar	1962	$30
SKYLARK			
❏ SKLP-19 [M]	Oscar Moore Trio	1954	$100
TAMPA			
❏ TP-22 [M]	Galivantin' Guitar	1957	$150
— Colored vinyl			
❏ TP-22 [M]	Galivantin' Guitar	1958	$150
— Black vinyl			
❏ TP-16 [M]	Oscar Moore Trio	1957	$150
— Colored vinyl			
❏ TP-16 [M]	Oscar Moore Trio	1958	$150
— Black vinyl			

MOORE, PHIL, JR.
Albums
ATLANTIC			
❏ SD1530	Right On	1969	$35

MOORE, PHIL
Pianist, male singer and composer.
Albums
CLEF			
❏ MGC-635 [M]	Music for Moderns	1954	$250
STRAND			
❏ SL-1004 [M]	Polynesian Paradise	1959	$40
❏ SLS-1004 [S]	Polynesian Paradise	1959	$50

MOORE, RALPH
Tenor and soprano saxophone player.

Albums
LANDMARK			
❏ LLP-1526	Furthermore	1990	$30
❏ LLP-1520	Images	1988	$25

MOORE, REGGIE
Pianist and keyboard player.
Albums
MAINSTREAM			
❏ MRL-380	Furioso	1972	$25
❏ MRL-341	Wishbone	1971	$50

MOORE, SHELLEY
Female singer.
Albums
ARGO			
❏ LP-4016 [M]	For the First Time	1962	$30
❏ LPS-4016 [S]	For the First Time	1962	$40

MOORE, WILD BILL
Tenor saxophone player.
Albums
JAZZLAND			
❏ JLP-54 [M]	Bottom Groove	1961	$30
❏ JLP-954 [S]	Bottom Groove	1961	$40
❏ JLP-38 [M]	Wild Bill's Beat	1961	$60
❏ JLP-938 [S]	Wild Bill's Beat	1961	$40

MOORMAN, DENNIS
Pianist.
Albums
INDIA NAVIGATION			
❏ IN-1055	Circles of Destiny	198?	$30

MORAN, GAYLE
Female singer.
Albums
WARNER BROS.			
❏ BSK3339	I Loved You Then, I Love You Now	1980	$12

MORAN, PAT
Female singer.
Albums
AUDIO FIDELITY			
❏ AFLP-1875 [M]	This Is Pat Moran	1958	$40
❏ AFSD-5875 [S]	This Is Pat Moran	1958	$50
BETHLEHEM			
❏ BCP-6007 [M]	Pat Moran Quartet	1956	$250
❏ BCP-6018 [M]	While at Birdland	1957	$250

MORATH, MAX
Pianist and male vocalist.
Albums
EPIC			
❏ LN24066 [M]	Celebrated Maestro	1963	$75
❏ BN26066 [S]	Celebrated Maestro	1963	$40
JAZZOLOGY			
❏ JCE-52 [M]	All Play Together	1969	$30
RCA VICTOR			
❏ LSO-1159	Max Morath at the Turn of the Century	1969	$30
SAVOY			
❏ MG-12091 [M]	Introducing Max Morath	196?	$25
VANGUARD			
❏ VSD-79378	Jonah Man and Others of the Bert Williams Era	1976	$25
❏ VSD-79391	Living a Ragtime Life: A One-Man Show	1977	$30
❏ VSD-79418	Max Morath in Jazz Country	1979	$25
❏ VSD-83/84	Max Morath Plays Ragtime	197?	$35
❏ VSD-79402	Ragtime Women	1977	$25
❏ VRS-39/40	The Best of Scott Joplin and Other Rag Classics	1972	$35
❏ VSD-73106	The Best of Scott Joplin and Other Rag Classics	198?	$30
❏ VSD-79429	The Great American Piano Bench	1980	$25
❏ VSD-310	The World of Scott Joplin	197?	$30
❏ VSD-351	The World of Scott Joplin, Vol. 2	197?	$30

Wes Montgomery, *Willow Weep for Me*, Verve V6-8765, **$35**.

Moondog, *Moondog and His Friends*, Epic LG 1002, 10-inch LP, **$300**.

Lee Morgan, *Lee Morgan Indeed!*, Blue Note BLP-1538, with New York, USA, address on label, **$2,000**.

Ella Mae Morse, *Barrelhouse Boogie and the Blues*, Capitol H 513, 10-inch LP, **$400**.

Number	Title	Yr	NM

MOREIRA, AIRTO
See AIRTO.

MOREL, TERRY
Female singer.

Albums

BETHLEHEM

Number	Title	Yr	NM
❏ BCP-47 [M]	Songs of a Woman in Love	1956	$250

MORELLO, JOE, AND GARY BURTON
Also see each artist's individual listing.

Albums

OVATION

Number	Title	Yr	NM
❏ OV-1714	Percussive Jazz	197?	$30

MORELLO, JOE
Drummer.

Albums

INTRO

Number	Title	Yr	NM
❏ 608 [M]	Joe Morello Sextet	1957	$150

OVATION

Number	Title	Yr	NM
❏ OV-1197	Joe Morello	197?	$35

RCA VICTOR

Number	Title	Yr	NM
❏ LPM-2486 [M]	It's About Time	1961	$30
❏ LSP-2486 [S]	It's About Time	1961	$30

MORGAN, DICK
Pianist.

Albums

RIVERSIDE

Number	Title	Yr	NM
❏ RLP 12-329 [M]	Dick Morgan at the Showboat	1960	$200
❏ RLP-1183 [S]	Dick Morgan at the Showboat	1960	$200
❏ RLP-347 [M]	See What I Mean?	1960	$200
❏ RS-9347 [S]	See What I Mean?	1960	$200
❏ RLP-383 [M]	Settin' In	1961	$200
❏ RS-9383 [S]	Settin' In	1961	$200

MORGAN, FRANK
Alto saxophone player.

Albums

ANTILLES

Number	Title	Yr	NM
❏ 91320	Mood Indigo	1989	$30

CONTEMPORARY

Number	Title	Yr	NM
❏ C-14026	Bebop Lives!	1987	$25
❏ C-14045	Double Image	1988	$25
❏ C-14013	Easy Living	198?	$25
❏ C-14021	Lament	1986	$25
❏ C-14039	Major Changes	1988	$25
❏ C-14052	Reflections	1989	$30
❏ C-14045	Yardbird Suite	1988	$25

GENE NORMAN

Number	Title	Yr	NM
❏ GNP-12 [M]	Frank Morgan	1955	$120

—Red vinyl

GNP CRESCENDO

Number	Title	Yr	NM
❏ GNPS-9014	Frank Morgan with Conte Candoli	197?	$25

SAVOY JAZZ

Number	Title	Yr	NM
❏ SJL-1201	Bird Calls	198?	$25

WHIPPET

Number	Title	Yr	NM
❏ WLP-704 [M]	Frank Morgan	1956	$100

MORGAN, LEE
Trumpeter. Also see JOHN COLTRANE; THE YOUNG LIONS.

Albums

BLUE NOTE

Number	Title	Yr	NM
❏ BLP-1590 [M]	Candy	1958	$350
—Regular edition, W. 63rd St. address on label			
❏ BST-1590 [S]	Candy	1959	$300
—Regular edition, W. 63rd St. address on label			
❏ BLP-1590 [M]	Candy	1963	$200
—New York, USA" address on label			
❏ BST-1590 [S]	Candy	1963	$140
—New York, USA" address on label			
❏ BST-84289	Caramba!	1969	$150
—A Division of Liberty Records" on label			
❏ BST-84312	Charisma	1969	$100
—A Division of Liberty Records" on label			
❏ BLP-1575 [M]	City Lights	1958	$3500
—Deep groove" version; W. 63rd St. address on label			
❏ BLP-1575 [M]	City Lights	1958	$200
—Regular edition, W. 63rd St. address on label			
❏ BST-1575 [S]	City Lights	1959	$300
—Regular edition, W. 63rd St. address on label			
❏ BLP-1575 [M]	City Lights	1963	$200
—New York, USA" address on label			
❏ BST-1575 [S]	City Lights	1963	$150
—New York, USA" address on label			
❏ BLP-4222 [M]	Cornbread	1967	$150
—New York, USA" on label			
❏ BST-84222 [S]	Cornbread	1967	$150
—New York, USA" address on label			
❏ BST-84222 [S]	Cornbread	1968	$60
—A Division of Liberty Records" on label			
❏ BLP-4243 [M]	Delightfulee Morgan	1967	$400
❏ BST-84243 [S]	Delightfulee Morgan	1967	$120
—New York, USA" address on label			
❏ BST-84243 [S]	Delightfulee Morgan	1968	$60
—A Division of Liberty Records" on label			
❏ BST-84243	Delightfulee Morgan	198?	$30
—The Finest in Jazz Since 1939" reissue			
❏ LT-1091	Infinity	1981	$40
❏ BST-84901	Lee Morgan	1972	$60
—A Division of Unted Artists" on blue and white labels			
❏ BLP-1541 [M]	Lee Morgan, Volume 2	1957	$2000
—Deep groove" version; Lexington Ave. address on label			
❏ BLP-1541 [M]	Lee Morgan, Volume 2	1963	$400
—New York, USA" address on label			
❏ BLP-1557 [M]	Lee Morgan, Volume 3	1957	$1200
—Deep groove" version; W. 63rd St. address on label			
❏ BLP-1557 [M]	Lee Morgan, Volume 3	1957	$500
—Regular edition, W. 63rd St. address on label			
❏ BLP-1557 [M]	Lee Morgan, Volume 3	1963	$200
—New York, USA" address on label			
❏ BST-89906	Lee Morgan at the Lighthouse	1970	$100
❏ BLP-1538 [M]	Lee Morgan Indeed!	1963	$2000
—New York, USA" address on label			
❏ BLP-1538 [M]	Lee Morgan Indeed!	200?	$100
—200-gram edition; distributed by Classic Records			
❏ BLP-4034 [M]	Lee-Way	1960	$800
—Deep groove" version; W. 63rd St. address on label			
❏ BLP-4034 [M]	Lee-Way	1960	$300
—Regular edition, W. 63rd St. address on label			
❏ BST-84034 [S]	Lee-Way	1960	$150
—Regular edition, W. 63rd St. address on label			
❏ BLP-4034 [M]	Lee-Way	1963	$200
—New York, USA" address on label			
❏ BST-84034 [S]	Lee-Way	1963	$40
—New York, USA" address on label			
❏ BST-84034 [S]	Lee-Way	1968	$60
—A Division of Liberty Records" on label			
❏ B1-32089	Lee-Way	1995	$50
❏ BN-LA224-G	Memorial Album	1974	$50
❏ BN-LA582-4047	Procrastinator	1977	$60
❏ BLP-4169 [M]	Search for the New Land	1965	$200
—New York, USA" on label			
❏ BST-84169 [S]	Search for the New Land	1965	$150
—New York, USA" address on label			
❏ BST-84169 [S]	Search for the New Land	1968	$60
—A Division of Liberty Records" on label			
❏ LT-987	Sonic Boom	1979	$60
❏ LT-1031	Taru	1980	$40
❏ B1-91138	The Best of Lee Morgan	1988	$35
❏ BLP-1578 [M]	The Cooker	1958	$1300
—Deep groove" version; W. 63rd St. address on label			
❏ BLP-1578 [M]	The Cooker	1958	$200
—Regular edition, W. 63rd St. address on label			
❏ BST-1578 [S]	The Cooker	1959	$2000
—Deep groove" version; W. 63rd St. address on label			
❏ BST-1578 [S]	The Cooker	1959	$200
—Regular edition, W. 63rd St. address on label			
❏ BLP-1578 [M]	The Cooker	1963	$200
—New York, USA" address on label			
❏ BST-1578 [S]	The Cooker	1963	$100
—New York, USA" address on label			
❏ BST-81578 [S]	The Cooker	1968	$60
—A Division of Liberty Records" on label			
❏ BLP-4212 [M]	The Gigolo	1966	$175
—New York, USA" on label			
❏ BST-84212 [S]	The Gigolo	1966	$150
—New York, USA" address on label			
❏ BST-84212 [S]	The Gigolo	1968	$60
—A Division of Liberty Records" on label			
❏ BST-84212	The Gigolo	1986	$30
—The Finest in Jazz Since 1939" reissue			
❏ B1-33579	The Procrastinator	1995	$50
❏ BST-84426	The Rajah	1984	$100
❏ BLP-4199 [M]	The Rumproller	1966	$175
—New York, USA" on label			
❏ BST-84199 [S]	The Rumproller	1966	$150
—New York, USA" address on label			
❏ BST-84199 [S]	The Rumproller	1968	$60
—A Division of Liberty Records" on label			
❏ BLP-4157 [M]	The Sidewinder	1964	$175
—New York, USA" on label			
❏ BST-84157 [S]	The Sidewinder	1964	$150
—New York, USA" address on label			
❏ BST-84157 [S]	The Sidewinder	1968	$60
—A Division of Liberty Records" on label			
❏ LN-10075	The Sidewinder	1981	$35
—Budget-line reissue			
❏ BST-84157	The Sidewinder	1985	$30
—The Finest in Jazz Since 1939" reissue			
❏ B1-46137	The Sidewinder	1997	$50
❏ BST-84335	The Sixth Sense	1969	$120
—A Division of Liberty Records" on label			
❏ LT-1058	Tom Cat	1980	$40

FANTASY

Number	Title	Yr	NM
❏ OJC-310	Take Twelve	198?	$30

GNP CRESCENDO

Number	Title	Yr	NM
❏ GNP-2079	Lee Morgan	1973	$50

JAZZLAND

Number	Title	Yr	NM
❏ JLP-80 [M]	Take Twelve	1962	$100
❏ JLP-980 [S]	Take Twelve	1962	$120

MOSAIC

Number	Title	Yr	NM
❏ MQ6-162 [B]	The Complete Blue Note Lee Morgan Fifties Sessions	1995	$1000

PRESTIGE

Number	Title	Yr	NM
❏ MPP-2510	Take Twelve	198?	$30

SAVOY

Number	Title	Yr	NM
❏ MG-12091 [M]	Introducing Lee Morgan	1956	$500

SUNSET

Number	Title	Yr	NM
❏ SUS-5269	All the Way	1969	$35

TRADITION

Number	Title	Yr	NM
❏ 2079	The Genius of Lee Morgan	1969	$50

TRIP

Number	Title	Yr	NM
❏ 5037	A Date with Lee	1974	$35
❏ 5041	Live Sessions	1975	$60
❏ 5029	One of a Kind	1974	$35
❏ 5020	Speedball	1974	$35
❏ 5003	Two Sides of Lee Morgan	1974	$60

VEE JAY

Number	Title	Yr	NM
❏ LP-3015 [M]	Expoobident	1960	$150
❏ SR-3015 [S]	Expoobident	1960	$200
❏ SR-3007 [S]	Here's Lee Morgan	1960	$150
❏ VJS-3007	Here's Lee Morgan	1986	$35
—Reissue on reactivated label			
❏ E-4000	Lee Morgan 1938-1972	198?	$50
❏ VJ-2508 [M]	Lee Morgan Quintet	1965	$120
❏ VJS-2508 [S]	Lee Morgan Quintet	1965	$150

MORGAN, LENNY

Albums

PALO ALTO

Number	Title	Yr	NM
❏ PA-8007	It's About Time	1981	$30

MORGAN, RUSS
Pianist, trombonist, bandleader and composer.

Albums

CAPITOL

Number	Title	Yr	NM
❏ T1703 [M]	Medleys in the Morgan Manner	1962	$60
❏ ST1703 [S]	Medleys in the Morgan Manner	1962	$75
❏ T2158 [M]	Music in the Country Manner	1964	$60
❏ ST2158 [S]	Music in the Country Manner	1964	$50

CIRCLE

Number	Title	Yr	NM
❏ CLP-87	Music in the Morgan Manner (1938)	198?	$25
❏ C-9	Russ Morgan and His Orchestra 1936	198?	$25

DECCA

Number	Title	Yr	NM
❏ DL8423 [M]	A Lovely Way to Spend an Evening (Songs of Jimmy McHugh)	1957	$120

—Black label, silver print

Number	Title	Yr	NM
❏ DL8423 [M]	A Lovely Way to Spend an Evening (Songs of Jimmy McHugh)	196?	$30
—Black label with color bars			
❏ DL8581 [M]	Cheerful Little Earful (Songs of Harry Warren)	195?	$25
—Black label, silver print			
❏ DL8581 [M]	Cheerful Little Earful (Songs of Harry Warren)	196?	$30
—Black label with color bars			
❏ DL5278 [10]	College Marching Songs	195?	$30
❏ DL8332 [M]	Does Your Heart Beat for Me	1956	$150
—Black label, silver print			
❏ DL8332 [M]	Does Your Heart Beat for Me	196?	$30
—Black label with color bars			
❏ DL4503 [M]	Does Your Heart Beat for Me	1964	$30
❏ DL74503 [S]	Does Your Heart Beat for Me	1964	$35
❏ DL8337 [M]	Everybody Dance	1956	$150
—Black label, silver print			
❏ DL8337 [M]	Everybody Dance	196?	$30
—Black label with color bars			
❏ DL5406 [10]	Everybody Dance to the Music of Russ Morgan	195?	$30
❏ DL8746 [M]	Kitten on the Keys	195?	$25
—Black label, silver print			
❏ DL8746 [M]	Kitten on the Keys	196?	$30
—Black label with color bars			
❏ DL5324 [10]	Morgan-Airs	1951	$200
❏ DL5098 [10]	Music in the Morgan Manner	1950	$120
❏ DL8828 [M]	Songs Everybody Knows	1958	$100
—Black label, silver print			
❏ DL8828 [M]	Songs Everybody Knows	196?	$30
—Black label with color bars			
❏ DL78828 [S]	Songs Everybody Knows	1958	$100
—Black label, silver print			
❏ DL78828 [S]	Songs Everybody Knows	196?	$35
—Black label with color bars			
❏ DL8336 [M]	Tap Dancing for Pleasure	1956	$150
—Black label, silver print			
❏ DL8336 [M]	Tap Dancing for Pleasure	196?	$30
—Black label with color bars			
❏ DXB196 [M]	The Best of Russ Morgan	1965	$25
❏ DXSB7196 [R]	The Best of Russ Morgan	1965	$35
❏ DL8642 [M]	Velvet Violins	1957	$120
—Black label, silver print			
❏ DL8642 [M]	Velvet Violins	196?	$30
—Black label with color bars			

EVEREST

❏ LPBR-5083 [M]	Dance Along	1960	$30
❏ SDBR-1083 [S]	Dance Along	1960	$35
❏ LPBR-5055 [M]	Let's All Sing with Russ Morgan and Eddie Wilser	1959	$30
❏ SDBR-1055 [S]	Let's All Sing with Russ Morgan and Eddie Wilser	1959	$35
❏ LPBR-5129 [M]	Morgan Time	1961	$30
❏ SDBR-1129 [S]	Morgan Time	1961	$35
❏ LPBR-5054 [M]	Music in the Morgan Manner	1959	$30
❏ SDBR-1054 [S]	Music in the Morgan Manner	1959	$35
❏ LPBR-5095 [M]	Russ Morgan and His Wolverine Band	1960	$30
❏ SDBR-1095 [S]	Russ Morgan and His Wolverine Band	1960	$35
❏ LPBR-5130 [M]	Russ Morgan at Catalina	1961	$30
❏ SDBR-1130 [S]	Russ Morgan at Catalina	1961	$35

GNP CRESCENDO

❏ GNPS-9015	The Best of Russ Morgan	197?	$25

HINDSIGHT

❏ HSR-145	Russ Morgan and His Orchestra 1937-38	198?	$25
❏ HSR-404	Russ Morgan and His Orchestra Play 22 Original Big Band Recordings	198?	$30

MCA

❏ 92	Golden Favorites	1973	$25
❏ 4036	The Best of Russ Morgan	197?	$30

PICKWICK

❏ PC-3030 [M]	Dance Along	196?	$25
❏ SPC-3030 [S]	Dance Along	196?	$30
❏ PC-3016 [M]	There Goes That Song	196?	$25
❏ SPC-3016 [S]	There Goes That Song	196?	$30

RUSS MORGAN PRESENTS

❏ RMP-1000	Russ Morgan Presents "Music in the Morgan Manner"	1967	$35

SEARS

❏ SPS-413 [R]	Does Your Heart Beat for Me?	196?	$25

SUNSET

❏ SUM-1142 [M]	Does Your Heart Beat for Me	1967	$30

Number	Title	Yr	NM
❏ SUS-5142 [S]	Does Your Heart Beat for Me	1967	$25

VEE JAY

❏ VJ-1125 [M]	His Greatest Hits	1964	$35
❏ VJS-1125 [S]	His Greatest Hits	1964	$25
❏ VJ-1139 [M]	Red Roses for a Blue Lady	1965	$35
❏ VJS-1139 [S]	Red Roses for a Blue Lady	1965	$25
❏ E-4009 [M]	Russ Morgan 1904-1969	1975	$35

VOCALION

❏ VL3695 [M]	Hoop-De-Doo Polkas and Waltzes	196?	$30
❏ VL3601 [M]	Let's Dance	195?	$30
❏ VL3792 [M]	Music in the Morgan Manner	196?	$30
❏ VL73792 [R]	Music in the Morgan Manner	196?	$25

MORRIS, AUDREY

Female singer.

Albums

BETHLEHEM

❏ BCP-6010 [M]	The Voice of Audrey Morris	1956	$250

MORRIS, MARLOWE

Pianist and organist.

Albums

COLUMBIA

❏ CL1819 [M]	Play the Thing	1962	$25
❏ CS8619 [S]	Play the Thing	1962	$30

MORRISON, SAM

Alto and soprano saxophone player.

Albums

CHIAROSCURO

❏ 184	Natural Layers	197?	$30

INNER CITY

❏ IC-6017	Dune	197?	$35

MORRISSEY, PAT

Albums

MERCURY

❏ MG-20197 [M]	I'm Pat Morrissey, I Sing	1957	$150

MORROW, BUDDY

Trombone player and bandleader.

Albums

EPIC

❏ LN24095 [M]	Big Band Beatlemania	1964	$60
❏ BN26095 [S]	Big Band Beatlemania	1964	$60
❏ LN24171 [M]	Campus After Dark	1965	$60
❏ BN26171 [S]	Campus After Dark	1965	$75

HINDSIGHT

❏ HSR-154	Buddy Morrow 1963-64	198?	$25

MERCURY

❏ MG-20764 [M]	A Collection of 33 All-Time Dance Favorites	1963	$100
❏ SR-60764 [S]	A Collection of 33 All-Time Dance Favorites	1963	$100
❏ MG-20204 [M]	A Salute to the Fabulous Dorseys	1957	$100
❏ MG-20221 [M]	Golden Trombone	1956	$100
❏ MG-20372 [M]	Just We Two	195?	$100
❏ SR-60018 [S]	Just We Two	1958	$100
❏ MG-20396 [M]	Night Train	195?	$100
❏ SR-60009 [S]	Night Train	1958	$100
❏ MG-20702 [M]	Night Train Goes to Hollywood	1962	$100
❏ SR-60702 [S]	Night Train Goes to Hollywood	1962	$100
❏ MG-20062 [M]	Shall We Dance?	195?	$100
❏ MG-20290 [M]	Tribute to Tommy Dorsey	1957	$100

RCA VICTOR

❏ LPM-2018 [M]	Big Band Guitar	1959	$30
❏ LSP-2018 [S]	Big Band Guitar	1959	$40
❏ LPM-1925 [M]	Dancing Tonight To Morrow	1958	$30
❏ LSP-1925 [S]	Dancing Tonight To Morrow	1958	$40
❏ LPM-2180 [M]	Double Impact	1960	$30
❏ LSP-2180 [S]	Double Impact	1960	$40
❏ LPM-2042 [M]	Impact	1959	$30
❏ LSP-2042 [S]	Impact	1959	$40
❏ LPM-1427 [M]	Night Train	1956	$40
❏ LPM-2208 [M]	Poe for Moderns	1960	$30
❏ LSP-2208 [S]	Poe for Moderns	1960	$40

WING

❏ MGW-12102 [M]	Dance Date	196?	$30
❏ SRW-16102 [R]	Dance Date	196?	$30
❏ MGW-12105 [M]	Tribute to a Sentimental Gentleman	196?	$30

MORSE, ELLA MAE

Female singer; in addition to jazz, she sang pop, country and R&B.

Albums

CAPITOL

❏ H513 [10]	Barrelhouse Boogie and the Blues	1954	$400
❏ T513 [M]	Barrelhouse Boogie and the Blues	1955	$300
❏ T1802 [M]	Hits of Ella Mae Morse and Freddie Slack	1962	$150
❏ ST1802 [S]	Hits of Ella Mae Morse and Freddie Slack	1962	$200
❏ M-11971 [M]	Hits of Ella Mae Morse and Freddie Slack	197?	$20
—Reissue			
❏ T898 [M]	Morse Code	1957	$250
—Turquoise label			

MORTIMER, AZIE

Albums

BETHLEHEM

❏ BLP-10006	The Feeling of Jazz	197?	$35

MORTON, BENNY / JIMMY HAMILTON

Morton was a trombonist. Also see JIMMY HAMILTON.

Albums

MOSAIC

❏ MR1-115	The Benny Morton and Jimmy Hamilton Blue Note Swingtets	199?	$60
—Limited edition of 7,500			

MORTON, JELLY ROLL

Pianist, male singer, arranger and composer.

Albums

BIOGRAPH

❏ 1004	Rare Piano Rolls 1924-1926	197?	$25

BLUEBIRD

❏ 6588-1-RB	Jelly Roll Morton & His Red Hot Peppers	1988	$30

CIRCLE

❏ L-14001 [M]	The Saga of Mr. Jelly Lord Volume 1: Jazz Started in New Orelans	1951	$120
❏ L-14002 [M]	The Saga of Mr. Jelly Lord Volume 2: Way Down Yonder	1951	$120
❏ L-14003 [M]	The Saga of Mr. Jelly Lord Volume 3: Jazz Is Strictly Music	1951	$120
❏ L-14004 [M]	The Saga of Mr. Jelly Lord Volume 4: The Spanish Tinge	1951	$120
❏ L-14005 [M]	The Saga of Mr. Jelly Lord Volume 5: Bad Man Ballads	1951	$120
❏ L-14006 [M]	The Saga of Mr. Jelly Lord Volume 6: Jazz Piano Soloist #1	1951	$120
❏ L-14007 [M]	The Saga of Mr. Jelly Lord Volume 7: Everyone Had His Style	1951	$120
❏ L-14008 [M]	The Saga of Mr. Jelly Lord Volume 8: Jelly and the Blues	1951	$120
❏ L-14009 [M]	The Saga of Mr. Jelly Lord Volume 9: Alabama Bound	1951	$120
❏ L-14010 [M]	The Saga of Mr. Jelly Lord Volume 10: Jazz Piano Soloist #2	1951	$120
❏ L-14011 [M]	The Saga of Mr. Jelly Lord Volume 11: In New Orleans	1951	$120
❏ L-14012 [M]	The Saga of Mr. Jelly Lord Volume 12: I'm the Winin' Boy	1951	$120

COMMODORE

❏ DL-30000 [M]	New Orleans Memories	1950	$100
❏ XFL-14942	New Orleans Memories	198?	$30

EVEREST ARCHIVE OF FOLK & JAZZ

❏ 267	Jelly Roll Morton	197?	$25

JAZZ PANORAMA

❏ 1804 [10]	Peppers	1951	$100
❏ 1810 [10]	Peppers	1951	$100

MAINSTREAM

❏ 56020 [M]	Jelly Roll Morton	1965	$30

Number	Title	Yr	NM
❑ S-6020 [R]	Jelly Roll Morton	1965	$30
MILESTONE			
❑ M-2003 [M]	Immortal Jelly Roll Morton	1970	$30
❑ 47018	Jelly Roll Morton 1923-24	197?	$35
RCA VICTOR			
❑ LPT-32 [10]	A Treasury of Immortal Performances	1952	$100
❑ LPV-524 [M]	Hot Jazz, Pop Jazz, Hokum and Hilarity	1965	$25
❑ LPV-559 [M]	I Thought I Heard Buddy Bolden Say	1966	$25
❑ LPV-546 [M]	Mr. Jelly Lord	1966	$25
❑ LPV-508 [M]	Stomps and Joys	1965	$25
❑ LPM-1649 [M]	The King of New Orleans Jazz	1957	$50
RIVERSIDE			
❑ RLP-1038 [10]	Classic Jazz Piano, Volume 1	1954	$300
❑ RLP-1041 [10]	Classic Jazz Piano, Volume 2	1954	$300
❑ RLP 12-111 [M]	Classic Piano Solos	1955	$300
❑ RLP 12-133 [M]	Jelly Roll Morton Plays and Sings	1956	$250
❑ RLP-1027 [10]	Jelly Roll Morton's Kings of Jazz: His Rarest Recordings	1954	$300
❑ RLP-9001 [M]	Library of Congress Recordings Volume 1	1955	$300
❑ RLP-9002 [M]	Library of Congress Recordings Volume 2	1955	$300
❑ RLP-9003 [M]	Library of Congress Recordings Volume 3	1955	$300
❑ RLP-9004 [M]	Library of Congress Recordings Volume 4	1955	$300
❑ RLP-9005 [M]	Library of Congress Recordings Volume 5	1955	$300
❑ RLP-9006 [M]	Library of Congress Recordings Volume 6	1955	$300
❑ RLP-9007 [M]	Library of Congress Recordings Volume 7	1955	$300
❑ RLP-9008 [M]	Library of Congress Recordings Volume 8	1955	$300
❑ RLP-9009 [M]	Library of Congress Recordings Volume 9	1955	$300
❑ RLP-9010 [M]	Library of Congress Recordings Volume 10	1955	$300
❑ RLP-9011 [M]	Library of Congress Recordings Volume 11	1955	$300
❑ RLP-9012 [M]	Library of Congress Recordings Volume 12	1955	$300
❑ RLP 12-132 [M]	Mr. Jelly Lord	1956	$250
❑ RLP 12-140 [M]	Rags and Blues	1956	$250
❑ RLP-1018 [10]	Rediscovered Solos	1953	$300
❑ RLP 12-128 [M]	The Incomparable Jelly Roll Morton	1956	$250
❑ RLP 12-102 [M]	The New Orleans Rhythm Kings with Jelly Roll Morton	1955	$300
TIME-LIFE			
❑ STL-J-07	Giants of Jazz	1979	$50
TRIP			
❑ J-1	Piano Roll Solos	197?	$25
X			
❑ LX-3008 [10]	Red Hot Peppers, Volume 1	1954	$100
❑ LVA-3028 [10]	Red Hot Peppers, Volume 2	1954	$100

MOSCA, SAL
Pianist.

Albums

Number	Title	Yr	NM
CHOICE			
❑ 1022	For You	1979	$30
INTERPLAY			
❑ 7712	Sal Mosca Music	197?	$30

MOSCHNER, PINGUIN
Tuba player.

Albums

Number	Title	Yr	NM
SOUND ASPECTS			
❑ 05	Tuba Love Story	1986	$30

MOSES, BOB
Drummer and percusssionist.

Albums

Number	Title	Yr	NM
GRAMAVISION			
❑ 8307	Visit with the Great Spirit	1983	$25
❑ 8203	When Elephants Dream of Music	198?	$25

MOSES, KATHRYN
Flutist.

Albums

Number	Title	Yr	NM
PM			
❑ 017	Music in My Heart	1979	$30

MOSHER, JIMMY
Saxophone player and flutist.

Albums

Number	Title	Yr	NM
DISCOVERY			
❑ 860	A Chick from Chelsea	1981	$25

MOSS, ANNE MARIE
Female singer.

Albums

Number	Title	Yr	NM
STASH			
❑ ST-211	Don't You Know Me	198?	$25

MOSSE, SANDY
Tenor and alto saxophone player.

Albums

Number	Title	Yr	NM
ARGO			
❑ LP-609 [M]	Chicago Scene	1957	$50
❑ LP-639 [M]	Relaxin' with Sandy Mosse	1959	$30
❑ LPS-639 [S]	Relaxin' with Sandy Mosse	1959	$40

MOST, ABE
Clarinetist.

Albums

Number	Title	Yr	NM
LIBERTY			
❑ LJH-6004 [M]	Mister Clarinet	1955	$60

MOST, SAM
Flutist, clarinetist and alto saxophone player. Also see DON ELLIOTT; HERBIE MANN; THE NUTTY SQUIRRELS.

Albums

Number	Title	Yr	NM
BETHLEHEM			
❑ BCP-18 [M]	I'm Nuts About the Most: East Coast Jazz, Volume 7	1955	$250
❑ BCP-6008 [M]	Musically Yours	1956	$250
❑ BCP-75 [M]	Sam Most Plays Bird, Bud, Monk and Miles	1957	$250
❑ BCP-78 [M]	The Amazing Sam Most with Strings	1958	$250
CATALYST			
❑ 7609	But Beautiful	1976	$30
DEBUT			
❑ DLP-11 [10]	Sam Most Sextet	1954	$350
VANGUARD			
❑ VRS-8014 [10]	Sam Most Sextet	1954	$80
XANADU			
❑ 141	Flute Flight	1977	$30
❑ 173	Flute Talk	1980	$30
❑ X-3001	Flute Talk	1980	$30
—*Audiophile edition*			
❑ 160	From the Attic of My Mind	198?	$25
❑ 133	Mostly Flute	1976	$30

MOTEN, BENNIE
Pianist , composer and bandleader.

Albums

Number	Title	Yr	NM
BLUEBIRD			
❑ 9768#NAME?	Bennie Moten's Kansas City Orchestra	1989	$30
HISTORICAL			
❑ 9	Bennie Moten's Kansas City Orchestra	1966	$25
RCA VICTOR			
❑ LPV-514 [M]	Bennie Moten's Great Band of 1930-32	1965	$25
X			
❑ LX-3004 [10]	Kansas City Jazz, Volume 1	1954	$60
❑ LVA-3025 [10]	Kansas City Jazz, Volume 2	1954	$60
❑ LVA-3038 [10]	Kansas City Jazz, Volume 3	1954	$60

MOTHER'S BOYS

Albums

Number	Title	Yr	NM
AUDIOPHILE			
❑ AP-100	Stompin' Hot! Singin' Sweet!	1970	$30

MOTIAN, PAUL
Drummer.

Albums

Number	Title	Yr	NM
ECM			
❑ 1028	Conception Vessel	197?	$35
❑ 1108	Dance	1977	$25
❑ 1283	It Should Have Happened a Long Time Ago	1985	$30
❑ 1138	Le Voyage	1979	$25
❑ 1222	Psalm	198?	$25
❑ 1048	Tribute	197?	$30
SOUL NOTE			
❑ SN-1124	Jack of Clubs	1986	$30
❑ 121224	One Time Out	1990	$35
❑ SN-1074	The Story of Maryam	1983	$30

MOULE, KEN
Pianist, composer and arranger.

Albums

Number	Title	Yr	NM
LONDON			
❑ LL1673 [M]	Ken Moule Arranges for…	1957	$50
—*Label calls this "Cool Moule*			

MOUZON, ALPHONSE
Drummer, percussionist, keyboard player, bass player and composer.

Albums

Number	Title	Yr	NM
BLUE NOTE			
❑ BN-LA058#NAME?	Essence of Mystery	1973	$35
❑ BN-LA222#NAME?	Funky Snakefoot	1974	$25
❑ BN-LA584#NAME?	Man Incognito	1976	$35
❑ BN-LA398#NAME?	Mind Transplant	1975	$35
OPTIMISM			
❑ OP-6003	Back to Jazz	198?	$25
❑ OP-6002	Early Spring	198?	$25
❑ OP-6001	Love, Fantasy	198?	$25
❑ OP-6004	Morning Sun	198?	$25
PAUSA			
❑ 7196	Back to Jazz	1986	$25
❑ 7087	By All Means	198?	$25
❑ 7107	Morning Sun	198?	$25
❑ 7182	The 11th House	1985	$25
❑ 7173	The Sky Is the Limit	1985	$25
❑ 7054	Virtue	197?	$25

MOVER, BOB
Alto saxophone player.

Albums

Number	Title	Yr	NM
CHOICE			
❑ 1015	On the Move	1977	$30
VANGUARD			
❑ VSD-79408	Bob Mover	1978	$25
XANADU			
❑ 187	In the True Tradition	198?	$25
❑ 194	Things Unseen	198?	$25

MOYE, DON
Drummer and percussionist. Also see ART ENSEMBLE OF CHICAGO.

Albums

Number	Title	Yr	NM
AECO			
❑ 01	Sun Percussion, Vol. 1	1980	$35

MOZIAN, ROGER KING
Trumpeter, arranger and bandleader.

Albums

Number	Title	Yr	NM
CLEF			
❑ MGC-166 [10]	The Colorful Music of Roger King Mozian	1954	$250

MOZZ, THE

Albums

Number	Title	Yr	NM
MESA			
❑ R1-79018	Mystique and Identity	1989	$35

Gerry Mulligan, *Gerry Mulligan and the Concert Jazz Band Presents a Concert in Jazz*, Verve V-8415, **$30**.

Gerry Mulligan, *Something Borrowed*, Something Blue, Limelight LS 86040, **$30**.

Gerry Mulligan, *Gerry Mulligan Quartet*, Fantasy 3-6, 10-inch album, red or green vinyl, **$200**. The black vinyl version goes for **$150**.

Gerry Mulligan and Shorty Rogers, *Modern Sounds*, Capitol T 691, mono, **$200**.

MRUBATA, MCCOY
Saxophone player.
Albums
JIVE

Number	Title	Yr	NM
❏ 1254-1-J	Firebird	1989	$30

MTUME UMOJA ENSEMBLE
Led by Mtume (drums, percussion, piano), who went on from this album to do some soul and funk albums, including the hit "Juicy Fruit."
Albums
STRATA-EAST

Number	Title	Yr	NM
❏ SES-1972-4	Alkebu-Lan, Land of the Blacks	1972	$50

MUHAMMAD, IDRIS
Drummer and percussionist.
Albums
FANTASY

Number	Title	Yr	NM
❏ F-9581	Foxhuntin'	1979	$35
❏ F-9598	Make It Count	1980	$35
❏ F-9566	You Ain't No Friend of Mine	1978	$35

KUDU

Number	Title	Yr	NM
❏ 38	Boogie to the Top	1978	$25
❏ 27	House of the Rising Sun	1976	$30
❏ 17	Power of Soul	1974	$30
❏ 34	Turn This Mutha Out	1977	$25

PRESTIGE

Number	Title	Yr	NM
❏ 10005	Black Rhythm Revolution	1971	$40
❏ 10036	Peace and Rhythm	1971	$30

THERESA

Number	Title	Yr	NM
❏ 110	Kabsha	198?	$35

MULLIGAN, GERRY, AND CHET BAKER
Also see each artist's individual listings.
Albums
CTI

Number	Title	Yr	NM
❏ 6054	The Carnegie Hall Concert, Volume 1	1976	$30
❏ 6055	The Carnegie Hall Concert, Volume 2	1976	$30

JAZZTONE

Number	Title	Yr	NM
❏ J-1253 [M]	Mulligan and Baker!	1957	$40

MULLIGAN, GERRY, AND SHORTY ROGERS
Also see each artist's individual listings.
Albums
CAPITOL

Number	Title	Yr	NM
❏ T691 [M]	Modern Sounds	1956	$200
❏ T2025 [M]	Modern Sounds	1963	$150
❏ DT2025 [R]	Modern Sounds	1963	$150

MULLIGAN, GERRY
Baritone saxophone player, pianist, soprano saxophone player, and occasional clarinetist and male singer. Also see CHET BAKER; BOOTS BROWN; STAN GETZ; THELONIOUS MONK; OSCAR PETERSON; SHORTY ROGERS; ANNIE ROSS; PHIL SUNKEL; TEDDY WILSON.
Albums
A&M

Number	Title	Yr	NM
❏ SP-3036	The Age of Steam	1971	$35

CAPITOL

Number	Title	Yr	NM
❏ H439 [10]	Gerry Mulligan and His Ten-Tette	1953	$300

CHIAROSCURO

Number	Title	Yr	NM
❏ 155	Idol Gossip	1977	$30

COLUMBIA

Number	Title	Yr	NM
❏ CL1932 [M]	Jeru	1963	$30
— Red label, "Guaranteed High Fidelity" at bottom			
❏ CS8732 [S]	Jeru	1963	$30
— Red label, "360 Sound Stereo" in black at bottom			
❏ CL1932 [M]	Jeru	1965	$15
— Red label, "360 Sound Mono" at bottom			
❏ CS8732 [S]	Jeru	1965	$35
— Red label, "360 Sound Stereo" in white at bottom			
❏ CL1932 [M]	Jeru	1963	$100
— Red and black label with six "eye" logos			
❏ JC34803	The Arranger (1946-57)	1977	$30
❏ CL1307 [M]	What Is There to Say?	1959	$40
— Red and black label with six "eye" logos			

Number	Title	Yr	NM
❏ CS8116 [S]	What Is There to Say?	1959	$40
— Red and black label with six "eye" logos			
❏ CL1307 [M]	What Is There to Say?	1963	$30
— Red label, "Guaranteed High Fidelity" or "360 Sound Mono" at bottom			
❏ CS8116 [S]	What Is There to Say?	1963	$35
— Red label, "360 Sound Stereo" at bottom			

CONCORD JAZZ

Number	Title	Yr	NM
❏ CJ-300	Soft Lights and Sweet Music	1986	$25

CROWN

Number	Title	Yr	NM
❏ CLP-5363 [M]	The Great Gerry Mulligan	196?	$35
❏ CST-363 [R]	The Great Gerry Mulligan	196?	$30

DRG

Number	Title	Yr	NM
❏ MRS-506	Gerry Mulligan and Dave Grusin	198?	$25
❏ SL-5194	Walk on the Water	1980	$25

EMARCY

Number	Title	Yr	NM
❏ MG-36101 [M]	Mainstream of Jazz	1956	$200
❏ MG-36056 [M]	Presenting the Gerry Mulligan Sextet	1955	$200

FANTASY

Number	Title	Yr	NM
❏ 3-6 [10]	Gerry Mulligan Quartet	1953	$200
— Green vinyl			
❏ 3-6 [10]	Gerry Mulligan Quartet	1953	$200
— Red vinyl			
❏ 3-6 [10]	Gerry Mulligan Quartet	1953	$150
— Black vinyl			
❏ OJC-003	Mulligan Plays Mulligan	1982	$25

GENE NORMAN

Number	Title	Yr	NM
❏ GNP-3 [10]	Gerry Mulligan Quartet	1952	$250

GRP

Number	Title	Yr	NM
❏ GR-1003	Little Big Horn	198?	$25

LIMELIGHT

Number	Title	Yr	NM
❏ LM-82004 [M]	Butterfly with Hiccups	1964	$30
❏ LS-86004 [S]	Butterfly with Hiccups	1964	$30
❏ LM-82030 [M]	Feelin' Good	1965	$30
❏ LS-86030 [S]	Feelin' Good	1965	$30
❏ LM-82021 [M]	If You Can't Beat 'Em, Join 'Em	1965	$30
❏ LS-86021 [S]	If You Can't Beat 'Em, Join 'Em	1965	$30
❏ LM-82040 [M]	Something Borrowed, Something Blue	1966	$25
❏ LS-86040 [S]	Something Borrowed, Something Blue	1966	$30

MERCURY

Number	Title	Yr	NM
❏ MG-20453 [M]	A Profile of Gerry Mulligan	1959	$100

MOBILE FIDELITY

Number	Title	Yr	NM
❏ 1-179	At the Village Vanguard	1985	$50
— Audiophile vinyl			
❏ 1-241	Blues in Time	1996	$50
— Audiophile vinyl			
❏ 1-234	Gerry Mulligan Meets Ben Webster	1995	$50
— Audiophile vinyl			

MOSAIC

Number	Title	Yr	NM
❏ MR5-102	The Complete Pacific Jazz and Capitol Recordings of the Original Gerry Mulligan Quartet and Tentette	198?	$150

ODYSSEY

Number	Title	Yr	NM
❏ 32160290	Jeru	1968	$30
❏ 32160258	What Is There to Say?	1968	$30

PACIFIC JAZZ

Number	Title	Yr	NM
❏ PJ-50 [M]	California Concerts	1962	$30
❏ PJ-1228 [M]	Gerry Mulligan at Storyville	1957	$150
❏ PJLP-1 [10]	Gerry Mulligan Quartet	1953	$300
❏ PJLP-5 [10]	Gerry Mulligan Quartet	1953	$300
❏ PJ-1201 [M]	Gerry Mulligan Sextet	1955	$150
❏ PJ-38 [M]	Konitz Meets Mulligan	1962	$30
❏ PJLP-10 [10]	Lee Konitz and the Gerry Mulligan Quartet	1954	$250
❏ PJLP-2 [10]	Lee Konitz Plays with the Gerry Mulligan Quartet	1953	$300
❏ PJM-406 [M]	Lee Konitz with the Gerry Mulligan Quartet	1956	$150
❏ PJ-1210 [M]	Paris Concert	1956	$150
❏ PJ-10102 [M]	Paris Concert	1966	$25
❏ ST-20102 [S]	Paris Concert	1966	$25
❏ PJ-47 [M]	Reunion with Chet Baker	1962	$30
❏ ST-47 [S]	Reunion with Chet Baker	1962	$30
❏ T90061 [M]	Reunion with Chet Baker	196?	$60
— Capitol Record Club edition			
❏ PJ-8 [M]	The Genius of Gerry Mulligan	1960	$40
❏ ST-20140 [R]	The Genius of Gerry Mulligan	1968	$35
❏ PJ-1207 [M]	The Original Mulligan Quartet	1955	$150
❏ PJ-75 [M]	Timeless	1963	$30

PAR

Number	Title	Yr	NM
❏ PAD-703	Symphonic Dreams	1987	$25

PAUSA

Number	Title	Yr	NM
❏ 9010	The Genius of Gerry Mulligan	198?	$25

PHILIPS

Number	Title	Yr	NM
❏ PHM200108 [M]	Night Lights	1963	$250
❏ PHS600108 [S]	Night Lights	1963	$300
❏ PHM200077 [M]	Spring Is Sprung	1963	$25

PRESTIGE

Number	Title	Yr	NM
❏ PRLP-120 [10]	Gerry Mulligan Blows	1952	$300
❏ PRLP-7251 [M]	Historically Speaking	1963	$40
— Yellow label			
❏ 24016	Mulligan/Baker	1972	$35
❏ PRLP-7006 [M]	Mulligan Plays Mulligan	1956	$100
— Yellow label			
❏ PRLP-141 [10]	Mulligan Too Blows	1953	$300

SUNSET

Number	Title	Yr	NM
❏ SUM-1117 [M]	Concert Days	1966	$35
❏ SUS-5117 [S]	Concert Days	1966	$30

TRIP

Number	Title	Yr	NM
❏ 5561	Gerry Mulligan Sextet	197?	$25
❏ 5531	Profile (1955-56)	197?	$25

UNITED ARTISTS

Number	Title	Yr	NM
❏ UAL-4085 [M]	Nightwatch	1960	$40
❏ UAS-5085 [S]	Nightwatch	1960	$50

VERVE

Number	Title	Yr	NM
❏ V-8478 [M]	Blues in Time	1962	$25
❏ V6-8478 [S]	Blues in Time	1962	$30
❏ V-8515 [S]	Gerry Mulligan '63 -- The Concert Jazz Band	1963	$25
❏ V6-8515 [S]	Gerry Mulligan '63 -- The Concert Jazz Band	1963	$30
❏ MGV-8388 [M]	Gerry Mulligan and the Concert Jazz Band	1960	$150
❏ V6-8388 [S]	Gerry Mulligan and the Concert Jazz Band	1961	$30
❏ V-8388 [M]	Gerry Mulligan and the Concert Jazz Band	1961	$25
❏ MGV-8396 [M]	Gerry Mulligan and the Concert Jazz Band at the Village Vanguard	1960	$150
❏ V6-8396 [S]	Gerry Mulligan and the Concert Jazz Band at the Village Vanguard	1961	$50
❏ V-8396 [M]	Gerry Mulligan and the Concert Jazz Band at the Village Vanguard	1961	$40
❏ UMV-2057	Gerry Mulligan and the Concert Jazz Band at the Village Vanguard	198?	$30
❏ V-8415 [M]	Gerry Mulligan and the Concert Jazz Band Presents a Concert in Jazz	1961	$30
❏ V6-8415 [S]	Gerry Mulligan and the Concert Jazz Band Presents a Concert in Jazz	1961	$30
❏ MGV-8343 [M]	Gerry Mulligan Meets Ben Webster	1959	$100
❏ MGVS-6104 [S]	Gerry Mulligan Meets Ben Webster	1960	$150
❏ V-8343 [M]	Gerry Mulligan Meets Ben Webster	1961	$25
❏ V-8534 [M]	Gerry Mulligan Meets Ben Webster	1963	$35
❏ V6-8534 [S]	Gerry Mulligan Meets Ben Webster	1963	$25
❏ UMJ-3093	Gerry Mulligan Meets Ben Webster	198?	$30
❏ MGV-8367 [M]	Gerry Mulligan Meets Johnny Hodges	1960	$150
❏ V6-8367 [S]	Gerry Mulligan Meets Johnny Hodges	1961	$30
❏ MGVS-6137 [S]	Gerry Mulligan Meets Johnny Hodges	1960	$0
— Canceled			
❏ V-8367 [M]	Gerry Mulligan Meets Johnny Hodges	1961	$25
❏ V-8536 [M]	Gerry Mulligan Meets Johnny Hodges	1963	$35
❏ V6-8536 [S]	Gerry Mulligan Meets Johnny Hodges	1963	$25
❏ V-8535 [M]	Gerry Mulligan Meets Stan Getz	1963	$35
❏ V6-8535 [S]	Gerry Mulligan Meets Stan Getz	1963	$25
❏ UMV-2652	Gerry Mulligan Presents a Concert in Jazz	198?	$30
❏ VSP-6 [M]	Gerry's Time	1966	$35
❏ VSPS-6 [R]	Gerry's Time	1966	$30
❏ MGV-8249 [M]	Getz Meets Mulligan in Hi-Fi	1958	$100
❏ MGVS-6003 [S]	Getz Meets Mulligan in Hi-Fi	1960	$150
❏ V-8249 [M]	Getz Meets Mulligan in Hi-Fi	1961	$25
❏ V6-8249 [S]	Getz Meets Mulligan in Hi-Fi	1961	$30
❏ VE-2-2537	Mulligan & Getz & Desmond	1980	$35

Number	Title	Yr	NM
❑ V-8567 [M]	The Essential Gerry Mulligan	1964	$30
❑ V6-8567 [S]	The Essential Gerry Mulligan	1964	$35
❑ V-8438 [M]	The Gerry Mulligan Concert Jazz Band On Tour with Guest Soloist Zoot Sims	1962	$30
❑ V6-8438 [S]	The Gerry Mulligan Concert Jazz Band On Tour with Guest Soloist Zoot Sims	1962	$30
❑ MGV-8246 [M]	The Gerry Mulligan-Paul Desmond Quartet	1958	$100
❑ V-8246 [M]	The Gerry Mulligan-Paul Desmond Quartet	1961	$25
❑ V-8466 [M]	The Gerry Mulligan Quartet	1962	$30
❑ V6-8466 [S]	The Gerry Mulligan Quartet	1962	$30

WHO'S WHO IN JAZZ

| ❑ 21007 | Lionel Hampton Presents Gerry Mulligan | 1978 | $30 |

WING

| ❑ MGW-12335 [M] | Night Lights | 1964 | $30 |
| ❑ SRW-16335 [S] | Night Lights | 1964 | $35 |

WORLD PACIFIC

❑ WP-1201 [M]	California Concerts	1958	$150
❑ WP-1228 [M]	Gerry Mulligan at Storyville	1958	$150
❑ ST-1006 [S]	Gerry Mulligan at Storyville	1958	$200
❑ WP-1273 [M]	Lee Konitz Plays with the Gerry Mulligan Quartet	1959	$150
—Reissue of 406			
❑ PJM-406 [M]	Lee Konitz with the Gerry Mulligan Quartet	1958	$150
❑ WP-1210 [M]	Paris Concert	1958	$150
❑ PJ-1241 [M]	Reunion with Chet Baker	1957	$250
❑ WP-1241 [M]	Reunion with Chet Baker	1958	$150
❑ ST-1007 [S]	Reunion with Chet Baker	1958	$150
❑ PJ-1237 [M]	The Gerry Mulligan Songbook, Volume 1	1957	$250
❑ WP-1237 [M]	The Gerry Mulligan Songbook, Volume 1	1958	$150
❑ ST-1001 [S]	The Gerry Mulligan Songbook, Volume 1	1958	$200
❑ WP-1207 [M]	The Original Mulligan Quartet	1958	$150

MULLIGAN, GERRY/BUDDY DEFRANCO
Also see each artist's individual listings.

Albums

GENE NORMAN

❑ GNP-26 [M]	The Gerry Mulligan Quartet with Chet Baker/Buddy DeFranco Quartet	1957	$80
—Combined reissue of two 10-inch LPs			
❑ GNP-56 [M]	The Gerry Mulligan Quartet with Chet Baker/Buddy DeFranco Quartet	196?	$40
—Reissue of 26			

GNP CRESCENDO

| ❑ GNPS-56 [R] | The Gerry Mulligan Quartet with Chet Baker/Buddy DeFranco Quartet | 196? | $25 |

MULLIGAN, GERRY/KAI WINDING/RED RODNEY
Also see each artist's individual listings.

Albums

NEW JAZZ

| ❑ NJLP-8306 [M] | Broadway | 1963 | $0 |
| —Canceled; reassigned to Status | | | |

STATUS

| ❑ ST-8306 [M] | Broadway | 1965 | $40 |

MULLIGAN, GERRY/PAUL DESMOND
Also see each artist's individual listings.

Albums

FANTASY

❑ 3220 [M]	Gerry Mulligan Quartet/Paul Desmond Quintet	1956	$80
—Red vinyl; combined reissue of two 10-inch LPs			
❑ 3220 [M]	Gerry Mulligan Quartet/Paul Desmond Quintet	1956	$40
—Black vinyl			

MULLINS, ROB
Pianist, saxophone player, guitarist, bass player and drummer/percussionist.

Albums

Number	Title	Yr	NM

FLYING PIANO

| ❑ FPR102 | Red Shoes | 1982 | $35 |

NOVA

| ❑ 8810 | 5th Gear | 1988 | $25 |

MULTIPLICATION ROCK (SOUNDTRACK)
More jazz than rock, it features the vocal and composing talents of BOB DOROUGH, with BLOSSOM DEARIE also involved.

Albums

CAPITOL

| ❑ SJA-11174 | Multiplication Rock | 1973 | $40 |

MUNOZ
Full name: Tisziji Munoz. Drummer and percussionist.

Albums

INDIA NAVIGATION

| ❑ IN-1034 | Rendezvous with Now | 1978 | $35 |

MURIBUS, GEORGE

Albums

CATALYST

| ❑ 7602 | Brazilian Tapestry | 1976 | $30 |
| ❑ 7619 | Trio '77 | 1977 | $30 |

MURPHY, JAC

Albums

MUSIC IS MEDICINE

| ❑ 9003 | Child's Gift | 1978 | $30 |
| ❑ 9016 | Erin Eileen | 198? | $30 |

MURPHY, LYLE
Saxophone, clarinet player and bandleader, but best-known as a composer and arranger.

Albums

CONTEMPORARY

| ❑ C-3506 [M] | Gone with the Woodwinds | 1955 | $200 |

GENE NORMAN

❑ GNP-9 [10]	Four Saxophones in Twelve Tones	1954	$120
❑ GNP-152 [M]	Four Saxophones in Twelve Tones	195?	$50
❑ GNP-33 [M]	New Orbits in Sound	1957	$50

INNER CITY

| ❑ IC-1133 | Ultimate Odyssey | 198? | $35 |

MURPHY, MARK
Male singer.

Albums

AUDIOPHILE

| ❑ AP-132 | Mark Murphy Sings Dorothy Fields and Cy Coleman | 197? | $25 |

CAPITOL

❑ T1299 [M]	Hip Parade	1960	$60
❑ ST1299 [S]	Hip Parade	1960	$60
❑ T1458 [M]	Playing the Field	1960	$60
❑ ST1458 [S]	Playing the Field	1960	$60
❑ T1177 [M]	This Could Be the Start of Something	1959	$60
❑ ST1177 [S]	This Could Be the Start of Something	1959	$60

DECCA

| ❑ DL8632 [M] | Let Yourself Go | 1958 | $100 |
| ❑ DL8390 [M] | Meet Mark Murphy | 1957 | $120 |

FANTASY

| ❑ OJC-141 | Rah | 198? | $25 |
| ❑ OJC-367 | That's How I Love the Blues | 198? | $25 |

FONTANA

| ❑ MGF-27537 [M] | A Swingin' Singin' Affair | 1965 | $25 |
| ❑ SRF-67537 [S] | A Swingin' Singin' Affair | 1965 | $30 |

MILESTONE

| ❑ M-9145 | Night Mood | 1987 | $25 |
| ❑ M-9154 | September Ballads | 1988 | $25 |

MUSE

❑ MR-5355	Beauty and the Beast	198?	$25
❑ MR-5253	Bop for Kerouac	1981	$30
❑ MR-5297	Brazil Song (Cancoes do Brasil)	1983	$25
❑ MR-5009	Bridging a Gap	197?	$30
❑ MR-5359	Kerouac, Then and Now	198?	$30
❑ MR-5345	Living Room	1986	$25
❑ MR-5041	Mark II	197?	$30
❑ MR-5078	Mark Murphy Sings	1975	$30

Number	Title	Yr	NM
❑ MR-5308	Mark Murphy Sings Nat's Choice	1985	$25
❑ MR-5320	Mark Murphy Sings Nat's Choice, Vol. 2	1986	$25
❑ MR-5213	Satisfaction Guaranteed	1980	$25
❑ MR-5102	Stolen Moments	1978	$30
❑ MR-5286	The Artistry of Mark Murphy	1982	$25

PAUSA

| ❑ 7023 | Midnight Mood | 1979 | $25 |
| ❑ 9042 | This Could Be the Start of Something | 1985 | $25 |

RIVERSIDE

❑ RLP-395 [M]	Rah	1961	$200
❑ RS-9395 [S]	Rah	1961	$200
❑ 6064	Rah	197?	$30
❑ 6091	That's How I Love the Blues	197?	$30
❑ RLP-441 [M]	That's How I Love the Blues!	1962	$150
❑ RS-9441 [S]	That's How I Love the Blues!	1962	$150

MURPHY, ROSE
Female singer.

Albums

AUDIOPHILE

| ❑ AP-70 | Rose Murphy | 198? | $30 |

MCA

| ❑ 1558 | Rose Murphy Sings Again | 1983 | $35 |

ROYALE

| ❑ VLP-6079 [10] | Chi-Chi Girl | 195? | $80 |
| ❑ 1835 [10] | Rose Murphy and Quartette | 195? | $80 |

UNITED ARTISTS

| ❑ UAJ-14025 [M] | Jazz, Joy and Happiness | 1962 | $50 |
| ❑ UAJS-15025 [S] | Jazz, Joy and Happiness | 1962 | $60 |

VERVE

| ❑ MGV-2070 [M] | Not Cha-Cha But Chi-Chi | 1957 | $150 |
| ❑ V-2070 [M] | Not Cha-Cha But Chi-Chi | 1961 | $30 |

MURPHY, TURK
Trombonist and bandleader. Also see GEORGE LEWIS.

Albums

ATLANTIC

| ❑ SD1613 | The Many Faces of Ragtime | 1972 | $30 |

COLUMBIA

❑ CL6257 [10]	Barrelhouse Jazz	1953	$50
❑ CL595 [M]	Barrelhouse Jazz	1954	$40
—Maroon label, gold print			
❑ CL595 [M]	Barrelhouse Jazz	1955	$40
—Red and black label with six "eye" logos			
❑ CL650 [M]	Dancing Jazz	1955	$50
—Maroon label, gold print			
❑ CL650 [M]	Dancing Jazz	1955	$40
—Red and black label with six "eye" logos			
❑ CL559 [M]	The Music of Jelly Roll Morton	1954	$40
—Maroon label, gold print			
❑ CL559 [M]	The Music of Jelly Roll Morton	1955	$40
—Red and black label with six "eye" logos			
❑ CL546 [M]	When the Saints Go Marching In	1953	$40
—Maroon label, gold print			
❑ CL546 [M]	When the Saints Go Marching In	1955	$75
—Red and black label with six "eye" logos			

FORUM

❑ F-9017 [M]	Turk Murphy and His Jazz Band at the Roundtable	196?	$30
—Reissue of Roulette R-25076			
❑ SF-9017 [S]	Turk Murphy and His Jazz Band at the Roundtable	196?	$35
—Reissue of Roulette SR-25076			

GHB

❑ 91	Turk Murphy, Volume 1	198?	$25
❑ 92	Turk Murphy, Volume 2	198?	$25
❑ 93	Turk Murphy, Volume 3	198?	$25

GOOD TIME JAZZ

❑ L-12026 [M]	San Francisco Jazz, Volume 1	1955	$50
❑ L-12027 [M]	San Francisco Jazz, Volume 2	1955	$50
❑ L-7 [10]	Turk Murphy with Claire Austin	1952	$50

MERRY MAKERS

| ❑ S-105 | Turk Murphy San Francisco Jazz Band | 197? | $35 |
| ❑ S-106 | Turk Murphy's Jazz Band | 197? | $35 |

MOTHERLODE

Number	Title	Yr	NM
❏ 0103	Turk Murphy's Jazz Band, Vol. 1	1973	$30
❏ 0104	Turk Murphy's Jazz Band, Vol. 2	1973	$30
MPS			
❏ MC-22097	Live!	197?	$35
RCA VICTOR			
❏ LPM-2501 [M]	Let the Good Times Roll	1962	$25
❏ LSP-2501 [S]	Let the Good Times Roll	1962	$30
ROULETTE			
❏ R-25088 [M]	Music for Wise Guys	1960	$25
❏ SR-25088 [S]	Music for Wise Guys	1960	$30
❏ R-25076 [M]	Turk Murphy and His Jazz Band at the Roundtable	1959	$25
❏ SR-25076 [S]	Turk Murphy and His Jazz Band at the Roundtable	1959	$30
SONIC ARTS			
❏ 14	Natural High	1979	$35
STOMP OFF			
❏ SOS-1161	Southern Stomps	1989	$25
❏ SOS-1155	Turk at Carnegie	1988	$25
VERVE			
❏ MGV-1013 [M]	Music for Losers	1957	$150
❏ V-1013 [M]	Music for Losers	1961	$25
❏ MGV-1015 [M]	Turk Murphy on Easy Street	1957	$100
❏ V-1015 [M]	Turk Murphy on Easy Street	1961	$25

MURRAY, DAVID
Tenor saxophone player and bass clarinetist.

Albums

Number	Title	Yr	NM
ADELPHI			
❏ 5002	Low Class Conspiracy	1976	$35
BLACK SAINT			
❏ BSR-0089	Children	1986	$30
❏ BSR-0055	Home	198?	$30
❏ BSR-0018	Interboogieology	198?	$35
❏ 120105	I Want to Talk About You	1990	$35
❏ BSR-0085	Live at Sweet Basil, Vol. 1	1985	$30
❏ 120095	Live at Sweet Basil, Vol. 2	1986	$30
❏ BSR-0045	Ming	198?	$30
❏ BSR-0075	Morning Song	1984	$30
❏ BSR-0065	Murray's Steps	1983	$30
❏ BSR-0039	Sweet Lovely	198?	$30
❏ 120110	The Hill	1990	$35
HAT ART			
❏ 2016	3D Family	1986	$35
HAT HUT			
❏ 0U/V	The Third Family	1979	$25
INDIA NAVIGATION			
❏ IN-1026	Flowers for Albert	197?	$35
❏ IN-1044	Live, Volume 2	1979	$35
❏ IN-1032	Live at the Ocean Club	1978	$35
PORTRAIT			
❏ OR44432	Ming's Samba	1989	$30
RED RECORD			
❏ VPA-129	Last of the Hipman	198?	$30

MURRAY, SUNNY
Drummer.

Albums

Number	Title	Yr	NM
ESP-DISK'			
❏ 1032 [M]	Sunny Murray	1966	$200
❏ S-1032 [S]	Sunny Murray	1966	$200
JIHAD			
❏ 663 [M]	Sunny's Time Now	1967	$200

MUSIC COMPANY, THE
Studio group led by pianist DON RANDI.

Albums

Number	Title	Yr	NM
CRESTVIEW			
❏ CRS-3057	Hard and Heavy	196?	$60
MIRWOOD			
❏ M-7002 [M]	Rubber Soul Jazz	1966	$50
❏ MS-7002 [S]	Rubber Soul Jazz	1966	$60

MUSIC IMPROVISATION COMPANY, THE
Members: Evan Parker (soprano sax); Derek Bailey (guitar); Hugh Davies (live electronics); Jamie Muir (percussion); Christine Jeffrey (vocals).

Albums

Number	Title	Yr	NM
ECM			
❏ 1005	The Music Improvisation Company	197?	$35

MUSRA, PHIL

Albums

Number	Title	Yr	NM
INTEX SOUND			
❏ 84 [B]	Creatorspaces	1974	$500

MUSSO, VIDO
Tenor saxophone player and occasional clarinetist.

Albums

Number	Title	Yr	NM
CROWN			
❏ CLP-5029 [M]	Teenage Dance Party	1957	$50
❏ CLP-5007 [M]	The Swingin'st	1957	$50
—Reissue of Modern LP			
MODERN			
❏ MLP-1207 [M]	The Swingin'st	1956	$100

MUSSULLI, BOOTS
Alto saxophone player.

Albums

Number	Title	Yr	NM
CAPITOL			
❏ H6506 [10]	Boots Mussulli	1955	$200
❏ T6506 [M]	Boots Mussulli	1955	$80

MYERS, AMINA CLAUDINE
Female singer, keyboard player and composer.

Albums

Number	Title	Yr	NM
BLACK SAINT			
❏ BSR-0078	Circle of Time	1984	$30
MINOR MUSIC			
❏ MM-012	Country Girl	1987	$25
❏ MM-002	Jumping in the Sugar Bowl	198?	$30
NOVUS			
❏ 3030-1-N	Amina	1988	$25
❏ 3064-1-N	In Touch	1989	$30

MYRICK, BERL

Albums

Number	Title	Yr	NM
STRATA-EAST			
❏ SES-102-74	Live 'n Well	1974	$30

MYSTERIOUS FLYING ORCHESTRA, THE

Albums

Number	Title	Yr	NM
RCA VICTOR			
❏ APL1-2137	The Mysterious Flying Orchestra	1977	$50

N

NAJEE
Saxophone player, also an occasional flutist and keyboard player.

Albums

Number	Title	Yr	NM
EMI			
❏ E1-92248	Tokyo Blue	1990	$12
EMI AMERICA			
❏ ST-17241	Najee's Theme	1986	$12
EMI MANHATTAN			
❏ E1-90096	Day By Day	1988	$12

NAKAMURA, TERUO
Bass player.

Albums

Number	Title	Yr	NM
POLYDOR			
❏ PD-1-6119	Manhattan Special	1977	$25
❏ PD-1-6097	Rising Sun	1977	$25

NAMYSLOVSKI, ZBIGNIEW
Alto saxophone player and arranger.

Albums

Number	Title	Yr	NM
INNER CITY			
❏ IC-1130	Air Condition	198?	$30
❏ IC-1048	Namyslovski	197?	$35

NANCE, RAY
Violinist.

NANTON, MORRIS
Pianist. Also see THE FIRST JAZZ PIANO QUARTET.

Albums

Number	Title	Yr	NM
PRESTIGE			
❏ PRLP-7345 [M]	Preface	1964	$25
❏ PRST-7345 [S]	Preface	1964	$30
❏ PRLP-7409 [M]	Something We've Got	1965	$25
❏ PRST-7409 [S]	Something We've Got	1965	$30
❏ PRLP-7467 [M]	Soul Fingers	1966	$25
❏ PRST-7467 [S]	Soul Fingers	1966	$30
WARNER BROS.			
❏ WS-1256 [S]	Flower Drum Song	1958	$30
❏ W-1279 [M]	The Original Jazz Performance of "Roberta	1959	$30
❏ WS-1279 [S]	The Original Jazz Performance of "Roberta	1959	$30

NAPOLEON, PHIL
Trumpeter. Also see PETE DAILY.

Albums

Number	Title	Yr	NM
CAPITOL			
❏ T1428 [M]	In the Land of Dixie	1961	$50
❏ ST1344 [S]	Phil Napoleon and the Memphis Five	1960	$50
❏ T1535 [M]	Tenderloin Dixieland	1961	$50
COLUMBIA			
❏ CL2505 [10]	Two-Beat	1955	$80
EMARCY			
❏ MG-26008 [10]	Dixieland Classics Vol. 1	1954	$200
❏ MG-26009 [10]	Dixieland Classics Vol. 2	1954	$200
JOLLY ROGER			
❏ 5006 [10]	Dixieland By Phil Napoleon	1954	$50
MERCURY			
❏ MG-25078 [10]	Dixieland Classics Vol. 1	1953	$150
❏ MG-25079 [10]	Dixieland Classics Vol. 2	1953	$150

NARAHARA, STEVE

Albums

Number	Title	Yr	NM
PAUSA			
❏ 7177	Odyssey	1985	$25
❏ 7153	Sierra	1982	$25

NARELL, ANDY
Steel pan player. Also see OPAFIRE.

Albums

Number	Title	Yr	NM
HIPPOCKET			
❏ HP-103	Light in Your Eyes	1983	$30
—Original issue			
❏ HP-105	Slow Motion	1985	$30
—Original issue			
❏ HP-101	Stickman	1981	$30
—Original issue			
INNER CITY			
❏ IC-1053	Hidden Treasure	1979	$35
WINDHAM HILL			
❏ WH-0103	Light in Your Eyes	1987	$25
—Reissue of HipPocket 103			
❏ WH-0120	Little Secrets	1989	$30
❏ WH-0105	Slow Motion	1987	$25
—Reissue of HipPocket 105			
❏ WH-0101	Stickman	1987	$25
—Reissue of HipPocket 101			
❏ WH-0107	The Hammer	1987	$25

NARK, VAUGHN
Trumpeter, fluegel horn player and valve trombonist.

Albums

Number	Title	Yr	NM
STATIRAS			
❏ SLP-8070	El Tigre	1985	$25

NASCIMENTO, MILTON
Guitarist, male singer and composer.

Albums

Number	Title	Yr	NM
A&M			
❏ SP-3019	Courage	1969	$25
❏ SP9-3019	Courage	198?	$35
—Audiophile reissue (clearly marked as such)			
❏ SP-4719	Journey to Dawn	1979	$35

Gerry Mulligan, *The Gerry Mulligan Songbook*, *Volume 1*, World Pacific PJ-1237, mono, **$250**.

Gerry Mulligan, *Gerry Mulligan and His Ten-Tette*, Capitol H 439, **$300**.

Mark Murphy, *Let Yourself Go*, Decca DL 8632, **$100**.

Rose Murphy featuring Slam Stewart, *Jazz, Joy and Happiness*, United Artists UAJ-14025, **$50**.

Number	Title	Yr	NM
❏ SP-4611	Milton	1976	$25
❏ LP-0(????) [M]	Milton Nascimento	1967	$30
❏ SP-0(????) [S]	Milton Nascimento	1967	$25

COLUMBIA

❏ FC45239	Miltons	1989	$30
❏ FC44277	Yauarate	1987	$25

INTUITION

❏ B1-90790	Milagre Dos Peixes	1988	$30

— *Originally issued in Brazil in 1973*

POLYDOR

❏ 827638-1	Encontros E Despedidas	1986	$30

VERVE

❏ 831349-1	A Barca Dos Amantes	1986	$30

NASH, PAUL
Guitarist and composer.

Albums

REVELATION

❏ 32	A Jazz Composer's Ensemble	1980	$35

SOUL NOTE

❏ SN-1107	Second Impression	1986	$30

NASH, TED & DICK
Dick Nash plays trombone. Also see TED NASH.

Albums

LIBERTY

❏ LJH-6011 [M]	The Brothers Nash	1956	$50

NASH, TED
Clarinetist, bass clarinetist, and tenor and alto saxophone player.

Albums

COLUMBIA

❏ CL989 [M]	Star Eyes	1957	$40

CONCORD JAZZ

❏ CJ-106	Conception	1980	$25

STARLITE

❏ LP-6001 [10]	Ted Nash	1954	$50

NASHVILLE JAZZ MACHINE, THE

Albums

AM-PM

❏ 14	Where's Eli?	1986	$25

NATAL, NANETTE
Female singer, composer and arranger.

Albums

BENYO

❏ BY-3335	Hi-Fi Baby	198?	$30
❏ BY-3334	Wild in Reverie	198?	$30

NATIONAL JAZZ ENSEMBLE
Led by bass player, arranger and composer Chuck Israels. Members included Jimmy Maxwell, Tom Harrell, Don Hayes, Dave Berger (trumpets); Jimmy Knepper, Rod Levitt, Joe Randazzo (trombones); Greg Herbert, Lawrence Feldman (alto sax); Sal Nistico, Dennis Anderson (tenor sax); Kenny Berger (baritone sax); Ben Aranov (piano); Steve Brown (guitar); Lyle Atkinson (bass); Bill Goodwin (drums); with guest soloists Lee Konitz (alto sax) and Bill Evans (piano).

Albums

CHIAROSCURO

❏ 140	National Jazz Ensemble	197?	$30
❏ 151	National Jazz Ensemble, Volume 2	197?	$25

NATIONAL YOUTH JAZZ ORCHESTRA
British band.

Albums

RCA VICTOR

❏ LPL1-5116	11 Plus	197?	$35

NATURAL ESSENCE
Fusion group led by drummer T.S. Monk (son of Thelonious).

Albums

FANTASY

❏ F-9440	In Search of Happiness	1974	$30

NATURAL LIFE
Also see MIKE ELLIOT.

Albums

ASI

❏ 5006	All Music	1977	$30
❏ 5001	Natural Life	1977	$30
❏ 5005	Unnamed Land	1977	$30

CELEBRATION

❏ 5001	Natural Life	197?	$35
❏ 5005	Unnamed Land	1975	$35

NATURAL PROGRESSIONS

Albums

PALO ALTO/TBA

❏ TBA-248	Rumor Has It	1989	$30

NAUGHTON, BOBBY
Vibraphone player.

Albums

OTIC

❏ 1009	Nauxtagram	1979	$30
❏ 1005	The Haunt	1976	$35
❏ 1003	Understanding	197?	$35

NAUSEEF, MARK
Drummer.

Albums

CMP

❏ CMP-16-ST	Personal Note	198?	$25
❏ CMP-21-ST	Sura	198?	$25
❏ CMP-25-ST	Wun Wun	1987	$25

NAVARRO, FATS
Trumpeter. Also see TADD DAMERON; MILES DAVIS; STAN GETZ; HOWARD McGHEE.

Albums

BLUE NOTE

❏ BLP-5004 [10]	Fats Navarro Memorial Album	1952	$1000
❏ BN-LA507-H2	Prime Source	1976	$35
❏ BLP-1531 [M]	The Fabulous Fats Navarro, Vol. 1	1956	$500

— *Deep groove" version; Lexington Ave. address on label*

❏ BLP-1531 [M]	The Fabulous Fats Navarro, Vol. 1	1956	$200

— *Deep groove" version, W. 63rd St. address on label*

❏ BLP-1531 [M]	The Fabulous Fats Navarro, Vol. 1	1963	$80

— *With "New York, USA" address on label*

❏ BST-81531 [R]	The Fabulous Fats Navarro, Vol. 1	196?	$30

— *With "A Divison of Liberty Records" on label*

❏ BST-81531	The Fabulous Fats Navarro, Vol. 1	1985	$30

— *The Finest in Jazz Since 1939" reissue*

❏ BLP-1532 [M]	The Fabulous Fats Navarro, Vol. 2	1956	$500

— *Deep groove" version; Lexington Ave. address on label*

❏ BLP-1532 [M]	The Fabulous Fats Navarro, Vol. 2	1956	$200

— *Deep groove" version, W. 63rd St. address on label*

❏ BST-81532 [R]	The Fabulous Fats Navarro, Vol. 2	196?	$30

— *With "A Divison of Liberty Records" on label*

❏ BST-81532	The Fabulous Fats Navarro, Vol. 2	1985	$30

— *The Finest in Jazz Since 1939" reissue*

RIVERSIDE

❏ RS-3019	Good Bait	1968	$100

SAVOY

❏ MG-12011 [M]	Fats Navarro Memorial	1955	$150
❏ MG-9005 [10]	New Sounds in Modern Music	1952	$400
❏ MG-9019 [10]	New Trends Of Jazz	1952	$400
❏ MG-12133 [M]	Nostalgia	1958	$100

SAVOY JAZZ

❏ SJL-2216	Fat Girl	197?	$30
❏ SJC-416	Memorial Album	1985	$25

NAVARRO, FATS/KAI WINDING/BREW MOORE
Also see each artist's individual listings.

Albums

SAVOY

❏ MG-12119 [M]	In the Beginning…Bebop	1957	$60

NAVARRO, JOEY
Keyboard player.

Albums

ANTILLES

❏ 90985	On the Rocks	1988	$25

NEELY, DON
Saxophone player, clarinetist, male singer and bandleader.

Albums

MERRY MAKERS

❏ 108	Don Neely's Royal Society Jazz Orchestra	197?	$25

STOMP OFF

❏ SOS-1208	Ain't That a Grand and Glorious Feeling?	1991	$30

NEELY, JIMMY
Pianist.

Albums

TRU-SOUND

❏ TRU-15002 [M]	Misirlou	1962	$40

NEIDLINGER, BUELL
Bass player.

Albums

ANTILLES

❏ AN-1014	Swingrass '83	1983	$25

NELL, BOB
Pianist.

Albums

CADENCE JAZZ

❏ CJR-1022	Chasin' a Classic	198?	$25

NELOMS, BOB
Pianist.

Albums

INDIA NAVIGATION

❏ IN-1050	Pretty Music	198?	$30

NELSON, LOUIS
Trombonist.

Albums

GHB

❏ 158	Everybody's Talkin' 'Bout the Piron Band	198?	$25
❏ GHB-25	The Big Four, Vol. 1	196?	$35
❏ GHB-26	The Big Four, Vol. 2	196?	$35

NELSON, OLIVER, AND LOU DONALDSON
Also see each artist's individual listings.

Albums

CHESS

❏ 2ACMJ-404	Back Talk	1976	$35
❏ CH2-92515	Back Talk	198?	$30

NELSON, OLIVER; KING CURTIS; JIMMY FORREST
Also see each artist's individual listings.

Albums

PRESTIGE

❏ PRLP-7223 [M]	Soul Battle	1962	$150

— *Yellow label*

❏ PRST-7223 [S]	Soul Battle	1962	$150

Number	Title	Yr	NM

NELSON, OLIVER
Alto (occasional tenor) saxophone player and composer. Also see CARL B. STOKES.

Albums
ABC IMPULSE!
| AS-9132 [S] | Happenings | 1968 | $200 |

—With Hank Jones; black label with red ring
| AS-9153 [S] | Live From Los Angeles | 1968 | $200 |

—Black label with red ring
| AS-9113 [S] | Michelle | 1968 | $200 |

—Black label with red ring
| AS-75 [S] | More Blues and the Abstract Truth | 1968 | $200 |

—Black label with red ring
| AS-75 [S] | More Blues and the Abstract Truth | 1975 | $30 |

—Green, blue, purple "target" label
| AS-9168 [S] | Soulful Brass | 1968 | $120 |

—Black label with red ring
| AS-9129 [S] | Sound Pieces | 1968 | $200 |

—Black label with red ring
| AS-5 [S] | The Blues and the Abstract Truth | 1968 | $200 |

—Black label with red ring
| AS-9144 [S] | The Kennedy Dream | 1968 | $200 |

—Black label with red ring
| AS-9147 [S] | The Spirit of '67 | 1968 | $200 |

—With Pee Wee Russell; black label with red ring
| IA-9335-2 | Three Dimensions | 1978 | $200 |

ARGO
| LP-737 [M] | Fantabulous | 1964 | $50 |
| LPS-737 [S] | Fantabulous | 1964 | $50 |

BLUEBIRD
| 6993-1-RB | Black, Brown and Beautiful | 1989 | $35 |

—Reissue of Flying Dutchman 10116

CADET
| LPS-737 [S] | Fantabulous | 1966 | $35 |

—Fading blue label
| LP-737 [M] | Fantabulous | 1966 | $60 |

—Fading blue label

FANTASY
OJC-227	Meet Oliver Nelson	198?	$30
OJC-089	Screamin' the Blues	198?	$30
OJC-325	Soul Battle	1988	$30
OJC-099	Straight Ahead	198?	$30

FLYING DUTCHMAN
| FD-10134 | Berlin Dialogue | 1972 | $60 |
| FD-10116 | Black, Brown and Beautiful | 1971 | $40 |

—Reissue of 116
FD-116	Black, Brown and Beautiful	1970	$60
CYL2-1449	Dream Deferred	1976	$60
BDL1-0592	Oliver Nelson in London	1974	$60
BDL1-0825	Skull Session	1975	$150

—Reproductions exist
| FD-10149 | Swiss Suite | 1973 | $60 |

GRP IMPULSE!
| IMP-212 | More Blues and the Abstract Truth | 1997 | $200 |

—Reissue on audiophile vinyl
| IMP-154 | The Blues and the Abstract Truth | 1995 | $35 |

—Reissue on audiophile vinyl

IMPULSE!
| A-9132 [M] | Happenings | 1967 | $160 |

—With Hank Jones
| AS-9132 [S] | Happenings | 1967 | $120 |

—With Hank Jones
AS-9153 [S]	Live From Los Angeles	1967	$120
A-9113 [M]	Michelle	1966	$120
AS-9113 [S]	Michelle	1966	$160
A-9129 [M]	Sound Pieces	1966	$160
AS-9129 [S]	Sound Pieces	1966	$160
A-5 [M]	The Blues and the Abstract Truth	1961	$200

—Original cover has an abstract painting and lists Bill Evans' name first
| AS-5 [S] | The Blues and the Abstract Truth | 1961 | $120 |

—Original cover has an abstract painting and lists Bill Evans' name first
| A-5 [M] | The Blues and the Abstract Truth | 196? | $160 |

—Later cover has Oliver Nelson clearly indicated as leader and features a photo of him at the right

| AS-5 [S] | The Blues and the Abstract Truth | 196? | $200 |

—Later cover has Oliver Nelson clearly indicated as leader and features a photo of him at the right
A-9144 [M]	The Kennedy Dream	1967	$160
AS-9144 [S]	The Kennedy Dream	1967	$120
A-9147 [M]	The Spirit of '67	1967	$200

—With Pee Wee Russell
| AS-9147 [S] | The Spirit of '67 | 1967 | $120 |

—With Pee Wee Russell

INNER CITY
| IC-6008 | Stolen Moments | 1977 | $35 |

MCA
| 29052 | More Blues and the Abstract Truth | 1980 | $25 |
| 5888 | More Blues and the Abstract Truth | 1987 | $25 |

—Another reissue
| 29063 | The Blues and the Abstract Truth | 1980 | $25 |
| 4148 | Three Dimensions | 1980 | $30 |

MCA IMPULSE!
| MCA-5888 | More Blues and the Abstract Truth | 1987 | $25 |
| MCA-5659 | The Blues and the Abstract Truth | 1985 | $30 |

MOODSVILLE
| MVLP-13 [M] | Nocturne | 1960 | $100 |

—Green label
| MVLP-13 [M] | Nocturne | 1965 | $50 |

—Blue label, trident logo at right

NEW JAZZ
| NJLP-8224 [M] | Meet Oliver Nelson | 1959 | $200 |

—Purple label
| NJLP-8224 [M] | Meet Oliver Nelson | 1965 | $150 |

—Blue label, trident logo at right
| NJLP-8243 [M] | Screamin' the Blues | 1960 | $200 |

—Purple label
| NJLP-8324 [M] | Screamin' the Blues | 1963 | $0 |

—Canceled
| NJLP-8243 [M] | Screamin' the Blues | 1965 | $150 |

—Blue label, trident logo at right
| NJLP-8255 [M] | Straight Ahead | 1961 | $200 |

—Purple label
| NJLP-8255 [M] | Straight Ahead | 1965 | $150 |

—Blue label, trident logo at right
| NJLP-8233 [M] | Takin' Care of Business | 1960 | $200 |

—Purple label
| NJLP-8233 [M] | Takin' Care of Business | 1965 | $150 |

—Blue label, trident logo at right

PRESTIGE
PRLP-7225 [M]	Afro/American Sketches	1962	$150
PRST-7225 [S]	Afro/American Sketches	1962	$150
P-24060	Images	1976	$50
PRLP-7236 [M]	Main Stem	1962	$150
PRST-7236 [S]	Main Stem	1962	$150

STATUS
| ST-8324 [M] | Screamin' the Blues | 1965 | $50 |

UNITED ARTISTS
| UAJ-14019 [M] | Impressions of Phaedra | 1962 | $50 |
| UAJS-15019 [S] | Impressions of Phaedra | 1962 | $80 |

VERVE
V-8508 [M]	Full Nelson	1963	$40
V6-8508 [S]	Full Nelson	1963	$50
V6-8743 [S]	Leonard Feather Presents the Sound of Feeling and the Sound of Oliver Nelson	1968	$100

NELSON, OZZIE
Bandleader. Best known for his 1950s TV sitcom with wife Harriet.

Albums
AIRCHECK
| 19 | Ozzie Nelson and His Orchestra On the Air | 198? | $25 |

HINDSIGHT
HSR-189	Ozzie Nelson and His Orchestra 1937	198?	$25
HSR-208	Ozzie Nelson and His Orchestra 1938	198?	$25
HSR-107	Ozzie Nelson and His Orchestra 1940-42	198?	$25

NELSON, RICK "COUGAR"
Trombonist.

Albums
JAZZOLOGY
| J-123 | Steppin' Out | 198? | $25 |

NEPTUNE, JOHN KAIZAN
Shakuhachi (type of Japanese flute) player.

Albums
FORTUNA
| 17030 | Dance for the One in Six | 198? | $25 |

INNER CITY
| IC-6077 | Bamboo | 198? | $30 |
| IC-6078 | Shogun | 198? | $30 |

MILESTONE
| M-9113 | West of Somewhere | 1981 | $30 |

NERO, PAUL
Violinist and composer.

Albums
SUNSET
| LP-303 [M] | Play the Music of Paul Nero and His Hi-Fiddles | 1956 | $60 |

NERO, PETER
Pianist. Best known for his pop and classical work, the below are jazz-oriented. The Mode LP was recorded under his real name, Bernie Nerow.

Albums
CONCORD JAZZ
| CJ-48 | Now | 1978 | $25 |

MODE
| LP-117 [M] | Bernie Nerow Trio | 1957 | $200 |

—As "Bernie Nerow"
PREMIER
| PM-2011 [M] | Just for You | 1963 | $50 |
| PS-2011 [R] | Just for You | 1963 | $30 |

NEROW, BERNIE
See PETER NERO.

NESTICO, SAMMY
Arranger and bandleader.

Albums
MARK
| 32244 | Swingaphonic | 1969 | $25 |

SEA BREEZE
| SBD-103 | Night Flight | 1986 | $25 |

NEUMANN, ROGER
Saxophone player, bandleader, composer and arranger.

Albums
SEA BREEZE
| SBD-102 | Introducing Roger Neumann's Rather Large Band | 1983 | $25 |

NEW AIR
See AIR.

NEW ART JAZZ ENSEMBLE, THE
See JOHN CARTER AND BOBBY BRADFORD.

NEW BLACK EAGLE JAZZ BAND
Members: Tony Pringle (trumpet); Pam Pameijer (drums); Peter Bullis (banjo); Eli Newberger (tuba); Stan Vincent (trombone); Stan MacDonald (clarinet, soprano sax); Norm Stowell (string bass); Bob Pilsbury (piano). Brian Ogilvie replaced MacDonald in 1980; Hugh Blackwell replaced Ogilvie in 1981; Billy Novick replaced Blackwell in 1986.

Albums
DIRTY SHAME
| 2002 | On the River | 197? | $25 |

GHB
| GHB-59 | New Black Eagle Jazz Band | 1973 | $30 |

PHILO

Number	Title	Yr	NM
❏ 1086	New Black Eagle Jazz Band at Symphony Hall: 10th Anniversary	198?	$30

STOMP OFF

❏ SOS-1147	Don't Monkey With It	1988	$25
❏ SOS-1065	Dreaming the Hours Away	1984	$25
❏ SOS-1048	Live at the World Music Concourse	198?	$25
❏ SOS-1054	Live at the World Music Concourse, Volume 2	198?	$25
❏ SOS-1091	Mt. Gretna Week-End, Vol. 1	1985	$25
❏ SOS-1092	Mt. Gretna Week-End, Vol. 2	1985	$25

NEW GLENN MILLER ORCHESTRA
MILLER ORCHESTRA (in the M's).

NEW HERITAGE KEYBOARD QUARTET

Albums

BLUE NOTE

❏ BN-LA099-F	New Heritage Keyboard Quartet	1973	$30

NEW McKINNEY'S COTTON PICKERS, THE
Fronted by banjo player and male singer Dave Wilborn, who was one of the original McKINNEY'S COTTON PICKERS.

Albums

BOUNTIFUL

❏ 38000	The New McKinney's Cotton Pickers	1972	$35
❏ 38001	You're Driving Me Crazy	1974	$35

NEW ORLEANS ALL STARS, THE
Among the members: Raymond Burke; Jack Delaney; George Gerard; Johnny St. Cyr.

Albums

DIXIELAND JUBILEE

❏ DJ-502	In Concert	196?	$35

NEW ORLEANS CREOLE ORCHESTRA

Albums

SOUTHLAND

❏ 234 [M]	New Orleans Creole Jazz Band	1962	$35

NEW ORLEANS HERITAGE HALL JAZZ BAND
Among the members: Alvin Alcorn; Louis Barbarin; Louis Cuttrell; "Frog" Joseph; Walter Lewis; Blanche Thomas.

Albums

DIXIELAND JUBILEE

❏ DJ-512	New Orleans Heritage Hall Jazz Band	197?	$30

NEW ORLEANS NIGHTHAWKS, THE

Albums

GHB

❏ 98	The New Orleans Nighthawks	1979	$25

NEW ORLEANS RAGTIME ORCHESTRA
Revival band led by Lars Edegran.

Albums

ARHOOLIE

❏ 1058	New Orleans Ragtime Orchestra	197?	$30

DELMARK

❏ DS-214	Grace and Beauty	197?	$30

VANGUARD

❏ VSD-69/70	New Orleans Ragtime Orchestra	197?	$35

NEW ORLEANS RASCALS, THE
Based in Osaka, Japan.

Albums

STOMP OFF

❏ SOS-1074	Love Song of the Nile	1984	$25
❏ SOS-1113	The New Orleans Rascals at Preservation Hall	1986	$25

NEW ORLEANS RHYTHM KINGS
Important early white jazz band; the first to make a racially mixed jazz record when JELLY ROLL MORTON joined on piano in 1923. Original members: Louis Black (banjo); GEORG BRUNIS (trombone); Alfred Loyacano (bass); Paul Mares (cornet); Leon Roppolo (clarinet); Elmer Schobel (piano); Frank Snyder (drums).

Albums

BRUNSWICK

❏ BL58011 [10]	Dixieland Jazz	1950	$120

KINGS OF JAZZ

❏ NLJ-18009/10	New Orleans Rhythm Kings Heritage	198?	$35

MILESTONE

❏ 47020	New Orleans Rhythm Kings	197?	$35

NEW ORLEANS SHUFFLERS, THE

Albums

KINGSWAY

❏ KL-700 [M]	The New Orleans Shufflers	1955	$50

NEW PAUL WHITEMAN ORCHESTRA
See PAUL WHITEMAN ORCHESTRA (in the W's).

NEW SUNSHINE JAZZ BAND

Albums

BIOGRAPH

❏ 12058	Too Much Mustard	197?	$30

FLYING DUTCHMAN

❏ BDL1-0549	Old Rags	1974	$30

NEW YANKEE RHYTHM KINGS, THE
Led by trombonist Bob Connors.

Albums

STOMP OFF

❏ SOS-1015	Jazz Band	198?	$25
❏ SOS-1050	Live at the Strata-Capitol	1982	$25
❏ SOS-1067	Together at Last	1984	$25

NEW YORK ART QUARTET, THE
Members: MILFORD GRAVES; ROSWELL RUDD; JOHN TCHICAI; Lewis Worrell (bass).

Albums

ESP-DISK'

❏ 1004 [M]	The New York Art Quartet	1965	$200
❏ S-1004 [S]	The New York Art Quartet	1965	$200

NEW YORK BASS VIOLIN CHOIR
Founded by Bill Lee. Other members: Lisle Atkinson, RON CARTER, RICHARD DAVIS, Michael Fleming, MILT HINTON, SAM JONES.

Albums

STRATA-EAST

❏ SES-8003	New York Bass Violin Choir	1980	$35

NEW YORK JAZZ GUITAR ENSEMBLE, THE
Among the members: PETER LEITCH; Paul Meyers.

Albums

CHOICE

❏ CRS-6831	4 On 6 x 5	1986	$30

NEW YORK JAZZ QUARTET, THE (1)
Members: HERBIE MANN; MAT MATTHEWS; WHITEY MITCHELL; JOE PUMA.

Albums

CORAL

❏ CRL57136 [M]	Music For Suburban Living	1958	$200
❏ CRL757136 [S]	Music For Suburban Living	1958	$150

ELEKTRA

❏ EKL-118 [M]	Gone Native	1957	$50
❏ EKL-115 [M]	The New York Jazz Quartet	1957	$50

SAVOY

❏ MG-12172 [M]	Adam's Theme	1960	$30
❏ MG-12175 [M]	Gone Native	1961	$30

NEW YORK JAZZ QUARTET, THE (2)
Members: ROLAND HANNA; George Mraz (bass); revolving drummers including Richard Pratt, MARVIN "SMITTY" SMITH and GRADY TATE; FRANK WESS.

Albums

ENJA

❏ 3083	Oasis	1981	$30

INNER CITY

❏ IC-3024	Blues for Sarka	1978	$35
❏ IC-3011	Surge	197?	$35

SALVATION

❏ 703	Concert in Japan	197?	$30

NEW YORK JAZZ REPERTORY COMPANY, THE
Directed by DICK HYMAN. Many jazz greats appeared in this band, which toured the world playing a tribute to Louis Armstrong.

Albums

ATLANTIC

❏ SD1671	The Music of Louis Armstrong	1975	$25

NEW YORK JAZZ SEXTET, THE
Members: RICHARD DAVIS; ART FARMER; TOMMY FLANAGAN; ALBERT HEATH; Tom McIntosh (trombone); JAMES MOODY.

Albums

SCEPTER

❏ S-526 [M]	New York Jazz Sextet	1964	$25
❏ SS-526 [S]	New York Jazz Sextet	1964	$30

NEW YORK MARY
Members: Joe Corsello (drums); Bruce Johnstone (baritone sax); Rick Petrone (bass).

Albums

ARISTA/FREEDOM

❏ AF1019	New York Mary	1975	$35
❏ AF1035	Piece of the Apple	1976	$35

NEW YORK ORIGINATORS, THE

Albums

PARAMOUNT

❏ RS-201 [10]	The New York Style	1952	$60

NEW YORK SAXOPHONE QUARTET, THE

Albums

20TH CENTURY FOX

❏ TFM-3150 [M]	The New York Saxophone Quartet	1964	$25
❏ TFS-3150 [S]	The New York Saxophone Quartet	1964	$30

MARK

❏ 32322	The New York Saxophone Quartet	1969	$25

STASH

❏ ST-220	An American Experience	198?	$25
❏ ST-210	New York Saxophone Quartet	198?	$25

NEW YORK VOICES
Vocal group: Peter Eldridge; Caprice Fox; Sara Krieger; Darmon Meader; Kim Nazarian. Lauren Kinhan replaced Krieger in 1992. Fox left in 1994.

Albums

GRP

❏ GR-9589	New York Voices	1989	$30

NEWBERGER, ELI, AND JIMMY MAZZY
Newberger plays tuba; Mazzy is a banjo player.

Albums

STOMP OFF

❏ SOS-1109	Shake It Down	1986	$25

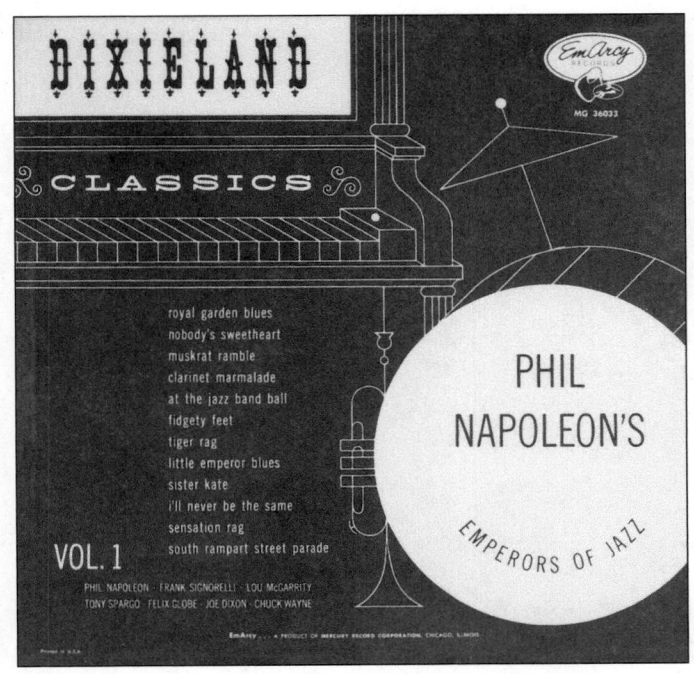

Phil Napoleon, *Dixieland Classics Vol. 1*, EmArcy MG 26008, **$200**.

Oliver Nelson, *Screamin' the Blues*, New Jazz NJLP-8243, purple label, **$200**.

Bernie Nerow, *Bernie Nerow Trio*, Mode LP-117, **$200**. He later recorded as "Peter Nero."

Joe Newman, *Joe's Hap'nin's*, Swingville SVST-2027, stereo, red label, **$60**.

NEWBORN, PHINEAS

Pianist. Also see ROY HAYNES; YOUNG MEN FROM MEMPHIS.

Albums

ATLANTIC

Number	Title	Yr	NM
❏ 1235 [M]	Here Is Phineas	1956	$300
— Black label			
❏ SD1235 [S]	Here Is Phineas	1958	$300
— Green label			
❏ 1235 [M]	Here Is Phineas	1961	$150
— Multicolor label, white "fan" logo at right			
❏ SD1235 [S]	Here Is Phineas	1961	$150
— Multicolor label, white "fan" logo at right			
❏ 1235 [M]	Here Is Phineas	1964	$35
— Multicolor label, black "fan" logo at right			
❏ SD1235 [S]	Here Is Phineas	1964	$30
— Multicolor label, black "fan" logo at right			
❏ SD1672	Solo Piano	1975	$30
❏ 90534	The Piano Artistry of Phineas Newborn	1986	$25

CONTEMPORARY

Number	Title	Yr	NM
❏ C-7648	Back Home	198?	$15
❏ M-3611 [M]	Great Jazz Piano	1962	$200
❏ S-7611 [S]	Great Jazz Piano	1962	$200
❏ S-7622 [S]	Please Send Me Someone to Love	1969	$75
❏ M-3615 [M]	The Newborn Touch	1964	$200
❏ S-7615 [S]	The Newborn Touch	1964	$200
❏ M-3600 [M]	The World of Piano!	1961	$200
❏ S-7600 [S]	The World of Piano!	1961	$200

FANTASY

Number	Title	Yr	NM
❏ OJC-175	A World of Piano	198?	$25
❏ OJC-388	Great Jazz Piano	1989	$30
❏ OJC-270	The Newborn Touch	1988	$25
❏ OJC-175	The World of Piano!	198?	$25

PABLO

Number	Title	Yr	NM
❏ 2310801	Look Out, Phineas Is Back	197?	$30

RCA VICTOR

Number	Title	Yr	NM
❏ LPM-1873 [M]	Fabulous Phineas	1958	$50
❏ LSP-1873 [S]	Fabulous Phineas	1958	$40
❏ LPM-1589 [M]	Phineas Newborn Plays Jamaica	1957	$50
❏ LPM-1421 [M]	Phineas' Rainbow	1957	$50
❏ LPM-1474 [M]	While the Lady Sleeps	1957	$100

ROULETTE

Number	Title	Yr	NM
❏ R-52043 [M]	I Love a Piano	1960	$30
❏ SR-52043 [S]	I Love a Piano	1960	$30
❏ R-52031 [M]	Piano Portraits	1959	$30
❏ SR-52031 [S]	Piano Portraits	1959	$30

NEWMAN, DAVID "FATHEAD

Tenor saxophone player; also plays alto sax and flute. Also see JAMES CLAY.

Albums

ATLANTIC

Number	Title	Yr	NM
❏ SD1505	Bigger and Better	1968	$25
❏ 1399 [M]	Fathead Comes On	1962	$150
❏ 81965	Fire! Live at the Village Vanguard	1989	$30
❏ 81725	Heads Up	1987	$25
❏ SD1489	House of David	1968	$25
❏ SD1600	Lonely Avenue	1972	$35
❏ SD1524	Many Facets	1969	$35
❏ SD1662	Newmanism	1974	$30
❏ 1304 [M]	Ray Charles Presents David "Fathead" Newman	1959	$300
— Black label			
❏ 1304 [M]	Ray Charles Presents David "Fathead" Newman	1961	$150
— Multicolor label with white "fan" logo			
❏ 1304 [M]	Ray Charles Presents David "Fathead" Newman	1964	$30
— Multicolor label with black "fan" logo			
❏ SD1304 [S]	Ray Charles Presents David "Fathead" Newman	1959	$300
— Green label			
❏ SD1304 [S]	Ray Charles Presents David "Fathead" Newman	1961	$150
— Multicolor label with white "fan" logo			
❏ SD1304 [S]	Ray Charles Presents David "Fathead" Newman	1964	$35
— Multicolor label with black "fan" logo			
❏ 1366 [M]	Straight Ahead	1961	$150
— Multicolor label with white "fan" logo			
❏ 1366 [M]	Straight Ahead	1964	$30
— Multicolor label with black "fan" logo			
❏ SD1366 [S]	Straight Ahead	1961	$150
— Multicolor label with white "fan" logo			
❏ SD1366 [S]	Straight Ahead	1964	$35
— Multicolor label with black "fan" logo			
❏ SD1590	The Best of David "Fathead" Newman	1972	$35
❏ SD1638	The Weapon	1973	$35

COTILLION

Number	Title	Yr	NM
❏ SD18002	Captain Buckles	1970	$25

MUSE

Number	Title	Yr	NM
❏ MR-5234	Resurgence	1981	$25
❏ MR-5283	Still Hard Times	1982	$25

PRESTIGE

Number	Title	Yr	NM
❏ 10104	Concrete Jungle	1978	$35
❏ 10106	Keep the Dream Alive	1978	$35
❏ 10108	Scratch My Back	1979	$35

WARNER BROS.

Number	Title	Yr	NM
❏ BS2984	Front Money	1977	$25
❏ BS2917	Mr. Fathead	1976	$25

NEWMAN, JOE, AND JOE WILDER

Also see each artist's individual listings.

Albums

CONCORD JAZZ

Number	Title	Yr	NM
❏ CJ-262	Joe Newman and Joe Wilder	1985	$30

NEWMAN, JOE

Trumpeter. Also see EDDIE BERT.

Albums

AMERICAN RECORDING SOCIETY

Number	Title	Yr	NM
❏ G-447 [M]	Basically Swing	1958	$40
❏ G-451 [M]	New Sounds In Swing	1958	$40

CORAL

Number	Title	Yr	NM
❏ CRL57208 [M]	Soft Swingin' Jazz	1958	$50
❏ CRL57121 [M]	The Happy Cats	1957	$50

FANTASY

Number	Title	Yr	NM
❏ OJC-185	Good 'N Groovy	1985	$25
❏ OJC-419	Jive At Five	1990	$30

JAZZTONE

Number	Title	Yr	NM
❏ J-1217 [M]	New Sounds In Swing	1956	$40
❏ J-1265 [M]	Swing Lightly	1957	$40
❏ J-1220 [M]	The Count's Men	1956	$40

MERCURY

Number	Title	Yr	NM
❏ MG-20696 [M]	Joe Newman At Count Basie's	1962	$100
❏ SR-60696 [S]	Joe Newman At Count Basie's	1962	$100

PRESTIGE

Number	Title	Yr	NM
❏ 2509	Jive At Five	198?	$30

RAMA

Number	Title	Yr	NM
❏ LP-1003 [M]	Locking Horns	1957	$400

RCA VICTOR

Number	Title	Yr	NM
❏ LPM-1118 [M]	All I Want To Do Is Swing	1955	$100
❏ LPM-1324 [M]	Salute To Satch	1956	$80

ROULETTE

Number	Title	Yr	NM
❏ R-52014 [M]	Joe Newman With Woodwinds	1958	$40
❏ SR-52014 [S]	Joe Newman With Woodwinds	1958	$30
❏ R-52009 [M]	Locking Horns	1958	$40
❏ SR-52009 [S]	Locking Horns	1958	$30

STASH

Number	Title	Yr	NM
❏ ST-219	In a Mellow Mood	198?	$25

STORYVILLE

Number	Title	Yr	NM
❏ STLP-905 [M]	I Feel Like a Newman	1956	$100
❏ STLP-318 [10]	Joe Newman and the Boys In the Band	1955	$150

SWINGVILLE

Number	Title	Yr	NM
❏ SVLP-2019 [M]	Good 'N Groovy	1961	$50
— Purple label			
❏ SVLP-2019 [M]	Good 'N Groovy	1965	$30
— Blue label, trident logo at right			
❏ SVLP-2011 [M]	Jive At Five	1961	$50
— Purple label			
❏ SVLP-2011 [M]	Jive At Five	1965	$30
— Blue label, trident logo at right			
❏ SVLP-2027 [M]	Joe's Hap'nin's	1961	$60
— Purple label			
❏ SVST-2027 [S]	Joe's Hap'nin's	1961	$60
— Red label			
❏ SVLP-2027 [M]	Joe's Hap'nin's	1965	$30
— Blue label, trident logo at right			
❏ SVST-2027 [S]	Joe's Hap'nin's	1965	$30
— Blue label, trident logo at right			

TRIP

Number	Title	Yr	NM
❏ 5548	Live at Basie's	197?	$12

VANGUARD

Number	Title	Yr	NM
❏ VRS-8007 [10]	Joe Newman and His Band	1954	$200

VIK

Number	Title	Yr	NM
❏ LX-1060 [M]	The Midgets	1957	$80

WORLD PACIFIC

Number	Title	Yr	NM
❏ WP-1288 [M]	Countin'	1960	$150
❏ ST-1288 [S]	Countin'	1960	$150

NEWMAN, JOE/RUBY BRAFF

Also see each artist's individual listings.

Albums

HALL OF FAME

Number	Title	Yr	NM
❏ 601	Swing Lightly	197?	$25

NEWPORT ALL STARS, THE

Organized by pianist GEORGE WEIN.

Albums

BASF

Number	Title	Yr	NM
❏ 20717	A Tribute to Duke	1972	$35

BLACK LION

Number	Title	Yr	NM
❏ 303	Newport All Stars	197?	$30

CONCORD JAZZ

Number	Title	Yr	NM
❏ CJ-343	European Tour	1988	$25
— As "The Newport Jazz Festival All-Stars			

NEWTON, CAM

Guitarist.

Albums

INNER CITY

Number	Title	Yr	NM
❏ IC-1059	The Motive Behind the Smile	1979	$35
❏ IC-1079	Welcome Aliens	1980	$35

NEWTON, JAMES

Flutist.

Albums

BLUE NOTE

Number	Title	Yr	NM
❏ BT-85109	The African Flower	1986	$30

CELESTIAL HARMONIES

Number	Title	Yr	NM
❏ CEL-012	Echo Canyon	1984	$30
❏ 13012	Echo Canyon	198?	$25
— Reissue with new number			
❏ 14030	James Newton in Venice	1988	$30

ECM

Number	Title	Yr	NM
❏ 1214	Axum	1981	$25

GRAMAVISION

Number	Title	Yr	NM
❏ 8205	James Newton	1982	$25
❏ GR-8304	Luella	1983	$25

INDIA NAVIGATION

Number	Title	Yr	NM
❏ IN-1046	Mystery School	1980	$30
❏ IN-1037	Paseo Del Mar	197?	$35
❏ IN-1051	Portraits	198?	$30

NEWTON, LAUREN

Female singer.

Albums

HAT HUT

Number	Title	Yr	NM
❏ 3511	Timbre	1982	$35

NGCUKANA, EZRA

Saxophone player and multi-instrumentalist from South Africa.

Albums

JIVE

Number	Title	Yr	NM
❏ 1250-1-J	You Think You Know Me	1989	$30

NHOP

See NIELS-HENNING ORSTED PEDERSEN.

NICHOLAS, ALBERT

Clarinetist and saxophone player.

Albums

DELMARK

Number	Title	Yr	NM
❏ DS-209	Albert Nicholas with Art Hodes' All-Star Stompers	1964	$25

GHB

Number	Title	Yr	NM
❏ 64	The Albert Nicholas/John Defferary Jazztet	197?	$30

Number	Title	Yr	NM

NICHOLAS, ALBERT/SIDNEY BECHET

Also see each artist's individual listings.

Albums

RIVERSIDE

❏ RLP-12-216 [M]	Creole Reeds	1956	$250
— *White label, blue print*			
❏ RLP-12-216 [M]	Creole Reeds	1959	$300
— *Blue label, microphone logo at top*			

NICHOLAS, GEORGE "BIG NICK"

Tenor saxophone player and male singer.

Albums

INDIA NAVIGATION

❏ IN-1061	Big and Warm	1985	$30
❏ IN-1066	Big Nick	1986	$30

NICHOLAS, JOSEPH "WOODEN JOE"

Cornet player.

Albums

AMERICA MUSIC

❏ 640 [10]	A Nite at Artesian Hall With Wooden Joe	1951	$60

NICHOLS, HERBIE

Pianist and composer.

Albums

BETHLEHEM

❏ BCP-81 [M]	Love Gloom Cash and Love	1957	$250
❏ BCP-6028	The Bethlehem Years	197?	$35
— *Distributed by RCA Victor*			

BLUE NOTE

❏ BLP-1519 [M]	Herbie Nichols Trio	1963	$500
— *With "New York, USA" address on label*			
❏ BST-81519 [R]	Herbie Nichols Trio	1967	$50
— *With "A Division of Liberty Records" on label*			
❏ BLP-1519 [M]	Herbie Nichols Trio	1971	$200
— *A Division of United Artists" on label*			
❏ BLP-5068 [10]	The Prophetic Herbie Nichols, Volume 1	1955	$1200
❏ BLP-5069 [10]	The Prophetic Herbie Nichols, Volume 2	1955	$1200
❏ BN-LA485-H2	Third World	1975	$40

MOSAIC

❏ MR5-118	The Complete Blue Note Recordings of Herbie Nichols	1987	$200
— *Limited edition of 7,500*			

NICHOLS, KEITH

Pianist.

Albums

STOMP OFF

❏ SOS-1159	Chitterlin' Strut	1988	$25
❏ SOS-1135	Doctors Jazz	1987	$25

NICHOLS, RED, AND THE FIVE PENNIES

Nichols played cornet. The Five Pennies were often more than five, and the membership changed often.

Albums

AUDIOPHILE

❏ AP-1 [M]	Red Nichols and Band	195?	$50
❏ AP-7 [M]	Syncopated Chamber Music, Volume 1	195?	$50
❏ AP-8 [M]	Syncopated Chamber Music, Volume 2	195?	$50

BRUNSWICK

❏ BL58008 [10]	Classics, Volume 1	1950	$80
❏ BL58009 [10]	Classics, Volume 2	1950	$80
❏ BL54008 [M]	For Collectors Only	1954	$50
❏ BL54047 [M]	The Red Nichols Story	1959	$50
❏ BL58027 [10]	Volume 3	1951	$80

CAPITOL

❏ T2065 [M]	Blues and Old-Time Rags	1963	$75
❏ ST2065 [S]	Blues and Old-Time Rags	1963	$40
❏ T1297 [M]	Dixieland Dinner Dance	1960	$75
❏ ST1297 [S]	Dixieland Dinner Dance	1960	$40
❏ T775 [M]	Hot Pennies	1956	$80
❏ H215 [10]	Jazz Time	1950	$150
❏ T1051 [M]	Parade of the Pennies	1958	$50
❏ ST1051 [S]	Parade of the Pennies	1958	$60
❏ T1803 [M]	The All-Time Hits of Red Nichols	1962	$75

Number	Title	Yr	NM
❏ ST1803 [S]	The All-Time Hits of Red Nichols	1962	$50

CIRCLE

❏ CLP-110	Red Nichols and His Orchestra 1936	1987	$25

CONCERT DISC

❏ CS-53	Red Nichols and His Five Pennies	1961	$25

HALL OF FAME

❏ 619	Red Nichols and His Five Pennies	197?	$25

JAZZOLOGY

❏ J-90	Red Nichols and His Five Pennies	198?	$25

MARK 56

❏ 612	Red Nichols and His Five Pennies	197?	$30

MCA

❏ 1518	The Rarest Brunswick Masters	198?	$25

PAUSA

❏ 9022	All Time Hits	198?	$25

PICCADILLY

❏ 3570	Big Band Series/Original Recordings	198?	$25

STARDUST

❏ SD-122 [M]	Red Nichols and His "Five Pennies	196?	$30
❏ SDS-122 [S]	Red Nichols and His "Five Pennies	196?	$30

SUNBEAM

❏ 12	Popular Concert 1928-32	197?	$30
❏ 137	Red Nichols and His Five Pennies 1929-31	1973	$25

NICHOLS-JACOBY DREAMLAND SYNCOPATORS

Albums

STOMP OFF

❏ SOS-1150	Territory Jazz	1988	$25

NIEBLA, EDUARDO, AND ANTONIO FORCIONE

Niebla and Forcione are guitarists.

Albums

VENTURE

❏ 90655	Celebration	1988	$25

NIEHAUS, LENNIE

Alto saxophone player and arranger.

Albums

CAMBRIA

❏ C-1016	Shades of Dring	1981	$50

CONTEMPORARY

❏ C-2513 [10]	Lennie Niehaus, Vol. 1: The Quintet	1954	$250
❏ C-2517 [10]	Lennie Niehaus, Vol. 2: The Octet	1954	$250
❏ C-3503 [M]	Lennie Niehaus, Vol. 3: The Octet No. 2	1955	$250
❏ C-3510 [M]	Lennie Niehaus, Vol. 4: Quintets & Strings	1956	$250
❏ C-3524 [M]	Lennie Niehaus, Vol. 5: The Sextet	1956	$250
❏ C-3518 [M]	The Lennie Niehaus Quintet	1956	$250

Number	Title	Yr	NM

❏ C-3540 [M]	Zounds! Lennie Niehaus, Vol. 2: The Octet	1957	$250

FANTASY

❏ OJC-319	The Lennie Niehaus Quintet	198?	$30

MERCURY

❏ MG-20555 [M]	I Swing for You	1960	$100
❏ SR-60123 [S]	I Swing for You	1960	$100

NIEMACK, JUDY, AND SIMON WETTENHALL

Niemack is a female singer; Wettenhall plays trumpet.

Albums

INNER CITY

❏ IC-1115	Night Sprite	198?	$30

SEA BREEZE

❏ 2001	By Heart	1980	$30

NIEWOOD, GERRY

Flutist.

Albums

A&M

❏ SP-3409	Slow, Hot Wind	1977	$25

HORIZON

❏ SP-719	Gerry Niewood and Timepiece	1976	$30

NIGHTWIND

Albums

PAUSA

❏ 7127	Casual Romance	198?	$25

NIMMONS, PHIL

Clarinetist, alto saxophone player and composer.

Albums

VERVE

❏ MGV-8376 [M]	Nimmons 'n' Nine	1960	$100
❏ MGVS-6153 [S]	Nimmons 'n' Nine	1960	$0
— *Canceled*			
❏ V-8376 [M]	Nimmons 'n' Nine	1961	$25
❏ MGV-8025 [M]	The Canadian Scene Via Phil Nimmons	1957	$150
❏ V-8025 [M]	The Canadian Scene Via Phil Nimmons	1961	$25

NINETEENTH WHOLE, THE

Jazz-funk group: Billy Wooten (vibraphone), Emmanuel Riggins (electric piano, organ), Harold Cardwell (drums, percussion).

Albums

EASTBOUND

❏ EB-9003	Smilin'	1970	$200

NISTICO, SAL
Tenor saxophone player.
Albums

Number	Title	Yr	NM
BEE HIVE			
❏ BH-7006	Neo/Nistico	1980	$30
JAZZLAND			
❏ JLP-66 [M]	Heavyweights	1962	$30
❏ JLP-966 [S]	Heavyweights	1962	$40
RIVERSIDE			
❏ RLP-457 [M]	Comin' On Up	1963	$150
❏ RS-9457 [S]	Comin' On Up	1963	$150

NOCK, MIKE
Pianist.
Albums

Number	Title	Yr	NM
ECM			
❏ 1220	Ondas	1981	$25
IAI			
❏ 373851	Almanac	197?	$35
TIMELESS			
❏ 313	In Out and Around	1978	$30
TOMATO			
❏ TOM-8009	Climbing	1979	$35

NO/GAP JAZZ BAND, THE
Albums

Number	Title	Yr	NM
NO/GAP			
❏ 7444001	Live	197?	$35
❏ 7444002	No/Gap Jazz Band	197?	$35

NOONE, JIMMIE
Clarinetist and soprano and alto saxophone player. Also see JOHNNY DODDS.
Albums

Number	Title	Yr	NM
BRUNSWICK			
❏ BL58006 [10]	The Apex Club Orchestra	1950	$50
MCA			
❏ 1313	Jimmie Noone and Earl Hines at the Apex Club	198?	$25

NOONE, JIMMY, JR.
Albums

Number	Title	Yr	NM
STOMP OFF			
❏ SOS-1121	Jimmy Remembers Jimmie	1986	$25

NORDINE, KEN
Spoken-word performer known for his so-called "word jazz."
Albums

Number	Title	Yr	NM
BLUE THUMB			
❏ BTS-33	How Are Things in Your Town?	1971	$60
❏ BTS-35	Ken Nordine	1972	$50
DECCA			
❏ DL8550 [M]	Concert in the Sky	1957	$150
DOT			
❏ DLP-3115 [M]	Love Words	1958	$200
❏ DLP-25115 [S]	Love Words	1959	$250
❏ DLP-3142 [M]	My Baby	1959	$100
❏ DLP-25142 [S]	My Baby	1959	$175
❏ DLP-3196 [M]	Next!	1959	$100
❏ DLP-25196 [S]	Next!	1959	$175
❏ DLP-25096 [S]	Son of Word Jazz	1959	$250
❏ DLP-25880	The Best of Word Jazz	1968	$80

Number	Title	Yr	NM
❏ DLP-3075 [M]	Word Jazz	1958	$300
❏ DLP-25075 [S]	Word Jazz	1959	$300

Number	Title	Yr	NM
❏ DLP-3301 [M]	Word Jazz, Vol. 2	1960	$250
❏ DLP-25301 [S]	Word Jazz, Vol. 2	1960	$300
FM			
❏ 304 [M]	Passion In the Desert	1963	$30
❏ S-304 [S]	Passion In the Desert	1963	$40
HAMILTON			
❏ HL-102 [M]	The Voice of Love	1964	$30
❏ HL-12102 [S]	The Voice of Love	1964	$40
PHILIPS			
❏ PHM200224 [M]	Colors	1966	$80
❏ PHM200258 [M]	Ken Nordine Does Robert Shure's "Twink	1967	$30
❏ PHS600258 [S]	Ken Nordine Does Robert Shure's "Twink	1967	$40
SNAIL			
❏ SR-1003	Grandson of Word Jazz	1987	$30
❏ SR-1001	Stare with Your Ears	1979	$30
VERSION			
❏ VLP101 [10]	Passion In the Desert	1957	$200

NORMAN, GENE, GROUP
Studio band formed by record company owner Norman.
Albums

Number	Title	Yr	NM
GNP CRESCENDO			
❏ GNP-2015 [M]	Dylan Jazz	1965	$25
❏ GNPS-2015 [S]	Dylan Jazz	1965	$30

NORRIS, WALTER, AND ALADAR PAGE
Page is a bass player. Also see WALTER NORRIS.
Albums

Number	Title	Yr	NM
INNER CITY			
❏ IC-3028	Synchronicity	1979	$35

NORRIS, WALTER, AND GEORGE MRAZ
Mraz is a bass player. Also see WALTER NORRIS.
Albums

Number	Title	Yr	NM
ENJA			
❏ 2044	Drifting	197?	$35

NORRIS, WALTER
Pianist.
Albums

Number	Title	Yr	NM
ENJA			
❏ 2044	Drifting	198?	$30
PROGRESSIVE			
❏ PRO-7039	Stepping on Cracks	198?	$30

NORVO, RED, AND ROSS TOMPKINS
Also see each artist's individual listings.
Albums

Number	Title	Yr	NM
CONCORD JAZZ			
❏ CJ-90	Red Norvo and Ross Tompkins	1979	$25

NORVO, RED
Vibraphone, xylophone and marimba player. Also an occasional pianist. Also see RED ALLEN; THE JAZZ PICKERS; CHARLIE PARKER; ART PEPPER; DINAH SHORE.
Albums

Number	Title	Yr	NM
ALLEGRO			
❏ 1739 [M]	Red Norvo Jazz Trio	195?	$40
BLUEBIRD			
❏ 6278-1-RB	Just a Mood	1987	$25
CAPITOL			
❏ T616 [M]	Classics in Jazz	1955	$150
CHARLIE PARKER			
❏ PLP-833 [M]	Pretty Is the Only Way To Fly	1962	$30
❏ PLP-833S [S]	Pretty Is the Only Way To Fly	1962	$30
CIRCLE			
❏ 3	Red Norvo and His Orchestra 1938	198?	$25
COMMODORE			
❏ FL-20023 [10]	Town Hall Concert, Volume 1	1952	$150
❏ FL-20027 [10]	Town Hall Concert, Volume 2	1952	$150
CONTEMPORARY			
❏ C-3534 [M]	Music To Listen To Red Norvo By	1957	$250
❏ S-7009 [S]	Music To Listen To Red Norvo By	1959	$250
CONTINENTAL			
❏ C-16005 [M]	Mainstream Jazz	1962	$35
❏ CS-16005 [S]	Mainstream Jazz	1962	$25
DECCA			
❏ DL5501 [10]	Dancing on the Ceiling	1953	$150
DIAL			
❏ LP-903 [M]	Fabulous Jazz Session	1951	$600
DISCOVERY			
❏ DL-3012 [10]	Red Norvo Trio	1950	$300
❏ DL-3018 [10]	Red Norvo Trio	1952	$300
❏ DL-4005 [M]	Red Norvo Trio, Volume 1	1951	$300
DOT			
❏ DLP-3126 [M]	Windjammer City Style	1958	$175
❏ DLP-25126 [S]	Windjammer City Style	1958	$80
EMARCY			
❏ MG-26002 [10]	Improvisation	1954	$200
ENCORE			
❏ EE-22009	Original 1933-38 Recordings	1968	$35
EPIC			
❏ LN3128 [M]	Red Norvo and His All Stars	1955	$100
FAMOUS DOOR			
❏ 116	Red Norvo in New York	197?	$30
❏ 108	Second Time Around	197?	$30
❏ 105	Vibes A La Red	197?	$30
FANTASY			
❏ OJC-155	Music To Listen To Red Norvo By	198?	$25
❏ 3-12 [10]	Red Norvo Trio	1953	$150
—Colored vinyl			
❏ 3-12 [10]	Red Norvo Trio	1953	$100
—Black vinyl			
❏ 3-19 [M]	Red Norvo Trio	1955	$80
—Red vinyl			
❏ 3-19 [M]	Red Norvo Trio	195?	$40
—Black vinyl			
❏ OJC-641	Red Norvo Trio	1991	$30
❏ 3218 [M]	Red Norvo With Strings	1956	$150
—Red vinyl			
❏ 3218 [M]	Red Norvo With Strings	195?	$40
—Black vinyl			
❏ 3244 [M]	The Red Norvo Trios	1957	$80
—Red vinyl			

Herbie Nichols, *The Prophetic Herbie Nichols*, Vol. 2, Blue Note BLP-5069, 10-inch LP, **$1,200**.

Lennie Niehaus, *Lenny Niehaus Volume 5: The Sextet*, Comtemporary C 3524, **$250**.

Ken Nordine, *Ken Nordine Does Robert Shure's "Twink,"* Philips PHM 200258, **$30**.

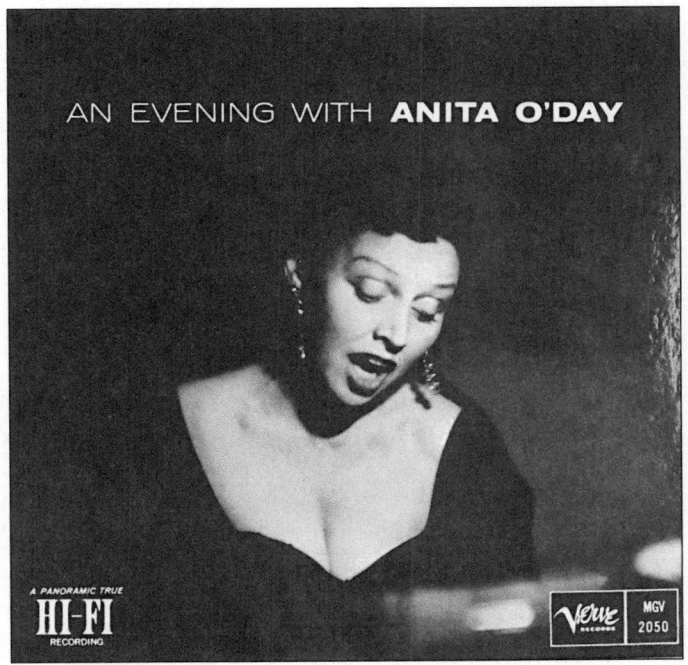

Anita O'Day, *An Evening with Anita O'Day*, Verve MGV-2050, **$100**.

Number	Title	Yr	NM
❑ 3244 [M]	The Red Norvo Trios	195?	$40
—Black vinyl			
LIBERTY			
❑ LRP-3035 [M]	Ad Lib	1957	$40
MERCURY			
❑ 830966-1	Improvisations	1987	$25
PAUSA			
❑ 9015	All Star Sessions	198?	$25
PRESTIGE			
❑ 24108	The Trios	198?	$35
RAVE			
❑ 101 [M]	Red Norvo Quintet	1956	$80
RCA VICTOR			
❑ LPM-1420 [M]	Hi Five	1957	$40
❑ LSP-1711 [S]	Red Norvo In Stereo	1958	$50
❑ LPM-1729 [M]	Red Plays the Blues	1958	$40
❑ LSP-1729 [S]	Red Plays the Blues	1958	$50
❑ LPM-1449 [M]	Some of My Favorites	1957	$40
REFERENCE RECORDINGS			
❑ RR-8	The Forward Look	1983	$25
❑ RR-8-UHGR	The Forward Look	1983	$40
RONDO-LETTE			
❑ A-28 [M]	Red Norvo Trio	1958	$30
SAVOY			
❑ MG-12093 [M]	Midnight On Cloud 69	1956	$80
❑ MG-12088 [M]	Move!	1956	$80
SAVOY JAZZ			
❑ SJL-2212	Red Norvo Trio	197?	$30
SPOTLITE			
❑ 107	Fabulous Jam	197?	$25
STASH			
❑ ST-230	Just Friends	1984	$25
STEREO RECORDS			
❑ S-7009 [S]	Music To Listen To Red Norvo By	1958	$50
TAMPA			
❑ TP-35 [M]	Norvo Naturally	1957	$200
—Colored vinyl			
❑ TP-35 [M]	Norvo Naturally	1958	$150
—Black vinyl			
TIME-LIFE			
❑ STL-J-14	Giants of Jazz	1980	$50
X			
❑ LXA-3034 [M]	Red's Blue Room	1955	$150
XANADU			
❑ 199	Time in His Hands	198?	$25

NORVO, RED/CAL TJADER
Also see each artist's individual listings.

Albums

Number	Title	Yr	NM
JAZZTONE			
❑ J-1277 [M]	Delightfully Light	195?	$40

NORVO, RED/GEORGIE AULD
Also see each artist's individual listings.

Albums

Number	Title	Yr	NM
GOLDEN ERA			
❑ 15016 [M]	The Great Dance Bands, Vol. 2	195?	$40

NOTHING, CHARLIE
Imagine if The Legendary Stardust Cowboy played sax...

Albums

Number	Title	Yr	NM
TAKOMA			
❑ C-1015	The Psychedelic Saxophone of Charlie Nothing	1967	$60

NOTO, SAM
Trumpeter.

Albums

Number	Title	Yr	NM
XANADU			
❑ 127	Act One	1976	$30
❑ 144	Notes to You	1977	$30
❑ 168	Noto-Riety	198?	$25

NOVAC, JERRY

Albums

Number	Title	Yr	NM
EMBRYO			
❑ 527	The 5th Word	1970	$30

NOW CREATIVE ARTS JAZZ ENSEMBLE, THE

Albums

Number	Title	Yr	NM
ARHOOLIE			
❑ 8002	Now	1969	$25

NOZERO, LARRY
Alto saxophone player.

Albums

Number	Title	Yr	NM
STRATA			
❑ 109-75	Time	1975	$25

NRG ENSEMBLE
See HAL RUSSELL.

NUBIN, KATI BELL
Female singer.

Albums

Number	Title	Yr	NM
VERVE			
❑ MGV-8372 [M]	Soul, Soul Searchin'	1960	$0
—Canceled			
❑ MGV-3004 [M]	Soul, Soul Searchin'	1960	$80
❑ MGVS-6147 [S]	Soul, Soul Searchin'	1960	$0
—Canceled			
❑ V-3004 [M]	Soul, Soul Searchin'	1961	$40
❑ V6-3004 [S]	Soul, Soul Searchin'	1961	$50

NUNEZ, FLIP
Pianist.

Albums

Number	Title	Yr	NM
CATALYST			
❑ 7603	My Own Time and Space	1976	$30

NUROCK, KIRK
Pianist and composer.

Albums

Number	Title	Yr	NM
LABOR			
❑ 13	Natural Sound	1981	$30

NUTTY SQUIRRELS, THE
Jazz counterpart to the Chpmunks, created by DON ELLIOTT with Sascha Burland (vocals) and a band of jazz all-stars: CANNONBALL ADDERLEY; BOBBY JASPAR; HAL McKUSICK; SAM MOST; Romeo Penque (flute); Sol Schlinger (baritone sax).

Albums

Number	Title	Yr	NM
COLUMBIA			
❑ CL1589 [M]	Bird Watching	1961	$60
HANOVER			
❑ HML-8014 [M]	The Nutty Squirrels	1960	$100
MGM			
❑ E-4272 [M]	A Hard Day's Night	1964	$60
❑ SE-4272 [S]	A Hard Day's Night	1964	$60

O

OAKLEY, LEON
Cornet player and bandleader.

Albums

Number	Title	Yr	NM
GHB			
❑ GHB-153	Leon Oakley and the Flying Duces	198?	$25
STOMP OFF			
❑ SOS-1013	New Orleans Joys	198?	$25

OBEIDO, RAY
Guitarist.

Albums

Number	Title	Yr	NM
WINDHAM HILL			
❑ WH-0115	Perfect Crime	1989	$30

O'BRIEN, HOD
Pianist.

Albums

Number	Title	Yr	NM
UPTOWN			
❑ 278	Bits and Pieces	198?	$25

O'BRYANT, JIMMY
Clarinet player and bandleader.

Albums

Number	Title	Yr	NM
BIOGRAPH			
❑ 12002 [M]	Jimmy O'Bryant's Washboard Wonders 1924-26	1968	$30

O'CONNELL, BILL
Pianist.

Albums

Number	Title	Yr	NM
INNER CITY			
❑ IC-1035	Searching	197?	$35

O'DAY, ALAN

Albums

Number	Title	Yr	NM
PACIFIC			
❑ PC4300	Appetizers	1977	$12
❑ PC4301	Oh Johnny!	1979	$12
VIVA			
❑ VV2679	Caress Me Pretty Music	1973	$20

O'DAY, ANITA
Female singer.

Albums

Number	Title	Yr	NM
ADVANCE			
❑ LSP-8 [10]	Anita O'Day Specials	1951	$250
AMERICAN RECORDING SOCIETY			
❑ G-426 [M]	For Oscar	1957	$40
BASF			
❑ MB20750	Recorded Live at the Berlin Jazz Festival	1973	$25
BOB THIELE MUSIC			
❑ BBM1-0595 [M]	Hi Ho Trailus Boot Whip	1974	$35
CLEF			
❑ MGC-130 [10]	Anita O'Day Collates	1953	$300
CORAL			
❑ CRL-56073 [10]	Singin' and Swingin'	1953	$150
DOCTOR JAZZ			
❑ FW39418	Hi Ho Trailus Boot Whip	198?	$25
EMILY			
❑ 13081	Angel Eyes	1981	$30
❑ 83084	A Song for You	1984	$30
❑ 92685	Big Band Concert 1985	1985	$30
❑ 11579	Live at Mingos	1979	$35
❑ 102479	Live at the City	1979	$35
❑ 42181	Live at the City: The Second Set	1981	$30
❑ 9579	Live at Tokyo	1979	$35
❑ 11279	My Ship	1979	$35
❑ 32383	The Night Has a Thousand Eyes	1983	$30
GLENDALE			
❑ 6001	Anita O'Day	197?	$30
❑ 6000	Once Upon a Summertime	197?	$30
GNP CRESCENDO			
❑ GNPS-2126	Mello' Day	197?	$25
NORGRAN			
❑ MGN-1057 [M]	An Evening With Anita O'Day	1956	$200
❑ MGN-1049 [M]	Anita O'Day	1955	$300
❑ MGN-30 [10]	Songs By Anita O'Day	1954	$150
PAUSA			
❑ 7092	Anita O'Day in Berlin	198?	$25
VERVE			
❑ V-8442 [M]	All the Sad Young Men	1962	$30
❑ V6-8442 [S]	All the Sad Young Men	1962	$40
❑ MGV-2050 [M]	An Evening With Anita O'Day	1957	$100
❑ V-2050 [M]	An Evening With Anita O'Day	1961	$25
❑ MGV-2000 [M]	Anita	1956	$150
❑ V-2000 [M]	Anita	1961	$60
❑ 829261-1	Anita	1986	$25
❑ V-2141 [M]	Anita O'Day and Billy May Swing Rodgers and Hart	1961	$60
❑ V6-2141 [S]	Anita O'Day and Billy May Swing Rodgers and Hart	1961	$60

Number	Title	Yr	NM
❏ V-8514 [M]	Anita O'Day and the Three Sounds	1963	$30
❏ V6-8514 [S]	Anita O'Day and the Three Sounds	1963	$30
❏ MGV-2113 [M]	Anita O'Day At Mr. Kelly's	1958	$150
❏ MGVS-6043 [S]	Anita O'Day At Mr. Kelly's	1960	$150
❏ V-2113 [M]	Anita O'Day At Mr. Kelly's	1961	$60
❏ V6-2113 [S]	Anita O'Day At Mr. Kelly's	1961	$60
❏ UMV-2550	Anita O'Day At Mr. Kelly's	198?	$30
❏ MGV-8283 [M]	Anita O'Day Sings the Winners	1958	$150
❏ MGVS-6002 [S]	Anita O'Day Sings the Winners	1960	$150
❏ V-8283 [M]	Anita O'Day Sings the Winners	1961	$60
❏ V6-8283 [S]	Anita O'Day Sings the Winners	1961	$60
❏ V-8485 [M]	Anita O'Day Sings the Winners	1962	$25
❏ V6-8485 [S]	Anita O'Day Sings the Winners	1962	$30
❏ UMV-2536	Anita O'Day Sings the Winners	198?	$30
❏ MGV-2118 [M]	Anita O'Day Swings Cole Porter	1959	$150
❏ MGVS-6059 [S]	Anita O'Day Swings Cole Porter	1960	$150
❏ V-2118 [M]	Anita O'Day Swings Cole Porter	1961	$60
❏ V6-2118 [S]	Anita O'Day Swings Cole Porter	1961	$60
❏ MGV-8259 [M]	Anita Sings the Most	1958	$150
❏ V-8259 [M]	Anita Sings the Most	1961	$60
❏ MGV-8312 [M]	Cool Heat -- Anita O'Day Sings Jimmy Giuffre Arrangements	1959	$100
❏ MGVS-6046 [S]	Cool Heat -- Anita O'Day Sings Jimmy Giuffre Arrangements	1960	$100
❏ V-8312 [M]	Cool Heat -- Anita O'Day Sings Jimmy Giuffre Arrangements	1961	$25
❏ V6-8312 [S]	Cool Heat -- Anita O'Day Sings Jimmy Giuffre Arrangements	1961	$30
❏ UMV-2679	Cool Heat -- Anita O'Day Sings Jimmy Giuffre Arrangements	198?	$30
❏ V-8572 [M]	Incomparable! Anita O'Day	1964	$30
❏ MGV-2154 [M]	I Remember Billie Holiday	1960	$0
—Canceled			
❏ MGV-2043 [M]	Pick Yourself Up With Anita O'Day	1957	$150
❏ V-2043 [M]	Pick Yourself Up With Anita O'Day	1961	$25
❏ VE-2-2534	The Big Band Sessions	1979	$35
❏ MGV-2049 [M]	The Lady Is a Tramp	1957	$150
❏ V-2049 [M]	The Lady Is a Tramp	1961	$25
❏ V-8483 [M]	This Is Anita	1962	$30
❏ V6-8483 [R]	This Is Anita	1962	$35
❏ V-8472 [M]	Time For Two	1962	$30
❏ V6-8472 [S]	Time For Two	1962	$40
❏ UMJ-3287	Time For Two	198?	$30
❏ MGV-2157 [M]	Trav'lin' Light	1960	$60
❏ V-2157 [M]	Trav'lin' Light	1961	$25
❏ V6-2157 [S]	Trav'lin' Light	1961	$30
❏ MGV-2145 [M]	Waiter, Make Mine Blues	1960	$60
❏ V-2145 [M]	Waiter, Make Mine Blues	1961	$25
❏ V6-2145 [S]	Waiter, Make Mine Blues	1961	$30

ODETTA
Female singer better known in the folk realm.

Albums
FANTASY

❏ OBC-509	Odetta and the Blues	198?	$25

—Reissue of Riverside LP

RIVERSIDE

❏ RLP-417 [M]	Odetta and the Blues	1962	$150
❏ RS-9417 [S]	Odetta and the Blues	1962	$150

ODRICH, RON
Bass clarinet player.

Albums
CLASSIC JAZZ

❏ 35	Blackstick	1978	$30

O'FARRILL, CHICO
Trumpeter, arranger, composer and bandleader.

Albums
ABC IMPULSE!

❏ AS-9135 [S]	Nine Flags	1968	$35

CLEF

Number	Title	Yr	NM
❏ MGC-131 [10]	Afro-Cuban	1953	$350
❏ MGC-132 [10]	Chico O'Farrill Jazz	1953	$350
❏ MGC-699 [M]	Chico O'Farrill Jazz	1956	$200

IMPULSE!

❏ AS-9135 [S]	Nine Flags	1967	$200
❏ A-9135 [M]	Nine Flags	1967	$120

NORGRAN

❏ MGN-31 [10]	Chico O'Farrill	1954	$150
❏ MGN-28 [10]	Latino Dance Sessions	1954	$200
❏ MGN-27 [10]	Mambo Dance Sessions	1954	$150
❏ MGN-9 [10]	The Second Afro-Cuban Jazz Suite	1954	$150

VERVE

❏ MGV-8083 [M]	Jazz North of the Border and South of the Border	1957	$150
❏ V-8083 [M]	Jazz North of the Border and South of the Border	1961	$30
❏ MGV-2003 [M]	Mambo/Latino Dances	1956	$200
❏ V-2003 [M]	Mambo/Latino Dances	1961	$30
❏ MGV-2024 [M]	Music From South America	1956	$200
❏ V-2024 [M]	Music From South America	1961	$30

OGERMAN, CLAUS, AND MICHAEL BRECKER
Also see each artist's individual listings.

Albums
ECM

❏ 23698	Cityscape	1982	$25

OGERMAN, CLAUS
Pianist, composer and arranger.

Albums
JAZZ MAN

❏ 5015	Aranjuez	198?	$30

RCA VICTOR

❏ LPM-3640 [M]	Saxes Mexicano	1966	$25
❏ LSP-3640 [S]	Saxes Mexicano	1966	$30
❏ LPM-3366 [M]	Soul Searchin'	1965	$25
❏ LSP-3366 [S]	Soul Searchin'	1965	$30
❏ LPM-3455 [M]	Watusi Trumpets	1965	$25
❏ LSP-3455 [S]	Watusi Trumpets	1965	$30

UNITED ARTISTS

❏ UAL-3206 [M]	Sing Along in German	1962	$25
❏ UAS-6206 [S]	Sing Along in German	1962	$30

WARNER BROS.

❏ BS3006	Gate of Dreams	1977	$25

OHLSON, CURTIS
Bass player.

Albums
INTIMA

❏ D1-73358	Better Than Ever	1989	$30
❏ SJE-73274	So Fast	1987	$25

OHNO, SHUNZO
Trumpeter.

Albums
INNER CITY

❏ IC-1108	Quarter Moon	198?	$30

OLAY, RUTH
Female singer.

Albums
ABC

❏ ABC-573 [M]	Soul In the Night	1966	$25
❏ ABCS-573 [S]	Soul In the Night	1966	$30

EMARCY

❏ MG-36125 [M]	Olay! The New Sound Of Ruth Olay	1958	$200

EVEREST

❏ LPBR-5218 [M]	Olay! OK	1963	$30
❏ SDBR-1218 [S]	Olay! OK	1963	$30

LAUREL

❏ 501	Ruth Olay Sings Jazz Today	198?	$30

MERCURY

❏ MG-20390 [M]	Easy Living	1959	$100
❏ SR-60069 [S]	Easy Living	1959	$100

UNITED ARTISTS

❏ UAL-3115 [M]	Ruth Olay In Person	1960	$30
❏ UAS-4115 [S]	Ruth Olay In Person	1960	$40

OLD AND NEW DREAMS
Members: Ed Blackwell (drums); DON CHERRY; CHARLIE HADEN; DEWEY REDMAN.

Albums
BLACK SAINT

Number	Title	Yr	NM
❏ 120113	A Tribute to Blackwell	1990	$35
❏ BSR-0013	Old and New Dreams	198?	$35

ECM

❏ ECM1-1154	Old and New Dreams	1979	$35

—Distributed by Warner Bros.

❏ ECM1-1205	Playing	1981	$35

—Distributed by Warner Bros.

O'LENO, LARRY
Pianist and male singer.

Albums
PAINTED SMILES

❏ 1348	Larry O'Leno Sings Billy Strayhorn	198?	$30

OLIPHANT, GRASELLA

Albums
ATLANTIC

❏ 1438 [M]	The Grass Roots	1965	$35
❏ SD-1438 [S]	The Grass Roots	1965	$25

OLIVER, KING
Cornet player, bandleader and composer, an important jazz pioneer. Also see LOUIS ARMSTRONG.

Albums
BRUNSWICK

❏ BL58020 [10]	King Oliver	1950	$120

DECCA

❏ DL79246	Papa Joe	1969	$35

EPIC

❏ LA16003 [M]	King Oliver and His Orchestra	1960	$60
❏ BA17003 [R]	King Oliver and His Orchestra	1960	$50
❏ LN3208 [M]	King Oliver Featuring Louis Armstrong	1956	$100

HERWIN

❏ 106	Zulus Ball/Working Man Blues	197?	$30

LONDON

❏ AL3510 [10]	King Oliver Plays the Blues	195?	$80

MCA

❏ 1309	Papa Joe	198?	$25

MILESTONE

❏ M-2006	The Immortal King Oliver	197?	$35

RCA VICTOR

❏ LPV-529 [M]	King Oliver In New York	1965	$30

X

❏ LVA-3018 [10]	King Oliver's Uptown Jazz	1954	$100

OLSEN, GEORGE
Violinist and bandleader.

Albums
RCA VICTOR

❏ LPV-549 [M]	George Olsen and His Music	1968	$25

OLSHER, LESLEY
Female singer.

Albums
VITAL

❏ VTL-011	Lesley	1993	$25

OLYMPIA BRASS BAND OF NEW ORLEANS

Albums
AUDIOPHILE

❏ AP-108	Olympia Brass Band of New Orleans	197?	$30

BASF

❏ 20678	New Orleans Street Parade	197?	$30

BIOGRAPH

❏ VPS-4	Here Come Da Great Olympia Jazz Band	197?	$30

Number	Title	Yr	NM

O'NEAL, JOHNNY
Male singer and pianist.

Albums

CONCORD JAZZ
| CJ-228 | Coming Out | 198? | $25 |

ONENESS OF JUJU
Led by saxophone player J. Plunky Branch. Other members on the Juju LPs: Ken Shabala (bass); Lon Moshe (vibraphone); Michael Babatunde Lea (percussion); Al-Hammel Rasul (piano); Jalongo Ngoma (percussion). Personnel changes included Ronnie Toler (drums), replacing Ngoma; Muzi Branch (bass), replacing Shabala; and a female singer, Lady Eka-Ete.

Albums

BLACK FIRE
| 0(# unknown) | Space Jungle Luv | 1976 | $60 |

STRATA-EAST
| SES-19735 | A Message from Mozambique | 1973 | $100 |

—As "Juju

| SES-7420 | Chapter 2: Nia | 1974 | $100 |

—As "Juju

OPA
Members: Hugo Fattoruso (keyboards, vocal, percussion); George Fattoruso (drums, vocal, percussion); Ringo Thielmann (electric bass, vocal).

Albums

MILESTONE
| M-9069 | Goldenwings | 1976 | $30 |
| M-9078 | Magic Time | 1977 | $30 |

OPAFIRE
Led by Norman Engeleitner (keyboards, guitar, percussion, composer). Other members include Christopher Hedge (keyboards, guitar, percussion, hammer dulcimer, mandolin, kalimba); Robert Powell (various guitars, banjo, mandolin); Michael Manning (bass); JEFF NARELL (steel pans).

Albums

NOVUS
| 3084-1-N | Opafire Featuring Norman Engeleitner | 1990 | $30 |

OPEN SKY
Members: David Liebman (soprano and tenor saxophone, flute, piano, percussion); Bob Moses (vibes, drums); Frank Tusa (bass).

Albums

PM
| PMR-001 | Open Sky | 1974 | $35 |
| PMR-003 | Spirit in the Sky | 1975 | $35 |

OPHELIA RAGTIME ORCHESTRA
Founded by Morten Gunnar Larsen in Oslo, Norway.

Albums

STOMP OFF
| SOS-1108 | Echoes from the Snowball Club | 1986 | $25 |

ORANGE THEN BLUE
Big band from Boston.

Albums

GM RECORDINGS
| GM-3006 | Music for Jazz Orchestra | 1987 | $25 |

ORCHESTRA OF THE EIGHTH DAY
Polish jazz/classical group led by Jan A.P. Kaczmarek.

Albums

FLYING FISH
| FF-292 | Music for the End | 1982 | $35 |

ORCHESTRA U.S.A.
Group of more than two dozen musicians led by JOHN LEWIS. Among the names listed elsewhere who appeared on one or more of the LPs are ERIC DOLPHY; GARY McFARLAND; ZOOT SIMS; and PHIL WOODS.

Albums

COLPIX
| CP-448 [M] | Orchestra U.S.A. Debut | 1964 | $150 |
| SCP-448 [S] | Orchestra U.S.A. Debut | 1964 | $150 |

COLUMBIA
| CL2247 [M] | Jazz Journey | 1963 | $30 |
| CS9047 [S] | Jazz Journey | 1963 | $30 |

RCA VICTOR
| LPM-3498 [M] | The Sextet Of Orchestra U.S.A. | 1965 | $25 |
| LSP-3498 [S] | The Sextet Of Orchestra U.S.A. | 1965 | $30 |

OREGON
Members include Paul McCandless (oboe, English horn, soprano saxophone); Glen Moore (bass); and Ralph Towner (guitar, piano, synthesizers).

Albums

ECM
| 25025 | Crossing | 1985 | $25 |
| 23796 | Oregon | 1983 | $25 |

ELEKTRA
AB-304	In Performance	1979	$35
6E-154	Out of the Woods	1978	$25
6E-224	Roots in the Sky	1979	$25

MOBILE FIDELITY
| 1-514 | Distant Hills | 198? | $125 |

—Audiophile vinyl

PORTRAIT
| OR44465 | 45th Parallel | 1989 | $30 |

TERRA
| T-1 | Music of Another Present Era | 1985 | $25 |

VANGUARD
VSD-79341	Distant Hills	1973	$30
VSQ-40031 [Q]	Distant Hills	1974	$40
VSD-79370	Friends	1976	$30
VSD-79358	In Concert	1975	$30
VSD-79419	Moon and Mind	1979	$30
VSD-79326	Music of Another Present Era	197?	$30
VSD-79432	Our First Record	1980	$30
VSD-109/10	The Essential Oregon	198?	$35
VSD-79397	Violin	1978	$30
VSD-79350	Winter Light	1974	$30

OREGON AND ELVIN JONES
Also see each artist's individual listings.

Albums

VANGUARD
| VSD-79377 | Together | 1977 | $30 |

ORGAN-IZERS, THE
See ODELL BROWN.

ORIGINAL CAMELLIA JAZZ BAND
Led by Clive Wilson (trumpet).

Albums

NEW ORLEANS
| 7207 | Original Camellia Jazz Band | 198? | $25 |

ORIGINAL DIXIELAND JAZZ BAND, THE
Artists on the first jazz record ever released, "Livery Stable Blues" backed with "Dixie Jass (sic) Band One Step," on the Victor label in 1917. The original members of the all-white group were Eddie Edwards (trombone); NICK LaROCCA (cornet); Yellow Nunez (clarinet); Henry Ragas (piano); Tony Sbarbaro (drums).

Albums

RCA VICTOR
| LPV-547 [M] | The Original Dixieland Jazz Band | 1968 | $25 |

X
| LX-3007 [M] | The Original Dixieland Jazz Band | 1954 | $50 |

ORIGINAL MEMPHIS FIVE, THE
Founded in 1917 by PHIL NAPOLEON and pianist Frank Signorelli. None of its revolving-door membership was from Memphis!

Albums

FOLKWAYS
| RBF-26 | The Original Memphis Five | 197? | $35 |

ORIGINAL SALTY DOGS, THE
Among the members: Lew Green Jr. (cornet); Tom Bartlett (trombone); Kim Cusack (clarinet); John Cooper (piano); Jack Kuncl (banjo); Mike Waldbridge (tuba).

Albums

BLACKBIRD
| 12003 | Traditional Classics | 1967 | $35 |

GHB
58	Free Wheeling	1968	$35
44	The Original Salty Dogs	1967	$35
62	The Right Track	197?	$30

STOMP OFF
| SOS-1115 | Honky Tonk Town | 1987 | $25 |

ORLANDO, JAY

Albums

DOBRE
| 1040 | Jay Orlando Loves Earl Bostic | 197? | $30 |

ORNBERG, THOMAS
Soprano saxophone player, clarinetist and bandleader.

Albums

STOMP OFF
| SOS-1043 | Come Back, Sweet Papa | 198? | $25 |

ORPHEON CELESTA
From France.

Albums

STOMP OFF
| SOS-1083 | Gare de Lyon | 1985 | $25 |
| SOS-1095 | Shim-Me-Sha-Wabble | 1985 | $25 |

ORSTED PEDERSEN, NIELS-HENNING, AND KENNETH KNUDSEN
Knudsen plays keyboards. Also see NIELS-HENNING ORSTED PEDERSEN.

Albums

STEEPLECHASE
| SCS-1068 | Pictures | 198? | $30 |

ORSTED PEDERSEN, NIELS-HENNING, AND SAM JONES
Also see each artist's individual listings.

Albums

INNER CITY
| IC-2055 | Double Bass | 197? | $35 |

STEEPLECHASE
| SCS-1055 | Double Bass | 198? | $30 |

ORSTED PEDERSEN, NIELS-HENNING
Bass player. Also see JOE ALBANY; MONTY ALEXANDER; PAUL BLEY; KENNY DREW; BOULOU FERRE.

Albums

INNER CITY
| IC-2041 | Jaywalkin' | 197? | $35 |

STEEPLECHASE
SCS-1125	Dancing on the Tables	1979	$30
SCS-1041	Jaywalkin'	198?	$30
SCS-1083	Trio 1	198?	$30
SCS-1093	Trio 2	198?	$30

ORTEGA, ANTHONY
Alto saxophone and clarinet player.

Albums

BETHLEHEM
| BCP-79 [M] | Jazz For Young Moderns | 1957 | $250 |

DISCOVERY
| 788 | Rain Dance | 1978 | $30 |

HERALD
| HLP-0101 [M] | A Man and His Horn | 1956 | $60 |

REVELATION
| REV-M3 [M] | New Dance | 1968 | $40 |
| REV-3 [S] | New Dance | 1968 | $25 |

VANTAGE
| VLP-2 [10] | Anthony Ortega | 1954 | $120 |

Number	Title	Yr	NM

ORTEGA, FRANKIE
Pianist.
Albums
DOBRE
| ❑ 1043 | Smokin' | 197? | $30 |

IMPERIAL
| ❑ LP-9025 [M] | Piano Stylings | 1956 | $150 |
| ❑ LP-12011 [S] | Piano Stylings | 1959 | $150 |

JUBILEE
❑ JLP-1106 [M]	77 Sunset Strip	1959	$30
❑ JGS-1106 [S]	77 Sunset Strip	1959	$40
❑ JGM-1112 [M]	Frankie Ortega at the Embers	1960	$25
❑ JGS-1112 [S]	Frankie Ortega at the Embers	1960	$30
❑ JLP-1080 [M]	Swingin' Abroad	1958	$30
❑ SDJLP-1080 [S]	Swingin' Abroad	1958	$30
❑ JLP-1051 [M]	Twinkling Pinkies	1958	$30

ORTEGA/DOMANICO/WEST/GOODWIN
ANTHONY ORTEGA; Chuck Domanico (bass); Bob West (bass); BILL GOODWIN.
Albums
REVELATION
| ❑ REV-7 [S] | Permutations | 1969 | $30 |

ORY, KID
Trombone player and bandleader. Under the name "Spike's Seven Pods of Pepper Orchestra," his group was the first black jazz band to make recordings.
Albums
COLUMBIA
| ❑ CL6145 [10] | Kid Ory & His Creole Dixieland Band | 1950 | $100 |
| ❑ CL835 [M] | Kid Ory | 1955 | $60 |

DIXIELAND JUBILEE
| ❑ DJ-519 | Kid Ory at the Dixieland Jubilee | 198? | $25 |

FOLKLYRIC
| ❑ 9008 | Kid Ory's Creole Jazz Band | 197? | $25 |

GOOD TIME JAZZ
❑ L-12022 [M]	Kid Ory's Creole Jazz Band, 1944-45	1955	$50
❑ L-21 [10]	Kid Ory's Creole Jazz Band, 1953	1954	$50
❑ L-12004 [M]	Kid Ory's Creole Jazz Band, 1954	1954	$40
❑ L-12008 [M]	Kid Ory's Creole Jazz Band, 1955	1955	$50
❑ L-12016 [M]	Kid Ory's Creole Jazz Band, 1956	1955	$50
❑ L-12041/2 [M]	Kid Ory's Favorites!	1961	$50
❑ M-12045 [M]	This Kid's the Greatest!	1962	$30

STORYVILLE
| ❑ 4064 | Kid Ory Plays the Blues | 198? | $25 |

VAULT
| ❑ 9006 | Kid Ory Live! | 196? | $35 |

VERVE
❑ MGV-1022 [M]	Dance with Kid Ory or Just Listen	1957	$150
❑ MGVS-6125 [S]	Dance with Kid Ory or Just Listen	1960	$100
❑ V-1022 [M]	Dance with Kid Ory or Just Listen	1961	$25
❑ V6-1022 [S]	Dance with Kid Ory or Just Listen	1961	$35
❑ MGV-1026 [M]	Dixieland Marching Songs	1957	$150
❑ V-1026 [M]	Dixieland Marching Songs	1961	$25
❑ V6-1026 [S]	Dixieland Marching Songs	1961	$35
❑ MGV-8254 [M]	Kid Ory In Europe	1958	$150
❑ V-8254 [M]	Kid Ory In Europe	1961	$25
❑ MGV-1017 [M]	Kid Ory Plays W.C. Handy	1957	$150
❑ MGVS-6061 [S]	Kid Ory Plays W.C. Handy	1960	$100
❑ V-1017 [M]	Kid Ory Plays W.C. Handy	1961	$25
❑ V6-1017 [S]	Kid Ory Plays W.C. Handy	1961	$35
❑ MGV-1030 [M]	Kid Ory Sings French Traditional Songs	1957	$150

—Canceled
❑ MGV-1014 [M]	Song of the Wanderer	1957	$150
❑ MGVS-6011 [S]	Song of the Wanderer	1960	$100
❑ V-1014 [M]	Song of the Wanderer	1961	$25
❑ V6-1014 [S]	Song of the Wanderer	1961	$35
❑ V6-8456 [M]	Storyville Nights	1962	$30
❑ V6-8456 [S]	Storyville Nights	1962	$25
❑ MGV-1016 [M]	The Kid From New Orleans	1957	$150
❑ V-1016 [M]	The Kid From New Orleans	1961	$25
❑ MGV-1023 [M]	The Original Jazz	1957	$150
❑ V-1023 [M]	The Original Jazz	1961	$25
❑ V6-1023 [S]	The Original Jazz	1961	$35

ORY, KID/JOHNNY WITTWER
Also see KID ORY.
Albums
JAZZ MAN
| ❑ LP-2 [10] | Kid Ory's Creole Band/ Johnny Wittwer Trio | 1954 | $50 |

OSBORNE, MARY
Guitarist and female singer.
Albums
STASH
| ❑ ST-215 | Now and Then | 198? | $25 |

WARWICK
| ❑ W-2004 [M] | A Girl and Her Guitar | 1960 | $100 |
| ❑ W-2004ST [S] | A Girl and Her Guitar | 1960 | $120 |

OSBORNE, WILL
Drummer, male singer and bandleader. He was one of the pioneers of the singing style known as "crooning."
Albums
AIRCHECK
| ❑ 37 | Will Osborne and His Orchestra On the Air | 198? | $25 |

HINDSIGHT
| ❑ HSR-197 | Will Osborne and His Orchestra 1936 | 198? | $25 |

OSTERWALD, HAZY
Vibraphone player and trumpeter.
Albums
BALLY
| ❑ BAL-12004 [M] | Swiss Jazz | 1956 | $40 |

OTB
Also known as "Out of the Blue." Original members: Ralph Bowen (tenor sax); KENNY GARRETT (alto sax); Robert Hurst (bass); Michael Philip Mossman (trumpet); Ralph Peterson (drums); Harry Pickens (piano). Personnel changes: Kenny Davis (bass) for Hurst; Billy Drummond (drums) for Peterson; Renee Rosnes (piano) for Pickens; Steve Wilson (alto sax) for Garrett.
Albums
BLUE NOTE
❑ BT-85128	Inside Track	1986	$30
❑ B1-85141	Live at Mt. Fuji	1987	$30
❑ BT-85118	Out of the Blue	1985	$30
❑ B1-93006	Spiral Staircase	1989	$35

OTTE, HANS
Pianist and composer.
Albums
KUCKUCK
| ❑ KU-069/70 | Das Buch der Klange | 1984 | $35 |

OUSLEY, HAROLD
Tenor saxophone player.
Albums
BETHLEHEM
| ❑ BCP-6059 [M] | Tenor Sax | 1961 | $200 |
| ❑ SBCP-6059 [S] | Tenor Sax | 1961 | $200 |

COBBLESTONE
| ❑ 9017 | The Kid! | 1971 | $30 |

MUSE
| ❑ MR-5141 | Sweet Double Hipness | 1979 | $30 |
| ❑ MR-5107 | The People's Groove | 197? | $35 |

OVERTON, HALL
See DUKE JORDAN; DAVE McKENNA.

OWENS, CHARLES
Tenor saxophone player.
Albums
DISCOVERY
| ❑ 811 | Music of Harry Warren, Volume 1 | 1980 | $30 |
| ❑ 787 | Two Quartets | 1978 | $30 |

VAULT
| ❑ LP-0 (# unknown) | I Stand Alone | 196? | $50 |

OWENS, JIMMY
Trumpeter and fluegel horn player.
Albums
ATLANTIC
| ❑ SD1491 | Jimmy Owens-Kenny Barron 1968 Quintet | | $25 |

—Multicolor label, black "fan" logo at right
| ❑ SD1491 | Jimmy Owens-Kenny Barron 1969 Quintet | | $35 |

—Red and green label
HORIZON
| ❑ SP-729 | Headin' Home | 1978 | $30 |
| ❑ SP-712 | Jimmy Owens | 197? | $30 |

OZONE, MAKOTO
Pianist.
Albums
COLUMBIA
❑ FC40240	After	1986	$25
❑ BFC39624	Makoto Ozone	1985	$25
❑ FC40676	Now You Know	1987	$25

P

PACE, JOHNNY
Male singer.
Albums
RIVERSIDE
| ❑ RLP 12-292 [M] | Chet Baker Introduces Johnny Pace | 1958 | $300 |
| ❑ RLP-1130 [S] | Chet Baker Introduces Johnny Pace | 1959 | $300 |

PACHECO, MIKE
Bongo drummer.
Albums
INTERLUDE
| ❑ MO-513 [M] | Hot Skins | 1959 | $40 |
| ❑ ST-1013 [S] | Hot Skins | 1959 | $30 |

TAMPA
| ❑ TP-30 [M] | Bongo Date | 1957 | $200 |

—Colored vinyl
| ❑ TP-30 [M] | Bongo Date | 1958 | $150 |

—Black vinyl
| ❑ TP-21 [M] | Bongo Session | 1957 | $200 |

—Colored vinyl
| ❑ TP-21 [M] | Bongo Session | 1958 | $150 |

—Black vinyl
| ❑ TP-10 [M] | Bongo Skins | 1957 | $200 |

—Colored vinyl
| ❑ TP-10 [M] | Bongo Skins | 1958 | $150 |

—Black vinyl

PACIFIC COAST RAGTIMERS, THE
Albums
CIRCLE
| ❑ CLP-1376 | The Pacific Coast Ragtimers | 199? | $30 |

PACKHAM, GREG
Guitarist.
Albums
STASH
| ❑ ST-242 | Action Reaction | 198? | $25 |

PADDOCK JAZZ BAND
Members: James Davis (trumpet, trombone); Bill Kelsey (clarinet, saxophones); Art Langston (bass); Walter Lewis (piano); Stan Williams (drums).
Albums
BIOGRAPH
| ❑ CEN-10 | Paddock Jazz Band | 197? | $25 |

Number	Title	Yr	NM

PAGE, HOT LIPS
Trumpeter, occasional mellophone player and male singer.
Albums
ONYX
❑ 207	After Hours	197?	$30

XANADU
❑ 107	Trumpet at Minton's	197?	$30

PAGE, PATTI
Female singer. Most of her material was in the pop or country-western field, but the following were released on Mercury's jazz label. For a more complete listing of her releases, see the Standard Catalog of American Records.
Albums
EMARCY
❑ MG-36074 [M]	In the Land of Hi-Fi	1956	$200
❑ SR-80000 [S]	In the Land of Hi-Fi	1959	$200
❑ MG-36116 [M]	The East Side	1957	$200
❑ MG-36136 [M]	The West Side	1957	$200

MERCURY
❑ SR-60114 [S]	The East Side	1959	$100
❑ SR-60113 [S]	The West Side	1959	$100

PAGE, SID, AND DAVID SHELANDER
Page is a violinist; Shelander is a pianist.
Albums
BAINBRIDGE
❑ 6257	Odyssey	198?	$25

PAICH, MARTY
Pianist, arranger and bandleader. Also see RUSS GARCIA.
Albums
BETHLEHEM
❑ BCP-44 [M]	Jazz City Workshop	1956	$250

CADENCE
❑ CLP-3010 [M]	Marty Paich Big Band	1958	$50

DISCOVERY
❑ 829	I Get A Boot Out of You	198?	$25
❑ 844	New York Scene	198?	$25
❑ DS-857	What's New	198?	$25

GENE NORMAN
❑ GNP-10 [10]	Marty Paich Octet	1955	$120
—Red vinyl			
❑ GNP-21 [M]	Marty Paich Octet	1956	$80

INTERLUDE
❑ MO-514 [M]	Like Wow -- Jazz 1960	1960	$30
❑ ST-1014 [S]	Like Wow -- Jazz 1960	1960	$30
❑ MO-509 [M]	Revel Without a Pause	1959	$30
❑ ST-1009 [S]	Revel Without a Pause	1959	$30

MODE
❑ LP-110 [M]	Jazz Band Ball	1957	$80
❑ LP-105 [M]	Marty Paich Trio	1957	$80

RCA VICTOR
❑ LPM-2164 [M]	Piano Quartet	1960	$25
❑ LSP-2164 [S]	Piano Quartet	1960	$30
❑ LPM-2259 [M]	Piano Quartet	1960	$25
❑ LSP-2259 [S]	Piano Quartet	1960	$30

REPRISE
❑ RS-6206 [S]	The Rock-Jazz Incident	1966	$35
❑ R-6206 [M]	The Rock-Jazz Incident	1966	$30

TAMPA
❑ TP-23 [M]	Hot Piano	1957	$250
—Probably the original title			
❑ TP-23 [M]	Jazz for Relaxation	1957	$300
—Colored vinyl			
❑ TP-23 [M]	Jazz for Relaxation	1958	$200
—Black vinyl			
❑ TP-28 [M]	Marty Paich Quintet Featuring Art Pepper	1957	$1000
—Red vinyl			
❑ TP-28 [M]	Marty Paich Quintet Featuring Art Pepper	1958	$400
—Black vinyl			

WARNER BROS.
❑ W1349 [M]	I Get A Boot Out of You	1959	$400
❑ WS1349 [S]	I Get A Boot Out of You	1959	$180

PALMER, JEFF
Organist.
Albums
AUDIOQUEST
❑AQ-LP-1014	Ease On	1993	$35

STATIRAS
❑ SLP-8081	Laser Wizzard	1987	$30

PALMER, ROY
Trombonist.
Albums
RIVERSIDE
❑ RLP-1020 [10]	Roy Palmer's State Street Ramblers	1953	$300

PALMER, SINGLETON
Bass and tuba player.
Albums
DIXIELAND JUBILEE
❑ DJ-513	At the Opera House	197?	$25
❑ DJ-511	Dixie by Gaslight	197?	$25

NORMAN
❑ NS-206 [S]	At the Opera House	1963	$35
❑ NL-106 [M]	At the Opera House	1963	$30
❑ NS-201 [S]	Dixie by Gaslight	1962	$35
❑ NL-101 [M]	Dixie by Gaslight	1962	$30
❑ NL-110 [M]	The Best Dixieland Band	1965	$30
❑ NS-210 [S]	The Best Dixieland Band	1965	$35

PALMIER, REMO
Guitarist.
Albums
CONCORD JAZZ
❑ CJ-76	Remo Palmier	1979	$25

PALMIERI, EDDIE
Pianist.
Albums
EPIC
❑ JE35523	Lucumi Macumba Voodoo	1978	$25

INTUITION
❑ C1-91353	Sueno	1989	$30

PAMEIJER, PAM
Drummer and percussionist.
Albums
STOMP OFF
❑ SOS-1134	Jelly Roll Morton: 100 Years	1987	$25
❑ SOS-1194	Little Bits	1989	$25
❑ SOS-1172	London Blues	1988	$25

PARAMOUNT JAZZ BAND OF BOSTON
Members: Jeff Hughes (cornet, trumpet, fluegel horn); Gary Rodberg (clarinet, soprano and alto sax); Jim Mazzy (banjo, vocals); Ray Smith (drums, leader); Robin Verdier (piano); Steve Wright (saxes, clarinets, cornet).
Albums
STOMP OFF
❑ SOS-1205	Ain't Cha Glad	1991	$25

PARAMOUNT THEATRE ORCHESTRA, THE
Albums
STOMP OFF
❑ SOS-1089	Lolly Pops	1985	$25

PARANOISE
Members: Lloyd Fonoroff (drums); Jim Matus (guitar); Miguel Ortiz (bass). Many jazz musicians were guests on the below LP.
Albums
ANTILLES
❑ 90986	Constant Fear	1988	$35

PARENTI, TONY
Clarinetist and baritone and alto saxophone player.
Albums
JAZZOLOGY
❑ J-11 [M]	Downtown Boys	1965	$35
❑ J-41	Jazz Goes Underground	197?	$25
❑ J-26	Jean Kittrell with Tony Parenti and His Blues Blowers	196?	$35
❑ J-31 [M]	Night at Jimmy Ryan's	196?	$35
❑ J-15	Ragtime	196?	$35
❑ J-21 [M]	Ragtime Jubilee	1967	$35
❑ J-71	The Final Bar	197?	$25
❑ J-1 [M]	Tony Parenti	1962	$35

Number	Title	Yr	NM
❑ JCE-1 [10]	Tony Parenti and His New Orleanians	1962	$25

RIVERSIDE
❑ RLP 12-205 [M]	Ragtime	1956	$250
—White label, blue print			
❑ RLP 12-205 [M]	Ragtime	195?	$30
—Blue label, microphone logo at top			

PARENTI, TONY/THE DIXIELAND RHYTHM KINGS
Also see each artist's individual listings.

PARHAM, TINY
Pianist, organist, celeste player, bandleader, arranger and composer.
Albums
FOLKLYRIC
❑ 9028	Hot Chicago Jazz	198?	$25

X
❑ LVA-3039 [10]	Tiny Parham's South Side Jazz	1955	$75

PARIS, JACKIE, AND ANNE MARIE MOSS
Also see each artist's individual listings.
Albums
DIFFERENT DRUMMER
❑ 1004	Maisonette	197?	$35

PARIS, JACKIE
Male singer.
Albums
ABC IMPULSE!
❑AS-17 [S]	The Song Is Paris	1968	$200

AUDIOPHILE
❑ 158	Jackie Paris	198?	$25

BRUNSWICK
❑ BL-54019 [M]	Skylark	1957	$100

CORAL
❑ CRL-56118 [10]	That Paris Mood	195?	$80

EASTWEST
❑ 4002 [M]	The Jackie Paris Sound	1958	$250

EMARCY
❑ MG-36095 [M]	Songs by Jackie Paris	1956	$200

IMPULSE!
❑ A-17 [M]	The Song Is Paris	1962	$120
❑ AS-17 [S]	The Song Is Paris	1962	$160

TIME
❑ T-70009 [M]	Jackie Paris Sings the Lyrics of Ira Gershwin	1959	$40
❑ ST-70009 [S]	Jackie Paris Sings the Lyrics of Ira Gershwin	1959	$50

WING
❑ MGW-60004 [M]	Songs by Jackie Paris	1956	$80

PARIS WASHBOARD
Four-piece band from France.
Albums
STOMP OFF
❑ SOS-1182	When We're Smiling	1988	$25

PARKER, BILLY (2)
Percussionist. Not to be confused with a country singer with the same name.
Albums
STRATA-EAST
❑ SES-19754	Freedom of Speech	1975	$30

PARKER, CHARLIE; DIZZY GILLESPIE; RED NORVO
Also see each artist's individual listings.
Albums
DIAL
❑ LP-903 [M]	Fabulous Jam Session	1951	$600

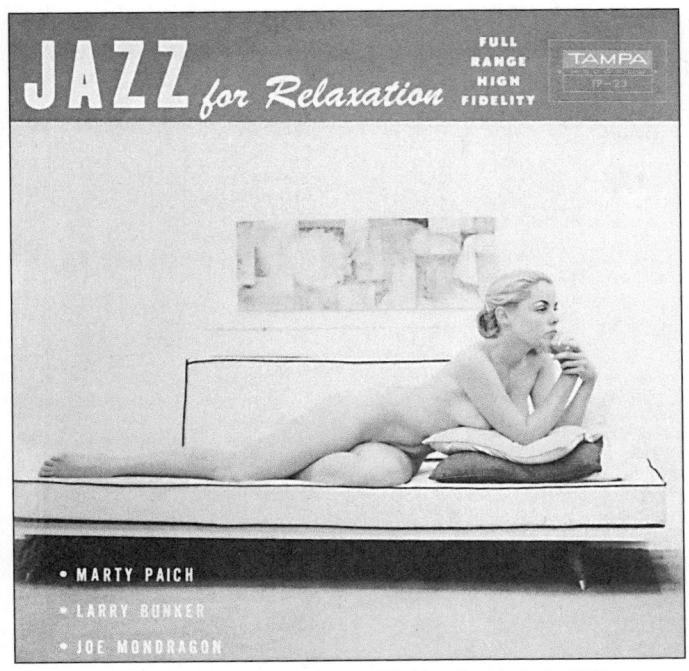

Marty Paich, *Jazz for Relaxation*, Tampa TP-23, colored vinyl, **$300**.

Charlie Parker, *Bird at St. Nick's*, Fantasy (Debut Series) 6012, **$60**.

Charlie Parker/Dizzy Gillespie, *Charlie Parker/Dizzy Gillespie*, Emus ES-12027, **$30**.

Charlie Parker, *Charlie Parker*, Dial LP-203, 10-inch LP, **$2,500**.

PARKER, CHARLIE

Alto saxophone player and composer. He was every bit as important to jazz in the second half of the 20th century as LOUIS ARMSTRONG was in the first half. Also see DIZZY GILLESPIE; THE QUINTET.

Albums

Number	Title	Yr	NM
ALAMAC			
❏ QSR2430	Charlie Parker's All Stars 1950	198?	$30
AMERICAN RECORDING SOCIETY			
❏ G-441 [M]	Now's the Time	1957	$100
BARONET			
❏ B-105 [M]	A Handful of Modern Jazz	1962	$50
❏ BS-105 [R]	A Handful of Modern Jazz	1962	$30
❏ B-107 [M]	The Early Bird	1962	$50
❏ BS-107 [R]	The Early Bird	1962	$30
BIRDLAND			
❏ 425 [10]	A Night at Carnegie Hall	1956	$300
BLUE NOTE			
❏ BT-85108	Charlie Parker at Storyville	198?	$30
BLUE RIBBON			
❏ 8011 [M]	The Early Bird	1962	$50
❏ S-8011 [R]	The Early Bird	1962	$30
CHARLIE PARKER			
❏ PLP-401 [M]	Bird Is Free	1961	$40
❏ PLP-407 [M]	Bird Symbols	1961	$40
❏ PLP-406 [M]	Charlie Parker	1961	$40
❏ CP-513 [M]	Charlie Parker Plus Strings	196?	$40
❏ PLP-701	Historical Masterpieces	196?	$120
❏ CP-2-502 [M]	Live at Rockland Palace, September 26, 1952	1961	$100
❏ PLP-408 [M]	Once There Was Bird	1961	$40
❏ PLP-404 [M]	The Happy Bird	1961	$40
CLEF			
❏ MGC-512 [10]	Bird and Diz	1954	$400
—Reissue of Mercury 512			
❏ MGC-157 [10]	Charlie Parker	1954	$400
❏ MGC-609 [10]	Charlie Parker Big Band	1954	$400
❏ MGC-501 [10]	Charlie Parker with Strings	1954	$400
—Reissue of Mercury 501			
❏ MGC-675 [10]	Charlie Parker with Strings	1955	$400
❏ MGC-101 [10]	Charlie Parker with Strings	1958	$0
—Canceled			
❏ MGC-509 [10]	Charlie Parker's with Strings, No. 2	1954	$400
—Reissue of Mercury 509			
❏ MGC-725 [M]	Night and Day	1956	$350
❏ MGC-513 [10]	South of the Border	1954	$400
—Reissue of Mercury 513			
❏ MGC-646 [M]	The Magnificent Charlie Parker	1955	$700
COLUMBIA			
❏ JC34832	Bird with Strings Live	1977	$30
❏ JG34808	One Night in Birdland	1977	$35
❏ C234808	One Night in Birdland	198?	$30
—Reissue with new prefix			
❏ JC34831	Summit Meeting	1977	$30
CONCERT HALL JAZZ			
❏ 1017 [10]	The Art of Charlie Parker, Vol. 2	1955	$120
❏ 1004 [10]	The Fabulous Bird	1955	$120
CONTINENTAL			
❏ 16004 [M]	Bird Lives	1962	$40
DEBUT			
❏ DEB-611 [M]	Bird on 52nd Street	196?	$150
DIAL			
❏ LP-904 [M]	Alternate Masters	1951	$600
❏ LP-905 [M]	Alternate Masters	1951	$1400
❏ LP-203 [10]	Charlie Parker	1949	$2500
❏ LP-201 [10]	Charlie Parker Quintet	1949	$1000
❏ LP-202 [10]	Charlie Parker Quintet	1949	$800
❏ LP-207 [10]	Charlie Parker Sextet	1949	$800
❏ LP-901 [M]	The Bird Blows the Blues	1949	$4000
—Limited edition of 300 copies on opaque red vinyl; designed as a mail-order offer; issued with a generic gray cover; also has a pale yellow Dial label similiar to the label's 78 rpm design			
❏ LP-901 [M]	The Bird Blows the Blues	1950	$600
—Commercial version of mail-order album			
ELEKTRA/MUSICIAN			
❏ 60019	One Night in Washington	1982	$25
ESP-DISK'			
❏ ESP-BIRD-2	Broadcast Performances 1948-1949, Vol. 2	1973	$150
EVEREST ARCHIVE OF FOLK & JAZZ			
❏ 214	Charlie Parker	1969	$30
❏ 254	Charlie Parker, Vol. 3	197?	$25
❏ 295	Charlie Parker, Vol. 4	197?	$25
❏ 315	Charlie Parker, Vol. 5	197?	$25

Number	Title	Yr	NM
❏ 232	Charlie Parker, Volume 2	1970	$25
FANTASY			
❏ 6012 [M]	Bird at St. Nick's	1964	$60
❏ OJC-041	Bird at St. Nick's	1983	$25
❏ 86012 [R]	Bird at St. Nick's	1964	$35
❏ 6011 [M]	Bird on 52nd St.	1964	$60
❏ 86011 [R]	Bird on 52nd St.	1964	$35
❏ OJC-114	Bird on 52nd St.	198?	$25
❏ OJC-044	Jazz at Massey Hall	198?	$25
HALL OF FAME			
❏ 617	Giants of Jazz	197?	$25
❏ 620	Takin' Off	197?	$25
JAZZTONE			
❏ J-1204 [M]	Giants of Modern Jazz	1955	$100
❏ J-0(# unknown) [M]	The Art of Charlie Parker, Vol. 2	1955	$100
❏ J-1214 [M]	The Fabulous Bird	1955	$100
❏ J-1240 [M]	The Saxes of Stan Getz and Charlie Parker	1957	$100
JAZZ WORKSHOP			
❏ JWS-500 [M]	Bird at St. Nick's	1958	$200
❏ JWS-501 [M]	Bird on 52nd Street	1958	$200
LES JAZZ COOL			
❏ 101 [M]	Les Jazz Cool, Volume 1	1960	$100
❏ 102 [M]	Les Jazz Cool, Volume 2	1960	$100
❏ 103 [M]	Les Jazz Cool, Volume 3	1960	$100
MERCURY			
❏ MGC-512 [10]	Bird and Diz	1952	$500
❏ MG-35010 [10]	Charlie Parker with Strings	1950	$600
❏ MGC-101 [10]	Charlie Parker with Strings	1950	$500
—Reissue of 35010			
❏ MGC-501 [10]	Charlie Parker with Strings	1951	$500
—Reissue of 101 with new number			
❏ MGC-109 [10]	Charlie Parker with Strings, Volume 2	1950	$500
❏ MGC-509 [10]	Charlie Parker with Strings, Volume 2	1952	$500
—Reissue of 109 with new number			
❏ MGC-513 [10]	South of the Border	1952	$500
MGM			
❏ M3G-4949	Archetypes	1974	$30
MOSAIC			
❏ MR10-129	The Complete Dean Benedetti Recordings of Charlie Parker	199?	$175
ONYX			
❏ 221	First Recordings with Jay McShann	197?	$30
PHOENIX			
❏ 10	New Bird	197?	$25
❏ 12	New Bird, Vol. 2	197?	$25
❏ 17	Yardbird in Lotusland	197?	$25
PICKWICK			
❏ SPC-3054 [R]	Yardbird	196?	$25
❏ PC-3054 [M]	Yardbird	196?	$30
PRESTIGE			
❏ 24009	Charlie Parker	197?	$35
❏ 24024	Parker/Powell/Mingus/Roach	197?	$35
ROOST			
❏ LP-2210 [M]	All Star Sextet	1958	$200
❏ LP-2257 [M]	The World of Charlie Parker	1963	$40
SAVOY			
❏ MG-12152 [M]	An Evening at Home with the Bird	196?	$40
❏ MG-12138 [M]	Bird's Night -- The Music of Charlie Parker	1958	$100
❏ MG-9000 [10]	Charlie Parker	1950	$1400
❏ MG-9001 [10]	Charlie Parker, Volume 2	1951	$500
❏ MG-9010 [10]	Charlie Parker, Volume 3	1952	$500
❏ MG-9011 [10]	Charlie Parker, Volume 4	1952	$500
❏ MG-12000 [M]	Charlie Parker Memorial	1955	$175
❏ MG-12009 [M]	Charlie Parker Memorial, Volume 2	1955	$175
❏ MG-12186 [M]	Newly Discovered Sides by the Immortal Charlie Parker	1966	$60
❏ MG-12179 [M]	The "Bird" Returns	196?	$60
❏ MG-12079 [M]	The Charlie Parker Story	1956	$175
❏ MG-12014 [M]	The Genius of Charlie Parker	1955	$175
❏ MG-12001 [M]	The Immortal Charlie Parker	1955	$175
SAVOY JAZZ			
❏ SJL-2201	Bird: The Savoy Recordings	1976	$35
❏ SJL-1108	Bird at the Roost	197?	$30
❏ SJL-1173	Bird at the Roost, Vol. 3	1987	$25
❏ SJL-2259	Bird at the Roost: The Complete Royal Roost Performances, Vol. 1	198?	$35
❏ SJL-2260	Bird at the Roost: The Complete Royal Roost Performances, Vol. 2	1986	$35
❏ SJL-1107	Encores	197?	$30
❏ SJL-1129	Encores, Vol. 2	198?	$25
❏ SJL-1132	One Night in Chicago	198?	$25

Number	Title	Yr	NM
❏ SJL-1208	Original Bird: The Best on Savoy	198?	$25
❏ SJL-5500	The Complete Savoy Studio Sessions	197?	$60
SPOTLITE			
❏ 101	Charlie Parker on Dial, Vol. 1	197?	$25
❏ 102	Charlie Parker on Dial, Vol. 2	197?	$25
❏ 103	Charlie Parker on Dial, Vol. 3	197?	$25
❏ 104	Charlie Parker on Dial, Vol. 4	197?	$25
❏ 105	Charlie Parker on Dial, Vol. 5	197?	$25
❏ 106	Charlie Parker on Dial, Vol. 6	197?	$25
STASH			
❏ ST-260	Birth of the Bebop	1986	$25
❏ ST-280	The Bird You Never Heard	1988	$25
TRIP			
❏ 5039	Birdology	197?	$35
❏ 5035	The Master	197?	$30
UPFRONT			
❏ UPF-172	Live Sessions	197?	$25
VERVE			
❏ MGV-8004 [M]	April in Paris (The Genius of Charlie Parker #2)	1957	$150
❏ V-8004 [M]	April in Paris (The Genius of Charlie Parker #2)	1961	$60
❏ V6-8004 [R]	April in Paris (The Genius of Charlie Parker #2)	196?	$30
❏ 50-5263 [M]	April in Paris (The Genius of Charlie Parker #2)	197?	$35
—Book-of-the-Month Club edition of 8004			
❏ 837176-1	Bird: The Original Recordings of Charlie Parker	1987	$25
❏ MGV-8006 [M]	Bird and Diz (The Genius of Charlie Parker #4)	1957	$150
❏ V-8006 [M]	Bird and Diz (The Genius of Charlie Parker #4)	1961	$60
❏ V6-8006 [R]	Bird and Diz (The Genius of Charlie Parker #4)	196?	$30
❏ 817442-1	Bird on Verve, Vol. 1: Charlie Parker with Strings	1985	$25
❏ 817443-1	Bird on Verve, Vol. 2: Bird and Diz	1985	$25
❏ 817444-1	Bird on Verve, Vol. 3: More Charlie Parker with Strings	1985	$25
❏ 817445-1	Bird on Verve, Vol. 4: Afro-Cuban Jazz	1985	$25
❏ 817446-1	Bird on Verve, Vol. 5: Charlie Parker	1985	$25
❏ 817447-1	Bird on Verve, Vol. 6: South of the Border	1985	$25
❏ 817448-1	Bird on Verve, Vol. 7: Big Band	1985	$25
❏ 817449-1	Bird on Verve, Vol. 8: Charlie Parker in Hi-Fi	1985	$25
❏ V6-8787 [R]	Bird Set	1969	$35
❏ VSP-23 [M]	Bird Wings	1966	$50
❏ VSPS-23 [R]	Bird Wings	1966	$30
❏ MGV-8007 [M]	Charlie Parker Plays Cole Porter (The Genius of Charlie Parker #5)	1957	$150
❏ V-8007 [M]	Charlie Parker Plays Cole Porter (The Genius of Charlie Parker #5)	1961	$60
❏ V6-8007 [R]	Charlie Parker Plays Cole Porter (The Genius of Charlie Parker #5)	196?	$30
❏ VE-2-2508	Charlie Parker Sides	197?	$35
❏ 833564-1	Charlie Parker Sides	198?	$25
❏ UMV-2562	Charlie Parker with Strings	198?	$25
❏ MGV-8008 [M]	Fiesta (The Genius of Charlie Parker #6)	1957	$150
❏ V-8008 [M]	Fiesta (The Genius of Charlie Parker #6)	1961	$60
❏ V6-8008 [R]	Fiesta (The Genius of Charlie Parker #6)	196?	$30
❏ UMV-2617	Jazz Perennial	198?	$25
❏ MGV-8009 [M]	Jazz Perennial (The Genius of Charlie Parker #7)	1957	$150
❏ V-8009 [M]	Jazz Perennial (The Genius of Charlie Parker #7)	1961	$60
❏ V6-8009 [R]	Jazz Perennial (The Genius of Charlie Parker #7)	196?	$30
❏ MGV-8003 [M]	Night and Day (The Genius of Charlie Parker #1)	1957	$150
❏ V-8003 [M]	Night and Day (The Genius of Charlie Parker #1)	1961	$60
❏ V6-8003 [R]	Night and Day (The Genius of Charlie Parker #1)	196?	$30
❏ UMV-2029	Now's the Time	198?	$25
❏ V6-8005 [R]	Now's the Time (The Genius of Charlie Parker #3)	196?	$30
❏ V-8005 [M]	Now's the Time (The Genius of Charlie Parker #3)	1961	$60
❏ MGV-8005 [M]	Now's the Time (The Genius of Charlie Parker #3)	1957	$150
❏ V3HB-8840	Return Engagement	197?	$35
❏ UMV-2030	Swedish Schnapps	198?	$25

Number	Title	Yr	NM
MGV-8010 [M]	Swedish Schnapps (The Genius of Charlie Parker #8)	1957	$150
V-8010 [M]	Swedish Schnapps (The Genius of Charlie Parker #8)	1961	$60
V6-8010 [R]	Swedish Schnapps (The Genius of Charlie Parker #8)	196?	$30
MGV-8100-3 [M]	The Charlie Parker Story	1957	$300
—Combines 8000, 8001 and 8002 in a box set			
V-8100-3 [M]	The Charlie Parker Story	1961	$120
—Combines 8000, 8001 and 8002 in a box set			
MGV-8000 [M]	The Charlie Parker Story, Volume 1	1957	$150
V-8000 [M]	The Charlie Parker Story, Volume 1	1961	$60
V6-8000 [R]	The Charlie Parker Story, Volume 1	196?	$30
MGV-8001 [M]	The Charlie Parker Story, Volume 2	1957	$150
V-8001 [M]	The Charlie Parker Story, Volume 2	1961	$60
V6-8001 [R]	The Charlie Parker Story, Volume 2	196?	$30
MGV-8002 [M]	The Charlie Parker Story, Volume 3	1957	$150
V-8002 [M]	The Charlie Parker Story, Volume 3	1961	$60
V6-8002 [R]	The Charlie Parker Story, Volume 3	196?	$30
823250-1	The Cole Porter Songbook	1986	$25
V-8409 [M]	The Essential Charlie Parker	1961	$60
V6-8409 [R]	The Essential Charlie Parker	196?	$30
VE-2-2501	The Verve Years 1948-50	197?	$35
VE-2-2512	The Verve Years 1950-51	197?	$35
VE-2-2523	The Verve Years 1952-54	197?	$35

VOGUE

LAE-12002 [M]	Memorial Album	1955	$150

WARNER BROS.

6BS3159	The Complete Dial Recordings	1977	$150
—Limited edition of 4,000 box sets			
2WB3198	The Very Best of Bird	1977	$50

ZIM

1006	Apartment Jam	197?	$30
1003	At the Pershing Ballroom, Chicago, 1950	197?	$30
1001	Lullaby in Rhythm	197?	$30

EASTWEST

4002 [M]	The Jackie Paris Sound	1958	$250

EMARCY

MG-36095 [M]	Songs by Jackie Paris	1956	$200

IMPULSE!

A-17 [M]	The Song Is Paris	1962	$120
AS-17 [S]	The Song Is Paris	1962	$160

TIME

T-70009 [M]	Jackie Paris Sings the Lyrics of Ira Gershwin	1959	$40
ST-70009 [S]	Jackie Paris Sings the Lyrics of Ira Gershwin	1959	$50

WING

MGW-60004 [M]	Songs by Jackie Paris	1956	$80

PARIS WASHBOARD

Four-piece band from France.

Albums

STOMP OFF

SOS-1182	When We're Smiling	1988	$25

PARKER, BILLY (2)

Percussionist. Not to be confused with a country singer with the same name.

Albums

STRATA-EAST

SES-19754	Freedom of Speech	1975	$30

PARKER, CHARLIE; DIZZY GILLESPIE; RED NORVO

Also see each artist's individual listings.

Albums

DIAL

LP-903 [M]	Fabulous Jam Session	1951	$600

PARKER, CHARLIE

Alto saxophone player and composer. He was every bit as important to jazz in the second half of the 20th century as LOUIS ARMSTRONG was in the first half. Also see DIZZY GILLESPIE; THE QUINTET.

Albums

ALAMAC

Number	Title	Yr	NM
QSR2430	Charlie Parker's All Stars 1950	198?	$30

AMERICAN RECORDING SOCIETY

G-441 [M]	Now's the Time	1957	$100

BARONET

B-105 [M]	A Handful of Modern Jazz	1962	$50
BS-105 [R]	A Handful of Modern Jazz	1962	$30
B-107 [M]	The Early Bird	1962	$50
BS-107 [R]	The Early Bird	1962	$30

BIRDLAND

425 [10]	A Night at Carnegie Hall	1956	$300

BLUE NOTE

BT-85108	Charlie Parker at Storyville	198?	$30

BLUE RIBBON

8011 [M]	The Early Bird	1962	$50
S-8011 [R]	The Early Bird	1962	$30

CHARLIE PARKER

PLP-401 [M]	Bird Is Free	1961	$40
PLP-407 [M]	Bird Symbols	1961	$40
PLP-406 [M]	Charlie Parker	1961	$40
CP-513 [M]	Charlie Parker Plus Strings	196?	$40
PLP-701	Historical Masterpieces	196?	$120
CP-2-502 [M]	Live at Rockland Palace, September 26, 1952	1961	$100
PLP-408 [M]	Once There Was Bird	1961	$40
PLP-404 [M]	The Happy Bird	1961	$40

CLEF

MGC-512 [10]	Bird and Diz	1954	$400
—Reissue of Mercury 512			
MGC-157 [10]	Charlie Parker	1954	$400
MGC-609 [10]	Charlie Parker Big Band	1954	$400
MGC-501 [10]	Charlie Parker with Strings	1954	$400
—Reissue of Mercury 501			
MGC-675 [M]	Charlie Parker with Strings	1955	$400
MGC-101 [10]	Charlie Parker with Strings	1958	$0
—Canceled			
MGC-509 [10]	Charlie Parker with Strings, No. 2	1954	$400
—Reissue of Mercury 509			
MGC-725 [M]	Night and Day	1956	$350
MGC-513 [10]	South of the Border	1954	$400
—Reissue of Mercury 513			
MGC-646 [M]	The Magnificent Charlie Parker	1955	$700

COLUMBIA

JC34832	Bird with Strings Live	1977	$30
JG34808	One Night in Birdland	1977	$35
C234808	One Night in Birdland	198?	$30
—Reissue with new prefix			
JC34831	Summit Meeting	1977	$30

CONCERT HALL JAZZ

1017 [10]	The Art of Charlie Parker, Vol. 2	1955	$120
1004 [10]	The Fabulous Bird	1955	$120

CONTINENTAL

16004 [M]	Bird Lives	1962	$40

DEBUT

DEB-611 [M]	Bird on 52nd Street	196?	$150

DIAL

LP-904 [M]	Alternate Masters	1951	$600
LP-905 [M]	Alternate Masters	1951	$1400
LP-203 [10]	Charlie Parker	1949	$2500
LP-201 [10]	Charlie Parker Quintet	1949	$1000
LP-202 [10]	Charlie Parker Quintet	1949	$800
LP-207 [10]	Charlie Parker Sextet	1949	$800
LP-901 [10]	The Bird Blows the Blues	1949	$4000
—Limited edition of 300 copies on opaque red vinyl; designed as a mail-order offer; issued with a generic gray cover; also has a pale yellow Dial label similiar to the label's 78 rpm design			
LP-901 [M]	The Bird Blows the Blues	1950	$600
—Commercial version of mail-order album			

ELEKTRA/MUSICIAN

60019	One Night in Washington	1982	$25

ESP-DISK'

ESP-BIRD-2	Broadcast Performances 1948-1949, Vol. 2	1973	$150

EVEREST ARCHIVE OF FOLK & JAZZ

214	Charlie Parker	1969	$30
254	Charlie Parker, Vol. 3	197?	$25
295	Charlie Parker, Vol. 4	197?	$25
315	Charlie Parker, Vol. 5	197?	$25
232	Charlie Parker, Volume 2	1970	$25

FANTASY

6012 [M]	Bird at St. Nick's	1964	$60
OJC-041	Bird at St. Nick's	1983	$25
86012 [R]	Bird at St. Nick's	1964	$35
6011 [M]	Bird on 52nd St.	1964	$60

Number	Title	Yr	NM
86011 [R]	Bird on 52nd St.	1964	$35
OJC-114	Bird on 52nd St.	198?	$25
OJC-044	Jazz at Massey Hall	198?	$25

HALL OF FAME

617	Giants of Jazz	197?	$25
620	Takin' Off	197?	$25

JAZZTONE

J-1204 [M]	Giants of Modern Jazz	1955	$100
J-0(# unknown) [M]	The Art of Charlie Parker, Vol. 2	1955	$100
J-1214 [M]	The Fabulous Bird	1955	$100
J-1240 [M]	The Saxes of Stan Getz and Charlie Parker	1957	$100

JAZZ WORKSHOP

JWS-500 [M]	Bird at St. Nick's	1958	$200
JWS-501 [M]	Bird on 52nd Street	1958	$200

LES JAZZ COOL

101 [M]	Les Jazz Cool, Volume 1	1960	$100
102 [M]	Les Jazz Cool, Volume 2	1960	$100
103 [M]	Les Jazz Cool, Volume 3	1960	$100

MERCURY

MGC-512 [10]	Bird and Diz	1952	$500
MG-35010 [10]	Charlie Parker with Strings	1950	$600
MGC-101 [10]	Charlie Parker with Strings	1950	$500
—Reissue of 35010			
MGC-501 [10]	Charlie Parker with Strings	1951	$500
—Reissue of 101 with new number			
MGC-109 [10]	Charlie Parker with Strings, Volume 2	1950	$500
MGC-509 [10]	Charlie Parker with Strings, Volume 2	1952	$500
—Reissue of 109 with new number			
MGC-513 [10]	South of the Border	1952	$500

MGM

M3G-4949	Archetypes	1974	$30

MOSAIC

MR10-129	The Complete Dean Benedetti Recordings of Charlie Parker	199?	$175

ONYX

221	First Recordings with Jay McShann	197?	$30

PHOENIX

10	New Bird	197?	$25
12	New Bird, Vol. 2	197?	$25
17	Yardbird in Lotusland	197?	$25

PICKWICK

SPC-3054 [R]	Yardbird	196?	$25
PC-3054 [M]	Yardbird	196?	$30

PRESTIGE

24009	Charlie Parker	197?	$35
24024	Parker/Powell/Mingus/Roach	197?	$35

ROOST

LP-2210 [M]	All Star Sextet	1958	$200
LP-2257 [M]	The World of Charlie Parker	1963	$40

SAVOY

MG-12152 [M]	An Evening at Home with the Bird	196?	$40
MG-12138 [M]	Bird's Night -- The Music of Charlie Parker	1958	$100
MG-9000 [10]	Charlie Parker	1950	$1400
MG-9001 [10]	Charlie Parker, Volume 2	1951	$500
MG-9010 [10]	Charlie Parker, Volume 3	1952	$500
MG-9011 [10]	Charlie Parker, Volume 4	1952	$500
MG-12000 [M]	Charlie Parker Memorial	1955	$175
MG-12009 [M]	Charlie Parker Memorial, Volume 2	1955	$175
MG-12186 [M]	Newly Discovered Sides by the Immortal Charlie Parker	1966	$60
MG-12179 [M]	The "Bird" Returns	196?	$60
MG-12079 [M]	The Charlie Parker Story	1956	$175
MG-12014 [M]	The Genius of Charlie Parker	1955	$175
MG-12001 [M]	The Immortal Charlie Parker	1955	$175

SAVOY JAZZ

SJL-2201	Bird: The Savoy Recordings	1976	$35
SJL-1108	Bird at the Roost	197?	$30
SJL-1173	Bird at the Roost, Vol. 3	1987	$25
SJL-2259	Bird at the Roost: The Complete Royal Roost Performances, Vol. 1	198?	$35
SJL-2260	Bird at the Roost: The Complete Royal Roost Performances, Vol. 2	1986	$35
SJL-1107	Encores	197?	$30
SJL-1129	Encores, Vol. 2	198?	$25
SJL-1132	One Night in Chicago	198?	$25
SJL-1208	Original Bird: The Best on Savoy	198?	$25
SJL-5500	The Complete Savoy Studio Sessions	197?	$60

SPOTLITE

Number	Title	Yr	NM
❑ 101	Charlie Parker on Dial, Vol. 1	197?	$25
❑ 102	Charlie Parker on Dial, Vol. 2	197?	$25
❑ 103	Charlie Parker on Dial, Vol. 3	197?	$25
❑ 104	Charlie Parker on Dial, Vol. 4	197?	$25
❑ 105	Charlie Parker on Dial, Vol. 5	197?	$25
❑ 106	Charlie Parker on Dial, Vol. 6	197?	$25

STASH

❑ ST-260	Birth of the Bebop	1986	$25
❑ ST-280	The Bird You Never Heard	1988	$25

TRIP

❑ 5039	Birdology	197?	$35
❑ 5035	The Master	197?	$30

UPFRONT

❑ UPF-172	Live Sessions	197?	$25

VERVE

❑ MGV-8004 [M]	April in Paris (The Genius of Charlie Parker #2)	1957	$150
❑ V-8004 [M]	April in Paris (The Genius of Charlie Parker #2)	1961	$60
❑ V6-8004 [R]	April in Paris (The Genius of Charlie Parker #2)	196?	$30
❑ 50-5263 [M]	April in Paris (The Genius of Charlie Parker #2)	197?	$35

—Book-of-the-Month Club edition of 8004

❑ 837176-1	Bird: The Original Recordings of Charlie Parker	1987	$25
❑ MGV-8006 [M]	Bird and Diz (The Genius of Charlie Parker #4)	1957	$150
❑ V-8006 [M]	Bird and Diz (The Genius of Charlie Parker #4)	1961	$60
❑ V6-8006 [R]	Bird and Diz (The Genius of Charlie Parker #4)	196?	$30
❑ 817442-1	Bird on Verve, Vol. 1: Charlie Parker with Strings	1985	$25
❑ 817443-1	Bird on Verve, Vol. 2: Bird and Diz	1985	$25
❑ 817444-1	Bird on Verve, Vol. 3: More Charlie Parker with Strings	1985	$25
❑ 817445-1	Bird on Verve, Vol. 4: Afro-Cuban Jazz	1985	$25
❑ 817446-1	Bird on Verve, Vol. 5: Charlie Parker	1985	$25
❑ 817447-1	Bird on Verve, Vol. 6: South of the Border	1985	$25
❑ 817448-1	Bird on Verve, Vol. 7: Big Band	1985	$25
❑ 817449-1	Bird on Verve, Vol. 8: Charlie Parker in Hi-Fi	1985	$25
❑ V6-8787 [R]	Bird Set	1969	$35
❑ VSP-23 [M]	Bird Wings	1966	$50
❑ VSPS-23 [R]	Bird Wings	1966	$30
❑ MGV-8007 [M]	Charlie Parker Plays Cole Porter (The Genius of Charlie Parker #5)	1957	$150
❑ V-8007 [M]	Charlie Parker Plays Cole Porter (The Genius of Charlie Parker #5)	1961	$60
❑ V6-8007 [R]	Charlie Parker Plays Cole Porter (The Genius of Charlie Parker #5)	196?	$30
❑ VE-2-2508	Charlie Parker Sides	197?	$35
❑ 833564-1	Charlie Parker Sides	198?	$25
❑ UMV-2562	Charlie Parker with Strings	198?	$25
❑ MGV-8008 [M]	Fiesta (The Genius of Charlie Parker #6)	1957	$150
❑ V-8008 [M]	Fiesta (The Genius of Charlie Parker #6)	1961	$60
❑ V6-8008 [R]	Fiesta (The Genius of Charlie Parker #6)	196?	$30
❑ UMV-2617	Jazz Perennial	198?	$25
❑ MGV-8009 [M]	Jazz Perennial (The Genius of Charlie Parker #7)	1957	$150
❑ V-8009 [M]	Jazz Perennial (The Genius of Charlie Parker #7)	1961	$60
❑ V6-8009 [R]	Jazz Perennial (The Genius of Charlie Parker #7)	196?	$30
❑ MGV-8003 [M]	Night and Day (The Genius of Charlie Parker #1)	1957	$150
❑ V-8003 [M]	Night and Day (The Genius of Charlie Parker #1)	1961	$60
❑ V6-8003 [R]	Night and Day (The Genius of Charlie Parker #1)	196?	$30
❑ UMV-2029	Now's the Time	198?	$25
❑ V6-8005 [R]	Now's the Time (The Genius of Charlie Parker #3)	196?	$30
❑ V-8005 [M]	Now's the Time (The Genius of Charlie Parker #3)	1961	$60
❑ MGV-8005 [M]	Now's the Time (The Genius of Charlie Parker #3)	1957	$150
❑ V3HB-8840	Return Engagement	197?	$35
❑ UMV-2030	Swedish Schnapps	198?	$25
❑ MGV-8010 [M]	Swedish Schnapps (The Genius of Charlie Parker #8)	1957	$150
❑ V-8010 [M]	Swedish Schnapps (The Genius of Charlie Parker #8)	1961	$60
❑ V6-8010 [R]	Swedish Schnapps (The Genius of Charlie Parker #8)	196?	$30
❑ MGV-8100-3 [M]	The Charlie Parker Story	1957	$300

—Combines 8000, 8001 and 8002 in a box set

❑ V-8100-3 [M]	The Charlie Parker Story	1961	$120

—Combines 8000, 8001 and 8002 in a box set

❑ MGV-8000 [M]	The Charlie Parker Story, Volume 1	1957	$150
❑ V-8000 [M]	The Charlie Parker Story, Volume 1	1961	$60
❑ V6-8000 [R]	The Charlie Parker Story, Volume 1	196?	$30
❑ MGV-8001 [M]	The Charlie Parker Story, Volume 2	1957	$150
❑ V-8001 [M]	The Charlie Parker Story, Volume 2	1961	$60
❑ V6-8001 [R]	The Charlie Parker Story, Volume 2	196?	$30
❑ MGV-8002 [M]	The Charlie Parker Story, Volume 3	1957	$150
❑ V-8002 [M]	The Charlie Parker Story, Volume 3	1961	$60
❑ V6-8002 [R]	The Charlie Parker Story, Volume 3	196?	$30
❑ 823250-1	The Cole Porter Songbook	1986	$25
❑ V-8409 [M]	The Essential Charlie Parker	1961	$60
❑ V6-8409 [R]	The Essential Charlie Parker	196?	$30
❑ VE-2-2501	The Verve Years 1948-50	197?	$35
❑ VE-2-2512	The Verve Years 1950-51	197?	$35
❑ VE-2-2523	The Verve Years 1952-54	197?	$35

VOGUE

❑ LAE-12002 [M]	Memorial Album	1955	$150

WARNER BROS.

❑ 6BS3159	The Complete Dial Recordings	1977	$150

—Limited edition of 4,000 box sets

❑ 2WB3198	The Very Best of Bird	1977	$50

ZIM

❑ 1006	Apartment Jam	197?	$30
❑ 1003	At the Pershing Ballroom, Chicago, 1950	197?	$30
❑ 1001	Lullaby in Rhythm	197?	$30

PARKER, CHARLIE/COLEMAN HAWKINS/GEORGIE AULD

Also see each artist's individual listings.

Albums

JAM

❑ 5006	Unearthed Masters, Vol. 1	198?	$25

PARKER, CHARLIE/DIZZY GILLESPIE

Albums

EMUS

❑ ES-12027 [R]	Charlie Parker / Dizzy Gillespie	197?	$30

PARKER, CHARLIE/DIZZY GILLESPIE/BUD POWELL/MAX ROACH

Also see each artist's individual listings.

Albums

SAVOY

❑ MG-9034 [10]	Bird, Diz, Bud, Max	1953	$600

PARKER, CHARLIE/STAN GETZ/WARDELL GRAY

Also see each artist's individual listings.

Albums

DESIGN

❑ DLP-183 [M]	Charlie Parker/Stan Getz/ Wardell Gray	196?	$35

PARKER, JACY

Pianist and singer.

Albums

VERVE

❑ V-8424 [M]	Spotlight On Jacy Parker	1962	$40
❑ V6-8424 [S]	Spotlight On Jacy Parker	1962	$50

PARKER, JOHN

Albums

GOLDEN CREST

❑ GC-3051	Dixieland	196?	$35

PARKER, KIM

Female singer; stepdaughter of Charlie.

Albums

SOUL NOTE

❑ SN-1063	Good Girl	1982	$30
❑ SN-1033	Havin' Myself a Time	1981	$30
❑ SN-1133	Sometimes I'm Blue	1986	$30

PARKER, KNOCKY, AND SMOKEY MONTGOMERY

Montgomery is a banjo player. Also see KNOCKY PARKER.

Albums

CIRCLE

❑ CLP-10001	Texas Swing, Vol. 1: The Barrelhouse	1987	$25
❑ CLP-10002	Texas Swing, Vol. 2: The Boogie-Woogie	1987	$25
❑ CLP-10003	Texas Swing, Vol. 3: … And the Blues	1987	$25
❑ CLP-10004	Texas Swing, Vol. 4: Smokey and the Bearkats	1987	$25

PARKER, KNOCKY

Pianist.

Albums

AUDIOPHILE

❑ AP-28 [M]	Boogie Woogie Maxine	1956	$40
❑ AP-102/5	The Complete Piano Works of Jelly Roll Morton	196?	$50

—In box with booklet; it's unknown whether the volumes also were issued individually

EUPHONIC

❑ 1216	Classic Rags and Nostalgia	198?	$25
❑ 1215	Eight on Eighty-Eight	198?	$25

GHB

❑ GHB-19	Knocky Parker	1967	$35
❑ 150	Knocky Parker and the Cake-Walkin' Jazz Band	1981	$25

JAZZOLOGY

❑ J-81	Cakewalk to Ragtime	197?	$25

PROGRESSIVE

❑ PLP-1 [10]	New Orleans Stomps	1954	$50

PARKER, LEO

Baritone saxophone player.

Albums

BLUE NOTE

❑ BLP-4087 [M]	Let Me Tell You 'Bout It	1961	$100

—With 61st St. address on label

❑ BST-84087 [S]	Let Me Tell You 'Bout It	1961	$80

—With 61st St. address on label

❑ BLP-4087 [M]	Let Me Tell You 'Bout It	1963	$60

—With "New York, USA" address on label

❑ BST-84087 [S]	Let Me Tell You 'Bout It	1963	$30

—With "New York, USA" address on label

❑ BST-84087 [S]	Let Me Tell You 'Bout It	1967	$35

—With "A Division of Liberty Records" on label

❑ LT-1076	Rollin' with Leo	1980	$25
❑ BLP-4095 [M]	Rollin' with Leo	1961	$0

—Canceled

❑ BST-84095 [S]	Rollin' with Leo	1986	$30

—Originally scheduled for 1961 release, this was the first issue on its originally assigned number

CHESS

❑ LPV-413	The Late, Great King of Baritone Sax	1971	$35

COLLECTABLES

❑ COL-5329	Back to the Baritones	198?	$25

SAVOY

❑ MG-9009 [10]	Leo Parker	1952	$250
❑ MG-9018 [10]	New Trends in Modern Music	1952	$250

PARKER, MAYNARD

Guitarist.

Albums

PRESTIGE

❑ 10054	Midnight Rider	1973	$25

Passport, *Heavy Nights*, Atlantic 81727, **$25**.

Art Pepper, *The Return of Art Pepper*, Jazz West JWLP-10, **$600**.

Art Pepper, *Gettin' Together!*, Contemporary M-3573, **$250**.

Art Pepper, *Art Pepper + Eleven: Modern Jazz Classics*, Contemporary M-3568, **$250**.

Number	Title	Yr	NM

PARKINS, LEROY
Woodwinds player.

Albums

BETHLEHEM
❏ BCP-6047 [M]	LeRoy Parkins and His Yazoo River Band	1960	$250
❏ SBCP-6047 [S]	LeRoy Parkins and His Yazoo River Band	1960	$250

PARLAN, HORACE
Pianist.

Albums

BLUE NOTE
❏ BST-84134	Happy Frame of Mind	1986	$30

—*The Finest in Jazz Since 1939" issue*
❏ BLP-4062 [M]	Headin' South	1963	$60

—*With "New York, USA" address on label*
❏ BST-84062 [S]	Headin' South	1963	$30

—*With "New York, USA" address on label*
❏ BST-84062 [S]	Headin' South	1967	$35

—*With "A Division of Liberty Records" on label*
❏ BLP-4028 [M]	Movin' and Groovin'	1963	$60

—*With "New York, USA" address on label*
❏ BST-84028 [S]	Movin' and Groovin'	1963	$30

—*With "New York, USA" address on label*
❏ BST-84028 [S]	Movin' and Groovin'	1967	$35

—*With "A Division of Liberty Records" on label*
❏ BLP-4074 [M]	On the Spur of the Moment	1961	$150

—*With W. 63rd St. address on label*
❏ BST-84074 [S]	On the Spur of the Moment	1961	$125

—*With 61st St. address on label*
❏ BLP-4074 [M]	On the Spur of the Moment	1961	$100

—*With 61st St. address on label*
❏ BST-84074 [S]	On the Spur of the Moment	1961	$200

—*With W. 63rd St. address on label*
❏ BLP-4074 [M]	On the Spur of the Moment	1963	$60

—*With "New York, USA" address on label*
❏ BST-84074 [S]	On the Spur of the Moment	1963	$30

—*With "New York, USA" address on label*
❏ BST-84074 [S]	On the Spur of the Moment	1967	$35

—*With "A Division of Liberty Records" on label*
❏ BST-4074	On the Spur of the Moment	199?	$30

—*Classic Records reissue on audiophile vinyl*
❏ BLP-4043 [M]	Speakin' My Piece	1960	$500

—*Deep groove" version (deep indentation under label on both sides)*
❏ BLP-4043 [M]	Speakin' My Piece	1960	$150

—*Regular version, W. 63rd St. address on label*
❏ BST-84043 [S]	Speakin' My Piece	1963	$30

—*With "New York, USA" address on label*
❏ BLP-4043 [M]	Speakin' My Piece	1963	$60

—*With "New York, USA" address on label*
❏ BST-84043 [S]	Speakin' My Piece	1960	$80

—*With W. 63rd St. address on label*
❏ BLP-4043 [M]	Speakin' My Piece	1963	$60

—*With "New York, USA" address on label*
❏ BST-84043 [S]	Speakin' My Piece	1967	$35

—*With "A Division of Liberty Records" on label*
❏ BLP-4082 [M]	Up and Down	1961	$100

—*With 61st St. address on label*
❏ BST-84082 [S]	Up and Down	1961	$125

—*With 61st St. address on label*
❏ BLP-4082 [M]	Up and Down	1963	$60

—*With "New York, USA" address on label*
❏ BST-84082 [S]	Up and Down	1963	$30

—*With "New York, USA" address on label*
❏ BST-84082 [S]	Up and Down	1967	$35

—*With "A Division of Liberty Records" on label*
❏ BLP-4037 [M]	Us Three	1960	$150

—*Regular version, W. 63rd St. address on label*
❏ BST-84037 [S]	Us Three	1960	$80

—*With W. 63rd St. address on label*
❏ BLP-4037 [M]	Us Three	1963	$60

—*With "New York, USA" address on label*
❏ BST-84037 [S]	Us Three	1967	$35

—*With "A Division of Liberty Records" on label*
❏ BST-84037 [S]	Us Three	1963	$30

—*With "New York, USA" address on label*

INNER CITY
❏ IC-2012	Arrival	197?	$35
❏ IC-2056	No Blues	197?	$35

MOSAIC

❏ MQ8-197	The Complete Horace Parlan Blue Note Sessions	2000	$150

STEEPLECHASE
❏ SCS-1012	Arrival	198?	$30
❏ SCS-1124	Blue Parlan	198?	$30
❏ SCS-1076	Frank-ly Speaking	198?	$30
❏ SCS-1194	Glad I Met You	198?	$30
❏ SCS-1178	Like Someone in Love	1983	$30
❏ SCS-1141	Musically Yours	198?	$30
❏ SCS-1056	No Blues	198?	$30
❏ SCS-1167	The Maestro	198?	$30

PASS, JOE, AND ARNOLD ROSS
Also see each artist's individual listings.

Albums

PACIFIC JAZZ
❏ PJ-48 [M]	Sounds of Synanon	1962	$30
❏ ST-48 [S]	Sounds of Synanon	1962	$30

PASS, JOE, AND JIMMY ROWLES
Also see each artist's individual listings.

Albums

PABLO
❏ 2310865	Checkmate	1982	$30

PASS, JOE, AND NIELS-HENNING ORSTED PEDERSEN
Also see each artist's individual listings.

Albums

PABLO
❏ 2310830	Chops	1979	$30

PABLO LIVE
❏ 2308811	North Sea Nights	1979	$30

PASS, JOE, AND PAULINHO DA COSTA
Also see each artist's individual listings.

Albums

PABLO
❏ 2310824	Tudo Bern!	1978	$30

PASS, JOE, AND ROBERT CONTI
Also see each artist's individual listings.

Albums

DISCOVERY
❏ 906	The Living Legends	1985	$30

PASS, JOE; TOOTS THIELMANS; NIELS-HENNING ORSTED PEDERSEN
Also see each artist's individual listings.

Albums

PABLO LIVE
❏ 2308233	Live in the Netherlands	1981	$30

PASS, JOE
Guitarist.

Albums

BASF
❏ 20738	Intercontinental	197?	$35

BLUE NOTE
❏ LT-1103	Joy Spring	1981	$25
❏ LT-1053	The Complete "Catch Me" Sessions	1980	$30

DISCOVERY
❏ DS-776	Guitar Interludes	197?	$30
❏ DS-906	The Living Legends	1986	$25

FANTASY
❏ OJC-602	I Remember Charlie Parker	1991	$30
❏ OJC-382	Montreux '77	1989	$25

PABLO
❏ 2310931	Blues for Fred	198?	$25
❏ 2310877	Eximious	198?	$30
❏ 2310752	Montreux '75	1976	$30
❏ 2310936	One for My Baby	1989	$30
❏ 2310716	Portrait of Duke Ellington	1975	$30
❏ 2310939	Summer Nights	1990	$35
❏ 2310593	The Best of Joe Pass	198?	$30
❏ 2405419	The Best of Joe Pass	198?	$25
❏ 2310788	Virtuoso #2	1976	$30
❏ 2310805	Virtuoso #3	1978	$30
❏ 2640102	Virtuoso #4	198?	$35
❏ 2310708	Virtuoso	1974	$35
❏ 2310912	Whitestone	198?	$25

PABLO LIVE
❏ 2308249	Joe Pass at Akron University	1987	$25
❏ 2620114	Joe Pass Trio Live at Donte's	198?	$35
❏ 2308239	Live at Long Beach City College	1987	$25
❏ 2308212	Montreux '77	1978	$30

PABLO TODAY
❏ 2312109	I Remember Charlie Parker	1979	$30
❏ 2312133	Joe Pass Loves Gershwin	198?	$30

PACIFIC JAZZ
❏ PJ-73 [M]	Catch Me!	1963	$30
❏ ST-73 [S]	Catch Me!	1963	$30
❏ PJ-85 [M]	For Django	1964	$30
❏ ST-85 [S]	For Django	1964	$30
❏ LN-10132	For Django	198?	$20

—*Budget-line reissue*
❏ LN-10086	Simplicity	198?	$20

—*Budget-line reissue*

PAUSA
❏ 7043	Intercontinental	198?	$25

WORLD PACIFIC
❏ WP-1844 [M]	A Sign of the Times	1966	$100
❏ ST-21844 [S]	A Sign of the Times	1966	$100
❏ WP-1865 [M]	Simplicity	1967	$100
❏ ST-21865 [S]	Simplicity	1967	$100
❏ WP-1854 [M]	The Stones Jazz	1967	$100
❏ ST-21854 [S]	The Stones Jazz	1967	$100

PASSPORT
Fusion group led by KLAUS DOLDINGER.

Albums

ATCO
❏ SD 36-107	Cross-Collateral	1975	$30
❏ SD 36-149	Iguacu	1977	$25
❏ SD 36-132	Infinity Machine	1976	$30
❏ SD7042	Looking Thru	1974	$30

ATLANTIC
❏ SD19304	Blue Tattoo	1981	$25
❏ SD18162	Doldinger Jubilee '75	1976	$30
❏ 80034	Earthborn	1982	$25
❏ SD19233	Garden of Eden	1979	$25
❏ 81727	Heavy Nights	1986	$25
❏ 80144	Man in the Mirror	1983	$25
❏ SD19265	Oceanliner	1980	$25
❏ 81251	Running in Real Time	1985	$25
❏ SD19177	Sky Blue	1978	$25
❏ 81937	Talk Back	1989	$25

REPRISE
❏ MS2143	Doldinger	1973	$35

PASTICHE
Vocal trio: Sandy Cressman; Jenny Meltzer; Becky West.

Albums

NOVA
❏ 8707	That's R & B-Bop	198?	$30

PASTOR, GUY
Male singer. Also see TONY PASTOR.

Albums

DISCOVERY
❏ DS-918	This Is It	1986	$25

PASTOR, TONY
Tenor saxophone player and bandleader.

Albums

CIRCLE
❏ CLP-121	Tony Pastor and His Orchestra 1942-47	198?	$25
❏ 31	Tony Pastor and His Orchestra 1944-47	198?	$25

EVEREST
❏ LPBR-5031 [M]	P.S. -- Plays and Sings Shaw	1959	$35
❏ SDBR-1031 [S]	P.S. -- Plays and Sings Shaw	1959	$25

FORUM
❏ F-9009 [M]	Let's Dance with Tony Pastor	196?	$30
❏ SF-9009 [S]	Let's Dance with Tony Pastor	196?	$30

ROULETTE
❏ R-25027 [M]	Guy Pastor and His Dad	1958	$60
❏ R-25024 [M]	Let's Dance	1958	$60

X
❏ LXA-3025 [10]	Tony Pastor's Best	1954	$100

Number	Title	Yr	NM

PASTORIUS, JACO
Bass player. Also see WEATHER REPORT.
Albums

WARNER BROS.
| ❏ BSK3535 [B] | Word of Mouth | 1981 | $60 |

PATCHEN, KENNETH, WITH THE CHAMBER JAZZ SEXTET
Beat poet Patchen recites with a jazz band playing behind him.
Albums

CADENCE
| ❏ CLP-3004 [M] | Kenneth Patchen Reads His Poetry | 1957 | $300 |

PATE, JOHNNY
Bass player, composer and arranger.
Albums

GIG
| ❏ GLP-100 [M] | Subtle Sounds | 1956 | $400 |

KING
❏ 611 [M]	A Date with Johnny Pate	1959	$80
❏ 561 [M]	Jazz Goes Ivy League	1958	$80
❏ 584 [M]	Swingin' Flute	1958	$80

STEPHENY
| ❏ 4002 [M] | Johnny Pate at the Blue Note | 1957 | $100 |

TALISMAN
| ❏ TLP-1 [10] | Johnny Pate Trio | 1956 | $120 |

PATITUCCI, JOHN
Bass player.
Albums

GRP
| ❏ GR-1049 | John Patitucci | 1988 | $25 |
| ❏ GR-9583 | On the Corner | 1989 | $30 |

PATTERSON, DON
Organist.
Albums

CADET
| ❏ LPS-787 [S] | Goin' Down Home | 1967 | $25 |
| ❏ LP-787 [M] | Goin' Down Home | 1967 | $30 |

MUSE
❏ MR-5121	Movin' Up	1977	$30
❏ MR-5005	The Return of Don Patterson	1974	$35
❏ MR-5032	These Are Soulful Days	1975	$35
❏ MR-5148	Why Not	1979	$30

PRESTIGE
❏ PRST-7772	Best of Jazz Giants	1971	$35
❏ PRST-7563	Boppin' and Burnin'	1968	$25
❏ PRST-7738	Brothers-4	1970	$35
❏ PRST-7816	Donnybrook	1971	$35
❏ PRST-7533 [S]	Four Dimensions	1967	$25
❏ PRLP-7533 [M]	Four Dimensions	1967	$30
❏ PRST-7613	Funk You	1969	$25
❏ PRST-7349 [S]	Hip Cake Walk	1965	$30
❏ PRLP-7349 [M]	Hip Cake Walk	1965	$30
❏ PRST-7415 [S]	Holiday Soul	1965	$30
❏ PRLP-7415 [M]	Holiday Soul	1966	$30
❏ PRST-7510 [S]	Mellow Soul	1967	$25
❏ PRLP-7510 [M]	Mellow Soul	1967	$30
❏ PRST-7640	Oh, Happy Days!	1969	$25
❏ PRST-7577	Opus De Don	1968	$25
❏ PRST-7381 [S]	Patterson's People	1965	$30
❏ PRLP-7381 [M]	Patterson's People	1965	$30
❏ PRST-7430 [S]	Satisfaction	1966	$30
❏ PRLP-7430 [M]	Satisfaction	1966	$30
❏ PRST-7484 [S]	Soul Happening!	1967	$25
❏ PRLP-7484 [M]	Soul Happening!	1967	$30
❏ PRST-7704	The Best of Don Patterson	1969	$35
❏ PRST-7466 [S]	The Boss Men	1967	$30
❏ PRLP-7466 [M]	The Boss Men	1967	$30
❏ PRST-7331 [S]	The Exciting New Organ of Don Patterson	1964	$30
❏ PRLP-7331 [M]	The Exiting New Organ of Don Patterson	1964	$30
❏ PRST-7852	Tune Up	1971	$35

PATTERSON, KELLEE
Female singer.
Albums

BLACK JAZZ
| ❏ QD-12 | Maiden Voyage | 1974 | $25 |

PATTON, "BIG" JOHN
Organist.
Albums

BLUE NOTE
| ❏ BST-84340 [S] | Accent on the Blues | 1970 | $30 |
| — With "A Division of Liberty Records" on label |
| ❏ BLP-4130 [M] | Along Came John | 1963 | $60 |
| ❏ BST-84130 [S] | Along Came John | 1963 | $40 |
| — With "New York, USA" address on label |
| ❏ BST-84130 [S] | Along Came John | 1967 | $35 |
| — With "A Division of Liberty Records" on label |
| ❏ BLP-4143 [M] | Blue John | 1963 | $0 |
| — Canceled |
| ❏ BST-84143 [S] | Blue John | 1986 | $30 |
| — The Finest in Jazz Since 1939" issue; originally scheduled for 1963 release, but canceled |
| ❏ BLP-4229 [M] | Got a Good Thing Goin' | 1966 | $60 |
| ❏ BST-84229 [S] | Got a Good Thing Goin' | 1966 | $30 |
| — With "New York, USA" address on label |
| ❏ BST-84229 [S] | Got a Good Thing Goin' | 1967 | $35 |
| — With "A Division of Liberty Records" on label |
| ❏ BLP-4239 [M] | Let 'Em Roll | 1966 | $60 |
| ❏ BST-84239 [S] | Let 'Em Roll | 1966 | $30 |
| — With "New York, USA" address on label |
| ❏ BST-84239 [S] | Let 'Em Roll | 1967 | $35 |
| — With "A Division of Liberty Records" on label |
| ❏ BLP-4192 [M] | Oh Baby! | 1964 | $60 |
| ❏ BST-84192 [S] | Oh Baby! | 1964 | $30 |
| — With "New York, USA" address on label |
| ❏ BST-84192 [S] | Oh Baby! | 1967 | $35 |
| — With "A Division of Liberty Records" on label |
| ❏ BST-84281 [S] | That Certain Feeling | 1968 | $30 |
| — With "A Division of Liberty Records" on label |
| ❏ BLP-4174 [M] | The Way I Feel | 1964 | $60 |
| ❏ BST-84174 [S] | The Way I Feel | 1964 | $30 |
| — With "New York, USA" address on label |
| ❏ BST-84174 [S] | The Way I Feel | 1967 | $35 |
| — With "A Division of Liberty Records" on label |
| ❏ BST-84306 [S] | Understanding | 1969 | $30 |
| — With "A Division of Liberty Records" on label |

PAULIN, DOC
Trumpeter and bandleader.
Albums

FOLKWAYS
| ❏ FA2856 | Doc Paulin's Marching Band | 198? | $30 |

PAULO, MICHAEL
Saxophone player.
Albums

MCA
| ❏ 42295 | One Passion | 1989 | $30 |

PAVAGEAU, ALCIDE "SLOW DRAG
Bass player and bandleader.
Albums

GHB
| ❏ GHB-54 | Half Fast Jazz Band | 196? | $35 |

PAXTON, GEORGE
Saxophone player, bandleader and arranger.
Albums

HINDSIGHT
| ❏ HSR-184 | George Paxton and His Orchestra 1944-45 | 198? | $25 |

PAYNE, BENNIE
Pianist and male singer.
Albums

KAPP
| ❏ KL-1004 [M] | Bennie Payne Plays and Sings | 1955 | $80 |

PAYNE, CECIL, AND DUKE JORDAN
Also see each artist's individual listings.
Albums

MUSE
| ❏ MR-5015 | Brooklyn Brothers | 1974 | $35 |

PAYNE, CECIL
Baritone saxophone (and sometimes alto saxophone) player. Also see RANDY WESTON.
Albums

CHARLIE PARKER
❏ PLP-801 [M]	Cecil Payne Performing Charlie Parker's Music	1962	$40
❏ PLP-801S [S]	Cecil Payne Performing Charlie Parker's Music	1962	$50
❏ PLP-506 [M]	Shaw Nuff	1962	$30
❏ PLP-506S [S]	Shaw Nuff	1962	$30

MUSE
| ❏ MR-5061 | Bird Gets the Worm | 1976 | $30 |

SAVOY
| ❏ MG-12147 [M] | Patterns of Jazz | 1959 | $80 |

SAVOY JAZZ
| ❏ SJL-1167 | Patterns | 1986 | $25 |

SIGNAL
| ❏ S-1203 [M] | Cecil Payne Quintet and Quartet | 1955 | $600 |

STRATA-EAST
| ❏ SES-19734 | The Zodiac | 1973 | $30 |

PAYNE, FREDA
Earlier material appears in the Goldmine Standard Catalog of American Records 1950-1975. (SC2) Female singer better known for her work in R&B and soul music.
Albums

ABC IMPULSE!
| ❏ AS-53 [S] | After the Lights Go Down Low…And Much More | 1968 | $35 |

IMPULSE!
| ❏ A-53 [M] | After the Lights Go Down Low…And Much More | 1964 | $200 |
| ❏ AS-53 [S] | After the Lights Go Down Low…And Much More | 1964 | $160 |

PAYNE, JOHN, AND LOUIS LEVIN
Payne plays flute and saxophone; Levin is a keyboard player.
Albums

ARISTA/FREEDOM
| ❏ AF1025 | Bedtime | 1976 | $30 |
| ❏ AF1036 | The Razor's Edge | 1976 | $30 |

MERCURY
| ❏ SRM-1-1166 | John Payne/Louis Levin Band | 1977 | $25 |

PEACOCK, GARY
Bass player.
Albums

ECM
❏ 1119	December Poems	1979	$30
❏ 1165	Shift in the Wind	1981	$25
❏ 1101	Tale of Another	1977	$30
❏ 1210	Voice from the Past	1982	$25

PEAGLER, CURTIS
Alto and tenor saxophone player.
Albums

PABLO
| ❏ 2310930 | I'll Be Around | 1988 | $25 |

PEARSON, DUKE
Pianist, composer and arranger.
Albums

ATLANTIC
❏ 3002 [M]	Honeybuns	196?	$35
❏ SD3002 [S]	Honeybuns	196?	$35
❏ SD3005	Prairie Dog	196?	$35

BLUE NOTE
❏ BST-84344	How Insensitive	1970	$50
❏ B1-35220	I Don't Care Who Knows It	1996	$30
❏ BST-84276	Introducing Duke Pearson's Big Band	1968	$60

Number	Title	Yr	NM
❏ BN-LA317-G	It Could Only Happen with You	1974	$35
❏ BST-84323	Merry Ole Soul	1970	$50
❏ BST-84308	Now Hear This	1969	$60
❏ BLP-4022 [M]	Profile -- Duke Pearson	1959	$400

—Deep groove" version (deep indentation under label on both sides)

❏ BLP-4022 [M]	Profile -- Duke Pearson	1959	$150

—Regular version with W. 63rd St. address on label

❏ BLP-4022 [M]	Profile -- Duke Pearson	1963	$100

—With New York, USA address on label

❏ BST-84022 [S]	Profile -- Duke Pearson	1959	$120

—With W. 63rd St. address on label

❏ BST-84022 [S]	Profile -- Duke Pearson	1963	$50

—With New York, USA address on label

❏ BST-84022 [S]	Profile -- Duke Pearson	1967	$30

—With "A Division of Liberty Records" on label

❏ BLP-4252 [M]	Sweet Honey Bee	1966	$100
❏ BST-84252 [S]	Sweet Honey Bee	1966	$60

—With New York, USA address on label

❏ BST-84252 [S]	Sweet Honey Bee	1967	$30

—With "A Division of Liberty Records" on label

❏ B1-89792	Sweet Honey Bee	1993	$30

—Reissue of 84252

❏ BLP-4035 [M]	Tender Feelin's	1960	$500

—Deep groove" version (deep indentation under label on both sides)

❏ BLP-4035 [M]	Tender Feelin's	1960	$150

—Regular version with W. 63rd St. address on label

❏ BLP-4035 [M]	Tender Feelin's	1963	$100

—With New York, USA address on label

❏ BST-84035 [S]	Tender Feelin's	1960	$120

—With W. 63rd St. address on label

❏ BST-84035 [S]	Tender Feelin's	1963	$50

—With New York, USA address on label

❏ BST-84035 [S]	Tender Feelin's	1967	$30

—With "A Division of Liberty Records" on label

❏ BST-84293	The Phantom	1969	$60
❏ BST-84267	The Right Touch	1968	$60
❏ B1-28269	The Right Touch	1994	$30

—Reissue of 84267

❏ BLP-4191 [M]	Wahoo!	1965	$100
❏ BST-84191 [S]	Wahoo!	1965	$60

—With New York, USA address on label

❏ BST-84191 [S]	Wahoo!	1967	$30

—With "A Division of Liberty Records" on label

❏ B1-84191	Wahoo!	1986	$30

—The Finest in Jazz Since 1939" reissue

JAZZTIME

❏ 33-02 [M]	Hush!	1962	$700

PRESTIGE

❏ PRST-7729	Dedication	1970	$35

PECORA, SANTO
Trombonist. Also see LU WATTERS.

Albums
CLEF

❏ MGC-123 [10]	Santo Pecora Collates	1953	$300

—With either Mercury or Clef cover; all labels are Clef

MERCURY

❏ MGC-123 [10]	Dixieland Jazz Band	1953	$0

—Canceled; released on Clef 123

SOUTHLAND

❏ SLP-213 [M]	Santo Pecora	1955	$60

VIK

❏ XLA-1081 [M]	Dixieland Mardi Gras	1957	$50

PEDICIN, MICHAEL, JR.
Saxophone player.

Albums
OPTIMISM

❏ OP-3211	Angles	1989	$30
❏ OP-3106	City Song	198?	$25

PEIFFER, BERNARD
Pianist and composer. Also see DON BYAS.

Albums
DECCA

❏ DL9203 [M]	Piano Ala Mood	1958	$100
❏ DL79203 [S]	Piano Ala Mood	1958	$100
❏ DL8626 [M]	The Astounding Bernard Peiffer	1958	$120
❏ DL9218 [M]	The Pied Peiffer of the Piano	1959	$80
❏ DL79218 [S]	The Pied Peiffer of the Piano	1959	$80

EMARCY

❏ MG-36080 [M]	Bernie's Tunes	1956	$200
❏ MG-26036 [10]	Le Most	1954	$200

LAURIE

❏ LLP-1008 [M]	Cole Porter's "Can Can	1960	$30
❏ SLP-1008 [S]	Cole Porter's "Can Can	1960	$30
❏ LLP-1006 [M]	Modern Jazz for People Who Like Original Music	1960	$250
❏ SLP-1006 [S]	Modern Jazz for People Who Like Original Music	1960	$250

NORGRAN

❏ MGN-11 [10]	Bernard Peiffer Et Son Trio	1954	$150

PELL, DAVE, AND JOE WILLIAMS
Also see each artist's individual listings.

Albums
GNP CRESCENDO

❏ GNPS-2124	Prez & Joe: In Celebration of Lester Young	1979	$25

PELL, DAVE
Saxophone player and clarinetist. Also see LUCY ANN POLK.

Albums
ATLANTIC

❏ 1216 [M]	Jazz and Romantic Places	1955	$300

—Black label

❏ 1216 [M]	Jazz and Romantic Places	1961	$150

—Multicolor label, white "fan" logo at right

❏ 1249 [M]	Love Story	1956	$300

—Black label

❏ 1249 [M]	Love Story	1961	$150

—Multicolor label, white "fan" logo at right

CAPITOL

❏ T925 [M]	I Had the Craziest Dream	1958	$60

—Turquoise label

❏ T1687 [M]	I Remember John Kirby	1962	$50
❏ ST1687 [S]	I Remember John Kirby	1962	$60
❏ T1512 [M]	Old South Wails	1961	$25
❏ ST1512 [S]	Old South Wails	1961	$60
❏ T1309 [M]	The Big Small Bands	1960	$40
❏ ST1309 [S]	The Big Small Bands	1960	$60

CORAL

❏ CRL57248 [M]	Swingin' School Songs	1958	$30
❏ CRL757248 [S]	Swingin' School Songs	1958	$30

GNP CRESCENDO

❏ GNPS-2122	Prez Conference	1978	$25

HEADFIRST

❏ 715	Live at Alfonse's	198?	$30

KAPP

❏ KL-1034 [M]	Dave Pell Plays Burke and Van Heusen	1956	$40
❏ KL-1036 [M]	Dave Pell Plays Irving Berlin	1957	$40
❏ KL-1025 [M]	Dave Pell Plays Rodgers and Hart	1956	$30

LIBERTY

❏ LRP-3321 [M]	Jazz Voices in Video	1963	$35
❏ LST-7321 [S]	Jazz Voices in Video	1963	$25
❏ LST-7631 [S]	Man-Ha-Man-Ha	1969	$35
❏ LST-7298 [S]	Today;s Hits in Jazz	1961	$25
❏ LRP-3298 [M]	Today's Hits in Jazz	1961	$35

PRI

❏ 3003 [M]	Dave Pell Plays Artie Shaw's Big Band Sounds	196?	$25
❏ 3004 [M]	Dave Pell Plays Benny Goodman's Big Band Sounds	196?	$25
❏ 3007 [M]	Dave Pell Plays Duke Ellington's Big Band Sounds	196?	$25
❏ 3002 [M]	Dave Pell Plays Harry James' Big Band Sounds	196?	$25
❏ 3005 [M]	Dave Pell Plays Lawrence Welk's Big Band Sounds	196?	$25
❏ 3009 [M]	Dave Pell Plays Mantovani's Big Band Sounds	196?	$25
❏ 3006 [M]	Dave Pell Plays Perez Prado's Big Band Sounds	196?	$25
❏ 3011 [M]	Dave Pell Plays the Big Band Sounds	196?	$25
❏ 3010 [M]	Dave Pell Plays the Dorsey Brothers' Big Band Sounds	196?	$25

RCA VICTOR

❏ LPM-1662 [M]	Campus Hop	1957	$50
❏ LPM-1320 [M]	Jazz Goes Dancing	1956	$50
❏ LPM-1524 [M]	Pell of a Time	1957	$50
❏ LPM-1394 [M]	Swingin' in the Ol' Corral	1957	$50

TREND

❏ TL-1003 [10]	Dave Pell Plays Irving Berlin	1953	$120
❏ TL-1501 [M]	Dave Pell Plays Rodgers and Hart	1954	$100

PEMBROKE, MIKE

Albums
JAZZOLOGY

❏ J-24	Mike Pembroke's Hot Seven	197?	$25

PENAZZI, ANDRE
Percussionist.

Albums
DAUNTLESS

❏ 7020 [S]	Organ Jazz Samba Percussion	1963	$25
❏ 2020 [M]	Organ Jazz Samba Percussion	1963	$35

PENSYL, KIM
Pianist.

Albums
OPTIMISM

❏ OP-3210	Pensyl Sketches #1	1988	$25

PENTAGON
Led by Cedar Walton.

Albums
EAST WIND

❏ 10002	Pentagon	1979	$50

PEPLOWSKI, KEN
Clarinetist, also an alto and tenor saxophone player.

Albums
CONCORD JAZZ

❏ CJ-344	Double Exposure	1988	$25
❏ CJ-376	Sonny Side	1989	$30

PEPPER, ART
Alto saxophone player; also a tenor sax man and clarinetist. Also see CHET BAKER.

Albums
ANALOGUE PRODUCTIONS

❏ AP 017	Art Pepper + Eleven: Modern Jazz Classics	199?	$30

—Reissue on audiophile vinyl

❏ AP 010	Art Pepper Meets the Rhythm Section	199?	$30

—Reissue on audiophile vinyl

❏ AP 012	Smack Up!	199?	$30

—Reissue on audiophile vinyl

❏ APR3013	So in Love	199?	$35
❏ APR3014	The Intimate Art Pepper	199?	$35
❏ APR3012	The New York Album	199?	$35

ARTISTS HOUSE

❏ AH9412	So in Love	1979	$35

BLUE NOTE

❏ BN-LA591-H2	Early Art	1976	$60
❏ LT-1064	Omega Alpha	1980	$50

CONTEMPORARY

❏ C-7650	Art Pepper at the Village Vanguard, Vol. 4: More for Les	1986	$35
❏ M-3568 [M]	Art Pepper + Eleven: Modern Jazz Classics	1959	$250
❏ S-7568 [S]	Art Pepper + Eleven: Modern Jazz Classics	1959	$250
❏ C-3532 [M]	Art Pepper Meets the Rhythm Section	1957	$700
❏ S-7532 [S]	Art Pepper Meets the Rhythm Section	1959	$250
❏ S-7643	Friday Night at the Village Vanguard	1980	$35
❏ M-3573 [M]	Gettin' Together!	1960	$250
❏ S-7573 [S]	Gettin' Together!	1960	$250
❏ M-3607 [M]	Intensity	1963	$200
❏ S-7607 [S]	Intensity	1963	$200
❏ S-7633	Living Legend	1975	$50
❏ S-7639	No Limit	1978	$50
❏ C-7644	Saturday Night at the Village Vanguard	198?	$35
❏ M-3602 [M]	Smack Up!	1961	$200
❏ S-7602 [S]	Smack Up!	1961	$200

Bill Perkins and Richie Kamuca, *Tenors Head-On*, Liberty LRP-3051, **$80**.

Oscar Peterson, *Night Train Vol. 2*, Verve V6-8740, **$35**.

Oscar Pettiford, *O.P.'s Jazz Men*, ABC Paramount ABCS-227, stereo, **$100**.

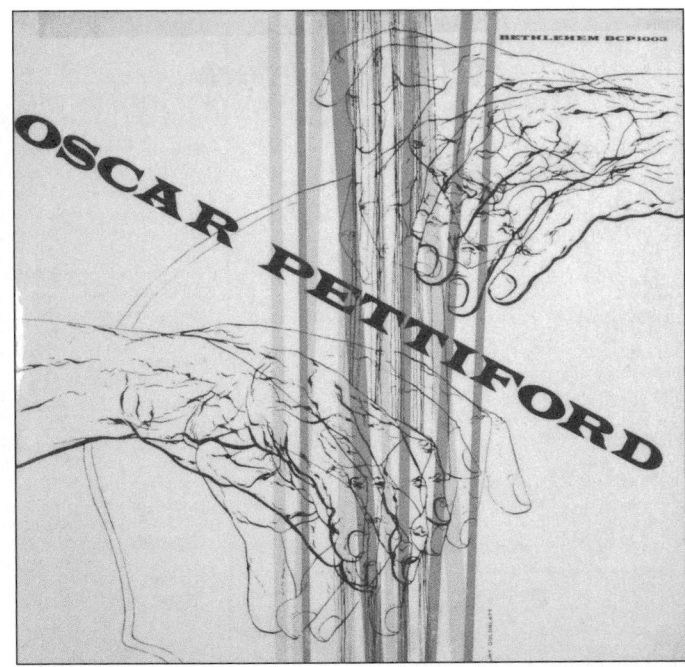

Oscar Pettiford, *Oscar Pettiford*, Bethlehem BCP-1003, 10-inch LP, **$250**.

Number	Title	Yr	NM
❏ S-7638	The Trip	1977	$50
❏ S-7630	The Way It Was!	1972	$50
—Originals have orange labels			
❏ S-7642	Thursday Night at the Village Vanguard	1979	$50
DISCOVERY			
❏ DS-837	Among Friends	1981	$50
❏ 3019 [10]	Art Pepper Quartet	1952	$600
❏ 3023 [10]	Art Pepper Quintet	1954	$600
FANTASY			
❏ OJC-338	Art Pepper Meets the Rhythm Section	198?	$30
❏ OJC-474	Art Pepper Today	1990	$35
❏ OJC-695	Friday Night at the Village Vanguard	199?	$30
❏ OJC-169	Gettin' Together	198?	$30
❏ OJC-387	Intensity	1989	$30
❏ OJC-408	Living Legend	1990	$35
❏ OJC-341	Modern Jazz Classics	198?	$30
❏ OJC-411	No Limit	1990	$35
❏ OJC-696	Saturday Night at the Village Vanguard	199?	$30
❏ OJC-176	Smack Up!	198?	$30
❏ OJC-475	Straight Life	1990	$35
❏ OJC-410	The Trip	1990	$35
❏ OJC-389	The Way It Was	1989	$30
GALAXY			
❏ GXY-5145	Art Lives	1983	$35
❏ GXY-5151	Art Pepper Quartet: The Maiden Voyage Sessions, Part 3	198?	$50
❏ GXY-5119	Art Pepper Today	1979	$35
❏ GXY-5148	Art Works	1984	$35
❏ GXY-5143	Goin' Home	1982	$35
❏ GXY-5128	Landscape	1980	$50
❏ GXY-5141	One September Afternoon	1981	$50
❏ GXY-5142	Roadgame	1982	$30
❏ GXY-5127	Straight Life	1979	$30
❏ GXY-5147	Tete-a-Tete	198?	$35
❏ GXY-5154	The New York Album	1985	$50
❏ GXY-5140	Winter Moon	1980	$35
INTERLUDE			
❏ MO-512 [M]	Art Pepper Quartet	1959	$50
❏ ST-1012 [S]	Art Pepper Quartet	1959	$40
INTERPLAY			
❏ 7718	Among Friends	1979	$50
INTRO			
❏ 606 [M]	Modern Art	1957	$2500
JAZZ WEST			
❏ JLP-10 [M]	The Return of Art Pepper	1956	$600
MOSAIC			
❏ MR3-105	The Complete Pacific Jazz Small Group Recordings of Art Pepper	198?	$80
ONYX			
❏ 219	Omega Man	197?	$25
	Omega Man		
PACIFIC JAZZ			
❏ PJ-60 [M]	The Artistry of Pepper	1962	$40
SAVOY			
❏ MG-12089 [M]	Surf Ride	1956	$100
SAVOY JAZZ			
❏ SJL-2217	Discoveries	197?	$35
SCORE			
❏ SLP-4030 [M]	Modern Art	1958	$250
❏ SLP-4031 [M]	The Art Pepper-Red Norvo Sextet	1958	$100
❏ SLP-4032 [M]	The Return of Art Pepper	1958	$100
STEREO RECORDS			
❏ S-7018 [S]	Art Pepper Meets the Rhythm Section	1958	$80
TAMPA			
❏ TP-20 [M]	Art Pepper Quartet	1957	$500
—Red vinyl			
❏ TP-20 [M]	Art Pepper Quartet	1958	$300
—Black vinyl			
❏ TS-1001 [S]	Art Pepper Quartet	1959	$1250
XANADU			
❏ 108	The Early Show	197?	$25
❏ 117	The Late Show	198?	$25

PEPPER, ART/SHELLY MANNE
Also see each artist's individual listings.

Albums

Number	Title	Yr	NM
CHARLIE PARKER			
❏ PLP-836 [M]	Pepper/Manne	1963	$30
❏ PLP-836S [S]	Pepper/Manne	1963	$30

Number	Title	Yr	NM

PEPPER, ART/SONNY REDD
Also see each artist's individual listings.

Albums

Number	Title	Yr	NM
REGENT			
❏ MG-6069 [M]	Two Altos	1959	$50
SAVOY			
❏ MG-12215 [M]	Art Pepper-Sonny Redd	1969	$25

PEPPER, JIM
Tenor saxophone player, composer and male singer.

Albums

Number	Title	Yr	NM
EMBRYO			
❏ SD-731	Pepper's Powwow	196?	$40

PERAZA, ARMANDO
Percussionist and occasional male singer.

Albums

Number	Title	Yr	NM
SKYE			
❏ S-5D	Wild Thing	1970	$35

PERIGEO
Fusion band from Italy: Franco D'Andrea (piano); Claudio Fassoli (tenor and soprano saxophones); Giovanni Tommaso (bass); others.

Albums

Number	Title	Yr	NM
RCA VICTOR			
❏ TPL1-1228	Fata Morgana	197?	$35
❏ TPL1-1080	Genealogia	197?	$35
❏ TPL1-1175	The Valley of the Temples	197?	$35
❏ APL1-1175	The Valley of the Temples	197?	$30
—Reissue with new prefix			

PERKINS, BILL, AND RICHIE KAMUCA
Also see each artist's individual listings.

Albums

Number	Title	Yr	NM
LIBERTY			
❏ LRP-3051 [M]	Tenors Head On	1957	$80

PERKINS, BILL, AND THE SAN FRANCISCANS

Albums

Number	Title	Yr	NM
FAMOUS DOOR			
❏ 128	The Other Bill	197?	$25

PERKINS, BILL; ART PEPPER; RICHIE KAMUCA
Also see each artist's individual listings.

Albums

Number	Title	Yr	NM
PACIFIC JAZZ			
❏ PJM-401 [M]	Just Friends	1956	$200
WORLD PACIFIC			
❏ PJM-401 [M]	Just Friends	1958	$250

PERKINS, BILL
Mostly a tenor saxophone player, but has played both soprano and baritone saxes on record. Also see AL COHN; THE FIVE.

Albums

Number	Title	Yr	NM
CONTEMPORARY			
❏ C-14011	Journey to the East	1985	$30
INTERPLAY			
❏ 7721	Confluence	1979	$60
❏ 8606	Remembrance of Dino's	1990	$30
LIBERTY			
❏ LRP-3293 [M]	Bossa Nova with Strings Attached	1963	$40
❏ LST-7293 [S]	Bossa Nova with Strings Attached	1963	$50
PACIFIC JAZZ			
❏ PJ-1221 [M]	The Bill Perkins Octet On Stage	1956	$120
RIVERSIDE			
❏ RS-3052	Quietly There	1969	$100
SEA BREEZE			
❏ SB-2006	Many Ways to Go	1980	$25
WORLD PACIFIC			
❏ WP-1221 [M]	The Bill Perkins Octet On Stage	1958	$150

Number	Title	Yr	NM

PERKINS, CARL (2)
Pianist. Not to be confused with the rock 'n' roll singer of the same name.

Albums

Number	Title	Yr	NM
DOOTO			
❏ DL-211 [M]	Introducing Carl Perkins	196?	$35
DOOTONE			
❏ DL-211 [M]	Introducing Carl Perkins	1956	$120
—Black vinyl			
❏ DL-211 [M]	Introducing Carl Perkins	1956	$200
—Red vinyl			

PERRI
Vocal quartet: Carolyn, Darlene, Lori and Sharon Perry.

Albums

Number	Title	Yr	NM
ZEBRA			
❏ ZEB-5684	Celebrate!	1986	$25
❏ ZR-5007	Perri	198?	$30
❏ ZEB-42017	The Flight	1987	$25

PERSIP, CHARLIE
Drummer. Also see THE MODERN JAZZ SEXTET.

Albums

Number	Title	Yr	NM
BETHLEHEM			
❏ BCP-6046 [M]	Charlie Persip and the Jazz Statesmen	1960	$200
❏ SBCP-6046 [S]	Charlie Persip and the Jazz Statesmen	1960	$200
❏ BCP-6046	Right Down Front	197?	$30
—Reissue, distributed by RCA Victor			
SOUL NOTE			
❏ SN-1079	In Case You Missed It	1985	$30
❏ 121179	No Dummies Allowed	1990	$35
STASH			
❏ ST-209	The Charlie Persip & Gerry LaFum Superband	198?	$25

PERSON, HOUSTON
Tenor saxophone player.

Albums

Number	Title	Yr	NM
20TH CENTURY			
❏ W-205	Houston Person	196?	$30
FANTASY			
❏ OJC-332	Goodness!	1988	$25
MERCURY			
❏ SRM-1-1151	Harmony	1977	$30
❏ SRM-1-1104	Pure Pleasure	1976	$30
MUSE			
❏ MR-5289	Always on My Mind	1986	$25
❏ MR-5344	Basics	1989	$30
❏ MR-5260	Heavy Juice	1982	$25
❏ MR-5376	Something in Common	1989	$30
❏ MR-5110	Stolen Sweets	1977	$30
❏ MR-5199	Suspicions	1980	$30
❏ MR-5136	The Big Horn	197?	$30
❏ MR-5178	The Nearness of You	197?	$30
❏ MR-5331	The Talk of the Town	1987	$25
❏ MR-5231	Very Personal	1981	$25
❏ MR-5433	Why Not!	1991	$35
❏ MR-5161	Wild Flower	1977	$30
PRESTIGE			
❏ 10044	Broken Windows, Empty Hallways	1972	$25
❏ PRST-7517	Chocomotive	1968	$25
❏ PRST-7678	Goodness!	1969	$25
❏ 10017	Houston Express	1971	$25
❏ 10003	Person to Person	1971	$30
❏ PRST-7621	Soul Dance!	1969	$25
❏ 10055	Sweet Buns and Barbeque	1973	$25
❏ PRST-7779	The Best of Houston Person	1970	$35
❏ PRST-7767	The Truth!	1970	$25
❏ PRST-7548	Trust in Me	1968	$25
❏ PRLP-7491 [M]	Underground Soul	1967	$30
❏ PRST-7491 [S]	Underground Soul	1967	$25
SAVOY			
❏ 14471	Gospel Soul	197?	$30
WESTBOUND			
❏ 213	Get Outa My Way	1975	$35
❏ 205	Houston Person '75	1975	$35

PERSSON, AAKE
Trombonist.

Albums

Number	Title	Yr	NM
EMARCY			
❏ MG-26039 [10]	Swedish Modern	1954	$200

PERSSON, AAKE/ARNE DOMNERUS
Also see each artist's individual listings.

Albums
PRESTIGE

Number	Title	Yr	NM
❏ PRLP-173 [10]	Aake Persson Swedish All Stars	1953	$350

PERSSON, BENT
Trumpeter and cornet player.

Albums
STOMP OFF

Number	Title	Yr	NM
❏ SOS-1167	Livin' High in London	198?	$25

PERUNA JAZZMEN, THE
Members: Mikael Zuschlag (first cornet); Peter Aller (second cornet); Claus Forchhammer (clarinet); Arne Hojberg (trombone, leader); Anette Strauss (piano, vocals); John Neess (banjo); Mik "Count" Schack (washboard); Leo Hechmann (sousaphone).

Albums
STOMP OFF

Number	Title	Yr	NM
❏ SOS-1003	Come On and Stomp, Stomp, Stomp	1981	$25
❏ SOS-1020	Mean Blues	198?	$25
❏ SOS-1105	Smoke House Blues	1986	$25

PETERSEN, EDWARD
Tenor saxophone player.

Albums
DELMARK

Number	Title	Yr	NM
❏ DS-445	Upward Spiral	1990	$30

PETERSON, HANNIBAL MARVIN
Trumpeter, percussionist and male singer.

Albums
ENJA

Number	Title	Yr	NM
❏ 3085	Angels of Atlanta	1981	$30

INNER CITY

Number	Title	Yr	NM
❏ IC-3020	Antibes	197?	$35

PETERSON, JEANNE ARLAND
Pianist and female singer.

Albums
CELEBRATION

Number	Title	Yr	NM
❏ 5004	Jeanne Arland Peterson	197?	$35

PETERSON, OSCAR, AND HERB ELLIS
Also see each artist's individual listings.

Albums
BASF

Number	Title	Yr	NM
❏ 20723	Hello Herbie	1969	$35

PAUSA

Number	Title	Yr	NM
❏ PR7085	Hello Herbie	1981	$25

—Reissue

PETERSON, OSCAR, AND MILT JACKSON

Albums
PABLO

Number	Title	Yr	NM
❏ 2310881	Two of the Few	1983	$30

PETERSON, OSCAR, AND STEPHANE GRAPPELLI
Also see each artist's individual listings.

Albums
JAZZ MAN

Number	Title	Yr	NM
❏ 5054	Time After Time	1983	$30

PABLO

Number	Title	Yr	NM
❏ 2310907	Violins No End	198?	$30

—With Stuff Smith

PRESTIGE

Number	Title	Yr	NM
❏ 24041	Oscar Peterson Featuring Stephane Grappelli	1974	$35

PETERSON, OSCAR
Pianist and bandleader. Also see LOUIS ARMSTRONG; BUDDY DeFRANCO; STAN GETZ; COLEMAN HAWKINS; BILL HENDERSON; SONNY STITT; BEN WEBSTER; LESTER YOUNG.

Albums
AMERICAN RECORDING SOCIETY

Number	Title	Yr	NM
❏ G-415 [M]	An Oscar for Peterson	1957	$40
❏ G-438 [M]	Oscar Peterson Trio at Newport	1957	$40

BASF

Number	Title	Yr	NM
❏ 20869	Another Day	1975	$35
❏ MC20668	A Rare Mood	1976	$35
❏ 25101	Exclusively for My Friends	1972	$35
❏ MC21281	Great Connection	1974	$35
❏ 25156	In a Mellow Mood	1973	$35
❏ 20905	In Tune	1973	$30
❏ 20713	Motions and Emotions	1972	$30
❏ 20908	Reunion Blues	1973	$35
❏ MC20879	Tracks	1974	$35
❏ 20734	Tristeza on Piano	1972	$30
❏ 20868	Walking the Line	1973	$150

BOOK-OF-THE-MONTH

Number	Title	Yr	NM
❏ 61-7546	Easy Does It	1984	$60

CLEF

Number	Title	Yr	NM
❏ MGC-698 [M]	An Evening with the Oscar Peterson Duo/Quartet	1956	$250
❏ MGC-697 [M]	Keyboard Music by Oscar Peterson	1956	$250
❏ MGC-695 [M]	Nostalgic Memories by Oscar Peterson	1956	$250
❏ MGC-107 [10]	Oscar Peterson at Carnegie Hall	1951	$350
❏ MGC-110 [10]	Oscar Peterson Collates	1952	$350
❏ MGC-127 [10]	Oscar Peterson Collates No. 2	1953	$300
❏ MGC-106 [10]	Oscar Peterson Piano Solos	1951	$300

—Reissue of Mercury 25024

Number	Title	Yr	NM
❏ MGC-603 [M]	Oscar Peterson Plays Cole Porter	1953	$300
❏ MGC-708 [M]	Oscar Peterson Plays Count Basie	1956	$250
❏ MGC-606 [M]	Oscar Peterson Plays Duke Ellington	1953	$300
❏ MGC-605 [M]	Oscar Peterson Plays George Gershwin	1953	$300
❏ MGC-649 [M]	Oscar Peterson Plays Harold Arlen	1955	$250
❏ MGC-648 [M]	Oscar Peterson Plays Harry Warren	1955	$250
❏ MGC-604 [M]	Oscar Peterson Plays Irving Berlin	1953	$300
❏ MGC-623 [M]	Oscar Peterson Plays Jerome Kern	1954	$250
❏ MGC-650 [M]	Oscar Peterson Plays Jimmy McHugh	1955	$250
❏ MGC-119 [10]	Oscar Peterson Plays Pretty	1952	$350
❏ MGC-155 [10]	Oscar Peterson Plays Pretty No. 2	1954	$300
❏ MGC-624 [M]	Oscar Peterson Plays Richard Rodgers	1954	$250
❏ MGC-625 [M]	Oscar Peterson Plays Vincent Youmans	1954	$250
❏ MGC-145 [10]	Oscar Peterson Sings	1954	$300
❏ MGC-694 [M]	Recital by Oscar Peterson	1956	$250
❏ MGC-696 [M]	Tenderly -- Music by Oscar Peterson	1956	$250
❏ MGC-116 [10]	The Oscar Peterson Quartet	1952	$350
❏ MGC-688 [M]	The Oscar Peterson Quartet	1956	$250

—Reissue of 116

Number	Title	Yr	NM
❏ MGC-168 [10]	The Oscar Peterson Quartet No. 2	1954	$300

DCC COMPACT CLASSICS

Number	Title	Yr	NM
❏ LPZ-2021	West Side Story	1996	$175

—Audiophile vinyl

EMARCY

Number	Title	Yr	NM
❏ 405	Oscar Peterson Trio Transition	1976	$35

FANTASY

Number	Title	Yr	NM
❏ OJC-383	Oscar Peterson and the Bassists -- Montreux '77	1989	$25
❏ OJC-378	Oscar Peterson Jam -- Montreux '77	1989	$25
❏ OJC-498	Skol	1991	$25
❏ OJC-627	The Good Life	1991	$25
❏ OJC-603	Trumpet Summit Meets the Oscar Peterson Big Four	1991	$25

LIMELIGHT

Number	Title	Yr	NM
❏ LM-82039 [M]	Blues Etude	1966	$35
❏ LS-86039 [S]	Blues Etude	1966	$35
❏ LM-82010 [M]	Canadiana Suite	1965	$35
❏ LM-82023 [M]	Eloquence	1965	$35
❏ LS-86023 [S]	Eloquence	1965	$50
❏ LM-82044 [M]	Soul Espanol	1967	$50
❏ LS-86044 [S]	Soul Espanol	1967	$35
❏ LM-82029 [M]	With Respect to Nat	1966	$35
❏ LS-86029 [S]	With Respect to Nat	1966	$50

MERCURY

Number	Title	Yr	NM
❏ MGC-107 [10]	Oscar Peterson at Carnegie Hall	1951	$300
❏ MGC-110 [10]	Oscar Peterson Collates	1952	$300
❏ MG-25024 [10]	Oscar Peterson Piano Solos	1950	$250
❏ MGC-106 [10]	Oscar Peterson Piano Solos	1951	$300
❏ MGC-603 [M]	Oscar Peterson Plays Cole Porter	1953	$300
❏ MGC-606 [M]	Oscar Peterson Plays Duke Ellington	1953	$300
❏ MGC-605 [M]	Oscar Peterson Plays George Gershwin	1953	$300
❏ MGC-604 [M]	Oscar Peterson Plays Irving Berlin	1953	$300
❏ MGC-119 [10]	Oscar Peterson Plays Pretty	1952	$300
❏ MG-20975 [M]	Oscar Peterson Trio + One	1964	$100
❏ SR-60975 [S]	Oscar Peterson Trio + One	1964	$100
❏ MGC-116 [10]	The Oscar Peterson Quartet	1952	$300

MGM

Number	Title	Yr	NM
❏ GAS-133	Oscar Peterson (Golden Archive Series)	1970	$30

MOBILE FIDELITY

Number	Title	Yr	NM
❏ 1-243	Very Tall	1995	$100

—Audiophile vinyl

PABLO

Number	Title	Yr	NM
❏ 2625705	A Salle Pleyel	1975	$35
❏ 2640101	Freedom Songbook	1983	$35
❏ 2310796	Giants	1977	$30
❏ 2625702	History of An Artist	1975	$35
❏ 2310895	History of An Artist, Volume 2	1983	$30
❏ 2310918	If You Could See Me Now	1987	$25
❏ 2310817	Jousts	1979	$30
❏ 2310940	Live	1990	$25
❏ 2310747	Montreux '75	1976	$30
❏ 2310742	Oscar Peterson and Clark Terry	1976	$30
❏ 2310740	Oscar Peterson and Dizzy Gillespie	1976	$30
❏ 2310741	Oscar Peterson and Harry Edison	1976	$30
❏ 2310743	Oscar Peterson and Jon Faddis	1976	$30
❏ 2310739	Oscar Peterson and Roy Eldridge	1976	$30
❏ 2310927	Oscar Peterson + Harry Edison + Eddie "Cleanhead" Vinson	1988	$25
❏ 2625711	Oscar Peterson in Russia	1976	$30
❏ 2310779	Porgy and Bess	1976	$30
❏ 2310701	The Trio	1975	$30

PABLO LIVE

Number	Title	Yr	NM
❏ 2308224	Digital at Montreux	1980	$30
❏ 2620115	Live at the Northsea Jazz Festival, 1980	1981	$35
❏ 2308231	Nigerian Marketplace	1982	$30
❏ 2308213	Oscar Peterson and the Bassists -- Montreux '77	1978	$30
❏ 2308208	Oscar Peterson Jam -- Montreux '77	1977	$30
❏ 2308232	Skol	1982	$30
❏ 2308241	The Good Life	1983	$30
❏ 2620111	The London Concert	1979	$35
❏ 2620112	The Paris Concert	1979	$35

PABLO TODAY

Number	Title	Yr	NM
❏ 2312129	A Royal Wedding Suite	198?	$30
❏ 2312108	Night Child	1979	$30
❏ 2313103	Silent Partner	1980	$30
❏ 2312135	The Personal Touch	1982	$30

PAUSA

Number	Title	Yr	NM
❏ PR7059	Action	1980	$25
❏ PR7135	Another Day	1983	$25

—Reissue of BASF 20869

Number	Title	Yr	NM
❏ PR7064	Girl Talk	1980	$25
❏ PR7113	Great Connection	1983	$25

—Reissue of BASF 21281

Number	Title	Yr	NM
❏ PR7073	In Tune	1980	$25

—Reissue of BASF 20905

Number	Title	Yr	NM
❏ PR7044	Mellow Mood	1979	$25
❏ PR7102	Motions and Emotions	1982	$25

—Reissue of BASF 20713

Number	Title	Yr	NM
❏ PR7069	My Favorite Instrument	1980	$25
❏ PR7099	Reunion Blues	1981	$25

—Reissue of BASF 20908

Number	Title	Yr	NM
❏ PR7080	The Way I Really Play	1981	$25
❏ PR7124	Tristeza on Piano	1983	$25

—Reissue of BASF 20734

PRESTIGE

Number	Title	Yr	NM
❏ PRST-7690	Easy Walker	1969	$35
❏ PRST-7649	Oscar Peterson Plays for Lovers	1969	$35
❏ PRST-7595	Soul-O!	1968	$35

Number	Title	Yr	NM
❏ PRST-7620	The Great Oscar Peterson on Prestige!	1969	$35

RCA VICTOR

Number	Title	Yr	NM
❏ LPT-3006 [10]	This Is Oscar Peterson	1952	$200

TRIP

Number	Title	Yr	NM
❏ 5560	Eloquence	197?	$25

VERVE

Number	Title	Yr	NM
❏ V-8516 [M]	Affinity	1963	$60
❏ V6-8516 [S]	Affinity	1963	$60
❏ MGV-2048 [M]	An Evening with Oscar Peterson	1957	$250
—Reissue of Clef 698			
❏ V-2048 [M]	An Evening with Oscar Peterson	1961	$50
❏ MGV-8287 [M]	A Night on the Town	1958	$120
❏ V-8287 [M]	A Night on the Town	1961	$50
❏ V6-8476 [S]	Bursting Out with the All Star Big Band!	1962	$60
❏ MGV-8399 [M]	Carnival	1960	$0
—Canceled			
❏ MGV-2002 [M]	In a Romantic Mood -- Oscar Peterson with Strings	1956	$200
❏ V-2002 [M]	In a Romantic Mood -- Oscar Peterson with Strings	1961	$50
❏ MGV-2047 [M]	Keyboard Music by Oscar Peterson	1957	$300
—Reissue of Clef 697			
❏ V-2047 [M]	Keyboard Music by Oscar Peterson	1961	$50
❏ MGV-8081 [M]	Keyboard Music by Oscar Peterson	1957	$150
—Canceled			
❏ 821289-1	Motions and Emotions	1984	$25
—Reissue			
❏ V-8538 [M]	Night Train	1963	$60
❏ V6-8538 [S]	Night Train	1963	$60
❏ BOMC 70-5601 [S]	Night Train	197?	$60
—Book-of-the-Month Club edition			
❏ V-8740 [M]	Night Train, Volume 2	1967	$50
❏ V6-8740 [S]	Night Train, Volume 2	1967	$35
❏ MGV-2045 [M]	Nostalgic Memories by Oscar Peterson	1957	$300
—Reissue of Clef 695			
❏ V-2045 [M]	Nostalgic Memories by Oscar Peterson	1961	$50
❏ MGV-8079 [M]	Nostalgic Memories by Oscar Peterson	1957	$150
—Canceled			
❏ UMV-2626	Oscar Peterson at the Concertgebouw	198?	$25
❏ UMV-2502	Oscar Peterson at the Stratford Shakespearean Festival	198?	$25
❏ MGV-2119 [M]	Oscar Peterson Plays "My Fair Lady	1958	$100
❏ MGVS-6060 [S]	Oscar Peterson Plays "My Fair Lady	1960	$100
❏ V-2119 [M]	Oscar Peterson Plays "My Fair Lady	1961	$50
❏ V6-2119 [S]	Oscar Peterson Plays "My Fair Lady	1961	$35
—Reissue of 6060			
❏ V-8581 [M]	Oscar Peterson Plays "My Fair Lady	1964	$35
❏ V6-8581 [S]	Oscar Peterson Plays "My Fair Lady	1964	$50
❏ MGV-8092 [M]	Oscar Peterson Plays Count Basie	1957	$300
—Reissue of Clef 708			
❏ V-8092 [M]	Oscar Peterson Plays Count Basie	1961	$50
❏ MGV-2052 [M]	Oscar Peterson Plays the Cole Porter Songbook	1957	$300
—Reissue of Clef 603			
❏ MGVS-6083 [S]	Oscar Peterson Plays the Cole Porter Songbook	1960	$100
❏ V6-2052 [S]	Oscar Peterson Plays the Cole Porter Songbook	1961	$35
—Reissue of 6083			
❏ V-2052 [M]	Oscar Peterson Plays the Cole Porter Songbook	1961	$50
❏ 821987-1	Oscar Peterson Plays the Cole Porter Songbook	1986	$25
—Reissue of 2053			
❏ MGV-2055 [M]	Oscar Peterson Plays the Duke Ellington Songbook	1957	$300
—Reissue of Clef 606			
❏ MGVS-6086 [S]	Oscar Peterson Plays the Duke Ellington Songbook	1960	$100
❏ V-2055 [M]	Oscar Peterson Plays the Duke Ellington Songbook	1961	$50
❏ V6-2055 [S]	Oscar Peterson Plays the Duke Ellington Songbook	1961	$35
—Reissue of 6086			
❏ MGV-2054 [M]	Oscar Peterson Plays the George Gershwin Songbook	1957	$300
—Reissue of Clef 605			
❏ MGVS-6085 [S]	Oscar Peterson Plays the George Gershwin Songbook	1960	$100
❏ V-2054 [M]	Oscar Peterson Plays the George Gershwin Songbook	1961	$50
❏ V6-2054 [S]	Oscar Peterson Plays the George Gershwin Songbook	1961	$35
—Reissue of 6085			
❏ 823249-1	Oscar Peterson Plays the George Gershwin Songbook	1985	$25
—Reissue of 2054			
❏ MGV-2060 [M]	Oscar Peterson Plays the Harold Arlen Songbook	1957	$300
—Reissue of Clef 649			
❏ MGVS-6091 [S]	Oscar Peterson Plays the Harold Arlen Songbook	1960	$100
❏ V-2060 [M]	Oscar Peterson Plays the Harold Arlen Songbook	1961	$50
❏ V6-2060 [S]	Oscar Peterson Plays the Harold Arlen Songbook	1961	$35
—Reissue of 6091			
❏ MGV-2059 [M]	Oscar Peterson Plays the Harry Warren Songbook	1957	$300
—Reissue of Clef 648			
❏ MGVS-6090 [S]	Oscar Peterson Plays the Harry Warren Songbook	1960	$100
❏ V-2059 [M]	Oscar Peterson Plays the Harry Warren Songbook	1961	$50
❏ V6-2059 [S]	Oscar Peterson Plays the Harry Warren Songbook	1961	$35
—Reissue of 6090			
❏ MGV-2053 [M]	Oscar Peterson Plays the Irving Berlin Songbook	1957	$300
—Reissue of Clef 604			
❏ MGVS-6084 [S]	Oscar Peterson Plays the Irving Berlin Songbook	1960	$100
❏ V-2053 [M]	Oscar Peterson Plays the Irving Berlin Songbook	1961	$50
❏ V6-2053 [S]	Oscar Peterson Plays the Irving Berlin Songbook	1961	$35
—Reissue of 6084			
❏ MGV-2056 [M]	Oscar Peterson Plays the Jerome Kern Songbook	1957	$300
—Reissue of Clef 623			
❏ MGVS-6087 [S]	Oscar Peterson Plays the Jerome Kern Songbook	1960	$100
❏ V-2056 [M]	Oscar Peterson Plays the Jerome Kern Songbook	1961	$50
❏ V6-2056 [S]	Oscar Peterson Plays the Jerome Kern Songbook	1961	$35
—Reissue of 6087			
❏ 825865-1	Oscar Peterson Plays the Jerome Kern Songbook	1985	$25
—Reissue of 2056			
❏ MGV-2061 [M]	Oscar Peterson Plays the Jimmy McHugh Songbook	1957	$300
—Reissue of Clef 650			
❏ MGVS-6092 [S]	Oscar Peterson Plays the Jimmy McHugh Songbook	1960	$100
❏ V-2061 [M]	Oscar Peterson Plays the Jimmy McHugh Songbook	1961	$50
❏ V6-2061 [S]	Oscar Peterson Plays the Jimmy McHugh Songbook	1961	$35
—Reissue of 6092			
❏ MGV-2057 [M]	Oscar Peterson Plays the Richard Rodgers Songbook	1957	$300
—Reissue of Clef 624			
❏ MGVS-6088 [S]	Oscar Peterson Plays the Richard Rodgers Songbook	1960	$100
❏ V-2057 [M]	Oscar Peterson Plays the Richard Rodgers Songbook	1961	$50
❏ V6-2057 [S]	Oscar Peterson Plays the Richard Rodgers Songbook	1961	$35
—Reissue of 6088			
❏ MGV-2058 [M]	Oscar Peterson Plays the Vincent Youmans Songbook	1957	$0
—Reissue planned but canceled			
❏ MGVS-6089 [S]	Oscar Peterson Plays the Vincent Youmans Songbook	1960	$0
—Canceled			
❏ V6-8775	Oscars -- Oscar Peterson Plays the Academy Awards	1969	$35
❏ MGV-2004 [M]	Pastel Moods by Oscar Peterson	1956	$200
❏ V-2004 [M]	Pastel Moods by Oscar Peterson	1961	$50
❏ MGV-8340 [M]	Porgy and Bess	1959	$100
❏ MGVS-6098 [S]	Porgy and Bess	1960	$0
—Canceled			
❏ V-8340 [M]	Porgy and Bess	1961	$50
❏ V6-8340 [S]	Porgy and Bess	1961	$35
❏ V-8660 [M]	Put On a Happy Face	1966	$35
❏ V6-8660 [S]	Put On a Happy Face	1966	$50
❏ MGV-2044 [M]	Recital by Oscar Peterson	1957	$200
—Reissue of Clef 694			
❏ V-2044 [M]	Recital by Oscar Peterson	1961	$50
❏ MGV-8078 [M]	Recital by Oscar Peterson	1957	$0
—Canceled			
❏ V3HB-8842	Return Engagement	1975	$35
❏ 833552	Return Engagement	198?	$30
—Reissue of 8842 (though the labels may still use the old number)			
❏ MGV-2012 [M]	Romance -- The Vocal Styling of Oscar Peterson	1956	$350
—Reissue of Clef 145			
❏ V-2012 [M]	Romance -- The Vocal Styling of Oscar Peterson	1961	$50
❏ MGV-2079 [M]	Soft Sands	1957	$100
❏ V-2079 [M]	Soft Sands	1961	$50
❏ V-8681 [M]	Something Warm	1966	$35
❏ V6-8681 [S]	Something Warm	1966	$50
❏ MGV-8334 [M]	Songs for a Swingin' Affair -- A Jazz Portrait of Sinatra	1959	$100
❏ MGVS-6071 [S]	Songs for a Swingin' Affair -- A Jazz Portrait of Sinatra	1960	$100
❏ V-8334 [M]	Songs for a Swingin' Affair -- A Jazz Portrait of Sinatra	1961	$50
❏ V6-8334 [S]	Songs for a Swingin' Affair -- A Jazz Portrait of Sinatra	1961	$35
—Reissue of 6071			
❏ 825769-1	Songs for a Swingin' Affair -- A Jazz Portrait of Sinatra	1985	$25
—Reissue of 8334			
❏ VSP-11 [M]	Stage Right	1966	$30
❏ VSPS-11 [S]	Stage Right	1966	$35
❏ MGV-8364 [M]	Swinging Brass with the Oscar Peterson Trio	1959	$100
❏ MGVS-6119 [S]	Swinging Brass with the Oscar Peterson Trio	1960	$80
❏ V-8364 [M]	Swinging Brass with the Oscar Peterson Trio	1961	$50
❏ V6-8364 [S]	Swinging Brass with the Oscar Peterson Trio	1961	$35
—Reissue of 6119			
❏ MGV-2046 [M]	Tenderly -- Music by Oscar Peterson	1957	$200
—Reissue of Clef 696			
❏ V-2046 [M]	Tenderly -- Music by Oscar Peterson	1961	$50
❏ MGV-8080 [M]	Tenderly -- Music by Oscar Peterson	1957	$0
—Canceled			
❏ MGV-8351 [M]	The Jazz Soul of Oscar Peterson	1959	$100
❏ V-8351 [M]	The Jazz Soul of Oscar Peterson	1961	$50
❏ V-8482 [M]	The Modern Jazz Quartet and the Oscar Petereson Trio at the Opera House	1962	$150
—Reissue of 8269			
❏ V6-8482 [S]	The Modern Jazz Quartet and the Oscar Petereson Trio at the Opera House	1962	$150
—Reissue of 8269			
❏ MGV-8366 [M]	The Music from "Fiorello!	1960	$80
❏ MGVS-6134 [S]	The Music from "Fiorello!	1960	$0
—Canceled			
❏ V-8366 [M]	The Music from "Fiorello!	1961	$50
❏ V3G-8828	The Newport Years	1974	$30
❏ V6-8810	The Oscar Peterson Collection	1972	$35
❏ 30-5606 [M]	The Oscar Peterson Quartet #1	197?	$30
—Book-of-the-Month Club edition			
❏ MGV-8072 [M]	The Oscar Peterson Quartet No. 1	1957	$150
❏ V-8072 [M]	The Oscar Peterson Quartet No. 1	1961	$50
❏ MGV-8368 [M]	The Oscar Peterson Trio at J.A.T.P.	1960	$100
❏ V-8368 [M]	The Oscar Peterson Trio at J.A.T.P.	1961	$50
❏ MGV-8268 [M]	The Oscar Peterson Trio at the Concertgebouw	1958	$100

Oscar Pettiford/Vinnie Burke, *Bass by Pettiford/Burke*, Bethlehem BCP-6, **$250**.

Oscar Pettiford/Red Mitchell, *Jazz Mainstream*, Bethlehem BCP-2, **$250**.

Flip Phillips, *Flip Phillips*, Mercury MGC-105, 10-inch LP, **$300**.

Nat Pierce, *Big Band at the Savoy Ballroom*, RCA Victor LPM-2543, **$30**.

Number	Title	Yr	NM
❏ V-8268 [M]	The Oscar Peterson Trio at the Concertgebouw	1961	$50
❏ MGV-8024 [M]	The Oscar Peterson Trio at the Stratford Shakespearean Festival	1957	$150
❏ V-8024 [M]	The Oscar Peterson Trio at the Stratford Shakespearean Festival	1961	$50
❏ V-8591 [M]	The Oscar Peterson Trio Plays	1964	$35
❏ V6-8591 [S]	The Oscar Peterson Trio Plays	1964	$50
❏ 825099-1	The Oscar Peterson Trio Set	1985	$25
❏ V-8562 [M]	The Oscar Peterson Trio with Nelson Riddle	1963	$60
❏ V6-8562 [S]	The Oscar Peterson Trio with Nelson Riddle	1963	$60
❏ MGV-8239 [M]	The Oscar Peterson Trio with Sonny Stitt, Roy Eldredge and Jo Jones at Newport	1958	$100
❏ V-8239 [M]	The Oscar Peterson Trio with Sonny Stitt, Roy Eldredge and Jo Jones at Newport	1961	$50
❏ MGV-8269 [M]	The Oscar Peterson Trio with the Modern Jazz Quartet at the Opera House	1958	$100
❏ MGVS-6069 [S]	The Oscar Peterson Trio with the Modern Jazz Quartet at the Opera House	1960	$100
❏ V-8269 [M]	The Oscar Peterson Trio with the Modern Jazz Quartet at the Opera House	1961	$50
❏ V6-8269 [S]	The Oscar Peterson Trio with the Modern Jazz Quartet at the Opera House	1961	$35
—Reissue of 6069			
❏ V-8480 [M]	The Sound of the Trio	1962	$60
❏ V6-8480 [S]	The Sound of the Trio	1962	$60
❏ V-8420 [M]	The Trio -- Live from Chicago	1961	$60
❏ V6-8420 [S]	The Trio -- Live from Chicago	1961	$60
❏ V-8700 [M]	Thoroughly Modern '20s	1967	$35
❏ V6-8700 [S]	Thoroughly Modern '20s	1967	$35
❏ 821849-1	Tracks	1985	$25
❏ 821663-1	Travelin' On	1985	$25
❏ V-8429 [M]	Very Tall	1962	$60
❏ V6-8429 [S]	Very Tall	1962	$60
❏ V-8606 [M]	We Get Requests	1965	$35
❏ V6-8606 [S]	We Get Requests	1965	$50
❏ 810047-1	We Get Requests	1986	$25
❏ V-8454 [M]	West Side Story	1962	$60
❏ V6-8454 [S]	West Side Story	1962	$60
WING			
❏ SRW16351	Canadiana Suite	1969	$30

PETERSON, OSCAR/GERRY MULLIGAN
Also see each artist's individual listings.

Albums

Number	Title	Yr	NM
VERVE			
❏ V-8559 [M]	The Oscar Peterson Trio and the Gerry Mulligan Four at Newport	1963	$60
❏ V6-8559 [S]	The Oscar Peterson Trio and the Gerry Mulligan Four at Newport	1963	$60

PETERSON, PAT
Male singer.

Albums

Number	Title	Yr	NM
ENJA			
❏ 4020	Introducing Pat Peterson	1982	$30

PETERSON, PETE
Bass player and bandleader.

Albums

Number	Title	Yr	NM
PAUSA			
❏ 7163	Jazz Journey	1984	$25
❏ 7191	Playin' in the Park	1986	$25
❏ 7143	Texas State of Mind	1982	$25

PETERSON, RALPH
Drummer.

Albums

Number	Title	Yr	NM
BLUE NOTE			
❏ B1-92750	Tri-Angular	1989	$30
❏ B1-91730	V	1989	$30

PETERSTEIN, SHORTY

Albums

Number	Title	Yr	NM
WORLD PACIFIC			
❏ WP-1274 [M]	The Wide Weird World of Shorty Petterstein	1959	$150

PETRUCCIANI, MICHEL
Pianist and composer.

Albums

Number	Title	Yr	NM
BLUE NOTE			
❏ B1-48679	Michel Plays Petrucciani	1988	$25
❏ B1-92563	Music	1989	$30
❏ BT-85124	Pianism	1987	$25
❏ BT-85133	Power of Three	1987	$25
GEORGE WEIN COLLECTION			
❏ GW-3001	100 Hearts	1984	$30
❏ GW-3006	Live at the Village Vanguard	1985	$30

PETTIFORD, OSCAR
Bass player and cellist. Also see SERGE CHALOFF; THE FOUR MOST; LES JAZZ MODES; THE MANHATTAN JAZZ SEPTETTE; LUCKY THOMPSON.

Albums

Number	Title	Yr	NM
ABC-PARAMOUNT			
❏ ABC-227 [M]	O.P.'s Jazz Men: Oscar Pettiford Orchestra in Hi-Fi, Vol. 2	1958	$120
❏ ABCS-227 [S]	O.P.'s Jazz Men: Oscar Pettiford Orchestra in Hi-Fi, Vol. 2	1958	$100
❏ ABC-135 [M]	Oscar Pettiford Orchestra in Hi-Fi	1956	$100
BETHLEHEM			
❏ BCP-1019 [10]	Basically Duke	1955	$250
❏ BCP-1003 [10]	Oscar Pettiford	1954	$250
❏ BCP-33 [M]	Oscar Pettiford Sextet	1955	$250
❏ BCP-6007	The Finest of Oscar Pettiford	197?	$35
—Reissue, distributed by RCA Victor			
DEBUT			
❏ DLP-8 [10]	Oscar Pettiford Sextet	1954	$500
FANTASY			
❏ 6010 [M]	My Little Cello	1964	$40
❏ 86010 [R]	My Little Cello	1964	$50
❏ 6015 [M]	The Essen Jazz Festival	1964	$40
❏ 86015 [R]	The Essen Jazz Festival	1964	$50
❏ OJC-112	The New Sextet	198?	$30
JAZZLAND			
❏ JLP-64 [M]	Last Recordings by the Late, Great Bassist	1962	$60
❏ JLP-964 [R]	Last Recordings by the Late, Great Bassist	1962	$40
JAZZ MAN			
❏ 5036	Blue Brothers	1981	$30
PRESTIGE			
❏ PRST-7813	Memorial Album	1971	$50
SAVOY JAZZ			
❏ SJL-1172	Discoveries	1986	$30

PETTIFORD, OSCAR/RED MITCHELL
Also see each artist's individual listings.

Albums

Number	Title	Yr	NM
BETHLEHEM			
❏ BCP-2 [M]	Jazz Mainstream	1957	$250

PETTIFORD, OSCAR/VINNIE BURKE
Also see each artist's individual listings.

Albums

Number	Title	Yr	NM
BETHLEHEM			
❏ BCP-6 [M]	Bass by Pettiford/Burke	1957	$250

PHILADELPHIA EXPERIMENT, THE
Members: Uri Caine (keyboards); Christian McBride (bass); and Ahmir Thompson (drums); with special guest PAT MARTINO.

Albums

Number	Title	Yr	NM
ATLANTIC			
❏ 93042	The Philadelphia Experiment	2001	$20

PHILLIPS, BARRE
Bass player.

Albums

Number	Title	Yr	NM
ECM			
❏ 1149	Barre Phillips II	198?	$30
❏ 1257	Call Me When You Get There	198?	$30
❏ 1076	Mountainscapes	1976	$30
❏ 1011	Music for Two Basses	197?	$35
OPUS ONE			
❏ 2	Journal Violone	197?	$35

PHILLIPS, ESTHER
Female singer. Best known for her work in R&B and soul, the below albums came out on jazz labels or numbering series.

Albums

Number	Title	Yr	NM
ATLANTIC			
❏ SD1565	Burnin'	1970	$60
❏ SD1680	Confessin' the Blues	1975	$35
❏ 90670	Confessin' the Blues	1987	$25
—Reissue of 1680			
MUSE			
❏ MR-5302	A Way to Say Goodbye	1986	$30
SAVOY JAZZ			
❏ SJL-2258	The Complete Savoy Recordings	1984	$25

PHILLIPS, FLIP, AND WOODY HERMAN
Also see each artist's individual listings.

Albums

Number	Title	Yr	NM
CENTURY			
❏ 1090	Together	1978	$35

PHILLIPS, FLIP
Tenor saxophone player and clarinetist.

Albums

Number	Title	Yr	NM
BRUNSWICK			
❏ BL58032 [10]	Tenor Sax Stylings	1953	$150
CHOICE			
❏ 1013	Phillips' Head	197?	$30
CLEF			
❏ MGC-693 [M]	Flip	1956	$300
❏ MGC-105 [10]	Flip Phillips	1953	$350
❏ MGC-109 [10]	Flip Phillips Collates	1953	$350
❏ MGC-133 [10]	Flip Phillips Collates No. 2	1953	$350
❏ MGC-691 [M]	Flip Wails	1956	$300
❏ MGC-158 [10]	Jumping Moods with Flip Phillips	1954	$350
❏ MGC-740 [M]	Rock with Flip	1956	$300
❏ MGC-692 [M]	Swinging with Flip Phillips and His Orchestra	1956	$300
❏ MGC-634 [M]	The Flip Phillips-Buddy Rich Trio	1954	$300
❏ MGC-637 [M]	The Flip Phillips Quintet	1954	$300
CONCORD JAZZ			
❏ CJ-358	A Real Swinger	1988	$25
❏ CJ-334	A Sound Investment	1988	$25
DOCTOR JAZZ			
❏ FW39419	A Melody from the Sky	198?	$25
MERCURY			
❏ MGC-105 [10]	Flip Phillips	1951	$300
❏ MGC-109 [10]	Flip Phillips Collates	1952	$300
❏ MGC-133 [10]	Flip Phillips Collates No. 2	1953	$0
—Canceled; issued on Clef			
❏ MG-25023 [10]	Flip Phillips Quartet	1950	$300
ONYX			
❏ 214	Flip Phillips in Florida	197?	$30
PROGRESSIVE			
❏ PRO-7063	Flipenstein	198?	$25
SUE			
❏ STLP-1035 [S]	Flip Phillips Revisited	1965	$40
❏ LP-1035 [M]	Flip Phillips Revisited	1965	$30
VERVE			
❏ MGV-8077 [M]	Flip	1957	$150
❏ V-8077 [M]	Flip	1961	$30
❏ MGV-8075 [M]	Flip Wails	1957	$150
❏ V-8075 [M]	Flip Wails	1961	$30
❏ MGV-8116 [M]	Rock with Flip	1957	$80
❏ V-8116 [M]	Rock with Flip	1961	$30
❏ MGV-8076 [M]	Swingin' with Flip	1957	$150
❏ V-8076 [M]	Swingin' with Flip	1961	$30

Number	Title	Yr	NM

PHILLIPS, SONNY
Organist and pianist.
Albums
MUSE
| MR-5157 | I Concentrate on You | 1979 | $30 |

PRESTIGE
PRST-7799	Black Magic	1970	$25
10007	Black On Black	1971	$25
PRST-7737	Sure 'Nuff	1970	$25

PHILLIPS, WOOLF
British bandleader and arranger.
Albums
CORAL
| CRL56036 [10] | Woolf Phillips Plays Duke Ellington Songs | 1951 | $100 |

PHOENIX SYMPHONY RAGTIME ENSEMBLE
Albums
WORLD JAZZ
| 12 | Phoenix Symphony Ragtime Ensemble | 197? | $25 |

PIANO CHOIR, THE
Created by STANLEY COWELL, it also featured HAROLD MABERN.
Albums
STRATA-EAST
| SES-19750 | Handscapes 2 | 1975 | $25 |

PIANO RED
Real name: William Perryman. Pianist. Also recorded as "Dr. Feelgood."
Albums
ARHOOLIE
| 1064 | William Perryman (Alone with Piano) | 197? | $30 |

EUPHONIC
| 1212 | Percussive Piano | 198? | $25 |

GROOVE
| LG-1001 [M] | Jump Man, Jump | 1956 | $0 |
— The existence of this LP has not been confirmed
| LG-1002 [M] | Piano Red in Concert | 1956 | $600 |

KING
| KS-1117 | Happiness Is Piano Red | 1970 | $50 |

RCA CAMDEN
| ACL1-0547 | Rockin' with Red | 1974 | $30 |

SOUTHLAND
| 8 | Willie Perryman-Piano Red- Dr. Feelgood | 1983 | $35 |

PIECES OF A DREAM
Members: James Lloyd (keyboards); Cedric Napoleon (bass, vocals); Curtis Harmon (drums).
Albums
ELEKTRA
60270	Imagine This	1984	$25
6E-350	Pieces of a Dream	1981	$25
60142	We Are One	1982	$25

MANHATTAN
| ST-53023 | Joyride | 1986 | $25 |

PIERANUNZI, ENRICO, AND ART FARMER
Also see each artist's individual listings.
Albums
SOUL NOTE
| SN-1021 | Isis | 198? | $30 |

PIERANUNZI, ENRICO
Pianist and occasional male singer.
Albums
SOUL NOTE
| 121221 | No Man's Land | 1990 | $35 |

PIERCE, BILLIE AND DEDE
Billie Pierce is a female singer and pianist. Also see DEDE PIERCE.
Albums
ARHOOLIE
| 2016 | New Orleans Music | 197? | $25 |

BIOGRAPH
| CEN-15 | Billie and Dede Pierce at Luthjen's | 197? | $25 |

JAZZOLOGY
| JCE-25 | New Orleans Legends Live, Vol. 15 | 196? | $35 |

RIVERSIDE
RLP-394 [M]	Blues and Tonks From the Delta	1961	$200
RS-9394 [R]	Blues and Tonks From the Delta	1961	$200
RLP-370 [M]	Blues in the Classic Tradition	1961	$200
RS-9370 [R]	Blues in the Classic Tradition	1961	$200

PIERCE, BILLY
Tenor and soprano saxophone player.
Albums
SUNNYSIDE
| SSC-1026 | Give and Take | 1988 | $25 |
| SSC-1013 | William the Conqueror | 1986 | $25 |

PIERCE, BOBBY
Keyboard player and male singer.
Albums
COBBLESTONE
| 9016 | Introducing Bobby Pierce | 197? | $35 |

MUSE
| MR-5030 | New York | 1974 | $30 |
| MR-5304 | Piercing | 198? | $25 |

PIERCE, DEDE
Trumpeter and male singer. Also see BILLIE AND DEDE PIERCE.
Albums
BIOGRAPH
| CEN-5 | Dede Pierce and the New Orleans Stompers | 197? | $25 |

PIERCE, NAT; DICK COLLINS; CHARLIE MARIANO
Also see each artist's individual listings.
Albums
FANTASY
| OJC-118 | Nat Pierce-Dick Collins Nonet/Charlie Mariano Sextet | 198? | $25 |
| 3224 [M] | Nat Pierce-Dick Collins Nonet/Charlie Mariano Sextet | 1956 | $120 |
— Red vinyl
| 3224 [M] | Nat Pierce-Dick Collins Nonet/Charlie Mariano Sextet | 195? | $60 |
— Black vinyl

PIERCE, NAT; MILT HINTON; BARRY GALBRAITH; OSIE JOHNSON
Also see each artist's individual listings.
Albums
MUSIC MINUS ONE
| Vol.1 [M] | Nat Pierce and Milt Hinton and Barry Galbraith and Osie Johnson | 1956 | $30 |
— With sheet music attached

PIERCE, NAT
Pianist and composer. Also see THE CAPP-PIERCE JUGGERNAUT.
Albums
CORAL
| CRL57128 [M] | Chamber Music for Moderns | 1957 | $50 |
| CRL57091 [M] | Kansas City Memories | 1957 | $50 |

FANTASY
| 3-14 [10] | Nat Pierce and the Herdsmen Featuring Dick Collins | 1954 | $80 |
— Red vinyl
| 3-14 [10] | Nat Pierce and the Herdsmen Featuring Dick Collins | 1954 | $80 |
— Blue vinyl

KEYNOTE
| LP-1101 [M] | Nat Pierce Octet and Tentette | 1955 | $80 |

RCA VICTOR
| LPM-2543 [M] | Big Band at the Savoy Ballroom | 1962 | $30 |
| LSP-2543 [S] | Big Band at the Savoy Ballroom | 1962 | $30 |

VANGUARD
| VRS-8017 [10] | Nat Pierce Bandstand | 1955 | $120 |

ZIM
| 2003 | Ballad of Jazz Street | 198? | $25 |
| 1005 | Nat Pierce and His Orchestra | 197? | $30 |

PIKE, DAVE
Vibraphone player.
Albums
ATLANTIC
| 1457 [M] | Jazz for the Jet Set | 1966 | $60 |
| SD1457 [S] | Jazz for the Jet Set | 1966 | $25 |

BASF
20739	Infra-Red	1972	$35
25112	Riff for Rent	1973	$25
21541	Salamao	1974	$35

COLUMBIA JAZZ ODYSSEY
| PC37011 | Pike's Peak | 1981 | $25 |
— Reissue of Epic 17025

DECCA
| DL4568 [M] | Manhattan Latin | 1965 | $35 |
| DL74568 [S] | Manhattan Latin | 1965 | $25 |

EPIC
| LA-16025 [M] | Pike's Peak | 1962 | $60 |
| BA-17025 [S] | Pike's Peak | 1962 | $60 |

MOODSVILLE
| MVLP-36 [M] | Dave Pike Plays the Jazz Version of "Oliver | 1963 | $50 |
— Green label
| MVLP-36 [M] | Dave Pike Plays the Jazz Version of "Oliver | 1965 | $30 |
— Blue label, trident logo at right

MUSE
MR-5203	Let the Minstrels Play On	1980	$25
MR-5261	Moon Bird	198?	$25
MR-5092	Times Out of Mind	197?	$30

NEW JAZZ
| NJLP-8281 [M] | Bossa Nova Carnival | 1962 | $150 |
— Purple label
| NJLP-8281 [M] | Bossa Nova Carnival | 1965 | $150 |
— Blue label, trident logo at right
| NJLP-8284 [M] | Limbo Carnival | 1962 | $150 |
— Purple label
| NJLP-8284 [M] | Limbo Carnival | 1965 | $150 |
— Blue label, trident logo at right

RIVERSIDE
| RLP-360 [M] | It's Time for David Pike | 1961 | $200 |
| RS-9360 [S] | It's Time for David Pike | 1961 | $200 |

TIMELESS
| LPSJP-302 | Bluebird | 1990 | $30 |

VORTEX
| 2007 | The Doors of Perception | 1970 | $25 |

PILHOFER, HERB
Pianist.
Albums
ARGO
| LP-657 [M] | Jazz | 1960 | $30 |
| LPS-657 [S] | Jazz | 1960 | $30 |

SOUND 80
| DLR103 | Spaces | 198? | $30 |

ZEPHYR
| ZP-12103-G [M] | Dick and Don Maw Present the Herb Pilhofer Octet -- Jazz from the North Coast, Volume 2 | 1959 | $60 |

Number	Title	Yr	NM

PILTZECKER, TED
Vibraphone player.
Albums
SEA BREEZE
| ❑ SB-2027 | Destinations | 1986 | $25 |

PINE, COURTNEY
Tenor and soprano saxophone player and flutist.
Albums
ANTILLES
❑ 510769-1	Closer to Home	1992	$50
❑ 90697	Destiny's Song + The Image	1987	$30
	of Pursuance		
❑ 8700	Journey to the Urge Within	1986	$35
❑ 91334	The Vision's Tale	1989	$30

PIRCHNER, WERNER; HARRY PEPI; JACK DeJOHNETTE
Pirchner plays accordion and vibes; Pepl is a guitarist. Also see JACK DeJOHNETTE.
Albums
ECM
| ❑ 1237 | Trio Recordings | 1985 | $30 |

PISANO, JOHNNY, AND BILLY BEAN
Pisano is a guitarist. Also see BILLY BEAN.
Albums
DECCA
❑ DL9206 [M]	Makin' It	1958	$100
❑ DL79206 [S]	Makin' It	1958	$100
❑ DL9219 [M]	Take Your Pick	1958	$100
❑ DL79219 [S]	Take Your Pick	1958	$100

PISTORIOUS, STEVE
Pianist.
Albums
JAZZOLOGY
| ❑ J-78 | Classic Piano Rags | 197? | $25 |

PIZZARELLI, BUCKY, AND BUD FREEMAN
Also see each artist's individual listings.
Albums
FLYING DUTCHMAN
| ❑ BDL1-1378 | Buck & Bud | 1976 | $30 |

PIZZARELLI, BUCKY, AND VINNIE BURKE
Also see each artist's individual listings.
Albums
SAVOY
| ❑ MG-12158 [M] | Music Minus Many Men | 1960 | $30 |

PIZZARELLI, BUCKY
Guitarist.
Albums
FLYING DUTCHMAN
| ❑ BDL1-1120 | Nightwings | 1975 | $30 |
MONMOUTH-EVERGREEN
❑ 7066	Bucky Pizzarelli Plays	197?	$35
❑ 7093	Beiderbecke, Challis, Kress Bucky Pizzarelli with the Care Pierre Trio	197?	$30
❑ 7082	Bucky's Bunch	197?	$30
❑ 7047	Green Guitar Blues	197?	$35
STASH
❑ ST-213	Love Songs	198?	$25
❑ ST-263	Solo Flight	1987	$25

PIZZARELLI, BUCKY AND JOHN JR.
Also see each artist's individual listings.
Albums
STASH
| ❑ ST-207 | 2 x 7 = Pizzarelli | 1980 | $30 |
| ❑ ST-239 | Swinging Sevens | 198? | $25 |

PIZZARELLI, JOHN JR.
Guitarist and male singer. Also see BUCKY PIZZARELLI.
Albums
STASH
❑ ST-256	Hit That Jive, Jack!	1985	$25
❑ ST-226	I'm Hip	1983	$25
❑ ST-267	Sing! Sing! Sing!	1987	$25

PIZZI, RAY
Tenor and soprano saxophone player.
Albums
DISCOVERY
| ❑ 853 | Espressivo | 1982 | $25 |
| ❑ 801 | The Love Letter | 1980 | $25 |
PABLO
| ❑ 2310795 | Conception | 197? | $30 |

PLANET, JANET
Female singer.
Albums
SEA BREEZE
| ❑ SB-2026 | Sweet Thunder | 1986 | $30 |

PLAXICO, LONNIE
Bass player.
Albums
MUSE
| ❑ MR-5389 | Plaxico | 1989 | $30 |

PLEASANT, BU
Organist, female singer and composer.
Albums
MUSE
| ❑ MR-5033 | Ms. Bu | 1975 | $30 |

PLONSKY, JOHN
Albums
GOLDEN CREST
| ❑ GC-3014 [M] | Cool Man, Cool | 1958 | $30 |

PLUMMER, BILL
Bass player.
Albums
ABC IMPULSE!
| ❑ A-9164 [M] | Bill Plummer and the Cosmic Brotherhood | 1968 | $160 |
| ❑ AS-9164 [S] | Bill Plummer and the Cosmic Brotherhood | 1968 | $200 |

PODEWELL, POLLY
Female singer.
Albums
AUDIOPHILE
| ❑ AP-136 | All of Me | 1980 | $25 |

POINDEXTER, PONY
Alto and soprano saxophone player.
Albums
EPIC
| ❑ LA-16035 [M] | Pony's Express | 1962 | $100 |
| ❑ BA-17035 [S] | Pony's Express | 1962 | $150 |
INNER CITY
| ❑ IC-1062 | Poindexter | 198? | $30 |
NEW JAZZ
❑ NJLP-8297 [M]	Gumbo	1963	$0
—Canceled			
❑ NJLP-8285 [M]	Pony Poindexter Plays the Big Ones	1962	$150
—Purple label			
❑ NJLP-8285 [M]	Pony Poindexter Plays the Big Ones	1965	$150
—Blue label, trident logo at right			
PRESTIGE
❑ PRLP-16001 [M]	Gumbo	1964	$40

POINTER, NOEL
Violinist.
Albums
BLUE NOTE
| ❑ BN-LA736-H | Phantazia | 1977 | $30 |
LIBERTY
❑ LT-1094	All My Reasons	1981	$25
❑ LN-10256	All My Reasons	198?	$20
—Budget-line reissue			
❑ LT-1050	Calling	1981	$20
—Reissue of United Artists 1050			
❑ LT-51123	Direct Hit	1982	$25
❑ LO-848	Hold On	1981	$20
—Reissue of United Artists 848			
❑ LN-10235	Hold On	198?	$20
—Budget-line reissue			
❑ LN-10236	Phantazia	198?	$20
—Budget-line reissue			
UNITED ARTISTS
❑ LT-1050	Calling	1980	$25
❑ UA-LA848-H	Hold On	1978	$25

POLAD, MIKE
Mostly a pianist, he also has played banjo, guitar, clarinet and saxophone.
Albums
JAZZOLOGY
| ❑ J-77 | The Cascades | 197? | $25 |

POLCER, ED
Cornet player and bandleader.
Albums
JAZZOLOGY
| ❑ J-150 | In the Condon Tradition | 1987 | $25 |

POLK, LUCY ANN
Female singer.
Albums
INTERLUDE
| ❑ MO-504 [M] | Easy Livin' | 1959 | $100 |
| ❑ ST-1004 [S] | Easy Livin' | 1959 | $80 |
MODE
| ❑ LP-115 [M] | Lucky Lucy Ann | 1957 | $150 |
TREND
| ❑ TL-1008 [10] | Lucy Ann Polk with Dave Pell | 1954 | $150 |

POLL WINNERS, THE
Members: RAY BROWN; BARNEY KESSEL; SHELLY MANNE.
Albums
CONTEMPORARY
❑ M-3581 [M]	Exploring the Scene	1960	$250
❑ S-7581 [S]	Exploring the Scene	1960	$250
❑ M-3576 [M]	Poll Winners Three	1960	$200
❑ S-7576 [S]	Poll Winners Three	1960	$200
❑ C-3535 [M]	The Poll Winners	1957	$250
❑ S-7535 [S]	The Poll Winners	1959	$250
❑ C-3556 [M]	The Poll Winners Ride Again	1958	$250
❑ S-7556 [S]	The Poll Winners Ride Again	1959	$250
STEREO RECORDS
❑ S-7010 [S]	The Poll Winners	1958	$50
❑ S-7029 [S]	The Poll Winners Ride Again	1958	$50

POLLACK, BEN
Drummer and bandleader.
Albums
BRUNSWICK
| ❑ BL58025 [10] | Ben Pollack | 1951 | $60 |
SAVOY
| ❑ MG-12207 [M] | Dixieland Strut | 196? | $25 |
| ❑ MG-12090 [M] | Pick a Rib Boys | 1956 | $50 |
X
| ❑ LX-3003 [10] | Ben Pollack and His Orchestra Featuring Benny Goodman | 1954 | $60 |

Number	Title	Yr	NM

POLLARD, TERRY
Vibraphone player.
Albums
BETHLEHEM

❏ BCP-1015 [10]	Terry Pollard	1954	$250

POLLARD, TERRY/BOBBY SCOTT
Also see each artist's individual listings.
Albums
BETHLEHEM

❏ BCP-1 [M]	Young Moderns	1957	$250

POMEROY, HERB
Trumpeter, fluegel horn player and bandleader.
Albums
ROULETTE

❏ R-52001 [M]	Life Is A Many Splendored Gig	1958	$120
❏ SR-52001 [S]	Life Is A Many Splendored Gig	1958	$100

SHIAH

❏ HP-1	Pramlatta's Hips	1980	$50

TRANSITION

❏ TRLP-1 [M]	Jazz in a Stable	1956	$400

— Deduct 25 percent if booklet is missing

UNITED ARTISTS

❏ UAL-4015 [M]	Band in Boston	1959	$150
❏ UAS-5015 [S]	Band in Boston	1959	$120

PONDER, JIMMY
Guitarist.
Albums
ABC IMPULSE!

❏ IA-9313	Illusions	197?	$30
❏ IA-9327	White Room	197?	$30

CADET

❏ CA-50048	While My Guitar Gently Weeps	1974	$30

MILESTONE

❏ M-9121	Down Here on the Ground	1984	$25
❏ M-9132	So Many Stars	1985	$25

MUSE

❏ MR-5347	Jump	1988	$25
❏ MR-5324	Mean Streets, No Bridges	1987	$25

PONTY, JEAN-LUC
Violinist and composer.
Albums
ATLANTIC

❏ SD19253	A Taste for Passion	1979	$25
❏ SD18163	Aurora	1976	$25
❏ SD19158	Aurora	1978	$20

— Reissue of 18163

❏ SD16020	Civilized Evil	1980	$25
❏ SD19189	Cosmic Messenger	1978	$25
❏ SD19110	Enigmatic Ocean	1977	$25
❏ 81276	Fables	1985	$20
❏ SD18195	Imaginary Voyage	1976	$25
❏ SD19136	Imaginary Voyage	1978	$20

— Reissue of 18195

❏ A1-80098	Individual Choice	1983	$20
❏ SD19229	Jean-Luc Ponty: Live	1979	$25
❏ SD19333	Mystical Adventures	1982	$25
❏ 80185	Open Mind	1984	$20
❏ SD18138	Upon the Wings of Music	1975	$25

BASF

❏ 21288	Open Strings	1973	$50
❏ 20645	Sunday Walk	1972	$50

BLUE NOTE

❏ BN-LA632-H2	Cantaloupe Island	1976	$50
❏ LWB-632	Cantaloupe Island	1981	$30

— Reissue of BN-LA632-H2

❏ LT-1102	Live at Donte's	1981	$25

COLUMBIA

❏ FC45252	Storytelling	1989	$35
❏ FC40983	The Gift of Time	1987	$20

DIRECT DISC

❏ SD-16603	Cosmic Messenger	1980	$60

— Audiophile vinyl

INNER CITY

❏ IC-1005	Jean-Luc Ponty and Stephane Grappelli	197?	$25

Number	Title	Yr	NM
❏ IC-1003	Live at Montreux: Sonata Erotica	1976	$35

PAUSA

❏ PR-7014	Jean-Luc Ponty Meets Giorgio Gaslini	1979	$25
❏ PR-7065	Open Strings	1980	$25

— Reissue of BASF 21288

❏ PR-7033	Sunday Walk	1980	$25

— Reissue of BASF 20645

❏ PA9001	The Jean-Luc Ponty Experience	1982	$50

PRESTIGE

❏ PRST-7676	Critic's Choice	1969	$50

WORLD PACIFIC

❏ ST-20156	Electric Connection	1969	$150
❏ ST-20134	More Than Meets the Ear	1969	$150

WORLD PACIFIC JAZZ

❏ ST-20172	King Kong -- Jean-Luc Ponty Plays the Music of Frank Zappa	1970	$150
❏ ST-20168	The Jean-Luc Ponty Experience	1969	$150

POOLE, BILLIE
Female singer.
Albums
RIVERSIDE

❏ RLP-458 [M]	Confessin' the Blues	1963	$150
❏ RS-9458 [S]	Confessin' the Blues	1963	$150
❏ RLP-425 [M]	Sermonette	1962	$150
❏ RS-9425 [S]	Sermonette	1962	$150

POPKIN, LENNY
Tenor saxophone player.
Albums
CHOICE

❏ 1027	Falling Free	198?	$25

PORT OF HARLEM JAZZMEN, THE
This all-star group recorded some of the first jazz on Blue Note Records.
Albums
MOSAIC

❏ MR1-108	The Complete Recordings of the Port of Harlem Jazzmen	198?	$25

PORTAL, MICHEL
Reeds player, often clarinet and bass clarinet.
Albums
HARMONIA MUNDI

❏ HM-5186	Turbulence	1987	$30

POTENZA, FRANK
Guitarist.
Albums
PALO ALTO/TBA

❏ TB-206	Sand Dance	198?	$25
❏ TB-222	Soft and Warm	1987	$25

POTTER, TOMMY
Bass player.
Albums
EASTWEST

❏ 4001 [M]	Tommy Potter's Hard Funk	1958	$350

POTTS, BILL
Pianist, arranger and composer.
Albums
COLPIX

❏ CP-451 [M]	Bye Bye Birdie	1963	$30
❏ SCP-451 [S]	Bye Bye Birdie	1963	$40

UNITED ARTISTS

❏ UAL-4032 [M]	The Jazz Soul of Porgy and Bess	1959	$30
❏ UAS-5032 [S]	The Jazz Soul of Porgy and Bess	1959	$40

Number	Title	Yr	NM

POWELL, BADEN
Guitarist.
Albums
BASF

❏ 25155	Canto on Guitar	197?	$25
❏ 29194	Estudios	197?	$35
❏ 29057	Images on Guitar	197?	$35
❏ 29623	Tristeza on Guitar	197?	$35

COLUMBIA

❏ KC32441	Solitude on Guitar	1974	$30

PAUSA

❏ 7078	Tristeza on Guitar	198?	$25

POWELL, BUD
Pianist. Also see CHARLIE PARKER; THE QUINTET; SONNY STITT.
Albums
BLACK LION

❏ 153	Invisible Cage	1974	$50

BLUE NOTE

❏ BST-84430	Alternate Takes	1985	$50
❏ BLP-1571 [M]	Bud!	1957	$300

— Regular version, W. 63rd St. address on label

❏ BST-1571 [S]	Bud!	1959	$250

— Regular version, W. 63rd St. address on label

❏ BLP-1571 [M]	Bud!	1963	$200

— With "New York, USA" address on label

❏ BST-1571 [S]	Bud!	1963	$100

— With "New York, USA" address on label

❏ BST-81571 [S]	Bud!	1967	$60

— With "A Division of Liberty Records" on label

❏ BST-81571 [S]	Bud!	1986	$30

— The Finest in Jazz Since 1939" reissue

❏ BLP-5003 [10]	The Amazing Bud Powell, Vol. 1	1951	$1000
❏ BLP-1503 [M]	The Amazing Bud Powell, Vol. 1	1955	$400

— Deep groove" version; Lexington Ave. address on label

❏ BLP-1503 [M]	The Amazing Bud Powell, Vol. 1	1958	$500

— Deep groove" version, W. 63rd St. address on label

❏ BLP-1503 [M]	The Amazing Bud Powell, Vol. 1	1963	$80

— With "New York, USA" address on label

❏ BST-81503 [R]	The Amazing Bud Powell, Vol. 1	1967	$50

— With "A Division of Liberty Records" on label

❏ B1-81503 [M]	The Amazing Bud Powell, Vol. 1	1989	$35

— The Finest in Jazz Since 1939" reissue

❏ BLP-5041 [10]	The Amazing Bud Powell, Vol. 2	1954	$1000
❏ BLP-1504 [M]	The Amazing Bud Powell, Vol. 2	1955	$500

— Deep groove" version; Lexington Ave. address on label

❏ BLP-1504 [M]	The Amazing Bud Powell, Vol. 2	1963	$80

— With "New York, USA" address on label

❏ BLP-1504 [M]	The Amazing Bud Powell, Vol. 2	1958	$250

— Deep groove" version, W. 63rd St. address on label

❏ BST-81504 [R]	The Amazing Bud Powell, Vol. 2	1967	$50

— With "A Division of Liberty Records" on label

❏ B1-81504 [M]	The Amazing Bud Powell, Vol. 2	1989	$35

— The Finest in Jazz Since 1939" reissue

❏ B1-93204	The Best of Bud Powell	1989	$35
❏ BLP-4009 [M]	The Scene Changes	1959	$200

— Regular version, W. 63rd St. address on label

❏ BST-4009 [S]	The Scene Changes	1959	$1250

— Deep groove" version; W. 63rd St. address on label

❏ BST-4009 [S]	The Scene Changes	1959	$150

— Regular version, W. 63rd St. address on label

❏ BLP-4009 [M]	The Scene Changes	1963	$80

— With "New York, USA" address on label

❏ BST-4009 [S]	The Scene Changes	1963	$40

— With "New York, USA" address on label

❏ BST-84009 [S]	The Scene Changes	1967	$50

— With "A Division of Liberty Records" on label

❏ BLP-1598 [M]	The Time Waits	1959	$400

— Deep groove" version; W. 63rd St. address on label

❏ BLP-1598 [M]	The Time Waits	1959	$250

Number	Title	Yr	NM
—Regular version, W. 63rd St. address on label			
☐ BST-1598 [S]	The Time Waits	1959	$250
—Deep groove" version; W. 63rd St. address on label			
☐ BST-1598 [S]	The Time Waits	1959	$150
—Regular version, W. 63rd St. address on label			
☐ BLP-1598 [M]	The Time Waits	1963	$80
—With "New York, USA" address on label			
☐ BST-1598 [S]	The Time Waits	1963	$40
—With "New York, USA" address on label			
☐ BST-81598 [S]	The Time Waits	1967	$50
—With "A Division of Liberty Records" on label			
CLEF			
☐ MGC-102 [10]	Bud Powell Piano Solos	1953	$0
—Canceled			
☐ MGC-502 [10]	Bud Powell Piano Solos	1954	$400
☐ MGC-507 [10]	Bud Powell Piano Solos, No. 2	1954	$400
☐ MGC-610 [M]	Bud Powell's Moods	1954	$350
☐ MGC-739 [M]	The Genius of Bud Powell	1956	$350
COLUMBIA			
☐ CL2292 [M]	A Portrait of Thelonious	1965	$40
☐ CS9092 [S]	A Portrait of Thelonious	1965	$50
—Red label with "360 Sound Stereo			
COLUMBIA JAZZ ODYSSEY			
☐ PC36805	A Portrait of Thelonious	1980	$25
COMMODORE			
☐ XFL-14943	The World Is Waiting	198?	$35
DEBUT			
☐ DLP-3 [10]	Jazz at Massey Hall, Volume 2	1953	$800
DELMARK			
☐ DL-406 [M]	Bouncing with Bud	1966	$40
☐ DS-9406 [S]	Bouncing with Bud	1966	$50
☐ DS-406	Bouncing with Bud	1987	$30
DISCOVERY			
☐ 830	Bud Powell in Paris	198?	$30
ELEKTRA/MUSICIAN			
☐ E1-60030	Inner Fires	1982	$30
ESP-DISK'			
☐ BUD-1	Broadcast Performances 1953	197?	$100
☐ 1066 [S]	Bud Powell at the Blue Note Café, Paris	1968	$150
FANTASY			
☐ 6006 [M]	Bud Powell Trio	1962	$80
—Red vinyl			
☐ 6006 [M]	Bud Powell Trio	1962	$40
—Black vinyl			
☐ 86006 [R]	Bud Powell Trio	1962	$40
—Blue vinyl			
☐ 86006 [R]	Bud Powell Trio	1962	$25
—Black vinyl			
☐ OJC-111	Jazz at Massey Hall, Volume 2	198?	$30
MAINSTREAM			
☐ MRL-385	Ups 'n' Downs	1973	$60
MERCURY			
☐ MG-35012 [10]	Bud Powell Piano	1950	$600
☐ MGC-102 [10]	Bud Powell Piano	1950	$500
☐ MGC-502 [10]	Bud Powell Piano Solos	1951	$500
☐ MGC-507 [10]	Bud Powell Piano Solos, No. 2	1951	$500
☐ MGC-610 [M]	Bud Powell's Moods	1953	$400
MOSAIC			
☐ MR5-116	The Complete Bud Powell Blue Note Recordings (1949-1958)	199?	$250
MYTHIC SOUND			
☐ MS-6002	Burning in the USA, 1953-55	199?	$30
☐ MS-6003	Cookin' at Saint-Germain, 1957-59	199?	$30
☐ MS-6001	Early Years of a Genius, 1944-48	199?	$30
☐ MS-6005	Groovin' at the Blue Note, 1959-61	199?	$30
☐ MS-6008	Holiday in Edenville, 1964	199?	$30
☐ MS-6004	Relaxin' at Home, 1961-64	199?	$30
☐ MS-6009	Return to Birdland, 1964	199?	$30
☐ MS-6007	Tribute to Thelonious, 1964	199?	$30
☐ MS-6006	Writin' for Duke, 1963	199?	$30
NORGRAN			
☐ MGN-1098 [M]	Bud Powell '57	1957	$350
☐ MGN-1064 [M]	Bud Powell's Moods	1956	$300
☐ MGN-23 [10]	Bud Powell Trio	1954	$500
☐ MGN-1063 [M]	Jazz Giant	1956	$300
☐ MGN-1017 [M]	Jazz Original	1955	$300
☐ MGN-1077 [M]	Piano Interpretations by Bud Powell	1956	$300
QUINTESSENCE			

Number	Title	Yr	NM
☐ 25381	Bud Powell	1980	$30
RCA VICTOR			
☐ LPM-1423 [M]	Strictly Powell	1957	$150
—Reproductions exist			
☐ LPM-1507 [M]	Swingin' with Bud	1957	$120
—Reproductions exist			
REPRISE			
☐ R-6098 [M]	Bud Powell in Paris	1964	$40
☐ R9-6098 [S]	Bud Powell in Paris	1964	$60
ROOST			
☐ LP-401 [10]	Bud Powell Trio	1950	$650
☐ LP-412 [10]	Bud Powell Trio	1953	$500
☐ LP-2224 [M]	Bud Powell Trio	1957	$150
ROULETTE			
☐ R-52115 [M]	The Return of Bud Powell – His First New Recordings Since 1958	1965	$30
☐ SR-52115 [S]	The Return of Bud Powell – His First New Recordings Since 1958	1965	$40
STEEPLECHASE			
☐ SCC-6001	Bud Powell at the Golden Circle, Vol. 1	198?	$35
☐ SCC-6002	Bud Powell at the Golden Circle, Vol. 2	198?	$35
☐ SCC-6009	Bud Powell at the Golden Circle, Vol. 3	198?	$35
☐ SCC-6014	Bud Powell at the Golden Circle, Vol. 4	198?	$35
☐ SCC-6017	Bud Powell at the Golden Circle, Vol. 5	198?	$35
VERVE			
☐ MGV-8218 [M]	Blues in the Closet	1958	$150
☐ V-8218 [M]	Blues in the Closet	1961	$30
☐ MGV-8185 [M]	Bud Powell '57	1957	$150
☐ V-8185 [M]	Bud Powell '57	1961	$30
☐ UMV-2571	Bud Powell '57	198?	$25
☐ MGV-8154 [M]	Bud Powell's Moods	1957	$150
☐ V-8154 [M]	Bud Powell's Moods	1961	$30
☐ MGV-8153 [M]	Jazz Giant	1957	$150
☐ V-8153 [M]	Jazz Giant	1961	$30
☐ MGV-8167 [M]	Piano Interpretations by Bud Powell	1957	$150
☐ V-8167 [M]	Piano Interpretations by Bud Powell	1961	$30
☐ UMV-2573	Piano Interpretations by Bud Powell	198?	$25
☐ MGV-8115 [M]	The Genius of Bud Powell	1957	$150
☐ V-8115 [M]	The Genius of Bud Powell	1961	$30
☐ VE-2-2506	The Genius of Bud Powell, Vol. 1	197?	$35
☐ VE-2-2526	The Genius of Bud Powell, Vol. 2	197?	$35
☐ VSP-34 [M]	The Jazz Legacy of Bud Powell	1966	$25
☐ VSPS-34 [R]	The Jazz Legacy of Bud Powell	1966	$30
☐ MGV-8301 [M]	The Lonely One…	1959	$100
☐ V-8301 [M]	The Lonely One…	1961	$30
☐ VSP-37 [M]	This Was Bud Powell	1966	$25
☐ VSPS-37 [R]	This Was Bud Powell	1966	$30
XANADU			
☐ 102	Bud in Paris	1975	$35

POWELL, JIMMY (2)
Alto saxophone player. Not to be confused with the British singer of the same name.

Albums

Number	Title	Yr	NM
JUBILEE			
☐ JGM8001 [M]	In a Sentimental Mood	1966	$35

POWELL, LOVEY
Female singer.

Albums

Number	Title	Yr	NM
TRANSITION			
☐ TRLP-1 [M]	Lovelady	1956	$100
—Deduct 25 percent if booklet is missing			

POWELL, MEL
Pianist, arranger and composer.

Albums

Number	Title	Yr	NM
CAPITOL			
☐ T615 [M]	Classics in Jazz	1955	$75
COMMODORE			
☐ XFL-14943	The World Is Waiting	1979	$25
PAUSA			
☐ 9023	The Unavailable Mel Powell	198?	$25
VANGUARD			

Number	Title	Yr	NM
☐ VRS-8015 [10]	Bandstand	1954	$80
☐ VRS-8501 [M]	Borderline	1954	$50
☐ VRS-8519 [M]	Easy Swing	1955	$100
☐ VRS-8004 [10]	Mel Powell Septet	1953	$80
☐ VRS-8506 [M]	Out on a Limb	1955	$100
☐ VRS-8502 [M]	Thigamagig	1954	$50

POWELL, ROGER
Pianist and synthesizer player.

Albums

Number	Title	Yr	NM
ATLANTIC			
☐ SD7251	Cosmic Furnace	1973	$35

POWELL, SELDON
Tenor saxophone player and flutist.

POWELL, SPECS
Drummer and percussionist.

Albums

Number	Title	Yr	NM
ROULETTE			
☐ R-52004 [M]	Movin' In	1958	$30
☐ SR-52004 [S]	Movin' In	1958	$30
STRAND			
☐ SL-1027 [M]	Specs Powell Presents Big Band Jazz	1961	$25
☐ SLS-1027 [S]	Specs Powell Presents Big Band Jazz	1961	$30

POWER TOOLS
Members: BILL FRISELL; Melvin Gibbs (bass); RONALD SHANNON JACKSON.

Albums

Number	Title	Yr	NM
ANTILLES			
☐ 90627	Strange Meeting	1987	$25

POWERS, CHRIS

Albums

Number	Title	Yr	NM
CIRCLE			
☐ CLP-89	Chris Powers and His Orchestra 1985	1986	$25

POWRIE, GLENNA
Pianist.

Albums

Number	Title	Yr	NM
MUSE			
☐ MR-5392	Ashja	1990	$30

PRADO, PEREZ
Bandleader, pianist and arranger. Known as "El Rey de Mambo" or "The King of the Mambo," he integrated traditional Cuban music with American jazz influences.

Albums

Number	Title	Yr	NM
RCA CAMDEN			
☐ CAL-547 [M]	Latino!	1960	$50
☐ CAL-409 [M]	Mambo Happy!	1957	$50
RCA VICTOR			
☐ LPM-2133 [M]	A Touch of Tabasco	1960	$50
☐ LSP-2133 [S]	A Touch of Tabasco	1960	$60
☐ LPM-2104 [M]	Big Hits by Prado	1959	$60
☐ LSP-2104 [S]	Big Hits by Prado	1959	$40
☐ LPM-3330 [M]	Dance Latino	1965	$35
☐ LSP-3330 [S]	Dance Latino	1965	$40
☐ LPM-1883 [M]	Dilo (Ugh!)	1958	$60
☐ LSP-1883 [S]	Dilo (Ugh!)	1959	$40
☐ LPM-2571 [M]	Exotic Suite	1962	$50
☐ LSP-2571 [S]	Exotic Suite	1962	$60
☐ LPM-1257 [M]	Havana 3 A.M.	1956	$40
☐ LPM-1459 [M]	Latin Satin	1957	$40
☐ LPM-3108 [10]	Mambo by the King	1953	$120
☐ LPM-1196 [M]	Mambo by the King	1956	$40
☐ LPM-1075 [M]	Mambo Mania	1955	$50
☐ LPM-21 [10]	Perez Prado Plays Mucho Mambo for Dancing	1951	$120
☐ LPM-2028 [M]	Pops and Prado	1959	$60
☐ LSP-2028 [S]	Pops and Prado	1959	$40
☐ LPM-1556 [M]	Prez	1958	$60
☐ LSP-1556 [S]	Prez	1959	$60
☐ ANL1-1941	Pure Gold	1975	$25
☐ LSP-2308 [M]	Rockambo	1961	$40
☐ LSP-2308 [S]	Rockambo	1961	$60
☐ LPM-3732 [M]	The Best of Perez Prado	1967	$50
☐ LSP-3732 [S]	The Best of Perez Prado	1967	$35
☐ LPM-2379 [M]	The New Dance La Chunga	1961	$50
☐ LSP-2379 [S]	The New Dance La Chunga	1961	$60

Nat Pierce, *Nat Pierce and the Herdsmen featuring Dick Collins*, Fantasy 3-14, 10-inch LP, red or blue vinyl, **$80**.

Herb Pilhofer, *Dick and Don Maw Present Jazz from the North Coast, Volume 2*, Zephyr ZP 12013 G, **$60**.

Lucy Ann Polk, *Easy Livin'*, Interlude ST-1004, **$80**.

Herb Pomeroy, *Life Is a Many Splendored Gig*, Roulette R 52001, **$120**.

Number	Title	Yr	NM
❏ LPM-2524 [M]	The Twist Goes Latin	1962	$50
❏ LSP-2524 [S]	The Twist Goes Latin	1962	$60
❏ VPS-6066	This Is Perez Prado	1972	$35
❏ LPM-1101 [M]	Voodoo Suite (and Six All-Time Greats)	1955	$50

UNITED ARTISTS

❏ LS-61032	Estas Si Viven (The Living End)	196?	$35

PREACHER ROLLO
Drummer and bandleader.

Albums
KING

❏ 295-101 [10]	Dixieland	195?	$120

MGM

❏ E-3259 [M]	Dixieland Favorites	1955	$60
❏ E-95 [10]	Preacher Rollo and the Five Saints	1951	$80
❏ E-217 [10]	Preacher Rollo at the Jazz Band Ball	1953	$80
❏ E-3403 [M]	Swanee River Jazz	1956	$50

PRESERVATION HALL JAZZ BAND
Among the most long-standing members: Percy Humphrey (trumpet); Willie Humphrey (clarinet); Frank Demond (trombone); Allan Jaffe (tuba).

Albums
CBS MASTERWORKS

❏ FM44856	New Orleans, Vol. 4	1989	$30
❏ FM37780	New Orleans, Volume 2	1982	$25
❏ FM38650	New Orleans, Volume 3	1983	$25
❏ FM44996	The Best of Preservation Hall Jazz Band	1989	$30

COLUMBIA MASTERWORKS

❏ M34549	Preservation Hall Jazz Band	1977	$30

PRESIDENT, THE
Led by WAYNE HORVITZ.

Albums
ELEKTRA/MUSICIAN

❏ 60799	Bring Yr Camera	1989	$30

PRESTER, ROB

Albums
ANTILLES

❏ 90967	Trillum	1988	$25

PRESTIGE BLUES SWINGERS, THE
Members: PEPPER ADAMS; RAY BRYANT; Buster Cooper (trombone); ART FARMER; JIMMY FORREST; TINY GRIMES; OSIE JOHNSON; WENDELL MARSHALL; JEROME RICHARDSON; IDRESS SULIEMAN; Jerry Valentine (trombone).

Albums
PRESTIGE

❏ PRST-7787	Outskirts of Town	1970	$35
❏ PRLP-7145 [M]	Outskirts of Town	1958	$250

SWINGVILLE

❏ SVLP-2013 [M]	Stasch	1960	$200
—Blue label, trident logo at right			
❏ SVLP-2013 [M]	Stasch	1965	$50
—Purple label			

PRESTIGE JAZZ QUARTET, THE
Members: TEDDY CHARLES; Addison Farmer (bass); Jerry Segal (drums); MAL WALDRON. Also see TEO MACERO.

Albums
PRESTIGE

❏ PRLP-7108 [M]	The Prestige Jazz Quartet	1957	$250

PREVIN, ANDRE, AND RUSS FREEMAN
Also see each artist's individual listings.

Albums
CONTEMPORARY

❏ C-3537 [M]	Double Play!	1957	$250
❏ S-7011 [S]	Double Play!	1959	$250

STEREO RECORDS

❏ S-7011 [S]	Double Play!	1958	$100

PREVIN, ANDRE; HERB ELLIS; SHELLY MANNE; RAY BROWN
Also see each artist's individual listings.

Albums
COLUMBIA

❏ CL2018 [M]	Four to Go	1963	$50
❏ CS8818 [S]	Four to Go	1963	$60

PREVIN, ANDRE
Pianist, composer and arranger. Also see SHORTY ROGERS.

Albums
ANGEL

❏ DS-37780	A Different Kind of Blues	1981	$25
❏ S-1-37799	It's a Breeze	1981	$25

COLUMBIA

❏ CL2034 [M]	Andre Previn in Hollywood	1963	$35
—Red label with "Guaranteed High Fidelity" at bottom			
❏ CS8834 [S]	Andre Previn in Hollywood	1963	$50
—Red label with "360 Sound Stereo" in black at bottom			
❏ CL2034 [M]	Andre Previn in Hollywood	1966	$30
—Red label with "360 Sound Mono" at bottom			
❏ CS8834 [S]	Andre Previn in Hollywood	1966	$35
—Red label with "360 Sound Stereo" in white at bottom			
❏ CL1649 [M]	A Touch of Elegance	1961	$50
—Red and black label with six "eye" logos			
❏ CS8449 [S]	A Touch of Elegance	1961	$60
—Red and black label with six "eye" logos			
❏ CL1569 [M]	Camelot	1961	$50
—Red and black label with six "eye" logos			
❏ CS8369 [S]	Camelot	1961	$60
—Red and black label with six "eye" logos			
❏ CL1569 [M]	Camelot	1963	$30
—Red label with "Guaranteed High Fidelity" or "360 Sound Mono" at bottom			
❏ CS8369 [S]	Camelot	1963	$35
—Red label with "360 Sound Stereo" at bottom			
❏ CL1786 [M]	Faraway Part of Town	1962	$50
—Red and black label with six "eye" logos			
❏ CS8586 [S]	Faraway Part of Town	1962	$60
—Red and black label with six "eye" logos			
❏ CL1786 [M]	Faraway Part of Town	1963	$30
—Red label with "Guaranteed High Fidelity" or "360 Sound Mono" at bottom			
❏ CS8586 [S]	Faraway Part of Town	1963	$35
—Red label with "360 Sound Stereo" at bottom			
❏ CL1530 [M]	Give My Regards to Broadway	1960	$50
—Red and black label with six "eye" logos			
❏ CS8330 [S]	Give My Regards to Broadway	1960	$60
—Red and black label with six "eye" logos			
❏ CL1530 [M]	Give My Regards to Broadway	1963	$30
—Red label with "Guaranteed High Fidelity" or "360 Sound Mono" at bottom			
❏ CS8330 [S]	Give My Regards to Broadway	1960	$35
—Red label with "360 Sound Stereo" at bottom			
❏ CL1437 [M]	Like Love	1960	$35
—Red and black label with six "eye" logos			
❏ CS8233 [S]	Like Love	1960	$50
—Red and black label with six "eye" logos			
❏ CL1437 [M]	Like Love	1963	$30
—Red label with "Guaranteed High Fidelity" or "360 Sound Mono" at bottom			
❏ CS8233 [S]	Like Love	1963	$35
—Red label with "360 Sound Stereo" at bottom			
❏ CL1741 [M]	Mack the Knife and Other Kurt Weill Music	1962	$50
—Red and black label with six "eye" logos			
❏ CS8541 [S]	Mack the Knife and Other Kurt Weill Music	1962	$60
—Red and black label with six "eye" logos			
❏ CL1741 [M]	Mack the Knife and Other Kurt Weill Music	1963	$30
—Red label with "Guaranteed High Fidelity" or "360 Sound Mono" at bottom			
❏ CS8541 [S]	Mack the Knife and Other Kurt Weill Music	1962	$35
—Red label with "360 Sound Stereo" at bottom			
❏ CL2195 [M]	My Fair Lady	1964	$35
—Red label with "Guaranteed High Fidelity" at bottom			
❏ CS8995 [S]	My Fair Lady	1964	$50
—Red label with "360 Sound Stereo" in black at bottom			
❏ CL2195 [M]	My Fair Lady	1966	$30
—Red label with "360 Sound Mono" at bottom			
❏ CS8995 [S]	My Fair Lady	1966	$35
—Red label with "360 Sound Stereo" in white at bottom			
❏ CL2294 [M]	Popular Previn	1965	$35
—Red label with "Guaranteed High Fidelity" at bottom			
❏ CS9094 [S]	Popular Previn	1965	$50
—Red label with "360 Sound Stereo" in black at bottom			
❏ CS9094 [S]	Popular Previn	1966	$35
—Red label with "360 Sound Stereo" in white at bottom			
❏ CL2294 [M]	Popular Previn	1966	$30
—Red label with "360 Sound Mono" at bottom			
❏ CL1495 [M]	Rhapsody in Blue	1960	$35
—Red and black label with six "eye" logos			
❏ CS8286 [S]	Rhapsody in Blue	1960	$50
—Red and black label with six "eye" logos			
❏ CS8286 [S]	Rhapsody in Blue	1963	$35
—Red label with "360 Sound Stereo" at bottom			
❏ CL1495 [M]	Rhapsody in Blue	1963	$30
—Red label with "Guaranteed High Fidelity" or "360 Sound Mono" at bottom			
❏ CS8733 [S]	Sittin' on a Rainbow: The Music of Harold Arlen	1963	$50
—Red label, "360 Sound Stereo" in black at bottom			
❏ CL1933 [M]	Sittin' on a Rainbow: The Music of Harold Arlen	1963	$35
—Guaranteed High Fidelity" on label			
❏ CL1888 [M]	The Light Fantastic	1962	$50
—Red and black label with six "eye" logos			
❏ CS8688 [S]	The Light Fantastic	1962	$60
—Red and black label with six "eye" logos			
❏ CL1888 [M]	The Light Fantastic	1963	$30
—Red label with "Guaranteed High Fidelity" or "360 Sound Mono" at bottom			
❏ CS8688 [S]	The Light Fantastic	1963	$35
—Red label with "360 Sound Stereo" at bottom			
❏ CL2114 [M]	The Soft and Swinging Music of Jimmy McHugh	1964	$35
—Red label with "Guaranteed High Fidelity" at bottom			
❏ CS8914 [S]	The Soft and Swinging Music of Jimmy McHugh	1964	$50
—Red label with "360 Sound Stereo" in black at bottom			
❏ CS8914 [S]	The Soft and Swinging Music of Jimmy McHugh	1966	$35
—Red label with "360 Sound Stereo" in white at bottom			
❏ CL2114 [M]	The Soft and Swinging Music of Jimmy McHugh	1966	$30
—Red label with "360 Sound Mono" at bottom			
❏ CL1595 [M]	Thinking of You	1961	$50
—Red and black label with six "eye" logos			
❏ CS8395 [S]	Thinking of You	1961	$60
—Red and black label with six "eye" logos			
❏ CL1595 [M]	Thinking of You	1963	$30
—Red label with "Guaranteed High Fidelity" or "360 Sound Mono" at bottom			
❏ CS8395 [S]	Thinking of You	1963	$35
—Red label with "360 Sound Stereo" at bottom			

CONTEMPORARY

❏ M-3586 [M]	Andre Previn Plays Harold Arlen	1960	$250
❏ S-7586 [S]	Andre Previn Plays Harold Arlen	1960	$250
❏ M-3567 [M]	Andre Previn Plays Jerome Kern	1959	$250
❏ S-7567 [S]	Andre Previn Plays Jerome Kern	1959	$250
❏ M-3558 [M]	Andre Previn Plays Vernon Duke	1959	$250
❏ S-7558 [S]	Andre Previn Plays Vernon Duke	1959	$250
❏ S-7548 [S]	Gigi	1959	$250
❏ M-3570 [M]	Jazz Trio, King Size	1959	$250
❏ S-7570 [S]	Jazz Trio, King Size	1959	$250
❏ M-3575 [M]	Like Previn	1960	$200
❏ S-7575 [S]	Like Previn	1960	$200
❏ C-3543 [M]	Pal Joey	1957	$250
❏ S-7543 [S]	Pal Joey	1959	$250
❏ M-3572 [M]	West Side Story	1960	$200
❏ S-7572 [S]	West Side Story	1960	$200

CORONET

❏ 170	Featuring Andre Previn	196?	$30
❏ 181	The Magic Sounds of Andre Previn	196?	$30

Number	Title	Yr	NM
DECCA			
❏ DL4115 [M]	Andre Previn Plays Pretty	1961	$30
❏ DL74115 [S]	Andre Previn Plays Pretty	1961	$35
❏ DL4350 [M]	But Beautiful	1963	$30
❏ DL74350 [S]	But Beautiful	1963	$35
❏ DL8341 [M]	Hollywood at Midnight	1957	$120
❏ DL8131 [M]	Let's Get Away from It All	1955	$150
EVEREST ARCHIVE OF FOLK & JAZZ			
❏ 247	Early Years	1970	$25
FANTASY			
❏ OJC-157	Double Play!	198?	$25
— Reissue of Contemporary 7011			
❏ OJC-170	Like Previn	198?	$25
— Reissue of Contemporary 7575			
❏ OJC-637	Pal Joey	1991	$30
❏ OJC-422	West Side Story	1990	$25
GUEST STAR			
❏ 1436	Piano Greats	196?	$30
HARMONY			
❏ HL7429 [M]	Camelot	1967	$30
❏ HS11229 [S]	Camelot	1967	$30
❏ HL7348 [M]	Misty	1965	$30
❏ HS11148 [S]	Misty	1965	$30
❏ HL7407 [M]	Starlight Piano	196?	$30
❏ HS11207 [S]	Starlight Piano	196?	$30
JAZZ ODYSSEY			
❏ 32160260	Mack the Knife and Other Kurt Weill Music	196?	$30
— Reissue of Columbia 8541			
MGM			
❏ E-4186 [M]	Andre Previn -- Composer, Conductor, Arranger, Pianist	1964	$35
❏ SE-4186 [S]	Andre Previn -- Composer, Conductor, Arranger, Pianist	1964	$50
❏ E-3811 [M]	Like Blue	1960	$50
❏ SE-3811 [S]	Like Blue	1960	$60
❏ E-3716 [M]	Secret Songs for Young Lovers	1959	$50
❏ SE-3716 [S]	Secret Songs for Young Lovers	1959	$60
MOBILE FIDELITY			
❏ Jan-0095	West Side Story	1982	$60
— Audiophile vinyl			
MONARCH			
❏ 203 [10]	All Star Jazz	1952	$150
❏ 204 [10]	Andre Previn Plays Duke	1952	$150
PRI			
❏ 3026 [S]	The World's Most Honored Pianist	1962	$60
— Issued on yellow vinyl			
RCA CAMDEN			
❏ CAL-792 [M]	Love Walked In	1964	$30
❏ CAS-792 [R]	Love Walked In	1964	$25
RCA VICTOR			
❏ LPM-3806 [M]	All Alone	1967	$35
❏ LSP-3806 [S]	All Alone	1967	$30
❏ LPM-36 [10]	Andre Previn By Request	1951	$150
❏ LPT-3002 [10]	Andre Previn Plays Harry Warren	1952	$150
❏ LPM-3491 [M]	Andre Previn Plays Music of the Young Hollywood Composers	1966	$30
❏ LSP-3491 [S]	Andre Previn Plays Music of the Young Hollywood Composers	1966	$35
❏ LPM-3551 [M]	Andre Previn with Voices	1966	$30
❏ LSP-3551 [S]	Andre Previn with Voices	1966	$35
❏ LPM-1011 [M]	Gershwin	1955	$50
❏ ANL1-2805	Pure Gold	1978	$25
❏ LPM-1356 [M]	Three Little Words	1957	$40
SPRINGBOARD			
❏ SPB-4053	After Dark	197?	$25
STEREO RECORDS			
❏ S-7020 [S]	Gigi	1958	$100
❏ S-7004 [S]	Pal Joey	1958	$100
STRAND			
❏ SL1074 [M]	Andre Previn Plays	1962	$30
❏ SLS1074 [S]	Andre Previn Plays	1962	$35
VERVE			
❏ V-8565 [M]	The Essential Andre Previn	1963	$30
❏ V6-8565 [S]	The Essential Andre Previn	1963	$35

PREVITE, ROBERT
Drummer, percussionist, keyboard player, guitarist and bass player.

Albums

Number	Title	Yr	NM
SOUND ASPECTS			
❏ SAS 008	Bump the Renaissance	1986	$30

PRICE, RUTH
Female singer.

Albums

Number	Title	Yr	NM
AVA			
❏ A-54 [M]	Live and Beautiful	1963	$40
❏ AS-54 [S]	Live and Beautiful	1963	$50
CONTEMPORARY			
❏ M-3590 [M]	Ruth Price with Shelly Manne at the Manne-Hole	1961	$200
❏ S-7590 [S]	Ruth Price with Shelly Manne at the Manne-Hole	1961	$200
KAPP			
❏ KL-1006 [M]	My Name Is Ruth Price. I Sing.	1955	$100
❏ KL-1054 [M]	The Party's Over	1957	$100
ROOST			
❏ LP-2217 [M]	Ruth Price Sings!	1956	$100

PRICE, SAMMY
Pianist and bandleader. Also see ROY ELDRIDGE.

Albums

Number	Title	Yr	NM
CIRCLE			
❏ 73	Sammy Price and His Musicians, 1944	1985	$25
CLASSIC JAZZ			
❏ 106	Fire	198?	$25
CONCERT HALL JAZZ			
❏ 1008 [10]	Barrelhouse and Blues	1955	$60
JAZZTONE			
❏ J-1207 [M]	Barrelhouse and Blues	1956	$40
❏ J-1236 [M]	Les Jeunesses Musicales	1956	$40
❏ J-1260 [M]	The Price Is Right	1957	$40
SAVOY			
❏ MG-14004	Rock	196?	$35
WORLD WIDE			
❏ 20016	Blues and Boogie	196?	$35

PRICE, VITO
Tenor and alto saxophone player.

PRIESTER, JULIAN
Trombonist.

Albums

Number	Title	Yr	NM
ECM			
❏ 1044	Love, Love	197?	$60
— Only issued in Germany?			
❏ 1098	Polarization	1977	$60
— Only issued in Germany?			
JAZZLAND			
❏ JLP-25 [M]	Spiritsville	1960	$50
❏ JLP-925 [S]	Spiritsville	1960	$125
RIVERSIDE			
❏ 6081	Keep Swingin'	197?	$35
❏ RLP 12-316 [M]	Keep Swingin'	1960	$200
❏ RLP1163 [S]	Keep Swingin'	1960	$200

PRIMA, LOUIS, AND KEELY SMITH
Also see each artist's individual listings.

Albums

Number	Title	Yr	NM
CAPITOL			
❏ T1160 [M]	Hey Boy! Hey Girl!	1959	$80
❏ T1531 [M]	The Hits of Louis and Keely	1961	$60
❏ ST1531 [S]	The Hits of Louis and Keely	1961	$60
❏ SM-1531	The Hits of Louis and Keely	197?	$12
— Reissue with new prefix			
CORONET			
❏ CX121 [M]	Louis Prima Digs Keely Smith	196?	$25
DOT			
❏ DLP-3210 [M]	Louis and Keely!	1959	$75
❏ DLP-25210 [S]	Louis and Keely!	1959	$80
❏ DLP-3266 [M]	Louis and Keely on Stage	1960	$75
❏ DLP-25266 [S]	Louis and Keely on Stage	1960	$75
❏ DLP-3263 [M]	Together	1960	$75
❏ DLP-25263 [S]	Together	1960	$75
FLEET			
❏ 101 [M]	Louis Prima Digs Keely Smith	196?	$25
RHINO			
❏ RNLP-70225	Zooma Zooma: The Best of Louis Prima Featuring Keely Smith	1986	$25
SPIN-O-RAMA			
❏ 74 [M]	Box of Oldies	196?	$20

PRIMA, LOUIS
Trumpeter, male singer and bandleader.

Albums

Number	Title	Yr	NM
BRUNSWICK			
❏ BL754183	The Prima Generation '72	1972	$80
CAPITOL			
❏ T1797 [M]	Lake Tahoe Prima Style	1962	$60
❏ ST1797 [S]	Lake Tahoe Prima Style	1962	$60
❏ T1010 [M]	Las Vegas Prima Style	1958	$80
❏ T1132 [M]	Strictly Prima	1959	$60
❏ T836 [M]	The Call of the Wildest	1957	$80
❏ T755 [M]	The Wildest	1956	$80
❏ T1723 [M]	The Wildest Comes Home	1962	$60
❏ ST1723 [S]	The Wildest Comes Home	1962	$60
❏ T908 [M]	The Wildest Show at Tahoe	1957	$80
COLUMBIA			
❏ CL1206 [M]	Breakin' It Up!	1959	$40
DOT			
❏ DLP-3385 [M]	Blue Moon	1961	$75
❏ DLP-25385 [S]	Blue Moon	1961	$75
❏ DLP-3410 [M]	Doin' the Twist	1961	$75
❏ DLP-25410 [S]	Doin' the Twist	1961	$75
❏ DLP-3262 [M]	His Greatest Hits	1960	$75
❏ DLP-25262 [S]	His Greatest Hits	1960	$75
❏ DLP-3264 [M]	Pretty Music Prima Style	1960	$75
❏ DLP-25264 [S]	Pretty Music Prima Style	1960	$75
❏ DLP-3392 [M]	Return of the Wildest!	1961	$75
❏ DLP-25392 [S]	Return of the Wildest!	1961	$75
❏ DLP-3272 [M]	The Wildest Clan	1960	$75
❏ DLP-25272 [S]	The Wildest Clan	1960	$75
❏ DLP-3352 [M]	Wonderland by Night	1960	$175
❏ DLP-25352 [S]	Wonderland by Night	1960	$175
GOLDEN TONE			
❏ 326 [M]	Italian Favorites	196?	$12
— Label calls this "Italian Songs"; one side is by Louis Prima, the other side by Phil Brito			
HANNA-BARBERA			
❏ HLP-8502 [M]	The Golden Hits of Louis Prima	1966	$30
MERCURY			
❏ MG-25142 [10]	Louis Prima Plays	1953	$150
PRIMA			
❏ ST 0074	Angelina	1973	$30
❏ PS3003 [S]	King of Clubs	1964	$100
❏ PM3003 [M]	King of Clubs	1964	$125
❏ PM3001 [M]	Prima Show in the Casbar	1963	$40
❏ PS3001 [S]	Prima Show in the Casbar	1963	$60
❏ ST 0072	The Prima Generation	1972	$50
RONDO-LETTE			
❏ A-25 [M]	Louis Prima Entertains	1959	$30
❏ A-9 [M]	Louis Prima in All His Moods	1959	$30
SAVOY JAZZ			
❏ SJL-2264	Play Pretty for the People	198?	$15
TOPS			
❏ 9759 [M]	Italian Favorites	195?	$20

PRINCE, BOB
Composer and bandleader.

Albums

Number	Title	Yr	NM
RCA VICTOR			
❏ LPM-2435 [M]	Opus Jazz	1961	$50
❏ LSP-2435 [S]	Opus Jazz	1961	$60
WARNER BROS.			
❏ W1276 [M]	Charleston 1970	1959	$50
❏ WS1276 [S]	Charleston 1970	1959	$60
❏ W1240 [M]	N.Y. Export: Op. Jazz from Ballets U.S.A.; Ballet Music from Leonard Bernstein's West Side Story	1958	$50
❏ WS1240 [S]	N.Y. Export: Op. Jazz from Ballets U.S.A.; Ballet Music from Leonard Bernstein's West Side Story	1958	$60

PRINCE, ROLAND
Guitarist.

Albums

Number	Title	Yr	NM
VANGUARD			
❏ VSD-79371	Color Visions	197?	$25
❏ VSD-79388	Free Spirit	197?	$25

PRINCE IGOR AND THE CZAR

Albums

Number	Title	Yr	NM
DIFFERENT DRUMMER			
❏ 1002	From Russia	197?	$35

Number	Title	Yr	NM

PRINCETON TRIANGLE JAZZ BAND
Albums
BIOGRAPH

Number	Title	Yr	NM
12014	College Jazz in the '20s	1969	$35

PRITCHARD, DAVID
Guitarist.
Albums
INNER CITY

Number	Title	Yr	NM
IC-1070	City Dreams	1979	$30
IC-1047	Light-Year	1978	$30

PRITCHETT, GEORGE
Guitarist.
Albums
KINNICKINNICK

Number	Title	Yr	NM
101	By Request	197?	$25

PROBERT, GEORGE
Alto and soprano saxophone player.
Albums
GHB

Number	Title	Yr	NM
GHB-70	The Incredible George Probert	197?	$25

PROCOPE, RUSSELL
Alto saxophone player and clarinetist.
Albums
DOT

Number	Title	Yr	NM
DLP3010 [M]	The Persuasive Sax of Russell Procope	1956	$80

PRYSOCK, ARTHUR
Male singer.
Albums
DECCA

Number	Title	Yr	NM
DL4628 [M]	Showcase	1965	$35
DL74628 [S]	Showcase	1965	$50
DL4581 [M]	Strictly Sentimental	1965	$35
DL74581 [S]	Strictly Sentimental	1965	$50

KING

Number	Title	Yr	NM
KS-1088	Fly My Love	1970	$30
KS-1064	The Country Side of Arthur Prysock	1969	$30
KS-1067	The Lord Is My Shepherd	1970	$30
KS-1134	Unforgettable	1971	$30
KS-1066	Where the Soul Trees Go	1970	$30

MCA

Number	Title	Yr	NM
3061	Here's To Good Friends	1978	$25

MGM

Number	Title	Yr	NM
SE-4694	Arthur Prysock	1970	$30
GAS-134	Arthur Prysock (Golden Archive Series)	1970	$30

MILESTONE

Number	Title	Yr	NM
M-9139	A Rockin' Good Way	1986	$25
M-9146	This Guy's in Love with You	1987	$25
M-9157	Today's Love Songs, Tomorrow's Blues	1988	$25

OLD TOWN

Number	Title	Yr	NM
LP-2009 [M]	A Double Header with Arthur Prysock	1965	$40
Dec-004	All My Life	1976	$30
LP-2006 [M]	A Portrait of Arthur Prysock	1963	$40
T-90604 [M]	A Portrait of Arthur Prysock	1965	$75

—Capitol Record Club edition

Number	Title	Yr	NM
ST-90604 [S]	A Portrait of Arthur Prysock	1965	$75

—Capitol Record Club edition

Number	Title	Yr	NM
Dec-001	Arthur Prysock '74	1973	$30
OT12005	Arthur Prysock Does It Again	1977	$30
LP-2004 [M]	Arthur Prysock Sings Only for You	1962	$100
LP-2005 [M]	Coast to Coast	1963	$40
LP-2007 [M]	Everlasting Songs for Everlasting Lovers	1964	$40
LP-2010 [M]	In a Mood	1965	$40
LP-2008 [M]	Intimately Yours	1964	$40
LP-102 [M]	I Worry About You	1962	$100
Dec-002	Love Makes It Right	1974	$30

POLYDOR

Number	Title	Yr	NM
PD-2-8901	Silk and Satin	1977	$35

VERVE

Number	Title	Yr	NM
V6-650	24 Karat Hits	1969	$35
V5-5012 [M]	A Portrait of Arthur Prysock	1967	$35
V6-5012 [S]	A Portrait of Arthur Prysock	1967	$35
V-5009 [M]	Art and Soul	1966	$30
V6-5009 [S]	Art and Soul	1966	$35
V6-5059	I Must Be Doing Something Right	1968	$30
V-5029 [M]	Love Me	1968	$35
V6-5029 [S]	Love Me	1968	$30
V-5014 [M]	Mister Prysock	1967	$35
V6-5014 [S]	Mister Prysock	1967	$35
V-5011 [M]	The Best of Arthur Prysock	1967	$30
V6-5011 [S]	The Best of Arthur Prysock	1967	$35
V-5038 [M]	The Best of Arthur Prysock, Number 2	1968	$50

—All mono copies appear to be yellow label promos

Number	Title	Yr	NM
V6-5038 [S]	The Best of Arthur Prysock, Number 2	1968	$30
V6-5070	This Is My Beloved	1969	$30
V-5048 [M]	To Love or Not to Love	1968	$60

—May be promo only

Number	Title	Yr	NM
V6-5048 [S]	To Love or Not to Love	1968	$30

PRYSOCK, ARTHUR/COUNT BASIE
Also see each artist's individual listings.
Albums
VERVE

Number	Title	Yr	NM
V-8646 [M]	Arthur Prysock/Count Basie	1966	$35
V6-8646 [S]	Arthur Prysock/Count Basie	1966	$50
827011-1	Arthur Prysock/Count Basie	1985	$20

—Reissue

PUCHO AND THE LATIN SOUL BROTHERS
Pucho's real name is Henry Brown; he is a percussionist.
Albums
PRESTIGE

Number	Title	Yr	NM
PRST-7555	Big Stick	1968	$30
PRST-7616	Dateline	1969	$30
PRST-7572	Heat!	1968	$30
PRLP-7471 [M]	Pucho and the Latin Soul Brothers	1967	$40
PRST-7471 [S]	Pucho and the Latin Soul Brothers	1967	$30
PRLP-7502 [M]	Saffron and Soul	1967	$40
PRST-7502 [S]	Saffron and Soul	1967	$30
PRLP-7528 [M]	Shuckin' and Jivin'	1967	$50
PRST-7528 [S]	Shuckin' and Jivin'	1967	$30
PRST-7679	The Best of Pucho and the Latin Soul Brothers	1969	$30

PUENTE, TITO
Timbales and vibraphone player, percussionist, composer and bandleader. A legend in Afro-Cuban music, he wrote "Oye Como Va," which was remade almost note-for-note by Santana in 1970. Also see WOODY HERMAN.
Albums
CONCORD PICANTE

Number	Title	Yr	NM
CJP-250	El Rey	1984	$25
CJP-283	Mambo Diablo	1985	$25
CP-207	On Broadway	1983	$25
CJP-354	Salsa Meets Jazz	1988	$25
CJP-301	Sensacion	1987	$25
CJP-329	Un Poco Loco	1987	$25

DECCA

Number	Title	Yr	NM
DL74910 [S]	Brasilia Nueve	1967	$25
DL4910 [M]	Brasilia Nueve	1967	$30

GNP CRESCENDO

Number	Title	Yr	NM
GNPS-2048 [S]	Puente Now!	197?	$25

—Reissue of 70

Number	Title	Yr	NM
GNP-70 [M]	The Exciting Tito Puente Band in Hollywood	196?	$30

RCA VICTOR

Number	Title	Yr	NM
LPM-2187 [M]	Cha Cha at Grossinger's	1959	$30
LSP-2187 [S]	Cha Cha at Grossinger's	1959	$40
LPM-1251 [M]	Cuban Carnival	1955	$60
LPM-1692 [M]	Dance Mania	1958	$30
LSP-1692 [S]	Dance Mania	1958	$40
LPM-1874 [M]	Dancing Under Latin Skies	1958	$30
LSP-1874 [S]	Dancing Under Latin Skies	1958	$40
LPM-1392 [M]	Let's Cha-Cha with Puente	1957	$40
LPM-1354 [M]	Mambo on Broadway	1957	$40
LPM-2113 [M]	Mucho Cha Cha Cha	1959	$30
LSP-2113 [S]	Mucho Cha Cha Cha	1959	$40
LPM-1479 [M]	Mucho Puente	1957	$40
LPM-1447 [M]	Night Beat	1957	$40
LPM-1312 [M]	Puente Goes Jazz	1956	$60
LPM-2299 [M]	Revolving Bandstand	1960	$30
LSP-2299 [S]	Revolving Bandstand	1960	$40
LPM-2257 [M]	Tambo	1960	$30
LSP-2257 [S]	Tambo	1960	$40
LPM-2974 [M]	The Best of Tito Puente	1964	$30
LSP-2974(e) [P]	The Best of Tito Puente	1964	$35
LSP-1617 [S]	Top Percussion	1958	$40
LPM-1617 [M]	Top Percussion	1958	$30

ROULETTE

Number	Title	Yr	NM
R-25193 [M]	Bossa Nova	1962	$25
SR-25193 [S]	Bossa Nova	1962	$30
R-25276 [M]	My Fair Lady" Goes Latin	1964	$25
SR-25276 [S]	My Fair Lady" Goes Latin	1964	$30

TICO

Number	Title	Yr	NM
LP-1151 [M]	20th Anniversary	1967	$30
SLP-1151 [S]	20th Anniversary	1967	$25
LP-1032 [M]	Basic Cha Cha Cha	1957	$50
LP-1127 [M]	Carnival in Harlem	196?	$25
SLP-1127 [S]	Carnival in Harlem	196?	$30
JMTS-1440	Ce' Magnifique	198?	$35
LP-128 [10]	Cha Cha Cha, Volume 1	195?	$80
LP-130 [10]	Cha Cha Cha, Volume 2	195?	$80
LP-134 [10]	Cha Cha Cha, Volume 3	195?	$80
LP-1025 [M]	Cha Cha Cha at the El Morocco	1956	$60
LP-1136 [M]	Cuba Y Puerto Ricon Son	196?	$25
SLP-1136 [S]	Cuba Y Puerto Ricon Son	196?	$30
JMTS-1439	Dance Mania 80's	198?	$35
LP-1010 [M]	Dance the Cha Cha Cha	195?	$60
LP-1116 [M]	De Mi Para Ti	196?	$30
SLP-1116 [S]	De Mi Para Ti	196?	$30
LP-1109 [M]	El Mundo Latino de Tito Puente	196?	$30
SLP-1109 [S]	El Mundo Latino de Tito Puente	196?	$30
SLP-1172	El Rey (The King)	1968	$25
LP-1086 [M]	El Rey Tito: Bravo Puente	1962	$30
SLP-1086 [S]	El Rey Tito: Bravo Puente	1962	$40

—This album contains the original version of "Oye Como Va," later a hit for Santana

Number	Title	Yr	NM
SLP-1154 [S]	El Rey Y Yo (The King and I)	1967	$25
LP-1154 [M]	El Rey Y Yo (The King and I)	1967	$30
LP-1106 [M]	Excitente Ritmo	196?	$25
SLP-1106 [S]	Excitente Ritmo	196?	$30
JMTS-1425	Homenaje a Beny More	1978	$35
LP-1131 [M]	Homenaje a Rafael Hernandez	196?	$25
SLP-1131 [S]	Homenaje a Rafael Hernandez	196?	$30
LP-133 [10]	Instrumental Mambos	195?	$80
JMTS-1430	La Pareja	1978	$35
LP-1003 [M]	Mambo and Me	1955	$75
LP-1001 [M]	Mamborama	1955	$75
LP-101 [10]	Mambos, Volume 1	1951	$100
LP-103 [10]	Mambos, Volume 2	1952	$80
LP-107 [10]	Mambos, Volume 3	195?	$80
LP-114 [10]	Mambos, Volume 4	195?	$80
LP-116 [10]	Mambos, Volume 5	195?	$80
LP-131 [10]	Mambos, Volume 8	195?	$80
LP-1006 [M]	Mambos for Lovers	1955	$75
LP-1115 [M]	Mucho Puente	196?	$30
SLP-1115 [S]	Mucho Puente	196?	$30
SLP-1083 [S]	Pachanga Con Puente	1961	$40
LP-1083 [M]	Pachanga Con Puente	1961	$30
SLP-1214	P'alante!	1970	$25
CLP-1301	Para Los Rumberos	1972	$30
LP-1058 [M]	Puente in Love	1959	$40
LP-1011 [M]	Puente in Percussion	1956	$60
SLP-1203	The Best of Tito Puente	1969	$25
LP-120 [10]	The King of the Mambo and His Orchestra	195?	$80
JMTS-1413	The Legend	1976	$35
CLP-1308	Tito Puente and His Concert Orchestra	1972	$35
LP-124 [10]	Tito Puente at the Vibes and His Rhythm Quartet	195?	$80
LP-1093 [M]	Tito Puente Bailables	1963	$30
SLP-1093 [S]	Tito Puente Bailables	1963	$30
SLP-1191	Tito Puente En El Puente (On the Bridge)	1969	$25
LP-1088 [M]	Tito Puente in Puerto Rico	1963	$30
SLP-1088 [S]	Tito Puente in Puerto Rico	1963	$30
SLP-1121 [S]	Tito Puente Swings/The Exciting Lupe Sings	196?	$30
LP-1121 [M]	Tito Puente Swings/The Exciting Lupe Sings	196?	$25
LP-1049 [M]	Tito Puente Swings/ Vicentico Valdes Sings	1958	$50
SLP-1125 [S]	Tu Y Yo (You 'n' Me)	196?	$30
LP-1125 [M]	Tu Y Yo (You 'n' Me)	196?	$25
CLP-1322	Unlimited Tito	1974	$35
LP-1085 [M]	Vaya Puente	1962	$30
SLP-1085 [S]	Vaya Puente	1962	$40

PUKWANA, DUDU
Alto and tenor saxophone player.
Albums
ARISTA/FREEDOM

Number	Title	Yr	NM
AF1041	Diamond	1977	$30

PULLEN, DON, AND MILFORD GRAVES
Also see each artist's individual listings.
Albums
PULLEN-GRAVES MUSIC

Number	Title	Yr	NM
0(# unknown)	Graves-Pullen Duo	1967	$50

S.R.P.

Number	Title	Yr	NM
LP-290	Nommo	1968	$40

Jean-Luc Ponty, *The Gift of Time*, Columbia FC 40983, **$20**.

Bud Powell, *Jazz Giant*, Norgran MGN-1063, **$300**.

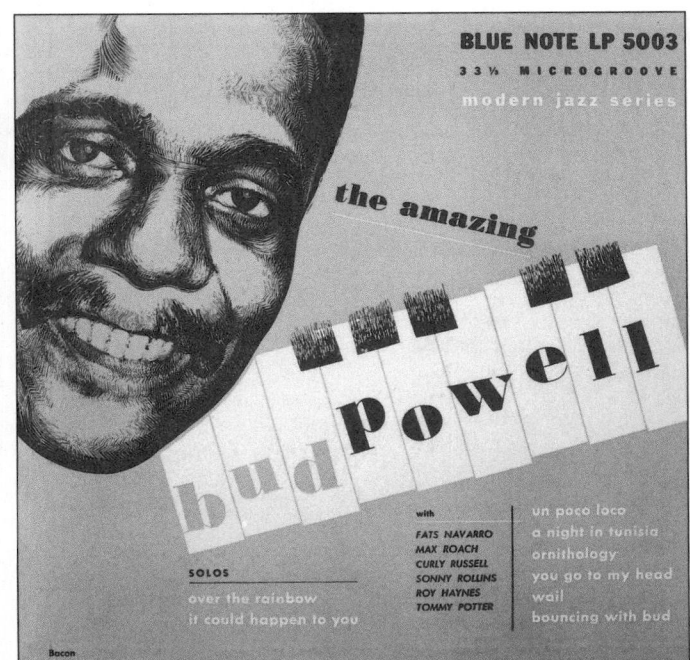

Bud Powell, *The Amazing Bud Powell*, Blue Note BLP-5003, 10-inch LP, **$1,000**.

Perez Prado, *Mambo by the King*, RCA Victor LPM-3108, 10-inch LP, **$120**.

Number	Title	Yr	NM

PULLEN, DON
Pianist.

Albums

ATLANTIC

Number	Title	Yr	NM
☐ SD8802	Montreux '77	1978	$30
☐ SD1699	Tomorrow's Promises	1977	$30

BLACK SAINT

☐ BSR-0004	Capricorn Rising	198?	$30
☐ BSR-0080	Evidence of Things Unseen	198?	$30
☐ BSR-0010	Healing Force	198?	$30
☐ BSR-0028	Milano Strut	198?	$30
☐ BSR-0038	The Magic Triangle	198?	$30
☐ BSR-0088	The Sixth Sense	1986	$30
☐ BSR-0019	Warriors	198?	$30

BLUE NOTE

| ☐ B1-91785 | New Beginnings | 1989 | $30 |

SACKVILLE

| ☐ 3008 | Solo Piano Record | 198? | $25 |

PUMA, JOE
Guitarist.

Albums

BETHLEHEM

| ☐ BCP-1012 [10] | East Coast Jazz 3 | 1954 | $250 |

COLUMBIA

| ☐ CL1618 [M] | Like Tweet | 1961 | $30 |
| ☐ CS8418 [S] | Like Tweet | 1961 | $40 |

DAWN

| ☐ DLP-1118 [M] | Wild Kitten | 1957 | $175 |

JUBILEE

| ☐ JLP-1070 [M] | Joe Puma Jazz | 1958 | $80 |

PUNCH & HANDY'S CALIFORNIA CRUSADERS
Led by PUNCH MILLER and CAP'N JOHN HANDY.

Albums

GHB

☐ 191	Punch & Handy's California Crusaders, Vol. 1	1985	$25
☐ 192	Punch & Handy's California Crusaders, Vol. 2	1985	$25
☐ 193	Punch & Handy's California Crusaders, Vol. 3	1985	$25

PURCELL, JOHN
Alto and baritone saxophone player and flutist.

Albums

MINOR MUSIC

| ☐ MM-006 | Third Kind of Blue | 1986 | $30 |

PURDIE, BERNARD
Drummer.

Albums

DATE

| ☐ TEM3006 [M] | Soul Drums | 1967 | $25 |
| ☐ TES4006 [S] | Soul Drums | 1967 | $25 |

PRESTIGE

| ☐ 10013 | Purdie Good | 1971 | $20 |
| ☐ 10038 | Shaft | 1972 | $25 |

PURIM, FLORA, AND AIRTO
Also see each artist's individual listings.

Albums

CROSSOVER

| ☐ CR-5001 | The Magicians | 1988 | $25 |
| ☐ CR-5003 | The Sun Is Out | 1989 | $35 |

GEORGE WEIN COLLECTION

| ☐ GW-3007 | Humble People | 1986 | $25 |

PURIM, FLORA
Female singer. Also see RETURN TO FOREVER.

Albums

FANTASY

☐ OJC-315	Butterfly Dreams	1988	$20
—*Reissue of Milestone 9052*			
☐ OJC-619	Stories to Tell	1991	$30
—*Reissue of Milestone 9058*			

MILESTONE

☐ M-9070	500 Miles High	1976	$30
☐ M-9052	Butterfly Dreams	1973	$35
☐ M-9077	Encounter	1977	$35
☐ M-9095	Love Reborn	1980	$30

Number	Title	Yr	NM
☐ M-9075	Nothing Will Be As It Was... Tomorrow	1977	$50
☐ M-9065	Open Your Eyes You Can Fly	1976	$35
☐ M-9058	Stories to Tell	1974	$35
☐ M-9081	That's What She Said	1978	$30

VIRGIN

| ☐ 90995 | The Midnight Sun | 1988 | $30 |

WARNER BROS.

☐ BSK3344	Carry On	1979	$35
☐ BSK3168	Everyday, Everynight	1978	$30
☐ BS2985	Nothing Will Be As It Was... Tomorrow	1977	$30

PURVIS, PAM, AND BOB ACKERMAN
Purvis is a female singer and keyboard player; Ackerman is a saxophone player, clarinetist and flutist.

Albums

BLACKHAWK

| ☐ BKH-51201 | Heart Song | 1986 | $25 |

Q

QUADRANT
Members: JOE PASS; MILT JACKSON; RAY BROWN; Mickey Roker (drums).

Albums

PABLO

| ☐ 2310837 | Quardrant | 1978 | $30 |

PABLO TODAY

| ☐ 2312117 | Quardrant Toasts Duke Ellington/All Too Soon | 1980 | $30 |

QUARTET, THE
See THE MODERN JAZZ QUARTET.

QUARTETTE TRES BIEN
Members: Percy James; Albert St. James; Richard Simmons; Jeter Thompson (keyboards).

Albums

ATLANTIC

| ☐ 1461 [M] | Bully! | 1966 | $30 |
| ☐ SD1461 [S] | Bully! | 1966 | $20 |

DECCA

☐ DL4547 [M]	Boss Tres Bien	1964	$30
☐ DL74547 [S]	Boss Tres Bien	1964	$25
☐ DL4958 [M]	Four of a Kind	1967	$20
☐ DL74958 [S]	Four of a Kind	1967	$30
☐ DL74893 [S]	Here It Is	1967	$30
☐ DL4791 [M]	In" Motion	1966	$30
☐ DL74791 [S]	In" Motion	1966	$20

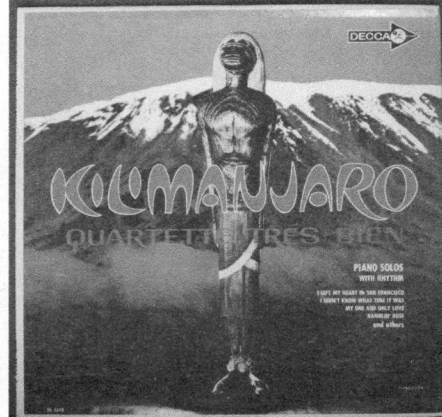

☐ DL4548 [M]	Kilimanjaro	1964	$30
☐ DL74548 [S]	Kilimanjaro	1964	$25
☐ DL75044	Our Thing	1969	$30
☐ DL4715 [M]	Sky High	1966	$30
☐ DL74715 [S]	Sky High	1966	$20
☐ DL4617 [M]	Spring Into Spring	1965	$30
☐ DL74617 [S]	Spring Into Spring	1965	$20
☐ DL4675 [M]	Stepping Out	1965	$30
☐ DL4822 [M]	Where It's At	1966	$30
☐ DL74822 [S]	Where It's At	1966	$35

GNP

| ☐ GNP-107 [M] | Kilimanjaro | 1963 | $25 |

Number	Title	Yr	NM
☐ GNPS-107 [S]	Kilimanjaro	1963	$30
☐ GNP-102 [M]	Quartette Tres Bien	1962	$25
☐ GNPS-102 [S]	Quartette Tres Bien	1962	$30

QUEBEC, IKE
Tenor saxophone player and pianist.

Albums

BLUE NOTE

☐ BST-84098 [S]	Blue and Sentimental	1962	$25
—*With "New York, USA" address on label*			
☐ BLP-4098 [M]	Blue and Sentimental	1962	$150
—*With 61st St. address on label*			
☐ BST-84098 [S]	Blue and Sentimental	1962	$60
—*With 61st St. address on label*			
☐ BST-84098 [S]	Blue and Sentimental	1967	$30
—*With "A Division of Liberty Records" on label*			

☐ BST-84098 [S]	Blue and Sentimental	1986	$25
—*The Finest in Jazz Since 1939" reissue*			
☐ BST-84114 [S]	Bossa Nova Soul Samba	1962	$40
—*With "New York, USA" address on label*			
☐ BST-84114 [S]	Bossa Nova Soul Samba	1967	$35
—*With "A Division of Liberty Records" on label*			
☐ BLP-4103 [M]	Easy Living	1962	$0
—*Canceled*			
☐ BST-84103 [S]	Easy Living	1987	$30
—*The Finest in Jazz Since 1939" issue; originally scheduled for 1962 release*			
☐ BLP-4093 [M]	Heavy Soul	1962	$60
—*With "New York, USA" address on label*			
☐ BST-84093 [S]	Heavy Soul	1961	$25
—*With "New York, USA" address on label*			
☐ BLP-4093 [M]	Heavy Soul	1961	$150
—*With 61st St. address on label*			
☐ BST-84093 [S]	Heavy Soul	1961	$60
—*With 61st St. address on label*			
☐ BST-84093 [S]	Heavy Soul	1967	$30
—*With "A Division of Liberty Records" on label*			
☐ B1-32090	Heavy Soul	1995	$35
—*The Finest in Jazz Since 1939" reissue*			
☐ BST-84105 [S]	It Might As Well Be Spring	1962	$40
—*With "New York, USA" address on label*			
☐ BST-84105 [S]	It Might As Well Be Spring	1967	$35
—*With "A Division of Liberty Records" on label*			
☐ BST-84114	Soul Samba	199?	$30
—*Classic Records reissue on audiophile vinyl*			
☐ LT-1052	With a Song in My Heart	1980	$25

MOSAIC

| ☐ MR3-121 | The Complete Blue Note 45 Sessions of Ike Quebec | 199? | $60 |
| ☐ MR4-107 | The Complete Blue Note Forties Recordings of Ike Quebec and John Hardee | 199? | $125 |

QUEEN CITY RAGTIME ENSEMBLE
From Cincinnati, Ohio: Hank Troy (piano/leader); Marl Shanahan (drums); Maurie Walker (banjo); Bill Clark (tuba).

Albums

STOMP OFF

| ☐ SOS-1138 | Everybody's Rag | 1987 | $25 |

Number	Title	Yr	NM

QUEST
Members: RICHIE BEIRACH; BILLY HART; DAVID LIEBMAN; RON McCLURE.

Albums

PATHFINDER
| ❏ PTF-8839 | Natural Selection | 1988 | $12 |

QUIGLEY, JACK

Albums

SAND
| ❏ C-30 [M] | Class In Session | 196? | $30 |

—*Red vinyl; may or may not exist on black vinyl*

❏ CS-30 [S]	Class In Session	196?	$25
❏ C-38 [M]	D'Jever	196?	$25
❏ CS-38 [S]	D'Jever	196?	$30
❏ C-28 [M]	Jack Quigley in Hollywood	196?	$30

—*Red vinyl; may or may not exist on black vinyl*

| ❏ CS-28 [S] | Jack Quigley in Hollywood | 196? | $25 |
| ❏ C-32 [M] | Listen! Quigley | 196? | $30 |

—*Red vinyl; may or may not exist on black vinyl*

| ❏ CS-32 [S] | Listen! Quigley | 196? | $25 |

QUILL, GENE
Alto saxophone player and occasional clarinetist. Also see THE FOUR MOST; MUNDELL LOWE; PHIL WOODS.

Albums

ROOST
| ❏ LP-2229 [M] | Three Bones and a Quill | 1958 | $50 |

QUINICHETTE, PAUL, AND FRANK FOSTER
Also see each artist's individual listings.

Albums

DECCA
| ❏ DL8058 [M] | Jazz Studio 1 | 1954 | $150 |

QUINICHETTE, PAUL
Tenor saxophone player. Also see JOHN COLTRANE; BENNIE GREEN; CHARLIE ROUSE; LESTER YOUNG.

Albums

BIOGRAPH
| ❏ BLP-12066 | The Kid from Denver | 199? | $60 |

DAWN
| ❏ DLP-1109 [M] | The Kid from Denver | 1956 | $100 |

EMARCY
❏ MG-36003 [M]	Moods	1955	$200
❏ MG-26035 [10]	Sequel	1954	$250
❏ MG-26022 [10]	The Vice 'Pres'	1954	$250

FANTASY
| ❏ OJC-076 | On the Sunny Side | 198? | $30 |

PRESTIGE
❏ PRLP-7147 [M]	Basie Reunion	1958	$300
❏ P-24109	Basie Reunions	198?	$35
❏ PRLP-7127 [M]	For Basie	1957	$300

—*Yellow label with W. 50th St. address*

| ❏ PRLP-7103 [M] | On the Sunny Side | 1957 | $350 |

—*Yellow label with W. 50th St. address*

STATUS
| ❏ ST-2036 [M] | For Basie | 1966 | $25 |

—*Reissue of Swingville 2036*

SWINGVILLE
| ❏ SVLP-2037 [M] | Basie Reunion | 1962 | $50 |

—*Purple label*

| ❏ SVLP-2037 [M] | Basie Reunion | 1965 | $30 |

—*Blue label, trident logo at right*

| ❏ SVLP-2036 [M] | For Basie | 1965 | $30 |

—*Blue label, trident logo at right*

| ❏ SVLP-2036 [M] | For Basie | 1962 | $50 |

—*Purple label*

TRIP
| ❏ TLP-5542 | The Vice 'Pres' | 197? | $60 |

UNITED ARTISTS
❏ UAL-4024 [M]	Like Basie	1959	$50
❏ UAS-5024 [S]	Like Basie	1959	$40
❏ UAL-4054 [M]	Like Who?	1959	$40
❏ UAS-5054 [S]	Like Who?	1959	$30
❏ UAL-4077 [M]	Paul Quinichette	1960	$40
❏ UAS-5077 [S]	Paul Quinichette	1960	$50

QUINICHETTE, PAUL/GENE ROLAND
Also see each artist's individual listings.

Albums

DAWN
| ❏ DLP-1112 [M] | Jazzville | 1957 | $100 |

QUINTET, THE
Members: DIZZY GILLESPIE; CHARLES MINGUS; CHARLIE PARKER; BUD POWELL; MAX ROACH.

Albums

DEBUT
| ❏ DLP-2 [10] | Jazz at Massey Hall | 1953 | $400 |
| ❏ DLP-4 [10] | Jazz at Massey Hall, Volume 3 | 1953 | $400 |

FANTASY
| ❏ 6006 [M] | Jazz at Massey Hall | 1962 | $50 |

—*Red vinyl*

| ❏ 6006 [R] | Jazz at Massey Hall | 1962 | $30 |

—*Black vinyl*

| ❏ 86006 [M] | Jazz at Massey Hall | 1962 | $30 |

—*Blue vinyl*

| ❏ 86006 [R] | Jazz at Massey Hall | 1962 | $25 |

—*Black vinyl*

| ❏ OJC-044 | Jazz at Massey Hall | 198? | $15 |

QUINTET OF THE HOT CLUB OF FRANCE, THE
Members: Joseph Chaput (rhythm guitar); Roget Chaput (rhythm guitar); STEPHANE GRAPPELLI; DJANGO REINHARDT; Louis Vola (bass).

Albums

CAPITOL
| ❏ T2045 [M] | Hot Club of France | 1964 | $60 |
| ❏ DT2045 [R] | Hot Club of France | 1964 | $40 |

DIAL
| ❏ LP-214 [10] | Django Reinhardt and the Hot Club Quintet | 1951 | $300 |
| ❏ LP-218 [10] | Django Reinhardt and the Quintet | 1951 | $300 |

LONDON
| ❏ LB-810 [10] | Hot Club Quintet | 1954 | $120 |
| ❏ LL1344 [M] | Swing from Paris | 1956 | $80 |

PRESTIGE
| ❏ PRST-7614 [R] | First Recordings | 1969 | $35 |

QUIRE

Albums

RCA VICTOR
| ❏ BGL1-1700 | Quire | 1976 | $30 |

R

RA, SUN
See SUN RA in the "S" section.

RACHABANE, BARNEY
Alto saxophone player.

Albums

JIVE
| ❏ 1253-1-J | Barney's Way | 1989 | $30 |

RADER, DON
Trumpeter.

Albums

DISCOVERY
| ❏ 796 | Wallflower | 1979 | $30 |

PBR
| ❏ 10 | Now | 197? | $30 |

RADKE, FRED, AND MIKE VAX
Both Radke and Vax are trumpeters, arrangers and bandleaders.

Albums

MUSIC IS MEDICINE
| ❏ 9052 | The First Reunion | 198? | $30 |

RAE, JOHN
Vibraphone player.

Albums

SAVOY
| ❏ MG-12156 [M] | Opus De Jazz, Volume 2 | 1960 | $40 |

RAEBURN, BOYD
Soprano saxophone player, arranger and bandleader.

Albums

AIRCHECK
| ❏ 20 | Rhythms by Boyd Raeburn | 197? | $25 |

CIRCLE
| ❏ 22 | Boyd Raeburn and His Orchestra 1944-45 | 198? | $25 |
| ❏ CLP-113 | More Boyd Raeburn and His Orchestra 1944-45 | 1987 | $25 |

COLUMBIA
❏ CL889 [M]	Dance Spectacular	1956	$40
❏ CL957 [M]	Fraternity Rush	1957	$40
❏ CL1073 [M]	Teen Rock	1958	$50

MUSICRAFT
| ❏ 505 | Experiments in Big Band Jazz 1945 | 198? | $25 |

SAVOY
❏ MG-12040 [M]	Boyd Meets Stravinsky	1955	$80
❏ MG-15010 [10]	Innovations by Boyd, Volume 1	1951	$150
❏ MG-15011 [10]	Innovations by Boyd, Volume 2	1951	$150
❏ MG-15012 [10]	Innovations by Boyd, Volume 3	1951	$150
❏ MG-12025 [M]	Man With the Horns	1955	$80

SAVOY JAZZ
| ❏ SJL-2250 | Jewels Plus | 1980 | $60 |
| ❏ SJC-406 | Man With the Horns | 1985 | $35 |

RAFF, RENEE
Female singer.

Albums

AUDIO FIDELITY
| ❏ AFLP-2142 [M] | Among the Stars | 1965 | $35 |
| ❏ AFSD-6142 [S] | Among the Stars | 1965 | $25 |

RAGTIME BANJO COMMISSION, THE

Albums

GHB
| ❏ GHB-154 | The Ragtime Banjo Commission | 1981 | $25 |

RAHIM, EMANUEL K., AND THE KAHLIQA
Percussionist.

Albums

COBBLESTONE
| ❏ 9014 | Total Submission | 1972 | $30 |

RAHMLEE
Full name: Rahmlee Michael Davis. Trumpeter and fluegel horn player.

Albums

HEADFIRST
| ❏ 9703 | Rise of the Phoenix | 198? | $30 |

RAI, VASANT
From India. Sarod player.

Albums

VANGUARD
| ❏ VSD-79414 | Autumn Song | 1978 | $30 |
| ❏ VSD-79379 | Spring Flowers | 197? | $30 |

RAINBOW (3)
Led by organist Will Boulware.

Albums

INNER CITY
| ❏ IC-6001 | Crystal Green | 197? | $35 |

Number	Title	Yr	NM

RAINER, TOM
Pianist.
Albums
MUSIC IS MEDICINE

❑ 9042	Night Music	198?	$30

RAINEY, CHUCK
Bass player.
Albums
COBBLESTONE

❑ 9008	Chuck Rainey Coalition	1972	$25

RAINEY, MA
Female singer, one of the pioneer blues singers.
Albums
BIOGRAPH

❑ LP-12001	Blues the World Forgot	1968	$20
❑ LP-12011	Oh My Babe Blues	197?	$15
❑ LP-12032	Queen of the Blues	197?	$15

MILESTONE

❑ 2008	Blame It on the Blues	196?	$20
❑ 2017	Down in the Basement	197?	$15
❑ 2001	Immortal Ma Rainey	1967	$20
❑ 47021	Ma Rainey	197?	$20

RIVERSIDE

❑ RLP 12-137 [M]	Broken Hearted Blues	1956	$250
❑ RLP 12-108 [M]	Ma Rainey	1955	$300
❑ RLP-1003 [10]	Ma Rainey, Vol. 1	1953	$300
❑ RLP-1016 [10]	Ma Rainey, Vol. 2	1953	$300
❑ RLP-1045 [10]	Ma Rainey, Vol. 3	1954	$300

RALKE, DON
Arranger and composer.
Albums
CROWN

❑ CLP-5019 [M]	Bongo Madness	1957	$30

WARNER BROS.

❑ W1321 [M]	Bourbon Street Beat	1959	$30
❑ WS1321 [S]	Bourbon Street Beat	1959	$30
❑ W1360 [M]	But You've Never Heard Gershwin with Bongos	1960	$25
❑ WS1360 [S]	But You've Never Heard Gershwin with Bongos	1960	$30
❑ W1398 [M]	The Savage and Sensuous Bongos	1960	$30
❑ WS1398 [S]	The Savage and Sensuous Bongos	1960	$30

RAMIREZ, RAM
Pianist and composer.
Albums
MASTER JAZZ

❑ 8122	Rampant Ram	1973	$30

RAMPART STREET PARADERS, THE
Members: Clyde Hurley (trumpet); Abe Lincoln (trombone); MARTY MATLOCK (clarinet); EDDIE MILLER (saxophones); GEORGE VAN EPS (guitar).
Albums
COLUMBIA

❑ CL785 [M]	Dixieland My Dixieland	1956	$60
❑ CL648 [M]	Rampart and Vine	1955	$50

—Maroon label, gold print

❑ CL648 [M]	Rampart and Vine	1956	$60

—Red and black label with six "eye" logos

❑ CL1061 [M]	Texas! U.S.A.	1957	$60

HARMONY

❑ HL7214 [M]	Real Dixieland	196?	$35

RANDI, DON
Pianist, arranger and composer. Also see THE MUSIC COMPANY.
Albums
CAPITOL

❑ ST-287	Love Theme from Romeo and Juliet	1969	$25

PALOMAR

❑ 24002 [M]	Don Randi!	1965	$35
❑ 34002 [S]	Don Randi!	1965	$25

POPPY

❑ PY-5701	Don Randi Trio at the Baked Potato	1972	$35

REPRISE

❑ R-6229 [M]	Revolver Jazz	1966	$25
❑ RS-6229 [S]	Revolver Jazz	1966	$30

VERVE

❑ V-8524 [M]	Last Night With the Don Randi Trio	1963	$30
❑ V6-8524 [S]	Last Night With the Don Randi Trio	1963	$35
❑ V-8469 [M]	Where Do We Go From Here?	1962	$30
❑ V6-8469 [S]	Where Do We Go From Here?	1962	$35

WORLD PACIFIC

❑ WP-1297 [M]	Feelin' Like Blues	1960	$100
❑ ST-1297 [S]	Feelin' Like Blues	1960	$100

RANELIN, PHIL
Trombonist, composer and arranger.
Albums
TRIBE

❑ PRSD-2226	Message from the Tribe	197?	$100
❑ TRCD4006	The Time Is Now!	1974	$80

RANEY, DOUG
Guitarist. Also see JIMMY AND DOUG RANEY.
Albums
STEEPLECHASE

❑ SCS-1191	Black and White	198?	$30
❑ SCS-1105	Cuttin' Loose	198?	$30
❑ SCS-1212	Guitar, Guitar, Guitar	198?	$30
❑ SCS-1166	I'll Close My Eyes	1982	$30
❑ SCS-1082	Introducing Doug Raney	1978	$30
❑ SCS-1200	Lazy Bird	198?	$30
❑ SCS-1144	Listen	1981	$30

RANEY, JIMMY
Guitarist and composer. Also see BOB BROOKMEYER; KENNY BURRELL; THE MANHATTAN JAZZ ALL-STARS; ZOOT SIMS.
Albums
ABC-PARAMOUNT

❑ ABC-129 [M]	Jimmy Raney Featuring Bob Brookmeyer	1956	$200
❑ ABC-167 [M]	Jimmy Raney in Three Attitudes	1957	$150

BIOGRAPH

❑ LP-12060	Too Marvelous for Words	198?	$30

DAWN

❑ DLP-1120 [M]	Jimmy Raney Visits Paris	1958	$100

FANTASY

❑ OJC-1706	Jimmy Raney/A	1985	$30

MUSE

❑ MR-5004	Strings and Swings	1973	$40

NEW JAZZ

❑ NJLP-1103 [10]	Jimmy Raney Ensemble	1953	$500
❑ NJLP-1101 [10]	Introducing Phil Woods Jimmy Raney Quartet Featuring Hall Overton	1953	$500

PAUSA

❑ 7021	Momentum	197?	$30

PRESTIGE

❑ PRLP-7089 [M]	Jimmy Raney/A	1957	$300

—Yellow label with W. 50th St. address

❑ PRLP-203 [10]	Jimmy Raney Ensemble	1955	$400
❑ PRLP-179 [10]	Jimmy Raney in Sweden	1954	$400
❑ PRLP-156 [10]	Jimmy Raney Plays	1953	$400
❑ PRLP-201 [10]	Jimmy Raney Quartet	1955	$400
❑ PRLP-199 [10]	Jimmy Raney Quintet	1954	$400

XANADU

❑ 116	Influence	197?	$60
❑ 132	Live in Tokyo	197?	$60
❑ 140	Solo	1977	$60

RANEY, JIMMY AND DOUG
Also see each artist's individual listings.
Albums
STEEPLECHASE

❑ SCS-1134	Duets	1980	$35
❑ SCS-1184	Nardis	198?	$35
❑ SCS-1118	Stolen Moments	198?	$35

RANEY, JIMMY/GEORGE WALLINGTON
Also see each artist's individual listings.
Albums
EMARCY

❑ MG-36121 [M]	Swingin' in Sweden	1958	$200

RANEY, SUE, AND BOB FLORENCE
Also see each artist's individual listings.
Albums
DISCOVERY

❑ DS-931	Flight of Fancy: A Journey of Alan and Marilyn Bergman	1987	$25
❑ DS-939	Quietly There	1988	$25

RANEY, SUE
Female singer.
Albums
CAPITOL

❑ T2032 [M]	All By Myself	1964	$75
❑ ST2032 [S]	All By Myself	1964	$50
❑ T1335 [M]	Songs for a Raney Day	1960	$50
❑ ST1335 [S]	Songs for a Raney Day	1960	$60

DISCOVERY

❑ DS-913	Ridin' High	1984	$25
❑ DS-875	Sue Raney Sings the Music of Johnny Mandel	1982	$25

IMPERIAL

❑ LP-9323 [M]	Alive and In Love	1966	$150
❑ LP-12323 [S]	Alive and In Love	1966	$150
❑ LP-9355 [M]	New and Now	1967	$150
❑ LP-12355 [S]	New and Now	1967	$150
❑ LP-9376 [M]	With a Little Help from My Friends	1968	$175
❑ LP-12376 [S]	With a Little Help from My Friends	1968	$150

RANGELL, NELSON
Soprano, alto and tenor saxophone player and flutist.
Albums
GRP

❑ GR-9593	Playing for Keeps	1989	$30

RATZER, KARL
Guitarist.
Albums
CMP

❑ CMP-13-ST	Dancing on a String	198?	$25

VANGUARD

❑ VSD-79407	In Search of the Ghost	1978	$30
❑ VSD-79423	Street Talk	1979	$30

RAULSTON, FRED
Vibraphone player and percussionist.
Albums
INNER CITY

❑ IC-1054	Open Stream	197?	$30
❑ IC-1085	Uncharted Waters	198?	$30

SEA BREEZE

❑ SBD-104	Fred's Rescue	1987	$25

RAVA, ENRICO
Trumpeter.
Albums
BLACK SAINT

❑ BSR-0011	Il Giro Del Giorno	198?	$30

ECM

❑ 1122	Enrico Rava Quartet	1978	$30
❑ 1224	Opening Night	1981	$25
❑ 1063	Pilgrim	197?	$30
❑ 1078	Plot	1976	$30

SOUL NOTE

❑ SN-1064	Andanada	198?	$30
❑ SN-1114	String Band	1985	$30

RAVAZZA, CARL
Male singer, violinist and bandleader.
Albums
HINDSIGHT

❑ HSR-117	Carl Ravazza and His Orchestra 1940-44	198?	$25

Julian Priester, *Keep Swingin'*, Riverside RLP 12-316, **$200**.

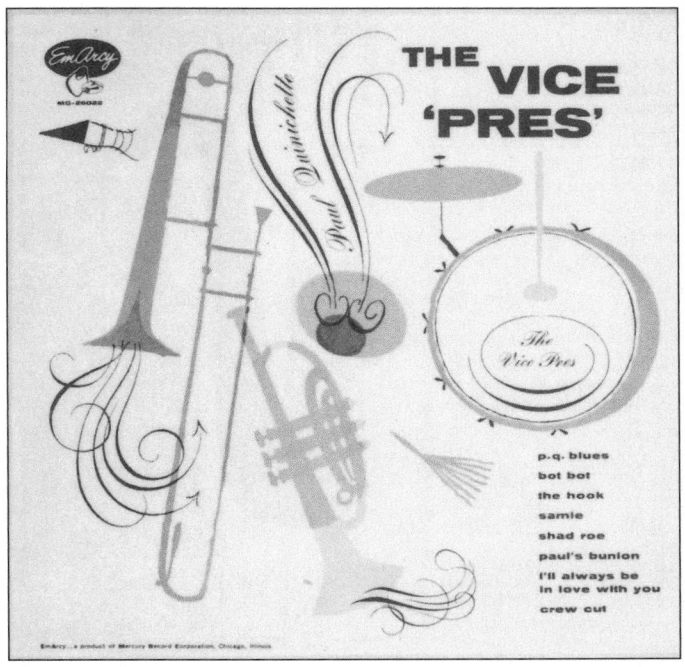

Paul Quinichette, *The Vice 'Pres'*, EmArcy MG 26022, 10-inch LP, **$250**.

Paul Quinichette, *On the Sunny Side*, Prestige PRLP-7103, yellow label with W. 50th St. address, **$350**.

The Quintet, *Jazz at Massey Hall*, Debut DLP-2, **$400**.

Number	Title	Yr	NM

RAWLINS, STEVE
Pianist.
Albums
SEA BREEZE
| ❑ SB-3003 | Step Right Up | 1985 | $25 |

RAWLS, LOU
Male singer. Has had hits in pop, R&B/soul and dance music as well as jazz.
7-Inch Extended Plays
CAPITOL CREATIVE PRODUCTS
| ❑ SU-479 | Another Saturday Night/ Chain Gang/Cool Night// Take Me for What I Am/Win Your Love/What Makes the Ending So Sad | 1970 | $15 |

— Stereo jukebox issue; small hole, plays at 33 1/3 rpm
| ❑ SU-479 [PS] | Bring It on Home | 1970 | $15 |
Albums
ALLEGIANCE
| ❑ AV-5016 | Trying As Hard As I Can | 198? | $12 |
BELL
| ❑ 1318 | She's Gone | 1974 | $15 |
BLUE NOTE
❑ B1-91937	At Last	1989	$15
❑ B1-93841	It's Supposed to Be Fun	1990	$18
❑ B1-91441	Stormy Monday	1990	$15
— Reissue of Capitol 1714

CAPITOL
❑ T1824 [M]	Black and Blue	1963	$25
❑ ST1824 [S]	Black and Blue	1963	$30
❑ ST-479	Bring It on Home	1970	$18
❑ SWBB-261	Close-Up	1969	$25
— Reissue of 1824 and 2042 in one package
❑ STBB-720	Down Here on the Ground/I'd Rather Drink Muddy Water	1971	$25
❑ T2864 [M]	Feelin' Good	1968	$30
❑ ST2864 [S]	Feelin' Good	1968	$18
❑ T2401 [M]	Lou Rawls and Strings	1965	$25
❑ ST2401 [S]	Lou Rawls and Strings	1965	$30
❑ T2632 [M]	Lou Rawls Carryin' On!	1966	$18
❑ ST2632 [S]	Lou Rawls Carryin' On!	1966	$25
❑ T2459 [M]	Lou Rawls Live!	1966	$18
❑ ST2459 [S]	Lou Rawls Live!	1966	$25
❑ SM-2459	Lou Rawls Live!	197?	$12
— Reissue with new prefix
| ❑ SN-16097 | Lou Rawls Live! | 1980 | $10 |
— Budget-line reissue
❑ T2566 [M]	Lou Rawls Soulin'	1966	$18
❑ ST2566 [S]	Lou Rawls Soulin'	1966	$25
❑ SM-2566	Lou Rawls Soulin'	197?	$12
— Reissue with new prefix
❑ ST2790 [S]	Merry Christmas, Ho, Ho, Ho	1967	$15
❑ T2790 [M]	Merry Christmas, Ho, Ho, Ho	1967	$18
❑ T2273 [M]	Nobody But Lou	1965	$25
❑ ST2273 [S]	Nobody But Lou	1965	$30
❑ T1714 [M]	Stormy Monday	1962	$25
❑ ST1714 [S]	Stormy Monday	1962	$30
❑ SM-1714	Stormy Monday	197?	$12
— Reissue with new prefix
❑ T2756 [M]	That's Lou	1967	$25
❑ ST2756 [S]	That's Lou	1967	$18
❑ SKBB-11585	The Best from Lou Rawls	1976	$15
❑ SKAO2948	The Best of Lou Rawls	1968	$18
❑ SM-2948	The Best of Lou Rawls	197?	$12
— Reissue with new prefix
| ❑ SN-16096 | The Best of Lou Rawls | 1980 | $10 |
— Budget-line reissue
❑ ST-122	The Way It Was	1969	$18
❑ ST-215	The Way It Was -- The Way It Is	1969	$18
❑ ST 8-0215	The Way It Was -- The Way It Is	1969	$25
— Capitol Record Club edition
❑ T2042 [M]	Tobacco Road	1964	$25
❑ ST2042 [S]	Tobacco Road	1964	$30
❑ T2713 [M]	Too Much!	1967	$25
❑ ST2927	You're Good for Me	1968	$18
❑ ST-325	Your Good Thing	1969	$18
❑ ST-427	You've Made Me So Very Happy	1970	$18

EPIC
❑ FE39403	Close Company	1984	$12
❑ FE40210	Love All Your Blues Away	1986	$12
❑ FE37448	Now Is the Time	1982	$12
❑ FE38553	When the Night Comes	1983	$12
MGM

❑ SE-4861	A Man of Value	1973	$15
❑ SE-4965	Live at the Century Plaza	1974	$15
❑ SE-4771	Natural Man	1971	$15
❑ SE-4809	Silk & Soul	1972	$15
PHILADELPHIA INT'L.
❑ PZ33957	All Things in Time	1976	$12
— No bar code on cover
| ❑ PZ33957 | All Things in Time | 198? | $10 |
— With bar code on cover
❑ FZ39285	Classics	1984	$12
❑ JZ36006	Let Me Be Good to You	1979	$12
❑ PZ36006	Let Me Be Good to You	198?	$10
— Budget-line reissue
❑ PZ235517	Lou Rawls Live	1978	$15
❑ JZ36774	Shades of Blue	1980	$12
❑ JZ36304	Sit Down and Talk to Me	1979	$12
❑ PZ36304	Sit Down and Talk to Me	198?	$10
— Budget-line reissue
| ❑ PZ34488 | Unmistakably Lou | 1977 | $12 |
| ❑ PZ34488 | Unmistakably Lou | 1986 | $10 |
— Budget-line reissue
| ❑ JZ35036 | When You Hear Lou, You've Heard It All | 1977 | $12 |
PICKWICK
| ❑ SPC-3156 | Come On In, Mr. Blues | 1971 | $12 |
| ❑ SPC-3228 | Gee Baby | 1972 | $12 |
POLYDOR
| ❑ PD-1-6086 | Naturally | 1976 | $12 |

RAY, JOHNNIE
Male singer. Most of his output is pop, but the below features jazz-group backing.
Albums
COLUMBIA
| ❑ CL1225 [M] | 'Til Morning | 1958 | $40 |
— Red and black label with six "eye" logos
| ❑ CL1225 [M] | 'Til Morning | 1963 | $25 |
— Red label with either "Guraranteed High Fidelity" or "360 Sound Mono" at bottom

REBILLOT, PAT
Pianist.
Albums
ATLANTIC
| ❑ SD1663 | Free Fall | 1974 | $30 |

REBIRTH BRASS BAND
Led by Keith Frazier (bass drum) and Philip Frazier (tuba).
Albums
ARHOOLIE
| ❑ 1092 | Here to Stay | 1986 | $25 |
— As "Rebirth Jazz Band of New Orleans
ROUNDER
| ❑ 2093 | Feel Like Funkin' It Up | 1989 | $30 |

RECOIL
Led by PAT COIL.
Albums
PAUSA
| ❑ 7117 | Pardon My Fantasy | 198? | $25 |
| ❑ 7168 | The Fantasy Continues | 1985 | $25 |

RED, SONNY
Alto saxophone player. Also see ART PEPPER.
Albums
BLUE NOTE
| ❑ BLP-4032 [M] | Out of the Blue | 1960 | $400 |
— Deep groove" version (deep indentation under label on both sides)
| ❑ BLP-4032 [M] | Out of the Blue | 1960 | $150 |
— Regular version, W. 63rd St. address on label
| ❑ ST-84032 [S] | Out of the Blue | 1960 | $60 |
— With W. 63rd St. address on label
| ❑ BLP-4032 [M] | Out of the Blue | 1963 | $60 |
— With "New York, USA" address on label
| ❑ ST-84032 [S] | Out of the Blue | 1963 | $25 |
— With "New York, USA" address on label
| ❑ ST-84032 [S] | Out of the Blue | 1967 | $35 |
— With "A Division of Liberty Records" on label

FANTASY
| ❑ OJC-148 | Images | 198? | $25 |
JAZZLAND
❑ JLP-32 [M]	Breezin'	1960	$30
❑ JLP-932 [M]	Breezin'	1960	$40
❑ JLP-74 [M]	Images	1962	$30
❑ JLP-974 [S]	Images	1962	$40
❑ JLP-59 [M]	The Mode	1961	$200
❑ JLP-959 [S]	The Mode	1961	$200
MAINSTREAM
❑ MRL-324	Sonny Red	1971	$35

RED ONION JAZZ BAND, THE
Albums
BIOGRAPH
| ❑ LP-12012 | There'll Be a Hot Time in the Old Town Tonight | 1969 | $35 |
RIVERSIDE
| ❑ RLP 12-260 [M] | Dance Off Both Your Shoes In Hi-Fi | 1958 | $300 |

RED ONIONS AND OTTILIE
From Berlin, Germany.
Albums
STOMP OFF
| ❑ SOS-1090 | Mad Dog | 1985 | $25 |

RED ROSE RAGTIME BAND
Led by Mike Schwimmer (washboard, vocals).
Albums
STOMP OFF
| ❑ SOS-1128 | A Rose Is a Rose Is a Rose | 1987 | $25 |

RED ROSELAND CORNPICKERS, THE
Albums
STOMP OFF
❑ SOS-1101	Double Talk	1985	$25
❑ SOS-1133	Handful of Keith	1987	$25
❑ SOS-1153	Red Hot Band	1988	$25
❑ SOS-1102	That's No Bargain	1985	$25

RED WING BLACKBIRDS RAGTIME BAND
Albums
STOMP OFF
| ❑ SOS-1018 | Two-Step Ball | 198? | $25 |

REDD, FREDDIE, AND HAMPTON HAWES
Also see each artist's individual listings.
Albums
FANTASY
| ❑ OJC-1705 | Piano: East/West | 1985 | $25 |
NEW JAZZ
| ❑ NJLP-8307 [M] | Movin' | 1963 | $0 |
— Canceled; reassigned to Status
PRESTIGE
| ❑ PRLP-7067 [M] | Piano: East/West | 1956 | $300 |
STATUS
| ❑ ST-8307 [M] | Movin' | 1965 | $40 |

REDD, FREDDIE
Pianist and composer.
Albums
BLUE NOTE
| ❑ BLP-4027 [M] | Music From "The Connection | 1960 | $300 |
— Deep groove" version (deep indentation under label on both sides)
| ❑ BLP-4027 [M] | Music From "The Connection | 1963 | $60 |
— With "New York, USA" address on label
| ❑ BST-84027 [S] | Music From "The Connection | 1967 | $20 |
— With "A Division of Liberty Records" on label
| ❑ BLP-4027 [M] | Music From "The Connection | 1960 | $200 |
— Regular version, W. 63rd St. address on label
| ❑ BST-84027 [S] | Music From "The Connection | 1960 | $100 |

Number	Title	Yr	NM
— With W. 63rd St. address on label			
❑ BST-84027 [S]	Music From "The Connection	1963	$50
— With "New York, USA" address on label			
❑ BLP-4045 [M]	Shades of Redd	1960	$1000
— Deep groove" version (deep indentation under label on both sides)			
❑ BLP-4045 [M]	Shades of Redd	1963	$300
— With "New York, USA" address on label			
❑ BST-84045 [S]	Shades of Redd	1960	$0
— Canceled			
❑ BLP-4045 [M]	Shades of Redd	1960	$300
— Regular version, W. 63rd St. address on label			
FANTASY			
❑ OJC-1748	San Francisco Suite For Jazz Trio	1990	$30
INTERPLAY			
❑ 7715	Straight Ahead	1979	$30
MOSAIC			
❑ MR3-124	The Complete Blue Note Recordings of Freddie Redd	199?	$30
PRESTIGE			
❑ PRLP-197 [10]	Introducing the Freddie Redd Trio	1954	$300
RIVERSIDE			
❑ RLP 12-250 [M]	San Francisco Suite For Jazz Trio	1957	$350
❑ 6184	San Francisco Suite For Jazz Trio	198?	$30

REDD, VI
Female singer and alto saxophone player.

Albums

Number	Title	Yr	NM
ATCO			
❑ 33-157 [M]	Lady Soul	1963	$30
❑ SD 33-157 [S]	Lady Soul	1963	$40
UNITED ARTISTS			
❑ UAJ-14016 [M]	Bird Call	1962	$40
❑ UAJS-15016 [S]	Bird Call	1962	$50

REDMAN, DEWEY, AND ED BLACKWELL
Blackwell played drums. Also see DEWEY REDMAN.

Albums

Number	Title	Yr	NM
BLACK SAINT			
❑ BSR-0093	Red and Black in Willisau	1985	$30

REDMAN, DEWEY
Tenor saxophone player, percussionist and male singer. Also see OLD AND NEW DREAMS.

Albums

Number	Title	Yr	NM
ABC IMPULSE!			
❑ AS-9300	Coincide	1974	$35
❑ AS-9250	The Ear of the Behearer	1973	$35
ARISTA/FREEDOM			
❑ AF1011	Look for the Black Star	1976	$30
BLACK SAINT			
❑ 120123	Living on the Edge	1990	$35
ECM			
❑ 1225	The Struggle Continues	1981	$25
GALAXY			
❑ 5118	Musics	1980	$30
❑ 5130	Soundsigns	198?	$30

REDMAN, DON
Multi-instrumentalist, male singer, bandleader and arranger.

Albums

Number	Title	Yr	NM
GOLDEN CREST			
❑ GC-3017 [M]	Park Avenue Patter	1958	$40
RCA VICTOR			
❑ LPV-520 [M]	Master of the Big Band	1965	$25
ROULETTE			
❑ R-25070 [M]	Dixieland in High Society	1960	$25
❑ SR-25070 [M]	Dixieland in High Society	1960	$30
STEEPLECHASE			
❑ SCC-6020	For Europeans Only	198?	$30

REDMAN, GEORGE
Drummer.

Albums

Number	Title	Yr	NM
SKYLARK			
❑ SKLP-20 [10]	The George Redman Group	1954	$150

REDMOND, EDGAR

Albums

Number	Title	Yr	NM
DISQUE-PHENOMENON			
❑ 2696 [10]	Edgar Redmond & the Modern String Ensemble	1965	$30

REDOLFI, MICHEL
Composer, arranger and electronic instrumentalist. The below album was recorded entirely underwater!

Albums

Number	Title	Yr	NM
HAT ART			
❑ 2002	Sonic Waters	1986	$35

REECE, DIZZY, AND TUBBY HAYES
Also see each artist's individual listings.

Albums

Number	Title	Yr	NM
SAVOY			
❑ MG-12111 [M]	Changing the Jazz at Buckingham Palace	1957	$100

REECE, DIZZY
Trumpeter.

Albums

Number	Title	Yr	NM
BEE HIVE			
❑ BH-7001	Manhattan Project	1978	$60
BLUE NOTE			
❑ BLP-4006 [M]	Blues in Trinity	1958	$150
— Regular version, W. 63rd St. address on label			
❑ BST-4006 [S]	Blues in Trinity	1959	$120
— Regular version, W. 63rd St. address on label			
❑ BLP-4006 [M]	Blues in Trinity	1963	$80
— With "New York, USA" address on label			
❑ BST-4006 [S]	Blues in Trinity	1963	$30
— With "New York, USA" address on label			
❑ BST-84006 [S]	Blues in Trinity	1967	$60
— With "A Division of Liberty Records" on label			
❑ B1-32093	Blues in Trinity	1995	$35
❑ BLP-4033 [M]	Soundin' Off	1960	$800
— Deep groove" version; W. 63rd St. address on label			
❑ BLP-4033 [M]	Soundin' Off	1960	$200
— Regular version, W. 63rd St. address on label			
❑ BST-84033 [S]	Soundin' Off	1960	$150
— With W. 63rd St. address on label			
❑ BLP-4033 [M]	Soundin' Off	1963	$100
— With "New York, USA" address on label			
❑ BST-84033 [S]	Soundin' Off	1963	$40
— With "New York, USA" address on label			

Number	Title	Yr	NM
❑ BST-84033 [S]	Soundin' Off	1967	$60
— With "A Division of Liberty Records" on label			
❑ BLP-4023 [M]	Star Bright	1959	$250
— Deep groove" version; W. 63rd St. address on label			
❑ BLP-4023 [M]	Star Bright	1959	$150
— Regular version, W. 63rd St. address on label			

Number	Title	Yr	NM
❑ BST-84023 [S]	Star Bright	1959	$120
— With W. 63rd St. address on label			
❑ BLP-4023 [M]	Star Bright	1963	$80
— With "New York, USA" address on label			
❑ BST-84023 [S]	Star Bright	1963	$40
— With "New York, USA" address on label			
❑ BST-84023 [S]	Star Bright	1967	$60
— With "A Division of Liberty Records" on label			
❑ BLP-4023 [M]	Star Bright	200?	$60
— 200-gram reissue; distributed by Classic Records			
DISCOVERY			
❑ DS-839	Moose the Mooche	1982	$50
IMPERIAL			
❑ LP-9043 [M]	London Jazz	1957	$175
NEW JAZZ			
❑ NJLP-8274 [M]	Asia Minor	1962	$150
— Purple label			
❑ NJLP-8274 [M]	Asia Minor	1965	$150
— Blue label, trident logo at right			

REED, LUCY
Female singer.

Albums

Number	Title	Yr	NM
FANTASY			
❑ 3212 [M]	The Singing Reed	1956	$150
— Red vinyl			
❑ 3212 [M]	The Singing Reed	195?	$80
— Black vinyl			
❑ 3243 [M]	This Is Lucy Reed	1957	$150
— Red vinyl			
❑ 3243 [M]	This Is Lucy Reed	195?	$80
— Black vinyl			

REED, WAYMON
Trumpeter.

Albums

Number	Title	Yr	NM
ARTISTS HOUSE			
❑ 10	46th and 8th	1980	$30

REESE, DELLA
Female singer. Earlier material appears in the Goldmine Standard Catalog of American Records.

Albums

Number	Title	Yr	NM
ABC			
❑ 612 [M]	Della on Strings of Blue	1967	$25
❑ S-612 [S]	Della on Strings of Blue	1967	$20
❑ 569 [M]	Della Reese Live	1966	$20
❑ S-569 [S]	Della Reese Live	1966	$25
❑ S-636	I Gotta Be Me…This Trip Out	1968	$20
❑ 589 [M]	One More Time	1967	$25
❑ S-589 [S]	One More Time	1967	$20
❑ AC-30002	The ABC Collection	1976	$20
ABC-PARAMOUNT			
❑ ABC-524 [M]	C'mon and Hear Della Reese	1965	$25
❑ ABCS-524 [S]	C'mon and Hear Della Reese	1965	$25
❑ ABC-540 [M]	I Like It Like Dat!	1966	$20
❑ ABCS-540 [S]	I Like It Like Dat!	1966	$25
AVCO EMBASSY			
❑ 33004	Black Is Beautiful	1969	$20
❑ 33017	Right Now	1970	$20
JAZZ A LA CARTE			
❑ 3	One of a Kind	1978	$20
JUBILEE			
❑ JLP-1071 [M]	A Date with Della Reese at Mr. Kelly's in Chicago	1959	$30
— Originals have blue labels			
❑ SDJLP-1071 [S]	A Date with Della Reese at Mr. Kelly's in Chicago	1959	$30
— Originals have blue labels			
❑ JGM-1071 [M]	A Date with Della Reese at Mr. Kelly's in Chicago	196?	$25
— Black label with all-silver print			
❑ JGM-1071 [M]	A Date with Della Reese at Mr. Kelly's in Chicago	1963	$25
— Black label, multi-colored spokes around "jubilee			
❑ SDJLP-1071 [S]	A Date with Della Reese at Mr. Kelly's in Chicago	1959	$30
— Black label with all-silver print			

Number	Title	Yr	NM
❏ SDJLP-1071 [S]	A Date with Della Reese at Mr. Kelly's in Chicago	1962	$25
—Black label, multi-colored spokes around "jubilee," yellow spoke goes almost to center hole			
❏ JGS-1071 [S]	A Date with Della Reese at Mr. Kelly's in Chicago	1965	$25
—Black label, multi-colored spokes around "jubilee," yellow spoke goes nowhere near center hole; new prefix			
❏ JLP-1083 [M]	Amen	1959	$30
❏ SDJLP-1083 [S]	Amen	1959	$30
❏ JLP-1116 [M]	And That Reminds Me	1960	$30
❏ JLP-1026 [M]	Melancholy Baby	1957	$30
❏ JGM-5002 [M]	The Best of Della Reese	196?	$20
❏ JGS-5002 [S]	The Best of Della Reese	196?	$25
❏ JLP-1095 [M]	The Story of the Blues	1960	$30
—Original labels are black with all-silver print			
❏ SDJLP-1095 [S]	The Story of the Blues	1960	$30
—Original labels are black with all-silver print			
❏ JLP-1095 [M]	The Story of the Blues	1960	$25
—Black label, multi-colored spokes around "jubilee," yellow spoke goes almost to center hole			
❏ JGM-1095 [M]	The Story of the Blues	1962	$25
—Black label, multi-colored spokes around "jubilee," yellow spoke goes almost to center hole; new prefix			
❏ JGS-1095 [S]	The Story of the Blues	1964	$25
—Black label, multi-colored spokes around "jubilee," yellow spoke goes nowhere near center hole			
❏ SDJLP-1095 [S]	The Story of the Blues	1962	$30
—Black label, multi-colored spokes around "jubilee," yellow spoke goes almost to center hole			
❏ JLP-1109 [M]	What Do You Know About Love	1960	$30
PICKWICK			
❏ SPC-3058	And That Reminds Me	196?	$15
RCA VICTOR			
❏ LPM-2157 [M]	Della	1960	$25
❏ LPM-2204 [M]	Della by Starlight	1960	$25
❏ LSP-2204 [S]	Della by Starlight	1960	$30
❏ LPM-2280 [M]	Della Della Cha-Cha-Cha	1961	$25
❏ LSP-2280 [S]	Della Della Cha-Cha-Cha	1961	$30
❏ LPM-2568 [M]	Della on Stage	1962	$25
❏ LSP-2568 [S]	Della on Stage	1962	$30
❏ LPM-2872 [M]	Della Reese at Basin Street East	1964	$25
❏ LSP-2872 [S]	Della Reese at Basin Street East	1964	$30
❏ LPM-2814 [M]	Moody	1963	$25
❏ LSP-2814 [S]	Moody	1963	$30
❏ LPM-2391 [M]	Special Delivery	1961	$25
❏ LSP-2391 [S]	Special Delivery	1961	$30
❏ LSP-4651	The Best of Della Reese	1972	$15
❏ LPM-2419 [M]	The Classic Della	1962	$25
❏ LSP-2419 [S]	The Classic Della	1962	$30
❏ LPM-2711 [M]	Waltz with Me, Della	1963	$25
❏ LSP-2711 [S]	Waltz with Me, Della	1963	$30

REEVES, DIANNE
Female singer and composer.

Albums
BLUE NOTE

Number	Title	Yr	NM
❏ BT-46906	Dianne Reeves	1987	$25
EMI			
❏ E1-92401	Never Too Far	1990	$30
PALO ALTO			
❏ PA-8026	Welcome to My Love	1983	$35
PALO ALTO/TBA			
❏ TB-203	For Every Heart	1984	$30

REHAK, FRANK/ALEX SMITH
Rehak played trombone.

Albums
DAWN

Number	Title	Yr	NM
❏ DLP-1107 [M]	Jazzville, Vol. 2	1956	$100

REICHMAN, JOE
Pianist and bandleader.

Albums
CIRCLE

Number	Title	Yr	NM
❏ CLP-84	The Pagliacci of the Piano	1986	$25
HINDSIGHT			
❏ HSR-166	Joe Reichman and His Orchestra 1944-49	198?	$25
RCA CAMDEN			
❏ CAL-230 [M]	Show Tunes of Broadway	1954	$40
❏ CAL-133 [M]	Tea for Two	195?	$35

REID, IRENE
Female singer.

Albums
MGM

Number	Title	Yr	NM
❏ E-4159 [M]	It's Only the Beginning for Irene Reid	1963	$25
❏ SE-4159 [S]	It's Only the Beginning for Irene Reid	1963	$30
POLYDOR			
❏ 24-4040	The World Needs What I Need	1971	$35
VERVE			
❏ V-8621 [M]	Room for One More	1965	$35
❏ V6-8621 [S]	Room for One More	1965	$25

REID, RUFUS
Bass player.

Albums
SUNNYSIDE

Number	Title	Yr	NM
❏ SSC-1010	Seven Minds	1985	$25
THERESA			
❏ 111	Perpetual Stroll	1980	$30

REILLY, JACK
Keyboard player, arranger and composer.

Albums
CAROUSEL

Number	Title	Yr	NM
❏ 1001	Blue-Sean-Green	197?	$35
❏ 1002	Tributes	197?	$35
REVELATION			
❏ 36	Brinksman	198?	$25
❏ 35	Together (Again)… For the First Time	198?	$25

REINHARDT, DJANGO
Highly influential guitarist. Also see DIZZY GILLESPIE; THE QUINTET OF THE HOT CLUB OF FRANCE.

Albums
ANGEL

Number	Title	Yr	NM
❏ ANG-36985	Django Reinhardt and the Quintet of the Hot Club of France	197?	$25
❏ ANG.60011 [10]	Django's Guitar	1955	$150
❏ ANG.60003 [10]	Le Jazz Hot	1954	$150
BLUEBIRD			
❏ 9988-1-RB	Djangology 49	1990	$30
CAPITOL			
❏ TBO10226 [M]	The Best of Django Reinhardt	1960	$80
—Black colorband labels, Capitol logo at left			
CLEF			
❏ MGC-516 [10]	The Great Artistry of Django Reinhardt	1954	$300
COLUMBIA			
❏ C31479	Swing It Lightly	1972	$30
❏ PC31479	Swing It Lightly	198?	$20
—Budget-line reissue			
EMARCY			
❏ 66004	Jazz Hot	1967	$100
EPITAPH			
❏ E-4002	Django Reinhardt 1910-1953	1975	$35
EVEREST ARCHIVE OF FOLK & JAZZ			
❏ FS-212 [R]	Django Reinhardt	1968	$25
❏ FS-255	Django Reinhardt, Vol. 3	197?	$25
❏ FS-306	Django Reinhardt, Vol. 4	197?	$25
❏ FS-230 [R]	Django Reinhardt, Volume II	1969	$25
GNP CRESCENDO			
❏ GNP-9031	Django Reinhardt 1934	197?	$25
❏ GNP-9023	Django Reinhardt 1935	197?	$25
❏ GNP-9019	Django Reinhardt 1935-39	197?	$25
❏ GNP-9001	Django Reinhardt and the Quintet of the Hot Club of France	196?	$25
❏ GNP-9039	Legendary Django Reinhardt	198?	$25
❏ GNP-9002	Parisian Swing	197?	$25
❏ GNP-9038	The Immortal Django Reinhardt	198?	$25
INNER CITY			
❏ IC-1106	Compositions	198?	$30
❏ IC-1104	Django Reinhardt and the Quintet of the Hot Club of France	198?	$30
❏ IC-1105	Solos/Duos/Trios, Vol. 2	198?	$30
❏ IC-7004	The Versatile Giant	198?	$30

Number	Title	Yr	NM
JAY			
❏ 3008 [10]	Django Reinhardt	1954	$180
MERCURY			
❏ MGC-516 [10]	The Great Artistry of Django Reinhardt	1953	$300
PERIOD			
❏ SPL-1100 [10]	Django Reinhardt Memorial, Volume 1	1954	$120
❏ SPL-1101 [10]	Django Reinhardt Memorial, Volume 2	1954	$120
❏ SPL-1102 [10]	Django Reinhardt Memorial, Volume 3	1954	$120
❏ SPL-1201 [M]	Django Reinhardt Memorial Album, Volume 1	1956	$50
❏ SPL-1201 [M]	Django Reinhardt Memorial Album, Volume 2	1956	$50
❏ SPL-1203 [M]	Django Reinhardt Memorial Album, Volume 3	1956	$50
❏ SPL-1204 [M]	The Best of Django Reinhardt	1956	$50
❏ SPL-2204 [R]	The Best of Django Reinhardt	196?	$30
PRESTIGE			
❏ PRST-7633 [R]	Django Reinhardt and American Jazz Giants	1969	$35
RCA VICTOR			
❏ LPM-2319 [M]	Djangology	1961	$40
❏ LSP-2319 [R]	Djangology	196?	$30
❏ LPM-1100 [M]	Django Reinhardt	1955	$100
REPRISE			
❏ R-6075 [M]	The Immortal Django Reinhardt	1963	$30
❏ R9-6075 [R]	The Immortal Django Reinhardt	1963	$35
SUTTON			
❏ SU-274 [M]	Django Reinhardt and His Guitar	1966	$25
❏ SSU-274 [R]	Django Reinhardt and His Guitar	1966	$30
SWING			
❏ SW-8420/7	Djangologie USA Volumes 1-7	1988	$60

REMINGTON, DAVE

Albums
JUBILEE

Number	Title	Yr	NM
❏ JLP-1017 [M]	Chicago Jazz Reborn	1956	$40

REMLER, EMILY
Guitarist.

Albums
CONCORD JAZZ

Number	Title	Yr	NM
❏ CJ-265	Catwalk	1985	$25
❏ CJ-356	East to Wes	1988	$25
❏ CJ-162	Firefly	1981	$25
❏ CJ-195	Take Two	1982	$25
❏ CJ-236	Transitions	1984	$25

RENA, KID
Trumpeter.

Albums
CIRCLE

Number	Title	Yr	NM
❏ L-409 [10]	Kid Rena Delta Jazz Band	1951	$80

RENAUD, HENRI
Pianist, composer and bandleader.

Albums
CONTEMPORARY

Number	Title	Yr	NM
❏ C-2502 [10]	The Henri Renaud All-Stars	1953	$250
PERIOD			
❏ SPL-1211 [M]	The Birdlanders	1954	$80
❏ SPL-1212 [M]	The Birdlanders	1954	$80

RENDELL, DON
Saxophone player (soprano, alto, tenor), clarinetist and flutist.

Albums
JAZZLAND

Number	Title	Yr	NM
❏ JLP-51 [M]	Roarin'	1961	$30
❏ JLP-951 [S]	Roarin'	1961	$40

RENE, HENRI
Accordion player, composer, arranger and bandleader.

Albums

Boyd Raeburn, *Innovations by Boyd Raeburn*, Volume 3, Savoy MG 15012, 10-inch LP, **$150**.

Jimmy Raney, *Jimmy Raney Quartet Featuring Hall Overton*, New Jazz NJLP-1101, 10-inch LP, **$500**.

Jimmy Raney/George Wallington, *Swingin' in Sweden*, EmArcy MG 36121, **$200**.

Dizzy Reece, *Blues in Trinity*, Blue Note BLP-4006, with W. 63rd St. address on label, **$150**.

Number	Title	Yr	NM
IMPERIAL			
❏ LP-9096 [M]	Swingin' 59	1960	$150
❏ LP-12040 [S]	Swingin' 59	1960	$150
❏ LP-9074 [M]	White Heat	1959	$175
❏ LP-12021 [S]	White Heat	1959	$175
RCA CAMDEN			
❏ CAL-312 [M]	In Love Again	195?	$35
❏ CAL-353 [M]	Melodic Magic	195?	$35
❏ CAL-130 [M]	Portfolio for Easy Listening	195?	$35
RCA VICTOR			
❏ LPM-1947 [M]	Compulsion to Swing	1958	$30
❏ LSP-1947 [S]	Compulsion to Swing	1958	$30
❏ LSA-2396 [S]	Dynamic Dimensions	1961	$30
❏ LPM-3076 [10]	Listen to Rene	1953	$40
❏ LPM-1046 [M]	Music for Bachelors	1955	$120
—*Cover model is Jayne Mansfield*			
❏ LPM-1583 [M]	Music for the Weaker Sex	1957	$30
❏ LPM-1033 [M]	Passion in Paint	1955	$80
❏ LPM-2002 [M]	Riot in Rhythm	1959	$25
❏ LSP-2002 [S]	Riot in Rhythm	1959	$30
❏ LPM-3049 [10]	Serenade to Love	1953	$40

RENTIE, DAMON

Albums

PALO ALTO/TBA			
❏ TB-212	Designated Hitter	198?	$25
❏ TB-219	Don't Look Back	1986	$25
❏ TB-230	Skyline	1987	$25

RENZI, MIKE
Pianist and arranger.

Albums

STASH			
❏ ST-273	A Beautiful Friendship	1988	$25

REPERCUSSION UNIT
Members: John Bergamo, Jim Hildebrandt, Gregg Johnson, Ed Mann, Lucky Mosko and Larry Stein. All play various percussion instruments and non-instruments.

Albums

CMP			
❏ CMP-31-ST	In Need Again	1987	$25

RESNICK, ART
Pianist and composer.

Albums

CAPRI			
❏ 74015	A Gift	198?	$25
SYMPOSIUM			
❏ 2005	Jungleopolis	197?	$35

RETURN TO FOREVER
Landmark fusion group led by CHICK COREA. Among the other members at various times: AIRTO; STANLEY CLARKE; AL DiMEOLA; JOE FARRELL; EARL KLUGH; FLORA PURIM; LENNY WHITE.

Albums

COLUMBIA			
❏ PC34682	Musicmagic	1977	$30
—*No bar code on cover*			
❏ PC34682	Musicmagic	1985	$20
—*Reissue with bar code*			
❏ PCQ34682 [Q]	Musicmagic	1977	$60
❏ JC35281	Return to Forever Live	1979	$25
❏ PC34076	Romantic Warrior	1976	$30
—*No bar code on cover*			
❏ PC34076	Romantic Warrior	198?	$20
—*Reissue with bar code*			
❏ JC36359	The Best of Return to Forever	1980	$30
❏ PC36359	The Best of Return to Forever	198?	$25
—*Budget-line reissue with new prefix*			
ECM			
❏ 1022ST	Return to Forever	197?	$35
—*Original issue; made in Germany*			
❏ ECM-1-1022	Return to Forever	197?	$30
—*Distributed by Polydor*			
POLYDOR			
❏ PD-5536	Hymn of the Seventh Galaxy	1973	$30
❏ 825336-1	Hymn of the Seventh Galaxy	198?	$20
—*Reissue*			

Number	Title	Yr	NM
❏ PD-5525	Light as a Feather	1973	$30
❏ PD-6512	No Mystery	1975	$30
❏ PD-6509	Where Have I Known You Before	1974	$30

REVELERS, THE
Male vocal group with piano.

Albums

RONDO-LETTE			
❏ A-50 [M]	Jazz at the Downstairs Club	1962	$25
❏ SA-50 [S]	Jazz at the Downstairs Club	1962	$30

REVERBERI
Italian group led by Gian Piero Reverberi.

Albums

PAUSA			
❏ 7003	Reverberi and ...	198?	$25
❏ 7016	Timer	198?	$25
UNITED ARTISTS			
❏ UA-LA813-H	Stairway to Heaven	1977	$30

REVOLUTIONARY ENSEMBLE, THE
Members: LEROY JENKINS; JEROME COOPER; Sirone (bass, trombone).

Albums

ESP-DISK'			
❏ S-3007	The Revolutionary Ensemble at Peace Church	196?	$120
HORIZON			
❏ SP-708	People's Republic	1975	$30
INDIA NAVIGATION			
❏ IN-1023	Manhattan Cycles	197?	$35
INNER CITY			
❏ IC-3016	The Revolutionary Ensemble	197?	$30

REXROTH, KENNETH, AND LAWRENCE FERLINGHETTI
Also see each artist's individual listings.

Albums

FANTASY			
❏ 7002 [M]	Poetry Readings from the Cellar	1957	$200
—*Red vinyl*			
❏ 7002 [M]	Poetry Readings from the Cellar	1957	$100
—*Black vinyl*			

REXROTH, KENNETH
Beat poet.

Albums

FANTASY			
❏ 7008 [M]	Poetry and Jazz at the Blackhawk	1958	$200
—*Red vinyl*			
❏ 7008 [M]	Poetry and Jazz at the Blackhawk	1958	$100
—*Black vinyl*			

REY, ALVINO
Guitarist, bandleader and arranger.

Albums

CAPITOL			
❏ T808 [M]	Aloha	1957	$60
❏ T1262 [M]	Ping Pong!	1959	$50
❏ ST1262 [S]	Ping Pong!	1959	$60
❏ T1085 [M]	Swinging Fling	1958	$60
❏ ST1085 [S]	Swinging Fling	1958	$60
❏ T1395 [M]	That Lonely Feeling	1960	$50
❏ ST1395 [S]	That Lonely Feeling	1960	$60
HINDSIGHT			
❏ HSR-196	Alvino Rey and His Orchestra 1940-41	198?	$25
❏ HSR-121	Alvino Rey and His Orchestra 1946	198?	$25
❏ HSR-167	Alvino Rey and His Orchestra 1946, Vol. 2	198?	$25

Number	Title	Yr	NM
REYNOLDS, TOMMY			
Clarinet player and bandleader.			
Albums			
AUDIO LAB			
❏ AL-1509 [M]	Dixieland All-Stars	1958	$100
KING			
❏ 395-510 [M]	Jazz for Happy Feet	1956	$80
ROYALE			
❏ 18117 [10]	Tommy Reynolds Orchestra with Bon Bon	195?	$80

REYS, RITA
Female singer.

Albums

COLUMBIA			
❏ CL903 [M]	The Cool Voice of Rita Reys with Art Blakey and the Jazz Messengers	1956	$150
EPIC			
❏ LN3522 [M]	Her Name Is Rita Reys	1957	$150
INNER CITY			
❏ IC-1157	Songs of Antonio Carlos Jobim	198?	$35

RHODES, GEORGE
Pianist.

Albums

GROOVE			
❏ LG-1005 [M]	Real George!	1956	$60

RHYNE, MEL
Organist.

Albums

JAZZLAND			
❏ JLP-16 [M]	Organizing	1960	$30
❏ JLP-916 [S]	Organizing	1960	$40

RHYTHM AND BLU
Violin trio: John Blake; DIDIER LOCKWOOD; MICHAL URBANIAK.

Albums

GRAMAVISION			
❏ 18-8608	Rhythm and Blu	1986	$30

RHYTHM COMBINATION, THE
German group led by Peter Herbolzheimer.

Albums

BASF			
❏ 25124	Power Play	197?	$35
❏ 21751	Waitaminute	197?	$35

RHYTHMIC UNION, THE
Led by percussionist Robert Chappell.

Albums

INNER CITY			
❏ IC-1100	Gentle Awakening	198?	$30

RICE, DARYLE
Female singer and guitarist.

Albums

AUDIOPHILE			
❏ AP-141	I Walk with Music	1980	$25

RICH, BUDDY, AND MAX ROACH
Also see each artist's individual listings.

Albums

MERCURY			
❏ MG-20448 [M]	Rich Versus Roach	1959	$200
❏ SR-60133 [S]	Rich Versus Roach	1959	$250

RICH, BUDDY, AND SWEETS EDISON
Also see each artist's individual listings.

Albums

VERVE			
❏ MGV-8129 [M]	Buddy and Sweets	1957	$200
—*Reissue of Norgran 1038*			
❏ V-8129 [M]	Buddy and Sweets	1961	$50

Number	Title	Yr	NM

RICH, BUDDY

Drummer, bandleader and male singer. Also see LIONEL HAMPTON; GENE KRUPA; FLIP PHILLIPS; LESTER YOUNG.

Albums

ARGO
❏ LP-676 [M]	Playtime	1961	$60
❏ LPS-676 [S]	Playtime	1961	$40

EMARCY
❏ EMS-2-402	Both Sides	1976	$35
❏ 66006	Driver	1967	$100

EVEREST ARCHIVE OF FOLK & JAZZ
❏ 260	Buddy Rich	197?	$35

GREAT AMERICAN
❏ 1030	Class of '78	1978	$50

— Direct-to-disc version of Gryphon 781

GROOVE MERCHANT
❏ 3307	The Big Band Machine	1976	$30
❏ 3303	The Last Blues Album, Vol. 1	1975	$30
❏ 528	The Roar of '74	1974	$30
❏ 4407	Tuff Dude!	197?	$35
❏ 3301	Very Live at Buddy's Place	1974	$30

GRYPHON
❏ 781	Class of '78	1978	$30

LIBERTY
❏ 11006	Keep the Customer Satisfied	1970	$35

MCA
❏ 5186	The Buddy Rich Band	1981	$25

MERCURY
❏ MG-20451 [M]	Richcraft	1959	$200
❏ SR-60136 [S]	Richcraft	1959	$250
❏ MG-20461 [M]	The Voice Is Rich	1959	$150
❏ SR-60144 [S]	The Voice Is Rich	1959	$200

NORGRAN
❏ MGN-26 [10]	Buddy Rich Swingin'	1954	$200
❏ MGN-1031 [M]	Sing and Swing with Buddy Rich	1955	$150
❏ MGN-1052 [M]	The Swingin' Buddy Rich	1955	$120

— Reissue of 26
❏ MGN-1088 [M]	This One's for Basie	1956	$250

PACIFIC JAZZ
❏ ST-20126	A New One	1968	$50
❏ PJ-10117 [M]	Big Swing Face	1967	$60
❏ ST-20117 [S]	Big Swing Face	1967	$50
❏ LN-10090	Big Swing Face	1981	$20

— Budget-line reissue
❏ PJ-10113 [M]	Swingin' New Big Band	1966	$60
❏ ST-20113 [S]	Swingin' New Big Band	1966	$50
❏ LN-10089	Swingin' New Big Band	1981	$20

— Budget-line reissue

PAUSA
❏ 9004	Buddy & Soul	1983	$25

QUINTESSENCE
❏ 25051	Mr. Drums	1978	$30

RCA VICTOR
❏ LSP-4593	A Different Drummer	1971	$30
❏ ANL1-1090	A Different Drummer	1975	$25

— Reissue of 4593
❏ CPL2-2273	Buddy Rich Plays & Plays & Plays	1977	$35
❏ LSP-4666	Rich in London	1972	$30
❏ AFL1-4666	Rich in London	1977	$25

— Reissue with new prefix
❏ APL1-1503	Speak No Evil	1976	$30
❏ LSP-4802	Stick It	1972	$30
❏ AFL1-4802	Stick It	1977	$25

— Reissue with new prefix

UNITED ARTISTS
❏ UXS-86	Buddy Rich Superpak	1972	$35

VERVE
❏ V-8712 [M]	Big Band Shout	1967	$50
❏ V6-8712 [S]	Big Band Shout	1967	$35
❏ V-8425 [M]	Blues Caravan	1962	$60
❏ V6-8425 [S]	Blues Caravan	1962	$60
❏ VSP-40 [M]	Buddy Rich at J.A.T.P.	1966	$35
❏ VSPS-40 [R]	Buddy Rich at J.A.T.P.	1966	$30
❏ MGV-8285 [M]	Buddy Rich in Miami	1958	$150
❏ V-8285 [M]	Buddy Rich in Miami	1961	$50
❏ MGV-2075 [M]	Buddy Rich Just Sings	1957	$150
❏ V-2075 [M]	Buddy Rich Just Sings	1961	$50
❏ MGV-2009 [M]	Buddy Rich Sings Johnny Mercer	1956	$150
❏ V-2009 [M]	Buddy Rich Sings Johnny Mercer	1961	$50
❏ V-8471 [M]	Burnin' Beat	1962	$60
❏ V6-8471 [S]	Burnin' Beat	1962	$60
❏ V-8484 [M]	Drum Battle: Gene Krupa vs. Buddy Rich	1962	$60
❏ V6-8484 [S]	Drum Battle: Gene Krupa vs. Buddy Rich	1962	$60
❏ V6-8824	Monster	1973	$35
❏ V6-8778	Super Rich	1969	$35
❏ MGV-8142 [M]	The Swingin' Buddy Rich	1957	$150

— Reissue of Norgran 1052
❏ V-8142 [M]	The Swingin' Buddy Rich	1961	$50
❏ MGV-8168 [M]	The Wailing Buddy Rich	1957	$200

— Reissue of Norgran 1078
❏ V-8168 [M]	The Wailing Buddy Rich	1961	$50
❏ MGV-8176 [M]	This One's for Basie	1957	$250

— Reissue of Norgran 1086
❏ V-8176 [M]	This One's for Basie	1961	$50

WHO'S WHO IN JAZZ
❏ 21006	Lionel Hampton Presents Buddy Rich	1978	$30

WORLD PACIFIC
❏ WPS-20158	Buddy & Soul	1969	$100
❏ WPS-20133	Mercy, Mercy	1968	$100
❏ WPS-20169	The Best of Buddy Rich	1970	$100
❏ WPS-20113	The Buddy Rich Big Band	1968	$100

RICH, LISA

Female singer.

Albums

DISCOVERY
❏ 908	Listen Here	1986	$25

TREND
❏ 541	Touch of the Rare	1986	$25

RICHARDS, ANN

Female singer.

Albums

ATCO
❏ 33-136 [M]	Ann, Man!	1961	$40
❏ SD 33-136 [S]	Ann, Man!	1961	$60

CAPITOL
❏ T1087 [M]	I'm Shooting High	1959	$80
❏ ST1087 [S]	I'm Shooting High	1959	$100
❏ T1406 [M]	The Many Moods of Ann Richards	1960	$100
❏ ST1406 [S]	The Many Moods of Ann Richards	1960	$150
❏ T1495 [M]	Two Much!	1961	$100
❏ ST1495 [S]	Two Much!	1961	$150

VEE JAY
❏ LP-1070 [M]	Live...At the Losers	1963	$40
❏ SR-1070 [S]	Live...At the Losers	1963	$50

RICHARDS, EMIL

Percussionist.

Albums

ABC IMPULSE!
❏ AS-9188 [S]	Journey to Bliss	1969	$200
❏ AS-9182 [S]	Spirit of '76	1968	$200

UNI
❏ 3008 [M]	New Sound	1967	$30
❏ 73008 [S]	New Sound	1967	$25
❏ 3003 [M]	New Time Element	1967	$30
❏ 73003 [S]	New Time Element	1967	$25

RICHARDS, JOHNNY

Tenor saxophone player, composer, arranger and bandleader.

Albums

BETHLEHEM
❏ BCP-6011 [M]	Something Else by Johnny Richards	1956	$250
❏ BCP-6032	Something Else by Johnny Richards	197?	$50

— Reissue, distributed by RCA Victor

CAPITOL
❏ T981 [M]	Experiments In Sound	1958	$60

— Turquoise label
❏ T885 [M]	Wide Range	1957	$200

— Turquoise label

CORAL
❏ CRL57304 [M]	Walk Softly/Run Wild	1959	$120
❏ CRL757304 [S]	Walk Softly/Run Wild	1959	$80

CREATIVE WORLD
❏ ST-1052	Wide Range	198?	$35

DISCOVERY
❏ DS-915	Je Vous Adore	1986	$60

ROULETTE
❏ SR-25351 [S]	Aqui Se Habla Espanol	1967	$30
❏ R-25351 [M]	Aqui Se Habla Espanol	1967	$30
❏ R-52114 [M]	My Fair Lady, My Way	1964	$60
❏ SR-52114 [S]	My Fair Lady, My Way	1964	$40
❏ R-52008 [M]	The Rites of Diablo	1958	$80
❏ SR-52008 [S]	The Rites of Diablo	1958	$60

RICHARDS, RED

Pianist.

Albums

SACKVILLE
❏ 2017	I'm Shooting High	198?	$30

WEST 54
❏ 8005	Mellow Tone	1980	$30
❏ 8000	Soft Buns	1979	$30

RICHARDS, TREVOR

Drummer.

Albums

STOMP OFF
❏ SOS-1222	The Trevor Richards New Orleans Trio	1991	$30

RICHARDSON, JEROME

Saxophone player (soprano, alto, tenor, baritone), flutist and piccolo player. Also see THE PRESTIGE BLUES SWINGERS.

Albums

NEW JAZZ
❏ NJLP-8205 [M]	Jerome Richardson Sextet	1958	$150

— Purple label
❏ NJLP-8205 [M]	Jerome Richardson Sextet	1965	$150

— Blue label, trident logo at right
❏ NJLP-8226 [M]	Roamin' with Richardson	1959	$400

— Purple label
❏ NJLP-8226 [M]	Roamin' with Richardson	1965	$150

— Blue label, trident logo at right

UNITED ARTISTS
❏ UAJ-14006 [M]	Going to the Movies	1962	$30
❏ UAJS-15006 [S]	Going to the Movies	1962	$40

VERVE
❏ V-8729 [M]	Groove Merchant	1967	$25
❏ V6-8729 [S]	Groove Merchant	1967	$35

RICHARDSON, JIMMY

Albums

STARDAY
❏ SLP-126 [M]	Sweet with a Beat	1960	$30

RICHARDSON, WALLY

Guitarist.

Albums

PRESTIGE
❏ PRST-7569	Soul Guru	1969	$25

RICHMOND, DANNIE

Drummer.

Albums

ABC IMPULSE!
❏ AS-98 [S]	Dannie Richmond	1968	$35

GATEMOUTH
❏ 1004	Dannie Richmond Quintet	1980	$30

IMPULSE!
❏ AS-98 [S]	Dannie Richmond	1966	$120
❏ A-98 [M]	Dannie Richmond	1966	$200

RED RECORD
❏ VPA-161	Dionysius	198?	$30

SOUL NOTE
❏ SN-1005	Ode to Mingus	198?	$30

RICHMOND, MIKE, AND ANDY LAVERNE

Also see each artist's individual listings.

Albums

STEEPLECHASE
❏ SCS-1101	For Us	198?	$30

RICHMOND, MIKE

Bass player.

Albums

INNER CITY
❏ IC-1065	Dream Waves	1978	$30

Number	Title	Yr	NM

RIDLEY, LARRY
Bass player.
Albums
STRATA-EAST
| ❏ SES-19759 | Sum of the Parts | 1975 | $30 |

RIEDEL, GEORGE /
Bass player, composer and arranger.
Albums
PHILIPS
| ❏ PHM200140 [M] | Jazz Ballet | 1964 | $35 |
| ❏ PHS600140 [S] | Jazz Ballet | 1964 | $25 |

RIEMANN, KURT
Electronic instrumentalist and composer.
Albums
INNOVATIVE COMMUNICATION
| ❏ KS 80.047 | Electronic Nightworks | 1987 | $30 |

RIFKIN, JOSHUA
Classical pianist, arranger and composer. Most of his work is outside the scope of this book, but the below LPs helped to re-acquaint the United States with the long-neglected music of Scott Joplin.
Albums
NONESUCH
| ❏ H-71248 | Piano Rags by Scott Joplin | 1970 | $30 |
| ❏ H-71264 | Piano Rags by Scott Joplin, Vol. 2 | 1971 | $30 |

RILEY, DOUG
Pianist and organist.
Albums
PM
| ❏ 07 | Dreams | 1977 | $30 |

RIMINGTON, SAMMY
Clarinetist, alto saxophone player and bandleader.
Albums
GHB
❏ GHB-181	Sammy Rimington and the Mouldy Five, Vol. 1	1985	$25
❏ GHB-182	Sammy Rimington and the Mouldy Five, Vol. 2	1985	$25
❏ GHB-94	Sammy Rimington Plays George Lewis Classics	198?	$25
JAZZ CRUSADE
❏ 1005	Sammy Rimington Plays George Lewis Classics	196?	$35
PROGRESSIVE
❏ PRO-7077	The Exciting Sax of Sammy Rimington	1987	$25

RIPPINGTONS, THE
Members: Russ Freeman (leader, guitar, keyboards); Brandon Fields (alto, tenor and soprano sax, flute); Steve Reid (percussion); Tony Morales (drums). They appeared on all four of the below albums; others came and went.
Albums
GRP
| ❏ GR-9588 | Tourist in Paradise | 1989 | $30 |
| ❏ GR-9618 | Welcome to the St. James Club | 1990 | $35 |
PASSPORT JAZZ
| ❏ PJ88042 | Kilimanjaro | 1988 | $30 |
| ❏ PJ88019 | Moonlighting | 1987 | $30 |

RITENOUR, LEE
Guitarist. Also see DAVE GRUSIN.
Albums
ELEKTRA
❏ 60358	Banded Together	1984	$25
❏ 6E-192	Feel the Night	1979	$25
❏ 6E-331	Rit	1981	$25
❏ 60186	Rit/2	1982	$25
❏ 6E-136	The Captain's Journey	1978	$25
ELEKTRA/MUSICIAN
❏ 60310	On the Line	1983	$25
❏ 60024	Rio	1982	$25
EPIC

Number	Title	Yr	NM

❏ PE34426	Captain Fingers	1977	$25
—Orange label			
❏ PE34426	Captain Fingers	1979	$20
—Dark blue label			
❏ PE33947	First Course	1976	$25
—Orange label			
❏ PE33947	First Course	1979	$20
—Dark blue label			
❏ JE36527	The Best of Lee Ritenour	1980	$25
❏ PE36527	The Best of Lee Ritenour	198?	$20
—Budget-line reissue			
GRP
❏ GR-9594	Color Rit	1989	$30
❏ GR-1021	Earth Run	1986	$25
❏ GR-9570	Festival	1988	$25
❏ GR-1042	Portrait	1987	$25
❏ GR-1017	Rio	1986	$20
❏ GR-9615	Stolen Moments	1990	$35
MOBILE FIDELITY
❏ 1-147	Captain Fingers	1985	$50
—Audiophile vinyl			
NAUTILUS
❏ NR-41	Rit	198?	$40
—Audiophile vinyl			

RITZ, LYLE
Ukulele and bass player.
Albums
VERVE
❏ MGV-8333 [M]	50th State Jazz	1959	$100
❏ MGVS-6070 [S]	50th State Jazz	1960	$120
❏ V-8333 [M]	50th State Jazz	1961	$30
❏ V6-8333 [S]	50th State Jazz	1961	$25
❏ MGV-2087 [M]	How About Uke?	1957	$150

RITZ, THE
Tenor saxophone player.
Albums
PAUSA
| ❏ 7190 | Born to Bop | 1986 | $25 |

RIVERS, JAMES
Albums
SPINDLETOP
| ❏ STP-101 | The Dallas Sessions | 1986 | $30 |

RIVERS, MAVIS
Female singer.
Albums
CAPITOL
| ❏ T1210 [M] | Take a Number | 1959 | $60 |
| ❏ ST1210 [S] | Take a Number | 1959 | $75 |
DELOS
| ❏ DMS-4002 | It's a Good Day | 1983 | $30 |
REPRISE
❏ R-2002 [M]	Mavis	1961	$30
❏ R9-2002 [S]	Mavis	1961	$40
❏ R-6074 [M]	Mavis Rivers Meets Shorty Rogers	1963	$30
❏ RS-6074 [S]	Mavis Rivers Meets Shorty Rogers	1963	$30
VEE JAY
❏ VJ-1132 [M]	We Remember Mildred Bailey	1964	$30
❏ VJS-1132 [S]	We Remember Mildred Bailey	1964	$40

RIVERS, RAY
Guitarist.
Albums
INSIGHT
| ❏ 202 | Let Me Hear Some Jazz | 198? | $25 |
PROJECT 3
| ❏ PR5110SD | Cool Cat on a Jazz Guitar | 1983 | $25 |

RIVERS, SAM, AND DAVE HOLLAND
Also see each artist's individual listings.
Albums
IAI

Number	Title	Yr	NM

| ❏ 373843 | Sam Rivers and Dave Holland | 197? | $35 |
| ❏ 373848 | Sam Rivers and Dave Holland, Vol. 2 | 1976 | $35 |

RIVERS, SAM
Saxophone player, flutist, pianist and composer.
Albums
ABC IMPULSE!
❏ AS-9286	Crystals	1974	$35
❏ AS-9302	Hues	1974	$35
❏ IA-9352	Sam Rivers Live	1978	$35
❏ AS-9316	Sizzle	1975	$35
❏ AS-9251	Streams	1973	$35
BLACK SAINT
❏ BSR-0064	Colours	1982	$30
BLUE NOTE
❏ BLP-4249 [M]	A New Conception	1966	$100
❏ BST-84249 [S]	A New Conception	1966	$60
—With "New York, USA" address on label			
❏ BST-84249 [S]	A New Conception	1967	$50
—With "A Division of Liberty Records" on label			
❏ BLP-4206 [M]	Contours	1965	$60
❏ BST-84206 [S]	Contours	1965	$30
—With "New York, USA" address on label			
❏ BST-84206 [S]	Contours	1967	$25
—With "A Division of Liberty Records" on label			
❏ BLP-4261 [M]	Dimensions and Extensions	1966	$0
—Canceled			
❏ BST-84261 [S]	Dimensions and Extensions	1986	$30
—The Finest in Jazz Since 1939' label; originally scheduled for 1966 release			
❏ BLP-4184 [M]	Fuchsia Swing Song	1964	$60
❏ BST-84184 [S]	Fuchsia Swing Song	1964	$30
—With "New York, USA" address on label			
❏ BST-84184 [S]	Fuchsia Swing Song	1967	$25
—With "A Division of Liberty Records" on label			
❏ BN-LA453-H2	Involution	1975	$35
ECM
❏ 1162	Contrasts	1980	$30
MCA
❏ 4149	Live Trio Session	198?	$30
PAUSA
❏ 7015	The Quest	198?	$25
RED RECORD
❏ VPA-106	The Quest	198?	$30
TOMATO
❏ TOM-8002	Waves	1979	$30

RIVERSIDE JAZZ STARS, THE
Members include JIMMY HEATH; BLUE MITCHELL; CLARK TERRY; BOBBY TIMMONS; JULIUS WATKINS.
Albums
RIVERSIDE
| ❏ RLP-397 [M] | A Jazz Version of "Kean | 1961 | $200 |
| ❏ RS-9397 [S] | A Jazz Version of "Kean | 1961 | $200 |

RIZZI, TONY
Guitarist.
Albums
MILAGRO
| ❏ 1000 | Tony Rizzi Plays Charlie Christian | 197? | $30 |
STARLITE
| ❏ 6002 [10] | Tony Rizzi Guitar | 1954 | $50 |

ROACH, FREDDIE
Organist and composer.
Albums
BLUE NOTE
❏ BLP-4190 [M]	All That's Good	1965	$60
❏ BST-84190 [S]	All That's Good	1965	$30
—With "New York, USA" address on label			
❏ BST-84190 [S]	All That's Good	1967	$35
—With "A Division of Liberty Records" on label			
❏ BLP-4168 [M]	Brown Sugar	1964	$60
❏ BST-84168 [S]	Brown Sugar	1964	$30
—With "New York, USA" address on label			
❏ BST-84168 [S]	Brown Sugar	1967	$35
—With "A Division of Liberty Records" on label			

Django Reinhardt, *Django Reinhardt*, RCA Victor LPM-1100, **$100**.

Django Reinhardt, Django's Guitar, Angel ANG.60011, 10-inch LP, **$150**.

Return to Forever, *Romantic Warrior*, Columbia PC 34076, no bar code on cover, **$30**.

Rita Reys, *Her Name Is Rita Reys*, Epic LN 3522, **$150**.

Number	Title	Yr	NM
❏ BLP-4113 [M]	Down to Earth	1962	$60
❏ BST-84113 [S]	Down to Earth	1962	$30
— With "New York, USA" address on label			
❏ BST-84113 [S]	Down to Earth	1967	$35
— With "A Division of Liberty Records" on label			
❏ BLP-4158 [M]	Good Move	1964	$60
❏ BST-84158 [S]	Good Move	1964	$30
— With "New York, USA" address on label			
❏ BST-84158 [S]	Good Move	1967	$35
— With "A Division of Liberty Records" on label			
❏ BLP-4128 [M]	Mo' Greens, Please	1963	$60
❏ BST-84128 [S]	Mo' Greens, Please	1963	$30
— With "New York, USA" address on label			
❏ BST-84128 [S]	Mo' Greens, Please	1967	$35
— With "A Division of Liberty Records" on label			

PRESTIGE
Number	Title	Yr	NM
❏ PRLP-7507 [M]	Mocha Motion	1967	$30
❏ PRST-7507 [S]	Mocha Motion	1967	$25
❏ PRLP-7521 [M]	My People -- Soul People	1967	$30
❏ PRST-7521 [S]	My People -- Soul People	1967	$25
❏ PRLP-7490 [M]	The Soul Book	1967	$30
❏ PRST-7490 [S]	The Soul Book	1967	$25

ROACH, MAX, AND ANTHONY BRAXTON
Also see each artist's individual listings.
Albums
HAT HUT
❏ 06	One in Two -- Two in One	1980	$50

ROACH, MAX, AND ARCHIE SHEPP
Also see each artist's individual listings.
Albums
HAT HUT
❏ 13	The Long March	1980	$50

ROACH, MAX, AND CECIL TAYLOR
Also see each artist's individual listings.
Albums
SOUL NOTE
❏ SN-1100/1	Historic Concerts	1985	$35

ROACH, MAX, AND CLIFFORD BROWN
See CLIFFORD BROWN.

ROACH, MAX, AND CONNIE CROTHERS
Also see each artist's individual listings.
Albums
NEW ARTISTS
❏ NA-1001	Swish	198?	$30

ROACH, MAX, AND STAN LEVEY
Also see each artist's individual listings.
Albums
LIBERTY
❏ LRP-3064 [M]	Drummin' the Blues	1957	$150

ROACH, MAX; SONNY CLARK; GEORGE DUVIVIER
Duvivier is a bass player. Also see SONNY CLARK; MAX ROACH.
Albums
TIME
❏ 52101 [M]	Max Roach, Sonny Clark, George Duvivier	1962	$60
❏ S-2101 [S]	Max Roach, Sonny Clark, George Duvivier	1962	$40

ROACH, MAX
Drummer. Also see DUKE ELLINGTON; THE JAZZ ARTISTS GUILD; M'BOOM; CHARLES MINGUS; CHARLIE PARKER; THE QUINTET; BUDDY RICH; SONNY ROLLINS.
Albums
ABC IMPULSE!
❏ AS-16 [S]	It's Time	1968	$160
❏ AS-8 [S]	Percussion Bitter Sweet	1968	$200

ARGO
❏ LP-623 [M]	Max	1958	$100
❏ LPS-623 [S]	Max	1958	$40

ATLANTIC
Number	Title	Yr	NM
❏ 1467 [M]	Drums Unlimited	1966	$50
❏ SD1467 [S]	Drums Unlimited	1966	$60
❏ SD1587	Lift Every Voice and Sing	1972	$30
❏ 1435 [M]	Max Roach Trio Featuring the Legendary Hasaan	1965	$50
❏ SD1435 [S]	Max Roach Trio Featuring the Legendary Hasaan	1965	$60
❏ SD1510 [S]	Members Don't Get Weary	1968	$50

BAINBRIDGE
❏ 1042	Max Roach	198?	$25
❏ 1044	Max Roach/George Duvivier/Sonny Clark	198?	$25

CANDID
❏ CD-8002 [M]	We Insist -- Freedom Now Suite	1960	$120
❏ CS-9002 [S]	We Insist -- Freedom Now Suite	1960	$120

DEBUT
❏ DLP-13 [10]	Max Roach Quartet Featuring Hank Mobley	1954	$400

EMARCY
Number	Title	Yr	NM
❏ MG-36108 [M]	Jazz in 3/4 Time	1957	$200
❏ SR-80002 [S]	Jazz in 3/4 Time	1959	$200
❏ 826456-1	Jazz in 3/4 Time	1986	$25
❏ MG-36132 [M]	Max Roach + 4 on the Chicago Scene	1958	$120
❏ MG-36098 [M]	Max Roach + 4	1957	$200
❏ SR-80001 [S]	Max Roach + 4	1959	$200
❏ MG-36140 [M]	Max Roach Plus Four At Newport	1958	$120
❏ SR-80010 [S]	Max Roach Plus Four At Newport	1959	$200
❏ MG-36144 [M]	Max Roach with the Boston Percussion Ensemble	1958	$120
❏ SR-80015 [S]	Max Roach with the Boston Percussion Ensemble	1959	$200
❏ 814190-1	Standard Time	198?	$30
❏ MG-36127 [M]	The Max Roach 4 Plays Charlie Parker	1958	$150
❏ SR-80019 [S]	The Max Roach 4 Plays Charlie Parker	1959	$200

FANTASY
❏ OJC-304	Deeds, Not Words	1988	$25
❏ OJC-202	Max Roach Quartet Featuring Hank Mobley	1985	$25
❏ 6007 [M]	Speak Brother, Speak	1963	$60
❏ 86007 [S]	Speak Brother, Speak	1963	$60

HAT ART
❏ 4026	The Long March	1986	$60

IMPULSE!
❏ A-16 [M]	It's Time	1962	$200
❏ AS-16 [S]	It's Time	1962	$200
❏ A-8 [M]	Percussion Bitter Sweet	1961	$200
❏ AS-8 [S]	Percussion Bitter Sweet	1961	$160

JAZZLAND
❏ JLP-79 [M]	Conversation	1962	$60
❏ JLP-979 [S]	Conversation	1962	$60

MCA
❏ 29053	It's Time	1980	$25

MERCURY
❏ MG-20539 [M]	Moon Faced and Starry-Eyed	1960	$100
❏ SR-60215 [S]	Moon Faced and Starry-Eyed	1960	$150
❏ MG-20760 [M]	Parisian Sketches	1962	$100
❏ SR-60760 [S]	Parisian Sketches	1962	$100
❏ MG-20491 [M]	Quiet As It's Kept	1959	$100
❏ SR-60170 [S]	Quiet As It's Kept	1959	$150
❏ MG-20911 [M]	The Many Sides of Max	1964	$100
❏ SR-60911 [S]	The Many Sides of Max	1964	$100

MILESTONE
❏ 47061	Conversations	198?	$35

RIVERSIDE
❏ RLP 12-280 [M]	Deeds, Not Words	1958	$300
❏ RLP-1122 [S]	Deeds, Not Words	1959	$300
❏ RS-3018 [S]	Deeds, Not Words	1968	$100

SOUL NOTE
❏ SN-1109	Easy Winners	1985	$30
❏ SN-1053	In the Light	1982	$30
❏ SN-1003	Pictures in a Frame	198?	$30
❏ SN-1103	Scott Free	1985	$30
❏ SN-1093	Survivors	1985	$30

TIME
❏ T-70003 [M]	Award Winning Drummer	1959	$150
❏ ST-70003 [S]	Award Winning Drummer	1959	$120
❏ 52087 [M]	Max Roach	1962	$40
❏ S-2087 [S]	Max Roach	1962	$40

TRIP
❏ TLP-5559	Jazz in 3/4 Time	197?	$30
❏ TLP-5522	Max Roach + 4	197?	$30

ROACH, MAX/ART BLAKEY
Also see each artist's individual listings.
Albums
BLUE NOTE
❏ BLP-5010 [10]	Max Roach Quintet / Art Blakey and His Band	1952	$1000

ROANE, STEPHEN
Bass player.
Albums
LABOR
❏ 2	Siblings	1980	$30

ROARING SEVEN JAZZBAND, THE
Albums
STOMP OFF
❏ SOS-1019	Hot Dance	198?	$25

ROBBINS, ADELAIDE/MARIAN MCPARTLAND/ BARBARA CARROLL
Robbins is a pianist. Also see BARBARA CARROLL; MARIAN McPARTLAND.
Albums
SAVOY
❏ MG-12097 [M]	Lookin' for a Boy	1957	$50

ROBERT, GEORGE
Alto saxophone player.
Albums
CONTEMPORARY
❏ C-14037	Sun Dance	1988	$25

ROBERTS, DAVID THOMAS
Pianist.
Albums
STOMP OFF
❏ SOS-1021	An Album of Early Folk Rags	198?	$25
❏ SOS-1132	The Amazon Rag	1986	$25
❏ SOS-1075	Through the Bottomlands	1985	$25

ROBERTS, HANK
Cello player. Also a fiddler and male singer.
Albums
JMT
❏ 834416-1	Black Pastels	1988	$25

ROBERTS, HOWARD
Guitarist.
Albums
ABC IMPULSE!
Number	Title	Yr	NM
❏ AS-9207	Antelope Freeway	1972	$35
❏ AS-9299	Equinox Express Elevator	1974	$35

CAPITOL
❏ T2609 [M]	All-Time Great Instrumental Hits	1966	$75
❏ ST2609 [S]	All-Time Great Instrumental Hits	1966	$50
❏ T1887 [M]	Color Him Funky	1963	$75
❏ ST1887 [S]	Color Him Funky	1963	$60
❏ T2400 [M]	Goodies	1965	$75
❏ ST2400 [S]	Goodies	1965	$50
❏ T2824 [M]	Guilty	1967	$50
❏ ST2824 [S]	Guilty	1967	$75
❏ SM-1961 [S]	H.R. Is A Dirty Guitar Player	1976	$25
—Reissue with new prefix			
❏ T1961 [M]	H.R. Is A Dirty Guitar Player	1963	$75
❏ ST1961 [S]	H.R. Is A Dirty Guitar Player	1963	$50
❏ T2716 [M]	Jaunty -- Jolly	1967	$60
❏ ST2716 [S]	Jaunty -- Jolly	1967	$75
❏ ST2901 [S]	Out Of Sight -- But In Mind	1968	$50
❏ T2214 [M]	Something's Cookin'	1965	$50
❏ ST2214 [S]	Something's Cookin'	1965	$50
❏ ST-11247	Sounds	1974	$30
❏ ST-336	Spinning Wheel	1970	$50
❏ T2478 [M]	Whatever's Fair	1966	$60
❏ ST2478 [S]	Whatever's Fair	1966	$50

CONCORD JAZZ
❏ CJ-53	The Real Howard Roberts	1978	$25

DISCOVERY
❏ 812	Turning to Spring	1980	$30

NORGRAN

Number	Title	Yr	NM
❏ MGN-1106 [M]	Mr. Roberts Plays Guitar	1955	$0
—Canceled			
VERVE			
❏ MGV-8305 [M]	Good Pickin's	1959	$100
❏ V-8305 [M]	Good Pickin's	1961	$30
❏ MGV-8192 [M]	Mr. Roberts Plays Guitar	1957	$150
❏ V-8192 [M]	Mr. Roberts Plays Guitar	1961	$30
❏ UMV-2673	Mr. Roberts Plays Guitar	198?	$30
❏ VSP-29 [M]	The Movin' Man	1966	$25
❏ VSPS-29 [R]	The Movin' Man	1966	$30
❏ V-8662 [M]	Velvet Groove	1966	$25
❏ V6-8662 [S]	Velvet Groove	1966	$35

ROBERTS, JUDY
Pianist and female singer.
Albums
INNER CITY			
❏ IC-1078	Judy Roberts Band	198?	$30
❏ IC-1138	Nights in Brazil	198?	$30
❏ IC-1088	The Other World	198?	$30
PAUSA			
❏ 7147	Judy Roberts Trio	198?	$25
❏ 7176	You Are There	1985	$25

ROBERTS, LUCKEY, AND WILLIE "THE LION" SMITH
Also see each artist's individual listings.
Albums
GOOD TIME JAZZ			
❏ L-12035 [M]	Harlem Piano Solos	1958	$40
❏ S-10035 [S]	Harlem Piano Solos	1958	$30

ROBERTS, LUCKEY
Pianist and composer.

ROBERTS, MARCUS
Pianist.
Albums
NOVUS			
❏ 3078-1-N	Deep in the Shed	1990	$35
❏ 3051-1-N	The Truth Is Spoken Here	1989	$30

ROBERTS, POLA
See GLORIA COLEMAN.

ROBERTS, WILLIAM NEIL
Harpsichordist.
Albums
KLAVIER			
❏ 510	Great Scott!	197?	$30
❏ 516	Scott Joplin Ragtime, Vol. 2	1974	$30

ROBERTSON, HERB
Trumpeter, cornet and fluegel horn player.
Albums
JMT			
❏ 834420-1	Shades of Bud Powell	1988	$25

ROBERTSON, PAUL
Albums
PALO ALTO			
❏ PA-8013	Old Friends, New Friends	1982	$25
❏ PA-8002	The Song Is You	1981	$25

ROBICHAUX, JOE
Pianist and bandleader.
Albums
FOLKLYRIC			
❏ 9032	Joe Robichaux and the Hot New Orleans Rhythm Boys	198?	$25

ROBINS, CAROL JOY
Female singer.
Albums
OPTIMISM			
❏ OP-3202	Joy Sings the Blues	1988	$25

ROBINSON, FREDDY
Guitarist.
Albums
ENTERPRISE			
❏ ENS-1025	Freddy Robinson at the Drive-In	1972	$30
PACIFIC JAZZ			
❏ ST-20176	Hot Fun in the Summertime	1971	$35
❏ ST-20162	The Coming Atlantis	1970	$35

ROBINSON, JIM, AND BILLIE AND DEDE PIERCE
Also see each artist's individual listings.
Albums
ATLANTIC			
❏ 1409 [M]	Jim Robinson and Billie & DeDe Pierce	1963	$50
❏ SD1409 [S]	Jim Robinson and Billie & DeDe Pierce	1963	$50

ROBINSON, JIM
Trombonist and bandleader.
Albums
BIOGRAPH			
❏ CEN-8	Jim Robinson and His New Orleans Band	197?	$25
❏ CEN-16	Jim Robinson and His New Orleans Joymakers	197?	$25
CENTER			
❏ PLP-1 [M]	Jim Robinson and His New Orleans Band	196?	$35
GHB			
❏ GHB-196	1944 Revisited	1986	$25
❏ GHB-185	Big Jim's Little Six	1986	$25
❏ GHB-28	Jim Robinson at the Jacinto Ballroom	197?	$30
JAZZ CRUSADE			
❏ 2015	1944 Revisited	196?	$35
❏ 2005	Jim Robinson	1965	$35
❏ 2010	Jim Robinson's Little Six	196?	$35
PEARL			
❏ PS-5	Economy Hall Breakdown	197?	$30
RIVERSIDE			
❏ RLP-393 [M]	Jim Robinson Plays Spirituals and Blues	1961	$200
❏ RS-9393 [R]	Jim Robinson Plays Spirituals and Blues	1961	$200
❏ RLP-369 [M]	Jim Robinson's New Orleans Band	1961	$200
❏ RS-9369 [R]	Jim Robinson's New Orleans Band	1961	$200

ROBINSON, PERRY
Clarinetist.
Albums
IAI			
❏ 373856	Kundalini	1978	$35
SAVOY			
❏ MG-12202 [M]	East of Suez	196?	$35
❏ MG-12177 [M]	Funk Dumpling	1962	$30
SAVOY JAZZ			
❏ SJL-1180	Funk Dumpling	198?	$25

ROBINSON, PETE
Keyboard player and composer.
Albums
TESTAMENT			
❏ 4401	Dialogues for Piano and Reeds	197?	$30

ROBINSON, PETER MANNING
Keyboard player and composer.
Albums
CMG			
❏ CML-8018	Phoenix Rising	1989	$30

ROBINSON, SPIKE, AND AL COHN
Also see each artist's individual listings.
Albums
CAPRI			
❏ 71787	Henry B. Meets Alvin G.	1987	$25

ROBINSON, SPIKE
Tenor saxophone player.
Albums
CAPRI			
❏ 72185	It's a Wonderful World	1985	$25
❏ 8984	London Reprise	1984	$25
❏ 71785	Spring Can Really Hang You Up the Most	1985	$25
DISCOVERY			
❏ 870	This Is Always: The Music of Harry Warren, Vol. 2	198?	$25

ROBINSON, SUGAR CHILE
Albums
CAPITOL			
❏ T589 [M]	Boogie Woogie	1955	$200

ROBINSON/LANGWORTHY/AXT JAZZ TRIO, THE
Members: Charlie Robinson (guitar); Lew Langworthy (drums); Kevin Axt (bass).
Albums
ASHLAND			
❏ 4963	The Robinson/Langworthy/Axt Jazz Trio	198?	$30

ROCHE, BETTY
Female singer.
Albums
BETHLEHEM			
❏ BCP-64 [M]	Take the "A" Train	1956	$250
❏ BCP-6026	Take the "A" Train	197?	$50
—Reissue, distributed by RCA Victor			
FANTASY			
❏ OJC-1718	Singin' and Swingin'	198?	$30
PRESTIGE			
❏ PRLP-7187 [M]	Singin' and Swingin'	1961	$200

ROCHESTER-VEASLEY BAND, THE
Led by Cornell Rochester (drums) and Gerald Veasley (bass, vocals).
Albums
GRAMAVISION			
❏ 18-8505	One Minute of Love	1986	$25

ROCKWELL, ROBERT
Albums
ASI			
❏ 5002	Androids	1977	$30
CELEBRATION			
❏ 5002	Androids	197?	$35

RODGER, MART
Clarinetist and bandleader.
Albums
GHB			
❏ GHB-224	Jazz Tale of Two Cities	198?	$25

RODGERS, GENE
Pianist and arranger.
Albums
EMARCY			
❏ MG-36145 [M]	Jazz Comes to the Astor	1958	$150

RODGERS, IKE
Trombonist.
Albums
RIVERSIDE			
❏ RLP-1013 [10]	The Trombone of Ike Rodgers	1953	$300

RODITI, CLAUDIO
Trumpeter and fluegel horn player.
Albums
MILESTONE			
❏ M-9158	Gemini Man	198?	$25
❏ M-9175	Slow Fire	198?	$25

Number	Title	Yr	NM
RODNEY, RED, AND IRA SULLIVAN			
Also see each artist's individual listings.			
Albums			
ELEKTRA/MUSICIAN			
❑ 60261	Sprint	198?	$25
❑ 60020	The Spirit Within	1982	$25
RODNEY, RED			
Trumpeter. Also see GERRY MULLIGAN.			
Albums			
ARGO			
❑ LP-643 [M]	Red Rodney Returns	1959	$50
❑ LSP-643 [S]	Red Rodney Returns	1959	$40
FANTASY			
❑ 3208 [M]	Modern Music from Chicago	1956	$200
—Red vinyl			
❑ 3208 [M]	Modern Music from Chicago	195?	$80
—Black vinyl			
❑ OJC-048	Modern Music from Chicago	198?	$25
MUSE			
❑ MR-5307	Alive in New York	1986	$25
❑ MR-5034	Bird Lives!	1975	$30
❑ MR-5371	Bird Lives!	1989	$25
❑ MR-5135	Home Free	197?	$30
❑ MR-5209	Live at the Village Vanguard	1980	$30
❑ MR-5274	Night and Day	1981	$25
❑ MR-5088	Red Tornado	1975	$30
❑ MR-5111	Red White and Blues	1977	$30
❑ MR-5046	Superbop	197?	$30
❑ MR-5290	The 3 R's	198?	$25
ONYX			
❑ 204	Red Arrow	197?	$30
PRESTIGE			
❑ PRLP-122 [10]	Red Rodney	1952	$350
SAVOY			
❑ MG-12148 [M]	Fiery Red Rodney	1959	$100
SIGNAL			
❑ S-1206 [M]	Red Rodney 1957	1957	$600
❑ S-1206 [S]	Red Rodney 1957	199?	$30
—Classic Records reissue on audiophile vinyl (in stereo)			
RODRIGUEZ, WILLIE			
Congas and bongos player.			
Albums			
RIVERSIDE			
❑ RLP-469 [M]	Flatjacks	1963	$150
❑ RS-9469 [S]	Flatjacks	1963	$150
RODRIGUEZ, BOBBY			
Bass player.			
Albums			
SEA BREEZE			
❑ SB-2030	Tell An Amigo	1986	$25
ROESSLER, GEORGE			
Guitarist.			
Albums			
EAGLE			
❑ SM-4195	Still Life and Old Dreams	1985	$25
ROGERS, BOB			
Vibraphone player.			
Albums			
INDIGO			
❑ 1501 [M]	All That and This, Too	1961	$40
ROGERS, SHORTY, AND ANDRE PREVIN			
Also see each artist's individual listings.			
Albums			
RCA VICTOR			
❑ LPM-1018 [M]	Collaboration	1954	$60
ROGERS, SHORTY, AND BUDD SHANK			
Also see each artist's individual listings.			
Albums			
CONCORD JAZZ			
❑ CJ-223	Yesterday, Today and Forever	1983	$25

Number	Title	Yr	NM
ROGERS, SHORTY			
Trumpeter, arranger and composer. Also see AL COHN; MAVIS RIVERS; BUD SHANK.			
Albums			
ATLANTIC			
❑ 1232 [M]	Martians, Come Back	1956	$300
—Black label			
❑ SD1232 [S]	Martians, Come Back	1958	$250
—Green label			
❑ 1232 [M]	Martians, Come Back	1961	$150
—Multicolor label, white "fan" logo at right			
❑ SD1232 [S]	Martians, Come Back	1961	$150
—Multicolor label, white "fan" logo at right			
❑ 1232 [M]	Martians, Come Back	1963	$25
—Multicolor label, black "fan" logo at right			
❑ SD1232 [S]	Martians, Come Back	1963	$35
—Multicolor label, black "fan" logo at right			
❑ 90042	The Swinging Mr. Rogers	1983	$25
❑ 1212 [M]	The Swinging Mr. Rogers	1955	$300
—Black label			
❑ 1212 [M]	The Swinging Mr. Rogers	1961	$150
—Multicolor label, white "fan" logo at right			
❑ 1212 [M]	The Swinging Mr. Rogers	1963	$25
—Multicolor label, black "fan" logo at right			
❑ 1270 [M]	Way Up There	1957	$300
—Black label			
❑ 1270 [M]	Way Up There	1961	$150
—Multicolor label, white "fan" logo at right			
❑ 1270 [M]	Way Up There	1963	$25
—Multicolor label, black "fan" logo at right			
BLUEBIRD			
❑ 5917-1-RB	Short Stops	1987	$35
CAPITOL			
❑ T1960 [M]	Gospel Mission	1963	$60
❑ ST1960 [S]	Gospel Mission	1963	$50
❑ H294 [10]	Modern Sounds	1952	$300
DISCOVERY			
❑ 843	Jazz Waltz	1982	$25
MGM			
❑ E-3798 [M]	Shorty Rogers Meets Tarzan	1960	$30
❑ SE-3798 [S]	Shorty Rogers Meets Tarzan	1960	$40
MOSAIC			
❑ MR6-125	The Complete Atlantic and EMI Jazz Recordings of Shorty Rogers	199?	$150
—Limited edition of 7,500			
PAUSA			
❑ 9016	14 Historic Arrangements and Performances	198?	$25
RCA VICTOR			
❑ LPM-1763 [M]	Afro-Cuban Influence	1958	$40
❑ LSP-1763 [S]	Afro-Cuban Influence	1958	$50
❑ LPM-1975 [M]	Chances Are It Swings	1959	$40
❑ LSP-1975 [S]	Chances Are It Swings	1959	$50
❑ LPM-1334 [M]	Collaboration	1956	$60
❑ LPM-3138 [10]	Cool and Crazy	1953	$200
❑ LPM-1696 [M]	Gigi Goes Jazz	1958	$50
❑ LSP-1696 [S]	Gigi Goes Jazz	1958	$60
❑ LPM-1564 [M]	Portrait of Shorty	1957	$60
❑ LPM-1195 [M]	Shorty Rogers and His Giants	1956	$125
❑ LJM-1004 [M]	Shorty Rogers Courts the Count	1954	$80
❑ LPM-3137 [10]	Shorty Rogers' Giants	1953	$200
❑ LPM-1428 [M]	Shorty Rogers Plays Richard Rogers	1957	$60
❑ LPM-1350 [M]	The Big Shorty Rogers Express	1957	$60
❑ LPM-2110 [M]	The Swingin' Nutcracker	1960	$40
❑ LSP-2110 [S]	The Swingin' Nutcracker	1960	$50
❑ LPM-1997 [M]	The Wizard of Oz	1959	$40
❑ LSP-1997 [S]	The Wizard of Oz	1959	$50
❑ LPM-1326 [M]	Wherever the Five Winds Blow	1956	$140
REPRISE			
❑ R-6050 [M]	Bossa Nova	1962	$25
❑ R9-6050 [S]	Bossa Nova	1962	$30
❑ R-6060 [M]	Jazz Waltz	1962	$25
❑ R9-6060 [S]	Jazz Waltz	1962	$30
WARNER BROS.			
❑ W1443 [M]	4th Dimension Jazz	1961	$60
❑ WS1443 [S]	4th Dimension Jazz	1961	$60
XANADU			
❑ 148	Popi	198?	$25

Number	Title	Yr	NM
ROLAND, GENE			
Trombonist, trumpeter, arranger and composer. Also see PAUL QUINICHETTE.			
Albums			
BRUNSWICK			
❑ BL54114 [M]	Swingin' Friends	1963	$40
❑ BL754114 [S]	Swingin' Friends	1963	$50
DAWN			
❑ DLP-1122 [M]	Jazzville, Volume 4	1958	$80
ROLAND, JOE			
Vibraphone player. Also see EDDIE SHU.			
Albums			
BETHLEHEM			
❑ BCP-17 [M]	Joe Roland Quintet	1955	$250
SAVOY			
❑ MG-15034 [10]	Joe Roland Quartet	1954	$120
❑ MG-15047 [10]	Joe Roland Quartet	1954	$120
❑ MG-12039 [M]	Joltin' Joe Roland	1955	$60
ROLDINGER, ADELHARD			
Bass player.			
Albums			
ECM			
❑ 1221	Schattseite	1981	$30
ROLLAND, BRIAN			
Guitarist.			
Albums			
WUMAT			
❑ WM-1001	Guitar Bazaar	198?	$30
ROLLINI, ADRIAN			
Bass saxophone player, pianist, vibraphone player, "goofus" (keyed harmonica) and "hot fountain pen" (miniature clarinet) player and bandleader.			
Albums			
MERCURY			
❑ MG-20011 [M]	Chopsticks	1953	$100
SUNBEAM			
❑ 134	Adrian Rollini and His Orchestra 1933-34	197?	$25
ROLLINS, SONNY; CLIFFORD BROWN; MAX ROACH			
Also see each artist's individual listings.			
Albums			
PRESTIGE			
❑ PRST-7821	Three Giants	1971	$30
❑ PRLP-7291 [M]	Three Giants	1964	$40
❑ PRST-7291 [R]	Three Giants	1964	$60
ROLLINS, SONNY			
Tenor saxophone player. Plays sax on the Rolling Stones' hit song "Waiting on a Friend" from 1981. Also see GARY BURTON; MILES DAVIS; ART FARMER; THELONIOUS MONK.			
Albums			
ABC IMPULSE!			
❑ AS-9121 [S]	East Broadway Run Down	1968	$35
—Black label with red ring			
❑ AS-9236	Reevaluation: The Impulse Years	1973	$200
❑ IA-9349	There Will Never Be Another You	1978	$35
ANALOGUE PRODUCTIONS			
❑ AP 008	Way Out West	199?	$60
—180-gram audiophile vinyl			
BLUEBIRD			
❑ 5634-1-RB	The Quartets Featuring Jim Hall	1986	$50
BLUE NOTE			
❑ BLP-1581 [M]	A Night at the Village Vanguard	1958	$1500
—Regular version, W. 63rd St. address on label			
❑ BLP-1581 [M]	A Night at the Village Vanguard	1963	$350
—With "New York, USA" address on label			
❑ BST-81581 [R]	A Night at the Village Vanguard	1967	$40

Ann Richards, *Two Much!*, Capitol T 1495, **$100**.

Ann Richards, *The Many Moods of Ann Richards*, Capitol T 1406, **$100**.

Johnny Richards, *Wide Range*, Capitol T 885, **$200**.

Max Roach, *Max Roach*, Time S/2087, **$40**.

Number	Title	Yr	NM
— With "A Division of Liberty Records" on label			
❏ BST-81581 [M]	A Night at the Village Vanguard, Vol. 1	1987	$30
— The Finest in Jazz Since 1939" reissue			
❏ BN-LA475-H2!	More from the Vanguard	1975	$35
❏ BLP-4001 [M]	Newk's Time	1958	$600
— Deep groove" version; W. 63rd St. address on label			
❏ BLP-4001 [M]	Newk's Time	1958	$150
— Regular version, W. 63rd St. address on label			
❏ BST-4001 [S]	Newk's Time	1959	$250
— Deep groove" version; W. 63rd St. address on label			
❏ BST-4001 [S]	Newk's Time	1959	$200
— Regular version, W. 63rd St. address on label			
❏ BLP-4001 [M]	Newk's Time	1963	$120
— With "New York, USA" address on label			
❏ BST-4001 [S]	Newk's Time	1963	$40
— With "New York, USA" address on label			
❏ BST-84001 [S]	Newk's Time	1967	$50
— With "A Division of Liberty Records" on label			
❏ BST-84001 [S]	Newk's Time	198?	$30
— The Finest in Jazz Since 1939" reissue			
❏ BLP-1542 [M]	Sonny Rollins	1957	$1200
— Deep groove" version; Lexington Ave. address on label			
❏ BLP-1542 [M]	Sonny Rollins	1958	$500
— Deep groove" version, W. 63rd St. address on label			
❏ BLP-1542 [M]	Sonny Rollins	1963	$150
— With "New York, USA" address on label			
❏ BST-81542 [R]	Sonny Rollins	1967	$35
— With "A Division of Liberty Records" on label			
❏ BN-LA401-H2	Sonny Rollins	1975	$60
❏ BST-81542 [M]	Sonny Rollins	1985	$30
— The Finest in Jazz Since 1939" reissue			
❏ BLP-1558 [M]	Sonny Rollins, Volume 2	1957	$1000
— Deep groove" version; W. 63rd St. address on label			
❏ BLP-1558 [M]	Sonny Rollins, Volume 2	1957	$400
— Regular version, W. 63rd St. address on label			
❏ BLP-1558 [M]	Sonny Rollins, Volume 2	1963	$150
— With "New York, USA" address on label			
❏ BST-81558 [R]	Sonny Rollins, Volume 2	1967	$35
— With "A Division of Liberty Records" on label			
❏ BST-81558 [R]	Sonny Rollins, Volume 2	1985	$30
— The Finest in Jazz Since 1939" reissue			
❏ B1-93203	The Best of Sonny Rollins	1989	$35
CONTEMPORARY			
❏ C-7651	Alternate Takes	1986	$35
❏ M-3564 [M]	Sonny Rollins and the Contemporary Leaders	1959	$250
❏ S-7564 [S]	Sonny Rollins and the Contemporary Leaders	1959	$250
❏ C-3530 [M]	Way Out West	1957	$250
❏ S-7530 [S]	Way Out West	1959	$300
DCC COMPACT CLASSICS			
❏ LPZ-2008	Saxophone Colossus	1995	$175
— 180-gram audiophile vinyl			
❏ LPZ-2022	Tenor Madness	1996	$150
— 180-gram audiophile vinyl			
EVEREST ARCHIVE OF FOLK & JAZZ			
❏ FS-220 [R]	Sonny Rollins with Guest Artist Thad Jones	1968	$30
FANTASY			
❏ OJC-067	Freedom Suite	198?	$30
❏ OJC-314	Horn Culture	198?	$30
❏ OJC-058	Moving Out	198?	$30
❏ OJC-620	Nucleus	1991	$35
❏ OJC-291	Saxophone Colossus	198?	$30
❏ OJC-348	Sonny Boy	198?	$30
❏ OJC-340	Sonny Rollins and the Contemporary Leaders	198?	$35
❏ OJC-214	Sonny Rollins Plays for Bird	198?	$30
❏ OJC-243	Sonny Rollins Plus 4	1987	$30
❏ OJC-011	Sonny Rollins with the Modern Jazz Quartet	1982	$30
❏ OJC-124	Tenor Madness	198?	$30
❏ OJC-468	The Cutting Edge: Montreux 1974	198?	$30
❏ OJC-312	The Next Album	1988	$30
❏ OJC=029	The Sound of Sonny	198?	$30
❏ OJC-337	Way Out West	198?	$30
❏ OJC-007	Work Time	1982	$30
GATEWAY			
❏ GS-7204	The Sound of Sonny	1977	$25
GRP IMPULSE!			
❏ IMP-161 [M]	East Broadway Run Down	199?	$100
— 180-gram audiophile reissue			
❏ IMP-223	Sonny Rollins On Impulse!	1997	$100
— 180-gram reissue			
IMPULSE!			

Number	Title	Yr	NM
❏ A-9121 [M]	East Broadway Run Down	1967	$160
❏ AS-9121 [S]	East Broadway Run Down	1967	$200
❏ A-91 [M]	Sonny Rollins On Impulse!	1966	$200
❏ AS-91 [S]	Sonny Rollins On Impulse!	1966	$160
JAZZLAND			
❏ JLP-86 [M]	Shadow Waltz	1962	$150
❏ JLP-986 [S]	Shadow Waltz	1962	$140
❏ JLP-72 [M]	Sonny's Time	1962	$150
❏ JLP-972 [S]	Sonny's Time	1962	$140
MCA			
❏ 4127	Great Moments with Sonny Rollins	198?	$30
❏ 29054	Sonny Rollins On Impulse!	1980	$25
❏ 29055	There Will Never Be Another You	1980	$25
MCA IMPULSE!			
❏ MCA-5655	Sonny Rollins On Impulse!	1986	$25
METROJAZZ			
❏ E-1002 [M]	Sonny Rollins and the Big Brass	1958	$350
❏ SE-1002 [S]	Sonny Rollins and the Big Brass	1958	$300
❏ E-1011 [M]	Sonny Rollins at Music Inn	1958	$350
❏ SE-1011 [S]	Sonny Rollins at Music Inn	1958	$350
MILESTONE			
❏ M-9155	Dancing in the Dark	1988	$30
❏ M-9090	Don't Ask	1979	$30
❏ M-55005	Don't Stop the Carnival	1978	$50
❏ M-9080	Easy Living	1977	$30
❏ M-9179	Falling in Love with Jazz	1990	$35
❏ M-47007	Freedom Suite Plus	1973	$50
❏ M-9150	G-Man	1987	$30
❏ M-9051	Horn Culture	1974	$30
❏ M-9098	Love at First Sight	1980	$30
❏ M-9104	No Problem	1981	$25
❏ M-9064	Nucleus	1975	$30
❏ M-9108	Reel Life	1982	$25
❏ M-9122	Sunny Days, Starry Nights	1984	$25
❏ M-9059	The Cutting Edge: Montreux 1974	1975	$30
❏ M-9042	The Next Album	197?	$30
❏ M-9074	The Way I Feel	1976	$30
PRESTIGE			
❏ PRLP-7058 [M]	Moving Out	1956	$750
— Yellow label with W. 50th St. address			
❏ PRLP-7058 [M]	Moving Out	1958	$250
— Yellow label with Bergenfield, N.J. address			
❏ PRLP-7079 [M]	Saxophone Colossus	1957	$2500
— Yellow label with W. 50th St. address			
❏ PRLP-7326 [M]	Saxophone Colossus	1964	$120
❏ PRST-7326 [R]	Saxophone Colossus	1964	$60
❏ P-24050	Saxophone Colossus and More	1974	$50
❏ PRLP-7269 [M]	Sonny and the Stars	1963	$150
❏ PRST-7269 [R]	Sonny and the Stars	1963	$40
❏ PRLP-7207 [M]	Sonny Boy	1961	$200
❏ PR-24004	Sonny Rollins	1972	$60
❏ PRLP-190 [10]	Sonny Rollins	1954	$600
❏ PRST-7553 [R]	Sonny Rollins Plays for Bird	1968	$60
❏ PRLP-7433 [M]	Sonny Rollins Plays Jazz Classics	1967	$175
❏ PRST-7433 [R]	Sonny Rollins Plays Jazz Classics	1967	$60
❏ PRLP-7038 [M]	Sonny Rollins Plus 4	1956	$400
— Yellow label with W. 50th St. address			
❏ PRLP-137 [10]	Sonny Rollins Quartet	1952	$800
❏ PRLP-186 [10]	Sonny Rollins Quartet	1954	$700
❏ PRLP-7029 [M]	Sonny Rollins with the Modern Jazz Quartet	1956	$750
— Orange cover; original edition has the wrong catalog number at upper left (PR 7020), but the record has the correct number			
❏ PRLP-7029 [M]	Sonny Rollins with the Modern Jazz Quartet	1956	$300
— Orange cover; second edition has the correct catalog number, "Prestige LP 7029," in upper left inside an orange box			
❏ PRLP-7029 [M]	Sonny Rollins with the Modern Jazz Quartet	1956	$300
— Brown and yellow cover; catalog number at upper left is "Prestige Hi-Fil LP 7029"; record has yellow label with W. 50th St. address			
❏ P-24082	Taking Care of Business	1978	$50
❏ PRLP-7047 [M]	Tenor Madness	1956	$300
— Yellow label with W. 50th St. address			
❏ PRST-7657 [R]	Tenor Madness	1969	$60
❏ PRLP-7047 [M]	Tenor Madness	1958	$200
— Yellow label with Bergenfield, N.J. address			
❏ PRST-7856	The First Recordings	1972	$30
❏ PRLP-7126 [M]	Tour de Force	1957	$250
— Yellow label with W. 50th St. address			
❏ P-24096	Vintage Sessions	1981	$50
❏ PRST-7750	Worktime	1970	$30
❏ PRLP-7020 [M]	Work Time	1956	$500
— Yellow label with W. 50th St. address			

Number	Title	Yr	NM
❏ PRLP-7246 [M]	Work Time	1962	$150
❏ PRST-7246 [R]	Work Time	1962	$40
QUINTESSENCE			
❏ QJ-25181	Green Dolphin Street	1978	$30
RCA VICTOR			
❏ LPM-2927 [M]	Now's the Time	1964	$60
❏ LSP-2927 [S]	Now's the Time!	1964	$60
❏ LSP-2927 [S]	Now's the Time!	199?	$60
— Classic Records reissue on audiophile vinyl			
❏ LPM-2612 [M]	Our Man In Jazz	1962	$60
❏ LSP-2612 [S]	Our Man In Jazz	1962	$120
❏ LSP-2612 [S]	Our Man In Jazz	199?	$60
— Classic Records reissue on audiophile vinyl			
❏ ANL1-2809	Pure Gold	1978	$25
❏ LPM-2712 [M]	Sonny Meets Hawk!	1963	$60
❏ LSP-2712 [S]	Sonny Meets Hawk!	1963	$120
❏ LSP-2712 [S]	Sonny Meets Hawk!	199?	$60
— Classic Records reissue on audiophile vinyl			
❏ LPM-2527 [M]	The Bridge	1962	$40
— Black label, dog on top, "Long 33 1/3 Play" at bottom			
❏ LSP-2527 [S]	The Bridge	1962	$140
— Black label, dog on top, "Living Stereo" at bottom			
❏ APL1-0859	The Bridge	1975	$50
— Reissue of LSP-2527; orange or tan label			
❏ AFL1-0859	The Bridge	1977	$30
— Reissue with new prefix; black label, dog at 1 o'clock			
❏ LSP-2527 [S]	The Bridge	199?	$60
— Classic Records reissue on audiophile vinyl			
❏ LSP-2527-45	The Bridge	1999	$120
— Classic Records reissue; 4 single-sided LPs that play at 45 rpm			
❏ LPM-3355 [M]	The Standard Sonny Rollins	1965	$60
❏ LSP-3355 [S]	The Standard Sonny Rollins	1965	$60
❏ LPM-2572 [M]	What's New?	1962	$60
❏ LSP-2572 [S]	What's New?	1962	$120
RIVERSIDE			
❏ RLP-258 [M]	Freedom Suite	1958	$300
❏ RS-3010 [S]	Freedom Suite	1968	$100
❏ SMJ-6044	Freedom Suite	1974	$50
❏ RLP 12-241 [M]	The Sound of Sonny	1957	$750
— White label, blue print			
❏ RLP 12-241 [M]	The Sound of Sonny	1959	$200
— Blue label, microphone logo at top			
❏ RLP-1124 [S]	The Sound of Sonny	1959	$200
STEREO RECORDS			
❏ S-7017 [S]	Way Out West	1958	$200
VERVE			
❏ V-8430 [M]	Sonny Rollins/Brass, Sonny Rollins/Trio	1962	$40
❏ V6-8430 [S]	Sonny Rollins/Brass, Sonny Rollins/Trio	1962	$60
❏ UMV-2555	Sonny Rollins/Brass, Sonny Rollins/Trio	198?	$25
❏ VSP-32 [M]	Tenor Titan	1966	$35
❏ VSPS-32 [S]	Tenor Titan	1966	$30

ROLLINS, SONNY/JIMMY CLEVELAND
Also see each artist's individual listings.

Albums

PERIOD

Number	Title	Yr	NM
❏ SPL-1204 [M]	Sonny Rollins Plays/Jimmy Cleveland Plays	1956	$2000

ROMAN NEW ORLEANS JAZZ BAND, THE

Albums

RCA VICTOR

Number	Title	Yr	NM
❏ LPT-3033 [10]	Around the World in Jazz -- Italy	1953	$40

ROMAO, DOM UM
Drummer and percussionist.

Albums

MUSE

Number	Title	Yr	NM
❏ MR-5013	Dom Um Romao	1974	$35
❏ MR-5049	Spirit of the Times	197?	$30

PABLO

Number	Title	Yr	NM
❏ 2310777	Hotmosphere	197?	$30

Number	Title	Yr	NM

ROMERO, RAOUL
Guitarist.
Albums
SEA BREEZE
| SB-2031 | The Music of Raoul Romero | 1987 | $25 |

RONEY, WALLACE
Trumpeter.
Albums
MUSE
MR-5346	Intuition	1989	$30
MR-5372	The Standard Bearer	1990	$30
MR-5335	Verses	1987	$25

ROSE, DAVID (2)
French violinist. Not to be confused with the American orchestra leader.
Albums
INNER CITY
| IC-1058 | The Distance Between Dreams | 197? | $30 |

ROSE, WALLY
Pianist.
Albums
BLACKBIRD
| 12007 | Wally Rose on Piano | 196? | $30 |
| 12010 | Whippin' the Keys | 197? | $30 |
COLUMBIA
| CL782 [M] | Cake Walk to Lindy Hop | 1956 | $40 |
| CL2535 [10] | Honky-Tonkin' | 1955 | $40 |
—House Party Series" reissue
| CL6260 [10] | Wally Rose | 1953 | $50 |
GOOD TIME JAZZ
| S-10034 [S] | Ragtime Classics | 1960 | $25 |
| L-12034 [M] | Ragtime Classics | 1960 | $35 |
STOMP OFF
| SOS-1057 | Wally Rose Revisited | 1982 | $25 |

ROSE
French-American jazz-rock group.
Albums
MILLENNIUM
| BXL1-7749 | Worlds Apart | 1979 | $35 |

ROSENGREN, BERNT
Tenor saxophone player.
Albums
STOMP OFF
| SOS-1177 | Surprise Party | 198? | $25 |

ROSEWOMAN, MICHELE
Pianist and female singer.
Albums
ENJA
| R1-79607 | Contrast High | 1990 | $35 |
SOUL NOTE
| SN-1072 | The Source | 1984 | $30 |

ROSIE O'GRADY'S GOOD TIME BAND
Albums
DIRECT DISK
| DD-103 | Dixieland | 1979 | $25 |
—Audiophile recording

ROSNES, RENEE
Pianist.
Albums
BLUE NOTE
| B1-93561 | Renee Rosnes | 1990 | $35 |

ROSOLINO, FRANK
Trombonist. Also see VINCE GUARALDI.
Albums
BETHLEHEM

| BCP-26 [M] | I Play Trombone | 1955 | $250 |
CAPITOL
T6509 [M]	Frankly Speaking	1955	$150
H6507 [10]	Frank Rosolino	1954	$250
T6507 [M]	Frank Rosolino	1955	$150
INTERLUDE
MO-500 [M]	The Legend of Frank Rosolino	1959	$80
ST-1000 [S]	The Legend of Frank Rosolino	1959	$60
MODE
LP-107 [M]	Frank Rosolino Quintet	1957	$150
REPRISE
R-6016 [M]	Turn Me Loose	1961	$60
R9-6016 [S]	Turn Me Loose	1961	$80
SACKVILLE
2014	Thinking About You	198?	$50
SPECIALTY
SPS-2161	Free for All	1974	$40

ROSS, ANNIE; DOROTHY DUNN; SHELBY DAVIS
All of the above are female singers. Also see ANNIE ROSS.
Albums
SAVOY
| MG-12060 [M] | Singin' 'N Swingin' | 1956 | $60 |

ROSS, ANNIE
Female singer. Also see LAMBERT, HENDRICKS AND ROSS.
Albums
DECCA
| DL4922 [M] | Fill My Heart with Song | 1967 | $40 |
| DL74922 [S] | Fill My Heart with Song | 1967 | $30 |
KIMBERLY
| 2018 [M] | Annie Ross Sings A Song With Mulligan! | 1963 | $40 |
| 11018 [S] | Annie Ross Sings A Song With Mulligan! | 1963 | $40 |
WORLD PACIFIC
WP-1285 [M]	A Gasser!	1960	$150
ST-1285 [S]	A Gasser!	1960	$150
WP-1253 [M]	Annie Ross Sings A Song With Mulligan!	1959	$250
ST-1020 [S]	Annie Ross Sings A Song With Mulligan!	1959	$150
WP-1808 [M]	Gypsy	1959	$150
ST-1028 [S]	Gypsy	1959	$150

ROSS, ARNOLD
Pianist, composer and bandleader. Also see JOE PASS; LENNIE TRISTANO.
Albums
CLEF
| MGC-134 [10] | Arnold Ross | 1953 | $0 |
—Evidently canceled
DISCOVERY
| DL-2006 [M] | Arnold Ross | 1954 | $300 |
MERCURY
| MGC-134 [10] | Arnold Ross | 1952 | $250 |

ROSS, RONNIE
Baritone saxophone player.
Albums
ATLANTIC
| 1333 [M] | The Jazz Makers | 1960 | $250 |
| SD1333 [S] | The Jazz Makers | 1960 | $250 |

ROSS-LEVINE BAND, THE
Members: Billy Ross (flute, saxophone) and Machael Levine (keyboards) with Pete Harris (guitar); Cookie Lopez (percussion) and Steve Rucker (drums).
Albums
HEADFIRST
| 9701 | That Summer Something | 198? | $30 |

ROUSE, CHARLIE, AND PAUL QUINICHETTE
Also see each artist's individual listings.
Albums
BETHLEHEM
| BCP-6021 [M] | The Chase Is On | 1958 | $200 |

ROUSE, CHARLIE
Tenor saxophone player. Also see LES JAZZ MODES.
Albums
BLUE NOTE
| BLP-4119 [M] | Bossa Nova Bacchanal | 1962 | $60 |
| BST-84119 [S] | Bossa Nova Bacchanal | 1962 | $40 |
—With "New York, USA" address on label
| BST-84119 [S] | Bossa Nova Bacchanal | 196? | $25 |
—With "A Division of Liberty Records" on label
DOUGLAS
| 7044 | Cinnamon Flower | 197? | $35 |
EPIC
LA16018 [M]	We Paid Our Dues	1961	$80
BA17018 [S]	We Paid Our Dues	1961	$100
LA16012 [M]	Yeah!	1960	$700
BA17012 [S]	Yeah!	1960	$200
BA17012 [S]	Yeah!	199?	$60
—Classic Records reissue on audiophile vinyl
FANTASY
| OJC-491 | Takin' Care of Business | 1991 | $30 |
JAZZLAND
| JLP-19 [M] | Takin' Care of Business | 1960 | $40 |
| JLP-919 [S] | Takin' Care of Business | 1960 | $50 |
LANDMARK
| LLP-1521 | Epistrophy | 1989 | $30 |
STORYVILLE
| 4079 | Moment's Notice | 198? | $25 |
STRATA-EAST
| SES-19746 | Two Is One | 1974 | $30 |

ROVA
Saxophone quartet named after the first initials of their surnames: Jon Raskin (baritone, alto); Larry Ochs (tenor, sopranino); Andrew Voigt (alto, soprano, sopranino); Bruce Ackley (soprano, tenor).
Albums
BLACK SAINT
| 120126 | Beat Kennel | 1987 | $30 |
| BSR-0076 | Rova Plays Lacy -- Favorite Street | 1984 | $30 |
HAT ART
| 2013 | Saxophone Diplomacy | 1986 | $35 |
| 2032 | The Crowd | 198? | $35 |
METALANGUAGE
118	As Was	1981	$35
101	Cinema Rovate	1978	$50
0(# unknown)	Daredevils	1979	$50
106	The Removal of Secrecy	1979	$50

ROWLES, JIMMY, AND GEORGE MRAZ
Mraz plays bass. Also see JIMMY ROWLES.
Albums
PROGRESSIVE
| PRO-7009 | Music's the Only Thing on My Mind | 1981 | $35 |

ROWLES, JIMMY
Pianist and male singer.
Albums
ANDEX
| A-3007 [M] | Weather in a Jazz Vane | 1958 | $50 |
| AS-3007 [S] | Weather in a Jazz Vane | 1958 | $40 |
CAPITOL
| T1831 [M] | Kinda Groovy! | 1963 | $100 |
| ST1831 [S] | Kinda Groovy! | 1963 | $75 |
CHOICE
| CRS1014 | Grandpaws | 1976 | $50 |
| CRS1023 | Paws That Refresh | 1979 | $35 |
COLUMBIA
| FC37639 | Jimmy Rowles Plays Duke Ellington and Billy Strayhorn | 1981 | $35 |
| JC34873 | Peacocks | 1979 | $35 |
CONTEMPORARY
| C-14032 | I'm Glad There Is You | 1988 | $30 |
| C-14016 | Jimmy Rowles/Red Mitchell Trio | 1986 | $30 |
HALCYON
| HAL110 | Special Magic | 197? | $25 |
INTERLUDE
| MO-515 [M] | Upper Classmen | 1959 | $60 |
| ST-1015 [S] | Upper Classmen | 1959 | $40 |
JAZZZ
| 103 | Jazz Is a Fleeting Moment | 1976 | $60 |

Number	Title	Yr	NM
LIBERTY			
❑ LRP-3003 [M]	Rare -- But Well Done	1955	$150
SIGNATURE			
❑ SM-6011 [M]	Fiorello Uptown, Mary Sunshine Downtown	1960	$120
❑ SS-6011 [S]	Fiorello Uptown, Mary Sunshine Downtown	1960	$150
STASH			
❑ ST-227	Peacocks	198?	$25
TAMPA			
❑ TP-8 [M]	Let's Get Acquainted with Jazz… For People Who Hate Jazz	1957	$300
—Colored vinyl			
❑ TP-8 [M]	Let's Get Acquainted with Jazz… For People Who Hate Jazz	1958	$250
❑ TPS-8 [S]	Let's Get Acquainted with Jazz… For People Who Hate Jazz	1958	$150
XANADU			
❑ 157	Make Such Beautiful Music Together	1980	$35

ROWLES, STACY AND JIMMY

Stacy is a trumpeter, fluegel horn player and female singer, and JIMMY ROWLES' daughter.

Albums

Number	Title	Yr	NM
CONCORD JAZZ			
❑ CJ-249	Tell It Like It Is	1984	$25

ROY, WILLIAM

Pianist, composer and arranger.

Albums

Number	Title	Yr	NM
AUDIOPHILE			
❑ AP-213	When I Sing Alone	1986	$25

ROYAL, ERNIE

Trumpeter.

Albums

Number	Title	Yr	NM
URANIA			
❑ UJLP-1203 [M]	Accent on Trumpet	1955	$150

ROYAL, MARSHALL

Alto saxophone player.

Albums

Number	Title	Yr	NM
CONCORD JAZZ			
❑ CJ-88	First Chair	1979	$25
❑ CJ-125	Royal Blue	1980	$25
EVEREST			
❑ LPBR-5087 [M]	Gordon Jenkins Presents Marshall Royal	1960	$30
❑ SDBR-1087 [S]	Gordon Jenkins Presents Marshall Royal	1960	$30

RUBIN, STAN

Bandleader, clarinetist and saxophone player.

Albums

Number	Title	Yr	NM
CORAL			
❑ CRL57185 [M]	Dixieland Goes Broadway	1959	$30
❑ CRL757185 [S]	Dixieland Goes Broadway	1959	$30
JUBLIEE			
❑ JLP-1003 [M]	College Jazz Comes to Carnegie Hall	1955	$50
❑ JLP-1024 [M]	Stan Rubin in Morocco	1956	$40
❑ JLP-1001 [M]	The College All Stars at Carnegie Hall	1955	$50
❑ JLP-4 [10]	The Tigertown Five, Vol. 1	1954	$50
❑ JLP-5 [10]	The Tigertown Five, Vol. 2	1954	$50
❑ JLP-6 [10]	The Tigertown Five, Vol. 3	1954	$50
❑ JLP-1016 [M]	Tigertown Five	1956	$40
PRINCETON			
❑ LP-102 [10]	The Stan Rubin Tigertown Five	1954	$60
RCA VICTOR			
❑ LPM-1200 [M]	Dixieland Bash	1956	$40
❑ LPM-3277 [10]	Stan Rubin's Dixieland Comes to Carnegie Hall	1955	$60

RUCKER, ELLYN

Pianist and female singer.

Albums

Number	Title	Yr	NM
CAPRI			
❑ 10187	Ellyn	1987	$30

RUDD, ROSWELL, AND STEVE LACY

Also see each artist's individual listings.

Albums

Number	Title	Yr	NM
SOUL NOTE			
❑ SN-1054	Regeneration	1982	$30

RUDD, ROSWELL

Trombonist and male singer.

Albums

Number	Title	Yr	NM
ABC IMPULSE!			
❑ AS-9126 [S]	Everywhere	1968	$35
ARISTA/FREEDOM			
❑ AF1006	Flexible Flyer	1975	$30
❑ AF1029	Inside Job	1976	$30
IMPULSE!			
❑ AS-9126 [S]	Everywhere	1967	$120
JCOA			
❑ 1007	The Numatik String Band	197?	$35

RUEDEBUSCH, DICK

Trumpeter.

Albums

Number	Title	Yr	NM
ASCOT			
❑ AM-13017 [M]	Dick Ruedebusch	1964	$30
❑ AS-16017 [S]	Dick Ruedebusch	1964	$35
JUBILEE			
❑ JGS-5015 [S]	Dick Ruedebusch Remembers the Greats	1962	$25
❑ JGM-5015 [M]	Dick Ruedebusch Remembers the Greats	1962	$35
❑ JGS-5008 [S]	Meet Mr. Trumpet	1962	$25
❑ JGM-5008 [M]	Meet Mr. Trumpet	1962	$35
❑ JGS-5021 [S]	Mr. Trumpet, Volume 2	1963	$25
❑ JGM-5021 [M]	Mr. Trumpet, Volume 2	1963	$35

RUFF, WILLIE

Bass and French horn player. Also see THE MITCHELL-RUFF DUO.

Albums

Number	Title	Yr	NM
COLUMBIA			
❑ CS9603	The Smooth Side of Willie Ruff	1968	$25
—Red "360 Sound" label			

RUGOLO, PETE

Arranger, composer and bandleader.

Albums

Number	Title	Yr	NM
COLUMBIA			
❑ CL604 [M]	Adventures in Rhythm	1955	$60
—Maroon label, gold print			
❑ CL604 [M]	Adventures in Rhythm	1956	$40
—Red and black label with six "eye" logos			
❑ CL6289 [10]	Introducing Pete Rugolo	1954	$60
❑ CL635 [M]	Introducing Pete Rugolo	1955	$60
—Maroon label, gold print			
❑ CL635 [M]	Introducing Pete Rugolo	1956	$40
—Red and black label with six "eye" logos			
❑ CL689 [M]	Rugolomania	1956	$40
—Red and black label with six "eye" logos			
EMARCY			
❑ MG-36082 [M]	Music for Hi-Fi Bugs	1956	$200
❑ MG-36115 [M]	Out on a Limb	1957	$200
❑ MG-36122 [M]	Percussion at Work	1958	$200
❑ MG-36143 [M]	Rugolo Plays Kenton	1958	$200
HARMONY			
❑ HL7003 [M]	New Sounds	195?	$35
MERCURY			
❑ PPS-2023 [M]	10 Saxophones and 2 Basses	196?	$125
❑ PPS-6023 [S]	10 Saxophones and 2 Basses	196?	$100
❑ PPS-6016 [S]	10 Trombones and 2 Guitars	196?	$100
❑ PPS-2016 [M]	10 Trombones and 2 Guitars	196?	$125
❑ PPS-6001 [S]	10 Trombones Like 2 Pianos	196?	$100
❑ PPS-2001 [M]	10 Trombones Like 2 Pianos	196?	$125

Number	Title	Yr	NM
❑ MG-0(# unknown) [M]	An Adventure in Sound: Reeds	1958	$150
❑ SR-60039 [M]	An Adventure in Sound: Reeds	1959	$150
❑ MG-20261 [M]	Brass in Hi-Fi	1958	$150
❑ SR-60044 [S]	Brass in Hi-Fi	1959	$100
❑ MG-20118 [M]	Music from Outer Space	1957	$100
❑ MG-20260 [M]	Reeds in Hi-Fi	1958	$150
❑ SR-60043 [S]	Reeds in Hi-Fi	1959	$100

RUIZ, HILTON

Pianist.

Albums

Number	Title	Yr	NM
INNER CITY			
❑ IC-2036	Piano Man	197?	$35
NOVUS			
❑ 3024-1-N	El Camino (The Road)	1988	$25
❑ 3011-1-N	Something Grand	1987	$25
❑ 3053-1-N	Strut	1989	$30
STASH			
❑ ST-248	Cross Currents	1985	$25
STEEPLECHASE			
❑ SCS-1078	Excitation	198?	$30
❑ SCS-1094	New York Hilton	198?	$30
❑ SCS-1036	Piano Man	198?	$30
❑ SCS-1158	Steppin' Into Beauty	198?	$30

RUIZ, JORGE LOPEZ

Bass player.

Albums

Number	Title	Yr	NM
CATALYST			
❑ 7908	Amor Buenos Aires	197?	$30

RUMMEL, JACK

Pianist and composer.

Albums

Number	Title	Yr	NM
STOMP OFF			
❑ SOS-1118	Back to Ragtime	1986	$25

RUMSEY, HOWARD

Bass player and bandleader.

Albums

Number	Title	Yr	NM
CONTEMPORARY			
❑ C-2506 [10]	Howard Rumsey's Lighthouse All-Stars	1953	$250
❑ C-3508 [M]	Howard Rumsey's Lighthouse All-Stars, Vol. 3	1955	$200
❑ C-3520 [M]	Howard Rumsey's Lighthouse All-Stars, Vol. 4: Oboe/Flute	1956	$200
❑ C-3504 [M]	Howard Rumsey's Lighthouse All-Stars, Vol. 6	1955	$200
❑ C-2513 [10]	Howard Rumsey's Lighthouse All-Stars, Volume 1: The Quintet	1954	$250
❑ C-2515 [10]	Howard Rumsey's Lighthouse All-Stars, Volume 2: The Octet	1954	$250
❑ C-2510 [10]	Howard Rumsey's Lighthouse All-Stars, Volume 4	1954	$250
❑ C-3517 [M]	In the Solo Spotlight	1956	$200
❑ C-14051	Jazz Invention	1989	$30
❑ C-3509 [M]	Lighthouse at Laguna	1955	$200
❑ C-3528 [M]	Music for Lighthousekeeping	1957	$250
❑ S-7008 [S]	Music for Lighthousekeeping	1959	$250
❑ C-2501 [10]	Sunday Jazz a la Lighthouse	1953	$250
❑ C-3501 [M]	Sunday Jazz a la Lighthouse	1955	$200
FANTASY			
❑ OJC-266	Howard Rumsey's Lighthouse All-Stars, Vol. 3	198?	$25
❑ OJC-154	Howard Rumsey's Lighthouse All-Stars, Vol. 4: Oboe/Flute	198?	$25
❑ OJC-386	Howard Rumsey's Lighthouse All-Stars, Vol. 6	1989	$25
❑ OJC-451	In the Solo Spotlight	1990	$30
❑ OJC-406	Lighthouse at Laguna	1989	$25
❑ OJC-151	Sunday Jazz a la Lighthouse	198?	$25
LIBERTY			
❑ LRP-3045 [M]	Double or Nothin'	1957	$50
❑ LST-7014 [S]	Double or Nothin'	1959	$40
LIGHTHOUSE			
❑ LP-300 [M]	Jazz Rolls-Royce	1958	$40
❑ LP-301 [M]	Sunday Jazz a la Lighthouse	1958	$40
—Red vinyl			
OMEGA			
❑ OML-5 [M]	Jazz Rolls-Royce	1960	$30

Max Roach, *Award-Winning Drummer*, Time ST/70003, **$150**.

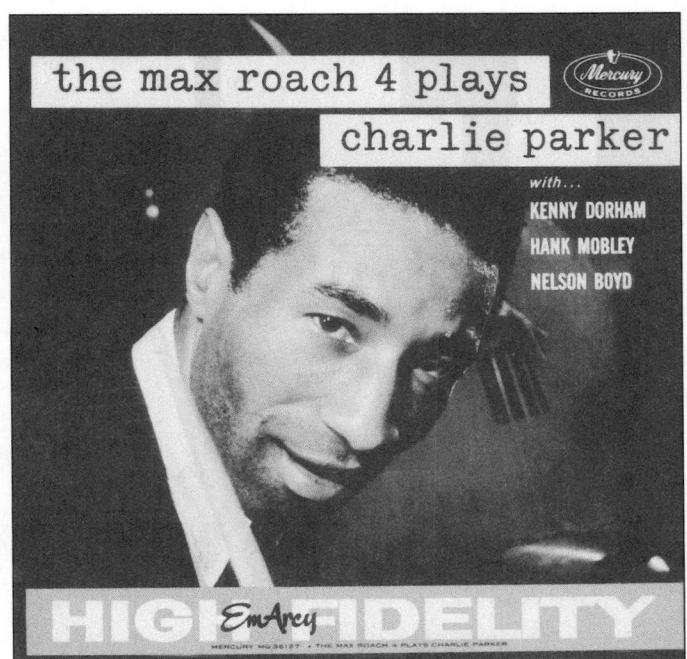

Max Roach, *The Max Roach 4 Plays Charlie Parker*, EmArcy MG 36127, **$150**.

Betty Roche, *Singin' & Swingin'*, Prestige PRLP-7187, yellow label, **$200**.

Shorty Rogers, *Cool and Crazy*, RCA Victor LPM-3138, 10-inch LP, **$200**.

Number	Title	Yr	NM
❏ OSL-5 [S]	Jazz Rolls-Royce	1960	$30
PHILIPS			
❏ PHM200012 [M]	Jazz Structures	1961	$25
❏ PHS600012 [S]	Jazz Structures	1961	$30
STEREO RECORDS			
❏ S-7008 [S]	Music for Lighthousekeeping	1958	$125

RUSHEN, PATRICE
Female singer.
Albums

Number	Title	Yr	NM
ARISTA			
❏ AL-8401	Watch Out!	1987	$12
ELEKTRA			
❏ 60465	Anthology of Patrice Rushen	1986	$12
❏ 6E-160	Patrice	1978	$12
❏ 60360	Patrice Rushen Now	1984	$12
❏ 6E-243	Pizzazz	1979	$12
❏ 6E-302	Posh	1980	$12
❏ 60015	Straight from the Heart	1982	$12
PRESTIGE			
❏ 10098	Before the Dawn	1976	$25
❏ 10110	Let There Be Funk	1980	$20
❏ 10089	Prelusion	1974	$25
❏ 10101	Shout It Out	1977	$20

RUSHING, JIMMY; ADA MOORE; BUCK CLAYTON
Also see each artist's individual listings.
Albums

Number	Title	Yr	NM
COLUMBIA			
❏ CL778 [M]	Cat Meets Chick	1956	$60

RUSHING, JIMMY
Singer and pianist.
Albums

Number	Title	Yr	NM
AUDIO LAB			
❏ AL-1512 [M]	Two Shades of Blue	1959	$120
BLUESWAY			
❏ BL-6005 [M]	Everyday I Have the Blues	1967	$25
❏ BLS-6005 [S]	Everyday I Have the Blues	1967	$25
❏ BLS-6017	Livin' the Blues	1968	$25
❏ BLS-6057	Sent for You Yesterday	1973	$20
COLPIX			
❏ CP-446 [M]	Five Feet of Soul	1963	$40
❏ SCP-446 [S]	Five Feet of Soul	1963	$60
— The existence of this record has been confirmed			
COLUMBIA			
❏ CL1605 [M]	Jimmy Rushing and the Smith Girls	1961	$30
❏ CS8405 [S]	Jimmy Rushing and the Smith Girls	1961	$40
❏ CL1152 [M]	Little Jimmy Rushing and the Big Brass	1958	$40
❏ CS8060 [S]	Little Jimmy Rushing and the Big Brass	1958	$50
❏ C236419	Mister Five by Five	1979	$15
❏ CL1401 [M]	Rushing Lullabies	1959	$40
❏ CS8196 [S]	Rushing Lullabies	1959	$50
❏ CL963 [M]	The Jazz Odyssey of James Rushing, Esq.	1957	$40
JAZZTONE			
❏ J-1244 [M]	Listen to the Blues	195?	$40
MASTER JAZZ			
❏ 8104	Gee, Baby	197?	$20
❏ 8120	Who Was It Sang That Song?	1971	$35
RCA VICTOR			
❏ LSP-4566	You and Me The Used to Be	1972	$35
VANGUARD			
❏ VRS-65/66	Essential Jimmy Rushing	197?	$20
❏ VRS-8518 [M]	Going to Chicago	1957	$80
❏ VRS-8513 [M]	If This Ain't the Blues	1957	$80
❏ VSD-2008 [S]	If This Ain't the Blues	1958	$100
❏ VRS-8011 [10]	Jimmy Rushing Sings the Blues	1955	$200
❏ VRS-8505 [M]	Listen to the Blues	1955	$100
❏ VSD-73007	Listen to the Blues	1967	$20

RUSSELL, GENE
Pianist. Founder of the Black Jazz record label.
Albums

Number	Title	Yr	NM
BLACK JAZZ			
❏ 1	New Direction	1972	$30
❏ QD-10	Talk to My Lady	1973	$30
OVATION			
❏ OV-1803	Listen Here	197?	$30
SEA BREEZE			
❏ SB-3001	Autumn Leaves	198?	$25

RUSSELL, GEORGE
Pianist, composer, arranger and bandleader.
Albums

Number	Title	Yr	NM
BASF			
❏ 25125	Live at Beethoven Hall	1973	$35
BLUE NOTE			
❏ BT-85132	So What	1987	$35
❏ BT-85103	The African Game	198?	$30
CONCEPT			
❏ 02	Listen to the Silence	197?	$30
DECCA			
❏ DL9220 [M]	George Russell at the Five Spot	1958	$120
❏ DL79220 [S]	George Russell at the Five Spot	1958	$120
❏ DL4183 [M]	George Russell in Kansas City	1961	$30
❏ DL74183 [S]	George Russell in Kansas City	1961	$40
❏ DL9219 [M]	Jazz in the Space Age	1958	$120
❏ DL79219 [S]	Jazz in the Space Age	1958	$120
❏ DL9216 [M]	New York, N.Y.	1958	$100
❏ DL79216 [S]	New York, N.Y.	1958	$100
FANTASY			
❏ OJC-070	Ezz-thetics	198?	$25
❏ OJC-232	Stratusphunk	198?	$25
❏ OJC-616	The Outer View	1991	$30
❏ OJC-365	The Stratus Seekers	198?	$25
FLYING DUTCHMAN			
❏ FD-10124	Electronic Sonata for Souls Loved by Nature	1971	$35
❏ FD-124	Electronic Sonata for Souls Loved by Nature	1970	$25
❏ FD-10122	Othello Ballet Suite/ Electronic Organ Sonata No. 1	1971	$35
❏ FD-122	Othello Ballet Suite/ Electronic Organ Sonata No. 1	1970	$25
MCA			
❏ 4017	New York, N.Y./Jazz in the Space Age	1974	$35
MGM			
❏ E-3321 [M]	George Russell Octets	1955	$80
MILESTONE			
❏ 47027	Outer Thoughts	197?	$35
PETE			
❏ 1107	Easy Listening	1969	$35
RCA VICTOR			
❏ LPM-1372 [M]	Jazz Workshop	1957	$80
❏ LPM-2534 [M]	Jazz Workshop	1962	$30
❏ LSP-2534 [R]	Jazz Workshop	1962	$35
RIVERSIDE			
❏ RLP-375 [M]	Ezz-thetics	1961	$200
❏ RS-9375 [S]	Ezz-thetics	1961	$200
❏ 6112	Ezz-thetics	197?	$30
❏ RS-3043	George Russell Sextet	1970	$100
❏ RLP-341 [M]	Stratusphunk	1960	$200
❏ RS-9341 [S]	Stratusphunk	1960	$200
❏ RLP-440 [M]	The Outer View	1963	$150
❏ RS-9440 [S]	The Outer View	1963	$150
❏ RS-3016	The Outer View	1968	$100
❏ RLP-412 [M]	The Stratus Seekers	1962	$150
❏ RS-9412 [S]	The Stratus Seekers	1962	$150
SOUL NOTE			
❏ SN-1034	Electronic Sonata for Souls Loved by Nature 1969	198?	$30
❏ SN-1009	Electronic Sonata for Souls Loved by Nature 1980	1980	$30
❏ SN-1024	Listen to the Silence (A Mass for Our Time)	198?	$30
❏ SN-1049	Live in an American Time Spiral	1983	$30
❏ SN-1039	New York Big Band	198?	$30
❏ SN-1014	Othello Ballet Suite	198?	$30
❏ SN-1044/5	The Essence of George Russell	198?	$35
❏ SN-1029	Trip to Pillar-Guri	198?	$30
❏ SN-1019	Vertical Form VI	198?	$30
STRATA-EAST			
❏ SES-19761	Electronic Sonata for Souls Loved by Nature	1976	$25

RUSSELL, HAL
Saxophone player and bandleader.
Albums

Number	Title	Yr	NM
NESSA			
❏ N-25	Generation	1982	$50
❏ N-21	NRG Ensemble	1981	$50

RUSSELL, JIMMY
Albums

Number	Title	Yr	NM
CUCA			
❏ 4100 [M]	Jimmy Russell Trio	1965	$30
DORIAN			
❏ 1020	The Swingin'est	1968	$35

RUSSELL, LUIS
Pianist and bandleader, a pioneer in swing music.
Albums

Number	Title	Yr	NM
COLUMBIA			
❏ CG32338	Luis Russell and the Louisiana Swing Orchestra	1973	$35
❏ PG32338	Luis Russell and the Louisiana Swing Orchestra	197?	$30
— Reissue with new prefix			

RUSSELL, PEE WEE, AND RUBY BRAFF
Also see each artist's individual listings.
Albums

Number	Title	Yr	NM
SAVOY			
❏ MG-12034 [M]	Jazz At Storyville, Volume 1	1955	$60
❏ MG-12041 [M]	Jazz at Storyville, Volume 2	1955	$60

RUSSELL, PEE WEE
Clarinetist and saxophone player. Also see RUBY BRAFF; COLEMAN HAWKINS; PEE WEE HUNT; JACK TEAGARDEN.
Albums
ABC IMPULSE!

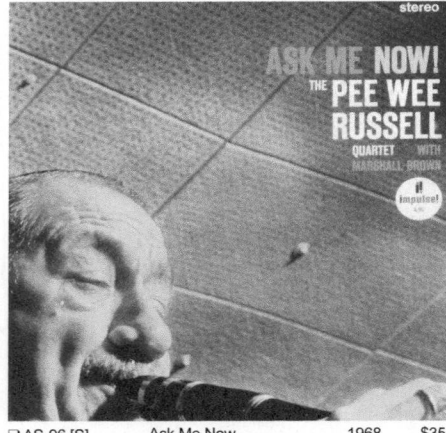

Number	Title	Yr	NM
❏ AS-96 [S]	Ask Me Now	1968	$35
❏ AS-9137 [S]	College Concert of Pee Wee Russell with Henry "Red" Allen	1968	$35
❏ IA-9359	Salute to Newport	1979	$35
ATLANTIC			
❏ ALS-126 [10]	Pee Wee Russell All Stars	1952	$350
BARNABY			
❏ BR-5018	Jazz Reunion	197?	$30
BELL			
❏ LP-42 [M]	Pee Wee Russell Plays Pee Wee	1961	$30
❏ LPS-42 [S]	Pee Wee Russell Plays Pee Wee	1961	$30
COLUMBIA			
❏ CL1985 [M]	New Groove	1963	$35
❏ CS8785 [S]	New Groove	1963	$25
COMMODORE			
❏ XFL-16440	Three Deuces and Hot Four: The Pied Piper of Jazz	198?	$25
COUNTERPOINT			
❏ 0(# unknown) [M]	Portrait of Pee Wee	1957	$60
DCC COMPACT CLASSICS			
❏ LPZ-2024	Portrait of Pee Wee	1996	$30
— Audiophile vinyl			
DISC			
❏ DLP-0(# unknown) [10]	Jazz Ensemble	195?	$120
DOT			
❏ DLP-3253 [M]	Pee Wee Russell Plays	1960	$75
❏ DLP-25253 [S]	Pee Wee Russell Plays	1960	$75
ESOTERIC			

Number	Title	Yr	NM
❑ 565 [M]	Pee Wee Russell All Stars	1959	$40
❑ 5565 [S]	Pee Wee Russell All Stars	1959	$30
EVEREST ARCHIVE OF FOLK & JAZZ			
❑ 233 [R]	Pee Wee Russell	1969	$25
FANTASY			
❑ OJC-1708	Rhythmakers and Teagarden	1985	$25
IMPULSE!			
❑ A-96 [M]	Ask Me Now	1966	$120
❑ AS-96 [S]	Ask Me Now	1966	$120
❑ A-9137 [M]	College Concert of Pee Wee Russell with Henry "Red" Allen	1967	$120
❑ AS-9137 [S]	College Concert of Pee Wee Russell with Henry "Red" Allen	1967	$200
MAINSTREAM			
❑ 56026 [M]	A Legend	1965	$35
❑ S-6026 [S]	A Legend	1965	$25
MCA			
❑ 4150	Salute to Newport	198?	$30
PRESTIGE			
❑ 24051	Jam Session in Swingville	198?	$35
❑ PRST-7672 [R]	The Pee Wee Russell Memorial Album	1969	$35
RIVERSIDE			
❑ RLP 12-141 [M]	Rhythmakers and Teagarden	1955	$300
SAVOY JAZZ			
❑ SJL-2228	The Individualism of Pee Wee Russell	197?	$35
STEREO-CRAFT			
❑ RTN-105 [M]	Pee Wee Plays Pee Wee	196?	$25
❑ RTS-105 [S]	Pee Wee Plays Pee Wee	196?	$30
STORYVILLE			
❑ STLP-308 [10]	Pee Wee Russell	1954	$80
❑ STLP-909 [M]	We're In the Money	1956	$50
SWINGVILLE			
❑ SVLP-2008 [M]	Swingin' with Pee Wee	1960	$50
— Purple label			
❑ SVLP-2008 [M]	Swingin' with Pee Wee	1965	$30
— Blue label, trident logo at right			
TIME-LIFE			
❑ STL-J-17	Giants of Jazz	1981	$50
XANADU			
❑ 192	Over the Rainbow	198?	$25

RUSSELL, PEE WEE/BILLY BANKS

Banks is a male singer. Also see PEE WEE RUSSELL.

Albums

Number	Title	Yr	NM
JAZZ PANORAMA			
❑ 1808 [10]	Pee Wee Russell / Billy Banks	1951	$80

RUSSIAN JAZZ QUARTET, THE

Albums

Number	Title	Yr	NM
ABC IMPULSE!			
❑ AS-80 [S]	Happiness	1968	$35
IMPULSE!			
❑ A-80 [M]	Happiness	1965	$200
❑ AS-80 [S]	Happiness	1965	$120

RUSSIN, BABE

Tenor saxophone player and clarinetist.

Albums

Number	Title	Yr	NM
DOT			
❑ DLP-3060 [M]	To Soothe the Savage	1956	$100

RUSSO, BILL

Trombonist, arranger, composer and bandleader. Also see STAN KENTON; SHELLY MANNE.

Albums

Number	Title	Yr	NM
ATLANTIC			
❑ 1241 [M]	The World of Alcina	1956	$300
— Black label			
❑ 1241 [M]	The World of Alcina	1961	$150
— Multicolor label, white "fan" logo at right			
DEE GEE			
❑ 1001 [10]	A Recital in New American Music	1952	$200
FM			

Number	Title	Yr	NM
❑ 302 [M]	Stereophony	1963	$30
❑ S-302 [S]	Stereophony	1963	$30
ROULETTE			
❑ R-52045 [M]	School of Rebellion	1960	$30
❑ SR-52045 [S]	School of Rebellion	1960	$30
❑ R-52063 [M]	Seven Deadly Sins	1960	$30
❑ SR-52063 [S]	Seven Deadly Sins	1960	$30

RUTHER, BULL

See MILT HINTON.

RUTHERFORD, PAUL

Trombonist and pianist.

Albums

Number	Title	Yr	NM
EMANEM			
❑ 3305	Gentle Harm of the Bourgeoisie	197?	$30

RYG, JORGEN

Trumpeter.

Albums

Number	Title	Yr	NM
EMARCY			
❑ MG-36099 [M]	Jorgen Ryg Jazz Quartet	1956	$200

RYPDAL, TERJE, AND DAVID DARLING

Also see each artist's individual listings.

Albums

Number	Title	Yr	NM
ECM			
❑ 23799	EOS	198?	$25

RYPDAL, TERJE

Guitarist, flutist and keyboard player.

Albums

Number	Title	Yr	NM
ECM			
❑ 1083	After the Rain	1977	$30
❑ 1303	Chaser	1986	$25
❑ 1144	Descendre	1979	$30
❑ 1067/8	Odyssey	1976	$35
❑ 1125	Terje Rypdal/Miroslav Vitous/Jack DeJohnette	1979	$30
❑ 1192	To Be Continued	198?	$25
❑ 1110	Waves	1978	$30
❑ 1031	What Comes After	1974	$35
❑ 1045	Whenever I Seem to Be Far Away	1975	$30

S

SABIEN, RANDY

Violinist and mandolin player.

Albums

Number	Title	Yr	NM
FLYING FISH			
❑ FF-297	In a Fog	198?	$25

SABU

Full name: Sabu Martinez. Percussionist (bongos and conga drums) and male singer.

Albums

Number	Title	Yr	NM
ALEGRE			
❑ 802 [M]	Jazz Espagnole	195?	$300
BLUE NOTE			
❑ BLP-1561 [M]	Palo Congo	1957	$350
— Regular version, W. 63rd St. address on label			
❑ BLP-1561 [M]	Palo Congo	1963	$150
— With "New York, USA" address on label			
❑ BST-81561 [R]	Palo Congo	1967	$35
— With "A Division of Liberty Records" on label			

SACBE

Mexican group: Eugenio Toussaint (piano, keyboards); Enrique Toussaint (bass); Fernando Toussaint (drums); Armando Montiel (percussion).

Albums

Number	Title	Yr	NM
DISCOVERY			
❑ 864	Street Corner	198?	$25
TREND			

Number	Title	Yr	NM
❑ TR-521	Aztlan	1979	$30
❑ TR-544	The Sleeping Lady	1986	$25

SACHS, AARON

Clarinetist, tenor and alto saxophone player and flutist.

Albums

Number	Title	Yr	NM
BETHLEHEM			
❑ BCP-1008 [10]	Aaron Sachs Quintet	1954	$250
DAWN			
❑ DLP-1114 [M]	Jazzville, Volume 3	1957	$80
RAMA			
❑ LP-1004 [M]	Clarinet and Co.	1957	$80

SACHS, AARON/HANK D'AMICO

Also see each artist's individual listings.

Albums

Number	Title	Yr	NM
BETHLEHEM			
❑ BCP-7 [M]	We Brought Our "Axes	1955	$250

SACKVILLE ALL-STARS, THE

The below album features BUDDY TATE; JIM GALLOWAY; JAY McSHANN; Don Thompson (bass); and Terry Clarke (drums).

Albums

Number	Title	Yr	NM
SACKVILLE			
❑ 3028	Saturday Night Function	198?	$25

SADI, FATS

Vibraphone player.

Albums

Number	Title	Yr	NM
BLUE NOTE			
❑ BLP-5061 [10]	The Swinging Fats Sadi Combo	1955	$300

SALIM, A.K.

Arranger, composer and bandleader.

Albums

Number	Title	Yr	NM
PRESTIGE			
❑ PRLP-7379 [M]	Afro-Soul Drum Orgy	1966	$30
❑ PRST-7379 [S]	Afro-Soul Drum Orgy	1966	$30
SAVOY			
❑ MG-12132 [M]	Blues Suite	1958	$50
❑ SST-13001 [S]	Blues Suite	1959	$40
❑ MG-12118 [M]	Pretty for the People	1957	$80
❑ MG-12102 [M]	The Flute Suite	1957	$80

SALIS, ANTONELLO

Pianist and accordion player.

Albums

Number	Title	Yr	NM
HAT HUT			
❑ 10	Orange Juice/Nice Food	1980	$35

SALT CITY FIVE, THE

Among the members: Jack Maheu (clarinet); Bill Rubenstein (piano).

Albums

Number	Title	Yr	NM
JUBILEE			
❑ JLP-13 [10]	Salt City Five	1955	$60
❑ JLP-1012 [M]	Salt City Five	1956	$40
❑ JLP-24 [10]	Salt City Five, Volume 2	1955	$60

SALUZZI, DINO

Bandoneon player, flutist and male singer.

Albums

Number	Title	Yr	NM
ECM			
❑ 1251	Kultrum	198?	$30
❑ 25042	Once Upon a Time… Far Away in the South	1986	$25

SALVADOR, DOM

Pianist and arranger.

Albums

Number	Title	Yr	NM
MUSE			
❑ MR-5085	My Family	1976	$30

Number	Title	Yr	NM

SALVADOR, SAL
Guitarist and bandleader.

Albums

BEE HIVE

Number	Title	Yr	NM
❑ BH-7009	Juicy Lucy	1979	$30
❑ BH-7002	Starfingers	1978	$30

BETHLEHEM

Number	Title	Yr	NM
❑ BCP-59 [M]	Frivolous Sal	1956	$250
❑ BCP-39 [M]	Shades of Sal Salvador	1956	$250
❑ BCP-74 [M]	Tribute to the Greats	1957	$250

BLUE NOTE

Number	Title	Yr	NM
❑ BLP-5035 [10]	Sal Salvador Quintet	1954	$300

CAPITOL

Number	Title	Yr	NM
❑ H6505 [10]	Sal Salvador	1954	$200
❑ T6505 [M]	Sal Salvador	1955	$150

DAUNTLESS

Number	Title	Yr	NM
❑ DM-4307 [M]	You Ain't Heard Nothin' Yet	1963	$60
❑ DS-6307 [S]	You Ain't Heard Nothin' Yet	1963	$40

DECCA

Number	Title	Yr	NM
❑ DL4026 [M]	Beat for This Generation	1959	$100
❑ DL74026 [S]	Beat for This Generation	1959	$100
❑ DL9210 [M]	Colors in Sound	1958	$120
❑ DL79210 [S]	Colors in Sound	1958	$120

GOLDEN CREST

Number	Title	Yr	NM
❑ GC-1001 [M]	Sal Salvador Quartet	1961	$30
❑ GCS-1001 [S]	Sal Salvador Quartet	1961	$30

GP

Number	Title	Yr	NM
❑ 5010	Live at the University of Bridgeport	197?	$30

ROULETTE

Number	Title	Yr	NM
❑ RS-25262 [S]	Music To Stop Smoking By	1964	$30

STASH

Number	Title	Yr	NM
❑ ST-224	In Our Own Sweet Way	198?	$25
❑ ST-251	Sal Salvador Plays Gerry Mulligan	1985	$25
❑ ST-234	Sal Salvador Plays the World's Greatest Standards	198?	$25

SAMPLE, JOE, AND DAVID T. WALKER
Also see each artist's individual listings.

Albums

CRUSADERS

Number	Title	Yr	NM
❑ 16004	Swing Street Café	198?	$50

—*Audiophile vinyl*

MCA

Number	Title	Yr	NM
❑ 5785	Swing Street Café	198?	$25

SAMPLE, JOE; RAY BROWN; SHELLY MANNE
Also see each artist's individual listings.

Albums

EAST WIND

Number	Title	Yr	NM
❑ 10001	The Three	1976	$50

INNER CITY

Number	Title	Yr	NM
❑ IC-6007	The Three	197?	$35

SAMPLE, JOE
Keyboard player. Also see THE CRUSADERS.

Albums

ABC

Number	Title	Yr	NM
❑ AA-1126	Carmel	1979	$30
❑ AA-1050	Rainbow Seeker	1978	$25

CRUSADERS

Number	Title	Yr	NM
❑ 16001	Carmel	198?	$50

—*Audiophile vinyl*

MCA

Number	Title	Yr	NM
❑ 37210	Carmel	198?	$20

—*Budget-line reissue*

Number	Title	Yr	NM
❑ AA-1126	Carmel	1979	$25

—*Reissue of ABC 1126*

Number	Title	Yr	NM
❑ 5481	Oasis	1985	$25
❑ AA-1050	Rainbow Seeker	1979	$20

—*Reissue of ABC 1050*

Number	Title	Yr	NM
❑ 5978	Roles	1987	$25
❑ 5397	The Hunter	1983	$25
❑ 5172	Voices in the Rain	1981	$25
❑ 27077	Voices in the Rain	198?	$20

—*Budget-line reissue*

MOBILE FIDELITY

Number	Title	Yr	NM
❑ Jan-0016	Rainbow Seeker	1979	$60

—*Audiophile vinyl*

STORYVILLE

Number	Title	Yr	NM
❑ 4000	Fancy Dance	1980	$30

WARNER BROS.

Number	Title	Yr	NM
❑ 26318	Ashes to Ashes	1990	$35
❑ 25781	Spellbound	1989	$30

SAMPSON, EDGAR
Alto saxophone player, clarinetist and violinist.

Albums

CORAL

Number	Title	Yr	NM
❑ CRL57049 [M]	Swing Softly Sweet Sampson	1957	$40

MCA

Number	Title	Yr	NM
❑ 1354	Sampson Swings Again	198?	$25

SAMS, GEORGE
Trumpeter.

Albums

HAT HUT

Number	Title	Yr	NM
❑ 3506	Nomadic Winds	198?	$30

SAMUELS, DAVID
Vibraphone player and timpanist.

Albums

MCA

Number	Title	Yr	NM
❑ 6328	Ten Degrees North	1988	$25

SANBORN, DAVID
Saxophone player (mostly alto). Also see BOB JAMES.

Albums

REPRISE

Number	Title	Yr	NM
❑ 25715	Close-Up	1988	$25

WARNER BROS.

Number	Title	Yr	NM
❑ 25479	A Change of Heart	1987	$25
❑ 23650	As We Speak	1982	$25
❑ 23906	Backstreet	1983	$25
❑ BSK3189	Heart to Heart	1978	$25
❑ BSK3379	Hideaway	1980	$25
❑ BS3051	Promise Me the Moon	1977	$25
❑ BS2957	Sanborn	1976	$25
❑ 25150	Straight from the Heart	1985	$25
❑ BS2873	Taking Off	1975	$25
❑ BSK3546	Voyeur	1981	$25

SANCHEZ, PONCHO
Percussionist.

Albums

CONCORD PICANTE

Number	Title	Yr	NM
❑ CJP-239	Bien Sabroso	198?	$25
❑ CJP-286	El Conguero	1985	$25
❑ CJP-340	Fuente	1988	$25
❑ CJP-369	La Familia	1989	$25
❑ CJP-310	Papa Gato	1987	$25
❑ CJP-201	Sonando	198?	$25

DISCOVERY

Number	Title	Yr	NM
❑ 799	Poncho	1979	$30
❑ 813	Straight Ahead	1980	$30

SANCIOUS, DAVID
Keyboard player. Formerly in Bruce Springsteen's band.

Albums

ELEKTRA/MUSICIAN

Number	Title	Yr	NM
❑ 60130	The Bridge	1982	$25

SANCTON, TOMMY
Clarinet player and bandleader.

Albums

GHB

Number	Title	Yr	NM
❑ GHB-52	Tommy Sancton's Galvanized Washboard Band	1969	$30

SANDERS, ANNETTE
Female singer.

Albums

SOVEREIGN

Number	Title	Yr	NM
❑ SOV-502	The Time Is Right	198?	$30

SANDERS, PHAROAH
Tenor saxophone player. Also see THE JAZZ COMPOSERS ORCHESTRA; SUN RA.

Albums

ABC IMPULSE!

Number	Title	Yr	NM
❑ AS-9219	Black Unity	1972	$35
❑ AQ-9219 [Q]	Black Unity	1974	$200
❑ AS-9261	Elevation	1974	$30
❑ AQ-9261 [Q]	Elevation	1974	$200
❑ AS-9190	Jewels of Thought	1970	$200
❑ AS-9181	Karma	1969	$200
❑ AS-9227	Live at the East	1973	$35
❑ AQ-9227 [Q]	Live at the East	1974	$200
❑ ASD-9280	Love in Us All	1975	$30
❑ AQ-9280 [Q]	Love in Us All	1975	$200
❑ AS-9199	Summun Bukmun Umyum	1970	$200
❑ A-9138 [M]	Tauhid	1967	$200
❑ AS-9138 [S]	Tauhid	1967	$200
❑ AS-9229	The Best of Pharoah Sanders	1973	$200
❑ AS-9206	Thembi	1971	$35
❑ AS-9254	Village of the Pharoahs	1974	$30
❑ AQ-9254 [Q]	Village of the Pharoahs	1974	$200
❑ AS-9233	Wisdom Through Music	1973	$35

ARISTA

Number	Title	Yr	NM
❑ AL4161	Love Will Find a Way	1978	$30

ESP-DISK'

Number	Title	Yr	NM
❑ 1003 [M]	Pharoah's First	1965	$120
❑ S-1003 [S]	Pharoah's First	1965	$120

GRP/IMPULSE!

Number	Title	Yr	NM
❑ IMP-219	Black Unity	199?	$35

—*Reissue on audiophile vinyl*

INDIA NAVIGATION

Number	Title	Yr	NM
❑ IN-1027	Pharoah	1977	$30

MCA

Number	Title	Yr	NM
❑ 29058	Jewels of Thought	1981	$20

—*Reissue of Impulse 9190*

Number	Title	Yr	NM
❑ 29057	Karma	1981	$20

—*Reissue of Impulse 9181*

Number	Title	Yr	NM
❑ 29056	Tauhid	1981	$20

—*Reissue of Impulse 9138*

Number	Title	Yr	NM
❑ 4151	The Best of Pharoah Sanders	1981	$30

—*Reissue of Impulse 9229*

Number	Title	Yr	NM
❑ 29059	Thembi	1981	$20

—*Reissue of Impulse 9206*

SIGNATURE

Number	Title	Yr	NM
❑ FA40952	Oh Lord, Let Me Do No Wrong	1989	$30

STRATA-EAST

Number	Title	Yr	NM
❑ 19733	Izipho Sam (My Gifts)	1973	$35

THERESA

Number	Title	Yr	NM
❑ 118	Heart Is a Melody	1986	$25
❑ 108/9	Journey to the One	1980	$35
❑ 116	Pharoah Sanders Live	1985	$25
❑ 112/13	Rejoice	1981	$35
❑ 121	Shukuru	1986	$25

TIMELESS

Number	Title	Yr	NM
❑ SJP-253	Africa	1990	$30

UPFRONT

Number	Title	Yr	NM
❑ 150	Spotlight	1973	$30

SANDKE, JORDAN
Trumpeter. Brother of Randy.

Albums

STASH

Number	Title	Yr	NM
❑ ST-259	Rhythm Is Our Business	1986	$25

SANDKE, RANDY
Trumpeter and fluegel horn player. Brother of Jordan.

Albums

STASH

Number	Title	Yr	NM
❑ ST-264	New York Stories	1987	$25

SANDOLE, DENNIS
Guitarist. Also see THE SANDOLE BROTHERS.

Albums

FANTASY

Number	Title	Yr	NM
❑ 3251 [M]	Compositions and Arrangements for Guitar	1958	$30

SANDOLE BROTHERS, THE
With DENNIS SANDOLE (guitar) and Adolphe Sandole (piano).

Albums

FANTASY

Number	Title	Yr	NM
❑ 3209 [M]	Modern Music from Philadelphia	1956	$200

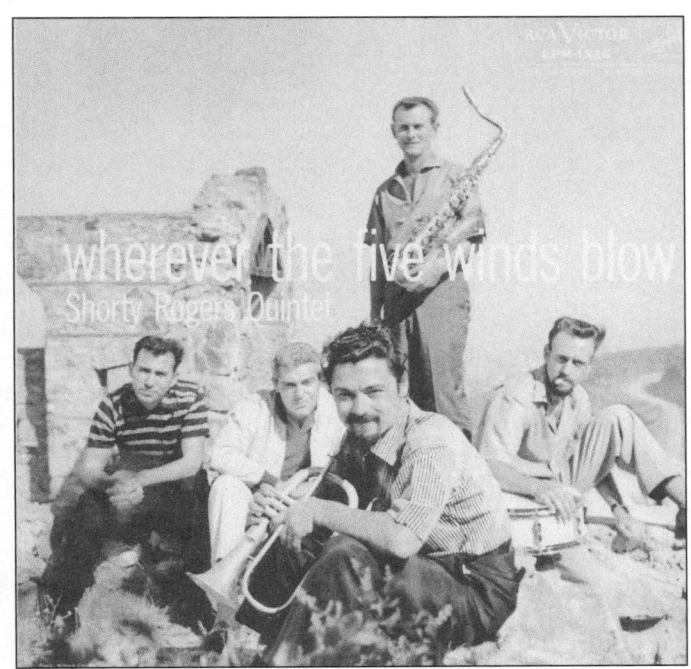

Shorty Rogers, *Wherever the Five Winds Blow*, RCA Victor LPM-1326, **$140**.

Shorty Rogers, *Shorty Rogers Courts the Count*, RCA Victor LJM-1004, **$80**.

Sonny Rollins, *Sonny Rollins On Impulse!*, Impulse! A-91, mono, **$200**.

Sonny Rollins, *Sonny Rollins with the Modern Jazz Quartet*, Prestige PRLP-7029, third cover, yellow label with W. 50th St. address, **$300**.

Number	Title	Yr	NM
— Red vinyl			
❏ 3209 [M]	Modern Music from Philadelphia	1957	$250
— Black vinyl			

SANDOVAL, ARTURO
Trumpeter. Also see IRAKERE.

Albums

GRP
| ❏ GR-9634 | Flight to Freedom | 1991 | $35 |

SANGUMA
From Papua New Guinea.

Albums

ODE NEW ZEALAND
| ❏ SODE-194 | Sanguma | 1986 | $30 |

SANTAMARIA, MONGO
Conga player and bandleader. His version of the HERBIE HANCOCK composition "Watermelon Man" was a top-10 pop hit in 1963.

Albums

ATLANTIC
❏ SD8252	Feelin' Alright	1970	$30
❏ SD1567	Mongo '70	1970	$30
❏ SD1593	Mongo at Montreux	1972	$30
❏ SD1581	Mongo's Way	1971	$30
❏ SD1621 [S]	Up from the Roots	1972	$30
❏ 1621 [M]	Up from the Roots	1972	$60
— Mono is white label promo only; "d/j copy monaural" sticker on stereo cover			

BATTLE
❏ B-6129 [M]	Mongo at the Village Gate	1964	$50
❏ BS-96129 [S]	Mongo at the Village Gate	1964	$60
❏ B-6120 [M]	Watermelon Man!	1963	$50
❏ BS-96120 [S]	Watermelon Man!	1963	$60

COLUMBIA
❏ CS9988	All Strung Out	1970	$35
❏ CL2411 [M]	El Bravo	1966	$30
❏ CS9211 [S]	El Bravo	1966	$35
❏ CL2298 [M]	El Pussy Cat	1965	$50
— With "Guaranteed High Fidelity" in black at bottom of red label			
❏ CS9098 [S]	El Pussy Cat	1965	$60
— With "360 Sound Stereo" in black at bottom of red label			
❏ CL2298 [M]	El Pussy Cat	1965	$30
— With "360 Sound Mono" in white at bottom of red label			
❏ CS9098 [S]	El Pussy Cat	1965	$35
— With "360 Sound Stereo" in white at bottom of red label			
❏ CL2473 [M]	Hey! Let's Party	1966	$30
❏ CS9273 [S]	Hey! Let's Party	1966	$35
❏ CL2375 [M]	La Bamba	1965	$35
❏ CS9175 [S]	La Bamba	1965	$50
❏ CL2612 [M]	Mongomania	1967	$35
❏ CS9412 [S]	Mongomania	1967	$30
❏ CL2770 [M]	Mongo Santamaria Explodes at the Village Gate	1967	$35
❏ CS9570 [S]	Mongo Santamaria Explodes at the Village Gate	1967	$30
❏ CS1060	Mongo's Greatest Hits	1970	$30
❏ PC1060	Mongo's Greatest Hits	198?	$20
— Reissue with new prefix			
❏ CL2375 [M]	Mr. Watermelon Man	196?	$30
— Retitled reissue			
❏ CS9175 [S]	Mr. Watermelon Man	196?	$35
— Retitled reissue			
❏ CS9653	Soul Bag	1968	$35
❏ CS9780	Stone Soul	1969	$35
❏ CS9937	Workin' on a Groovy Thing	1969	$35

CONCORD JAZZ
| ❏ CJ-387 | Ole Ola | 1989 | $30 |

CONCORD PICANTE
| ❏ CJP-362 | Soca Me Nice | 1988 | $25 |
| ❏ CJP-327 | Soy Yo | 1987 | $25 |

FANTASY
❏ 3324 [M]	Arriba!	1961	$40
— Red vinyl			
❏ 3324 [M]	Arriba!	1961	$60
— Black vinyl			
❏ 8067 [S]	Arriba!	1962	$60
— Blue vinyl			
❏ 8067 [S]	Arriba!	1962	$50
— Black vinyl			
❏ 3328 [M]	Mas Sabroso	1962	$40
— Red vinyl			

Number	Title	Yr	NM
❏ 3328 [M]	Mas Sabroso	1962	$60
— Black vinyl			
❏ 8071 [S]	Mas Sabroso	1962	$60
— Blue vinyl			
❏ 8071 [S]	Mas Sabroso	1962	$50
— Black vinyl			
❏ 8351 [S]	Mighty Mongo	1963	$50
❏ 3351 [M]	Mighty Mongo	1963	$35
❏ 3291 [M]	Mongo	1959	$40
— Red vinyl			
❏ 3291 [M]	Mongo	1959	$60
— Black vinyl			
❏ 8032 [S]	Mongo	1962	$60
— Blue vinyl			
❏ 8032 [S]	Mongo	1962	$50
— Black vinyl			
❏ OJC-490	Mongo at the Village Gate	1991	$30
— Reissue of Riverside 93529			
❏ 3311 [M]	Mongo in Havana	1960	$40
— Red vinyl			
❏ 3311 [M]	Mongo in Havana	1960	$60
— Black vinyl			
❏ 8055 [S]	Mongo in Havana	1962	$60
— Blue vinyl			
❏ 8055 [S]	Mongo in Havana	1962	$50
— Black vinyl			
❏ 8373	Mongo Santamaria's Greatest Hits	1967	$30
❏ MPF-4529	Mongo Santamaria's Greatest Hits	198?	$20
— Budget-line reissue			
❏ 9431	Mongo Y La Lupe	1974	$30
❏ 3302 [M]	Our Man in Havana	1960	$40
— Red vinyl			
❏ 3302 [M]	Our Man in Havana	1960	$60
— Black vinyl			
❏ 8045 [S]	Our Man in Havana	1962	$60
— Blue vinyl			
❏ 8045 [S]	Our Man in Havana	1962	$50
— Black vinyl			
❏ 3314 [M]	Sabroso	1960	$40
— Red vinyl			
❏ 3314 [M]	Sabroso	1960	$60
— Black vinyl			
❏ 8058 [S]	Sabroso	1962	$60
— Blue vinyl			
❏ 8058 [S]	Sabroso	1962	$50
— Black vinyl			
❏ OJC-281	Sabroso	1987	$25
— Reissue of 8058			
❏ OJC-626	Summertime	1991	$30
— Reissue of Pablo 2308 229			
❏ 3335 [M]	Viva Mongo!	1962	$40
— Red vinyl			
❏ 3335 [M]	Viva Mongo!	1962	$60
— Black vinyl			
❏ 8087 [S]	Viva Mongo!	1962	$60
— Blue vinyl			
❏ 8087 [S]	Viva Mongo!	1962	$50
— Black vinyl			
❏ 3267 [M]	Yambu	1959	$40
— Red vinyl			
❏ 3267 [M]	Yambu	1959	$60
— Black vinyl			
❏ 8012 [S]	Yambu	1962	$60
— Blue vinyl			
❏ 8012 [S]	Yambu	1962	$50
— Black vinyl			
❏ OJC-276	Yambu	1987	$25
— Reissue of 8012			

HARMONY
| ❏ H30291 | The Dock of the Bay | 1971 | $25 |

MILESTONE
| ❏ 47038 | Skins | 1976 | $35 |
| ❏ 47012 | Watermelon Man | 1974 | $35 |

PABLO
| ❏ 2308229 | Summertime | 1980 | $30 |

PRESTIGE
| ❏ 24018 | Afro Roots | 1973 | $35 |

RIVERSIDE
| ❏ R-3008 [M] | Explosion | 1967 | $100 |
| ❏ RS-3008 [S] | Explosion | 1968 | $100 |

Number	Title	Yr	NM
❏ RM-3008 [M]	Explosion	1968	$100
❏ RLP-423 [M]	Go, Mongo!	1962	$150
❏ RS-9423 [S]	Go, Mongo!	1962	$150
❏ RM-3529 [M]	Mongo at the Village Gate	1963	$150
❏ RS-93529 [S]	Mongo at the Village Gate	1963	$150
❏ RM-3523 [M]	Mongo Introduces La Lupe	1963	$150
❏ RS-93523 [S]	Mongo Introduces La Lupe	1963	$150
❏ RM-3530 [M]	Mongo Santamaria Explodes!	1964	$150
❏ RS-93530 [S]	Mongo Santamaria Explodes!	1964	$150
❏ RS-3045	Mongo Soul	1969	$100

TICO
❏ LP-137 [10]	Chango	1955	$150
❏ LP-1037 [M]	Chango: Mongo Santamaria's Drums and Chants	1957	$120
❏ LP-1149 [M]	Mongo Santamaria's Drums and Chants	1967	$50

SANTANA, CARLOS, AND MAHAVISHNU JOHN MCLAUGHLIN
Santana is a guitarist whose other work is outside the scope of this book. Also see JOHN McLAUGHLIN.

Albums

COLUMBIA
❏ KC32034	Love Devotion Surrender	1973	$25
❏ PC32034	Love Devotion Surrender	197?	$20
— Reissue with new prefix			

SANTIAGO, MIKE
Guitarist.

Albums

CHIAROSCURO
| ❏ 193 | White Trees | 1978 | $30 |

SANTOS, MOACIR
Saxophone player, clarinetist, composer and arranger.

Albums

BLUE NOTE
❏ BN-LA483-G	Carnival of the Spirits	1975	$35
❏ BN-LA007-F	Maestro	1972	$25
❏ BN-LA260-G	Saudade	1974	$35

DISCOVERY
| ❏ 795 | Opus 3, No. 1 | 1979 | $30 |

SANTOS BROTHERS, THE

Albums

METROJAZZ
| ❏ E-1015 [M] | Jazz For Two Trumpets | 1958 | $120 |
| ❏ SE-1015 [S] | Jazz For Two Trumpets | 1958 | $120 |

SARACHO
Full name: Gary Saracho. Keyboard player.

Albums

ABC IMPULSE!
| ❏ AS-9247 | En Medio | 1974 | $35 |

SARBIB, SAHEB
Bass player.

Albums

CADENCE JAZZ
❏ CJR-1010	Aisha	198?	$25
❏ CJR-1001	Live at the Public Theatre	198?	$25
❏ CJR-1008	U.F.O. -- Live on Tour	198?	$25

SOUL NOTE
| ❏ SN-1098 | It Couldn't Happen Without You | 198? | $30 |
| ❏ SN-1048 | Sessions | 198? | $30 |

Number	Title	Yr	NM

SASH, LEON
Accordion player, guitarist and vibraphone player.

Albums

DELMARK
| DS-9416 | I Remember Newport | 1968 | $35 |

STORYVILLE
| STLP-917 [M] | Leon Sash Quartet | 1956 | $50 |

SATCHMO LEGACY BAND, THE
Members: Alvin Batiste (clarinet, vocals); RED CALLENDER (bass, tuba, vocals), AL CASEY (guitar, vocals); Alan Dawson (drums); CURTIS FULLER (trombone, vocals); FREDDIE HUBBARD (trumpet, fluegel horn, vocals); KIRK LIGHTSEY (piano, vocals).

Albums

SOUL NOTE
| 121116 | Salute to Pops, Vol. 1 | 1990 | $35 |

SATOH, MASAHIKO
Pianist. Last name also spelled "Sato."

Albums

ENJA
| 2008 | Trinity | 197? | $35 |

PORTRAIT
| OR44194 | Amorphism | 1989 | $30 |

SATTERFIELD, ESTHER
Female singer.

Albums

A&M
| SP-3408 | Once I Loved | 1974 | $25 |
| SP-3411 | The Need to Be | 1975 | $25 |

SAUNDERS, HERM
Pianist.

Albums

VOGUE
| 101 [10] | Music at the Bantam Cock | 1953 | $200 |

WARNER BROS.
| W1269 [M] | That Celestial Feeling | 1959 | $25 |
| W1234 [M] | The Tinkling Piano in the Next Apartment | 1958 | $30 |

SAUNDERS, MERL
Keyboard player. Frequent collaborator with Jerry Garcia of the Grateful Dead.

Albums

CRYSTAL CLEAR
| 5006 | Do I Move You | 1980 | $50 |

—Direct-to-disc recording

FANTASY
| 9421 | Fire Up | 1973 | $50 |

— With Jerry Garcia and Tom Fogerty

8421	Heavy Turbulence	1972	$35
MPF-4533	Keystone Encores, Vol. 1	1988	$30
MPF-4534	Keystone Encores, Vol. 2	1988	$30
9503	Leave Your Hat On	1976	$30
79002	Live at the Keystone	198?	$50
MPF-4535	Live at the Keystone, Vol. 1	1988	$30
MPF-4536	Live at the Keystone, Vol. 2	1988	$30
9460	Saunders	1974	$35

GALAXY
| 8209 | Soul Grooving | 197? | $35 |

SAUNDERS, TEDDY
Pianist.

Albums

DISCOVERY
| 809 | Sue Blue | 1980 | $30 |

SAUNDERS, TOM
Cornet player and bandleader.

Albums

BOUNTIFUL
| 38002 | Tom Saunders' Surf Side Six | 197? | $35 |

SAUSSY, TUPPER
Also see THE NEON PHILARMONIC. (LP)
Pianist. In the pop-rock world, he was composer for The Neon Philharmonic, who had one hit, "Morning Girl," in 1969.

Albums

MONUMENT
MLP-8034 [M]	A Swinger's Guide to "Mary Poppins	1965	$25
SLP-18034 [S]	A Swinger's Guide to "Mary Poppins	1965	$30
MLP-8004 [M]	Discover Tupper Saussy	1964	$25
SLP-18004 [S]	Discover Tupper Saussy	1964	$30
MLP-8027 [M]	Said I to Shostakovitch	1965	$25
SLP-18027 [S]	Said I to Shostakovitch	1965	$30

SAUTER-FINEGAN; CHICAGO SYMPHONY ORCHESTRA (FRITZ REINER, CONDUCTOR)

Albums

RCA VICTOR RED SEAL
| LM-1888 [M] | Concerto for Jazz Band and Orchestra | 1954 | $60 |

SAUTER-FINEGAN
Eddie Sauter (trumpet, arranger) and Bill Finegan (pianist, arranger). Also see RAY McKINLEY.

Albums

GOLDEN ERA
| 15071 | Sauter-Finegan Orchestra Revisited | 198? | $25 |

RCA VICTOR
LPM-1240 [M]	Adventure In Time	1956	$120
LPM-1051 [M]	Concert Jazz	1955	$120
LJM-1003 [M]	Inside Sauter-Finegan	1954	$150
LPM-2473 [M]	Inside Sauter-Finegan Revisited	1961	$60
LSP-2473 [S]	Inside Sauter-Finegan Revisited	1961	$40
LPM-1634 [M]	Memories of Goodman and Miller	1958	$100
LPM-3115 [10]	New Directions in Music	1953	$200
LPM-1227 [M]	New Directions in Music	1956	$120
LPM-1104 [M]	Sons of Sauter-Finegan	1955	$120
LPM-1497 [M]	Straight Down the Middle	1957	$100
LPM-1009 [M]	The Sound of Sauter-Finegan	1954	$150
LPM-1341 [M]	Under Analysis	1957	$100

UNITED ARTISTS
| WWR3511 [M] | The Return of the Doodletown Fifers | 1959 | $40 |
| WWS7511 [S] | The Return of the Doodletown Fifers | 1959 | $100 |

SAVITT, JAN
Violinist and bandleader.

Albums

HINDSIGHT
| HSR-213 | Jan Savitt and His Top Hatters 1939 | 198? | $25 |

SAYE, JOE
Pianist.

Albums

EMARCY
MG-36147 [M]	A Double Shot of Saye	1958	$200
SR-80022 [S]	A Double Shot of Saye	1958	$200
MG-36112 [M]	A Wee Bit of Jazz	1957	$200
MG-36072 [M]	Scotch on the Rocks	1956	$200

MERCURY
| SR-60052 [S] | A Wee Bit of Jazz | 1959 | $150 |

SAYLES SILVER LEAF RAGTIME

Albums

GHB
| GHB-8 | Sayles Sugar Leaf Ragtime | 196? | $35 |

SCALETTA, DON
Pianist.

Albums

CAPITOL
T2328 [M]	All in Good Time	1965	$75
ST2328 [S]	All in Good Time	1965	$50
T2204 [M]	Any Time, Any Groove	1965	$75
ST2204 [S]	Any Time, Any Groove	1965	$50

VERVE
| V-5027 [M] | Sunday Afternoon at the Trident | 1967 | $25 |
| V6-5027 [S] | Sunday Afternoon at the Trident | 1967 | $35 |

SCANIAZZ
Swedish band.

Albums

STOMP OFF
SOS-1056	It's Right Here for You	198?	$25
SOS-1004	Messin' Around	198?	$25
SOS-1038	Sunset Café Stomp	198?	$25

SCHAEFER, HAL
Pianist.

Albums

DISCOVERY
| DS781 | Extraordinary Jazz Pianist | 1979 | $30 |

RCA VICTOR
| LPM-1106 [M] | Just Too Much | 1955 | $120 |
| LPM-1199 [M] | The RCA Victor Jazz Workshop | 1956 | $120 |

RENAISSANCE
| 1000 | Extraordinary Jazz Pianist | 197? | $35 |

UNITED ARTISTS
| UAL-3021 [M] | Ten Shades of Blue | 1959 | $60 |
| UAS-6021 [S] | Ten Shades of Blue | 1959 | $50 |

SCHAERLI, PETER
Trumpeter.

Albums

HAT ART
| 2037 | Schnipp Schnapp | 1987 | $35 |

SCHECKTER, JANE
Female singer.

Albums

DRG
| MRS-711 | I've Got My Standards | 1989 | $30 |

SCHEER MUSIC

Albums

PALO ALTO
| TB-204 | High Rise | 198? | $30 |
| PA-8025 | Rappin' It Up | 198? | $30 |

SCHIFRIN, LALO
Pianist, composer and conductor. Much of his work for movies and TV is listed below.

Albums

AMERICAN INT'L.
| AILP3003 | The Amityville Horror | 1979 | $25 |

AUDIO FIDELITY
AFLP-1981 [M]	Bossa Nova -- New Brazilian Jazz	1962	$50
AFSD-5981 [S]	Bossa Nova -- New Brazilian Jazz	1962	$60
AFLP-2117 [M]	Eso Es Latino Jazz	1963	$50
AFSD-6117 [S]	Eso Es Latino Jazz	1963	$60
AFSD-6195	The Other Side of Lalo Schifrin	1968	$35

COLGEMS
| COMO-5003 [M] | Murderer's Row | 1967 | $100 |
| COSO-5003 [S] | Murderer's Row | 1967 | $175 |

CTI
| 5000 | Black Widow | 1976 | $30 |
| 5003 | Towering Toccata | 1977 | $30 |

DOT
DLP-3833 [M]	Cool Hand Luke	1968	$200
DLP-25833 [S]	Cool Hand Luke	1968	$200
DLP-3831 [M]	Music from Mission: Impossible	1967	$175
DLP-25831 [S]	Music from Mission: Impossible	1967	$80
DLP-25852	There's a Whole Lot of Schifrin Goin' On	1968	$100

DRG
| SBL-12591 | The Fourth Protocol | 1987 | $35 |

ENTR'ACTE
| ERS-6510 | The Eagle Has Landed/The Four Musketeers | 1980 | $30 |

Number	Title	Yr	NM
❏ ERS-6508	Voyage of the Damned	1977	$60
MCA			
❏ 25137	Liquidator	1966	$20
❏ 2374	Nunzio	1978	$30
❏ 2284	Rollercoaster	1977	$35
❏ 25012	The Cincinnati Kid	1986	$20
❏ 5185	The Competition	1980	$25
MGM			
❏ E-4156 [M]	Between Broadway and Hollywood	1963	$35
❏ SE-4156 [S]	Between Broadway and Hollywood	1963	$50
❏ E-4413ST [M]	Liquidator	1966	$50
❏ SE-4413ST [S]	Liquidator	1966	$60
❏ SE-4742	Medical Center and Other Great Themes	1971	$50
❏ E-4110 [M]	Piano, Strings and Bossa Nova	1963	$35
❏ SE-4110 [S]	Piano, Strings and Bossa Nova	1963	$50
❏ E-4313 [M]	The Cincinnati Kid	1965	$50
❏ SE-4313 [S]	The Cincinnati Kid	1965	$60
NAUTILUS			
❏ NR-51	Ins and Outs	198?	$40
—Audiophile vinyl			
PALO ALTO			
❏ 8055	Ins and Outs	1983	$30
PARAMOUNT			
❏ PAS-5004	Mannix	1969	$60
❏ PAS-5002	More Music from Mission: Impossible	1969	$40
ROULETTE			
❏ R52088 [M]	Lalo Brilliance	1962	$50
❏ SR52088 [S]	Lalo Brilliance	1962	$60
❏ SR-42013	Lalole" -- The Latin Sound	1968	$35
TABU			
❏ JZ35436	Gypsies	1978	$30
❏ JZ36091	No One Home	1979	$30
TETRAGRAMMATON			
❏ T-5006	Che!	1969	$60
TICO			
❏ LP-1070 [M]	Piano Espanol	1960	$60
❏ LPS-1070 [S]	Piano Espanol	1960	$60
VARESE SARABANDE			
❏ STV-81198	The Osterman Weekend	1983	$25
VERVE			
❏ V6-8785	Insensatez	1968	$35
❏ V-8601 [M]	New Fantasy	1964	$35
❏ V6-8601 [S]	New Fantasy	1964	$50
❏ V-8624 [M]	Once a Thief and Other Themes	1965	$35
❏ V6-8624 [S]	Once a Thief and Other Themes	1965	$50
❏ V6-8801	Rock Requiem	1971	$30
❏ V-8543 [M]	Samba Paros Dos	1963	$35
— With Bob Brookmeyer			
❏ V6-8543 [S]	Samba Paros Dos	1963	$50
— With Bob Brookmeyer			
❏ V-8654 [M]	The Dissection and Reconstruction of Music from the Past	1966	$35
❏ V6-8654 [S]	The Dissection and Reconstruction of Music from the Past	1966	$50
WARNER BROS.			
❏ BSK3328	Boulevard Nights	1979	$25
❏ WS1777	Bullitt	1968	$120
❏ BS2727	Enter the Dragon	1973	$120

SCHNEIDER, ERIC, AND EARL HINES

Also see each artist's individual listings.

Albums

GATEMOUTH
❏ 1003	Eric and Earl	1980	$30

SCHNEIDER, ERIC

Alto, tenor and soprano saxophone player and clarinetist.

Albums

GATEMOUTH
❏ 1005	Eric's Alley	1981	$30

SCHNEIDER, KENT

Albums

DELMARK
❏ DS-418	Celebration for Modern Man	197?	$30

Number	Title	Yr	NM

SCHNITTER, DAVID

Tenor saxophone player.

Albums

MUSE
❏ MR-5222	Glowing	1980	$30
❏ MR-5153	Goliath	1977	$30
❏ MR-5108	Invitation	197?	$30
❏ MR-5197	Thundering	1979	$30

SCHOEN, VIC

Bandleader and arranger, best known for his studio work with BING CROSBY and the Andrews Sisters, among others, for Decca. Also see LES BROWN AND VIC SCHOEN.

Albums

DECCA
| ❏ DL8132 [M] | Letter to Laura | 195? | $60 |
| ❏ DL8081 [M] | Music for a Rainy Night | 195? | $60 |
KAPP
| ❏ KL-1097 [M] | Great Songs from All Over the World | 1959 | $50 |
| ❏ K-1097-S [S] | Great Songs from All Over the World | 1959 | $60 |
MAINSTREAM
❏ 56036 [M]	Corcovado Trumpets	196?	$50
❏ S-6036 [S]	Corcovado Trumpets	196?	$50
❏ MMS705	Girls with Brass	197?	$30
RCA VICTOR
❏ LPM-2344 [M]	Brass Laced with Strings	196?	$35
❏ LSA-2344 [S]	Brass Laced with Strings	196?	$60

SCHOOF, MANFRED

Trumpeter and fluegel horn player.

Albums

ECM
❏ 19004	Scales	1980	$30

SCHULLER, GUNTHER

Horn player, bandleader, composer and arranger.

Albums

ANGEL
| ❏ S-36060 | Joplin | 197? | $30 |
ATLANTIC
❏ SD1368 [S]	Jazz Abstractions	1963	$50
—Multicolor label, black "fan" logo at right			
❏ 1368 [M]	Jazz Abstractions	1961	$150
—Multicolor label, white "fan" logo at right			
❏ SD1368 [S]	Jazz Abstractions	1961	$150
—Multicolor label, white "fan" logo at right			
❏ 1368 [M]	Jazz Abstractions	1963	$50
—Multicolor label, black "fan" logo at right			
GM RECORDINGS
❏ GM-3010	Jumpin' in the Future	1989	$30
GOLDEN CREST
❏ 31043	Happy Feet: A Tribute to Paul Whiteman	197?	$30
❏ 31042	The Road from Rags to Jazz	197?	$35

SCHUUR, DIANE

Female singer and pianist.

Albums

GRP
❏ GR-1010	Deedles	1984	$25
❏ GR-1039	Diane Schuur and the Count Basie Orchestra	1987	$25
❏ GR-9628	Pure Schuur	1991	$35
❏ GR-1022	Schuur Thing	1985	$25
❏ GR-9567	Talkin' 'Bout You	1988	$25
❏ GR-9591	The Diane Schuur Collection	1989	$30
❏ GR-1030	Timeless	1986	$25
MUSIC IS MEDICINE
❏ 9057	Pilot of My Destiny	1982	$25

SCHWARTZ, CHARLES

Composer and conductor.

Albums

INNER CITY
| ❏ IC-1015 | Professor Jive | 197? | $35 |
| ❏ IC-1164 | Solo Brothers | 198? | $30 |
PABLO TODAY
| ❏ 2312115 | Mother--! Mother--! | 1980 | $35 |

Number	Title	Yr	NM

SCHWARTZ, JONATHAN

Albums

MUSE
❏ MR-5325	Anyone Would Love You	1986	$25

SCHWARTZ, THORNEL

Guitarist.

Albums

ARGO
| ❏ LP-704 [M] | Soul Cookin' | 1962 | $30 |
| ❏ LPS-704 [S] | Soul Cookin' | 1962 | $30 |

SCHWEIZER, IRENE, AND RUDIGER CARL

Scweizer is a pianist and drummer. Carl plays accordion, clarinet and saxophone and also is an arranger and composer.

Albums

HAT HUT
❏ 0X	The Very Centre of Middle Europe	1979	$35

SCIANNI, JOSEPH

Pianist.

Albums

SAVOY
❏ MG-12185 [M]	New Concepts	1965	$30

SCOBEY, BOB

Trumpeter.

Albums

AMERICAN RECORDING SOCIETY
| ❏ G-408 [M] | Bob Scobey's Frisco Band | 1956 | $40 |
DOWN HOME
| ❏ MGD-1 [M] | Bob Scobey's Frisco Band with Clancy Hayes | 1954 | $50 |
GOOD TIME JAZZ
❏ L-22 [10]	Bob Scobey's Frisco Band	1954	$50
❏ L-12032 [M]	Bob Scobey's Frisco Band, Volume 1	1957	$40
❏ L-12033 [M]	Bob Scobey's Frisco Band, Volume 2	1957	$40
❏ L-14 [10]	Bob Scobey's Frisco Band Vol. 2	1954	$50
❏ L-12006 [M]	Bob Scobey's Frisco Band with Clancy Hayes	1955	$50
❏ L-12009 [M]	Scobey and Clancy	1955	$50
JANSCO
❏ 6250	The Great Bob Scobey, Volume 1	1967	$35
❏ 6252	The Great Bob Scobey, Volume 2	1967	$35
❏ 5231	The Great Bob Scobey, Volume 3	1967	$35
RCA VICTOR
❏ LPM-1344 [M]	Beauty and the Beat	1957	$40
❏ LPM-1567 [M]	Between 18th and 19th on Any Street	1957	$40
❏ LPM-1700 [M]	College Classics	1958	$40
❏ LPM-2086 [M]	Rompin' and Stompin'	1959	$30
❏ LSP-2086 [S]	Rompin' and Stompin'	1959	$40
❏ LPM-1889 [M]	Something's Always Happening on the River	1958	$40
❏ LSP-1889 [S]	Something's Always Happening on the River	1958	$60
❏ LPM-1448 [M]	Swingin' on the Golden Gate	1957	$40
VERVE
❏ MGV-1001 [M]	Bob Scobey's Band	1956	$200
❏ V-1001 [M]	Bob Scobey's Band	1961	$25
❏ MGV-1009 [M]	Music from Bourbon Street	1956	$200
❏ V-1009 [M]	Music from Bourbon Street	1961	$25
❏ MGV-1011 [M]	The San Francisco Jazz of Bob Scobey	1957	$80
❏ V-1011 [M]	The San Francisco Jazz of Bob Scobey	1961	$25

SCOFIELD, JOHN

Guitarist, bass player and bandleader.

Albums

ARISTA/NOVUS
| ❏ AN3018 | Who's Who? | 1980 | $30 |
BLUE NOTE
| ❏ B1-92894 | Time on My Hands | 1990 | $35 |
ENJA
| ❏ 4038 | Out Like a Light | 1982 | $30 |
| ❏ 4004 | Shinola | 1981 | $30 |

Sonny Rollins, *Saxophone Colossus*, Prestige PRLP-7079, yellow label with W. 50th St. address, **$2,500**.

Frank Rosolino, *Frank Rosolino*, Capitol H 6507, 10-inch LP, **$250**.

Jimmy Rowles, *Rare – But Well Done*, Liberty LRP 3003, **$150**.

Annie Ross, *Gypsy*, World Pacific WP-1808, **$150**.

Number	Title	Yr	NM

GRAMAVISION
❏ 18-8702-1	Blue Matter	1987	$25
❏ GR-8405	Electric Outlet	1984	$25
❏ R1-79400	Flat Out	1989	$30
❏ 18-8508-1	Still Warm	1985	$25

INNER CITY
❏ IC-3022	John Scofield Live	197?	$35
❏ IC-3030	Rough House	1979	$30

SCOOBY DOO

Albums

ZEPHYR
❏ ZMP-12002 [M]	Jerry Leiber Presents Scooby Doo	1959	$100

SCOTT, BOBBY
Pianist, male singer and composer. His best-known composition is "A Taste of Honey."

Albums

ABC-PARAMOUNT
❏ ABC-148 [M]	Bobby Scott and Two Horns	1957	$50
❏ ABC-102 [M]	Scott Free	1956	$50

ATLANTIC
❏ 1355 [M]	A Taste of Honey	1960	$250
— Multicolor label, white "fan" logo at right			
❏ SD1355 [M]	A Taste of Honey	1960	$250
— Multicolor label, white "fan" logo at right			
❏ 1341 [M]	The Compleat Musician	1960	$250
— Multicolor label, white "fan" logo at right			
❏ SD1341 [M]	The Compleat Musician	1960	$250
— Multicolor label, white "fan" logo at right			

BETHLEHEM
❏ BCP-1004 [10]	Great Scott	1954	$250
❏ BCP-8 [M]	The Compositions of Bobby Scott	1957	$250
❏ BCP-1009 [10]	The Compositions of Bobby Scott, Volume 1	1954	$250
❏ BCP-1029 [10]	The Compositions of Bobby Scott, Volume 2	1955	$250

MERCURY
❏ MG-20854 [M]	108 Pounds of Heartache	1963	$100
❏ SR-60854 [S]	108 Pounds of Heartache	1963	$100
❏ MG-20995 [M]	I Had a Ball	1964	$100
❏ SR-60995 [S]	I Had a Ball	1964	$100
❏ MG-20701 [M]	Joyful Noises	1962	$100
❏ SR-60701 [S]	Joyful Noises	1962	$100
❏ MG-20767 [M]	When the Feeling Hits You	1963	$100
❏ SR-60767 [S]	When the Feeling Hits You	1963	$100

VERVE
❏ MGV-8326 [M]	Bobby Scott Plays the Music of Leonard Bernstein	1959	$150
❏ MGVS-6065 [S]	Bobby Scott Plays the Music of Leonard Bernstein	1960	$120
❏ V-8326 [M]	Bobby Scott Plays the Music of Leonard Bernstein	1961	$30
❏ V6-8326 [S]	Bobby Scott Plays the Music of Leonard Bernstein	1961	$25
❏ MGV-2106 [M]	Bobby Scott Sings the Best of Lerner and Loewe	1958	$150
❏ MGVS-6030 [S]	Bobby Scott Sings the Best of Lerner and Loewe	1960	$120
❏ V-2106 [M]	Bobby Scott Sings the Best of Lerner and Loewe	1961	$30
❏ V6-2106 [S]	Bobby Scott Sings the Best of Lerner and Loewe	1961	$25
❏ MGV-8297 [M]	Serenate -- Bobby Scott, Pianist	1959	$100
❏ MGVS-6031 [S]	Serenate -- Bobby Scott, Pianist	1960	$100
❏ V-8297 [M]	Serenate -- Bobby Scott, Pianist	1961	$30
❏ V6-8297 [S]	Serenate -- Bobby Scott, Pianist	1961	$25

SCOTT, CLIFFORD, AND LES McCANN
Also see each artist's individual listings.

Albums

PACIFIC JAZZ
❏ PJ-66 [M]	Out Front	1963	$40
— Colored vinyl			
❏ PJ-66 [M]	Out Front	1963	$25
— Black vinyl			
❏ ST-66 [S]	Out Front	1963	$50
— Colored vinyl			
❏ ST-66 [S]	Out Front	1963	$30
— Black vinyl			

SCOTT, CLIFFORD
Tenor saxophone player and flutist.

Albums

WORLD PACIFIC
❏ WP-1825 [M]	Lavender Sax	1964	$100
❏ ST-1825 [S]	Lavender Sax	1964	$150
❏ WP-1811 [M]	The Big Ones	1964	$100
— Black vinyl			
❏ ST-1811 [S]	The Big Ones	1964	$100
— Black vinyl			
❏ WP-1811 [M]	The Big Ones	1964	$150
— Green vinyl			
❏ ST-1811 [S]	The Big Ones	1964	$150
— Green vinyl			

SCOTT, HAZEL
Pianist and female singer.

Albums

CAPITOL
❏ H364 [10]	Late Show	1953	$150

COLUMBIA
❏ CL6090 [10]	Great Scott	1950	$80

CORAL
❏ CRL56057 [10]	Hazel Scott	1952	$80

DEBUT
❏ DLP-16 [10]	Relaxed Piano Moods	1955	$300

DECCA
❏ DL8474 [M]	'Round Midnight	1957	$120
❏ DL5130 [10]	Swinging the Classics	1950	$150

FANTASY
❏ OJC-1702	Relaxed Piano Moods	1985	$25

TIOCH
❏ TD-1013	Afterhours	198?	$25

SCOTT, JIMMY
Male singer.

Albums

SAVOY
❏ MG-12181 [M]	If You Only Knew	1963	$40
❏ MG-12150 [M]	The Fabulous Little Jimmy Scott	1959	$40
❏ MG-12301 [M]	The Fabulous Songs of Jimmy Scott	1969	$35
❏ MG-12302 [M]	The Fabulous Voice of Jimmy Scott	1969	$35
❏ MG-12027 [M]	Very Truly Yours	1955	$75
❏ MG-12300 [M]	Very Truly Yours	1969	$35

TANGERINE
❏ TRC-1501 [M]	Falling in Love Is Wonderful	1963	$200
❏ TRCS-1501 [S]	Falling in Love Is Wonderful	1963	$250

SCOTT, LIZABETH

Albums

VIK
❏ LX-1130 [M]	Lizabeth	1958	$100

SCOTT, ROBERT WILLIAM

Albums

WARNER BROS.
❏ WS1886	Robert William Scott	1970	$35

SCOTT, SHIRLEY, AND CLARK TERRY
Also see each artist's individual listings.

Albums

ABC IMPULSE!
❏ AS-9133 [S]	Soul Duo	1968	$35

IMPULSE!
❏ A-9133 [M]	Soul Duo	1967	$120
❏ AS-9133 [S]	Soul Duo	1967	$200

SCOTT, SHIRLEY
Organist, pianist and female singer.

Albums

ABC IMPULSE!
❏ AS-73 [S]	Everybody Loves a Lover	1968	$35
❏ AS-51 [S]	For Members Only	1968	$35
❏ AS-9141	Girl Talk	1967	$35
❏ AS-67 [S]	Great Scott!	1968	$35
❏ AS-93 [S]	Latin Shadows	1968	$35
❏ AS-9109	On a Clear Day	1968	$35
❏ AS-81 [S]	Queen of the Organ	1968	$35
❏ AS-9119	Shirley Scott Plays the Big Bands	1968	$35
❏ IA-9341	The Great Live Sessions	1978	$35

ATLANTIC
❏ SD1561	Something	1970	$35
❏ SD1532	Soul Saxes	1969	$35
❏ SD1515	Soul Song	1968	$35

CADET
❏ CA-50025	Lean On Me	1972	$30
❏ CA-50009	Mystical Lady	1972	$30
❏ CA-50036	Superstition	1973	$30

FANTASY
❏ OJC-328	Blue Flames	1988	$25

IMPULSE!
❏ A-73 [M]	Everybody Loves a Lover	1964	$200
❏ AS-73 [S]	Everybody Loves a Lover	1964	$120
❏ A-51 [M]	For Members Only	1963	$200
❏ AS-51 [S]	For Members Only	1963	$120
❏ A-9141 [M]	Girl Talk	1967	$120
❏ AS-9141 [S]	Girl Talk	1967	$200
❏ A-67 [M]	Great Scott!	1964	$200
❏ AS-67 [S]	Great Scott!	1964	$120
❏ A-93 [M]	Latin Shadows	1965	$200
❏ AS-93 [S]	Latin Shadows	1965	$120
❏ A-9109 [M]	On a Clear Day	1967	$200
❏ AS-9109 [S]	On a Clear Day	1967	$120
❏ A-81 [M]	Queen of the Organ	1965	$200
❏ AS-81 [S]	Queen of the Organ	1965	$120
❏ A-9119 [M]	Shirley Scott Plays the Big Bands	1966	$200
❏ AS-9119 [S]	Shirley Scott Plays the Big Bands	1966	$120

MCA
❏ 4152	The Great Live Sessions	1980	$30

MOODSVILLE
❏ MVLP-19 [M]	Like Cozy	1961	$50
— Green label			
❏ MVST-19 [S]	Like Cozy	1961	$50
— Green label			
❏ MVLP-19 [M]	Like Cozy	1965	$30
— Blue label, trident logo at right			
❏ MVST-19 [S]	Like Cozy	1965	$30
— Blue label, trident logo at right			
❏ MVLP-5 [M]	Shirley Scott Trio	1960	$50
— Green label			
❏ MVLP-5 [M]	Shirley Scott Trio	1965	$30
— Blue label, trident logo at right			

MUSE
❏ MR-5388	Oasis	1990	$30

PRESTIGE
❏ PRLP-7338 [M]	Blue Flames	1965	$30
❏ PRST-7338 [S]	Blue Flames	1965	$30
❏ PRLP-7376 [M]	Blue Seven	1965	$30
❏ PRST-7376 [S]	Blue Seven	1965	$30
❏ PRLP-7305 [M]	Drag 'Em Out	1964	$40
❏ PRST-7305 [S]	Drag 'Em Out	1964	$50
❏ PRLP-7143 [M]	Great Scott!	1958	$300
❏ PRLP-7262 [M]	Happy Talk	1963	$40
❏ PRST-7262 [S]	Happy Talk	1963	$50
❏ PRLP-7205 [M]	Hip Soul	1961	$200
— Yellow label, Bergenfield, NJ address			
❏ PRLP-7205 [M]	Hip Soul	1965	$25
— Blue label, trident logo at right			
❏ PRLP-7226 [M]	Hip Twist	1962	$150
— Yellow label, Bergenfield, NJ address			
❏ PRST-7226 [S]	Hip Twist	1962	$150
— Silver label, Bergenfield, NJ address			
❏ PRLP-7226 [M]	Hip Twist	1965	$25
— Blue label, trident logo at right			
❏ PRST-7226 [S]	Hip Twist	1965	$30
— Blue label, trident logo at right			
❏ PRLP-7182 [M]	Mucho, Mucho	1960	$200
❏ PRLP-7440 [M]	Now's the Time	1967	$30
❏ PRST-7440 [S]	Now's the Time	1967	$30
❏ PRLP-7283 [M]	Satin Doll	1963	$40
❏ PRST-7283 [S]	Satin Doll	1963	$50
❏ PRLP-7155 [M]	Scottie	1959	$200
❏ PRLP-7163 [M]	Scottie Plays Duke	1959	$200
❏ PRLP-7240 [M]	Shirley Scott Plays Horace Silver	1962	$150
❏ PRST-7240 [S]	Shirley Scott Plays Horace Silver	1962	$150
❏ PRLP-7195 [M]	Shirley's Sounds	1961	$200
❏ PRST-7195 [S]	Shirley's Sounds	1961	$200
❏ PRLP-7173 [M]	Soul Searching	1960	$200
❏ PRLP-7312 [M]	Soul Shoutin'	1964	$40
— Yellow label, Bergenfield, NJ address			
❏ PRST-7312 [S]	Soul Shoutin'	1964	$50
— Silver label, Bergenfield, NJ address			
❏ PRLP-7312 [M]	Soul Shoutin'	1965	$25
— Blue label, trident logo at right			

Number	Title	Yr	NM
❑ PRST-7312 [S]	Soul Shoutin'	1965	$30
—Blue label, trident logo at right			
❑ PRLP-7392 [M]	Soul Sisters	1965	$30
❑ PRST-7392 [S]	Soul Sisters	1965	$30
❑ PRST-7456 [S]	Stompin'	1968	$30
❑ PRLP-7360 [M]	Sweet Soul	1965	$30
❑ PRST-7360 [S]	Sweet Soul	1965	$30
❑ PRST-7773	The Best for Beautiful People	1970	$25
❑ PRST-7707 [S]	The Best of Shirley Scott and Stanley Turrentine	1969	$25
❑ PRLP-7267 [M]	The Soul Is Willing	1963	$40
— Yellow label, Bergenfield, NJ address			
❑ PRST-7267 [S]	The Soul Is Willing	1963	$50
— Silver label, Bergenfield, NJ address			
❑ PRLP-7267 [M]	The Soul Is Willing	1965	$25
—Blue label, trident logo at right			
❑ PRST-7267 [S]	The Soul Is Willing	1965	$30
—Blue label, trident logo at right			
❑ PRST-7845	The Soul Is Willing	1971	$35
❑ PRLP-7328 [M]	Travelin' Light	1964	$30
❑ PRST-7328 [S]	Travelin' Light	1964	$30
❑ PRLP-7424 [M]	Workin'	1966	$60
❑ PRST-7424 [S]	Workin'	1966	$60

STRATA-EAST

Number	Title	Yr	NM
❑ SES-7430	One for Me	197?	$25

SCOTT, TOM

Saxophone player and flutist.

Albums

A&M

Number	Title	Yr	NM
❑ SP-4330	Great Scott!	1972	$35

ABC IMPULSE!

| ❑ AS-9171 | Rural Still Life | 1968 | $200 |

ATLANTIC

| ❑ 80106 | Target | 1983 | $25 |

COLUMBIA

❑ FC37419	Apple Juice	1981	$25
❑ JC35557	Intimate Strangers	1978	$25
❑ PC35557	Intimate Strangers	198?	$20
—Budget-line reissue			
❑ JC36137	Street Beat	1979	$25
❑ JC36352	The Best of Tom Scott	1980	$25

ELEKTRA/MUSICIAN

| ❑ 60162 | Desire | 1982 | $25 |

FLYING DUTCHMAN

❑ 106	Hair	1969	$50
❑ 114	Paint Your Wagon	1970	$50
❑ BDL1-0833	Tom Scott in L.A.	1975	$30
❑ AYL1-3875	Tom Scott in L.A.	1980	$20
—Best Buy Series" reissue			
❑ BXL1-0833	Tom Scott in L.A.	197?	$25
—Second edition; new prefix, "RE" on cover			

GRP

| ❑ GR-9571 | Flashpoint | 1988 | $25 |
| ❑ GR-1044 | Streamlines | 1987 | $25 |

MCA

| ❑ 29060 | Rural Still Life | 198? | $20 |
| —Reissue of Impulse 9171 | | | |

ODE

❑ PE34966	Blow It Out	1977	$25
❑ SP-77033	New York Connection	1976	$25
❑ PE34959	New York Connection	1977	$20
—Reissue of 77033			
❑ SP-77029	Tom Cat	1975	$25
❑ PE34956	Tom Cat	1977	$20
—Reissue of 77029			
❑ SP-77021	Tom Scott and the L.A. Express	1974	$25
❑ PE34952	Tom Scott and the L.A. Express	1977	$20
—Reissue of 77021			

SOUNDWINGS

| ❑ SW-202 | Tom Scott | 1986 | $25 |

SCOTT, TONY, AND JIMMY KNEPPER

Also see each artist's individual listings.

Albums

CARLTON

Number	Title	Yr	NM
❑ LP-12-113 [M]	Free Blown Jazz	1959	$50
❑ ST-12-113 [S]	Free Blown Jazz	1959	$50

SCOTT, TONY, AND MAT MATTHEWS

Also see each artist's individual listings.

Albums

BRUNSWICK

Number	Title	Yr	NM
❑ BL58057 [10]	Jazz for GI's	1954	$120

SCOTT, TONY, AND TERRY GIBBS

Also see each artist's individual listings.

Albums

BRUNSWICK

Number	Title	Yr	NM
❑ BL58058 [10]	Hi-Fi Jazz	1955	$120

SCOTT, TONY

Clarinetist, baritone saxophone player and pianist. Also see THE MODERN JAZZ SOCIETY; ZOOT SIMS.

Albums

ABC-PARAMOUNT

Number	Title	Yr	NM
❑ ABC-235 [M]	South Pacific	1958	$30
❑ ABCS-235 [S]	South Pacific	1958	$30

BRUNSWICK

❑ BL58040 [10]	Music After Midnight	1953	$120
❑ BL54021 [M]	Tony Scott In Hi-Fi	1957	$80
❑ BL58056 [10]	Tony Scott Quartet	1954	$120
❑ BL54056 [M]	Tony Scott Quartet	1957	$120

CORAL

| ❑ CRL57239 [M] | 52nd Street Scene | 1958 | $50 |
| ❑ CRL757239 [S] | 52nd Street Scene | 1958 | $40 |

MUSE

| ❑ MR-5230 | Golden Moments | 198? | $25 |
| ❑ MR-5266 | I'll Remember | 198? | $25 |

PERFECT

| ❑ PL-12010 [M] | My Kind of Jazz | 1960 | $40 |
| ❑ PL-14010 [S] | My Kind of Jazz | 1960 | $50 |

RCA VICTOR

❑ LPM-1353 [M]	A Touch of Tony Scott	1956	$80
❑ LPM-1268 [M]	Both Sides of Tony Scott	1956	$80
❑ LJM-1022 [M]	Scott's Fling	1955	$80
❑ LPM-1452 [M]	The Complete Tony Scott	1957	$80

SEECO

❑ SLP-428 [M]	Hi-Fi Land of Jazz	1959	$150
❑ SLP-4280 [S]	Hi-Fi Land of Jazz	1959	$150
❑ SLP-425 [M]	The Modern Art of Jazz	1959	$250
❑ SLP-4250 [S]	The Modern Art of Jazz	1959	$250

SIGNATURE

| ❑ SM-6001 [M] | Gypsy | 1959 | $50 |
| ❑ SS-6001 [S] | Gypsy | 1959 | $40 |

SOUL NOTE

| ❑ SN-1083 | African Bird: Come Back! Mother Africa | 1984 | $30 |

SUNNYSIDE

| ❑ SSC-1015 | Sung Heroes | 1987 | $25 |

VERVE

❑ V6-8788 [S]	Homage to Lord Krishna	1969	$35
❑ V-8742 [M]	Music for Yoga Meditation and Other Joys	1967	$25
❑ V6-8742 [S]	Music for Yoga Meditation and Other Joys	1967	$35
❑ V-8634 [M]	Music for Zen Meditation	1965	$35
❑ V6-8634 [S]	Music for Zen Meditation	1965	$25

SCOTT-HERON, GIL

lMale singer (proto-rapper), pianist and composer.

Albums

ARISTA

Number	Title	Yr	NM
❑ AL9514	1980	1980	$25
❑ AL4147	Bridges	1977	$25
❑ AL4044	From South Africa to South Carolina	1975	$25
❑ A2L5001	It's Your World	1976	$30
❑ AL9606	Moving Target	1982	$25
❑ AL9540	Real Eyes	1980	$25
❑ AL9566	Reflections	1981	$25
❑ AB4189	Secrets	1978	$25
❑ ALB6-8306	The Best of Gil Scott-Heron	1985	$20
—Reissue of 8248			
❑ AL8248	The Best of Gil Scott-Heron	1984	$25
❑ AL4030	The First Minute of a New Day	1975	$25
❑ AL8301	The Mind of Gil Scott-Heron	1980	$35

BLUEBIRD

| ❑ 6994-RB-1 | The Revolution Will Not Be Televised | 1988 | $30 |

FLYING DUTCHMAN

❑ FD-10153	Free Will	1972	$50
❑ FD-10143	Pieces of a Man	1971	$50
❑ BXL1-2834	Pieces of a Man	1978	$30
—Reissue of 10143			

Number	Title	Yr	NM
❑ AYL1-3819	Pieces of a Man	1980	$20
—Best Buy Series" reissue			
❑ BXL1-0613	The Revolution Will Not Be Televised	1978	$30
—Reissue with new prefix			
❑ AYL1-3818	The Revolution Will Not Be Televised	1980	$20
—Best Buy Series" reissue			

STRATA-EAST

| ❑ SES-19742 | Winter in America | 1974 | $60 |

SEALY, JOE

Pianist and composer.

Albums

SACKVILLE

Number	Title	Yr	NM
❑ 4007	Clear Vision	198?	$25

SEARS, AL

Tenor saxophone player.

Albums

AUDIO LAB

Number	Title	Yr	NM
❑ AL-1540 [M]	Dance Music with a Swing Beat	1959	$120

SWINGVILLE

❑ SVLP-2018 [M]	Swing's the Thing	1961	$50
—Purple label			
❑ SVLP-2018 [M]	Swing's the Thing	1965	$30
—Blue label, trident logo at right			

SEBESKY, DON

Composer, arranger and trombonist.

Albums

CTI

Number	Title	Yr	NM
❑ CTX-6031/2	Giant Box	1974	$35
❑ 6061	The Rape of El Morro	197?	$30

DOCTOR JAZZ

| ❑ FW40155 | Moving Lines | 1986 | $25 |

GNP CRESCENDO

| ❑ GNPS-2164 | Full Circle | 198? | $25 |

GRYPHON

| ❑ 791 | Three Works for Jazz Soloists and Symphony Orchestra | 1980 | $35 |

MOBILE FIDELITY

| ❑ 1-503 | Three Works for Jazz Soloists and Symphony Orchestra | 198? | $60 |
| —Audiophile vinyl | | | |

VERVE

| ❑ V6-8756 | Don Sebesky and the Jazz-Rock Syndrome | 1968 | $25 |

SEEGER, BERT

Pianist.

Albums

ANTILLES

Number	Title	Yr	NM
❑ AN-7088	Because They Can	198?	$25
❑ AN-7086	Time to Burn	198?	$25

SEGAL, GEORGE

Banjo player. Better known as an actor.

Albums

PHILIPS

Number	Title	Yr	NM
❑ PHM200242 [M]	The Yama-Yama Man	1967	$50
❑ PHS600242 [S]	The Yama-Yama Man	1967	$50

SIGNATURE

| ❑ BSL1-0654 | A Touch of Ragtime | 1976 | $35 |

SEIFERT, ZBIGNIEW

Violinist.

Albums

CAPITOL

Number	Title	Yr	NM
❑ ST-11618	Zbigniew Seifert	197?	$30

PAUSA

| ❑ 7077 | Man of the Light | 1979 | $25 |

Number	Title	Yr	NM

SENENSKY, BERNIE
Pianist.
Albums
PM

❏ 021	Free Spirit	1986	$25
❏ 06	New Life	197?	$30

SERRANO, PAUL
Trumpeter.
Albums
RIVERSIDE

❏ RLP-359 [M]	Blues Holiday	1961	$200
❏ RS-9359 [S]	Blues Holiday	1961	$200

SERRY, JOHN
Keyboard player.
Albums
CHRYSALIS

❏ CHS1279	Jazziz	1979	$25

SERTL, DOUG
Trombonist.
Albums
DISCOVERY

❏ 920	Groovin'	1986	$25

SETE, BOLA
Guitarist. Also see VINCE GUARALDI.
Albums
ANALOGUE PRODUCTIONS

❏ APR3003	Tour de Force	199?	$35

COLUMBIA

❏ KC32375	Goin' to Rio	1973	$30

DANCING CAT

❏ DC-3005	Jungle Suite	1985	$30

FANTASY

❏ OJC-290	Autentico!	1987	$25
❏ 3375 [M]	Autentico!	1966	$35
❏ 8375 [S]	Autentico!	1966	$25
❏ OJC-286	Bossa Nova	1987	$25
❏ 3349 [M]	Bossa Nova	1963	$35
❏ 8417	Shebaba	1971	$15
❏ OJC-288	The Incomparable Bola Sete	1987	$25
❏ 3364 [M]	The Incomparable Bola Sete	1965	$35
❏ 8364 [S]	The Incomparable Bola Sete	1965	$25
❏ 3369 [M]	The Solo Guitar of Bola Sete	1966	$35
❏ 8369 [S]	The Solo Guitar of Bola Sete	1966	$25
❏ 7358 [S]	Tour de Force	1965	$50
❏ 3358 [M]	Tour de Force	1965	$35

LOST LAKE ARTS

❏ LL-82	Ocean	1981	$25

— Reissue of Takoma LP

PARAMOUNT

❏ PAS-5011	Workin' on a Groovy Thing	1970	$35

TAKOMA

❏ C-1049	Ocean	1975	$30

VERVE

❏ V-8689 [M]	Bola Sete At the Monterey Jazz Festival	1967	$25
❏ V6-8689 [S]	Bola Sete At the Monterey Jazz Festival	1967	$35

SETZER, BRIAN
Guitarist formerly with rockabilly revival band Stray Cats, Setzer helped spur the late-1990s "swing" revival.
Albums
INTERSCOPE

❏ 90183	The Dirty Boogie	1998	$35

— As "The Brian Setzer Orchestra

SURFDOG

❏ 67124	Ignition!	2001	$35

— As "Brian Setzer '68 Comeback Special"; red vinyl

SEVENTH AVENUE
Members: Vincent Green (saxophones); Kenery Smith (bass); Ben Johnson (drums); Phillip Seed (guitar).
Albums
I.T.I.

❏ JL-022	Heads Up	1986	$30

SEVENTH AVENUE STOMPERS
Albums
SAVOY JAZZ

❏ SJL-1139	Fidgety Feet	198?	$25

SEVERINSON, DOC
Trumpeter and bandleader.
Albums
ABC

❏ X-771	Trumpets, Crumpets	1973	$25

AMHERST

❏ AMH-3319	Facets	1988	$25
❏ AMH-3311	The Tonight Show Band with Doc Severinson	1986	$25
❏ AMH-3312	The Tonight Show Band with Doc Severinson, Vol. II	1987	$25

COMMAND

❏ RS 33-904 [M]	Command Performances	1966	$30
❏ RS904SD [S]	Command Performances	1966	$35
❏ RS937SD	Doc Severinson with Strings	1969	$30
❏ RS 33-893 [M]	Fever!	1966	$30
❏ RS893SD [S]	Fever!	1966	$35
❏ QD-40003 [Q]	Fever!	1972	$40
❏ RS 33-883 [M]	High, Wide and Wonderful	1965	$35
❏ RS883SD [S]	High, Wide and Wonderful	1965	$50
❏ RS 33-901 [M]	Live!	1966	$30
❏ RS901SD [S]	Live!	1966	$35
❏ RS 33-909 [M]	Swinging and Singing	1967	$35
❏ RS909SD [S]	Swinging and Singing	1967	$30
❏ RS819SD [S]	Tempestuous Trumpet	1961	$50
❏ RS952SD	The Best of Doc Severinson	1970	$30
❏ RS 33-837 [M]	The Big Band's Back in Town	1962	$35
❏ RS837SD [S]	The Big Band's Back in Town	1962	$50
❏ RS950SD	The Closet	1970	$30
❏ RS927SD	The Great Arrival	1968	$30
❏ RS 33-917 [M]	The New Sound	1967	$35
❏ RS917SD [S]	The New Sound	1967	$30
❏ RS 33-859 [M]	Torch Songs for Trumpet	1963	$35

EPIC

❏ PE34925	A Brand New Thing	1977	$25
❏ PE34078	Night Journey	1976	$25

EVEREST ARCHIVE OF FOLK & JAZZ

❏ 334	Doc Severinson and Friends	1978	$25

FIRSTLINE

❏ FDLP5001	London Sessions	1980	$30

JUNO

❏ 1001	I Feel Good	1970	$30

MCA

❏ 4168	The Best of Doc Severinson	198?	$25

PICKWICK

❏ SPC3627	Tempestuous Trumpet	1978	$20
❏ SPC-3608	Torch Songs for Trumpet	1978	$20

RCA VICTOR

❏ LSP-3627	Brass Roots	1971	$30
❏ LSP-4669	Doc	1972	$30
❏ AFL1-4669	Doc	1977	$25

— Reissue with new prefix

❏ APL1-0273	Rhapsody for Now!	1973	$30

SEVERSON, PAUL
Trombonist.
Albums
ACADEMY

❏ MWJ-1 [M]	Midwest Jazz	1956	$50

SEVILLA, JORGE
Guitarist.
Albums
VERVE

❏ MGV-8342 [M]	The Incredible Guitar of Jorge Sevilla	1959	$150
❏ MGVS-6103 [S]	The Incredible Guitar of Jorge Sevilla	1960	$100
❏ V-8342 [M]	The Incredible Guitar of Jorge Sevilla	1961	$30
❏ V6-8342 [S]	The Incredible Guitar of Jorge Sevilla	1961	$25

SHAKATAK
Members: Bill Sharpe (keyboards); Keith Winter (guitar); Roger Odell (drums); Jill Saward (vocals); George Anderson (bass).
Albums
POLYDOR

❏ 823017-1	Drivin' Hard	1987	$25
❏ 839578-1	Manic and Cool	1989	$30

SHANK, BUD
Alto saxophone player and flutist. Also see LAURINDO ALMEIDA; CHET BAKER.
Albums
BAINBRIDGE

❏ CRS-6830	Live at the Haig	1985	$25

CONCORD CONCERTO

❏ CC-2002	Explorations 1980: Suite for Flute and Piano	1981	$25

CONCORD JAZZ

❏ CJ-126	Crystal Comments	1980	$25
❏ CJ-58	Heritage	1979	$30
❏ CJ-20	Sunshine Express	1976	$30

CONTEMPORARY

❏ C-14027	Bud Shank at Jazz Alley	1987	$25
❏ C-14012	California Concert	1985	$25
❏ C-14031	Serious Swingers	1988	$25

— With the Bill Perkins Quartet

❏ C-14019	That Old Feeling	1986	$25
❏ C-14048	Tomorrow's Rainbow	1989	$25

CROWN

❏ CLP-5311 [M]	Bud Shank	1963	$35
❏ CST-311 [R]	Bud Shank	1963	$30

KIMBERLY

❏ 2025 [M]	The Talents of Bud Shank	1963	$25
❏ 11025 [S]	The Talents of Bud Shank	1963	$30

MUSE

❏ 5309	This Bud's for You	198?	$25

NOCTURNE

❏ NLP-2 [10]	Compositions of Shorty Rogers	1953	$200

PACIFIC JAZZ

❏ PJ-58 [M]	Bossa Nova Jazz Samba	1962	$30
❏ ST-58 [S]	Bossa Nova Jazz Samba	1962	$30
❏ PJ-64 [M]	Brassamba Bossa Nova	1963	$25
❏ ST-64 [S]	Brassamba Bossa Nova	1963	$30
❏ PJLP-20 [10]	Bud Shank and Bob Brookmeyer	1954	$120
❏ PJ-89 [M]	Bud Shank and His Brazilian Friends	1965	$25
❏ ST-89 [S]	Bud Shank and His Brazilian Friends	1965	$30
❏ PJ-10110 [M]	Bud Shank and the Sax Section	1966	$35
❏ ST-20110 [S]	Bud Shank and the Sax Section	1966	$25
❏ LN-10091	Bud Shank and the Sax Section	198?	$25
❏ PJ-4 [M]	Bud Shank Plays Tenor	1960	$30
❏ ST-4 [S]	Bud Shank Plays Tenor	1960	$30
❏ PJ-1205 [M]	Bud Shank/Shorty Rogers	1955	$80
❏ PJLP-14 [10]	Bud Shank with Three Trombones	1954	$120
❏ PJ-1226 [M]	Flute 'n Oboe	1957	$60
❏ PJ-1219 [M]	Jazz at Cal-Tech	1956	$60
❏ PJ-21 [M]	New Groove	1961	$30
❏ ST-21 [S]	New Groove	1961	$30
❏ PJ-1213 [M]	Strings and Trombones	1956	$80
❏ PJ-1215 [M]	The Bud Shank Quartet	1956	$80
❏ PJ-1230 [M]	The Bud Shank Quartet	1957	$60
❏ PJM-411 [M]	The Swing's to TV	1957	$60
❏ ST-20157	Windmills of Your Mind	1969	$35

SUNSET

❏ SUM-1132 [M]	I Hear Music	1967	$50
❏ SUS-5132 [S]	I Hear Music	1967	$30

WORLD PACIFIC

❏ ST-21868	A Spoonful of Jazz	1968	$100
❏ WP-1855 [M]	Brazil! Brazil! Brazil!	1967	$100
❏ ST-21855 [S]	Brazil! Brazil! Brazil!	1967	$100
❏ WP-1864 [M]	Bud Shank Plays Music from Today's Movies	1967	$100
❏ ST-21864 [S]	Bud Shank Plays Music from Today's Movies	1967	$100
❏ WP-1205 [M]	Bud Shank/Shorty Rogers	1958	$150
❏ WP-1845 [M]	California Dreaming	1966	$100
❏ ST-21845 [S]	California Dreaming	1966	$100
❏ WP-1827 [M]	Flute, Oboe and Strings	1965	$100
❏ ST-21827 [S]	Flute, Oboe and Strings	1965	$100
❏ WP-1286 [M]	Flute 'n Alto	1960	$100
❏ ST-1286 [S]	Flute 'n Alto	1960	$150
❏ WP-1226 [M]	Flute 'n Oboe	1958	$150
❏ WP-1819 [M]	Folk 'n Flute	1965	$100
❏ ST-21819 [S]	Folk 'n Flute	1965	$100
❏ WP-1853 [M]	Girl in Love	1967	$100
❏ ST-21853 [S]	Girl in Love	1967	$100
❏ WP-1259 [M]	Holiday in Brazil	1959	$150
❏ ST-1018 [S]	Holiday in Brazil	1959	$150
❏ WP-1251 [M]	I'll Take Romance	1958	$150
❏ WP-1416 [M]	Improvisations	1961	$100
❏ WP-1219 [M]	Jazz at Cal-Tech	1958	$150
❏ WP-1299 [M]	Koto 'n Flute	1960	$150
❏ ST-1299 [S]	Koto 'n Flute	1960	$150
❏ WP-1424 [M]	Koto 'n Flute	1962	$100
❏ WP-1281 [M]	Latin Contrasts	1959	$150
❏ ST-1281 [S]	Latin Contrasts	1959	$100
❏ ST-20170	Let It Be	1970	$100
❏ ST-21873	Magical Mystery Tour	1968	$100
❏ WP-1840 [M]	Michelle	1966	$100

Hal Schaefer, *The RCA Victor Jazz Workshop*, RCA Victor LPM-1199, **$120**.

Lizabeth Scott, *Lizabeth*, Vik LX-1130, **$100**.

Shirley Scott, *Shirley's Sounds*, Prestige PRLP-7195, **$200**.

Tony Scott and Jimmy Knepper, *Free Blown Jazz*, Carlton LP-12/113, **$50**.

Number	Title	Yr	NM
❏ ST-21840 [S]	Michelle	1966	$100
❏ WP-1215 [M]	The Bud Shank Quartet	1958	$150
❏ WP-1230 [M]	The Bud Shank Quartet	1958	$150
❏ WPM-411 [M]	The Swing's to TV	1958	$150
❏ ST-1002 [S]	The Swing's to TV	1959	$100
❏ PJM-411 [M]	The Swing's to TV	1958	$150

SHANK, BUD/CHET BAKER
Also see each artist's individual listings.

Albums

KIMBERLY
❏ 2016 [M]	Swinging Soundtrack	1963	$25
❏ 11016 [S]	Swinging Soundtrack	1963	$30

SHANKAR
10-string double violin player, percussionist and male singer.

Albums

ECM
❏ 25016	Song for Everyone	1985	$25
❏ 25039	The Epidemics	1986	$25
❏ 25004	Vision	1985	$25
❏ 1195	Who's to Know	198?	$30

SHARON, RALPH
Pianist and composer.

Albums

ARGO
❏ LP-635 [M]	2:38 A.M.	1958	$40

BETHLEHEM
❏ BCP-13 [M]	Mr. & Mrs. Jazz	1955	$250
❏ BCP-41 [M]	Ralph Sharon Trio	1956	$250

COLUMBIA
❏ CL2321 [M]	Do I Hear a Waltz?	1965	$30
❏ CS9121 [S]	Do I Hear a Waltz?	1965	$30

GORDY
❏ G-903 [M]	Modern Innovations on Country & Western Themes	1963	$200

LONDON
❏ LB-842 [10]	Autumn Leaves	1954	$50
❏ LB-733 [10]	Spring Fever	1953	$50
❏ LL1339 [M]	Spring Fever/Autumn Leaves	1955	$50

RAMA
❏ RLP-1001 [M]	Jazz Around the World	1957	$50

SHARROCK, SONNY
Guitarist.

Albums

VORTEX
❏ 2014	Black Woman	1970	$25

SHAVERS, CHARLIE
Trumpeter, male singer, composer and arranger. Also see JONAH JONES; HAL SINGER.

Albums

AAMCO
❏ 310 [M]	The Most Intimate Charlie Shavers	1959	$40

BETHLEHEM
❏ BCP-27 [M]	Gershwin, Shavers and Strings	1955	$250
❏ BCP-1007 [10]	Horn o' Plenty	1954	$250
❏ BCP-67 [M]	The Complete Charlie Shavers with Maxine Sullivan	1957	$250
❏ BCP-6005 [M]	The Finest of Charlie Shavers: The Most Intimate	1976	$30

—Reissue, distributed by Caytronics

❏ BCP-1021 [10]	The Most Intimate Charlie Shavers	1955	$250
❏ BCP-5002 [M]	The Most Intimate Charlie Shavers	1958	$200

CAPITOL
❏ T1883 [M]	Excitement Unlimited	1963	$40
❏ ST1883 [S]	Excitement Unlimited	1963	$60

EVEREST
❏ LPBR-5070 [M]	Girl of My Dreams	1960	$25
❏ SDBR-1070 [S]	Girl of My Dreams	1960	$30
❏ LPBR-5108 [M]	Here Comes Charlie	1960	$25
❏ SDBR-1108 [S]	Here Comes Charlie	1960	$30
❏ LPBR-5127 [M]	Like Charlie	1961	$25
❏ SDBR-1127 [S]	Like Charlie	1961	$30

JAZZTONE
❏ J-1229 [M]	Flow Gently, Sweet Rhythm	1956	$40

MGM
❏ E-3809 [M]	Charlie Digs Dixie	1960	$30
❏ SE-3809 [S]	Charlie Digs Dixie	1960	$30
❏ E-3765 [M]	Charlie Digs Paree	1959	$30

Number	Title	Yr	NM
❏ SE-3765 [S]	Charlie Digs Paree	1959	$30

PERIOD
❏ SPL-1113 [10]	Flow Gently, Sweet Rhythm	1955	$120

PHOENIX
❏ 21	Trumpet Man	197?	$25

SHAW, ARTIE
Clarinet player, composer and bandleader.

Albums

AIRCHECK
❏ 11	Artie Shaw and His Orchestra 1939-40	197?	$25

ALLEGRO
❏ 1405 [M]	An Hour with Artie Shaw	1955	$50
❏ 1466 [M]	Artie Shaw Hour	1955	$50

ALLEGRO EILTE
❏ 4023 [10]	Artie Shaw Plays	195?	$40
❏ 4107 [10]	Artie Shaw Plays Cole Porter	195?	$40

BLUEBIRD
❏ AXM2-5580	The Complete Artie Shaw, Volume 7: Retrospective	198?	$35
❏ AXM2-5517	The Complete Artie Shaw, Volume 1 (1938-39)	197?	$35
❏ AXM2-5533	The Complete Artie Shaw, Volume 2 (1939)	197?	$35
❏ AXM2-5556	The Complete Artie Shaw, Volume 3 (1939-40)	1979	$35
❏ AXM2-5572	The Complete Artie Shaw, Volume 4 (1940-41)	1980	$35
❏ AXM2-5576	The Complete Artie Shaw, Volume 5 (1941-42)	198?	$35
❏ AXM2-5579	The Complete Artie Shaw, Volume 6 (1942-45)	198?	$35
❏ 7637-1-RB	The Complete Gramercy Five Sessions	1989	$30

CAPITOL
❏ ST2992	Artie Shaw Re-Creates His Great '38 Band	1968	$75

CLEF
❏ MGC-159 [10]	Artie Shaw and His Gramercy Five, Volume 1	1954	$200
❏ MGC-160 [10]	Artie Shaw and His Gramercy Five, Volume 2	1954	$200
❏ MGC-630 [M]	Artie Shaw and His Gramercy Five, Volume 3	1954	$200
❏ MGC-645 [M]	Artie Shaw and His Gramercy Five, Volume 4	1955	$200

COLUMBIA MASTERWORKS
❏ ML4260 [M]	Modern Music for Clarinet	1950	$250

DECCA
❏ DL5286 [10]	Artie Shaw Dance Program	195?	$50
❏ DL8309 [M]	Did Someone Say Party?	1956	$150

—Black label, silver print

❏ DL5524 [10]	Speak to Me of Love	195?	$50

ENCORE
❏ EE22023	Free for All	196?	$35

EPIC
❏ LG1102 [10]	Artie Shaw	1955	$100
❏ LN3150 [M]	Artie Shaw and His Orchestra	1955	$80
❏ LG1006 [10]	Artie Shaw with Strings	1954	$100
❏ LN3112 [M]	Artie Shaw with Strings	1955	$80
❏ LG1017 [10]	Non-Stop Flight	1954	$100

EVEREST ARCHIVE OF FOLK & JAZZ
❏ 248	Artie Shaw	1970	$25

HINDSIGHT
❏ HSR-139	Artie Shaw and His Orchestra, 1938	198?	$25
❏ HSR-140	Artie Shaw and His Orchestra, 1938, Volume 2	198?	$25
❏ HSR-176	Artie Shaw and His Orchestra, 1938-39	198?	$25
❏ HSR-148	Artie Shaw and His Orchestra, 1939	198?	$25
❏ HSR-149	Artie Shaw and His Orchestra, 1939, Volume 2	198?	$25
❏ HSR-401	Artie Shaw and His Orchestra Play 22 Original Big Band Recordings	198?	$30

INSIGHT
❏ 204	Artie Shaw and His Orchestra (1938-39)	198?	$25

LION
❏ L-70058 [M]	Artie Shaw Plays Irving Berlin and Cole Porter	1958	$30

MCA
❏ 4081	The Best of Artie Shaw	197?	$30

MGM

Number	Title	Yr	NM
❏ E-517 [10]	Artie Shaw Plays Cole Porter	1950	$50

MUSICRAFT
❏ 503	Artie Shaw and His Orchestra, Volume 1	198?	$25
❏ 507	Artie Shaw and His Orchestra, Volume 2	198?	$25

PAIR
❏ PDL2-1012	Original Recordings	1986	$30

RCA CAMDEN
❏ ACL1-0509	Greatest Hits	1974	$25
❏ CAL-584 [M]	One Night Stand	1959	$25
❏ CAL-908 [M]	September Song and Other Favorites	196?	$25
❏ CAL-465 [M]	The Great Artie Shaw	195?	$25

RCA VICTOR
❏ LPM-1648 [M]	A Man and His Dream	1957	$40
❏ LPM-1241 [M]	Artie Shaw and His Gramercy Five	1956	$40
❏ LPT-28 [10]	Artie Shaw Favorites	195?	$50
❏ LPM-1217 [M]	Back Bay Shuffle	1956	$40
❏ ANL1-2151	Backbay Shuffle	1977	$25
❏ LPM-30 [10]	Four Star Favorites	1955	$60
❏ LPT-6000 [M]	In the Blue Room/In the Café Rouge	195?	$50

—Originals are in a box; silver labels; red print

❏ LPM-1244 [M]	Moonglow	1956	$40
❏ LPT-1020 [M]	My Concerto	195?	$40
❏ ANL1-1089	The Best of Artie Shaw	1975	$25
❏ LPM-3675 [M]	The Best of Artie Shaw	1967	$25
❏ LSP-3675 [R]	The Best of Artie Shaw	1967	$30
❏ LPT-3013 [10]	This Is Artie Shaw	1952	$50
❏ VPM-6039	This Is Artie Shaw	197?	$35
❏ VPM-6062	This Is Artie Shaw, Volume 2	1972	$35
❏ VPM-6062	This Is Artie Shaw, Volume 2	1976	$30

—Black labels, dog near top

ROYALE
❏ 18135 [10]	The Best in Dance Music	195?	$30

SUNBEAM
❏ 207	New Music 1936-37	197?	$25

TIME-LIFE
❏ STBB-06	Big Bands: Artie Shaw	1983	$35
❏ STBB-26	Big Bands: Encore: Artie Shaw	1986	$35

VERVE
❏ MGV-2014 [M]	I Can't Get Started	1956	$200
❏ V-2014 [M]	I Can't Get Started	1961	$25
❏ MGV-2015 [M]	Sequence in Music	1956	$200
❏ V-2015 [M]	Sequence in Music	1961	$25

SHAW, BOBO
Drummer.

Albums

BLACK SAINT
❏ BSR-0021	Junk Trap	198?	$30

MUSE
❏ MR-5268	Bugle Boy Bop	198?	$30
❏ MR-5232	P'NKJ'ZZ	198?	$35

SHAW, GENE
Trumpeter.

Albums

ARGO
❏ LP-707 [M]	Breakthrough	1962	$30
❏ LPS-707 [S]	Breakthrough	1962	$30
❏ LP-743 [M]	Carnival Sketches	1964	$30
❏ LPS-743 [S]	Carnival Sketches	1964	$30
❏ LP-726 [M]	Debut In Blues	1963	$150
❏ LPS-726 [S]	Debut In Blues	1963	$150

CHESS
❏ CH-91564	Debut In Blues	198?	$25

SHAW, GEORGE
Trumpeter.

Albums

PALO ALTO/TBA
❏ TBA-218	Encounters	1986	$25
❏ TBA-223	Let Yourself Go	1987	$25

SHAW, LEE
Pianist.

Albums

CADENCE JAZZ
❏ CJR-1021	OK!	198?	$25

Number	Title	Yr	NM

SHAW, MARLENA
Female singer.

Albums
BLUE NOTE

Number	Title	Yr	NM
❏ BN-LA143-F	From the Depths of My Soul	1974	$35
❏ BN-LA606-G	Just a Matter	1976	$35
❏ BST-84422	Marlena	1972	$35
❏ BN-LA397-G	Who Is This Bitch, Anyway?	1975	$35

CADET

❏ LPS-803	Different Bags	1968	$50
❏ LPS-833	Spice of Life	1969	$50

COLUMBIA

❏ JC35073	Acting Up	1978	$30
❏ PC34458	Sweet Beginnings	1977	$30
❏ JC35632	Take a Bite	1979	$30
❏ JC36367	The Best of Marlena Shaw	1980	$25

VERVE

❏ 831438-1	It Is Love	1987	$25
❏ 837312-1	Love Is In Flight	1988	$25

SHAW, WOODY
Trumpeter.

Albums
COLUMBIA

❏ FC36383	For Sure	1980	$30
❏ JC35309	Rosewood	1977	$30
❏ JC35560	Stepping	1978	$30
❏ FC36519	The Best of Woody Shaw	1980	$25
❏ JC35977	Woody III	1979	$30

CONTEMPORARY

❏ C-7627/8	Blackstone Legacy	1971	$75
❏ C-7632	Song of Songs	197?	$35

ELEKTRA/MUSICIAN

❏ 60131	Master of the Art	1983	$25
❏ 60299	Night Music	1984	$25

ENJA

❏ 4018	Lotus Flower	1982	$30

FANTASY

❏ OJC-180	Song of Songs	198?	$25

MOSAIC

❏ MR4-142	The Complete CBS Studio Recordings of Woody Shaw	199?	$80

MUSE

❏ MR-5139	Concert Ensemble '76	1977	$30
❏ MR-5338	Imagination	1988	$25
❏ MR-5298	In the Beginning	198?	$25
❏ MR-5074	Love Dance	1976	$30
❏ MR-5058	Moontrane	1975	$30
❏ MR-5103	Red's Fantasy	197?	$30
❏ MR-5318	Setting Standards	198?	$25
❏ MR-5329	Solid	1987	$25
❏ MR-5160	The Iron Men	198?	$30

RED RECORD

❏ VPA-168	The Time Is Right	198?	$30

SHAY, SHERYL

Albums
LAUREL

❏ LR-506	Sophisticated Lady	1985	$30

SHEA, TOM
Pianist.

Albums
STOMP OFF

❏ SOS-1022	Little Wabash Special	198?	$25

SHEARING, GEORGE, AND MEL TORME
Also see each artist's individual listings.

Albums
CONCORD JAZZ

❏ CJ-294	An Elegant Evening	1985	$25
❏ CJ-248	An Evening at Charlie's	1984	$25
❏ CJ-190	An Evening with George Shearing and Mel Torme	1982	$25
❏ CJ-341	A Vintage Year	1988	$25
❏ CJ-219	Top Drawer	1983	$25

SHEARING, GEORGE, AND THE MONTGOMERY BROTHERS
Also see each artist's individual listings.

Albums
FANTASY

❏ OJC-040	George Shearing and the Montgomery Brothers	198?	$25

JAZZLAND

Number	Title	Yr	NM
❏ JLP-55 [M]	Love Walked In	1961	$60
— Cover has Shearing and the brothers			
❏ JLP-55 [M]	Love Walked In	1962	$60
— Cover has a woman			
❏ JLP-955 [S]	Love Walked In	1961	$40
— Cover has Shearing and the brothers			
❏ JLP-955 [S]	Love Walked In	1962	$60
— Cover has a woman			

RIVERSIDE

❏ 6087	George Shearing and the Montgomery Brothers	197?	$25

— Reissue of Jazzland LP

SHEARING, GEORGE
Pianist, arranger, composer and bandleader. Also see NAT KING COLE; MARIAN McPARTLAND.

45s
CAPITOL

❏ XE 3-1715 [S]	Be-Bop Irishman/I'll Be Around	1962	$60
— Small hole, plays at 33 1/3 rpm			
❏ XE 4-1715 [S]	Jumpin' with Symphony Sid/ Cocktails for Two	1962	$60
— Small hole, plays at 33 1/3 rpm			
❏ XE 5-1715 [S]	Lullaby of Birdland (Part 1)/(Part 2)	1962	$60
— Small hole, plays at 33 1/3 rpm			
❏ XE 2-1715 [S]	Monophraseology/My New Mambo	1962	$60
— Small hole, plays at 33 1/3 rpm			
❏ XE 1-1715 [S]	The Outlaw/When April Comes Again	1962	$60
— Small hole, plays at 33 1/3 rpm			

Albums
BASF

❏ MC-25612	Continental Experience	1975	$30
❏ 25340	Light, Airy and Swinging	1973	$30
❏ 25351	The Way We Are	1974	$30

CAPITOL

❏ T858 [M]	Black Satin	1957	$100
— Turquoise label			
❏ T858 [M]	Black Satin	1959	$80
— Black label with colorband, logo on left			
❏ T858 [M]	Black Satin	1962	$75
— Black label with colorband, logo on top			
❏ ST858 [S]	Black Satin	1959	$80
— Black label with colorband, logo on left			
❏ ST858 [S]	Black Satin	1962	$75
— Black label with colorband, logo on top			
❏ SM-11800	Black Satin	1978	$25
❏ T1124 [M]	Blue Chiffon	1959	$80
— Black label with colorband, logo on left			
❏ T1124 [M]	Blue Chiffon	1962	$75
— Black label with colorband, logo on top			
❏ ST1124 [S]	Blue Chiffon	1959	$100
— Black label with colorband, logo on left			
❏ ST1124 [S]	Blue Chiffon	1962	$80
— Black label with colorband, logo on top			
❏ T1873 [M]	Bossa Nova	1963	$75
❏ ST1873 [S]	Bossa Nova	1963	$80
❏ T1038 [M]	Burnished Brass	1958	$80
— Black label with colorband, logo on left			
❏ T1038 [M]	Burnished Brass	1962	$75
— Black label with colorband, logo on top			
❏ ST1038 [S]	Burnished Brass	1959	$100
— Black label with colorband, logo on left			
❏ ST1038 [S]	Burnished Brass	1962	$80
— Black label with colorband, logo on top			
❏ T1755 [M]	Concerto for My Love	1962	$75
❏ ST1755 [S]	Concerto for My Love	1962	$80
❏ T2143 [M]	Deep Velvet	1964	$60
❏ ST2143 [S]	Deep Velvet	1964	$75
❏ ST-181	Fool on the Hill	1969	$60
❏ T1187 [M]	George Shearing On Stage	1959	$80
— Black label with colorband, logo on left			
❏ T1187 [M]	George Shearing On Stage	1962	$75
— Black label with colorband, logo on top			
❏ ST1187 [S]	George Shearing On Stage	1959	$100
— Black label with colorband, logo on left			
❏ ST1187 [S]	George Shearing On Stage	1962	$80
— Black label with colorband, logo on top			

Number	Title	Yr	NM
❏ T2699 [M]	George Shearing Today	1967	$75
❏ ST2699 [S]	George Shearing Today	1967	$60
❏ T2372 [M]	Here and Now	1965	$60
❏ ST2372 [S]	Here and Now	1965	$75
❏ T1992 [M]	Jazz Concert	1963	$75
❏ ST1992 [S]	Jazz Concert	1963	$80
❏ T1827 [M]	Jazz Moments	1963	$75
❏ ST1827 [S]	Jazz Moments	1963	$80
❏ T1275 [M]	Latin Affair	1960	$80
— Black label with colorband, logo on left			
❏ T1275 [M]	Latin Affair	1962	$75
— Black label with colorband, logo on top			
❏ ST1275 [S]	Latin Affair	1960	$100
— Black label with colorband, logo on left			
❏ ST1275 [S]	Latin Affair	1962	$80
— Black label with colorband, logo on top			
❏ T737 [M]	Latin Escapade	1957	$100
— Turquoise label			
❏ T737 [M]	Latin Escapade	1959	$80
— Black label with colorband, logo on left			
❏ T737 [M]	Latin Escapade	1962	$75
— Black label with colorband, logo on top			
❏ DT737 [R]	Latin Escapade	196?	$60
❏ SM-11454	Latin Escapade	197?	$25
❏ T1082 [M]	Latin Lace	1958	$80
— Black label with colorband, logo on left			
❏ T1082 [M]	Latin Lace	1962	$75
— Black label with colorband, logo on top			
❏ ST1082 [S]	Latin Lace	1958	$100
— Black label with colorband, logo on left			
❏ ST1082 [S]	Latin Lace	1962	$80
— Black label with colorband, logo on top			
❏ T2326 [M]	Latin Rendezvous	1965	$60
❏ ST2326 [S]	Latin Rendezvous	1965	$75
❏ T1567 [M]	Mood Latino	1961	$80
— Black label with colorband, logo on left			
❏ T1567 [M]	Mood Latino	1962	$75
— Black label with colorband, logo on top			
❏ ST1567 [S]	Mood Latino	1961	$100
— Black label with colorband, logo on left			
❏ ST1567 [S]	Mood Latino	1962	$80
— Black label with colorband, logo on top			
❏ T943 [M]	Night Mist	1957	$100
— Turquoise label			
❏ T2048 [M]	Old Gold and Ivory	1964	$60
❏ ST2048 [S]	Old Gold and Ivory	1964	$50
❏ T1416 [M]	On the Sunny Side of the Strip	1960	$80
— Black label with colorband, logo on left			
❏ T1416 [M]	On the Sunny Side of the Strip	1962	$50
— Black label with colorband, logo on top			
❏ ST1416 [S]	On the Sunny Side of the Strip	1960	$100
— Black label with colorband, logo on left			
❏ ST1416 [S]	On the Sunny Side of the Strip	1962	$80
— Black label with colorband, logo on top			
❏ T2272 [M]	Out of the Woods	1965	$60
❏ ST2272 [S]	Out of the Woods	1965	$50
❏ T2447 [M]	Rare Form	1965	$60
❏ ST2447 [S]	Rare Form	1965	$50
❏ T1715 [M]	San Francisco Scene	1962	$50
❏ ST1715 [S]	San Francisco Scene	1962	$80
❏ T1628 [M]	Satin Affair	1961	$80
— Black label with colorband, logo on left			
❏ T1628 [M]	Satin Affair	1962	$50
— Black label with colorband, logo on top			
❏ ST1628 [S]	Satin Affair	1961	$100
— Black label with colorband, logo on left			
❏ ST1628 [S]	Satin Affair	1962	$80
— Black label with colorband, logo on top			
❏ T909 [M]	Shearing Piano	1957	$100
— Turquoise label			
❏ T909 [M]	Shearing Piano	1959	$80
— Black label with colorband, logo on left			
❏ T2567 [M]	That Fresh Feeling	1966	$60
❏ ST2567 [S]	That Fresh Feeling	1966	$50
❏ T2104 [M]	The Best of George Shearing	1964	$60
❏ ST2104 [S]	The Best of George Shearing	1964	$75
❏ SM-2104	The Best of George Shearing	1977	$25
— Reissue with new prefix			
❏ SKAO-139	The Best of George Shearing, Vol. 2	1969	$60
❏ T648 [M]	The Shearing Spell	1956	$100

Number	Title	Yr	NM
—Turquoise label			
❏ T648 [M]	The Shearing Spell	1959	$80
—Black label with colorband, logo on left			
❏ T1472 [M]	The Shearing Touch	1961	$80
—Black label with colorband, logo on left			
❏ T1472 [M]	The Shearing Touch	1962	$50
—Black label with colorband, logo on top			
❏ ST1472 [S]	The Shearing Touch	1961	$100
—Black label with colorband, logo on left			
❏ ST1472 [S]	The Shearing Touch	1962	$80
—Black label with colorband, logo on top			
❏ SM-1472	The Shearing Touch	1977	$25
—Reissue with new prefix			
❏ T1874 [M]	Touch Me Softly	1963	$50
❏ ST1874 [S]	Touch Me Softly	1963	$80
❏ T720 [M]	Velvet Carpet	1956	$100
—Turquoise label			
❏ T720 [M]	Velvet Carpet	1959	$80
—Black label with colorband, logo on left			
❏ T720 [M]	Velvet Carpet	1962	$50
—Black label with colorband, logo on top			
❏ DT720 [R]	Velvet Carpet	196?	$50
❏ T1334 [M]	White Satin	1960	$80
—Black label with colorband, logo on left			
❏ T1334 [M]	White Satin	1962	$60
—Black label with colorband, logo on top			
❏ ST1334 [S]	White Satin	1960	$100
—Black label with colorband, logo on left			
❏ ST1334 [S]	White Satin	1962	$80
—Black label with colorband, logo on top			
CONCORD CONCERTO			
❏ CC-2010	George Shearing and Barry Tuckwell Play the Music of Cole Porter	1986	$25
CONCORD JAZZ			
❏ CJ-171	Alone Together	1981	$25
❏ CJ-357	A Perfect Match	1988	$25
—With Ernestine Anderson			
❏ CJ-110	Blues Alley Jazz	1980	$25
❏ CJ-335	Breakin' Out	1988	$25
❏ CJ-346	Dexterity	1988	$25
❏ CJ-177	First Edition	1982	$25
❏ CJ-388	George Shearing in Dixieland	1989	$30
❏ CJ-281	Grand Piano	1985	$25
❏ CJ-246	Live at the Café Carlyle	1984	$25
❏ CJ-318	More Grand Piano	1987	$25
❏ CJ-132	On a Clear Day	1981	$25
—With Brian Torff			
❏ CJ-400	Piano	1989	$30
❏ CJ-371	The Spirit of 176	1989	$30
—With Hank Jones			
DISCOVERY			
❏ DL-3002 [10]	George Shearing Quintet	1950	$300
EVEREST ARCHIVE OF FOLK & JAZZ			
❏ 236	The Early Years, Vol. 2	1969	$25
❏ 223	Young George Shearing	1968	$25
LONDON			
❏ LL1343 [M]	By Request	1956	$60
❏ LL295 [10]	Souvenirs	1951	$120
MGM			
❏ E-252 [10]	An Evening with George Shearing	1954	$100
❏ E-90 [10]	A Touch of Genius	1951	$100
❏ E-155 [10]	I Hear Music	1952	$100
❏ E-3266 [M]	I Hear Music	1955	$75
❏ E-4041 [M]	Satin Latin	1962	$35
❏ SE-4041 [R]	Satin Latin	1962	$30
❏ E-3175 [M]	Shearing Caravan	1955	$75
❏ E-3293 [M]	Shearing in Hi-Fi	1955	$75
❏ E-4043 [M]	Smooth and Swinging	1962	$35
❏ SE-4043 [R]	Smooth and Swinging	1962	$30
❏ E-4042 [M]	Soft and Silky	1962	$35
❏ SE-4042 [R]	Soft and Silky	1962	$30
❏ E-4169 [M]	The Very Best of George Shearing	1963	$35
❏ SE-4169 [R]	The Very Best of George Shearing	1963	$30
❏ E-3265 [M]	Touch of Genius	1955	$75
❏ E-226 [10]	When Lights Are Low	1953	$100
❏ E-3264 [M]	When Lights Are Low	1955	$75
❏ GAS-143	You're Hearing George Shearing	1970	$30
❏ E-3216 [M]	You're Hearing George Shearing	1955	$75
❏ E-3796 [M]	You're Hearing the Best of George Shearing	1960	$35
❏ E-518 [10]	You're Hearing the George Shearing Quartet	1950	$120
MOSAIC			

Number	Title	Yr	NM
❏ MQ7-157	The Complete Capitol Live Recordings of George Shearing	199?	$300
PAUSA			
❏ 7072	500 Miles High	1979	$25
❏ 7088	Getting in the Swing of Things	1981	$25
❏ 9036	Jazz Moments	1985	$25
❏ 9065	Latin Affair	1986	$25
❏ 7035	Light, Airy and Swinging	1977	$25
❏ 7116	On Target	198?	$25
❏ PR7049	The Reunion	1977	$25
—With Stephane Grappelli			
❏ 9030	The Shearing Touch	198?	$25
PICKWICK			
❏ SPC-3039	Lullaby of Birdland	197?	$25
❏ SPC-3100	You Stepped Out of a Dream	197?	$25
SAVOY			
❏ MG-15003 [10]	Piano Solo	1951	$120
SAVOY JAZZ			
❏ SJL-1117	So Rare	198?	$25
SHEBA			
❏ 105	As Requested	197?	$30
❏ 107	GAS	197?	$30
❏ 104	George Shearing Quartet	197?	$30
❏ 103	George Shearing Trio	197?	$30
❏ 106	Music to Hear	197?	$30
❏ 101	Out of This World	197?	$30
VERVE			
❏ VSP-9 [M]	Classic Shearing	1966	$35
❏ VSPS-9 [R]	Classic Shearing	1966	$30
❏ 827977-1	Lullaby of Birdland	1986	$30
❏ 821664-1	My Ship	198?	$25

SHEEN, MICKEY
Drummer.

Albums

Number	Title	Yr	NM
HERALD			
❏ HLP-0105 [M]	Have Swing, Will Travel	1956	$60

SHELDON, JACK
Trumpeter.

Albums

Number	Title	Yr	NM
CAPITOL			
❏ T1851 [M]	Out!	1963	$50
❏ ST1851 [S]	Out!	1963	$50
❏ T2029 [M]	Play Buddy, Play!	1966	$50
❏ ST2029 [S]	Play Buddy, Play!	1966	$50
CONCORD JAZZ			
❏ CJ-339	Hollywood Heroes	1988	$25
❏ CJ-229	Stand By for Jack Sheldon	1983	$25
GENE NORMAN			
❏ GNP-60 [M]	Jack's Groove	1961	$40
GNP CRESCENDO			
❏ GNPS-60	Jack's Groove	196?	$30
❏ GNPS-9036	Jack Sheldon and His All-Star Band	197?	$25
❏ GNPS-2029 [S]	Play, Buddy, Play!	1966	$30
❏ GNP-2029 [M]	Play, Buddy, Play!	1966	$35
JAZZ WEST			
❏ JWLP-1 [10]	Get Out of Town	1955	$400
❏ JWLP-2 [10]	Jack Sheldon Quintet	1955	$400
❏ JWLP-6 [M]	The Quartet and the Quintet	1956	$800
REAL TIME			
❏ 303	Playin' It Straight	1981	$35
REPRISE			
❏ R-2004 [M]	A Jazz Profile of Ray Charles	1961	$30
❏ R9-2004 [S]	A Jazz Profile of Ray Charles	1961	$30

SHELDON, NINA

Albums

Number	Title	Yr	NM
PLUG			
❏ PLUG-2	Secret Places	1986	$30

SHEPARD, TOMMY
Trombonist.

Albums

Number	Title	Yr	NM
CORAL			
❏ CRL57110 [M]	Shepard's Flock	1957	$80

SHEPHERD, CYBILL
Female singer. Better known as an actress.

Number	Title	Yr	NM
Albums			
PARAMOUNT			
❏ PAS-1018	Cybill Does It...to Cole Porter	1974	$50
—With poster			

SHEPP, ARCHIE, AND BILL DIXON
Also see each artist's individual listings.

Albums

Number	Title	Yr	NM
SAVOY			
❏ MG-12184 [M]	Archie Shepp and the New Contemporary 5/The Bill Dixon 7-Tette	1964	$200
—White bordered cover			
❏ MG-12184 [M]	Archie Shepp and the New Contemporary 5/The Bill Dixon 7-Tette	1965	$150
—Purple bordered cover			
❏ MG-12178 [M]	The Archie Shepp-Bill Dixon Quartet	1962	$30

SHEPP, ARCHIE, AND DOLLAR BRAND
Also see ARCHIE SHEPP; ABDULLAH IBRAHIM.

Albums

Number	Title	Yr	NM
DENON			
❏ 7532	Duet	197?	$35

SHEPP, ARCHIE, AND HORACE PARLAN
Also see each artist's individual listings.

Albums

Number	Title	Yr	NM
STEEPLECHASE			
❏ SCS-1079	Goin' Home	197?	$30
❏ SCS-1139	Trouble in Mind	1980	$30

SHEPP, ARCHIE
Tenor saxophone player, pianist and male singer.

Albums

Number	Title	Yr	NM
ABC IMPULSE!			
❏ AS-9222	Africa Blues	197?	$35
❏ AS-9231	Cry of My People	1973	$35
❏ AS-86 [S]	Fire Music	1968	$35
❏ AS-9188	For Losers	1970	$200
❏ AS-71 [S]	Four for Trane	1968	$35
❏ AS-9262	Kwanza	1974	$35
❏ AS-9118 [S]	Live In San Francisco	1968	$35
❏ AS-9134 [S]	Mama Too Tight	1968	$35
❏ AS-97 [S]	On This Night	1968	$35
❏ AS-9154 [S]	The Magic of Ju Ju	1968	$200
❏ AS-9170 [S]	The Way Ahead	1969	$200
❏ AS-9212	Things Have Got to Change	197?	$35
❏ AS-9162 [S]	Three for a Quarter, One for a Dime	1968	$200
ARISTA/FREEDOM			
❏ AF1027	Montreux 1	197?	$30
❏ AF1034	Montreux 2	197?	$30
❏ AF1016	There's a Trumpet in My Soul	1975	$30
BASF			
❏ 20651	Donaueschingen Festival	197?	$35
BLACK SAINT			
❏ BSR-0002	A Sea of Faces	198?	$30
DELMARK			
❏ DL-409 [M]	Archie Shepp in Europe	1968	$30
❏ DS-9409 [S]	Archie Shepp in Europe	1968	$25
DENON			
❏ 7543	Lady Bird	197?	$35
❏ 7538	Live in Tokyo	197?	$35
GRP/IMPULSE!			
❏ IMP-218	Four for Trane	199?	$35
—Reissue on audiophile vinyl			
IMPULSE!			
❏ A-86 [M]	Fire Music	1965	$120
❏ AS-86 [S]	Fire Music	1965	$120
❏ A-71 [M]	Four for Trane	1964	$120
❏ AS-71 [S]	Four for Trane	1964	$120
❏ A-9118 [M]	Live In San Francisco	1967	$120
❏ AS-9118 [S]	Live In San Francisco	1967	$120
❏ A-9134 [M]	Mama Too Tight	1967	$120
❏ AS-9134 [S]	Mama Too Tight	1967	$120
❏ A-97 [M]	On This Night	1966	$120
❏ AS-97 [S]	On This Night	1966	$120
INNER CITY			
❏ IC-1001	Doodlin'	197?	$35
❏ IC-3002	Steam	1976	$30
PRESTIGE			

Ben Sidran, *Too Hot to Touch*, Windham Hill WH-0108, **$30**.

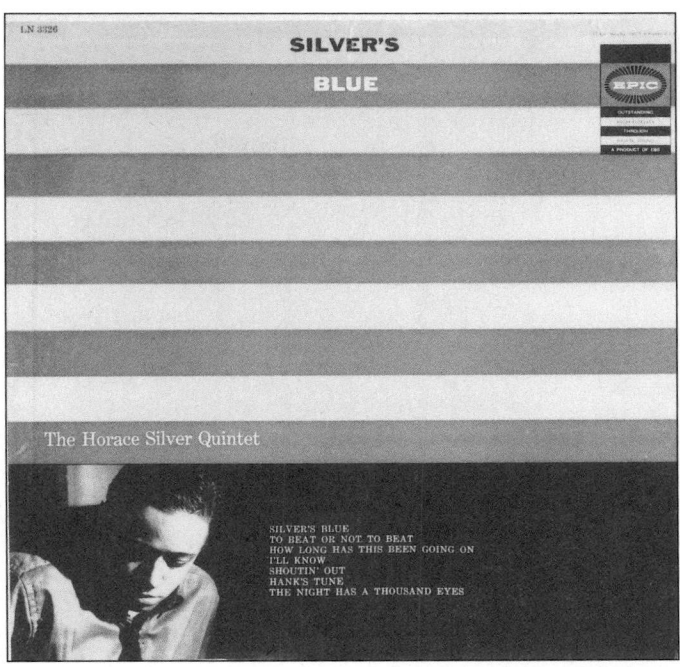

Horace Silver, *Silver's Blue*, Epic LN 3326, original cover and catalog number, **$300**.

Horace Silver, *Doin' the Thing at the Village Gate*, Blue Note BLP-4076, "New York, USA" on label, **$150**.

Horace Silver, *6 Pieces of Silver*, Blue Note BLP-1539, "deep groove" edition with W. 63rd St. address on label, **$600**.

Number	Title	Yr	NM
❏ 10034	Black Gypsy	197?	$35
❏ 10066	Coral Rock	197?	$35
SACKVILLE			
❏ 3026	I Know About the Life	198?	$25
SOUL NOTE			
❏ SN-1102	Down Home in New York	1985	$30
STEEPLECHASE			
❏ SCS-1149	Looking at Bird	198?	$30
❏ SCS-1169	Mama Rose	1982	$30
❏ SCS-6013	The House I Live In	198?	$30
TIMELESS			
❏ SJP-287	Lover Man	1990	$30
VARRICK			
❏ VR-005	The Good Life	198?	$25

SHEPPARD, ANDY
Tenor and soprano saxophone player.
Albums
ANTILLES

Number	Title	Yr	NM
❏ 90692	Andy Sheppard	1988	$25

SHERMAN, MARK
Vibraphone player, pianist and composer.
Albums
COLUMBIA

❏ BFC40360	A New Balance	1986	$25

SHERRILL, JOYA
Female singer and composer.
Albums
20TH CENTURY FOX

Number	Title	Yr	NM
❏ TFL-3170 [M]	Joya Sherrill Sings Duke Ellington	196?	$30
❏ TFS-4170 [S]	Joya Sherrill Sings Duke Ellington	196?	$30
COLUMBIA			
❏ CL1378 [M]	Sugar and Spice	1959	$30
❏ CS8178 [S]	Sugar and Spice	1960	$30
DESIGN			
❏ DLP-22 [M]	Joya Sherrill Jumps with Sammy Davis, Jr.	196?	$30

SHERWOOD, BOBBY
Guitarist, trumpeter, trombonist, pianist, composer, arranger and bandleader.
Albums
CAPITOL

Number	Title	Yr	NM
❏ H463 [10]	Bobby Sherwood	1954	$80
❏ H320 [10]	Classics in Jazz	1952	$100
❏ T320 [M]	Classics in Jazz	1955	$75
IAJRC			
❏ LP35	Out of Sherwood's Forest	198?	$25
JUBILEE			
❏ JLP-1040 [M]	I'm an Old Cowhand	1957	$30
❏ JLP-1061 [M]	Pal Joey	1958	$30
❏ SDJLP-1061 [S]	Pal Joey	1959	$30

SHEW, BOBBY, AND BILL MAYS
Also see each artist's individual listings.
Albums
JAZZ HOUNDS

❏ 03	Telepathy	198?	$25

SHEW, BOBBY, AND CHUCK FINDLEY
Findley is a trumpeter. Also see BOBBY SHEW.
Albums
DELOS

❏ DMS-4003	Trumpets No End	1984	$25

SHEW, BOBBY
Trumpeter.
Albums
INNER CITY

Number	Title	Yr	NM
❏ IC-1077	Outstanding in His Field	197?	$30
JAZZ HOUNDS			
❏ 02	Play Song	1980	$25
PAUSA			
❏ 7171	Breakfast Wine	1985	$25
❏ 7198	Shewhorn	1986	$25

SHIELDS, BILL
Keyboard player.
Albums
OPTIMISM

Number	Title	Yr	NM
❏ OP-9001	Shieldstone	198?	$25

SHIELDS, ROGER
Mostly a classical pianist, this is his one jazz-related LP.
Albums
TURNABOUT

❏ 34579	The Age of Ragtime	197?	$25

SHIHAB, SAHIB
Baritone and alto saxophone player and flutist.
Albums
ARGO

Number	Title	Yr	NM
❏ LP-742 [M]	Summer Dawn	1964	$400
❏ LPS-742 [S]	Summer Dawn	1964	$30
CHESS			
❏ CH-91563	Summer Dawn	198?	$25
SAVOY			
❏ MG-12124 [M]	Jazz Sahib	1957	$50
SAVOY JAZZ			
❏ SJL-2245	All-Star Sextets	197?	$30
❏ SJC-409	Jazz Sahib	1985	$25

SHIHAB, SAHIB/HERBIE MANN
Also see each artist's individual listings.
Albums
SAVOY

❏ MG-12112 [M]	The Jazz We Heard Last Summer	1957	$50

SHOEMAKE, CHARLIE, AND BILL HOLMAN
Also see each artist's individual listings.
Albums
PAUSA

❏ 7180	Collaboration	1985	$25

SHOEMAKE, CHARLIE, AND HAROLD LAND
Also see each artist's individual listings.
Albums
CMG

❏ CML-8016	Stand-Up Guys	1989	$30

SHOEMAKE, CHARLIE
Vibraphone player and bandleader.
Albums
DISCOVERY

Number	Title	Yr	NM
❏ 856	Away from the Crowd	198?	$25
❏ 894	Charlie Shoemake Plays the Music of David Raksin	1986	$25
❏ 924	I Think We're Almost There	1987	$25
MUSE			
❏ MR-5221	Blue Shoe	1979	$30
❏ MR-5193	Sunstroke	1978	$30

SHORE, DINAH
Female singer. Most of her output is pop, but the below was done with RED NORVO.
Albums
CAPITOL

Number	Title	Yr	NM
❏ T1354 [M]	Dinah Sings Some Blues with Red	1960	$60
❏ ST1354 [S]	Dinah Sings Some Blues with Red	1960	$60

SHORT, BOBBY
Male singer.
Albums
ATLANTIC

Number	Title	Yr	NM
❏ 81715	50 from Bobby Short	1987	$60
❏ 1230 [M]	Bobby Short	1956	$300
—Black label			
❏ 1230 [M]	Bobby Short	1961	$250
—White "fan" logo at right of label			
❏ 1230 [M]	Bobby Short	1963	$50
—Black "fan" logo at right of label			
❏ SD 2-610	Bobby Short Celebrates Rodgers and Hart	197?	$35
❏ SD 2-608	Bobby Short Is K-RA-Z-Y for Gershwin	1973	$35
❏ SD 2-606	Bobby Short Loves Cole Porter	1972	$50
❏ 81778	Guess Who's in Town: The Lyrics of Andy Razaf	1988	$25
❏ SD1535	Jump for Joy	1969	$30
❏ SD 2-609	Live at the Café Carlyle	1974	$35
❏ SD 2-607	Mad About Noel Coward	1972	$50
❏ SD1574	Nobody Else But Me	1971	$30
❏ 1321 [M]	On the East Side	1960	$250
—Black label			
❏ 1321 [M]	On the East Side	1961	$150
—White "fan" logo at right of label			
❏ 1321 [M]	On the East Side	1963	$35
—Black "fan" logo at right of label			
❏ SD1321 [S]	On the East Side	1960	$250
—Green label			
❏ SD1321 [S]	On the East Side	1961	$150
—White "fan" logo at right of label			
❏ SD1321 [S]	On the East Side	1963	$50
—Black "fan" logo at right of label			
❏ SD1689	Personal	1977	$30
❏ 1285 [M]	Sing Me a Swing Song	1958	$300
—Black label			
❏ 1285 [M]	Sing Me a Swing Song	1961	$150
—White "fan" logo at right of label			
❏ 1285 [M]	Sing Me a Swing Song	1963	$35
—Black "fan" logo at right of label			
❏ 1214 [M]	Songs by Bobby Short	1955	$300
—Black label			
❏ 1214 [M]	Songs by Bobby Short	1961	$150
—White "fan" logo at right of label			
❏ 1214 [M]	Songs by Bobby Short	1963	$35
—Black "fan" logo at right of label			
❏ 1262 [M]	Speaking of Love	1958	$300
—Black label			
❏ 1262 [M]	Speaking of Love	1961	$150
—White "fan" logo at right of label			
❏ SD1262 [S]	Speaking of Love	1959	$300
—Green label			
❏ SD1262 [S]	Speaking of Love	1961	$150
—White "fan" logo at right of label			
❏ 1302 [M]	The Mad Twenties	1959	$300
—Black label			
❏ 1302 [M]	The Mad Twenties	1961	$150
—White "fan" logo at right of label			
❏ 1302 [M]	The Mad Twenties	1963	$35
—Black "fan" logo at right of label			
❏ SD1302 [S]	The Mad Twenties	1959	$300
—Green label			
❏ SD1302 [S]	The Mad Twenties	1961	$150
—White "fan" logo at right of label			
❏ SD1302 [S]	The Mad Twenties	1963	$50
—Black "fan" logo at right of label			
❏ SD1664	The Mad Twenties	1974	$30
❏ SD1620	The Very Best of Bobby Short	1973	$30
ELEKTRA			
❏ E1-60002	Moments Like This	1982	$25

SHORTER, ALAN
Trumpeter and fluegel horn player.
Albums
VERVE

❏ V6-8769	Orgasm	1969	$25

SHORTER, WAYNE
Tenor and soprano saxophone player, arranger and composer. Also see WEATHER REPORT; THE YOUNG LIONS.
Albums
BLUE NOTE

Number	Title	Yr	NM
❏ BST-84232	Adam's Apple	1967	$50
❏ BST-84232	Adam's Apple	1985	$25
—The Finest in Jazz Since 1939" reissue			
❏ LT-1056	Etcetera	1980	$30
❏ B1-33581	Etcetera	1995	$35
❏ BLP-4182 [M]	Juju	1965	$100
❏ BST-84182 [S]	Juju	1965	$60
—With New York, USA address on label			
❏ BST-84182 [S]	Juju	1967	$35

Number	Title	Yr	NM
— With "A Division of Liberty Records" on label			
❏ BST-84182	Juju	198?	$25
—The Finest in Jazz Since 1939" reissue			
❏ BN-LA014-G	Moto Grosso Feio	1973	$35
❏ BLP-4173 [M]	Night Drreamer	1964	$100
❏ BST-84173 [S]	Night Drreamer	1964	$60
— With New York, USA address on label			
❏ BST-84173 [S]	Night Drreamer	1967	$35
— With "A Division of Liberty Records" on label			
❏ BST-84297	Schizophrenia	1969	$50
❏ B1-32096	Schizophrenia	1995	$35
❏ BLP-4194 [M]	Speak No Evil	1966	$100
❏ BST-84194 [S]	Speak No Evil	1966	$60
— With New York, USA address on label			
❏ BST-84194 [S]	Speak No Evil	1967	$35
— With "A Division of Liberty Records" on label			
❏ B1-46509	Speak No Evil	1997	$35
—Reissue on 180-gram vinyl			
❏ BST-84332	Super Nova	1970	$50
❏ BLP-4219 [M]	The All Seeing Eye	1966	$100
❏ BST-84219 [S]	The All Seeing Eye	1966	$60
— With New York, USA address on label			
❏ BST-84219 [S]	The All Seeing Eye	1967	$35
— With "A Division of Liberty Records" on label			
❏ B1-29100	The All Seeing Eye	1994	$35
❏ B1-91141	The Best of Wayne Shorter	1988	$25
❏ BST-84363	The Odyssey of Iska	1971	$35
❏ LT-988	The Soothsayer	1979	$30
COLUMBIA			
❏ FC40055	Atlantis	1985	$25
❏ FC44110	Joy Ryder	1988	$25
❏ PC33418	Native Dancer	1975	$30
— Originals have no bar code			
❏ PC33418	Native Dancer	198?	$20
— Reissue with bar code			
❏ FC40373	Phantom Navigator	1987	$25
GNP CRESCENDO			
❏ GNPS-2075	Wayne Shorter	1973	$35
TRIP			
❏ 5009	Shorter Moments	1974	$30
VEE JAY			
❏ LP-3006 [M]	Introducing Wayne Shorter	1960	$40
❏ SR-3006 [S]	Introducing Wayne Shorter	1960	$100
❏ VJS-3006	Introducing Wayne Shorter	1986	$30
— 1980s reissue on thinner vinyl			
❏ LP-3057 [M]	Second Genesis	1963	$60
❏ SR-3057 [S]	Second Genesis	1963	$40
❏ VJS-3057	Second Genesis	198?	$30
— 1980s reissue on thinner vinyl			
❏ LP-3029 [M]	Wayning Moments	1962	$60
❏ SR-3029 [S]	Wayning Moments	1962	$40
❏ VJS-3029	Wayning Moments	198?	$30
— 1980s reissue on thinner vinyl			

SHQ
Czech group led by Karel Velebny.

Albums

ESP-DISK'

❏ 1080 [S]	The Uhu Sleeps Only During the Day	1969	$120

SHU, EDDIE
Tenor saxophone player, trumpeter and male singer.

Albums

BETHLEHEM

❏ BCP-1013 [10]	I Only Have Eyes For Shu	1954	$250

SHU, EDDIE/BOB HARDAWAY
Also see each artist's individual listings.

SHU, EDDIE/JOE ROLAND/"WILD" BILL DAVIS
Also see each artist's individual listings.

Albums

MERCER

❏ LP-1002 [10]	New Stars, New Sounds, Volume 1	1951	$150

SHULMAN, JOEL

Albums

JAMAL

❏ 5162	Peninah	197?	$50

Number	Title	Yr	NM

SHUMATE, TED, AND IRA SULLIVAN
Shumate is a guitarist. Also see IRA SULLIVAN.

Albums

PAUSA

❏ 7188	Gulfstream	1986	$25

SIDMAN, DAVID
Guitarist, composer and bandleader.

Albums

CADENCE JAZZ

❏ CJR-1033	Shades of Meaning	1988	$25

SIDRAN, BEN
Keyboard player, pianist and male singer.

Albums

ANTILLES

| ❏ AN-1012 | Bop City | 1984 | $30 |
| ❏ AN-1004 | Old Songs for the New Depression | 1981 | $35 |

ARISTA

❏ AB4178	A Little Kiss in the Night	1978	$35
❏ AL4081	Free in America	1976	$30
❏ AB4218	Live at Montreux	1979	$30
❏ AL4131	The Doctor Is In	1977	$30

BLUEBIRD

| ❏ 6575-1-RB | That's Life I Guess | 1990 | $35 |

BLUE THUMB

❏ BTS-6012	Don't Let Go	1974	$50
❏ BTS-40	I Lead a Life	1972	$40
❏ BTS-55	Puttin' In Time on Planet Earth	1973	$50

CAPITOL

| ❏ ST-825 | Feel Your Groove | 1971 | $80 |

HORIZON

| ❏ SP-741 | The Cat and the Hat | 1980 | $30 |

MAGENTA

| ❏ MA-0204 | On the Cool Side | 1985 | $25 |
| ❏ MA-0206 | On the Live Side | 1986 | $25 |

WINDHAM HILL

| ❏ WH-0108 | Too Hot to Touch | 1988 | $30 |

SIEGEL, DAN
Keyboards player.

Albums

CBS ASSOCIATED

| ❏ OZ44490 | Late One Night | 1989 | $30 |
| ❏ BZ44026 | Northern Nights | 1987 | $25 |

INNER CITY

❏ IC-1046	Nite Ride	197?	$30
❏ IC-1134	Oasis	198?	$30
❏ IC-1111	The Hot Shot	198?	$30

PAUSA

❏ 7164	Another Time	1984	$25
❏ 7179	On the Edge	1985	$25
❏ 7142	Reflections	198?	$25

SIGNATURES, THE
Vocal and instrumental quintet: Bunny Phillips (lead voice); Ruth Alcivar (vocals, drums); Lee Humes (vocals, bass, trombone); Bob Alcivar (vocals, piano, arranger); Hal Curtis (vocals, trumpet).

Albums

WARNER BROS.

❏ W1353 [M]	Prepare to Flip!	1959	$60
❏ WS1353 [S]	Prepare to Flip!	1959	$40
❏ W1250 [M]	The Signatures Sing In	1958	$60
❏ WS1250 [S]	The Signatures Sing In	1958	$40

WHIPPET

| ❏ WLP-702 [M] | The Signatures -- Their Voices and Instruments | 1957 | $120 |

SIGNORELLI, FRANK
Pianist and composer.

Albums

DAVIS

| ❏ JD-103 [M] | Piano Moods | 1951 | $100 |

SILVA, ALAN
Bass player.

Albums

CHIAROSCURO

Number	Title	Yr	NM
❏ 2015	The Shout: Portrait for a Small Woman	197?	$30
ESP-DISK'			
❏ 1091 [S]	Alan Silva	1969	$120

SILVA, MARCOS
Keyboard player.

Albums

CROSSOVER

| ❏ CR-5004 | Here We Go | 1987 | $25 |
| ❏ CR-5006 | White and Black | 1989 | $30 |

SILVEIRA, RICARDO
Guitarist.

Albums

VERVE FORECAST

| ❏ 835054-1 | Long Distance | 1988 | $25 |
| ❏ 837696-1 | Sky Light | 1989 | $30 |

SILVER, HORACE
Pianist, bandleader and composer. Also see STAN GETZ.

Albums

BLUE NOTE

❏ BLP-4017 [M]	Blowin' the Blues Away	1959	$200
— Regular edition, W. 63rd St. address on label			
❏ BLP-4017 [M]	Blowin' the Blues Away	1963	$80
— New York, USA" address on label			
❏ BST-84017 [S]	Blowin' the Blues Away	1959	$200
— W. 63rd St. address on label			
❏ BST-84017 [S]	Blowin' the Blues Away	1963	$40
— New York, USA" address on label			
❏ BST-84017 [S]	Blowin' the Blues Away	1967	$60
— A Division of Liberty Records" on label			
❏ BST-84017	Blowin' the Blues Away	1985	$30
— The Finest in Jazz Since 1939" reissue			
❏ BLP-4076 [M]	Doin' the Thing at the Village Gate	1961	$150
— W. 63rd St. address on label			
❏ BLP-4076 [M]	Doin' the Thing at the Village Gate	1963	$150
— New York, USA" address on label			
❏ BST-84076 [S]	Doin' the Thing at the Village Gate	1961	$200
— W. 63rd St. address on label			
❏ BST-84076 [S]	Doin' the Thing at the Village Gate	1963	$150
— New York, USA" address on label			
❏ BST-84076 [S]	Doin' the Thing at the Village Gate	1967	$60
— A Division of Liberty Records" on label			
❏ B1-84076	Doin' the Thing at the Village Gate	1989	$30
— The Finest in Jazz Since 1939" reissue			
❏ BLP-4008 [M]	Finger Poppin'	1959	$200
— Regular edition, W. 63rd St. address on label			
❏ BLP-4008 [M]	Finger Poppin'	1963	$80
— New York, USA" address on label			
❏ BST-4008 [S]	Finger Poppin'	1959	$175
— Regular edition, W. 63rd St. address on label			
❏ BST-4008 [S]	Finger Poppin'	1963	$40
— New York, USA" address on label			
❏ BST-84008 [S]	Finger Poppin'	1967	$50
— With "A Division of Liberty Records" on label			
❏ B1-84008	Finger Poppin'	198?	$30
— The Finest in Jazz Since 1939" reissue			
❏ BLP-1589 [M]	Further Explorations	1958	$400
— Regular edition, W. 63rd St. address on label			
❏ BLP-1589 [M]	Further Explorations	1963	$150
— New York, USA" address on label			
❏ BST-1589 [S]	Further Explorations	1959	$1000
— Deep groove" version; W. 63rd St. address on label			
❏ BST-1589 [S]	Further Explorations	1959	$350
— Regular edition, W. 63rd St. address on label			
❏ BST-1589 [S]	Further Explorations	1963	$150
— New York, USA" address on label			
❏ BST-81589 [S]	Further Explorations	1967	$50
— With "A Division of Liberty Records" on label			
❏ BLP-4042 [M]	Horace-Scope	1960	$200
— Regular edition, W. 63rd St. address on label			
❏ BLP-4042 [M]	Horace-Scope	1963	$80

SILVER, HORACE

Number	Title	Yr	NM
—New York, USA" address on label			
❏ BST-84042 [S]	Horace-Scope	1960	$200
—W. 63rd St. address on label			
❏ BST-84042 [S]	Horace-Scope	1963	$40
—New York, USA" address on label			
❏ BST-84042 [S]	Horace-Scope	1967	$60
—A Division of Liberty Records" on label			
❏ BN-LA402-H2	Horace Silver	1975	$60
❏ BLP-1518 [M]	Horace Silver and the Jazz Messengers	1956	$300
—Deep groove" edition, W. 63rd St. address on label			
❏ BLP-1518 [M]	Horace Silver and the Jazz Messengers	1963	$200
—New York, USA" address on label			
❏ BST-81518 [R]	Horace Silver and the Jazz Messengers	1967	$60
—A Division of Liberty Records" on label			
❏ BST-81518	Horace Silver and the Jazz Messengers	1985	$35
—The Finest in Jazz Since 1939" reissue			
❏ BLP-5058 [10]	Horace Silver Quintet	1955	$700
❏ BLP-5062 [10]	Horace Silver Quintet	1955	$700
❏ BLP-5034 [10]	Horace Silver Trio, Vol. 2	1954	$800
❏ BLP-5018 [10]	New Faces	1953	$800
❏ BST-84420	Phase Three "All	1972	$100
—A Division of United Artists Records" on blue and white label			
❏ BST-84277	Serenade to a Soul Sister	1968	$150
—A Division of Liberty Records" on label			
❏ LWB-1033	Silver and Strings Play Music of the Spheres	1980	$60
❏ BN-LA406-G	Silver 'n' Brass	1975	$50
❏ BN-LA853-H	Silver 'n' Percussion	1978	$35
❏ BN-LA708-G	Silver 'n' Voices	1977	$50
❏ BN-LA581-G	Silver 'n' Wood	1976	$60
❏ BLP-4131 [M]	Silver's Serenade	1963	$175
—New York, USA" on label			
❏ BST-84131 [S]	Silver's Serenade	1963	$150
—New York, USA" address on label			
❏ BST-84131 [S]	Silver's Serenade	1967	$60
—A Division of Liberty Records" on label			
❏ BLP-1539 [M]	Six Pieces of Silver	1957	$1000
—Deep groove" version; Lexington Ave. address on label			
❏ BLP-1539 [M]	Six Pieces of Silver	1957	$600
—Deep groove" edition, W. 63rd St. address on label			
❏ BLP-1539 [M]	Six Pieces of Silver	1963	$200
—New York, USA" address on label			
❏ BST-81539 [R]	Six Pieces of Silver	1967	$50
—With "A Division of Liberty Records" on label			
❏ B1-81539	Six Pieces of Silver	1988	$30
—The Finest in Jazz Since 1939" reissue			
❏ B1-46548	Song for My Father	1997	$35
—Reissue on 180-gram vinyl			
❏ BLP-4185 [M]	Song for My Father (Cantiga Para Meu Pai)	1965	$175
—New York, USA" on label			
❏ BST-84185 [S]	Song for My Father (Cantiga Para Meu Pai)	1965	$140
—New York, USA" address on label			
❏ BST-84185 [S]	Song for My Father (Cantiga Para Meu Pai)	1967	$60
—A Division of Liberty Records" on label			
❏ BST-84185	Song for My Father (Cantiga Para Meu Pai)	1985	$30
—The Finest in Jazz Since 1939" reissue			
❏ BLP-1520 [M]	Spotlight on Drums	1956	$600
—Deep groove" version; Lexington Ave. address on label			
❏ BLP-1520 [M]	Spotlight on Drums	1956	$300
—Deep groove" edition, W. 63rd St. address on label			
❏ BLP-1520 [M]	Spotlight on Drums	1963	$200
—New York, USA" address on label			
❏ BST-81520 [R]	Spotlight on Drums	1967	$50
—With "A Division of Liberty Records" on label			
❏ BN-LA945-H	Sterling Silver	1979	$35
❏ BST-84352	That Healin' Feelin' (Phase 1)	1970	$150
—A Division of Liberty Records" on label			
❏ BST-84325	The Best of Horace Silver	1970	$60
—A Division of Liberty Records" on label			
❏ B1-91143	The Best of Horace Silver	1988	$30
❏ B1-93206	The Best of Horace Silver, Vol. 2	1989	$30
❏ BLP-4220 [M]	The Cape Verdean Blues	1965	$175
❏ BST-84220 [S]	The Cape Verdean Blues	1965	$140
—New York, USA" address on label			
❏ BST-84220 [S]	The Cape Verdean Blues	1967	$60
—A Division of Liberty Records" on label			

Number	Title	Yr	NM
❏ B1-81520	The Horace Silver Trio	1989	$30
—The Finest in Jazz Since 1939" reissue			
❏ BLP-4250 [M]	The Jody Grind	1966	$150
—A Division of Liberty Records" on label			
❏ BST-84250 [S]	The Jody Grind	1966	$120
—New York, USA" address on label			
❏ BST-84250 [S]	The Jody Grind	1967	$60
—A Division of Liberty Records" on label			
❏ BN-LA054-F	The Pursuit of the 27th Man	1973	$35
—Dark blue label with black stylized "b" at upper right			
❏ BLP-1562 [M]	The Stylings of Silver	1957	$1250
—Deep groove" version; W. 63rd St. address on label			
❏ BLP-1562 [M]	The Stylings of Silver	1957	$200
—Regular edition, W. 63rd St. address on label			
❏ BLP-1562 [M]	The Stylings of Silver	1963	$200
—New York, USA" address on label			
❏ BST-1562 [S]	The Stylings of Silver	1959	$1200
—Deep groove" version; W. 63rd St. address on label			
❏ BST-1562 [S]	The Stylings of Silver	1959	$175
—Regular edition, W. 63rd St. address on label			
❏ BST-1562 [S]	The Stylings of Silver	1963	$80
—New York, USA" address on label			
❏ BST-81562 [S]	The Stylings of Silver	1967	$50
—With "A Division of Liberty Records" on label			
❏ BLP-4110 [M]	The Tokyo Blues	1962	$175
—New York, USA" on label			
❏ BST-84110 [S]	The Tokyo Blues	1962	$150
—New York, USA" address on label			
❏ BST-84110 [S]	The Tokyo Blues	1967	$60
—A Division of Liberty Records" on label			
❏ BST-84368	Total Response (Phase 2)	1971	$175
❏ BST-84309	You Gotta Take a Little Love	1969	$100
—A Division of Liberty Records" on label			
EPIC			
❏ LN3326 [M]	Silver's Blue	1956	$300
❏ LA16006 [M]	Silver's Blue	1959	$250
—Reissue with new cover			
❏ BA17006 [R]	Silver's Blue	196?	$100

SIMEON, OMER
Clarinetist. Also see SIDNEY BECHET.

Albums

CONCERT HALL JAZZ

Number	Title	Yr	NM
❏ 1014 [10]	Clarinet A La Creole	195?	$50
DISC			
❏ DLP-748 [10]	Omer Simeon Trio With James P. Johnson	195?	$200

SIMMONS, NORMAN
Pianist and composer.

Albums

Number	Title	Yr	NM
ARGO			
❏ LP-607 [M]	Norman Simmons Trio	1956	$40
CREATIVE			
❏ LP-607 [M]	Interpolations	1956	$80
MILLJAC			
❏ MLP-1002	I'm the Blues	1981	$35
❏ MLP-1001	Midnight Creeper	1979	$35

SIMMONS, SONNY
Alto saxophone player.

Albums

Number	Title	Yr	NM
ARHOOLIE			
❏ 8003 [S]	Manhattan Egos	1969	$35
CONTEMPORARY			
❏ S-7625/6	Burning Spirits	1970	$75
❏ M-3623 [M]	Rumasuma	1966	$150
❏ S-7623 [S]	Rumasuma	1966	$150
ESP-DISK'			
❏ 1043 [M]	Music from the Spheres	1967	$120
❏ S-1043 [S]	Music from the Spheres	1967	$120
❏ 1030 [M]	Sonny Simmons	1966	$120
❏ S-1030 [S]	Sonny Simmons	1966	$120

SIMON, ALAN
Pianist.

Albums

Number	Title	Yr	NM
CADENCE JAZZ			
❏ CJR-1027	Rainsplash	198?	$25

SIMON, FRED
Pianist and keyboard player. Also see SIMON AND BARD.

Albums

Number	Title	Yr	NM
WNDHAM HILL			
❏ WH-1071	Usually/Always	1988	$25

SIMON, RALPH
Tenor, soprano and alto saxophone player.

Albums

Number	Title	Yr	NM
GRAMAVISION			
❏ 8002	Time Being	1981	$25

SIMON AND BARD
FRED SIMON (keyboards, composer) and Michael Bard (saxophones).

Albums

Number	Title	Yr	NM
FLYING FISH			
❏ FF-243	Musaic	1980	$25
❏ FF-262	Tear It Up	1982	$25
❏ FF-321	The Enormous Radio	198?	$25

SIMONE, NINA
Female singer.

Albums

Number	Title	Yr	NM
ACCORD			
❏ SN-7108	In Concert	1981	$25
BETHLEHEM			
❏ BCP-6028 [M]	Jazz As Played in an Exclusive Side Street Club	1959	$200
❏ SBCP-6028 [S]	Jazz As Played in an Exclusive Side Street Club	1959	$200
❏ BCP-6041 [M]	Nina Simone and Her Friends	1960	$250
❏ SBCP-6041 [S]	Nina Simone and Her Friends	1960	$250
—With Carmen McRae and Chris Connor			
❏ BCP-6003	Nina Simone's Finest	197?	$30
❏ BCP-6028 [M]	The Original Nina Simone	1961	$1500
—Retitled reissue			
❏ SBCP-6028 [S]	The Original Nina Simone	1961	$1500
—Retitled reissue			
CANYON			
❏ 7705	Gifted and Black	1971	$35
COLPIX			
❏ CP-465 [M]	Folksy Nina	1964	$60
❏ SCP-465 [S]	Folksy Nina	1964	$60
❏ CP-419 [M]	Forbidden Fruit	1961	$60
❏ SCP-419 [S]	Forbidden Fruit	1961	$60
❏ CP-412 [M]	Nina at Newport	1960	$60
❏ SCP-412 [S]	Nina at Newport	1960	$60
❏ CP-409 [M]	Nina at Town Hall	1960	$60
❏ SCP-409 [S]	Nina at Town Hall	1960	$60
❏ CP-443 [M]	Nina's Choice	1963	$60
❏ SCP-443 [S]	Nina's Choice	1963	$60
❏ CP-455 [M]	Nina Simone at Carnegie Hall	1963	$60
❏ SCP-455 [S]	Nina Simone at Carnegie Hall	1963	$60
❏ CP-421 [M]	Nina Simone at the Village Gate	1961	$60
❏ SCP-421 [S]	Nina Simone at the Village Gate	1961	$60
❏ CP-425 [M]	Nina Sings Ellington	1962	$60
❏ SCP-425 [S]	Nina Sings Ellington	1962	$60
❏ CP-496 [M]	Nina with Strings	1966	$60
❏ SCP-496 [S]	Nina with Strings	1966	$60
❏ CP-407 [M]	The Amazing Nina Simone	1959	$60
❏ SCP-407 [S]	The Amazing Nina Simone	1959	$60
CTI			
❏ 7084	Baltimore	1978	$30
PHILIPS			
❏ PHM200148 [M]	Broadway...Blues...Ballads	1964	$35
❏ PHS600148 [S]	Broadway...Blues...Ballads	1964	$50
❏ PHM200172 [M]	I Put a Spell on You	1965	$35
❏ PHS600172 [S]	I Put a Spell on You	1965	$400
❏ PHM200202 [M]	Let It All Out	1966	$35
❏ PHS600202 [S]	Let It All Out	1966	$50
❏ PHM200135 [M]	Nina Simone In Concert	1964	$35
❏ PHS600135 [S]	Nina Simone In Concert	1964	$50
❏ PHM200187 [M]	Pastel Blues	1965	$35
❏ PHS600187 [S]	Pastel Blues	1965	$50
❏ PHS600298	The Best of Nina Simone	1969	$50
❏ 822846-1	The Best of Nina Simone	198?	$25
❏ PHM200219 [M]	The High Priestess of Soul	1967	$35
❏ PHS600219 [S]	The High Priestess of Soul	1967	$50
❏ PHM200207 [M]	Wild Is the Wind	1966	$35
❏ PHS600207 [S]	Wild Is the Wind	1966	$50
PM			
❏ 018	A Very Rare Evening	1979	$30
QUINTESSENCE			

Horace Silver, *Horace Silver and the Jazz Messengers*, Blue Note BLP-1518, "deep groove" edition, **$300**.

Zoot Sims, *The Modern Art of Jazz*, Dawn DLP-1102, **$300**.

The Six, *The View from Jazzbo's Head*, Bethlehem BCP-87, **$250**.

Carol Sloane, *Live at 30th Street*, Columbia CS 8723, **$80**.

Number	Title	Yr	NM
❏ 25421	Silk and Soul	1979	$25
RCA VICTOR			
❏ LSP-4248	Black Gold	1970	$35
❏ LSP-4757	Emergency Ward!	1972	$35
❏ LSP-4536	Here Comes the Sun	1971	$35
❏ AFL1-4536	Here Comes the Sun	1977	$25
— Reissue with new prefix			
❏ APL1-0241	It Is Finished -- Nina 1974	1974	$30
❏ AFL1-0241	It Is Finished -- Nina 1974	1977	$25
— Reissue with new prefix			
❏ LSP-4102	Nina Simone and Piano	1968	$35
❏ LPM-3789 [M]	Nina Simone Sings the Blues	1967	$60
❏ LSP-3789 [S]	Nina Simone Sings the Blues	1967	$35
❏ LSP-4065	'Nuff Said	1968	$35
❏ APL1-1788	Poets	1976	$30
❏ AFL1-1788	Poets	1977	$25
— Reissue with new prefix			
❏ LPM-3837 [M]	Silk and Soul	1967	$60
❏ LSP-3837 [S]	Silk and Soul	1967	$35
❏ LSP-4374	The Best of Nina Simone	1970	$35
❏ AFL1-4374	The Best of Nina Simone	1977	$25
— Reissue with new prefix			
❏ LSP-4152	To Love Somebody	1969	$35
SALSOUL			
❏ SA-8546	Little Girl Blue	1982	$25
TRIP			
❏ 8021	Black Is the Color	1973	$30
❏ 8020	Live in Europe	1973	$30
❏ 9521	Portrait	197?	$25
VERVE			
❏ 831437-1	Let It Be Me	1987	$25

SIMONE
Female singer from Brazil.

Albums

COLUMBIA

❏ FC44275	Vicio	1988	$30

SIMPKINS, ANDY, AND DAVE MacKAY
Simpkins plays bass. Also see DAVID MacKAY.

Albums

STUDIO 7

❏ 403	Happying	197?	$30

SIMPSON, CAROLE
Female singer.

Albums

CAPITOL

❏ T878 [M]	All About Carole	1957	$150

TOPS

❏ L-1732 [M]	Singin' and Swingin'	1960	$30

SIMPSON, CASS
Pianist.

Albums

ABC-PARAMOUNT

❏ ABC-103 [M]	Cass Simpson	1956	$40

SIMS, ZOOT, AND BUDDY RICH
Also see each artist's individual listings.

Albums

QUINTESSENCE

❏ 25041	Air Mail Special	197?	$30

SIMS, ZOOT, AND HARRY "SWEETS" EDISON
Also see each artist's individual listings.

Albums

FANTASY

❏ OJC-499	Just Friends	1991	$30

PABLO

❏ 2310841	Just Friends	198?	$25

SIMS, ZOOT, AND JIMMY ROWLES
Also see each artist's individual listings.

Albums

PABLO

❏ 2310803	Lucky	1977	$30

SIMS, ZOOT; JIMMY RANEY; JIM HALL
Also see each artist's individual listings.

Albums

MAINSTREAM

Number	Title	Yr	NM
❏ MRL-358	Otra Vez	1972	$30
❏ 56013 [M]	Two Jims and Zoot	1965	$25
❏ S-6013 [S]	Two Jims and Zoot	1965	$30

SIMS, ZOOT; TONY SCOTT; AL COHN
Also see each artist's individual listings.

Albums

JAZZLAND

❏ JLP-11 [M]	East Coast Sounds	1960	$40
❏ JLP-911 [S]	East Coast Sounds	1960	$40

SIMS, ZOOT
Tenor saxophone player. Also see PEPPER ADAMS; BOB BROOKMEYER; AL COHN; ROY ELDRIDGE; THE FOUR BROTHERS; STAN GETZ; JUTTA HIPP; THE MANHATTAN ALL-STARS; GERRY MULLIGAN; ORCHESTRA USA.

Albums

ABC IMPULSE!

❏ AS-9131 [S]	The Waiting Game	1968	$120
— Black label with red ring			

ABC-PARAMOUNT

❏ ABC-155 [M]	Zoot Sims Plays Alto, Tenor and Baritone	1957	$150
❏ ABC-198 [M]	Zoot Sims Plays Four Altos	1957	$150

ARGO

❏ LP-608 [M]	Zoot	1956	$700
— Color cover			
❏ LP-608 [M]	Zoot	1957	$150
— Black and white cover			

BETHLEHEM

❏ BCP-6027	Down Home	197?	$50
— Reissue, distributed by RCA Victor			
❏ BCP-6051 [M]	Down Home	1960	$500
❏ SBCP-6051 [S]	Down Home	1960	$250

BIOGRAPH

❏ 12062	One to Blow On	198?	$25

CADET

❏ LP-608 [M]	Zoot	1966	$50
— Fading blue label			

CHOICE

❏ 1006	Party	197?	$35

CLASSIC JAZZ

❏ 21	Zoot Sims and Bucky Pizzarelli	197?	$30

COLPIX

❏ CP-435 [M]	New Beat Bossa Nova	1962	$40
❏ SCP-435 [S]	New Beat Bossa Nova	1962	$50
❏ CP-437 [M]	New Beat Bossa Nova, Volume 2	1962	$40
❏ SCP-437 [S]	New Beat Bossa Nova, Volume 2	1962	$50

DAWN

❏ DLP-1102 [M]	The Modern Art of Jazz	1956	$300
❏ DLP-1115 [M]	Zoot Sims Goes to Jazzville	1957	$200

DISCOVERY

❏ DL-3015 [10]	The Zoot Sims Quartet In Paris	1951	$300

FAMOUS DOOR

❏ HL-2000	At Ease	197?	$35

FANTASY

❏ OJC-444	The Gershwin Brothers	1990	$35
❏ OJC-228	Zoot!	198?	$30
❏ OJC-242	Zoot Sims Quartets	1987	$30

GROOVE MERCHANT

❏ 533	Nirvana	197?	$35

IMPULSE!

❏ A-9131 [M]	The Waiting Game	1967	$200
❏ AS-9131 [S]	The Waiting Game	1967	$200

JAZZLAND

❏ JLP-2 [M]	Zoot Sims Quintet	1960	$40
❏ JLP-92 [S]	Zoot Sims Quintet	1960	$60

MCA

❏ 29069	Zoot Sims Plays Four Altos	1980	$25

NEW JAZZ

❏ NJLP-8280 [M]	Good Old Zoot	1962	$150
❏ NJLP-8309 [M]	Koo Koo	1963	$0
— Canceled; reassigned to Status			
❏ NJLP-8302 [M]	Trotting	1963	$0
— Canceled; reassigned to Status			

Number	Title	Yr	NM
❏ NJLP-1102 [10]	Zoot Sims in Hollywood	1954	$350
PABLO			
❏ 2310783	Hawthorne Nights	197?	$30
❏ 2310868	I Wish I Were Twins	198?	$25
❏ 2310903	Quietly There	198?	$25
❏ 2310770	Soprano Sax	197?	$30
❏ 2310898	Suddenly It's Spring	198?	$25
❏ 2310861	Swinger	198?	$25
❏ 2405406	The Best of Zoot Sims	198?	$25
❏ 2310744	The Gershwin Brothers	197?	$30
❏ 2310872	The Innocent Years	198?	$25
❏ 2310831	Warm Tenor	1979	$30
PABLO TODAY			
❏ 2312120	Zoot Sims Plays Duke Ellington/Passion Flower	1980	$30
PACIFIC JAZZ			
❏ PJ-20 [M]	Choice	1961	$40
PRESTIGE			
❏ PRST-7817	First Recordings!	1970	$35
❏ PRLP-117 [10]	Swingin' with Zoot Sims	1951	$300
❏ PRLP-118 [10]	Tenor Sax Favorites	1951	$300
❏ PRLP-16009 [M]	Trotting	1963	$60
❏ P-24061	Zootcase	197?	$50
❏ PRLP-138 [10]	Zoot Sims All Stars	1953	$300
❏ PRLP-7026 [M]	Zoot Sims Quartets	1956	$300
— Yellow label with W. 50th St. address			
❏ PRLP-202 [10]	Zoot Sims Quintet	1955	$300
RIVERSIDE			
❏ 6103	Zoot	197?	$30
❏ RLP 12-228 [M]	Zoot!	1957	$300
SEECO			
❏ CELP-452 [M]	The Modern Art of Jazz	1960	$250
❏ CELP-4520 [S]	The Modern Art of Jazz	1960	$250
STATUS			
❏ ST-8280 [M]	Good Old Zoot	1965	$40
❏ ST-8309 [M]	Koo Koo	1965	$40
SWING			
❏ SW-8417	Zoot Sims in Paris	1987	$25
TRIP			
❏ 5548	You 'n Me	197?	$25
UNITED ARTISTS			
❏ UAL-4040 [M]	A Night at the Half Note	1959	$40
❏ UAS-5040 [S]	A Night at the Half Note	1959	$50
❏ UAJ-14013 [M]	Zoot Sims in Paris	1962	$40
❏ UAJS-15013 [S]	Zoot Sims in Paris	1962	$100
ZIM			
❏ 1008	Nash-ville	198?	$25

SINATRA, FRANK
Male singer. Highly influenced by jazz, and highly influential on jazz as well, we have decided to include all his known American albums here rather than be selective. Also see TOMMY DORSEY; HARRY JAMES.

Albums

ARTANIS

❏ ARZ101	Sinatra '57 In Concert	1999	$0
— Canceled			

BOOK-OF-THE-MONTH

❏ (# unknown)	Tommy Dorsey/Frank Sinatra: The Complete Sessions	1983	$175

CAPITOL

❏ W894 [M]	A Jolly Christmas from Frank Sinatra	1957	$75
— Original mono with gray label			
❏ W894 [M]	A Jolly Christmas from Frank Sinatra	1958	$100
— Black colorband label, logo at left			
❏ W1538 [M]	All the Way	1961	$80
❏ SW1538 [S]	All the Way	1961	$100
❏ SN-16205	All the Way	198?	$20
— Budget-line reissue			
❏ W803 [M]	A Swingin' Affair!	1957	$100
— Gray label			
❏ W803 [M]	A Swingin' Affair!	1957	$80
— Black label with colorband			
❏ DW803 [R]	A Swingin' Affair!	196?	$60
❏ SM-11502	A Swingin' Affair!	1976	$25
❏ W789 [M]	Close to You	1957	$100
— Gray label			
❏ W789 [M]	Close to You	1959	$80
— Black label with colorband			
❏ DW789 [R]	Close to You	196?	$60
❏ DWBB-254 [R]	Close-Up	196?	$60
— Reissue in one package of "This Is Sinatra" and "This Is Sinatra, Volume Two"			
❏ W1069 [M]	Come Dance with Me!	1959	$80
❏ SW1069 [S]	Come Dance with Me!	1959	$100

Number	Title	Yr	NM
❑ SN-16203	Come Dance with Me!	198?	$20
—Budget-line reissue			
❑ W920 [M]	Come Fly with Me	1958	$60
—Gray label			
❑ W920 [M]	Come Fly with Me	1959	$80
—Black label with colorband			
❑ SW920 [S]	Come Fly with Me	1959	$100
❑ SM-920	Come Fly with Me	197?	$20
❑ SY-4528 [S]	Come Fly with Me	197?	$25
—Reissue of SW 920 with orange label and "Capitol" at bottom			
❑ SM-11801	Come Swing with Me!	1978	$25
❑ W1594 [M]	Come Swing with Me!	1961	$80
❑ SW1594 [S]	Come Swing with Me!	1961	$100
❑ C1-89611	Duets	1993	$80
❑ T2602 [M]	Forever Frank	1966	$80
❑ DT2602 [R]	Forever Frank	1966	$60
❑ T735 [M]	Frank Sinatra Conducts Tone Poems of Color	1956	$200
—Turquoise label			
❑ T735 [M]	Frank Sinatra Conducts Tone Poems of Color	1959	$60
—Black label with colorband			
❑ PRO-2974/5 [DJ]	Frank Sinatra Minute Masters	1965	$60
—Edited version of 20 songs			
❑ DKAO-374 [R]	Frank Sinatra's Greatest Hits	1969	$60
❑ W1053 [M]	Frank Sinatra Sings for Only the Lonely	1958	$60
—Gray label			
❑ W1053 [M]	Frank Sinatra Sings for Only the Lonely	1959	$80
—Black label with colorband			
❑ SW1053 [S]	Frank Sinatra Sings for Only the Lonely	1959	$100
—Originals do not include "It's a Lonesome Old Town" and "Spring Is Here"			
❑ SW1053 [S]	Frank Sinatra Sings for Only the Lonely	196?	$100
—Later releases restore "It's a Lonesome Old Town" and "Spring Is Here"			
❑ SN-16202	Frank Sinatra Sings for Only the Lonely	198?	$20
—Budget-line reissue			
❑ SY-4533 [S]	Frank Sinatra Sings for Only the Lonely	197?	$25
—Reissue of SW-1053 on orange label with "Capitol" at bottom			
❑ W581 [M]	In the Wee Small Hours	1955	$75
—Gray label original			
❑ W581 [M]	In the Wee Small Hours	1959	$100
—Black label with colorband			
❑ DW581 [R]	In the Wee Small Hours	196?	$60
❑ SM-581	In the Wee Small Hours	197?	$20
❑ H1-581 [10]	In the Wee Small Hours, Part 1	1955	$250
❑ H2-581 [10]	In the Wee Small Hours, Part 2	1955	$250
❑ W1164 [M]	Look to Your Heart	1959	$100
❑ DW1164 [R]	Look to Your Heart	196?	$60
❑ N-16148	Look to Your Heart	198?	$20
—Budget-line reissue			
❑ N-16112	My One and Only Love	198?	$20
—Budget-line reissue			
❑ STBB-724	My One and Only Love/ Sentimental Journey	1971	$50
	My One and Only Love/ Sentimental Journey	197?	$50
—Columbia Record Club edition of STBB-724			
❑ W1417 [M]	Nice 'N' Easy	1960	$80
❑ SN-16204	Nice 'N' Easy	198?	$20
—Budget-line reissue			
❑ W1221 [M]	No One Cares	1959	$80
❑ SW1221 [S]	No One Cares	1959	$100
❑ SM-1221	No One Cares	197?	$20
❑ ST-11309	One More for the Road	1973	$25
❑ W1676 [M]	Point of No Return	1962	$80
❑ SW1676 [S]	Point of No Return	1962	$100
❑ SM-1676	Point of No Return	197?	$20
❑ SABB-11367 [P]	Round #1	1974	$50
❑ PRO-2163/4/5/6 [DJ]	Selections from Sinatra, The Great Years	1962	$75
❑ W90986 [M]	Sentimental Journey	1966	$100
—Capitol Record Club issue			
❑ DW90986 [R]	Sentimental Journey	1966	$50
—Capitol Record Club issue			
❑ SN-16113	Sentimental Journey	198?	$20
—Budget-line reissue			
❑ WCO1762 [M]	Sinatra, The Great Years	1962	$100
❑ SWCO1762 [P]	Sinatra, The Great Years	1962	$75

Number	Title	Yr	NM
❑ W1729 [M]	Sinatra Sings…Of Love and Things	1962	$80
❑ SW1729 [P]	Sinatra Sings…Of Love and Things	1962	$80
❑ SN-16149	Sinatra Sings…Of Love and Things	198?	$20
—Budget-line reissue			
❑ W1825 [M]	Sinatra Sings Rodgers and Hart	1963	$80
❑ DW1825 [R]	Sinatra Sings Rodgers and Hart	1963	$60
❑ STBB-95191	Sinatra Sings the Great Ones	1973	$80
—Longines Symphonette (formerly Capitol) Record Club issue			
❑ W2301 [M]	Sinatra Sings the Select Cole Porter	1965	$80
❑ DW2301 [R]	Sinatra Sings the Select Cole Porter	1965	$60
❑ T2123 [M]	Sinatra Sings the Select Harold Arlen	1964	$150
—Only released in Canada, Australia and the UK			
❑ W1994 [M]	Sinatra Sings the Select Johnny Mercer	1963	$80
❑ DW1994 [R]	Sinatra Sings the Select Johnny Mercer	1963	$60
❑ W1491 [M]	Sinatra's Swingin' Session!!!	1961	$80
❑ SW1491 [S]	Sinatra's Swingin' Session!!!	1961	$100
❑ SM-1491	Sinatra's Swingin' Session!!!	197?	$20
❑ W653 [M]	Songs for Swingin' Lovers!	1956	$150
—Gray label; cover has Sinatra facing away from the embracing couple			
❑ W653 [M]	Songs for Swingin' Lovers!	1956	$75
—Gray label; cover has Sinatra facing toward the embracing couple			
❑ W653 [M]	Songs for Swingin' Lovers!	1959	$100
—Black label with colorband			
❑ DW653 [R]	Songs for Swingin' Lovers!	196?	$60
❑ SM-653	Songs for Swingin' Lovers!	197?	$20
❑ DQBO91261 [R]	Songs for the Young at Heart	196?	$100
—Capitol Record Club issue			
❑ H488 [10]	Songs for Young Lovers	1954	$200
❑ W1432 [M]	Songs for Young Lovers	1960	$80
❑ DW1432 [R]	Songs for Young Lovers	1960	$60
❑ H528 [10]	Swing Easy	1954	$200
❑ W1429 [M]	Swing Easy	1960	$80
❑ DW1429 [R]	Swing Easy	1960	$60
❑ W587 [M]	Swing Easy/Songs for Young Lovers	1955	$75
—Gray label original; 12-inch version of two 10-inch LPs			
❑ W587 [M]	Swing Easy/Songs for Young Lovers	1959	$100
—Black label with colorband			
❑ T1919 [M]	Tell Her You Love Her	1963	$80
❑ DT1919 [R]	Tell Her You Love Her	1963	$60
❑ DKAO2900 [R]	The Best of Frank Sinatra	1968	$35
❑ SN-16109	The Best of Frank Sinatra	198?	$20
—Budget-line reissue			
❑ C1-94777	The Capitol Years	1990	$250
—With book and wraparound banner. Only 5,000 were pressed			
❑ TFL2814 [M]	The Frank Sinatra Deluxe Set	1968	$250
❑ STFL2814 [P]	The Frank Sinatra Deluxe Set	1968	$200
❑ T2036 [M]	The Greatest Hits of Frank Sinatra	1964	$80
❑ DT2036 [R]	The Greatest Hits of Frank Sinatra	1964	$60
❑ T2700 [M]	The Movie Songs	1967	$80
❑ DT2700 [R]	The Movie Songs	1967	$60
❑ SN-16111	The Night We Called It a Day	198?	$20
—Budget-line reissue			
❑ T894 [M]	The Sinatra Christmas Album	196?	$80
—Reissue of A Jolly Christmas with Frank Sinatra with same contents; some copies have this cover and "A Jolly Christmas" labels			
❑ SM-894 [R]	The Sinatra Christmas Album	197?	$20
—Reissue in rechanneled stereo; any color label			
❑ DT894 [R]	The Sinatra Christmas Album	196?	$25
—Rechanneled reissue of A Jolly Christmas with Frank Sinatra with same contents; some copies have this cover and "A Jolly Christmas" labels			
❑ DNFR7630 [P]	The Sinatra Touch	19??	$200
❑ T768 [M]	This Is Sinatra!	1956	$100
—Turquoise label			
❑ T768 [M]	This Is Sinatra!	196?	$80

Number	Title	Yr	NM
—Black "Starline" label			
❑ T768 [M]	This Is Sinatra!	196?	$50
—Gold "Starline" label			
❑ DT768 [R]	This Is Sinatra!	196?	$60
❑ M-11883	This Is Sinatra!	1979	$25
❑ W982 [M]	This Is Sinatra, Volume Two	1958	$75
—Gray label			
❑ W982 [M]	This Is Sinatra, Volume Two	1959	$80
—Black label with colorband, logo at left			
❑ DW982 [R]	This Is Sinatra, Volume Two	196?	$60
❑ DN-16268	This Is Sinatra, Volume Two	198?	$20
—Budget-line reissue			
❑ W982 [M]	This Is Sinatra, Volume Two	1963	$50
—Black label with colorband, logo at top			
❑ DN-16110	What Is This Thing Called Love	198?	$20
—Budget-line reissue			
❑ STBB-529	What Is This Thing Called Love?/The Night We Called It a Day	1970	$60
❑ SN-16267	Where Are You	198?	$20
—Budget-line reissue			
❑ W855 [M]	Where Are You?	1957	$100
—Gray label			
❑ W855 [M]	Where Are You?	1959	$80
—Black label with colorband			
❑ SW855 [S]	Where Are You?	1959	$75
—Originals do not include "I Cover the Waterfront"			
❑ SW855 [S]	Where Are You?	196?	$100
—Later releases restore "I Cover the Waterfront"			

CAPITOL PICKWICK SERIES

Number	Title	Yr	NM
❑ PC-3457 [M]	Just One of Those Things	196?	$60
❑ SPC-3457 [R]	Just One of Those Things	196?	$25
❑ PC-3463 [M]	My Cole Porter	196?	$60
❑ SPC-3463 [R]	My Cole Porter	196?	$40
❑ PC-3456 [M]	Nevertheless	196?	$60
❑ SPC-3456 [R]	Nevertheless	196?	$25
❑ PC-3450 [M]	The Nearness of You	196?	$60
❑ SPC-3450 [R]	The Nearness of You	196?	$25
❑ PC-3458 [M]	This Love of Mine	196?	$60
❑ SPC-3458 [R]	This Love of Mine	196?	$25
❑ PC-3452 [M]	Try a Little Tenderness	196?	$60
❑ SPC-3452 [R]	Try a Little Tenderness	196?	$25

COLUMBIA

Number	Title	Yr	NM
❑ CL953 [M]	Adventures of the Heart	1957	$60
❑ PC40707	Christmas Dreaming	1987	$60
—Reissue of CL 1032 with an extra track			
❑ CL1032 [M]	Christmas Dreaming	1957	$150
❑ CL6019 [10]	Christmas Songs by Sinatra	1948	$175
—With "gingerbread man" cover			
❑ CL6019 [10]	Christmas Songs by Sinatra	1949	$150
—With green vinylite cover			
❑ CL2542 [M]	Christmas with Sinatra	1955	$120
—House Party Series" release			
❑ CL1359 [M]	Come Back to Sorrento	1959	$60
❑ CL6096 [10]	Dedicated to You	1952	$175
—Three of the tracks on this LP are alternate takes unavailable on vinyl anywhere else			
❑ CL606 [M]	Frankie	1955	$75
—Cover has drawing of Frank Sinatra wearing a hat			
❑ CL606 [M]	Frankie	1955	$75
—Cover has Frank with Debbie Reynolds			
❑ CL6059 [10]	Frankly Sentimental	1951	$120
❑ CL884 [M]	Frank Sinatra Conducts Music of Alec Wilder	1956	$40
—Reissue of Columbia Masterworks ML 4271			
❑ CL2913 [M]	Frank Sinatra in Hollywood	1968	$150
❑ CS9713 [R]	Frank Sinatra in Hollywood	1968	$30
❑ CL2521 [10]	Get Happy	1955	$120
—House Party Series" release			
❑ CL2474 [M]	Greatest Hits, The Early Years, Vol. 1	1966	$35
❑ CS9274 [R]	Greatest Hits, The Early Years, Vol. 1	1966	$25
❑ PC9274	Greatest Hits, The Early Years, Vol. 1	197?	$20
❑ CL2572 [M]	Greatest Hits, The Early Years, Vol. 2	1966	$35
❑ CS9372 [R]	Greatest Hits, The Early Years, Vol. 2	1966	$25
❑ PC9372	Greatest Hits, The Early Years, Vol. 2	197?	$20
❑ C2X40897	Hello Young Lovers	1988	$60
❑ KG31358	In the Beginning	1971	$40
—Original edition; titles of songs at left on front cover			
❑ PG31358	In the Beginning	197?	$30
—Revised version; titles of songs at right on front cover			
❑ CL6290 [10]	I've Got a Crush on You	1954	$120
❑ CL2539 [10]	I've Got a Crush on You	1955	$120

—House Party Series" release; different contents from CL 6290

Number	Title	Yr	NM
❑ CL1241 [M]	Love Is a Kick	1958	$60
❑ CL1136 [M]	Put Your Dreams Away	1958	$60
❑ CL1448 [M]	Reflections	1959	$120
❑ PC44238 [M]	Sinatra Rarities	1989	$40
❑ CL6143 [10]	Sing and Dance with Frank Sinatra	1953	$120
❑ CL6087 [10]	Songs by Sinatra, Volume 1	1952	$120
❑ CL902 [M]	That Old Feeling	1956	$60
❑ CL1297 [M]	The Broadway Kick	1958	$60
❑ S3L42 [M]	The Essential Frank Sinatra	1966	$175
❑ S3S42 [R]	The Essential Frank Sinatra	1966	$100
❑ CL2739 [M]	The Essential Frank Sinatra, Volume 1	1967	$60
❑ CS9539 [R]	The Essential Frank Sinatra, Volume 1	1967	$30
❑ CL2740 [M]	The Essential Frank Sinatra, Volume 2	1967	$60
❑ CS9540 [R]	The Essential Frank Sinatra, Volume 2	1967	$30
❑ CL2741 [M]	The Essential Frank Sinatra, Volume 3	1967	$60
❑ CS9541 [R]	The Essential Frank Sinatra, Volume 3	1967	$30
❑ C2L6 [M]	The Frank Sinatra Story	1958	$60
❑ CL743 [M]	The Voice	1956	$60
❑ CL743 [M]	The Voice	1999	$60

—Classic Records reissue on audiophile vinyl

Number	Title	Yr	NM
❑ C6X40343	The Voice: The Columbia Years 1943-1952	1986	$150
❑ CAS2475 [DJ]	The Voice: The Columbia Years Sampler	1986	$40
❑ CL6001 [10]	The Voice of Frank Sinatra	1949	$140

—Original in pink paper cover

Number	Title	Yr	NM
❑ CL6001 [10]	The Voice of Frank Sinatra	1950	$120

—Blue cardboard cover

COLUMBIA MASTERWORKS

Number	Title	Yr	NM
❑ ML4271 [M]	Frank Sinatra Conducts Music of Alec Wilder	1955	$175

HARMONY

Number	Title	Yr	NM
❑ HS11390 [R]	Frank Sinatra	1969	$35
❑ KH30318 [R]	Greatest Hits, Early Years	1971	$35
❑ HL7400 [M]	Have Yourself a Merry Little Christmas	1967	$60
❑ HS11200 [R]	Have Yourself a Merry Little Christmas	1967	$50

—At least two different cover designs exist

Number	Title	Yr	NM
❑ HL7405 [M]	Romantic Scenes from the Early Years	1967	$60
❑ HS11205 [R]	Romantic Scenes from the Early Years	1967	$30
❑ HS11277 [R]	Someone to Watch Over Me	1968	$35

LONGINES SYMPHONETTE

Number	Title	Yr	NM
❑ LS-308A	Sinatra: The Works	1972	$150
❑ LS-309A	Sinatra: The Works	1973	$40

—Abridged version of LS-308A

Number	Title	Yr	NM
❑ SYS-5637	Sinatra Like Never Before	1972	$60

—Bonus LP with purchase of LS-308A

MOBILE FIDELITY

Number	Title	Yr	NM
❑ 1-135 [M]	A Jolly Christmas from Frank Sinatra	1984	$100

—Audiophile vinyl using the original title

Number	Title	Yr	NM
❑ Jan-0086	Nice 'N' Easy	1981	$40

—Audiophile vinyl

Number	Title	Yr	NM
❑ SC-1	Sinatra	1983	$800

—Audiophile vinyl; only two of the 16 records in this box were released individually

PAIR

Number	Title	Yr	NM
❑ PDL2-1027	All-Time Classics	1986	$30
❑ PDL2-1122	Classic Performances	1986	$30
❑ PDL2-1028	Timeless	1986	$30

QWEST

Number	Title	Yr	NM
❑ 25145	L.A. Is My Lady	1984	$30

RCA VICTOR

Number	Title	Yr	NM
❑ LPT-3063 [10]	Fabulous Frankie	1953	$120
❑ LPM-1569 [M]	Frankie and Tommy	1957	$120

—First issue of this LP

Number	Title	Yr	NM
❑ AFL1-4741 [R]	Radio Years (Sinatra/ Dorsey/Stordahl)	1983	$35
❑ CPL2-4334	The Sinatra/Dorsey Sessions, Vol. 1	1982	$60
❑ CPL2-4335	The Sinatra/Dorsey Sessions, Vol. 2	1982	$60
❑ CPL2-4336	The Sinatra/Dorsey Sessions, Vol. 3	1982	$60
❑ LPV-583 [M]	This Love of Mine	1971	$40
❑ LPM-1569 [M]	Tommy Plays, Frankie Sings	1957	$40

—Second issue with new title

Number	Title	Yr	NM
❑ LPM-1632 [M]	We Three	1958	$120

—First issue

Number	Title	Yr	NM
❑ LPM-1632 [M]	We Three	1958	$40

—Second issue, "RE" on cover

Number	Title	Yr	NM
❑ APL1-0497 [R]	What'll I Do	1974	$30
❑ ANL1-1050 [R]	What'll I Do	1976	$25

REPRISE

Number	Title	Yr	NM
❑ F1007 [M]	All Alone	1962	$35
❑ R91007 [S]	All Alone	1962	$50
❑ FS1030	A Man Alone & Other Songs of Rod McKuen	1969	$35
❑ FS1030	A Man Alone & Other Songs of Rod McKuen	1969	$400

—Signed copies with gatefold cover and hardbound book; 400 made

Number	Title	Yr	NM
❑ SMAS-92081	A Man Alone & Other Songs of Rod McKuen	1969	$80

—Capitol Record Club edition

Number	Title	Yr	NM
❑ 2F1016 [M]	A Man and His Music	1965	$50
❑ 2FS1016 [S]	A Man and His Music	1965	$60
❑ 5004 [DJ]	A Man and His Music, Part II	1966	$300

—Promotional album for use by Budweiser

Number	Title	Yr	NM
❑ 2F/2FS1016	A Man and His Music Special Box	1965	$200

—Blue slipcase with embossed silver front, raised letters, plus 4-page booklet and a signed card (deduct 50% if card missing). Add this to LP value.

Number	Title	Yr	NM
❑ FS1027	Cycles	1969	$35
❑ F1011 [M]	Days of Wine and Roses, Moon River, and Other Academy Award Winners	1964	$35
❑ FS1011 [S]	Days of Wine and Roses, Moon River, and Other Academy Award Winners	1964	$50
❑ FS1024	Francis A. and Edward K.	1968	$50
❑ F1021 [M]	Francis Albert Sinatra & Antonio Carlos Jobim	1967	$30
❑ FS1021 [S]	Francis Albert Sinatra & Antonio Carlos Jobim	1967	$35
❑ R173798 [S]	Francis Albert Sinatra & Antonio Carlos Jobim	2004	$35

—180-gram reissue

Number	Title	Yr	NM
❑ FS1025	Frank Sinatra's Greatest Hits	1968	$35
❑ FS1034	Frank Sinatra's Greatest Hits, Vol. 2	1972	$35
❑ FS4-1034 [Q]	Frank Sinatra's Greatest Hits, Vol. 2	1974	$40
❑ F1022 [M]	Frank Sinatra (The World We Knew)	1967	$35
❑ FS1022 [S]	Frank Sinatra (The World We Knew)	1967	$35
❑ F1006 [M]	Great Songs from Great Britain	1962	$80

—Only released in the UK

Number	Title	Yr	NM
❑ R91006 [S]	Great Songs from Great Britain	1962	$100

—Only released in the UK

Number	Title	Yr	NM
❑ F1003 [M]	I Remember Tommy	1961	$50
❑ R91003 [S]	I Remember Tommy	1961	$60
❑ 5409 [DJ]	I Sing the Songs	1976	$100
❑ F1012 [M]	It Might As Well Be Swing	1964	$35
❑ FS1012 [S]	It Might As Well Be Swing	1964	$50
❑ F1018 [M]	Moonlight Sinatra	1966	$35
❑ FS1018 [S]	Moonlight Sinatra	1966	$50
❑ F1015 [M]	My Kind of Broadway	1965	$35
❑ FS1015 [S]	My Kind of Broadway	1965	$50
❑ FS1029	My Way	1969	$35
❑ FS41029 [Q]	My Way	1974	$40
❑ FS2155	Ol' Blue Eyes Is Back	1973	$30
❑ FS42155 [Q]	Ol' Blue Eyes Is Back	1974	$40
❑ F1001 [M]	Ring-a-Ding-Ding!	1961	$50
❑ F1014 [M]	September of My Years	1965	$35
❑ FS1014 [S]	September of My Years	1965	$50
❑ R173799 [S]	September of My Years	2004	$35

—180-gram reissue

Number	Title	Yr	NM
❑ FS2305	She Shot Me Down	1981	$30
❑ F1004 [M]	Sinatra & Strings	1962	$35
❑ R91004 [S]	Sinatra & Strings	1962	$50
❑ R6167 [M]	Sinatra '65	1965	$35
❑ RS6167 [S]	Sinatra '65	1965	$50
❑ FS1033	Sinatra and Company	1971	$35
❑ F1005 [M]	Sinatra and Swingin' Brass	1962	$35
❑ R91005 [S]	Sinatra and Swingin' Brass	1962	$50
❑ 2F1019 [M]	Sinatra at the Sands	1966	$50
❑ 2FS1019 [S]	Sinatra at the Sands	1966	$60
❑ F1008 [M]	Sinatra-Basie	1963	$35
❑ R91008 [S]	Sinatra-Basie	1963	$50
❑ F6045 [M]	Sinatra Conducts Music from Pictures and Plays	1962	$60
❑ R96045 [S]	Sinatra Conducts Music from Pictures and Plays	1962	$40
❑ FS1028	SinatraJobim	1969	$4000

—Unreleased; test pressings exist (value is for one of these). 8-track tapes also exist and are 10% of this value; VG value 1000; VG+ value 1000

Number	Title	Yr	NM
❑ R-1010 [M]	Sinatra's Sinatra	1963	$35

—Gatefold jacket; some copies have a large photo of Sinatra holding a pack of Lucky Strikes at the right side of the inside gatefold; we don't yet know the relative rarity of these variations, or which came first, or whether they also exist on stereo copies

Number	Title	Yr	NM
❑ R-1010 [M]	Sinatra's Sinatra	1963	$35

—Gatefold jacket; some copies have eight photos of previous Frank Sinatra Reprise LPs at the right side of the inside gatefold; we don't yet know the relative rarity of these variations, or which came first, or whether they also exist on stereo copies

Number	Title	Yr	NM
❑ R91010 [S]	Sinatra's Sinatra	1963	$50
❑ F1002 [M]	Sinatra Swings	1961	$80

—Retitled version of "Swing Along with Me"; Capitol threatened legal action because of its "Come Swing With Me!" collection

Number	Title	Yr	NM
❑ R91002 [S]	Sinatra Swings	1961	$100

—Retitled version of "Swing Along with Me"; Capitol threatened legal action because of its "Come Swing With Me!" collection

Number	Title	Yr	NM
❑ FS2207	Sinatra -- The Main Event Live	1974	$30
❑ F1013 [M]	Softly, As I Leave You	1964	$35
❑ FS1013 [S]	Softly, As I Leave You	1964	$50
❑ FS2195	Some Nice Things I've Missed	1974	$30
❑ FS42194 [Q]	Some Nice Things I've Missed	1974	$40
❑ 5230 [DJ]	Songbook, Vol. 1	1971	$100
❑ 5267 [DJ]	Songbook, Vol. 2	1972	$175
❑ F1017 [M]	Strangers in the Night	1966	$30
❑ FS1017 [S]	Strangers in the Night	1966	$35
❑ F1002 [M]	Swing Along with Me	1961	$40

—Original title

Number	Title	Yr	NM
❑ R91002 [S]	Swing Along with Me	1961	$100

—Original title

Number	Title	Yr	NM
❑ F1020 [M]	That's Life	1966	$30
❑ FS1020 [S]	That's Life	1966	$35
❑ F1009 [M]	The Concert Sinatra	1963	$35
❑ R91009 [S]	The Concert Sinatra	1963	$60

—Original pressings declare this was recorded in "35mm Stereo

Number	Title	Yr	NM
❑ R91009 [S]	The Concert Sinatra	196?	$50

—Without cover reference to "35mm Stereo

Number	Title	Yr	NM
❑ FS1023	The Sinatra Christmas Album	1967	$175

—Album never released; value is for cover slick

Number	Title	Yr	NM
❑ 3FS2300	Trilogy: Past, Present, Future	1980	$50
❑ FS1031	Watertown	1970	$60

—With gatefold and poster

Number	Title	Yr	NM
❑ SMAS-93119	Watertown	1970	$100

—Capitol Record Club edition; does not contain poster

TIME-LIFE

Number	Title	Yr	NM
❑ SLGD-02	Legendary Singers: Frank Sinatra	1985	$60

SINGER, HAL, AND CHARLIE SHAVERS

Singer plays tenor saxophone. Also see CHARLIE SHAVERS.

Albums

PRESTIGE

Number	Title	Yr	NM
❑ PRLP-7153 [M]	Blue Stompin'	1959	$200

SWINGVILLE

Number	Title	Yr	NM
❑ SVLP-2023 [M]	Blue Stompin'	1961	$50

—Purple label

Number	Title	Yr	NM
❑ SVLP-2023 [M]	Blue Stompin'	1965	$30

—Blue label, trident logo at right

SINGERS UNLIMITED, THE

Vocal quartet: Gene Puerling; Don Shelton (both formerly of THE HI-LO'S); Len Dresslar; and Bonnie Herman.

Albums

BASF

Number	Title	Yr	NM
❑ 21852	The Four of Us	197?	$30
❑ 20903	Try to Remember	197?	$30

PAUSA

Number	Title	Yr	NM
❑ 7100	A Cappella I	198?	$25
❑ 7101	A Cappella II	198?	$25
❑ 7076	A Cappella III	1979	$25
❑ 7062	A Special Blend	197?	$25
❑ 7136	Composer's Corner: The Singers Unlimited Sing Music of Lennon, McCartney and Ellington	198?	$30
❑ 7109	Easy to Love	198?	$25
❑ 7118	Eventide	198?	$25
❑ 7068	Feeling Free	197?	$25
❑ 7121	Four of Us	198?	$25
❑ 7039	Friends	197?	$25

Number	Title	Yr	NM
❑ 7048	Just in Time	197?	$25
❑ 7056	The Singers Unlimited with Rob McConnell and the Boss Brass	197?	$25
VERVE			
❑ 815671-1	A Cappella	1985	$25
❑ 821859-1	Christmas	198?	$30
❑ 817486-1	The Singers Unlimited with Rob McConnell and the Boss Brass	198?	$25

SINGLETON, ZUTTY/ART TATUM

Singleton played drums. Also see ART TATUM.

Albums

Number	Title	Yr	NM
BRUNSWICK			
❑ BL58038 [10]	Battle of Jazz, Vol. 2	1953	$50

SIRAVO, GEORGE

Reeds player, bandleader and arranger.

Albums

Number	Title	Yr	NM
AD-LIB			
❑ 226 [M]	Out on a Limb	196?	$35
❑ S-226 [S]	Out on a Limb	196?	$25
COLUMBIA			
❑ CL6146 [10]	Your Dance Date with George Siravo	1951	$40
DECCA			
❑ DL8464 [M]	Portraits in Hi-Fi	1957	$120
EPIC			
❑ LN3803 [M]	Everything Goes	1961	$75
❑ BN607 [S]	Everything Goes	1961	$40
KAPP			
❑ KL-1016 [M]	Polite Jazz	1956	$30
MERCURY			
❑ MG-20327 [M]	Darling, Please Forgive Me	1958	$150
RCA CAMDEN			
❑ CAL-505 [M]	Siravo Swing Session	1959	$35
❑ CAS-505 [S]	Siravo Swing Session	1959	$25
RCA VICTOR			
❑ LPM-1970 [M]	Swingin' in Hi-Fi in Studio A	1959	$30
❑ LSP-1970 [S]	Swingin' in Hi-Fi in Studio A	1959	$30
TIME			
❑ 52115 [M]	And Then I Wrote Richard Rodgers	196?	$35
❑ S-2115 [S]	And Then I Wrote Richard Rodgers	196?	$25
❑ S-2019 [S]	Seductive Strings	196?	$25
❑ 52019 [M]	Seductive Strings	196?	$35
VIK			
❑ LX-1091 [M]	Old But New	1957	$30
❑ LX-1125 [M]	Swing Hi, Swing Fi	1958	$30

SIVUCA

Albums

Number	Title	Yr	NM
VANGUARD			
❑ VSD-79352	Live at the Village Gate	197?	$30
❑ VSD-79337	Sivuca	197?	$35

SIVUKA

Accordion player, guitarist, keyboard player and male singer.

SIX, THE

Members: Bill Britto; JOHN GLASEL; BOB HAMMER; Eddie Phufe; Sonny Truitt; BOB WILBER.

Albums

Number	Title	Yr	NM
BETHLEHEM			
❑ BCP-28 [M]	The Six	1955	$250
❑ BCP-57 [M]	The View From Jazzbo's Head	1956	$250

SIX AND SEVEN-EIGHTHS STRING BAND, THE

Albums

Number	Title	Yr	NM
FOLKWAYS			
❑ FP-2671 [M]	The Six and Seven-Eighths String Band	195?	$40
❑ FP-671 [M]	The Six and Seven-Eighths String Band	1951	$50

SKJELBRED, RAY

Pianist.

Albums

Number	Title	Yr	NM
EUPHONIC			
❑ 1223	Chicago High Life	198?	$25
STOMP OFF			
❑ SOS-1097	Gin Mill Blues	1985	$25
❑ SOS-1124	Stompin' 'Em Down	1987	$25

SKYWALK

Six-piece Canadian fusion band. Among the members: Kat Hendrikse (drums); Harris Van Berkel (guitar); Rene Worst (bass).

Albums

Number	Title	Yr	NM
ZEBRA			
❑ ZEB-42204	Paradiso	1988	$25
❑ ZEB-5680	Silent Witness	1986	$25
—Reissue of 5004			
❑ ZR5004	Silent Witness	1984	$30
❑ ZEB-5715	The Bohemians	1986	$25

SLACK, FREDDIE

Pianist and bandleader.

Albums

Number	Title	Yr	NM
EMARCY			
❑ MG-36094 [M]	Boogie-Woogie on the 88	1956	$200
PAUSA			
❑ 9027	Behind the Eight-Beat	198?	$25

SLAGLE, STEVE

Alto and soprano saxophone player, clarinetist, flutist and male singer.

Albums

Number	Title	Yr	NM
ATLANTIC			
❑ 81657	Rio Highlife	1986	$25

SLEET, DON

Trumpeter.

Albums

Number	Title	Yr	NM
JAZZLAND			
❑ JLP-45 [M]	All Members	1961	$30
❑ JLP-945 [S]	All Members	1961	$30

SLICKAPHONICS

Members: Ray Anderson (trombone, vocals); Steve Elson (saxophones, vocals); Allan Jaffe (guitar, vocals); Mark Helias (bass, vocals); Jim Payne (drums, vocals).

Albums

Number	Title	Yr	NM
ENJA			
❑ 4024	Wow Bag	1982	$30

SLIDER-GLENN

Albums

Number	Title	Yr	NM
I.T.I.			
❑ JL-031	A Whispered Warning	1986	$25
REEL DREAMS			
❑ 1007	A Whispered Warning	1983	$35

SLINGER, CEES

Pianist and composer.

Albums

Number	Title	Yr	NM
TIMELESS			
❑ LPSJP-225	Sling Shot	1990	$30

SLOANE, CAROL

Female singer.

Albums

Number	Title	Yr	NM
AUDIOPHILE			
❑ AP-195	Sophisticated Lady	1985	$25
CHOICE			
❑ 1025	Cottontail	1979	$35
COLUMBIA			
❑ CL1923 [M]	Carol Sloane Live at 30th Street	1963	$60
❑ CS8723 [S]	Carol Sloane Live at 30th Street	1963	$80
❑ CL1766 [M]	Out of the Blue	1962	$60
❑ CS8566 [S]	Out of the Blue	1962	$80
CONTEMPORARY			
❑ C-14049	Love You Madly	1989	$35
❑ C-14060	The Real Thing	1990	$35

Number	Title	Yr	NM
PROGRESSIVE			
❑ PRO-7047	Carol Sings	1978	$30

SMALL HERD, THE

See CHUBBY JACKSON.

SMALLEY, JUNE

Albums

Number	Title	Yr	NM
CIRCLE			
❑ C-6	June Smalley Swings America	1979	$25

SMALLS, CLIFF

Pianist.

Albums

Number	Title	Yr	NM
MASTER JAZZ			
❑ 8131	Swing and Things	197?	$30

SMART SET, THE

Vocal group.

Albums

Number	Title	Yr	NM
WARNER BROS.			
❑ W-1203 [M]	A New Experience in Vocal Styles	1958	$30
❑ WS-1203 [S]	A New Experience in Vocal Styles	1958	$40

SMIAROWSKI, MIKE

Albums

Number	Title	Yr	NM
SMEAR			
❑ SMR-891	Island Fantasy	1990	$35

SMITH, BARTON

Albums

Number	Title	Yr	NM
FOLKWAYS			
❑ FSP-33856	Realizations	198?	$30

SMITH, BESSIE

Female singer and composer, one of the first recorded female blues singers.

Albums

Number	Title	Yr	NM
COLUMBIA			
❑ CG30126	Any Woman's Blues	1971	$35
❑ CG30818	Empress	1972	$35
❑ CG30450	Empty Bed Blues	1971	$35
❑ CG31093	Nobody's Blues But Mine	1972	$35
❑ GL503 [M]	The Bessie Smith Story, Volume 1	1951	$50
—Maroon label, gold print			
❑ CL855 [M]	The Bessie Smith Story, Volume 1	1956	$30
—Red and black label with six "eye" logos			
❑ CL855 [M]	The Bessie Smith Story, Volume 1	1963	$35
—Red label with "Guaranteed High Fidelity" or "360 Sound Mono			
❑ GL504 [M]	The Bessie Smith Story, Volume 2	1951	$50
—Maroon label, gold print			
❑ CL856 [M]	The Bessie Smith Story, Volume 2	1956	$30
—Red and black label with six "eye" logos			
❑ CL856 [M]	The Bessie Smith Story, Volume 2	1963	$35
—Red label with "Guaranteed High Fidelity" or "360 Sound Mono			
❑ GL505 [M]	The Bessie Smith Story, Volume 3	1951	$50
—Maroon label, gold print			
❑ CL857 [M]	The Bessie Smith Story, Volume 3	1956	$30
—Red and black label with six "eye" logos			
❑ CL857 [M]	The Bessie Smith Story, Volume 3	1963	$35
—Red label with "Guaranteed High Fidelity" or "360 Sound Mono			
❑ GL506 [M]	The Bessie Smith Story, Volume 4	1951	$50

Number	Title	Yr	NM
—Maroon label, gold print			
❏ CL858 [M]	The Bessie Smith Story, Volume 4	1956	$30
—Red and black label with six "eye" logos			
❏ CL858 [M]	The Bessie Smith Story, Volume 4	1963	$35
—Red label with "Guaranteed High Fidelity" or "360 Sound Mono			
❏ C247091	The Complete Recordings Volume 1: Empress of the Blues	1991	$25
—Box set; none of the subsequent volumes came out on vinyl			
❏ GP33	The World's Greatest Blues Singer	1970	$25
COLUMBIA MASTERWORKS			
❏ ML4801 [M]	The Bessie Smith Story, Volume 1	1954	$40
❏ ML4802 [M]	The Bessie Smith Story, Volume 2	1954	$40
❏ ML4809 [M]	The Bessie Smith Story, Volume 3	1954	$40
❏ ML4810 [M]	The Bessie Smith Story, Volume 4	1954	$40
TIME-LIFE			
❏ STL-J-28	Giants of Jazz	1982	$50

SMITH, BILL
Clarinetist and composer.
Albums

Number	Title	Yr	NM
CONTEMPORARY			
❏ M-3591 [M]	Folk Jazz	1961	$200
❏ S-7591 [S]	Folk Jazz	1961	$200
ONARI			
❏ 04	Pick a Number	198?	$30

SMITH, BUSTER
Alto saxophone player. Also played clarinet and guitar.
Albums

Number	Title	Yr	NM
ATLANTIC			
❏ 1323 [M]	The Legendary Buster Smith	1960	$250
—Black label			
❏ 1323 [M]	The Legendary Buster Smith	1961	$150
—Multi-color label, white "fan" logo			
❏ SD1323 [S]	The Legendary Buster Smith	1960	$250
—Green label			
❏ SD1323 [S]	The Legendary Buster Smith	1961	$150
—Multi-color label, white "fan" logo			

SMITH, CARRIE
Female singer.
Albums

Number	Title	Yr	NM
AUDIOPHILE			
❏ AP-164	Fine and Mellow	198?	$25
CLASSIC JAZZ			
❏ 139	Do Your Duty	197?	$35
WEST 54			
❏ 8002	Carrie Smith	197?	$35

SMITH, DAN
Albums

Number	Title	Yr	NM
BIOGRAPH			
❏ LP-12036	God Is Not Dead	197?	$25

SMITH, DEREK
Pianist. Also see DICK KATZ.
Albums

Number	Title	Yr	NM
PROGRESSIVE			
❏ PRO-7055	Derek Smith Plays Jerome Kern	198?	$25
❏ PRO-7002	Love for Sale	197?	$30
❏ PRO-7035	The Man I Love	197?	$30

SMITH, DWAYNE, AND ART JOHNSON
Smith is a pianist; Johnson plays guitar.
Albums

Number	Title	Yr	NM
CAFÉ			
❏ L-729	Heartbound	1985	$25

SMITH, GREG AND BEV
Both are baritone saxophone players. Greg also plays soprano sax and clarinet; Bev also plays bass clarinet and flute.
Albums

Number	Title	Yr	NM
INTIMA			
❏ SJE-73291	Mr. and Mrs. Smith: No Baggage	1987	$30

SMITH, HAL
Drummer and bandleader.
Albums

Number	Title	Yr	NM
JAZZOLOGY			
❏ J-136	Hal Smith and His Rhythmakers with Butch Thompson	1985	$25
STOMP OFF			
❏ SOS-1078	Do What Ory Say!	1985	$25

SMITH, JABBO
Trumpeter.
Albums

Number	Title	Yr	NM
MCA			
❏ 1347	Ace of Rhythm	198?	$25
MELODEON			
❏ 7326	Trumpet Ace of the 20s, Vol. 1	197?	$30
❏ 7327	Trumpet Ace of the 20s, Vol. 2	197?	$30

SMITH, JIMMY, AND WES MONTGOMERY
Also see each artist's individual listings.
Albums

Number	Title	Yr	NM
VERVE			
❏ V-8678 [M]	Jimmy and Wes, The Dynamic Duo	1967	$50
❏ V6-8678 [S]	Jimmy and Wes, The Dynamic Duo	1967	$35
❏ UMV-2069	Jimmy and Wes, The Dynamic Duo	198?	$25
—Reissue of 8678			
❏ V6-8766	The Further Adventures of Jimmy Smith and Wes Montgomery	1969	$35

SMITH, JIMMY
Organist. Also see BEVERLY KENNEY.
Albums

Number	Title	Yr	NM
BLUE NOTE			
❏ BLP-1547 [M]	A Date with Jimmy Smith, Vol. 1	1957	$1000
—Regular edition, W. 63rd St. address on label			
❏ BLP-1547 [M]	A Date with Jimmy Smith, Vol. 1	1963	$200
—With New York, USA address on label			
❏ BST-81547 [R]	A Date with Jimmy Smith, Vol. 1	1967	$30
❏ BLP-1548 [M]	A Date with Jimmy Smith, Vol. 2	1957	$800
—Regular edition, W. 63rd St. address on label			
❏ BLP-1548 [M]	A Date with Jimmy Smith, Vol. 2	1963	$300
—With New York, USA address on label			
❏ BST-81548 [R]	A Date with Jimmy Smith, Vol. 2	1967	$30
❏ BLP-4117 [M]	Back at the Chicken Shack	1963	$100
❏ BST-84117 [S]	Back at the Chicken Shack	1963	$60
—With New York, USA address on label			
❏ BST-84117 [S]	Back at the Chicken Shack	1967	$35
—With "A Division of Liberty Records" on label			
❏ BST-84117	Back at the Chicken Shack	1985	$25
—The Finest in Jazz Since 1939" reissue			
❏ BLP-4235 [M]	Bucket!	1966	$100
❏ BST-84235 [S]	Bucket!	1966	$60
—With New York, USA address on label			
❏ BST-84235 [S]	Bucket!	1967	$35
—With "A Division of Liberty Records" on label			
❏ LT-992	Confirmation	1979	$25
❏ LT-1054	Cool Blues	1980	$25
❏ BLP-4030 [M]	Crazy Baby	1960	$150
—Regular edition, W. 63rd St. address on label			
❏ BLP-4030 [M]	Crazy Baby	1963	$100
—With New York, USA address on label			
❏ BST-84030 [S]	Crazy Baby	1960	$100
—With W. 63rd St. address on label			
❏ BST-84030 [S]	Crazy Baby	1963	$50
—With New York, USA address on label			
❏ BST-84030 [S]	Crazy Baby	1967	$35
—With "A Division of Liberty Records" on label			
❏ B1-84030	Crazy Baby	1988	$25
—The Finest in Jazz Since 1939" reissue			
❏ B1-85125	Go For Whatcha Know	198?	$25
❏ BLP-1585 [M]	Groovin' at Small's Paradise, Vol. 1	1958	$300
—Regular edition, W. 63rd St. address on label			
❏ BLP-1585 [M]	Groovin' at Small's Paradise, Vol. 1	1963	$200
—With New York, USA address on label			
❏ BST-1585 [S]	Groovin' at Small's Paradise, Vol. 1	1959	$200
—Regular edition, W. 63rd St. address on label			
❏ BST-1585 [S]	Groovin' at Small's Paradise, Vol. 1	1963	$150
—With New York, USA address on label			
❏ BST-81585 [S]	Groovin' at Small's Paradise, Vol. 1	1967	$35
❏ BST-81586 [S]	Groovin' at Small's Paradise, Vol. 1	1967	$35
❏ BLP-1586 [M]	Groovin' at Small's Paradise, Vol. 2	1958	$300
—Regular edition, W. 63rd St. address on label			
❏ BLP-1586 [M]	Groovin' at Small's Paradise, Vol. 2	1963	$200
—With New York, USA address on label			
❏ BST-1586 [S]	Groovin' at Small's Paradise, Vol. 2	1959	$200
—Regular edition, W. 63rd St. address on label			
❏ BST-1586 [S]	Groovin' at Small's Paradise, Vol. 2	1963	$150
—With New York, USA address on label			
❏ BLP-4050 [M]	Home Cookin'	1961	$200
—With W. 63rd St. address on label			
❏ BST-84050 [S]	Home Cookin'	1961	$100
—With W. 63rd St. address on label			
❏ BST-84050 [S]	Home Cookin'	1963	$50
—With New York, USA address on label			
❏ BST-84050 [S]	Home Cookin'	1967	$35
—With "A Division of Liberty Records" on label			
❏ BLP-4002 [M]	House Party	1959	$150
—Regular edition, W. 63rd St. address on label			
❏ BLP-4002 [M]	House Party	1963	$100
—With New York, USA address on label			
❏ BST-4002 [S]	House Party	1959	$100
—Regular edition, W. 63rd St. address on label			
❏ BST-4002 [S]	House Party	1963	$50
—With New York, USA address on label			
❏ BST-84002 [S]	House Party	1967	$35
❏ BST-84002	House Party	1985	$25
—The Finest in Jazz Since 1939" reissue			
❏ BLP-4255 [M]	I'm Movin' On	1967	$100
❏ BST-84255 [S]	I'm Movin' On	1967	$50
❏ BN-LA400-H2	Jimmy Smith	1975	$35
❏ BLP-1512 [M]	Jimmy Smith at the Organ, Vol. 1	1956	$850
—Regular edition, Lexington Ave. address on label			
❏ BLP-1512 [M]	Jimmy Smith at the Organ, Vol. 1	1963	$100
—With New York, USA address on label			
❏ BLP-1551 [M]	Jimmy Smith at the Organ, Vol. 1	1957	$250
—Regular edition, W. 63rd St. address on label			
❏ BLP-1551 [M]	Jimmy Smith at the Organ, Vol. 1	1963	$200
—With New York, USA address on label			
❏ BST-81512 [R]	Jimmy Smith at the Organ, Vol. 1	1967	$30
❏ BST-81551 [R]	Jimmy Smith at the Organ, Vol. 1	1967	$30
❏ BLP-1514 [M]	Jimmy Smith at the Organ, Vol. 2	1956	$1000
—Regular edition, Lexington Ave. address on label			
❏ BLP-1514 [M]	Jimmy Smith at the Organ, Vol. 2	1963	$150
—With New York, USA address on label			
❏ BLP-1552 [M]	Jimmy Smith at the Organ, Vol. 2	1957	$250
—Regular edition, W. 63rd St. address on label			

Sonny Stitt, *Sonny Stitt Now!*, Impulse! A-43, mono, **$200**.

Sonny Stitt, *The Hard Swing*, Verve MGV-8306, **$100**.

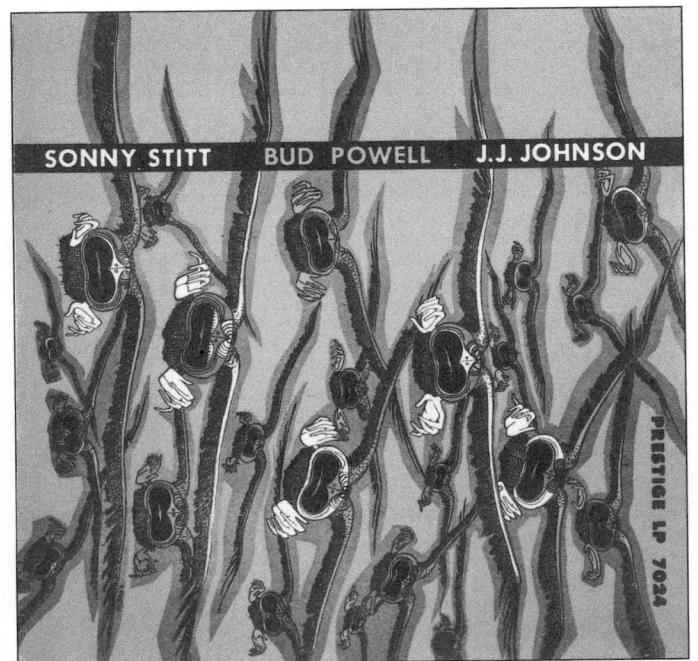

Sonny Stitt, Bud Powell, J.J. Johnson, *Sonny Stitt, Bud Powell, J.J. Johnson*, Prestige PRLP-7024, yellow label with W. 50th St. address, **$450**.

Ira Sullivan, *Horizons*, Atlantic 1476, mono, **$30**.

Number	Title	Yr	NM
❑ BLP-1552 [M]	Jimmy Smith at the Organ, Vol. 2	1963	$200
— With New York, USA address on label			
❑ BST-81514 [R]	Jimmy Smith at the Organ, Vol. 2	1967	$30
❑ BST-81552 [R]	Jimmy Smith at the Organ, Vol. 2	1967	$30
❑ BLP-4100 [M]	Jimmy Smith Plays Fats Waller	1962	$200
— With 61st St. address on label			
❑ BLP-4100 [M]	Jimmy Smith Plays Fats Waller	1963	$100
— With New York, USA address on label			
❑ BST-84100 [S]	Jimmy Smith Plays Fats Waller	1962	$100
— With 61st St. address on label			
❑ BST-84100 [S]	Jimmy Smith Plays Fats Waller	1963	$50
— With New York, USA address on label			
❑ BST-84100 [S]	Jimmy Smith Plays Fats Waller	1967	$35
— With "A Division of Liberty Records" on label			
❑ BLP-1563 [M]	Jimmy Smith Plays Pretty Just for You	1957	$150
— Regular edition, W. 63rd St. address on label			
❑ BLP-1563 [M]	Jimmy Smith Plays Pretty Just for You	1963	$0
— With New York, USA address on label			
❑ BST-1563 [S]	Jimmy Smith Plays Pretty Just for You	1959	$100
— Regular edition, W. 63rd St. address on label			
❑ BST-1563 [S]	Jimmy Smith Plays Pretty Just for You	1963	$150
— With New York, USA address on label			
❑ BST-81563 [S]	Jimmy Smith Plays Pretty Just for You	1967	$35
❑ BST-89901	Jimmy Smith's Greatest Hits!	1969	$60
❑ LWB-89901	Jimmy Smith's Greatest Hits!	198?	$35
❑ BLP-4078 [M]	Midnight Special	1961	$200
— With 61st St. address on label			
❑ BLP-4078 [M]	Midnight Special	1963	$100
— With New York, USA address on label			
❑ BST-84078 [S]	Midnight Special	1961	$100
— With 61st St. address on label			
❑ BST-84078 [S]	Midnight Special	1963	$50
— With New York, USA address on label			
❑ BST-84078 [S]	Midnight Special	1967	$35
— With "A Division of Liberty Records" on label			
❑ B1-84078	Midnight Special	1989	$25
— The Finest in Jazz Since 1939" reissue			
❑ LT-1092	On the Sunny Side	1981	$25
❑ BST-84269	Open House	1968	$50
❑ BST-84296	Plain Talk	1969	$50
❑ BLP-4164 [M]	Prayer Meetin'	1964	$100
❑ BST-84164 [S]	Prayer Meetin'	1964	$60
— With New York, USA address on label			
❑ BST-84164 [S]	Prayer Meetin'	1967	$35
— With "A Division of Liberty Records" on label			
❑ B1-84164	Prayer Meetin'	1988	$25
— The Finest in Jazz Since 1939" reissue			
❑ BLP-4141 [M]	Rockin' the Boat	1963	$100
❑ BST-84141 [S]	Rockin' the Boat	1963	$60
— With New York, USA address on label			
❑ BST-84141 [S]	Rockin' the Boat	1967	$35
— With "A Division of Liberty Records" on label			
❑ BLP-4200 [M]	Softly as a Summer Breeze	1965	$100
❑ BST-84200 [S]	Softly as a Summer Breeze	1965	$60
— With New York, USA address on label			
❑ BST-84200 [S]	Softly as a Summer Breeze	1967	$35
— With "A Division of Liberty Records" on label			
❑ B1-91140	The Best of Jimmy Smith	1988	$25
❑ BLP-1528 [M]	The Incredible Jimmy Smith at Club Baby Grand, Wilmington, Delaware, Vol. 1	1956	$1000
— Deep groove" version (deep indentation under label on both sides)			
❑ BLP-1528 [M]	The Incredible Jimmy Smith at Club Baby Grand, Wilmington, Delaware, Vol. 1	1956	$800
— Regular edition, Lexington Ave. address on label			
❑ BLP-1528 [M]	The Incredible Jimmy Smith at Club Baby Grand, Wilmington, Delaware, Vol. 1	1963	$100
— With New York, USA address on label			

Number	Title	Yr	NM
❑ BST-81528 [R]	The Incredible Jimmy Smith at Club Baby Grand, Wilmington, Delaware, Vol. 1	1967	$30
❑ BLP-1529 [M]	The Incredible Jimmy Smith at Club Baby Grand, Wilmington, Delaware, Vol. 2	1956	$1000
— Deep groove" version (deep indentation under label on both sides)			
❑ BLP-1529 [M]	The Incredible Jimmy Smith at Club Baby Grand, Wilmington, Delaware, Vol. 2	1956	$755
— Regular edition, Lexington Ave. address on label			
❑ BLP-1529 [M]	The Incredible Jimmy Smith at Club Baby Grand, Wilmington, Delaware, Vol. 2	1963	$150
— With New York, USA address on label			
❑ BST-81529 [R]	The Incredible Jimmy Smith at Club Baby Grand, Wilmington, Delaware, Vol. 2	1967	$30
❑ BLP-1525 [M]	The Incredible Jimmy Smith at the Organ, Vol. 3	1956	$150
— Deep groove" version (deep indentation under label on both sides)			
❑ BLP-1525 [M]	The Incredible Jimmy Smith at the Organ, Vol. 3	1956	$175
— Regular edition, Lexington Ave. address on label			
❑ BLP-1525 [M]	The Incredible Jimmy Smith at the Organ, Vol. 3	1963	$100
— With New York, USA address on label			
❑ BST-81525 [R]	The Incredible Jimmy Smith at the Organ, Vol. 3	1967	$30
❑ BLP-4011 [M]	The Sermon	1959	$200
— Deep groove" version (deep indentation under label on both sides)			
❑ BLP-4011 [M]	The Sermon	1959	$150
— Regular edition, W. 63rd St. address on label			
❑ BLP-4011 [M]	The Sermon	1963	$100
— With New York, USA address on label			
❑ BST-4011 [S]	The Sermon	1959	$150
— Deep groove" version (deep indentation under label on both sides)			
❑ BST-4011 [S]	The Sermon	1959	$100
— Regular edition, W. 63rd St. address on label			
❑ BST-4011 [S]	The Sermon	1963	$50
— With New York, USA address on label			
❑ BST-84011 [S]	The Sermon	1967	$35
❑ BLP-1556 [M]	The Sounds of Jimmy Smith	1957	$2000
— Deep groove" version (deep indentation under label on both sides)			
❑ BLP-1556 [M]	The Sounds of Jimmy Smith	1957	$250
— Regular edition, W. 63rd St. address on label			
❑ BLP-1556 [M]	The Sounds of Jimmy Smith	1963	$200
— With New York, USA address on label			
❑ BST-81556 [R]	The Sounds of Jimmy Smith	1967	$30
ELEKTRA/MUSICIAN			
❑ 60301	Keep On Comin'	1984	$25
❑ 60175	Off the Top	1983	$25
GUEST STAR			
❑ G1914 [M]	Jimmy Smith	196?	$30
❑ 1344 [M]	Jimmy Smith	196?	$30
INNER CITY			
❑ 1121	The Cat Strikes Again	1981	$25
MERCURY			
❑ SRM-1-1189	It's Necessary	1977	$25
❑ SRM-1-1127	Sit On It!	1976	$25
❑ SRM-1-3716	Unfinished Business	1978	$25
METRO			
❑ M-521 [M]	Jimmy Smith at the Village Gate	1965	$150
❑ MS-521 [S]	Jimmy Smith at the Village Gate	1965	$150
❑ M-568 [M]	Live In Concert/The Incredible Jimmy Smith	196?	$150
❑ M-568 [S]	Live In Concert/The Incredible Jimmy Smith	196?	$150
MGM			
❑ SE-4751	I'm Gon' Git Myself Together	1971	$30
❑ GAS-107	Jimmy Smith (Golden Archive Series)	1970	$35
❑ SE-4709	The Other Side	1970	$30
MILESTONE			
❑ M-9176	Prime Time	198?	$25
MOSAIC			
❑ MQ5-154 [B]	The Complete February 1957 Jimmy Smith Blue Note Sessions	199?	$1000
PICKWICK			

Number	Title	Yr	NM
❑ SPC-3023	Stranger in Paradise	196?	$25
PRIDE			
❑ 6011	Black Smith	1974	$30
SUNSET			
❑ SUM-1175 [M]	Jimmy Smith Plays the Standards	1967	$35
❑ SUS-5175 [S]	Jimmy Smith Plays the Standards	1967	$30
❑ SUS-5316	Just Friends	1971	$30
VERVE			
❑ V6-652-2	24 Karat Hits	196?	$35
❑ V6-8552 [S]	Any Number Can Win	1963	$60
❑ 823308-1	Bashin'	1986	$25
— Reissue of 8474			
❑ V6-8809	Bluesmith	1973	$30
❑ V-8604 [M]	Christmas '64	1964	$50
❑ V6-8604 [S]	Christmas '64	1964	$60
❑ V6-8666 [M]	Christmas Cookin'	1966	$50
❑ V6-8666 [S]	Christmas Cookin'	1966	$60
❑ V-8641 [M]	Got My Mojo Workin'	1966	$35
❑ V6-8641 [S]	Got My Mojo Workin'	1966	$50
❑ MAS-90751 [M]	Got My Mojo Workin'	1966	$80
— Capitol Record Club edition			
❑ SMAS-90751 [S]	Got My Mojo Workin'	1966	$60
❑ V6-8794	Groove Drops	1970	$35
❑ V6-8814	History of Jimmy Smith	1973	$30
❑ V6-8667 [M]	Hoochie Coochie Man	1966	$35
❑ V6-8667 [S]	Hoochie Coochie Man	1966	$50
❑ V6-8750	Livin' It Up!	1968	$35
❑ V-8628 [M]	Organ Grinder Swing	1965	$35
❑ V6-8628 [S]	Organ Grinder Swing	1965	$50
❑ UMV-2073	Organ Grinder Swing	198?	$25
— Reissue of 8628			
❑ V-8652 [M]	Peter and the Wolf	1966	$50
❑ V6-8652 [S]	Peter and the Wolf	1966	$60
❑ V6-8800	Plain Brown Wrapper	1971	$30
❑ V6-8832	Portuguese Soul	1974	$30
❑ V-8705 [M]	Respect	1967	$50
❑ V6-8705 [S]	Respect	1967	$35
❑ V6-8806	Root Down	1972	$30
❑ V6-8745 [S]	Stay Loose	1968	$35
❑ V-8721 [M]	The Best of Jimmy Smith	1967	$50
❑ V6-8721 [S]	The Best of Jimmy Smith	1967	$35
❑ V6-8770	The Boss	1969	$35
❑ V6-8587 [S]	The Cat	1964	$60
❑ V-8618 [M]	The Monster	1965	$35
❑ V6-8618 [S]	The Monster	1965	$50
❑ SMAS-90643 [S]	The Monster	1965	$100
— Capitol Record Club edition			
❑ V-8583 [M]	Who's Afraid of Virginia Woolf?	1964	$50
❑ V6-8583 [S]	Who's Afraid of Virginia Woolf?	1964	$60

SMITH, JOHNNY "HAMMOND
See JOHNNY HAMMOND.

SMITH, JOHNNY
Guitarist and composer; he wrote "Moonlight in Vermont." Also see JERI SOUTHERN.

Albums

Number	Title	Yr	NM
LEGENDE			
❑ 1401 [10]	Annotations of the Muses	1955	$100
ROOST			
❑ R-410 [10]	A Three-Dimension Sound Recording of Jazz at NBC with the Johnny Smith Quintet	1953	$150
❑ LP-2239 [M]	Dear Little Sweetheart	1960	$30
❑ SLP-2239 [S]	Dear Little Sweetheart	1960	$40
❑ LP-2238 [M]	Designed for You	1960	$30
❑ SLP-2238 [S]	Designed for You	1960	$40
❑ LP-2233 [M]	Easy Listening	1959	$40
❑ SLP-2233 [S]	Easy Listening	1959	$30
❑ LP-2237 [M]	Favorites	1959	$40
❑ SLP-2237 [S]	Favorites	1959	$30
❑ LP-2231 [M]	Flower Drum Song	1958	$40
❑ SLP-2231 [S]	Flower Drum Song	1958	$30
❑ LP-2242 [M]	Guitar and Strings	1960	$30
❑ SLP-2242 [S]	Guitar and Strings	1960	$40
❑ LP-2254 [M]	Guitar World	1963	$30
❑ SLP-2254 [S]	Guitar World	1963	$30
❑ R-421 [10]	In a Mellow Mood	1954	$100
❑ R-424 [10]	In a Sentimental Mood	1954	$100
❑ LP-2223 [M]	Johnny Smith Foursome, Volume 1	1956	$50
❑ LP-2228 [M]	Johnny Smith Foursome, Volume 2	1957	$50
❑ LP-2201 [M]	Johnny Smith Plays Jimmy Van Heusen	1955	$80
❑ LP-2250 [M]	Johnny Smith Plays Jimmy Van Heusen	1963	$30
❑ SLP-2250 [S]	Johnny Smith Plays Jimmy Van Heusen	1963	$30
❑ LP-2243 [M]	Johnny Smith Plus the Trio	1960	$30
❑ SLP-2243 [S]	Johnny Smith Plus the Trio	1960	$40

Number	Title	Yr	NM
❏ LP-2203 [M]	Johnny Smith Quartet	1955	$80
❏ R-413 [10]	Johnny Smith Quintet	1953	$120
❏ LP-2248 [M]	Man with the Blue Guitar	1962	$30
❏ SLP-2248 [S]	Man with the Blue Guitar	1962	$40
❏ LP-2215 [M]	Moods	1956	$60
❏ LP-2211 [M]	Moonlight in Vermont	1956	$80
❏ LP-2216 [M]	New Quartet	1956	$60
❏ LP-2259 [M]	Reminiscing	1965	$30
❏ SLP-2259 [S]	Reminiscing	1965	$30
❏ LP-2246 [M]	The Sound of the Johnny Smith Guitar	1961	$30
❏ SLP-2246 [S]	The Sound of the Johnny Smith Guitar	1961	$40

VERVE

Number	Title	Yr	NM
❏ V-8692 [M]	Johnny Smith	1967	$30
❏ V6-8692 [S]	Johnny Smith	1967	$25
❏ V-8737 [M]	Johnny Smith's Kaleidoscope	1968	$30
❏ V6-8737 [S]	Johnny Smith's Kaleidoscope	1968	$25
❏ V6-8767 [S]	Phase II	1969	$25

SMITH, KEELY

Female singer. Also see LOUIS PRIMA AND KEELY SMITH.

Albums

CAPITOL

Number	Title	Yr	NM
❏ W914 [M]	I Wish You Love	1957	$80
—Turquoise label			
❏ W914 [M]	I Wish You Love	1959	$60
—Black label with colorband, Capitol logo at left			
❏ W914 [M]	I Wish You Love	1962	$40
—Black label with colorband, Capitol logo at top			
❏ SW914 [S]	I Wish You Love	1959	$60
—Black label with colorband, Capitol logo at left			
❏ SW914 [S]	I Wish You Love	1962	$40
—Black label with colorband, Capitol logo at top			
❏ T1073 [M]	Politely!	1958	$75
—Black label with colorband, Capitol logo at left			
❏ T1073 [M]	Politely!	1962	$40
—Black label with colorband, Capitol logo at left			
❏ ST1073 [S]	Politely!	1959	$80
—Black label with colorband, Capitol logo at left			
❏ ST1073 [S]	Politely!	1962	$50
—Black label with colorband, Capitol logo at top			
❏ T1145 [M]	Swingin' Pretty	1959	$75
—Black label with colorband, Capitol logo at left			
❏ T1145 [M]	Swingin' Pretty	1962	$40
—Black label with colorband, Capitol logo at top			
❏ ST1145 [S]	Swingin' Pretty	1959	$80
—Black label with colorband, Capitol logo at left			
❏ ST1145 [S]	Swingin' Pretty	1962	$50
—Black label with colorband, Capitol logo at top			

DOT

Number	Title	Yr	NM
❏ DLP-3345 [M]	A Keely Christmas	1961	$75
❏ DLP-25345 [S]	A Keely Christmas	1961	$75
❏ DLP-3415 [M]	Because You're Mine	1962	$75
❏ DLP-25415 [S]	Because You're Mine	1962	$75
❏ DLP-3241 [M]	Be My Love	1959	$75
❏ DLP-25241 [S]	Be My Love	1959	$75
❏ DLP-3460 [M]	Cherokeely Swings	1962	$75
❏ DLP-25460 [S]	Cherokeely Swings	1962	$75
❏ DLP-3287 [M]	Dearly Beloved	1961	$75
❏ DLP-25287 [S]	Dearly Beloved	1961	$75
❏ DLP-3265 [M]	Swing, You Lovers	1960	$75
❏ DLP-25265 [S]	Swing, You Lovers	1960	$75
❏ DLP-3423 [M]	Twist with Keely Smith	1962	$75
❏ DLP-25423 [S]	Twist with Keely Smith	1962	$75
❏ DLP-3461 [M]	What Kind of Fool Am I	1962	$75
❏ DLP-25461 [S]	What Kind of Fool Am I	1962	$75

HARMONY

Number	Title	Yr	NM
❏ HS11333	That Old Black Magic	1968	$15

REPRISE

Number	Title	Yr	NM
❏ R-6142 [M]	Keely Smith Sings the John Lennon/Paul McCartney Songbook	1964	$30
❏ RS-6142 [S]	Keely Smith Sings the John Lennon/Paul McCartney Songbook	1964	$30
❏ R-6086 [M]	Little Girl Blue, Little Girl New	1963	$25
❏ R9-6086 [S]	Little Girl Blue, Little Girl New	1963	$30
❏ R-6175 [M]	That Old Black Magic	1965	$25
❏ RS-6175 [S]	That Old Black Magic	1965	$30
❏ R-6132 [M]	The Intimate Keely Smith	1964	$25
❏ RS-6132 [S]	The Intimate Keely Smith	1964	$30

SMITH, KEITH

Trumpeter and bandleader.

Albums

GHB

Number	Title	Yr	NM
❏ GHB-27	Keith Smith's Climax Jazz Band	196?	$30

SMITH, LAVERGNE

Female singer.

Albums

COOK

Number	Title	Yr	NM
❏ LP-1081 [10]	Angel in the Absinthe House	1955	$150

SAVOY

Number	Title	Yr	NM
❏ MG-12031 [M]	New Orleans Nightingale	1955	$60

VIK

Number	Title	Yr	NM
❏ LX-1056 [M]	La Vergne Smith	1956	$50

SMITH, LEO

Trumpeter, fluegel horn player, flutist and percussionist.

Albums

BLACK SAINT

Number	Title	Yr	NM
❏ BSR-0053	Go in Numbers	198?	$30

ECM

Number	Title	Yr	NM
❏ 1143	Divine Love	1979	$30

KABELL

Number	Title	Yr	NM
❏ CM-1	Creative Music-1	197?	$35

NESSA

Number	Title	Yr	NM
❏ N-19	Spirit Catcher	1980	$35

SACKVILLE

Number	Title	Yr	NM
❏ 3030	Rastafari	198?	$25

SMITH, LONNIE

Organist.

Albums

BLUE NOTE

Number	Title	Yr	NM
❏ BST-84351	Drives	1971	$35
❏ B1-28266	Drives	1994	$35
❏ B1-31880	Live at Club Mozambique	1995	$35
❏ BST-84326	Move Your Hand	1970	$35
❏ B1-31249	Move Your Hand	1996	$35
❏ BST-84290	Think!	1968	$50
❏ BST-84313	Turning Point	1969	$50

CHIAROSCURO

Number	Title	Yr	NM
❏ 2019	When the Night Is Right	1979	$30

COLUMBIA

Number	Title	Yr	NM
❏ CL2696 [M]	Finger-Lickin' Good Soul Organ	1967	$60
❏ CS9496 [S]	Finger-Lickin' Good Soul Organ	1967	$50

GROOVE MERCHANT

Number	Title	Yr	NM
❏ 3308	Afro-Desia	1975	$30
❏ 3312	Keep On Lovin'	1976	$30

KUDU

Number	Title	Yr	NM
❏ 02	Mama Wailer	1972	$30

SMITH, LONNIE LISTON

Pianist and keyboard player.

Albums

BLUEBIRD

Number	Title	Yr	NM
❏ 6996-1-RB	Golden Dreams	1988	$25

COLUMBIA

Number	Title	Yr	NM
❏ JC35654	Exotic Mysteries	1979	$25
❏ JC36373	Love Is the Answer	1980	$25
❏ JC35332	Loveland	1978	$25
❏ JC36141	Song for the Children	1979	$25
❏ JC36366	The Best of Lonnie Liston Smith	1980	$25

DOCTOR JAZZ

Number	Title	Yr	NM
❏ FW38447	Dreams of Tomorrow	1983	$25
❏ FW40063	Rejuvenation	1985	$25
❏ FW39420	Silhouettes	1984	$25

FLYING DUTCHMAN

Number	Title	Yr	NM
❏ 10163	Astral Travelling	1973	$30
❏ BDL1-0591	Cosmic Funk	1974	$30
❏ BXL1-0591	Cosmic Funk	1978	$20
—Reissue with new prefix			
❏ BDL1-0934	Expressions	1975	$30
❏ BXL1-0934	Expressions	1978	$20
—Reissue with new prefix			
❏ BDL1-1460	Reflections of a Golden Dream	1976	$30
❏ BXL1-1460	Reflections of a Golden Dream	1978	$20
—Reissue with new prefix			
❏ BDL1-1196	Visions of a New World	1975	$30
❏ BXL1-1196	Visions of a New World	1978	$20
—Reissue with new prefix			

RCA VICTOR

Number	Title	Yr	NM
❏ APL1-2433	Live!	1977	$25
❏ AFL1-2433	Live!	1978	$20
—Reissue with new prefix			
❏ APL1-1822	Renaissance	1976	$25
❏ AFL1-1822	Renaissance	1978	$20
—Reissue with new prefix			
❏ AFL1-2897	The Best of Lonnie Liston Smith	1978	$25

STARTRAK

Number	Title	Yr	NM
❏ STA-4021	Love Goddess	198?	$25

SMITH, LOUIS

Trumpeter and fluegel horn player.

Albums

BLUE NOTE

Number	Title	Yr	NM
❏ BST-81584 [S]	Here Comes Louis Smith	1967	$35
— With "A Division of Liberty Records" on label			
❏ BLP-1594 [M]	Smithville	1958	$1500
—Deep groove" version (deep indentation under label on both sides)			
❏ BLP-1594 [M]	Smithville	1958	$1500
— Regular version, W. 63rd St. address on label			
❏ BST-1594 [S]	Smithville	1959	$800
—Deep groove" version (deep indentation under label on both sides)			
❏ BST-1594 [S]	Smithville	1959	$600
— Regular version, W. 63rd St. address on label			
❏ BST-81594 [S]	Smithville	1967	$35
— With "A Division of Liberty Records" on label			

STEEPLECHASE

Number	Title	Yr	NM
❏ SCS-1096	Just Friends	198?	$30
❏ SCS-1121	Prancin'	1979	$30

SMITH, MARVIN "SMITTY"

Drummer.

Albums

CONCORD JAZZ

Number	Title	Yr	NM
❏ CJ-325	Keeper of the Drums	1987	$25
❏ CJ-379	The Road Less Traveled	1989	$30

SMITH, MICHAEL

Albums

STORYVILLE

Number	Title	Yr	NM
❏ 4014	Reflection on Progress	1980	$30

SMITH, MIKE

Alto saxophone player.

Albums

DELMARK

Number	Title	Yr	NM
❏ DS-444	Unit 7: A Tribute to Cannonball Adderley	1990	$30

SMITH, OSBORNE

Male singer.

Albums

ARGO

Number	Title	Yr	NM
❏ LP-4000 [M]	Eyes of Love	1960	$30
❏ LPS-4000 [S]	Eyes of Love	1960	$40

SMITH, PAUL; RAY BROWN; LOUIS BELLSON

Also see each artist's individual listings.

Albums

DISCWASHER

Number	Title	Yr	NM
❏ 001	Intensive Care	1979	$25

SMITH, PAUL

Pianist and organist.

Albums

CAPITOL

Number	Title	Yr	NM
❏ T665 [M]	Cascades	1955	$75
❏ T757 [M]	Cool and Sparkling	1956	$60
❏ T1017 [M]	Delicate Jazz	1958	$60
❏ ST1017 [S]	Delicate Jazz	1958	$60
❏ H493 [10]	Liquid Sounds	1954	$150

Number	Title	Yr	NM
❑ T829 [M]	Softly, Baby	1957	$75
DISCOVERY			
❑ DL-3009 [10]	Paul Smith	1950	$300
❑ DL-3017 [10]	Paul Smith Trio	1952	$300
MGM			
❑ E-4057 [M]	Memories of Paris	1962	$25
❑ SE-4057 [S]	Memories of Paris	1962	$30
OUTSTANDING			
❑ 09	Heavy Jazz	197?	$30
❑ 011	Heavy Jazz, Vol. 2	1978	$30
❑ 024	Jazz Spotlight on Ellington and Rodgers	1980	$35
❑ 023	Jazz Spotlight on Porter and Gershwin	1980	$35
❑ 04	The Art Tatum Touch	197?	$30
❑ 07	The Art Tatum Touch, Vol. 2	197?	$30
❑ 05	The Ballad Touch	197?	$30
❑ 02	The Master Touch	197?	$30
❑ 012	This One Cooks!	197?	$30
PAUSA			
❑ 7172	Paul Smith Plays Steve Allen	1985	$25
SAVOY			
❑ MG-12094 [M]	By the Fireside	1956	$50
SKYLARK			
❑ SKLP-13 [10]	Paul Smith Quartet	1954	$120
TAMPA			
❑ TP-9 [M]	Fine, Sweet and Tasty	1957	$200
— Colored vinyl			
❑ TP-9 [M]	Fine, Sweet and Tasty	1958	$150
— Black vinyl			
VERVE			
❑ MGV-4051 [M]	Carnival! In Percussion	1961	$30
❑ V-4051 [M]	Carnival! In Percussion	1961	$25
❑ V6-4051 [S]	Carnival! In Percussion	1961	$30
❑ MGV-2148 [M]	Latin Keyboards and Percussion	1960	$100
❑ V-2148 [M]	Latin Keyboards and Percussion	1961	$25
❑ V6-2148 [S]	Latin Keyboards and Percussion	1961	$35
❑ MGV-2130 [M]	The Big Men	1960	$150
❑ MGVS-6135 [S]	The Big Men	1960	$150
❑ V-2130 [M]	The Big Men	1961	$25
❑ V6-2130 [S]	The Big Men	1961	$35
❑ MGV-2128 [M]	The Sound of Music	1960	$80
❑ MGVS-6128 [S]	The Sound of Music	1960	$80
❑ V-2128 [M]	The Sound of Music	1961	$25
❑ V6-2128 [S]	The Sound of Music	1961	$35
VOSS			
❑ VLP1-42937	The Good Life	1988	$25

SMITH, PINE TOP
Pianist and male singer.

Albums

BRUNSWICK			
❑ BL58003 [10]	Pine Top Smith	1950	$120

SMITH, PLATO

Albums

LAND O' JAZZ			
❑ 1972	Dixieland Dance Date	1972	$25

SMITH, RAY
Pianist.

Albums

STOMP OFF			
❑ SOS-1012	Jungle Blues	198?	$30

SMITH, RICHARD
Guitarist.

Albums

CMG			
❑ CML-8011	Puma Creek	1988	$25

SMITH, STEVE
Drummer.

Albums

COLUMBIA			
❑ FC44334	Fiafiaga	1988	$25
❑ FC38955	Vital Information	1983	$25

SMITH, STUFF
Violinist and male singer.

Albums

Number	Title	Yr	NM
20TH FOX			
❑ FTM-3008 [M]	Sweet Singin' Stuff	1959	$30
❑ FTS-3008 [S]	Sweet Singin' Stuff	1959	$30
BASF			
❑ 20650	Black Violin	197?	$35
EVEREST ARCHIVE OF FOLK & JAZZ			
❑ 238	Stuff Smith/Guest Artist: Stphane Grappelly	1970	$25
PRESTIGE			
❑ PRST-7691 [R]	The Stuff Smith Memorial Album	1969	$35
STORYVILLE			
❑ 4087	Swingin' Stuff	198?	$25
VERVE			
❑ MGV-8339 [M]	Cat on a Hot Fiddle	1959	$150
❑ MGVS-6097 [S]	Cat on a Hot Fiddle	1960	$100
❑ V-8339 [M]	Cat on a Hot Fiddle	1961	$25
❑ V6-8339 [S]	Cat on a Hot Fiddle	1961	$35
❑ MGV-8282 [M]	Have Violin, Will Swing	1958	$100
❑ V-8282 [M]	Have Violin, Will Swing	1961	$25
❑ MGV-8206 [M]	Soft Winds	1958	$100
❑ V-8206 [M]	Soft Winds	1961	$25
❑ MGV-8270 [M]	Stephane Grappelli With Stuff Smith	1958	$0
— Canceled			
❑ MGV-2041 [M]	Stuff Smith	1957	$0
— Canceled			

SMITH, TOMMY
Alto and soprano saxophone player.

Albums

BLUE NOTE			
❑ B1-91930	Step by Step	1989	$30
STOMP OFF			
❑ SOS-1162	South Side Strut: A Tribute to Don Ewell	1989	$25

SMITH, WILLIE "THE LION", AND DON EWELL
Also see each artist's individual listings.

Albums

SACKVILLE			
❑ 2004	Grand Piano	198?	$25

SMITH, WILLIE "THE LION"
Pianist, composer and male singer. Also see LUCKEY ROBERTS.

Albums

BLACK LION			
❑ 156	Pork and Beans	197?	$35
BLUE CIRCLE			
❑ 1500-33 [10]	Willie "The Lion" Smith	1952	$150
CHIAROSCURO			
❑ 104	Live at Blues Alley	197?	$35
COMMODORE			
❑ DL-30004 [M]	The Lion of the Piano	1951	$100
❑ XFL-15775	Willie "The Lion" Smith	198?	$25
DIAL			
❑ LP-305 [10]	Harlem Memories	1953	$250
DOT			
❑ DLP-3094 [M]	The Lion Roars	1958	$100
GNP CRESCENDO			
❑ GNP-9011	Willie "The Lion" Smith	197?	$25
GRAND AWARD			
❑ GA-33-368 [M]	The Legend of Willie Smith	1956	$50
MAINSTREAM			
❑ 56027 [M]	A Legend	1965	$30
❑ S-6027 [R]	A Legend	1965	$35
RCA VICTOR			
❑ LSP-6016	Memoirs	1968	$25
URANIA			
❑ UJLP-1207 [M]	Accent On Piano	1955	$250

SMITH, WILLIE
Alto saxophone player. Also a bariton sax player, clarinetist and male singer.

Albums

EMARCY			
❑ MG-26000 [10]	Relaxin' After Hours	1954	$100
GNP CRESCENDO			

Number	Title	Yr	NM
❑ GNPS-2055	The Best -- Alto Saxophone Supreme	196?	$25
MERCURY			
❑ MG-25075 [10]	Alto Sax Artistry	1950	$200

SMITH-GLAMANN QUINTET
Members: Barry Galbraith (guitar); Betty Glamann (harp); Rufus Smith (bass); Nick Perito (accordion); Frank Garisto (drums).

Albums

BETHLEHEM			
❑ BCP-22 [M]	Smith-Glamann Quintet	1955	$250

SMITHSONIAN JAZZ REPERTORY ENSEMBLE, THE
Members: PANAMA FRANCIS; Jack Gale (trombone); Major Holley (bass); DICK HYMAN; JIMMIE MAXWELL; DICK WELLSTOOD; BOB WILBER.

Albums

SMITHSONIAN			
❑ N-021	The Music of Fats Waller and James P. Johnson	1988	$35

SMOKER, PAUL
Trumpeter.

Albums

SOUND ASPECTS			
❑ SAS-006	Mississippi River Rat	1985	$30

SNOW, VALAIDA
Trumpeter and female singer.

Albums

SWING			
❑ SW-8455/6	Swing Is the Thing	198?	$30

SNOWDEN, ELMER
Banjo player and bandleader.

Albums

FANTASY			
❑ OJC-1756	Harlem Banjo	198?	$25
IAJRC			
❑ LP12	Elmer Snowden 1924-63	198?	$25
RIVERSIDE			
❑ RLP-348 [M]	Harlem Banjo	1960	$200
❑ RS-9348 [S]	Harlem Banjo	1960	$200

SOCOLOW, FRANK
Tenor and alto saxophone player.

Albums

BETHLEHEM			
❑ BCP-70 [M]	Sounds By Socolow	1957	$250

SOFTWARE
Led by Peter Mergener and Michael Weissner.

Albums

HEADFIRST			
❑ 9707	Marbles	198?	$30
INNOVATIVE COMMUNICATION			
❑ KS 80.050	Chip-Meditation	1987	$35
❑ D1-74766	Digital Dance	1988	$30
❑ KS 80.055	Electronic Universe	1987	$50
❑ IC 80.064	Syn-Code/Live in Concert	1988	$35

SOLAL, MARTIAL
Pianist; also a composer, clarinetist and saxophone player. Also see SIDNEY BECHET.

Albums

CAPITOL			
❑ T10261 [M]	Martial Solal	1960	$60
❑ ST10261 [S]	Martial Solal	1960	$60
❑ T10354 [M]	Vive La France! Viva La Jazz! Vive Solal!	1961	$50
❑ ST10354 [S]	Vive La France! Viva La Jazz! Vive Solal!	1961	$60
CONTEMPORARY			
❑ C-2512 [10]	French Modern Sounds	1954	$250
LIBERTY			
❑ LRP-3335 [M]	Martial Solal in Concert	1963	$35
❑ LST-7335 [S]	Martial Solal in Concert	1963	$25
MILESTONE			

Number	Title	Yr	NM
❑ CJ-277	Na Pali Coast	1985	$25

XANADU
Number	Title	Yr	NM
❑ 184	Bird Raga	198?	$25
❑ 176	Dance of the Universe	1980	$30
❑ 193	Message Sent on the Wind	1982	$25
❑ 183	The Path	1981	$25

SPRING STREET STOMPERS, THE

Albums

JUBILEE
Number	Title	Yr	NM
❑ JLP-1004 [M]	I Go, Hook, Line and Sinker	1955	$200
❑ JLP-1002 [M]	The Spring Street Stompers at Carnegie Hall	1955	$50

SPYRO GYRA
Many personnel changes over the years, but the two constants have been Jay Beckenstein (saxophones) and Tom Schuman (keyboards).

Albums

AMHERST
Number	Title	Yr	NM
❑ AMH-1014	Spyro Gyra	1978	$35

GRP
Number	Title	Yr	NM
❑ GR-9608	Fast Forward	1990	$35

INFINITY
Number	Title	Yr	NM
❑ INF-9004	Morning Dance	1979	$30

MCA
Number	Title	Yr	NM
❑ 6893	Access All Areas	1984	$30
❑ 5606	Alternating Currents	1985	$25
❑ 5753	Breakout	1986	$25
❑ 37176	Carnaval	198?	$20
— Budget-line reissue			
❑ 5149	Carnaval	1981	$25
❑ 16010	Catching the Sun	1982	$40
— Audiophile vinyl			
❑ 5108	Catching the Sun	1980	$25
❑ 1445	City Kids	1986	$20
— Budget-line reissue			
❑ 5431	City Kids	1983	$25
❑ 5238	Freetime	1981	$25
❑ 5368	Incognito	1982	$25
❑ 37148	Morning Dance	198?	$20
— Reissue of Infinity LP			
❑ 6309	Point of View	1989	$30
❑ 6235	Rites of Summer	1988	$25
❑ 37149	Spyro Gyra	198?	$20
— Reissue of Amherst LP			
❑ 42046	Stories Without Words	1987	$25

NAUTILUS
Number	Title	Yr	NM
❑ NR-9	Morning Dance	1979	$40
— Audiophile vinyl			

SQUIRES, ROSEMARY

Albums

MGM
Number	Title	Yr	NM
❑ E3597 [M-DJ]	My Love is a Wanderer		$1000

SQUIRREL NUT ZIPPERS
Neo-swing band founded by Jim Mathus (vocals, guitar, trombone) and Katharine Whalen (vocals, banjo) in 1993.

Albums

MAMMOTH
Number	Title	Yr	NM
❑ MR 0137	Hot	1996	$10
❑ MR 0169	Perennial Favorites	1998	$10
❑ MR 0105	The Inevitable	1995	$10

ST. CLAIRE, BETTY
Female singer.

Albums

JUBILEE
Number	Title	Yr	NM
❑ JLP-23 [10]	Cool and Clearer	1955	$100
❑ JLP-15 [10]	Hal McKusick Plays — Betty St. Clair Sings	1955	$150
❑ JLP-1011 [M]	What Is There to Say?	1956	$50

SEECO
Number	Title	Yr	NM
❑ SLP-456 [M]	Betty St. Claire at Basin Street	1960	$125
❑ SLP-4560 [S]	Betty St. Claire at Basin Street	1960	$125

ST. CYR, JOHNNY
Banjo player and guitarist. Also see PAUL BARBARIN.

Albums

SOUTHLAND
Number	Title	Yr	NM
❑ 212	Johnny St. Cyr and His Hot Five	196?	$50

ST. LOUIS RAGTIMERS, THE
Members: Don Franz (tuba); Bill Mason (cornet, washboard); Al Stricker (banjo, vocals); Trebor Jay Tichenor (piano); Ed Freund (drums); Glenn Meyer (clarinet).

Albums

AUDIOPHILE
Number	Title	Yr	NM
❑ AP-122	Songs of the Showboat Era	197?	$25
❑ AP-116	The St. Louis Ragtimers	1977	$25

STACY, JESS
Pianist.

Albums

AIRCHECK
Number	Title	Yr	NM
❑ 26	Jess Stacy On the Air	198?	$25

ATLANTIC
Number	Title	Yr	NM
❑ 1225 [M]	A Tribute to Benny Goodman	1956	$300
— Black label			
❑ 90664	A Tribute to Benny Goodman	1988	$25

BRUNSWICK
Number	Title	Yr	NM
❑ BL58029 [10]	Piano Solos	1951	$80
❑ BL54017 [M]	Piano Solos	1956	$50

CHIAROSCURO
Number	Title	Yr	NM
❑ 177	Stacy's Still Swinging	1978	$30
❑ 133	Stacy Still Swings	197?	$30

COLUMBIA
Number	Title	Yr	NM
❑ CL6147 [10]	Piano Moods	1950	$100

COMMODORE
Number	Title	Yr	NM
❑ XFL-15358	Jess Stacy and Friends	198?	$25

HANOVER
Number	Title	Yr	NM
❑ HL-8010 [M]	The Return of Jess Stacy	1964	$35
❑ HS-8010 [S]	The Return of Jess Stacy	1964	$25

JAZZOLOGY
Number	Title	Yr	NM
❑ JCE-90	Blue Notion	198?	$25

STADLER, HEINER
Composer.

Albums

LABOR
Number	Title	Yr	NM
❑ 7001	Brains on Fire	197?	$35
❑ 7002	Brains on Fire, Vol. 2	1974	$35
❑ 7003	Ecstasy	197?	$35
❑ 7006	Jazz Alchemy	197?	$35

STAETER, TED

Albums

ATLANTIC
Number	Title	Yr	NM
❑ 1218 [M]	Ted Staeter's New York	1955	$300
— Multicolor label, white "fan" logo at right			
❑ 1218 [M]	Ted Staeter's New York	1961	$150
— Black label			

STAFFORD, JO, AND GORDON MACRAE
MacRae is a male singer not otherwise listed in this book. Also see JO STAFFORD.

Albums

CAPITOL
Number	Title	Yr	NM
❑ T423 [M]	Memory Songs	1955	$80
❑ H247 [10]	Sunday Evening Songs	1952	$100
❑ T1916 [M]	There's Peace in the Valley	1963	$50
❑ ST1916 [S]	There's Peace in the Valley	1963	$60
❑ T1696 [M]	Whispering Hope	1962	$80
❑ ST1696 [S]	Whispering Hope	1962	$100

STAFFORD, JO
Female singer.

Albums

BAINBRIDGE
Number	Title	Yr	NM
❑ 6234	Look at Me Now	1982	$12

CAPITOL
Number	Title	Yr	NM
❑ H75 [10]	American Folk Songs	1950	$100
❑ T1653 [M]	American Folk Songs	1962	$50
❑ ST1653 [S]	American Folk Songs	1962	$60

Number	Title	Yr	NM
❑ H197 [10]	Autumn in New York	195?	$100
❑ T197 [M]	Autumn in New York	1955	$80
— Turquoise or gray label			
❑ T197 [M]	Autumn in New York	1959	$60
— Black colorband label, Capitol logo at left			
❑ T423 [M]	Memory Songs	1955	$80
— Turquoise or gray label			
❑ T423 [M]	Memory Songs	1959	$60
— Black colorband label, Capitol logo at left			
❑ H247 [10]	Songs for Sunday Evening	195?	$100
❑ H9014 [10]	Songs of Faith	1950	$100
❑ H435 [10]	Starring Jo Stafford	1953	$100
❑ T435 [M]	Starring Jo Stafford	1955	$80
— Turquoise or gray label			
❑ T435 [M]	Starring Jo Stafford	1959	$60
— Black colorband label, Capitol logo at left			
❑ T2069 [M]	Sweet Hour of Prayer	1964	$50
❑ ST2069 [S]	Sweet Hour of Prayer	1964	$60
❑ T1921 [M]	The Hits of Jo Stafford	1963	$50
❑ ST1921 [S]	The Hits of Jo Stafford	1963	$60
❑ SM-11889	The Hits of Jo Stafford	1979	$12
❑ T2166 [M]	The Joyful Season	1964	$40
❑ ST2166 [S]	The Joyful Season	1964	$60
❑ SM-1696	Whispering Hope	1977	$25
— Reissue with new prefix			

COLUMBIA
Number	Title	Yr	NM
❑ CL2591 [10]	A Gal Named Jo	1955	$50
❑ CL6210 [10]	As You Desire Me	1952	$50
❑ CL1339 [M]	Ballad of the Blues	1959	$30
❑ CS8139 [S]	Ballad of the Blues	1959	$40
❑ CL6286 [10]	Garden of Prayer	1954	$50
❑ CL691 [M]	Happy Holiday	1955	$75
❑ CL1262 [M]	I'll Be Seeing Me	1959	$30
❑ CS8080 [S]	I'll Be Seeing You	1959	$40
❑ CL1561 [M]	Jo + Jazz	1960	$40
❑ CS8361 [S]	Jo + Jazz	1960	$60
❑ CL1228 [M]	Jo Stafford's Greatest Hits	1958	$40
— Red and black label with six "eye" logos			
❑ CL1228 [M]	Jo Stafford's Greatest Hits	1963	$25
— Red label with "Guaranteed High Fidelity" in black			
❑ CL1228 [M]	Jo Stafford's Greatest Hits	1965	$25
— Red label with "360 Sound Mono" in white			
❑ CL6238 [10]	Jo Stafford Sings Broadway's Best	1953	$50
❑ CL584 [M]	Jo Stafford Sings Broadway's Best	1954	$40
— Maroon label, gold print			
❑ CL584 [M]	Jo Stafford Sings Broadway's Best	1955	$40
— Red and black label with six "eye" logos			
❑ CL6274 [10]	My Heart's in the Highland	1954	$50
❑ CL578 [M]	New Orleans	1954	$40
— Maroon label, gold print			
❑ CL6268 [10]	New Orleans	1954	$50
❑ CL578 [M]	New Orleans	1955	$40
— Red and black label with six "eye" logos			
❑ CL968 [M]	Once Over Lightly	1957	$40
❑ CL910 [M]	Ski Trails	1956	$40
❑ CL2501 [10]	Soft and Sentimental	1955	$50
❑ CL1124 [M]	Swingin' Down Broadway	1958	$40

CORINTHIAN
Number	Title	Yr	NM
❑ COR-118	Broadway Revisited	198?	$12
❑ COR-119	By Request	198?	$12
❑ COR-105	G.I. Jo	1977	$12
❑ COR-106	Greatest Hits	1977	$12
❑ COR-115	International Hits	197?	$12
❑ COR-114	Jo + Blues	197?	$12
❑ COR-112	Jo + Broadway	197?	$12
❑ COR-108	Jo + Jazz	197?	$12
❑ COR-110	Jo Stafford Sings American Folk Songs	197?	$12
❑ COR-123	Music of My Life	1986	$12
❑ COR-113	Ski Trails	197?	$12
❑ COR-111	Songs of Faith, Hope and Love	197?	$12

DECCA
Number	Title	Yr	NM
❑ DL74973	Jo Stafford's Greatest Hits	1968	$20

DOT
Number	Title	Yr	NM
❑ DLP-3673 [M]	Do I Hear a Waltz?	1966	$60
❑ DLP-25673 [S]	Do I Hear a Waltz?	1966	$75
❑ DLP-3745 [M]	This Is Jo Stafford	1967	$60
❑ DLP-25745 [S]	This Is Jo Stafford	1967	$75

REPRISE
Number	Title	Yr	NM
❑ R-6090 [M]	Getting Sentimental Over Tommy Dorsey	1963	$25
❑ R9-6090 [S]	Getting Sentimental Over Tommy Dorsey	1963	$30

STANYAN
Number	Title	Yr	NM
❑ 10073	Look at Me Now	197?	$15

TIME-LIFE
Number	Title	Yr	NM
❑ SLGD-14	Legendary Singers: Jo Stafford	1986	$20

Number	Title	Yr	NM
❏ MSP-9014	On Home Ground	1969	$35
❏ MLP-1001 [M]	Solal!	1967	$30
❏ MSP-9001 [S]	Solal!	1967	$35
PAUSA			
❏ 7061	Four Keys	197?	$25
❏ 7103	Movability	198?	$25
RCA VICTOR			
❏ LPM-2777 [M]	Martial Solal at Newport '63	1963	$35
❏ LSP-2777 [S]	Martial Solal at Newport '63	1963	$25
SOUL NOTE			
❏ SN-1060	Bluesine	1983	$30

SOLAR PLEXUS
Swedish fusion group.

Albums

Number	Title	Yr	NM
INNER CITY			
❏ IC-1087	Earth Songs	1980	$30
❏ IC-1067	Solar Plexus	1979	$30

SOLOFF, LEW
Trumpeter.

Albums

Number	Title	Yr	NM
PROJAZZ			
❏ PAD-601	Hanalei Bay	1986	$25

SOLUTION, THE
Members: Tom Barlage (sax and flute); Willem Ennes (keyboards); Ad Kooi (bass, replaced by Peter van der Sande, who was then replaced by Guus Willemse); Ap Alberts (sax); Frits Lagerwerff (trumpet); Frank de Graaf (vocals); Frits Schmidt (drums, replaced by Hans Waterman).

Albums

Number	Title	Yr	NM
FIRST AMERICAN			
❏ 7776	It's Only Just Begun	198?	$25

SOMMERS, JOANIE
Female singer. Best known for her pop records (not included here).

SOMOA

Albums

Number	Title	Yr	NM
PROJAZZ			
❏ PAD-645	No Band Is an Island	1987	$25

SONDHEIM, ALAN

Albums

Number	Title	Yr	NM
ESP-DISK'			
❏ 1048 [S]	Ritual-All-7-70	1969	$100
❏ 1082 [S]	T'Other Little Tune	1969	$100

SONN, LARRY
Trumpeter and pianist.

Albums

Number	Title	Yr	NM
CORAL			
❏ CRL57057 [M]	The Sound of Sonn	1956	$40
DOT			
❏ DLP-9005 [M]	Jazz Band Having a Ball	1958	$75
❏ DLP-29005 [S]	Jazz Band Having a Ball	1958	$75

SONS OF BIX, THE
Members: Tom Pletcher (cornet); Don Ingle (valve trombone); John Harker (clarinet); Russ Whitman (bass saxophone); Dave Miller (guitar, banjo); Don Gibson (piano); Wayne Jones (drums).

Albums

Number	Title	Yr	NM
JAZZOLOGY			
❏ J-99	Copenhagen	1983	$25
❏ J-59	Ostrich Walk	1979	$25

SOPRANO SUMMIT
Led by KENNY DAVERN and BOB WILBER on soprano sax.

Albums

Number	Title	Yr	NM
CHIAROSCURO			
❏ 149	Chalumeau Blue	197?	$30
❏ 178	Crazy Rhythm	1977	$30
CONCORD JAZZ			
❏ CJ-52	Live at Concord '77	1977	$30
❏ CJ-29	Soprano Summit in Concert	1976	$30
JAZZOLOGY			
❏ J-56	Live at Big Horn Jazzfest	197?	$25

SOSKIN, MARK
Pianist.

Albums

Number	Title	Yr	NM
PRESTIGE			
❏ 10109	Rhythm Vision	1979	$35

SOSSON, MARSHALL
Violinist.

Albums

Number	Title	Yr	NM
TOWN HALL			
❏ M-26	Virtuoso Jazz Violin Classics	197?	$30

SOUCHON, DR. EDMOND
Guitarist and bandleader.

Albums

Number	Title	Yr	NM
GHB			
❏ GHB-6	Dr. Edmond Souchon	1963	$35
❏ GHB-131	Dr. Edmond Souchon and the Milneburg Boys	1969	$30
GOLDEN CREST			
❏ GC-3021	Dixieland of New Orleans	196?	$35
❏ GC-3065	Minstrel Days	196?	$35
SOUTHLAND			
❏ 231	Dr. Edmond Souchon and the Milneburg Boys	1962	$35

SOUL FLUTES
The "flutes" on this album were played by Joel Kaye, HERBIE MANN, George Marge, Romeo Penque and Stan Webb.

Albums

Number	Title	Yr	NM
A&M			
❏ SP-3009	Trust in Me	1968	$25

SOULFUL STRINGS, THE
Arranged by RICHARD EVANS.

Albums

Number	Title	Yr	NM
CADET			
❏ LPS-805	Another Exposure	1968	$30
❏ 50022	Best of the Soulful Strings	1973	$30
❏ LPS-846	Gamble-Huff	1971	$25
❏ LPS-796	Groovin' with the Soulful Strings	1967	$30
❏ LPS-820	In Concert/Back by Demand	1969	$30
❏ LP-776 [M]	Paint It Black	1967	$35
❏ LPS-776 [S]	Paint It Black	1967	$30
❏ LPS-834	String Fever	1969	$30
❏ LPS-814	The Magic of Christmas	1968	$30

SOUND OF FEELING

Albums

Number	Title	Yr	NM
LIMELIGHT			
❏ LS-86063	Spleen	1969	$25

SOUNDS ORCHESTRAL
British studio group. The hit single "Cast Your Fate to the Wind," an almost note-for-note remake of VINCE GUARALDI's original, featured Johnny Pearson on piano.

Albums

Number	Title	Yr	NM
PARKWAY			
❏ SP7046 [S]	Cast Your Fate to the Wind	1965	$50
❏ SP7050 [S]	Impressions of James Bond	1966	$60
❏ SP7047 [S]	The Soul of Sounds Orchestral	1965	$50

SOUNDSTAGE ALL-STARS, THE

Albums

Number	Title	Yr	NM
DOT			
❏ DLP-3204 [M]	More "Peter Gunn"	1959	$75
❏ DLP-25204 [S]	More "Peter Gunn"	1959	$75

SOUTER, EDDIE
See RAY McKINLEY.

SOUTH, EDDIE
Violinist.

Albums

Number	Title	Yr	NM
CHESS			
❏ ACMJ-415	South Side Jazz	197?	$30
MERCURY			
❏ MG-20401 [M]	The Distinguished Violin of Eddie South	1959	$100
❏ SR-60070 [S]	The Distinguished Violin of Eddie South	1959	$100
SWING			
❏ SW-8405	Eddie South	1985	$25
TRIP			
❏ 5803	Dark Angel of the Fiddle	197?	$25

SOUTH FRISCO JAZZ BAND, THE
Formed in 1956 by Vince Saunders (banjo).

Albums

Number	Title	Yr	NM
SFJB			
❏ 2-1978	Diggin' Clams	1978	$35
STOMP OFF			
❏ SOS-1180	Broken Promises	1988	$25
❏ SOS-1103	Jones Law Blues	1985	$25
❏ SOS-1027	Live at Earthquake McGoon's	198?	$25
❏ SOS-1143	Sage Hen Strut	1987	$25
❏ SOS-1035	These Cats Are Diggin' Us	198?	$25
VAULT			
❏ S-9008	Hot Tamale Man	196?	$35

SOUTHERN, JERI
Female singer and pianist.

Albums

Number	Title	Yr	NM
CAPITOL			
❏ T1278 [M]	Jeri Southern at the Crescendo	1960	$60
—Black colorband label, Capitol logo at left			
❏ ST1278 [S]	Jeri Southern at the Crescendo	1960	$75
—Black colorband label, Capitol logo at left			
❏ T1278 [M]	Jeri Southern at the Crescendo	1963	$75
—Black colorband label, Capitol logo at top			
❏ ST1278 [S]	Jeri Southern at the Crescendo	1963	$50
—Black colorband label, Capitol logo at top			
❏ T1173 [M]	Jeri Southern Meets Cole Porter	1959	$60
—Black colorband label, Capitol logo at left			
❏ ST1173 [S]	Jeri Southern Meets Cole Porter	1959	$75
—Black colorband label, Capitol logo at left			
❏ T1173 [M]	Jeri Southern Meets Cole Porter	1963	$75
—Black colorband label, Capitol logo at top			
❏ ST1173 [S]	Jeri Southern Meets Cole Porter	1963	$50
—Black colorband label, Capitol logo at top			
DECCA			
❏ DL5531 [10]	Intimate Songs	1954	$150
❏ DL8472 [M]	Jeri Southern Gently Jumps	1957	$120
❏ DL8745 [M]	Prelude to a Kiss	1958	$100
❏ DL8761 [M]	Southern Hospitality	1958	$100
❏ DL8055 [M]	Southern Style	1955	$150
❏ DL8394 [M]	When Your Heart's on Fire	1956	$150
❏ DL8214 [M]	You Better Go Now	1956	$150
FORUM			
❏ F-9030 [M]	Jeri Southern Meets Johnny Smith	196?	$30
❏ SF-9030 [S]	Jeri Southern Meets Johnny Smith	196?	$35
PAUSA			
❏ PR9054	Jeri Southern Meets Cole Porter	1986	$25
—Reissue of Capitol ST 1173			
ROULETTE			
❏ R-25039 [M]	Coffee, Cigarettes and Memories	1958	$40
❏ R-52016 [M]	Jeri Southern Meets Johnny Smith	1958	$40
❏ RS-52016 [S]	Jeri Southern Meets Johnny Smith	1958	$50
❏ R-52010 [M]	Southern Breeze	1958	$40
❏ RS-52010 [S]	Southern Breeze	1958	$50
STANYAN			
❏ SR10106	You Better Go Now	1974	$35
—Reissue of Decca DL 8214			

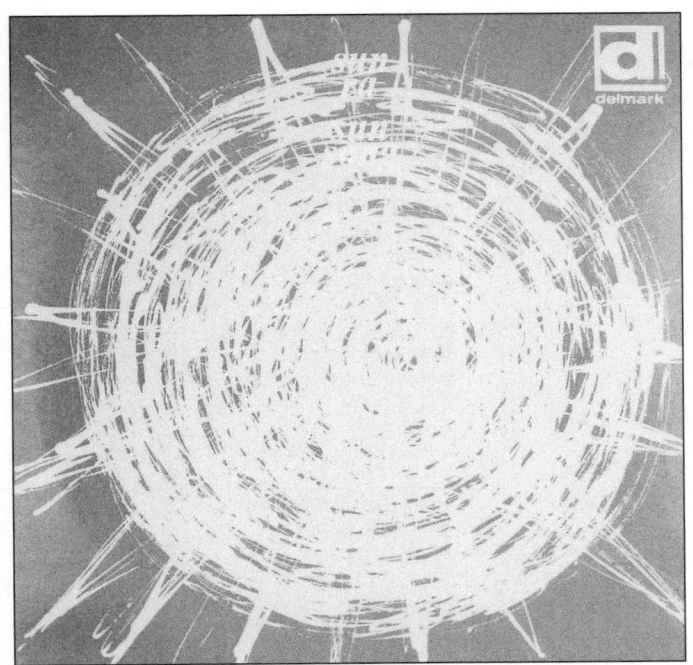

Sun Ra, *Sun Song*, Delmark DL-411, **$250**.

Phil Sunkel, *Gerry Mulligan and Bob Brookmeyer Play Phil Sunkel's Jazz Concerto Grosso*, ABC-Paramount ABC-225, **$60**.

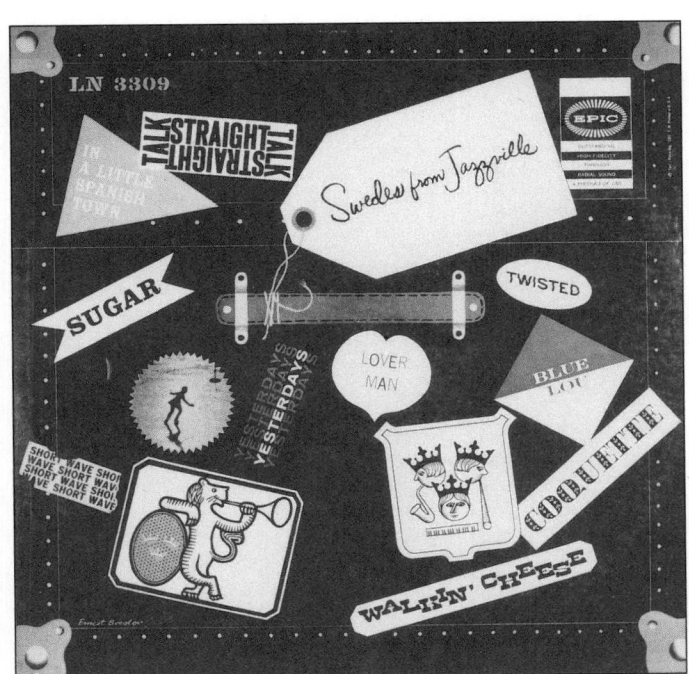

Swedes from Jazzville, *Swedes from Jazzville*, Epic LN 3309, **$100**.

Thomas Talbert, *Bix Fats Duke Interpreted* by Thomas Talbert, Atlantic 1250, black label, **$300**.

Number	Title	Yr	NM

SOUTHERN STOMPERS, THE

Albums

STOMP OFF

❏ SOS-1215	Echoes of King Oliver's Jazz Band	1991	$25

SOUTHERN UNIVERSITY JAZZ BAND ENSEMBLE

Albums

JAZZSTRONAUTS

❏ LP1 [B]	Live at the 1971 American College Jazz Festival	1971	$1000

SPACE

Featuring ROSCOE MITCHELL and Gerald Oshita (saxophones).

Albums

1750 ARCH

❏ 1806	An Interesting Breakfast Conversation	198?	$30

SPANIER, MUGGSY

Cornet player and bandleader.

Albums

AVA

❏ A-12 [M]	Columbia, the Gem of the Ocean	1963	$30
❏ AS-12 [S]	Columbia, the Gem of the Ocean	1963	$35

COMMODORE

❏ FL-30016 [M]	Chicago Jazz	1957	$50
❏ XFL-15777	Muggsy Spanier at Nick's New York, April 1944	198?	$25
❏ FL-20009 [10]	Spanier's Ragtimers	1950	$100

DECCA

❏ DL5552 [10]	Hot Horn	1955	$150

EMARCY

❏ MG-26011 [10]	Muggsy Spanier and His Dixieland Band	1954	$100

EVEREST ARCHIVE OF FOLK & JAZZ

❏ 226	Muggsy Spanier	1968	$25
❏ 326	Muggsy Spanier, Vol. 2	197?	$25

GLENDALE

❏ GLS6024	One of a Kind	198?	$25

JAZZ ARCHIVES

❏ JA-44	Jazz from California	198?	$25
❏ JA-30	Little David Play Your Harp	198?	$25

JAZZOLOGY

❏ J-33	Muggsy Spanier	197?	$25
❏ J-115	Relaxin' at Touro -- 1952	198?	$25

LONDON

❏ AL-3503 [S]	Muggsy, Tesch and the Chicagoans	195?	$30
❏ LL3528 [M]	Muggsy Spanier and the Bucktown Five	1959	$40

MERCURY

❏ MG-25095 [10]	Muggsy Spanier and His Dixieland Band	1953	$200
❏ MG-20171 [M]	Muggsy Spanier and His Dixieland Band	1956	$100

RCA VICTOR

❏ LPM-3043 [10]	Ragtime Favorites	195?	$120
❏ LPM-1295 [M]	The Great 16	1956	$50

RIVERSIDE

❏ RLP 12-107 [M]	Classic Early Recordings	1955	$300
❏ RLP-1004 [10]	Muggsy Spanier and Frank Teschemacher	1953	$300
❏ RLP-1035 [10]	Muggsy Spanier and His Bucktown Five	1954	$300

RKO

❏ ULP130 [M]	Chicago Jazz	195?	$25

STINSON

❏ SLP30 [M]	Muggsy Spanier's Ragtimers, Vol. 1	1962	$50

— Red vinyl

❏ SLP30 [M]	Muggsy Spanier's Ragtimers, Vol. 1	1962	$30

— Black vinyl

❏ SLP31 [M]	Muggsy Spanier's Ragtimers, Vol. 2	1962	$50

— Red vinyl

❏ SLP31 [M]	Muggsy Spanier's Ragtimers, Vol. 2	1962	$30

— Black vinyl

STORYVILLE

❏ 4053	Hot Horn	198?	$25
❏ 4020	Muggsy Spanier	198?	$25
❏ 4056	Muggsy Spanier at Club Hangover	198?	$25

TRIP

❏ 5532	Dixieland Session	197?	$25

WEATHERS INDUSTRIES

❏ W-5401 [M]	Dynamic Dixie	1954	$60

ZEE GEE

❏ 101 [10]	Muggsy Spanier's Ragtimers, Vol. 1	195?	$120
❏ 102 [10]	Muggsy Spanier's Ragtimers, Vol. 2	195?	$120

SPANN, LES

Guitarist and flutist.

Albums

JAZZLAND

❏ JLP-35 [M]	Gemini	1961	$30
❏ JLP-935 [S]	Gemini	1961	$30

SPARKS, MELVIN

Guitarist.

Albums

MUSE

❏ MR-5248	Sparkling	1981	$35

PRESTIGE

❏ 10039	Akilah!	1973	$25
❏ 10016	Spark Plug	1972	$25
❏ 10001	Sparks!	1971	$25

WESTBOUND

❏ 204	Melvin Sparks '75	1975	$25

SPAULDING, JAMES

Alto saxophone player and flutist.

Albums

MUSE

❏ MR-5369	Brilliant Corners	1989	$25
❏ MR-5413	Gotstabe a Better Way!	1990	$30

STORYVILLE

❏ 4034	Jame Spaulding Plays the Legacy of Duke	1980	$30

SPECIAL EFX

Members: George Jinda (percussion); Chieli Minucci (guitar).

Albums

GRP

❏ GR-9581	Confidential	1989	$30
❏ GR-1048	Double Feature	1988	$25
❏ GR-1014	Modern Manners	1986	$25
❏ GR-1033	Mystique	1987	$25
❏ GR-1025	Slice of Life	1987	$25
❏ GR-1007	Special EFX	1986	$25

SPENCER, LEON, JR.

Organist.

Albums

PRESTIGE

❏ 10042	Bad Walking Woman	1973	$25
❏ 10033	Louisiana Slim	1972	$25
❏ 10011	Sneak Preview!	1971	$25
❏ 10063	Where I'm Coming From	197?	$35

SPHERE (1)

Albums

STRATA

❏ 103-74	Inside Ourselves	1974	$35

SPHERE (2)

Tribute group to THELONIOUS MONK, including KENNY BARRON (piano); Ben Riley (drums); CHARLIE ROUSE (saxophones); Buster Williams (bass).

Albums

ELEKTRA/MUSICIAN

❏ 60313	Flight Path	1984	$25
❏ 60166	Four in One	1982	$25

RED RECORD

❏ VPA-191	Sphere On Tour	1986	$30

VERVE

❏ 837032-1	Bird Songs	198?	$25
❏ 831674-1	Four for All	1987	$25

SPHEROE

French fusion group: Michel Perez (guitar); Gerard Maimone (keyboards); Rido Bayonne (bass, percussion); Patrick Cactus Garel (drums).

Albums

INNER CITY

❏ IC-1034	Spheroe	197?	$35

SPIEGEL, VICTOR

Pianist.

Albums

EAGLE

❏ SM-4197	Wind on the Water	1985	$30

SPINOZZA, DAVID

Guitarist and electric sitar player.

Albums

A&M

❏ SP-4677	Spinozza	1978	$25

SPIRIT OF NEW ORLEANS JAZZ BAND, THE

Led by LOUIS COTTRELL.

Albums

GHB

❏ GHB-247	The Spirit of New Orleans Jazz Band	198?	$25

SPITFIRE BAND, THE

Founded by Jackie Rae in 1981.

Albums

COLUMBIA

❏ FC39891	Flight III	1985	$25

SPIVAK, CHARLIE

Trumpeter and bandleader.

Albums

CIRCLE

❏ 17	Charlie Spivak and His Orchestra: Now!	1981	$25
❏ 16	Charlie Spivak and His Orchestra 1942	198?	$25
❏ CLP-80	Charlie Spivak and His Orchestra 1946	1985	$25

HINDSIGHT

❏ HSR-188	Charlie Spivak and His Orchestra 1941	198?	$25
❏ HSR-105	Charlie Spivak and His Orchestra 1943-46	198?	$25

INSIGHT

❏ 215	Charlie Spivak and His Orchestra 1943-46	198?	$25

SPIVAK, DUBBY

Male singer.

Albums

AUDIOPHILE

❏ AP-189	Dubby Swings Lightly	1986	$25

SPONTANEOUS MUSIC ENSEMBLE, THE

Members on the below LP: John Stevens (drums, percussion, cornet, vocals); Trevor Watts (soprano saxophone).

Albums

EMANEM

❏ 303	Face to Face	1974	$25

SPOTTS, ROGER HAMILTON

Albums

SEA BREEZE

❏ SB-5004	Roger Hamilton Spotts and His Big Band	1986	$25

SPRAGUE, PETER

Guitarist.

Albums

CONCORD JAZZ

❏ CJ-237	Musica Del Mar	1984	$25

Number	Title	Yr	NM
VOCALION			
❏ VL73856 [R]	Happy Holidays	1968	$15
❏ VL73892	In the Mood for Love	1970	$15
❏ VL73866 [R]	Sweet Singer of Songs	1969	$15

STAFFORD, MARILYN, AND THE ERNIE CARSON BAND

Albums

Number	Title	Yr	NM
CIRCLE			
❏ C-66	Jazz Goes Country	198?	$25

STALLINGS, MARY, AND CAL TJADER
Stallings is a female singer. Also see CAL TJADER.

Albums

Number	Title	Yr	NM
FANTASY			
❏ 3325 [M]	Cal Tjader Plays, Mary Stallings Sings	1962	$50
—Red vinyl			
❏ 3325 [M]	Cal Tjader Plays, Mary Stallings Sings	1962	$30
—Black vinyl			
❏ 8068 [S]	Cal Tjader Plays, Mary Stallings Sings	1962	$40
—Blue vinyl			
❏ 8068 [S]	Cal Tjader Plays, Mary Stallings Sings	1962	$25
—Black vinyl			

STAMM, MARVIN
Trumpeter.

Albums

Number	Title	Yr	NM
PALO ALTO			
❏ PA-8022	Stampede	198?	$25
VERVE			
❏ V6-8759	Machinations	1968	$25

STANDBACK

Albums

Number	Title	Yr	NM
SEA BREEZE			
❏ SB-3004	Norwegian Wood	198?	$25

STANKO, TOMASZ
Trumpeter.

Albums

Number	Title	Yr	NM
ECM			
❏ 1071	Balladyna	1976	$30

STARR, KAY
Female singer.

Albums

Number	Title	Yr	NM
ABC			
❏ S-631	When the Lights Go On Again	1968	$30
CAPITOL			
❏ T1468 [M]	All Starr Hits	1961	$60
❏ ST1468 [S]	All Starr Hits	1961	$60
❏ T1681 [M]	I Cry by Night	1962	$50
❏ ST1681 [S]	I Cry by Night	1962	$60
❏ T580 [M]	In a Blue Mood	1955	$80
❏ T1795 [M]	Just Plain Country	1962	$40
❏ ST1795 [S]	Just Plain Country	1962	$60
❏ ST-8-1795 [S]	Just Plain Country	196?	$60
—Capitol Record Club edition			
❏ T1438 [M]	Kay Starr, Jazz Singer	1960	$60
❏ ST1438 [S]	Kay Starr, Jazz Singer	1960	$75
❏ ST-11323	Kay Starrs Again	1974	$12
❏ SM-11323	Kay Starrs Again	1977	$10
—Reissue with new prefix			
❏ T1303 [M]	Losers Weepers	1960	$60
❏ ST1303 [S]	Losers Weepers	1960	$60
❏ T1254 [M]	Movin'	1959	$60
❏ ST1254 [S]	Movin'	1959	$60
❏ SM-11880	Movin'	1979	$12
❏ T1374 [M]	Movin' on Broadway	1960	$60
❏ ST1374 [S]	Movin' on Broadway	1960	$60
❏ T1358 [M]	One More Time	1960	$60
❏ ST1358 [S]	One More Time	1960	$60
❏ H211 [10]	Songs by Starr	1950	$200
❏ T211 [M]	Songs by Starr	1955	$80
❏ T2550 [M]	Tears and Heartaches/Old Records	1966	$40
❏ ST2550 [S]	Tears and Heartaches/Old Records	1966	$40

Number	Title	Yr	NM
❏ T2106 [M]	The Fabulous Favorites	1964	$80
❏ ST2106 [S]	The Fabulous Favorites	1964	$25
❏ H415 [10]	The Hits of Kay Starr	1953	$200
❏ T415 [M]	The Hits of Kay Starr	1955	$80
—Turquoise or gray label			
❏ T415 [M]	The Hits of Kay Starr	1958	$60
—Black label with colorband, Capitol logo at left			
❏ T415 [M]	The Hits of Kay Starr	1962	$25
—Black label with colorband, Capitol logo at top			
❏ DT415 [R]	The Hits of Kay Starr	196?	$50
❏ H363 [10]	The Kay Starr Style	1953	$200
❏ T363 [M]	The Kay Starr Style	1955	$80
CORONET			
❏ CX-106 [M]	Kay Starr Sings	196?	$15
❏ CXS-106 [S]	Kay Starr Sings	196?	$15
GNP CRESCENDO			
❏ GNPS-2090	Back to the Roots	1975	$12
❏ GNPS-2083	Country	1974	$12
HINDSIGHT			
❏ HSR-214	Kay Starr 1947	1985	$12
LIBERTY			
❏ LRP-9001 [M]	Swingin' with the Starr	1956	$50
❏ LRP-3280 [M]	Swingin' with the Starr	1963	$30
—Reissue of 9001			
PARAMOUNT			
❏ PAS-5001	How About This	1969	$15
RCA CAMDEN			
❏ CAL-567 [M]	Kay Starr	196?	$15
RCA VICTOR			
❏ LPM-1549 [M]	Blue Starr	1957	$30
❏ LPM-2055 [M]	I Hear the Word	1959	$30
❏ LSP-2055 [S]	I Hear the Word	1959	$30
❏ ANL1-1311	Pure Gold	1976	$10
❏ LPM-1720 [M]	Rockin' with Kay	1958	$50
❏ LPM-1149 [M]	The One and Only Kay Starr	1955	$40
RONDO-LETTE			
❏ A-3 [M]	Them There Eyes	1958	$30
SUNSET			
❏ SUM-1126 [M]	Portrait of a Starr	196?	$25
❏ SUS-5126 [R]	Portrait of a Starr	196?	$12

STARR, KAY/ERROLL GARNER
Also see each artist's individual listings.

Albums

Number	Title	Yr	NM
CROWN			
❏ CLP-5003 [M]	Singin' Kay Starr, Swingin' Erroll Garner	1957	$30
MODERN			
❏ MLP-1203 [M]	Singin' Kay Starr, Swingin' Erroll Garner	1956	$80

STARSHIP ORCHESTRA
Led by NORMAN CONNORS.

Albums

Number	Title	Yr	NM
COLUMBIA			
❏ NJC36456	Celestial Sky	1980	$25

STATE STREET ACES, THE

Albums

Number	Title	Yr	NM
STOMP OFF			
❏ SOS-1106	Old Folks Shuffle	198?	$25
❏ SOS-1041	Pass Out Lightly	198?	$25
❏ SOS-1011	Stuff	198?	$25

STATE STREET RAMBLERS, THE
Studio group of varying musicians led by JIMMY BLYTHE.

Albums

Number	Title	Yr	NM
HERWIN			
❏ 104	The State Street Ramblers, Vol. 1	197?	$30
❏ 105	The State Street Ramblers, Vol. 2	197?	$30

STATON, DAKOTA
Female singer.

Albums

Number	Title	Yr	NM
CAPITOL			
❏ T1387 [M]	Ballads and the Blues	1960	$100
—Black label with colorband, Capitol logo at left			
❏ ST1387 [S]	Ballads and the Blues	1960	$60
—Black label with colorband, Capitol logo at left			
❏ T1387 [M]	Ballads and the Blues	1962	$75

Number	Title	Yr	NM
—Black label with colorband, Capitol logo at top			
❏ ST1387 [S]	Ballads and the Blues	1962	$80
—Black label with colorband, Capitol logo at top			
❏ T1170 [M]	Crazy He Calls Me	1959	$100
—Black label with colorband, Capitol logo at left			
❏ T1170 [M]	Crazy He Calls Me	1962	$75
—Black label with colorband, Capitol logo at top			
❏ ST1170 [S]	Crazy He Calls Me	1959	$60
—Black label with colorband, Capitol logo at left			
❏ ST1170 [S]	Crazy He Calls Me	1962	$80
—Black label with colorband, Capitol logo at top			
❏ T1490 [M]	Dakota	1961	$100
—Black label with colorband, Capitol logo at left			
❏ T1490 [M]	Dakota	1962	$75
—Black label with colorband, Capitol logo at top			
❏ ST1490 [S]	Dakota	1961	$60
—Black label with colorband, Capitol logo at left			
❏ ST1490 [S]	Dakota	1962	$80
—Black label with colorband, Capitol logo at top			
❏ T1649 [M]	Dakota at Storyville	1962	$80
❏ ST1649 [S]	Dakota at Storyville	1962	$100
❏ T1054 [M]	Dynamic!	1958	$100
—Black label with colorband, Capitol logo at left			
❏ T1054 [M]	Dynamic!	1962	$75
—Black label with colorband, Capitol logo at top			
❏ ST1054 [S]	Dynamic!	1959	$60
—Black label with colorband, Capitol logo at left			
❏ ST1054 [S]	Dynamic!	1962	$80
—Black label with colorband, Capitol logo at top			
❏ T1003 [M]	In the Night	1958	$150
—Turquoise or gray label			
❏ T1003 [M]	In the Night	1959	$100
—Black label with colorband, Capitol logo at left			
❏ M-1003	In the Night	1976	$25
—Reissue with new prefix			
❏ T1325 [M]	More Than the Most	1960	$100
—Black label with colorband, Capitol logo at left			
❏ T1325 [M]	More Than the Most	1962	$75
—Black label with colorband, Capitol logo at top			
❏ ST1325 [S]	More Than the Most	1960	$75
—Black label with colorband, Capitol logo at left			
❏ ST1325 [S]	More Than the Most	1962	$80
—Black label with colorband, Capitol logo at top			
❏ T1597 [M]	'Round Midnight	1961	$100
—Black label with colorband, Capitol logo at left			
❏ T1597 [M]	'Round Midnight	1962	$50
—Black label with colorband, Capitol logo at left			
❏ ST1597 [S]	'Round Midnight	1961	$75
—Black label with colorband, Capitol logo at left			
❏ ST1597 [S]	'Round Midnight	1962	$80
—Black label with colorband, Capitol logo at top			
❏ T1427 [M]	Softly	1961	$100
—Black label with colorband, Capitol logo at left			
❏ T1427 [M]	Softly	1962	$50
—Black label with colorband, Capitol logo at top			
❏ ST1427 [S]	Softly	1961	$75
—Black label with colorband, Capitol logo at left			
❏ ST1427 [S]	Softly	1962	$80
—Black label with colorband, Capitol logo at top			
❏ T876 [M]	The Late, Late Show	1957	$150
—Turquoise or gray label			
❏ T876 [M]	The Late, Late Show	1959	$100
—Black label with colorband, Capitol logo at left			
❏ T876 [M]	The Late, Late Show	1962	$75
—Black label with colorband, Capitol logo at top			
❏ DT876 [R]	The Late, Late Show	196?	$60
❏ SM-876	The Late, Late Show	1977	$25
—Reissue with new prefix			
❏ T1241 [M]	Time to Swing	1959	$100
—Black label with colorband, Capitol logo at left			
❏ T1241 [M]	Time to Swing	1962	$50
—Black label with colorband, Capitol logo at top			
❏ ST1241 [S]	Time to Swing	1959	$75
—Black label with colorband, Capitol logo at left			
❏ ST1241 [S]	Time to Swing	1962	$80
—Black label with colorband, Capitol logo at top			
GROOVE MERCHANT			
❏ 4410	Confessin'	197?	$35
❏ 521	I Want a Country Man	1973	$30
❏ 510	Madame Foo-Foo	1972	$30
❏ 532	Ms. Soul	1974	$30
LONDON			

Number	Title	Yr	NM
LL3495 [M]	Dakota '67	1967	$50
PS495 [S]	Dakota '67	1967	$35
MUSE			
MR-5401	Dakota Staton	1991	$35
UNITED ARTISTS			
UAL-3355 [M]	Dakota Staton with Strings	1964	$50
UAS-6355 [S]	Dakota Staton with Strings	1964	$60
UAL-3292 [M]	From Dakota with Love	1963	$50
UAS-6292 [S]	From Dakota with Love	1963	$60
UAL-3312 [M]	Live and Swinging	1963	$50
UAS-6316 [S]	Live and Swinging	1963	$60
VERVE			
V6-8799	I've Been There	1971	$35

STEELE, JOAN, AND JOHN MAGALDI

Albums

Number	Title	Yr	NM
AUDIOPHILE			
AP-156	Lonesome No More	198?	$25

STEELE, JOAN

Albums

Number	Title	Yr	NM
AUDIOPHILE			
AP-94	'Round Midnight	1975	$30

STEIG, JEREMY, AND EDDIE GOMEZ

Also see each artist's individual listings.

Albums

Number	Title	Yr	NM
CMP			
CMP-3-ST	Lend Me Your Ears	198?	$25
CMP-6-ST	Music for Flute and Double Bass	198?	$25
CMP-12-ST	Rain Forest	198?	$25
ENJA			
2098	Outlaws	198?	$30
INNER CITY			
IC-3015	Outlaws	197?	$30

STEIG, JEREMY

Flutist.

Albums

Number	Title	Yr	NM
BLUE NOTE			
BST-84354	Wayfaring Stranger	1970	$25
CAPITOL			
SM-662	Energy	1976	$25
—Reissue with new prefix			
ST-662	Energy	1971	$35
COLUMBIA			
CL2136 [M]	Flute Fever	1964	$30

Number	Title	Yr	NM
CS8936 [S]	Flute Fever	1964	$35
KC32579	Monium	1974	$30
KC33297	Temple of Birth	1975	$30
CTI			
7075	Firefly	1977	$30
GROOVE MERCHANT			
2204	Fusion	197?	$35
SOLID STATE			
SS-18068	Legwork	1970	$35
SS-18059	This Is Jeremy Steig	1969	$35

STEIN, ANDY

Violinist.

Albums

Number	Title	Yr	NM
STOMP OFF			
SOS-1146	Goin' Places	1987	$25

STEIN, HAL, AND WARREN FITZGERALD

Stein plays alto and tenor saxophone; Fitzgerald plays trumpet.

Albums

Number	Title	Yr	NM
PROGRESSIVE			
PLP-1002 [M]	Hal Stein-Warren Fitzgerald Quintet	1955	$500

STEIN, LOU

Pianist.

Albums

Number	Title	Yr	NM
AUDIOPHILE			
AP-198	Solo Piano	1984	$25
BRUNSWICK			
BL58053 [10]	Lou Stein	1953	$100
CHIAROSCURO			
CR-2027	Temple of the Gods	1979	$35
140	Tribute to Tatum	197?	$30
CORAL			
CRL57201 [M]	Sing Around the Piano	1958	$50
CRL57003 [M]	Sweet and Lovely	195?	$30
DREAMSTREET			
DR-106	Lou Stein Trio Live at the Dome	1986	$25
EPIC			
LN3186 [M]	From Broadway to Paris	1955	$80
LG3101 [M]	House Top	1955	$80
LN3148 [M]	Three, Four and Five	1955	$80
JUBILEE			
JLP-1019 [M]	Eight for Kicks, Four for Laughs	1956	$40
JLP-8 [10]	Six for Kicks	1954	$100
MASTERSEAL			
MS33-1812 [M]	Mood Music for Beer and Pretzels	1957	$35
MERCURY			
SR-60054 [S]	Honky Tonk Piano	1959	$100
MG-20364 [M]	Honky Tonk Piano	195?	$20
MG-20159 [M]	Honky Tonk Piano	195?	$25
MG-20469 [M]	Honky Tonk Piano and a Hot Banjo	1960	$100
SR-60151 [S]	Honky Tonk Piano and a Hot Banjo	1960	$100
MG-20271 [M]	Saloon Favorites	195?	$20
MUSICOR			
MM-2057 [M]	Hey Louie! Play Melancholy Baby!	1967	$35
MS-3057 [S]	Hey Louie! Play Melancholy Baby!	1967	$30
WING			
SRW-16219 [S]	The Lou Stein-Way of Piano Pleasure	196?	$35
MGW-12219 [M]	The Lou Stein-Way of Piano Pleasure	196?	$30
WORLD JAZZ			
WJLPS-17	Lou Stein and Friends	1980	$30

STEPS AHEAD

Fusion supergroup: MICHAEL BRECKER (tenor sax); Steve Gadd (drums, replaced by PETER ERSKINE); EDDIE GOMEZ (bass); MIKE MAINIERI (vibes); DON GROLNICK (piano, replaced by ELIANE ELIAS, who was replaced by WARREN BERNHARDT).

Albums

Number	Title	Yr	NM
ELEKTRA/MUSICIAN			
60441	Magnetic	1986	$25
60351	Modern Times	1985	$25
60168	Steps	1983	$25

STERLING, ARNOLD

Alto saxophone player.

Albums

Number	Title	Yr	NM
JAM			
010	Here's Brother Sterling	198?	$30

STERN, LENI

Guitarist.

Albums

Number	Title	Yr	NM
ENJA			
R1-79602	Secrets	1989	$30

STERN, MIKE

Guitarist.

Albums

Number	Title	Yr	NM
ATLANTIC			
82027	Jigsaw	1990	$30
81840	Time in Place	1988	$25
81656	Upside Downside	1986	$25

STEVENS, CLIVE

Tenor and soprano saxophone player and flutist.

Albums

Number	Title	Yr	NM
CAPITOL			
ST-11263	Atmospheres	1973	$35
SM-11675	Atmospheres	1976	$25
ST-11320	Voyage to Uranus	1974	$35
SM-11676	Voyage to Uranus	1976	$25

STEVENS, LEITH

Pianist, composer and conductor.

Albums

Number	Title	Yr	NM
CORAL			
CRL57283 [M]	Jazz Themes for Cops and Robbers	1958	$50
DECCA			
DL5515 [10]	Jazz Themes in "The Wild One	1954	$150

STEVENS, MIKE

Saxophone and keyboard player.

Albums

Number	Title	Yr	NM
NOVUS			
3042-1-N	Light Up the Night	1988	$25
3080-1-N	Set the Spirit Free	1990	$30

STEWARD, HERB

Tenor, alto and baritone saxophone player. Also see THE FOUR BROTHERS.

Albums

Number	Title	Yr	NM
AVA			
A-9 [M]	So Pretty	1962	$30
AS-9 [S]	So Pretty	1962	$30
FAMOUS DOOR			
139	Three Horns of Herb Steward	1981	$30

STEWART, BOB

Tuba player.

Albums

Number	Title	Yr	NM
DAWN			
DLP-1103 [M]	Let's Talk About Love	1956	$50
JMT			
834414-1	First Line	1988	$25
STASH			
ST-266	In a Sentimental Mood	1987	$25

STEWART, HELYNE

Female singer.

Albums

Number	Title	Yr	NM
CONTEMPORARY			
M-3601 [M]	Love Moods	1962	$200
S-7601 [S]	Love Moods	1962	$200

STEWART, JIMMY

Guitarist.

Albums

Number	Title	Yr	NM
BLACKHAWK			
BKH-50301	The Touch	1986	$25
CADENCE JAZZ			
CJR-1018	An Engineer of Sounds	198?	$25
CATALYST			
7621	Fire Flower	1977	$30

Art Tatum, *The Genius of Art Tatum 10*, Clef MGC-661, **$200**.

Art Tatum, *The Art Tatum Trio*, Capitol H 408, 10-inch LP, **150**.

Billy Taylor, *Billy Taylor Trio Vol. 2*, Prestige PRLP-7016, **$300**.

Billy Taylor, *In Concert at Town Hall*, December 17, 1954, Prestige PRLP-194, 10-inch LP, **$300**.

STEWART, REX, AND DICKIE WELLS
Also see each artist's individual listings.
Albums

Number	Title	Yr	NM
RCA VICTOR			
❏ LPM-2024 [M]	Chatter Jazz	1959	$30
❏ LSP-2024 [S]	Chatter Jazz	1959	$30

STEWART, REX
Cornet and trumpet player.
Albums

Number	Title	Yr	NM
AMERICAN RECORDING SOCIETY			
❏ G-448 [M]	The Big Challenge	1958	$40
ATLANTIC			
❏ 1209 [M]	Big Jazz	1956	$300
CONCERT HALL JAZZ			
❏ 1202 [M]	Dixieland On Location	1954	$80
DIAL			
❏ LP-215 [10]	Ellingtonia	1951	$250
FELSTED			
❏ 7001 [M]	Rendezvous with Rex	1958	$40
❏ 2001 [S]	Rendezvous with Rex	1958	$30
GRAND AWARD			
❏ GA 33-414 [M]	Just for Kicks	195?	$40
HALL OF FAME			
❏ 624	Reunion	197?	$25
JAZZOLOGY			
❏ J-36	The Irrepressible Rex Stewart	197?	$30
JAZZTONE			
❏ J-1202 [M]	Dixieland Free-for-All	1956	$40
❏ J-1268 [M]	The Big Challenge	1957	$60
❏ J-1285 [M]	The Big Reunion	1957	$60
MASTER JAZZ			
❏ 8123	Rendezvous with Rex	197?	$30
PRESTIGE			
❏ PRST-7728	Memorial Album	1970	$35
❏ PRST-7812	Trumpet Jive!	1971	$35
— With Wingy Manone			
SWING			
❏ SW-8414	Porgy and Bess Revisited	1986	$25
SWINGVILLE			
❏ SVLP-2006 [M]	The Happy Jazz of Rex Stewart	1960	$50
— Purple label			
❏ SVLP-2006 [M]	The Happy Jazz of Rex Stewart	1965	$30
— Blue label, trident logo at right			
UNITED ARTISTS			
❏ UAL-4009 [M]	Henderson Homecoming	1959	$40
❏ UAS-5009 [S]	Henderson Homecoming	1959	$30
URANIA			
❏ UJLP-2012 [M]	Cool Fever	1955	$150
WARNER BROS.			
❏ W1260 [M]	Porgy and Bess Revisited	1958	$40
❏ WS1260 [S]	Porgy and Bess Revisited	1958	$30
X			
❏ LX-3001 [10]	Rex Stewart and His Orchestra	1954	$100

STEWART, REX/ILLINOIS JACQUET
Also see each artist's individual listings.
Albums

Number	Title	Yr	NM
GRAND AWARD			
❏ GA 33-315 [M]	Rex Stewart Plays Duke/ Uptown Jazz	1955	$50

STEWART, REX/PEANUTS HUCKO
Also see each artist's individual listings.
Albums

Number	Title	Yr	NM
JAZZTONE			
❏ J-1250 [M]	Dedicated Jazz	1957	$40

STEWART, SANDY
Female singer. On the below LP, she is accompanied by DICK HYMAN on piano.
Albums

Number	Title	Yr	NM
AUDIOPHILE			
❏ AP-205	Sandy Stewart Sings Songs of Jerome Kern	1985	$25
— Accompanied by Dick Hyman on piano			
COLPIX			
❏ CP-441 [M]	My Coloring Book	1963	$60
❏ SCP-441 [S]	My Coloring Book	1963	$60

STEWART, SLAM, AND BUCKY PIZZARELLI
Also see each artist's individual listings.
Albums

Number	Title	Yr	NM
STASH			
❏ ST-201	Dialogue	1978	$30

STEWART, SLAM
Bass player and male singer.
Albums

Number	Title	Yr	NM
JAZZ MAN			
❏ 5010	Slam Stewart with Milt Buckner and Jo Jones	198?	$25
SAVOY			
❏ MG-12067 [M]	Bowin' Singin' Slam	1956	$40

STEWART, TOM
Tenor horn and bass trumpet player.
Albums

Number	Title	Yr	NM
ABC-PARAMOUNT			
❏ ABC-117 [M]	Tom Stewart Sextette/ Quintet	1956	$50

STEWART, TOMMY
Albums

Number	Title	Yr	NM
PROGRESSIVE			
❏ PRO-7009	Tommy Stewart and His Orchestra	198?	$25

STILES, DANNY, AND BILL WATROUS
Stiles is a trumpeter. Also see BILL WATROUS.
Albums

Number	Title	Yr	NM
FAMOUS DOOR			
❏ HL-103	In Tandem	1974	$50
❏ 126	In Tandem -- Into the 80s	1980	$35
❏ HL-112	One More Time	1977	$50

STITT, SONNY, AND GENE AMMONS
See GENE AMMONS AND SONNY STITT.

STITT, SONNY
Alto, tenor and baritone saxophone player. Also see STAN GETZ; THE MODERN JAZZ SEXTET; OSCAR PETERSON.
Albums

Number	Title	Yr	NM
ABC IMPULSE!			
❏ AS-52 [S]	Salt and Pepper	1968	$200
— With Paul Gonsalves; black label with red ring			
❏ AS-43 [S]	Sonny Stitt Now!	1968	$200
— Black label with red ring			
❏ AS-43 [S]	Sonny Stitt Now!	1975	$30
— Green, purple, blue "target" label			
ARGO			
❏ LP-661 [M]	Burnin'	1960	$40
❏ LPS-661 [S]	Burnin'	1960	$100
❏ LP-730 [M]	Move On Over	1964	$40
❏ LPS-730 [S]	Move On Over	1964	$100
❏ LP-744 [M]	My Main Man	1965	$40
❏ LPS-744 [S]	My Main Man	1965	$100
❏ LP-709 [M]	Rearin' Back	1962	$40
❏ LPS-709 [S]	Rearin' Back	1962	$100
❏ LP-629 [M]	Sonny Stitt	1958	$100
❏ LP-683 [M]	Sonny Stitt at the D.J. Lounge	1961	$40
❏ LPS-683 [S]	Sonny Stitt at the D.J. Lounge	1961	$100
ATLANTIC			
❏ SD3008	Deuces Wild	1970	$50
❏ 1395 [M]	Sonny Stitt and the Top Brass	1962	$150
❏ SD1395 [S]	Sonny Stitt and the Top Brass	1962	$150
❏ 90139	Sonny Stitt and the Top Brass	198?	$30
❏ 1418 [M]	Stitt Plays Bird	1964	$60
❏ SD1418 [S]	Stitt Plays Bird	1964	$40
BLACKHAWK			
❏ 528	Good Life	1982	$30
BLACK LION			
❏ 307	Night Work	197?	$30
CADET			
❏ LP-661 [M]	Burnin'	1966	$50
— Fading blue label			
❏ LPS-661 [S]	Burnin'	1966	$60
— Fading blue label			
❏ CA-661	Burnin'	197?	$30
— Yellow and pink label			
❏ 2CA-50039	I Cover the Waterfront	1974	$60
❏ LP-760 [M]	Inter-Action	1966	$60
— Fading blue label			
❏ LPS-760 [S]	Inter-Action	1966	$40
— Fading blue label			
❏ LP-730 [M]	Move On Over	1966	$50
— Fading blue label			
❏ LPS-730 [S]	Move On Over	1966	$60
— Fading blue label			
❏ CA-730 [S]	Move On Over	197?	$30
— Yellow and pink label			
❏ CA-50026	Mr. Bojangles	1973	$40
❏ LP-744 [M]	My Main Man	1966	$50
— Fading blue label			
❏ LPS-744 [S]	My Main Man	1966	$60
— Fading blue label			
❏ CA-60040	Never Can Say Goodbye	1975	$50
❏ LP-709 [M]	Rearin' Back	1966	$50
— Fading blue label			
❏ LPS-709 [S]	Rearin' Back	1966	$60
— Fading blue label			
❏ CA-709	Rearin' Back	197?	$30
— Yellow and pink label			
❏ CA-50060	Satan	1974	$50
❏ LP-629 [M]	Sonny Stitt	1966	$50
— Fading blue label			
❏ CA-629 [R]	Sonny Stitt	197?	$25
— Yellow and pink label			
❏ LP-683 [M]	Sonny Stitt at the D.J. Lounge	1966	$50
— Fading blue label			
❏ LPS-683 [S]	Sonny Stitt at the D.J. Lounge	1966	$60
— Fading blue label			
❏ CA-683	Sonny Stitt at the D.J. Lounge	197?	$30
— Yellow and pink label			
❏ LP-770 [M]	Soul In the Night	1966	$60
— Fading blue label			
❏ LPS-770 [S]	Soul In the Night	1966	$40
— Fading blue label			
CATALYST			
❏ 7608	Forecast	1976	$50
— With Red Holloway			
❏ 7616	I Remember Bird	1977	$50
❏ 7620	Tribute to Duke Ellington	1977	$35
CHESS			
❏ 2ACMJ-405	Interaction	197?	$50
— With Zoot Sims			
❏ CH-9317	Sonny Stitt	1990	$30
❏ CH-91523	Sonny Stitt at the D.J. Lounge	198?	$30
COBBLESTONE			
❏ CST-9021	Constellation	1973	$50
❏ CST-9013	Tune-Up	1972	$60
COLPIX			
❏ CP-499 [M]	Broadway Soul	1964	$60
❏ SCP-499 [S]	Broadway Soul	1964	$40
DELMARK			
❏ DS-426	Made for Each Other	1972	$50
FANTASY			
❏ OJC-060	Kaleidoscope	198?	$30
❏ OJC-009	Sonny Stitt/Bud Powell/J.J. Johnson	198?	$30
FLYING DUTCHMAN			
❏ BDL1-1197	Dumpy Mama	1975	$60
❏ BDL1-1538	Stomp Off Let's Go	1976	$50
GALAXY			
❏ 8204	In the Beginning	197?	$50
GRP/IMPULSE!			
❏ IMP-210	Salt and Pepper	1997	$35
— Reissue on audiophile vinyl			
IMPULSE!			
❏ A-52 [M]	Salt and Pepper	1964	$160
❏ AS-52 [S]	Salt and Pepper	1964	$200
— With Paul Gonsalves			
❏ A-43 [M]	Sonny Stitt Now!	1963	$200
❏ AS-43 [S]	Sonny Stitt Now!	1963	$200
JAZZLAND			
❏ JLP-71 [M]	Low Flame	1962	$40

Number	Title	Yr	NM
❑ JLP-971 [S]	Low Flame	1962	$100

JAZZ MAN

Number	Title	Yr	NM
❑ 5040	Night Work	198?	$30

—Reissue of Black Lion LP

JAZZTONE

Number	Title	Yr	NM
❑ J-1231 [M]	Early Modern	1956	$150
❑ J-1263 [M]	Early Modern	1957	$120

MUSE

Number	Title	Yr	NM
❑ MR-5006	12!	1973	$35
❑ MR-5129	Blues for Duke	1978	$30
❑ MR-5323	Constellation	1986	$35

—Reissue of Cobblestone 9021

Number	Title	Yr	NM
❑ MR-5228	In Style	1982	$30
❑ MR-5067	Mellow	1975	$50
❑ MR-5091	My Buddy: Sonny Stitt Plays for Gene Ammons	1976	$35
❑ MR-5204	Sonny's Back	1981	$35
❑ MR-5023	The Champ	1974	$35
❑ MR-5269	The Last Stitt Sessions, Vol. 1	1983	$35
❑ MR-5280	The Last Stitt Sessions, Vol. 2	1984	$35
❑ MR-5334	Tune-Up	1987	$35

—Reissue of Cobblestone 9013

NEW JAZZ

Number	Title	Yr	NM
❑ NJLP-103 [10]	Sonny Stitt and Bud Powell	1950	$500

PACIFIC JAZZ

Number	Title	Yr	NM
❑ PJ-71 [M]	My Mother's Eyes	1963	$150
❑ ST-71 [S]	My Mother's Eyes	1963	$150

PAULA

Number	Title	Yr	NM
❑ 4004	Soul Girl	1974	$30

PHOENIX

Number	Title	Yr	NM
❑ 19	Battles	197?	$25
❑ 15	Superstitt	197?	$25

PRESTIGE

Number	Title	Yr	NM
❑ PRLP-7248 [M]	All God's Chillun Got Rhythm	1962	$150

—Yellow label with Bergenfield, N.J. address

Number	Title	Yr	NM
❑ PRLP-7248 [M]	All God's Chillun Got Rhythm	1964	$40

—Blue label with trident logo

Number	Title	Yr	NM
❑ PRST-7248 [R]	All God's Chillun Got Rhythm	1962	$150
❑ PRST-7769	Best for Lovers	1970	$60
❑ P-10032	Black Vibrations	1972	$60
❑ PRST-7839	Bud's Blues	1974	$50
❑ PRLP-126 [10]	Favorites, Volume 1	1952	$400
❑ PRLP-148 [10]	Favorites, Volume 2	1953	$400
❑ P-24044	Genesis	1974	$50
❑ 10048	Goin' Down Slow	1973	$60
❑ PRLP-7077 [M]	Kaleidoscope	1957	$300

—Yellow label with W. 50th St address

Number	Title	Yr	NM
❑ PRLP-111 [10]	Mr. Saxophone	1951	$400
❑ PRLP-7436 [M]	Night Crawler	1966	$40

—Blue label, trident logo at right

Number	Title	Yr	NM
❑ PRST-7436 [S]	Night Crawler	1966	$100

—Blue label, trident logo at right

Number	Title	Yr	NM
❑ PRST-7759	Night Letter	1970	$50
❑ PRLP-7452 [M]	'Nuther Fu'ther	1966	$40

—Blue label, trident logo at right

Number	Title	Yr	NM
❑ PRST-7452 [S]	'Nuther Fu'ther	1966	$100

—Blue label, trident logo at right

Number	Title	Yr	NM
❑ PRST-7452 [S]	'Nuther Fu'ther	197?	$60

—Green label

Number	Title	Yr	NM
❑ PRLP-7459 [M]	Pow!	1967	$100

—Blue label, trident logo at right

Number	Title	Yr	NM
❑ PRST-7459 [S]	Pow!	1967	$40

—Blue label, trident logo at right

Number	Title	Yr	NM
❑ PRLP-7302 [M]	Primitive Soul!	1964	$150

—Yellow label with Bergenfield, N.J. address

Number	Title	Yr	NM
❑ PRLP-7302 [M]	Primitive Soul!	1965	$40

—Blue label with trident logo

Number	Title	Yr	NM
❑ PRST-7302 [S]	Primitive Soul!	1964	$140

—Silver label

Number	Title	Yr	NM
❑ PRST-7302 [S]	Primitive Soul!	1965	$40

—Blue label with trident logo

Number	Title	Yr	NM
❑ PRLP-7332 [M]	Shangri-La	1964	$40

—Blue label, trident logo at right

Number	Title	Yr	NM
❑ PRST-7332 [S]	Shangri-La	1964	$100

—Blue label, trident logo at right

Number	Title	Yr	NM
❑ P-10074	So Doggone Good	1974	$35
❑ PRLP-103 [10]	Sonny Stitt Plays	1951	$400
❑ PRLP-7024 [M]	Sonny Stitt with Bud Powell and J.J. Johnson	1956	$450
❑ PRST-7635	Soul Electricity	1969	$60
❑ PRLP-7372 [M]	Soul People	1965	$40

—Blue label, trident logo at right

Number	Title	Yr	NM
❑ PRST-7372 [S]	Soul People	1965	$100

—Blue label, trident logo at right

Number	Title	Yr	NM
❑ PRST-7372 [S]	Soul People	197?	$60

—Green label

Number	Title	Yr	NM
❑ PRLP-7297 [M]	Soul Shack	1964	$150

—Yellow label with Bergenfield, N.J. address

Number	Title	Yr	NM
❑ PRLP-7297 [M]	Soul Shack	1965	$40

—Blue label with trident logo

Number	Title	Yr	NM
❑ PRST-7297 [S]	Soul Shack	1964	$140

—Silver label with Bergenfield, N.J. address

Number	Title	Yr	NM
❑ PRST-7297 [S]	Soul Shack	1965	$40

—Blue label with trident logo

Number	Title	Yr	NM
❑ PRLP-7244 [M]	Stitt Meets Brother Jack	1962	$150

—Yellow label with Bergenfield, N.J. address

Number	Title	Yr	NM
❑ PRLP-7244 [M]	Stitt Meets Brother Jack	1964	$40

—Blue label with trident logo

Number	Title	Yr	NM
❑ PRST-7244 [S]	Stitt Meets Brother Jack	1962	$150
❑ PRLP-7133 [M]	Stitt's Bits	1958	$200
❑ PRST-7585	Stitt's Bits, Volume 1	1968	$60
❑ PRST-7612	Stitt's Bits, Volume 2	1969	$60
❑ PRST-7701	The Best of Sonny Stitt with Brother Jack McDuff	1969	$60
❑ P-10012	Turn It On	1971	$60

PROGRESSIVE

Number	Title	Yr	NM
❑ PRO-7034	Sonny Stitt Meets Sadik Hakim	1978	$60

ROOST

Number	Title	Yr	NM
❑ LP-2219 [M]	37 Minutes and 48 Seconds with Sonny Stitt	1957	$150
❑ LP-2235 [M]	A Little Bit of Stitt	1959	$140
❑ SLP-2235 [S]	A Little Bit of Stitt	1959	$120
❑ LP-1203 [M]	Battle of Birdland	1955	$200
❑ LP-2247 [M]	Feelin's	1962	$120
❑ SLP-2247 [S]	Feelin's	1962	$120
❑ LP-418 [10]	Jazz at the Hi-Hat	1954	$400
❑ LP-2245 [M]	Sonny Side Up	1960	$150
❑ SLP-2245 [S]	Sonny Side Up	1960	$150
❑ LP-1208 [M]	Sonny Stitt	1956	$200
❑ LP-2208 [M]	Sonny Stitt	1957	$200
❑ LP-2253 [M]	Sonny Stitt Goes Latin	1963	$100
❑ SLP-2253 [S]	Sonny Stitt Goes Latin	1963	$100
❑ LP-2252 [M]	Sonny Stitt in Orbit	1963	$100
❑ SLP-2252 [S]	Sonny Stitt in Orbit	1963	$100
❑ LP-415 [10]	Sonny Stitt Plays Arrangements from the Pen of Johnny Richards	1952	$400
❑ LP-2204 [M]	Sonny Stitt Plays Arrangements of Quincy Jones	1957	$150
❑ LP-2226 [M]	Sonny Stitt with the New Yorkers	1958	$150
❑ LP-2244 [M]	Stittsville	1960	$140
❑ SLP-2244 [S]	Stittsville	1960	$150
❑ LP-2230 [M]	The Saxophone of Sonny Stitt	1959	$140
❑ SLP-2230 [S]	The Saxophone of Sonny Stitt	1959	$120
❑ LP-2240 [M]	The Sonny Side of Stitt	1960	$140
❑ SLP-2240 [S]	The Sonny Side of Stitt	1960	$120

ROULETTE

Number	Title	Yr	NM
❑ R-25348 [M]	I Keep Comin' Back	1967	$40
❑ SR-25348 [S]	I Keep Comin' Back	1967	$60
❑ SR-42035	Make Someone Happy	1969	$50
❑ SR-25354 [S]	Parallel-O-Stitt	1968	$60
❑ R-25354 [M]	Parallel-O-Stitt	1968	$100
❑ SR-42048	Stardust	1970	$50
❑ SR-5002	Stardust	197?	$35

—Reissue of 42048

Number	Title	Yr	NM
❑ R-25339 [M]	The Matadors Meet the Bull	1965	$40
❑ SR-25339 [S]	The Matadors Meet the Bull	1965	$100
❑ R-25343 [M]	What's New?	1966	$60
❑ SR-25343 [S]	What's New?	1966	$40

SAVOY

Number	Title	Yr	NM
❑ MG-9006 [10]	All Star Series: Sonny Stitt	1953	$300
❑ MG-9012 [10]	New Sounds in Modern Music	1953	$300
❑ MG-9014 [10]	New Trends Of Jazz	1953	$300

SAVOY JAZZ

Number	Title	Yr	NM
❑ SJL-1165	Symphony Hall Swing	1986	$35

SOLID STATE

Number	Title	Yr	NM
❑ SS-18057	Come Hither	1969	$50
❑ SS-18047	Little Green Apples	1968	$50

TRIP

Number	Title	Yr	NM
❑ TLX-5008	Two Sides of Sonny Stitt	1974	$35

UPFRONT

Number	Title	Yr	NM
❑ UPF-196	Sonny's Blues	197?	$30

VERVE

Number	Title	Yr	NM
❑ MGV-8219 [M]	New York Jazz	1957	$150
❑ V-8219 [M]	New York Jazz	1961	$60
❑ UMV-2558	New York Jazz	198?	$30
❑ MGV-8250 [M]	Only the Blues	1958	$100
❑ V-8250 [M]	Only the Blues	1961	$60
❑ UMV-2634	Only the Blues	198?	$30
❑ MGV-8324 [M]	Personal Appearance	1959	$100
❑ V-8324 [M]	Personal Appearance	1961	$60
❑ V6-8837	Previously Unreleased Recordings	1974	$30
❑ MGV-8377 [M]	Saxophone Supremacy	1960	$100
❑ MGVS-6154 [S]	Saxophone Supremacy	1960	$0

—Canceled

Number	Title	Yr	NM
❑ V-8377 [M]	Saxophone Supremacy	1961	$60
❑ V-8380 [M]	Sommy Stitt Swings the Most	1961	$60
❑ MGV-8262 [M]	Sonny Side Up	1958	$120
❑ V-8262 [M]	Sonny Side Up	1961	$60
❑ MGV-8403 [M]	Sonny Stitt	1960	$0

—Canceled

Number	Title	Yr	NM
❑ MGV-8374 [M]	Sonny Stitt Blows the Blues	1960	$100
❑ MGVS-6149 [S]	Sonny Stitt Blows the Blues	1960	$100
❑ V-8374 [M]	Sonny Stitt Blows the Blues	1961	$60
❑ V6-8374 [S]	Sonny Stitt Blows the Blues	1961	$50
❑ MGVS-6149	Sonny Stitt Blows the Blues	1996	$40

—Audiophile reissue by Classic Records

Number	Title	Yr	NM
❑ MGVS-6149-45	Sonny Stitt Blows the Blues	1999	$40

—Audiophile reissue by Classic Records; plays at 45 rpm

Number	Title	Yr	NM
❑ MGV-8309 [M]	Sonny Stitt Plays Jimmy Giuffre Arrangements	1959	$100
❑ MGVS-6041 [S]	Sonny Stitt Plays Jimmy Giuffre Arrangements	1960	$100
❑ V-8309 [M]	Sonny Stitt Plays Jimmy Giuffre Arrangements	1961	$60
❑ V6-8309 [S]	Sonny Stitt Plays Jimmy Giuffre Arrangements	1961	$50
❑ MGV-8344 [M]	Sonny Stitt Sits In with the Oscar Peterson Trio	1959	$100
❑ MGVS-6108 [S]	Sonny Stitt Sits In with the Oscar Peterson Trio	1960	$100
❑ V-8344 [M]	Sonny Stitt Sits In with the Oscar Peterson Trio	1961	$60
❑ V6-8344 [S]	Sonny Stitt Sits In with the Oscar Peterson Trio	1961	$50
❑ MGV-8380 [M]	Sonny Stitt Swings the Most	1960	$100
❑ MGVS-6162 [S]	Sonny Stitt Swings the Most	1960	$0

—Canceled

Number	Title	Yr	NM
❑ MGV-8306 [M]	The Hard Swing	1959	$100
❑ MGVS-6038 [S]	The Hard Swing	1960	$100
❑ V-8306 [M]	The Hard Swing	1961	$60
❑ V6-8306 [S]	The Hard Swing	1961	$50
❑ V-8451 [M]	The Sensual Sound of Sonny Stitt	1962	$50
❑ V6-8451 [S]	The Sensual Sound of Sonny Stitt	1962	$60

WHO'S WHO IN JAZZ

Number	Title	Yr	NM
❑ 21022	Sonny, Sweets and Jaws	1981	$35
❑ 21025	The Bubba's Sessions	1982	$35

STOKES, CARL B.

Stokes was the first black mayor of a major American city (Cleveland, Ohio). This album consists of a Stokes press conference on Side 1, and him doing narration on Side 2 over music by OLIVER NELSON.

Albums

FLYING DUTCHMAN

Number	Title	Yr	NM
❑ FD-130	The Mayor and the People	1970	$100

STOLTZMAN, RICHARD

Clarinetist.

Albums

RCA

Number	Title	Yr	NM
❑ 5944-1-RC	New York Counterpoint	1987	$25

RCA VICTOR

Number	Title	Yr	NM
❑ AML1-7124	Begin Sweet World	1986	$25

STONE ALLIANCE

Primary members: Don Alias (drums, percussion); Steve Grossman (tenor saxophone); Gene Perla (bass). Also see MARCIO MONTARROYOS.

Albums

PM

Number	Title	Yr	NM
❑ 015	Con Amigos	197?	$30
❑ 020	Heads Up	197?	$30
❑ 013	Stone Alliance	197?	$30

STOPAK, BERNIE

Albums

STASH

Number	Title	Yr	NM
❑ ST-274	Remember Me	1988	$25

STORYVILLE STOMPERS, THE

Albums

TROPICANA

Number	Title	Yr	NM
❑ 1204 [M]	New Orleans Jazz	195?	$40

Number	Title	Yr	NM

STOVER, SMOKEY
Trumpeter and bandleader.
Albums

ARGO
LP-652 [DJ]	Smokey Stover's Original Firemen	1960	$60
—White label, multi-color vinyl			
LP-652 [M]	Smokey Stover's Original Firemen	1960	$30
LPS-652 [S]	Smokey Stover's Original Firemen	1960	$30

JAZZOLOGY
| J-53 | Smokey Stover and the Original Firemen | 197? | $25 |

STOWELL, JOHN
Guitarist.
Albums

INNER CITY
| IC-1030 | Golden Delicious | 197? | $30 |

STRAND, LES
Organist and pianist.
Albums

FANTASY
3242 [M]	Jazz Classics on the Baldwin Organ	1956	$50
—Red vinyl			
3242 [M]	Jazz Classics on the Baldwin Organ	195?	$25
—Black vinyl			
3231 [M]	Les Strand on the Baldwin Organ	1956	$50
—Red vinyl			
3231 [M]	Les Strand on the Baldwin Organ	195?	$25
—Black vinyl			

STRATTON, DON
Trumpeter.
Albums

ABC-PARAMOUNT
| ABC-118 [M] | Modern Jazz with Dixieland Roots | 1956 | $200 |

STRAYHORN, BILLY
Pianist, arranger and composer most closely associated with the DUKE ELLINGTON Orchestra. Among the many songs he wrote were "Take the 'A' Train" and "Lush Life."
Albums

FELSTED
| 7008 [M] | Billy Strayhorn Septet | 1958 | $80 |
| 2008 [S] | Billy Strayhorn Septet | 1958 | $60 |

MASTER JAZZ
| 8116 | Cue for Sax | 197? | $35 |

MERCER
| LP-1005 [10] | Billy Strayhorn and All-Stars | 1951 | $200 |
| LP-1001 [10] | Billy Strayhorn Trio | 1951 | $200 |

ROULETTE
| R-52119 [M] | Live! | 1965 | $25 |
| SR-52119 [S] | Live! | 1965 | $30 |

SOLID STATE
| SS-18031 | The Peaceful Side of Billy Strayhorn | 1968 | $35 |

UNITED ARTISTS
| UAJ-14010 [M] | The Peaceful Side of Billy Strayhorn | 1962 | $40 |
| UAJS-15010 [S] | The Peaceful Side of Billy Strayhorn | 1962 | $50 |

STRAZZERI, FRANK
Pianist.
Albums

CATALYST
| 7607 | After the Rain | 1976 | $30 |
| 7623 | Straz | 1977 | $30 |

CREATIVE WORLD
| ST-3003 | View From Within | 197? | $30 |

DISCOVERY
| DS-933 | Kat Dancin' | 1987 | $25 |

Number	Title	Yr	NM

GLENDALE
| 6002 | Frames | 197? | $30 |

REVELATION
| REV-10 | That's Him and This Is New | 1969 | $30 |

SEA BREEZE
| SB-1007 | Relaxin' | 198? | $30 |

STREETDANCER
Albums

DHARMA
| 807 | Rising | 197? | $35 |

FUTURE
| 2001 | Streetdancer | 197? | $35 |

STRING TRIO OF NEW YORK
Members: Diane Monroe (violin); James Emery (guitar); John Lindberg (bass).
Albums

BLACK SAINT
BSR-0048	Area Code 212	198?	$30
BSR-0058	Common Goal	198?	$30
BSR-0031	First String	198?	$30
BSR-0068	Rebirth of a Feeling	1984	$30

STROLLERS, THE
Members: PLAS JOHNSON (flute); Earl Palmer (drums); AL VIOLA (guitar); Wilfred Middlebrooks (bass).
Albums

SCORE
| SLP-4026 [M] | Swinging Flute in Hi-Fi | 1958 | $100 |

STROZIER, FRANK
Alto saxophone player and composer. Also see THE YOUNG LIONS; YOUNG MEN FROM MEMPHIS.
Albums

INNER CITY
| IC-2066 | Remember Me | 197? | $35 |

JAZZLAND
JLP-56 [M]	Long Night	1961	$30
JLP-956 [S]	Long Night	1961	$30
JLP-70 [M]	March of the Siamese Children	1962	$30
JLP-970 [S]	March of the Siamese Children	1962	$30

STEEPLECHASE
| SCS-1066 | Remember Me | 198? | $30 |

VEE JAY
| LP-3005 [M] | Fantastic Frank Strozier | 1960 | $30 |
| SR-3005 [S] | Fantastic Frank Strozier | 1960 | $40 |

STRUNZ & FARAH
Guitarists Jorge Strunz and Ardeshir Farah.
Albums

MILESTONE
| M-9123 | Frontera | 1984 | $25 |
| M-9136 | Guitarras | 1985 | $25 |

STUART, RORY
Guitarist.
Albums

CADENCE JAZZ
| CJR-1016 | Nightwork | 1983 | $25 |

SUNNYSIDE
| SSC-1021 | Hurricane | 1988 | $25 |

STUBBLEFIELD, JOHN
Tenor and soprano saxophone player.
Albums

SOUL NOTE
| SN-1095 | Confessin' | 1985 | $30 |

STORYVILLE
| 4011 | Prelude | 197? | $30 |

STUBO, THORGEIR
Guitarist.
Albums

CADENCE JAZZ
| CJR-1036 | End of a Tune | 1988 | $25 |
| CJR-1030 | Rhythm-A-Ning | 1987 | $25 |

Number	Title	Yr	NM

STUERMER, DARYL
Guitarist.
Albums

GRP
| GR-9573 | Steppin' Out | 1988 | $25 |

SUBRAMANIAM, DR. L.
Violinist.
Albums

CRUSADERS
| 16003 | Blossom | 198? | $25 |
| —Audiophile vinyl | | | |

DISCOVERY
| DS-202 | Indian Classical Music | 198? | $30 |

MCA
| 5784 | Blossom | 1986 | $25 |

MILESTONE
M-9130	Conversations	1985	$25
M-9138	Mani & Co.	1986	$25
M-9114	Spanish Wave	198?	$30

STORYVILLE
| 4075 | Garland | 198? | $25 |

TREND
| 524 | Fantasy Without Limits | 1980 | $30 |

SUDHALTER, DICK
Trumpeter and fluegel horn player.
Albums

AUDIOPHILE
| AP-159 | Friends with Pleasure | 1981 | $25 |

STOMP OFF
| SOS-1207 | Get Out and Get Under the Moon | 1991 | $30 |

SUDLER, MONETTE
Guitarist.
Albums

INNER CITY
| IC-2062 | Time for a Change | 197? | $35 |

STEEPLECHASE
SCS-1087	Brighter Days for You	198?	$30
SCS-1102	Live in Europe	198?	$30
SCS-1062	Time for a Change	198?	$30

SULIEMAN, IDREES
Trumpeter and fluegel horn player. Also see THE PRESTIGE BLUES SWINGERS.
Albums

NEW JAZZ
NJLP-8202 [M]	Roots	1958	$150
—Purple label			
NJLP-8202 [M]	Roots	1958	$200
—Yellow label			
NJLP-8202 [M]	Roots	1965	$150
—Blue label, trident logo at right			

STEEPLECHASE
| SCS-1202 | Bird's Grass | 198? | $30 |
| SCS-1052 | Now Is the Time | 198? | $30 |

SULLIVAN, CHARLES
Trumpeter.
Albums

INNER CITY
| IC-1012 | Genesis | 1975 | $35 |

SULLIVAN, FRANK
Pianist.
Albums

REVELATION
| 34 | First Impressions | 1981 | $25 |

SULLIVAN, IRA
Trumpeter, fluegel horn player, alto and tenor saxophone player, and flutist.
Albums

ATLANTIC
| 1476 [M] | Horizons | 1967 | $30 |

Billy Taylor, *Cross Section*, Prestige PRLP-7071, **$300**.

Clark Terry, *Serenade to a Bus Seat*, Riverside RLP 12-237, white label with blue print, original, **$350**.

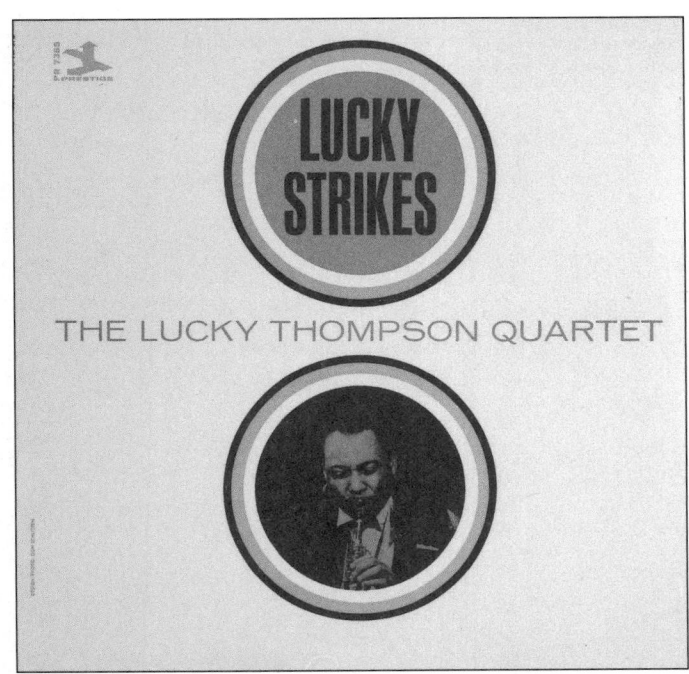

Lucky Thompson, *Lucky Strikes*, Prestige PRLP-7365, mono, **$50**.

Claude Thornhill, *Claude Thornhill Plays the Great Jazz Arrangements of Gerry Mulligan and Ralph Aldrich*, Trend TL-1002, 10-inch LP, **$120**.

Number	Title	Yr	NM
❏ SD-1476 [S]	Horizons	1967	$35
DELMARK			
❏ DL-402 [M]	Blue Stroll	1961	$30
❏ DS-402 [S]	Blue Stroll	1961	$40
❏ DS-422	Nicky's Tune	1970	$50
DISCOVERY			
❏ 873	Horizons	1983	$30
—Reissue of Atlantic SD 1476			
FLYING FISH			
❏ FF-27075	Ira Sullivan	198?	$25
—Reissue			
❏ FF-075	Ira Sullivan	1978	$30
GALAXY			
❏ 5137	Multimedia	198?	$30
❏ 5114	Peace	1979	$30
HORIZON			
❏ SP-706	Ira Sullivan	1976	$30
MUSE			
❏ MR-5242	Ira Sullivan Does It All!	1981	$35
PAUSA			
❏ 7169	Strings Attached	1985	$30
STASH			
❏ ST-208	The Incredible Ira Sullivan	1980	$50
VEE JAY			
❏ VJS-3003 [S]	Bird Lives!	198?	$30
—Reissue with new prefix on thinner vinyl			
❏ LP-3003 [M]	Bird Lives!	1960	$50
❏ SR-3003 [S]	Bird Lives!	1960	$60

SULLIVAN, JOE
Pianist.

Albums

Number	Title	Yr	NM
CAPITOL			
❏ T636 [M]	Classics in Jazz	1955	$75
DOWN HOME			
❏ MGD-2 [M]	Mr. Piano Man: The Music of Joe Sullivan	1956	$50
EPIC			
❏ LG1003 [10]	Joe Sullivan Plays Fats Waller Compositions	1954	$150
FOLKWAYS			
❏ FJ-2851	Joe Sullivan Piano	197?	$30
RIVERSIDE			
❏ RLP 12-202 [M]	New Solos by an Old Master	1955	$300
TIME-LIFE			
❏ STL-J-27	Giants of Jazz	1982	$50
VERVE			
❏ MGV-1002 [M]	Mr. Piano Man: The Music of Joe Sullivan	1957	$150
❏ V-1002 [M]	Mr. Piano Man: The Music of Joe Sullivan	1961	$25

SULLIVAN, MAXINE, AND BOB WILBER
Also see each artist's individual listings.

Albums

Number	Title	Yr	NM
MONMOUTH-EVERGREEN			
❏ 6917	Bob & Maxine	1969	$35
❏ 6919	Maxine Sullivan and Bob Wilber	1969	$30

SULLIVAN, MAXINE
Female singer.

Albums

Number	Title	Yr	NM
ATLANTIC			
❏ 81783	Together	1987	$25
AUDIOPHILE			
❏ AP-193	Good Morning, Life!	1986	$25
❏ AP-185	It Was Great Fun	1984	$25
❏ AP-167	Maxine	198?	$25
❏ AP-154	Maxine Sullivan and the Ike Isaacs Trio	198?	$25
❏ AP-128	We Just Couldn't Say Goodbye	1979	$25
CIRCLE			
❏ 47	Maxine Sullivan and John Kirby 1940	198?	$25
CONCORD JAZZ			
❏ CJ-288	Uptown	1986	$25
EVEREST ARCHIVE OF FOLK & JAZZ			
❏ 307	Maxine Sullivan with Jack Teagarden	197?	$25

MONMOUTH-EVERGREEN

Number	Title	Yr	NM
❏ 7038	Sullivan, Shakespeare and Hyman	197?	$35
PERIOD			
❏ SPL-1207 [M]	Maxine Sullivan, Volume 2	1956	$50
❏ RL-1909 [M]	Maxine Sullivan 1956	1956	$50
STASH			
❏ ST-257	Maxine Sullivan Sings the Music of Burton Lane	1986	$25
❏ ST-244	The Great Songs from the Cotton Club by Harold Arlen and Ted Koehler	1985	$25

SULLIVAN, PAT, JAZZ ORCHESTRA

Albums

Number	Title	Yr	NM
PJS			
❏ WRC1-2536	Stairway Down to the Stars	1985	$25

SUMMERLIN, ED
Composer, arranger and conductor. Also a tenor saxophone player.

Albums

Number	Title	Yr	NM
ECCLESIA			
❏ ER-101 [M]	Liturgical Jazz	1959	$60

SUMMERS, BILL
Percussionist.

Albums

Number	Title	Yr	NM
PRESTIGE			
❏ 10103	Cayenne	1977	$35
❏ 10102	Feel the Heat	1977	$35
❏ 10105	Straight to the Bank	1978	$35

SUN RA
Pianist, keyboard player, composer and bandleader (assorted Arkestras). The albums on the Saturn label are difficult to arrange into any sensible order - they are roughly numerical below, ignoring most punctuation, though some may not be. They also are much more difficult to find than the prices indicate. Rarely do any of them come up for sale, and when they do, the prices vary widely. We've opted to go on the side of caution, but be aware that a Sun Ra fanatic can pay a LOT more for some of these LPs. There are also many more variations than even listed below; if you have to know more, see Robert Campbell's The Earthy Recordings Of Sun Ra (Cadence Jazz Books; a new edition available on the website www.cadencebuilding.com).

Albums

Number	Title	Yr	NM
A&M			
❏ SP-5260 [B]	Blue Delight	1989	$150
ABC IMPULSE!			
❏ AS-9245 [B]	Angels and Demons at Play	1974	$300
❏ AS-9294	Art Forms from Dimensions Tomorrow	1974	$0
—Canceled?			
❏ AS-9255 [B]	Astro Black	1973	$300
❏ AS-9239 [B]	Atlantis	1973	$300
❏ AS-9291	Cosmic Tones for Mental Therapy	1974	$0
—Canceled?			
❏ AS-9297	Crystal Spears	1974	$0
—Canceled?			
❏ AS-9296	Cymbals	1974	$0
—Canceled?			
❏ AS-9270	Fate in a Pleasant Mood	1974	$200
❏ ASD-9265 [B]	Jazz in Silhouette	1974	$1200
❏ AS-9295	Monorails and Satellites	1974	$0
—Canceled?			
❏ AS-9289	My Brother the Wind	1974	$0
—Canceled?			
❏ AS-9287	Night of the Purple Moon	1974	$0
—Canceled?			
❏ AS-9293	Other Planes of There	1974	$0
—Canceled?			
❏ ASD-9298	Pathways to Unknown Worlds	1975	$250
❏ AS-9288	Planet Earth	1974	$0
—Canceled?			
❏ AS-9290	Sound Sound Pleasure	1974	$0
—Canceled?			
❏ AS-9271	Super Sonic Sounds	1974	$200
❏ ASD-9276 [B]	The Bad and the Beautiful	1974	$300
❏ AS-9243	The Magic City	1973	$200
❏ AS-9242 [B]	The Nubians of Plutonia	1974	$1200
❏ 1974 [B]	Welcome to Saturn	1974	$250

Number	Title	Yr	NM
❏ ASD-9292	We Travel the Spaceways	1974	$300
—May only exist as a promo or test pressing			
AFFINITY			
❏ AFF10	The Solar-Myth Approach Volume I	1978	$250
❏ AFF76	The Solar-Myth Approach Volume II	1978	$250
BASF			
❏ 20748	It's After the End of the World	1971	$250
BLACK LION			
❏ 106	Pictures of Infinity	197?	$250
BLACK SAINT			
❏ 120111	Hours After	1990	$150
❏ 120101	Reflections in Blue	1987	$200
DELMARK			
❏ DS-414 [R]	Sound of Joy	1968	$250
❏ DL-411 [M]	Sun Song	1967	$250
❏ DS-411 [R]	Sun Song	1967	$250
—Reissue of Transition 10			
DIW			
❏ DIWP-2 [PD]	Cosmo Omnibus Imaginable Illusion: Live at Pit-Inn	1988	$300
—Picture disc; limited to under 1,000 copies			
❏ 8024 [B]	Cosmo Omnibus Imaginable Illusion: Live at Pit-Inn	1988	$200
ESP-DISK'			
❏ S-1045 [S]	Nothing Is	1969	$250
❏ 1014 [M]	The Heliocentric Worlds of Sun Ra, Volume 1	1966	$300
❏ S-1014 [S]	The Heliocentric Worlds of Sun Ra, Volume 1	1966	$300
—Reproductions exist of this LP			
❏ 1017 [M]	The Heliocentric Worlds of Sun Ra, Volume 2	1966	$300
—With voices overdubbed on "The Sun Myth"			
❏ S-1017 [S]	The Heliocentric Worlds of Sun Ra, Volume 2	1966	$300
—With voices overdubbed on "The Sun Myth"			
❏ 1017 [M]	The Heliocentric Worlds of Sun Ra, Volume 2	1966	$300
—Without voices overdubbed on "The Sun Myth"			
❏ S-1017 [S]	The Heliocentric Worlds of Sun Ra, Volume 2	1966	$300
—Without voices overdubbed on "The Sun Myth"			
HAT ART			
❏ 2017	Sunrise in Different Directions	1986	$200
HAT HUT			
❏ 17	Sunrise in Different Directions	1980	$200
HORO			
❏ HDP-25/26	New Steps	1978	$200
❏ HDP-23/24	Other Voices, Other Blues	1978	$250
❏ HDP-19/20	Unity	1978	$250
IAI			
❏ 373850	Solo Piano Volume 1	197?	$250
❏ 373858	St. Louis Blues	1978	$250
INNER CITY			
❏ IC-1020	Cosmos	1978	$250
—Original edition; reproductions exist			
❏ IC-1039	Live at Montreux	1978	$250
JIHAD			
❏ 1968 [S]	A Black Mass	1968	$500
—Black and white cover			
❏ 1968 [S]	A Black Mass	1968	$800
—Color cover			
LEO			
❏ LR-154	Love in Outer Space: Live in Utrecht	1988	$200
MELTDOWN			
❏ MPA-1	John Cage Meets Sun Ra	1987	$200
PHILLY JAZZ			
❏ PJ-666	Lanquidity	1978	$250
—Reproductions exist			
❏ PJ-1007	Of Mythic Worlds	1980	$250
PRAXIS			
❏ CM110	Live at Praxis 84 Volume 3	1985	$200
❏ CM108	Live at Praxis Volume 1	1984	$250
❏ CM106	Sun Ra Arkestra Meets Salah Ragab in Egypt	1983	$250
RECOMMENDED			
❏ RR-11	Nuits de la Fondation Maeght Volume I	1981	$250
—Reissue of Shandar 10.001; plays at 45 rpm			

Number	Title	Yr	NM
ROUNDER			
❑ 3035	Strange Celestial Road	1982	$250
— Reproductions exist			
SATURN			
❑ A/B-1984SG-9 [B]	A Fireside Chat with Lucifer	1984	$1200
❑ 19841 [B]	A Fireside Chat with Lucifer	1984	$500
❑ SR-9956-2/O/P [M]	Angels and Demons at Play	1965	$800
— Red label; metallic gold cover			
❑ LP-407 [M]	Angels and Demons at Play	196?	$400
— Chicago address on label; reproductions exist			
❑ SR-9956 [M]	Art Forms of Dimensions Tomorrow	1965	$1200
— Red label; reproductions exist			
❑ LP-404 [M]	Art Forms of Dimensions Tomorrow	1969	$500
— Chicago address on label; reproductions exist			
❑ ESR-507 [S]	Atlantis	1969	$800
— El Saturn" label			
❑ 527-529-530 [B]	A Tonal View of Times Tomorrow		$2000
❑ 10480 [B]	Aurora Borealis	1980	$500
❑ 123180 [B]	Beyond the Purple Star Zone	1981	$500
❑ C/D-1984SG-9 [B]	Celestial Love	1984	$1300
❑ 19842 [B]	Celestial Love	1984	$500
❑ ESR-520 [B]	Continuation	1969	$800
❑ LP-520 [B]	Continuation	1970	$500
❑ LP-408 [S]	Cosmic Tones for Mental Therapy	1967	$1200
— Red label; Sun Ra art on cover; reproductions exist			
❑ KH-2772 [S]	Cosmic Tones for Mental Therapy	196?	$800
— Blue cover; Chicago address on label			
❑ 1981 [B]	Dance of Innocent Passion	1981	$1200
❑ 72579 [B]	Days of Happiness		$1500
— hand pasted sleeve			
❑ LP-485 [B]	Deep Purple	1973	$1000
❑ LP-538 [B]	Discipline 27-II	1973	$750
❑ CMIJ78 [B]	Disco 3000	1978	$750
❑ SR-9956-2/A/B [M]	Fate in a Pleasant Mood	1965	$800
— Red label; reproductions exist			
❑ LP-202 [M]	Fate in a Pleasant Mood	196?	$400
— Chicago address on label			
❑ 72579 [B]	God Is More Than Love Can Ever Be	1979	$500
❑ 13188III/12988II [B]	Hidden Fire 1	1988	$400
❑ 13088A/12988B [B]	Hidden Fire 2	1988	$400
❑ 101185 [B]	Hiroshima	1985	$500
❑ ESR-508 [S]	Holiday for Soul-Dance	1969	$600
— El Saturn" label; reproductions exist			
❑ LP-849 [B]	Horizon	1974	$500
❑ 1217718 [B]	Horizon	1974	$500
❑ 6680 [B]	I, Pharaoh	1980	$750
— El Saturn" label			
❑ LP-203 [M]	Interstellar Low Ways	1969	$750
— Chicago address on label; reproductions exist			
❑ 144000 [B]	Invisible Shield	197?	$1200
❑ LP-5786 [M]	Jazz in Silhouette	1958	$1500
— Yellow label			
❑ LP-205 [M]	Jazz in Silhouette	1967	$500
— Red label			
❑ LP-205 [M]	Jazz in Silhouette	1967	$300
— Green label			
❑ 1984A/B [B]	Just Friends	1984	$250
❑ MS87976 [B]	Live at Montreux	1976	$750
❑ 1272 [B]	Live in Egypt 1	1973	$800
❑ 19783 [B]	Media Dream	1978	$1000
❑ 1978 [B]	Media Dream	1978	$500
❑ LP-509 [M]	Monorails and Satellites	1968	$800
— El Saturn" label; reproductions exist			
❑ LP-519 [S]	Monorails and Satellites, Vol. II	1969	$800
— El Saturn" label			
❑ ESR-1970 [B]	My Brother the Wind	1970	$750
❑ ESR-521 [B]	My Brother the Wind	1970	$750
— Reproductions exist			
❑ LP-521 [B]	My Brother the Wind	197?	$500
❑ SRA-2000 [B]	My Brother the Wind, Volume II	1971	$750
❑ ESR-523 [B]	My Brother the Wind, Volume II	1971	$750
— Reproductions exist			
❑ 77771	Nidhamu	197?	$250
❑ 7771	Nidhamu	197?	$250
❑ 1982 [B]	Nuclear War	1982	$250

Number	Title	Yr	NM
❑ IX SR72881	Oblique Parallax	1981	$200
❑ 91379 [B]	Omniverse	1979	$1200
❑ 101679 [B]	On Jupiter	1979	$800
— El Saturn" label			
❑ KH-98766 [M]	Other Planes of There	1966	$1000
— Red label; reproductions exist			
❑ LP-206 [M]	Other Planes of There	1967	$800
— Chicago address on label			
❑ 61674 [B]	Out Beyond the Kingdom Of	1974	$750
❑ 9121385	Outer Reach Intensity-Energy	1985	$200
❑ LP-530	Outer Spaceways Incorporated	1974	$200
— Chicago address on label			
❑ LP-530	Outer Spaceways Incorporated	1974	$350
— Philadelphia address on label			
❑ LP-564	Pathways to Unknown Worlds	1974	$0
— Canceled?			
❑ IX/1983-220 [B]	Ra to the Rescue	1983	$350
❑ SR-9956-2-M/N [M]	Rocket #9 Take Off For the Planet Venus	1966	$500
— Cover has "burning candle" logo			
❑ GH-9954-E/F [M]	Secrets of the Sun	1965	$1500
— Red label			
❑ LP-208 [M]	Secrets of the Sun	196?	$1000
— Chicago address on label			
❑ 11179 [B]	Sleeping Beauty	1979	$800
❑ LP-747	Some Blues But Not the Kind That's Blue	1977	$200
❑ 1014077 [B]	Some Blues But Not the Kind That's Blue	1977	$750
❑ 101477 [B]	Some Blues But Not the Kind That's Blue	1977	$750
❑ 7877	Somewhere Over the Rainbow	1977	$200
❑ LP-487	Song of the Stargazers	1979	$250
❑ 6161 [B]	Song of the Stargazers	1979	$2000
❑ 19782 [B]	Sound Mirror	1978	$750
❑ LP-512 [B]	Sound Sun Pleasure!!	1970	$600
— Reproductions exist			
❑ LP-527 [B]	Space Probe	197?	$750
❑ 14200-A/B [B]	Space Probe	197?	$600
❑ LP-502 [S]	Strange Strings	1967	$800
— Red label; reproductions exist			
❑ 92074 [B]	Sub Underground	1974	$600
❑ IHNY-165 [B]	Sun Ra and His Arkestra Featuring Pharoah Sanders and Black Harold	1976	$750
❑ SR-9956-11A/B [M]	Sun Ra Visits Planet Earth	1966	$800
— Red label; reproductions exist			
❑ LP-207 [M]	Sun Ra Visits Planet Earth	1968	$500
— Minneapolis address on label			
❑ LP-207 [M]	Sun Ra Visits Planet Earth	196?	$600
— El Saturn" label			
❑ SRLP-0216 [M]	Super-Sonic Jazz	1958	$1250
— Purple "keyboard" cover			
❑ SRLP-0216 [M]	Super-Sonic Jazz	1965	$800
— Blue or green cover			
❑ LP-204 [M]	Super-Sonic Sounds	1968	$750
— Blue or green cover; Chicago address on label			
❑ LP-772 [B]	Taking a Chance on Chances	1977	$500
❑ 92074 [B]	Temple U		$750
— hand drawn sleeve			
❑ 81774 [B]	The Antique Blacks	1974	$700
❑ ESR-532 [B]	The Bad and the Beautiful	196?	$1000
— Chicago address on label; reproductions exist			
❑ LP-529 [B]	The Invisible Shield	1974	$750
— Philadelphia address on label			
❑ LP-529	The Invisible Shield	1974	$200
— Chicago address on label			
❑ SR-9956-11E/F [M]	The Lady with the Golden Stockings	1966	$600
— Cover is generic and says "Tonal Views of Times Tomorrow"			
❑ LPB-711 [M]	The Magic City	1966	$800
— Red label; reproductions exist			
❑ LP-403 [M]	The Magic City	196?	$600
— Chicago address on label			
❑ LP-522 [B]	The Night of the Purple Moon	197?	$400
— Reproductions exist			
❑ LP-406 [M]	The Nubians of Plutonia	1969	$400
— Chicago address on label; reproductions exist			
❑ LP-771	The Soul Vibrations of Man	1977	$200

Number	Title	Yr	NM
❑ ESR-5000 [B]	Universe in Blue	1972	$750
❑ LP-200 [B]	Universe in Blue	197?	$500
❑ 91780 [B]	Voice of the Eternal Tomorrow	1980	$350
❑ HK-5445 [M]	We Travel the Spaceways	1966	$800
— Red label			
❑ LP-409 [M]	We Travel the Spaceways	196?	$600
— El Saturn" label; reproductions exist			
❑ LP-539 [B]	What's New?	197?	$1500
❑ 752 [B]	What's New?	197?	$800
❑ 52375 [B]	What's New?	197?	$500
❑ LP-405	When Angels Speak of Love	196?	$300
❑ LP-1966 [M]	When Angels Speak of Love	1966	$1200
— Red cover with a "sideways" image of Sun Ra			
❑ 101485	When Spaceships Appear	1985	$300
❑ LP-402 [B]	When Sun Comes Out	196?	$400
❑ LP-2066 [M]	When Sun Comes Out	1963	$400
— Blank cover			
❑ LP-2066 [M]	When Sun Comes Out	1963	$500
— Green cover with yellow sun			
❑ LP-2066 [M]	When Sun Comes Out	1963	$500
— Black ameboid figure on cover			
❑ LP-2066 [M]	When Sun Comes Out	1967	$300
— Spaceman at piano cover; reproductions exist			
SATURN/RECOMMENDED			
❑ SRRD-1 [B]	Cosmo Sun Connection	1985	$800
SAVOY			
❑ MG-12169 [M]	The Futuristic Sounds of Sun Ra	1961	$300
SAVOY JAZZ			
❑ SJL-1141	We Are in the Future	1984	$250
SHANDAR			
❑ SR 10.001	Nuits de la Fondation Maeght Volume I	1971	$250
❑ SR 10.003	Nuits de la Fondation Maeght Volume II	1971	$250
SWEET EARTH			
❑ SER1003	The Other Side of the Sun	1979	$250
— Reproductions exist			
THOTH INTERGALACTIC			
❑ KH-2772 [S]	Cosmic Tones for Mental Therapy	1969	$300
❑ KH-1272	Live in Egypt 1	1973	$6300
❑ 7771	Nidhamu	197?	$250
❑ KH-98766 [M]	Other Planes of There	1969	$250
❑ KH-5472 [M]	Strange Strings	196?	$300
❑ LPB-711 [M]	The Magic City	1969	$250
❑ IR-1972	The Night of the Purple Moon	1970	$300
TOTAL ENERGY			
❑ NER3029	It Is Forbidden	2001	$150
— Green vinyl			
❑ NER3026	Life Is Beautiful	1999	$150
❑ NER3021	Outer Space Employment Agency	1999	$150
TRANSITION			
❑ TLP-10 [M]	Jazz by Sun Ra	1957	$2500
— With booklet (deduct 1/5 if missing)			

SUNDBOM, LARS "SUMPEN

Trumpeter.

Albums

Number	Title	Yr	NM
GHB			
❑ GHB-148	Hemma Hos Sumpen	1979	$25

SUNKEL, PHIL

Trumpeter, cornet player and composer.

Albums

Number	Title	Yr	NM
ABC-PARAMOUNT			
❑ ABC-225 [M]	Gerry Mulligan and Bob Brookmeyer Play Phil Sunkel's Jazz Concerto Grosso	1958	$60
❑ ABCS-225 [S]	Gerry Mulligan and Bob Brookmeyer Play Phil Sunkel's Jazz Concerto Grosso	1958	$50
❑ ABC-136 [M]	Jazz Band	1956	$80

SUNSHINE, MONTY

Clarinet player best known for his playing on the CHRIS BARBER hit "Petite Fleur."

Albums

Number	Title	Yr	NM
STOMP OFF			
❑ SOS-1110	New Orleans Hula	1986	$25

SUPERBLUE
Members at the time of the below LP: Don Sickler (trumpet); Roy Hargrove (trumpet); Frank Lacy (trombone); Bobby Watson (alto sax); Billy Pierce (tenor sax); Mulgrew Miller (piano); Bob Hurst (bass); Kenny Washington (drums).

Albums

BLUE NOTE

Number	Title	Yr	NM
❏ B1-91731	Superblue	1989	$35

SUPERSAX
Formed by Buddy Clark and MED FLORY. The band's premise was to arrange CHARLIE PARKER solos for a band.

Albums

CAPITOL

Number	Title	Yr	NM
❏ ST-11177	Supersax Plays Bird	1973	$25
❏ ST-11271	Supersax Plays Bird, Volume 2/Salt Peanuts	1974	$25
❏ ST-11371	Supersax Plays Bird with Strings	1975	$25

COLUMBIA

❏ FC44436	Stone Bird	1989	$30
❏ FC39140	Supersax and L.A. Voices	1984	$25
❏ FC39925	Supersax and L.A. Voices, Vol. 2	1985	$25
❏ FC40547	Supersax and L.A. Voices Volume 3: Straighten Up and Fly Right	1986	$25

MOBILE FIDELITY

| ❏ 1-511 | Supersax Plays Bird | 1981 | $40 |

—*Audiophile vinyl*

PAUSA

❏ 7038	Chasin' the Bird	1977	$25
❏ 7082	Dynamite!	1979	$25
❏ 9028	Supersax Plays Bird, Volume 2/Salt Peanuts	198?	$20

SURMAN, JOHN
Saxophone player, clarinetist, keyboard player and percussionist.

Albums

ANTILLES

| ❏ AN-7004 | Morning Glory | 197? | $30 |

ECM

❏ 1148	Reflection	197?	$30
❏ 23795	Such Winters of Memory	1983	$25
❏ 1193	The Amazing Adventures of Simon Simon	1981	$30
❏ 1295	Withholding Pattern	1986	$30

SUSSMAN, RICHARD
Pianist and keyboard player.

Albums

INNER CITY

| ❏ IC-1045 | Free Fall | 1978 | $30 |
| ❏ IC-1068 | Tributaries | 1979 | $30 |

SUTTON, DICK
Trumpeter, composer and bandleader.

Albums

JAGUAR

| ❏ JP-802 [10] | Jazz Idiom | 1954 | $80 |
| ❏ JP-804 [10] | Progressive Dixieland | 1954 | $80 |

SUTTON, RALPH
Trumpeter, composer and bandleader.

Albums

ANALOGUE PRODUCTIONS

| ❏ AP 018 | Partners in Crime | 199? | $30 |

—*Audiophile vinyl*

AUDIOPHILE

| ❏ AP-163 | Off the Cuff | 198? | $25 |

CIRCLE

| ❏ L-413 [10] | Ralph Sutton | 1951 | $80 |

COLUMBIA

| ❏ CL6140 [10] | Piano Moods | 1950 | $80 |

COMMODORE

| ❏ XFL-16570 | Bix Beiderbecke Suite and Jazz Portraits | 198? | $25 |
| ❏ FL-30001 [M] | Ralph Sutton | 1951 | $80 |

DECCA

| ❏ DL5498 [10] | I Got Rhythm | 1953 | $150 |

DOWN HOME

| ❏ MGD-4 [M] | Backroom Piano: The Ragtime Piano of Ralph Sutton | 1955 | $75 |
| ❏ DH-1003 [10] | Ragtime Piano Solos | 1953 | $80 |

HARMONY

| ❏ HL7109 [M] | Tribute to Fats | 1958 | $30 |

JAZZ ARCHIVES

| ❏ JA-45 | Ralph Sutton and the All-Stars | 198? | $25 |

JAZZOLOGY

| ❏ JCE-92 | Alligator Crawl | 197? | $25 |

OMEGA

| ❏ OML-51 [M] | Jazz At the Olympics | 196? | $35 |
| ❏ OSL-51 [S] | Jazz At the Olympics | 196? | $25 |

PROJECT 3

| ❏ PR5040SD | Knocked Out Nocturne | 1969 | $30 |

RIVERSIDE

| ❏ RLP 12-212 [M] | Classic Jazz Piano | 1956 | $250 |

ROULETTE

| ❏ R-25232 [M] | Ragtime, U.S.A. | 1963 | $35 |
| ❏ SR-25232 [S] | Ragtime, U.S.A. | 1963 | $25 |

SACKVILLE

| ❏ 2012 | Piano Solos | 198? | $25 |

STORYVILLE

| ❏ 4013 | Ralph Sutton Quartet | 198? | $25 |

VERVE

| ❏ MGV-1004 [M] | Backroom Piano: The Ragtime Piano of Ralph Sutton | 1956 | $150 |

SVENSSON, REINHOLD
Pianist, organist and composer.

Albums

PRESTIGE

❏ PRLP-155 [10]	New Sounds from Sweden, Volume 8	1953	$300
❏ PRLP-129 [10]	Reinhold Svensson, Volume 2: Favorites	1952	$350
❏ PRLP-106 [10]	Reinhold Svensson Piano	1951	$250

SVENSSON, REINHOLD/BENGT HALLBERG
Also see each artist's individual listings.

Albums

PRESTIGE

| ❏ PRLP-174 [10] | Piano Moderns | 1953 | $300 |

SWALLOW, STEVE
Bass player.

Albums

ECM

| ❏ 1160 | Home | 1979 | $30 |

SWANSON, RIC

Albums

ARMERICAN GRAMAPHONE

| ❏ AG-600 | Urban Surrender | 1985 | $25 |

OPTIMISM

| ❏ OP-3220 | Renewal | 198? | $30 |

SWARTZ, HARVIE
Bass player.

Albums

GRAMAVISION

| ❏ 8202 | Underneath It All | 198? | $25 |
| ❏ 18-8503-1 | Urban Earth | 1986 | $25 |

SWEDES FROM JAZZVILLE
Among the members: REINHOLD SVENSSON and ARNE DOMNERUS.

Albums

EPIC

| ❏ LN3309 [M] | Swedes from Jazzville | 195? | $100 |

SWEDISH JAZZ KINGS, THE
Formed by Tomas Ornberg (clarinet, soprano sax) in 1985.

Albums

STOMP OFF

| ❏ SOS-1188 | After Midnight | 1987 | $25 |
| ❏ SOS-1122 | What Makes Me Love You So? | 1986 | $25 |

SWEET EMMA
See EMMA BARRETT.

SWIFT, DUNCAN
Pianist.

Albums

BLACK LION

| ❏ 301 | Piano Ragtime: Joplin and Morton | 197? | $30 |

SWINGING SWEDES, THE

Albums

TELEFUNKEN

| ❏ LGX-66050 [M] | The Swinging Swedes | 195? | $100 |

SWINGING SWEDES, THE/THE COOL BRITONS

Albums

BLUE NOTE

| ❏ BLP-5019 [10] | New Sounds from the Olde World | 1951 | $300 |

SWINGLE SINGERS, THE
Formed by Ward Swingle of THE DOUBLE SIX OF PARIS. The basic premise was to take scat singing and apply it to classical works. Original members: Jean-Claude Briodin, Anne Germain, Jean Cussac, Claudine Meunier, Claude Germain, Christiane Legrand, Ward Swingle, Jeanette Baucomont. Many changes since.

Albums

COLUMBIA

| ❏ PC34194 | Rags and All That Jazz | 1976 | $25 |

COLUMBIA MASTERWORKS

| ❏ M33013 | Love Songs for Madrigals and Madriguys | 1976 | $25 |

MMG

| ❏ 1125 | Folio | 198? | $20 |
| ❏ 1115 | Swingle Skyliner | 198? | $20 |

PHILIPS

❏ PHM200149 [M]	Anyone for Mozart?	1965	$25
❏ PHS600149 [S]	Anyone for Mozart?	1965	$30
❏ PHS 2-5400	Bachanalia	1972	$30

—*Reissue of 600-197 and 600-126 in same package*

❏ PHM200097 [M]	Bach's Greatest Hits	1963	$25
❏ PHS600097 [S]	Bach's Greatest Hits	1963	$30
❏ PHS600288	Back to Bach	1968	$25
❏ PHM200225 [M]	Encounter	1966	$30

—*With the Modern Jazz Quartet*

| ❏ PHS600225 [S] | Encounter | 1966 | $35 |

—*With the Modern Jazz Quartet*

❏ PHM200191 [M]	Getting Romantic	1965	$25
❏ PHS600191 [S]	Getting Romantic	1965	$30
❏ PHM200126 [M]	Going Baroque	1964	$25
❏ PHS600126 [S]	Going Baroque	1964	$30
❏ 824544-1	Jazz Sebastian Bach	1985	$20
❏ 824545-1	Place Vendome	1985	$20

—*With the Modern Jazz Quartet; reissue of 600-225*

❏ PHM200214 [M]	Rococo A-Go-Go	1966	$25
❏ PHS600214 [S]	Rococo A-Go-Go	1966	$30
❏ PHM200261 [M]	Spanish Masters	1967	$25
❏ PHS600261 [S]	Spanish Masters	1967	$30
❏ PHS700004	The Joy of Singing	1973	$25

SYMPHONY JAZZ ENSEMBLE

Albums

QCA

| ❏ 364 | Carmen | 197? | $35 |
| ❏ 378 | Eastside Corridor | 197? | $35 |

SYMS, SYLVIA
Female singer.

Albums

20TH CENTURY FOX

Claude Thornhill, *Claude Thornhill Encores*, Columbia CL 6164,
10-inch LP, **$80**.

Bobby Timmons, *The Bobby Timmons Trio In Person – Recorded "Live"*
at the Village Vanguard, Riverside RLP-391, **$200**.

Cy Touff, *Touff Assignment*, Argo LPS-641, **$30**.

Cy Touff, *Cy Touff, His Octet & Quintet*, Pacific Jazz PJ-1211, **$150**.

Number	Title	Yr	NM
❏ TFM-4123 [M]	The Fabulous Sylvia Syms	1963	$30
❏ TFS-4123 [S]	The Fabulous Sylvia Syms	1963	$30
ATLANTIC			
❏ALS-137 [10]	Songs by Sylvia Syms	1952	$350
❏ 1243 [M]	Songs by Sylvia Syms	1956	$300
—Black label			
❏ 1243 [M]	Songs by Sylvia Syms	1960	$250
—Multicolor label, white "fan" logo at right			
COLUMBIA			
❏ CL1447 [M]	Torch Song	1960	$30
—Red and black label with six "eye" logos			
❏ CS8243 [S]	Torch Song	1960	$40
—Red and black label with six "eye" logos			
DECCA			
❏ DL8639 [M]	Songs of Love	1958	$100
—Black label, silver print			
❏ DL8188 [M]	Sylvia Syms Sings	1955	$150
—Black label, silver print			
KAPP			
❏ KL-1236 [M]	That Man -- Love Songs to Frank Sinatra	1961	$30
❏ KS-3236 [S]	That Man -- Love Songs to Frank Sinatra	1961	$40
MOVIETONE			
❏ 2022 [M]	In a Sentimental Mood	1967	$25
❏ 72022 [S]	In a Sentimental Mood	1967	$35
PRESTIGE			
❏ PRLP-7489 [M]	For Once in My Life	1967	$30
❏ PRST-7489 [S]	For Once in My Life	1967	$25
❏ PRLP-7439 [M]	Sylvia Is!	1965	$25
❏ PRST-7439 [S]	Sylvia Is!	1965	$30
VERSION			
❏ VLP-103 [10]	After Dark	1954	$80

SYNTHESIS

Albums

CHIAROSCURO			
❏ 172	Six by Six	197?	$30

SZABO, GABOR
Guitarist.

Albums

ABC IMPULSE!			
❏ AS-9105	Gypsy 66	1968	$30
❏ AS-9204	His Great Hits	1971	$35
❏ AS-9128	Jazz Raga	1968	$30
❏ AS-9159	Light My Fire	1968	$35
❏ AS-9167	More Sorcery	1968	$35
❏ AS-9123	Spellbinder	1968	$30
❏ AS-9173	The Best of Gabor Szabo	1968	$35
❏ AS-9146	The Sorcerer	1968	$30
❏ AS-9151	Wind, Sky and Diamonds	1968	$35
BLUE THUMB			
❏ BTS-28	High Contrast	1972	$30
—With Bobby Womack			
❏ 6014	Live	1974	$30
❏ BTS-8823	Magical Connection	1971	$30
BUDDAH			
❏ 20-SK	Blowin' Some Old Smoke	1971	$30
❏ 18-SK	Watch What Happens	1970	$30
CTI			
❏ 6026	Mizrab	1973	$30
❏ 6035	Rambler	1974	$30
GRP/IMPULSE!			
❏ IMP-211	The Sorcerer	199?	$35
—Reissue on audiophile vinyl			
IMPULSE!			
❏ A-9105 [M]	Gypsy 66	1966	$200
❏ AS-9105 [S]	Gypsy 66	1966	$200
❏ A-9128 [M]	Jazz Raga	1967	$200
❏ AS-9128 [S]	Jazz Raga	1967	$200
❏ A-9123 [M]	Spellbinder	1966	$200
❏ AS-9123 [S]	Spellbinder	1966	$200
❏ A-9146 [M]	The Sorcerer	1967	$200
❏ AS-9146 [S]	The Sorcerer	1967	$200
❏ AS-9151	Wind, Sky and Diamonds	1968	$200
—This exists on the pre-ABC Impulse! label, though theoretically it shouldn't. Other titles may exist on that label also.			
MCA			
❏ 4155	His Great Hits	198?	$30
MERCURY			
❏ SRM-1-1141	Faces	1977	$25
❏ SRM-1-1091	Nightflight	1976	$25
PEPITA			
❏ 707	Femme Fatalo	198?	$25

Number	Title	Yr	NM
SALVATION			
❏ 704	Macho	1975	$30
SKYE			
❏ SK-3 [S]	Bacchanal	1968	$35
❏ MK-3 [M]	Bacchanal	1968	$40
—Mono is promo only; "Monaural Promotion Copy" sticker on stereo cover			
❏ SK-7	Dreams	1969	$35
❏ SK-9	Gabor Szabo 1969	1969	$35
❏ SK-15	Lena & Gabor	1970	$35
—With Lena Horne			

SZABO, RICH
Trumpeter.

Albums

BBW			
❏ 2001	Best of Both Worlds	198?	$30

SZAJNER, BOB

Albums

RMS			
❏ 77004	Afterthoughts	198?	$30
❏ 77003	Sound Ideas	198?	$30
SEEDS & STEMS			
❏ SSH-7802	Jazz Opus 20/40	1979	$30

SZAKCSI
Pianist.

Albums

GRP			
❏ GR-9577	Mystic Dreams	1989	$30
❏ GR-1045	Sa-chi	1988	$25

SZOBEL, HERMANN

Albums

ARISTA			
❏ AL4058	Szobel	1976	$30

T

T-SQUARE
Japanese fusion group: Masahiro Andoh (guitars); Takeshi Itoh (saxophones); Hirotaka Izumi (piano, keyboards); Hiroyuke Noritake (drums); Mitsuru Sutoh (bass).

Albums

PORTRAIT			
❏ FR44193	Truth	1988	$25

TABACKIN, LEW
Saxophone player and flutist.

Albums

INNER CITY			
❏ IC-1028	Dual Nature	1976	$30
❏ IC-6052	Rites of Pan	197?	$35
❏ IC-1038	Tabackin	1977	$30
❏ IC-6048	Tenor Gladness	197?	$35
JAM			
❏ 5005	Black and Tan Fantasy	198?	$30

TABOR, ERON
Male singer.

Albums

STUDIO ONE			
❏ S-104	Eron Tabor	196?	$25

TACUMA, JAMAALADEEN
Bass player.

Albums

GRAMAVISION			
❏ 18-8803	Jukebox	1988	$25
❏ 18-0(# unknown)	Music World	1986	$25
❏ GR-8308	Renaissance Man	1984	$25
❏ GR-8301	Showstopper	1983	$30

Number	Title	Yr	NM
TAILGATE RAMBLERS, THE			

Members: Wild Bill Davison; Bruce Gerletti; John McDonald; Bob Butler; Eddie Collins; Jim Joseph; Frank Foguth.

Albums

JAZZOLOGY			
❏ J-32	Pause	1968	$30
❏ J-43	Swing	197?	$30

TALBERT, THOMAS
Pianist, composer and arranger.

Albums

ATLANTIC			
❏ 1250 [M]	Bix Fats Duke Interpreted by Thomas Talbert	1957	$300
—Black label			
❏ SD1250 [S]	Bix Fats Duke Interpreted by Thomas Talbert	1958	$300
—Green label			
❏ 1250 [M]	Bix Fats Duke Interpreted by Thomas Talbert	1961	$250
—Multicolor label, white "fan" logo at right			
❏ SD1250 [S]	Bix Fats Duke Interpreted by Thomas Talbert	1961	$250
—Multicolor label, white "fan" logo at right			
SEA BREEZE			
❏ SB-2038	Things As They Are	198?	$25
—As "Tom Talbert			

TAMBA 4, THE
From Brazil. Members: Luis Eca (piano, organ); Dorio (bass, guitar, percussion); Ohana (drums, jawbone, percussion); Bebeto (flute, bass, vocals).

Albums

A&M			
❏ SP-3013	Samba Blim	1969	$30
❏ SP-3004	We and the Sea	1968	$30

TAPSCOTT, HORACE
Pianist and composer.

Albums

FLYING DUTCHMAN			
❏ FDS-107	The Giant Is Awakened	1969	$25
❏ FD-10107	The Giant Is Awakened	197?	$35
INTERPLAY			
❏ 7724	Horace Tapscott in New York	197?	$30
❏ 7714	Songs of the Unsung	197?	$30

TARIKA BLUE

Albums

CHIAROSCURO			
❏ 141	Blue Path	197?	$35

TATE, BUDDY, AND DOLLAR BRAND
Also see ABDULLAH IBRAHIM; BUDDY TATE.

Albums

CHIAROSCURO			
❏ 165	Buddy Tate and Dollar Brand	1977	$30

TATE, BUDDY
Tenor saxophone and clarinet player. Also see BUCK CLAYTON.

Albums

BASF			
❏ 20740	Unbroken	197?	$35
BLACK LION			
❏ 312	Kansas City Woman	197?	$35
CHIAROSCURO			
❏ 123	Buddy Tate and His Buddies	1973	$35
CONCORD JAZZ			
❏ CJ-163	The Great Buddy Tate	1981	$25
FANTASY			
❏ OJC-184	Tate-A-Tate	1985	$25
FELSTED			
❏ 7004 [M]	Swinging Like Tate	1958	$80
❏ 2004 [S]	Swinging Like Tate	1958	$80
MASTER JAZZ			
❏ 8127	Swinging Like Tate	197?	$30
❏ 8128	Texas Twister	197?	$30
MUSE			

Number	Title	Yr	NM
MR-5198	Buddy Tate and the Muse All-Stars Live at Sandy's	1979	$25
MR-5249	Hard Blowin': Live at Sandy's	198?	$25
PAUSA			
7030	Unbroken	198?	$25
SACKVILLE			
3027	Buddy Tate Quartet	198?	$25
3017	Sherman Shuffle	198?	$25
3034	The Ballad of Artistry	198?	$25
SWINGVILLE			
SVLP-2029 [M]	Groovin' with Buddy Tate	1961	$50
—Purple label			
SVLP-2029 [M]	Groovin' with Buddy Tate	1965	$30
—Blue label, trident logo at right			
SVLP-2014 [M]	Tate-A-Tate	1960	$50
—Purple label			
SVLP-2014 [M]	Tate-A-Tate	1965	$30
—Blue label, trident logo at right			
SVLP-2003 [M]	Tate's Date	1960	$50
—Purple label			
SVLP-2003 [M]	Tate's Date	1965	$30
—Blue label, trident logo at right			

TATE, GRADY
Drummer and percussionist.

Albums

Number	Title	Yr	NM
ABC IMPULSE!			
ASD-9330	The Master	197?	$30
BUDDAH			
BDS-5623	By Special Request	1973	$30
JANUS			
7010	Movin' Day	197?	$30
3050	She Is My Lady	197?	$30
SKYE			
SK-17	After the Long Ride Home	197?	$35
SK-1007	Feeling Life	197?	$35
SK-4	Windmills of My Mind	1969	$50

TATRO, DUANE
Saxophone player, arranger and composer.

Albums

Number	Title	Yr	NM
CONTEMPORARY			
C-3514 [M]	Jazz for Moderns	1956	$200

TATUM, ART, AND BUDDY DEFRANCO
Also see each artist's individual listings.

Albums

Number	Title	Yr	NM
AMERICAN RECORDING SOCIETY			
G-412 [M]	The Art Tatum-Buddy DeFranco Quartet	1956	$40
VERVE			
MGV-8229 [M]	The Art Tatum-Buddy DeFranco Quartet	1958	$150
V-8229 [M]	The Art Tatum-Buddy DeFranco Quartet	1961	$60

TATUM, ART; BENNY CARTER; LOUIS BELLSON
Also see each artist's individual listings.

Albums

Number	Title	Yr	NM
CLEF			
MGC-643 [M]	Tatum-Carter-Bellson	1955	$200
VERVE			
MGV-8227 [M]	Makin' Whoopee	1958	$120
V-8227 [M]	Makin' Whoopee	1961	$25
MGV-8013 [M]	The Three Giants	1957	$100
V-8013 [M]	The Three Giants	1961	$25

TATUM, ART; ROY ELDRIDGE; ALVIN STOLLER; JOHN SIMMONS

Albums

Number	Title	Yr	NM
CLEF			
MGC-679 [M]	The Art Tatum-Roy Eldridge-Alvin Stoller-John Simmons Quartet	1955	$300
VERVE			
MGV-8064 [M]	The Art Tatum-Roy Eldridge-Alvin Stoller-John Simmons Quartet	1957	$150
V-8064 [M]	The Art Tatum-Roy Eldridge-Alvin Stoller-John Simmons Quartet	1961	$60

TATUM, ART
Pianist. Also see LIONEL HAMPTON; ZUTTY SINGLETON.

Albums

Number	Title	Yr	NM
20TH CENTURY FOX			
S-4162 [R]	This Is Art Tatum, Volume 1	196?	$30
3162 [M]	This Is Art Tatum, Volume 1	196?	$35
S-4163 [R]	This Is Art Tatum, Volume 2	196?	$30
3163 [M]	This Is Art Tatum, Volume 2	196?	$35
20TH FOX			
FTM-102-2 [M]	Piano Discoveries	1961	$200
FTS-102-2 [R]	Piano Discoveries	1961	$200
FTM-3029 [M]	Piano Discoveries Vol. I	1960	$200
FTS-3029 [R]	Piano Discoveries Vol. I	1960	$200
FTM-3033 [M]	Piano Discoveries Vol. II	1960	$200
FTS-3033 [R]	Piano Discoveries Vol. II	1960	$200
AIRCHECK			
21	Radio Broadcasts	197?	$25
ASCH			
ALP-356 [10]	Art Tatum	1950	$150
AUDIOPHILE			
AP-88	The Remarkable Art Tatum	198?	$25
BOOK-OF-THE-MONTH			
51-5400	The One and Only	1980	$30
BRUNSWICK			
BL58023 [10]	Art Tatum Piano Solos	1950	$100
BL58013 [10]	Art Tatum Trio	1950	$100
BL54004 [M]	Here's Art Tatum	1955	$120
CAPITOL			
H216 [10]	Art Tatum	1950	$150
T216 [M]	Art Tatum	1955	$150
—Turquoise label			
M-11028	Art Tatum	1972	$30
T216 [M]	Art Tatum	1959	$60
—Black colorband label, logo at left			
T216 [M]	Art Tatum	196?	$50
—Black colorband label, logo at top			
H269 [10]	Art Tatum Encores	1951	$150
H408 [10]	Art Tatum Trio	1953	$150
CLEF			
0(no cat #) [M]	Art Tatum	1954	$350
—Boxed set with volumes 2, 3, 4 and 5 of The Genius of Art Tatum			
MGC-746 [M]	Presenting the Art Tatum Trio	1955	$0
—Canceled			
MGC-612 [M]	The Genius of Art Tatum #1	1954	$200
MGC-613 [M]	The Genius of Art Tatum #2	1954	$200
MGC-614 [M]	The Genius of Art Tatum #3	1954	$200
MGC-615 [M]	The Genius of Art Tatum #4	1954	$200
MGC-618 [M]	The Genius of Art Tatum #5	1954	$200
MGC-657 [M]	The Genius of Art Tatum #6	1955	$200
MGC-658 [M]	The Genius of Art Tatum #7	1955	$200
MGC-659 [M]	The Genius of Art Tatum #8	1955	$200
MGC-660 [M]	The Genius of Art Tatum #9	1955	$200
MGC-661 [M]	The Genius of Art Tatum #10	1955	$200
MGC-712 [M]	The Genius of Art Tatum #11	1956	$200
CMS/SAGA			
6915	The Rarest Solos	197?	$25
COLUMBIA			
CL6301 [10]	An Art Tatum Concert	1954	$80
GL101 [10]	Gene Norman Concert at Shrine Auditorium, May 1949	1952	$150
CS9655 [S]	Piano Starts Here	1968	$25
—Red "360 Sound" label			
CS9655	Piano Starts Here	1971	$25
—Orange label			
PC9655	Piano Starts Here	198?	$20
—Reissue with new prefix			
CS9655	Piano Starts Here	1968	$40
—Mono is white label promo only with stereo number; "Special Mono Radio Station Copy" sticker on cover			
CL2565 [10]	The Tatum Touch	1956	$50
DECCA			
DL5086 [10]	Art Tatum Piano Solos	1950	$150
DL8715 [M]	The Art of Tatum	1958	$120
DIAL			
LP-206 [10]	Art Tatum Trio	1950	$250
EMARCY			
826129-1	20th Century Piano Genius	1986	$30
FOLKWAYS			
FL-33 [10]	Art Tatum Trio	1951	$100
F-12293	Footnotes to Jazz	197?	$30
GNP CRESCENDO			
GNP-9025	Art Tatum at the Crescendo, Vol. 1	197?	$25
GNP-9026	Art Tatum at the Crescendo, Vol. 2	197?	$25
HARMONY			
HL7006 [M]	An Art Tatum Concert	1957	$30
JAZZ MAN			
5030	Get Happy	198?	$25
5024	The Genius	198?	$25
JAZZZ			
101	Works of Art	197?	$30
MCA			
42327	Solos	1990	$30
4019	Tatum Masterpieces	197?	$30
MOVIETONE			
2021 [M]	The Legendary Art Tatum	1967	$35
72021 [R]	The Legendary Art Tatum	1967	$30
ONYX			
205	God Is in the House	197?	$30
PABLO			
2310887	The Best of Art Tatum	198?	$25
2405418	The Best of Art Tatum	198?	$25
2625706	The Tatum Group Masterpieces	197?	$60
—Boxed set with eight volumes (except 2310 775) included			
2310732	The Tatum Group Masterpieces with Benny Carter, Vol. 1	197?	$25
2310733	The Tatum Group Masterpieces with Benny Carter, Vol. 2	197?	$25
2310737	The Tatum Group Masterpieces with Ben Webster	197?	$25
2310736	The Tatum Group Masterpieces with Buddy DeFranco	197?	$25
2310735	The Tatum Group Masterpieces with Jo Jones	197?	$25
2310720	The Tatum Group Masterpieces with Lionel Hampton, Buddy Rich	197?	$25
2310775	The Tatum Group Masterpieces with Lionel Hampton, Buddy Rich, Vol. 2	198?	$25
2310731	The Tatum Group Masterpieces with Lionel Hampton, Sweets Edison, Barney Kessel	197?	$25
2310734	The Tatum Group Masterpieces with Roy Eldredge	197?	$25
2625703	The Tatum Solo Masterpieces	1974	$150
—Box set with all 13 volumes included			
2310723	The Tatum Solo Masterpieces, Vol. 1	197?	$25
2310729	The Tatum Solo Masterpieces, Vol. 2	197?	$25
2310730	The Tatum Solo Masterpieces, Vol. 3	197?	$25
2310789	The Tatum Solo Masterpieces, Vol. 4	197?	$25
2310790	The Tatum Solo Masterpieces, Vol. 5	197?	$25
2310791	The Tatum Solo Masterpieces, Vol. 6	197?	$25
2310792	The Tatum Solo Masterpieces, Vol. 7	197?	$25
2310793	The Tatum Solo Masterpieces, Vol. 8	198?	$25
2310835	The Tatum Solo Masterpieces, Vol. 9	198?	$25
2310862	The Tatum Solo Masterpieces, Vol. 10	198?	$25
2310864	The Tatum Solo Masterpieces, Vol. 11	198?	$25
2310870	The Tatum Solo Masterpieces, Vol. 12	198?	$25
2310875	The Tatum Solo Masterpieces, Vol. 13	198?	$25
PAUSA			
9017	The Legend	198?	$25
REM HOLLYWOOD			
LP-3 [10]	Piano Virtuoso	1950	$120
—The number "2" is on the front cover, but "LP-3" appears on the label			
STINSON			
SLP-40 [M]	Art Tatum Solos and Trio	195?	$40
SLP-40 [10]	Art Tatum Trio	1950	$150
STORYVILLE			
4108	Masters of Jazz, Vol. 8	199?	$30

Number	Title	Yr	NM
TIME-LIFE			
❏ STL-J-24	Giants of Jazz	1982	$50
VARESE SARABANDE			
❏ VC81021	The Keystone Sessions	197?	$35
VERVE			
❏ MGV-8101-5 [M]	Art Tatum, Volume 1	1957	$250
—Boxed set with volumes 1-5 of The Genius of Art Tatum			
❏ MGV-8102-5 [M]	Art Tatum, Volume 2	1957	$250
—Boxed set with volumes 6-10 of The Genius of Art Tatum			
❏ MGV-8347 [M]	More of the Greatest Piano of Them All	1959	$100
❏ V-8347 [M]	More of the Greatest Piano of Them All	1961	$25
❏ MGV-8118 [M]	Presenting the Art Tatum Trio	1957	$100
❏ V-8118 [M]	Presenting the Art Tatum Trio	1961	$25
❏ MGV-8360 [M]	Still More of the Greatest Piano of Them All	1960	$80
❏ V-8360 [M]	Still More of the Greatest Piano of Them All	1961	$25
❏ VSP-33 [M]	The Art of Art	1966	$35
❏ VSPS-33 [R]	The Art of Art	1966	$30
❏ MGV-8220 [M]	The Art Tatum-Ben Webster Quartet	1958	$350
❏ V-8220 [M]	The Art Tatum-Ben Webster Quartet	1961	$60
❏ V-8433 [M]	The Essential Art Tatum	1962	$25
❏ MGV-8036 [M]	The Genius of Art Tatum #1	1957	$150
❏ V-8036 [M]	The Genius of Art Tatum #1	1961	$25
❏ MGV-8037 [M]	The Genius of Art Tatum #2	1957	$150
❏ V-8037 [M]	The Genius of Art Tatum #2	1961	$25
❏ MGV-8038 [M]	The Genius of Art Tatum #3	1957	$150
❏ V-8038 [M]	The Genius of Art Tatum #3	1961	$25
❏ MGV-8039 [M]	The Genius of Art Tatum #4	1957	$150
❏ V-8039 [M]	The Genius of Art Tatum #4	1961	$25
❏ MGV-8040 [M]	The Genius of Art Tatum #5	1957	$150
❏ V-8040 [M]	The Genius of Art Tatum #5	1961	$25
❏ MGV-8055 [M]	The Genius of Art Tatum #6	1957	$150
❏ V-8055 [M]	The Genius of Art Tatum #6	1961	$25
❏ MGV-8056 [M]	The Genius of Art Tatum #7	1957	$150
❏ V-8056 [M]	The Genius of Art Tatum #7	1961	$25
❏ MGV-8057 [M]	The Genius of Art Tatum #8	1957	$150
❏ V-8057 [M]	The Genius of Art Tatum #8	1961	$25
❏ MGV-8058 [M]	The Genius of Art Tatum #9	1957	$150
❏ V-8058 [M]	The Genius of Art Tatum #9	1961	$25
❏ MGV-8059 [M]	The Genius of Art Tatum #10	1957	$150
❏ V-8059 [M]	The Genius of Art Tatum #10	1961	$25
❏ MGV-8095 [M]	The Genius of Art Tatum #11	1957	$150
❏ V-8095 [M]	The Genius of Art Tatum #11	1961	$25
❏ V-8323 [M]	The Greatest Piano of Them All	1961	$25
❏ MGV-8332 [M]	The Incomparable Music of Art Tatum	1959	$150
❏ V-8332 [M]	The Incomparable Music of Art Tatum	1961	$25

TATUM, ART/ERROLL GARNER
Also see each artist's individual listings.

Albums

Number	Title	Yr	NM
JAZZTONE			
❏ J-1203 [M]	Kings of the Keyboard	1956	$40
ROOST			
❏ LP-2213 [M]	Giants of the Piano	1956	$50

TATUM, ART/JAMES P. JOHNSON
Also see each artist's individual listings.

Albums

Number	Title	Yr	NM
MCA			
❏ 4112	Tatum Masterpieces Vol. 2/ Johnson Plays Fats Waller	197?	$30

TATUM, ART/MARY LOU WILLIAMS
Also see each artist's individual listings.

Albums

Number	Title	Yr	NM
HALL OF FAME			
❏ 607	King and Queen	197?	$25
JAZZTONE			
❏ J-1280 [M]	The King and Queen	1958	$40

TAYLOR, ART
Drummer. Also see LES JAZZ MODES.

Albums

Number	Title	Yr	NM
BLUE NOTE			
❏ BLP-4047 [M]	A.T.'s Delight	1960	$180
—Regular version, W. 63rd St. address on label			
❏ BST-84047 [S]	A.T.'s Delight	1960	$160
—W. 63rd St. address on label			
❏ BST-84047 [S]	A.T.'s Delight	1985	$1220
—"The Finest in Jazz Since 1939" reissue			

Number	Title	Yr	NM
FANTASY			
❏ OJC-094	Taylor's Wailers	198?	$25
NEW JAZZ			
❏ NJLP-8219 [M]	Taylor's Tenors	1959	$150
—Purple label			
❏ NJLP-8219 [M]	Taylor's Tenors	1965	$150
—Blue label, trident logo at right			
PRESTIGE			
❏ PRLP-7117 [M]	Taylor's Wailers	1957	$650

TAYLOR, BILLY
Pianist. Also see ERROLL GARNER; JOE HOLIDAY; MUNDELL LOWE.

Albums

Number	Title	Yr	NM
ABC IMPULSE!			
❏ AS-71 [S]	My Fair Lady Loves Jazz	1968	$35
ABC-PARAMOUNT			
❏ ABC-134 [M]	Billy Taylor At the London House	1956	$100
❏ ABC-162 [M]	Billy Taylor Introduces Ira Sullivan	1957	$100
❏ ABC-112 [M]	Evergreens	1956	$100
❏ ABC-177 [M]	My Fair Lady Loves Jazz	1957	$100
❏ ABC-226 [M]	The New Trio	1958	$100
❏ ABCS-226 [S]	The New Trio	1958	$40
ARGO			
❏ LP-650 [M]	Taylor Made Flute	1959	$100
❏ LPS-650 [S]	Taylor Made Flute	1959	$40
ATLANTIC			
❏ 1329 [M]	One for Fun	1960	$250
—Black label			
❏ SD1329 [S]	One for Fun	1960	$250
—Green label			
❏ ALR-113 [10]	Piano Panorama	1951	$250
❏ 1277 [M]	The Billy Taylor Touch	1958	$300
—Black label			
❏ 1277 [M]	The Billy Taylor Touch	1961	$250
—Multicolor label, white "fan" logo at right			
BELL			
❏ S-6049	OK Billy!	1970	$35
CAPITOL			
❏ T2302 [M]	Midnight Piano	1965	$80
❏ ST2302 [S]	Midnight Piano	1965	$100
❏ T2039 [M]	Right Here, Right Now	1963	$80
❏ ST2039 [S]	Right Here, Right Now	1963	$100
CONCORD JAZZ			
❏ CJ-145	Where've You Been	1981	$25
FANTASY			
❏ OJC-1730	Cross Section	198?	$25
❏ OJC-015	The Billy Taylor Trio with Candido	1982	$25
IMPULSE!			
❏ A-71 [M]	My Fair Lady Loves Jazz	1965	$200
❏ AS-71 [S]	My Fair Lady Loves Jazz	1965	$200
MERCURY			
❏ MG-20722 [M]	Impromptu	1962	$100
❏ SR-60722 [S]	Impromptu	1962	$100
MONMOUTH-EVERGREEN			
❏ 7089	Jazz Alive	1978	$30
MOODSVILLE			
❏ MVLP-16 [M]	Interlude	1961	$100
—Green label			
❏ MVLP-16 [M]	Interlude	1965	$60
—Blue label, trident logo at right			
NEW JAZZ			
❏ NJLP-8313 [M]	Live! At Town Hall	1963	$0
—Canceled; reassigned to Status			
PAUSA			
❏ 7096	Sleeping Bee	198?	$25
PRESTIGE			
❏ PRLP-7001 [M]	A Touch of Taylor	1955	$300
❏ PRST-7664 [R]	A Touch of Taylor	1969	$35
❏ PRLP-184 [10]	Billy Taylor Trio	1954	$300
❏ PRLP-188 [10]	Billy Taylor Trio	1954	$300
❏ PRLP-139 [10]	Billy Taylor Trio, Volume 1	1953	$300
❏ PRLP-7015 [M]	Billy Taylor Trio, Volume 1	1956	$300
❏ PRLP-165 [10]	Billy Taylor Trio, Volume 2	1953	$300
❏ PRLP-7016 [M]	Billy Taylor Trio, Volume 2	1956	$300
❏ PRLP-168 [10]	Billy Taylor Trio, Volume 3	1953	$300
❏ PRLP-7093 [M]	Billy Taylor Trio at Town Hall	1957	$300
❏ PRLP-194 [10]	Billy Taylor Trio In Concert at Town Hall, December 17, 1954	1955	$300
❏ PRLP-7071 [M]	Cross Section	1956	$300
❏ 16-2 [M]	Let's Get Away from It All	1957	$500
—This album plays at 16 2/3 rpm and is marked as such; white label			

Number	Title	Yr	NM
❏ PRLP-7051 [M]	The Billy Taylor Trio with Candido	1956	$300
❏ PRST-7762	Today!	1970	$35
RIVERSIDE			
❏ RLP 12-319 [M]	Billy Taylor Trio Uptown	1960	$200
❏ RLP 12-306 [M]	Billy Taylor with Four Flutes	1959	$300
❏ RLP 12-339 [M]	Warming Up	1960	$200
ROOST			
❏ R-406 [10]	Jazz at Storyville	1952	$200
❏ R-409 [10]	Taylor Made Jazz	1952	$200
SAVOY			
❏ MG-9035 [10]	Billy Taylor Piano	1953	$200
SESAC			
❏ N-3001 [M]	Custom Taylored	1959	$120
❏ SN-3001 [S]	Custom Taylored	1959	$100
STATUS			
❏ ST-8313 [M]	Live! At Town Hall	1965	$40
SURREY			
❏ S-1033 [M]	Easy Life	1966	$60
❏ SS-1033 [S]	Easy Life	1966	$60
TOWER			
❏ ST-5111 [S]	I Wish I Knew	1968	$60
WEST 54			
❏ 8008	Live at Storyville	198?	$30

TAYLOR, CECIL
Pianist and composer. Also see DONALD BYRD; JAZZ COMPOSERS ORCHESTRA.

Albums

Number	Title	Yr	NM
A&M			
❏ 7502152861	In Florescence	1990	$30
AMERICAN RECORDING SOCIETY			
❏ G-437 [M]	Modern Jazz	195?	$40
ARISTA/FREEDOM			
❏ AF1038	Indent	197?	$30
❏ AF1905	Nefertiti	197?	$35
❏ AF1005	Silent Tongues	1975	$30
BARNABY			
❏ Z30562	Cecil Taylor Quartet	1971	$35
❏ KZ31035	New York City R&B	1972	$35
BLUE NOTE			
❏ BLP-4260 [M]	Conquistador	1967	$60
❏ BST-84260 [S]	Conquistador	1967	$30
—With "A Division of Liberty Records" on label			
❏ B1-84260 [S]	Conquistador	1989	$30
—"The Finest in Jazz Since 1939" reissue			
❏ BST-84260 [S]	Conquistador	197?	$20
—Reissue with newer label; with "A Division of United Artists Records" on label			
❏ BN-LA458-H2	In Transition	197?	$35
❏ BLP-4237 [M]	Unit Structures	1966	$60
❏ BST-84237 [S]	Unit Structures	1966	$30
—With "New York, USA" on label			
❏ BST-84237 [S]	Unit Structures	1967	$35
—With "A Division of Liberty Records" on label			
CANDID			
❏ CD-8006 [M]	The World of Cecil Taylor	1960	$50
CONTEMPORARY			
❏ C-3562 [M]	Looking Ahead!	1959	$250
❏ S-7562 [S]	Looking Ahead!	1959	$250
FANTASY			
❏ 6014 [M]	Live At the Café Montmarte	1964	$25
❏ 86014 [S]	Live At the Café Montmarte	1964	$30
❏ OJC-452	Looking Ahead	1990	$30
HAT ART			
❏ 1993/4	Garden	1986	$35
—Reissue of Hat Hut 1993/4			
❏ 3011	One Too Many Salty Swift & Not Goodbye	1986	$25
—Reissue of Hat Hut 02			
❏ 2036	The Eight	1987	$35
HAT HUT			
❏ 3508	Calling It the 8th	1981	$30
❏ 1993/4	Garden	198?	$25
❏ 16	It Is In the Brewing Luminous	198?	$35
❏ 02	One Too Many Salty Swift & Not Goodbye	197?	$30
INNER CITY			
❏ IC-3021	Air Above Mountains (Buildings Within)	1977	$35
❏ IC-3001	The Dark to Themselves	197?	$35
JAZZ MAN			
❏ 5031	New York R & B	198?	$25
❏ 5026	The World of Cecil Taylor	198?	$25
JCOA			

Number	Title	Yr	NM
1002	Cecil Taylor with the Jazz Composers Orchestra	197?	$35

MOSAIC

Number	Title	Yr	NM
MR6-127	The Complete Candid Recordings of Cecil Taylor and Buell Neidlinger	199?	$100

NEW WORLD

Number	Title	Yr	NM
201	Cecil Taylor	1978	$30
303	Three Phasis	197?	$30

PAUSA

Number	Title	Yr	NM
7108	Fly! Fly! Fly!	198?	$25
7053	Live in the Black Forest	198?	$25

PRESTIGE

Number	Title	Yr	NM
34003	Great Concert	197?	$25

SOUL NOTE

Number	Title	Yr	NM
121150	For Olim	199?	$30
SN-1089	Winged Serpent (Sliding Quadrants)	1986	$30

TRANSITION

Number	Title	Yr	NM
TRLP-19 [M]	Jazz Advance	1956	$750

— With booklet (deduct 1/4 if missing)

UNIT CORE

Number	Title	Yr	NM
30551	Spring of Two Blue-J's	197?	$25

UNITED ARTISTS

Number	Title	Yr	NM
UAL-4014 [M]	Hard Driving Jazz	1959	$50
UAL-4046 [M]	Love for Sale	1959	$50
UAS-5046 [S]	Love for Sale	1959	$40
UAS-5014 [S]	Stereo Drive	1959	$40

TAYLOR, CREED
Arranger and producer, best known for his hand in other people's recordings. The below albums are generally conceded to have been recorded by a group led by Kenyon Hopkins.

Albums
ABC-PARAMOUNT

Number	Title	Yr	NM
ABC-308 [M]	Lonelyville "The Nervous Beat	1960	$30
ABCS-308 [S]	Lonelyville "The Nervous Beat	1960	$30
ABC-259 [M]	Shock Music in Hi-Fi	1958	$40
ABCS-259 [S]	Shock Music in Hi-Fi	1958	$60
ABC-317 [M]	The Best of the Barracks Ballads	1960	$30
ABCS-317 [S]	The Best of the Barracks Ballads	1960	$30

TAYLOR, DICK
Trombonist.

Albums
SKYLARK

Number	Title	Yr	NM
SKLP-18 [10]	Blue Moon	1954	$80

TAYLOR, JOE
Drummer.

Albums
PROJAZZ

Number	Title	Yr	NM
PAD-635	Mystery Walk	1988	$25

TAYLOR, LYNN

Albums
GRAND AWARD

Number	Title	Yr	NM
GA-33-0(# unknown) [M]	Lynn Taylor Sings	195?	$300

TAYLOR, MARTIN
Guitarist.

Albums
CONCORD JAZZ

Number	Title	Yr	NM
CJ-184	Skye Boat	198?	$25

TAYLOR, RUSTY

Albums
STOMP OFF

Number	Title	Yr	NM
SOS-1082	Give Me a Call	1985	$25
SOS-1028	Good Old Bad Old Days	198?	$25
SOS-1186	Let's Misbehave	1988	$25

TAYLOR, SAM "THE MAN"
Tenor and baritone saxophone player and clarinetist.

Albums

DECCA

Number	Title	Yr	NM
DL4417 [M]	It's a Blue World	1963	$35
DL74417 [S]	It's a Blue World	1963	$25
DL4302 [M]	Misty Mood	1962	$35
DL74302 [S]	Misty Mood	1962	$25
DL4573 [M]	Somewhere in the Night	1964	$35
DL74573 [S]	Somewhere in the Night	1964	$25

LION

Number	Title	Yr	NM
L-70054 [M]	Sam "The Man" Taylor	1958	$30

METROJAZZ

Number	Title	Yr	NM
E-1008 [M]	Jazz for Commuters	1958	$120
SE-1008 [S]	Jazz for Commuters	1958	$120

MGM

Number	Title	Yr	NM
E-3292 [M]	Blue Mist	1955	$75

— Yellow label

Number	Title	Yr	NM
E-3973 [M]	Blue Mist	1961	$30
SE-3973 [S]	Blue Mist	1961	$30

— Possibly a re-recording of 3292

Number	Title	Yr	NM
E-3607 [M]	Lush Life	1957	$0

— Canceled

Number	Title	Yr	NM
E-3783 [M]	More Blue Mist	1959	$30
SE-3783 [S]	More Blue Mist	1959	$40
E-3482 [M]	Music for Melancholy Babies	1957	$60

— Yellow label

Number	Title	Yr	NM
E-293 [10]	Music with the Big Beat	195?	$100
E-3473 [M]	Music with the Big Beat	1956	$80

— Yellow label

Number	Title	Yr	NM
E-3380 [M]	Out of This World	1956	$60

— Yellow label

Number	Title	Yr	NM
E-3573 [M]	Prelude to Blues	1957	$60

— Yellow label

Number	Title	Yr	NM
E-3553 [M]	Rockin' Sax and Rollin' Organ	1957	$60

— Yellow label

Number	Title	Yr	NM
GAS-146	Sam "The Man" Taylor (Golden Archive Series)	1970	$35
E-3967 [M]	Sam "The Man" Taylor Plays Hollywood	1960	$30
SE-3967 [S]	Sam "The Man" Taylor Plays Hollywood	1960	$40

MOODSVILLE

Number	Title	Yr	NM
MVLP-24 [M]	The Bad and the Beautiful	1962	$50

— Green label

Number	Title	Yr	NM
MVLP-24 [M]	The Bad and the Beautiful	1965	$30

— Blue label, trident logo at right

TCHICAI, JOHN, AND PIERRE DERGE
Also see each artist's individual listings.

Albums
STEEPLECHASE

Number	Title	Yr	NM
SCS-1174	Ball at Louisiana	1982	$30

TCHICAI, JOHN
Saxophone player and composer. Many guest appearances, including, bizarrely, on the John Lennon/Yoko Ono album Unfinished Music No. 2: Life with the Lions. Also see THE NEW YORK ART QUINTET.

Albums
BLACK SAINT

Number	Title	Yr	NM
120094	Timo's Message	1990	$30

STEEPLECHASE

Number	Title	Yr	NM
SCS-1075	The Real Tchical	198?	$30

TEAGARDEN, JACK
Trombonist and occasional male singer. Also see RED ALLEN; BENNY GOODMAN; LIONEL HAMPTON.

Albums
AIRCHECK

Number	Title	Yr	NM
9	Jack Teagarden and Frankie Trumbauer	197?	$25
24	Jack Teagarden on the Air	198?	$25

BETHLEHEM

Number	Title	Yr	NM
BCP-32 [M]	Jazz Great	1955	$250
BCP-6040	Meet Me Where They Play the Blues	1978	$30

— Distributed by Caytronics" reissue

BIOGRAPH

Number	Title	Yr	NM
C-2	Great Soloist	197?	$25

BLUEBIRD

Number	Title	Yr	NM
9986-1-RB	That's a Serious Thing	1990	$30

CAPITOL

Number	Title	Yr	NM
T1095 [M]	Big T's Dixieland Band	1959	$40
ST1095 [S]	Big T's Dixieland Band	1959	$60
T1143 [M]	Shades of Night	1959	$50
ST1143 [S]	Shades of Night	1959	$60
T820 [M]	Swing Low Sweet Spiritual	1957	$75
T721 [M]	This Is Teagarden	1956	$75

COLUMBIA SPECIAL PRODUCTS

Number	Title	Yr	NM
JSN6044 [M]	King of the Blues Trombone	197?	$30

COMMODORE

Number	Title	Yr	NM
20015 [10]	Big T	195?	$80

DECCA

Number	Title	Yr	NM
DL8304 [M]	Big T's Jazz	1956	$150
DL4540 [M]	The Golden Horn of Jack Teagarden	1964	$35
DL74540 [R]	The Golden Horn of Jack Teagarden	1964	$30

EPIC

Number	Title	Yr	NM
SN6044 [M]	King of the Blues Trombone	1963	$150
LN24045 [M]	King of the Blues Trombone, Vol. 1	1963	$60
LN24046 [M]	King of the Blues Trombone, Vol. 2	1963	$60
LN24047 [M]	King of the Blues Trombone, Vol. 3	1963	$60

EVEREST ARCHIVE OF FOLK & JAZZ

Number	Title	Yr	NM
352	Big Band Jazz	198?	$25
FS-335	Original Dixieland	198?	$25

FOLKWAYS

Number	Title	Yr	NM
FJ-2819	The Big Band Sound of Jack Teagarden and Bunny Berigan	198?	$30

IAJRC

Number	Title	Yr	NM
LP-19	Sincerely, Jack Teagarden	198?	$35

JAZZTONE

Number	Title	Yr	NM
J-1222 [M]	Big T	195?	$30

— Reissue of Period material

JOLLY ROGER

Number	Title	Yr	NM
5026 [10]	Jack Teagarden	1955	$60

MCA

Number	Title	Yr	NM
227	The Golden Horn of Jack Teagarden	1973	$25

— Black rainbow label

MOSAIC

Number	Title	Yr	NM
MQ6-168	The Complete Capitol Fifties Jack Teagarden Sessions	199?	$150

PERIOD

Number	Title	Yr	NM
SLP-1106 [10]	Meet Me Where They Play the Blues	1955	$80
SLP-1110 [10]	Original Dixieland	1955	$80

RCA VICTOR

Number	Title	Yr	NM
LPV-528 [M]	Jack Teagarden	1965	$25

RONDO-LETTE

Number	Title	Yr	NM
A-18 [M]	The Blues and Dixie	1958	$30

ROULETTE

Number	Title	Yr	NM
R-25177 [M]	Dixie Sound	1962	$35
SR-25177 [S]	Dixie Sound	1962	$25
R-25091 [M]	Jack Teagarden at the Round Table	1960	$35
SR-25091 [S]	Jack Teagarden at the Round Table	1960	$25
R-25119 [M]	Jazz Maverick	1961	$35
SR-25119 [S]	Jazz Maverick	1961	$25
R-25243 [M]	Portrait of Mr. T	1963	$35
SR-25243 [S]	Portrait of Mr. T	1963	$25

ROYALE

Number	Title	Yr	NM
18156 [10]	The Blues	195?	$80

SAVOY JAZZ

Number	Title	Yr	NM
SJL-1162	Varsity Sides	1986	$25

SOUNDS

Number	Title	Yr	NM
S-1203	Jack Teagarden in Concert	197?	$35

TIME-LIFE

Number	Title	Yr	NM
STL-J-08	Giants of Jazz	1979	$50

TRIP

Number	Title	Yr	NM
6	Jack Teagarden	197?	$25

URANIA

Number	Title	Yr	NM
UJLP-1002 [10]	Jack Teagarden Sings and Plays	1954	$300
UJLP-1001 [10]	Meet the New Jack Teagarden	1954	$300

VERVE

Number	Title	Yr	NM
V-8495 [M]	Jack Teagarden!!	1962	$35
V6-8495 [S]	Jack Teagarden!!	1962	$25
V-8416 [M]	Mis'ry and the Blues	1961	$35
V6-8416 [S]	Mis'ry and the Blues	1961	$25
V-8465 [M]	Think Well of Me	1962	$35
V6-8465 [S]	Think Well of Me	1962	$25

Number	Title	Yr	NM

TEAGARDEN, JACK/BOBBY HACKETT
Also see each artist's individual listings.

Albums

COMMODORE
| ❏ FL-30012 [M] | Jack Teagarden and Bobby Hackett | 1959 | $30 |

TEAGARDEN, JACK/JONAH JONES
Also see each artist's individual listings.

Albums

AAMCO
| ❏ ALP-309 [M] | Two Boys from Dixieland | 196? | $30 |
—*Reissue of Bethlehem material*

BETHLEHEM
| ❏ BCP-6042 [M] | Dixieland | 1959 | $200 |

TEAGARDEN, JACK/MAX KAMINSKY
Also see each artist's individual listings.

Albums

COMMODORE
| ❏ XFL-14940 | Big T and Mighty Max | 198? | $25 |

HALL OF FAME
| ❏ 616 | Jack and Max | 197? | $25 |

TEAGARDEN, JACK/PEE WEE RUSSELL
Also see each artist's individual listings.

Albums

FANTASY
| ❏ OJC-1708 | Jack Teagarden's Big Eight / Pee Wee Russell's Rhythmakers | 1985 | $25 |

RIVERSIDE
| ❏ RLP 12-141 | Jack Teagarden's Big Eight / Pee Wee Russell's Rhythmakers | 1956 | $250 |

TEDESCO, TOMMY
Six- and 12-string guitarist. Best known for his session work on Phil Spector-produced records, among others.

Albums

DISCOVERY
❏ 928	Hollywood Gypsy	1986	$12
❏ 851	My Desiree	1982	$12
❏ 789	When Do We Start	1978	$30

IMPERIAL
❏ LP-9321 [M]	Calypso Soul	1966	$100
❏ LP-12321 [S]	Calypso Soul	1966	$150
❏ LP-9295 [M]	Guitars	1965	$100
❏ LP-12295 [S]	Guitars	1965	$150
❏ LP-9263 [M]	The Electric 12 String Guitar of Tommy Tedesco	1964	$100
❏ LP-12263 [S]	The Electric 12 String Guitar of Tommy Tedesco	1964	$150

TREND
| ❏ TR-517 | Alone at Last | 1979 | $25 |
—*Direct-to-disc recording*
| ❏ TR-514 | Autumn | 1978 | $25 |
—*Direct-to-disc recording*

TEITELBAUM, RICHARD
Synthesizer player and composer.

Albums

ARISTA/FREEDOM
| ❏ AF1037 | Time Zones | 197? | $30 |

TEMIZ, OKAY
Drummer and percussionist.

Albums

FINNADAR
| ❏ 9032 | Drummer of Two Worlds | 198? | $35 |

TEMPERLEY, JOE, AND JIMMY KNEPPER
Temperley is a baritone, tenor and alto saxophone player and clarinetist. Also see JIMMY KNEPPER.

Albums

HEP
| ❏ 2003 | Just Friends | 198? | $25 |

TEMPLETON, ALEC
Pianist and composer.

Albums

ATLANTIC
| ❏ 1222 [M] | The Magic Piano | 1956 | $300 |
—*Black label*
| ❏ 1222 [M] | The Magic Piano | 1961 | $150 |
—*Multicolor label, white "fan" logo at right*

TEMPLIN, RAY

Albums

EUPHONIC
| ❏ 1219 | A Flash at the Piano | 198? | $25 |

TERRACE, PETE
Percussionist and bandleader.

Albums

FANTASY
| ❏ 3203 [M] | Going Loco | 1956 | $60 |
—*Red vinyl*
| ❏ 3203 [M] | Going Loco | 195? | $30 |
| ❏ 3215 [M] | Invitation to the Mambo | 1956 | $60 |
—*Red vinyl*
| ❏ 3215 [M] | Invitation to the Mambo | 195? | $30 |
| ❏ 3234 [M] | The Pete Terrace Quintet | 1957 | $60 |
—*Red vinyl*
| ❏ 3234 [M] | The Pete Terrace Quintet | 195? | $30 |

FORUM
| ❏ F-9041 [M] | Cole Porter in Latin America | 196? | $35 |
| ❏ SF-9041 [S] | Cole Porter in Latin America | 196? | $30 |

TICO
❏ LP-1023 [M]	A Night in Mambo Jazzland	1956	$40
❏ SLP-1082 [S]	Bella Pachanga	1961	$30
❏ LP-1082 [M]	Bella Pachanga	1961	$30
❏ LP-1036 [M]	Cha Cha Cha in New York	1957	$50
❏ LP-1063 [M]	Cole Porter in Latin America	1959	$30
❏ LP-1057 [M]	My One and Only Love	1959	$30
❏ LP-1050 [M]	Pete with a Latin Beat	1958	$30
❏ LP-1028 [M]	The Nearness of You	1956	$40

TERRY, BUDDY
Tenor and soprano saxophone player and flutist.

Albums

MAINSTREAM
❏ MRL-336	Awareness	1972	$35
❏ MRL-391	Lean On Him	1974	$30
❏ MRL-356	Pure Dynamite	1973	$35

PRESTIGE
❏ PRLP-7525 [M]	Electric Soul	1967	$30
❏ PRST-7525 [S]	Electric Soul	1967	$30
❏ PRLP-7541 [M]	Natural Soul	1967	$30
❏ PRST-7541 [S]	Natural Soul	1967	$30

TERRY, CLARK
Trumpeter and fluegel horn player. Also see GARY BURTON; KENNY DORHAM; COLEMAN HAWKINS; THE RIVERSIDE JAZZ STARS; SHIRLEY SCOTT.

Albums

20TH CENTURY FOX
| ❏ TFM-3137 [M] | What Makes Sammy Swing | 1963 | $25 |
| ❏ TFS-4137 [S] | What Makes Sammy Swing | 1963 | $30 |

ABC IMPULSE!
❏ AS-9157 [S]	It's What's Happenin'	1968	$200
❏ AS-9127 [S]	Spanish Rice	1968	$35
❏ AS-64 [S]	The Happy Horn of Clark Terry	1968	$35

ARGO
| ❏ LP-620 [M] | Out on a Limb | 1957 | $60 |

CAMEO
❏ CS-1064 [S]	More	1964	$40
❏ C-1071 [M]	Tread Ye Lightly	1964	$30
❏ CS-1071 [S]	Tread Ye Lightly	1964	$40

CANDID
| ❏ CD-8009 [M] | Color Changes | 1960 | $50 |
| ❏ CS-9009 [S] | Color Changes | 1960 | $40 |

EMARCY
| ❏ MG-36007 [M] | Clark Terry | 1955 | $250 |
| ❏ MG-36093 [M] | The Jazz School | 1956 | $200 |

ETOILE
| ❏ CPR-1 | Clark Terry's Big Bad Band | 197? | $25 |

FANTASY
❏ OJC-229	Duke with a Difference	1990	$30
❏ OJC-302	In Orbit	1988	$30
❏ OJC-604	Memories of Duke	1991	$30
❏ OJC-066	Serenade to a Bus Seat	198?	$30

IMPULSE!
❏ A-9127 [M]	Spanish Rice	1966	$120
❏ AS-9127 [S]	Spanish Rice	1966	$120
❏ A-64 [M]	The Happy Horn of Clark Terry	1964	$120
❏ AS-64 [S]	The Happy Horn of Clark Terry	1964	$120

JAZZ MAN
| ❏ 5046 | Color Changes | 198? | $25 |

MAINSTREAM
❏ MRL-347	Angyumaluma	1972	$35
❏ MRL-373	Clark Terry and the W.B. Brookmeyer Quintet	1973	$35
❏ 56043 [M]	Clark Terry Tonight	1965	$25
❏ S-6043 [S]	Clark Terry Tonight	1965	$30
❏ S-6086	Clark Terry with Bob Brookmeyer	196?	$25
❏ 56066 [M]	Mumbles	1966	$25
❏ S-6066 [S]	Mumbles	1966	$30
❏ MRL-320	Straight No Chaser	1971	$35
❏ 56054 [M]	The Power of Positive Swinging	1965	$25
❏ S-6054 [S]	The Power of Positive Swinging	1965	$30
❏ MRL-803	What'd He Say	197?	$25

MILESTONE
| ❏ 47032 | Cruising | 197? | $35 |

MOODSVILLE
| ❏ MVLP-20 [M] | Everything's Mellow | 1961 | $50 |
—*Green label*
| ❏ MVLP-20 [M] | Everything's Mellow | 1965 | $30 |
—*Blue label, trident logo at right*
| ❏ MVLP-26 [M] | The Jazz Version of "All American" | 1962 | $50 |
—*Green label*
| ❏ MVLP-26 [M] | The Jazz Version of "All American" | 1965 | $30 |
—*Blue label, trident logo at right*

PABLO TODAY
❏ 2312105	Ain't Misbehavin'	1979	$30
❏ 2312118	Memories of Duke	1980	$30
❏ 2313127	Yes, the Blues	1981	$30

PAUSA
| ❏ 7131 | Wham! | 198? | $25 |

POLYDOR
| ❏ 24-5002 | Clark Terry at Montreux Jazz Festival | 1970 | $35 |

RIVERSIDE
❏ 6167	Clark Terry and Thelonious Monk in Orbit	198?	$30
❏ RM-3009 [M]	C.T. Meets Monk	1967	$100
❏ RS-3009 [S]	C.T. Meets Monk	1967	$100
❏ RLP 12-246 [M]	Duke with a Difference	1957	$250
❏ RLP-1108 [S]	Duke with a Difference	1959	$300
❏ RLP 12-271 [M]	In Orbit	1958	$300
❏ RLP 12-237 [M]	Serenade to a Bus Seat	1957	$350
—*White label, blue print*
| ❏ RLP 12-237 [M] | Serenade to a Bus Seat | 1957 | $350 |
—*Blue label, microphone logo at top*
❏ 6209	Serenade to a Bus Seat	198?	$30
❏ RLP 12-295 [M]	Top and Bottom Brass	1959	$200
❏ RLP-1137 [S]	Top and Bottom Brass	1959	$200

SWING
| ❏ 8406 | Paris 1960 | 1985 | $25 |

TRIP
| ❏ 5528 | Swahili | 197? | $25 |

VANGUARD
❏ VSD-79365	Clark Terry and His Jolly Giants	197?	$30
❏ VSD-79373	Clark Terry Big Band Live at Buddy's Place	1976	$30
❏ VSD-79355	Clark Terry Big Band Live at Wichita Fest '74	1975	$30
❏ VSD-79393	Globetrotter	1977	$30

VERVE
| ❏ V6-8836 | Previously Unreleased Recordings | 197? | $35 |

WING
| ❏ MGW-60002 [M] | The Jazz School | 1955 | $80 |

TERRY, CLARK/COLEMAN HAWKINS
Also see each artist's individual listings.

Albums

COLPIX
| ❏ SCP-450 [S] | Eddie Costa Memorial Concert | 1963 | $50 |

Nick Travis, *The Panic Is On*, RCA Victor LJM-1010, **$120**.

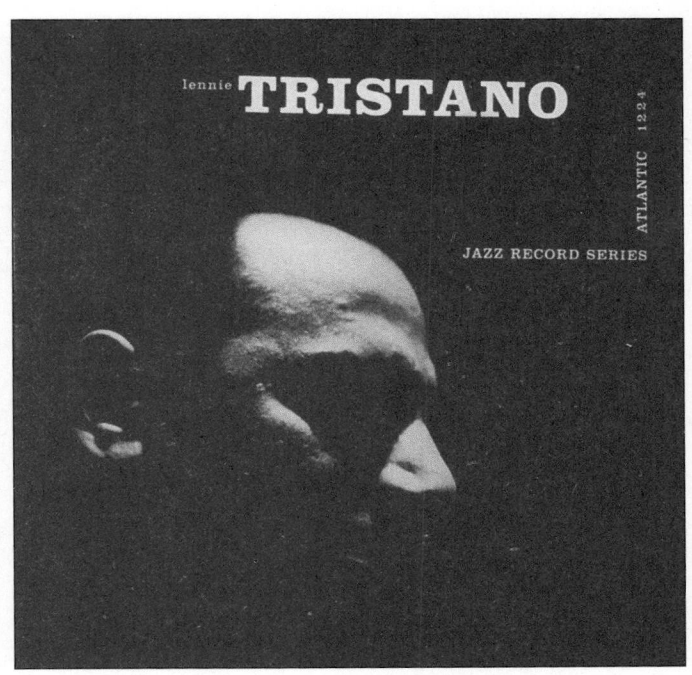

Lennie Tristano, *Lennie Tristano*, Atlantic 1224, black label, **$300**.

The Trombones, Inc., *They Met at the Continental Divide*, Warner Bros. W 1272, mono, **$50**.

Bobby Troup, *Bobby Swings Tenderly*, Mode LP-111, **$100**.

Number	Title	Yr	NM

TERRY, LILLIAN

Albums

SOUL NOTE
❑ SN-1047	A Dream Comes True	198?	$30
❑ SN-1147	Oo-Shoo-Be-Doo-Be…Oo…	1986	$30
	Oo…Oo…Oo		

TERRY, PAT, JR.
Banjo player.

Albums

CIRCLE
❑ C-54	All Jazzed Up	1981	$25

TESCHEMACHER, FRANK
Clarinetist, alto saxophone player, violinist and banjo player.

Albums

BRUNSWICK
❑ BL58017 [10]	Tesch Plays Jazz Classics	1950	$80

TIME-LIFE
❑ STL-J23	Giants of Jazz	1982	$25

THESAURUS RHYTHM MAKERS

Albums

SUNBEAM
❑ 101	The Thesaurus Rhythm Makers, Vol. 1	197?	$25
❑ 102	The Thesaurus Rhythm Makers, Vol. 2	197?	$25
❑ 103	The Thesaurus Rhythm Makers, Vol. 3	197?	$25

THESELIUS, GOSTA
Tenor saxophone player and pianist.

Albums

BALLY
❑ BAL-12002 [M]	Swedish Jazz	1956	$50

THEUS, FATS
Tenor saxophone player.

Albums

CTI
❑ 1005	Black Out	1972	$35

THIELEMANS, TOOTS
Harmonica player.

Albums

A&M
❑ SP-3613	Yesterday and Today	1974	$30

ABC-PARAMOUNT
❑ ABC-482 [M]	The Whistler and His Guitar	1965	$30
❑ ABCS-482 [S]	The Whistler and His Guitar	1965	$30

CHOICE
❑ 1007	Captured Alive	197?	$35

COLUMBIA
❑ CL658 [M]	The Sound	1955	$60

COMMAND
❑ RS 33-906 [M]	Contrasts	1967	$25
❑ RS906SD [S]	Contrasts	1967	$35
❑ RS 33-918 [M]	Guitars and Strings… And Things	1967	$25
❑ RS918SD [S]	Guitars and Strings… And Things	1967	$35
❑ RSSD978-2	The Salient One	1973	$35
❑ RS930SD	Toots!	1968	$35

CONCORD JAZZ
❑ CJ-355	Only Trust Your Heart	1988	$25

DECCA
❑ DL9204 [M]	Time Out for Toots	1958	$100
❑ DL79204 [S]	Time Out for Toots	1958	$100

FANTASY
❑ OJC-1738	Man Bites Harmonica	198?	$25

INNER CITY
❑ IC-1145	Live	198?	$30
❑ IC-1146	Live 2	198?	$30
❑ IC-1147	Live 3	198?	$30
❑ IC-1148	Spotlight	198?	$30

JAZZ MAN
❑ 5016	Slow Motion	198?	$25

RIVERSIDE
❑ RLP 12-257 [M]	Man Bites Harmonica	1958	$300

SIGNATURE
❑ SM-6006 [M]	The Soul of Toots Thielmans	1960	$80
❑ SS-6006 [S]	The Soul of Toots Thielmans	1960	$60

THIGPEN, ED
Drummer and percussionist.

Albums

GNP CRESCENDO
❑ GNPS-2098	Action Re-Action	197?	$25

VERVE
❑ V-8663 [M]	Out of the Storm	1966	$25
❑ V6-8663 [S]	Out of the Storm	1966	$30

THILO, JESPER
Danish tenor saxophone player.

Albums

STORYVILLE
❑ 4065	Swingin' Friends	198?	$25
❑ 4072	Tribute to Frog	198?	$25

THOMAS, DAVID
Pianist.

Albums

STOMP OFF
❑ SOS-1072	Through the Bottomlands	1984	$12

THOMAS, GARY
Tenor and soprano saxophone player and flutist.

Albums

ENJA
❑ R1-79604	Code Violations	1989	$30

JMT
❑ 834432-1	By Any Means Necessary	198?	$25

THOMAS, JEANNIE
Female singer.

Albums

STRAND
❑ SL-1030 [M]	Jeannie Thomas Sings for the Boys	1961	$40
❑ SLS-1030 [S]	Jeannie Thomas Sings for the Boys	1961	$50

THOMAS, JOE (1)
Trumpeter; among others, he played in FLETCHER HENDERSON's early orchestras. See VIC DICKENSON.

THOMAS, JOE (2), AND JAY MCSHANN
Also see each artist's individual listings.

Albums

UPTOWN
❑ 2712	Blowin' In from Kansas City	198?	$30

THOMAS, JOE (2)
Tenor saxophone player.

Albums

UPTOWN
❑ 271	Raw Meat	198?	$30

THOMAS, JOE (3), AND BILL ELLIOTT
Elliott is a drummer. Also see JOE THOMAS (3).

Albums

SUE
❑ LP-1025 [M]	Speak Your Piece	1964	$50

THOMAS, JOE (3)
Tenor saxophone player and flutist. Not to be confused with Joe Thomas (2), who was a tenor saxophone player with the JIMMIE LUNCEFORD orchestra.

Albums

CHIAROSCURO
❑ 2018	Flash	1979	$30

GROOVE MERCHANT
❑ 504	Joy of Cookin'	197?	$50
❑ 3310	Masada	197?	$35

THOMAS, KID
See KID THOMAS in the letter K.

THOMAS, LEON
Male singer.

Albums

FLYING DUTCHMAN
❑ FD-10155	Blues and the Soulful Truth	197?	$35
❑ FD-10164	Facets	1973	$35
❑ FD-10167	Full Circle	197?	$35
❑ FD-10115	Spirits Known and Unknown	1969	$25
❑ FD-10132	The Leon Thomas Album	197?	$25

MEGA
❑ M51-5003	Gold Sunrise on Magic Mountain	197?	$25

PORTRAIT
❑ FR44161	The Leon Thomas Blues Band	1988	$25

THOMAS, PAT
Male singer.

Albums

MGM
❑ E-4103 [M]	Desafinado	1962	$35
❑ SE-4103 [S]	Desafinado	1962	$50
❑ E-4206 [M]	Moody's Mood	1964	$50
❑ SE-4206 [S]	Moody's Mood	1964	$60

STRAND
❑ SL-1015 [M]	Jazz Patterns	1961	$40
❑ SLS-1015 [S]	Jazz Patterns	1961	$100

THOMAS, RENE
Guitarist.

Albums

FANTASY
❑ OJC-1725	Guitar Groove	198?	$25

JAZZLAND
❑ JLP-27 [M]	Guitar Groove	1960	$30
❑ JLP-927 [S]	Guitar Groove	1960	$40

THOMAS, WALTER "FOOTS"
Alto, tenor and baritone saxophone player, clarinetist and bandleader.

Albums

PRESTIGE
❑ PRST-7584	Walter "Foots" Thomas All-Stars	196?	$35

THOMPSON, BOB
Pianist and keyboard player.

Albums

INTIMA
❑ SJ-73284	7 In, 7 Out	1987	$25

—Reissue of Rainbow 2010
❑ SJ-73238	Brother's Keeper	1987	$25
❑ D1-73331	Say What You Want	1988	$25
❑ D1-73519	Wilderness	1989	$30

RAINBOW
❑ 2010	7 In, 7 Out	1986	$50

THOMPSON, BUTCH, AND CHET ELY
Also see each artist's individual listings.

Albums

JAZZOLOGY
❑ J-79	Jelly Rolls On	197?	$25

THOMPSON, BUTCH, AND HAL SMITH
Also see each artist's individual listings.

Albums

STOMP OFF
❑ SOS-1075	Echoes from Storyville, Vol. 1: If You Don't Shake	1985	$25
❑ SOS-1116	Echoes from Storyville, Vol. 2: Milenberg Joys	1986	$25

THOMPSON, BUTCH
Pianist and bandleader.

Albums

JAZZOLOGY

Number	Title	Yr	NM
❑ J-146	Butch Thompson and His Boys in Chicago	1986	$25
STOMP OFF			
❑ SOS-1037	A' Solas	198?	$25

THOMPSON, CHESTER
Organist.
Albums

Number	Title	Yr	NM
BLACK JAZZ			
❑ 6	Powerhouse	197?	$30

THOMPSON, DON
Pianist, bass player, vibraphone player, arranger and composer.
Albums

Number	Title	Yr	NM
CONCORD JAZZ			
❑ CJ-243	Beautiful Friendship	198?	$25
PM			
❑ 08	Country Place	1976	$30

THOMPSON, LES
Albums

Number	Title	Yr	NM
RCA VICTOR			
❑ LPT-3102 [10]	Gene Norman Presents "Just Jazz	1952	$150

THOMPSON, LUCKY
Tenor and soprano saxophone player. Also see THE MODERN JAZZ SOCIETY.
Albums

Number	Title	Yr	NM
51 WEST			
❑ Q16072	Back to the World	198?	$30
ABC IMPULSE!			
❑ ASH-9307-2	Dancing Sunbeam	1975	$60
ABC-PARAMOUNT			
❑ ABC-111 [M]	Lucky Thompson Featuring Oscar Pettiford, Volume 1	1956	$120
❑ ABC-171 [M]	Lucky Thompson Featuring Oscar Pettiford, Volume 2	1957	$120
BIOGRAPH			
❑ BLP-12061	Lullaby in Rhythm	1979	$60
DAWN			
❑ DLP-1113 [M]	Lucky Thompson	1957	$100
FANTASY			
❑ OJC-194	Lucky Strikes	1985	$30
GROOVE MERCHANT			
❑ GM-508	Goodbye Yesterday	1973	$60
❑ GM-4411	Illuminations	197?	$30
❑ GM-517	I Offer You	1974	$60
INNER CITY			
❑ IC-7016	Lucky Thompson	1976	$35
LONDON			
❑ D-93098 [10]	Recorded in Paris '56	1956	$100
MOODSVILLE			
❑ MVLP-39 [M]	Lucky Thompson Plays Jerome Kern and No More	1963	$60
— Green label			
❑ MVST-39 [S]	Lucky Thompson Plays Jerome Kern and No More	1963	$80
— Green label			
❑ MVLP-39 [M]	Lucky Thompson Plays Jerome Kern and No More	1965	$30
— Blue label, trident logo at right			
❑ MVST-39 [S]	Lucky Thompson Plays Jerome Kern and No More	1965	$40
— Blue label, trident logo at right			
NESSA			
❑ N-13	Body and Soul	197?	$60
PRESTIGE			
❑ PRLP-7394 [M]	Happy Days Are Here Again	1965	$50
— Blue label, trident logo at right			
❑ PRST-7394 [S]	Happy Days Are Here Again	1965	$60
— Blue label, trident logo at right			
❑ PRLP-7365 [M]	Lucky Strikes	1965	$50
— Blue label, trident logo at right			
❑ PRST-7365 [S]	Lucky Strikes	1965	$60
— Blue label, trident logo at right			
RIVOLI			
❑ 44 [M]	Kinfolk's Corner	1965	$100
❑ S-44 [S]	Kinfolk's Corner	1965	$120
❑ 40 [M]	Lucky Is Back!	1965	$100

Number	Title	Yr	NM
❑ S-40 [S]	Lucky Is Back!	1965	$120
SWING			
❑ 8404	Paris 1956, Vol. 1	1985	$25
TOPS			
❑ L-928 [10]	Jazz at the Auditorium	1954	$150
TRANSITION			
❑ TRLP-21 [M]	Lucky Strikes	1956	$500
— With booklet (deduct 1/5 if missing)			
URANIA			
❑ UJLP-1206 [M]	Accent on Tenor Sax	1955	$350
XANADU			
❑ 204	Brown Rose	1985	$35

THOMPSON, MALACHI
Trumpeter.

Albums

Number	Title	Yr	NM
DELMARK			
❑ DS-442	Spirit	1989	$30

THOMPSON, SIR CHARLES
Pianist, organist, bandleader and arranger. Also see THE MANHATTAN JAZZ ALL-STARS.

Albums

Number	Title	Yr	NM
AMERICAN RECORDING SOCIETY			
❑ G-447 [M]	Basically Swing	1957	$30
APOLLO			
❑ 103 [10]	Sir Charles Thompson and His All Stars	1951	$400
COLUMBIA			
❑ CL1663 [M]	Rockin' Rhythm	1961	$30
❑ CS8463 [S]	Rockin' Rhythm	1961	$30
❑ CL1364 [M]	Sir Charles Thompson and the Swing Organ	1959	$30
❑ CS8205 [S]	Sir Charles Thompson and the Swing Organ	1959	$30
EUPHONIC			
❑ 1221	The Neglected Professor	198?	$25
SACKVILLE			
❑ 3037	Portrait of a Piano	199?	$30
VANGUARD			
❑ VRS-8009 [10]	Sir Charles Thompson and His Band	1954	$150
❑ VRS-8006 [10]	Sir Charles Thompson Quartet	1954	$100
❑ VRS-8003 [10]	Sir Charles Thompson Sextet	1953	$100
❑ VRS-8018 [10]	Sir Charles Thompson Trio	1955	$120

THORNE, FRAN
Pianist.

Albums

Number	Title	Yr	NM
TRANSITION			
❑ TRLP-27 [M]	Piano Reflections	1956	$200
— With booklet (deduct 1/4 if missing)			

THORNHILL, CLAUDE
Pianist, bandleader, composer and arranger.

Albums

Number	Title	Yr	NM
CIRCLE			
❑ CLP-19	Claude Thornhill and His Orchestra 1941 & 1947	1981	$30
COLUMBIA			
❑ CL6164 [10]	Claude Thornhill Encores	1951	$80
❑ CL6050 [10]	Dance Parade	1949	$80
❑ CL709 [M]	Dancing After Midnight	1955	$50
❑ CL6035 [10]	Piano Reflections	1949	$80
❑ KG32906	The Memorable Claude Thornhill	1974	$35
— Original issue			
❑ PG32906	The Memorable Claude Thornhill	197?	$30
— Reissue with new prefix; some may have bar codes			
DECCA			
❑ DL8722 [M]	Claude on a Cloud	1958	$120
❑ DL78722 [S]	Claude on a Cloud	1958	$120
❑ DL8878 [M]	Dance to the Sound of Claude Thornhill	1958	$120
❑ DL78878 [S]	Dance to the Sound of Claude Thornhill	1958	$120
DESIGN			

Number	Title	Yr	NM
❑ DLP-50 [M]	Sleepy Serenade	196?	$25
HARMONY			
❑ HL7088 [M]	The Thornhill Sound	1957	$30
HINDSIGHT			
❑ HSR-108	Claude Thornhill and His Orchestra 1947	198?	$30
INSIGHT			
❑ IN-207	Claude Thornhill and His Orchestra	198?	$30
KAPP			
❑ KL-1058 [M]	Two Sides of Claude Thornhill	1958	$30
❑ KS-3058 [S]	Two Sides of Claude Thornhill	1958	$30
MONMOUTH-EVERGREEN			
❑ 7024	Claude Thornhill at Glen Island Casino 1941	198?	$25
❑ MR-6606	Snowfall -- A Memory of Claude Thornhill	197?	$35
RCA CAMDEN			
❑ CAL-307 [M]	Dinner for Two	1958	$30
TREND			
❑ TL-1002 [10]	Claude Thornhill Plays the Great Jazz Arrangements of Gerry Mulligan and Ralph Aldrich	1953	$120
❑ TL-1001 [10]	Dream Stuff	1953	$120

THORNTON, ARGONNE
See SADIK HAKIM.

THORNTON, CLIFFORD
Trumpeter.

Albums

Number	Title	Yr	NM
JCOA			
❑ 1008	Gardens of Harlem	197?	$35
THIRD WORLD			
❑ 12372	Communications Network	197?	$35
❑ 9636 [S]	Freedom and Unity	1969	$30

THORNTON, TERI
Female singer.

Albums

Number	Title	Yr	NM
COLUMBIA			
❑ CL2094 [M]	Open Highway	1963	$30
❑ CS8894 [S]	Open Highway	1963	$40
DAUNTLESS			
❑ DM-4306 [M]	Somewhere in the Night	1963	$30
❑ DS-6306 [S]	Somewhere in the Night	1963	$30
RIVERSIDE			
❑ RLP-352 [M]	Devil May Care	1961	$200
❑ RS-9352 [S]	Devil May Care	1961	$200
❑ 6142	Devil May Care	198?	$30
❑ RM-3525 [M]	Lullabye of the Leaves	1964	$150
❑ RS-93525 [S]	Lullabye of the Leaves	1964	$150

THREADGILL, HENRY
Alto and tenor saxophone player, clarinetist and bass flutist. Also see AIR.

Albums

Number	Title	Yr	NM
ABOUT TIME			
❑ 1005	Just the Facts and Pass the Bucket	198?	$30
❑ 1004	When Was That?	198?	$30
NOVUS			
❑ 3025-1-N	Easily Slip Into Another World	1988	$25
❑ 3052-1-N	Rag, Bush and All	1989	$25
❑ 3013-1-N	You Know the Number	1987	$25

THREE
Members: KHAN JAMAL; JOHNNY DYANI; PIERRE DORGE.

Albums

Number	Title	Yr	NM
STEEPLECHASE			
❑ SCS-1201	Three	198?	$30
— Khan Jamal; Johnny Dyani; Pierre Dorge			

THREE DEUCES, THE

Albums

Number	Title	Yr	NM
STOMP OFF			
❑ SOS-1185	Stompin' 'n' Slidin'	1988	$25

Number	Title	Yr	NM

THREE JOLLY MINERS, THE

Albums

HISTORICAL
❑ 23 [M]   The Three Jolly Miners 1925-28   1968 $35

THREE SOULS, THE

Members: Henry Cain; Albert Coleman; Will Scott.

Albums

ARGO
❑ LP-4005 [M]   Almost Like Being In Love   1960 $0
—Canceled
❑ LPS-4005 [S]   Almost Like Being In Love   1960 $0
—Canceled
❑ LP-4036 [M]   Dangerous Dan Express   1964 $50
❑ LPS-4036 [S]   Dangerous Dan Express   1964 $60
❑ LP-4044 [M]   Soul Sounds   1965 $50
❑ LPS-4044 [S]   Soul Sounds   1965 $60

THREE SOUNDS, THE

Members: GENE HARRIS (piano); Bill Dowdy (drums); Andrew Simpkins (bass). Harris later recorded as "Gene Harris and the Three Sounds" with studio musicians; those albums are listed under Harris' name.

Albums

BLUE NOTE
❑ BLP-4155 [M]   Black Orchid   1963 $60
❑ BST-84155 [S]   Black Orchid   1963 $30
—With "New York, USA" address on label
❑ BST-84155 [S]   Black Orchid   1967 $35
—With "A Division of Liberty Records" on label
❑ BLP-4014 [M]   Bottoms Up   1959 $150
—Regular version, W. 63rd St. address on label
❑ BST-4014 [S]   Bottoms Up   1959 $60
—Regular version, W. 63rd St. address on label
❑ BLP-4014 [M]   Bottoms Up   1963 $60
—With "New York, USA" address on label
❑ BST-4014 [S]   Bottoms Up   1963 $25
—With "New York, USA" address on label
❑ BST-84014 [S]   Bottoms Up   1967 $35
—With "A Division of Liberty Records" on label
❑ BST-84285 [S]   Coldwater Flat   1968 $25
—With "A Division of Liberty Records" on label
❑ BST-84301 [S]   Elegant Soul   1968 $25
—With "A Division of Liberty Records" on label
❑ BLP-4072 [M]   Feelin' Good   1961 $150
—With W. 63rd St. address on label
❑ BST-84072 [S]   Feelin' Good   1961 $50
—With W. 63rd St. address on label
❑ BLP-4072 [M]   Feelin' Good   1963 $60
—With "New York, USA" address on label
❑ BST-84072 [S]   Feelin' Good   1963 $25
—With "New York, USA" address on label
❑ BST-84072 [S]   Feelin' Good   1967 $35
—With "A Division of Liberty Records" on label
❑ BLP-4020 [M]   Good Deal   1959 $150
—Regular version, W. 63rd St. address on label
❑ BST-84020 [S]   Good Deal   1959 $50
—With W. 63rd St. address on label
❑ BLP-4020 [M]   Good Deal   1963 $60
—With "New York, USA" address on label
❑ BST-84020 [S]   Good Deal   1963 $25
—With "New York, USA" address on label
❑ BST-84020 [S]   Good Deal   1967 $35
—With "A Division of Liberty Records" on label
❑ BLP-4088 [M]   Here We Come   1961 $150
—With 61st St. address on label
❑ BST-84088 [S]   Here We Come   1961 $50
—With 61st St. address on label
❑ BLP-4088 [M]   Here We Come   1963 $60
—With "New York, USA" address on label
❑ BST-84088 [S]   Here We Come   1963 $25
—With "New York, USA" address on label
❑ BST-84088 [S]   Here We Come   1967 $35
—With "A Division of Liberty Records" on label
❑ BLP-4102 [M]   Hey! There   1962 $60
❑ BST-84102 [S]   Hey! There   1962 $30
—With "New York, USA" address on label
❑ BST-84102 [S]   Hey! There   1967 $35
—With "A Division of Liberty Records" on label

❑ BLP-1600 [M]   Introducing the Three Sounds   1958 $150
—Regular version, W. 63rd St. address on label
❑ BST-1600 [S]   Introducing the Three Sounds   1959 $60
—Regular version, W. 63rd St. address on label
❑ BLP-1600 [M]   Introducing the Three Sounds   1963 $60
—With "New York, USA" address on label
❑ BST-1600 [S]   Introducing the Three Sounds   1963 $25
—With "New York, USA" address on label
❑ BST-81600 [S]   Introducing the Three Sounds   1967 $35
—With "A Division of Liberty Records" on label
❑ BLP-4120 [M]   It Just Got To Be   1963 $60
❑ BST-84120 [S]   It Just Got To Be   1963 $30
—With "New York, USA" address on label
❑ BST-84120 [S]   It Just Got To Be   1967 $35
—With "A Division of Liberty Records" on label
❑ BLP-4265 [M]   Live at the Lighthouse   1967 $60
❑ BST-84265 [S]   Live at the Lighthouse   1967 $25
—With "A Division of Liberty Records" on label
❑ BLP-4044 [M]   Moods   1960 $150
—Regular version, W. 63rd St. address on label
❑ BST-84044 [S]   Moods   1960 $50
—With W. 63rd St. address on label
❑ BLP-4044 [M]   Moods   1963 $60
—With "New York, USA" address on label
❑ BST-84044 [S]   Moods   1967 $35
—With "A Division of Liberty Records" on label
❑ BST-84044 [S]   Moods   1963 $25
—With "New York, USA" address on label
❑ BLP-4197 [M]   Out of This World   1965 $60
❑ BST-84197 [S]   Out of This World   1965 $30
—With "New York, USA" address on label
❑ BST-84197 [S]   Out of This World   1967 $35
—With "A Division of Liberty Records" on label
❑ BST-84197 [S]   Out of This World   1970 $35
—With "Liberty/UA, Inc." on label
❑ BST-84341 [S]   Soul Symphony   1969 $25
—With "A Division of Liberty Records" on label
❑ BLP-4248 [M]   Vibrations   1966 $60
❑ BST-84248 [S]   Vibrations   1966 $30
—With "New York, USA" address on label
❑ BST-84248 [S]   Vibrations   1967 $35
—With "A Division of Liberty Records" on label

LIMELIGHT
❑ LM-82026 [M]   Beautiful Friendship   1965 $25
❑ LS-86026 [S]   Beautiful Friendship   1965 $30
❑ LM-82014 [M]   Three Moods   1965 $25
❑ LS-86014 [S]   Three Moods   1965 $30

MERCURY
❑ MG-20776 [M]   Jazz On Broadway   1963 $100
❑ SR-60776 [S]   Jazz On Broadway   1963 $100
❑ MG-20921 [M]   Live at the Living Room   1963 $100
❑ SR-60921 [S]   Live at the Living Room   1963 $100
❑ MG-20839 [M]   Some Like It Modern   1963 $100
❑ SR-60839 [S]   Some Like It Modern   1963 $100

VERVE
❑ V-8513 [M]   Blue Genes   1963 $30
❑ V6-8513 [S]   Blue Genes   1963 $30

THURSDAY GROUP, THE

Members: Douglas Lichterman (guitar); Clayton Englar (tenor, soprano and bass sax, flute); Jim Kerwin (bass); Vinnie Johnson (drums, replaced by Tony Manno).

Albums

PATHFINDER
❑ PTF-8307   The Thursday Group   198? $30
❑ PTF-8807   Uncle Mean   198? $30

TIBBETTS, STEVE

Guitarist, kalimba player and synthesizer player.

Albums

ECM
❑ 1218   Northern Song   198? $25
❑ 25002   Safe Journey   1984 $25

TICHENOR, TREBOR

Pianist. Also see THE ST. LOUIS RAGTIMERS.

Albums

DIRTY SHAME
❑ 2001   King of Folk Ragtime   197? $30

TILLES, NURIT

Pianist.

Albums

JAZZOLOGY
❑ JCE-87   Ragtime, Here and Now!   1982 $25

TIMELESS ALL-STARS, THE

Members: CURTIS FULLER; BILLY HIGGINS; BOBBY HUTCHERSON; HAROLD LAND; CEDAR WALTON; BUSTER WILLIAMS.

Albums

TIMELESS
❑ LPSJP-178   It's Timeless   1988 $25

TIMMENS, JIM, AND HIS JAZZ ALL-STARS

Arranger and conductor. Some of the musicians on this album were KENNY BURRELL; DONALD BYRD; and JOE VENUTO.

Albums

WARNER BROS.
❑ W1278 [M]   Gilbert and Sullivan Revisited   1958 $30
❑ WS1278 [S]   Gilbert and Sullivan Revisited   1958 $30

TIMMONS, BOBBY

Pianist. Also see JOE ALEXANDER; JOHN JENKINS; THE RIVERSIDE JAZZ STARS; THE YOUNG LIONS.

Albums

FANTASY
❑ OJC-364   Bobby Timmons In Person   198? $25
❑ OJC-104   This Here Is Bobby Timmons   198? $25

MILESTONE
❑ MSP-9020   Do You Know the Way   1969 $25
❑ MSP-9011   Got to Get It   1969 $25
❑ 47031   Moanin'   197? $35

PRESTIGE
❑ PRLP-7429 [M]   Chicken and Dumplin's   1966 $30
❑ PRST-7429 [S]   Chicken and Dumplin's   1966 $30
❑ PRLP-7351 [M]   Chun-King   1965 $30
❑ PRST-7351 [S]   Chun-King   1965 $30
❑ PRLP-7414 [M]   Holiday Soul   1966 $30
❑ PRST-7414 [S]   Holiday Soul   1966 $40
❑ PRLP-7335 [M]   Little Barefoot Soul   1964 $30
❑ PRST-7335 [S]   Little Barefoot Soul   1964 $30
❑ PRLP-7483 [M]   Soul Food   1967 $60
❑ PRST-7483 [S]   Soul Food   1967 $50
❑ PRLP-7465 [M]   Soul Man   1967 $60
❑ PRST-7465 [S]   Soul Man   1967 $50
❑ PRST-7780   The Best of Soul Piano   1970 $50
❑ PRLP-7387 [M]   Workin' Out   1966 $60
❑ PRST-7387 [S]   Workin' Out   1966 $60

RIVERSIDE
❑ R-6110   Bobby Timmons In Person   197? $35
❑ RLP-468 [M]   Born to Be Blue!   1963 $150
❑ RS-9468 [S]   Born to Be Blue!   1963 $150
❑ RLP-363 [M]   Easy Does It   1961 $200
❑ RS-9363 [S]   Easy Does It   1961 $200
❑ RS-3053   From the Bottom   196? $35
❑ RLP-334 [M]   Soul Time   1960 $200
❑ RS-9334 [S]   Soul Time   1960 $200
❑ RLP-422 [M]   Sweet and Soulful Sounds   1962 $150
❑ RS-9422 [S]   Sweet and Soulful Sounds   1962 $150
❑ RLP-391 [M]   The Bobby Timmons Trio In Person -- Recorded "Live" at the Village Vanguard   1961 $200
❑ RS-9391 [S]   The Bobby Timmons Trio In Person -- Recorded "Live" at the Village Vanguard   1961 $200
❑ RLP 12-317 [M]   This Here Is Bobby Timmons   1960 $200
❑ RLP-1164 [S]   This Here Is Bobby Timmons   1960 $200
❑ R-6050   This Here Is Bobby Timmons   197? $35

TIRABASSO, JOHN

Drummer.

Albums

DISCOVERY
❑ DS-884   Live at Dino's   198? $25

DOBRE
❑ 1022   Diamond Cuff Links and Mink   197? $35

TISO, WAGNER

Pianist, keyboard player, arranger and composer.

Number	Title	Yr	NM

Albums

PHILIPS

| 834632-1 | Manu Carue | 1989 | $30 |

VERVE

| 831819-1 | Giselle | 1987 | $25 |

TJADER, CAL, AND CARMEN MCRAE

Also see each artist's individual listings.

Albums

CONCORD JAZZ

| CJ-189 | Heat Wave | 1982 | $25 |

TJADER, CAL, AND CHARLIE BYRD

Also see each artist's individual listings.

Albums

FANTASY

| 9453 | Tambu | 1974 | $30 |

TJADER, CAL, AND STAN GETZ

Also see each artist's individual listings.

Albums

FANTASY

8348 [S]	Cal Tjader-Stan Getz Quartet	1963	$30
—Reissue of 8005			
3266 [M]	Cal Tjader-Stan Getz Sextet	1958	$100
—Red vinyl			
3266 [M]	Cal Tjader-Stan Getz Sextet	1958	$60
—Black vinyl, red label, non-flexible vinyl			
3266 [M]	Cal Tjader-Stan Getz Sextet	196?	$35
—Black vinyl, red label, flexible vinyl			
3348 [M]	Cal Tjader-Stan Getz Sextet	1963	$35
—Reissue of 3266			
8005 [S]	Cal Tjader-Stan Getz Sextet	196?	$60
—Blue vinyl			
8005 [S]	Cal Tjader-Stan Getz Sextet	196?	$50
—Black vinyl, blue label, non-flexible vinyl			
8005 [S]	Cal Tjader-Stan Getz Sextet	196?	$30
—Black vinyl, blue label, flexible vinyl			

TJADER, CAL

Vibraphone player. The most prominent non-Latino in the Latin jazz realm. Also see DAVE BRUBECK; DON ELLIOTT; MARY STALLINGS.

Albums

CONCORD JAZZ

| CJ-159 | The Shining Sea | 1981 | $25 |

CONCORD PICANTE

CJP-176	A Fuego Vivo	1981	$25
CJP-247	Good Vibes	1983	$25
CJP-133	Gozame! Pero Ya…	1980	$30
CJP-113	La Onda Va Bien	1979	$30

CRYSTAL CLEAR

| 8003 | Huracan | 1978 | $60 |
| —Direct-to-disc recording | | | |

FANTASY

8416	Agua Dulce	1971	$30
9502	Amazonas	1975	$30
3283 [M]	A Night at the Blackhawk	1959	$100
—Red vinyl			
3283 [M]	A Night at the Blackhawk	1959	$60
—Black vinyl, red label, non-flexible vinyl			
3283 [M]	A Night at the Blackhawk	196?	$35
—Black vinyl, red label, flexible vinyl			
8026 [S]	A Night at the Blackhawk	196?	$60
—Blue vinyl			
8026 [S]	A Night at the Blackhawk	196?	$50
—Black vinyl, blue label, non-flexible vinyl			
8026 [S]	A Night at the Blackhawk	196?	$30
—Black vinyl, blue label, flexible vinyl			
OJC-278	A Night at the Blackhawk	1987	$25
—Reissue of 8026			
9521	At Grace Cathedral	1977	$30
3253 [M]	Cal Tjader	1958	$120
—Red vinyl			
3253 [M]	Cal Tjader	1958	$40
—Black vinyl, non-flexible vinyl			
3315 [M]	Cal Tjader Live and Direct	1961	$40
—Red vinyl			

Number	Title	Yr	NM

3315 [M]	Cal Tjader Live and Direct	1961	$60
—Black vinyl, red label, non-flexible vinyl			
3315 [M]	Cal Tjader Live and Direct	196?	$35
—Black vinyl, red label, flexible vinyl			
8059 [S]	Cal Tjader Live and Direct	1962	$60
—Blue vinyl			
8059 [S]	Cal Tjader Live and Direct	1962	$50
—Black vinyl, blue label, non-flexible vinyl			
8059 [S]	Cal Tjader Live and Direct	196?	$30
—Black vinyl, blue label, flexible vinyl			
3330 [M]	Cal Tjader Plays the Harold Arlen Songbook	1961	$40
—Red vinyl			
3330 [M]	Cal Tjader Plays the Harold Arlen Songbook	1961	$60
—Black vinyl, red label, non-flexible vinyl			
3330 [M]	Cal Tjader Plays the Harold Arlen Songbook	196?	$35
—Black vinyl, red label, flexible vinyl			
8072 [S]	Cal Tjader Plays the Harold Arlen Songbook	1962	$60
—Blue vinyl			
8072 [S]	Cal Tjader Plays the Harold Arlen Songbook	1962	$50
—Black vinyl, blue label, non-flexible vinyl			
8072 [S]	Cal Tjader Plays the Harold Arlen Songbook	196?	$30
—Black vinyl, blue label, flexible vinyl			
OJC-285	Cal Tjader Plays the Harold Arlen Songbook	1987	$25
—Reissue of 8072			
3227 [M]	Cal Tjader Quartet	1956	$175
—Red vinyl			
3307 [M]	Cal Tjader Quartet	1960	$40
—Red vinyl			
3307 [M]	Cal Tjader Quartet	1960	$60
—Black vinyl, red label, non-flexible vinyl			
3307 [M]	Cal Tjader Quartet	196?	$35
—Black vinyl, red label, flexible vinyl			
8083 [R]	Cal Tjader Quartet	1962	$60
—Blue vinyl			
8083 [R]	Cal Tjader Quartet	1962	$50
—Black vinyl, blue label, non-flexible vinyl			
8083 [R]	Cal Tjader Quartet	1962	$30
—Black vinyl, blue label, flexible vinyl			
3313 [M]	Cal Tjader Quintet	1961	$40
—Red vinyl; evidently a different album than 3232			
3313 [M]	Cal Tjader Quintet	1961	$60
—Black vinyl, red label, non-flexible vinyl			
3313 [M]	Cal Tjader Quintet	196?	$35
—Black vinyl, red label, flexible vinyl			
8084 [S]	Cal Tjader Quintet	1962	$60
—Blue vinyl; stereo version of 3313			
8084 [S]	Cal Tjader Quintet	1962	$50
—Black vinyl, blue label, non-flexible vinyl			
8084 [S]	Cal Tjader Quintet	1962	$30
—Black vinyl, blue label, flexible vinyl			
3366 [S]	Cal Tjader's Greatest Hits	1965	$35
8366 [S]	Cal Tjader's Greatest Hits	1965	$30
MPF-4527	Cal Tjader's Greatest Hits	1987	$25
—Reissue of 8366			
3374 [M]	Cal Tjader's Greatest Hits, Violume 2	1966	$35
8374 [S]	Cal Tjader's Greatest Hits, Volume 2	1966	$30
MPF-4530	Cal Tjader's Greatest Hits, Volume 2	1987	$25
—Reissue of 8374			
3275 [M]	Cal Tjader's Latin Concert	1958	$100
—Red vinyl			
3275 [M]	Cal Tjader's Latin Concert	1958	$60
—Black vinyl, red label, non-flexible vinyl			
3275 [M]	Cal Tjader's Latin Concert	196?	$35
—Black vinyl, red label, flexible vinyl			
8014 [S]	Cal Tjader's Latin Concert	196?	$60
—Blue vinyl			
8014 [S]	Cal Tjader's Latin Concert	196?	$50
—Black vinyl, blue label, non-flexible vinyl			
8014 [S]	Cal Tjader's Latin Concert	196?	$30
—Black vinyl, blue label, flexible vinyl			
OJC-643	Cal Tjader's Latin Concert	1991	$30
—Reissue of 8014			
3295 [M]	Concert by the Sea	1959	$100

Number	Title	Yr	NM

—Red vinyl			
3295 [M]	Concert by the Sea	1959	$60
—Black vinyl, red label, non-flexible vinyl			
3295 [M]	Concert by the Sea	196?	$35
—Black vinyl, red label, flexible vinyl			
8038 [S]	Concert by the Sea	196?	$60
—Blue vinyl			
8038 [S]	Concert by the Sea	196?	$50
—Black vinyl, blue label, non-flexible vinyl			
8038 [S]	Concert by the Sea	196?	$30
—Black vinyl, blue label, flexible vinyl			
3341 [M]	Concert by the Sea, Volume 2	1962	$40
—Red vinyl			
3341 [M]	Concert by the Sea, Volume 2	1962	$60
—Black vinyl, red label, non-flexible vinyl			
3341 [M]	Concert by the Sea, Volume 2	196?	$35
—Black vinyl, red label, flexible vinyl			
8098 [S]	Concert by the Sea, Volume 2	1962	$60
—Blue vinyl			
8098 [S]	Concert by the Sea, Volume 2	1962	$50
—Black vinyl, blue label, non-flexible vinyl			
8098 [S]	Concert by the Sea, Volume 2	196?	$30
—Black vinyl, blue label, flexible vinyl			
3299 [M]	Concert on the Campus	1960	$40
—Red vinyl			
3299 [M]	Concert on the Campus	1960	$60
—Black vinyl, red label, non-flexible vinyl			
3299 [M]	Concert on the Campus	196?	$35
—Black vinyl, red label, flexible vinyl			
8044 [S]	Concert on the Campus	196?	$60
—Blue vinyl			
8044 [S]	Concert on the Campus	196?	$50
—Black vinyl, blue label, non-flexible vinyl			
8044 [S]	Concert on the Campus	196?	$30
—Black vinyl, blue label, flexible vinyl			
OJC-279	Concert on the Campus	1987	$25
—Reissue of 8044			
3309 [M]	Demasiado Caliente	1960	$40
—Red vinyl			
3309 [M]	Demasiado Caliente	1960	$60
—Black vinyl, red label, non-flexible vinyl			
3309 [M]	Demasiado Caliente	196?	$35
—Black vinyl, red label, flexible vinyl			
8053 [S]	Demasiado Caliente	196?	$60
—Blue vinyl			
8053 [S]	Demasiado Caliente	196?	$50
—Black vinyl, blue label, non-flexible vinyl			
8053 [S]	Demasiado Caliente	196?	$30
—Black vinyl, blue label, flexible vinyl			
9533	Guarabe	1977	$30
3241 [M]	Jazz at the Blackhawk	1957	$100
—Red vinyl			
3241 [M]	Jazz at the Blackhawk	1957	$60
—Black vinyl, red label, non-flexible vinyl			
3241 [M]	Jazz at the Blackhawk	196?	$35
—Black vinyl, red label, flexible vinyl			
8096 [R]	Jazz at the Blackhawk	1962	$60
—Blue vinyl			
8096 [R]	Jazz at the Blackhawk	1962	$50
—Black vinyl, blue label, non-flexible vinyl			
8096 [R]	Jazz at the Blackhawk	196?	$30
—Black vinyl, blue label, flexible vinyl			
OJC-436	Jazz at the Blackhawk	1990	$25
—Reissue of 8096			
9446	Last Bolero in Berkeley	1974	$30
9482	Last Night When We Were Young	1975	$30
8019	Latin for Dancers	196?	$175
—Blue vinyl; the existence of this has been confirmed. Black vinyl copies of 8019 are unknown.			
8019 [S]	Latin for Dancers	196?	$200
—A red vinyl copy with this number is known to exist also, probably pressed in error			
3279 [M]	Latin for Lovers	1958	$100
—Red vinyl			
3279 [M]	Latin for Lovers	1958	$60

Number	Title	Yr	NM
—Black vinyl, red label, non-flexible vinyl			
❏ 3279 [M]	Latin for Lovers	196?	$35
—Black vinyl, red label, flexible vinyl			
❏ 8016 [S]	Latin for Lovers	196?	$60
—Blue vinyl			
❏ 8016 [S]	Latin for Lovers	196?	$50
—Black vinyl, blue label, non-flexible vinyl			
❏ 8016 [S]	Latin for Lovers	196?	$30
—Black vinyl, blue label, flexible vinyl			
❏ 3250 [M]	Latin Kick	1957	$100
—Red vinyl			
❏ 3250 [M]	Latin Kick	1957	$60
—Black vinyl, red label, non-flexible vinyl			
❏ 3250 [M]	Latin Kick	196?	$35
—Black vinyl, red label, flexible vinyl			
❏ 8033 [S]	Latin Kick	196?	$60
—Blue vinyl			
❏ 8033 [S]	Latin Kick	196?	$50
—Black vinyl, blue label, non-flexible vinyl			
❏ 8033 [S]	Latin Kick	196?	$30
—Black vinyl, blue label, flexible vinyl			
❏ OJC-642	Latin Kick	1991	$30
—Reissue of 8033			
❏ 3339 [M]	Latino	1962	$40
—Red vinyl			
❏ 3339 [M]	Latino	1962	$60
—Black vinyl, red label, non-flexible vinyl			
❏ 3339 [M]	Latino	196?	$35
—Black vinyl, red label, flexible vinyl			
❏ 8079 [S]	Latino	1962	$60
—Blue vinyl			
❏ 8079 [S]	Latino	1962	$50
—Black vinyl, blue label, non-flexible vinyl			
❏ 8079 [S]	Latino	196?	$30
—Black vinyl, blue label, flexible vinyl			
❏ 9409	Live at the Funky Quarters	1970	$30
❏ 24712	Los Ritmos Caliente	197?	$35
❏ 3326 [M]	Mambo	1961	$40
—Red vinyl			
❏ 3326 [M]	Mambo	1961	$60
—Black vinyl, red label, non-flexible vinyl			
❏ 3326 [M]	Mambo	196?	$35
—Black vinyl, red label, flexible vinyl			
❏ 8057 [S]	Mambo	1962	$60
—Blue vinyl			
❏ 8057 [S]	Mambo	1962	$50
—Black vinyl, blue label, non-flexible vinyl			
❏ 8057 [S]	Mambo	196?	$30
—Black vinyl, blue label, flexible vinyl			
❏ 3202 [M]	Mambo with Tjader	1955	$175
—Red vinyl			
❏ 3202 [M]	Mambo with Tjader	1956	$100
—Black vinyl, red label, non-flexible vinyl			
❏ 3202 [M]	Mambo with Tjader	196?	$60
—Black vinyl, red label, flexible vinyl			
❏ 9424	Mambo with Tjader	1973	$30
❏ OJC-271	Mambo with Tjader	1987	$25
—Reissue of 3202			
❏ 3262 [M]	Mas Ritmo Caliente	1958	$100
—Red vinyl			
❏ 3262 [M]	Mas Ritmo Caliente	1958	$60
—Black vinyl, red label, non-flexible vinyl			
❏ 3262 [M]	Mas Ritmo Caliente	196?	$35
—Black vinyl, red label, flexible vinyl			
❏ 8003 [S]	Mas Ritmo Caliente	196?	$60
—Blue vinyl			
❏ 8003 [S]	Mas Ritmo Caliente	196?	$50
—Black vinyl, blue label, non-flexible vinyl			
❏ 8003 [S]	Mas Ritmo Caliente	196?	$30
—Black vinyl, blue label, flexible vinyl			
❏ 9422	Primo	1972	$30
❏ 9463	Puttin' It Together	1974	$30
❏ 3-17 [10]	Ritmo Caliente	1954	$150
—Any of various non-black vinyl pressings			
❏ 3-17 [10]	Ritmo Caliente	1954	$175
—Black vinyl			
❏ 3216 [M]	Ritmo Caliente	1956	$175
—Red vinyl			
❏ 3216 [M]	Ritmo Caliente	1956	$100
—Black vinyl, red label, non-flexible vinyl			
❏ 3216 [M]	Ritmo Caliente	196?	$60
—Black vinyl, red label, flexible vinyl			
❏ 8077 [R]	Ritmo Caliente	1962	$60
—Blue vinyl			
❏ 8077 [R]	Ritmo Caliente	1962	$50
—Black vinyl, blue label, non-flexible vinyl			
❏ 8077 [R]	Ritmo Caliente	196?	$30
—Black vinyl, blue label, flexible vinyl			
❏ 3271 [M]	San Francisco Moods	1958	$100
—Red vinyl			
❏ 3271 [M]	San Francisco Moods	1958	$60
—Black vinyl, red label, non-flexible vinyl			
❏ 3271 [M]	San Francisco Moods	196?	$35
—Black vinyl, red label, flexible vinyl			
❏ 8017 [S]	San Francisco Moods	196?	$60
—Blue vinyl			
❏ 8017 [S]	San Francisco Moods	196?	$50
—Black vinyl, blue label, non-flexible vinyl			
❏ 8017 [S]	San Francisco Moods	196?	$30
—Black vinyl, blue label, flexible vinyl			
❏ OJC-277	San Francisco Moods	1987	$25
—Reissue of 8017			
❏ 3232 [M]	The Cal Tjader Quintet	1956	$175
—Red vinyl			
❏ 3232 [M]	The Cal Tjader Quintet	1956	$100
—Black vinyl, red label, non-flexible vinyl			
❏ 3232 [M]	The Cal Tjader Quintet	196?	$60
—Black vinyl, red label, flexible vinyl			
❏ 8085 [R]	The Cal Tjader Quintet	196?	$60
—Blue vinyl; stereo version of 3232			
❏ 8085 [R]	The Cal Tjader Quintet	196?	$50
—Black vinyl, blue label, non-flexible vinyl			
❏ 8085 [R]	The Cal Tjader Quintet	196?	$30
—Black vinyl, blue label, flexible vinyl			
❏ 3-9 [10]	The Cal Tjader Trio	1953	$300
—Any of various non-black vinyl pressings			
❏ 3-9 [10]	The Cal Tjader Trio	1953	$175
—Black vinyl			
❏ 8406	Tjader	1970	$30
❏ 3289 [M]	Tjader Goes Latin	1959	$100
—Red vinyl			
❏ 3289 [M]	Tjader Goes Latin	1959	$60
—Black vinyl, red label, non-flexible vinyl			
❏ 3289 [M]	Tjader Goes Latin	196?	$35
—Black vinyl, red label, flexible vinyl			
❏ 8030 [S]	Tjader Goes Latin	196?	$60
—Blue vinyl			
❏ 8030 [S]	Tjader Goes Latin	196?	$50
—Black vinyl, blue label, non-flexible vinyl			
❏ 8030 [S]	Tjader Goes Latin	196?	$30
—Black vinyl, blue label, flexible vinyl			
❏ 3221 [M]	Tjader Plays Mambo	1956	$175
—Red vinyl			
❏ 3221 [M]	Tjader Plays Mambo	1956	$100
—Black vinyl, red label, non-flexible vinyl			
❏ 3221 [M]	Tjader Plays Mambo	196?	$60
—Black vinyl, red label, flexible vinyl			
❏ OJC-274	Tjader Plays Mambo	1987	$25
—Reissue of 3221			
❏ 3-18 [10]	Tjader Plays Mambo	1954	$300
—Red vinyl			
❏ 3211 [M]	Tjader Plays Tjazz	1956	$175
—Red vinyl			
❏ 3211 [M]	Tjader Plays Tjazz	1956	$100
—Black vinyl, red label, non-flexible vinyl			
❏ 3278 [M]	Tjader Plays Tjazz	1958	$100
—Red vinyl; reissue of 3211			
❏ 3278 [M]	Tjader Plays Tjazz	196?	$35
—Black vinyl, red label, flexible vinyl			
❏ 8097 [R]	Tjader Plays Tjazz	1962	$60
—Blue vinyl			
❏ 8097 [R]	Tjader Plays Tjazz	1962	$50
—Black vinyl, blue label, non-flexible vinyl			
❏ 8097 [R]	Tjader Plays Tjazz	196?	$30
—Black vinyl, blue label, flexible vinyl			
❏ 3310 [M]	West Side Story	1960	$40
—Red vinyl			
❏ 3310 [M]	West Side Story	1960	$60
—Black vinyl, red label, non-flexible vinyl			
❏ 3310 [M]	West Side Story	196?	$35
—Black vinyl, red label, flexible vinyl			
❏ 8054 [S]	West Side Story	196?	$60
—Blue vinyl			
❏ 8054 [S]	West Side Story	196?	$50
—Black vinyl, blue label, non-flexible vinyl			
❏ 8054 [S]	West Side Story	196?	$30
—Black vinyl, blue label, flexible vinyl			
❏ 8379	West Side Story	1967	$30
—Reissue of 8054			

GALAXY

Number	Title	Yr	NM
❏ 5107	Breathe Easy	1977	$30
❏ 5121	Here	1978	$30

MGM

| ❏ 10008 | Sonido Nuevo | 197? | $35 |

PRESTIGE

| ❏ 24026 | The Monterey Concerts | 1973 | $35 |

SAVOY

| ❏ MG-9036 [10] | Cal Tjader -- Vibist | 1954 | $175 |

SKYE

❏ SK-10	Cal Tjader Plugs In	1969	$50
❏ SK-1	Solar Heat	1968	$50
❏ SK-19	Tjader-Ade	1970	$35

VERVE

❏ V-8671 [M]	Along Comes Cal	1966	$35
❏ V6-8671 [S]	Along Comes Cal	1966	$50
❏ V-8575 [M]	Breeze from the East	1964	$50
❏ V6-8575 [S]	Breeze from the East	1964	$60
❏ V-8651 [M]	El Soni Do Nuevo -- The New Soul Sound	1966	$35
❏ V6-8651 [S]	El Soni Do Nuevo -- The New Soul Sound	1966	$50
❏ V-8730 [M]	Hip Vibrations	1967	$50
❏ V6-8730 [S]	Hip Vibrations	1967	$35
❏ V-8419 [M]	In a Latin Bag	1961	$50
❏ V6-8419 [S]	In a Latin Bag	1961	$60
❏ V-8459 [M]	Saturday Night...Sunday Night at the Blackhawk	1962	$50
❏ V6-8459 [S]	Saturday Night...Sunday Night at the Blackhawk	1962	$60
❏ V-8507 [M]	Several Shades of Jade	1963	$50
❏ V6-8507 [S]	Several Shades of Jade	1963	$60
❏ V-8531 [M]	Sona Libre	1963	$50
❏ V6-8531 [S]	Sona Libre	1963	$60
❏ V-8626 [M]	Soul Bird: Whippenpoof	1965	$50
❏ V6-8626 [S]	Soul Bird: Whippenpoof	1965	$60
❏ V-8637 [M]	Soul Burst	1965	$50
❏ V6-8637 [S]	Soul Burst	1965	$60
❏ V-8614 [M]	Soul Sauce	1965	$50
❏ V6-8614 [S]	Soul Sauce	1965	$60
❏ 827756-1	Soul Sauce	1986	$25
—Reissue of 8614			
❏ V-8725 [M]	The Best of Cal Tjader	1967	$35
❏ V6-8725 [S]	The Best of Cal Tjader	1967	$50
❏ V-8470 [M]	The Contemporary Music of Mexico and Brazil	1962	$200
❏ V6-8470 [S]	The Contemporary Music of Mexico and Brazil	1962	$200
❏ V6-8769	The Prophet	1969	$35
❏ V-8585 [M]	Warm Wave	1964	$50
❏ V6-8585 [S]	Warm Wave	1964	$60

TJADER, CAL/DON ELLIOTT

Also see each artist's individual listings.

Albums

SAVOY

| ❏ MG-12054 [M] | Vib-Rations | 1956 | $40 |
| —Reissue of 9036 and 9033 | | | |

TODD, RICHARD

French horn player.

Albums

GM RECORDINGS

| ❏ 2010 | New Ideas | 1986 | $30 |

TOGASHI, MASAHIKO

Drummer and bandleader.

Albums

INNER CITY

| ❏ IC-6011 | Spiritual Nature | 197? | $35 |

TOGAWA, PAUL

Drummer and bandleader.

Albums

MODE

| ❏ LP-104 [M] | Paul Togawa Quartet | 1957 | $80 |

TOLLIVER, CHARLES

Trumpeter and composer.

Albums

Stanley Turrentine, *Up at Minton's*, Volume 2, Blue Note BLP-84070, with W. 63rd St. address on label, **$200**.

Sarah Vaughan, *Sarah Slightly Classical*, Roulette SR 52123, **$50**.

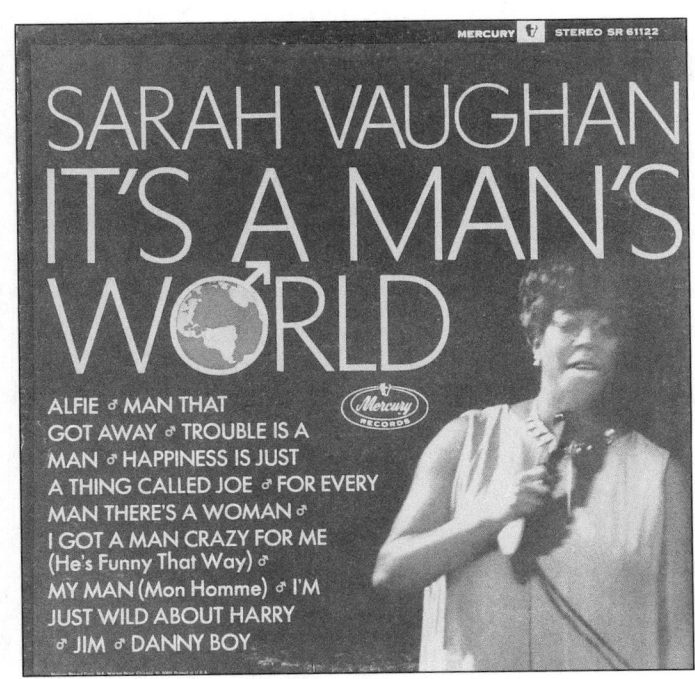

Sarah Vaughan, *It's a Man's World*, Mercury SR 61122, **$100**.

Sarah Vaughan, *All Time Favorites by Sarah Vaughan*, Wing MGW-12123, **$30**.

Number	Title	Yr	NM
ARISTA/FREEDOM			
❏ AF1002	Paper Man	1975	$30
❏ AF1017	The Ringer	1975	$30
STRATA-EAST			
❏ SES-8001	Compassion	1980	$30
❏ SES-19757	Impact	1975	$35
❏ SES-1972	Live at Slugs'	1972	$25
❏ SES-19720	Live at Slugs', Vol. 2	1972	$25
❏ SES-19740/1	Live at the Loosdrecht Jazz Festival	1974	$30
❏ SES-19745	Live in Tokyo	1974	$25
❏ SES-1971	Music Inc.	1971	$25

TOLONEN, JUKKA

Albums

Number	Title	Yr	NM
TERRA			
❏ T-6	Touch Wood	1985	$30

TOMPKINS, FRED

Composer and conductor.

Albums

Number	Title	Yr	NM
FESTIVAL			
❏ 9001	Compositions	197?	$30
❏ 9002	Somesville	1975	$30
F.K.T.			
❏ 103	Cecile	1980	$30
❏ 101	Compositions	1980	$25
❏ 102	Somesville	1980	$25

TOMPKINS, ROSS, AND JOE VENUTI

Also see each artist's individual listings.

Albums

Number	Title	Yr	NM
CONCORD JAZZ			
❏ CJ-51	Live '77	1978	$30

TOMPKINS, ROSS

Pianist.

Albums

Number	Title	Yr	NM
CONCORD JAZZ			
❏ CJ-117	Festival Time	198?	$25
❏ CJ-46	Lost in the Stars	1977	$30
❏ CJ-65	Ross Tompkins and His Good Friends	1978	$30
❏ CJ-28	Scrimshaw	1976	$30
FAMOUS DOOR			
❏ HL-153	In the Swing of Things	1987	$25
❏ HL-151	L.A. After Dark	1986	$25
❏ HL-143	Street of Dreams	198?	$25
❏ HL-146	Symphony	198?	$25

TONIGHT SHOW BAND, THE

See DOC SEVERINSON.

TORFF, BRIAN

Bass player and composer.

Albums

Number	Title	Yr	NM
AUDIOPHILE			
❏ AP-182	Manhattan Hoe-Down	1983	$25
OPTIMISM			
❏ OP-2601	Hitchhiker of Karoo	198?	$25

TORKANOWSKY, DAVID

Organist and pianist.

Albums

Number	Title	Yr	NM
ROUNDER			
❏ 2090	Steppin' Out	198?	$25

TORME, MEL, AND BUDDY RICH

Also see each artist's individual listings.

Albums

Number	Title	Yr	NM
CENTURY			
❏ 1100	Together Again -- For the First Time	1978	$30

— Direct-to-disc recording

Number	Title	Yr	NM
GRYPHON			
❏ G-903	Together Again -- For the First Time	1978	$25

TORME, MEL

Male singer, pianist, drummer and composer, best known probably for his "The Christmas Song," made popular by NAT KING COLE.

Albums

Number	Title	Yr	NM
ALLEGRO ELITE			
❏ 4117 [10]	Mel Torme Sings	195?	$30
ATLANTIC			
❏ 8069 [M]	Comin' Home Baby	1962	$150
❏ SD8069 [S]	Comin' Home Baby	1962	$150
❏ SD18129	Live at the Maisonette	1975	$30
❏ 8066 [M]	Mel Torme at the Red Hill Inn	1962	$150
❏ SD8066 [S]	Mel Torme at the Red Hill Inn	1962	$150
❏ 80078	Songs of New York	1982	$12
❏ 8091 [M]	Sunday in New York	1963	$30
❏ SD8091 [S]	Sunday in New York	1963	$40
AUDIOPHILE			
❏ 67	Mel Torme Sings About Love	198?	$25
BETHLEHEM			
❏ BCP6016 [M]	California Suite	1957	$250
❏ BCP-34 [M]	It's a Blue World	1956	$250
❏ BCP-52 [M]	Mel Torme and the Marty Paich Dektette	1956	$250
❏ BCP6020 [M]	Mel Torme Live at the Crescendo	1958	$200
❏ BCP6013 [M]	Mel Torme Sings Fred Astaire	1957	$250
❏ BCP6031 [M]	Songs for Any Taste	1959	$200
❏ BCP6042	The Torme Touch	1978	$15

— Reissue of BCP 52

Number	Title	Yr	NM
CAPITOL			
❏ ST-313	A Time for Us	1969	$40
❏ P200 [M]	California Suite	1950	$150
❏ ST-430	Raindrops Keep Falling on My Head	1970	$15
COLUMBIA			
❏ CL2535 [M]	Mel Torme Right Now	1966	$30
❏ CS9335 [S]	Mel Torme Right Now	1966	$35
❏ CL2318 [M]	That's All -- A Lush Romantic Album	1965	$35
❏ CS9118 [S]	That's All -- A Lush Romantic Album	1965	$25
COLUMBIA SPECIAL PRODUCTS			
❏ P13090	That's All	1976	$30
CONCORD JAZZ			
❏ CJ-382	In Concert Tokyo	1989	$25

— Above two with the Marty Paich Dek-Tette

Number	Title	Yr	NM
❏ CJ-306	Mel Torme with Rob McConnell and the Boss Brass	1986	$25
❏ CJ-360	Reunion	1988	$25
CORAL			
❏ CRL57012 [M]	Gene Norman Presents Mel Torme "Live" at the Crescendo	1955	$60
❏ CRL57044 [M]	Musical Sounds Are the Best Songs	1956	$50
DISCOVERY			
❏ 910	Sings His California Suite	1986	$12

— Reissue of Capitol 200

Number	Title	Yr	NM
EVEREST ARCHIVE OF FOLK & JAZZ			
❏ 324	The Velvet Fog	1976	$12
FINESSE			
❏ W2X37484	Mel Torme & Friends Recorded at Marty's, New York City	1981	$15
GLENDALE			
❏ 6018	Easy to Remember	1979	$12
❏ 6007	Mel Torme	1978	$12
GRYPHON			
❏ G-916	A New Album	1980	$12
LIBERTY			
❏ LST-7560 [S]	A Day in the Life of Bonnie and Clyde	1968	$25
❏ LRP-3560 [M]	A Day in the Life of Bonnie and Clyde	1968	$40

— Stock copy mono inside stereo cover with "Audition Mono LP Not for Sale" sticker

Number	Title	Yr	NM
METRO			
❏ M-532 [M]	I Wished on the Moon	1965	$150
❏ MS-532 [S]	I Wished on the Moon	1965	$250
MGM			
❏ E552 [10]	Mel Torme Sings	1952	$100
MUSICRAFT			
❏ 2005	Gone with the Wind	1986	$12
❏ 510	It Happened in Monterey	1983	$12
❏ 508	Mel Torme, Volume 1	1983	$12

Number	Title	Yr	NM
STASH			
❏ ST-252	'Round Midnight	1985	$12
STRAND			
❏ SL-1076 [M]	Mel Torme Sings	1960	$25
❏ SLS-1076 [S]	Mel Torme Sings	1960	$30
TIME-LIFE			
❏ SLGD-13	Legendary Singers: Mel Torme	1986	$20
TOPS			
❏ L-1615 [M]	Prelude to a Kiss	1958	$60
VENISE			
❏ 10021 [M]	The Touch of Your Lips	196?	$25

— Yellow vinyl; reissue of Tops L-1615 without patter in between songs

Number	Title	Yr	NM
VERVE			
❏ MGV2120 [M]	Back in Town	1959	$150
❏ V-2120 [M]	Back in Town	1961	$25

— Reissue

Number	Title	Yr	NM
❏ MGVS6063 [S]	Back in Town	1960	$150
❏ V6-2120 [S]	Back in Town	1961	$30

— Reissue

Number	Title	Yr	NM
❏ UMV-2675	Back in Town	1982	$25
❏ MGV2146 [M]	Broadway, Right Now	1961	$50
❏ V-2146 [M]	Broadway, Right Now	1961	$25

— Reissue

Number	Title	Yr	NM
❏ V6-2146 [S]	Broadway, Right Now	1961	$30
❏ MGV2153 [M]	I Dig the Duke! I Dig the Count!	1961	$0

— Canceled; moved to 8491

Number	Title	Yr	NM
❏ V-8491 [M]	I Dig the Duke! I Dig the Count!	1962	$30
❏ V6-8491 [S]	I Dig the Duke! I Dig the Count!	1962	$30
❏ MGV2132 [M]	Mel Torme Swings Schubert Alley	1960	$100
❏ V-2132 [M]	Mel Torme Swings Shubert Alley	1961	$25

— Reissue

Number	Title	Yr	NM
❏ MGVS6146 [S]	Mel Torme Swings Shubert Alley	1960	$100
❏ V6-2132 [S]	Mel Torme Swings Shubert Alley	196?	$30

— Reissue of 62132

Number	Title	Yr	NM
❏ UMV-2521	Mel Torme Swings Shubert Alley	1981	$25
❏ MGVS62132 [S]	Mel Torme Swings Shubert Alley	196?	$40

— Early reissue of 6146

Number	Title	Yr	NM
❏ V-8440 [M]	My Kind of Music	1962	$30
❏ V6-8440 [S]	My Kind of Music	1962	$30
❏ MGV2117 [M]	Ole Torme! Mel Torme Goes South of the Border with Billy May	1959	$100
❏ V-2117 [M]	Ole Torme! Mel Torme Goes South of the Border with Billy May	1961	$25

— Reissue

Number	Title	Yr	NM
❏ MGVS6058 [S]	Ole Torme! Mel Torme Goes South of the Border with Billy May	1960	$100
❏ V6-2117 [S]	Ole Torme! Mel Torme Goes South of the Border with Billy May	1961	$30

— Reissue

Number	Title	Yr	NM
❏ MGV2144 [M]	Swingin' on the Moon	1960	$80
❏ V-2144 [M]	Swingin' on the Moon	1961	$25

— Reissue

Number	Title	Yr	NM
❏ V6-2144 [S]	Swingin' on the Moon	1961	$30

— Reissue of 62144

Number	Title	Yr	NM
❏ MGVS62144 [S]	Swingin' on the Moon	1960	$80
❏ 823248-1	The Duke Ellington and Count Basie Songbooks	1984	$12

— Reissue of Verve 8491

Number	Title	Yr	NM
❏ V-2105 [M]	Torme	1961	$25

— Reissue

Number	Title	Yr	NM
❏ MGVS6015 [S]	Torme	1960	$60
❏ V6-2105 [S]	Torme	1961	$30

— Reissue

Number	Title	Yr	NM
❏ V-8593 [M]	Verve's Choice -- The Best of Mel Torme	1964	$30
❏ V6-8593 [S]	Verve's Choice -- The Best of Mel Torme	1964	$35
VOCALION			
❏ VL73905	The Velvet Fog	197?	$25

Number	Title	Yr	NM

TORN, DAVID, AND GEOFFREY GORDON
Torn is a guitarist; Gordon a percussionist.
Albums
ECM
| □ 1284 | Best Laid Plans | 1985 | $30 |

TORRES, NESTOR
Flutist.
Albums
VERVE FORECAST
| □ 839387-1 | Morning Ride | 1989 | $30 |

TOSHIKO
See TOSHIKO AKIYOSHI.

TOUFF, CY
Bass trumpet player.
Albums
ARGO
□ LP-606 [M]	Doorway To Dixie	1956	$40
□ LP-641 [M]	Touff Assignment	1959	$30
□ LPS-641 [S]	Touff Assignment	1959	$30
PACIFIC JAZZ
□ PJ-1211 [M]	Cy Touff, His Octet and Quintet	1956	$150
□ PJ-42 [M]	Keester Parade	1962	$60
WORLD PACIFIC
□ PJM-410 [M]	Havin' A Ball	1958	$200

TOWNER, RALPH, AND GARY BURTON
Also see each artist's individual listings.
Albums
ECM
| □ 1056 | Matchbook | 1975 | $30 |
| □ 25038 | Slide Show | 1986 | $25 |

TOWNER, RALPH, AND GLEN MOORE
Also see each artist's individual listings.
Albums
ECM
| □ 1025 | Trios/Solos | 197? | $30 |

TOWNER, RALPH, AND JOHN ABERCROMBIE
Also see each artist's individual listings.
Albums
ECM
| □ 1207 | Five Years Later | 198? | $25 |

TOWNER, RALPH
Guitarist, pianist, synthesizer player, French horn player, cornet player and percussionist.
Albums
ECM
□ 1121	Batik	1978	$30
□ 23788	Blue Sun	1983	$25
□ 1032	Diary	1973	$35
□ 1153	Old Friends, New Friends	197?	$25
□ 1173	Solo Concert	1979	$25
□ 1060	Solstice	197?	$30
□ ECM-1-1095	Sound and Shadows	1977	$30

TRACEY, STAN, AND KEITH TIPPETT
Tippett also plays piano. Also see STAN TRACEY.
Albums
EMANEM
| □ 3307 | TNT | 1975 | $35 |

TRACEY, STAN
Pianist and composer.
Albums
LONDON
| □ LL3107 [M] | Showcase | 195? | $40 |

TRAUT, ROSS
Guitarist. Also see TRAUT/RODBY DUO.
Albums
HEADFIRST
| □ 9709 | Ross Traut | 198? | $35 |

TRAUT/RODBY
ROSS TRAUT (guitar) and Steve Rodby (bass).
Albums
COLUMBIA
| □ FC44472 | The Great Lawn | 1989 | $30 |

TRAVIS, NICK
Trumpeter. Also see THE MANHATTAN JAZZ ALL-STARS.
Albums
RCA VICTOR
| □ LJM-1010 [M] | The Panic Is On | 1954 | $120 |

TREVOR, JEANNIE
Female singer.
Albums
MAINSTREAM
| □ 56075 [M] | Jeannie Trevor Sings!! | 1965 | $30 |
| □ S-6075 [S] | Jeannie Trevor Sings!! | 1965 | $30 |

TRIO, THE
Members: KENNY CLARKE; HANK JONES; WENDELL MARSHALL.
Albums
SAVOY
| □ MG-12023 [M] | The Trio | 1955 | $100 |

TRISTANO, LENNIE; JO BUSHKIN; BOBBY SCOTT; MARIAN MCPARTLAND
Also see each artist's individual listings.
Albums
SAVOY
| □ MG-12043 [M] | The Jazz Keyboards of Lennie Tristano, Joe Bushkin, Bobby Scott & Marian McPartland | 1955 | $80 |

TRISTANO, LENNIE
Pianist and composer. Also see LEE WILEY.
Albums
ATLANTIC
| □ 1224 [M] | Lennie Tristano | 1955 | $300 |
— Black label
| □ 1224 [M] | Lennie Tristano | 1960 | $250 |
—Multicolor label, white "fan" logo at right
| □ 1224 [M] | Lennie Tristano | 1964 | $35 |
—Multicolor label, black "fan" logo at right
□ SD 2-7006	Lennie Tristano Quartet	198?	$35
□ SD 2-7003	Requiem	1980	$35
□ 1357 [M]	The New Tristano	1960	$250
—Multicolor label, white "fan" logo at right
| □ 1357 [M] | The New Tristano | 196? | $35 |
—Red and purple label, black "fan" logo at right
ELEKTRA/MUSICIAN
| □ 60264 | New York Improvisations | 1984 | $30 |
INNER CITY
| □ IC-6002 | Descent Into the Maelstrom | 197? | $60 |
JAZZ
□ JR-6	Continuity	1985	$30
□ JR-1	Live at Birdland 1949	198?	$30
□ JR-5	Live in Toronto 1952	198?	$30
MOSAIC
□ MQ10-174	The Complete Atlantic Recordings of Lennie Tristano, Lee Konitz and Warne Marsh	199?	$300
NEW JAZZ
□ NJLP-101 [10]	Lennie Tristano with Lee Konitz	1950	$600
PRESTIGE
□ PRLP-101 [10]	Lennie Tristano with Lee Konitz	1951	$500

TRISTANO, LENNIE/ARNOLD ROSS
Also see each artist's individual listings.
Albums
EMARCY
| □ MG-26029 [10] | Holiday in Piano | 1953 | $400 |

TRISTANO, LENNIE/BUDDY DEFRANCO
Also see each artist's individual listings.
Albums
CAPITOL
| □ M-11060 | Cross Currents | 1972 | $100 |
—Capitol Jazz Classics, Vol. 14"; original edition does not have an "All Rights Reserved" disclaimer in the perimeter print
| □ M-11060 | Cross Currents | 1975 | $35 |
— Capitol Jazz Classics, Voil. 14"; yellow label with "Capitol" at bottom; "All Rights Reserved" in perimeter print

TROMBONES, INC., THE
All-star group featuring as many as 18 different trombonists.
Albums
WARNER BROS.
| □ W1272 [M] | They Met at the Continental Divide | 1959 | $50 |
| □ WS1272 [S] | They Met at the Continental Divide | 1959 | $60 |

TROMBONES UNLIMITED
Albums
LIBERTY
□ LRP-3494 [M]	Big Boss Bones	1967	$25
□ LST-7494 [S]	Big Boss Bones	1967	$20
□ LST-7592	Grazing in the Grass	1968	$20
□ LRP-3527 [M]	Holiday for Trombones	1967	$25
□ LST-7527 [S]	Holiday for Trombones	1967	$20
□ LRP-3549 [M]	One of Those Songs	1968	$30
□ LST-7549 [S]	One of Those Songs	1968	$20
□ LRP-3449 [M]	These Bones are Made for Walking	1966	$20
□ LST-7449 [S]	These Bones are Made for Walking	1966	$25
□ LRP-3472 [M]	You're Gonna Hear From Me	1966	$35
□ LST-7472 [S]	You're Gonna Hear From Me	1966	$50

TROUP, BOBBY
Pianist, male singer and composer. His best-known song was "Route 66."
Albums
AUDIOPHILE
| □ AP-98 | In a Class Beyond Compare | 198? | $25 |
BETHLEHEM
□ BCP-1030 [10]	Bobby Troup	1955	$250
□ BCP-19 [M]	Bobby Troup Sings Johnny Mercer	1955	$250
□ BCP-35 [M]	The Distinctive Style of Bobby Troup	1955	$250
CAPITOL
□ H484 [10]	Bobby	1953	$150
□ T484 [M]	Bobby	1955	$80
INTERLUDE
□ MO-501 [M]	Cool	1959	$40
□ ST-1001 [S]	Cool	1959	$40
LIBERTY
□ LRP-3002 [M]	Bobby Troup and His Trio	1955	$60
□ LRP-3026 [M]	Do Re Mi	1957	$50
□ LRP-3078 [M]	Here's to My Lady	1958	$50
MODE
□ LP-111 [M]	Bobby Swings Tenderly	1957	$100
PAUSA
□ 9032	Bobby Troup	198?	$25
RCA VICTOR
□ LPM-1959 [M]	Bobby Troup and His Jazz All-Stars	1959	$40
□ LSP-1959 [S]	Bobby Troup and His Jazz All-Stars	1959	$50

TRUMPET KINGS, THE
Members: ROY ELDRIDGE; DIZZY GILLESPIE; CLARK TERRY.
Albums
ANALOGUE PRODUCTIONS
| □ APR-3010 | Alternate Blues | 199? | $35 |
PABLO
| □ 2310754 | Montreux '75 | 1975 | $30 |

Number	Title	Yr	NM

TRUMPET SUMMIT
Members: DIZZY GILLESPIE; FREDDIE HUBBARD; CLARK TERRY.

Albums

PABLO TODAY

❏ 2312114	Trumpet Summit Meets the Oscar Peterson Big 4	198?	$30

TRYFOROS, BOB
Guitarist.

Albums

PURITAN

❏ 5002	Joplin on Guitar	197?	$30

TRYNIN, JENNIFER
Female singer, guitarist and composer. After a recording hiatus, she returned as a more pop-oriented singer for the Warner Bros. label.

Albums

PATHFINDER

❏ PTF-8827 [EP]	Trespassing	1988	$20

TUCK & PATTI
Tuck Andress (guitar) and Patti Cathcart (vocals).

Albums

WINDHAM HILL

❏ WH-0116	Love Warriors	1989	$30
❏ WH-0111	Tears of Joy	1988	$25

TUCKER, MICKEY
Pianist.

Albums

MUSE

❏ MR-5174	Mister Mysterious	1978	$30
❏ MR-5223	The Crawl	1979	$30

XANADU

❏ 143	Sojourn	1977	$30
❏ 128	Triplicity	1976	$30

TUCKER, SOPHIE
Female singer. Known as "The Last of the Red Hot Mamas," she is definitely borderline when it comes to jazz. But she did spend some time in the 1920s calling herself "The Queen of Jazz."

Albums

COLUMBIA

❏ CL2604 [M]	Last of the Red Hot Mamas	1966	$35

DECCA

❏ DL5371 [10]	A Collection of Songs She Has Made Famous	1951	$200
❏ DL4942 [M]	Greatest Hits	1968	$60
❏ DL74942 [R]	Greatest Hits	1968	$30
❏ DL8355 [M]	The Great Sophie Tucker	195?	$60

MCA

❏ 263	Greatest Hits	1973	$25

MERCURY

❏ MG20267 [M]	Bigger and Better Than Ever	1957	$100
❏ MG20046 [M]	Cabaret Days	1955	$100
❏ MG20073 [M]	Her Latest and Greatest Spicy Songs	1956	$100
❏ MG20567 [M]	In Person -- Adults Only	1960	$100
❏ SR60227 [S]	In Person -- Adults Only	1960	$100
❏ MG20035 [M]	My Dream	1955	$100

WING

❏ MGW12176 [M]	Bigger and Better Than Ever	196?	$30
❏ MGW12213 [M]	Cabaret Days	196?	$30
❏ SRW16213 [R]	Cabaret Days	196?	$25
❏ MGW12167 [M]	Her Latest and Greatest Spicy Songs	196?	$30

TUCKER, TOMMY
Male singer and bandleader.

Albums

CIRCLE

❏ CLP-124	Tommy Tucker and His Californians 1933	1991	$30
❏ C-15	Tommy Tucker and His Orchestra 1942-1947	198?	$25

TURNER, JIM
Pianist.

Albums

EUPHONIC

❏ 1222	Old Fashioned Love: A Tribute to James P. Johnson	198?	$25

TURNER, JOE, AND PETE JOHNSON
Johnson was the pianist for vocalist Joe Turner in his early days.

Albums

EMARCY

❏ MG-36014 [M]	Joe Turner and Pete Johnson	1955	$300

TURNER, JOE
Male singer, sometimes known as "Big Joe Turner." Also popular in rhythm & blues.

Albums

ARHOOLIE

❏ 2004 [M]	Jumpin' the Blues	1962	$50

ATCO

❏ 33-376 [M]	Joe Turner -- His Greatest Recordings	1971	$35

ATLANTIC

❏ 8033 [M]	Big Joe Is Here	1959	$300
— Black label			
❏ 8033 [M]	Big Joe Is Here	1960	$300
— White "bullseye" label			
❏ 8033 [M]	Big Joe Is Here	1963	$50
— Black "fan" logo on label			
❏ 8033 [M]	Big Joe Is Here	1960	$300
— White "fan" logo on label			
❏ 1332 [M]	Big Joe Rides Again	1959	$300
— Black label			
❏ SD1332 [S]	Big Joe Rides Again	1959	$300
— Green label			
❏ 1332 [M]	Big Joe Rides Again	1963	$50
— Black "fan" logo on label			
❏ SD1332 [S]	Big Joe Rides Again	1963	$50
— Black "fan" logo on label			
❏ 1332 [M]	Big Joe Rides Again	1960	$300
— White "fan" logo on label			
❏ SD1332 [S]	Big Joe Rides Again	1960	$300
— White "fan" logo on label			
❏ SD8812	Boss of the Blues	1981	$25
— Reissue of 1234			
❏ 81752	Greatest Hits	1987	$25
❏ 8005 [M]	Joe Turner	1957	$300
— Black label			
❏ 8005 [M]	Joe Turner	1963	$50
— Black "fan" logo on label			
❏ 8005 [M]	Joe Turner	1961	$150
— White "fan" logo on label			
❏ 8023 [M]	Rockin' the Blues	1958	$300
— Black label			
❏ 8023 [M]	Rockin' the Blues	1963	$35
— Black "fan" logo on label			
❏ 8023 [M]	Rockin' the Blues	1960	$250
— White "fan" logo on label			
❏ 8081 [M]	The Best of Joe Turner	1963	$100
❏ 1234 [M]	The Boss of the Blues	1956	$300
— Black label			
❏ SD1234 [S]	The Boss of the Blues	1959	$300
— Green label			
❏ 1234 [M]	The Boss of the Blues	1960	$300
— White "bullseye" label			
❏ SD1234 [S]	The Boss of the Blues	1960	$400
— White "bullseye" label			
❏ 1234 [M]	The Boss of the Blues	1963	$50
— Black "fan" logo on label			
❏ SD1234 [S]	The Boss of the Blues	1963	$50
— Black "fan" logo on label			
❏ 1234 [M]	The Boss of the Blues	1961	$250
— White "fan" logo on label			
❏ SD1234 [S]	The Boss of the Blues	1961	$150
— White "fan" logo on label			

BLUES SPECTRUM

❏ BS-104	Great Rhythm and Blues Oldies Vol. 4	197?	$35

BLUESTIME

❏ 9002 [M]	The Real Boss of the Blues	196?	$40
❏ 29002 [S]	The Real Boss of the Blues	196?	$60

BLUESWAY

❏ S-6060	Roll 'Em	1973	$35
❏ BL6006 [M]	Singing the Blues	1967	$50
❏ BLS-6006 [S]	Singing the Blues	1967	$60

DECCA

❏ DL8044 [M]	Joe Turner Sings Kansas City Jazz	1953	$250

FANTASY

❏ OJC-497	Trumpet Kings Meet Joe Turner	1991	$30

INTERMEDIA

❏ QS-5036	Everyday I Have the Blues	198?	$25
❏ QS-5008	Rock This Joint	198?	$25
❏ QS-5043	Roll Me Baby	198?	$25
❏ QS-5030	The Blues Boss -- Live	198?	$25
❏ QS-5026	The Very Best of Joe Turner -- Live	198?	$25

KENT

❏ KST-542	Joe Turner Turns On the Blues	1973	$35

MCA

❏ 1325	Early Big Joe	198?	$25

MUSE

❏ MR-5293	Blues Train	198?	$25
— With Roomful of Blues and Dr. John			

PABLO

❏ 2310818	Every Day I Have the Blues	198?	$30
❏ 2310937	Flip, Flop and Fly	1989	$30
❏ 2310863	Have No Fear, Joe Turner Is Here	1983	$30
❏ 2310776	In the Evening	197?	$30
❏ 2310760	Nobody in Mind	197?	$30
❏ 2310913	Patcha, Patcha, All Night Long	198?	$30
❏ 2310883	Singing the Same, Sad, Happy, Forever Blues	1983	$30
❏ 2405404	The Best of "Big" Joe Turner	198?	$30
❏ 2310848	The Best of Joe Turner	1980	$30
❏ 2310800	Things That I Used to Do	197?	$30
❏ 2310717	Trumpet Kings Meet Joe Turner	197?	$30

SAVOY

❏ MG-14012 [M]	Blues'll Make You Happy	1958	$300
❏ MG-14106 [M]	Careless Love	1963	$150

SAVOY JAZZ

❏ SJC-406	Blues'll Make You Happy	1985	$25
— Reissue of Savoy 14012			
❏ SJL-2223	Have No Fear	197?	$35

TURNER, JOE (2)
Frequently confused with the above Joe Turner, this is the stride pianist.

Albums

CHIAROSCURO

❏ 147	King of Stride	1976	$35

CLASSIC JAZZ

❏ 138	Effervescent	1976	$35

PABLO

❏ 2310763	Another Epoch Stride Piano	197?	$30

TURNER, RAY
Pianist.

Albums

CAPITOL

❏ H306 [10]	Kitten on the Keys	1952	$80

TURRE, STEVE
Trombonist.

Albums

STASH

❏ ST-275	Fire and Ice	1988	$25
❏ ST-270	Viewpoint	1987	$25

TURRENTINE, STANLEY
Tenor saxophone player. Also see SHIRLEY SCOTT.

Albums

BAINBRIDGE

❏ BT-1038	Stan the Man	1981	$30

BLUE NOTE

❏ BLP-4150 [M]	A Chip Off the Old Block	1963	$120
❏ BST-84150 [S]	A Chip Off the Old Block	1963	$200
— With New York, USA address on label			

Number	Title	Yr	NM
BST-84150 [S]	A Chip Off the Old Block	1967	$150

— With "A Division of Liberty Records" on label

Number	Title	Yr	NM
LT-1095	Ain't No Way	1981	$35
BST-84298	Always Something There	1968	$40

— A Division of Liberty Records" on label

BST-84336	Another Story	1969	$40

— A Division of Liberty Records" on label

BLP-4057 [M]	Blue Hour	1961	$300

— With W. 63rd St. address on label

BLP-4057 [M]	Blue Hour	1963	$80

— With New York, USA address on label

BST-84057 [S]	Blue Hour	1961	$200

— With W. 63rd St. addresss on label

BST-84057 [S]	Blue Hour	1963	$40

— With New York, USA address on label

BST-84057 [S]	Blue Hour	1967	$60

— With "A Division of Liberty Records" on label

BST-84057 [S]	Blue Hour	1971	$50

— With "A Division of United Artists" on label

BST-84057	Blue Hour	1986	$30

— The Finest in Jazz Since 1939" label reissue

B1-84065	Comin' Your Way	1988	$35

— The Finest in Jazz Since 1939" label; first issue of LP

BLP-4065 [M]	Comin' Your Way	1961	$0

— Canceled

BST-84065 [S]	Comin' Your Way	1961	$0

— Canceled

BST-84315	Common Touch!	1969	$60

— A Division of Liberty Records" on label

BLP-4081 [M]	Dearly Beloved	1961	$200

— With W. 63rd St. address on label

BLP-4081 [M]	Dearly Beloved	1963	$80

— With New York, USA address on label

BST-84081 [S]	Dearly Beloved	1961	$200

— With W. 63rd St. address on label

BST-84081 [S]	Dearly Beloved	1963	$100

— With New York, USA address on label

BST-84081 [S]	Dearly Beloved	1967	$60

— With "A Division of Liberty Records" on label

BLP-4268 [M]	Easy Walker	1967	$175

— A Division of Liberty Records" on label

BST-84268 [S]	Easy Walker	1967	$100

— A Division of Liberty Records" on label

BLP-4162 [M]	Hustlin'	1964	$120
BST-84162 [S]	Hustlin'	1964	$120

— With New York, USA address on label

BST-84162 [S]	Hustlin'	1967	$60

— With "A Division of Liberty Records" on label

BST-84162 [S]	Hustlin'	1970	$35

— With "A Division of United Artists" on label

LT-1037	In Memory Of...	1980	$60
BLP-4201 [M]	Joyride	1965	$200
BST-84201 [S]	Joyride	1964	$120

— With New York, USA address on label

BST-84201 [S]	Joyride	1967	$60

— With "A Division of Liberty Records" on label

BST-84201	Joyride	1984	$30

— The Finest in Jazz Since 1939" label reissue

BLP-4122 [M]	Jubilee Shout!!!	1963	$0

— Canceled

BN-LA883-4047	Jubilee Shout!!	1977	$60
BST-84122	Jubilee Shout!!	1986	$35

— The Finest in Jazz Since 1939" label; first issue of LP

B1-90261	La Place	1989	$35

— The Finest in Jazz Since 1939" on label

BLP-4039 [M]	Look Out!	1960	$150

— Regular version with W. 63rd St. address on label

BLP-4039 [M]	Look Out!	1963	$80

— With New York, USA address on label

BST-84039 [S]	Look Out!	1960	$120

— With W. 63rd St. addresss on label

BST-84039 [S]	Look Out!	1963	$40

— With New York, USA address on label

BST-84039 [S]	Look Out!	1967	$60

— With "A Division of Liberty Records" on label

LT-1075	Mr. Natural	1980	$35
BLP-4129 [M]	Never Let Me Go	1963	$120
BST-84129 [S]	Never Let Me Go	1963	$120

— With New York, USA address on label

BST-84129 [S]	Never Let Me Go	1967	$60

— With "A Division of Liberty Records" on label

LT-993	New Time Shuffle	1979	$35

BLP-4240 [M]	Rough 'n Tumble	1966	$200
BST-84240 [S]	Rough 'n Tumble	1966	$100

— With New York, USA address on label

BST-84240 [S]	Rough 'n Tumble	1967	$60

— With "A Division of Liberty Records" on label

BLP-4234 [M]	Stanley Turrentine	1965	$0

— Canceled

BST-84234 [S]	Stanley Turrentine	1965	$0

— Canceled

BN-LA394-H2	Stanley Turrentine	1975	$50
BT-85105	Straight Ahead	1984	$30

— The Finest in Jazz Since 1939" on label

BLP-4096 [M]	That's Where It's At	1962	$200

— With W. 63rd St. address on label

BLP-4096 [M]	That's Where It's At	1963	$120

— With New York, USA address on label

BST-84096 [S]	That's Where It's At	1962	$200

— With W. 63rd St. address on label

BST-84096 [S]	That's Where It's At	1963	$100

— With New York, USA address on label

BST-84096 [S]	That's Where It's At	1967	$60

— With "A Division of Liberty Records" on label

BST-84096	That's Where It's At	1986	$30

— The Finest in Jazz Since 1939" reissue

B1-93201	The Best of Stanley Turrentine	1989	$35

— The Finest in Jazz Since 1939" on label

BST-84286	The Look of Love	1968	$60

— With "A Division of Liberty Records" on label

BST-84286	The Look of Love	1971	$50

— With "A Division of United Artists" on label

BLP-4256 [M]	The Spoiler	1967	$150

— A Division of Liberty Records" on label

BST-84256 [S]	The Spoiler	1967	$40

— A Division of Liberty Records" on label

BLP-4069 [M]	Up at Minton's, Volume 1	1961	$200

— With W. 63rd St. addresss on label

BLP-4069 [M]	Up at Minton's, Volume 1	1963	$80

— With New York, USA address on label

BST-84069 [S]	Up at Minton's, Volume 1	1961	$200

— With W. 63rd St. addresss on label

BST-84069 [S]	Up at Minton's, Volume 1	1963	$40

— With New York, USA address on label

BST-84069 [S]	Up at Minton's, Volume 1	1967	$60

— With "A Division of Liberty Records" on label

BLP-4070 [M]	Up at Minton's, Volume 2	1961	$200

— With W. 63rd St. addresss on label

BLP-4070 [M]	Up at Minton's, Volume 2	1963	$80

— With New York, USA address on label

BST-84070 [S]	Up at Minton's, Volume 2	1961	$200

— With W. 63rd St. addresss on label

BST-84070 [S]	Up at Minton's, Volume 2	1963	$40

— With New York, USA address on label

BST-84070 [S]	Up at Minton's, Volume 2	1967	$60

— With "A Division of Liberty Records" on label

BT-85140	Wonderland	1987	$30

— The Finest in Jazz Since 1939" on label

BST-84424	Z.T.'s Blues	1985	$30

— The Finest in Jazz Since 1939" on label

CTI

6017	Cherry	1972	$50
8010	Cherry	1981	$30

— Reissue of 6017

6030	Don't Mess with Mister T.	1973	$35
8011	Don't Mess with Mister T.	1981	$30

— Reissue of 6030

CTSQ-6030 [Q]	Don't Mess with Mister T.	1973	$150
6010	Salt Song	1971	$50
8008	Salt Song	1981	$30

— Reissue of 6010

6005	Sugar	1971	$50
8006	Sugar	1981	$30

— Reissue of 6005

6048	The Baddest Turrentine	1974	$35
6052	The Sugar Man	1975	$50

ELEKTRA

6E-217	Betcha	1979	$25
60201	Home Again	1982	$30
6E-269	Inflation	1980	$25
5E-534	Tender Togetherness	1981	$30

FANTASY

F-9508	Everybody Come On Out	1976	$35
F-9493	Have You Ever Seen the Rain	1975	$35

F-9478	In the Pocket	1975	$35
F-9534	Nightwings	1977	$35
FPM-4002 [Q]	Pieces of Dreams	1974	$40
F-9465	Pieces of Dreams	1974	$35
F-9519	The Man with the Sad Face	1976	$35
F-9604	Use the Stairs	1980	$30
F-9548	West Side Highway	1978	$35
F-9563	What About You!	1978	$30

MAINSTREAM

56041 [M]	Tiger Tail	1965	$40
S-6041 [S]	Tiger Tail	1965	$100

PHOENIX 10

PHX-317	Yester-Me, Yester-You	198?	$30

SUNSET

SUS-5255	The Soul of Stanley Turrentine	196?	$30

TIME

52086 [M]	Stan the Man	1962	$175
S-2086 [S]	Stan the Man	1962	$200

TRIP

TLX-5006	Yester-Me, Yester-You	197?	$35

UPFRONT

UPF-147	Stanley Turrentine	197?	$30

TURRENTINE, TOMMY

Trumpeter.

Albums

BAINBRIDGE

BT-1047	Tommy Turrentine	198?	$30

TIME

T-70008 [M]	Tommy Turrentine	1960	$80

— Reproductions exist

ST-70008 [S]	Tommy Turrentine	1960	$100

TURTLE ISLAND STRING QUARTET

Members: Darol Anger (violin, fiddle); David Balakrishnan (violin, baritone violin); Irene Sazer (viola); Mark Summer (cello).

Albums

WINDHAM HILL

WH-0114	Metropolis	1989	$30
WH-0110	Turtle Island String Quartet	1988	$25

TUSA, FRANK

Bass player.

Albums

ENJA

2056	Father Time	197?	$35

TWARDZIK, RICHARD

Pianist. Also see RUSS FREEMAN.

Albums

PACIFIC JAZZ

PJ-37 [M]	The Last Set	1962	$60

TYLE, TEDDY

Tenor saxophone player.

Albums

GOLDEN CREST

GC-3060 [M]	Moon Shot	1959	$40

TYLER, ALVIN "RED

Tenor saxophone player and composer.

Albums

ACE

LP-1006 [M]	Rockin' and Rollin'	1960	$150
LP-1021 [M]	Twistin' with Mr. Sax	1962	$120

ROUNDER

2061	Graciously	1987	$25
2047	Heritage	1986	$30

TYLER, CHARLES

Alto and baritone saxophone player and clarinetist.

Albums

ADELPHI

5011	Sixty Minute Man	1980	$30

ESP-DISK'

S-1059 [S]	Eastern Man Alone	1968	$100
1029 [M]	The Charles Tyler Ensemble	1966	$100
S-1029 [S]	The Charles Tyler Ensemble	1966	$100

NESSA

Number	Title	Yr	NM
❑ N-16	Saga of the Outlaws	197?	$35
SILKHEART			
❑ SH-118	Autumn in Paris	199?	$30
STORYVILLE			
❑ 4098	Definite, Vol. 1	198?	$25

TYNER, MCCOY
Pianist.

Albums

ABC IMPULSE!

Number	Title	Yr	NM
❑ IA-9338	Early Trios	1978	$35
❑ AS-18	Inception	1968	$30
❑ AS-48	McCoy Tyner Live at Newport	1968	$30
❑ AS-79	McCoy Tyner Plays Duke Ellington	1968	$30
❑ AS-39	Nights of Ballads and Blues	1968	$30
❑ AS-33	Reaching Fourth	1968	$30
❑ IA-9235	Reevaluation: The Impulse! Years	197?	$35
❑ AS-63	Today and Tomorrow	1968	$30

BLUE NOTE

Number	Title	Yr	NM
❑ BN-LA223-G	Asante	1974	$35
❑ BST-84338	Expansions	1969	$50
— With "A Division of Liberty Records" on label			
❑ BST-84338	Expansions	1970	$30
— With United Artists distribution			
❑ BST-84338	Expansions	1984	$25
— The Finest in Jazz Since 1939" label			
❑ BN-LA022-F	Extensions	1973	$35
❑ B1-91651	Revelations	1989	$30
❑ BST-84275	Tender Moments	1968	$50
— With "A Division of Liberty Records" on label			
❑ BST-84275	Tender Moments	1970	$30
— With United Artists distribution			
❑ BST-84275	Tender Moments	1985	$25
— The Finest in Jazz Since 1939" label			
❑ BLP-4264 [M]	The Real McCoy	1967	$100
❑ BST-84264 [S]	The Real McCoy	1967	$50
— With "A Division of Liberty Records" on label			
❑ BST-84264	The Real McCoy	1970	$30
— With United Artists distribution			
❑ BLP-84264	The Real McCoy	1987	$60
— The Finest in Jazz Since 1939" label			
❑ BST-84307	Time for Tyner	1969	$50
— With "A Division of Liberty Records" on label			
❑ BLP-84307	Time for Tyner	1987	$60
— The Finest in Jazz Since 1939" label			

COLUMBIA

Number	Title	Yr	NM
❑ FC37375	La Leyenda de la Hora (The Legend of the Hour)	1981	$25
❑ FC38053	Looking Out	1982	$25

ELEKTRA/MUSICIAN

Number	Title	Yr	NM
❑ 60350	Dimensions	1984	$25

FANTASY

Number	Title	Yr	NM
❑ OJC-650	Echoes of a Friend	1991	$25
— Reissue of Milestone 9055			
❑ OJC-311	Sahara	1988	$25
— Reissue of Milestone 9039			
❑ OJC-313	Song for My Lady	1988	$25
— Reissue of Milestone 9044			
❑ OJC-618	Song of the New World	1991	$25
— Reissue of Milestone 9049			

GRP/IMPULSE!

Number	Title	Yr	NM
❑ 220	Inception	1997	$200
— Reissue on audiophile vinyl			
❑ 216	McCoy Tyner Plays Duke Ellington	1997	$200
— Reissue on audiophile vinyl			
❑ 221	Nights of Ballads and Blues	1997	$200
— Reissue on audiophile vinyl			

IMPULSE!

Number	Title	Yr	NM
❑ A-18 [M]	Inception	1962	$200
❑ AS-18 [S]	Inception	1962	$200
❑ A-48 [M]	McCoy Tyner Live at Newport	1963	$200
❑ AS-48 [S]	McCoy Tyner Live at Newport	1963	$200
❑ A-79 [M]	McCoy Tyner Plays Duke Ellington	1965	$200
❑ AS-79 [S]	McCoy Tyner Plays Duke Ellington	1965	$200
❑ A-39 [M]	Nights of Ballads and Blues	1963	$200
❑ AS-39 [S]	Nights of Ballads and Blues	1963	$200
❑ A-33 [M]	Reaching Fourth	1963	$200
❑ AS-33 [S]	Reaching Fourth	1963	$200

Number	Title	Yr	NM
❑ A-63 [M]	Today and Tomorrow	1964	$200
❑ AS-63 [S]	Today and Tomorrow	1964	$200
MCA			
❑ 4157	Early Trios	1981	$30
— Reissue of Impulse! 9338			
❑ 4126	Great Moments with McCoy Tyner	1981	$30
❑ 4156	Reevaluation: The Impulse Years	1981	$30
— Reissue of Impulse! 9235			

MILESTONE

Number	Title	Yr	NM
❑ 55007	4 x 4	1980	$30
❑ 9102	13th House	1981	$25
❑ 55002	Atlantis	1975	$30
❑ 9055	Echoes of a Friend	1974	$25
❑ 55001	Enlightenment	1973	$30
❑ 9067	Fly with the Wind	1976	$25
❑ 9072	Focal Point	1977	$25
❑ 9094	Horizon	1980	$25
❑ 9079	Inner Voices	1978	$25
❑ 9091	Passion Dance	1979	$25
❑ M-47062	Reflections	1981	$25
❑ 9039	Sahara	197?	$25
❑ 9056	Sama Layuca	1974	$25
❑ 9044	Song for My Lady	197?	$25
❑ FPM-4006 [Q]	Song of the New World	197?	$60
❑ 9049	Song of the New World	197?	$25
❑ 55003	Supertrios	1977	$30
❑ 9085	The Greeting	1978	$25
❑ 9087	Together	1979	$25
❑ 9063	Trident	1975	$25
❑ 9167	Uptown/Downtown	1988	$25

PALO ALTO

Number	Title	Yr	NM
❑ PA-8083	Just Feelin'	1985	$25

PAUSA

Number	Title	Yr	NM
❑ 9007	Time for Tyner	198?	$20
— Reissue of Blue Note 84307			

QUICKSILVER

Number	Title	Yr	NM
❑ QS-4010	Just Feelin'	1990	$25
— Reissue of Palo Alto LP			

TIMELESS

Number	Title	Yr	NM
❑ SJP-260	Bon Voyage	1990	$25

U

UEMATSU, YOSHITAKA
See JEFF HITMAN.

ULANO, SAM

Albums

LANE

Number	Title	Yr	NM
❑ LP-140 [M]	Sam Ulano	195?	$50
❑ LP-151 [M]	Sam Ulano Is Mr. Rhythm	195?	$50

ULMER, JAMES "BLOOD"
Guitarist and male singer.

Albums

ARTISTS HOUSE

Number	Title	Yr	NM
❑ 13	Are You Glad to Be in America?	1980	$50

BLUE NOTE

Number	Title	Yr	NM
❑ BT-85136	America -- Do You Remember the Love?	1987	$30

CARAVAN OF DREAMS

Number	Title	Yr	NM
❑ CDP85004	Live at the Caravan of Dreams	1986	$35

COLUMBIA

Number	Title	Yr	NM
❑ ARC38285	Black Rock	1982	$50
❑ BFC38900	Odyssey	1983	$30

IN+OUT

Number	Title	Yr	NM
❑ 7007	Revealing	1990	$30

UNCLE FESTIVE
Members: John Pondel (guitar); Ron Pedley (keyboards); Bud Harner (drums); Marc Levine (bass).

Albums

NOVA

Number	Title	Yr	NM
❑ 8703-1	Money's No Object	198?	$25

OPTIMISM

Number	Title	Yr	NM
❑ OP-3107	Say Uncle	1988	$25

UPCHURCH, PHIL
Guitarist and bandleader. His "You Can't Sit Down" was a hit single in the early 1960s.

Albums

BLUE THUMB

Number	Title	Yr	NM
❑ BTS-6005	Darkness, Darkness	1971	$50
❑ BTS-59	Lovin' Feelin'	1973	$30

BOYD

Number	Title	Yr	NM
❑ B-398 [M]	You Can't Sit Down	1961	$150
❑ BS-398 [S]	You Can't Sit Down	1961	$175

CADET

Number	Title	Yr	NM
❑ LPS-840	The Way I Feel	1970	$35
❑ LPS-826	Upchurch	1969	$35

JAM

Number	Title	Yr	NM
❑ 07	Free and Easy	198?	$30

KUDU

Number	Title	Yr	NM
❑ 22	Phil Upchurch and Tennyson Stevens	1975	$30

MARLIN

Number	Title	Yr	NM
❑ 2209	Phil Upchurch	1978	$30

MILESTONE

Number	Title	Yr	NM
❑ MSP-9010	Feeling Blue	1968	$35

UNITED ARTISTS

Number	Title	Yr	NM
❑ UAL-3175 [M]	Big Hit Dances	1962	$60
❑ UAS-6175 [S]	Big Hit Dances	1962	$60
❑ UAL-3162 [M]	You Can't Sit Down, Part 2	1961	$60

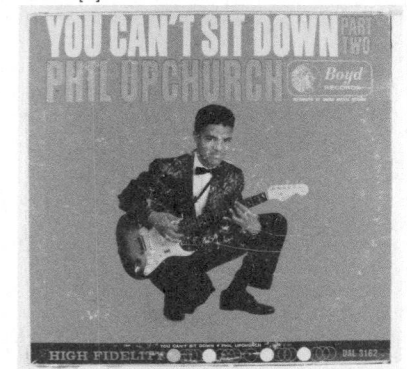

Number	Title	Yr	NM
❑ UAS-6162 [S]	You Can't Sit Down, Part 2	1961	$40

UPTOWN LOWDOWN JAZZ BAND
Founded and led by Bert Barr (cornet) in 1971.

Albums

GHB

Number	Title	Yr	NM
❑ GHB-159	Hauling Ash	1981	$25
❑ GHB-149	Uptown Lowdown Jazz Band	1979	$25

STOMP OFF

Number	Title	Yr	NM
❑ SOS-1030	Uptown Lowdown Jazz Band in Colonial York, Pa.	1982	$25

ULJB

Number	Title	Yr	NM
❑ UL-0(# unknown)	Jingle Jazz	1989	$25
❑ UL-0(# unknown)	Seattle Style	1985	$25
❑ UL-101	Uptown Lowdown Jazz Band	197?	$25

UPTOWN STRING QUARTET, THE
Members: Eileen Folson (cello); Diane Monroe (violin); Maxine Roach (viola); Lesa Terry (violin).

Albums

PHILIPS

Number	Title	Yr	NM
❑ 838358-1	Max Roach Presents the Uptown String Quartet	1989	$30

URBAN EARTH FEATURING HARVIE SWARTZ
Also see HARVIE SWARTZ.

URBANIAK, MICHAL
Violinist.

Albums

ARISTA

Number	Title	Yr	NM
❑ AL4086	Body English	1976	$30

CATALYST

Number	Title	Yr	NM
❑ 7909	Beginning	197?	$35

COLUMBIA

Number	Title	Yr	NM
❑ KC33184	Atma	1975	$30
❑ KC32852	Fusion	1974	$30

Number	Title	Yr	NM
❏ PC33542	Fusion III	1975	$30
EASTWEST			
❏ 90992	Urban Express	1989	$30
INNER CITY			
❏ IC-1036	Urbaniak	1977	$30
JAM			
❏ 5004	Jam at Sandy's	198?	$30
OPTIMISM			
❏ OP-5012	Milky Way	198?	$25
PAUSA			
❏ 7114	Daybreak	198?	$25
❏ 7047	Heritage	197?	$25
STEEPLECHASE			
❏ SCS-1159	My One and Only Love	1981	$30
❏ SCS-1195	Take Good Care of My Heart	198?	$30

URSO, PHIL
Tenor saxophone player.

Albums
SAVOY

Number	Title	Yr	NM
❏ MG-15041 [10]	Bob Brookmeyer with Phil Urso	1954	$150
❏ MG-12056 [M]	The Philosophy of Urso	1956	$50

URTREGER, RENE
See DICK KATZ.

US3
Created by Geoff Wilkinson (producer) and Mel Simpson (producer, keyboards), this jazz-rap melange spawned a hit single, "Cantaloop (Flip Fantasia)." Its extensive samples from the Blue Note back catalog, much of which still had not been reissued on CD in 1993, helped revive interest in the legendary label.

Albums
BLUE NOTE

Number	Title	Yr	NM
❏ B1-30027	Broadway & 52nd	1997	$18
❏ B1-80883	Hand on the Torch	1993	$18

USSELTON, BILLY
Tenor saxophone player.

Albums
KAPP

Number	Title	Yr	NM
❏ KL-1051 [M]	Bill Usselton -- His First Album	1957	$50

V

V.S.O.P. QUINTET
See HERBIE HANCOCK.

VACHE, ALLAN, AND CHUCK HUGHES
Hughes also plays clarinet. Also see ALLAN VACHE.

Albums
JAZZOLOGY

Number	Title	Yr	NM
❏ J-131	Clarinet Climax	198?	$25

VACHE, ALLAN
Clarinetist and saxophone player.

Albums
AUDIOPHILE

Number	Title	Yr	NM
❏ AP-192	High Speed Swing	1986	$25
❏ AP-176	Vache's Jazz Moods	1983	$25

VACHE, WARREN
Cornet and fluegel horn player.

Albums
AUDIOPHILE

Number	Title	Yr	NM
❏ AP-196	First Time Out	1986	$25
CONCORD JAZZ			
❏ CJ-323	Easy Going	1987	$25
❏ CJ-153	Iridescence	1981	$25
❏ CJ-87	Jillian	1979	$25
❏ CJ-203	Midtown Jazz	1982	$25
❏ CJ-98	Polished Brass	1980	$25
❏ CJ-392	Warm Evenings	1989	$30

Number	Title	Yr	NM
DREAMSTREET			
❏ 101	Blues Walk	197?	$35
MONMOUTH-EVERGREEN			
❏ 7081	First Time Out	197?	$35

VALENTIN, DAVE
Flutist.

Albums
GRP

Number	Title	Yr	NM
❏ GR-1016	Jungle Garden	198?	$25
❏ GR-1009	Kalahari	198?	$25
❏ GR-1028	Light Struck	198?	$25
❏ GR-9568	Live at the Blue Note	1988	$25
❏ GR-1043	Mind Time	1988	$25
GRP/ARISTA			
❏ GL5006	Hawk	1979	$25
❏ GL5511	In Love's Time	198?	$25
❏ GL5001	Legends	1978	$30
❏ GL5505	Pied Piper	198?	$25

VAN DAMME, ART
Accordion player.

Albums
BASF

Number	Title	Yr	NM
❏ 22016	Invitation	197?	$35
❏ 21755	Squeezing Art and Tender Flutes	197?	$35
❏ 25257	Star Spangled Rhythm	197?	$25
❏ 25113	The Many Moods of Art Van Damme	197?	$25
CAPITOL			
❏ H178 [10]	Cocktail Capers	1950	$80
❏ T178 [M]	Cocktail Capers	1954	$60
❏ L300 [10]	More Cocktail Capers	1952	$80
❏ T300 [M]	More Cocktail Capers	1954	$75
COLUMBIA			
❏ CL1563 [M]	Accordion A La Mode	1960	$30
❏ CS8363 [S]	Accordion A La Mode	1960	$30
❏ CL2013 [M]	A Perfect Match	1963	$35
❏ CS8813 [S]	A Perfect Match	1963	$25
❏ CL1794 [M]	Art Van Damme Swings Sweetly	1962	$35
❏ CS8594 [M]	Art Van Damme Swings Sweetly	1962	$25
❏ CL1382 [M]	Everything's Coming Up Music	1959	$30
❏ CS8177 [S]	Everything's Coming Up Music	1959	$30
❏ CL801 [M]	Manhattan Time	1956	$30
❏ CL6265 [10]	Martini Time	1953	$40
❏ CL630 [M]	Martini Time	1955	$40
❏ CL876 [M]	The Art of Van Damme	1956	$30
❏ CL2585 [10]	The Art Van Damme Quintet	1956	$40
❏ CL2192 [M]	The New Sound Of the Art Van Damme Septet	1964	$30
❏ CS8992 [S]	The New Sound Of the Art Van Damme Septet	1964	$35
❏ CL544 [M]	The Van Damme Sound	1955	$40
❏ C2L7 [M]	They're Playing Our Song	1958	$40
DESIGN			
❏ DLP-905 [M]	3 of a Kind	196?	$30
❏ SDLP-905 [R]	3 of a Kind	196?	$20
HARMONY			
❏ HL-7439 [M]	Music for Lovers	196?	$30
❏ HS-11439 [S]	Music for Lovers	196?	$25
PAUSA			
❏ 7151	Art Van Damme and Friends	198?	$25
❏ 7027	Blue World	197?	$25
❏ 7066	Invitation	197?	$25
❏ 7104	Keep Going	198?	$25
❏ 7126	Squeezing Art and Tender Flutes	198?	$25
PICKWICK			
❏ PC-3009 [M]	Lover Man!	196?	$30
❏ PCS-3009 [R]	Lover Man!	196?	$20
SONIC ARTS			
❏ 12	By Request	1980	$30

VAN DER GELD, TOM
Vibraphone player.

Albums
ECM

Number	Title	Yr	NM
❏ 1134	Path	1979	$30
❏ 1113	Patience	1977	$30

VAN DYKE, LOUIS
Pianist.

Albums
COLUMBIA MASTERWORKS

Number	Title	Yr	NM
❏ M34511	'Round Midnight	1977	$25

VAN EPS, GEORGE
Seven-string guitarist. Also see EDDIE MILLER; THE RAMPART STREET PARADERS.

Albums
CAPITOL

Number	Title	Yr	NM
❏ T2533 [M]	My Guitar	1966	$50
❏ ST2533 [S]	My Guitar	1966	$40
❏ ST2783	Seven String Guitar	1968	$50
❏ ST-267	Soliloquy	1969	$50
COLUMBIA			
❏ CL929 [M]	Mellow Guitar	1956	$40
CORINTHIAN			
❏ 121	Mellow Guitar	198?	$25

VAN'T HOF, JASPER
Pianist.

Albums
PAUSA

Number	Title	Yr	NM
❏ 7084	Live in Montreux	1979	$25

VARNER, TOM
French horn player.

Albums
SOUL NOTE

Number	Title	Yr	NM
❏ SN-1067	Motion/Stillness	198?	$30
❏ SN-1017	TV	198?	$30

VASCONCELOS, NANA
Percussionist and male singer.

Albums
ANTILLES

Number	Title	Yr	NM
❏ 90698	Bush Dance	1987	$25
ECM			
❏ 1147	Saudades	1979	$30

VAUGHAN, SARAH, AND BILLY ECKSTINE
Also see each artist's individual listings.

Albums
EMARCY

Number	Title	Yr	NM
❏ 822526-1	The Irving Berlin Songbook	1984	$25
LION			
❏ L-70088 [M]	Billy and Sarah	195?	$30
MERCURY			
❏ MG-20316 [M]	Sarah Vaughan and Billy Eckstine Sing the Best of Irving Berlin	1959	$100
❏ SR-60002 [S]	Sarah Vaughan and Billy Eckstine Sing the Best of Irving Berlin	1959	$100

VAUGHAN, SARAH, AND COUNT BASIE
Also see each artist's individual listings.

Albums
PABLO

Number	Title	Yr	NM
❏ 2312130	Send In the Clowns	1980	$25
ROULETTE			
❏ R52061 [M]	Count Basie and Sarah Vaughan	1960	$60
❏ SR52061 [S]	Count Basie and Sarah Vaughan	1960	$60
❏ SR42018	Count Basie and Sarah Vaughan	1968	$35

VAUGHAN, SARAH; DINAH WASHINGTON; JOE WILLIAMS
Also see each artist's individual listings.

Albums
ROULETTE

Number	Title	Yr	NM
❏ R52108 [M]	We Three	1964	$35
❏ SR52108 [S]	We Three	1964	$50

VAUGHAN, SARAH

Female singer, one of the great interpreters of popular song.

Albums

ACCORD

Number	Title	Yr	NM
❑ SN-7195	Simply Divine	1981	$25

ALLEGRO

Number	Title	Yr	NM
❑ 3080 [10]	Early Sarah	195?	$80
❑ 1592 [M]	Sarah Vaughan	1955	$100
❑ 1608 [M]	Sarah Vaughan	1955	$100

ALLEGRO ELITE

Number	Title	Yr	NM
❑ 4106 [10]	Sarah Vaughan Sings	195?	$30

ATLANTIC

Number	Title	Yr	NM
❑ SD16037	Songs of the Beatles	1981	$30

BRYLEN

Number	Title	Yr	NM
❑ BN4411	Desires	198?	$25

—Last name is misspelled "Vaughn

CBS MASTERWORKS

Number	Title	Yr	NM
❑ FM42519	Brazilian Romance	1987	$25
❑ FM37277	Gershwin Live!	1982	$25

—With the Los Angeles Philharmonic Orchestra

COLUMBIA

Number	Title	Yr	NM
❑ CL660 [M]	After Hours with Sarah Vaughan	1955	$100
❑ CL914 [M]	Linger Awhile	1956	$100
❑ CL6133 [10]	Sarah Vaughan	1950	$200
❑ CL745 [M]	Sarah Vaughan in Hi-Fi	1956	$100

COLUMBIA SPECIAL PRODUCTS

Number	Title	Yr	NM
❑ P14364	Linger Awhile	1978	$25

—Reissue of Columbia 914

Number	Title	Yr	NM
❑ P13084	Sarah Vaughan in Hi-Fi	1976	$25

—Reissue of Columbia 745

CONCORD

Number	Title	Yr	NM
❑ 3018 [M]	Sarah Vaughan Concert	1957	$60

CORONET

Number	Title	Yr	NM
❑ 277	Sarah Vaughan Belts the Hits	196?	$35

EMARCY

Number	Title	Yr	NM
❑ MG-26005 [10]	Images	1954	$200
❑ MG-36058 [M]	In the Land of Hi-Fi	1956	$200
❑ 826454-1	In the Land of Hi-Fi	1986	$25

—Reissue of 36058

Number	Title	Yr	NM
❑ MG-36004 [M]	Sarah Vaughan	1955	$200
❑ EMS-2-412	Sarah Vaughan Live	197?	$30
❑ MG-36089 [M]	Sassy	1956	$200
❑ MG-36109 [M]	Swingin' Easy	1957	$200
❑ 814187-1	The George Gershwin Songbook	1983	$30
❑ 824864-1	The Rodgers & Hart Songbook	1985	$25

EVEREST ARCHIVE OF FOLK & JAZZ

Number	Title	Yr	NM
❑ 250	Sarah Vaughan	197?	$25
❑ 271	Sarah Vaughan, Volume 2	1973	$25
❑ 325	Sarah Vaughan, Volume 3	197?	$25

FORUM

Number	Title	Yr	NM
❑ F-9034 [M]	Dreamy	196?	$30

HARMONY

Number	Title	Yr	NM
❑ HL7158 [M]	The Great Sarah Vaughan	196?	$30

LION

Number	Title	Yr	NM
❑ L70052 [M]	Tenderly	1958	$60

MAINSTREAM

Number	Title	Yr	NM
❑ MRL379	Feelin' Good	1973	$35
❑ MRL419	More Sarah Vaughan from Japan	1974	$35
❑ MRL2401	Sarah Vaughan "Live" In Japan	1973	$50
❑ MRL404	Sarah Vaughan and the Jimmy Rowles Quintet	1974	$35
❑ MRL361	Sarah Vaughan/Michel Legrand	1972	$35
❑ MRL340	Time in My Life	1972	$35

MERCURY

Number	Title	Yr	NM
❑ SR-60020 [S]	After Hours at the London House	1959	$150
❑ MG-20383 [M]	After Hours at the London House	1958	$150
❑ MG-20580 [M]	Close to You	1960	$100
❑ SR-60240 [S]	Close to You	1960	$100
❑ MG-25188 [10]	Divine Sarah	1955	$300
❑ MGP-2-100 [M]	Great Songs from Hit Shows	1957	$200
❑ MG-20244 [M]	Great Songs from Hit Shows, Vol. 1	1958	$100
❑ SR-60041 [S]	Great Songs from Hit Shows, Vol. 1	1959	$100
❑ MG-20245 [M]	Great Songs from Hit Shows, Vol. 2	1958	$100
❑ SR-60078 [S]	Great Songs from Hit Shows, Vol. 2	1959	$100
❑ MG-20223 [M]	In a Romantic Mood	1957	$100
❑ MG-21122 [M]	It's a Man's World	1967	$100
❑ SR-61122 [S]	It's a Man's World	1967	$100
❑ MG-20617 [M]	My Heart Sings	1961	$100
❑ SR-60617 [S]	My Heart Sings	1961	$100
❑ MG-20441 [M]	No 'Count Sarah	1959	$100
❑ SR-60116 [S]	No 'Count Sarah	1959	$100
❑ MG-21069 [M]	Pop Artistry	1966	$100
❑ SR-61069 [S]	Pop Artistry	1966	$100
❑ MG-20326 [M]	Sarah Vaughan and Her Trio at Mr. Kelly's	1958	$100
❑ MG-20094 [M]	Sarah Vaughan at the Blue Note	1956	$100
❑ MG-20645 [M]	Sarah Vaughan's Golden Hits	1961	$100
❑ SR-60645 [S]	Sarah Vaughan's Golden Hits	1961	$100

—Original black label version

Number	Title	Yr	NM
❑ SR-60645 [S]	Sarah Vaughan's Golden Hits	1965	$100

—Red label version with white "MERCURY" alone at top

Number	Title	Yr	NM
❑ SR-60645 [S]	Sarah Vaughan's Golden Hits	1968	$100

—Red label with multiple Mercury logos along the label edge

Number	Title	Yr	NM
❑ MGP-2-101 [M]	Sarah Vaughan Sings George Gershwin	1957	$200
❑ MG-20310 [M]	Sarah Vaughan Sings George Gershwin, Vol. 1	1958	$100
❑ SR-60045 [S]	Sarah Vaughan Sings George Gershwin, Vol. 1	1959	$100
❑ MG-20311 [M]	Sarah Vaughan Sings George Gershwin, Vol. 2	1958	$100
❑ SR-60046 [S]	Sarah Vaughan Sings George Gershwin, Vol. 2	1959	$100
❑ MG-21009 [M]	Sarah Vaughan Sings the Mancini Songbook	1965	$100
❑ SR-61009 [S]	Sarah Vaughan Sings the Mancini Songbook	1965	$100
❑ MG-21116 [M]	Sassy Swings Again	1967	$100
❑ SR-61116 [S]	Sassy Swings Again	1967	$100
❑ MG-20831 [M]	Sassy Swings the Tivoli	1962	$100
❑ SR-60831 [S]	Sassy Swings the Tivoli	1962	$100
❑ 826320-1	The Complete Sarah Vaughan on Mercury Vol. 1: Great Jazz years (1954-56)	1986	$40
❑ 826327-1	The Complete Sarah Vaughan on Mercury Vol. 2: Great American Songs (1956-57)	1986	$40
❑ 826333-1	The Complete Sarah Vaughan on Mercury Vol. 3: Great Show on Stage (1954-56)	1986	$40
❑ 830721-1	The Complete Sarah Vaughan on Mercury Vol. 4 Part 1: Live in Europe (1963-64)	1987	$40
❑ 830726-1	The Complete Sarah Vaughan on Mercury Vol. 4 Part 2: Sassy Swings Again	1987	$40
❑ MG-25213 [10]	The Divine Sarah Sings	1955	$300
❑ MG-20540 [M]	The Divine Sarah Vaughan	1960	$100
❑ SR-60255 [S]	The Divine Sarah Vaughan	1960	$100
❑ MG-20438 [M]	The Magic of Sarah Vaughan	1959	$100
❑ SR-60110 [S]	The Magic of Sarah Vaughan	1959	$100
❑ MG-21079 [M]	The New Scene	1966	$100
❑ SR-61079 [S]	The New Scene	1966	$100
❑ MG-20370 [M]	Vaughan and Violins	1958	$100
❑ SR-60038 [S]	Vaughan and Violins	1959	$100
❑ MG-20882 [M]	Vaughan with Voices	1963	$100
❑ SR-60882 [S]	Vaughan with Voices	1963	$100
❑ MG-20941 [M]	Viva Vaughan	1964	$100
❑ SR-60941 [S]	Viva Vaughan	1964	$100
❑ MG-20219 [M]	Wonderful Sarah	1957	$100

METRO

Number	Title	Yr	NM
❑ M-539 [M]	Tenderly	1965	$150
❑ MS-539 [S]	Tenderly	1965	$250

MGM

Number	Title	Yr	NM
❑ E-544 [10]	Sarah Vaughan Sings	1951	$200
❑ E-165 [10]	Tenderly	1950	$200

MUSICRAFT

Number	Title	Yr	NM
❑ 504	Divine Sarah	197?	$25
❑ MVS-2006	Lover Man	1986	$25
❑ MVS-2002	The Man I Love	1986	$25

PABLO

Number	Title	Yr	NM
❑ 2312125	Copacabana	1981	$25
❑ 2310821	How Long	1978	$25
❑ 2312101	I Love Brazil	1978	$25
❑ 2310885	The Best of Sarah Vaughan	1983	$25
❑ 2405416	The Best of Sarah Vaughan	1990	$25
❑ 2312111	The Duke Ellington Songbook One	1979	$25
❑ 2312116	The Duke Ellington Songbook Two	1980	$25

PABLO TODAY

Number	Title	Yr	NM
❑ 2312137	Crazy and Mixed Up	1982	$25

PALACE

Number	Title	Yr	NM
❑ 5191 [M]	Sarah Vaughan Sings	195?	$30

PICKWICK

Number	Title	Yr	NM
❑ PCS-3035	Fabulous Sarah Vaughan	197?	$25

REMINGTON

Number	Title	Yr	NM
❑ RLP-1024 [10]	Hot Jazz	1953	$200

RIVERSIDE

Number	Title	Yr	NM
❑ RLP2511 [10]	Sarah Vaughan Sings with John Kirby	1955	$300

RONDO-LETTE

Number	Title	Yr	NM
❑ A-53 [M]	Sarah Vaughan Sings	1959	$60
❑ A-35 [M]	Songs of Broadway	1958	$60

ROULETTE

Number	Title	Yr	NM
❑ R52070 [M]	After Hours	1961	$60
❑ SR52070 [S]	After Hours	1961	$60
❑ R52060 [M]	Divine One	1960	$60
❑ SR52060 [S]	Divine One	1960	$60
❑ R52046 [M]	Dreamy	1960	$60
❑ SR52046 [S]	Dreamy	1960	$40
❑ RE-103	Echoes of an Era: The Sarah Vaughan Years	197?	$35
❑ R52104 [M]	Lonely Hours	1963	$35
❑ SR52104 [S]	Lonely Hours	1963	$50
❑ R52118 [M]	Sarah Plus Two	1965	$35
❑ SR52118 [S]	Sarah Plus Two	1965	$50
❑ R52116 [M]	Sarah Sings Soulfully	1965	$35
❑ SR52116 [S]	Sarah Sings Soulfully	1965	$50
❑ R52123 [M]	Sarah Slightly Classical	1966	$35
❑ SR52123 [S]	Sarah Slightly Classical	1966	$50
❑ R52091 [M]	Snowbound	1962	$50
❑ SR52091 [S]	Snowbound	1962	$60
❑ R52100 [M]	Star Eyes	1963	$35
❑ SR52100 [S]	Star Eyes	1963	$50
❑ R52112 [M]	Sweet 'N Sassy	1964	$35
❑ SR52112 [S]	Sweet 'N Sassy	1964	$50
❑ R52092 [M]	The Explosive Side of Sarah	1962	$50
❑ SR52092 [S]	The Explosive Side of Sarah	1962	$60
❑ K-105 [M]	The Sarah Vaughan Years	196?	$50
❑ SK-105 [S]	The Sarah Vaughan Years	196?	$60
❑ K-105 [M]	The Sarah Vaughan Years	196?	$50
❑ R52109 [M]	The World of Sarah Vaughan	1964	$35
❑ SR52109 [S]	The World of Sarah Vaughan	1964	$50
❑ R52082 [M]	You're Mine	1962	$60
❑ SR52082 [S]	You're Mine	1962	$60

—Black vinyl

Number	Title	Yr	NM
❑ SR52082 [S]	You're Mine	1962	$120

—Red vinyl

ROYALE

Number	Title	Yr	NM
❑ 18129 [10]	Sarah Vaughan and Orchestra	195?	$30
❑ 18149 [10]	Sarah Vaughan and Orchestra	195?	$30

—Includes recordings made on the Musicraft label in the 1940s

SCEPTER CITATION

Number	Title	Yr	NM
❑ CTN-18029	The Best of Sarah Vaughan	1972	$30

SPIN-O-RAMA

Number	Title	Yr	NM
❑ 73 [M]	Sweet, Sultry and Swinging	196?	$40
❑ S-73 [S]	Sweet, Sultry and Swinging	196?	$100
❑ 114 [M]	The Divine Sarah Vaughan	196?	$40
❑ S-114 [S]	The Divine Sarah Vaughan	196?	$100

TIME-LIFE

Number	Title	Yr	NM
❑ SLGD-09	Legendary Singers: Sarah Vaughan	1985	$35

TRIP

Number	Title	Yr	NM
❑ 5523	In the Land of Hi-Fi	197?	$25
❑ 5501	Sarah Vaughan	197?	$25
❑ 5517	Sassy	197?	$25
❑ 5551	Swingin' Easy	197?	$25

WING

Number	Title	Yr	NM
❑ MGW-12123 [M]	All Time Favorites	1963	$30
❑ SRW-16123 [S]	All Time Favorites	1963	$35
❑ MGW-12280 [M]	The Magic of Sarah Vaughan	1964	$30
❑ SRW-16280 [S]	The Magic of Sarah Vaughan	1964	$35

VAUGHN, FATHER TOM

Pianist.

Albums

CONCORD JAZZ

Number	Title	Yr	NM
❑ CJ-16	Joyful Jazz	1976	$30

RCA VICTOR

Number	Title	Yr	NM
❑ LPM-3708 [M]	Cornbread (Meat Loaf, Greens and Deviled Eggs)	1967	$50
❑ LSP-3708 [S]	Cornbread (Meat Loaf, Greens and Deviled Eggs)	1967	$35
❑ LPM-3577 [M]	Jazz In Concert at the Village Gate	1966	$35
❑ LSP-3577 [S]	Jazz In Concert at the Village Gate	1966	$50
❑ LPM-3845 [M]	Motor City Soul	1967	$50
❑ LSP-3845 [S]	Motor City Soul	1967	$35

Sarah Vaughan, *Sarah Vaughan's Golden Hits!!!*, Mercury SR 60645, original black label, **$100**.

Sarah Vaughan, *Echoes of an Era: The Sarah Vaughan Years*, Roulette RE-103, two-record set, **$35**.

Charlie Ventura, *Charlie Ventura's Carnegie Hall Concert*, Norgran MGN-1041, **$200**.

Charlie Ventura, *Charlie Ventura in a Jazz Mood*, Norgran MGN-1073, **$200**.

Number	Title	Yr	NM

VAZQUEZ, ROLAND
Drummer, percussionist and composer.
Albums
GRP/ARISTA

| ❏ GL5002 | Roland Vazquez and the Urban Ensemble | 1978 | $35 |

HEADFIRST

| ❏ 9710 | Feel Your Dream | 198? | $30 |

SOUNDWINGS

| ❏ SW-2106 | The Tides of Time | 1988 | $25 |

VEGA, AL
Pianist.
Albums
PRESTIGE

| ❏ PRLP-152 [10] | Al Vega Piano Solos With Bongos | 1953 | $250 |

VELEBNY, KAREL
See SHQ.

VELEZ, GLEN
Drummer and percussionist.
Albums
CMP

❏ CMP-42-ST	Assyrian Rose	1989	$25
❏ CMP-23-ST	Internal Combustion	1987	$25
❏ CMP-30-ST	Seven Heaven	1988	$25

VENTURA, CAROL
Female singer.
Albums
PRESTIGE

❏ PRLP-7358 [M]	Carol!	1965	$30
❏ PRST-7358 [S]	Carol!	1965	$30
❏ PRLP-7405 [M]	I Love to Sing!	1965	$30
❏ PRST-7405 [S]	I Love to Sing!	1965	$30

VENTURA, CHARLIE, AND MARY ANN MCCALL
Also see each artist's individual listings.
Albums
NORGRAN

❏ MGN-20 [10]	An Evening with Mary Ann McCall and Charlie Ventura	1954	$200
❏ MGN-1053 [M]	An Evening with Mary Ann McCall and Charlie Ventura	1955	$200
❏ MGN-1013 [M]	Another Evening with Charlie Ventura and Mary Ann McCall	1954	$300

VERVE

| ❏ MGV-8143 [M] | An Evening with Mary Ann McCall and Charlie Ventura | 1957 | $100 |
| ❏ V-8143 [M] | An Evening with Mary Ann McCall and Charlie Ventura | 1961 | $30 |

VENTURA, CHARLIE
Saxophone player (tenor, alto, baritone, bass). Also see GENE KRUPA.
Albums
BATON

| ❏ 1202 [M] | New Charlie Ventura in Hi-Fi | 1957 | $50 |

BRUNSWICK

| ❏ BL54025 [M] | Here's Charlie | 1957 | $80 |

CLEF

| ❏ MGC-117 [10] | Charlie Ventura Collates | 1953 | $350 |

CORAL

| ❏ CRL56067 [10] | Open House | 1952 | $150 |

CRAFTSMAN

| ❏ 8039 [M] | Charlie Ventura Plays for the People | 1960 | $30 |

CRYSTALETTE

| ❏ 5000 [10] | Stomping With the Sax | 1950 | $200 |

EMARCY

| ❏ MG-26028 [10] | F.Y.I. Ventura | 1954 | $200 |
| ❏ MG-36015 [M] | Jumping with Ventura | 1955 | $200 |

FAMOUS DOOR

| ❏ 115 | Chazz '77 | 1977 | $25 |

GENE NORMAN

| ❏ GNP-1 [M] | Charlie Ventura In Concert | 1954 | $100 |

GNP CRESCENDO

| ❏ GNP-1 [M] | Charlie Ventura In Concert | 196? | $30 |
| ❏ GNPS-1 [R] | Charlie Ventura In Concert | 196? | $25 |

HALL OF FAME

| ❏ 605 | Charlie Ventura Quintet | 197? | $25 |

IMPERIAL

| ❏ IM-3002 [10] | Charlie Ventura and His Sextet | 1953 | $250 |

KING

| ❏ 543 [M] | Adventure with Charlie Ventura | 1958 | $80 |

MCA

| ❏ 42330 | Gene Norman Presents a Charlie Ventura Concert | 1990 | $30 |

MERCURY

| ❏ MGC-117 [10] | Charlie Ventura Collates | 1952 | $300 |

MOSAIC

| ❏ MQ9-182 | The Complete Verve/Clef Charlie Ventura/Flip Phillips Studio Sessions | 199? | $300 |

NORGRAN

❏ MGN-1075 [M]	Blue Saxophone	1956	$80
❏ MGN-1103 [M]	Charley's Parley	1956	$200
❏ MGN-1073 [M]	Charlie Ventura in a Jazz Mood	1956	$200
❏ MGN-8 [10]	Charlie Ventura Quartet	1953	$250
❏ MGN-1041 [M]	Charlie Ventura's Carnegie Hall Concert	1955	$200

PHOENIX

| ❏ 6 | Charlie Boy | 197? | $25 |

RCA VICTOR

| ❏ LPM-1135 [M] | It's All Bop to Me | 1955 | $120 |

REGENT

| ❏ MG-6064 [M] | East of Suez | 1958 | $50 |

SAVOY JAZZ

| ❏ SJL-2243 | Euphoria | 198? | $30 |

TOPS

| ❏ L-1528 [M] | Charlie Ventura Plays Hi-Fi Jazz | 1958 | $30 |

TRIP

| ❏ 5536 | Jumping with Ventura | 197? | $25 |

VERVE

❏ V-8165 [M]	Blue Saxophone	1961	$30
❏ MGV-8165 [M]	Blue Saxophone	1957	$150
❏ V-8132 [M]	Charlie Ventura'a Carnegie Hall Concert	1961	$30
❏ MGV-8163 [M]	Charlie Ventura in a Jazz Mood	1957	$150
❏ V-8163 [M]	Charlie Ventura in a Jazz Mood	1961	$30
❏ MGV-8132 [M]	Charlie Ventura's Carnegie Hall Concert	1957	$150

ZIM

| ❏ 1004 | Charlie Ventura in Chicago | 197? | $25 |

VENTURA, CHARLIE/CHARLIE KENNEDY
Charlie Kennedy played alto saxophone. Also see CHARLIE VENTURA.
Albums
REGENT

| ❏ MG-6047 [M] | Crazy Rhythms | 1957 | $60 |

SAVOY

| ❏ MG-12200 | Crazy Rhythms | 197? | $30 |

VENTURA, JOE, AND DAVE MCKENNA
Also see each artist's individual listings.
Albums
CHIAROSCURO

| ❏ 160 | Alone at the Palace | 1977 | $30 |

VENTURA, JOE, AND EARL HINES
Also see each artist's individual listings.
Albums
CHIAROSCURO

| ❏ 145 | Hot Sonatas | 1975 | $30 |

VENUTI, JOE, AND GEORGE BARNES
Also see each artist's individual listings.
Albums
CONCORD JAZZ

| ❏ CJ-14 | Gems | 197? | $30 |
| ❏ CJ-30 | Live at the Concord Summer Festival | 197? | $30 |

VENUTI, JOE, AND LOUIS PRIMA
Also see each artist's individual listings.
Albums
DESIGN

| ❏ DLP-54 [M] | Hi-Fi Lootin' | 195? | $25 |

VENUTI, JOE, AND MARIAN MCPARTLAND
Also see each artist's individual listings.
Albums
HALCYON

| ❏ 112 | Maestro and Friend | 197? | $30 |

VENUTI, JOE, AND ZOOT SIMS
Also see each artist's individual listings.
Albums
CHIAROSCURO

| ❏ 128 | Joe and Zoot | 197? | $35 |
| ❏ 142 | Joe Venuti and Zoot Sims | 1975 | $30 |

VENUTI, JOE
Violinist, basically the first to use the instrument in jazz.
Albums
AUDIOPHILE

| ❏ AP-118 | Incredible | 197? | $25 |

CHIAROSCURO

| ❏ 134 | Blue Four | 1975 | $30 |
| ❏ 203 | The Best of Joe Venuti | 1979 | $25 |

EVEREST ARCHIVE OF FOLK & JAZZ

| ❏ 349 | Joe Venuti and the Dutch Swing College Band | 197? | $25 |

FLYING FISH

| ❏ FF-077 | Joe in Chicago, 1978 | 1979 | $30 |

GOLDEN CREST

| ❏ GC-3100 [M] | Joe Venuti Plays Gershwin | 1959 | $30 |
| ❏ GC-3101 [M] | Joe Venuti Plays Jerome Kern | 1959 | $30 |

GRAND AWARD

| ❏ GA-33-351 [M] | Fiddle on Fire | 1956 | $40 |

PAUSA

| ❏ 7034 | Doin' Things | 197? | $25 |

TOPS

| ❏ L923 [10] | Twilight on the Trail | 195? | $30 |

VANGUARD

| ❏ VSD-79405 | Jazz Violin | 197? | $25 |
| ❏ VSD-79396 | Joe Venuti in Milan | 197? | $25 |

YAZOO

| ❏ 1062 | Violin Jazz | 198? | $25 |

VENUTI, JOE/EDDIE LANG
Also see each artist's individual listings.
Albums
COLUMBIA

| ❏ C2L24 [M] | Swinging the Blues | 1965 | $25 |

— Red labels with "360 Sound Mono" on labels

| ❏ C2L24 [M] | Swinging the Blues | 1963 | $30 |

— Guaranteed High Fidelity" on labels

COLUMBIA SPECIAL PRODUCTS

| ❏ JC2L24 [M] | Swinging the Blues | 1975 | $35 |

— Reissue of C2L 24

X

| ❏ LVA-3036 [M] | Joe Venuti and Eddie Lang | 1955 | $50 |

VER PLANCK, BILLY
Trombonist and composer.
Albums
SAVOY

| ❏ MG-12101 [M] | Dancing Jazz | 1957 | $40 |
| ❏ MG-12121 [M] | Jazz for Playgirls | 1957 | $40 |

VER PLANCK, MARLENE
Female singer.
Albums
AUDIOPHILE

❏ AP-160	A New York Singer	1980	$25
❏ AP-169	A Warmer Place	1981	$25
❏ AP-186	I Like to Sing	1984	$25
❏ AP-138	Marlene Ver Planck Loves Johnny Mercer	197?	$25

Number	Title	Yr	NM
❑ AP-218	Marlene Ver Planck Sings Alec Wilder	1986	$25
❑ AP-235	Pure and Natural	1988	$25
❑ AP-121	You'd Better Love Me	197?	$25
MOUNTED			
❑ 108	A Breath of Fresh Air	1968	$35
❑ 114	This Happy Feeling	197?	$35
SAVOY			
❑ MG-12058 [M]	I Think of You with Every Breath I Take	1956	$100

—As "Marlene

VERGARI, MADELINE
Female singer.

Albums
SEA BREEZE			
❑ SB-108	This Is My Lucky Day	198?	$25

VERHEYEN, CARL
Guitarist.

Albums
CMG			
❑ CML-8012	No Borders	198?	$25

VERNON, MILLI
Female singer.

Albums
STORYVILLE			
❑ STLP-910 [M]	Introducing Milli Vernon	1956	$300

VERY SPECIAL ENVOY

Albums
ROULETTE			
❑ SR-42003	Very Special Envoy	1968	$25

VESALA, EDWARD
Drummer, composer and arranger.

Albums
ECM			
❑ 1088	Satu	197?	$30

VIBRATION SOCIETY, THE
Among the members: Steve Turre (trombone); Hilton Ruiz (piano).

Albums
STASH			
❑ ST-261	The Music of Rahsaan Roland Kirk	1986	$25

VICK, HAROLD
Tenor saxophone player.

Albums
BLUE NOTE			
❑ BST-84138 [S]	Steppin' Out	1963	$50

— With "New York, USA" address on label
❑ BST-84138 [S]	Steppin' Out	196?	$35

— With "A Division of Liberty Records" on label
MUSE			
❑ MR-5054	Commitment	197?	$30
RCA VICTOR			
❑ LPM-3761 [M]	Straight Up	1967	$25
❑ LSP-3761 [S]	Straight Up	1967	$35
❑ LPM-3677 [M]	The Caribbean Suite	1966	$35
❑ LSP-3677 [S]	The Caribbean Suite	1966	$25
STRATA-EAST			
❑ SES-7431	Don't Look Back	197?	$25

VIDEO ALL STARS, THE
Organized and led by Skip Martin. Some of the musicians were BOB COOPER; SHELLY MANNE; RED MITCHELL; and FRANK ROSOLINO.

Albums
SOMERSET			
❑ SF-8800 [M]	The Video All Stars Play TV Jazz Themes	1956	$120

VIENNA ART ORCHESTRA
Led and conducted by Mathias Ruegg.

Albums
HAT HUT			
❑ 1980/1	Concerto Piccolo	1980	$50
❑ 1999/2000	From No Time to Rag Time	1982	$50
❑ 2024	Perpetuum Mobile	1985	$35
❑ 1991/2	Suite for the Green Eighties	1981	$50
❑ 2005	The Minimalism of Erik Satie	1984	$35

VIG, TOMMY
Percussionist.

Albums
DISCOVERY			
❑ 780	Encounter with Time	197?	$25
DOBRE			
❑ 1015	1978	1978	$30
MILESTONE			
❑ MSP-9007	Sounds of the Seventies	1968	$25

VILLAGE STOMPERS, THE
Dixieland-style band from New York. Their hit was "Washington Square."

Albums
EPIC			
❑ LN24109 [M]	Around the World with the Village Stompers	1964	$60
❑ BN26109 [S]	Around the World with the Village Stompers	1964	$60
❑ LN24180 [M]	A Taste of Honey	1965	$60
❑ BN26180 [S]	A Taste of Honey	1965	$75
❑ LN24090 [M]	More Sounds of Washington Square	1964	$75
❑ BN26090 [S]	More Sounds of Washington Square	1964	$100
❑ LN24129 [M]	New Beat on Broadway!	1964	$60
❑ BN26129 [S]	New Beat on Broadway!	1964	$75
❑ LN24235 [M]	One More Time	1966	$60
❑ BN26235 [S]	One More Time	1966	$75
❑ LN24161 [M]	Some Folk, a Bit of Country and a Whole Lot of Dixie	1965	$60
❑ BN26161 [S]	Some Folk, a Bit of Country and a Whole Lot of Dixie	1965	$75
❑ LN24318 [M]	The Village Stompers' Greatest Hits	1967	$60
❑ BN26318 [S]	The Village Stompers' Greatest Hits	1967	$75
❑ LN24078 [M]	Washington Square	1963	$75
❑ BN26078 [S]	Washington Square	1963	$100

VILLEGAS
Full name: Enrique Mono Villegas. Pianist.

Albums
COLUMBIA			
❑ CL787 [M]	Introducing Villegas	1956	$30
❑ CL877 [M]	Very, Very Villegas	1956	$30

VINNEGAR, LEROY
Bass player.

Albums
CONTEMPORARY			
❑ C-3542 [M]	Leroy Walks!	1957	$250
❑ S-7003 [S]	Leroy Walks!	1959	$250
❑ S-7542 [S]	Leroy Walks!	197?	$30
❑ M-3608 [M]	Leroy Walks Again!	1962	$200
❑ S-7608 [S]	Leroy Walks Again!	1962	$200
FANTASY			
❑ OJC-160	Leroy Walks!	198?	$25
❑ OJC-454	Leroy Walks Again!	1990	$25
LEGEND			
❑ 1001	Glass of Water	197?	$35
PBR			
❑ 6	The Kid	197?	$30
STEREO RECORDS			
❑ S-7003 [S]	Leroy Walks!	1958	$60
VEE JAY			
❑ LP-2502 [M]	Jazz's Great Walker	1964	$30
❑ LPS-2502 [S]	Jazz's Great Walker	1964	$30

VINSON, EDDIE "CLEANHEAD"/ JIMMY WITHERSPOON
Also see each artist's individual listings.

Albums
KING			
❑ 634 [M]	Battle of the Blues, Volume 3	1960	$1500

VINSON, EDDIE "CLEANHEAD
Alto saxophone player and male singer.

Albums
BETHLEHEM			
❑ BCP-6036	Back in Town	1978	$35
❑ BCP-5005 [M]	Eddie "Cleanhead" Vinson Sings	1957	$250
BLUESWAY			
❑ BL-6007 [M]	Cherry Red	1967	$60
❑ BLS-6007 [S]	Cherry Red	1967	$60
CIRCLE			
❑ CLP-57	Kidney Stew	1983	$30
DELMARK			
❑ 631	Old Kidney Stew Is Fine	1980	$30
FLYING DUTCHMAN			
❑ 31-1012	You Can't Make Love Alone	197?	$35
KING			
❑ KS-1087	Cherry Red	1969	$60
MUSE			
❑ MR-5282	Cleanhead and Roomful of Blues	1982	$30
❑ MR-5243	Eddie "Cleanhead" Vinson and the Muse All-Stars: Hold It Right There	198?	$30
❑ MR-5208	Eddie "Cleanhead" Vinson and the Muse All-Stars: Live at Sandy's	1979	$30
❑ MR-5310	Eddie "Cleanhead" Vinson Sings the Blues	198?	$30
❑ MR-5116	The Clean Machine	1978	$35
PABLO			
❑ 2310866	I Want a Little Girl	198?	$30
REGGIES			
❑ 1000	Rollin' Over the Devil	1981	$30
RIVERSIDE			
❑ RLP-502 [M]	Back Door Blues	1965	$150
❑ RLS-9502 [S]	Back Door Blues	1965	$150

VIOLA, AL
Guitarist.

Albums
LEGEND			
❑ 1002	Alone Again	197?	$35
MODE			
❑ LP-121 [M]	Solo Guitar	1957	$80
PBR			
❑ 11	Prelude to a Kiss	197?	$30
❑ 7	Salutations F.S.	197?	$30

VISION

Albums
MUSIC IS MEDICINE			
❑ 9027	Vision	198?	$30

VISITORS, THE
Members: Earl Grubbs (soprano saxophone); Carl Grubbs (alto sax).

Albums
COBBLESTONE			
❑ 9010	Neptune	197?	$25
MUSE			
❑ MR-5024	In My Youth	197?	$30
❑ MR-5094	Motherland	1976	$30
❑ MR-5195	Neptune	197?	$25
❑ MR-5047	Rebirth	197?	$30

VITOUS, MIROSLAV
Bass player. Also see WEATHER REPORT.

Albums
ARISTA			
❑ AL4099	Majesty Music	197?	$25
ARISTA/FREEDOM			
❑ AF1040	Vitous	1976	$30
ATLANTIC			
❑ SD1622	Mountain in the Clouds	1972	$30
ECM			
❑ 1145	First Meeting	1979	$30
❑ 1185	Miroslav Vitous Group	198?	$30
EMBRYO			
❑ SD524	Infonite Search	1970	$35
WARNER BROS.			
❑ BS2925	Magical	1976	$25

VITRO, ROSEANNA
Female singer.
Albums

Number	Title	Yr	NM
SKYLINE			
❏ SKYP-1001	A Quiet Place	1987	$25
TEXAS ROSE			
❏ TRM-1001	Listen Here	1984	$25

VIZZUTTI, ALLEN
Trumpeter.
Albums

Number	Title	Yr	NM
BAINBRIDGE			
❏ 6246	Red Metal	198?	$25
HEADFIRST			
❏ 9700	Vizzutti	198?	$30

VOCAL JAZZ INCORPORATED
Albums

Number	Title	Yr	NM
GRAPEVINE			
❏ 3310	Vocal Jazz Incorporated	197?	$30

VOLLENWEIDER, ANDREAS
Harpist.
Albums

Number	Title	Yr	NM
CBS/FM			
❏ FM42255	Down to the Moon	1986	$25
❏ FM39963	White Winds	1985	$25
CBS MASTERWORKS			
❏ FM37793	…Behind the Gardens… Behind the Wall…Under the Tree…	1984	$25
❏ FM37827	Caverna Magica (…Under the Tree-In the Cave…)	1984	$25
COLUMBIA			
❏ OC45154	Dancing with the Lion	1989	$30

VON OHLEN, JOHN "THE BARON"
Drummer.
Albums

Number	Title	Yr	NM
CREATIVE WORLD			
❏ ST-3001	The Baron	197?	$25

VON SCHLIPPENBACH, ALEXANDER
Pianist.
Albums

Number	Title	Yr	NM
ENJA			
❏ 2012	Payan	197?	$35

VUCKOVICH, LARRY
Pianist, arranger and composer.
Albums

Number	Title	Yr	NM
INNER CITY			
❏ IC-1096	Blue Balkan	198?	$30
PALO ALTO			
❏ PA-8012	City Sounds	1981	$25

W

WACKER, FRED
Drummer and bandleader.
Albums

Number	Title	Yr	NM
CADET			
❏ LPS-4050 [S]	Fred Wacker Swings Cool	1966	$35
❏ LP-4050 [M]	Fred Wacker Swings Cool	1966	$30
DOLPHIN			
❏ 9 [M]	Freddy Wacker and His Windy City Seven	195?	$50

WADDELL, STEVE
Waddell (trombone, vocals) leads a trad jazz band called Creole Bells.
Albums

Number	Title	Yr	NM
STOMP OFF			
❏ SOS-1172	Frisco Comes to Melbourne	1987	$25

WADUD, ABDUL
Cellist.
Albums

Number	Title	Yr	NM
RED RECORD			
❏ VPA-147	Straight Ahead/Free at Last	198?	$30

WAGNER, LARRY
Albums

Number	Title	Yr	NM
A44			
❏ AP-501 [10]	Larry Wagner	1954	$60

WALCOTT, COLLIN
Sitar and tabla player, violinist, percussionist and male singer. Also see CODONA.
Albums

Number	Title	Yr	NM
ECM			
❏ 1062	Cloud	1976	$30
❏ 1096	Grazing	1977	$30

WALD, JERRY
Clarinetist and bandleader.
Albums

Number	Title	Yr	NM
KAPP			
❏ KL-1043 [M]	Listen to the Music of Jerry Wald	1956	$40
LION			
❏ L-70014 [M]	Tops in Pops -- Designed for Dancing	1958	$30

WALDEN, NARADA MICHAEL
Drummer, male singer and producer.
Albums

Number	Title	Yr	NM
ATLANTIC			
❏ SD19222	Awakening	1979	$25
❏ SD19351	Confidence	1981	$25
❏ SD19141	I Cry, I Smile	1978	$25
❏ SD19259	The Dance of Life	1979	$25
❏ SD19279	Victory	1980	$25
❏ 80058	You, Looking at Me	1982	$25
REPRISE			
❏ 25694	Divine Emotion	1988	$25
WARNER BROS.			
❏ 25176	The Nature of Things	1984	$25

WALDO, TERRY
Pianist and male singer. Also see WALDO'S GUTBUCKET SYNCOPATORS; WALDO'S RAGTIME ORCHESTRA.
Albums

Number	Title	Yr	NM
DIRTY SHAME			
❏ 1237	Snookums Rag	197?	$30
STOMP OFF			
❏ SOS-1120	Terry Waldo and the Gotham City Band	1987	$25
❏ SOS-1002	Wizard of the Keyboard	198?	$25

WALDO'S GUTBUCKET SYNCOPATORS
Also see TERRY WALDO.
Albums

Number	Title	Yr	NM
BLACKBIRD			
❏ 12009	Jazz in the Afternoon	197?	$30
❏ 6002	Ohio Theatre Concert	197?	$25
STOMP OFF			
❏ SOS-1001	Feelin' Devilish	198?	$25
❏ SOS-1036	Presents	198?	$25

WALDO'S RAGTIME ORCHESTRA
Also see TERRY WALDO.
Albums

Number	Title	Yr	NM
STOMP OFF			
❏ SOS-1007	Smiles and Chuckles	198?	$25
❏ SOS-1069	Spectacular Ragtime	198?	$25

WALDRON, MAL, AND GARY PEACOCK
Also see each artist's individual listings.
Albums

Number	Title	Yr	NM
CATALYST			
❏ 7906	First Encounter	197?	$30

WALDRON, MAL, AND STEVE LACY
Also see each artist's individual listings.
Albums

Number	Title	Yr	NM
HAT ART			
❏ 2038	Let's Call This	1987	$35
INNER CITY			
❏ IC-3010	One-upsmanship	197?	$30
SOUL NOTE			
❏ 121170	Sempre Amore	1990	$35

WALDRON, MAL
Pianist and composer. Also see THE PRESTIGE JAZZ QUARTET.
Albums

Number	Title	Yr	NM
ARISTA/FREEDOM			
❏ AF1013	Blues for Lady Day	1975	$30
❏ AF1042	Signals	1977	$30
BETHLEHEM			

Number	Title	Yr	NM
❏ BCP-6045 [M]	Left Alone	1960	$1200
—maroon label, deep groove			
❏ SBCP-6045 [S]	Left Alone	1960	$250
ENJA			
❏ 2004	Black Glory	197?	$35
❏ 2050	Hard Talk	197?	$35
❏ 3075	Mingus Lives	198?	$30
❏ 2034	Up Popped the Devil	197?	$35
❏ 4010	What It Is	198?	$30
FANTASY			
❏ OJC-132	Impressions	198?	$25
❏ OJC-611	Mal/1	1991	$30
❏ OJC-082	The Quest	198?	$25
INNER CITY			
❏ IC-3018	Moods	1979	$35
MUSE			
❏ MR-5305	Encounters	198?	$25
MUSIC MINUS ONE			
❏ 4005 [M]	Blue Drums	1961	$25
❏ 4007 [M]	For Pianists Only	1961	$25
❏ 1018 [M]	For Singers 'N Singer	1960	$25
❏ 175 [M]	Fun With Brushes	1960	$25
❏ 1017 [M]	Mal Waldron	1960	$25
❏ 1012 [M]	Moonglow and Stardust	1960	$25
❏ 1015 [M]	Music of Duke Ellington	1960	$25
❏ 1016 [M]	Music of McHugh	1960	$25
❏ 4008 [M]	They Laughed When I Sat Down to Play	1961	$25
NEW JAZZ			
❏ NJLP-8242 [M]	Impressions	1960	$150
—Purple label			
❏ NJLP-8242 [M]	Impressions	1965	$150
—Blue label, trident logo at right			
❏ NJLP-8201 [M]	Mal/3: Sounds	1958	$150
—Purple label			
❏ NJLP-8201 [M]	Mal/3: Sounds	1958	$200
—Yellow label			
❏ NJLP-8201 [M]	Mal/3: Sounds	1965	$150
—Blue label, trident logo at right			
❏ NJLP-8208 [M]	Mal/4: Trio	1958	$150
—Purple label			
❏ NJLP-8208 [M]	Mal/4: Trio	1965	$150
—Blue label, trident logo at right			
❏ NJLP-8269 [M]	The Quest	1962	$150
—Purple label			
❏ NJLP-8269 [M]	The Quest	1965	$150
—Blue label, trident logo at right			

George Wallington, *Jazz for the Carriage Trade*, Prestige PRLP-7032, **$800**.

George Wallington, *George Wallington Trio*, Progressive PLP 3001, 10-inch LP, **$500**.

George Wallington, *Variations*, Verve MGV-2017, **$200**.

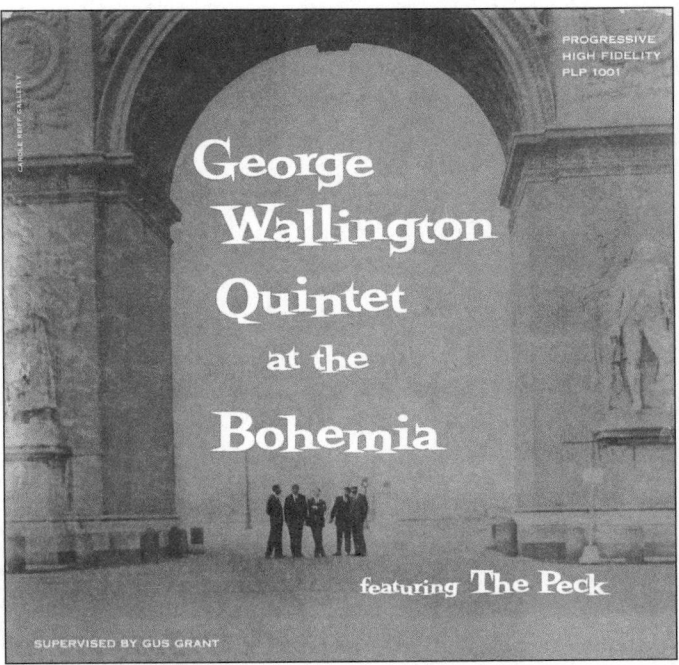

George Wallington, *George Wallington Quintet at the Bohemia*, Progressive PLP 1001, **$1,500**.

Number	Title	Yr	NM
PALO ALTO			
❑ PA-8014	One Entrance, Many Exits	1982	$25
PAULA			
❑ LPS-4000	Mal Waldron on the Steinway	197?	$30
PRESTIGE			
❑ 24107	After Hours	197?	$35
❑ PRLP-7090 [M]	Mal/1	1957	$300
❑ PRLP-7111 [M]	Mal/2	1957	$650
❑ 24068	Mal Waldron/1 and 2	197?	$35
❑ PRST-7579 [S]	The Quest	1969	$25
SOUL NOTE			
❑ 121118	The Go-Go -- Live at the Vilalge Gate	1989	$30
❑ 121148	The Seagulls of Kristiansund	1990	$35
❑ 121130	Update	1989	$30
STATUS			
❑ ST-8316 [M]	The Dealers	1965	$40
WEST 54			
❑ 8010	Live/Left Alone	1980	$30

WALI AND THE AFRO-CARAVAN

Albums

Number	Title	Yr	NM
SOLID STATE			
❑ SS-18065	Home Lost and Found	1969	$25

WALKER, KIT

Keyboard player, composer and producer.

Albums

Number	Title	Yr	NM
WINDHAM HILL			
❑ WH-0109	Dancing on the Edge of the World	1987	$25
❑ WH-0117	Fire in the Lake	1989	$30

WALKER, T-BONE

Guitarist and male singer. Earlier material appears in the Goldmine Standard Catalog of American Records.

Albums

Number	Title	Yr	NM
ATLANTIC			
❑ SD8256	T-Bone Blues	1970	$50
BLUE NOTE			
❑ BN-LA533-H2	Classics	1975	$50
BLUESTIME			
❑ 29010	Blue Rocks	1969	$60
❑ 29004	Everyday I Have the Blues	1968	$60
BLUESWAY			
❑ BLS-6058	Dirty Mistreater	1973	$35
❑ BLS-6014	Funky Town	1968	$60
BRUNSWICK			
❑ BL754126	The Truth	1968	$60
CAPITOL			
❑ H370 [10]	Classics in Jazz	1953	$1000
❑ T370 [M]	Classics in Jazz	1953	$350
DELMARK			
❑ D-633 [M]	I Want a Little Girl	1967	$40
❑ DS-633 [S]	I Want a Little Girl	1967	$100
IMPERIAL			
❑ LP-9146 [M]	I Get So Weary	1961	$300
❑ LP-9116 [M]	Singing the Blues	1960	$250
❑ LP-9098 [M]	T-Bone Walker Sings the Blues	1959	$300
MOSAIC			
❑ MR9-130	The Complete Recordings of T-Bone Walker 1940-1954	199?	$300

—Limited edition of 7,500

Number	Title	Yr	NM
REPRISE			
❑ 2RS6483	Very Rare	1973	$50
WET SOUL			
❑ 1002	Stormy Monday Blues	1967	$100

WALL, DAN

Organist.

Albums

Number	Title	Yr	NM
AUDIOPHILE			
❑ AP-143	Dan Wall Trio	198?	$25
PROGRESSIVE			
❑ PRO-7016	The Trio	198?	$30

WALLACE, BENNIE

Tenor saxophone player.

Albums

Number	Title	Yr	NM
AUDIOQUEST			
❑ AQLP-1017	The Old Songs	1993	$35
BLUE NOTE			
❑ BT-48014	Border Town	1988	$30
❑ BT-85107	Twilight Time	198?	$30
ENJA			
❑ 4028	Bennie Wallace and Chick Corea	1982	$30
❑ 4046	Big Jim's Tango	1982	$30
❑ 3091	Wallace Plays Monk	198?	$30
INNER CITY			
❑ IC-3025	Fourteen Bar Blues	1979	$30
❑ IC-3034	Live at the Public Theater	1979	$30

WALLER, FATS

Pianist, organist, male singer and composer.

Albums

Number	Title	Yr	NM
BIOGRAPH			
❑ 1002	Rare Piano Rolls	197?	$25
❑ 1005	Rare Piano Rolls, Volume 2	197?	$25
❑ 1015	Rare Piano Rolls, Volume 3	197?	$25
BLUEBIRD			
❑ AXM2-5518	Piano Solos	197?	$35
❑ AXM2-5511	The Complete Fats Waller, Volume 1	197?	$35
❑ AXM2-5575	The Complete Fats Waller, Volume 2	198?	$35
❑ AXM2-5583	The Complete Fats Waller, Volume 3	198?	$35
❑ 5905-1-RB	The Complete Fats Waller, Volume 4	1987	$35
❑ 6288-1-RB	The Joint Is Jumpin'	1987	$30
❑ 9983-1-RB	The Last Years: Fats Waller and His Rhythm, 1940-1943	198?	$30
BULLDOG			
❑ BDL-2004	20 Golden Pieces of Fats Waller	198?	$25
EVEREST ARCHIVE OF FOLK & JAZZ			
❑ 337	Ain't Misbehavin'	197?	$25
❑ 319	Fats Waller Plays Fats Waller	197?	$25
GIANTS OF JAZZ			
❑ GOJ-1035	Live, Volume 2	198?	$25
❑ GOJ-1029	Live at the Yacht Club	198?	$25
MUSICAL HERITAGE SOCIETY			
❑ MHS4937	Fats" Waller at the Organ	1981	$25
RCA VICTOR			
❑ LPV-562 [M]	African Ripples	1969	$25
❑ LPM-1246 [M]	Ain't Misbehavin'	1956	$50
❑ CPL1-2904	A Legendary Performer	1979	$25
❑ LPM-6000 [M]	Fats	1960	$80
❑ LPT-8 [10]	Fats Waller 1934-42	1951	$150
❑ LPV-516 [M]	Fats Waller '34/'35	1965	$25
❑ LPT-14 [10]	Fats Waller Favoites	1951	$150
❑ LPT-1001 [M]	Fats Waller Plays and Sings	1954	$80
❑ LPT-6001 [M]	Fats Waller Radio Transcriptions	1954	$120

— Boxed set with booklet

Number	Title	Yr	NM
❑ LPM-1502 [M]	Handful of Keys	1957	$50
❑ LPM-1503 [M]	One Never Knows, Do One?	1959	$50
❑ LPV-550 [M]	Smashing Thirds	1968	$25
❑ LPT-3040 [10]	Swingin' the Organ	1953	$120
❑ LPV-473 [M]	The Real Fats Waller	1965	$30
❑ LPV-525 [M]	Valentine Stomp	1966	$25
RIVERSIDE			
❑ RLP-1021 [10]	Fats Waller at the Organ	1953	$300
❑ RLP-1010 [10]	Rediscovered Fats Waller Piano Solos	1953	$300
❑ RLP 12-109 [M]	The Amazing Mr. Waller	1955	$300
❑ RLP-1022 [10]	The Amazing Mr. Waller Vol. 2: Jivin' with Fats	1953	$150

— Black vinyl

Number	Title	Yr	NM
❑ RLP-1022 [10]	The Amazing Mr. Waller Vol. 2: Jivin' with Fats	1953	$350

—Red vinyl

Number	Title	Yr	NM
❑ RLP 12-103 [M]	The Young Fats Waller	1955	$300
STANYAN			
❑ 10057	The Undiscovered Fats Waller	197?	$25
SWING			
❑ SW-8442/3	Fats Waller in London	198?	$30
TIME-LIFE			
❑ STL-J-15	Giants of Jazz	1980	$50
TRIP			
❑ 5042	A Legend in His Lifetime	197?	$30
❑ J-4	Fats Waller on the Air	197?	$25
X			
❑ LVA-3035 [10]	The Young Fats Waller	1955	$150

WALLINGTON, GEORGE

Pianist and composer. Also see JAMES MOODY; JIMMY RANEY.

Albums

Number	Title	Yr	NM
ATLANTIC			
❑ 1275 [M]	Knight Music	1958	$300
—Black label			
❑ SD1275 [S]	Knight Music	1958	$250
— Green label			
❑ 1275 [M]	Knight Music	1961	$150
— Multicolor label, white "fan" logo at right			
❑ SD1275 [S]	Knight Music	1961	$150
— Multicolor label, white "fan" logo at right			
BLUE NOTE			
❑ BLP-5045 [10]	George Wallington and His All-Star Band	1954	$1000
EAST-WEST			
❑ 4004 [M]	The Prestidigitator	1958	$250
FANTASY			
❑ OJC-1704	Jazz for the Carriage Trade	1985	$30
❑ OJC-1754	The George Wallington Trios	198?	$30
NEW JAZZ			
❑ NJLP-8207 [M]	The New York Scene	1965	$150
—Blue label, trident logo at right			
NORGRAN			
❑ MGN-1010 [M]	George Wallington with Strings	1954	$250
❑ MGN-24 [10]	The Workshop of the George Wallington Trio	1954	$200
PRESTIGE			
❑ PRST-7820	At Café Bohemia '55	1971	$35
❑ PRLP-7032 [M]	Jazz for the Carriage Trade	1956	$800
❑ P-24093	Our Delight	197?	$35
❑ PRLP-136 [10]	The George Wallington Trio	1952	$500
❑ PRLP-158 [10]	The George Wallington Trio, Volume 2	1953	$500
❑ PRST-7587 [R]	The George Wallington Trios	1968	$35
PROGRESSIVE			
❑ PRO-7001	The George Wallington Quintet at the Café Bohemia, 1955	198?	$25
❑ PLP-3001 [10]	The George Wallington Trio	1952	$500
SAVOY			
❑ MG-12122 [M]	Jazz at Hotchkiss	1957	$100
❑ MG-15037 [10]	The George Wallington Trio	1954	$150
❑ MG-12081 [M]	The George Wallington Trio	1956	$100
SAVOY JAZZ			
❑ SJL-1122	Dance of the Infidels	198?	$30
VERVE			
❑ MGV-2017 [M]	Variations	1956	$200

WALRATH, JACK

Trumpeter and composer.

Albums

Number	Title	Yr	NM
BLUE NOTE			
❑ BT-46905	Master of Suspense	1987	$30
❑ B1-91101	Neohippus	1989	$30
GATEMOUTH			
❑ 1002	Demons in Pursuit	1979	$30
MUSE			
❑ MR-5362	Wholly Trinity	198?	$25
RED RECORD			
❑ VPA-182	Live at Umbria Jazz Festival, Vol. 1	1986	$30
❑ VPA-186	Live at Umbria Jazz Festival, Vol. 2	1986	$30
STASH			
❑ ST-223	A Plea for Sanity	198?	$25
❑ ST-221	Revenge of the Fat People	198?	$25
STEEPLECHASE			
❑ SCS-1172	Jack Walrath in Europe	1982	$30

WALTER, CY

Pianist and composer.

Albums

Number	Title	Yr	NM
ATLANTIC			
❑ 1236 [M]	Rodgers Revisited	1956	$300
—Black label			
❑ 1236 [M]	Rodgers Revisited	1961	$150
— Multicolor label, white "fan" logo at right			
MGM			
❑ E-4393 [M]	Cy Walter at the Drake	1966	$30
❑ SE-4393 [S]	Cy Walter at the Drake	1966	$35
WESTMINSTER			
❑ WST-15054 [S]	Dry Martini, Please	195?	$30

Number	Title	Yr	NM

WALTON, CEDAR, AND HANK MOBLEY
Also see each artist's individual listings.
Albums
MUSE
| ❏ MR-5132 | Breakthrough | 197? | $30 |

WALTON, CEDAR
Pianist and composer.
Albums
CLEAN CUTS
| ❏ 704 | Solos | 1980 | $35 |

COBBLESTONE
| ❏ 9011 | Breakthrough | 197? | $35 |

COLUMBIA
| ❏ JC36285 | Soundscapes | 1980 | $25 |

FANTASY
| ❏ OJC-462 | Cedar! | 1990 | $25 |
| ❏ OJC-6002 | Cedar Walton Plays Cedar Walton | 1988 | $25 |

INNER CITY
| ❏ IC-6019 | Pit Inn | 198? | $30 |
| ❏ IC-6009 | The Pentagon | 197? | $30 |

MUSE
❏ MR-5010	A Night at Boomer's, Vol. 1	1973	$30
❏ MR-5022	A Night at Boomer's, Vol. 2	1973	$30
❏ MR-5059	Firm Roots	197?	$35
❏ MR-5244	The Maestro	1981	$25

PRESTIGE
❏ PRLP-7519 [M]	Cedar!	1967	$30
❏ PRST-7519 [S]	Cedar!	1967	$25
❏ PRST-7693	Soul Cycle	1970	$25
❏ PRST-7591	Spectrum	1968	$25
❏ PRST-7618	The Electric Boogaloo Song	1969	$25

RCA VICTOR
| ❏ APL1-1435 | Beyond Mobius | 1976 | $25 |

RED RECORD
| ❏ VPA-179 | Cedar's Blues | 1986 | $30 |

STEEPLECHASE
| ❏ SCS-1085 | First Set | 198? | $30 |
| ❏ SCS-1179 | Third Set | 198? | $30 |

WALTON, FRANK
Albums
DELMARK
| ❏ DS-436 | Reality | 197? | $25 |

WALTON, JON
Albums
GATEWAY
| ❏ 7006 | Jon Walton Swings Again | 1964 | $35 |

WANDERLEY, WALTER
Organist. His "Summer Samba" was a top-40 hit in 1966.
Albums
A&M
| ❏ SP-3022 | Moondreams | 1969 | $30 |
| ❏ SP-3018 | When It Was Done | 1969 | $30 |

CANYON
| ❏ 7711 | Return of the Original Sound | 196? | $30 |

GNP CRESCENDO
| ❏ GNPS-2137 | Brazil's Greatest Hits | 197? | $25 |
| ❏ GNPS-2142 | Perpetual Motion Love | 197? | $25 |

MGM LATINO SERIES
| ❏ LAT10010 [S] | Cheganca | 197? | $35 |
— Reissue of Verve V6-8676

PHILIPS
❏ PHM200227 [M]	Brazilian Blend	1967	$30
❏ PHS600227 [S]	Brazilian Blend	1967	$35
❏ PHM200233 [M]	Organ-ized	1967	$30
❏ PHS600233 [S]	Organ-ized	1967	$35

TOWER
❏ T5047 [M]	From Rio with Love	1966	$35
❏ ST5047 [S]	From Rio with Love	1966	$35
❏ T5058 [M]	Murmurio	1967	$35
❏ ST5058 [S]	Murmurio	1967	$35

VERVE
❏ V-8706 [M]	Batucada	1967	$50
❏ V6-8706 [S]	Batucada	1967	$35
❏ V-8676 [M]	Cheganca	1966	$35
❏ V6-8676 [S]	Cheganca	1966	$50
❏ V-8739 [M]	Kee-Ka-Roo	1967	$50
❏ V6-8739 [S]	Kee-Ka-Roo	1967	$35
❏ V6-8658 [S]	Rain Forest	1966	$50

WORLD PACIFIC
❏ WP-1866 [M]	Quarteto Bossamba	1967	$150
❏ ST-21866 [S]	Quarteto Bossamba	1967	$100
❏ WP-1856 [M]	Samba So!	1967	$150
❏ ST-21856 [S]	Samba So!	1967	$100

WAR
R&B group; the below album, which is not much different than their usual material, was, until the mid-1990s, the only gold record in the history of the Blue Note label.
Albums
BLUE NOTE
| ❏ BN-LA690-G [(2)] | Platinum Jazz | 1977 | $18 |

WARBURTON, PAUL, AND DALE BRUNING
Warburton is a bass player, Bruning is a guitarist.
Albums
CAPRI
| ❏ 7986 | Our Delight | 198? | $25 |

WARD, HELEN
Female singer.
Albums
COLUMBIA
| ❏ CL-6271 [10] | It's Been So Long | 1954 | $50 |

PAX
| ❏ 6004 [10] | Wild Bill Davison with Helen Ward | 1954 | $120 |

RCA VICTOR
| ❏ LPM-1464 [M] | With a Little Bit of Swing | 1957 | $40 |

WARDELL, ROOSEVELT
Pianist.
Albums
RIVERSIDE
| ❏ RLP-350 [M] | The Revelation | 1960 | $200 |
| ❏ RS-9350 [S] | The Revelation | 1960 | $200 |

WARE, DAVID S.
Tenor saxophone player and composer.
Albums
HAT HUT
| ❏ W | Birth of a Being | 1978 | $35 |

WARE, WILBUR; JOHNNY GRIFFIN; JUNIOR MANCE
Also see each artist's individual listings.
Albums
JAZZLAND
| ❏ JLP-12 [M] | The Chicago Cookers | 1960 | $40 |

WARE, WILBUR
Bass player.
Albums
FANTASY
| ❏ OJC-1737 | The Chicago Sound | 198? | $25 |

RIVERSIDE
| ❏ RLP 12-252 [M] | The Chicago Sound | 1957 | $400 |
| ❏ 6048 | The Chicago Sound | 197? | $30 |

WARREN, EARLE
Alto saxophone player and clarinetist.
Albums
MUSE
| ❏ MR-5312 | Earle Warren and the Count's Men | 198? | $25 |

WARREN, FRAN
Female singer.
Albums
AUDIO FIDELITY
| ❏ AFSD-6207 | Come Into My World | 1968 | $30 |

MGM
| ❏ E-3394 [M] | Mood Indigo | 1956 | $50 |
— Yellow label

VENISE

| ❏ 7019 [M] | Come Rain or Come Shine | 195? | $30 |
| ❏ 10019 [S] | Come Rain or Come Shine | 195? | $50 |
— Yellow vinyl

WARWICK
| ❏ W-2012 [M] | Something's Coming | 1960 | $30 |

WARREN, PETER
Bass player.
Albums
ENJA
| ❏ 2018 | Bass Is | 197? | $35 |

WASHINGTON, DINAH, AND BROOK BENTON
Benton is a male singer not otherwise listed in this book. Also see DINAH WASHINGTON.
Albums
MERCURY
❏ MG-20588 [M]	The Two of Us	1960	$100
❏ SR-60244 [S]	The Two of Us	1960	$100
❏ 824823-1	The Two of Us	1985	$20
— Reissue

WASHINGTON, DINAH
Earlier material appears in the Goldmine Standard Catalog of American Records. Female singer and occasional vibraphone player. Also see SARAH VAUGHAN.
Albums
ACCORD
| ❏ SN-7207 | Retrospective | 1982 | $25 |

COLLECTABLES
| ❏ COL-5200 | Golden Classics | 1989 | $25 |

DELMARK
| ❏ DL-451 | Mellow Mama | 1992 | $50 |

EMARCY
| ❏ MG-26032 [10] | After Hours with Miss D | 1954 | $300 |
| ❏ MG-36028 [M] | After Hours with Miss D | 1955 | $250 |
— Reissue of 26032
❏ MG-36065 [M]	Dinah	1956	$200
❏ MG-36000 [M]	Dinah Jams	1955	$250
❏ MG-36130 [M]	Dinah Washington Sings Bessie Smith	1957	$200
❏ MG-36119 [M]	Dinah Washington Sings Fats Waller	1957	$200
❏ MG-36011 [M]	For Those in Love	1955	$300
❏ 826453-1	In the Land of Hi-Fi	1986	$25
❏ EMS-2-401	Jazz Sides	197?	$35
❏ 824883-1	Jazz Sides	198?	$30
— Reissue of 401
❏ MG-36141 [M]	Newport '58	1958	$200
❏ 814184-1	Slick Chick (On the Mellow Side)	1983	$30
❏ MG-36104 [M]	The Swingin' Miss "D	1956	$200

EVEREST ARCHIVE OF FOLK & JAZZ
| ❏ FS-297 | Dinah Washington | 197? | $30 |

GRAND AWARD
| ❏ GA 33-318 [M] | Dinah Washington Sings the Blues | 1955 | $100 |
— Add 50% if removable wrap-around cover is still there

HARLEM HIT PARADE
| ❏ 8002 | Finer Dinah | 197? | $25 |

MERCURY
❏ MG-25140 [10]	Blazing Ballads	1952	$300
❏ MG-21119 [M]	Dinah Discovered	1967	$100
❏ SR-61119 [S]	Dinah Discovered	1967	$100
❏ MG-25060 [10]	Dinah Washington	1950	$250
❏ MG-20525 [M]	Dinah Washington Sings Fats Waller	1960	$150
— Reissue of EmArcy 36119
❏ SR-60202 [S]	Dinah Washington Sings Fats Waller	1960	$100
❏ MG-25138 [10]	Dynamic Dinah	1952	$250
❏ MG-20614 [M]	For Lonely Lovers	1961	$100
❏ SR-60614 [S]	For Lonely Lovers	1961	$100
❏ MG-20604 [M]	I Concentrate on You	1961	$100
❏ SR-60604 [S]	I Concentrate on You	1961	$100
❏ MG-20729 [M]	I Wanna Be Loved	1962	$100
❏ SR-60729 [S]	I Wanna Be Loved	1962	$100
❏ MG-20120 [M]	Music for Late Hours	1957	$150
❏ MG-20523 [M]	Newport '58	1960	$150
— Reissue of EmArcy 36141
❏ SR-60200 [S]	Newport '58	1960	$100
❏ MG-20638 [M]	September in the Rain	1961	$100
❏ SR-60638 [S]	September in the Rain	1961	$100
❏ MG-20661 [M]	Tears and Laughter	1962	$100
❏ SR-60661 [S]	Tears and Laughter	1962	$100
❏ MG-20247 [M]	The Best in Blues	1958	$150
❏ MG-20829 [M]	The Good Old Days	1963	$100

Number	Title	Yr	NM
❑ SR-60829 [S]	The Good Old Days	1963	$100
❑ MG-20439 [M]	The Queen	1959	$100
❑ SR-60111 [S]	The Queen	1959	$100
❑ MG-20928 [M]	The Queen and Quincy	1965	$100
❑ SR-60928 [S]	The Queen and Quincy	1965	$100
❑ MGP-2-103 [M]	This Is My Story	1963	$100
—Combines 20788 and 20789 in one package			
❑ MGP-2-603 [S]	This Is My Story	1963	$100
—Combines 60788 and 60789 in one package			
❑ MG-20788 [M]	This Is My Story -- Dinah Washington's Golden Hits, Volume 1	1963	$100
❑ SR-60788 [S]	This Is My Story -- Dinah Washington's Golden Hits, Volume 1	1963	$100
❑ 822867-1	This Is My Story -- Dinah Washington's Golden Hits, Volume 1	1985	$20
—Reissue			
❑ MG-20789 [M]	This Is My Story -- Dinah Washington's Golden Hits, Volume 2	1963	$100
❑ SR-60789 [S]	This Is My Story -- Dinah Washington's Golden Hits, Volume 2	1963	$100
❑ MG-20572 [M]	Unforgettable	1961	$100
❑ SR-60232 [S]	Unforgettable	1961	$100
❑ MG-20479 [M]	What a Diff'rence a Day Makes!	1960	$100
❑ SR-60158 [S]	What a Diff'rence a Day Makes!	1960	$100
❑ 818815-1	What a Diff'rence a Day Makes!	198?	$20
—Reissue			
PICKWICK			
❑ SPC-3043	Dinah Washington	196?	$25
❑ SPC-3536	Greatest Hits	197?	$25
❑ SPC-3230	I Don't Hurt Anymore	197?	$25
ROULETTE			
❑ R25253 [M]	A Stranger on Earth	1964	$35
❑ SR25253 [S]	A Stranger on Earth	1964	$50
❑ R25189 [M]	Back to the Blues	1963	$35
❑ SR25189 [S]	Back to the Blues	1963	$50
❑ R25170 [M]	Dinah '62	1962	$35
❑ SR25170 [S]	Dinah '62	1962	$50
❑ R25220 [M]	Dinah '63	1963	$35
❑ SR25220 [S]	Dinah '63	1963	$50
❑ R25269 [M]	Dinah Washington	1964	$35
❑ SR25269 [S]	Dinah Washington	1964	$50
❑ R25183 [M]	Drinking Again	1962	$35
❑ SR25183 [S]	Drinking Again	1962	$50
❑ RE104	Echoes of an Era	196?	$35
❑ R25180 [M]	In Love	1962	$35
❑ SR25180 [S]	In Love	1962	$50
❑ R25244 [M]	In Tribute	1963	$35
❑ SR25244 [S]	In Tribute	1963	$50
❑ RE117	Queen of the Blues	1971	$35
❑ R25289 [M]	The Best of Dinah Washington	1965	$35
❑ SR25289 [S]	The Best of Dinah Washington	1965	$50
❑ 42014	The Best of Dinah Washington	1968	$30
—Reissue of 25289			
❑ RE125	The Immortal Dinah Washington	1973	$35
TRIP			
❑ 5516	After Hours	1973	$25
❑ 5500	Dinah Jams	1973	$25
❑ 5556	Dinah Washington Sings Bessie Smith	197?	$30
❑ TLX9505	Sad Songs -- Blue Songs	197?	$30
❑ 5524	Tears and Laughter	1974	$25
❑ 5565	The Swingin' Miss D	197?	$25
VERVE			
❑ 818930-1	The Fats Waller Songbook	1984	$25
WING			
❑ MGW-12271 [M]	Dinah Washington Sings Fats Waller	1964	$30
❑ SRW-16271 [S]	Dinah Washington Sings Fats Waller	1964	$30
❑ MGW-12140 [M]	The Late Late Show	1963	$30
❑ SRW-16140 [S]	The Late Late Show	1963	$30
❑ PKW-2-121	The Original Queen of Soul	1969	$50
❑ SRW-16386	The Original Soul Sister	196?	$30

WASHINGTON, EARL
Pianist and composer.

Albums

JAZZ WORKSHOP			
❑ JWS-202 [M]	All Star Jazz	1963	$60
❑ JWS-213 [M]	Reflections	1963	$60

Number	Title	Yr	NM

WASHINGTON, ERNESTINE
Female singer best known in the gospel realm.

Albums

DISC			
❑ DLP-712 [10]	Ernestine Washington with Bunk Johnson	195?	$200

WASHINGTON, GROVER, JR.
Saxophone player. Very popular in the 1970s into the early 1980s, his biggest hit (with a vocal assist from R&B singer Bill Withers) was "Just the Two of Us." Earlier material appears in the Goldmine Standard Catalog of American Records.

Albums

COLUMBIA			
❑ C48530	Next Exit	1992	$50
❑ FC40510	Strawberry Moon	1987	$25
❑ OC44256	Then and Now	1988	$25
❑ OC45253	Time Out of Mind	1989	$25
ELEKTRA			
❑ 60415	Anthology of Grover Washington, Jr.	1985	$25
❑ 5E-562	Come Morning	1981	$25
❑ 60318	Inside Moves	1984	$25
❑ 6E-182	Paradise	1979	$25
❑ 60215	The Best Is Yet to Come	1982	$25
❑ 6E-305	Winelight	1980	$25
KUDU			
❑ KU-07	All the King's Horses	1972	$30
❑ KU-32	A Secret Place	1976	$30
❑ KU-24	Feels So Good	1975	$30
❑ KU-03	Inner City Blues	1971	$30
❑ KUX-3637	Live at the Bijou	1977	$35
❑ KU-20	Mister Magic	1975	$30
❑ KUX-1213	Soul Box	1973	$35
—The two records also were issued separately			
❑ KU-13	Soul Box, Vol. 2	1973	$30
MOTOWN			
❑ M5-186V1	All the King's Horses	1981	$20
—Reissue of Kudu 07			
❑ M9-961A2	Anthology	1981	$35
❑ M5-165V1	A Secret Place	1981	$20
—Reissue of Kudu 32			
❑ M9-940	Baddest	1980	$35
❑ M5-177V1	Feels So Good	1981	$20
—Reissue of Kudu 24			
❑ 5307ML	Greatest Performances	1983	$25
❑ 6126ML	Grover Washington Jr. at His Best	198?	$25
❑ M5-189V1	Inner City Blues	1981	$20
—Reissue of Kudu 03			
❑ M8-239	Live at the Bijou	1982	$30
—Reissue			
❑ M5-175V1	Mister Magic	1981	$20
—Reissue of Kudu 20			
❑ M7-910	Reed Seed	1978	$25
❑ 5236ML	Reed Seed	1982	$20
—Reissue of 910			
❑ M7-933	Skylarkin'	1980	$25
❑ 5232ML	Skylarkin'	1982	$20
—Reissue of 933			
❑ M5-184V1	Soul Box, Vol. 1	1981	$20
—Reissue of half of Kudu 1213			
❑ M5-187V1	Soul Box, Vol. 2	1981	$20
—Reissue of half of Kudu 1213			
NAUTILUS			
❑ NR-39	Winelight	1981	$100
—Audiophile vinyl			

WASHINGTON, TUTS
Pianist.

Albums

ROUNDER			
❑ 2041	New Orleans Piano Professor	198?	$25

WASHINGTON, TYRONE
Tenor saxophone player.

Albums

BLUE LABOR			
❑ 102	Do Right	197?	$25
BLUE NOTE			
❑ BST-84274	Natural Essence	1968	$30

Number	Title	Yr	NM

WASSERMAN, ROB
Bass player.

Albums

MCA			
❑ 42131	Duets	1988	$25
ROUNDER			
❑ 0179	Solo	198?	$30

WATANABE, KAZUMI
Guitarist.

Albums

GRAMAVISION			
❑ R1-79415	Kilowatt	1989	$30
❑ 18-8506	Mobo Club	1985	$25
❑ GR-8404	Mobo I	1984	$30
❑ GR-8406	Mobo II	1984	$30
❑ 18-8602	Mobo Splash	1986	$25
❑ 18-8706	Spice of Life	1987	$25
❑ 18-8810	Spice of Life Too	1988	$25
INNER CITY			
❑ IC-6071	Mermaid Boulevard	198?	$30

WATANABE, SADAO
Saxophone player (alto, soprano, sopranino) and flutist.

Albums

CATALYST			
❑ 7911	Sadao Watanabe and Charlie Mariano	197?	$30
COLUMBIA			
❑ C2X36818	How's Everything	1980	$30
❑ FC37433	Orange Express	1981	$25
ELEKTRA			
❑ 60748	Birds of Passage	1987	$25
❑ 60816	Elis	1988	$25
❑ 60906	Front Seat	1989	$30
❑ 60431	Maisha	1986	$25
❑ 60475	Parker's Mood	1986	$25
❑ 60803	Selected Sadao Watanabe	1989	$35
ELEKTRA/MUSICIAN			
❑ 60297	Fill Up the Night	1984	$25
❑ 60371	Rendezvous	1985	$25
INNER CITY			
❑ IC-6064	Autumn Blow	198?	$30
❑ IC-6061	Bird of Paradise	198?	$30
❑ IC-6062	California Shower	197?	$30
❑ IC-6015	I'm Old Fashioned	1978	$30
❑ IC-6060	Morning Island	198?	$30
❑ IC-6063	My Dear Life	198?	$30
VANGUARD			
❑ VSD-79344	Round Trip	1974	$30

WATERGATE SEVEN PLUS ONE, THE

Albums

STOMP OFF			
❑ SOS-1165	Ostrich Walk and Alligator Crawl	1989	$25

WATERS, BENNY
Saxophone player, clarinetist and male singer.

Albums

MUSE			
❑ MR-5340	From Paradise (Small's) to Shangri-La	1987	$25
STOMP OFF			
❑ SOS-1210	Memories of the Twenties	1991	$25

WATERS, ETHEL
Female singer, a pioneer of the blues.

Albums

BIOGRAPH			
❑ 12022	Ethel Waters 1921/24	197?	$25
❑ 12025	Jazzin' Babies Blues	197?	$25
COLUMBIA			
❑ KG31571	Her Greatest Years	1972	$35
❑ PG31571	Her Greatest Years	197?	$30
—Reissue with new prefix			
❑ CL2792 [M]	On Stage and Screen 1925-1940	1968	$35
GLENDALE			
❑ GL-9011	Ethel Waters	198?	$25
MERCURY			
❑ MG-20051 [M]	Ethel Waters	1954	$100
MONMOUTH-EVERGREEN			

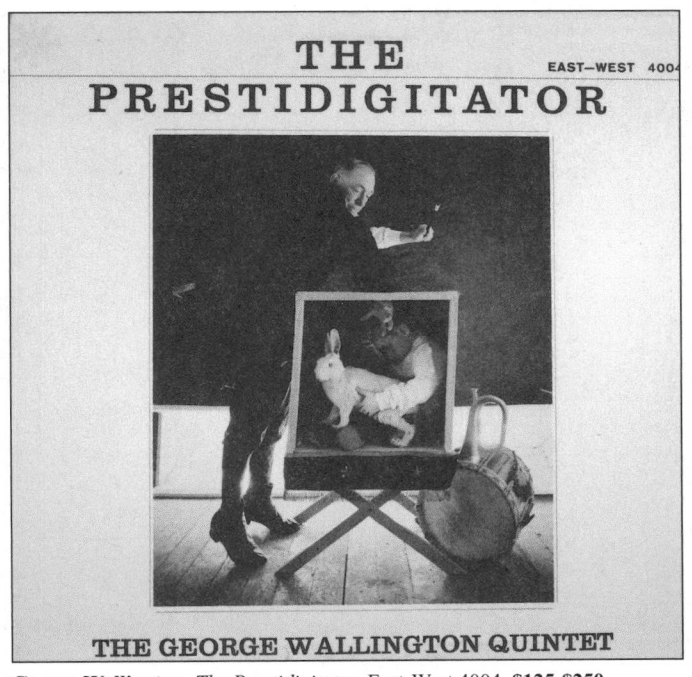

George Wallington, *The Prestidigitator*, East-West 4004, **$125-$250**.

Dinah Washington, *The Queen*, Mercury MG 20439, **$100**.

Dinah Washington, *Dinah Washington*, Mercury MG 25060, 10-inch LP, **$250**.

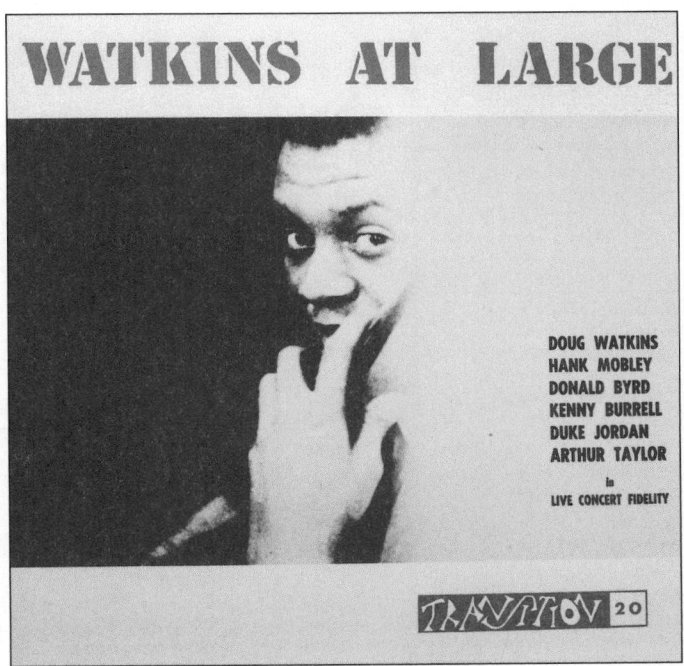

Doug Watkins, *Watkins at Large*, Transition TRLP-20, with booklet, **$1,200**.

Number	Title	Yr	NM
❑ 6812	Miss Ethel Waters	1968	$30
REMINGTON			
❑ RLP-1025 [10]	Ethel Waters	1950	$50
WORD			
❑ WST-8044	His Eye Is On the Sparrow	197?	$30
❑ W-3100LP [M]	His Eye Is On the Sparrow	196?	$35
X			
❑ LVA-1009 [M]	Ethel Waters	1955	$60

WATERS, KIM
Soprano and alto saxophone player.

Albums

Number	Title	Yr	NM
WARLOCK			
❑ WAR-2720	All Because of You	1990	$30
❑ WAR-2713	Sweet and Saxy	1989	$30

WATERS, PATTY
Female singer.

Albums

Number	Title	Yr	NM
ESP-DISK'			
❑ 1055 [S]	Patty Waters College Tour	1968	$100
❑ 1025 [M]	Patty Waters Sings	1966	$100
❑ S-1025 [S]	Patty Waters Sings	1966	$100

WATKINS, DOUG
Bass player. Also see THE MANHATTAN JAZZ ALL-STARS.

Albums

Number	Title	Yr	NM
NEW JAZZ			
❑ NJLP-8238 [M]	Soulnik	1960	$150
—Purple label			
❑ NJLP-8238 [M]	Soulnik	1965	$150
—Blue label, trident logo at right			
PHILIPS			
❑ PHM200001 [M]	French Horns for My Lady	1962	$25
❑ PHS600001 [S]	French Horns for My Lady	1962	$30
TRANSITION			
❑ TRLP-20 [M]	Watkins at Large	1956	$1200
—Deduct 1/10 if booklet is missing			

WATKINS, JOE
Drummer and occasional male singer.

Albums

Number	Title	Yr	NM
GHB			
❑ GHB-74	Last Will and Testament	197?	$25

WATKINS, JULIUS
French horn player and composer. Also see LES JAZZ MODES.

Albums

Number	Title	Yr	NM
BLUE NOTE			
❑ BLP-5053 [10]	Julius Watkins Sextet	1954	$400
❑ BLP-5064 [10]	Julius Watkins Sextet, Volume 2	1955	$400

WATKINS, MARY
Female singer

Albums

Number	Title	Yr	NM
OLIVIA			
❑ LF-919	Something Moving	1978	$25
PALO ALTO			
❑ PA-8030	Wind of Change	1982	$25
REDWOOD			
❑ R-8506	Spiritsong	1985	$25

WATKINS, MITCH
Guitarist.

Albums

Number	Title	Yr	NM
ENJA			
❑ R1-79603	Underneath It All	1989	$30

WATROUS, BILL
Trombonist.

Albums

Number	Title	Yr	NM
COLUMBIA			
❑ PC36977	Bill Watrous	1981	$30
❑ KC33090	Manhattan Wildlife Refuge	1974	$50
❑ PC33701	Tiger of San Pedro	1975	$50
FAMOUS DOOR			

Number	Title	Yr	NM
❑ HL-101	Bone Straight Ahead	1973	$60
❑ HL-136	Coronary Trombossa	1981	$25
❑ HL-134	I'll Play for You	1980	$30
❑ HL-137	La Zorra	1981	$25
❑ HL-144	Roarin' Back Into New York	1982	$25
❑ HL-147	The Best of Bill Watrous	198?	$25
❑ HL-127	Watrous in Hollywood	1979	$30
SOUNDWINGS			
❑ SW-2104	Reflections	1987	$35
❑ SW-2100	Someplace Else	1986	$35

WATSON, BOBBY
Alto saxophone player.

Albums

Number	Title	Yr	NM
BLUE NOTE			
❑ B1-90262	No Question About It	1988	$30
❑ B1-91915	The Inventor	1990	$30
RED RECORD			
❑ VPA-184	Appointment in Milano	1986	$30
❑ VPA-173	Perpetual Groove (Live in Europe)	198?	$30

WATT, TOMMY
British bandleader.

Albums

Number	Title	Yr	NM
BETHLEHEM			
❑ BCP-6052 [M]	Watts Cooking	1961	$200

WATTERS, LU
Trumpeter and bandleader. Also see BOB HELM; BUNK JOHNSON.

Albums

Number	Title	Yr	NM
CLEF			
❑ MGC-103 [10]	Lu Watters Jazz	1954	$0
—Canceled			
❑ MGC-503 [10]	Lu Watters Jazz	1954	$250
DOWN HOME			
❑ MGD-5 [10]	Lu Watters and His Yerba Buena Jazz Band	1955	$75
GOOD TIME JAZZ			
❑ L-12007 [M]	1942 Series	1955	$50
❑ L-12001 [M]	Dawn Club Favorites	1954	$40
❑ L-8 [10]	Lu Watters and His Yerba Buena Jazz Band	1952	$50
❑ L-12002 [M]	Originals and Ragtime	1954	$40
❑ L-0A [M]	San Francisco Style	195?	$60
❑ L-12003 [M]	Stomps, Etc. and the Blues	1954	$40
HOMESPUN			
❑ 103	Live Recordings from Hambone Kelly's	197?	$25
❑ 107	Lu Watters and the Yerba Buena Jazz Band, 1941	197?	$25
❑ 101	Lu Watters and the Yerba Buena Jazz Band, Vol. 1	197?	$25
❑ 102	Lu Watters and the Yerba Buena Jazz Band, Vol. 2	197?	$25
❑ 104	Lu Watters and the Yerba Buena Jazz Band, Vol. 4	197?	$30
❑ 106	Lu Watters and the Yerba Buena Jazz Band, Vol. 6	197?	$25
❑ 105	Memories of the Bodega Battle	197?	$30
MERCURY			
❑ MGC-510 [10]	Lu Watters and His Yerba Buena Jazz Band	1952	$200
❑ MG-35013 [10]	Lu Watters and the Yerba Buena Jazz Band	1950	$250
❑ MGC-103 [10]	Lu Watters and the Yerba Buena Jazz Band	1950	$200
❑ MGC-503 [10]	Lu Watters Jazz	1951	$200
RIVERSIDE			
❑ RLP-2513 [10]	Lu Watters 1947	1955	$300
❑ RLP 12-213 [M]	San Francisco Style	1956	$250
VERVE			
❑ MGV-1005 [M]	Lu Watters and His Yerba Buena Jazz Band	1956	$200
❑ V-1005 [M]	Lu Watters and His Yerba Buena Jazz Band	1961	$25

WATTERS, LU/SANTO PECORA
Also see each artist's individual listings.

Albums

Number	Title	Yr	NM
VERVE			
❑ MGV-1008 [M]	Dixieland Jamboree	1956	$150
❑ V-1008 [M]	Dixieland Jamboree	1961	$30

WATTS, CHARLIE
Drummer, best known as a member of The Rolling Stones.

Albums

Number	Title	Yr	NM
COLUMBIA			
❑ FC40570	The Charlie Watts Orchestra Live Fulham Town Hall	1986	$35
CONTINUUM			
❑ 19308	From One Charlie	1990	$60
—Box set with LP, book ("Ode to a High Flying Bird") and photo of Charlie Parker			

WATTS, ERNIE
Tenor saxophone player.

Albums

Number	Title	Yr	NM
ELEKTRA			
❑ 6E-285	Look in Your Heart	1980	$25
PACIFIC JAZZ			
❑ PJ-20155	Planet Love	1969	$30
QWEST			
❑ 25283	Musician	1985	$25
VAULT			
❑ LP-9011	Wonderbag	1968	$50

WATTS, MARZETTE
Bass clarinetist and soprano and alto saxophone player.

Albums

Number	Title	Yr	NM
ESP-DISK'			
❑ 1044 [S]	Marzette Watts and Company	1971	$75
SAVOY			
❑ MG-12193 [M]	The Marzette Watts Ensemble	1968	$25

WAVE, THE

Albums

Number	Title	Yr	NM
ATLANTIC			
❑ 81883	Second Wave	1988	$25

WAYLAND QUARTET, THE

Albums

Number	Title	Yr	NM
4 CORNERS OF THE WORLD			
❑ FCS-4249	Jazz Bach	1968	$35

WAYNE, CHUCK, AND JOE PUMA
Also see each artist's individual listings.

Albums

Number	Title	Yr	NM
CHOICE			
❑ 1004	Interactions	197?	$30

WAYNE, CHUCK
Guitarist.

Albums

Number	Title	Yr	NM
FOCUS			
❑ FL-333 [M]	Tapestry	1964	$30
❑ FS-333 [S]	Tapestry	1964	$30
PRESTIGE			
❑ PRLP-7367 [M]	Morning Mist	1965	$25
❑ PRST-7367 [S]	Morning Mist	1965	$30
PROGRESSIVE			
❑ 3003 [10]	The Chuck Wayne Quintet	1953	$200
❑ PRO-7008	Traveling	1976	$30
SAVOY			
❑ MG-12077 [M]	The Jazz Guitarist	1956	$50
SAVOY JAZZ			
❑ SJL-1144	Tasty Pudding	198?	$25
VIK			
❑ LX-1098 [M]	String Fever	1957	$50

WAYNE, FRANCES
Female singer.

Albums

Number	Title	Yr	NM
ATLANTIC			
❑ 1263 [M]	The Warm Sound	1957	$300
—Black label			
❑ 1263 [M]	The Warm Sound	1961	$150
—White "fan" logo at right of label			

Number	Title	Yr	NM
BRUNSWICK			
❏ BL54022 [M]	Frances Wayne	1958	$40
CORAL			
❏ CRL56019 [10]	Salute to Ethel Waters	195?	$60
EPIC			
❏ LN3222 [M]	Songs for My Man	1956	$100

WEATHER REPORT

Important fusion band whose "Birdland," from the Heavy Weather album, has become a jazz standard. The constants were JOE ZAWINUL (keyboards) and WAYNE SHORTER (saxophones). Among those who came and went were AIRTO; VICTOR BAILEY; ALPHONSE MOUZON; JACO PASTORIUS; and MIROSLAV VITOUS.

Albums

Number	Title	Yr	NM
ARC			
❏ PC236030	8:30	1979	$35
❏ JC35358	Mr. Gone	1978	$25
—Original issue; no bar code on cover			
❏ PC35358	Mr. Gone	1980	$20
—Budget-line reissue; bar code on back cover			
❏ JC36793	Night Passage	1980	$25
❏ PC36793	Night Passage	198?	$20
—Budget-line reissue			
❏ FC37616	Weather Report	1982	$25
❏ HC47616	Weather Report	1982	$40
—Half Speed Mastered" on cover			
❏ PC37616	Weather Report	198?	$20
—Budget-line reissue			
COLUMBIA			
❏ PC34099	Black Market	1976	$30
—No bar code on cover			
❏ PC34099	Black Market	1980	$20
—With bar code on cover			
❏ FC39147	Domino Theory	1984	$25
❏ PC34418	Heavy Weather	1977	$25
—No bar code on cover			
❏ PC34418	Heavy Weather	198?	$20
—Budget-line reissue; bar code on back cover			
❏ HC44418	Heavy Weather	198?	$40
—Half-Speed Mastered" on cover			
❏ KC31352	I Sing the Body Electric	1972	$30
—Original edition; no bar code on cover			
❏ PC31352	I Sing the Body Electric	1977	$20
—Reissue; with or without bar code on cover			
❏ KC32494	Mysterious Traveller	1974	$30
—Original issue; no bar code on cover			
❏ PC32494	Mysterious Traveller	1977	$20
—Reissue; with or without bar code on cover			
❏ CQ32494 [Q]	Mysterious Traveller	1974	$40
❏ FC38427	Procession	1983	$25
❏ FC39908	Sportin' Life	1985	$25
❏ KC32210	Sweetnighter	1973	$30
—Original edition; no bar code on back cover			
❏ PC32210	Sweetnighter	1977	$20
—Reissue with new prefix; with or without bar code on cover			
❏ PC33417	Tale Spinnin'	1975	$30
—Original edition; no bar code on cover			
❏ PC33417	Tale Spinnin'	1977	$20
—Budget-line reissue; with or without bar code			
❏ PCQ33417 [Q]	Tale Spinnin'	1975	$40
❏ FC40280	This Is This	1986	$30
❏ C30661	Weather Report	1971	$30
—Original edition; no bar code on cover			
❏ KC30661	Weather Report	1974	$25
—Reissue of C 30661			
❏ PC30661	Weather Report	1977	$20
—Reissue; with or without bar code on cover			

WEATHERBIRD JAZZ BAND, THE

Albums

Number	Title	Yr	NM
STOMP OFF			
❏ SOS-1034	Fireworks	198?	$25

WEATHERBURN, RONN

Pianist.

Albums

Number	Title	Yr	NM
STOMP OFF			
❏ SOS-1107	After the Ball	198?	$25

WEBB, ART

Flutist.

Albums

Number	Title	Yr	NM
ATLANTIC			
❏ SD18226	Love Eyes	197?	$25
❏ SD18212	Mr. Flute	197?	$25

WEBB, CHICK

Drummer and bandleader.

Albums

Number	Title	Yr	NM
CIRCLE			
❏ CLP-81	Stompin' at the Savoy, 1936	198?	$25
COLUMBIA			
❏ CL2639 [M]	The Immortal Chick Webb	1967	$30
❏ CS9439 [R]	The Immortal Chick Webb	1967	$30
DECCA			
❏ DL9223 [M]	Chick Webb 1937-39	1958	$120
❏ DL79223 [R]	Chick Webb 1937-39	1958	$120
FOLKWAYS			
❏ FJ-2818	Chick Webb Featuring Ella Fitzgerald	197?	$30
MCA			
❏ 1327	Ella Swings the Band	198?	$25
❏ 1303	Legend	198?	$25
❏ 1348	Princess of the Savoy	198?	$25
❏ 4107	The Best of Chick Webb	197?	$30
TRIP			
❏ J-5	On the Air	197?	$25

WEBB, GEORGE

One of the leaders of the British "trad jazz" movement.

Albums

Number	Title	Yr	NM
JAZZOLOGY			
❏ J-122	George Webb's Dixielanders	1985	$25

WEBB, ROGER

Albums

Number	Title	Yr	NM
SWAN			
❏ SLP-516 [M]	John, Paul and All That Jazz	1964	$30

WEBER, EBERHARD

Bass player.

Albums

Number	Title	Yr	NM
ECM			
❏ 1288	Chorus	1985	$30
❏ 1042	Colours of Chloe	197?	$35
❏ 1137	Fluid Rustle	1979	$25
❏ 1086	Following Morning	197?	$30
❏ 1231	Later That Evening	198?	$25
❏ 1188	Little Movements	1980	$25
❏ 1107	Silent Feet	1978	$25
❏ 1066	Yellow Fields	197?	$30

WEBER, HAJO, AND ULRICH INGENBOLD

Albums

Number	Title	Yr	NM
ECM			
❏ 1235	Winterreise	198?	$30

WEBSTER, BEN, AND COLEMAN HAWKINS

Also see each artist's individual listings.

Albums

Number	Title	Yr	NM
COLUMBIA			
❏ KG32774	Giants of the Tenor Saxophone	1973	$35
VERVE			
❏ VE-2-2520	Tenor Giants	197?	$35

WEBSTER, BEN, AND DON BYAS

Also see each artist's individual listings.

Albums

Number	Title	Yr	NM
COMMODORE			
❏ XFL-14938	Kings of Tenor Sax	198?	$25

WEBSTER, BEN, AND HARRY "SWEETS" EDISON

Also see each artist's individual listings.

Albums

Number	Title	Yr	NM
COLUMBIA			
❏ CL1891 [M]	Ben Webster-Sweets Edison	1962	$30
❏ CS8691 [S]	Ben Webster-Sweets Edison	1962	$30
COLUMBIA JAZZ MASTERPIECES			

Number	Title	Yr	NM
❏ CJ40853	Ben and "Sweets	1987	$25
COLUMBIA JAZZ ODYSSEY			
❏ PC37036	Ben and "Sweets	1981	$25

WEBSTER, BEN, AND JOE ZAWINUL

Also see each artist's individual listings.

Albums

Number	Title	Yr	NM
FANTASY			
❏ OJC-109	Soulmates	198?	$25
MILESTONE			
❏ 47056	Trav'lin' Light	198?	$30
RIVERSIDE			
❏ RLP-476 [M]	Soulmates	1964	$150
❏ RS-9476 [S]	Soulmates	1964	$150

WEBSTER, BEN

Tenor saxophone player, pianist and arranger. Also see DON BYAS; BENNY CARTER; COLEMAN HAWKINS; ILLINOIS JACQUET; GERRY MULLIGAN; ART TATUM.

Albums

Number	Title	Yr	NM
ABC IMPULSE!			
❏ AS-65 [S]	See You at the Fair	1968	$35
ANALOGUE PRODUCTIONS			
❏ AP 011	Ben Webster at the Renaissance	199?	$30
BASF			
❏ 20658 [B]	Ben Webster Meets Don Byas	197?	$150
BLACK LION			
❏ 111	Atmosphere for Lovers and Thieves	197?	$35
❏ 190	Duke's in Bed!	197?	$30
❏ 302	Saturday Montmartre	197?	$30
BRUNSWICK			
❏ BL58031 [10]	Tenor Sax Stylings	1952	$600
CIRCLE			
❏ 41	The Horn	198?	$25
❏ 42	The Horn -- Alternate Takes	198?	$25
DISCOVERY			
❏ 818	The Warm Moods of Ben Webster	198?	$25
EMARCY			
❏ MG-26006 [10]	The Big Tenor	1954	$300
❏ 824836-1	The Complete Ben Webster on EmArcy	1986	$35
ENJA			
❏ 2038	Live at Pio's	197?	$30
FIDELIO			
❏ FL-4475	Gentle Ben	198?	$25
IMPULSE!			
❏ A-65 [M]	See You at the Fair	1964	$120
❏ AS-65 [S]	See You at the Fair	1964	$120
INNER CITY			
❏ IC-2008	My Man	197?	$35
JAZZ ARCHIVES			
❏ JA-15	Ben: A Tribute to a Great Jazzman	198?	$25
❏ JA-35	Ben and the Boys	198?	$25
JAZZ MAN			
❏ 5007	Atmosphere for Lovers	198?	$25
NESSA			
❏ N-8	Did You Call?	197?	$25
NORGRAN			
❏ MGN-1039 [M]	Ben Webster Plays Music with Feeling	1955	$200
❏ MGN-1089 [M]	King of the Tenors	1956	$300
❏ MGN-1018 [M]	Music for Loving	1955	$300
❏ MGN-1001 [M]	The Consummate Artistry of Ben Webster	1954	$400
PRESTIGE			
❏ 24031	At Work in Europe	197?	$35
REPRISE			
❏ R-2001 [M]	The Warm Moods of Ben Webster	1961	$30
❏ R9-2001 [S]	The Warm Moods of Ben Webster	1961	$30
STEEPLECHASE			
❏ SCS-1008	My Man	198?	$30
TIME-LIFE			
❏ STL-J-21	Giants of Jazz	1981	$50
VERVE			
❏ VE-2-2530	Ballads	197?	$35
❏ 833550-1	Ballads	198?	$30
❏ MGV-8318 [M]	Ben Webster and Associates	1959	$150
❏ MGVS-6056 [S]	Ben Webster and Associates	1959	$150
❏ V-8318 [M]	Ben Webster and Associates	1961	$30

Number	Title	Yr	NM
❏ V6-8318 [S]	Ben Webster and Associates	1961	$25
❏ UMV-2515	Ben Webster and Associates	198?	$30
❏ MGV-8349 [M]	Ben Webster Meets Oscar Peterson	1959	$150
❏ V-8349 [M]	Ben Webster Meets Oscar Peterson	1961	$30
❏ V6-8349 [S]	Ben Webster Meets Oscar Peterson	1961	$25
❏ MGV-8020 [M]	King of the Tenors	1957	$150
❏ V-8020 [M]	King of the Tenors	1961	$30
❏ UMV-2081	King of the Tenors	198?	$25
❏ MGV-8130 [M]	Music with Feeling -- Ben Webster with Strings	1957	$150
❏ V-8130 [M]	Music with Feeling -- Ben Webster with Strings	1961	$30
❏ MGV-2026 [M]	Sophisticated Lady -- Ben Webster with Strings	1956	$200
❏ V-2026 [M]	Sophisticated Lady -- Ben Webster with Strings	1961	$30
❏ MGV-8274 [M]	Soulville	1958	$450
❏ V-8274 [M]	Soulville	1961	$30
❏ VE-2-2536	Soulville	1980	$35
❏ 833551-1	Soulville	198?	$30
❏ MGV-8359 [M]	The Soul of Ben Webster	1960	$50
❏ V-8359 [M]	The Soul of Ben Webster	1961	$30

WECHTER, JULIUS
Vibraphone player and percussionist. Best known for creating the Baja Marimba Band, which is outside the scope of this book.

Albums
JAZZ: WEST

Number	Title	Yr	NM
❏ LP-9 [M]	Linear Sketches	1956	$200

WEED, BUDDY
Pianist and bandleader.

Albums
COLUMBIA

Number	Title	Yr	NM
❏ CL6160 [10]	Piano Moods	1951	$50

CORAL

Number	Title	Yr	NM
❏ CRL57087 [M]	Piano Solos with Rhythm Accompaniment	1957	$40

WEEKS, ANSON
Bandleader and composer. Popular in the 1920s and early 1930s, he came out of retirement in the 1950s to make the series of albums for Fantasy.

Albums
FANTASY

Number	Title	Yr	NM
❏ 3306 [M]	Cruisin' with Anson	1960	$30
—Red vinyl			
❏ 3306 [M]	Cruisin' with Anson	1960	$35
—Black vinyl			
❏ 8051 [S]	Cruisin' with Anson	1960	$30
—Blue vinyl			
❏ 8051 [S]	Cruisin' with Anson	1960	$30
—Black vinyl			
❏ 3333 [M]	Dancin' at Anson's	1961	$15
—Black vinyl			
❏ 8076 [S]	Dancin' at Anson's	1961	$25
—Black vinyl			
❏ 3333 [M]	Dancin' at Anson's	1961	$60
—Red vinyl			
❏ 8076 [S]	Dancin' at Anson's	1961	$60
—Blue vinyl			
❏ 3258 [M]	Dancin' with Anson	1958	$30
—Red vinyl			
❏ 3258 [M]	Dancin' with Anson	1958	$35
—Black vinyl			
❏ 8001 [S]	Dancin' with Anson	1960	$30
—Blue vinyl			
❏ 8001 [S]	Dancin' with Anson	1960	$30
—Black vinyl			
❏ 8001 [S]	Dancin' with Anson	1960	$30
—Red vinyl (error pressing?)			
❏ 3269 [M]	Memories	1958	$30
—Red vinyl			
❏ 3269 [M]	Memories	1958	$35
—Black vinyl			
❏ 8006 [S]	Memories	1960	$30
—Blue vinyl			
❏ 8006 [S]	Memories	1960	$30
—Black vinyl			
❏ 3297 [M]	More Dancin' with Anson	1959	$30
—Red vinyl			

Number	Title	Yr	NM
❏ 3297 [M]	More Dancin' with Anson	1959	$35
—Black vinyl			
❏ 8043 [S]	More Dancin' with Anson	1960	$30
—Blue vinyl			
❏ 8043 [S]	More Dancin' with Anson	1960	$30
—Black vinyl			
❏ 3338 [M]	Old Favorites and New	1962	$30
—Red vinyl			
❏ 3338 [M]	Old Favorites and New	1962	$30
—Black vinyl			
❏ 8090 [S]	Old Favorites and New	1962	$30
—Blue vinyl			
❏ 8090 [S]	Old Favorites and New	1962	$35
—Black vinyl			
❏ 8355 [S]	Reminiscing at the Mark	1964	$35
❏ 3355 [M]	Reminiscing at the Mark	1964	$30

HINDSIGHT

Number	Title	Yr	NM
❏ HSR-146	Anson Weeks and the Hotel Mark Hopkins Orchestra 1932	198?	$25

WEIN, GEORGE
Pianist, male singer and bandleader.

Albums
ATLANTIC

Number	Title	Yr	NM
❏ SD1533 [S]	George Wein and the Newport All-Stars	1969	$35
❏ 1221 [M]	Wein, Women and Song	1955	$300
—Black label			
❏ 1221 [M]	Wein, Women and Song	1961	$150
—Multicolor label, white "fan" logo at right			

BETHLEHEM

Number	Title	Yr	NM
❏ BCP-6050 [M]	George Wein and the Storyville Sextet -- Jazz at the Modern	1960	$300
❏ SBCP-6050 [S]	George Wein and the Storyville Sextet -- Jazz at the Modern	1960	$300

COLUMBIA

Number	Title	Yr	NM
❏ CS9631 [S]	Alive and Well in Mexico	1968	$35

IMPULSE!

Number	Title	Yr	NM
❏ A-31 [M]	George Wein and the Newport All-Stars	1963	$200

RCA VICTOR

Number	Title	Yr	NM
❏ LPM-1332 [M]	The Magic Horn of George Wein	1956	$40

WEISBERG, TIM
Flutist. Earlier material appears in the Goldmine Standard Catalog of American Records.

Albums
A&M

Number	Title	Yr	NM
❏ SP-3045	Dreamspeaker	1973	$25
❏ SP-4352	Hurtwood Edge	1972	$30
❏ SP-4545	Listen to the City	1975	$25
❏ SP-4600	Live at Last!	1976	$25
❏ SP-4749	Smile/The Best of Tim Weisberg	1979	$25
❏ SP-3261	Smile/The Best of Tim Weisberg	198?	$20
—Budget-line reissue			
❏ SP-3039	Tim Weisberg	1971	$30
❏ SP-3658	Tim Weisberg 4	1974	$25
❏ SP-3121	Tim Weisberg 4	198?	$20
—Budget-line reissue			

CYPRESS

Number	Title	Yr	NM
❏ 661112-1	High Risk	1986	$25
❏ YL-0123	Outrageous Temptations	1989	$30

DESERT ROCK

Number	Title	Yr	NM
❏ DR-001	High Risk	1985	$35

LIBERTY

Number	Title	Yr	NM
❏ LN-10029	Rotations	198?	$20
—Budget-line reissue			
❏ LN-10031	The Tim Weisberg Band	198?	$20
—Budget-line reissue			

MCA

Number	Title	Yr	NM
❏ 3084	Night-Rider!	1979	$25
❏ 5125	Party of One	1980	$25
❏ 5245	Travelin' Light	1981	$25

UNITED ARTISTS

Number	Title	Yr	NM
❏ UA-LA857-H	Rotations	1978	$25
❏ UA-LA773-G	The Tim Weisberg Band	1977	$25

WELCH, ELISABETH
Female singer.

Albums
DRG

Number	Title	Yr	NM
❏ SL-5202	Where Have You Been?	1987	$25

WELDON, MAXINE
Female singer.

Albums
MAINSTREAM

Number	Title	Yr	NM
❏ MRL-339	Chilly Wind	1972	$30
❏ MRL-319	Right On	1971	$30

WELLS, DICKY
Trombonist. Also see REX STEWART.

Albums
FELSTED

Number	Title	Yr	NM
❏ FAJ-7006 [M]	Bones for the King	1958	$40
❏ SJA-2006 [S]	Bones for the King	1958	$40
❏ FAJ-7009 [M]	Trombone Four in Hand	1958	$40
❏ SJA-2009 [S]	Trombone Four in Hand	1958	$40

MASTER JAZZ

Number	Title	Yr	NM
❏ 8118	Trombone Four-in-Hand	197?	$30

PRESTIGE

Number	Title	Yr	NM
❏ PRST-7593 [R]	Dicky Wells in Pais 1937	1968	$30

UPTOWN

Number	Title	Yr	NM
❏ 277	Lonesome Road	198?	$25

WELLSTOOD, DICK, AND CLIFF JACKSON
Jackson is a pianist. Also see DICK WELLSTOOD.

Albums
SWINGVILLE

Number	Title	Yr	NM
❏ SVLP-2026 [M]	Uptown and Downtown	1961	$50
—Purple label			
❏ SVLP-2026 [M]	Uptown and Downtown	1965	$30
—Blue label, trident logo at right			

WELLSTOOD, DICK
Pianist.

Albums
CHIAROSCURO

Number	Title	Yr	NM
❏ 129	Dick Wellstood Featuring Kenny Davern	197?	$30
❏ 109	From Ragtime On	197?	$30
❏ 139	One-Man Jazz Machine	1975	$30

CLASSIC JAZZ

Number	Title	Yr	NM
❏ 10	From Dixie to Swing	197?	$25

JAZZOLOGY

Number	Title	Yr	NM
❏ JCE-73	Alone	197?	$25

PICKWICK

Number	Title	Yr	NM
❏ SPC-3376	Music from "The Sting	197?	$25
❏ SPC-3575	Ragtime Music of Scott Joplin	197?	$25

RIVERSIDE

Number	Title	Yr	NM
❏ RLP-2506 [10]	Dick Wellstood	1955	$300

WERNER, KEN
Pianist.

Albums
FINNADAR

Number	Title	Yr	NM
❏ SR9019	The Piano Music of Bix Beiderbecke - Duke Ellington - George Gershwin - James P. Johnson	1978	$25

INNER CITY

Number	Title	Yr	NM
❏ IC-3036	Beyond the Forest of Mirkwood	198?	$30

WESS, FRANK, AND JOHNNY COLES
Also see each artist's individual listings.

Albums
UPTOWN

Number	Title	Yr	NM
❏ 2714	Two at the Top	198?	$25

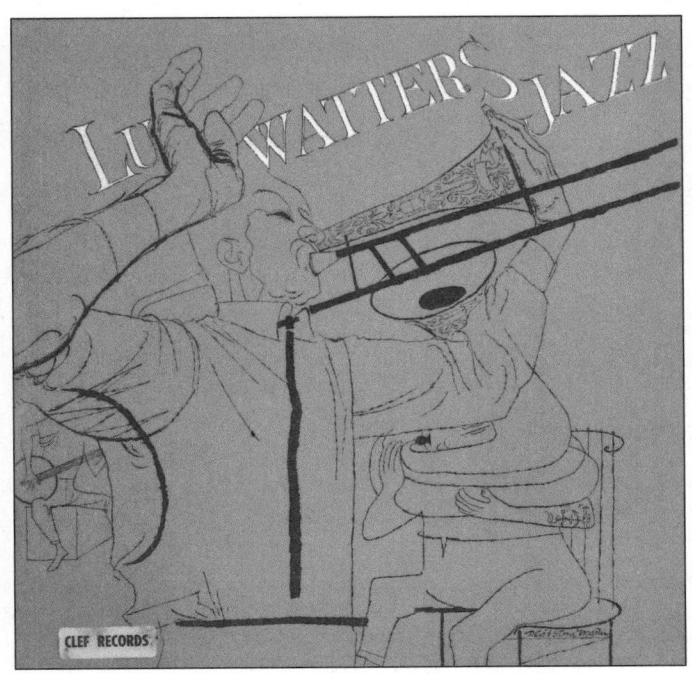

Lu Watters, *Lu Watters Jazz*, Clef MGC-503, 10-inch LP, **$250**.

Frances Wayne, *The Warm Sound*, Atlantic 1263, mono, **$300**.

Ben Webster, *Tenor Sax Stylings*, Brunswick BL 58031, **$600**.

Ben Webster, *Ben Webster Meets Oscar Peterson*, Verve MGV-8349, **$150**.

Number	Title	Yr	NM

WESS, FRANK, AND KENNY BURRELL
Also see each artist's individual listings.

Albums

PRESTIGE
❏ PRLP-7278 [M]	Steamin'	1963	$40
❏ PRST-7278 [R]	Steamin'	1963	$30

WESS, FRANK, AND THAD JONES
Also see each artist's individual listings.

Albums

NEW JAZZ
❏ NJLP-8310 [M]	Touche	1963	$0

—Canceled; reassigned to Status

STATUS
❏ ST-8310 [M]	Touche	1965	$40

WESS, FRANK
Tenor saxophone player and flutist.

Albums

COMMODORE
❏ FL-20032 [10]	Frank Wess	1952	$120
❏ FL-20031 [10]	Frank Wess Quintet	1952	$120

ENTERPRISE
❏ 5001	To Memphis	197?	$35

MAINSTREAM
❏ 56033 [M]	Award Winner	1965	$30
❏ S-6033 [R]	Award Winner	1965	$30

MOODSVILLE
❏ MVLP-8 [M]	Frank Wess Quartet	1960	$50

—Green label
❏ MVLP-8 [M]	Frank Wess Quartet	1965	$30

—Blue label, trident logo at right

PRESTIGE
❏ PRLP-7231 [M]	Southern Comfort	1962	$150
❏ PRST-7231 [S]	Southern Comfort	1962	$150
❏ PRLP-7266 [M]	Yo Ho! Poor You, Little Me	1963	$40
❏ PRST-7266 [S]	Yo Ho! Poor You, Little Me	1963	$100

PROGRESSIVE
❏ PRO-7057	Flute Juice	198?	$25

SAVOY
❏ MG-12022 [M]	Flutes and Reeds	1955	$80
❏ MG-12095 [M]	Jazz for Playboys	1956	$80
❏ MG-12072 [M]	North, South, East, Wess	1956	$80

SAVOY JAZZ
❏ SJL-1136	I Hear Ya Talkin'	198?	$25

STATUS
❏ ST-7266 [S]	Yo Ho! Poor You, Little Me	1965	$50

WEST, ALVY
Alto saxophone player and bandleader.

Albums

COLUMBIA
❏ CL6062 [10]	Alvy West and His Little Band	1949	$60

WEST END JAZZ BAND

Albums

STOMP OFF
❏ SOS-1085	Chicago Breakdown	1985	$25
❏ SOS-1042	Red Hot Chicago	1982	$25

WESTBROOK, FORREST
Keyboard player.

Albums

REVELATION
❏ REV-11	This Is Their Time, Oh Yes	197?	$35

WESTBROOK, MIKE
Pianist, composer and bandleader.

Albums

HAT ART
❏ 2031	Love for Sale	198?	$35
❏ 2012	On Duke's Birthday	1986	$35
❏ 2040	Westbrook-Rossini	1987	$35

WESTCHESTER WORKSHOP, THE
Among the members was trombonist EDDIE BERT.

Albums

UNIQUE
❏ LP-103 [M]	Unique Jazz	1957	$50

WESTON, PAUL
Pianist, bandleader and arranger whose Music for Dreaming, first issued on 78s in 1944, is considered the first "mood music" or "lounge" album.

Albums

CAPITOL
❏ T1153 [M]	Floatin' Like a Feather	1959	$80
❏ T1154 [M]	Music for Dreaming	1959	$50
❏ ST1154 [S]	Music for Dreaming	1959	$40
❏ H222 [10]	Music for Dreaming	195?	$75
❏ T1222 [M]	Music for Memories	1959	$50
❏ ST1222 [S]	Music for Memories	1959	$40
❏ T1563 [M]	Music for My Love	1961	$50
❏ ST1563 [S]	Music for My Love	1961	$40
❏ T1192 [M]	Music for the Fireside	1959	$40
❏ ST1192 [S]	Music for the Fireside	1959	$40
❏ ST-91212	Romantic Reflections	196?	$40

—Capitol Record Club exclusive

COLUMBIA
❏ CL572 [M]	Caribbean Cruise	1955	$40
❏ CL977 [M]	Crescent City	1956	$30
❏ CL1112 [M]	Hollywood	1958	$30
❏ CL794 [M]	Love Music from Hollywood	1956	$30
❏ CL693 [M]	Mood for 12	1955	$40
❏ CL909 [M]	Moonlight Becomes You	1956	$30
❏ CL879 [M]	Solo Mood	1956	$30
❏ CL6232 [10]	Whispers in the Dark	195?	$40

CORINTHIAN
❏ 107	Cinema Cameos	198?	$10
❏ 116	Crescent City	198?	$10
❏ 109	Easy Jazz	198?	$10

HARMONY
❏ KH31578	Paul Weston Plays Jerome Kern	1972	$12
❏ KH31603	Paul Weston Plays Jerome Kern, Vol. 2	1972	$12

WESTON, RANDY, AND CECIL PAYNE
Also see each artist's individual listings.

Albums

JAZZLAND
❏ JLP-13 [M]	Greenwich Village Jazz	1960	$40

WESTON, RANDY
Pianist and composer.

Albums

1750 ARCH
❏ 1802	Blue	198?	$30

ARISTA/FREEDOM
❏ AF1026	Berkshire Blues	197?	$30
❏ AF1014	Blues Africa	197?	$30
❏ AF1004	Carnival	1975	$30

ATLANTIC
❏ SD1609	African Cookbook	197?	$35

COLPIX
❏ CP-456 [M]	Highlight	1963	$30
❏ SCP-456 [S]	Highlight	1963	$60

CTI
❏ 6016	Blue Moses	197?	$30

DAWN
❏ DLP-1116 [M]	The Modern Art of Jazz	1957	$300

FANTASY
❏ OJC-1747	Jazz A La Bohemia	1990	$25

INNER CITY
❏ IC-1013	African Nite	1975	$30

JAZZLAND
❏ JLP-4 [M]	Zulu!	1960	$40

JUBILEE
❏ JLP-1060 [M]	Piano A La Mode	1957	$40

MILESTONE
❏ 7206	Zulu	197?	$35

PAUSA
❏ PR7017	Randy Weston	198?	$35

POLYDOR
❏ PD-5055	Tanjah	197?	$30

RIVERSIDE
❏ RLP-2508 [10]	Cole Porter in a Modern Mood	1954	$300
❏ RLP 12-203 [M]	Get Happy	1956	$250
❏ 6063	Get Happy	197?	$30
❏ RLP 12-232 [M]	Jazz A La Bohemia	1957	$250
❏ RLP-2515 [10]	Randy Weston Trio	1955	$300
❏ RLP 12-227 [M]	Randy Weston Trio and Solo	1957	$350
❏ 6208	Trio and Solo	198?	$25
❏ RLP 12-214 [M]	With These Hands…	1956	$250

ROULETTE
❏ R-65001 [M]	Uhuru Afrika	1960	$100
❏ RS-65001 [S]	Uhuru Afrika	1960	$120

TRIP
❏ 5033	Blues	197?	$25

UNITED ARTISTS
❏ UAL-4045 [M]	Destry Rides Again	1959	$40
❏ UAS-5045 [S]	Destry Rides Again	1959	$50
❏ UAL-4011 [M]	Little Niles	1959	$40
❏ UAS-5011 [S]	Little Niles	1959	$50
❏ UAL-4066 [M]	Live at the Five Spot	1959	$40
❏ UAS-5066 [S]	Live at the Five Spot	1959	$50

WESTON, RANDY/LEM WINCHESTER
Also see each artist's individual listings.

Albums

METROJAZZ
❏ SE-1005 [S]	New Faces at Newport	1958	$120

WETMORE, DICK
Violinist.

Albums

BETHLEHEM
❏ BCP-1035 [10]	Dick Wetmore	1955	$250

WETTLING, GEORGE
Drummer.

Albums

COLUMBIA
❏ CL2559 [10]	George Wettling's Jazz Band	1956	$50

—House Party Series" issue
❏ CL6189 [10]	George Wettling's Jazz Band	1951	$80

—Original issue

HARMONY
❏ HL7080 [M]	Dixieland in Hi-Fi	1957	$30

KAPP
❏ KL-1028 [M]	Jazz Trios	1956	$40
❏ KL-1005 [M]	Ragtime Duo	1955	$50

WEATHERS INDUSTRIES
❏ 5501 [M]	High Fidelity Rhythms	1955	$50

WGJB (WORLD'S GREATEST JAZZ BAND)
See YANK LAWSON AND BOB HAGGART; THE WORLD'S GREATEST JAZZ BAND.

WHALUM, KIRK
Player of various saxophones and keyboards.

Albums

COLUMBIA
❏ FC40812	And You Know That!	1988	$25
❏ FC40221	Floppy Disk	1985	$25
❏ FC45215	The Promise	1989	$30

WHEELER, CLARENCE
Saxophone player.

Albums

ATLANTIC
❏ SD1551	Doin' What We Wanna	1970	$100
❏ SD1636	New Chicago Blues	1973	$50
❏ SD1585	The Love I've Been Looking For	1971	$60

WHEELER, KENNY
Trumpeter, fluegel horn player and cornet player.

Albums

ECM
❏ 1156	Around 6	1979	$25
❏ 1102	Deer Wan	1977	$25
❏ 25000	Double, Double You	1984	$25
❏ 1069	Gnu High	197?	$30

Number	Title	Yr	NM

WHIGHAM, JIGGS
Trombonist.

Albums

PAUSA
| ❏ 7134 | Hope | 198? | $25 |

WHITCOMB, IAN, AND DICK ZIMMERMAN
Zimmerman is a pianist. Also see IAN WHITCOMB.

Albums

AUDIOPHILE
| ❏ AP-225 | Steppin' Out | 1987 | $25 |

STOMP OFF
| ❏ SOS-1017 | Don't Say Goodbye Miss Ragtime | 198? | $30 |
| ❏ SOS-1049 | My Wife Is Dancing Mad | 198? | $30 |

WHITCOMB, IAN
Male singer and accordion and ukulele player. Best known as a rock star during the British Invasion of the mid-1960s (his big hit was "You Turn Me On"), from the 1970s on he has been an aficionado of more traditional forms of music.

Albums

AUDIOPHILE
| ❏ AP-147 | At the Ragtime Ball | 1983 | $30 |
| ❏ AP-115 | Treasures of Tin Pan Alley | 197? | $30 |

FIRST AMERICAN
❏ 7704	Crooner Tunes	1979	$25
❏ 7789	In Hollywood	1982	$25
❏ 7751	Instrumentals	1981	$25
❏ 7725	Red Hot "Blue Heaven"	1980	$25
❏ 7729	The Rock and Roll Years	1981	$25

RHINO
| ❏ RNLP-127 | The Best of Ian Whitcomb (1964-1968) | 1986 | $20 |

SIERRA
| ❏ 8708 | Pianomelt | 1980 | $25 |

TOWER
❏ T5042 [M]	Mod, Mod Music Hall	1966	$35
❏ ST5042 [S]	Mod, Mod Music Hall	1966	$50
❏ ST5100	Sock Me Some Rock	1968	$50
❏ T5071 [M]	Yellow Underground	1967	$35
❏ ST5071 [S]	Yellow Underground	1967	$50
❏ T5004 [M]	You Turn Me On	1965	$60

| ❏ DT5004 [R] | You Turn Me On | 1965 | $50 |

UNITED ARTISTS
| ❏ UA-LA021-F | Under the Ragtime Moon | 1972 | $25 |

WHITE, ANDREW
Tenor saxophone player who, in addition to his vast catalog on his own label, has transcribed and published the solos of JOHN COLTRANE and ERIC DOLPHY in book form. Also see THE J.F.K. QUINTET.

Albums

ANDREW'S MUSIC
❏ AM-1	Andrew Nathaniel White III	197?	$50
❏ AM-33	Bionic Saxophone	1978	$30
❏ AM-14	Collage	1975	$35
❏ AM-25	Countdown	1976	$35
❏ AM-28	Ebony Glaze	1977	$30
❏ AM-2	Live at the "New Thing"	197?	$60
❏ AM-8	Live at the Foolery, Vol. 1	1975	$35
❏ AM-9	Live at the Foolery, Vol. 2	1975	$35
❏ AM-10	Live at the Foolery, Vol. 3	1975	$35
❏ AM-11	Live at the Foolery, Vol. 4	1975	$35

❏ AM-12	Live at the Foolery, Vol. 5	1975	$35
❏ AM-13	Live at the Foolery, Vol. 6	1975	$35
❏ AM-3	Live in Bucharest	197?	$50
❏ AM-31	Live in New York Vol. 1	1977	$30
❏ AM-32	Live in New York Vol. 2	1977	$30
❏ AM-15	Marathon' 75, Vol. 1	1976	$35
❏ AM-16	Marathon' 75, Vol. 2	1976	$35
❏ AM-17	Marathon' 75, Vol. 3	1976	$35
❏ AM-18	Marathon' 75, Vol. 4	1976	$35
❏ AM-19	Marathon' 75, Vol. 5	1976	$35
❏ AM-20	Marathon' 75, Vol. 6	1976	$35
❏ AM-21	Marathon' 75, Vol. 7	1976	$35
❏ AM-22	Marathon' 75, Vol. 8	1976	$35
❏ AM-23	Marathon' 75, Vol. 9	1976	$35
❏ AM-29	Miss Ann	1977	$35
❏ AM-5	Passion Flower	197?	$50
❏ AM-42	Profile: White	1983	$30
❏ AM-26	Red Top	1977	$30
❏ AM-36	Saxophonitis	1979	$30
❏ AM-30	Seven Giant Steps for Coltrane	1977	$35
❏ AM-6	Songs for a French Lady	197?	$50
❏ AM-24	Spotts, Maxine and Brown	1976	$35
❏ AM-7	Theme	1975	$50
❏ AM-27	Trinkle, Trinkle	1977	$30
❏ AM-37	Weekend at One Step, Vol. 1: Fonk Update	1980	$30
❏ AM-38	Weekend at One Step, Vol. 2: I Love Japan	1980	$30
❏ AM-39	Weekend at One Step, Vol. 3: Have Band Will Travel	1980	$30
❏ AM-4	Who Got Da Funk?	197?	$50

WHITE, BRIAN, AND ALAN GRESTY
White is a clarinetist and male singer; Gresty is a trumpeter.

Albums

JAZZOLOGY
| ❏ J-116 | Muggsy Remembered | 1988 | $25 |

WHITE, CARLA
Female singer.

Albums

STASH
| ❏ ST-237 | Andruline | 1983 | $25 |

WHITE, JOHN
Percussionist and male singer.

Albums

MAINSTREAM
| ❏ MRL-330 | John White | 1972 | $30 |

WHITE, KITTY
Female singer.

Albums

EMARCY
| ❏ MG-36020 [M] | A New Voice in Jazz | 1955 | $200 |
| ❏ MG-36068 [M] | Kitty White | 1955 | $200 |

PACIFICA
| ❏ PL-802 [10] | Kitty White | 1955 | $100 |

WHITE, LENNY
Drummer. His group Twennynine was popular in R&B circles in the early 1980s. Also see RETURN TO FOREVER.

Albums

ELEKTRA
❏ 6E-121	Adventures of Astral Pirates	1978	$25
❏ 6E-223	Best of Friends	1979	$25
❏ 5E-551	Just Like Dreamin'	1981	$25
❏ 6E-164	Streamline	1978	$25
❏ 6E-304	Twennynine with Lenny White	1980	$25

NEMPEROR
| ❏ SD441 | Big City | 1977 | $30 |
| ❏ SD435 | Venusian Summer | 1975 | $30 |

WHITE, MICHAEL
Violinist.

Albums

ABC IMPULSE!
❏ AS-9268	Father Music, Mother Dance	1974	$35
❏ ASD-9281	Go with the Flow	1974	$35
❏ AS-9241	Land of Spirit and Light	1973	$35
❏ AS-9221	Pneuma	197?	$35
❏ AS-9215	Spirit Dance	197?	$35

ELEKTRA
| ❏ 6E-138 | X Factor | 1978 | $25 |

WHITE, MIKE

Albums

SEECO
| ❏ SLP-442 [M] | Dixieland Jazz | 1960 | $125 |
| ❏ SLP-4420 [S] | Dixieland Jazz | 1960 | $125 |

WHITE, STEVE
Tenor saxophone player.

Albums

LIBERTY
| ❏ LJH-6006 [M] | Jazz Mad – The Unpredictable Steve White | 1955 | $60 |

WHITE EAGLE JAZZ BAND, THE

Albums

GHB
| ❏ GHB-204 | The White Eagle Jazz Band | 1988 | $25 |

WHITEMAN, PAUL, ORCHESTRA
New recordings of arrangements used by the original PAUL WHITEMAN Orchestra. Conceived by trumpeter Dick Sudhalter and conducted by Alan Cohen.

Albums

MONMOUTH-EVERGREEN
| ❏ 7078 | Live in '75 | 1975 | $30 |
| ❏ 7074 | The Classic Arrangements of Challis, Satterfield, Hayton | 197? | $30 |

WHITEMAN, PAUL
Violinist and bandleader. The self-proclaimed "King of Jazz," his band's highly polished and arranged music was a forerunner to the big bands. Many of his musicians were jazz greats (TOMMY DORSEY, BIX BEIDERBECKE and JOE VENUTI just to name several), and he helped make BING CROSBY a star.

Albums

CAPITOL
❏ T622 [M]	Classics in Jazz	1955	$80
❏ T1678 [M]	Paul Whiteman Conducts George Gershwin	1962	$50
❏ DT1678 [R]	Paul Whiteman Conducts George Gershwin	1962	$60

COLUMBIA
| ❏ CL2830 [M] | Paul Whiteman Featuring Bing Crosby | 1968 | $35 |

CORAL
| ❏ CRL57021 [M] | The Great Gershwin | 1955 | $40 |

GRAND AWARD
❏ GA-33-412 [M]	Cavalcade of Music	1960	$25
❏ GA-244SD [S]	Cavalcade of Music	1960	$30
❏ GA-33-351 [M]	Fiddle on Fire	195?	$30
❏ GA-33-502 [M]	Great Whiteman Hits	195?	$30
❏ GA-33-356 [M]	Hawaiian Magic	1958	$30
❏ GA-208SD [S]	Hawaiian Magic	1958	$30
❏ GA-33-901 [M]	Paul Whiteman/50th Anniversary	1956	$50
❏ GA-33-503 [M]	The Greatest Stars of My Life	195?	$50
— In red velvet jacket			
❏ GA-33-409 [M]	The Night I Played at 666 Fifth Ave.	1960	$25
❏ GA-241SD [S]	The Night I Played at 666 Fifth Ave.	1960	$30

MARK 56
| ❏ 761 [M] | Tribute to Gershwin 1936 | 197? | $30 |

RCA VICTOR
| ❏ LPV-555 [M] | Paul Whiteman, Volume 1 | 195? | $35 |

SUNBEAM
| ❏ 18 [M] | In Concert 1927-32 | 197? | $30 |

X
| ❏ LVA-3040 [10] | Paul Whiteman's Orchestra Featuring Bix Beiderbecke | 1955 | $80 |

WHITING, MARGARET, AND JIMMY WAKELY

Albums

HILLTOP
| ❏ JM-6053 [M] | I'll Never Slip Around Again | 196? | $30 |
| ❏ JS-6053 [R] | I'll Never Slip Around Again | 196? | $30 |

Number	Title	Yr	NM

WHITING, MARGARET
Female singer.

Albums

AUDIOPHILE

Number	Title	Yr	NM
❑ AP-173	Come a Little Closer	198?	$25
❑ AP-207	This Lady's in Love with You	1986	$25
❑ AP-152	Too Marvelous for Words	198?	$25

CAPITOL

❑ T685 [M]	For the Starry-Eyed	1955	$75
❑ T410 [M]	Love Songs	1954	$75
❑ H209 [10]	Margaret Whiting Sings Rodgers and Hart Songs	1950	$150
❑ H234 [10]	Songs	1950	$150
❑ H163 [10]	South Pacific	1950	$150

DOT

❑ DLP3072 [M]	Goin' Places	1957	$150
❑ DLP3337 [M]	Just a Dream	1960	$75
❑ DLP25337 [S]	Just a Dream	1960	$100
❑ DLP3113 [M]	Margaret	1958	$75
❑ DLP25113 [S]	Margaret	1958	$100
❑ DLP3176 [M]	Margaret Whiting's Great Hits	1959	$75
❑ DLP25176 [S]	Margaret Whiting's Great Hits	1959	$100
❑ DLP3235 [M]	Ten Top Hits	1960	$75
❑ DLP25235 [S]	Ten Top Hits	1960	$100

HAMILTON

❑ HLP143 [M]	My Ideal	196?	$30
❑ HLP12143 [S]	My Ideal	196?	$35

LONDON

❑ LL3510 [M]	Maggie Isn't Margaret Anymore	1967	$50
❑ PS510 [S]	Maggie Isn't Margaret Anymore	1967	$35
❑ PS527	Pop Country	1968	$35
❑ LL3497 [M]	The Wheel of Hurt	1967	$50
❑ PS497 [S]	The Wheel of Hurt	1967	$35

MGM

❑ E-4006 [M]	Past Midnight	1961	$35
❑ SE-4006 [S]	Past Midnight	1961	$50

VERVE

❑ V-4038 [M]	The Jerome Kern Song Book	1960	$100
❑ V6-4038 [S]	The Jerome Kern Song Book	1960	$100

WHITNEY, DAVE
Trumpeter and bandleader.

Albums

JAZZOLOGY

❑ J-68	Dave Whitney and His Jazz Band	198?	$25

WHYTE, RONNIE
Male singer and pianist.

Albums

AUDIOPHILE

❑ AP-127	I Love a Piano	198?	$25
❑ AP-151	Ronnie Whyte at the Conservatory	198?	$25
❑ AP-204	Soft Whyte	1986	$25

MONMOUTH-EVERGREEN

❑ 7088	New York State of Mind	197?	$30

PROGRESSIVE

❑ PRO-7075	Something Wonderful	1986	$25

WIDESPREAD DEPRESSION ORCHESTRA, THE
Swing revival band about 20 years ahead of its time. Members: Dean Nicyper (tenor sax); Michael Hashim (alto sax); David Lillie (baritone sax); Jordan Sandke (trumpet); Tim Atherton (trombone); Phil Flanagan (bass); John Ellis (drums); Michael LeDonne (piano); Jonny Holtzman (vocals).

Albums

STASH

❑ ST-206	Boogie in the Barnyard	1980	$25
❑ ST-203	Downtown Uproar	1979	$25
❑ ST-212	Time to Jump and Shout	198?	$25

WIDESPREAD JAZZ ORCHESTRA
Among the members were Dan Barrett (trombone).

Albums

ADELPHI

❑ 5015	Swing Is the Thing	198?	$25

COLUMBIA

❑ FC40034	Paris Blues	1985	$25

WIGGINS, GERALD
Pianist.

Albums

CHALLENGE

Number	Title	Yr	NM
❑ CHP-604 [M]	The King and I	1957	$60

CLASSIC JAZZ

❑ 117	Wig Is Here	198?	$25

CONTEMPORARY

❑ M-3595 [M]	Relax and Enjoy It	1961	$200
❑ S-7595 [S]	Relax and Enjoy It	1961	$200

DIG

❑ LP-102 [M]	Gerald Wiggins Trio	1956	$60

DISCOVERY

❑ DL-2003 [10]	Gerald Wiggins Trio	1953	$300

FANTASY

❑ OJC-173	Relax and Enjoy It	198?	$25

HIFI

❑ J-618 [M]	Wiggin' Out	1961	$60
❑ JS-618 [S]	Wiggin' Out	1961	$40

MOTIF

❑ 504 [M]	Reminiscin' with Wig	1956	$60

SPECIALTY

❑ SP-2101 [S]	Around the World	1969	$25

TAMPA

❑ TP-33 [M]	Gerald Wiggins Trio	1957	$200
—Colored vinyl			
❑ TP-33 [M]	Gerald Wiggins Trio	1958	$150
—Black vinyl			
❑ TP-1 [M]	The Loveliness of You	1957	$200
—Colored vinyl			
❑ TP-1 [M]	The Loveliness of You	1958	$150
—Black vinyl			

WIGGS, JOHNNY, AND RAYMOND BURKE
Also see each artist's individual listings.

Albums

S/D

❑ LP-1001 [10]	Chamber Jazz	1955	$60

WIGGS, JOHNNY
Cornet player.

Albums

GHB

❑ GHB-100	Johnny Wiggs and the New Orleans Kids	197?	$25

NEW ORLEANS

❑ 7206	Congo Square	197?	$25
❑ 47045	Congo Square	197?	$25

PARAMOUNT

❑ CJS107 [10]	Johnny Wiggs' New Orleanians Playing Jazz Favorites and Featuring Ray Burke	195?	$60

SOUTHLAND

❑ LP-200 [10]	Johnny Wiggs	1954	$50
❑ LP-200 [M]	Johnny Wiggs	195?	$30

WILBER, BOB, AND KENNY DAVERN
Also see each artist's individual listings.

Albums

WORLD JAZZ

❑ WJLP-S-5	Soprano Summit	1974	$35

WILBER, BOB, AND SCOTT HAMILTON
Also see each artist's individual listings.

Albums

CHIAROSCURO

❑ 171	Bob Wilber and Scott Hamilton	1977	$30

WILBER, BOB
Clarinetist and soprano saxophone player. Also see SOPRANO SUMMIT.

Albums

CIRCLE

❑ L-406 [10]	Bob Wilbur Jazz Band	1951	$50
❑ CLP-98	Reflections	1986	$25

CLASSIC JAZZ

❑ 9	Blowin' the Blues Away	197?	$25

Number	Title	Yr	NM
❑ 8	New Clarinet in Town	197?	$25
❑ 5	Spreadin' Joy	197?	$25

JAZZOLOGY

❑ J-44	Bob Wilber and His Famous Jazz Band	198?	$25
❑ J-141	Live at Bechet's	1986	$25
❑ J-142	Ode to Bechet	1986	$25

MONMOUTH-EVERGREEN

❑ 6917	The Music of Hoagy Carmichael	197?	$30

RIVERSIDE

❑ RLP-2501 [10]	Young Men With Horns	1952	$300

WILCOX, LARRY
Arranger.

Albums

COLUMBIA

❑ CL2147 [M]	Hot Rod Jazz	1964	$30
❑ CS8947 [S]	Hot Rod Jazz	1964	$40

COLUMBIA SPECIAL PRODUCTS

❑ CSRP8947 [M]	Hot Rod Jazz	196?	$25

WILDER, ALEC
Composer. Also see FRANK SINATRA.

Albums

COLUMBIA

❑ CL6181 [10]	Alec Wilder Octet	1951	$60

MERCURY

❑ MG25008 [10]	Alec Wilder and His Octet	1949	$100

WILDER, JOE
Trumpeter.

Albums

COLUMBIA

❑ CL1319 [M]	Jazz from "Peter Gunn	1959	$40
—Red and black label with six "eye" logos			
❑ CS8121 [S]	Jazz from "Peter Gunn	1959	$60
—Red and black label with six "eye" logos			
❑ CL1372 [M]	The Pretty Sound of Joe Wilder	1959	$50
—Red and black label with six "eye" logos			
❑ CS8173 [S]	The Pretty Sound of Joe Wilder	1959	$100
—Red and black label with six "eye" logos			

SAVOY

❑ MG-12063 [M]	'N' Wilder...	1956	$50

SAVOY JAZZ

❑ SJL-1191	Softly with Feeling	1989	$30

WILEY, LEE
Female singer. Also see ELLIS LARKINS.

Albums

ALLEGRO ELITE

❑ 4019 [10]	Lee Wiley Sings -- Lennie Tristano Plays	195?	$100

AUDIOPHILE

❑ AP-1	Lee Wiley Sings Ira and George Gershwin and Cole Porter	1986	$25
❑ AP-10	Lee Wiley Sings the Songs of Richard Rodgers and Lorenz Hart and Harold Arlen	1990	$30

COLUMBIA

❑ CL6216 [10]	Lee Wiley Sings Irving Berlin	1952	$100
❑ CL6215 [10]	Lee Wiley Sings Vincent Youmans	1952	$100
❑ CL6169 [10]	Night in Manhattan	1951	$120
❑ CL656 [M]	Night in Manhattan	1955	$80

JAZZTONE

❑ J-1248 [M]	The Songs of Rodgers and Hart -- Intimate Jazz	1956	$50

JJC

❑ M-2003 [M]	The Classic Interpretations of the Immortal Cole Porter	195?	$50
❑ M-2002 [M]	The One and Only Lee Wiley	195?	$50

LIBERTY MUSIC SHOP

❑ 1003 [10]	Cole Porter Songs by Lee Wiley	195?	$300
❑ 1004 [10]	George Gershwin Songs by Lee Wiley	195?	$300

Randy Weston, *Randy Weston Trio and Solo with Art Blakey*, Riverside RLP 12-227, **$350**.

Dick Wetmore, *Dick Wetmore*, Bethlehem BCP 1035, 10-inch LP, **$250**.

Lee Wiley, *West of the Moon*, RCA Victor LPM-1408, **$80**.

Lee Wiley, *Night in Manhattan*, Columbia CL 6169, 10-inch LP, **$120**.

Number	Title	Yr	NM

MONMOUTH-EVERGREEN
7041	Back Home Again	1971	$30
6807	Lee Wiley Plays Rodgers & Hart/Harold Arlen	1968	$35
7034	Lee Wiley Sings Gershwin & Porter	1970	$30

RCA VICTOR
| LPM-1566 [M] | Touch of the Blues | 1957 | $60 |
| LPM-1408 [M] | West of the Moon | 1957 | $80 |

RIC
| M-2002 [M] | The One and Only Lee Wiley | 1964 | $25 |
| S-2002 [S] | The One and Only Lee Wiley | 1964 | $30 |

STORYVILLE
| STLP-312 [10] | Lee Wiley Sings Rodgers and Hart | 1954 | $200 |

TOTEM
| 1021 | Lee Wiley on the Air | 197? | $25 |
| 1033 | Lee Wiley on the Air, Vol. 2 | 198? | $25 |

WILKERSON, DON
Tenor saxophone player.

Albums

BLUE NOTE
BLP-4121 [M]	Elder Don	1963	$60
BST-84121 [S]	Elder Don	1963	$40
— With "New York, USA" address on label			
BST-84121 [S]	Elder Don	1967	$25
— With "A Division of Liberty Records" on label			
BLP-4107 [M]	Preach, Brother!	1962	$60
BST-84107 [S]	Preach, Brother!	1962	$40
— With "New York, USA" address on label			
BST-84107 [S]	Preach, Brother!	1967	$25
— With "A Division of Liberty Records" on label			
BLP-4145 [M]	Shoutin'	1963	$60
BST-84145 [S]	Shoutin'	1963	$40
— With "New York, USA" address on label			
BST-84145 [S]	Shoutin'	1967	$25
— With "A Division of Liberty Records" on label			

RIVERSIDE
| RLP-332 [M] | Texas Twister | 1960 | $200 |
| RLP-1186 [S] | Texas Twister | 1960 | $200 |

WILKES, RAY
Guitarist.

Albums

INNER CITY
| IC-1051 | Dark Blue Man | 197? | $30 |

WILKINS, ERNIE
Tenor and alto saxophone player, arranger and composer. Also see KENNY CLARKE.

Albums

EVEREST
LPBR-5077 [M]	Here Comes the Swingin' Mr. Wilkins	1959	$30
SDBR-1077 [S]	Here Comes the Swingin' Mr. Wilkins	1959	$30
LPBR-5104 [M]	The Big New Band of the '60s	1960	$30
SDBR-1104 [S]	The Big New Band of the '60s	1960	$30

MAINSTREAM
| MRL-305 | Hard Mother Blues | 1971 | $35 |
| MRL-806 | Screaming Mothers | 197? | $35 |

RCA CAMDEN
| CAL-543 [M] | The Greatest Songs Ever Swung | 195? | $35 |

SAVOY
| MG-12044 [M] | Top Brass Featuring 5 Trumpets | 1955 | $75 |

STEEPLECHASE
| SCS-1190 | Montreux | 198? | $30 |

STORYVILLE
| 4051 | Ernie Wilkins and the Almost Big Band | 198? | $25 |

WILKINS, JACK
Guitarist.

Albums

CHIAROSCURO
| 156 | Merge | 1977 | $30 |

Number	Title	Yr	NM

| 185 | You Can't Live Without It | 1978 | $30 |

MAINSTREAM
| MRL-396 | Windows | 197? | $30 |

WILLETTE, BABY FACE
Organist.

Albums

ARGO
LP-749 [M]	Behind the 8-Ball	1965	$30
LPS-749 [S]	Behind the 8-Ball	1965	$30
LP-739 [M]	No Rock	1964	$30
LPS-739 [S]	No Rock	1964	$30

BLUE NOTE
BLP-4068 [M]	Face to Face	1961	$150
— With W. 63rd St. address on label			
BST-84068 [S]	Face to Face	1961	$120
— With W. 63rd St. address on label			
BLP-4068 [M]	Face to Face	1963	$60
— With "New York, USA" address on label			
BST-84068 [S]	Face to Face	1963	$25
— With "New York, USA" address on label			

BST-84068 [S]	Face to Face	1967	$35
— With "A Division of Liberty Records" on label			
BLP-4084 [M]	Stop and Listen	1962	$120
— With 61st St. address on label			
BST-84084 [S]	Stop and Listen	1962	$100
— With 61st St. address on label			
BLP-4084 [M]	Stop and Listen	1963	$60
— With "New York, USA" address on label			
BST-84084 [S]	Stop and Listen	1963	$25
— With "New York, USA" address on label			
BST-84084 [S]	Stop and Listen	1967	$35
— With "A Division of Liberty Records" on label			

CADET
LP-749 [M]	Behind the 8-Ball	1966	$30
LPS-749 [S]	Behind the 8-Ball	1966	$35
LPS-739 [S]	No Rock	1966	$35
LP-739 [M]	No Rock	1966	$30

WILLIAMS, AL

Albums

RENAISSANCE
| 9565 | Sandance | 1976 | $30 |

WILLIAMS, ANN
Female singer.

Albums

CHARLIE PARKER
| PLP-807 [M] | First Time Out | 1963 | $40 |
| PLP-807S [S] | First Time Out | 1963 | $40 |

WILLIAMS, ANTHONY
See TONY WILLIAMS.

WILLIAMS, BILLY
Male singer.

Albums

CORAL
| CRL57184 [M] | Billy Williams | 1957 | $120 |
| CRL57251 [M] | Half Sweet, Half Beat | 1959 | $100 |

Number	Title	Yr	NM

CRL757251 [S]	Half Sweet, Half Beat	1959	$150
CRL57343 [M]	The Billy Williams Revue	1960	$100
CRL757343 [S]	The Billy Williams Revue	1960	$120

MERCURY
| MG20317 [M] | Oh Yeah! | 1958 | $200 |

MGM
| E-3400 [M] | The Billy Williams Quartet | 1957 | $120 |

WING
| MGW-12131 [M] | Vote for Billy Williams | 1959 | $40 |

WILLIAMS, BUSTER
Bass player.

Albums

BUDDAH
| BDS-5728 | Dreams Come True | 1980 | $30 |

MUSE
MR-5171	Heartbeat	1979	$30
MR-5080	Pinnacle	1975	$30
MR-5101	Reflections	1976	$30

WILLIAMS, CHARLES
Alto saxophone player.

Albums

MAINSTREAM
| MRL-381 | Stickball | 1973 | $30 |
| MRL-345 | Trees and Grass and Things | 1972 | $30 |

WILLIAMS, CLARENCE
Pianist, male singer, bandleader, composer and arranger.

Albums

BIOGRAPH
| 12038 | Clarence Williams Volume 1, 1927-28 | 197? | $25 |
| 12006 | Clarence Williams Volume 1, 1927-29 | 197? | $25 |

MCA
| 1349 | Music Mann | 198? | $25 |

RIVERSIDE
| RLP-1033 [10] | Clarence Williams and Orchestra | 1954 | $300 |

WILLIAMS, CLAUDE
Violinist and male singer.

Albums

CLASSIC JAZZ
| 135 | Fiddler's Dream | 198? | $25 |

WILLIAMS, COOTIE
Trumpeter.

Albums

HALL OF FAME
| 602 | The Big Challenge | 197? | $25 |

JARO
| JAM-5001 [M] | Around Midnight | 1959 | $100 |
| JAS-8001 [S] | Around Midnight | 1959 | $80 |

MOODSVILLE
MVLP-27 [M]	The Solid Trumpet of Cootie Williams	1962	$50
— Green label			
MVLP-27 [M]	The Solid Trumpet of Cootie Williams	1965	$30
— Blue label, trident logo at right			

PHOENIX
| 1 | Cootie Williams Sextet and Orchestra | 197? | $25 |

RCA VICTOR
| LPM-1718 [M] | Cootie Williams in Hi-Fi | 1958 | $80 |
| LSP-1718 [S] | Cootie Williams in Stereo | 1958 | $150 |

WARWICK
| W-2027 [M] | Do Nothing Till You Hear From Me | 1960 | $40 |
| W-2027ST [S] | Do Nothing Till You Hear From Me | 1960 | $60 |

WILLIAMS, COOTIE/JIMMY PRESTON
Preston was a male singer and alto saxophone player. Also see COOTIE WILLIAMS.

Albums

ALLEGRO ELITE
| 4109 [10] | Rock 'N' Roll | 195? | $50 |

Number	Title	Yr	NM

WILLIAMS, DAVID "FAT MAN"
Pianist and male singer.
Albums
NEW ORLEANS
❏ 7204 | Apple Tree | 197? | $25

WILLIAMS, GEORGE
Composer, arranger and bandleader.
Albums
BRUNSWICK
❏ BL54020 [M] | The Fox | 1957 | $50
RCA VICTOR
❏ LPM-1301 [M] | Rhythm Was His Business | 1956 | $40
❏ LPM-1205 [M] | We Could Make Such Beautiful Music | 1956 | $40

WILLIAMS, GRIFF
Pianist and bandleader.
Albums
HINDSIGHT
❏ HSR-175 | Griff Williams and His Orchestra 1946-1951 | 198? | $25

WILLIAMS, HERBIE
Trumpeter.
Albums
WORKSHOP JAZZ
❏ WSJ-216 [M] | The Soul and Sound of Herbie Williams | 1963 | $60

WILLIAMS, JAMES
Pianist.
Albums
CONCORD JAZZ
❏ CJ-104 | Everything I Love | 1980 | $25
❏ CJ-140 | Images (Of the Things to Come) | 1981 | $25
❏ CJ-192 | The Arioso Touch | 1982 | $25
EMARCY
❏ 834368-1 | Magical Trio 2 | 1989 | $30
❏ 832859-1 | The Magical Trio | 1988 | $25
SUNNYSIDE
❏ SSC-1007 | Alter Ego | 1985 | $25
❏ SSC-1012 | Progress Report | 1986 | $25
ZIM
❏ 2005 | Flying Colors | 1977 | $30

WILLIAMS, JESSICA
Pianist.
Albums
ADELPHI
❏ 5005 | Portraits | 197? | $35
❏ 5003 | The Portal of Antrim | 1976 | $35
BLACKHAWK
❏ BKH-51301 | Nothin' But the Truth | 1986 | $25
CLEAN CUTS
❏ 703 | Orgonomic Music | 198? | $30
❏ 701 | Rivers of Memory | 1979 | $30
❏ 706 | Update | 1982 | $30

WILLIAMS, JOE
Male singer. Also see COUNT BASIE; SARAH VAUGHAN.
Albums
BLUEBIRD
❏ 6464-1-RB | The Overwhelming Joe Williams | 1988 | $25
BLUE NOTE
❏ BST-84355 | Worth Waiting For | 1970 | $35
DELOS
❏ DMS-4001 | Nothin' But the Blues | 1984 | $30
FANTASY
❏ F-9441 | Joe Williams Live | 1974 | $30
❏ OJC-438 | Joe Williams Live | 1990 | $25
FORUM
❏ F-9033 [M] | That Kind of Woman | 196? | $30
❏ SF-9033 [S] | That Kind of Woman | 196? | $35
JASS
❏ J-6 | Chains of Love | 198? | $25
PAUSA
❏ PR9008 | Worth Waiting For | 1982 | $25

RCA VICTOR
❏ LPM-2762 [M] | Joe Williams at Newport '63 | 1963 | $30
❏ LSP-2762 [S] | Joe Williams at Newport '63 | 1963 | $30
❏ LPM-2713 [M] | Jump for Joy | 1963 | $30
❏ LSP-2713 [S] | Jump for Joy | 1963 | $30
❏ LPM-2879 [M] | Me and the Blues | 1964 | $30
❏ LSP-2879 [S] | Me and the Blues | 1964 | $30
❏ LPM-3461 [M] | The Exciting Joe Williams | 1965 | $25
❏ LSP-3461 [S] | The Exciting Joe Williams | 1965 | $30
❏ LPM-3433 [M] | The Song Is You | 1965 | $25
❏ LSP-3433 [S] | The Song Is You | 1965 | $30
REGENT
❏ MG-6002 [M] | Everyday | 1956 | $50
ROULETTE
❏ R-52005 [M] | A Man Ain't Supposed to Cry | 1958 | $30
❏ SR-52005 [S] | A Man Ain't Supposed to Cry | 1958 | $40
❏ SR-42016 | A Man Ain't Supposed to Cry | 1968 | $35
❏ R-52071 [M] | Have a Good Time with Joe Williams | 1961 | $30
❏ SR-52071 [S] | Have a Good Time with Joe Williams | 1961 | $40
❏ R-52030 [M] | Joe Williams Sings About You! | 1959 | $30
❏ SR-52030 [S] | Joe Williams Sings About You! | 1959 | $40
❏ R-52105 [M] | New Kind of Love | 1964 | $30
❏ SR-52105 [S] | New Kind of Love | 1964 | $30
❏ R-52102 [M] | One Is a Lonesome Number | 1963 | $30
❏ SR-52102 [S] | One Is a Lonesome Number | 1963 | $30
❏ R-52066 [M] | Sentimental and Melancholy | 1961 | $30
❏ SR-52066 [S] | Sentimental and Melancholy | 1961 | $40
❏ R-52085 [M] | Swingin' Night at Birdland | 1962 | $30
❏ SR-52085 [S] | Swingin' Night at Birdland | 1962 | $30
❏ R-52039 [M] | That Kind of Woman | 1960 | $30
❏ SR-52039 [S] | That Kind of Woman | 1960 | $40
❏ R-52069 [M] | Together | 1961 | $30
❏ SR-52069 [S] | Together | 1961 | $40
— With Harry "Sweets" Edison
SAVOY
❏ MG-12216 [M] | Joe Williams Sings | 196? | $35
— Reissue of Regent LP
SAVOY JAZZ
❏ SJL-1140 | Everyday I Have the Blues | 198? | $25
SHEBA
❏ 102 | Heart and Soul | 197? | $30
SOLID STATE
❏ SM-17008 [M] | Presenting Joe Williams and the Jazz Orchestra | 1967 | $30
❏ SS-18008 [S] | Presenting Joe Williams and the Jazz Orchestra | 1967 | $25
❏ SS-18015 [S] | Something Old, New and Blue | 1968 | $25
TEMPONIC
❏ 29561 | With Love | 197? | $35
VERVE
❏ 833236-1 | Every Night | 1987 | $25
❏ 837932-1 | In Good Company | 1989 | $30

WILLIAMS, JOHN
Bass player.
Albums
EMARCY
❏ MG-26047 [10] | John Williams | 1955 | $200
❏ MG-36061 [M] | John Williams Trio | 1956 | $200

WILLIAMS, JOHN TOWNER
Pianist, composer and arranger. This is the John Williams who became famous for his film scores and as conductor of the Boston Pops Orchestra.
Albums
BETHLEHEM
❏ BCP-6025 [M] | World on a String | 1958 | $200

WILLIAMS, KEITH
Trumpeter, arranger and bandleader.
Albums
EDISON INTERNATIONAL
❏ SDP-501 [S] | Big Band Jazz Themes | 1960 | $30
❏ 501 [M] | Big Band Jazz Themes | 1960 | $25
LIBERTY
❏ LRP-3040 [M] | The Dazzling Sound | 1957 | $30

WILLIAMS, MARY LOU, AND CECIL TAYLOR
Also see each artist's individual listings.
Albums
PABLO LIVE
❏ 2620108 | Embraced | 1978 | $35

WILLIAMS, MARY LOU, AND DON BYAS
Also see each artist's individual listings.
Albums
GNP CRESCENDO
❏ GNP-9030 | Mary Lou Williams and Don Byas | 197? | $25

WILLIAMS, MARY LOU, AND DON BYAS/ BUCK CLAYTON AND ALIX COMBELLE
Combelle played tenor saxophone. Also see DON BYAS; BUCK CLAYTON; MARY LOU WILLIAMS.
Albums
STORYVILLE
❏ STLP-906 [M] | Messin' 'Round in Montmarte | 1956 | $50

WILLIAMS, MARY LOU
Pianist and composer. Also see BARBARA CARROLL; AL HAIG; ART TATUM.
Albums
ASCH
❏ ALP-345 [10] | Mary Lou Williams Trio | 1950 | $200
ATLANTIC
❏ ALR-114 [10] | Piano Panorama, Volume 2 | 1951 | $250
AUDIOPHILE
❏ AP-8 [M] | Roll 'Em | 1988 | $25
CHIAROSCURO
❏ 103 | From the Heart | 197? | $30
❏ 146 | Live at the Cookery | 197? | $30
CIRCLE
❏ 412 [10] | Piano Contempo | 1951 | $120
CONCERT HALL JAZZ
❏ 1007 [10] | A Keyboard History | 1955 | $60
CONTEMPORARY
❏ C-2507 [10] | Piano '53 | 1953 | $250
EMARCY
❏ MG-26033 [10] | Mary Lou | 1954 | $200
FOLKWAYS
❏ FS-2860 [M] | History of Jazz | 197? | $30
❏ FS-32843 [R] | Mary Lou Williams | 196? | $30
❏ FS-2843 [M] | Mary Lou Williams | 196? | $40
❏ FP-32 [10] | Rehearsal -- Jazz Session/ Footnotes to Jazz, Vol. 3 | 1951 | $120
❏ FJ-2966 | The Asch Recordings 1944-1947 | 197? | $35
❏ FJ-32844 | Zodiac Suite | 196? | $30
GNP CRESCENDO
❏ GNPS-9029 | Mary Lou Williams in London | 198? | $25
INNER CITY
❏ IC-2043 | Free Spirits | 197? | $35
JAZZTONE
❏ J-1206 [M] | A Keyboard History | 1955 | $50
KING
❏ 295-85 [10] | Progressive Piano Stylings | 1953 | $150
MARY
❏ 32843 [M] | Black Christ of the Andes | 1964 | $30
❏ 32843 [S] | Black Christ of the Andes | 1964 | $30
❏ 101 | Black Christ of the Andes | 197? | $35
— Reissue with new number
❏ 102 | Mary Lou's Mass | 197? | $35
❏ 282489 [M] | Music for Peace | 1964 | $30
❏ 282489 [S] | Music for Peace | 1964 | $30
❏ 103 | Zoning | 1974 | $35
PABLO
❏ 2310819 | My Mama Pinned a Rose | 1978 | $30
❏ 2405412 | The Best of Mary Lou Williams | 198? | $25
PABLO LIVE
❏ 2308218 | Solo Recital/Montreux Jazz Festival 1978 | 1979 | $30
STEEPLECHASE
❏ SCS-1043 | Free Spirits | 198? | $30
STINSON
❏ SLP-29 [10] | Jazz Variation | 1950 | $150
❏ SLP-24 [M] | Mary Lou Williams | 195? | $30
❏ SLP-24 [10] | Mary Lou Williams | 1950 | $150

WILLIAMS, MARY LOU/JUTTA HIPP
Also see each artist's individual listings.
Albums
SAVOY JAZZ
❏ SJL-1202 | First Ladies of Jazz | 1990 | $30

Number	Title	Yr	NM

WILLIAMS, MARY LOU/RALPH BURNS
Also see each artist's individual listings.
Albums
JAZZTONE

| ❏ J-1255 [M] | Composers -- Pianists | 1956 | $40 |

WILLIAMS, NORMAN
Alto saxophone player. Known as "Bishop."
Albums
THERESA

❏ 105	One for Bird	1980	$30
❏ 101	The Bishop	1979	$30
❏ 102	The Bishop's Bag	1979	$30

WILLIAMS, PATRICK
Composer, arranger and conductor.
Albums
ALLEGIANCE

| ❏ AV-443 | Dreams and Themes | 1985 | $25 |
— *Reissue of PCM album*
CAPITOL
| ❏ ST-11242 | Threshold | 1974 | $25 |
COLUMBIA
| ❏ JC36318 | An American Concerto | 1979 | $25 |
PAUSA
| ❏ 7060 | Theme | 1980 | $25 |
PCM
| ❏ PAA1001 | Dreams and Themes | 1984 | $30 |
SOUNDWINGS
| ❏ SW-2103 | 10th Avenue | 1987 | $25 |
| ❏ SW-2107 | Threshold | 1988 | $25 |

WILLIAMS, RICHARD
Trumpeter, fluegel horn player and composer.
Albums
BARNABY

| ❏ BR-5014 | New Horn in Town | 197? | $25 |
CANDID
| ❏ CD-8003 [M] | New Horn in Town | 1960 | $40 |
| ❏ CS-9003 [S] | New Horn in Town | 1960 | $50 |

WILLIAMS, ROD
Pianist.
Albums
MUSE

| ❏ MR-5380 | Hanging in the Balance | 198? | $25 |

WILLIAMS, TONY (2)
Drummer. Not to be confused with the Tony Williams who was one of the lead voices in the R&B group The Platters in the 1950s and early 1960s.
Albums
BLUE NOTE

❏ BT-48494	Angel Street	1988	$30
❏ BT-85138	Civilization	1987	$30
❏ BT-85119	Foreign Intrigue	198?	$30
❏ BLP-4180 [M]	Life Time	1964	$60
❏ BST-84180 [S]	Life Time	1964	$30
— *With "New York, USA" address on label*
| ❏ BST-84180 [S] | Life Time | 1967 | $35 |
— *With "A Division of Liberty Records" on label*
❏ B1-93170	Native Heart	1990	$30
❏ BLP-4216 [M]	Spring	1965	$60
❏ BST-84216 [S]	Spring	1965	$30
— *With "New York, USA" address on label*
| ❏ BST-84216 [S] | Spring | 1967 | $35 |
— *With "A Division of Liberty Records" on label*
| ❏ BST-84216 [S] | Spring | 1985 | $25 |
— *The Finest in Jazz Since 1939" reissue*
COLUMBIA
| ❏ PC33836 | Believe It | 1975 | $25 |
| ❏ HC45705 | Joy of Flying | 198? | $50 |
— *Half-speed mastered edition*
❏ JC35705	Joy of Flying	1979	$25
❏ PC34263	Million Dollar Legs	1976	$25
❏ JC36397	The Best of Tony Williams	1980	$25
POLYDOR
❏ PD-4065	Ego	197?	$30
❏ 25-3001	Emergency	1969	$50
❏ PD-4017	Emergency, Vol. 1	197?	$30
❏ PD-5040	The Old Bum's Rush	1973	$30

Number	Title	Yr	NM
❏ PD-4021	Turn It Over	197?	$30

VERVE
| ❏ VE-2-2541 | Once in a Lifetime | 198? | $30 |

WILLIAMS, VALDO
Pianist.
Albums
SAVOY

| ❏ MG-12188 [M] | New Advanced Jazz | 1967 | $30 |

WILLIAMSON, CLAUDE
Pianist.
Albums
BETHLEHEM

| ❏ BCP-54 [M] | Claude Williamson | 1956 | $200 |
| ❏ BCP-69 [M] | 'Round Midnight | 1957 | $250 |
CAPITOL
❏ H6502 [10]	Claude Williamson	1954	$200
❏ H6511 [10]	Keys West	1955	$200
❏ T6511 [M]	Keys West	1956	$150
— *Turquoise label*
CONTRACT
| ❏ 15003 [M] | Theatre Party | 196? | $30 |
| ❏ 15001 [M] | The Fabulous Claude Williamson Trio | 196? | $30 |
CRITERION
| ❏ 601 [M] | Claude Williamson Mulls the Mulligan Scene | 1958 | $80 |
DISCOVERY
| ❏ 862 | La Fiesta | 198? | $25 |
INTERPLAY
❏ 7708	Holography	1977	$30
❏ 7727	La Fiesta	1979	$30
❏ 7717	New Departure	1978	$30

WILLIAMSON, STU
Trumpeter and valve trombonist.
Albums
BETHLEHEM

❏ BCP-55 [M]	Stu Williamson	1956	$250
❏ BCP-1024 [10]	Stu Williamson Plays	1955	$250
❏ BCP-31 [M]	Stu Williamson Plays	1955	$250

WILLIS, LARRY
Pianist.
Albums
GROOVE MERCHANT

| ❏ 514 | Inenr Crisis | 197? | $35 |

WILLIS, PETE
Albums
CIRCLE

| ❏ C-45 | The One and Only Pete Willis | 1982 | $25 |
PROGRESSIVE
| ❏ PRO-7013 | The One and Only Pete Willis | 198? | $25 |

WILLS, BOB
Bandleader, composer and fiddler. Founded "The Texas Playboys," among the earliest purveyors of the melding of jazz and country music known as "Western swing."
Albums
ANTONES

| ❏ 6000 [10] | Old Time Favorites | 195? | $500 |
— *Fan club release*
| ❏ 6010 [10] | Old Time Favorites | 195? | $500 |
— *Fan club release*
CAPITOL
| ❏ SKBB-11550 | Bob Wills and His Texas Playboys in Concert | 1976 | $25 |
COLUMBIA
| ❏ KG32416 | Anthology | 1973 | $25 |
| ❏ CL9003 [10] | Bob Wills Round-Up | 1949 | $300 |
DECCA
| ❏ DL8727 [M] | Bob Wills and His Texas Playboys | 1957 | $150 |
— *Black label, silver print*

Number	Title	Yr	NM
❏ DL8727 [M]	Bob Wills and His Texas Playboys	1961	$40
— *Black label with color bars*
| ❏ DL78727 [R] | Bob Wills and His Texas Playboys | 196? | $25 |
| ❏ DL5562 [10] | Dance-O-Rama #2 | 1955 | $300 |
DELTA
| ❏ DLP-1149 | Bob Wills and His Texas Playboys On Stage | 1982 | $12 |
HARMONY
| ❏ HL7036 [M] | Bob Wills Special | 1957 | $40 |
— *Maroon label*
| ❏ HL7036 [M] | Bob Wills Special | 196? | $25 |
— *Black label*
| ❏ HL7304 [M] | The Best of Bob Wills | 1963 | $30 |
| ❏ HL7345 [M] | The Great Bob Wills | 1965 | $25 |
KAPP
❏ KS-3639	Bob Wills in Person	1970	$25
❏ KL-1506 [M]	From the Heart of Texas	1966	$25
❏ KS-3506 [S]	From the Heart of Texas	1966	$30
❏ KL-1542 [M]	Here's That Man Again	1968	$50
— *Mono is white label promo only; in stereo cover with "Mono" sticker*
❏ KS-3542 [S]	Here's That Man Again	1968	$30
❏ KL-1523 [M]	King of Western Swing	1967	$30
❏ KS-3523 [S]	King of Western Swing	1967	$30
❏ KS-3641	The Best of Bob Wills	1971	$25
❏ KS-3601	The Greatest String Band Hits	1969	$25
❏ KS-3587	The Living Legend	1969	$25
❏ KS-3569	Time Changes Everything	1969	$25
LIBERTY
❏ LRP-3303 [M]	Bob Wills Sings and Plays	1963	$30
❏ LST-7303 [S]	Bob Wills Sings and Plays	1963	$40
❏ LRP-3182 [M]	Living Legend	1961	$30
❏ LST-7182 [S]	Living Legend	1961	$40
❏ LRP-3194 [M]	Mr. Words and Mr. Music	1961	$30
❏ LST-7194 [S]	Mr. Words and Mr. Music	1961	$40
❏ LRP-3173 [M]	Together Again	1960	$30
❏ LST-7173 [S]	Together Again	1960	$40
LONGHORN
❏ LP-001 [M]	My Keepsake Album	1965	$80
MGM
❏ GAS-141	A Tribute (Golden Archive Series)	1971	$30
❏ E-91 [10]	Ranch House Favorites	1951	$300
❏ E-3352 [M]	Ranch House Favorites	1956	$150
STARDAY
❏ SLP-375 [M]	San Antonio Rose	1965	$40
TIME-LIFE
❏ STW-119	Country Music	1981	$12
UNITED ARTISTS
❏ LST-7303 [S]	Bob Wills Sings and Plays	1978	$20
— *Reissue of Liberty 7303 on "sunrise" label; tan label variations may exist but are unconfirmed*
| ❏ UAS-9962 | Legendary Masters | 1971 | $30 |
VOCALION
| ❏ VL3735 [M] | Western Swing Band | 1965 | $25 |

WILSON, CASSANDRA
Female singer and composer.
Albums
JMT

❏ 834419-1	Blue Skies	1988	$25
❏ 834412-1	Days Aweigh	1987	$25
❏ 860004-1	Point of View	1986	$35
— *Original edition*
| ❏ 834404-1 | Point of View | 1987 | $25 |

WILSON, CLIVE
Trumpeter.
Albums
NEW ORLEANS

| ❏ NOR-7210 | Clive Wilson Plays New Orleans Jazz | 1986 | $25 |

WILSON, GERALD
Trumpeter, composer and arranger.
Albums
AUDIO LAB

| ❏ AL-1538 [M] | Big Band Modern | 1959 | $150 |
DISCOVERY
| ❏ 872 | Corcovado | 1983 | $25 |
| ❏ 833 | Lomelin | 1981 | $25 |
FEDERAL
| ❏ 295-93 [10] | Gerald Wilson | 1953 | $300 |

Claude Williamson, *Claude Williamson*, Capitol H 6502, 10-inch LP, **$200**.

Stu Williamson, *Stu Williamson Plays*, Bethlehem BCP-31, **$250**.

Joe Wilder, *N' Wilder*, Savoy MG 12063, **$50**.

Teddy Wilson, *Soft Moods with Teddy Wilson*, Clef MGC-156, 10-inch LP, **$350**.

Number	Title	Yr	NM

PACIFIC JAZZ

Number	Title	Yr	NM
❏ ST-20135 [S]	California Soul	1969	$35
❏ ST-20160 [S]	Eternal Equinox	1969	$35
❏ ST-20132 [S]	Everywhere	1968	$35
❏ PJ-10099 [M]	Feelin' Kinda Blue	1964	$35
❏ ST-20099 [S]	Feelin' Kinda Blue	1966	$25
❏ LN-10101	Feelin' Kinda Blue	1981	$20
—Budget-line reissue			
❏ PJ-88 [M]	Gerald Wilson on Stage	1964	$30
❏ ST-88 [S]	Gerald Wilson on Stage	1964	$30
❏ LN-10100	Gerald Wilson on Stage	1981	$20
—Budget-line reissue			
❏ PJ-10111 [M]	Golden Sword	1966	$35
❏ ST-20111 [S]	Golden Sword	1966	$25
❏ PJ-10118 [M]	Live and Swinging	1967	$25
❏ ST-20118 [S]	Live and Swinging	1967	$35
❏ PJ-61 [M]	Moment of Truth	1962	$30
❏ LN-10098	Moment of Truth	1981	$20
—Budget-line reissue			
❏ PJ-80 [M]	Portraits	1964	$30
❏ ST-80 [S]	Portraits	1964	$30
❏ ST-20174	The Best of Gerald Wilson	1970	$35
❏ PJ-LA889-H	The Best of the Gerald Wilson Orchestra	1978	$25
❏ PJ-34 [M]	You Better Believe It	1961	$60
❏ ST-34 [S]	You Better Believe It	1961	$60
❏ LN-10097	You Better Believe It	1981	$20
—Budget-line reissue			

TREND

Number	Title	Yr	NM
❏ TR-537	Calafia	1985	$30

WILSON, GLENN

Baritone saxophone player.

Albums

CADENCE JAZZ

Number	Title	Yr	NM
❏ CJR-1023	Impasse	198?	$25

SUNNYSIDE

Number	Title	Yr	NM
❏ SSC-1030	Elusive	1988	$25

WILSON, JACK

Pianist.

Albums

ATLANTIC

Number	Title	Yr	NM
❏ 1406 [M]	Jack Wilson Quartet	1963	$50
❏ SD1406 [S]	Jack Wilson Quartet	1963	$50
❏ 1427 [M]	The Two Sides of Jack Wilson	1964	$30
❏ SD1427 [S]	The Two Sides of Jack Wilson	1964	$40

BLUE NOTE

Number	Title	Yr	NM
❏ BST-84270 [S]	Easterly Winds	1968	$25
—With "A Division of Liberty Records" on label			
❏ BLP-4251 [M]	Something Personal	1967	$80
❏ BST-84251 [S]	Something Personal	1967	$30
—With "New York, USA" address on label			
❏ BST-84251 [S]	Something Personal	1967	$25
—With "A Division of Liberty Records" on label			
❏ BST-84328 [S]	Song for My Daughter	1969	$25
—With "A Division of Liberty Records" on label			

DISCOVERY

Number	Title	Yr	NM
❏ 872	Corcovado	198?	$25
❏ 777	Innovations	1977	$35
❏ 805	Margo's Theme	1979	$30

VAULT

Number	Title	Yr	NM
❏ LP-9001 [M]	Brazilian Mancini	1964	$30
❏ LPS-9001 [S]	Brazilian Mancini	1964	$30
❏ LP-9008 [M]	Jazz Organs	1965	$30
❏ LPS-9008 [S]	Jazz Organs	1965	$30
❏ LP-9002 [M]	Ramblin'	1964	$30
❏ LPS-9002 [S]	Ramblin'	1964	$30

WILSON, JOE LEE

Male singer.

Albums

INNER CITY

Number	Title	Yr	NM
❏ IC-1042	Secrets from the Sun	197?	$30
❏ IC-1064	Without a Song	197?	$30

OBLIVION

Number	Title	Yr	NM
❏ 5	Livin' High Off Nickels and Dimes	197?	$35

SURVIVAL

Number	Title	Yr	NM
❏ 110	What Would It Be	1975	$30

WILSON, LESETTE

Albums

HEADFIRST

Number	Title	Yr	NM
❏ 9708	Now That I've Got Your Attention	198?	$30

WILSON, MARIE

Albums

DESIGN

Number	Title	Yr	NM
❏ DLP-76 [M]	Gentlemen Prefer Marie Wilson	1959	$40

STASH

Number	Title	Yr	NM
❏ ST-250	I Thought About You	1985	$25

WILSON, NANCY, AND CANNONBALL ADDERLEY

Also see each artist's individual listings.

Albums

CAPITOL

Number	Title	Yr	NM
❏ T1657 [M]	Nancy Wilson/Cannonball Adderley	1962	$100
—Black label with colorband, Capitol logo on left			
❏ ST1657 [S]	Nancy Wilson/Cannonball Adderley	1962	$100
—Black label with colorband, Capitol logo on left			
❏ ST1657 [S]	Nancy Wilson/Cannonball Adderley	1962	$80
—Black label with colorband, Capitol logo on top			
❏ T1657 [M]	Nancy Wilson/Cannonball Adderley	1962	$50
—Black label with colorband, Capitol logo on top			
❏ SM-1657	Nancy Wilson/Cannonball Adderley	197?	$25
—Reissue			

WILSON, NANCY

Female singer. Earlier material appears in the Goldmine Standard Catalog of American Records.

Albums

CAPITOL

Number	Title	Yr	NM
❏ ST-11317	All in Love Is Fair	1974	$30
❏ T2495 [M]	A Touch of Today	1966	$50
❏ ST2495 [S]	A Touch of Today	1966	$80
❏ SM-2495	A Touch of Today	197?	$25
—Reissue			
❏ T1828 [M]	Broadway My Way	1963	$75
❏ ST1828 [S]	Broadway My Way	1963	$80
❏ SM-1828	Broadway My Way	197?	$25
—Reissue			
❏ SY-4575	Broadway My Way	197?	$25
—Odd reissue			
❏ ST-798	But Beautiful	1971	$35
❏ SM-798	But Beautiful	197?	$25
—Reissue			
❏ ST-429	Can't Take My Eyes Off You	1970	$35
❏ SM-12031	Can't Take My Eyes Off You	1980	$25
—Reissue of 429			
❏ SWBB-256	Close-Up	1969	$80
—Combines 1828 and 1934 into one package			
❏ ST-11386	Come Get to This	1975	$30
❏ SM-11819	Come Get to This	1978	$25
—Reissue of 11386			
❏ ST2909	Easy	1968	$75
❏ SM-11802	Easy	1978	$25
—Reissue of 2909			
❏ STBB-727	For Once in My Life/Who Can I Turn To	1971	$80
❏ T2433 [M]	From Broadway with Love	1966	$75
❏ T2433 [S]	From Broadway with Love	1966	$80
❏ T2351 [M]	Gentle Is My Love	1965	$75
❏ ST2351 [S]	Gentle Is My Love	1965	$80
❏ T1767 [M]	Hello Young Lovers	1962	$80
❏ ST1767 [S]	Hello Young Lovers	1962	$100
❏ T1934 [M]	Hollywood My Way	1963	$75
❏ ST1934 [S]	Hollywood My Way	1963	$80
❏ SM-1934	Hollywood My Way	197?	$25
—Reissue			
❏ T2155 [M]	How Glad I Am	1964	$75
❏ ST2155 [S]	How Glad I Am	1964	$80
❏ SM-11767	How Glad I Am	1978	$25
—Reissue of 2155			
❏ ST-353	Hurt So Bad	1969	$75
❏ ST-11131	I Know I Love Him	1972	$30
❏ ST-11659	I've Never Been to Me	1977	$30
❏ T2712 [M]	Just for Now	1967	$60
❏ ST2712 [S]	Just for Now	1967	$80
❏ ST-842	Kaleidoscope	1971	$35
❏ ST-11943	Life, Love and Happiness	1979	$30
❏ T1319 [M]	Like in Love	1960	$100
—Black label with colorband, Capitol logo on left			
❏ ST1319 [S]	Like in Love	1960	$100
—Black label with colorband, Capitol logo on left			
❏ T1319 [M]	Like in Love	1960	$75
—Black label with colorband, Capitol logo on top			
❏ ST1319 [S]	Like in Love	1960	$80
—Black label with colorband, Capitol logo on top			
❏ T2757 [M]	Lush Life	1967	$80
❏ ST2757 [S]	Lush Life	1967	$75
❏ SMAS-11786	Music on My Mind	1978	$30
❏ ST-148	Nancy	1969	$50
❏ T2634 [M]	Nancy -- Naturally	1967	$50
❏ ST2634 [S]	Nancy -- Naturally	1967	$80
❏ SM-11884	Nancy -- Naturally	1979	$25
—Reissue of 2634			
❏ ST-541	Now I'm a Woman	1970	$50
❏ T1440 [M]	Something Wonderful	1960	$100
—Black label with colorband, Capitol logo on left			
❏ ST1440 [S]	Something Wonderful	1960	$100
—Black label with colorband, Capitol logo on left			
❏ T1440 [M]	Something Wonderful	1960	$50
—Black label with colorband, Capitol logo on top			
❏ ST-234	Son of a Preacher Man	1969	$50
❏ ST-12055	Take My Love	1980	$30
❏ T2555 [M]	Tender Loving Care	1966	$50
❏ ST2555 [S]	Tender Loving Care	1966	$80
❏ SKAO2947	The Best of Nancy Wilson	1968	$75
❏ SN-16128	The Best of Nancy Wilson	198?	$20
—Budget-line reissue			
❏ KAO2136 [M]	The Nancy Wilson Show!	1965	$50
❏ SKAO2136 [S]	The Nancy Wilson Show!	1965	$80
❏ ST-763	The Right to Love	1971	$50
—Retitled reissue of 2757			
❏ ST2970	The Sound of Nancy Wilson	1968	$50
❏ T1524 [M]	The Swingin's Mutual	1961	$100
—Black label with colorband, Capitol logo on left			
❏ ST1524 [S]	The Swingin's Mutual	1961	$100
—Black label with colorband, Capitol logo on left			
❏ T1524 [M]	The Swingin's Mutual	1961	$50
—Black label with colorband, Capitol logo on top			
❏ ST1524 [S]	The Swingin's Mutual	1961	$80
—Black label with colorband, Capitol logo on top			
❏ SM-1524 [S]	The Swingin's Mutual	1976	$25
—With George Shearing; reissue			
❏ ST-11518	This Mother's Daughter	1976	$30
❏ T2082 [M]	Today, Tomorrow, Forever	1964	$50
❏ ST2082 [S]	Today, Tomorrow, Forever	1964	$80
❏ T2321 [M]	Today -- My Way	1965	$50
❏ ST2321 [S]	Today -- My Way	1965	$80
❏ T2844 [M]	Welcome to My Love	1968	$100
❏ ST2844 [S]	Welcome to My Love	1968	$60
❏ T2012 [M]	Yesterday's Love Songs/Today's Blues	1964	$60
❏ ST2012 [S]	Yesterday's Love Songs/Today's Blues	1964	$80

COLUMBIA

Number	Title	Yr	NM
❏ FC40787	Forbidden Lover	1987	$25
❏ FC40330	Keep You Satisfied	1986	$25
❏ FC44464	Nancy Now!	1989	$25

PAUSA

Number	Title	Yr	NM
❏ PR-9041	Nancy -- Naturally	1985	$25

PICKWICK

Number	Title	Yr	NM
❏ SPC-3273	Goin' Out of My Head	197?	$25
❏ SPC-3348	The Good Life	197?	$25

WILSON, PHIL, AND RICH MATTESON

Matteson plays valve trombone. Also see PHIL WILSON.

Albums

ASI

Number	Title	Yr	NM
❏ 203	Sound of Wasp	197?	$30
❏ 5000	Sound of Wasp	197?	$25
—Reissue of 203			

WILSON, PHIL

Trombonist.

Albums

FAMOUS DOOR

Number	Title	Yr	NM
❏ HL-133	Boston-New York Axis	1980	$30
❏ HL-109	That's All	197?	$30

OUTRAGEOUS

Number	Title	Yr	NM
❏ 1	Getting It All Together	197?	$35

Number	Title	Yr	NM

WILSON, PHILLIP
Drummer and percussionist.

Albums

HAT HUT
| ❏ 0Q | Esoteric | 197? | $35 |

WILSON, REG

Albums

HERALD
| ❏ HLP-0104 [M] | All By Himself | 1956 | $50 |

WILSON, REUBEN
Organist and composer.

Albums

BLUE NOTE
❏ BST-84343	Blue Mode	1970	$30
❏ BST-84365	Groovy Situation	1971	$30
❏ BST-84317	Love Bug	1969	$30

— With "A Division of Liberty Records" on label
| ❏ BST-84295 | On Broadway | 1968 | $30 |

— With "A Division of Liberty Records" on label
| ❏ BST-84377 | Set Us Free | 1972 | $30 |

CADET
| ❏ CA-60033 | Got to Get Your Own | 1975 | $35 |

GROOVE MERCHANT
❏ 4404	Bad Stuff	197?	$25
❏ 511	Sweet Life	1973	$25
❏ 523	The Cisco Kid	1974	$35

WILSON, TEDDY, AND MARIAN MCPARTLAND
Also see each artist's individual listings.

Albums

HALCYON
| ❏ 106 | Elegant Piano | 197? | $30 |

WILSON, TEDDY
Pianist.

Albums

ALLEGRO
| ❏ 4024 [10] | All Star Sextet | 1954 | $100 |
| ❏ 4031 [10] | All Star Sextet | 1954 | $100 |

BLACK LION
❏ 177	Moonglow	197?	$30
❏ 209	Runnin' Wild Montreux	197?	$30
❏ 308	Striding After Fats	197?	$30

CAMEO
| ❏ C-1059 [M] | Teddy Wilson 1964 | 1964 | $30 |
| ❏ SC-1059 [S] | Teddy Wilson 1964 | 1964 | $30 |

CHIAROSCURO
❏ 168	Teddy Martin Revamps	197?	$30
❏ 150	Rodgers and Hart	197?	$30
	Teddy Wilson and the		
	All-Stars		
❏ 111	With Billie in Mind	1973	$30

CLASSIC JAZZ
| ❏ 32 | Live at Santa Tecia | 1976 | $25 |
| ❏ 101 | Three Little Words | 197? | $25 |

CLEF
❏ MGC-156 [10]	Soft Moods with Teddy	1954	$350
	Wilson		
❏ MGC-140 [10]	The Didactic Mr. Wilson	1953	$350

COLUMBIA
❏ CL1442 [M]	And Then They Wrote	1960	$30
❏ CS8242 [S]	And Then They Wrote	1960	$40
❏ CS8160 [S]	Gypsy	1959	$40
❏ CL1352 [M]	Gypsy in Jazz	1959	$30
❏ CL748 [M]	Mr. Wilson	1956	$60
❏ CL1318 [M]	Mr. Wilson and Mr. Gershwin	1959	$40
❏ CL6153 [10]	Piano Moods	1950	$120
❏ KG31617	Teddy Wilson and His	1973	$35
	All-Stars		
❏ CL6098 [10]	Teddy Wilson and His Piano	1950	$250
❏ CL6040 [10]	Teddy Wilson Featuring	1949	$400
	Billie Holiday		

COMMODORE
| ❏ FL-20029 [10] | Town Hall Concert | 1952 | $200 |

DIAL
| ❏ LP-213 [10] | Teddy Wilson All Stars | 1950 | $300 |

GNP CRESCENDO
| ❏ GNP-9014 | Teddy Wilson | 197? | $25 |

JAZZ ARCHIVES
| ❏ JA-28 | Teddy Wilson Sextet 1944, | 198? | $25 |
| | Vol. 1 | | |

| ❏ JA-36 | Teddy Wilson Sextet 1944, | 198? | $25 |
| | Vol. 2 | | |

JAZZOLOGY
| ❏ J-86 | Teddy's Choice | 198? | $25 |

MERCURY
| ❏ MG-25172 [10] | Piano Pastries | 1953 | $200 |

MGM
| ❏ E-129 [10] | Runnin' Wild | 1951 | $200 |

MOSAIC
❏ MQ8-173	The Complete Verve	199?	$150
	Recordings of the Teddy		
	Wilson Trio		

MUSICRAFT
❏ 2007	As Time Goes By	1986	$25
❏ 2008	Sunny Morning	1986	$25
❏ 502	Teddy Wilson and His All	198?	$25
	Stars, Vol. 1		

NORGRAN
| ❏ MGN-1019 [M] | The Creative Teddy Wilson | 1955 | $200 |

PRESTIGE
| ❏ PRST-7696 [S] | The Teddy Wilson Trio in | 1969 | $35 |
| | Europe | | |

QUICKSILVER
| ❏ QS-9002 | Into the Sky | 198? | $25 |

ROYALE
| ❏ 18169 [10] | Teddy Wilson and His All | 195? | $100 |
| | Stars | | |

SACKVILLE
| ❏ 2005 | Teddy Wilson in Tokyo | 198? | $25 |

STORYVILLE
| ❏ 4046 | Teddy Wilson Revisits the | 198? | $25 |
| | Goodman Years | | |

TIME-LIFE
| ❏ STL-J-20 | Giants of Jazz | 1981 | $60 |

VERVE
❏ MGV-2029 [M]	For Quiet Lovers	1956	$150
❏ V-2029 [M]	For Quiet Lovers	1961	$30
❏ MGV-2073 [M]	I Got Rhythm	1957	$150
❏ V-2073 [M]	I Got Rhythm	1961	$25
❏ MGV-2011 [M]	Intimate Listening	1956	$200
❏ V-2011 [M]	Intimate Listening	1961	$25
❏ MGV-8272 [M]	The Impeccable Mr. Teddy	1958	$120
	Wilson		
❏ V-8272 [M]	The Impeccable Mr. Teddy	1961	$25
	Wilson		
❏ MGV-8299 [M]	These Tunes Remind Me	1959	$100
	of You		
❏ V-8299 [M]	These Tunes Remind Me	1961	$25
	of You		
❏ MGV-8330 [M]	The Touch of Teddy Wilson	1959	$100
❏ V-8330 [M]	The Touch of Teddy Wilson	1961	$25

WHO'S WHO IN JAZZ
| ❏ 21009 | Lionel Hampton Presents | 1979 | $25 |
| | Teddy Wilson | | |

WILSON, TEDDY/GERRY MULLIGAN
Also see each artist's individual listings.

Albums

VERVE
❏ V6-8827	Newport Years	197?	$30
❏ MGV-8235 [M]	The Teddy Wilson Trio and	1958	$150
	the Gerry Mulligan Quartet		
	at Newport		
❏ V-8235 [M]	The Teddy Wilson Trio and	1961	$25
	the Gerry Mulligan Quartet		
	at Newport		
❏ UMV-2622 [M]	The Teddy Wilson Trio and	198?	$30
	the Gerry Mulligan Quartet		
	at Newport		

WINCHESTER, LEM
Vibraphone player. Also see RANDY WESTON.

Albums

ARGO
❏ LPS-642 [S]	Lem Winchester with the	1959	$40
	Ramsey Lewis Trio		
❏ LP-642 [M]	Lem Winchester with the	1959	$50
	Ramsey Lewis Trio		

FANTASY
| ❏ OJC-1719 | Winchester Special | 198? | $25 |

METROJAZZ
| ❏ E-1005 [M] | New Faces at Newport | 1958 | $120 |

MOODSVILLE
| ❏ MVLP-11 [M] | Lem Winchester with | 1960 | $50 |
| | Feeling | | |

— Green label

| ❏ MVLP-11 [M] | Lem Winchester with | 1965 | $30 |
| | Feeling | | |

— Blue label, trident logo at right

NEW JAZZ
| ❏ NJLP-8244 [M] | Another Opus | 1960 | $150 |

— Purple label
| ❏ NJLP-8244 [M] | Another Opus | 1965 | $150 |

— Blue label, trident logo at right
| ❏ NJLP-8239 [M] | Lem's Beat | 1960 | $150 |

— Purple label
| ❏ NJLP-8239 [M] | Lem's Beat | 1965 | $150 |

— Blue label, trident logo at right
| ❏ NJLP-8223 [M] | Winchester Special | 1959 | $200 |

— Purple label
| ❏ NJLP-8223 [M] | Winchester Special | 1965 | $150 |

— Blue label, trident logo at right

WIND CHILL FACTOR

Albums

QCA
| ❏ 372 | City Streets | 1978 | $30 |

WINDHURST, JOHNNY
Trumpeter.

Albums

JAZZOLOGY
| ❏ J-3 | The Imaginative Johnny | 1963 | $35 |
| | Windhurst | | |

TRANSITION
| ❏ TRLP-2 [M] | Jazz at Columbus Ave. | 1956 | $200 |

— Deduct 1/4 if booklet is missing

WINDING, KAI, AND SONNY STITT
Also see each artist's individual listings.

Albums

HALL OF FAME
| ❏ 612 | Early Modern | 197? | $25 |

WINDING, KAI
Trombonist and composer. Best known for his hit instrumental recording of "More (Theme from Mondo Cane)." Also see STAN GETZ; J.J. JOHNSON; GERRY MULLIGAN; FATS NAVARRO.

Albums

A&M
| ❏ SP-3008 | Israel | 1969 | $30 |

ABC IMPULSE!
| ❏ AS3 [S] | The Incredible Kai Winding | 1968 | $30 |
| | Trombones | | |

— Black and red label

COLUMBIA
❏ CL1329 [M]	Dance to the City Beat	1959	$40
❏ CS8136 [S]	Dance to the City Beat	1959	$60
❏ CL1264 [M]	Swingin' State	1958	$100
❏ CS8062 [S]	Swingin' State	1958	$40
❏ CL999 [M]	Trombone Panorama	1957	$100
❏ CL936 [M]	Trombone Sound	1956	$100

GATEWAY
| ❏ 7022 | Jazz Showcase | 1979 | $25 |

GLENDALE
| ❏ 6004 | Caravan | 1977 | $25 |
| ❏ 6003 | Danish Blue | 1976 | $25 |

HARMONY
| ❏ HL7341 [M] | The Great Kai Winding | 1962 | $35 |
| | Sound | | |

IMPULSE!
❏ A3 [M]	The Incredible Kai Winding	1960	$200
	Trombones		
❏ AS3 [S]	The Incredible Kai Winding	1960	$200
	Trombones		

— Orange and black label

MCA
| ❏ 29062 | Incredible Kai Winding | 198? | $25 |
| | Trombones | | |

— Reissue of Impulse! 3

PICKWICK
| ❏ SPC-3004 | Trombones | 196? | $30 |

RED RECORD
| ❏ VPA-143 | Duo Bones | 198? | $30 |

ROOST

Number	Title	Yr	NM
❏ LP408 [10]	Kai Winding All Stars	1952	$200
SAVOY			
❏ MG-12119 [M]	In the Beginning	196?	$35
❏ MG-9017 [10]	New Trends Of Jazz	1952	$200
VERVE			
❏ V-8661 [M]	Dirty Dog	1966	$30
❏ V6-8661 [S]	Dirty Dog	1966	$35
❏ V-8427 [M]	Kai Ole	1962	$60
❏ V6-8427 [S]	Kai Ole	1962	$60
❏ V-8525 [M]	Kai Winding Solo	1963	$60
❏ V6-8525 [S]	Kai Winding Solo	1963	$60
❏ V-8602 [M]	Modern Country	1964	$150
❏ V6-8602 [S]	Modern Country	1964	$150
❏ V-8573 [M]	Mondo Cane #2	1964	$60
❏ V6-8573 [S]	Mondo Cane #2	1964	$60
❏ V-8551 [M]	More!!!	1963	$60
❏ V6-8551 [S]	More!!!	1963	$60
❏ V-8657 [M]	More Brass	1966	$30
❏ V6-8657 [S]	More Brass	1966	$35
❏ V-8691 [M]	Penny Lane and Time	1967	$35
❏ V6-8691 [S]	Penny Lane and Time	1967	$30
❏ V-8620 [M]	Rainy Day	1965	$35
❏ V6-8620 [S]	Rainy Day	1965	$50
❏ V-8493 [M]	Suspense Themes in Jazz	1962	$60
❏ V6-8493 [S]	Suspense Themes in Jazz	1962	$60
❏ V-8639 [M]	The "In" Instrumentals	1965	$35
❏ V6-8639 [S]	The "In" Instrumentals	1965	$50
❏ V-8556 [M]	The Lonely One	1963	$60
❏ V6-8556 [S]	The Lonely One	1963	$60
WHO'S WHO IN JAZZ			
❏ 21001	Lionel Hampton Presents Kai Winding	1978	$25

WINDMILL SAXOPHONE QUARTET
Formed by Clayton Englar (saxophonist, flutist, composer, arranger) in 1984. Other members: Jesse Meman, Ken Plant, and Tom Monroe, all of whom play various saxophones plus flutes and clarinets.

Albums

Number	Title	Yr	NM
PATHFINDER			
❏ PTF-8801	Very Scary	1988	$25

WINDOWS
Members: Skipper Wise (bass, guitar); Tim Timmermans (drums, percussion, keyboards); Ed Cohen (acoustic and electric keyboards, percussion); Michael Acosta (tenor and soprano saxes).

Albums

Number	Title	Yr	NM
CYPRESS			
❏ YL-0214	The French Laundry	1989	$30
INTIMA			
❏ SJ-73218	Is It Safe	1987	$25
❏ D1-73298	Mr. Bongo	1988	$25
❏ SJ-73219	Windows	1987	$25
—Reissue of self-titled debut album			
(LABEL UNKNOWN)			
❏ 0(# unknown)	Windows	1985	$50

WINDY CITY BANJO BAND, THE

Albums

Number	Title	Yr	NM
PINNACLE			
❏ 107	The Windy City Banjo Band	1963	$35

WINDY CITY SEVEN, THE
See FRED WACKER.

WINKLER, MARK
Male singer and composer.

Albums

Number	Title	Yr	NM
CMG			
❏ CML-7207	Ebony Rain	1988	$25
❏ CML-8021	Hottest Night of the Year	1989	$30

WINSTON, GEORGE
Pianist.

Albums

Number	Title	Yr	NM
LOST LAKE ARTS			
❏ LL-0081	Ballads and Blues 1972	1981	$40
—Reissue of Takoma recordings			
TAKOMA			
❏ 9016	Piano Solos	1973	$40
WINDHAM HILL			
❏ WH-1012	Autumn	1984	$25
—Reissue with A&M distribution			

Number	Title	Yr	NM
❏ C-1012	Autumn	1980	$30
—Original issue			
❏ WH-1025	December	1984	$25
—Distributed by A&M Records; "December" in raised white letters			
❏ C-1025	December	1982	$35
—NOT distributed by A&M Records; "December" in black letters			
❏ WH-1019	Winter Into Spring	1984	$25
—Reissue, distributed by A&M Records			
❏ C-1019	Winter Into Spring	1982	$30
—Original issue			

WINSTON, MURIEL
Female singer.

Albums

Number	Title	Yr	NM
STRATA-EAST			
❏ SES-7411	A Fresh Viewpoint	197?	$35

WINSTON, SHERRY
Flutist.

Albums

Number	Title	Yr	NM
HEADFIRST			
❏ 634	Do It for Love	198?	$25
WARLOCK			
❏ WAR-2724	Love Is	1991	$30

WINTER, PAUL, AND PAUL HALLEY
Halley is a pianist and organist. Also see PAUL WINTER.

Albums

Number	Title	Yr	NM
LIVING MUSIC			
❏ LM-0013	Whales Alive!	1987	$25

WINTER, PAUL
Saxophone player, clarinetist, composer and bandleader - first a sextet, then the Paul Winter Consort. He was an early advocate of "world music," which has since been lumped in with the "new age" movement. Members of the Consort since 1980 are EUGENE FRIESEN (cello); Paul Halley (piano, organ); and Glen Velez (percussion).

Albums

Number	Title	Yr	NM
A&M			
❏ SP-4698	Common Ground	1978	$15
❏ SP-4653	Earthdance	1977	$15
❏ SP-4207	Something in the Wind	1969	$35
❏ SP-4279	The Road	1970	$35
❏ SP-4170	The Winter Consort	1968	$35
COLUMBIA			
❏ CL1925 [M]	Jazz Meets the Bossa Nova	1962	$35
❏ CS8725 [S]	Jazz Meets the Bossa Nova	1962	$25
❏ CL2155 [M]	Jazz Meets the Folk Song	1964	$35
❏ CS8955 [S]	Jazz Meets the Folk Song	1964	$25
❏ CL1997 [M]	Jazz Premiere: Washington	1963	$35
❏ CS8797 [S]	Jazz Premiere: Washington	1963	$25
❏ CL2064 [M]	New Jazz on Campus	1963	$35
❏ CS8864 [S]	New Jazz on Campus	1963	$25
❏ CL2315 [M]	Rio	1965	$35
❏ CS9115 [S]	Rio	1965	$25
❏ CL2272 [M]	The Sound of Ipanema	1965	$35
❏ CS9072 [S]	The Sound of Ipanema	1965	$25
EPIC			
❏ KE31643	Icarus	1972	$60
❏ PE31643	Icarus	197?	$25
—Reissue			
LIVING MUSIC			
❏ LMR-1	Callings	1980	$25
—With 20-page booklet			
❏ LM-0001	Callings	198?	$20
—Reissue of LMR-1			
❏ LMR-6	Canyon	1986	$15
❏ LMR-5	Concert for the Earth Live at the United Nations	1985	$15
❏ LM-0015	Earthbeat	1987	$12
❏ LMR-4	Icarus	1985	$25
—Reissue of Epic LP			
❏ LM-0004	Icarus	198?	$12
—Reissue of LMR-4			
❏ LMR-2	Missa Gaia/Earth Mass	1983	$25
❏ LMR-3	Sun Singer	1984	$15
❏ LM-0003	Sun Singer	198?	$12
—Reissue of LMR-3			
❏ LM-0012	Wintersong	1986	$25

WINTER, RAYMOND

Albums

Number	Title	Yr	NM
INNER CITY			
❏ IC-1135	Tropic Woods	198?	$30

WINTERS, JERRI
Female singer.

Albums

Number	Title	Yr	NM
BETHLEHEM			
❏ BCP-76 [M]	Somebody Loves Me	1957	$250
FRATERNITY			
❏ F-1001 [M]	Winter's Here	1955	$120

WINTERS, PINKY

Albums

Number	Title	Yr	NM
ARGO			
❏ LP-604 [M]	Lonely One	1956	$650
CREATIVE			
❏ LP-604 [M]	Lonely One	1956	$60
VANTAGE			
❏ VLP-3 [10]	Pinky Winters	1954	$1000

WINTERS, SMILEY
Drummer.

Albums

Number	Title	Yr	NM
ARHOOLIE			
❏ 8004/5	Smiley Etc.	1969	$25

WISHFUL THINKING
Members: Tim Weston (guitar); David Garibaldi (drums); Chris Boardman (keyboards); Jerry Watts Jr. (bass); Dave Shank (vibes, percussion).

Albums

Number	Title	Yr	NM
PAUSA			
❏ 7205	Think Again	1987	$30
❏ 7187	Wishful Thinking	1986	$25
SOUNDWINGS			
❏ SW-2109	Way Down West	1988	$25

WISNER, JIMMY
Pianist.

Albums

Number	Title	Yr	NM
CHANCELLOR			
❏ CHJ-5014 [M]	Aper-Sepshun	1960	$60
❏ CHJS-5014 [S]	Aper-Sepshun	1960	$60
FELSTED			
❏ FL-7509 [M]	Blues for Harvey	1962	$60
❏ FL-2509 [S]	Blues for Harvey	1962	$60

WITHERSPOON, JIMMY, AND BEN WEBSTER
Also see each artist's individual listings.

Albums

Number	Title	Yr	NM
VERVE			
❏ V6-8835	Previously Unreleased Recordings	197?	$35

WITHERSPOON, JIMMY, AND GERRY MULLIGAN
Also see each artist's individual listings.

Albums

Number	Title	Yr	NM
EVEREST ARCHIVE OF FOLK & JAZZ			
❏ 264	Jimmy Witherspoon and Gerry Mulligan	197?	$30

WITHERSPOON, JIMMY, AND RICHARD "GROOVE" HOLMES
Also see each artist's individual listings.

Albums

Number	Title	Yr	NM
OLYMPIC GOLD MEDAL			
❏ 7107	Groovin' and Spoonin'	1974	$30
SURREY			
❏ S-1106 [M]	Blues for Spoon and Groove	1965	$60
❏ SS-1106 [S]	Blues for Spoon and Groove	1965	$60

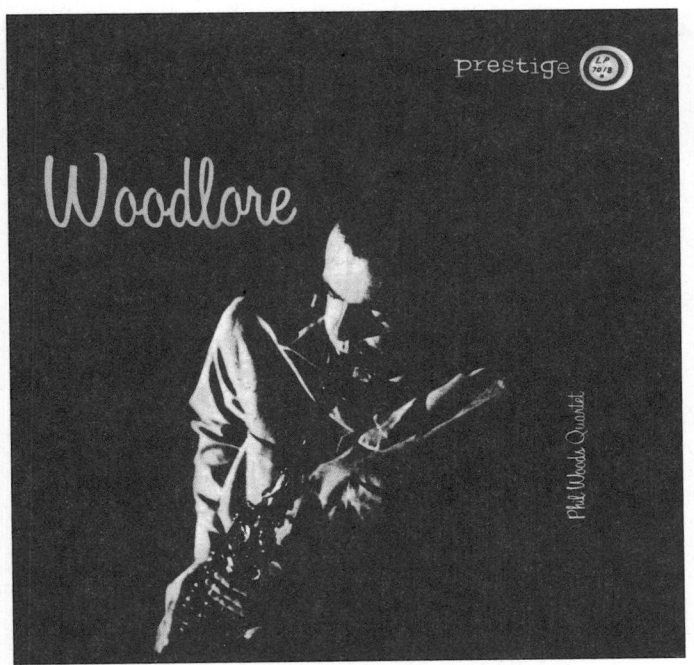

Phil Woods, *Woodlore*, Prestige PRLP-7018, yellow label with W. 50th St. address, **$500**.

Phil Woods, *Bird Feathers*, Prestige (New Jazz) 8204, yellow label, **$350**.

John Wright, *South Side Soul*, Prestige PRLP-7190, **$200**.

Lester Young, *The President Plays with the Oscar Peterson Trio*, Verve MGV-8144, **$100**.

WITHERSPOON, JIMMY

Male singer. Also see EDDIE "CLEANHEAD" VINSON. Earlier material appears in the Goldmine Standard Catalog of American Records.

Albums

Number	Title	Yr	NM
ABC			
❏ 717	Handbags and Gladrags	1970	$60
ANALOGUE PRODUCTIONS			
❏ APR3008	Evenin' Blues	199?	$35
BLUE NOTE			
❏ BN-LA534-G	Spoonful	1976	$30
BLUESWAY			
❏ BLS-6026	Blues Singer	1969	$60
❏ BLS-6040	Hunh	1970	$60
❏ BLS-6051	The Best of Jimmy Witherspoon	1970	$60
CAPITOL			
❏ ST-11360	Love Is a Five Letter Word	1975	$30
CHESS			
❏ CH-93003	Spoon So Easy: The Chess Years	1990	$30
CONSTELLATION			
❏ CM1422 [M]	Take This Hammer	1964	$100
❏ CMS1422 [R]	Take This Hammer	1964	$60
CROWN			
❏ CLP-5156 [M]	Jimmy Witherspoon	1959	$150
—Black label, silver print			
❏ CLP-5156 [M]	Jimmy Witherspoon	1961	$60
—Gray label, black print			
❏ CLP-5192 [M]	Jimmy Witherspoon Sings the Blues	1959	$150
—Black label, silver print			
❏ CLP-5192 [M]	Jimmy Witherspoon Sings the Blues	1961	$60
—Gray label, black print			
❏ CST-215 [S]	Jimmy Witherspoon Sings the Blues	1961	$150
—Red vinyl; contrary to prior reports, this album -- at least the red vinyl version -- is in true stereo!			
❏ CST-215 [S]	Jimmy Witherspoon Sings the Blues	1961	$175
—Black vinyl; this value assumes that this is in true stereo, as the red vinyl version is, but this has not been confirmed			
FANTASY			
❏ OBC-527	Baby, Baby, Baby	1990	$30
—Reissue of Prestige 7290			
❏ OBC-511	Evenin' Blues	1988	$30
—Reissue of Prestige 7300			
❏ 9660	Rockin' L.A.	1989	$30
❏ 24701	The 'Spoon Concerts	1972	$50
HIFI			
❏ R-421 [M]	At the Monterey Jazz Festival	1959	$175
❏ SR-421 [S]	At the Monterey Jazz Festival	1959	$120
❏ R-422 [M]	Feelin' the Spirit	1959	$175
❏ SR-422 [S]	Feelin' the Spirit	1959	$120
❏ R-426 [M]	Jimmy Witherspoon at the Renaissance	1959	$175
❏ SR-426 [S]	Jimmy Witherspoon at the Renaissance	1959	$120
JAZZ MAN			
❏ 5013	Jimmy Witherspoon Sings the Blues	1980	$30
LAX			
❏ PW37115	Love Is a Five Letter Word	1981	$25
—Reissue of Capitol LP			
MUSE			
❏ MR-5288	Jimmy Witherspoon Sings the Blues	1983	$25
❏ MR-5327	Midnight Lady Called the Blues	1986	$25
PRESTIGE			
❏ PRLP-7290 [M]	Baby, Baby, Baby	1963	$40
❏ PRST-7290 [S]	Baby, Baby, Baby	1963	$40
❏ PRLP-7314 [M]	Blues Around the Clock	1964	$40
❏ PRST-7314 [S]	Blues Around the Clock	1964	$40
❏ PRLP-7475 [M]	Blues for Easy Livers	1967	$60
❏ PRST-7475 [S]	Blues for Easy Livers	1967	$50
❏ PRLP-7327 [M]	Blue Spoon	1964	$40
❏ PRST-7327 [S]	Blue Spoon	1964	$40
❏ PRLP-7300 [M]	Evenin' Blues	1964	$40
❏ PRST-7300 [S]	Evenin' Blues	1964	$40
❏ 7855	Mean Old Frisco	1974	$35
❏ PRLP-7356 [M]	Some of My Best Friends Are the Blues	1965	$60
❏ PRST-7356 [S]	Some of My Best Friends Are the Blues	1965	$60
❏ PRLP-7418 [M]	Spoon in London	1966	$60
❏ PRST-7418 [S]	Spoon in London	1966	$60
❏ PRST-7713	The Best of Jimmy Witherspoon	1969	$50
RCA VICTOR			
❏ LPM-1639 [M]	Goin' to Kansas City Blues	1957	$175
❏ ANL1-1048	Goin' to Kansas City Blues	1976	$25
—Reissue			
REPRISE			
❏ R-6012 [M]	Hey, Mrs. Jones	1961	$40
❏ R9-6012 [S]	Hey, Mrs. Jones	1961	$120
❏ R-6059 [M]	Roots	1962	$40
❏ R9-6059 [S]	Roots	1962	$120
❏ R-2008 [M]	Spoon	1961	$40
❏ R9-2008 [S]	Spoon	1961	$120
UNITED			
❏ 7715	A Spoonful of Blues	197?	$30
VERVE			
❏ V-5050 [M]	A Spoonful of Soul	1968	$60
❏ V6-5050 [S]	A Spoonful of Soul	1968	$50
❏ V-5007 [M]	Blue Point of View	1966	$50
❏ V6-5007 [S]	Blue Point of View	1966	$60
❏ V-5030 [M]	Blues Is Now	1967	$60
❏ V6-5030 [S]	Blues Is Now	1967	$50
WORLD PACIFIC			
❏ WP-1267 [M]	Singin' the Blues	1959	$300
❏ WP-1402 [M]	There's Good Rockin' Tonight	1961	$250
—Reissue of 1267			

WITTWER, JOHNNY

Pianist. Also see KID ORY.

Albums

Number	Title	Yr	NM
STINSON			
❏ SLP-58	Piano Rags	195?	$25

WOFFORD, MIKE

Pianist.

Albums

Number	Title	Yr	NM
DISCOVERY			
❏ 784	Afterthoughts	1978	$35
❏ 778	Bird of Paradise	1977	$35
❏ 808	Mike Wofford Plays Jerome Kern	1979	$25
❏ 816	Mike Wofford Plays Jerome Kern, Volume 2	1980	$25
❏ 827	Mike Wofford Plays Jerome Kern, Volume 3	198?	$25
EPIC			
❏ LN24225 [M]	Strawberry Wine	1967	$40
❏ BN26225 [S]	Strawberry Wine	1967	$75
FLYING DUTCHMAN			
❏ BDL1-1372	Joplin: Interpretations '76	1976	$30
MILESTONE			
❏ MPS-9012	Summer Night	1968	$25
TREND			
❏ TR-552	Funkalero	1988	$25

WOFSEY, GARY

Trumpet and flugel horn player, sometimes playing both simultaneously! Also a bandleader (The Contemporary Jazz Orchestra).

Albums

Number	Title	Yr	NM
AMBI			
❏ 1521	Kef's Pool	198?	$30
❏ 1520	Mel	198?	$30
❏ 1519	My Grandfather's Clock	198?	$30

WOLFE, NEIL, AND NOAH YOUNG

Also see each artist's individual listings.

Albums

Number	Title	Yr	NM
WK			
❏ 101	I Am Music/I Am Song	197?	$35

WOLFE, NEIL

Pianist.

Albums

Number	Title	Yr	NM
COLUMBIA			
❏ CL2378 [M]	Out of This World	1965	$30
❏ CS9178 [S]	Out of This World	1965	$35
❏ CS9600	Piano for Barbra	1968	$30
❏ CL2239 [M]	Piano -- My Way	1964	$30
❏ CS9039 [S]	Piano -- My Way	1964	$35
IMPERIAL			
❏ LP-9169 [M]	Neil Swings Nicely	1962	$150
❏ LP-12084 [S]	Neil Swings Nicely	1962	$150
❏ LP-9192 [M]	One Order of Blues	1962	$150
❏ LP-12192 [S]	One Order of Blues	1962	$150

WOLFE, STEVE, AND NANCY KING

Wolfe is a tenor saxophone player, pianist, flutist and oboist. King is a female singer.

Albums

Number	Title	Yr	NM
INNER CITY			
❏ IC-1049	First Date	197?	$30

WOLLMAN, TERRY

Guitarist.

Albums

Number	Title	Yr	NM
NOVA			
❏ 8706	Bimini	1987	$25

WOOD, BOOTY

Trombonist.

Albums

Number	Title	Yr	NM
MASTER JAZZ			
❏ 8102	Hang In There	197?	$35

WOOD, JOHN

Albums

Number	Title	Yr	NM
LOS ANGELES			
❏ 1001	Freeway of Love	197?	$35
❏ 1002	Until Goodbye	1976	$35
RANWOOD			
❏ RLP-8036	Introducing the John Wood Trio	1969	$35

WOODARD, LYMAN

Keyboard player.

Albums

Number	Title	Yr	NM
STRATA			
❏ 105-75	Saturday Night Special	197?	$35

WOODEN JOE

See WOODEN JOE NICHOLAS.

WOODING, SAM

Pianist and bandleader.

Albums

Number	Title	Yr	NM
BIOGRAPH			
❏ 12026	Chocolate Dandies	197?	$25

WOODS, CHRIS

Alto saxophone player and flutist.

Albums

Number	Title	Yr	NM
DELMARK			
❏ DS-437	Modus Operandi	1979	$25
❏ DS-434	Somebody Stole My Blues	197?	$30

WOODS, JIMMY

Alto and tenor saxophone player.

Albums

Number	Title	Yr	NM
CAPITOL			
❏ ST-654	Essence	1971	$20
CONTEMPORARY			
❏ M-3605 [M]	Awakening	1962	$200
❏ S-7605 [S]	Awakening	1962	$200
❏ M-3612 [M]	Conflict	1963	$200
❏ S-7612 [S]	Conflict	1963	$200

WOODS, PHIL, AND CHRIS SWANSON

Swanson is a trombonist. Also see PHIL WOODS.

Albums

Number	Title	Yr	NM
SEA BREEZE			
❏ SB-2008	Crazy Horse	198?	$25
❏ SB-2019	Piper at the Gates of Dawn	1984	$25

Number	Title	Yr	NM

WOODS, PHIL, AND GENE QUILL
Also see each artist's individual listings.
Albums
COLUMBIA JAZZ ODYSSEY
❑ PC36806 — Phil Talks with Quill — 1980 — $25
EPIC
❑ LN3521 [M] — Phil Talks with Quill — 1959 — $100
❑ BN554 [S] — Phil Talks with Quill — 1959 — $80
❑ BN554 [S] — Phil Talks with Quill — 199? — $60
— Classic Records reissue on audiophile vinyl
FANTASY
❑ OJC-215 — Phil and Quill with Prestige — 198? — $25
PRESTIGE
❑ 2508 — Four Altos — 198? — $30
❑ PRLP-7115 [M] — Phil and Quill with Prestige — 1957 — $250
RCA VICTOR
❑ LPM-1284 [M] — The Woods-Quill Sextet — 1956 — $80

WOODS, PHIL, AND GENE QUILL/JACKIE MCLEAN AND JOHN JENKINS/HAL MCKUSICK
Also see each artist's individual listings.
Albums
NEW JAZZ
❑ NJLP-8204 [M] — Bird Feathers — 1958 — $350
— Yellow Prestige label
❑ NJLP-8204 [M] — Bird Feathers — 1959 — $150
— Purple label
❑ NJLP-8204 [M] — Bird Feathers — 1965 — $150
— Blue label, trident logo at right

WOODS, PHIL, AND LEW TABACKIN
Also see each artist's individual listings.
Albums
OMNISOUND
❑ 1033 — Phil Woods and Lew Tabackin — 198? — $25

WOODS, PHIL
Alto and soprano saxophone player, clarinetist and male singer. Also see THE MANHATTAN JAZZ ALL-STARS; ORCHESTRA USA; JIMMY RANEY.
Albums
ABC IMPULSE!
❑ AS-9143 [S] — Greek Cooking — 1968 — $35
ADELPHI
❑ 5010 — More Live — 198? — $25
ANTILLES
❑ AN-1013 — At the Vanguard — 198? — $25
❑ AN-1006 — Birds of a Feather — 1982 — $25
BARNABY
❑ KZ31036 — Rights of Swing — 1972 — $30
❑ BR-5016 — Rights of Swing — 197? — $25
— Reissue
BLACKHAWK
❑ BKH-50401 — Heaven — 1986 — $25
CANDID
❑ CD-8016 [M] — Rights of Swing — 1960 — $40
❑ CS-9016 [S] — Rights of Swing — 1960 — $50
CENTURY
❑ 1050 — Songs for Sisyphus — 197? — $25
CLEAN CUTS
❑ 702 — Phil Woods Quartet, Vol. 1 — 1979 — $30
CONCORD JAZZ
❑ CJ-345 — Bop Stew — 1988 — $25
❑ CJ-377 — Bouquet — 1989 — $30
❑ CJ-361 — Evolution — 1988 — $25
EMBRYO
❑ SD530 — Phil Woods at the Frankfurt Jazz Festival — 197? — $35
ENJA
❑ 3081 — Three for All — 1981 — $30
FANTASY
❑ OJC-1735 — Bird Feathers — 198? — $30
❑ OJC-092 — Paring Off — 198? — $30
❑ OJC-1732 — The Young Bloods — 198? — $30
❑ OJC-052 — Woodlore — 1982 — $30
GRYPHON
❑ 788 — I Remember — 1979 — $30
❑ 782 — Sisyphus — 1978 — $30
IMPULSE!
❑ A-9143 [M] — Greek Cooking — 1967 — $60
❑ AS-9143 [S] — Greek Cooking — 1967 — $60

Number	Title	Yr	NM

INNER CITY
❑ IC-1002 — European Rhythm Machine — 197? — $35
JAZZ MAN
❑ 5001 — Rights of Swing — 1982 — $25
MGM
❑ SE-4695 — Phil Woods at the Montreux Jazz Festival — 197? — $35
MOSAIC
❑ MQ7-159 — The Phil Woods Quartet/Quintet 20th Anniversary Set — 199? — $120
MUSE
❑ MR-5037 — Musique de Bois — 1974 — $30
NEW JAZZ
❑ NJLP-1104 [10] — Phil Woods New Jazz Quintet — 1954 — $500
❑ NJLP-8291 [M] — Pot Pie — 1962 — $200
— Purple label
❑ NJLP-8291 [M] — Pot Pie — 1965 — $150
— Blue label, trident logo at right
❑ NJLP-8304 [M] — Sugan — 1963 — $0
— Canceled, reassigned to Status
PALO ALTO/TBA
❑ PA-8084 — Live from New York — 1985 — $25
PRESTIGE
❑ 24065 — Altology — 197? — $35
❑ PRST-7673 [R] — Early Quintets — 1969 — $35
❑ PRLP-7046 [M] — Paring Off — 1956 — $400
❑ PRLP-191 [10] — Phil Woods New Jazz Quartet — 1954 — $400
❑ PRLP-204 [10] — Phil Woods New Jazz Quintet — 1955 — $400
❑ PRLP-7080 [M] — The Young Bloods — 1957 — $300
❑ PRLP-7018 [M] — Woodlore — 1956 — $500
— Yellow label with W. 50th St. address
QUICKSILVER
❑ QS-4011 — Live from New York — 1991 — $30
RCA VICTOR
❑ BGL1-1800 — Floresta — 1976 — $30
❑ BXL1-1800 — Floresta — 1978 — $25
— Reissue with new prefix
❑ BGL1-1027 — Images — 1975 — $30
❑ BXL1-1027 — Images — 1978 — $25
— Reissue with new prefix
❑ BGL2-2202 — Live from the Showboat — 1977 — $35
❑ BGL1-1391 — The New Album — 1976 — $30
❑ BXL1-1391 — The New Album — 1978 — $25
— Reissue with new prefix
RED RECORD
❑ VPA-163 — European Tour Live — 198? — $30
❑ VPA-177 — Integrity — 1985 — $35
SAVOY JAZZ
❑ SJL-1179 — Bird Calls: Vol. 1 — 1987 — $25
STATUS
❑ ST-8304 [M] — Sugan — 1965 — $40
TESTAMENT
❑ 4402 — New Music — 197? — $35
VERVE
❑ V6-8791 — Round Trip — 1969 — $35

WORLD BASS VIOLIN ENSEMBLE
Members: Phil Bowler; Greg Maker; Rufus Reid; Bob Cunningham; Brian Smith; Fred Hopkins.
Albums
BLACK SAINT
❑ BSR-0063 — Basically Yours — 198? — $30

WORLD RHYTHM BAND
Albums
DISCOVERY
❑ 865 — Ibex — 198? — $25

WORLD SAXOPHONE QUARTET
Members: JULIUS HEMPHILL (soprano, alto, tenor saxes, flute); OLIVER LAKE (soprano, alto, tenor saxes, flute); DAVID MURRAY (tenor sax, bass clarinet); HAMIET BLUIETT (baritone sax, alto clarinet, alto flute).
Albums
BLACK SAINT
❑ BSR-0077 — Live in Zurich — 198? — $30
❑ BSR-0056 — Revue — 198? — $30
❑ BSR-0027 — Steppin' — 198? — $30
❑ BSR-0046 — W.S.Q. — 198? — $30
ELEKTRA/MUSICIAN

Number	Title	Yr	NM

❑ 60864 — Rhythm and Blues — 1989 — $30
ELEKTRA/NONESUCH
❑ 79164 — Dances and Ballads — 1988 — $25
❑ 79137 — World Saxophone Quartet Plays Duke Ellington — 1987 — $25

WORLD'S GREATEST JAZZ BAND, THE
Continuation of the listings of YANK LAWSON AND BOB HAGGART.
Albums
EVEREST ARCHIVE OF FOLK & JAZZ
❑ 314 — The World's Greatest Jazz Band — 197? — $25
FLYING DUTCHMAN
❑ BDL1-1371 — The World's Greatest Jazz Band In Concert — 1976 — $30
WORLD JAZZ
❑ 1 — Century Plaza — 197? — $30
❑ 2 — Hark the Herald Angels Swing — 197? — $30
❑ 3 — The World's Greatest Jazz Band in Concert, Vol. 1 — 197? — $30
❑ 4 — The World's Greatest Jazz Band in Concert, Vol. 2 — 197? — $30
❑ 8 — The World's Greatest Jazz Band On Tour — 197? — $30
❑ 10 — The World's Greatest Jazz Band On Tour II — 197? — $30
❑ 6 — The World's Greatest Jazz Band Plays Cole Porter — 197? — $30
❑ 9 — The World's Greatest Jazz Band Plays Duke Ellington — 197? — $30
❑ 11 — The World's Greatest Jazz Band Plays George Gershwin — 1978 — $30
❑ 7 — The World's Greatest Jazz Band Plays Rodgers and Hart — 197? — $30

WRICE, LARRY "WILD"
Albums
PACIFIC JAZZ
❑ PJ-24 [M] — Wild! — 1961 — $60
❑ ST-24 [S] — Wild! — 1961 — $60

WRIGHT, BERNARD
Keyboard player and male singer.
Albums
ARISTA
❑ ALB8-8103 — Funky Beat — 198? — $25
GRP/ARISTA
❑ GL5011 — 'Nard — 1980 — $30
MANHATTAN
❑ ST-53014 — Mr. Wright — 1985 — $25

WRIGHT, DEMPSEY
Guitarist.
Albums
ANDEX
❑ A-3006 [M] — The Wright Approach — 1958 — $60
❑ AS-3006 [S] — The Wright Approach — 1958 — $50

WRIGHT, FRANK
Tenor saxophone player.
Albums
CHIAROSCURO
❑ 2014 — Kevin, My Dear Son — 1979 — $30
ESP-DISK'
❑ 1023 [M] — Frank Wright Trio — 1966 — $100
❑ S-1023 [S] — Frank Wright Trio — 1966 — $100
❑ 1053 [S] — Your Prayer — 1968 — $100

WRIGHT, JOHN
Pianist.
Albums
FANTASY
❑ OJC-1743 — South Side Soul — 1990 — $30
NEW JAZZ
❑ NJLP-8322 [M] — The Last Amen — 196? — $0
— Canceled; reassigned to Status
PRESTIGE

Number	Title	Yr	NM
❏ PRLP-7212 [M]	Makin' Out	1961	$200
❏ PRLP-7233 [M]	Mr. Soul	1962	$150
❏ PRST-7233 [S]	Mr. Soul	1962	$150
❏ PRLP-7197 [M]	Nice 'N' Nasty	1961	$200
❏ PRLP-7190 [M]	South Side Soul	1960	$200
STATUS			
❏ ST-8322 [M]	The Last Amen	1965	$80

WRIGHT, LEO
Alto saxophone player, flutist and clarinetist.
Albums
ATLANTIC

❏ 1358 [M]	Blues Shout	1960	$300

—*Multicolor label, white "fan" logo at right*

❏ SD1358 [S]	Blues Shout	1960	$300

—*Multicolor label, white "fan" logo at right*

❏ 1358 [M]	Blues Shout	196?	$35

—*Multicolor label, black "fan" logo at right*

❏ SD1358 [S]	Blues Shout	196?	$25

—*Multicolor label, black "fan" logo at right*

❏ 1393 [M]	Suddenly the Blues	1962	$150

—*Multicolor label, black "fan" logo at right*

❏ SD1393 [S]	Suddenly the Blues	1962	$150

—*Multicolor label, black "fan" logo at right*

ROULETTE			
❏ SR-5007	Evening Breeze	1977	$25
VORTEX			
❏ 2011	Soul Talk	197?	$25

WRIGHT, MARVIN "LEFTY"
Pianist.
Albums
X

❏ LXA-3028 [10]	Boogie Woogie Piano	1954	$60

WRIGHT, NAT
Male singer.
Albums
WARWICK

❏ W-2040 [M]	The Biggest Voice in Jazz	1961	$50
❏ W-2040ST [S]	The Biggest Voice in Jazz	1961	$80

WYNN, ALBERT
Trombonist and bandleader.
Albums
RIVERSIDE

❏ RLP-426 [M]	Albert Wynn and His Gutbucket Seven	1962	$200
❏ RS-9426 [R]	Albert Wynn and His Gutbucket Seven	1962	$200

Y

YAGED, SOL
Clarinetist.
Albums
HERALD

❏ HLP-0103 [M]	It Might As Well Be Swing	1956	$50
LANE			
❏ LP-149 [M]	Live at the Gaslight Club	195?	$50
❏ LPS-154 [S]	One More Time	195?	$50
❏ LP-155 [M]	Sol Yaged at the Gaslight Club	195?	$50
❏ LPS-155 [S]	Sol Yaged at the Gaslight Club	195?	$50
PHILIPS			
❏ PHM200002 [M]	Jazz at the Metropole	1961	$35

YALE DIXIELAND BAND, THE
Albums
COLUMBIA

❏ CL736 [M]	Eli's Chosen Six	1955	$50

YAMA YAMA JAZZ BAND, THE
Albums
JAZZOLOGY

❏ J-78	New Orleans Jazz -- Australian Style, Vol. 1	198?	$25
❏ J-79	New Orleans Jazz -- Australian Style, Vol. 2	198?	$25

YAMAMOTO, TSUYOSHI
Pianist and composer.
Albums
CONCORD JAZZ

❏ CJ-218	Zephyr	1981	$25
THREE BLIND MICE			
❏ TBM-23	Midnight Sugar	1995	$30

—*Audiophile vinyl*

❏ TBM-30	Misty	199?	$30

—*Audiophile vinyl*

YAMASHITA, STOMU
Percussionist.
Albums
KUCKUCK

❏ KU-072	Sea and Sky	198?	$30

YANCEY, JIMMY
Albums
ATLANTIC

❏ ALS-134 [10]	Piano Solos	1952	$350
❏ 1283 [M]	Pure Blues	1958	$300

—*Black label*

❏ 1283 [M]	Pure Blues	1961	$150

—*Multicolor label, white "fan" logo at right*

❏ 1283 [M]	Pure Blues	1964	$35

—*Multicolor label, black "fan" logo at right*

❏ ALS-103 [10]	Yancey Special	1950	$250
❏ ALS-130 [10]	Yancey Special	1952	$350
JAZZOLOGY			
❏ J-51	In the Beginning	197?	$25
PARAMOUNT			
❏ CJS-101 [10]	Yancey Special	1951	$175
PAX			
❏ LP-6011 [10]	1943 Mixture	1954	$80
❏ LP-6012 [10]	Evening With the Yanceys	1954	$80
RIVERSIDE			
❏ RLP-1028 [10]	Lost Recording Date	1954	$300
❏ RLP 12-124 [M]	Yancey's Getaway	1956	$250

YANCEY, MAMA, AND ART HODES
Yancey is a female singer. Also see ART HODES.
Albums
VERVE FOLKWAYS

❏ FVS-9015 [S]	Blues	1965	$35
❏ FV-9015 [M]	Blues	1965	$35

YANKEE RHYTHM KINGS
Formed in 1974 in Boston. Among the members: Bob Connors (trombone); Jeff Hughes (cornet, trumpet, fluegel horn); Jim Mazzy (banjo, vocals).
Albums
GHB

❏ GHB-151	Classic Jazz of the 20s	1980	$25
❏ GHB-97	Classic Jazz of the 20s	1978	$25
❏ GHB-83	Yankee Rhythm Kings, Vol. 1	197?	$25

YARBROUGH, CAMILLE
Female singer and composer.
Albums
VANGUARD

❏ VSD-79356	The Iron Pot Cooker	197?	$30

YAZ-KAZ
Albums
GRAMAVISION

❏ 18-7013	Jonon-Sho	198?	$30

YELL CHASERS, THE
Albums
REALTIME

❏ 822	I've Got My Fingers	197?	$25

—*Direct-to-disc recording; plays at 45 rpm*

YELLIN, PETE
Alto saxophone player and flutist.
Albums
MAINSTREAM

❏ MRL-363	Dance of Allegra	197?	$35
❏ MRL-397	It's the Right Thing	1974	$35

YELLOWJACKETS
Members: Russell Ferrante (keyboards); Jimmy Haslip (bass); Mark Russo (alto sax through 1990); Ricky Lawson (drums, replaced by William Kennedy in 1986); Robben Ford (guitar through 1983).
Albums
MCA

❏ 5994	Four Corners	1987	$25
❏ 6236	Politics	1988	$25
❏ 5752	Shades	1986	$25
❏ 6304	The Spin	1989	$30
WARNER BROS.			
❏ 23813	Mirage A Trois	1983	$25
❏ 25204	Samurai Samba	1985	$25
❏ BSK3573	The Yellowjackets	1982	$25

YERBA BUENA JAZZ BAND, THE
See LU WATTERS.

YORK, BETH
Pianist.
Albums
LADYSLIPPER

❏ LR-104	Transformations	1986	$30

YOST, PHIL
Bass player, soprano saxophone player, flutist, guitarist and banjo player. On the below albums, he played all the instruments.
Albums
TAKOMA

❏ C-1016	Bent City	196?	$50
❏ C-1021	Fog-Hat Ramble	196?	$50

YOSUKA, YAMASHITA
Pianist and keyboard player.
Albums
WEST 54

❏ 8009	Breathtake	1980	$30

YOUNG, CECIL
Trumpeter.
Albums
AUDIO LAB

❏ AL-1516 [M]	Jazz on the Rocks	1959	$80
KING			
❏ 295-1 [10]	A Concert of Cool Jazz	1952	$100

YOUNG, DAVID
Tenor saxophone player.
Albums
MAINSTREAM

❏ MRL-323	David Young	1972	$35

YOUNG, ELDEE
Bass player; was a member of the classic RAMSEY LEWIS Trio of the 1960s. Also see YOUNG-HOLT UNLIMITED.
Albums
ARGO

❏ LPS-1003 [S]	Eldee Young and Company	1962	$30
❏ LPS-699 [S]	Just for Kicks	1962	$25

YOUNG, JOHN
Pianist.

Albums
ARGO

Number	Title	Yr	NM
❑ LP-713 [M]	A Touch of Pepper	1962	$30
❑ LPS-713 [S]	A Touch of Pepper	1962	$30
❑ LP-692 [M]	Themes and Things	1962	$30
❑ LPS-692 [S]	Themes and Things	1962	$30
❑ LP-612 [M]	Young John Young	1957	$40

CADET

Number	Title	Yr	NM
❑ LPS-692 [S]	Themes and Things	1966	$35
❑ LP-692 [M]	Themes and Things	1966	$30

DELMARK

Number	Title	Yr	NM
❑ DL-403 [M]	The John Young Trio	1961	$30
❑ DS-403 [S]	The John Young Trio	1961	$40

VEE JAY

Number	Title	Yr	NM
❑ VJS-3060	Opus de Funk	1974	$25

YOUNG, LARRY
Organist and composer.

Albums
ARISTA

Number	Title	Yr	NM
❑ AL4072	Spaceball	1976	$30

BLUE NOTE

Number	Title	Yr	NM
❑ BLP-4266 [S]	Contrasts	1967	$80
❑ BST-84266 [S]	Contrasts	1967	$30
— With "A Division of Liberty Records" on label			
❑ BST-84304 [S]	Heaven on Earth	1968	$30
— With "A Division of Liberty Records" on label			
❑ BLP-4187 [M]	Into Somethin'	1964	$60
❑ BST-84187 [S]	Into Somethin'	1964	$40
— With "New York, USA" address on label			
❑ BST-84187 [S]	Into Somethin'	1967	$25
— With "A Division of Liberty Records" on label			
❑ LT-1038	Mother Ship	1980	$30
❑ BLP-4242 [M]	Of Love and Peace	1966	$60
❑ BST-84242 [S]	Of Love and Peace	1966	$40
— With "New York, USA" address on label			
❑ BST-84242 [S]	Of Love and Peace	1967	$25
— With "A Division of Liberty Records" on label			
❑ BST-84221 [S]	Unity	1966	$40
— With "New York, USA" address on label			
❑ BST-84221 [S]	Unity	1967	$25
— With "A Division of Liberty Records" on label			
❑ BST-84221	Unity	198?	$25
— The Finest in Jazz Since 1939" reissue			

MOSAIC

Number	Title	Yr	NM
❑ MR9-137	The Complete Blue Note Recordings of Larry Young	199?	$200

NEW JAZZ

Number	Title	Yr	NM
❑ NJLP-8249 [M]	Testifying	1960	$150
— Purple label			
❑ NJLP-8249 [M]	Testifying	1965	$150
— Blue label, trident logo at right			
❑ NJLP-8264 [M]	Young Blues	1961	$200
— Purple label			
❑ NJLP-8264 [M]	Young Blues	1965	$150
— Blue label, trident logo at right			

PRESTIGE

Number	Title	Yr	NM
❑ PRLP-7237 [M]	Groove Street	1962	$150
❑ PRST-7237 [S]	Groove Street	1962	$150

YOUNG, LESTER, AND PAUL QUINICHETTE
Also see each artist's individual listings.

Albums
EMARCY

Number	Title	Yr	NM
❑ MG-26021 [10]	Pres Meets Vice-Pres	1954	$250

YOUNG, LESTER; ROY ELDRIDGE; HARRY "SWEETS" EDISON
Also see each artist's individual listings.

Albums
VERVE

Number	Title	Yr	NM
❑ MGV-8298 [M]	Going for Myself	1959	$100
❑ V-8298 [M]	Going for Myself	1961	$30
❑ MGV-8316 [M]	Laughin' to Keep from Cryin'	1960	$100
❑ V-8316 [M]	Laughin' to Keep from Cryin'	1961	$30
❑ MGVS-6054 [S]	Laughin' to Keep from Cryin'	1960	$150
❑ V6-8316 [S]	Laughin' to Keep from Cryin'	1961	$30
❑ UMV-2694	Laughin' to Keep from Cryin'	198?	$25
❑ MGVS-6054 [S]	Laughin' to Keep from Cryin'	199?	$30
— Classic Records reissue on audiophile vinyl			

YOUNG, LESTER
Tenor saxophone player, clarinetist and male singer. His nickname "Pres" was coined by BILLIE HOLIDAY. Also see COLEMAN HAWKINS.

Albums
ALADDIN

Number	Title	Yr	NM
❑ LP-706 [10]	Easy Does It	1954	$700
❑ LP-801 [M]	Lester Young and His Tenor Sax, Volume 1	1956	$400
❑ LP-802 [M]	Lester Young and His Tenor Sax, Volume 2	1956	$300
❑ LP-705 [10]	Lester Young Trio	1953	$300

AMERICAN RECORDING SOCIETY

Number	Title	Yr	NM
❑ G-417 [M]	Pres and Teddy	1957	$50

BLUE NOTE

Number	Title	Yr	NM
❑ BN-LA456-H2	Pres: The Aladdin Sessions	1975	$35

CHARLIE PARKER

Number	Title	Yr	NM
❑ CLP-402 [M]	Pres	1961	$50
❑ CLP-405 [M]	Pres Is Blue	1961	$50

CLEF

Number	Title	Yr	NM
❑ MGC-108 [10]	Lester Young Collates	1953	$350
❑ MGC-124 [10]	Lester Young Collates No. 2	1953	$350
— Some copies of this have Mercury covers; no difference in value			
❑ MGC-104 [10]	The Lester Young Trio	1953	$350
❑ MGC-135 [10]	The Lester Young Trio No. 2	1953	$350

COLUMBIA

Number	Title	Yr	NM
❑ JG33502	The Lester Young Story, Vol. 1	1975	$35
❑ JG34837	The Lester Young Story, Vol. 2: Romance	1976	$35
❑ JG34840	The Lester Young Story, Vol. 3: Enter Count	1976	$35

COMMODORE

Number	Title	Yr	NM
❑ XFL-15352	A Complete Session	198?	$25
❑ FL-20021 [10]	Kansas City Style	1952	$300
❑ FL-30014 [M]	Kansas City Style	1959	$100
❑ XFL-14937	The Kansas City Six and Five	198?	$25

CROWN

Number	Title	Yr	NM
❑ CLP-5305 [M]	Nat "King" Cole Meets Lester Young	196?	$30
❑ CST-305 [R]	Nat "King" Cole Meets Lester Young	196?	$30

EMARCY

Number	Title	Yr	NM
❑ SRE-66010	Lester Young At His Very Best	1967	$100

EPIC

Number	Title	Yr	NM
❑ LN3107 [M]	Lester Leaps In	1956	$200
❑ SN6031 [M]	Lester Young Memorial Album	1959	$300
❑ LN3576 [M]	Lester Young Memorial Album, Volume 1	1959	$100
❑ LN3577 [M]	Lester Young Memorial Album, Volume 2	1959	$100
❑ LN3168 [M]	Let's Go to Pres	1956	$200

EVEREST ARCHIVE OF FOLK & JAZZ

Number	Title	Yr	NM
❑ 287	Pres	197?	$25

IMPERIAL

Number	Title	Yr	NM
❑ LP-9187-A [M]	The Great Lester Young, Volume 2	1962	$175
❑ LP-12187-A [R]	The Great Lester Young, Volume 2	196?	$150
❑ LP-9181-A [M]	The Immortal Lester Young	1962	$175
❑ LP-12181-A [R]	The Immortal Lester Young	196?	$150

INTRO

Number	Title	Yr	NM
❑ LP-602 [M]	Swinging Lester Young	1957	$100
❑ LP-603 [M]	The Greatest	1957	$100

JAZZ ARCHIVES

Number	Title	Yr	NM
❑ JA-18	Jammin' with Lester, Vol. 1	198?	$25
❑ JA-34	Jammin' with Lester, Vol. 2	198?	$25
❑ JA-42	Lester Young and Charlie Christian 1939-40	198?	$25

MAINSTREAM

Number	Title	Yr	NM
❑ 56009 [M]	52nd Street	1965	$30
❑ S-6009 [R]	52nd Street	1965	$30
❑ 56008 [M]	Chairman of the Board	1965	$30
❑ S-6008 [R]	Chairman of the Board	1965	$30
❑ 56012 [M]	Prez	1965	$30
❑ S-6012 [R]	Prez	1965	$30
❑ 56002 [M]	The Influence of Five	1965	$30
❑ S-6002 [R]	The Influence of Five	1965	$30
❑ 56004 [M]	Town Hall Concert	1965	$30
❑ S-6004 [R]	Town Hall Concert	1965	$30

MERCURY

Number	Title	Yr	NM
❑ MGC-108 [10]	Lester Young Collates	1951	$300
❑ MGC-124 [10]	Lester Young Collates No. 2	1953	$0
— Canceled			
❑ MGC-104 [10]	The Lester Young Trio	1951	$300

NORGRAN

Number	Title	Yr	NM
❑ MGN-1071 [M]	Lester's Here	1956	$200
❑ MGN-1093 [M]	Lester Swings Again	1956	$200
❑ MGN-1022 [M]	Lester Young	1955	$200
❑ MGN-1100 [M]	Lester Young	1956	$200
❑ MGN-1074 [M]	Lester Young and the Buddy Rich Trio	1956	$200
❑ MGN-5 [10]	Lester Young with the Oscar Peterson Trio No. 1	1954	$500
❑ MGN-6 [10]	Lester Young with the Oscar Peterson Trio No. 2	1954	$500
❑ MGN-1072 [M]	Pres	1956	$100
❑ MGN-1043 [M]	Pres and Sweets	1955	$200
❑ MGN-1005 [M]	The President	1954	$350
❑ MGN-1054 [M]	The President Plays with the Oscar Peterson Trio	1955	$100

ONYX

Number	Title	Yr	NM
❑ 218	Prez in Europe	197?	$30

PABLO

Number	Title	Yr	NM
❑ 2405420	The Best of Lester Young	198?	$25

PABLO LIVE

Number	Title	Yr	NM
❑ 2308219	Lester Young in Washington, D.C., at Olivia Davis', Vol. 1	1979	$30
❑ 2308225	Lester Young in Washington, D.C., at Olivia Davis', Vol. 2	1980	$30
❑ 2308228	Lester Young in Washington, D.C., at Olivia Davis', Vol. 3	198?	$25
❑ 2308230	Lester Young in Washington, D.C., at Olivia Davis', Vol. 4	198?	$25

PICKWICK

Number	Title	Yr	NM
❑ SPC-5015	Prez Leaps Again	197?	$25

SAVOY

Number	Title	Yr	NM
❑ MG-12068 [M]	Blue Lester	1956	$80
❑ MG-9002 [10]	Lester Young (All Star Be Bop)	1951	$300
❑ MG-12155 [M]	The Immortal Lester Young	1959	$60
❑ MG-12071 [M]	The Master's Touch	1956	$80

SAVOY JAZZ

Number	Title	Yr	NM
❑ SJL-1133	Master Takes	198?	$25
❑ SJL-1109	Pres Lives	1977	$25
❑ SJL-2202	The Complete Lester Younbg (1944-49)	197?	$35

SCORE

Number	Title	Yr	NM
❑ SLP-4019 [M]	Lester Young / The King Cole Trio	1958	$80
❑ SLP-4028 [M]	Swinging Lester Young	1958	$80
❑ SLP-4029 [M]	The Great Lester Young	1958	$80

SUNSET

Number	Title	Yr	NM
❑ SUS-5181	Giant of Jazz	1967	$30

TIME-LIFE

Number	Title	Yr	NM
❑ STL-J-13	Giants of Jazz	1980	$50

TRIP

Number	Title	Yr	NM
❑ 5519	Pres at His Best	197?	$25

VERVE

Number	Title	Yr	NM
❑ VSP-30 [M]	Giants 3	1966	$30
— With Buddy Rich and Nat King Cole			
❑ VSPS-30 [R]	Giants 3	1966	$30
❑ MGV-8187 [M]	It Don't Mean a Thing (If It Ain't Got That Swing)	1957	$150
❑ V-8187 [M]	It Don't Mean a Thing (If It Ain't Got That Swing)	1961	$30
❑ VE-2-2527	Jazz Giants '56	197?	$35
❑ MGV-8161 [M]	Lester's Here	1957	$150
❑ V-8161 [M]	Lester's Here	1961	$30
❑ VE-2-2516	Lester Swings	197?	$35
❑ 833554-1	Lester Swings	198?	$30
❑ MGV-8181 [M]	Lester Swings Again	1957	$150
❑ V-8181 [M]	Lester Swings Again	1961	$30
❑ MGV-8164 [M]	Lester Young and the Buddy Rich Trio	1957	$150
❑ V-8164 [M]	Lester Young and the Buddy Rich Trio	1961	$30
❑ VSPS-41 [R]	Lester Young at J.A.T.P.	196?	$30
❑ VSP-41 [M]	Lester Young at J.A.T.P.	196?	$35
❑ MGV-8378 [M]	Lester Young in Paris	1960	$100
❑ V-8378 [M]	Lester Young in Paris	1961	$30
❑ VE-2-2538	Mean to Me	197?	$35
❑ VE-2-2502	Pres & Teddy & Oscar	197?	$35
❑ MGV-8162 [M]	Pres	1957	$100
❑ V-8162 [M]	Pres	1961	$30
❑ UMV-2672	Pres	198?	$25
❑ VSP-27 [M]	Pres and His Cabinet	1966	$30
❑ VSPS-27 [R]	Pres and His Cabinet	1966	$30
❑ MGV-8134 [M]	Pres and Sweets	1957	$100
❑ V-8134 [M]	Pres and Sweets	1961	$30
❑ UMV-2528	Pres and Sweets	198?	$25
❑ MGV-8205 [M]	Pres and Teddy	1957	$100
❑ V-8205 [M]	Pres and Teddy	1961	$30
❑ MGV-8398 [M]	The Essential Lester Young	1961	$60
❑ V-8398 [M]	The Essential Lester Young	1961	$30
❑ MGV-8308 [M]	The Lester Young Story	1959	$100
❑ V-8308 [M]	The Lester Young Story	1961	$30
❑ MGV-8144 [M]	The President Plays with the Oscar Peterson Trio	1957	$100
❑ V-8144 [M]	The President Plays with the Oscar Peterson Trio	1961	$30

YOUNG, LESTER/CHU BERRY
Also see each artist's individual listings.

Albums

JAZZTONE

Number	Title	Yr	NM
❏ J-1218 [M]	Tops on Tenor: Pres and Chu	1956	$125

YOUNG, LESTER/COUNT BASIE
Also see each artist's individual listings.

Albums

MERCURY

Number	Title	Yr	NM
❏ MG-25015 [10]	Lester Young Quartet/Count Basie Seven	1950	$300

YOUNG, NOAH
Bass player.

Albums

LAUGHING ANGEL

Number	Title	Yr	NM
❏ LAR33	Unicorn Dream	1981	$35

YOUNG, SNOOKY
Trumpeter and fluegel horn player.

Albums

CONCORD JAZZ

Number	Title	Yr	NM
❏ CJ-91	Horn of Plenty	1979	$30
❏ CJ-55	The Snooky Young/Marshal Royal Album	1977	$30

MASTER JAZZ

Number	Title	Yr	NM
❏ 8130	Dayton	197?	$30

YOUNG, STERLING
Violinist and bandleader.

Albums

HINDSIGHT

Number	Title	Yr	NM
❏ HSR-113	Sterling Young and His Orchestra 1939-1949	198?	$25

YOUNG, WEBSTER
Trumpeter.

Albums

FANTASY

Number	Title	Yr	NM
❏ OJC-1716	For Lady	198?	$25

PRESTIGE

Number	Title	Yr	NM
❏ PRLP-7106 [M]	For Lady	1957	$650

YOUNG-HOLT UNLIMITED
Group formed by RED HOLT and ELDEE YOUNG after they left the RAMSEY LEWIS Trio. In late 1968-early 1969, they had a Top 10 hit single with the instrumental "Soulful Strut."

Albums

ATLANTIC

Number	Title	Yr	NM
❏ SD1634	Oh Girl	1973	$30

BRUNSWICK

Number	Title	Yr	NM
❏ BL754141	Funky But!	1968	$50
❏ BL754150	Just a Melody	1969	$35
❏ BL54125 [M]	On Stage	1967	$50

—As "Young-Holt Trio"

Number	Title	Yr	NM
❏ BL754125 [S]	On Stage	1967	$50

—As "Young-Holt Trio"

Number	Title	Yr	NM
❏ BL754144	Soulful Strut	1968	$35
❏ BL54128 [M]	The Beat Goes On	1967	$60
❏ BL754128 [S]	The Beat Goes On	1967	$50
❏ BL54121 [M]	Wack-Wack	1966	$50

—As "Young-Holt Trio"

Number	Title	Yr	NM
❏ BL754121 [S]	Wack-Wack	1966	$50

—As "Young-Holt Trio"

CADET

Number	Title	Yr	NM
❏ LPS-791 [S]	Feature Spot	1967	$50

—As "Eldee Young and Red Holt (of the Ramsey Lewis Trio)"

Number	Title	Yr	NM
❏ LP-791 [M]	Feature Spot	1967	$60

COTILLION

Number	Title	Yr	NM
❏ SD18004	Born Again	1972	$30
❏ SD18001	Mellow Dreamin'	1971	$30

PAULA

Number	Title	Yr	NM
❏ LPS-4002	Super Fly	1973	$50

YOUNG LIONS, THE (1)
Members: Bob Cranshaw; LOUIS HAYES; ALBERT HEATH; LEE MORGAN; WAYNE SHORTER; BOBBY TIMMONS.

Albums

TRIP

Number	Title	Yr	NM
❏ 5011	Lions of Jazz	197?	$30

VEE JAY

Number	Title	Yr	NM
❏ VJS-3013 [S]	The Young Lions	197?	$25

—Reissue on thinner, more flexible vinyl

Number	Title	Yr	NM
❏ SR-3013 [S]	The Young Lions	1960	$50

YOUNG LIONS, THE (2)
Approximately 17 young musicians in a gig recorded live at Carnegie Hall.

Albums

ELEKTRA/MUSICIAN

Number	Title	Yr	NM
❏ 60196	The Young Lions	1984	$30

YOUNG MEN FROM MEMPHIS
Members: BOOKER LITTLE, Louis Smith (trumpet); FRANK STROZIER (alto sax); GEORGE COLEMAN (tenor sax); PHINEAS NEWBORN (piano); Calvin Newborn (guitar); George Joyner, aka Jamil Nasser (bass); Charles Crosby (drums).

Albums

UNITED ARTISTS

Number	Title	Yr	NM
❏ UAL-4029 [M]	Down Home Reunion	1959	$50
❏ UAS-5029 [S]	Down Home Reunion	1959	$40

YOUNG TUXEDO BRASS BAND, THE
Members at the time of recording: John Casimir (E-flat clarinet, leader); Andrew Anderson (trumpet), John "Pickey" Brunious (trumpet); Albert "Fernandez" Walters (trumpet); Clement Tervalon (trombone), Jim Robinson (trombone), Herman Sherman (alto sax), Andrew Morgan (tenor sax), Wilbert Tillman (sousaphone), Emile Knox (bass drum), Paul Barbarin (snare drum).

Albums

ATLANTIC

Number	Title	Yr	NM
❏ 1297 [M]	Jazz Begins	1958	$300

—Black label

Number	Title	Yr	NM
❏ SD-1297 [M]	Jazz Begins	1958	$300

—Green label

Number	Title	Yr	NM
❏ 1297 [M]	Jazz Begins	1961	$150

—Multicolor label, white "fan" logo at right

Number	Title	Yr	NM
❏ SD-1297 [M]	Jazz Begins	1961	$150

—Multicolor label, white "fan" logo at right

Number	Title	Yr	NM
❏ 1297 [M]	Jazz Begins	1964	$35

—Multicolor label, black "fan" logo at right

Number	Title	Yr	NM
❏ SD-1297 [M]	Jazz Begins	1964	$30

—Multicolor label, black "fan" logo at right

YOUR FRIENDLY NEIGHBORHOOD BIG BAND
See MATT CATINGUB.

YUTAKA
Keyboard player.

Albums

GRP

Number	Title	Yr	NM
❏ GR-1046	Yutaka	1988	$25

Z

ZACK, GEORGE
Pianist and male singer.

Albums

COMMODORE

Number	Title	Yr	NM
❏ FL-20001 [10]	Party Piano of the Roaring '20s	1950	$50

ZAHARA

Albums

ANTILLES

Number	Title	Yr	NM
❏ AN-1011	Flight of the Spirit	198?	$30

ZAPPA, FRANK
Guitarist, keyboard player, composer, bandleader and male vocalist, Zappa is prominent as a rock musician, but he's impossible to pigeonhole. Many of his albums, especially on the Barking Pumpkin and Bizarre labels, are jazzy. Zappa was chosen by jazz critics to the Down Beat Magazine Jazz Hall of Fame in 1994.

Albums

ANGEL

Number	Title	Yr	NM
❏ DS-38170	Boulez Conducts Zappa: The Perfect Stranger	1983	$30

BARKING PUMPKIN

Number	Title	Yr	NM
❏ D1-74218	Broadway the Hard Way	1988	$25
❏ ST-74202	Francesco Zappa	1985	$25
❏ ST-74203	Frank Zappa Meets the Mothers of Prevention	1985	$25
❏ D1-74212	Guitar	1988	$25
❏ ST-74205	Jazz from Hell	1986	$25
❏ 74206	Joe's Garage, Acts 1, 2 and 3	1986	$100

—Box set, two gatefolds, with insert

Number	Title	Yr	NM
❏ FW38820	London Symphony Orchestra	1983	$30
❏ SJ-74207	London Symphony Orchestra, Volume 2	1987	$25
❏ FW38403	Man from Utopia	1983	$30
❏ FW38066	Ship Arriving Too Late to Save a Drowning Witch	1982	$30
❏ SVBO-74200	Them Or Us	1984	$35
❏ SWCO-74201	Thing-Fish	1984	$50
❏ PW237336	Tinsel Town Rebellion	1981	$50
❏ AS995 [DJ]	Tinsel Town Rebellion	1981	$50

—Promo-only sampler

Number	Title	Yr	NM
❏ PW237537	You Are What You Is	1981	$50
❏ AS1294 [DJ]	You Are What You Is Special Clean Cuts Edition	1981	$50
❏ R174213	You Can't Do That on Stage Anymore Sampler	1988	$30
❏ D1-74213	You Can't Do That on Stage Anymore Sampler	1988	$25
❏ D1-74217	You Can't Do That on Stage Anymore Vol. 2	1988	$25

BIZARRE

Number	Title	Yr	NM
❏ MS-2030	Chunga's Revenge	1970	$60

—Blue label original

Number	Title	Yr	NM
❏ MS-2030	Chunga's Revenge	1973	$35

—Reissue with brown Reprise label

Number	Title	Yr	NM
❏ MS-2042	Fillmore East, June 1971	1973	$35

—Reissue with brown Reprise label

Number	Title	Yr	NM
❏ RS-6356	Hot Rats	1969	$100

—Blue label original

Number	Title	Yr	NM
❏ RS-6356	Hot Rats	1973	$35

—Reissue with brown Reprise label

Number	Title	Yr	NM
❏ MS2075	Just Another Band from L.A.	1973	$35

—Reissue with brown Reprise label

Number	Title	Yr	NM
❏ MS2093	The Grand Wazoo	1973	$35

—Reissue with brown Reprise label

Number	Title	Yr	NM
❏ MS-2024	Uncle Meat	1973	$50

—Reissue with brown Reprise label

COLUMBIA

Number	Title	Yr	NM
❏ (no #) [DJ]	Lather	1977	$750

—Test pressing only; parts of this LP are on DSK 2291, 2292 and 2294; released as a whole only after Zappa's death, with vinyl only coming out in Japan

DISCREET

Number	Title	Yr	NM
❏ DS2175	Apostrophe (')	1974	$35
❏ DS42175 [Q]	Apostrophe (')	1974	$100
❏ DS2175	Apostrophe (')	1974	$100

—White label promo

Number	Title	Yr	NM
❏ DSK2289	Apostrophe (')	1977	$30

—Reissue with new number

Number	Title	Yr	NM
❏ DS2234	Bongo Fury	1975	$35
❏ DS2216	One Size Fits All	1975	$35
❏ DSK2294	Orchestral Favorites	1978	$35
❏ MS42149 [Q]	Over-Nite Sensation	1973	$100
❏ DSK2288	Over-Nite Sensation	1977	$30

—Reissue of DiscReet 2149 with new number

Number	Title	Yr	NM
❏ 2DS2202	Roxy and Elsewhere	1974	$60
❏ DSK2292	Sleep Dirt	1978	$35
❏ DSK2291	Studio Tan	1978	$35
❏ 2D2290 [DJ]	Zappa in New York	1978	$400

—Test pressing with "Punky's Whips"

Number	Title	Yr	NM
❏ 2D2290	Zappa in New York	1978	$250

—Stock copy with "Punky's Whips" erroneously listed on jacket

Number	Title	Yr	NM
❏ 2D2290	Zappa in New York	1978	$50

MCA

Number	Title	Yr	NM
❑ 4183	200 Motels (movie soundtrack)	1986	$35

—Reissue

MGM

| ❑ GAS-112 [DJ] | The Mothers of Invention | 1970 | $175 |

— Yellow label promo

| ❑ GAS-112 | The Mothers of Invention | 1970 | $100 |
| ❑ SE-4754 [DJ] | The Worst of the Mothers | 1971 | $300 |

— Yellow label promo

| ❑ SE-4754 | The Worst of the Mothers | 1971 | $100 |

RHINO/DEL-FI

| ❑ RNEP-604 | Rare Meat: The Early Productions of Frank Zappa | 1984 | $40 |

— With original cover

UNITED ARTISTS

| ❑ UAS-9956 | 200 Motels (movie soundtrack) | 1971 | $100 |

VERVE

| ❑ V6-5055 | Cruising with Ruben and the Jets | 1968 | $120 |
| ❑ V-5005-2 [M] | Freak Out! | 1966 | $400 |

— White label promo

| ❑ V-5005-2 [M] | Freak Out! | 1966 | $200 |

—Cover version 1: Has blurb on inside gatefold on how to get a map of "freak-out hot spots" in L.A.

| ❑ V6-5005-2 [S] | Freak Out! | 1966 | $300 |

— Yellow label promo

| ❑ V6-5005-2 [S] | Freak Out! | 1966 | $150 |

— Cover version 1: Has blurb on inside gatefold on how to get a map of "freak-out hot spots" in L.A.

| ❑ V6-8741 [DJ] | Lumpy Gravy | 1968 | $200 |

— Yellow label promo

| ❑ V6-5068 [DJ] | Mothermania -- The Best of the Mothers | 1969 | $150 |

— Yellow label promo

| ❑ V6-5074 [DJ] | The XXXX of the Mothers | 1969 | $300 |

— Yellow label promo

| ❑ V6-5074 | The XXXX of the Mothers | 1969 | $100 |
| ❑ V6-5045 [S] | We're Only in It for the Money | 1968 | $120 |

— Un-censored version, with cut-outs

WARNER BROS.

| ❑ BS-2970 | Zoot Allures | 1976 | $35 |

ZAPPA

❑ SRZ-1-1603	Joe's Garage, Act I	1979	$35
❑ SRZ-2-1502	Joe's Garage, Acts II and III	1980	$50
❑ MK-129 [DJ]	Joe's Garage Acts I, II and III Sampler	1980	$150
❑ SRZ-2-1501	Sheik Yerbouti	1979	$50
❑ MK-78 [DJ]	Sheik Yerbouti Clean Cuts	1979	$150

ZAWINUL, JOE

Keyboard player and composer (wrote "Mercy, Mercy, Mercy" and "Birdland"). Two of the albums on Columbia were released as "Zawinul Syndicate." Also see WEATHER REPORT; BEN WEBSTER.

Albums

ATLANTIC

❑ SD1694	Concerto	1976	$35
❑ 3004 [M]	Money in the Pocket	1966	$50
❑ SD3004 [S]	Money in the Pocket	1966	$60
❑ SD1579	Zawinul	1970	$50

COLUMBIA

❑ FC44316	Black Water	1989	$30
❑ FC40081	Dialects	1986	$25
❑ FC40969	Immigrants	1988	$25

VORTEX

| ❑ 2002 [S] | The Rise and Fall of the 3rd Stream | 1968 | $50 |

ZEITLIN, DENNY, AND CHARLIE HADEN

Also see each artist's individual listings.

Albums

ECM

| ❑ 1239 | Time Remembers One Time Once | 1981 | $30 |

ZEITLIN, DENNY

Pianist.

Albums

1750 ARCH

| ❑ 1758 | Expansions | 197? | $35 |
| ❑ 1770 | Soundings | 1979 | $35 |

Number	Title	Yr	NM
❑ 1759	Syzygy	197?	$35

COLUMBIA

❑ CL2340 [M]	Carnival	1965	$25
❑ CS9140 [S]	Carnival	1965	$30
❑ CL2182 [M]	Cathexis	1964	$25
❑ CS8982 [S]	Cathexis	1964	$30
❑ CL2463 [M]	My Shining Hour	1966	$35
❑ CS9263 [S]	My Shining Hour	1966	$25
❑ CL2748 [M]	Zeitgeist	1966	$35
❑ CS9548 [S]	Zeitgeist	1966	$50

LIVING MUSIC

| ❑ LM-0011 | Homecoming | 1986 | $25 |

WINDHAM HILL

| ❑ WH-0112 | Denny Zeitlin Trio | 1988 | $25 |
| ❑ WH-0121 | In the Moment | 1989 | $30 |

ZENITH HOT STOMPERS, THE

British group.

Albums

STOMP OFF

| ❑ SOS-1191 | 20th Anniversary Album | 1991 | $30 |

ZENITH SIX, THE

British group, it once shared a bill with The Beatles at the Cavern Club in Liverpool (October 13, 1962, to be exact).

Albums

GHB

| ❑ GHB-12 | The Zenith Six, Vol. 1 | 196? | $30 |
| ❑ GHB-13 | The Zenith Six, Vol. 2 | 196? | $30 |

ZENTNER, SI

Bandleader and trombonist.

Albums

LIBERTY

❑ LMM-13009 [M]	A Great Band with Great Voices	1961	$30
❑ LSS-14009 [S]	A Great Band with Great Voices	1961	$35
❑ LMM-13017 [M]	A Great Band with Great Voices Swing the Great Voices of the Great Bands	1962	$30
❑ LSS-14017 [S]	A Great Band with Great Voices Swing the Great Voices of the Great Bands	1962	$35
❑ LRP-3197 [M]	Big Band Plays the Big Hits	1961	$30
❑ LST-7197 [S]	Big Band Plays the Big Hits	1961	$35
❑ LRP-3350 [M]	Big Big Band Hits	1964	$30
❑ LST-7350 [S]	Big Big Band Hits	1964	$35
❑ LRP-3273 [M]	Desafinado	1963	$30
❑ LST-7273 [S]	Desafinado	1963	$35
❑ LRP-3353 [M]	From Russia with Love	1964	$30
❑ LST-7353 [S]	From Russia with Love	1964	$35
❑ LRP-3326 [M]	More	1963	$30
❑ LST-7326 [S]	More	1963	$35
❑ LRP-3457 [M]	The Best of Si Zentner	1966	$30
❑ LST-7457 [S]	The Best of Si Zentner	1966	$30
❑ LRP-3247 [M]	The Stripper and Other Big Band Hits	1962	$30
❑ LST-7247 [S]	The Stripper and Other Big Band Hits	1962	$35
❑ LRP-3216 [M]	Up a Lazy River (Big Band Plays the Big Hits: Vol. 2)	1962	$30
❑ LST-7216 [S]	Up a Lazy River (Big Band Plays the Big Hits: Vol. 2)	1962	$35
❑ LRP-3284 [M]	Waltz in Jazz Time	1963	$30
❑ LST-7284 [S]	Waltz in Jazz Time	1963	$35

SMASH

❑ MGS-27007 [M]	Presenting Si Zentner	1961	$35
❑ SRS-67007 [S]	Presenting Si Zentner	1961	$50
❑ MGS-27013 [M]	Swing Fever	1962	$35
❑ SRS-67013 [S]	Swing Fever	1962	$50

SUNSET

| ❑ SUM-1110 [M] | Big Band Brilliance | 196? | $25 |
| ❑ SUS-5110 [S] | Big Band Brilliance | 196? | $30 |

ZETTERLUND, MONICA

Female singer.

Albums

INNER CITY

| ❑ IC-1082 | It Only Happens Every Time | 197? | $35 |

ZIMMERMAN, DICK

See IAN WHITCOMB.

Number	Title	Yr	NM

ZINN'S RAGTIME STRING QUARTET

Albums

CLASSIC JAZZ

| ❑ 13 | Zinn's Ragtime String Quartet | 197? | $25 |

ZITO, PHIL

Drummer and bandleader.

Albums

COLUMBIA

| ❑ CL6110 [10] | International City Dixielanders | 1950 | $50 |

ZITRO, JAMES

Drummer and composer. Also see ZYTRON.

Albums

ESP-DISK'

| ❑ 1052 [S] | Zitro | 1968 | $120 |

ZOLLER, ATTILA

Guitarist.

Albums

EMARCY

| ❑ SPE-66013 [S] | The Horizon Beyond | 1968 | $100 |

INNER CITY

| ❑ IC-3008 | Dream Bells | 1976 | $20 |

ZONJIC, ALEXANDER

Flutist.

Albums

OPTIMISM

❑ OP-3206	Elegant Evening	198?	$25
❑ OP-3207	Romance with You	198?	$25
❑ OP-3102	When Is It Real	198?	$25

ZORN, JOHN

Horn player, composer and bandleader.

Albums

ELEKTRA

| ❑ 60844 | Spy vs. Spy | 1989 | $30 |

ELEKTRA/NONESUCH

❑ 79238	Naked City	1990	$30
❑ 79172	Spillane/Two-Lane Highway/ Forbidden Fruit	1987	$25
❑ 79139	The Big Gundown	1987	$25

HAT ART

| ❑ 2034 | Cobra | 1987 | $35 |

ZOTTOLA, GLENN

Trumpeter.

Albums

DREAMSTREET

| ❑ 105 | Live at Eddie Condon's | 1980 | $30 |
| ❑ 107 | Steamin' Mainstream | 1986 | $25 |

FAMOUS DOOR

| ❑ HL-141 | Secret Love | 1981 | $30 |
| ❑ HL-149 | Stardust | 1983 | $30 |

ZUNIGER, RICK

Guitarist.

Albums

HEADFIRST

| ❑ 675 | New Frontier | 198? | $30 |

ZURKE, BOB

Pianist.

Albums

RCA VICTOR

| ❑ LPM-1013 [M] | The Tom Cat on the Keys | 1955 | $80 |

ZYTRON

Led by JAMES ZITRO and DAVE LIEBMAN.

Albums

PACIFIC ARTS

| ❑ B7-120 | New Moon in Zytron | 197? | $35 |

Number	Title	Yr	NM

Original Cast Recordings

AIN'T MISBEHAVIN'
❏ RCA Victor CBL2-2965 — 1978 — 15.00
—New recordings of the music of Fats Waller

ALL NIGHT STRUT!
❏ Playhouse Square PHS-CLE 1S-1001 — 1976 — 80.00

CLARA (BEG, BORROW OR STEAL)
❏ Commentary CYN-02 [M] — 1960 — 120.00

MY PEOPLE
❏ Contact C-1 [M] — 1966 — 50.00
❏ Contact CS-1 [S] — 1966 — 60.00

Soundtracks

ABSOLUTE BEGINNERS
❏ EMI America SV-17182 — 1986 — 15.00
❏ EMI America SV-517182 — 1986 — 15.00
—Columbia House record club edition

ALFIE
❏ ABC Impulse! AS-9111 [S] — 1968 — 35.00
❏ Impulse! A-9111 [M] — 1966 — 120.00
❏ Impulse! AS-9111 [S] — 1966 — 120.00

ALL NIGHT LONG
❏ Epic LA16032 [M] — 1962 — 80.00
❏ Epic BA17032 [S] — 1962 — 200.00

ALL THAT JAZZ
❏ Casablanca NBLP-7198 — 1979 — 12.00

AMERICAN FLYERS
❏ GRP 2001 — 1985 — 15.00

ANATOMY OF A MURDER
❏ Columbia CL1360 [M] — 1959 — 40.00
❏ Columbia CS8166 [S] — 1959 — 100.00

BABY DOLL
❏ Columbia CL958 [M] — 1956 — 120.00
—Ads for other Columbia LPs on back cover
❏ Columbia CL958 [M] — 195? — 50.00
—No ads for LPs on back cover

BAREFOOT ADVENTURE
❏ Pacific Jazz PJ-35 [M] — 1961 — 40.00
❏ Pacific Jazz ST-35 [S] — 1961 — 120.00

BAREFOOT IN THE PARK
❏ Dot DLP-3803 [M] — 1967 — 25.00
❏ Dot DLP-25803 [S] — 1967 — 30.00

THE BARKLEYS OF BROADWAY
❏ MGM E-503 [10] — 1949 — 80.00

BARRY LYNDON
❏ Warner Bros. BS2903 — 1975 — 18.00

BATMAN
❏ Warner Bros. 25977 — 1989 — 25.00
—Music composed and conducted by Danny Elfman

BILLY JACK
❏ Warner Bros. WS1926 — 1971 — 30.00
—Original; green "WB" label
❏ Warner Bros. BJS-1001 — 1973 — 20.00
—Reissue; "Burbank" palm trees label

BIRD
❏ Columbia SC44299 — 1988 — 20.00

BLACK ORPHEUS
❏ Epic LN3672 [M] — 1959 — 80.00
❏ Fontana MGF-27520 [M] — 1963 — 50.00
❏ Fontana SRF-67520 [R] — 1963 — 35.00

BLACK RAIN
❏ Virgin 91292 — 1989 — 12.00
—Includes UB40, Iggy Pop

BLACULA
❏ RCA Victor LSP-4806 — 1972 — 60.00

BLADE RUNNER
❏ Full Moon/Warner Bros. 23748 — 1982 — 25.00

BLESS THE BEASTS AND CHILDREN
❏ A&M SP-4322 — 1971 — 30.00

BLOOD AND SAND
❏ Decca DL5380 [10] — 1952 — 80.00

BLOOMER GIRL
❏ Decca DL8015 [M] — 1950 — 30.00

BLOW-UP
❏ MGM E-4447 [M] — 1967 — 40.00
❏ MGM SE-4447 [S] — 1967 — 100.00

THE BLUE MAX
❏ Mainstream 56081 [M] — 1966 — 40.00
❏ Mainstream S-6081 [S] — 1966 — 80.00

BLUE VELVET
❏ Varese Sarabande STV-81292 — 1986 — 30.00

BOBO
❏ Warner Bros. W1711 [M] — 1967 — 25.00
❏ Warner Bros. WS1711 [S] — 1967 — 25.00

THE BODYGUARD
❏ Arista 18699 — 1992 — 15.00

BODY HEAT
❏ Label X LXSE-1-002 — 1983 — 120.00

BOEING, BOEING
❏ RCA Victor LOC-1121 [M] — 1965 — 30.00
❏ RCA Victor LSO-1121 [S] — 1965 — 30.00

BONNIE AND CLYDE
❏ Warner Bros. W1742 [M] — 1968 — 40.00
❏ Warner Bros. WS1742 [S] — 1968 — 30.00
—Originals have green labels with "W7" logo in a square at top
❏ Warner Bros. ST-91414 [S] — 1968 — 30.00
—Capitol Record Club issue

BORA, BORA
❏ American Int'l. STA-1029 — 1970 — 30.00

BORDER RADIO
❏ Enigma ST-73221 — 1987 — 15.00
—Includes John Doe

BORN FREE
❏ MGM E-4368 [M] — 1966 — 18.00
❏ MGM SE-4368 [S] — 1966 — 25.00

BORN ON THE FOURTH OF JULY
❏ MCA 6340 — 1989 — 15.00
—Includes Edie Brickell and New Bohemians

BORSALINO
❏ Paramount PAS-5019 — 1970 — 30.00

THE BOY FRIEND
❏ MGM 1SE-32 — 1971 — 25.00

A BOY NAMED CHARLIE BROWN
❏ Columbia Masterworks OS3500 — 1970 — 50.00

BOY ON A DOLPHIN
❏ Decca DL8580 [M] — 1957 — 60.00
—Black label with silver print, or pink label with black print (promo)
❏ Decca DL8580 [M] — 196? — 25.00
—Black label with color bars

THE BOYS FROM SYRACUSE
❏ Capitol TAO1933 [M] — 1963 — 30.00
❏ Capitol STAO1933 [S] — 1963 — 30.00

THE BOY WHO COULD FLY
❏ Varese Sarabande STV-81299 — 1986 — 25.00

BOYZ 'N THE HOOD
❏ Warner Bros. PRO-A-4996 [DJ] — 1991 — 25.00
—Promo-only vinyl release

THE BRAVE ONE
❏ Decca DL8344 [M] — 1956 — 40.00

BREAKIN'
❏ Polydor 821919-1 — 1984 — 12.00
—Includes Re-Flex

BRIGHT LIGHTS, BIG CITY
❏ Warner Bros. R100483 — 1988 — 15.00
—Includes M/A/R/R/S, Depeche Mode, New Order, Prince; BMG Direct Marketing edition
❏ Warner Bros. 25688 — 1988 — 12.00
—Includes M/A/R/R/S, Depeche Mode, New Order, Prince

BRIMSTONE & TREACLE
❏ A&M SP-4915 — 1982 — 12.00
—Includes Sting, The Police, Go-Go's, Squeeze

BRONCO BILLY
❏ Elektra 5E-512 — 1980 — 12.00

BROTHER ON THE RUN
❏ Perception PLP-45 — 1973 — 40.00

THE BROTHERS
❏ Warner Bros. 48058-1 — 2001 — 25.00

BUCCANEER
❏ Columbia CL1278 [M] — 1958 — 30.00
❏ Columbia CS8096 [S] — 1958 — 40.00

BULL DURHAM
❏ Capitol C1-90586 — 1988 — 12.00
—Includes Los Lobos, The Blasters, House of Schock

BULLITT
❏ Warner Bros. WS1777 — 1968 — 60.00

BUNDLE OF JOY

❏ RCA Victor LPM-1399 [M] — 1956 — 40.00

BUNNY LAKE IS MISSING
❏ RCA Victor LOC-1115 [M] — 1965 — 40.00
❏ RCA Victor LSO-1115 [S] — 1965 — 70.00

BUNNY O'HARE
❏ American Int'l. STA-1041 — 1971 — 25.00

BUONA SERA, MRS. CAMPBELL
❏ United Artists UAS-5192 — 1969 — 30.00

BURGLAR
❏ MCA 6201 — 1987 — 12.00
—Includes Belinda Carlisle, The Belle Stars, The Smithereens

THE BURGLARS
❏ Bell 1105 — 1971 — 40.00

BUSTER
❏ Atlantic 81905 — 1988 — 12.00
—Includes The Searchers ("Sweets for My Sweet")

BUTTERFIELD-8
❏ MGM E-3952 [M] — 1960 — 25.00
❏ MGM SE-3952 [S] — 1960 — 30.00

BYE BYE BIRDIE
❏ RCA Victor LOC-1081 [M] — 1963 — 30.00
—First cover without Ann-Margret on the front
❏ RCA Victor LOC-1081 [M] — 196? — 25.00
—Second cover with Ann-Margret on front, but with no credits underneath
❏ RCA Victor LOC-1081 [M] — 196? — 18.00
—Third cover with Ann-Margret on front and with credits underneath
❏ RCA Victor LSO-1081 [S] — 1963 — 30.00
—First cover without Ann-Margret on the front
❏ RCA Victor LSO-1081 [S] — 196? — 30.00
—Second cover with Ann-Margret on front, but with no credits underneath
❏ RCA Victor LSO-1081 [S] — 196? — 25.00
—Third cover with Ann-Margret on front and with credits underneath
❏ RCA Victor AYL1-3947 [S] — 1980 — 10.00
—Best Buy Series" reissue

CABARET
❏ ABC ABCD-752 — 1972 — 25.00
❏ MCA 37125 — 198? — 10.00
—Reissue; blue label with rainbow

THE CAINE MUTINY
❏ RCA Victor LOC-1013 [M] — 1954 — 10000.00
—VG value 4000; VG+ value 7000
❏ RCA Victor LOC-1013 [M] — 1993 — 200.00
—Very limited edition (100 copies) reproduction of the original LP

CALIFORNIA SUITE
❏ Columbia JC35727 — 1978 — 12.00
—Full name: "Neil Simon's California Suite

CALL ME MADAM
❏ Decca DL5465 [10] — 1953 — 50.00

CALL ME MISTER
❏ Decca DLP7005 [10] — 1950 — 100.00

CAMELOT
❏ Warner Bros. B1712 [M] — 1967 — 30.00
❏ Warner Bros. BS1712 [S] — 1967 — 25.00
—Gold label original
❏ Warner Bros. SW-91347 — 1968 — 30.00
—Capitol Record Club edition
❏ Warner Bros. BS1712 [S] — 1968 — 18.00
—Green label, "W7" box logo at top
❏ Warner Bros. BS1712 [S] — 1970 — 15.00
—Green label, "WB" shield logo at top
❏ Warner Bros. BS1712 [S] — 1973 — 12.00
—Burbank" palm trees label
❏ Warner Bros. BSK3102 [S] — 1977 — 10.00
—Reissue with new number

CAN-CAN
❏ Capitol W1301 [M] — 1960 — 25.00
❏ Capitol SW1301 [S] — 1960 — 30.00

CANDY
❏ ABC ABCS-OC-9 — 1968 — 30.00

CAPTIVE
❏ Virgin 90609 — 1987 — 18.00
—Music by The Edge and Larry Mullen of U2

THE CARDINAL
❏ RCA Victor LOC-1084 [M] — 1963 — 40.00
❏ RCA Victor LSO-1084 [S] — 1963 — 60.00

THE CARE BEARS MOVIE

Number	Title	Yr	NM

Kid Stuff 3901 — 1985 — 25.00

THE CARETAKERS
- Ava A-31 [M] — 1963 — 25.00
- Ava AS-31 [S] — 1963 — 30.00

CAROUSEL
- Capitol W694 [M] — 1956 — 30.00
— *Gray label*
- Capitol W694 [M] — 1959 — 25.00
— *Black colorband label, logo at left*
- Capitol W694 [M] — 1962 — 18.00
— *Black colorband label, logo at top*
- Capitol SW694 [S] — 1962 — 25.00
— *Black colorband label*
- Capitol SW694 [S] — 1969 — 18.00
— *Lime green label*
- Capitol SW694 [S] — 1973 — 15.00
— *Orange label*

THE CARPETBAGGERS
- Ava A-45 [M] — 1964 — 30.00
- Ava AS-45 [S] — 1964 — 40.00

CARRY IT ON
- Vanguard VSD-79313 — 1971 — 30.00

CASINO ROYALE
- Colgems COMO-5005 [M] — 1967 — 30.00
- Colgems COSO-5005 [S] — 1967 — 100.00
- Colgems COSO-5005 [S] — 1999 — 30.00
— *Classic Records reissue on audiophile vinyl*
- Colgems COSO-5005-45 — 199? — 40.00
— *Classic Records reissue on four 12-inch 45 rpm records*

THE CATHERINE WHEEL
- Sire SRK3645 — 1981 — 15.00
— *Includes David Byrne, who also composed all the music*

CAT PEOPLE
- Backstreet BSR6107 — 1982 — 25.00

A CERTAIN SMILE
- Columbia CL1194 [M] — 1958 — 40.00
- Columbia CS8068 [S] — 1958 — 80.00

THE CHAIRMAN
- Tetragrammaton T-5007 — 1969 — 30.00

CHARLOTTE'S WEB
- Paramount PAS-1008 — 1973 — 30.00

THE CHASE
- Columbia Masterworks OL6560 [M] — 1966 — 40.00
- Columbia Masterworks OS2960 [S] — 1966 — 60.00

CHINATOWN
- ABC ABDP-848 — 1974 — 40.00

CHITTY CHITTY BANG BANG
- United Artists UAS-5188 — 1968 — 30.00

CHRISTIANE F.
- RCA ABL1-4239 — 1981 — 18.00
— *Includes David Bowie ("Helgen (Heroes)")*

THE CHRISTMAS RACCOONS
- Starland Music 1031 — 1982 — 15.00
— *Story record with Rich Little, Rita Coolidge and Rupert Holmes as the star voices*

THE CHRISTMAS THAT ALMOST WASN'T
- RCA Camden CAL-1086 [M] — 1966 — 30.00
- RCA Camden CAS-1086 [S] — 1966 — 40.00

CINDERELLA
- Disneyland WDL-4007 [M] — 1957 — 200.00
— *Original issue, gatefold cover*
- Disneyland DQ-1207 [M] — 1959 — 40.00
— *Second issue, white back cover with ads for nine other LPs*
- Disneyland DQ-1207 [M] — 1963 — 30.00
— *Third issue, pink back cover*
- Disneyland DQ-1207 [M] — 1987 — 30.00
— *Fifth issue, high gloss cover with prince putting slipper on Cinderella's foot*
- Disneyland 3107 [PD] — 1981 — 30.00
— *Fourth issue, picture disc*

CINDERFELLA
- Dot DLP-8001 [M] — 1960 — 60.00
- Dot SLP-38001 [S] — 1960 — 100.00
— *Gatefold cover with many extras including game board, spinner, booklet, music stand.*

CITY HEAT
- Warner Bros. 25219 — 1984 — 15.00
— *Incidental music by Lennie Niehaus*

CLEOPATRA
- 20th Century Fox FXG-5008 [M] — 1963 — 30.00
- 20th Century Fox SXG-5008 [S] — 1963 — 40.00

CLEOPATRA JONES

Warner Bros. BS2719 — 1973 — 30.00

CLOCKERS
- MCA 11304 — 1995 — 12.00
— *Includes Seal*

CLOSE ENCOUNTERS OF THE THIRD KIND
- Arista AL9500 — 1977 — 30.00
— *Includes one 12-inch record and one 7-inch record. Deduct 50 percent if the 7-inch record is missing.*

THE CLOWNS
- Columbia S30772 — 1971 — 40.00

C'MON, LET'S LIVE A LITTLE
- Liberty LRP-3430 [M] — 1966 — 30.00
- Liberty LST-7430 [S] — 1966 — 30.00

COAL MINER'S DAUGHTER
- MCA 5107 — 1980 — 18.00

COFFY
- Polydor PD-5048 — 1973 — 100.00

THE COLLECTOR
- Mainstream 56053 [M] — 1965 — 30.00
- Mainstream S-6053 [S] — 1965 — 50.00

COLLEGE CONFIDENTIAL
- Chancellor CHL-5016 [M] — 1960 — 40.00
- Chancellor CHLS-5016 [S] — 1960 — 100.00

THE COLOR PURPLE
- Qwest 25336 — 1985 — 25.00
— *Regular gatefold edition; records are still on purple vinyl*
- Qwest 25289 — 1985 — 30.00
— *Box set "limited edition" on purple vinyl with booklet*

COLORS
- Sire R154136 — 1988 — 15.00
— *Includes Ice-T ("Colors")*
- Warner Bros. 25713 — 1988 — 12.00
— *Includes Ice-T, Salt-N-Pepa*

COMANCHE
- Coral CRL57046 [M] — 1956 — 400.00

COME BACK CHARLESTON BLUE
- Atco SD7010 — 1972 — 30.00

COME BLOW YOUR HORN
- Reprise R-6071 [M] — 1963 — 30.00
- Reprise R9-6071 [S] — 1963 — 50.00

COMETOGETHER
- Apple SW-3377 — 1971 — 25.00

THE CONNECTION
- Charlie Parker PLP-806 [M] — 1962 — 60.00
- Charlie Parker PLP-806S [S] — 1962 — 40.00
- Felsted 7512 [M] — 1960 — 200.00
- Felsted 2512 [S] — 1960 — 300.00

CONVOY
- United Artists UA-LA910-H — 1978 — 15.00

COOLEY HIGH
- Motown M7-840R2 — 1975 — 25.00

THE CORRUPT ONES
- United Artists UAL-4158 [M] — 1967 — 40.00
- United Artists UAS-5158 [S] — 1967 — 40.00

COTTON COMES TO HARLEM
- United Artists UAS-5211 — 1970 — 30.00

COURIER
- Virgin 90954 — 1989 — 15.00
— *Includes U2, Elvis Costello (as Declan MacManus), Hothouse Flowers*

THE COURT JESTER
- Decca DL8212 [M] — 1956 — 70.00
— *Black label, silver print, or pink label, black print promo copy*
- Decca DL8212 [M] — 196? — 30.00
— *Black label with color bars*

THE COWBOY
- Decca DL8684 [M] — 1958 — 60.00
— *Black label, silver print, or pink label, black print promo copy*
- Decca DL8684 [M] — 196? — 25.00
— *Black label with color bars*

CRADLE 2 THE GRAVE
- Def Jam 44063615-1 — 2002 — 25.00

CRIME IN THE STREETS
- Decca DL8376 [M] — 1956 — 60.00
— *Black label, silver print, or pink label, black print promo copy*
- Decca DL8376 [S] — 196? — 30.00
— *Black label with color bars*

THE CROSS AND THE SWITCHBLADE
- Light LS-5550 — 1970 — 30.00

CRUISING
- Columbia JS36410 — 1980 — 40.00

CUSTER OF THE WEST

- ABC ABC-OC-5 [M] — 1968 — 80.00
- ABC ABCS-OC-5 [S] — 1968 — 100.00

CYCLE SAVAGES
- American Int'l. STA-1033 — 1970 — 30.00

CYRANO DE BERGERAC
- Capitol S283 [M] — 1951 — 30.00
— *Originals have red labels with Capitol logo at top*

DAKTARI
- Leo the Lion CH-1043 [M] — 1967 — 50.00
- MGM CH-1043 [M] — 1967 — 50.00

THE DAMNED
- Warner Bros. WS1829 — 1969 — 30.00

DAMN THE DEFIANT!
- Colpix CP511 [M] — 1962 — 30.00
- Colpix SCP511 [S] — 1962 — 60.00

DAMN YANKEES
- RCA Victor LOC-1047 [M] — 1958 — 40.00
— *Original pressing with "Long Play" on label*

DANCE CRAZE
- Chrysalis CHR1299 — 1981 — 25.00
— *Includes The Specials, The Selecter, Bad Manners, Madness, The English Beat, The Bodysnatchers; a great introduction to 2-Tone ska*

DANGEROUSLY CLOSE
- Enigma SJ-73204 — 1986 — 12.00
— *Includes The Smithereens, Lords of the New Church*

DARKMAN
- MCA 10094 — 1990 — 15.00
— *Composed and conducted by Danny Elfman*

THE DARK OF THE SUN
- MGM SE-4544 — 1968 — 40.00

DARLING LILI
- RCA Victor LSPX-1000 — 1969 — 25.00

DAWN OF THE DEAD
- Varese Sarabande VC-81106 — 1979 — 30.00

DAYDREAMER
- Columbia Masterworks OL6540 [M] — 1966 — 30.00
- Columbia Masterworks OS2940 [S] — 1966 — 40.00

DAY OF ANGER
- RCA Victor LSO-1165 — 1969 — 25.00

THE DAY OF THE DOLPHIN
- Avco AV-11014 — 1973 — 30.00

DAYS OF HEAVEN
- Pacific Arts PAC8-128 — 1978 — 40.00

DAYS OF THUNDER
- DGC 24294 — 1990 — 25.00

THE DAY THE FISH CAME OUT
- 20th Century Fox TF-3194 [M] — 1967 — 30.00
- 20th Century Fox TFS-4194 [S] — 1967 — 40.00

DEADFALL
- 20th Century Fox S-4203 — 1968 — 60.00

THE DEADLY AFFAIR
- Verve V-8679 [M] — 1966 — 60.00
- Verve V6-8679 [S] — 1966 — 60.00

DEAD MAN WALKING
- Columbia C367989 — 1997 — 200.00

DEAR JOHN
- Dunhill OCD-55001 [M] — 1966 — 25.00
- Dunhill OCDS-55001 [S] — 1966 — 30.00

THE DECLINE OF WESTERN CIVILIZATION
- Slash 105 — 1981 — 25.00

THE DEEP
- Casablanca NBLP-7060 — 1977 — 18.00
— *Blue vinyl*

DEEP IN MY HEART
- MGM E-3153 [M] — 1955 — 40.00
- MGM E-3153 [M] — 1955 — 50.00

DE SADE
- Tower ST-5170 — 1969 — 30.00

DESIRE UNDER THE ELMS
- Dot DLP-3095 [M] — 1958 — 100.00

DESTINATION MOON
- Columbia CL6151 [10] — 1950 — 200.00
- Omega OL-3 [M] — 1959 — 40.00

THE DEVIL AT 4 O'CLOCK
- Colpix CP509 [M] — 1962 — 40.00
- Colpix SCP509 [S] — 1962 — 70.00

THE DEVIL IN MISS JONES
- Janus JLS-3059 — 1973 — 30.00

THE DEVIL'S BRIGADE
SOUNDTRACKS — 1968 — 25.00

DIAMOND HEAD
- Colpix CP-440 [M] — 1963 — 30.00

Number	Title	Yr	NM
❑ Colpix SCP440 [S]	1963	60.00

DIAMONDS ARE FOREVER
| ❑ United Artists UAS-5520 | 1971 | 25.00 |
| ❑ United Artists UA-LA301-G | 1974 | 15.00 |

—Reissue of 5520

THE DIARY OF ANNE FRANK
| ❑ 20th Fox FOX-3012 [M] | 1959 | 50.00 |
| ❑ 20th Fox SFX-3012 [S] | 1959 | 80.00 |

DIRTY DANCING
| ❑ RCA 6408-1-R | 1987 | 12.00 |
| ❑ RCA 6965-1-R | 1988 | 18.00 |

—Album's title is "More Dirty Dancing"; original editions of the LP have instrumental selections entitled "Baby's Walk" and "The Lifts in the Lake Theme (Finale)"
| ❑ RCA 6965-1-R-A | 1988 | 12.00 |

—Album's title is "More Dirty Dancing"; revised editions of the LP have the two instrumental selections, but they are retitled "(I've Had) The Time of My Life (Instrumental Version)"

—

DIRTY GAME
| ❑ Laurie LLP-2034 [M] | 1966 | 30.00 |
| ❑ Laurie SLP-2034 [S] | 1966 | 30.00 |

DIVORCE AMERICAN STYLE
| ❑ United Artists UAL-4163 [M] | 1967 | 25.00 |
| ❑ United Artists UAS-5163 [S] | 1967 | 25.00 |

DIVORCE ITALIAN STYLE
| ❑ United Artists UAL-4106 [M] | 1962 | 40.00 |
| ❑ United Artists UAS-5106 [S] | 1962 | 50.00 |

D.O.A.
| ❑ Varese Sarabande 704.610 | 1988 | 40.00 |

DOCTOR DETROIT
| ❑ Backstreet 6120 | 1983 | 12.00 |

—Includes Devo (2)

DOCTOR DOLITTLE
| ❑ 20th Century Fox TCF-5101 [M] | 1967 | 25.00 |
| ❑ 20th Century Fox TCS-5101 [S] | 1967 | 25.00 |

DOCTOR GOLDFOOT AND THE GIRL BOMBS
| ❑ Tower T5053 [M] | 1966 | 25.00 |
| ❑ Tower DT5053 [R] | 1966 | 30.00 |

DOCTOR ZHIVAGO
| ❑ MCA 39042 | 198? | 10.00 |

—Reissue
❑ MGM 1E-6 [M]	1965	18.00
❑ MGM S1E-6ST [S]	1965	25.00
❑ MGM SWAE-90620 [S]	1965	25.00

—Capitol Record Club issue

A DOG OF FLANDERS
| ❑ 20th Fox FOX-3026 [M] | 1959 | 80.00 |
| ❑ 20th Fox SFX-3026 [S] | 1959 | 300.00 |

DOGS IN SPACE
| ❑ Atlantic 81789 | 1987 | 15.00 |

—Includes Iggy Pop, Michael Hutchense (of INXS), Brian Eno, etc.

$ (DOLLARS)
| ❑ Reprise MS2051 | 1971 | 25.00 |

DON'T MAKE WAVES
| ❑ MGM E-4483 [M] | 1967 | 30.00 |
| ❑ MGM SE-4483 [S] | 1967 | 30.00 |

THE DOORS
| ❑ Elektra E1-61047 | 1991 | 100.00 |

—Only vinyl edition in US released through Columbia House

DO THE RIGHT THING
| ❑ Motown 6272 | 1989 | 12.00 |

—Includes Public Enemy

DOWN AND OUT IN BEVERLY HILLS
| ❑ MCA 6160 | 1986 | 12.00 |

—Includes Andy Summers (6)

DRAGNET
| ❑ MCA 6210 | 1987 | 12.00 |

—Includes Art of Noise

DRANGO
| ❑ Liberty LRP-3036 [M] | 1957 | 150.00 |

A DREAM OF KINGS
| ❑ National General NG-1000 | 1969 | 30.00 |

DR. NO
| ❑ Liberty LT-50275 | 1981 | 10.00 |

—Reissue of United Artists 275
❑ United Artists UAL-4108 [M]	1963	40.00
❑ United Artists UAS-5108 [S]	1963	50.00
❑ United Artists UA-LA275-G	1974	12.00

—Reissue of 5108

DR. PHIBES
| ❑ American Int'l. A-1040 | 1971 | 60.00 |

DUCK, YOU SUCKER
| ❑ United Artists UAS-5221 | 1972 | 40.00 |

DUDES
| ❑ MCA 6212 | 1987 | 12.00 |

—Includes Jane's Addiction

DUEL AT DIABLO
| ❑ United Artists UAL-4139 [M] | 1966 | 30.00 |
| ❑ United Artists UAS-5139 [S] | 1966 | 30.00 |

DUMBO
| ❑ Disneyland WDL-4013 [M] | 1957 | 200.00 |

—Original issue, gatefold cover
| ❑ Disneyland DQ-1204 [M] | 1959 | 30.00 |

—Second issue, back cover has ads for nine other LPs
| ❑ Disneyland DQ-1204 [M] | 1963 | 18.00 |

—Third issue, four black & white photos on back cover
| ❑ Disneyland 1204 [M] | 197? | 12.00 |

—Fourth issue, yellow rainbow label, flying Dumbo on back cover
| ❑ Disneyland ST-4904 [M] | 1963 | 200.00 |

—Special issue with pop-up figures in gatefold

DUNE
| ❑ Polydor 823770-1 | 1984 | 30.00 |

THE DUNWICH HORROR
| ❑ American Int'l. STA-1028 | 1970 | 40.00 |

EARTH GIRLS ARE EASY
| ❑ Sire 25835 | 1989 | 12.00 |

—Includes The B-52's, Depeche Mode, The Jesus and Mary Chain, Julie Brown (2), Stewart Copeland

EASTER PARADE
| ❑ MGM E-502 [10] | 1950 | 80.00 |

EAST SIDE, WEST SIDE
| ❑ Columbia CL2123 [M] | 1963 | 150.00 |
| ❑ Columbia CS8923 [S] | 1963 | 150.00 |

EASY MONEY
| ❑ Columbia JS38968 | 1983 | 12.00 |

—Includes Nick Lowe

EASY RIDER
| ❑ ABC Dunhill DSX-50063 | 1969 | 30.00 |

EATING RAOUL
| ❑ Varese Sarabande STV81164 | 1982 | 15.00 |

—Includes Los Lobos

ECCO
| ❑ Warner Bros. W1600 [M] | 1965 | 30.00 |
| ❑ Warner Bros. WS1600 [S] | 1965 | 30.00 |

THE EDDY DUCHIN STORY
| ❑ Decca DL8289 [M] | 1956 | 40.00 |

—Original cover with Tyrone Power and Kim Novak at a piano
| ❑ Decca DL8289 [M] | 1959 | 25.00 |

—Reissue cover with Tyrone Power and Kim Novak kissing
| ❑ Decca DL78289 [S] | 1959 | 30.00 |

—Maroon label, silver print, "Full Stereo" on front cover
| ❑ Decca DL9121 [M] | 196? | 15.00 |

—Reissue of 8289
| ❑ Decca DL79121 [S] | 196? | 18.00 |

—Reissue of 78289
| ❑ MCA 2041 | 1973 | 12.00 |

—Reissue of 79121; black label with rainbow
| ❑ MCA 37088 | 198? | 10.00 |

—Reissue of 2041

THE EDUCATION OF SONNY CARSON
| ❑ Paramount PAS-1045 | 1974 | 25.00 |

THE EGYPTIAN
| ❑ Decca DL9014 [M] | 1954 | 60.00 |
| ❑ Decca DL79014 [R] | 196? | 25.00 |

EIGHT MEN OUT
| ❑ Varese Sarabande 704.600 | 1988 | 30.00 |

8 MILE, MORE MUSIC FROM
| ❑ Shady/Interscope 004450979-1 | 2002 | 30.00 |

—U.S. edition comes in generic black sleeve with center hole and sticker across top of cover

84 CHARING CROSS ROAD
| ❑ Varese Sarabande STV81306 | 1987 | 15.00 |

EL CID
| ❑ MGM E-3977 [M] | 1962 | 40.00 |
| ❑ MGM SE-3977 [S] | 1962 | 50.00 |

EL DORADO
| ❑ Epic FLM-13114 [M] | 1967 | 50.00 |
| ❑ Epic LFS-15114 [S] | 1967 | 70.00 |

ELECTRA GLIDE IN BLUE
| ❑ United Artists UA-LA062-H | 1973 | 40.00 |

—With booklet and two posters

ELEPHANT STEPS
| ❑ Columbia Masterworks M2X33044 | 1975 | 25.00 |

ELMER GANTRY
| ❑ United Artists UAL-4069 [M] | 1960 | 40.00 |
| ❑ United Artists UAS-5069 [S] | 1960 | 50.00 |

EL TOPO
| ❑ Apple SWAO-3388 | 1972 | 40.00 |

THE EMPIRE STRIKES BACK
| ❑ RSO RS-2-4201 | 1980 | 25.00 |

—With booklet

ENTER THE DRAGON
| ❑ Warner Bros. BS2727 | 1973 | 60.00 |

E.T. THE EXTRA-TERRESTRIAL
| ❑ MCA 6109 | 1982 | 12.00 |
| ❑ MCA 6113 [PD] | 1982 | 30.00 |

—Picture disc in plastic envelope
| ❑ MCA 16014 | 1982 | 40.00 |

—Audiophile edition
| ❑ MCA 70000 | 1982 | 80.00 |

—Boxed version with booklet; story narrated by Michael Jackson

EVERYTHING I HAVE IS YOURS
| ❑ MGM E-187 [10] | 1953 | 40.00 |

EVERY WHICH WAY BUT LOOSE
| ❑ Elektra 5E-503 | 1978 | 15.00 |

EVIL DEAD
| ❑ Varese Sarabande STV-81199 | 1984 | 25.00 |

EXODUS
| ❑ RCA Victor LOC-1058 [M] | 1960 | 25.00 |

—"Long Play" on label
| ❑ RCA Victor LSO-1058 [S] | 1960 | 30.00 |

—"Living Stereo" on label

THE EXORCIST
| ❑ Warner Bros. W2774 | 1974 | 30.00 |

A FACE IN THE CROWD
| ❑ Capitol W872 [M] | 1957 | 50.00 |

THE FALCON AND THE SNOWMAN
| ❑ EMI America SV-17150 | 1985 | 25.00 |

—Includes David Bowie ("This Is Not America")

THE FALL OF THE ROMAN EMPIRE
| ❑ Columbia Masterworks OL6060 [M] | 1964 | 40.00 |
| ❑ Columbia Masterworks OS2460 [S] | 1964 | 60.00 |

THE FAMILY WAY
| ❑ London M76007 [M] | 1967 | 100.00 |

—No promo sticker on front cover (deduct 20 percent for promo)
| ❑ London ST82007 [S] | 1967 | 120.00 |

—No promo sticker on front cover (deduct 20 percent for promo)

FANNY
| ❑ Warner Bros. W1416 [M] | 1961 | 30.00 |
| ❑ Warner Bros. WS1416 [S] | 1961 | 30.00 |

FANTASIA
| ❑ Buena Vista WDX-101 [M] | 1961 | 30.00 |

—Second issue, blue labels, includes 24-page booklet
| ❑ Buena Vista STER-101 [S] | 1961 | 40.00 |

—First stereo issue, black and yellow rainbow labels, includes 24-page booklet
| ❑ Buena Vista 101 [S] | 1982 | 25.00 |

—Stereo reissue, two records, no booklet
| ❑ Buena Vista V-104 | 1982 | 30.00 |

—Digitally re-recorded music track, Mickey Mouse as The Sorcerer on cover
| ❑ Disneyland WDX-101 | 1957 | 60.00 |

—Original issue, maroon/red labels, includes 24-page booklet

FANTASIA: NIGHT ON BALD MOUNTAIN; PASTORAL SYMPHONY; AVE MARIA
| ❑ Disneyland WDL-4101C [M] | 1958 | 25.00 |
| ❑ Disneyland STER-4101C [S] | 1958 | 30.00 |

FANTASIA: RITE OF SPRING; TOCCATA AND FUGUE
| ❑ Disneyland WDL-4101A [M] | 1958 | 25.00 |
| ❑ Disneyland STER-4101A [S] | 1959 | 30.00 |

FANTASIA: THE NUTCRACKER SUITE; DANCE OF THE HOURS
| ❑ Disneyland WDL-4101B [M] | 1958 | 25.00 |
| ❑ Disneyland STER-4101B [S] | 1959 | 30.00 |

THE FANTASTIC PLASTIC MACHINE
| ❑ Epic BN26469 | 1969 | 30.00 |

A FAREWELL TO ARMS
| ❑ Capitol W918 [M] | 1957 | 50.00 |

FAR FROM THE MADDING CROWD

Number	Title	Yr	NM
❑ MGM 1E-11 [M]		1967	30.00
❑ MGM S1E-11 [S]		1967	30.00

THE FASTEST GUITAR ALIVE
❑ MGM SE-4475		1968	30.00

FAST TIMES AT RIDGEMONT HIGH
❑ Full Moon/Asylum 60158		1982	18.00

— Includes Go-Go's, Oingo Boingo

FATHOM
❑ 20th Century Fox TFM-4195 [M]		1967	40.00
❑ 20th Century Fox TFS-4195 [S]		1967	50.00

FELLINI SATYRICON
❑ United Artists UAS-5208		1969	30.00

FELLINI'S ROMA
❑ United Artists UA-LA052-F		1972	30.00

THE FEMALE PRISONER
❑ Columbia Masterworks OS3320		1969	30.00

FIDDLER ON THE ROOF
❑ United Artists UAS-10900		1971	25.00

— With booklet

55 DAYS AT PEKING
❑ Columbia CL2028 [M]		1963	40.00
❑ Columbia CS8828 [S]		1963	70.00

THE FIGHTER
❑ Decca DL5414 [10]		1952	80.00

THE FINAL COUNTDOWN
❑ Casablanca NBLP-7232		1980	40.00

A FINE MESS
❑ Motown 6180		1986	12.00

— Includes Los Lobos

FINIAN'S RAINBOW
❑ Warner Bros. BS2550		1968	25.00

FIRE DOWN BELOW
❑ Decca DL8597 [M]		1957	70.00

FIRSTBORN
❑ EMI America ST-517144		1984	15.00

— Includes Wang Chung, Talk Talk, Re-Flex; Columbia House edition
❑ EMI America ST-17144		1984	12.00

— Includes Wang Chung, Talk Talk, Re-Flex

A FISTFUL OF DOLLARS
❑ RCA Victor LOC-1135 [M]		1967	25.00
❑ RCA Victor LSO-1135 [S]		1967	30.00

— Black label, dog on top
❑ RCA Victor LSO-1135 [S]		1969	15.00

— Orange label, tan label, or black label with dog at 1 o'clock

FITZWILLY
❑ United Artists UAL-4173 [M]		1967	25.00
❑ United Artists UAS-5173 [S]		1967	30.00

FIVE EASY PIECES
❑ Epic KE30456		1971	30.00

THE FIVE PENNIES
❑ Dot DLP-9500 [M]		1959	150.00
❑ Dot DLP-29500 [S]		1959	200.00

THE FLAMINGO KID
❑ Motown 6131ML		1984	12.00

— Commonly distributed issue
❑ Varese Sarabande STV-81232		1984	40.00

— Original issue

FLASHDANCE
❑ Casablanca 811492-1		1983	12.00

A FLEA IN HER EAR
❑ 20th Century Fox TFS-4200		1968	30.00

FLETCH
❑ MCA 6142		1985	12.00

— Includes The Fixx, Kim Wilde

FLOWER DRUM SONG
❑ Decca DL9098 [M]		1961	25.00
❑ Decca DL79098 [S]		1961	30.00
❑ MCA 2069		1973	12.00

— Reissue; black label with rainbow

THE FOG
❑ Varese Sarabande STV-81191		1980	30.00

FOLIES BERGERE
❑ Decca DL8571 [M]		1958	30.00

FOLLOW ME
❑ Uni 73056		1969	30.00

FOOTLOOSE
❑ Columbia JS39242		1984	12.00
❑ Columbia 9C939404 [PD]		1984	25.00

— Picture disc version

FOR A FEW DOLLARS MORE
❑ United Artists UAL-3608 [M]		1967	25.00

Number	Title	Yr	NM
❑ United Artists UAS-6608 [S]		1967	30.00

FORBIDDEN ZONE
❑ Varese Sarabande STV81170		1983	15.00

— Includes Oingo Boingo (as The Mystical Knights of the Oingo Boingo); composed by Danny Elfman

FOR LOVE OF IVY
❑ ABC SOC-7		1968	30.00

FOR THE FIRST TIME
❑ RCA Victor Red Seal LSC-2338 [S]		1959	25.00

— Shaded dog" and smaller "RCA Victor" lettering
❑ RCA Victor Red Seal LSC-2338 [S]		1965	18.00

— White dog" and larger "RCA Victor" lettering
❑ RCA Victor Red Seal LSC-2338 [S]		1969	15.00

— Red label, no dog
❑ RCA Victor Red Seal LM-2338 [M]		1959	18.00

40 POUNDS OF TROUBLE
❑ Mercury MG-20784 [M]		1963	30.00
❑ Mercury SR-60784 [S]		1963	40.00

FOR YOUR EYES ONLY
❑ Liberty LOO-1109		1981	30.00

THE FOUR HORSEMEN OF THE APOCALYPSE
❑ MGM E-3993 [M]		1962	25.00
❑ MGM SE-3993 [S]		1962	30.00

FOUR IN THE MORNING
❑ Roulette OS805 [M]		1966	40.00
❑ Roulette OSS805 [S]		1966	50.00

THE FOX
❑ Warner Bros. W1738 [M]		1968	40.00
❑ Warner Bros. WS1738 [S]		1968	30.00

THE FOX AND THE HOUND
❑ Disneyland 3106 [PD]		1981	30.00

— Disney Picture Disc" series
❑ Disneyland ST-3823		1981	25.00

— Non-picture disc version

FOXY BROWN
❑ Motown M7-811		1974	25.00

FRANCIS OF ASSISI
❑ 20th Fox FOX-3053 [M]		1961	200.00
❑ 20th Fox SFX-3053 [S]		1961	250.00

THE FRENCH LINE
❑ Mercury MG-25182 [10]		1954	80.00

FRIDAY
❑ Priority P1-53959		1995	18.00

— Includes Ice Cube, Dr. Dre, other gangsta rappers

FRIENDLY PERSUASION
❑ RKO Unique LP-110 [M]		1956	75.00

FRIGHT NIGHT
❑ Private I SZ40087		1985	15.00

— Includes Devo ("Let's Talk")

FRITZ THE CAT
❑ Fantasy F-9406		1972	30.00

FROM RUSSIA WITH LOVE
❑ United Artists UAL-4114 [M]		1964	25.00
❑ United Artists UAS-5114 [S]		1964	30.00

THE FUGITIVE KIND
❑ United Artists UAL-4065 [M]		1959	100.00
❑ United Artists UAS-5065 [S]		1959	140.00

FUNERAL IN BERLIN
❑ RCA Victor LOC-1136 [M]		1966	30.00
❑ RCA Victor LSO-1136 [S]		1966	50.00

FUNNY GIRL
❑ Columbia Masterworks SQ30992 [Q]		1971	50.00
❑ Columbia Masterworks BOS3220		1968	18.00

— Gray "360 Sound" label; record is removed from inside the gatefold; liner notes on a black background
❑ Columbia Masterworks BOS3220		1968	15.00

— Gray "360 Sound" label; record is removed from inside the gatefold; liner notes on a tan background
❑ Columbia Masterworks BOS3220		1970	12.00

— Olive label with "Columbia" encircling the edge

A FUNNY THING HAPPENED ON THE WAY TO THE FORUM
❑ United Artists UAL-4144 [M]		1966	15.00
❑ United Artists UAS-5144 [S]		1966	18.00
❑ United Artists UA-LA284-G		1974	12.00

— Reissue of 5144

GAILY, GAILY
❑ United Artists UAS5202		1969	30.00

THE GAME IS OVER
❑ Atco 33-205 [M]		1967	25.00
❑ Atco SD 33-205 [S]		1967	30.00

THE GAMES
❑ Viking LPS-105		1970	200.00

Number	Title	Yr	NM

GAY PURR-EE
❑ Warner Bros. B1479 [M]		1963	25.00
❑ Warner Bros. BS1479 [S]		1963	30.00

GEISHA BOY
❑ Jubilee JLP-1096 [M]		1958	50.00
❑ Jubilee JGS-1096 [S]		1959	80.00

THE GENE KRUPA STORY
❑ Verve MGV-15010 [M]		1959	100.00
❑ Verve MGVS-6105 [S]		1959	175.00

— Original issue
❑ Verve V6-15010 [S]		1963	150.00

— Early reissue
❑ Verve V-15010 [M]		1961	50.00

GENGHIS KHAN
❑ Liberty LRP-3412 [M]		1965	40.00
❑ Liberty LST-7412 [S]		1965	60.00

GENTLEMEN MARRY BRUNETTES
❑ Coral CRL57013 [M]		1955	70.00

GENTLEMEN PREFER BLONDES
❑ MGM E-208 [M]		1953	120.00

THE GENTLE RAIN
❑ Mercury MG-21016 [M]		1966	100.00
❑ Mercury SR-61016 [S]		1966	100.00

GET CRAZY
❑ Morocco 6065		1983	14.00

— Includes Ramones, Marshall Crenshaw, Lou Reed, Fear

GETTING STRAIGHT
❑ Colgems COSO-5010		1970	30.00

GET YOURSELF A COLLEGE GIRL
❑ MGM E-4273 [M]		1965	25.00
❑ MGM SE-4273 [S]		1965	40.00

GHOSTBUSTERS
❑ Arista AL8-8246		1984	18.00

— First pressing has smaller print on front and eight photos on back
❑ Arista AL8-8246		1984	12.00

— Later pressings have large print on front and seven photos on back

GHOSTBUSTERS II
❑ MCA R151964		1989	15.00

— BMG Direct Marketing edition
❑ MCA 6306		1989	12.00

GIANT
❑ Capitol W773 [M]		1956	40.00

— Turquoise or gray label
❑ Capitol W773 [M]		1959	30.00

— Black colorband label, logo at left
❑ Capitol W773 [M]		1962	18.00

— Black colorband label, logo at top
❑ Capitol DW773 [R]		196?	15.00

GIDGET GOES HAWAIIAN
❑ Colpix CP418 [M]		1961	50.00

GIGI
❑ MCA 39045		1986	10.00

— Reissue
❑ MGM W90523 [M]		1965	15.00

— Capitol Record Club edition
❑ MGM SW90523 [S]		1965	18.00
❑ MGM E-3641 [M]		1958	25.00

— Yellow label
❑ MGM SE-3641 [S]		1959	30.00

— Yellow label
❑ MGM E-3641 [M]		1960	15.00

— Black label
❑ MGM SE-3641 [S]		1960	18.00

— Black label
❑ MGM SE-3641 [S]		1968	15.00

— Blue and gold label

GIGOT
❑ Capitol W1754 [M]		1962	30.00
❑ Capitol SW1754 [S]		1962	40.00

THE GIRL IN THE BIKINI
❑ Poplar PLP 33-1002 [M]		1952	400.00

THE GIRL MOST LIKELY
❑ Capitol W930 [M]		1957	60.00

GIRL ON A MOTORCYCLE
❑ Tetragrammaton T-5000		1969	30.00

GIRLS JUST WANT TO HAVE FUN
❑ Mercury 824510-1		1985	12.00

— Includes Animotion

THE GLENN MILLER STORY
❑ Decca DL5519 [10]		1954	150.00
❑ Decca DL8226 [M]		1956	150.00

Number	Title	Yr	NM
❏ Decca DL9123 [M]		196?	50.00

—*Reissue of 8226*

❏ Decca DL79123 [R]		196?	35.00
❏ MCA 2036		1973	25.00
❏ MCA 1624		198?	35.00

—*This reissue is a bit more desirable because it was issued in true stereo*

GLORY

❏ Virgin 91329		1989	30.00
❏ Virgin 91329		1998	25.00

—*Classic Records edition; audiophile reissue; cover is noticeably less sharp than the originals*

THE GLORY STOMPERS

❏ Sidewalk DT5910 [R]		1968	50.00

GO, GO, GO WORLD

❏ Musicor MM-2059 [M]		1965	40.00
❏ Musicor MS-3059 [S]		1965	60.00

GO, JOHNNY, GO!

❏ (no label) (no number) [DJ]		1959	1000.00

—*Only exists as a promo*

THE GODFATHER

❏ Paramount PAS-1003		1972	25.00

—*Original cover with triple gatefold*

THE GODFATHER PART II

❏ ABC ABDP-856		1975	25.00

THE GODFATHER PART III

❏ Columbia C47078		1990	25.00

GOD'S LITTLE ACRE

❏ United Artists UAL-4002 [M]		1958	150.00

GOLD

❏ ABC ABCD-855		1975	30.00

GOLDEN BOY

❏ Colpix CP-478 [M]		1964	50.00
❏ Colpix SCP-478 [S]		1964	60.00

THE GOLDEN BREED

❏ Capitol ST2886		1967	30.00

THE GOLDEN CHILD

❏ Capitol SJ-12544		1986	12.00

—*Includes Martha Davis*

THE GOLDEN COACH

❏ MGM E-3111 [M]		1954	150.00

THE GOLDEN SCREW

❏ Atco 33-208 [M]		1967	30.00
❏ Atco SD 33-208 [S]		1967	40.00

GOLDFINGER

❏ United Artists UAL-4117 [M]		1964	18.00
❏ United Artists UAS-5117 [S]		1964	25.00

GOLIATH AND THE BARBARIANS

❏ American Int'l. 1001-M [M]		1960	40.00
❏ American Int'l. 1001-S [S]		1960	70.00

GONE WITH THE WAVE

❏ Colpix CP-492 [M]		1965	40.00
❏ Colpix SCP-492 [S]		1965	120.00

GONE WITH THE WIND

❏ MGM 1E-10 [M]		1967	25.00

—*Gatefold edition with 32-page booklet*

❏ MGM S1E-10 [S]		1967	25.00

—*Gatefold edition with 32-page booklet*

GOODBYE, CHARLIE

❏ 20th Century Fox TFM-3165 [M]		1964	30.00
❏ 20th Century Fox TFS-4165 [S]		1964	30.00

GOODBYE, MR. CHIPS

❏ MCA 39006		1986	10.00

—*Reissue*

❏ MGM 1SE-19		1969	25.00

GOODBYE AGAIN

❏ United Artists UAL-4091 [M]		1961	30.00
❏ United Artists UAS-5091 [S]		1961	40.00

GOOD MORNING, VIETNAM

❏ A&M R154001		1987	15.00

—*Includes The Searchers; BMG Direct Marketing edition*

GOOD NEWS

❏ MGM E-504 [10]		1950	50.00

THE GOONIES

❏ Epic SE40067		1985	12.00

—*Includes Cyndi Lauper (2), Bangles*

GORDON'S WAR

❏ Buddah BDS-5137		1973	40.00

THE GOSPEL ACCORDING TO ST. MATTHEW

❏ Mainstream 54000 [M]		1966	30.00
❏ Mainstream S-4000 [S]		1966	100.00

GOTCHA!

❏ MCA Curb 5596		1985	15.00

—*Includes Joan Jett and the Blackhearts, Bronski Beat*

GOTHIC

❏ Virgin 90607		1987	25.00

GOYA

❏ Decca DL8236 [M]		1959	150.00

THE GRADUATE

❏ CBS Masterworks JS3180 [S]		198?	10.00

—*CBS Masterworks" replaces "Columbia" along outer edge of label*

❏ Columbia Masterworks OS3180 [S]		1968	15.00

—*Original stereo edition: Gray label, "360 Sound Stereo" in white*

❏ Columbia Masterworks OL6780 [M]		1968	50.00

—*"Mono" on label*

❏ Columbia Masterworks OS3180 [S]		1971	12.00

—*Olive label, "Columbia" along outer edge*

❏ Columbia Masterworks JS3180 [S]		197?	10.00

—*Reissue with new prefix*

GRAND PRIX

❏ MGM 1E-8 [M]		1967	25.00
❏ MGM 1SE-8 [S]		1967	30.00

THE GREAT ESCAPE

❏ United Artists UAL-4107 [M]		1963	30.00
❏ United Artists UAS-5107 [S]		1963	30.00

THE GREATEST SHOW ON EARTH

❏ RCA Victor LPM-3018 [10]		1952	200.00

THE GREATEST STORY EVER TOLD

❏ United Artists UAL-4120 [M]		1965	30.00
❏ United Artists UAS-5120 [S]		1965	30.00

THE GREAT GATSBY

❏ Paramount 2-3001		1974	25.00

THE GREAT OUTDOORS

❏ Atlantic 81859		1988	12.00

—*Includes Pop Will Eat Itself*

GREMLINS

❏ Geffen GHSP24044 [EP]		1984	12.00

—*Includes Peter Gabriel*

GROUNDS FOR MARRIAGE

❏ MGM E-536 [M]		1950	80.00

GUESS WHO'S COMING TO DINNER

❏ Colgems COM-108 [M]		1968	30.00
❏ Colgems COS-108 [S]		1968	30.00

GULLIVER'S TRAVELS BEYOND THE MOON

❏ Mainstream 54001 [M]		1965	30.00
❏ Mainstream S-4001 [S]		1965	40.00

GUNS FOR SAN SEBASTIAN

❏ MGM SE-4565		1968	60.00

THE GUNS OF NAVARONE

❏ Columbia CL1655 [M]		1961	25.00
❏ Columbia C8455 [S]		1961	50.00

GURU

❏ RCA Victor LSO-1158		1969	25.00

GYPSY

❏ Warner Bros. B1480 [M]		1962	25.00
❏ Warner Bros. BS1480 [S]		1962	30.00

GYPSY GIRL

❏ Mainstream 56090 [M]		1966	30.00
❏ Mainstream S-6090 [S]		1966	40.00

HALLELUJAH THE HILLS

❏ Fontana MGF-27524 [M]		1964	30.00
❏ Fontana SRF-67524 [S]		1964	30.00

THE HALLELUJAH TRAIL

❏ United Artists UAL-4127 [M]		1965	25.00
❏ United Artists UAS-5127 [S]		1965	30.00

HAMMERHEAD

❏ Colgems COS-110		1968	40.00

HAMMERSMITH IS OUT

❏ Capitol SW-861		1972	30.00

HANG 'EM HIGH

❏ United Artists UAS-5179		1968	30.00

THE HAPPENING

❏ Colgems COMO-5006 [M]		1967	30.00
❏ Colgems COSO-5006 [S]		1967	50.00

THE HAPPIEST MILLIONAIRE

❏ Buena Vista BV-5001 [M]		1967	18.00
❏ Buena Vista STER-5001 [S]		1967	25.00

HARD COUNTRY

❏ Epic SE37367		1981	12.00

THE HARD RIDE

❏ Paramount PAS-6005		1971	30.00

HARPER

❏ Mainstream 56078 [M]		1966	25.00
❏ Mainstream S-6078 [S]		1966	30.00

THE HARRAD EXPERIMENT

❏ Capitol ST-11182		1973	30.00

HARRAD SUMMER

❏ Capitol ST-11338		1974	30.00

HAWAII

❏ United Artists UAL-4143 [M]		1966	25.00
❏ United Artists UAS-5143 [S]		1966	30.00
❏ United Artists SW-90935 [S]		1966	30.00

—*Capitol Record Club issue*

THE HEART IS A LONELY HUNTER

❏ Warner Bros. WS1759		1968	30.00

HEART OF DIXIE

❏ A&M SP-3930		1989	25.00

HEAVENLY BODIES

❏ Private I SZ39930		1985	12.00

—*Includes The Tubes*

HEAVENLY BODIES SAMPLER

❏ Private I AS1965 [DJ]		1984	10.00

—*Includes The Tubes; promo-only 4-song sampler*

HEAVY METAL

❏ Full Moon/Asylum DP-90004		1981	25.00

—*Contains two LPs of pop/rock music*

HEAVY METAL, THE SCORE

❏ Full Moon/Asylum 5E-547		1981	50.00

—*Contains Elmer Bernstein's instrumental music*

HEAVY TRAFFIC

❏ Fantasy F-9436		1973	60.00

HEIDI'S SONG

❏ K-Tel NU5310		1982	25.00

THE HELEN MORGAN STORY

❏ RCA Victor LOC-1030 [M]		1957	60.00

HELLCATS

❏ Tower ST5124		1968	30.00

HELLO-GOODBYE

❏ 20th Century Fox S-4210		1970	40.00

HELL'S ANGELS '69

❏ Capitol SKAO-303		1969	30.00

HELL'S ANGELS ON WHEELS

❏ Smash MGS-27094 [M]		1967	30.00
❏ Smash SRS-67094 [S]		1967	30.00

HELL'S BELLS

❏ Sidewalk ST5919		1969	30.00

HELL TO ETERNITY

❏ Warwick W2030 [M]		1960	200.00
❏ Warwick WST2030 [S]		1960	200.00

HELL UP IN HARLEM

❏ Motown M802V1		1974	30.00

HEMINGWAY'S ADVENTURES OF A YOUNG MAN

❏ RCA Victor LOC-1074 [M]		1962	40.00
❏ RCA Victor LSO-1074 [S]		1962	70.00

HERCULES

❏ Varese Sarabande STV-81187		1983	25.00

THE HERO

❏ Capitol SW-11098		1972	25.00

A HERO AIN'T NOTHIN' BUT A SANDWICH

❏ Columbia PS35046		1978	25.00

HEROES OF TELEMARK

❏ Mainstream 56064 [M]		1965	25.00
❏ Mainstream S-6064 [S]		1965	30.00

HEY, LET'S TWIST

❏ Roulette R-25168 [M]		1962	30.00
❏ Roulette SR-25168 [S]		1962	30.00

HEY THERE, IT'S YOGI BEAR!

❏ Colpix CP-472 [M]		1964	50.00
❏ Colpix SCP-472 [S]		1964	80.00

HIDING OUT

❏ Virgin R163706		1987	12.00

—*Includes Pretty Poison ("Catch Me I'm Falling"), Boy George ("Live My Life"); Public Image Ltd. ("Seattle")*

❏ Virgin 90661		1987	10.00

—*Includes Pretty Poison ("Catch Me I'm Falling"), Boy George ("Live My Life"); Public Image Ltd. ("Seattle")*

HIGH SOCIETY

❏ Capitol W750 [M]		1956	30.00

—*Gray label original*

❏ Capitol W750 [M]		1959	25.00

—*Black colorband label, logo at left*

❏ Capitol W750 [M]		1962	18.00

—*Black colorband label, logo at top*

❏ Capitol SW750 [S]		1959	30.00

—*Black colorband label, logo at left*

❏ Capitol SW750 [S]		1962	25.00

—*Black colorband label, logo at top*

Number	Title	Yr	NM
THE HOBBIT			
❑ Buena Vista 103		1977	30.00
❑ Buena Vista 103A		1977	40.00
—*Special edition sold at Sears stores, with four decals and poster*			
❑ Disneyland ST-3819		1978	30.00
HOLIDAY INN			
❑ Decca DL4256		1962	30.00
❑ MCA 25205		1987	10.00
—*Reissue of Decca LP*			
HOMER AND EDDIE			
❑ Apache D1-71654		1989	30.00
HONKYTONK MAN			
❑ Warner Bros. 23739		1982	12.00
HOOSIERS			
❑ Polydor 831475-1		1987	30.00
HOOTENANNY HOOT			
❑ MGM E-4172 [M]		1963	25.00
❑ MGM SE-4172 [S]		1963	30.00
THE HORSEMEN			
❑ Sunflower SNF-5007		1971	40.00
THE HORSE SOLDIERS			
❑ United Artists UAL-4035 [M]		1959	60.00
❑ United Artists UAS-5035 [S]		1959	150.00
HOTEL PARADISO			
❑ MGM E-4419 [M]		1966	25.00
❑ MGM SE-4419 [S]		1966	30.00
THE HOT ROCK			
❑ Prophesy SD8055		1972	25.00
HOT ROD RUMBLE			
❑ Liberty LRP-3048 [M]		1957	150.00
THE HOUR OF THE GUN			
❑ United Artists UAL-4166 [M]		1967	40.00
❑ United Artists UAS-5166 [S]		1967	70.00
HOUSEBOAT			
❑ Columbia CL1222 [M]		1958	50.00
A HOUSE IS NOT A HOME			
❑ Ava A-50 [M]		1964	30.00
❑ Ava AS-50 [S]		1964	30.00
HOUSE PARTY			
❑ Motown 9296		1990	15.00
—*Includes L.L. Cool J, Flavor Flav (of Public Enemy)*			
HOWARD THE DUCK			
❑ MCA 6173		1986	25.00
HOW SWEET IT IS			
❑ RCA Victor LSP-4037		1968	25.00
HOW THE WEST WAS WON			
❑ MCA 39043		1986	10.00
—*Reissue*			
❑ MGM 1E-5 [M]		1963	18.00
❑ MGM 1SE-5 [S]		1963	25.00
HOW TO BEAT THE HIGH COST OF LIVING			
❑ Columbia JS36741		1981	35.00
HOW TO MURDER YOUR WIFE			
❑ United Artists UAL-4119 [M]		1965	18.00
❑ United Artists UAS-5119 [S]		1965	25.00
HOW TO SAVE A MARRIAGE AND RUIN YOUR LIFE			
❑ Columbia Masterworks OS3140		1968	25.00
HOW TO STEAL A MILLION			
❑ 20th Century Fox TFM-3183 [M]		1966	40.00
❑ 20th Century Fox TFS-4183 [S]		1966	50.00
HOW TO STUFF A WILD BIKINI			
❑ Wand 671 [M]		1965	30.00
❑ Wand S-671 [S]		1965	40.00
HOW TO SUCCEED IN BUSINESS WITHOUT REALLY TRYING			
❑ United Artists UAL-4151 [M]		1967	25.00
❑ United Artists UAS-5151 [S]		1967	30.00
HUGO THE HIPPO			
❑ United Artists UA-LA637-G		1976	25.00
THE HUNGER			
❑ Varese Sarabande STV-81184		1984	12.00
—*Includes David Bowie*			
❑ Varese Sarabande STV-81184		1983	25.00
THE HUNT FOR RED OCTOBER			
❑ MCA 6428		1990	30.00
HURRICANE			
❑ Elektra 5E-504		1979	25.00
HURRY SUNDOWN			
❑ RCA Victor LOC-1133 [M]		1967	30.00
❑ RCA Victor LSO-1133 [S]		1967	40.00
THE HUSTLER			
❑ Kapp KL-1264 [M]		1961	60.00
❑ Kapp KS-3264 [S]		1961	120.00
ICEMAN			
❑ Southern Cross SCRS-1006		1983	25.00
ICE STATION ZEBRA			
❑ MGM S1E-14ST		1968	40.00
IF HE HOLLERS, LET HIM GO			
❑ Tower ST5152		1968	40.00
I'LL NEVER FORGET WHAT'S 'IS NAME			
❑ Decca DL9163 [M]		1967	30.00
❑ Decca DL79163 [S]		1967	30.00
I LOVE MELVIN			
❑ MGM E-190 [10]		1953	50.00
I'M GONNA GIT YOU SUCKA			
❑ Arista AL-8574		1988	12.00
—*Includes Fishbone (with Curtis Mayfield)*			
IMITATION OF LIFE			
❑ Decca DL8879 [M]		1959	50.00
❑ Decca DL78879 [S]		1959	80.00
IN A SHALLOW GRAVE			
❑ Varese Sarabande STV-81359		1988	40.00
INCHON			
❑ Regency RI-8502		1982	30.00
INDIANA JONES AND THE TEMPLE OF DOOM			
❑ Polydor 821592-1		1984	25.00
THE INDISCRETION OF AN AMERICAN WIFE			
❑ Columbia CL6277 [10]		1954	80.00
I NEVER SANG FOR MY FATHER			
❑ Bell 1204		1970	40.00
IN HARM'S WAY			
❑ RCA Victor LOC-1100 [M]		1965	40.00
❑ RCA Victor LSO-1100 [S]		1965	80.00
IN LIKE FLINT			
❑ 20th Century Fox 4193 [M]		1967	40.00
❑ 20th Century Fox S-4193 [S]		1967	80.00
INNERSPACE			
❑ Geffen GHS24161		1987	12.00
—*Includes Wang Chung, Berlin*			
THE INN OF THE SIXTH HAPPINESS			
❑ 20th Century Fox FOX-3011 [M]		1958	50.00
❑ 20th Century Fox SFX-3011 [S]		1958	70.00
IN SEARCH OF THE CASTAWAYS			
❑ Disneyland ST-3916 [M]		1962	70.00
INSIDE DAISY CLOVER			
❑ Warner Bros. W1616 [M]		1965	25.00
❑ Warner Bros. WS1616 [S]		1965	30.00
INSPECTOR CLOUSEAU			
❑ MCA 25107		1986	10.00
—*Reissue*			
❑ United Artists UAS-5186		1968	30.00
INTERLUDE			
❑ Colgems COSO-5007		1968	40.00
THE INTERNS			
❑ Colpix CP427 [M]		1962	60.00
❑ Colpix SCP427 [S]		1962	40.00
IN THE GOOD OLD SUMMERTIME			
❑ MGM E-169 [10]		1949	100.00
IN THE HEAT OF THE NIGHT			
❑ United Artists UAL-4160 [M]		1967	18.00
❑ United Artists UAS-5160 [S]		1967	25.00
INVITATION TO THE DANCE			
❑ MGM E-3207 [M]		1956	50.00
THE IPCRESS FILE			
❑ Decca DL9124 [M]		1965	30.00
❑ Decca DL79124 [S]		1965	40.00
IRMA LA DOUCE			
❑ United Artists UAL-4109 [M]		1963	25.00
❑ United Artists UAS-5109 [S]		1963	30.00
THE ISLAND			
❑ Varese Sarabande VC-81147		1979	25.00
THE ISLAND AT THE TOP OF THE WORLD			
❑ Disneyland ST-3814		1974	30.00
ISLAND IN THE SKY			
❑ Decca DL7029 [10]		1953	300.00
IS PARIS BURNING?			
❑ Columbia Masterworks OL6630 [M]		1966	30.00
❑ Columbia Masterworks OS3030 [S]		1966	40.00
THE ITALIAN JOB			
❑ Paramount PAS-5007		1969	40.00
IT'S ALWAYS FAIR WEATHER			
❑ MCA 25018		1986	12.00
—*Reissue*			
❑ MGM E-3241 [M]		1955	50.00
IT'S A MAD, MAD, MAD, MAD WORLD			
❑ MCA 39076		198?	10.00
—*Reissue of United Artists 276*			
❑ United Artists UAL-4110 [M]		1963	25.00
❑ United Artists UAS-5110 [S]		1963	30.00
❑ United Artists UA-LA276-G		1974	12.00
—*Reissue of 5110*			
IT STARTED IN NAPLES			
❑ Dot DLP-3324 [M]		1960	60.00
❑ Dot DLP-25324 [S]		1960	100.00
❑ Varese Sarabande STV-81122		1982	18.00
—*Reissue of Dot 25324*			
I WANT TO LIVE			
❑ United Artists UAL-4005 [M]		1958	60.00
—*Orchestral music by Johnny Mandel*			
❑ United Artists UAS-4005 [S]		1958	40.00
—*Orchestral music by Johnny Mandel*			
❑ United Artists UAL-4006 [M]		1958	60.00
—*Jazz music by Gerry Mulligan, Shelly Manne and Art Farmer*			
❑ United Artists UAS-4006 [S]		1958	40.00
—*Jazz music by Gerry Mulligan, Shelly Mann and Art Farmer*			
❑ United Artists UXL1 [M]		1958	120.00
—*Combines 4005 and 4006 into one package*			
❑ United Artists UXS51 [S]		1958	150.00
—*Combines 5005 and 5006 into one package*			
I WAS A TEENAGE ZOMBIE			
❑ Enigma SJ-73296		1987	15.00
—*Includes The Fleshtones, The Del Fuegos, the dB's, The Dream Syndicate, Violent Femmes, The Waitresses, The Smithereens, Los Lobos*			
JACK THE RIPPER			
❑ RCA Victor LPM-2199 [M]		1960	30.00
❑ RCA Victor LSP-2199 [S]		1960	50.00
JAMBOREE!			
❑ Warner Bros. (no #) [M]		1957	1200.00
—*Album has been counterfeited. Originals have front cover slicks and back cover notes printed on the cardboard, and the records have "Jam 1" and "Jam 2" stamped (not etched) in the dead wax.*			
THE JAMES DEAN STORY			
❑ Capitol W881 [M]		1957	200.00
❑ Kimberly 2016 [M]		1960	40.00
❑ Kimberly 11016 [S]		1960	200.00
—*Reissue of World Pacific 2005*			
❑ World Pacific P-2005 [M]		1958	300.00
JAWS			
❑ MCA 2087		1975	25.00
❑ MCA 1660		198?	10.00
—*Reissue of 2087*			
JEAN DE FLORETTE			
❑ TVT 3004		1986	25.00
JEREMIAH JOHNSON			
❑ Warner Bros. BS2902		1972	25.00
—*Green label*			
JESSICA			
❑ United Artists UAL-4096 [M]		1962	25.00
❑ United Artists UAS-5096 [S]		1962	30.00
THE JOE LOUIS STORY			
❑ MGM E-221 [10]		1953	80.00
JOHNNY COOL			
❑ United Artists UAL-4111 [M]		1963	25.00
❑ United Artists UAS-5111 [S]		1963	30.00
JOHNNY TREMAIN			
❑ Disneyland WDL-4014 [M]		1957	50.00
JOHN PAUL JONES			
❑ Varese Sarabande STV-81146		1981	18.00
—*Reissue of Warner Bros. WS 1293*			
❑ Warner Bros. W1293 [M]		1959	60.00
❑ Warner Bros. WS1293 [S]		1959	120.00
JUD			
❑ Ampex A-50101		1971	25.00
JUDGMENT AT NUREMBERG			
❑ MCA 39055		198?	12.00
—*Reissue of United Artists 5095*			
❑ United Artists UAL-4095 [M]		1961	25.00
❑ United Artists UAS-5095 [S]		1961	50.00
JUDITH			
❑ RCA Victor LOC-1119 [M]		1966	18.00
❑ RCA Victor LSO-1119 [S]		1966	30.00
JUICE			
❑ MCA 10577		1992	12.00
—*Includes Naughty By Nature, others; issude in generic sleeve with sticker*			
JULIET OF THE SPIRITS			
❑ Mainstream 56062 [M]		1965	30.00
❑ Mainstream S-6062 [S]		1965	60.00
JULIUS CAESAR			

Number	Title	Yr	NM

❑ MGM E-3033 [M] — 1953 — 40.00

JUMBO (BILLY ROSE'S)
❑ Columbia Masterworks OL5860 [M] — 1962 — 25.00
❑ Columbia Masterworks OS2260 [S] — 1962 — 30.00

JUMPIN' JACK FLASH
❑ Mercury 830545-1 — 1986 — 12.00
— *Includes Bananarama*

THE JUNGLE BOOK
❑ Buena Vista BV-4041 [M] — 1967 — 18.00
❑ Buena Vista STER-4041 [S] — 1967 — 30.00
❑ Disneyland 3105 [PD] — 1981 — 30.00
— *Disney Picture Disc" series*

JURASSIC PARK
❑ MCA/BMG (no #) [PD] — 1993 — 1500.00
— *Custom-made picture disc; promo only*

JUSTINE
❑ Monument SLP-18123 — 1969 — 30.00

JUST ONE OF THE GUYS
❑ Elektra 60426 — 1985 — 12.00
— *Includes Berlin*

KALEIDOSCOPE
❑ Warner Bros. W1663 [M] — 1966 — 25.00
❑ Warner Bros. WS1663 [S] — 1966 — 30.00

THE KARATE KID
❑ Casablanca 822213-1 — 1984 — 15.00
— *Includes The Flirts (with Jan & Dean), Gang of Four*

KELLY'S HEROES
❑ MGM S1E-23 — 1970 — 30.00

THE KEY
❑ Columbia CL1185 [M] — 1958 — 80.00

KILLERS THREE
❑ Tower ST-5141 — 1968 — 25.00

THE KING AND I
❑ Capitol W740 [M] — 1956 — 30.00
— *Gray label*
❑ Capitol W740 [M] — 1959 — 18.00
— *Black colorband label, logo at left*
❑ Capitol W740 [M] — 1962 — 15.00
— *Black colorband label, logo at top*
❑ Capitol SW740 [S] — 1959 — 25.00
— *Black colorband label, logo at left*
❑ Capitol SW740 [S] — 1962 — 18.00
— *Black colorband label, logo at top*
❑ Capitol SW740 [S] — 1969 — 15.00
— *Lime green label*
❑ Capitol SW740 [S] — 1973 — 12.00
— *Orange label*
❑ Capitol SW740 [S] — 1978 — 10.00
— *Purple label*

KING KONG
❑ Reprise MS2260 — 1976 — 25.00

KING KONG LIVES
❑ MCA 6203 — 1987 — 30.00

THE KING OF COMEDY
❑ Warner Bros. 23765 — 1983 — 12.00
— *Includes The Pretenders ("Back on the Chain Gang"), Talking Heads, Ric Ocasek*

KING OF KINGS
❑ MCA 39056 — 198? — 10.00
— *Reissue of MGM S1E-2*
❑ MGM 1E-2 [M] — 1961 — 30.00
— *Boxed version with hardbound book and four 8x10 photos*
❑ MGM S1E-2 [S] — 1961 — 40.00
— *Boxed version with hardbound book and four 8x10 photos*
❑ MGM 1E-2 [M] — 1961 — 18.00
— *Standard cover*
❑ MGM S1E-2 [S] — 1961 — 25.00
— *Standard cover*

KING RAT
❑ Mainstream 56061 [M] — 1965 — 30.00
❑ Mainstream S-6061 [S] — 1965 — 50.00

KINGS GO FORTH
❑ Capitol W1063 [M] — 1958 — 150.00

KING SOLOMON'S MINES
❑ Restless 72106 — 1985 — 25.00

KISMET
❑ MCA 1424 — 198? — 10.00
— *Reissue of MGM 3281*
❑ Metro M-526 [M] — 1965 — 15.00
— *Reissue of MGM E-3281 with one fewer track*
❑ Metro MS-526 [R] — 1955 — 12.00
— *Rechanneled reissue of MGM E-3281 with one fewer track*
❑ MGM E-3281 [M] — 1955 — 25.00
— *Yellow label*
❑ MGM E-3281 [M] — 1960 — 18.00
— *Black label*

KISS ME, KATE
❑ MCA 25003 — 1986 — 12.00
— *Reissue of MGM 3077*
❑ Metro M-525 [M] — 1965 — 15.00
— *Reissue of MGM 3077, but with only 10 songs*
❑ Metro MS-525 [R] — 1965 — 12.00
— *Rechanneled reissue of MGM 3077, but with only 10 songs*
❑ MGM E-3077 [M] — 1953 — 25.00
— *Yellow label*
❑ MGM E-3077 [M] — 1959 — 18.00
— *Black label*

KRULL
❑ Southern Cross SCRS-1004 — 1983 — 25.00

KRUSH GROOVE
❑ Warner Bros. 25295 — 1985 — 12.00
— *Includes Beastie Boys, L.L. Cool J, Krush Groove All-Stars, Debbie Harry*

KWAMINA
❑ Mercury MG-20654 [M] — 1961 — 100.00
❑ Mercury SR-60654 [S] — 1961 — 100.00

LA BAMBA
❑ Slash/Warner Bros. R120062 — 1987 — 15.00
— *BMG Direct Marketing version*
❑ Slash/Warner Bros. 25605 — 1987 — 12.00

LABYRINTH
❑ EMI America SV-17206 — 1986 — 12.00
— *Includes David Bowie*

LADY AND THE TRAMP
❑ Decca DL5557 [10] — 1955 — 60.00
❑ Decca DL8462 [M] — 1957 — 70.00
❑ Disneyland 3103 [PD] — 1981 — 30.00
— *Disney Picture Disc" edition*

LADYHAWKE
❑ Atlantic 81248 — 1985 — 25.00

THE LANDLORD
❑ United Artists UAS-5209 — 1970 — 25.00

THE LAST AMERICAN VIRGIN
❑ Columbia JS38279 — 1982 — 40.00

THE LAST EMBRACE
❑ Varese Sarabande STV-81166 — 1983 — 25.00

THE LAST EMPEROR
❑ Virgin 90690 — 1987 — 12.00
— *One side of music by David Byrne*

THE LAST OF THE SECRET AGENTS
❑ Dot DLP-3714 [M] — 1966 — 25.00
❑ Dot DLP-25714 [S] — 1966 — 30.00

THE LAST RUN
❑ MCA 25116 — 1986 — 10.00
— *Reissue of MGM 1SE-30*
❑ MGM 1SE-30 — 1971 — 30.00

THE LAST STARFIGHTER
❑ Southern Cross SCRS-1007 — 1984 — 30.00

LAST SUMMER
❑ Warner Bros. WS1791 — 1969 — 25.00

THE LAST VALLEY
❑ ABC-Dunhill DSX-50102 — 1971 — 40.00

LAWRENCE OF ARABIA
❑ Arista ABM-4009 — 1975 — 12.00
— *Reissue of Bell 1205*
❑ Bell 1205 — 1971 — 12.00
— *Reissue of Colgems COSO-5004*
❑ Colgems COMO-5004 [M] — 1967 — 15.00
— *Reissue of Colpix CP-514*
❑ Colgems COSO-5004 [S] — 1967 — 18.00
— *Reissue of Colpix SCP-514*
❑ Colpix CP-514 [M] — 1962 — 25.00
❑ Colpix SCP-514 [S] — 1962 — 30.00

LEAN ON ME
❑ Warner Bros. 25843 — 1987 — 12.00
— *Includes Guns N' Roses ("Welcome to the Jungle")*

LENNY
❑ United Artists UA-LA359-H [(2)] — 1974 — 50.00

THE LEOPARD
❑ 20th Century Fox FXG-5015 [M] — 1963 — 30.00
❑ 20th Century Fox SXG-5015 [S] — 1963 — 40.00
❑ Varese Sarabande STV-81190 — 1982 — 18.00
— *Reissue of 20th Century Fox SXG-5015*

LES LIAISONS DANGEREUSES
❑ Charlie Parker PLP-813 [M] — 1962 — 60.00
❑ Charlie Parker PLP-813S [S] — 1962 — 60.00
❑ Epic LA16022 [M] — 1961 — 80.00
❑ Epic BA17022 [S] — 1961 — 100.00
❑ Fontana MGF-27539 [M] — 1965 — 50.00
❑ Fontana SRF-67539 [R] — 1965 — 35.00

LESS THAN ZERO
❑ Def Jam SC44042 — 1987 — 12.00
— *Includes Bangles, Joan Jett and the Blackhearts, Glenn Danzig, Publ;ic Enemy, L.L. Cool J, Oran "Juice" Jones*

LETHAL WEAPON
❑ Warner Bros. 25561 — 1987 — 12.00
— *Includes Honeymoon Suite*

LET'S MAKE LOVE
❑ Columbia CL1527 [M] — 1960 — 30.00
❑ Columbia CS8327 [S] — 1960 — 50.00

LETTER TO BREZHNEV
❑ MCA/London 6162 — 1985 — 12.00
— *Includes Fine Young Cannibals, Bronski Beat*

LET THE GOOD TIMES ROLL
❑ Bell 9002 — 1973 — 30.00

LEVIATHAN
❑ Varese Sarabande VS-5226 — 1989 — 25.00

THE LIFE AND TIMES OF JUDGE ROY BEAN
❑ Columbia Masterworks S31948 — 1972 — 30.00

LIFEFORCE
❑ Varese Sarabande STV-81249 — 1985 — 30.00

LIGHT FANTASTIC
❑ 20th Century Fox FXG-5016 [M] — 1963 — 25.00
❑ 20th Century Fox SXG-5016 [S] — 1963 — 30.00

LIGHT OF DAY
❑ Blackheart SZ40654 — 1986 — 15.00
— *Includes The Barbusters (Joan Jett and the Blackhearts), Dave Edmunds*

LI'L ABNER
❑ Columbia Masterworks OL5460 [M] — 1959 — 30.00
— *Credits within photo*
❑ Columbia Masterworks OL5460 [M] — 196? — 25.00
— *Credits in red strip at bottom of photo*
❑ Columbia Masterworks OS2021 [S] — 1959 — 40.00
— *Credits within photo*
❑ Columbia Masterworks OS2021 [S] — 196? — 30.00
— *Credits in red strip at bottom of photo*

LILIES OF THE FIELD
❑ Epic LN24094 [M] — 1964 — 25.00
❑ Epic BN26094 [S] — 1964 — 30.00

THE LION
❑ London M-76001 [M] — 1962 — 400.00

LIONHEART
❑ Varese Sarabande STV-81304 — 1987 — 25.00

LIONHEART (MORE MUSIC FROM THE FILM)
❑ Varese Sarabande STV-81311 — 1987 — 50.00

THE LION IN WINTER
❑ Columbia Masterworks OS3250 — 1969 — 25.00

LITTLE BIG MAN
❑ Columbia Masterworks S30545 — 1970 — 25.00

LITTLE SHOP OF HORRORS
❑ Geffen GHS-24125 — 1986 — 25.00

LIVE AND LET DIE
❑ Liberty LMAS-100 — 1981 — 15.00
— *Gray label; reissue of United Artists 100 with gatefold cover*
❑ Liberty LT-50100 — 1982 — 15.00
— *Gray label; reissue of Liberty 100 with standard cover*
❑ United Artists UA-LA100-G — 1973 — 25.00
— *Tan label; cover corner is not clipped off*
❑ United Artists SWAO-95120 — 1973 — 30.00
— *Longines (formerly Capitol) Record Club edition*
❑ United Artists UA-LA100-G — 1973 — 12.00
— *Tan label; cover corner is clipped*
❑ United Artists UA-LA100-G — 1977 — 12.00
— *Sunrise" label with this number on both jacket and label*
❑ United Artists LMAS-100 — 1979 — 12.00
— *Sunrise" label with this number on label (jacket still has UA-LA100-G)*

LIVE FOR LIFE
❑ United Artists UAL-4165 [M] — 1967 — 25.00
❑ United Artists UAS-5165 [S] — 1967 — 25.00

THE LIVELY SET
❑ Decca DL9119 [M] — 1964 — 30.00
❑ Decca DL79119 [S] — 1964 — 40.00

LOGAN'S RUN
❑ MGM MG-1-5302 — 1976 — 30.00

Number	Title	Yr	NM

LOLITA
❏ MCA 39067 — 198? — 10.00
—Reissue of MGM SE-4050
❏ MGM E-4050 [M] — 1962 — 25.00
❏ MGM SE-4050 [S] — 1962 — 30.00

THE LOLLIPOP COVER
❏ Mainstream 56067 [M] — 1966 — 25.00
❏ Mainstream S-6067 [S] — 1966 — 30.00

THE LONGEST DAY
❏ 20th Century Fox FXG-5007 [M] — 1962 — 25.00
❏ 20th Century Fox SXG-5007 [S] — 1962 — 30.00

THE LONG HOT SUMMER
❏ Roulette R-25026 [M] — 1958 — 75.00

LONG JOHN SILVER
❏ RCA Victor LPM-3279 [10] — 1954 — 300.00

THE LONG SHIPS
❏ Colpix CP-517 [M] — 1964 — 50.00
❏ Colpix SCP-517 [S] — 1964 — 60.00

LORD JIM
❏ Colpix CP-521 [M] — 1965 — 30.00
❏ Colpix SCP-521 [S] — 1965 — 40.00

LORD LOVE A DUCK
❏ United Artists UAL-4137 [M] — 1966 — 25.00
❏ United Artists UAS-5137 [S] — 1966 — 30.00

THE LORD OF THE RINGS
❏ Fantasy LOR-1 — 1978 — 25.00
❏ Fantasy LOR-PD2 — 1978 — 30.00
—Two picture discs

THE LORDS OF FLATBUSH
❏ ABC ABCD-828 — 1974 — 30.00

A LOSS OF INNOCENCE
❏ Colpix CP-508 [M] — 1961 — 40.00

LOST ANGELS
❏ A&M SP-3926 — 1989 — 15.00
—Includes The Cure, Soundgarden, The Pogues, Soul Ayslum, Happy Mondays

THE LOST BOYS
❏ Atlantic 81767 — 1987 — 12.00
—Includes INXS and Jimmy Barnes, Echo and the Bunnymen

THE LOST CONTINENT
❏ MGM E-3635 [M] — 1957 — 200.00

LOVE IN 4 DIMENSIONS
❏ Request RLP-8090 [M] — 1966 — 30.00
❏ Request SRLP-8090 [S] — 1966 — 30.00

LOVE LIFE
❏ Heritage 600 [M] — 195? — 60.00

LOVERS AND OTHER STRANGERS
❏ ABC ABCS-OC-15 — 1970 — 25.00
❏ ABC SW-93479 — 1971 — 30.00
—Capitol Record Club edition

M*A*S*H
❏ Columbia Masterworks OS3520 — 1970 — 50.00
—Original copies do not have the theme song done by Ahmad Jamal
❏ Columbia Masterworks S32753 — 1973 — 25.00
—Reissue with the movie's theme performed by Ahmad Jamal

MACARTHUR
❏ MCA 2287 — 1977 — 25.00

THE MAD ADVENTURES OF RABBI JACOB
❏ London PS652 — 1974 — 25.00
—Cover is intact with no cut-out markings
❏ London PS652 — 1974 — 12.00
—Cover has cut-out markings (usually a hole punch or a cut-off corner)

MADAME BOVARY
❏ MGM E-3507 [M] — 195? — 150.00

MADE IN USA
❏ Chrysalis OV41566 — 1987 — 12.00
—Includes Timbuk 3, World Party, Sonic Youth, Mojo Nixon & Skid Roper

THE MAGIC CHRISTIAN
❏ Commonwealth United CU-6004 — 1970 — 30.00

MAGNIFICENT OBSESSION
❏ Decca DL8078 [M] — 1954 — 60.00
—Black label, gold print
❏ Decca DL8078 [M] — 1955 — 50.00
—Black label, silver print
❏ Decca DL8078 [M] — 196? — 30.00
—Black label with color bars
❏ Varese Sarabande STV-81118 — 1981 — 15.00
—Reissue of Decca 8078

MAJOR DUNDEE

❏ Columbia Masterworks OL6380 [M] — 1965 — 25.00
❏ Columbia Masterworks OS2780 [S] — 1965 — 30.00

MAJOR LEAGUE
❏ Curb 10402 — 1989 — 15.00
—Includes X, Beat Farmers, Lyle Lovett

MALAMONDO
❏ Epic LN24126 [M] — 1964 — 30.00
❏ Epic BN26126 [S] — 1964 — 40.00

MALLRATS
❏ MCA 11294 — 1995 — 12.00
—Includes Weezer, Elastica, Belly, etc.

MAME
❏ Warner Bros. W2773 — 1974 — 18.00
❏ Warner Bros. PRO580 [DJ] — 1973 — 50.00
—Promo-only gatefold edition with Lucille Ball in Christmas hat on the cover

A MAN AND A WOMAN (UN HOMME ET UNE FEMME)
❏ United Artists UAL-4147 [M] — 1966 — 18.00
❏ United Artists UAS-5147 [S] — 1966 — 25.00
❏ United Artists SW-91032 [S] — 1967 — 30.00
—Capitol Record Club edition

A MAN CALLED ADAM
❏ Reprise R6180 [M] — 1966 — 35.00
❏ Reprise RS6180 [S] — 1966 — 50.00

A MAN CALLED DAGGER
❏ MGM E-4516 [M] — 1967 — 18.00
❏ MGM SE-4516 [S] — 1967 — 25.00

A MAN CALLED FLINTSTONE
❏ Hanna-Barbera HLP-2055 [M] — 1967 — 100.00

A MAN COULD GET KILLED
❏ Decca DL4750 [M] — 1966 — 18.00
❏ Decca DL74750 [S] — 1966 — 25.00

A MAN FOR ALL SEASONS
❏ RCA Victor VDM-116 [M] — 1966 — 30.00

MAN FROM SHAFT
❏ MGM SE-4836 — 1972 — 30.00

MANIAC
❏ Varese Sarabande STV-81143 — 1980 — 25.00

MAN IN THE MIDDLE
❏ 20th Century Fox TFM-3128 [M] — 1965 — 30.00
❏ 20th Century Fox TFS-4128 [S] — 1965 — 50.00

THE MAN OF A THOUSAND FACES
❏ Decca DL8623 [M] — 1957 — 50.00
—Black label, silver print, or pink label, black print promos
❏ Decca DL8623 [M] — 196? — 30.00
—Black label with color bars
❏ Varese Sarabande STV-81121 — 1981 — 15.00
—Reissue of Decca 8623

MAN OF LA MANCHA
❏ United Artists UAS-9906 — 1972 — 25.00
—Cover is intact with no cut corners
❏ United Artists UAS-9906 — 1972 — 12.00
—Cover has cut-out marking such as a cut-off corner

THE MAN WHO WOULD BE KING
❏ Capitol SW-11474 — 1975 — 25.00

THE MAN WITH THE GOLDEN ARM
❏ Decca DL8257 [M] — 1956 — 120.00
❏ Decca DL78257 [R] — 196? — 50.00
❏ MCA 2043 [R] — 1973 — 25.00
—Reissue of Decca 78257; black label with rainbow
❏ MCA 1528 — 198? — 10.00
—Reissue of MCA 2043

THE MAN WITH THE GOLDEN GUN
❏ United Artists UA-LA358-G — 1974 — 25.00

MARACAIBO
❏ Decca DL8756 [M] — 1958 — 40.00
—Black label, silver print, or pink label, black print promos
❏ Decca DL8756 [M] — 196? — 25.00
—Black label with color bars

MARCO THE MAGNIFICENT
❏ Columbia Masterworks OS2870 [S] — 1966 — 40.00
❏ Columbia Masterworks OL6470 [M] — 1966 — 30.00

MARIE WARD
❏ Varese Sarabande STV-81268 — 1985 — 50.00

MARJORIE MORNINGSTAR
❏ RCA Victor LOC-1044 [M] — 1958 — 40.00
—"RE" next to label number
❏ RCA Victor LOC-1044 [M] — 1958 — 60.00
—An Original Soundtrack Recording" on spine

MARRIED TO THE MOB
❏ Reprise 25763 — 1988 — 15.00

—Includes New Order, Sinead O'Connor, Chris Isaak, Debbie Harry, Brian Eno, The Feelies, Tom Tom Club

MARRY ME, MARRY ME
❏ RCA Victor LSO-1160 — 1969 — 25.00

MARY, QUEEN OF SCOTS
❏ Decca DL79186 — 1972 — 30.00

MARY POPPINS
❏ Buena Vista BV-4026 [M] — 1964 — 15.00
—Originals have gatefold covers
❏ Buena Vista STER-4026 [S] — 1964 — 18.00
—Originals have gatefold covers
❏ Buena Vista STER-5005 [S] — 1973 — 12.00
—Reissue with new number and no gatefold
❏ RCA Victor COP-111 [M] — 1964 — 18.00
—With gatefold; RCA Record Club edition
❏ RCA Victor CSO-111 [S] — 1964 — 25.00
—With gatefold; RCA Record Club edition

THE MASK
❏ Chaos 6455 [DJ] — 1994 — 25.00
—Generic cover; no other U.S. vinyl

MASKED AND ANONYMOUS
❏ Columbia CSK90618-1 — 2006 — 30.00
—Classic Records issue on 140-gram vinyl; CD issued in 2003

MASTER OF THE WORLD
❏ Varese Sarabande VC-81070 — 1978 — 18.00
—Reissue of Vee Jay 4000
❏ Vee Jay LP-4000 [M] — 1961 — 30.00
❏ Vee Jay SR-4000 [S] — 1961 — 40.00

MASTERS OF THE UNIVERSE
❏ Varese Sarabande STV-81333 — 1987 — 25.00

MCLINTOCK!
❏ United Artists UAL-4112 [M] — 1963 — 60.00
❏ United Artists UAS-5112 [S] — 1963 — 80.00

ME AND THE COLONEL
❏ RCA Victor LOC-1046 [M] — 1958 — 50.00

MEDITERRANEAN HOLIDAY
❏ London M-76003 [M] — 1964 — 50.00
❏ London MS-82003 [S] — 1964 — 80.00

MEET ME IN ST. LOUIS
❏ AEI 3101 — 1978 — 15.00
—Reissue of Decca LP
❏ Decca DL8498 [M] — 1957 — 30.00
—LP reissue of 78 rpm album from 1944; B-side of LP is "The Harvey Girls.

MEMORIES AUX BRUXELLES
❏ Carlton LP-112 [M] — 1959 — 30.00
❏ Carlton LP-12112 [S] — 1959 — 40.00

MENACE II SOCIETY
❏ Jive 41522 [DJ] — 1993 — 25.00
—Vinyl is promo only

MEN IN WAR
❏ Imperial LP-9032W [M] — 1957 — 150.00

MERRY ANDREW
❏ Capitol T1016 [M] — 1958 — 50.00

MERRY CHRISTMAS, MR. LAWRENCE
❏ MCA 6125 — 1983 — 15.00
—Includes David Sylvian
❏ MCA 6125 — 1983 — 12.00
—Music by Ryuichi Sakamoto. David Bowie stars in the movie, but does not sing on the LP.

METROPOLIS
❏ Columbia JS39526 — 1984 — 12.00
—Includes Adam Ant

MICKEY ONE
❏ MGM E-4312 [M] — 1965 — 50.00
❏ MGM SE-4312 [S] — 1965 — 60.00

MIDNIGHT COWBOY
❏ United Artists UAS-5198 — 1969 — 25.00

MIDNIGHT EXPRESS
❏ Casablanca NBLP-7114 — 1978 — 25.00

THE MIGHTY QUINN
❏ A&M SP-3924 — 1989 — 12.00
—Includes UB40, Yello

A MILANESE STORY
❏ Atlantic 1388 [M] — 1962 — 150.00
❏ Atlantic SD1388 [S] — 1962 — 150.00

THE MINX
❏ Amsterdam 12007 — 1970 — 120.00

THE MISFITS
❏ United Artists UAL-4087 [M] — 1961 — 50.00

Number	Title	Yr	NM
❏ United Artists UAS-5087 [S]	1961	100.00
❏ United Artists UA-LA273-G [S]	1974	15.00
—Reissue of 5087		

THE MISSOURI BREAKS
❏ MCA 25113	1986	12.00
—Reissue of United Artists UA-LA623-G		
❏ United Artists UA-LA623-G	1976	30.00

MISS SADIE THOMPSON
| ❏ Mercury MG-25181 [10] | 1954 | 75.00 |
| ❏ Mercury MG-20123 [M] | 1956 | 150.00 |

MOBY DICK
| ❏ RCA Victor LPM-1247 [M] | 1956 | 120.00 |

MODERN GIRLS
| ❏ Warner Bros. 25526 | 1986 | 12.00 |
| —Includes Depeche Mode, Toni Basil, Icehouse, The Jesus and Mary Chain | | |

MODERN TIMES
| ❏ United Artists UAL-4049 [M] | 1959 | 30.00 |
| ❏ United Artists UAS-5049 [R] | 196? | 25.00 |

MODESTY BLAISE
| ❏ 20th Century Fox TFM-3182 [M] | 1966 | 30.00 |
| ❏ 20th Century Fox TFS-4182 [S] | 1966 | 50.00 |

MOHAMMAD, MESSENGER OF GOD
| ❏ Namara 79001 | 1977 | 30.00 |

MONDO CANE
| ❏ United Artists UAL-4105 [M] | 1963 | 18.00 |
| ❏ United Artists UAS-5105 [S] | 1963 | 25.00 |

MONDO CANE NO. 2
| ❏ 20th Century Fox TFM-3147 [M] | 1964 | 30.00 |
| ❏ 20th Century Fox TFS-4147 [S] | 1964 | 40.00 |

MOON OVER PARADOR
| ❏ MCA 6249 | 1988 | 30.00 |

THE MOON SPINNERS
| ❏ Buena Vista BV-3323 [M] | 1964 | 40.00 |

MORE AMERICAN GRAFFITI
| ❏ MCA MCA2-11006 | 1979 | 25.00 |
| —Tan labels | | |

MR. BUDDWING
| ❏ Verve V-8638 [M] | 1965 | 35.00 |
| ❏ Verve V6-8638 [S] | 1965 | 60.00 |

MR. MAGOO: 1001 ARABIAN NIGHTS
| ❏ Colpix CP-410 [M] | 1959 | 50.00 |
| ❏ Colpix SCP-410 [S] | 1959 | 150.00 |

MURDER INC.
| ❏ Canadian American CALP-1003 [M] | 1960 | 100.00 |

MUSCLE BEACH PARTY PLUS MERLIN JONES AND THE SCRAMBLED EGGHEAD
| ❏ Buena Vista BV-3314 [M] | 1964 | 60.00 |
| ❏ Buena Vista STER-3314 [S] | 1964 | 120.00 |

THE MUSIC MAN
❏ Warner Bros. B1459 [M]	1962	18.00
❏ Warner Bros. BS1459 [S]	1962	25.00
—Gold label originals		
❏ Warner Bros. BS1459 [S]	1968	15.00
—Green label with "W7" box logo at top		
❏ Warner Bros. BS1459 [S]	1970	12.00
—Green label with "WB" shield logo at top		
❏ Warner Bros. BS1459 [S]	1973	10.00
—Burbank" palm trees label or later white label		

MUTINY ON THE BOUNTY
❏ MCA 25007	1986	10.00
—Reissue of MGM 1SE-4		
❏ MGM 1E-4 [M]	1962	30.00
—Boxed set with book and painting		
❏ MGM S1E-4 [S]	1962	40.00
—Boxed set with book and painting		
❏ MGM 1E-4 [M]	196?	15.00
—Standard cover		
❏ MGM S1E-4 [S]	196?	18.00
—Standard cover		

MY FAIR LADY
| ❏ Columbia Masterworks KOL8000 [M] | 1964 | 15.00 |
| ❏ Columbia Masterworks KOS2600 [S] | 1964 | 18.00 |

MY GEISHA
| ❏ RCA Victor LOC-1070 [M] | 1962 | 50.00 |
| ❏ RCA Victor LSO-1070 [S] | 1962 | 100.00 |

MY SIDE OF THE MOUNTAIN
| ❏ Capitol ST-245 | 1969 | 30.00 |

MY STEPMOTHER IS AN ALIEN
| ❏ Polydor 837798-1 | 1988 | 12.00 |
| —Includes Animotion, M/A/R/R/S | | |

MY WILD IRISH ROSE
| ❏ RCA Victor LPM-3036 [10] | 1952 | 40.00 |

NAKED ANGELS
| ❏ Straight STS-1056 | 1969 | 30.00 |

THE NAKED MAJA
| ❏ United Artists UAL-4031 [M] | 1959 | 30.00 |
| ❏ United Artists UAS-5031 [S] | 1959 | 40.00 |

NANCY GOES TO RIO
| ❏ MGM E-508 [10] | 1950 | 60.00 |

NASHVILLE
| ❏ ABC ABCD-893 | 1975 | 25.00 |

NATIONAL LAMPOON'S ANIMAL HOUSE
❏ MCA 3046	1978	15.00
—Tan label original		
❏ MCA 3046	1980	12.00
—Blue label with rainbow		
❏ MCA 1692	198?	10.00
—Reissue; blue label with rainbow		

NATIONAL LAMPOON'S VACATION
| ❏ Warner Bros. 23909 | 1983 | 25.00 |

NATIVE SON
| ❏ MCA 6198 | 1986 | 25.00 |

NAVAJO JOE
| ❏ United Artists UA-LA292-G | 1974 | 30.00 |

NED KELLY
❏ United Artists UAS-5213	1970	30.00
❏ United Artists UA-LA300-G	1974	15.00
—Reissue of 5213		

NEVADA SMITH
| ❏ Dot DLP-3718 [M] | 1966 | 30.00 |
| ❏ Dot DLP-25718 [S] | 1966 | 40.00 |

THE NEVER ENDING STORY
| ❏ EMI America ST-17139 | 1984 | 25.00 |

NEVER ON SUNDAY
❏ United Artists UAL-4070 [M]	1960	18.00
❏ United Artists UAS-5070 [S]	1960	25.00
❏ United Artists SW-90834 [S]	196?	25.00
—Capitol Record Club edition		

THE NEW INTERNS
| ❏ Colpix CP-473 [M] | 1964 | 30.00 |
| ❏ Colpix SCP-473 [S] | 1964 | 40.00 |

NEW JACK CITY
| ❏ Giant 24409 | 1991 | 15.00 |
| —Includes Ice-T | | |

A NEW KIND OF LOVE
| ❏ Mercury MG-20859 [M] | 1963 | 100.00 |
| ❏ Mercury SR-60859 [S] | 1963 | 100.00 |

THE NEW MESSIAH
| ❏ Columbia KC31713 | 1972 | 25.00 |

NEW YORK STORIES
| ❏ Elektra Musician 60857 | 1988 | 15.00 |
| —Includes Kid Creole and the Coconuts, Transvision Vamp | | |

NICHOLAS AND ALEXANDRA
| ❏ Bell 1103 | 1971 | 30.00 |

A NIGHT IN HEAVEN
| ❏ A&M SP-4966 | 1983 | 15.00 |
| —Includes The English Beat | | |

A NIGHTMARE ON ELM STREET
| ❏ Varese Sarabande STV-81236 | 1984 | 18.00 |

A NIGHTMARE ON ELM STREET 2: FREDDY'S REVENGE
| ❏ Varese Sarabande STV-81275 | 1986 | 15.00 |

A NIGHTMARE ON ELM STREET 3: DREAM WARRIORS
| ❏ Varese Sarabande STV-81314 | 1987 | 18.00 |

A NIGHTMARE ON ELM STREET 4: THE DREAM MASTER
❏ Chrysalis R100504	1988	18.00
—BMG Direct Marketing edition		
❏ Chrysalis OV41673	1988	18.00
—Various-artists song collection		
❏ Varese Sarabande VS-5203	1988	18.00
—Orchestral and incidental music		

A NIGHTMARE ON ELM STREET 5: THE DREAM CHILD
| ❏ Jive 1258-1-J | 1989 | 15.00 |
| —Various-artists song collection | | |

NIGHT OF THE GENERALS
| ❏ Colgems COMO-5002 [M] | 1967 | 40.00 |
| ❏ Colgems COSO-5002 [S] | 1967 | 70.00 |

THE NIGHT OF THE HUNTER
| ❏ RCA Victor LPM-1136 [M] | 1955 | 250.00 |

THE NIGHT THE LIGHTS WENT OUT IN GEORGIA
| ❏ Mirage SD16051 | 1981 | 12.00 |

9 1/2 WEEKS
❏ Capitol SV-12470	1986	12.00
❏ Capitol SV-512470	1986	18.00
—Columbia House edition		

NINE HOURS TO RAMA
| ❏ London M-76002 [M] | 1963 | 300.00 |

1969
| ❏ Polydor R100724 | 1988 | 12.00 |
| —Includes Pretenders ("Windows of the World") | | |

9 TO 5
| ❏ 20th Century T-627 | 1980 | 12.00 |

NOTHING BUT THE BEST
| ❏ Colpix CP-477 [M] | 1964 | 25.00 |
| ❏ Colpix SCP-477 [S] | 1964 | 30.00 |

NOT WITH MY WIFE, YOU DON'T
| ❏ Warner Bros. W1668 [M] | 1966 | 18.00 |
| ❏ Warner Bros. WS1668 [S] | 1966 | 25.00 |

NO WAY TO TREAT A LADY
| ❏ Dot DLP-25846 | 1968 | 30.00 |

A NUN'S STORY
| ❏ Warner Bros. B1306 [M] | 1959 | 60.00 |
| ❏ Warner Bros. BS1306 [S] | 1959 | 100.00 |

O BROTHER, WHERE ART THOU?
| ❏ Lost Highway 088170069-1 | 2003 | 25.00 |

OBSESSION
| ❏ London Phase 4 SPC-21160 | 1976 | 30.00 |

OCTOPUSSY
| ❏ A&M SP-4967 | 1983 | 25.00 |

THE ODD COUPLE
| ❏ Dot DLP-25862 | 1968 | 25.00 |

ODDS AGAINST TOMORROW
| ❏ United Artists UAL-4061 [M] | 1959 | 60.00 |
| ❏ United Artists UAS-5061 [S] | 1959 | 100.00 |

OF LOVE AND DESIRE
| ❏ 20th Century Fox FXG-5014 [M] | 1963 | 30.00 |
| ❏ 20th Century Fox SXG-5014 [S] | 1963 | 30.00 |

OH, ROSALINDA!
| ❏ Mercury MG-20145 [M] | 1957 | 50.00 |

OH DAD, POOR DAD, MAMMA'S HUNG YOU IN THE CLOSET AND I'M FEELIN' SO SAD
| ❏ RCA Victor LPM-3750 [M] | 1967 | 25.00 |
| ❏ RCA Victor LSP-3750 [S] | 1967 | 30.00 |

OIL TOWN, U.S.A.
| ❏ RCA Victor LFM-2000 [10] | 1953 | 60.00 |

OKLAHOMA!
❏ Capitol WAO595 [M]	1955	30.00
—Purple or dark red label		
❏ Capitol WAO595 [M]	1956	25.00
—Gray label		
❏ Capitol WAO595 [M]	1959	18.00
—Black colorband label, logo at left		
❏ Capitol WAO595 [M]	1962	15.00
—Black colorband label, logo at top		
❏ Capitol SWAO595 [S]	1959	25.00
—Black colorband label, logo at left		
❏ Capitol SWAO595 [S]	1962	18.00
—Black colorband label, logo at top		
❏ Capitol SWAO595 [S]	1969	15.00
—Lime green label		
❏ Capitol SWAO595 [S]	1973	12.00
—Orange label		

OLD BOYFRIENDS
| ❏ Columbia Masterworks JS36072 | 1979 | 50.00 |

THE OLD MAN AND THE SEA
| ❏ Columbia CL1183 [M] | 1958 | 30.00 |
| ❏ Columbia CS8013 [S] | 1958 | 60.00 |

OLD YELLER
❏ Disneyland WDL-3024 [M]	1957	50.00
—First edition		
❏ Disneyland WDL-1024 [M]	1960	40.00
—Second edition		
❏ Disneyland 1024 [M]	1974	30.00
—Reissue with no prefix		

OLIVER AND COMPANY
| ❏ Disney 64101 | 1988 | 30.00 |

ONCE UPON A TIME IN THE WEST
| ❏ RCA Victor LSP-4736 | 1969 | 30.00 |

THE ONE AND ONLY, GENUINE, ORIGINAL FAMILY BAND
| ❏ Buena Vista BV-5002 [M] | 1968 | 18.00 |
| ❏ Buena Vista STER-5002 [S] | 1968 | 25.00 |

THE ONE-EYED JACKS
| ❏ Liberty LOM-16001 [M] | 1961 | 30.00 |

Number	Title	Yr	NM
❏ Liberty LOS-17001 [S]		1961	50.00
ONE FLEW OVER THE CUCKOO'S NEST			
❏ Fantasy F-9500		1975	25.00
❏ Fantasy MPF-4531		198?	12.00
—Budget-line reissue of 9500			
101 DALMATIONS			
❏ Disneyland ST-4903 [M]		1963	150.00
—Gatefold cover with pop-up scene in center			
❏ Disneyland ST-3931 [M]		1965	40.00
❏ Disneyland DQ-1308 [M]		1966	25.00
❏ Disneyland ST-1908 [M]		1960	30.00
ON HER MAJESTY'S SECRET SERVICE			
❏ United Artists UAS-5204		1969	25.00
❏ United Artists UA-LA299-G		1974	15.00
—Reissue of 5204			
ON THE BEACH			
❏ Roulette R-25098 [M]		1959	80.00
❏ Roulette SR-25098 [S]		1959	150.00
THE OPTIMISTS			
❏ Paramount PAS-1015		1973	30.00
ORCHESTRA WIVES			
❏ RCA Victor LPT-3065 [10]		1954	120.00
THE OSCAR			
❏ Columbia Masterworks OL6550 [M]		1966	25.00
❏ Columbia Masterworks OS2950 [S]		1966	30.00
OTLEY			
❏ Colgems COS-112		1969	30.00
OUR MAN FLINT			
❏ 20th Century Fox TFM-3179 [M]		1966	40.00
❏ 20th Century Fox TFS-4179 [S]		1966	60.00
OUTLAND			
❏ Warner Bros. HS3551		1981	30.00
OUTLAW BLUES			
❏ Capitol ST-11691		1977	18.00
THE OUTLAW JOSEY WALES			
❏ Warner Bros. BS2956		1976	30.00
THE OUTLAW RIDERS			
❏ MGM 1SE-26		1970	25.00
OUT OF AFRICA			
❏ MCA 6158		1985	25.00
❏ MCA 11327		1995	25.00
—Limited edition on "Heavy Vinyl"			
OUT OF SIGHT			
❏ Decca DL4751 [M]		1966	25.00
❏ Decca DL74751 [S]		1966	30.00
OVER THE EDGE			
❏ Warner Bros. HS3335		1979	12.00
—Includes The Ramones, The Cars			
PAGAN LOVE SONG			
❏ MGM E-534 [M]		1950	40.00
PAINT YOUR WAGON			
❏ MCA 37099		198?	10.00
—Reissue of Paramount 1001			
❏ Paramount PMS-1001		1969	25.00
—With booklet			
THE PAJAMA GAME			
❏ Columbia Masterworks OL5210 [M]		1957	30.00
—Gray and black label with six "eye" logos			
PAL JOEY			
❏ Capitol W912 [M]		1957	25.00
—Gray label			
❏ Capitol W912 [M]		1959	18.00
—Black colorband label, logo at left			
❏ Capitol W912 [M]		1962	15.00
—Black colorband label, logo on top			
❏ Capitol DW912 [R]		196?	12.00
—Black colorband label			
❏ Capitol SM-912 [R]		1977	10.00
—Reissue with new prefix			
PANIC BUTTON			
❏ Musicor MM-2026 [M]		1964	80.00
❏ Musicor MS-3026 [S]		1964	120.00
PAPER MOON			
❏ Paramount PAS-1012		1973	50.00
PAPER TIGER			
❏ Capitol SW-11475		1975	25.00
PAPILLON			
❏ Capitol ST-11260		1973	25.00
THE PARENT TRAP!			
❏ Buena Vista BV-3309 [M]		1961	40.00
❏ Buena Vista STER-3309 [S]		1961	60.00
—B-side of the above two: Camerata Conducts Themes from Great Motion Pictures			

Number	Title	Yr	NM
PARIS BLUES			
❏ United Artists UAL-4092 [M]		1961	60.00
❏ United Artists UAS-5092 [S]		1961	60.00
PARIS HOLIDAY			
❏ United Artists UAL-4001 [M]		1958	50.00
PARIS WHEN IT SIZZLES			
❏ Reprise R6113 [M]		1964	30.00
❏ Reprise RS6113 [S]		1964	40.00
PARRISH			
❏ Warner Bros. W1413 [M]		1961	30.00
❏ Warner Bros. WS1413 [S]		1961	80.00
—B-side of the above two: Popular Piano Concertos by George Greeley			
PARTY PARTY			
❏ A&M SP-3212		1982	18.00
—Includes Elvis Costello, Dave Edmunds ("Run Rudolph Run"), Bananarama, Midge Ure, Bad Manners, etc.			
A PATCH OF BLUE			
❏ Mainstream 56068 [M]		1965	25.00
❏ Mainstream S-6068 [S]		1965	30.00
❏ Mainstream ST-90805 [S]		1965	30.00
—Capitol Record Club edition			
PATTON			
❏ 20th Century Fox S-4208		1970	25.00
PATTY			
❏ Stang 1026		1976	25.00
PENELOPE			
❏ MGM E-4426 [M]		1966	25.00
❏ MGM SE-4426 [S]		1966	30.00
PENTHOUSE			
❏ United Artists UAL-4170 [M]		1967	25.00
❏ United Artists UAS-5170 [S]		1967	25.00
THE PEOPLE NEXT DOOR			
❏ Avco AV-11002		1970	30.00
PEPE			
❏ Colpix CP-507 [M]		1960	25.00
❏ Colpix SCP-507 [S]		1960	30.00
PERFECT			
❏ Arista R163614		1985	15.00
—Includes Wham! ("Wham Rap")			
❏ Arista AL98278		1985	12.00
—Includes Wham! ("Wham Rap")			
PERFORMANCE			
❏ Warner Bros. WS1846		1970	1500.00
—Original issue; has a completely different cover to the more common 2554			
❏ Warner Bros. BS2554		1970	25.00
—Second issue			
PERMANENT RECORD			
❏ Epic E40879		198?	15.00
—Includes Joe Strummer (5 tracks), Lou Reed, The Stranglers			
PETE KELLY'S BLUES			
❏ Columbia CL690 [M]		1955	50.00
❏ Decca DL8166 [M]		1955	150.00
—Black label, silver print			
PETE'S DRAGON			
❏ Capitol SW-11704		1977	25.00
PET SEMATARY			
❏ Varese Sarabande VS-5227		1989	18.00
PETULIA			
❏ Warner Bros. WS1755		1968	30.00
PEYTON PLACE			
❏ RCA Victor LOC-1042 [M]		1958	30.00
—Long Play" at bottom of label			
❏ RCA Victor LOC-1042 [M]		1965	30.00
—Monaural" at bottom of label			
❏ RCA Victor LSO-1042 [S]		1958	100.00
—Living Stereo" at bottom of label			
❏ RCA Victor LSO-1042 [S]		1965	60.00
—Stereo" at bottom of label			
PHAEDRA			
❏ United Artists UAL-4102 [M]		1962	25.00
❏ United Artists UAS-5102 [S]		1962	30.00
THE PHILADELPHIA EXPERIMENT			
❏ Rhino RNSP-306		1984	30.00
PICNIC			
❏ Decca DL8320 [M]		1956	30.00
—Black label, silver print			
❏ Decca DL8320 [M]		196?	18.00
—Black label with color bars			
❏ Decca DL78320 [S]		1959	30.00
—Maroon or all-black label			

Number	Title	Yr	NM
❏ Decca DL78320 [S]		196?	18.00
—Black label with color bars			
❏ MCA 2049		1973	12.00
—Reissue of Decca 78320; black label with rainbow			
❏ MCA 1527		198?	10.00
—Reissue of 2049			
A PIECE OF THE ACTION			
❏ Curtom CU5019		1977	25.00
PINK CADILLAC			
❏ Warner Bros. 25922		1989	12.00
PINOCCHIO			
❏ Disneyland WDL-4002 [M]		1956	250.00
—Original edition			
❏ Disneyland ST-4905 [M]		1963	150.00
—Gatefold cover with pop-up center graphics			
❏ Disneyland DQ-1202 [M]		1959	30.00
—Second edition			
❏ Disneyland DQ-1202MO [M]		1963	25.00
—Third edition			
❏ Disneyland 3102 [PD]		1981	30.00
—Disney Picture Disc" edition			
PIRANHA			
❏ Varese Sarabande STV-81126		1979	25.00
THE PIRATE			
❏ MGM E-21 [10]		1951	70.00
PLANET OF THE APES			
❏ Project 3 PR-5023SD		1968	30.00
—Gatefold cover			
❏ Project 3 PR-5023SD		1968	25.00
—Regular cover			
PLAYING FOR KEEPS			
❏ Atlantic 81678		1986	12.00
—Includes Arcadia			
THE PLEASURE SEEKERS			
❏ RCA Victor LOC-1101 [M]		1964	50.00
❏ RCA Victor LSO-1101 [S]		1964	100.00
POLLYANNA			
❏ Disneyland ST-1906 [M]		1960	50.00
❏ Disneyland DQ-1307 [M]		1967	30.00
POLTERGEIST			
❏ MGM MG-1-5408		1982	40.00
POLTERGEIST III			
❏ Varese Sarabande 704.620		1988	80.00
PORGY AND BESS			
❏ Columbia Masterworks OL5410 [M]		1959	18.00
❏ Columbia Masterworks OS2016 [S]		1959	25.00
PORKY'S REVENGE			
❏ Columbia CAS2034 [DJ]		1985	15.00
—Promo-only sampler; includes Dave Edmunds, Jeff Beck and George Harrison			
❏ Columbia JS39983		1985	15.00
—Includes Dave Edmunds			
THE POWER			
❏ Cerberus CST-0211		1984	25.00
PRET-A-PORTER			
❏ Miramax CAS6700 [DJ]		1994	30.00
—Promo only vinyl			
PRETTY BOY FLOYD			
❏ Audio Fidelity AFLP-1936 [M]		1960	60.00
❏ Audio Fidelity AFSD-5936 [S]		1960	80.00
PRETTY IN PINK			
❏ A&M R144487		1986	12.00
—Includes Orchestral Manoeuvres in the Dark ("If You Leave"); Psychedelic Furs ("Pretty in Pink"); etc.			
PRETTY WOMAN			
❏ EMI E1-93492		1990	15.00
—Includes David Bowie, Go West, Red Hot Chili Peppers, Jane Wiedlin			
THE PRIDE AND THE PASSION			
❏ Capitol W873 [M]		1957	60.00
THE PRINCESS BRIDE			
❏ Warner Bros. 25610		1987	25.00
THE PRISONER OF ZENDA			
❏ United Artists UA-LA374-G		1974	25.00
PRIVATE HELL 36			
❏ Coral CRL56122 [10]		1954	175.00
THE PRODUCERS			
❏ RCA Victor LPM-4008 [M]		1968	50.00
❏ RCA Victor LSP-4008 [S]		1968	30.00
❏ RCA Victor ANL1-1132		1975	12.00
—Reissue of LSP-4008			

Number	Title	Yr	NM
THE PROFESSIONALS			
❏ Colgems COMO-5001 [M]		1966	60.00
❏ Colgems COSO-5001 [S]		1966	150.00
A PROMISE AT DAWN			
❏ Polydor 24-5502		1970	30.00
THE PROPER TIME			
❏ Contemporary M-3587 [M]		1960	200.00
❏ Contemporary S-7587 [S]		1960	200.00
PROVIDENCE			
❏ DRG SL-9502		1977	25.00
PRUDENCE AND THE PILL			
❏ 20th Century Fox S-4199		1968	25.00
PSYCHO II			
❏ MCA 6119		1983	25.00
Q THE WINGED SERPENT			
❏ Cerberus CST-0206		1983	25.00
QUEST FOR FIRE			
❏ RCA Victor ABL1-4274		1982	25.00
THE QUIET MAN			
❏ Decca DL5411 [10]		1952	120.00
THE QUILLER MEMORANDUM			
❏ Columbia Masterworks OL6660 [M]		1966	30.00
❏ Columbia Masterworks OS3060 [M]		1966	60.00
QUO VADIS?			
❏ MCA 39075		198?	10.00
—Reissue of MGM 3524			
❏ MGM E-103 [10]		1951	40.00
—Music soundtrack only			
❏ MGM E-134 [10]		1951	60.00
—Box set of two discs; includes dialogue			
❏ MGM E-3524 [M]		1957	30.00
—Yellow label; has both music and dialogue			
RAGTIME			
❏ Elektra 5E-565		1981	25.00
RAIDERS OF THE LOST ARK			
❏ Columbia JS37373		1981	15.00
—Original issue; music only			
❏ Columbia JS37696		1981	15.00
—Music and dialogue			
❏ DCC Compact Classics LPZ 2-2009		1995	30.00
—Audiophile edition; includes music not on other releases of the soundtrack			
❏ Polydor 821583-1		1984	12.00
—Reissue			
THE RAILWAY CHILDREN			
❏ Capitol SW-871		1972	25.00
THE RAINMAKER			
❏ RCA Victor LPM-1434 [M]		1956	100.00
RAINTREE COUNTY			
❏ RCA Victor LOC-6000 [M]		1957	120.00
❏ RCA Victor LOC-1038 [M]		1958	30.00
❏ RCA Victor LSO-1038 [S]		1958	50.00
RAN			
❏ Fantasy FSP-21004		1985	25.00
THE RAT RACE			
❏ Dot DLP-3306 [M]		1960	80.00
❏ Dot DLP-25306 [S]		1960	200.00
RED DAWN			
❏ Intrada RVF-6001		1985	40.00
RED GARTERS			
❏ Columbia CL6282 [10]		1954	50.00
RED HEAT			
❏ Virgin Movie Music 90891		1988	30.00
THE RED PONY			
❏ Columbia Masterworks ML5983 [M]		196?	30.00
❏ Columbia Masterworks MS6583 [R]		196?	30.00
❏ Varese Sarabande STV-81259		1986	30.00
REDS			
❏ Columbia Masterworks BJS37960		1981	25.00
THE RED TENT			
❏ Paramount PAS-6019		1971	30.00
RENT-A-COP			
❏ Intrada MAS-7002		1988	25.00
THE REPORTER			
❏ Columbia CL2269 [M]		1963	60.00
❏ Columbia CS9069 [S]		1963	40.00
THE RESCUERS			
❏ Disneyland ST-3816		1977	25.00
RETURN OF SUPERFLY			
❏ Capitol C1-94244		1990	15.00
—Includes Ice-T			
RETURN TO PARADISE			
❏ Decca DL5489 [10]		1953	200.00
THE REVOLUTION			

Number	Title	Yr	NM
❏ United Artists UAS-5185		1968	30.00
❏ United Artists UA-LA296-G		1974	15.00
—Reissue of 5185			
RHAPSODY OF STEEL			
❏ U.S. Steel JB-502/3		1958	100.00
RICH, YOUNG AND PRETTY			
❏ MGM E-86 [10]		1951	40.00
RIDER ON THE RAIN			
❏ Capitol ST-584		1970	30.00
RIKKI AND PETE			
❏ DRG SBL-12593		1988	15.00
—Includes Crowded House			
RIOT ON SUNSET STRIP			
❏ Tower T5065 [M]		1967	25.00
❏ Tower DT5065 [R]		1967	30.00
ROADIE			
❏ Warner Bros. 2HS3441		1980	18.00
—Includes Blondie			
ROAD TO HONG KONG			
❏ Liberty LOM-16002 [M]		1962	25.00
❏ Liberty LOS-17002 [S]		1962	40.00
THE ROBE			
❏ Decca DL9012 [M]		1953	30.00
—Maroon label			
❏ Decca DL79012 [R]		196?	15.00
❏ MCA 1529		198?	10.00
—Reissue of MCA 2052			
❏ MCA 2052		1973	12.00
—Reissue of Decca 79012; black label with rainbow			
ROBIN AND THE SEVEN HOODS			
❏ Reprise F2021 [M]		1964	50.00
❏ Reprise FS2021 [S]		1964	60.00
ROBIN HOOD			
❏ Disneyland ST-3810		1973	30.00
ROCK, PRETTY BABY			
❏ Decca DL8429 [M]		1957	120.00
—Black label, silver print; also includes pink label promo			
❏ Decca DL8429 [M]		196?	30.00
—Black label with color bars			
ROCK, ROCK, ROCK			
❏ Chess LP-1425 [M]		1958	200.00
❏ (no label) (no #) [M]		1958	1500.00
—Demo version, 20 tracks			
ROCK ALL NIGHT			
❏ Mercury MG-20293 [M]		1957	100.00
ROCK 'N' ROLL HIGH SCHOOL			
❏ Sire QSR-6070		1980	18.00
—Includes The Ramones (title song), Devo			
ROMANCE OF A HORSETHIEF			
❏ Allied Artists AAS-110-100		1971	50.00
ROME ADVENTURE			
❏ Warner Bros. W1458 [M]		1962	25.00
❏ Warner Bros. WS1458 [S]		1962	30.00
ROMEO AND JULIET			
❏ Capitol SWDR-289		1969	30.00
—From the 1968 Franco Zeffirelli remake; contains dialogue and music			
❏ Capitol ST-2993		1968	15.00
—From the 1968 Franco Zeffirelli remake; contains the music; black label with colorband			
❏ Capitol ST-400		1970	18.00
—From the 1968 Franco Zeffirelli remake; edited version of 289			
❏ Epic LC3126 [M]		1954	60.00
❏ Epic FLM13104 [M]		1966	30.00
—Reissue of 3126			
❏ Epic FLS15104 [R]		1966	30.00
ROOTS OF HEAVEN			
❏ 20th Fox FOX-3005 [M]		1958	300.00
ROSE MARIE			
❏ MGM E-229 [10]		1954	40.00
ROSEMARY'S BABY			
❏ Dot DLP-25875		1968	25.00
THE ROSE TATTOO			
❏ Columbia CL727 [M]		1955	50.00
THE ROYAL WEDDING			
❏ MGM E-543 [10]		1951	50.00
THE RULING CLASS			
❏ Avco AV-11003		1972	30.00
RUMBLE FISH			
❏ A&M SP-6-4983		1983	12.00
—Includes Stewart Copeland (ex-Police)			

Number	Title	Yr	NM
RUN, ANGEL, RUN			
❏ Epic BN26474		1969	25.00
THE RUN OF THE ARROW			
❏ Decca DL8620 [M]		1957	60.00
—Black label, silver print, or pink label, black print promo			
❏ Decca DL8620 [M]		196?	30.00
—Black label with color bars			
RUN WILD, RUN FREE			
❏ SGC SD5003		1969	25.00
RUSTLERS' RHAPSODY			
❏ Warner Bros. 25284		1985	12.00
RYAN'S DAUGHTER			
❏ MGM 1SE-27		1970	30.00
SACCO AND VANZETTI			
❏ RCA Victor LSP-4612		1971	25.00
THE SACRED IDOL			
❏ Capitol T1293 [M]		1960	30.00
❏ Capitol ST1293 [S]		1960	30.00
THE SAINT			
❏ Virgin SPRO-12261 [DJ]		1997	30.00
SAINT JOAN			
❏ Capitol W865 [M]		1957	30.00
SALLAH			
❏ Philips PHM200177 [M]		1965	25.00
❏ Philips PHS600177 [S]		1965	30.00
SALOME			
❏ Decca DL6026 [10]		1953	120.00
SALVATION			
❏ Giant GR-16002		1988	15.00
—Includes New Order, Cabaret Voltaire			
SAMSON AND DELILAH			
❏ Decca DL6007 [10]		1952	60.00
THE SAND CASTLE			
❏ Columbia CL1455 [M]		1961	18.00
❏ Columbia CS8249 [S]		1961	25.00
THE SAND PEBBLES			
❏ 20th Century Fox 3189 [M]		1966	30.00
❏ 20th Century Fox S-4189 [S]		1966	50.00
THE SANDPIPER			
❏ Mercury MG-21032 [M]		1965	30.00
❏ Mercury SR-61032 [S]		1965	30.00
SANTA AND THE 3 BEARS			
❏ Mr. Pickwick SPC1501		196?	25.00
—With "Santa" cutout intact			
SANTA CLAUS THE MOVIE			
❏ EMI America SJ-17177		1985	12.00
SATAN IN HIGH HEELS			
❏ Charlie Parker PLP-406 [M]		1962	100.00
—Gatefold cover			
❏ Charlie Parker PLP-406S [S]		1962	120.00
—Gatefold cover			
❏ Charlie Parker PLP-406 [M]		1962	60.00
—Standard cover			
❏ Charlie Parker PLP-406S [S]		1962	40.00
—Standard cover			
SATAN'S SADISTS			
❏ Smash SRS-67127		1969	30.00
SATURDAY NIGHT FEVER			
❏ RSO RS-2-4001		1977	18.00
—First editions have the studio version of "Jive Talkin'" by the Bee Gees on side 3			
❏ RSO RS-2-4001		1978	15.00
—Later editions have a live version of "Jive Talkin'" by the Bee Gees on side 3 ("REV" is in the Side 3 trail-off wax)			
❏ RSO 825389-1		198?	12.00
—Reissue with new number			
SATURDAY NIGHT FEVER/GREASE			
❏ RSO RPO1011 [DJ]		1978	30.00
—Side 1 has "The Best of Saturday Night Fever" (side 1 of original LP); Side 2 has "The Best of Grease" (side 1 of original LP)			
THE SAVAGE SEVEN			
❏ Atco 33-245 [M]		1968	30.00
❏ Atco SD 33-245 [S]		1968	30.00
SAVAGE WILD			
❏ American Int'l. STA-1032		1970	25.00
SAYONARA			
❏ RCA Victor LOC-1041 [M]		1957	50.00
❏ RCA Victor LSO-1041 [S]		1957	70.00
SAY ONE FOR ME			
❏ Columbia CL1337 [M]		1959	40.00
❏ Columbia CS8147 [S]		1959	80.00
THE SCALPHUNTERS			

Number	Title	Yr	NM
❏ MCA 25042		1986	12.00
— *Reissue of United Artists 5176*			
❏ United Artists UAL-4176 [M]		1968	30.00
❏ United Artists UAS-5176 [S]		1968	40.00
SCARFACE			
❏ MCA 6126		1984	25.00
THE SCARLET AND THE BLACK			
❏ Cerberus CEM-0120		1983	30.00
SCENT OF MYSTERY			
❏ Ramrod T-6001 [M]		1960	50.00
❏ Ramrod ST-6001 [S]		1960	100.00
SCROOGE			
❏ Columbia Masterworks S30258		1970	30.00
❏ Columbia Special Products P14077		1977	15.00
— *Special Products reissue*			
SCROOGED			
❏ A&M SP-3921		1988	12.00
— *Includes the following Christmas songs:*			
SEARCH FOR PARADISE			
❏ RCA Victor LOC-1034 [M]		1957	40.00
SEASIDE SWINGERS			
❏ Mercury MG-21031 [M]		1965	25.00
❏ Mercury SR-61031 [S]		1965	30.00
SEBASTIAN			
❏ Dot DLP-3845 [M]		1968	50.00
❏ Dot DLP-25845 [S]		1968	25.00
THE SECRET OF SANTA VITTORIA			
❏ MCA 25034		1986	12.00
— *Reissue of United Artists 5200*			
❏ United Artists UAS-5200		1969	30.00
SERGEANTS 3			
❏ Reprise R-2013 [M]		1962	30.00
❏ Reprise RS-2013 [S]		1962	50.00
THE SERPENT AND THE RAINBOW			
❏ Varese Sarabande STV-81362		1988	40.00
SERPICO			
❏ Paramount PAS-1016		1973	30.00
SEVEN BRIDES FOR SEVEN BROTHERS			
❏ MGM E-244 [10]		1954	40.00
SEVEN GOLDEN MEN			
❏ United Artists UAS-5193		1969	30.00
THE SEVEN LITTLE FOYS			
❏ RCA Victor LPM-3275 [10]		1955	70.00
1776			
❏ Columbia S31741		1972	25.00
THE SEVENTH DAWN			
❏ United Artists UAL-4115 [M]		1964	30.00
THE 7TH DAWN			
❏ United Artists UAL-4115 [M]		1964	30.00
THE SEVENTH DAWN			
❏ United Artists UAS-5115 [S]		1964	40.00
THE 7TH DAWN			
❏ United Artists UAS-5115 [S]		1964	40.00
THE 7TH VOYAGE OF SINBAD			
❏ Colpix CP-504 [M]		1958	200.00
❏ Varese Sarabande STV-81135		1983	25.00
SEX AND THE SINGLE GIRL			
❏ Warner Bros. W1572 [M]		1964	18.00
❏ Warner Bros. WS1572 [S]		1964	25.00
SHAFT IN AFRICA			
❏ ABC ABCX-793		1973	30.00
SHAFT'S BIG SCORE			
❏ MGM 1SE-36		1972	30.00
SHAG			
❏ Sire 25800		1989	12.00
— *Includes k.d. lang, Chris Isaak*			
SHAKE HANDS WITH THE DEVIL			
❏ United Artists UAL-4043 [M]		1959	30.00
❏ United Artists UAS-5043 [S]		1959	50.00
SHALAKO			
❏ Philips PHS600286		1968	30.00
SHEBA BABY			
❏ Buddah BDS-5634		1975	30.00
SHE-DEVIL			
❏ Polydor 841583-1		1989	30.00
SHENANDOAH			
❏ Decca DL9125 [M]		1965	30.00
❏ Decca DL79125 [S]		1965	40.00
SHE'S OUT OF CONTROL			
❏ MCA 6281		1989	12.00
— *Includes Oingo Boingo*			
THE SHINING			
❏ Warner Bros. HS3449		1980	25.00

Number	Title	Yr	NM
THE SHOP ON MAIN STREET			
❏ Mainstream 56082 [M]		1966	30.00
❏ Mainstream S-6082 [S]		1966	40.00
SHORT EYES			
❏ Curtom CU5017		1977	30.00
THE SHOW			
❏ Def Jam 529021-1		1995	15.00
— *Includes L.L. Cool J, etc.*			
SHOW BOAT			
❏ MGM E-559 [10]		1951	30.00
THE SICILIAN CLAN			
❏ 20th Century Fox S-4209		1970	50.00
SID & NANCY			
❏ MCA 6181		1986	12.00
— *Includes Joe Strummer (ex-Clash), John Cale, The Pogues, Steve Jones (ex-Pistols)*			
THE SIDEHACKERS			
❏ Amaret ST-5004		1969	25.00
THE SILENCERS			
❏ RCA Victor LOC-1120 [M]		1966	30.00
❏ RCA Victor LSO-1120 [S]		1966	50.00
SILENT RUNNING			
❏ Decca DL79188		1972	40.00
❏ Varese Sarabande STV-81072		1980	18.00
— *Reissue*			
SILK STOCKINGS			
❏ MCA 39074		198?	12.00
— *Reissue*			
❏ MGM E-3542 [M]		1957	30.00
SILVERADO			
❏ Geffen GHS24080		1985	25.00
SINGIN' IN THE RAIN			
❏ MCA 39044		198?	12.00
❏ Metro M-599 [M]		1966	18.00
— *Reissue of MGM LP*			
❏ Metro MS-599 [R]		1966	15.00
❏ MGM E-113 [10]		1952	30.00
SINGLE ROOM FURNISHED			
❏ Sidewalk ST-5917		1968	40.00
THE 633 SQUADRON			
❏ United Artists UA-LA305-G		1974	30.00
SKATEDANCER			
❏ Mira LP-3004 [M]		1966	25.00
❏ Mira LPS-3004 [S]		1966	30.00
SKI ON THE WILD SIDE			
❏ MGM E-4439 [M]		1967	30.00
❏ MGM SE-4439 [S]		1967	50.00
SLAUGHTERHOUSE-FIVE			
❏ Columbia Masterworks S31333		1972	30.00
SLAUGHTER ON 10TH AVENUE			
❏ Decca DL8657 [M]		1957	30.00
— *Black label, silver print*			
❏ Decca DL78657 [S]		1957	30.00
— *Black label, silver print*			
❏ Decca DL8657 [M]		1960	15.00
— *Black label with color bars*			
❏ Decca DL78657 [S]		1960	18.00
— *Black label with color bars*			
SLAVES			
❏ Skye SK-11		1969	60.00
THE SLAVE TRADE IN THE WORLD TODAY			
❏ London M-76006 [M]		1964	200.00
SLEEPING BEAUTY			
❏ Disneyland WDL-4018 [M]		1959	30.00
❏ Disneyland STER-4018 [S]		1959	40.00
❏ Disneyland STER-4036 [S]		1970	25.00
— *Reissue of STER-4018*			
SLEUTH			
❏ Columbia Masterworks S32154		1973	25.00
SLIPPERY WHEN WET			
❏ World Pacific WP-1265 [M]		1959	200.00
SLUMBER PARTY '57			
❏ Mercury SRM-1-1097		1976	30.00
A SMASHING TIME			
❏ ABC ABC-OC-6 [M]		1967	25.00
❏ ABC ABCS-OC-6 [S]		1967	30.00
❏ ABC SW-91399 [S]		1967	30.00
— *Capitol Record Club edition*			
SMOKEY AND THE BANDIT			
❏ MCA 2099		1977	15.00
SMOKEY AND THE BANDIT 2			
❏ MCA 6101		1980	12.00
SMOKEY AND THE BANDIT 3			

Number	Title	Yr	NM
❏ MCA 36006		1983	12.00
SNOOPY COME HOME			
❏ Columbia Masterworks S31451		1972	25.00
THE SNOW QUEEN			
❏ Decca DL8977 [M]		1959	40.00
❏ Decca DL78977 [S]		1959	60.00
SNOW WHITE AND THE SEVEN DWARFS			
❏ Buena Vista 102		1975	50.00
— *Entire movie on three LPs; TV mail-order item*			
❏ Disneyland WDL-4005 [M]		1956	200.00
— *Gatefold cover*			
❏ Disneyland DQ-1201 [M]		1959	50.00
— *Reissue of 4005; whirlpool-like designs on cover*			
❏ Disneyland DQ-1201 [M]		1968	30.00
— *Reissue; with same cover as 4005, but no gatefold*			
❏ Disneyland DQ-1201 [M]		1987	30.00
— *Reissue; high-gloss cover with cel photos on back*			
❏ Disneyland 3101 [PD]		1981	30.00
— *Disney Picture Disc" edition*			
SNOW WHITE AND THE THREE STOOGES			
❏ Columbia CL1650 [M]		1961	60.00
❏ Columbia CS8450 [S]		1961	100.00
SODOM AND GOMORRAH			
❏ RCA Victor LOC-1076 [M]		1963	80.00
❏ RCA Victor LSO-1076 [S]		1963	100.00
SOL MADRID			
❏ MGM SE-4541ST		1968	30.00
SOLOMON AND SHEBA			
❏ MCA 1425		198?	10.00
— *Reissue*			
❏ United Artists UAL-4051 [M]		1959	50.00
— *First cover with silky finish*			
❏ United Artists UAL-4051 [M]		1959	30.00
— *Second, regular cover*			
❏ United Artists UAS-5051 [S]		1959	120.00
— *First cover with silky finish*			
❏ United Artists UAS-5051 [S]		1959	60.00
— *Second, regular cover*			
SOMEBODY LOVES ME			
❏ RCA Victor LPM-3097 [10]		1952	50.00
SOME CAME RUNNING			
❏ Capitol W1109 [M]		1958	30.00
❏ Capitol SW1109 [S]		1958	80.00
SOME LIKE IT HOT			
❏ United Artists UAL-4030 [M]		1959	50.00
❏ United Artists UAS-5030 [S]		1959	75.00
❏ United Artists UA-LA272-G		1974	15.00
— *Reissue of 5030*			
SOMETHING WILD			
❏ MCA 6194		1986	12.00
— *Includes New Order*			
SOMEWHERE IN TIME			
❏ MCA 5154		1980	25.00
SONG OF THE SOUTH			
❏ Disneyland WDL-4001 [M]		1956	300.00
— *Yellow label (first pressing)*			
❏ Disneyland WDL-4001 [M]		1957	200.00
— *Red/maroon label (second pressing)*			
SONG OF THE SOUTH (UNCLE REMUS)			
❏ Disneyland DQ-1205 [M]		1959	30.00
SONG WITHOUT END			
❏ Colpix CP-506 [M]		1960	25.00
❏ Colpix SCP-506 [S]		1960	30.00
THE SONS OF KATIE ELDER			
❏ Columbia Masterworks OL6420 [M]		1965	50.00
❏ Columbia Masterworks OS2820 [S]		1965	100.00
SO THIS IS LOVE			
❏ RCA Victor LOC-3000 [10]		1953	80.00
SO THIS IS PARIS			
❏ Decca DL5553 [10]		1955	50.00
SOUL MAN			
❏ A&M SP-3903		1986	10.00
— *Includes Lou Reed, Martha Davis*			
THE SOUL OF NIGGER CHARLEY			
❏ MGM 1SE-46		1973	25.00
THE SOUND AND THE FURY			
❏ Decca DL8885 [M]		1959	30.00
❏ Decca DL78885 [S]		1959	70.00
THE SOUND OF MUSIC			
❏ RCA Victor LOCD-2005 [M]		1965	18.00
— *With booklet; back cover lists "I Have Confidence" as "I Have Confidence in Me"*			

Number	Title	Yr	NM

❑ RCA Victor LSOD-2005 [S] — 1965 — 25.00
—*With booklet; back cover lists "I Have Confidence" as "I Have Confidence in Me*
❑ RCA Victor LOCD-2005 [M] — 1965 — 15.00
—*With booklet; back cover lists "I Have Confidence" correctly*
❑ RCA Victor LSOD-2005 [S] — 1965 — 18.00
—*With booklet; back cover lists "I Have Confidence" correctly*
❑ RCA Victor LSOD-2005 [S] — 1969 — 15.00
—*No booklet; gatefold cover, record comes out from inside; orange or tan label*
❑ RCA Victor LSOD-2005 [S] — 1977 — 12.00
—*Gatefold cover, record comes out from outside; black label with dog at 1 o'clock*

SOUTH CENTRAL
❑ Hollywood 61403 [DJ] — 1992 — 25.00
—*Vinyl is promo only*

SOUTHERN STAR
❑ Colgems COSO-5009 — 1969 — 60.00

SOUTH PACIFIC
❑ RCA Victor LOC-1032 [M] — 1958 — 25.00
—*Long Play" on label; no "Academy Award Winner" on front cover*
❑ RCA Victor LSO-1032 [S] — 1958 — 30.00
—*Living Stereo" on label; no "Academy Award Winner" on front cover*
❑ RCA Victor LOCD-2000 [M] — 1958 — 40.00
—*Gatefold cover with photos inside*
❑ RCA Victor LOC-1032 [M] — 196? — 15.00
—*Long Play" or "Mono" on label; with "Academy Award Winner" on front cover*
❑ RCA Victor LSO-1032 [S] — 196? — 18.00
—*Living Stereo" or "Stereo" on black label; with "Academy Award Winner" on front cover*
❑ RCA Victor LSO-1032 [S] — 1958 — 15.00
—*Orange label*
❑ RCA Victor AYL1-3681 — 1981 — 10.00
—*Best Buy Series" reissue*

SPACEBALLS
❑ Atlantic 81770 — 1987 — 12.00
—*Includes Berlin*

SPACECAMP
❑ RCA Victor ABL1-5856 — 1986 — 40.00

SPACE JAM, MUSIC FROM AND INSPIRED BY
❑ Warner Sunset/Atlantic 82961 — 1997 — 18.00

A SPANISH AFFAIR
❑ Dot DLP-3078 [M] — 1958 — 100.00

SPARKLE
❑ Atlantic SD18176 — 1976 — 25.00

SPARTACUS
❑ Decca DL9092 [M] — 1960 — 25.00
—*Black label, silver print*
❑ Decca DL79092 [S] — 1960 — 30.00
—*Maroon label, silver print*
❑ Decca DL9092 [M] — 1961 — 15.00
—*Black label with color bars*
❑ Decca DL79092 [S] — 1961 — 18.00
—*Black label with color bars*
❑ MCA 2068 — 1973 — 15.00
—*Reissue of 79092; black label with rainbow*
❑ MCA 1534 — 198? — 12.00
—*Reissue of 2068*

THE SPIRIT OF ST. LOUIS
❑ RCA Victor LPM-1472 [M] — 1957 — 50.00

SPLASH
❑ Cherry Lane 00301 — 1984 — 30.00
—*With poster of Daryl Hannah*

THE SPY WHO CAME IN FROM THE COLD
❑ RCA Victor LOC-1118 [M] — 1965 — 25.00
❑ RCA Victor LSO-1118 [S] — 1965 — 40.00

THE SPY WITH A COLD NOSE
❑ Columbia Masterworks OL6670 [M] — 1966 — 25.00
❑ Columbia Masterworks OS3070 [S] — 1966 — 30.00

STAGECOACH
❑ Mainstream 56077 [M] — 1966 — 25.00
❑ Mainstream S-6077 [S] — 1966 — 30.00
❑ Mainstream T-90802 [M] — 1966 — 30.00
—*Capitol Record Club edition*
❑ Mainstream ST-90802 [S] — 1966 — 30.00
—*Capitol Record Club edition*

STAR!
❑ 20th Century Fox DTCS-5102 — 1968 — 25.00

THE STARS AND STRIPES FOREVER
❑ MGM E-176 [10] — 1952 — 30.00

STAR TREK -- THE MOTION PICTURE
❑ Columbia JS36334 — 1979 — 25.00

STATE FAIR
❑ Dot DLP-9011 [M] — 1962 — 30.00
❑ Dot DLP-29011 [S] — 1962 — 30.00

THE STERILE CUCKOO
❑ Paramount PAS-5009 — 1970 — 25.00

STILETTO
❑ Columbia Masterworks OS3360 — 1969 — 25.00

THE STING
❑ MCA 2040 — 197? — 25.00
❑ MCA 37091 — 1981 — 20.00
❑ MCA 390 — 1973 — 30.00
—*Original edition*

ST. LOUIS BLUES
❑ Capitol W993 [M] — 1958 — 150.00
—*Turquoise or gray label*
❑ Capitol W993 [M] — 1959 — 100.00
—*Black colorband label, logo at left*
❑ Capitol W993 [M] — 196? — 80.00
—*Black colorband label, logo at top*

ST. LOUIS WOMAN
❑ Capitol L355 [10] — 1955 — 250.00

THE STRANGE ONE
❑ Coral CRL57132 [M] — 1957 — 140.00

THE STRAWBERRY STATEMENT
❑ MGM 2SE-14 — 1970 — 30.00

A STREETCAR NAMED DESIRE
❑ Capitol L289 [10] — 1951 — 50.00

STREETS OF FIRE
❑ MCA 5492 — 1984 — 12.00
—*Includes The Fixx, The Blasters*

STRICTLY BUSINESS
❑ MCA 10428 — 1991 — 12.00
—*Includes L.L. Cool J*

A STUDY IN TERROR
❑ Roulette OS-801 [M] — 1965 — 40.00
❑ Roulette OSS-801 [S] — 1965 — 80.00

THE STUNT MAN
❑ 20th Century T-626 — 1980 — 30.00

THE SUBTERRANEANS
❑ MGM E-3812ST [M] — 1960 — 40.00
❑ MGM SE-3812ST [S] — 1960 — 80.00

SUMMER AND SMOKE
❑ RCA Victor LOC-1067 [M] — 1961 — 50.00
❑ RCA Victor LSO-1067 [S] — 1961 — 70.00

SUMMER HOLIDAY
❑ Epic LN24063 [M] — 1963 — 30.00
❑ Epic BN26063 [S] — 1963 — 30.00

SUMMER LOVE
❑ Decca DL8714 [M] — 1958 — 60.00
—*Black label, silver print, or pink label, black print promo*
❑ Decca DL8714 [M] — 196? — 30.00
—*Black label with color bars*

SUMMER MAGIC
❑ Buena Vista BV-4025 [M] — 1963 — 40.00
❑ Buena Vista STER-4025 [S] — 1963 — 60.00

SUMMER STOCK
❑ MGM E-519 [10] — 1950 — 40.00

THE SUN ALSO RISES
❑ Kapp KDL-7001 [M] — 1957 — 60.00

THE SUNNY SIDE OF THE STREET
❑ Mercury MG-25100 [10] — 1951 — 60.00

SUN VALLEY SERENADE
❑ RCA Victor LPT-3064 [10] — 1954 — 120.00

SURFER GIRLS
❑ Oakwood SUS-1001 — 1978 — 100.00

SURF PARTY
❑ 20th Century Fox TFM-3131 [M] — 1964 — 30.00
❑ 20th Century Fox TFS-4131 [S] — 1964 — 30.00

THE SWAN
❑ MCA 25086 — 1986 — 12.00
—*Reissue of MGM 3399*
❑ MGM E-3399 [M] — 1956 — 70.00

THE SWARM
❑ Warner Bros. BSK3208 — 1978 — 30.00

SWEDISH HEAVEN AND HELL
❑ Ariel ARS-15000 — 1969 — 30.00

SWEET CHARITY
❑ Decca DL71502 — 1969 — 25.00

SWEET LOVE, BITTER

ABC Impulse! AS-9141 [S]
❑ ABC Impulse! AS-9141 [S] — 1968 — 35.00
❑ Impulse! A-9141 [M] — 1967 — 160.00
❑ Impulse! AS-9141 [S] — 1967 — 120.00

THE SWEET RIDE
❑ 20th Century Fox S-4198 — 1968 — 25.00

THE SWEET SMELL OF SUCCESS
❑ Decca DL8610 [M] — 1957 — 120.00

SWEET SWEETBACK'S BADASSSSSS SONG
❑ Stax STS-3001 — 1971 — 30.00

SWEPT AWAY
❑ Peters International PLD1005 — 1957 — 40.00

THE SWIMMER
❑ Columbia Masterworks OS3210 — 1968 — 30.00

SWINGER'S PARADISE
❑ Epic LN24145 [M] — 1965 — 25.00
❑ Epic BN26145 [S] — 1965 — 30.00

A SWINGIN' SUMMER
❑ Hanna-Barbera HLP-8500 [M] — 1966 — 30.00
❑ Hanna-Barbera HST-9500 [S] — 1966 — 30.00

SYLVIA
❑ Mercury MG-21004 [M] — 1965 — 25.00
❑ Mercury SR-61004 [S] — 1965 — 30.00

TAKE THIS JOB AND SHOVE IT!
❑ Epic SE37177 — 1981 — 15.00

TAPEHEADS
❑ Island 91030 — 1988 — 12.00
—*Includes Devo ("Baby Doll" sung in Swedish!), Fishbone*

TARAS BULBA
❑ United Artists UAL-4100 [M] — 1962 — 30.00
❑ United Artists UAS-5100 [S] — 1962 — 50.00

TAXI DRIVER
❑ Arista AL4079 — 1976 — 25.00
❑ Arista AL8179 — 198? — 18.00
—*Reissue of 4079*

TEENAGE CRUISERS
❑ Rhino RNLP-016 — 197? — 18.00
—*Includes The Blasters, many others*

TEENAGE REBELLION
❑ Sidewalk T-5903 [M] — 1967 — 25.00
❑ Sidewalk ST-5903 [S] — 1967 — 30.00

TELL ME THAT YOU LOVE ME, JUNIE MOON
❑ Columbia Masterworks OS3540 — 1970 — 25.00

THE TEN COMMANDMENTS
❑ Dot DLP-3054 [M] — 1956 — 40.00
❑ Dot DLP-25054 [S] — 1959 — 30.00
—*Re-recording of the original soundtrack in stereo*
❑ MCA 4159 — 198? — 18.00
—*Reissue of Paramount set*
❑ Paramount PAS-1006 — 1973 — 25.00
—*Reissue of Dot 25054*

TENDER IS THE NIGHT
❑ 20th Century Fox FOX-3054 [M] — 1962 — 150.00
❑ 20th Century Fox SFX-3054 [S] — 1962 — 200.00

THE TENTH VICTIM
❑ Mainstream 56071 [M] — 1965 — 40.00
❑ Mainstream S-6071 [S] — 1965 — 50.00

TEQUILA SUNRISE
❑ Capitol C1-91185 — 1988 — 15.00
—*Includes Crowded House, Duran Duran*

THANK GOD IT'S FRIDAY
❑ Casablanca NBLP-7099-3 — 1978 — 25.00
—*Two full-length LPs plus a bonus 12-inch single by Donna Summer with blank B-side*

THAT DARN CAT
❑ Buena Vista BV-3334 [M] — 1965 — 25.00
❑ Buena Vista STER-3334 [S] — 1965 — 30.00

THAT MAN IN ISTANBUL
❑ Mainstream 56072 [M] — 1966 — 25.00
❑ Mainstream S-6072 [S] — 1966 — 30.00

THAT'S ENTERTAINMENT!
❑ MCA 11002 — 1974 — 25.00
—*Film credits in small print on back cover, and list of songs omits "That's Entertainment*
❑ MCA 11002 — 1976 — 18.00
—*Film credits in larger print on back cover, and list of songs includes "That's Entertainment*

THERE'S NO BUSINESS LIKE SHOW BUSINESS
❑ Decca DL8091 [M] — 196? — 25.00
—*Black label with color bars*
❑ Decca DL8091 [M] — 1954 — 30.00
—*Black label with silver print*

THEY CALL IT AN ACCIDENT
❑ Island ILPS9757 — 1982 — 12.00

Number	Title	Yr	NM

— Includes U2 (two versions of "October")

THEY SHOOT HORSES, DON'T THEY?
❏ ABC ABCS-OC-10 — 1969 — 25.00

THIEF OF HEARTS
❏ Casablanca 822942-1 — 1984 — 25.00

THE THIN BLUE LINE
❏ Nonesuch 79209-1 — 1988 — 25.00

THIS COULD BE THE NIGHT
❏ MGM E-3530 [M] — 1957 — 50.00

THIS EARTH IS MINE
❏ Decca DL8915 [M] — 1959 — 80.00
❏ Decca DL78915 [S] — 1959 — 100.00
❏ Varese Sarabande VC-81076 — 1979 — 18.00

— Reissue of Decca 78915

THIS PROPERTY IS CONDEMNED
❏ Verve V-8664 [M] — 1966 — 50.00
❏ Verve V6-8664 [S] — 1966 — 60.00

THE THOMAS CROWN AFFAIR
❏ United Artists UAS-5182 — 1968 — 25.00
❏ United Artists UA-LA295-G — 1974 — 15.00

— Reissue of 5182

THOROUGHLY MODERN MILLIE
❏ Decca DL1500 [M] — 1967 — 25.00
— With bound-in booklet
❏ Decca DL71500 [S] — 1967 — 25.00
— With bound-in booklet

THOSE GLORIOUS MGM MUSICALS: DEEP IN MY HEART/WORDS AND MUSIC
❏ MGM 2-SES-54-ST — 1973 — 25.00

THOSE GLORIOUS MGM MUSICALS: EVERYTHING I HAVE IS YOURS/SUMMER STOCK/I LOVE MELVIN
❏ MGM 2-SES-52-ST — 1973 — 25.00

THOSE GLORIOUS MGM MUSICALS: GOOD NEWS/IN THE GOOD OLD SUMMERTIME/TWO WEEKS WITH LOVE
❏ MGM 2-SES-49-ST — 1973 — 25.00

THOSE GLORIOUS MGM MUSICALS: LOVELY TO LOOK AT/BRIGADOON
❏ MGM 2-SES-50-ST — 1973 — 25.00

THOSE GLORIOUS MGM MUSICALS: NANCY GOES TO RIO/RICH, YOUNG AND PRETTY/ROYAL WEDDING
❏ MGM 2-SES-53-ST — 1973 — 25.00

THOSE GLORIOUS MGM MUSICALS: ROSE MARIE/SEVN BRIDES FOR SEVEN BROTHERS
❏ MGM 2-SES-41-ST — 1973 — 25.00

THOSE GLORIOUS MGM MUSICALS: SHOW BOAT/ANNIE GET YOUR GUN
❏ MGM 2-SES-42-ST — 1973 — 25.00

THOSE GLORIOUS MGM MUSICALS: SINGIN' IN THE RAIN/EASTER PARADE
❏ MGM 2-SES-40-ST — 1973 — 25.00

THOSE GLORIOUS MGM MUSICALS: THE BAND WAGON/KISS ME, KATE
❏ MGM 2-SES-44-ST — 1973 — 25.00

THOSE GLORIOUS MGM MUSICALS: THE BARKLEYS OF BROADWAY/LES GIRLS
❏ MGM 2-SES-51-ST — 1973 — 25.00

THOSE GLORIOUS MGM MUSICALS: THE PIRATE/PAGAN LOVE SONG/HIT THE DECK
❏ MGM 2-SES-43-ST — 1973 — 40.00

THOSE GLORIOUS MGM MUSICALS: TILL THE CLOUDS ROLL BY/THREE LITTLE WORDS
❏ MGM 2-SES-45-ST — 1973 — 25.00

THREE BITES OF THE APPLE
❏ MCA 25010 — 198? — 10.00
— Reissue of MGM SE-4444
❏ MGM E-4444 [M] — 1967 — 30.00
❏ MGM SE-4444 [S] — 1967 — 25.00

THREE FOR THE SHOW
❏ Mercury MG-25204 [M] — 1955 — 60.00

THREE IN THE ATTIC
❏ Sidewalk S-5918 — 1968 — 30.00

THREE LITTLE WORDS
❏ MGM E-516 [10] — 1959 — 60.00

THE THREEPENNY OPERA
❏ RCA Victor LOC-1086 [M] — 1964 — 150.00
— With rare original cover: White background, pink and black drawing, characters underneath
❏ RCA Victor LOC-1086 [M] — 1964 — 18.00
— Reissue cover: White background, orange drawing, Sammy

Davis Jr. in foreground, "RE" at bottom
❏ RCA Victor LSO-1086 [S] — 1964 — 200.00
— With rare original cover: White background, pink and black drawing, characters underneath
❏ RCA Victor LSO-1086 [S] — 1964 — 25.00
— Reissue cover: White background, orange drawing, Sammy Davis Jr. in foreground, "RE" at bottom

THE THREE WORLDS OF GULLIVER
❏ Colpix CP-414 [M] — 1960 — 60.00

THUNDER ALLEY
❏ Sidewalk T-5902 [M] — 1967 — 25.00
❏ Sidewalk ST-5902 [S] — 1967 — 30.00

THUNDERBALL
❏ United Artists UAL-4132 [M] — 1965 — 25.00
❏ United Artists UAS-5132 [S] — 1965 — 30.00
❏ United Artists SW-90820 [S] — 1965 — 40.00
— Capitol Record Club edition

TICK…TICK…TICK
❏ MGM SE-4667 [M] — 1970 — 30.00

TILL THE CLOUDS ROLL BY
❏ MCA 25000 — 1986 — 12.00
❏ Metro M-578 [M] — 1966 — 15.00
— Reissue of MGM 501
❏ Metro MS-578 [R] — 1966 — 12.00
❏ MGM E-501 [10] — 1950 — 50.00

TIMES SQUARE
❏ RSO RS-2-4203 — 1980 — 18.00
— Includes The Ramones ("I Wanna Be Sedated"), Talking Heads ("Life During Wartime"), XTC, Patti Smith, The Cure, etc.

TIMES SQUARE SAMPLER
❏ RSO RPO1026 [DJ] — 1980 — 15.00
— Includes Talking Heads, Roxy Music, Pretenders, two others

A TIME TO LOVE AND A TIME TO DIE
❏ Decca DL8778 [M] — 1958 — 100.00
❏ Varese Sarabande VC-81075 — 1979 — 18.00
— Reissue of Decca 8778

TO BED… OR NOT TO BED
❏ London M-76005 [M] — 1963 — 40.00

TO KILL A MOCKINGBIRD
❏ Ava A-20 [M] — 1962 — 30.00
❏ Ava AS-20 [S] — 1962 — 30.00

TOKYO OLYMPIAD
❏ Monument MLP-8046 [M] — 1966 — 18.00
❏ Monument SLP-18046 [S] — 1966 — 25.00

TOM JONES
❏ United Artists UAL-4113 [M] — 1963 — 25.00
❏ United Artists UAS-5113 [S] — 1963 — 30.00

TOMMY
❏ Polydor PD 2-9502 — 1975 — 25.00

TOM SAWYER
❏ United Artists UA-LA057-F — 1973 — 25.00

TOO MUCH TOO SOON
❏ Mercury MG-20381 [M] — 1958 — 30.00
❏ Mercury SR-60019 [S] — 1958 — 80.00

TOP GUN
❏ Columbia SC40323 — 1986 — 12.00

TOPKAPI
❏ MCA 25118 — 1986 — 12.00
❏ United Artists UAL-4118 [M] — 1964 — 25.00
❏ United Artists UAS-5118 [S] — 1964 — 30.00

TO SIR, WITH LOVE
❏ Fontana MGF-27569 [M] — 1967 — 25.00
❏ Fontana SRF-67569 [S] — 1967 — 30.00

THE TOUCHABLES
❏ 20th Century Fox S-4206 — 1969 — 25.00

TO WONG FOO, THANKS FOR EVERYTHING! JULIE NEWMAR
❏ MCA 11231 — 1995 — 15.00
— Includes Cyndi Lauper, Salt-N-Pepa

THE TRAIN
❏ United Artists UAL-4122 [M] — 1965 — 25.00
❏ United Artists UAS-5122 [S] — 1965 — 40.00

TRANSYLVANIA 6-5000
❏ Varese Sarabande STV-81267 — 1985 — 25.00

THE TRAP
❏ Atco 33-204 [M] — 1966 — 40.00
❏ Atco SD 33-204 [S] — 1966 — 70.00

TRAPEZE
❏ Columbia CL870 [M] — 1956 — 30.00

THE TRAPP FAMILY
❏ 20th Fox FOX-3044 [M] — 1961 — 30.00
❏ 20th Fox STX-3044 [S] — 1961 — 40.00

THE TREASURE OF SAN GENNARO
❏ Buddah BDS-5011 — 1968 — 40.00

THE TRIP
❏ Sidewalk T-5908 [M] — 1967 — 30.00
❏ Sidewalk ST-5908 [S] — 1967 — 40.00

TRIPLE CROSS
❏ United Artists UAL-4162 [M] — 1967 — 25.00
❏ United Artists UAS-5162 [S] — 1967 — 30.00

TROUBLE IN MIND
❏ Island 90501 — 1986 — 12.00
— Includes Marianne Faithfull

THE TROUBLE WITH ANGELS
❏ Mainstream 56073 [M] — 1966 — 40.00
❏ Mainstream S-6073 [S] — 1966 — 80.00

TRUE GRIT
❏ Capitol ST-263 — 1969 — 30.00
❏ Capitol ST-8-0263 — 1969 — 40.00
— Capitol Record Club edition

TRUE LIFE ADVENTURES
❏ Disneyland WDL-4011 [M] — 1957 — 70.00

TRUE STORIES, SOUNDS FROM
❏ Sire 25515 — 1986 — 12.00
— Includes individual members of Talking Heads…not to be confused with the Talking Heads album True Stories.

THE TRUE STORY OF THE CIVIL WAR
❏ Coral CRL59100 [M] — 1958 — 80.00

TWO MULES FOR SISTER SARA
❏ Kapp KRS-5512 — 1970 — 30.00

TWO WEEKS WITH LOVE
❏ MGM E-530 [10] — 1950 — 40.00

ULYSSES
❏ RCA Victor LOC-1138 [M] — 1967 — 30.00
❏ RCA Victor LSO-1138 [S] — 1967 — 30.00

THE UMBRELLAS OF CHERBOURG (LES PARAPLUIES DE CHERBOURG)
❏ Philips PCC216 [M] — 1965 — 25.00
❏ Philips PCC616 [S] — 1965 — 30.00

THE UNBEARABLE LIGHTNESS OF BEING
❏ Fantasy FSP-21006 — 1988 — 25.00

UNCLE TOM'S CABIN
❏ Philips PHS600272 — 1968 — 40.00

THE UNFORGIVEN
❏ United Artists UAL-4068 [M] — 1960 — 40.00
❏ United Artists UAS-5068 [S] — 1960 — 70.00

THE UNSINKABLE MOLLY BROWN
❏ MCA 25011 — 1986 — 12.00
— Reissue of MGM 4232
❏ MGM E-4232 [M] — 1964 — 18.00
❏ MGM SW-90048 [S] — 1964 — 18.00
— Capitol Record Club edition
❏ MGM W-90048 [M] — 1964 — 15.00
— Capitol Record Club edition
❏ MGM SE-4232 [S] — 1964 — 25.00

UP IN THE CELLAR
❏ American Int'l. A-1036 — 1970 — 25.00

UP THE DOWN STAIRCASE
❏ United Artists UAL-4169 [M] — 1967 — 25.00
❏ United Artists UAS-5169 [S] — 1967 — 40.00

UP THE JUNCTION
❏ Mercury SR-61159 — 1968 — 30.00

URBAN COWBOY
❏ Full Moon/Asylum DP-90002 — 1980 — 15.00

URBAN COWBOY II (MORE MUSIC FROM THE ORIGINAL SOUNDTRACK)
❏ Full Moon/Epic SE36291 — 1980 — 12.00

URGH! A MUSIC WAR
❏ A&M SP-6019 — 1981 — 15.00
— Includes live tracks by The Police, Joan Jett and the Blackhearts, Wall of Voodoo, XTC, Go-Go's, Orchestral Manouvres in the Dark, Pere Ubu, Devo, Gary Numan, X, Gang of Four, The Cramps, etc.

VALENTINO
❏ United Artists UA-LA810-H — 1977 — 30.00

VALLEY GIRL
❏ Epic FE38623 — 1983 — 80.00
❏ Roadshow RS-101 — 1983 — 120.00

VALLEY OF THE DOLLS
❏ 20th Century Fox TF-4196 [M] — 1968 — 30.00
❏ 20th Century Fox TFS-4196 [S] — 1968 — 30.00
❏ 20th Century Fox SW-91374 [S] — 1968 — 30.00
— Capitol Record Club edition

VANILLA SKY
❏ Reprise RTH-2002 — 2002 — 40.00
— Classic Records edition on 180-gram vinyl ; contains a packet with a piece of film from the movie

THE VANISHING POINT

Number	Title	Yr	NM
Amos AAS-8002		1971	25.00
THE VANISHING PRAIRIE			
Columbia CL6332 [10]		1954	80.00
VERTIGO			
Mercury MG-20384 [M]		1958	150.00
THE VICTORS			
Colpix CP-516 [M]		1963	25.00
Colpix SCP-516 [S]		1963	30.00
VICTOR/VICTORIA			
MGM MG-1-5407		1982	30.00
Polydor MG-1-5407		198?	12.00
— Reissue of MGM release			
A VIEW TO A KILL			
Capitol SJ-12413		1985	25.00
THE VIKINGS			
United Artists UAL-4003 [M]		1958	30.00
United Artists UAS-5003 [S]		1958	40.00
VILLA RIDES!			
Dot DLP-25870		1968	40.00
THE V.I.P.S			
MGM E-4184 [M]		1963	50.00
MGM SE-4184 [S]		1963	60.00
— Music by Bill Evans			
VISION QUEST			
Geffen R153920		1985	12.00
— Includes Madonna ("Crazy for You," "Gambler")			
VIVA MARIA!			
United Artists UAL-4135 [M]		1965	25.00
United Artists UAS-5135 [S]		1965	30.00
VIVA MAX!			
RCA Victor LSP-4275		1969	25.00
THE VIXEN			
Beverly Hills BHS-22		1968	50.00
VOYAGE EN BALLON			
Philips PHM200029 [M]		1960	30.00
Philips PHS600029 [S]		1960	40.00
WALK DON'T RUN			
Mainstream 56080 [M]		1966	25.00
Mainstream S-6080 [S]		1966	40.00
WALK ON THE WILD SIDE			
Ava A-4-ST [M]		1962	25.00
Ava AS-4-ST [S]		1962	40.00
Choreo A-4-ST [M]		1962	30.00
Choreo AS-4-ST [S]		1962	50.00
A WALK WITH LOVE AND DEATH			
Citadel CT-6025		1969	80.00
THE WANDERERS			
Warner Bros. BSK3359		1979	30.00
WAR AND PEACE			
Columbia CL930 [M]		1956	30.00
Melodiya/Capitol SWAO2918		1968	40.00
THE WARLOCK			
Intrada MAF-7003		1990	25.00
THE WAR LORD			
Decca DL9149 [M]		1965	30.00
Decca DL79149 [S]		1965	50.00
WARNING SHOT			
Liberty LRP-3498 [M]		1967	30.00
Liberty LST-7498 [S]		1967	40.00
WATERLOO			
Paramount PAS-6003		1971	30.00
Paramount SW-93729		1971	30.00
— Capitol Record Club edition			
WATERMELON MAN			
Beverly Hills BHS-26		1970	30.00
WATERSHIP DOWN			
Columbia JS35707		1978	30.00
WAY…WAY OUT			
20th Century Fox 3192 [M]		1966	30.00
20th Century Fox S-4192 [S]		1966	40.00
WEDDING IN MONACO			
Mercury MG-20149 [M]		1956	250.00
WEST SIDE STORY			
Columbia Masterworks OL5670 [M]		1961	25.00
— Originals have gatefold covers and gray and black labels with six "eye" logos			
Columbia Masterworks OS2070 [S]		1961	30.00
— Originals have gatefold covers and gray and black labels with six "eye" logos			
Columbia Masterworks OS2070 [S]		1963	18.00
— Gatefold cover; gray "360 Sound Stereo" label			
Columbia Masterworks OS2070 [S]		196?	15.00
— Regular cover; gray "360 Sound Stereo" label			
Columbia Masterworks OS2070 [S]		1971	12.00
— Regular cover; olive label with "Columbia" continuously			

Number	Title	Yr	NM
around edge			
Columbia Masterworks OL5670 [M]		1963	15.00
— Gatefold cover; gray "360 Sound Stereo" label			
Columbia Masterworks OL5670 [M]		196?	12.00
— Regular cover; gray "360 Sound Stereo" label			
WHAT A WAY TO GO!			
20th Century Fox TFM-3143 [M]		1964	25.00
20th Century Fox TFS-4143 [S]		1964	40.00
WHAT'S NEW PUSSYCAT?			
United Artists UAL-4128 [M]		1965	25.00
United Artists UAS-5128 [S]		1965	30.00
United Artists UA-LA278-G		1974	15.00
— Reissue of 5128			
WHEN HARRY MET SALLY…			
Columbia SC45319		1989	15.00
WHEN THE BOYS MEET THE GIRLS			
MCA 25013		1986	12.00
— Reissue of MGM 4334			
MGM E-4334 [M]		1965	18.00
MGM SE-4334 [S]		1965	30.00
WHEN THE WIND BLOWS			
Virgin 90599		1987	12.00
— Includes David Bowie, Squeeze			
WHERE EAGLES DARE			
MCA 25082		1986	12.00
— Reissue of MGM S1E-16			
MGM S1E-16ST		1969	30.00
WHERE'S JACK?			
Paramount PAS-5005		1969	30.00
WHERE'S POPPA?			
United Artists UAS-5216		1970	30.00
WHERE THE BUFFALO ROAM			
Backstreet 5126		1980	15.00
— Includes Neil Young			
THE WHISPERERS			
MCA 25041		1986	12.00
— Reissue of United Artists 5161			
United Artists UAL-4161 [M]		1967	25.00
United Artists UAS-5161 [S]		1967	30.00
WHITE CHRISTMAS			
Decca DL8083		1954	50.00
Decca ED819 [PS]		1954	12.00
— Box for 3-EP set			
WHITE CHRISTMAS (PART 1)			
Decca (# unknown)		1954	10.00
— Contents unknown			
WHITE CHRISTMAS (PART 2)			
Decca (# unknown)		1954	10.00
— Contents unknown			
WHITE CHRISTMAS (PART 3)			
Decca (# unknown)		1954	10.00
— Contents unknown			
WHO FRAMED ROGER RABBIT?			
Buena Vista 64100		1988	25.00
WHO'S AFRAID OF VIRGINIA WOOLF?			
Warner Bros. B1656 [M]		1966	30.00
Warner Bros. BS1656 [S]		1966	30.00
Warner Bros. 2B1657 [M]		1966	40.00
— Above (1657) is the complete film, not just the music and some dialogue			
WHO'S THAT GIRL			
Sire R100761		1987	12.00
— Includes Madonna ("Who's That Girl," "Causing a Commotion," "The Look of Love," "Can't Stop"); Scritti Politti ("Best Thing Ever")			
WILD, WILD WINTER			
Decca DL4699 [M]		1966	25.00
Decca DL74699 [S]		1966	30.00
THE WILD BUNCH			
Varese Sarabande STV-81145		1981	18.00
— Reissue of Warner Bros. 1814			
Warner Bros. WS1814		1969	100.00
THE WILD EYE			
RCA Victor LSP-4003		1968	30.00
WILD GEESE			
A&M SP-4730		1978	25.00
WILD IN THE STREETS			
Tower SKAO5099		1968	30.00
WILD IS THE WIND			
Columbia CL1090 [M]		1957	30.00
THE WILD ONE			
Decca DL5515 [10]		1954	150.00

Number	Title	Yr	NM
Decca DL8349 [M]		1956	150.00
WILD ON THE BEACH			
RCA Victor LPM-3441 [M]		1965	30.00
RCA Victor LSP-3441 [S]		1965	40.00
THE WILD RACERS			
Sidewalk ST-5914		1968	30.00
WILD WHEELS			
RCA Victor LSO-1156		1969	25.00
WILLIE DYNAMITE			
MCA 393		1974	25.00
WILLOW			
Virgin Movie Music 90939		1988	30.00
WILLY WONKA AND THE CHOCOLATE FACTORY			
MCA 37124		198?	12.00
— Reissue of Paramount 6012			
Paramount PAS-6012		1971	40.00
THE WITCHES OF EASTWICK			
Warner Bros. 25607		1987	30.00
WITH A SONG IN MY HEART			
Capitol L309 [10]		1952	40.00
Capitol T309 [M]		195?	30.00
THE WIZARD OF OZ			
MCA 39046		198?	12.00
— Reissue of MGM 3996			
MGM E-3464 [M]		1956	50.00
— Yellow label			
MGM E-3996 [M]		1962	18.00
— Gatefold cover, black label			
MGM SE-3996 [R]		196?	18.00
— Gatefold cover, black label			
WOMEN OF THE WORLD			
Decca DL9112 [M]		1963	25.00
Decca DL79112 [S]		1963	30.00
WONDERFUL COUNTRY			
United Artists UAL-4050 [M]		1959	50.00
United Artists UAS-5050 [S]		1959	100.00
WONDERFUL TO BE YOUNG			
Dot DLP-3474 [M]		1962	30.00
Dot DLP-25474 [S]		1962	40.00
THE WONDERFUL WORLD OF THE BROTHERS GRIMM			
MGM 1E-3 [M]		1962	30.00
— With box and hardback book			
MGM S1E-3 [S]		1962	40.00
— With box and hardback book			
WORDS AND MUSIC			
MCA 25029		1986	15.00
— Reissue of MGM 505 with the addition of "Slaughter on Tenth Avenue," which does not appear on either the 10-inch LP or the budget-line Metro reissues			
Metro M-580 [M]		1966	15.00
Metro MS-580 [R]		1966	12.00
MGM E-505 [10]		1950	50.00
THE WORLD OF SUZIE WONG			
RCA Victor LOC-1059 [M]		1960	25.00
RCA Victor LSO-1059 [S]		1960	50.00
THE WRAITH			
Scotti Bros. SZ40429		1986	12.00
— Includes Honeymoon Suite			
WRITTEN ON THE WIND			
Decca DL8424 [M]		1956	40.00
— Black label, silver print, or pink label, black print promo			
Decca DL8424 [M]		196?	25.00
— Black label with color bars			
Varese Sarabande VC-81074		1979	15.00
— Reissue of Decca 8424			
THE WRONG BOX			
Mainstream 56088 [M]		1966	100.00
Mainstream S-6088 [S]		1966	150.00
WUTHERING HEIGHTS			
American Int'l. A-1039		1971	30.00
W.W. AND THE DIXIE DANCEKINGS			
20th Century ST-103		1975	30.00
THE YELLOW CANARY			
Verve V-8548 [M]		1963	50.00
Verve V6-8548 [S]		1963	60.00
THE YELLOW ROLLS-ROYCE			
MGM T90424 [M]		1965	18.00
— Capitol Record Club edition			
MGM ST90424 [S]		1965	18.00
— Capitol Record Club edition			
MGM E-4292 [M]		1965	25.00
MGM SE-4292 [S]		1965	30.00

Number	Title	Yr	NM

YES, GEORGIO
❏ London PDV9001 — 1982 — 12.00
—Contains one Christmas song:

YESTERDAY, TODAY AND TOMORROW
❏ Warner Bros. W1552 [M] — 1964 — 40.00
❏ Warner Bros. WS1552 [S] — 1964 — 50.00

YOJIMBO
❏ MGM E-4096 [M] — 1962 — 100.00
❏ MGM SE-4096 [S] — 1962 — 150.00

YOU ARE WHAT YOU EAT
❏ Columbia Masterworks OS3240 — 1968 — 25.00

YOUNG BILLY YOUNG
❏ MCA 25031 — 1986 — 25.00
—Reissue of United Artists 5199
❏ United Artists UAS-5199 — 1969 — 60.00

YOUNG DOCTORS IN LOVE
❏ Regency RI-8501 — 1982 — 25.00

YOUNG EINSTEIN
❏ A&M SP-3929 — 1988 — 12.00
—Includes Mental As Anything, The Saints, Icehouse, Models

YOUNG FRANKENSTEIN
❏ ABC ABCD-870 — 1975 — 25.00

THE YOUNG GIRLS OF ROCHEFORT
❏ Philips PCC 2-226 [M] — 1968 — 25.00
❏ Philips PCC 2-626 [S] — 1968 — 30.00

THE YOUNG LIONS
❏ Decca DL8719 [M] — 1958 — 30.00
❏ Decca DL78719 [S] — 1958 — 80.00
❏ Varese Sarabande STV-81115 — 1981 — 18.00
—Reissue of Decca 78719

YOUNG LOVERS
❏ Columbia Masterworks OL7010 [M] — 1964 — 25.00
❏ Columbia Masterworks OS2510 [S] — 1964 — 30.00

YOUNG MAN WITH A HORN
❏ Columbia CL6106 [10] — 1950 — 175.00
❏ Columbia CL582 [M] — 1950 — 40.00

THE YOUNG SAVAGES
❏ Columbia CL1672 [M] — 1961 — 30.00
❏ Columbia CS8472 [S] — 1961 — 100.00

YOUNG WINSTON
❏ Angel SFO-36901 — 1972 — 30.00

YOU ONLY LIVE TWICE
❏ United Artists UAL-4155 [M] — 1967 — 25.00
❏ United Artists UAS-5155 [S] — 1967 — 30.00
❏ United Artists UA-LA289-G — 1974 — 15.00
—Reissue of 5155

YOURS, MINE AND OURS
❏ MCA 1434 — 198? — 10.00
—Reissue of United Artists 5181
❏ United Artists UAS-5181 — 1968 — 25.00

Z
❏ Columbia Masterworks OS3370 — 1970 — 25.00

ZABRISKIE POINT
❏ MCA 25032 — 1986 — 12.00
—Reissue of MGM 4468
❏ MGM SE-4468 — 1970 — 25.00

ZACHARIAH
❏ ABC ABCS-OC-13 — 1970 — 30.00

ZOOT SUIT
❏ MCA 5267 — 1981 — 25.00

ZORBA THE GREEK
❏ 20th Century T-903 — 1973 — 15.00
—Reissue of 20th Century Fox 4167
❏ 20th Century Fox TFM-3167 [M] — 1965 — 25.00
❏ 20th Century Fox TFS-4167 [S] — 1965 — 30.00
❏ Casablanca 826245-1 — 198? — 10.00
—Reissue of 20th Century 903

ZULU
❏ United Artists UAL-4116 [M] — 1964 — 40.00
❏ United Artists UAS-5116 [S] — 1964 — 70.00

Television

A CHARLIE BROWN CHRISTMAS
❏ Charlie Brown 3701 — 1977 — 25.00
—Complete soundtrack with dialogue, plus music by Vince Guaraldi; includes 12-page bound-in booklet with script and illustrations

THE MUSIC FROM M SQUAD
❏ RCA Victor LPM-2062 [M] — 1959 — 60.00
❏ RCA Victor LSP-2062 [S] — 1959 — 40.00

RICHARD DIAMOND
❏ EmArcy MG-36162 [M] — 1959 — 200.00

❏ EmArcy SR-80045 [S] — 1959 — 200.00

77 SUNSET STRIP
❏ Warner Bros. W1289 [M] — 1959 — 60.00
❏ Warner Bros. WS1289 [S] — 1959 — 40.00

THE SOUND OF JAZZ
❏ Columbia CL1098 [M] — 1958 — 60.00
❏ Columbia CS8040 [S] — 1958 — 40.00

THRILLER
❏ Time 52034 [M] — 1960 — 60.00
❏ Time S-2034 [S] — 1960 — 40.00

Various Artists Collections

ACCENT ON TROMBONE
❏ Urania UJLP-1205 [M] — 1955 — 150.00

AC-DC BLUES
❏ Stash ST-106 — 197? — 25.00

ADD-A-PART JAZZ
❏ Columbia CL908 [M] — 1956 — 60.00

AFRO-COOL
❏ GNP Crescendo GNP-48 [M] — 1959 — 50.00

AFRO-CUBAN JAZZ
❏ Verve 833561-1 — 198? — 30.00
❏ Verve VE-2-2522 — 197? — 35.00

AFRO SUMMIT
❏ BASF 20675 — 197? — 50.00
❏ Pausa 7026 — 198? — 25.00

AFTER HOUR JAZZ
❏ Epic LN(# unk) [M] — 1955 — 100.00

AFTER HOURS BLUES, 1949
❏ Biograph 12010 — 1969 — 30.00

ALIVEMUTHERFORYA
❏ Columbia JC35349 — 1977 — 30.00
— With Billy Cobham, Alphonso Johnson, Steve Khan, Tom Scott

ALL DAY LONG
❏ Prestige PRLP-7081 [M] — 1957 — 300.00
— Reissued as Prestige 7277; see KENNY BURRELL.

ALL NIGHT LONG
❏ Prestige PRLP-7073 [M] — 1957 — 300.00
— Reissued as Prestige 7289; see KENNY BURRELL.

ALL-STAR DATES
❏ RCA Victor LPT-21 [10] — 1951 — 100.00

ALL STAR JAZZ
❏ Halo 50223 [M] — 195? — 30.00

ALL STAR SESSIONS
❏ Capitol M-11031 — 1973 — 30.00

ALL-STAR STOMPERS
❏ Circle L-402 [M] — 1951 — 40.00

ALL STAR SWING GROUPS
❏ Savoy Jazz SJL-2218 — 198? — 30.00

ALL STAR TRIBUTE TO TATUM
❏ American Recording Society G-424 [M] — 1957 — 60.00

ALTO ALTITUDE
❏ EmArcy MG-36018 [M] — 1955 — 250.00

ALTO ARTISTRY
❏ Trip 5543 — 197? — 25.00

ALTO SAXES
❏ Norgran MGN-1035 [M] — 1955 — 300.00
❏ Verve MGV-8126 [M] — 1957 — 150.00
❏ Verve V-8126 [M] — 1961 — 60.00

ALTO SUMMIT
❏ Prestige PRLP-7684 — 1969 — 35.00

AMERICANS ABROAD, VOL. 1
❏ Pax LP-6009 [10] — 1955 — 70.00

AMERICANS ABROAD, VOL. 2
❏ Pax LP-6015 [10] — 1955 — 70.00

AMERICANS IN EUROPE, VOL. 1
❏ ABC Impulse! AS-36 [S] — 1968 — 30.00
❏ Impulse! A-36 [M] — 1963 — 100.00
❏ Impulse! AS-36 [S] — 1963 — 120.00

AMERICANS IN EUROPE, VOL. 2
❏ ABC Impulse! AS-37 [S] — 1968 — 30.00
❏ Impulse! A-37 [M] — 1963 — 100.00
❏ Impulse! AS-37 [S] — 1963 — 120.00

AMERICA'S GREATEST JAZZMEN PLAY COLE

PORTER
❏ Moodsville MVLP-34 [M] — 1963 — 40.00
— Green label
❏ Moodsville MVST-34 [S] — 1963 — 40.00
— Green label
❏ Moodsville MVLP-34 [M] — 1965 — 50.00
— Blue label, trident logo at right
❏ Moodsville MVST-34 [S] — 1965 — 50.00
— Blue label, trident logo at right

AMERICA'S GREATEST JAZZMEN PLAY GEORGE GERSHWIN
❏ Moodsville MVLP-33 [M] — 1963 — 40.00
— Green label
❏ Moodsville MVST-33 [S] — 1963 — 40.00
— Green label
❏ Moodsville MVLP-33 [M] — 1965 — 50.00
— Blue label, trident logo at right
❏ Moodsville MVST-33 [S] — 1965 — 50.00
— Blue label, trident logo at right

AMERICA'S GREATEST JAZZMEN PLAY RICHARD RODGERS
❏ Moodsville MVLP-35 [M] — 1963 — 40.00
— Green label
❏ Moodsville MVST-35 [S] — 1963 — 40.00
— Green label
❏ Moodsville MVLP-35 [M] — 1965 — 50.00
— Blue label, trident logo at right
❏ Moodsville MVST-35 [S] — 1965 — 50.00
— Blue label, trident logo at right

AMERICA'S GREATEST JAZZMEN PLAY THE BROADWAY SCENE
❏ Moodsville MVLP-38 [M] — 1963 — 40.00
— Green label
❏ Moodsville MVST-38 [S] — 1963 — 40.00
— Green label
❏ Moodsville MVLP-38 [M] — 1965 — 50.00
— Blue label, trident logo at right
❏ Moodsville MVST-38 [S] — 1965 — 50.00
— Blue label, trident logo at right

ANNIVERSARY
❏ Xanadu 201 — 1986 — 25.00

ANOTHER MONDAY NIGHT AT BIRDLAND
❏ Roulette R52022 [M] — 1959 — 60.00
❏ Roulette RS52022 [S] — 1959 — 60.00

AN ANTHOLOGY OF CALIFORNIA MUSIC
❏ Jazz: West Coast JWC-500 [M] — 1955 — 300.00

AN ANTHOLOGY OF CALIFORNIA MUSIC, VOL. 2
❏ Jazz: West Coast JWC-501 [M] — 1956 — 300.00

ANTHROPOLOGY
❏ Zim 1002 — 197? — 30.00

THE ART OF JAZZ PIANO
❏ Epic LN3295 [M] — 1956 — 100.00

THE ART OF THE BALLAD
❏ Verve VSP-17 [M] — 1966 — 35.00
❏ Verve VSPS-17 [R] — 1966 — 25.00

THE ART OF THE BALLAD 2
❏ Verve VSP-38 [M] — 1966 — 35.00
❏ Verve VSPS-38 [R] — 1966 — 25.00

THE ART OF THE JAM SESSION: MONTREUX '77
❏ Pablo Live 2620106 — 1978 — 125.00

ASIAN JOURNAL
❏ Music of the World H-303 — 198? — 25.00

ASSORTED FLAVORS OF PACIFIC JAZZ
❏ Pacific Jazz HFS-1 [M] — 1956 — 100.00

THE ATLANTIC FAMILY LIVE AT MONTREUX
❏ Atlantic SD-2-3000 — 1977 — 35.00

ATLANTIC JAZZ
❏ Atlantic 81712 — 1987 — 250.00
—Boxed set with 12 volumes in 15 records, liner notes and credits

ATLANTIC JAZZ: BEBOP
❏ Atlantic 81702 — 1987 — 25.00

ATLANTIC JAZZ: FUSION
❏ Atlantic 81711 — 1987 — 25.00

ATLANTIC JAZZ: INTROSPECTION
❏ Atlantic 81710 — 1987 — 25.00

ATLANTIC JAZZ: KANSAS CITY
❏ Atlantic 81701 — 1987 — 25.00

ATLANTIC JAZZ: MAINSTREAM
❏ Atlantic 81704 — 1987 — 25.00

ATLANTIC JAZZ: NEW ORLEANS

Number	Title	Yr	NM
☐ Atlantic 81700		1987	25.00
ATLANTIC JAZZ: PIANO			
☐ Atlantic 81707		1987	30.00
ATLANTIC JAZZ: POST BOP			
☐ Atlantic 81705		1987	25.00
ATLANTIC JAZZ: SINGERS			
☐ Atlantic 81706		1987	30.00
ATLANTIC JAZZ: SOUL			
☐ Atlantic 81708		1987	30.00
ATLANTIC JAZZ: THE AVANT-GARDE			
☐ Atlantic 81709		1987	25.00
ATLANTIC JAZZ: WEST COAST			
☐ Atlantic 81703		1987	25.00
ATLANTIC RECORDS: GREAT MOMENTS IN JAZZ			
☐ Atlantic 81907		1989	30.00
AUDIO MASTER PLUS SAMPLER			
☐ A&M SP6-3000		1983	30.00
AUDIO MASTER PLUS SAMPLER II			
☐ A&M SP6-3021		1984	30.00
AUTOBIOGRAPHY IN JAZZ			
☐ Debut DEB-198 [M]		1955	350.00
☐ Fantasy OJC-115		198?	12.00
AWARD ALBUM JAZZ VOCALS			
☐ Bethlehem BCP-6060 [M]		1961	250.00
BACKGROUNDS OF JAZZ, VOL. 1: THE JUG BANDS			
☐ X LX-3009 [10]		1954	150.00
BACKGROUNDS OF JAZZ, VOL. 2: COUNTRY & URBAN BLUES			
☐ X LVA-3016 [10]		1954	150.00
BACKGROUNDS OF JAZZ, VOL. 3: KINGS OF THE BLUES			
☐ X LVA-3032 [10]		1955	150.00
BACKWOOD BLUES			
☐ Riverside RLP-1039 [10]		1954	300.00
BALLROOM BANDSTAND			
☐ Columbia CL611 [M]		1955	75.00
BARGAIN DAY			
☐ EmArcy MG-36087 [M]		1956	200.00
BARRELHOUSE BOOGIE			
☐ Bluebird 8334-1-RB		198?	25.00
BARREL HOUSE PIANO			
☐ Brunswick BL58022 [10]		1951	120.00
BARRELHOUSE PIANO 1927-36			
☐ Yazoo 1028		197?	25.00
THE BASS			
☐ ABC Impulse! AS-9284		197?	100.00
BATTLE OF BANDS			
☐ Capitol H235 [10]		1950	150.00
BATTLE OF JAZZ, VOL. 3			
☐ Brunswick BL58039 [10]		1953	100.00
BATTLE OF THE BIG BANDS			
☐ Capitol T667 [M]		1956	100.00
☐ Trip 5527		197?	25.00
BATTLE OF THE SAXES-TENOR ALL STARS			
☐ EmArcy MG-36023 [M]		1955	250.00
BEBOP BOYS			
☐ Savoy Jazz SJL-2225		198?	30.00
THE BEBOP ERA			
☐ Columbia Jazz Masterpieces CJ40972		1988	25.00
THE BE-BOP ERA			
☐ RCA Victor LPV-519		1965	50.00
BEBOP REVISITED, VOL. 1			
☐ Xanadu 120		197?	25.00
BEBOP REVISITED, VOL. 2			
☐ Xanadu 124		197?	25.00
BEBOP REVISITED, VOL. 3			
☐ Xanadu 172		197?	25.00
BEBOP REVISITED, VOL. 4			
☐ Xanadu 197		197?	25.00
BEBOP REVISITED, VOL. 5			
☐ Xanadu 205		1986	25.00
BEBOP REVISITED, VOL. 6			
☐ Xanadu 208		1987	25.00
BE-BOP SINGERS			
☐ Prestige PRST-7828		1971	30.00
BE OUR GUEST			
☐ Gene Norman GNP-20 [M]		1955	75.00
BEST COAST JAZZ			
☐ EmArcy MG-36039 [M]		1955	250.00
BEST FROM THE WEST: MODERN SOUNDS FROM CALIFORNIA, VOL. 1			
☐ Blue Note BLP-5059 [10]		1955	200.00

Number	Title	Yr	NM
BEST FROM THE WEST: MODERN SOUNDS FROM CALIFORNIA, VOL. 2			
☐ Blue Note BLP-5060 [10]		1955	200.00
THE BEST OF ARGO JAZZ			
☐ Argo ALPS-1 [M]		1961	60.00
THE BEST OF BLUE NOTE, VOL. 1			
☐ Blue Note BST-84429		197?	50.00
THE BEST OF BLUE NOTE, VOL. 2			
☐ Blue Note BST-84433		197?	50.00
BEST OF DIXIELAND			
☐ RCA Victor ANL1-1431		1976	12.00
THE BEST OF DIXIELAND			
☐ RCA Victor LPM-2982 [M]		1965	50.00
☐ RCA Victor LSP-2982 [R]		1965	30.00
BEST OF THE BIG NAME BANDS			
☐ RCA Camden CAL-368 [M]		1958	60.00
BETHLEHEM'S BEST			
☐ Bethlehem EXLP-6 [M]		1958	400.00
—Box set of 82, 83, and 84			
BETHLEHEM'S BEST, VOLUME 1			
☐ Bethlehem BCP-82 [M]		1958	250.00
BETHLEHEM'S BEST, VOLUME 2			
☐ Bethlehem BCP-83 [M]		1958	250.00
BETHLEHEM'S BEST, VOLUME 3			
☐ Bethlehem BCP-84 [M]		1958	250.00
BETHLEHEM'S GRAB BAG			
☐ Bethlehem EXLP-2 [M]		1958	200.00
THE BIG 18 -- LIVE ECHOES OF THE SWINGING BANDS			
☐ RCA Victor LSP-1921 [S]		1959	50.00
☐ RCA Victor LPM-1921 [M]		1959	40.00
BIG BAND CONTRAST			
☐ Bethlehem BCP-6037 [M]		1960	200.00
BIG BAND JAZZ			
☐ Brunswick BL58050 [10]		1953	100.00
BIG BAND JAZZ: TULSA TO HARLEM			
☐ Delmark DL-439		1989	25.00
BIG BANDS			
☐ Capitol STFL-293		1969	100.00
—One album each by Les Brown, Glen Gray, Duke Ellington, Benny Goodman, Harry James and Woody Herman			
BIG BANDS!			
☐ Onyx 202		197?	30.00
BIG BANDS: BIG BAND BASH			
☐ Time-Life STBB-15		1984	20.00
BIG BANDS: ON THE ROAD			
☐ Time-Life STBB-18		1985	20.00
BIG BANDS: THE SMALL GROUPS			
☐ Time-Life STBB-21		1985	20.00
BIG BANDS: UPTOWN			
☐ Time-Life STBB-20		1985	20.00
BIG BANDS: WORLD WAR II			
☐ Time-Life STBB-28		1986	20.00
THE BIG BANDS 1933			
☐ Prestige PRLP-7645		1969	35.00
BIG BANDS ARE BACK			
☐ Commodore J2-15596		198?	30.00
BIG BANDS' GREATEST HITS			
☐ Columbia G30009		1970	50.00
—Red "360 Sound" labels			
☐ Columbia G30009		1970	35.00
—Orange labels			
☐ Columbia CG30009		197?	30.00
—CG" prefix is a reissue of "G			
BIG BANDS' GREATEST HITS, VOL. 2			
☐ Columbia G31213		1972	35.00
☐ Columbia CG31213		197?	30.00
—CG" prefix is a reissue of "G			
BIG BANDS OF THE SINGING YEARS, VOLUME 1			
☐ Collectables COL-5096		198?	25.00
BIG BANDS OF THE SINGING YEARS, VOLUME 2			
☐ Collectables COL-5097		198?	25.00
BIG BANDS OF THE SWING YEARS			
☐ Everest Archive of Folk & Jazz 359		198?	25.00
BIG BAND STEREO			
☐ Capitol SW1055 [S]		1959	100.00
BIG BANDS UPTOWN			
☐ MCA 1323		198?	25.00
BIG BANDS UPTOWN, VOL. 1			
☐ Decca DL79242		1969	30.00
THE BIG BEAT			
☐ Milestone 47016		1990	35.00

Number	Title	Yr	NM
BIG LITTLE BANDS			
☐ Onyx 220		197?	30.00
BIG NAME DIXIE			
☐ Score SLP-4024 [M]		1958	100.00
BILL EVANS: A TRIBUTE			
☐ Palo Alto PA-8028		1982	35.00
BILLIE, ELLA, LENA, SARAH!			
☐ Columbia Jazz Odyssey PC36811		198?	25.00
BILLIE HOLIDAY REVISITED			
☐ Mainstream MRL-409		197?	30.00
BIRDLAND ALL STARS AT CARNEGIE HALL			
☐ Roulette RE-127		197?	30.00
BIRDLANDERS			
☐ Everest Archive of Folk & Jazz 275		197?	25.00
THE BIRDLAND STARS ON TOUR, VOL. 1			
☐ RCA Victor LPM-1327 [M]		1956	40.00
THE BIRDLAND STARS ON TOUR, VOL. 2			
☐ RCA Victor LPM-1328 [M]		1956	40.00
THE BIRDLAND STORY			
☐ Roulette RB-2 [M]		1961	40.00
☐ Roulette SRB-2 [S]		1961	40.00
BIRD'S NIGHT: A CELEBRATION OF THE MUSIC OF CHARLIE PARKER, LIVE AT THE FIVE SPOT			
☐ Savoy Jazz SJL-2257		198?	30.00
BIRD'S NIGHT -- THE MUSIC OF CHARLIE PARKER			
☐ Savoy MG-12138 [M]		1958	100.00
THE BIRTH OF BOP, VOL. 1			
☐ Savoy MG-9022 [10]		1953	300.00
THE BIRTH OF BOP, VOL. 2			
☐ Savoy MG-9023 [10]		1953	300.00
THE BIRTH OF BOP, VOL. 3			
☐ Savoy MG-9024 [10]		1953	300.00
THE BIRTH OF BOP, VOL. 4			
☐ Savoy MG-9025 [10]		1953	300.00
THE BIRTH OF BOP, VOL. 5			
☐ Savoy MG-9026 [10]		1953	300.00
BLACK AND WHITE RAGTIME, 1921-39			
☐ Biograph 12047		197?	30.00
BLACKBERRY JAM 1943-45			
☐ Sunbeam 214		197?	25.00
BLACK CALIFORNIA, VOL. 1			
☐ Savoy Jazz SJL-2215		198?	30.00
BLACK CALIFORNIA, VOL. 2			
☐ Savoy Jazz SJL-2242		198?	30.00
BLACK GIANTS			
☐ Columbia CG33402		197?	35.00
BLACK LION AT MONTREUX			
☐ Black Lion 213		197?	35.00
THE BLACK SWING TRADITION			
☐ Savoy Jazz SJL-2246		198?	30.00
BLOWIN' SESSIONS			
☐ Blue Note BN-LA521-H2		1975	50.00
BLOWOUT AT MARDI GRAS			
☐ Cook LP-1084 [M]		1955	50.00
THE BLUE NOTE 50TH ANNIVERSARY COLLECTION VOL. 1: FROM BOOGIE TO BOP, 1939-1956			
☐ Blue Note B1-92465		1989	35.00
THE BLUE NOTE 50TH ANNIVERSARY COLLECTION VOL. 2: THE JAZZ MESSAGE, 1956-1965			
☐ Blue Note B1-92468		1989	35.00
THE BLUE NOTE 50TH ANNIVERSARY COLLECTION VOL. 3: FUNK AND BLUES, 1956-1967			
☐ Blue Note B1-92471		1989	35.00
THE BLUE NOTE 50TH ANNIVERSARY COLLECTION VOL. 4: OUTSIDE IN, 1964-1989			
☐ Blue Note B1-92474		1989	35.00
THE BLUE NOTE 50TH ANNIVERSARY COLLECTION VOL. 5: LIGHTING THE FUSE, 1970-1989			
☐ Blue Note B1-92477		1989	35.00
BLUE NOTE '86: A GENERATION OF JAZZ			
☐ Blue Note BQ-85127		1986	30.00
BLUE NOTE CLASSICS			
☐ Blue Note B-6509 [M]		1969	35.00
BLUE NOTE LIVE AT THE ROXY			
☐ Blue Note BN-LA663-4047		1976	35.00
BLUE NOTE MEETS THE L.A. PHILHARMONIC			
☐ Blue Note BN-LA870-H		1977	35.00

Soundtrack, *Pete Kelly's Blues*, Decca DL 8166, black label with silver print, **$150**.

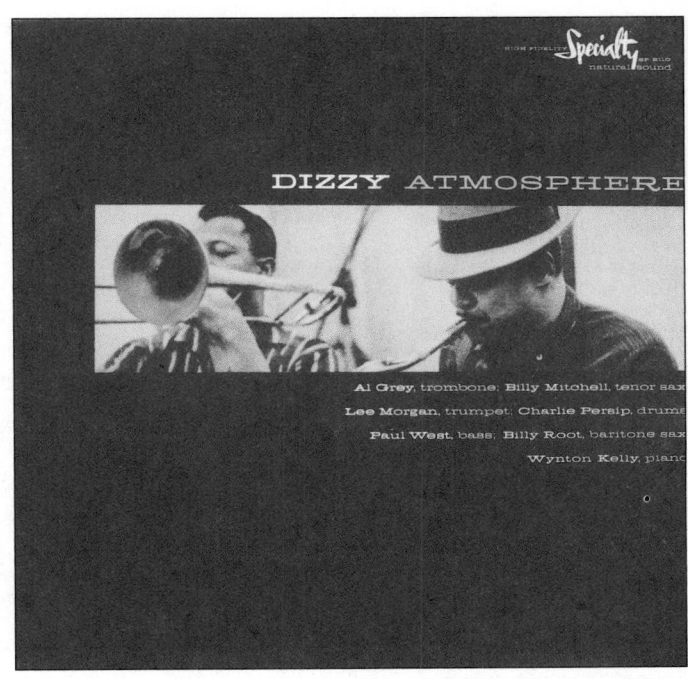

Various Artists, *Dizzy Atmosphere*, Specialty LP-2110, original issue, **$40**.

Various Artists, *Jam Session #6*, Clef MGC-4006, **$250**.

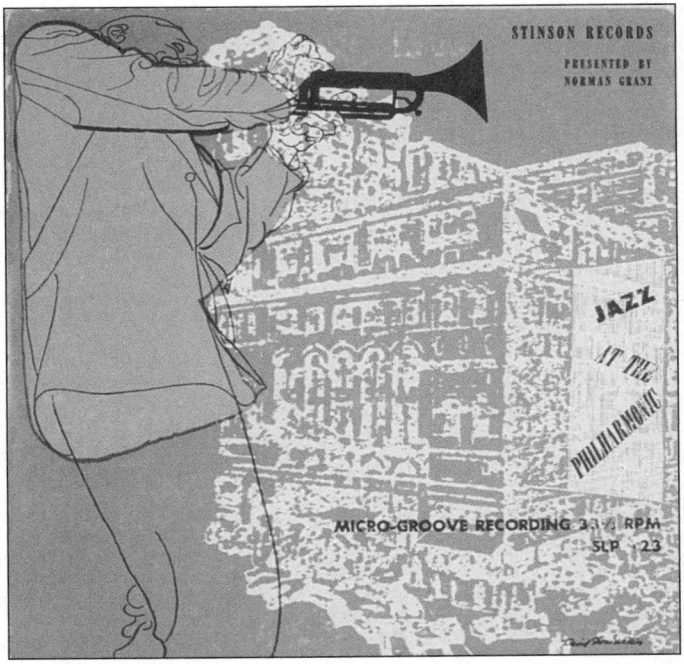

Various Artists, *Jazz at the Philharmonic*, Stinson SLP-23, 10-inch LP on see-through red vinyl, **$200**.

Number	Title	Yr	NM

THE BLUES, VOL. 2
❑ Pacific Jazz JWC-502 [M] — 1956 — 100.00
❑ World Pacific JWC-502 [M] — 1958 — 150.00

THE BLUES, VOL. 2: HAVE BLUES, WILL TRAVEL
❑ World Pacific JWC-509 [M] — 1958 — 150.00

THE BLUES, VOL. 3: BLOWIN' THE BLUES
❑ World Pacific JWC-512 [M] — 1958 — 150.00
❑ World Pacific ST-1029 [S] — 1959 — 150.00

THE BLUES AND ALL THAT JAZZ
❑ MCA 1353 — 198? — 25.00

BLUES FOR TOMORROW
❑ Fantasy OJC-030 — 1982 — 12.00
❑ Riverside RLP 12-243 [M] — 1957 — 250.00

BLUES IN CONCERT
❑ Groove Merchant 4405 — 197? — 25.00

THE BLUES IN MODERN JAZZ
❑ Atlantic 1337 [M] — 1961 — 250.00
—Multicolor label, white "fan" logo at right
❑ Atlantic 1337 [M] — 1963 — 50.00
—Multicolor label, black "fan" logo at right
❑ Atlantic SD1337 [R] — 1969 — 30.00

THE BLUES IN STEREO
❑ World Pacific ST-1021 [S] — 1959 — 150.00

BODY AND SOUL
❑ RCA Victor LPV-501 — 1964 — 50.00

BONING UP ON 'BONES
❑ EmArcy MG-36038 [M] — 1955 — 250.00

BOOGIE WOOGIE
❑ Decca DL5248 [10] — 1950 — 150.00

BOOGIE WOOGIE KINGS AND QUEENS
❑ Decca DL5249 [10] — 1950 — 150.00

BOOGIE WOOGIE PIANO
❑ Brunswick BL58018 [10] — 1950 — 120.00

BOOGIE WOOGIE PIANOS
❑ Columbia KC32708 — 197? — 25.00

BOOGIE WOOGIE RARITIES (1927-43)
❑ Milestone M-2009 — 197? — 30.00

BOOGIE WOOGIE TRIO
❑ Storyville 4006 — 198? — 25.00

BOOTY
❑ Mainstream MRL-413 — 1974 — 60.00

BOP CITY: EVIDENCE
❑ Boplicity BOPM-12 — 198? — 25.00

BOP CITY: MIDNIGHT
❑ Boplicity BOPM-9 — 198? — 25.00

BOP CITY: STRAIGHT AHEAD
❑ Boplicity BOPM-10 — 198? — 25.00

BOP CITY: THINGS ARE GETTING BETTER
❑ Boplicity BOPM-11 — 198? — 25.00

BOP LIVES
❑ Pickwick SPC-5011 — 197? — 25.00

BRASS FEVER
❑ ABC Impulse! AS-9308 — 1975 — 35.00

BRASS FEVER: TIME IS RUNNING OUT
❑ ABC Impulse! AS-9319 — 197? — 35.00

BRITISH FESTIVAL OF JAZZ CONCERT
❑ Decca DL5422 [10] — 1952 — 200.00

BRITISH JAZZ FESTIVAL
❑ Decca DL5424 [10] — 1952 — 200.00

BROTHERS AND OTHER MOTHERS
❑ Savoy Jazz SJL-2210 — 198? — 30.00

BROTHERS AND OTHER MOTHERS, VOL. 2
❑ Savoy Jazz SJL-2236 — 198? — 30.00

BUSHKIN-SAFRANSKI-WILSON GROUPS
❑ Allegro 1590 [10] — 1955 — 100.00

CAFÉ SOCIETY
❑ Onyx 210 — 197? — 30.00

CALIFORNIA CONCERT
❑ CTI CTX22 — 197? — 35.00

CATS AND JAMMER KIDS
❑ Angel ANG-60007 [10] — 1955 — 100.00

CATS VS. CHICKS
❑ MGM E-255 [10] — 1954 — 100.00

A CELEBRATION OF DUKE
❑ Fantasy OJC-605 — 1991 — 30.00
❑ Pablo Today 2312119 — 197? — 35.00

CENTRAL AVENUE BREAKDOWN, VOL. 1
❑ Onyx 212 — 197? — 30.00

CENTRAL AVENUE BREAKDOWN, VOL. 2
❑ Onyx 215 — 197? — 30.00

THE CHANGING FACE OF HARLEM
❑ Savoy Jazz SJL-2208 — 198? — 30.00

THE CHANGING FACE OF HARLEM, VOL. 2
❑ Savoy Jazz SJL-2224 — 198? — 30.00

CHARLIE PARKER 10TH MEMORIAL CONCERT
❑ Limelight LM-82017 [M] — 1965 — 35.00
❑ Limelight LS-86017 [S] — 1965 — 50.00
❑ Trip 5510 — 197? — 25.00

CHARLIE PARKER MEMORIAL CONCERT
❑ Cadet 2CA-60002 — 1971 — 50.00
❑ Chess CH-92510 — 198? — 15.00

CHICAGO: THE LIVING LEGENDS, VOL. 1
❑ Riverside RLP-389 [M] — 196? — 50.00
❑ Riverside RS-9389 [R] — 196? — 30.00

CHICAGO: THE LIVING LEGENDS, VOL. 2
❑ Riverside RLP-390 [M] — 196? — 50.00
❑ Riverside RS-9390 [R] — 196? — 30.00

CHICAGO AND ALL THAT JAZZ!
❑ Verve V-8441 [M] — 1961 — 60.00
❑ Verve V6-8441 [S] — 1962 — 60.00

THE CHICAGOANS
❑ Decca DL79231 — 1968 — 30.00

CHICAGO / AUSTIN HIGH SCHOOL
❑ RCA Victor LPM-1508 [M] — 1957 — 60.00

CHICAGO JAZZ, 1923-29
❑ Biograph 12005 — 1968 — 30.00

CHICAGO JAZZ, VOLUME 2, 1925-29
❑ Biograph 12043 — 197? — 30.00

CHICAGO JAZZ ALBUM
❑ Decca DL8029 [M] — 1954 — 150.00

CHICAGO'S BOSS TENORS
❑ Chess CHV-414 — 1970 — 35.00

CHICAGO SOUTH SIDE
❑ Historical 10 — 1968 — 25.00

CHICAGO SOUTH SIDE, VOL. 2
❑ Historical 30 — 1969 — 25.00

CHOCOLATE DANDIES, 1928-1933
❑ Swing SW-8448 — 198? — 25.00

CLAMBAKE ON BOURBON STREET
❑ Cook LP-1085 [10] — 1955 — 100.00

CLASSIC BLUES ACCOMPANISTS
❑ Riverside RLP-1052 [10] — 1955 — 300.00

CLASSIC CAPITOL JAZZ SESSIONS
❑ Mosaic MQ19-170 — 199? — 400.00

THE CLASSIC COLLECTION -- CONTEMPORARY: THE GREAT JAZZ MEN/VOL. 2
❑ Dot DLP-25879 — 1968 — 75.00

THE CLASSIC COLLECTION -- TRADITIONAL: THE GREAT JAZZ MEN/VOL. 1
❑ Dot DLP-25878 — 1968 — 75.00

CLASSIC JAZZ PIANO STYLES
❑ RCA Victor LPV-544 [M] — 1967 — 50.00

CLASSIC PIANOS
❑ Doctor Jazz FW38851 — 198? — 25.00

CLASSICS IN JAZZ
❑ Capitol T320 [M] — 1954 — 60.00

CLASSICS IN JAZZ: COOL AND QUIET
❑ Capitol H371 [10] — 1953 — 150.00

CLASSICS IN JAZZ: DIXIELAND STYLISTS
❑ Capitol H321 [10] — 1952 — 150.00

CLASSICS IN JAZZ: SMALL COMBOS
❑ Capitol H322 [10] — 1952 — 150.00

CLASSIC TENORS, VOL. 2
❑ Doctor Jazz FW39519 — 198? — 25.00

COLLECTORS' ITEMS, 1922-30
❑ Historical 11 — 1967 — 25.00

COLLECTORS' ITEMS, 1925-29
❑ Historical 20 — 1968 — 25.00

COLLECTORS ITEMS, VOL. 2
❑ Riverside RLP-1040 [10] — 1954 — 300.00

COLLECTOR'S JACKPOT, VOL. 1
❑ Jazz Archives JA-21 — 198? — 25.00

COLLECTOR'S JACKPOT, VOL. 2
❑ Jazz Archives JA-40 — 198? — 25.00

COLLEGE JAZZ: DIXIELAND
❑ Columbia CL736 [M] — 1956 — 50.00

COLORADO JAZZ PARTY
❑ BASF 25099 — 197? — 50.00

COLUMBIA JAZZ FESTIVAL
❑ Columbia JJ-1 [M] — 1959 — 60.00

COLUMBIA'S ALL NEW TIME-RELEASE CAPSULE
❑ Columbia AS247 [DJ] — 1977 — 35.00
—Promo-only sampler

COMBO JAZZ
❑ Jazztone J-1221 [M] — 1956 — 60.00

COMPARATIVE BLUES
❑ Hall of Fame 603 — 197? — 25.00
❑ Jazztone J-1258 [M] — 1957 — 60.00

THE COMPLETE COMMODORE JAZZ RECORDINGS, VOLUME I
❑ Mosaic M23-123 — 199? — 400.00

THE COMPLETE COMMODORE JAZZ RECORDINGS, VOLUME II
❑ Mosaic M23-128 — 199? — 400.00

THE COMPLETE COMMODORE JAZZ RECORDINGS, VOLUME III
❑ Mosaic M20-134 — 199? — 300.00

THE COMPLETE KEYNOTE COLLECTION
❑ Keynote 830121-1 — 1986 — 250.00

THE COMPLETE MASTER JAZZ PIANO SERIES
❑ Mosaic M6-140 — 199? — 100.00

COMPOSERS AT PLAY: HAROLD ARLEN AND COLE PORTER
❑ X LVA-1003 [M] — 1955 — 50.00

THE COMPOSITIONS OF BENNY GOLSON
❑ Riverside RLP-3505 [M] — 1962 — 200.00
❑ Riverside RS-93505 [S] — 1962 — 200.00

THE COMPOSITIONS OF BOBBY TIMMONS
❑ Riverside RLP-3512 [M] — 1962 — 200.00
❑ Riverside RS-93512 [S] — 1962 — 200.00

THE COMPOSITIONS OF CHARLIE PARKER
❑ Riverside RLP-3506 [M] — 1962 — 200.00
❑ Riverside RS-93506 [S] — 1962 — 200.00

THE COMPOSITIONS OF COLE PORTER
❑ Riverside RM-3515 [M] — 1963 — 150.00
❑ Riverside RS-93515 [S] — 1963 — 150.00

THE COMPOSITIONS OF DIZZY GILLESPIE
❑ Riverside RLP-3508 [M] — 1962 — 200.00
❑ Riverside RS-93508 [S] — 1962 — 200.00

THE COMPOSITIONS OF DUKE ELLINGTON
❑ Riverside RLP-3507 [M] — 1962 — 200.00
❑ Riverside RS-93507 [S] — 1962 — 200.00

THE COMPOSITIONS OF DUKE ELLINGTON, VOL. 2
❑ Riverside RLP-3510 [M] — 1962 — 200.00
❑ Riverside RS-93510 [S] — 1962 — 200.00

THE COMPOSITIONS OF GEORGE GERSHWIN
❑ Riverside RM-3517 [M] — 1963 — 150.00
❑ Riverside RS-93517 [S] — 1963 — 150.00

THE COMPOSITIONS OF HAROLD ARLEN
❑ Riverside RM-3518 [M] — 1963 — 150.00
❑ Riverside RS-93518 [S] — 1963 — 150.00

THE COMPOSITIONS OF HORACE SILVER
❑ Riverside RLP-3509 [M] — 1962 — 200.00
❑ Riverside RS-93509 [S] — 1962 — 200.00

THE COMPOSITIONS OF IRVING BERLIN
❑ Riverside RM-3519 [M] — 1963 — 150.00
❑ Riverside RS-93519 [S] — 1963 — 150.00

THE COMPOSITIONS OF JEROME KERN
❑ Riverside RM-3516 [M] — 1963 — 150.00
❑ Riverside RS-93516 [S] — 1963 — 150.00

COMPOSITIONS OF LIONEL HAMPTON
❑ Crown CLP-5107 [M] — 195? — 30.00

THE COMPOSITIONS OF MILES DAVIS
❑ Riverside RLP-3504 [M] — 1962 — 200.00
❑ Riverside RS-93504 [S] — 1962 — 200.00

THE COMPOSITIONS OF RICHARD RODGERS
❑ Riverside RM-3514 [M] — 1963 — 150.00
❑ Riverside RS-93514 [S] — 1963 — 150.00

THE COMPOSITIONS OF TADD DAMERON
❑ Riverside RLP-3511 [M] — 1962 — 200.00
❑ Riverside RS-93511 [S] — 1962 — 200.00

THE COMPOSITIONS OF THELONIOUS MONK
❑ Riverside RLP-3503 [M] — 1962 — 200.00
❑ Riverside RS-93503 [S] — 1962 — 200.00

CONCEPTION
❑ Prestige PRLP-7013 [M] — 1956 — 300.00

CONCERT IN ARGENTINA
❑ Halcyon 113 — 197? — 35.00

CONCERT IN JAZZ
❑ Tops L-1532 [M] — 1958 — 50.00

CONCERT JAZZ
❑ Brunswick BL54027 [M] — 1956 — 60.00

A CONCORD JAM
❑ Concord Jazz CJ-142 — 1981 — 25.00

A CONCORD JAM, VOL. 2
❑ Concord Jazz CJ-180 — 1982 — 25.00

A CONCORD JAM, VOL. 3: A GREAT AMERICAN EVENING
❑ Concord Jazz CJ-220 — 1984 — 25.00

CONCORD JAZZ GUITAR COLLECTION, VOL. 1 AND 2
❑ Concord Jazz CJ-160 — 198? — 30.00

THE CONCORD SOUND, VOL. 1

Number	Title	Yr	NM
❑ Concord Jazz CJ-278		1985	25.00
COOL AND CAREFREE			
❑ Columbia Special Products CSP119 [M]		1963	30.00
—Sold only by Carrier air conditioner dealers			
COOL CALIFORNIA			
❑ Savoy Jazz SJL-2254		198?	30.00
COOL EUROPE			
❑ MGM E-3157 [M]		1955	75.00
COOLIN'			
❑ New Jazz NJLP-8216 [M]		1959	200.00
—Purple label			
❑ New Jazz NJLP-8216 [M]		1965	150.00
—Blue label, trident logo at right			
COOL JAZZ			
❑ Seeco CELP-465 [M]		1960	125.00
COOL JAZZ FROM HOLLAND			
❑ Epic LN1126 [10]		1955	80.00
COPULATIN' BLUES			
❑ Stash ST-101		197?	35.00
COPULATIN' BLUES, VOL. 2			
❑ Stash ST-122		198?	35.00
COPULATIN' RHYTHM			
❑ Jass J-3		198?	35.00
COPULATIN' RHYTHM, VOL. 2			
❑ Jass J-5		198?	35.00
THE CORE OF JAZZ			
❑ MGM SE-4737		1970	30.00
COTTON CLUB STARS			
❑ Stash ST-124		198?	30.00
CRITICS' CHOICE			
❑ Dawn DLP-1123 [M]		1958	150.00
CRUISIN'			
❑ Jazzland JLP-7 [M]		1960	60.00
❑ Jazzland JLP-97 [S]		1960	60.00
CTI SUMMER JAZZ AT THE HOLLYWOOD BOWL: LIVE ONE			
❑ CTI 7076		197?	30.00
CTI SUMMER JAZZ AT THE HOLLYWOOD BOWL: LIVE THREE			
❑ CTI 7078		197?	30.00
CTI SUMMER JAZZ AT THE HOLLYWOOD BOWL: LIVE TWO			
❑ CTI 7077		197?	30.00
CYLINDER JAZZ			
❑ Saydisc SDL-334		198?	25.00
DANCE, BE HAPPY!			
❑ Columbia CL967 [M]		1957	50.00
DANCE BAND HITS			
❑ RCA Victor LPT-2 [10]		1951	40.00
DANCE TO THE BANDS			
❑ Capitol TBO727 [M]		1956	60.00
❑ Capitol T977 [M]		1958	80.00
DANCING WITH THE STARS			
❑ Epic LN3136 [M]		1955	100.00
DAS IS JAZZ!			
❑ Decca DL8229 [M]		1956	150.00
A DATE WITH GREATNESS			
❑ Imperial LP-12188A [R]		1962	175.00
❑ Imperial LP-9188A [M]		1962	300.00
—Features Aladdin tracks by Coleman Hawkins, Howard McGhee and Lester Young			
A DATE WITH RIVERSIDE			
❑ Riverside S-4 [M]		195?	40.00
DECADE OF JAZZ, VOLUME 1, 1939-49			
❑ Blue Note BN-LA158-G2 [(2)]		1974	35.00
DECADE OF JAZZ, VOLUME 2, 1949-59			
❑ Blue Note BN-LA159-G2 [(2)]		1974	35.00
DECADE OF JAZZ, VOLUME 3, 1959-69			
❑ Blue Note BN-LA160-G2 [(2)]		1974	35.00
THE DEFINITIVE JAZZ SCENE, VOL. 1			
❑ ABC Impulse! AS-99 [S]		1968	30.00
❑ Impulse! A-99 [M]		1966	35.00
❑ Impulse! AS-99 [S]		1966	100.00
THE DEFINITIVE JAZZ SCENE, VOL. 2			
❑ ABC Impulse! AS-100 [S]		1968	30.00
❑ Impulse! A-100 [M]		1966	35.00
❑ Impulse! AS-100 [S]		1966	100.00
THE DEFINITIVE JAZZ SCENE, VOL. 3			
❑ ABC Impulse! AS-9101 [S]		1968	30.00
❑ Impulse! A-9101 [M]		1966	35.00
❑ Impulse! AS-9101 [S]		1966	100.00
DIGITAL III AT MONTREUX			
❑ Pablo Live 2308223		1980	30.00
DIXIE, LONDON STYLE			
❑ London LL1337 [M]		1956	50.00
DIXIELAND AT CARNEGIE HALL			
❑ Forum SF-9011 [S]		196?	60.00
❑ Forum F-9011 [M]		196?	50.00
❑ Roulette R25038 [M]		1958	60.00
—Originals have a black label			
❑ Roulette R25038 [M]		1959	50.00
—Second pressings have a white label with colored spokes			
DIXIELAND AT ITS BEST			
❑ RCA Camden CAL-838 [M]		1964	30.00
❑ RCA Camden CAS-838 [R]		1964	25.00
DIXIELAND AT JAZZ, LTD.			
❑ Atlantic 1261 [M]		1957	300.00
—Black label			
❑ Atlantic 1261 [M]		1961	150.00
—Multicolor label, white "fan" logo at right			
DIXIELAND AT JAZZ, LTD., VOL. 1			
❑ Atlantic ALS-139 [10]		1952	250.00
DIXIELAND AT JAZZ, LTD., VOL. 2			
❑ Atlantic ALS-140 [10]		1952	250.00
DIXIELAND CLASSICS			
❑ Jazztone J-1216 [M]		1956	60.00
DIXIELAND CONTRASTS			
❑ Jazzman LJ-334 [M]		1954	60.00
DIXIELAND FESTIVAL, VOL. 1			
❑ Vik LX-1057 [M]		1956	60.00
DIXIELAND HITS			
❑ Swingville SVLP-2040 [M]		1962	40.00
—Purple label			
❑ Swingville SVLP-2040 [M]		1965	50.00
—Blue label, trident logo at right			
DIXIELAND IN OLD NEW ORLEANS			
❑ Golden Crest GC-3021 [M]		1958	50.00
DIXIELAND JAZZ			
❑ Audiophile XL-325 [M]		1954	60.00
❑ Audiophile XL-330 [M]		1954	60.00
❑ Grand Award GA 33-310 [M]		1955	120.00
—With wrap-around outer cover			
❑ Grand Award GA 33-310 [M]		1955	75.00
—Without wrap-around outer cover			
DIXIELAND JAZZ CLASSICS			
❑ Herwin H-116		1980	30.00
DIXIELAND JAZZ GEMS			
❑ Commodore FL-20010 [10]		1950	100.00
DIXIELAND MAIN STREAM			
❑ Savoy MG-12213 [M]		196?	50.00
DIXIELAND -- NEW ORLEANS			
❑ Mainstream 56003 [M]		1965	60.00
❑ Mainstream S-6003 [R]		1965	30.00
DIXIELAND RHYTHM KINGS			
❑ Paradox LP-6002 [10]		1951	100.00
DIXIE LAND U.S.A.			
❑ Promenade 2134 [M]		195?	20.00
DIXIELAND VS. BIRDLAND			
❑ MGM E-231 [10]		1954	150.00
DIZZY ATMOSPHERE			
❑ Specialty LP-2110 [M]		1957	40.00
—Original edition, heavier vinyl			
❑ Specialty LP-2110 [M]		198?	50.00
—Reissue on lighter vinyl			
DOUBLE BARREL JAZZ			
❑ Bethlehem BCP-87 [M]		1958	200.00
DOWN BEAT JAZZ CONCERT			
❑ Dot DLP-9003 [M]		1958	150.00
❑ Dot DLP-29003 [S]		1958	150.00
DOWN BEAT JAZZ CONCERT, VOL. 2			
❑ Dot DLP-3188 [M]		1959	150.00
❑ Dot DLP-25188 [S]		1959	150.00
DOWN BEAT'S HALL OF FAME, VOL. 1			
❑ Verve MGV-8320 [M]		1959	100.00
❑ Verve V-8320 [M]		1961	50.00
DREAMING ON THE RIVER TO NEW ORLEANS			
❑ Southland SLP-238		1963	35.00
THE DRUMS			
❑ ABC Impulse! AS-9272		197?	100.00
THE EARL BAKER CYLINDERS			
❑ Jazz Archives JA-43		198?	25.00
EARLY AND RARE: CLASSIC JAZZ "COLLECTORS ITEMS			
❑ Riverside RLP 12-134 [M]		1957	250.00
EARLY JAZZ GREATS, VOL. 1			
❑ Jazztone J-1249 [M]		1957	60.00
EARLY JAZZ GREATS, VOL. 2			
❑ Jazztone J-1252 [M]		1957	60.00
EARLY MODERN			
❑ Milestone M-9035		197?	30.00
EARLY VIPER JIVE			
❑ Stash ST-105		197?	25.00
EARTHY!			
❑ Prestige PRLP-7102 [M]		1957	500.00
THE EAST COAST JAZZ SCENE, VOL. 1			
❑ Coral CRL57035 [M]		1956	100.00
EASY LISTENING			
❑ Audiophile AP-27 [M]		1953	60.00
❑ Audiophile AP-38 [M]		1953	60.00
❑ Audiophile XL-327 [M]		1954	60.00
ECHOES OF AN ERA			
❑ Elektra 60021		1982	25.00
—With Stanley Clarke, Chick Corea, Chaka Khan and Joe Henderson			
ECHOES OF AN ERA VOLUME 2: THE CONCERT			
❑ Elektra/Musician 60165		1983	25.00
ECHOES OF ENJA			
❑ Enja 4000		197?	30.00
ECHOES OF NEW ORLEANS			
❑ Southland SLP-239		1963	35.00
EIGHT WAYS TO JAZZ			
❑ Riverside RLP 12-272 [M]		1958	300.00
THE ELVIS PRESLEY YEARS			
❑ Reader's Digest RBA-236A		1991	100.00
ENCYCLOPEDIA OF JAZZ IN THE '60'S, VOL. 1			
❑ Verve V-8677 [M]		1966	35.00
❑ Verve V6-8677 [S]		1966	50.00
THE ENCYCLOPEDIA OF JAZZ IN THE 70S			
❑ RCA Victor APL2-1984		1977	35.00
THE ENCYCLOPEDIA OF JAZZ ON RECORDS			
❑ Decca DXF140 [M]		1957	275.00
—Box set; individually issued as Decca 8398, 8399, 8400 and 8401			
THE ENCYCLOPEDIA OF JAZZ ON RECORDS, VOL. 1: JAZZ OF THE TWENTIES			
❑ Decca DL8398 [M]		1957	150.00
THE ENCYCLOPEDIA OF JAZZ ON RECORDS, VOL. 1 AND 2: JAZZ OF THE TWENTIES/JAZZ OF THE THIRTIES			
❑ MCA 4061		197?	20.00
THE ENCYCLOPEDIA OF JAZZ ON RECORDS, VOL. 2: JAZZ OF THE THIRTIES			
❑ Decca DL8399 [M]		1957	150.00
THE ENCYCLOPEDIA OF JAZZ ON RECORDS, VOL. 3: JAZZ OF THE FORTIES			
❑ Decca DL8400 [M]		1957	150.00
THE ENCYCLOPEDIA OF JAZZ ON RECORDS, VOL. 3 AND 4: JAZZ OF THE FORTIES/JAZZ OF THE FIFTIES			
❑ MCA 4062		197?	20.00
THE ENCYCLOPEDIA OF JAZZ ON RECORDS, VOL. 4: JAZZ OF THE FIFTIES			
❑ Decca DL8401 [M]		1957	150.00
THE ENCYCLOPEDIA OF JAZZ ON RECORDS, VOL. 5: JAZZ OF THE SIXTIES			
❑ MCA 4063		197?	20.00
ENERGY ESSENTIALS			
❑ ABC Impulse! ASD-9228		197?	100.00
ERA OF THE CLARINET			
❑ Mainstream S-6011 [R]		1965	30.00
❑ Mainstream 56011 [M]		1965	60.00
ESCAPADE REVIEWS THE JAZZ SCENE			
❑ Liberty SL-9005 [M]		1957	60.00
ESCAPE			
❑ Gene Norman GNP-27 [M]		1958	60.00
ESQUIRE'S 2ND ANNUAL ALL-AMERICAN JAZZ CONCERT			
❑ Sunbeam 219		197?	30.00
ESQUIRE'S ALL-AMERICAN HOT JAZZ			
❑ RCA Victor LPV-544 [M]		1967	50.00
ESQUIRE'S WORLD OF JAZZ			
❑ Capitol TBO1970 [M]		1963	80.00
❑ Capitol STBO1970 [S]		1963	80.00
THE ESSENTIAL JAZZ VOCALS			
❑ Verve V-8505 [M]		1963	50.00
❑ Verve V6-8505 [R]		1963	30.00
AN EVENING OF JAZZ			
❑ Norgran MGN-1065 [M]		1956	300.00
❑ Verve MGV-8155 [M]		1957	100.00

Number	Title	Yr	NM
❏ Verve V-8155 [M]		1961	50.00
FANTASY SAMPLER			
❏ Fantasy FS-654 [M]		195?	25.00
—Red vinyl			
THE FEMININE TOUCH			
❏ Decca DL5486 [10]		1953	150.00
❏ Decca DL8316 [M]		1956	150.00
FESTIVAL JAZZ, VOL. 1			
❏ Jim Taylor Presents 106		197?	30.00
FESTIVAL JAZZ, VOL. 2			
❏ Jim Taylor Presents 107		197?	30.00
FIFTEEN STAR SAXOPHONES			
❏ Bethlehem BCP-6035 [M]		1959	200.00
52ND STREET, VOL. 1			
❏ Onyx 203		197?	30.00
52ND STREET, VOL. 2			
❏ Onyx 217		197?	30.00
52ND STREET JAZZ			
❏ Waldorf Music Hall MH 33-148 [10]		195?	175.00
50 YEARS OF JAZZ GREATS			
❏ Columbia Musical Treasury P3S5932		197?	50.00
50 YEARS OF JAZZ GUITAR			
❏ Columbia CG33566		1973	35.00
FILL YOUR HEAD WITH JAZZ			
❏ Columbia G30217		1971	35.00
FIRE INTO MUSIC			
❏ CTI CTS-2		197?	35.00
FIRST ALBUM OF JAZZ			
❏ Folkways FP-712 [10]		1951	120.00
FIVE BIRDS AND A MONK			
❏ Galaxy 5134		1979	30.00
FIVE FEET OF SWING			
❏ Decca DL8045 [M]		1954	150.00
FOOTNOTES TO JAZZ, VOL. 2: ANATOMY OF A JAZZ COMPOSITION			
❏ Folkways FP-31 [10]		1951	120.00
FOR DANCERS ONLY			
❏ Epic LN3120 [M]		1955	100.00
FOREMOST!			
❏ Onyx 201		197?	30.00
FOR JAZZ LOVERS			
❏ EmArcy MG-36086 [M]		1956	200.00
FOUNDATIONS			
❏ MCA 4153		198?	30.00
FOUNDATIONS OF MODERN JAZZ			
❏ Everest Archive of Folk & Jazz 229		196?	25.00
FOUR ALTOS			
❏ Prestige PRLP-7116 [M]		1957	300.00
FOUR DECADES OF JAZZ			
❏ Xanadu 5001		197?	35.00
FOUR FRENCH HORNS			
❏ Savoy MG-12173 [M]		1961	100.00
THE FOUR MOST GUITARS			
❏ ABC-Paramount ABC-109 [M]		1956	60.00
❏ Paramount LP-109 [10]		1954	120.00
THE FOUR ROSES DANCE PARTY			
❏ Columbia Special Products XTV68933/4 [M]		1961	35.00
FOUR TO GO			
❏ Columbia CL2018 [M]		1963	50.00
❏ Columbia CS8818 [S]		1963	60.00
FOUR TROMBONES… THE DEBUT RECORDINGS			
❏ Prestige 24097		197?	150.00
FRANK BULL AND GENE NORMAN PRESENT DIXIELAND JUBILEE			
❏ Decca DL7022 [10]		1952	150.00
FRENCH FESTIVAL			
❏ Classic Jazz 133		197?	30.00
FRENCH TOAST			
❏ Angel ANG-60009 [10]		1956	100.00
FRIDAY THE 13TH, COOK COUNTY JAIL			
❏ Groove Merchant 515		197?	35.00
FROM CANADA WITH LOVE			
❏ PM 011		198?	25.00
FROM SPIRITUALS TO SWING			
❏ Vanguard VMS-73131		197?	25.00
❏ Vanguard VSD-47/48		197?	35.00
FUNKY BLUES NO. 2			
❏ American Recording Society G-404 [M]		1956	60.00
FUN ON THE FRETS: EARLY JAZZ GUITAR			
❏ Yazoo 1061		197?	25.00
GARY MOORE PRESENTS "MY KIND OF MUSIC"			
❏ Columbia CL717 [M]		1956	60.00
GEMS OF JAZZ, VOL. 1			
❏ Decca DL5133 [10]		1950	150.00
❏ Decca DL8039 [M]		1954	150.00
GEMS OF JAZZ, VOL. 2			
❏ Decca DL5134 [10]		1950	150.00
❏ Decca DL8040 [M]		1954	150.00
GEMS OF JAZZ, VOL. 3			
❏ Decca DL5383 [10]		1952	150.00
❏ Decca DL8041 [M]		1954	150.00
GEMS OF JAZZ, VOL. 4			
❏ Decca DL5384 [10]		1952	150.00
❏ Decca DL8042 [M]		1954	150.00
GEMS OF JAZZ, VOL. 5			
❏ Decca DL8043 [M]		1954	150.00
GET IT TOGETHER			
❏ Mainstream MRL-350		197?	30.00
GIANTS OF BOOGIE WOOGIE			
❏ Riverside RLP 12-106 [M]		1956	250.00
GIANTS OF JAZZ			
❏ American Recording Society G-401 [M]		1956	60.00
THE GIANTS OF JAZZ			
❏ Columbia CL1970 [M]		1963	60.00
GIANTS OF JAZZ			
❏ George Wein Collection GW-3004		198?	25.00
GIANTS OF JAZZ, VOL. 2			
❏ Who's Who in Jazz 21014		197?	25.00
GIANTS OF JAZZ, VOLUME 1			
❏ Who's Who in Jazz WWLP21012		1977	25.00
GIANTS OF JAZZ: THE GUITARISTS			
❏ Time-Life STL-J-12		1980	35.00
GIANTS OF JAZZ ORGAN			
❏ King 837 [M]		1963	200.00
GIANTS OF JAZZ VOL. 2			
❏ American Recording Society G-444 [M]		1957	60.00
GIANTS OF SMALL BAND SWING, VOL. 1			
❏ Fantasy OJC-1723		1990	12.00
❏ Riverside RLP 12-143 [M]		1957	250.00
GIANTS OF SMALL BAND SWING, VOL. 2			
❏ Fantasy OJC-1724		1990	12.00
❏ Riverside RLP 12-145 [M]		1957	250.00
GIANTS OF THE BLUES TENOR SAX			
❏ Prestige 24101		197?	35.00
GIANTS OF THE FUNK TENOR SAX			
❏ Prestige 24102		197?	35.00
GIANTS OF TRADITIONAL JAZZ			
❏ Savoy Jazz SJL-2251		198?	30.00
THE GIRLS SING			
❏ Savoy MG-12220 [M]		196?	50.00
GOD REST YE MERRY, JAZZMEN			
❏ Columbia FC37551		1981	30.00
—7-inch 33 1/3 rpm single with small hole; distributed by various banks			
❏ Columbia PC37551		198?	20.00
—Budget-line reissue			
GOLDEN JAZZ INTRSUMENTALS			
❏ Bethlehem BCP-6065 [M]		1962	200.00
THE GREAT BAND ERA			
❏ Reader's Digest RD-25 [M]		1965	50.00
—Box set with flip-open top			
❏ Reader's Digest RD-25 [R]		1965	35.00
—Box set with flip-open top			
THE GREAT BANDS			
❏ Columbia Musical Treasury P2M5267		1968	50.00
GREAT BLUES			
❏ Riverside RLP-1074 [10]		1955	300.00
GREAT BLUES SINGERS			
❏ Riverside RLP 12-121 [M]		1957	250.00
THE GREAT BLUES SINGERS			
❏ Riverside RLP-1032 [10]		1954	300.00
GREATEST HITS			
❏ Harmony HL7255 [M]		1960	35.00
THE GREATEST JAZZ CONCERT EVER			
❏ Prestige 24024		197?	35.00
THE GREATEST JAZZ CONCERT IN THE WORLD			
❏ Pablo 2625704		197?	30.00
THE GREATEST NAMES IN JAZZ			
❏ Verve PR2-3		196?	50.00
—Box set			
GREAT GUITARS AT THE WINERY			
❏ Concord Jazz CJ-131		1980	30.00
—Original issue			
GREAT GUITARS OF JAZZ			
❏ MGM SE-4691		1970	30.00
GREAT JAZZ			
❏ Rondo-lette A-31 [M]		195?	30.00
THE GREAT JAZZ ALBUM			
❏ Project 3 PR6009/10		197?	35.00
THE GREAT JAZZ ALBUM, VOLUME 2			
❏ Project 3 PR6023/24		197?	35.00
GREAT JAZZ BRASS			
❏ RCA Camden CAL-383 [M]		1958	60.00
GREAT JAZZ PIANISTS			
❏ RCA Camden CAL-328 [M]		1958	60.00
GREAT JAZZ PIANISTS OF OUR TIME			
❏ RCA Camden CAL-882 [M]		1965	35.00
❏ RCA Camden CAS-882 [R]		1965	25.00
GREAT JAZZ REEDS			
❏ RCA Camden CAL-339 [M]		1958	60.00
THE GREAT JAZZ SINGERS			
❏ Halo 50269 [M]		1957	35.00
THE GREAT SWING BANDS			
❏ Jazztone J-1245 [M]		1957	60.00
GREAT SWING BANDS OF THE FORTIES			
❏ Audio Lab AL-1530 [M]		1959	150.00
THE GREAT TENOR JAZZMEN			
❏ Allegro 1634 [M]		195?	40.00
GREAT TRUMPET ARTISTS			
❏ RCA Victor LPT-26 [10]		1951	100.00
❏ RCA Victor LPT-35 [10]		1952	100.00
GRETSCH DRUM NIGHT, VOLUME 2			
❏ Roulette R52067 [M]		1961	60.00
❏ Roulette SR52067 [S]		1961	60.00
GRETSCH DRUM NIGHT AT BIRDLAND			
❏ Roulette R52049 [M]		1960	60.00
❏ Roulette SR52049 [S]		1960	60.00
THE GRIFFITH PARK COLLECTION			
❏ Elektra/Musician 60025		1982	25.00
—All-star session with STANLEY CLARKE; CHICK COREA; JOE HENDERSON; FREDDIE HUBBARD; LENNY WHITE			
THE GRIFFITH PARK COLLECTION VOL. 2: THE CONCERT			
❏ Elektra/Musician 60262		198?	30.00
A GRP CHRISTMAS COLLECTION			
❏ GRP GR-9574		1988	30.00
GRP LIVE IN SESSION			
❏ GRP GR-1023		1985	25.00
GRP SAMPLER, VOL. 1			
❏ GRP F-7701		198?	25.00
GRP SUPER LIVE IN CONCERT			
❏ GRP GR-2-1650		1988	30.00
GUIDE TO JAZZ			
❏ RCA Victor LPM-1393 [M]		1956	60.00
GUITAR PLAYER			
❏ MCA 6002		197?	35.00
❏ MCA 8012		197?	35.00
GUITAR PLAYER PRESENTS JAZZ GUITAR CLASSICS			
❏ Fantasy OJC-6012		1990	35.00
GUITAR PLAYERS			
❏ Mainstream MRL-410		197?	30.00
GUITAR SESSION			
❏ Inner City IC-6050		198?	30.00
GUITAR WORKSHOP			
❏ Pausa 7089		198?	25.00
HANDFUL OF COOL JAZZ			
❏ Bethlehem BCP-90 [M]		1959	200.00
HAPPY JAZZ			
❏ Jazztone J-1215 [M]		1956	60.00
THE HARD SWING			
❏ Pacific Jazz JWC-508 [M]		1957	100.00
❏ World Pacific JWC-508 [M]		1958	150.00
HARLEM COMES TO LONDON			
❏ Swing SW-8444		198?	25.00
HARLEM JAZZ 1930			
❏ Brunswick BL58024 [10]		1951	100.00
HARLEN ODYSSEY			
❏ Xanadu 112		197?	25.00
HEAD START -- BOB THIELE EMERGENCY			
❏ Flying Dutchman FDS-104		1969	30.00
HERE AND NOW			
❏ Catalyst 7613		197?	25.00
HERE COME THE GIRLS			
❏ Verve MGV-2036 [M]		1956	200.00
❏ Verve V-2036 [M]		1961	50.00
HERE COME THE SWINGING BANDS			
❏ Verve MGV-8207 [M]		1957	150.00
❏ Verve V-8207 [M]		1961	50.00
HI-FI JAZZ			

Various Artists, *Jazz Committee for Latin American Affairs*, FM LP-303, **$100**.

Various Artists, *The Mellow Moods*, RCA Victor LPM-1365, **$40**.

Various Artists, *New Sounds from Sweden Vol. 1*, Prestige PRLP-119, 10-inch LP, **$400**.

Various Artists, *Opus de Jazz*, Savoy MG 12036, **$150**.

Number	Title	Yr	NM
❑ Brunswick BL58058 [10]		1954	100.00
HI-FI JAZZ SESSION			
❑ Masterseal MSLP5013 [M]		1957	60.00
A HI-FI SALUTE TO THE GREAT ONES			
❑ MGM E-3325 [M]		1956	60.00
A HI-FI SALUTE TO THE GREAT ONES, VOL. 2			
❑ MGM E-3354 [M]		1956	60.00
HIGHLIGHTS IN JAZZ: TWELFTH ANNIVERSARY CONCERT			
❑ Stash ST-254		1985	25.00
THE HISTORIC DONAUESCHINGEN JAZZ CONCERT 1957			
❑ Pausa 7081		198?	25.00
HISTORIC JAZZ CONCERT AT MUSIC INN			
❑ Atlantic 1298 [M]		1958	300.00
—Black label			
❑ Atlantic 1298 [M]		1961	150.00
—Multicolor label, white "fan" logo at right			
❑ Atlantic 1298 [M]		1963	50.00
—Multicolor label, black "fan" logo at right			
HISTORY OF CLASSIC JAZZ			
❑ Riverside SDP-11 [M]		1956	300.00
—Five-record set in leatherette album with booklet; records were available separately as Riverside 112, 113, 114, 115 and 116.			
HISTORY OF CLASSIC JAZZ, VOL. 1			
❑ Riverside RLP 12-112 [M]		1957	250.00
HISTORY OF CLASSIC JAZZ, VOL. 2			
❑ Riverside RLP 12-113 [M]		1957	250.00
HISTORY OF CLASSIC JAZZ, VOL. 3			
❑ Riverside RLP 12-114 [M]		1957	250.00
HISTORY OF CLASSIC JAZZ, VOL. 4			
❑ Riverside RLP 12-115 [M]		1957	250.00
HISTORY OF CLASSIC JAZZ, VOL. 5			
❑ Riverside RLP 12-116 [M]		1957	250.00
HISTORY OF JAZZ, VOL. 1: NEW ORLEANS ORIGINS			
❑ Capitol T793 [M]		1956	100.00
HISTORY OF JAZZ, VOL. 1: THE SOLID SOUTH			
❑ Capitol H239 [10]		1950	150.00
HISTORY OF JAZZ, VOL. 2: THE GOLDEN ERA			
❑ Capitol H240 [10]		1950	150.00
HISTORY OF JAZZ, VOL. 2: THE TURBULENT '20S			
❑ Capitol T794 [M]		1956	100.00
HISTORY OF JAZZ, VOL. 3: EVERYBODY SWINGS			
❑ Capitol T795 [M]		1956	100.00
HISTORY OF JAZZ, VOL. 3: THEN CAME SWING			
❑ Capitol H241 [10]		1950	150.00
HISTORY OF JAZZ, VOL. 4: ENTER THE COOL			
❑ Capitol H242 [10]		1950	150.00
❑ Capitol T796 [M]		1956	100.00
THE HITS ARE ON VERVE			
❑ Verve V-201 [M]		1964	35.00
❑ Verve V6-201 [S]		1964	50.00
HODGE PODGE OF OFF-BEAT JAZZ			
❑ Sunbeam 1		197?	25.00
HODGE PODGE OF OFF-BEAT JAZZ, VOL. 2			
❑ Sunbeam 5		197?	25.00
HOLIDAY IN SAX			
❑ EmArcy MG-26019 [10]		1954	200.00
HOLIDAY IN TRUMPET			
❑ EmArcy MG-26015 [10]		1954	200.00
HONKERS AND BAR WALKERS			
❑ Delmark DL-438		198?	25.00
HOT CANARIES			
❑ Columbia CL2534 [10]		1954	60.00
HOT CLARINETS			
❑ Historical 25		1969	25.00
THE HOT ONES			
❑ Columbia Special Products CSP-107 [M]		1963	50.00
—Available only from Johnson Sea Horse boat dealers			
HOT PIANOS			
❑ Historical 29		1969	25.00
HOT TRUMPETS			
❑ Historical 28		1969	25.00
HOT VS. COOL: A BATTLE OF JAZZ			
❑ MGM E-211 [10]		1953	100.00
HOUSE RENT PARTY			
❑ Savoy MG-12199 [M]		1961	100.00
HOW BLUE CAN YOU GET? GREAT BLUES VOCALS IN THE JAZZ TRADITION			
❑ Bluebird 6758-1-RB		1989	30.00

Number	Title	Yr	NM
HOW HIGH THE MOON			
❑ Clef MGC-Vol.1 [M]		1955	250.00
—Reissue of 608			
❑ Clef MGC-608 [M]		1955	250.00
—Reissue of Mercury 608			
❑ Mercury MGC-608 [M]		1953	250.00
—Reissue of Vol. 1			
❑ Mercury MG-35001 [10]		1950	250.00
❑ Mercury MGC-Vol.1 [10]		1951	200.00
—Reissue of 35001			
(I GOT NO KICK AGAINST) MODERN JAZZ			
❑ GRP GR-9827		1995	35.00
—Jazz artists do songs made famous by the Beatles			
I LIKE JAZZ!			
❑ Columbia JZ1 [M]		1955	75.00
IMPULSE ARTISTS ON TOUR			
❑ ABC Impulse! AS-9264		197?	30.00
IMPULSIVELY!			
❑ ABC Impulse! AS-9266		197?	35.00
I'M WILD ABOUT MY LOVIN'			
❑ Historical 32		1969	25.00
IN CONCERT, VOL. 2			
❑ CTI 6049		197?	30.00
INDIVIDUALS			
❑ Columbia CG36213		197?	30.00
INFORMAL SESSION AT SQUIRREL'S BY THE SONS OF BIX			
❑ Paramount LP-104 [10]		1954	150.00
IN FROM THE STORM: THE MUSIC OF JIMI HENDRIX			
❑ RCA Victor 68233-1 [PD]		1995	30.00
—Includes Sting (with many jazz and rock musicians); limited edition picture disc (no regular U.S. vinyl exists)			
INTERCOLLEGIATE MUSIC FESTIVAL, VOL. 1			
❑ ABC Impulse! AS-9145 [S]		1968	30.00
❑ Impulse! A-9145 [M]		1967	100.00
❑ Impulse! AS-9145 [S]		1967	35.00
INTERNATIONAL JAM SESSIONS			
❑ Xanadu 122		197?	25.00
INTERNATIONAL JAZZ WORKSHOP			
❑ EmArcy MGE-26002 [M]		1964	100.00
❑ EmArcy SRE-66002 [S]		1964	100.00
INTERPLAY FOR TWO TRUMPETS AND TWO TENORS			
❑ Fantasy OJC-292		1988	25.00
❑ Prestige PRLP-7112 [M]		1957	300.00
INTRODUCTION TO JAZZ			
❑ Decca DL8244 [M]		1956	150.00
I REMEMBER BEBOP			
❑ Columbia C235381		197?	35.00
IRREPRESSIBLE IMPULSES			
❑ ABC Impulse! IMP-1972		1972	35.00
ISLES OF JAZZ			
❑ Discovery DL-2010 [10]		1954	250.00
ITALIAN JAZZ STARS			
❑ Angel ANG-60001 [10]		1955	100.00
IVY LEAGUE JAZZ			
❑ Decca DL8282 [M]		1956	150.00
❑ Golden Crest GC-3039 [M]		1958	50.00
JAMMING AT RUDI'S, VOL. 1			
❑ Circle L-407 [M]		1951	40.00
JAMMING AT RUDI'S, VOL. 2			
❑ Circle L-410 [M]		1951	40.00
JAMMIN' IN SWINGVILLE			
❑ Prestige 24051		197?	35.00
JAM SESSION #1			
❑ Clef MGC-4001 [M]		1953	250.00
❑ Clef MGC-601 [M]		1954	200.00
❑ Clef MGC-651 [M]		1955	200.00
—Reissue of 4001			
❑ Mercury MGC-601 [M]		1953	250.00
❑ Verve MGV-8049 [M]		1956	350.00
—Reissue of Clef 651			
JAM SESSION #2			
❑ Clef MGC-4002 [M]		1953	250.00
❑ Clef MGC-652 [M]		1955	200.00
—Reissue of 4002			
❑ Clef MGC-602 [M]		1954	200.00
❑ Mercury MGC-602 [M]		1953	250.00
❑ Verve MGV-8050 [M]		1956	350.00
—Reissue of Clef 652			
JAM SESSION #3			
❑ Clef MGC-653 [M]		1955	200.00
—Reissue of 4003			

Number	Title	Yr	NM
❑ Clef MGC-4003 [M]		1953	250.00
❑ Verve MGV-8051 [M]		1956	350.00
—Reissue of Clef 653			
JAM SESSION #4			
❑ Clef MGC-654 [M]		1955	200.00
—Reissue of 4004			
❑ Clef MGC-4004 [M]		1953	250.00
❑ Verve MGV-8052 [M]		1956	350.00
—Reissue of Clef 654			
JAM SESSION #5			
❑ Clef MGC-655 [M]		1955	200.00
—Reissue of 4005			
❑ Clef MGC-4005 [M]		1953	250.00
❑ Verve MGV-8053 [M]		1956	350.00
—Reissue of Clef 655			
JAM SESSION #6			
❑ Clef MGC-656 [M]		1955	200.00
—Reissue of 4006			
❑ Clef MGC-4006 [M]		1953	250.00
❑ Verve MGV-8054 [M]		1956	350.00
—Reissue of Clef 656			
JAM SESSION #7			
❑ Clef MGC-677 [M]		1955	200.00
❑ Verve MGV-8062 [M]		1957	300.00
—Reissue of Clef 677			
JAM SESSION #8			
❑ Clef MGC-711 [M]		1955	200.00
❑ Verve MGV-8094 [M]		1957	300.00
—Reissue of Clef 711			
JAM SESSION #9			
❑ Verve MGV-8196 [M]		1957	150.00
JAM SESSION			
❑ Clef MGC-4001/7 [M]		1953	350.00
—Boxed set containing 4001-4007			
❑ EmArcy MG-36002 [M]		1954	200.00
JAM SESSION, VOL. 2			
❑ Skylark SKLP-12 [10]		1954	250.00
JAM SESSION AT CARNEGIE HALL			
❑ Columbia CL557 [M]		1954	60.00
JAM SESSION AT COMMODORE			
❑ Commodore FL-30006 [M]		1951	40.00
JAM SESSION COAST TO COAST			
❑ Columbia CL547 [M]		1954	60.00
THE JAM SESSIONS: MONTREUX '77			
❑ Fantasy OJC-385		1989	25.00
❑ Pablo Live 2620105		1978	35.00
THE JATP ALL-STARS: FUNKY BLUES			
❑ Verve V-8486 [M]		1962	50.00
❑ Verve V6-8486 [S]		1962	60.00
THE JATP ALL STARS: HOW HIGH THE MOON			
❑ Verve VSP-15 [M]		1966	30.00
❑ Verve VSPS-15 [R]		1966	20.00
THE JATP ALL STARS: PERDIDO			
❑ Verve VSP-16 [M]		1966	30.00
❑ Verve VSPS-16 [R]		1966	20.00
THE JATP ALL-STARS AT THE OPERA HOUSE			
❑ Verve MGV-8267 [M]		1958	120.00
❑ Verve MGVS-6029 [S]		1960	100.00
❑ Verve V-8267 [M]		1961	40.00
❑ Verve V6-8267 [S]		1961	30.00
❑ Verve V-8489 [M]		1962	50.00
❑ Verve V6-8489 [S]		1962	60.00
JAZZ			
❑ Halo 50242 [M]		1957	35.00
❑ Mainstream MRL-408		197?	30.00
❑ Royale 1883 [10]		195?	30.00
JAZZ, SKIFFLE AND JUG STYLE			
❑ Herwin 113		197?	30.00
JAZZ, VOL. 1: THE SOUTH			
❑ Folkways FP-53/4 [M]		1951	150.00
❑ Folkways FJ-2801 [M]		197?	30.00
JAZZ, VOL. 2: THE BLUES			
❑ Folkways FP-55/6 [M]		1951	40.00
❑ Folkways FJ-2802 [M]		197?	30.00
JAZZ, VOL. 3: NEW ORLEANS			
❑ Folkways FP-57/8 [M]		1951	40.00
❑ Folkways FJ-2803 [M]		197?	30.00
JAZZ, VOL. 4: JAZZ SINGERS			
❑ Folkways FP-59/60 [M]		1951	40.00
❑ Folkways FJ-2804 [M]		197?	30.00
JAZZ, VOL. 5: CHICAGO			
❑ Folkways FP-63/4 [M]		1951	40.00
❑ Folkways FJ-2805 [M]		197?	30.00
JAZZ, VOL. 6: CHICAGO #2			
❑ Folkways FP-65/6 [M]		1951	40.00
❑ Folkways FJ-2806 [M]		197?	30.00

Number	Title	Yr	NM

JAZZ, VOL. 7: NEW YORK 1922-1934
- ❏ Folkways FP-67/8 [M] — 1951 — 40.00
- ❏ Folkways FJ-2807 [M] — 197? — 30.00

JAZZ, VOL. 8: BIG BANDS BEFORE 1938
- ❏ Folkways FP-69/70 [M] — 1951 — 40.00
- ❏ Folkways FJ-2808 [M] — 197? — 30.00

JAZZ, VOL. 9: PIANO
- ❏ Folkways FP-71/2 [M] — 1951 — 40.00
- ❏ Folkways FJ-2809 [M] — 197? — 30.00

JAZZ, VOL. 10: BOOGIE WOOGIE, JUMP, KANSAS CITY
- ❏ Folkways FP-73/4 [M] — 1951 — 40.00
- ❏ Folkways FJ-2810 [M] — 197? — 30.00

JAZZ, VOL. 11: ADDENDA
- ❏ Folkways FP-75/6 [M] — 1951 — 40.00
- ❏ Folkways FJ-2811 [M] — 197? — 30.00

JAZZ: THE 60S, VOLUME 1
- ❏ Pacific Jazz PJ-LA893-H — 1977 — 25.00

JAZZ: THE 60S, VOLUME 2
- ❏ Pacific Jazz PJ-LA895-H — 1977 — 25.00

JAZZ A LA MIDNIGHT
- ❏ Hall of Fame 608 — 197? — 12.00
- ❏ Jazztone J-1282 [M] — 1957 — 60.00

JAZZ A LA MOOD
- ❏ Jazztone J-1254 [M] — 1957 — 60.00

JAZZ ALL STARS, VOL. 1
- ❏ Who's Who in Jazz 21010 — 197? — 30.00

JAZZ AMERICANA
- ❏ Tampa TP-11 [M] — 1957 — 300.00
—Colored vinyl
- ❏ Tampa TP-11 [M] — 1958 — 150.00
—Black vinyl

JAZZ AND POPS FROM THE SOVIET UNION
- ❏ Colosseum CRLP-171 [M] — 1955 — 40.00

JAZZ ANTHOLOGY OF WEST COAST JAZZ
- ❏ Jazztone J-1243 [M] — 1957 — 300.00
- ❏ Mercury MG-35002 [10] — 1950 — 250.00
—Reissue of Arco 4

JAZZ AT CARNEGIE HALL, VOLUME 2
- ❏ Arco AL-8 [10] — 195? — 80.00

JAZZ AT COLUMBIA -- COLLECTORS ITEMS
- ❏ Columbia CB-16 [M] — 195? — 25.00
—Columbia Record Club "bonus record" in generic sleeve with die-cut circle in middle

JAZZ AT COLUMBIA -- DIXIELAND
- ❏ Columbia CB-8 [M] — 195? — 25.00
—Columbia Record Club "bonus record" in generic sleeve with die-cut circle in middle

JAZZ AT JAZZ LTD.
- ❏ Atlantic 1338 [M] — 1961 — 150.00
—Multicolor label, white "fan" logo at right

JAZZ AT PRESERVATION HALL
- ❏ Atlantic 1408 [M] — 1964 — 30.00
- ❏ Atlantic SD1408 [S] — 1964 — 35.00

JAZZ AT PRESERVATION HALL, VOL. 2
- ❏ Atlantic 1409 [M] — 1964 — 30.00
- ❏ Atlantic SD1409 [S] — 1964 — 35.00

JAZZ AT PRESERVATION HALL, VOL. 3
- ❏ Atlantic 1410 [M] — 1964 — 30.00
- ❏ Atlantic SD1410 [S] — 1964 — 35.00

JAZZ AT STORYVILLE
- ❏ Paradox LP-6003 [10] — 1951 — 100.00
- ❏ Storyville STLP-319 [10] — 1955 — 150.00

JAZZ AT STORYVILLE, VOL. 3
- ❏ Savoy MG-15019 [10] — 1953 — 150.00

JAZZ AT STORYVILLE, VOL. 4
- ❏ Savoy MG-15020 [10] — 1953 — 150.00

JAZZ AT THE BOSTON ARTS FESTIVAL
- ❏ Storyville STLP-311 [10] — 1954 — 150.00

JAZZ AT THE HOLLYWOOD BOWL
- ❏ Verve MGV-8231-2 [M] — 1958 — 100.00
- ❏ Verve V-8231-2 [M] — 1961 — 60.00

JAZZ AT THE NEW SCHOOL
- ❏ Chiaroscuro 110 — 197? — 35.00

JAZZ AT THE PHILHARMONIC
- ❏ Stinson SLP-23 [10] — 195? — 80.00
—Black vinyl
- ❏ Stinson SLP-23 [10] — 195? — 80.00
—Opaque red vinyl
- ❏ Stinson SLP-23 [10] — 1950 — 200.00
—See-through red vinyl; the first pressing of the first volume to be issued
- ❏ Stinson SLP-23 [10] — 195? — 25.00

JAZZ AT THE PHILHARMONIC, NEW VOLUME 2

- ❏ Clef MGC-Vol.2 [M] — 1955 — 250.00
—Side 1 is the 10-inch Vol. 2; Side 2 is the 10-inch Vol. 3

JAZZ AT THE PHILHARMONIC, NEW VOLUME 3
- ❏ Clef MGC-Vol.3 [M] — 1955 — 250.00
—Side 1 is the 10-inch Vol. 4; Side 2 is the 10-inch Vol. 5

JAZZ AT THE PHILHARMONIC, NEW VOLUME 4
- ❏ Clef MGC-Vol.4 [M] — 1955 — 250.00
—Combines the 10-inch Vol. 6 and Vol. 14 on one record

JAZZ AT THE PHILHARMONIC, NEW VOLUME 5
- ❏ Clef MGC-Vol.5 [M] — 1955 — 250.00
—Combines the 10-inch Vol. 7, 10 and 11 on one record

JAZZ AT THE PHILHARMONIC, NEW VOLUME 6
- ❏ Clef MGC-Vol.6 [M] — 1955 — 250.00
—Combines the 10-inch Vol. 8 and Vol. 9 on one record

JAZZ AT THE PHILHARMONIC, NEW VOLUME 7
- ❏ Clef MGC-Vol.7 [M] — 1955 — 250.00
—Combines the 10-inch Vol. 12 and 13 on one record

JAZZ AT THE PHILHARMONIC, VOL. 2
- ❏ Verve MGV-Vol.2 [M] — 1957 — 300.00
—Reissue of 12-inch Clef Vol. 2

JAZZ AT THE PHILHARMONIC, VOL. 3
- ❏ Verve MGV-Vol.3 [M] — 1957 — 300.00
—Reissue of 12-inch Clef Vol. 3

JAZZ AT THE PHILHARMONIC, VOL. 4
- ❏ Verve MGV-Vol.4 [M] — 1957 — 300.00
—Reissue of 12-inch Clef Vol. 4

JAZZ AT THE PHILHARMONIC, VOL. 5
- ❏ Verve MGV-Vol.5 [M] — 1957 — 300.00
—Reissue of 12-inch Clef Vol. 5

JAZZ AT THE PHILHARMONIC, VOL. 6
- ❏ Verve MGV-Vol.6 [M] — 1957 — 300.00
—Reissue of 12-inch Clef Vol. 6

JAZZ AT THE PHILHARMONIC, VOL. 7
- ❏ Verve MGV-Vol.7 [M] — 1957 — 300.00
—Reissue of 12-inch Clef Vol. 7

JAZZ AT THE PHILHARMONIC, VOL. 8
- ❏ Verve MGV-Vol.8 [M] — 1957 — 300.00
—Reissue of Clef Vol. 15

JAZZ AT THE PHILHARMONIC, VOL. 9
- ❏ Verve MGV-Vol.9 [M] — 1957 — 300.00
—Reissue of Clef Vol. 16

JAZZ AT THE PHILHARMONIC, VOL. 10
- ❏ Verve MGV-Vol.10 [M] — 1957 — 300.00
—Reissue of Clef Vol. 17

JAZZ AT THE PHILHARMONIC, VOL. 11
- ❏ Verve MGV-Vol.11 [M] — 1957 — 300.00
—Reissue of Clef Vol. 18
- ❏ Clef MGC-Vol.2 [10] — 1953 — 350.00
—Reissue of Mercury Vol. 2
- ❏ Mercury MGC-Vol.2 [10] — 1951 — 200.00
—Reissue of 35003
- ❏ Mercury MG-35003 [10] — 1950 — 250.00
—Reissue of Arco 1
- ❏ Clef MGC-Vol.3 [10] — 1953 — 350.00
—Reissue of Mercury Vol. 3
- ❏ Mercury MGC-Vol.3 [10] — 1951 — 200.00
—Reissue of 35004
- ❏ Mercury MG-35004 [10] — 1950 — 250.00
—Reissue of Arco 2

JAZZ AT THE PHILHARMONIC, VOLUME 4
- ❏ Clef MGC-Vol.4 [10] — 1953 — 350.00
—Reissue of Mercury Vol. 4
- ❏ Mercury MGC-Vol.4 [10] — 1951 — 200.00
—Reissue of 35005
- ❏ Mercury MG-35005 [10] — 1950 — 250.00

JAZZ AT THE PHILHARMONIC, VOLUME 5
- ❏ Clef MGC-Vol.5 [10] — 1953 — 350.00
—Reissue of Mercury Vol. 5
- ❏ Mercury MGC-Vol.5 [10] — 1951 — 200.00
—Reissue of 35006
- ❏ Mercury MG-35006 [10] — 1950 — 250.00

JAZZ AT THE PHILHARMONIC, VOLUME 6
- ❏ Clef MGC-Vol.6 [10] — 1953 — 350.00
—Reissue of Mercury Vol. 6
- ❏ Mercury MGC-Vol.6 [10] — 1951 — 200.00
—Reissue of 35007
- ❏ Mercury MG-35007 [10] — 1950 — 250.00

JAZZ AT THE PHILHARMONIC, VOLUME 7
- ❏ Clef MGC-Vol.7 [10] — 1953 — 350.00
—Reissue of Mercury Vol. 7
- ❏ Mercury MGC-Vol.7 [10] — 1951 — 200.00
—Reissue of 35008
- ❏ Mercury MG-35008 [10] — 1950 — 250.00

JAZZ AT THE PHILHARMONIC, VOLUME 8
- ❏ Clef MGC-Vol.8 [10] — 1953 — 350.00
—Reissue of Mercury Vol. 8
- ❏ Mercury MGC-Vol.8 [10] — 1951 — 200.00
—Reissue of 35000
- ❏ Mercury MG-35000 [10] — 1950 — 250.00

JAZZ AT THE PHILHARMONIC, VOLUME 9
- ❏ Clef MGC-Vol.9 [10] — 1953 — 350.00
—Reissue of Mercury Vol. 9
- ❏ Mercury MGC-Vol.9 [10] — 1951 — 200.00
—Reissue of 35009
- ❏ Mercury MG-35009 [10] — 1950 — 250.00

JAZZ AT THE PHILHARMONIC, VOLUME 10
- ❏ Clef MGC-Vol.10 [10] — 1953 — 350.00
—Reissue of Mercury Vol. 10
- ❏ Mercury MGC-Vol.10 [10] — 1951 — 200.00
—Reissue of 35010
- ❏ Mercury MG-35010 [10] — 1950 — 300.00

JAZZ AT THE PHILHARMONIC, VOLUME 11
- ❏ Clef MGC-Vol.11 [10] — 1953 — 350.00
—Reissue of Mercury Vol. 11
- ❏ Mercury MGC-Vol.11 [10] — 1951 — 200.00
—Reissue of 35011
- ❏ Mercury MG-35011 [10] — 1950 — 250.00

JAZZ AT THE PHILHARMONIC, VOLUME 12
- ❏ Clef MGC-Vol.12 [10] — 1953 — 350.00
—Reissue of Mercury Vol. 12
- ❏ Mercury MGC-Vol.12 [10] — 1951 — 200.00

JAZZ AT THE PHILHARMONIC, VOLUME 13
- ❏ Clef MGC-Vol.13 [10] — 1953 — 350.00
—Reissue of Mercury Vol. 13
- ❏ Mercury MGC-Vol.13 [10] — 1951 — 200.00

JAZZ AT THE PHILHARMONIC, VOLUME 14
- ❏ Clef MGC-Vol.14 [10] — 1953 — 350.00
—Reissue of Mercury Vol. 14
- ❏ Mercury MGC-Vol.14 [10] — 1951 — 200.00

JAZZ AT THE PHILHARMONIC, VOLUME 15
- ❏ Clef MGC-Vol.15 [10] — 1954 — 300.00
—Boxed set of new material with program
- ❏ Clef MGC-Vol.15 [10] — 1953 — 350.00
—Reissue of Mercury Vol. 15
- ❏ Mercury MGC-Vol.15 [10] — 1951 — 200.00

JAZZ AT THE PHILHARMONIC, VOLUME 16
- ❏ Clef MGC-Vol.16 [M] — 1954 — 300.00
—Boxed set of new material with program

JAZZ AT THE PHILHARMONIC, VOLUME 17
- ❏ Clef MGC-Vol.17 [M] — 1955 — 300.00
—Boxed set of new material with photo booklet

JAZZ AT THE PHILHARMONIC, VOLUME 18
- ❏ Clef MGC-Vol.18 [M] — 1955 — 300.00
—Boxed set of new material with booklet

JAZZ AT THE PHILHARMONIC: BIRD & PRES, CARNEGIE HALL 1949
- ❏ Verve 815150-1 — 1984 — 25.00

JAZZ AT THE PHILHARMONIC: BIRD & PRES, THE '46 CONCERTS
- ❏ Verve 833565-1 — 198? — 30.00
- ❏ Verve VE-2-2518 — 197? — 35.00

JAZZ AT THE PHILHARMONIC: BLUES IN CHICAGO, 1955
- ❏ Verve 815155-1 — 1984 — 25.00

JAZZ AT THE PHILHARMONIC: CARNEGIE BLUES
- ❏ Verve 825101-1 — 1985 — 25.00

JAZZ AT THE PHILHARMONIC: HARTFORD 1953
- ❏ Pablo Live 2308240 — 198? — 25.00

JAZZ AT THE PHILHARMONIC: HISTORIC RECORDINGS
- ❏ Verve VE-2-2504 — 197? — 35.00

JAZZ AT THE PHILHARMONIC: IN TOKYO 1983
- ❏ Pablo Live 2620117 — 1984 — 25.00

JAZZ AT THE PHILHARMONIC: LONDON 1969
- ❏ Pablo Live 2620119 — 198? — 30.00

JAZZ AT THE PHILHARMONIC: MONTREUX '75
- ❏ Pablo 2310748 — 197? — 35.00

JAZZ AT THE PHILHARMONIC: NORGRAN BLUES

Number	Title	Yr	NM

1950
- Verve 815151-1 — 1984 — 25.00

JAZZ AT THE PHILHARMONIC: ONE O'CLOCK JUMP 1953
- Verve 815153-1 — 1984 — 25.00

JAZZ AT THE PHILHARMONIC: THE 1940S
- Verve UMV-9070/2 — 197? — 30.00

JAZZ AT THE PHILHARMONIC: THE CHALLENGES, 1954
- Verve 815154-1 — 1984 — 25.00

JAZZ AT THE PHILHARMONIC: THE COLEMAN HAWKINS SET
- Verve 815148-1 — 1984 — 25.00

JAZZ AT THE PHILHARMONIC: THE DRUM BATTLE
- Verve 815146-1 — 1984 — 25.00

JAZZ AT THE PHILHARMONIC: THE ELLA FITZGERALD SET
- Verve 815147-1 — 1984 — 25.00

JAZZ AT THE PHILHARMONIC: THE EXCITING BATTLE -- STOCKHOLM '55
- Pablo 2310713 — 197? — 30.00

JAZZ AT THE PHILHARMONIC: THE GETZ & J.J. SET
- Verve 825100-1 — 1985 — 25.00

JAZZ AT THE PHILHARMONIC: THE OSCAR PETERSON SET
- Verve 825099-1 — 1985 — 25.00

JAZZ AT THE PHILHARMONIC: THE RAREST CONCERTS
- Verve 815149-1 — 1984 — 25.00

JAZZ AT THE PHILHARMONIC: TRUMPET BATTLE, 1952
- Verve 815152-1 — 1984 — 25.00

JAZZ AT THE PHILHARMONIC ALL STARS
- American Recording Society G-416 [M] — 1957 — 60.00

JAZZ AT THE PHILHARMONIC IN EUROPE
- Verve V6-8823 — 197? — 50.00

JAZZ AT THE PHILHARMONIC IN EUROPE, VOL. 1
- Verve V-8539 [M] — 1963 — 40.00
- Verve V6-8539 [S] — 1963 — 50.00

JAZZ AT THE PHILHARMONIC IN EUROPE, VOL. 2
- Verve V-8540 [M] — 1963 — 40.00
- Verve V6-8540 [S] — 1963 — 50.00

JAZZ AT THE PHILHARMONIC IN EUROPE, VOL. 3
- Verve V-8541 [M] — 1963 — 40.00
- Verve V6-8541 [S] — 1963 — 50.00

JAZZ AT THE PHILHARMONIC IN EUROPE, VOL. 4
- Verve V-8542 [M] — 1963 — 40.00
- Verve V6-8542 [S] — 1963 — 50.00

JAZZ AT THE PHILHARMONIC IN TOKYO
- Pablo Live 2620104 — 198? — 30.00

JAZZ AT THE SANTA MONICA CIVIC '72
- Pablo 2625701 — 197? — 30.00

JAZZ BAND BALL
- Good Time Jazz L-12005 [M] — 1954 — 50.00

JAZZ BANDS 1926-30
- Historical 16 — 1967 — 25.00

JAZZ CITY PRESENTS
- Bethlehem BCP-80 [M] — 1957 — 250.00

JAZZ COMMITTEE FOR LATIN AMERICAN AFFAIRS
- FM LP-303 [M] — 1963 — 100.00
- Vee-Jay LP-303 [S] — 196? — 50.00
—All-black label with Vee Jay "brackets" logo and "STEREO" on label; most likely a reissue

JAZZ CONCERT
- Jazztone J-1219 [M] — 1956 — 60.00
- Mercury MGJC-1 [M] — 1953 — 300.00
—Combines 601 and 602 in a box
- Norgran MGN-3501-2 [M] — 1956 — 300.00
—Reissue of Mercury MGJC-1

JAZZ CONCERT WEST COAST
- Savoy MG-12012 [M] — 1955 — 150.00
- Savoy MG-12196 [M] — 1961 — 100.00

JAZZ CONFIDENTIAL
- Crown CLP-5056 [M] — 1959 — 50.00

JAZZ CORNUCOPIA
- Coral CRL57149 [M] — 1958 — 60.00

JAZZ CRITICS' CHOICE
- Columbia Jazz Odyssey PC36807 — 198? — 25.00

JAZZ CRITICS' CHOICE: GREAT JAZZ CRITICS CHOOSE HISTORIC PERFORMANCES
- Columbia CL2126 [M] — 1964 — 30.00

JAZZ CRYSTALLIZATIONS
- Pausa 7020 — 198? — 25.00

JAZZ DANCE
- Jaguar JP-801 [10] — 1954 — 100.00

JAZZ DUPLEX
- Pax LP-6006 [10] — 1954 — 60.00

JAZZ FESTIVAL
- Imperial LP-9233 [M] — 1963 — 175.00
- Imperial LP-12233 [S] — 1963 — 175.00
- Kapp KS-1 [M] — 1956 — 50.00

JAZZ FESTIVAL, VOLUME 2
- Imperial LP-9238 [M] — 1963 — 175.00
- Imperial LP-12238 [S] — 1963 — 175.00

JAZZ FESTIVAL IN HI-FI: NEAR IN AND FAR OUT
- Warner Bros. W1281 [M] — 1959 — 60.00

JAZZ FESTIVAL IN STEREO: NEAR IN AND FAR OUT
- Warner Bros. WS1281 [S] — 1959 — 60.00

JAZZ FOR ART'S SAKE
- Dotted Eighth 101 [M] — 195? — 40.00

JAZZ FOR A SUNDAY AFTERNOON
- Solid State SS-18027 — 1968 — 35.00

JAZZ FOR A SUNDAY AFTERNOON, VOL. 2
- Solid State SS-18028 — 1968 — 35.00

JAZZ FOR A SUNDAY AFTERNOON, VOL. 3
- Solid State SS-18037 — 1968 — 35.00

JAZZ FOR A SUNDAY AFTERNOON, VOL. 4
- Solid State SS-18052 — 1969 — 35.00

JAZZ FOR HI-FI LOVERS
- Dawn DLP-1124 [M] — 1958 — 150.00

JAZZ FOR LOVERS
- Riverside RLP 12-244 [M] — 1957 — 300.00

JAZZ FOR PEOPLE WHO HATE JAZZ
- RCA Victor LJM-1008 [M] — 1954 — 100.00

JAZZ FOR PLAYBOYS
- Savoy Jazz SJC-412 — 1985 — 25.00

JAZZ FOR PLAYGIRLS
- Savoy Jazz SJC-413 — 1985 — 25.00

JAZZ FOR SURF-NIKS
- Bethlehem BCP-6073 [M] — 1961 — 250.00

JAZZ FROM DOWN UNDER
- Jaguar JP-803 [10] — 1954 — 100.00

JAZZ FROM NEW YORK, 1928-32
- Historical 33 — 1969 — 25.00

JAZZ FROM SWEDEN
- Discovery DL-2002 [10] — 1953 — 300.00

JAZZ FROM THE FAMOUS DOOR
- GHB GHB-116 — 197? — 25.00

JAZZ GALA CONCERT
- Atlantic SD1693 — 197? — 30.00

JAZZ GIANTS
- Biograph 3002 — 196? — 30.00

THE JAZZ GIANTS
- Norgran MGN-1056 [M] — 1956 — 500.00

JAZZ GIANTS, VOL. 1
- EmArcy MG-36048 [M] — 1955 — 200.00
- Trip 5504 — 197? — 25.00

JAZZ GIANTS, VOL. 2: THE PIANO PLAYERS
- EmArcy MG-36049 [M] — 1955 — 200.00

JAZZ GIANTS, VOL. 2 (REEDS)
- Trip 5518 — 197? — 25.00

JAZZ GIANTS, VOL. 3
- Trip 5538 — 197? — 25.00

JAZZ GIANTS, VOL. 3: REEDS, PART 1
- EmArcy MG-36050 [M] — 1955 — 200.00

JAZZ GIANTS, VOL. 3: REEDS, PART 2
- EmArcy MG-36051 [M] — 1955 — 200.00

JAZZ GIANTS, VOL. 3 (REEDS)
- Trip 5555 — 197? — 25.00

JAZZ GIANTS, VOL. 4: FOLK BLUES
- EmArcy MG-36052 [M] — 1955 — 200.00

JAZZ GIANTS, VOL. 5: BRASS
- EmArcy MG-36053 [M] — 1955 — 200.00

JAZZ GIANTS, VOL. 6: MODERN SWEDES
- EmArcy MG-36054 [M] — 1955 — 200.00

JAZZ GIANTS, VOL. 7: DIXIELAND
- EmArcy MG-36055 [M] — 1955 — 200.00

JAZZ GIANTS, VOL. 8: DRUM ROLE
- EmArcy MG-36071 [M] — 1956 — 200.00

JAZZ GIANTS '56
- Verve UMV-2511 — 197? — 15.00

THE JAZZ GIANTS '56
- Verve MGV-8146 [M] — 1957 — 150.00
- Verve V-8146 [M] — 1961 — 50.00

JAZZ GIANTS '58
- Verve MGV-8248 [M] — 1958 — 100.00
- Verve V-8248 [M] — 1961 — 60.00
- Verve UMV-2540 — 197? — 30.00

JAZZ GOES TO BROADWAY
- Kapp KL-1007 [M] — 1956 — 50.00

JAZZ GREATS
- Gateway 10111 — 197? — 30.00
- Tops L-1508 [M] — 1958 — 50.00

JAZZ GREATS!
- Allegro 737 [M] — 1958 — 60.00

JAZZ GREATS, VOL. 2
- Columbia Special Products P13230 — 1976 — 25.00
—Custom manufactured for Radio Shack

JAZZ GREATS 2
- Gateway 10112 — 197? — 30.00

JAZZ GREATS 3
- Gateway 10113 — 197? — 30.00

JAZZ HALL OF FAME, VOL. 2
- Design DLP-113 [M] — 196? — 50.00

A JAZZ HOLIDAY
- MCA MCA2-4018 — 1973 — 35.00
—Black label with rainbow

THE JAZZ HOUR
- Savoy MG-12126 [M] — 1957 — 100.00

JAZZ IN A VERTICAL GROOVE, 1925-28
- Biograph 12057 — 197? — 25.00

JAZZ IN HOLLYWOOD
- Liberty LJH-6001 [M] — 1955 — 75.00

JAZZ INTERPLAY
- Prestige PRLP-7341 [M] — 1964 — 40.00
- Prestige PRLP-7341 [R] — 1964 — 60.00

JAZZ IN THE THIRTIES
- Swing SW-8457/8 — 198? — 30.00

JAZZ IN TRANSITION
- Transition TRLP-30 [M] — 1956 — 200.00
—With booklet (deduct 1/4 if missing)

JAZZ IS BUSTING OUT ALL OVER
- Savoy MG-12123 [M] — 1957 — 100.00
- Savoy Jazz SJC-408 — 198? — 12.00

JAZZ JAMBOREE
- Halo 50229 [M] — 1957 — 50.00

JAZZ LAB
- Starlite ST-7003 [M] — 1955 — 100.00

THE JAZZ LIFE
- Candid CD-8019 [M] — 1960 — 40.00
- Candid CS-9019 [S] — 1960 — 60.00

JAZZ LIFE!
- Barnaby BR-5021 — 197? — 30.00

JAZZ LTD.
- Regal LP-11 [10] — 1951 — 100.00

THE JAZZ MAKERS
- Columbia CL1036 [M] — 1957 — 50.00

JAZZMEN -- DETROIT
- Savoy MG-12083 [M] — 1956 — 150.00

JAZZ MONTAGE
- Liberty LRP-3292 [M] — 1963 — 35.00
- Liberty LST-7292 [S] — 1963 — 50.00

JAZZ MUSIC FOR BIRDS
- Bethlehem BCP-6039 [M] — 1959 — 200.00

JAZZ MUSIC FOR PEOPLE WHO DON'T CARE ABOUT MONEY
- Bethlehem BCP-88 [M] — 1958 — 200.00

JAZZ ODYSSEY: THE SOUND OF CHICAGO
- Columbia C3L32 [M] — 1964 — 40.00

JAZZ ODYSSEY: THE SOUND OF HARLEM
- Columbia C3L33 [M] — 1964 — 40.00

JAZZ ODYSSEY: THE SOUND OF NEW ORLEANS
- Columbia C3L30 [M] — 1964 — 40.00

JAZZ OF THE FORTIES, VOL. 1
- Folkways FJ-2841 — 197? — 30.00

JAZZ OF THE ROARING 20'S
- Riverside RLP 12-801 [M] — 195? — 50.00

JAZZ OF THE ROARING TWENTIES: DANCE MUSIC OF THE CHARLESTON ERA
- Riverside RLP 12-108 [M] — 1956 — 250.00

JAZZ OF THE SIXTIES
- Vee Jay VJS-2-1008 — 1974 — 50.00

JAZZ OF TWO DECADES
- EmArcy DEM-2 [M] — 1956 — 200.00

THE JAZZOLOGY POLL WINNERS 1964
- GHB GHB-200 — 1986 — 25.00

JAZZ OMNIBUS

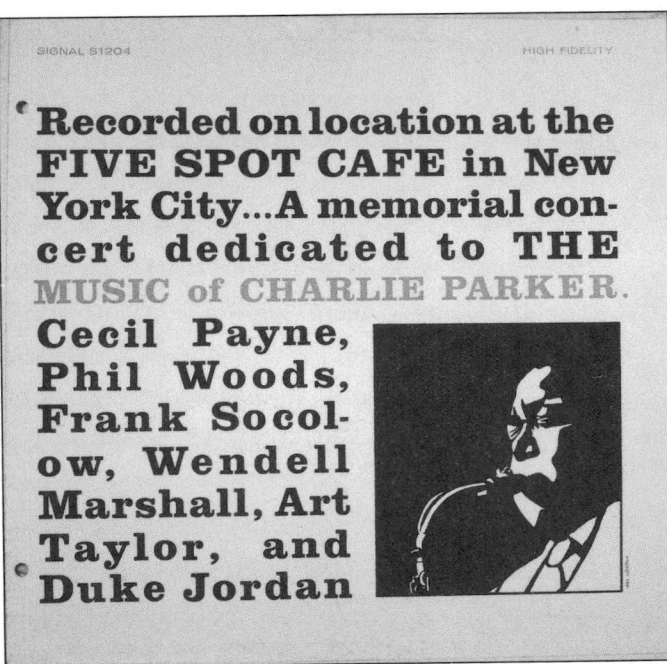

Various Artists, *Recorded on Location at the Five Spot Café in New York City… A Memorial Concert Dedicated to the Music of Charlie Parker*, Signal S1204, **$200**.

Various Artists, *Saxes, Inc.*, Warner Bros. W 1336, **$100**.

Various Artists, *The Smithsonian Collection of Classic Jazz*, Smithsonian/CSP P6-11891, six-record box set, **$40**.

Various Artists, *Something for Both Ears!*, World Pacific HFS-2, **$150**.

Number	Title	Yr	NM

Columbia CL1020 [M] — 1957 — 50.00

JAZZ ON THE AIR
Brunswick BL58048 [10] — 1953 — 100.00

JAZZ ON THE SCREEN
Fontana MGF-27532 [M] — 1965 — 40.00
Fontana SRF-67532 [S] — 1965 — 40.00

JAZZ PIANISTS GALORE
Jazz: West Coast JWC-506 [M] — 1956 — 150.00

THE JAZZ PIANO
RCA Victor LPM-3499 [M] — 1966 — 50.00
RCA Victor LSP-3499 [S] — 1966 — 60.00

A JAZZ PIANO ANTHOLOGY
Columbia PG32355 — 197? — 35.00

JAZZ PIANO GREATS
Folkways FJ-2852 — 197? — 30.00

JAZZ PIONEERS 1933-36
Prestige PRLP-7647 — 1969 — 35.00

JAZZ POLL WINNERS
Columbia CL1610 [M] — 1960 — 50.00

JAZZ POTPOURRI
Audiophile AP-24 [M] — 1953 — 60.00

THE JAZZ RECORD STORY
Jazzology J-82 — 197? — 25.00

THE JAZZ-ROCK-SOUL PROJECT
Riverside 3048 — 197? — 50.00

THE JAZZ ROUND
Verve VSP-24 [M] — 1966 — 35.00
Verve VSPS-24 [R] — 1966 — 25.00

A JAZZ SALUTE TO FREEDOM
Core 100 [M] — 196? — 60.00

THE JAZZ SCENE
American Recording Society G-419 [M] — 1957 — 60.00
Clef MGC-674 [M] — 1955 — 200.00
—Reissue of 4007
Clef MGC-4007 [M] — 1953 — 250.00
Clef Special Edition (no #) [10] — 1953 — 350.00
—Two 10-inch LPs in box. Buyers had the option of purchasing a collection of photos that had been used in the original 78 rpm album; add another 50 percent if these photos are included
Verve MGV-8060 [M] — 1957 — 300.00
—Reissue of Clef 674
Verve V-8060 [M] — 1961 — 40.00

JAZZ SET
Columbia Special Products CSP-217S [S] — 1965 — 25.00
—Special item for Zenith
Columbia Special Products CSP-217M [M] — 1965 — 30.00

THE JAZZ SINGERS
Prestige 24113 — 197? — 35.00

JAZZ SOUL OF "CLEOPATRA"
New Jazz NJLP-8292 [M] — 1962 — 150.00
—Purple label
New Jazz NJLP-8292 [M] — 1965 — 150.00
—Blue label, trident logo at right

THE JAZZ SOUND
Columbia Special Products CSP298 [M] — 1966 — 25.00

THE JAZZ STORY
Coral CJE-100 [M] — 195? — 100.00
—Box set; narrated by Steve Allen

JAZZ SUPER HITS
Atlantic SD1528 — 1969 — 60.00

JAZZ SUPER HITS, VOL. 2
Atlantic SD1559 — 1970 — 50.00

JAZZ SURPRISE
Crown CLP-5008 [M] — 1957 — 50.00

JAZZ SWINGS BROADWAY
Pacific Jazz PJM-404 [M] — 1956 — 100.00
World Pacific PJM-404 [M] — 1958 — 150.00

JAZZTIME, U.S.A.
MCA 4113 — 197? — 30.00

JAZZ TIME U.S.A. -- VOLUME 1
Brunswick BL54000 [M] — 1952 — 60.00

JAZZ TIME U.S.A. -- VOLUME 2
Brunswick BL54001 [M] — 1953 — 60.00

JAZZ TIME U.S.A. -- VOLUME 3
Brunswick BL54002 [M] — 1954 — 60.00

JAZZTONE SAMPLER
Jazztone J-SPEC-100 [10] — 1955 — 100.00
—With booklet

JAZZ TRUMPET, VOL. 1
Prestige 24111 — 198? — 35.00

THE JAZZ TRUMPET, VOL. 2
Prestige 24112 — 198? — 35.00

JAZZ VARIATIONS, VOL. 1
Stinson SLP-20 [10] — 195? — 60.00
Stinson SLP-20 [M] — 196? — 60.00

JAZZ VARIATIONS, VOL. 2
Stinson SLP-29 [M] — 196? — 60.00

JAZZVILLE, VOL. 1
Dawn DLP-1101 [M] — 1956 — 150.00

JAZZ VIOLINS OF THE 40S
Folkways FJ-2854 — 197? — 30.00

JAZZVISIONS: ALL STRINGS ATTACHED
Verve 841291-1 — 1989 — 30.00

JAZZVISIONS: BRIZILIAN KNIGHTS AND A LADY
Verve 841292-1 — 1989 — 30.00

JAZZVISIONS: ECHOES OF ELLINGTON, VOL. 1
Verve 841288-1 — 1989 — 30.00

JAZZVISIONS: ECHOES OF ELLINGTON, VOL. 2
Verve 841289-1 — 1989 — 30.00

JAZZVISIONS: JUMP THE BLUES AWAY
Verve 841287-1 — 1989 — 30.00

JAZZVISIONS: LATIN FAMILIA
Verve 841290-1 — 1989 — 30.00

JAZZVISIONS: RIO REVISITED
Verve 841286-1 — 1989 — 30.00

JAZZVISIONS: THE MANY FACES OF BIRD
Verve 841285-1 — 1989 — 30.00

JAZZ VOCALS AWARD ALBUM
Bethlehem BCP-6068 [M] — 1963 — 200.00

JAZZ WEST COAST, VOL. 1
Pacific Jazz JWC-500 [M] — 1956 — 100.00
World Pacific JWC-500 [M] — 1958 — 150.00

JAZZ WEST COAST, VOL. 2
Pacific Jazz JWC-501 [M] — 1956 — 100.00
World Pacific JWC-501 [M] — 1958 — 150.00

JAZZ WEST COAST, VOL. 3
Pacific Jazz JWC-507 [M] — 1957 — 100.00
World Pacific JWC-507 [M] — 1958 — 150.00

JAZZ WEST COAST, VOL. 4
World Pacific JWC-510 [M] — 1958 — 150.00
World Pacific ST-1009 [S] — 1959 — 150.00

JAZZ WEST COAST, VOL. 5
World Pacific JWC-511 [M] — 1958 — 150.00

JAZZ -- WEST COAST VOL. III
Jazztone J-1274 [M] — 195? — 30.00

JAZZ WIZARDS, VOL. 1
Herwin 106 — 197? — 30.00

JAZZ WIZARDS, VOL. 2
Herwin 107 — 197? — 30.00

JAZZ WOMEN: A FEMINIST RETROSPECTIVE
Stash ST-109 — 197? — 35.00

THE JAZZ WORLD
Columbia Special Products CSS524 [S] — 1967 — 25.00

JAZZ YEARS: 25TH ANNIVERSARY
Atlantic SD-2-316 — 197? — 35.00

A JAZZY WONDERLAND
Columbia 1P8120 — 1990 — 35.00
—Available on vinyl through Columbia House only

JINGLE BELL JAZZ
Columbia CL1893 [M] — 1962 — 50.00
Columbia CS8693 [S] — 1962 — 35.00
Columbia PC36803 — 1980 — 12.00
—Reissue of Harmony KH 32529 on the "Jazz Odyssey" series
Harmony KH32529 — 1973 — 30.00
—Reissue of CS 8693 with one track changed

JOHN COLTRANE IN THE WINNER'S CIRCLE
Bethlehem BCP-6066 [M] — 1961 — 150.00
—Reissue of 6024 with new title

JOHN HAMMOND PRESENTS "FROM SPIRITUALS TO SWING" AT CARNEGIE HALL 1938
Vanguard VRS-8523 [M] — 1959 — 120.00

JOHN HAMMOND PRESENTS "FROM SPIRITUALS TO SWING" AT CARNEGIE HALL 1939
Vanguard VRS-8524 [M] — 1959 — 120.00

JOURNEYS INTO JAZZ, VOL. 1
GHB GHB-65 — 197? — 25.00

JOURNEYS INTO JAZZ, VOL. 2
GHB GHB-66 — 197? — 25.00

JUST JAZZ
Imperial LP-9246 [M] — 1963 — 175.00
Imperial LP-12246 [S] — 1963 — 175.00

KANSAS CITY IN THE '30S
Capitol T1057 [M] — 1958 — 100.00

KANSAS CITY JAZZ
Decca DL8044 [M] — 1954 — 150.00

KANSAS CITY PIANO
Decca DL9226 [M] — 1967 — 60.00
Decca DL79226 [R] — 1967 — 30.00

KBIG CHOICES
World Pacific KBIG-1 [S] — 1964 — 150.00

KELLOGG'S PRESENTS…BIG BAND CLASSICS
RCA Special Products DPL1-0438(e) — 1980 — 25.00

KEYBOARD KINGS
MGM E-100 [10] — 1951 — 100.00

KEYBOARD KINGS OF JAZZ
RCA Victor LPT-4 [10] — 1951 — 40.00

KINGS AND QUEENS OF IVORY
MCA 1329 — 198? — 25.00

KINGS OF CLASSIC JAZZ
Riverside RLP 12-131 [M] — 1957 — 300.00

KINGS OF SWING
Pickwick PTP-2072 — 197? — 30.00

KINGS OF THE KEYBOARD
American Recording Society G-406 [M] — 1956 — 60.00

KNOW YOUR JAZZ
ABC-Paramount ABC-115 [M] — 1956 — 60.00

LEGENDARY BLACK JAZZ STARS IN THEIR FIRST FILMS
Biograph M-3 — 198? — 25.00

LENNY TRISTANO MEMORIAL CONCERT
Jazz Records JR-3 — 198? — 40.00

LEONARD FEATHER'S ENCYCLOPEDIA OF JAZZ
Vee Jay VJSP-400 — 1977 — 30.00

LEONARD FEATHER'S ENCYCLOPEDIA OF JAZZ, VOLUME ONE: GIANTS OF THE SAXOPHONE
Vee Jay LP-2501 [M] — 1964 — 50.00
Vee Jay VJS-2501 [S] — 1964 — 60.00

LEONARD FEATHER'S ENCYCLOPEDIA OF JAZZ OF THE '60S: BLUES BAG
Vee Jay LP-2506 [M] — 1964 — 50.00

LIGHTS OUT SAN FRANCISCO
Blue Thumb BT6004 — 1970 — 60.00

LISTEN TO OUR STORY
Brunswick BL59001 [10] — 1950 — 120.00

LISTEN TO OUR VISION
Gramavision 18-8509 — 1986 — 25.00

LIVE AT THE FESTIVAL
Enja 2030 — 197? — 35.00

THE LIVELY SOUND OF UNIVERSITY
Capitol Custom (no #) [M] — 1966 — 80.00
—"Mustang Sweepstakes Prize Winner" on front cover

LIVING MUSIC COLLECTION '86
Living Music LM-0006 — 1986 — 25.00

LOADED
Savoy MG-12074 [M] — 1956 — 100.00

LONDON BROIL
Angel ANG-60004 [10] — 1955 — 100.00

A LOOK AT YESTERDAY
Mainstream 56025 [M] — 1965 — 60.00
Mainstream S-6025 [R] — 1965 — 30.00

A LOT OF YARN BUT A WELL-KNITTED JAZZ ALBUM
Bethlehem BCP-91 [M] — 1958 — 200.00

LULLABY OF BIRDLAND
RCA Victor LPM-1146 [M] — 1955 — 100.00

LUSTY MOODS
Moodsville MVLP-37 [M] — 1963 — 40.00
—Green label
Moodsville MVST-37 [S] — 1963 — 40.00
—Green label
Moodsville MVLP-37 [M] — 1965 — 50.00
—Blue label, trident logo at right
Moodsville MVST-37 [S] — 1965 — 50.00
—Blue label, trident logo at right
Status ST-8319 — 1965 — 60.00

THE MAGIC HORN
RCA Victor LPM-1332 [M] — 1956 — 40.00

MAGNAVOX PRESENTS A REPRISE OF GREAT HITS
Reprise PRO578 — 1973 — 25.00

MAMBO JAZZ
Prestige PRLP-135 [10] — 1952 — 300.00

MANASSAS JAZZ FESTIVAL
Jazzology J-17 — 196? — 25.00

THE MAN WITH A HORN
Decca DL5191 [10] — 1950 — 100.00

THE MANY FACES OF THE BLUES
Savoy MG-12125 [M] — 1957 — 100.00

Number Title	Yr	NM
MASTER JAZZ PIANO		
❏ Master Jazz 8105	197?	30.00
MASTER JAZZ PIANO, VOL. 2		
❏ Master Jazz 8108	197?	30.00
MASTER JAZZ PIANO, VOL. 3		
❏ Master Jazz 8117	197?	30.00
MASTER JAZZ PIANO, VOL. 4		
❏ Master Jazz 8129	197?	30.00
MASTERS OF THE MODERN PIANO		
❏ Verve VE-2-2514	197?	35.00
THE MELLOW MOODS		
❏ RCA Victor LPM-1365 [M]	1956	40.00
MELLOW THE MOOD/JAZZ IN A MELLOW MOOD		
❏ Blue Note BLP-5001 [10]	1951	200.00
MEMORABLE SESSIONS IN JAZZ		
❏ Blue Note BLP-5026 [10]	1953	200.00
MEMPHIS JAZZ FESTIVAL		
❏ Jazzology J-134	198?	25.00
THE MERCURY 40TH ANNIVERSARY V.S.O.P. ALBUM		
❏ Mercury 824116-1	1985	100.00
THE METRONOME ALL-STARS		
❏ Columbia CL2528 [10]	1954	60.00
METRONOME ALL-STARS		
❏ Harmony HL7044 [M]	1957	60.00
❏ RCA Camden CAL-426 [M]	1958	60.00
METRONOME ALL STARS 1956		
❏ Clef MGC-743 [M]	1956	200.00
❏ Verve MGV-8030 [M]	1957	150.00
❏ Verve V-8030 [M]	1961	50.00
MIDNIGHT JAZZ AT CARNEGIE HALL		
❏ Verve MGV-8189-2 [M]	1957	150.00
❏ Verve V-8189-2 [M]	1961	60.00
MILESTONE JAZZSTARS IN CONCERT		
❏ Milestone M-55006	198?	35.00
MILESTONE TWOFER GIANTS		
❏ Milestone MSP-1	197?	35.00
MISSING LINKS		
❏ MCA 42206	1988	25.00
THE MODERN IDIOM		
❏ Capitol H325 [10]	1952	200.00
MODERN JAZZ		
❏ London LL1185 [M]	1955	250.00
❏ Tops L-1521 [M]	1958	250.00
MODERN JAZZ CONCERT		
❏ Adventures in Sound WL-127 [M]	1958	250.00
MODERN JAZZ FESTIVAL		
❏ Harmony HL7196 [M]	1958	250.00
MODERN JAZZ GALLERY		
❏ Kapp KXL-5001 [M]	195?	25.00
MODERN JAZZ GREATS		
❏ Crown CLP-5212 [M]	196?	35.00
MODERN JAZZ HALL OF FAME		
❏ Design DLP-29 [M]	196?	30.00
❏ Design DLPS-29 [R]	196?	20.00
MODERN JAZZ PIANO		
❏ RCA Camden CAL-384 [M]	1958	250.00
MODERN JAZZ PIANO ALBUM		
❏ Savoy Jazz SJL-2247	198?	30.00
MODERN JAZZ SPECTACULAR		
❏ Jazztone J-1231 [M]	1956	200.00
MODERN JAZZ SURVEY 1: NEW YORK JAZZ		
❏ Prestige 16-5	1957	600.00
— This album plays at 16 2/3 rpm and is marked as such; white label		
MODERN JAZZ SURVEY 2: BARITONES AND FRENCH HORNS		
❏ Prestige 16-6	1957	600.00
— This album plays at 16 2/3 rpm and is marked as such; white label		
MODERN JAZZ TRUMPETS		
❏ Prestige PRLP-113 [10]	1951	250.00
MODERN MOODS		
❏ Moodsville MVLP-2 [M]	1961	150.00
— Green label		
❏ Moodsville MVLP-2 [M]	1965	80.00
— Blue label, trident logo at right		
MONARCH ALL STAR JAZZ, VOL. 1		
❏ Monarch LP-201 [10]	1952	100.00
MONARCH ALL STAR JAZZ, VOL. 2		
❏ Monarch LP-202 [10]	1952	100.00
MONARCH ALL STAR JAZZ, VOL. 3		
❏ Monarch LP-203 [10]	1952	100.00

Number Title	Yr	NM
MONARCH ALL STAR JAZZ, VOL. 4		
❏ Monarch LP-204 [10]	1952	100.00
MONARCH ALL STAR JAZZ, VOL. 5		
❏ Monarch LP-205 [10]	1952	100.00
MONDAY NIGHT AT BIRDLAND		
❏ Roulette R52015 [M]	1958	60.00
❏ Roulette SR52015 [S]	1959	60.00
MONTAGE		
❏ Savoy MG-12029 [M]	1955	150.00
THE MONTREUX '77 COLLECTION		
❏ Pablo Live 2620107	1978	125.00
THE MONTREUX COLLECTION		
❏ Pablo 2625707	197?	35.00
MONTREUX SUMMIT		
❏ Columbia JG35005	1978	35.00
MONTREUX SUMMIT, VOLUME 2		
❏ Columbia JG35090	1978	35.00
MOOD IN BLUE		
❏ Urania UJLP-1209 [M]	1955	150.00
MOOD TO BE WOOED		
❏ Cadet LP-784 [M]	1967	50.00
❏ Cadet LPS-784 [S]	1967	35.00
MORE DRUMS ON FIRE		
❏ World Pacific WP-1261 [M]	1960	150.00
❏ World Pacific ST-1022 [S]	1960	150.00
MORE LIVE ECHOES OF THE SWINGING BANDS		
❏ RCA Victor LSP-1983 [S]	1959	100.00
❏ RCA Victor LPM-1983 [M]	1959	40.00
THE MOST		
❏ Forum Circle FC-9079 [M]	1963	30.00
❏ Forum Circle FCS-9079 [S]	1963	30.00
THE MOST, VOLUME 1		
❏ Roulette R52050 [M]	1960	50.00
❏ Roulette SR52050 [S]	1960	60.00
THE MOST, VOLUME 2		
❏ Roulette R52053 [M]	1960	50.00
❏ Roulette SR52053 [S]	1960	60.00
THE MOST, VOLUME 3		
❏ Roulette R52057 [M]	1961	50.00
❏ Roulette SR52057 [S]	1961	60.00
THE MOST, VOLUME 4		
❏ Roulette R52062 [M]	1961	50.00
❏ Roulette SR52062 [S]	1961	60.00
THE MOST, VOLUME 5		
❏ Roulette R52075 [M]	1961	50.00
❏ Roulette SR52075 [S]	1961	60.00
MOTOR CITY SCENE		
❏ Bethlehem BCP-6056 [M]	1961	200.00
A MUSICAL HISTORY OF JAZZ		
❏ Grand Award GA 33-322 [M]	1955	60.00
MUSIC FOR THE BOY FRIEND…HE REALLY DIGS JAZZ		
❏ Decca DL8314 [M]	1956	120.00
MUSIC FROM THE DANCING YEARS		
❏ RCA Victor PR-112 [M]	1961	35.00
— Created for Dole Pineapple		
MUSIC FROM THE SOUTH, VOL. 1: COUNTRY BRASS BANDS		
❏ Folkways FA-2650 [M]	195?	30.00
THE MUSIC OF NEW ORLEANS, VOL. 1		
❏ Folkways FA-2461 [M]	1959	60.00
THE MUSIC OF NEW ORLEANS, VOL. 2		
❏ Folkways FA-2462 [M]	1959	60.00
THE MUSIC OF NEW ORLEANS, VOL. 3: DANCE HALLS		
❏ Folkways FA-2463 [M]	1959	60.00
THE MUSIC OF NEW ORLEANS, VOL. 4: THE BIRTH OF JAZZ		
❏ Folkways FA-2464 [M]	1959	60.00
THE MUSIC OF NEW ORLEANS, VOL. 5: NEW ORLEANS JAZZ		
❏ Folkways FA-2465 [M]	1959	60.00
❏ Status ST-8315 [M]	1965	60.00
THE NAMES OF DIXIELAND		
❏ Baronet B-108 [M]	195?	25.00
NATIVE NEW ORLEANS JAZZ		
❏ Dot DLP-3009 [M]	1956	175.00
NEW AMERICAN MUSIC VOL. 1: JAZZ		
❏ Folkways FA-33901	197?	30.00
NEW BLUE HORNS		
❏ Fantasy OJC-256	198?	25.00
❏ Riverside RLP 12-294 [M]	1958	300.00
THE NEW BREED		
❏ ABC Impulse! IA-9339	197?	35.00
NEW CHAMBER JAZZ		

Number Title	Yr	NM
❏ Epic LN1124 [10]	1955	100.00
NEW FACES AT NEWPORT		
❏ Metrojazz E-1005	1958	150.00
❏ Metrojazz SE-1005 [S]	1958	120.00
NEW MUSIC: SECOND WAVES		
❏ Savoy Jazz SJL-2235	198?	30.00
NEW ORLEANS: THE LIVING LEGENDS		
❏ Riverside RLP-356/7 [M]	196?	100.00
— Two records in gatefold jacket		
NEW ORLEANS: THE LIVING LEGENDS, VOL. 1		
❏ Riverside RLP-356 [M]	196?	50.00
❏ Riverside RS-9356 [R]	196?	30.00
NEW ORLEANS: THE LIVING LEGENDS, VOL. 2		
❏ Riverside RLP-357 [M]	196?	50.00
❏ Riverside RS-9357 [R]	196?	30.00
NEW ORLEANS ALL-STARS		
❏ GHB GHB-35	196?	30.00
NEW ORLEANS BRASS BANDS: DOWN YONDER		
❏ Rounder 2062	198?	25.00
NEW ORLEANS DIXIELAND		
❏ Southland SLP-216 [M]	1955	75.00
NEW ORLEANS ENCORE		
❏ Riverside RLP-2503 [10]	1954	300.00
NEW ORLEANS EXPRESS		
❏ EmArcy MG-36022 [M]	1955	200.00
NEW ORLEANS HORNS		
❏ Riverside RLP-1005 [10]	1953	300.00
NEW ORLEANS JAZZ		
❏ Decca DL5483 [10]	1953	150.00
❏ Decca DL8283 [M]	1956	120.00
NEW ORLEANS JAZZ AND HERITAGE FESTIVAL, 10TH ANNIVERSARY		
❏ Flying Fish FF-089	198?	25.00
NEW ORLEANS JAZZ AND HERITAGE FESTIVAL, 1976		
❏ Rhino R1-71111	1989	35.00
NEW ORLEANS JAZZ AT THE KITTY HALLS		
❏ Arhoolie 1013	198?	25.00
NEW ORLEANS JAZZ BABIES		
❏ Southland SLP-214 [M]	1955	75.00
NEW ORLEANS JAZZ KINGS		
❏ Southland SLP-217 [M]	1955	75.00
NEW ORLEANS JAZZ STARS		
❏ Southland SLP-211 [M]	1955	75.00
NEW ORLEANS LEGENDS		
❏ Riverside RLP 12-119 [M]	1957	350.00
NEW ORLEANS REVIVAL		
❏ Riverside RLP-1047 [10]	1954	300.00
NEW ORLEANS RHYTHM KINGS		
❏ Riverside RLP 12-102 [M]	195?	60.00
— Also see NEW ORLEANS RHYTHM KINGS in the main A-Z listings.		
NEW ORLEANS STYLE		
❏ X LVA-3029 [10]	1954	150.00
NEW ORLEANS TO LOS ANGELES		
❏ Southland SLP-215 [M]	1955	75.00
NEWPORT JAZZ FESTIVAL		
❏ RCA Victor LPM-3369 [M]	1965	35.00
❏ RCA Victor LSP-3369 [S]	1965	50.00
NEWPORT JAZZ FESTIVAL: LIVE		
❏ Columbia C238262	198?	30.00
NEWPORT JAZZ FESTIVAL ALL STARS		
❏ Atlantic SD1331 [S]	1961	150.00
— Multicolor label, white "fan" logo at right		
NEWPORT JAZZ FESTIVAL ALL-STARS		
❏ Atlantic 1331 [M]	1961	150.00
— Multicolor label, white "fan" logo at right		
NEW SOUNDS FROM SWEDEN, VOL. 1: THE DARING YOUNG SWEDES		
❏ Prestige PRLP-119 [10]	1951	400.00
A NEW VISION FROM GRAMAVISION		
❏ Gramavision 18-8510	1986	25.00
NEW VOICES		
❏ Dawn DLP-1125 [M]	1956	150.00
THE NEW WAVE IN JAZZ		
❏ ABC Impulse! AS-90 [S]	1968	30.00
❏ Impulse! A-90 [M]	1966	35.00
❏ Impulse! AS-90 [S]	1966	100.00
NEW YORK JAZZ OF THE TWENTIES		
❏ Riverside RLP-1048 [10]	1954	300.00
THE 1930S, VOL. 1		
❏ Aircheck 1	197?	25.00
1944 ESQUIRE JAZZ ALL-STARS		

Number	Title	Yr	NM
❑ Aircheck 27		197?	25.00
1947 WNEW SATURDAY NIGHT SWING SESSION			
❑ Everest Archive of Folk & Jazz 231		196?	25.00
1959 MONTEREY JAZZ FESTIVAL			
❑ Everest Archive of Folk & Jazz 239		196?	25.00
NO 'COUNT			
❑ Savoy MG-12078 [M]		1956	120.00
NO ENERGY CRISIS			
❑ ABC Impulse! AS-9267		1974	100.00
NORMAN GRANZ JAM SESSION			
❑ Verve VE-2-2508		197?	35.00
NORMAN GRANZ JAZZ CONCERT			
❑ Norgran MGN-2502 [M]		1954	300.00
❑ Norgran MGN-2501 [M]		1954	300.00
NO SOUR GRAPES, JUST PURE JAZZ			
❑ Bethlehem BCP-92 [M]		1958	200.00
NOTHING CHEESY ABOUT THIS JAZZ			
❑ Bethlehem BCP-85 [M]		1958	200.00
THE OFFICIAL GRAMMY AWARDS ARCHIVE COLLECTION (JAZZ VOCALISTS)			
❑ Franklin Mint GRAM-13		1985	60.00
THE OFFICIAL GRAMMY AWARDS ARCHIVE COLLECTION (THE BIG BAND SOUND)			
❑ Franklin Mint GRAM-7		1985	60.00
OLEO			
❑ Pausa 7025		198?	25.00
OLIO			
❑ Prestige PRLP-7084 [M]		1957	500.00
— Yellow label with W. 50th St. address			
ONE NIGHT STAND: A KEYBOARD EVENT			
❑ Columbia KC237100		198?	15.00
—Half-Speed Mastered" edition			
❑ Columbia HC247100		198?	50.00
ONE NIGHT WITH BLUE NOTE PRESERVED			
❑ Blue Note BTDK-85117		1985	60.00
ONE NIGHT WITH BLUE NOTE PRESERVED, VOL. 1			
❑ Blue Note BT-85113		1985	30.00
ONE NIGHT WITH BLUE NOTE PRESERVED, VOL. 2			
❑ Blue Note BT-85114		1985	30.00
ONE NIGHT WITH BLUE NOTE PRESERVED, VOL. 3			
❑ Blue Note BT-85115		1985	30.00
ONE NIGHT WITH BLUE NOTE PRESERVED, VOL. 4			
❑ Blue Note BT-85116		1985	30.00
—Box set containing all 4 volumes			
ONE WORLD JAZZ			
❑ Adventures in Sound WL-162 [M]		1959	100.00
❑ Adventures in Sound WS-314 [S]		1959	40.00
ON-THE-ROAD JAZZ			
❑ Riverside RLP 12-127 [M]		1957	350.00
ON THE TRAIL			
❑ Pausa 7024		198?	25.00
OPUS DE BLUES			
❑ Savoy MG-12142 [M]		1959	120.00
OPUS DE JAZZ			
❑ Savoy MG-12036 [M]		1955	150.00
OPUS IN SWING			
❑ Savoy MG-12085 [M]		1956	120.00
THE ORCHESTRA "HOUSE OF SOUND			
❑ Brunswick BL54003 [M]		1954	60.00
ORIGINAL BLUE NOTE JAZZ, VOL. 1			
❑ Blue Note B-6504		1969	50.00
ORIGINAL BLUE NOTE JAZZ, VOL. 2			
❑ Blue Note B-6506		1970	50.00
THE ORIGINAL SOUND OF THE 20'S			
❑ Columbia C3L35		1965	40.00
OUR BEST			
❑ Clef MGC-639 [M]		1955	250.00
❑ Norgran MGN-1021 [M]		1955	250.00
OUT CAME THE BLUES			
❑ MCA 1352		198?	25.00
PABLO ALL-STARS JAM: MONTREUX '77			
❑ Fantasy OJC-380		1989	25.00
❑ Pablo Live 2308210		197?	35.00
PANORAMA OF BRITISH JAZZ			
❑ Discovery DL-2001 [10]		1953	300.00
PARAMOUNT CORNET BLUES RARITIES CHICAGO 1924-27			
❑ Herwin 111		197?	30.00

Number	Title	Yr	NM
PARAMOUNT HOT JAZZ RARITIES 1926-28			
❑ Herwin 110		197?	30.00
PARLOR PIANO: BLUES AND STOMPS			
❑ Biograph 1001		197?	25.00
PARTY AFTER HOURS			
❑ Aladdin LP-703 [10]		1950	8000.00
— Red vinyl			
❑ Aladdin LP-703 [10]		1950	4000.00
— Black vinyl			
PERCUSSION PROFILES			
❑ ECM 19002		1977	30.00
PERCUSSION UNABRIDGED			
❑ Kimberly 2022 [M]		1963	50.00
❑ Kimberly 11022 [S]		1963	60.00
PERFECT FOR DANCING: ALL TEMPOS			
❑ RCA Victor LPM-1072 [M]		1954	60.00
PERFECT FOR DANCING: FOX TROTS			
❑ RCA Victor LPM-1070 [M]		1954	60.00
PERFECT FOR DANCING: JITTERBUG OR LINDY			
❑ RCA Victor LPM-1071 [M]		1954	60.00
PERIOD'S JAZZ DIGEST			
❑ Period SPL-302 [M]		1956	100.00
PERIOD'S JAZZ DIGEST VOL. 2			
❑ Period SPL-304 [M]		1955	100.00
PIANISTS GALORE			
❑ Pacific Jazz JWC-506 [M]		1957	100.00
❑ World Pacific JWC-506 [M]		1958	150.00
PIANO ARTISTRY			
❑ Audiophile AP-28 [M]		1953	60.00
PIANO GIANTS			
❑ Prestige 24052		197?	20.00
PIANO IN STYLE			
❑ MCA 1332		198?	12.00
PIANO INTERPRETATIONS			
❑ Norgran MGN-1036 [M]		1955	250.00
❑ Verve MGV-8125 [M]		1957	150.00
❑ Verve V-8125 [M]		1961	50.00
PIANO JAZZ, VOLUME 1			
❑ Brunswick BL54014 [M]		1955	75.00
PIANO JAZZ, VOLUME 2			
❑ Brunswick BL54015 [M]		1955	75.00
PIANO MODERN			
❑ Verve VSP-13 [M]		1966	35.00
❑ Verve VSPS-13 [R]		1966	25.00
PIANO MUSIC FOR PARTIES			
❑ Columbia CL603 [M]		1955	75.00
PIANO MUSIC FOR TWO			
❑ Columbia CL602 [M]		1955	75.00
PIANO ONE			
❑ Private Music 2004-1-P		1986	25.00
THE PIANO PLAYERS			
❑ Xanadu 171		197?	30.00
PIANO RAGTIME OF THE FORTIES			
❑ Herwin 403		197?	30.00
PIANO RAGTIME OF THE TEENS, TWENTIES AND THIRTIES			
❑ Herwin 402		197?	30.00
PIANO RAGTIME OF THE TEENS, TWENTIES AND THIRTIES, VOL. 2			
❑ Herwin 405		197?	30.00
PIANO RAGTIME OF THE TEENS, TWENTIES AND THIRTIES, VOL. 3			
❑ Herwin 406		197?	30.00
PIANO ROLL HALL OF FAME			
❑ Sounds 1202		196?	30.00
PIANO ROLL TRANSCRIPTIONS			
❑ Riverside RLP 12-110 [M]		1956	250.00
❑ Riverside RLP 12-126 [M]		1957	350.00
PIANO STYLISTS			
❑ Capitol H323 [10]		1952	150.00
PIANO TWO			
❑ Private Music 2027-1-P		1988	25.00
PICK UP THE BEAT			
❑ Epic LN3127 [M]		1955	100.00
PIONEERS OF BOOGIE WOOGIE			
❑ Riverside RLP-1009 [10]		1953	300.00
PIONEERS OF BOOGIE WOOGIE, VOL. 2			
❑ Riverside RLP-1034 [10]		1954	300.00
PIONEERS OF THE JAZZ GUITAR			
❑ Yazoo 1057		197?	25.00
PLAYBOY ALL STARS VOLUME 1			
❑ Playboy PB-1957 [M]		1957	40.00
PLAYBOY ALL STARS VOLUME 2			
❑ Playboy PB-1958 [M]		1958	40.00

Number	Title	Yr	NM
PLAYBOY ALL STARS VOLUME 3			
❑ Playboy PB-1959 [M]		1959	120.00
THE PLAYERS' ASSOCIATION			
❑ Vanguard VSD-79384		197?	30.00
POP PARADE			
❑ MGM E-194 [10]		1953	100.00
POPULAR FAVORITES			
❑ Columbia CL6057 [10]		1949	40.00
PORGY AND BESS			
❑ Bethlehem EXLP-1 [M]		1956	250.00
❑ Bethlehem BCP-6040 [M]		1959	200.00
PORTRAITS IN JAZZ			
❑ Reprise R-6084 [M]		1963	30.00
❑ Reprise R9-6084 [S]		1963	35.00
POT, SPOON, PIPE AND JUG			
❑ Stash ST-102		197?	25.00
A POTPOURRI OF JAZZ			
❑ Verve MGV-2032 [M]		1956	200.00
❑ Verve V-2032 [M]		1961	50.00
POWER, GLORY AND MUSIC			
❑ Salvation 1000		197?	35.00
PRESTIGE CLASSIC JAM SESSIONS, VOL. 1			
❑ Prestige 24107		198?	35.00
PRESTIGE GROOVY GOODIES, VOL. 1			
❑ Prestige PRLP-7298 [M]		1964	60.00
❑ Prestige PRST-7298 [R]		1964	50.00
PRESTIGE SOUL MASTERPIECES			
❑ Fantasy OJC-1201		1988	30.00
PRESTIGE TWOFER GIANTS, VOL. 1			
❑ Prestige PRP-1		197?	35.00
PRESTIGE TWOFER GIANTS, VOL. 2			
❑ Prestige PRP-2		197?	35.00
PRIMITIVE PIANO			
❑ Tone 1 [M]		195?	30.00
PROGRESSIVE PIANO			
❑ RCA Victor LJM-3001 [10]		1952	100.00
THE PROGRESSIVE RECORDS ALL STAR TENOR SAX SPECTACULAR			
❑ Progressive PRO-7019		1978	30.00
THE PROGRESSIVE RECORDS ALL STAR TROMBONE SPECTACULAR			
❑ Progressive PRO-7018		1978	30.00
THE PROGRESSIVE RECORDS ALL STAR TRUMPET SPECTACULAR			
❑ Progressive PRO-7015		1978	30.00
THE PROGRESSIVE RECORDS ALL STAR TRUMPET SPECTACULAR, VOL. 2			
❑ Progressive PRO-7017		1978	30.00
THE PROGRESSIVES			
❑ Columbia KG31574		1973	50.00
❑ Columbia CG31574		197?	30.00
—CG" prefix is a reissue of "KG			
RAGTIME PIANO ROLL, VOL. 1			
❑ Riverside RLP-1006 [10]		1953	300.00
RAGTIME PIANO ROLL, VOL. 2			
❑ Riverside RLP-1025 [10]		1954	300.00
RAGTIME PIANO ROLL, VOL. 3			
❑ Riverside RLP-1049 [10]		1954	300.00
RAGTIMERS' IMMORTAL PERFORMANCES			
❑ RCA Victor LPT-1000 [M]		1954	60.00
RARE BANDS OF THE 20S, VOL. 1			
❑ Historical ASC-3		1966	30.00
RARE BANDS OF THE 20S, VOL. 2			
❑ Historical ASC-6		1966	30.00
RARE BANDS OF THE 20S, VOL. 3			
❑ Historical ASC-7		1966	30.00
RARE HOT CHICAGO JAZZ			
❑ Herwin 109		197?	30.00
RARE VERTICAL JAZZ			
❑ Historical ASC-8		1966	30.00
THE RCA VICTOR ENCYCLOPEDIA OF RECORDED JAZZ, ALBUM 1			
❑ RCA Victor LEJ-1 [10]		1956	40.00
THE RCA VICTOR ENCYCLOPEDIA OF RECORDED JAZZ, ALBUM 2			
❑ RCA Victor LEJ-2 [10]		1956	40.00
THE RCA VICTOR ENCYCLOPEDIA OF RECORDED JAZZ, ALBUM 3			
❑ RCA Victor LEJ-3 [10]		1956	40.00
THE RCA VICTOR ENCYCLOPEDIA OF RECORDED JAZZ, ALBUM 4			
❑ RCA Victor LEJ-4 [10]		1956	40.00
THE RCA VICTOR ENCYCLOPEDIA OF			

Various Artists, *Straight No Chaser*, Blue Note B1-28263, two-record set, **$60**.

Various Artists, *A Swingin' Gig*, Tampa TP-2, black vinyl, **$200**.

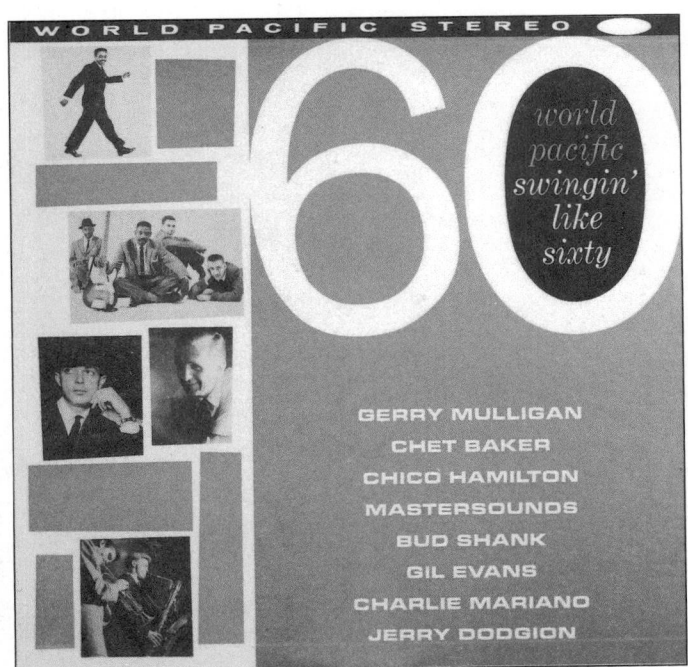

Various Artists, *Swingin' Like Sixty*, World Pacific ST-1289, **$150**.

Various Artists, *West Coast vs. East Coast*, MGM E-3390, **$250**.

Number Title	Yr	NM
RECORDED JAZZ, ALBUM 5		
❏ RCA Victor LEJ-5 [10]	1956	40.00
THE RCA VICTOR ENCYCLOPEDIA OF RECORDED JAZZ, ALBUM 6		
❏ RCA Victor LEJ-6 [10]	1956	40.00
THE RCA VICTOR ENCYCLOPEDIA OF RECORDED JAZZ, ALBUM 7		
❏ RCA Victor LEJ-7 [10]	1956	40.00
THE RCA VICTOR ENCYCLOPEDIA OF RECORDED JAZZ, ALBUM 8		
❏ RCA Victor LEJ-8 [10]	1956	40.00
THE RCA VICTOR ENCYCLOPEDIA OF RECORDED JAZZ, ALBUM 9		
❏ RCA Victor LEJ-9 [10]	1956	40.00
THE RCA VICTOR ENCYCLOPEDIA OF RECORDED JAZZ, ALBUM 10		
❏ RCA Victor LEJ-10 [10]	1956	40.00
THE RCA VICTOR ENCYCLOPEDIA OF RECORDED JAZZ, ALBUM 11		
❏ RCA Victor LEJ-11 [10]	1956	40.00
THE RCA VICTOR ENCYCLOPEDIA OF RECORDED JAZZ, ALBUM 12		
❏ RCA Victor LEJ-12 [10]	1956	40.00
THE REAL AMBASSADORS		
❏ Columbia CL5850 [M]	1962	50.00
❏ Columbia OS2250 [S]	1962	60.00
REBIRTH OF BEALE STREET		
❏ Beale Street BS-1	1983	200.00
—Limited edition of 1,000 made for the city of Memphis		
RECORDED IN NEW ORLEANS, VOL. 1		
❏ Good Time Jazz L-12019 [M]	1955	60.00
RECORDED IN NEW ORLEANS, VOL. 2		
❏ Good Time Jazz L-12020 [M]	1955	60.00
RECORDED ON LOCATION AT THE FIVE SPOT CAFE IN NEW YORK CITY...A MEMORIAL CONCERT DEDICATED TO THE MUSIC OF CHARLIE PARKER		
❏ Signal S-1204 [M]	1957	200.00
RECORD HOP		
❏ Decca DL8067 [M]	1955	150.00
RED HOT AND BLUE JAZZ		
❏ Waldorf Music Hall MH 33-141 [10]	195?	200.00
REEFER SONGS		
❏ Stash ST-100	197?	35.00
RELAXED SAXOPHONE MOODS		
❏ Prestige PRLP-141 [10]	1953	300.00
REMEMBERING CHRISTMAS WITH THE BIG BANDS		
❏ RCA Special Products DPM1-0506 [M]	1981	30.00
REQUESTED BY YOU		
❏ Columbia CL607 [M]	1955	75.00
RHYTHM & BLUES		
❏ RCA Camden CAL-371 [M]	1958	60.00
RHYTHM, BLUES AND BOOGIE-WOOGIE		
❏ Decca DL4011 [M]	1960	60.00
RHYTHM PLUS ONE		
❏ Epic LN3297 [M]	1956	100.00
THE RHYTHM SECTION		
❏ Epic LN3271 [M]	1956	100.00
RIDIN' IN RHYTHM		
❏ Swing SW-8453/4	198?	30.00
RINGSIDE AT CONDON'S		
❏ Savoy MG-15029 [10]	1954	150.00
RINGSIDE AT CONDON'S VOL. 2		
❏ Savoy MG-15030 [10]	1954	150.00
RIVERBOAT JAZZ		
❏ Brunswick BL58026 [10]	1951	100.00
RIVERSIDE DRIVE		
❏ Riverside RLP 12-267 [M]	1958	300.00
RIVERSIDE MODERN JAZZ SAMPLER		
❏ Riverside S-3 [M]	1956	250.00
THE ROARING 20'S		
❏ Saydisc SDL-344	198?	25.00
—Compilation of seven versions of the title song, released not long after the movie of the same name		
RODGERS AND HART GEMS		
❏ Pacific Jazz JWC-504 [M]	1956	100.00
❏ World Pacific JWC-504 [M]	1958	150.00
ROOST 5TH ANNIVERSARY ALBUM		
❏ Roost RST-1201 [M]	1955	100.00
THE ROOTS OF DIXIELAND JAZZ		
❏ Everest Archive of Folk & Jazz 274	197?	25.00

Number Title	Yr	NM
THE ROOTS OF DIXIELAND JAZZ, VOL. 2		
❏ Everest Archive of Folk & Jazz 320	198?	25.00
'ROUND MIDNIGHT		
❏ Milestone M-9144	1986	30.00
SAXES, INC.		
❏ Warner Bros. W1336 [M]	1959	100.00
❏ Warner Bros. WS1336 [S]	1959	150.00
SAX GREATS		
❏ Everest Archive of Folk & Jazz 331	198?	25.00
THE SAXOPHONE		
❏ ABC Impulse! AS-9253	197?	100.00
SAXOPHONE REVOLT		
❏ Riverside RLP 12-284 [M]	1958	300.00
THE SAX SECTION		
❏ Epic LN3278 [M]	1956	80.00
SAX STYLISTS		
❏ Capitol H328 [10]	1952	150.00
A SCRAPBOOK OF BRITISH JAZZ, 1926-1956		
❏ London LL1444 [M]	1956	50.00
SECOND SESSION AT SQUIRREL'S		
❏ Paramount LP-108 [10]	1954	120.00
SESSION AT MIDNIGHT		
❏ Capitol T707 [M]	1956	100.00
SESSION AT RIVERSIDE		
❏ Capitol T761 [M]	1956	300.00
THE SEVEN AGES OF JAZZ		
❏ Metrojazz 2-E-1009 [M]	1959	175.00
❏ Metrojazz 2-SE-1009 [S]	1959	150.00
THE 77 SESSIONS		
❏ GHB GHB-250	198?	25.00
SHADES OF NEW ORLEANS		
❏ GHB GHB-140	198?	25.00
❏ Southland SLP-240	1963	35.00
SHOUTIN', SWINGIN' AND MAKIN' LOVE		
❏ Chess CHV-412	1970	35.00
SIGNALS		
❏ Savoy Jazz SJL-2231	198?	30.00
SILVER BLUE		
❏ Xanadu 137	197?	30.00
THE SILVER YEARS: COMMEMORATING CAPITOL'S 25 YEARS IN THE RECORDING INDUSTRY		
❏ Capitol SNP-91097 [S]	1967	60.00
—Custom silver label		
❏ Capitol NP-91097 [M]	1967	60.00
—Custom silver label		
❏ Savoy MG-12217 [M]	196?	50.00
SINGIN' THE BLUES		
❏ MCA 4064	197?	30.00
SITTIN' IN		
❏ Verve MGV-8225 [M]	1958	100.00
❏ Verve V-8225 [M]	1961	60.00
SMALL COMBO HITS		
❏ RCA Victor LPT-3 [10]	1951	40.00
SMART, LUSCIOUS, BEAUTIFUL		
❏ Bethlehem BCP-6034 [M]	1960	250.00
THE SMITHSONIAN COLLECTION OF CLASSIC JAZZ		
❏ Smithsonian/CSP P611891	1973	40.00
❏ Smithsonian/CSP P719477	1987	40.00
—Revised version of 1973 original		
SMOKE RINGS		
❏ RCA Victor LPT-13 [10]	1951	40.00
SMOOTH & SWINGING JAZZ		
❏ Verve PM-12 [M]	1964	35.00
—Custom edition for Whyte & Mackay's Blended Scotch Whiskey		
SOFT PEDAL		
❏ Columbia CL2511 [10]	1954	60.00
SOLID STATE DEMONSTRATION RECORD		
❏ Solid State SS93 [DJ]	1966	35.00
—Sampler from six Solid State LP releases		
SOLO FLIGHT		
❏ Pacific Jazz JWC-505 [M]	1956	100.00
❏ World Pacific JWC-505 [M]	1958	150.00
SOME LIKE IT COOL		
❏ United Artists X-71 [M]	1959	40.00
❏ United Artists SX-71 [S]	1959	40.00
SOMETHING FOR BOTH EARS		
❏ World Pacific HFS-2 [S]	1958	150.00
—Stereo sampler		
SOMETHING NEW, SOMETHING BLUE		
❏ Columbia CL1388 [M]	1959	50.00

Number Title	Yr	NM
SONGS BY RODGERS AND HART AND JOHNNY GREEN		
❏ Discovery DL-3014 [10]	1951	300.00
SOUL JAZZ, VOL. 1		
❏ Bluesville BVLP-1009 [M]	1960	100.00
—Blue label, silver print		
❏ Bluesville BVLP-1009 [M]	1965	60.00
—Blue label, trident logo at right		
SOUL JAZZ, VOL. 2		
❏ Bluesville BVLP-1010 [M]	1960	100.00
—Blue label, silver print		
❏ Bluesville BVLP-1010 [M]	1965	60.00
—Blue label, trident logo at right		
SOUL JAZZ GIANTS		
❏ Prestige PRST-7791	1970	35.00
THE SOUL OF JAZZ		
❏ Riverside S-5 [M]	1957	300.00
❏ World Wide MGS-20002 [S]	1958	150.00
THE SOUL OF JAZZ PERCUSSION		
❏ Warwick W5003 [M]	1961	60.00
❏ Warwick W5003ST [S]	1961	40.00
THE SOUL OF JAZZ PIANO		
❏ Riverside 9S-7 [S]	196?	60.00
THE SOUND OF BIG BAND JAZZ IN HI-FI		
❏ World Pacific WP-1257 [M]	1960	150.00
THE SOUND OF BIG BAND JAZZ IN STEREO		
❏ World Pacific ST-1015 [S]	1960	150.00
THE SOUND OF PICANTE		
❏ Concord Picante CJP-295	1986	25.00
SOUNDS IN SPACE		
❏ RCA Victor SP-33-13 [S]	1958	50.00
—Narrated by Ken Nordine with songs by various artists		
SOUTH SIDE JAZZ		
❏ Chess CHV-415	1971	30.00
THE SPANISH SIDE OF JAZZ		
❏ Roulette SR-42001	1968	50.00
SPIRITUALS TO SWING: JOHN HAMMOND'S 30TH ANNIVERSARY CONCERT 1967		
❏ Columbia G30776	1971	35.00
❏ Columbia CG30776	197?	30.00
—CG" prefix is a reissue of "G		
STABLE MATES		
❏ Savoy MG-12115 [M]	1957	100.00
STARS OF JAZZ '61		
❏ Jazzland JLP-1001 [M]	1961	60.00
STARS OF THE APOLLO		
❏ Columbia G30788	1971	35.00
❏ Columbia CG30788	197?	30.00
—CG" prefix is a reissue of "G		
THE STASH CHRISTMAS ALBUM		
❏ Stash 125	1980	35.00
ST. LOUIS JAZZ, 1925-27		
❏ Herwin 114	197?	30.00
STRAIGHT NO CHASER		
❏ Blue Note B1-28263	1994	60.00
—Compilation of original recordings that were sampled by US3, plus others		
STRETCHING OUT		
❏ United Artists UAL-4023 [M]	1959	400.00
❏ United Artists UAS-5023 [S]	1959	300.00
STRICTLY BEBOP		
❏ Capitol M-11059	1973	30.00
STRICTLY FROM DIXIE		
❏ MGM E-3262 [M]	1956	60.00
A STRING OF SWINGIN' PEARLS		
❏ RCA Victor LPM-1373 [M]	1956	60.00
SUMMIT MEETING		
❏ Vanguard VSD-79390	1977	30.00
❏ Vee Jay LP-3026 [M]	1961	50.00
❏ Vee Jay SR-3026 [S]	1961	60.00
SWEDES FROM JAZZVILLE		
❏ Epic LN3309 [M]	1957	200.00
SWEDISH PASTRY		
❏ Discovery DL-2008 [10]	1954	250.00
SWING 1946		
❏ Prestige PRLP-7604	1969	35.00
SWING AGAIN!		
❏ Capitol T1386 [M]	1960	80.00
❏ Capitol DT1386 [R]	196?	60.00
SWING CLASSICS 1935		
❏ Prestige PRLP-7646	1969	35.00
THE SWING ERA, VOL. 1		
❏ X LVA-3030 [10]	1955	150.00

Number	Title	Yr	NM

SWING GOES DIXIE
❏ American Recording Society G-420 [M] | 1957 | 60.00

SWING GUITARS
❏ Norgran MGN-1033 [M] | 1955 | 150.00
❏ Verve MGV-8124 [M] | 1957 | 150.00
❏ Verve V-8124 [M] | 1961 | 50.00

SWING HI, SWING LO
❏ Blue Note BLP-5027 [10] | 1953 | 200.00
❏ Blue Note B-6507 [M] | 1969 | 35.00

SWINGIN': BIG BAND SWING AND JAZZ FROM THE 1930S AND 1940S
❏ Folkways FJ-2861 | 1986 | 30.00

SWINGING BROADWAY
❏ Kimberly 2024 [M] | 1963 | 50.00
❏ Kimberly 11024 [S] | 1963 | 60.00

SWINGING FOR THE KING
❏ Mercury MG-20133 [M] | 1956 | 150.00

A SWINGIN' GIG
❏ Tampa TP-2 [M] | 1957 | 300.00
— Colored vinyl
❏ Tampa TP-2 [M] | 1958 | 200.00
— Black vinyl

SWINGING SMALL BANDS
❏ MCA 1324 | 198? | 25.00

SWINGING SOUNDTRACK
❏ Kimberly 2016 [M] | 1963 | 50.00
❏ Kimberly 11016 [S] | 1963 | 60.00

SWINGIN' LIKE SIXTY, VOL. 1
❏ World Pacific WP-1289 [M] | 1960 | 150.00
❏ World Pacific ST-1289 [S] | 1960 | 150.00

SWINGIN' LIKE SIXTY, VOL. 2
❏ World Pacific ST-1290 [S] | 1960 | 150.00

SWINGIN' LIKE SIXTY, VOL. 3
❏ World Pacific ST-1291 [S] | 1960 | 150.00

SWINGIN' SOUNDS
❏ Columbia Special Products XTV82030 [M] | 1962 | 60.00
— Issued for the W.A. Sheaffer Pen Co.

SWING LIGHTLY
❏ Jazztone J-1265 [M] | 1957 | 60.00

SWING… NOT SPRING!
❏ Savoy MG-12062 [M] | 1956 | 100.00

SWING POTPOURRI
❏ Audiophile AP-23 [M] | 1953 | 60.00

SWINGTIME JIVE
❏ Stash ST-108 | 197? | 25.00

THE SWINGVILLE ALL-STARS
❏ Swingville SVLP-2010 [M] | 1960 | 40.00
— Purple label
❏ Swingville SVLP-2010 [M] | 1965 | 50.00
— Blue label, trident logo at right

A TASTE OF JAZZ
❏ Concord Jazz CJ-93 | 1979 | 25.00

TEA PAD SONGS, VOL. 1
❏ Stash ST-103 | 197? | 25.00

TEA PAD SONGS, VOL. 2
❏ Stash ST-104 | 197? | 25.00

TENOR CONCLAVE
❏ Prestige PRLP-7074 [M] | 1957 | 175.00
— Reissued as Prestige 7249; see JOHN COLTRANE.

TENOR JAZZ
❏ Mercury MG-20016 [10] | 1950 | 300.00
— Issued in a paper sleeve

TENORS ANYONE?
❏ Dawn DLP-1126 [M] | 1958 | 200.00

TENOR SAX
❏ Concord 3012 [M] | 195? | 40.00

TENOR SAXES
❏ Norgran MGN-1034 [M] | 1955 | 250.00
❏ Verve MGV-8127 [M] | 1957 | 150.00
❏ Verve V-8127 [M] | 1961 | 50.00

TENOR SAX SOLOS, VOL. 1
❏ Savoy MG-9008 [10] | 1952 | 300.00

TENOR SAX SOLOS, VOL. 2
❏ Savoy MG-9013 [10] | 1952 | 300.00

TENOR SAX SOLOS, VOL. 3
❏ Savoy MG-9021 [10] | 1953 | 300.00

TERRITORY BANDS 1926-31
❏ Historical 26 | 1969 | 25.00

TERRITORY BANDS 1929-33
❏ Historical 24 | 1968 | 25.00

THAT'S THE WAY I FEEL NOW
❏ A&M SP-6600 | 1984 | 35.00
— Includes Joe Jackson

THAT'S THE WAY I FEEL NOW (A TRIBUTE TO THELONIOUS MONK)
❏ A&M SP-6006 | 198? | 35.00

THEME SONGS
❏ Columbia CL6016 [10] | 1949 | 40.00
❏ RCA Victor LPT-1 [10] | 1951 | 40.00

THESAURUS OF CLASSIC JAZZ
❏ Columbia C4L18 | 1961 | 100.00

THEY ALL PLAYED RAGTIME
❏ Jazzology JCE-52 | 197? | 25.00

THEY ALL PLAYED THE MAPLE LEAF RAG
❏ Herwin 401 | 197? | 30.00

A THIRD SESSION AT SQUIRREL'S
❏ Paramount LP-110 [10] | 1954 | 120.00

THIS COULD LEAD TO LOVE
❏ Riverside RLP 12-808 [M] | 195? | 50.00

THIS IS THE BIG BAND ERA
❏ RCA Victor VPM-6043 | 197? | 35.00

THIS IS THE BLUES
❏ Kimberly 2020 [M] | 1963 | 50.00
❏ Kimberly 11020 [S] | 1963 | 60.00

THIS IS THE BLUES, VOL. 1
❏ Pacific Jazz PJ-13 [M] | 1961 | 60.00

THIS IS THE BLUES, VOL. 2
❏ Pacific Jazz PJ-30 [M] | 1962 | 60.00
❏ Pacific Jazz ST-30 [M] | 1962 | 60.00

THIS IS THEIR TIME, OH YEAH
❏ Revelation REV-11 | 1970 | 35.00

THREE DECADES OF MUSIC, 1939-49, VOL. 1
❏ Blue Note BST-89902 | 1969 | 60.00

THREE DECADES OF MUSIC, 1949-59, VOL. 1
❏ Blue Note BST-89903 | 1969 | 60.00

THREE DECADES OF MUSIC, 1959-69, VOL. 1
❏ Blue Note BST-89904 | 1969 | 60.00

THREE ROADS TO JAZZ
❏ American Recording Society LP-100 [M] | 1956 | 60.00

TIME SPEAKS: DEDICATED TO THE MEMORY OF CLIFFORD BROWN
❏ Timeless LPSJP-187 | 1990 | 30.00
— With Benny Golson, Freddie Hubbard, Woody Shaw, Kenny Barron, Cecil McBee, Ben Riley

TOOTIN' THROUGH THE ROOF, VOL. 1
❏ Onyx 209 | 197? | 30.00

TOOTIN' THROUGH THE ROOF, VOL. 2
❏ Onyx 213 | 197? | 30.00

TOWN HALL CONCERT
❏ Mainstream S-6004 [R] | 1965 | 30.00
❏ Mainstream 56004 [M] | 1965 | 60.00

TRADITIONAL JAZZ
❏ London LL1242 [M] | 1955 | 60.00

TRADITIONAL JAZZ AT THE ROYAL FESTIVAL HALL
❏ London LL1184 [M] . | 1955 | 60.00

TRIBUTE TO CHARLIE PARKER FROM THE NEWPORT JAZZ FESTIVAL
❏ RCA Victor LPM-3738 [M] | 1967 | 60.00
❏ RCA Victor LSP-3738 [S] | 1967 | 50.00

A TRIBUTE TO DUKE
❏ Concord Jazz CJ-50 | 197? | 30.00

TRIBUTE TO MONK AND BIRD
❏ Tomato TOM-9002 | 1979 | 35.00

TROMBONE BAND STAND
❏ Bethlehem BCP-6036 [M] | 1960 | 250.00

TROMBONES
❏ Savoy MG-12086 [M] | 1956 | 120.00

TROMBONE SCENE
❏ Vik LX-1087 [M] | 1957 | 60.00

TRUE BLUE
❏ Xanadu 136 | 197? | 25.00

THE TRUMPET ALBUM
❏ Savoy Jazz SJL-2237 | 198? | 30.00

TRUMPET BLUES 1925-29
❏ Historical 27 | 1969 | 25.00

TRUMPETER'S HOLIDAY
❏ Epic LN3252 [M] | 1956 | 100.00

TRUMPET INTERLUDE
❏ EmArcy MG-36017 [M] | 1955 | 200.00
❏ Savoy MG-12096 [M] | 1957 | 120.00

TRUMPET STYLISTS
❏ Capitol H326 [10] | 1952 | 150.00

TRUMPET TRIBUTE TO FATS NAVARRO, CLIFFORD BROWN, BOOKER LITTLE
❏ Trip 5036 | 197? | 30.00

24 KARAT GOLD FOR GROOVIN'
❏ Verve V6-6654 | 1968 | 50.00

25 YEARS OF PRESTIGE
❏ Prestige 24046 | 197? | 35.00

UNDER ONE ROOF
❏ EmArcy MG-36088 [M] | 1956 | 200.00

UNEXPURGATED JAZZ
❏ Audiophile AP-43 [M] | 1953 | 60.00

UNFORGETTABLE PERFORMANCES BY THE JAZZ IMMORTALS
❏ Dot DLP-3444 [M] | 196? | 75.00

UPRIGHT AND LOWDOWN
❏ Columbia CL685 [M] | 1955 | 60.00

UP SWING
❏ RCA Victor LPT-12 [10] | 1951 | 40.00

THE VERVE COMPENDIUM OF JAZZ, NO. 1
❏ Verve MGV-8194 [M] | 1957 | 100.00
❏ Verve V-8194 [M] | 1961 | 50.00

THE VERVE COMPENDIUM OF JAZZ, NO. 2
❏ Verve MGV-8195 [M] | 1957 | 100.00
❏ Verve V-8195 [M] | 1961 | 50.00

VERY SAXY
❏ Fantasy OJC-458 | 1990 | 15.00
❏ Prestige PRST-7790 | 1971 | 50.00
— Reissue of 7167
❏ Prestige PRLP-7167 | 1959 | 200.00

VICEROY CIGARETTES CAMPUS JAZZ FESTIVAL
❏ RCA Custom KO7P-1544 [M] | 1959 | 60.00
— Available thoruigh Viceroy cigarettes

THE VIOLIN SUMMIT
❏ Prestige PRLP-7631 | 1969 | 35.00

VOODOO DRUMS IN HI-FI
❏ Atlantic 1296 [M] | 1958 | 300.00
— Black label
❏ Atlantic 1296 [M] | 1961 | 150.00
— Multicolor label, white "fan" logo at right
❏ Atlantic 1296 [M] | 1963 | 50.00
— Multicolor label, black "fan" logo at right

WASHBOARD RHYTHM KINGS, VOL. 1
❏ X LVA-3021 [10] | 1954 | 300.00

WE CUT THIS ALBUM FOR BREAD
❏ Bethlehem BCP-86 [M] | 1958 | 200.00

WEED: A RARE BATCH
❏ Stash ST-107 | 197? | 30.00

WE LIKE BANDS
❏ Coral CRL57229 [M] | 195? | 15.00

WEST COAST JAZZ, VOL. 2
❏ Jazztone J-(# unk) [M] | 1957 | 60.00

WEST COAST VS. EAST COAST
❏ MGM E-3390 [M] | 1956 | 250.00

WE'VE BUILT A JAZZ ALBUM FOR YOU
❏ Bethlehem BCP-89 [M] | 1958 | 200.00

WHEELIN' AND DEALIN'
❏ Prestige PRLP-7131 [M] | 1957 | 350.00
— Reissued as Status 8327; see JOHN COLTRANE.

THE WIDE, WIDE WORLD OF JAZZ
❏ RCA Victor LPM-1325 [M] | 1956 | 60.00

WILDFLOWERS: NEW YORK LOFT JAZZ 1
❏ Douglas 7045 | 1976 | 30.00

WILDFLOWERS: NEW YORK LOFT JAZZ 2
❏ Douglas 7046 | 1976 | 30.00

WILDFLOWERS: NEW YORK LOFT JAZZ 3
❏ Douglas 7047 | 1976 | 30.00

WILDFLOWERS: NEW YORK LOFT JAZZ 4
❏ Douglas 7048 | 1976 | 30.00

WILDFLOWERS: NEW YORK LOFT JAZZ 5
❏ Douglas 7049 | 1976 | 30.00

WINNERS ALL! THE DOWN BEAT JAZZ POLL '64
❏ Verve V-8579 [M] | 1964 | 50.00
❏ Verve V6-8579 [S] | 1964 | 60.00

WINNER'S CIRCLE
❏ Bethlehem BCP-6024 [M] | 1958 | 200.00

WINNERS CIRCLE LIMITED EDITION
❏ Columbia GB-4 [M] | 1959 | 60.00

THE WOMEN IN JAZZ
❏ Storyville STLP-916 [M] | 1956 | 100.00

WOMEN IN JAZZ, VOL. 1: ALL-WOMAN GROUPS
❏ Stash ST-111 | 198? | 25.00

WOMEN IN JAZZ, VOL. 2: PIANISTS
❏ Stash ST-112 | 198? | 25.00

WOMEN IN JAZZ, VOL. 3: SWINGTIME TO MODERN

Number	Title	Yr	NM
❑ Stash ST-113		198?	25.00

THE WORLD OF SWING
| ❑ Columbia KG32945 | | 1974 | 35.00 |

THE WORLD'S GREATEST MUSIC SERIES 'POP'
-- JAZZ
| ❑ Artia-Parliament WGM2AB | | 196? | 175.00 |

—*Box set of material from the Roulette label; also issued as two five-record boxes*
| ❑ Artia-Parliament WGM2B | | 196? | 100.00 |

—*Second of two five-record sets*
| ❑ Artia-Parliament WGM-2A [M] | | 196? | 100.00 |
| ❑ Artia-Parliament WGM(S)-2A [S] | | 196? | 120.00 |

XANADU AT MONTREUX, VOL. 1
| ❑ Xanadu 162 | | 198? | 25.00 |

XANADU AT MONTREUX, VOL. 2
| ❑ Xanadu 163 | | 198? | 25.00 |

XANADU AT MONTREUX, VOL. 3
| ❑ Xanadu 164 | | 198? | 25.00 |

XANADU AT MONTREUX, VOL. 4
| ❑ Xanadu 165 | | 198? | 25.00 |

XANADU IN AFRICA
| ❑ Xanadu 180 | | 1981 | 30.00 |

YAZOO'S HISTORY OF JAZZ
| ❑ Yazoo 1070 | | 197? | 25.00 |

YESTERDAY
| ❑ Mainstream MRL-364 | | 197? | 30.00 |

THE YOUNG AT BOP
| ❑ EmArcy MG-26001 [10] | | 1954 | 350.00 |

THE YOUNG ONES OF JAZZ
| ❑ EmArcy MG-36085 [M] | | 1956 | 200.00 |

YOURS
| ❑ Harmony HL7042 [M] | | 1957 | 50.00 |

YOU'VE GOT TO HEAR IT TO BELIEVE IT
| ❑ Solid State SS-94 | | 1966 | 50.00 |

YULE STRUTTIN' -- A BLUE NOTE CHRISTMAS
| ❑ Blue Note 1P8119 | | 1990 | 30.00 |

—*Available on vinyl through Columbia House only*

ZENITH SALUTES THE SWINGIN' BANDS
| ❑ Columbia Special Products CSS525 [M] | | 1967 | 35.00 |

—*Available from Zenith dealers*

ALABAMA

Excalibur Vintage and Vinyl
215 Second Ave., Unit 2, Decatur, AL 35601
Phone: 256-345-0988
E-mail: excaliburvintageandvinyl@gmail.com

Mobile Records
140 S. Sage Ave., No. B, Mobile, AL 36606
Phone: 251-479-0096
E-mail: kglassal@aol.com

OZ Music
506 14th St., Tuscaloosa, AL 35401
Phone: 205-758-1222

ALASKA

Beat Garden
3300 College Road, Fairbanks, AK 99709-3707

Hoitts Music
1698 Airport Way, Fairbanks, AK 99701-4004

Mammoth Music
500 E. 5th Ave., Anchorage, AK
https://mammothmusicak.wordpress.com

ARKANSAS

Sound Warehouse
17 N. Block Ave., Fayetteville, AR 72702
Phone: 479-442-4822

Vintage Stock-Rogers
4505 W. Walnut, Suite 5, Rogers, AR 72756
Phone: (479) 936-5881

ARIZONA

Renfield Record Exchange
403 Clark St., Suite B11, Jerome, AZ 86331
Phone: 928-634-1615
E-mail: renfieldrecordexchange@hotmail.com

Revolver Records
918 N. Second St., Phoenix, AZ 85001
Phone: 602-795-4980

Rockzone Records
2155 E. University, No. 104, Tempe, AZ 85281
Phone: 480-964-6301
E-mail: rockzonerecords@yahoo.com

Stinkweeds
12 W. Camelback Road,
Phoenix, AZ 85013-2518
Phone: 602-248-9461

Tracks in Wax Records
4741 N. Central Ave., Phoenix, AZ 85001
Phone: 602-274-2660
E-mail: tracksinwax44@cox.net

CALIFORNIA

Amoeba Music Hollywood
6400 Sunset Blvd., Los Angeles, CA 90028
Web: www.amoeba.com

Amoeba Music
2455 Telegraph Ave., Berkeley, CA 94704a
Phone: 510-549-1125

Aquarius Records
1055 Valencia St., San Francisco, CA 94110
Web: www.aquariusrecords.org

Dr. Strange Records
7136 Amethyst Ave., Alta Loma, CA 91701
Phone: 909-944-1778

Dyzzy Vinyl
3004 E. Seventh St., Long Beach, CA 90804
Phone: 562-438-8928

Folk Arts Rare Records
3072 El Cajon Blvd, San Diego, CA 92104
Phone: 619-282-7833
Web: folkartsrarerecords.com

Kool Kat Jazz Records
97 Linden St., Oakland, CA 94607
Phone: 510-291-1223

The Last Record Store
1899 A-Mendocino Ave., Santa Rosa, CA 95401
Phone: 7070-525-1963

Rasputin Music
2401 Telegraph Ave., Berkeley, CA 94720
Phone: 800-350-8700

The Record Collector
7809 Melrose Ave., Hollywood, CA 90046
Web: www.therecordcollector.net

The Record Parlour
6408 Selma Avenue, Hollywood, CA 90028
Web: www.therecordparlour.com

Record Surplus
12436 Santa Monica Blvd.,
Los Angeles, CA 90025
Phone: 310-979-4577
Web: www.recordsurplusla.com

Rockaway Records
2395 Glendale Blvd., Los Angeles, CA 90039
Web: http://www.rockaway.com

Streetlight Records
2350 Market St., San Francisco, CA
Phone: 888-396-2350
Web: http://www.streetlightrecords.com

Streetlight Records
980 S. Bascom Ave., San Jose, CA
Phone: 888-330-7776

Streetlight Records
939 S. Pacific Ave., Santa Cruz, CA
Phone: 888-648-9201

Vinyl Revolution
230 Lighthouse Ave., Monterey, CA 93940
Phone: 831-646-9020
E-mail: vinylrev@sbcglobal.net

Vinyl Solution Records
151 West 25th Ave., San Mateo, CA. 94403
http://www.vinylsolutionrecords.com

Zoinks Records
226 S. Main St., Pomona, CA
Phone: 909-865-4755

COLORADO

Absolute Vinyl Records and Stereo
4474 N. Broadway St., Boulder, CO 80304-0506
Phone: 303-955-1519
E-mail: fortherecords@cs.com

Albums on the Hill
1128 13th St., Boulder, CO 80302
Phone: 303-447-0159
E-mail: albums2001@comcast.net

Finest Record Store
1129 W. Elizabeth St., Fort Collins, CO 80527
Phone: 970-484-6446
E-mail: finest74@yahoo.com

The Leechpit
708 N. Weber St., Colorado Springs, CO 80903
Phone: 719-634-3675
E-mail: adam@csindy.com

LPHound's Vinyl House
6235 E. 14th Ave., Denver, CO 80220
Phone: 303-593-2540
E-mail: LPHounds@gmail.com

CONNECTICUT

Brass City Records (and Old Tools)
489 Meadow St, Waterbury, CT 06702
www.brasscityrecords.com

Disc & Dat
107 Greenwood Ave., Bethel, CT 06801-2528
Phone: 203-797-0067

Exile on Main St.
267 E. Main St., Branford, CT 06405

Gerosa Records
246 Federal Rd C16, Brookfield, CT 06804
www.gerosarecords.com

Johnny's Records
45 Tokeneke Road, Darien, CT 06820
Phone: 203-655-0157

Merle's Record Rack
307 Racebrook Road, Orange, CT 06477

Mystic Disc
10 Steamboat Wharf, Mystic, CT
Phone: 860-536-1312
E-mail: dandisc@sbcglobal.net

Redscroll Records
24 N Colony Rd, Wallingford, CT 06492
www.redscrollrecords.com

Replay Records
2586 Whitney Ave., Hamden, CT 06518
Phone: 203-980-1277
E-mail: davidelliott87@gmail.com

Tumbleweeds
325 Main St., Niantic, CT 06357
Web: http://www.tumbleweedst.com

Willimantic Records
744 Main Street, Willimantic, CT 06226 USA
Phone: 860-450-7000

DELAWARE

Bert's Music
2501 Concord Pike, Wilmington, DE 19803
Phone: 302-478-3724

Rainbow Music & Books
54 E. Main St., Newark, DE 19702
Phone: 302-368-7738
E-mail: chrisavino@gmail.com

Vintage Vinyl at The Barn Shops at Five Points
18388 Coastal Highway, Unit 6,
Lewes, DE 19958
Phone: 410-960-2919
Facebook: https://www.facebook.com/pages/
Vintage-Vinyl-at-the-Barn-Shops-at-Five-
Points

FLORIDA

Hot Wax
1524 E 7th Ave., Tampa, FL 33605
Phone: 813-248-6999
E-mail: hotwax1200@aol.com

Rock & Roll Heaven Inc.
1814 N. Orange Ave., Orlando, FL 32804
www.rock-n-rollheaven.com

Remember Wynn Records
7007 Lanier Drive, Pensacola, FL 32504
Phone: 800-476-8630
E-mail: rememberwynn@bellsouth.net

GEORGIA

Low Yo Yo Stuff
261 W. Washington St., Athens, GA 30601
Phone: 706-606-0842
E-mail: chris@chrisrazz.com

Wax 'n' Facts
432 Moreland Ave. NE, Atlanta, GA 30307
Phone: 404-525-2275
E-mail: waxnfacts@gmail.com

Wuxtry Records
197 E. Clayton St., Athens, GA 30601
Phone: 706-369-9428

HAWAII

Hungry Ear Records
418 Kuulei Road, Kailua, HI 96734
Phone: 808-262-2175
Web: www.hungryear.com

Jelly's Hawaii
670 Auahi Stree I-19, Honolulu, HI 96813
Phone: 808-587-7001
E-mail: pb.hawaii.1983@gmail.com

Stylus Honolulu
2615 S. King St. No, A-301, Honolulu, HI 96826
Phone: 808-951-4500

IDAHO

Big Hole Music
60 East Little Ave., Driggs, ID
E-mail: bigholemusic@hotmail.com

Budget Tapes & Records
416 S. Fifth St., Pocatello, ID 83201
Phone: 208-233-9650
E-mail: budgetrecords@gmail.com

The Long Ear
2405 N. Fourth St., Coeur d Alene, ID 83814
Phone: 208-765-3472
E-mail: thelongear@frontier.com

The Record Exchange
1105 W. Idaho St., Boise, ID 83702
Phone: 208-343-0107, Ext. 1

ILLINOIS

Blue Jay Way Records 14 W. Peru St.
Princeton, IL 61356
www.facebook.com/pages/
Blue-Jay-Way-Records

Deadwax
3819 N. Lincoln, Chicago, IL 60613
Phone: 773-529-1932

Jazz Record Mart
27 E. Illinois, Chicago, IL 60610
Web site: http://www.jazzmart.com

Reverberation Vinyl
1302 N. Main St., Bloomington, IL 61701
Website: www.reverberationvinyl.com

Rich's Record Emporium
131 W. Main St. Collinsville IL
www.richsrecordemporium.com

INDIANA

Alpha Records and Music
Indianapolis
Web site: www.alpha.gemm.com

Dan's Downtown Records
219 W. Main St., Muncie, IN 47305
Phone: 765-284-7611

Indy CD & Vinyl
806 Broad Ripple Ave., Indianapolis, IN 46220
Phone: 317-259-1012

Karma Records
2606 Shelden St, Warsaw, IN 46582
Phone: 574-267-2080
Fax: 574-267-0091
E-mail: karma12@embarqmail.com

Landlocked Music
202 N. Walnut St., Bloomington, IN 47404
Phone: 812-339-2574

IOWA

Metro Records
807 E. 18th St., Cedar Falls, IA 50613
Phone: 319-266-5539

Record Collector
116 S. Linn St., Iowa City, IA 52240
Phone: 319-337-5029

Vinyl Cafe
303 Kellogg Ave., Ames, IA 50010
Phone: 515-230-4574
E-mail: amesvinylcafe@gmail.com

Weird Harold's
411 Jefferson ST., Burlington, IA 52601-5319
Web: http://weirdharolds.com

Zzz Records
2200 Ingersoll, Des Moines, IA 50312
Web: http://www.zzzrecords.com

KANSAS

The Flipside
11212 W. 75th St., Shawnee, KS 66214
Phone: 913-602-8660

Keep N It Real Records
1700 State Ave., Kansas City, KS 66102
Phone: 913-514-0901
E-mail: burnett-mike@sbcglobal.net

Sisters of Sound Records/SOS Music
1214 Moro St. (Aggieville U Clothing Co.)
Manhattan, KS 66502
Phone: 785-770-9767

KENTUCKY

Ear X-Tacy
2226 Bardstown Road, Louisville, KY 40205
Phone: 502.452.1799

The Great Escape Bowling Green
2945 Scottsville Road,
Bowling Green, KY 42104
Phone: 270-782-8092

The Great Escape Louisville
2433 Bardstown Road, Louisville, KY 40205
Phone: 502-456-2216

Ticket to Ride
Flealand 229, London, KY
Phone: 606-309-1389

Underground Sounds
2003 Highland Ave., Louisville, KY 40204
Phone: 502-485-0174

LOUISIANA

Euclid Records NOLA
3401 Chartres St., New Orleans, LA 70117
Phone: 504-947-4348
Web site: www.euclidnola.com

Louisiana Music Factory
210 Decatur, New Orleans, LA 70130
Phone: (504) 586-1094

Odyssey Records
1012 Canal St., New Orleans, LA 70112
Phone: 504-523-3506
E-mail: mistaodyssey@aol.com

Spazz Records
231 Trenton St., West Monroe, LA, LA 71291,
Phone: (318) 805-6337
E-mail: popshop.monroe@gmail.com

Atomic Pop Shop
2963 Government St., Baton Rouge, LA 70806
Phone: 225-771-8455
http://www.atomicpopshop.com

Vinylville, LA
3011 NW Evangeline Throughway,
Lafayette, LA 70507

Phone: 337-349-1932
E-mail: vinylvillela@gmail.com

MAINE

Bill O'Neil's House of Rock 'n' Roll
840 Portland Road, Saco, ME 04072
Phone: 207-283-1966

The Record Connection
252 Main St., Waterville, ME 04901
Phone: 207-873-1798
E-mail: recconn@roadrunner.com

MARYLAND

Blinding Sun Records
332 N. Market St., Frederick, MD 21701
Phone: 410-279-8869

Joe's Record Paradise
8216 Georgia Ave., Silver Spring, MD 20910
Phone: 3015853269
E-mail: timsheamusic@live.com

KA-CHUNK!! Records
78 Maryland Ave., Annapolis, MD 21401
Phone: (410) 571-5047
E-mail: kachunkrecords@gmail.com

MASSACHUSETTS

Armageddon Records
12 B Eliot St., Cambridge, MA 02909
Phone: 617-492-1235
E-mail: armageddonshop@gmail.com

Planet Records, CDs, Tapes
54-B JFK Street, Cambridge, MA 02138
Phone: 617-492-0693
E-mail: planet@tiac.net

Rhythm and Muse
470 Centre St., Jamaica Plain, MA 02130
Phone: 617-524-6622
Fax: 617-524-6039
E-mail: muse3@comcast.net

That's Entertainment
244 Park Ave., Worcester, MA 01609
Phone: 508-755-4207
E-mail: pete@thatse.com

Turn It Up!
5 Pleasant St., Northampton, MA 01060
Phone: 413-582-1885

MICHIGAN

Dearborn Music
22501 Michigan Ave., Dearborn, MI
313-561-1000

Flat Black & Circular
541 E. Grand River, East Lansing, MI 48823

PJ's Used Records
617 Packard St., Ann Arbor, MI 48104

Slick Disc
1625 West Road, Trenton, MI 48183
Phone: 734-692-1881
E-mail: SlickDisc@hotmail.com

Underground Sounds
255 E. Liberty St. Suite 249,
Ann Arbor, MI 48104
Phone: 734-327-9239
E-mail: undergroundsoundsmi@gmail.com

MINNESOTA

Dusty Pixels
2443 Hennepin Ave. S.,
Minneapolis, MN 55405
Phone: 612-377-3371

Electric Fetus Records (three locations)
• 2000 Fourth Ave. S., Minneapolis, MN 55404
Phone: 612-870-9300
• 12 E. Superior St., Duluth, MN 55802
Phone: 218-722-9970
• 28 S. Fifth Ave., St. Cloud, MN 56301
Phone: 320-251-2569
Web: http://www.electricfetus.com

Hymie's Vintage Records
3820 E. Lake St., Minneapolis, MN 55406
Phone: 612-729-8890

Mother's Music
431 Main Ave, Moorhead, MN 56560
Phone: (218)287-9601

Record Collectors' Co-op
3755 Bloomington Ave.,
Minneapolis, MN 55407
Phone: 612-724-7070

MISSISSIPPI

Be-Bop Record Shop
1220 E. Northside Drive No. 160,
Jackson, MS 39211
Phone: 601-981-5000
E-mail: bkstgrock@yahoo.com

Cat Head Delta Blues & Folk Art
252 Delta Ave., Clarksdale, MS 38614
Phone: 662-624-5992

MISSOURI

Earwaxx Records & More
6408 N. Oak Trafficway, Gladstone, MO 64118
Phone: 816-436-9299
E-mail: earwaxxrecords@att.net

Euclid Records
601 East Lockwood Ave., St. Louis, MO 63119
Phone: 314-961-8978
Web site: www.euclidrecords.com

Vintage Vinyl
6610 Delmar Blvd, St Louis, MO 63130-4503
Phone: (314) 721-4096

MONTANA

Cactus Records & Gifts
29 W. Main St., Bozeman, MT 59715
Phone: 406-587-0245
E-mail: cactusrecords@yahoo.com

Ear Candy Music
624 S. Higgins Ave., Missoula, MT 59807
Phone: 406-542-5029
E-mail: earcandymusic@live.com

Rockin' Rudy's
237 Blaine, Missoula, MT 59801
Phone: 406-542-0077

NEBRASKA

Backtrack Records
1549 N. Cotner Blvd., Studio A,
Lincoln, NE 68505-1627
Phone: 402-464-4567

Drastic Plastic
1209 Howard St., Omaha, NE 68139
Phone: 402-346-8843

Recycled Sounds
909 O Street, Lincoln, NE 68508
Phone: 402-476-8240

Spindle Records
122 N. 14th St, Lincoln, NE 68508
Phone: 402-435-8350

NEVADA

Discology CDs, DVDs, LPs
11 N. Sierra St. No. 100, Reno, NV 89504
Phone: 775-323-2121
E-mail: discology@sbcglobal.net

Wax Trax Records Inc.
2909 S. Decatur Blvd.,
Las Vegas, NV 89102-7043
Phone: 702-362-4300
E-mail: waxtraxinc@aol.com

Zia Records – Eastern
4225 S. Eastern Ave., Las Vegas, NV 89119
Phone: 702-735-4942

Zia Records – Sahara
4503 W. Sahara Ave., Las Vegas, NV 89102
Phone: 702-233-4942

NEW HAMPSHIRE

Metro City Records
691 Somerville St., Manchester, NH 03103
Phone: 603-665-9889

Pitchfork Records
2 S. Main St., Concord, NH 03301
Phone: 603-224-6700
E-mail: pfork3@aol.com

Spun
266 Central Ave., Dover, NH 03820
Phone: 603-742-6939
E-mail: spunmusicllc@yahoo.com

NEW JERSEY

21st Century Music
121 Gertrude Ave., Paramus, NJ 07652
Web: http://www.21centurymusic.com

Groovy Graveyard
658 Cookman Ave., Asbury Park, N.J. 07712
Web: www.groovygraveyard.com

Holdfast Records and Clothing
639 Cookman Ave., Asbury Park, NJ 07712

Phone: 732-988-0066

Princeton Record Exchange
20 S. Tulane St., Princeton, NJ 08542
Phone: 609-921-0881

Vintage Vinyl
51 LaFayette Road, Fords, NJ 08863
Phone: 732-225-7717

Zig Zag
2367 Highway 36, Atlantic Highlands, NJ 07752
Phone: 732 708 1666

NEW MEXICO

Guy in the Groove
215 N. Guadalupe (inside Constellation)
Santa Fe, NM 87501
Phone: 505-699-3332
E-mail: GuyInTheGroove@aol.com

Mecca Records
1404 Central Ave. SW, Albuquerque, NM 87104
Phone: 505 243-5041
E-mail: meccaworld@gmail.com

Taosound Tape and CD
314F Paseo del Pueblo Norte, Taos, NM 87571
Phone: 575-758-0323
Fax: 575-758-0323
E-mail: taosound@taosnet.com

NEW YORK

A1 Records
439 E 6th St, New York, NY 10009
Phone: 212-473-2870

Academy LPs
415 E. 12th St., New York, NY 10116
Phone: 212-780-9166

Academy Record Annex
85 Oak St, Brooklyn, NY 11222
Phone: 718-218-8200

Academy Records & CDs
12 W. 18th St., New York, NY 10011
Phone: 212-242-3000

Black Gold Records
461 Court St., Brooklyn, NY 11231
Phone: 347-227-8227

Bleecker Street Records
188 West 4th Street, New York, NY 10014
Phone: 212-255-7899

Colony Records
1619 Broadway, corner of Fourth and Broadway
New York, NY 10019
Web: www.colonymusic.com

CO-OP 87 Records
87 Guernsey St, Brooklyn, NY 11222
Phone: 347-294-4629

Darkside Records & Gallery
782 Main St., Poughkeepsie, NY 12603
www.darksiderecordsandgallery.com

Earwax Records
218 Bedford Ave., Brooklyn, NY 11211
Phone: 718-486-3771

Generation Records
210 Thompson St, New York, NY 10012
Phone: 212-254-1100

Gimme Gimme Records
325 E. Fifth St., New York, NY 10003
Phone: 212-475-2955
E-mail: dc@raremusic.com

Good Records
218 East 5th Street, New York, NY 10003
www.goodrecordsnyc.com

Heaven Street
167 N 9th St., Brooklyn, NY 11211
Phone: 718-486-3771

Human Head Records
168 Johnson Ave., Brooklyn, NY 11206
Phone: 347-987-3362

In Living Stereo
2 Great Jones St., New York, NY 10012
Phone: 929-600-2008

Infinity Records
510 Park Blvd., Massapequa Park, NY 11762
Web site: http://www.infinityrecords.net

Jazz Record Center
236 W 26th #804, New York, NY 10001
Phone:212-675-4480

Music Matters
413 7th Ave., Brooklyn, NY 11215

Phone: 718-369-7087

Other Music
15 East 4th Street, New York, NY 10003
www.othermusic.com

Rhino Records of New Paltz
3 Church St., New Paltz, NY 12561
Phone: 845-255-0230

Rough Trade
64 North 9th Street, Brooklyn, NY 11249
www.roughtradenyc.com

Spiral Scratch Records
2531 Delaware Ave., Buffalo, NY 14216
Phone: 716-873-1484
E-mail: spiralscratchrecords@yahoo.com

The Thing
1001 Manhattan Ave., Brooklyn, NY 11222
Phone: 718-349-8234

Westsider Records
233 W 72nd St., New York, NY 10023
Phone: 212-874-1588

Woodstock Music Shop
6 Rock City Road, Woodstock, NY 12498
Phone: 845-679-3224

Ye Olde Hippie Shoppe of Woodstock
69 Tinker Street, Woodstock, NY 12498
Phone: 845-679-2650

NORTH CAROLINA

The Birdsnest
102 B S. Main St., Davidson, NC 28036
Phone: 704-990-6378

Bull City Records
1916 Perry St., Durham, NC 27705, USA
Phone: (919)286-9640

Gravity Records LLC
125 S. Kerr Ave. Suite No. 1,
Wilmington, NC 28403
Phone: 910.392.2414

Green Eggs and Jam
740 W. King St., Boone, NC 28608
Phone: 828-264-3233
E-mail: greeneggsandjam@gmail.com

Lunchbox Records
1419-A Central Ave., Charlotte, NC 28205
Phone: 704-331-0788

NORTH DAKOTA

Orange Records
641 First Ave. N., Fargo, ND 58102
Phone: 701-478-6240
E-mail: matthewoland@gmail.com

Whole Wheat Records & Comics
2 N. Third St., Grand Forks, ND 58203
Phone: 701-215-8557
E-mail: upauat@msn.com

OHIO

A Separate Reality Records
2678 W. 14th St., Cleveland, OH 44113
Phone: 216-644-7934
E-mail: Augustuspayne@gmail.com
Web: www.aseparaterealityrecords.com

Checkered Records
1954 Whipple Ave. NW, Canton, OH 44708
Phone: 3304799576
E-mail: dcheckeredrecor@neo.rr.com

Elizabeth's Records
3037 Indianola Ave., Columbus, Ohio 43202
Phone: 614-569-6009

Everybody's Records
6106 Montgomery Road, Cincinnati, OH 45213

Evil Empire Records at What The Rock!?
1194 N. High St., Columbus, OH 43234
Phone: 614-294-WHAT

Moles Records and CD
111 Calhoun St., Cincinnati, OH 45219
Phone: 513-861-6291
Email: molesrecords@fuse.net

MusicSaves.com
15801 Waterloo Road, Cleveland, OH 44110
Web: www.musicsaves.com

OKLAHOMA

Guestroom Records
125 E. Main St., Norman, OK 73070
Phone: 405-701-5974
E-mail: guestroomrecords@gmail.com

RECORD STORE DIRECTORY

Guestroom Records
3701 N. Western Ave.,
Oklahoma City, OK 73113
Phone: 405-601-3859
E-mail: guestroomrecords@gmail.com

Omega Music
318 E. Fifth St., Dayton, OH 45402
Phone: 937-275-9949
Web: http://www.omegamusicdayton.com

Randy's M&M'S
3200 S. Blvd., Edmond, OK 73113
Phone: (405) 340-0404
E-mail: krisabt@swbell.net

Reggie's Records
110 S. 4th St., Ponca City, OK 74601
Phone: 580-762-2544
E-mail: r.records@att.net

Starship Records
1241 S. Lewis Ave., Tulsa, OK 74104
Phone: 918-583-0638
E-mail: starshiprecordz@yahoo.com

OREGON

Exiled Records
4628 SE Hawthorne Blvd., Portland, OR 97215
Phone: 503.232.0751
E-mail: exiledrecords@gmail.com

Jackpot Records
203 SW Ninth Ave., Portland, OR 97205
503-222-0990

Mississippi Records
5202 N. Albina Ave., Portland, OR 97217
Phone: 503-282-2990

Off the Record
2227 B Newmark Ave., North Bend, OR 97459
Phone: 1-541-751-0301

PENNSYLVANIA

A.K.A. Music
27 North Second St., Philadelphia, PA 08101
Phone: 215-922-3855
Fax: 215-922-3852
E-mail: aka-music@hotmail.com

Angry Young & Poor
356 W. Orange St., Lancaster, PA 17603
Phone: 717-397-6116

Double Decker
808 Saint John St., Allentown, PA 18103
Phone: 610-439-3600
E-mail: doubledeckerrecords@gmail.com

Main St. Jukebox
606 Main St., Stroudsburg, Pa 18360
Phone: 570-424-2246

Musical Energi
59 N. Main St., Wilkes-Barre, PA 18701
Phone: 570-829-2929
Web site: www.musicalenergi.com

Record Connection
550 N. Reading Road, Ephrata, PA 17522
Phone: 717-733-1641
Website: www.recordconnectionpa.com

Sound Stage Direct
212 Decatur St., Doylestown, PA18901
Website: www.soundstagedirect.com

RHODE ISLAND

Armageddon Shop
436 Broadway, Providence, RI 02909
Phone: 401-521-6667

In Your Ear
462 Main St., Warren, RI 02885
Phone: 401-245-9840
E-mail: inyourear@fullchannel.net

What Cheer!
7 S. Angell St., Providence, RI 02906
Phone: 401-861-4244
E-mail: what_cheer_records@yahoo.com

SOUTH DAKOTA

Ernie November
1319 W. Main St., Rapid City, SD 57701
Phone: 605-341-0768

Ernie November
1918 w. 41st, Sioux Falls, SD 57105
Phone: 605-221-0621
E-mail: ernienovember@hotmail.com

Last Stop CD Shop
3508 W. 41 St., Sioux Falls, SD 57106

Phone: 605-361-4416
E-mail: onlyfactor@hotmail.com

Mind Machine Records
29 N. Broadway, Watertown, SD 57201
Phone: 605-886-4337

SOUTH CAROLINA

BJ MUSIC
1430 Augusta St., Greenville, SC 29604
Phone: 864-242-0500
E-mail: bjmusic1@hotmail.com

Rainbow Records
2705-B N. Main St., Anderson, SC 29622
Phone: 864-225-0725
E-mail: dynamorecords@hotmail.com

Scratch N Spin Records
513 12th St., West Columbia, SC 2916
Phone: 803 794 8888
Fax: 803 794 8002
E-mail: scratchnspin@aol.com

TENNESSEE

Chad's Records
321 Vine St., Chattanooga, TN 37403
Phone: 423-756-7563

Disc Exchange
2615 Chapman Highway, Knoxville, TN 37920
Phone: 865-573-9691, x12

For The Record
1 Northgate Mall, Chattanooga, TN 37421
Phone: 423-504-9589

Lost and Found Records
3714 Walker Blvd., Knoxville, TN 37917
Phone: 865-687-5556
Email: albumhunter@comcast.net

TEXAS

All That Music & Video
6800 Gateway East, Suite 1B, El Paso, TX 79915
Web: http://www.allthatmusic.com/

Cactus Records
2110 Portsmouth, Houston, TX 77098
Phone:713-526-9272

Encore Records
1745 W. Anderson Lane, Austin, TX 78757
Phone: (512) 451-8111
E-mail: encoremusic@austin.rr.com

Forever Young Records
2955 S. Highway 360, Grand Prairie, TX 75052

Good Records
1808 Greenville Ave., Dallas, TX 75206-7437
Phone: 214-752-4663

Jukebox Records
Irving, TX 75060
Phone: 972-278-4333

Snake Eyes Vinyl
1101 Navasota Suite 3, Austin, TX 78765
Phone: 512-600-6950

Vinyl Edge Records
13171 Veterans Memorial Drive,
Houston, TX 77014

UTAH

Graywhale
208 S. 1300 E., Salt Lake City, UT 84102

Graywhale
1775 W. 4700 S., Taylorsville, UT 84118

Graywhale
4066 Riverdale Road, Ogden, UT 84107

Graywhale
575 E. University Parkway, Orem, UT

Graywhale
390 North 500 W., Bountiful UT 84010

Graywhale
1670 W. 9000 SW, Jordan, UT 84088
Phone: 801-712-5457
E-mail: jon@fatfin.com

Positively 4th Street Music
249 E. 400 S., Salt Lake City, UT 84110
Phone: 801-531-8181
E-mail: fourthstmusic@yahoo.com

Sgt. Peppers Music & Video
59 S. Main St. No. 1, Moab, UT 84532
Phone: 435-259-4405

VERMONT

BCA Records
East Arlington Antique Center
1223 E. Arlington Road, Arlington, VT

Phone: 802-375-6144

Burlington Records
170 Bank St., Burlington, VT 05402
Phone: 802-881-0303
E-mail: saiddone@hotmail.com

Exile On Main Street
94 North Main St., Barre, VT 05670
Phone: (802) 479-3107
E-mail: exile@vtlink.net

Pure Pop Records
115 S. Winooski Ave., Burlington, VT 05402
Phone: 802 658 2652
E-mail: purepop@myfairpoint.net

VIRGINIA

American Oldies Records
14333 Warwick Blvd.,
Newport News, VA 23602
Phone: (757)877-6877
E-mail: crane4533@aol.com

Birdland Music
951 Providence Square Shopping Center
Virginia Beach, VA 23464

Blue Groove Soundz
5852 N. Washington Blvd., Arlington, VA 22205
Phone: 703-270-9075

Chester Records
185 N. Loudoun St., Winchester, VA 22601
Phone: (540) 667-3444
E-mail: n8rhodes@gmail.com

Sidetracks Music
310 Second St. SE, Unit A,
Charlottesville, VA 22902
Phone: 434-295-3080
E-mail: calicotunes@mail.com

Skinnies Records
2119 Colonial Ave., Norfolk, VA 23517
Phone: 757 622-2241
E-mail: Steveathey@prodigy.net

WASHINGTON

Avalon Music
1330 Railroad Ave., Bellingham, WA 98227
Phone: 1-360-676-9573
E-mail: Avalonrecords@hotmail.com

Bop Street Records
2220 NW Market St., Seattle, WA 98107
www.bopstreetrecords.com

The Business
402 Commercial Ave., Anacortes, WA 98221
Phone: 360-293-9788
E-mail: lizatthebiz@hotmail.com

Easy Street Records & Cafe
4559 California Ave SW No. 200, Seattle, WA
Phone: (206) 938-EASY(3279)

Easy Street Records
20 Mercer St., Seattle, WA
Phone: (206) 691-EASY(3279)

Everyday Music
115 E. Magnolia, Bellingham, WA 98225
Phone: 360-676-1404
E-mail: shefte@everydaymusic.com

Exploding Planet Records
320 N. Callow Ave., Bremerton, WA 98312
Phone: 8602946165
E-mail: explodingplanetrecords@gmail.com

Four Thousand Holes
1610 N Monroe St., Spokane, WA 99205
Phone: (509) 325-1914
https://www.facebook.com/Bob4000Angel

Groove Merchants
905 W Garland Ave., Spokane, WA 99205
Phone: (509) 998-0410
http://www.groovemerchantsspokane.com/

House of Records / Turn Table Treasures
608 N. Prospect, Tacoma, WA 98406
http://www.facebook.com/
HouseOfRecordsTacomaSundays
Phone: 253-272-9229 or 888-300-2902

Off the Record
901 Summitview, Suite 180, Yakima, WA 98902
Hours: 9 a.m.-8 p.m. Monday-Saturday;
11 a.m.-6 p.m. Sunday
Phone: 509-453-9652
E-mail: rich@offtherecord.com
Web: www.offtherecord.com
Facebook: https://www.facebook.com/pages/

Off-the-Record/413543865952?fref=ts

Recorded Memories
1902 N Hamilton St., Spokane, WA 99207
Phone: (509) 483-4753
Online: http://richardsrecordedmemories.com/

Sounds Great
3007 Judson St., Gig Harbor, WA 98335
Phone: 253 851 8986
E-mail: Soundsgreat@harbornet.com

WEST VIRGINIA

Cheap Thrills Records
102 Galleria Plaza, Beckley, WV 25801
Phone: 304-252-DISC
E-mail: chpthrlls@earthlink.net

Cheap Thrills Records
1130 Stafford Drive, Princeton, WV 24740
Phone: 304-487-0404

Now Hear This
1101 Fourth Ave., Huntington, WV 25701
Phone: 3045220021
E-mail: vincehebert03@gmail.com

WISCONSIN

B-Side Records
436 State St., Madison, WI 53702, USA
Phone: 608-255-1977

Bullseye Records
1627 E. Irving Place, Milwaukee, WI 53202
Phone: 414-223-3177

Inner Sleeve Records (Mike's Still Here!)
209 Scott St., Wausau, WI 54403
715-842-8297

The Exclusive Company
770 West Northland Ave., Appleton, WI 54914
Web: http://www.exclusivecompany.com

The Exclusive Company
144 N. Main St., West Bend, WI 53095
Web: http://www.exclusivecompany.com

The Exclusive Company
318 N. Main St., Oshkosh, WI 54901
Web: http://www.exclusivecompany.com

The Exclusive Company
423 Dousman St., Green Bay, WI 54303
Phone: 920-435-0880
Web: http://www.exclusivecompany.com

The Exclusive Company
1259 Milton Ave., Janesville, WI 53545
Web: http://www.exclusivecompany.com

The Exclusive Company
5026 S. 74th St., Greenfield, WI 53220
Web: http://www.exclusivecompany.com

The Exclusive Company
1669 N. Farwell, Milwaukee, WI 53202
Web: http://www.exclusivecompany.com

The Exclusive Company
508 State St., Madison, WI 53703
Phone: 608-255-2433
Web: http://www.exclusivecompany.com

MadCity Music Exchange
600 Williamson St. (inside the Gateway Mall)
Madison, WI 53703
E-mail: mcmxchange@gmail.com

Rush Mor Records
2635 S. Kinnickinnic Ave.,
Milwaukee, WI 53207
Phone: 414-481-6040
E-mail: rushmor@rushmor.com

Radio Kaos
968 Main St., Stevens Point, WI 54481

Strictly Discs
1900 Monroe St., Madison, WI 53711
Phone: 6082599179
E-mail: angie@strictlydiscs.com

Sugar Shack Records
2301 Atwood Ave., Madison, WI 53708, USA
Phone: 608-256-7155
E-mail: sgrshack@sbcglobal.net

WYOMING

Mammoth Music Inc.
318 E. Main, Riverton, WY 82501
Phone: 307-856-0258

Sonic Rainbow CDs
140 S. Center, Casper, WY 82601
Phone: 307-577-5947

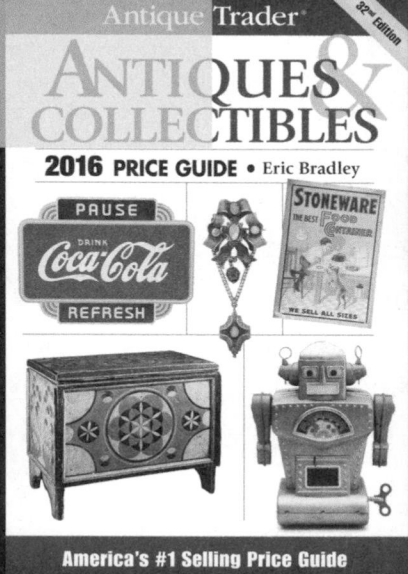

SUBSCRIBE

and receive 1 year (25 issues)
of Antique Trader print or digital version.

Antique Trader is a magazine in which your interest and passion for antiques and collectibles is encouraged, celebrated and expanded. Every issue contains exclusive content from industry-leading authors and experts in bottles, fine art, dolls, furniture, antiques business, and lamps, among others. Plus, you'll also find current antique market trends and values, profiles of fellow collectors and their treasures, expert appraisals, as well as in-depth insights on niche collectibles.

To subscribe to Antique Trader, call our customer service team at 1-855-864-2579 (M-F, 8 a.m.-5 p.m. CT) or visit subscribe.antiquetrader.com.